Penguin Handbooks

The Complete Penguin Stereo Record and Cassette Guide

Edward Greenfield has been Record Critic of the *Guardian* since 1954 and from 1964 Music Critic too. At the end of 1960 he joined the reviewing panel of *Gramophone*, specializing in operatic and orchestral issues. He is a regular broadcaster on music and records for the BBC, and has a weekly record programme on the BBC World Service. In 1958 he published a monograph on the operas of Puccini. More recently he has written studies on the recorded work of Joan Sutherland and André Previn. He has been a regular juror on International Record awards and has appeared with such artists as Elisabeth Schwarzkopf and Joan Sutherland in public interviews.

Robert Layton studied at Oxford with Edmund Rubbra for composition and with the late Egon Wellesz for the history of music. He spent two years in Sweden at the universities of Uppsala and Stockholm. He joined the BBC Music Division in 1959 and has been responsible for such programmes as *Interpretations on Record.* He has contributed 'A Quarterly Retrospect' to *Gramophone* for a number of years, and he has written books on Berwald and Sibelius and has specialized in Scandinavian music. His recent publications include a monograph on the Dvořák symphonies and concertos for the BBC Music Guides, of which he is series General Editor, and the first volume of his translation of Erik Tawaststjerna's definitive study of Sibelius.

Ivan March is an ex-professional musician. He studied at Trinity College of Music, London, and later at the Royal Manchester College. After service in the RAF Central Band, he played the horn professionally for the BBC and has also travelled with the Carl Rosa and D'Oyly Carte opera companies. Now director of the Long Playing Record Library, the largest commercial lending library for classical music on LP, CD and cassette tapes in the British Isles, he is a well-known lecturer, journalist, and personality in the world of recorded music. He is a regular contributor (reviewing both cassettes and records) to *Gramophone.*

Edited by Ivan March

The Complete Penguin Stereo Record and Cassette Guide

Edward Greenfield Robert Layton Ivan March

Penguin Books

Penguin Books Ltd, Harmondsworth, Middlesex, England
Viking Penguin Inc., 40 West 23rd Street, New York, New York 10010, U.S.A.
Penguin Books Australia Ltd, Ringwood, Victoria, Australia
Penguin Books Canada Ltd, 2801 John Street, Markham, Ontario, Canada L3R 1B4
Penguin Books (N.Z.) Ltd, 182–190 Wairau Road, Auckland 10, New Zealand

First published 1984
Reprinted 1985

Reproduced, printed and bound in Great Britain by
Hazell Watson & Viney Limited,
Member of the BPCC Group,
Aylesbury, Bucks
Set in Monophoto Times

Contents

Preface

The role of the recording industry in the musical world of the mid-1980s continues to be of fundamental importance, bringing to the musical public a repertoire coverage far wider and therefore more influential than is possible in the 'live' concert hall and musical theatre. The many treasures – some only recently discovered, others which have been hitherto the sole province of the musical scholar – form a continuously expanding source of great fascination and enjoyment. The distillation of four hundred years of great music is readily available to everyone at remarkably low cost but, even for the experienced, some guidance is essential.

Recordings inevitably focus the listener's attention on the character of the performance itself, heard against a background historical perspective which now extends over more than half a century of electric recording. The established masterpieces of the concert hall and opera house enjoy a constant renewal which is just as essential as the expansion of musical horizons, for each generation's performances have fresh insights to offer.

At the present time a great deal of emphasis is being placed on 'authentic' presentation, particularly with regard to music from the baroque and early classical eras (a practice which was often of much less concern to previous generations of performers). While it is undoubtedly valuable to have an educated opinion of what the music sounded like in the composer's own time, sometimes considerations of scholarship – however dedicated – seem to inhibit the spirit of the music-making. Advocates of the 'authentic' school often seem to regard any kind of expressive licence as reactionary, whereas music-making that deprives itself of conscious beauty of phrase and texture has only limited rewards to offer the listener. There is also a sense of paradox in the modern revival of primitive older instruments which musicians of early periods had to strive to make sound adequate. It seems reasonable to assume that a composer's vision is not confined by the inadequacies of performances and instruments available to him in his own lifetime. It is difficult to believe that Beethoven, for instance, would have preferred the effect of his later piano sonatas when heard on an early pianoforte, as compared with the modern Steinway, with its richer dynamic shading and fuller sonority.

Yet in music there is no turning back the clock. The astringent freshness of the English Concert in Bach, or the revelatory experience of the Academy of Ancient Music in the symphonies of Mozart, obviously represent something new and valuable to generations which have experienced a profound reaction to the *fin de siècle* excesses of the romantic era, reflecting a special mood of our time, when rose-tinted spectacles are completely out of favour. Nevertheless, it is good to see that the 'old-fashioned' traditional approach to the Haydn and Mozart orchestral repertoire remains healthy. The vitality of a Mozart symphony or a baroque concerto grosso may be enhanced by vibrato-less string playing with plenty of edge on the timbre, but the music's balancing elegance, warmth and humanity sometimes emerge more readily when modern instruments are used, allowing their players greater flexibility of execution.

The collector can make up his own mind about these matters, for the gramophone already offers more than one generation of 'authenticity', with further fresh views undoubtedly still to come. Indeed this quest for new ways of approaching old music seems to be one method of filling the vacuum left by the contemporary music scene. An increasingly experienced and educated musical public continues to find very little late-twentieth-century music with which it can identify. As the distinguished American composer and critic Virgil Thomson has said, 'Everything had happened before the 1914–1918 War – after that it was downhill all the way.'

The coming of the compact disc (CD) seems likely to produce a further recording renaissance, although the finest recordings of the analogue era – many of them now available on less expensive labels – are unlikely to be eclipsed artistically or sonically in the immediate future. The best of them deserve to be digitally remastered for CD issue. The musical riches currently available in terms of stereo recording remain one of the great blessings of civilized society in the mid-1980s, and we hope our book will open new doors for the reader who wants both to explore and to discover a fresh awareness of familiar masterpieces.

The Musicassette and the Compact Digital Disc (a reappraisal)

From the earliest days of Edison's cylinder phonograph, it was obvious to all listeners that the recorded sound offered only an approximation of the real thing. Some of the original distortions of the musical recording system, together with others added at the adoption of electronic techniques, have persisted to a diminishing extent right up to the present day. Unwanted background noises, compression of dynamic and frequency ranges, slight fluctuations in constancy of pitch, and clouding of detail (which experts call non-linear distortion) are all features of the reproduction chain with which readers will be familiar. Moreover the vast improvement in the quality of the modern hi-fi reproducer itself has, in certain respects, been a mixed blessing. During the early gramophone era, the record groove contained much more information than primitive play-back machines could truthfully transmit. Today's super-sensitive modern pick-ups can reproduce virtually everything on the disc, but they cannot distinguish between the musical wave forms and groove debris, and they also faithfully transmit pressing imperfections to produce clicks and pops that can wreck the listener's concentration.

Undoubtedly the record manufacturers have achieved considerable success in improving the standard of their pressing operation to meet modern requirements. Yet a long-playing record which on first hearing is silent-surfaced can too easily develop background disturbances when it has been played a few times, and stored under normal domestic conditions. It is this which has caused collectors over the last few years to turn in increasing numbers to the musicassette as a partial or complete replacement of the LP disc for their source of recorded music. The case for the tape cassette was argued fully in *The Penguin Cassette Guide*, and it is sufficient to say here that since that book was published in 1979 the quality and reliability of musicassettes have become impressively consistent. Moreover, during the early 1980s the major manufacturers have moved steadily towards the consistent use of chrome tape (in the place of ferric-based stock), and at the end of 1982 chrome began to be employed in the duplication of upper-mid-price reissue material as well as the newer digital recordings. (A curious exception to this comes from EMI, who have simultaneously moved away from chrome – whose acceptance they did so much to promote – and back to ferric stock, using a new process called XDR. This involves a special monitoring of the level at which the Dolby pre-emphasis is applied to the cassette master-tape, whilst strict quality control ensures that the transfer level matches the potential of each recording. However, EMI plan to launch a new advanced tape formation within the lifetime of this book.)

It can now be argued that the technical advantages enjoyed by the LP in comparison with the cassette have steadily narrowed to the point where the difference is so small as to be of little musical consequence while, in certain cases, the balance of sound on tape can be preferable to the equivalent disc. For younger ears, the presence of a degree of background hiss – for the Dolby noise-reduction circuitry almost never produces absolute silence – can still be irritating, but at least it is constant and much easier for the ear to tolerate than sporadic rustles, clicks and pops. Another considerable advantage of cassettes is that they offer little or no appreciable deterioration of quality over hundreds of playings, while the convenience, portability and lack of ritual in use, which distinguish the tape medium, make impressive bonus points. The latest industry projection for the tape market suggests that pre-recorded cassettes could achieve parity sales in unit terms with the LP by mid-1985 and already – especially in the bargain and mid-price field – there are many classical issues where tape outsells disc. The coming of the miniature personalized stereo cassette reproducer with comfortable earphones (which can surround the listener in an agreeable cocoon of sound and minimize background noise almost to the point of non-existence) must also have a profound effect on the medium in which collectors will choose to purchase their recorded music in the future. Yet at the very moment of the emergence of tape as a front runner, the record industry decided to place its faith in a completely new conception of disc recording.

The digital compact disc – developed jointly by Philips and Sony – is a quite different conception from previous systems, with its technology firmly placed in the second half of the twentieth century. The disc is truly compact in size, measuring 12 cm (4¾ inches) in diameter. While it has a potential for containing music on both sides, in the event only the underside is used for the recording, the upper face featuring label details. The earliest 78 r.p.m. discs were single-sided, so one senses here an almost sentimental link with the gramophone's original development. However, while the first shellac disc contained only about four minutes of information, the CD offers up to eighty minutes' playing time, long enough to contain Beethoven's *Choral symphony*. As we go to press, the American Denon company have achieved a place in history by issuing the first CD of this work (**C37-7021**). It is not an outstanding version, either musically or technically, but, in running for seventy-one minutes, it effectively outstrips all current CD rivals in playing time and challenges other companies to present this epic symphony in the same way. Yet most CDs issued so far slavishly follow the content of their equivalent LPs, and the musical public is still waiting for a major company to pioneer the use of the extra groove space of CDs in an imaginative way. For instance, Bach's *Goldberg variations* will not fit on to a single LP if all marked repeats are included, yet it should be possible to devise an alternative method of editing a digital recording of this work so that the CD version can carry a much fuller performance. The cassette, of course, could match the CD rather than the LP.

The CD's recorded information is cut on to a single spiral track in the form of pits instead of wave forms, and this information is read by a laser beam. The speed at which the disc rotates is very fast (300–500 r.p.m.) and the recorded information is read at a constant velocity. The disc starts at the inner radius where it is revolving at its highest r.p.m. As the beam moves outwards, the angular speed is reduced to maintain constant track speed. The disc itself is moulded in clear PVC, but has additional covering laminations of mirror-like micro-thin aluminium, and finally a protective lacquer. There is no wear or deterioration in use and, given reasonable handling care, the lifetime of a compact digital disc has no foreseeable limit. It was originally thought that CDs were robust enough to withstand unfriendly treatment of any kind, but experience suggests that the playing surface should be treated with care and kept free of grease and dust. A diametrical scratch could well offer no problems, but grease-bonded foreign matter running parallel with the groove might, in certain circumstances, interrupt the pulse code modulation in the groove which maintains the tracking laser beam on its course.

The main features of digital reproduction using the CD system give the following advantages:

a silent background for the music;
a breadth of dynamic range to equal that experienced at a live concert;
a frequency range covering the complete audio spectrum discernible by the human ear;
an absence of non-linear and other distortions;
absolute pitch security;
no loss of quality in the mastering or pressing process.

It all sounds elysian, but of course microphones are still needed to pick up the sound, and, as readers will know, this in itself is a source of many problems of balance. Human fallibility is not cancelled out by the digital process. At the time of going to press, a catalogue of only a few hundred classical CDs is available in the UK. The instantaneous world-wide success of the new system caught the industry unprepared, and demand continues to outstrip supply, with only one European factory able to manufacture these records under the necessary stringent clean-air conditions. As CD players gradually become less expensive and the catalogue expands, there seems no doubt that the CD system will gradually take over from the LP and cassette as the principal sound source for new recordings of classical music intended for serious domestic listening. The total security from unwanted extraneous noise is a primary advantage, and it seems a universal human experience at a first audition of CDs to be pleasurably taken aback at the complete silence which surrounds the music. This contributes to the accompanying manifestation of the almost uncanny sense of presence afforded to the performance, as if a gauze veil has been lifted between the listener and the musical image. But if, at its best, the CD offers a remarkable illusion of reality, it also cruelly shows up flaws and artificialities in the recording balance far more critically than LPs or the more kindly cassettes; any extraneous noise in the recording studio, or made by the performing artists themselves, is also projected with crystal clarity.

As the CD era unfolds, all these problems will be met and dealt with, and already there are a handful of CDs (to which we have given a special accolade) which demonstrate the sense of greater tangibility and vividly defined realism, within a believable acoustic, which we shall eventually come to expect as normal. Of course, older LPs and precious 78 r.p.m. discs will in no way be compatible with the new system, so one's older record-player must be retained for a pre-digital collection. Record collectors are used to starting afresh; yet one more interesting question-mark hangs over the durability of the new system. A paper presented at the 71st Convention of the Audio Engineering Society in Montreux, in March 1982, set out the principles for a digital reproducing method, based on a standard audio musicassette, achieved with a thin film multi-track recording head with a recording potential of thirty-seven tracks! It is claimed that this new system can match the quality and playing time of the compact digital disc, and that by further technology it should be possible for the areal recording density to be doubled by using the tape in both directions. We shall see.

Introduction

The object of *The Complete Penguin Stereo Record and Cassette Guide* is to provide the serious collector with a comprehensive guide to the finest stereo records, cassettes and compact discs of permanent music available in the United Kingdom. This new complete edition includes concert and recital collections, and we have taken the opportunity of adding a few really outstanding reissues from the mono era. Our survey, so far as possible, covers all the more important issues of the major international companies, although in the case of RCA we have been restricted by the recent withdrawal of the bulk of this company's back classical catalogue from the UK and the lack of further information about future plans.

In addition we have included a more arbitrary selection from the major European domestic labels, plus some American digital material. Here we have concentrated on repertoire which is unique to its country of origin, subject to its being available through specialist importers. The most enterprising and efficient of these is Conifer Records who have taken over distribution of Telefunken from Decca plus EMI's European catalogue, alongside other important European recordings, notably from France and Scandinavia, while Harmonia Mundi distribute further comparable labels in parallel with their own output. Discs from the Eastern European Supraphon and Hungaroton series are now also much easier to obtain. Much rare and worthwhile repertoire is appearing in this way and we are glad to be able to discuss its merits within these pages. Another welcome feature of the mid-1980s is the survival and expansion of smaller British companies like Abbey, ASV, Chandos, Hyperion, Meridian and Pearl, each of which has found a special niche in the market place and continues to enrich the recording scene by its enterprise in choice of music, often featuring performing artists of high musical calibre who have not yet achieved 'star' status.

Meanwhile the majors continue to balance the flood of new digital material by reissuing the finest earlier analogue recordings at very competitive prices, while in the bargain range Classics for Pleasure and Pickwick/Contour are as active as ever. Readers will find therefore that the scope of this volume is wider than ever before and it contains many treasures.

The sheer number of available records of artistic merit causes considerable problems in any assessment of overall and individual excellence. While in the case of a single popular repertoire work it might be ideal for the discussion to be conducted by a single reviewer, it was not always possible for one person to have access to every version, and division of reviewing responsibility inevitably leads to some clashes of opinion. Also there are certain works and certain recorded performances for which one or another of our team has a special affinity. Such a personal identification can often carry with it a special perception too. We feel that it is a strength of our basic style to let such conveyed pleasure or admiration for the merits of an individual recording come over directly to the reader, even if this produces a certain ambivalence in the matter of choice between competing recordings. Where disagreement is profound (and this has rarely happened), then readers will find an indication of this difference of opinion in the text.

We have considered and rejected the use of initials against individual reviews, since this is essentially a team project. The occasions for disagreement generally concern matters of aesthetics, for instance in the manner of recording balance, where a contrived effect may trouble some ears more than others, or in the matter of style, where the difference between robustness and refinement of approach produces controversy, rather than any question of artistic integrity.

EVALUATION

Unlike the early LPs, nearly all records issued now by the major companies are of a high technical standard, and most offer performances of a quality at least as high as is heard in the average concert hall. In deciding to adopt a starring system for the evaluation of records we have felt it necessary to use a wider margin than has sometimes been practised in the past, making use of from one to three stars.

The symbols (M) and (B) indicate whether a record is issued in the UK at medium or bargain price. Where no bracketed initial precedes the starring it can be taken that the issue is on a premium-priced label (currently ranging from about £5.50 to £7.00, although some imported digital LPs can cost twice as much as this; CDs usually cost about £10).

The key to our indications is as follows:
(M) Medium-priced label: in the price-range between £2.75 and £4.50.
(B) Bargain-priced label: between £2.00 and £2.60.

It is possible that, in current inflationary times, prices may rise during the life of this book, so that the above limitations become unrealistic, but the major manufacturers usually maintain the price ratios between labels when an overall increase is made.

Dig. This indicates that the master recording was digitally encoded.

*** An outstanding performance and recording in every way.
** A good performance and recording of today's normal high standard.
* A fair performance, reasonably well or well recorded.

Brackets round one or more of the stars indicate some reservations about its inclusion and readers are advised to refer to the text.

Our evaluation is normally applied to the record as a whole, unless there are two main works, or groups of works, on each side of the disc, and by different composers. In this case each is dealt with separately in its appropriate place. In the case of a collection of shorter works we feel there is little point in giving a different starring to each item, even if their merits are uneven, since the record can only be purchased as a complete programme.

ROSETTES

To a very few records and cassettes we have awarded a rosette: ❀.

Unlike our general evaluation, where we have tried to be consistent, a rosette is a quite arbitrary compliment by a member of the reviewing team to a recorded performance which, he finds, shows special illumination, a magic, or spiritual quality that places it in a very special class. The choice is essentially a personal one (although often it represents a shared view), and in some cases it is applied to an issue where certain reservations must also be mentioned in the text of the review. The rosette symbol is placed immediately before the normal evaluation and record number. It is quite small – we do not mean to imply an 'Academy award' but a personal token of appreciation for something uniquely valuable. We hope that once the reader has discovered and perhaps acquired a 'rosette' record, CD or tape, its special qualities will soon become apparent.

COMPACT DISC ACCOLADE

To an even fewer number of recordings we have awarded a compact disc accolade: **C**.

This suggests that the recording gives a sense of natural presence and realism beyond that which we have previously experienced, and that balance problems have been satisfactorily solved, liberating the musical image to give a convincing illusion of a real performance within a believable acoustic. Certain of the compact disc numbers included in our listings have been provided by manufacturers at the time of going to press and have been included for the convenience of readers who are already collecting compact discs, even though we have not been able to sample them. Obviously some may well deserve an accolade but this could not be given without an audition. However, if a recording is highly praised in its LP or cassette formats, the compact disc will almost certainly reflect a similar degree of excellence.

LAYOUT OF TEXT

We have aimed to make our style as simple as possible, even though the catalogue numbers of recordings are no longer as straightforward as they once were. Almost all records listed are 12-inch LPs which play at 33⅓ r.p.m.; but a very few play at 45 r.p.m. and this is clearly indicated in each instance. Immediately after the evaluation and before the catalogue numbers the record make and label are given, usually in abbreviated form (a key to the abbreviations is provided on pp. xxi–xxiii). In the relatively few instances where there is a compact disc available, its catalogue number then follows, printed in bold type. (In the case of CBS recordings where CD, LP and cassette have an identical number, the letters **CD** indicate that there is a CD version available, distinguished by this additional prefix.) Otherwise the catalogue number for the LP is given first, then (where available) the cassette equivalent in *italics*. Often the digits are the same for both, and the alphabetical prefixes indicate disc or cassette. Here is a typical example:

Decca Dig. **400 055-2**; SXDL/*KSXDC*7562.

This indicates that the **CD** number is **400 055-2**; the LP is SXDL 7562 and the cassette is *KSXDC 7562*.

Sometimes the cassette uses the full record number with an added prefix, e.g. HMV Dig. **CDC 747002-2**; ASD/*TCC-ASD* 4059; or CBS **CD**; 35826/*40-*.

Here the **CD**s are: **CDC 747002-2**
CD 35826
the LPs: ASD 4059
35826
and the cassettes: *TCC-ASD 4059*
40-35826

Where the catalogue number is entirely in digits, often the first four change to indicate the cassette, e.g. DG Priv. 2535/*3335* 176. This means that the LP number is 2535 176 and the tape equivalent *3335 176*.

With the move towards international numbering of recordings, further complications have arisen. For instance the Polygram group (Decca, DG and Philips) are now beginning to use the same basic catalogue number for the recording in all three media, indicating which by the final additional digit:

1 = LP;
2 = CD;
4 = cassette.

In this case our listing would be, for example: DG Dig. **410 507-2**; 410 507-1/*4*.
To complicate matters even further, EMI use different final digits to indicate a set. Here is an example where two LPs have as equivalent a single double-length cassette: HMV Dig. SLS/*TC-SLS* 143484-3/*9*. This means that the LP number is SLS 143484-3 and the cassette number *TC-SLS 143484-9*.

The numbers which follow in square brackets are US catalogue numbers; here a similar differentiation is made between disc (in roman type) and cassette issues (in italics), while the abbreviation [id.] indicates that the American number is identical with the European.

ABBREVIATIONS

To save space we have adopted a number of standard abbreviations in listing orchestras and performing groups (a list is provided below), and the titles of works are often shortened, especially where they are listed several times. Artists' christian names are omitted where they are not absolutely necessary for identification purposes. We have also usually omitted details of the contents of operatic highlights collections. These can be found in the *Gramophone Classical Catalogue*, published quarterly by *Gramophone* magazine.

We have followed common practice in the use of the original language for titles where it seems sensible. In most cases English is used for orchestral and instrumental music and the original language for vocal music and opera. There are exceptions, however; for instance, the Johann Strauss discography uses the German language in the interests of consistency.

ORDER OF MUSIC

The order of music under each composer's name broadly follows that adopted by the *Gramophone Classical Catalogue*: orchestral music, including concertos and symphonies; chamber music; solo instrumental music (in some cases with keyboard and organ music separated); vocal and choral music; opera; vocal collections; miscellaneous collections.

The *Gramophone Classical Catalogue* now usually elects to include stage works alongside opera; we have not generally followed this practice, preferring to list, for instance, ballet music and incidental music (where no vocal items are involved) in the general orchestral group. Within each group our listing follows an alphabetical sequence, and couplings within a single composer's output are *usually* discussed together instead of separately with cross-references. Occasionally and inevitably because of this alphabetical approach, different recordings of a given work can become separated when a record is listed and discussed under the first work of its alphabetical sequence. A cross-reference is then usually given (either within the listing or in the review) to any important alternative versions. The editor feels that alphabetical consistency is essential if the reader is to learn to find his way about.

CONCERTS AND RECITALS

Most collections of music intended to be regarded as concerts or recitals involve many composers and it is quite impractical to deal with them within the alphabetical composer index. They are grouped separately, at the end of the book, in three sections. In each section, recordings are usually arranged in alphabetical order of the performers' names: concerts of orchestral and concertante music under the name of the orchestra, ensemble or, if more important, conductor or soloist; instrumental recitals under the name of the instrumentalist; operatic and vocal recitals under the principal singer or vocal group as seems appropriate.

In certain cases where the compilation features many different performers it is listed alphabetically under its collective title, or the key word in that title (so *Favourite operatic duets* is listed under 'Operatic duets'). Sometimes for complicated collections only brief details of contents and performers are given; fuller information can usually be found in the *Gramophone Classical Catalogue*.

RECORD NUMBERS

Enormous care has gone into the checking of record and cassette numbers and contents to ensure that all details are correct, but the editor and publishers cannot be held responsible for any mistakes that may have crept in despite all our zealous checking. When ordering records or cassettes, readers are urged to provide their record-dealer with full details of the music and performers as well as the catalogue number.

DELETIONS

During the whole time we have been working on this book, the deletions axe has been falling all round us. Inevitably more records and cassettes will have been withdrawn in the period before we appear in print, and many others are likely to disappear during the lifetime of the book. Sometimes copies may still be found in specialist shops, and there remains the compensation that most really important and desirable recordings are eventually reissued, often on a less expensive label.

REVISED CATALOGUE NUMBERS

In the latter part of 1984 the Polygram group (including Decca, DG and Philips) has been altering catalogue numbers of some important older issues. The reissue usually features a price reduction. Readers are therfore urged to double-check with their source of supply if a major recording is reported as unobtainable.

ACKNOWLEDGEMENTS

The editor and authors express herewith their gratitude to Roger Wells for his help in the preparation of this volume, and also to E. T. Bryant, M.A., F.L.A., for his assistance with the task of proof-correcting. The editor also wishes to thank his wife, Kathleen March, for her zealous checking of the finished copy before it was delivered to Roger Wells and thence the printers. He would also like to acknowledge the expert assistance of Raymond Cooke, O.B.E., the Managing Director of KEF Electronics, in the preparation of the information about the compact digital disc and the possibility of a cassette alternative. The authors would also like gratefully to acknowledge many letters from readers which have helped to make the present text freer from errata than its predecessor.

For American Readers

American catalogue numbers are included throughout this survey where they are known at the time of going to press. In each case the American domestic listing is given in square brackets immediately after the British catalogue number. The abbreviation [id.] indicates that the American and British numbers are identical. The addition of (d) immediately before the American number indicates some difference in the contents of the American issue; and sometimes a recording available on a single disc in the UK is only issued within an album collection in the USA or vice versa. The initials PSI or SI (short for Polygram Special Import or Special Import) indicate that recording may not be continuously available. We have taken care to check catalogue information as far as possible, but as all the editorial work has been done in England there is always the possibility of error and American readers are invited, when ordering records locally, to take the precaution of giving their dealer the fullest information about the music and recordings they want.

The indications (M) and (B) immediately before the starring of a disc refer only to the British record, as pricing systems are not always identical on both sides of the Atlantic.

Where no American catalogue number is given this does not necessarily mean that a record is not available in the USA; the transatlantic issue may not have been made at the time of the publication of this *Guide*. Readers are advised to check the current *Schwann* catalogue and consult their local record store.

One of the more significant roles played by the international recording industry is to provide recordings of contemporary scores, and in this way the gramophone record becomes fundamental in establishing the reputation of music written in our own time. However, for understandable commercial reasons, the greater part of this output is permanently accessible only in its country of origin. Those recordings that are exported seldom remain available abroad for long periods (although there are honourable exceptions). A great deal of important twentieth-century American music is not readily obtainable in recorded form in Great Britain, whilst modern British and European composers are much more generously favoured. The reflection of this imbalance within these pages is obviously not the choice of the authors. However, our coverage of the American musical scene in the present volume is more comprehensive than hitherto, and we plan to make a further expansion in future editions to embrace some of the smaller American labels.

An International Mail-order Source for Recordings

Readers are urged to support a local dealer if he is prepared and able to give a proper service, and to remember that many records and cassettes involve a great deal of perseverance to obtain. If, however, difficulty is experienced in ordering recordings, we suggest the following mail-order alternative, which operates world-wide:

Squires Gate Music Centre,
Squires Gate Station Approach,
Blackpool,
Lancashire,
England.

Scrupulous care is taken in the visual inspection of records exported by this organization (which is operated under the direction of the Editor of *The Penguin Stereo Record and Cassette Guide*), and a full guarantee is made of safe delivery of any order undertaken. Please write for more details, enclosing a stamped, addressed envelope if within the UK.

American readers seeking a domestic mail-order source may write to the following address where a new supply service is being set up (to handle both American and European labels) concurrent with the publication of this book. Please write for more details (enclosing a stamped, addressed envelope) to:

Squires Gate (US A),
PO Box 406,
Fairfax,
Virginia [illegible],
US A.

Abbreviations

Ac.	Academy
AcAM	Academy of Ancient Music
Acc.	Accolade
Ace	Ace of Diamonds
Amb. S.	Ambrosian Singers
Ang.	Angel
Ara.	Arabesque
Arc.	Archive
ASMF	Academy of St Martin-in-the-Fields
ASV	Academy Sound and Vision
Bar.	Baroque
Bav.	Bavarian
Bay.	Bayreuth
Blue.	Bluebell
Cal.	Calliope
Cam. Ac.	Camerata Academica
Camb.	Cambridge
Cap.	Caprice
Cath.	Cathedral
CBSO	City of Birmingham Symphony Orchestra
CfP	Classics for Pleasure
Ch.	Choir; Choral; Chorus
Chan.	Chandos
CO	Chamber Orchestra
Col.	Cologne
Coll.	Collegium
Coll. Aur.	Collegium Aureum
Coll. Mus.	Collegium Musicum
Con.	Contour
Concg. O	Concertgebouw Orchestra of Amsterdam
cond.	conductor
Cons.	Consort
DG	Deutsche Grammophon
Dig.	digital recording
E.	England, English
ECO	English Chamber Orchestra

Em.	Eminence
Ens.	Ensemble
Fest.	Festival
Fr.	French
GO	Gewandhaus Orchestra
Gold	Gold Label
Gr. Écurie	La Grande Écurie et la Chambre du Roy
Green.	Greensleeve
HM	Harmonia Mundi
HMV	His Master's Voice
Hung.	Hungaroton
Hyp.	Hyperion
Jub.	Jubilee
L.	London
Lon.	London (Record Company)
LACO	Los Angeles Chamber Orchestra
LAPO	Los Angeles Philharmonic Orchestra
Liszt CO	Ferenc Liszt Chamber Orchestra
Liv.	Liverpool
LOP	Lamoureux Orchestra of Paris
LPO	London Philharmonic Orchestra
LSO	London Symphony Orchestra
Lux.	Luxembourg
Lyr.	Lyrita
Mer.	Meridian
Moz.	Mozart
MfP	Music for Pleasure
movt	movement
Mun.	Munich
Mus. Ant.	Musica Antiqua
N.	North
Nat.	National
Neth.	Netherlands
None.	Nonesuch
NY	New York
O	Orchestra, Orchestre
Odys.	Odyssey
O-L	Oiseau-Lyre
Op.	Opera
orch.	orchestrated
Ph.	Philips
Phd.	Philadelphia
Philh.	Philharmonia

Philomus.	Philomusica
Pick.	Pickwick
PO	Philharmonic Orchestra
Pres.	Presence
Priv.	Privilege
PRT	Precision Records & Tapes
Quint	Quintet
Qt	Quartet
R.	Radio
Ref.	Reference
ROHCG	Royal Opera House, Covent Garden
RPO	Royal Philharmonic Orchestra
RSO	Radio Symphony Orchestra
S.	South
Salz.	Salzburg
Sar.	Sarabande
SCO	Stuttgart Chamber Orchestra
Seq.	Sequenza
Ser.	Serenata
Sera.	Seraphim
Sig.	Signature
Sinf.	Sinfonietta
SNO	Scottish National Orchestra
SO	Symphony Orchestra
Soc.	Society
Sol. Ven.	I Solisti Veneti
SRO	Suisse Romande Orchestra
Sup.	Supraphon
Symph.	Symphonica
Tel.	Telefunken
Th.	Theatre
Turn.	Turnabout
Uni.	Unicorn-Kanchana
V.	Vienna
Van.	Vanguard
Var.	Varese
VCM	Vienna Concentus Musicus
VPO	Vienna Philharmonic Orchestra
VSO	Vienna Symphony Orchestra
W.	West
World	World Records

Adam, Adolphe (1803–56)

Le Diable à quatre (ballet): complete.
*** Decca SXL 6188 [Lon. CS 6454]. LSO, Bonynge.

Le Diable à quatre was the seventh of Adam's thirteen ballets, arriving in 1845, four years after *Giselle*. Throughout the score Adam's felicitous sense of orchestral colouring (even more sophisticated here than in *Giselle*) adds to one's pleasure in the slight, but continuously melodic writing. This is a highly enjoyable disc, made the more so by Richard Bonynge's stylish pointing of the elegant writing for the upper strings. The mid-1960s recording is up to Decca's best ballet quality.

Giselle (original score): complete.
** Decca SET 433/4 [Lon. CSA 2226]. Monte Carlo Op. O, Bonynge.

Giselle (older European score): complete.
(M) *(**) Mercury SRI/*MRI* 77003 (2) [id.]. LSO, Fistoulari.

Giselle (older European score): highlights.
(M) **(*) Decca Jub. JB/*KJBC* 14 [Lon. CS 6251]. VPO, Karajan.

(i) *Giselle* (ed. Henri Büsser); (ii) *Overture: Si j'étais roi*.
(M) *** Decca SPA 384. Paris Conservatoire O, (i) Martinon; (ii) Wolff.

Adam's famous score – the first of the great romantic ballets – has been heard in various forms since its first performance in 1841, but for the ordinary ballet-lover the various interpolations and alterations of orchestration will not be of prime importance. The Büsser version has the great advantage of fitting on to a single disc and yet including all the important music. Jean Martinon's performance is an ideal one, warm and full of poetry, with lovely string playing. The recording here is early (1959), but it is vintage Decca sound and has fine atmosphere, tonal bloom and crispness of focus. Decca's alternative of the original score complete on two discs is much less desirable. The Monte Carlo Orchestra is competent enough, and so, of course, is Richard Bonynge, but the orchestral playing here does not really merit the SET price-range, and the recording, although more modern than the Martinon issue, does not yield to it, except that the newer version is more ample in texture. Apart from the price advantage the inclusion of a stylish account of the *Si j'étais roi overture* (conducted by Albert Wolff) makes an attractive bonus.

However, Philips have now reissued the famous Fistoulari Mercury set from the early 1960s which (like Karajan's Jubilee highlights) draws on the score which was in general European use before the war. This was also the basis of the Sadler's Wells version, but apparently the Royal Ballet have now adopted a more authentic score from Russia. Fistoulari was unquestionably among the most distinguished of all ballet conductors in the post-war era and under his direction the LSO play most beautifully. One might miss the French accent of the wind playing, but few will count this a disadvantage. While this particular score also incorporates music which is not by Adam at all – some of it not of the highest quality either – the magical Fistoulari touch consistently beguiles the ear and this makes a fine entertainment. Unfortunately the balance is very bass-oriented and over-resonant, with the bass-drum swamping the sound in one or two tuttis.

Karajan's Vienna disc is lovingly played, with the suave blandishments of the Karajan baton guiding the famous orchestra to produce a reading of beauty and elegance. The glowing Decca recording (with a matching tape) is first-rate and as the legend of the Wilis (the ghosts of dead girls jilted by their lovers) on which *Giselle* is based is a German one, to have a distinct impression of Austrian peasantry and hunting music will seem to many very appropriate. But the lighter, French style of Martinon's account remains preferable.

Albéniz, Isaac (1860–1909)

Iberia (suite): *Evocación; El Corpus en Sevilla; Triana; El Puerto; El Albaicín* (orch. Arbós). *Navarra* (arr. Séverac and orch. Arbós).
*** HMV Dig. ASD/*TCC-ASD* 4160 [Ang. DS/*4XS* 37878]. LSO, Bátiz.

Splendid playing and glittering and sensuously telling recorded sound. Bátiz balances atmosphere with spectacle – *El Corpus en Sevilla* has genuine grandeur. Sometimes the last degree of extrovert excitement is missing, but the vividness of the orchestral image – on disc and chrome cassette alike – is a pleasure in itself.

Suite española (arr. Frühbeck de Burgos).
*** Decca SXL 6355 [Lon. CS 6581]. New Philh. O, Frühbeck de Burgos.

This is light music of the best kind. Tuneful, exotically scored (by the conductor, Rafael Frühbeck de Burgos), and giving orchestra and recording engineers alike a chance to show their paces, the *Suite española* makes highly entertaining listening. We are given here seven pieces from Albéniz's original piano suite plus *Cordoba*, which is from the same composer's *Cantos de España*. As this has a very fetching tune to end the record graciously, no one is likely to complain. But try the opening *Castilla* for its glittering castanets or the *Asturias* with its eloquent and sonorous brass chords to offset the flurry of strings.

Cantos de España: Cordoba, Op. 232/4; Mallorca (Barcarolla), Op. 202; Piezas caracteristicas: Zambra Granadina; Torre bermeja, Op. 92/7, 12; Suite española: Granada; Sevilla; Cádiz; Asturias, Op. 47/1, 3–5
*** CBS Dig. **CD;** 36679/*41*- [M/*HMT* 36679]. Williams (guitar).

Some of Albéniz's more colourful miniatures are here, and John Williams plays them most evocatively. His mood is slightly introvert, and the underlying technical skill is hidden in his concern for atmosphere. A most beguiling recital, recorded with great faithfulness and not over-projected. The chrome cassette is the equal of the disc, if not the CD.

Cantos de España: Cordoba, Op. 232/4; Mallorca Op. 202. Suite española, Op. 47: Cádiz; Granada; Sevilla.
C ❀ *** RCA Dig. **RCD 14378**; RS/*RSK* 9008 [ARL 14378]. Bream. GRANADOS: *Collection.**** **C** ❀

Julian Bream is in superb form in this splendid recital, his own favourite record, vividly recorded in the pleasingly warm acoustic of Wardour Chapel, near his home in Wiltshire. The normal LP and cassette both convey the illusion of live music-making very convincingly, but the compact disc, with its background of complete silence, is electrifying, giving an uncanny impression of the great guitarist sitting and making music just beyond the loudspeakers. Perhaps the image is a fraction larger than life, but the effect is remarkable, and this issue is undoubtedly a landmark in recorded realism. The playing itself has wonderfully communicative rhythmic feeling, great subtlety of colour, and its spontaneity increases the impression that one is experiencing a 'live' recital. The performance of the haunting *Cordoba*, which ends the group, is unforgettable.

Iberia: complete; *Cantos de España; Navarra.*
*** Decca SXL 6586/7 [Lon. CSA 2235]. Larrocha.

Alicia de Larrocha brings a special authority to this repertoire and has few rivals here. Apart from the familiar *Evocación Fête-Dieu à Séville, Triana* and one or two other pieces, there is a lot of first-rate and highly colourful music that will be new to many music-lovers. Alicia de Larrocha's fingerwork invites admiration for the clarity of her articulation and rhythmic attack. She plays with full-blooded temperament and fire, though there are occasionally touches of wilful rubato. The piano recording has extraordinary realism and range; on both artistic and technical grounds this issue is uncommonly rewarding.

Albinoni, Tommaso
(1671–1750)

Adagio in G min. for organ and strings (arr. Giazotto).
*** Ph. Dig. **410 001-2**; 6514/*7337* 370 [id.]. I Musici – (with *Concert of baroque music****).
(M) ** EMI Em. EMX/*TC-EMX* 2037 [Sera. S/*4XG* 60271]. Toulouse CO, Auriacombe – CORELLI: *Christmas concerto;* MOZART: *Serenade 13;* PACHELBEL: *Canon.***

I Musici give the famous *Adagio* its compact disc debut in an outstanding performance with nicely judged, expressive feeling, giving the melodic line a kind of restrained nobility.

An acceptable performance from Auriacombe, not seeking a genuine baroque sensibility; indeed the melody is very much 'on the G string', with a weighty bass line. But it is agreeable enough within a popular collection of this kind and the sound is rich, with little to choose between disc and cassette. There are of course other versions of this notoriously anachronistic piece listed below and in the Concerts section, notably an enticingly plushy Karajan/Berlin Philharmonic performance within an anthology using the Giazotto piece as its sobriquet (2530 267/*3300 317*).

Adagio in G min. (arr. Giazotto); *Oboe concerto in D min., Op. 9/2; Trumpet concerto in D, Op. 7/6; Sinfonia in B flat; Sonata à 5 in G min.*
**(*) Erato STU/*MCE* 70231. Chambon, André, Saar R. CO, Ristenpart.

This record originates from the mid-1960s and offers the splendid *D minor Oboe concerto*, Op. 9/2, as well as another from Op. 7, here presented on Maurice André's trumpet. The Giazotto arrangement of the famous *Adagio* acts as a bait, but those who succumb will be rewarded by some inventive and often beautiful music given in thoroughly stylish performances. This is a good Albinoni anthology and the quality both of the playing under the late Karl Ristenpart and of the Erato recording is fully acceptable. There is an excellent, high-level cassette, quite as vivid as the disc.

Adagio in G min. (arr. Giazotto). *Oboe concertos: Op. 9/3* (for 2 oboes); *Op. 9/8. Violin concertos: Op. 9/1; Op. 10/8.*
(M) ** Ph. Seq. 6527/*7311* 107. I Musici.

This collection remains attractive and still sounds well (it offers strikingly fresh quality in the cassette version). With Heinz Holliger the principal oboe soloist, the playing is distinguished (although the two oboes remain too forwardly balanced in the *Double concerto*). The *Adagio* sounds rather thin-textured: those seeking this particular piece might do better with one of the many recordings available which do not seek to permeate Giazotto's arrangement with baroque feeling.

12 Concerti a cinque, Op. 5.
*** Ph. Dig. 6769/*7654* 082 (2) [id.]. I Musici.

Albinoni has been quite unjustly overshadowed by many of his contemporaries. His invention is unfailingly fresh and vital, which cannot always be said of Vivaldi, and this body of concertos has variety and resource to commend it. I Musici and Pina Carmirelli as the solo player are every bit as fresh as the music, and they are accorded altogether first-rate sound. This is one of the best sets of its kind in recent years and those prepared to stray beyond the handful of well-worn baroque concertos will be well rewarded.

The cassette transfer is hardly less successful and has a clarity and presence that puts some of the concertos (in particular those on the second sides of each tape) right into the demonstration bracket.

Oboe concertos, Op. 7, Nos. 2 (for 2 oboes); *3; 5* (for 2 oboes); *6; 8* (for 2 oboes); *9; 11* (for 2 oboes); *12.*
*** DG Arc. 2533 409 [id.]. Holliger, Elhorst, Camerata Bern.

This record contains eight of the twelve concertos comprising Albinoni's Op. 7, which were published in Amsterdam in 1715. Four of them are oboe concertos, four others are for two oboes, and the remainder are for strings. Though not to be played all at one sitting, this is definitely a record to acquire. The music itself is fresh, inventive and original; it is far removed from the general-purpose baroquerie all too often exhumed for the gramophone. The ideas are memorable and there is a touching charm about many of the slow movements. The playing of Heinz Holliger, Hans Elhorst and the Camerata Bern is refined, persuasive and vital, and the recording could hardly be more truthful or better detailed. This is a most distinguished issue.

Oboe concertos, Op. 7: Nos. 3 and 6.
(B) *** PRT GSGC/*ZCGC* 2003. Rothwell, Pro Arte O, Barbirolli – CIMAROSA and MARCELLO: *Concertos.****

There are two outstanding collections of oboe concertos recorded by Evelyn Rothwell with her husband conducting, and while both are equally desirable they are also quite different in character. This is partly caused by the recording, which here balances Miss Rothwell fairly well forward, gives her a more ample tone than on the companion disc (Haydn; Corelli; Pergolesi) and reproduces the orchestra with a pithy athleticism. This suits Sir John's strong classical style. Miss Rothwell's line in the two slow movements is ravishing without being too romantic, while the spiccato playing in the opening movement of Op. 7/6 and the crispness in the same work's finale are a joy. There is a good cassette transfer, the focus only marginally less sharp than on the disc.

Concerti a cinque, Op. 9: Nos. 2 in D min.; 5 in C; 8 in G min.; 11 in B flat.
(M) *** Ph. 9502/*7313* 012 [id.]. Holliger, I Musici.

This issue offers all the solo oboe concertos in Albinoni's Op. 9. They are played with characteristic finesse and style and are sympathetically accompanied. The recording is excellent for its period (the late 1960s), and the cassette transfer is admirably fresh and clean.

Concerti a cinque, Op. 9: Nos. 3 in F; 6 in G; 9 in C; 12 in D.
(M) **(*) Ph. 9502/*7313* 042 [id.]. Holliger, Bourgue, I Musici.

These performances come from a complete boxed set issued at the end of 1968 and quickly withdrawn. The four double concertos are grouped here. With well-matched soloists they are played crisply and stylishly, if not always too flexibly. The balance is good and the recorded sound clear and clean, if a little dry. The cassette transfer is first-class.

12 Concerti (Opera Decima), Op. 10.
*** Erato STU/*MCE* 71311 (2). Toso, Carmignola. Sol. Ven., Scimone.

Although the existence of this set of concertos was long known and was listed by the Amsterdam publisher, Le Cène, their rediscovery is relatively recent. They came to light as late as the 1960s when Michael Talbot found them in a Swedish library at the castle of Leufsta. They were immediately recorded by I Musici but now appear in a two-record set from I Solisti Veneti under Claudio Scimone. Four of the set are violin concertos (6, 8, 10 and 12) and three are concerti grossi with a small concertino group (2, 3 and 4), while the remainder are without soloists and have non-fugal last movements. They were composed in the mid-1730s, thirteen years after Op. 9 and after the composer had been absorbed by operatic ventures. Although they are of special interest in showing the development of the solo violin writing by the side of his earlier sets, it is for their lyricism and warmth that these concertos will be cherished. They radiate vitality and love of life, and a youthful exuberance that belie the composer's age. The playing is warm and musical, and the recording, made in an ample acoustic, though reverberant is still very agreeable. The discs are cut at a fairly high level so that suitable adjustment of the controls is necessary. The set has an informative note by Roger-Claude Travers. The cassette transfer is of good quality.

Alfvén, Hugo (1872–1960)

Symphony No. 3 in E flat, Op. 23.
** Swedish Soc. SLT 33161. Stockholm PO, Grevillius.

Alfvén was more at home in folk-inspired tone poems such as the *Midsummer watch* or the *Dalecarlian rhapsody* or miniatures such as are to be found in the music to *King Gustaf II Adolf* (SLT 33173) than in any of the symphonies. The style which lies somewhere between Svendsen, Grieg and Strauss can easily become overblown when stretched to symphonic proportions. Leif Segerstam has recorded the *First Symphony* with the Swedish Radio Orchestra (SLT 33213) and the *Second* with the Stockholm Philharmonic (SLT 33211) in excellent modern sound, and has secured a sensitive response from his players. Yet even his persuasive accounts do not really convince one of Alfvén's ability to master a symphonic canvas. The *Third Symphony*, which Nils Grevillius and the Stockholm orchestra recorded in the early days of stereo, is perhaps the first to deserve wider attention. Although the ideas lack the refinement of a Stenhammar, they have a certain vitality and are well held together in this authoritative performance. Alfvén himself recorded it with the same orchestra in 1950 and this, together with his performance of the *Dalarapsodi* (*Dalecarlian rhapsody*) made ten years earlier, have been transferred to LP (EMI 4E 053-34620). The *Symphony* sounds surprisingly clean and fresh, and readers for whom stereo is not the first consideration may well choose this in preference.

Symphony No. 4 in C min. (Från Havsbandet), Op. 39.
**(*) Blue. BELL 107 [Turn. TVS 34778/ *CT 4778*]. Söderström, Winbergh, Stockholm PO, Westerberg.
** Swedish Soc. SLT 33186. Malmborg, Vikstrom, Stockholm PO, Grevillius.

This long and somewhat self-indulgent symphony dates from 1919 and its subtitle is probably best translated as 'from the outermost skerries of the archipelago'. It evokes the other-worldly atmosphere of the beautiful archipelago that stretches out from Stockholm into the Baltic. There is a highly romantic programme which plots the emotions of two lovers, and which rather shocked contemporary opinion in Sweden as being excessively sensual. The musical language stems from Strauss and Wagner, and there is a considerable orchestral apparatus, quadruple woodwind, eight horns, two harps, celesta and piano, etc. It is more successful in its evocation of nature than in its expression of feeling: the vocalise has distinctly Wagnerian overtones. In the Bluebell version the tenor is rather hard and unpleasing, and Söderström's vibrato is wide, but though the music is sometimes derivative, there is much that is colourful and atmospheric, and the recording is in the demonstration class, with marvellously detailed sound and great presence. The orchestral playing is altogether excellent, too, and though the work outstays its welcome it is difficult to imagine a more committed performance.

The soprano in the earlier version made under Nils Grevillius in 1962 is Gunilla von Malmborg who has a less obtrusive vibrato than Söderström. The recording made for Swedish Decca sounds remarkably good, even though it is more than twenty years old. Grevillius had authority and evident rapport with his players, and though this must yield to the newcomer on technical grounds, those wanting this self-indulgent score could do worse than invest in this version.

Swedish rhapsody No. 1 (Midsummer Watch), Op. 19.
(M) (**) CBS 61266 [(d) MS 7674]. Phd. O, Ormandy – GROFÉ: *Grand Canyon suite.**(*)

Ormandy's performance is immensely vivid

and likeable. There is a superb sense of bravura from the orchestra, who obviously enjoy the folksy dance rhythms. Unfortunately the CBS recording is brittle and shrill, especially in the work's final climax. This can be recommended only to those wanting the *Grand Canyon suite*, which is rather better engineered. However, this is now available in several superior versions.

Alkan, Charles (1813–88)

Barcarolle; Gigue, Op. 24; March, Op. 37; Nocturne No. 2; Saltarelle, Op. 23; Scherzo diabolico; Sonatine, Op. 61.
(M) *** HM HMB 927/*40*. Ringeissen.

Bernard Ringeissen is slightly less flamboyant than Smith (see below) but he is fully equal to the cruel demands of this music. The *Sonatine*, incidentally, an extended, big-boned piece, is the only item on this record that duplicates Ronald Smith's discography. All this music is of interest, though none of it rewards repeated hearing. The recording is more than just acceptable; it has splendid presence and body. Though none of this is great music in the true sense of the word, it has strong personality and a vein of genuine poetry that makes one regret its neglect in the concert hall. The cassette is transferred at a very high level indeed and fortissimos tend to lose their clarity of focus in consequence.

Grande sonate (*Les quatre âges*), *Op. 33.*
(M) *** HMV HQS 1326 [Ara. 8140/*9140*]. Ronald Smith.

The *Grande sonate* dates from 1847, some six years before the Liszt *Sonata*, and is a rather extraordinary piece. Its four movements describe four decades of a man's life: his twenties, thirties, forties and fifties, each getting progressively slower. The first movement is a whirlwind of a scherzo whose difficulties Mr Smith almost nonchalantly bestrides; the second, *Quasi-Faust*, is the most Lisztian, perhaps, while the last two are the most searching and individual. The piano sound is admirably realistic and clean (it could perhaps have done with a shade more resonance, though it is by no means dry), and it goes without saying that Mr Smith's performance is a remarkable piece of virtuosity.

3 Petites Fantaisies, Op. 41; 12 Studies in all minor keys, Op. 39; 12 Studies in all major keys, Op. 35: No. 5, Allegro barbaro (only); *25 Preludes, Op. 31: No. 8, La Chanson de la folle au bord de la mer* (only).
*** HMV SLS 5100 (3) [Ara. 8127-3/*9127-3*]. Ronald Smith.

The *Twelve Studies in all the minor keys* include the *Symphony for piano* (Studies 4–7), the *Concerto for piano* (Studies 8–10) and *Le Festin d'Ésope* (No. 12); only the very first, *Comme le vent* (*Like the wind . . .*), could be reasonably described as a study in the normal sense of the word. These twelve pieces occupy five sides; the *Trois Petites Fantaisies* and two shorter pieces (the *Song of the Mad Woman on the Sea Shore* and the *Allegro barbaro*) complete the sixth. Some of this music is quite astonishing; much of it is prophetic, remarkably so when one recalls that the *Song of the Mad Woman* dates from 1847, and the Op. 41 fantasies even appear to presage Prokofiev. Ronald Smith plays it all with consummate ease. As in his earlier Alkan recordings the virtuosity is remarkable, and his understanding of this repertoire is beyond question. The recording too is appropriately vivid and realistic.

Allegri, Gregorio (1582–1652)

Miserere.
(B) *** CfP CFP/*TC-CFP* 40339. Tallis Scholars, Phillips – MUNDY: *Vox Patris caelestis* ***; PALESTRINA: *Missa Papae Marcelli.***(*)

Allegri's motet makes an indelible effect on the listener by the repetition of a short but ravishing sequence, dominated by a soaring treble line. It was a liturgical 'pop' of its day, and its success persuaded the Vatican authorities to guard the manuscript and thus restrict performances solely to the Sistine Chapel. However, the piece made such an impression on Mozart that he wrote it out from memory so that it could be performed elsewhere. On record it has long been famous in a King's performance on Argo (SPA/*KCSP* 245), with an arresting account of the treble line from Roy Goodman. In this new CfP version the treble solo is taken by a girl, Alison Stamp (the Tallis Scholars are a mixed choir). Her performance is no less outstanding, and the effect of her memorable contribution is enhanced by the recording itself, which is superb. Peter Phillips emphasizes his use of a double choir by placing the solo group in the echoing distance of Merton College Chapel, Oxford, and the main choir directly in front of the listener. The contrasts are dramatic and hugely effective, the ethereal quality of the distanced singers clearly focused by the soaring treble line. This is music ideally suited to cassette (with its freedom from intrusive noises) and the tape quality is every bit the equal of the disc.

Collectors of compact discs must be reminded that the Westminster Cathedral Choir under Stephen Cleobury have given the *Miserere* its digital debut (Argo **410 005-2**). The virtue of a completely silent background for this music is obvious and the recording is uncannily realistic, but, alas, the Westminster treble soloist is insecure and no match for his competitors in the King's and Tallis versions.

Alwyn, William (born 1905)

Autumn Legend; Concerto grosso No. 2 in G; (i) *Lyra Angelica* (concerto for harp).
*** Lyr. SRCS 108. LPO, composer, (i) with Ellis.

Alwyn's music is avowedly and unashamedly romantic, yet though the idiom is accessible the music is far from wanting in substance. The *Concerto grosso*, like the Elgar *Introduction and allegro*, is for string quartet contrasted with full strings and, though traditional in outlook, it is nonetheless distinctive in utterance. 'Originality does not come by rejection of one's heritage; individuality is founded on the past.' The *Autumn Legend* pays homage to Bax, though it is envisaged as 'a very personal tribute to Rossetti'; the *Lyra Angelica* is inspired by a less well-known poet, Giles Fletcher. It is a reflective piece, ideal for late-night listening, eloquently played by Osian Ellis and the LPO under the composer's authoritative direction, and recorded with splendid clarity and range.

Derby Day: overture.
*** Lyr. SRCS 95. LPO, composer – *Concert (Overtures).****

This lively performance is part of an attractive anthology discussed in the Concerts section below.

Symphony No. 1.
*** Lyr. SRCS 86. LPO, composer.

The first of Alwyn's symphonies dates from 1950 and is a work of considerable power and maturity. Its gestures are occasionally overblown, particularly in the finale, and offer echoes of the film scores of which Alwyn is so consummate a master. But the work is not only expertly wrought and marvellously scored, but genuinely imaginative and often moving. Alwyn is a *natural* musician, and his ideas flow effortlessly. The LPO responds splendidly and the recording is in the demonstration category, with superb presence and clarity to recommend it.

Symphony No. 2; Sinfonietta for strings.
*** Lyr. SRCS 85. LPO, composer.

The *Second Symphony* dates from 1953 and is a powerfully inventive work that shows an original cast of mind. Its language is not 'exploratory' either in terms of new harmonies or of sonorities, but it is coherent and personal. The symphony is a two-movement work and is magnificently scored: every detail is tellingly captured by the engineers, and the playing of the LPO under the composer's own direction is thoroughly committed. The *Sinfonietta for strings* is a later piece, written in 1970, and is expertly laid out. Its slow movement is particularly beautiful. This music can be warmly recommended to any collector with a taste for Walton or Bax, though it differs from them both. The recording is quite outstanding and fulfils the high expectations with which one approaches a Lyrita disc. An excellent introduction to Alwyn's music.

Symphony No. 3; The Magic Island: symphonic prelude.
*** Lyr. SRCS 63. LPO, composer.

The *Third Symphony* was the result of a BBC commission and was first performed by the BBC Symphony Orchestra under Sir Thomas Beecham. It is a well-argued and imaginative score, richly coloured and at times even reminiscent of Bax. The scoring is opulent and masterly, and though the insistence on the four-note figure (D, E, F, A flat) is somewhat obtrusive and inhibiting, the work exhibits a genuine organic coherence. The performance is authoritative, and the recording has enormous presence and clarity. The prelude is a fine piece, too, and the two works make a most welcome coupling.

Symphonies Nos. 4; 5 (*Hydriotaphia*).
*** Lyr. SRCS 76. LPO, composer.

The *Fourth* is the longer of these works, spilling over to the second side, and is undeniably impressive. Those not attuned to the English symphonic tradition will probably not respond to its rhetoric, but others will warm to its lyricism and its willingness to tackle a large symphonic canvas. The *Fifth* dates from 1973, and its title derives from Sir Thomas Browne, whose *Urn Burial* or *Hydriotaphia* is its source of inspiration. It is a short one-movement work that falls into four sections, and is cogently argued and often eloquent. Both symphonies benefit from the composer's authoritative direction and the fine orchestral playing of the LPO. Like most recent orchestral records from Lyrita, this disc falls into the demonstration class as far as sound quality is concerned. Strongly recommended.

String quartet Nos. 1 in D min.; 2 (*Spring waters*).
**(*) Chan. Dig. ABRD/*ABTD* 1063. Qt of London.

Both quartets are works of substance. The First comes from the mid-1950s and immediately precedes the *Third Symphony*, while its companion comes twenty years later and derives its sub-title, *Spring waters*, from Turgenev: *'My careless years, my precious days, like the waters of springtime have melted away'*. Its theme is the daunting prospect of old age, and there is a note of disillusion and resignation running through its pages. Both pieces are well played, even if the performance of the First is not quite as accomplished as that by the Gabrieli Quartet on Unicorn (now deleted). The performances are thoroughly committed, however, and the digital recording has clarity and presence. A rewarding issue, and in its chrome-cassette form the sound is of demonstration quality with all the vividness of the disc.

Miss Julie (opera): complete.
*** Lyr. SRCS 121/2. Gomez, Luxon, Della Jones, Mitchinson, Philh. O, Tausky.

As a highly successful film composer William Alwyn is a master of atmosphere and dramatic timing. Strindberg's chilling study of Miss Julie's sudden infatuation for her father's manservant, adapted by the composer himself, is given the punch and power of verismo opera, with much learnt from Puccini above all. Alwyn introduces an extra character, the gamekeeper Ulrik, and instead of having a pet bird killed by Jean, the manservant, Alwyn – much less chillingly – has a pet dog killed by the gamekeeper. But the operatic gestures are big, and though the melodies hardly match Puccini's, Alwyn's score is rich and confident, passionately performed by the Philharmonia under Tausky's direction. Jill Gomez sings ravishingly as Miss Julie and Benjamin Luxon gives a most convincing characterization of the manservant lover, with roughness a part of the mixture. Della Jones's mezzo is not contrasted enough with the heroine's soprano, but she sings warmly, and it is good to have as powerful a tenor as John Mitchinson in the incidental role of Ulrik. Excellent recording.

Anderson, Leroy (born 1908)

Belle of the ball; Blue Tango; Bugler's Holiday; Fiddle-faddle; Forgotten Dreams; Jazz Pizzicato/Jazz Legato; Plink, plank, plunk; Promenade; Sandpaper Ballet; Saraband; Serenata; Sleigh ride; Song of the Bells; Syncopated Clock; A Trumpeter's Lullaby; The Typewriter.

(M) *** MCA MCL/*MCLC* 1690 [MCA 531]. O, composer.

Bugler's Holiday; Forgotten Dreams; Irish Suite; Penny whistle Song; Sandpaper Ballet; Serenata; Sleigh Ride; A Trumpeter's Lullaby.

(M) *** Mercury SRI/*MRI* 75013 [id.]. Eastman-Rochester Pops O, Fennell.

Leroy Anderson, who studied under both Walter Piston and George Enesco, has in his varied musical career been bandmaster, church organist, choir master, double-bass player and orchestral conductor. At the beginning of the 1950s he was asked by Arthur Fiedler to provide a series of specially written orchestral 'lollipops' for use as encores at the Boston Pops Concerts. In response he produced a series of instantly memorable vignettes, wittily scored and often melodically indelible. Over two decades he wrote some two dozen such pieces in the best traditions of American popular music and the finest of them are as freshly attractive as the day they were written. The composer's own recorded collection is admirable, with spontaneous, sparkling orchestral playing and vivid vintage stereo from the early 1960s.

The *Irish Suite* was commissioned by the Boston Eire Society in 1947. Some very familiar Irish tunes are used and the composer's melodic decorations impress his personality firmly on the music, without spoiling the folksy freshness of the melodic ideas. The highlight is a masterly arrangement of *The Minstrel Boy* in the form of a gentle and haunting funeral march. Fennell gives polished and cultured performances of both the suite and some of the most famous orchestral miniatures, which have become standard hits, played all over the world. The Mercury recording again has a vintage flavour, slightly studio-ish and a little too bass-resonant, but with a sharp, clear upper range. Both discs are highly recommended.

Arnaud, Leo (born 1904)

3 Fanfares

*** Telarc Dig. DG 10050 [id.]. Cleveland Symphonic Winds, Fennell – GRAINGER: *Lincolnshire Posy* etc.; VAUGHAN WILLIAMS: *Folksongs suite* etc.***

Arnaud, a pupil of Ravel and d'Indy, now lives in the USA. His *Three Fanfares* (*Olympic theme, La Chasse* and *Olympiad*) are admirably succinct, with a total playing time of just over three minutes. They use traditional material and are brilliantly scored, the use of antiphonal horns and trumpets a striking feature. The playing here is marvellous and the recording spectacularly demonstration-worthy, crisp and clear, yet with the brass realistically recessed.

Arne, Thomas (1710–78)

6 Favourite concertos: Nos. 4 in B flat (for organ); *5 in G min.* (for harpsichord).

(M) ** DG Arc. Priv. 2547/*3347* 054. Salter, Lucerne Fest. Strings, Baumgartner – BOYCE: *Symphonies.****

These Arne concertos, written for the composer's son Michael (who was a prodigy), date from the end of the baroque era, and they have a certain interest in that Arne was well placed historically to look backward as well as forward in the matter of style. The music is amiable and lively if not especially memorable; here the organ concerto projects more readily than the harpsichord concerto, because of the balance. The recordings come from the mid-1960s and still sound vivid; the cassette transfer is admirably done.

8 Overtures: Nos. 1 in E min.; 2 in A; 3 in G; 4 in F; 5 in D; 6 in B flat; 7 in D; 8 in G min.
** O-L DSLO 503 [id.]. Ac AM, Hogwood.

Arne's *Overtures*, besides showing a pleasing individuality of invention, are formally imaginative too in not slavishly following either the traditional French or the newer Italian patterns. The performances here, recorded in a resonant but not inflated acoustic, are well made and spirited. However, while the use of authentic instruments (especially when skilfully played) has much in its favour, to offer an 'impossible' fanfare-like passage on open horn harmonics (as in *Overture No. 4*) seems grotesque when modern instruments could encompass the music without assaulting the ears of the listener. This blemish apart, the disc makes enjoyable listening. It is beautifully presented in a handsome sleeve with good insert notes.

Symphonies Nos. 1 in C; 2 in F; 3 in E flat; 4 in C min.
(M) *** HMV Green. ESD/*TC-ESD* 106024-1/*-4*. Bournemouth Sinf., Montgomery – WESLEY: *Symphony in D major*.***

Late in his career Arne, faced by the newfangled symphonies of the Mannheim school and others, suddenly seems to have said to himself that he could beat the youngsters at their own game. He did so in these superb, exciting symphonies, as electric in their way as those of Haydn's middle period, with Arne embracing the new *galant* style and generally forgetting or at least toning down his earlier baroque manners. Amazingly these works remained totally unknown until they were published in a scholarly edition in 1973. There is evidence to suggest that the *C minor*, the most ambitious of the group, was not even performed in Arne's lifetime. This superb record, which can be warmly recommended to specialist and non-specialist alike, makes ample amends with stylish, resilient playing from the Bournemouth Sinfonietta. The coupling is well worth investigating too. Warm, vivid recording. There is an excellent cassette, well focused, yet resonant and full-bodied.

Harpsichord sonatas Nos. 1 in F; 2 in E min.; 3 in G; 4 in D min.; 5 in B flat; 6 in G min.; 7 in A; 8 in G.
*** O-L DSLO 502 [id.]. Hogwood.

A considerable part of the pleasure afforded by this record comes from the superb recording of the two harpsichords used, a 1766 Kirckman on side one, and a 1744 Blasser on side two. There are so few really truthful solo harpsichord records available that this one must be welcomed with open arms, particularly as Christopher Hogwood's playing is so spontaneous and full of character. The music itself, although rather eclectic in style, has plenty of personality; the *Sonata No. 7* is an especially vivid piece. No. 8 is a set of variations on a very Handelian tune which is so familiar that one doubts the information in the insert note that it is 'reputedly taken from Rameau'. A most enjoyable record, presented in a delightful picture-sleeve which is the stylish format of the attractive Oiseau-Lyre Florilegium series.

Arnold, Malcolm (born 1921)

Beckus the Dandipratt: overture (see also below).
*** Lyr. SRCS 95. LSO, Braithwaite – *Concert* (*Overtures*).***

One of the colourful descriptive miniatures

which established Malcolm Arnold's reputation for skilful manipulation of the orchestral palette. This brilliant performance, splendidly recorded, is part of a useful collection discussed in the Concerts section below.

(i; ii) *Beckus the Dandipratt: overture;* (iii; ii) *4 Cornish dances;* (i; iv) *8 English dances;* (iii; ii) *Peterloo: overture;* (i; ii) *Solitaire: Saraband; Polka.*
(M) *** HMV Green. ESD/*TC-ESD* 107780-1/*4*. (i) Bournemouth SO; (ii) composer; (iii) CBSO; (iv) Groves.

Arnold is above all a miniaturist and his shorter pieces show his orchestral and melodic flair to best advantage. *Beckus the Dandipratt* is given a delightfully nonchalant portrayal here, with the jazzy secondary theme gently and wittily understated. The rhetoric of *Peterloo* (written for the T.U.C.) does not quite come off, but the feeling of approaching menace at the opening is unforgettable. Best of all are the *English dances*, played by Groves with an admirable mixture of expressive feeling and gusto. What indelible little masterpieces they are. The *Solitaire* items (almost equally effective) were additional numbers added to turn the *Dances* into a ballet in 1956. A splendid anthology, vividly recorded, with the sound often approaching demonstration quality. The cassette is vivid, but loses just a little of the sharpness and refinement of the upper range, although on side two – where the level rises a little – the *English dances* project well.

Guitar concerto, Op. 67.
(M) *** RCA Gold GL/*GK* 13883 [AGL 1/*AGK 1* 3883]. Bream, Melos Ens., composer – GIULIANI: *Concerto.****
*** CBS 76715/*40*- [M/*MT* 36680]. Williams, L. Sinf., Howarth – BROUWER: *Concerto.****

It was Julian Bream who pioneered Malcolm Arnold's *Guitar concerto* in the recording studio, and his performance has the freshness of new discovery. This version dates from 1961, although it was not released in stereo until 1970. The medium-price reissue wears its years lightly and the balance is good. With the composer directing, authenticity in matters of tempo is assured. The cassette transfer is fresh and clean.

The CBS issue makes a splendid alternative. The recording is analytical and finely detailed, though John Williams is a shade larger than life, albeit not unacceptably so. Slightly more ambience might have given the orchestral timbre a shade more freshness, but in any event this is a first-class recording with great immediacy and presence. Julian Bream gives the more romantic, dreamier performance, but John Williams has concentration and eloquence. A finely characterized reading with good support from Elgar Howarth and the London Sinfonietta. The cassette transfer is faithful, though it has not quite the range of the disc.

Harmonica concerto.
*** Argo ZRG 905. Reilly, L. Sinf., Atherton – BENJAMIN and VILLA-LOBOS: *Concertos.****

Malcolm Arnold wrote this concerto for Larry Adler, who recorded a charismatic performance (now deleted) on RCA. Tommy Reilly's is also a fine performance. He has the advantage of a much more natural balance, and he plays the music with understanding and warmth. The superb Argo recording and the fine accompaniment under David Atherton yield their own pleasures.

4 Cornish dances, Op. 91; 8 English dances; 4 Scottish dances, Op. 59.
*** Lyr. SRCS 109. LPO, composer.

Starting with his first set of *English dances*, Malcolm Arnold has developed the most attractive genre in these sharply memorable pieces, all of them strong in character with immediate tuneful appeal. Arnold himself is his own best advocate (he was once an orchestral player in this very orchestra) and he presents swaggeringly effective performances, brilliantly recorded.

Serenade for guitar and string orchestra.
**(*) CBS 76634/*40*- [M35172]. Williams, ECO, Groves – CASTELNUOVO-TEDES-

CO: *Concerto*; DODGSON: *Concerto No. 2*.**(*)

This is a short, beguiling piece, beautifully laid out for guitar and strings, and played with great poetry and charm by John Williams and the ECO. The sound is warm and pleasing, even if the balance favours the distinguished soloist unduly. The cassette is well managed, though not especially extended in range.

Sinfonietta No. 1, Op. 49.
*** Lyr. SRCS 115. LSO, Braithwaite – BENJAMIN: *Cotillon;* BUSH: *Symphony No. 1*.***

The *Sinfonietta No. 1* is one of Malcolm Arnold's most popular and frequently heard pieces. It comes from 1955 and is scored for modest forces (two oboes and horns, and string orchestra). Its textures are clean and the melodic invention is fertile and gracefully written for the instruments. Two quick movements flank a slower middle movement of a reflective character, tinged with flashes of melancholy that are soon dispelled by a scatter-brained finale. The middle movement has moments of real poetry. Lively playing from the LSO and fine recording, as one would expect from this source.

Symphony for brass, Op. 123.
(*) Argo ZRG 906 [id.]. Jones Brass Ens. – PREMRU: *Music* *; SALZEDO: *Capriccio*.**

A longish piece, lasting some twenty-six minutes, and, as one would expect from a former trumpeter, expertly scored for his unusual forces (horn, tuba, four trumpets and four trombones). Ultimately, the ideas remain a shade facile and the invention wanting the last ounce of distinction, but there are powerful sonorities here. The Philip Jones group plays with stunning ensemble and precision, and is superbly recorded. For those who respond to Arnold's muse, this will be a three-star issue.

Arriaga, Juan (1806–26)

String quartets Nos. 1 in D min.; 2 in A; 3 in E flat.
*** CRD CRD 1012/3/*CRDC 4012/3* [id.]. Chilingirian Qt.

Arriaga's three quartets serve admirably to demonstrate the strength of his musical personality. The *First* has a memorable slow movement that immediately evokes Haydn, and the opening movement of the *Second* shows a quite remarkable impulse and maturity. None of these three quartets has a bar of music not worthy of a musical mind of the highest order. The Chilingirian Quartet is one of the most polished and stylish to have emerged in the last decade, and these performances impressively present a case for regarding these works as weightier than we have generally thought. If Arriaga stands at a pivotal point between the eighteenth and nineteenth centuries, the Chilingirians firmly plant him in a world that knew Beethoven. Quite apart from completeness and ample recording, these CRD performances – notably of the *Andante* of the *D minor*, here very measured – bring new illumination to a lost genius. The cassette quality is first class; the tape coupling Nos. 2 and 3 approaches a demonstration standard in its vividness and excellent detail.

Attenburg, Kurt (1887–1974)

Symphony No. 2 in F, Op. 6.
** Swedish Soc. SLT 33179. Swedish R. SO, Westerberg.

Atterberg is still best remembered for his *Sixth Symphony*, which won the Schubert centenary prize in 1928. The *Second* comes from 1912 when it was in two movements, but the composer added a third the following year.

Best is the slow movement, which enfolds the scherzo within its structure, as Berwald had in the *Sinfonie singulière*, which had received its première only seven years earlier. It is more evocative and distinctively Scandinavian in feeling than the outer movements, and has a delicate and poetic opening. The piece as a whole is heavily indebted to the German romantic tradition (Schumann, Wagner and so on) and it is true to say that in the outer movements Attenberg had not found his personal voice. This he was to do only a few years later in the *Suite No. 3 for violin, viola and strings* (Swedish Soc. SLT 33167), a most lovely work well worth investigating. The *Second Symphony* is persuasively and sensitively played and well recorded, but it is not essential listening.

The *Suite* has a gentle modal flavouring that almost reminds one of Vaughan Williams, though there is a more pervasive sense of melancholy. There is no modern recording of the *Sixth Symphony*, but Beecham's old mono set from 1929 has been transferred to LP (both in the Beecham centenary box and separately on EMI 7C-037-35982) and collectors will be astonished by the vividness of the sound for its period as well as the vitality of this neo-romantic score.

Auber, Daniel (1782–1871)

Fra Diavolo.
**(*) Fonit/Cetra LMA 3013 (3). Serra, Dupuy, Raffanti, Portella, Camb. University Chamber Ch., Martina Franca Fest. O, Zedda.

Auber's operas are known outside France only by their overtures (and isolated arias), so their rediscovery by the gramophone is welcome. *Fra Diavolo* was used in 1933 as a vehicle for a Laurel and Hardy film and the tenor aria, *On yonder rock reclining*, almost became a hit at the time. The inept pair of bandits, Beppo and Giacomo, portrayed so delightfully in the film by the great comedy-duo, are a genuine part of the original and add an enjoyable touch of comic relief to the melodrama. This Fonit/Cetra set, which at the time of going to press may take some perseverance to obtain in the UK, is virtually complete, with traditional cuts opened out by the conductor, Alberto Zedda. He is a Rossini scholar and he finds much in common with that other master's work.

The performance was recorded live at the Martina Franca Festival in August 1981 (which accounts for the ability of a Cambridge Choir to attend), and inevitably that means the performance and recording lack studio finesse. The dry recording acoustic is initially distracting, but grows more acceptable. The bright, clear tone of the coloratura soprano, Luciana Serra – quite the most striking member of the cast – loses some of its bloom. Her agility in Zerlina's aria at the start of Act II is rightly greeted with cheering. The rest of the cast is never less than acceptable, and the music itself – of which tempting samples will already be familiar from the well-known overture – is generally a delight. Orchestral playing is not always crisp, but the set is well worth investigating.

Manon Lescaut (complete).
**(*) EMI 2C 167 14056/8. Mesplé, Orliac, Runge, Bisson, Greger, Ch. and O Lyrique of R. France, Marty.

Ending, like Puccini's setting of the same story, in 'a desert in Lousiana', Auber's opera, written in the 1850s when he was already seventy-four, bears little relationship to that example of high romanticism. Born ten years before Rossini, Auber died two years after Berlioz. Here he demonstrated that the liveliness we know from his overtures persisted to the end. Scribe's libretto is a free and often clumsy adaptation of the Prévost novel, but the sequence of arias and ensembles, conventional in their way, restores some of the original poetry. Manon herself is a coloratura soprano (here the tweety but agile Mady Mesplé) and Des Grieux a lyric tenor (here the lightweight Jean-Claude Orliac). A recording as lively as this with first-rate sound is very welcome.

Auric, Georges
(born 1899)

Imaginées 1–6.
** EMI 2C 069 16287. Debost, Desurmont, Command, Lodeon, Parrenin Qt, Cazauran, Collard, Ens., Myrat.

Georges Auric's music has never gained the public following that Honegger, Milhaud and Poulenc command. *Imaginées* is a series of six works, begun in 1968, for various combinations: the first is for flute, the second for cello, the third for clarinet, all with piano; the fourth and sixth include a singer and are separated by a solo piano piece. The music is well crafted and intelligently resourceful, as one would expect, but no strong distinctive personality emerges; indeed, some of the pieces are moderately tedious. However, these are accomplished performances and are well recorded.

Avison, Charles
(1709–70)

12 Concerti grossi after Scarlatti.
*** Ph. 6769 018 (3) [id.]. ASMF, Marriner.

A handful of Avison's original concertos have become known on record, but it was a brilliant idea of Neville Marriner to delve into these endlessly refreshing concertos which Avison based on Scarlatti harpsichord sonatas. His transcriptions for strings were attractively free (borrowing was always acceptable for composers in the eighteenth century) and he varied the Scarlatti-based movements with original ones of his own. The playing is both refined and resilient under Marriner, and the recording is beautifully balanced.

Bach, Carl Philipp Emanuel
(1714–88)

(i) *Cello concerto in A min., Wq. 170;* (ii) *Quartet for flute, violin, cello and piano in A min., Wq. 93; Trio for bass recorder, viola and continuo in F, Wq. 163.*
(M) **(*) DG Arc. 2547/*3347* 070. (i) Storck, Berlin Chamber Music Group, Lange; (ii) Linde, Seiler, Zartner, Storck.

The original Sackville-West/Shawe-Taylor *Record Guide* declared that Carl Philipp Emanuel, the second of Bach's three sons, 'probably inherited the largest share of his father's genius'. He was greatly admired in the eighteenth century, and now the gramophone is giving us an opportunity to re-assess the adventurous originality and strong personality of his best music. The present collection comes from the mid-1960s and its sound is slightly dated (although not distractingly so, and there is a clear, lively cassette). Its return to the catalogue is welcome. The playing is sophisticated and elegant and quite strong in character. The unusual scoring of the *Quartet* shows the composer's individuality at its most engaging; the *Trio* is slightly less striking. The *Cello concerto* is suavely done; a little more bite would have been welcome, but the music is enjoyable.

Cello concerto in A, Wq. 172.
(M) ** Uni. UNS 207. Paul Tortelier, L. CO – HAYDN: *Concerto in D.***

(i) *Cello concerto in A, Wq. 172;* (ii) *Flute concerto in D min., Wq. 22.*
(M) **(*) HM HM 545/*40-*. (i) Bex, (ii) Rampal, CO, Boulez.

Boulez is perhaps an unlikely figure to find directing C. P. E. Bach, but these are enjoyably spirited performances and the coupling is convenient. He has excellent soloists: Jean-Pierre Rampal gives a distinguished account of the *Flute concerto* and Robert Bex – forwardly balanced – provides warmth and vigour in the *Cello concerto* and is fully equal to the expressively contoured *Largo*. In both finales (especially the *Allegro di molto* of the *Flute concerto*, which is taken literally) Boulez chooses strikingly fast tempi, but the orchestral playing is equal to his pacing and the recording, both full and transparent, (with an excellent matching cassette) allows good detail and balances the continuo (Hugette Dreyfus) convincingly.

Although not one of Tortelier's more memorable records, this is a useful coupling, respectably recorded. The soloist's tone and manner suggest restraint, perhaps too much so in the slow movement. It is curious that Tortelier should appear to draw back from the suggestion of nineteenth-century ripeness in his playing and yet at the same time take liberties with the musical text, with octave transpositions included. The accompaniment, directed by the soloist, is satisfactory.

Flute concerto in D min., Wq. 22.

(M) ** Decca Ser. SA/*KSC* 8. Nicolet, Stuttgart CO, Münchinger – CIMAROSA: *Double flute concerto.***

(M) ** ASV ACM/*ZCACM* 2020 [None. 71388]. Dingfelder, ECO, Mackerras, – HOFFMEISTER: Flute concerto No. 6.**

Flute concertos: in D min., Wq. 22; in G, Wq. 169.

(M) *** DG Arc. Priv. 2547/*3347* 021. Linde, Lucerne Fest. Strings, Baumgartner.

A pair of most engaging works, nimbly and imaginatively played by Hans-Martin Linde with a stylishly conceived accompaniment under Rudolf Baumgartner. The string playing is both spirited and makes sensitive use of light and shade. The disc wears its years lightly and the sound on tape is first-class, quite its equal in every way.

On Decca Serenata a beautifully recorded and elegant performance of the *D minor Concerto*, Wq. 22, with its gracious slow movement and brilliant finale, marked *Allegro di molto*. Aurèle Nicolet is fully equal to both its musical and its technical demands, and Münchinger accompanies attentively. Devotees of 'authentic timbres', however, may feel that the sound here (equally rich and spacious on disc and cassette) is rather too ample and lacking in any kind of spikiness.

Similarly the ASV performance is recorded in a resonant acoustic and the full orchestral textures may not suit every taste. But the playing of Ingrid Dingfelder is both spirited and stylish, and Mackerras's accompaniments match polish with vigour. The high-level cassette transfer matches the technical excellence of the disc.

Flute concertos: in A min.; in B flat, Wq. 166/7.

**(*) DG Arc. 2533 455 [id.]. Preston, E. Concert, Pinnock.

Stephen Preston plays a period instrument, which is inevitably less strong in the bottom octave than the modern flute. He gives performances of considerable accomplishment and virtuosity; he makes much of the introspection of the slow movement of the *A minor* and tosses off the finales with enormous facility. He receives excellent support from the English Concert under Trevor Pinnock, and the recording quality is very good too. However, some ears may find this record, with its slightly abrasive upper string sound, a little lacking in charm.

Harpsichord concertos: in A, Wq. 8; in D, Wq. 18.

**(*) None. Dig. D 79015 [id.]. Hamilton, LACO, Schwarz.

As their numbers in the Wotquenne catalogue indicate, these are early works; the *A major Concerto* comes from 1741 and its companion 1745, when Bach was at the court of Frederick the Great. They are not otherwise available on record. As early works, they are free from the idiosyncrasies he subsequently developed, and concentrate on display and charm, both of which qualities they possess. The slow movement of the *A major* is very beguiling with its muted strings, though the invention in the *D major* is probably more consistent in quality. Malcolm Hamilton is an accomplished player and makes out an excellent case for these pieces, and the Los Angeles orchestra has welcome body and vigour, though their playing is good rather than distinguished. There is a most admirably judged balance between the soloist and orchestra, and the timbre is very lifelike.

Harpsichord concertos: in E, Wq. 14; in G, Wq. 43/5.
*** CRD CRD 1011/*CRDC 4011* [Van. 71265]. Pinnock, E. Concert – MOZART: *Harpsichord concerto.****

The *E major Harpsichord concerto* is one of the most ambitious that C. P. E. Bach left us, with an expansive first movement, an intense slow movement with some fascinating chromatic writing and an exuberant finale. Trevor Pinnock and his talented group of players, using original-style instruments and little vibrato, give an admirable performance, nicely balancing the claims of modern ears and total authenticity. First-rate recording with a lively chrome cassette, although there is a difference in transfer level between sides (side one is smoother, but less vivid; side two needs a degree of taming in the upper range).

Harpsichord concertos, Wq. 43/1–6.
*** HMV Dig. SLS/*TC-SLS* 143486-3/9 (2) [Ang. SB 3829]. Van Asperen, Melante 81 O.

The six *'Hamburg' concertos* were written in the years after 1768 when C. P. E. Bach escaped from the restrictions of the Prussian court in Berlin and went to Hamburg, succeeding Telemann as municipal composer. His new freedom encouraged him to exploit his taste for making an audience sit up in surprise. So in the *D major Concerto*, No. 2 of this set, he suddenly interrupts the dashing orchestral tutti with a low note that sounds like a rude noise and then inconsequentially gets the harpsichord soloist to weave a leisurely *Andante* before carrying on with the movement. Bob Asperen's light and lively readings bring out the spring-like freshness of the writing, presented on original instruments with clarity and no excessive abrasiveness. Warm, full recording, less sharply focused on tape.

Double harpsichord concerto in F, Wq. 46.
(M) *(*) HM 29367. Leonhardt, Curtis, Coll. Aur. – J. S. BACH: *Harpsichord concerto No. 1.**(*)

This concerto is earlier than the more celebrated concerto in E flat for fortepiano and harpsichord. It dates from 1740 and is scored for strings, horns and continuo. Good but not memorable playing from the distinguished soloists and the Collegium Aureum and acceptable but not outstanding recording, which dates from the mid-1960s.

Concerto for 4 harpsichords and strings in F, Wq. 46 (adapted and arr. Leppard).
(M) **(*) Decca Ser. 410 136-1 [Lon. STS 15075]. Malcolm, Aveling, Parsons, Preston, ECO, Leppard – J. S. BACH: *Concertos* **(*); MALCOLM: *Variations.****

This offers an interesting example (from the late 1960s) of an attempt to record four harpsichords clearly and without jangle. It succeeds, but the quieter keyboard figurations sound insubstantial. In the days of C. P. E. Bach, orchestral tone was much less ample than it is today, and problems of balance with a harpsichord did not arise. Here they do, and one has to turn the volume well up to get the harpsichord image right. Having said this, let it be added that this is a fine work, arranged by Leppard from the *Double harpsichord concerto* listed above, and the excellent performance here gives a stronger character to the music (especially the first movement) than does the account of the original by the Collegium Aureum – see above.

Organ concertos: in G, Wq. 34; in E flat, Wq. 35; Fantasia and fugue in C min., Wq. 119/7.
**(*) Erato STU/*MCE* 71115. Alain, Paillard CO, Paillard.

The G major concerto, which also exists in a version for the flute, dates from the mid-1750s, and its companion was composed four years later. The slow movement of the latter is particularly powerful and expressive, but all the music here is representative of C. P. E. Bach at something like his very best. Marie-Claire Alain plays with excellent style, and the orchestra produces a rich and well-focused sound even if ensemble is not always impeccable. One or two minor disturbances of pitch may worry some listeners, but, generally speaking, this is a welcome issue. The cassette transfer is made at a high level, and is both full and attractively vivid, its upper range only fractionally less refined than the disc.

Sinfonias: in C, Wq. 174; in D, Wq. 176; 6 Sinfonias, Wq. 182/1–6.
*** O-L DSLO 557/8 [id.]. AcAM, Hogwood.

6 Sinfonias, Wq. 182/1–6.
*** DG Arc. 2533 449 [id./*3310 449*]. E. Concert, Pinnock.
**(*) HM 1C 065 99691 (Nos. 2–5 only). Coll. Aur.

The sharp originality of C. P. E. Bach was never more apparent than in these symphonies. The six for strings, Wq. 182, written after he had left the employ of the Emperor of Prussia and could at last please himself in adventurous writing, are particularly striking in their unexpected twists of imagination, with wild, head-reeling modulations and sudden pauses which suggest the twentieth century rather than the eighteenth. The abrasiveness of such music comes out sharply in an authentic performance like that of the Academy of Ancient Music and, though the angularity may not make it relaxing listening, Hogwood continually has one responding as to new music, not least in the dark, bare slow movements. The two symphonies with wind (on side four) are marginally less original; but, with superb recording, it is a remarkable and refreshing set.

The performing style of the English Concert is less abrasive than that of its rival and has more concern for eighteenth-century poise and elegance without losing any degree of authenticity. This issue also has the advantage of fitting the six symphonies Wq. 182 on two sides instead of three. Excellent recording.

The Collegium Aureum disc (originally issued in the UK on BASF) was the début recording of these works on 'original instruments'. The playing has grip and impulse, and the resilient yet slightly grainy sound has virility and bite, and a strikingly fresh beauty too. The acoustic is both resonant and clean, and the continuo comes through in perfect overall balance. But, fine though this LP is, it has the irredeemable disadvantage of offering only four of the six symphonies.

4 Sinfonias, Wq. 183/1–4.
(M) *** Ph. 9502 013. ECO, Leppard.

This record is devoted to four symphonies published in Hamburg in 1780. The music is not merely historically interesting but is often characterized by an emotional insistence that is disturbing and a capacity to surprise that is quite remarkable. The playing is splendid, lively and vital, and the recording is exemplary, both in quality of sound and in balance.

Chamber and instrumental music

Fantasy in C; Quartets for flute, viola, cello and piano in A min., D, and G, Wq. 93/5.
*** O-L DSLO 520. McGegan, Mackintosh, Pleeth, Hogwood.

The three quartets come from the last year of Bach's life and are all beautifully fashioned, civilized pieces with many of the expressive devices familiar from this composer. There is a highly chromatic slow movement for the D major work, and some of the outer movements are unpredictable and inventive. The *Fantasy* dates from the mid-1780s and is roughly contemporary with Mozart's *C minor Fantasy*. All the performances are first-rate: Christopher Hogwood uses a fortepiano rather than harpsichord and secures a wide dynamic range and clean intelligent articulation. The recorded sound could hardly be bettered.

Flute sonata in A min.
*** RCA RL/*RK* 25315 [ARL 1/*ARK 1* 3858]. Galway – STAMITZ: *Flute concertos.* **(*)

This sonata for unaccompanied flute is an inspired and characteristically original piece, and James Galway gives it a marvellous performance, as striking for its insight as for its spontaneity. He is well recorded on both disc and cassette, but the couplings offer more conventional music.

Trio sonata in E, Wq. 162.
*** O-L DSLO 518 [id.]. Preston, McGegan,

Ryan, Pleeth, Hogwood – J. S. BACH: *Trio sonata* ***; W. F. BACH: *Duo* etc.**

Stephen Preston and Nicholas McGegan play on period instruments and show why the flute was so cultivated at Potsdam as the instrument of sensibility. This sonata is an original and eloquent piece, well crafted and structured, with an expressive, inward-looking slow movement. It is persuasively played and truthfully recorded. The J. S. Bach coupling is an added attraction, though the fill-ups by W. F. Bach are less interesting.

Essay on the True Art of Playing Keyboard Instruments: 6 Sonatas, Wq. 63/1–6; 6 Sonatine nuove, Wq. 63/7–12.
*** O-L DSLO 589. Hogwood.

This record contains the twelve keyboard sonatas that C. P. E. Bach published with the first part of his *Essay on the True Art of Playing Keyboard Instruments* in 1753. These were to wield enormous influence for the remainder of the century on composers such as Haydn, Mozart and Beethoven. Despite their didactic intention, they are pieces of great expressive power and are played by Christopher Hogwood not only with virtuosity but with a rare vein of poetic feeling. He uses a 1761 Haas clavichord of great beauty and is recorded excellently, though the disc should be played at low level.

Vocal music

Magnificat, Wq. 215.
*** Argo ZRG 853 [id.]. Palmer, Watts, Tear, Roberts, King's College Ch., ASMF, Ledger.
** HM 1C 065 99624. Ameling, Lehane, Altmeyer, Hermann, Tölz Ch., Coll. Aur., Kurt Thomas.

One would have thought that the example of father Johann Sebastian in setting the *Magnificat* would be daunting to his son; but just before old Bach died, C.P.E. produced a setting which in terms of the *galant* style conveyed startling involvement. The magnificent opening chorus (repeated later in the setting of the *Gloria*) presents King's College Choir at its most exhilarating. This irresistible movement, here taken challengingly fast, leads to a whole series of sharply characterized numbers, including a sparkling tenor aria on *Quia fecit*. The whole is rounded off in a choral fugue as energetic as Handel's best, with barely a nod in father's direction. With vividly atmospheric recording the performance under Philip Ledger comes electrically to life, with choir, soloists and orchestra all in splendid form.

The Harmonia Mundi version is enjoyable, and Elly Ameling is outstanding among the soloists. But the performance overall has not the vitality of the Argo version, and although the splendour of the closing *Sicut erat* comes over impressively the resonant recording does not provide much inner detail.

Bach, Johann Christian
(1735–82)

Six 'favourite' overtures: Nos. 1–3 in D; 4 in C; 5–6 in G.
*** O-L DSLO/*DSLC* 525 [id.]. AcAM, Hogwood.

J. C. Bach's *Six 'favourite' overtures* were published as a set in London in 1763 for use in the concert hall, although their original derivation was theatrical. They are all short and succinct Italian-style pieces in three movements (fast–slow–fast), and they show great variety of invention and imaginative scoring (using double wind, horns and strings). The performances here are characteristically alert and vivid and there are many features to stay in the mind: the trio for wind instruments in the finale of No. 1; the attractively robust outer movements of No. 3; the Vivaldi-like figuration of the finale of No. 4; the tripping strings in the *Andante* of No. 5. This is not an issue to play all at once but, when dipped into, it offers delightful music played in a refreshingly spirited (and stylish) way. The recording is excellent on disc, and the tape transfer is very good indeed, if fractionally mellower on side one than side two.

6 Sinfonias, Op. 3 (ed. Erik Smith).
(M) *** Ph. 9502/*7313* 001 [id.]. ASMF, Marriner.

These Op. 3 symphonies are recorded here for the first time. They were first played in 1765 'at Mrs Cornelys's' in Carlisle House, Soho Square. Erik Smith, who has edited them, describes them as 'in essence Italian overtures, though with an unusual wealth of singing melody'. They are beguilingly played by the Academy of St Martin-in-the-Fields under Neville Marriner and beautifully recorded. None of this can be called great music but it has an easy-going and fluent charm. The tape transfer is of excellent quality, fresh and transparent.

(i) *6 Sinfonias Op. 3* (ed. Smith); (ii) *6 Sinfonias Op. 6; Sinfonias Op. 8, Nos. 2 in G; 3 in D; 4 in F; Sinfonias Op. 9, Nos. 1 in B flat; 2 in E flat; 3 in B flat; 6 Sinfonias Op. 18; Overture: La calamità de cuori. Sinfonia concertante in F for oboe, cello and orchestra.*
(M) **(*) Ph. 6768 336 (5). (i) ASMF, Marriner; (ii) Netherlands CO, Zinman.

This five-record set consists of reissue material drawn together to mark the bicentenary of the composer in 1982. The Op. 3 symphonies are scored for strings with oboes and horns in subsidiary roles. The performances are expert and fresh and the recordings eminently well balanced. For the remainder of the set, Philips draw on recordings by the Netherlands Chamber Orchestra made in the late 1970s, who are also splendidly recorded with particularly good separation in the concertos for double orchestra. David Zinman secures good lively playing from the Netherlanders and few will quarrel with the results. A case could be made for giving some of the outer movements less elegance and greater weight. Memories of Raymond Leppard's Op. 6 set made in the late 1960s are not entirely banished for he brought greater intensity and sense of style to them. But if there are times when one feels that Zinman is too brisk, there are many more when he gives pleasure with the vigour of his presentation of the outer movements and the charm of the slower ones. This set has many first-class performances and would form a valuable corner-stone for any collector about to embark on this composer.

Sinfonias, Op. 6/6; Op. 18/4 and 6.
** HM 1C 065/*265* 99759. Coll. Aur.

The Collegium Aureum are less successful with the music of J. C. Bach than in their disc of sinfonias by Carl Philipp. But they are not helped by the recording which, though full and pleasing, lacks brilliance. The playing itself is elegant but rather unsmiling. The slow movement of the G minor symphony, Op. 6/6, which is the longest work, with a side to itself, has more emotional depth than is revealed here.

Sinfonia in E flat, Op. 9/2; Sinfonia concertante in C (for flute, oboe, violin, cello and orchestra).
(M) *(*) Decca Ser. SA 24 [Lon. STS 15510]. ECO, Bonynge (with SALIERI: *Sinfonia; Double concerto* **).

There is some careful attention to detail in these performances but they do not show the same sureness of style that marks Leppard's or Zinman's recordings. A pity, since the *Sinfonia concertante* is not at present available in an alternative version and there is, of course, some fine playing from the soloists. The Salieri coupling is not important music but performances and recording are of comparable quality.

(i) *Sinfonia concertante in A, for violin, cello and orchestra. Sinfonia in E flat for double orchestra, Op. 18/1.*
*(*) HM 1C 065 99827. Coll. Aur., (i) with Maier, May.

This record offers poor value: the two-movement *Sinfonia concertante* is an agreeable work, with an attractively inventive rondo finale, but it lasts only 15′36″. Its soloists are balanced very closely, which makes their period instruments sound unnecessarily husky and minimizes the expressive effect of their playing. The *Sinfonia* on side two is a splendid piece. It has a fine central *Andante*, with a strong Mozartian flavour. The performance is lively and sympathetic, but the reverberant acoustic does not fully exploit the work's antiphonal possibilities. Side two plays for just 12′21″.

Symphonies (for wind sextet) *Nos. 1 in E flat; 2 in B flat; 3 in E flat; 4 in B flat; 5 in E flat; 6 in B flat.*
(B) **(*) PRT GSGC/*ZCGC* 2033. Camden Wind Ens.

These six sextets were probably written for Vauxhall and they certainly would make attractive open-air music. The combination of clarinets, horns and bassoons was also that of many mid-eighteenth-century military bands. This and the fact that marches replace minuets in a number of the works may indicate that Bach composed them for some regimental band. Attractive period music, but if the writing has plenty of surface charm there is little real substance. However, for relaxed and undemanding listening it can be recommended.

The highly regarded Decca set by the London Wind Soloists under Jack Brymer is currently out of the catalogue, though no doubt it will return shortly on Decca's Serenata label. The earlier version by the Camden Wind Ensemble – recorded when the great bassoonist Archie Camden was still active – has rather more astringent recording but the sound is full of character, and there is a good tape (slightly sharper in focus on the second side). Until the Decca returns, this PRT alternative is well worth considering in the bargain price-range.

4 Sonatas and 2 Duets, Op. 18 (for flute and fortepiano): *Sonatas Nos. 1 in C; 2 in D; 3 in E flat; 4 in G; Duets Nos. 1 in A; 2 in F.*
**(*) O-L DSLO 516. McGegan, Hogwood or Tilney (fortepiano).

These sonatas have nothing whatever to do with the Op. 18 *Sinfonias*. They were first published in France in about 1780, and are played on an Adlam Burnett fortepiano, based on a south German instrument of the period, and a George Astor flute of 1790. The flute is very much the accompanying instrument here, and it would be idle to pretend that the music, obviously intended for amateur performance, is of any great substance. It is, however, undeniably pleasing, particularly as presented in these stylish performances and in this exemplary and truthful recording.

Bach, Johann Sebastian
(1685–1750)

The Art of Fugue; Brandenburg concertos Nos. 1–6; The Musical Offering; Orchestral suites Nos. 1–4.
(M) ** Ph. 6768 232 (6). ASMF, Marriner.

Marriner and the St Martin's Academy are refined interpreters of Bach, but the two major offerings here – the idiosyncratic earlier set of the *Brandenburgs*, using Thurston Dart's idea of the original text, and the self-conscious readings of the *Suites* – are less sympathetic than most of their records. Consistently good recording.

The Art of fugue, BWV 1080 (see also organ and harpsichord versions).
*** Ph. 6747 172/*7699 007* (2) [id.]. ASMF, Marriner.
(M) ** Sup. 1411 2971/2. Ars Rediviva CO, Munclinger.

How to perform *The Art of fugue* has always presented problems, since Bach's own indications are so sparse. The very fact that (with the exception of the items for two harpsichords) the whole complex argument can be compassed by ten fingers on one keyboard points to that option, but there is no doubt that for the listener at large, not following the score, a more varied instrumentation is both easier on the ear and clearer in its presentation of argument.

Neville Marriner in the edition he prepared with Andrew Davis has varied the textures most intelligently, giving a fair proportion of the fugues and canons to keyboard instruments, organ as well as harpsichord. In each instance the instrumentation has been chosen as specially suitable to that particular movement. So the opening fugue is given to plain string quartet, the second to the full orchestra of strings (two violins, viola, cello and violone) and woodwind (two oboes, cor anglais and bassoon), and so on. The fugue for two harpsichords and its inversion are exhilarating as performed by Andrew Davis and Christopher Hogwood, while the final quadruple fugue, which Bach never completed, is left achingly in mid-air at the end, a valid procedure on record at least. Marriner's style of performance is profoundly satisfying, with finely judged tempi, unmannered phrasing and resilient rhythms. The recording is beautifully refined on disc, rather less reliably so on cassette (7699 007), although still impressive.

Milán Munclinger's arrangement of *The Art of fugue* is for a small string band of seventeen players, supplemented by four wind instruments (oboe, oboe d'amore, two bassoons) and two harpsichords. The wind instruments are used to define the different versions of the subject rather than for reasons of colour or sonority. Contrapunctus 18 is allotted, as specified, to the two harpsichords. There is some adjustment of the order of the fugues and Munclinger does include the unfinished fugue in its incomplete form. The overall effect is more severe than other orchestral transcriptions have been, save, perhaps, for Marriner's version with the Academy, who enjoy the advantage of more vivid recording. Not a first choice by any means – but at the same time not negligible.

Brandenburg concertos Nos. 1–6, BWV 1046/51; Orchestral suites Nos. 1–4, BWV 1066/9.
(M) ** HM 1C 97 5300-30 (4). Coll. Aur.

The Collegium Aureum helped to pioneer the return to authentic textures with 'original instruments', but they sugared the pill a little by the use of a widely reverberant acoustic, which added a mellowing effect to the instrumental timbres, especially in the *Suites*. Here their recordings of Bach's major orchestral works are gathered together in a box at medium price. The performances are considered in more detail below; the sound quality itself is warmly beautiful.

Brandenburg concertos Nos. 1–6.
*** DG Arc. Dig. **410 500/1-2**; 2742/*3383* 003 (2) [id.]. E. Concert, Pinnock.
*** Ph. Dig. **400 076/7-2**; 6769/*7654* 058 (2) [id.]. ASMF, Marriner.
*** Ph. 6747 166 (2) [id.]. ECO, Leppard.
(M) *** EMI Em. EMX/*TC-EMX* 41 2043/4-1/*4*. Polish CO, Maksymiuk.
(M) *** HMV SXDW/*TC-SXDW* 3054 (2) [Ang. S/*4X2S* 3787]. Bath Fest. O, Menuhin.
*** Erato STU 70801/2 [CRL 2 5801]. Jean-François Paillard CO, Paillard.
(M) **(*) Decca Ser. SA/*KSC 26* and 410 132-1/*4* [Lon. 42005]. ECO, Britten.
**(*) HMV Dig. SLS/*TCC-SLS* 5256 [Ang. DXB/4X253930]. Linde Cons., Linde.
(M) **(*) ASV ACM 2038/9. Northern Sinf., Malcolm.
(M) **(*) Ph. 9502 014/5 [id.]. ASMF, Marriner.
(M) **(*) Ph. Seq. 6527/*7311* 053/4. Berlin RSO, Maazel.
(M) ** Decca Jub. JB/*KJBC* 61/2 [Lon. STS 15366/7]. SCO, Münchinger.
** DG 2707 112 (2)/*3370 030* [id.]; also 2531/*3301* 332 (Nos. 1–3); 2531/*3301* 333 (Nos. 4–6) [id.]. Berlin PO, Karajan.
(B) ** Con. CC/*CCT* 7535 and 7541. Stuttgart Chamber Soloists, Couraud.
** HM IC 151 99643/4. Coll. Aur.
** Tel. Dig. AZ6/*CX4* 42823 and 42840 [2635620]. VCM, Harnoncourt.
(M) *(*) Tel. Ref. AQ6/*CQ4* 41191/2 [2635/*2435* 043]. VCM, Harnoncourt.
**(*) CBS 79227/*40-* (2). Carlos (synthesizer).

For the *Brandenburg concertos* there is now a joint principal recommendation shared between Pinnock on DG-Archiv and Marriner on Philips. Pinnock's is the most exhilarating set of the Brandenburgs, whether on original or modern instruments. It represents the very peak of his achievement as an advocate of authentic performance with sounds that are clear and refreshing but not too abrasive. Interpretatively he tends to opt for fast speeds in outer movements, relatively slow in *Andantes* with a warm but stylish degree of expressiveness – as in the lovely account of the slow movement of No. 6 – but from first to last there is no routine. Soloists are outstanding, and so is the recording. The chrome cassettes too are vivid and clear, if marginally less cleanly focused than the LPs. The compact disc is made at a very high level, giving the sound great immediacy.

For those who still cannot quite attune their ears to the style of string playing favoured by the authentic school, Marriner's ASMF set should prove an ideal alternative. Above all, these performances communicate warmth and enjoyment. In three of the concertos Marriner introduces such distinguished soloists as Henryk Szeryng, Jean-Pierre Rampal and Michala Petri, adding individuality without breaking the consistency of beautifully sprung performances. George Malcolm is an ideal continuo player. With superb playing, well-chosen speeds and refined recording, this is now on balance the best choice for those not insisting on the use of period instruments. The sound is equally natural on both LP and cassette. The compact discs, available individually, appear to have been separately mastered. The first, containing *Concertos Nos. 1–3*, has each concerto separately banded, whereas the second has additional bands for individual movements. The sound is first-class, but very slightly more refined in the later concertos, with No. 5 sounding exceptionally realistic and the strings in No. 6 captured more successfully than ever before on disc. In the earlier concertos the ear more readily notices artificial balances, and the trumpet in No. 2 is rather too bright and forward; the strings, however, in No. 3 sound very natural and, taken as a whole, this analogue recording has responded well to its digital re-mastering.

Although Leppard's set is also placed near the top of the list, there is an element of controversy about the consistently fast tempi that he adopts throughout. Certainly the sparkling contribution from the ECO soloists is splendidly alive and buoyant, and the recording is beautifully balanced as well as vivid. The secure horns in No. 1 with their easy roulades and trills; the impeccable, crisp accuracy of John Wilbraham's trumpet in No. 2, matched by some delightful oboe playing; a characteristically piquant account of the recorder solos in No. 4 from the late David Munrow: all these give consistent pleasure to the listener. Leppard's own harpsichord solo in No. 5, however, seems curiously rigid. The sound is very good indeed, fresh and with fine body, yet with the inner detail admirably clear. To some ears this is all irresistible; others find that Leppard's vivacity can sometimes seem a little too insistent. Nevertheless this stands very high indeed among the current versions on disc, and even though the tape transfer is slightly variable in freshness of focus, it is still fully acceptable.

But if Leppard's approach may seem too brisk at times the HMV Polish set of *Brandenburgs* (recorded when the orchestra was on tour in England in 1977) is surely the fastest on record. Some will undoubtedly resist, especially in No. 3, yet the crisp articulation and the buoyancy of the playing are exhilarating, here and elsewhere. The orchestra is augmented with English recorder soloists, who obviously enjoy themselves, as does the trumpeter, who is called to even greater flights of virtuosity than usual in No. 2. In No. 3 a slow movement from a G major violin sonata is interpolated between the two regular movements. No. 5 has a first-class contribution from the solo harpsichord player, Wladyslaw Klosiewicz. The balance throughout is excellent and the recording is admirably full and clear, with the cassettes matching the discs fairly closely although on each the level drops on the second side, bringing some loss in the upper range. Each of the two discs and tapes is available separately with *Concertos No. 1, 3* and *4* and *2, 5* and *6* grouped together.

The reissue of Menuhin's 1959 set (in a folding double-sleeve) on HMV's mid-priced Concert Classics label is most welcome. The recording has been slightly freshened, but has not lost its bloom. The hint of overloading from the horns in No. 1 is perhaps slightly more noticeable (especially on the cassettes, which have less upper range than the discs), but otherwise the sound is well-balanced and clean. Rarely have the *Brandenburg* rhythms been sprung more joyfully, and tempi are uncontroversially apt. The soloists are outstanding, and there is a spontaneity here that is consistently satisfying.

Of its kind, Paillard's set, on Erato, is very good indeed. It is old-fashioned in the sense that we have flutes in No. 4, for example, instead of recorders, and we are given readings in the received tradition of the 1950s rather than the questing, scholarly interpretations of Dart. But there is an admirable robustness of spirit and some vital playing here, as well as admirably vivid recording. The trumpet soloist in No. 2 is Maurice André, and the flautists in No. 4 are Jean-Pierre Rampal and Alain Marion, so that there is some distinguished playing. Another point to consider is that no concerto is split over two sides; 1 and 5 have a side each, 2 and 4 have a third, and 3 and 6 the last.

Britten made his recording in the Maltings Concert Hall not long before the serious fire there. The engineers had not quite accustomed themselves to the reverberant acoustic, and to compensate they put the microphones rather close to the players. The result is big sound that in its way goes well with Britten's interpretations, which are not quite what one would expect. The disappointing element is the lack of delicacy in the slow movements of Nos. 1, 2 4 and 6. However, the bubbling high spirits of the outer movements are hard to resist and Philip Ledger, the harpsichordist, follows the pattern he set in live Britten performances, with extra Britten-inspired elaborations a continual delight. The cassette transfer is very successful.

The Linde Consort is one of the most stylish and responsive of authentic performing groups working in Europe and in general their HMV set can be warmly recommended with its sprung rhythms and generally well-chosen tempi. The recorded sound is first-rate, but in almost every way the DG Archiv set of Trevor Pinnock is even finer.

George Malcolm's Northern Sinfonia set offers highly enjoyable, amiable performances, undoubtedly competitive in the medium price-range. They are very well recorded, although it might be felt that the balance in No. 4 makes the harpsichord too dominant. Malcolm's direction ensures rhythmic resilience throughout, and, more clearly than in many more brilliant performances, the players here convey the joy of Bach's inspiration. Much of the solo playing – for instance the oboe – is most sensitive, but by the highest international standards there is sometimes a shortfall in polish and precision.

On 9502 014/5 Marriner used an edition prepared by Thurston Dart which aims at recreating the first version of these works, long before Bach thought of sending them to the Margrave of Brandenburg. So No. 1, for example, has only three movements; there is a horn instead of a trumpet in No. 2, and maddeningly squeaky sopranino recorders in No. 4. Often the sounds are delightful, but this is not the definitive set, and Marriner's newest recording is much more successful.

Maazel's set dates from 1966 and makes a good companion for his equally lively recording of the Bach *Suites*. Those who enjoy Bach played with the fuller textures of a modern orchestra will find these alert, stylish performances solve most of the problems inherent in such an approach. The balances are cleverly manipulated, so that in No. 5 a chamber conception is maintained with the solo harpsichord coming through strongly. In No. 3 the string playing is splendidly resilient with exhilarating bravura of articulation in the brisk finale. Solo playing throughout is of high quality with Maurice André making a distinguished contribution to No. 2. The expressive balance between purity and warmth in slow movements is particularly attractive. The sound is glowingly resonant but detail is not obscured, while a high-level cassette transfer brings a close match with the discs.

Münchinger's recording is of Decca's best, and this Jubilee set also offers fresh and clean cassette transfers, as sophisticated as any available. The performances are stylish and have plenty of vitality, if not the detailed imagination of some of the finest rival versions.

Over the years Karajan's approach to Bach has been modified, at least in such relatively intimate works. These are not the inflated, over-smooth performances one might expect. The playing is highly polished, the rhythms resilient and, whatever the authenticists may say, the viola melody of the slow movement of No. 6 is a joy to the ear when played as sweetly as this. There are fresher performances than these, but they show Karajan in attractively lively mood, and the recording is full and vivid. The cassette box has a curious layout, with Nos. 1 and 5 coupled together on the first tape, and 2 and 4 backing 3 and 6 on the second. The sound is of high quality, smooth and sleek rather than sharply detailed. The transfer level is modest, but there is no appreciable lack of range.

The Contour set is recorded very acceptably, with full, if rather resonant, sound. The horns are backwardly balanced in No. 1 and inner detail is blurred by the acoustic. The performances are variable; the rhythms of the first-movement allegros are generally well-sprung though not as irresistible as in some other versions. The trumpet soloist in No. 2 is excellent and so are the flutes in No. 4. Martin Galling's continuo is sensitive, and the recording allows his contribution to make its mark. The cassettes are less refined than the discs, but at bargain price this may be worth considering.

Of the other recordings using original instruments, that by the Collegium Aureum (first issued here by BASF and now on Harmonia Mundi) is to be preferred to either of the Harnoncourt versions. Here the recorders create some engaging sounds, and No. 3 is buoyant and alert, with clean inner lines. No. 5 is strikingly fresh and clear, and although the bravura harpsichord contribution tends to dominate the texture too much the overall quality is beautiful. In No. 2 the balance does not unduly favour the trumpet, and the piquant timbres of the other instruments are freshly enjoyable.

It is a sign of the maturing art of authentic performance that Harnoncourt – a pioneer in the field – in his newest digital recording for Telefunken, now sounds so laboured. Speeds are slow, rhythms heavy. There is some expert playing, both solo and ensemble, but the artificially bright and clinically clear recording gives an aggressive projection to the music-making. The chrome tapes tend to exaggerate this still further and the very high transfer level of the first cassette brings roughness to the solo trumpet's upper partials in *Concerto No. 2*.

Harnoncourt's earlier set (reissued at medium price) was recorded in the Great Hall of the Schönbrun Palace in Vienna. The close placing of the microphones resulted in a consistently forward sound picture, with nothing like a real pianissimo at any time, even in slow movements. Generally tempi are traditional, but here and there the pacing is less convincing and the balance too has variable success. The cassettes match the discs closely, but neither this nor the later set (above) can compare with Pinnock's on DG.

The wit of Carlos in transcribing baroque music on the Moog synthesizer was never clearer than in his first essays on *Brandenburg concertos*. Over the years he completed a whole cycle (echoing the interpretative idiosyncrasies of other versions in different movements). There are diminishing returns on his wit, but there is no denying the liveliness.

Flute concertos in A min. (*from BWV 1056;* ed. Galway); *E min.* (*from BWV 1059 and BWV 35;* ed. Radeke); *Suite No. 2 in B min., BWV 1067.*

*** RCA RL/*RK* 25119 [ARL 1/*ARK 1* 2907]. Galway, Zagreb Soloists, Ninic.

The two arranged concertos (one a reconstruction) prove an admirable vehicle for James Galway, and he plays the famous slow-movement cantilena of BWV 1056 (the *F minor Harpsichord concerto*) as beautifully as one would expect. He is balanced forwardly, and is in consequence slightly larger than life. In the *Suite in B minor* the orchestral textures are a little less transparent, but generally the sound is excellent on disc, and the transfer to tape is first-class in every way, with body as well as range and detail.

(i; v) *Flute concerto in G min.* (*from BWV 1056*); (ii; iii; v) *Double concerto in D min. for violin, oboe and strings* (*from BWV 1060*); (ii; iv; v) *Triple violin concerto in D* (*from BWV 1064*).

*** Argo ZRG/*KZRC* 820 [id.]. (i) Bennett, (ii) Kaine, (iii) Miller, (iv) Thomas, Studt, (v) ASMF, Marriner.

The idea behind this disc and its companion (ZRG/*KZRC* 821 – see below) is to present Bach harpsichord concertos in reconstructions for alternative instruments that either did exist or might have existed. The purist may throw up his hands in horror, but the sparkle, charm and sensitivity of all these performances under Marriner, with soloists from among early Academy members, should silence all but the severest Bachians. For identification BWV

1056 is the *F minor Harpsichord concerto* (here for flute), BWV 1060 is the *Double harpsichord concerto in C minor* (here for violin and oboe), and BWV 1064 is the *Triple harpsichord concerto No. 3* (here for three violins). Christopher Hogwood's realizations are admirably stylish. The recording is most beautiful, and the cassette is also of excellent quality, crisper and more leonine in sound than the LP.

Flute concerto in G min. (from BWV 1056); Suite No. 2 in B min. for flute and strings, BWV 1067.

(M) *** Argo ZK 82. Bennett, ASMF, Marriner – VIVALDI: *Flute and Piccolo concertos.****

A mid-priced re-coupling of much-praised performances that is self-recommending if the chosen repertoire is required.

Harpsichord concertos Nos. 1–7, BWV 1052/8; Double harpsichord concertos Nos. 1–3, BWV 1060/2; Triple harpsichord concertos Nos. 1 and 2, BWV 1063/4; Quadruple harpsichord concerto in A min., BWV 1065.

*** DG Arc. 2723 077 (4) [id.]. Pinnock, Gilbert, Mortensen, Kraemer, E. Concert, Pinnock.

Harpsichord concertos Nos. 1 in D min.; 2 in E; 3 in D, BWV 1052/4.

*** DG Arc. 2533/*3310* 466 [id.]. Pinnock (from above).

Harpsichord concertos Nos. 4 in A; 5 in F; 6 in F; 7 in G min., BWV 1055/8.

*** DG Arc. 2533/*3310* 467 [id.]. Pinnock (from above).

A useful and often distinguished set. Trevor Pinnock plays with real panache, his scholarship tempered by excellent musicianship. There are occasions when one feels his tempi are a little too fast and unrelenting, but for the most part there is little cause for complaint. On the contrary, the performances give much pleasure and the period instruments are better played than on most issues of this kind. Two of the records are digital and have the advantage of great clarity of texture, and all four discs sound excellent. Apart from the very quick tempi (particularly in the finale of BWV 1055) which strike an unsympathetic note – and baroque violins are not to every taste – this set is thoroughly recommendable. The separate issues of the solo concertos are welcome, with their cassette equivalents, although the tape transfers are made at only a modest level and, with iron oxide rather than chrome stock in use, the upper range is less sharply focused than on the discs.

Harpsichord concerto No. 1 in D min., BWV 1052.

(M) *(*) HM 29367. Leonhardt, Coll. Aur. – C. P. E. BACH: *Double concerto.**(*)

Gustav Leonhardt's account of the *D minor Concerto* dates from the mid-1960s and shows the Dutch master at his least beguiling. Rhythms are metronomic and after a promisingly alert opening become rigid. While it would be an exaggeration to call this routine and uninspired, it gives a good deal less pleasure than many of its rivals, and for that matter Leonhardt's other records. The slow movement in particular is dull and the reading as a whole is disappointing.

Harpsichord concertos Nos. 1; 2 in E, BWV 1052/3.

(M) *** Decca Jub. JB/*KJBC* 9. Malcolm, SCO, Münchinger.

Harpsichord concertos Nos. 1 and 2; 4 in A, BWV 1052/3, and 1055.

(M) *** Ph. 9502/*7313 002* [id.]. Leppard, ECO.

Harpsichord concertos Nos. 1 and 4; 5 in F min., BWV 1056.

(M) *** DG Arc. Priv. 2547/*3347* 010 [id.]. Kirkpatrick, Lucerne Fest. Strings, Baumgartner.

Taken from Leppard's deleted set of the concertos, this medium-price Philips issue makes an outstanding recommendation, generously filled with three concertos and including the greatest, the *D minor*. The recording is excellent. The DG Archive disc is also highly recommendable. Dating from 1959/60 these recordings were models of their period, with fresh, clean performances, beautifully scaled. The Lucerne players match the liveliness of Kirkpatrick, who hits an admirable balance between expressiveness and classical detachment. Fine sound, lacking only a little in range.

On cassette George Malcolm's coupling of the first two concertos remains technically first choice, the sound being of demonstration quality in its body and clarity. Münchinger, however, is a less imaginative accompanist than either Leppard or Baumgartner, and offers only two concertos. Both the Philips and DG tape transfers are of good quality: the Philips is fresh and transparent; the DG is especially vivid in the *D minor Concerto*, but with a lower level on side two, there is slightly less presence and detail in the other two works.

Clavier concertos Nos. 1, 4 and 5, BWV 1052, 1055/6.
*** Denon Dig. 7182 [id.]. Schiff (piano), ECO, Malcolm.

If Bach's keyboard concertos are to be given on the piano rather than the harpsichord – and there are many listeners for whom the substitution is an agreeable one – they could hardly be more persuasively presented than here. The recording is beautifully balanced, the sound absolutely truthful, fresh, vivid and clean. Andras Schiff never tries to pretend that he is not using a modern piano, and the lightness of his touch and his control of colour are a constant delight to the ear. Malcolm's accompaniments are both alert and resilient, and the actual sound of the strings is perfectly in scale. Outer movements have splendid vigour and transparency; slow movements are expressive and evocative in their control of atmosphere. Schiff's decoration in the *Larghetto* of the *A major* (No. 4) is admirable, as is his simple eloquence in the famous cantilena of the *F minor Concerto* (No. 5). This is highly recommended, and it is an example of digital recording at its most impressive.

Clavier concertos Nos. 1; 7 in G min., BWV 1052 and 1058.
**(*) HMV ASD/*TC-ASD* 4312. Gavrilov, Moscow CO, Nikolayevsky.

Gavrilov, the most naturally inspired Soviet pianist of his generation, has been making tantalizingly few visits to the West and tantalizingly few records. Following his recording of the Handel *Suites* in partnership with Sviatoslav Richter he tackles more classical repertory, choosing unusually slow speeds for the middle movements but restraining his taste for espressivo. If you want Bach concertos on the piano, these versions are as fine as almost any, with first-rate playing and recording. A good cassette, with a higher level bringing a slightly crisper focus on side two (No. 7).

Harpsichord concertos Nos. 3 in D; 6 in F; 7, BWV 1054 and 1057/8.
**(*) Ph. 9500/*7300* 962 [id.]. Leppard, ECO.

These concertos are better known in other forms: the *D major* and *G minor Concertos* are the *Violin concertos in E major* and *A minor* respectively, transposed so as to accommodate the solo line within the compass of the keyboard while the *F major* is a transcription of the *Fourth Brandenburg*, the keyboard part drawing almost entirely on the solo violin line. This is probably the most interesting of the three and includes material that is new. In the slow movements of the two violin concertos Raymond Leppard adopts (not unnaturally since the harpsichord is not a singing instrument) rather quicker tempi than that favoured by many soloists, but this lends greater fluency and concentration to these readings. The balance of the recording is exemplary and does not attempt to give the solo instrument excessive prominence. The sound on the cassette is also first-class, full, clean and transparent. An interesting issue.

Clavier concerto No. 5, BWV 1056.
*** Decca SXL/*KSXC* 6952 [Lon. CS/5-7180]. Larrocha (piano), L. Sinf., Zinman – HAYDN: *Concerto in D*; MOZART: *Concerto No. 12.****

David Zinman has recorded the *D minor Concerto* (BWV 1052) for Decca with Ashkenazy, like Alicia de Larrocha here, using a piano instead of a harpsichord. His robust accompaniments, rhythmically strong and alert, are matched by Miss de Larrocha with her clean, firm articulation, and their partnership is eminently satisfying, particularly in the famous and beautiful slow movement, which is shaped with a cool and moving simplicity. The Decca recording is first-class on disc and cassette alike, and as the generous couplings include a highly recommendable version of Mozart's K.414 and a lively performance of Haydn's most famous keyboard concerto, the Bach might be regarded as a bonus.

Double harpsichord concertos Nos. 1 in C min.; 2 in C; 3 in C min., BWV 1060/2.

**(*) DG Arc. Dig. 2534/*3311* 002 [id.]. Pinnock, Gilbert, E. Concert.

Double harpsichord concertos Nos. 1 and 2; Harpsichord concerto No. 5 in F min., BWV 1056.

(M) *** Ph. 9502/*7313* 017. Leppard, Andrew Davis, ECO.

Both these issues derive from boxed sets (the Philips collection was issued in 1974 and is now withdrawn). The famous *F minor* solo concerto probably comes from a violin concerto; it and the *C minor Double concerto*, BWV 1060, based on a work envisaging two violins or a violin and oboe, occupy the first side of the Philips disc. On the reverse is the *C major Double concerto*, BWV 1061; it seems likely that this was conceived for two keyboards alone and that the strings were an afterthought in the outer movements. Leppard and Davis play with skill and flair, and the ECO shows plenty of life. It is less incisive than the English Concert under Pinnock, but the performances overall have resilience and communicate such joy in the music that criticism is disarmed. The Philips balance is first-class, the harpsichords not too forward and the strings clear and fresh. The cassette – though not transferred at the highest level – is one of Philips' best, full and clean.

The character of the Pinnock performances is altogether more robust, with the balance forward and the performances very strongly projected. The combination of period instruments and playing of determined vigour certainly makes a bold impression, but the relatively unrelaxed approach to the slow movements will not appeal to all ears. The third of the double concertos, BWV 1062, is an alternative version of the *Concerto for two violins*, BWV 1043, and though the keyboard format has a certain fascination it is no match for the original, especially in the beautiful slow movement, with – as here – squeezed accompanying chords. The lively recording is equally effective on disc and cassette.

Triple harpsichord concertos Nos. 1 in D min.; 2 in C, BWV 1063/4; Quadruple harpsichord concerto in A min., BWV 1065.

(*) DG Arc. Dig. **400 041-2; 2534/*3311* 001 [id.]. Pinnock, Gilbert, Mortensen, Kraemer, E. Concert.

(M) **(*) Decca Ser. 410 136-1 [Lon. STS 15075] (omitting BWV 1064). Malcolm, Aveling, Parsons, Preston, ECO, Leppard – C. P. E. BACH: *Concerto* **(*); MALCOLM: *Variations.****

Like the *Double concertos* above, this is taken from Pinnock's integral boxed set, and again the music was originally conceived for other instruments. *The C major Concerto*, BWV 1064, was based on a triple violin concerto, and in the *Quadruple concerto* Bach drew on Vivaldi's Op. 3/10, originally for four violins. The slightly aggressive style of the music-making – everything alert, vigorously paced and forwardly projected – emphasizes the bravura of Bach's conceptions. The sound too has striking presence and clarity, yet is not without atmosphere. The cassette matches the disc very closely. The compact disc adds to the feeling of presence and the sound has added depth, but the aggressive feeling remains and the listener is the more conscious that the balance is artificial and microphone-aided.

The alternative analogue recording reissued on Decca Serenata solves the problems of clarity and balance rather less readily, the solo instruments lacking presence. However, the recording is otherwise better integrated than the C. P. E. Bach coupling and the performances are excellent. At lower-medium price this is well worth considering for those not requiring BWV 1064.

Oboe concerto in F (from BWV 1053); Oboe d'amore concerto in A (from BWV 1055); Triple concerto in D min. for violin, oboe, flute and strings (from BWV 1063).

*** Argo ZRG/*KZRC* 821 [id.]. Black, Kaine, Bennett, ASMF, Marriner.

This second instalment of Bach harpsichord concertos in conjectural realizations for different instruments is just as attractive as the first (see above: ZRG/*KZRC* 820). Whatever the arguments about whether they could actually have existed in this form in Bach's time, there is no doubt of the charm of hearing, for example, the *Triple harpsichord concerto in D minor* arranged for violin, oboe and flute. Most beautiful is the *Oboe d'amore concerto in F*, arranged from the *E major Harpsichord concerto.* Beautiful recording quality, both on disc and on cassette.

Violin concertos Nos. 1–2, BWV 1041/2.
(M) *** Ph. Seq. 6527/*7311* 120 [id.]. Grumiaux, ECO, Leppard – HAYDN: *Violin concerto.****

Violin concertos Nos. 1 in A min.; 2 in E; Double violin concerto in D min., BWV 1041/3.
*** HMV Dig. **CDC 747011-2**; ASD/*TC-ASD* 143520-1/*4* [Ang. DS/*4XS* 37989]. Mutter, Accardo, ECO, Accardo.
*** DG Arc. Dig. **410 646–2;** 410 646-1/*4* [id.]. Standage, Wilcock, E. Concert, Pinnock.
(M) *** HMV ED 290188-1/*4*. Menuhin, Ferras, Bath Fest. CO.
(M) **(*) Ph. 9502/*7313* 016 [Quin. 7084]. Szeryng, Rybar, Winterthur Coll. Mus.
**(*) DG 138820 [id.]. D. and I. Oistrakh, VSO; RPO, Goossens.
** Ph. 9500 226/*7300 537* [id.]. Szeryng, Hasson, ASMF, Marriner.
*(**) O-L Dig. **400 080-2**; DSLO/*KDSLC* 702 [id.]. Schroder, Hirons, AcAM, Hogwood.
(B) ** Con. CC/*CCT* 7548. Ayo, Michelucci, I Musici.

(i) *Double violin concerto;* (ii) *Double concerto in D min. for violin and oboe, BWV 1060.*
(M) **(*) DG. Priv. 135082. (i) D. and I. Oistrakh, RPO, Goossens; (ii) Shann, Buchner, Mun. Bach O, Richter – VIVALDI: *Double concertos.***(*)

Double violin concerto.
*** DG Dig. 2741/*3382* 026 (2) [id.]. Stern, Mintz, Israel PO, Mehta – MOZART: *Sinfonia concertante, K.364* ⊛ VIVALDI: *Four Seasons* and *Concerto, Op. 3/10.****
(M) ** DG Priv. 2535/*3335* 176 [id.]. D. and I. Oistrakh, RPO, Goossens – BRUCH: *Concerto No. 1.***

(i) *Violin concerto No. 2;* (ii) *Violin concerto in G min.* (*from BWV 1056*)*;* (i; ii) *Double violin concerto, BWV 1043.*
*** HMV ASD/*TC-ASD* 2783 [Ang. S/*4XS* 36841]. (i) Perlman, (ii) Zukerman, ECO, Barenboim.

(i) *Violin concerto No. 2;* (i; ii) *Double violin concerto, BWV 1043;* (i; iii) *Double concerto in D min. for violin and oboe, BWV 1060.*
**(*) HMV Dig. ASD/*TCC-ASD* 4207 [Ang. DS 37896]. (i) Menuhin: (ii) Li; (iii) Camden, with LSO.

Double violin concerto, BWV 1043; Double concerto for violin and oboe, BWV 1060.
** CBS Dig. 37278/*40-* [id.]. Zukerman, Stern, Killmer, St Paul CO, James – VIVALDI: *L'estro armonico: Double concerto.***

Double concerto in D min. for violin and oboe, BWV 1060.
(M) *** HMV SXLP/*TC-SXLP* 30294 [Ang. S 36103]. Menuhin, Goossens, Bath Fest. CO – HANDEL and VIVALDI: *Concertos.****

Double concerto for violin and oboe in D min., BWV 1060; Triple concerto in A min. for flute, violin and harpsichord, BWV 1044.
** HMIC 065 99639. Maier, Hucke, Kuijken, Van Asperen, Coll. Aur.

Readers will have to determine their own priorities in making a choice from the various collections listed above. The two greatest violin concertos, the *E major* and the *Double concerto*, are also included in two of the miscellaneous compilations, notably the Perlman/Zukerman HMV LP, which should suit those who find the Mutter/Accardo version of the *Double concerto* too overtly expressive in the slow movement, while the Stern/Minz version of the latter work is included in a two-disc concert, recorded live in Israel.

It is not currently fashionable to play Bach with the degree of romantic warmth that Anne-Sophie Mutter adopts, but her range of tone as well as the imagination of her phrasing is extremely compelling. Her performance of the slow movement of the *E major Concerto* is finer than any other version, with marvellous shading within a range of hushed tones. Accardo's accompaniment here (as throughout this collection) is splendidly stylish and alert, as the opening of the first movement of *BWV 1042* readily shows. In principle the slow movement of the *Double concerto* – where Accardo takes up his bow to become a solo partner, scaling down his timbre – is too slow, but the result could hardly be more beautiful, helped by warm EMI recording which gives richness and body to the small ECO string band. The soloists are rather forwardly balanced, but in all other respects this issue is technically outstanding and the equivalent cassette (though not chrome) is one of EMI's best. The level drops slightly on side two, but the sound remains full and vivid. The CD is strikingly fresh and clear and gives the artists great presence.

If you want the three favourite Bach *Violin concertos* on original instruments, then Pinnock's disc is the one to go for. Rhythms are crisp and lifted at nicely chosen speeds – not too fast for slow movements – but, as so often with authentic performances of violin concertos, the edge will not please everyone. Good, clear recording.

Menuhin's (1960) record was made when he was in excellent technical form. He directs the orchestra besides appearing as principal soloist and it is in the accompaniments that these accounts fall slightly short, with outer movements not as rhythmically resilient as Accardo's. Nevertheless Menuhin's playing still gives much pleasure, with its balance of humanity and classical sympathy. Ferras matches his timbre to Menuhin's perfectly in the *Double concerto* and their playing cannot be faulted on minor points of style. HMV have freshened the recording, losing something in bass resonance, but providing a sound picture that belies the record's age.

Perlman and Zukerman with their friend and colleague, Barenboim, are inspired to give a magic performance of the great *Double concerto*, one in which their artistry is beautifully matched in all its intensity. The slow movement in particular has rarely sounded so ravishing on record. Perlman is also most impressive in the slow movement of the *E major* solo *Violin concerto*, but neither he nor Zukerman in the *G minor Concerto* (arranged from the *F minor Harpsichord concerto* with its sublime *Arioso* slow movement) is quite so impressive without the challenge of the other. Nonetheless, with fine accompaniment from the ECO, this is a Bach record to cherish. There is a good cassette.

Grumiaux's performances of the two solo concertos come from 1964, but the warmly resonant recording does not sound dated. This playing from one of the most musical and sensitive soloists of our time is extremely satisfying. It has a purity of line and an expressive response that communicate very positively and the crisply stylish accompaniments under Leppard have striking buoyancy. Try the opening of the *E major Concerto* to sample the rhythmic spring of Bach at his most communicative. Those for whom the coupling is suitable will find this highly recommendable, for the Haydn performance is no less memorable. The excellent cassette matches the disc closely.

Menuhin's newer collection omits the A minor solo concerto and substitutes the *Double concerto for violin and oboe* which he also recorded successfully in the 1960s with Leon Goossens (see below). Technically his playing on the new record is not as smooth as in earlier versions, yet his artistic sensibility remains as strong as ever and he is at his most sympathetic here, challenged in one double concerto by the bright yet restrained artistry of Anthony Camden, principal oboe of the LSO, and on the other by Jin Li, from Shanghai, only 12 at the time of the recording and training at the Menuhin School in Surrey. Menuhin early in his recording career partnered George Enesco in the *Double violin concerto*, and though his individuality was more marked than that of Jin Li, the two interpretations share a warm, natural expressiveness that transcends fashion. The same might be said too of the solo *Violin concerto*. Warm but clear recording to match and an identically bright chrome cassette.

The reissue of Szeryng's performances with the Winterthur group, dating from the mid-1960s, can be recommended at medium price. Szeryng plays the two solo concertos with dignity and classical feeling; the slow movements are particularly fine. Peter Rybar proves an excellent partner in the *Double concerto*. The accompaniments are sympathetic and lively, and the sound (if rather resonant) is fresh and full, the tape focus only fractionally less clean than the disc.

Szeryng's later record with the ASMF under Marriner has the advantage of a sumptuous, modern recording, which produces an excellent balance between the soloists and orchestra and a warm spread of sound. But in spontaneity the performances show no advance on the earlier versions and in depth of feeling and understanding they do not displace the finest of the rival accounts.

The partnership of Stern and Mintz in the *Double concerto* was achieved by making a live digital recording (of high quality) at the Huberman Festival in Israel in December 1982. The performance is essentially classical in feeling with an attractive element of restraint in the slow movement, which is nevertheless played most beautifully. Mehta directs a lively and sympathetic accompaniment and the performance carries the full intensity of a real concert, yet not at the sacrifice of polish. The chrome cassette matches the disc in quality – this is altogether an admirable set.

The styles of David and Igor Oistrakh are different enough to provide a suitable contrast of timbre in their performance of the *Double concerto*; at the same time the musical partnership provided by father and son is an understanding one. The performance is available coupled to sympathetic versions of the solo concertos on an early full-priced issue. But with its somewhat dated sound this issue, for all its merits, seems less desirable than the Menuhin collection. However, the *Double concerto* is also available on Privilege, coupled either to Bruch, or more appropriately to Vivaldi and the *Concerto for violin and oboe*, BWV 1060. The star here is the oboist, Edgar Shann. The violin soloist, Otto Buchner, supports him capably if with rather less distinction. The sound in both works is dated, but fully acceptable when the somewhat fizzy treble is smoothed.

With authentic sound uncompromisingly abrasive and speeds generally brisk and inflexible, the Academy of Ancient Music's version of the *Violin concertos* is the opposite of Mutter's expressive approach. For some it apparently stands as a refreshing revelation, but sample the slow movement of the *Double concerto* – like a siciliana – before you buy. Bright and clear recording to match with the edge of string sound unrelenting. There is little to choose between LP and cassette, while the compact disc with its silent background puts the music-making into even sharper relief.

On the bargain-priced Contour issue it is Felix Ayo who plays the *E major Concerto*, and with rather more flair than his colleague Roberto Michelucci shows in the *A minor*; but the two players join for a spirited account of the *Double concerto*. The clear, unaffected approach to all three works gives pleasure, and the only snag is the reverberant acoustic, which rarely allows the harpsichord continuo to come through with any bite. But the sound itself is pleasing, and this is fair value.

Zukerman – who is the music director of the St Paul Chamber Orchestra – has made this group a fair rival in its musical achievement to the Minneapolis Orchestra in the other city of the yoked pair of 'twins'. Unfortunately the recording of his CBS digital collection underlines the weightiness of the bass which is uncomfortably heavy for Bach. Solo work is a delight, but there are better versions of all these concertos.

Menuhin's earlier version of the *Concerto for violin and oboe*, however, remains very attractive. This recording dates from 1962 but wears its years lightly, although the oboe is too backwardly balanced in the outer movements. But this is a vintage performance with both Menuhin and Leon Goossens on top form. The slow movement cantilena is most beautifully played. The couplings (especially the Handel) are highly recommendable, and the cassette transfer is immaculate, matching the disc closely.

From Maier and his Collegium Aureum players come enjoyably spontaneous performances using original instruments within a warmly reverberant acoustic so that nothing sounds acerbic. The slow movements are well judged and the balance is convincing. The cassette can be recommended alongside the disc.

Triple concerto in A min. for flute, violin and harpsichord, BWV 1044.

*** DG Arc. 2533 410 [id./*3310 410*]. Preston,

Standage, Pinnock, E. Concert – *Suite No. 2*.**(*)

Stephen Preston and Simon Standage both use baroque instruments and there is a suitable matching harpsichord timbre. All the artists play with genuine warmth and plenty of vitality too. Tempi are well judged and there is no want of style. This concerto is derived from borrowed material (the A minor *Prelude and fugue*, BWV 894, and the *Trio sonata*, BWV 527, both for organ) but it could not sound more persuasive than it does here.

Violin concerto No. 1 in A min., BWV 1041; Violin concerto in D min., BWV 1052 (alternative version of *Harpsichord concerto*); (i) *Double concerto in D min. for violin and oboe, BWV 1060.*

*** HMV ASD 3076 [Ang. S/*4XS* 37076]. Perlman (violin), ECO, Barenboim, (i) with Black.

These are performances of genuine excellence, and they are beautifully recorded. Perlman plays Bach with great naturalness of feeling, and his account of the *A minor Concerto* can scarcely be faulted, even if his tempi will not be to all tastes. The *D minor Concerto* is a 'restoration' of the keyboard concerto in the same key, while the companion concerto is a transcription of the *C minor Concerto for two harpsichords*. Outer movements tend to be fastish and slow movements expressive and eloquent. Barenboim provides most sympathetic support in all three works, and Neil Black is the distinguished oboist in the double concerto. The engineers provide a warm and agreeable ambience that preserves an excellent balance between soloists and orchestra.

The Musical Offering, BWV 1079.

*** Ph. 9500 585 [id.]. ASMF, Marriner.

*** EMI 1C-065 43045. Linde Cons.

(M) **(*) Decca Ser. SA 29 [Lon. STS 15063]. SCO, Münchinger.

*(*) DG Arc. 2533 422 [id.]. Col. Mus. Ant., Goebel.

Neville Marriner uses his own edition and instrumentation: strings with three solo violins, solo viola and a solo cello; a flute and organ and harpsichord. He places the three-part *Ricercar* at the beginning (scored for organ) and the six-part *Ricercar* at the very end, scored for strings. As the centrepiece comes the *Trio sonata* (flute, violin and continuo) and on either side the canons. A snag is that this arrangement requires a turn-over in the middle of the *Trio sonata*. Thurston Dart advocated playing the three-part *Ricercar* on the fortepiano (as it was probably heard in Potsdam). The actual performance here is of high quality, though some of the playing is a trifle bland. It is, however, excellently recorded and generally must be numbered among the most successful accounts of the work.

Hans-Martin Linde draws on the thinking of the American scholar, Ursula Kirkendale, whose conclusion favours the same sequence of movements as that adopted by Spitta, not that this is necessarily a first consideration since, with a little effort, the listener can exercise his own preferences in playing the disc. Generally speaking, Linde is as stylish and accomplished as any of his rivals, and he and his six colleagues are to be preferred to the Musica Antiqua, Köln, and have a warmer sound too.

Münchinger's latest version of this score – now economically re-issued on Serenata – is strikingly well recorded. It has excellent presence and detail. Moreover the performance itself is far from negligible; indeed there is playing of genuine breadth and eloquence here, particularly in the *Trio sonata*. The canons are grouped together and come off well. Not that this is entirely free from the heavy-handedness that sometimes disfigures Münchinger's art, but the performance has many fine qualities and its cost is reasonable.

There are some good things on the Archive issue. The *Ricercars* open and close the work, but, unlike Marriner, Reinhard Goebel places the canons together and follows them with the *Trio sonata*, in which there is no side-turn. The *Ricercars* are played on the harpsichord by Henk Boum, an impressive artist who is somewhat austere in making no registration changes, but has a strong grasp of the architecture. The six-part *Ricercar* is particularly fine, and the canons are also very successful. However, the centrepiece of the *Musical Offering* is the *Trio sonata*, and this reading is simply too mannered and self-conscious (particularly in the slow movement) to be recommended.

Orchestral suites Nos. 1–4, BWV 1066/9.
(M) *** Ph. 6768 028/*7699 165* (2) [id.]. ECO, Leppard.
*** Argo ZRG/*KZRC* 687/8 [id.]. ASMF, Marriner.
*** HMV SLS/*TC-SLS* 143484-3/9 (2) [Ang. SB 3943]. Linde Cons., Linde.
**(*) DG Arc. 2723 072 (2)/*3310 175* [id.]. E. Concert, Pinnock.
**(*) HM Dig. 1C 165 99930/1. Petite Bande, Kuijken.
**(*) Ph. 6769 012 (2)/*7699 087* [id.]. ASMF, Marriner.
(M) **(*) HM 20353/4. Coll. Aur.
(M) ** Tel. DX6. 35046 (2) [2635 046]. VCM, Harnoncourt.
(M) (***) EMI mono 2C 151 03960/1. Busch Chamber Players.

Suites Nos. 1 and 3.
**(*) DG Arc. 2533/*3310* 411 [id.]. E. Concert, Pinnock.

Suite No. 2 (for flute and strings).
(*) DG Arc. 2533 410 [id./*3310 410*]. Preston, E. Concert, Pinnock – *Triple concerto.**
(M) **(*) Decca Ser. SA/*KSC* 13 [Lon. STS 15561]. Rampal, SCO, Münchinger – PERGOLESI: *Flute concertos.****

Suites Nos. 2–3.
*** Argo ZRG/*KZRC* 948 [id.]. ASMF, Marriner.
(M) * DG Priv. 2535/*3335* 138. [id.]. Berlin PO, Karajan.

Suites Nos. 2–3; Cantata No. 12: Sinfonia; Cantata No. 131: Sonata.
(M) ** Decca VIV/*KVIC* 8 [Lon. STS 15541/5-]. SRO, Ansermet.

Leppard's exhilarating performances have never been surpassed. In this mid-priced reissue, with first-rate sound, they cannot be bettered, sparklingly played and brilliantly recorded. There is excellent solo playing throughout, not least the sprightly and elegant flute of Richard Adeney in No. 2, while the less familiar No. 4 with its spirited wind and brass contributions is more strongly characterized than usual. Overall, Leppard's conception balances gravitas and elegance with spirited baroque ebullience and the recording, on both disc and cassette, is naturally balanced and projected.

The Argo set – also dating from the beginning of the 1970s – remains at premium price and to emphasize this an additional coupling of the two most popular *Suites*, also at full-price, was made in the autumn of 1983. Certainly the performances are highly characterized and they are slightly more vividly recorded than the Philips issue, with lively cassettes to match the discs, although in the separate issue of *Suites Nos. 2* and *3* (KZRC 687) the transfer of No. 3 is rather rough. Great care went into their preparation with Thurston Dart's imaginative, scholarly mind searching always for a compromise between the truth of the original score and what is sensible in terms of modern re-creative performance. Hence not only the ornamentation comes into the picture but even the lightening of the scoring itself to favour the baroque practice of altering the colouring on repeats. This is especially noticeable in *Suites 3* and *4* in the use of the trumpets (which Thurston Dart tells us in his excellent notes did not appear in Bach's original). The set is a splendid memorial to Dart himself, and because the music-making is so exuberant and alive, it is the most joyous memorial; no one could ask for better. Indeed the playing throughout is quite marvellous, expressive without being romantic, buoyant and vigorous and yet retaining the music's strength and weight. William Bennett is the agile and sensitive flute soloist in the *Second Suite*, even providing decoration in the famous *Badinerie*, with splendid bravura. Throughout the performances the baroque spirit is realized at its most colourful.

The Linde Consort's version on EMI's Reflexe label makes an excellent choice for anyone wanting a performance on original instruments. The string style is less abrasive than that of the English Concert on the rival DG Archiv version, and the rhythmic spring in allegros generally lighter, with a preference for fast speeds. Linde – himself the flute soloist in No. 2 – encourages a hint of stringendo in the virtuoso display of the final *Badinerie*, yet the grandeur of the music is not missed either, for against a warm acoustic the intimate scale readily accommodates the panoply of trumpets in Nos. 3 and 4. The famous *Air*, on the fast side, is pointed and elegant. Good warm recording. The tapes are not recommended.

Trevor Pinnock boldly encourages a more abrasive style than most in the Bach *Suites*, with string tone which within its lights is beautifully controlled, but which to the unprepared listener could well sound disagreeable, with a bright edge to the squeezed vibrato-less timbre. Any feeling of baroque grandeur of the kind Marriner conveys in his Argo set is minimized here. Nevertheless, with a refreshingly alert approach to each movement in turn – not least to the slow introductions, which, as one would expect, are anything but ponderous – these are invigorating performances, beautifully sprung and splendidly recorded on disc. In the *B minor Suite*, although there could be more contrast in feeling, there is no sense that reverence for supposed authenticity is stifling musical spontaneity. When these performances first appeared the couplings seemed unnecessarily complicated, but now they have been reissued as a set, with a matching double-length tape which offers all four works at what is in effect half-price. Unfortunately the transfer is made at a very low level and the substance and range are diminished.

Kuijken with La Petite Bande shows that authentic performance need not be acidly over-abrasive. Set against a warm acoustic – more comfortable for the trumpet-sound if not always helpful to clarity – these are brightly attractive performances with their just speeds and well-sprung rhythms. Solo work is most stylish, though ensemble is not always immaculate. An excellent alternative to Pinnock and the English Concert if you are looking for performances on original instruments. Issued on a single, extended-length cassette, the tape transfer is generally satisfactory, the textures fresh and clear, although the trumpets offer slight problems in the *Third Suite*.

Fine as it is, Marriner's second recording of the *Suites* is no match for his first. The movements where he has changed his mind – for example, the famous *Air* from the *Suite No. 3*, which is here ponderously slow – are almost always less convincing, and that reflects an absence of the very qualities of urgency and spontaneity which made the earlier Argo version so enjoyable. The recording is refined, but in some ways less aptly balanced than the Argo. That set remains a better choice for those not insisting on period instruments.

In contrast to the Pinnock set, the approach of the Collegium Aureum, also using original instruments, is comparatively expressive; the famous *Air*, for example, is restrained but not without feeling. Tempi are often similar to modern practice, although the slow introductions are not as crisply dotted and the pulse is less measured. The woodwind instruments make some delightful baroque sounds, especially in Nos. 1 and 4. With the early trumpets, however, one has to accept moments of poor intonation in the upper register. But despite any reservations, this set is enjoyable for stopping short of the ruthless authenticity of Pinnock and avoiding the heavy German rhythmic pulse of Münchinger.

Harnoncourt sounds altogether more academic. His approach is clean and literal, and the acoustic of the Telefunken recording is brighter and harder than that given to the Collegium Aureum. The result is not always sweet to the ear, and the prevailing mezzo forte becomes monotonous. But these are livelier, more compelling performances than those of the *Brandenburgs* on the same label. Slow introductions are taken fast in allemande-style, minuets are slow and – hardest point to accept – there is no concession to expressiveness in the *Air* from *Suite No. 3*. The *Sarabande* of No. 2 may sound a little disconcerting with its use of notes inégales, but the *Gigue* of No. 3, and for that matter all the fast movements and the fugues, are splendidly alert. Good Telefunken recording.

The Busch performances come from the mid-1930s and serve as a reminder that those 'inauthentic' years have something to teach us. For all the period limitations, string portamenti, sweet-toned vibrato, piano continuo and so on, these readings have a radiance and a joy in music-making that completely transcend their sonic shortcomings – which, it is worth noting, are remarkably few, given the provenance. There is a naturalness of musical expression, a marvellous musicality from Marcel Moyse, the flautist in the *B minor Suite*, and a richness of feeling on the part of all concerned that make this a special document. One wonders whether future music-lovers coming to the standard versions in our present catalogue from the vantage-point of five decades on will discover as much joy and illumination in Marriner, Leppard, Pinnock and others as we can in the Adolf Busch Chamber Players.

Rampal's first-class playing in the *Second suite* was one of the highlights of Münchinger's 1962 complete set, at present out of the catalogue. With bright Decca recording this makes a useful coupling for some attractive Pergolesi *Flute concertos*.

Ansermet's Bach is warm-hearted, not for purists but not seriously unstylish. The performances do not lack freshness, although the full body of strings tends to swamp the continuo. There is some nimble and elegant solo flute playing from André Pepin in the *B minor Suite*. The bonuses are not memorable: Roger Reversy, the oboe soloist in the *Sinfonia* from *Cantata No. 12*, is accomplished but phrases rather stiffly. The sound remains good, and there is little to choose between disc and cassette.

Karajan seems to think of Bach harmonically rather than contrapuntally, and the rich, glossy textures are matched by similarly unstylish rhythms. Although there is some superb flute playing in the *B minor Suite*, this cannot be recommended.

CHAMBER AND INSTRUMENTAL MUSIC

(Unaccompanied) *Cello suites Nos. 1–6, BWV 1007/12.*

*** HMV Dig. SLS/*TC-SLS* 107772-3/5 (3). Tortelier.

(M) *** HMV SLS 798 (3). Tortelier.

*** Ph. 6770 005 (3) [id.]. Gendron.

Recorded in the reverberant acoustic of the Temple Church in London, Tortelier's 1983 performances of the *Suites* present clear contrasts with his version of twenty years earlier. His approach remains broadly romantic by today's purist standards, but this time the rhythms are steadier, the command greater, with the preludes of each suite strongly characterized to ensnare the attention even in simple chattering passagework. Some will prefer a drier acoustic than this, but the digital sound is first-rate, with little to choose in quality between the discs and the excellent XDR cassettes.

In his earlier set issued in 1971, Tortelier's rhythmic grip is strong, his technique masterly and his intonation true. Yet at the same time there are touches of reticence – one is almost tempted to say inhibition: it is as if he is consciously resisting the temptation to give full rein to his musical and lyrical instinct. Comparing his *Sarabande* from the *D minor Suite* (No. 2) with Casals leaves no doubts as to the greater freedom, range and inwardness of the latter. Tortelier sounds dull by comparison. Nonetheless the faster movements are splendidly played and the prelude to the *E flat major Suite* finds him at his most imposing. The set is good value and the recording, though made in the first half of the 1960s, is extremely fine.

No one artist holds all the secrets in this repertoire, but few succeed in producing such consistent beauty of tone as Maurice Gendron. He has, of course, the advantage of an excellent and truthful recording. His phrasing is unfailingly musical, and although Roger Fiske, writing in *Gramophone*, spoke of the sobriety of these readings (save for No. 6, which he thought stunning), their restraint and fine judgement command admiration. They do not displace Tortelier or Fournier (DG – at present out of the catalogue) but can certainly be recommended alongside them, particularly as the recorded sound is so natural and vivid. The surfaces, too, are quite impeccable. No one has come near to the depth and imagination shown by Casals in his pre-war pioneering set, now transferred to mono LP and very much in a class of its own (HMV RLS 712).

Flute sonatas Nos. 1 in B min.; 2 in E flat; 3 in A; 4 in C; 5 in E min.; 6 in E, BWV 1030/5; Partita in A min., BWV 1013.

*** CRD CRD 1014/5. Preston, Pinnock, Savall.

(M) *(*) ASV ACD/*ZCACD* 251 (2). Bennett, Malcolm.

Using an authentic one-key baroque flute, Stephen Preston plays Bach's flute music with a rare delicacy. By its nature the instrument can only cope with a limited dynamic range, but Preston is finely expressive, not least in the splendid *Partita* for solo flute. Of the works with continuo the two minor-key sonatas are particularly fine. A reconstruction of the first movement of the *A major*, where bars are missing, is included. Fine continuo playing and well-balanced recording.

The ASV set gives us the sonatas in expertly turned performances by William Bennett and George Malcolm. The flautist looms much larger in the aural picture than does the harpsichord, and his tone has a rich bloom with no want of the expressive vibrato that is now much out of favour in this repertoire. Rather more disturbing perhaps is the absence of any cello continuo support for the bass line in the first three sonatas. The playing is enormously accomplished and the traditional approach of these artists will not inhibit the pleasure of many collectors. All six sonatas are conveniently accommodated on one single cassette whose quality is very good. Not a first choice all the same.

Guitar transcriptions: *Chorale: Wachet auf* (from *Cantata No. 140*); *English suite No. 2: Bourrée. English suite No. 3: Gavotte; Musette. French suite No. 5: Gigue; French suite No. 6: Allemande. Fugue à la gigue, BWV 577. Italian concerto, BWV 971: 1st movement. Pastorale, BWV 587: Adagio. Violin sonata No. 4, BWV 1017: Adagio. Trio, BWV 1027a. Trio sonata No. 6, BWV 530*
*(*) CBS Dig. 37250/*40*- [id.]. Williams, Hurford.

Although the casting is illustrious, this is in the last resort not a very stylish collection. Lively movements tend to be more effective than slow ones. But all the music is attractive and perhaps such a programme will tempt a wider public than usual. The sound is good on both disc and chrome cassette, although the latter needs a bass cut.

Guitar transcriptions: *Prelude in C min., BWV 999; Prelude, fugue and allegro in E flat, BWV 998; Lute suite No. 1 in E min., BWV 996; Sarabande in E min. Unaccompanied violin sonata No. 1 in G min., BWV 1001: Fugue in A min. Partita No. 1 in B min., BWV 1002: Sarabande and Double. Partita No. 2 in D min., BWV 1004: Chaconne.*
(B) *** Con. CC/*CCT* 7519. Yepes.

Those who enjoy Bach on the guitar will find this a distinguished and enjoyable recital. Narciso Yepes is on top form and brings all the music to life compellingly, without romantic exaggeration. The programme includes the famous *Chaconne*, which is splendidly projected here. The sound is first-class, and the cassette transfer has only marginally less life at the top than the disc.

Lute music transcribed for guitar

Suites Nos. 1 in E min.; 2 in C min., BWV 996/7; 3 in A min., BWV 995; 4 in E, BWV 1006a; Prelude, fugue and allegro in E flat, BWV 998; Prelude in C min., BWV 999; Fugue in A min., BWV 1000.
*** CBS 79203/*40*- [M2-33510]. Williams (guitar).

John Williams's rhythmic vitality and sense of colour tell. His is a first-class set in every way; the control of line and the ornamentation are equally impressive, and the presence of the recording is in no doubt. There is also a good cassette transfer.

Lute suites Nos. 1–2, BWV 996/7.
*** DG Dig. 410 643-1/*4*. Söllscher (guitar).

Göran Söllscher is a highly musical player; his style is fluent and there is judicious use of light and shade. The flowing opening of the *C minor Suite* (*No. 2*) is particularly attractive. He is realistically recorded too and the effect is suitably intimate. This is consistently sensitive playing.

Lute suites Nos. 1 in E min., BWV 996; 2 in C min., BWV 997. Trio sonatas Nos. 1 in E flat, BWV 525; 5 in C, BWV 529 (ed. Bream). *Fugue in A* (trans. from BWV 1001); *Prelude in C min.* (trans. D min.), *BWV 999.*
**(*) RCA RL 42378 (2) [(d) LSC 2896]. Bream, Malcolm.

This compilation comes from records made in the late 1960s. The first disc includes two of the *Lute suites*, played with great subtlety and mastery on the guitar; the second contains arrangements for lute and harpsichord of the *Trio sonatas in E flat* and *C* for organ. One may prefer the latter on the original instrument, but these transcriptions still give pleasure, for they are elegantly played and crisply recorded. Perhaps the harpsichord is a little less well defined in the bass register than is ideal.

Lute arrangements: *Fugue in G min., BWV 1000; Prelude in C min., BWV 999; Prelude, fugue and allegro in E flat, BWV 998; Suite* (arr. from *Partita for unaccompanied violin*) *in E, BWV 1006a.*
(M) ** DG Arc. Priv. 2547/*3347* 063. Yepes.

Yepes uses a baroque lute. He plays very musically and there is a good deal to enjoy here as the recording is excellent. However, this collection does not have quite the degree of lively communication of his earlier programme recorded on the guitar – see above.

(*Organ*) *Trio sonatas Nos. 1 in E flat, BWV 525; 5 in C, BWV 529* (arr. for lute and harpsichord).
(M) **(*) RCA Gold GL/*GK* 14139 [AGL/*AGK1* 4139]. Bream, Malcolm – VIVALDI: Sonatas.**(*)

These recordings date from the late 1960s and are arrangements of the *Trio sonatas in E flat* and *C* for organ. One may prefer the latter on the original instrument but these transcriptions still give pleasure. The sound is good with a matching chrome tape.

Trio sonatas Nos. 1–4, BWV 1036/9.
*** DG Arc. 2533 448. Col. Mus. Ant.

Polished accounts of all four pieces. The *G major*, BWV 1038, is thought by some authorities to be a student work by Carl Philipp Emanuel Bach, and the *C major*, BWV 1037, is likewise variously attributed to Bach and to his pupil Johann Gottlieb Goldberg. However, the *G major*, BWV 1039, is indisputably by Bach, but the *D minor* is again probably by Wilhelm Friedemann or Carl Philipp Emanuel. In any event, these are lively and eminently well-recorded accounts that can be confidently recommended. No other disc currently on the market assembles all four together.

Trio sonatas Nos. 3 and 4 in G, BWV 1038/9; The Musical Offering, BWV 1079: Trio sonata in C.
*** RCA RL/*RK* 25280. Galway, Kyung-Wha Chung, Moll, Welsh.

With two such individual artists as Galway and Chung, both given to highly personal expressiveness, you might expect their Bach to be too wilful, but not so. These are refreshing performances of the two *Trio sonatas* with flute and of the comparable sonata from *The Musical Offering*, which some may even count slightly understated. The recording is fresh and clean on disc and cassette alike.

Trio sonata No. 4, BWV 1039.
*** O-L DSLO 518 [id.]. Preston, McGegan, Ryan, Pleeth, Hogwood – C. P. E. BACH: *Trio sonata* ***; W. F. BACH: *Duo* etc.**

The *Trio sonata in G major* is probably better known in its alternative form for viola da gamba and continuo. Stephen Preston and Nicholas McGegan, playing period instruments, leave one in no doubt as to its expressive power, particularly in the chromatic lines of the slow movement. They are excellently recorded, and C. P. E. Bach's *E major Trio sonata* is a valuable coupling.

Viola da gamba sonatas Nos. 1–3, BWV 1027/9.
(M) *** HM 22225. Kuijken, Leonhardt.
*** CBS 37794/*40*- [id.]. Yo Yo Ma (cello), Cooper.
(M) *(*) Ph. 9502 003 [id.]. Cervera, Puyana.

The three sonatas for viola da gamba and harpsichord come from Bach's Cöthen period, and the G minor is arguably the highest peak in this particular literature. Wieland Kuijken and Gustav Leonhardt are both sensitive and scholarly, their tempi well judged and their artistry in good evidence. Their phrasing is finely shaped and natural, and there is no sense of the relentless flow that can so often impair the faster movements. The slow movement of the G minor is very slow but the tempo obviously springs from musical conviction and as a result *feels* right. This is the best account of these sonatas to have appeared on the market for some years, and the recorded sound is faithful; it may be too immediate for some tastes, but adjustment of the controls gives a satisfactory result.

Yo Yo Ma plays with great eloquence and natural feeling and an inborn understanding of this music. His tone is warm and refined, and his technical command remains as ever irreproachable. Kenneth Cooper is a splendid partner, too, so readers who want the cello rather than the viola da gamba need not hesitate. The balance favours Yo Yo Ma a little but not at the expense of clarity. The colour of the cello does not blend with the harpsichord as naturally as a gamba and there is a case still to be made for the modern piano as a more appropriate partner. The chrome cassette is not quite as well focused as the disc on side one (where the harpsichord lacks presence), but on side two the level rises and with it comes extra definition.

The performances by Marçal Cervera and Rafael Puyana are much less attractive. These works need cleaner, more stylish playing if they are not to sound muddy and dull. The recording in this mid-priced Philips reissue is good but not outstanding.

(Unaccompanied) *Violin sonatas Nos. 1–3, BWV 1001, 1003 and 1005; Violin partitas Nos. 1–3, BWV 1002, 1004 and 1006.*
*** ASV ALHB 306 (3). Shumsky.
*** DG 270 047/*3371 030* (3) [id.]. Milstein.
**(*) Uni. Dig. DKP 9010/12. Ricci.
* Ph. 6769/*7654* 053 (3) [id.]. Kremer.

Partitas Nos. 2 in D min.; 3 in E.
**** DG 2530 730. Milstein.

Partita No. 2; Sonata No. 3 in C.
** Decca SXL 6721 [Lon. CS 6940]. Kyung-Wha Chung.

Shumsky's clean attack and tight vibrato, coupled with virtuosity of the highest order, make for strong and refreshing readings, full of flair and imagination. If you want big-scale playing of Bach, this supplies the need splendidly, though the dry, close acoustic reduces the scale and undermines tenderness. Nevertheless this now makes a clear first choice in this repertoire.

Every phrase is beautifully shaped and keenly alive in the Milstein set; there is a highly developed feeling for line, and no want of virtuosity. Milstein is excellently served by the DG engineers, and the sound is natural and lifelike. The tape set is outstanding too.

Ricci gives good old-fashioned readings. Speeds in movements both fast and slow are measured, the tone is romantically ripe and full, but the expressive style is not exaggerated. The recordings were made without editing. Occasional flaws occur, but they are generally balanced out by the warm concentration. Excellent sound, with the violin tone given bloom against a comfortably reverberant acoustic.

Kyung-Wha Chung is so commanding an artist that one hardly expects anything other than total mastery. However, the natural warmth of her approach here brings a feeling of romanticism that will not appeal to all ears. There are extremes of dynamics, touches of rubato that some will not find convincing and, for all the technical assurance, some traces of less than secure intonation, though these are rare. She is superbly recorded by the Decca engineers.

Gidon Kremer is an impressive player and there are no doubts about the sheer facility and accuracy of his readings, nor the technical excellence of the recordings. But he conveys little sense of musical enjoyment, dispatching the faster movements with an unfeeling and joyless brilliance. There is also an aggressive edge to his double-stopping and a general want of imagination in matters of phrasing. The discs are excellently produced and include a reproduction of the autograph MS. All the same, this set gives only limited pleasure. The layout on two cassettes, against three discs, is ill-conceived, as works are split between sides. The high-level transfer gives the violin presence, although there is a degree of fierceness on the first tape (especially on side two).

Violin and harpsichord sonatas Nos. 1–6, BWV 1014/9.
*** HM IC 151 1998203. Kuijken, Leonhardt.
*** EMI 2C 181 43236/7. Menuhin, Malcolm, Gauntlett.

Sigiswald Kuijken uses a baroque violin, and both he and Gustav Leonhardt give us playing of rare eloquence. This issue is an admirable instance of the claims of authenticity and musical feeling pulling together rather than apart. The violinist does not shrink from an intelligent use of vibrato, and both artists demonstrate in every bar that scholarship is at their service and not an inhibiting task-master. As so often from this source, the harpsichord is extremely well recorded and the texture is lighter and cleaner than in many issues of this repertoire. This version is unlikely to be superseded for a very long time.

Menuhin, who is so often at his best in Bach, made his recording in the early 1960s, when he was still in peak form. He achieves a splendid partnership with Malcolm, and Ambrose Gauntlett on the viola da gamba provides an imaginative continuo, not always doubling the bass part of the harpsichord – the keyboard instrument usually has two contrapuntal lines – but resting now and then or adjusting the line to suit his instrument in true eighteenth-century tradition. The performances have that special combination of humanity and classical feeling for which Menuhin is famous, and the recording is truthful and well balanced.

KEYBOARD MUSIC

(All played on the harpsichord unless otherwise stated)

The Art of Fugue, BWV 1080.
*** HM IC 165 1997933. Leonhardt.

Versions of *The Art of Fugue* in instrumental transcriptions of various kinds as well as on the organ have not been rare, but harpsichord performances are few. Gustav Leonhardt argues most convincingly in the leaflet accompanying this set that a 'glance at the compass of the alto voice (down to B, second octave below middle C) in the first twelve fugues suffices to make sure that none of Bach's nevertheless richly varied ensemble groups can be used for the *Art of Fugue*'. The notation of polyphonic textures in full as opposed to short score was common in the seventeenth and eighteenth centuries (and even as early as 1580), and it has only been in the twentieth century that musicians have taken *The Art of Fugue* as 'ensemble music'. Leonhardt uses a copy by Martin Skowroneck of a Dulcken harpsichord of 1745, a responsive and beautiful instrument. Convincing though Leonhardt's scholarly essay is, it is his playing that clinches the truth of his musical argument. Every strand in the texture emerges with clarity and every phrase is allowed to speak for itself. In the 12th and 18th fugues Leonhardt is joined by Bob van Asperen. The great Dutch artist-scholar argues that from the 'unsustained instruments with keyboard range larger than four octaves, the harpsichord claims first place in *The Art of Fugue* (Bach left five harpsichords and no clavichord on his death), though organ and clavichord are not to be totally excluded, especially for certain pieces'. Leonhardt does not include the unfinished fugue, but that will be the only reservation to cross the minds of most listeners. This is a very impressive and rewarding set, well recorded and produced.

Capriccio in B flat (on the departure of a beloved brother), BWV 992; Chromatic fantasia and fugue in D min., BWV 903; Fantasia in C min., BWV 906; Italian concerto in F, BWV 971; Toccata in G, BWV 916.
(M) ** DG Arc. 2547/*3347* 031. Kirkpatrick.

Ralph Kirkpatrick is a scholar of international repute and a fine musician, with a strong rhythmic grip and a highly developed sense of style. Here he plays a modern Neupert harpsichord and uses it to maximum effect in the *Chromatic fantasia*, with an impressive increase in tension at the climax of the fugue. The *Toccata* (from Bach's Weimar period) also brings well-realized opportunities for bravura. The *Capriccio*, BWV 992, is in essence a six-movement miniature suite with programmatic implications. It includes an engaging 'departure' section, with a posthorn motif implanted in the texture which Kirkpatrick plays with a nice rhythmic point. Elsewhere he sounds more pedantic, and the *Italian concerto* is frankly dull. The recordings date from the late 1950s/early 1960s and have considerable clarity and presence (the cassette transfer is bold and clear, matching the disc closely). Some ears might prefer a rather more recessed balance.

Chaconne (arr. Busoni) from *Unaccompanied Violin partita No. 2 in D min., BWV 1004.*
*** Decca SXL 6669 [Lon. CS 6866]. Larrocha (piano) – MOZART: *Fantasy in C minor* etc.***

In Alicia de Larrocha's record the Bach–Busoni is the odd-man-out in a Mozart recital. She is an artist of strong temperament and good taste, and is admirably served by the Decca engineers. This is currently the only version of the Busoni arrangement in the catalogue.

Chromatic fantasia and fugue in D min., BWV 903; 4 Duets, BWV 802/5; Goldberg variations, BWV 988.
*** Decca D 275 D 2. Schiff (piano).

Andras Schiff as a boy in Hungary heard a record of Glenn Gould and from that moment was a passionate devotee of Bach on the piano. Like Gould he uses a wide range of piano tone, exploiting the instrument rather than imitating the harpsichord. Like Gould he has natural magnetism in whatever he does, so that the darkly intense 25th variation of the *Goldberg* set becomes an emotional peak; but unlike Gould he is rarely idiosyncratic. Unlike Gould, too, he observes all the repeats, often providing pointful variants the second time. The fourth side brings a valuable extra in the four rare *Duets* and the *Chromatic fantasia and fugue*. The recording, made in Kingsway Hall, is full and atmospheric.

Chromatic fantasia and fugue in D min., BWV 903; Fantasia in C min., BWV 906; Prelude and fugue in A min., BWV 894; Toccatas Nos. 1 in F sharp min., BWV 910; 3 in D, BWV 912.
** DG Arc. 2533 402 [id./*3310 402*]. Pinnock.

As in the companion record of *Toccatas*, Trevor Pinnock's sense of style is matched by his technical expertise. Sometimes his approach is rather literal, but at others he allows himself more expressive latitude. The playing is always rhythmically alive, but the close recording of the harpsichord and the high level combine to create a somewhat unrelentless dynamic, without a great deal of light and shade.

Chromatic fantasia and fugue in D min., BWV 903; Italian concerto in F, BWV 971; Partita No. 1 in B flat, BWV 825.
(M) *** Ph. 9502/*7313* 087. Verlet.

Miss Verlet uses two different harpsichords here and they sound splendid, the recording equally vivid on disc and the excellent high-level tape. She is at her finest in the *Chromatic fantasia* which is played quite flamboyantly with a nice feeling for its rhapsodic character. The fugue is clear and positive. The instruments are French, here a restored Hemsch, whereas the rest of the programme is given on a Rubio. The playing throughout is musical and never rigid, although at times a little matter-of-fact, noticeable in the *Andante* of the *Italian concerto* and in the *Partita*. Nevertheless this is a spontaneous recital and, with such good recording (a little forward perhaps), cannot fail to make a good impression.

Chromatic fantasia and fugue in D min., BWV 903; French suite No. 5 in G, BWV 816; Italian concerto in F, BWV 971; Toccata in D, BWV 912.
(M) *** Decca Ser. SA/*KSC* 11 [Lon. STS 15491]. Malcolm.

A well-regarded recital from the beginning of the 1960s that wears its years lightly (although the – for Decca – surprisingly low transfer level of the cassette means that the recording has less presence on tape). Highlights are the buoyant *Toccata* and the genial, even lyrical approach to the *French suite*. The *Chromatic fantasia and fugue* is rather more didactic, but still makes a strong effect, especially the culmination of the fugue.

English suites Nos. 1–6, BWV 806/11.
*** HM HM 1074-5/*40* [id.]. Gilbert.

Kenneth Gilbert uses a Couchet-Taskin of 1788 and is given a first-class recording. His playing has a fine sense of style, the rubato flowing naturally and never self-conscious, the ornamentation nicely judged. He is inconsistent in the matter of repeats, but this may be due to the desire to fit the six suites economically on to four sides. As the price is slightly lower than the premium range, this is excellent value, particularly as the recording itself is so realistic. The cassettes are transferred at the highest level and while the sound is admirably vivid, care will have to be taken with the volume control if a truthful image is to be obtained.

English suite No. 2 in A min., BWV 807; Partita No. 2 in C min., BWV 826; Toccata in C min., BWV 911.
*** DG 2531/*3301* 088 [id.]. Argerich (piano).

It is good to see Bach returning to the piano after more than two decades when pianists have tended to leave this repertoire to their harpsichord colleagues. One critic thought this style 'too dated for any but the most reactionary of Bach lovers'; so expectations of a genuine musical experience are naturally aroused. Martha Argerich does not disappoint: her playing is alive, keenly rhythmic but wonderfully flexible and rich in colour. There is none of the didacticism that marks Tureck, and her finger control is no less impressive. The textures are always varied and clean, and there is an intellectual and musical vitality here that is refreshing. Moreover, Miss Argerich is beautifully recorded on both disc and cassette.

French suites Nos. 1–6, BWV 812/17.
(M) **(*) Decca Ser. SA/*KSC* 5. Dart (clavichord).
* CBS 73393 [M 32347]. Gould (piano).

By cutting the repeats, Thurston Dart managed to get all six suites on to a single medium-priced LP. The choice of the clavichord for works of this scale is questionable, as its tiny voice has a restricted range of timbre as well as dynamic. But Dart's playing is impeccable in style and has plenty of spontaneity. The balance tends to make the intimate clavichord image larger than life, but if the volume is cut well back a truthful image can be obtained. The admirable cassette transfer is ideal in this respect, as at the level necessary for faithful reproduction there is virtually no background noise.

Brilliant though Glenn Gould's playing is, it is far too idiosyncratic to justify an unqualified recommendation. Needless to say, there are revealing touches, marvellously clear part-writing and much impressive finger dexterity. There are some odd tempi and a lot of very detached playing that inspires more admiration that conviction. The recording is acceptable.

French suite No. 5 in G, BWV 816; Italian concerto in F, BWV 971; Partita No. 7 in B min., BWV 831.
(M) *** Decca Ace SDD 564. Schiff (piano).

Andras Schiff belongs to the school of young Hungarian pianists that includes Zoltan Kocsis and Dezsö Ránki, and, judging from this Bach recital, he is fully their equal. In addition to producing a wide range of keyboard colour, he is scrupulous in his observance of the correct conventions in the interpretation of Bach, and in this respect compares favourably with many harpsichordists. His playing is musically alive and imaginative: indeed, the *Italian concerto* is arguably the finest available on either harpsichord or piano, and the whole programme is an outstanding success. This was Schiff's first solo record on a UK label and will surely not be his last. The sound is very good indeed: the recording emanates from Japan.

Goldberg variations, BWV 988.
*** HM 1C 065 99710. Leonhardt.
*** DG Arc. 2533/*3310* 425 [id.]. Pinnock.
(M) **(*) DG Arc. Priv. 2547/*3347* 050 [198020]. Kirkpatrick.

(M) **(*) DG Acc. 2542/*3342* 160. Kempff (piano).
*(**) CBS **CD**; 37779/40- [id.]. Gould (piano).

The great Dutch harpsichordist Gustav Leonhardt has recorded the *Goldberg* three times, and his last version, though the most beautifully recorded, will not necessarily enjoy universal appeal. This is an introvert and searching performance, at times very free rhythmically – indeed almost mannered. The *Black Pearl* variation is a case in point; but the reading is so thoughtful that no one can fail to find some illumination from it. His instrument is a Dowd copy of a Blanchet and tuned a semitone flat, as opposed to the Skowroneck copy of a Dulcken at our present-day pitch he used in his 1967 record (Tel. AW 6.41198). The sound is altogether mellower and more appealing, and though no repeats are observed, this version is fresher and more personal than his Das Alte Werk record.

Trevor Pinnock uses a Ruckers dating from 1646, modified over a century later by Taskin and restored most recently in 1968 by Hubert Bédard. He retains repeats in more than half the variations, which seems a good compromise in that variety is maintained yet there is no necessity for a third side. The playing is eminently vital and intelligent, with alert, finely articulated rhythm. If tempi are generally brisk, there are few with which listeners are likely to quarrel, and Pinnock shows himself flexible and imaginative in the inward-looking variations such as No. 25. The recording is very truthful and vivid, though it benefits from a slightly lower level setting than usual. In any event this can be recommended alongside Leonhardt's Harmonia Mundi version.

Ralph Kirkpatrick's recording comes from the late 1950s and on its first appearance the *Stereo Record Guide* found it impressive: Kirkpatrick 'delights in light and subtle registration, and the music benefits both in clarity and colour . . . the playing is lively where it should be, controlled and steady in the slow, stately, contrapuntal variations'. It also sounds extremely fresh in spite of the passage of time. Generally speaking, the account he gives sounds less pedantic than some of his other Bach records of this period. Kirkpatrick is a scholarly rather than an intuitive player and his thoughts are rarely without interest. Though not a first choice, this version is still worth considering, particularly as it has a price advantage over some of its rivals. The cassette transfer is first-class, softer in treble outline than the LP, but wholly natural.

Kempff's version is not for purists, but it has a special magic of its own. Ornaments are ignored altogether in the outlining of the theme, and the instances of anachronisms of style are too numerous to mention. Yet for all that the sheer musicianship exhibited by this great artist fascinates, and even where he seems quite wilfully nineteenth-century in his approach, there is a musical impulse and conviction behind it. Readers should certainly hear this for themselves, and libraries should acquire it. The recording is of good quality and the cassette matches the disc.

Glenn Gould made his recording début with the *Goldberg Variations* way back in the mid-1950s and this latest version was among the last he made. As in his earlier account, there are astonishing feats of prestidigitation and the clarity he produces in the part-writing is often little short of extraordinary. In his earlier record he made no repeats, now he repeats a section of almost half of them and also joins some pairs together (6 and 7, 9 and 10, for example). Yet, even apart from his vocalise he does a number of weird things, fierce staccatos, brutal accents and so on, that inhibit one from suggesting this as a first recommendation even among piano versions. The recording is, as usual with this artist, inclined to be dry and forward (he engineers his own records and admires this kind of sound) which aids clarity. A thought-provoking rather than a satisfying reading – an award-winning disc, too; but for all that, many readers will find the groans and croons intolerable and be bewildered by many things he does. The withdrawn, rapt opening *Aria* is rather beautiful but why, one wonders, does he emphasize the third part in many of the canons? The chrome cassette matches the disc faithfully. The CD has admirable presence but emphasizes the vocalise.

15 2-part Inventions, BWV 772/786; 15 3-part Inventions, BWV 787/801.

(M) (**) CBS 60254/*40*- [MS 6622]. Gould (piano).

Gould pairs each of the *Two-* and *Three-part* inventions (with each pair in identical keys). The listener is conscious he is in the presence of a penetrating musical mind throughout these performances and the clarity of the individual strands is remarkable. The rhythmic line, however, is slightly eccentric at times, and the ear cannot fail to be exasperated by the vocalizations. There is much to admire, yet in the last resort this is difficult to live with. One longs at least for vocal silence. The recording is dry but clear and believable within its chosen acoustic, and there is no appreciable difference between chrome tape and disc.

Partitas Nos. 1–6 BWV 825/30.
*** HM 1C 149 99840/2. Leonhardt.

This set was not conceived as an entity but recorded over a longish period (1964–71). The *Second Partita* is heard at today's pitch, the others are recorded a semitone lower, and there are some variations of quality in the recordings of different partitas. Nevertheless, these are searching and often profound readings. There are occasional exaggerations (the *Allemande* of the *First Suite*) and some of the dotted rhythms are over-emphatic – or stiff might be a better expression. Yet this still remains an impressive achievement, for the thoughts of this scholar–musician are always illuminating and his artistry compels admiration.

Partitas Nos. 1–6, BWV 825/30; 7 Toccatas, BWV 910/6.
*(*) CBS 79409 (4). Gould (piano).

Glenn Gould recorded the *Partitas* in the early 1970s and there is no questioning his keyboard mastery. The articulation and clarity of part-writing is remarkable and there is formidable intelligence evident in each movement. This artist favours a very dry-sounding acoustic and the recording is shallow in timbre, though the blame for this is not wholly to be laid at the doors of the CBS engineers. These are thought-provoking readings that will make many pianists listen with fresh ears, but are too idiosyncratic to carry an unqualified recommendation. The piano does not resemble any instrument one is likely to encounter in real life and the vocalise is tiresome. The *Toccatas* are of later provenance and combine the most fastidious pianism with some characteristically mannered touches. As with the *Partitas*, the playing is of no mean order of expertise, and in terms of linear clarity and coherence, it would be difficult to fault him. The dry sound does, of course, help to ensure that the various contrapuntal strands register to maximum effect. If the stimulus afforded by these readings were matched by aural satisfaction, these could be more warmly recommended. As it is, this handsomely produced set is for initiates rather than the general collector.

Toccatas Nos. 1 in F sharp min.; 3 in D; 4 in D min., BWV 910, 912/13.
*(*) CBS 76881 [M/*MT* 35144]. Gould (piano).

Toccatas Nos. 2 in C min.; 4 in D min.; 5 in E min.; 6 in G min.; 7 in G, BWV 911, 913/16.
** DG Arc. 2533 403 [id.]. Pinnock.

Toccatas Nos. 2 and 5–7.
** CBS 76984 [M/*MT* 35831]. Gould (piano).

Trevor Pinnock is a highly gifted artist and brings to this repertoire both scholarship and technical prowess. Rhythms are alive, and there are times when he almost seems relentless. Yet there are moments of great expressive freedom, and the rhapsodic quality of the slow sections in the *Toccatas* is vividly brought to life. Unfortunately pleasure is diminished by the rather close recorded sound, cut at too high a level and rather unrelieved in range.

Glenn Gould's first set combines the most fastidious and remarkable pianism with some impulsive, not to say wilful, touches. Though the playing is of the highest distinction, the actual piano tone is not, and the poor recorded sound, plus the tiresome vocalise on which this artist seems to insist, somewhat dampen one's enthusiasm for this release. In the second set there is some impressive playing, with contrapuntal strands being beautifully balanced and clarified. The recording is rather wanting in depth and colour (on disc and chrome cassette alike), but that is not unusual from this source.

The Well-tempered Clavier (*48 Preludes and fugues*), *BWV 846/893*.
** DG Arc. 2723 054 (5) [2714 004]. Walcha.
** HM 1C 153 99752/6. Leonhardt.

No single survey of *The Well-tempered Clavier* is likely to give universal satisfaction throughout all the *Forty-eight*. Walcha recorded them earlier on EMI's short-lived Baroque label (HQS 1042–7), but these are a good deal more satisfactory, even though traces of pedantry can still be found. This reading first appeared as part of the DG Archive Bach Edition in the mid-1970s: Book I is recorded on a restored Ruckers and Book II on a Hemsch. There is no question of the great German organist's keyboard mastery and his wonderful sense of control. He is at his best in those preludes and fugues that do not call for any vein of poetic feeling, for textures are unfolded with compelling clarity and impressive command of detail. There is an intellectual rigour that is undeniably imposing but he is at times somewhat inflexible (for example, in the *Prelude in B flat*, Book I) and rarely permits imagination and fantasy to take full wing in the more contemplative pieces. However, the overall picture is positive and he is excellently recorded.

Gustav Leonhardt also chooses the harpsichord for the *Forty-eight*, playing a copy of a Taskin by David Rubio for Book I and an instrument of Martin Skowroneck for Book II. It must be said straight away that the attractions of this issue are much diminished by the quality of the recorded sound. Both instruments are closely balanced and even when the volume is reduced the perspective seems unnatural, as if one were leaning into the instrument itself. Tastes in matters of 'registration' are bound to differ, but there is little with which to quarrel and much to admire. This distinguished player and scholar possesses both the effortless technique and the musical insights that are required, and even if there are moments that seem a trifle pedantic – the *C sharp major Fugue* of Book II is rather 'spelt out' – this version offers more rewarding interpretative insights than most of the previously available rivals. Were the sound more sympathetic and appealing, this would be a first recommendation, for Leonhardt combines scholarship, technique and sensibility in no small measure.

ORGAN MUSIC

Adagio in C (from *BWV 565*); *Chorales: Herzlich tut mich verlangen, BWV 727; Liebster Jesu, BWV 730; Wachet auf, BWV 645; Fantasia and fugue in G min., BWV 542; Fugue in E flat* (*St Anne*), *BWV 552; Passacaglia and fugue in C min., BWV 582; Toccata and fugue in D min., BWV 565.*
*** Argo ZRG/*KZRC* 943 [id.]. Hurford (various organs).

An admirable popular sampler for Peter Hurford's outstanding Bach series. Performances are consistently alive and the vivid recording (the high-level tape every bit as impressive as the disc) projects them strongly. A self-recommending issue that will surely tempt any purchaser to go on and explore the whole series.

Allabreve in D, BWV 589; Canonic variations on Vom Himmel hoch, BWV 769; Chorale partita: Sei gegrüsset, Jesu gütig, BWV 768; Chorale preludes, BWV 726, 728/32, 735, 737; 6 Schübler chorale preludes, BWV 645/50; Concerto No. 6 in E flat, BWV 597; Fugue in B min., BWV 579; Preludes and fugues, BWV 544/5; Sonatas Nos. 1 in E flat, BWV 525; 3 in D min., BWV 527; Trio in D min., BWV 588.
(M) ❀ *** Argo D 150 D 3/*K 150 K 32* [id.]. Hurford (Wolff/Casavant organ, Our Lady of Sorrows, Toronto; Sharp organ of Knox Grammar School, Sydney, Australia; Grant, Degens and Bradbeer organ, New College, Oxford; Dutch organ, Eton College).

This is the third (as released) of Peter Hurford's recital-styled collections in his complete recording of Bach's organ music for Argo. Hurford's approach is in its way as revolutionary in gramophone terms as Dorati's reappraisal of the Haydn *Symphonies* or the musical adventures of the Academy of Ancient Music in the baroque world (including the symphonies of Mozart). Hurford's playing has a comparable freshness. Rather than adhere to the German tradition, which favours sober registration and lets Bach's musical argument unfold in a controlled, sometimes tensionless manner to let the fugal detail register as clearly as the acoustic will allow, Hurford takes an almost orchestral approach, seeking to bring out all the music's colour and emotional resource. He uses several organs in each programme, grouping the pieces to match the character of each (often with uncanny aptness), and he receives consistent support from the Argo recording engineers. They provide superb sound, which has weight and, where necessary, a sense of spectacle and grandeur, yet always reveals inner detail with remarkable transparency. Moreover the cassettes match the discs closely and are a demonstration of the breadth and range of recording possible when the boundaries of transferring technology are pressed to their limit.

This third box is exceptionally attractive; indeed it could well make a starting-point for a beginner in this repertoire. The choice of organs is characteristically imaginative and Hurford's registration gives endless pleasure. The *Sei gegrüsset* variations are a model of Bach exposition, cool yet never dull; the *Schübler chorales* are splendidly done, with the most remarkable variety of colour; and at the end of the recital the *Sonata in D minor*, BWV 527, with its deliciously dazzling finale, and the *E flat Concerto*, BWV 597, are no less engaging. The superb recording handles the closing section of the *Partita* (BWV 768) with impressive freedom and weight. On cassette, for some reason, the bass seems over-emphasized in the opening *Schübler chorale*, which is at the beginning of side three (there are two cassettes instead of three discs, which seems no great advantage); but elsewhere the sound balance, on tape and disc alike, is first-class. A token Rosette is awarded as a mark of the distinction of the complete series.

Allabreve in D, BWV 589; Canzone in D min., BWV 588; Chorale preludes Nos. 1–45 (Orgelbüchlein), BWV 599/644; 6 Schübler chorale preludes, BWV 645/50; Chorales, BWV 690, 691, 706, 709, 711, 714, 731, 738; Chorale fughettas, BWV 696/9, 701, 703/4; Fugues: in C min., BWV 575; in G; in G min.; in B min., BWV 577/9; Pastorale in F, BWV 590; Preludes and fugues, BWV 536, 541, 543/8.

(M) ** HM HM 523 (6). Rogg (Silbermann organ, Arlesheim).

This is the least attractive of Lionel Rogg's three boxes of Bach's organ music recorded at Arlesheim. As in the other sets the recording is generally consistent in its body and clarity (though the *Preludes in C major and minor*, BWV 545/6, each have a hint of congestion at their openings). Rogg lays out the music with reliable clarity and structural control. His registration is apt if conventional; often one feels that he could have been more imaginative in this respect, especially in the *Orgelbüchlein*. There is the occasional exception: *In dulci jubilo* has striking colour and the *Pastorale* which opens the first disc is no less effective. But so often the playing seems too circumspect. Try the opening Schübler choral (*Wachet auf*) which is curiously stiff. During the *Preludes and fugues* the listener's concentration is tempted to falter, as the music is allowed to unfold with no attempt to increase or vary the basically low level of tension.

Aria, BWV 587; Canzone in D min., BWV 588; Chorale variations: Ach, was soll ich Sünder machen; Allein Gott in der Höh' sei Ehr', BWV 770/71; Fantasias: in C min., BWV 562; in G, BWV 571; Fugue in C min. on a theme of Legrenzi, BWV 574; Fugues: in G, BWV 576; in G min., BWV 578; Passacaglia and fugue in C min., BWV 582; Pastorale in F, BWV 590; Pedal-Exercitium, BWV 598; Preludes: in A min., BWV 569; in C, BWV 567; Preludes and fugues: in C min.; in C, BWV 546/7; Trio in G, BWV 1027a.

(M) *** Argo D 177 D 3/*K 177 K 32* [id.]. Hurford.

In Volume 4 of his series Peter Hurford uses three organs, chosen with characteristic skill to show the music to its best advantage. The superb recording lets every detail register and gives each instrument an individual character on both discs and cassettes. The first collection uses the organ of Melk Abbey, Austria, and Hurford's registration in the serene *Pastorale*, BWV 590, is matched by the piquancy of colour he finds in the *Fantasia in G major*, with its effective use of light and shade. In the *Chorale variations* on *Ach, was soll*, BWV 770, Hurford keeps the melody firmly in front of the listener and at the same time achieves an almost orchestral variety in his characterization. The division between groups of pieces and the organs on which they are played is made using six sides on disc and (less attractively) four on tape. Recital two was recorded in the cathedral of St Poulten (also in Austria), and its highlights include a splendid account of the *Fugue in G minor*, BWV 578, played with great spontaneity and clarity, and a powerful and strongly rhythmic *Canzone in D minor*. After the deliciously registered lightweight *Trio in G*, BWV 1027a, there is a massive contrast with the granite-hewn *Prelude and fugue in C minor*, BWV 546. The third section includes a major set of variations on the Trinity hymn *Allein Gott in der Höh'*, with a highly imaginative variety of treatments (Hurford omits Variations 3 and 8 as being unsuitable for organ, rather than keyboard), and closes with a masterly account of the famous *Passacaglia and fugue in C minor*, played with a tough cumulative force, yet with every detail clear. (On cassette this is one of the most impressive demonstrations of transferring technology in the entire series.) The third organ is a Canadian instrument in Toronto already used in Volume 3 (see above); heard alongside the Austrian instruments it proves to be every bit their equal in this repertoire. Overall this set contains many rarities which are often ignored, and many of them are very rewarding.

Canonic variations on Vom Himmel hoch, BWV 769; Chorale fantasias and variations, BWV 720, 727, 734, 736/7; 18 Leipzig chorale preludes, BWV 651/8; Chorale partitas, BWV 766/7; Fantasias: in C min., BWV 562; in G, BWV 572; Fugue on the Magnificat, BWV 722; Preludes and fugues; in C, BWV 531; in C min., BWV 549; in D, BWV 532; in D min., BWV 539; in E min., BWV 533; in F min., BWV 534; in G, BWV 550; in G min., BWV 535; Toccata and fugue in E, BWV 566; Trio in D min., BWV 583.

(M) **(*) HMHM 522 (6). Rogg (Silbermann organ, Arlesheim).

Rogg is at his very best in the Arnstadt *Preludes and fugues*, early works of great character which inspire performances of communicating vigour. In the chorales too his clear registration, with the theme kept unexaggeratedly to the fore, gives pleasure, but as so often with Rogg's performances the listener is inclined – in the Leipzig set in particular – to reflect that a more flamboyant approach would not be out of place. Some of the other large-scale works sound very pedantic, the approach measured and apparently uninvolved. Yet everything is beautifully clear and controlled, and those who do not seek conscious bravura and an extrovert style in this music should be well satisfied with the recorded sound, which is first-class. So are the pressings, but the accompanying booklet is in French.

Chorale partita: Christ, der du bist, BWV 766; Chorale preludes, BWV 715, 720, 722, 738; Concertos Nos. 3 in C, BWV 594; 5 in D min., BWV 596; Fantasias and fugues: in C, BWV 570 and 946; in C min., BWV 537; in G, BWV 577; Kleines harmonisches Labyrinth, BWV 591; 8 Short Preludes and fugues, BWV 553/60; Preludes and fugues: in D, BWV 532; in F min., BWV 534; Sonata No. 6 in G, BWV 530; Toccatas and fugues: in D min., BWV 538 (Dorian) and 565; Trio in G min., BWV 584.

(M) *** Argo D 207 D 3/*K 207 K 33* [id.]. Hurford.

In Volume 5 Argo have sensibly reverted to a three-cassette layout, to match the discs. The recital opens with an arresting account of the powerful *Prelude and fugue in D*, which shows the spectacular range of the organ of Ratzeburg Cathedral in West Germany. This instrument is no less effective in the most famous of all Bach's organ works, the *Toccata and fugue in D minor*, BWV 565. Opening with a superbly rhythmic flourish Hurford makes effective use of spatial and dynamic contrast, and the exhilaratingly paced fugue brings a suggestion of orchestral colour that recalls Stokowski's famous transcription in Disney's *Fantasia*. The *Sonata in G* shows a similar orchestral feeling; the attractive *Concerto*, BWV 596, after Vivaldi, and the fascinatingly titled *Kleines harmonisches Labyrinth* evoke an appropriately less extrovert style and again demonstrate Hurford's apt colouristic registration. These are both played on the Toronto organ, which was used to great effect in Volumes 3 and 4 of the series, and this instrument proves also a perfect choice for the *Eight Short Preludes and fugues*, BWV 533/60, presented with appealing simplicity, and the captivating *Fugue à la gigue*, BWV 577, which is irresistibly gay and buoyant. The way Hurford keeps all the music alive and constantly engages the ear with the sounds he creates (in the mellow *Fantasia in C*, for instance) continues to recommend this series above other Bach organ issues. The sound is first-class, whether one chooses cassettes or discs. (There is just a hint of roughness at the opening of the *Prelude*, BWV 532, on the first tape, but it lasts for a few bars only and is of little consequence. Careless editing, however, has divided the booklet accompanying the cassettes into 'record' sides.)

Chorale partita on Sei gegrüsset, Jesu gütig, BWV 768; Fugue à la gigue, BWV 577; Toccata and fugue in F, BWV 540.

(B) *** PRT GSGC/*ZCGC* 2014. Downes (organ of the Royal Festival Hall, London) – WIDOR: *Toccata*.***

This extraordinarily fine record dates from the very earliest days of stereo, being (in its original full-priced form) among the first disc-stereo pressings available in the UK. It would be difficult to guess from the sound, however, that it was not recorded relatively recently. Ralph Downes helped to design the Festival Hall organ, which because of its wide spatial layout is ideal for stereo recording. But it is not only the antiphonal and tonal qualities of the recording which recommend this bargain reissue, but the excellence of the performances too. The *Fugue 'à la gigue' in G major* is given a delightfully spirited reading; the elaborate *Toccata in F major* is spontaneous and invigorating; and the extended chorale variations are registered with flair and musicianship nicely balanced. There is an excellent cassette too, clear and without congestion.

Chorale preludes, BWV 717, 725 (Te Deum), 739/41, 747, 755, 758, 765; Herr Christ, der einig Gottes-Sohn, Ahn. 55; Fugue in C min., BWV 575; Preludes and fugues: in A min., BWV 551; in C, BWV 531; in C min., BWV 549 and 575; in E min., BWV 548; in G, BWV 550; in G min., BWV 535; Sonata No. 2 in C min., BWV 526; Toccata, adagio and fugue in C, BWV 564; Trio in C min., BWV 585.

(M) *** Argo D 226 D 3/*K 226 K 33* (3) [id.]. Hurford (organs of Ratzeburg Cath.; Our Lady of Sorrows, Toronto; Eton College).

Peter Hurford opens Volume 6 of his series with a massively unrelenting performance of the *Toccata and fugue in F* and then makes a suitable contrast with the lighter-textured *Sonata in C minor*. Highlights of this set include a splendid, dashing account of the *G major Prelude and fugue*, BWV 550, and a superb version of the *Toccata, adagio and fugue in C*, powerful yet relaxed. Elsewhere the playing is more deliberate than usual, notably so in the *A minor* and *G minor Preludes and fugues*, which come together on side five. The clear, unforced momentum reminds one of Lionel Rogg and in the spacious *Te Deum* setting (*Herr Gott, dich loben wir*) Hurford seems almost overawed by the religious implications of the music. The chorale preludes gathered together to close the recital are beautifully registered; every strand of texture is transparently clear. The recording of the three organs is up to the high standards of the series, on disc and tape alike. However, the otherwise admirable booklet with the tapes does not make it clear how the programme is divided among the instruments used. As in Volume 5, the tape layout matches the discs.

Chorale prelude: In dir ist Freude, BWV 615; Fantasia in G, BWV 572; Fugue in G min., BWV 578; Pedal-exercitium in G min., BWV 598; Prelude and fugue in B min., BWV 544; Toccata, adagio and fugue in C, BWV 564.

*** RCA RL/*RK* 25369. Curley (organ of Vangede Church, Copenhagen).

Carlo Curley is better known for more flamboyant repertoire, but here, playing a magnificent Frobenius organ, he shows himself a first-class advocate of Bach's organ music. The performances throughout are tingling with life and colour. They have strength and character too – as the splendid *Toccata, adagio and fugue* readily shows – but above all they communicate, and this is essentially a record for the non-organ specialist. There is even humour in the choice of registration for *In dir ist Freude* (a demonstration item), while the bravura at the opening and close of the *Fantasia in G major* is breathtaking. No less impressive is the control of detail and momentum of the *Fugue in G minor*. This is a very enjoyable and highly recommendable disc, and the cassette too is brilliantly transferred (indeed a slight tempering of the treble is useful on side two) and is clear and undistorted.

Chorale preludes: Alle Menschen müssen sterben, BWV 643; Vater unser in Himmelreich, BWV 737; Fantasia and fugue in G min., BWV 542; Passacaglia and fugue in C min., BWV 582; Toccata in F, BWV 540.
(*) Telarc Dig. **CD 80049; DG 10049 [id.]. Murray (organ at Methuen Memorial Hall, Mass.).

The sound here is first-class, of course, especially on the compact disc, though not more impressive and certainly not clearer than Peter Hurford's analogue Argo records. The acoustic is fairly reverberant, and this is an organ obviously intended by its builders to produce a wide panoply of sound rather than crystal-clear inner detail. It reproduces naturally and one feels the engineers have not sought spectacle for its own sake. The most impressive performance is of the *Passacaglia and fugue in C minor*, well placed and powerful with an effectively wide dynamic range. Michael Murray's approach to the *Fantasia and fugue* and *Toccata* is rather measured. But he clearly understands the structure of all this music. The chorale preludes are given serene and, it must be admitted, slightly static performances, but the sense of repose of *Alle Menschen müssen sterben*, which ends the recital, is enhanced by the clean focus of the compact disc, although the background is not quite silent, for the organ contributes its own characteristic sound as the air goes through the pipes.

Chorale preludes: Erbarm' dich mein, BWV 721; Wo soll fliehen hin, BWV 646; Chorale: Jesu joy of man's desiring (from *Cantata No. 147*); *Concerto No. 4 in C, BWV 595* (after Ernst): Excerpt. *Schübler chorale prelude: Nun freut euch, BWV 734; Sinfonia* (from *Cantata No. 29*); *Suite No. 3 in D, BWV 1068; Air* (both arr. Curley); *Toccata and fugue in D min., BWV 565.*
** RCA Dig. RL/*RK* 25412. Curley.

This tends to be a collection of bits and pieces, although the opening *Toccata and fugue in D minor* is resplendently done. All Carlo Curley's playing is strongly communicative and full of character, not always of the right kind, as the famous *Air* and the chorale, *Jesu joy of man's desiring*, demonstrate. Yet the Frobenius pipe-organ makes some attractive sounds, for the registration is lively and imaginative. There is a good chrome cassette, only marginally less clean in detail than the disc, and it handles the cadential climax in BWV 565 with aplomb.

Chorale preludes: In dulci jubilo, BWV 751; Vor deinen Thron, BWV 668; Wachet auf, BWV 645; Fantasia in G, BWV 572; Fantasia and fugue in G min., BWV 542; Fugue in E flat (*St Anne*), *BWV 552; Passacaglia and fugue in C min., BWV 582; Toccata, adagio and fugue in C, BWV 564; Toccatas and fugues: in D min., BWV 565; in F, BWV 540.*
(M) *** HMV *TCC2-POR 54288.* Rogg.

Rogg's admirable collection is recorded on four different organs (two Metzler and two Anderson). It is superbly engineered and offers an example of chrome tape used to very best advantage. (EMI's *'Portrait of the Artist'* series is only available in cassette format.) They are heavyweight performances, but the playing is strong and authoritative. On side one, three well-known chorales are used to add contrast between the major works. On side two we get three big works in a row, and some lighter relief might have been a good idea. In all other respects this hour-and-a-half of Bach can be recommended.

Chorale preludes: Kommst du nun, Jesu, BWV 650; Wachet auf, BWV 645; Fantasia and fugue in G min., BWV 542; Prelude and fugue in E flat, BWV 552; Toccata and fugue in D min., BWV 565.

(M) *** DG Priv. 2535/*3335* 611. Karl Richter (organ of Jaegersborg Church, Copenhagen).

This compilation, taken from recordings made in 1964 and 1967, represents Richter's Bach playing at its finest. The performance of the famous *Toccata and fugue in D minor* is outstanding, matching weight with vigour, and splendidly paced, while the other pieces are presented spontaneously and with a deceptive simplicity that disguises the underlying control. The *E flat Prelude and fugue*, which uses a very famous hymn for its fugal subject, is brought off especially well. The recording of the Danish organ is superb; it sounds slightly more reedy on disc than on tape, but both are of demonstration quality, with the pedal opening of BWV 542 caught without a ripple of distortion.

(i) *Chorale preludes: Kommst du nun, BWV 650; Wachet auf, BWV 645;* (ii) *Concerto No. 2 in A min.* (*after Vivaldi, Op. 3/8*), *BWV 593;* (iii) *Passacaglia in C min., BWV 582; Toccata and fugue in D min.* (*Dorian*), *BWV 538;* (i) *Toccata and fugue in D min., BWV 565.*

(M) ** DG Sig. 2543/*3343* 537. Karl Richter (organs at (i) Copenhagen; (ii) Arlesheim; (iii) Freiberg).

This is a regrouping of Richter performances from three different recitals. The most successful items are those recorded in Copenhagen and they are praised above. The *Concerto* arrangement of Vivaldi has a memorably registered *Adagio*, but the organ at Freiberg is a less attractive instrument than the other two and Richter's account of the famous *Passacaglia* – taken at a very measured pace – does not maintain its tension consistently. The recording is faithful, on disc and tape alike, and sounds especially impressive in Copenhagen.

Chorale preludes and variations, BWV 690/713, 727, 734, 736; Concertos Nos. 1 in G; 2 in A min., BWV 592/3; Fantasia in G, BWV 572; Fantasia and fugue in G min., BWV 542; Preludes and fugues: in A, BWV 536; in E min., BWV 533; in G, BWV 541; Trio sonatas Nos. 4 in E min.; 5 in C, BWV 528/9.

(M) *** Argo D 120 D 3/*K 120 33* [id.]. Hurford.

This was the first box to be issued in Peter Hurford's projected complete recording of Bach's organ music. It set the standards for the series by combining lively and engrossing performances – giving the listener the impression of hearing the music for the first time – and first-class recording. The layout (over either three discs or two cassettes) presents the various works intermixed, recital-style. Thus instead of (for instance) placing all the *Preludes and fugues* together they are separated by groups of chorales, and the *Trio sonatas* and transcribed solo *Concertos* are fitted within the overall scheme to enhance the stylistic contrast. It works well. Two different modern organs are used: for most of the programme Hurford plays on the Casavant instrument at the Church of Our Lady of Sorrows, Toronto, but in two of the *Preludes and fugues*, one of the *Concertos*, the *Trio sonatas* and certain of the *Chorales* he changes to the Ronald Sharp organ at Knox Grammar School, Sydney. Both instruments produce sound that is internally clear yet has admirable baroque colouring. Indeed the piquancy of the registration, often reedily robust in the *Chorales*, is a constant source of delight. The playing itself is fresh, vigorous and imaginative throughout, but the bigger set-pieces have no want of breadth. Hurford's technical control is never in doubt, and a concern to bring the music to tingling life is the overriding feature of his interpretations. The recording is clean and sparkling, the sound never weighted down by puddingy bass, yet there is no lack of range at the bottom end. (On tape the resonance in the pedals may be very slightly reduced in the interest of preventing cross-modulation effects, but never enough to spoil the overall balance.)

Clavierübung, Part 3: German organ Mass.

(B) *** PRT GSGC/*ZCGC* 2046/7. Downes (Festival Hall organ).

This Ralph Downes set comes from the mid-1960s, but the recording is as fresh as the day it was made. It is clear and smooth, has remarkable detail and effectively conveys the spatial layout of the Festival Hall organ. The cassette transfers too are expertly managed and virtually the equal of the discs, in range and immediacy. Downes' registration is splendidly chosen and adds exactly the right degree of colour to music-making which can be dramatic, yet for most of the time has a simple, direct eloquence. The pacing is often measured, but the playing is never dull, and with such good sound this remains a first-class bargain.

Clavierübung, Part 3: German organ Mass; Chorale preludes, BWV 710/13, 718; Chorale variations, BWV 717 and 740; Fantasias and fugues: in C min., BWV 536; in G min., BWV 542; Passacaglia and fugue in C min., BWV 582; Toccatas and fugues: in D min., BWV 538 and 565; in F, BWV 540; Toccata, adagio and fugue in C, BWV 564; Trio sonatas Nos. 1–6, BWV 525/30.

(M) **(*) HM HM 521 (6). Rogg (Silbermann organ, Arlesheim).

Like the other two Harmonia Mundi albums in Lionel Rogg's second integral recording, this music is superbly recorded and the pressings are immaculate. The first disc opens with the *Passacaglia and fugue in C minor*, and Rogg's grave, indeed sombre, mood immediately establishes his seriousness of purpose. The music is laid before the listener in the simplest manner; there is no conscious bravura, and the tension is held at a comparatively low level. In the so-called *German organ Mass*, where one might have expected a more expressive style, Rogg is content to let the music speak for itself. He does not seek to achieve a cumulative emotional force, even at the end of the fugues. The variety of the registration is impressive, but even in the chorales there is never any suggestion of using colour for its own sake. As in the companion issues, the accompanying booklet is in French only.

Clavierübung, Part 3: German organ Mass; Chorale preludes and variations, BWV 714, 716, 719, 721, 723/4; Fantasia in B min., BWV 563; Fugue on the Magnificat, BWV 733; Prelude and fugue in A min., BWV 543; Toccata and fugue in E (C), BWV 566.

(M) *** Argo D 138 D 3/*K 138 K 32* [id.]. Hurford (organs of New College Chapel, Oxford; Knox Grammar School, Sydney, Australia).

Peter Hurford's performance of the so-called *Organ Mass* is uncompromisingly direct. The music itself is essentially reflective, with powerful contrasts made between weight and serenity. Hurford's account makes concessions only in the choice of registrations, which give colour to the expressive writing and lively detail to the more complex polyphony. The opening *Prelude* is massively presented and the *Fugue* is no less forceful, the two pieces making a kind of bracket to enclose the twenty-five diverse inner movements. The use of two different organs successfully adds variety of texture. We are then offered three major works to round off the recital; the closing *Prelude and fugue in A minor* is especially compelling. The sound is first-class; on tape one or two cadential climaxes have momentary hints of congestion, but never for more than a bar or two.

Fantasias and fugues: in C min., BWV 537; in G min., BWV 542; Passacaglia and fugue in C min., BWV 582; Toccata and fugue in D min., BWV 565.

(M) ** HM HM 771. Rogg (Silbermann organ, Arlesheim).

An excellent sampler of Rogg's literal way with Bach and of the fine recording of the Arlesheim organ. The playing is assured and strong, but rather pedantic; the two *Preludes and fugues* are very literal indeed.

Fantasia in G, BWV 572; Preludes and fugues: in C, BWV 545; in C min.; in G, BWV 549/50; in G min., BWV 535; Toccata and fugue in D min., BWV 565.

(M) *** Ph. Seq. 6527/*7311* 109. Rübsam (organ of Frauenfeld, Switzerland).

A splendid collection of early works, nearly all dating from Bach's Arnstadt and Weimar periods and full of exuberance of spirit. The

Fugue in G, BWV 550, is especially memorable, but undoubtedly the highlight of the recital is the superb performance of the *Fantasia in G*. It opens with an exhilarating *Très vitement* and after a massive *Grave* middle section comes a brilliantly lightweight bravura finale. Wolfgang Rübsam's articulation is deliciously pointed. The recording of the Metzler organ has a fairly long reverberation period, and Rübsam anticipates this in his playing most successfully. The quality of the recorded sound is splendid, on tape as well as disc. Highly recommended.

Fantasia and fugue in G min., BWV 542; Passacaglia and fugue in C min., BWV 582; Prelude and fugue in E min., BWV 548; Toccata and fugue in D min., BWV 565.
(M) ** Decca Ser. SA/*KSC* 2. Karl Richter (organ of Victoria Hall, Geneva).

Richter's recital has been in and out of the catalogue several times. It is essentially severe in character with fairly massive sound, generally well accommodated on disc and cassette but with a hint of congestion at one or two climaxes. The highlight is the performance of the *Passacaglia and fugue in C minor* which Richter controls very impressively. There are more exciting accounts available of BWV 565, although Richter's is perfectly acceptable.

Fantasia and fugue in G min., BWV 542; Passacaglia and fugue in C min., BWV 582; Toccata, adagio and fugue in C, BWV 564; Toccata and fugue in D min., BWV 565.
(M) *** HMV SXLP 30274. Germani (organ of the Royal Festival Hall, London).

This HMV reissue again demonstrates how well suited is the Festival Hall organ to stereo recording. Its 8,000 pipes are widely spread, and while there is only a suggestion here of point source in the sound, one can enjoy the impression of music originating from different sections of a broad area. The acoustic too means that the quality of the sound itself is clear, yet full-blooded. The performances are first-class. The listener can hear every detail of the registration, and Fernando Germani's control of tension skilfully lets each fugue slowly build itself to an impressive climax. This especially applies to the *Passacaglia and fugue in C minor*, a riveting performance.

Fantasia and fugue in G min., BWV 542; Passacaglia and fugue in C min., BWV 582; Toccatas and fugues in D min., BWV 538 (Dorian) and 565.
(M) **(*) DG Arc. Priv. 2547/*3347* 011. Walcha (organ of St Laurenskerk, Alkmaar).

Lucid, well-controlled performances, beautifully laid out and effectively if soberly registered, but somewhat lacking in tension. The recording is first-class on disc, marginally less clean on tape, but fully acceptable.

Prelude and fugue in E flat, BWV 552; Prelude, Largo (BWV 529/2) and fugue in C, BWV 545; Toccata and fugue in D min., BWV 565.
** Ph. Dig. **410 038-2**; 6514/*7337* 274 [id.]. Chorzempa (organ).

Daniel Chorzempa is splendidly recorded on compact disc, LP and the excellent chrome tape, but the performances are very measured as is obvious from the famous *D minor fugue*. In the big E flat work, the effect is massive but static and the performance is too deliberate by half. The compact disc with its silent background creates a most spectacular impression on the listener and it is a pity that the organ-début in this medium offers playing of relatively little flair.

6 Schübler chorale preludes, BWV 645/50; Pastorale in F, BWV 590; Prelude and fugue in B min., BWV 544.
** Abbey LPB 760. Lumsden (organ of New College, Oxford).

A fine, musicianly account of the *Schübler chorales*, well contrasted in colour and expertly recorded. The tempi throughout are finely judged, though the registration in the *Pastorale*, BWV 590, could perhaps have been more varied. It is difficult to fault this playing, for David Lumsden is a distinguished musician; but at the same time it must be said that there are more compelling accounts of the *B minor Prelude and fugue* on the market. Good recording.

Toccata and fugue in D min., BWV 565; Trio sonata No. 2 in C min., BWV 526; Preludes and fugues: in D, BWV 532; in G min., BWV 534.
*** DG 138 907 [id.]. Karl Richter (organ).

One of Richter's very finest records and given a superlative recording, which is in a vintage class. Even a sustained pedal note (which causes a feeling of strain) is handled by the engineers with aplomb, and the sound remains clear in the spectacular cadences. The organ is a fairly new one at Jaegersborg, near Copenhagen. The builders have attempted to simulate the principals and action of a baroque instrument, and the result is highly effective. Richter's registration is perceptive in its choice of the right timbres for each piece (notably so in the *Trio sonata*), and his control of the fugues is no less impressive. This is one of the finest available accounts of the famous *Toccata and fugue in D minor*, and if Richter does not show Hurford's exuberance in BWV 532, both this and BWV 534 have a splendid feeling of weight and power.

ORGAN AND VOCAL MUSIC

(i) *18 Leipzig Chorale preludes, BWV 651/68. Chorale partita: O Gott, du frommer Gott; Chorale variations: Christ lag in Todesbanden, BWV 718; Concerto No. 4 in C, BWV 595; Fantasia and fugue in A min., BWV 561; Fugues: in G, BWV 580/1; in G min., BWV 131a; Prelude in G, BWV 568; Prelude and fugue in G min., BWV 539; Trio in G, BWV 586.*
(M) **(*) Argo D 227 D 3/*K 227 K 33* (3). Hurford, (i) with Alban Singers.

For two-thirds of the content of Volume 7 of Peter Hurford's series, Argo have returned to his 1976 integral recording of the *Leipzig Chorale preludes*, where each of the organ performances is preceded by an admirably expressive (and often very beautiful) sung version of the chorale by the Alban Singers. The chorale preludes are played on the excellent Rieger organ of All Souls Unitarian Church, Washington, DC. The playing is impressive, but slightly less telling than the performances we have come to take for granted in this series. Tempi are sometimes relaxed, and the use of a tremolando stop with a rather wide beat will not appeal to all tastes. The alternation of voices and organ is highly effective, although the organ recording is not quite as crisp in focus as the later recordings. This is readily demonstrated when for sides five and six Hurford returns to the organs of Our Lady of Sorrows, Toronto, and Eton College, Windsor, where the sound is as crisp as the playing is buoyant. As usual the tape and disc quality is virtually identical.

(i) *Orgenbüchlein* (*chorale preludes*) *BWV 599–644* (with original vocal chorales); (ii) *Chorale preludes: Ach Herr, mich armen Sünder, BWV 742; Ach was ist doch unser Leben, BWV 743;* (ii) *Auf meinen lieben Gott, BWV 744; Aus der Tiefe rufe ich, BWV 745; Christ ist erstanden, BWV 746; Christus, der uns selig macht, BWV 620a; Gott der Vater wohn' uns bei, BWV 748; In dulci jubilo, BWV 751; Jesu, der du meine Seele, BWV 752; Liebster Jesu, BWV 754; O Herre Gott, BWV 757; O Lamm Gottes unschuldig, NBA; Schmücke dich, O liebe Seele, BWV 759; Vater unser im Himmelreich* (3 settings, *BWV 760/2*); *Wie schöne leuchtet, BWV 763. Prelude and fugue in G min., BWV 535a; Prelude, trio and fugue in B flat, BWV 545b; Ricercar in C min., BWV 1079/5.*
*** Argo D 228 D 4/*K 228 K 44* (4) [id.]. (i) Peter Hurford (organ of Church of Our Lady of Sorrows, Toronto), St John's College Ch., Camb.; (ii) Organ of St Catherine's College, Camb.

In the final box, Volume 8, Peter Hurford crowns his achievement by combining highly imaginative performance of the chorale preludes from the *Orgelnbüchlein* with radiantly expressive singing of the chorales themselves by the St John's College Choir. On the final side there is a short recital to conclude an enterprise that is in every way outstanding, by far the most rewarding assessment of Bach's organ music ever committed to record. The sound remains superb on both disc and tape, with a most beautifully resonant, yet not blurring, ambient effect for the choir.

VOCAL AND CHORAL MUSIC

Cantatas

Sinfonias from Cantatas Nos. 29, 35, 49, 146, 169, 188.
** Erato STU/*MCE* 71116. Alain, Paillard CO, Paillard.

This interesting record is a programme of concerto movements for organ and orchestra culled from various cantatas. The sinfonia from Cantata No. 29 is a transcription of the *Prelude* from the *E major Partita for solo violin*; the one from Cantata No. 35 reconstructs the *D minor Concerto*, BWV 1059, with the organ instead of harpsichord as soloist. The second side is an organ version of the great *D minor Harpsichord concerto*, using the first two movements of Cantata No. 146 and the first of No. 188. The performances are generally of good quality (the organ is of the church of St-Donat in south-east France) and though greater polish would not come amiss from the orchestra, there is little to quarrel with. The recording is well-balanced and lively, and the programme amounts to more than a mere compilation of popular cantata movements.

Cantatas Nos. 1–75.
**(*) [(*1–4*): Tel. 2635 027 (2). VCM, Harnoncourt; (*5–8*): 2635 028 (2). VCM, Harnoncourt and Leonhardt Cons., Leonhardt; (*9–11*): 2635 029 (2). Harnoncourt and Leonhardt; (*12–14; 16*): 2635 030 (2). Leonhardt; (*17–20*): 2635 031 (2). Harnoncourt; (*21–3*): 2635 032 (2). Harnoncourt and Leonhardt; (*24–7*): 2635 033 (2). Harnoncourt; (*28–30*): 2635 034 (2). Harnoncourt; (*31–4*): 2635 035 (2). Harnoncourt and Leonhardt; (*35–8*): 2635 036 (2). Harnoncourt; (*39–42*): 2635 269 (2). Harnoncourt and Leonhardt; (*43–6*): 2635 283 (2). Harnoncourt and Leonhardt; (*47–50*): 2635 284 (2). Harnoncourt; (*51–2; 54–6*): 2635 304 (2): Leonhardt; (*57–60*): 2635 305 (2). Harnoncourt; (*61–4*): 2635 306 (2). Harnoncourt; (*65–8*): 2635 335 (2). Harnoncourt and Leonhardt; (*69–9a; 70–1*): 2635 340 (2). Harnoncourt; (*73–5*): 2635 341 (2). Leonhardt.]

This admirable enterprise, which got under way in the early 1970s during the life of the first *Penguin Stereo Record Guide*, continues to enrich the catalogue, and whatever qualifications one may make, it maintains a consistent and dedicated approach to the greatest repertory of its kind. Briefly, the series aims at the highest authenticity in terms of performance practice, observing the accepted conventions of the period and using authentic instruments or replicas. Boys replace women not only in the choruses but also as soloists, and the size of the musical forces is confined to what we know Bach himself would have expected. Naturally, the absence of famous soloists in the soprano roles will be regretted by many collectors; these can be found in alternative versions. There are advantages in escaping from the sheer beauty of the glamorous celebrities in rival sets, for the imperfect yet other-worldly quality some of the boy soloists possess serves to focus interest on the music itself rather than on the voices. Less appealing perhaps is the quality of the violins, which eschew vibrato – and it would sometimes seem any kind of timbre! Each of the two-record volumes contains copious documentation: the texts of the cantatas in English and French translations, scholarly notes and copies of the scores either in the old Bach Gesellschaft editions or, where available, the Neue-BGG scores. It is probably true to say that the series has grown in strength over the past five years, and much of the self-conscious, slightly inhibited flavour of the earliest sets has gone. Although in most cases we would not wish to see the Leonhardt and Harnoncourt versions as the only recordings in the field, they have so much to recommend them that nearly all the newcomers reviewed below should be investigated by everyone who has the means and inclinations to do so.

Volumes Nos. 1–19 which include the first seventy-five Cantatas have been withdrawn from the British Telefunken catalogue as distributed by Decca, but as we go to press we hear that they will soon become available again through Conifer. They are listed above in the American catalogue number format. In Europe the first two digits (26) are replaced with the prefix EX 6.

Cantata No. 10: Meine Seele erhebt den Herren.
*** Decca SXL 6400 [Lon. CSA 26103]. Ameling, Watts, Krenn, Rintzler, V. Ac. Ch., SCO, Münchinger – *Magnificat.****

This performance is discussed under its coupling.

Cantatas Nos. 11: Lobet Gott in seinen Reichen; 34: O ewiges Feuer.
**(*) HMV ASD/*TC-ASD* 4055. Marshall, Hodgson, Hill, Roberts, King's College Ch., ECO, Ledger.

Apart from boys' voices, the forces used here are traditional. In No. 11 (sometimes known as the *Ascension oratorio*) we encounter the theme Bach was to use later in the *Agnus Dei* of the *B minor Mass*. The solo singing is often impressive, though it could have been more prominently balanced (particularly Martyn Hill in *O ewiges Feuer*). Philip Ledger breaks up the phrases in the *Ach bleibe doch, mein Liebstes leben* in a way that draws attention to itself and inhibits the music's sweep and dignity. But there is some excellent singing and playing in the choruses, and though we have heard more compelling accounts of both cantatas this makes an attractive coupling, with a vivid cassette that matches the disc fairly closely.

Cantatas Nos. 11: Lobet Gott in seinen Reichen; 58: Ach Gott, wie manches Herzeleid; 78: Jesu, der du meine Seele; 198: Lass, Fürstin, lass noch einen Strahl (*Funeral*).
**(*) Erato STU 71099 (2). Girod, Elwes, Ihara, Huttenlocher, Lausanne Chamber Vocal Ens. and O, Corbóz.

The finest cantata here is the so-called Funeral cantata, *Lass, Fürstin*, written for the memorial service to the Princess Christiane Eberhardine, Electress of Saxony and Queen of Poland. Corbóz and his Swiss forces bring a fresh approach to bear, though their interpretation does not eclipse memories of the Jürgens account from the late 1960s, and the recording is not so transparent as the earlier Telefunken. There are some odd details, for instance discrepancies in note values (the choir singing in even notes while the accompaniment is dotted), and the contralto aria is wanting in real intensity. However, there are good things too. The performance of *Lobet Gott* is first-class, and the overall effect, in spite of the less than well-focused detail, is fresh and pleasing.

Cantatas Nos. 53: Schlage doch, gewünschte Stunde; 54: Widerstehe doch der Sünde; 169: Gott soll allein mein Herze haben.
* Erato STU 71161. Finnilä, Paillard CO, Paillard.

The best thing here is the performance of *Gott soll allein*, which finds Birgit Finnilä in good voice. Cantata No. 53 is not authentic, but it is a charming enough piece, if charm is the appropriate term for a funeral aria! Unfortunately the orchestral playing is not really distinguished, and string intonation in *Widerstehe doch der Sünde* is decidedly vulnerable. Here there is no organ continuo, though it is, of course, present in No. 169, whose sinfonia is familiar as the first movement of the *Harpsichord concerto in E.*

Cantatas Nos. (i) *56: Ich will den Kreuzstab gerne tragen;* (ii) *82: Ich habe genug.*
(M) **(*) Ph. 9502/*7313* 094. Souzay, Berlin Capella, German Bach Soloists, Winschermann.
(M) ** Tel. AQ 6.42579. (i) Schopper, V. Boys' Ch., Leonhardt Cons., Leonhardt; (ii) Huttenlocher, VCM, Harnoncourt.

Souzay's recording comes from the beginning of the 1970s. Fischer-Dieskau recorded this coupling too at about the same time, but his version has not yet been reissued. But in many ways Souzay's approach with its greater simplicity of feeling is to be preferred. The recording sounds fresh, but Winschermann alternates harpsichord and organ continuo, which will irritate some listeners. There are attractive oboe obbligati in both works. Winschermann is the soloist in No. 56, but in No. 82 Gunther Zörn takes over and his contribution is memorably beautiful. The sound is generally very good with quite a high-level tape transfer (higher on side one, with a gain in presence in No. 56). On Telefunken Cantata No. 56 is a highly successful performance, with fine solo singing from the bass, Michael Schopper, and some sensitive obligato oboe playing. *Ich habe genug*, however, has been performed more impressively on other recordings. Philippe Huttenlocher, though intelligent and thoughtful, is not always secure. The recording is well up to standard.

Cantata No. 60: O Ewigkeit, du Donnerwort.
(M) *(*) Sup. 50804. Mrázová, English, Polster, Musici Pragenses, Czech Philharmonic Ch., Turnovsky – BERG: *Violin concerto.****

It was a good idea to couple Suk's beautiful performance of the Berg *Violin concerto* with the Bach work from which Berg took his chorale theme, though in fact the Czech interpretation of Bach is far less stylish than the playing of the modern work. Martin Turnovsky does not avoid rhythmic lumpiness with his slab-sided continuo-playing, and though the soloists are good, there is not enough variety of expression among the instrumentalists. The recording is well spread in stereo.

Cantatas Nos. (i) *73: Herr wie du willt, so schicks mit mir;* (ii) *94: Was frag' ich nacht der Welt.*
(M) ** Tel. AQ 6.42664. (i) Erler, Equiluz, Van Egmond, Hanover Boys' Ch., Coll. Vocale, Gent, Leonhardt Cons., Leonhardt; (ii) Wiedl, Treble soloists from Tölz Ch., Esswood, Equiluz, Huttenlocher, Tölz Ch., VCM, Harnoncourt.

No. 73 is an Epiphany cantata and has some strikingly original invention. The performance, however, with rather sedate tempi and uneven solo singing, is not up to the finest standards of this series. No. 94, in Harnoncourt's hands, is a consistently fine account with excellent solo singing and plenty of life in the accompaniments, with excellent obligato playing from the flute and oboe.

Cantatas Nos. (i) *76: Die Himmel erzählen die Ehre Gottes;* (ii) *77: Du sollst Gott, deinen Herrn, lieben;* (i) *78: Jesu, der du meine Seele;* (ii) *79: Gott, der Herr, ist Sonn' und Schild.*
**(*) Tel. EX 6.35362 (2) [id.]. Esswood, (i) Wiedl, Equiluz, Van der Meer, Tölz Ch., VCM, Harnoncourt; (ii) Bratschke, Krauss, Van Egmond, Hanover Boys' Ch., Leonhardt Cons., Leonhardt.

Two of the cantatas in Volume 20 are not otherwise recorded at present, and all four are of outstanding interest. As always in authentic performances one is aware of constraints, and the ear longs for the bolder colours and greater power of modern instruments. However, there is too much good music here for such reservations to worry us for long. Two of the cantatas (77 and 79) are given by Gustav Leonhardt and sound excellent. There is some superb playing from Don Smithers in *Du sollst Gott, deinen Herrn, lieben* and some beautifully pure singing from the boy treble, Detlef Bratschke. The Harnoncourt performances are a little less satisfying and one feels the want of grandeur in the opening of No. 78 (*Jesu, der du meine Seele*), but again there are too many things to admire for small reservations to weigh too much in the balance. The quality of sound is very good indeed.

Cantatas Nos. 80: Ein' feste Burg; 81: Jesus schläft; 82: Ich habe genug; 83: Erfreute Zeit.
*(*) Tel. EX 6.35363 (2) [id.]. V. Boys' Ch. treble soloists, Esswood, Equiluz, Van Egmond, Huttenlocher, Van der Meer, Ch. Viennensis, Tölz Ch., VCM, Harnoncourt.

This is one of the less successful issues in the Telefunken series. *Ich habe genug* has been performed more impressively on other recordings, and Philippe Huttenlocher, though intelligent and thoughtful, is not always secure. Some of the choral singing elsewhere in this volume could do with more polish and incisiveness too. *Ein' feste Burg* is given minus the trumpets and drums thought to have been added by Wilhelm Friedemann, and here the gain in textural clarity is considerable. The singing of the treble is excellent in this cantata. No. 83 is an older recording, dating from the late 1960s; No. 81 is more impressive instrumentally than vocally. As all but one of these cantatas are available in other versions, this set has less strong claims than its immediate neighbours in the series. Those collecting the whole series will know what to expect.

Cantatas Nos. 80: Ein' feste Burg; 140: Wachet auf.

(M) ** DG Arc. Priv. 2547/*3347* 024 [198 407/ *924 007*]. Giebel, Töpper, Schreier, Adam, Leipzig Thomanerchor and GO, Mauersberger.

** Ph. 6514/7337 097 [id.]. Ameling, Finnie, Baldin, Ramey, London Voices, ECO, Leppard.

Serviceable rather than distinguished accounts of these two well-known cantatas from Mauersberger. *Ein' feste Burg* is performed without the trumpets and drums of Wilhelm Friedemann, but with harpsichord rather than organ continuo. The recordings were made in the mid-1960s in Bach's own St Thomas's, Leipzig. Boys are used in the choruses; their intonation is not perfect. The solo singing is predictably good, and the recording has admirable clarity and definition. But Mauersberger does not bring the highest sensitivity to bear on the phrasing, and some of the obbligati are routine. There is enough here to warrant a recommendation at medium price, but the qualifications should be noted. The tape transfer is fresh and clear, with good choral focus, although the level is rather low on side two (No. 140).

In *Ein' feste Burg* Leppard uses the parts for three trumpets and drums that Wilhelm Friedemann added to the score after his father's death. It is a well-prepared, straightforward account with good playing from the ECO and some responsive singing from the chorus. *Wachet auf* is the less successful and, even apart from the rather too measured tempo of the first of the duets, Elly Ameling's intonation is not completely true. There are good things, of course, and the actual sound is extremely fine. It is to be preferred to Karl Richter's pedestrian account from his 1978 box which was similarly coupled, and makes a useful complement to the Mauersberger version. The cassette transfer is satisfactory, quite lively on top, although the choral sound is rather grainy.

Cantatas Nos. 82: Ich habe genug; 169: Gott soll allein mein Herze haben.

(M) *** HMV *TCC2-POR 154592-9*. Baker, Amb. S., Bath Fest. O, Menuhin – *Arias.****

Ich habe genug is one of the best-known of Bach's cantatas, while No. 169 is a comparative rarity. The performances are expressive and intelligent, though Dame Janet Baker does not achieve quite the same heights of inspiration here as in her Jubilee record of No. 159. Recording is admirably lifelike and reproduces smoothly. The chrome tape transfer too is immaculate, clean and clear, with a natural bloom on the voice. The disc version is now withdrawn, but the coupling of this special double-length cassette issue is very attractive – see below.

Cantatas Nos. (i) *82: Ich habe genug;* (ii) *202: Weichet nur, betrübte Schatten.*

*(*) Hyp. A/*KA* 66036. (i) Thomas; (ii) Kirkby; Taverner Players, Parrott.

In *Ich habe genug* David Thomas gives a good but not inspired account of the solo part and although the odd intonation blemish is of little importance, memories of Hotter, Souzay, Fischer-Dieskau and others who have recorded it in the past are not banished. Emma Kirkby is more successful in *Weichet nur, betrübte Schatten* and as usual delights the listener though some may feel that the excellent Taverner Players under Andrew Parrott could bring greater flair and lightness of touch to this felicitous score. Good recording and sensibly balanced. The cassette is made at fractionally too high a level and the upper range is confused in focus.

Cantatas Nos. (i) *84: Ich bin vergnügt; 85: Ich bin ein guter Hirt; 86: Wahrlich, wahrlich, ich sage euch; 87: Bisher habt ihr nichts gebeten in meinem Namen;* (ii) *88: Siehe, ich will viel Fischer aussenden; 89: Was soll ich aus dir machen; 90: Es reifet euch ein schrecklich Ende.*

** Tel. EX 6.35364 (2) [id.]. Esswood, Equiluz, (i) Wiedl, Van der Meer, Tölz Ch., VCM, Harnoncourt; (ii) Klein, Van Egmond, Hanover Boys' Ch., Ghent Coll. Vocale, Leonhardt Cons., Leonhardt.

On the first record Harnoncourt directs polished but often uncommitted performances, though there is brave singing from the treble Wilhelm Wiedl in some cruelly demanding solo writing (*Ich bin vergnügt*). Leonhardt's performances are more effectively characterized, and there is some particularly fine obbligato trumpet playing from Don Smithers and eloquent singing from Max van Egmond. If the performances are of variable quality, the musical inspiration is not, and the set is worth acquiring for the sake of this neglected music, much of which is otherwise unobtainable.

Cantatas Nos. (i) *91: Gelobet seist du, Jesus Christ; 92: Ich hab' in Gottes Herz und Sinn;* (ii) *93: Wer nur den lieben Gott lässt walten; 94: Was frag' ich nach der Welt.*
*** Tel. EX 6.35441 (2) [id.]. Esswood, Equiluz, (i) Bratschke, Van Egmond, Hanover Boys' Ch., Ghent Coll. Vocale, Leonhardt Cons., Leonhardt; (ii) Wiedl, Van der Meer, Huttenlocher, Tölz Ch., VCM, Harnoncourt.

One of the most desirable of these Bach sets, with assured and confident playing and singing from all concerned. Cantata No. 91 is not otherwise available, and while No. 94 is also issued on a single disc, coupled with No. 73, the above compilation is preferable. These cantatas, though not among Bach's greatest, include some marvellous and neglected music.

Cantatas Nos. (i) *95: Christus, der ist mein Leben; 96: Herr Christ, der ein'ge Gottessohn; 97: In allen meinen Taten;* (ii) *98: Was Gott tut.*
*** Tel. EX 6.35442 (2) [id.]. (i) Wiedl, Esswood, Equiluz, Huttenlocher, Van der Meer, Tölz Ch., VCM, Harnoncourt; (ii) Lengert, Equiluz, Esswood, Van Egmond, Hanover Boys' Ch., Ghent Coll. Vocale, Leonhardt Cons., Leonhardt.

Apart from No. 96, which was included in Richter's deleted set of cantatas for the last ten Sundays after Trinity, these cantatas are not otherwise represented in the current catalogue. There are occasional weaknesses here (Philippe Huttenlocher is not altogether happy in No. 96), but the set is still well worth having. Harnoncourt is more stylistically assured and polished than Richter and the opening chorus is more imaginatively handled here. No. 95, on the theme of imminent death and the soul's departure from earth, is a wonderful piece, full of striking invention, and it fares excellently in these artists' hands.

Cantatas Nos. (i) *99: Was Gott tut;* (ii) *100: Was Gott tut;* (i) *101: Nimm von uns, Herr; 102: Herr, deine Augen sehen nach dem Glauben.*
** Tel. EX 6.35443 (2) [id.]. (i) Wiedl, Esswood, Equiluz, Huttenlocher, Tölz Ch., VCM, Harnoncourt; (ii) Bratschke, Esswood, Equiluz, Van Egmond, Hanover Boys' Ch., Ghent Coll. Vocale, Leonhardt Cons., Leonhardt.

With this album Telefunken come to the twenty-fifth volume of the cantatas and pass the century! This is no mean achievement, and though inevitably there is unevenness in the series, it is still one of the triumphs of the recording industry. In this volume, Cantata No. 99 fares less well than the others, and the boy soloist, Wilhelm Wiedl, is not his usual self; nor is the Tölz choir at its most positive. Greater expressive intensity would not have come amiss in the chorus of No. 101, but it would be curmudgeonly to dwell on the shortcomings of this box – or of the series as a whole, for it serves to introduce collectors to unfamiliar works. Cantatas Nos. 100 and 102 were included in Richter's now deleted DG set; Nos. 99 and 101 are not otherwise available elsewhere.

Cantatas Nos. (i; ii) *103: Ihr werdet weinen und heulen;* (iii; iv) *104: Du Hirte Israel, höre;* (v; vi) *105: Herr, gehe nicht ins Gericht;* (vi; ii) *106: Gottes Zeit* (*Actus tragicus*).
*** Tel. EX 6.35558 (2) [id.]. (i) Esswood, Equiluz, Van Egmond; (ii) Hanover Boys' Ch., Coll. Vocale, Leonhardt Cons., Leonhardt; (iii) Esswood, Huttenlocher; (iv) Tölz Boys' Ch., VCM, Harnoncourt; (v) Wiedl, Equiluz, Van der Meer; (vi) Klein, Harten, Van Altena, Van Egmond.

Gustav Leonhardt directs Nos. 103 and 106, and Nikolaus Harnoncourt the other two. The best-known and most deeply moving is the 'Actus Tragicus' (*Gottes Zeit ist die allerbeste Zeit*), which receives an exemplary performance that surpasses Leonhardt's account in the mid-1960s for Das Alte Werk, much praised by Alec Robertson. There is an excellent boy soloist and, as in the earlier disc, Franz Brüggen is one of the masterly recorder players. *Ihr werdet weinen und heulen* has rarely been put on disc and is a poignant and expressive piece that rewards attention. Both these performances are among the very finest to have reached us in this series. No. 105, *Herr, gehe nicht ins Gericht*, is arguably one of the very deepest of all Bach cantatas, and since Ansermet's account was deleted, the only alternative version was by Richter. But this too has now gone. The Harnoncourt is perhaps wanting in expressive weight, but neither this fact nor the reservations one might feel about his account of No. 104, which is not otherwise available, diminishes the value of this excellent box, which comes with the usual notes and score.

Cantata No. 106: Gottes Zeit (*Actus tragicus*).
(M) *** HM 21441. Ameling, Lehane, Equiluz, McDaniel, Aachen Domchor, Coll. Aur., Pohl – TELEMANN: *Funeral cantata*.***

Cantatas Nos. 106; 140: Wachet auf.
** Mer. E 77016. Rödin, Hallin, Björkegren, Hagegård, Stockholm Bach Ch. and Bar. Ens., Ohrwall.

Cantatas Nos. 106; 182: Himmelskönig, sei willkommen.
(M) *** Tel. AQ 6.41060. Falk, Van t'Hoff, Villisech, Hamburg Monteverdi Ch., Leonhardt Cons., Jürgens.

Bach's *Funeral cantata* probably owes its existence to the death of his uncle, Tobias Lämmerhirt, in 1707. Bach's feelings must have been mixed, as he was left a small legacy. At any rate, if this was for the uncle, Bach did him proud, with writing of great poignancy. In fact *Gottes Zeit* is one of the most inspired of all Bach cantatas. Its opening sinfonia is positively sublime and it is played with great feeling and imagination here. It is no surprise to learn from the Telefunken sleeve that Franz Brüggen is one of the recorder players. Throughout, the performance is as sensitive as it is stylish, and the recording is beautifully balanced and splendidly spacious. No. 182 is a Palm Sunday cantata, not one of Bach's finest, but there are, of course, good things in it, and it is most persuasively performed. The recording is spacious yet well-defined, and the disc is worth having for *Gottes Zeit* alone.

The Pohl recording dates from the late 1960s, and it can be recommended alongside the Telefunken version by Jürgen Jürgens, though the latter has a slightly more transparent and revealing sound. There is fine solo singing here, but the boys of the Aachen Cathedral Choir are not always as sure and firm as Jürgens's forces. The Collegium Aureum provide a thoroughly musical support on their authentic instruments, and the warm acoustic flatters all concerned. The coupling is particularly attractive too; no need for hesitation here.

The version from Stockholm has the merits of freshness and vitality, and there is excellent singing from Margot Rödin and Håkan Hagegård, as well as some musical and sensitive instrumental playing. *Wachet auf* is less impressive vocally (the often brilliant Margareta Hallin is not strongly cast in this repertoire), and the choral singing could perhaps be a little more strongly characterized. The good recording helps, but for both cantatas this is a useful alternative rather than a first choice.

Cantatas Nos. (i) *107: Was willst du dich betrüben;* (ii) *108: Es ist euch gut; 109: Ich glaube, lieber Herr; 110: Unser Mund sei voll Lachens.*
*** Tel. EX 6.35559 (2) [id.]. (i) Klein, Equiluz, Van Egmond, Hanover Boys' Ch., Ghent Coll. Vocale, Leonhardt Cons., Leonhardt; (ii) Wiedl, Frangoulis, Stumpf, Lorenz, Esswood, Equiluz, Van der Meer, Tölz Ch., VCM, Harnoncourt.

Gustav Leonhardt gets splendid results in the expressive chorus which opens Cantata No. 107, and the singing throughout is of a high order. The cantatas all date from the period 1724–5; No. 110 borrows the overture from the *Suite No. 4 in D*, which is effectively used to accompany a four-part vocal texture. This is a festive cantata produced for Christmas Day in Leipzig in 1725 and again three years later, and is scored for relatively large forces. The high standards of this series are maintained throughout this volume, and that applies to performance, recording, pressings and presentation.

Cantata No. 110: Unser Mund sei voll Lachens.

*(*) HM 1C 065 99750. Hinterreiter, Stein, Altmeyer, Nimsgern, Tölz Ch., Coll. Aur., Maier – *Magnificat*.*(*)

This is the only available recording of the joyful Christmas Day cantata other than Harnoncourt's, and it is given a serviceable performance here, well recorded. But use of authentic instruments does provide problems of intonation (and the solo singing is not immaculate in this respect either). The performance of the *Magnificat* shares this defect. Its style is robust, and the lack of refinement together with a jerky contribution from the chorus do not recommend it very highly.

Cantata No. 118: O Jesu Christ mein's Lebens Licht.

(M) *(*) Uni. UNS 248. Soloists, L. Bach Soc. Ch., Steinitz Bach Players, Steinitz – *Magnificat*.*(*)

See below under the coupling.

Cantatas Nos. (i; iii; iv) *115: Mache dich, mein Geist, bereit; 116: Du Friedefürst, Herr Jesu Christ:* (ii; v; vi) *117: Sei Lob und Ehr dem höchsten Gut;* (i; iii; vii) *119: Preise, Jerusalem, den Herrn.*

*** Tel. EX 6.35577 (2) [id.]. (i) Tölz Ch., VCM, Harnoncourt; (ii) Hanover Boys' Ch., and Collegium Vocale, Leonhardt Cons.; (ii) directed Leonhardt, with Equiluz; (iii) Esswood; (iv) Huttenlocher; (v) Jacobs; (vi) Van Egmond; (vii) Holl.

Considering its high quality of melodic inspiration, it is astonishing that *Mache dich, mein Geist, bereit* has been so neglected by the gramophone. It comes from 1724 and is richly inventive. Particularly felicitous is the aria for soprano, flute and violoncello piccolo which, despite a moment of uncertainty from Markus Huber, is most affectingly done. Its companion, *Du Friedefürst, Herr Jesu Christ*, is close both in provenance and theme (the approaching Day of Judgement), and opens with a lively A major chorus that is given with plenty of vigour and spirit. There is a demanding trio for boy soprano, tenor and bass that taxes the soloists (and in particular their intonation) but rewards the listener with invention of great contrapuntal refinement (the middle section is in triple counterpoint with permutations). *Sei Lob und Ehr dem höchsten Gut* is later, written probably between 1728 and 1731, and is an imposing piece. This is the only one conducted by Gustav Leonhardt whose tempi are excellently judged (one grumble is the detached delivery of the chorale which sounds unnecessarily jerky). The last cantata, *Preise, Jerusalem, den Herrn*, dates from 1723, Bach's first year at Leipzig, and is rich in colouring: the tenor aria, *Wohl dir, du Volk der Linden*, with its accompaniment of two *oboi de caccia* with organ and bassoon continuo is rudely interrupted by a recitative with four trumpets, timpani and provides just one of the contrasts of texture that make this so fascinating a piece. Harnoncourt is in good form and the recording is excellently balanced and splendidly truthful. The presentation including scores and notes by Ludwig Finscher is up to the standards we expect from this enterprise.

Cantatas Nos. 120: Gott, man lobet dich in der Stille; 121: Christum wir sollen loben; 122: Das neugebor'ne Kindelein; 123: Liebster Immanuel, Herzog der Frommen.

*** Tel. EX 6.35578 (2) [id.]. Treble soloists from Tölz Ch., Esswood, Equiluz, Huttenlocher or Holl, Tölz Ch., VCM, Harnoncourt.

Gott, man lobet dich in der Stille includes a movement that Bach later adapted for use in the *Credo* of the *B minor Mass*. The cantata, like BWV 119, was written for the Leipzig Town Council Election, but some five or six years later. Though it is not quite as imposing, it is far from inconsiderable and its opening aria, with its ritornelli for two oboes d'amore, is a delight. *Christum wir sollen loben* and *Das neugebor'ne Kindelein*, both from the second cycle of Leipzig cantatas (1724), are both rewarding even if the bass aria in No. 121 has been more effectively done on record. *Liebster Immanuel, Herzog der Frommen* is based on Ahasuerus Fritsch's hymn (1679) and the melody of the opening movement derives from the courante. Alec Robertson called it 'an intimate and tender meditation on the "beloved Emmanuel" ', and it is a haunting movement. No serious grumbles about any of the performances, even if one or two numbers fall short of perfection. The recordings are exemplary in every way and those who have followed the series – and at present there is no other way of acquiring these cantatas – need not hesitate. As usual there are scholarly notes, texts and miniature scores provided.

Cantatas Nos. (i) *124: Meinen Jesum lass ich nicht; 125: Mit Fried und Freud ich fahr dahin; 126: Erhalt uns, Herr, bei deinem Wort;* (ii) *127: Herr Jesu Christ wahr' Mensch.*
*** Tel. EX 6.35602 (2) [id.]. (i) Bergius, Rampf, Esswood, Equiluz, Thomaschke, Tölz Ch., VCM, Harnoncourt; (ii) Hennig, Van Egmond, Hanover Boys' Ch., Coll. Vocale, Leonhardt Cons., Leonhardt.

These all come from the second cycle of cantatas that Bach wrote for Leipzig and which, until Easter 1725, consisted entirely of chorale cantatas. No. 124, *Meinen Jesum lass ich nicht*, an Epiphany work, is a piece of strong melodic vitality and is full of colour too. Apart from the almost romantic tenor aria with its inspired oboe d'amore part, there is also a glorious duet for treble and alto charmingly sung by Alan Bergius and Stefan Rampf, which also haunts the memory. This is an excellent piece and its neglect by the gramophone remains unaccountable. As with the case of Nos. 125 and 126, there is no alternative version. *Mit Fried und Freud ich fahr dahin* is even finer and would alone justify the cost of this set. The opening chorus is little short of inspired, and the alto solo which follows is wonderfully expressive and receives eloquent treatment, too, from Paul Esswood. This is a grave, elevated work that is quite affecting. No. 126 is based on a Lutheran hymn and the bellicose spirit of the first verse inspires Bach to write real battle music, and include a demanding trumpet part. No. 127, *Herr Jesu Christ wahr' Mensch und Gott*, is another cantata of striking richness and inspiration, and the soprano aria, *Die Seele ruht in Jesu Händen*, depicting the soul summoned to Jesus' keeping, is extraordinarily beautiful (the plucked strings are heard against a lyrical figure, a texture comprising oboe and two recorders). It is an altogether marvellous piece and very well performed, too. This is a set that collectors who are not automatically acquiring the complete series should not overlook.

Cantatas Nos. 136: Erforsche mich Gott; 137: Lobe den Herren; 138: Warum betrübst du dich; 139: Wohl dem, der sich auf seinem Gott.
**(*) Tel. EX 6.35608 (2) [id.]. Bergius, Rampf, Esswood, Equiluz, Holl, Heldwein, Hartinger, Tolz Ch., VCM, Harnoncourt.

Cantata No. 136 belongs to Bach's first Leipzig cycle in 1723, though Gerhard Schuhmacher suggests in the excellent notes that Bach had recourse to earlier, no longer extant, compositions. There is a fine alto aria, *Es kömmt ein Tag*, and an imposing final chorale, but otherwise this does not rank among the greatest of the cantatas, nor is the playing impeccable either, though the singing is generally good. In No. 137 there is a marvellous performance from Paul Esswood in his aria, *Lobe den Herren*, and from the boy soprano, Alan Bergius, in the duet with bass that follows. But the real discovery in this set is No. 138, *Warum betrübst du dich, mein Herz?*, which is something of a rarity on record. Its astonishing opening movement is in itself worth the price of the set, for it is Bach at his most inspired. In part, the text is based on a hymn of fourteen stanzas attributed to Hans Sachs, but the resource and ingenuity of this movement are as formidable as its profound originality. It quite overshadows everything else in the cantata. No. 139 is another fine piece and its opening chorus, though not in the same class as its predecessor, is still a good one, though the arias that follow for tenor and bass are even finer. The autograph does not survive and Bach experts believe that a second violin part is missing and, according to Alfred Dürr, the violin part in the bass aria,

Das Unglück schlägt auf allen Seiten, was added by Bach's pupil and son-in-law, Johann Christoph Altnikol. Although not all is perfect and Harnoncourt's direction may at times strike some listeners as a little too literal, there is enough here to reward the collector of this invaluable series. As usual throughout the set, there are scores provided. Impeccably silent surfaces.

Cantata No. 147: Herz und Mund und Tat und Leben. Motets: *Fürchte dich nicht, BWV 228; Der Geist hilft unsrer, BWV 226; Loben den Herrn, BWV 230.*

(M) ** HMV HQS 1254 [Ang. S 36804]. Ameling, Baker, Partridge, Shirley-Quirk, King's College Ch., ASMF, Willcocks.

This issue has the advantage of a mid-priced label and excellent soloists. The motets are rather less successful than the cantata (as a performance, not the music itself), but this is still a refreshing coupling. The cantata is, of course, the source of the famous chorale, *Jesu joy of man's desiring*. The recording is of a high quality.

Cantatas Nos. 159: Sehet, wir geh'n hinauf gen Jerusalem; 170: Vergnügte Ruh'.

(M) ❀ *** Decca Jub. 410 170-1/*4* [id.]. Baker, Tear, Shirley-Quirk, St Anthony S., ASMF, Marriner.

Sehet, wir geh'n hinauf gen Jerusalem is one of Bach's most inspired cantatas and surely ranks high on any short list of the essential Bach. Particularly glorious is the penultimate meditation, *Es ist vollbracht* (*It is finished*), with its poignant oboe obbligato. Both Dame Janet Baker and John Shirley-Quirk are in marvellous voice, and performance and recording are of high quality. The coupling, *Vergnügte Ruh'*, makes a worthy companion, and it is equally superbly performed. This is among the half dozen or so cantata records that ought to be in every collection.

Cantata No. 210: O! holder Tag, erwunschte Zeit.

** None. Dig. D/*DI* 79013 [id.]. Nelson, Bach Ens., Rifkin.

O! holder Tag, erwunschte Zeit is something of a rarity on record. It is a late work, composed in the late 1730s, and intended for a wedding celebration. The score makes considerable demands on the soprano soloist and, though it is not alone among the cantatas in so doing, it is more extended than many others: there are five recitatives and five arias. Judith Nelson copes with the taxing solo role bravely, even if she betrays the odd moment of strain, and Joshua Rifkin and his Bach Ensemble give fluent support. The digital recording is clean and the acoustic decent. Not an indispensable cantata for the non-specialist collector, but a rewarding one all the same.

Cantatas Nos. 211: Schweigt stille (*Coffee*)*; 212: Mer hahn eine neue Oberkeet* (*Peasant*).

*** HMV Dig. ASD/*TC-ASD* 146743-1/*4* [Ang. S/*4XS* 37984]. Hofmann, De Mey, Reinhardt, Linde Cons., Linde.

Bach at his most genial is presented here in authentic performances which are also warmly communicative. Linde is as light and lively here as he is in his recordings of the orchestral suites, and though the voices are recorded with a lively ambience the result is intimate. The singers are all splendid at bringing out the charm and humour of both pieces with vivid pointing of words. On tape the choral focus is less sharp than on disc.

Christmas oratorio, BWV 248.

*** HMV SLS/*TC-SLS* 5098 (3) [Ang. SC 3840]. Ameling, Baker, Tear, Fischer-Dieskau, King's College Ch., ASMF, Ledger.

**(*) Tel. FK 6.35022/*MO4 35022* (3) [3635022]. Treble soloists from V. Boys' Ch., Esswood, Equiluz, Nimsgern, V. Boys' Ch., Ch. Viennensis, VCM, Harnoncourt.

**(*) DG Arc. 2710 024 (3)/*3376 012* [id.]. Hopfner, Hillebrand, Regensburg Ch. treble and alto soloists, Coll. St Emmeram, Schneidt.

With generally brisk tempi (controversially so in the alto's cradle song, *Schlafe mein Liebster*, in Part II) Philip Ledger directs an intensely refreshing performance which grows more winning the more one hears it.

It was Ledger who played the harpsichord continuo in many of Benjamin Britten's performances of this work, and some of Britten's imagination comes through here, helped by four outstanding and stylish soloists. The King's acoustic gives a warm background to the nicely scaled performances of choir and orchestra; the timpani at the very start sound spectacularly impressive. However, the reverberant acoustic has obviously caused problems in the cassette transfer, and the recording on tape is not always well-focused in fortissimos and is generally without the edge of brilliance that this joyful work needs.

Harnoncourt in his search for authenticity in Bach performance has rarely been more successful than here. It will not be to everyone's taste to have a boy treble and male counter-tenor instead of women soloists, but the purity of sound of these singers is most affecting. Above all Harnoncourt in this instance never allows his pursuit of authentic sound to weigh the performance down. It has a lightness of touch which should please everyone. The sound, as usual from this source, is excellent.

On the Archive recording conducted by Hans-Martin Schneidt it may seem incongruous to hear the Virgin Mary's cradle song sung by a piping boy treble, but that is how Bach must have heard it, and here the easy authenticity makes for performance which, from the joyful fanfares of the opening sinfonia of the first cantata, is celebratory on an intimate scale. Ensemble is not always flawless, but the spirit is consistently compelling. Excellent recording; the tape transfer is generally smooth and pleasing, but lacks the last degree of range at the top, which seldom sparkles.

Christmas oratorio: choruses and arias.
(M) **(*) DG Priv. 2535 369 [id.]. Janowitz, Ludwig, Wunderlich, Crass, Mun. Bach Ch. and O, Richter.

This is a good selection of items from a long work; they are taken mainly from the first, second and fourth cantatas of the six. Karl Richter's direction has its prosaic moments, but the solo and choral singing is first-rate. The 1965 recording is good for its period.

Christmas oratorio: highlights.
(M) ** Ph. Seq. 6527/*7311* 070. Ameling, Fassbaender, Laubenthal, Prey, Bav. R. Ch. and SO, Jochum.

This fairly generous sampler from Jochum's complete set tends rather to emphasize its stylistic shortcomings; its overall warmth and dedication are less striking when the music is presented piecemeal (although the selection is well balanced). The singing is excellent and the recording sounds very natural.

Easter oratorio, BWV 249.
(M) **(*) Ph. Seq. 6527/*7311* 084 [id.]. Donath, Reynolds, Haefliger, Talvela, Berlin RIAS Chamber Ch., Berlin RSO, Maazel.

Maazel produces an enjoyably lively account, of this surprisingly under-recorded work, with a good team of soloists and a spirited contribution from the chorus. The orchestral playing is also first-class – there is a beautifully played oboe solo (Gunter Zorn) in the opening *Sinfonia* and later the obbligato woodwind are very good too, notably the flute (Karl Bernhard) who embroiders Helen Donath's lovely *Seele deine Spezereien* skilfully. The sound of the 1966 recording remains fresh (the cassette is strikingly wide in range and has excellent detail and bite) and if at times Maazel shows a somewhat conventional rhythmic feeling, the performance communicates readily throughout.

Magnificat in D, BWV 243.
*** Decca SXL 6400 [Lon. OS 26103]. Ameling, Van Bork, Watts, Krenn, Krause, V. Ac. Ch., SCO, Münchinger – *Cantata No. 10.****
(*) Argo ZRG/*KZRC* 854 [id. LP only]. Palmer, Watts, Tear, Roberts, King's College Ch., ASMF, Ledger – VIVALDI: *Magnificat.(*)*
** DG 2531/*3301* 048 [id.]. Tomowa-Sintow, Baltsa, Schreier, Luxon, German Op. Ch., Berlin PO, Karajan – STRAVINSKY: *Symphony of Psalms.***
(M) *(*) Uni. UNS 248. Molyneux, Esswood, Partridge, Noble, L. Bach Soc. Ch., Steinitz Bach Players, Steinitz – *Cantata No. 118.*(*)*

*(*) HM 1C 065 99750. Gampert, Hinterreiter, Stein, Altmeyer, Nimsgern, Tolz Boys' Ch., Coll. Aur., Maier – *Cantata No. 110.**(*)

Magnificat in E flat (original version), *BWV 243a.*
*** O-L DSLO/*KDSLC* 572. Nelson, Kirkby, C. Watkinson, Elliot, D. Watkinson, Christ Church Ch., AcAM, Preston – KUHNAU: *Der Gerechte kommt um.****

The original version of the *Magnificat* is textually different in detail (quite apart from being a semitone higher) and has four interpolations for the celebration of Christmas. Preston and the Academy of Ancient Music present a characteristically alert and fresh performance, and the Christ Church Choir is in excellent form. One might quibble at the use of women soloists instead of boys, but these three specialist singers have just the right incisive timbre and provide the insight of experience. The fill-up is a welcome rarity. Excellent recording and an outstandingly good tape transfer.

The better-known D major version of the *Magnificat* receives a performance and recording from Münchinger and Decca as impressive as any in the catalogue. The soloists are uniformly good, and so are the contributions of the Vienna Academy Choir and the Stuttgart Orchestra. Münchinger tends to stress the breadth and spaciousness of the *Magnificat*, and the Decca engineers have captured the detail with admirable clarity and naturalness. The recording is finer than Ledger's or Karajan's, and the performance is deeply considered. The *Cantata* too is very well performed and makes an excellent coupling.

On Argo, Philip Ledger directs a lively and dramatic account. The warm acoustic of King's College Chapel creates problems of balance but surprisingly few of clarity, and with its apt and unusual coupling this is a most attractive version, highly recommendable if boys' voices are preferred in the chorus. The women soloists are outstanding, as is the St Martin's Academy. The four Christmas interpolations provide an additional attraction. However, the cassette is not one of Argo's best.

Karajan's reading of the *Magnificat* makes it an orchestral work with subsidiary chorus, and though the ingredients are polished and refined, the result is artificial. The soloists are excellent, but with its curious coupling this is not a competitive version.

Steinitz directs a characteristically energetic performance, also using the Christmas interpolations; but, apart from the contributions of the male soloists, it is not a sufficiently polished account to compete with the best. The *Funeral cantata*, No. 118, makes a good fill-up, and except for some odd balances the recording quality is good.

The Harmonia Mundi Collegium Aureum version is discussed under its coupling.

Mass in B min., BWV 232.
*** HMV Dig. SLS/*TCC-SLS* 5215 (3/*2*) [Ang. DSC/*4X3S* 3904]. Donath, Fassbaender, Ahnsjö, Holl, Bav. R. Ch. and SO, Jochum.
*** Ph. 6769 002/*7699 076* [id.]. Marshall, Baker, Tear, Ramey, Ch. and ASMF, Marriner.
**(*) Decca SET 477/8 [Lon. OSA 1287]. Ameling, Minton, Watts, Krenn, Krause, Stuttgart Chamber Ch. and O, Münchinger.
*** None. Dig. **CD 79036-2**; D 79036/*D4-* [id.]. Nelson, Baird, Dooley, Minter, Hoffmeister, Brownless, Opalach, Schultze, Bach Ens., Rifkin.
** Tel. FK 6.35019/*MH2-4.35019* (3) [3635019]. Hansmann, Iiyama, Watts, Equiluz, Van Egmond, V. Boys' Ch., Ch. Viennensis, VCM, Harnoncourt.
** DG 2740 112 (3) [2709049]. Janowitz, Ludwig, Schreier, Kerns, Ridderbusch, Vienna Singverein, Berlin PO, Karajan.
** HMV SLS/*TC-SLS* 930 (3/*2*) [Ang. 3720]. Giebel, Baker, Gedda, Prey, Crass, BBC Ch., New Philh. O, Klemperer.

Jochum's memorably dedicated performance, marked by resilient rhythms – made clearer by the atmospheric digital recording – is the most completely satisfying yet recorded. It is a magnificent reading which more than any of its rivals captures the grandeur of the work. Gilded with bright trumpets, the *Gloria* is irresistibly joyful and, as is apt in this piece, the choral numbers stand as the corner-stones.

The quintet of soloists is firmly satisfying, with Brigitte Fassbaender the most characterful. The close microphone balance for the soloists takes away a little of the vocal bloom. Claes Ahnsjö, with cleanly focused tenor tone, fares better than his male colleagues. *Quoniam* goes to the baritone, Roland Herman, *Crucifixus* to the bass, Robert Holl, both lacking a little in weight. The chrome transfer, on two cassettes as against three discs, offers demonstration quality, the balance between sharpness of focus and detail and overall bloom if anything more impressive.

For Neville Marriner this was a larger recording project than he had undertaken before, and he rose superbly to the challenge. Predictably many of the tempi are daringly fast; *Et resurrexit*, for example, has the Academy chorus on its toes, but the rhythms are so resiliently sprung that the result is exhilarating, never hectic. An even more remarkable achievement is that in the great moments of contemplation such as *Et incarnatus* and *Crucifixus* Marriner finds a degree of inner intensity to match the gravity of Bach's inspiration, with tempi often slower than usual. That dedication is matched by the soloists, the superb soprano Margaret Marshall as much as the longer-established singers. This is a performance which finds the balance between small-scale authenticity and recognition of massive inspiration, neither too small nor too large, and with good atmospheric recording, not quite as defined as it might be on inner detail; this is fully recommendable. The cassette transfer, made at a modest level, lacks the last degree of upper range, but is naturally balanced.

Münchinger's is a strong, enjoyable performance with an exceptionally fine quintet of soloists and first-rate recording. That it comes on four sides instead of six adds to its attractiveness, and on balance it makes a fair recommendation; but with fastish tempi and a generally extrovert manner, it is efficient rather than inspiring. The chorus sings well, but is placed rather backwardly.

Whether or not you subscribe to the controversial theories behind the performance under Joshua Rifkin, the result is undeniably refreshing and often exhilarating. Rifkin – best known for playing Scott Joplin rags but a classical scholar too – here presents Bach's masterpiece in the improbable form of one voice to a part in the choruses. There are scholarly arguments in favour of suggesting that Bach, even for such grand choruses, had that smallest possible ensemble. Certainly one gets a totally new perspective when, at generally brisk speeds, the complex counterpoint is so crisp and clean with original instruments in the orchestra (relatively gentle) adding to the freshness and intimacy. The soprano, Judith Nelson, is already well known in the world of authentic performance, and the other soloists too sing with comparable brightness, freshness and precision, even if lack of choral weight means that dramatic contrasts are less sharp than usual. An exciting pioneering set, crisply and vividly recorded, which rightly won *Gramophone*'s choral award in 1983. Not a first choice, perhaps, but a refreshing alternative view of Bach's masterpiece. The iron-oxide cassettes are of good quality, but the sound is somewhat bland and lacking bite, making the singing sound rather chaste.

As with Harnoncourt's other records of Bach, reactions will vary widely. Harnoncourt has very strictly rationed himself to authentic numbers as well as authentic instruments, and with boys' voices in the choir, the effect is more of a chamber performance – fatal in the great *Sanctus*. But Harnoncourt's dedication comes over, and in its way this is a successful issue. Good solo singing, particularly from Helen Watts.

Karajan's performance is marked by his characteristic smoothness of Bach style. He conveys intensity, even religious fervour, but the sharp contours of Bach's majestic writing are often missing. The very opening brings an impressive first entry of the choir on *Kyrie*, but then after the instrumental fugue the contrapuntal entries are sung in a self-consciously softened tone. But there is a strong sense of the work's architecture, and the highly polished surfaces do not obscure the depths of this music.

Klemperer is disappointing. The sobriety of the reading, with plodding tempi, and a dogged observance of the *Neue Bach-Ausgabe* (Bärenreiter) utterly unornamented, were no doubt predictable. Only when the drama of the mass takes over in the *Crucifixus* and *Et resurrexit* does the majesty of Klemperer's conception become apparent. Dame Janet

Baker stands out among the soloists, with superb accounts of the *Qui sedes* and *Agnus Dei*. Whatever the initial shortcomings, Klemperer's *Sanctus* (faster than usual) has wonderful momentum, the *Osanna* is genuinely joyful, and the concluding sections of the sublime work come vividly alive. The choral recording is, however, none too clear and the quality overall is good rather than outstanding. However, remastering has cleaned up the sound on disc, and the cassettes are well laid out and excellently transferred.

American readers will want to be reminded of Somary's Vanguard set [71190/2] which is not at present available in the UK. In every bar Somary inspires his authentically small choir to superbly incisive singing; the vocal soloists are as fine as on any rival set and the ECO play most stylishly. Throughout, the music-making conveys the feeling of a live performance, its tensions and resolutions, and the recording is first-rate, bright and clear.

Mass in B min.: highlights.
(M) **(*) Ph. Seq. 6527/*7311* 099 [id.]. (from above set, cond. Marriner).

This set of excerpts concentrates on the choral music from the *B minor Mass*; there are only three solo items. It provides a fair sampler of Marriner's style, rhythmically crisp in the fast passages yet with the fullest intensity when the music is contemplative. But this can only be seriously recommended for those whose budgets simply will not stretch to the complete work.

Masses in F, BWV 233; in A, BWV 234.
*** Argo ZRG 873 [id.]. Eathorne, Esswood, Jenkins, Hickox Singers and O, Hickox.

Following the success of their earlier recording of the two Lutheran Masses BWV 235/6 (see below), Richard Hickox and his colleagues now turn to the others. The performances are expressive but always in excellent style, and the soloists bring conviction and fine musicianship to their parts. The *A major Mass*, which draws on Cantata No. 67 for its *Gloria*, is the more inspired of the two, but both offer many beauties. The relative neglect of these 'short' Masses is hard to understand when they are treated so persuasively, and they are finely recorded with a warm acoustic, well-balanced soloists and exemplary perspective.

(Short) *Masses: in G min., BWV 235; in G, BWV 236.*
**(*) Argo ZRG 829 [id.]. Eathorne, Esswood, Langridge, Roberts, Hickox Singers and O, Hickox; Ross (organ).

Richard Hickox is a distinguished choir-trainer, and in these two 'short' masses drawing their material from the cantatas, it is the contribution of the choir which shines out. An excellent and apt coupling, with fine atmospheric recording helped by the acoustic of St John's, Smith Square.

Motets: *Fürchte dich nicht, BWV 228; Jesu meine Freude, BWV 227; Loben den Herrn, BWV 230; Singet dem Herrn, BWV 225.*
** ASV ALH/*ZCALH* 828. Christ Church Cath. Ch., Oxford, Grier.

The first of two discs devoted to Bach's motets finds Christ Church Cathedral Choir under Francis Grier giving fresh and lively but surprisingly rough performances. The matching and occasionally the intonation are suspect, but the brightness of the treble sound is well caught in the digital recording, closely placed in a lightly ecclesiastical acoustic. Supporting bass is provided by the organ, clearly defined like all the other strands. The cassette quality is bright and lively, although the level rises appreciably on side two and brings a hint of peaking.

Motet: *Jesus priceless treasure* (*Jesu, meine Freude*). Sacred part songs: *Die bitt're Leidenszeit; Brunnquell aller Güter; Es ist vollbracht; Gott lebet noch; Herr, nicht schicke deine Rache; Jesus ist das schönste Licht; O Jesuslein süss* (sung in English).
(M) *** Argo ZK 67. King's College Ch., Willcocks.

There is a place in the catalogue for an English-language version of *Jesu, meine Freude*, and this performance surpasses any of the German-text recordings made on the continent which have been available at various times. The famous King's atmosphere is caught in a characteristic Argo manner, yet the words are clear, and the balance with the continuo of organ, cello and bass is admirable. David Willcocks and his choir have also recorded the work in German (HMV HQS 1254, coupled to other motets and the Cantata No. 147), and some may prefer that (unaccompanied) version. The items from the Schemelli hymn-book which are included on the Argo disc are, however, not otherwise available in recommendable versions. They are of fine musical quality and beautifully sung. Recommended.

St John Passion, BWV 245.
**(*) DG Arc. 2710 027 (3) [id.]. Hopfner, Baldin, Hillebrand, Ahrens, Regensburg Cath. Ch., Coll. St Emmeram, Schneidt.
**(*) Erato STU 71151 (3). Palmer, Finnilä, Equiluz, Van der Meer, Huttenlocher, Lausanne Vocal Ens. and CO, Corbóz.

The Archive set may not have quite the innocent exhilaration of Schneidt's recording of the *Christmas oratorio* (see above), but it too presents an unaggressively authentic performance on an attractively intimate scale. There is less bite in the drama than in many other versions of whatever degree of authenticity, but with the fresh tones of the Regensburg Domspatzen and the generally gentle tones of the instrumental ensemble, this version has a distinctive place. It is beautifully recorded.

Those who resist the idea of the new authenticity with its characteristic instrumental timbres will be well-pleased by Corbóz's middle-of-the-road reading with its fresh and lively choral singing and accomplished team of soloists. Corbóz is excellent in telling the Passion story, bringing out the drama of Bach's concept in a work more compact, less contemplative than the *St Matthew*. Kurt Equiluz with his distinctive high tenor makes an urgently effective Evangelist, always agile, and the recording is first-rate.

St John Passion, BWV 245 (sung in English).
(M) **(*) Argo Ace GOS 628/30. Pears, Harwood, Watts, Young, Alan, Ward, King's College Ch, L. Philomus., Willcocks.

Willcock's Ace of Diamonds set comes from the very beginning of the 1960s and makes a generally good recommendation for those seeking an English-language recording. The singing of the King's College Choir combines purity and freshness, the soloists make a fine team in all respects, while the recording hardly sounds its age in this re-issue. Only the big opening chorus falls a little short of the rest in intensity.

St Matthew Passion (sung in German).
*** DG Arc. 2723 067/*3376 016* [2712 005/id.]. Schreier, Fischer-Dieskau, Mathis, Baker, Salminen, Regensburg Cath. Ch., Mun. Bach Ch. and O, Karl Richter.
*** HMV SLS 827 (4)/*TC-SLS 827*. Pears, Fischer-Dieskau, Schwarzkopf, Ludwig, Gedda, Berry, Hampstead Parish Church Boys' Ch., Philh. Ch. and O, Klemperer.
*** Decca SET 288/91 [Lon. CSA 1431]. Pears, Prey, Ameling, Höffgen, Wunderlich, Krause, Stuttgart Hymnus Boys' Ch., SCO, Münchinger.
** Tel. FK 6.35047/*MR3-4.35047* (4) [4635047]. Equiluz, Esswood, Sutcliffe, Bowman, Rogers, Ridderbusch, Van Egmond, Schopper, Regensburger Ch., V. Boys' Ch. solo trebles, King's Coll. Ch., VCM, Harnoncourt.
** DG 2720 070/*3371 007* (4) [2711 012/id.]. Schreier, Fischer-Dieskau, Janowitz, Ludwig, V. Singverein, V. Boys' Ch., German Op. Ch., Berlin PO, Karajan.
** HMV SLS/*TCC-SLS* 5257 (4). Garrison, Britten, Laki, Murray, Ahrens, Stamm, Luxon, N. German R. Ch. and O, Leppard.

Richter used to be thought a somewhat dry, even prosaic interpreter of Bach, but this fine, expressive, but always stylish reading tells of warmth and affection. The new purists will object to Richter's rallentandos and the fluid approach to chorales, but in sum this has the feeling of a great spiritual experience flowing spontaneously, with outstanding contributions from soloists, choir and orchestra. If it seems odd that the performance appears on the Archive label, dedicated to scholarly authenticity, this only reflects developing standards; by the lights of a few years ago the scale and general approach are anything but romantic, only the expression. Peter Schreier makes a strong and intense Evangelist, Fischer-Dieskau is deeply committed as Jesus, with Matti Salminen darkly contrasted. Edith Mathis is sweet in tone if not always flawless of line, but best of all is Dame Janet Baker, whose rendering of *Erbarme dich* crowns what from first to last is an unusually impressive recording. The sound is spacious and generally well-balanced on disc, and the tape transfer is of excellent quality. The choral sound is less incisive than on LP (noticeably at the opening), but the wide dynamic range is encompassed without loss of amplitude, and the solo voices and orchestra are vividly and freshly projected.

While Richter's new Archive set may seem the more obvious first recommendation, Klemperer's 1962 Philharmonia recording is by no means superseded. It has recently been re-mastered and issued on tape alongside the discs. The performance represents one of Klemperer's greatest achievements on record, an act of devotion of such intensity that points of style and interpretation dwindle into insignificance. Klemperer's approach is, according to the latest dictates, old-fashioned. He takes the chorales slowly, with pauses at the end of each line; he makes no concessions to scholarship on the question of introducing ornamentation. On the face of it this could have been a very dull, plodding performance indeed, but instead, through Klemperer's genius, captured at white heat from first to last, we have a monument of the gramophone. The whole cast managed to share Klemperer's own intense feelings, and one can only sit back and share them too, whatever one's preconceptions.

Klemperer's dedication is immediately apparent in the first great chorus, *Kommt, ihr Töchter*, with the chorale *O Lamm Gottes unschuldig* given to trebles in ripieno. Stereo allows clear separation between the first and second choruses on left and right, while ringing out from the centre is the pure tone of the boys of the Hampstead choir. There is a matchless team of soloists, with Peter Pears at his peak in the role of Evangelist and Fischer-Dieskau deeply expressive as Jesus. The Philharmonia Choir (not the amateur Philharmonia Chorus) sings with the finest focus, and in this reissue the recorded sound remains astonishingly vivid. The cassette transfer is on three chrome tapes with Part I complete on the first. The level ideally might have been just a little higher – at mezzo forte the choral focus is a shade bland, but climaxes expand clearly and the sound overall is well balanced and full, the solo voices naturally caught.

There is no direct conflict between Münchinger's version and Klemperer's colossal conception. Münchinger's direction does not reach such heights, but his performance is consistently fresh and alert, and above all has greater authenticity. All the soloists are excellent, with Peter Pears again showing that no tenor in the world today rivals his insight as the Evangelist. Elly Ameling is sweet-toned and sensitive. The recording is first-class, clear, brilliant and beautifully balanced, though some may object to the deliberate closeness with which the voice of Hermann Prey as Jesus has been recorded.

Harnoncourt's authentic approach means that his version of the *St Matthew Passion* can be compared with no other. The instrumental sound is different (the strings, for instance, use a vibrato-less tone production); the vocal sound is almost revolutionary in its total reliance on male voices (including boy trebles); the choral singing is incisive and lightweight. For many, the emotional kernel of Bach's work lies in the solo contributions and here these are variable, with Karl Ridderbusch (as Christus) and Paul Esswood outstanding. Some of the other contributions are less reliable. The use of solo boy trebles from the Vienna Choir for the soprano arias produces a strangely detached effect, although the singing itself is usually technically good.

Karajan's Bach, always polished, grows smoother still with the years. His account of the *St Matthew Passion* is plainly aimed at devotees – of Karajan as much as of Bach. The result, concentrated in refinement, faithfully reflects the live performances which he has given in Berlin. With excellent singing and playing and with reverberant recording moulded to the interpretation, it represents an individual view pursued in the face of the current fashion, and many will enjoy it.

Leppard's account is disappointingly lacking in just the qualities one expects of him. A German venue seems to have prevented him from giving the rhythmic lift and impulse coupled with expressive warmth which mark his best work on record. Though modest forces are used, the result is surprisingly laboured with Jon Garrison an uninspired and unmellifluous Evangelist. There is good work from other soloists and the chorales fare better than the big choruses, but other sets are preferable. The digital recording is oddly balanced, while the two cassettes, transferred on ferric stock, have a restricted upper range which produces a woolly choral focus, although tape two at a higher level is clearer than tape one.

St Matthew Passion, BWV 244 (sung in English).
**(*) Decca D 139 D 4/*K 139 K 44*. Tear, Shirley-Quirk, Loft, Hodgson, Jenkins, Roberts, Bach Ch., St Paul's Cath. Ch. Boys, Thames CO, Willcocks.

It is a comment on current taste (of record companies if not perhaps the public) that the newest Decca set, conducted by Sir David Willcocks, was the first complete recording of the *St Matthew Passion* to be made in English for thirty years. The pity is that the performance fails to lift quite as it ought, remaining earthbound and conscientious where it should have the qualities of a spiritual experience. Willcocks, most experienced of choirmasters, draws light and rhythmic singing from his choirs in the choruses, and the chorales avoid heaviness. There is a good team of soloists, headed by Robert Tear, but Peter's denial – usually a supremely moving moment – is here prosaic. The recording is clean and well-balanced, and the cassette transfer is admirably fresh and clear; solo voices are well-projected and the choral textures are full and, if fractionally husky at times, for the most part very cleanly focused.

St Matthew Passion: Arias and choruses.
(M) ** Decca SPA/*KCSP* 596 (from above set, cond. Willcocks).

A representative and generous selection from the Willcocks set, enjoyable if lacking something in vitality. Cassette and disc are closely matched, the choral focus marginally less sharp on tape.

Vocal collections

Arias: *Bist du bei mir*. Cantata arias: *No. 6: Hochgelobter Gottessohn; No. 11: Ach bleibe doch; No. 34: Wohl euch ihr auserwählten Seelen; No. 129: Gelobet sei der Herr; No. 161: Kommn, du süsse Todesstunde; No. 190: Lobe Zion, deinen Gott. Christmas oratorio: Bereite dich. Easter oratorio: Saget, saget mir geschwinde. Magnificat: Et exultavit. St John Passion: Es ist vollbracht.*
*** [Ang. S 37229]. Baker, ASMF, Marriner.
(M) *** HMV *TCC 2-POR 154592-9*. (As above) – *Cantatas Nos. 82 and 169.****

Predictably Dame Janet Baker gives beautiful and deeply felt performances of a fine collection of Bach arias. Sweet contemplative arias predominate, and an excellent case is made for including the alternative cantata version, *Ach bleibe doch*, of what became the *Agnus Dei* in the *B minor Mass*. The accompaniments could hardly be more understanding (the gamba solo in *Es ist vollbracht* adding extra poignancy), and the recording is rich and warm. The alternative tape-only issue in HMV's '*Portrait of the Artist*' series, which is on chrome stock, is even more vivid. Here the arias are coupled with two fine performances of Cantatas which are not otherwise available. The single LP issue has been withdrawn in the UK.

Mass in B min.: Agnus Dei; Qui sedes. St John Passion: All is fulfilled. St Matthew Passion: Grief for sin.
(M) *** Decca SPA/*KCSP* 531. Ferrier, LPO, Boult – HANDEL: *Arias.****

Decca have reissued this famous Kathleen Ferrier disc on their cheapest label. With a splendidly transferred cassette to match, it sounds remarkably vivid. Readers may remember that in the early days of stereo Sir Adrian Boult and the LPO re-recorded the accompaniments with such skill and devotion that the new orchestral sound completely masked the old. Even the voice seems to have the extra presence of the newer techniques.

St John Passion: (i) *All is fulfilled;* (ii) *Rest calm, O body pure and holy; The dear angel*

send. (iii) *St Matthew Passion: Come, ye daughters; O sacred head; In tears of grief.*
(M) *** Decca SPA/*KCSP* 588. (i) Ferrier, LPO, Boult; (ii) King's College Ch., L. Philomus., Willcocks; (iii) Bach Ch., St Paul's Cath. Boys' Ch., Thames CO, Willcocks – HANDEL: *Messiah excerpts.****

An excellent and well-planned disc of Bach and Handel sung in English. Kathleen Ferrier's noble performance of *All is fulfilled* (with the famous added accompaniment in real stereo) is framed by freshly sung chorus and chorales taken from the Willcocks complete sets of the *Passions.* The sound is first-class, with no perceptible difference between tape and disc.

COLLECTIONS

Flute concerto in G min., BWV 1056; Oboe concerto in F, BWV 1053; Oboe d'amore concerto in A, BWV 1055; Double concerto for violin and oboe in D min., BWV 1060; Triple concerto for violin, oboe and flute in D min., BWV 1063; Triple violin concerto in D, BWV 1064; Suite No. 3 in D, BWV 1068. (i) *Cantata No. 170; Vergnügte Ruh'.*
(M) *** Argo D 241 D 3 (3)/*K 241 K 33.* Soloists, ASMF, Marriner, (i) with Baker.

The concertos included here (drawn from Argo ZRG/*KZRC* 820-21 – see above) are conjectural reconstructions of Bach harpsichord concertos for alternative instruments that either did exist or might have existed in Bach's time. The purist may resist, but the attractions of these performances tend to disarm criticism, for every concerto makes delightful listening. To make up this excellent medium-priced anthology, Dame Janet Baker's distinguished performances of the cantata *Vergnügte Ruh'* and the Academy's outstanding version of the *Third Orchestral suite* are added. The recording is of Argo's highest quality on disc and cassette alike, although on tape there is a degree of roughness on top in the tuttis of the *Suite.*

'Classics': (i) *Brandenburg concerto No. 3.* (ii) *Violin concerto No. 2 in E min.; Double violin concerto; Orchestral suite No. 2, BWV 1067: Badinerie. Suite No. 3, BWV 1068: Air.* (iii) *Violin Partita No. 3: Prelude.* (iv) *Italian concerto.* (v) *Well-tempered Clavier: Prelude and fugue No. 5 in D.* (vi) *Schübler chorale: Wachet auf.* (vii) *Toccata and fugue in D min., BWV 565. Chorales: Ein feste Burg.* (viii) *Jesu, joy of man's desiring.* (ix) *Sheep may safely graze.*
(M) *** HMV *TC2-COS* 54253. (i) LPO, Boult; (ii) Menuhin, CO, (with Ferras); (iii) Suk; (iv) Malcolm; (v) Ogdon; (vi) Willcocks; (vii) Germani; (viii) King's College Ch., Willcocks; (ix) Goossens, Thalben-Ball.

A most successful double-length (iron-oxide) tape, equally suitable for in-car listening or for the late evening. With Boult's excellent, if slightly old-fashioned, full string version of the *Third Brandenburg* and the distinguished Menuhin recordings of the *Violin concertos* as ballast, the shorter pieces leaven the collection very attractively, and the inclusion of *Sheep may safely graze* with a contribution from Leon Goossens was a happy idea. The sound is consistently good.

'The world of Bach': (i) *Brandenburg concerto No. 2; Orchestral suite No. 2, BWV 1067: Badinerie; Suite No. 3, BWV 1068: Air.* (ii) *Italian concerto:* 1st movement. (iii) *Toccata and fugue in D min., BWV 565.* (iv) *Chorales: Jesu, joy of man's desiring.* (v) *Sheep may safely graze.* (i; vi) *Christmas oratorio: Jauchzet, Frohlocket.* (vii) *Mass in B min.: Agnus Dei.* (i; viii) *St Matthew Passion: Wir setzen uns mit Tränen nieder* (chorus).
(M) *** Decca SPA/*KCSP* 322. SCO, Münchinger; (ii) Malcolm; (iii) Karl Richter; (iv) St John's College Ch., Guest; (v) Flagstad; LPO, Boult; (vi) Lübecker Cantorei; (vii) Ferrier, LPO, Boult; (viii) Stuttgart Hymnus Boys' Ch.

A characteristically skilful Decca anthology that is even more than the sum of its parts, which itself is considerable. The juxtaposition of pieces is managed with perfect taste so that each seems to follow on spontaneously. The *Second Brandenburg concerto* and the other short orchestral items show the Stuttgart team at their best, but the real highlights here are vocal, notably Kathleen Ferrier's beautiful contribution, and the oratorio excerpts. The recording is consistently good throughout on both disc and cassette. A satisfying concert in its own right, but one that should tempt inexperienced listeners to explore further.

ARRANGEMENTS

Bach–Stokowski

Arioso (from *Cantata No. 165*); *Chorales: Ein feste Burg, BWV 720; Komm süsser Tod* (*from BWV 229*); *Wachet auf, BWV 645; Fugue in G min., BWV 577; Orchestral suite No. 3, BWV 1068: Air.* (Violin) *Partita No. 2, BWV 1004: Chaconne. Partita No. 3, BWV 1006: Preludio.*

(M) *** RCA GL/*GK* 42921 [AGL1/*AGK1* 3656]. LSO, Stokowski.

In his vintage days in Philadelphia Stokowski made many records of his own Bach transcriptions, inflated but flamboyantly convincing. This is a gloriously enjoyable collection of some of the ripest, recorded by the LSO under a nonagenarian Stokowski with opulent stereo adding to the splendour. Not for the purist, but highly enjoyable for everyone else. With the medium-priced reissue on Gold Seal has come a cassette, but, though acceptable, it does not match the LP in richness; the upper range is less refined and there is an element of constriction at a couple of climaxes. (N.B.: As we go to press, the continued availability of this issue in the UK is uncertain.)

Adagio, BWV 564; Chorales, BWV 4; BWV 680; Komm süsser Tod, BWV 478; Fugue in G min., BWV 578; Passacaglia and fugue in C min., BWV 582; Toccata and fugue in D min., BWV 565 (all arr. Stokowski).

* Chan. ABRD/*ABTD* 1055. Sydney SO, Pikler.

A disappointing collection. Stokowski's famous transcriptions are made to sound remarkably unglamorous, partly the fault of the recording which gives an unflatteringly thin sound to the strings of the Sydney Orchestra. The playing too is less than first-class and Robert Pikler's very free treatment of the famous *Toccata and fugue* fails to convince. The chorales, *Christ lag in Todesbanden* and *Kom süsser Tod* come off best: here the playing is pleasingly expressive. The cassette and disc are fairly closely matched, the tape somewhat smoother on top.

Miscellaneous arrangements

'Switched-on Bach' (electronic realizations by Walter Carlos and Benjamin Folkman): *Brandenburg concerto No. 3 in G. Cantatas Nos. 29: Sinfonia; 147: Jesu, joy of man's desiring. Chorale prelude: Wachet auf. Suite No. 3 in D: Air. Two-part inventions in B flat; D min.; F. The Well-tempered Clavier: Preludes and fugues Nos. 2 in C min.; 7 in E flat.*

*** CBS 63501 [MS 7194/*16 11 0092*]. Carlos (Moog synthesizer).

The Moog synthesizer has now become quite an accepted item in the recording studio, but this highly individual record was the one which above all established Moog's claims as a popularizer in the classical field. The purist will certainly wince, but almost any of these arrangements for computer sound has a hypnotic quality, attested by the phenomenal success the disc had in America and by the way that non-Bachians tend to take to it. The interpretation of the *Third Brandenburg* is allegedly based – with all the subtleties of rubato and phrasing – on two classic recordings of the past, though Carlos rightly takes ultimate responsibility. The stereo effects are elaborate, many of them not just gimmicks but attempts to clarify what Bach wrote without altering his notes. In most ways this is a brilliantly successful record, the best of its kind.

Bach, Wilhelm Friedemann
(1710–84)

Duo in F; Trio in A min.
** O-L DSLO 518 [id.]. Preston, McGegan, Ryan, Pleeth, Hogwood – C. P. E. BACH and J. S. BACH: *Trio sonatas.****

Wilhelm Friedemann is an interesting figure, but the *Duo* for two flutes (a combination much favoured at the time) is not particularly memorable or distinguished, though it is certainly well played. So, too, is the single-movement *A minor Trio*. But this is fill-up material for two more substantial pieces.

Bainbridge, Simon (born 1952)

Viola concerto.
*** Uni. Dig. RHD 400. Trampler, Philh. O, Tilson Thomas – KNUSSEN: *Symphony No. 3* etc.***

Simon Bainbridge is an exact contemporary of Oliver Knussen with whose *Third Symphony* and *Ophelia dances* this concerto is coupled. Like Knussen he studied with John Lambert and later with Gunther Schuller. Though Bainbridge's idiom is uncompromising, he allows himself open romantic melodies in both of the extended movements of his fine *Viola concerto*. The work dates from 1976 and is an eloquent and atmospheric piece. One senses a nostalgia for the uninhibited romanticism of the greatest of twentieth-century viola concertos, Walton's. It is perhaps more impressive in its inward, reflective sections than in the vigorous orchestral tutti, and there is an appealing gentleness in the slow movement. Though less dense in argument than the Knussen works with which it is coupled, this makes an excellent contrasted companion piece. No praise could be too high for the quality of the performance and recording here; both are outstanding. An issue well worth the attention of those who think they do not like contemporary music.

Baird, Tadeusz (1928–81)

Elegeia for orchestra.
(M) *** Sup. 1410 2734. Prague RSO, Kasprzk – LUTOSLAWSKI: *Mi-Parti;* PENDERECKI: *Anaklasis* etc.***

A useful anthology of contemporary Polish music. Baird attracted attention in the early 1960s with his *Four Essays* for orchestra, highly evocative and inventive and well worth a place in the catalogue. Baird's style is expressionist, and the music arises from genuine feeling. This *Elegy*, which was composed in 1973, is perhaps less haunting than the *Essays*, but it too is atmospheric. It is well served by the recording engineers, and the Prague Radio Orchestra play with total commitment under Kasprzyk.

Balfe, Michael (1808–70)

The Bohemian Girl (opera): highlights.
** HMV CSD 3651. Dunne, Deanne, Hinds, O, Nelson – BENEDICT: *The Lily of Killarney*; WALLACE: *Maritana.***

This disc enterprisingly collects together music from three operas, two by Irish composers and the third set in Ireland, which some wag has cynically christened 'the Irish *Ring*'. It is proper that a whole side should be given to Balfe's *Bohemian Girl*, for this is the most famous of the three. First staged at Drury Lane in 1843, it has been often revived, and was a favourite of Sir Thomas Beecham. The music is corny but so sure of itself that when sung and played with gusto it has an undeniable success in the theatre. The conductor here well understands this and the *Overture*, *Waltz* and *Galop* are very successful indeed. The singing is more variable: Eric Hinds makes a suitably dolorous Count, Veronica Dunne is better in the second verse of the famous *I dreamt that I dwelt* than she is in the first (which she oversings), and the tenor is lyrically-minded if somewhat weak. But the anthology on this disc reminds us that these were the only British operas to hold the stage between Arne and Sullivan, and for those who can listen with tongue in cheek, this is irresistible. The recording, made in Dublin, has clarity and a splendid overall bloom.

Barber, Samuel (1910–81)

Adagio for strings.

*** Argo ZRG/*KZRC* 845 [id.]. ASMF, Marriner – COPLAND: *Quiet City;* COWELL: *Hymn*; CRESTON: *Rumor*; IVES: *Symphony No. 3.****

*** DG Dig. **413 343-2**; 2532/*3302* 083 [id.]. LAPO, Bernstein – BERNSTEIN: *Candide overture;* COPLAND: *Appalachian spring;* SCHUMAN: *American festival overture.****

(B) **(*) RCA VICS/*VK* 2001 [AGL 1/*AGK 1* 3790]. Boston SO, Munch – ELGAR: *Introduction and allegro;* TCHAIKOVSKY: *Serenade.***(*)

(i) *Adagio for strings, Op. 11; 2nd Essay for orchestra, Op. 17; Medea's Meditation and Dance of Vengeance, Op. 23a; The School for Scandal: overture.* (ii) *Dover Beach, Op. 3.*

(M) **(*) CBS 61898/*40*- [Odys.Y/*YT* 33230]. (i) NYPO, Schippers; (ii) Fischer-Dieskau, Juilliard Qt.

Samuel Barber's *Adagio for strings* is a transcription of the slow movement of his fine *String quartet*, Op. 11, and brought him international fame in its pioneer recording by Toscanini and the NBC Orchestra. Marriner's performance all but matches Toscanini's intensity and has enormous eloquence and conviction. It is arguably the most satisfying version we have had since the war. The quality of the recorded sound is altogether superb, never excessively analytical, but splendidly detailed and rich. The rest of the programme on this LP of twentieth-century American music has been chosen with skill. The cassette equivalent also offers sound of the highest quality.

The alternative version from Bernstein is no less rewarding, if quite different in character. Moreover Bernstein's couplings – including a superb account of the concert version of Copland's *Appalachian spring* and William Schuman's engaging *American festival overture*, are also highly desirable. His reading of the *Adagio* has something of the expansiveness of his interpretation of another slow movement with valedictory associations forced on it, *Nimrod* from Elgar's *Enigma*. In Barber, Bernstein's expressiveness is more restrained and elegiac, but his control of the climax – in what is substantially a live recording – is unerring. Recording somewhat close, but full and clear. The chrome cassette is exceptionally successful, extremely rich and vivid.

Munch too finds a spacious nobility at the climax of the *Adagio*, and his broad conception is fully convincing. The RCA recording is full if slightly dated now, but the couplings make this issue worth considering in the bargain price-range.

Drawn from earlier sources, the CBS mid-price collection made for the composer's seventieth birthday is a good anthology, including some of his most memorable works, not just the famous *Adagio* but the coolly atmospheric setting of Matthew Arnold (with Fischer-Dieskau immaculate in his English, treating the piece rightly like Lieder) and other short orchestral works. The recording quality is somewhat hard. But it has transferred quite vividly to cassette, lacking only the last degree of upper range, and that not always disadvantageously. However, on tape the voice in *Dover Beach* lacks edge and presence.

Cello concerto, Op. 22.

*** Chan. Dig. ABRD/*ABTD* 1085. Wallfisch, ECO, Simon – SHOSTAKOVICH: *Cello concerto No. 1.****

Barber's *Cello concerto* dates from the end of the war years (following after the *Second Symphony* of 1944). It had its first performance in Boston in 1946 and the soloist on that occasion, Raya Garbousova, has since recorded it in the USA [Varese Sara. 81057]. The composer himself made a mono record of it for Decca during a visit to London in 1951 (LX 3048, long deleted). His soloist was Zara Nelsova, and while her performance had undoubted insights, the Sackville-West/Shawe-Taylor *Record Guide* thought her playing of the bravura passages sounded 'rather scratchy'. That is certainly not a criticism that can be applied to Raymond Wallfisch, whose tone in this splendid new Chandos recording is admirably focused. He is forwardly balanced, but the recording is truthful and the orchestra is vividly detailed both on disc and the excellent chrome tape. It is an impressive and eloquent reading and the elegiac slow movement is especially fine. With its excellent Shostakovich coupling, this must receive the strongest recommendation.

(i) *Piano concerto, Op. 38;* (ii) *Violin concerto, Op. 14.*
(M) **(*) CBS Classics 61621/*40*-. (i) Browning, Cleveland O, Szell; (ii) Stern, NYPO, Bernstein.

Barber's career has a number of parallels with that of William Walton: a vein of acid-tinged romanticism; comparatively sparse output, mainly of major works; a comparative failure to maintain full intensity in later work. The *Piano concerto*, written for John Browning, is one of those later works, and though technically it is most impressive and the seriousness cannot be denied, it never quite adds up to the sum of its parts. The seven-in-a-bar finale is the most immediately attractive movement, and will provide firm enjoyment from the start; the weighty first movement and intermezzo-like middle movement improve on acquaintance. The *Violin concerto* is more consistently inspired. It has warmth, freshness and humanity, and the slow movement is genuinely beautiful. Both performances here are of superlative quality, and if the characteristic CBS forward balance for the soloists is less than ideal, the recording is otherwise good. An impressive disc, recommended to all who care about twentieth-century music. There is a good cassette.

(i) *Violin concerto, Op. 14. Music for a scene from Shelley.* (ii) *Knoxville: Summer of 1915.*
(M) *** Uni. UNS 256. W. Australian SO, Measham, with (i) Thomas, (ii) McGurk.

Ronald Thomas captures the youthful innocence and rapture of Barber's heart-warming *Concerto*, and though the performance may lack the glamour and power of Stern and Bernstein (see above), there is an unforced eloquence and naturalness that are deeply satisfying. The sound is well-balanced and completely truthful, and no one coming to this performance is likely to be unmoved. The concerto is coupled with *Knoxville* for soprano and orchestra, one of Barber's most evocative pieces, and an underrated early work, *Music for a scene from Shelley*, whose rich romantic textures are never overripe but seem to relate to genuinely felt experience. While the Stern/Bernstein version of the *Concerto* is available, it must perhaps remain a first recommendation for its splendid panache and virtuosity, yet readers who enjoy purposeful, relaxed and committed music-making and excellent recorded sound should not overlook this fine Unicorn issue.

Symphony No. 1, Op. 9; Essays for orchestra Nos. 1, Op. 12; 2, Op. 17; Night Flight, Op. 19a.
*** Uni. RHS 342. LSO, Measham.

Barber's *First Symphony*, originally recorded on 78 by Bruno Walter and the New York Philharmonic, has been shamefully neglected in the age of LP. It has admittedly become a period work – written in the late 1930s in a somewhat Waltonian style and in a one-movement form that recalls Sibelius's *Seventh* – but Barber has rarely matched the vitality and memorability of the writing. David Measham, principal second violin of the LSO before he launched into conducting, proves a superb advocate, securing a passionately committed performance, brilliantly recorded. The two *Essays for orchestra* were written respectively in 1938 and 1942; the hauntingly evocative movement, *Night Flight*, is all that the composer has allowed to survive of his fine *Symphony No. 2*.

Ballade, Op. 46; 4 Excursions, Op. 20; Nocturne (Homage to John Field), Op. 33; Sonata, Op. 26.
**(*) Hyp. A 66016. Brownridge.

This record performs a useful function in the catalogue: it accommodates Barber's entire output for the piano on two sides, offering the only available versions of the *Ballade* (1972), and the endearing *Four Excursions*. These are not quite so crisp or characterful as in the old Andor Foldes mono record from the 1950s but in some details are more sensitive. Angela Brownridge gives a good account of herself in the dazzling *Sonata*. Though she may not perhaps possess the transcendental virtuosity of a Horowitz (or of Van Cliburn, who also recorded it in the 1960s), nor is her performance quite as strongly characterized as that of Ruth Laredo – see below; nevertheless she is fully equal to its demands. The recording is not first-class; the resonant acoustic makes the piano sound slightly unfocused, yet the ear soon adjusts.

Piano sonata in E flat min., Op. 26; Nocturne (Homage to John Field), Op. 33; Souvenirs (ballet), Op. 28.
**(*) None. Dig. D/*D4* 79032 [id.]. Laredo.

The toughness of Ruth Laredo's piano style suits the virtuoso demands of Barber's *Sonata*, originally written with Horowitz in mind. It is a formidable performance, well recorded if with a touch of hardness in digital sound. The coupling is a lightweight suite of genre pieces – *Waltz, Schottische, Pas de deux* and so on – arranged for solo piano by Barber himself from a two-piano original. That and the gentle pastiche of a *Nocturne* are affectionately played by Miss Laredo.

Barraqué, Jean (1928–73)

Piano sonata.
(M) *** Uni. UNS 263. Woodward.

This performance of Barraqué's *Sonata* by Roger Woodward, recorded in the early 1970s, earned the imprimatur of the composer himself. Barraqué's idiom is not readily accessible but there is a sense of creative urgency and purpose here. Some may find the language tortuous and convoluted, but there can be no doubt that Woodward makes as good a case for it as anyone and he is assisted by excellent and well-focused recorded sound. This is highly specialized in its appeal but can be recommended to those interested in the avant-garde.

Barrios, Agustin (1885–1944)

Aconquija; Aire de Zamba; La catedral; Choro de saudade; Cueca; Estudio; Una limosna el amor de Dios; Madrigal (Gavota); Maxixa; Mazurka apassionata; Minuet; Preludio; Sueño en la floresta; Valse No. 3; Villancico de Navidad.
**(*) CBS 76662/*40*- [M/*MT* 35145]. Williams.

Agustin Barrios is a little-known Paraguayan guitarist and composer who had the distinction of making (in 1909) the first known recording of a guitar. His music essentially belongs to the previous century. Its invention is fresh, if sometimes ingenuous, and the pieces here are well varied in style. In the expert hands of John Williams the collection provides a very entertaining recital, ideal for late-evening listening. Try the charming opening *La catedral* (sweet but not sugary) or the irresistible *Sueño en la floresta*, which ends the side in a breathtaking haze of fluttering figurations that remind one of Tarrega's *Recuerdos de la Alhambra*. The recording is excellent, both on disc and on cassette.

Bartók, Béla (1881–1945)

Concerto for orchestra.
(M) *** CBS 60141/*40*- [MY/*MYT* 37259]. NYPO, Boulez.
(B) **(*) RCA VICS/*VK* 2005 [AGL1 2909). Chicago SO, Reiner.
(*) Dell'Arte 45 r.p.m. DA 9013. Houston SO, Stokowski – CANNING: *Fantasy on a hymn tune.**
(M) ** DG 2535/*3335* 202 [id.]. Berlin PO, Karajan.

Concerto for orchestra; Dance suite.
*** Decca Dig. **400 052-2**; SXDL/*KSXDC* 7536 [Lon. LDR/*5*- 71036]. Chicago SO, Solti.
(M) *** Decca Jub. JB/*KJBC* 144. LSO, Solti.
(M) **(*) Ph. Seq. 6527/*7311* 140. Concg. O, Haitink.

Concerto for orchestra; 2 Images, Op. 10.
**(*) DG 2531/*3301* 269 [id.]. Berlin PO, Maazel.

(i) *Concerto for orchestra;* (ii) *Rumanian folk dances.*
(M) *** Mercury SRI 75105. (i) LSO; (ii) Minneapolis SO; Dorati.

Bartók's *Concerto for orchestra* is now exceptionally well served by the gramophone, with an excellent choice in each price-range. If first recommendation lies with Solti, Boulez, Reiner and Haitink all have different insights to offer in this most popular of Bartók's orchestral works. Solti's newest Decca recording is also available on a brilliantly clear compact disc, with the silent background increasing the projection of the music-making and (with superb definition in the bass) helping to create the listener's feeling of anticipation in the atmospheric opening bars. The upper range of the sound, however, is very brightly lit indeed, which brings an aggressive feeling to the upper strings. Undoubtedly this suits the reading, fierce and biting on the one hand, exuberant on the other. With superlative playing from Solti's own Chicago orchestra and such vivid sound – equally impressive on LP and the strikingly brilliant chrome tape – this will be an obvious choice for most readers, particularly as Decca offer in addition a generous and apt coupling in the *Dance suite*, performed with a similar combination of sympathy and incisiveness. In the *Concerto* Solti has consulted original sources to suggest a faster speed than usual in the second movement, and this he makes entirely convincing. Otherwise these are marginally straighter readings than those in his 1966 coupling of these same works, now reissued on Jubilee.

There will be those who will prefer the earlier version, for though the 1960s recording – outstanding in its day – shows its age a little in the string tone, in all other respects it is of high quality with a matching chrome tape. The performance has all the fire and passion one could want, but also a touch more of wit and idiosyncrasy than the later version. One senses Solti's Hungarian upbringing more readily here for he allows himself certain rubato effects not strictly marked in the score, absorbing the inflections of Hungarian folk song, very much an influence on Bartók's last-period lyricism.

Dorati's Mercury version of the *Concerto* is one of his most exciting records. He secures outstandingly brilliant and committed playing from the LSO, who open the work evocatively and combine bite with a fiery ardour in the *Allegro*. With the central movements strongly characterized and an exhilarating finale – the brass producing an electrifying burst of excitement near the close – this makes a strong recommendation at medium price. The brilliantly lit recording has a tendency to shrillness, but it also has a wide dynamic range and combines atmosphere with vivid colouring. There is a lower voltage in the *Rumanian dances*, but Dorati is naturally understanding in these folk-derived miniatures. The pressing is immaculate.

Though Boulez does not draw such precise ensemble from his New York players as many of his rivals do with other orchestras in this virtuoso music, this is an urgent, highly enjoyable performance, very much more consciously expressive than the accounts of the piece that he has directed live in London. The sessions were set up with quadraphonic sound very much in mind, but the ordinary stereo pressing sounds both clear and atmospheric, though it is rather dry in the bass. The high-level cassette sounds vivid and slightly richer than the disc, but on our copy there was some loss of refinement in the higher partials of the woodwind timbre.

Not unexpectedly in the Haitink version the orchestral playing is of the highest quality, more polished than with Boulez, and the recording, always truthful and atmospheric, now sounds clearer, with a brighter texture, than on the original, full-priced disc. The performance is more subtle, less tense than in Solti's similar mid-priced coupling, although the element of dramatic contrast is not missing. Haitink's touch of emotional restraint brings a gentle character to the *Elegy* and the close of the *Allegretto*. Thus the contrasts of the furious bravura of the opening of the finale and the splendour of the work's closing pages are the more telling. There is superb playing and fine recording too in the *Dance suite*, which has a natural rhythmic impulse.

Maazel's reading of the *Concerto*, exciting and very well played, has warmth as well as bite, but lacks wit in such a movement as the *Play of the couples*. The recording is spectacular, full and wide-ranging, but for some reason the trumpet is balanced absurdly far back. The unusual coupling further recommends this issue, two early pieces which in different ways anticipate much later developments in Bartók's last, relatively mellow period. The cassette transfer is sophisticated, with good body and detail, and it is a pity that the relatively low transfer level has marginally reduced the bite in the treble.

Reiner's performance was recorded in the early days of stereo, but the sound is remarkably good, spacious and vivid. The performance is most satisfying, surprisingly straightforward from one brought up in central Europe, but with plenty of cutting edge. For those with limited budgets this is well worth considering. The chrome tape is first-class.

Originally issued on the American Everest label, Stokowski's disc has been carefully remastered at 45 r.p.m. and the sound is clear and well-balanced, if not opulent. Stokowski's approach has romantic leanings, but is in no way eccentric; and it makes an impressive effect, especially in the central movements. The main interest of this record is the Canning *Fantasia*, a splendid piece which shows the conductor in his finest form.

On DG Privilege the Berlin Philharmonic, in superb form, gives a performance that is rich, romantic and smooth – for some ears perhaps excessively so. Karajan is right in treating Bartók emotionally, but the comparison with Solti on Decca Jubilee immediately points the contrast between Berlin romanticism and earthy red-blooded Hungarian passion. Both conductors allow themselves a fair degree of rubato but Solti's is linked with the Hungarian folk-song idiom, where Karajan's moulding of phrases is essentially of the German tradition. The DG cassette offers a bonus, not included on the LP, a performance of the *Dance suite* directed by György Lehel. But this account, although idiomatic, is not given the bite and presence by the recording that the Decca engineers afford to Solti.

Piano concertos Nos. (i) *1 in A;* (ii) *2 in G;* (i) *3 in E;* (iii) *Sonata for 2 pianos and percussion.*
(M) *** Ph. 6768 053 (2) [id.]. Bishop-Kovacevich, with (i) LSO, (ii) BBC SO, Colin Davis, (iii) Argerich, Goudswaard, De Roo.

Piano concertos Nos. 1–2.
*** DG 2530/*3300* 901 [id.]. Pollini, Chicago SO, Abbado.

Piano concertos Nos. 2–3.
*** Decca SXL/*KSXC* 6937 [Lon. CS/*5*-7167]. Ashkenazy, LPO, Solti.

Piano concerto No. 3.
(M) **(*) HMV SXLP/*TC-SXLP* 30514. Ogdon, New Philh. O, Sargent – SHOSTAKOVICH: *Piano concerto No. 2.****

Bartók's piano concertos are well represented in the current catalogue, with a wide permutation of couplings; but the partnership of Ashkenazy and Solti, combined with superb Decca sound, has set new standards in this repertoire. Their first issue, coupling the *Second* and *Third Concertos*, sparks off the energy and dash one would expect only at a live performance. With the Slavonic bite of the soloist beautifully matching the Hungarian fire of the conductor, the readings of both works are wonderfully urgent and incisive. The tempi tend to be fast, but the clarity of focus is superb, and the slow movements bring a hushed inner concentration, beautifully captured in exceptionally refined recording. With red-blooded Hungarian qualities underlined, these two works from very different periods of Bartók's career, the later one more mellow, seem far more closely akin than usual. The cassette offers demonstration sound of quite extraordinary vividness. If anything, the *Third Concerto* is even more lively than the *Second.*

On Philips, Bishop-Kovacevich's readings of the three concertos, direct and incisive, are superbly matched by an electrifying account of the *Sonata for two pianos and percussion*, in which he is challenged by the more volatile artistry of Martha Argerich. It was originally coupled differently (see below), but this is both logical and satisfying. Most impressive of all is the pianist's handling of Bartók's often spare and always intense slow movements, here given concentrated power to compare with late Beethoven. Good clean Philips recording of mid-1970s vintage.

The newest DG issue forms a partnership between two of the most distinguished Italian musicians of the day, collaborating in performances of two formidable works which in their exuberance sweep away any idea that this might be forbidding music. Virtuosity goes with a sense of spontaneity. Rhythms in fast movements are freely and infectiously sprung to bring out bluff Bartókian humour rather than any brutality. The Chicago orchestra, vividly recorded, is in superb form. The cassette transfer offers bold, clear piano tone, and the atmosphere and detail of the slow movement are well caught. In the outer movements the reverberation loses some of the crispness of the orchestral focus, but there is good range.

Ogdon's performance of the *Third Concerto* was originally coupled to an impressive version of the *Sonata for two pianos and percussion*, in which he was joined by his wife, Brenda Lucas. Ogdon gives a fine performance of the *Concerto*, and although Sargent's accompaniment lacks the last degree of brilliance and intensity, this makes an enjoyable coupling for an outstanding version of Shostakovich's *Second Concerto*. The 1968 recording has come up well, especially on the bright, crisply transferred cassette.

Violin concertos Nos. 1 (1908); 2 in B min. (1938).

(M) *** HMV SXLP/*TC-SXLP* 30533. Menuhin, New Philh. O, Dorati.

Yehudi Menuhin was closely associated with Bartók in the last few years of the composer's life and made the pioneering commercial records of the 1938 concerto with Dorati and the Dallas Symphony Orchestra. His HMV version, though not quite as fresh as that very first account, is thoroughly committed and beautifully recorded. It has a price advantage over both Itzhak Perlman and Kyung-Wha Chung (see below) and the additional attraction of including the early concerto that Bartók wrote for Stefi Geyer, which at the time of writing is not otherwise available. The cassette is every bit the equal of the disc, the quality full, yet strikingly clean and clearly detailed.

Violin concerto No. 2 in B min.

*** HMV ASD 3014 [Ang. S/*4XS* 37014]. Perlman, LSO, Previn.

*** Decca SXL/*KSXC* 6802 [Lon. CS/*5*-7023]. Kyung-Wha Chung, LPO, Solti.

** Argo ZRG 936. Iona Brown, Philh. O, Rattle.

Perlman's is a superb performance, totally committed and full of youthful urgency, with the sense of spontaneity that comes more readily when performers have already worked together on the music in the concert hall. The contrasts are fearlessly achieved by both soloist and orchestra, with everyone relishing virtuosity in the outer movements. The slow movement is deliberately understated by the soloist, with the fragmentation of the theme lightly touched in, but even there the orchestra has its passionate comments. With no coupling the disc is rather short measure, but no finer version of this masterly concerto has ever been available. The recording is rich and lively.

The combination of Chung and Solti produces a fiery, diamond-bright performance in which the Hungarian inflections are sharply brought out. Where the Perlman/Previn performance is warm and rich in confidence, treating this work (validly enough) as a successor to the great romantic concertos, Chung and Solti interpret it less comfortably. Though the angularity will not please everyone, it is an equally characterful reading. Bright Decca sound with forward violin, vivid on both disc and cassette alike.

Iona Brown gives a clean-cut and stylish performance superbly recorded, yet ultimately in sheer character and individuality it has to yield before such superb readings as Perlman's on HMV and Chung's on Decca, which have the benefit of recording almost equally full and brilliant.

Dance suite; 2 Portraits, Op. 5; Rumanian dances, Nos. 1–7.
** Decca SXL 6121. SRO, Ansermet.

If anything, Ansermet is too sensitive, too refined in the *Dance suite*, but it goes without saying that the Decca recording is excellent, and the *Two Portraits*, Op. 5 (the first of which is now better known as the first movement of the rediscovered *Violin concerto No. 1*), plus the *Rumanian dances* make an excellent coupling.

Divertimento for strings; Music for strings, percussion and celesta (see also below).
*** Argo ZRG 657 [id.]. ASMF, Marriner.
(M) **(*) EMI Em. EMX/*TC-EMX* 2029. ECO, Barenboim.
(M) ** Ph. Seq. 6527/*7311* 139. (i) BBC SO; (ii) Philh. Hungarica, Dorati.

On a vintage (1970) Argo record Neville Marriner and the St Martin's Academy provide a superlative Bartók coupling. The composer originally intended the *Music for strings, percussion and celesta* to be performed by a chamber-sized orchestra, and certainly, compared with the recorded performances using full orchestras (Solti and Bernstein, both impressive), this one reveals extra detail, extra expressiveness, extra care for tonal and dynamic nuances. There is of course a comparative lack of body in some of the big climaxes, but that is not a big price to pay. Marriner, for example, observes meticulously in the slow opening fugue the instruction to keep the music down to a pianissimo as far as bar 26, and there is no sense of cold, uncommitted playing. Quite the opposite. In the second movement the terracing of subtly different tempi is much more adeptly managed than usual, and all the playing reflects the working together beforehand in democratic conference which generally preceded a St Martin's performance at that time. The *Divertimento* is given a similarly vivid performance, and the recording is outstandingly good.

The contrasts between Barenboim and Marriner are very clearly marked. They are most obvious in the *Divertimento*, where Barenboim's earthiness contrasts with the point and refinement of Marriner. Ensemble is wilder, but the results are just as convincing. In the *Music for strings* Barenboim's romanticism will be too extreme for some, with a very slow expressive opening fugue and wild urgency in second and fourth movements. If the *Divertimento* is your first concern, then this could be a first choice even over Marriner. The recording is full-blooded and vivid. The cassette has rather less range at the top, but the treble is smoother and slightly richer, and there is no serious lack of bite.

Dorati's Sequenza issue is a re-coupling. The *Divertimento*, apart from a slightly too steady account of the finale, is interpreted with characteristically red-blooded Hungarian passion, with the BBC orchestra adopting a convincingly authentic Hungarian accent. The *Music for strings, percussion and celesta* is a little disappointing. The performance is surprisingly relaxed and the second and fourth movements lose something of their bite and brilliance, although in its remastered version the recording has more projection than the original. The espressivo warmth of the opening slow fugue is however most convincing, but this is much less attractive than the more temperamental Barenboim coupling in the same price-range. The Philips cassette transfer is lively and full.

(i) *The Miraculous Mandarin* (complete ballet); (ii) *2 Portraits, Op. 5.*
*** DG Dig. 410 598-1/*4* [id.]. (i) Amb. S., LSO, Abbado; (ii) with Mintz.
** Decca SXL 6882. VPO, Dohnányi; (ii) with Binder.

Abbado directs a fiercely powerful performance of Bartók's barbarically furious ballet – including the wordless chorus in the finale – but one which, thanks to the refinement of the recording, is texturally clear and unclouded. That makes the aggressiveness of the writing more acceptable even while it loses nothing in power. The LSO has rarely given a better performance on record for its music director, and the fill-up, with Mintz a warm and at times over-sweet soloist, is apt and attractive. The very opening of the ballet on the chrome cassette lacks something in crispness of focus because of the resonance but, taken as a whole, the tape transfer is very good, encompassing a wide dynamic range with vivid detail at piano level and plenty of impact in climaxes.

Dohnányi's direction of *The Miraculous Mandarin* is clean, precise and often beautiful. It is far less violent and weighty than usual, and not éveryone will respond to what one could almost describe as an unsuspected neoclassical element in the score. Dohnányi's Bartók style is more obviously suited to the *Two Portraits*, the first of which is used also as the first movement of the *Violin concerto No. 1*. The playing of the Vienna Philharmonic is radiantly beautiful, helped by spacious recording. Erich Binder is a first-class soloist in the *Portraits*.

The Miraculous Mandarin: suite; Music for strings, percussion and celesta.
*** Decca SXL 6111. LSO, Solti.
*** *TC-ASD 3655* [Ang. SZ 37608]. Phd. O, Ormandy.

Music for strings, percussion and celesta.
(M) *** CBS 60259 [(d) MS 6956]. NYPO, Bernstein – BERIO: *Sinfonia.****
(M) **(*) HMV SXLP/*TC-SXLP* 30536 [Ang. S 35949]. Berlin PO, Karajan – HINDEMITH: *Mathis der Maler.****
(M) **(*) DG Acc. 2542/*3342* 134 [2530 065]. Berlin PO, Karajan – STRAVINSKY: *Apollon Musagète.****

Solti and the LSO at their very finest, and how fine that is. The streak of ruthlessness in Solti's make-up that sometimes mars performances of less barbaric music is here given full rein in *The Miraculous Mandarin suite*, and that same unrelenting urgency makes this a most exciting account of the *Music for strings, percussion and celesta*. For all the nervous drive, Solti's control of dynamic and rhythm is most precise, though he loses some of the mystery of the weird third movement. The recording is superb.

Ormandy and the Philadelphia Orchestra have recorded *The Miraculous Mandarin* before, but this new version does full justice to the opulence of the Philadelphia strings and the rich sonorities of their cellos and basses. *The Miraculous Mandarin suite* is dazzling and the only reservation to make concerns the *Music for strings, percussion and celesta*, where greater mystery is needed (at least in the first and third movements). There is no want of eloquence and passion, but the dynamic range at the pianissimo end of the spectrum leaves something to be desired. That apart, there is so much to enjoy and admire here that this issue can be strongly recommended: the orchestral playing as such and the recording too are of the very first order. Curiously, in the UK the LP has been withdrawn, leaving only the cassette available. But the transfer is admirably vivid and clean. However, Solti's Decca coupling is by no means pushed into second place by the newer issue. Ormandy has the advantage of finer orchestral playing and an obviously more modern recording, but Solti shows a special feel for these scores.

Bernstein's recording of the *Music for strings, percussion and celesta* comes from the end of the 1960s and shows the New York Philharmonic at their finest. The playing combines power with atmospheric feeling in the most compelling way, and the performance has striking spontaneity. The recording, too, is one of the best from this source, forwardly balanced, but both full and vivid. With its coupling this is one of the most rewarding of the CBS 'Portrait' reissue series. Chrome cassette and disc are very closely matched.

Karajan first recorded the *Music for strings, percussion and celesta* with the Philharmonia Orchestra in 1949 (Columbia LX 1371-74); the HMV version comes from 1960. Though not as well recorded as the 1969 remake for DG, this is a tellingly atmospheric and committed account, in some ways fresher and more spontaneous than the later version. The sound needs more body and colour in the middle and upper register but it is still perfectly acceptable and in view of the excellence of the performance (and the coupling) this should not deter readers from investing in it. There is a good cassette.

Karajan's Accolade version has the advantage of excellent sound and a luxuriant Stravinsky coupling that is no less attractive than the Hindemith on the HMV record. Karajan's view of the Bartók has remained essentially romantic. He avoids undue expressiveness in the opening slow fugue (except in a big rallentando at the end), but the third movement is given a performance in soft focus. Nevertheless the playing of the Berlin strings is a delight to the ear and at medium price this remains worthwhile. There is a first-class cassette, clear and well detailed.

Miraculous Mandarin: suite.
** Mercury SRI 75030 [id.]. BBC SO, Dorati – PROKOFIEV: *Love of 3 oranges*, etc.**(*)

The suite is taken from Dorati's complete recording of the mid-1960s. The performance is a fine one, but the resonance tends to blunt the orchestra's upper range and the upper strings lack edge. Otherwise the sound is vivid.

Chamber music

(i) *Contrasts; Rumanian folk dances* (arr. Szekely); *Rhapsodies Nos. 1 and 2; Violin sonatas Nos. 1 and 2.*
*** None. Dig. DB 79021 (2) [id.]. Luca, Schoenfield; (i) with Shifrin.

These two records collect all of Bartók's music for violin and piano and throw in the *Contrasts* of 1938 for good measure (with the excellent David Shifrin as clarinet). The two *Sonatas*, composed in the early 1920s, make exacting demands on both players, and neither work finds Sergiu Luca and Paul Schoenfield wanting either artistically or technically. They are no less authoritative in the later and more immediately accessible *Rhapsodies* of 1928. The balance is well-judged in the recording and the digital technique secures clarity without loss of warmth. Highly recommendable.

44 Duos.
*** HMV ASD 4011 [Ang. SZ/*4ZS* 37540]. Perlman, Zukerman.

Though intended for educational use, and arranged in ascending order of difficulty, these miniatures emerge as little jewels of inspiration – the heart of Bartók revealed – when played with such warmth and intensity as here. Few will want to hear all forty-four at a single sitting, so it is a pity that the banding is not identified. The recording is warm and immediate, to enhance the compelling performances.

Sonata for two pianos and percussion.
*** Ph. 9500 434/*7300 644*. Argerich, Bishop-Kovacevich, Goudswaard, De Roo – DEBUSSY: *En blanc et noir*; MOZART: *Andante.****

A strongly atmospheric and finely characterized performance (also available coupled to the *Piano concertos*: see above). This is most imaginative playing and is afforded a recording of exceptionally wide range and truthfulness. It would be difficult to imagine a more eloquent or better recorded account of this powerful work. The tape transfer, however, is made at a low level (the opening is recessed) and there is a lack of transient bite.

(i) *Sonata for two pianos and percussion;* (ii) *Violin sonata* (for solo violin).
*** Accord **CD** 149 047. (i) Wyttenbach Duo, Schmid, Huber; (ii) Schneeberger.

The sound is astonishingly natural and lifelike in both works though the two pianos could with advantage be freer from the speaker areas. Hansheinz Schneeberger is little known outside Switzerland where he recorded the Willy Burkhard *Concerto*, but he is fully equal to the demands of Bartók's late sonata. There are the odd blemishes of intonation and the occasional unrefined dynamic nuance, but there is much to admire. He plays the alternative opening to the finale with its microtones. The *Sonata for two pianos and percussion* is given with great relish and attack by Jürg and Janka Wyttenbach and the two brilliant percussion players. It is an exhilarating account though not as pianistically imaginative as that of Bishop-Kovacevich and Argerich who bring exceptional flair and colour to this work. Thoroughly recommendable all the same.

String quartets Nos. 1–6.
*** DG 2740 235 (3) [id.]. Tokyo Qt.
*** ASV Dig. DCAB 301 (3). Lindsay Qt.
(M) ** CBS Dig. D3 37857 (3) [id.]. Juilliard Qt.
**(*) DG Priv. 2733 001 (3) [2728/*3373* 011]. Hungarian Qt.

String quartets Nos. 1–2.
*** ASV Dig. DCA/*ZCDCA* 510. Lindsay Qt.
(M) **(*) CBS 61118 [M 31196]. Juilliard Qt.

String quartets Nos. 3–4.
*** ASV Dig. DCA/*ZCDCA* 509. Lindsay Qt.
(M) **(*) CBS 61119 [M 31197]. Juilliard Qt.

String quartets Nos. 5–6.
*** ASV Dig. DCA/*ZCDCA* 504. Lindsay Qt.
(M) **(*) Sup. 1111 2846. Talich Qt.
(M) **(*) CBS 61120 [M 31198]. Juilliard Qt.

It was the Tokyo Quartet's records of the *Second* and *Sixth* Bartók quartets (DG 2530 658 – now withdrawn in the UK) that alerted us to an exceptional group. These performances brought an almost ideal combination of fire and energy with detailed point and refinement. When, several years later, the group went on to record the rest of the cycle, the performances proved just as consistently satisfying, outshining direct rivals in almost every way. Though the polish is higher than in other versions – helped by splendid recording – the sense of commitment and seeming spontaneity is greater too. So the range of expression includes in the fullest measure not only the necessary Bartókian passion but the sparkle and wit, each interpretative problem closely considered and solved with finesse and assurance.

The Lindsay Quartet on ASV have the advantage of first-class digital sound, warmly atmospheric but nicely focused, and these are the only recordings available on cassette. The quality of the tape transfers is outstanding, combining presence with body and homogeneity of timbre, and giving excellent detail at piano and pianissimo levels. The discs are available separately or in a box with a modest price reduction. Searching and powerfully expressive, the Lindsay Quartet give strongly projected readings which can be recommended alongside though not in preference to the Tokyo set. Artistically the claims of both sets are very finely balanced, although the Lindsay readings, direct and committed, lack the last degree of pointed detail which makes those of the Tokyo players so compelling.

The Juilliard Quartet was the first group to record a complete cycle of the Bartók *Quartets* on LP, and it was that early issue – appearing in Europe on Philips, in the United States on the Columbia label – which alerted us to the arrival of a fine new quartet group. Since then they have re-recorded the music twice in stereo, and the latest CBS set is a vivid digital version. The playing is distinguished. Though only the leader remains the same as in that first mono set, there is a natural expressiveness here, dramatic and red-blooded. Only *No. 2* seriously disappoints, but in other quartets too there is an occasional lack of repose. With no competition this would be an excellent contender, but there are several versions preferable, and recorded with more refinement too.

The Juilliards' first stereo recordings of 1970 remain available separately. The style of the playing was then, as now, essentially romantic, full-blooded and warmly expressive rather than hushed and introspective, but vividly conveying the earthiness of Bartók's inspiration. The forward balance of the recording takes something away from the music's atmospheric quality, but there is no doubt whatever about the conviction behind the playing all through.

The DG set by the Hungarian Quartet also has considerable authority: the Hungarians were the first to record *Nos. 5* and *6*, and their leader gave the première of the *Violin concerto*. But if they are more refined than the Juilliard players, they do not quite convey the full intensity that distinguishes the best rival versions. The DG recording is excellent for its age (1962).

The Talich Quartet on Supraphon do not disturb current recommendations. They are fine players and their version of the *Sixth* is beautifully shaped and by far the better of the two. The *Fifth* is really too well bred by comparison with the best of the competition and the recording quality, too, is not in the same league as the DG or ASV sets.

Violin sonatas Nos. 1–2.
*(**) CBS Dig. 36697 [id.]. Zukerman, Neikrug.

Highly accomplished performances of these demanding sonatas come from this impressive partnership. Both artists are completely inside this music and play with imagination and flair. Since the musical interest of the two parts is equal in balance, it is a pity that the CBS engineers have chosen to focus the violinist in an almost solo spotlight, relegating the piano to the role of an accompanist.

Piano music

Allegro barbaro; 4 Dirges, Op. 9a; 3 Hungarian folksongs from the Czik District; 15 Hungarian peasant songs; 8 Improvisations on Hungarian peasant songs, Op. 20; 7 Sketches, Op. 9b.
*** Ph. 9500/*7300* 876 [id.]. Kocsis.

A marvellous recital, with playing of exceptional sensitivity and range. Zoltán Kocsis is always thoughtful, and his performance of the *Dirges* is penetrating and moving. He discovers a world of colour that leaves no doubt of the quality of his imagination and musicianship. Yet there is no want of drama and power when required. The *Songs from the Czik District* are exquisitely done, and so, for that matter, are all the pieces here. This is one of the finest Bartók recitals in the catalogue: it makes the old Andor Foldes set seem very monochrome indeed. The recording is stunningly lifelike; as piano sound, this is in the demonstration class. The cassette too is of Philips' best quality, full-bodied and clear.

Mikrokosmos (complete).
(M) ** HM HM 968/70. Helffer (with Austbö).

Claude Helffer gives an intelligent account, though he tends to invest detail with greater expressive emphasis than this mostly simple music can bear. Greater simplicity would have yielded stronger artistic results, though this is not to deny that there is some fine playing during the course of the six sides. In the pieces requiring a second player Helffer is joined by Haakon Austbö (some artists such as Ránki play with the second part pre-recorded). The sound is realistic and fully acceptable.

Out of Doors (suite); *Piano sonata; Suite, Op. 14.*
*** CBS 76650 [M/*MT* 36704]. Perahia.

Murray Perahia brings to this repertoire a muscularity and fire that will exhilarate – and surprise – those who know only his Mozart concerto records. He attacks the keyboard with total yet disciplined abandon (if that is not a contradiction in terms) and gives us playing of exceptional imaginative vision. In *Out of Doors* there are delicate glints of light, scarcely perceptible rustling of foliage and insect chirrups, and Perahia does not pull his punches in the *Chase* or obscure the peasant earthiness of the *Musettes* movement. As in everything this artist gives us on record, there is total commitment; no phrase is ever given less than its full weight, yet here is no self-indulgent overstatement. Indeed these performances have so complete a ring of authenticity that one soon forgets to think of the player – in almost the same way as with Schnabel's Beethoven sonatas Op. 110 or Op. 111. The recording does not do full justice to Perahia's tone (judging from his Bartók performances in the concert hall): the acoustic is dry and the studio obviously smaller than the one used in Kocsis's much-admired Philips disc (see above). As a result the sound is a trifle metallic and wanting in bloom (though that is not entirely unsuited to this music). Were the recorded sound as good as for Kocsis, this would rate a rosette.

5 Songs, Op. 16.
*** Decca SXL 6964. Sass, Schiff – LISZT: *Lieder.****

Darkly beautiful, these settings of poems by Endre Ady come from the period leading up to Bartók's *Second Quartet*. The mood is tragic, the technique often adventurous, but the result seductive. Sylvia Sass and Andras

Schiff, Hungarians both, give intense, persuasive performances, beautifully recorded.

OPERA

Bluebeard's Castle (sung in Hungarian).
*** CBS 76518/*40-* [M 34217]. Troyanos, Nimsgern, BBC SO, Boulez.
*** Decca SET 311. Ludwig, Berry, LSO, Kertesz.
**(*) Decca SET 630 [Lon. OSA 1174]. Sass, Kovats, LPO, Solti.
(*) Hung. Dig. **MCD 12254; SLPD/*MK* 12254 [id.]. Obraztsova, Nesterenko, Hungarian State Op. O, Ferencsik.
*(*) DG 2531 172 [id.]. Varady, Fischer-Dieskau, Bav. State Op. O, Sawallisch.

Bartók's idea of portraying marital conflict in an opera was as unpromising as could be, but in the event *Bluebeard's Castle* is an enthralling work with its concentration on mood, atmosphere and slow development as Bluebeard's wife finds the key to each new door. Its comparative absence of action makes it an ideal work for the gramophone, and there have been a surprising number of attempts to record it (so conveniently filling a single LP). Kertesz set new standards in his version with Christa Ludwig and Walter Berry, not only in the playing of the LSO at its peak, in the firm sensitivity of the soloists and the brilliance of recording, but in the natural Hungarian inflections inspired by the conductor.

Then, some years later, Boulez made his recording, and though there is still a case for preferring the reading conducted by a Hungarian, the later version has the balance of advantage. Here more than ever Boulez reveals what warmth has developed in his character as an interpreter; the soloists are even more vibrantly committed than their counterparts, and the recording is outstandingly vivid, among the very finest on this label. Unlike the Decca it presents the singers in a slightly contrasted acoustic, as though on a separate stage. Boulez has rarely if ever made so fine a record.

Solti directs a richly atmospheric reading of Bartók's ritualistic opera, not as searingly dramatic as one might have expected but with recording of spectacular range. The performance is introduced by the Hungarian verses which are printed in the score. The Hungarian soloists are tangily authentic, though their voices are not always perfectly steady, and Sylvia Sass is very appealing with her exquisite pianissimo singing. The recording – less analytical than is normal from Decca – produces a rich carpet of sound. The result is a more romantic effect than usual, and even reveals an affinity with Richard Strauss.

With two distinguished Soviet singers taking the roles of Bluebeard and Judith, Ferencsik's Hungaraton version (his fourth recording of the work) is vocally resonant and delicately atmospheric with the hushed pianissimo of the opening tellingly caught. Yet in musical weight and intensity, not to mention dramatic detail and technical virtuosity, this inevitably yields before the finest versions using western orchestras. The digital recording is full and faithful.

The two soloists on the DG version – in real life husband and wife – bring Lieder-like intensity to the almost ritualistic exchanges of Bluebeard and Judith. The pity is that their voices are recorded too close and the orchestral contribution lacks the bite and drama which are essential to this sharply structured piece.

Bax, Arnold (1883–1953)

The Garden of Fand (symphonic poem).
(B) ** PRT GSGC/*ZCGC* 2059. Hallé O, Barbirolli – BUTTERWORTH: *Shropshire Lad;* VAUGHAN WILLIAMS: *Symphony No. 8.***

The Garden of Fand; The Happy forest; November woods; Summer music.
C *** Chan. Dig. **CHAN 8307**; ABRD/*ABTD* 1066 [id.]. Ulster O, Bryden Thomson.

This excellent, highly enjoyable Chandos collection of Bax tone poems is intended as the first of a series and represents the work of the Ulster Orchestra at its very finest. The

Celtic twilight in Bax's music is ripely and sympathetically caught in the first three items, while *Summer Music*, dedicated to Sir Thomas Beecham and here given its first ever recording, brings an intriguing kinship with the music of Delius. The Chandos recording is superb, full, vivid and natural with no unnatural close-ups. The chrome cassette has striking range and projection, but the massed upper strings lack body compared with the LP. The compact disc is outstanding, the bass firm and clean, while the sound has exceptional detail and range.

Barbirolli's vintage recording of *The Garden of Fand* offers a performance of striking spontaneity and feeling. The 1957 recording lacks range but remains adequate and the cassette is satisfactory too. This remains worthwhile at bargain price as both couplings show Barbirolli at his finest.

Symphonic variations in E for piano and orchestra.
*** Concert Artist *FED-TC-001*. Hatto, Guildford PO, Handley.

Bax's *Symphonic variations for piano and orchestra* dates from 1917, a particularly productive period when he also wrote *Tintagel* and *November woods*. (*The garden of Fand* had come the year before.) It is an ambitious work, on the largest scale, with the most luxuriant romantic feeling; the six movements are titled: *Youth*; *Nocturne*; *Strife*; *The Temple*; *Intermezzo*; *Triumph*. The present performance was recorded (using a fully professional body of players) in EMI's Abbey Road studios, and the sound is admirably full-blooded to suit the extrovert romanticism of the score. Joyce Hatto is a committed advocate and Handley makes a thoroughly sympathetic partner. Baxians will not want to miss this issue, though others might feel that the piece might have gained if it had been more concise. But that was not Bax's way at this period of his career. The 'real-time' cassette is admirably transferred; at present there is no equivalent LP.

Symphony No. 4; Tintagel.
*** Chan. **CHAN 8312;** ABRD/*ABTD* 1091. Ulster O, Bryden Thomson.

The *Fourth Symphony* was written in 1930–31; part of the first movement was worked out at Bax's Irish refuge in Glencolumcille, but the seascapes that the score brings to mind are mainly those of the coast and islands of the Western Highlands where Bax spent each winter during the 1930s. The copious flow of ideas in the best of his symphonies (2, 3, 5 and 6) does not always go hand in hand with organic coherence, and the overall impression remains of a series of related episodes rather than a growing musical organism. This is not to belittle their power or originality but merely to underline what one critic has said, that a Bax symphony is 'like an instinctive drama of the emotions rather than a logically sustained argument'. *No. 4* is the least concentrated and most hedonistic of the seven and flaunts the 'unashamed Romanticism' which Bax so often proclaimed. The ideas may not be quite as memorable as those of the *Third* and *Fifth* but the moods are still powerful and the colours vivid. The performance is altogether splendid; Bryden Thomson encourages his players to a scrupulous observance of dynamic nuance as well as a sensitive projection of atmosphere. The recording is in the demonstration bracket. *Tintagel* need not fear comparison with Barbirolli and the LSO, or Boult and the LPO, artistically, and is technically even finer. This is reflected in the excellent chrome tape which sounds superb in the tone poem, and first-rate elsewhere.

Symphony No. 6 in C.
**(*) Lyr. SRCS 35. New Philh. O, Del Mar.

The *Sixth Symphony* (1934) has some of the wild beauty of Inverness-shire, where Bax wrote it. He seems to have found his inspiration in the dark, brooding landscapes of the North and West, and there is a passionate fervour about it that offsets its somewhat sprawling architecture. Although the *Sixth* is not as imaginative as the *Second Symphony* or as fresh and original as the *Third*, it is a welcome addition to Bax's growing representation in the catalogue. Norman Del Mar's performance with the New Philharmonia is committed, though a greater attention to dynamic nuance would have been welcome.

The balance, too, is less than ideal and far too close at times. Bax's woodwind writing is very distinctive and blends into the orchestral texture to highly personal ends: it is a pity that the aural perspective shifts to highlight it. The same happens to some of the delicate colouristic effects in the trio section of the finale. Nonetheless, these are not major defects, and one hopes that readers will not be put off investigating this fine British symphony.

Tintagel.
(M) *** HMV Green. ESD/*TC-ESD* 7092 [Ang. S 36415]. LSO, Barbirolli – DELIUS: *Collection;* IRELAND: *London overture.****

Barbirolli's performance of *Tintagel* was the first to be issued in stereo, and its reissue on HMV Greensleeve is most welcome. The sound is fresh and the splendid cassette matches the disc in its brightness and clarity. The performance is characteristically full-blooded. The sea vistas (with their musical reminders of Debussy as well as Wagner) are magnificently painted by players and recording engineers alike and Sir John sees that the memorable principal tune is given a fine romantic sweep. If the couplings are attractive this is highly recommendable.

Clarinet sonata.
** Chan. Dig. ABRD/*ABTD* 1078. Hilton, Swallow – BLISS: *Clarinet quintet*; VAUGHAN WILLIAMS: *6 Studies.****

Both artists are rather closely balanced in a very ample acoustic but they play the *Sonata* with sensitivity and conviction. It comes from 1934, the same year as the *Sixth Symphony*, and, despite its rhapsodic air, is a well-fashioned and succinct piece. For all its overt romanticism, it is not the best Bax and does not compare with the *Nonet* or the *Oboe quintet*, but its vein of lyricism and undoubted warmth will win it a following. The coupling, the *Clarinet quintet* of Bliss, enhances the attraction of the disc. The chrome cassette is of the highest Chandos quality, vivid and well balanced.

Rhapsodic ballad (for unaccompanied cello).
*** Pearl SHE 547. Saram – L. BERKELEY and BRIDGE: *Trios.***

One does not associate Bax with so austere a medium as the unaccompanied cello. This dates from the beginning of the Second World War and is a passionately argued work, which uses as its point of departure the opening theme from Bax's 1929 *Overture, elegy and rondo.* It throws new light on the composer, who was not usually so concentrated in utterance. It is played with masterly command by Rohan de Saram, whose range of tone and colour does much to win over the most sceptical of critics. The recording is a shade close but fully acceptable, and the interest of this disc outweighs other considerations.

Piano sonata No. 2 in G; Appleblossom time; The princess's rose garden; Scherzo; Slave dance.
** Pearl SHE 565. Binns.

Though Bax was a formidable pianist, none of his output for the instrument has won more than a peripheral hold on the repertory. Malcolm Binns gives a persuasive enough account of the second of his sonatas written in 1919. Lewis Foreman reminds us in his excellent sleeve note that its successor (1921–2) eventually turned into the *First Symphony*, and there is undoubtedly much in the present score that would sound more effective were the texture orchestral rather than keyboard. The other smaller pieces are equally well played and it is good to have them on disc. However, the recording balances the instrument rather more closely than is desirable in an acoustic setting which is cramped and a little dry.

Bedford, David (born 1937)

The Tentacles of the Dark Nebula.
(*) Decca HEAD 3 [id.]. Pears, L. Sinf., composer – BERKELEY: *Ronsard sonnet*(*); LUTOSLAWSKI: *Paroles.****

Peter Pears was the inspirer of each of the three works on an unexpectedly varied disc coupling Bedford, Berkeley and Lutoslawski. The Bedford work presents the soloist in a narrative from a science-fiction story by Arthur C. Clarke, the images and situations vividly illustrated by Bedford's finely textured score. Whether the musical argument as such holds together is another matter, but on the level of illustration it is a more communicative piece than most. The performance and recording are excellent.

Beethoven, Ludwig van

(1770–1827)

(i) *Piano concertos Nos. 1–5;* (ii) *Violin concerto, Op. 61;* (iii) *Triple concerto, Op. 56; 2 Romances, Opp. 40 and 50.*

(M) **(*) DG Priv. 2721 128 (6). (i) Kempff; (ii) Ferras; (iii) Schneiderhan, Fournier, Anda; Berlin PO, Leitner, Karajan, or Fricsay or RPO, Goossens.

Piano concertos Nos. 1–5; (i) *Triple concerto, Op. 56.*

(M) *** Ph. 6768 350 (6) [id.]. Arrau, Concg. O, Haitink; (i) Arrau, Szeryng, Starker, New Philh. O, Inbal.

Piano concertos Nos. 1–5; (i) *Choral fantasia, Op. 80.*

*** Ph. 6767 002 (5)/*7699 061* [id.]. Brendel, LPO, Haitink, (i) with LPO Ch.

(M) *** HMV SLS/*TC-SLS* 5180 (4). Barenboim, New Philh. O, Klemperer, (i) with John Alldis Ch.

(B) **(*) CfP CFP 78253 (4). Lill, SNO, Gibson, (i) with Ch.

(i) *Piano concertos Nos. 1–5. Andante favori; Für Elise; Polonaise in C, Op. 89; Variations in F, Op. 34.*

(M) (***) World mono SHB/*TC-SHB* 64 (4). Schnabel, (i) with LPO, Sargent.

Piano concertos Nos. 1–5.

(M) *** Ph. 6747 104 (4). Bishop-Kovacevich, BBC SO, Davis.

*** Decca SXLG 6594/*7K 44 K 43* [Lon. CSA 2404]. Ashkenazy, Chicago SO, Solti.

** DG 2740 284/*3378 142* (4/*3*) [id.]. Pollini, VPO, Boehm or Jochum.

The available range of boxed sets of the Beethoven *Concertos* is remarkable and any of those listed will give much satisfaction. Kempff's recordings are currently only available in boxed format within a grouping of other concerto records, but they are also, of course, available separately at mid-price – see below. Kempff's cycle of the piano concertos is to the 1960s what Solomon's was for the preceding decade. They sound astonishingly fresh in Kempff's hands: the *B flat* possesses a classical poise and sparkle that immediately disarms criticism, while in the *Fourth* there is an impressive sense of repose and spirituality. What a fine accompanist Leitner was in this cycle, drawing playing of great warmth and humanity from the Berlin Philharmonic. The quality of these transfers is so fine that one could be forgiven for thinking the recordings were made in the 1970s. Ferras's account of the *Violin concerto* is not among the very best but worth hearing all the same, and the *Triple concerto* (with soloists too forward – the piano is marvellously balanced in Kempff's recordings) receives a distinguished reading.

Technically the Brendel recordings are superb and must be numbered among the best concerto recordings available in cassette or disc form. Given an artist of Brendel's distinction, it would be surprising if this set were not in the first flight artistically, even though there are moments (for instance in the *Emperor*) when one's mind returns to his earlier Turnabout recordings, which sound less studied. Elsewhere there is no lack of spontaneity, and generally speaking the performances are as satisfying as the recording is rich. The perspective between soloist and orchestra is perfectly judged and the piano tone itself is remarkably lifelike, clean and well-focused throughout its register. There is general consent that these performances are among the finest in the market, and as sound they certainly head the list.

Stephen Bishop-Kovacevich's is a dedicated

set of performances to put alongside Kempff's. In freshness and directness, they have rarely been surpassed, yet the depth of introspection in slow movements confirms the expressive range. Equally Colin Davis in each concerto is at his most inspired. These are central readings, finely recorded, that can be recommended without reservation.

Hardly less rewarding is the fine Barenboim/Klemperer set recorded at the end of the 1960s and still sounding very well indeed, both on disc and in the bold, high-level cassette transfers. Indeed the tape box offers the ideal presentation of the music, with each of the concertos complete on one cassette side (the *Emperor* backed by the *Choral fantasia*). No more individual performances of the Beethoven concertos have ever been put on record. The combination of Barenboim and Klemperer is nothing if not inspired, and for every wilfulness of a measured Klemperer there is a youthful spark from the spontaneously-combusting Barenboim. That may imply a lack of sympathy between conductor and soloist, but plainly this is not so. These recordings were made much more quickly than usual, with long takes allowing a sense of continuity rare on record. Some may not like an apparently spontaneous performance for repeated listening (in the *Emperor*, for example, Barenboim has some slight fluffs of finger) but the concentration is formidable and especially compelling in the slow movements, whether in the earliest concerto, No. 2 – here given an interpretation that is anything but Mozartian, and splendidly strong – or in the later concertos. No. 3 brings the most obviously wilful slow tempi, but, with fine rhythmic points from soloist and orchestra, the result is still vivid and compelling. No. 4 is anything but a delicate, feminine work, with basic tempi slow enough to avoid the need for much slowing when the lyrical countersubjects emerge. The *Choral fantasia* too is given an inspired performance, with the weaknesses of Beethoven's writing wonderfully concealed when the music-making is so intense.

The partnership of Ashkenazy and Solti is no less fascinating. Where Solti is fiery and intense, Ashkenazy provides an introspective balance. No better example of this can be found than in the slow movement of the *Fourth Concerto*. The 'masculine/feminine' dialogue has rarely been so strongly contrasted on record, Solti strong and commanding, Ashkenazy's reply exquisitely gentle, yet never losing the argument. Ashkenazy brings a hushed, poetic quality to every slow movement, while Solti's urgency maintains a vivid forward impulse in the outer movements. Sometimes, as in the *C minor Concerto*, one feels that the music-making is too intense. Here a more relaxed, lyrical approach can find in the first movement a warmth of humanity that Solti misses. But for the most part the listener is given an overriding impression of vitality and freshness, and the *Emperor* performance, while on the grandest scale, has a marvellously individual moment in the first movement when Ashkenazy lingers over his presentation of the second subject. The Chicago orchestral playing is characteristically brilliant, and the very bright recording (with not as rich piano tone as Decca usually provides) is inclined to be fierce to emphasize the driving quality of the orchestral contribution. The tape transfer is excellent.

Unlike his alternative box of the *Piano concertos* on four records (Philips 6770 014), this listed Arrau set has been remastered and sounds even fresher and wide-ranging. Made in the mid-1960s, the concertos are most beautifully recorded with each concerto being accommodated on one record – and the *Triple Concerto*, in which Arrau is joined by Szeryng and Starker, included as well. The balance in the latter places the three soloists far too forward but the *Piano concertos* still sound marvellous and do not compare unfavourably with many more recent recordings. The merits of these performances are well known: Arrau produces tone of consistent beauty and refinement, and his approach is aristocratic without ever being aloof. At its eminently reasonable price, this deserves a full star rating.

John Lill has never been more impressive on record than in his set of the Beethoven concertos; in each of the works he conveys a sense of spontaneity and a vein of poetry that in the studio have too often eluded him. Gibson and the Scottish National Orchestra provide strong, direct support, helped by good modern recording, and though there have been more strikingly individual readings than these, as a set they make a very impressive cycle. The records are issued in their original sleeves but within an attractively robust box, and the value for money is obvious.

In the Pollini set for DG the last three concertos brought the unexpected but generally fruitful collaboration of this inspired but temperamental pianist with the veteran Boehm, and similarly in the first two concertos – recorded after Boehm's death – Jochum provides a sheet-anchor of tradition in accompaniments superbly judged. Pollini is sometimes wilful and rarely warm in expressiveness, but always fresh and spontaneously communicative. As a set this hardly compares with the finest cycles, but is a characterful reminder of a highly individual pianist. The cassettes are clear and well balanced to match the discs, the sound sometimes rather dry. Nos. 1 and 3 and 2 and 4 are back to back in the tape set.

Schnabel's performances fall into a special category. The concertos were recorded in 1932–3, save for the *B flat*, which dates from 1935; the solo pieces come from 1938 and some were unpublished. They are not to be confused with Schnabel's post-war cycle with Galliera and Dobrowen or his wartime accounts of Nos. 4 and 5, made in Chicago. His playing has such enormous character that it transcends the limitations of sound that are inevitable at this period, the only possible exception being the *Emperor*. The orchestral playing is occasionally lacking the finesse that we take for granted nowadays, but Schnabel's impulsive, searching and poetic playing offers special rewards. Not everything is equally successful: there is some roughness in the first movement of No. 3, but there are some marvellously spirited touches. Schnabel may not be so illuminating in the concertos as he was in, say, the late *Piano sonatas*, but that is comparing one peak with another higher one. Among historic collections Solomon's has a surpassing claim on the collector, and Schnabel, though he often penetrates deeper, seldom attains the latter's poise. Nonetheless, these revealing performances are to be treasured, whether on disc or on the expertly transferred tapes, where the sound is consistently crisp and lively.

Piano concerto No. 1 in C, Op. 15.

(M) *** DG Acc. 2542/*3342* 188 [id.]. Kempff, Berlin PO, Leitner.

(M) *** Ph. Seq. 6527/*7311* 174 [id.]. Bishop-Kovacevich, BBC SO, Davis.

*** Ph. 9500 252/*7300 563* [id.]. Brendel, LPO, Haitink.

*** Decca SXL/*KSXC* 6653 [Lon. CS 6853/*5*-]. Ashkenazy, Chicago SO, Solti (with *Sonata No. 8, Pathétique* ***).

(*) DG Dig. **410 511-2; 2532/*3302* 103 [id.]. Pollini, VPO, Jochum.

(M) ** DG Priv. 2535 273 [id.]. Eschenbach, Berlin PO, Karajan.

*(*) DG 2531/*3301* 302 [id.]. Michelangeli, VSO, Giulini.

Piano concerto No. 1; 12 Variations on a Russian theme.

(M) ** HMV SXLP/*TC-SXLP* 30540. Gilels, Cleveland O, Szell.

With both Kempff and Bishop-Kovacevich at medium price in excellent remastered pressings, a first choice must be dictated by personal inclination. Leitner's contribution to the DG version is especially distinguished and there is memorable orchestral playing throughout and especially in the slow movement. Kempff's sense of repose is remarkable in this concerto. The slow movement is in fact a shade faster than in Kempff's earlier version. Yet the very profundity of Kempff's sense of calm creates the illusion of something much slower. In the Finale, the playing sparkles joyously. The recording is good, with the piano balanced rather farther back than is common with DG. The cassette is naturally balanced, but the upper range is not as open as the disc. Nevertheless, with a truthful piano image, the tape is still fully acceptable.

The combination of Bishop-Kovacevich and Sir Colin Davis rarely fails to produce an exceptionally satisfying reading, and this performance, which combines clarity of articulation and deep thoughtfulness, is among the very finest versions of this concerto. Maybe Bishop-Kovacevich misses some of the exuberance of Kempff, but the unforced rightness of the interpretation may be judged from the fact that, though he keeps the pulse remarkably steady in the slow movement, the result still conveys spontaneity with no feeling of rigidity. An advantage over Kempff (among others) is that Bishop-Kovacevich uses the longest and most challenging of the cadenzas that Beethoven wrote for the first movement. The recording is beautifully refined in the Philips manner, and the cassette quality is both lively and full-bodied.

There is a spontaneity about Brendel's playing in his Philips set of the Beethoven concertos that puts most of his performances rather in contrast with his concentrated but rather more studied accounts of the *Piano sonatas* on the same label. Nowhere is this spontaneity more compelling than in the *First Concerto*, though in places neither the solo nor the orchestral playing is quite as tidy as one would expect of these performers. Very good recording, with a matching cassette, rather over-ample in bass.

Ashkenazy has the advantage of a bold, modern recording of considerable depth and power. The sound is notably resonant in the middle range, imparting a slight huskiness to the orchestral image in the first movement. The performance is characteristic of the Ashkenazy/Solti partnership, with a strong large-scale opening *tutti* balanced by the comparative reticence of the soloist's lyricism. Solti, however, ensures that the woodwind comments when Ashkenazy is taking the dominating role have no lack of delicacy. The hushed slow movement is very beautiful, and taken as a whole this is most satisfying. Many will be attracted by the substantial coupling, a major performance, with its calm *Adagio cantabile* and cool, flowing finale making a perfect balance with the opening movement.

The clarity and tonal range of Gilels's playing excites unfailing admiration. The slow movement in particular is searching and illuminating; the first is broad and unhurried with a trace of sobriety and, like the finale, perhaps a little wanting in spontaneity. Szell is businesslike and efficient and does not match Gilels's sense of poetry (as in the closing bars of the finale) and there is not the same rapport between the two artists as there was in earlier Beethoven records Gilels made with Sanderling, Leopold Ludwig and André Cluytens. Good but not distinguished recording. The fill-up, the *Wranitzky variations*, are quite superb and the cassette quality is also very good indeed.

Pollini is sometimes wilful, but with refreshing clarity of articulation his is a performance, brisk rather than poetic, which vividly reflects the challenge of an unexpected partnership between pianist and conductor. The recording was taken from live performances, but betrays little sign of that. There is a good if not outstanding cassette.

Eschenbach and Karajan choose a slow tempo for the first movement, and though the concentration holds the attention, the result here is closer to a chamber approach. A beautiful performance of the slow movement and a lightweight finale. The performance is attractive and interesting, but in its concentration on refinement (Karajan's doing?) it misses any sort of greatness. The recording is good.

Recorded at a live concert, the partnership of Michelangeli and Giulini is intensely disappointing, with Michelangeli strangely metrical – a fault accentuated by the forward balance and clangorous tone of the piano. Against such competition the contribution of Giulini and the orchestra is undistinguished.

Piano concertos Nos. 1–2.

*** Decca Dig. SXDL/*KSXDC* 7502 [Lon. LDR 10006]. Lupu, Israel PO, Mehta.

(M) **(*) Decca SPA/*KCSP* 401. Backhaus, VPO, Schmidt-Isserstedt.

Lupu couples the two early concertos in an exceptionally generous digital disc. (Indeed such a coupling offers stiff competition, even to bargain-priced issues.) The readings find Lupu and Mehta favouring fast resilient speeds. The slow movements are treated with lightness too and throughout it is the pianist who dominates. Lupu's playing has both sparkle and sensitivity and its poetry is ever apparent. He never tries to invest detail with undue expressive intensity, nor does he view early Beethoven through the eyes of his maturity. These are marvellously articulated readings, and if the playing of the Israel Philharmonic is sometimes not very refined it is always sympathetic. The digital recording is outstandingly successful (both on disc and on the cassette, which is of demonstration standard). The balance is excellently judged and the sound combines comfort with great clarity. No attempt to be spectacular is made and the effect is consistently pleasing.

Backhaus's recording career spanned fifty

of the most important years of the gramophone's history. It was he who made the first serious attempt at recording a major piano concerto (the Grieg, issued during the First World War and condensed to two twelve-inch 78 r.p.m. sides), and the evidence of these fine records, made at the end of the 1950s, is that his vitality stayed unimpaired. Indeed it is the sheer vigour of the solo playing that impresses the listener so much, to say nothing of the excellence of the recording, which has come up fresh and sparkling in these new transfers, not in the least dated. Some might feel that the brisk manner Backhaus adopts in the *First Concerto* suggests superficiality, but this is by no means the case, and repeated listenings yield increasing pleasure: the almost brusque way the pianist treats the slow movement falls into place within the reading as a whole. The *Second Concerto* is even finer. Here the soloist is more generous in his variations of touch, and the flowing spontaneity of the music-making brings a feeling of youthful freshness. The finale is particularly successful. This disc is a good bargain, and so is the matching cassette.

Piano concerto No. 2 in B flat, Op. 19.

*** Ph. 9500 471/*7300 628* [id.]. Brendel, LPO, Haitink – *Choral fantasia.****

(M) *** DG Acc. 2542/*3342* 136 [id.]. Kempff, Berlin PO, Leitner – *Concerto No. 4.****

(M) *** Ph. Seq. 6527/*7311* 175 [id.]. Bishop-Kovacevich, BBC SO, Davis – *Concerto No. 4.****

*** Decca SXL/*KSXC* 6652 [Lon. CS 6854/5-]. Ashkenazy, Chicago SO, Solti (with *Sonata No. 21, Waldstein****).

(M) **(*) HMV SXLP/*TC-SXLP* 30515 [(d) Ang. S 36030]. Gilels, Cleveland O, Szell – *Concerto No. 4.***(*)*

(M) ** Ph. Seq. 6527/*7311* 028. Haebler, New Philh. O, Galliera – *Concerto No. 4.***

Brendel and Haitink convey both the strength and the charm of the young Beethoven's first mature essay in piano concerto writing. The spontaneity of the playing is a delight, not least in the capriciousness of the finale, though the slow movement could be more gently treated – partly the fault of the recording's acoustic. The *Choral fantasia* makes an excellent coupling, with Brendel inspired in the opening cadenza. Vivid, immediate sound, with an excellent tape transfer of the *Concerto*, which is beautifully balanced. In the *Choral fantasia*, however, one might wish the level of transfer had been a little higher. Here, although the quality is refined, the choral detail lacks the last degree of crispness of focus.

There is intense competition in the medium price-range. Kempff's account of the *Second Concerto*, attractively coupled with the *Fourth*, has long been a favourite choice. Like No. 4, it is a less individual performance than on Kempff's earlier mono LP, but his playing is unmistakable in almost every bar and Leitner's conducting is both strong and sympathetic. The recording, from the early 1960s, still sounds well and the tape was one of the best of DG's early transfers, although it has not been remastered for the reissue.

For those who find Kempff's coupling too personal, Stephen Bishop-Kovacevich provides the ideal answer in a direct, thoughtful reading, with fine accompaniment from Sir Colin Davis and the BBC orchestra, and refined Philips recording, more modern than the DG, with clear, pellucid piano timbre. The sound is lighter in the bass than the other issues in this series, but that is the only indication of the length of the sides. The tape transfer is well managed too, clear and clean.

Those for whom the coupling of the *Waldstein sonata* is suitable need look no further than the splendid Decca recording by Ashkenazy and Solti, which shows this fine partnership at its most rewarding. Here the poetry of the solo playing is perfectly balanced by the orchestral response. The slow movement is particularly beautiful and its hushed close creates a memorable feeling of repose before the sparkling finale. The recording is first-class in every way. Ashkenazy's *Waldstein* is satisfying too, clear and direct. The great tune of the finale does not steal in quite so magically as with Kempff, for instance, but the performance overall is certainly one of the finest on disc. The cassette sounds well too.

Gilels is an incomparable Beethoven player and we have long cherished his seraphic account of the *G major Concerto* with Leopold Ludwig (now deleted). He is unfailingly illuminating and poetic, his playing consistently a matter for marvel. Szell is a less sympathetic accompanist. He keeps everything on a rather tight rein and rarely matches the humanity and vision of his soloist. The recording too is dry and clear rather than expansive. The cassette is of first-class quality, matching the disc closely.

The sensibility of Ingrid Haebler's playing always gives pleasure and this is a highly musical performance, very well recorded on both disc and cassette and given sympathetic accompaniments under Galliera. But in the last resort this playing is not memorable, the slow movement, without idiosyncrasy, is coolly beautiful, especially in the closing pages, but like the neatly played finale lacking the imaginative touches a pianist like Kempff can bring to it.

Piano concerto No. 3 in C min., Op. 37.

(M) *** Ph. Seq. 6527/*7311* 176 [id.]. Bishop-Kovacevich, BBC SO, Davis.

(M) *** DG Acc. 2542/*3342* 210 [id.]. Kempff, Berlin PO, Leitner.

(M) *** Ph. Seq. 6527/*7311* 090 [id.]. Haskil, Lamoureux O, Markevitch.

**(*) DG 2531/*3301* 057 [id.]. Pollini, VPO, Boehm.

**(*) Ph. 9500 253/*7300 564* [id.]. Brendel, LPO, Haitink.

**(*) Decca SXL/*KSXC* 6653 [Lon. CS 6855/5-]. Ashkenazy, Chicago SO, Solti (with *Sonata No. 26, Les Adieux* **(*)).

(M) **(*) Decca SPA/*KCSP* 402. Backhaus, VPO, Schmidt-Isserstedt (with *Sonata No. 14, Moonlight* *(*)).

(B) *(*) Con. CC/*CCT* 7509. Eschenbach, LSO, Henze.

Piano concerto No. 3; 2 Rondos, Op. 51/1–2.

**(*) Decca Dig. SXDL/*KSXDC* 7507 [Lon. LDR 10000]. Lupu, Israel PO, Mehta.

(i) *Piano concerto No. 3; 32 variations on an original theme in C min., G.191; 6 Variations on the Turkish march from The Ruins of Athens, Op. 76.*

(M) **(*) HMV SXLP/*TC-SXLP* 143649-1/*4* [Ang. (d) RL/*4RL* 32074]. Gilels, Cleveland O, Szell.

Bishop-Kovacevich's performance has stood the test of time and remains among the most satisfying available accounts of the *C minor Concerto*. The recording is clear and refined, and the tape matches the disc closely.

Kempff's stereo recording of the *Third Concerto* made in 1961 is more measured and serious than an earlier mono version, but, in its unforced way, happily lyrical, diamond-bright in articulation, it still sparkles refreshingly. Kempff may characteristically adopt a flowing speed for the slow movement, but his natural thoughtfulness gives it the necessary gravity and intensity. The recording in this mid-price reissue still sounds well, not least the piano sound, and the cassette is of DG's best quality, full and clear.

Haskil, in a clean, muscular style, gives a most refreshing performance, one of her relatively rare records made not long before she died in 1960. Her first entry establishes that feminine delicacy is not her style. Intellectual concentration married to sharp articulation (most remarkable in the left hand) characterize a performance where even the delicate pianissimos at the end of the slow movement convey strength rather than poetry. The recording is excellent for its period. The cassette transfer is admirable, well-balanced, full and lively.

The single-minded clarity of Pollini's reading is no less refreshing. Boehm's strong and sober accompaniment adds to the purposefulness, though charm is never present and warmth not often. Nonetheless the concentration of playing, beautifully recorded (there is no appreciable difference between tape and disc), makes this a strong and individual version.

In contrast Brendel and Haitink give an easy, relaxed account of the first movement, spontaneous-sounding, like the rest of the set, with the timpani taps of the coda even more measured and mysterious than usual. If the other two movements are less tense, with the finale thrown off in a mercurial manner, this adds up to a strong, persuasive performance, beautifully recorded.

The one controversial performance in the Ashkenazy/Solti set is created by the almost fierce intensity of the orchestral tuttis of the outer movements. The strength of the playing is in no doubt, but some will need a more relaxed atmosphere. The slow movement is finely done, and the bold performance of the *Les Adieux sonata* makes an appropriate fill-up. There is a first-class cassette.

Radu Lupu has the benefit of digital recording and very good it is too, on tape and disc alike. His reading of the concerto is forthright and dramatic, yet attentive to every detail of colour and dynamic nuance. He is unfailingly perceptive and musical, though unsmiling at those moments where a gentle poetry surfaces. In every sense a powerfully conceived reading, somewhat let down by the orchestral support: the first desks of the Israel Philharmonic strings are not heard to flattering effect and the wind playing, though not insensitive, is far from distinguished. Were the orchestral response as impressive as either Lupu or the Decca engineers, this would be a strong front-runner, and Lupu offers an immaculately played fill-up. However, Bishop-Kovacevich, Pollini and Brendel, among the more modern recordings, remain preferable.

Gilels's fine cycle of Beethoven concertos with Szell, recorded at the very end of that conductor's career, have had disappointingly limited circulation. This account of No. 3 is strong and direct rather than sparkling. It is generously coupled with the two sets of variations superbly done. Good 1970 recording, but the cassette is slightly disappointing – rather soft-grained in the treble.

After the *Emperor*, SPA 402 is the most obviously attractive performance in the Backhaus canon. The opening tutti is magisterial, but the basic mood is essentially classical, and the lyrical flow of the first movement's development section is memorable. The freshness of the recording suits the playing, and the only hint that the disc is not freshly minted is to be found in the upper string tone, which is sparer in texture than one would expect today. The piano tone is attractively bright, but with no lack of depth. In the slow movement Backhaus refuses to yield to any romantic impulses, but his mood of classical restraint is balanced by the vigorous rhythms of the finale. The approach to the first movement of the *Moonlight sonata*, which acts as a filler, is characteristically severe, but, in spite of some technical fluffs in the finale, this is still a performance that obstinately remains in the mind. The cassette is of Decca's best quality.

Eschenbach plays with imagination and poetry; the opening of the slow movement is magical. But the performance is hopelessly weighed down by the accompaniment under Hans Werner Henze, who seems unable to produce more than the most routine conducting in Beethoven. Despite the fine contribution of the soloist and full recording (more opaque on cassette than disc), this is not a strong competitor, even at bargain price.

Piano concerto No. 4 in G, Op. 58.

(M) *** DG Acc. 2542/*3342* 136 [id.]. Kempff, Berlin PO, Leitner – *Concerto No. 2.****

(M) *** CBS 60149/*40-* [(d) YT 34590]. Fleisher, Cleveland O, Szell – MOZART: *Concerto No. 25.****

(M) *** Ph. Seq. 6527/*7311* 175 [id.]. Bishop-Kovacevich, BBC SO, Davis – *Concerto No. 2.****

(M) *** Decca Jub. JB 41. Gulda, VPO, Stein (with *Sonata No. 24***).

(M) **(*) RCA Gold GL/*GK* 14369 [AGL1/*AGK1* 4369]. Rubinstein, Boston SO, Leinsdorf.

**(*) DG 2530/*3300* 791 [id.]. Pollini, VPO, Boehm.

(M) **(*) HMV SXLP/*TC-SXLP* 30515 [(d) Ang. S 36030]. Gilels, Cleveland O, Szell – *Concerto No. 2.***(*)

**(*) Ph. 9500 254/*7300 600* [id.]. Brendel, LPO, Haitink.

(M) ** Ph. Seq. 6527/*7311* 028. Haebler, New Philh. O, Galliera – *Concerto No. 2.***

(M) *(*) Decca SPA/*KCSP* 403. Backhaus, VPO, Schmidt-Isserstedt (with *Sonata No. 8, Pathétique* *(*)).

Piano concerto No. 4; Overture Leonora No. 3.

*** Decca SXL/*KSXC* 6654 [Lon. CS 6856/*5-*]. Ashkenazy, Chicago SO, Solti.

Although Kempff's delicacy of fingerwork and his shading of tone colour are as effervescent as ever, this is not as personal a reading as his earlier mono version. The stereo version also allows some speed variation, but the increased sense of unity owes much, it is plain, to the fine control of the conductor, Leitner. The recording still sounds full and clear, though the cassette transfer is not quite as crisp in outline as in the coupling.

Fleisher's is a magical performance, memorable in every bar, to rival even Kempff's version. Starting with the genuine tension of a live performance and displaying throughout a commanding control of argument from soloist and conductor alike – the orchestral playing is superb – this is among the finest recordings of the work ever committed to disc. Fleisher's half-tones are most beautiful and his finger-work dazzling without ever giving the slightest impression of mere slickness. In some ways this is even preferable to Kempff's more idiosyncratic approach, although the 1959 CBS sound is less agreeable than the DG recording. Nevertheless it can be made to sound well (the lively cassette also needs taming) and with its impressive coupling demands consideration by all serious collectors.

Bishop-Kovacevich's reading is intense and deeply thoughtful. He opens the concerto very gently, and the orchestral response matches his delicacy of feeling. Yet in seeking a balance between classicism and romanticism he leans further towards the former than Kempff. The slow movement matches poetic serenity with a firm orchestral contrast, and leads naturally to a swelling of pianistic fervour at the climax. The finale is joyfully alert, mercurial and lyrical, with bursts of sheer energy from the orchestra. The sound is satisfying, with excellent detail, the long side bringing a slightly reduced bass resonance compared with other issues in this fine series. The cassette transfer is clear and clean.

The Ashkenazy/Solti performance of the *G major Concerto* is one of the finest of their complete series, the contrast between the musical personalities of soloist and conductor bringing new insights to this masterly score. The performance of the overture is fresh and dramatic, and this record can be recommended alongside those of Kempff, Fleisher and Bishop-Kovacevich. There is an excellent cassette, clear and full.

On Decca Jubilee the freshness and poetry of Gulda's playing make for an exceptionally compelling reading, full of strong contrasts which have the excitement of the moment, never sounding forced. In the slow movement Gulda is deeply thoughtful without ever falling into sentimentality, and the finale is clean in its directness and strength. The piano sound is somewhat shallow on top, but the orchestral recording is excellent. The short *F sharp Sonata* is not a very generous coupling, and Gulda's tempi here are controversially fast; but this issue remains highly recommendable in the medium price-range.

Rubinstein's Boston recording with Leinsdorf is spread over two sides, but in the medium price-range remains competitive. The performance has a spring-like freshness, with Rubinstein's combination of crisp, firm articulation and delicacy of touch bringing out the lyricism. The slow movement is less dramatic than usual but the finale sparkles. The recording is light-textured but firm, and the Boston acoustic has been captured without more than a hint of harshness in tuttis. There is a spontaneity about this playing which is impossible to resist.

Pollini's account of the concerto is another distinguished one. More aristocratic playing would be hard to find, save perhaps from Gilels. Since Kempff, Bishop-Kovacevich, Katchen and others offer the *Second Concerto* as a coupling, this is short measure; but given playing of this stature, in which classical poise and poetic sensitivity are so delicately balanced, the disc remains competitive. Boehm is a faithful accompanist, and the sound is of excellent quality. The cassette transfer is admirable, fractionally dry in the bass, but with fine range, body and presence.

Gilels's Cleveland performance offers solo playing of the highest order. His slow movement is no less magical and searching than in his earlier account with Ludwig (HMV SXLP 30086 (now deleted), but in the outer movements Szell's rather hard-driven support and a somewhat dryish recording diminish the overall impact of this otherwise very distinguished issue. The cassette is of first-class quality, matching the disc closely.

Brendel gives a tough and strong reading, not as immaculate as one might expect on detail but presenting an almost impressionistic thrust of urgency in the first movement. With Brendel the slow movement is rapt in its simplicity and the finale is treated almost flippantly, with mercurial strokes of individuality which, with some slips of ensemble, suggest the immediacy of a live performance rather than the care of a studio recording. On tape the low-level transfer provides sound that is basically warm and natural, and the beauty of the recording is caught; nevertheless there is a lack of sparkle at the top, and inner detail is slightly masked, notably in the first movement. With no coupling this issue cannot be given a top recommendation on either tape or disc.

An enjoyable performance from Haebler, well accompanied with an excellent modern recording. But the performance, although highly musical, is almost entirely without any real idiosyncrasy and the slow movement, in particular, lacks a sense of participation from both soloist and conductor in the drama inherent in the music's contrasts. The cassette is well managed.

Backhaus's gruff manner in this most lyrical of concertos will not be to all tastes, yet there is a strength and integrity to the performance which offer some compensation for the starkness of approach. The famous dialogue between piano and orchestra in the slow movement is played in an exceedingly deadpan manner, yet, if anything, this serves to underline Beethoven's contrasts even more than in a romantic performance. There are moments in the finale when the playing is not as cleanly accurate, but even these can be forgiven, and so can the sound, which is brilliantly clear – to match the music-making – but not as warm as in others of this series. The *Sonata* is even more literal than the *Concerto*. The cassette version can be considered alongside the disc.

Piano concertos Nos. 4 and 5 (Emperor), Op. 73; Piano sonatas Nos. 14 (Moonlight), Op. 27/2; 19, Op. 49/1.

(M) *** HMV *TCC2-POR 154594-9*. Gieseking, Philh. O, Galliera.

These Gieseking stereo recordings from the late 1950s of the *G major* and *Emperor concertos* are here issued for the first time, on a superior double-length chrome tape. The sound is astonishingly good, and Gieseking's incandescently bright timbre is captured truthfully, while the orchestra is full-bodied and well detailed. The performances are admirably fresh and imbued with classical feeling. Gieseking's playing is appealingly spontaneous and, with such impressive recording, admirers of this artist will not be disappointed, although the two *Sonatas* are rather cool. Each concerto is complete on one cassette side, with a sonata used to balance out each.

Piano concerto No. 5 in E flat (Emperor), Op. 73.

(M) *** DG Acc. 2542/*3342* 190 [id.]. Kempff, Berlin PO, Leitner.

(M) *** Ph. Seq. 6527/*7311* 177 [id.]. Bishop-Kovacevich, LSO, Davis.

(M) *** HMV SXLP/*TC-SXLP* 30223 [Ang. S 36031]. Gilels, Cleveland O, Szell.

(M) *** Ph. Seq. 6527/*7311* 055 [id.]. Arrau, Concg. O, Haitink.

*** Telarc Dig. **CD 80065**; DG 10065 [id.]. Serkin, Boston SO, Ozawa.

*** Decca SXL 6655/*KSXC* 16655 [Lon. CS/5- 6857]. Ashkenazy, Chicago SO, Solti (with *Egmont* or *Coriolan overture****).

(M) *** Decca SPA/*KCSP* 452. Backhaus, VPO, Schmidt-Isserstedt.

(M) *** EMI Em. EMX/*TC-EMX* 412014-1/*4*. Gelber, New Philh. O, Leitner.

(M) *** Decca VIV/*KVIC* 14. Katchen, LSO, Gamba (with *Egmont overture****).

(*) Decca Dig. **400 050-2; SXDL/*KSXDC* 7503 [Lon. LDR/5- 10005]. Lupu, Israel PO, Mehta.

**(*) HMV Dig. ASD/*TCC-ASD* 143433-1/*4*. [Ang. DS 37958]. Egorov, Philh. O, Sawallisch.

(B) **(*) CfP CFP/*TC-CFP* 40087. Lill, SNO, Gibson.

(M) **(*) Decca SPA/*KCSP* 334 [Lon. JL/5-41020]. Curzon, VPO, Knappertsbusch.

**(*) HMV ASD/*TC-ASD* 2500. Barenboim, New Philh. O, Klemperer.

(B) **(*) Con. CC/*CCT* 7547 [Odys. 32160326]. Casadesus, Concg. O, Rosbaud.

**(*) DG 2531/*3301* 194 [id.]. Pollini, VPO, Boehm.

**(*) Ph. 9500 243/*7300 542* [id.]. Brendel, LPO, Haitink.

(M) **(*) Decca Jub. JB/*KJBC* 18. Gulda, VPO, Stein.

**(*) Decca SXL/*KSXC* 6899 [Lon. CS/5-7121]. Larrocha, LAPO, Mehta.

(M) *(**) CBS 60122/*40*- [M/*MT* 31807]. Serkin, NYPO, Bernstein.

(M) *(*) RCA Gold GL/*GK* 14220 [AGL1/*AGK1* 4220]. Rubinstein, Boston SO, Leinsdorf.

* DG 2531/*3301* 385 [id.]. Michelangeli, VSO, Giulini.

Even amid the wealth of fine *Emperor* performances Kempff's version stands out as among the most refreshing and imaginative of all. The interests of the musical argument always take precedence over the demands of virtuosity. Beside less thoughtful pianists Kempff's interpretation may at times sound comparatively small-scale: there is no attempt at the big bow-wow approach. But strength there is in plenty, and excitement too. As ever Kempff's range of tone colour is extraordinarily wide, from the merest half-tone as though the fingers are barely brushing the keys to the crisp impact of a dry fortissimo. Leitner's orchestral contribution is of high quality and the Berlin orchestral playing has vigour and warmth. The recording on disc has been freshened, but remains naturally balanced. The bass is resonant but clear. The cassette, however, has an over-ample bass response without a comparably extended treble range. It is acceptable, but ideally needs remastering.

Those wanting a more modern recording might turn to Bishop-Kovacevich who also offers one of the most deeply satisfying versions of this much-recorded concerto ever made. His is not a brash, extrovert way. With alert, sharp-edged accompaniment from Sir Colin Davis, he gives a clean, dynamic performance of the outer movements, then in the central slow movement finds a depth of intensity that completely explodes any idea of this as a lighter central resting point. Even so he avoids weighing the simple plan down with unstylistic mannerisms: he relies simply on natural, unforced concentration in the most delicate, hushed tones. Fine recording, full-bodied, yet clear on both disc and tape.

Of the many other versions available, few are more superb than Gilels's; here strength is matched with poetry in no small measure. It goes without saying that Szell has tremendous grip and that the playing of the Cleveland Orchestra is beyond reproach. Memories of Gilels's earlier recording with the Philharmonia Orchestra under Leopold Ludwig are not completely banished (it had even greater humanity in some ways) but, make no mistake, this is a performance that must be numbered among the very finest on the market. Listening to it reaffirms one's conviction that Gilels is one of the very greatest Beethoven pianists of the present age. At Concert Classics price, this is very competitive indeed.

Hardly less commanding is Arrau's magnificent version. It originally appeared as part of a complete cycle (see above), and it is remarkable how much more spontaneous Arrau sounds here than in his previous account of the work, an early Columbia record. The slow movement in particular conveys the tension of a live performance – it sounds as though it might have been done in a single unedited take. Arrau is at his most authoritative in the outer movements, and the finale is stylishly played. The recording is first-rate and, even without consideration of the reasonable price, this is one of the very finest available versions on any count. The tape is splendid, with boldly resonant piano tone.

With extraordinarily vivid recording Serkin's Telarc *Emperor* offers sound of spectacular realism. The great pianist is almost as commanding as ever, with fire and brilliance in plenty in the outer movements, yet there is also a degree of relaxation, of conscious enjoyment, that increases the degree of communication. The hushed expressive pianism that provides the lyrical contrast in the first movement is matched by the poised refinement of the *Adagio*; the finale is vigorously joyful. While this record is undoubtedly expensive, the sound could justify the price for those seeking to establish an exclusively digital or CD collection. Ozawa's accompaniment is first-class.

Ashkenazy and Solti combine to give an excitingly dramatic performance on the largest possible scale, yet one which is consistently imbued with poetry. Alongside the *Fourth Concerto* this represents the peak of achievement of their complete cycle. With the *Egmont overture* a successful bonus, and brilliant recording, this can be cordially recommended as another very rewarding and individual performance of Beethoven's masterpiece. The cassette includes the *Coriolan overture*. The sound on tape is slightly less well-focused in the orchestra but the piano timbre is clear.

There is absolutely no question about the power and authority of Backhaus's *Emperor*. The performance is at once vigorous and forthright. It does not lack the grand manner, yet there is lyrical feeling too. There is even a touch of exuberance in the finale. In short, this is the best of both Backhaus and Schmidt-Isserstedt; and what a fine conductor he has proved throughout this series of recordings, providing a firm, yet often mellow strength against which Backhaus's sometimes uncompromising solo playing is set in bold relief. Some might feel that more variety of colour might be appropriate in the slow movement, yet Backhaus's restraint does not stem from insensitivity, and this is undoubtedly a performance to uncover new facets of a much-played masterpiece. The recording is splendidly bold and resonant to match this genuinely large-scale conception, and the cassette transfer is of high quality.

Comparing Gelber – the young Buenos Aires pianist – directly with Kempff shows how astonishingly alike the two performances are. There is a wonderful hushed intensity in the slow movement and a willingness elsewhere to relax into half-tones whenever the music demands it. The bravura is clean and dramatic, the accompaniment first-rate and this is an outstanding bargain. The recording is rich and full-bodied, though the quality on cassette is drier and brighter than the disc with a markedly lower transfer level on the second side.

The 1964 Katchen/Gamba version has been reissued on Decca's mid-priced label, Viva, and the sound remains impressively full and clear, although the cassette is less recommendable, with a slightly narrower dynamic range. It is an excellent performance, full of characteristic animal energy. The first and last movements are taken at a spanking pace but not so fast that Katchen sounds at all rushed. Plainly he enjoyed himself all through, and with this pianist who had sometimes seemed too rigid in his recorded playing, it is good to find that here he seemed to be coaxing the orchestra to match his own delicacy. The slow movement is very relaxed but, with the tension admirably sustained, it contrasts well with the extreme bravura of the finale. The filler is a welcome and brightly played performance of the *Egmont overture*.

Lupu's version was the first to be issued on compact disc and the clarity of detail is remarkable in this format. The upper range is over-bright but the orchestral layout is convincing and if the piano image seems a trifle near it gives a commanding presence to the solo playing. Lupu gives a performance which, without lacking strength, brings thoughtfulness and poetry even to the magnificence of the first movement, with classical proportions made clear. The slow movement has delicacy and fantasy, the finale easy exhilaration, though neither conductor nor orchestra quite matches the soloist's distinction. The cassette (unusually for Decca) is disappointing, with a lack of refinement in the orchestral tuttis of the first movement.

Yuri Egorov in his first concerto recording gives a refreshingly direct but still individual account of the opening *Allegro*, helped by authoritative conducting from Sawallisch, and the finale too has splendid drive and attack, helped by full and rich digital sound. The slow movement is the controversial point, taken at a very measured *Adagio*, which might have flowed better had Egorov adopted a more affectionate style of phrasing. The chrome cassette is of good quality, though rather bass-orientated on side one; side two is brighter.

John Lill has too often seemed inhibited by the recording process, but here his rare combination of power and poetry is captured with seeming spontaneity. With first-rate modern recording quality (only marred by a lack of edge on the violin tone) this is an excellent version, even making no allowance for the modest price. There is quite a good cassette though it is marginally less refined than the disc.

Curzon's is a refined, thoughtful reading of the *Emperor*, almost Mozartian in the delicacy of the finale but with keen intelligence and inner concentration working throughout. The recording, one of Decca's earliest stereo issues, has been revamped well, but on top there is a limited range, and the orchestral quality has moments of slight roughness. Even so, this is a strongly competitive issue.

Barenboim's and Klemperer's account of the *Emperor* is individual almost to the point of perverseness. Many Beethovenians will resist it violently, but with its dry style and measured speeds coupled to a degree of concentration from pianist and conductor rarely caught on record, it provides an astonishingly fresh experience. The technical demands of the solo part, the sheer power, are somehow brought out more vividly, not less, when one has a pianist who, in the best sense, has to struggle to be master – no unthinking pile-driver but a searching voyager. The performance – with a number of unimportant 'fluffs' unedited – has the spontaneous quality of the rest of the cycle.

Casadesus and Rosbaud give a most beautiful interpretation, satisfyingly detailed and refined with a wonderfully serene *Adagio*. Though Arrau, with the same orchestra, is even more searching and better recorded, at bargain price this Contour issue is well worth considering. There is little to choose between disc and cassette; both are full and clear.

The clarity of Pollini's vision in his dedicated reading is never in doubt, and if at times his playing verges on the chilly, the strong and wise accompaniment of Boehm and the Vienna Philharmonic provides compensation. The slow movement is elegant, lacking the depth which the finest versions give it, and the finale is urgent and energetic rather than joyful. Excellent recording, with a first-class cassette transfer (one of the finest of the *Emperor*), combining fullness with brilliance.

Brendel's *Emperor* is among the very best recordings as such at present on the market. The sound is vivid, full-bodied and beautifully balanced, with wide range and warmth. It goes without saying that there is much to admire from the artistic point of view too. The reading is spaciously conceived, and the phrasing has no lack of eloquence. But generally it is less spontaneous in feeling than Brendel's earlier Turnabout recording with Mehta, although that is not nearly so well recorded. Undoubtedly the new version will give satisfaction, but there is a studied quality about the music-making that keeps this performance from being at the top of the list. The tape transfer, made at rather a low level, is full and natural but lacks sparkle, particularly in the finale.

With its dramatically recorded opening (the tone of the Bösendorfer piano extremely vivid) Gulda's account of the first movement does not lack a robust quality, yet he plays less for excitement than for poetry. The passages in his reading of the *Emperor* that latch in the memory are the gentle ones, whether the half-tones of the second subject in the first movement or the serene phrases of the slow movement, here given with real *Innigkeit*. Although there are more individual performances available, this is not likely to disappoint. The tape matches the disc closely, apart from a slight slip of focus at the opening of the slow movement.

The easy command of Alicia de Larrocha makes for a strong and convincing account, lacking a little in refinement – not least in the slow movement, where she misses a genuine pianissimo – but natural and completely unpompous. The recording is excellent and the cassette transfer clear and clean, although there is a touch of dryness in the orchestral strings and the upper range of the finale becomes slightly fierce.

Serkin gives a characteristically noble and commanding performance, sympathetically supported by Bernstein and the New York Philharmonic. But it is not just the somewhat coarse recording quality which prevents this from being among the most refined as well as the most powerful versions: both soloist and orchestra fall short on occasion.

Rubinstein's performance is disappointing; Leinsdorf proves a less stimulating partner than Barenboim (who accompanied his later set with the LPO). The playing is not without insights, but it lacks spontaneity.

It is sad, when by any reckoning Michelangeli is one of the very greatest pianists of this age, one who moreover exposes himself to the public disappointingly seldom, that his account of the *Emperor concerto*, like that of Beethoven's *First* from the same performers, should be so casual and uninvolving. The result, surprisingly, is superficial, a travesty of the work of both pianist and conductor, and the harsh recording is similarly unsympathetic. The cassette is bottom-heavy and unattractively boomy in the bass.

(i) *Piano concerto No. 5 (Emperor)*; (ii) *Violin concerto, Op. 61*; (iii) *Fidelio overture, Op. 72b*.
(B) *** DG Walkman *413 145-4*. (i) Eschenbach, Boston SO, Ozawa; (ii) Schneiderhan, Berlin PO, Jochum; (iii) Dresden State O, Boehm.

This was among the first issues in DG's Walkman series, specifically designed to capture the rapidly expanding market offered by the miniaturized cassette reproducer with headphones. Here are outstanding versions of two of Beethoven's greatest concertos, each uninterrupted, with the *Fidelio overture* used to fill out the space at the end of side two (after the *Emperor*). Both transfers are made at a high level on chrome tape, and in the case of the *Emperor* the reverberant acoustic appears to offer no serious problems. Although detail is not as sharp as in some versions, the sound has splendid weight and richness with the piano timbre appropriately firm and bold. Eschenbach gives a deeply satisfying interpretation, helped by the equally youthful urgency of the accompanist. With thoughtfulness, power and bravura nicely balanced, this interpretation has nothing to fear from its rivals, and it does not lack imaginative individuality. The recording dates from 1974, whereas the coupling – sounding hardly less full-bodied – is from 1962. Schneiderhan's stereo version of the *Violin concerto* is among the greatest recordings of this work. The serene spiritual beauty of the slow movement, and the playing of the second subject in particular, have never been surpassed on record and the orchestra under Jochum provides a background tapestry of breadth and dignity. It is a noble reading with an innate sense of classicism, yet the first movement offers wonderful lyrical intensity. As an added point of interest, Schneiderhan uses cadenzas provided for the transcription of the work for piano and orchestra. The first-movement cadenza is impressive in scale and adds a solo part for the timpani. In all, an astonishing bargain (with no disc equivalent).

Violin concerto in D, Op. 61.

*** HMV Dig. **CDC 747002-2**; ASD/*TCC-ASD* 4059 [Ang. DS/*4XS* 37471]. Perlman, Philh. O, Giulini.

(M) *** Ph. Seq. 6527/*7311* 126. Krebbers, Concg. O, Haitink.

*** CRD CRD 1053/*CRDC 4053*. Ronald Thomas, Bournemouth Sinf.

(M) **(*) CBS 60123/*40-* [M/*MT* 31805]. Stern, NYPO, Bernstein.

**(*) DG 2531/*3301* 250 [id.]. Mutter, Berlin PO, Karajan.

(M) **(*) HMV SXLP/*TC-SXLP* 30168 [Ang. S 35780]. D. Oistrakh, French Nat. RO, Cluytens.

** Argo ZRG/*KZRC* 929. Iona Brown, ASMF, Marriner.

** Ph. 9500 407/*7300 615* [id.]. Accardo, Leipzig GO, Masur.

C ** Decca Dig. **400 048-2**; SXDL/*KSXDC* 7508 [Lon. LDR/*5-* 10010]. Kyung-Wha Chung, VPO, Kondrashin.

** HMV Dig. ASD/*TCC-ASD* 4280 [Ang. DS/*4XS* 37890]. Menuhin, Leipzig GO, Masur.

(B) ** Con. CC/*CCT* 7568 [Quin. 7076]. Szeryng, LSO, Schmidt-Isserstedt.

*(*) Ph. Dig. 6514/*7337* 075 [id.]. Kremer, ASMF, Marriner.

Violin concerto; Overture: Coriolan, Op. 62.

(B) *** CfP CFP/*TC-CFP* 41 4409 [Van. S 353]. Suk, New Philh. O, Boult.

(i) *Violin concerto;* (ii) *2 Romances, Opp. 40 and 50.*

(M) *** DG Sig. 2543/*3343* 520 [2530/*3300* 903 (without *Romances*)]. Zukerman, (i) Chicago SO, Barenboim; (ii) LPO, Abbado.

Perlman's outstanding HMV digital recording of Beethoven's *Violin concerto* must be counted among the great recordings of this work alongside those of Kreisler (1926), Wolfgang Schneiderhan (1953 – a performance of profound beauty and unique classical serenity, recently available on DG Heliodor, but now deleted), and of course the Krebbers version, below.

Perlman's is the most commanding reading. The violin emerges in the first movement almost imperceptibly, rising gently from the orchestra, but there and throughout the performance the element of slight understatement, the refusal to adopt too romantically expressive a style makes for a compelling strength, perfectly matched by Giulini's thoughtful, direct accompaniment. Steadiness of pulse is a mark of this version, but there is never a feeling of rigidity, and the lyrical power of the music-making is a vital element. The beautiful slow movement has a quality of gentle rapture, almost matching Schneiderhan's sense of stillness and serenity, and the finale, joyfully, exuberantly fast, is charged with the fullest excitement. The digital recording is satisfyingly full and spacious, yet admirably clear, with an outstanding matching cassette. The compact disc is one of the finest so far to come from EMI, adding extra presence and refining detail.

There are a number of fine recordings of Beethoven's *Violin concerto*, but we are agreed that there is something very special about the Krebbers Philips issue. As a soloist, Krebbers has not quite the commanding 'star' quality of, for instance, David Oistrakh, but he plays with a wonderful naturalness and a totally unforced spontaneity. The slow movement has a tender simplicity which is irresistible, and it is followed by a delightfully relaxed and playful reading of the finale. In the first movement Haitink and his soloist form a partnership that brings out the symphonic strength more than any other reading, except perhaps Perlman's with Giulini. Krebbers is more meticulous than most virtuosi in playing *a tempo*, even in passagework. With a lesser artist that could have meant a dull result, but Krebbers's artistry is magnetic and his technique flawless. Altogether this is a memorable issue and the recording is excellent; the balance of the soloist is a fraction too close, but no matter, the sound itself is first-rate. The cassette transfer, too, is admirable, one of Philips's best.

Another highly recommendable version is the DG recording by Zukerman and Barenboim, who also take a spacious and persuasive view of the first movement, stretched to the limit but still held in complete concentration. If warmth and tonal richness are the qualities most wanted, then this is the ideal version, with the immaculate playing of the Chicago orchestra ripely recorded. Reissued on DG's upper mid-price Signature label, with fine accounts of the two *Romances* as a considerable bonus, this remains very competitive. The chrome cassette is wide-ranging and clear, although the transfer level is not especially high. The layout, with the *G major Romance* placed first, is not ideal for cassette presentation.

On a different scale but no less rewarding is the account recorded by CRD in Bournemouth. Ronald Thomas, directing from the violin, gives a thoughtful and direct reading which in its beauty and poise is most refreshing, particularly as the recorded sound is excellent and the playing of the Bournemouth Sinfonietta first-rate. Thomas may miss the finest flights of individual poetry, but the unity of the performance is totally compelling. The cassette transfer is clean and vivid; a little smoothing at the top is advantageous, but the solo violin has truthful timbre and presence.

Suk's version with the New Philharmonia under Boult – now reissued on Classics for Pleasure – is extremely well recorded. As with Mutter and Karajan, the first movement is taken at an unusually slow tempo, and some may feel that there is not enough urgency and concentration to sustain the conception. But Suk's playing is both noble and spacious. The performance is classical in style, although Suk, like Kreisler, pulls back at the G minor section in the development of the first movement. It is the breadth and grandeur of design that emerge. Sir Adrian observes the revisions in the score brought to light in Alan Tyson's edition. The eloquence of the slow movement and the lightness and sparkle of the finale are in no doubt. And though no one buys a record of the *Violin concerto* for the sake of the *Coriolan overture*, it would almost be worth it for Boult's impressively played account. The recording has striking body and excellent balance, and this makes a fine bargain in all respects.

The reissue of Issac Stern's earlier performance on CBS shows the intense creative relationship established between Stern and Bernstein. Stern's reading has a tremendous onward flow, his personality projected strongly, yet Bernstein keeps the orchestra well in the picture (in spite of the forward balance of the soloist), and the energy of the music-making is compulsive. The close CBS recording means that a real pianissimo in the slow movement is not possible, but the intensity is in no doubt, and the finale is comparably vigorous.

The slow basic tempi of Anne-Sophie Mutter's beautiful reading on DG were her own choice, she claims, and certainly not forced on her by her super-star conductor. The first two movements have rarely if ever on record been more expansively presented, but the purity of the solo playing and the concentration of the whole performance make the result intensely convincing. The finale is relaxed too but is well pointed, at a fair tempo, and presents the necessary contrast. Good atmospheric recording against the warm acoustic of the Philharmonie in Berlin. On cassette, however, while the first two movements sound vivid, the orchestral focus slips somewhat in the finale.

David Oistrakh's strong, aristocratic reading on HMV Concert Classics is also a fine one. The HMV recording still sounds well, with a spacious acoustic and resonant orchestral tone. The balance, however, places the soloist unnaturally forward, although he is truthfully recorded. The reading is characteristically assured, the soloist's phrasing and sense of line impeccable, but for some ears there is a suggestion of aloofness in the slow movement. The cassette transfer is admirably vivid, full and well focused.

Iona Brown, a fine orchestral leader and director, gives an honest, clean-cut and always sympathetic account, never overfaced by the challenge, but with unusually analytic sound the chamber scale is not all gain here. Inevitably it seems a smaller work, in a way that it does not with Ronald Thomas. The recording is of the highest quality on disc and cassette alike.

Accardo is not only an artist of impeccable technique but a musician of genuine insight and spirituality. He gives a wholy dedicated and faithful account of the concerto, lacking only the last ounce of *Innigkeit*. Full justice is not done to his tone by the engineers, and it is necessary to tamper with the controls if a certain shrillness is to be removed. There is no doubt that, once this is done, the performance will give great pleasure, but it is not to be numbered among the greatest of the Beethoven concerto or of Accardo's records. Masur produces excellent results from the Leipzig orchestra, but the engineers have not secured the cleanest bass sound. The cassette has been transferred at a high level and also needs a degree of smoothing at the top.

Miss Chung gives a measured and thoughtful reading which lacks the compulsion one would have predicted. That is largely due to the often prosaic conducting of Kondrashin. There is poetry in individual moments – the minor-key episode of the finale, for example, which alone justifies the unusually slow tempo – but with too little of the soloist's natural electricity conveyed and none of her volatile imagination, it must not be counted her final statement on a masterpiece. The digital recording is impressive on LP, but outstanding on the compact disc which is wonderfully transparent and real. The clarity and presence – and the silent background – are a joy and the balance is most natural. The cassette too is of demonstration quality and it is a pity that the performance is so relatively uninvolving.

Menuhin had recorded this concerto four times before this latest version was made in Leipzig, with Kurt Masur conducting. His previous conductors have been more individualistic, Klemperer and Silvestri among them, but most memorable of all, Furtwaengler (twice). His splendid mono LP is still available as a special import (EMI 2C 051 1570) as is the earlier 78 r.p.m. transfer (EMI 1C 047 0117), which some listeners count finest of all. Compared with these versions, the newest recording is disappointing. It is Menuhin's slowest performance yet, on the face of it almost a parody of caution, yet, helped by magically beautiful sounds from the Leipzig orchestra, Menuhin makes the work a unique meditation. It is not the full story, not a definitive version, but with Menuhin quickly recovering from an edgy first entry it provides unquestionable evidence of his unique sensibility. There is a vivid chrome tape (the orchestral focus marginally less clean on the second side), but Menuhin's art is better remembered with one of his earlier records.

Szeryng's account – reissued on Contour – is let down somewhat in the first movement by Schmidt-Isserstedt's accompaniment which sounds rather too weighty and considered, but the conductor is sympathetic in the slow movement – where Szeryng's hushed lyricism is very effective, and he lightens the finale effectively. This might be considered at bargain price, were not the excellent Suk version available on Classics for Pleasure.

The point of controversy which for most will completely rule out the Kremer version is his use of the Schnittke cadenza with its facile avant-garde effects – including what one supposes are imitations of electronic music – which is totally out of style. Otherwise the soloist's playing is sweet and generally sympathetic and the playing of the Academy under Marriner admirably transparent, not at all lacking in power. Excellent recording on disc, but the chrome cassette is bass-heavy.

Triple concerto for violin, cello and piano in C, Op. 56.

**(*) HMV ASD/*TC-ASD* 2582 [Ang. S/*4XS* 36727]. D. Oistrakh, Rostropovich, Sviatoslav Richter, Berlin PO, Karajan.

*** Ph. 9500 382/*7300 604* [id.]. Beaux Arts Trio, LPO, Haitink.
*** DG 2531/*3301* 262 [id.]. Mutter, Zeltser, Ma, Berlin PO, Karajan.
(M) **(*) EMI Em. EMX/*TC-EMX* 2035. D. Oistrakh, Knushevitzky, Oborin, Philh. O, Sargent – BRAHMS: *Double concerto*.***
**(*) HM 1C 065 99700. Maier, Bijlsma, Badura-Skoda, Coll. Aur.
(M) ** Ph. Seq. 6527/*7311* 121 [id.]. Szeryng, Starker, Arrau, New Philh. O, Inbal.
(M) ** DG Priv. 2535 153 [id.]. Scheiderhan, Fournier, Anda, Berlin RO, Fricsay.

Even in these days of star-studded recordings the roster of soloists on the HMV disc is breathtaking (EMI plotted for a long time to capture the magic trio), and to have so spectacular a conductor as Karajan in addition is almost too good to be true. The results are aptly opulent, with Beethoven's priorities between the soloists well preserved in the extra dominance of Rostropovich over his colleagues. This is warm, expansive music-making that confirms even more clearly than before that the old view of this as one of Beethoven's weaker works is wrong. The three Soviet soloists revel in the multiplicity of ideas, with Richter in the spare piano part providing a tautening influence. The recording is rather too reverberant, and suffers from loss of focus in some climaxes, but this is not too serious. The cassette matches the disc closely.

The world's most distinguished regular piano trio is a natural choice when it comes to soloists for this great but wayward concerto. If the Beaux Arts cellist, Bernard Greenhouse, lacks the full vibrant character of a Rostropovich in his first entries on each theme, he is more clearly coordinated with his colleagues, and consistently the joy of this performance – with the soloists sharply focused in front of the orchestra – is to relish the interplay between the instruments. The result adds up to a really satisfying structure instead of a series of separate and memorable passages. Haitink's splendid direction helps too, with powerful tuttis and fine rhythmic pointing in the polacca rhythms of the finale. The engineers as ever have found the problems of balance impossible to solve, with the orchestra damped down during solo passages, but the sound has the beauty and refinement of the best Philips offerings. The cassette is acceptable.

On DG, after an exceptionally positive account of the opening tutti, with Karajan building up a formidable crescendo, the soloists may seem rather small-scale, but there are benefits from the unity brought by the conductor when each of the young soloists has a positive contribution to make, no less effectively when the recording balance for once in this work does not unduly favour the solo instruments. Yo Yo Ma's playing is not immaculate, and he does not dominate each thematic statement, but the urgency, spontaneity and – in the slow movement – the depth of expressiveness make for an outstanding version, beautifully recorded on disc. On cassette the orchestral tuttis are rather opaque (this is most noticeable at the opening of the first movement) but the solo detail matches the disc closely.

The earlier EMI recording also featuring distinguished Russian soloists dates from the early days of stereo, yet the sound is excellent for its period and the balance (with Walter Legge producing) perhaps the most successful this concerto has received in the recording studio. Sargent does not direct the proceedings with Karajan's flair, but he is authoritative and musical and his soloists make a good team as well as displaying plenty of individual personality. The slow movement is strikingly eloquent. At lower-medium price with an outstanding version of the Brahms *Double concerto* as coupling, the bargain status is obvious. The cassette is closely matched to the disc, although on tape the focus of the solo instruments is marginally less sharp.

The Harmonia Mundi issue seeks to re-establish the sound Beethoven might have expected to hear, and the tinny quality of the Broadwood grand of 1816 is initially disconcerting. Yet like other Beethoven interpretations by the Collegium Aureum this has individual points of revelation, not least in the way one can register the relationship of the work to the *concerto grosso*, then not long defunct. Recording is good, but not all detail is clear.

Arrau and his colleagues, adopting very unhurried tempi, run the risk of losing concentration, but this version, almost on a chamber scale, with fine rhythmic pointing, is still enjoyable at medium price and is helped by refined (if artificially balanced) recording. Starker's dedicated and spacious reading of the great cello solo in the brief slow movement has rarely been matched. The level of the cassette transfer is only modest and the inner focus of the recording is poorly defined. Not recommended on tape.

The balance is much better integrated on the DG Privilege issue. The solo players are still well forward (and clearly separated) but the relationship with the orchestra is more convincing here than on the Philips Sequenza issue. The performance has breadth and a genuine grasp of structure, with a fine contribution from each of the distinguished soloists. Only in the first movement does one sense a slight want of spontaneity, but in all other respects this is satisfactory, although it now seems short measure, compared with the Eminence version.

Overtures: The Consecration of the House, Op. 124; Coriolan, Op. 62; The Creatures of Prometheus, Op. 43; Egmont, Op. 84; Fidelio, Op. 72c; King Stephen, Op. 117; Namensfeier, Op. 115; Leonora Nos. 1–3, Opp. 138; 72a; 72b; The Ruins of Athens, Op. 113.

(M) *** DG Priv. 2726 079 (2) [2707 046]. Berlin PO, Karajan.

These two records come from the box of three that DG issued during the Beethoven Year under the title *Music for the stage*. The *Leonora No. 3* and *Fidelio* overtures come from the mid-1960s, however. There is a fastidiousness about some of the phrasing (for example in *Leonora No. 2*) and a smoothness of texture that sometimes seem out of character. Nonetheless one cannot but marvel at the superlative playing of the Berlin Philharmonic and the no less excellent recorded sound. There are impressive and exciting things about these performances and they have undoubted atmosphere. At Privilege price the set is excellent value.

Overtures: Coriolan, Op. 62; The Creatures of Prometheus, Op. 43; Egmont, Op. 84; Fidelio, Op. 72c; King Stephen, Op. 117; Leonora No. 3, Op. 72b.

*** DG 2531/*3301* 347 [id.]. VPO, Bernstein.

These lively, sympathetic performances were originally the fill-ups for Bernstein's set of the Beethoven symphonies. They are well recorded and make an excellent collection. The sound on cassette is first-class too; even though the level is not especially adventurous, there is both body and brilliance.

Overtures: Coriolan, Op. 62; Egmont, Op. 84; Fidelio, Op. 72c; Leonora No. 3, Op. 72b; The Ruins of Athens, Op. 113.

(M) *** DG Acc. 2542/*3342* 141. Berlin PO, Karajan.

Impressive performances that can stand comparison with the finest now in the catalogue. Karajan's accounts of all these overtures show an imposing command of structure and detail as well as the customary virtuosity one expects from him and the Berlin Philharmonic. The only notable reservation is in *Leonora No. 3*, where the tempo Karajan chooses in the coda strikes one as very brisk indeed. The recording is eminently acceptable even if it is not in the demonstration class. The cassette matches the disc very closely indeed.

Overtures: *Egmont, Op. 84; Fidelio, Op. 72c; King Stephen, Op. 117; Leonora Nos. 1–3, Opp. 138; 72a; 72b.*

(M) *(*) CBS 60255/*40-*. Cleveland O, Szell.

Some of these performances by the Cleveland Orchestra were recorded in London when the players were on a European tour. The sound was originally good, but this reissue has made it harsher and more limited. In Szell's intense way the performances are excellent.

Romances for violin and orchestra Nos. 1 in G, Op. 40; 2 in F, Op. 50.

*** CRD CRD 1069/*CRDC 4069*. Ronald Thomas, Bournemouth Sinf. – MENDELSSOHN: *Concerto;* SCHUBERT: *Konzertstück*.***

The purity of Ronald Thomas's intonation (particularly important in the double stopping at the start of Op. 40) makes for clean-cut, direct readings which with the Schubert make a good if unexpected coupling for his refreshing account of the Mendelssohn concerto. The recording is first-rate on disc and tape alike.

SYMPHONIES

Symphonies Nos. 1–9; Overtures: *The Consecration of the House; Coriolan; The Creatures of Prometheus; Egmont* (with incidental music); *Fidelio; King Stephen; Leonora Nos. 1–3.*

(B) **(*) HMV SLS/*TC-SLS* 788 (9). Philh. O, Klemperer (with soloists and chorus).

Symphonies Nos. 1–9. Overtures: *Coriolan; The Creatures of Prometheus; Egmont; Fidelio.*

**(*) HMV Dig. SLS/*TC-SLS* 5239 (8) [id. – import]. Philh. O, Sanderling (with Armstrong, Finnie, Tear, Tomlinson, Philh. Ch.).

Symphonies Nos. 1–9; Overtures: *Coriolan; Egmont; Leonora No. 3.*

**(*) Decca 11 BB 188/96 (9)/*K 3 F 10/11* [Lon. CSP 9]. Chicago SO, Solti (with soloists and chorus).

(M) **(*) ASV ALHB 803 (8). Hallé O, Loughran (with Buchanan, Hodgson, Mitchinson, Howell, Hallé Ch.).

Symphonies Nos. 1–9.

*** DG 2740 172 (8)/*3378 070* [id.]. Berlin PO, Karajan (with Tomowa-Sintow, Baltsa, Schreier, Van Dam).

(M) *** DG 2740 216 (8)/*3378 090* [id.]. VPO, Bernstein (with Jones, Schwarz, Kollo, Moll, V. State Op. Ch.).

Some fifteen years after his first Beethoven cycle with the Berlin Philharmonic, Karajan recorded the nine symphonies again for the same company, and once more presented a series of extraordinary consistency, superbly played and recorded. Just as the cycle of 1962 established standards which were hard for any rival to match, let alone outshine, so the 1977 cycle, different in emphasis on certain symphonies, is if anything more satisfying, thanks largely to richer, fuller and more immediate sound.

Interpretatively, Karajan's views on Beethoven have changed relatively little – consistency has always been one of his most striking qualities, almost to the fault of predictability – but some of the modifications are significant. In the first two symphonies it is partly a question of recording quality, but the earlier feeling of eighteenth-century elegance has given way to genuine Beethovenian strength and urgency, applied even in these early works. The *Eroica* – given a superlative performance in the earlier set – presents the one major disappointment of the new cycle, at least in the outer movements. These are faster than before, with a more brittle, slightly rushed manner, though the *Funeral march* remains very similar, measured and direct. To compensate for that disappointment, the first movement of the *Pastoral*, angular and tense in the earlier cycle, has elegance and joyfulness at a tempo barely any slower, while the other movements too avoid the tense manner of the earlier version. Otherwise the middle symphonies remain very much as they were in the earlier cycle. Finales tend to be a little faster than before, though not so much that they sound breathless.

Most important of all, the *Ninth* is given a superlative performance. In the first movement the precision of the individual notes of the tremolo at the start points the first important change, and the recording, exceptionally rich and forward, underlines an extra toughness and intensity. The scherzo is a fraction slower than before and more lilting, while the slow movement is warmer and more relaxed, less metrical by a tiny but vital margin. As for the finale, it benefits from a more passionate view of the recitatives (both instrumental and vocal), while the two men soloists, Peter Schreier and José van Dam, easily outshine their rivals of 1962. The coda, taken very fast indeed, brings an exciting culmination.

Though the outer movements of the *Eroica* remain a noticeable drawback, and Karajan observes far fewer repeats than is nowadays customary (in expositions only in Nos. 1, 5 and 8), this is a set which for many will be a first choice. The cassettes are well engineered, although levels are not always high and there is occasional slight recession of image at pianissimo. Symphonies 4 and 5 are back-to-back and so are 6 and 7.

Bernstein's cycle, dramatic, perceptive, rich

in emotion but never sentimental, has a natural spontaneous quality that stems in part from his technique of recording. As in other recordings for D G, Bernstein opted to have live performances recorded and then – with some tidying of detail – edited together. Those who remember the electrifying account of the first movement in the *Eroica* in his earlier New York cycle may be disappointed that the voltage here is lower, but with Bernstein's electricity matched against the traditional warmth of Viennese playing the results are consistently persuasive, culminating in a superb, triumphant account of the *Ninth* with a fast, tense first movement, a resilient scherzo, a hushed expansive reading of the *Adagio* and a dramatic account of the finale. Balances are not always perfect, with microphones placed in order to eliminate audience noise, but the results are generally undistracting. The cassette transfers are exceptionally successful, the sound fresh, open at the top and refined in detail. There is plenty of body too, and although the level is relatively modest, hiss is not a problem. The *Choral symphony* sounds unusually refined, with a good balance and the most natural, well-focused quality for chorus and soloists alike. The layout, with Nos. 1 and 2, 4 and 5, and 6 and 7 all back-to-back, is beyond criticism. With such enjoyable performances this could be a first recommendation for tape collectors.

Solti's epic Beethoven cycle with his own Chicago orchestra has a firm centrality to it. The recording of symphonies 1 to 8 followed on the outstandingly successful version of the *Ninth* with which Solti started his cycle. The performance of the *Eroica* has comparable qualities, with expansive, steady tempi and a dedicated, hushed account of the slow movement. Here and elsewhere Solti shows his new-found ability to relax as well as to press dramatically forward, and there is plenty of sunshine in the even-numbered symphonies, though Nos. 1 and 8 are arguably too weighty in their tone of voice. The recording has Decca's characteristic brilliance and sharpness of focus (best in Nos. 6 and 7, recorded at the Sofiensaal in Vienna), and one powerful point of distinction is that for the very first time every single repeat is observed. The set is also available on cassettes of high quality.

Klemperer's set is priced very reasonably, and on any count it provides outstanding value for money in showing Klemperer's achievement in the Beethoven orchestral music. There are some disappointments, notably in symphonies 1, 5, 7, 8 and 9 (in varying degrees), but Klemperer is never less than interesting. The performances of symphonies 2, 3, 4 and 6 are among the very finest ever recorded, and the overtures too are generally very successful in their magisterial way. The recordings have been freshened and generally sound well if inevitably sometimes slightly dated. Originally the cassettes were spoilt by a restricted dynamic range, but we understand they have now been successfully remastered.

The likenesses between Sanderling and Klemperer as Beethoven interpreters – both of them taking a rugged, unvarnished view – were underlined in the H M V cycle sponsored by the cigarette firm Du Maurier. Much of it is very fine, with the strong, forthright reading of the *Eroica*, the spaciously lilting account of the *Pastoral* and the direct and measured view of the *Ninth* the obvious high points. The first two symphonies are weighty in a very nineteenth-century way, and the *Fifth* – lacking a little in spontaneity – is on the heavy side. The disappointment is the *Seventh*, where slow speeds convey little of the work's dance-like qualities. The digital recording is clear but rather over-bright, with the violins of the Philharmonia often presented unflatteringly. The chrome tapes are of high quality, clean and clear, yet full, the brightness of the upper strings tempered just a little compared with the discs. Detail is excellent. The only disappointment is the *Ninth*, dry and light in the bass, with the choral focus far from sharp. The presentation has one eccentricity: No. 2 is put at the beginning of the first cassette, with the turn-over coming before the finale, and No. 1 then follows on.

Loughran's cycle finds a natural place even among the more obviously glamorous cycles from Solti, Karajan, Bernstein and others, though success is not even between all the symphonies and the recorded sound is sometimes lacking in impact. Loughran's readings are remarkable for their total directness, their refusal to embroider, not just in being unusually meticulous about Beethoven's markings and keeping tempi steady, but in refusing, to a remarkable degree, even to allow agogic hesitations or the exaggeration of dotted rhythms or sprung compound time. The ruggedness of the *Eroica* funeral march might be taken as typical: sober, sombre and weighty. It is sad that largely through lack of brightness and clarity the recording of the *Ninth* prevents the culminating symphony from having its full impact, but that need not deter those who prefer their Beethoven sober and rather severe.

Symphonies Nos. 1; 3 (*Eroica*)*; 4; 5; 6* (*Pastoral*)*. Overtures: Coriolan; Egmont.*

(M) **(*) Chan. CBR/*CBT* 4001 (4). Sydney SO, Otterloo.

It is a weird idea to issue these records as a box since we are offered only five symphonies. Willem van Otterloo enjoyed much esteem in the 1950s for his Philips record of the *Symphonie fantastique* and it is evident that he was a fine Beethoven conductor too. The *Fourth Symphony* can hold its own against all comers; rhythms are taut yet never square, and there is a splendid sense of momentum without any loss of feeling for detail. What emerges from these readings is the subtlety of his rhythmic control; his tempi are steady and the musical flow undisturbed by any agogic mannerisms. The overall impression these performances leave in the mind is almost comparable with Weingartner's Beethoven – lean textures, lithe rhythms, a sense of rightness. (The only exception is, perhaps, the slow movement of the *Pastoral.*) The Sydney Orchestra responds with discipline and enthusiasm and though the upper strings could do with more bloom, the sound is eminently satisfactory both on disc and cassette. These discs should be made available separately for they are highly competitive. A slightly higher level of transfer would have been advantageous in the cassette format but Nos. 1, 3 and 5 are still vivid and the balance throughout the set is always musically judged and truthful in perspective.

Symphonies Nos. 1 in C, Op. 21; 2 in D, Op. 36.

(M) *** DG Acc. 2542/*3342* 102 [2535/*3335* 301]. Berlin PO, Karajan.

(M) *** EMI Em. EMX/*TC-EMX* 2015. LSO, Jochum.

(M) *** Ph. Seq. 6527/*7311* 074. ASMF, Marriner.

**(*) DG 2531/*3301* 101 [id.]. Berlin PO, Karajan.

(M) **(*) DG Sig. 410 836-1/*4*. VPO, Bernstein.

(B) **(*) CfP CFP/*TC-CFP* 4406. Munich PO, Kempe.

**(*) HMV Dig. ASD/*TCC-ASD* 4151. Philh. O, Sanderling.

(M) ** Decca Jub. JB/*KJBC* 3. VPO, Schmidt-Isserstedt.

Refinement and strength are combined in Karajan's 1962 readings (now reissued on Accolade), which are consistently resilient and exciting. The fast tempi for the slow movements of both symphonies give an eighteenth-century quality, not inappropriate. The recording, finely balanced, hardly sounds its age, with little perceptible difference between tape and disc. Karajan's 1977 performances are just as exciting, polished and elegant as those of 1962, with firm lines giving the necessary strength. The manner is a degree weightier, with less controversial tempi for the slow movements. The recording, less well balanced, is weightier too, with close-up effects which are less believable. On the tape, which matches the disc closely, there is a feeling of slight recession of the orchestral image in piano and pianissimo passages.

Jochum takes a relatively large-scale view of both symphonies. No. 2 with exposition repeat observed in the first movement comes first, with three movements on side one, the finale on side two, leaving room for No. 1 as fill-up, also with repeats observed. Jochum's weight of tone never degenerates into mere heaviness, for rhythms are well sprung and the playing of the LSO is first-rate, notably the woodwind. An excellent choice at its reasonable price if you prefer these works to look forward rather than back. Excellent recording. On our copy the cassette transfer of No. 1 was slightly disappointing with a somewhat restricted upper range, but No. 2 better balanced and brighter.

Marriner presents the first two symphonies authentically with a Mozart-sized orchestra, and the result is lithe and fresh, with plenty of character but few if any quirks or mannerisms. Nor are the dramatic contrasts underplayed, for the chamber scale is most realistically captured in the excellent recording. The cassette too is first-class, lively and full-bodied. This is a most satisfying issue.

Bernstein presents the first two symphonies as large-scale works with fast allegros made sharply rhythmic and exposition repeats observed. So the young Beethoven's syncopations – as in the finale of the *First* or the first movement of the *Second* – are pointed with clean emphasis. Slow introductions are carefully moulded, as are the two slow movements. Recording with little loss from having No. 2 squeezed on to a single side. The chrome cassette is faithful, though the level might have been higher.

Kempe's direct view of Beethoven goes for generally spacious speeds, so that even the introduction of No. 1 is weighty. Otherwise the crisp articulation of the Munich woodwind (Kempe himself was an oboist before he became a conductor) makes for refreshing results in the allegros of both symphonies. The strings of the Munich Orchestra are not the most refined, but the tone is sweet, notably in the slow movements. The 1974 recording is full and well-rounded, a first-rate bargain. The sound on cassette is wide-ranging but the upper strings are rather thin and edgy in No. 1.

Sanderling presents the early symphonies with the weight of the nineteenth century already in them. Speeds in No. 1 are sprightlier than in No. 2, where Sanderling's spacious approach runs the risk – as Klemperer's did – of seeming too heavy. Clean but over-bright digital recording and an excellent cassette equivalent.

For both symphonies 1 and 2 Schmidt-Isserstedt adopts unusually slow tempi, giving each movement a hint of ponderousness. In the finales the measured approach is a pure delight, revealing detail normally submerged and with nicely pointed playing from the Vienna Philharmonic. Though these are natural, unforced performances to give much pleasure, the Karajan coupling with its direct manner and crisp tempi is a safer recommendation than this for those not wanting Marriner's smaller scale. The Decca cassette is admirably clean and fresh.

Symphonies Nos. 1 and 4.
*** DG 2531/*3301* 308 [id.]. VPO, Bernstein.

Except for Toscanini in mono, no other conductor offers the coupling of Nos. 1 and 4, and Bernstein's readings are both strong and dramatic. Mock pomposity in the introduction to No. 1 leads to a challengingly fast account of the *Allegro*, obviously influenced by the presence of an audience, though at other times – as in the blaring brass of the finale – that spur brings just a hint of vulgarity. In No. 4 Bernstein's taut manner brings out the compactness of argument. The development is especially fine: in context one registers it as the message of No. 1 retold in the language of the *Fifth*. The live recording, not ideally balanced, is very acceptable, on both tape and disc, although the cassette transfer is made at rather a low level.

Symphonies Nos. 1 and 8.
**(*) Decca SXL/*KSXC* 6760 [Lon. CS/5-6926]. Chicago SO, Solti.
** ASV ALH/*ZCALH* 917. Hallé O, Loughran.

Though both the Solti performances are vigorous and dramatic, this is not the record with which to convert anyone to Solti's Beethoven. Other discs offering this coupling in the past have had a more genial air, though Solti's urgency is most persuasive. Bright recording, and an excellent cassette transfer.

The ruggedness of Loughran's Beethoven style comes out from the start even in the *First Symphony*. The first movement is plain and straight, lacking a little in delicacy, and the second movement is rugged and on the slow side too. The *Eighth Symphony* gains more from such treatment, for the outer movements are given a weight apt for a much bigger symphony, which by implication this is, first cousin of the *Seventh*. The middle movements lack charm, suffering from some lack of refinement in the playing. Recording fair, with an element of harshness in the cassette transfer on side one.

Symphony No. 2 in D, Op. 36; Overture; The Creatures of Prometheus.
**(*) DG 2531/*3301* 309 [id.]. VPO, Bernstein.

Symphony No. 2; Overtures: Fidelio; King Stephen.
(M) *** Decca SPA/*KCSP* 584 [Lon. STS/*5-*15518]. LSO, Monteux.

Symphony No. 2; Overture: *Egmont, Op. 84.*
*** Decca SXL 6761 [Lon. 6927]. Chicago SO, Solti.

One of the finest of Monteux's Beethoven series, the Decca reissue of his recording from the mid-1960s is excellent value in the lower-medium price-range. The alertness of the LSO playing makes it strong and enjoyable. There is no first-movement exposition repeat, but Monteux structures the movement overall to take this into account. The overtures are well done too, although *Fidelio* is a little under-powered at the opening. The recording is full, lively and realistic on both disc and tape.

Solti's is a performance of extremes. Though this is early Beethoven, the young composer was intent on writing a symphony on a scale never attempted before, and Solti clearly conveys that absence of apology. The slow introduction is massive and measured, leading to a fast and weighty account of the *Allegro*. The *Larghetto* has spacious refinement, and the last two movements bring performances that are tough, bold and fast. Big, bold recording to match.

Bernstein's Vienna version at full price offers rather short measure for coupling, but the performance has touches that obviously stemmed from the inspiration of the moment, and the tension rises superbly at the end of the finale. Bernstein seems intent on emphasizing how much bigger a symphony this is than No. 1, and though the ensemble is not always flawless and the recording has a rather boomy bass, the liveness is captivating. The cassette transfer is sophisticated, but the level is too low for maximum bite at the top.

Symphonies Nos. 2 and 4.
**(*) ASV ALH/*ZCALH* 909. Hallé O, Loughran.

Lacking a little in rhythmic subtlety and refinement of detail, Loughran yet directs strong and convincing readings of both symphonies. In No. 4 the bluffness of the allegro in the first movement gives way to a plain view of the soaring lyricism of the slow movement which yet is admirably light. When this is a most desirable and generous coupling not otherwise available, Loughran's readings should not be ignored. The cassette benefits from a bass cut; otherwise disc and tape are fairly closely matched.

Symphony No. 3 in E flat (Eroica), Op. 55.
(M) *** DG Acc. 2542/*3342* 103 [2535/*3335* 302]. Berlin PO, Karajan.
C *** Ph. Dig. **410 044-2**; 6514/*7337* 314 [id.]. ASMF, Marriner.
*** Decca SXL 6829 [Lon. CS 6049]. Chicago SO, Solti.
*** ASV ALH/*ZCALH* 901. Hallé O, Loughran.
**(*) DG 2531/*3301* 310 [id.]. VPO, Bernstein.
(B) **(*) CfP CFP/*TC-CFP* 41 4410-1/*-4*. Munich PO, Kempe.
(*) DG. Dig. **410 028-2; 2532/*3302* 123 [id.]. LAPO, Giulini.
*(**) DG 2531/*3301* 103 [id.]. Berlin PO, Karajan.

Symphony No. 3; Overture: Coriolan.
(B) ** Con. CC/*CCT* 7545. BBC SO, Sir Colin Davis.

Symphony No. 3; Overture: Egmont.
(M) *** EMI Em. EMX/*TC-EMX* 2016 [Ang. S/*4XS* 37410]. LSO, Jochum.

Symphony No. 3; Overture: Fidelio.
(M) *** HMV SXLP/*TC-SXLP* 30310. Philh. O, Klemperer.
**(*) HMV Dig. ASD/*TCC-ASD* 4152. Philh. O, Sanderling.

The *Eroica* is a symphony in which only a few conductors have given their finest. Klemperer, Karajan and Jochum are certainly among them and so is Bernstein (although his newest version is no match for the earlier New

York recording). Loughran, Sanderling and Solti all make a strong response to this remarkable symphony, but while first choice probably remains between Karajan's 1962 recording and Jochum's splendid LSO performance, Marriner's St Martin's Academy account should not be forgotten for, on compact disc, it represents technically the most realistic recording of any Beethoven symphony so far.

Karajan's Accolade *Eroica* is refreshing and urgent, without the hint of excessive tension which makes the first movement of his 1977 performance slightly controversial. The refinement of detail never gets in the way of the dramatic urgency, and this is an outstandingly safe, central recommendation, with the Berlin Philharmonic on top form. The cassette matches the disc closely, although side two is transferred at a slightly lower level and has marginally less bite, and more hiss. The tape, however, has the advantage of a bonus not included on the disc, a fine performance of the *Coriolan overture*.

Jochum's too is a magnificent reading, direct in outline and manner, but with keen refinement of detail. Tempi are all centrally convincing and though the exposition repeat is observed in the first movement, making the side extremely long, the sound is still both full and lively. The glory of the performance lies above all in the dedicated account of the *Funeral march*, never overstated but darkly intense. Coupled with a fine version of the *Egmont overture*, this is as recommendable on disc as it is on the tape, which matches it closely, although the upper range is somewhat less sharply focused.

It is widely felt that Klemperer's second reading of the *Eroica* with the Philharmonia lacked something of the incandescence of his earlier mono performance, but the concentration was just as keen, with even slower tempo given natural unforced weight, most strikingly of all in the stoically intense account of the *Funeral march*. Only in the coda of the finale does the slow tempo bring some slackness. Well-balanced recording of early-1960s vintage and a vivid tape transfer. The overture, however, has a degree of congestion at its closing climax (on tape only).

Marriner's version is in every way outstanding, for although the Academy may use fewer strings, the impression is of weight and strength ample for Beethoven's mighty inspiration, coupled with a rare transparency of texture and extraordinary resilience of rhythm. The dance-rhythms of the fast movements are brought out captivatingly with sforzandos made clean and sharp to have one transferring to the *Eroica* Wagner's famous remark about the *Seventh*, 'the apotheosis of the dance'. The *Funeral march* may emerge less grave and dark than it can be, but Marriner's unforced directness is most compelling. The recorded sound is among the best ever in a Beethoven symphony, most impressive of all in the compact disc version, which in the slow movement gains greatly from the absence of background.

Unquestionably this is one of the finest performances from the Solti complete set. The power and weight of the reading are apparent from the very opening bars. The forward momentum is strong and positive. The tempo is comparatively relaxed, and this is matched by a very slow speed for the *Funeral march*. Yet the concentration creates an electric degree of tension, which is naturally resolved in the sparkling scherzo and the vigorous lyricism of the finale. The recording is of Decca's best.

Loughran began his projected cycle of Beethoven symphonies with an account of the *Eroica* which has all the rhythmic urgency and sense of spontaneity that make his Brahms cycle so compelling. This is a performance with minor flaws – the Hallé violins are not always sweet-toned – but it is an exceptionally compelling one, with finely chosen tempi forthrightly maintained and a resilience of pulse in the first movement that is memorable. The recording quality is full and warm, but the closeness of balance in a relatively narrow stereo spectrum hardly does justice to the hushed playing in the *Funeral march*, and occasionally exposes individual instruments. An ingenious and original solution has been devised to get round the problem of including the first-movement exposition repeat and yet not making a break in the middle of the slow movement. This is achieved by having the first movement begin in mid-side. Then one turns over for movements two and three and back again for the finale. The cassette, of course, does not need to do this and plays straightforwardly. The transfer is clear, but the upper range is fierce, with a lack of bloom on the violins.

Sanderling too is at his finest in the *Eroica.* This more than anything sets the pattern for his complete cycle in its rugged honesty, marked by plain, unhurried speeds. There are more dramatic readings, more intense ones too, but with its inclusion of the exposition repeat, as well as bright, clean digital sound and a good fill-up it is a fair recommendation. The cassette and disc are closely matched.

Bernstein's 1966 recording (still available in the US on M/*MT* 31822, but withdrawn in the UK) was electrically intense, with a first movement almost as fast as Toscanini's – maintaining the tension over a fuller span by the inclusion of the exposition repeat – and a darkly tragic *Funeral march.* Compared with that, there is a degree of disappointment about his new Vienna version, with less incandescence in the first movement and a hard, clattering sound for the opening chords. The exposition repeat is still observed, however, and this is undoubtedly a strong, dramatic reading, with a superb, dedicated account of the *Funeral march.* This emerges as more clearly a march than before, yet very measured indeed, its intensity enhanced by the presence of an audience. Both disc and tape offer a good sound.

Kempe takes a spacious view of the first movement. Initially it may sound unexciting, but then, as with Klemperer, the structure builds up strongly and compellingly. The *Funeral march* is subdued and inward, spontaneous-sounding in its concentration up to the hushed disintegration of the main theme. The oboe solos are beautiful. Fast speeds and fine articulation in the last two movements, though violin-tone lacks bloom. Excellent value at CfP price.

With an extraordinarily measured view of the first movement Giulini's is an outstandingly refined and individual reading. If at first the performance seems lacking a little in tension, one comes to appreciate the long-breathed concentration which, without forcing, compels one to listen afresh. The playing is comparably refined and the recording undistracting, not at all recognizable as coming from this orchestra. The tape matches the disc fairly closely.

Not everyone will readily identify with the fiery intensity of fast tempi in the outer movements of Karajan's 1977 performance. Contrasts are heightened, with, if anything, an even more intense account of the *Funeral march* than in his earlier recordings. A point to consider is the absence of the exposition repeat in the first movement (until recent years rarely observed in recordings), but this is among the most polished as well as the most dramatic accounts available. The sound is full-blooded, though there are some intrusive close-up effects, and the cassette matches the disc closely.

On the Contour reissue a strong account from Davis, the conception broadly satisfying, and the playing excellent throughout. But with such an approach and a very slow tempo for the *Funeral march*, a higher degree of concentration is needed and, good though this is, the sense of urgency here is lacking. The Overture is a successful bonus, but this is not among the great performances of the *Eroica*, even though it is undoubtedly enjoyable and well-recorded.

Symphony No. 4 in B flat, Op. 60.
*** DG 2531/*3301* 104 [id.]. Berlin PO, Karajan.
(M) *** DG 2542/*3342* 104 [2535/*3335* 303]. Berlin PO, Karajan.
(*) Decca SXL 6830 [Lon. CS 7050]. Chicago SO, Solti – WEBER: *Oberon overture.*(*)*

Symphony No. 4; Overture: Egmont.
**(*) HMV Dig. ASD/*TCC-ASD* 4153. Philh. O, Sanderling.

Symphony No. 4; Overture: Leonora No. 3.
(M) *** EMI Em. EMX/*TC-EMX* 2017 [Ang. S/*4XS* 37529]. LSO, Jochum.
(B) **(*) CfP CFP/*TC-CFP* 4407. Munich PO, Kempe.

Symphony No. 4; (i) *Ah! Perfido.*
*** CBS Dig. 37209/*40-* [id.]. ECO, Tilson Thomas; (i) Marton.

As can be seen above, the *Fourth* is well served at both full and medium price, and many collectors will reflect that the Karajan versions, fine though they are, seem expensive on disc with no couplings (although, curiously, the Accolade tape includes the *Egmont overture*). But first choice probably rests with Jochum.

Jochum's reading of the *Fourth* has been splendidly caught three times over, and the latest version with the LSO has even greater breadth, while bringing out the work's free, natural lyricism. The EMI recording is full and clear, and the weighty account of the *Leonora No. 3 overture* makes a substantial coupling. The cassette is of acceptable quality, full-bodied certainly, but it does not match the upper range of the disc.

Karajan's two versions are closely matched. The earlier 1962 reading is splendid, with the dynamic contrasts heavily underlined in the outer movements. In the slow movement there is a lyrical feel to the playing that suggests Schubert. The recording still sounds well, although the tape is less lively than the disc. In the later, 1977 version the balance is even closer, exposing every flicker of tremolando. Yet the precision of the Berlin Philharmonic is a thing of wonder, and if anything Karajan conveys more weight and strength than before, with more emphasis on the *Adagio*. Only the extremely fast tempo for the finale marks a questionable development, but even there the brilliance and excitement are never in doubt. On tape the orchestral image is full-blooded and clear, but again the ear notices the tendency for the strings to recede in pianissimos.

Michael Tilson Thomas's project of recording all the Beethoven symphonies with the English Chamber Orchestra brings an admirable version of the *Fourth*. The outer movements are vigorous and urgent, the scherzo nicely paced to allow less slowing than usual in the trio. Though the strings may be fewer in number than usual, the stereo spread is wide with second violins on the right presented in antiphony with the firsts, particularly important in this symphony. The dramatic account of *Ah! perfido* features the powerful Hungarian soprano, Eva Marton, to make a useful fill-up. Excellent digital sound. The chrome tape is admirably bright and clean, without loss of body.

Sanderling has specifically related the mood of the big slow introduction to a misty early morning in summer, and the weight and concentration are immediately impressive. The *Allegro*, characteristically measured, is less successful, relatively unsprung, but this is a powerful, undistracting reading, brightly recorded on disc and tape alike.

Solti gives an unashamedly large-scale reading of the *Fourth*, vigorous, even exuberant, but not strong on charm: it is not one to make you love the work as representing Beethoven in restrained mood. With Solti the *Fourth* clearly points forward to the *Seventh Symphony*, which in structure it strikingly resembles on such points as the slow introduction and the extra sections in the scherzo. The Chicago playing is flawless, with a highly polished violin tone sustaining the poised beauty of the *Adagio*. The finale has superb vitality, but one wishes that the playing smiled more readily.

Kempe directs a tough rather than affectionate performance, easy-going in the first movement, with no exposition repeat. The lovely slow movement with its soaring cantilena is forthright rather than refined. This remains a strong, well-articulated reading with first-rate 1974 sound, well worth its CfP price. The Overture (also well done) comes first, an order no doubt encouraged by the need on the cassette to even out the sides. Side one of the tape, transferred at a high level, is brighter than side two, which is fuller; the sound of the disc comes somewhere in between.

Symphony No. 5 in C min., Op. 67.

*** DG Dig. **410 028-2**; 2532/*3302* 049 [id.]. LAPO, Giulini.

*** DG 2530 516/*3300* 472 [id.]. VPO, Kleiber.

*** DG 2531/*3301* 105 [id.]. Berlin PO, Karajan.

(M) *** DG Acc. 2542/*3342* 105 [2535/*3335* 304]. Berlin PO, Karajan.

*** DG 2531/*3301* 311 [id.]. VPO, Bernstein.

(M) **(*) CBS 60106/*40*- [MY/*MYT* 36719]. NYPO, Bernstein – SCHUBERT: *Symphony No. 8 (Unfinished)*.**(*)

(M) ** DG Sig. 2543/*3343* 506. VPO, Boehm – SCHUBERT: *Symphony No. 8 (Unfinished)*.***

* Decca VIC/*KVIC* 24 [Lon. JL/5- 41016]. VPO, Solti.

Symphony No. 5; Overture: Coriolan.

**(*) HMV Dig. ASD/*TCC-ASD* 4136. Philh. O, Sanderling.

Symphony No. 5; Overtures: Coriolan; Egmont.
**(*) ASV ALH/*ZCALH* 908. Hallé O, Loughran.

Symphony No. 5; Overture: Egmont.
(M) **(*) Decca SPA/*KCSP* 585. LSO, Monteux.
*(*) Telarc **CD 80060**; DG 10060 [id.]. Boston SO, Ozawa.

Symphony No. 5; Overture: Fidelio.
(M) *** EMI Em. EMX/*TC-EMX* 2018 [Ang. S/*4XS* 37463]. LSO, Jochum.
(B) **(*) Con. CC/*CCT* 7526. Bav. RSO, Jochum.

Symphony No. 5; Overture: Leonora No. 3.
*** Decca Dig. **400 060-2**; SXDL/*KSXDC* 7540 [LDR/*5*- 71040]. Philh. O, Ashkenazy.
*** Decca SXL/*KSXC* 6762 [Lon. CS/*5*-6930]. Chicago SO, Solti.

Beethoven's *Fifth* has often been recorded and the present catalogue has distilled a high degree of excellence among some half-dozen versions, so that a first choice is not readily made. Both the Karajan readings are marvellously played and, while lacking neither weight nor warmth in the *Andante*, they engender a rush of adrenalin in the outer movements that is difficult to resist. Yet among recent versions, Giulini's stands out, and his new digital recording is impressively full and brilliant, especially on compact disc.

At times one cannot escape the feeling that Giulini has thought too deeply about the music he conducts and has pondered over every phrase, over the weight of sonority on every chord, to such an extent that his very search for truth inhibits its complete realization. Yet this account of the *Fifth Symphony* must be numbered among his unqualified successes. It possesses majesty in abundance, and conveys the power and vision of this inexhaustible work. It is the finest version to appear on record since Carlos Kleiber's account with the VPO from the mid-1970s. Good recording too. The chrome cassette is first-class, wide-ranging and full-bodied, and the compact disc with its combination of clarity of detail and truthful textures makes all the more impact, heard against a background of silence.

Carlos Kleiber's famous record still dominates the rest of the catalogue as did his father Erich's famous performance two decades earlier. In his hands the first movement is electrifying, but has a hushed intensity too. Where Karajan, also outstanding, with a very similar overall approach, and speeds in the Toscanini tradition, suggests swaggering extroversion, the hero striding forward, Carlos Kleiber finds darker, more disturbed emotions. The slow movement is tender and delicate, with dynamic contrasts underlined but not exaggerated. The horns, like the rest of the VPO, are in superb form, and the finale, even more than usual, releases the music into pure daylight. The gradation of dynamics from the hushed pianissimo of the close of the scherzo to the weight of the great opening statement of the finale has not been heard on disc with such overwhelming effect since Toscanini. There is an equally impressive cassette of this performance, not quite as clean as the disc, but encompassing the wide dynamics with startling ease.

Karajan's 1977 version is magnificent in every way, tough and urgently incisive, with fast tempi, bringing weight as well as excitement but no unwanted blatancy, even in the finale. The recording is satisfyingly wide-ranging in frequency and dynamic on both disc and tape.

Karajan's 1962 version with the same players is hardly less powerful and incisive than his later account and the recording is more naturally balanced. So heroic a reading makes an excellent recommendation at medium price. The cassette is not only well managed (only marginally less lively than the LP) but offers the *Leonora No. 3* and *Fidelio* overtures as a very considerable bonus; these come first, then the first movement of the symphony, with the remaining three movements on side two.

The Eminence reissue of Jochum's LSO recording remains a very strong competitor, and at medium-price may be preferred over the Karajan versions. The sound combines body with good detail and is most realistically balanced (the cassette quite close to the LP although side one is cleaner than side two). It is usual enough for a conductor to treat Beethoven's *Fifth* as an epic work, but Jochum's idea of the epic here is massive rather than compressed, and in this he is aided not only by superbly chiselled playing from the LSO but by the opulent recording. The first movement is strong and central in the German tradition, with big contrasts, but it is the *Andante* which especially marks this newest Jochum reading out. It is spacious and poised yet fresh and unmannered, with no hint of the German band in the brassy fortissimos. With Jochum they frame the moments of hushed intensity, so that the pianissimo hints at the motto rhythm take on a key importance. The scherzo is taken slower than usual, easy and light at the very start, then weighty; the finale enters as an expression not of bombast but of pure joy. The expansiveness is underlined by Jochum's observance of the exposition repeat. As a coupling Jochum again offers the *Fidelio overture* (as on his earlier Contour issue) in a brilliant performance, rather less sumptuously recorded than the symphony.

Bernstein in his Vienna version re-thought his reading of the *Fifth*, giving it resonance and spaciousness as well as drama. Some of the Toscanini-like tension of his earlier New York reading has evaporated from the first movement, but the warmth and conviction of the whole performance are most persuasive, ending with a blazing account of the finale. The recording, made at live concerts, is good though not ideal, and the cassette matches the disc closely, with plenty of body and impact.

Ashkenazy's is a vivid and urgent reading of the *Fifth*, with well-chosen speeds for all four movements, though the *Andante con moto* is on the slow side, and the finale is on the fast side, with joyful exuberance a fair substitute for grandeur. The Overture too, also fast, finds Ashkenazy at his freshest. The impact of these performances is enhanced by the richness and ample spread of the recording set against a warm Kingsway Hall acoustic. The chrome cassette is lively and full-bodied with excellent detail. The compact disc is a degree richer than the LP (there is an impressively full bass) but only marginally clearer. Here the Symphony comes before the Overture, whereas on the LP it is the other way about.

Solti gives a big and bold reading of No. 5, tense but not neurotic, with a warm expansive reading of the slow movement, a surprisingly measured view of the scherzo and a really joyful account of the finale. With resonant playing and recording to match, it makes a fair recommendation, including as it does *Leonora No. 3*, dramatically performed, if with less immediacy than the symphony. The cassette too is excellent.

Loughran continues his Beethoven series with an exceptionally vibrant account of the *Fifth*. His first movement is leonine rather than massive, but by observing the repeats in both outer movements he underlines the scale of the symphony as well as its strength. After a direct yet lyrical *Andante* comes a fast scherzo, with nimble playing from the lower strings; and the release of exultant energy in the finale caps a performance which is notable above all for its vigour and forward impulse. The overtures too are splendidly played. The lively recording has transferred to tape with admirable presence and detail. It sounds best with a slight treble reduction.

Sanderling's reading of the *Fifth* is typical of his whole cycle, powerful and direct, lacking a little in rhythmic subtlety, almost too plain, but generally conveying a Klemperer-like ruggedness. A detailed point is that Sanderling at the start has – with fair justification – a shorter pause after the first knock of fate than after the second. The opening statement of the finale is massive rather than incisively dramatic. The digital sound is bold and clear, and the cassette is striking in its combination of body and a brilliant upper range.

Bernstein's New York version on CBS is a strong dramatic reading, not quite so memorable as the *Eroica* he recorded at the same period, but concentrated and vital, with a balancing warmth in the slow movement. The recording is not distinguished, but although it lacks the widest dynamic range it has a fairly convincing ambient depth. Coupled with a dramatic and individual account of Schubert's *Unfinished* this lays fair claim to its place in this CBS 'Great performances' series. However, to fit the Symphony on a single side repeats have been cut, which some consider rather cavalier of CBS. The cassette transfer is very successful, coping well with the reverberation.

Jochum's early DG recording makes a fine bargain in this Contour reissue. Although the opening bars are less dramatic than in some versions, Jochum launches into a finely vigorous reading, warmly lyrical in the slow movement, yet unmarred throughout by any romantic exaggerations. He includes the first-movement exposition repeat, and the whole performance is gripping in a totally natural, unforced way. The recording hardly shows its age and the lively performance of the Overture makes a fine bonus. As usual in this series the cassette has less energy in the upper range than the disc, which reduces the dynamic contrast.

Monteux's Beethoven performances on record tended to be straight and direct, but here – in a previously unissued recording – the volatile Frenchman plays his part in a performance which has strength and drive as well as an element of waywardness. Unashamedly he presents the fate theme at the very start more slowly and weightily than the very fast basic tempo of the movement, an effect which requires sleight of hand there and elsewhere. It is a personal reading but a compelling one in all four movements, with fine articulation from the LSO, though the brassiness of the finale is a little aggressive. *Egmont* has comparable urgency but less polish. The recording is excellent for its early-1960s vintage. The cassette is of demonstration quality, matching the disc very closely indeed.

Boehm's equable approach to Beethoven wears well, particularly when you are listening at home. His version of the *Fifth*, here recoupled as a sampler for his Beethoven and Schubert cycles, lacks the dramatic power which this of all Beethoven symphonies really needs, but it is a characteristic example of his work. The recording wears well, and there is little to choose between disc and the excellent chrome tape.

Ozawa's Telarc recording with the Boston Symphony Orchestra is well played and has impressively rich and well-balanced sound. But the reading, with fast outer movements and an uneventful *Andante*, seriously lacks electricity. Considering the wide dynamic range possible with digital techniques the opening of the finale is surprisingly wanting in drama. In a competitive field this expensive issue is a non-starter.

In the Viva reissue Solti's 1959 recording sounds strikingly full and vivid, but otherwise this record does little to further the conductor's reputation. The first movement is exciting in its way with a fast tempo and precise, efficient playing. But one senses that the music-making is a little forced and in the slow movement the overall effect is of ponderousness, with exaggerated climaxes.

Symphonies Nos. 5–6 (Pastoral); Egmont overture.
(B) *** DG Walkman *413 144–4*. VPO, Boehm.

This second in DG's new Walkman series, like the coupling of the *Violin concerto* and the *Emperor*, offers extraordinary value. The transfers on to chrome tape are remarkably vivid. Boehm's account of the *Fifth* may not be the most powerful available; but with excellent playing and recording, rich and weighty in the bass as well as lively on top, it is a good version to live with. It pairs naturally with the *Pastoral* in its display of positive feeling and absence of neurosis. The latter is as fine as any version listed at full-price, except perhaps Ashkenazy's newest Decca, and is successfully transferred at a high level. Each symphony is offered uninterrupted, and an excellent account of the *Egmont overture* balances the two sides. In DG's lowest price-range, yet offering nearly ninety minutes of music, this tape is a bargain in every sense of the word.

Symphonies Nos. 5 and 8.
(M) **(*) Decca Jub. JB/*KJBC* 5. VPO, Schmidt-Isserstedt.
(B) **(*) CfP CFP/*TC-CFP* 41 4415-1/*4*. Munich PO, Kempe.

The coupling of *Symphonies 5* and *8* is a happy idea, and on Decca Schmidt-Isserstedt offers strong readings of both; this is a fine disc with generous sides and first-rate recording. Schmidt-Isserstedt makes no allowances and includes exposition repeats in both the first movements. The first movement of the *Eighth* is slower than usual in the interests of emphasizing that this is not simply Beethoven's 'little one' but a powerful, symphonic argument. There is a crisp, light *Allegretto* and a minuet more heavily pointed than usual, with a Brahmsian touch in the trio. But it is the performance of the *Fifth* that stands out in a first movement that has both bite and breathing space, a nicely measured *Andante* and a triumphant finale. Only the scherzo invites controversy in its slow tempo, but logic plays its part in the choice in that it allows the double-basses in the trio to play their scampering part without either stumbling or having the conductor slow for them. The cassette transfer is vividly managed.

Kempe's is an outstanding and generous coupling at CfP price. The *Fifth*, recorded on a relatively intimate scale with violins a little thin-sounding, lacks excitement at the start, but builds up splendidly in spontaneous-sounding strength. The approach is direct and unforced in all four movements, and only the failure to point the entry of the great brass theme which opens the finale is disappointing. The *Eighth*, with speeds faster than usual and rhythms well lifted, is given an exhilarating performance, strongly argued, lacking only a little in detail of expression though textural detail is commendably clear in the fresh-sounding 1974 recording.

Symphony No. 6 in F (Pastoral), Op. 68.
*** Decca Dig. **410 003-2**; SXDL/*KSXDC* 7578 [Lon. LDR/*5-* 71078]. Philh. O, Ashkenazy.
*** DG 2530 142/*3300 476* [id.]. VPO, Boehm.
(M) *** CBS 60107/*40-* [MY/*MYT* 36720]. Columbia SO, Walter.
(B) *** CfP CFP/*TC-CFP* 40017. Berlin PO, Cluytens.
*** HMV [Ang. S/*4ZS* 36739]. Phd. O, Muti.
*** ASV ALH/*ZCALH* 902. Hallé O, Loughran.
(M) *** EMI Em. EMX/*TC-EMX* 2019 [Ang. S/*4XS* 37530]. LSO, Jochum.
*** HMV ASD/*TCC-ASD* 4154. Philh. O, Sanderling.
(M) *** Ph. Seq. 6527/*7311* 045. Concg. O, Jochum.
**(*) CBS 76825/*40-* [M/*MT* 35169]. ECO, Tilson Thomas.
**(*) DG 2531/*3301* 312 [id.]. VPO, Bernstein.
**(*) Decca SXL 6763 [Lon. CS 6931]. Chicago SO, Solti.
(B) ** CfP CFP/*TC-CFP* 41 4419-1/*4*. Munich PO, Kempe.
(B) ** Con. CC/*CCT* 7546. BBC SO, Sir Colin Davis.
** DG 2531/*3301* 106 [id.]. Berlin PO, Karajan.
** DG 2531/*3301* 266 [id.]. LAPO, Giulini.
(M) *(*) Decca SPA 113 [Lon. STS 15161]. VPO, Monteux.
(M) * DG Acc. 2542/*3342* 106 [2535/*3335* 305]. Berlin PO, Karajan.

Symphony No. 6; Overture: Egmont.
(M) *(*) Decca Jub. JB/*KJBC* 2. VPO, Schmidt-Isserstedt.

Ashkenazy's is a genial reading, almost totally unmannered to the point where some may feel it lacking in individuality. But the performance has a beguiling warmth and it communicates readily. With generally spacious tempi (although not as measured as Jochum's in the first movement) the feeling of lyrical ease and repose is most captivating, thanks to the response of the Philharmonia players and the richness of the recording, made in the Kingsway Hall. After a *Storm* that is civilized rather than frightening, the performance is crowned by a radiant account of the *Shepherds' thanksgiving*. The sound, with its fairly reverberant acoustic, is particularly impressive on the excellent compact disc, but the chrome cassette too is of demonstration quality. On tape there is slightly less edge on the strings, yet no loss of detail, and the balance suits the music-making admirably.

Boehm's 1972 recording still sounds well on both disc and tape, if not as full-textured as the new Decca version. But the performance has great character, and for that some will prefer it to Ashkenazy's relatively self-effacing account. Boehm gives a beautiful, unforced reading of the *Pastoral*, one of the best played (even if Vienna violins are not quite as splendid on this showing as those of Berlin) and certainly one of the best recorded. In the first movement he observes the exposition repeat (not many versions do); and though the dynamic contrasts are never underplayed and the phrasing is affectionate, there is a feeling of inevitable rightness about Boehm's approach, no sense of an interpreter enforcing his will. Only the slow movement with its even stressing raises any reservation, and that very slight.

Bruno Walter was always famous for his interpretation of the *Pastoral symphony*. It was the only Beethoven symphony he recorded twice in the 78 r.p.m. era (although his second version with the Philadelphia Orchestra was disappointing). The present version dates from the beginning of the 1960s and represents the peak of his Indian summer in the American recording studios. The whole performance glows, and the gentle warmth of phrasing is comparable with Klemperer's famous version. The slow movement is taken slightly fast, but there is no sense of hurry, and the tempo of the *Shepherds' thanksgiving* is less controversial than Klemperer's. It is an affectionate and completely integrated performance from a master who thought and lived the work all his life. The sound is surprisingly full (with a good cassette) and hardly dates, making this a classic reissue, fully worthy of the 'Great performances' sobriquet that distinguishes this CBS medium-price series.

Cluytens's recording is intensely warm-hearted and atmospheric. On analysis alone one might object to the occasional idiosyncrasy, the very affectionate phrasing and a few speed changes. But the obvious spontaneity makes the whole performance most compelling, so that one finds oneself playing it again and again for sheer delight. Each movement has a glow which can only come from complete sympathy between players and conductor, and the final *Shepherds' hymn after the storm* shines out as an apotheosis. In the linking passage after the storm Beethoven's picture of a world freshened by rain is most vivid and from there to the end the sense of joyous release increases in triumphant crescendo. With good sound (on tape and disc alike) and at bargain price it should not be missed.

With the first two movements youthfully urgent, Muti's is an exhilarating performance, fresh and direct. It is a strong symphonic view, rather than a programmatic one. The recording is rich and wide-ranging, though high violins do not always live up to the 'Philadelphia sound'. The tape transfer is full, clear and clean. This version has been deleted in the UK.

Loughran's performance shows him at his most persuasive, conveying the joy of Beethoven's arrival in the countryside with seeming spontaneity, so that the whole performance carries forward in a single sweep. The slow movement is especially fine; in the scherzo the horns sing out exuberantly, so that after the storm the dewy radiance of the finale is the more refreshing. The Hallé is on peak form, and the recording is rich and bright. The cassette transfer is bold and clear, but in spite of a basic resonant warmth the upper strings lack bloom.

Jochum's Eminence version is among the most distinctive. His tempo for the first movement is exceptionally slow (slower than in his earlier recording for Philips), but the rhythms are so exquisitely sprung that the result has more the flavour of a country dance than usual, with a hint of rustic tone in some of the wind solos (presumably, with these LSO players, that is by intent). There is a dance element too in Jochum's *Scene by the brook*, with the lapping triplet rhythms pointed as delectably as by Klemperer. The scherzo is jaunty and sharp-hitting, the *Storm* is given classical strength, and the *Shepherds' thanksgiving* is fresh and innocent, again with a persuasive lilt. This will not be everyone's first choice, but with full and finely balanced recording it is a most compelling reading. It has transferred smoothly to tape, the sound retaining its bloom and a good deal of detail.

Sanderling's characteristically slow speeds give an easy geniality to the *Pastoral*. Like Jochum he omits the exposition repeat in the first movement, marring the balance of movements, but otherwise this is a warm, glowing account which rises in the *Shepherds' hymn* from rugged honesty to rapt dedication. Bright digital recording, with very little difference between disc and chrome tape.

Jochum's Philips recording of the *Pastoral* dates from the end of the 1960s. It still sounds extremely well, resonantly full-bodied, vivid and clear. Like his newer EMI recording this is a leisurely reading, the countryside relaxing in the sunshine. In the first movement Jochum is essentially undramatic until the radiant final climax in the coda, which he links with the similar burst of energy in the finale. The slow movement has an Elysian stillness and repose; the *Storm* is not over-romanticized. With beautiful playing from the Concertgebouw Orchestra, the reading is sustained without a hint of lethargy and makes a splendid medium-priced alternative view of Beethoven's ever-fresh symphony. There is little appreciable difference in sound between the disc and the excellent cassette.

With the body of strings reduced to a size such as Beethoven would have expected, Tilson Thomas adopts generally fast tempi and makes them sound lithe and exhilarating, not at all hectic. It is a strong, attractive reading, but with close-up recording, many will not notice much difference from big-orchestra sound. The high-level tape transfer is bright to the point of fierceness, although it does not lack weight in the bass. But the *Storm* seems excessively brilliant, and side two generally is more aggressive-sounding than side one.

Joy and serenity are not qualities one would normally associate with any American conductor, even Bernstein, but here he draws those qualities from the Vienna Philharmonic in a warm, persuasive reading, not perfect of ensemble (this was made at live concerts) but very enjoyable. The balance seems slightly over-resonant in the bass on disc, but the high-level tape transfer produces vivid sound throughout.

Solti gives a bright, fresh, resilient performance which consistently conveys the composer's joy at arriving in the countryside. The contrasts are big and bold, with resonant tone from the Chicago orchestra, and they are splendidly caught by the Decca engineers working in their favourite haunt of the Sofiensaal. This is a performance about which there is a divergence of views; some ears find Solti not quite relaxed and the orchestral playing marginally high-powered for the essentially lyrical quality of Beethoven's inspiration.

Kempe, adopting relatively brisk speeds, gives a plain, rather unvarnished reading, lacking a little in poetry but full of energy and beautifully clear in texture, thanks to the 1974 recording quality. Kempe may lack the magic of his CfP predecessor in Beethoven, Cluytens, but you hear far more.

The bargain-priced Contour version by the BBC Symphony Orchestra under Sir Colin Davis was recorded as recently as 1976 and has splendidly full and well-balanced sound, with disc and cassette very closely matched. The performance is broader and more expansive than Davis's earlier record with the LSO. The controversial point about the later account is the very measured reading of the fourth movement, the *Storm*. Though the playing is refined, inevitably it lacks something in excitement. Nonetheless it matches Davis's relaxed approach to the whole work.

Karajan's 1977 performance brought a more congenial reading than his earlier excessively tense 1962 recording with the same orchestra. It is fresh and alert, consistent with the rest of the cycle, a good dramatic version with polished playing and recording which is wide-ranging but suffers from the odd balances which mark the 1977 cycle. The tape transfer matches the disc but is marginally brighter on side two.

Giulini's New Philharmonia version, recorded in the mid-1960s, was better balanced than his much later Los Angeles account. However, Giulini's measured view makes a stronger and more convincing effect in his second recording in Los Angeles. But the DG engineers produce disappointing results and the balances and mixing make the sound unrealistic. (The cassette matches the disc closely.)

Schmidt-Isserstedt's Jubilee reissue is in the last analysis disappointing. It is well recorded and offers a good, clean, straightforward classical account. But there is somehow a lack of atmosphere and warmth, in the approach rather than the playing, and certainly an absence of charm.

Monteux's version too is disappointing, in spite of good sound. Plainly the Vienna Philharmonic were not in the form they were for this conductor's account of the *Eroica*, and it is sad to find so little lilt in the first movement.

Karajan's 1962 version of the *Pastoral* was by far the least appealing of his first Berlin Beethoven cycle, with hectically fast tempi. The playing is very refined, but even at medium price there are far more persuasive versions.

Symphony No. 7 in A, Op. 92.

*** DG 2531/*3301* 313 [id.]. VPO, Bernstein.

(M) *** DG Acc. 2542/*3342* 107 [2535/*3335* 306]. Berlin PO, Karajan.

(M) *** HMV SXLP 20038. RPO, Sir Colin Davis.

(M) *** CBS 60126 [MY/*MYT* 37233]. Marlboro Fest. O, Casals.

**(*) DG 2531/*3301* 107 [id.]. Berlin PO, Karajan.
**(*) ASV ALH/*ZCALH* 904. Hallé O, Loughran.
(M) **(*) Decca SPA/*KCSP* 586 [Lon. STS 15520]. LSO, Monteux.
**(*) DG Sig. 410 932/1-*4* [id.]. VPO, Kleiber.
**(*) HMV ASD/*TC-ASD* 3646 [Ang. S/*4XS* 37538]. Phd. O, Muti.
**(*) HM 1C 067 99872. Col. Aur., Maier.
(M) ** Ph. Seq. 6527/*7311* 141 [id.]. LSO, Sir Colin Davis.
(B) * Con. CC/*CCT* 7502 [Lon. STS 15107]. VPO, Karajan.

Symphony No. 7; Overture: Coriolan.
(M) *** EMI Em. EMX/*TC-EMX* 2020 [Ang. S/*4XS* 37531]. LSO, Jochum.
*** Decca SXL 6764 [Lon. CS 6932]. Chicago SO, Solti.

Symphony No. 7; Overture: The Creatures of Prometheus.
*(*) HMV Dig. ASD/*TCC-ASD* 4155. Philh. O, Sanderling.

Symphony No. 7; Overture: Egmont.
(B) **(*) CfP CFP/*TC-CFP* 4408. Munich PO, Kempe.

Symphony No. 7; Overture: Leonora No. 3.
(M) *** Decca Jub. JB/*KJBC* 4. VPO, Schmidt-Isserstedt.

As in the *Eroica* the Beethovenian tensions in Bernstein's Vienna performance of the *Seventh* are less marked than in his earlier New York recording, but that makes for extra spring and exhilaration in the lilting rhythms of the first movement, while the *Allegretto* is reposeful without falling into an ordinary *Andante*, and the last two movements have the adrenalin flowing with a greater sense of occasion than in most of this Bernstein series. One almost regrets the lack of applause. The recording is among the best and brightest in the set, the cassette marginally less refined at the top than the disc (noticeable in the first tutti of the opening movement's *Allegro*) but well balanced and lively.

Karajan is nothing if not consistent, and his 1962 and 1977 versions of the *Seventh* are remarkably similar. The 1962 version tingles with excitement. It is hard-driven in the Toscanini manner and never less than compelling, lacking only the last degree of resilience that slightly slower tempi might have allowed. There is not quite the lift to the dance rhythms that the Italian Toscanini managed to retain even when driving at his hardest. With excellent recording for its period it makes an attractive Accolade reissue, with a good equivalent tape, slightly less bright than the disc but with plenty of body and good detail.

Karajan's 1977 version is similarly tense, with the conductor emphasizing the work's dramatic rather than its dance-like qualities. The slow introduction, taken at a fastish tempo, is tough rather than monumental, and the main *Allegro* is fresh and bright and not very lilting in its 6/8 rhythm, though it is more sharply pointed here than in the earlier 1962 version. The *Allegretto* is this time a little weightier, but the consistency with the earlier reading is still a point to emphasize. With good, full recording, the tape as vivid as the disc, this can be recommended alongside the earlier account, which is, of course, less expensive.

Sir Colin Davis has recorded the *Seventh* twice, once for HMV and again for Philips. It is the earlier version that has stood the test of time and it still rivals any performance ever recorded. Here is an ideal illustration of the difference between a studio run-through and a performance that genuinely takes one forward compellingly from bar to bar. Admittedly the opening of the slow introduction is a shade lacking in weight, but from there on there is barely a blemish. The first movement, with delicious pointing of the dotted rhythm, has both stylishness and strength. The slow movement, taken at a measured speed, is beautifully controlled not only in the detailed phrasing but over the architectural span of the whole movement. The scherzo, with all the repeats taken for once, is wonderfully rumbustious, with some superb woodwind playing. The finale, taken very fast indeed, barely allows one to breathe for excitement. The recording from the early 1960s still sounds well.

Casals's is undoubtedly a great performance. It suffers from relatively undistinguished sound, but it can be made to reproduce satisfactorily. It emanates from a live performance given in Marlboro in 1969, when Casals was ninety-three. Every single phrase is vibrant with musical feeling, and the slow movement is among the most beautiful and moving on record. Right from the outset, the listener is gripped by this record, and the less than vivid sound is soon forgotten. In matters musical there is no substitute for genuinely felt phrasing, and it is this that makes Casals's reading so revealing and compelling. There is a wonderful humanity about this performance that gives it special claims in a less than humane world.

Jochum's is a distinguished reading of the *Seventh*, particularly impressive in the first movement, where after a weighty but lyrically compelling slow introduction, the main *Allegro* is given the affectionate pointing of a country dance. The exposition repeat is observed to give extra, necessary weight. The second movement is taken at a genuine *Allegretto*, and the remaining two movements are refreshingly vigorous, though this Eminence reissue has brought a lightening of bass, and with it a touch of fierceness at the top on violin tone. The cassette is smoother, without loss of vividness, and many will prefer it.

Solti is immensely powerful and energetic but always resilient to bring out the dance-like qualities of the music. The hushed and measured account of the introduction sets the tone of seriousness, but joy is in the skipping rhythms of the *Allegro*, while the lyrical breadth of the *Allegretto* is most persuasive. Solti's observance of all the repeats underlines the massiveness of scale. The recording, made in the Sofiensaal in Vienna, is among the finest in the Solti cycle.

Schmidt-Isserstedt gives a magnetic performance that compels attention from first bar to last, with vivid recording quality. Tempi are generally judged with perfect regard for the often conflicting requirements of symphony and dance – not too ponderous, not too hectic. The generous fill-up is most welcome, a dramatic performance of *Leonora No. 3*. For both symphony and overture the Vienna Philharmonic is in outstanding form. There is an excellent cassette.

Loughran's Beethoven is rugged and energetic. The energy shines through, even when – as in the outer movements – he chooses basic tempi a degree more relaxed than is common. Like his Brahms performances for CfP, this account of the *Seventh* conveys an immediate spontaneity, with light and shade fully contrasted. The playing of the Hallé is not always quite so refined as that on the finest rival versions, but this is a powerful contender, with full, atmospheric recording. All repeats are observed. The sound on cassette is full-bodied, but has slightly less range and refinement on top than the LP.

Monteux opens with a powerful slow introduction, followed by a hard-driven 6/8 *Allegro* but with the rhythms nicely pointed, and a fast *Allegretto*, to recall the famous early mono LP by Erich Kleiber. Then comes a wide speed change for the trio after the scherzo, and an absolute headlong finale, with the kind of excitement one usually finds only in a live performance. The effect is ultimately somewhat lightweight, although certainly charismatic. The recording is bright and quite full, but not as clean as the companion records of the *Second* and *Fifth* symphonies. The tape is first-class.

Of all the recordings of Beethoven's *Seventh Symphony* that have been issued in recent years none has caused more interest or controversy than the version by the VPO under Carlos Kleiber. By some voices it has been hailed as the finest since Toscanini; others find it unrelenting; like Toscanini, certainly, but with less lyricism – and certainly this is a performance where symphonic argument never yields to the charms of the dance. Kleiber's incisively dramatic approach is marked instead with sharp dynamic contrasts and thrustful rhythms. Another controversial point is that Kleiber, like his father, maintains the pizzicato for the strings on the final brief phrase of the *Allegretto*, a curious effect. About the recording there is less argument: the quality has a constriction to it and it is much less open than one expects from DG working in Vienna. Yet even this is not all loss, for the spare, leonine quality of the sound somehow matches the intensity and urgency of the argument. This could not sensibly be suggested as a first recommendation for an only purchase, but it is not a record to ignore. The cassette version offers a generally less refined sound than the LP, and there is a hint of coarseness in the very first tutti of the first movement.

The slow introduction of No. 7 in Kempe's version is very measured indeed, and seems the more so, coming after the *Egmont overture*. The main *Allegro* is then attractively relaxed in its dance rhythms (no exposition repeat). The *Allegretto* is kept moving in obedience to that marking, lacking a little in delicacy. Despite clean violin articulation in the finale (taken fast and fiercely) the finale has its roughness too. A bluff attractive reading, well worth its CfP price, with first-rate 1974 sound. The high-level cassette is not as clean in the upper range as the disc, but is admirably vivid. Side two is slightly smoother than side one.

The vigour and drive of Muti's account of the *Seventh* are never in doubt, but, surprisingly, the ensemble of the Philadelphia Orchestra is less than immaculate. There is spontaneity, but it is paid for in lack of precision, which puts this below the very finest versions. It is a fair example of EMI's 'new Philadelphia sound'. The high-level cassette transfer brings a touch of roughness at the opening and close of the symphony and a degree of rawness to the upper string timbre. However, a cutback of treble improves matters considerably.

Maier with the Collegium Aureum aims at an authentic approach with a string group of 19 players merely (6, 5, 3, 3, 2) using gut strings and original instruments. Maier does not favour the abrasiveness of non-vibrato performance, and the result is fresh and direct thanks not only to the transparent textures but to Maier's unforced and unmannered reading. All repeats are observed.

Sir Colin Davis re-recorded the *Seventh* in the mid-1970s for Philips. The performance is more refined than the earlier one and does not lack freshness. The slow introduction, now more weighty, leads to an account of the first movement strikingly crisp in rhythm. This time, too, all the repeats are observed. But the Philips recording has been remastered in an attempt to give more brilliance to the sound, and at fortissimos the focus is not as clean as it was originally, on either disc or cassette. This is still a rewarding performance but the earlier HMV version wears its years more lightly and makes a stronger impact.

Sanderling's reading is disappointing, unsprung and heavy to the point of turgidity in the first movement and lacking intensity elsewhere, with generally slow speeds. The bright digital recording, with a corresponding chrome cassette, is well up to the standard of this series.

Karajan's 1960 recording of the *Seventh*, originally made for Decca, has been reissued at bargain price on Contour, the recording still sounding wide-ranging and full-bodied (on cassette it is bass-heavy, especially in the finale). It is interesting to compare it with the exciting Berlin version on Accolade, made only a year or so later. The effect in Vienna is massive rather than incandescent; the performance refuses to catch fire and the result is heartless.

Symphony No. 8 in F, Op. 93.

(B) *** Con. CC/*CCT* 7503. VPO, Abbado – SCHUBERT: *Symphony No. 8.****

At bargain price Abbado's Contour reissue makes a splendid recommendation. The fresh, alert performance underlines the sun in this symphony. The tempi are all well chosen, the rhythms beautifully sprung and such key moments as the gentle pay-off to the first movement delicately pointed. Some of the abrasiveness of Beethoven is missing, but not the resilience. Coupled with an equally sunny account of Schubert's *Unfinished* and given first-rate recording, which in no way sounds dated, this is one of the highlights of the Contour catalogue. The cassette lacks the upper range of the disc, and the bass sounds muddy.

Symphonies Nos. 8; 9 in D min. (Choral), Op. 125.

** DG 2707/*3370* 109 (2) [id.]. Tomowa-Sintow, Baltsa, Schreier, Van Dam, V. Singverein, Berlin PO, Karajan.

(M) *** DG Acc. 2725/*3372* 101 (2). Janowitz, Rössl-Majdan, Kmentt, Berry, V. Singverein, Berlin PO, Karajan.

*** DG 2707 124/*3370 037* (2) [id.]. Jones, Schwarz, Kollo, Moll, V. State Op. Ch., VPO, Bernstein.

(M) *** EMI Em. EMX/*TC-EMX* 2040 (2) [SZ/*4Z2S* 3880]. Te Kanawa, Hamari, Burrows, Holl, LSO Ch., LSO, Jochum.

**(*) HMV Dig. SLS/*TCC-SLS* 5244 (2). Armstrong, Finnie, Tear, Tomlinson, Philh. Ch. and O, Sanderling.

Symphony No. 9 in D min. (*Choral*), *Op. 125.*
(M) *** Decca 6BB 121/2 *KBB2 7041* [Lon. CSP 8]. Lorengar, Minton, Burrows, Talvela, Chicago Symphony Ch. and SO, Solti.
*** DG Dig. 2741/*3382* 009 (2) [id.]. Norman, Fassbaender, Domingo, Berry, Concert Singers of V. State Op., VPO, Boehm.
(M) *** Decca VIV/*KVIC* 1 [Lon. SPA 21043/5-]. Harper, Watts, Young, McIntyre, LSO Ch., LSO, Stokowski.
(B) *** CfP CFP/*TC-CFP* 41 4418-1/*4*. Koszut, Fassbaender, Gedda, McIntyre, Mun. Philharmonic Ch., Mun. Motet Ch., Mun. PO, Kempe.
(M) *** Decca Jub. JB/*KJBC* 1 [Lon. JL 41004]. Sutherland, Horne, King, Talvela, V. State Op. Ch., VPO, Schmidt-Isserstedt.
** ASV ALH/*ZCALH* 903, Buchanan, Hodgson, Mitchinson, Howell, Hallé Ch. and O, Loughran.
(M) *(*) CBS 60134/*40-* [M/*MT* 31818]. Amara, Chookasian, Alexander, Macurdy, Mormon Tabernacle Ch., Phd. O, Ormandy.
(*) Denon **C37-7021** [id.]. Hajossyova, Priew, Buchner, Schenk, Berlin R. Ch. and State O, Suitner.

Fine as Karajan's earlier reading of the *Ninth* with the Berlin Philharmonic is, his 1977 performance reveals even greater insight, above all in the *Adagio*, where he conveys spiritual intensity at a slower tempo than before. In the finale the concluding eruption has an animal excitement rarely heard from this highly controlled conductor, and the soloists make an excellent team, with contralto, tenor and bass all finer than their predecessors. What is less satisfactory is the balance of the recording. The result may be wider in range but it is less atmospheric and less realistic than before, with the solo voices in the finale unnaturally close.

On the fourth side Karajan directs an electrically tense performance of the *Eighth*, missing some of the joy of Beethoven's 'little one', but justifying his brisk tempi in the brilliant playing of the orchestra. The cassette transfer of both works is of the highest quality: this is one of the very finest-sounding recordings of the *Choral symphony* on tape.

The earlier Karajan version has been reissued at medium price on Accolade and remains excellent value. When recording his 1962 cycle Karajan, in a concentrated series of sessions, kept till the end the biggest challenge of all. The last two symphonies on the list were the *Eroica* and finally the *Ninth*. One senses that feeling of a challenge accepted in triumph throughout this incandescent reading of the symphony, one of the finest ever recorded. Though the great *Adagio* has received more intense readings, the hush of pianissimo has never been recorded with greater purity than here, and the electricity of the finale has all the tension of Karajan at his most inspired. The recording still sounds very well, spaced on three sides. Karajan's sharply dramatic reading of the *Eighth* makes an excellent fill-up. The tape transfer is clear and realistic, although the choral focus in the finale of No. 9 is somewhat grainy.

Boehm was one of the select handful of conductors who made records of the *Choral symphony* during the 78 r.p.m. era. Later he recorded it on mono LP for Philips and more recently as part of his 1972 complete set for DG. Just a few months before he died, he made his final statement on the work in this resplendent new digital set. With generally slow tempi his reading is spacious and powerful – the first movement even has a certain stoic quality – and in its broad concept it has much in common with Klemperer's famous version. Yet overall there is a transcending sense of a great occasion, and the concentration is unfailing, reaching its peak in the glorious finale, where ruggedness and strength well over into inspiration, and that in spite of a pacing nearly as individual as that of Stokowski, notably in the drum and fife march, which is much more serious in feeling than usual. But with an outburst of joy in the closing pages the listener is left in no doubt that this recording was the culmination of a long and distinguished career. With a fine, characterful team of soloists, and a freshly incisive chorus formed from singers of the Vienna State Opera this is strongly recommendable, and many will like the layout, with one movement complete on each side. The chrome cassettes match the discs very closely indeed (the choral focus and transients in the finale are very impressive).

Bernstein's characterful account of the

Ninth superbly crowns his Beethoven series, and in this two-disc set, coupled with a sympathetic account of the *Eighth*, it makes an excellent recommendation. The very start conveys immediate electricity, reflecting the presence of an audience, and the first movement is presented at white heat from first to last, with only a slight rallentando detracting from the thrust. The scherzo is resilient, the *Adagio* deeply convincing in its distinctive contrasting of inner meditation in a very slow first theme with lighter carefree interludes in a fast-flowing *Andante*. In the finale Gwyneth Jones's soprano is as well controlled as it ever has been on record, and otherwise this is a superb account, sung and played with dedication, if a fraction less intense than the earlier movements. The recording, unlike some others in the series, needs no apology: it is bright and immediate. The cassette transfer, however, has been made at rather a low level; the *Eighth Symphony* lacks upper range, and although No. 9 sounds more lively, the choral focus is not absolutely sharp, though the sound itself is bright.

Jochum's reading of the *Ninth* is in the grand German tradition, crowning the whole of a distinguished cycle with the LSO. Uncharacteristically for Jochum, speeds tend to be on the fast side with the massive structures of the first and third movements seamlessly held together. By contrast the scherzo is almost violent in its urgency, and the choral finale too has fierceness in its generally fast speeds with youthful-sounding voices among the soloists as well as in the chorus. In its upper-bargain bracket, this two-disc set makes an excellent choice with its first-rate sound of 1980 vintage. The format means that the slow movement is unbroken. The *Eighth Symphony* on side four brings a strong reading too, for characteristically Jochum refuses to treat it as a lightweight work, linking it more closely than is common with the *Seventh*. The cassettes (packaged in a double-width hinged box) match the discs closely: the choral focus is admirably sharp.

Solti's recording of the *Ninth* is one of his outstanding gramophone achievements. If you regard the sublime slow movement as the key to this epic work, then Solti clearly is with you. With spacious measured tempi he leads the ear on, not only with his phrasing but with his subtle shading of dynamic down to whispered pianissimo. Here is *Innigkeit* of a concentration rarely heard on record, even in the *Ninth*. Solti in the first movement is searing in his dynamic contrasts, maybe too brutally so, while the precision of the finale, with superb choral work and solo singing, confirms this as one of the very finest *Ninth*s on record. Superb recording quality, clean yet coordinated, with an excellent matching double-length cassette.

Stokowski's version, reissued on Decca's newest budget label, Viva, makes an impressive first choice for the *Ninth* in the lower price-range. The recording – originally Phase Four – is excellent, only losing marginally in lower bass amplitude on three-sided versions, and remaining full and vivid. The cassette matches the disc closely. Unmistakably this is a great, compelling account of the *Ninth*. There is the sort of tension about this recorded performance which one expects from a great conductor in the concert hall, and that compulsion carries one over all of Stokowski's idiosyncrasies, including a fair amount of touching up in the orchestration. The first movement is strong and dramatic, taken at a Toscanini pace; the scherzo is light and pointed, with timpani cutting through; the slow movement has great depth and *Innigkeit*, and that perhaps more than anything confirms the greatness of the performance, for the finale, with some strangely slow tempi, is uneven, despite fine singing.

Kempe's fine Munich version, generally plain in manner but exhilarating in impact, appeared originally on three sides, but in this bargain two-sided transfer it has lost nothing at all in quality, for the sound of the orchestra as in the rest of the series is fresh and cleanly detailed. The precision of the shimmering tremolo strings leads to an account of the first movement which is strong and direct but not cataclysmic, though it builds in strength as it progresses. The scherzo is fast and crisply articulated with excellent timpani, the slow movement unaffected in its simple expressiveness. The choral finale then crowns the reading as it should in a spontaneous-sounding expression of joy with a first-rate team of singers.

Schmidt-Isserstedt, with no exaggeration and few if any high-flown purple passages, gives a most satisfying reading of the *Ninth*, which in many ways is easier to live with than more monumental, more obviously great performances. The approach associates the work more readily than most with Beethoven's earlier symphonic achievements – the link with the *Pastoral* at the end of the slow movement, for example – but it is the fine singing of soloists and chorus in the finale that above all makes this one of the keenest current recommendations. All four soloists are in peak form, and few rival versions match the beauty and balance of ensemble. Despite the length of sides the recording quality is outstandingly good. The cassette transfer is of first-class quality, matching the disc closely in weight and detail until the coda of the finale, where there is a miscalculation and the entry of the bass drum muddles the texture unattractively and spoils the work's closing pages.

Sanderling's recorded cycle with the Philharmonia developed out of a live series of concerts. The performances of the *Eighth* and *Ninth symphonies* have a rugged directness – an unvarnished honesty, as one commentator put it – which makes special links here with the Philharmonia Klemperer versions. Like Klemperer, Sanderling prefers slowish tempi, maintained steadily. The *Ninth*, in clear digital sound, may lack mystery at the start, and the finale is dangerously slow; but the power of the work is splendidly caught. The soloists make an excellent team, but the Philharmonia Chorus is just below its best form, the singing of the sopranos not always well supported. The sound on tape matches the discs until the finale, where the choral focus is disappointing.

Loughran gives a direct and unaffected reading of the *Ninth* which may not scale the heights but which makes a fine culmination to his very recommendable series. The single-disc format means both that the turn-over in the slow movement is at an uncomfortable point and that the recording lacks a little in immediacy. But with an interpretation which calls attention to the music rather than to any idiosyncrasy, no one will be disappointed who has ever responded to Loughran's Beethoven. All the repeats are observed in the scherzo. Soloists and choir in the finale are first-rate. The cassette transfer is full-bodied and clear, although in the finale soloists and chorus lack something in presence.

Ormandy, fast and clear-cut even on the opening tremolos, makes it clear that mystery plays no part in his concept of the *Ninth*. Though the resonance of the Philadelphia players, particularly the strings, is as ever impressive, with superb articulation in the scherzo, Beethoven's deeper qualities are smoothed over, above all in the slow movement. Among the soloists the bass is disappointing. Fair if restricted recording.

Suitner's performance of the *Choral symphony* brought the first compact disc lasting over seventy minutes. Otherwise it is as undistinguished a version of this supreme masterpiece as could be imagined, plodding and unimaginative, indifferently played and poorly recorded.

Wellington's victory (sometimes called the *Battle symphony*), *Op. 91*.

(*) CBS Dig. **CD/37252 [id.]. VPO, Maazel – TCHAIKOVSKY: *1812*. *(*).

(M) ** DG Priv. 2538 142 [2536 298]. Berlin PO, Karajan – TCHAIKOVSKY: *1812*.**(*)

(M) *(*) Mercury SRI/*MRI* 75142. LSO, Dorati – TCHAIKOVSKY: *1812*.*(*)

(B) RCA VICS/*VK* 2035 [AGL1/*AGK1* 2700]. O, Gould – TCHAIKOVSKY: *1812*. (***)

Potentially by far the finest recording of Beethoven's flamboyant piece is Morton Gould's Victrola reissue with the opposing forces marching in on the left and right independently and a spectacular expansion of sound for *Rule Britannia*. But after the line-up is completed to the strains of *Marlborough* the recording deteriorates into distortion and obviously the master-tape was hopelessly over-modulated. This is almost worth buying for the first few minutes as the *1812* coupling is thrilling, although the sound again is coarse.

The opening is produced with rather less flair on CBS, but the acoustic is well judged and the performance is certainly engaging with the fanfares and battle noises realistically interpolated. On the compact disc everything is even clearer; but the drawback to this issue is the coupling which is rather harshly recorded.

Karajan's version is very professional and well played and recorded, but there is no sense of occasion and the opening assembly is unimaginatively produced.

Dorati's recording is spoilt by poor balance. After the line-up of troops, clearly separated to the left and right by what is virtually double mono recording, the battle noises swamp the orchestra which retires to the background. The actual musketry sounds like a glorified fireworks display and the cannon produce muddy bass noises. The fanfares are well done, but later in the piece the elegant orchestral playing seems too subdued and refined to be entirely suitable for the occasion.

CHAMBER MUSIC

Cello sonatas Nos. 1–5; Variations, G. 158; Op. 66; G. 157 (for cello and piano); *Violin sonatas Nos. 1–10; Rondo in G, G. 155.*
(M) *** DG 2721 132 (6). Fournier, Menuhin, Kempff.

Fournier's distinguished readings of the *Cello sonatas* were recorded live in Paris and are compulsively alive. Menuhin and Kempff too are much and rightly admired, even though they do not displace the Grumiaux–Haskil mono accounts or challenge the stimulating series Perlman and Ashkenazy have committed to disc for Decca. At only approximately £3 per record, however, these are good value.

Cello sonatas Nos. 1–5, Opp. 5/1–2; Op. 69; Op. 102/1–2.
*** Ph. 6700 027 [835182/3]. Rostropovich, Sviatoslav Richter.
*** HMV SLS 836 (2). Tortelier, Heidsieck.
*(**) CBS Dig. 37251 [id.]. Yo Yo Ma, Ax.

With Jacqueline du Pré's inspirational set with her husband, Daniel Barenboim – recorded live for the BBC during the Edinburgh Festival of 1970 – temporarily withdrawn from the EMI catalogue, choice rests between Rostropovich and Tortelier.

The Philips is an excellent set that has stood the test of time, showing a true partnership between two giants among today's performing artists. There is a considerable difference in style between the music of Op. 5 and Op. 102, written some twenty years later, but the two players are fully equal to such subtleties. Above all these performances are spontaneous and committed. They are well recorded too.

From Tortelier, distinguished performances that make a useful alternative to Rostropovich's set with Richter and are probably slightly better-recorded than the Philips set, which dates from 1964.

Yo Yo Ma plays with extraordinary sensitivity and imagination – so, for that matter, does his partner who has the more brilliant part. Unfortunately the recording balance is very far from ideal and the piano often masks the refined lines that Yo Yo Ma draws. Though the artists have the benefit of truthful digital recording in every other respect, the dominance of the piano is an irritant. No criticism attaches to the pianist whose dynamic range is both wide and consistent. Even if these are sonatas 'with obbligato cello', Yo Yo Ma scales down his playing sufficiently without the need of further assistance. One sometimes despairs at the insensitivity of the CBS recording engineers in this respect, for undoubtedly some ears will find this balance intolerable for repeated listening.

Cello sonata No. 3 in A, Op. 69.
*** HMV Dig. ASD/*TCC*-ASD 4075. Tortelier, De la Pau – SCHUBERT: *Arpeggione sonata.* ***

Unaffected and natural playing that conveys the sense of chamber music-making in the home – for pleasure! There is little sense of the public platform and no attempt to make profound interpretative points. This may not be a great performance but it is very enjoyable and recorded with great fidelity and wide dynamic range. The treble is very slightly restricted in the otherwise excellent chrome cassette transfer but the disc is extraordinarily lifelike.

Clarinet trio in B flat, Op. 11; Piano trios Nos. 1–7; Trio No. 14 in E flat (1784); *Trio in E flat* (1790/91); *14 Variations in E flat, Op. 44; 10 Variations on Müller's 'Ich bin der Schneider Kakadu', Op. 121a.*

(M) **(*) EMI 1C 137 02046/50. Barenboim, du Pré, Zukerman, de Peyer.

The Barenboim/Zukerman/du Pré set of Beethoven's music for piano trio was recorded in an intensive series of sessions spread over a week at the EMI Abbey Road studios. Even more than usual for Barenboim, the individual takes involved long spans of music, often complete movements, sometimes even a complete work. The result is playing of rare concentration, spontaneity and warmth. Any tendency to self-indulgence (and this is an aspect of the playing R.L. finds obtrusive), plus a certain leaning towards romantic expressiveness, are counterbalanced by the urgency and intensity of the playing. Speeds tend to be extreme in both directions, and the *Innigkeit* of some of the slow movements, especially in the *Ghost trio*, Op. 70/1, has the depth of really mature artistry, extraordinary in the work of such young musicians. The first movement of the *Archduke trio* offers the most controversial performance. The speed is uncharacteristically slow, and the music's weight seems minimized. But this is counterbalanced by a slow movement of great depth and eloquence and an exuberant finale. The extra items include an early work in E flat (1784) and another written in 1790–91. Of the variations, the *Kakadu* set is given a superlative performance, and Gervase de Peyer joins the team for the *Clarinet trio*, which is played most beautifully. The recording is excellent throughout, and although these performances will not suit all tastes (and at the moment one has to purchase the whole set), there is no question about their integrity.

Clarinet trio in B flat, Op. 11; Piano trios Nos. 1–6 and 10; in E flat, WoO. 38; in E flat; (Variations), Op. 44; 10 Variations on Müller's 'Ich bin der Schneider Kakadu', Op. 121a; Piano quartets Nos. 1–3.

(M) *** DG 2721 132 (6). Leister, Kempff, Szeryng, Fournier, Eschenbach, members of the Amadeus Qt.

This compilation scores over its rival in offering the early *Piano quartets* played by Eschenbach and the Amadeus. It also includes the Op. 11 *Trio* with Karl Leister as clarinet, though the EMI set with Zukerman, du Pré and Barenboim includes this, too. The Kempff, Szeryng and Fournier performances are eminently civilized and enjoyable and there is not much to choose between them and the Beaux Arts (see below).

Clarinet trio in B flat, Op. 11.

*** Ph. 9500 670/*7300 826* [id.]. Pieterson, Pressler, Greenhouse – BRAHMS: *Clarinet trio.****

*** HMV Dig. ASD/*TC-ASD* 146784-1/*4*. Meyer, Buchbinder, Schiff – BRAHMS: *Clarinet trio.****

(M) *** Decca Ace SDD 528. Schmidl, New V. Octet (members) – *Septet.****

**(*) CRD CRD 1045 (with *Clarinet trio* by Archduke Rudolph of Austria). Nash Ens.

This *Trio* comes from 1798 and its last movement consists of a set of variations on a theme from Weigl's opera *L'Amor marinaro*. Beethoven later thought sufficiently well of the work to consider writing another finale for it and letting the variations stand on their own as a separate entity. George Pieterson is the first clarinet of the Concertgebouw Orchestra, and his playing is distinguished by refined tone and sensitive phrasing; Menahem Pressler, the pianist of the Beaux Arts Trio, is no less vital and imaginative than he is in the sparkling set of Haydn *Trios*, and the Op. 11 *Trio* sounds very persuasive. This is a distinguished and enjoyable record, and the tape transfer is excellent too, warm and vivid.

However, the HMV version is by no means outclassed and some may prefer it. The digital recording has striking presence and clarity, yet the sound has warmth and realism while the high-level cassette transfer is in the demonstration class. Sabine Meyer is very impressive indeed, and if Heinrich Schiff projects a little less personality than his rival in the Beaux Arts, there is still much fine musicianship in evidence and the playing is both fresh and well integrated.

The New Vienna Octet also make a better case for the Op. 11 *Trio* than most previous rivals. The playing is wonderfully alert and has both sparkle and warmth. In this repertoire couplings tend to determine choice, and in that respect this Decca Ace of Diamonds issue cannot be faulted; taken on artistic merit alone, this is second to none. The sound is first-rate.

The Nash Ensemble's account has a royal rarity as coupling; Archduke Rudolph was a son of an Austrian emperor. But his claim to fame is as a pupil and friend of Beethoven; he was a good enough pianist to take part in the *Triple concerto* and he subscribed to the fund that gave support to Beethoven after the onset of his deafness. His *Clarinet trio* is incomplete: of the closing rondo, only a fragment survives, and this performance ends with the slow movement, a set of variations on a theme by yet another prince, Louis Ferdinand of Prussia. The music may be no great shakes but it is more than just a curiosity, and its inclusion on this record is welcome. The playing is thoroughly persuasive, with some attractive pianism from the excellent Clifford Benson. Much the same goes for the performance of the Beethoven *Trio*, and though obviously not an indispensable issue, this is well worth investigating for interest.

Clarinet trio; Horn sonata in F, Op. 17; 7 Variations on Mozart's 'Bei Männern' from 'Die Zauberflöte', WoO. 46.
*** ASV ACA 1005. Music Group of L.

Well-recorded and finely played versions of some less important Beethoven pieces. This is natural, unaffected playing – thoroughly musical and unfailingly intelligent, and the sound quality is faithful. In Alan Civil's hands the *Horn sonata* holds its own against some distinguished rival versions, and the performance of the *Clarinet trio*, with Keith Puddy in excellent form, also has much to commend it.

Cor anglais sonata in F, Op. 17. Trio in C, Op. 87; Variations on Mozart's 'Là ci darem', WoO, 28 (both for 2 oboes and cor anglais).
*** Ph. 9500 672/*7300 767* [id.]. Holliger, Elhorst, Bourgue, Wyttenbach.

An enterprising issue. The *C major Trio*, Op. 87, occupies one side. Despite its late opus number, it is an early work dating from 1794, and its scale is larger than its neglect would lead one to expect. There are four movements, which show no mean degree of organic cohesion and an awareness of formal design. The *Là ci darem Variations* were performed in 1797 but not published until the present century. They are also ingeniously written and often diverting. The *Horn sonata*, Op. 17, which is somewhat later (1800), transposes to the cor anglais quite effectively. It goes without saying that these artists make the most of the possibilities here and are accorded excellent and well-balanced sound. None of this is major Beethoven but the catalogues are richer for its appearance. The cassette transfer matches the disc closely: it is strikingly fresh and clear.

Piano trios Nos. 1–11; Trio in E flat (from *Septet*), *Op. 38; Trio in D* (from *Symphony No. 2*)*; Trio movement in E flat.*
** Ph. 6725/*7655* 035 (7/5). Beaux Arts Trio.

Unlike their earlier set made in the late 1960s and accommodated at mid-price on four records – see below – the present box offers absolutely everything Beethoven composed (or arranged) for this medium and runs to seven records. The performances are as accomplished and musical as one would expect from this celebrated team and the recordings, too, are very good. However, those who possess the earlier set can rest content, for it has a freshness and sparkle that these new accounts do not wholly match. Four of the recordings are digital and these have matching chrome tapes; the other cassettes are satisfactorily transferred on ferric stock and the sound remains refined, although the level is not especially high.

Piano trios: Nos. 1–6; in B flat, Op. 11; in B flat (*in one movement*), *Op. posth.; in E flat* (*Variations*), *Op. 44; 10 Variations, Op. 121a.*
(M) **(*) Ph. 6747 142 (4) [id.]. Beaux Arts Trio.

The Beaux Arts are let down a little by the ungenerous tone of their leader, Daniel Guilet, but the spritely and sensitive playing of Menahem Pressler is a constant source of delight. Tempi are admirably chosen (save for the *Ghost trio*, which is too brisk), and phrasing is marvellously alive. Ultimately the Beaux Arts score on account of the chamber-music quality of their playing. They convey the sense of superb music-making in the home rather than the concert hall. The recording is excellently balanced.

Piano trios: in B flat, Op. 11; No. 4 in D (Ghost), Op. 70/1; 10 Variations on 'Ich bin der Schneider Kakadu', Op. 121a.
(M) *** Ph. 6527/*7311* 077. Beaux Arts Trio.

Piano trio No. 4.
(M) ** HMV SXLP/*TC-SXLP* 30523. H. and Y. Menuhin, Gendron – SCHUBERT: *Trout quintet.***

Piano trios Nos. 4; 5 in E flat, Op. 70/1–2.
(M) **(*) DG Acc. 2542/*3342* 125. Kempff, Szeryng, Fournier.

Piano trio No. 6 in B flat (Archduke).
(M) **(*) Ph. 6570/*7310* 917. Beaux Arts Trio.
(M) **(*) DG Acc. 2542/*3342* 118. Kempff, Szeryng, Fournier.
** Ph. 9500/*7300* 895 [id.]. Beaux Arts Trio.

Piano trio No. 6 (Archduke); 10 in B flat, G. 154.
*** HMV Dig. ASD/*TCC-ASD* 4315. Ashkenazy, Perlman, Harrell.
** (*) HMV ASD/*TC-ASD* 2572. Barenboim, Zukerman, du Pré.

No need for hesitation in considering the Ashkenazy–Perlman–Harrell recording of the *Archduke*. This is in every respect a most musical and masterly performance and is excellently recorded. Even in a highly competitive field, this is very much a front runner; there is spontaneity, warmth and a feeling for architecture. In its cassette format, the sound is equally wide-ranging and vivid, as it is on the LP.

The outstanding quality of the performance by Barenboim, Zukerman and du Pré is its sense of spontaneity – not surprising when it was recorded in very long takes of more than one movement at a time. The slow movement, so hushed and intense one catches one's breath, provides the peak of the experience. The first movement is rather wayward, but rhythmic point grips the attention, and the second and fourth movements are nothing less than sparkling. The early *B flat Trio* makes a brief but worthwhile fill-up. Good recording. The cassette, issued more recently than the disc, is transferred at a high level and has striking immediacy and presence, although there is also a hint of brittleness on the piano timbre.

The earlier Beaux Arts recording of the *Archduke* dates from 1965 but does not sound its age. The recording indeed is admirably natural with an attractive bloom on the sound, yet detail is clear. The approach is not unlike that of the later version, but has more spontaneity, and the overall feeling is of lightness and grace. The scherzo is a delight and elsewhere there is an attractive pervading lyricism. Some might like a weightier approach, but this is highly rewarding in its own way and very easy to live with. The cassette is of high quality, matching the disc fairly closely.

The later version was designed as a twenty-fifth anniversary issue, but sadly it proved one of the least compelling recordings from that superb group. The first movement, at a very slow tempo, sounds self-conscious and mannered; the scherzo fails to maintain its spring and so does the finale. The slow variations have little sense of flow. The recording quality is excellent, and as ever the ensemble is immaculate. The cassette is of excellent quality, if without quite the sharpness of internal focus of the disc.

The other Beaux Arts issue is an economical and attractive rearrangement of performances that originally appeared in different couplings. The Op. 11 trio, which is split over two sides of the disc, is usually heard in its clarinet version. The Beaux Arts players are on excellent form here, and they project the drama and intensity of the *Ghost trio* to brilliant effect. The *Kakadu variations* are played with characteristic elegance too. The recordings date from the mid-1960s (when Daniel Guilet was the violinist) but they still sound fresh and lifelike. Good value, particularly at medium price. The cassette transfer is natural and well balanced.

Kempff and his colleagues give a crystalline reading of the *Archduke*. It is the clarity and imagination of Kempff's playing which set the tone of the whole performance. He it is who grips the listener's attention with his individual touches of genius, so that by comparison Szeryng and Fournier sound less than inspired. An interesting but not a definitive version. In the coupling of the two

Op. 70 *Trios* the performances are again comparatively restrained. As a whole these are sweet and lyrical rather than dramatic readings, but they are naturally recorded. Both issues are available in excellent cassette versions, with fresh, clean transfers.

On the HMV mid-priced disc the *Ghost trio* makes a generous coupling for the *Trout quintet*. This performance dates from the mid-1960s, and on its first appearance we deplored the fact that the piano part was outweighed by the closer balance given to violin and cello; and we still feel that this diminishes the attractions of a good performance. The sound is also rather dry, and this is especially noticeable on the cassette, where the violin timbre lacks bloom.

Piano and wind quintet in E flat, Op. 16.

*** Decca SXL 6252 [Lon. CS 6494]. Ashkenazy, L. Wind Soloists – MOZART: *Quintet*.***

*** CRD CRD 1067/*CRDC 4067*. Nash Ens. – MOZART: *Quintet*.***

(M) *(*) Ph. 6570/*7310* 881. Haebler, members of Bamberg Wind Quintet – MOZART: *Quintet*.*(*)

The Beethoven is less interesting than the Mozart *Quintet* which plainly inspired it, except from the pianist's standpoint. Of these two recommended versions, Ashkenazy and the London Wind Soloists secure the greater measure of brilliance, and the performance has great spontaneity; the Decca recording too has admirable presence and immediacy.

The Nash Ensemble (with Ian Brown as pianist) gives a fresh and intelligent account of the *Quintet*, which makes an excellent alternative. This *Quintet* is no masterpiece and may need the greater projection that the Decca team brings to it, but this is natural and unforced playing that yields equally musical rewards. The recording balance is less forward than Decca's, and the overall result is more pleasing. The cassette is first-class too.

The Philips performance is disappointing. Ingrid Haebler makes a considerable contribution, but the supporting wind group are not especially imaginative and the finale lacks impetus. There is a good cassette.

Septet in E flat, Op. 20.

(M) *** Decca Ace SDD 528. New V. Octet (members) – *Clarinet trio*.***

(M) **(*) Con. CC/*CCT* 7589. Melos Ens.

**(*) Ph. 9500/*7300* 873 [id.]. ASMF Chamber Ens.

(M) ** DG Priv. 2535/*3335* 328. Berlin Octet (members) – MOZART: *Sonata for bassoon and cello*.**

** HM IC 065 99713. Coll. Aur.

(M) ** Ph. Seq. 6527/*7311* 066. Berlin Philharmonic Octet (members).

The older Vienna Octet's recording (also on Decca Ace of Diamonds, but now withdrawn) held sway in the catalogue for more than two decades. It had great lightness of touch and spontaneity and the *Penguin Stereo Record Guide* forecast that it would be 'a long time before [this] work receives a better all-round performance'. Like the earlier ensemble, the New Vienna Octet consists of the first desks of the VPO. This later version has all the elegance of the earlier one but conveys a sparkle and a sense of enjoyment that are thoroughly exhilarating. In terms of spirit and exuberance it is altogether special. The recording is first-class.

The Melos recording, reissued on Contour, dates from the beginning of the 1960s, but the recording has remarkable presence and immediacy and indeed tape collectors may consider this a first choice (the Decca cassette has been withdrawn) as it is expertly transferred and is quite the equal of the disc. The performance is more tensely organized, bright rather than mellifluous in tone, urgent rather than leisurely. There is less of a sense of fun than in the Decca version, but there is some magnificent playing here (the group includes Gervase de Peyer, William Waterhouse, Neil Saunders Emanuel Hurwitz and Cecil Aronowitz) and the freshness of the music-making offsets the tautness.

The Academy players give a highly accomplished and thoroughly musical account of the *Septet* which has the merit of excellent balance and truthful recording, the cassette only marginally less clean and lively than the disc. It is completely enjoyable and thoroughly recommendable, and were competition not quite so stiff it would rate an unqualified three stars. But it does not have quite the same sense of character or profile as its rivals.

Made in the mid-1960s, the Berlin Octet's Privilege version has much to recommend it, not least the highly accomplished wind playing. By comparison with its rivals, however, it seems a shade self-aware and is not free from expressive point-making. The recording is excellent on disc and cassette alike.

The Collegium Aureum retains some modern practices (a little vibrato and the occasional expressive bulge) but plays with plenty of life. The clarinet is less smooth than in our day, and the horn somewhat uneven (had it been even, there would have been no need for the valve horn). It seems a paradox that our age should revive instruments that musicians of the period found inadequate. The playing is splendidly accomplished and admirably recorded, and collectors wishing to sample the *Septet* on period instruments need not hesitate. For the non-specialist collector there are better and cheaper records.

On the Philips Sequenza reissue the Berlin players take a somewhat solemn view. This is a refined performance, beautifully recorded, but next to the Decca version it lacks wit and sparkle. The high-level tape transfer produces excellent quality, and there is little to choose between tape and disc.

Wind music

(i) *Flute trio* (for flute, bassoon, piano) *in G*; (ii) *Horn sonata in F, Op 17*; (iii; v) *Piano and wind quintet, Op. 16*; (iv) *Serenade in D for flute, violin and viola, Op. 25*; (v) *Septet, Op. 20*; *Sextet in E flat, Op. 81b; Wind octet in E flat, Op. 103*; *Wind sextet in E flat, Op. 71.*

(M) *** DG 2721 129 (5). (i) Kontarsky, Zöller, Thunemann; (ii) Seifert, Demus; (iii) Demus; (iv) Zöller, Brandis, Ueberschaer; (v) members of the Berlin PO.

These are beautifully alert, civilized performances, and they are recorded with the utmost clarity and definition. There is no rival compilation currently on the market, and even if there were, it is difficult to imagine it surpassing the present set.

String quartets

String quartets Nos. 1–16; Grosse Fuge, Op. 133.

*** Ph. 6747 272 (10) [id.]. Italian Qt.

(M) **(*) HMV SLS 857 (10) [Sera. SIC 6005/6 and 510 6007]. Hungarian Qt.

String quartets Nos. 1–16; String quartet in F (transcription of *Piano sonata No. 9, Op. 14/1*)*: Grosse Fuge, Op. 133;* (i) *String quintet in C, Op. 29.*

(M) ** DG 2721 130 (11) [(d) 2720 110]. Amadeus Qt, (i) with Aronowitz.

The Italians took a decade to complete their odyssey through the Beethoven quartets, and this box is arguably the finest complete cycle ever to appear. The Végh Quartet (see below) at times penetrate more deeply, particularly in the late quartets, but they are not as well recorded, nor do they possess the purity of intonation, perfection of ensemble, beauty and richness of tone that distinguish the Italians. The recording is absolutely superb, totally lifelike and with fine body. There may be individual misses here and there but, taken overall, this is a very fine achievement.

The Hungarians' readings are sound and unmannered and in the late quartets a good deal more perceptive than the Amadeus's. The recording too is lively and vivid; but the Italians are to be preferred both as performances and certainly as recordings.

The Amadeus are at their best in the Op. 18 quartets, where their mastery and polish are heard to good advantage. In the middle-period and late quartets their sumptuous tone and refinement of balance are always in evidence, but they do not always penetrate very far beneath the surface. Norbert Brainin's vibrato often sounds disturbing and a shade self-regarding, and the readings, particularly of the late quartets, no longer sound freshly experienced as they did when this ensemble was first before the public. There is some superb quartet playing in this cycle, but there are more searching accounts of the late quartets to be found.

String quartets Nos. 1–6, Op. 18/1–6.

(M) *** ASV ALHB 304 (3). Lindsay Qt.

*** HMV SLS/*TC-SLS* 5217 (3). Alban Berg Qt.
(M) *** Ph. 6703 081 (3) [id.]. Italian Qt.
*** Valois CMB 31 (3). Végh Qt.
(M) **(*) Decca Dig. D 280 D 3 (3). Gabrieli Qt.
*(*) CBS 3-37868 Juilliard Qt.
*(*) CBS Dig. D 3-37868 (3) [id.]. Juilliard Qt.

The great merit of the Lindsay Quartet in Beethoven is the natural expressiveness of the playing, most strikingly of all in slow movements, where even in these early works such movements as the D minor *Adagio affetuoso* of No. 1 has a hushed inner quality too rarely caught on record. The sense of spontaneity brings the obverse quality that these are not as precise performances as those in the finest rival sets, but there are few Beethoven quartet recordings that so convincingly bring out the humanity of the writing, its power to communicate warmly and immediately. Others are more immaculate, but the Lindsays have more to say with imaginative detail in every phrase. The recording, set against a fairly reverberant acoustic, is warm and realistic.

Otherwise the Alban Berg set of the Op. 18 quartets is a strong front-runner. The affectation that we noted in this Quartet's set of the *Rasumovskys* (the tendency to exaggerate dynamic extremes) is less obtrusive here, and the overall sense of style is so sure and the technical accomplishment so satisfying, that few readers are likely to be disappointed. Moreover, the quality of the recorded sound is altogether excellent, and in this respect, for some collectors the clarity and body may well tip the scales in the Berg Quartet's favour. It can certainly be recommended alongside the Italian Quartet issue, and this has the advantage of an excellent cassette alternative.

The Italian Quartet's performances are in superb style and are beautifully recorded. The Cleveland [ARL3-3485] (not available in the UK) offer a coherent and thoughtful account of the Op. 18 quartets, perhaps more impetuous than the Végh and the Italian performances and, in the long run, probably less satisfying. But the Cleveland players have obviously thought deeply about these quartets, and in the accompanying notes they argue coherently for the accuracy of Beethoven's metronome markings. They are unusual in that they repeat the second halves of the first movements of the *A major* and *B flat Quartets* (the latter is taken at an enormous speed). The readings as a whole are not free from expressive point-making, and there are some pretty controversial interpretative decisions: the development of the first movement of the *C minor* is too symphonic in feeling and the introduction to the finale is rushed. Both the Italian and the Végh Quartets are more reposeful and humane: the Cleveland sometimes seem to try too hard to make detail come alive and they indulge in agogic exaggerations, albeit of a musical and legitimate nature. The playing is enormously accomplished; the recording is a little too hard in climaxes.

The performances of Op. 18 from the Végh Quartet have been much and rightly admired. They combine strength and warmth in equal measure, and even in the slow movement of No. 1 they penetrate further than most of their rivals. Some readers may be slightly put out by the leader's vibrato, but, this apart, the performances can be highly recommended. The sound is firm and full.

The first two quartets in the Gabrieli set appeared in the mid-1970s on Ace of Diamonds analogue recording (see below) while the remaining four come in new digital sound. Phrasing is alive, rhythmic articulation well-defined and they are responsive to the overall shape of the architecture. The first side of the set has now been re-cut though there is a trace of rumble at the close of the slow movement. Nos. 3 and 4 are recorded in the somewhat reverberant acoustic of St Barnabas Church and Nos. 5 and 6 revert to Kingsway Hall. The recordings are very good and faithfully reproduce the fine-grained sound this ensemble produces in the concert hall. The Gabrielis give a good account of the *D Major* (No. 3) and are eminently sane and sound; they make no attempt to invest detail with excessive significance, yet at the same time are not wanting in personality. There is a trace of blandness in the slow movement and the leader could characterize his theme in the trio section of the third movement to greater effect. In the stormy first movement of the *C minor* (No. 4), the Gabrielis are suitably dark and impassioned and it would be difficult to flaw their reading. Yet other ensembles (the Alban

Berg with its greater tonal bloom, or the Quartetto Italiano) bring greater intensity to this music: the Gabrielis are enormously accomplished and well-paced, but rival groups are better projected and more compelling. No. 5 fares better: the first movement is beautifully played and the leader floats the line with splendid freedom. (They are better in tune than, say, the Lindsays, and more polished than the Végh.) They are beautifully suave in the slow movement – one of the best things in the whole set – and their account of No. 6 is also successful with a spirited and winning first movement, and it certainly holds its own as a performance and recording with its rivals.

Summing up, taken on their merits, these performances are very satisfying in spite of minor quibbles and they are well-recorded. They are more polished though less characterful than the Lindsays but, though they can be recommended, it would not be in preference to the Quartetto Italiano, the Alban Berg or Végh ensembles. There is no cassette version.

The Juilliard box is newly recorded and derives not from their earlier complete cycle of the mid-1970s but from 'live' performances at the Library of Congress, Washington, in 1982. The sound quality is dry and one could well be forgiven for thinking that the venue was a fairly small studio. Although the playing is of a high order of accomplishment, it is not the equal of the Végh, the Quartetto Italiano or the Alban Berg – or in fact any of the current alternatives who enjoy infinitely superior sound.

String quartets Nos. 1 in F; 2 in G, Op. 18/1–2.
(M) *** Ph. 6503/*7303* 059. Italian Qt.
(M) *** Decca Ace SDD 478 [Lon. STS 15398]. Gabrieli Qt.
*** Cal. CAL 1631/*4631* [id.]. Talich Qt.

This is the first of what is presumably to be the reissue of all the Italian versions of the *Op. 18 Quartets* on individual records and represents a sensible re-coupling. The performances are in superb style and immaculately recorded with a splendid cassette transfer of demonstration quality.

The Gabrielis are a well-balanced and intelligent team whose readings of both quartets hold their own against stiff competition. In No. 1 they show consistent vitality and imagination; their phrasing is alive, rhythmic articulation is well-defined, and they are responsive to the overall shape of the structure. There is an appealing freshness about their playing, and the slow movement fares particularly well. It has gentleness and reticence, and its melodic line is most sensitively shaped without the slightest trace of exaggerated expressive feeling. In No. 2 they give a no less impressive account of themselves, and although their rivals are at times more authoritative, the freshness and naturalness of their playing as well as the excellence of the Decca recording make this a most competitive issue.

The Talich versions too are first-class performances with well-judged tempi, a real feeling for architecture and sensitivity to detail. The Talich produce finely blended tone and the recording enables detail to come across with warmth and clarity though some may find it a little bottom-heavy. At times (in the slow movement of the *G major*, for example) the leader, Petr Messiereur, is a little too reticent, and in the first movement of the *F major* they are perhaps more measured and more restrained in feeling than such rivals as the Gabrielis and the Alban Berg. Generally speaking, however, these are finely characterized and keenly-felt performances that can be warmly recommended. We have not heard the cassette.

String quartets Nos. 7 in F; 8 in E min.; 9 in C (Rasumovsky Nos. 1–3), Op. 59/1–3; 10 in E flat (Harp), Op. 74; 11 in F min., Op. 95.
*** Valois CMB 32 (3). Végh Qt.
(M) *** Ph. 6747 139 (2) [id.]. Italian Qt.
*** Cal. CAL 163436 (3) *CAL 4636/7* and *8* [id.]. Talich Qt.
(M) **(*) HMV SLS/*TC-SLS* 5171 (3) [Sera. SIC 6122]. Alban Berg Qt.
** [ARL4 3010] (available in USA only). Cleveland Qt.

String quartets Nos. 7–9.
(M) *** Decca Ace D 214 D 2 (2). Gabrieli Qt.

String quartets Nos. 8 and 11.
*** Cal. CAL 1634/*CAL 4634* [id.]. Talich Qt.

String quartet No. 9.
**(*) DG 410 652-1/*4* [id.]. Amadeus Qt – HAYDN: *String quartet No. 76.* **(*)

String quartets Nos. 10 and 11.
(M) *** Ph. 6570/*7310* 746. Italian Qt.
**(*) ASV ACA/*ZCACA* 1012. Lindsay Qt.
(M) *(*) Argo ZK 81. Allegri Qt.

The Végh performances were originally issued on the Telefunken label, but have now reverted to an import label, Valois, so may need some perseverance to obtain. But on balance, the Végh Quartet gives us by far the most searching and thoughtful account of the middle-period quartets, and for once it is possible to speak of one set being the best. These performances may not always have the high technical finish that distinguishes the Italians or other rivals, but they possess abundant humanity and insight. Végh himself commands great beauty of tone and range of colour; his phrases breathe naturally and yet he constantly surprises one by the imaginative way he shapes a line or the sheer quality and range of the pianissimo tone on which he can draw. He is occasionally under the note, but this is rarely disturbing. At no point does one feel, either from him or from his colleagues, that beauty of tone is the first and overriding consideration. Beauty is the by-product, as it were, of the search for truth and never an end in itself. All the way through, right from the opening of Op. 59/1, one feels they offer the tempo giusto, and throughout they show the same alertness of articulation and rhythmic grasp, yet with a flexibility and subtlety that are masterly. Only in the slow movement of Op. 59/1 does one feel that the Italian Quartet is more searching, though it is undoubtedly the more perfect quartet in many ways.

The Italians have the advantage of much finer recording, and no one listening to two excerpts side by side would doubt their superiority in terms of sheer quartet playing: purity of intonation, perfectly blended tone and superb ensemble and attack. Their tempi are perfectly judged, and every phrase is shaped sensitively. Yet there is no attempt to 'beautify' Beethoven, and given the superb quality of the recorded sound these are in some ways a safer recommendation. Végh is a little recessed at times: the recording is less well balanced and is a bit bottom-heavy. But reservations should not diminish the strength of one's recommendation for the Végh set: there are many places where one feels that they offer more illumination and wisdom than do their distinguished colleagues.

The Talich Quartet was formed in the 1960s and takes its name from its violist, Jan Talich, nephew of the great Czech conductor. These performances have the air of authority and the fine musical judgement that distinguishes their versions of the late quartets. The recordings are similar too, with a tendency to be a little bottom-heavy (as, for that matter, are those of the Végh Quartet). Tempi are sensible throughout, and the phrasing is unfailingly musical. The cassettes (available separately) are transferred at a high level and the sound is lively and full, the upper range slightly less sharp than the discs.

The Gabrieli Quartet gives an account of the three *Rasumovskys* that can hold its own with the very best of its rivals. The layout of the two records differs from its immediate rivals: the Italians accommodate Op. 59/1 and the first movement of Op. 59/2 on the first record, and the rest on the second. The Gabrielis begin with the *E minor*, observing the exposition repeat in the first movement, and then proceed to the first movement of Op. 59/1. Although the ensemble of the Italians is superior in one or two places and their tonal blend is more finely integrated, this playing is still extremely impressive and often really distinguished. The recording is warm and vivid. This can be recommended alongside (but not in preference to) the Végh, Talich, or Italian Quartets.

The Alban Berg Quartet is an assured and alert group with finely blended tone and excellent attack. They have been particularly successful in their Mozart and Schubert issues and have an enviable reputation – rightly so. Generally speaking, they favour rather brisk tempi in the first movements, which they dispatch with exemplary polish and accuracy of intonation. Indeed, an almost unsmiling momentum is maintained when they reach the quaver theme in thirds in the first movement of Op. 59/1, where almost every other quartet relaxes just a little. The slow movement of Op. 59/1 is free from excessive point-making of the kind that mars the Cleveland version, and throughout this quartet and its companions there is much perceptive music-making. Rhythms are marvellously sprung and every phrase is vividly characterized. One generalization can be made: there is a distinct tendency to exaggerate dynamic extremes. The introduction to Op. 59/3 suffers in this respect, and the results sound self-conscious. In the first movements of Op. 59/2 and Op. 95 the brilliance of the attack almost draws attention to itself, and perhaps the recording quality, which is a little closely balanced, gives it a slightly more aggressive quality than it really has. As quartet playing, however, this is superlative and in some respects (such as ensemble and intonation) it would be difficult to fault. But this is not the whole picture, and while this remains the most accomplished and generally successful *Rasumovsky* set to appear since our last volume, it does not dislodge either the Végh or the Italians. The Végh are by no means as perfect in terms of ensemble and they are not as well recorded but both they and the excellently recorded Philips set of the Italians inhabit a world far more closely related to the deep humanity and vision of this music. The Alban Berg recordings of the *Rasumovskys* are alone in the tape catalogue; the cassette transfers are of admirable quality, rich and clear.

The Cleveland Quartet is an accomplished body with a well-integrated approach to these scores, a splendid unanimity of ensemble and fine intonation. Dynamic nuances are faithfully observed and there is a wide range of colour as well as a distinctive surface polish. As a body, however, these players favour an overtly (and, perhaps, overly) expressive style that will not be to all tastes. The leader's tone is sweet but a little wanting in richness, though the lack of warmth in the overall sound quality may enhance this impression. At times the Cleveland's sonority is impressively big and symphonic, as if they were relating this music to Beethoven's middle-period orchestral output. There is a lot of expressive point-making, particularly in the slow movements of Op. 59/1 and 2, and again in the first movement of Op. 95, where they pull back for the D flat theme, which is then sentimentalized. There is no doubting the virtuosity of the group (the finale of Op. 59/3 is played with tremendous attack and brilliance) but the humanity and depth of these scores are better revealed elsewhere. The recordings, too, are a little wanting in warmth, though there is clarity and separation.

The Amadeus account of the *Third Rasumovsky quartet*, coupled with Haydn's Op. 76/2, comes from a public concert given at the Wigmore Hall in January 1983 to mark their thirty-fifth anniversary; hence tuning and applause are included, and the performance has the feel of a living musical experience. Doubtless there would have been an attempt to cover certain inelegances were this a studio performance, but the loss in terms of a sense of occasion and real musical flow far outweighs any blemishes. Brainin's vibrato is very personal and does not appeal to all listeners but, this apart, collectors will find much more to admire than to cavil at.

At mid-price and in freshly-minted pressings, the Italians' coupling of Op. 74 and Op. 95 retains its hold on the collector's allegiance. The Quartetto Italiano give beautifully shaped readings in both pieces, as eloquent as they are unmannered. There is a superb polish to their playing and the sound is as refined and vivid as you could wish. The cassette is in the demonstration class.

There is much to admire in the Lindsay coupling of Opp. 74 and 95. They take an unhurried view of the slow movements where they are generally penetrating but there are some rough edges, tonally speaking, elsewhere. They are not quite as well recorded as the Gabrielis – nor in fact as the somewhat older Quartetto Italiano. The cassette is also of good quality, though it is not as lively in the upper range as the disc.

There is some sensitive playing from the Allegri Quartet in the slow movements of the *Harp* and Op. 95 and no want of musical intelligence. But the playing can also be a little heavy-handed and wanting in refinement, though some of this impression may be due to a rather bottom-heavy recording.

String quartets Nos. 12 in E flat, Op. 127; 13 in B flat, Op. 130; 14 in C sharp min., Op. 131; 15 in A min., Op. 132; 16 in F, Op. 135; Grosse Fuge, Op. 133.

(M) *** ASV ALHB 403 (4). Lindsay Qt.
*** Valois CMB 33 (4). Végh Qt.
(M) **(*) Ph. *7656 348* [id.]. Italian Qt.
(M) (***) HMV mono RLS/*TC-RLS* 7707 (4). Hollywood Qt.

(M) ** DG Priv. 2734 006 (4). Amadeus Qt.

String quartets Nos. 12–13; 16; Grosse Fuge.
(M) *** Ph. 6768 341 (2) [id.]. Italian Qt.

String quartets Nos. 12 and 16.
*** HMV ASD/*TC-ASD* 4305. Alban Berg Qt.
*** Cal. 1640/*4640* [id.]. Talich Qt.

String quartet No. 13; Grosse Fuge.
*** Cal. CAL 1637/*4637* [id.]. Talich Qt.
**(*) HMV ASD/*TC-ASD* 143563-1/*4*. Alban Berg Qt.
**(*) ASV ACA/*ZCACA* 1006. Lindsay Qt.

String quartet No. 14.
*** Cal. CAL 1638/*4638* [id.]. Talich Qt.

String quartets Nos. 14–15.
(M) **(*) Ph. 6768 347 (2) [id.]. Italian Qt.

String quartet No. 15.
*** Cal. CAL 1639/*4639* [id.]. Talich Qt.

The Lindsays get far closer to the essence of this great music than many more illustrious ensembles and offer performances that are distinctly superior to their earlier records of Op. 18. They have the benefit of better balanced recording than the Végh and the Talich which are both a little bottom-heavy: the sound on the ASV set is more present and vivid on disc and cassette alike. They seem to find tempi that somehow strike the listener as completely right and which enable them to convey so much both of the letter and of the spirit. Finding the tempo that completely matches an artist's conception both of detail and of the overall architecture and vision of a piece is crucial, for it enables a phrase to breathe in a way that harmonizes exactly with the interpreters' intentions, and it is this that gives the impression of complete naturalness. The slow movement of Op. 135 is much broader than, say, the Alban Berg Quartet who produce the more integrated and beautiful sound, yet do not penetrate quite the same depths as the Lindsays. In terms of tonal blend and refinement of ensemble, the Alban Berg are probably superior in Op. 127, but the Lindsays bring such richness of characterization and musical strength. The first movement is excellently paced: everything seems so completely natural, and dynamic markings, which are scrupulously observed, never seem extreme. There is some wonderfully rapt playing in the slow movement too. Everywhere in the set the listener is carried along by the sheer spirit of the playing which at times quite properly places truth before beauty as, for example, in the finale of Op. 131 or in the *Grosse Fuge* where risks are taken with beauty of sound for the sake of truth of character.

Some minor (and not so minor) points: in the *molto adagio* middle section of the *Heiliger Dankgesang*, the leader eschews vibrato while his colleagues do not and the effect is not wholly convincing. Yet tone is often beautifully matched elsewhere. The turnover point in Op. 131 occurs in the middle of the fourth movement whereas rivals such as the Végh and the Italians accommodate the first four movements on one side. Moreover – and this is more serious – the Lindsays omit the alternative finale of Op. 130, a needless and self-inflicted handicap. This apart, the Lindsays must be included among the very finest versions to have been made in the last few years.

Sandor Végh and his colleagues bring qualities of great insight and humanity to these masterpieces, and the set challenges the fine and perceptive readings by the Italian Quartet, which are widely and rightly admired. There are some moments of discomfort as far as Végh's intonation is concerned, but they are few and trivial in comparison with the wisdom and richness of experience that his playing communicates. These are deeply impressive readings and are finely recorded, though the Philips engineers produce a more transparent and detailed sound for the Italians. However, this is without doubt a most useful and distinguished alternative to the Italian set, and some readers may well prefer it.

Of the modern accounts of the late quartets, the Talich versions were the first that can match those of the Végh and Italian Quartets. One is immediately gripped by the purity of the sound these artists produce and the effortlessness of their phrasing. As a quartet, their ensemble and intonation are impeccable and they possess both depth of feeling and insight. Their reading of Op. 132 brings one close to the heart of this music, particularly in the *Heiliger Dankgesang*, where they show great inwardness. There is little to fault elsewhere;

the readings unfold with a totally unforced naturalness; tempi have that feeling of rightness one recognizes in masterly performances, and the dynamic range is wide without being exaggerated. They can be recommended alongside the Italians, though the latter have the advantage of more transparent and vivid recording. As in the Végh Quartet's recordings, the sound here is just a shade bottom-heavy, but at the same time both ensembles bring a rich humanity to bear on these masterpieces. The cassettes match the discs closely, and are only marginally less refined in the upper range.

The late quartets were the first to appear in the Quartetto Italiano's complete cycle and have dominated the field since the late 1960s. At mid-price but split into two double-packs, they still remain highly competitive. The Op. 127 is a powerful reading that compels admiration on account of its finely-blended and firm tone and accuracy of intonation and ensemble. It is a useful alternative to the Alban Berg or the less vividly recorded Végh and Talich quartets. In the *B flat*, Op. 130, they are also highly impressive and few readers will find cause to quarrel with the excellent quality of the sound.

Fine though it is, the Italians' Op. 131 may worry some collectors on account of the rather slow tempo of the opening fugue and the variation movement. The espressivo playing in the former might strike some as a little exaggerated by comparison with more recent rivals – such as the Talich Quartet, for example. We have always rated it very highly, however, and still find it impressive. Op. 132 still remains one of the most distinguished versions around and few are likely to regret its acquisition, and the sound, as usual in this Philips Chamber Music series, is remarkably good. The Italian performances of the late *Quartets* have also been issued in a tape box with each work (including the *Grosse Fuge*) complete on one of six sides. For some reason, side one is transferred at a higher level than the remainder, which brings a touch of shrillness, but generally the quality is lively and the hint of edginess elsewhere is easily tamed.

The Hollywood set enjoyed classic status in the late 1950s and early 1960s. Had it not been that it was made in the last days of mono, it would have remained much longer in circulation. The members of the quartet all belonged to various Hollywood studio ensembles and they possessed superb attack, generally flawless intonation and beautifully blended tone. Op. 127 is superbly played and its slow movement inspires them to real heights. The E major variation (*Adagio molto espressivo*) is little short of sublime and there is a wonderful sense of awe at the C sharp minor section of the movement. The sound occasionally strikes the ears as a shade overblown, almost too 'symphonic' and it is advisable not to play the discs at too high a level: the recordings were not made in a large studio and though the sound is well-focused and lifelike, a slightly lower level setting removes some of the glare from Felix Slatkin's tone above the stave, as well as the impression of excessive projection.

Op. 132 has a finely-paced and well-held-together first movement though the *Heiliger Dankgesang* is a shade too fast: it is less penetrating than the famous pre-war Busch set (alas not currently available) though more commanding technically. The *Alla marcia* is deliberate and impressive and the finale is impeccably played and has wonderful restraint. The first five movements of Op. 130 are accommodated on one side so that the listener can complete the work as he wishes with the *Grosse Fuge* or the final *Allegro* which is placed second (thus encouraging choice). Feeling is never overstated and the playing of the *Grosse Fuge* can only be called stunning.

The opening fugue of Op. 131 could perhaps have had more *Innigkeit* though it has marvellous tone and feeling. Even if there are moments when one feels things are overdriven or larger than life, there are so many more where admiration is unqualified and one simply relishes the splendour and purity of this wonderful quartet's playing. No need for apologies for the quality of sound either and the cassettes are first-class, with plenty of body and atmosphere. The image is cleanly focused with no exaggeration on top. These are performances of stature and come with admirable notes from Desmond Shawe-Taylor.

Incidentally, admirers of the pioneering Busch pre-war set of *Quartets Nos. 12, 14, 15* and *16*, which still give immense satisfaction, can still obtain them in LP transfers, as an EMI import – 1C 147 01668/70.)

The Amadeus provide refined performances, and there is much subtle playing of a very high technical standard. The refinement does not prevent vigour when needed, and the performance of the *Grosse Fuge* may surprise some with the strength of the Amadeus playing. But in the last analysis these performances suffer from a lack of the 'inner' quality which should make the slow movements experiences beyond anything else in music. There is a case for the Amadeus's forthrightness in attacking the slow fugue which opens the *C sharp minor*, Op. 131; but not one of the adagios is taken quite slowly enough, and the great *Cavatina* of the Op. 130 sounds almost casual at a swinging andante. The recording still sounds fresh.

The Alban Berg coupling of Opp. 127 and 135 is their best Beethoven record so far. Their *Rasumovsky* was just a shade too self-aware, with rather exaggerated dynamic contrasts that draw attention to themselves and away from the music. These performances are much more direct and totally unaffected. Of course, the Alban Berg Quartet are highly polished in matters of ensemble and tonal blend, but the shining surfaces do not, as it were, come between Beethoven and the listener. They allow the music to speak for itself far more naturally than in, say, the *E minor Rasumovsky*, Op. 59, No. 2, and though they do not displace the Végh, the Talich and the Italians, who are all wonderfully perceptive and thoughtful, they can be recommended alongside them. The recording as such is absolutely first-class and better than any of its rivals. The cassette is of demonstration presence and realism.

The Alban Berg version of Op. 130 can be warmly commended and, in terms of tonal blend, accuracy of intonation and keen musical intelligence, this ensemble is second to none. They play the quartet with the *Grosse Fuge* as finale as do the Lindsays, and add the real finale at the end of the second side. Those who want to hear the quartet in Beethoven's definitive form have to leap up and move the stylus on, using some care as there is only a six-second gap between the two finales. Their playing is magnificent throughout and in some ways more polished than that of the Lindsays, though they do not penetrate so deeply in the *Cavatina*. The *Presto* second movement is very fast indeed and superbly played – and thoroughly convincing. They do not observe exposition repeats in the first and last movements. If the Talich and Végh find greater depths and move one more, the Berg has the advantage of a well-balanced and very 'present' recording. The cassette is extremely vivid too, though there is a degree of fierceness on fortissimos on side one.

The Lindsay recording of Op. 130 plus the *Grosse Fuge* preceded their account of the complete late quartets. It is a fine and concentrated reading with an unusually slow but eloquent account of the *Cavatina*. They play Beethoven's original finale, the *Grosse Fuge* – and magnificent it is, too, in their hands, but omit the alternative finale that he composed later. If you can accept this, there is no doubt that the Lindsays play with superb commitment and real insight. There is a first-class cassette.

String quartet No. 14 (arr. for string orch.).
(***) DG 2531 077 [id.]. VPO, Bernstein.

Bernstein is not the first to perform late Beethoven quartets in this fashion: Toscanini recorded two movements of Op. 135, and Mitropoulos conducted Op. 131 in the 1940s, a performance which Bernstein attended and now emulates. Obviously the added weight and the different colour that the full strings offer make for losses as well as gains; the intimacy of private feeling becomes transformed into the outpouring of public sentiment. There is no doubt as to the commitment and depth of feeling that Bernstein brings to this performance, dedicated to the memory of his wife; nor are there doubts as to the quality of the response he evokes from the Vienna Philharmonic strings. This is not a record about which we are in agreement: many collectors would never play it more than once. What one can agree about is that, if this is to be done at all, it could not be given more eloquent advocacy than it is here. The recording has excellent range and clarity.

String trios

String trios Nos. 1 in E flat, Op. 3; 2 in G; 3 in D; 4 in C min., Op. 9/1–3; Serenade in D (for string trio), *Op. 8*.

(M) *** DG Priv. 2721 131 (3). Italian String Trio.

Beethoven's *String trios* are sadly neglected, but in vitality and imagination they match the Op. 18 quartets. When the Italian and Grumiaux Trio sets first appeared they served to draw attention from each other. At present Grumiaux's set is no longer available. The Italian Trio is no less distinguished or profoundly musical than its rival, and the DG recording is certainly vivid. This is a most attractive set.

Violin sonatas Nos. 1–10.
❀ *** Decca D 92 D 5/*K 92 K 53* [Lon. CSA/5- 2501]. Perlman, Ashkenazy.
(M) *** Ph. 6768 036 (4). D. Oistrakh, Oborin.

The Ashkenazy/Perlman set is unlikely to be surpassed on disc or cassette for many years to come. Perlman and Ashkenazy are for the 1970s what Kreisler and Rupp were for the 1930s and 1940s, Grumiaux and Haskil for the 1950s and Oistrakh and Oborin for the 1960s. These performances offer a blend of classical purity and spontaneous vitality that is irresistible. Their musicianship and judgement are matched by a poise and elegance that give consistent pleasure. It would be difficult to improve on the balance between the two instruments, both of which are recorded with vivid realism and truthfulness of timbre on disc and cassette alike.

The versions by David Oistrakh and Lev Oborin are also performances to treasure. There is a relaxed joy in music-making, an almost effortless lyricism and an infectious sparkle. At times the Grumiaux/Haskil (mono) set (now deleted) went deeper, and there is none of the tension that marks (some would say disfigures) the Heifetz/Bay set (also now withdrawn). The recording is rather wider in separation than we favour nowadays, but it is a beautiful sound in every other respect.

Violin sonatas Nos. 1 in D, Op. 12/1; 10 in G, Op. 96.
*** Decca **411 948-2**; SXL/*KSXC* 6790 [Lon. CS/5- 7013]. Perlman, Ashkenazy.

Perlman and Ashkenazy offer the first and last of the sonatas in performances that could scarcely be improved upon. No phrase is unimaginatively handled or too lovingly caressed; their approach strikes a perfect balance between classical virtue and expressive spontaneity. Excellent recording, with a matching cassette.

Violin sonatas Nos. 2 in A, Op. 12/2; 9 in A (Kreutzer), Op. 47.
*** Decca SXL/*KSXC* 6632 [Lon. CS/5- 6845]. Perlman, Ashkenazy.

A superb performance of the *Kreutzer sonata*, undoubtedly the finest available. The strong first movement is followed by a wonderfully eloquent account of the variations. The beauty of Perlman's lyrical playing in the closing pages makes one catch one's breath, and the hushed answering chords from Ashkenazy show how complete is the rapport between these two artists. The lilting rhythms of the finale are irresistible. The coupling is no less strongly characterized, and the recording has the truthfulness of timbre and balance characteristic of this admirable series. The tape transfer is extremely vivid, the extremely high level on side one contributing a slight dryness of texture and needing a careful balance of the controls.

Violin sonatas Nos. 3 in E flat, Op. 12/3; 8 in G, Op. 30/3.
*** Decca SXL/*KSXC* 6789 [Lon. CS/5- 7012]. Perlman, Ashkenazy.

The Perlman–Ashkenazy Beethoven series is most distinguished. The *E flat Sonata* has exemplary warmth and naturalness; tempi are excellently judged and articulation could hardly be more alive. The *G Major* is no less finely characterized, and there is plenty of dramatic contrast in the first movement. The Decca recording has immediacy and presence. A winner. The cassette transfer is of demonstration quality.

Violin sonatas Nos. 4 in A min., Op. 23; 5 in F (Spring), Op. 24.
*** Decca SXL/*KSXC* 6736 [Lon. CS/5- 6958]. Perlman, Ashkenazy.

Perlman and Ashkenazy, a superb team, give sparkling, alert performances full of vitality and imagination. There is no question of virtuoso performers inflating the music or adopting unstylish mannerisms. The manner is youthful, the style classical. The degree of restraint never obstructs the dynamism, and with outstanding recording quality the record can be warmly recommended, even though it provides rather short value for money. Like its companions, this has a splendid equivalent cassette.

Violin sonatas Nos. 5 in F (Spring); 9 (Kreutzer).

*** Decca **410 554-2**; SXL/*KSXC* 6990. Perlman, Ashkenazy.

(M) *** HMV SXLP 31064. Yehudi and Hephzibah Menuhin.

An obvious recoupling from the Perlman/Ashkenazy series. The manner has a youthful freshness, yet the style is classical. The dynamism is there but never becomes too extrovert, and the music unfolds naturally and spontaneously. The recording quality is outstanding on both disc and tape, and especially on the excellent compact disc.

The coupling by the Menuhin brother and sister of the *Spring* and *Kreutzer sonatas* is also in a special class. Menuhin's playing does not always offer absolutely immaculate technique. A slightly sharp note in a cadential phrase, perhaps, or a quick passage not perfectly controlled might catch the ear, but these are lost and forgotten in the nobility and warmth of the readings as a whole. The playing has great spontaneity – the wonderful flow of the opening pastoral melody of the *Spring sonata*, the sustained tension of the *Adagio* of the same work, or the beautiful closing pages of the variations in the *Kreutzer*: these are high spots in music-making which remains on a consistently high level. The recording is drier than the original full-priced issue, but is still of excellent quality. The balance is very good.

Violin sonatas Nos. 6 in A; 7 in C min., Op. 30/1–2.

*** Decca SXL/*KSXC* 6791 [Lon. CS/5-7014]. Perlman, Ashkenazy.

This, the last of the Decca series to be issued separately, is well up to the standard of the others; discernment is matched by spontaneity, and the recording is immaculate on both disc and cassette.

PIANO MUSIC

Piano sonatas

(i) *Piano sonatas Nos. 1–32; Andante favori in F, G.170; 6 Bagatelles, Op. 126; 6 Ecossaises in E flat; Für Elise; Rondo à capriccio in G (Rage over a lost penny), Op. 129; 6 Variations on Paisiello's duet 'Nel cor più' in G; 2 Rondos, Op. 51/1–2.* (ii) *33 Variations in C on a waltz by Diabelli, Op. 120.* (iii) (Piano duet) *Grosse Fuge, Op. 134; 3 Marches, Op. 45; Sonata for piano duet (Ich denke dein), Op. 6; 8 Variations on a theme by Waldstein.*

(M) *** DG 2721 134 (14). (i) Kempff; (ii) Anda; (iii) Demus and Shetler.

Kempff's Beethoven has been providing a deeply spiritual experience for record-collectors since the 1920s, and though there may be argument about his clear and refreshing style in Beethoven, there is no doubt whatever of the inner compulsion which holds all these performances together. Kempff more than any pianist has the power to make one appreciate and understand Beethoven in a new way, and that is so, however many times one has heard him. It makes a fascinating study to compare the interpretations not only with those of other pianists but with his own previous ones. Above all, these magnificent records never fail to reveal his own spontaneity in the studio, his ability to rethink the reading on each occasion.

Kempff's classic survey of the 32 *Sonatas* was available on eleven records (2740 130, now deleted). Here, for little extra outlay, we are also given his account of the *Op. 126 Bagatelles*, the six *Ecossaises* and other pieces, and Géza Anda's recording of the *Diabelli variations*, as well as some of the earlier music for piano duo, played by Joerg Demus and Norman Shetler. Curiously enough, DG omit the *Eroica variations*, the *F major Variations*, Op. 34, the *Thirty-two Variations in C minor*, the *Kurfurstein sonatas*, as well as the *Bagatelles*, Opp. 33 and 116. The *Sonata* recordings all date from the early to mid-1960s, and are to that decade what Schnabel's were to the pre-war years, in other words performances that represent a yardstick by which all others are judged. The recordings as such have less bloom and freshness than Barenboim's, but they have a commanding stature. Kempff is occasionally fast (for example, in the slow movements of Opp. 26 and 110) but invariably illuminating and has many felicitous touches. Of the boxed sets of Beethoven's *Sonatas* now before the public, this would be a first choice for many collectors.

Piano sonatas Nos. 1–32; Eroica Variations; 32 Variations in C min., Op. 34; 5 Variations in F, Op. 34.
(M) **(*) Ph. 6768 351 (14) [id.]. Arrau.

This is one of the compilations issued to mark the eightieth birthday of the great Chilean pianist and it offers the sonata cycle, which he recorded in the 1960s, in transfers of admirable freshness, together with the 1969 account of the *Eroica variations*. As always there is an unfailing beauty of tone here and, as the late Alec Robertson put it, 'intellectual power and individuality of outlook'. There is an aristocratic finesse and a range of tonal subtleties that always hold the listener, even if there are occasions when one cannot share his view of a phrase. When he is on the highest plane as in the slow movement of the *Hammerklavier* or the *D Minor*, Op. 31, No. 2, there are illuminating things. Elsewhere he can seem a little wanting in spontaneity. There are some idiosyncratic (some would say personal) touches but there are also marvellous insights and the sound wears its years well.

Piano sonatas Nos. 1–32.
*** Decca D 258 D 12 (12) (with *Andante favori*). Ashkenazy.
(B) *** DG mono 2740 228 (10). Kempff.
(B) *** HMV SLS 794 (12). Barenboim.

Piano sonatas Nos. 1–3, 5–8, 13–14, 16–17, 18–20, 23–4, 28.
(M) ** ASV ACMB 601 (6). Lill.

Piano sonatas Nos. 4, 9–12, 15, 21–2, 25–7, 29–32.
(M) ** ASV ACMB 602 (6). Lill.

No need to say much about Ashkenazy's self-recommending set, which has occupied him over the best part of a decade or more. These are eminently sound, well-recorded performances that deserve to rank alongside the best. Crisply articulated, intelligently shaped, not always inspired but never less than musically satisfying – and with consistently lifelike recording to boot.

The Kempff cycle, the earlier of the two that he recorded for DG, is the more personal, the more individual, at times the more wilful; but for any listener who responds to Kempff's visionary concentration it is a magical series of interpretations. No other set of the sonatas so clearly gives the impression of new discovery, of fresh inspiration in the composer as in the pianist.

In the early sonatas Kempff's clarity presents an ideal (though the very opening movement of the *First Sonata* is controversially slow); but he has sometimes been accused of being too light in the big sonatas of the middle period. What this set demonstrates is that sharpness of impact makes for a toughness to compensate for any lack of sheer volume, while the inspirational manner brings out the quirky turns of last-period invention with incisive inevitability.

Even the first movement of the *Hammerklavier* has one marvelling not just at the concentration and power but at the beauty of sound, while the fugal finale brings the most remarkable example of Kempff's clarity, a towering performance, no less powerful for not being thunderous. Such personal performances will not please everyone, but for those who respond the experience is unique. The mid-1950s' mono sound has been beautifully transferred, with only a slight lightness of bass. It compares favourably with the later stereo set.

Barenboim's set is also available at a very reasonable price, making it a most attractive bargain, with good truthful recording and unique interpretations. The readings are sometimes idiosyncratic, with unexpected tempi both fast and slow, but the spontaneous style is unfailingly compelling. This is a keenly thoughtful musician thinking through Beethoven's great piano cycle with an individuality that already puts him in the line of master pianists. Often Barenboim's playing of the early and middle-period sonatas reflects an unusual weight of utterance that makes one rethink the aims and achievements of the young, revolutionary composer, and even if one disagrees with a tempo at the start of a movement, the concentration of the playing has one sympathizing, even thinking there is no alternative by the end. All three of the wonderful Sonatas, Op. 10, are given superb performances, with telling illumination of detail, quite apart from the overall structural control. No. 11, Op. 22, is exceptionally compelling and, in the *Funeral march* of Op. 26, Barenboim clearly hints at the *Eroica* ahead. Sometimes his unconventional tempi (as in the outer movements of the *Waldstein* and the first movement of Op. 110) will not appeal to all tastes, but both these interpretations are remarkable for their expansiveness. At other times his approach is mercurial, with an element of fantasy, a degree of warmth and romanticism, a charm missing in Brendel, for instance. Yet the performance of *Les Adieux*, one of the finest in the cycle, is made to sound stronger than usual and the last sonatas show remarkable concentration, with the *Hammerklavier* providing a fitting culmination to the series. The first movement is surprisingly rhapsodic, with rallentandos underlined, yet holds together most convincingly. The slow movement is taken for once at a true expansive *Adagio*, and there is clarity and fire in the finale.

John Lill's forthright, uncompromising way with Beethoven – almost entirely lacking in charm – will not be to all tastes, but his playing has both strength and spontaneity. The manner is always direct and determined, with extreme speeds in both directions. There are some parallels here with the solo playing of Backhaus; the tendency to brusqueness and the non-romantic response are offset by a sometimes elemental communication of the composer's fiery spirit. The recording is generally truthful in timbre and balance, though sometimes sounding very close.

Piano sonatas Nos. 1–7.
*** Nimbus D/C 901 (4). Roberts.
(M) **(*) O-L D 182 D 3 (3). Binns (fortepiano).
(M) (***) HMV mono RLS/*TC-RLS* 753 (3). Schnabel.

Bernard Roberts's integral recording of the Beethoven sonatas is a most remarkable achievement, for each sonata was recorded complete at a single sitting. The direct-cut recording technique meant that there was no possibility of pausing between movements, yet, so far from being inhibited, Roberts with his direct, clean-cut Beethoven style conveys a keener electricity the more he is challenged. The readings have a freshness and intensity which are most compelling. Roberts, an outstanding chamber music pianist, deliberately adopts a less idiosyncratic style here than do most of his rivals, and the result is intensely refreshing, helped by the vivid, amply reverberant recording.

Malcolm Binns is an underrated artist whose musicianship and intelligence have made a strong impression both in the concert hall and in the recording studio. It would be a pity if his interest in period instruments, as evidenced here and in the Hummel sonatas he has recorded, were to stand in the way of his recording early Beethoven on a modern Steinway. He plays the three Op. 2 sonatas on an instrument by Heilmann of Mainz, reputed to be the finest German piano-builder after Stein, and Opp. 7 and 10 on a Broadwood. The Heilmann is an instrument of the kind that Haydn, Mozart and Beethoven would have played. Its lighter action and colouring serve to clarify the texture of this familiar music, and the same must be said of the Broadwood, though its bass is richer. Malcolm Binns shows himself equal both in artistry and in technical fluency to the special problems this repertoire poses, and the recording engineers have secured sound that is in every way truthful and clean. In recommending this, there is no point in denying that our preference for the richer dynamic range and fuller sonority of a modern Steinway remains unshaken, and it is to the impressive surveys of the sonatas by Ashkenazy, Brendel, Kempff, Gilels (alas, still incomplete) and other masters that the majority of collectors will turn.

At last the pioneering Beethoven Sonata Society records made by Artur Schnabel are back in circulation and in excellent transfers. Schnabel somehow penetrated deeper than any other pianist into the spirit of Beethoven, even though others offer greater beauty of sound. His technical limitations are well known but even they are turned to advantage here: these performances centre so much on things of the spirit that the occasional lack of finish seems in character, reflecting the impatience of the spirit with the flesh. The earlier sonatas are generally not so fine as the late: the *A major*, Op. 2/2, is ungainly at times, but – particularly in the slow movements – there is scarcely anything not illuminated. The cassettes match the discs closely; the familiar brittle quality of the original 78s is immediately apparent, but often the sound has surprising body too, and the timbre in slow movements has plenty of colour and bloom.

Piano sonatas Nos. 1 in F min.; 2 in A, Op. 2/1; 19 in G min., Op. 49/1.
*** Ph. 6514/*7337* 173 [id.]. Brendel.

Both early sonatas come off splendidly and leave one in no doubt that we are embarking on an altogether new century. Brendel is at his very finest and is not at present surpassed either artistically or in terms of recorded sound.

Piano sonatas Nos. 1; 7 in D, Op. 10/3.
*** Decca SXL/*KSXC* 6960 [Lon. CS/*5-7190*]. Ashkenazy.

Ashkenazy made an earlier recording of Op. 10/3 in 1973 (it was coupled to the *Appassionata* on SXL 6603); now he has had second thoughts, and this new performance has more unity without loss of spontaneity. In the *F minor Sonata* his way is mercurial yet thrusting and has fine lyric feeling when the music is in repose. The recording maintains the high standard of the series, and the cassette is full-bodied and clear.

Piano sonatas Nos. 1; 24 in F sharp, Op. 78; 28 in A, Op. 101.
(M) ** ASV ACM/*ZCACM* 2028. Lill.

This first record of John Lill's series offers some of the finest (and most characteristic) performances in the cycle. Lill's deliberation at the opening of the Sonata No. 1 gives the first movement great character, and the slow movement too is eloquently played. The *Adagio* of No. 28 again shows the keen grip and intelligence of Lill's approach. The piano is recorded very close and has remarkable presence (on disc and cassette alike), and while the timbre has both body and colour the upper range is inclined to harden in fortissimos.

Piano sonatas Nos. 2 in A; 3 in C, Op. 2/2–3.
*** Decca SXL/*KSXC* 6808 [Lon. CS/*5-7028*]. Ashkenazy.
(M) ** ASV ACM/*ZCACM* 2023. Lill.

Ashkenazy brings to these two early sonatas the concentrated unaffected qualities which make his recordings of the *Violin sonatas* with Perlman so eminently convincing. Interpretatively the manner is strong and direct, treating the young Beethoven rightly as a fully mature composer, no imitator of Mozart and Haydn; but the important point is that, whether in fast music or slow, the pianist conveys the feeling of new discovery and ready communication. The recording captures the piano sound with vivid reality, percussive but not clangorous, and there is an equally fine cassette.

There is a directness of utterance about John Lill's Beethoven which is undoubtedly compulsive, particularly as the recording has great presence and the tone is admirably secure and realistic, on disc and tape alike. Lill brings a formidable technique to both sonatas, and the first movement of Op. 2/2 is crisply articulated, though at times it could do with greater lightness of touch. The slow movement of Op. 2/3 makes a strong impression, though some will feel that the fortissimo outbursts are over-characterized. John Lill is not strong on charm, yet there is an integrity about his playing that the listener cannot fail to notice. These performances may seem quite attractive in their mid-priced reissue, but it would be idle to pretend that they compete with Ashkenazy.

Piano sonatas Nos. 3; 13 in E flat, Op. 27/1; 24.
*** Ph. 6514/*7337* 176 [id.]. Brendel.

Previously coupled with his masterly Op. 22, Brendel's fresh and sparkling account of the early *C Major* is now harnessed to eminently satisfactory versions of the *E flat*, Op. 27, No. 1 and the *F sharp Major*, Op. 78, all of which can be numbered among the very best versions made in the 1970s. The high-level cassette transfer is first-class and offers completely lifelike piano timbre, full and cleanly focused, with perhaps a slight bass heaviness on the second side.

Piano sonatas Nos. 3; 15 in D (Pastoral), Op. 28.
*(*) DG Dig. 2532/*3302* 078 [id.]. Gilels.

As with the Sonatas, Op. 31, Nos. 2 and 3, the DG engineers elect for a close balance. It is as if one is observing the instrument from the vantage point of the keyboard itself, or at least very near it. There is clarity and impact but the percussive qualities of the instrument are emphasized on disc and tape alike. It is very different from the sound one would expect to hear at a Gilels recital in the concert hall, and there is a hardness in fortissimo passages that one is unaware of in a less forward balance. The first movement of the *C major Sonata* almost seems overdriven though the old Gilels re-emerges in the searching slow movement. However the fortissimo tone at bar 53 is ugly and percussive. The *Pastoral* is very strange indeed – a laboured, almost hectoring first movement, very deliberate in tempo and character with little sense of flow, and only occasional glimpses of the wisdom and humanity one associates with this great artist.

Piano sonata No. 4 in E flat, Op. 7.
(M) * DG 2543/*3343* 505 [id.]. Michelangeli.

Short measure even at mid-price. Curiously aloof and detached as if the artist is viewing the sonata's progress without ever involving himself in its evolution. The matching cassette is clear but transferred at only a modest level.

Piano sonatas Nos. 4; 9 in E; 10 in G, Op. 14/1–2.
*** Decca SXL/*KSXC* 6961 [Lon. CS 7191]. Ashkenazy.

A superb disc, one of the very finest in Ashkenazy's memorably poetic series. Warmth and intelligence are matched, and Ashkenazy is especially persuasive in the two Op. 14 sonatas, producing elegant, crisply articulated performances of striking character. The cassette is of demonstration quality, outstanding in its presence: the piano seems to be in the room.

Piano sonatas Nos. 4; 11 in B flat, Op. 22.
*** CBS 76995/*40*- [M/*MT* 36695]. Perahia.

These performances are as vibrant and ardent as any of Perahia's Mozart and Schumann on record. Perhaps the first movement of the *B flat Sonata*, Op. 22, is a shade brisk but one warms to its urgency and drive. They are performances of fine intelligence and the keenest sensibility and although the recording is not quite as impressive as the sound that Philips gives Brendel, it is more than adequate and does not diminish the strong appeal of this coupling. The cassette is transferred at a good level and produces a fine sense of presence and depth to the piano tone.

Piano sonatas Nos. 4; 21 in C (Waldstein), Op. 53.
(M) ** ASV ACM/*ZCACM* 2018. Lill.

In these two large-scale sonatas Lill's clean-cut, incisive style makes for performances that are generally refreshing but lacking a little in gentler qualities; even the rather formal slow movement of Op. 7 is given an uncompromising quality. The articulation from fingers of steel is thrilling, but the rhythms too rarely spring. The recording is bright and clean to match the performances; the cassette transfer is first-class, full, bold and clear.

Piano sonatas Nos. 5 in C min.; 6 in F; 7 in D, Op. 10/1–3.
(M) * ASV ACM/*ZCACM* 2031. Lill.

These are among the more disappointing of Lill's Beethoven sonata readings, rather square and charmless. The great D minor slow movement of Op. 10/3 is taken challengingly slowly, but there is little feeling of flow. Bright recording to match others in the series; the well-focused realism is equally striking on disc and cassette.

Piano sonatas Nos. 5–6; 15 in D (Pastoral).
*** Decca SXL/*KSXC* 6804 [Lon. CS/5-7024]. Ashkenazy.

Ashkenazy gives characteristically thoughtful and alert performances of an attractive grouping of three early sonatas. At times the tempi are questionably fast (the finale of Op. 10/2) or slow (the first movement of Op. 28), but Ashkenazy's freshness of manner silences criticism, and like the others in the series this is an outstanding issue, particularly as the recording is again first-rate on both disc and cassette.

Piano sonata No. 7; 15 Variations and fugue on a theme from Prometheus in E flat (Eroica variations), Op. 35.
*** DG Dig. 2532/*3302* 024 [id.]. Gilels.

Artistic wisdom is in abundant evidence in this coupling. Gilels draws a tonal colour all his own from the keyboard and yet it is Beethoven who speaks. The slow movement of the sonata has never seemed more searching and affecting, yet there is no sense in which Gilels is ever seen to strain after depth. Yet if his insights are penetrating, the results are fresh; phrases are articulated with inflections that seem to give them a new meaning and the question that launches the flow of ideas at the beginning of the finale has never been more coaxing and gentle. There are magisterial accounts elsewhere of Op. 35 but this seems to storm the heavens. Good sound, with a very vivid and lifelike cassette.

Piano sonatas Nos. 7; 23 in F min. (Appassionata), Op. 57.
*** Decca SXL 6603 [Lon. CS 6821]. Ashkenazy.

Ashkenazy's *Appassionata* is a superb one, and it is linked with a thoughtful and masterly account of the *D major Sonata*, Op. 10/3. However, those who feel strongly about matters of tempo may well find Ashkenazy a little too free in the first movement of the *Appassionata*. The sound is firm and well defined.

Piano sonatas Nos. 8–15.
**(*) Nimbus D/C 902 (4). Roberts.
(M) (***) HMV mono RLS/*TC-RLS* 754 (3). Schnabel.

Bernard Roberts's survey continues, maintaining the same high standards of the first two volumes, with recording that matches presence and realism with immaculate direct-cut pressings. The readings do not have the penetration of Schnabel's, but they have genuine breadth, and if the *Moonlight* and *Pathétique* (for instance) have received more memorable treatment in other hands, Roberts's playing is not without individuality; moreover his performances give genuine pleasure and satisfaction.

Schnabel's Beethoven (as we have said above) is unfailingly illuminating, and the second volume of transfers of his pre-war Sonata Society recordings equals the standards of the first. The slow movements in particular penetrate more deeply than with almost any other artist, and technical shortcomings such as rushed triplets and the odd unevenness are warts on the most lifelike Beethoven we have. In terms of artistic truth these are the performances by which others are measured, and the transfers have never sounded as good. The tapes are at a slightly lower level than in Volume 1 and the piano has slightly less presence, though the *Pathétique* sounds well and so do Opp. 22 and 26.

Piano sonatas Nos. 8 in C min. (Pathétique), Op. 13; 14 in C sharp min. (Moonlight), Op. 27/2; 17 in D min. (Tempest), Op. 31/2; 21 (Waldstein); 23 in F min. (Appassionata), Op. 57; 26 in E flat (Les Adieux), Op. 81a.
(M) *** DG Priv. 2726 042 (2). Kempff.

This collection of favourite named sonatas reveals the essence of Kempff's approach to Beethoven, above all its refreshing clarity. To hear every note clearly of such a movement as the finale of the *Moonlight* or of the *Appassionata* shows exactly what Kempff has to offer beyond superficially more exciting readings. Even those who know these sonatas well may be surprised at the revelations that Kempff has to give. He never falls into convention or routine. Fair recording.

Piano sonatas Nos. 8 (Pathétique); 13; 14 (Moonlight).

*** DG Dig. **400 036-2**; 2532/*3302* 008 [id.]. Gilels.

Gilels is served by superb sound, and, as always, his performances leave the overriding impression of wisdom. Yet this disc, coupling the two Op. 27 sonatas together on one side and the *Pathétique* on the other, does not quite rank among his very best (such as the *Waldstein* and Op. 101). The opening movement of the *Moonlight* is wonderfully serene, and there are many felicities. But the first movement of the *E flat Sonata* is strangely reserved (the wonderful change to C major so subtly illuminated by Schnabel goes relatively unremarked here), as if Gilels feared the charge of self-indulgence or out-of-period sentiment. However, such are the strengths of this playing that few will quarrel with the magnificence of his conceptions of all three pieces. The digital recording is marvellously lifelike on the compact disc and the background silence benefits the opening of the *Moonlight* very strikingly. This would have earned a technical accolade, were not the balance so close (which brings a touch of hardness on fortissimos), but even so the presence of the piano is remarkable. The chrome tape is first-class also.

Piano sonatas Nos. 8 (Pathétique); 14 (Moonlight); 23 (Appassionata).

*** Decca **410 260-2**; SXL/*KSXC* 7012 [Lon. CS/*5-* 7247]. Ashkenazy.
*** DG 139 300/*3300 506* [id.]. Kempff.
*** Ph. **411 470-2**; 9500/*7300* 899 [id.]. Brendel.
(M) **(*) HMV HQS/*TC-HQS* 1076. Barenboim.
**(*) Ph. 6599 308 [id.]. Arrau.
**(*) O-L DSLO/*KDSLC* 603 [id.]. Binns (fortepiano).
(M) **(*) EMI Em. EMX/*TC-EMX* 2036. Gelber.
(M) ** Decca SPA/*KCSP* 69. Backhaus.
(M) ** CBS 60118/40- [MY/*MYT* 37219]. Serkin.
(M) *(*) ASV ACM/*ZCACM* 2015. Lill.

Ashkenazy's coupling is one of the most impressive of those currently available and those wanting him need have no grounds for holding back. The merits of his readings are discussed in their alternative couplings and he is well served by the engineers on disc and chrome tape alike, while the compact disc is even more impressive, even though it is made from analogue masters.

Kempff's disc shows so well his ability to rethink Beethoven's music within the recording studio. He coupled these three works together in a (no less successful) early stereo LP. Here the slow movement of the *Pathétique*, for example, is slower and more expressively romantic than before, but still restrained. The *Appassionata* is characteristically clear, and if anything more classically 'straight' than it was before (in the same way that the *Waldstein* – on another disc – is cooler and clearer, with a wonderful classical purity in the rippling quavers). The opening of the *Moonlight* is gently atmospheric, the scherzo poised, with admirable contrast in the finale. Everything Kempff does has his individual stamp, and above all he never fails to convey the deep intensity of a master in communion with Beethoven. The recording is a little shallow sometimes – one notices this more in a work like the *Pathétique* with a slow movement that makes special use of the piano's sustaining quality – but still faithful enough. The cassette transfer seems marginally fuller in timbre than the disc. It includes a bonus, not present on the LP, of the *'Nel cor più' Variations* played with telling simplicity. This acts as a short prelude to the performance of the *Appassionata* on side two.

Among the other additions to the records and cassettes combining the three most popular named sonatas, only Brendel's, offering undeniably impressive performances and excellent recording, could be advocated as an alternative to present recommendations. The cassette quality is natural and full to match the disc closely, with only a fractional loss in upper range.

Barenboim's coupling of three named sonatas showed at once the sort of inspiration he can convey. The first movement of the *Pathétique*, for example, taken rather fast, has a natural wildness about it, but it is so compelling that one forgives minor blemishes. The second movement brings a tempo so slow that the result could have seemed too static had not Barenboim's control of line been so confident. The *Appassionata* too is rather wild and rhapsodic in the first movement, and again the slow speed for the central variations brings a simple, natural intensity, which contrasts well with the lightness and clarity of the finale. The cassette has been successfully remastered (it was first issued in non-Dolby format) and the sound is first-class, with excellent sonority and a warm colouring of the piano's middle register.

Arrau's thoughtful and individual cycle of the Beethoven sonatas is well represented by a sampler disc of the three most popular sonatas. Plainly this is the playing of a master, sometimes wayward but deeply felt. The recording is good, but the extra alertness and spontaneity of Barenboim's coupling make that a better general choice in the middle price-range.

Even with an authentic cycle of Beethoven sonatas performed on historic instruments, it is welcome to have a sampler of three of the most popular sonatas. Binns gives refreshing performances of all three, at times cramped rhythmically by the mechanical limitations of the early instruments but providing an excellent idea of a fine series, superbly recorded.

Bruno-Leonardo Gelber enjoyed some exposure on the EMI label in the late 1960s and he is a far from unimpressive contender in this coupling. Indeed, impulse buyers alighting on this record will find no cause for regret and, though it is half the price of such celebrities as Ashkenazy and Brendel, it is more than half as good! The recording is in the highest flight. On cassette the piano image is softer-grained with less edge, but it is still realistically balanced.

Decca issued this separate disc of favourite sonatas from Backhaus's stereo cycle as a cheap sampler to tempt buyers to the rest which is now long deleted. It is amazing that an octogenarian could produce such positive, alert, imaginative playing, but by the standards of Barenboim, let alone Brendel, his style is wilful, with a touch of heaviness that is not always cancelled out by the electric concentration. All the same, at lower-medium price it is worth any Beethovenian's while to sample the greatness of Backhaus.

Serkin has recorded remarkably few of the Beethoven sonatas, considering how eminent a Beethoven pianist he is. Instead he has concentrated on the popular named works and these three in particular, each recorded by him several times before. The result this time is as incisive and dramatic as before, and as with all master pianists one has dozens of points of new insight emerging as well as one or two points of personal mannerism that may or may not irritate. The piano tone is acceptable in a slightly hard American way, with the cassette matching the disc quite closely.

John Lill plays the opening of the *Moonlight* more evocatively, and then makes a striking contrast in the finale, which is taken with furious bravura. The slow movement of the *Pathétique* is thoughtful but lacks something in poetic feeling. This is strong, intelligent playing, but at times one has the impression that the drama is overdone. The piano image has striking realism and forward projection – some will feel the balance is a shade too close – with a first-class tape transfer that matches the disc closely.

Piano sonatas Nos. 8; 14 in C sharp min. (Moonlight), Op. 27/2; 21 in C (Waldstein), Op. 53.

(M) ** Decca Jub. JB/*KJBC* 105. Lupu.
(B) ** Con. CC/*CCT* 7529. Firkusny.

Radu Lupu is an unfailingly sensitive artist, and he has the undoubted gift of creating spontaneity in the recording studio; but sometimes his playing can seem mannered, as in his rather deliberate approach to the famous slow movement of the *Pathétique sonata*, or at the opening of the *Moonlight*. But the playing carries conviction, and the performances of both these works are individual and enjoyable. Lupu is less successful in holding the concentration of the *Waldstein* finale, after having prepared the opening beautifully, and it is this that lets down an otherwise impressive issue. The Decca recording is first-rate in every way, sonorous and clear, a real piano sound; and the cassette too offers demonstration quality.

Rudolf Firkusny's Contour reissue has a Decca Phase Four source and the recording is characteristically close and immediate. It is truthfully balanced, however, the timbre full and natural, slightly warmer on cassette but with a sharper focus on disc, though there is not too much difference between them. The performances are eminently musical and well shaped, though lacking in drama. The opening of the *Moonlight* and the slow movement of the *Pathétique* are appealing, but the account of the *Waldstein* is under-characterized.

Piano sonatas Nos. 8 (Pathétique); 19–20, Op. 49/1 and 2; 23 (Appassionata).
*** Decca SXL/*KSXC* 6994. Ashkenazy.

No quarrels with this playing, and in particular an admirable *Appassionata.* Ashkenazy does not always find as much in the two Op. 49 pieces as, say, Brendel or Richter (in his now deleted disc from the 1960s) but, for many collectors, this may not be a bad thing. These have been removed from the latest transfer (see above), which replaces them with the *Moonlight.* But both records can be recommended. The cassette transfer is bold and clear, a natural image but with a touch of hardness on the treble.

Piano sonatas Nos. 8 (Pathétique); 21 (Waldstein); 26 (Les Adieux).
*** Decca SXL/*KSXC* 6706 [Lon. CS/5-6921]. Ashkenazy.

Taking a broadly lyrical view, Ashkenazy gives a deeply satisfying reading of the *Waldstein sonata.* His degree of restraint, his occasional hesitations, intensify his thoughtful approach, never interrupt the broader span of argument. The *Pathétique*, perhaps understated for so ebulliently youthful a work, with the finale unusually gentle, conveys the underlying power, and *Les Adieux* brings a vehement first movement and memorable concentration. Excellent recording. The cassette transfer is good but the quality tends to harden and become brittle on side two.

Piano sonatas Nos. 9–10, Op. 14/1–2; 30 in E, Op. 109.
(M) *(*) ASV ACM/*ZCACM* 2026. Lill.

For the two small-scale early sonatas Lill scales down the aggressiveness in his approach to Beethoven. The results are clear and refreshing if lacking in charm. There is not much fun, for example, in the finale of the *G major.* Op. 109 is given a somewhat four-square performance, the structural freedom of the first movement underplayed and put in a strict sonata frame. Bright, clear recording, as in the rest of this series, and the tape transfer is admirable, firm and with good presence.

Piano sonatas Nos. 11; 12 in A flat (Funeral march), Op. 26.
**(*) Decca SXL/*KSXC* 6929 [Lon. CS 7162]. Ashkenazy.

Ashkenazy's account of Op. 22 is expert but less perceptive than Brendel's. The latter finds more wit and poetry, though Ashkenazy is handicapped by a less revealing recording. There are some fine things in the Op. 26 sonata, even though again he does not search out the subtleties of the opening variation movement as do Gilels, Richter and Brendel. Of course, the playing is still impressive, particularly in the scherzo and the finale, and this side is better recorded too. But generally speaking, this is one of the less successful of Ashkenazy's cycle. The cassette transfer is of very high quality, matching the disc closely.

Piano sonatas Nos. 11; 17 in D (Tempest), Op. 31/2.
*** Ph. 6514/*7337* 175 [id.]. Brendel.

A recoupling of performances originally issued on Philips 9500 540 and 9500 503. Except in the late sonatas, Brendel's was the most satisfying of the Beethoven sonata cycles to have appeared in the 1970s both musically and as far as recorded sound is concerned. The *D Minor* is finely conceived and thoroughly compelling, not as flamboyantly dramatic as Richter's was but powerful all the same, while his Op. 22 is among the very best now on record. The sound is first-class and the cassette too is of excellent quality; a little more level would have put it in the demonstration class.

Piano sonatas Nos. 11; 32 in C min., Op. 111.
(M) ** ASV ACM/*ZCACM* 2013. Lill.

This is one of the most convincing records in the Lill series. No. 11 is strongly characterized and the concentration in the *C Minor* is well sustained with the variations especially successful. The sound is characteristically vivid. There is a degree of brittleness on the cassette transfer of Op. 111, but No. 11 in B flat is bold and clear.

Piano sonatas Nos. 12 (Funeral march); 18 in E flat, Op. 31/3; 20.
*** Ph. 6514/*7337* 174 [id.]. Brendel.

Brendel's version of No. 12 was earlier coupled with Op. 31, No. 1, (No. 16) when we found it 'surpassingly beautiful', which it remains. The *E flat*, Op. 31, No. 3, is marvellously responsive to the changing character of the invention and is as aware of all the interpretative pitfalls and how to solve them! Very truthful piano sound. The cassette transfer is of good quality but the sonatas on side two (Nos. 12 and 20) have rather more immediacy than No. 18, where the transfer level is somewhat lower.

Piano sonatas Nos. 12; 22 in F, Op. 54; 25 in G, Op. 79; 31 in A flat, Op. 110.
(M) ** ASV ACM/*ZCACM* 2027. Lill.

Charm plays no part at all in John Lill's Beethoven; that is clear not just in the rugged account of the *Funeral march* of Op. 26 but in the first two movements as well, the lyrical variations and the sparkling scherzo. There is no compromise either in the two small sonatas; the first movement of Op. 79 is brutally fast. Even the lyrical first movement of Op. 110, very slow and square, keeps to the pattern of ruggedness, though the intensity of Lill's playing is never in doubt, and the bright recording matches his readings. The cassette, like the disc, has striking presence.

Piano sonatas Nos. 13; 14 (Moonlight), Op. 27/1 and 2.
*** None. Dig. H 73177 [id.]. Bilson (fortepiano) – MOZART: *Rondos.****

Malcolm Bilson uses a modern copy by Philip Belt of Pawcatuck, Connecticut, rather than the original Walter of Vienna (1785) which Mozart owned or the Dulcken from the following decade. The result is rather more satisfactory in terms of evenness and (at times even) sonority than the real thing. Professor Bilson does not feel obliged to eschew rubato in Op. 27, No. 2, and approaches both this and its companion with scholarship tempered by imagination. Indeed, after a few moments for the ear to accustom itself to the timbre of the instrument, one listens to what the artist is saying rather than the medium which he is using – which is what it should be. Some may find the opening movement of Op. 27, No. 1 just a shade too fast, but for the most part these are performances that excite admiration for their authority and musicianship. What is likeable here is that Bilson attacks the finale of the *Moonlight* with the same temperament and fire as he would were he playing a modern grand piano. A low level setting is desirable if the most natural sound is to be achieved.

Piano sonatas Nos. 13; 14 (Moonlight); 16 in G, Op. 31/1.
*** Decca SXL/*KSXC* 6889 [Lon. CS/5-7111]. Ashkenazy.

There is a difference in acoustic between the two Op. 27 sonatas, which occupy the same side. Ashkenazy's account of Op. 31/1 is perhaps the strongest of the three performances, though there is much to admire throughout; his growing interest in the baton does not seem to have impaired his prowess at the keyboard. In the opening of Op. 27/1 he does not find the depths that distinguished the old Schnabel set, but in every other respect this is formidable playing; the *G major* is thoughtful and compelling, though it does not quite achieve the stature of Gilels's classic DG account. The tape transfer is impressively wide in range but the fortissimos are inclined to harden under pressure; otherwise the sound is full and clear.

Piano sonatas Nos. 13; 17 (Tempest); 19.
(M) ** ASV ACM/*ZCACM* 2029. Lill.

Lill's account of No. 13 is thoughtful, but not really imaginative enough, and memories of the marvellous range of colour that Schnabel produced in the first movement flood back.

There is no want of fire in No. 17 but it is in no sense a performance of real stature. The two-movement *G minor Sonata* is played with effective simplicity. The piano tone is firm and secure, somewhat hard on top, especially in the clear cassette version.

Piano sonatas Nos. 14 (Moonlight); 17 (Tempest); 26 (Les Adieux).
*** DG Priv. 2535/*3335* 316 [id.]. Kempff.

Kempff's individuality in Beethoven is nowhere more clearly established than in this coupling; the understated clarity of his playing gives an otherworldly quality to the outer movements of the *Moonlight*, both the opening *Adagio* (more flowing than usual) and the rushing finale (more measured and clearer). The so-called *Tempest Sonata* and *Les Adieux* may be less weightily dramatic than in other readings, but the concentration is irresistible. The recording is clear and not lacking in colour; the tape transfers are well managed (although the level is modest): the sound in the *Tempest* is comparatively shallow, but there is no lack of bloom on Op. 27/2.

Piano sonatas Nos. 15 (Pastoral); 21 (Waldstein).
*** Ph. 6514/*7337* 111 [id.]. Brendel.

The *Pastoral* is radiant, subtly coloured and beautifully shaped with every detail fitting in harmoniously with the artist's conception of the whole. His earlier *Waldstein* (on Turnabout 34394) has claims to be considered among the very finest on record, alongside those of Schnabel and Gilels. This is hardly less fine and certainly better recorded. The cassette is excellent, marginally brighter and more sharply focused on side two (No. 15).

Piano sonatas Nos. 15 (Pastoral); 26 (Les Adieux); 27 in E min., Op. 90.
(M) ** ASV ACM/*ZCACM* 2014. Lill.

As sound this is undeniably impressive, and though the sound picture slightly favours the bass end of the instrument the treble has no lack of clarity. John Lill adopts very deliberate tempi in the *Pastoral sonata*, where one feels some want to flow, yet *Les Adieux* is a distinct success, though Brendel's performance has even more character, and at no time is Gilels challenged, either in *Les Adieux* or in the *E minor* work, even though Lill is obviously at home in this too, and all three sonatas here show his thoughtful musicianship at its most communicative. The cassette transfer is first-class, matching the disc closely.

Piano sonatas Nos. 16–22; 24.
(M) (***) HMV mono RLS/*TC-RLS* 755 (3). Schnabel.

Schnabel is in a special category and, for all his idiosyncrasies, he can no more be ignored in this repertoire than Weingartner, Toscanini or Furtwängler in the symphonies. Few artists are more searching in the slow movement of the *Waldstein* or as characterful in its first movement. Music-making of outsize personality which readers should hear, no matter how many rival accounts they may have. Exemplary transfers from the original 78s; the cassettes too – made at the highest level – are the finest in the series so far, offering remarkable presence.

Piano sonatas Nos. 16–25.
**(*) Nimbus D/C 903 (4). Roberts.

Bernard Roberts brings sound good sense to everything he does. He has become something of a vogue pianist: he is every bit as good as he was a few years ago when no one was putting him on disc or on the radio and he deserves much of his present exposure. These performances are recorded in one take and cut direct to disc, and the sound is both immediate and clean; in fact, it is very lifelike indeed. Generally speaking, the playing is robust, alive, sensitive, well proportioned and always intelligent, though in such sonatas as the *Appassionata* and the *Waldstein* Roberts's insights and finesse are not superior to those of, say, Brendel, Kempff and Gilels.

Piano sonatas Nos. 16; 18; 20.
(M) ** ASV ACM/*ZCACM* 2022. Lill.

The first movement of No. 16 is keenly alive

and cleanly articulated here, if somewhat aggressive. The slow movement is characteristically direct and there are some sensitive touches. In the *E flat Sonata* (No. 18) there is much to admire, and Op. 49/2 (No. 20) again shows Lill's strong yet emotionally reserved way with Beethoven, minimizing charm and indeed warmth. The recording has striking truthfulness and presence, especially on the cassette, which is of demonstration quality.

Piano sonatas Nos. 17 (Tempest); 18.
*** Decca SXL/*KSXC* 6871 [Lon. CS 7088]. Ashkenazy.
**(*) DG Dig. 2532/*3302* 061 [id.]. Gilels.

These are among the best of Ashkenazy's Beethoven cycle. He brings concentration of mind together with a spontaneity of feeling that illumine both works. The command of keyboard colour is as always impressive, and, both in terms of dramatic tension and the sense of architecture, these are thoroughly satisfying performances. The recorded sound is also of high quality and the cassette is exceptionally vivid and clear, with bold transients and a natural underlying sonority.

Gilels's performances have excited universal acclaim – and rightly so. They have enormous pianistic and musical distinction. Some ears will not care for the quality of the sound, however, and find the balance far too close. The listener seems to be standing on the platform beside the pianist: there is tremendous clarity and impact, but one is all too aware of the percussive qualities of the instrument. Despite the hardness of timbre, this is nonetheless a record to have for the sake of Gilels's artistry and insights.

Piano sonatas Nos. 22; 24–5; 27.
*** Decca SXL/*KSXC* 6962 [Lon. CS 7192]. Ashkenazy.

Another worthwhile addition to the catalogue. Ashkenazy is in top form, and his readings of these sonatas are as masterly and penetrating as anything he has given us. He is splendidly recorded, and the cassette transfer is of the highest quality, projecting a piano image that is natural and firm.

Piano sonatas Nos. 23 (Appassionata); 25; 26 (Les Adieux); 27–8; 29 (Hammerklavier); 30–32.
❀ (***) HMV mono RLS/*TC-RLS* 758 (4). Schnabel.

Of all the Schnabel sets this is the most indispensable. No performance of the later sonatas, Opp. 109–111, has surpassed these, not even Schnabel's own RCA recordings of Opp. 109 and 111 made in the 1940s. The *Arietta* of Op. 111, the first movement of Op. 110 and . . . one could go on – have a depth and authority that remain unrivalled. If Schnabel's pianism was not always immaculate (there are plenty of wrong notes in the *Hammerklavier*), he brings one closer to the spirit of this music than any other artist. No self-respecting collector should be without this powerful and searching document. The sound is remarkably good, and the cassette transfers are beautifully clean and clear. On tape each sonata is offered uninterrupted, with the nine works spread over four sides. Sometimes, as in the first movement of Op. 79 (at the beginning of side three), there is a slightly brittle quality, but the slow movements of the late sonatas are strikingly full in timbre, Schnabel's subtle control of colour faithfully caught.

Piano sonatas Nos. 24–32.
(M) **(*) O-L D 185 D 3 (3). Binns.

This is a set to investigate, for it gives us the late sonatas on instruments that Beethoven himself knew (but could not, of course, have heard). But those who like their Beethoven on a modern Steinway and whose minds and ears are closed to contemporary instruments should give this box a miss. Binns uses a Graf for Op. 111 and a Haschka for the *Hammerklavier*, both Viennese instruments. He chooses a Dulcken of about 1785 for the earlier sonatas, Broadwoods for Opp. 109 and 110 (albeit of slightly different periods – 1814 and 1819 respectively), a Clementi for Op. 90, and an Erard for Op. 101. There is an excellent booklet describing each instrument in some detail. The differences between them are often quite striking, and space does not permit discussion of them here; the basic test is whether one would want Binns playing Beethoven sonatas if the added dimension of period instrumental colour were removed, or whether this is merely a guided tour around the Colt Collection using Beethoven sonatas by way of illustration. Malcolm Binns satisfies the listener musically as well as historically, although played on period instruments the most searching of Beethoven's thoughts (in Opp. 110 and 111) seem to lose something of their depth and mystery. Yet the exercise is undoubtedly illuminating and given the modest price – and the excellent value (no other three-record box offers all the sonatas from Op. 78 onwards) – it can be confidently recommended. It goes without saying that few would consider it as their *only* version of these great works, but as a supplement it is revealing and thought-provoking.

Piano sonatas Nos. 26–32.
*** Nimbus D/C 904 (5). Roberts.

With their few idiosyncrasies Bernard Roberts's readings of the late sonatas can consistently be registered as the listener's own inner vision from Beethoven turned into sound. Roberts's achievement in recording even the *Hammerklavier* and Op. 111 direct-to-disc in single takes is nothing less than astonishing, and though some will positively demand more personal, more idiosyncratic readings, there is none of the lack of concentration which afflicts other would-be scalers of these peaks, nor even any feeling of cautiousness. With the exception that Roberts, forthright in everything, is reluctant to allow a gentle pianissimo, the revelation here is consistently satisfying. The sound is outstandingly fine.

Piano sonatas Nos. 27–32.
*** DG 2740 166/*3371 033* [id.]. Pollini.

Here is playing of the highest order of mastery. Pollini's *Hammerklavier* is among the best to have been recorded in recent years. Hardly less impressive is the eloquent account of Op. 111, which has a peerless authority and expressive power. Joan Chissell spoke of the 'noble purity' of these performances, and that telling phrase aptly sums them up. The slow movement of Op. 110 may be a trifle fast for some tastes, and in the *A major* work Gilels has the greater poetry and humanity. But, taken by and large, this series is a magnificent achievement and as sheer pianism it is quite stunning. The recording has excellent body and transparency and there is little to choose between the disc and cassette, so impressive is the latter. This set won the 1977 *Gramophone* Critics' Award for instrumental music, and rightly so.

Piano sonatas Nos. 28; 30.
*** Decca SXL/*KSXC* 6809 [Lon. CS/*5-7029*]. Ashkenazy.

Distinguished performances of both sonatas, as one would expect, and an impressive sense of repose in the slow movement of Op. 109. Perhaps Gilels found greater depth in Op. 101, but this is not to deny that Ashkenazy is searching and masterly too. The sound is of excellent quality, with exceptional dynamic range. The cassette transfer too is admirably clear and clean, with only a minor degree of hardening on fortissimos.

Piano sonatas Nos. 26 (Les Adieux); 29 in B flat (Hammerklavier), Op. 106.
**(*) Ph. 6514/*7337* 110 [id.]. Brendel.

Piano sonata No. 29 (Hammerklavier).
*** DG Dig. **410 527-2**; 410 527-1/*4* [id.]. Gilels.
** Decca SXL 6355 [Lon. CS 6563]. Ashkenazy.
*(*) ASV ACM/*ZCACM* 2032. Lill.

Piano sonata No. 29 (Hammerklavier); Andante favori, WoO 57.
**(*) Decca SXL/*KSXC* 7011. Ashkenazy.

Gilels's *Hammerklavier* is a performance of supreme integrity, Olympian, titanic, subtle, imperious, one of the finest accounts ever recorded. Speeds for the outer movements are surprisingly spacious and relaxed with clarity of texture and refinement of detail brought out. Yet the concentration brings the most powerful impact – not just in those movements but all four. The recording is close and bright and harder than ideal: hearing Gilels play the work in London in 1984 left one in no doubt that there is more to the sound he produces in real life than the overlit quality the DG engineers have achieved. The chrome tape matches the disc quite faithfully but the recording is at its most effective on compact disc. Whichever format is chosen, this is still an indispensable issue and no collector need hesitate on artistic grounds.

Brendel's recording of the *Hammerklavier* for Philips came early in his re-recording of the whole Beethoven sonata cycle, and there are still signs of a self-consciousness which make it less powerful than his earlier recording for Vox Turnabout [34392]. Yet thanks to fine recording he conveys a deep, hushed concentration in the slow movement. Though this may not be quite worthy of a pianist who has become one of the great visionary Beethovenians of our time, it remains a fine version, more attractively coupled than on its first issue, with *Les Adieux*. There is an excellent, full-bodied cassette transfer, though side two benefits from a bass cut.

Ashkenazy's earlier reading of the *Hammerklavier* (on SXL 6355) is thoughtful, but misses greatness. One admires almost everything individually, but the total experience is less than monumental. His second recording was made to include in his collected edition of the complete Beethoven sonatas. It is curiously coupled with the *Andante favori*, but the performance is fresher and more spontaneous-sounding than the earlier version, not quite so immaculate in the playing but still strong and direct with power and speed in the outer movements. The recording is good but clangs a little on some notes. The ferric cassette is every bit the equal of the disc, wide-ranging, full, with excellent presence.

John Lill's speed in the great slow movement is so slow that ASV have resorted to the device of putting the finale at the beginning of side one, before the first movement, so that the slow movement can be contained on side two without a break. Unfortunately Lill does not convey the necessary concentration, and though the outer movements pack tremendous virtuoso punch, this does not compare with the finest versions. The recording is a little clangy. The cassette, which is laid out straightforwardly, faithfully matches the disc, clean but shallower than the best of this series.

Piano sonatas Nos. 31, Op. 110; 32, Op. 111.
*** Decca SXL/*KSXC* 6632 [Lon. CS 6843]. Ashkenazy.

Ashkenazy plays the last two sonatas with a depth and spontaneity which put the record among the very finest available. In the slow movement of Op. 111 Ashkenazy matches the concentration at the slowest possible speed which marks out the reading of his friend Barenboim, but there is an extra detachment. If anything, the interpretation of Op. 110 is even more remarkable, consistently revealing. The recording is a little clangorous, but the ear quickly adjusts. There is an outstanding cassette transfer.

Piano sonata No. 32, Op. 111.
(*) DG Dig. **410 520-2; 2532/*3302* 036 [id.]. Pogorelich – SCHUMANN: *Études symphoniques* etc.**(*)

Ivo Pogorelich produces consistent beauty of tone throughout the sonata, and his account of this masterpiece contains many felicities. It is imposing piano playing and impressive music-making. At times he seems to view Beethoven through Lisztian eyes, but there is much that is powerful here. Pogorelich has a strong personality and will provoke equally strong reactions. There are self-indulgent touches here and there but also moments of illumination. The sound is truthful on both disc and tape. The compact disc is admirably clear and realistically balanced, but the clarity of the recording and its background silence tend to emphasize the slightly dry bass quality.

Miscellaneous piano music

7 Bagatelles, Op. 33; 11 Bagatelles, Op. 119; 6 Bagatelles, Op. 126; Fantasia in G min., Op. 77; Für Elise, WoO 50; Minuet in E flat, WoO 82; Rondos: *in A, WoO 49; in C, Op. 51/1; Rondo à capriccio, Op. 129; 15 Variations in E flat (Eroica), Op. 35; 33 Variations on a waltz by Diabelli, Op. 120.*
(M) (***) HMV mono RLS/*TC-RLS* 769 (3). Schnabel.

The remaining Beethoven Sonata Society

volumes from the 1930s reappear in excellent transfers by Keith Hardwick, including Schnabel's *Diabelli variations*. No one has seen deeper into these and although there are masterly successors from Brendel, Bishop-Kovacevich and others, his insights are formidable. Of course, as the old *Record Guide* of Edward Sackville-West and Desmond Shawe-Taylor put it, 'his great virtues of intellect and insight are accompanied by certain temperamental and technical eccentricities, notably a tendency to rush rapid passages, to the detriment of steady rhythm and clarity of outline'. Some of these surface now and again in this set but, warts and all, no one better conveys the spirit of Beethoven's art. One almost sees the composer himself, bad-tempered and impatient at the limitations of the medium, before one's very eyes. The set includes Op. 119 *Bagatelles* which remained unissued at the time, and it reproduces Eric Blom's notes accompanied by lavish music-type examples. The sound is as usual dryish but very clear, and the cassette transfers are made at a good level and are of high quality, matching the piano timbre found on the LPs.

7 Bagatelles, Op. 33.
*** Decca SXL 6951 [Lon. CS 7179]. Larrocha – MOZART: *Sonatas Nos. 4 and 8.****

7 Bagatelles, Op. 33; 11 Bagatelles, Op. 119; 6 Bagatelles, Op. 126.
(M) *** Turn. TV/*KC* 334077 [34077]. Brendel.

Beethoven's *Bagatelles*, particularly those from Opp. 119 and 126, have often been dismissed as chips from the master's workbench. Brendel treats them as worthwhile miniatures, and he shapes them with care and precision. His taste can never be faulted, and he is supported by mostly excellent recording. The treble is sometimes on the brittle side, but the focus is exact in all but the most complicated moments, when there is a slight excess of reverberation, not in the overall acoustic but in the piano's basic texture. (This is now available from Conifer in the UK in an imported American pressing.)

Alicia de Larrocha displays her usual finesse in the Op. 33 *Bagatelles*, and her articulation in the faster pieces is exhilaratingly crisp and clean. Her playing is consistently polished and sympathetic, and each of these miniatures is surely characterized. She is beautifully recorded, and, with its fine Mozart coupling, this can be recommended.

33 Variations on a waltz by Diabelli.
(M) *** Ph. Seq. 6527/*7311* 178. Bishop-Kovacevich.
**(*) Ph. 9500 381 [id.]. Brendel.
(M) **(*) Turn. TV/*KC* 334 139 [34139]. Brendel.
**(*) DG Dig. 2532/*3302* 048 [id.]. Barenboim.

Bishop-Kovacevich's marvellous interpretation of this most formidable of piano works does not make for easy listening. His manner is generally austere but, as he has repeatedly proved in the concert hall, he has the firmest possible grasp of the massive structure, and the end result, less immediately exciting than some others as it may be, is ultimately the most satisfying of all. Unlike Brendel on Turnabout Bishop does not allow himself unmarked accelerandos in each half of the fast crescendo variations, but his use of sharp dynamic contrasts is fearless, and in the ultimate test of the concluding variations he surpasses even his earlier achievement – the simple gravity of No. 31 leading to an exultant release in the bravura of the fugue, the deepest *Innigkeit* on the repeated chords in diminuendo which conclude it and a further magical release into the final minuet. A beautiful performance, cleanly recorded. The cassette transfer is faithful and clear, but the level might ideally have been a little higher.

Recorded live, Alfred Brendel's later Philips version of the *Diabelli variations* has an energy and urgency lacking in some of his other Philips recordings. The playing is understandably not flawless, but the tensions are superbly conveyed. The sound is first-rate, though not as delicate in dynamic range as in a studio recording.

The earlier Vox/Turnabout version is now available in an imported American pressing with cassette equivalent (which we have not heard). It offers a powerful, commanding performance of Beethoven's most taxing piano work. As in his live performances Brendel builds up the variations unerringly, but it is surprising to find to what degree he indulges in little accelerandos in each half of those variations which involve crescendos. Broadly his approach is romantic, with the adagio variation, No. 29, made into a moving lament. Few, if any, performances of this work on record convey its continuity so convincingly. The recording is faithful enough, but not really soft enough in pianissimos.

Barenboim's is an intensely personal reading, one which seems to stem from a purely spontaneous response to Beethoven's vast structure. Barenboim gives the illusion of an improvisation with expressive exaggerations in both directions, which may initially strike the listener as mannered, but which – caught by the engineer on the inspiration of the moment – have genuine magic. The sound is excellent.

VOCAL MUSIC

(i–iii) *Ah perfido!, Op. 65;* (iv–v) *Lieder* (complete, including *An die ferne Geliebte, Op. 98);* (v–vi; ii–iii) *Choral fantasia, Op. 80;* (vi–viii; ii) *Christus am Ölberge, Op. 85;* (iv; ix) *Folksong arrangements* (complete); (vi; ii–iii) *Meeresstille und glückliche Fahrt* (*Calm Sea and Prosperous Voyage*), *Op. 112*.

(M) *** DG 2721 138 (7) (i) Nilsson; (ii) VSO; (iii) Leitner; (iv) Fischer-Dieskau; (v) Demus; (vi) V. Singverein; (vii) Harwood, King, Crass; (viii) Klee; (ix) Mathis, Hamari, Young, Berlin RIAS Chamber Ch., Röhn, Donderer, Engel.

Obviously this set is a must. It collects all the songs from *An die ferne Geliebte* to the *Gellert lieder*, the folksong arrangements, the *Choral fantasia, Christ on the Mount of Olives*, and the cantata *Meeresstille und glückliche Fahrt* in exemplary performances on seven records. This is a set that cannot easily be compiled from alternative sources at so reasonable a cost, and it is to be recommended with all possible enthusiasm.

(i) *Ah perfido!;* (ii) *Cantata on the death of Emperor Joseph II, WoO 87*.

(M) ** CBS 60289/*40*-. (i) Crespin; (ii) Arroyo, Diaz, Camerata Singers, NYPO, Schippers.

A Beethoven curiosity, written in 1790 but not performed until 1884, after the composer's death. The piece is mainly of interest in including a theme he was to use again for the climax of *Fidelio* when the hero is freed. The performance here is lively but fails to make a case for returning the work to the repertoire. Régine Crespin's *Ah perfido!* is powerful, but its very forthright style is somewhat overwhelming, as the singing is not always too well focused. The recording is good, and there is a matching chrome cassette.

Choral fantasia in C, Op. 80.

*** Ph. 9500 471/*7300 628* [id.]. Brendel (piano), LPO Ch., LPO, Haitink – *Piano concerto No. 2*.***

This is discussed above under the coupling.

Christus am Ölberge, Op. 85.

(M) ** [Turn. 34458/*CT 2252*]. Rebmann, Bartel, Messthaler, S. German Ch., Stuttgart PO, Bloser.

With Beethoven depicting Christ (a tenor) as another Florestan, this oratorio is a stronger and more interesting work than has often been thought. This is not a high-powered performance, but it is convincingly spontaneous and live, and very welcome on a mid-price label. The recording is a little dated but fully acceptable. It is not currently available in the UK.

Egmont (incidental music), *Op. 84; The Creatures of Prometheus overture, Op. 43.*

(M) *** Decca Jub. JB 119. Lorengar, Wussow, VPO, Szell.

The problems of performing Beethoven's incidental music for Goethe's *Egmont* in its original dramatic context are partially solved here by drawing on a text by the Austrian poet Franz Grillparzer and using the *melodrama* of the final peroration from Goethe, vibrantly spoken by Klausjuergen Wussow. The snag is that, whereas the experience of listening to the music is eminently renewable, even German listeners find repetition of the text unrewarding. So for this reissue the narrative has been cut well back, though Goethe's *melodrama* remains. It is a fair compromise; Szell is a gripping advocate, and the songs are movingly sung by Pilar Lorengar. Abbado's performance of the *Prometheus overture* is an excellent make-weight.

Folksong arrangements: *The British Light Dragoons; Cease your fuming; Come Darby dear; Farewell song; Sally in our alley; Shepherd's song; The soldier; Sympathy; To the Aeolian harp.*
*** HM 1C 069 99940. Griffett, Maier, Mandalka, Tracey – HAYDN: *Folk-songs.***(*)

Beethoven's folksong settings written for George Thomson of Edinburgh are recognizably more than the pot-boilers some have called them. James Griffett's bright, fresh style, helped by the clearest possible diction, is excellently suited to Beethoven's lively manner and the twanging of a fortepiano along with violin and cello adds to the attraction. Excellent selection of items; first-rate recording.

(i) *Mass in C, Op. 86;* (ii) *Missa solemnis in D, Op. 123.*
** EMI 1C 149 52675/7 [Ang. S 36775 and SB 3836]. (i) Ameling, Baker, Altmeyer, Rintzler; (ii) Harper, Baker, Tear, Sotin; New Philh. Ch. and O, Giulini.
(M) ** DG 2721 135 (3). (i) Soloists, Munich Bach Ch. and O, Karl Richter; (ii) Soloists, V. Singverein, Berlin PO, Karajan.

Giulini directs the *C major Mass* without apology. After all it is only the dazzling splendour of the *Missa solemnis* that prevents this from being acclaimed as a Beethoven masterpiece, and in a performance as inspired, polished and intense as Giulini's, with a fine quartet of soloists and a superb choir, the gramophone can make ample amends for its neglect in the concert hall. With so splendid a team one expected even more from his set of the *Missa solemnis.* The recording is vivid, but it rarely conveys any kind of hushed tension, an essential quality in this of all choral works, and the ensemble of the chorus is far from perfect; the excellent soloists are all balanced very close.

The DG box is the least attractive of the Beethoven Edition sets. Those who want Karajan's earlier recording of the *Missa solemnis,* notable for its beauty of sound rather than for spiritual strength, can opt for the Privilege reissue. Richter's account of the *C major Mass* is somewhat earthbound.

Mass in C, Op. 86.
(M) **(*) Decca Jub. JB/*KJBC* 129. Palmer, Watts, Tear, Keyte, St John's College, Cambridge Ch., ASMF, Guest.

George Guest's reading is designedly intimate and his performance continually reminds us that this work was specifically intended as a successor to the late great Haydn masses, like them being commissioned for the Princess Esterhazy's name day. Naturally with boys' voices in the choir and a relatively small band of singers the results are incisive rather than dramatic, but with excellent recording this remains attractive in its own way. There is an impressively vivid cassette, one of Decca's best, with good detail and a generally clean focus.

Missa solemnis in D, Op. 123.
*** DG 2707 110/*3370 029* (2) [id.]. Moser, Schwarz, Kollo, Moll, Netherlands Ch., Concg. O, Bernstein.
(B) *** CfP CFP/*TC-CFP* 414420–3/*5* [Ang. SB 3821]. Janowitz, Baltsa, Schreier, Van Dam, V. Singverein, Berlin PO, Karajan.
**(*) HMV SLS/*TC-SLS* 922 (2). Söderström, Hoffgen, Kmennt, Talvela, New Philh. Ch. and O, Klemperer.
(M) **(*) DG 413 191-1/*4* (2) [id.]. Price, Ludwig, Ochman, Talvela, V. State Op. Ch., VPO, Boehm.
(M) ** DG 2726 048 (2) [2707 030]. Janowitz, Ludwig, Wunderlich, Berry, V. Singverein, Berlin PO, Karajan.

Bernstein's DG version with the Concertgebouw was edited together from tapes of two live performances, and the result has a spiritual intensity matched by very few rivals. Edda Moser is not an ideal soprano soloist, but the others are outstanding, and the *Benedictus* is made angelically beautiful by the radiant playing of the Concertgebouw concertmaster, Hermann Krebbers. The recording is a little light in bass, but outstandingly clear as well as atmospheric. On cassette, although the balance is somewhat recessed, the transfer is impressively clear, full-bodied and free from distortion.

Karajan's EMI version is notably more colourful and dramatic than his earlier DG account with the same orchestra, chorus and soprano. Though the reverberant recording obscures some detail, the urgency of Karajan's view here is most compelling. There is no feeling that he is skating over the surface of a spiritual experience, and the soloists are excellent. This makes a real bargain in its CfP reissue, with the sound on LP fresh yet full, and the cassettes remarkably successful too, with no distortion and very little loss of upper range compared with the discs. They are ingeniously packed in a double-thickness hinged plastic box with both top and bottom lids.

Klemperer's set has also been successfully remastered and HMV have taken the opportunity to issue a tape box alongside the discs. The whole work is accommodated on one double-length cassette, but the wide dynamic range has dictated a fairly unadventurous transfer level and while the climaxes open up well, the detail at pianissimo levels is less well projected and there is a degree of hiss. Tape collectors might do better with the CfP set. The glory of Klemperer's version is the superb choral singing of the New Philharmonia Chorus. It is not just their purity of tone and their fine discipline but the real fervour with which they sing that make the choral passages so moving. The orchestra too is in fine form. The soloists are less happily chosen. Waldemar Kmennt seems unpleasantly hard, and Elisabeth Söderström does not sound as firm as she can be.

Boehm's is a clean intelligent reading, but there is surprisingly little sense of occasion. Generally measured tempi and square rhythms undermine Beethoven's vividness of illustration, his sense of drama. It is a fine reading, but not an inspired one.

In response to Karajan's EMI version, DG reissued his earlier Berlin version on the mid-price Privilege label, and though its relative superficiality and detachment prevent an enthusiastic recommendation, the beauty is undeniable; and there is an exceptionally fine team of soloists and refined recording.

OPERA

Fidelio (complete).

*** HMV SLS/*TC-SLS* 5006 (3) [Ang. SCL 3625]. Ludwig, Vickers, Frick, Berry, Crass, Philh. Ch. and O, Klemperer.

(M) *** HMV SLS/*TC-SLS* 5231 (2) [Ang. SCL 3773]. Dernesch, Vickers, Ridderbusch, Van Dam, Kelemen, German Op. Ch., Berlin PO, Karajan.

*** DG 2709 082/*3371* 039 (3) [id.]. Janowitz, Kollo, Jungwirth, Sotin, Fischer-Dieskau, V. State Op. Ch., VPO, Bernstein.

** Decca Dig. D 178 D3/*K178 K32* [Lon. LDR/*5*- 10017]. Behrens, Hofmann, Sotin, Adam, Ghazarian, Kuebler, Howell, Chicago Ch. and SO, Solti.

(M) *(*) DG 2721 136 (3) [2709 031]. Jones, King, Talvela, Crass, Adam, Leipzig R. Ch., Dresden State Op. Ch. and State O, Boehm.

Klemperer's great set of *Fidelio* has been remastered and reissued with improved sound. It is a massive performance but one with wonderful incandescence and spiritual strength, and with a final scene in which, more than in any other performance ever recorded, the parallel with the finale of the *Choral symphony* is underlined. The cassette issue offers somewhat different quality on each of the two cassettes. Act I on tape one offers full, rich sound with both bloom and presence on the voices; in Act II the quality is rather more vibrant and sharply defined because of a higher transfer level, which is effective for the opera's climax.

Karajan's splendid 1971 recording has been reissued on two discs (or tapes), providing what amounts almost to a bargain-priced version to challenge the famous Klemperer set. Comparison between Karajan's strong and heroic reading and Klemperer's version is fascinating. Both have very similar merits, underlining the symphonic character of the work with their weight of utterance. Both may miss some of the sparkle of the opening scenes; but it is better that seriousness should enter too early than too late. Since seriousness is the keynote it is rather surprising to find Karajan using bass and baritone soloists lighter than usual. Both the Rocco (Ridderbusch) and the Don Fernando (Van Dam) lack something in resonance in their lower range. Yet they sing dramatically and intelligently and there is the advantage that the Pizarro of Zoltan Kelemen sounds the more biting and powerful as a result – a fine performance. Jon Vickers as Florestan is if anything even finer than he was for Klemperer, and though Helga Dernesch as Leonore does not have quite the clear-focused mastery of Christa Ludwig in the Klemperer set, this is still a glorious, thrilling performance, far outshining lesser rivals than Ludwig. The orchestral playing is superb. The cassette quality is admirably bright, clear and vivid. Unlike the Klemperer tapes, the side divisions are not tailored to match the ends of Acts, but the sharpness of focus of the sound is striking: the *Abscheulicher*, with its vibrant horns, and the following scene with the *Prisoners' chorus* have splendid presence and projection, yet there is no suspicion of peaking.

Bernstein, as one would expect, directs a reading of *Fidelio* full of dramatic flair. The recording was made in conjunction with live performances by the same cast at the Vienna State Opera, and the atmosphere in the domestic scenes at the start might almost come from a predecessor of the stage musical (compliment intended), with Lucia Popp as Marzelline particularly enchanting. The spoken dialogue is splendidly produced too. The Canon Quartet in Act I has warmth and humanity rather than monumental qualities; and though Bernstein later rises splendidly to the high drama of Act II (the confrontation with Pizarro in the Quartet is as exciting as in Klemperer's classic reading), it remains a drama on a human scale. Gundula Janowitz sings most beautifully as Leonore, shading her phrases in the long opening section of the *Abscheulicher*, coping superbly with the intricacies of the *Allegro* and falling short only at the very end, in a less than triumphant payoff. Kollo as Florestan is intelligent and musicianly but indulges in too many intrusive aitches, and there is some coarseness of tone. Hans Sotin as Pizarro sings with superb projection, and the size of voice makes up for its not sounding villainous. Manfred Jungwirth makes an engaging Rocco, though his singing is not always perfectly steady. Fischer-Dieskau – once an incomparable Pizarro – here makes a noble Don Fernando in the final scene. In keeping with Bernstein's approach the voices are placed rather close, and the balance is not always quite consistent, though the sound is vivid. The cassette transfer is made at a comparatively modest level, which means that there is some lack of range in the orchestral sound of the overture. As soon as the opera itself begins, however, the refinement of the recording, both of voices and of background orchestral detail, is quite striking, although the level of the transfer varies a little between sides. The tape layout matches the three discs.

Solti's set was the first-ever digital recording of an opera. The sound is full, clean and vividly atmospheric, matched by the conductor's urgent and intense direction. With fine choral singing the ensembles are excellent, but the solo singing is too flawed for comfort. Hildegard Behrens seems ungainly in the great *Abscheulicher*, the voice sounding less beautiful than usual; and both Peter Hofmann as Florestan and Theo Adam as Pizarro too often produce harsh unattractive tone. The cassette transfer is extremely sophisticated, matching the clarity and excellence of the discs. The layout, with one act on each of the two cassettes, is superior and the libretto/booklet is well designed and clearly printed.

Boehm, returning to the orchestra he directed in the 1930s, brings a mature warmth to the score; but there are too many flaws in the singing for the set to compete seriously. Gwyneth Jones produces too many squally notes to be a satisfying Leonore, and James King is an uninspired Florestan. Theo Adam as Pizarro is no more appealing to the ear. Good, warm recording.

Fidelio: highlights.
** Decca Dig. SXDL/*KSXDC* 7529 (from above set cond. Solti).

Choosing highlights from Solti's flawed performance of *Fidelio* inevitably underlines the weaknesses, when Behrens lacks full control in the first part of the *Abscheulicher* and Theo Adam is so gritty a Pizzaro. But the selection is generous, and it is good to have the end of the finale included. The digital recording is excellent, although on cassette the choral focus is not quite as sharp as on disc.

Bellini, Vincenzo (1801–35)

Oboe concerto in E flat.
(M) *** DG Priv. 2535/*3335* 417 [139152]. Holliger, Bamberg SO, Maag – CIMAROSA, DONIZETTI, SALIERI: *Concertos.****

Bellini's *Oboe concerto* seems too brief, so beautifully is it played here. It is part of an irresistible anthology, immaculately recorded on both disc and cassette. Highly recommended.

Night Shadow (ballet, arr. Rieti).
(M) ** HMV Green. ESD/*TC-ESD* 7148. L. Fest. Ballet O, Kern – DRIGO: *Le Corsaire* *(*); HELSTED: *La Fête.***

Bellini's music is tastefully scored by Vittorio Rieti (for Balanchine) and, played with style and sparkle, makes enjoyable if not memorable listening. The recording is excellent with a matching cassette.

OPERA

Beatrice di Tenda: complete.
**(*) Decca SET 320/2 [Lon. OSA 1384]. Sutherland, Veasey, Pavarotti, Ward, Opthof, Amb. Op. Ch., LSO, Bonynge.

Beatrice di Tenda was Bellini's last but one opera, coming after *Sonnambula* and *Norma* and before *I Puritani* (the latter written for Paris). It had an unfortunate birth, for the composer had to go to the law-courts to wring the libretto from his collaborator, Romani, and the result is not exactly compelling dramatically. The story involves a whole string of unrequited loves – X loves Y who loves Z who loves . . . and so on, and the culminating point comes when the heroine, Beatrice, wife of Filippo, Duke of Milan, is denounced falsely for alleged infidelity. There is an impressive trial scene – closely based on the trial scene of Donizetti's *Anna Bolena* – and the unfortunate Beatrice is condemned to death and executed despite the recantation of false witnesses. Bellini always intended to revise the score, but failed to do so before his death. As it is, the piece remains essentially a vehicle for an exceptional prima donna with a big enough voice and brilliant enough coloratura. Joan Sutherland has naturally made it her own, and though in this recorded version she indulges in some of the 'mooning' one hoped she had left behind, the many dazzling examples of her art on the six sides are a real delight. The other star of the set is Sutherland's husband, Richard Bonynge, whose powers as a Bellini conductor are most impressive. The supporting cast could hardly be better, with Pavarotti unusually responsive for a modern tenor. Outstanding recording.

I Capuleti e i Montecchi: complete.
**(*) EMI 2C 167 02713/5 [Ang. SCLX/*4X3X* 3824]. Sills, Baker, Gedda, Herincx, Lloyd, Alldis Ch., New Philh. O, Patané.

Bellini's setting of the Romeo and Juliet story makes a strange opera, enjoyable as long as you can forget any parallel with Shakespeare. The decision to give the role of Romeo to a mezzo-soprano is itself controversial, but here, with Janet Baker responding richly to the unfailing lyricism of Bellini, Romeo's music provides the focus of interest in an opera where the material is spread somewhat thinly. Much of the inspiration brings reminders of early Verdi – the exciting opening of the overture, for example – and the whole score is well worth the attention of Bellinians. Beverly Sills has her moments of shrillness, but the rest of the singing is very commendable, and the conducting of Giuseppe Patané is beautifully sprung. Good atmospheric recording, with a cassette version available in the USA.

Norma: complete.
*** Decca SET 424/6/*K 21 K 32* [Lon. OSA/*5-* 1394]. Sutherland, Horne, Alexander, Cross, LSO Ch., LSO, Bonynge.
*** HMV SLS/*TC-SLS* 5186 (3) [Ang. SCL 3615]. Callas, Corelli, Zaccaria, Ludwig, Palma, Ch. and O of La Scala, Milan, Serafin.
** [CBS M3X 35902]. Scotto, Giacomini, Troyanos, Plishka, Crook, Murray, Ambrosian Op. Ch., Nat. PO, Levine.

The combination of Sutherland and Marilyn Horne – whose control of florid singing is just as remarkable – is formidable here in a score which makes great technical demands on both female principals. But fine as Horne's contribution is, Sutherland's marked a new level of achievement in her recording career. Accepting the need for a dramatic approach in very much the school of Callas, she then ensures at the same time that something as near as possible to musical perfection is achieved. The old trouble of diction with the words masked is occasionally present, and on the whole Sutherland's old account of *Casta diva* on her early recital disc, *The art of the prima donna*, (see Recitals) is fresher than this. But basically this is a most compelling performance, musically and dramatically, and in this Sutherland is helped by the conducting of Richard Bonynge. In the many conventional accompaniment figures he manages to keep musical interest alive with sprung rhythm and with the subtlest attention to the vocal line. The other soloists are all very good indeed, John Alexander and Richard Cross both young, clear-voiced singers. The recording, made at Walthamstow, has the usual fine qualities of Decca opera recording. The tape transfer is good, but the high level brings some occasional 'peaking' on the soprano voices at climaxes.

By the time Callas recorded her stereo version of *Norma* in the early 1960s, the tendency to hardness and unsteadiness in the voice above the stave, always apparent, had grown more serious; but the interpretation was as sharply illuminating as ever, a unique assumption helped – as the earlier mono performance was not – by a strong cast. Christa Ludwig as Adalgisa brings not just rich firm tone but a real feeling for Italian style, and despite moments of coarseness Corelli sings heroically. Serafin as ever is the most persuasive of Bellini conductors, and the recording is good for its period, with an excellent cassette transfer. The layout is on two cassettes, with no attempt made to apportion Acts to sides; the reduction of the libretto gives very small print. (Callas's earlier 1954 mono set is also available (HMV SLS/*TC-SLS* 5115), offering a unique reminder of the diva at her vocal peak, but the rest of the cast is flawed.)

Renata Scotto as Norma has many beautiful moments, but above pianissimo in the upper register the voice too regularly acquires a heavy beat, and the sound becomes ugly. The close recording does not help, any more than it does with Tatiana Troyanos as Adalgisa, whose vibrato is exaggerated. Giuseppe Giacomini sings with fair style but little imagination, and Levine's conducting is far too brutal for such a piece, favouring aggressively fast tempi. (This set has been withdrawn in the UK.)

Duets from *Norma:* Act I: *O rimembranza! . . . O, non tremare;* Act II: *Deh! con te . . . Mira, o Norma . . . Sì, fino all'ore estreme.*

(*) Decca SET 456 [Lon. OS 26168]. Sutherland, Horne, LSO, Bonynge – ROSSINI: *Semiramide duets.**

The collaboration of Joan Sutherland and Marilyn Horne is a classic one, and it was a good idea to collect the great duets from *Semiramide* as well as from *Norma*, a feast for vocal collectors. *Mira, o Norma* is taken rather slowly, with a degree more of mannerism than the singers might currently allow themselves.

I Puritani: complete.

*** Decca SET 587/9 [Lon. OSA/*5*-13111]. Sutherland, Pavarotti, Cappuccilli, Ghiaurov, ROHCG Ch. and O, Bonynge.

(M) **(*) HMV SLS 5201 [Ang. SZCX/*4Z3X* 3881]. Caballé, Kraus, Manuguerra, Amb. Op. Ch., Philh. O, Muti.

Ten years after her first recording of *I Puritani*, made in Florence, Joan Sutherland returned to this limpidly lyrical music. 'Opera must make people weep, shudder, die through the singing,' wrote Bellini to his librettist, and this sharply committed performance – much crisper of ensemble than the earlier one, with Bonynge this time adopting a more urgently expressive style – breathes life into what can seem a rather limp story about Cavaliers and Roundheads. Where the earlier set was recorded when Sutherland had adopted a soft-grained style, with consonants largely eliminated and a tendency to lag behind the beat, this time her singing is fresher and brighter. The lovely aria *Qui la voce* is no longer a wordless melisma, and though the great showpiece *Son vergin vezzosa* is now taken dangerously fast, the extra bite and tautness are exhilarating. Pavarotti, possessor of the most radiantly beautiful of tenor voices, shows himself a remarkable Bellini stylist, rarely if ever coarsening a legato line, unlike so many of his Italian colleagues. Ghiaurov and Cappuccilli make up an impressive cast, and the only disappointing contributor is Anita Caminada in the small role of Enrichetta – Queen Henrietta Maria in disguise. Vivid, atmospheric recording. The tape transfer is of high quality in Acts I and III, but slightly less perfect in focus in Act II.

In the HMV version of *I Puritani* Riccardo Muti's contribution is the most distinguished. As the very opening demonstrates, his attention to detail and pointing of rhythm make for refreshing results, and the warm but luminous recording is excellent. But both the principal soloists – Bellini stylists on their day – indulge in distracting mannerisms, hardly allowing even a single bar to be presented straight in the big numbers, pulling and tugging in each direction, rarely sounding spontaneous in such deliberate expressiveness. The big ensemble *A te, o cara*, in its fussiness at slow speed, loses the surge of exhilaration which the earlier Decca set with Sutherland and Pavarotti shows so strongly.

Il Pirata (opera): complete.
** EMI 3C 165 02108/10. Caballé, Rafanelli, Martí, Baratti, Cappuccilli, Raimondi, Rome Radiotelevisione Ch., and O, Gavazzeni.

Bellinians will welcome this first complete recording of *Il Pirata*, the composer's third opera, written for La Scala to a libretto by Romani. By Caballé's standards there is some carelessness here – clumsy changes of register and less than usual beauty of tonal contrast. Nor is the conducting and presentation sparkling enough to mask the comparative poverty of Bellini's invention at this early stage of his career. Bellinians will undoubtedly lap it up, but for others there must be reservations about recommending an opera that is very long for its material. Bernabé Martí, Caballé's husband, makes a fair stab at the difficult part of the Pirate himself: not many current rivals could even manage the range. The recording is full-blooded and realistic.

La Sonnambula (complete).
*** Decca Dig. D 230 D 3/*K 230 K 33* (3) [Lon. LDR/5- 73004]. Sutherland, Pavarotti, Della Jones, Ghiaurov, L. Op. Ch., Nat. PO, Bonynge.
(M) ** HMV SLS/*TC-SLS* 5134 (2). Callas, Monti, Cossotto, Zaccaria, Ratti, Ch. and O of La Scala, Milan, Votto.

Sutherland in her second complete recording sings with richness and ease in even the most spectacular coloratura, matched in the tenor role this time by an equal (if not always so stylish) star. Ensembles as well as display arias have an authentic Bellinian surge. Excellent recording, with matching chrome tapes.

Substantially cut, the Callas version was recorded in mono in 1957, yet it gives a vivid picture of the diva at the peak of her powers. By temperament she may not have related closely to Bellini's heroine, but the village girl's simple devotion through all trials is touchingly caught, most of all in the recitatives.

Benda, Jiří Antonín (1722–95)

Harpsichord concertos: in C; D; F; G; G min.; Divertimento in G.
(M) ** Sup. 1111 2761/2. Hála, Novák Quintet.

Jiří Antonín, the younger brother of Franz (František) Benda, made his reputation as a composer of melodramas (music with spoken dialogue), the best-known of which are *Ariadne auf Naxos*, *Medea* and *Pygmalion*. These concertos reflect something of the influence of C. P. E. Bach, with whom Benda came into contact during his formative years at the Prussian court. Not all the pieces recorded here with single strings are of equal interest; intelligently laid out though they are, the melodic inspiration is not always distinctive enough to engage one's whole-hearted sympathy. The performances are alert and well recorded, though the first violin is rather too prominently placed.

Benedict, Julius (1804–85)

The Lily of Killarney (opera): highlights.
** HMV CSD 3651. Dunne, Deane, Hinds, O, Nelson – BALFE: *Bohemian Girl;* WALLACE: *Maritana.***

Benedict's music has a soft Irish lilt and also a strong rhythmic flavour of Sullivan. Its pastel shades make a pleasing contrast with the primary colours of Wallace's *Maritana* selection, which precedes it on the present L.P. *The Moon hath raised* is typical, but the other three numbers here are equally pleasant and they bring out the best in the soloists, who do not attempt to oversing them. Especially charming is Veronica Dunne's performance of *I'm alone*. The opera, which has a rustic plot with mistaken accusations of murder, has a happy ending. It was first produced at Covent Garden in 1862.

Benjamin, Arthur (1893–1960)

Harmonica concerto.
*** Argo ZRG 905. Reilly, L. Sinf., Atherton – ARNOLD and VILLA-LOBOS: *Concertos.****

Arthur Benjamin's engaging *Harmonica concerto* was written for Larry Adler who has made an RCA recording of it – not at present available – but the RCA recorded balance is less than ideal. The Argo sound is infinitely finer, and in the beautiful slow movement, which has a strong hint of Vaughan Williams (who prompted Benjamin to write the work), there is far more depth and atmosphere. Tommy Reilly plays with great sympathy and he is more naturally balanced with the orchestra.

Cotillon: suite of English dance tunes.
*** Lyr. SRCS 115. LSO, Braithwaite – ARNOLD: *Sinfonietta No. 1* ***; BUSH: *Symphony No. 1.****

Arthur Benjamin was gifted with much natural facility and readers who know the *Concerto for harmonica* and the *Overture to an Italian Comedy* will not need reminding that, at its best, his invention approached real distinction. If his music does not always bear an individual stamp, it is nearly always unpretentious and well-crafted. However, *Cotillon*, an arrangement of melodies found in *The Dancing Master* by W. Pearson and John Young in London in 1719 and made for a fairly large orchestra, hardly seems worth while putting on record. The tunes themselves are not unattractive but the arrangement strikes us as less than elegant. However, it is very well played and recorded.

Bennett, Richard Rodney (born 1936)

(i) *Aubade for orchestra;* (ii) *Spells.*
**(*) Argo ZRG 907. Philh. O, (i) Atherton, (ii) Willcocks, with Manning, Bach Ch.

Spells is an ambitious choral work, a setting of verses by Kathleen Raine, which skilfully gets an amateur choir singing confidently in a serial idiom. Not that the Bach Choir is as dramatic and colourful as the music really demands, and it is Jane Manning who, above all in *Love Spell*, the longest of the six movements, conveys the work's magical flavour. *Aubade* is one of Bennett's most attractive shorter orchestral works, here well conducted by David Atherton. The recording is good, though the choral sound could be clearer.

Bentzon, Niels (born 1919)

Symphonies Nos. 3, Op. 46; 5 (Ellipsis), Op. 61; 7 (The Three Versions), Op. 83.
*** Danish Music Anthology DMAO 56/7. Aarhus City O, Schmidt.

Niels Viggo Bentzon is enormously prolific and can match such figures as Milhaud and Villa-Lobos in this respect. There are 14 symphonies, 15 piano concertos, dozens of sonatas for various instruments and an opus list extending to 450 entries. Though his output is uneven, the late 1940s and early 1950s (when these symphonies were composed) show his powers at their height. The *Third Symphony* has a gentle pastoral opening which gives rise to a great variety of themes, none of which ever outstays its welcome. The listener is engaged throughout and amazed by the fertility and facility of the ideas. At every playing this symphony grows in strength and its world, which at first seems to derive from Nielsen with a touch of Hindemith and Stravinsky, soon assumes its rightful individual identity. Bentzon has (at least at this stage in his career) strong classical instincts which surface even more powerfully in the *Fourth* (*Metamorphosis*) and *Sixth Symphonies*, as well as the *Fifth* recorded here. They serve to discipline an abundant musical imagination teeming with vital invention. The most impressive of the three symphonies recorded here (and the handful we have heard) is the *Seventh* whose vision is keener and more vivid than the other two. There is a boldness of conception, a plenitude of melodic interest and a vivid harmonic and orchestral palette. At times the luminous woodwind chords that are sustained in the background behind the main burden of the musical argument remind one of the effect in the *Prelude* to Sibelius's *Tempest*, of distant lights glimpsed on the horizon as the storm subsides. The neglect of this composer who is infinitely more substantial than many much more celebrated figures can only be explained in terms of his fertility and unevenness. Save only for Holmboe, these are the most impressive Scandinavian symphonies to have appeared since the war. Those who like Nielsen, and wish that he had not stopped at No. 6, should investigate these original pieces which are played with total dedication and conviction, and excellently recorded.

Berg, Alban (1885–1935)

Chamber concerto for piano, violin and 13 wind.
*** Argo ZRG 937 [id.]. Crossley, Pauk, L. Sinf., Atherton – STRAVINSKY: *Agon.****

As a birthday tribute to his friend and teacher Schoenberg, Berg wrote the *Chamber concerto*, his most concentratedly formalized work, a piece that can very easily seem cold and inexpressive. Atherton rightly takes the opposite view that for all its complexity it is romantic at heart, so that one hears it as a melodic work full of warmth and good humour, and the waltz rhythms are given a genuine Viennese flavour. Pauk and Crossley are outstanding soloists, the Sinfonietta plays with precision as well as commitment, and the recording is excellent, with the difficult balance problems intelligently solved.

Violin concerto.
*** DG 2531/*3301* 110 [id.]. Perlman, Boston SO, Ozawa – STRAVINSKY: *Concerto.****
(M) *** Sup. 50804. Suk, Czech PO, Ančerl – BACH: *Cantata No. 60.**(*)

Perlman's performance of the Berg *Violin concerto* is totally commanding. The effortless precision of the playing goes with great warmth of expression, so that the usual impression of 'wrong-note romanticism' gives way to total purposefulness. The Boston orchestra accompanies superbly, and though the balance favours the soloist, the recording is excellent, with a faithful tape transfer.

Suk's moving account is aptly coupled with the Bach cantata from which Berg took the chorale theme for the culmination of his finale. The soloist's sweet unforced style brings out the work's lyrical side without ever exaggerating the romanticism. The arrival of the chorale is most delicately achieved, and the final coda has rarely if ever sounded so tender and hushed on record. A most beautiful performance, very well recorded.

Lyric suite: 3 Pieces; 3 Pieces for orchestra, Op. 6.
*** DG 2711 014 (4) [id.]. Berlin PO, Karajan – SCHOENBERG and WEBERN: *Orchestral pieces.****

Karajan's purification process gives wonderful clarity to these often complex pieces, with expressive confidence bringing out the romantic overtones. No more persuasive view could be taken, though next to Schoenberg and Webern Berg appears here as the figure who overloaded his music, rather than as the most approachable of the Second Viennese School. Beautiful, refined recording.

Lyric suite.
(*) CBS 76305/*40*– [M 35166]. NYPO, Boulez – SCHOENBERG: *Verklaerte Nacht.*(*)

Boulez offers the *Lyric suite* spread over one side (short measure at only fifteen minutes). He is not as sumptuously recorded as Karajan, nor is his reading as subtle or refined, and the pianissimo tone of the New Yorkers does not match that of the Berlin Philharmonic. However, this is fine playing (dodecaphony with a human face), and some will prefer the greater urgency and emotional strength of Boulez's approach. The CBS recording is perfectly acceptable and the cassette transfer is quite vivid.

Lulu (original version).
*** Decca D 48 D 3/*K 48 K 32* (3) [Lon. OSA/*5*- 13120]. Silja, Fassbaender, Berry, Hopferweiser, Moll, Krenn, VPO, Dohnányi.

Lulu (with orchestration of Act III completed by Cerha).
*** DG 2740 213/*3378* 086 (4) [id.]. Stratas, Minton, Schwarz, Mazura, Blankenheim, Riegel, Tear, Paris Op. O, Boulez.

The full three-act structure of Berg's *Lulu*, first unveiled by Boulez in his Paris Opéra production and here treated to studio recording, was a revelation with few parallels. The third Act, musically even stronger than the first two and dramatically essential in making sense of the stylized plan based on a palindrome, transforms the opera. Although it ends with a lurid portrayal of Jack the Ripper's murder of Lulu – here recorded with hair-raising vividness – the nastiness of the subject is put in context, made more acceptable artistically. The very end of the opera, with Yvonne Minton singing the Countess Geschwitz's lament, is most moving, though Lulu remains to the last a repulsive heroine. Teresa Stratas's bright, clear soprano is well recorded, and there is hardly a weak link in the cast. The recording is a little lacking in clarity and atmosphere compared with the Decca version of Acts I and II. On tape, although the transfer level is modest, the naturalness and detail of the sound demonstrate DG's best standards, and the climaxes are accommodated without strain. The layout on four cassettes follows the discs, with side eight given to commentaries on the work by Douglas Jarman (in English), Friedrich Cerha (in German) and Pierre Boulez (in French); translations are provided in the booklet libretto (easier to read in the disc than the characteristic narrow DG tape format). Altogether this is a historic issue, presenting an intensely involving performance of a work which in some ways is more lyrically approachable than *Wozzeck*.

Recordings earlier than the Decca set on disc were made during live performances, so Dohnányi was the first to achieve anything like precision. The pity is that he was not able to record the completed Act III, for which

Boulez had first recording rights. Instead, Dohnányi follows traditional practice in using the two movements of the *Lulu suite* as a replacement. Anja Silja is vividly in character, attacking the stratospheric top notes with ease, always singing with power and rarely falling into her usual hardness. Walter Berry too is exceptionally strong as Dr Schön, aptly sinister, and even the small roles are cast from strength. The Vienna Philharmonic plays ravishingly, underlining the opera's status – whatever the formal patterns behind the notes, and whatever the subject – as an offshoot of romanticism. The cassettes, like the discs, set new standards, with sound of amazing richness and depth.

Lulu: symphonic suite.
(M) ** CBS 60258/*40*-. De Sett, Phd. O, Ormandy – SCHOENBERG: *Theme and variations*; WEBERN: *3 Pieces*.**

Lulu: symphonic suite. 3 Pieces for orchestra, Op. 6; 5 Orchestral songs, Op. 4.
(M) *** DG Sig. 2543 804 [id.]. M. Price; LSO, Abbado.

Though the need for the so-called *Symphonic suite* (using material from the uncompleted Act III) has sharply diminished since the completion of the whole opera has been heard, this DG record offers a superb rendering from conductor, soloist and orchestra. Abbado makes it clear above all how beautiful Berg's writing is, not just in the *Lulu* excerpts but in the early *Opus 4 Songs* and the *Opus 6 Orchestral pieces*, among which even the formidable march movement has sumptuousness as well as power. The recording from the early 1970s is still outstanding, rich and refined.

Fine playing from the Philadelphia Orchestra, but not as subtle or as well recorded as the LSO. The sound is full and the strings are rich-textured, but the overall effect is a little glamorized and the texture less transparent than that offered by DG for Abbado where climaxes expand more comfortably. The soprano, Luisa de Sett, tackles her demanding part very well indeed but Margaret Price is even better. The clear, full-bodied chrome cassette matches the disc fairly closely.

Lulu: suite. Wozzeck: 3 scenes.
(M) **(*) Mercury SRI 75065 [id.]. Pilarczyk; LSO, Dorati.

Though dating from 1962, the Mercury recording of the *Lulu suite* and three excerpts from *Wozzeck* is still impressive as sound, not just for powerful performances. The restoration of the full Act III of *Lulu* undermines the need for this suite, but it provides a vivid reminder of some of the most striking passages in the opera, neatly reworked, as do the *Wozzeck* scenes – Marie watching the parade, Marie reading the Bible, and the watery death of Wozzeck, followed by the scene of his child playing. Pilarczyk, balanced rather close, gives positive performances whether as Marie or in the *Lulu* last movement as Lulu (shrieking her last) and Countess Geschwitz (lamenting).

Wozzeck (complete).
*** Decca Dig. D 231 D 2/*K 231 K 22* [Lon. LDR 72007]. Waechter, Silja, Winkler, Laubenthal, Jahn, Malta, Sramek, VPO, Dohnányi.
** DG 2707 023 (2) [id.]. Lear, Melchert, Stolze, Wunderlich, Fischer-Dieskau, Kohn, Schoenberger Sängerknaben, Ch. and O of German Op., Berlin, Boehm.

Dohnányi, with refined textures and superb playing from the Vienna Philharmonic, presents an account of *Wozzeck* that is not only more accurate than any other on record but also more beautiful. It may lack some of the bite of Pierre Boulez's CBS version (now deleted) and some of the romantic warmth of Karl Boehm's set, but with superb digital sound the Decca set stands as first choice. Unfortunately the beauty of the performance does not extend to Eberhard Waechter's vocal quality in the name part, but he gives a thoughtful, sensitive performance. The edge of Anja Silja's voice and her natural vibrancy of character make her a memorable Marie, first cousin to Lulu. An excellent supporting cast too. As usual with Decca, the cassette transfer is of admirable quality, the sound richly atmospheric as well as clear and vivid.

Boehm finds more beauty in Berg's score than one ever thought possible, just as Fischer-Dieskau finds more nobility in the hero's character. Thanks largely to the timbre of Fischer-Dieskau's voice and to the intensity of projection in his words, one can hardly picture Wozzeck here as in any way moronic. His situation is much closer to conventional tragedy than one imagines Berg, or for that matter Büchner, original creator of the character, ever conceived. The result may be unconventional, unauthentic even, but it certainly makes one listen to the opera afresh, and on record there is a case for a performance which brings out clarity, precision and beauty, even in a work like this. Evelyn Lear is a far more convincing Marie than her CBS rival (though still not ideal), and generally the supporting cast is vocally more assured than Boulez's Paris singers.

Berio, Luciano (born 1925)

A-Ronne; Cries of London.
*** Decca HEAD 15. Swingle II, composer.

A-Ronne, literally 'A to Z', is an extraordinary setting of a multilingual poem by Edoardo Sanguinetti. From time to time the eight voices break into singing briefly, but for the most part the characteristic musical collage consists of shouts, snarls and organized crowd noises, with the fragmentary word-sequence run through some twenty times. This definitive recording was used for a memorable BBC television film, and many of the techniques are directly related to film camera-work. Berio himself calls the piece a documentary on Sanguinetti's poem. It may not be so concentrated as earlier Berio works, but it is just as fascinating in its way. The *Cries of London*, adapted from a piece originally written for the King's Singers, is almost equally surrealistic, an updating of the cries used by Elizabethan madrigal composers but with musical references to medieval patterns rather than Elizabethan. There is some jokiness (as when to the words *Some go down* the bass gets lower and lower and finally coughs out of his last note), but much of the music in this cycle of seven vocal pieces is immediately beautiful. The performances by Swingle II are nothing less than brilliant, and are recorded with stunning immediacy.

Sinfonia.
(M) *** CBS 60259/*40*-. Swingle Singers, NYPO, composer – BARTÓK: *Music for strings, percussion and celesta.****

Berio's *Sinfonia* was commissioned by the New York Philharmonic Orchestra. It is a highly successful work that readily communicates to the listener. The longest movement is a musical collage using material from Mahler's *Second symphony*, Beethoven's *Pastoral symphony*, Ravel's *La valse*, Wagner's *Das Rheingold* and Strauss's *Der Rosenkavalier*, among other items. The Swingle Singers add their own comments (subconscious thoughts, perhaps?) to the proceedings, and the whole thing is highly spontaneous. The other movements are simple, more static, but contain the kernel of the work's musical thought. The recording is first-class, with a matching chrome tape.

Berkeley, Lennox (born 1903)

Antiphon.
(M) **(*) Uni. UNS 260. Westminster Cath String O, Mawby – M. BERKELEY: *Meditations*; IRELAND: *Concertino pastorale.***(*)

Written for the St Martin's Academy to play at the Cheltenham Festival in 1973, Sir Lennox Berkeley's *Antiphon* presents a skilful set of variations on a plainchant theme, not a strongly characterized piece but a satisfyingly thoughtful one. The strings here could be more polished, but the coupling is apt and attractive.

(i) *Flute concerto, Op. 36;* (ii) *Flute sonatina; Flute sonata, Op. 97.*
*** RCA RS/*RSK* 9011. Galway; (i) LPO, composer; (ii) Moll (piano).

None of this music is 'important' but it has great charm, and admirers of Berkeley's elegant and finely crafted *Concerto* will be delighted with Galway's presentation of it and that of the early *Sonatina*, originally intended for the recorder. Civilized and refreshing music, excellently recorded too. The orchestra, over which the composer himself presides, play with sympathy and enthusiasm. There is an excellent chrome cassette.

Guitar concerto.
*** RCA ARL1 1181/*RK 11734* [ARL1/*ARK1* 1181]. Bream, Monteverdi O, Gardiner – RODRIGO: *Concierto de Aranjuez.****

When it was originally performed as part of the City of London Festival of 1974, this concertante work for Julian Bream was described as a concertino. Though the orchestral writing was light, that diminutive title was unfair to an extended work which presents a serious as well as an attractive argument, with elegant architecture and a stylish brand of guitar-writing that never leans barrenly on Spanish models. Bream's performance is superb, and the recording vivid. An attractive if out-of-the-way coupling for the most popular of all guitar concertos. There is an effective cassette transfer.

(i) *Piano concerto in B flat, Op. 29;* (ii) *Symphony No. 2, Op. 51.*
*** Lyr. SRCS 94. (i) Wilde, New Philh. O; (ii) LPO; both cond. Braithwaite.

Sir Lennox Berkeley's *Second Symphony* dates from 1957, though he made some small revisions in 1976, not long before this record was made. It is the work of a sophisticated and cultured musical mind; textures are clean and the ideas are beautifully laid out. This is civilized music and its originality is all the more rewarding for the restrained expressive means. The *Piano concerto* is a much earlier piece, written in the immediate wake of the war, and though it is more traditional in layout, it is by no means less rewarding. It is every bit as well performed here as the symphony, and the Lyrita recording has impeccable clarity, depth and realism. A valuable addition to the discography of English music.

(i) *Double piano concerto, Op. 30; Symphony No. 1.*
*** Lyr. SRCS 80. LPO, Del Mar, (i) with Beckett, McDonald.

The *Symphony* is a beautifully fashioned work which reflects Berkeley's Gallic sympathies as well as his admiration for Stravinsky. It is distinctly individual, memorable and finely proportioned and the scoring has a pale, luminous quality that is most appealing. The *Symphony* dates from 1940 and the *Concerto*, no less finely wrought and rewarding, comes from 1948. The playing of the LPO under Norman Del Mar and the contribution of the two soloists merit the warmest plaudits, and the engineering maintains the high standards of the Lyrita series. An altogether admirable issue.

Divertimento in B flat, Op. 18; Partita for chamber orchestra, Op. 66; Serenade for strings, Op. 12; Sinfonia concertante for oboe and chamber orchestra, Op. 84: Canzonetta (only).
*** Lyr. SRCS 74. LPO, composer.

This beautifully planned Lyrita disc brings together some of the most elegant and enjoyable music that Berkeley has written. The *Divertimento* is enchanting with its four stylish and often witty movements, while the *String serenade*, similarly in four sections, brings a beautiful closing slow movement. The fourth movement from the *Sinfonia concertante* is a splendid makeweight, while another relatively recent work, the *Partita*, belies in its rather weightier tone of voice the fact that it was written originally with a youth orchestra in mind. Excellent performances, splendid recording.

Sinfonietta.
*** Lyr. SRCS 111. ECO, Del Mar – BRITTEN: *Sinfonietta*; RAWSTHORNE: *Divertimento*; TIPPETT: *Divertimento.****

Berkeley's *Sinfonietta* is a delightful example of his genius for the miniature. Perfectly crafted, it says much in the shortest possible span, lightly but with no feeling of triviality. It is well-matched with other sinfoniettas and divertimentos by his contemporaries, and is beautifully performed and recorded.

CHAMBER MUSIC

Diversions, Op. 63; Oboe quartet, Op. 70; Sextet, Op. 47; Palm Court waltz, Op. 81/2 (piano duet version)*; Piano Sonatina, Op. 39.*
*** Hyp. A 66086. Stott, Nash Ens.

The Nash Ensemble's eightieth-birthday tribute to Sir Lennox is delightful. Though the *Palm Court waltz* is not quite as charming as one hopes, it is fun, and goes well with the elegant *Sonatina* as well as the more important chamber pieces, which show Berkeley at his most effective and characteristically refined. Of the soloists the oboist, Michael Collins, deserves special mention, and the recording is first-rate with woodwind balanced a little forward of strings.

(i) *Piano and wind quintet, Op. 90; 6 Preludes, Op. 23; Scherzo, Op. 32/2.* (ii) *Another Spring* (3 songs), *Op. 93.*
**(*) Mer. E 77017. Horsley, with (i) Lord, Fell, Baker, Kerry Camden; (ii) Loring.

Berkeley's *Quintet* is, as its opus number suggests, a late piece, dating from 1974. It was commissioned by the Chamber Music Society of Lincoln Center. It is fluent, inventive music, well laid out for the medium, and is nicely played here by Colin Horsley and his wind players. There is a substantial first movement, perhaps the best of the four, and a fine set of variations as finale. The piano *Preludes* come off attractively, and so do the appealing Walter de la Mare settings (Op. 93). Berkeley's meticulous craftsmanship is always in evidence, and the recording, though not distinguished (there is too much reverberance in the piano pieces), is fully acceptable.

String trio, Op. 19.
** Pearl SHE 547. Georgiadis, Hawkins, Cummings – BAX: *Rhapsodic ballad* ***; BRIDGE: *Trio.***

Berkeley's *Trio* comes from 1944 and is as expertly crafted and musically rewarding as one expects from this fastidious and sensitive master. Its elegance is well conveyed by the three artists recorded here, and though the piece may not have the darker overtones of its companions, it is far from merely lightweight in character. The recording is slightly closer than is ideal, but the interest of this disc outweighs any such reservations.

Andantino, Op. 21/2b; Fantasia, Op. 92; 3 Pieces, Op. 72/1.
*** Hyp. Dig. A 66061. Bate (organ of St James' Church, Muswell Hill) – DICKINSON: *Organ pieces.****

It is not surprising to find Lennox Berkeley, the most fastidious British composer of his generation, turning to the organ and producing pieces of Gallic refinement. The impulse is never strong or urgent, but with superb playing on a resonant organ, magnificently recorded, the result is highly recommendable to organ-lovers.

4 Ronsard sonnets (chamber orchestra version).
(*) Decca HEAD 3 [id.]. Pears, L. Sinf., composer – BEDFORD: *Tentacles of the Dark Nebula* **(*); LUTOSLAWSKI: *Paroles.**

These settings of Ronsard, written for Peter Pears, date from 1963. Berkeley's sympathy with the poet is very evident in each song, with a finely drawn vocal line and well-shaped accompaniment. Like the other works on the disc, this one benefits from Pears's fine artistry and the understanding accompaniment of the composer. Excellent recording.

Berkeley, Michael

(born 1948)

Meditations.

(M) **(*) Uni. UNS 260. Westminster Cath. String O, Mawby – L. BERKELEY: *Antiphon;* IRELAND: *Concertino pastorale.***(*)

Michael Berkeley's *Meditations* won the Guinness Prize for Composition. It is a thoughtful, beautifully written piece, which, like his father's *Antiphon*, has links with plainchant. This performance could be more polished but is persuasive enough.

Berlioz, Hector

(1803–69)

(i; ii) *Harold in Italy, Op. 16;* (ii) *Marche funèbre pour la dernière scène de Hamlet, Op. 18/3;* (iii) *Symphonie fantastique, Op. 14;* (ii; iv; v) *Roméo et Juliette, Op. 17;* (ii; v) *Symphonie funèbre et triomphale, Op. 15;* (ii) *Les Troyens: Prelude.*

(M) **(*) Ph. 6747 271 (5). (i) Imai; (ii) LSO; (iii) Concg. O, (iv) Kern, Tear, Shirley-Quirk; (v) Alldis Ch., Sir Colin Davis.

In an album these performances (issued at medium price) make a fairly impressive collection, showing both the strengths and weaknesses of Davis's Berlioz cycle. The recording is consistently impressive, as are the surfaces, in this set of pressings.

Harold in Italy, Op. 16.

(M) **(*) CBS 61091/*40-*. Lincer, NYPO, Bernstein.

(M) **(*) HMV SXLP/*TC-SXLP* 30314 [Ang. RL/*4RL* 32077]. Menuhin, Philh. O, Sir Colin Davis.

**(*) Ph. 9500 026/*7300 441* [id.]. Imai, LSO, Sir Colin Davis.

(B) *(*) RCA VICS/*VK* 2004. Primrose, Boston SO, Munch.

With Barenboim's ripely romantic and highly dramatic reading – Zukerman the resonant soloist – withdrawn in the UK (though still available in the USA on M/*MT* 34541) CBS have reissued instead Bernstein's outstanding version from the early 1960s. It is most convincing and the finale is breathlessly exciting, helped by an extremely vivid CBS recording. The upper range is very brightly lit (though as usual tempered a little in the cassette transfer) but it suits the performance. Bernstein drives hard, but the dramatic tension is complete justification, and the reverberant stereo provides the sense of atmosphere. William Lincer – an excellent player – does not emerge as a strong personality, rather as the first among equals in the orchestra; but this prevents any conflict between soloist and conductor.

Barenboim proves a more forceful conductor in this work than Sir Colin Davis, who may perhaps in his earlier HMV version have been overfaced by his viola soloist. The fact is that the Menuhin/Philharmonia recording openly treats the work as a concerto, with the soloist often dictating the rhythm which the orchestra has to follow. But this remains an enjoyable version, now more competitive in this medium-priced reissue. The sound is full and lively on disc, rather more bland on tape (although side two has more edge than side one and the finale springs readily to life).

Those who value quality of recorded sound most should turn to Davis's more recent version for Philips, with an exceptionally talented viola soloist from Japan. There is no question here of the soloist taking precedence; in fact many will find that her relative reticence takes something away from the performance's sense of spontaneity. With this richly distinctive score the benefit of such excellent, refined stereo is enormous. The cassette version is disappointing, slightly overmodulated, with lack of refinement in tuttis.

Primrose's stereo recording with Munch does not match his earlier mono record (with Koussevitzky). Munch's direction of the outer movements is tense without creating real electricity, and the inner movements lack charm.

Overtures: *Béatrice et Bénédict; Benvenuto Cellini; Le Carnaval Romain; Le Corsaire; Les Francs-juges, Op. 30.*
(M) **(*) HMV Green. ESD/*TC-ESD* 290030-1/*4* [Ang. S 37170]. LSO, Previn.

Overtures: *Béatrice et Bénédict; Le Carnaval romain, Op. 9; Le Corsaire, Op. 21; Rob Roy; Le Roi Lear, Op. 4.*
(*) Chan. Dig. **CHAN 8316; ABRD/*ABTD* 1067. SNO, Gibson.

Overture: Béatrice et Bénédict. L'Enfance du Christ, Op. 25. Part 2: Prelude; (i) *Funeral march for the last scene of Hamlet; Roméo et Juliette, Op. 17: Love scene.* (i) *Les Troyens: Royal hunt and storm.*
** Chan. ABR/*ABT* 1059. Sydney SO, Pikler (i) with NSW Conservatorium Op. Ch.

Overtures: *Benvenuto Cellini; Le Carnaval romain; Le Corsaire; Les Francs-juges, Op. 3.*
**(*) Erato STU/*MCE* 71409. Strasbourg PO, Lombard.

Overtures: *Le Carnaval romain; Le Corsaire; Les Francs-juges; Le Roi Lear; Waverley, Op. 2b.*
(M) **(*) Ph. Seq. 6527/*7311* 179. LSO, Sir Colin Davis.

In the absence of Munch's early RCA collection (which includes a wonderfully atmospheric account of the *Royal hunt and storm* from *Les Troyens*), Sir Colin Davis's record stands out. The recording is not ideally balanced, but the sound has been freshened, the upper range is livelier than it was, and the woodwind detail remains well-integrated. The playing has fire and brilliance and the performance of *King Lear* is outstanding, challenging comparison with Beecham. The cassette is vividly transferred. It has not quite the range of the disc, notably on side two, where the transfer level drops a little.

Rob Roy is the rarity of Gibson's Berlioz collection. It adds an aptly Scottish tinge to the record, even when traditional melodies – *Scots wha hae* at the opening – are given distinctly Berliozian twists. It is if anything even wilder than the other pieces, and with its anticipations of *Harold in Italy* finds Gibson and the SNO at their most dashingly committed. *King Lear*, another rarity, also comes out most dramatically, and though *Béatrice et Bénédict* is not quite so polished, the playing is generally excellent. With first-rate digital recording it can be generally recommended. The chrome tape is strikingly vivid but lacks something in the middle range.

As the Strasbourg Philharmonic demonstrates, there is a febrile quality about French string playing that catches the atmosphere of Berlioz's music effectively; there is warmth of timbre too, and the charismatic nature of Berlioz's invention is not missed. The finest performance here is *Les Francs-juges* with a massively strong brass contribution. The recording is vivid; the cassette has not quite the upper range of the disc.

Under Previn *Béatrice et Bénédict* fizzes and the swing-along melody of *Les Francs-juges* swaggers boldly. The recorded sound is spectacular, yet there is a special response to Berlioz displayed by Davis which Previn does not quite equal. Nevertheless there is real panache here.

In spite of generally good playing, with the Sydney strings producing an agreeable body of tone in the overture, Pikler's collection is disappointingly studio-bound and the temperature seldom rises very high, not even in the *Royal hunt and storm*, although here the closing pages are evocative. The recording is good; the cassette, transferred at a low level, lacks range.

Romance, rêverie et caprice, Op. 8.
*** DG Dig. **400 032–2**; 2532/*3302* 011 [id.]. Perlman, Orchestre de Paris, Barenboim – LALO: *Symphonie espagnole* ***

Berlioz's short concertante work for violin and orchestra uses material originally intended for *Benvenuto Cellini*. Perlman's ripely romantic approach to the *Rêverie* brings out the individuality of the melody, and with a sympathetic accompaniment from Barenboim the work as a whole is given considerable substance. First-rate digital recording, with disc and cassette closely matched. The sound on the compact disc is very similar to the standard LP, with the additional advantage of background silence.

Symphonie fantastique, Op. 14.
*** DG Dig. **410 895-2**; 410 895-1/*4* [id.]. Chicago SO, Abbado.

(M) *** HMV SXLP/*TC-SXLP* 30295 [Sera. S/*4XG* 60165]. French Nat. RO, Beecham.
*** DG 2530 597/*3300 498* [id.]. Berlin PO, Karajan.
*** Ph. 6500 774/*7300 313* [id.]. Concg. O, Sir Colin Davis.
(B) **(*) PRT GSGC/*ZCGC* 2025. Hallé O, Barbirolli.
(B) **(*) CfP CFP/*TC-CFP 4401* [Ang. S/*4XS* 37485]. LSO, Previn.
**(*) Decca SXL/*KSXC* 6938 [Lon. CS/*5*-7168]. VPO, Haitink.
** Decca Dig. **400 046-2**; SXDL/*KSXDC* 7512 [Lon. LDR/5- 10013]. NYPO, Mehta.
(M) **(*) EMI Em. EMX/*TC-EMX* 2030. Philh. O, Klemperer.
(M) ** Ph. Seq. 6527/*7311* 081. LSO, Sir Colin Davis.
(M) *(*) DG Priv. 2535/*3335* 256 [id.]. Berlin PO, Karajan.
(M) *(*) DG Sig. 2543/*3343* 534. (as above, cond. Karajan) – WEBER: *Invitation to the dance*.***
(M) *(*) Decca Jub. JB/*KJBC* 135 [Lon. CS/*5*- 6790]. Chicago SO, Solti.
* ASV ABM/*ZCABM* 754. Philh. O, Ling Tung.

Abbado brings the right dreamy atmosphere and feverish intensity to this score and the playing of the Chicago Symphony Orchestra has all the polish and finesse one could expect. There is much poetic feeling and the slow movement is outstandingly fine. This is a performance that can hold its own alongside those of Beecham, Karajan and Davis. There are two special points of interest: first, Abbado observes the exposition repeat in the first movement (also in the *March to the scaffold*); secondly, he incorporates the cornet part, which Klemperer was the first to include in his Philharmonia version. The DG recording is rich in texture but the balance is less than ideal (notably so in the oboe solo at fig. 16 in the first movement and at the opening of the *March*). The effect is recessed and as the LP is not cut at a high level this may offer problems of background noise in the hushed, rapt pianissimo passages of the slow movement which are magically played. The chrome cassette, transferred at quite a good level, solves this problem to a considerable extent, but the compact disc provides a more complete answer, for while the balance problems remain, the completely silent background enables the most refined pianissimo to register fully. CD collectors will find this version infinitely preferable artistically to Mehta's Decca account.

Beecham's account still enjoys classic status, though it is now over twenty years old. The sound is amazingly fresh and vivid, while the performance has a demonic intensity that is immediately compelling. Gounod wrote that 'with Berlioz, all impressions, all sensations – whether joyful or sad – are expressed in extremes to the point of delirium', and Beecham brought to this score all the fire and temperament, all the magic and affection in his armoury. He drew from the French National Radio Orchestra playing of great rhythmic subtlety; the waltz has never sounded more elegant. This is an indispensable record, and the clear, bright tape transfer is admirable.

Karajan's newer performance (not to be confused with his old one on Privilege) is urgently compelling. The very opening reveals the greater depth (compared to the earlier account), the extra intensity in hushed pianissimo; and the beautiful DG recording brings out every nuance of the Berlin orchestra's unusually subtle tone colours. The immensely dramatic finale too sends the adrenalin racing, and for some ears this issue will be first choice although, unlike Davis, Karajan does not observe the first-movement repeat.

Sir Colin Davis chose the *Symphonie fantastique* for his first recording with the Concertgebouw Orchestra. The interpretation is very similar to his earlier account with the LSO (see below), only the performance has even more energy, life and colour. The slow movement too is more atmospheric than before, if not quite as fine as Abbado's outstanding performance. It is not helped by Philips's crude side-break. In all other respects the engineering is strikingly brilliant, although on tape the sound is rather lacking in sparkle with side two better than side one.

Barbirolli provides a reading which not only is exciting but has a breadth and flair missing in many other performances. He builds the first-movement climax with care, and the same thoughtfulness can be felt in the slow movement, which is most beautifully played. The thunder at the end, on the timpani, bursts into the room and anticipates the mood of the *March to the scaffold.* This is again spacious in style, rather than rhythmically pointed, and in the finale there is a strong feeling of atmosphere, helped by the fullest realization of Berlioz's orchestration. Fortunately the Pye stereo recording is good, and there is a matching cassette. At bargain price, this is a vintage reissue, for Barbirolli's account of this work is justly famous.

Helped by modern EMI sound of high quality, André Previn presents the *Symphonie fantastique* as above all a symphonic structure. Some may find him not atmospheric or volatile enough – the last two movements are without the rhythmic impetus of some versions, but on its own direct terms it is a most compelling reading, one which almost completely avoids vulgarity. It is a performance which gains in impact on repetition and its reissue is made the more attractive at bargain price on the CfP label. The cassette has been remastered and is very closely matched to the disc.

Haitink with the Vienna Philharmonic may sound a little unidiomatic in French music, but the freshness and refinement of the reading, helped by clean, atmospheric sound, will suit those who prefer a degree of detachment even in this high romantic symphony. The cassette transfer is not one of Decca's very best; it has not quite the upper range of the disc, and in the finale the bass drum offers minor problems.

Mehta's reading is fresh and direct but not specially illuminating. The disc's chief claim to attention lies in the digital recording (Decca's first with this orchestra), which is wide-ranging and atmospheric. The cassette too is extremely vivid, but it has a less spectacular dynamic range: the big climaxes fail to expand as dramatically as in some versions. The compact disc is outstanding. The clarity and transparency of detail are very striking indeed and the *March to the scaffold* has demonstration potential. However, overall the performance is stronger on extrovert brilliance than poetic feeling and it has little sense of fantasy.

Weight is the keynote of Klemperer's reading, so individual that some will regard it as merely perverse in its avoidance of conventional thrusting excitement. But from the first movement onwards – far more clearly symphonic than usual – Klemperer conveys a rugged strength, which in the massiveness of the *Witches' sabbath* for example brings you close to Satan himself. The *March to the scaffold* too is given commanding power, and the close is made the more impressive by recording superb for its period, still sounding excellent now. Disc and cassette are very much the same.

Sir Colin Davis's earlier recording has been reissued in an admirably fresh transfer on Philips's new medium-priced label. The quality is slightly dry and gives a less massive, less atmospheric sound picture than in Davis's re-recording with the Concertgebouw Orchestra. The first movement begins with a fine sense of anticipation, but the tension is not always maintained throughout the movement, and the *Adagio*, although beautifully played, is a little detached. The final two movements are very exciting. In the *March to the scaffold* Davis gives the rhythm exactly the right spring, and by doing the rarely heard repeat he adds to our pleasure. The finale is gripping to the last bar, with really taut orchestral playing and clear projection from the recording. The cassette is clear and clean, with vivid brass and string detail.

Karajan's earlier performance (now on both Signature and Privilege) was altogether too erratic to be entirely convincing and Solti's version is no more successful, in spite of extremely vivid sound, on disc and cassette alike. Hardly a semiquaver is out of place, but the spirit of the music eludes the conductor.

The finale is the most impressive part of Ling Tung's bargain-priced ASV issue. The rest, though well played, is lacking in any kind of panache. This cannot compare with Barbirolli or Previn in the lower price-range.

La Damnation de Faust, Op. 24.

*** Ph. 6703 042 (3) [id.]. Veasey, Gedda, Bastin, Van Allan, Amb. S., Wandsworth School Boys' Ch., LSO Ch. and LSO, Sir Colin Davis.

*** Decca Dig. D 259 D 3/*K 259 K 33* (3)

[Lon. LDR/5- 73007]. Von Stade, Riegel, Van Dam, King, Chicago Ch. and SO, Solti.

Of these two versions of *The Damnation of Faust* the Philips set is on balance the finer. Both Gedda as Faust and Bastin as Mephistopheles are impressive, and the response of the orchestra and chorus is never less than intelligent and in the quieter passages highly sensitive. The recording is altogether outstanding: its perspective is extraordinarily natural and realistic, every nuance truthfully reflected in relation to the aural picture, and the balance could not be improved on. The LSO plays marvellously for Davis and the surfaces are particularly silent. All in all, this is a most satisfying and idiomatic account of the work.

Solti's performance, searingly dramatic, is given stunning digital sound (and matching chrome tapes) to make the ride to Hell supremely exciting. But, with Von Stade singing tenderly, this is a warmly expressive performance too; and the *Hungarian march* has rarely had such sparkle and swagger. This makes an admirable alternative to Davis and it certainly communicates vividly.

La Damnation de Faust: Minuet of the Will-o'-the-wisps; Hungarian march; Dance of the sylphs.

** Ph. Dig. 6769/*7654* 089 [id.]. Concg. O, Dorati – LISZT: *Faust symphony**; WAGNER: *Faust overture.***

Dorati's *Faust* programme assembles Wagner and Liszt as well. Although the Berlioz pieces are neatly done and are probably the best thing about this set, the Liszt symphony is really not competitive enough to hold its own in the catalogue. The Concertgebouw Orchestra play beautifully as always but the performance is not well held together. Dorati is, however, on better form in these Berlioz excerpts, which have sparkle. The recording is good and the chrome-tape transfer offers generally refined quality to match the sound on disc.

La Damnation de Faust: Dance of the sylphs.

(M) *** Decca Jub. JB/*KJBC* 136. LSO, Stokowski – DEBUSSY: *La Mer;* RAVEL: *Daphnis: suite No. 2.****

This was recorded as a *bonne bouche* at the end of the *La Mer* sessions and the performance, although slow, is captivating – Stokowski at his most magical. The sound is very good indeed.

L'Enfance du Christ, Op. 25.

*** Ph. 6700 106/*7699 058* (2) [id.]. Baker, Tappy, Langridge, Allen, Herincx, Rouleau, Bastin, John Alldis Ch., LSO, Sir Colin Davis.

(M) *** Argo D 248 D 2 (2). Morison, Pears, Fleet, Cameron, Frost, Rouleau, St Anthony Singers, Goldsbrough O, Sir Colin Davis.

Davis characteristically directs a fresh and refined reading for Philips of one of Berlioz's most directly appealing works. The beautifully balanced recording intensifies the colour and atmosphere of the writing, so that for example the *Nocturnal march* in the first part is wonderfully mysterious. There is a fine complement of soloists, and though Eric Tappy's tone as narrator is not always sweet, his sense of style is immaculate. Others are not always quite so idiomatic, but Dame Janet Baker and Thomas Allen, as ever, both sing beautifully. Good cassette sound, although the transfer level is very low. On disc the contrast with Davis's earlier set, now reissued on Argo, is not as clear-cut as one might expect, for at times the earlier performance was fresher and more urgent; the recording remains remarkably bright and clean for its early-1960s vintage, and Pears was a sweeter-toned, more characterful narrator. Elsie Morison and John Cameron are perfectly cast as Mary and Joseph, and Joseph Rouleau makes an impressive contribution as the Ishmaelite father. Not all the French pronunciations are immaculate, but Davis and his singers revel in the sheer originality of the melody and such moments as the angelic hosannas which end Part 2 are ravishingly beautiful. At medium-price this remains a fine alternative.

Herminie; La Mort de Cléopâtre, Op. 18/1 (scènes lyriques) – see also below.

*** Ph. 9500 683/*7300 778* [id.]. Baker, LSO, Sir Colin Davis.

These two dramatic scenas make an apt coupling: both were written as entries for the Prix de Rome, early works which yet give many hints of the mature Berlioz, even presenting specific hints of material later used in the *Symphonie fantastique* (the *idée fixe*) and the *Roman Carnival overture* (the melody of the introduction). Dame Janet Baker sings with passionate intensity, while Davis draws committed playing from the LSO. Excellent recording on both disc and cassette.

(i) *La Mort de Cléopâtre* (see also above); (ii) *Les Nuits d'été, Op. 7* (see also below).
*** DG Dig. **410 966-2**; 2532/*3302* 047 [id.]. (i) Norman, (ii) Te Kanawa, O de Paris, Barenboim.

The coupling of Jessye Norman in the scena, and Kiri Te Kanawa in the song-cycle makes for one of the most ravishing of Berlioz records with each singer at her very finest. Jessye Norman has natural nobility and command as the Egyptian queen in this dramatic scena, while Kiri Te Kanawa compasses the challenge of different moods and register in *Les Nuits d'été* more completely and affectingly than any singer on record in recent years, more so than Jessye Norman in her beautiful but rather bland recording with Davis. Excellent DG recording for Barenboim and first-rate playing from the Paris Orchestra. There is a good chrome tape, although the chosen transfer level brings a degree of background hiss.

Les Nuits d'été (song cycle), *Op. 7*.
*** HMV ASD 2444 [Ang. S 36505]. Baker, New Philh. O, Barbirolli – RAVEL: *Shéhérazade*.***
*** Decca Jub. JB/*KJBC* 15 [Lon. OS/5-25821]. Crespin, SRO, Ansermet – RAVEL: *Shéhérazade*.***
(*) Ph. 9500 783/*7300* 857 [id.]. Norman, LSO, Sir Colin Davis – RAVEL: *Shéhérazade*.(*)

The collaboration of Dame Janet Baker and Sir John Barbirolli in what is probably the most beautiful of all orchestral song cycles produces ravishing results. Admittedly the wide range demanded of the soloist puts some strain on Dame Janet, particularly in the first song, *Villanelle*, but she is so immersed in the mood of this and the other highly contrasted songs that it is always the musical line which holds attention, never any flaw. The half-tones in the middle songs are exquisitely controlled, and the elation of the final song, *L'île inconnue*, with its vision of an idyllic island, has never been more rapturously captured on record. An outstandingly beautiful record, perfectly coupled.

The alternative version from Decca is also superb in a different, more direct way. Crespin's sheer richness of tone and a style which has an operatic basis do not prevent her from bringing out the subtlety of Berlioz's writing. *Le spectre de la rose* (a wonderful song), for instance, has a bigness of style and colouring and an immediate sense of drama that immediately conjure up the opera house. But this is not a criticism. With Ansermet brilliantly directing the accompaniment, this glowing performance is a *tour de force*. Decca's sound too is marvellous, and there is a fine cassette, vivid and clear.

Jessye Norman is in fine voice here but does not get fully inside this most magical of orchestral song cycles. There is no lack of voluptuousness, but the word meanings are less subtly registered than in the finest rival versions. Davis's tempi too are sometimes over-deliberate. The recording is pleasing, atmospheric on both disc and cassette.

Lélio, Op. 14b (without dialogue); *Tristia* (*Méditation religieuse; La mort d'Ophélie; Marche funèbre pour la dernière scène de Hamlet*), *Op. 18/1–3*.
*** Ph. 9500/*7300* 444 [id.]. Carreras, Allen, Alldis Ch., LSO, Sir Colin Davis.

Lélio, Op. 14b (complete).
(M) *** CBS 60280/*40*- Barrault (nar.), Mitchinson, Shirley-Quirk, LSO Ch. and O, Boulez.

By not using the spoken dialogue Davis is able to include on his record not only the music of *Lélio* – a work which was designed as a companion-piece to the *Symphonie fantastique* but which in the repertory falls between many stools – but the three evocative pieces he called *Tristia*, two of them also Shakespeare-inspired – *Méditation religieuse, La mort d'Ophélie* and *Funeral March for the last scene of Hamlet*. That last piece makes the perfect introduction to *Lélio* with its *Hamlet* obsessions, for the cantata (if that is what it is) otherwise starts most ineffectively as though in the middle. It is altogether a strange piece, uneven in inspiration, but is here given a direct, well-sprung reading with complex textures clarified, thanks also to excellent Philips recording. Stylish performances from everyone, though some might prefer tougher, weightier treatment. The chrome cassette is not transferred at the highest possible level and there is some clouding of the climax of the *Hamlet Marche funèbre*, while the choral focus could be generally sharper. Otherwise the sound is acceptable.

The mid-price reissue in CBS's Masterworks Portrait series of the Boulez version of 1967 provides a valuable alternative to the Davis issue. Boulez, unlike Davis, has this strange piece introduced – as the composer intended – with plentiful passages of spoken dialogue in French. For repetition it may not be ideal for everyone, but if any French voice can present these words persuasively then it is Jean-Louis Barrault's. The performance is exciting and red-blooded rather than transparent and refined, and that suits a rough-hewn work well, with rhythms pressed home strongly. Mitchinson and Shirley-Quirk make aptly firm and strong soloists. The recording remains extraordinarily vivid, with a matching chrome tape. This has far more adrenalin than Davis's version, and Berlioz's quirky invention, especially in the *Chanson de Brigands*, is splendidly projected.

Requiem Mass (*Grande Messe des Morts*), *Op. 5*.

*** HMV Dig. SLS/*TCC-SLS* 5209 [Ang. DSB 3907]. Tear, LPO Ch., LPO, Previn.

**(*) CBS 79205 (2) [M2/*MT* 34202]. Burrows, Ch. of R. France, O Nat. de France, O Philharmonique, Bernstein.

**(*) Ph. 6700 019/*7699 008* (2) [id.]. Dowd, Wandsworth School Boys' Ch., LSO Ch., LSO, Sir Colin Davis.

** DG 2707 119 (2) [id.]. Domingo, Ch. and O de Paris, Barenboim.

(M) ** HMV ESDW/*TC2-ESDW* 718 (2). Tear, CBSO Ch., CBSO, Frémaux.

Previn's version of Berlioz's great choral work is the most impressive so far put on disc or tape. Spectacular digital sound allows the registration of the extremes of dynamic in this extraordinary work for massed forces. The gradations of pianissimo against total pianissimo are breathtakingly caught, making the great outbursts all the more telling. There is fine bloom on the voices, and the separation of sound gives a feeling of reality to the massed brass and multiple timpani, even though current digital techniques still fall short of conveying the full expansive glory experienced in a big cathedral. The double-length chrome cassette matches the discs closely. It catches the full amplitude of the climaxes without problems; only in the pianissimo passages (especially at the very opening of the work) is the sharpness of focus marginally less firm than with the LPs, and even here the difference is marginal. Previn's view is direct and incisive (like that of Sir Colin Davis on his long-established version), not underlining expressiveness but concentrating on rhythmic qualities. So the *Rex tremendae* is given superb buoyancy, even if Previn misses some of the animal excitement captured by other conductors, such as Bernstein (see below). Robert Tear is a sensitive soloist, though the voice is balanced rather close. The cassette is presented in a box (with booklet) like the discs.

None of the alternative versions is nearly as successful technically as the Previn HMV set, but Bernstein's acoustic is reasonably ample, and this allows the chorus to sound bigger than Davis's forces. Characteristically Bernstein adopts a more moulded, more consciously persuasive style than Davis, and the result is more atmospheric and often more dramatic too. In *Rex tremendae*, for example, Bernstein's expansiveness is well in scale with the music, where Davis's clean, taut account is altogether less tremendous. In the *Lacrymosa* Bernstein is faster and more urgent, with an irresistible wave-like rhythm, while Davis is angular in precision. There is a case for both views, but Bernstein is notable for warmth and expressiveness, Davis for fine precision and close focus.

Davis went to Westminster Cathedral for the recording sessions, which should have been atmospheric enough, but then the engineers were allowed to produce a sound which minimizes the massiveness of forces in anything but the loudest fortissimos, thanks to the closeness of the microphones. In many passages one can hear individual voices in the choir. Once that is said, the performance itself is a fine one, though still not as full of mystery as it might be. The large-scale brass sound is formidably caught with not a trace of distortion, and the choral fortissimos are glorious, helped by the fresh cutting edge of the Wandsworth Boys' Choir. It was Davis's idea, not Berlioz's, to have boys included, but it is entirely in character. Their brilliance rather shows up the adult singers. The LSO provides finely incisive accompaniment. The Philips cassettes are made at a low level which brings too much hiss and a restricted range.

With its distant sound, transferred at a lowish level, it is hard to obtain from the Barenboim version the sort of impact which marks out Previn's forward and direct reading in digital sound. This is an expressive reading but, unlike Bernstein who similarly takes an expressive view, Barenboim tends to prefer measured tempi, with fewer stringendi. It is a performance which conveys the mystery and awe of the piece rather than its brazen drama, though it certainly has plenty of power, and the singing of the chorus (trained by Arthur Oldham) is outstandingly fine, with no raw tone from any section even under stress.

It is disappointing too, that for Frémaux's performance the EMI engineers fell into the same trap as their Philips colleagues in the Davis set, only rather more so. The choir and orchestra are recorded relatively close, to make the result seem too small-scale for such a work. Detail is clarified, and there is a typical bloom on the sound, but the absence of true pianissimos is just as serious as the failure to expand in the big climaxes, making a potentially fine performance far less effective than it might have been. The chorus work is surprisingly variable. This is now a medium-priced set, but Previn's version is well worth the extra cost. The Frémaux tape issue is on a single cassette (in a plastic hinged box). The quality is generally good, though not outstanding.

Roméo et Juliette, Op. 17.

*** DG 2707 115/*3370 036* [id.]. Minton, Araiza, Bastin, Ch. and O de Paris, Barenboim.

*** Ph. 6700 032 (2). Kern, Tear, Shirley-Quirk, Alldis Ch., LSO Ch., LSO, Sir Colin Davis.

*** Decca SET 570/1 [Lon. OSA 12102]. Ludwig, Senechel, Ghiaurov, V. State Op. Ch., L'ORTF Ch., VPO, Maazel.

These three sets are each rewarding in different ways and readers can follow their own inclination. Certainly Barenboim's reading is as warmly romantic as anyone could wish. He takes a very flexible view of such great set-pieces as the love scene, which here sounds very Wagnerian in a *Tristan*-like way. Though Barenboim's own magnetic purposefulness holds the work together, the playing of the Paris Orchestra has its lapses, for example in the *Queen Mab scherzo*, which misses something in mercurial lightness. With a first-rate team of soloists and warmly atmospheric recording on disc and tape alike, it nevertheless makes an excellent choice.

Colin Davis has a rare sympathy with this score and secures playing of great vitality and atmosphere from the LSO. The recording is excellent; it is natural in tone and balance and has been recut to give added presence.

The Maazel performance on Decca is a fine one too, and the recording reproduces detail with superb clarity and definition. The Philips engineers get a more natural perspective, however, and also a greater sense of atmosphere and space.

Roméo et Juliette: orchestral music.

(M) *** DG Sig. 2543/*3343* 536 [id.]. Boston SO, Ozawa.

Ozawa's fine complete set has been withdrawn in the UK but is still available in America [DG 2709 089 PSI]. However, DG have now reissued a single LP containing all the orchestral music (and at least one short contribution from the New England Conservatory Chorus) including the great love scene, splendidly built over the longest span with a tempo not too expansive, and the *Queen Mab Scherzo*. It is a warmly dramatic performance, showing this conductor at his finest and the richly atmospheric recording serves the music-making admirably. Disc and chrome tape sound virtually identical.

Roméo et Juliette: Love scene.
(M) *** DG Priv. 2535/*3335* 422 [2530 308/*3300 284*]. San Francisco SO, Ozawa – PROKOFIEV and TCHAIKOVSKY: *Romeo and Juliet.****

Ozawa's Privilege issue attractively couples three very contrasted views of Shakespeare's lovers. The Berlioz has all the warmth and glow required in this vision of the great love scene and it is very well recorded on both disc and cassette.

Te Deum, Op. 22.
*** DG Dig. **410 696-2**; 2532/*3302* 044 [id.]. Araiza, LSO Ch., LPO Ch., Woburn Singers, Boys' Ch., European Community Youth O, Abbado.
*** Ph. LY 839 790 [id.]. Tagliavini, Wandsworth School Boys' Ch., LSO Ch., LSO, Sir Colin Davis.

The newest DG recording from Abbado is very impressive. The sound is wide-ranging with striking dynamic contrasts and a much greater sense of presence than its predecessors. Artistically, too, it is of considerable merit: Abbado brings great tonal refinement and dignity to this performance, and the spacious sound helps. Francisco Araiza is altogether first-class and has eloquence as well as tonal beauty to commend him. The choirs are responsive as are the young players Abbado has assembled and there is no need for readers to hold back. Memories of Beecham in mono and Colin Davis on the Philips label are not banished, however, and Sir Colin has a natural feeling for the pace of this work and his reading is perhaps the more moving. In some respects Abbado's version is superior (certainly as far as the soloist is concerned) and collectors acquiring it are unlikely to be disappointed. In its cassette format, the wide dynamic range poses some problems. The chrome tape is not quite as free as the disc, though; on the copies submitted for review, side two has a slightly sharper focus than side one. But there are no serious grumbles here. On compact disc the quality is very impressive indeed, bringing extra gain in definition and spatial feeling.

The Davis version (first issued in 1969) still sounds extremely well. In its day it stood out even among his other Berlioz centenary recordings. He conveys the massiveness without pomposity, the drama without unwanted excesses of emotion, and his massed forces – not as numerous as the 950 reported to have taken part at the first performance in Paris in 1855, but still very large – respond superbly. The recording is aptly brilliant and atmospheric. It was a visit to London that persuaded the composer to add children's voices to the score, and the glorious fresh tone of the Wandsworth boys certainly confirms the wisdom of that decision. The only disappointment comes in the singing of Tagliavini, reasonably restrained by the standards of most Italian tenors, but not really in style with the others or, for that matter, Berlioz.

OPERA

Béatrice et Bénédict (complete).
*** Ph. 6700 121 (2) [id.]. Baker, Tear, Eda-Pierre, Allen, Lloyd, Van Allen, Watts, John Alldis Ch., LSO, Colin Davis.
** DG 2707 130 (2) [id.]. Minton, Domingo, Cotrubas, Fischer-Dieskau, Ch. and O de Paris, Barenboim.

Well produced for records, with a smattering of French dialogue between numbers, *Béatrice et Bénédict* here reveals itself as less an opera than a dramatic symphony, one of the important Berlioz works (like *Romeo and Juliet*) which refuse to fit in a conventional category. The score presents not just witty and brilliant music for the hero and heroine (Dame Janet Baker and Robert Tear at their most pointed) but sensuously beautiful passages such as the duet for Hero and Ursula at the end of Act I and the trio they later share with Beatrice, both incidental to the drama but very important for the musical structure. First-rate solo and choral singing, brilliant playing and outstanding recording. Davis's earlier Oiseau-Lyre set (at present out of the catalogue) is not entirely superseded, but the new Philips version takes pride of place.

Barenboim's version of *Béatrice et Bénédict* is seriously marred by the spoken dialogue in French which links the numbers of this off-beat adaptation of Shakespeare. It is done by Geneviève Page in the over-intimate manner of a French film. Nor is the musical performance as fresh and stylish as that for Davis on Philips, though it is good to hear Bénédict's part sung with such ringing tone by Domingo. Minton is less warm and less characterful than Baker for Davis, and Fischer-Dieskau is miscast as Somarone (the comic role added by Berlioz to replace Dogberry and Verges). The beauty of the score is caught rather than its point and wit. Apart from the discrepancy between the narration and the rest, the recorded quality is first-rate.

Benvenuto Cellini (complete).
*** Ph. 6707 019 (4) [id.]. Gedda, Eda-Pierre, Bastin, Massard, Blackwell, Berbié, ROHCG Ch., BBC SO, Sir Colin Davis.

Benvenuto Cellini is just the sort of opera – almost impossibly ambitious in its vision for the stage, unconventionally structured – which comes superbly alive on record. Davis here achieves one of his most brilliantly incisive recorded performances ever, drawing electric playing and singing from his Covent Garden cast. The compelling success of the venture is crowned by the classic performance of Gedda in the title role. He has made dozens of superb records, but rarely has he sounded so confidently heroic as here, so deeply conscious of the overtones of characterization. The clarity and balance of the Philips recording can hardly be faulted in the slightest detail – a great achievement all round. For a sample, try the eavesdropping scene in Act I, or the scene of the casting of Cellini's statue at the end.

Les Troyens (complete).
*** Ph. 6709 002 (5) [id./*7699 142* (*3*)]. Veasey, Vickers, Lindholm, Glossop, Soyer, Partridge, Wandsworth School Boys' Ch., ROHCG Ch. and O, Sir Colin Davis.

The complete recording of Berlioz's great epic opera was an achievement to outshine all other centenary offerings to this composer, indeed to outshine almost all other recording projects whatever. Davis had long preparation for the task, both in his concert performances and in his direction of the Covent Garden production, on which this recording is firmly based. The result is that, even more than in most of his other Berlioz recordings, he conveys the high dramatic tension of the music. Throughout this long and apparently disjointed score Davis compels the listener to concentrate, to appreciate its epic logic. His tempi are generally faster than in the theatre, and the result is exhilarating with no hint of rush. Only in the great love scene of *O nuit d'ivresse* would one have welcomed the more expansive hand of a Beecham. It is interesting too to find Davis pursuing his direct, dramatic line even in Dido's death scene at the end.

Veasey on any count, even next to Dame Janet Baker, makes a splendid Dido, single-minded rather than seductive, singing always with fine heroic strength. Of the rest, Berit Lindholm as Cassandra, in the first half of the opera, is the only soloist who falls short – the voice is not quite steady – but otherwise one cannot imagine a more effective cast, with Vickers as a ringing Aeneas. The Covent Garden Chorus and Orchestra excel themselves in virtuoso singing and playing. The recording quality is outstandingly fine, brilliant, atmospheric and refined.

Les Troyens: highlights.
(M) *** Ph. Seq. 410 458-1/*4*. (from above recording).

Choosing excerpts from so wide-ranging a work as *Les Troyens* is impossibly difficult. Any choice inevitably leaves out favourite items – the immolation of the women at the end of Act I or the great love duet, *O nuit d'ivresse*, are both omitted here – but what is included provides a superb sampler of the five-disc set, with the magnificent drama of the Trojan horse scene, the *Royal hunt and storm* with choral comment, Aeneas's magnificent Act V aria and Dido's death aria. There is the same superb quality of recording here as in the complete set.

Les Troyens: Trojan march; Royal hunt and storm.
(M) *** HMV SXLP 30260. Beecham Ch. Soc., RPO, Beecham – BIZET: *Symphony*; DELIBES: *Le Roi s'amuse.****

Beecham's version of the *Royal hunt and storm* has splendid panache and atmosphere, and the *Trojan march* is characteristically ebullient. The recordings are good – though the choral focus in the former piece is not very clean. A most attractive compilation.

Berners, Lord (Gerald)
(1883–1950)

Piano music: *Dispute entre le papillon et le crapaud; Fragments psychologiques; Le poisson d'or; Polka; Trois Petites Marches funèbres.* Piano duet: *Valses bourgeoises.* Vocal music: *Come on, Algernon; Dialogue between Tom Filuter and his man; 3 English songs; Lieder album: 3 Songs in the German manner; Red roses and red noses; 3 Sea songs; Trois chansons.*
*** Uni. RHS 355. Peter and Meriel Dickinson, Dickerson, Bradshaw, Bennett.

Berners was a vintage English eccentric, as a composer something of an English Satie. These pieces often have a comparably haunting quality, so that in the end the immediate joke matters less than the musical invention, limited as it is. The musicians here have all performed these pieces in concert, and the results can hardly be faulted, even if one would sometimes welcome a more sparkling manner. A valuable and enjoyable collection, well recorded.

Fantaisie espagnole; Trois morceaux.
** Auracle AUC 1001. Lawson, Scott – LAMBERT: *3 Pièces nègres*; LANE: *Badinages.***

Berners was an accomplished pasticheur and a many-sided artist (a painter and a man of letters whose autobiography has great charm and brilliance) whose fame rests on his ballet, *The Triumph of Neptune*, composed for Diaghilev in the mid-1920s. (Its absence from the catalogue is to be regretted; neither of Beecham's records of it with the LPO and the Philadelphia Orchestra is currently in circulation.) The *Fantaisie espagnole* was composed in Rome in 1919 for orchestra and subsequently arranged for piano duet; and the *Trois morceaux* were written the same year. These pieces are slight and entertaining, closer in spirit to *Les six* than any English precursors. They are neatly played, though the studio is small and the instrument a bit close.

Bernstein, Leonard
(born 1918)

Candide: overture.
*** DG Dig. **413 342-2**; 2532/*3302* 083 [id.]. LAPO, Bernstein – BARBER: *Adagio*; COPLAND: *Appalachian spring*; SCHUMAN: *American festival overture.****

Bernstein's *Candide overture* is one of the most dazzlingly brilliant of the century, and the composer directs it in this live recording with tremendous flair, his speed a fraction slower than in his New York studio recording for CBS. One item in an outstanding collection of American music.

(i) *Candide overture; Fancy Free; On the Town: 3 Dances.* (ii) *Prelude, fugue and riffs.*
(M) *** CBS 61816/*40*- [MS 6677]. (i) NYPO, composer; (ii) Benny Goodman, Columbia Jazz Combo.

This collection of some of Leonard Bernstein's most approachable works, most of them with jazz overtones and including both of the sailor-based dramatic pieces, makes an excellent mid-price issue. The overture to *Candide* is an equivalent to Rossini. The recording is aptly hard and bright, and the performances irrepressible. The cassette is acceptable but has less range than the disc.

Divertimento for orchestra; Facsimile; A Musical toast; On the Town (3 Dance episodes); Slava! (A political overture).
*** DG Dig. 2532/*3302* 052 [id.]. Israel PO, composer.

Musically Bernstein encompasses many worlds, and this charming record, full of vigour, reflects above all his love of Broadway and a popular American idiom. *Facsimile* is the least popular style, a choreographic essay for Jerome Robbins, ending with a poignantly beautiful coda representing a 'woman alone, still unfulfilled'. The three dance episodes from *On the Town* bring a vivid reminder of one of the most brilliant of all American film musicals. The other side has three more recent works that show how little of the flair has been lost, each written as an occasional piece, *Divertimento*, written for the Boston Symphony Orchestra, *A Musical Toast* for André Kostelanetz and *Slava* (a 'political overture, fast and flamboyant') to celebrate Rostropovich in Washington. A collection of party pieces recorded live in fizzing performances. The high-level cassette is wide-ranging and clear and does not lack the necessary transient bite.

Dybbuk (ballet): *Suites Nos. 1 and 2.*
*** DG 2531 348 [id.]. Sperry, Fifer, NYPO, composer.

These two suites between them are no shorter than the original ballet (one of Bernstein's toughest works, on the sinister subject of a lost spirit), dividing the original score broadly between passages involving vocal elements and those purely instrumental. The first suite is the longer and more dramatic, the second the more contemplative. Even the jazzy dance sequences typical of Bernstein (often in seven-in-a-bar rhythms) acquire a bitter quality. Bernstein directs strong, colourful performances, cleanly recorded, with excellent vocal contributions from Paul Sperry and Bruce Fifer.

Facsimile (choreographic essay from ballet score of same name).
** CBS 72374 [Col. MS 6792]. NYPO, composer – *Chichester Psalms.***

The *Facsimile* ballet score, written in 1946 for Jerome Robbins, tells of two boys and a girl and their balletic flirtations, culminating in their realization that 'they couldn't care less'. It is an inventive and resourceful score: eclectic perhaps, but with no want of atmosphere here and imagination. The performance is first-class, the recording good.

Fancy Free (ballet); (i) *Serenade after Plato's Symposium* (for solo violin, string O, harp and percussion).
*** DG 2531 196 [id.]. Israel PO, composer, (i) with Kremer.

There are earlier versions of both works, but this DG record surpasses any of them. Perhaps Isaac Stern was a more extrovert protagonist in his pioneering mono recording of the *Serenade* (never available in the UK) but Gidon Kremer has all the nervous intensity and vibrant energy to do justice to this powerful and inventive score. The *Serenade* must rank among Bernstein's most resourceful and inspired creations, full of ideas, often thrilling and exciting, and equally often moving. The ballet, *Fancy Free*, one of Bernstein's earliest successes, written in 1944, is an attractive example of his freely eclectic style, raiding Stravinsky, Copland or Gershwin and putting the result effectively together thanks to his exuberant sense of colour and rhythm. Though the Israel Philharmonic does not match the New York orchestra (see above) in its sheer virtuosity or its command of jazz rhythms, it still plays with tremendous spirit and also enjoys the merit of outstanding recording quality. Both performances have the spontaneity of a live occasion, and cannot be too strongly recommended.

(i) *Halil* (*Nocturne for flute and orchestra*); (ii) *Mass* (*3 Meditations for cello and orchestra*); *On the Waterfront: symphonic suite.*
**(*) DG Dig. 2532/*3302* 051 [id.]. (i) Rampal; (ii) Rostropovich; Israel PO, composer.

This brings together Bernstein pieces from three different periods of his career. In the suite *On the Waterfront*, he glories in his youthful virtuosity, picking up music that would otherwise have been left on the floor of the dubbing-room. In the *Meditations* from the *Mass* he develops the spiritual message which has increasingly led him to build links with his Jewish background and Israel, as in *Halil*, written for Rampal in 1981, a piece which uses a 12-note theme melodically yet echoes Hebrew music. Bernstein with his chosen performers inspires dedicated readings. With a high-level matching chrome cassette these live recordings are generally atmospheric and reasonably well-balanced.

Symphonies Nos. 1 (Jeremiah); 2 (The Age of Anxiety); 3 (Kaddish). Chichester Psalms.
*** DG 2709 077 (3) [id.]. Ludwig, Foss, Caballé; Wager (speaker), V. Boys' Ch., Israel PO, composer.

Bernstein's musical invention is always memorable if at times a little too facile to match the ambitiousness of his symphonic aim, but the compelling confidence of his writing speaks of a genius stretching himself to the limit. The *Jeremiah symphony* dates from Bernstein's early twenties and ends with a moving passage from *Lamentations* for the mezzo soloist. As its title suggests, the *Second Symphony* was inspired by the poem of W. H. Auden, with the various movements directly reflecting dramatic passages from it, though no words are set in this work for orchestra alone. The *Third Symphony*, written in memory of President Kennedy, is the most impressive of all, and is here recorded in a revised version which concentrates the original concept of a dialogue between man and God, a challenge from earth to heaven. The revision has a male speaker instead of female, and the result is less self-conscious. These performances with the Israel Philharmonic are not always quite as polished or forceful as those Bernstein recorded earlier in New York, but with excellent recording they never fail to reflect the warmth of Bernstein's writing.

Vocal music

Chichester Psalms.
*** HMV ASD 3035 [Ang. S 37119]. Bowman, Lancelot, Corkhill, Ellis, King's Coll. Ch., Ledger – BRITTEN: *Festival Te Deum* etc.***
*** CBS 72374 [MS 6792]. Bogart, Camerata Singers, NYPO, composer – *Facsimile*.**

Bernstein wrote his *Chichester Psalms* in response to a commission from the Dean of Chichester, the Very Reverend Walter Hussey, who when he was at Northampton prompted notable works of art of all kinds. The occasion was the Southern Cathedrals Festival of July 1965, but Bernstein was not deterred from using the original Hebrew for the actual psalm texts instead of the Bible or Prayer-Book versions. It is the central setting of *Psalm 100* with jazz rhythms reminiscent of *West Side Story* that is the most obviously appealing section, but the a cappella setting of *Psalm 133* has a distinctive beauty, and whatever one's doubts about the music's ultimate value, it makes an attractive choral piece. Bernstein naturally secures a vivid performance from singers and players alike; but the version from the King's College Choir is even more distinctive, using the original accompaniment of organ, harp and percussion. The choir, under their director, Philip Ledger, are wonderfully incisive and jaunty in the jazzy rhythms, but the palm goes to the countertenor James Bowman, who revels in the blues overtones of the setting of *Psalm 23*. Splendid recording.

Mass (for the death of President Kennedy): complete.
*** CBS 77256 (2) [M2-31008]. Titus (celebrant), Scribner Ch., Berkshire Boy Ch., Rock Band and O, composer.

Bernstein is nothing if not ambitious. Composed for the opening of the Kennedy Center for the Performing Arts in Washington, this is a full-length 'entertainment', outrageously eclectic in its borrowings from pop and the avant-garde, and with a scenario that boldly defies all sense of good taste, with the celebrant smashing the holy vessel before the altar. Its impact wanes demonstrably on repetition, but still it presents an extraordinary example of Bernstein's irresistible energy. To a remarkable degree he succeeds despite everything, and it is worth hearing these records to experience a unique, brave phenomenon.

Songfest (cycle of American poems for 6 singers and orch.).
*** DG 2531 044 [id.]. Dale, Elias, Williams, Rosenshein, Reardon, Gramm, Nat. SO of Washington, composer.

Songfest, one of Bernstein's most richly varied works, is a sequence of poems which creatively uses all six singers solo and in various combinations. Not only the plan but the writing too is ingenious, one song using strict serialism in the most approachable, idiomatically American way. Characteristically, Bernstein often chooses controversial words to set, and by his personal fervour welds a very disparate group of pieces together into a warmly satisfying whole, comparable with Britten's *Serenade, Nocturne* or *Spring symphony*. Outstanding performance and recording.

Stage works

Candide: Overture and excerpts.
(M) ❀ *** CBS 60337/*40*- [OS/*ST* 2350]. Adrian, Cook, Rounseville and original New York cast, Krachmalnick.

Bernstein's *Candide* was a Broadway flop on its first appearance in 1956, and in spite of an outstanding cast and a highly praised production by Tyrone Guthrie, it ran for only 23 performances. It has since been more successfully revived in a new format, but this marvellous record encapsulates the original and should be snapped up by all who care about the musical theatre, before it is withdrawn. The music with its eclectic derivations is irresistibly spontaneous. Its highlight, the Rossini-styled *Glitter and be gay*, is given a scintillating coloratura performance here by Barbara Cook. Max Adrian is hardly less memorable and the Gilbert and Sullivan influences will surely endear the score to British listeners. The lyrics, by Richard Wilbur, give pleasure in themselves and the LP (complete with its original sleeve-note) is a collector's item. There is also a vivid cassette, but without the documentation. Not to be missed.

West Side Story.
(M) *** CBS 32193/*40*- [JS/*JST* 32603]. Original Broadway cast.
*** CBS 70006/*40*- [JS/*JST* 3270]. Film soundtrack cast.

It would seem perverse – although our coverage does not normally extend to Musicals – to omit a reference to Bernstein's greatest score, just because it is not normally performed in the opera house. It contains several of the finest popular tunes of the post-war era: *Tonight*, *Maria* and *Somewhere*, among others, are unforgettable. The virility of the music is remarkable; the ballet sequences although noisy are as fresh now as on the day they were written. It is fashionable to prefer the original Broadway cast with Carol Lawrence, Larry Kerr and Chita Rivera (musical director, Max Goberman), and the recording uses stereo effectively enough in the dance sequences. But there is nothing much wrong with the film soundtrack version, except that it is still on CBS's top-priced label. Both tape transfers are successful. The film soundtrack has all the singers projected very forwardly in aural 'close-up', so it is not surprising that the voices are vividly clear. The balance in the original-cast version has a convincing theatrical ambience and perspectives are well caught without loss of clarity: the stereo is remarkably natural on cassette, as it is on LP.

West Side Story: Symphonic dances.
*** DG Dig. **410 025-2**; 2532/*3302* 082 [id.]. LAPO, composer – GERSHWIN: *Rhapsody in blue* etc.**(*)
(M) *** DG 2535/*3335* 210 [id.]. San Francisco SO, Ozawa – GERSHWIN: *Piano concerto*. ***

West Side Story: Symphonic dances; On the Waterfront: Symphonic suite.
(M) ** CBS 61096/*40*-[MS 6251]. NYPO, composer.

Bernstein, recorded live, is at his most persuasive conducting a highly idiomatic account of the orchestral confection devised from his most successful musical. It may not be quite so crisp of ensemble as his earlier New York version, but it has more spirit with the players contributing the necessary shouts in the *Mambo* representing a street fight. Vivid if close-up sound, with a first-class chrome cassette. The compact disc is very good too, but shows no marked difference from the standard issues, although the resonance is controlled more cleanly.

Ozawa's performance is highly seductive, with an approach which is both vivid and warm, yet conceals any sentimentality. The sound is very good on both disc and cassette.

Bernstein's earlier NYPO version is certainly vibrant and superbly played, but the close-up recording is less agreeable than either of the DG records. The score from *On the Waterfront* is film music pure and simple, and expertly though it may underline the film's action, it does not bear too much repetition on its own. Bernstein's later Israeli recording sounds richer than this – see above.

Berwald, Franz (1797–1868)

(i) *Piano concerto in D;* (ii) *Violin concerto in C sharp min. Play of the elves; Serious and joyful fancies* (tone poems).
*** EMI 7C 061 35471. (i) Migdal; (ii) Tellefsen, RPO, Björlin.

With EMI's important Berwald box (including the four symphonies, two concertos and orchestral music) now withdrawn from EMI's domestic catalogue – although it apparently still remains in the USA on Serafin SID 6113 – we are left with a pair of discs extracted from it. The *Violin concerto* is an early work, dating from 1820 when Berwald was still active as a violinist. It is slight but pleasing, well worth hearing when it is persuasively played as it is here by the Norwegian violinist, Arve Tellefsen. It explores no great depths and its melodic invention is somewhat bland, but there is a good deal of charm to recommend it. The *Piano concerto*, a late work dating from the mid-1850s, is a strange piece. The soloist plays throughout: there is not a bar's rest and the score bears a note to the effect that the concerto can be performed without orchestra. Marian Migdal, a Polish-born pianist, plays it with poetry, sensitivity and panache; he is scrupulous in his observance of dynamic markings, and his command of keyboard colour is most impressive. So, too, is his handling of rubato, which is most musical and natural. Playing that is so affectionate and perceptive cannot fail to win friends for this concerto, which in spite of its Chopinesque gestures has a quiet and persuasive individuality. The recording is first-class.

Symphonies Nos. 1 in G min. (*Sinfonie sérieuse*)*; 3 in C* (*Sinfonie singulière*).
[M] **(*) HMV Green. ESD/*TC-ESD* 135470-1/*4*. RPO, Björlin.

Now that Ehrling's coupling of the *Singulière* and the *E flat Symphony*, made with the LSO for Decca, is out of circulation, this is the only available UK recording of either work. Berwald's symphonies come from the early 1840s and are really quite remarkable. The *Singulière* is, by general consent, the finest and is quite unlike anything else in the music of its time (or indeed any other). Although the musical language is predominantly diatonic, both this and the *Sérieuse* have a refreshing life and an imaginative vitality that step well outside the comparatively pale atmosphere of the Scandinavian musical world of the mid-nineteenth century. Berwald is a highly original figure and a distinctive voice who rewards investigation. The playing here could do with more bite and vigour (the recordings were made during a heat-wave) but sufficient of the music's character is conveyed for this to be a most welcome reissue, particularly at mid-price. The sound – from the mid-1970s – is very good indeed in its disc format, but the XDR ferric-cassette transfer has slight problems with the resonance, bringing a degree of bass-orientation in the sound balance and less freshness on top.

Grand septet in B flat.
*** CRD CRD 1004/*CRDC 4044*. Nash Ens. – HUMMEL: *Septet*.***

Berwald's only *Septet* is a work of genuine quality and deserves a secure place in the repertory instead of on its periphery. It dates from 1828 and is for the same forces as the Beethoven and Kreutzer *Septets*; the invention is lively and the ideas have charm. It is eminently well played by the Nash Ensemble and finely recorded. The cassette (as is usual with CRD) is an altogether excellent transfer, matching the disc closely.

String quartet in G min.
*** CRD CRD 1061/*CRDC 4061*. Chilingirian Qt – WIKMANSON: *Quartet*.***

Berwald composed four quartets: two in 1849 after the symphonies, and two in his mid-twenties. The *G minor Quartet*, and a companion in B flat which has not survived, date from 1818. This work did not appear in print until the 1940s, when the parts of the middle movements were discovered during stocktaking at the Royal Swedish Academy of Music. It is, as one would expect from an accomplished violinist, a remarkably assured piece, and the first movement is full of modulatory audacities. If the thematic substance has not the same quality of inspiration as in Arriaga's quartets, it is still both characterful and appealing. The trio of the scherzo has a touching charm that is almost Schubertian, though it is impossible that Berwald could have been aware of his great contemporary. This is a highly interesting and often bold quartet, and the Chilingirian players give a well-shaped and sensitive account of it. They are truthfully recorded, and the coupling – another Swedish quartet – enhances the attractions of this issue. The cassette transfer is outstandingly fresh and clear. Strongly recommended.

Birtwistle, Harrison (born 1934)

Punch and Judy (opera).
*** Decca HEAD 24/5 [id.]. Bryn-Julson, DeGaetani, Langridge, Roberts, Wilson-Johnson, Tomlinson, L. Sinf., Atherton.

Punch and Judy is a brutal ritualistic piece, 'the first modern English opera' as it was called when it first appeared at the Aldeburgh Festival in 1968. Characteristically, in setting the traditional puppet story Birtwistle has adopted a sharp, abrasive style, the more angular because Stephen Pruslin's libretto has a stylized patterning based on nursery rhymes and children's games. It may not make easy listening, but it is not easy to forget either, for behind the aggressiveness Birtwistle's writing has a way of touching an emotional chord, just as Stravinsky's so often does. Heard on record, Punch's war-cry and first murder (his wife Judy battered to death) have an impact that reminds one of the shower-bath murder in the film *Psycho*, itself intensified by music. Stephen Roberts is outstanding as Punch, and among the others there is not a single weak link. David Atherton, conductor from the first performances, excels himself with the Sinfonietta. Clear vivid recording.

Bizet, Georges (1838–75)

L'Arlésienne (incidental music): *suites Nos. 1–2; Carmen: suites Nos. 1–2.*
(M) *** CBS 60142/*40*- [MY/*MYT* 60142]. Nat. PO, Stokowski.
(M) *** Mercury SRI/*MRI* 75060. Detroit SO, Paray.
**(*) Ph. 9500 566/*7300 715* [id.]. LSO, Marriner.
(M) **(*) Ph. Seq. 6527/*7311* 083. LOP, Markevitch.

L'Arlésienne: suites Nos. 1–2; Carmen: suite No. 1.

(M) *** HMV SXLP/*TC-SXLP* 30276. RPO, Beecham.
*** DG 2531/*3301* 329 [id.]. LSO, Abbado.
(M) *** EMI Em. EMX/*TC-EMX* 2028. Philh. O, Karajan.

L'Arlésienne: suites Nos. 1–2; Jeux d'enfants.
**(*) Decca SXL/*KSXC* 6903 [Lon. CS 7127]. Cleveland O, Maazel.
** CBS Dig. 36713 [id.]. Toronto SO, Andrew Davis.

Carmen: suites Nos. 1–2.
(*) Telarc Dig. **CD 80048; DG 10048 [id.]. St Louis SO, Slatkin – GRIEG: *Peer Gynt.***(*)

Among recent couplings of *L'Arlésienne* and *Carmen*, Abbado's DG recording with the LSO stands out. The orchestral playing is characteristically refined, the wind solos cultured and elegant, especially in *L'Arlésienne*, where the pacing of the music is nicely judged. A vibrant accelerando at the end of the *Farandole* only serves to emphasize the obvious spontaneity of the music-making. There is warmth too, of course, and in the opening *Prélude* of the *Carmen suite* plenty of spirit. With vivid, truthful recording, this is very attractive. The sound of the cassette is virtually identical with that of the disc, though there is a very slight loss of transient bite on side two.

However the catalogue is currently extremely rich in mid-price reissues. Leading them is Stokowski's outstanding CBS record, made in 1977 during the great conductor's Indian summer in the recording studios, not long before he died. It offers recording of demonstration quality, with ripely resonant sound, with a beguiling bloom on wind and strings alike. The polish and vitality of the playing are striking from the opening bar of the *Carmen Prélude*, taken at a cracking pace, but never sounding rushed. Stokowski's affectionately romantic approach to both scores communicates in every number, yet he never sentimentalizes, and the panache of the music-making is headily enjoyable. The selection is generous in offering four suites, the only omission being the *Intermezzo* from the second suite of *L'Arlésienne*. The cassette is well managed but does not match the disc in technical distinction.

Looking further back, to the early days of stereo, there are excellent records from Karajan, with the Philharmonia Orchestra in peak form, and Paray in a vintage Mercury coupling, one of the first to be made in the excellent acoustics of the Ford Auditorium in Detroit. The sound is glowing and natural, weighty and brilliant and in no way dated, and there is a very good cassette. Paray's performances are strongly rhythmic (the famous string tune in *L'Arlésienne*) and very positive; the *Minuet* in the second suite is brisk and light. The playing is first-class, and the recording another colourful demonstration of the flair of the Mercury engineers at the beginning of the 1960s. Paray has the advantage over Karajan in including six items from the two *Carmen* suites, whereas the EMI disc offers only the first four. Yet Karajan's record, too, is very attractive, with solo wind playing at times even more distinguished than that afforded by the excellent Detroit players. Some of Karajan's tempi are unusual (in this respect Paray is rather more convincing – there is a Gallic feel to his set) with the *Carillon* from *L'Arlésienne* taken fast and the *Pastorale* very spacious. But the playing combines finesse and spontaneity and with warm, vivid sound this is very enjoyable. The cassette has a slightly less brilliant upper range than the disc (because of the resonance), but does not lack life at the top and is well balanced.

Markevitch's Philips selection is also highly recommendable, well played and vividly characterized with French wind soloists. The recording is rich and colourful, rather more reverberant in *Carmen* than in *L'Arlésienne*, which is brighter and more forwardly balanced, both on disc and the excellent matching cassette.

However, Beecham's performances have been successfully reissued on HMV and they have a very special place in the catalogue. Besides the beauty and unique character of the wind solos, Beecham's deliciously sprightly *Minuet* from *L'Arlésienne* and his gently affectionate way with the lovely *Adagietto* are irresistibly persuasive, as is the characteristic swagger in the opening *Carmen Prélude*, the cymbals marvellously telling. The recording sounds astonishingly full and vivid, and there is no appreciable difference between disc and cassette (the transients just marginally sharper on the former, the latter displaying slightly more fullness).

Maazel's Cleveland coupling of *L'Arlésienne* and the delightful *Jeux d'enfants* is also outstanding. Maazel coaxes some real pianissimo playing from the Cleveland Orchestra, who respond to this music with relish. They are especially good in *Jeux d'enfants*; its miniature qualities and colour are engagingly caught, and the closing *Galop* is delightfully vivacious. Maazel chooses fast tempi in *L'Arlésienne*, and the famous saxophone solo in the *Prélude* does not achieve the haunting quality famous in the Beecham version. But the Decca recording is extremely vivid, and the cassette is only marginally less crisp than the disc.

Andrew Davis's similar coupling is disappointing. It is all well played, and the digital recording – if a little artificial in balance – is impressively firm and brilliant. But there is a curious lack of vivacity, although *Jeux d'enfants* has more sparkle than *L'Arlésienne*.

Marriner's collection is exceptionally generous, offering eleven items from *Carmen* and both *L'Arlésienne suites*, missing out only the *Intermezzo* from the second. The recording too is attractively rich and naturally balanced. But the musical characterization – in spite of fine LSO solo playing, notably from the flautist, Peter Lloyd – is sometimes lacking in flair and indeed brio. There are minor touches of eccentricity – Marriner's tempo suddenly quickens for the middle section of the *Minuet* from the *Second L'Arlésienne suite*, and although there is much to ravish the ear, the orchestrations of the vocal numbers from *Carmen* are not always convincing. The cassette transfer is good; there is some lack of glitter, and the inner focus of fortissimos is less sharp than on disc.

The Telarc digital recordings of the *Carmen* orchestral suites made in St Louis have a self-conscious glittering brilliance. But there is a natural perspective, and the orchestral colour is very telling, helped by good playing, if with no special sophistication. Audiophiles will undoubtedly respond to the range and vividness of the sound: the only snag is that the bass drum is over-recorded and muddies the texture at one or two climaxes. The pressing itself is immaculate.

Symphony in C.

(M) *** HMV SXLP 30260 [(d) Sera. S 60192]. French Nat. RO, Beecham – BERLIOZ: *Troyens: excerpts;* DELIBES: *Le Roi s'amuse.****

(M) *** Decca Jub. 410 167-1/*4*. ASMF, Marriner – PROKOFIEV: *Symphony No. 1.****

(M) **(*) CBS 60112/*40*- [MY/*MYT* 36725]. NYPO, Bernstein – PROKOFIEV: *Symphony No. 1* etc.**

Symphony in C; L'Arlésienne: suite No. 1; suite No. 2: Menuet; Farandole.

(B) ** Con. CC/*CCT* 7562. SRO, Gibson.

Symphony in C; The Fair maid of Perth: suite; Jeux d'enfants.

(M) *** Ph. Seq. 6527/*7311* 180 [id.]. LSO, Benzi.

Symphony in C; Jeux d'enfants.

*** Ph. 9500 443/*7300 649* [id.]. Concg O, Haitink.

Symphony in C; Jeux d'enfants; Patrie: overture.

**(*) HMV Dig. ASD/*TCC-ASD* 143339-1/*4* [Ang. DS/*4XS* 37928]. O Nat. de France, Ozawa.

Marriner's performance is beautifully played and richly recorded, in a warm, resonant acoustic. Perhaps there is a trifle too much reverberation, but it is easy to adjust, and the wit of the finale is not blunted: this is irrepressibly gay and high-spirited. With an equally successful coupling this is a very desirable record, particularly now it has been reissued at medium price on Decca's Jubilee label. The chrome cassette is also of the highest quality.

Beecham's reissued version from the beginning of the 1960s is no less attractive if the couplings are suitable. No one has ever quite matched Sir Thomas in the way he brought out the spring-like qualities in this youthful work. The playing of the French orchestra is not quite so polished as that of Marriner's group, but Beecham's panache more than makes amends, and the slow movement is delightful. The resonant recording still sounds well.

Haitink's version is also very fine, though the Philips coupling is not very generous. His reading obviously takes into account the reverberant Amsterdam acoustic, for it is essentially broad and spacious. The slow movement is particularly eloquent, with a beautiful oboe solo. *Jeux d'enfants* is also delectably played. Demonstration-worthy Philips recording, slightly less crisp on tape than on disc.

Roberto Benzi has made too few records. He has the gift of bringing music fully alive in the recording studio and his 1966 Philips version of the *Symphony* is most attractive, standing comparison with both Marriner and Beecham. He is supported by first-rate LSO playing with the oboe distinctive in the slow movement. The personality of the orchestra comes through strongly in the vividly played couplings, although Benzi has not quite Beecham's panache in *The Fair maid of Perth*. In *Petit mari, petite femme* from *Jeux d'enfants* the leading string parts are played as cello and violin solos, which is not the composer's idea, but works very well. The sound is admirable, fresh and bright, yet full. If this coupling is convenient, this can be recommended. The cassette is one of Philips's best and is especially lively in the *Symphony*.

A generous enough offering in terms of playing time and eminently good performances from the Orchestre National de France and Ozawa. However, these do not displace such splendid records as the Haitink, which has a most lifelike and natural recording, or the Beecham with the same orchestra which has a charm and elegance all its own. The cassette is strikingly successful, vivid and wide-ranging, full-bodied and clear.

Bernstein's CBS recording has been remastered, and though it is still rather brightly lit it can be made to yield a satisfactory balance. The performance is characteristically brilliant, and the high spirits of the orchestral response bring a sense of exhilaration which is especially attractive in the last two movements. The slow movement is affectionately done, with a fine oboe solo, the contrast in the middle section heightened by the precision of the playing. Originally this was coupled with *The Sorcerer's Apprentice* as well as the Prokofiev; now the measure is slightly shorter.

Gibson's performances are given a first-rate, Decca sourced recording, but in the last analysis the presentation of the music, though stylish, is a little faceless and even at Contour bargain-price this is not really competitive when Beecham, Marriner and Benzi cost only a little more.

Jeux d'enfants (*Children's Games*): *Suite*.
(B) *** CfP CFP/*TC-CFP* 40086. SNO, Gibson – SAINT-SAËNS: *Carnival****; RAVEL: *Ma Mère l'Oye*.**(*)

From Classics for Pleasure a fresh recording and lively orchestral playing. The lyrical movements, shaped with gentle affection, give much pleasure and with good couplings this is an excellent bargain. Both disc and cassette sound equally vivid.

Piano music

Jeux d'enfants (for piano duet), *Op. 22*.
* DG 2531/*3301* 389 [id.]. Kontarsky Duo – FAURÉ: *Dolly;* MILHAUD: *Scaramouche*.*

The complete *Jeux d'enfants* is an enchanting score and a comparative rarity on record. (It does exist in a 3-record anthology on Arion played by Christian Ivaldi and Noël Lee.) However, this present version will not do: the sound is dry and forward, and this serves to undermine what little charm the Kontarskys bring to it. Disc and chrome tape sound virtually identical.

Premier Nocturne; Variations chromatiques.
(M) ** CBS 60290/*40*-. Gould – GRIEG: *Sonata*.*

Glenn Gould stakes a claim on the sleeve for Bizet's *Variations chromatiques* as one of the very few masterpieces for the solo piano to emerge in the third quarter of the last century. Be that as it may, he plays it as if it is, and almost convinces one that he is right. It is an early piece and a resourceful one, but the invention is not quite fresh enough nor does it bear the distinctive stamp of the early symphony. The *Premier Nocturne* is not without charm and, despite the somewhat dry recorded sound that this artist favoured, this is a satisfying issue: it is a pity that his account of the Grieg on the reverse side, though intensely musical, is too eccentric to be competitive. The excellent chrome tape matches the disc closely.

VOCAL MUSIC

Te Deum.
(*) Argo Dig. ZRDL/*KZRDC* 1010. Greenberg, Winbergh, Lausanne Pro Arte Ch., Swiss R. Ch., SRO, Lopez-Cobos – POULENC: *Gloria.*(*)

Bizet's *Te Deum* is a product of his youth and was written while he was still at Rome: indeed it was composed for the Rodrigues Prize which was only open to winners of the Prix de Rome and this *Te Deum* of 1858 did not win. It is very much a student work with little of the effortless mastery that distinguishes the even earlier *Symphony*, and there is much that is derivative. There are some entertaining moments in the course of its twenty-five minutes, along with some obviously manufactured ideas not all of which are effective. Both the performance and recording are good, and the work is not otherwise available. There is a very good cassette, lively and fresh in focus though not quite as refined in the upper end of the range as the disc.

OPERA

Carmen (complete).
*** DG Dig. **410 088-2**; 2741/*3382* 025 (3) [id.]. Baltsa, Carreras, Van Dam, Ricciarelli, Barbaux, Paris Op. Ch., Schoneberg Boys' Ch., Berlin PO, Karajan.
*** Decca D 11 D 3/*K 11 K 33* (3) [Lon. OSA/*5*- 13115]. Troyanos, Domingo, Van Dam, Te Kanawa, Alldis Ch., LPO, Solti.
*** DG 2709 083/*3371 040* (3) [id.]. Berganza, Domingo, Cotrubas, Milnes, Amb. S., LSO, Abbado.
*** [DG 2709 043/*3371 006* (3)]. Horne, McCracken, Krause, Maliponte, Manhattan Op. Ch., Metropolitan Op. O, Bernstein.
*** HMV SLS/*TC-SLS* 5021 (3) [Ang. SCL 3613]. Los Angeles, Gedda, Blanc, Micheau, Fr. R. Ch. and O, Petits Chanteurs de Versailles, Beecham.
**(*) [RCA LSC 6199/*ARK 3* 2542 (3)]. Price, Corelli, Merrill, Freni, V. State Op. Ch., V. Boys' Ch., VPO, Karajan.
(M) ** HMV SLS 913 (3) [Ang. SCLX/*4X3X* 3650]. Callas, Gedda, Massard, Guiot, Paris Op. Ch. and O, Prêtre.
*(*) Erato Dig. **ECD 88037**; NUM/*MCE* 75113 (3). Film soundtrack recording with: Migenes Johnson, Domingo, Raimondi, Esham, Watson, Fr. R. Ch. and Children's Ch., Fr. Nat. O, Maazel.

A clear first choice for *Carmen* is impossible. Readers will have their own inclinations, for it has been a very successful opera on record, after Beecham had set a standard against which other versions might be measured at the very beginning of the 1960s. Yet the new DG set, with first-class compact discs also available, finds a natural place at the top of the list.

Affection beams from this newest Karajan version as well as high tension and high polish. Where in his earlier RCA version he used the old text with added recitatives, here he uses the Oeser edition with its extra passages and spoken dialogue. That may account in part for the differences of approach, more intimate in the presentation of the drama, less extreme over certain controversial tempi.

In Carreras he has a Don José, lyrical and generally sweet-toned, who is far from a conventional hero-figure, more the anti-hero, an ordinary man caught up in tragic love. The *Flower Song* is exquisitely beautiful in its half-tones. The Micaela of Katia Ricciarelli is similarly scaled down, with the big dramatic voice kept in check. José van Dam – also the Escamillo for Solti – is incisive and virile, the public hero-figure, which leaves Agnes Baltsa as a vividly compelling Carmen, tough and vibrant yet musically precise and commanding. Where on stage (as at Covent Garden) Baltsa tends to exaggerate the characterization, here Karajan encourages her to be positively larger than life but still a believable figure, with tenderness under the surface. In her brief exchanges with Escamillo before the final scene, you are made to believe her love for the bullfighter.

As for Karajan, he draws richly resonant playing from the Berlin Philharmonic, sparkling and swaggering in the bullfight music but delicate and poetic too. The digital recording is bright and atmospheric if not always ideally balanced. The spoken dialogue distractingly sounds like the soundtrack of a French film. The cassettes follow the layout of the discs. The use of chrome stock means that the sound is refined in detail and vivid, with everything naturally focused. In spite of the modest level of transfer, hiss is not really a problem and both solo voices and chorus are clear, with very marginal loss of range compared with the discs. The dialogue is boldly projected. The compact disc version brings benefit in extra clarity, but it also brings out more noticeably the degree of close-up aggressiveness in the recording.

By the side of the newest digital sound the Solti discs (though not the cassettes) sound less strikingly brilliant than they seemed on first appearance. But this Decca performance, apart from making a satisfactory solution of the vexed question of text, is remarkable for its new illumination of characters whom everyone thinks to know inside out. Tatiana Troyanos is quite simply the subtlest Carmen on record. The blatant sexuality which is so often accepted as the essential ingredient in Carmen's character is here replaced by a far more insidious fascination, for there is a degree of vulnerability in this heroine. You can understand why she falls in love and then out again. Escamillo too is more readily sympathetic, not just the flashy matador who steals the hero's girl, in some ways the custodian of rationality, whereas Don José is revealed as weak rather than just a victim. Troyanos's singing is delicately seductive too, with no hint of vulgarity, while the others make up the most consistent singing cast on record to date. Solti like Karajan uses spoken dialogue and a modification of the Oeser edition, deciding in each individual instance whether to accept amendments to Bizet's first thoughts. Fine as other versions are of a much-recorded opera, this dramatic and sensitive account from Solti holds its place, high among recommended versions. The cassette transfer is outstanding, losing nothing of the tingling immediacy and drama of the discs.

Superbly disciplined, Abbado's performance nails its colours to the mast at the very start in a breathtakingly fast account of the opening prelude. Through the four Acts there are other examples of idiosyncratic tempi, but the whole entertainment hangs together with keen compulsion, reflecting the fact that these same performers – Sherrill Milnes as Escamillo excepted – took part in the Edinburgh Festival production directly associated with this recording project. Conductor and orchestra can take a large share of credit for the performance's success, for though the singing is never less than enjoyable, it is on the whole less characterful than on some rival sets. Teresa Berganza is a seductive if somewhat unsmiling Carmen – not without sensuality, and producing consistently beautiful tone, but lacking some of the flair which makes for a three-dimensional portrait. If you want a restrained and thoughtful view, then Tatiana Troyanos in Solti's set (see above), also opposite the admirably consistent Placido Domingo, is preferable. Ileana Cotrubas as Micaela is not always as sweetly steady as she can be; Milnes makes a heroic matador. The spoken dialogue is excellently produced, and the sound is vivid, betraying not at all that the sessions took place in different studios (in London as well as Edinburgh). The focus on cassette is less sharp than on disc.

Bernstein's recording – now withdrawn in the UK – was recorded at the New York Metropolitan Opera, the first major opera recording undertaken there for many years. It was based on the Met's spectacular production, with the same cast and conductor as on record, and the sessions plainly gained from being interleaved with live performances. Bizet scholars may argue about details of the text used in the performances: Bernstein adopted the original version of 1875 with spoken dialogue but with variations designed to suit a stage production. Some of his slow tempi will be questioned too, but what really matters is the authentic tingle of dramatic tension which impregnates the whole entertainment. Never before, not even in Beecham's classic set, had the full theatrical flavour of Bizet's score been conveyed, and Marilyn Horne – occasionally coarse in expression – gives a most fully satisfying reading of the heroine's role, a great vivid characterization, warts and all. The rest of the cast similarly works to Bernstein's consistent overall plan. The singing is not all perfect, but it is always vigorous and colourful, and so (despite often poor French accents) is the spoken dialogue. A presentation hard to resist, with generally atmospheric recording. The DG cassette transfer was a very early one and lacked brilliance and life.

Beecham's approach to Bizet's well-worn score is no less fresh and revealing. Like Bernstein's, his speeds are not always conventional but they always *sound* right. And unlike so many strong-willed conductors in opera Beecham allows his singers room to breathe and to expand their characterizations. It seems he specially chose de los Angeles to be his Carmen although she had never sung the part on the stage before making the recording. He conceived the *femme fatale* not as the usual glad-eyed character, but as someone far more subtly seductive, winning her admirers not so much by direct assault and high voltage as by genuine charm and real femininity. De los Angeles suits this conception perfectly: her characterization of Carmen is absolutely bewitching, and when in the Quintet scene she says *Je suis amoureuse* one believes her absolutely. Naturally the other singers are not nearly so dominant as this, but they make admirable foils; Gedda is pleasantly light-voiced as ever, Janine Micheau is a sweet Micaela, and Ernest Blanc makes an attractive Escamillo. The stereo recording does not add to things in the way that the best Decca opera recordings do, and there seems to have been little attempt at stage production, but in the newest transfer the sound is quite full and almost over-brilliant, and the recording does not too greatly show its age. The cassette transfer is also successful, although on our copy of the first cassette (not the second) some taming of an over-fierce treble is needed.

With Karajan's earlier RCA version – not currently available in the UK – much depends on the listener's reaction to the conductor's tempi and to Leontyne Price's smoky-toned Carmen, but if you are looking for a heroine who is a sexual threat as well as a charmer, Price is the more convincing. Corelli has moments of coarseness, but his is still a heroic performance. Robert Merrill sings with gloriously firm tone, while Freni is, as ever, enchanting as Micaela. With more spectacular recording than is given to Beecham, this set remains quite a keen competitor, with Karajan always inspired in a much-played score. The RCA cassettes have been remastered and give acceptable sound, although the transients are a little blunted by the resonance.

The Callas set is something of a disappointment. Fire is there in plenty, of course. Callas is Carmen, the advertisements said, but rather Callas is Callas, for the diva's interpretation gives only half the story, both dramatically and musically. Musically Callas has all her usual faults of sourness and wobbling; but what is more, there are few of those individual touches in phrasing which make one catch the breath. This is a spiteful, malicious, even evil Carmen, not nearly as sexual as Price's. When Prêtre's conducting is relentless and the playing of the French orchestra less than brilliant, the issue is hardly in doubt. Gedda is a fair enough Don José, as he was in the Beecham set, but the voice has not the big heroic ring. All the other soloists are most disappointing.

The glory of Maazel's Erato version is the Don José of Placido Domingo, freer and more spontaneously expressive than in his two previous recordings, not least in the lovely account of the *Flower song*. Julia Migenes Johnson is a fresh-toned Carmen, not very subtle on detail but convincing. Ruggero Raimondi as Escamillo is less resonant than usual but sings cleanly, where Faith Esham is a shrill and thin-toned Micaela. Maazel's conducting is generally strong and dramatic but not very tender. The recording is fair, to make this a set mainly recommendable to those who enjoyed the film.

Carmen: highlights.

(M) *** HMV Green. ESD/*TC-ESD* 7047 (from above set, cond. Beecham).

(B) **(*) Con. CC/*CCT* 7580. Horne, Molese and soloists, RPO, Henry Lewis.

*** DG 2537/*3306* 049 (from above set, cond. Abbado).

(M) ** Decca SPA/*KCSP* 539. Resnik, Del Monaco, Sutherland, Krause, Geneva Ch., SRO, Schippers.

Any collection of 'highlights' from *Carmen* is bound to leave out favourite items, but Beecham's compilation, on HMV's Greensleeve label, has the advantage of economy and is a delightful collection of plums from Bizet's masterly score. The sound is excellent, though the tape is slightly less refined than the disc.

But perhaps the most fascinating disc of Carmen excerpts is the (originally Decca Phase Four) Contour reissue with Marilyn Horne, made some years before her complete New York recording. She it was who was the singing voice behind Dorothy Dandridge in the film *Carmen Jones*; and here, with a decade more of experience, she is even more searingly compelling as the fire-eating heroine. There is not only dramatic presence but musical control too, and the flair of the performance is striking. The side-lengths are not generous, but the sparkle of the recording makes some amends, and Henry Lewis's conducting has no lack of flair.

The DG selection also is not as generous as some but it makes a good sampler of Abbado's forceful, sharply etched reading, with first-rate recording (although the tape is less cleanly focused than the disc).

On Decca's cheapest label the excerpts from the Schippers version are worth considering for the contribution of Joan Sutherland as Micaela. Resnik is a characterful Carmen, but the microphone is not always kind to the voice, and Del Monaco is a coarse Don José.

Carmen: excerpts.
(M) *** Decca GRV/*KGRC* 22. Domingo, Troyanos, Te Kanawa, LPO, Solti – OFFENBACH: *Contes d'Hoffmann:* excerpts.***

These excerpts centre on Placido Domingo and with the attractive *Tales of Hoffmann* coupling are issued in Decca's 'Grandi voci' series. Certainly the singing demonstrates his vibrant timbre admirably. The items include the duet, *Carmen! sur les pas nous . . . Ma mère, je la vois*, the *Flower song*, and the final scene with Troyanos. Disc and tape are both of excellent quality.

Carmen: ballet (arr. from the music of the opera by Rodion Shchedrin).
*** HMV Dig. ASD/*TCC-ASD* 4194 [Ang. DS/*4XS* 37337]. LA CO, Schwartz.

Rodion Shchedrin's very free adaptation of Bizet's *Carmen* music has not been universally well received. What he has done to create his ballet score is to take Bizet's tunes, complete with harmony, and rework them into a new orchestral tapestry, using only strings and a wide variety of percussion. To the listener very familiar with Bizet's note-for-note sequence the breaking up and rearrangement of many of the melodic ideas (some, of course, survive pretty well intact) is disconcerting to say the least. And the free use of percussive effects like the vibraphone involves the element of taste. Let it be said that the whole thing is brilliantly done, with a marvellous ear for the colour possibilities of the orchestral string section. The playing here is first-class, Schwartz more relaxed and smiling than the earlier Russian Melodiya version, but not less lively. If you like sparkling sound, and have not too strongly conceived notions about the 'sacredness' of accepted masterpieces, you may find this very much to your taste. But it is strictly not for purists. The vivid tape matches the disc closely.

Les Pêcheurs de Perles (complete).
** HMV SLS/*TC-SLS* 5113 (2) [Ang. SBLX/*4X2X* 3856]. Cotrubas, Vanzo, Sarabia, Soyer, Paris Op. Ch. and O, Prêtre.
(M) ** HMV SLS 877 (2) [Ang. SBL 3603]. Micheau, Gedda, Blanc, Mars, Paris Opéra-Comique Ch. and O, Dervaux.

This is one of Bizet's most appealing works, not so much for the story (about pearl fishers and a priestess in medieval Ceylon) as for the relaxed charm of the score and in particular the soaring lyricism of five or six superb numbers. More than anything it needs affectionate treatment from the conductor (and a reasonable degree of technical accomplishment from the singers). Neither of these two HMV recordings meets these demands fully.

Prêtre's set is a mixed success. Ileana Cotrubas is superb as the high priestess, Leila, projecting character as well as singing beautifully. The tenor, Alain Vanzo, is also most stylish, but after that the snags begin, not just with the singing (Sarabia a variably focused baritone) but with the conducting (Prêtre is generally fast, unlilting and unfeeling) and with the recording (not sufficiently atmospheric). In principle it may seem a positive gain to have the original 1863 score reinstated, but it is hard not to feel disappointed when the great duet for the pearl fishers culminates not in a rich reprise of the big melody but in a tinkly little waltz theme. The cassettes are well managed, smooth and detailed.

The alternative Paris Opéra-Comique version is hardly more inspiring. Pierre Dervaux is an efficient conductor, but one suspects it is largely his fault that the soloists do not acquit themselves better. Gedda in his romance *Je crois entendre encore* is rather lumpy and graceless; and it does not take comparison with Gigli and De Luca to realize that the great, thrilling duet *Au fond du temple saint* is below par. Ernest Blanc has an attractive voice, but there is comparatively little imagination here, and Janine Micheau is not so graceful as she has been on records in the past. The recording does not sound too dated – it is acceptably warm and generally well-balanced.

Les Pêcheurs de perles: highlights.
(M) *(*) HMV SXLP/*TC-SXLP* 30304. Micheau, Gedda, Blanc, Paris Opéra-Comique Ch. and O, Dervaux – GOUNOD: *Roméo:* highlights.*(*)

Gedda and Blanc are in ringing voice for the pearl fishers' duet, but it is not a subtle reading, and too many of these excerpts from a not very distinguished complete set are similarly disappointing. But as a medium-price selection, interestingly coupled, it may be worth considering. Early-1960s recording.

Blake, David (born 1936)

(i) *Violin concerto;* (ii) *In Praise of Krishna.*
*** Argo ZRG 922. (i) Brown, Philh. O, Del Mar; (ii) Cahill, Northern Sinf., composer.

The lyricism of Blake's *Violin concerto* within a broadly serial framework, together with challenging bravura, reflect the qualities of the dedicatee, Iona Brown, who here gives a passionately committed performance. Each of the two movements is sharply divided into contrasted halves, slow–fast followed by fast–slow, with the art and landscape of Italy a direct inspiration. The cantata to Bengali words, *In Praise of Krishna,* is even more sensuous in its idiom, with Teresa Cahill a sweet-toned soloist.

Bliss, Arthur (1891–1975)

Checkmate: 5 Dances.
(*) Chan. ABR/*ABT* 1018. W. Australian SO, Schönzeler – RUBBRA: *Symphony No. 5.*(*)

Checkmate was Arthur Bliss's first ballet score and was composed for the Royal Ballet's first visit to Paris in 1937. The idea of a ballet based on chess, with all its opportunities for symbolism and heraldic splendour, appealed to Bliss, and the score he produced remains one of his most inventive creations. The five dances on the Chandos issue are well played under Hans-Hubert Schönzeler, and otherwise not represented in the catalogue at present. (Nor, for that matter, is the coupling, Edmund Rubbra's *Fifth Symphony.*) If the performance is not in the very first flight, it is still well worth having. The cassette transfer of the Bliss is made at a low level and the sound is disappointing, with poor transients.

(i) *Piano concerto. March of Homage; Welcome the Queen.*
*** Uni. Kanchana Dig. DKP 9006. Royal Liv. PO, Atherton, (i) with Fowke.

The concerto was written for British Week at the New York World Fair in 1939, and Bliss attempted a bravura work on a very large scale. From the dashing double octaves at the start the pianistic style throughout has much of Rachmaninov and Liszt in it, though the idiom is very much Bliss's own, with some of his most memorable material. It is a work which needs a passionately committed soloist, and that is what it finds here in Philip Fowke, urgent and expressive, well matched by David Atherton and the Liverpool orchestra. The two occasional pieces are given lively performances and full-blooded sound. The digital recording is full and vivid, with the piano naturally balanced, less forward than is common. There is a tendency for the acoustic to be a shade over-resonant in the concerto (especially noticeable at the opening), which produces less internal clarity of focus than one expects with a digital master. But this is a first-class and rewarding issue.

A Colour symphony; Things to Come (incidental music for H. G. Wells film).
*** HMV ASD 3416. RPO, Groves.

Bliss's *Colour symphony* dates from 1922, and this is its first recording since the composer's own, made in the mid-1950s. Inspired by a chance encounter with a book on heraldry, Bliss conceived this series of mood pictures on the theme of the symbolic meanings associated with the primary colours. The work is too episodic to be truly symphonic but it is nonetheless highly effective and is expertly scored. It comes into its own in this sympathetic performance. *Things to Come* is given in an extended form admirably assembled by Christopher Palmer, who has also scored the opening *Prologue*, since the full score and parts do not survive. This work dates more than the *Symphony* and its style is at times somewhat eclectic. But its invention is always attractive, and the splendid *March* offers what is perhaps the single most memorable idea to come from the pen of its composer. Sir Charles Groves and the RPO are splendid advocates, and the HMV engineers lavish on it their richest and most natural sound. Admirers of Bliss need not hesitate.

Clarinet quintet.
*** Chan. Dig. ABRD/*ABTD* 1078. Hilton, Lindsay Qt – BAX: *Clarinet sonata***; VAUGHAN WILLIAMS: *Studies.****

The *Clarinet quintet*, composed in the early 1930s, is arguably Bliss's masterpiece and the present performance is a worthy successor to the 1963 recording by Gervase de Peyer and members of the Melos Ensemble. These artists have the measure of its autumnal melancholy, the recording is natural and well focused and the chrome cassette is of the highest quality. On both disc and tape this is technically an outstanding issue.

Morning Heroes.
(M) **(*) HMV Green. ESD 7133. Westbrook (narrator), Royal Liv. PO and Ch., Groves.

Morning Heroes is an elegiac work, written as a tribute to the composer's brother and all who fell in the First World War. The sincerity of the writing is never in doubt, but there is less contrast here than in comparable war-inspired works by Vaughan Williams and Britten. One misses both the anger of those other composers and their passages of total simplicity, but it is good that one of Bliss's most ambitious works should be available in so strong a performance. Good recording.

(i) *Pastoral* (*Lie strewn the white flocks*); (ii) *A knott of riddles.*
(B) *** PRT GSGC/*ZCGC* 2042. (i) Michelow, Bruckner-Mahler Ch. of L.; (ii) Shirley-Quirk, L. CO; Wyn Morris.

Bliss's eightieth year produced a good crop of first recordings of his work. These are two attractive song cycles that show his art at its least demanding. He conceived the *Pastoral* as a classical fantasy, linking verse from widely different sources, and using mezzo-soprano, chorus, flute (beautifully played here by Norman Knight), timpani and strings. *A knott of riddles* is just as easy on the ear – arguably too easy – with English riddles translated from the Anglo-Saxon and provided with a solution by the soloist after each one. This is a much more recent work, written for the Cheltenham Festival in 1963. It is here sung with fine point by John Shirley-Quirk. Good recording. The cassette is fully acceptable, but side two (*A knott of riddles*) is at a higher level and gives the singing more range and presence; on side one the choral sound is not sharply focused.

Bloch, Ernest (1880–1959)

Concerti grossi Nos. 1 and 2.
(M) *** Mercury SRI 75017 [id.]. Eastman-Rochester O, Hanson.

Bloch's two *Concerti grossi* were written in 1925 and 1952 respectively, but although separated by more than a quarter of a uniquely fast-moving century, they are surprisingly similar in style. They may not be among Bloch's most deeply personal works but they are thoroughly enjoyable. The neoclassical style brings a piano continuo in the baroque manner in No. 1; the second, for strings alone, is more intense in feeling. The performances here are admirable, lively and sympathetic and the slightly spiky tinge to the otherwise full Mercury sound is like an attractive condiment.

Schelomo: Hebrew rhapsody (for cello and orchestra).
(M) ** DG Priv. 2535/*3335* 201 [id.]. Fournier, Berlin PO, Wallenstein – ELGAR: *Cello concerto.***

Schelomo; Voice in the wilderness.
**(*) Decca SXL 6440 [Lon. CS 6661]. Starker, Israel PO, Mehta.

The lush scores of *Schelomo* and *Voice in the wilderness* were once coupled together by Nelsova with the LPO under Ansermet on an early Decca mono LP. *Voice in the wilderness* is a rather diffuse piece which at times sounds for all the world like the soundtrack of a Hollywood Biblical epic, while at others its textures are so vivid and imaginative that such unworthy thoughts are promptly banished. *Schelomo* is the more disciplined work, arguably Bloch's masterpiece. Compared with Feuermann's marvellously full-blooded account on 78s (which should be transferred to LP), Starker and Mehta seem a little lacking in intensity and fire, though they are certainly well recorded. The Decca engineers have not succumbed to the temptation of making the soloist sound larger than life, though the wind is fractionally forward.

In spite of the fervent advocacy of Fournier, the recording lets his account of *Schelomo* down. Fournier is closely balanced and the orchestral detail is not fully revealed. Even so the sound is otherwise impressive, and this performance is easy to enjoy. The tape is well managed too.

Sinfonia breve.
(*) Mercury SRI 75116 [id.]. Minneapolis SO, Dorati – MCPHEE: *Tabuh-Tabuhan* **(*); SCHULLER: *7 Studies on themes of Paul Klee.**

Bloch's *Sinfonia breve* dates from 1953. It is a sombre piece and the slow movement broods inexorably. Both performance and recording here are first-class and the Mercury pressing flawless, but the main interest of this compilation lies in the engaging Schuller *Klee studies.*

Sacred service.
** Chan. ABR/*ABT* 1001. Berkman, L. Chorale and Concord Singers, LSO, Simon.

Bloch's *Sacred Service* has been neglected by the gramophone since the composer's own pioneering record and Leonard Bernstein's version made in the 1960s (still available in the US [Col. MS 6221] but not in the UK). Its reappearance in the catalogue must be welcomed, particularly in such vivid sound. The singing is perhaps wanting in ardour and intensity, and there could be greater attention to dynamic nuances. However, it would be unfair to dwell on the shortcomings of this performance in the light of so much that is good, not least of which is the orchestral playing. The recording is spacious and well-focused. The cassette too is a distinct success and well balanced, although its upper range is slightly restricted compared with the disc.

Blomdahl, Karl-Birger
(1916–68)

Symphony No. 3 (Facetter).
*** Cap. CAP 1251. Stockholm PO, Ehrling – BROMAN: *Overture*; ROSENBERG: *Marionettes (dance suite)*.***

Blomdahl was the most influential figure to emerge in the post-war Swedish scene, and his *Third Symphony* caused something of a stir when it appeared in 1950. There is an imaginative intensity here that draws one immediately into its world. The 'facets' to which the title refers are the various tonal possibilities that arise from the opening 12-note series. There is a sense of organic purpose as well as a brooding fantasy that exercises a powerful if dark spell. The recording has marvellous presence and impact though the aural image is a bit too forward. Ehrling and this orchestra recorded the symphony in the early 1960s when it was coupled with an imaginative and powerfully wrought symphony of Hilding Rosenberg. The present coupling (some dance movements from his opera, *Marionettes* (1939)) is less substantial though more immediately attractive, while the Broman overture is well enough fashioned but lacks a distinctive profile. A one-sided record in some ways.

Blow, John (1649–1708)

Organ voluntary in A; Echo voluntary in G; Evening service in G; Let thy hand be strengthened; O pray for the peace of Jerusalem; Salvator mundi.
** Mer. E 77013. Ely Cath. Ch., Wills (organ) – PURCELL: *Collection*.**

As Purcell's mentor (both preceding and succeeding him as organist at Westminster Abbey), Blow was a master of English church music, overshadowed though he was by his pupil. This single side of anthems and voluntaries is a good successor to the fine Blow record from King's College Choir (Argo ZRG 767, recently deleted), though it cannot match it in polish or finesse. Good atmospheric recording, but the organ balance is variable.

Boccherini, Luigi (1743–1805)

Cello concerto in B flat (arr. Grützmacher; see also below).
(M) ** DG Arc. Priv. 2547/*3347* 046 [(d) 2523/*3335* 179]. Fournier, Lucerne Fest. Strings, Baumgartner – TARTINI and VIVALDI: *Concertos*.**

Fournier plays splendidly; the slow movement is beautifully done, and the finale maintains the same level. He is recorded, however, with a balance that gives a nasal quality to the cello's upper register and exaggerates the upper partials. A strong treble cut is needed. This fault is much less insistent on the tape, which otherwise has both life and warmth: a clear case where the sound on the cassette is preferable to the disc.

Cello concerto No. 2 in D.
(M) *** DG Sig. 2543/*3343* 517 [2530/*3300* 974]. Rostropovich, Zürich Coll. Mus., Sacher – TARTINI and VIVALDI: *Concertos*.***

Cello concertos Nos. 2; 3 in G.
*** Erato STU/*MCE* 71369. Lodéon, Lausanne CO, Jordan.

Although essentially a performance in the grand manner (with Rostropovich providing his own cadenzas), the music-making in the DG issue also has tremendous vitality, with extremely lively outer movements to balance the eloquence of the *Adagio*. The forceful nature of the performance is short on charm and so perhaps a little out of character for an essentially elegant composer like Boccherini; but Rostropovich is so compelling that reservations are swept aside. He is given an alert accompaniment by Sacher, and the recording has fine body and presence. The chrome tape transfer too has excellent range and detail.

Frédéric Lodéon is a young French player, barely thirty years of age, and obviously an artist of accomplishment. His playing has genuine style and real eloquence, and in the *G major Concerto*, unearthed by Maurice Gendron, he is wonderfully fresh and fervent. The Lausanne orchestra gives him excellent support, but the balance does tend to favour the soloist. That apart, there is little to fault in these performances of music that has more to commend it than meets the eye; the slow movement of the *D major Concerto* has genuine tenderness and depth. In the cassette format the high-level transfer has brought an emphasis on the upper range which is particularly noticeable in the *Concerto No. 3 in G*, but adjustment of the controls will produce pleasing results.

Cello concerto No. 9 in B flat (original version, with cadenzas by Gendron).
(M) *** Ph. Seq. 6527/*7311* 124 [id.]. Gendron, LOP, Casals – HAYDN: *Cello concerto in D.****

Cello concertos Nos. 9 (original version); *10 in D, Op. 34.*
*** Erato STU/*MCE* 70997. Lodéon, Bournemouth Sinf., Guschlbauer.

It was Gendron who pioneered the stereo recording of the original version of the famous *B flat Concerto* and now his coupling with a fine account of the Haydn *D major Concerto* is restored to the catalogue. Boccherini's concerto in this form is a totally different work from the Grützmacher, which such artists as Fournier (see above) and Jacqueline du Pré have recorded. (Grützmacher totally redrafted the outer movements, using material from other Boccherini pieces; his middle movement was drawn from yet another source and is even less related to the original.) Gendron's performance is in the front rank. The playing is warmly elegant and his own cadenzas display some impressive bravura. With Casals providing an authoritative accompaniment this is highly recommendable. The recording is good too, and one can forgive the forward balance of the soloist in a work of this nature. The cassette too is well managed, fresh and clear.

Lodéon plays splendidly in both this and the *D major Concerto* on the reverse (which is not to be confused with the *D major Concerto* above). Thoroughly musical playing throughout from the Bournemouth Sinfonietta and well-balanced recorded sound; this is a most desirable issue. There is a good cassette. The *D major Concerto* is especially full and vivid; side one is a little drier in quality.

Minuet (from *String quintet in E, Op. 13/5*).
*** Ph. Dig. **410 001-2**; 6514/*7337* 370 [id.]. I Musici (with concert of baroque music ***).

Boccherini's most famous piece is played here very persuasively and made to sound completely unhackneyed by the freshness of its treatment. The sound is first-class in all media and the rest of the programme is almost all equally successful.

CHAMBER MUSIC

Cello quintet, Op. 37/7 (Pleyel).
*** Argo ZRG 569 [id.]. ASMF – MENDELSSOHN: *Octet.****

This is an inspired piece. It would be worth getting for its own sake, and the performance of the Mendelssohn *Octet* is a particularly fine one.

Guitar quintets Nos. 1–7, G.446/51; 9, G.453.
*** Ph. 6768 268 (3). Romero, Iona Brown, Latchem, Shingles, Vigay.

Boccherini wrote or arranged twelve *Guitar quintets*, but only the present eight have survived, plus another version of G.448. Although some of the music is bland it is nearly all agreeably tuneful in an unostentatious way, and there are some highly imaginative touches, with attractive hints of melancholy and underlying passion. These performances by Pepe Romero (often willing to take a relatively minor role) and members of the ASMF Chamber Group are wholly admirable, and Philips are especially good at balancing textures of this kind in the most natural way, the guitar able to be assertive when required without overbalancing the ensemble. This is a delightfully undemanding set to dip into in the late evening.

Guitar quintets Nos. 1 in D min.; 2 in E, G.445/6; 7 in E min., G.451.
*** Ph. 9500/*7300* 985 [id.] (from above set).

All three quintets here were reworked by the composer from piano quintets. The guitar's role is for the most part a subsidiary one, although it often adds spice to the texture (as is apparent near the very beginning of No. 7, which opens the recital). There are touches of blandness, but there are attractive movements in all three works. G.446 has a *Polacca* for its finale, but the most consistently inventive piece is the *E minor Quintet*, G.451. The performances are unfailingly warm and sensitive, and the recording is first-class, with an immaculate cassette.

Guitar quintets Nos. 3 in B flat, G.447; 9 in C (La Ritirata di Madrid), G.453.
*** Ph. 9500 789/*7300 861* [id.] (from above set).

Both works here are arrangements. No. 3 comes from the *Piano quintet*, Op. 57/2; the first three movements of No. 9 originate in the *Piano quintet*, Op. 56/3, and the finale which gives it its subtitle, *La Ritirata di Madrid*, is familiar from a string quintet, Op. 30/6. This picturesque evocation of Spanish life is created with a set of twelve short variations set in a long, slow crescendo, followed by a similarly graduated decrescendo, a kind of Spanish patrol with the 'night watch' disappearing into the distance at the close. Both works are melodically engaging in Boccherini's elegant rococo style, and they are beautifully played and recorded, the guitar balanced within the string group, yet able to dominate when required. The cassette needs a bass cut, then matches the disc fairly closely, although the sound is slightly less transparent.

Guitar quintets Nos. 4 in D (Fandango); 5 in D; 6 in G, G.448/50.
*** Ph. 9500 621/*7300 737* [id.] (from above set).

Guitar quintets Nos. 5–6, G.449/50.
*** CBS Dig. 36671/*41-*. Williams, L. Qt – GUASTAVINO: *Las Presencias.****

Two of the *Quintets* recorded here are new to the gramophone: the *D major*, and *G major*, Nos. 449–50 in the Gérard catalogue. Both are arrangements of other works made for the benefit of the Marquis of Benavent, and only in the *D major* does the guitar emerge into the foreground. Boccherini's music often reveals unsuspected depths and has a melancholy and pathos that colour its polite discourse in subtle but memorable ways. The three quintets on the Philips issue show him at his most bland, and though they make pleasant listening, they possess no darker undercurrents. The performances are thoroughly effective and are well recorded. The cassette, though smooth and well balanced, has some loss of range at the top (the transfer level is unadventurous, in spite of the modest instrumentation).

On CBS the two quintets G.449/50 are impeccably played, though the recording favours a rather forward balance with little acoustic ambience. The sound is most musically judged and reproduces a fully acceptable result, though the effect is more natural if reproduced at a lower level setting than normal, since the digital recording is cut at a high level. The high-level chrome tape transfer has plenty of range; although there is a slight over-emphasis at the bass end, the treble is fresh and bright. Good performances, though the rival Romero set offers the advantage of a third Boccherini quintet rather than the somewhat uninteresting Guastavino fill-up.

Guitar quintets Nos. 4; 7; 9 (La Ritirata di Madrid).
(M) *** DG Acc. 2542/*3342* 170. Yepes, Melos Qt (with Tena, castanets in No. 9).

The playing on this DG compilation is expert and the recording excellent, with a lively yet full-bodied cassette. This has the advantage of economy and although the Philips versions have slightly more modern recording the gain is marginal. All these records give pleasure.

6 Oboe quintets, Op. 45.
(M) *** Argo ZK 93. Francis, Allegri Qt.

An attractive medium-price record. The quintets, written in 1797, were published as Op. 45 though Boccherini's own catalogue lists them as 55. They have a sunny grace that is altogether beguiling, and a gentle, wistful lyricism that is unfailing in its appeal. Excellent playing and recording.

String quartets: in D; in E flat, Op. 6/1 and 3; in E flat, Op. 58/2.
(M) *** Ph. 6503/*7303* 060 [9500 305]. Italian Qt.

The Italian Quartet recorded the *D major Quartet*, Op. 6/1, in the days of 78s, when they were still known as the 'New Italian Quartet', and were rightly hailed for their freshness and refinement of tone as well as their wide dynamic range. They include this and another from the same set – a remarkably beautiful piece it is, too – plus a much later quartet from the 1790s. Boccherini is all too readily dismissed as *la femme de Haydn*, but underneath the surface charm and elegance that one associates with him, there are deeper currents and an altogether special pathos to disturb the attentive listener. The Italian Quartet give excellently vital and sensitive performances and they are eminently well recorded, even if the sound image could with advantage be more recessed.

Boellmann, Leon (1862–97)

Symphonic variations (for cello and orch.), *Op. 23.*
*** HMV ASD 3728. Paul Tortelier, RPO, Yan-Pascal Tortelier – BRUCH: *Kol Nidrei****; SCHUMANN: *Concerto.***(*)

Boellmann's main interest as a composer lay in organ music, but this set of variations, when played so persuasively by his compatriot Tortelier, makes a most attractive unexpected item in a romantic concerto anthology. The cellist's son draws comparably sympathetic playing from the RPO, well recorded.

Boieldieu, François (1775–1834)

Harp concerto in 3 tempi, in C.
*** Argo ZRG/*KZRC* 930 [id.]. Robles, ASMF, Iona Brown – DITTERSDORF and HANDEL: *Concertos.****

Boieldieu's *Harp concerto* has been recorded before, but never more attractively. Iona Brown and the Academy set the scene with an alert, vigorous introduction and Miss Robles provides contrasting delicacy. Much play is made of the possibilities of light and shade, the harp providing gentle echo effects in repeated phrases; some might feel this is overdone but it is certainly engaging. The slow movement is delightful and the lilt of the finale irresistible. The recording is first-class, with a most convincing balance, and the cassette is of demonstration quality, one of Argo's finest.

Boito, Arrigo (1842–1918)

Sinfonia in A min.
*** Erato STU 71040. Monte Carlo Op. O, Scimone – PUCCINI: *Capriccio sinfonico* etc.***

An interesting if unimportant novelty included with a fascinating collection of Puccini's orchestral music. Performance and recording are excellent.

Mefistofele (opera): *Prologue*.
** DG 2707 100 (2) [id.]. Ghiaurov, V. State Op. Ch., VPO, Bernstein – LISZT: *Faust symphony*.***

Although there are two recordings of the complete opera, the only other complete version of the *Prologue* to *Mefistofele* is Toscanini's classic account from 1954 (now long deleted). This recording was made in Vienna and finds Ghiaurov in excellent form. The sound is wide in range but could generally be described as acceptable rather than distinguished.

OPERA

Mefistofele (complete).
**(*) Decca Dig. D 270 D 3/*K 270 K 32* (3/2) [Lon. LDR/5- 73010]. Ghiaurov, Pavarotti, Freni, Caballé, L. Op. Ch., Trinity Boys' Ch., Nat. PO, Fabritiis.
(M) **(*) Decca Ace GOS 591/3. Siepi, Del Monaco, Tebaldi, St Cecilia Ac., Rome Ch. and O, Serafin.

Boito's *Mefistofele* is a strange episodic work to come from the hand of the master-librettist of Verdi's *Otello* and *Falstaff*, but it has many fine moments. The modern digital recording given to the Fabritiis set brings obvious benefits in the extra weight of brass and percussion – most importantly in the heavenly prologue. With the principal soloists all at their best – Pavarotti most seductive in *Dai campi, dai prati*, Freni finely imaginative on detail, Caballé consistently sweet and mellifluous as Elena, Ghiaurov strongly characterful if showing some signs of strain – this is a highly recommendable set, though Fabritiis in his last recording lacks a little in energy, and the chorus is placed rather distantly. The chrome tapes are in the demonstration class – notably in the *Prologue*, with its excellent sense of perspective, and in the dramatically vivid Walpurgis-night scene (which opens side three in the tape layout, which is preferable to the discs).

Serafin, the most persuasive of Italian opera conductors of his day, draws glorious sounds from his performers, even Mario del Monaco, who is here almost sensitive. Tebaldi is a rich-toned Margherita – almost too rich-toned for so frail a heroine – and Siepi makes an excellent Mefistofele. With excellent sound for its day, this makes a good mid-priced alternative.

Mefistofele: highlights.
(M) **(*) HMV Green. ESD/*TC-ESD* 102717-1/*4*. Treigle, Domingo, Caballé, Wandsworth School Ch., Amb. Op. Ch., LSO, Rudel.

HMV's mid-1970s recording has many strong points, notably the Faust of Placido Domingo. This selection features the formidable Mefistofele of Norman Treigle, who made the part his own at the New York City Opera. Where he leans towards over-expressiveness Caballé lacks something in feeling for detail in *L'altra notte*, but the Faust/Margherita duet is most beautifully done. Good recording on disc, though the XDR ferric tape does not cope with the wide dynamic range too well, bringing some peaking at fortissimo level and indistinct detail at the other end of the spectrum.

Bolling, Claude (born 1930)

California suite: Suite for flute and jazz piano.
*** RCA Dig. RL/*RK* 25348 [XRL/*XRC*1 4148]. Duran, Holloway, Walley, Ganley, Kain.

Suite for flute and jazz piano.
*** CBS 73900/*40*- [Col. M/*MT* 35864]. Rampal, composer, Sabiani, Hédiguer.

Claude Bolling's *California suite* is a collection of incidental music from Neil Simon's film of the same name. Bolling's own recording (now deleted) included slightly more music and ran for about twelve minutes longer than the RCA selection. But in this kind of composition, which implies an improvisatory element from the performing musicians, the differences between the two versions are rather more than that of quantity. Obviously the composer's performance has extra authority and Hubert Laws, his flautist, makes a splendid partner.

However, for most collectors the singular advantage of the RCA record is its inclusion of the engaging *Suite for flute and jazz piano*, offering a full hour of music in excellent digital sound (with a fine cassette to match the disc closely). Virtually all the important music from the film score is included (*Hanna, Beverly Hills* and *Love theme* are all nostalgically memorable) and both here and in the *Suite* Elena Duran proves an immensely gifted soloist. Her playing is sprightly, vivacious and beguilingly expressive in feeling. Laurie Holloway, her pianist, also makes an excellent contribution, not always matching the composer, perhaps, but always sympathetic and stylish. He is especially good in his gentle arpeggios accompanying the reprise of the *Love theme*.

Bolling's own version of the *Suite for flute and jazz piano* is greatly helped by the splendid flute playing of Jean-Pierre Rampal, whose phrasing of the two lyrical movements, *Sentimentale* and *Irlandaise*, is very persuasive. The rhythmic background (Marcel Sabiani, drums, and Max Hédiguer, string bass) acts as a modern equivalent of the baroque continuo, and the two movements which look back towards this period, *Baroque and blue* and *Fugace*, are attractively cultivated. The composer's own contribution is authoritative and the CBS sound excellent; but the more economical RCA version is very good too.

Concerto for classic guitar and jazz piano.
**(*) EMI Dig. EMD/*TC-EMD* 5535 [Ang. DS/*4ZS* 37327]. Romero, Shearing, Manne, Brown.

Bolling's concertante piece is in effect a suite in seven movements with titles like *Hispanic dance*, *Mexicaine*, *Serenade* and so on. Its invention is quite lively, with one catchy theme, although the work tends as a whole to outstay its welcome. It certainly has a jazzy flavour and is likely to appeal to those whose tastes find stimulation in that area and who enjoy the combination of guitar, piano (George Shearing in very good form), drums and string bass. The performance is undoubtedly spontaneous and the recording vivid, with an excellent cassette.

Bonporti, Francesco (1672–1749)

Violin concertos, Op. 11/4, 6, 8–9.
(M) *** Ph. 9502 004 [id.]. Michelucci, I Musici.

Bonporti's Op. 11 concertos come from 1720 or thereabouts and show the influence of Corelli; they have dignity, vitality and imagination. These performances by Roberto Michelucci and I Musici date from 1970 and sound as immaculate now as they did then.

Borodin, Alexander (1833–87)

'The world of Borodin': (i) *In the Steppes of Central Asia;* (ii) *Symphony No. 2 in B min.;* (iii) *String quartet No. 2: Nocturne;* (i; iv) *Prince Igor: Polovtsian dances.*
(M) *** Decca SPA 281. (i) SRO, Ansermet, (iv) with chorus; (ii) LSO, Martinon; (iii) Borodin Qt.

An extraordinarily successful disc that will provide for many collectors an inexpensive summation of the art of Borodin. There can be few collections of this kind that sum up a composer's achievement so succinctly or that make such a rewarding and enjoyable concert. Martinon's performance of the *Symphony* is notable for its fast tempo for the famous opening theme, but the strong rhythmic thrust suits the music admirably, and the slow movement, with a beautifully played horn solo, is most satisfying. The recording has remarkable presence and sparkle, and only in the massed violin tone (which is good) is there a suggestion that the recording dates from the early 1960s. Side two opens with *In the Steppes of Central Asia*, a vivid rather than an atmospheric reading; then follows the *Nocturne*, so effectively that one might have thought it the composer's own plan. The disc ends generously with the complete set of *Polovtsian dances*, reliably done, if not breathtakingly exciting, and very well recorded. A remarkable bargain indeed.

Symphonies Nos. 1 in E flat; 2 in B min.; 3 in A min. (Unfinished); Prince Igor: Overture; (i) *Polovtsian dances.*
** CBS 79214 (2) [Col. M2 34587]. Toronto SO, Andrew Davis, (i) with Mendelssohn Ch.

Symphony No. 2.
(B) **(*) Con. CC/*CCT* 7533. SRO, Varviso – TCHAIKOVSKY: *Francesca da Rimini.***

Though the *Second* is the best-known of Borodin's symphonies, both its companions deserve popularity. The *First* is colourful and ebullient, with a particularly appealing scherzo, while the pastoral two-movement torso completed from sketches by Glazounov is a delight. Andrew Davis is not lacking in imagination, but the quality of the playing in Toronto and the CBS sound fall short of the ideal, so this set must be regarded as a stopgap until something more fully recommendable arrives.

Varviso's Contour reissue of the *Second* has the advantage of a vintage Decca recording from the late 1960s which is first-class: vivid, rich and well detailed. The performance has plenty of life and colour (it is less individual in control of tempi than Martinon's – see above) and the Suisse Romande Orchestra is in good form, providing a full romantic sweep when the big tune comes back at the end of the slow movement. The scherzo too has plenty of sparkle, and though the coupling is less spontaneous as a performance this is competitive at bargain price. The cassette was originally less recommendable, with a more limited range, but may have been remastered by now.

String quartets Nos. 1 in A; 2 in D.
❀ *** HMV ASD/*TC-ASD* 4100. Borodin Qt.
*** Decca SXL 6983 [Lon. CS 7239]. Fitzwilliam Qt.

String quartet No. 2.
(M) *** Ph. 6503/*7303* 109. Italian Qt – DVOŘÁK: *Quartet No. 12.****
(M) *** Decca Eclipse ECS 795 [Lon. STS 15046]. Borodin Qt – SHOSTAKOVICH: *Quartet No. 8.****

Although the Fitzwilliam Quartet's account of the two Borodin quartets is eminently satisfying on all counts, it must yield to the identical coupling from the eponymous Borodin Quartet. Their performance strikes one as completely effortless and idiomatic; indeed, so total is their sense of identification with these scores that one is scarcely conscious of the intervention of the interpreter. The sound quality achieved by the Melodiya engineers has no less clarity than the Decca and has a natural ambience and warmth that should ensure this record an unchallenged position for many years to come. The Borodin's account of the *Second Quartet* will give unalloyed delight. The XDR ferric tape is warm, refined and well balanced, but has not quite the presence and range of the disc.

Those wanting just the *Second Quartet* (famous because themes were taken from it for *Kismet*) will find that the playing of the Italians is in the front rank, while the excellent recording makes for a safe recommendation, as the Dvořák coupling (the *American quartet*) is equally fine. The earlier Borodin performance on Decca is no less masterly and some might prefer the forward, rich-textured recording Decca provided. It has the advantage of economy too, and the imaginative coupling is certainly desirable. The Philips recording, however, offers a first-class tape equivalent.

Prince Igor: Overture; Polovtsian dances.
*** Telarc Dig. **CD 80039**; DG 10039 [id.]. Atlanta Ch. and SO, Shaw – STRAVINSKY: *Firebird suite.***(*)
(M) ** Mercury SRI 75016. LSO Ch., LSO, Dorati – RIMSKY-KORSAKOV: *Le Coq d'Or.****

Prince Igor: Polovtsian dances.
*** Decca Dig. 410 121-1/*4*. Best, L. Op. Ch., Philh. O, Ashkenazy – MUSSORGSKY: *Pictures.***
(M) *** HMV SXLP/*TC-SXLP* 30445. Philh. O, Karajan – MUSSORGSKY: *Pictures* etc.***

Even though a British chorus is featured, the singing has striking fervour under Ashkenazy's direction, with solo interjections from Matthew Best (normally not included) to bring an added edge of excitement. It is a pity that the percussion-led opening dance is omitted; otherwise this is first-rate and the recording is splendid on disc and chrome tape alike.

It would be churlish not to give the remarkable Telarc digital recording of the *Polovtsian dances* a full recommendation. The choral singing is less clearly focused in the lyrical sections of the score than at climaxes, but the singers undoubtedly rise to the occasion. The entry of the bass drum is riveting and the closing section very exciting. The vivid sound balance is equally impressive in the overture, and if the Atlanta orchestra does not possess the body of string timbre to make the very most of the sweeping second subject, the playing has vitality and spontaneity in its favour. Robert Shaw's overall direction is thoroughly musical.

Karajan's version, with the Philharmonia on top form, is played with such virtuosity and élan that the ear hardly misses the chorus. The recording is from the early 1960s and sounds extremely vivid on both disc and tape.

Dorati's Mercury disc is a little earlier in provenance and the recording, although not restricted at the top, has a too ample bass resonance, so that in the *Polovtsian dances* the bass drum tends to swamp the texture. But the climax is exhilarating and this remains another vintage reissue, for the Rimsky-Korsakov coupling is strikingly lustrous.

Bottesini, Giovanni (1821–89)

Music for double bass: *Capriccio bravura; Fantasia on Beatrice di Tenda; Grande allegro di concerto; Introduzione e gavotta; Romanza drammatica.*
**(*) ASV ALH/*ZCALH* 939. Martin, Halstead.

The mechanical limitations of the double-bass mean that harmonics performed with scientific accuracy are out of tune. Thomas Martin is a superb virtuoso of the instrument, who relishes these display pieces, but some of the high melodies are oddly painful. A curiosity record with first-rate sound and excellent accompaniment from Anthony Halstead, better known as a fine horn-player. There is a good ferric tape, slightly less extended in upper range than the disc.

Boughton, Rutland (1878–1960)

The Immortal hour (opera): complete.
*** Hyp. Dig. A 66101/2. Kennedy, Dawson, Wilson-Johnson, Davies, Geoffrey Mitchell Ch., ECO, Melville.

This gently lyrical evocation of Celtic twilight hit London by storm in the 1920s and early 1930s, with four extended runs. There is far more to it than the still-celebrated *Faery song*, which hauntingly is heard first at the end of Act I, sung by a chorus in the distance. Analysed closely, much of it may seem like Vaughan Williams and water, but this fine performance conducted by a lifelong Boughton devotee brings out the hypnotic quality which had 1920s music-lovers attending performances many times over. The simple tunefulness goes with a fine feeling for atmosphere. The excellent cast of young singers includes the Ferrier prizewinner, Anne Dawson, as the heroine Princess Etain and Maldwyn Davies headily beautiful in the main tenor rendering of the *Faery song*. Warm, reverberant recording.

Boulanger, Lili (1893–1918)

(i; ii) *Cortège;* (i) *D'un jardin clair;* (i; ii; iii) *D'un matin de printemps; D'un soir triste;* (i) *D'un vieux jardin;* (i; iii) *Harmonies du soir;* (i; ii) *Nocturne.*
*** Uni. Dig. DKP 9021. (i) Parkin; (ii) Griffiths; (iii) Harvey – DELIUS: *Cello sonata* etc.***

Lili Boulanger, who died in 1918 at the age of 24, might well have become the greatest woman composer of her time. The first two of these brief chamber works suggest something of the power which had already developed in her music, for though the scale may be small, the expression is intense. The longest piece, *D'un soir triste*, for piano trio is especially fine. Eric Parkin, who contributes also two solo pieces, is a naturally persuasive advocate, beautifully matched by Barry Griffiths and Keith Harvey. An authoritative note by Christopher Palmer neatly links Boulanger and Delius.

Boyce, William (1710–79)

Concerti grossi: in B flat; in B min.; in E min.; Overture in F.
*** Chan. ABR/*ABT* 1005. Cantilena, Shepherd.

Though these *Concerti grossi* have not quite the consistent originality which makes the Boyce symphonies so refreshing, the energy of the writing – splendidly conveyed in these performances – is recognizably the same, with fugal passages that turn in unexpected directions. The overture which complements these three *Concerti grossi* (all that Boyce completed) was written for the New Year's Ode in 1762, a French overture with fugue. Good recording; the high-level cassette transfer is full and natural yet has not quite the range at the top of the disc, although side two is noticeably livelier than side one.

12 Overtures.
**(*) Chan. DBR/*DBT* 2002 (2). Cantilena, Shepherd.

The eight Boyce symphonies have been recorded many times, but this collection, put together ten years later in 1770 though including at least one work from as early as 1745, has much of comparable vigour. Unfortunately the first overture is not one of the best, but each has its attractions, and those which bring out the brass are most exciting. In 1770 Boyce, already deaf, was regarded as old-fashioned and was never given a proper hearing with this music. Cantilena's performances are not always as crisp and vigorous as they might be, but they certainly convey enough of the freshness of Boyce's inspiration, and the recording, though oddly balanced, is convincingly atmospheric. On cassette the sound is much brighter (to the point of fierceness) on the first tape than on the second, which is better balanced without loss of vividness.

Symphonies Nos. 1–8.
*** CRD CRD 1056/*CRDC 4056*. Bournemouth Sinf., Ronald Thomas.
*** Argo ZRG/*KZRC* 874 [id.]. ASMF, Marriner.

Even against such strong competition as the catalogue provides in these superb symphonies, Thomas and the Bournemouth Sinfonietta are outstanding, with buoyant playing set against a recording which captures the full bloom of the orchestra. The tempi are often rather brisker than those adopted by Marriner. This is an excellent set, highly recommendable, and the cassette is first-rate too, the sound vivid and rich, with little loss of inner clarity.

Marriner also treats these superb examples

of English baroque to exhilarating performances, with the rhythmic subtleties in both fast music and slow guaranteed to enchant. The recording, ample and full in the acoustic of St John's, Smith Square, is of demonstration quality on disc, though the cassette is drier and needs a reduction of treble and an increase of bass to sound its best.

Symphonies Nos. 4 in F; 5 in D; 8 in D min.
(M) *** DG Arc. Priv. 2547/*3347* 054. Lucerne Fest. O, Baumgartner – ARNE: *Concertos.***

Baumgartner offers three of the most attractive *Symphonies* coupled to a pair of Arne concertos. Arne and Boyce were contemporaries; on the evidence here, Boyce was the more interesting composer, although the comparison is well worth making. Performances are sound and have plenty of life, and the mid-1960s recording is fresh and vivid on disc and cassette.

Anthems: *I have surely built thee an house; O be joyful; O give thanks; Save me, O God; Turn thee unto me.*
** Abbey ABY 811. Soloists, Worcester Cath. Ch. and Academy, Hunt.

Though not as polished or as pure-toned as the great collegiate choirs, that of Worcester Cathedral has built up a strong reputation in English music such as these magnificent anthems of Boyce. Some of the solo contributions are slightly insecure, but with a naturally balanced recording, fresh and clear in detail, this can be recommended.

(i) *Organ voluntaries Nos. 1, 2, 4 and 10;* (ii) Anthems: *By the waters of Babylon; I have surely built thee an house; O where shall wisdom be found; Turn unto me, O Lord.*
(M) *** Saga 5440. (i) Wills; (ii) Ely Cathedral Ch., Wills; Gifford (organ).

It may seem strange to hear formal eighteenth-century settings of biblical texts set dramatically much later by Sir William Walton, but the music of Boyce is most compelling. The anthems in particular make this a highly valuable issue, not least because it comes at budget price and is generally well recorded. The organ voluntaries are a welcome makeweight.

Brahms, Johannes (1833–97)

Academic festival overture, Op. 80; Tragic overture, Op. 81; Variations on a theme of Haydn, Op. 56a; (i) *Alto rhapsody, Op. 53.*
(B) ** Precision GSGC/*ZCGC* 2030. LPO, Boult; (i) with Monica Sinclair, Croydon Philharmonic Ch.

Dating from as early as 1959, the generous group of works offered on the Precision Collector reissue shows Boult ever a reliable Brahmsian, securing lively imaginative playing from the LPO and full textures. Monica Sinclair makes a direct and vibrant contribution to the *Alto rhapsody* and the Croydon choral group is well-balanced. A bargain. The tape equivalent is well-managed, matching the disc fairly closely.

(i) *Piano concertos Nos. 1–2;* (ii) *Violin concerto;* (iii) *Double concerto for violin and cello.*
** DG 2740 276/*3378 121* (4) [id.]. (i) Pollini, VPO, Boehm or Abbado; (ii) Mutter, Berlin PO, Karajan; (iii) Kremer, Maisky, VPO, Bernstein.

This is the second volume of DG's mammoth collected edition of all Brahms's major works, and it is one of the least successful. Although Pollini and the Vienna Philharmonic under Karl Boehm are given finely detailed recording in the *First Piano concerto*, one need look no further than the Gilels set on the same label for greater wisdom and humanity. Not that Pollini is wanting in keyboard command, but he is a little short on tenderness and poetry. He seems all too often to have switched on the automatic pilot here, and although the *B flat Concerto* under Abbado is much fresher and offers some masterly pianism, there are warmer and more spontaneous accounts to be had. Anne-Sophie Mutter's version of the *Violin concerto* with Karajan and the Berlin Philharmonic is both individual and powerful and can hold its own with many distinguished rivals; but the newcomer, the *Double concerto* with Gidon Kremer and Mischa Maisky, is hard to take. Maisky is obviously a superb player who possesses wonderful tonal finesse and a wide dynamic range. Indeed, some may find these dynamic extremes too self-consciously expressive, as if he is unable to allow the melodic line to speak for itself. Mind you, he is nowhere near so narcissistic and self-aware as Kremer, who constantly harnesses his sweetness of tone and technical mastery in such a way as to draw attention to himself rather than to Brahms. The first movement is an allegro and although Bernstein is not alone in taking a measured approach to this movement (twice as slow as the classic Thibaud and Casals set from 1929), there is a disturbing want of momentum. The slow movement is also a bit self-indulgent in this respect, though detail is lovingly shaped. The finale is probably the best thing here and there is a real sense of exhilaration. However, one can do better by picking and choosing elsewhere, and none of these performances would be a first choice.

There is an identical chrome tape box, which offers somewhat variable technical quality. The *Violin concerto* is splendidly transferred at a high level and loses little as against the LP; the *Double concerto* is almost equally impressive, but the *First Piano concerto* sounds bass heavy (in spite of a digital source) and while the *Second* is much better-balanced and quite satisfactory, it is still less lively in sound than the rest. No attempt has been made to issue each work unbroken on a single side.

(i) *Piano concertos Nos. 1–2; Ballades, Op. 10; Scherzo, Op. 4; Sonatas Nos. 2 and 3; Variations and fugue on a theme by Handel, Op. 24; Variations on a theme by Paganini, Op. 35.*
(M) **(*) Ph. 6768 356 (5) [id.]. Arrau, (i) Concg. O, Haitink.

The merits of these performances are detailed under their separate listings. This box merely collects all of Arrau's performances of Brahms over the past decade or more in a more economical format and with some saving of cost. Impeccable pressings.

Piano concertos Nos. 1–2.
(M) *** DG 413 229-1/*4* (2). Gilels, Berlin PO, Jochum.
(B) **(*) CfP CFPD/*TC-CFPD* 414430-3/*5* (2). Tirimo, LPO, Sanderling or Levi.
(M) **(*) ASV ALHB 202 (2). Lill, Hallé O, Loughran.
** DG 2707 127/*3370 039* (2) [id.]. Pollini, VPO, Boehm or Abbado.
(M) ** Ph. 6770/*7650* 006. Brendel, Concg. O, Schmidt-Isserstedt.

Those wanting the two Brahms *Piano concertos* linked together will find the Gilels performances very satisfying, although they are now, of course, also available separately at mid-price (see below). There are chrome tapes.

Tirimo chooses slow basic tempi in both concertos. In No. 1 the stopwatch indicates how slow the pacing is in all three movements, and the opening tutti initially suggests heaviness, but Sanderling and his soloist amply justify their straight, measured manner in the thoughtful concentration of the whole reading. One has no feeling of the performance dragging, for crisp, lifted rhythms prevent that in the outer movements and the slow movement has a rapt quality to compare with that of Barenboim (HMV) or Arrau (Philips) – see below – holding one's attention as a live performance would. In No. 2, with the young Israeli Yoel Levi conducting, the reading is commanding and spacious, with the first movement not always quite tidy in its occasional impulsiveness. In the remaining two movements the clarity of articulation gives sharpness of focus to conceal the measured tempi, and both are made exuberant and joyful. With modern (1979) stereo and a truthful balance (especially so in No. 2), this makes an excellent bargain. The cassettes are well balanced, but the upper strings sound fresher on disc.

As in Lill's account of the *First Concerto* (see separate listing), the *Second* is a well thought-out and finely paced account without the slightest shred of self-indulgence. (There are some odd things – an ugly riposte to the strings at bar 89 in the first movement, and the rather spacious tempo he adopts has the effect of making him sound a little ponderous from bar 146 onwards – but, in general, the strengths of the set far outweigh the weaknesses.) The recorded sound is eminently well-balanced, though the timpani are a shade obtrusive. A good set.

Pollini's accounts of the two *Piano concertos* are unevenly matched; his version of the *First* under Boehm does not command the listener's response as his fine version of the *Second* with Abbado does (see below).

Brendel is a powerful, positive pianist and these were the last recordings made by Schmidt-Isserstedt, who provides very positive direction, especially in the *First Concerto* – no mere accompaniment but a forceful symphonic partnership with the soloist. This is the more successful of the two performances, for though the central slow movement could be more hushed and intense, the outer movements, with fair freedom of tempo, are impressively dramatic. The balance, however, is not ideal, with the piano unusually close for Philips. The *Second Concerto* is more realistic in this respect, but the performance falls a little below expectations. Brendel seems too judicious and adopts a deliberately restrained approach, so keen is he to eschew the grand manner. The results, though always commanding respect, are not wholly convincing. On cassette the sound is full and natural (the transfers are made at quite a high level), but orchestral detail is less telling than on disc. The second tape, however, offers a bonus of two *Hungarian dances* (which are not mentioned in the accompanying notes).

Piano concerto No. 1 in D min., Op. 15.

(M) *** DG Acc. 2542/*3342* 126 [2530 258]. Gilels, Berlin PO, Jochum.

(M) *** Decca Jub. JB/*KJBC* 102. Curzon, LSO, Szell.

(M) *** HMV SXLP/*TC-SXLP* 30283. Barenboim, New Philh. O, Barbirolli.

*** Decca Dig. **410 009-2**; SXDL/*KSXDC* 7552 [LDR/*5*- 71052]. Ashkenazy, Concg. O, Haitink.

**(*) ASV ALH/*ZCALH* 916. Lill, Hallé O, Loughran.

(M) **(*) Ph. Seq. 6527/*7311* 181 [id.]. Arrau, Concg. O, Haitink.

*(**) Ph. 9500/*7300* 871. Bishop-Kovacevich, LSO, Sir Colin Davis.

(M) *(*) Decca Jub. JB/*KJBC* 137 [Lon. CS/*5*- 7018]. Rubinstein, Israel PO, Mehta.

*(*) DG 2531/*3301* 294 [id.]. Pollini, VPO, Boehm.

The new Ashkenazy digital recording of the Brahms *First Concerto* was obviously intended by Decca to provide a version for the 1980s to compare with Curzon's famous record made two decades earlier. But for all its merits it fails to displace current recommendations and the sound on the compact disc, although for the most part admirably faithful, only serves to emphasize the forward balance and the not quite convincing quality of the piano timbre as recorded.

Choice remains with Gilels, Curzon and Barenboim, whose recording with Barbirolli has inspirational qualities absent from his remake with Mehta for CBS – now deleted.

From Gilels comes a combination of magisterial strength and a warmth, humanity and depth that are altogether inspiring. Jochum is a superb accompanist, and the only reservation is the recording, which though warm does not focus the piano and orchestra in truthful proportion. For all that, however, this remains an outstanding performance artistically. On cassette the focus at the very opening is less than sharp, but the quality immediately settles down to give vivid orchestral sound and a firm, rich piano image.

Curzon has a leonine power that fully matches Brahms's keyboard style and penetrates both the reflective inner world of the slow movement and the abundantly vital and massive opening movement. This is among the very best versions available, though the recording gives evidence of close-microphone techniques, used within a reverberant acoustic. The strings have a tendency to fierceness, especially in the powerful opening tutti of the first movement, yet there is no doubt of the vivid projection this gives to the music-making, and the piano balance is satisfying. The cassette transfer is outstandingly vivid, wide in range, with the opening cleanly caught; this is every bit the equal of the disc.

Barenboim and Barbirolli are very well recorded on disc, and their playing is heroic and marvellously spacious. Tempi are broad and measured, but the performance is sustained by its intensity of concentration. The recording has not transferred comfortably to tape; the piano timbre is convincing, but the orchestra lacks focus and warmth.

Ashkenazy gives a commanding and magisterial account of the solo part that is full of poetic imagination. All the different facets of the score, its combative energy, its strength and tenderness, are fully delineated. In the slow movement the atmosphere is not quite as rapt or hushed as in the Barenboim and Arrau versions but, taken as a whole, the performance is very impressive indeed and there is superlative playing from the Concertgebouw Orchestra. The recording is enormously vivid though the balance may worry some collectors. The forward placing of the soloist gives the lower and middle registers of the piano a disproportionate amount of aural space and one or two octaves appear not to be absolutely true. The cassette is extremely vivid, though the very forward balance brings a slightly aggressive quality to the strings and the piano timbre hardens on fortissimos.

Lill's playing is unfailingly impressive and scrupulous in its observance of every dynamic marking and expressive nuance. He is given warm and spirited support from Loughran and the Hallé, even though in one or two places woodwind intonation is not wholly above reproach. Although he has the measure of its fire and drama, John Lill's conception is fundamentally classical. Masterly and commanding playing, though there is a cool, marmoreal quality that inhibits unqualified admiration. The recording is very fine without being in the demonstration category. The cassette is transferred at a very high level and while the sound is vivid and wide-ranging, the ear is given the feeling that saturation point is near, using iron-oxide stock; the bass too is excessively resonant and needs cutting.

Arrau's reading has vision and power, and though there are some characteristic agogic distortions that will not convince all listeners, he is majestic and eloquent. There is never an ugly sonority even in moments of the greatest vehemence. By the side of Curzon he seems idiosyncratic, particularly in the slow movement, but given the excellence of the recorded sound and the warmth of Haitink's support, this is well worth considering in the medium-price range. The cassette has been remastered and is now one of Philips's best, vivid, full and clear, the transfer level quite high.

If recording quality is a secondary consideration, Stephen Bishop-Kovacevich's account of the concerto should figure high in the lists. He plays with great tenderness and lyrical feeling, and in the slow movement he achieves striking inwardness of response and poetry. There is no attention-seeking expressive point-making and no attempt either to exaggerate or to understate the combative, leonine side of the solo part. He is sympathetically supported by the LSO under Sir Colin Davis, though woodwind intonation is not always perfect. Unfortunately, the sound is opaque and bottom-heavy, and is not in the same league as the very best versions. The cassette is not especially well focused.

With more than a sprinkling of wrong notes, Rubinstein's Israel recording may not provide a general recommendation, but the character and drive of the man in his late eighties emerge vividly. To hear such a performance once in the concert hall one would readily pay far more. Unfortunately the recording balances the piano far too forwardly, so that the orchestral sound, clean enough on its own, becomes submerged even behind Rubinstein's most casual passagework. The high-level cassette transfer is first-class, characteristic of Decca's highest reissue standard, wide-ranging and full-bodied. But this issue does not displace Rubinstein's 1954 Chicago version (still available in the USA – ARL 1/*ARK 1* 2044), a poetic and essentially lyrical reading of some distinction, helped by Reiner's volatile, imaginative accompaniment. The sound is good, too.

With Pollini there is always much to admire, not least the masterly pianism. But he brings little spontaneity or tenderness to this concerto and this performance in no way matches his admired account of the *Second*. This is uncommitted and wanting in passion. Good recording.

Piano concerto No. 2 in B flat, Op. 83.
(M) *** DG Acc. 2542/*3342* 151 [2530 259]. Gilels, Berlin PO, Jochum.
*** Ph. 9500 682/*7300 777* [id.]. Bishop-Kovacevich, LSO, Sir Colin Davis.
*** DG 2530/*3300* 790 [id.]. Pollini, VPO, Abbado.
(M) **(*) Decca Jub. JB/*KJBC* 94 [Lon. JL/*5*- 41032]. Backhaus, VPO, Boehm.
**(*) Decca Dig. 410 199-1/*4*. Ashkenazy, VPO, Haitink.
(M) *(**) CBS 61040/*40*- [MY/*MYT* 37258]. Serkin, Cleveland O, Szell.
(M) **(*) Ph. 6527/*7311* 182 [id.]. Arrau, Concg. O, Haitink.
**(*) ASV ALH/*ZCALH* 910. Lill, Hallé O, Loughran.
** Decca SXL 6309. Ashkenazy, LSO, Mehta.
(M) *(*) EMI Em. EMX/*TC-EMX* 2039 [Ang. RL/*4RL* 32041]. Sviatoslav Richter, O de Paris, Maazel.

Brahms's *B flat Concerto* is well served on record. The partnership of Gilels and Jochum produces music-making of rare magic, and if the resonant recording has some want of sharpness of focus (and causes the occasional marginal slip of refinement in tuttis on cassette), the spacious acoustic and rich piano timbre seem well suited to this massive concerto.

Stephen Bishop-Kovacevich is better served in his account of the *Second* than he was in No. 1. Indeed, his version must be numbered among the very finest now before the public. The performance combines poetic feeling and intellectual strength, and reflects an unforced, natural eloquence that compels admiration. The first movement simply unfolds without any false urgency; the second is sparkling and fresh, and in the slow movement there is a rapt, poetic quality that almost matches Gilels. The finale has wit and delicacy, and Sir Colin Davis provides wholly sympathetic support throughout; the unnamed cellist in the slow movement plays with both tenderness and nobility. This is the best version we have had since the Gilels/Jochum and can be recommended alongside it. The recording is finely detailed and naturally balanced on disc, but the cassette has less range and is very much second-best.

Pollini's account is powerful and is in many ways more classical in feeling than Gilels or Barenboim. He has the measure of its scale and breadth, and is given excellent support by the Vienna Philharmonic under Abbado. Pollini may not possess the rich humanity of Gilels or create the degree of intensity which distinguished the Barenboim/Barbirolli partnership, but he has unfailing perception and never invests detail with excessive significance. This is among the more impressive versions now in the catalogue and is excellently recorded on both disc and cassette.

Backhaus was always a controversial artist, inspiring fervent allegiance from his admirers and indifference from others. His playing even before the war had an element of didacticism, and some of his performances in later years were literal and dry. He recorded the Brahms in his eighties and the rugged strength of his conception is matched by playing of remarkable power, even though there are moments of untidiness. His is a broad, magisterial account with, perhaps, too little poetry for some Brahms-lovers but much compensating strength. Tempi are inclined to be spacious but there is no loss of momentum or architectural grip. The recording wears its years remarkably well: it was made in the mid-1960s and sounds very fresh and finely detailed. The cassette offers a sound that is suitably rich and expansive but lacks the last degree of upper range.

Ashkenazy's new performance with Haitink, spacious in conception and thoughtful in detail, is curiously lacking in impulse with cautious speeds and overtly expressive in the lyrical episodes of the second movement. The slow movement is very beautiful and the finale offers the proper contrast but in the last resort, in spite of excellent recording, this is slightly disappointing.

Serkin's version would be much higher up the list were the recording more acceptable. It was his third LP of the work (the first in mono) and represented a great advance on his earlier stereo version with Ormandy. Indeed, it is an electrifying performance which grips the listener from the opening bars. There is a strength and purposefulness about the playing throughout and, with the help of Szell, Serkin achieves an ideal balance between directness and expressiveness. In the opening cadenza, for example, he has all the weight one could want, but he still manages to point the dotted rhythm very winningly and achieve remarkable clarity. In the scherzo he is again strong, but manages to convey more lilt than many of his rivals, while the slow movement has a genuine inner intensity with some wonderfully expressive playing from the Cleveland first cellist. Serkin chooses a comparatively slow speed for the finale (nearly as slow as Backhaus), but the flow and energy of the music are not impaired and the Hungarian motifs of the second subject sparkle with point and wit. This is undoubtedly a great and memorable account and it triumphs over the coarse recorded sound, with the piano inclined to be shallow and clattery and the upper strings crudely shrill. The cassette, too, loses refinement in being transferred at too high a level; tuttis are overblown and not absolutely clean. Yet the sound on tape is somewhat richer than the LP and there is less edge on top. With all its technical shortcomings, the music-making is so riveting as to cause the listener (if he can) to make the necessary allowances.

Arrau's account of the concerto is competitive at medium price. There are one or two idiosyncratic touches (bars 89–91 in the first movement) and some detail is underlined expressively in this artist's characteristic way; but the playing has a splendid combination of aristocratic finesse and warmth of feeling, and Haitink and the Concertgebouw Orchestra give excellent support. The engineers strike the right balance between the piano and orchestra, and the orchestral texture is better focused and cleaner than in the earlier Arrau recording. Although this is not a first choice, it must figure high on the list and should not be missed by admirers of the great Chilean pianist. As with the *First Concerto*, the cassette has been remastered and given quite a high transfer level for Philips, so that the sound is full and vivid, with a bold, natural piano image.

John Lill first recorded the *Second Concerto* not long after winning the Moscow Tchaikovsky Competition. This newer version with the Hallé Orchestra under James Loughran is in many ways a strong account, well thought-out, finely paced and without the slightest trace of self-indulgence. The opening has a powerful masculine ring, particularly the build-up just before the orchestral tutti, and it is the space and power of Brahms's conception that are given priority rather than his poetry. Not that the performance is wanting in feeling or imagination. There is a stronger sense of the philosopher musing than the poet dreaming. The recorded sound is eminently well balanced, though climaxes do not open out as much as they might. Recommendable though it is, it does not displace Gilels or Bishop-Kovacevich. The cassette is first-class, bold, full and clear.

Ashkenazy's earlier version was recorded in conjunction with a live performance at the Festival Hall, the sessions taking place (at Kingsway Hall) immediately after the concert. That being so, it is surprising to find that the chief shortcoming of the account, compared with the main rival versions, is a lack of tension. With much beautiful detail and some wonderfully poetic playing from Ashkenazy the performance still fails to come alive as it should. Naturally Ashkenazy is most successful in the lighter moments, but one is continually left uninvolved. The recording quality is outstandingly good, though the LSO strings are inclined to sound edgy.

Richter's second stereo version of the *Second Concerto* for EMI does not match his splendid early RCA recording with Leinsdorf in Chicago. Maazel seems unable to match (as Leinsdorf did) the orchestral contribution to Richter's mercurial impetuosity, and the result sounds unspontaneous, particularly in the first movement. The EMI recording is excellent (though the tape is not quite as fresh as the disc in the upper range, especially on side one) but the RCA version is far more enjoyable. It is still available in the USA [AGL1/*AGK1* 1267].

Violin concerto in D, Op. 77.

*** DG Dig. **400 064-2**; 2532/*3302* 032 [id.]. Mutter, Berlin PO, Karajan.

(M) *** HMV SXLP/*TC-SXLP* 30186. Menuhin, Berlin PO, Kempe.

*** HMV ASD/*TC-ASD* 3385 [Ang. S/*4XS* 37286]. Perlman, Chicago SO, Giulini.

(M) *** Ph. Seq. 6527/*7311* 197 [id.]. Grumiaux, New Philh. O, Sir Colin Davis.

(M) **(*) CBS 60144/*40-* [MY/*MT* 37262]. Stern, Phd. O, Ormandy.

(B) *** CfP CFP/*TC-CFP* 4398 [Ang. RL/*4RL* 32031]. D. Oistrakh, French Nat. RO, Klemperer.

(M) *** EMI Em. EMX/*TC-EMX* 2041 [Ang. RL/*4RL* 32096]. D. Oistrakh, Cleveland O, Szell.
(M) **(*) DG Sig. 2543/*3343* 515 [2530/*3300* 592]. Milstein, VPO, Jochum.
(M) **(*) DG Acc. 2542/*3342* 117 [138 930]. Ferras, Berlin PO, Karajan.
(M) *(**) RCA Conifer 26.48055 (2) [VCS 7058]. Heifetz, Chicago SO, Reiner – MENDELSSOHN (***) and TCHAIKOVSKY: *Concertos* (***).
** DG 2531/*3301* 251 [id.]. Zukerman, O de Paris, Barenboim.
** DG Dig. **410 029-2**; 2532/*3302* 088 [id.]. Kremer, VPO, Bernstein.
(B) * Con. CC/*CCT* 7523. Szeryng, LSO, Dorati.

It is an extraordinary achievement that the youthful Anne-Sophie Mutter should, so early in her career, provide a performance of the Brahms *Concerto* as commanding as any, matching fiery bravura with a glowing expressive quality, in a reading that is freshly spontaneous in every bar. In many ways her playing combines the unforced lyrical feeling of Krebbers (whose highly recommendable version is currently out of the catalogue) with the flair and individuality of Perlman. There is a lightness of touch, a gentleness in the slow movement that is highly appealing, while in the finale the incisiveness of the solo playing is well displayed by the clear (yet not clinical) digital recording. Needless to say, Karajan's accompaniment is strong in personality and the Berlin Philharmonic play beautifully, but he is by no means the dominant musical personality; the performance represents a genuine musical partnership between youthful inspiration and eager experience. The recording on disc is matched by the excellent chrome cassette, but the compact disc is finest of all, although its clarity emphasizes the close balance of the soloist, and there is a touch of fierceness in the orchestral upper range in tuttis. There is no increase in bass response, compared with the LP.

The recording made by Menuhin with Kempe and the Berlin Philharmonic at the end of the 1950s was one of his supreme achievements in the recording studio. He was in superb form, producing tone of resplendent richness, and the reading is also memorable for its warmth and nobility. He was splendidly accompanied by Kempe, and the Berlin Philharmonic was inspired to outstanding playing – the oboe solo in the slow movement is particularly beautiful. The sound is remarkably satisfying and well balanced and it has transferred equally well to cassette, the spacious qualities of the recording well caught, the soloist given presence without added edge.

A distinguished account of the solo part from Perlman, finely supported by Giulini and the Chicago Symphony Orchestra, a reading of darker hue than is customary, with a thoughtful, searching slow movement rather than the autumnal rhapsody which it so often becomes. Giulini could be tauter, perhaps, in the first movement but the songful playing of Perlman always holds the listener. The recording places the soloist rather too forward, and the orchestral detail could be more transparent. Admirers of Perlman, however, need not hesitate; granted a certain want of impetus in the first movement, this is an impressive and convincing performance. There is a good cassette (recently remastered).

Grumiaux's performance, it goes without saying, is full of insight and lyrical eloquence, and Sir Colin Davis lends his soloist the most sympathetic support. Grumiaux is a wonderful player and (at mid-price) this account might well be first choice for many readers, particularly in view of the excellence of the Philips sound, which is firm, detailed and refined without any loss of presence. The cassette transfer is of good quality, clear and full, although the transfer level is not especially high. Nevertheless the solo image is well-focused and the sound does not lack body or liveliness.

Stern's 1960 recording with Ormandy was made when this artist was at the peak of his career. The solo playing is ripely red-blooded and Ormandy contributes a wonderfully positive Brahmsian warmth to a reading that carries the listener forward in its expressive spontaneity and fire. It is undoubtedly a great performance which one can return to again and again with increasing satisfaction. The musical rewards of this account are slightly undermined by a recording which is somewhat coarse in the CBS manner of this period, and which highlights the soloist. But the remastered pressings can be made to produce a very satisfactory sound (there is no lack of body) although our copy of the cassette demonstrated poor quality-control, with the violin's upper partials occasionally discoloured. In its disc format this must be numbered among the very finest of all available recorded performances, with the inspiration of the occasion caught on the wing.

Each of the two stereo recordings that David Oistrakh made for EMI (one at the beginning of the 1960s with Klemperer, the second with Szell a decade later) has its own character. In each case the recording has been remastered and, perhaps surprisingly, the earlier version sounds better; in Cleveland there is a degree of fierceness on the orchestral tuttis.

The conjunction of two such positive artists as Oistrakh and Klemperer made for a reading characterful to the point of idiosyncrasy, monumental and strong rather than sweetly lyrical; the opening of the first movement has a feeling of engulfing power. The slow movement is particularly fine, and the French oboist plays beautifully. Oistrakh sounds superbly poised and confident, and in the finale, if the tempo is a shade deliberate, the total effect is one of clear gain. The recording is excellent and the tape transfer full-bodied yet clear. It is slightly smoother on top than the LP, and many will prefer it.

The performance with Szell is full of controlled feeling and disciplined vitality, and even though the sound quality is not of the finest for its period, playing of this order (and the Cleveland Orchestra is magnificent, to match the soloist) is not to be dismissed, especially at mid-price. This will well suit those for whom the greater idiosyncrasy of the account with Klemperer is less attractive than a straighter, less individual approach. The cassette is smoother than the disc on side one (with no serious loss of vividness); on side two, the level drops and the finale is less cleanly focused.

To praise Milstein's version for the refinement and beauty of the accompaniment may sound like a backhanded compliment, and so perhaps it is, when for all the beauty and brilliance of the playing this is not quite the flawless Milstein reading of the Brahms that he had put on record for other companies. The hint of unease in the soloist is only relative, and those who want to hear him in the finest possible recorded sound can be safely directed here. Jochum secures playing of great warmth and distinction from the Vienna Philharmonic. Moreover the recording is of very high quality, offering a most natural balance with both soloist and orchestra slightly recessed, giving a concert-hall effect that is far too rare in concerto recordings. There is no appreciable difference between the sound on LP and on chrome tape.

Much depends on one's attitude to Ferras's tone colour whether the Ferras/Karajan version is a good recommendation or not. DG have placed him close, so that the smallness of tone that in the concert hall is disappointing is certainly not evident here. Moreover there is a jewelled accuracy about the playing that is most appealing, and Karajan conducts vividly. The recording is of good quality and the high-level cassette transfer is of demonstration liveliness.

Heifetz's 78 r.p.m. gramophone performances were always something of an occasion, and his early re-recording of the Brahms *Concerto* (not previously available in stereo) has something of this quality. Technically the recording is not good, with rough patches in the louder orchestral moments and the violin spotlighted; the close microphoning gives a harsh quality to the strongly bowed passages. But there is a fine partnership here between Heifetz and Reiner. The interpretation is a satisfying one and it has some wonderful moments of lyrical strength and beauty. The close of the first movement is one such passage, where the melting beauty of tone shows the soloist's technique at its most moving; so is the passionate climax of the slow movement (which Reiner too opens exceptionally well); and the bravura of the finale triumphs over the less than ideal quality of the recording.

Zukerman is rightly famed for his sweetness of tone, and his general approach can often seem a little bland by comparison with the greatest artists. This is a well-conceived reading that has finish and facility yet ultimately leaves the listener untouched by any feeling that he is in contact with great music. Zukerman is exposed to a close balance, but this does not mask the Orchestre de Paris under Barenboim, who give excellent support and receive a well-detailed recording in spite of the unrealistic perspective. On cassette the balance for the soloist sounds much less forward; otherwise the quality for both soloist and orchestra is good, although there is a slight loss of focus in the tuttis of the finale.

Gidon Kremer's version of the Brahms is powerful in attack and has remarkably clean articulation and fine rhythmic buoyancy. His view of the first movement is considerably tauter than in his earlier version, made in the mid-1970s with Karajan. He replaces the Joachim cadenza with a longer one by Reger (his *Prelude in D minor*, *Op. 117*, *No. 6* for solo violin) – at least it isn't Schnittke – but this will undoubtedly diminish its appeal for many collectors. His second movement is hardly a true *Adagio* and Bernstein is much broader than the soloist who tries to move things on. His finale is very fast indeed – the 'ma non troppo vivace' marking being ignored. Bernstein generally produces sumptuous results from the Vienna Philharmonic and the recording has plenty of body, but ultimately Kremer is too narcissistic and idiosyncratic to carry a firm recommendation.

Szeryng made his earlier version of the Brahms *Concerto* for RCA (now out of the catalogue), but the conductor was then Monteux. That alone may help to explain the disappointment of his later Philips recording with Dorati, now reissued on Contour. It is generally unconvincing, and often cold, though inevitably the detail is admirably managed. The recording quality is not especially kind to Szeryng's distinctive tone-colour.

Double concerto for violin and cello in A min., Op. 102.

*** HMV ASD/*TC-ASD* 3905 [Ang. S/*4XS* 36062]. Perlman, Rostropovich, Concg. O, Haitink.

*** HMV ASD/*TC-ASD* 3312 [(d) Ang. SFO/*4XS* 36032]. D. Oistrakh, Rostropovich, Cleveland O, Szell – DVOŘÁK: *Slavonic dances Nos. 3 and 10.****

(M) *** EMI Em. EMX/*TC-EMX* 2035. D. Oistrakh, Fournier, Philh. O, Galliera – BEETHOVEN: *Triple concerto.***(*)

Double concerto; Academic festival overture.

**(*) CBS 74003 [M/*HMT* 35894]. Zukerman, Harrell, NYPO, Mehta.

Double concerto; Tragic overture.

*** DG Dig. **410 603-2**; -1/*4* [id.]. Mutter, Meneses, Berlin PO, Karajan.

(M) **(*) CBS 60130/*40*- [MY/*MYT* 37237]. Francescatti, Fournier, Columbia SO, Bruno Walter.

Double concerto; Variations on a theme of Haydn.

** Ph. 9500 623/*7300 728* [id.]. Accardo, Schiff, Leipzig GO, Masur.

The Brahms *Double concerto* has been lucky in its recordings since the earliest days of stereo, as the listed records conducted by Galliera and Bruno Walter readily demonstrate. Now the era of the digital compact disc produces a version which sets new standards. With two young soloists, Karajan conducts an outstandingly spacious and strong performance. If from Antonio Meneses the opening cello cadenza seems to lack something in urgency and command, that is a deceptive start, for from then on the concentration and power of the piece are built up superbly. As in her commanding performance of the Brahms *Violin concerto* – also with Karajan and the Berlin Philharmonic – Anne-Sophie Mutter conveys a natural authority comparable to Karajan's own, and the precision and clarity of Meneses' cello as recorded make an excellent match. (The chrome cassette is equally clear.) The central slow movement in its spacious way has a wonderful Brahmsian glow, and all these qualities come out the more vividly in the CD version, though the relatively close balance of the soloists – particularly the cellist – is more evident too.

Perlman and Rostropovich present their solo roles in giant size. This is partly a result of the recording balance but is also due to their strong, positive playing, which yet is not over-romantic or wilful. Haitink is the stabilizing force that holds the reading together with generally steady tempi, and though the orchestra is placed rather at a distance, the EMI engineers, on their first visit to the Concertgebouw, have generally coped well with the notorious problems of the Amsterdam hall. The format on two full sides is extravagant, but the fullness of the tonal spectrum justifies it. The cassette transfer is admirably clear and clean, without loss of amplitude:

Rostropovich's tone is strikingly rich and resonant.

The HMV reissue of the (1970) Oistrakh/Rostropovich account has been successfully remastered and the recording is full, yet has plenty of detail and sounds smoother than the original. This too is a powerful account, splendidly played, and deserves to be considered alongside Rostropovich's later version with Perlman. The cassette is quite well managed, but not as impressive as the tape of the later version.

David Oistrakh's first stereo recording with Fournier dates from 1959, but the recording was balanced by Walter Legge and the sound remains remarkably satisfying. The performance is distinguished, strong and lyrical – the slow movement particularly fine – and with Galliera and the Philharmonia providing excellent support this version, coupled to Beethoven's *Triple concerto*, makes an ideal choice for bargain-hunters. Disc and tape are closely matched in sound; the upper range of the LP is marginally sharper in focus.

There is much to admire in the performance by Pinchas Zukerman and Lynn Harrell, who are more truthfully balanced than are many others (namely Perlman and Rostropovich, or Schneiderhan and Starker). The soloists – especially Lynn Harrell – play with much beauty of tone and sensitivity, though there are moments when one feels that they almost make too much of dynamic contrasts and expressive detail at the expense of continuity of line. The orchestral support is less refined, though it is in no way inadequate and has plenty of spirit. In addition to the good balance between soloists and orchestra, the sound is finely judged and clean, though wanting the transparency and bloom of the finest rivals.

At mid-price, Francescatti and Fournier are competitive. Fournier is magnificent, and if one can adjust to Francescatti's rather nervous vibrato there is much to admire. Bruno Walter draws playing of great warmth from the Columbia orchestra, and the sound, though not first-class, is perfectly acceptable. CBS have now restored the original coupling, the *Tragic overture*, and Walter gives a fine account of it.

Salvatore Accardo and Heinrich Schiff bring warmth, lyricism and imagination to the *Double concerto*, and though this may not be the most exciting account of it on the market, it is surely among the most thoughtful and refined. There is nothing here that is not completely felt, but, unlike the Perlman/Rostropovich version, there is no hint of too much projection (the only reservation that one might in time feel about that superb account). Everything here seems unforced. The orchestral playing is admirably shaped and always responsive, but the balance is distinctly recessed. The soloists are forward, though not excessively so, but the orchestral detail is by no means as well defined as one would like. The texture should be better ventilated and the tuttis need firmer body.

There is also a bargain PRT disc (GSGC/*ZCGC* 2029) coupling the concerto with the *Academic festival overture*. The soloists are Campoli and Navarra with the Hallé Orchestra. Campoli is not on his (usually fine) form and is not helped by the balance. Nor is Navarra as authoritative as in his recording with Suk and Ančerl on Supraphon (now deleted). Despite keen admiration for both, not to mention Sir John Barbirolli himself, this is a disc that carries only a qualified recommendation. The sound does not match the rival EMI Eminence issue (the tape is brighter on side two than on side one) which also offers another concerto for only a modest extra outlay.

Hungarian dances Nos. 1–21 (complete).
*** Ph. Dig. **411 426-2**; 6514/*7337* 305 [id.]. Leipzig Gewandhaus O, Masur.
*** DG Dig. **410 615-2**; 410 615-1/*4* [id.]. VPO, Abbado.

Hungarian dances Nos. 1, 2, 5, 6, 10, 12, 15.
(M) *** Ph. Seq. 6527/*7311* 032 [from Mercury 72024]. LSO, Dorati – DVOŘÁK: *Slavonic dances.***

Hungarian dances Nos. 1, 3, 5–6.
(M) **(*) DG Priv. 2535/*3335* 628. Berlin PO, Karajan – LISZT: *Hungarian rhapsodies* etc.***

Hungarian dances Nos. 1, 5–7, 12–13, 19, 21.
(M) *** Decca VIV/*KVIC* 18 [Lon. STS 15009]. VPO, Reiner – DVOŘÁK: *Slavonic dances.****

Hungarian Dances Nos. 1, 3, 5, 6, 10, 12, 13, 19, 21.
(M) *** Decca Jub. 411 725-1/*4*. LSO, Boskovsky – DVOŘÁK: *Slavonic Dances.****

In Nos. 5 and 6 Masur uses Parlow's scoring instead of Martin Schmelling (as preferred by Abbado) and in Nos. 7 and 8 he opts for Schollum rather than Hans Gál. Masur is just a shade more relaxed and smiling and the timbre of the strings is generally richer and warmer than that achieved by the DG engineers in Vienna. Abbado has great sparkle and lightness, but the Leipzig orchestra is hardly less dazzling than the Viennese. The Philips issue has the finer sound (though the chrome tape has less sparkle than the disc and tends to be slightly middle-orientated), and sounds glowingly full on CD.

Boskovsky's performances sparkle and the (1975) recording is first-class to match the vivacious and polished playing. This is first choice for those wanting a coupling with Dvořák.

Dorati's selection has a Mercury source. His conducting is fierce, like Karajan's, but, more than Karajan, Dorati captures a true Hungarian spirit. When he takes a piece faster than expected, one does not feel he is being wilful or intent on showing off, but simply that he and his players are enjoying it better that way. The recording is brilliant and the cassette transfer is first-class.

Karajan's performances certainly have panache; but, with very brightly lit recording, their character is of extrovert brilliance rather than warmth. But the Liszt couplings (Fricsay's splendid version of *Les Préludes* as well as two *Hungarian rhapsodies*) are outstanding, and this is an attractive collection. The cassette tempers the upper range slightly, without losing the sparkle.

Reiner's collection was a favourite record of the late John Culshaw, and the recording (from the beginning of the 1960s) wears its years lightly. Reiner indulges himself in rubato and effects of his own (witness No. 12); but the affection of the music-making is obvious, and the sound balances brilliance with ambient warmth. The cassette matches the disc.

Serenade No. 1 in D, Op. 11.
(M) *** Decca Jub. JB/*KJBC* 86 [Lon. 6567]. LSO, Kertesz.
*** Ph. 9500 322 [id./*7300 584*]. Concg. O, Haitink.
**(*) DG Dig. 410 654-1/*4* [id.]. Berlin PO, Abbado.

The late Istvan Kertesz gives a beautifully relaxed and warm-hearted account of this marvellous score, whose comparative neglect is unaccountable. The playing is as fresh as is the recorded sound. The engineers provide an excellently balanced and vivid recording, and the Decca reissue has the advantage on price. The cassette transfer is of excellent quality, warm, yet fresh and clear.

A finely proportioned, relaxed yet vital account from Haitink and the Concertgebouw Orchestra. The wind-playing is particularly distinguished, and while the players obviously relish the many delights of this underrated score, the architecture is firmly held together without the slightest trace of expressive indulgence. The balance places the listener fairly well back, but the perspective is true to life and the sound blends admirably.

Abbado's performance is very fine indeed, vital, imaginative and sensitive, but the recording is good rather than distinguished: there is more air round the various sections of the orchestra in the Kertesz and Haitink versions. The chrome cassette is wide-ranging and clear, matching the disc closely.

Serenade No. 2 in A, Op. 16.
(M) *** Decca Jub. JB/*KJBC* 87. LSO, Kertesz – DVOŘÁK: *Serenade.****

'I was in a perfectly blissful mood. I have rarely written music with such delight', wrote Brahms to Joachim when arranging this delectable *Serenade* for piano duet. The work has surprisingly autumnal colourings, and one would not be surprised to learn that it was a late rather than an early work. It was in fact begun before Brahms had finished the *D major Serenade* and thus dates from his mid-twenties. Kertesz gives an alert yet at the same time relaxed account of it. Moreover, this offers excellent value by including the Dvořák *Wind serenade* in an altogether admirable reading. The cassette quality has an attractive warmth; indeed a slight bass cut may improve the balance.

SYMPHONIES

(i) *Symphonies Nos. 1–4; Tragic overture; Variations on a theme of Haydn, Op. 56a.* (ii) *Academic festival overture; 21 Hungarian dances; Serenades Nos. 1–2.*
**(*) DG 2740 275 (7) [id.]. (i) Berlin PO, Karajan; (ii) Berlin or VPO, Abbado.

Symphonies Nos. 1–4; Tragic overture; Variations, Op. 56a.
**(*) DG *3378 120* (4) [id.]. Berlin PO, Karajan.

Karajan's accounts of the symphonies are among the best in the catalogue (see below) and those who already possess them will not be interested in this new box just for the sake of the *Serenades.* To be frank, the new account of the *D major Serenade* under Abbado does not sound as spacious or as fresh as its companion (not digital and made in the 1960s by the same forces). The *A major Serenade* is marvellously done and well held together with dynamic nuances scrupulously observed. The *Hungarian dances* with the Vienna Philharmonic are very well played indeed. The *Brahms edition* has the benefit of luxury presentation with informative articles by such scholars as Ludwig Finscher, Constantin Floros and Robert Pascall. It is beautifully illustrated. However, the *D major Serenade* is available in better versions (Haitink etc.) and many readers may well prefer to get the earlier Karajan box of the symphonies mentioned below and look elsewhere for the *Serenades.* The cassette box concentrates on the *Symphonies* plus fillers. Nos. 1 and 4 which have a digital source produce first-class tapes, but although chrome is used for Nos. 2 and 3 the sound here is marginally less well focused, though still very good.

Symphonies Nos. 1–4; Academic festival overture; Tragic overture; Variations on a theme of Haydn.
** DG 2741/*3378* 023 (4); also **410 081/4-2** (available separately) [id.]. VPO, Bernstein.

Symphonies Nos. 1–4; Academic festival overture; Tragic overture; (i) *Alto rhapsody, Op. 53.*
(M) *** HMV SLS 5009 (4). LPO or LSO, Boult; (i) with Baker, Alldis Ch.

Symphonies Nos. 1–4; Academic festival overture; Tragic overture.
*** EMI 1C 137 50034/7. Philh. O, Klemperer.
**(*) Decca D 151 D 4/*K 151*/*K 44* (4) [Lon. CSA/*5*- 2406]. Chicago SO, Solti.

Symphonies Nos. 1–4; Tragic overture.
*** DG 2740 193/*3371 041* (4) [id.]. Berlin PO, Karajan.

Broadly, Karajan's 1978 cycle shows that his readings of the Brahms symphonies, with lyrical and dramatic elements finely balanced, have changed little over the years, though it is worth noting that his approach to No. 3 is now stronger and more direct, with less mannered phrasing in the third movement. The playing of the Berlin Philharmonic remains uniquely sweet, and the ensemble is finely polished. If the results are not always as incisively alert or as warm in texture as Karajan's earlier Berlin performances, that is partly due to less flattering recorded sound. Balance and top response are not always kind to the exposed violins, though in this the cassette version is preferable to the discs.

Apart from No. 2, Boult's individual records of the Brahms symphonies are no longer available separately. All but one of them were given three stars when first issued. The exception was No. 4 which, though finely recorded, is sober almost to a fault. The remainder are noble, straightforward readings that always come up fresh. It is ironic to remember that the whole cycle was started by accident, when Boult – in his crisp efficiency – had completed his schedule with two sessions to spare, and elected to do Brahms's *Third* as an unplanned extra. With Janet Baker in the *Alto rhapsody* the fill-up items are welcome, but note that the Brahms *Haydn variations* are not included.

Klemperer's set is also highly competitive; the sound is refurbished and these classical readings have commanding strength and integrity to commend them. No. 2 is particularly fine, and although some collectors may have individual reservations (R.L. has never really enjoyed this *Fourth*), the box is a worthwhile recommendation.

Sir Georg Solti came to the Brahms symphonies after a quarter-century of experience in the recording studio, having purposely left them aside over the years. His study was intensely serious, and that is reflected in his often measured but always forceful renderings. Those who think of Solti as a conductor who always whips up excitement may be surprised at the sobriety of the approach, but in a way these performances are the counterparts of those he recorded of the Beethoven symphonies, important and thoughtful statements, lacking only a degree of the fantasy and idiosyncrasy which make fine performances great. Superb playing and recording; on cassette the bass balance is slightly over-resonant at times, but generally the sound is massively rich and full-blooded, with characteristic Decca vividness and detail.

Bernstein's set of Brahms has – like many of his latterday recordings for DG – been edited together from live performances and with the exception of the *Third Symphony*, which at slow speeds loses impulse, it represents a warmly spontaneous response to much-loved music. Unfortunately, as Brahmsian, Bernstein is a Jekyll and Hyde figure. Though the thrust and urgency of the playing are rarely in doubt, Bernstein often dallies self-indulgently – as in the drawn-out account of the main theme in the finale of the *First Symphony* or the extreme allargando on the chorale motif at the end, or the Elgarian moulding in the slow movement of the *Fourth*. Like any Bernstein live performances, these are fascinating to listen to once, but hardly recommendable as a general set. Digital recording of excellent range but of variable balance and clarity. The chrome tapes are of DG's best quality, and have excellent body and warmth, refined detail and a clear bright upper range. Nos. 3 and 4 are back-to-back. The symphonies are also available separately in compact disc form, with the usual advantages of added clarity of focus and background silence. Compact disc collectors might consider the acquisition of the *Fourth Symphony* (**410 084-2**), undoubtedly the finest performance in the cycle, still idiosyncratic in control of tempo, but carrying its own special conviction – see below.

Symphony No. 1 in C min., Op. 68.

*** DG 2531/*3301* 131 [id.]. Berlin PO, Karajan.

(M) *** DG Acc. 2542/*3342* 166. Berlin PO, Karajan.

(M) *** HMV SXLP 30217 [Ang. S 35481]. Philh. O, Klemperer.

(M) *** EMI Em. EMX/*TC-EMX* 41 2023-1/*4*. LPO, Jochum.

**(*) Decca SXL/*KSXC* 6924 [Lon. CS 7198]. Chicago SO, Solti.

(M) **(*) Decca Jub. JB/*KJBC* 82 [Lon. JL/*5*- 41033]. VPO, Kertesz.

(*) DG Dig. **410 023-2; 2532/*3302* 056 [id.]. LAPO, Giulini.

(*) DG Dig. **410 081-2; 410 081-1/*4* [id.]. VPO, Bernstein.

(B) ** Con. CC/*CCT* 7514. Berlin PO, Boehm.

(M) * Decca VIV/*KVIC* 35 [Lon. STS 15194]. VPO, Karajan.

Symphony No. 1; (i) *Alto rhapsody.*

(B) *** CfP CFP/*TC-CFP* 4387. Hallé O, Loughran; (i) with B. Greevy and Hallé Ch.

When Karajan has performed the four Brahms symphonies as a cycle in concert, he has always put No. 1 last, a sign that it is the one with which he most completely identifies. So it is in this performance, his fifth on record, if anything even bigger in scale than his earlier Berlin version of 1964. He has grown more direct in his Brahmsian manner too, but the Berlin solo playing has never been more persuasive. Recording balance is somewhat close, giving edge to the high violins, but it remains an outstanding version. The tape transfer is full and clear. Yet the earlier performance is still highly recommendable. Perhaps the newer version is bigger-boned and longer-breathed but differences are marginal, and the sound in this mid-priced version is still amazingly good, although on cassette the bass resonance seems rather over-ample.

In its medium-priced reissue, Klemperer's monumental performance is very competitive indeed. The reading is tremendously compelling, and from the first bar of the introduction, with its thundering, relentless timpani strokes, Klemperer's conception moves with a single momentum to the final C major chord of the last movement. Here is real greatness, and even the listener who finds this approach too overwhelming must be aware of it. The sound too is admirably fresh in this new pressing.

The high drama of the *First Symphony* finds Jochum at his most persuasive, giving the illusion of live communication in ebb and flow of tension and natural flexibility. He is not as free as Furtwängler was – a specially revered master with him – but the warmth and lyricism go with comparable inner fire. He observes the rarely heard exposition repeat in the first movement. With fine playing from the LPO and very good EMI recording, it makes an excellent mid-priced choice to consider alongside Klemperer, and Karajan on Accolade. The sound is more modern than either of these versions, although the upper string timbre is a little thin on disc. This is slightly less noticeable on tape, especially on side two where the level drops and brings a mellower upper range.

With the Chicago orchestra's playing as refined as any on record, Solti here directs a performance both spacious and purposeful, with the first movement given modular consistency between sections by a single pulse preserved as far as possible. Some will want more relaxation, for the tension and electricity remain here even when tempi are expansive. The recording is both atmospheric and clear, and the cassette is outstandingly rich and full without loss of range at the top, although there is some excessive bass resonance to cut back.

On Classics for Pleasure Loughran provides a fully recommendable bargain version, the first to observe the exposition repeat in the first movement. The reading from first to last is as refreshing as Boult's HMV recording (no longer available separately). The second and third movements both have a spring-like quality, and the slow movement is less sweet than usual, while the 6/8 trio of the third movement is taken for once at a speed which allows the climax not to sound breathless. The introduction to the finale is unusually slow, weighty and concentrated, while the great string melody is not smoothed over at all. The entry of the chorale at the end finds Loughran characteristically refusing to slow down to half speed. Though some of the woodwind playing is not ideally responsive, the whole orchestra, particularly the strings, shows a natural feeling for Brahms's style. The reissue offers a fine performance of the *Alto* rhapsody as a not inconsiderable bonus. Greevy gives a forthright account of the solo part, not subtle but warmly enjoyable. On cassette the *Alto rhapsody* (which comes first) is vibrant and clear, but the first movement of the symphony has markedly less upper range than the disc. On side two disc and tape are much more closely matched.

Kertesz is beautifully recorded, and the orchestral playing is equally fine. But while anyone would be happy with this record, the reading is marginally under-characterized. The cassette is acceptable but not one of Decca's best.

Giulini takes a spacious view of the *First*, consistently choosing speeds slower than usual. Generally his keen control of rhythm means that slowness does not deteriorate into heaviness, but the speed for the big C major theme in the finale is so slow that it sounds self-conscious, not *Allegro ma non troppo* at all. That movement as a result loses its concentration, even with Giulini's magnetic control. It remains a noble, serene view of a heroic symphony, beautifully played and recorded. The chrome cassette too is of excellent quality, although at the very opening the resonant bass brings a slight ripple in the texture from the drum beats. The compact disc, however, is strikingly free and clear.

The finale in Bernstein's version, even more than with Giulini, brings a highly idiosyncratic reading with the great melody of the main theme presented first at a speed very much slower than the main part of the movement. On reprise it never comes back to the slow tempo, until the coda brings the most extreme slowing for the chorale motif. These two points are exaggerations of accepted tradition, and though Bernstein's electricity makes the results compelling, this is hardly a version for constant repetition. Good recording on both disc and chrome tape, with the compact disc bringing the usual extra refinement.

Boehm's Berlin Philharmonic version of the *First* comes from the early 1960s (he recorded it again later with the VPO). It is a centrally recommendable version, with tempi that are steady rather than volatile, but, with polished playing from the Berliners, the performance is effective in its way. It makes a fair recommendation on the bargain-priced Contour label. The recording is well-balanced although it begins to show its age. The cassette transfer is rather more opaque than the disc, but remains acceptable. (Indeed, it may have been remastered by now, as recent Contour issues show a much livelier sound than the earlier ones.)

Karajan's VPO recording made by Decca at the beginning of the 1960s is strangely mannered and, unlike most Karajan interpretations, fails to carry conviction. Everything is lacking in tension, and though towards the end of the finale the conductor cannot help creating excitement, this is dissipated in what must be the slowest chorale reference in the coda on record. The recording is spacious and brilliant; but this cannot be recommended.

Symphony No. 2 in D., Op. 73.
*** DG 2531/*3301* 132 [id.]. Berlin PO, Karajan.
(M) *** HMV SXLP 30513. Philh. O, Karajan – SCHUBERT: *Symphony No. 8.****
(M) *** DG Acc. 2542/*3342* 167. Berlin PO, Karajan.
(M) *** EMI Em. EMX/*TC-EMX* 41 2024-1/*4*. LPO, Jochum.
(*) DG Dig. **400 066-2; 2532/*3302* 014 [id.]. LAPO, Giulini.
(M) **(*) Decca Jub. JB/*KJBC* 83. VPO, Kertesz.

Symphony No. 2; Academic festival overture.
(B) *** CfP CFP/*TC-CFP* 4388. Hallé O, Loughran.
(*) DG Dig. **410 082-2; 410 082-1/*4* [id.]. VPO, Bernstein.

Symphony No. 2; Tragic overture.
**(*) Decca SXL/*KSXC* 6925 [Lon. CS/*5*-7199]. Chicago SO, Solti.

Symphony No. 2; (i) *Alto rhapsody.*
(M) *** HMV SXLP/*TC-SXLP* 30529. LPO, Boult; (i) with Baker, Alldis Ch.

For many British readers Boult's version will occupy a special place of honour. It has warmth, dignity and nobility and offers playing of great expressive power and a striking sense of spontaneity. The 1971 recording was of HMV's highest quality, and as the fill-up is a memorable account of the *Alto rhapsody* from Dame Janet Baker, the claims of this medium-priced reissue are indeed strong. The cassette too has been remastered and is highly successful; the *Rhapsody* is notably clear and clean.

Karajan's commanding new Berlin Philharmonic version, fresh and generally direct, is helped by superb playing from the Berlin orchestra. In the third movement this latest reading from Karajan is less affectionate than before and the finale is now very fast, challenging even the Berlin players. The recording, in the latterday Karajan/Berlin manner, is balanced relatively close but with lively atmosphere. The cassette is first-class in every way.

However, the reissue on HMV of Karajan's 1957 account with the Philharmonia Orchestra, very generously coupled at medium price, must also be seriously considered. In this splendid earlier performance the symphony unfolds with an unforced naturalness that is warmly compelling. The first movement is marvellously spacious and the horn solo (bars 455–77) is hauntingly poetic, more so than in either of the later records Karajan has made. Yet for all the relaxed atmosphere the grip that both his Berlin accounts have shown is strongly evident here. The slight blemishes (intonation between wind and strings at the beginning of the development, and a tape-join later on) will worry no one. The recording has slightly less range than the modern accounts, but it is rich and beautifully balanced. Despite its age, this is one of the best disc versions of the *Second* on the market, and the substantial Schubert bonus is no less recommendable.

Karajan's 1964 account was among the sunniest and most lyrical readings of the *Second Symphony*, and its sound is fully competitive even now, although the cassette (as with the companion Accolade reissue of the *First*) is rather bass-heavy. It fully justifies its position high in our recommendations list, though the recording does not quite match the later Karajan in terms of range, and it is without the bonus provided by the 1957 HMV version. However, it remains in every way a satisfying reissue.

Jochum's is a warmly lyrical reading, expansive in the first movement (with exposition repeat) allowing extremes of expression, fast and exciting in the finale. The combination of natural fervour and spontaneity is most compelling, justifying the natural flexibility. Excellent playing and recording, more modern than Boult's, but with no filler. Nevertheless at mid-price this is first-class value, although the cassette – which otherwise matches the LP fairly closely – is transferred at a lower level on the second side, and loses some of its bite.

The restraint which made Giulini's recording of Beethoven's *Eroica symphony* with the same orchestra so individual yet so compelling is evident in Brahms too. The result is less immediately magnetic, particularly in the first movement, and the recording is not one of DG's most vivid; but admirers of this conductor will find many points of fresh illumination. The chrome cassette is of matching quality, but again not one of DG's finest; the upper range is not quite as extended as some. However, this is an example where the compact disc is markedly superior in sound to either LP or chrome cassette. The quality is much fresher and more transparent and the effect is to give more projection and much better detail to the first movement and to give the whole performance something of a lift.

As a Brahmsian, James Loughran is a master of transition, and his account of No. 2, like those in the rest of his excellent Brahms cycle with the Hallé, has a natural, warm flow, carrying the listener on, even while the basic approach is direct and unfussy. On interpretation his reading (with exposition repeat included) matches and even outshines any in the catalogue, at whatever price, and the modern CFP recording is warm and naturally balanced, though there are one or two noticeable tape-joins. The Hallé ensemble and string tone are not always quite as polished as in the versions from metropolitan orchestras, but the sense of spontaneity is ample compensation. The reissue offers a bonus of the *Academic festival overture* – a fine performance after a rather limp start. The cassette is well-balanced and full, but has less range and bite at the top than the disc.

Bernstein in his live recording directs a warm and expansive account of No. 2, notably less free and idiosyncratic than the others in the series yet comparably rhythmic and equally spontaneous-sounding. Good recording, considering the limitations at a live concert. There is a good chrome tape, though the transfer level is not especially high. The compact disc sounds well.

A powerful, weighty performance from Solti, its lyrical feeling passionately expressed in richly upholstered textures. The reading displays a broad nobility, but the charm and delicately gracious qualities of the music are much less part of Solti's view. Yet the lyric power of the playing is hard to resist, especially when the recording is so full-blooded and brilliant. Solti includes the first-movement exposition repeat and offers a splendidly committed account of the *Tragic overture* as a bonus. The cassette is of comparable quality, full-bodied and bright, though there is some excessive bass resonance in the overture.

Kertesz's account is as direct and honest as it is attractive. The playing of the Vienna Philharmonic is absolutely first-class, and the Decca recording has brilliance, clarity and warmth. Kertesz also observes the exposition repeat, and the performance has a splendid freshness and youthful vigour. At the same time, it must be conceded that this is in no sense a performance of commanding stature. There is a good matching cassette, perhaps a trifle over-resonant in the bass.

Symphony No. 3 in F, Op. 90.
(B) **(*) RCA VICS/*VK* 2043. Chicago SO, Reiner.

Symphony No. 3; Academic festival overture.
(M) *** HMV SXLP/*TC-SXLP* 30255. Philh. O, Klemperer.
*** Decca SXL/*KSXC* 6902 [Lon. CS 7200]. Chicago SO, Solti.

Symphony No. 3; Tragic overture.
*** DG 2531/*3301* 133 [id.]. Berlin PO, Karajan.
(M) *** EMI Em. EMX/*TC-EMX* 41 2025-1/*4*. LPO, Jochum.
(B) *** CfP CFP/*TC-CFP* 4389. Hallé O, Loughran.

Symphony No. 3; Variations on a theme of Haydn.
(M) **(*) Decca Jub. JB/*KJBC* 84. VPO, Kertesz.
(M) **(*) DG Acc. 2542/*3342* 168. Berlin PO, Karajan.
*(*) DG Dig. **410 083-2**; 410 083-1/*4* [id.]. VPO, Bernstein.

In his newest recording Karajan gives superb grandeur to the opening of No. 3, but then characteristically refuses to observe the exposition repeat, which in this of all Brahms's first movements is necessary as a balance with the others. Comparing this 1978 reading with Karajan's earlier 1964 version, one finds him more direct, noticeably less mannered in his treatment of the third movement and strikingly more dynamic and compelling. The overture too is superbly done, and though one may criticize the recording balance, the result is powerful and immediate. The cassette matches the disc fairly closely (the texture is a little less clean at the opening). However, the level drops slightly on side two, with a corresponding marginal loss of immediacy.

Jochum's account with the LPO of the *Third Symphony* represents the peak of his cycle and this is among the most rewarding versions of this work, irrespective of price. Jochum conveys the full weight and warmth of the work with generally spacious speeds freely moulded. The first movement is magnificent (exposition repeat observed), leading to a passionate coda. In the central movements there is an engaging autumnal feeling and then in the finale, starting from hushed expectancy in the opening pianissimo, he builds powerfully and exuberantly in natural spontaneity and then creates a feeling of elegy in the closing pages. Both performance and recording are first-rate and this is a real bargain at mid-price, well coupled with a fine account of the *Tragic overture*. Disc and tape sound very much alike, although on side two of the cassette the level drops slightly, with marginal loss of upper range.

Klemperer's account is even more individual than his other Brahms symphony performances. With slow speeds and all repeats taken, his timing is much more extended than usual. But for all his expansiveness Klemperer does not make the music sound opulent. There is a severity about his approach which may at first seem unappealing, but which comes to underline the strength of the architecture. The recording is excellent for its period, and the cassette transfer has been remastered to produce clean, vivid textures with plenty of weight and breadth.

With dynamic contrasts heightened – helped by the gloriously resonant playing of the Chicago orchestra – and with unusually spacious tempi in the middle movements (the second is more an *Adagio* than an *Andante*), Solti takes a big-scale view of the *Third*, by far the shortest of the Brahms symphonies. The epically grand opening, Solti seems to say, demands an equivalent status for the rest; and the result, lacking a little in Brahmsian idiosyncrasy, is most compelling. Solti's Brahms should not be underestimated and with wonderfully rich sound this gives much satisfaction. The cassette transfer is wide in range and full, but there is some edginess on the upper strings and an excess of bass resonance.

Loughran, so urgently spontaneous in the other three Brahms symphonies, takes an unexpectedly measured view of No. 3. Though initially his slow tempi for all four movements may seem to undermine tension, on repetition this emerges as an unusually satisfying reading, presenting the symphony as an autumnal work with lighter scoring than in the other symphonies. The total impression is of toughness and restraint set alongside flowing lyricism. As is habitual with Loughran, the exposition repeat is observed in the first movement, an important point in this of all the Brahms symphonies. Full atmospheric recording: a welcome bargain recommendation. The cassette, however, is disappointing, especially on side two. Transferred at a low level, the orchestral texture lacks bite in the upper range.

It is a pity that Reiner's performance, which dates from the late 1950s, is not given a more refined recording. Nevertheless its reappearance on the RCA budget label is most welcome. It is a glowing, marvellously proportioned account, yet there is no want of momentum in the outer movements and lyrical intensity and warmth in the slow movement. The sound is acceptable rather than distinguished and, although the balance is good, climaxes are not reproduced as smoothly as they would be in a modern recording of quality, but this should not be enough to deter the serious collector, for this is a performance of stature, and the Chicago orchestra has never been better than it was in the days of Reiner.

Kertesz's version has the benefit of first-rate Decca engineering, with a good cassette too. It is a richly Brahmsian sound, marked by warm Viennese string tone. The performance is unaffected and natural, even though in the last analysis it is under-characterized and cannot compare with Reiner in this respect. However, the performance of the *Variations*, which are beautifully played, is very persuasive, smiling and lyrical.

Karajan's 1964 DG version is very good but not quite so compelling as his earlier No. 1 and No. 2. He takes the opening expansively, which makes it surprising that he omits the exposition repeat, and the movement is left rather short. The third movement too is very slow; overall, his more recent version is preferable. The cassette transfer of the Accolade version is first-class, the sound at once rich and vivid.

Bernstein's account of No. 3 was recorded live like the others in the series, but with speeds in the first three movements so slow as to sound sluggish, it lacks the very quality of flow one hopes to find in a concert performance. The result is disappointingly self-conscious, and only the finale at an aptly fast speed brings Bernstein's usual incisiveness. There is a satisfactory chrome tape and the compact disc brings the usual advantages.

Symphony No. 4 in E min., Op. 98.
*** DG 2531/*3301* 134 [id.]. Berlin PO, Karajan.
(M) *** HMV SXLP/*TC-SXLP* 30503. Philh. O, Karajan.
*** DG Dig. 2532/*3302* 003 [id.]. VPO, Carlos Kleiber.
*** Decca SXL/*KSXC* 6890 [Lon. CS 7201]. Chicago SO, Solti.
(M) *** Decca Jub. JB/*KJBC* 85 [Lon. JL/*5*-41055]. VPO, Kertesz.
(M) **(*) DG Acc. 2542/*3342* 169. Berlin PO, Karajan.
(M) ** Ph. Seq. 6527/*7311* 143 [id.]. Concg. O, Haitink.
(B) ** PRT GSGC/*ZCGC* 2027. Hallé O, Barbirolli.

Symphony No. 4; Academic festival overture.
(M) *** EMI Em. EMX/*TC-EMX* 2026. LPO, Jochum.

Symphony No. 4; Tragic overture.
*** DG Dig. **410 084-2**; 410 084-1/*4*. [id.]. VPO, Bernstein.

Symphony No. 4; Variations on a theme of Haydn.
(B) *** CfP CFP/*TC-CFP* 4390. Hallé O, Loughran.

Brahms's *Fourth Symphony* is now extremely well represented. Indeed, one might say that there are interpretations and recordings to suit every taste, and the medium price-range is especially well served, not only by Karajan but also by Kertesz and, notably, Jochum whose Eminence version is striking for its lyrical eloquence and richness of texture.

In his newest DG recording Karajan refuses to overstate the first movement, starting with deceptive reticence. His easily lyrical style, less moulded in this 1978 reading than in his 1964 (DG) account, is fresh and unaffected, and highly persuasive. The scherzo, fierce and strong, leads to a clean, weighty account of the finale. The overall performance is very satisfying. The recording is of a piece with the others in the series, with balances not quite natural. The cassette transfer is of outstanding quality, in many ways preferable to the disc; it is rich and clear, with excellent detail and a fine body to the string tone.

Jochum's disc opens with an exuberant account of the *Academic festival overture*. When the symphony begins, the very opening phrase establishes the reading as warmly affectionate and, as in Bruckner, Jochum combines a high degree of expressive flexibility with a rapt concentration which holds the symphonic structure strongly together. Though the orchestra is British – the LPO in fine form – this represents the German tradition at its most communicative; but, more than that, it demonstrates Jochum's passionate feeling for Brahms, with its spirit of soaring lyricism and – in the finale especially – a strong, even irresistible forward momentum. Although the performance has its idiosyncrasies of tempo, it is highly compelling in every bar, and with sound that admirably combines richness with bite and clear detail, it makes a first-rate recommendation, irrespective of its very reasonable price. The cassette is rather less wide-ranging in the treble than the disc, but this is more noticeable in the overture than the symphony, which is well-balanced.

Karajan's glowing HMV account from the mid-1950s holds its own with his mid-1960s Berlin version, and is in many ways to be preferred to several more recent issues. The keynote of the performance is its complete naturalness; the symphony unfolds at an unforced pace and possesses a glowing eloquence that is unfailingly impressive. The sound is amazingly fine, given that it is nearly thirty years old: the strings have a more natural timbre and sonority than they do even in the Kleiber digital recording. Naturally the range is not as wide as in a modern record, but the sound has refreshing warmth and the balance is excellently judged, though, compared with the disc, the tape is a little thick-textured and is less refined at both ends of the spectrum. The Philharmonia play marvellously for Karajan, and both artistically and technically this is to be preferred to the Klemperer version made only a year or two later.

Any record from Carlos Kleiber is an event and his is a performance of real stature. Everything is shaped with the attention to detail one would expect from this great conductor. Apart from one moment of expressive emphasis at bar 44 in the first movement, his reading is completely free from eccentricity. The digital recording is impressive, but the strings above the stave sound a little shrill and glassy, while at the other end of the spectrum one feels a want of opulence in the bass. A gripping and compelling performance, though not more impressive than Karajan's last Berlin version. The cassette transfer (on chrome tape) is outstanding in its body and clarity, if anything a little kinder than the disc to the upper string timbre.

Bernstein's Vienna version, recorded live, is exhilaratingly dramatic in fast music, while the slow movement brings richly resonant playing from the Vienna strings, not least in the great cello melody at bar 41, which with its moulded rubato comes to sound surprisingly like Elgar. This is the finest of Bernstein's Vienna cycle and, with good sound on both LP and cassette, is well worth considering. Like the others in the set, the compact disc gains in clarity, definition and range and gives the orchestra fine presence, although in the slow movement the LP offers slightly more warmth.

After a full twenty-five years recording for Decca, Solti at last came round to Brahms, and this account of No. 4 was the first result of that project. The most distinctive point about the reading, after a very direct, fast and steady first movement, is that the *Andante moderato* of the second movement is very slow indeed, more an *Adagio*. It is not just that it starts slowly, as in some other versions; Solti characteristically maintains that speed with complete concentration. Not everyone will like the result, but it is unfailingly pure and strong, not only in the slow movement but throughout. The playing of the Chicago orchestra is magnificent – note the cellos in the second subject of the first movement, and the articulation of the anapaestic rhythms in the scherzo – and the recording is full and precise. The high-level cassette transfer matches the disc in its massive richness of texture, although the very resonant bass needs cutting back.

Loughran's account, like Barbirolli's before him with the same orchestra, is outstanding. At bargain price and with excellent sound, and the *Haydn variations* as a bonus, it should not be missed. Loughran's approach is unobtrusively direct. He is rarely if ever concerned to underline interpretative points, yet as the concentration grows after the deceptively gentle start, so one appreciates more and more the satisfying assurance with which he solves every problem. His tempi – except perhaps for a relatively slow account of the scherzo – are unexceptionable, and like Barbirolli he believes in adopting expressive phrasing within a basically steady tempo. The Hallé strings are in excellent form, beautifully recorded, and so for that matter are all the sections of the orchestra. The cassette is quite lively and full, but does not match the disc in bite at the top.

Kertesz has the advantage of first-class modern Decca recording. This is a distinguished performance, the finest of his Brahms cycle. It is a serious, straight-faced reading, powerful yet resilient, with the slow movement emerging as an elegy – aptly enough, since this was one of the last records that Kertesz made before his tragic death. On the one hand there is dignity and grandeur, on the other delicacy and lyricism. At Jubilee price this remains competitive with a first-class cassette equivalent – admirably full and brilliant.

Karajan's mid-1960s version, now on Accolade, is also an impressive reading and certainly one of the finer versions of this work. The *Passacaglia* has splendid grip in his hands, and so too does the eloquent slow movement. The recording does not sound its age.

The Philips Sequenza issue offers a good balance, although the recording now begins to show its age in the timbre of the upper strings. But Haitink is not at his most penetrating in this symphony; although the playing of the Concertgebouw Orchestra is first-class and while the reading, direct and straightforward, is not without appeal, this has much less character (as well as less idiosyncrasy) than Jochum in the same price-range. The cassette transfer is lively, especially on side two.

Barbirolli's PRT version makes another fair bargain recommendation. The playing lacks some brilliance – for example the brass in the last movement – but generally this is a most satisfying performance, with the first movement pressed ahead with just the right degree of urgency, and the second warm and romantic. The recording, though not outstanding, is still acceptable, although the cassette is more sharply focused (and sounds brighter) on side two.

Tragic overture, Op. 81; Variations on a theme of Haydn (St Anthony chorale), Op. 56a; (i) *Alto rhapsody, Op. 53.*

(B) **(*) Con. CC/*CCT* 7536. VPO, Boehm, (i) with Ludwig, V. Singverein.

The spacious account of the *Alto rhapsody* is the gem of Boehm's collection of shorter Brahms pieces. Christa Ludwig is wonderfully intense in her illumination of both words and music, producing glorious tone-colours despite the extra strain on breath-control from the slow tempi. The *Tragic overture* is given a strong traditional reading; but, with the violin section somewhat unflatteringly recorded, the *Variations* have their disappointments, very much in the heavyweight German tradition and with generally slow tempi made heavier by even stressing. Note too that no room was found for the *Academic festival overture*. However, at bargain price this is well worth considering for the beautiful performance of the *Rhapsody*, and there are surprisingly few available versions of the *Variations* not coupled to one of the symphonies. The cassette transfer is perfectly acceptable although it lacks some of the bright upper range of the LP (not necessarily a disadvantage). The turn-over comes, irritatingly, in the middle of the *Variations*, but the break is not clumsy.

Variations on a theme of Haydn (St Anthony chorale), Op. 56a.

(M) *** Decca SPA/*KCSP* 121. LSO, Monteux – ELGAR: *Enigma variations.****

** Decca SXL 7004. Chicago SO, Solti – SCHOENBERG: *Variations.***

Monteux offers a fresh, enjoyable performance to match his *Enigma variations* on the reverse. The orchestral playing is excellent, and the vigorous style gives the music a splendid forward impulse. The bright recording still sounds well. There is a fairly good cassette transfer of Monteux's performance, but it is not among this company's best.

Solti gives a performance of high tension and keen control, helped by immaculate playing from the Chicago orchestra. There are few accounts more dramatic but many more affectionate. It made a better coupling as a fill-up for Solti's recording of the *German Requiem* than it does here for a controversial version of the Schoenberg *Variations*. Excellent Decca sound.

CHAMBER MUSIC

(i) *Cello sonatas Nos. 1–2;* (ii; iii) *Clarinet quintet;* (iv) *Clarinet sonatas Nos. 1–2;* (v) *Horn trio;* (vi; vii) *Piano quartets Nos. 1–3;* (vi) *Piano trios Nos. 1–3;* (viii) *Piano quintet;* (iii) *String quartets Nos. 1–3;* (iii; ix) *String quintets Nos. 1–2;* (iii; ix; x) *String sextets Nos. 1–2;* (xi) *Violin sonatas Nos. 1–3.*

** DG 2740 277 (15)/*3378 122* (4) – see below [id.]. (i) Rostropovich, Serkin; (ii) Leister; (iii) Amadeus Qt; (iv) Leister, Demus; (v) Hauptmann, Brandis, Vásáry; (vi) Vásáry, Brandis, Borwitzky; (vii) Christ; (viii) Pollini; Italian Qt; (ix) Aronowitz; (x) Pleeth; (xi) Zukerman, Barenboim.

About ten years ago, DG issued a fifteen-record set devoted to the Brahms chamber music; five of the records included here are inherited from it. These are the *Clarinet sonatas* and the *Quintet*, which Karl Leister recorded in the 1960s, the *String quintets*, Opp. 88 and 111 with the Amadeus Quartet and Cecil Aronowitz as second viola, and the two *Sextets*, Opp. 18 and 36 which are also all from the 1960s. The three *Violin sonatas* are offered by Zukerman and Barenboim who give expansive, songful accounts that may strike some listeners as overripe, but there is much to admire here, and the recordings are first-class. These come from the 1970s, as do the LaSalle accounts of the *String quartets* which are well-drilled, streamlined but unsympathetic readings that convey scant pleasure. The engineers do not help matters by a rather too forward balance, which gives no space round the sound. Things are worse in the *F minor Piano quintet* in which Pollini is so forward that the Quartetto Italiano is masked. Masterly playing, if lacking in spontaneity and tenderness.

The remaining six records are new, and all have been made using digital techniques. The three *Piano quartets* are in the capable hands of Tamás Vásáry, and three principals of the Berlin Philharmonic, and the *Piano trios* are from the same artists (minus viola). The performances are handicapped by forward and unnatural recording: it is as if you are listening to the players in the enclosed space of your living-room without there being sufficient room for the sound to expand. (True, the Beaux Arts Trio on Philips are a bit close, but the sound is not quite so unnatural.) The piano sounds artificial and not integrated with its partners; and the bright, forward sound of the stringed instruments is achieved at the expense of a natural tonal bloom. Things are somewhat better in the *Horn trio* in which Norbert Hauptmann shines. Best of all is the disc coupling the two *Cello sonatas* in which Rostropovich and Serkin produce a glorious wealth of tone. (Listeners must be prepared for the occasional moan from the participants.) The engineers get better results here.

The four chrome cassettes offer the *Cello sonatas*, the *Violin sonatas*, Opp. 78 and 100, the *First Piano trio*, the *Clarinet trio*, the Op. 51 *String quartets*, the *Piano quintet*, *Clarinet quintet* and the Op. 18 *Sextet*. Transfers are fresh, vivid and clean, levels good, if somewhat variable between works. Three of the eight sides include two works, but only one piece is split between sides, the Opus 51/2 *String quartet*.

Cello sonatas Nos. 1 in E min., Op. 38; 2 in F, Op. 99.

*** DG Dig. **410 510-2**; 2532/*3302* 073 [id.]. Rostropovich, Serkin.

**(*) Decca SXL/*KSXC* 6979 [Lon. CS/*5-7208*]. Harrell, Ashkenazy.

Cello sonata No. 1.

*(*) Nimbus 2111. Fleming, Parsons – SCHUBERT: *Arpeggione sonata.***

The partnership of the wild, inspirational Russian cellist and the veteran Brahmsian pianist is a challenging one, devised to give glamour to DG's *Brahms edition*. It proves an outstanding success with inspiration mutually enhanced, whether in the lyricism of Opus 38 or the heroic energy of Opus 99. Good if close recording with a matching chrome cassette. The balance is emphasized by the clarity of the compact disc, and the cello sounds almost as if coming from immediately inside the speakers. The various grunts and noises made by the participants also come over only too clearly. But the music-making, with all its fervour, is tellingly projected and listening becomes a very involving experience.

Harrell and Ashkenazy give almost ideal performances of the two Brahms *Cello sonatas*, strong and passionate as well as poetic. But although they are naturally recorded and well balanced, the acoustic is resonant and the imagery lacks the last degree of sharpness of focus. The cassette transfer is first-class but reflects the slightly hazy quality of the disc.

Amaryllis Fleming and Geoffrey Parsons play with passionate commitment but without any excessive rubato or expressive indulgence. There is a good sense of forward movement and a keen awareness of the importance of phrasing. Geoffrey Parsons has enormous vitality yet never swamps his partner. Unfortunately the Nimbus recording is simply not expansive enough, though the quadrophonic encoding may in part account for this.

Clarinet quintet in B min., Op. 115.
(M) *** Ph. 6570/*7310* 918. Berlin PO Octet (members) – DVOŘÁK: *Bagatelles.****
*** Chan. ABR/*ABT* 1035. Hilton, Lindsay Qt.
(M) *** Decca Ace SDD 575. Schmidl, New V. Octet (members) – WEBER: *Introduction* etc.***
(M) **(*) Decca Ace SDD 249 [Lon. STS 15408]. Boskovsky, Vienna Octet (members) – WAGNER: *Adagio.****
(M) **(*) Argo ZK/*KZKC* 62. Brymer, Allegri Qt – WAGNER: *Adagio.***(*)
(*) Decca SXL 6998. Hacker, Fitzwilliam Qt – WOLF: *Italian serenade.* *
(B) *(*) PRT GSGC/*ZCGC* 2015. Brymer, Prometheus Ens.

The Philips reissue offers a substantial coupling and first-class recording, with a matching cassette of demonstration quality. It also has the advantage of being in the medium-price bracket. The Berlin performance is exceptionally beautiful and faithful to Brahms's intentions, an outstanding version in every way. The delicacy with which the 'Hungarian' middle section of the great *Adagio* is interpreted gives some idea of the insight of these players. It is an autumnal reading, never overforced, and is recorded with comparable refinement. With its unusual and attractive coupling it makes an excellent first recommendation.

The Decca version with Peter Schmidl and members of the New Vienna Octet has very strong attractions, but the performance by Janet Hilton and the Lindsay Quartet has an individuality that makes it even more memorable. At times Janet Hilton is bolder than Schmidl, especially in the Zigeuner interlude at the centre of the *Adagio*, where she provides an exciting burst of bravura. Her lilting syncopations in the third movement are delightful, and the theme and variations of the finale are full of character. The recording has striking presence, with a realistic overall balance, and the cassette transfer is of the highest quality; there is little appreciable difference between disc and tape, the former showing only a hint of extra range at the top.

But at medium price and with an engaging coupling the Decca version can also be recommended warmly. Schmidl gives an altogether stronger performance than Alfred Boskovsky's earlier Ace of Diamonds version. The soaring opening clarinet theme establishes the passionate commitment of the playing, and the degree of contrast between the *Andantino* third movement and the finale is particularly successful. The *Adagio* is played tenderly and expressively; the element of nostalgia (which dominates Boskovsky's approach) is not missing here, although it is held in balance with the other emotional demands of the music. Schmidl has a warmly luminous tone which he colours with considerable subtlety, and the silkily serene Viennese string playing is equally sympathetic. The recording is splendid.

Boskovsky has a warm, luscious tone, and it suits the relaxed atmosphere of the whole performance. Perhaps it is a shade too relaxed. The first movement could be tauter than this, and the slow movement is on the gentle side. But with its fascinating coupling (hardly a lost masterpiece) it is an excellent disc.

Jack Brymer gives a masterly and finely poised account which in terms of polish and finesse can hold its own with the very best. Apart from Brymer's well-characterized playing, the Allegri Quartet are also in excellent shape, and they are given the benefit of eminently truthful recording, with an admirable cassette transfer to match. But it must be conceded that something of the nostalgia and the melancholy of this score which the Berlin players catch so well, eludes them, and the Hilton and Schmidl versions are more searching.

Alan Hacker and the Fitzwilliam Quartet give a finely paced and beautifully integrated account of the *Quintet*, and there is no lack of sensitivity or imagination. The recording is rather forward, and as a result, less atmospheric than the rival Viennese version and at times has a tendency to harden. However, this is not serious enough to deter a recommendation, for musically this is as good as any.

Jack Brymer's earlier account with the Prometheus Ensemble is on PRT's bargain Collector label, but the performance does not challenge his later Argo version nor the recordings made in Berlin or Vienna. The solo playing is often beautiful, but the reading as a whole is a trifle wanting in real character, and does not find these admirable artists at their best.

A more recent recording by Karl Leister with the Vienna String Quartet is available to collectors in the Far East on the Camerata label (CMT-1071) which is remarkably full-bodied and rich in tone and, though closely balanced, produces most musical results. As a performance it can hold its own with any of those listed in the European catalogues and the surfaces are spectacularly silent, helped no doubt by the high level at which it is cut.

Clarinet sonatas Nos. 1 in F min.; 2 in E flat, Op. 120/1–2.
*** Chan. ABR/*ABT* 1020. Hilton, Frankl.

Janet Hilton and Peter Frankl give attractively straightforward accounts of the *Clarinet sonatas*. They seem at first sight less sophisticated and idiosyncratic than some previous rivals (notably Gervase de Peyer and Daniel Barenboim) but nonetheless they offer considerable artistic rewards. At times one feels that perhaps the pianist's phrasing could be more imaginative, but for the most part these performances have warmth and good musical sense, and the recording is natural, forward without being obtrusively close. The cassette is most successful too, with a high-level transfer giving presence to both artists and fine body of tone within an attractively warm acoustic.

Clarinet trio in A, Op. 114.
*** Ph. 9500 670/*7300 826* [id.]. Pieterson, Pressler, Greenhouse – BEETHOVEN: *Clarinet trio.****
*** HMV Dig. ASD/*TC-ASD* 146784-1/*4*. Meyer, Buchbinder, Schiff – BEETHOVEN: *Clarinet trio.****

(i) *Clarinet trio;* (ii) *Horn trio.*
** DG Dig. 2532/*3302* 097 [id.]. (i) Leister; (ii) Hauptmann; with Brandis, Borwitzky, Vásáry.

Horn trio in E flat, Op. 40.
*** Decca SXL/*KSXC* 6408 [Lon. CS 6628]. Tuckwell, Perlman, Ashkenazy – FRANCK: *Violin sonata.****

The *Clarinet trio* is not generously represented on record, but this issue by George Pieterson and members of the Beaux Arts Trio is unlikely to be surpassed either as a performance or recording for many years. Masterly playing from all three artists. The cassette transfer is enjoyably warm and natural.

Sabine Meyer is no less excellent on HMV and the recording is much better balanced than the Leister–Vásáry–Borwitzky version on DG. Everything is played with great inner vitality and freshness, and there is not a breath of routine anywhere. An eminently satisfactory alternative to the Beaux Arts and, though not musically superior to the DG, it is to be preferred as giving the more pleasing and natural sound. The cassette too is first-class in every way.

A superb performance of Brahms's marvellous *Horn trio* from Tuckwell, Perlman and Ashkenazy. They realize to the full the music's passionate impulse, and the performance moves forward from the gentle opening, through the sparkling scherzo (a typical Brahmsian inspiration, broad in manner as well as vivacious, with a heart-warming trio), the more introspective but still outgiving *Adagio* and the gay, spirited finale. The recording is worthy of the playing, although the engineers in their care not to out-balance the violin with the horn have placed the horn rather backwardly. They should have trusted Brahms: he knew what he was doing when he invented this unusual but highly effective combination. The cassette transfer of the Decca performance is disappointing by this company's usually high standards. The level is rather low and this seems to affect adversely the recording balance in favour of the solo horn. The Franck coupling is much better.

The DG coupling first appeared in the *Brahms edition*. The playing is excellent, but the forwardly balanced sound picture, especially in the *Clarinet trio*, is much less praiseworthy. On the whole the chrome tape sounds better than the disc, as the sound is mellowed a little by the transfer, especially the *Horn trio* which is more recessed because of a lower level. All the same it would be perverse to recommend this in preference to the separate Philips and Decca versions listed above.

Piano quartet No. 1 in G min., Op. 25.
(M) **(*) DG Acc. 2542/*3342* 140 [2530 133]. Gilels, Amadeus Qt.

As might be expected, Gilels's account of the *G minor Quartet* with members of the Amadeus has much to recommend it. The great Soviet pianist is in impressive form and most listeners will respond to the withdrawn delicacy of the scherzo and the gipsy fire of the finale. The slow movement is perhaps somewhat wanting in ardour and the Amadeus do not sound as committed and fresh as their keyboard partner. At medium price, however, this version enjoys an additional advantage, and in any event rival versions are hardly thick on the ground. The DG recording is well-balanced and clean, and admirers of these distinguished artists need not hesitate. The high-level cassette transfer is first-class, vivid, wide-ranging and well-balanced.

(i) *Piano quintet; String quartets Nos. 1–3.*
(M) **(*) Ph. 6717/*7671* 010 (3) [id.]. (i) Pollini; Italian Qt.

Piano quintet in F min., Op. 34.
**(*) DG 2531/*3301* 197 [id.]. Pollini, Italian Qt.
(M) ** DG Priv. 2535/*3335* 418 [139 397]. Eschenbach, Amadeus Qt.
(M) * CBS 60261/*40-* [MS 6631]. Serkin, Budapest Qt.

There is some electrifying and commanding playing from Pollini, and the Italian Quartet is eloquent too. The balance, however, is very much in the pianist's favour; he dominates the texture rather more than is desirable, and occasionally masks the lower strings. There are minor agogic exaggerations but neither these nor the other reservations need necessarily put off prospective purchasers. The cassette offers admirable quality, cleanly focused and well-balanced, to match the disc closely.

Christoph Eschenbach gives a powerful – sometimes overprojected – account of his part and the Amadeus provide impressive support. This version is by no means to be dismissed at medium price, for the recording is excellent. The high-level cassette transfer too is outstandingly successful, full-bodied and clear.

Any performance in which Serkin participates is bound not to be without merit, but the close, thin-textured CBS sound precludes a recommendation. Disc and chrome cassette are closely matched.

The Italian Quartet's set of the *String quartets* is quite simply the best, but they are available separately – see below – and readers must decide for themselves whether or not they want a package-deal to include the *Piano quintet.*

Piano trios Nos. 1 in B, Op. 8; 2 in C, Op. 87; 3 in C min., Op. 101; 4 in A, Op. posth.
(M) *** Ph. 6770/*7650* 007 (2) [id.]. Beaux Arts Trio.
*** Chan. Dig. DBRD/*DBTD* 2005 (2) (without *No. 4*). Borodin Trio.

Piano trios Nos. 1 and 3.
(M) *** Decca Ace SDD 540. Katchen, Suk, Starker.

Piano trio No. 2; Cello sonata No. 2, Op. 99.
(M) *** Decca Ace SDD 541. Katchen, Suk, Starker.

The Beaux Arts set was originally issued on two separate full-priced discs at the beginning of 1968. Now they are together in a box with an excellent tape equivalent. The set includes the *A major Trio*, which may or may not be authentic, but is certainly rewarding. The performances are splendid, with strongly paced, dramatic allegros, consistently alert, and thoughtful, sensitive playing in slow movements. Characterization is positive (yet not over-forceful), and structural considerations are well judged: each reading has its own special individuality. The sound is first-class, and the cassettes offer demonstration quality, the resonance of Bernard Greenhouse's cello richly caught without any clouding of the focus.

The Borodin Trio give most musical and sensitive accounts of the three trios that convey the sense of music-making in the home. Theirs are not high-powered performances in the manner of Brandis–Vásáry–Borwitzky and they are accorded infinitely more natural recording. There is strength when it is called for, lightness of touch and a sense of repose. They are not always perfectly in tune (the opening of the slow movement of Op. 8 is an example – and there are suspicions elsewhere) and this might well prove tiresome on repetition. Although the Beaux Arts Trio recordings are older (and not quite as good as this excellent new set), they remain the safer recommendation. Moreover, while Op. 8 occupies two sides in the Chandos set, Philips have managed to find room for the doubtful *A major*, Op. posth. The chrome cassettes have no lack of body and range, and reproduce the piano tone most beautifully. However, there is some fizziness at the very top.

Julius Katchen and his team judge the tempi admirably and resist the temptation to dwell too lovingly on detail. In addition they are given really excellent recording. SDD 541 represents the results of Katchen's last recording sessions before his untimely death. They were held at the Maltings, and the results have a warmth that did not always characterize Katchen's recording of Brahms. The coupling may be unconventional, but both the tough *C major Trio* and the epic, thrustful *Cello sonata* are given strong and characterful performances.

String quartets Nos. 1–3.
(M) *** Ph. 6703 029 (3) [id.]. Italian Qt – SCHUMANN: *Quartets Nos. 1–3.****
(M) *(*) Sup. 1111 3451/2. Prague Qt.

String quartets Nos. 1 in C min.; 2 in A min., Op. 51/1 and 2.
(M) *** Ph. 6570/*7310* 919. Italian Qt.
(M) ** Argo ZK 89. Allegri Qt.

String quartet No. 3 in B flat, Op. 67.
(M) *** Ph. 6503/*7303* 061. Italian Qt – SCHUMANN: *Quartet No. 2.****
*(*) DG 2531/*3301* 343 [id.]. LaSalle Qt – SCHUMANN: *Piano quintet.**(*)

The recordings by the Italian Quartet are available either in a package with Schumann, or separately as above. Marvellously played, with detail sensitively observed, they are also admirably recorded and there are excellent cassette equivalents of the individual issues. The coupling of the two Op. 51 *Quartets* is especially fine, with a searching and penetrating reading of the *C minor*, revealing depths that elude other performers. The *A minor* is hardly less fine.

Both the Allegri and the Prague players are preferable to the LaSalle Quartet, but the Prague Quartet is let down by indifferent recording, although the playing is very musical, relaxed, without in any sense being wanting in concentration, but perhaps without the last ounce of distinction.

The Allegri players are warmer and more humane and their accounts of these masterpieces are eminently well served by the engineers. Their playing falls short of the elegance that their finest rivals can command, but this is a serviceable and recommendable coupling.

The LaSalle Quartet give efficient, streamlined accounts of both quartets but convey little sense of feeling or tenderness. These are not performances that bring one closer to the music, though there is no question of the polish and expertise of these players, or the quality of the recording, which is equally impressive on both disc and tape.

String quintets Nos. 1 in F, Op. 88; 2 in G, Op. 111.
(M) *** Ph. 6503/*7303* 110. Berlin PO Octet (members).
(M) ** Argo ZK 94. Allegri Qt, Ireland.

These splendid works are admirably served by this Philips reissue. The performances by the Berlin Philharmonic group are searching and artistically satisfying, combining freshness with polish, warmth with well-integrated detail. The sound, though not entirely transparent, is full and well balanced, the richness of texture suiting the music very well, on both the disc and the excellent cassette, which is one of Philips's best. Indeed the transfer of *No. 1*, made at the highest level, is in the demonstration class.

Ardent playing from the Allegris who adopt relaxed tempi and convey real pleasure in their music-making. Some listeners may be a little worried by excessive vibrato: the slow movement of the *G major* in particular suffers in this respect from both the leader and the first viola. However, these are generally pleasing performances.

String sextet No. 1 in B flat, Op. 18.
*** CRD CRD 1034/*CRDC 4034*. Augmented Alberni Qt – SCHUBERT: *String quartet No. 12 (Quartettsatz).****

Brahms-lovers who normally fight shy of his chamber music are urged to try this work (scored for two violins, two violas and two cellos) with its richly orchestral textures. The second-movement theme and variations is immediately attractive, while the *Ländler*-like trio of the scherzo will surely find a ready response in any lover of Viennese-style melody. In short this is a most rewarding piece, especially when it is played as eloquently as it is here, with a ripely blended recording to match the warmth of the playing. At times one might feel that a degree more fire would be welcome, but the performance does not lack spontaneity. The tape transfer is immaculate and beautifully balanced.

String sextets Nos. 1–2.
(M) **(*) Ph. 6570/*7310* 570. Berlin Philharmonic Octet (members).

The Berlin performances of the two *String sextets* were originally issued on separate discs. Now they are coupled together in Philips's 'Musica da Camera' mid-priced chamber-music series. The Berlin ensemble respond readily to the glories of the *Second Sextet*, playing with warmth and eloquence; the *First* is slightly less committed, but still shows a greater degree of feeling than either the Amadeus or the Menuhin versions (available on EMI 1C 063 2015). The original recordings, spacious and well balanced, still sound tonally satisfactory and there are quite good cassette transfers, although the sound has a touch of shrillness and the balance gains from a top cut and bass lift.

String sextet No. 2 in G, Op. 36.
*** CRD CRD 1046/*CRDC 4046*. Augmented Alberni Qt – BRUCKNER: *Intermezzo and trio.****

A splendid account of the *Second String sextet* to match the excellence of the *First* by this same group. Both works have proved elusive in the recording studio, but now we have thoroughly recommendable versions on disc and tape. The playing is splendidly alive and succeeds in matching expressive feeling with vigour. The finale is especially spirited. On tape the sound is full-blooded, with a fresh, clean treble.

(i; ii) *Violin sonatas Nos. 1 in G, Op. 78; 2 in A, Op. 100; 3 in D min., Op. 108; Scherzo in C min.* (i) *4 Ballades, Op. 10; 7 Fantasias, Op. 116.* (i; iii) *21 Hungarian dances.* (i) *3 Intermezzi, Op. 117; 8 Pieces, Op. 76; 6 Pieces, Op. 118; 4 Pieces, Op. 119; Scherzo in E flat min., Op. 4. Piano sonatas: in C, Op. 1; in F sharp min., Op. 2; in F min., Op. 5; Variations and fugue on a theme by Handel, Op. 24; Variations on an original theme, Op. 21/1; Variations on a Hungarian song, Op. 21/2; Variations on a theme by Paganini, Op. 35; Variations on a theme by Schumann, Op. 9; 16 Waltzes, Op. 39.*
(M) *** Decca Ace SDDA 261/9. (i) Katchen; (ii) Suk; (iii) Marty.

The content of this album is discussed below under the separate reissues. Only the *Scherzo in C minor* is a new addition. The album makes a fine investment at Ace of Diamonds price. Brahms brought out the best in Julius Katchen; he is particularly good in the impulsive early music. If at times one could make small criticisms, the spontaneity and understanding are always there, and of course the excitement that comes when bravura is controlled by a sensitive and musical mind. The clear Decca sound is consistent throughout.

Violin sonatas Nos. 1–3.
(M) *** Decca Ace SDD 542. Suk, Katchen.
(M) ** Ph. 6570/*7310* 880. Grumiaux, Sebok.
* HMV SLS/*TCC-SLS* 143443-3/9 (2). Mutter, Weissenberg – FRANCK: *Sonata.**

Decca have squeezed all three sonatas on a single disc with no loss in quality; indeed the recording of the violin is especially smooth and real and the piano tone has both amplitude and clarity. The balance is excellent. Suk's personal blend of romanticism and the classical tradition is warmly attractive but small in scale. These are intimate performances, with much less of the grand manner than Szeryng and Rubinstein found in their readings on RCA. But in their own way they are most enjoyable, and they are a first choice.

On Philips too the three Brahms sonatas are now accommodated on one as opposed to two discs so as to compete with the long-serving

Suk–Katchen set on the Decca mid-price label. Mellifluous playing from Grumiaux, expertly partnered by György Sebok, but the overall effect is perhaps a shade bland. The recording is eminently acceptable, full and round on the disc, though in the cassette format the level is a shade too low.

On HMV the three sonatas occupy a side each, as opposed to the rival versions which accommodate all three on one record. This gifted young violinist scores over her rivals in the vividness of the recorded sound on disc and cassette alike, but the attractions of the set end there. Her playing is accomplished enough and not wanting in ardour or imagination, but the pianist is insensitive and lacking in feeling. He conveys little pleasure – and there are few performances in the concert hall or on record that have less magic. Not recommended.

PIANO MUSIC

(i) *4 Ballades, Op. 10; Chaconne* (Bach) *for the left hand; Scherzo in E flat min., Op. 4; Sonatas Nos. 1–3; Theme and variations in D min.* (trans. from *Sextet, Op. 18*). (ii) *Fantasias, Op. 116; Intermezzi, Op. 117; Pieces, Opp. 118/9; 2 Rhapsodies, Op. 79.* (iii) *Pieces, Op. 76; Variations: on a theme by Schumann, Op. 9; on an original theme, Op. 21/2; on a Hungarian song, Op. 24; on a theme by Paganini, Op. 35; Variations and fugue on a theme by Handel, Op. 24;* (iv) (Piano duos): *21 Hungarian dances; Sonata, Op. 34b; Souvenir de la Russie; Variations: on a theme by Schumann, Op. 23; on a theme by Haydn, Op. 56a; 16 Waltzes, Op. 39.* (v) (Organ) *11 Chorale preludes; Chorale prelude: O Traurigkeit; Fugue in A flat; Preludes and fugues: in A min.; A flat min.; G min.*

**(*) DG 2740 278 (11)/*3378 123* (4) – see below [id.]. (i) Zimerman; (ii) Kempff; (iii) Vásáry; (iv) Kontarsky Duo; (v) Planyavsky.

These eleven records encompass all Brahms's keyboard music including his output for organ and two pianos. The three *Sonatas* are allotted to Krystian Zimerman who gives powerful and concentrated accounts of all three. His version of the *F minor*, Op. 5, is particularly commanding and is worthy to stand alongside the great performances of the past. There is a leonine strength, tempered with great poetic feeling. Zimerman is well-recorded though there could be a little more space round the instrument. He also gives masterful and satisfying performances of the transcription of Bach's *D minor Chaconne* for the left hand, naturally more austere than the familiar Busoni and not otherwise available on record, and there is no want of tenderness as well as strength in the Op. 10 *Ballades*.

The variations are entrusted to Tamás Vásáry whose account of the Paganini sets sounds marvellously fresh and sparkling. His virtuosity is effortless and unostentatious as one would expect from this impressive artist. There are one or two mannerisms: in the thirteenth of the *Handel variations, Op. 24*, he inserts an expressive comma between the third and fourth beats which could prove irksome on repetition. Generally speaking, he is well-recorded too. For the late piano pieces, Opp. 116–119, DG turn to Kempff's recordings from the 1960s which still sound first-class: they are in some ways better balanced than some of the newer ones, and the playing is incomparable.

In the Op. 34b *Sonata* (its intermediate stage between string quintet and piano quintet) the Kontarsky brothers achieve their customary clarity of texture and unanimity of ensemble. They make heavy weather of much of it and are prone to interrupt the flow of the music by the odd mannerism. The *Hungarian dances* are spirited enough but as usual they are encumbered with a close and dry recording which underlines the impression of sobriety rather than charm. They also give us some transcriptions Brahms made in 1849 and published under another name – quite rightly, as they are of scant interest! The set is completed by a well-recorded disc of the complete organ music made by Peter Planyavsky.

On the whole this is an impressive survey which can hold its own against most competition, even when one considers each disc on its merits. In its cassette format, the selection is restricted to piano music only and includes the Opus 5 *Sonata*, the *Ballades*, Op. 10; *Chaconne*, *Pieces*, Opp. 76 and 117/8; *Fantasias*, Op. 116; *Intermezzi*, Op. 117; *Rhapsodies*, Op. 79; *Scherzo in E flat*, the *Handel* and *Paganini variations* plus those on an original theme, and piano duo recordings of the *Haydn variations*, *Hungarian dances* and *Waltzes*. The transfers are of good quality, but the modern digital recordings are more successful than the Kempff reissues where, although the sound is generally good, the low transfer level brings attendant hiss.

4 Ballades, Op. 10.
*** DG Dig. **400 043-2**; 2532/*3302* 017 [id.]. Michelangeli – SCHUBERT: *Sonata No. 4*.**

4 Ballades; 2 Rhapsodies, Op. 79; Waltzes, Op. 39.
(M) **(*) Decca Ace SDD 535 [Lon. STS 15527]. Katchen.
*(*) CBS Dig. **CD**; 37800/*40*- [id.]. Gould.

Fantasia, Op. 116; Pieces, Op. 76.
(M) *** HMV HQS 1439. Alexeev.
(M) ** Decca Ace SDD 533. Katchen.

Michelangeli plays an instrument made in the 1910s which produces a wonderfully blended tone and a fine mellow sonority. The *Ballades* are given a performance of the greatest distinction and without the slightly aloof quality that at times disturbs his readings. Gilels had the greater insight and inwardness, perhaps, but there is no doubt that this is very fine playing, and it is superbly recorded, with the chrome cassette matching the disc closely. The compact disc is even more impressive, and approaches demonstration standard.

Dmitri Alexeev also enjoys the advantage of really first-class piano sound, full-bodied and totally natural. As his earlier record of Opp. 117–19 showed (and it appeared after we had gone to press in 1977 and was deleted before the next edition appeared), he is a Brahms pianist to note. His playing has authority and produces an ideally weighted sonority with the right blend of colour. His mastery of rubato is consummate and these performances generally hold their own with any now before the public; indeed, they will be hard to beat.

Katchen's style in Brahms is distinctive. It sometimes has a slightly unyielding quality that suits some works better than others. In general the bigger, tougher pieces come off better than the gentle *Intermezzi*, which lack the sort of inner tension that Curzon or Kempff can convey. But such pieces as the two *Rhapsodies*, Op. 79, are splendidly done, and so are the *Ballades*. The *Waltzes*, brief trivial ideas but on the whole extrovert, come somewhere in between. Katchen misses some of the magic with his uncoaxing style, but the brightness is still attractive. The recording of the whole cycle can be recommended in Decca's bright, slightly percussive manner of the mid-1960s.

Glenn Gould seems reluctant to let the *D minor Ballade* speak for itself and indulges in much exaggeration, lingering over cadences and losing any sense of natural movement. He has many insights of interest to offer but, overall, his view is too idiosyncratic to be widely recommended, and certainly not as an only version. The sound is dry and shallow, which is presumably what this artist likes, since his name is billed as co-producer. LP and chrome cassette sound very similar. The CD has added presence.

Hungarian dances Nos. 1–21 (for piano duet).
(M) **(*) Decca Ace SDD 536. Katchen, Marty.
** Ph. 6514/*7337* 107 [id.]. Katia and Marielle Labèque.

Katchen and Marty are first-rate, offering playing with real sparkle, and the recording is suitably brilliant. But Katchen plays Book 1 in Brahms's later arrangement for piano solo, so this is an alternative choice.

The Labèque sisters give a superb demonstration of their precision of ensemble in an almost immaculate account of these vigorous and colourful dances. But the expressive freedom and range of rubato are extreme to the point where the result sounds unspontaneous and mannered. This is better than rigidity in this music, but affection must always be heard to come from the heart. First-rate sound.

3 Intermezzi, Op. 117; 6 Pieces, Op. 118; 4 Pieces, Op. 119.
(M) ** Decca Ace SDD 532. Katchen.

3 Intermezzi, Op. 117; 2 Rhapsodies, Op. 79; Variations and fugue on a theme of Handel, Op. 24.
(B) *** PRT GSGC/*ZCGC* 2048. Vazsonyi.

6 Pieces, Op. 118; 4 Pieces, Op. 119; Rhapsody in G min., Op. 79/2.
*** Decca SXL 6831 [Lon. CS 7051]. Lupu.

6 Pieces, Op. 118; 2 Rhapsodies, Op. 79; 12 Waltzes, Op. 39.
*** Ph. Dig. 6514/*7337* 229 [id.]. Bishop-Kovacevich.

4 Pieces, Op. 119; Variations and fugue on a theme of Handel.
** CBS 76913/*40*- [Col. M/*MT* 35177]. Serkin.

Radu Lupu's late Brahms is quite outstanding in every way. He brings to this repertoire both concentration and depth of feeling. There is great intensity and inwardness when these qualities are required, and a keyboard mastery that is second to none. The quality of the recorded sound is wide in range and splendidly immediate, and his delicacy of colouring is most truthfully conveyed. This is undoubtedly one of the best Brahms recitals currently before the public, and no connoisseur of this repertoire should overlook it.

Bishop-Kovacevich gives performances of these shorter pieces by Brahms which are not only thoughtful but full of the sharpest contrasts. Even the gentle inspiration of the much-loved set of *Waltzes*, Op. 39 has him using the fullest range of dynamic and expression. The result is most compelling both there and in the later, more demanding pieces. Fine piano tone well caught by the engineers. The chrome cassette, however, does not quite match the disc in upper range, with the balance orientated to the middle.

Vazsonyi's recital too offers splendid Brahms playing. It is secure technically and the contrasts of mood of the three *Intermezzi* are nicely judged. There is a similar balance between the two *Rhapsodies*, but most rewarding of all is the finely characterized set of *Handel variations*. The variety of style and colour within this work is masterly. The slightly dry, but admirably full, bold recording suits the playing, and at medium price this is a formidable bargain. The cassette has not quite the upper range of the disc, but it is well-balanced and full in timbre.

Katchen is at his best in the stronger, more intense pieces; in the gentler music he is sometimes less persuasive, though his playing is never devoid of sensitivity. He is clearly if not very luminously recorded.

There are perceptive touches from Serkin in the Op. 119 *Intermezzi*, though the *B minor* has some curiously heavy-handed accents. The account of the *Handel variations* is also a compound of penetration and some curiously ugly mannerisms. Serkin is always an artist who inspires some awe for his quality of mind, and students of the piano and of Brahms should seek this out. The sound quality, however, is rather shallow and clangorous (the tape matches the disc); the studio obviously poses problems; and on these grounds Radu Lupu is to be preferred in Op. 119 and Vazsonyi in the *Variations*.

Piano sonatas Nos. 1 in C, Op. 1; 2 in F sharp min., Op. 2.
*** DG 2531 252 [id.]. Zimerman.
(M) ** Decca Ace SDD 534. Katchen.

Piano sonata No. 3 in F min., Op. 5; Intermezzi: in E flat, Op. 117/1; in C, Op. 119/3.
(M) *** Decca Ace SDD 498 [Lon. STS 15272]. Curzon.

Piano sonata No. 3; Scherzo in E flat min., Op. 4.
(M) ** Decca Ace SDD 539. Katchen.

Piano sonata No. 3; Theme and variations in D min. (from *String sextet, Op. 18*).
*** Decca Dig. SXDL 7561 [Lon. LDR 71061]. Lupu.

Curzon's account of the *F minor Sonata* is special. His approach is both perceptive and humane and his playing has great intensity and freshness. Technically too, this record is of the finest Decca vintage, and with Curzon at his peak, powerful and sensitive and above all spontaneous-sounding, this continues to hold its place at the head of the list.

The other two early sonatas have been well served by Katchen, Arrau and others, but never better than by Krystian Zimerman. He brings to them qualities of mind and spirit that more than justify the plaudits which greeted his record on its first appearance. The perfection of his technique can be taken for granted, but there is also a surpassing artistry that leaves no doubt that one is in the presence of a master. At the same time, such is its quality that attention is exclusively concentrated on Brahms and not Zimerman. Those who have hitherto regarded the *C major Sonata*, with its echoes of the *Hammerklavier*, as an uninteresting piece should lose no time in hearing Zimerman's performance. The work emerges with an altogether fresh urgency and expressive power, and the young Polish pianist has the qualities of intellect and temperament to do it full justice. The recorded sound is very good indeed.

Noble, dignified and spacious are the adjectives that spring to mind when listening to Lupu's Op. 5. He does not, perhaps, have the youthful ardour of Kocsis or the communicative qualities of Krystian Zimerman's account (which DG will surely make available separately during the lifetime of this book). At times in the first movement one feels the need for a greater sense of forward movement: Lupu's view is inward, ruminative and always beautifully rounded. His account does not displace the 1963 Curzon performance but makes a useful alternative to it. The *Variations* are at present only otherwise available in Zimerman's DG version, which some listeners might well prefer.

Katchen's playing of the first two sonatas hardly achieves the same compelling intensity as Zimerman, but the result is always exciting. These performances are brilliant and assured, and Katchen's account of Op. 5 is similarly commanding. The recording is excellent. But in the *F minor Sonata* Curzon, also on Ace of Diamonds, remains first choice.

Souvenir de la Russie; Variations on a theme by Schumann, Op. 23; Waltzes Nos. 1–16, Op. 39 (all for piano, 4 hands).

** DG Dig. 410 714-1/4 [id.]. Alfons and Aloys Kontarsky.

The *Souvenir de la Russie* is very lightweight and Brahms did not publish it under his own name. The *Schumann variations* are, of course, another matter as are the *Waltzes*, though the performances are a little short on charm.

Variations and fugue on a theme by Handel, Op. 24.

*** Decca SXL 6969 [Lon. CS 7197]. Bolet – REGER: *Telemann variations*.***.

Variations and fugue on a theme by Handel, Op. 24; Variations on a theme by Paganini, Op. 35.

(M) *(*) Decca Ace SDD 538 [Lon. STS 15150]. Katchen.

This first record by Bolet under a new Decca contract represents an exciting development, when this Philadelphia-trained Klavier-tiger has to be recognized as one of the most exciting representatives of an older school of virtuosi, an artist too little appreciated on record and in Europe. His playing in Brahms's best-loved set of piano variations is incisive and brightly revealing, intensely refreshing and concentrated. With excellent sound there is no finer version, and the coupling is fascinating too.

Brilliant though Katchen's performances are, they are not the finest of his impressive cycle. Oddly enough, for all their sheer pyrotechnical display, they remain curiously uncompelling. One admired the *Ballades* and the *Schumann variations* much more; these sound comparatively unspontaneous by their side.

There is also (on Sheffield Lab 4) a version of the Handel variations by Lincoln Mayorga which has been much admired by audiophiles. The interest of this record resides in its technique: it is a live performance directly cut on to disc with no possibility of retakes. The idea of prefacing the Brahms *Handel variations* with the Handel movement from which its theme derives is a good one but since the sides do not exceed seventeen minutes, a turn-over in the middle of the Brahms is inevitable. The sound is realistic enough but not better than – and in some cases not as good as – ordinary analogue tape-to-disc recordings. Mayorga's playing has clarity and good fingerwork to commend it, but on the evidence of this he is not the most imaginative of pianists, and the Brahms is not really competitive when placed alongside such artists as Katchen, Rogé, Arrau and Bishop-Kovacevich who have all recorded this in recent years. Besides the *Air with variations* from Handel's *Suite in B flat*, this record also includes Chopin's *Mazurka in A minor*, Op. 17/4.

Variations on a Hungarian song, Op. 21/2; Variations on an original theme, Op. 21/1; Variations on a theme by Schumann, Op. 9.
(M) *** Decca Ace SDD 537. Katchen.

One of the most worthwhile of the complete Brahms cycle that Julius Katchen recorded. The *Schumann* is a neglected work and so are the others, and they are played with the utmost persuasiveness and artistry by Katchen, who is also given the benefit of a vivid recording. This is a most compelling issue.

Variations on a theme by Paganini, Op. 35.
** HMV Dig. ASD/*TC-ASD* 143627-1/*4* [Ang. DS/*4XS* 38075]. Sgouros – SCHUMANN: *Études symphoniques.***

Dmitris Sgouros possesses a formidable technique and strong fingers. He is indeed something of a phenomenon and this memento of his playing at the age of fourteen has its place in the catalogue. However, this is basically a record designed to show off this youngster's ardent personality rather than a serious contender. It is perhaps going a little too far to call his playing brash but he does not resist temptations to play too fast and loud. Vásáry or Katchen are to be preferred. The recording is bold and clear. The LP has a slightly sharper focus than the tape.

ORGAN MUSIC

11 Chorale preludes, Op. 22; Choral prelude and fugue on 'O Traurigkeit, O Herzeleid'; Fugue in A flat min.; Preludes and fugues: in A min.; G min.
*** CRD Dig. CRDD 1104/*CRDC 4104*. Danby.

Danby gives restrained, clean-cut readings of this collection of Brahms's complete organ works, refreshingly at home both in the early and amiable *Preludes and fugues* – piano style not completely translated – and in the very late *Eleven chorale preludes* from the period of the *Four serious songs*. The sound of the Farm Street organ, beautifully recorded, is incisive rather than warm. The chrome tape is impressively faithful and well-balanced, the focus nearly always clean.

VOCAL MUSIC

(i) *Alto rhapsody, Op. 53;* (ii; iii) *German requiem, Op. 45; Nänie, Op. 82;* (iv) *Rinaldo, Op. 50; Song of destiny, Op. 54; Song of the Fates, Op. 89;* (iii) *Song of triumph, Op. 55.*
*** DG Dig. 2741 019 (4) [id.]. (i) Fassbaender; (ii) Popp; (iii) Wolfgang Brendel; (iv) Kollo; Prague P. Ch., Czech PO, Sinopoli.

Sinopoli's box of the choral music with orchestra for DG's *Brahms edition* brings performances both challenging and controversial which – particularly in the rare works – are a revelation. The *German requiem* is given a performance of extremes, generally very measured but consistently positive. Fassbaender makes a strong, noble soloist in the *Alto rhapsody*, but it is the other works which command first attention in such a collection, not least the one generally dismissed as mere occasional music, the *Triumphlied* of 1870 which, Elgar-like, had Brahms doing his patriotic bit. Sinopoli, helped by incandescent singing from the Czech choir, gives it Handelian exhilaration. There is freshness and excitement too in the other rare works, with Sinopoli lightening rhythms and textures. In *Rinaldo* for example – the nearest that Brahms came to writing an opera – Sinopoli moulds the sequence of numbers dramatically to make the 1970 Abbado recording for Decca sound square and heavy by comparison. René Kollo is the near-operatic soloist. The recording of the whole box, made in Prague, is warm and sympathetic with the orchestra incisively close and the chorus atmospherically behind if sometimes a little confusedly so. There is also a separate box containing the three best-known works from the above compilation.

(i) *Alto rhapsody, Op. 53; German requiem, Op. 45; Nänie, Op. 82; Song of destiny, Op. 54; Song of the Fates, Op. 89.* (ii) Choral music: *Ave Maria, Op. 12; Fest und Gedenksprüche, Op. 109; 8 German folk songs; 2 Motets, Op. 74; Songs, Opp. 17 and 104.*
*** DG *3382 018* (4) [id.]. (i) from above collection; (ii) from choral collection below; cond. Jena.

Tape collectors need not hesitate in acquiring this splendid box – a happy selection from the two larger collections on disc (see above and below). The transfers are of DG's highest quality, using chrome tape to its best advantage to secure the widest dynamic range and fine body and clarity. In the major works climaxes open up splendidly and most effectively, and the choral focus is always excellent. The shorter pieces (especially Op. 17) are delightful and again the sound is of demonstration standard.

Alto rhapsody, Op. 53.
*** HMV ASD 3260 [Ang. RL/*4RL* 32017]. Baker, Alldis Ch., LPO, Boult – R. STRAUSS: *Lieder***(*); WAGNER: *Wesendonk Lieder.****

Dame Janet Baker's devoted performance of the *Alto rhapsody* with Sir Adrian Boult (originally a fill-up to the *Second Symphony*) is well re-coupled in a mixed recital with the *Wesendonk Lieder* of Wagner and four Strauss songs. The Brahms remains meditative, even though the tempo is unlingering, and the manner totally unindulgent. Beautifully warm recording.

Alto rhapsody, Op. 53; Nänie, Op. 82; Song of triumph, Op. 55.
*** DG Dig. 410 864-1/*4* [id.]. Fassbaender, Wolfgang Brendel, Prague Philharmonic Ch., Czech PO, Sinopoli.

Taken from Sinopoli's collection of music for chorus and orchestra in DG's *Brahms edition*, this is a specially valuable coupling, presenting two highly enjoyable rarities including the exhilarating Handelian celebration of Prussian victory in 1870, the *Triumphlied.* Though Fassbaender has often sounded more tender on record, the *Alto rhapsody* is also given a fresh and compelling reading, set against the warm Prague acoustic. The chrome tape is transferred at only a modest level in the *Alto rhapsody* which sounds rather recessed. The *Song of triumph*, however, does not lack vividness, with the chorus generally well-focused.

Choral music – Female chorus: *Ave Maria, Op. 12; 13 Canons, Op. 113; Psalm 113, Op. 27; 3 Sacred choruses, Op. 37; 4 Songs, Op. 17; 12 Songs and Romances, Op. 44.* Male chorus: *7 Canons; Little wedding cantata; Songs, Op. 41; 23 German folk songs.* Mixed chorus: *Begrabnisgesang, Op. 13; Fest und Gedenksprüche, Op. 109; Marienlieder, Op. 22a; Motets, Opp. 29; 74; 110; Sacred songs, Op. 30; Songs, Opp. 42; 62; 104; Songs and Romances, Op. 93a; Tafellied Dank der Damen, Op. 93b.*
❀ *** DG Dig. 2741 018 (6). Hamburg N. German Broadcasting Corporation Ch., Jena.

This six-record collection of Brahms's unaccompanied choral music ranges wide, representing all periods of his career in intimate, warmly characterful writing, whether in motets, part-songs, canons or folksong settings. Like other boxes in DG's *Brahms edition*, it contains much buried treasure, not least the fine *Motets for double chorus*, Opp. 109 and 110, which – particularly in Op. 109 in biblical settings – find Brahms using that elaborate medium in joyful complexity and understanding. The box also includes pieces such as the *Songs, Op. 17* for women's voices, two horns and harp, with limited accompaniment, ravishing pieces. The Hamburg Choir gives radiant performances beautifully and atmospherically recorded with no hint of routine. Highly recommended.

Duets, Opp. 20; 28; 61; 66; Quartets, Opp. 31; 64; 92; 112; Ballades and Romances, Op. 85; Liebeslieder waltzes, Opp. 52 and 65; Zigeuner Lieder, Op. 103; 14 Children's folk songs; 49 Deutsche Volkslieder.
*** DG 2740 280 (5). Mathis, Fassbaender, Schreier, Fischer-Dieskau, Engel, Sawallisch, Kahl.

This box from DG's *Brahms edition* contains all his vocal ensembles for solo voices with piano, and they receive fresh, brightly affectionate performances from an almost ideally chosen quartet of distinguished singers accompanied by excellent, imaginative pianists. The writing here represents Brahms at his most engagingly domestic, though – as in the famous set of *Liebeslieder waltzes* – his imagination quickly took him beyond the normal capabilities of an amateur household.

Even so, you find an essentially domestic delight in the lovely folksong settings of the *Deutsche Volkslieder* and *Volks-Kinderlieder*, originally devised for the family of Robert and Clara Schumann. There is treasure to be found in all ten sides. Excellent recording.

Deutsche Volkslieder (42 German folksong settings).
*** EMI 1C 153 00054/5. Schwarzkopf, Fischer-Dieskau, Moore.

This collection of German folk-songs, published only three years before Brahms's death in 1897, represents the love of a lifetime. Particularly during his last years, when the creative springs ran less generously, he loved to set the folk-songs he had collected over the years – usually with straight, undistracting accompaniment, but almost always with some hint of genuine Brahms. Having so many short songs sung consecutively may seem too much of a good thing, but few singers in the world today could match Schwarzkopf and Fischer-Dieskau in their musical imagination and depth of understanding. It may well be wisest to take the collection a side at a time, but there are few folksong collections of any nation that can rival this in breadth of expression. The fact that the great classical masters tended to base their idiom on German folk-style should not prevent us from appreciating it as the voice of the country people. Gerald Moore proved the ideal accompanist, and the recording quality is rich and vivid, with some enchanting conversation-pieces between the two soloists.

German requiem, Op. 45; Tragic overture; Variations on a theme of Haydn.
(B) **(*) CfP CFP/*TC-CFP* 414422-3/*5* (2) [Ang. SB/*4XBS* 3838]. Tomowa-Sintow, Van Dam, V. Singverein, Berlin PO, Karajan.

German requiem; Variations on a theme of Haydn.
** Decca D 135 D 2/*K 135 K 22* (2) [Lon. OSA/*5*- 12114]. Te Kanawa, Weikl, Chicago Ch. and SO, Solti.
(M) ** DG Priv. 2726 078 (2) [2707 018]. Janowitz, Waechter, V. Singverein, Berlin PO, Karajan.

(i) *German requiem; Tragic overture;* (ii) *Alto rhapsody.*
*** HMV SLS/*TC-SLS* 821 (2) [Ang. SBL 3624]. (i) Schwarzkopf, Fischer-Dieskau; (ii) Ludwig; both with Philh. Ch. and O, Klemperer.

German requiem; Song of destiny, Op. 54.
(*) Ph. Dig. **411 436-2; 6769/*7654* 055 (2) [id.]. Janowitz, Krause, V. State Op. Ch., VPO, Haitink.

German requiem; Song of destiny; Song of the Fates, Op. 89.
**(*) DG Dig. 410 697-1/*4* (2) [id.]. Popp, Wolfgang Brendel, Prague Philharmonic Ch., Czech PO, Sinopoli.

Measured and monumental, Klemperer's performance would clearly have roused Bernard Shaw's Wagnerian derision, but, as so often, Klemperer's four-square honesty defies preconceived doubts. The speeds are consistently slow – too slow in the vivace of the sixth movement, where Death has little sting – but with dynamic contrasts underlined, the result is uniquely powerful. The solo singing is superb, and though the chorus is backwardly placed, the Philharmonia singers were at the peak of their form. Excellent recording well-refurbished, providing the additional benefit of generous fill-ups including a fine account of the *Alto rhapsody* from Christa Ludwig. Not long before we went to press, EMI made available a generally excellent tape transfer, issued on a single chrome tape in a box. The sound has plenty of body and quite good range, but one has to turn up the volume at the side-turn (which is well placed).

At about the same time, CfP reissued the 1977 Karajan set in excellent remastered pressings and with a cassette equivalent that is even more successful than Klemperer's. The chorus is both full and clearly focused and soloists and orchestral detail are vividly projected. Indeed the principal difference between Karajan's EMI version of the *Requiem* and his earlier DG set lies in the choral sound, altogether warmer, bigger and closer, with sharper dramatic contrasts. As a reading it is characteristically smooth and moulded, a complete contrast to Klemperer's four-square account. The soloists are both excellent.

Tomowa-Sintow sings with rich, creamy tone colour, while José van Dam is equally expressive, with smooth, firm tone. The fill-ups are given excellent performances, well worthy of Karajan.

Sinopoli's version, taken from his complete *Brahms edition* box, brings a performance of strong contrasts set against a warm, reverberant acoustic, very hushed, slow and intense in the first two movements, wild and energetic in the fugue of the third, building to a most exciting conclusion in the sixth movement, before the warm resolution of the seventh. Beautiful solo singing from Popp, but with Brendel rather unsteady. An excellent and unusual coupling of two rare choral works. The tape transfer level is, however, disappointingly low and pianissimos register less effectively than on LP.

Haitink (like Solti) chooses very slow tempi in the *German requiem*. There is a rapt quality in this glowing performance that creates an atmosphere of simple dedication; at slow speed *Denn alles Fleisch* (*All flesh is grass*) is made the more relentless when, with total concentration, textures are so sharply clarified. The digital recording offers beautiful sound on disc (the cassettes, transferred at a low level, are disappointingly amorphous and bass-heavy), and with outstanding soloists – Gundula Janowitz notably pure and poised – this is very persuasive, even if Klemperer shows even more grip. The fill-up is the rarely recorded *Schicksalslied* (*Song of destiny*), which is most welcome and is admirably sung and played.

Even more strikingly than in his set of the Brahms symphonies Solti here favours very expansive tempi, smooth lines and refined textures. There is much that is beautiful, even if the result overall is not as involving as it might be. Kiri Te Kanawa sings radiantly, but Bernd Weikl with his rather gritty baritone is not ideal. Fine recording, glowing and clear, with an excellent tape equivalent, full-blooded and only fractionally less cleanly detailed in the choral pianissimos.

On Privilege Karajan directs a refined performance of Brahms's big choral work, but though there are many beauties, it does not oust the magnificent Klemperer performance from first place. The solo singing is good, and some may prefer Gundula Janowitz's fresh style in *Ihr habt nun Traurigkeit* to Schwarzkopf's more coaxing, more deliberately beautiful manner. But generally both Schwarzkopf and Fischer-Dieskau are preferable, and the EMI recording is more forward. The fourth side brings a magnificent performance of the Brahms *St Anthony variations*, but that hardly sways the balance.

Liebeslieder waltzes, Op. 52; New Liebeslieder waltzes, Op. 65; 3 Quartets, Op. 64.

*** DG Dig. 2532/*3302* 094 [id.]. Mathis, Fassbaender, Schreier, Fischer-Dieskau; Engel and Sawallisch (pianos).

DG for its *Brahms edition* assembled these characterful yet well-matched voices. This sample from the complete set has one of the most successful recordings yet of the two seductive but surprisingly difficult sets of *Liebeslieder waltzes*. The chrome tape transfer offers demonstration quality; there is little to choose between disc and tape for presence and clarity.

Lieder, Opp. 3; 6; 7; 19; 43; 46–49; 57–59; 63; 69–72; (i) *91* (with viola)*; 94–97; 105–107; Mondnacht Lieder und Romanzen, Opp. 14; 32; Magelone Romanzen, Op. 33; Romanzen und Lieder, Op. 84; Zigeuner Lieder; Vier ernste Gesange, Op. 121.*

*** DG 2740 279 (10)/*3378 124* (4) – see below [id.]. Norman, Fischer-Dieskau, Barenboim; (i) Christ (viola).

Song-writing was for Brahms as natural as breathing, and this glorious collection, spanning the fullest breadth of his career, consistently bears witness to his unique genius, more as an exuberant songsmith than as a practitioner of the German Lied. For him, melody lay at the very heart of song-writing and, even more than Schubert, his songs go straight to the heart of German folk-song. Through most of his career he was more concerned with the immediate musical challenge of a poem rather than its literary merit, but this magnificent collection, recorded with love and understanding and not a suspicion of routine, effectively establishes that the Brahmsian approach in the world of Lieder provides a valid and important alternative to that of ostensibly subtler Lieder-composers such as his friend, Schumann, or Hugo Wolf. Fischer-Dieskau's 1972 recording of the culminating *Four serious songs* provides a superb conclusion, but for the rest this vast project brings entirely new recordings. Jessye Norman, full and golden of tone, consistently reveals how her art has developed, in most ways matching even the imagination of Fischer-Dieskau. Not the least important element is the playing of Barenboim, one who in accompanying Lieder gives an impression almost of improvisation, of natural fluidity and pianistic sparkle to match every turn of the singer's expression. Beautiful, faithful recording to match.

The cassette box offers four extended-length chrome cassettes of high quality and distils some of the finest songs including Opp. 3, 7, 32, 43, 47, 49, 59, 63, 86, the two *Songs with viola*, Op. 91, and the *Four serious songs*. On the final side are the *4 Vocal duets*, Op. 61 and the *Liebeslieder waltzes*, Op. 52 (see above). The quality is consistently sophisticated; transfer levels are slightly variable, but the balance is good and the solo voices are always vividly projected.

Die Botschaft. (i) *2 Songs with viola, Op. 91* (*Gestillte Sehnsucht; Geistliches Wiegenlied*). *Immer leiser; Die Mainacht; Meine Liebe ist grün; O komme, holde Sommernacht; Ständchen; Therese; Der Tod das ist die kühle Nachte; Von ewiger Liebe; Wie Melodien zieht es mir*.
**(*) Ph. 9500 785/*7300 859*. Norman, Parsons, with (i) von Wrochem.

The scale and tonal range of Jessye Norman's voice are ideal for many of these songs, but in some of them there is a studied quality which makes the result a little too static. That is particularly so in the most ambitious of the songs, *Von ewiger Liebe*, which mistakenly is put first. Nonetheless, there is much distinguished singing and playing here, and it is superbly recorded. The cassette has not quite the refinement of the disc, the voice losing something in presence at low level, and becoming slightly fierce at fortissimo.

Mädchenlieder; Zigeunerlieder, Op. 100.
*** Mer. E 77042. Walker, Vignoles – DVOŘÁK: *Folksongs* etc.***

It was Brahms's own suggestion to put together four of his songs on maidenly themes. Sarah Walker sings them with fine characterful tone and rich insight. The *Zigeunerlieder* too are most satisfyingly done if with fewer magic touches than one might expect from this remarkable singer. Excellent accompaniment from Roger Vignoles and truthful recording.

Rinaldo (cantata), *Op. 50*.
*** DG Dig. 410 865-1/*4* [id.]. Kollo, Prague Philharmonic Ch., Czech PO, Sinopoli.

Rinaldo; Song of destiny (*Schicksalslied;* for chorus and orchestra), *Op. 54*.
** Decca SXL 6386 [Lon. CS 26106]. King, Ambrosian Ch., New Philharmonia O, Abbado.

The cantata *Rinaldo* gives some idea of what a Brahms opera might have been like, but unfortunately for dramatic impact the text provides no music for the seducing Armida, and the score has only the one soloist. It is a rich and enjoyable work, nonetheless, the more so in Sinopoli's warmly persuasive reading with fine heroic singing from René Kollo and naturally reverberant recording.

The alternative Decca version offers the *Song of destiny* as a bonus with refined contributions from the Ambrosian Chorus in both works. Abbado directs strongly, but unfortunately James King is far from ideal in the role of Rinaldo. His Wagnerian Heldentenor is really too coarse for music that is much more easily lyrical than Wagner.

Die Schöne Magelone (15 Romances), *Op. 33*.
*** DG Dig. 410 644-1/*4* [id.]. Fischer-Dieskau, Barenboim.

Fischer-Dieskau's performance of this sequence of romances illustrating Ludwig Tieck's *The Love story of Fair Magelone and Count Peter of Provence* is taken from the big Lieder box of DG's *Brahms edition*. Not only does the singer bring his detailed expressiveness to every change of mood but, with the understanding encouragement of his accompanist, exceptional warmth. Other fine versions have been deleted, but this admirably takes their place, with excellent recording. The chrome tape is very good too, smooth and refined, with a higher level bringing added presence on side two.

4 Serious songs, Op. 121; Lieder: *Am Sonntag Morgen; Blinde Ku; Da unten im Thale* (folk-song); *Dein Blaues Auge; Die Mainacht; Mir ist ein schön's braun's Maidelein* (folk-song); *Sonntag.*
(B) ** PRT GSGC/*ZCGC* 2044. Forster, Schmidt.

A worthwhile reissue from the late 1960s. Norman Foster's rich bass-baritone voice brings a variety of colour to this well-planned recital which includes two charming folk-songs alongside major repertoire. Heinrich Schmidt provides good support, and those looking for an inexpensive but sympathetic version of the *Four serious songs* will not be disappointed. The recording is lifelike and well-balanced and the tape transfer generally well managed, although the upper range is not as wide-ranging as the disc. This expressive singing, essentially lyrical in style, communicates strongly.

Brian, Havergal (1876–1972)

Symphonies Nos. 6 ('Sinfonia tragica'); 16.
*** Lyr. SRCS 67. LPO, Fredman.

The cause of Havergal Brian has been ill served on records and this is the first wholly professional performance to reach us. It is stunningly well recorded and excellently played by the LPO under Myer Fredman. The opening of the *Sixteenth Symphony* (1960) is quite magical, and one is never unmindful of the presence of a stern and powerful imagination. It is the moments of stillness and tranquillity in Brian's music that leave the strongest impression. The years of neglect that he suffered served to stiffen his artistic backbone and deepened his view of life, but they also involved losses that might have been rectified had he heard more of his music in performance. Not all the awkwardness is the product of bluntness of utterance, and rhythmically he is not fleet of foot. But both these symphonies have genuine depths and a wholly personal vision. The *Sixth* (1948) withstands the test of time extremely well and will repay study. Let us hope that the *Eighth*, *Ninth* and *Eleventh* will be put on record; their power and eloquence are fully comparable. The recording has amazing clarity and body: the perspective is most musically judged, but there is no loss of vividness, presence or impact in getting a concert-hall balance. The sound is of demonstration standard.

Symphonies Nos. (i) *10 in C min.;* (ii) *21 in E flat.*
(M) ** Uni. UNS 265. Leicestershire Schools SO, (i) Loughran, (ii) Pinkett.

It was left to a small company and an amateur orchestra to make this first recording of a Brian symphony. Both are works of his old age; No. 10, a powerfully wrought and original one-movement work, dates from 1953–4 and is the more immediately appealing of the two. No. 21 was composed when he was in his late eighties and is in four movements. There need be no serious reservations about the recording, and the performances are astonishingly accomplished.

Songs: *Care – Charmer sleep; The chimney sweeper; The defiled sanctuary; Farewell; The Land of dreams; Lady Ellayne; Love is a merry game; The message; On parting; Piping down the valleys wild; Renunciation; Since love is dead; Sorrow song; The soul of steel; Take, O take, those lips away; When icicles hang by the wall; Why dost thou wound, and break my heart.*
**(*) Auracle AUC 1003. Rayner Cook, Vignoles.

If ever there was a compulsive composer, it was Havergal Brian, and it is refreshing to have here his immediate responses to a wide range of English lyric poetry over a wide range of moods. As his operas indicate, Brian had a sense of humour, and that comes out here, though, as in his symphonies, seriousness prevails. Brian Rayner Cook's baritone may not always be well-suited to recording, but he sings sensitively and intelligently and is beautifully matched by Roger Vignoles at the piano. Well-balanced sound.

Bridge, Frank (1879–1941)

Cherry Ripe; Enter Spring (rhapsody); *Lament; The Sea* (suite); *Summer* (tone poem).
*** HMV ASD 3190. Royal Liverpool PO, Groves.

This fine record spans the whole range of Frank Bridge's orchestral output from early to late. Writing in the early years of the century, the composer confidently produced a magnificent seascape in the wake of Debussy, *The Sea*, but already by 1914 his responses were subtler, more original. *Summer*, written in that fateful year, was free of the conventional pastoral moods of what has been called the 'cowpat' school, while in the last and greatest of Bridge's tone poems, *Enter Spring*, he was responding to still wider musical horizons in experimentation that matches that of European contemporaries. It was in that last period that Bridge, himself neglected, acted as mentor to a younger genius, Benjamin Britten, and instilled a comparable sense of economy and self-criticism. Even so, there is little direct likeness of style between Bridge and Britten, master and pupil. Groves's warm advocacy adds to the impressiveness. First-rate recording.

Elegy for cello and piano.
*** ASV ACA/*ZCACA* 1001. Lloyd Webber, McCabe – BRITTEN: *Suite* ***; IRELAND: *Sonata.***(*)

Though written as early as 1911, the *Elegy*, darkly poignant, points forward to the sparer, more austere style of later Bridge. It is good to have this important miniature included on this richly varied disc. The performance is deeply committed, though the recording balance strongly favours the cello. The cassette matches the disc closely.

Isabella (symphonic poem)*; A Prayer; 3 Tagore songs.*
*** Pearl SHE 568 [id.]. Walker, Chelsea Op. Group Ch. and O; Prospect Music Group, William Williams.

If you respond to Ravel's Mallarmé songs or even *Shéhérazade*, you should investigate the *Three Tagore Songs* (1922–5). They are highly imaginative works, beautifully fashioned and expertly scored with some of the hothouse exoticism of Scriabin and Szymanowski. They alone are worth the price of the record. The two companion pieces are also welcome additions to the catalogue: *Isabella*, based on Keats, is an early tone-poem which Henry Wood launched at the 1908 Prom season, and its language derives from such models as Liszt and Tchaikovsky. *A Prayer*, Bridge's only work for chorus and orchestra, dates from the war years and is an eloquent piece, a setting of Thomas à Kempis' prayer which, given Bridge's depression at the slaughter and carnage of the war and his strong pacifist instincts, obviously struck a deeply responsive chord. All three works are given with total commitment and much sensitivity by these artists and, apart from the reticent balance of the chorus, the engineering is excellent with a natural and lifelike perspective. There is an informative and helpful sleeve-note and our only grumble is at the design of the cover which is not as attractive as the record's contents.

(i) *Oration: Concerto elegiaco for cello and orchestra. Allegro moderato* (from unfinished *Symphony for strings*)*; 2 Poems.*
*** Lyr. SRCS 104. LPO, Braithwaite, (i) with Lloyd Webber.

Oration is one of Bridge's most searching and ambitious works, a full-scale cello concerto in a single movement half an hour long. It was inspired by the tragedy of the First World War, in which some of Bridge's closest friends had been killed. Julian Lloyd Webber gives a passionately committed performance, and although Braithwaite does not hold the massive structure together with quite the consistent tension it needs (slow music outlasts fast by a substantial margin) the mastery of the piece is not in doubt. The couplings are excellent, guaranteed to fascinate and equally extending our appreciation of a highly individual and long-neglected composer. Excellent recording.

Phantasm: Rhapsody for piano and orchestra.
*** Lyr. SRCS 91. Wallfisch, LPO, Braithwaite – MOERAN: *Rhapsody*.***

An excellent performance and recording of *Phantasm*, which dates from 1931 and finds Bridge at his most searching and exploratory. There are echoes of Berg and Scriabin, and the music is unfailingly thought-provoking and deeply felt.

There Is a Willow Grows Aslant a Brook.
(M) *** HMV Green. ESD/*TC-ESD* 7100. E. Sinfonia, Dilkes – *Concert* (English music).***

Bridge's 'impression', beautifully played, is a highlight in an excellent concert of English music, warmly recorded on both disc and cassette (see the Concerts section below).

Cello sonata.
*** Decca SXL 6426 [Lon. CS 6449]. Rostropovich, Britten – SCHUBERT: *Arpeggione sonata*.**(*)
** Nimbus 2117. Hocks, Jones – KODÁLY: *Sonata*.*(*)

Bridge wrote his *Cello sonata* during the First World War. At first sight it bears all the imprints of the English pastoral school with its pastel colourings and gentle discursive lines as well as a nod in the direction of Debussy. It has a sturdy independence of outlook nonetheless and a personality to which one increasingly warms. The craftsmanship is distinguished, the lines delicately traced, and the modulations are often personal. The playing is of an altogether rare order even by the exalted standards of Rostropovich and Britten, and the recording has immediacy, warmth and great presence.

The young cellist Christian Hocks brings freshness and commitment to Bridge's *Sonata*. He is forwardly placed by comparison with the pianist, who plays with great sensitivity and imagination, but the recording is acceptable, albeit not distinguished. But while the recording by Rostropovich and Benjamin Britten on Decca remains available it is a first choice both artistically and for recorded quality.

Phantasie quartet in F; (i) *Sextet for strings.*
*** Pearl SHE 570 [id.]. Hanson Qt (i) with Handy and Tees.

The *Sextet*, long under-appreciated, is one of Bridge's finest chamber works, not as dramatic or sharply original as the late quartets for example, but as felicitously apt for the rare medium of six strings as Brahms's masterpieces. It dates from 1912, before Bridge's idiom grew really spare and concentrated. It is well-matched on this fine record by the *Phantasie quartet in F minor* of 1905, one of the most successful works inspired by the prize set up by W. W. Cobbett, to link twentieth-century chamber music to the tradition represented by the free Fantasy form of the Elizabethans. Excellent recording.

String quartet No. 2 in G min.; An Irish melody; Christmas dance; Londonderry air; 2 Old English songs (*Sally in our alley; Cherry ripe*)*; Sir Roger de Coverley.*
*** Chan. Dig. ABRD/*ABTD* 1073. Delmé Qt.

As more of Bridge's works are recorded, so his stature seems to grow greater. The *String quartet No. 2* develops on the formula of the *Phantasie quartet* encouraged by W. W. Cobbett in the prize he founded, bringing together a sequence of movements thematically linked, each of which has a wide range of moods and tempi, phantasy-style. Not one of the three is strictly a slow movement, but the result is yet beautifully balanced and meticulously worked with memorable material to produce a satisfying and original structure. Though by 1915 disillusion had not set in to sour and darken Bridge's range of expression, his idiom here is quite distinctive. His series of four quartets may one day come to seem a landmark of English chamber music, and it is good to have this one in a generally first-rate performance, beautifully recorded on disc and chrome tape (which approaches demonstration quality and has fine range without an exaggerated treble response). The very enjoyable coupling offers five of his finely crafted and original pieces, based on folk tunes.

Trio (*Rhapsody*).
** Pearl SHE 547 [id.]. Georgiadis, Hawkins, Watson – BAX: *Rhapsodic ballad****; BERKELEY: *Trio.***

The *Trio* is for the unusual combination of two violins and viola, and comes from 1928, the period of the *Third Quartet* and the *Second Piano trio*. It is exploratory, questing and powerfully inventive, though not in every respect satisfying. It is played with conviction and some passion by these three players, and only the dryness of the recording lets things down.

Britten, Benjamin (1913–76)

(i) *Canadian carnival, Op. 19;* (i; ii; iii) *Scottish ballad, Op. 26;* (ii; iv) *Young Apollo, Op. 16;* (v; i) *4 French songs.*
❀ *** HMV ASD/*TCC-ASD* 4177 [DS/*4XS* 37919]. (i) CBSO, Rattle; (ii) Donohoe; (iii) Fowke; (iv) Kok, Ballard, Cole, Kaznowski; (v) Gomez.

This is a superb collection of early works of Britten, all of them previously neglected on record. *Canadian carnival* nods in the direction of Copland, but is still highly individual. The *Scottish ballad* (with two piano soloists) brings a caricature of what Scottish music represents, bagpipes and all, while *Young Apollo* (with piano and string quartet as soloists) is a fascinating exercise in colourings, a tour de force with barely any change of harmony. It directly echoes *Les Illuminations*.

Those are all works of Britten's early manhood, but the gem of the collection is the fourth of the works, written at the age of fourteen, the *Four French songs*, settings of Hugo and Verlaine, which have amazing maturity and emotional depth with flashes of genius worthy of Britten at his finest, as in Hugo's poem *L'enfance* where the child's song by the deathbed of its mother is recurringly represented by a poignantly gambolling flute solo.

The orchestration is amazingly original and assured, and though stylistically these lovely songs – which could well be called the *Four First songs* in parallel to the comparably beautiful *Four Last songs* of Strauss – owe much to the French impressionists, the depth of feeling is never in doubt.

Performances are all outstanding, with Rattle at his most inspired and Jill Gomez radiant in the songs. Recording of demonstration quality to match, with a splendid matching cassette, no less vivid.

Piano concerto, Op. 13.
(*) Chan. ABR/*ABT* 1061. Lin, Melbourne SO, John Hopkins – COPLAND: *Piano concerto.*(*)

(i; iii) *Piano concerto;* (ii; iii) *Violin concerto, Op. 15.*
*** Decca SXL 6512 [Lon. CS 6723]. (i) Sviatoslav Richter; (ii) Lubotsky; (iii) ECO, composer.

Violin concerto, Op. 15.
(M) *** Sup. 50959. Grumlikova, Prague SO, Maag – VAUGHAN WILLIAMS: *Concerto accademico.****

Both these works come from early in Britten's career, but as the Decca performances amply confirm, there is nothing immature or superficial about them. Richter – a regular visitor to Aldeburgh – is incomparable in interpreting the *Piano concerto*, not only the thoughtful introspective moments but the

Liszt-like bravura passages (many of them surprising from this composer). The *Violin concerto* is constructed in three movements, but the manner and idiom are subtler. With its highly original violin sonorities it makes a splendid vehicle for another Soviet artist, the young violinist Mark Lubotsky, whose Soviet-made recording (not available in the West) persuaded the composer that here was his ideal interpreter. Recorded in the Maltings, the playing of the ECO under the composer's direction matches the inspiration of the soloists.

Gillian Lin provides a useful alternative to Richter's classic recording. Miss Lin cannot match the Soviet master in detailed imagination, but from her sharp attack on the opening motif onwards she gives a strong and satisfying reading, well accompanied by Hopkins and the Melbourne orchestra. The recorded sound is wide-ranging and well-balanced and there is a lively cassette. It makes a fair alternative if you need the Copland coupling.

Nina Grumlikova's performance of the *Violin concerto* is outstanding and the work's final *Passacaglia* is played most movingly. The recording is one of Supraphon's best, and the coupling is equally desirable. Highly recommended, in spite of a grotesquely translated sleeve-note which tells us that 'usually slow movement is supplied here with vivace with a vivid stream of technique in double stopping and harmonics'.

(i) *Violin concerto;* (ii) *Sinfonia da requiem; Variations and fugue on a theme of Purcell, Op. 34;* (iii) *Variations on a theme of Frank Bridge, Op. 10;* (ii; iv) *Spring symphony, Op. 44;* (ii) *Peter Grimes: 4 Sea interludes and Passacaglia.*

(M) *** HMV SLS/*TCC-SLS* 5266. (i) Haendel, Bournemouth SO, Berglund; (ii) LSO, Previn; (iii) Bath Fest. O, Menuhin; (iv) with Armstrong, Baker, Tear, St Clement Dane's School Boys' Ch., LSO Ch.

One associates Britten's music above all with the Decca label – thanks to his own unique series of recordings – but this compilation of HMV recordings brings together fine performances, in generally full and excellent sound, of six works spanning the years when Britten emerged in full maturity, from the *Frank Bridge variations* of 1937 to the *Spring symphony* of 1949, years when he sought first to find a home in the United States but then in the midst of war found the need to return.

Previn is the conductor on the first two records. On one, the *Spring symphony* is a straight reissue of his fine, clean-cut and dramatic reading. On the other, the *Sinfonia da requiem* is generously coupled not only with the *Peter Grimes interludes* but the *Young person's guide,* all strongly and colourfully done. Ida Haendel's warmly expressive account of the *Violin concerto* is then coupled with a rather older but still acceptable recording, Menuhin conducting the *Frank Bridge variations*. The cassette transfers, on chrome tape, are extremely sophisticated (with the *Four Sea interludes* matching the demonstration quality of the LP). The *Spring symphony* is placed, uninterrupted, on side four.

Matinées musicales, Op. 25; Soirées musicales, Op. 9.

*** Decca Dig. **410 139-2**; SXDL/*KSXDC* 7539 [Lon. LDR/5- 71039]. Nat. PO, Bonynge – ROSSINI: *La Boutique fantasque.**** **C**

Matinées musicales; Soirées musicales; Variations on a theme of Frank Bridge, Op. 10.

*** HMV ASD/*TCC-ASD* 4388. SNO, Gibson.

A demonstration disc from HMV as far as quality is concerned, with string tone of extraordinary realism in the *Frank Bridge variations*. The ECO play well for Alexander Gibson and readers requiring this particular coupling need not hesitate either on artistic or on technical grounds. Both the *Matinées musicales* and the *Soirées* are comparative rarities in the concert hall, and their charm and high spirits are splendidly conveyed. The (iron-oxide) tape is good too, but does not quite match the upper range and thus the definition of the LP.

Bonynge's versions of the two sets of *Musicales* are also brightly played and extremely vividly recorded in the Decca manner. They are quite the equal of Gibson's and on the compact disc the sparkle in the upper range and the vivid orchestral detail are very striking indeed. The balance is forward but there is no lack of ambience. The chrome tape, transferred at a modest level for Decca, is disappointing – there is much less glitter than on the LP, to say nothing of the compact disc.

Men of goodwill; Young person's guide to the orchestra, Op. 34; Peter Grimes: 4 Sea interludes.
**(*) HMV Dig. ASD/*TC-ASD* 143628-1/*4* [Ang. DS/*4XS* 38049]. Minnesota O, Marriner.

The brief orchestral piece, *Men of goodwill*, a set of variations on *God rest ye merry gentlemen*, was constructed from music which Britten wrote in 1947 for a BBC radio feature. It is a slight but attractive piece. The Minnesota performances of the well-known music are a little stiff but enjoyable enough. First-rate digital sound and a vivid tape, although the focus on cassette is very slightly less sharp, notably at the climax of the *Young person's guide*.

The Prince of the Pagodas (ballet).
(M) *** Decca Ace GOS 558/9 [Lon. STS 15081/2]. ROHCGO, composer.

Britten wrote this lovely ballet score immediately after a tour of the Far East, where he had encountered the enchantment of the Balinese gamelan orchestra. That Eastern influence was finally to find expression in his *Parables for church performance*, notably *Curlew River*; but immediately, in this lighter, fairy-tale context, he drew on its influence and devised an enchanting idea for the pagoda music. This recording was originally made after the first performances at Covent Garden in January 1957. The stereo version sounds astonishingly well, with Britten's many offbeat fanfares ringing out superbly. Highly recommended; Britten's music, more than that of most long ballets, is concentrated enough in its argument to stand gramophone repetition.

The Prince of the Pagodas, Op. 57b: Prelude and dances.
(*) Uni. Dig. KP 8007. Adelaide SO, Measham – *Folksong arrangements.*(*)

The Prince of the Pagodas: Prelude and dances. Gloriana: suite.
**(*) HMV ASD/*TCC-ASD* 4073 [Ang. DS/*4XS* 37882]. Bournemouth SO, Segal.

David Measham here adds to his list of impressive records for Unicorn with an attractive coupling of the strongly characterized suite from Britten's full-length ballet and the first recording of Britten's own orchestral arrangements of his folksong settings, eight British, five French. Often the lightness of the original piano accompaniments must be counted preferable (particularly when the composer himself was playing), but orchestral sound gives extra dimensions in power and colour, notably in such a pay-off song as *Oliver Cromwell*. Gerald English is a first-rate soloist in the authentic Pears tradition, only occasionally overpointing, and Measham's own West Australian Symphony Orchestra (of which he was principal conductor for five years) plays spiritedly. The Adelaide orchestra is here not quite so incisive, but the suite is still given a strong and well-balanced performance. First-rate recording.

The HMV record pairs the ballet suite with music from *Gloriana* which by concentrating on the pageant sequence (the selection was made and prepared by the composer) may give a misleading idea of what is in reality a deep and moving work, but it is a fair stop-gap when, scandalously, the full opera still lacks a complete recording.

The suite from the ballet, described as *Prelude and dances*, was prepared by Norman Del Mar and accepted by the composer. That too bears witness to the intense imagination of the score, more than just memorable and colourful. The playing of the Bournemouth orchestra is not quite so crisp of ensemble as in some of its finest records, but these are both warmly understanding performances, vividly recorded. The chrome cassette too is outstandingly brilliant.

Simple symphony (for strings), *Op. 4.*
(*) Abbey ABY 810. Scottish Bar. Ens., Friedman – ELGAR: *Serenade*; WARLOCK: *Capriol suite*; WILLIAMSON: *English lyrics.***(*)

The Scottish Baroque Ensemble gives an energetic, warm-hearted performance of the youthful Britten inspiration, well recorded but not as polished as most of its rivals. The *Sentimental saraband* is particularly successful, played with feeling yet with the right degree of restraint, and the *Playful pizzicato* shows real high spirits.

By far the finest recording of the *Simple symphony* is the composer's own with the ECO, originally contained within an outstanding collection called *'Britten conducts English music'* (SXL 6405 – see below). The performance is also available in cassette format in another almost equally attractive miscellaneous compilation of English music played by various artists, called *'Greensleeves'* (see below). It is additionally reissued, as we go to press, recoupled to the *Spring symphony* – see under Vocal music.

(i) *Sinfonia da requiem, Op. 20;* (ii) *Symphony for cello and orchestra, Op. 68.*
*** Decca SXL 6641. (i) New Philh. O, (ii) Rostropovich, ECO; both cond. composer.

Sinfonia da requiem; Peter Grimes: 4 Sea interludes and Passacaglia.
֍ *** HMV ASD 3154 [Ang. S 37142]. LSO, Previn.

In Previn's HMV disc the *Sinfonia da requiem*, the most ambitious of Britten's early orchestral works, written after the death of his parents, there is the same passionate intensity as in his St Louis version on CBS (now deleted), but with far greater subtlety of inflection and execution. It is a warmer reading than the composer's own, less sharply incisive but presenting a valid alternative. So too in the *Four Sea interludes*, here – unlike the composer's own recording – presented in their concert form with tailored endings. Previn springs the bouncing rhythms of the second interlude – the picture of Sunday morning in the Borough – even more infectiously than the composer himself. These superb performances are presented in a sumptuous recording of demonstration quality. Indeed this is one of the very finest analogue recordings ever issued (particularly striking in the *Peter Grimes interludes*). The recording is not available on cassette, except within the boxed set of Britten's works – see above.

The composer's recording of the *Sinfonia da requiem* was first issued coupled to the *Cantata misericordium.* The performance is a definitive one and the recording excellent. Many may prefer the new coupling of the *Cello symphony*, which is also available coupled to Haydn's *C major Concerto.* The performance of the *Cello symphony* is everything one could ask for, and with the help of the score it immediately dispels any lingering doubts about the music. The initial impression of aridity was misleading. The style is perhaps not so immediately approachable as that of Britten's earlier works, but the same clarity of argument, the same magical use of sound is everywhere, and if at moments there is an echo of Shostakovich (deliberate compliment to the Russian?) or in the main theme of the finale a seemingly direct imitation of Copland's open-air style, the Britten characteristics are always uppermost. Though the work lasts a full thirty-five minutes, the recording is magnificent, and the English Chamber Orchestra fully justify the choice of players with splendid support for Rostropovich.

Sinfonietta, Op. 1.
*** Lyr. SRCS 111. ECO, Del Mar – BERKELEY: *Sinfonietta*; RAWSTHORNE: *Divertimento*; TIPPETT: *Divertimento.****

Britten's Opus 1 was written when he was in his teens and already a composer with a formidable list of works which have proved more than juvenilia. It has some Britten fingerprints, but points uncharacteristically towards central Europe – reflection no doubt of his desire at the time to study with Berg in Vienna. In this version with full strings, its astringency is tempered, but its seriousness and assurance are the more convincing, particularly in a performance as fine as this. Excellent recording.

Suite on English folksongs (*A time there was*), *Op. 30; Peter Grimes: 4 Sea interludes and Passacaglia.*
**(*) CBS 76640 [Col. M/*MT* 34529]. NYPO, Bernstein.

On the face of it Britten's *Suite on English folksongs* with its title quoted from Hardy is a relatively lightweight work, but this performance, like the première at the Maltings in 1975, reveals a darkness and weight of expression behind the seemingly trivial plan. The third movement, *Hankin Booby*, written for the opening of the Queen Elizabeth Hall in London, is an angular piece in which woodwind squeals in imitation of medieval manners. The other movements are less abrasive. For violins alone, *Hunt the squirrel* is brief, brilliant and witty; the final movement, *Lord Melbourne*, with its extended cor anglais solo, is plainly music written in the shadow of death. Bernstein's performance misses a little of the wit, but is warmly sympathetic, and the dramatic account of the *Grimes interludes* makes a fair coupling. Recording is good but not as full-ranging in the *Interludes* as, for example, the Previn HMV version.

Variations on a theme of Frank Bridge, Op. 10.
(M) ❀ *** HMV mono XLP/*TC-XLP* 60002. Philh. O, Karajan – VAUGHAN WILLIAMS: *Tallis fantasia.****

Variations on a theme of Frank Bridge, Op. 10.
*** Argo ZRG/*KZRC* 860 [id.]. ASMF, Marriner – BUTTERWORTH: *Banks of green willow* etc.***

Variations on a theme of Frank Bridge; The Young person's guide to the orchestra (*Variations and fugue on a theme of Purcell*), *Op. 34.*
*** Decca SXL 6450 [Lon. CS 6671]. ECO or LSO, composer.

If all stereo issues of the 1980s sounded like this Karajan mono-recording of the mid-1950s, there would be no need for a *Penguin Stereo Record Guide*! The sound is astonishingly fresh and vivid, and the playing of the Philharmonia strings is of the highest order of distinction. They produce beautifully blended tone, rich and full-bodied yet marvellously delicate at the pianissimo end of the dynamic spectrum. Karajan's reading is unaffected yet impassioned, quite electrifying in the *Funeral march*. The quality on cassette is at the very least as impressive as the disc (at times even more so) and one can hardly believe this is not real stereo. Indeed the recording compares well with some of the finest digital stereo issues of the 1980s. This is an issue that should never be out of the catalogue.

Britten goes more for half-tones and he achieves an almost circumspect coolness in the waltz-parody of the *Romance*. In the Viennese waltz section later, Britten is again subtly atmospheric, and in the *Funeral march* the composer is more solemn than Menuhin, showing here, as in the finale, that this is music to be taken seriously for all the lighthearted mood of the opening sections of the work. With its superb sound – a little under-recorded, but very natural – this is another example of Britten at his most convincing and spontaneous in the recording studio.

Though not even Marriner quite matches the natural warmth of expression of the composer himself in this music – compare the *Funeral march*, for example – his is a superb performance, if anything even more polished, and recorded with a vividness that sets new standards. With the beautiful Butterworth pieces for coupling it is a warmly attractive disc. The cassette transfer is vivid but slightly hard-edged.

The Young person's guide to the orchestra (*Variations and fugue on a theme of Purcell*), *Op. 34.*
*** Decca SXL 6110 (without narration). LSO, composer – *Serenade.****
*** HMV ASD/*TC-ASD* 2935 [Ang. S/*4XS* 36962]. Previn, LSO, Previn – PROKOFIEV: *Peter and the Wolf.****
(M) *** HMV Green. ESD/*TC-ESD* 7114 (without narration). Royal Liv. PO, Groves – PROKOFIEV: *Peter*; SAINT-SAËNS: *Carnival.****
(B) **(*) Con. CC/*CCT* 7519. Connery, RPO, Dorati – PROKOFIEV: *Peter.****
(M) ** Decca VIV/*KVIC* 40 (without narration). RPO, Dorati – PROKOFIEV: *Peter*; R. STRAUSS: *Till Eulenspiegel.****
(B) ** CfP CFP/*TC-CFP* 185. Richard Baker, New Philh. O, Leppard – PROKOFIEV: *Peter.***
** RCA RL/*RK* 12743 [ARL1/*ARK1* 2743] (without narration). Phd. O, Ormandy – PROKOFIEV: *Peter.***(*)

Britten takes a very brisk view of his *Variations*, so brisk that even the LSO players cannot always quite match him. But every bar has a vigour which makes the music sound even more youthful than usual, and the headlong, uninhibited account of the final fugue (trombones as vulgar as you like) is an absolute joy. An unexpected coupling for the *Serenade* on the reverse, but a marvellous one for old and young alike. Outstanding recording, except that at one point the trumpet is pushed from one side to the other: but only a very technically minded listener need worry about that.

Quite apart from the brilliance of the LSO's playing and the ripe realism of the recording, Previn's account of the *Young person's guide* is characterized by his own dry microphone manner in the narration. This is obviously directed at older children than those to whom Mia Farrow is talking in *Peter and the Wolf*, but it still makes a delightful coupling. The cassette transfer has plenty of impact and detail is quite good. The refinement only slips momentarily at the sumptuous opening statement and at the final climax of the fugue.

Groves's recording has been imaginatively and generously recoupled (at medium price) with excellent versions of *Peter and the Wolf* and the *Carnival of the Animals*, making a superb anthology for children of all ages. Groves's performance of the *Variations* is lively and genial; if it lacks the last degree of finesse, it has both high spirits and a fine sense of pace. The trumpet variation displays splendid bravura, and the flute and clarinet variations too are engagingly extrovert. The recording is first-class, vividly colourful and full-bodied, with an outstandingly brilliant cassette transfer to match the disc in clarity of focus.

The Sean Connery/Dorati version is obviously aimed at the listener whose knowledge of the orchestra is minimal. Connery's easy style is attractive and this version should go down well with young people, even if some of the points are made rather heavily. The orchestral playing is generally first-rate. This is perhaps not a version for everyone, but many will like it for its spontaneity, to which Connery contributes not a little. The recording was originally made using Decca's Phase Four techniques, which can – and do – bring forward solo instruments. But in this instance such a balance seems justifiable and the sound is clear, with instrumental timbres slightly exaggerated by the close microphones. As so often with early Contour reissues, the cassette has a restricted range; here the transients are unacceptably blunted. The Decca Viva version of the same recording has been re-edited to omit the narration, and once or twice the ear senses that the continuity is slightly affected, although it is a marginal impression. The performance remains a good one and the sound is vivid, with the new cassette transfer especially successful. It has fine body and range and a greatly improved overall focus. The couplings are both highly recommendable.

The rather cosy narration by Richard Baker on CfP tends to hold up the flow of the music. The orchestral playing is lively and the recording good, but one feels that there are too many words here and this is not a version to stand constant repetition, although it would be suitable for school use. The cassette transfer is very successful.

Ormandy's performance is straightforward and very well played. It has no special individuality, and the recording is brilliant rather than sumptuous, although not dry. There is some blurring on the cassette at the opening and close of the work.

The Young person's guide to the orchestra; Peter Grimes: 4 Sea interludes.

(M) **(*) HMV SXLP 30240 [Ang S 36215] (without narration). Philh. O, Giulini.

The sound here is astonishingly fine for a recording dating from the mid-1960s, with excellent bloom and atmosphere and vivid detail. Giulini's manner is rather literal and detached, and the first three *Peter Grimes interludes* do not come so readily to life here as they do under Previn (see above). But the Philharmonia playing is superb, and in the final storm interlude there is no lack of excitement. Similarly the *Variations* take a little while to warm up, but with the Philharmonia in fine form there is much to enjoy; the bassoon and harp variations are especially memorable.

CHAMBER AND INSTRUMENTAL MUSIC

Alla marcia; 3 Divertimenti; 2 Insect pieces; Phantasy oboe quartet, Op. 2; Phantasy string quintet; Temporal variations.
**(*) Uni. Dig. DKP 9020. Wickens, Constable, Augmented Gabrieli Qt.

Derek Wickens, formerly principal oboe of the RPO and a consummate artist, should record much more. Here his contributions to the *Phantasy oboe quartet* as well as the two rediscovered works, the *Temporal variations* and the *Insect pieces*, are incisive and classically poised rather than deeply expressive. The Gabrieli Quartet too plays with a degree of restraint, and that works rather better in the works for strings alone, three other pieces long buried. The *Phantasy in F minor* won the Cobbett Prize for 1932 for its teenage composer, and was broadcast the following year. It is a finely wrought piece but not so striking as the *Oboe quartet* in its material. Striking material is there in plenty in the *Alla marcia* of 1933 and three *Divertimenti* of 1936, both for string quartet, some of the material pointing forward to the song cycle *Les Illuminations*. Clear recording to match the performances.

Cello sonata in C, Op. 65.
(M) *** Decca Jub. 410 168-1/*4*. Rostropovich, composer – DEBUSSY: *Sonata*; SCHUMANN: *Funf Stücke*.***

This strange, five-movement work was written specially for Rostropovich's appearance at the Aldeburgh Festival of 1961, and the recording was made soon after the first performance. It is unlike anything Britten had written previously. The idiom itself is unexpected, sometimes recalling Soviet models as in the spiky *March*, perhaps out of tribute to the dedicatee. Then although technically it demands fantastic feats from the cellist it is hardly a display piece. Each of the five movements is poised and concentrated. It is an excellent work to wrestle with on a record, particularly when the performance is never likely to be outshone. The recording is superb in every way and its reissue on Jubilee, with a fine tape equivalent, is most welcome.

2 Insect pieces for oboe and piano; 6 Metamorphoses after Ovid for solo oboe, Op. 49; Phantasy quartet, Op. 2; Temporal variations for oboe and piano.
**(*) Phoenix DGS 1022. Canter; Hendry; Bochmann Qt.

This Phoenix issue brings together all the music Britten wrote for solo oboe, including several pieces which lay buried till after his death. Robin Canter and members of the Bochmann Quartet give a warmly expressive reading of the *Phantasy quartet* for oboe and strings of 1932, written for Leon Goossens, and one of the first works of his own which Britten agreed to recognize. Canter and Linn Hendry then give a strongly characterized performance too of the *Temporal variations* of 1936, a theme and nine variations which look forward in sharp wit and brilliance to the set of variations for string orchestra which Britten wrote the following year on a theme by his master, Frank Bridge. The *Six Metamorphoses for solo oboe* readily transcend the limitations of a single wind instrument, and the *Insect pieces* of 1935, written for an oboist friend but then kept private, make a spikily characterful fill-up. Good recording, but variable surfaces.

Lachrymae (for viola and piano), *Op. 48.*
(M) *** Sup. 1111 2694. Kodousek, Novotná – CLARKE and ECCLES: *Sonatas*.***

Britten's *Lachrymae* dates from 1950 and is a much underrated piece inspired by Dowland (it is subtitled *Reflections on a song by John Dowland*). Its dark-toned melancholy is finely conveyed by Josef Kodousek and his sensitive partner, Kveta Novotná, and the coupling is undoubtedly enterprising.

String quartet No. 1 in D, Op. 25.
(*) CRD CRD 1051/*CRDC 4051*. Alberni Qt – SHOSTAKOVICH: *Piano quintet*.(*)

String quartets Nos. 2 in C, Op. 36; 3, Op. 94.
*** Decca SXL 6893. Amadeus Qt.
*** CRD CRD 1095/*CRDC 4095*. Alberni Qt.

The well-recorded and conscientiously played reading of the *First* on CRD makes an admirable choice. The Alberni Quartet have good ensemble and intonation, and the sound is well detailed. The cassette transfer is of CRD's usual outstanding quality, with a high-level transfer bringing wide range, body and detail.

The *Third String quartet*, written for the Amadeus Quartet at the very end of the composer's life, is a spare, seemingly wayward work that reveals its depth of feeling with the repetition possible on record. The brooding *Passacaglia* shows clearly enough that, despite Britten's serious illness during his final years, his individual inspiration still burned. That movement is here strikingly contrasted with the forceful *Chaconne* which ends the *Second Quartet*, written in 1945 to commemorate the 250th anniversary of Purcell's death. The Amadeus recording, made in 1963, is the perfect coupling for their newly recorded version of the *Third*. The recorded sound is excellent in both.

The Alberni performances are a degree less refined than those by the Amadeus. The ensemble and tonal matching of the music-making is not quite so polished. But in No. 3 – one of Britten's last works written after his serious illness had made him an invalid – their sharp appreciation of the seemingly fragmentary pattern of argument provides compensation for a slight lack of meditative intensity. This is playing from the heart, vividly recorded and strongly characterized. The cassette is well up to CRD's usual high standard.

Suites for unaccompanied cello Nos. 1, Op. 72; 2, Op. 80.
*** Decca SXL 6393 [Lon. CS 6617]. Rostropovich.

This is rough, gritty music in Britten's latterday manner. It is characteristic of him that, not content with tackling the almost insoluble problem of writing for solo cello in a single work, he wrote a sequel. The *First Suite*, with its clean-cut genre pieces, remains the more strikingly memorable of the two; but Rostropovich gives such an inspired account of the *Second* that its even grittier manner reveals more and more with repetition on record. Fine recording; superlative performances.

Suite for unaccompanied cello No. 3, Op. 87.
*** ASV ACA/*ZCACA* 1001. Lloyd Webber – BRIDGE: *Elegy* ***; IRELAND: *Sonata*.**(*)

The *Third Suite* which Britten wrote for Rostropovich may be less ambitious in plan than its predecessors, but in such a performance as Lloyd Webber's the very directness and lyrical approachability in the sharply characterized sequence of pieces – *Marcia*, *Canto*, *Barcarolla*, *Dialogo*, *Fuga* etc. – make for the extra emotional impact. With Lloyd Webber the climax of the extended final *Passacaglia* is extraordinarily powerful, and all through he brings out what might be described as the schizophrenic side of the work, the play between registers high and low. These sharp contrasts are used not just to imply full orchestral textures but to interweave opposing ideas as the movements merge. The recording is full and warm; the cassette balance is wholly natural (although the level could have been a little higher).

Suite for violin and piano, Op. 6.
(B) **(*) PRT GSGC/*ZCGC* 2050. Nemet, Wruble – WALTON: *Violin sonata*.*(*)

Britten's *Suite for violin and piano* dates from 1935, but already shows much of that mastery which later works have proved time and time again. The contrast between this Britten work, written when the composer was in his early twenties, and the rather overripe Walton work on the reverse of the Pye disc is astonishing. The Walton is expansive to the point of luxuriance, while from the very opening this *Suite* is sharp and commanding, and every idea is crisply and cleanly placed without fuss. Its style suits Nemet and Wruble very well: the wit and brilliance are brought out, as well as the deeper underlying emotions that even the youthful Britten could not conceal. First-rate recording and a good cassette without quite the upper range of the disc.

VOCAL MUSIC

Collection: (i) *Prelude and fugue on a theme of Vittoria.* (ii) *Festival Te Deum; Hymn of St Columba.* (iii) *Hymn to St Cecilia.* (ii) *Hymn to St Peter; Hymn to the Virgin; Jubilate Deo; Missa brevis.*

(M) *** Argo ZK 19. (i) Preston (organ); (ii) St John's College Ch., Guest; Runnett (organ); (iii) LSO Ch., Malcolm.

A useful anthology of some of Britten's shorter choral works. The *Vittoria Prelude and fugue* is Britten's only solo organ piece and it is excellently played and recorded here. The recordings of the *Festival Te Deum*, *Hymn to the Virgin* and *Jubilate Deo* were originally presented within a highly praised collection of twentieth-century English church music, with the St John's Choir in superb form. While the *Hymn to the Virgin* was an early work, written in 1930, the *Hymn to St Cecilia* is a much more ambitious piece, written just before the war, when Britten's technique was already prodigious. The setting exactly matches the imaginative, capricious words of Auden. A highly recommendable and generous disc.

Canticles Nos. 1, My beloved is mine, Op. 40; 2, Abraham and Isaac, Op. 51; 3, Still falls the rain, Op. 55; 4, Journey of the Magi, Op. 86; 5, Death of St Narcissus, Op. 89.

*** Argo ZRG 946. Pears, Hahessy, Bowman, Shirley-Quirk, Tuckwell, Ellis, composer (piano).

This brings together on a single record all five of the miniature cantatas to which Britten gave the title 'Canticle', most of them performed by their original interpreters. They date from 1947 to 1974, but all share the spiritual intensity which stemmed from the composer's religious faith. A beautiful collection as well as a historical document, with recording that still sounds well.

(i; ii; iii) *Cantata academica, Op. 62;* (ii; iv) *Cantata misericordium, Op. 69;* (v) *Voices for today, Op. 75;* (ii; iii) *Gloriana: Choral dances.*

**(*) Argo ZRG 947. (i) Vyvyan, Watts, Pears, Brannigan; (ii) LSO Ch. and LSO; (iii) cond. Malcolm; (iv) Pears, Fischer-Dieskau, cond. composer; (v) King's College and Cambridge University Ch., Willcocks.

This makes an attractive compilation of choral recordings either made by or approved by the composer. Both the *Cantata academica* written for Basel with its deft use of a 12-note row and the *Cantata misericordium* written for the centenary of the Red Cross – using the Good Samaritan story simply but most movingly – go well with the cantata, *Voices for today*, written for the United Nations, a recording originally published in an Aldeburgh Festival celebration set. *Gloriana* still awaits a much-needed complete recording: these *Choral dances* provide a tempting sample. Recordings not of the most modern but very acceptable.

A Ceremony of Carols, Op. 28.

(M) *** Argo SPA/*KCSP* 164. St John's College Ch., Cambridge, Guest; Robles (with Collection: *'The world of Christmas'* ***).

A Ceremony of Carols; The Golden Vanity (vaudeville); *Missa brevis, Op. 63.*

(B) * PRT GSGC/*ZCGC* 2043. Winchester Cathedral Ch., Neary; Robles.

A Ceremony of Carols; Hymn to St Cecilia, Op. 17; Hymn to St Peter; Hymn to the Virgin; Te Deum in C.

**(*) ASV ALH/*ZCALH* 923. Christ Church Cathedral, Oxford, Ch., Grier; Kelly.

A Ceremony of Carols; Hymn to St Cecilia; Missa brevis.

(M) **(*) HMV HQS 1285 [Sera. S 60217]. King's College Ch., Willcocks; Ellis.

A Ceremony of Carols; Missa brevis; Rejoice in the Lamb (*Festival cantata*), *Op. 30.*

*** Argo ZRG 5440 [id.]. Tear, Forbes Robinson, St John's College Ch., Guest; Robles; Runnett.

A Ceremony of Carols, Op. 28 (with carols arr. Ellis: *Away in a manger; Coventry carol; Deck the hall; Ding dong merrily on high; I saw three ships; Once in Royal David's city; We've been awhile a-wandering*).

**(*) RCA RL/*RK* 30467 [ARL 1/*ARK 1* 3437]. V. Boys' Ch., Harrer; Ellis (harp).

Argo have provided us with a definitive recording of the *Ceremony of Carols*, one of Britten's freshest and most spontaneous works. This St John's performance has tingling vitality, spacious sound, and a superb contribution from Marisa Robles, who plays with masterly sensitivity, especially in her solo *Interlude*. The performance of *Rejoice in the Lamb* is very similar to Britten's own but much better recorded, and the *Missa brevis* has the same striking excellence of style. As can be seen above, the *Ceremony of Carols* is also available on Argo's medium-price label coupled to a delectable selection of traditional carols and modern settings. This is one of the finest records of Christmas music in the catalogue, with a matching cassette.

On ASV Christ Church Cathedral Choir under a relatively new choirmaster gives attractively vigorous performances, full of the right sort of rhythmic energy, of these strongly characterful choral works. There is an earthy quality which reflects the composer's own rejection of over-refined choirboy tone, but the *Hymn to St Cecilia* with its setting of a brilliant Auden poem (text not included) is a degree too rough, and it loses some impact when the choir is rather backwardly balanced. The coupling however is apt and most desirable, and for the rest the sound is excellent. On side one of the tape the transfer level is disappointingly low, which emphasizes the poor projection for the choir and especially the solos. But on side two the level rises dramatically and there is a marked improvement.

There was a time when Britten's insistence on earthily boyish tone among trebles seemed at the farthest remove from the King's tradition. But towards the end of David Willcocks's stay at Cambridge, a happy accommodation was achieved not only in appearances of the choir at the Aldeburgh Festival but in this excellent HMV record, conveniently coupling three of Britten's most appealing choral pieces. The King's trebles may still have less edge in the *Ceremony of Carols* than their rivals in Cambridge at St John's College, and the *Missa brevis* can certainly benefit from throatier sound, but the results here are dramatic as well as beautiful. Fine recording.

The Vienna Boys – for whom Britten wrote his *Golden Vanity* – give a brisk and fresh account of the *Ceremony of Carols*, beautifully tuned and not marred by the fruity tones which sometimes come from this choir. The processionals at the beginning and end are not very atmospheric, but the recording is fresh to match the voices. Osian Ellis, who accompanies in the Britten work, then provides some fancy arrangements of British carols with harp accompaniment, shouts and contrived dissonances.

With the composer's own version of *The Golden Vanity* currently out of the catalogue, the Winchester recording might have been very welcome. But it is little more than a stopgap, lacking a real projection of drama and without a sense of fun. The treble soloists are unimpressive, both here and in the *Ceremony of Carols*, which is also undistinguished for similar reasons. The recording is good, but the cassette lacks range and bite.

(i; ii) *A Charm of Lullabies, Op. 41;* (iii; ii) *On this Island, Op. 11;* (iii; iv) *Our Hunting Fathers, Op. 8.*

(***) BBC mono REGL 417. (i) Watts, (ii) composer (piano); (iii) Pears, (iv) LSO, composer.

These historic broadcast performances come in limited mono sound, sometimes marred (as in Helen Watts' superb account of the Lullaby sequence) by heavy background. Pears sings the Auden song-cycle as persuasively as one would expect, and the strange cantata on an anti-bloodsport theme comes over with bite and power despite the recording, with Pears again the most persuasive of interpreters.

Festival Te Deum, Op. 32; Jubilate Deo; Rejoice in the Lamb (Festival cantata), Op. 30; Te Deum in C.

*** HMV ASD 3035 [Ang. S 37119]. Bowman, King's College Ch., Ledger; Lancelot (organ), Corkhill (percussion) – BERNSTEIN: *Chichester Psalms.****

It was apt that Philip Ledger, for long active at the Aldeburgh Festival, should devote most of his first record as director of King's College Choir to the music of Britten. He scores a notable first in using here a new version of the cantata, *Rejoice in the Lamb*, with timpani and percussion added to the original organ part. The differences are minor, but they add to the weight and drama of this haunting setting of the words of the mad poet Christopher Smart. The biting climaxes are sung with passionate incisiveness, while the soloists make an attractive contrast one with another – James Bowman the counter-tenor in the delightful passage which tells you that 'the mouse is a creature of great personal valour'. The *Te Deum* settings and the *Jubilate* make an excellent coupling along with Bernstein's *Chichester Psalms*. First-rate recording.

Folksong arrangements: *The ash grove; La belle est au jardin d'amour; The bonny Earl o'Moray; The brisk young widow; Ca' the yowes; Come you not from Newcastle?; The foggy, foggy dew; The Lincolnshire poacher; Little Sir William; The minstrel boy; O can ye sew cushions; Oliver Cromwell; O waly, waly; The plough boy; Quand j'étais chez mon père; Le roi s'en va-t'en chasse; The Sally Gardens; Sweet Polly Oliver; The trees they grow so high.*

(M) *** HMV HQS 1341. Tear, Ledger.

Folksong arrangements: *La belle est au jardin d'amour; The bonnie Earl o'Moray; Come you not from Newcastle?; Eho! Eho!; Fileuse; Little Sir William; O can ye sew cushions; Oliver Cromwell; O waly, waly; The plough boy; Quand j'étais chez mon père; Le roi s'en va-t'en chasse; The Sally Gardens.*

(*) Uni. Dig. KP 8007. English, West Australian SO, Measham – *Prince of the Pagodas*.(*)

Close as Robert Tear's interpretations are to those of Peter Pears, he has a sparkle of his own, helped by resilient accompaniment from Philip Ledger. In any case some of these songs are unavailable in Pears versions, and the record is a delight on its own account. *Oliver Cromwell* is among the most delectable of pay-off songs ever written. Fine recording.

The alternative Unicorn collection using orchestral accompaniments is discussed under its coupling – see above.

(i) *Les Illuminations* (song cycle), *Op. 18;* (ii) *Serenade for tenor, horn and strings, Op. 31.*

*** Decca SXL 6449 [Lon. OS 26161]. (i) Pears, ECO, composer; (ii) with Tuckwell.

*** DG 2531 199 [id.]. Tear, cond. Giulini, with (i) Philh. O, (ii) Clevenger, Chicago SO.

(M) *** HMV SXLP 30194. (i) Harper, (ii) Tear, Civil, both with Northern Sinf. O, Marriner.

The superb interpretation of the *Serenade* by Peter Pears appeared first in the alternative coupling with Britten's *Young person's guide*, but this pairing with the earlier song cycle is clearly more logical. Pears's voice is so ideally suited to this music, his insight into word-meaning as well as into phrase-shaping so masterly, that for once one can use the word 'definitive'. With dedicated accompaniment under the composer's direction and superb recording, this is a disc to recommend to all who have yet to discover the magic of Britten's music.

Tear is very much in the Aldeburgh tradition set by Pears, but in his 1971 HMV recording gives a new, positive slant to each of Britten's lovely songs in the *Serenade*, with the Jonson *Hymn to Diana* given extra jollity, thanks partly to the brilliant galumphing of Alan Civil on the horn. *Les Illuminations*, originally written with the soprano Sophie Wiess in mind, is more headily beautiful with glorious tone from Heather Harper. Good, resonant recording.

In 1980 Robert Tear recorded both cycles for DG with Giulini who has long been a persuasive advocate of Britten's music. The fact that these two excellent performances were recorded on opposite sides of the Atlantic adds to the attractions, for the Philharmonia produces playing of warmth and resonance to match that of the Chicago orchestra. Without apology Giulini presents both cycles as full-scale orchestral works, and though some detail may be lost, the strength of Britten's writing amply justifies it. Tear is at his finest in both cycles, more open than in his earlier recording of the *Serenade*. Dale Clevenger is a superb horn-player, and though in places some may find him unidiomatic it is good to have a fresh view in such music. Soloists are balanced rather close, in an otherwise excellent, vivid recording.

(i) *Nocturne;* (ii) *Peter Grimes: 4 Sea interludes and Passacaglia.*

*** Decca SXL 2189 [Lon. CS 6179]. (i) Pears, wind soloists, LSO strings; (ii) soloists, Ch. and O of ROHCG, composer.

In this wide-ranging cycle on the subject of night and sleep, Britten chose from a diverse selection of poems – Coleridge, Tennyson, Wordsworth, Wilfred Owen and Keats, finishing with a Shakespeare sonnet. It is a work full – as so much of Britten's output is – of memorable moments. One thinks of the 'breathing' motif on the strings which links the different songs, the brilliant dialogue for flute and clarinet in the Keats setting, and above all the towering climax of the Wordsworth excerpt. Each song has a different obbligato instrument (with the ensemble unified for the final Shakespeare song), and each instrument gives the song it is associated with its own individual character. The Decca performance is as nearly definitive as anything could be. Pears as always is the ideal interpreter, the composer a most efficient conductor, and the fiendishly difficult obbligato parts are played superbly. The recording is brilliant and clear, with just the right degree of atmosphere. The *Sea interludes* and *Passacaglia* are taken from the complete recording. This means that odd extracts from the vocal parts are included and the general effect is not so tidy as in the concert version. But that proviso apart, these are wonderfully vital accounts of some superbly atmospheric music.

Noye's Fludde.

(M) *** Argo ZK 1. Brannigan, Rex, Anthony, East Suffolk Children's Ch. and O, English Op. Group O, Del Mar.

Even when Britten has long been renowned as the supreme master of deceptive simplicity it is easy to be fooled into underrating the musical value of this children's oratorio to words from the Chester Miracle Play. You can play through the piano score from beginning to end and wonder what the fuss was about, but the record brilliantly captures the flavour of a live performance together with the intense emotion hidden only just below the surface. There are a number of moments when the sheer felicity is liable to strike home and overwhelm the listener – the entry of the animals into the Ark, the sound of *Eternal Father* rising above the storm, the atmospheric moments after the storm.

All the effects have been miraculously well captured, particularly the entry into the Ark. In a church the children dressed as animals rush down the centre aisle, singing, shouting or squeaking their *Kyrie Eleisons* as they go to the Ark, while from the porch a bugle band blares out fanfares which finally turn into a rollicking march. All this has been caught in a way which makes this one of the finest examples of analogue stereo. Another excellent passage to sample is the syncopated little song that Noah's children sing as the Ark is built. The recording was made during the 1961 Aldeburgh Festival and not only the professional soloists but the children too have the time of their lives to the greater glory of God. A wonderful record, and an irresistible bargain in its mid-price reissue.

Our Hunting Fathers, Op. 8; Folksong arrangements: *The bonny Earl o'Moray; Come you not from Newcastle?; Little Sir William; Oliver Cromwell; O waly, waly; The plough boy.*

**(*) HMV ASD/*TCC-ASD* 4397. Söderström, Welsh Nat. Op. O, Armstrong.

Inexplicably *Our Hunting Fathers* – Britten's first major work using full orchestra, written for the Norwich Festival in 1936 – was neglected by the record companies until this valuable, strongly presented interpretation. W. H. Auden put together the sequence of poems on an anti-bloodsport theme designing it to shock the Norwich audience (which it did) and providing two of the poems himself. The piece with its obvious acerbities – like the shrieks in *Rats away* – still has a power to shock, and this performance finds Söderström a committed soloist. Yet those who have heard the BBC Records disc-transfer of a 1961 broadcast in mono (see above) will appreciate that Sir Peter Pears proved that a tenor suits this work even more. The folk-songs make an attractive but ungenerous fill-up. First-rate recording and a wide-ranging, vivid chrome cassette.

(i–iii) *Phaedra, Op. 93;* (iv) *Sacred and Profane (8 medieval lyrics), Op. 91; Shepherd's carol; Sweet was the song; The sycamore tree; Wealden trio* (*Christmas song*)*;* (ii; v) *Prelude and fugue for eighteen-part string orchestra, Op. 29.*
*** Decca SXL 6847 [Lon. OS 26527]. (i) Baker; (ii) ECO; (iii) cond. Bedford; (iv) Wilbye Cons., Pears; (v) cond. composer.

Phaedra was the work which Britten wrote at the very end of his life for Dame Janet Baker. Setting words from Robert Lowell's fine translation of Racine's play, the composer encapsulated the character of the tragic heroine, and provided vocal writing which brings out every glorious facet of her voice. The use of harpsichord in the recitatives linking the sections of this scena is no mere neo-classical device but a sharply atmospheric and dramatic stroke. *Sacred and Profane*, a collection of settings of medieval words that are curiously ironic in some of their overtones, is another highly imaginative product of Britten's last period, while the *Prelude and fugue* provides a welcome example, previously unissued, of Britten's own conducting. The ingenuity of this tribute to the Boyd Neel Orchestra is submerged by the music's energy as the composer interprets it. A fine collection with superb performances and first-class sound.

Saint Nicholas (cantata), *Op. 42.*
*** HMV ASD 2637 [Sera. 60296]. Tear, Russell, King's College Ch., ASMF, Willcocks.

Britten's own recording of this charming cantata for children – precursor of the first church opera, *Noye's Fludde* – was made in mono only, and there was clearly room for a version in modern stereo. Though the balancing of the solo voices – St Nicholas respectively as a boy and as a man – is rather too close, the actual performance is vivid and dramatic, with particularly fine contributions from the boys of King's College Choir, belying the old idea that their style was too pure to be adapted to rugged modern works. A delightful issue.

Serenade for tenor, horn and strings, Op. 31.
*** Decca SXL 6110. Pears, Tuckwell, ECO, composer – *Young person's guide.****

This performance is discussed above under its alternative coupling, *Les Illuminations.*

Spring symphony, Op. 44.
*** HMV ASD/*TC-ASD* 3650 [Ang. S 37562]. Armstrong, Baker, Tear, St Clement Dane's School Boys' Ch., LSO Ch., LSO, Previn.

(i) *Spring symphony; Simple symphony for strings.*
(M) *** Decca Jub. 410 171-1/*4*. (i) Vyvyan, Proctor, Pears, Wandsworth School Boys' Ch., Ch. and O of ROHCG; (ii) ECO; composer.

In 1961 Decca took advantage of a BBC performance with the same forces to obtain a recording of unusual brilliance and strength. If the title 'Symphony' is misleading – the work is much more an anthology akin to the *Serenade* and the *Nocturne* – Britten again shows by the subtlest of balancing that unity and cohesion are not just a matter of formal patterns. The four parts do come to have the coherence of balanced movements. But it is the freshness of Britten's imagination in dozens of moments that makes this work as memorable as it is joyous. Who but Britten would have dared use so unexpected an effect as boys whistling? Who but he would have introduced a triumphant C major *Sumer is icumen in* at the end, the boys' voices ringing out over everything else? Here of course a recording helps enormously. Thanks to the Decca engineers one hears more than is usually possible in a live performance. Jennifer Vyvyan and Peter Pears are both outstanding, and Britten shows that no conductor is more vital in his music than he himself. The Jubilee reissue couples the work to Britten's joyful account of his delightful *Simple symphony*, with the rich Maltings acoustic making the *Playful pizzicato* resonate gloriously as in no other version. There is a first-class chrome cassette.

Just as Sir Colin Davis's interpretation of *Peter Grimes* provides a strikingly new view of a work of which the composer seems the natural interpreter, so André Previn's reading of the *Spring symphony* is valuably distinctive. Like Britten, Previn makes this above all a work of exultation, a genuine celebration of spring; but here more than in Britten's recording the kernel of what the work has to say comes out in the longest of the solo settings, using Auden's poem *Out on the lawn I lie in bed.* With Janet Baker as soloist it rises above the lazily atmospheric mood of the opening to evoke the threat of war and darkness. Perhaps surprisingly, it is Britten who generally adopts faster tempi and a sharper rhythmic style, whereas Previn is generally the more atmospheric and mysterious, grading the climaxes and shading the tones over longer spans. He also takes more care over pointing Britten's pay-offs, often with the help of Robert Tear's sense of timing, as at the very end on *I cease.* Rich, atmospheric recording with glorious bass resonances, and a good cassette, clear and full, if not quite as ample at the bottom end of the spectrum. The choral climaxes are well caught.

War requiem, Op. 66.

*** Decca SET 252-3/*K 27 K 22* [Lon. OSA/*5-* 1255]. Vishnevskaya, Pears, Fischer-Dieskau, Bach Ch., LSO Ch., Highgate School Ch., Melos Ens., LSO, composer.

*** HMV Dig. SLS/*TC-SLS* 107757-3/*9* (2) [Ang. DSB/*4X2S* 3939]. Söderström, Tear, Allen, Trebles of Christ Church Cath. Ch., Oxford, CBSO Ch., CBSO, Rattle.

This most successful project hardly needs a recommendation. With the composer's own choice of forces under his direction, and with all the technical care of the Decca engineers, it has deserved all its success, and it is worth noting that in an important respect the gramophone has been able to fulfil the composer's directions even more completely than any live performance. Britten pointed the contrast between the full choir and orchestra in the settings of the *Requiem* and the tenor, baritone and chamber orchestra in the intervening settings of the Wilfred Owen poems. But what a recording can do that is impossible in a cathedral or concert hall is to modify the acoustic for each, and this has been done most sensitively and effectively by the Decca engineers. The Owen settings strike one more sharply than the Latin settings, but gradually as the work progresses the process of integration is accomplished, and the way the soloists' cries of *Let us sleep now* fade into the final chorus is almost unbearably moving on record as in performance. The recorded performance comes near to the ideal, but it is a pity that Britten insisted on Vishnevskaya for the soprano solos. Having a Russian singer was emotionally right, but musically Heather Harper would have been so much better still.

The cassette issue offers sound of amazing depth and clarity. The work's closing pages are wonderfully effective heard against an almost silent background, with no possible danger of intrusive clicks and pops.

The most striking difference between Rattle's interpretation and that of Britten himself lies in the relationship between the settings of Owen's poems and the setting of the liturgy in Latin. With Söderström a far more warmly expressive soloist than the oracular Vishnevskaya, the human emotions behind the Latin text come out strongly with less distancing than from the composer. One registers the more clearly the meaning of the Latin. Tear and Allen are fine soloists, though at times balanced too forwardly. If Tear does not always match the subtlety of Pears on the original recording, Allen sounds more idiomatic than Fischer-Dieskau. Rattle's approach is warm, dedicated and dramatic, with fine choral singing (not least from the Christ Church Cathedral trebles). The dramatic orchestral contrasts are superbly brought out as in the blaze of trumpets on *Hosanna.* The various layers of perspective are impressively managed by the superb digital recording with little to choose in definition between the discs and the first-rate XDR tape, except that the layout on cassette has the advantage of added continuity with the music spaced over two sides (as against four on LP). Yet in its combination of imaginative flair with technical expertise, the Culshaw recording of two decades earlier is by no means surpassed by this new HMV venture; indeed in sophistication of acoustic and detail it remains in a class of its own.

OPERA

Albert Herring (complete).
**(*) Decca SET 274/6 [Lon. OSA 1378]. Pears, Fisher, Noble, Brannigan, Cantelo, ECO, Ward, composer.

Comic opera performances on record are curiously unpredictable; the absence of an audience is often disturbing. This account of *Albert Herring* under the composer is as impressive musically as could be imagined, but somehow genuine gaiety is rather lacking. It is partly the fault of the libretto. In the theatre, with plenty of visual amusements to watch, one hardly notices the stiltedness of much of the language, but on record there are many lines that are just folksy and embarrassing. But with that reservation, there is everything to commend, and it is good to have Peter Pears's Albert so beautifully recorded. Sylvia Fisher makes a magnificent gorgon of a Lady Billows, and one welcomes the chance to hear so many excellent British singers on record who are normally neglected by the companies: Sheila Rex, for example, whose tiny portrait of Albert's mother is very funny indeed. Recording excellent.

Billy Budd (complete).
*** Decca SET 379/81 [Lon. OSA 1390]. Glossop, Pears, Langdon, Shirley-Quirk, Wandsworth School Boys' Ch., Ambrosian Op. Ch., LSO, composer.

This was the last opera recording supervised for Decca by John Culshaw. By then he was already in his new BBC role, but with the keenest enjoyment he returned for this long-cherished project, and successfully capped his earlier outstanding achievements in Wagner as well as Britten. The opera itself, daring in its use of an all-male cast without any lack of variety of texture, emerges magnificently. The libretto by E. M. Forster and Eric Crozier is more skilled than those Britten has usually set, and the range of characterization – so apparently limited in a tale of good and evil directly confronting one another – is masterly, with Peter Pears's part of Captain Vere presenting the moral issue at its most moving. Here, as in the opera house, Britten's masterstroke of representing the confrontation of Vere and the condemned Billy in a sequence of 34 bare common chords is irresistible, and the many richly imaginative strokes – atmospheric as well as dramatic – are superbly managed. An ideal cast, with Glossop a bluff heroic Billy, and Langdon a sharply dark-toned Claggart, making these symbol-figures believable. Magnificent sound.

Death in Venice (complete).
*** Decca SET 581/3 [Lon. OSA 13109]. Pears, Shirley-Quirk, Bowman, Bowen, Leeming, English Op. Group Ch., ECO, Bedford.

Even Britten has rarely chosen so offbeat an opera subject as Thomas Mann's novella which made an expansively atmospheric film far removed from the world of Mann, and here makes a surprisingly successful opera, totally original in its alternation of monologue for the central character, Aschenbach (on two levels, inner and external), and colourful set pieces showing off the world of Venice and the arrival of the plague. Britten's inspiration, drawing together threads from all his earlier operas from *Peter Grimes* to the *Church parables*, is nothing less than exuberant, with the chamber orchestra producing the richest possible sounds. Pears's searching performance in the central role is set against the darkly sardonic singing of John Shirley-Quirk in a sequence of roles as the Dionysiac figure who draws Aschenbach on to his destruction. The recording is gloriously vivid, and though Steuart Bedford's assured conducting lacks some of the punch that Britten would have brought, the whole presentation (including a finely produced libretto) makes this a set to establish the work as the very culmination of Britten's cycle of operas.

A Midsummer Night's Dream (complete).
*** Decca SET 338/40 [Lon. OSA 1385]. Deller, Harwood, Harper, Veasey, Watts, Shirley-Quirk, Brannigan, Choirs of Downside and Emanuel Schools, LSO, composer.

Britten and Pears together prepared the libretto for this opera by careful compression and rearrangement of the Shakespeare words. What this recording confirms – with the aid of the score – more than any live performance is how compressed the music is, as well as the words. At first one may regret the comparative absence of rich, memorable tunes, but there is no thinness of argument, and the atmosphere of every scene is brilliantly re-created in the most evocative orchestral sounds. The beauty of instrumental writing comes out in this recording even more than in the opera house, for John Culshaw, the recording manager, put an extra halo round the fairy-music, not to distort or confuse but to act as substitute for visual atmosphere. The problem of conveying the humour of the play-scene at the end with the 'rude mechanicals' cavorting about the stage proved more intractable. Humour is there all right, but the laughter of the stage audience is too ready for comfort. Britten again proves himself an ideal interpreter of his own music, and draws virtuoso playing from the LSO (marvellous trumpet-sounds for Puck's music). Among the singers Peter Pears has shifted from his original role of Flute (the one who has the Donizetti mad-scene parody to sing) to the straight role of Lysander. The mechanicals are admirably led by Owen Brannigan as Bottom; and among the lovers Josephine Veasey (Hermia) is outstanding. Deller, with his magical male alto singing, is the eerily effective Oberon.

Owen Wingrave (complete).
*** Decca SET 501/2 [Lon. OSA 1291]. Pears, Fisher, Harper, Vyvyan, Baker, Luxon, Shirley-Quirk, ECO, composer.

Britten's television opera had a bigger audience for its world-wide first performance than most composers receive for all the performances of all their operas put together. It marked a return after the *Church parables* to the mainstream Britten pattern of opera with a central character isolated from society. Each of the seven characters is strongly conceived, with the composer writing specially for the individual singers chosen for the television and gramophone presentations. This recording was made immediately after the trials of the television recording, and the result is even more concentrated and compelling. Strangely enough the drama, based on a short story by Henry James, seems less contrived when one has to imagine the setting instead of having it presented on the screen, particularly as the recording is so atmospheric and the production so sensitive. It is particularly good to hear Britten's highly original orchestral writing in high fidelity.

Peter Grimes (complete).
❀ *** Decca SXL 2150-2/*K 71 K 33* (2) [Lon. OSA/*5*- 1305]. Pears, Watson, Pease, Jean Watson, Nilsson, Brannigan, Evans, Ch. and O of ROHCG, composer.
*** Ph. 6769 014/*7699 089* (3) [id.]. Vickers, Harper, Summers, Bainbridge, Robinson, ROHCG Ch. and O, Sir Colin Davis.

The Decca recording of *Peter Grimes* was one of the first great achievements of the stereo era. Few opera recordings can claim to be so definitive, with Peter Pears, for whom it was written, in the name part, Owen Brannigan (another member of the original team) and a first-rate cast. One was a little apprehensive about Claire Watson as Ellen Orford, a part which Joan Cross made her own, but in the event Miss Watson gives a most sympathetic performance, and her voice records beautifully. Another member of the cast from across the Atlantic, James Pease, as the understanding Captain Balstrode, is brilliantly incisive musically and dramatically; but beyond that it becomes increasingly unfair to single out individual performances. Britten conducts superbly and secures splendidly incisive playing, with the whole orchestra on its toes throughout. The recording, superbly atmospheric, has so many felicities that it would be hard to enumerate them, and the Decca engineers have done wonders in making up aurally for the lack of visual effects. There is a splendidly atmospheric cassette version of demonstration quality.

Colin Davis takes a fundamentally darker, tougher view of *Peter Grimes* than the composer himself. In some ways the result is even more powerful if less varied and atmospheric, with the Borough turned into a dark place full of Strindbergian tensions and Grimes himself, powerful physically (no intellectual misplaced), turned into a Hardy-like figure. It was Jon Vickers's heroic interpretation in the Met. production in New York which first prompted Davis to press for a new recording, and the result sheds keen new illumination on what arguably remains the greatest of Britten's operas. In no way can it be said to supplant the composer's own unique recording on Decca; and Peter Pears's richly detailed and keenly sensitive performance in the name part remains unique too, even though Vickers is so plainly closer in frame and spirit to Crabbe's rough fisherman. Slow-spoken and weighty, Vickers is frighteningly intense. On the Davis set Heather Harper as Ellen Orford is far more moving than her opposite number on Decca, and generally the Philips cast is younger-voiced and fresher, with especially fine contributions from Jonathan Summers as Balstrode (a late choice) and Thomas Allen as Ned Keene. It is a pity the recording producer did not favour the sort of atmospheric effects which set the seal on the Decca version as a riveting experience, but this reinforces Davis's point about the actual notes needing no outside aid. The recording, made at All Saints, Tooting Graveney (not the ideal venue), is rich and vivid, with fine balancing. The Philips tape transfer is of excellent quality, warmly atmospheric and with natural vocal timbre. But the Decca set remains one of the great achievements of the stereo era. Few opera recordings have such claims to be definitive, and the superbly atmospheric recording is as effective on cassette as it is on disc.

Peter Grimes: 4 Sea interludes.
(M) *** Ph. Seq. 6527/*7311* 112. ROHCGO, Colin Davis – TIPPETT: *Midsummer Marriage: Dances.****

Davis recorded the *Four Sea interludes* as a dry run before his complete recording of Britten's opera. In many ways these performances are even more spontaneously convincing than the later ones, beautifully played. Well-coupled with the Tippett, they make an excellent medium-price issue. The cassette is of good quality but transferred at a rather low level.

The Rape of Lucretia (complete).
*** Decca SET 492/3 [Lon. OSA 1288]. Pears, Harper, Shirley-Quirk, Baker, Luxon, ECO, composer.

This is outstanding even among the many fine opera recordings that Britten made. In particular the performance of Janet Baker as Lucretia underlines the depth of feeling behind a work which in its formal classical frame may on the face of it seem to hide emotion. The logical problems of the story remain – why *should* Lucretia feel so guilty? – but with Janet Baker the heart-rending tragedy of the heroine is conveyed with passionate conviction, her glorious range of tone colours, her natural feeling for words and musical phrase used with supreme artistry. Benjamin Luxon too makes the selfish Tarquinius into a living, believable character. As the Male Chorus, Peter Pears astonishingly matches his own achievement of a quarter-century earlier in an abbreviated recording, and Heather Harper's creamy tones as the Female Chorus are beautifully poised. The stylization of the drama with its frame of Christian comment comes over even more effectively when imagined rather than seen. The seductive beauty of the writing – Britten at his early peak – is gloriously caught, the melodies and tone colours as ravishing as any that he ever conceived. A lovely set.

The Turn of the screw (complete).
**(*) Ph. Dig. 410 426-1/*4* (2) [id.]. Donath, Tear, Harper, June, Watson, Ginn, Ch. and O of ROHCG, Sir Colin Davis.

Sir Colin Davis's Covent Garden recording of *The Turn of the screw* has the benefit of spacious and atmospheric digital sound, but the composer's own mono recording of nearly thirty years earlier (Decca GOM 560/1) is in some ways better balanced and clearer on detail. Britten's own reading is a degree tougher and at times more intense, but Davis's extra ability to relax, to vary the expression, brings many dividends. As before, there is no weak link in the singing cast, with Tear underlining the devilish side of Peter Quint's character, more forcefully sinister than was Sir Peter Pears, but at times too melodramatic. Helen Donath sings feelingly as the Governess, making her a neurotic character, but she hardly erases memories of Jennifer Vyvyan. The treble, Michael Ginn, as Miles, is excellent, and Heather Harper as Miss Jessel is a warmly persuasive ghost. The playing of the Covent Garden orchestra is superb, to bring out the formidable compression of the piece.

Brouwer, Leo (born 1939)

Guitar concerto.
*** CBS 76715/*40*- [M/*MT* 36680]. Williams, L. Sinf., Howarth – ARNOLD: *Concerto.****

Leo Brouwer is a Cuban composer with the kind of avant-garde credentials and fashionable advocacy that inspire vigilance. The intelligent sleeve-note speaks of his being inspired by Ives, Cage, Nono and Xenakis, as well as the ideals of the Cuban revolution! His *Guitar concerto* is strangely powerful and haunting, yet it is not easy to describe it in a way that conveys its character. Its atmosphere is redolent of a jungle-like landscape in which half-real and half-imagined whispers mingle with the cries of exotic birds and the crackle of a living, insect-infested undergrowth. Yet this makes it sound colourful and attractive like some wild Villa-Lobos piece. In fact there is something dark, sour and disturbing about this music. John Williams and the ensemble play as if they believed every note of it, and though it may have less substance than appears, it is undeniably thought-provoking and imaginative. The recording is of good quality; the cassette is less wide-ranging than the disc.

Bruch, Max (1838–1920)

Adagio appassionato, Op. 57; Violin concerto No. 3 in D min., Op. 58; Romanze, Op. 42.
*** Ph. 9500 589/*7300 711* [id.]. Accardo, Leipzig GO, Masur.

No one could pretend that the *D minor Concerto* is as inventive or as concentrated as the famous *G minor*, and to be truthful there is much here that is unmemorable. Such is the quality of the playing, however, that the listener is beguiled into thinking it a better work than it is. The melodic invention in the *Adagio appassionato* and the *Romanze* is not particularly distinguished either but Accardo and this fine orchestra make out an excellent case for them. The recording is superb. The cassette is slightly less refined in the upper range than the LP, with a tendency to fierceness; but it yields to the controls.

Violin concerto No. 1 in G min., Op. 26.
*** HMV ASD/*TC-ASD* 2926 [Ang. S/*4XS* 36963]. Perlman, LSO, Previn – MENDELSSOHN: *Concerto.****
*** DG 2531/*3301* 304 [id.]. Mintz, Chicago SO, Abbado – MENDELSSOHN: *Concerto.***(*)*
*** DG Dig. **400 031-2**; 2532/*3302* 016 [id.]. Mutter, Berlin PO, Karajan – MENDELSSOHN: *Concerto.****
*** HMV ASD/*TC-ASD* 334. Menuhin, Philh. O, Susskind – MENDELSSOHN: *Concerto.****
(M) *** Decca SPA/*KCSP* 88 [Lon. STS 15402]. Ricci, LSO, Gamba – MENDELSSOHN: *Concerto.****
(*) Erato STU/*MCE* 71164. Amoyal, RPO, Scimone – GLAZOUNOV: *Concerto.**
(M) ** DG Priv. 2535/*3335* 176 [id.]. I. Oistrakh, RPO, D. Oistrakh – BACH: *Double concerto.***
(B) ** CfP CFP/*TC-CFP* 40374. Milstein, Philh. O, Barzin – MENDELSSOHN: *Concerto.***
(M) *(*) DG Priv. 2535/*3335* 294 [id.]. Yong Uck Kim, Bamberg SO, Kamu – MENDELSSOHN: *Concerto.***

Bruch's *First Violin concerto* is lucky in its recordings, and many of the above discs will satisfy in different ways. In discussing individual performances, that by Kyung-Wha Chung must be considered among the very finest – it is mentioned below coupled to the *Scottish fantasia.* Of the others among the finest is Perlman's. There is perhaps the faintest reservation about this reading, a glowing, powerful account that is almost too sure of itself. With Previn and the LSO backing him up richly, this is a strong, confident interpretation, forthrightly masculine – the contrast with Kyung-Wha Chung's inner qualities is very striking. The opulent, full recording suits the performance, and the Mendelssohn coupling is outstanding among many fine versions of that concerto. The cassette has been remastered to have its full dynamic range restored, but the tape orchestral focus is slightly less sharp than the disc.

Shlomo Mintz is a Russian-born player who studied in Israel and then at the Juilliard. This was his first commercial record and makes an exciting début; his account of the Bruch is exceptionally exciting and warm-blooded. No doubt some of the sheer size of his tone can be attributed to the flattering forward balance, which also means that dynamic shading is less evident than it might be. Mintz certainly makes the listener hang on to every phrase and his playing is undoubtedly compelling. The vibrato is wide (one notices it at the pianissimo opening of the *Adagio*) and for some ears there may be an impression of over-projection and a lack of the kind of inner communion that Perlman conveys so effectively. Nevertheless this approach is so distinctive and interesting that few listeners will not be fired. The Chicago Symphony Orchestra plays with great brilliance and enthusiasm and Abbado's direction is sympathetic. Marvellously vivid recording (if one accepts the forward balance of the soloist), which has more presence than many digital discs. On cassette, however, the resonance brings a lack of refinement in the orchestral tuttis.

In Anne-Sophie Mutter's hands the concerto has an air of chaste sweetness, shedding much of its ripe, sensuous quality but retaining its romantic feeling. There is a delicacy and tenderness here which is very appealing, and, although the tuttis have plenty of fire, Karajan sensitively scales down his accompaniment in the lyrical passages to match his soloist. There is no doubt of the dedication and conviction of the solo playing or of its natural spontaneity. The digital recording provides a natural balance and a vivid orchestral texture. Though not as rich in timbre as Mintz's performance, this has a pervading freshness that gives much pleasure. The tape is first-class and while the compact disc does not bring the degree of improvement over the normal issue that the finest examples of this new medium readily provide, the opening of the concerto obviously gains from the background silence. The balance is not wholly convincing (though the soloist is cleanly focused in front) and woodwind detail is not as freshly delineated as on the more impressive Decca CDs.

Menuhin's performance has long held an honoured place in the catalogue. The recording is beginning to show its age now, but Menuhin was in good form when he made the disc and his playing is much more technically secure than in his later version, coupled to Bruch's *Second Concerto* (see below). The performance has a fine spontaneity, the work's improvisatory quality skilfully caught, and there is no doubt about the poetry Menuhin finds in the slow movement, or the sparkle in the finale. The cassette – originally non-Dolby – has been successfully remastered. The bright, forward sound has a tendency to fierceness (as has the LP) in tuttis, but responds to a treble reduction.

Ricci has an outstanding technique and he has also a very characteristic tone, which alongside Perlman's rich sound, for instance, is more open and uncovered. But the performance here has a fine intensity and there is a natural warmth which brings out the music's temperament without indulging it. The stereo recording matches the playing with well-defined quality and plenty of depth, and the cassette transfer is very successful. An excellent medium-priced recommendation.

Pierre Amoyal is an eloquent player whose purity of tone and intonation and generosity of feeling make him a joy to listen to. In the Bruch he lacks something of the panache of Perlman or Mintz; he is closer to Yong Uck Kim (whose playing is underrated), but he has a fine sense of line. The RPO under Scimone give good support and the recording has plenty of detail and body, even if the soloist is placed rather further forward than is ideal. The effortless, unsensational musicianship of the playing gives much pleasure and the Glazounov coupling is highly desirable. The cassette transfer is made at a good level and is lively and full, although the big orchestral climax to the first movement is muddied by the resonance.

The Oistrakhs' DG Privilege version has been recoupled with the Bach *Double concerto*, a fine performance featuring the same partnership, but hardly an imaginative choice. The Bruch is passionately done, father and son combining to make the close of the *Adagio* swell up into a surge of feeling. The first movement is well shaped and the finale has splendid rhythmic verve. The snag is the recording, which is aggressively brilliant and slightly harsh, lacking opulence. The cassette has a smoother upper range (without loss of definition) and is preferable to the disc.

Milstein's aristocratic and lyrical playing undoubtedly gives pleasure and he is well supported. The recording is good, although it could be fresher and more expansive. However, at bargain price this is certainly excellent value. Disc and cassette are closely matched.

Yong Uck Kim's performances of both the Bruch and the Mendelssohn impress by their purity of style and understated feeling. But such an approach is rather less successful in this ripely romantic work than in the coupling, which readily responds to such delicacy of feeling. Unfortunately the orchestral accompaniment does not match the solo playing in finesse, but the recording is good and well balanced; the tape is slightly less transparent than the disc.

Violin concertos Nos. 1; 2 in D min., Op. 44.
**(*) HMV ASD 2852 [Ang. S 36920]. Menuhin, LSO, Boult.

Were not the Bruch *First Violin concerto* such a striking masterpiece the *Second* might be better known. Its melodies have less individuality, but its romanticism is unforced and attractive and it is strong in atmosphere. Menuhin is persuasive in the warmth and obvious affection of his interpretation, but he tends to be somewhat sketchy in the detail of the solo part, and the intonation and focus of his playing are far from exact. Yet it says a great deal for the strength of his musical personality that, in spite of the technical lapses, the performance is so enjoyable. Boult's accompaniment is equally sympathetic and many will feel this a worthwhile addition to the catalogue. With the *G minor Concerto*, Menuhin is on familiar ground, but there is no sign of over-familiarity, and the lovely slow movement is given a performance of great warmth and spiritual beauty. The orchestra accompanies admirably and the recording is excellent throughout the disc.

Violin concerto No. 1; Scottish fantasia, Op. 26.
*** Decca SXL/*KSXC* 6573 [Lon. CS 6795]. Kyung-Wha Chung, RPO, Kempe.
(M) ** Ph. Seq. 6527/*7311* 122 [id.]. Grumiaux, New Philh. O, Wallberg.

Violin concerto No. 2; Scottish fantasia.
*** HMV ASD 3310 [Ang. S/*4XS* 37210]. Perlman, New Philh. O, Lopez-Cobos.

The magic of Kyung-Wha Chung, a spontaneously inspired violinist if ever there was one, comes over beguilingly in this very desirable Bruch coupling. There may be more glossily perfect accounts of the famous *G minor Concerto*, but Kyung-Wha Chung goes straight to the heart, finding mystery and fantasy as well as more extrovert qualities. Just as strikingly in the *Scottish fantasia* she transcends the episodic nature of the writing to give the music a genuine depth and concentration, above all in the lovely slow movement. Kempe and the Royal Philharmonic, not always perfectly polished, give sympathetic accompaniment, well caught in a glowing recording. The cassette is good too, but not quite as richly recorded as the disc.

Superlative playing from Perlman invests the first movement of the *Second Violin concerto* with such warmth that it compares favourably with the more famous G minor work. In Perlman's hands both the main themes are given a soaring memorability, and the coda is exquisitely managed. If the rest of the work has a lower level of inspiration, it is still richly enjoyable, and Perlman's account of the delightful *Scottish fantasia* is wholly delectable, showing the same degree of stylish lyricism and eloquence of phrasing. For those who already have a record of the *First Concerto* this coupling will be ideal, and the EMI recording is fully worthy of the performances.

Grumiaux brings all his beauty of tone and expressive technique to both the concerto and the *Scottish fantasia*. Eminently civilized performances, yet a shade cool; Miss Chung has the greater fervour and flair, and she is more vividly recorded. The cassette is lively and vivid but the bass is rather explosive in the tuttis of the *Concerto* and in the *Scottish fantasia* the focus is not absolutely crisp.

Kol Nidrei, Op. 47.

*** HMV ASD 3728. Tortelier, RPO, Yan-Pascal Tortelier – BOELLMANN: *Symphonic variations* ***; SCHUMANN: *Concerto.***(*)

(*) Decca Dig. **410 144-2; SXDL/*KSXDC* 7608 [Lon. LDR/5- 71108]. Harrell, Philh. O, Ashkenazy – DVOŘÁK: *Cello concerto.***(*)

(B) *(*) Con. CC/*CCT* 7585 [Mercury 75045]. Starker, LSO, Dorati – DVOŘÁK: *Concerto.**(*)

The withdrawn, prayerful Bruch piece makes a good contrast with the more ambitious works on the HMV issue, all well played and recorded.

Lynn Harrell's account with Ashkenazy is both eloquent and atmospheric and certainly very well recorded, especially in its compact disc format. But other accounts of this work, including Tortelier's, have been even more memorable and the Dvořák coupling is somewhat disappointing.

Starker's recording has a Mercury source. The opening is rather stiff and the performance as a whole lacks the romantic urgency that this work needs.

Konzertstück, Op. 84; Scottish fantasia, Op. 46.

*** Ph. 9500 423/*7300 641* [id.]. Accardo, Leipzig GO, Masur.

The *Konzertstück* dates from 1911 and is one of Bruch's last works. As in the case of the *Serenade*, Bruch had toyed with the idea of calling it a violin concerto, but he finally decided on *Konzertstück* as the piece has only two movements. This is its first complete recording, but the American violinist Maud Powell made a disc of part of the slow movement in Bruch's lifetime. The composer wrote in horror to a friend: 'She appears to have played the *Adagio*, shortened by half, into a machine. I really gave her a piece of my mind about this.' One wonders what he would have thought of the present version. Neither this nor the *Scottish fantasia*, written more than three decades earlier, is great music, but it is made the most of by Accardo and the Leipzig orchestra, and is superbly recorded. The cassette transfer is lively but the upper range lacks the refinement of the disc.

Septet, Op. posth.

*** DG Dig. 2532/*3302* 077 [id.]. Berlin PO (members) – MENDELSSOHN: *Octet.***

Bruch's *Septet* came to light as recently as 1981 and is a product of his childhood. Indeed it is an astonishing achievement for a boy of eleven even in an age of such prodigies as Mendelssohn and Rossini. His admiration for Beethoven is evident and although the thematic substance is not particularly memorable, save for the scherzo which is delightful, it is still all rather remarkable. One can hardly expect it to have the individuality of the mature composer or the young Mendelssohn with whose *Octet* it is, appropriately enough, coupled. Good playing and good, if closely balanced, recording. The chrome cassette is of demonstration quality.

Bruckner, Anton
(1824–96)

Symphonies Nos. 0; 1–9.

(M) **(*) Ph. 6717 002 (12). Concg. O, Haitink.

(M) **(*) DG 2740 253 (12). Chicago SO, Barenboim.

Symphonies Nos. 1–9.

*** DG 2740 264 (11) [id.]. Berlin PO, Karajan.

*** HMV SLS 5252 (11). Dresden State O, Jochum.

Symphonies Nos. 1–9; (i) *Te Deum.*

(M) **(*) DG 2740 136 (11). Bav. RSO or Berlin PO, Jochum (i) with soloists and chorus.

It is a pity that Karajan does not include the *Nullte* in his cycle, and No. 6 is less concentrated than the rest. But with its spacious speeds, dramatic contrasts and refined playing the cycle overall sets new standards, even if the digital recording for Nos. 1–3 has the orchestral sound closer and less alluring than the rest.

Barenboim's cycle has many excellent things, not least the account of No. 8 (see below), an admirable *Sixth* and a more than serviceable version of the *Ninth*. Barenboim gives us the underrated *Nullte* (see below), though here he is less successful than Haitink. He brings keener and deeper responses in No. 3, and although these performances are not to be recommended in preference to Karajan and Jochum, at their best – as in the *Eighth* – they deserve to rank alongside them, which is no mean achievement. In Nos. 1–3 and 8 Barenboim has the advantage of excellent digital sound. No one investing in this set is likely to be greatly disappointed, though the Karajan cycle will give deeper satisfaction.

As a Brucknerian Eugen Jochum has special magnetism. Whatever the reservations that may be made on detailed points of style – Jochum believes in a free variation of tempo within a movement – his natural affinity of temperament with the saintly, innocent Austrian gives these massive structures an easy, warm, unforced concentration which brings out their lyricism as well as their architectural grandeur. So it is in all these fine performances with the Dresden orchestra. As in his earlier cycle for DG with the Berlin Philharmonic and Bavarian Radio orchestras he uses the Nowak edition which, in *No. 8* for example, means that the span of the finale is less spacious. The playing of the Dresden orchestra cannot always quite match that of the West German rivals of a decade and more earlier, but with opulent, wide-ranging recording from EMI it makes a superb collection, as warmly convincing in its way as any direct rival.

Whether as a box or taken individually Haitink's accounts of the ten Bruckner symphonies he has recorded have all the classical virtues. They are well-shaped, free from affectation and any kind of agogic distortion; Haitink's grasp of the architecture is strong and his feeling for beauty of detail refined. Perhaps he has a less developed sense of mystery and atmosphere than Jochum, whose readings have a spiritual dimension at which Haitink only hints.

Jochum's earlier set for DG (which includes also the *Te Deum*) remains worth considering at medium-price. There is a strong sense of ambience in the performances and those who look for spiritual qualities and a feeling of mystery will find Jochum's approach more subtle than Haitink's though Haitink's judgements on matters of text are more likely to please the scholar. The playing of the Berlin Philharmonic and Bavarian Radio orchestras is consistently fine and the sound remains very good for its period.

Symphony No. 1 in C min.

**(*) DG Dig. 2532/*3302* 062 [id.]. Berlin PO, Karajan.

(M) ** Ph. Seq. 6527/*7311* 142. Concg. O, Haitink.

Karajan's digital recording for this early symphony is brighter and less sympathetic than that for the later symphonies recorded in analogue sound. It is still a powerful and incisive reading of a work which may come at the beginning of a massive symphony cycle but which is in no sense an immature piece, written as it was when the composer was already in his forties. Karajan as a Brucknerian, here as elsewhere, has a clear-headed concentration, making light of the problems of coordinating arguments which in lesser hands can seem rambling. The chrome cassette is smoother on top and has less bite and impact than the LP.

Haitink's Philips recording has been remastered and the sound, though brightly projected and well detailed, has lost a good deal of its richness and is dry in the bass. There is some eloquent playing from the Concertgebouw Orchestra, particularly in the wind departments, and Haitink's performance is well structured, but the sound is less attractive than it was at full price. There is a matching cassette.

Symphony No. 2 in C min.

(M) *** Ph. 6527/*7311* 183. Concg. O, Haitink.

**(*) DG Dig. 2532/*3302* 063 [id.]. Berlin PO, Karajan.

Haitink uses the fuller version favoured by Haas. Characteristically Haas takes the view that Bruckner agreed to cuts with the thought that performance would be brought nearer and that left to himself he would not have favoured them. Most dedicated Brucknerians will probably agree, and this fine performance, clear-headed, direct, unmannered, presents the work in the freshest possible light. One sometimes misses Jochum's more persuasive manner, but no one wanting Bruckner's fullest thoughts in this powerful and noble work will be disappointed here. Clear Philips recording, which emerges freshly in this new transfer. There is a good tape too, clear, full and vivid.

Karajan's reading is not only powerful and polished, it is distinctive both on matters of tempi and of text. He modifies the Nowak edition by opening out some of the cuts, but by no means all. He starts reticently, only later opening out in grandeur. The scherzo at a fast speed is surprisingly lightweight, the finale relatively slow and spacious. It is a noble reading, not always helped by rather fierce digital recording. However the chrome tape is much smoother than the disc, and seems fuller too.

Symphony No. 3 in D min.
*** DG Dig. **413 362-2**; 2532/*3302* 007 [id.]. Berlin PO, Karajan.
(M) **(*) Decca Jub. JB/*KJBC* 126. VPO, Boehm.

Karajan's account of the *Third Symphony* is very impressive indeed. He opts for the Nowak edition of 1888–9 as opposed to the fuller 1878 version favoured by such Bruckner authorities as Robert Simpson and the late Deryck Cooke. One cannot fail to be awe-struck by the eloquence and beauty of the orchestral playing and the command of architecture that Karajan shows. His digital recording is marvellously spacious and refined. Karajan achieves a sense of majesty in the opening movement and an other-worldliness and spirituality in the slow movement that cannot fail to move the listener. We are not short of superb accounts of this score yet the Karajan is second to none and will be a first choice for many. Haitink used the 1878 edition in his set but must yield to Karajan in terms of sheer atmosphere. Disc and cassette are very closely matched.

Boehm's Vienna Philharmonic version has been reissued at mid-price on Jubilee. The Decca recording is excellent with splendid detail and firm sonority, and the performance is admirably free from eccentricity. Like Karajan and Jochum he opts for the Nowak text and if his version is less imaginative than either of theirs it still offers fine playing and makes a good mid-priced alternative. There is an excellent cassette, though the slow movement break remains.

Symphony No. 4 in E flat (*Romantic*).
*** DG 2530/*3300* 674 [id.]. Berlin PO, Karajan.
(M) *** DG Priv. 2535 111. Berlin PO, Jochum.
*** Decca Dig. **410 550-2**; SXDL/*KSXDC* 7538 [Lon. LDR/*5*- 71038]. Chicago SO, Solti.
(M) *** Decca Jub. JB/*KJBC* 120. VPO, Boehm.
(M) *** Ph. Seq. 6527/*7311* 101 [id.]. Concg. O, Haitink.
**(*) HMV Dig. SLS/*TCC-SLS* 5279 (2) [Ang. DSB/*4X2S* 3935]. Berlin PO, Tennstedt.
(M) **(*) HMV SXLP 30167 [Ang. RL/*4RL* 32059]. Philh. O, Klemperer.
** HM 1C 065 99738 [Pro. PAC/*P4C* 1044]. Cologne RSO, Wand.
(M) *(*) DG Sig. 410 835-1/*4* [2530 336 PSI]. Chicago SO, Barenboim.
(M) * Decca VIV/*KVIC* 53. LAPO, Mehta.

Choice for Bruckner's *Fourth* is wider than for any other of his symphonies and many of these recordings will give satisfaction in different ways. Karajan has recorded the work twice. His HMV record is now withdrawn but the DG version, recorded five years after the HMV, is tauter and more crisply disciplined, while keeping all the qualities of strength and mystery. In the slow movement Karajan's lyricism is simpler and more natural, less consciously expressive than before, and the DG recording quality is both rich and refined, superb in every way despite the very long sides. The cassette is clear but rather dry in the bass.

Jochum's way with Bruckner is unique. So gentle is his hand that the opening of each movement or even the beginning of each theme emerges into the consciousness rather than starting normally. And when it is a matter of leading from one section to another over a difficult transition passage – as in the lead-in to the first-movement recapitulation – no one can match Jochum in his subtlety and persuasiveness. The purist may object that to do this Jochum reduces the speed far below what is marked, but Jochum is for the man who wants above all to love Bruckner.

As a Brucknerian Solti can hardly be faulted, choosing admirable tempi, keeping concentration taut through the longest paragraphs, and presenting the architecture of the work in total clarity. Raptness is there too, and only the relative lack of Brucknerian idiosyncrasy will disappoint those who prefer a more loving, personal approach. Like Klemperer, Haitink and Boehm, Solti prefers the Nowak edition with the opening motif brought back on the horns at the end of the finale. The tape transfer is one of Decca's finest, with impressive clarity and amplitude and, like the digital LP, has no lack of ambient feeling. The compact disc immediately establishes its advantage at the atmospheric opening horn call over shimmering strings, the more magnetizing when heard against silence. The slow movement gains similarly and the overall clarity and presence is the more striking in climaxes. Yet the slightly artificial brightness of the sound picture is more apparent too; this is not a mellow, cultured aural tapestry that one expects, for instance, from the Concertgebouw. But those who like plenty of brilliance from their Bruckner will find Solti's version meets their needs admirably. It could hardly be more different from Jochum's conception.

Boehm's very compelling version is beautifully shaped, finely played and splendidly recorded on disc and cassette alike. At medium price it deserves the strongest recommendation.

Haitink's performance has been reissued again on the mid-priced Sequenza label. It is noble and unmannered; the recording is excellent, and the orchestral playing eloquent. The tape is good. Excellent value.

Tennstedt's version is the first of a projected series of Bruckner symphonies with the Berlin Philharmonic, following up his Mahler cycle for EMI. Generously HMV presents it on two records for the price of one, matched by an excellent single double-length cassette (in a box) of high quality. The breadth of the recording is admirable, if with digital 'edge' on the high violins. This is a reading that combines concentration and a degree of ruggedness, less moulded than Karajan or Jochum in their very different ways. Here plainness goes with pure beauty and natural strength in the first two movements. The scherzo is urgent, the finale resplendent. With one or two modifications, the Haas edition is used. Not a first choice, but compelling all the same.

Klemperer's performance with the Philharmonia is for those who primarily seek architectural strength. The reading is magisterial and the finale has an impressive weight and cogency. Some ears find this performance wanting in atmosphere and too marmoreal, but there is no question about its power or the vividness of the remastered HMV recording.

Günter Wand's reading has been much acclaimed in some quarters. His tempi are inclined to be a little brisker than usual, which serves to hold the architecture together more tautly than is sometimes the case. The orchestral playing is good though not in the top drawer, and the recording is fully acceptable. This is a good, serviceable and often perceptive account, but it falls short of the highest distinction.

Barenboim's version offers excellent sound but in such a competitive field must be passed over. The Chicago orchestra play magnificently, but the reading is mannered and the insights confined to the surface.

Mehta's version, too, is very well recorded, on disc and cassette alike, but the performance is without any real depth of feeling, though quite well played.

Symphony No. 5 in B flat.

*** DG 2707 101/*3370 025* (2) [id.]. Berlin PO, Karajan.

**(*) Decca Dig. D 221 D 2/*K 221 K 22* (2) [Lon. LDR 10031]. Chicago SO, Solti.

*(*) DG 2707 113 (2) [id.]. Chicago SO, Barenboim.

Symphony No. 5; (i) *Te Deum.*
(M) *** Ph. 6725/*7655* 021 (2). Concg. O, Haitink (i) with Ameling, Reynolds, Hoffman, Hoekman, Netherlands R. Ch.

Haitink's fine version has been reissued at medium price on three sides with his blazing account of the *Te Deum* – one of the best things he has given us – on the fourth. Haitink's view of the symphony may lack the last ounce of atmosphere and mystery, but it undoubtedly conveys the grandeur and sweep of this noble symphony. It is free from egocentric mannerisms but the orchestral playing has eloquence and the sound is sonorous, even though the upper strings, as so often in the Concertgebouw's recordings, are a little wanting in bloom. The cassettes are issued in a single hinged plastic box of double width. The recording is impressively refined, with the big climax of the finale opening up splendidly. In the *Te Deum* there is plenty of life in the choral sound.

Karajan's reading is not just poised and polished; it is superbly structured on every level, clear on detail as well as on overall architecture. Maybe the slow movement lacks some of the simple dedication which makes Jochum's reading with the same orchestra (currently not available separately) so compelling, but here as in his other Bruckner performances for DG, Karajan takes a patrician view of this great and individual symphonist. The playing of the Berlin Philharmonic is magnificent and the recording rich and opulent to match, more spacious than some other recent offerings from this source. The cassette transfer is sophisticated and refined in detail (although, as usual in Karajan DG recordings, the perspective changes slightly in the pianissimos).

Even in Bruckner Solti's conducting tends to give off electric sparks, and the precise control of this performance underlines dramatic contrasts, helped by the clarity and brilliance of the digital recording. The slow movement finds the necessary warmth, with Solti in what for him might be counted Elgarian mood. Like the discs the cassette transfer offers sound which is sharply defined in its clarity of focus, and the biggest climaxes bring no hint of congestion.

Daniel Barenboim's account with the Chicago Symphony Orchestra falls short on many counts and offers no challenge to Karajan's masterly version. It is disfigured by some curiously self-conscious touches: why, for instance, the loss of momentum before the entry of the chorale in the finale? There is some good playing from the Chicago orchestra, but Barenboim does not seem to have the measure of the work's architecture or vision, strange in an artist whose Brucknerian credentials have been amply demonstrated elsewhere in this cycle.

Symphony No. 6 in A.
(M) *** HMV SXLP 30448. New Philh. O, Klemperer.
**(*) DG 2531/*3301* 295 [id.]. Berlin PO, Karajan.
**(*) Decca SXL/*KSXC* 6946 [Lon. CS/*5-*7173]. Chicago SO, Solti.

Starting with a spacious account of the first movement, grandly majestic, sharply architectural, Klemperer directs a characteristically strong and direct reading. It is disarmingly simple rather than expressive in the slow movement (faster than usual) but is always concentrated and strong, with splendid playing from the orchestra and recording that hardly shows its early-1960s vintage. Bruckner's massive climaxes are accommodated without strain – in spite of the high level – and the inner detail is excellent. The brass is very telling (particularly the horns) and the string tone is warm and clear.

In this less expansive Bruckner symphony, posing a lesser challenge, Karajan is not so commanding as usual in his Bruckner recordings. It is still a compelling performance, tonally very beautiful and with a glowing account of the slow movement that keeps it in proportion – not quite the match of the sublime slow movements of Nos. 8 and 9. The cassette transfer is brilliant without being fierce; it is cleanly focused, slightly dry in the bass.

Solti offers a strong, rhetorical reading, powerfully convincing in the outer movements and helped by playing and recording of outstanding quality. Where he is less persuasive is in the slow movement, which fails to flow quite as it should; the expressiveness does not sound truly spontaneous. The cassette transfer is first-class, with fine body, transparency of detail and a complete absence of congestion.

Symphony No. 7 in E.

*** DG 2707 102/*3370 023* (2) [id.]. Berlin PO, Karajan – WAGNER: *Siegfried idyll.* ***

*** Ph. 6769 028/*7699 113* (2) [id.]. Concg. O, Haitink – WAGNER: *Siegfried idyll.****

(M) *** DG Priv. 2726 054 (2). Berlin PO, Jochum – WAGNER: *Parsifal: Prelude and Good Friday music.***(*)

(M) ** Ph. 6833 253. Concg. O, Haitink.

*(*) Uni. RHS/*UKC* 356. Danish State RO, Sanderling.

Like Bruckner's *Fourth*, Karajan recorded the *Seventh* for HMV five years before his DG version. The earlier reading showed a superb feeling for the work's architecture, and the playing of the Berlin Philharmonic was gorgeous. Yet in the newer DG version Karajan draws even more compelling playing from them, and this version shows even greater power and nobility. It is undoubtedly a great performance and is splendidly served by the engineers, with a richly textured string quality matched by brass timbres of comparable bite and sonority. The cassette transfer too is very impressive, nearly matching the discs in refinement.

Haitink's later reading of the *Seventh* is more searching and spacious than the version he recorded in the 1960s. The first movement is considerably slower and gains in mystery and atmosphere, and the *Adagio* expands in vision too. Yet there is nothing studied here; both movements grow with an unforced naturalness that is deeply impressive, and there is an altogether richer world of feeling. The Concertgebouw Orchestra play with their accustomed opulence of tone and marvellously blended ensemble, and the recording is wider in range and has greater presence. This goes to the top of the list and can be recommended alongside the Karajan, which is similarly coupled. The tape transfer is comparably sophisticated; the great slow-movement climax, resplendently capped with its cymbal clash, is caught without strain. There is just a hint of roughness in the closing fortissimo of the finale, but not enough to spoil the listener's pleasure.

Jochum's approach to the *Seventh* is entirely characteristic, with a relaxed manner and generally slow tempi in all four movements. But the concentration is never in doubt; such a passage as the transition into the second subject in the slow movement is characteristic of the magic that the conductor distils in this marvellous score. With no serious textual problems to worry about, this Privilege reissue stands high among the contrasted recorded performances of this symphony. The fill-up, originally coupled to the *Fifth Symphony*, is also recommendable.

Haitink's one-disc version of the *Seventh* has the merits of directness and grasp of architecture. It is by no means as expansive, spacious – or for that matter expensive – as his two-record version made in 1979, and though this is well balanced and finely conceived, the later version has far greater sensitivity to atmosphere. At medium price Jochum's DG version (see above) still holds its own and does not need a turn-over in the slow movement.

Symphony No. 8 in C min.

*** DG 2707 085/*3370 019* (2) [id.]. Berlin PO, Karajan.

(B) *** CfP CFPD/*TC-CFPD* 414434-3/*5* (2). Berlin PO, Karajan.

*** Ph. Dig. 6769/*7654* 080 (2) [id.]. Concg. O, Haitink.

*** HMV Dig. SLS/*TCC-SLS* 5290 [Ang. OSB/*4X2S* 3936]. LPO, Tennstedt.

Symphony No. 8. (i) *Te Deum.*

*** DG Dig. 2741/*3382* 007 (2). Chicago SO, Barenboim, (i) with Norman, Minton, Rendall, Ramey, Ch.

Even in Bruckner's most expansive symphony there is a volatile element in Barenboim's reading. The passionate manner which expresses itself in flexible phrasing and urgent stringendi takes something from the ruggedness of the work. At times it is almost as though Bruckner were being given a neurotic streak, reviving the false old idea of a link with Mahler. But that may exaggerate the point, for, with superb playing and digital recording which, apart from some thinness on high violin tone, is excellent, this is a fine, concentrated version. The chrome tape offers demonstration quality. In the *Symphony* the bloom and clarity of the strings is matched by the resonance and bite of the brass; the *Te Deum* sounds remarkably fresh and incisive, yet full-bodied, losing little on the disc in the fullest choral climaxes.

There is amazingly little to choose between Karajan's 1958 EMI recording (now reissued on CfP) and his 1976 DG set as far as sound is concerned. The CfP pressings have splendid definition and a sense of spaciousness as well as great presence. The newer DG set has greater richness and refinement of texture, but both performances are noble and searching and it is interesting to observe the consistency of Karajan's approach to the score over the years. The newer version has the greater depth and it is this which in the end tips the scales in its favour. Majestic, massive in scale, yet immaculate in detail. But in the earlier account the performance of the slow movement is very fine indeed and it has the advantage of economy, for it costs about half as much as the later issue. The DG cassettes are very successful. There is a warmth to the sound and a beautiful sheen on the high strings which gives special distinction here and the expansive climaxes are handled without strain until the closing pages of the finale, where the refinement slips fractionally.

Haitink's is a noble reading of this massive symphony using the extended Haas edition. Never one to force the pace, Haitink's degree of restraint will please those who find Karajan too powerfully concentrated. The spaciousness of the slow movement brings a rare clarity and refinement; the tempo relentlessly steady, even slower than Karajan's. The recording is refined and well-balanced to match. The cassettes are impressively clear and spacious, of Philips's best quality.

The plainness and honesty of Tennstedt in Bruckner is well illustrated in his fine account of the *Eighth*. It may not have the visionary exaltation which marked the performance which Tennstedt conducted with this same orchestra at the Proms of 1983, somewhat after the recording, but the inwardness and hushed beauty of the great *Adagio* in particular are superbly conveyed in unforced concentration. Though Karajan and Jochum both convey more of the work's power, Tennstedt in his relative reticence carries equal conviction. Where generally in the other symphonies Tennstedt prefers the Haas editions to those of Nowak, here he is firmly in favour of Nowak without the additional material in the recapitulation. Fine, well-balanced recording but with a transfer at rather a low level. The single chrome tape (supplied in a box-album) is of demonstration quality, wide-ranging, clear and beautiful. For some this will be first choice.

Symphony No. 9 in D min.

(M) *** DG Acc. 2542/*3342* 129 [2535/*3335* 342]. Berlin PO, Karajan.

*** HMV ASD 4218 [Ang. S/*4XS* 37700]. Dresden State O, Jochum.

*** Ph. Dig. **410 039-2**; 6514/*7337* 191 [id.]. Concg. O, Haitink.

*** DG 2530/*3300* 828 [id.]. Berlin PO, Karajan.

(M) **(*) Decca Jub. JB/*KJBC* 108. VPO, Mehta.

(M) *(*) HMV SXLP/*TC-SXLP* 30546 [Ang. S/*4XS* 37287]. Chicago SO, Giulini.

The Accolade reissue offers a glorious performance of Bruckner's last, uncompleted symphony, moulded in a way that is characteristic of Karajan, with a simple, direct nobility that is sometimes missing in his work. Here he seems not to feel it necessary to underline, but with glowing playing from the Berlin Philharmonic and superb recording he gives the illusion of letting the music speak for itself. Yet no one has a clearer idea of Bruckner's architecture, and as one appreciates the subtle gradation of climax in the concluding slow movement, one knows how firmly Karajan's sights have been set on this goal all along. Even in a competitive field this stands out. The differences between this superlative version from the late sixties and Karajan's later one (DG 2530/*3300* 828), recorded with the same orchestra eight years later, are relatively small. The clue lies principally in the differences of recording quality, sharper and closer in the latter version to suggest that Karajan wanted to convey a tougher impression. Where the earlier version brings natural gravity and profound contemplation in greater measure, with manners a degree more affectionate, the newer one concentrates on strength and impact. As before, the playing of the Berlin Philharmonic is immaculate. The Accolade cassette is generally well managed. Although the transfer level is not really high, the recording's atmosphere and the detail are well captured, and the only real drawback is the splitting of the scherzo, which turns over for the reprise of the first section, so unnecessary on a cassette.

The warmth as well as the power of Jochum in Bruckner set his readings apart, and this Dresden account of the last, uncompleted symphony is a splendid example of his art, with the Dresden strings made to sound weighty and sonorous in a fine digital recording. Jochum far more than is fashionable these days allows himself a wide degree of flexibility over tempi. Here he is at his most persuasive, giving an impression of spontaneity such as you would expect in the concert hall.

The extremely measured speed of the first movement in Haitink's pure and dedicated reading may be taken as a deciding factor. He underlines the elegiac mood. Though the great dynamic contrasts are superbly and fearlessly caught – with compact disc even more immediate and involving than LP or cassette – this is not so thrustful an interpretation as Jochum's or Karajan's. The spaciousness of the sound against an ambient Concertgebouw acoustic gives a degree of distancing which matches the interpretation. It is the more effective on CD, adding to the feeling of tangible presence. On CD the absence of background and the bite of fortissimos are specially impressive, as well as the clarity and refinement of light textures. The chrome cassette is fresh and refined, spacious and full, but registers detail rather less sharply than the disc versions.

Mehta's reading has moments of considerable power and orchestral playing of great splendour. There is a touch of febrile, oversweet vibrato on the strings at the opening of the finale, which is somewhat tiresome on repetition, but this remains a satisfying version even if it does not match Karajan's Accolade version in overall cogency. Decca's recording is up to the high standards of the house; the cassette transfer is first-class too.

Giulini's version is a good deal less persuasive than its rivals. There is no lack of power or grandeur, and, predictably, Giulini expends enormous care over detail, fashioning each phrase with care and thought. Indeed, that may lie at the heart of the problem, for in some way the sheer mystery of this noble score seems to elude him, even though he uncovers much beauty of detail. The recording on both disc and tape has a fine, spacious sound. But something goes awry in the horn parts in the first movement (bars 551 onwards), and this issue cannot challenge Karajan's.

Intermezzo and trio for string quintet.
*** CRD CRD 1046/*CRDC 4046*. Augmented Alberni Qt – BRAHMS: *Sextet No. 2.****

Bruckner wrote this attractive *Intermezzo and trio* as an alternative movement for the scherzo of his *Quintet in F major*, which was considered 'too difficult'. Following on after the vigorous finale of the Brahms *Sextet* the autumnal feeling of the Bruckner with its lighter (but still rich) textures makes a most pleasing encore. The recording is excellent and the tape transfer is freshly vivid, with fine range and detail.

VOCAL MUSIC

(i) *Heligoland; Psalm 150;* (ii) *Te Deum.*
(M) **(*) DG Sig. 410 650-1. (i) Welting; (ii) Norman, Minton, Rendall, Ramey; (i; ii) Chicago SO Ch. and O, Barenboim.

This neatly couples works previously issued as fill-ups to symphonies in Barenboim's Chicago series. The magnificent *Te Deum* and *Psalm 150* are majestically done, though Ruth Welting is too shallow in the *Psalm* and David Rendall too tight of tone in the *Te Deum. Heligoland* is the valuable rarity, a cantata in which the islanders pray to be spared from the marauding Romans. A storm saves them in this brief but graphic piece. The Chicago forces sing and play with heart-warming resonance, and are spaciously recorded.

Mass No. 3 in F min.
(M) **(*) DG Sig. 2543/*3343* 815. Stader, Hellmann, Haefliger, Borg, Bav. R. Ch. and SO, Jochum.
**(*) EMI 1C 047 28962. Lorengar, Ludwig, Traxel, Berry, St Hedwig's Cathedral Ch., Berlin SO, Forster.

The *F minor Mass* was completed in 1868, though Bruckner and Schalk made a number of later revisions. It is a highly rewarding work, but has not received a satisfactory modern recording to replace these two versions from the 1960s. Jochum has the finer team of soloists, but both he and Forster direct convincing accounts, with the EMI sound rather more spacious and resonant than the DG.

Motets: *Afferentur regi; Ave Maria; Christus factus est; Ecce sacerdos magnus; Inveni David; Locus iste; Os justi medititur; Pange lingua; Tota pulchra es; Vexilla regis; Virga Jesse.*
** Hyp. A 66062. Salmon, Corydon Singers, Best; Trotter (organ).

A much more resonant acoustic setting than the one which DG provided for Jochum in the late 1960s: his erred on the side of dryness but were it restored to circulation, it would take precedence over this record. The Corydon Singers under Matthew Best are not quite so well blended or as homogeneous in tone as were the Bavarian Radio Chorus, but Best's direction is often imaginative and he achieves a wide tonal range. The Motets span the best part of Bruckner's creative life, though given their devotional character, they are best heard two or three at a time rather than at one sitting.

Te Deum.
*** DG 2530/*3300* 704 [id.]. Tomowa-Sintow, Baltsa, Krenn, Schreier, Van Dam, V. Singverein, Berlin PO, Karajan – MOZART: *Mass No. 16.***(*)

Karajan's account is spacious and strong, bringing out the score's breadth and drama. This is very satisfying, and if the coupling is suitable this is self-recommending. Unfortunately the cassette transfer has some problems with the breadth and amplitude of the score and is not free from minor congestion.

Bruhns, Nikolaus (*c.* 1665–97)

Preludes Nos. 1 in G; 2–3 in E min.; Variations on 'Nun komm, der heiden Heiland'.
(M) ❀ *** Argo ZK 65. Weir (organ of Clare College, Camb.) – SCHEIDT: *Passamezzo variations.**** ❀

Bruhns died young and left only five organ works, of which four are recorded here. His individuality is striking, and so is the quirky originality of his musical style, which freely interchanges fugal passages and sections of fantasia using the most florid bravura. Gillian Weir has the full measure of this music, finding a perfect balance between the fantasy and the structural needs of each piece. She dazzles the ear not only with her vigour and virtuosity but also with some quite delicious registration on an organ that seems exactly right for the music. The recording is superb.

Buller, John born 1927

Proença (Provençal).
(M) *** Uni. UNS 266. Sarah and Timothy Walker, BBC SO, Elder.

Exuberance, energy and speed are not qualities one can often associate with new music, but they certainly apply to this masterly evocation of medieval Provence written in 1977, a work confidently large both in length and in the forces used. The sequence of settings of troubadour songs, often wild, often sensuous, brings out a surprising modernity in the attitudes of the original poets, relevant still after 700 years. So a love poem by a woman poet speaks with an absence of inhibition which even now sounds daring, and that is reflected in the music, with Sarah Walker a passionately committed soloist. Another layer is provided in the occasional contributions on electric guitar from Timothy Walker, adding a wild, amplified dimension to the sound. Mark Elder in his first recording superbly confirms the promise he has shown in the concert hall and opera house. The recording is aptly spectacular.

Burgon, Geoffrey (born 1941)

Requiem.
*** Argo Dig. ZRDL 1007 [id.]. Jennifer Smith, Murray, Rolfe Johnson, LSO Ch., Woburn Singers, City of L. Sinf., Hickox.

Geoffrey Burgon is now in his forties and has more than sixty works to his credit. He is best known for his incidental music to John le Carré's *Tinker, Tailor, Soldier, Spy* and Waugh's *Brideshead Revisited* on television. In idiom, this work owes much to Benjamin Britten and perhaps early Messiaen. Much of the writing is static in feeling but highly atmospheric. The composer has shown considerable resource in his handling of texture and though the melodic invention is unmemorable, the overall impression is quite powerful. The work enjoys committed advocacy from these artists and remarkably fine recording quality. Although the aspirations of this music may not quite be matched by its substance, this score has the power to fascinate the listener and it is well worth investigating.

Bush, Geoffrey (born 1920)

Symphony No. 1.
*** Lyr. SRCS 115. LSO, Braithwaite – ARNOLD: *Sinfonietta*; BENJAMIN: *Cotillon.****

Geoffrey Bush was a pupil of John Ireland, traces of whose influence can be discerned in his output and, like Ireland, he has shown great sensitivity in his setting of words. The finest of his songs, among which are his Herrick settings, are distinguished by a refined sense of line and feeling for atmosphere. The *First* of his two symphonies dates from 1954 and exhibits the traditional values of fine craftsmanship and directness of utterance by which he – and, for that matter, his companions on this record – set such store. He does not shrink from the notion that music should entertain and the main body of the first movement as well as the finale are much lighter in character than many contemporary British symphonists. At times one is reminded of Constant Lambert whose death inspired the slow movement, *Elegiac Blues*, which actually quotes from *The Rio Grande*. An alert performance and excellent recording in the best traditions of the house.

(i) *The end of love; Greek love songs;* (ii; iii) *A Little love music;* (iii) *3 Songs of Ben Jonson; Song of wonder.*
*** Chan. Dig. ABRD/*ABTD* 1053 [id.]. (i) Luxon; (ii) Cahill; (iii) Partridge; composer.

Geoffrey Bush has a particularly sensitive ear for the cadences of the English language and shows no lack of musical resource in their setting. He works within the tradition of John Ireland, with whom he studied, and Benjamin Britten, and his musical language is diatonic yet fresh. The repertoire ranges from his early Jonson settings (1952) through to the relatively recent cycle, *A Little love music* (1976) which are economical in style and touching in their directness of utterance. They are eminently well performed and though words are included, such is the clarity of these artists' diction that none are needed. Let us hope that the success of this record, which is splendidly balanced and very lifelike, will encourage some company to record the Herrick settings. The cassette transfer is admirably fresh and natural with good range.

Busoni, Ferruccio (1866–1924)

(i) *Piano concerto, Op. 39. Elegy No. 4 (Turandots Frauengemach); Sonatina No. 6 (Chamber fantasy on Bizet's 'Carmen'); 9 Variations on a Chopin prelude, Op. 22.*

(M) *** HMV SXDW 3053. Ogdon, (i) with John Alldis Ch., RPO, Revenaugh.

Busoni's *Piano concerto* is a strange and totally unconventional work, cast in five movements, the last of which incorporates a setting of lines from Oehlenschläger's *Aladdin*. Busoni composed it between 1902 and 1904 at a time when he had toyed with the idea of an opera based on *Aladdin*. The concerto runs to sixty-eight minutes and spreads over three sides. It is a commonplace to speak of Busoni bestriding two cultures, north and south of the Alps, but although there are Italian songs in the fourth movement, it is to Brahms that our thoughts turn in the Prologue, even if it is a Brahms suffused with Mediterranean light. This is not Busoni's greatest work but it has much striking and powerful invention, particularly in the first three movements. In Dent's words, it is more often the orchestra which 'seems possessed of the composer's prophetic inspiration', while Busoni sits at the piano, 'listens, comments, decorates and dreams'. John Ogdon has the measure of this extraordinary piece, and his magisterial and enthusiastic advocacy does much for it. The John Alldis Choir is first-rate in the final *Cantico*, and the orchestral support is thoroughly sympathetic. The recording dates from the late 1960s and is wonderfully clean and wide-ranging. No less impressive is the EMI transfer of part of Ogdon's début recital over twenty years ago, which brings three otherwise unobtainable Busoni rarities back into circulation. The playing is brilliant and exhilarating, and judging from the sound could have been recorded yesterday. At medium price this issue is an outstanding bargain, and though the concerto is certainly uneven it is well worth investigating.

Doktor Faust (opera): complete.
(M) *** DG 2740 273 (3). Fischer-Dieskau, Cochran, De Ridder, Hillebrecht, Kohn, Bav. R. Ch. and O, Leitner.

Busoni did not live to complete *Doktor Faust*, which crowns his creative career, and the task of finishing it was undertaken by his pupil Philipp Jarnach. It is a work of astonishing vision and originality whose fascination cannot be over-emphasized. This performance was recorded in conjunction with a broadcast mounted by the European Broadcasting Union, for the complexities of putting on a work of such importance are numerous. Fischer-Dieskau is, of course, a masterly Faust and dominates the proceedings (not that his is the only fine performance in the set), and the music is so deeply imaginative and richly rewarding that no one should lose the opportunity of investing in this recording. We are never likely to get another so that even the irritation one feels at the small but tiresome cuts made (presumably for the broadcast) and fury that these should all be applied to Busoni's text while Jarnach's completion is untouched, and the less than ideal casting for the Duchess of Parma, should not be allowed to qualify a recommendation. This is an enormously rewarding score, and DG give us recording quality of high standard, though the voices at times mask some of the orchestral detail.

Butterworth, George (1885–1916)

The Banks of Green Willow (idyll); *2 English idylls; A Shropshire Lad* (rhapsody).
*** Argo ZRG/*KZRC* 860 [id.]. ASMF, Marriner – BRITTEN: *Variations on a theme of Frank Bridge*.***

The Banks of Green Willow; A Shropshire Lad.
(M) *** HMV Green. ESD/*TC-ESD* 7100. E. Sinfonia, Dilkes – *Concert* (*English music*).***

A Shropshire Lad.
(B) ** PRT GSGC/*ZCGC* 2059. Hallé O, Barbirolli – BAX: *Garden of Fand*; VAUGHAN WILLIAMS: *Symphony No. 8*.**

Butterworth's *Shropshire Lad* represents the English folksong school at its most captivatingly atmospheric, and the other works are in a similarly appealing pastoral vein. Whether Butterworth would have gone on, had he lived through the First World War, to develop as his friend Vaughan Williams did is an interesting point, but the delicate genius here is displayed at its most rewarding.

Marriner's performances with the Academy are comparably beautiful, without the last degree of finesse, but very fine indeed, with vivid, wide-ranging recording quality. An excellent recommendation for those who prefer the Britten coupling to the Dilkes collection.

The performances by Dilkes and the English Sinfonia are also sensitive, and with fine, ripe recording on both disc and cassette this makes an excellent recommendation; the couplings include music by Bax, Frank Bridge and Harty (see the Concerts section below).

Barbirolli brings characteristic ardour to his wonderfully expressive performance, and as part of a vintage collection of English music at bargain price, this should not be dismissed. The recording is restricted (especially on cassette), but the sound has bloom and the playing has great character.

Songs: *Bredon Hill; Folk songs from Sussex: A lawyer he went out; The true lover's farewell; Roving in the dew. I fear thy kisses; I will make you brooches; O fair enough are sky and plain; On the idle hill of summer; Requiescat; When the lad for longing sies; With rue my heart is laden.*

(*) Hyp. A 66037. Trew, Vignoles – VAUGHAN WILLIAMS: *Songs of travel.*

This generous collection of Butterworth songs intelligently sung and well recorded makes a splendid coupling for the Vaughan Williams *Songs of Travel* on the reverse. Butterworth's creative spark was not always so original a one as that of his friend, Vaughan Williams, but these happily lyrical settings of Housman and others point the loss from his death in the First World War. His response to English lyric verse was easy and perceptive, and songs such as these should be accepted, as Lieder settings are in Germany. Trew's voice is on the dry side, but is well recorded. Vignoles makes an ideal accompanist.

Love Blows as the Wind (3 songs).

*** HMV ASD 3896. Tear, CBSO, Handley – ELGAR: *Songs* ***; VAUGHAN WILLIAMS: *On Wenlock Edge.***(*)

These charming songs to words by W. E. Henley provide an excellent makeweight for a mixed bag of orchestral songs based on the first recording of Vaughan Williams's cycle in its orchestral form. The sound is enjoyably warm and atmospheric.

A Shropshire Lad (song cycle).

(*) Pearl SHE 527. Carol Case, Ibbott – SOMERVELL: *Maud.**

A Shropshire Lad; Bredon Hill (song cycle).

*** Argo ZRG 838. Luxon, Willison – FINZI: *Earth and Air and Rain.****

Benjamin Luxon gives powerful, dramatic performances of songs which can take such treatment, not quite such miniatures as they may sometimes seem. But while he can project his tone and the words with great power, his delicate half-tones are equally impressive. In both the six songs in the regular *Shropshire Lad* cycle and the other Housman settings (which make an ideal companion set), Luxon underlines the aptness of the music to words often set by British composers but never more understandingly than here. Well-balanced recording. John Carol Case's fresh and sensitive version, slightly understated, makes an excellent alternative – an attractive fill-up to the major Somervell cycle which takes up most of the record. Excellent recording.

Buxtehude, Diderik

(*c.* 1637–1707)

Trio sonatas for violin, viola da gamba and harpsichord: in A. min., Op. 1/3; in B flat, Op. 1/4; in G min., Op. 2/3; in E, Op. 2/6 (*BuxWV 254–5; 261; 264*).

(M) *** HM HMB 1089. Boston Museum Trio.

The four *Sonatas* on this record come from the two collections published in his lifetime in 1694 and 1696. These are hardly represented in the catalogue at present though three were included in the Musica Antiqua Köln anthology published on Archive (*Deutsche Kammermusik vor Bach*), overlapping in only one instance with the present issue. The Boston Museum Trio are a highly accomplished group though not quite so subtle as the Musica Antiqua. Nonetheless, there is an exemplary feeling for style and the music is unfailingly inventive and, despite the obvious Italianate elements, distinctive. Not only are the playing, recording and presentation of high quality but the cost is modest. But even at full price, this would be worth the money.

Chorales: *Ach Herr, mich armen Sunder, BuxWV 178; Erhalt uns Herr, BuxWV 185; Es ist das Heil, BuxWV 186; Gott der Vater, BuxWV 190; Herr Jesu Christ, BuxWV 193; In dulci jubilo, BuxWV 197; Jesus Christus unser Heiland, BuxWV 198; Kommt her zu mir, BuxWV 201. Lobt Gott, ihr Christen allzugleich, BuxWV 202. Canzona in G, BuxWV 170; Fugue in C (Gigue), BuxWV 174; Passacaglia in D min., BuxWV 161; Preludes and fugues: in D, BuxWV 139; in E, BuxWV 141; in F sharp, BuxWV 146.*

*** Argo Dig. ZRDL 1004 [id.]. Hurford (organ of Church of Our Lady of Sorrows, Toronto).

Turning to survey a wider baroque field Peter Hurford here alights on Buxtehude, who, the story goes, Bach walked two hundred miles to visit. Each side opens with an impressively structured *Prelude and fugue* and there are some agreeable, mellifluous chorales. But what catches the ear engagingly are the delightful *Canzona in G* and the captivating *'Gigue' Fugue in C*, uncannily like Bach's *Fugue à la gigue in G, BWV 577*. Hurford's registration in both these pieces is agreeably apt, giving both a piquant bite to offset the blander sounds he creates for the chorale preludes. A distinguished recital, played with skill and understanding, on a splendid organ, but not one to suggest that Buxtehude's music is generally on a par with his illustrious contemporary.

Chorales: *Erschienen ist der herrliche Tag; Lobt Gott, ihr Christen allzugleich; Nun bittern wir der heiligen Geist; Preludes and fugues: in E; E min.; G.* Cantatas: *In dulci jubilo; Jubilate domino.*

(M) **(*) HM HMB 929/40. Saorgin; Deller, Deller Consort, Perulli, Chapuis.

Any anthology combining vocal and instrumental music is essentially arbitrary, but the organ pieces here show Buxtehude at his finest, particularly the opening *Prelude and fugue in G minor*, fully worthy of the young J. S. Bach. They are splendidly played by René Saorgin. *In dulci jubilo* is a florid piece for four voices with instrumental accompaniment while *Jubilate domino* is a solo cantata accompanied by viola da gamba and organ continuo. Deller is in good form here and altogether this disc or tape (which is excellently transferred) makes a serviceable introduction to a composer more written about than listened to.

Byrd, William (1543–1623)

Consort music: *Browning à 5; Christe redemptor à 4; Fantasias: à 3; à 4(2); à 5; à 6; In nomine à 4(2); In nomine à 5(2) Pavane and Galliard à 6; Prelude and Ground à 5.*

*** O-L DSLO 599. Cons. of Musicke, Trevor Jones.

This selection from the consort music of Byrd brings ample evidence of his contrapuntal mastery, most vividly and movingly of all in the six-part *Fantasia*. The Consort of Musicke using original instruments takes a relatively severe view, eliminating vibrato more than some of its rivals, but the sharpness and clarity go well with pieces that stand among the finest ever written for strings by an Englishman. Excellent recording.

My Ladye Nevells Booke, 1591 (42 keyboard pieces).

❀ *** O-L D 29 D 4 (4) [id.]. Hogwood (virginal, harpsichord, or chamber organ).

This collection of Byrd's keyboard music was compiled by John Baldwin of Windsor, 'a gentleman of the Chapel Royal', and must be reckoned the finest collection of keyboard music in Europe of the sixteenth century. Christopher Hogwood rings the changes by using a variety of instruments, a virginal, two harpsichords (one Flemish and the other Italian), and a fine chamber organ, all of which he plays with sympathy and vitality. Hogwood's scholarly gifts are shown in the fine notes that accompany the set, but, more important, his masterly keyboard technique and artistic sensitivity are sustained throughout the eight excellently recorded sides.

My Ladye Nevells Booke: excerpts (*4th Pavan and galliards; Qui passe; The Jewell; Sellinger's round; Monsieur's alman; Hugh Ashton's ground; A galliard's gigge; The second ground; 5th Pavan and galliard; The Carman's Whistle; A voluntary*).
*** O-L DSLO 566 [id.]. Hogwood (chamber organ, virginal or harpsichord).

This recital is a selection from Christopher Hogwood's impressive complete recording of *My Ladye Nevells Booke*, offering a dozen or so of its forty-two numbers. Hogwood's expert and sensitive performances on a variety of period instruments cannot be praised too highly, and this offering gives an excellent taste of his achievement.

Motets: *Beata es; Beati mundo corde; Confirma hoc Deus; Gaudeamus omnes; Iustorum animae; Non vos relinquam; Salve, sancta parens; Senex puerum; Tribulationes civitatum; Visita, quaesumus Domine.*
(M) **(*) Ph. 9502 030 [id.]. William Byrd Ch., Gavin Turner.

With one exception all these pieces come from the two books of the *Gradualia* (1602 and 1607). The Byrd Choir give well-blended performances that resist the temptation to linger expressively and are at times rather emphatically spirited. Gavin Turner moves the music along vigorously; there is room for a more relaxed, reposeful approach to many of these pieces. The recording is made in a sympathetic acoustic and is well balanced.

Mass for three voices; Mass for four voices; Mass for five voices; Ave verum corpus; Great service; Magnificat; Nunc dimittis.
(M) *** Argo ZK 53/4 [id.]. King's College Ch., Willcocks.

Mass for three voices; Mass for four voices.
❀ (M) *** Argo 411 723-1/*4*. King's College Ch., Wilcocks.

Mass for four voices; Mass for five voices.
*** Argo ZRG 858 [id.]. Christ Church Cathedral Ch., Oxford, Preston.

Mass for five voices.
*** HMV ASD/*TC-ASD* 4104. King's College, Camb., Ch., Ledger – TYE: *Euge Bone Mass.****

Mass for five voices. Motets: *Alleluia, cognoverunt discipuli; Ave Maria; Christe qui lux es et dies; Civitas sancti tui; Laetentur coeli; Miserere mei; Ne irascaris, Domine.*
(M) *** HM HM 211/13 [Van. HM 7]. Deller Cons.

In the Argo King's performances of the *Mass for five voices*, *Ave verum* and *Great service*, which were recorded in 1960, the style is more reticent, less forceful than in the famous coupling of the *Masses for three* and *four voices*, made three years later. These beautiful settings are sustained with an inevitability of phrasing and a control of sonority and dynamic that completely capture the music's spirit and emotional feeling. The recording of all this music is wonderfully clean and atmospheric, the acoustic perfectly judged so that the music seems to float in space yet retain its substance and clarity of focus.

Though the couplings are different, it is fascinating to compare the Christ Church performances of both Masses with those of King's College Choir, recorded over a decade earlier. In the four-part *Mass* the Oxford choir's more forthright, less moulded style is most refreshing, but sounds relatively square in rhythm. In the five-part *Mass*, on the other hand, the Christ Church choristers outshine their Cambridge rivals with a sharper, more dramatic performance, which is superbly resilient in the often complex cross-rhythms. The recording is gloriously clear and atmospheric with the voices sharply distinguished across the stereo spectrum.

Ledger in his last year as choirmaster at King's made a series of superb recordings with what must still be counted the premier collegiate/cathedral choir. The richest and most complex of Byrd's settings of the Mass here receives a superbly poised yet deeply expressive reading, atmospherically set against a warm, reverberant acoustic. Ledger combines the contemplative intensity that his predecessor, Sir David Willcocks, instilled in this choir, with an extra rhythmic urgency. The coupling of earlier Tudor music is apt and attractive. The chrome cassette offers demonstration quality, strikingly full and clear.

Whether or not it is historically correct for Byrd's five-part Mass to be sung by solo voices, the great merit of this Deller performance is its clarity, exposing the miracle of Byrd's polyphony, even though the tonal matching is not always flawless. The motets on the reverse are well chosen to illustrate the range of Byrd's religious music. This is perhaps the finest of the Deller Consort's records made for Harmonia Mundi in the years before Alfred Deller's death. It is very cleanly recorded.

Psalmes, Sonets and Songs of sadness: All as a sea; Care for thy soul; Come to me grief; If women could be fair; In fields abroad; Lullaby; The match that's made; O God give ear; O Lord how long; O that most rare breast; Susanna fair; What a pleasure to have great Princes.
*** O-L DSLO 596 [id.]. Cons. of Musicke, Rooley.

Byrd's *Psalmes, Sonets and Songs of sadness* of 1588 enjoyed such popularity in their time that they were reprinted twice in the first year of publication. They are more than just a collection of madrigals, as the title suggests, and are given exemplary performances here. Anthony Rooley gives many of them as consort pieces, some with their full number of repeated stanzas, where the artists discreetly embellish. This is a first-class issue, excellently recorded and an invaluable addition to the Byrd discography.

Caccini, Giulio (1550–1618)

Euridice (complete).
*** Arion ARN 238023 (2). Diestchy, Foronda, Dextre, Fuente, Mok, Santos, Encabo, Chapinal, Ch. and Instrumental Ens., Zayas.

Caccini's *Euridice* enjoys the distinction of being the first *published* opera, as opposed to the first to be staged, and has taken longer than almost any other to reach the gramophone: 380 years to be exact, though practical difficulties stood in its way for the best part of that time! This performance derives from three live occasions at Rennes in January 1980 and the cast is largely Spanish. So too is the conductor, Rodrigo de Zayas, who has also edited the score and plays the continuo part on the theorbo. His handling of the score is the soul of taste and he secures excellent singing from his cast, with the possible exception of Inigo Foronda, who betrays unsteadiness at times. Nonetheless, this is an enterprising and highly interesting venture, and extremely well recorded. Caccini's opera is not long (well under two hours) and it has moments of tender lyricism which make it well worth having and which more than compensate for its want of dramatic flair.

Cage, John (born 1912)

Concerto for prepared piano and orchestra.
(M) ** None. H 71201 [id.]. Takahashi, Buffalo PO, Foss – FOSS: *Baroque variations.***

However hard John Cage presses his crusade for 'the depersonalization of music', a work like this (written in 1951, rather before his more extreme experiments) shows the deeply personal results of almost any musical self-expression. Wispy as the sound is, with the prepared piano contributing sounds of oriental delicacy, the result – taken from a live performance in Buffalo in 1958 – has a clear enough concentration to compare with more conventional music. Much is owed to the performance, not only of Foss and the orchestra, but of the fine Japanese pianist Takahashi, best known for his interpretations of the music of Xenakis.

Piano sonatas (for prepared piano) *Nos. 1–4; 1st Interlude; 5–8; 2nd Interlude; 3rd Interlude; 9–12; 4th Interlude; 13–14; No. 15* (*'Gemini', after the work of Richard Lippold*)*; No. 16.*
*** Decca HEAD 9 [id.]. Tilbury (prepared piano).

This is among the most persuasive of Cage's music yet issued, sensitively performed and beautifully recorded, with the peculiar sounds of Cage's prepared piano vividly caught. The sonatas follow each other in groups of four, each group separated by an interlude, but the results tend to be hallucinatory, as eastern music can be. Sympathy with Indian music, the composer explains, lies behind this music, which he wrote in 'controlled improvisation'. It may be just a twitter, but it is an agreeable twitter.

Campion, Thomas (1567–1620)

Ayres: *All looks be pale; The cypress curtain of the night; Fain would I wed; Fair, if you expect admiring; Fire, fire; Harden now thy tired heart; I care not for these ladies; It fell on a summer's day; Jack and Joan they think no ill; Never love unless you can; Never weather-beaten sail; So sweet is thy discourse; Sweet, exclude me not; What if a day* (2 versions). Masque music: *Come ashore, merry mates; Move now with measured sound; Now hath Flora rob'd her bowers; While dancing rests.*
(M) *** Mer. E 77009. L. Camerata, Simpson or Mason.

As poet as well as composer Thomas Campion was one of the most sensitive of the Elizabethans, and this charming disc of intensely refreshing performances gives a splendid cross-section of his vocal work, including several settings of his words by other hands, including Coperario. It is a pity the texts are not provided; but Glenda Simpson with her bright boyish soprano is a most sympathetic interpreter, ably supported by the talented group she directs. The recording is first-rate.

Campra, André (1660–1744)

Requiem Mass.
*** Erato STU/*MCE* 71310. Nelson, Harris, Orliac, Evans, Roberts, Monteverdi Ch., E. Bar. Soloists, Gardiner.

The music of André Campra, who came from Provence and had Italian blood, often possesses a genial lyricism that seems essentially Mediterranean. Although he is best-known now for *L'Europe galante* and other *opéras-ballets*, he wrote a large quantity of sacred music, psalm settings and motets. This *Requiem* is a lovely work, with luminous textures and often beguiling harmonies, and its neglect is difficult to understand. John Eliot Gardiner and his team of fine singers and players have clearly lavished much affection on this performance, and they bring to it intelligence and sensitivity. Campra is one of the most delightful composers of this period and this admirably recorded disc should go some way towards gaining him a rightful place in the repertoire. The cassette is first-class, full and excellently focused – one of Erato's finest tapes.

Te Deum; Ecce panis angelorum.
(M) *** Erato Pres. EPR/*MCE* 15509. Monteil, Jelden, Mallabrera, Abdoun, Caillard Ch., Monte Carlo Op. O, Frémaux.

The Campra *Te Deum* sets out with a ceremonial D major introduction in the style of

Lully, Charpentier or Lalande, but it is not long before an individual voice emerges, and though the melodic invention is not on a consistently sustained level, there are some inspired ideas (the instrumental preface to the duet of the two tenors at the end of side one is both enchanting and original). The manuscript bears the date 1729 but scholars believe the work to be of earlier provenance. *Ecce panis angelorum* comes from the fifth Book of Motets published in 1720 and has considerable charm. The performances date from the early 1960s and sound very different in style from what we expect these days, but they are accomplished and musical. The recording is a little two-dimensional though the acoustic is reasonably ample, but the music is rewarding enough to outweigh such reservations. There is an impressive cassette, bringing presence and good detail and focus to singers and orchestra, with only a very slight loss of sharpness and refinement at the top (the obbligato trumpet is not quite as clean, but the choral focus remains good). Recommended.

L'Europe galante (opéra-ballet).
*** HM HM 20319. Yakar, Kweksilber, Jacobs, Petite Bande, Leonhardt.

The sheer tunefulness of *L'Europe galante* has ensured its appeal over the years: Roger Désormière recorded a suite from it for Oiseau-Lyre in the days of 78s, and Raymond Leppard gave us rather more in the late 1960s. This record, the first with period instruments, dates from 1973 and gives us the complete entertainment – and very delightful it is. Small wonder that Milhaud drew on Campra for his delightful *Suite Provençale*, for not only do they share the same birthplace, Aix, but have the sunny geniality and melodic freshness of the region. Like Couperin's *Les Nations*, though in very different fashion, the divertissement attempts to portray various national characteristics – the French, in which Lully's shades still loom (he died only ten years before *L'Europe galante* was staged in 1697), the Spanish, the Italian (Campra had Italian blood) and the Turkish are all featured in this enchanting score. The three soloists, Rachel Yakar, Marijanne Kweksilber and René Jacobs, all shine and the instrumentalists, led by Sigiswald Kuijken and conducted by Gustav Leonhardt, are both expert and spirited. The recording, too, is of excellent quality and is very acceptably balanced.

Canning, Thomas (born 1911)

Fantasy on a hymn tune by Justin Morgan.
*** Dell Arte 45 r.p.m. DA 9013. Houston SO, Stokowski – BARTÓK: *Concerto.***(*)

The full title of this fascinating piece is *Fantasy on a hymn tune by Justin Morgan for double string quartet and string orchestra*, and anyone with even a passing awareness of the Vaughan Williams *Tallis fantasia* will suspect this is something of a crib. Canning, born in Brookville, Pennsylvania, is a professor of composition at the Eastman School of Music (where this work was first performed in 1946). Justin Morgan was one of a group of eighteenth-century American hymnodists popular among New England settlers. The *Fantasy* may be remarkably like the famous Vaughan Williams work in structure and feeling, but it is a thoroughly worthwhile piece in its own right, atmospheric and eloquently scored, and in Stokowski's committed performance has an almost medieval resonance. He secures the most radiant sounds from the Houston strings and the 1960 recording (which has an Everest source and was made originally on 35mm magnetic film) is clear and full, within a warm ambience that suits the music admirably.

Canteloube, Marie-Joseph (1879–1957)

Chants d'Auvergne: L'Antouèno; Baïlèro; 3 Bourrées; 2 Bourrées; Brezairola; Lou coucout; Chut, chut; La Delaïssádo; Lo Fiolairé; Oï ayaï; Passo pel prat; Pour l'enfant; Tè, l'co, tè; Uno jionto postouro.

**(*) CBS Dig. 37299/*40*- [id.]. Von Stade, RPO, Almeida.

Canteloube, pupil of Vincent d'Indy, made a collection of charming folk-songs from the Auvergne, which he then presented within a framework of seductive orchestral opulence. The most famous of them, *Baïlèro*, (by becoming the accompaniment to a TV commercial) has drawn the attention of the wider musical public to this delightful repertoire.

Fine as Frederica von Stade's singing is, she is stylistically and temperamentally far less at home in Canteloube's lovely folksong settings than Kiri Te Kanawa, whose record of a slightly different selection appeared almost simultaneously with this (see below). Words are clearer here, but, thanks in part to the more abrasive recording, the result is far less persuasively sensuous. The chrome cassette is clear with comparable presence.

Chants d'Auvergne: L'Antouèno; Baïlèro; 3 Bourrées; 2 Bourrées; Brezairola; La Delaïssádo; Lo Fïolairé; Lou Boussu; Malurous qu'o uno fenno; La pastrouletta è lou Chibalie; Passo pel prat; La pastoura als camps; Pastourelle.

C ❀ *** Decca Dig. **410 004-2**; SXDL/*KSXDC* 7604 [Lon. LDR/*5*- 71104]. Te Kanawa, ECO, Tate.

Kiri Te Kanawa's is a ravishing recording of a selection from Canteloube's luscious settings. *Baïlèro*, the most famous of the songs, is taken extremely slowly, but one hardly registers that, when with sumptuous recording against a warm background the result is hypnotically compelling. In such an atmosphere the quick songs lose a little in bite, but, thanks in great measure to masterful and sympathetic accompaniment from the ECO under Jeffrey Tate, the compulsion of the whole sequence is irresistible. One wallows in Canteloube's uninhibited treatment, worrying little over matters of authenticity. The recording is of demonstration quality, most vivid and atmospheric. There is a splendid chrome cassette which vies with the compact disc for the lead in technical excellence (it is very slightly smoother on top), but the latter has the singular advantage of a completely silent background.

Chants d'Auvergne: Baïlèro; 3 Bournées; La Delaïssádo; Lo Fïolairé; Passo pel prat; Brezairola; Chut chut.

*** HMV ASD/*TC-ASD* 2826 [Ang. S 36897]. Los Angeles, LOP, Jacquillat – CHAUSSON: *Poème de l'amour et de la mer.****

'Pastorale' (More *Chants d'Auvergne*)*: La pastoura als camps: L'Antouèno: La pastrouletta è lou Chibalie; Lo Calhé; Lou Boussu; Malurous qu'o uno fenno; Oï ayaï; Pour l'enfant; Pastourelle; Lou coucout; Obal, din lo coumbelo; La haut, sur le rocher; Hé! beyla-z-y dáu fé; Tè, l'co, tè; Uno jionto.*

*** HMV ASD 3134 [Ang. S 36898]. Los Angeles, LOP, Jacquillat.

It was Victoria de los Angeles who made the pioneering stereo recordings of the Auvergne arrangements and her two EMI LPs (with a good matching cassette for ASD 2826) have been EMI best-sellers for some years. There is additionally available in America (and sporadically in Great Britain) a justly admired two-disc set by Natania Davrath [Vanguard T 713/4] which is folksier in feeling, with an edgier, very characterful vocal production, but the warmth of Los Angeles' tone matches exactly the allure of the settings of her two selections. There is also issued in the US a shorter selection of seven songs in radiant performances by Anna Moffo, given sumptuous accompaniments by Stokowski. With an attractive Villa-Lobos coupling, this makes a fine supplementary disc [RCA AGL 1 4877].

Carissimi, Giacomo (1605–74)

Cantatas: *Amor mio, che cosa è questo?; Apritevi, inferni; Bel tempo per me se n'andò; Deh, memoria; In un mar di pensieri; No, no, mio core; Suonerà l'ultima tromba; V'intendo, v'intendo, occhi.*

**(*) O-L DSLO 547 [id.]. Hill, Spencer, Jones, Hogwood.

Such works as *Jephte* and *Baltazar* have been well represented over the years, but Carissimi's cantatas, which number about 150, are relative rarities on disc. They have expressive power allied to musical purity (Carissimi has been called the Bernini of music), and the eight solo cantatas recorded here offer striking instances of word-painting and dramatic harmonic colouring. There is no want of chromaticism when the images of the texts inspire such treatment. There are numerous vocal challenges to which Martyn Hill rises gallantly, though greater dramatic range and variety might have helped at times. This music needs projection, but no collector need feel that these excellently recorded cantatas are merely of historical interest. They are often very beautiful indeed, and the instrumental support is admirably restrained and expert.

Duets: *A piè d'un verde alloro; Desta la cativa; Il mio core; Lungi omai.*
(M) (***) HMV mono HLM 7267. Schwarzkopf, Seefried, Moore – DVOŘÁK: *Moravian duets*; MONTEVERDI: *Duets*.(***)

In the mid-1950s it was a surprising choice for Schwarzkopf and Seefried to sing duets of Carissimi, and there is no attempt at what we would now regard as an 'authentic' approach. But the items are touchingly beautiful and the singing irresistible. Limited mono recording.

Carter, Elliott (born 1908)

(i) *Double concerto for harpsichord, piano and two chamber orchestra;* (ii) *Duo for violin and piano.*
** None. H 71314 [id.]. (i) Jacobs, Kalish, Contemporary Chamber Ens., Weisberg; (ii) Zukovsky, Kalish.

Carter uses two opposing orchestras (to say nothing of antiphonal percussion) in his *Double concerto*, and this adds to the appeal of his score, which is at once complex and dramatic. The performance is highly confident, and to complain that the balance between the two solo instruments is not always perfect (the piano obviously the stronger) would be churlish when similar difficulties would obviously arise at a live concert. In the case of the *Duo*, however, the forward placing of the violin (a little too near to the microphone for complete comfort) is much less excusable. Nevertheless, this is a valuable issue.

(i) *Cello sonata;* (ii) *Sonata for flute, cello and harpsichord.*
**(*) None. H 71234 [id.]. (i) Krosnick, Jacobs; (ii) Sollbergerl, Kuskin, Sherry, Jacobs.

Carter wrote his *Cello sonata* in the late 1940s, at a time when he had yet to develop his most uncompromising manner. The four movements, alternately lyrical and energetic, are immediately attractive yet also immediately reveal the seriousness of their argument. The *Sonata* for baroque ensemble gets away from neoclassic conventions in purposeful music, strongly argued in this performance. The balance in the *Cello sonata* is unkind to the piano, but the sound is more than faithful enough to let the music communicate.

String quartets Nos. 1 and 2.
*** None. H 71249 [id.]. Composers' Qt.

Elliott Carter, tough and uncompromising, making severe demands on the concentration of even the most skilled and sympathetic listeners (let alone on performers), is well suited to the genre of the string quartet. These are works which naturally follow on where Bartók and Schoenberg left off, and though you may feel that Carter's personality is not so universally communicative as those two twentieth-century masters, his music never fails to present a challenge worth taking – and never more so than in these strong works, which are superbly performed here.

Castellanos-Yumar, Gonzalo
(born 1926)

Violin concerto.
*** ASV Dig. DCA 519. Hanson, LSO, composer.

The Venezuelan composer and conductor, Gonzalo Castellanos-Yumar, wrote this formidable *Violin concerto* for his adopted countryman, Maurice Hanson, in 1972–4 when he was already in his late forties. He composed in London, but until this record appeared, his name was hardly known in England, and that is shocking when in its late romantic idiom – Walton slightly updated – it is an attractive as well as a strong work. At 47 minutes it is too long for its material, and the lyrical warmth of the sonata-form first movement rather puts the other two movements in the shade; but this is an outstanding performance beautifully recorded, and will please those looking for a rarity.

Castelnuovo-Tedesco, Mario
(1895–1968)

Guitar concerto in D, Op. 99.
*** HMV Dig. ASD 4171 [Ang. DS/*4XS* 37880]. Romero, ECO, Tórroba – TÓRROBA: *Homenaje.****
(B) *** Con. CC/*CCT* 7510. Behrend, Berlin PO, Peters – RODRIGO: *Concierto de Aranjuez.****
(*) CBS 76634/*40*- [Col. M 35172]. Williams, ECO, Groves – ARNOLD: *Serenade*; DODGSON: *Concerto No. 2.*(*)

Angel Romero's new HMV digital recording of Castelnuovo-Tedesco's slight but engaging concerto is less assertive than Behrend's, but the warmly sympathetic playing (especially in the *Andantino* with its melody which has a striking affinity with an even more famous tune) and atmospheric digital recording place it at the top of the list, particularly in view of its worthwhile coupling.

Behrend's is an attractive performance, the finest available after Romero's, now that John Williams's earlier version with Ormandy has been withdrawn by CBS in favour of his later partnership with Groves. Behrend's playing is strong in personality, and with a bright recording (sounding nearly as well on cassette as on the excellent disc) this is highly enjoyable. Reinhard Peters, the conductor, lets the impetus fall off marginally in the finale but this is not serious, and elsewhere he accompanies very effectively, with first-rate playing from the Berlin Philharmonic. As the coupling is one of the best available versions of the Rodrigo, this is a real bargain.

Though the newer CBS version is more vividly recorded, John Williams's earlier account, with Ormandy and the Philadelphia Orchestra, was fresher and had more pace. He is placed far forward here, so that it is not always possible to locate him in relation to his colleagues. But if the sound is synthetic as far as perspective is concerned, it is by no means unpleasing. These artists make the most of the slow movement's poetry, and the concerto has no want of charm. The attractions of the collection are the two accompanying works, particularly Stephen Dodgson's *Second Concerto.* The cassette transfer is satisfactory but has rather less range than the disc.

Catalani, Alfredo (1854–93)

La Wally (opera): complete.
** Decca SET 394/6 [id. PSI]. Tebaldi, Del Monaco, Cappuccilli, Diaz, Turin Lyric Ch., Monte Carlo Nat. Op. O, Cleva.

Catalani's *La Wally* produced one well-known aria – the heroine's *Ebben? Ne andro lontana* – and otherwise has languished outside Italy. Yet Verdi and Toscanini were among Catalani's enthusiastic admirers (Toscanini named his children after characters in this opera), and the neglect may in part be due to the composer's lamentably early death before the age of forty. It is good to have a lavishly presented performance of this, his most famous opera, but it does bring out clearly enough that the plot is curiously weak, with dramatic effects repeated in parallel, and that fundamentally, for all the romantic attractiveness of the idiom, Catalani was not a very distinctive melodist. Fausto Cleva directs a strong performance, in which Tebaldi sings with much of her old richness, power and feeling, and after an unpleasantly coarse start del Monaco provides some attractively ringing singing. Excellent recording.

Cavalli, Francesco (1602–76)

La Calisto (opera): complete (freely arranged performing version by Raymond Leppard).
*** Argo ZNF 11/12 [id.]. Cotrubas, Baker, Bowman, Cuénod, Davia, Gottlieb, Glyndebourne Festival Ch., LPO, Leppard.

No more perfect Glyndebourne entertainment has been devised than this freely adapted version of an opera written for Venice in the 1650s but never heard since. Even more than Leppard's other Cavalli confection, *L'Ormindo*, it exactly relates that permissive society of the seventeenth century to our own. It is the more delectable because of the brilliant part given to the goddess Diana, taken by Janet Baker. In Leppard's version she has a dual task: portraying the chaste goddess herself but then in the same costume switching immediately to the randy Jupiter disguised as Diana, quite a different character. Add to that a bad-tempered ageing nymph, hilariously portrayed by Hugues Cuénod, and parts for such singers as James Bowman that draw out their finest qualities, and the result is magic. No one should miss Janet Baker's heartbreakingly intense singing of her tender aria *Amara servitù*. The recording, made at Glyndebourne, is gloriously atmospheric.

Ercole amante (complete).
*** Erato STU 71328 (3). Alliot-Lugaz, Hill-Smith, Palmer, Hardy, Crouzat, Cold, Tomlinson, Miller, Lewis, Cassinelli, Corbóz, E. Bach Festival Ch. and Bar. O, Corbóz.

Originally commissioned for the wedding celebrations of Louis XIV but finally performed (with little success) some two years later, *Ercole amante* is one of Cavalli's later and greatest operas. Its profundity, with moving laments and monumental choral passages, brings it closer to the operas of Monteverdi than the other Cavalli works so far recorded. The snag is the libretto, but on record that drawback is minimized. This fine performance under Michel Corbóz was a direct result of the enterprise of Lina Lalandi and her English Bach Festival. Ulrik Cold, with his clean-cut bass, makes a fine Hercules, and the rest of the cast is excellent, with outstanding contributions from John Tomlinson in three roles and Patricia Miller as Dejanira. First-rate recording.

Certon, Pierre
(d. 1572)

Mass: *Sur le pont d'Avignon*. Chansons: *Amour a tort; Ce n'est a vous; C'est grand pityé; De tout le mal; En espérant; Entre vous gentilz hommes; Heilas ne fringuerons nous; Je l'ay aymé; Je ne veulx poinct; Martin s'en alla; Plus ne suys; Que n'est-elle auprès de moy; Si ta beaulté; Ung jour que Madame dormait.*
(M) *** HM HMA/40 1034. Boston Camerata, Cohen.

Pierre Certon is hardly a familiar name but this Mass and the accompanying secular songs give him strong claims to attention. He was active in Paris during the period 1530–70 and held the title of master of the choir at the Sainte-Chapelle in Paris. (He also gets a mention from Rabelais in the *Nouveau Prologue* to the second book of *Pantagruel*.) The Mass *Sur le pont d'Avignon* has genuine appeal, and the chansons with which it is coupled also exercise a real charm over the listener. The Mass is performed a cappella, and the chansons enjoy instrumental support. In both sacred and secular works the Boston Camerata bring musical accomplishment and stylistic understanding to bear, and they are well served by the engineers. Enterprising and interesting.

Cesti, Antonio (1623–69)

Orontea (opera): complete.
❀ *** HM HM/*40* 1100/02 [id.]. Müller-Molinari, Cadelo, Poulenard, Feldman, Reinhart, Jacobs, James, Sarti, Bierbaum, Giacinta Instrumental Ens., Jacobs.

As performed here under the singer and musicologist, René Jacobs, this early Italian opera – written in various versions from 1656 onwards – emerges as far more than an interesting historical curiosity. Its vigour and colour and – perhaps most important of all – its infectious sense of humour in treating a conventional classical subject make it a delight even today. It was – after the operas of Monteverdi and Cavalli – the most popular Venetian opera of its day, and those who know Cavalli will recognize similar fingerprints. This performance using singers who both sing authentically and characterize strongly presents the piece very much as a dramatic entertainment, and the vividly immediate recording gives an excellent sense of presence in a small-scale domestic performance. Outstanding among the singers are Helga Müller-Molinari, David James, Gastoni Sarti and Jacobs himself. The cassettes, transferred at the highest level, are in the demonstration class, every bit the equal of the discs.

Chabrier, Emmanuel (1841–94)

Bourrée fantastique; España; Gwendoline overture; Marche joyeuse; Le Roi malgré lui: Danse slave. Suite pastorale.
*** Erato Dig. **ECD 88018**; NUM/*MCE* 75079 [id.]. Fr. Nat. PO, Jordan.

A sparkling collection to provide Chabrier's compact disc debut. The playing is admirably spirited, even boisterous in the *Marche joyeuse*, and the melodramatic *Gwendoline overture* is relished with proper gusto. Perhaps Paray's account of the engaging *Suite pastorale* is that bit more distinctive, but here the tempo of the third movement, *Sous bois*, is less controversial. *España* has infectious élan, yet rhythms are nicely relaxed so that the gaiety is never forced. The recording is generally first-class, with the body and range of the CD especially telling. The balance of sound on tape is thinner, although there is no lack of liveliness.

España (rhapsody).
*** HMV Dig. ASD/*TCC-ASD* 3902 [Ang. DS/*4XS* 37742]. Phd. O, Muti – FALLA: *Three-cornered hat*; RAVEL: *Rapsodie*.***
** Decca SXL/*KSXC* 6956. LAPO, Lopez-Cobos – FALLA: *Three-cornered hat* **(*); RIMSKY-KORSAKOV: *Capriccio*.**

Muti's manner is brisk but lilting in Chabrier's dance rhythms, an apt make-weight for two other works inspired by the Spanish sun. The digital recording is one of the best from Philadelphia, with the reverberation clouding detail only slightly. The chrome cassette transfer shows striking range and brilliance (the brass has thrilling presence), balanced by a clear, resonant bass.

An enjoyable, more relaxed performance from Lopez-Cobos, with no lack of rhythmic resilience, and attractive in its way. It is very well recorded on disc and tape alike, but it lacks the excitement and glitter of Muti's version.

España; Marche joyeuse; Suite pastorale; Le Roi malgré lui (opera): *Danse slave; Fête polonaise.*
(M) **(*) Decca Jub. JB 10. SRO, Ansermet.

Extremely brilliant recording, typical of Decca's best in terms of amplitude (and percussion and bass drum) but with rather more edge to the treble than on some recordings from this source. The performances are all good, with a certain Gallic accent coming through in places, but *España* lacks the uninhibited exuberance that Beecham, for instance, brought to it. Those who like this touch of reserve will also like the *Suite pastorale*, which is rather restrained, especially in the third movement, *Sous Bois*. However, by the second side Ansermet seems to have warmed up. The *Marche joyeuse* certainly offers its measure of high spirits; the *Danse slave* has an agreeable panache, and the *Fête polonaise* goes splendidly. With all one's reservations, as a whole this disc offers an enjoyable selection of Chabrier's most attractive music.

Suite pastorale.
(M) **(*) Mercury SRI 75029. Detroit SO, Paray – CHAUSSON: *Symphony.****

A delightful account of Chabrier's engaging suite, given playing that is at once warm and polished, neat and perfectly in scale. The only reservation concerns the third movement, *Sous Bois*, which is taken at breakneck speed, which some ears find exhilarating, others simply too fast.

PIANO MUSIC

Air de ballet; Aubade; Ballabile; Bourrée fantasque; Caprice; Capriccio; Cortège burlesque; Feuillet d'album; Habañera; Impromptu; Joyeuse marche; Marche des Cipayes; Petite valse; 10 Pièces pittoresques; Ronde champêtre; Souvenirs de Brunehaut; Suite de valses. (i) (Piano, 4 hands): *Souvenirs de Munich:* (*Quadrille on themes from Wagner's Tristan und Isolde*); *Trois valses romantiques.*
*** Erato STU 714983 (3). Barbizet; (i) with Hubeau.

The delectable Gallic joke of doing quadrilles on themes from Wagner's *Tristan* may be what first attracts the new listener (those piano duets come on side six), but here Barbizet records for the very first time another Wagner joke, an elaborate waltz called *Souvenirs de Brunehaut* (Brünnhilde). Vigorous, jolly music makes up a high proportion of this collection, and Barbizet in his tough, brightly rhythmic style is excellently suited, recorded in first-rate sound with the piano close and real. Chabrier can be a poet too, and perhaps the only warning to give is that this is not a set to play at one sitting.

Chadwick, George (1854–1931)

Symphonic sketches (suite for orchestra).
(M) ** Mercury SRI 75050 [id.]. Eastman-Rochester SO, Hanson – PISTON: *Incredible flutist.***(*)

George Whitefield Chadwick belongs to the same generation as Elgar and Janáček (he was born the same year as Janáček and died three years after him). He studied at (and subsequently became director of) the New England Conservatory. The first two movements, *Jubilee* and *Noel*, come from 1895 and were written in the wake of Dvořák's visit, while the finale and the third movement were composed later: indeed, the third movement, *Hobgoblin*, did not see the light of day until 1904. It is well-made but ultimately unmemorable music: David Hall calls it 'a spirited blend of the Dvořák–Brahms manner with Americanistic overtones'. It is well played, but it is a pity that Piston's exhilarating and delightful ballet is not more appealingly coupled.

Chaminade, Cécile (1857–1944)

Concertino for flute and orchestra, Op. 107.
*** RCA RL/*RK* 25109 [ARL 1/*ARK 1* 3777]. Galway, RPO, Dutoit – FAURÉ: *Fantaisie*; IBERT: *Concerto*; POULENC: *Sonata*.***

The Chaminade *Concertino* undoubtedly has great charm. The principal theme of the first movement is of the kind that insinuates itself irresistibly into the subconscious, and the work has a delightful period atmosphere. It is splendidly played by James Galway, who is given excellent support by the RPO under Charles Dutoit. The recording is admirably spacious and finely detailed, and it has also transferred to cassette with excellent presence and no lack of bloom. Altogether this is a most desirable and enjoyable anthology.

Charpentier, Marc-Antoine (1634–1704)

Les Antiennes 'O' de l'Avent-Noëls pour les instruments; Canticum in nativitatem D.N.J.C.
❀ *** HM HM 5124/*40*. Les Arts Florissants Vocal and Instrumental Ens., Christie.

Charpentier wrote numerous works in celebration of Christmas and set the words of the *Canticum in nativitatem Domini* four times, and there are the delightful *Dialogus inter Angelos et Pastores Judae* as well as the *Midnight Mass* which is the most familiar of his works for the Festive Season, at least as far as the UK is concerned. These *'O' Antiphons* are so called because of their opening invocation – *O salutaris hostia*, *O Sapientia* etc. Charpentier explained in his manuscript that custom demanded that Noëls were performed between these solemn *'O' Antiphons*, which are sung on the days preceding the Nativity. Charpentier places the emphasis on the opening invocations in his settings with often striking results, and the pastoral interludes form a refreshing contrast. It would be difficult to overemphasize the musical delights here. The coupling, the *Canticum in nativitatem Domini*, was composed for Marie de Lorraine, Duchesse de Guise, whose ensemble Charpentier directed until her death in 1688. It is very different from the Antiphons, having much more of the character of an oratorio (indeed the term *Canticum* was loosely used to indicate both the Motet and the Oratorio) and affirms the composer's debt to his master, Carissimi. The invention in both works has great appeal and variety, and the artists who give so convincing an account of *Actéon* (see below) are no less persuasive here. The same high standards of performance and recording prevail, and the disc can be warmly recommended to readers investigating Charpentier's art. The cassette – transferred at the highest level – is hardly less successful. Indeed it is in the demonstration class.

Beatus vir; Le Jugement dernier (oratorio).
*** Erato STU 71222. Vieira, Brunner, Ihara, Zaepffel, Ramirez, Huttenlocher, Lisbon Gulbenkian Foundation Ch. and O, Corbóz.

A welcome addition to the growing representation of Charpentier on record. Performances and recording are admirable, and *Le Jugement dernier*, which occupies the first side, is an imposing work. Charpentier's teacher, Carissimi, had set the same text, and the oratorio form, though he never used that name, occupied an important place in Charpentier's output: he produced no fewer than thirty-four. They are more diverse in character than Carissimi's; in fact, they are closer to French operatic recitative in the narrative sections than to the Italian style.

Caecilia, Virgo et Martyr; Filius prodigus (oratorios).
(M) *** HM HM 10 066 [id.]. Grenat, Benet, Laplenie, Reinhard, Studer, Instrumental Ens., Christie.

As the sleeve-note puts it, these Latin oratorios or dramatic motets of Charpentier occupy 'an isolated, if elevated position in French seventeenth-century music'. The two works recorded here come from different periods of his life: *Caecilia, Virgo et Martyr* was composed for the Duchesse de Guise in 1675, when he wrote a number of works on the subject of St Cecilia; the second, on the theme of the Prodigal Son, dates from the later period when Charpentier was *maître de chapelle* at St Louis-le-Grand (1684–98), and is richer in expressive harmonies and poignant dissonances. The music could scarcely find more eloquent advocates than these artists under William Christie; its stature and nobility is fully conveyed here. An altogether splendid coupling, beautifully recorded too.

Grand Magnificat; Te Deum.
(M) ** Erato Pres. EPR/*MCE* 15508. Angelici, Chamonin, Mallabrera, Corazza, Abdoun, Mars, Paillard CO, Martini.

The *Te Deum* is an imposing ceremonial work and the *Grand Magnificat* has some beautiful things in it, too. The recordings were made in 1963 and issued in the early 1970s on the Vanguard label. The editions used are by Guy Lambert and though ideas on performance practice may have changed in the last two decades, there is still much pleasure to be had from this issue. The sound shows its age a little but the performances are alive and musical.

Judith (oratorio).
** Erato STU 71282. Alliot-Lugaz, Russell, York-Skinner, Roden, Goldthorpe, Jackson, Tomlinson, E. Bach Fest. Ch., and O.

As a pupil of Carissimi, Charpentier's interest in the oratorio, the short narrative choral pieces that when brought to France were known as *histoires sacrées*, was a natural development, and he was one of its most celebrated exponents. This work tells the story of Judith and Holofernes, and it inspires some characteristically individual music from Charpentier's pen. His harmonic style is richer and more resourceful than Lully and many other French baroque composers before Rameau, and here, in spite of a performance that is a little wanting in dramatic flair, readers will find no lack of musical rewards. The recording is well balanced, and if the performance had slightly more character, this would be a three-star recommendation. No conductor is named.

Leçons de ténèbres.
(M) *** HM **CD 90-1005**; HM/*HM40* 1005/7. Jacobs, Nelson, Verkinderen, Kuijken, Christie, Junghänel.

Charpentier was an almost exact contemporary of Lully whom he outlived but whose shadow served to obscure him during his lifetime. These *Leçons de ténèbres* are eloquent and moving pieces, worthy of comparison with Purcell and more substantial musically than Couperin's later setting. Since the falsetto tradition was weak, it seems unlikely that any of the music was intended for male alto, a fact that the counter-tenor René Jacobs readily concedes in his notes. Yet his performance (like that of his colleagues) is so authentic in every respect that it is difficult to imagine it being surpassed. The pursuit of authenticity often produces inhibited phrasing and over-careful voice production, but here the results are a tribute both to musicianship and to scholarship. This music has depth and these artists reveal its stature to fine effect. The recording is as distinguished as the performances; the cassette transfer too is admirable (although it needs a bass cut), and the packaging is excellent, with bilingual notes, clearly printed.

Magnificat; Pastorale sur la naissance de notre Seigneur Jesus Christ.
*** HM HM/*40* 1082 [id.]. Les Arts Florissants Voc. and Instrumental Ens., Christie.

Like the *Canticum in nativitatem Domini* (see above), the *Pastorale* is one of the Christmas pieces that Charpentier composed for the Duchesse de Guise, and its charm and grace continue to win one over to this eminently resourceful composer. One thing that will immediately strike the listener is the delicacy and finesse of the scoring, both in the *Pastor-*

ale and the *Magnificat* for three voices. There is an almost Purcellian flavour to the latter. The *Pastorale* is not new to the gramophone, but this version supersedes its predecessor (in the edition of Guy Lambert) from which William Christie's departs. The present issue contains music that was not included in the Guy Lambert edition which contained a different second part that had been intended for use at the Jesuit College in the Rue Saint-Antoine, Paris. This series, undertaken by William Christie, seems almost self-recommending, so high are the standards of performance and recording, and so fertile is Charpentier's invention. A momentary lapse of intonation fairly early on by the shepherdess should not put anyone off, for it is a minor blemish on an otherwise delightful achievement.

Missa Assumpta est Maria. Dialogus inter Christum et peccatores.
**(*) Erato STU 71281. Nelson, Alliot-Lugaz, Russell, York-Skinner, Goldthorpe, Jackson, Rayner Cook, E. Bach Festival Ch. and Bar. O.

An unusually interesting record, even though it is flawed. The Mass is an expressive and beautiful work composed for the Sainte-Chapelle in Paris in 1699, not long before Charpentier's death. It is among the finest specimens of its kind in French music of this period, and its directness of utterance and depth of feeling give it a special claim to the collector's attention. It is for six-part choir and an orchestra of strings, flutes, continuo and organ, and although this performance may be wanting in finish it reveals much sensitivity and an awareness of the beauties of the score. The fill-up on the second side, the *Dialogus inter Christum et peccatores*, is one of the *histoires sacrées* that blend elements of the French and Italian styles (notably that of Carissimi). The performance here is marred by the obtrusive vibrato of the two sopranos, but the record as a whole is rewarding and the sound quality is good. No conductor is named.

Mors Saulis et Jonathae (oratorio); *Canticum: In honorem Sancti Ludovici.*
*** Erato STU/*MCE* 71466. Degelin, Mols, Strumphier, James, Devos, Caals, Meersman, Widmer, Bastin, Ghent Madrigal Ch. and Cantabile, Musica Polyphonica, Devos.

Mors Saulis et Jonathae (*The Death of Saul and Jonathan*) is thought to antedate *David et Jonathas* of 1688 and comes from the period in which he served as Master of Music at the Collège Louis-le-Grand. The oratorio is a narrative presentation of the biblical story as opposed to the dramatic one that emerges in the *opéra-sacré*. The invention is of the usual high standard one has come to expect from this composer and the performance is both sensitive and compelling. There are some striking things in it: the poignant chorus, *O sors! sors infelix et acerba*, has some highly individual false relations and the simplicity of David's lament, *Doleo, doleo super te*, has touching purity of utterance. The singers, including the incomparable Jules Bastin, are totally inside the idiom and the only small reservation one can envisage concerns the rather rapid vibrato of Jan Caals's soldier. However, he is an expressive and intelligent singer. The other work, *Canticum in honorem Sancti Ludovici*, is much later, and is one of several he composed during the last years of his life as Master at Sainte-Chapelle. It is richly scored and this lends force to the view that it was written for the visit of the King and Queen of England in 1698. It is a splendid piece and a typical *Grand Motet* of the period, full of variety. A most rewarding and impressive record. The cassette is transferred at quite a high level and has immediacy and plenty of body. Because of the resonance, the upper focus is not always as refined as the disc – though fully acceptable – and this is especially noticeable on side one at the entry of the trumpets, which are not caught quite cleanly.

OPÉRA

Actéon (complete).
*** HM **CD 90-1095**; HM 1095/*40* [id.]. Visse, Mellon, Laurens, Feldman, Paut, Les Arts Florissants Vocal and Instrumental Ens., Christie.

Actéon serves to confirm the growing impression that Charpentier was very much the greatest French composer of his day. It is a short work in six scenes, and the exact date of its composition remains unknown. As in so many other works which Harmonia Mundi and Erato are now investigating, the sheer fecundity and, above all, quality of invention take one by surprise though, by this time, one should take for granted Charpentier's extraordinarily rich imagination. Actéon is particularly well portrayed by Dominique Visse; his transformation in the fourth tableau and his feelings of horror are almost as effective as anything in nineteenth-century opera! William Christie has devoted such energy and scholarship to this composer that the authority of his direction ensures the success of this venture. Although scholarship is an important ingredient in this undertaking, musicianship and flair are even more important, and these are in welcome evidence. The other singers are first-rate, in particular the Diane of Agnès Mellon. Alert playing and an altogether natural recording which is truthfully balanced and sounds splendidly fresh, as well as excellent presentation, make this a most desirable record. The chrome cassette too is outstanding, of demonstration clarity and range.

Les Arts Florissants (opéra et idyle en musique). *Ouverture de la Comtesse d'Escarbagnes et intermèdes nouveaux du mariage forcé.*
*** HM HM/*40* 1083 [id.]. Les Arts Florissants Vocal and Instrumental Ens., Christie.

Charpentier was kept away from the principal Parisian stage as a result of Lully's monopoly and *Les Arts Florissants* which he called variously an opera and an 'idyll in music' was composed for Marie of Lorraine, Duchesse de Guise, who maintained a small group of musicians and mounted little chamber operas there. *Les Arts Florissants* is a short entertainment in five scenes, and the libretto tells of a conflict between the Arts who flourish under the rule of Peace, and the forces of war, personified by Discord and the Furies. (In the first performance, Charpentier himself sang one of the roles, representing the art of Painting.) This and the little Interlude that completes the second side contain some invigorating and fresh invention, performed very well indeed by this eponymous group under the expert direction of William Christie. Period instruments are used but intonation is always good, and the recording is excellent both as regards timbre and balance.

David et Jonathas (opera): complete.
*** Erato STU 71435 (3) [id.]. Alliot-Lugaz, Huttenlocher, Soyer, David, Jacobs, Lyons Op. Ch., E. Bach Fest. O, Corbóz.

David et Jonathas comes from 1688, the year after Lully's death had brought to an end his monopoly of the musical stage, and precedes Charpentier's only real opera, *Médée* (1693). Although the formula and the instrumental layout are thoroughly Lullian, Charpentier's music has greater imagination and musical substance than Lully's. The action follows the biblical narrative in broad outline, and much of the music (which is new to the gramophone) is fresh and inventive, remarkably free from period cliché. It confirms the impression made by many other Charpentier records during the last few years, that in him France has one of her most inspired baroque masters. This performance is marked by some good singing, though there are passages whch would, one feels, benefit from greater finish. But Michel Corbóz gets excellent results from his artists generally and is well recorded. One or two sides are short (one is 16′ 40″ only) but no matter: this rarity is still worth the price.

Charpentier, Gustave
(1860–1956)

Louise (opera): complete.
*** CBS 79302 (3) [M 3-34207]. Cotrubas, Berbié, Domingo, Sénéchal, Bacquier, Ambrosian Op. Ch., New Philh. O, Prêtre.

Even more than Mascagni and Leoncavallo, Gustave Charpentier is a one-work composer, and one might be forgiven for thinking that that work, the opera *Louise*, is a one-aria opera. No other melody in the piece may quite match the soaring lyricism of the heroine's *Depuis le jour*, but this fine atmospheric recording, the first in stereo, certainly explains why *Louise* has long been a favourite opera in Paris. It cocoons the listener in the atmosphere of Montmartre in the 1890s, with Bohemians more obviously proletarian than Puccini's, a whole factory of seamstresses and an assorted range of ragmen, junkmen, pea-sellers and the like making up a highly individual cast-list.

Only four characters actually matter in a plot that remains essentially simple, even though the music (not counting intervals) lasts close on three hours. Louise is torn between loyalty to her parents and her love of the Bohemian, Julien. The opera starts with a love duet and from there meanders along happily, enlivened mainly by the superb crowd scenes. One of them, normally omitted but included here, proves as fine as any, with Louise's fellow seamstresses in their workroom (cue for sewing-machines in the percussion department) teasing her for being in love, much as Carmen is teased in Bizet's quintet. The love duets too are enchanting, and though the confrontations with the boring parents are far less appealing, thc atmosphere carries one over. Ileana Cotrubas makes a delightful heroine, not always flawless technically but charmingly girlish. Placido Domingo is a relatively heavyweight Julien, and Jane Berbié and Gabriel Bacquier are excellent as the parents. Under Georges Prêtre, far warmer than usual on record, the ensemble is rich and clear, with refined recording every bit as atmospheric as one could want. A set which splendidly fills an obvious gap in the catalogue.

Chausson, Ernest (1855–99)

Concerto for violin, piano and string quartet, Op. 21.

*** CBS Dig. 37814 [IM/*IMT* 37814]. Perlman, Bolet, Juilliard Qt.

**(*) Telarc Dig. DG 10046 [id.]. Maazel, Margalit, Cleveland O Qt.

Since the pioneering records by Thibaud and Cortot, versions of the Chausson *Concerto* have hardly been thick on the ground.

Things have ironically improved and the catalogue now offers two digital versions, one very good, the other excellent. The CBS version is not only artistically more satisfying but also gives a better-integrated aural picture. The sound is natural yet well observed, and the playing of Perlman and Bolet is exemplary. In short this rather beautiful work has never been better served on record.

In the spectacular Telarc recording there is a wide range of dynamics, and though there are times when one would have welcomed more emotional restraint, the performance is both sensitive and accomplished. Maazel's vibrato in the slow movement may not be to all tastes but it would be ungenerous to withhold a star, particularly in view of the spectacular clarity and presence of the recording.

Poème for violin and orchestra.

*** HMV ASD 3125 [Ang. S/*4XS* 37118]. Perlman, O de Paris, Martinon – RAVEL: *Tzigane*; SAINT-SAËNS: *Havanaise* etc.***

*** Decca SXL/*KSXC* 6851 [Lon. CS/5-7073]. Kyung-Wha Chung, RPO, Dutoit – RAVEL: *Tzigane*; SAINT-SAËNS: *Havanaise* etc.***

Chausson's beautiful *Poème* has been generously represented on disc. Perlman's account with the Orchestre de Paris under the late Jean Martinon is to the 1970s what the youthful Menuhin's was to the 1930s or Grumiaux's was in the 1960s: it is the classic account by which newcomers are measured. What a glorious and inspired piece it is when played with such feeling! It comes on a particularly distinguished anthology which has a brilliant account of *Tzigane*, also available in Martinon's Ravel anthology, and the inevitable (and eternally fresh) Saint-Saëns pieces so much loved by virtuosi. The recording is particularly opulent and well-balanced.

Chung's performance is deeply emotional; some will prefer a more restrained approach, but with committed accompaniment from the orchestra and excellent recording, this makes an admirable foil for the virtuoso concertante pieces with which it is coupled. The tape transfer is successful; a slight treble reduction is useful, but then the sound has pleasing bloom and detail.

Symphony in B flat, Op. 20.
(M) *** Mercury SRI 75029. Detroit SO, Paray – CHABRIER: *Suite pastorale.***(*)

Symphony in B flat; Soir de Fête, Op. 32.
** EMI 2C 069 14086 [Sera. S 60310]. Toulouse Capitole O, Plasson.

Michel Plasson gives a sensitive account of the Chausson *Symphony* and, particularly in the powerful introduction and the somewhat *Tristanesque* slow movement, secures playing of real feeling from the Toulouse orchestra. This is an eloquent performance and were the recording more detailed and refined, it would be a first recommendation, particularly as the coupling, *Soir de Fête*, is something of a rarity. Written the year before his death, this character sketch remained unpublished for many years as Chausson had intended to revise it. It is the poetic middle section which finds him at his best. The recordings are made in a somewhat reverberant acoustic and detail could be better focused. The upper strings have an unpleasing edge though acceptable results can be secured by manipulation of the controls.

Paray's recording was made twenty years earlier in the late 1950s and is better detailed and more clearly defined. The acoustic is drier and the overall sound, though not outstanding by modern standards, gives greater pleasure. The performance is powerful and committed and has both energy and poetic feeling. The Detroit orchestra manage to produce an almost Gallic sound at times. Given the bargain price, it is worth three stars, even though collectors should make allowances for the dated sound.

Poème de l'amour et de la mer.
❀ *** HMV ASD/*TC-ASD* 3455 [Ang. S 37401]. Baker, LSO, Previn – DUPARC: *Mélodies.* *** ❀
*** HMV ASD/*TC-ASD* 2826 [Ang. S 36897]. Los Angeles, LOP, Jacquillat – CANTELOUBE: *Chants d'Auvergne.****

Dame Janet Baker, always at her most inspired in French music, gives a glorious, heart-felt performance, both radiant and searching, so that this picture of love in two aspects, first emergent, then past, has a sharpness of focus often denied it. She is superbly supported by Previn and the London Symphony Orchestra, with clarity and warmth combined; the recording is of demonstration quality, and the cassette transfer is glowingly atmospheric.

The voice of Victoria de los Angeles is also ideally suited to Chausson's warm and evocative piece, a work unjustly neglected on record for not being the right length for LP. Coupled here with Canteloube's charming folksong settings, it can be enthusiastically recommended alongside Dame Janet Baker's version. On tape the sound is marginally less clearly focused than in the coupling.

Chávez, Carlos (1899–1978)

Symphony No. 2 (Sinfonia India).
(M) *** HMV Dig. Green. ESD/*TCC-ESD* 7146 [Var. Sara 704220]. Mexican State SO, Bátiz (with concert of Mexican music ***).

The *Sinfonia India* is striking for its exoticism and brilliant scoring, well captured here by good playing and a vivid digital recording – see the Concerts section, below.

Zarabanda for strings.
(M) *** HMV Green. ESD/*TC-ESD* 165105-1/*4*. Mexican State SO, Bátiz – PONCE: *Concierto del sur* **(*); SOLER: *Sonatas.***

Apart from the *Sinfonia India* (1936), Chávez is rarely heard these days in the concert hall and now that his own record of three of his symphonies has disappeared from view along with the *Piano concerto* (once available on HMV), his representation is scant. The *Zarabanda for strings* comes from a ballet commissioned for Martha Graham in 1943 on the subject of *Medea*. Chávez subsequently made a suite from the work, scored for full orchestra. This movement is for strings alone and is rather beautiful, meditative in character and grave in feeling. Despite its brevity, just under six minutes, it is probably the must substantial piece on this record, and it is eloquently played and excellently recorded, on both disc and tape.

Cherubini, Luigi (1760–1842)

Symphony in D.
(*) None. Dig. D/*D4* 79023 [id.]. LAPO, Schwarz – ROSSINI: *Sinfonia; Overture.**

Cherubini's *D major Symphony*, written for the Philharmonic Society of London in 1816, may not have the weight of Viennese equivalents, but it is a fine example of the work of a composer whom Beethoven admired. Toscanini many years ago made a superb recording of it, but this is a strong, well-disciplined performance with plenty of drive, if a little lacking in charm. The digital recording is bright and vivid with a fine sense of immediacy and presence.

String quartets Nos. 1 in E flat; 2 in C.
(M) *** DG Arc. Priv. 2547/*3347* 067 [id.]. Melos Qt.

This record comes from a (now deleted) boxed set of all the Cherubini quartets which are new to the catalogue. No. 1 was composed when Cherubini was already in his fifties; No. 2 is a reworking of his *Symphony in D* (see above), though Cherubini composed a fresh slow movement. The present disc has the advantage of authentic performing texts (the published Eulenberg scores are corrupt in some instances and others did not appear in print during the composer's lifetime). Listening to them makes one realize the justice of Beethoven's admiration for this composer, for Cherubini's art is informed by lofty ideals and often noble musical invention. His melodic inspiration is often distinguished and instinctive, though there are times when it falls short of true memorability. There is always a fine musical intelligence and polished craftsmanship in evidence. The Melos Quartet play these quartets with real commitment and authority and the sound is first-class, vivid and clear; indeed, the bright cassette transfer benefits from a little smoothing of the treble.

Requiem in C min.
*** HMV Dig. ASD 4071. Amb. S., Philh. O, Muti.

Muti directs a tough and incisive reading of Cherubini's most dramatic setting of the *Requiem* to remind one that this was a work which Toscanini too recorded some three decades ago. Muti in the religious music of his own country believes in underlining the drama. This was a work which even the unfriendly Berlioz recognized as impressive, and it may even have influenced his own *Grande messe des morts*. Muti is well served both by his orchestra and by his relatively small professional choir, and the full, clear recording is most satisfying.

Requiem in D min.
*** HMV ASD 3073 [Ang. S 37096]. Amb. S., New Philh. O, Muti.
*** Decca Dig. SXDL 7518 [Lon. LDR 10034]. Ch. de Brassus, SRO and Lausanne PA Choirs, SRO, Stein.

The darkness of tone in the use of male voices in Cherubini's *D minor Requiem* goes with much solemn minor-key music (a little inflated by Beethovenian standards) and some striking anticipations of Verdi. In this fine, committed performance under Muti, the listener forgets the scarcity of really memorable melodies, and relishes the drama and the distinctive textures, particularly as the recording is outstandingly fine.

Stein's performance on Decca provides an excellent alternative, and the digital recording is if anything even more impressive, helping to bring out the dramatic side of the work, the scale that of a cathedral rather than a church. The singing of the Brassus choir is less incisive than that of the Ambrosian Singers on the HMV version, though the balance is more forward.

Chopin, Frédéric (1810–49)

CONCERTANTE AND ORCHESTRAL MUSIC

(i) *Piano concertos Nos. 1–2; Andante spianato et grande polonaise brillante, Op. 22; Fantasia on Polish airs, Op. 13; Krakowiak, Op. 14; Variations on La ci darem, Op. 2. 4 Ballades; Barcarolle, Op. 60; Fantaisie, Op. 49; 4 Impromptus; 21 Nocturnes; 24 Preludes, Op. 28; Preludes, Op. 45 and posth.; Waltzes.*
(M) ** Ph. 6768 354 (9). Arrau, (i) LPO, Inbal.

Philips have repackaged Arrau's Chopin in two forms. This 9-record set includes the two concertos and the other works for piano and orchestra plus the *Impromptus*. The remaining 5 records (the *Ballades*, *Barcarolle*, *Fantaisie in F minor*, the *Nocturnes*, *Preludes*, Opp. 28 and 45 and the *Waltzes*) are common to both sets (see also below). The concertos are immaculately aristocratic though the expressive hesitations do not always grow naturally out of what has gone before and Arrau's rubato will inevitably convince some listeners less than others. Moreover, the balance gives the distinguished soloist undue prominence though the overall sound is reasonably fresh and truthful in timbre.

Piano concerto No. 1 in E min., Op. 11.
(M) *** HMV SXLP/*TC-SXLP* 30160 [Sera. S/*4XG* 60066]. Pollini, Philh. O, Kletzki.
*** DG 2531/*3301* 125 [id.]. Zimerman, LAPO, Giulini.
(M) **(*) CBS 60033/*40-* [Odys. Y/*YT* 32369]. Gilels, Phd. O, Ormandy.
*(**) CBS 76970/*40-* [M/*MT* 35893]. Perahia, NYPO, Mehta.

Piano concerto No. 1; Ballade No. 1 in G min., Op. 23; Nocturnes Nos. 4 in F; 5 in F sharp, Op. 15/1 and 2; 7 in C sharp min.; 8 in D flat, Op. 27/1 and 2; Polonaises Nos. 5 in F sharp min., Op. 44; 6 in A flat, Op. 53.
(M) *** HMV *TCC2-POR 54275.* Pollini (with *Concerto* as above).

Piano concerto No. 1; Mazurkas Nos. 5 in B flat, Op. 7/1; 46 in C, Op. 67/3; 47 in A min., Op. 68/2; 54 in D, Op. posth.
(B) ** Contour CC/*CCT* 7564 [DG 2535 206]. Vásáry, Berlin PO, Semkow.

Pollini's classic recording, made shortly after he won the Warsaw Prize in 1959 as a youth of eighteen, still remains the best, particularly now that the sound has been improved. One would not in fact guess the date of this recording, so fresh, well-defined and detailed is the sound picture. This is playing of such total spontaneity, poetic feeling and refined judgement that criticism is silenced. It is so marvellously sparkling and the rubato so superbly judged that one forgets about the performers and thinks only of Chopin. This performance is also available on a chrome cassette which couples the *Concerto* with Pollini's first solo recital for HMV (now withdrawn in disc form) which is as well-planned as it is superbly played, with admirably truthful recording. This double-length tape is one of EMI's '*Portrait of the Artist*' series and it certainly encapsulates the distinctive quality of Pollini's playing. The transfer both here and in the single-cassette format of the *Concerto* is very well managed.

Krystian Zimerman's is arguably the finest version of the *First Concerto* to have appeared in the 1970s, and is worthy to stand alongside Pollini's classic account and Gilels's famous recording from the mid-1960s on CBS. He is fresh, poetic and individual in his approach, and is afforded a cleanly detailed recording by the DG engineers. A sparkling, beautifully characterized reading with a first-rate tape.

Gilels also offers one of the most thoughtful and poetic accounts, with every phrase breathing naturally, although the recorded sound does not flatter him or Ormandy's fine accompaniment.

The Contour LP of Vásáry's performance sounds well, with a good balance and excellent piano tone. Vásáry's manner is somewhat self-effacing: the gentle poetry of the solo playing is in distinct contrast with the much more extrovert orchestral contribution under Semkow. But soloist and orchestra match their styles in the slow movement, which is beautifully done, and the finale has no lack of vivacity and sparkle. This is good value.

Murray Perahia produces some wonderfully poetic playing, with an unforced naturalness and sense of grace that one expects from an artist of his quality. But there are inevitable hazards in partnering him with a conductor of Zubin Mehta's calibre, and even if there are moments of that special insight that illumines everything Perahia does, it would be idle to pretend that this is the success for which one had hoped. From Perahia one would expect a Chopin *E minor Concerto* of altogether rare delicacy and flair, of the kind he has given us in the concert hall, but the orchestral playing is so coarse-grained in tutti and shows such little real sensitivity elsewhere that it is neither worthy of nor inspiring for this soloist. Given better casting, Perahia could give us an account of this concerto as fine as any on record, but this is not it. The tape transfer is first-class, one of CBS's best, vivid and clear and quite the equal of the disc.

Piano concerto No. 2 in F min., Op. 21.

(M) *** Decca VIV/*KVIC* 43 [(d) Lon. CS/*5-*6733]. De Larrocha, SRO, Comissiona – SCHUMANN: *Concerto.***

** ASV ALH/*ZCALH* 931. Vásáry, Northern Sinf. – SCHUMANN: *Concerto.**(*)*

Piano concerto No. 2; Andante spianato et grande polonaise brillante, Op. 22.

*** DG 2531/*3301* 126 [id.]. Zimerman, LAPO, Giulini.

(M) *** DG Priv. 2535/*3335* 221 [id.]. Vásáry, Berlin PO, Kulka.

Piano concerto No. 2; Krakowiak (rondo), Op. 14.

(*) Ph. Dig. **410 042-2; 6514/*7337* 259 [id.]. Davidovich, LSO, Marriner.

Piano concerto No. 2; Ballade No. 3 in A flat, Op. 47; Barcarolle, Op. 60; Nocturne No. 17 in B, Op. 62/1; Scherzo No. 3 in C sharp min., Op. 39.

*** Decca SXL 6693 [(d) Lon. CS/*5-* 6440]. Ashkenazy, LSO, Zinman.

Piano concerto No. 2; Polonaise No. 5 in F sharp min., Op. 44.

* DG **410 507-2**/1/*4* [id.]. Pogorelich, Chicago SO, Abbado.

Krystian Zimerman's version of the *F minor Concerto* has won much acclaim and rightly so. It combines qualities of freshness and poetic sensibility with effortless pianism. Elegant, aristocratic, sparkling – all these adjectives spring to mind: this has youthful spontaneity and at the same time a magisterial authority. In discussing the *E minor Concerto* we spoke of the DG recording being 'cleanly detailed' without perhaps sufficiently stressing the fact that the balance favoured the soloist a little too much. In this respect the *F minor* is an improvement, though the piano is still marginally too close to do full justice to the magic this remarkable young artist achieves in the concert hall. Among recent versions this leads the field without question. The tape transfer is first-class in every way, though (like the *First Concerto*) it benefits from a slight bass cut.

Ashkenazy's account was originally – rather inappropriately – coupled with Bach (and that issue remains available in the USA). But Decca soon reissued the performance within a recital of some of Chopin's most famous solo pieces, which seems much more suitable. Ashkenazy's sympathy with the music is very obvious, and his sophisticated use of light and shade in the opening movement, and the subtlety of phrasing and rubato, are a constant source of pleasure. The recitativo section in the *Larghetto*, which can often sound merely rhetorical, is here shaped with mastery, and there is a delicious lightness of touch in the finale. David Zinman and the players of the LSO are obviously in full contact with the soloist, and the recording is one of Decca's very best.

At medium-price, both De Larrocha and Vásáry remain competitive. De Larrocha's performance is highly poetic, and is supported by a strongly characterful accompaniment from Comissiona. There is much to admire here, including the fine Decca engineering; if the coupling (a fascinating version of the Schumann *Concerto* from Backhaus) is attractive, this is highly recommendable. There is a first-class cassette, every bit the equal of the LP.

Vásáry's DG performance is one of his finest Chopin recordings; moreover it is splendidly recorded. The balance is exceptionally convincing and the sound itself first-class, equally impressive on disc and tape. The slow movement is played most beautifully, and in the outer movements the orchestral direction has striking character and vigour. The fillers are generous; the *Andante spianato* is especially beguiling. There is a good tape.

Bella Davidovich's is a very musical reading, and there is undoubted poetry in the slow movement. She is beautifully recorded, both on LP and cassette, and the compact disc offers a particularly natural sound picture, warmly ambient, yet with excellent definition and detail. This is a pleasure to listen to, yet it must be admitted that alongside Ashkenazy, Zimerman or De Larrocha, the performance is somewhat undercharacterized. However, the attractions of this issue are increased by Davidovich's delightful account of the engaging *Krakowiak rondo*, sparkling and fresh, a very real bonus.

Vásáry's newest recording on ASV in which he not only plays but directs the Northern Sinfonia from the keyboard has the advantage of fresher and well-balanced sound, but the playing, while it has much delicacy and refinement, is not so boldly characterized nor as full of ardour and flair as was his earlier account – and there seems little case for his dividing his attentions between the keyboard and the orchestra whose contribution is pale by comparison with the Berliners. There are lovely things and some highly sensitive touches, and the sound is well-balanced and cleanly recorded. There is also a good cassette.

Listening to Pogorelich's account of the *Second concerto*, one can well understand what antagonized the jury at the Warsaw Chopin Competition in 1980, who did not admit him to the finals (just as his Prokofiev *Sixth sonata* makes one appreciate Argerich's championship of him on that occasion). This is pianism of no mean order – 'charismatic' is the word one is tempted to use – but at the service of a wholly narcissistic sensibility. It is Pogorelich's keyboard command and beauty of tone that his every gesture invites us to admire, while Chopin doesn't get too much of a look-in. It is all superbly played and recorded, but the prospect of repeating the experience of hearing it is not to be contemplated without mixed feelings. True, one cannot but be bowled over by the sounds he produces, but it is difficult to be persuaded by their sense. There is a first-class chrome cassette, matching the disc very closely.

A Month in the Country (ballet; arr. Lanchbery); *Barcarolle, Op. 60; Waltz in E, Op. posth.*

(M) ** HMV Green. ESD/*TC-ESD* 7037. Gammon, ROHCGO, Lanchbery.

John Lanchbery's score for Sir Frederick Ashton's ballet based on Turgenev's *A Month in the Country* is constructed from concertante works that Chopin wrote in his late teens, the *Fantasy on Polish airs*, the *Grande polonaise brillante* (which the composer joined to the *Andante spianato* years later) and the *Là ci darem variations* (using Mozart's air from *Don Giovanni*). Lanchbery comments – not unfairly – that Chopin's scoring is 'slender and at times sketchy', and so he has added his own touching up (although it does not seem to make a great deal of difference). The result is a very lightweight score which needs a pianist like Rubinstein to bring it fully to life. Philip Gammon's playing is musical and accomplished, and the orchestral accompaniment is tasteful. The recording is good.

Les Sylphides (ballet; orch. Douglas).

(M) *** DG Priv. 2535/*3335* 189 [136 257]. Berlin PO, Karajan – DELIBES: *Coppélia*.***

** Decca Dig. SXDL/*KSXDC* 7583. Nat. PO, Bonynge – THOMAS: *Hamlet: ballet music*.***

*(*) Ph. Dig. 6514/*7337* 070 [id.]. Rotterdam PO, Zinman – GOUNOD: *Faust: ballet suite*.**

Karajan has the advantage of limpid and svelte playing from the Berlin Philharmonic Orchestra, and he evokes a delicacy of texture which consistently delights the ear. The woodwind solos are played gently and lovingly and one can feel the conductor's touch on the phrasing. The upper register of the strings is clearly focused, the recording is warm and atmospheric, and this is one of Karajan's finest lighter discs. At Privilege price it is unbeatable, and there is a good cassette too.

Bonynge's version of *Les Sylphides* is rather disappointing, and does not match Karajan's in either flair or warmth. There are even moments of less than exact orchestral ensemble, although the solo wind playing is of high quality. The Decca sound is brilliant and full, obviously more modern than the DG issue which dates from 1977, yet that still sounds well. The Decca cassette has the wide range associated with chrome, but is not quite as smooth on top.

A perfectly acceptable version from Zinman and the Rotterdam orchestra, but there is more magic in this score than is revealed here. The digital recording is naturally balanced; the chrome cassette quite faithful but not vivid.

INSTRUMENTAL MUSIC

Cello sonata in G min., Op. 65.
*(*) HMV ASD 2587. Tortelier, Ciccolini – RACHMANINOV: *Cello sonata.**(*)

Cello sonata in G min., Op. 65; Introduction and polonaise brillante in C, Op. 3.
*** DG 2531/*3301* 201 [id.]. Rostropovich, Argerich – SCHUMANN: *Adagio and allegro.****

With such characterful artists as Rostropovich and Argerich challenging each other, this is a memorably warm and convincing account of the *Cello sonata*, Chopin's last published work, a piece which clicks into focus in such a performance. The contrasts of character between expressive cello and brilliant piano are also richly caught in the *Introduction and polonaise*, and the recording is warm to match. The cassette transfer is faithful and refined, although the modest level means that the cello timbre has rather less bite than on disc.

Tortelier's performance is obviously committed but rather lacks elegance and polish. Better vitality than perfumery, certainly, but Chopin's work needs grace as well as nervous tension. The recording is acceptable.

Piano trio in G min., Op. 8.
(M) *** Ph. 6570/*7310* 920. Beaux Arts Trio – SMETANA: *Piano trio.****

The *Piano trio* is an early work and not wholly characteristic of Chopin, but students of the composer will not fail to find it of interest. Moreover it is coupled with Smetana's excellent essay in the same medium, and the performance by the Beaux Arts Trio (particularly their admirable pianist, Menahem Pressler) could hardly be improved on; and the sound is life-like. The cassette transfer is remarkably faithful, but it is a pity the level is not higher.

SOLO PIANO MUSIC

Allegro de concert, Op. 46; Impromptu in F sharp, Op. 36; Mazurka in A min. (Notre temps); Nocturnes: in G min.; in G, Op. 37/1 and 2; Trois Nouvelles études 1–3; Polonaise in F sharp min., Op. 44; Waltzes: No. 5 in A flat, Op. 42; in E flat (Sostenuto).
*** Decca Dig. SXDL/*KSXDC* 7593 [Lon. LDR/5- 71093]. Ashkenazy.

Ashkenazy is recording the complete Chopin piano music, but instead of adopting the usual generic approach he is compiling a series of mixed programmes that have the benefit of musical contrast and show something of Chopin's development. Volume Six covers the years 1838–41 and includes a superb account of the *Allegro de concert* – originally (in 1832) planned as part of a projected *Third piano concerto*. Collectors will only need to know that the programme here is well up to the standards Ashkenazy and the Decca engineers have set in earlier volumes – see below. The playing is full of imaginative insights and often produces the spontaneity of a live recital. The cassette is first-class, matching the disc in its natural presence and colour, with a firm, warm bass response.

Andante spianato and grande polonaise brillante, Op. 22; Impromptus Nos. 1–3; Fantaisie-impromptu, Op. 66; Polonaise (Fantaisie) in A flat, Op. 61.
**(*) RCA SB 6649 [(d) in LSC 7037]. Rubinstein.

In Chopin piano music generally Rubinstein has no superior, and when it comes to polonaise rhythms he is in a class by himself. The great *Polonaise fantaisie*, Op. 61, is given a stunning performance, and one has only to listen to the snap of dotted rhythms in the Rubinstein manner to realize what made him so individual. The *Andante spianato and grande polonaise* is a curious but memorable piece that again inspires Rubinstein, and his clear and relaxed accounts of the *Impromptus* make most other interpretations sound forced by comparison. The recording is not ideal, rather too hard for European taste, but with such playing it need not get in the way of enjoyment.

Ballades Nos. 1–4; Fantasia, Op. 49; Nocturnes Nos. 1–21; Preludes Nos. 1–26; Waltzes Nos. 1–14.
(M) **(*) Ph. 6768 233 (5). Arrau.

The *Preludes* were the first of the five discs to be recorded; they date from the mid-1970s and remain available on the medium-priced Sequenza label – see below. The *Ballades* are particularly impressive. As always with this great artist, there is unfailing beauty of sound and a strong sense of personality. Some of the rubato he adopts in the *Nocturnes* may strike some listeners as just a shade too personal, but his artistry is unique and he is eminently well served by the engineers.

Ballades Nos. 1 in G min., Op. 23; 2 in F, Op. 38; 3 in A flat, Op. 47; 4 in F min., Op. 52.
**(*) RCA Conifer 26.41053 [LSC 2370]. Rubinstein.
* Nimbus 2110. Perlemuter.

Ballades Nos. 1–4; Allegro de concert, Op. 46; Introduction and variations on 'Je vends des scapulaires' in B flat, Op. 12.
*** CRD CRD 1060/*CRDC 4060*. Milne.

Ballades Nos. 1–4; Fantasy in F min., Op. 49.
*** Ph. 9500 393/*7300 605* [id.]. Arrau.

Ballades Nos. 1–4; Impromptus Nos. 1–3; Fantaisie-impromptu.
(M) **(*) DG Priv. 2535/*3335* 284 [id.]. Vásáry.

Ballades Nos. 1–4; Nouvelles études, Op. posth.
*** Decca SXL/*KSXC* 6143 [Lon. CS/5-6422]. Ashkenazy.

Rubinstein's readings are unique, a miracle of creative imagination. From the hushed half-tones of the tiny coda of the *Second Ballade* to the romantic splendour of the great heroic theme of the *Ballade in G minor*, Rubinstein is at his most inspired. The recording is shallow by the best European standards, but with a reinforcement of bass it can be made to sound quite well.

There is no technical reservation about Ashkenazy's finely recorded Decca disc. Indeed the recording here is admirably natural and satisfying. The readings are thoughtful and essentially unflashy. The rubato arises naturally from Ashkenazy's personal approach to the music. The intimacy of the recording allows him to share this with the listener. The openings of the *First* and *Fourth Ballades* show this quality well; the music unfolds naturally and without emphasis. There is occasionally a touch of magic in the Rubinstein performances that Ashkenazy, with his seriousness, misses (the beginning of the *F major Ballade*, for instance) but on the whole this is a most satisfying disc, with beautiful performances of the *Nouvelles études* thrown in for good measure. There is a good cassette too.

Distinguished performances from Arrau, as one would expect, beautifully recorded by the Philips engineers. There is scant evidence of Arrau's advancing years, though in his youth there would have been a more thrilling sense of exhilaration and virtuosity. But there is breadth and perception in abundance here all the same. This does not displace Ashkenazy's set, but it will not disappoint Arrau's admirers. The rich colouring and weight of the recording are equally impressive on disc and cassette.

Hamish Milne gives thoughtful and individual performances of the *Ballades*. They may initially sound understated, but in their freshness and concentration they prove poetic and compelling. Similarly he plays the two rarities with total conviction, suggesting that the *Allegro de concert* at least (originally a sketch for a third piano concerto) is most unjustly neglected. The recorded sound is first-rate, and that with very long sides indeed. The cassette transfer too is first-class; there is minimal difference between tape and disc.

From DG a generous and on the whole attractive coupling. Vásáry is rather matter-of-fact in the *Impromptus*, but the *Ballades* are imaginatively played, and the performances, although personal, offer poetry as well as bravura. The *G minor* is outstanding, with a fine romantic sweep, but Nos. 2, 3 and 4 are each individual and rewarding. The recording is rather dry but faithful and clear on both LP and the equivalent tape.

Vlado Perlemuter's reputation as an interpreter of Chopin is legendary, and it is a pity that the Nimbus recording of the *Ballades*, made when the French pianist was in his seventies, offers only a glimpse of his stature. The range of colour and dynamic shading and the overall sense of mastery are not what they once were, at least on this evidence, and in any case the recording is too unfocused and unflattering to be competitive.

Ballade No. 3; Fantaisie in F min., Op. 49; Mazurkas, Op. 50/1–3; Nocturnes, Op. 48, Nos. 1 in C min.; 2 in F sharp min.; Prelude in C sharp min., Op. 45; Tarantelle, Op. 43.
*** Decca SXL/*KSXC* 6922 [Lon. CS/5-7150]. Ashkenazy.

With Volume Five Ashkenazy comes to the years 1840–41, which offer two of the very greatest works, the third *Ballade* and the *F minor Fantasy*. Both are played with exceptional warmth and sonority; incidentally, the former is a new performance and not a reissue of Ashkenazy's mid-1960s account, available in various formats and couplings ever since. The *Mazurkas* are beautifully done too, and each side is sensibly planned. The recording maintains the high standard of the series, and the cassette transfer is of outstanding quality, the piano timbre warm and full with excellent range at both ends of the spectrum.

Barcarolle in F sharp, Op. 60; Berceuse in D flat, Op. 57; Boléro in C, Op. 19; Fantaisie in F min., Op. 49; 3 Nouvelles études, Op. posth.; Tarantelle in A flat, Op. 43.
*** RCA SB 6683 [LSC 2889]. Rubinstein.

When regarded in relation to Chopin's complete works – so neatly docketed into *Nocturnes*, *Mazurkas*, *Waltzes* and so on – these pieces seem like the rag-bag elements, but in fact they contain some of Chopin's finest inspirations, notably the magnificent *Barcarolle* and *Berceuse*. The *Tarantelle* may be musically less interesting and not very characteristic, but in Rubinstein's hands it is a glorious piece, full of bravura. Rubinstein's way with Chopin is endlessly fascinating. Like almost all his other Chopin records, this collection is highly recommendable. Recording bright and a little clangy in the RCA manner.

Barcarolle, Op. 60; Impromptus Nos. 1–3; 4 (Fantaisie-impromptu); Waltzes Nos. 15–19, Op. posth.
*** Ph. 9500/*7300* 963 [id.]. Arrau.

Although Arrau's Chopin is seldom mercurial it is never inflexible and it has its own special insights. The *Fantaisie-impromptu*, with its nobly contoured central melody, is a highlight here. The richly coloured piano timbre, warm in the middle, resonant in the bass, contributes a good deal to the character of this record. The cassette transfer too is outstanding; there is little appreciable difference between disc and tape.

Barcarolle, Op. 60; Mazurkas, Op. 63/1–3; Op. 67/2 and 4; Op. 68/4; Nocturnes, Op. 61/1–2; Polonaise fantaisie, Op. 61; Waltzes, Op. 64/1–3.
*** Decca SXL/*KSXC* 6801 [Lon. CS/5-7022]. Ashkenazy.

Continuing his chronological survey of Chopin's output, Ashkenazy here brings us music from 1845–6 to the end of Chopin's life. The sound quality is impressively lifelike (with a first-class cassette equivalent) and has considerable depth in the bass. (The recording was made in All Saints' Church, Petersham.) The performances have strong personality and an aristocratic poise, even though one takes issue with the odd tempo; the *Waltzes* are a little fast.

3 Écossaises, Op. 72/3; Introduction and variations on a German air, 'Der Schweizerbub';

Polonaises Nos. 8 in D min., Op. 71/1; 11 in B flat min. (Adieu); 13 in G min.; 14 in B flat; 15 in A flat; 16 in G sharp min.; Rondo in F, Op. 5; Rondo in C min., Op 1.
*** Decca SXL/*KSXC* 6981. Ashkenazy.

The *Polonaise in G minor* is Chopin's earliest known composition, and this fifth volume of Ashkenazy's collected edition covers very early works, written between 1817 (when he was only seven) and 1826, the year of the *Variations* and *B flat minor Polonaise*. Ashkenazy's performances are magical, fresh and direct, but full of touches of insight. Superb recorded sound and a matching cassette, notably well focused at the top.

Études, Op. 10/1–12; Op. 25/1–12.
*** DG 2530 291/*3300 287* [id.]. Pollini.
*** Decca SXL/*KSXC* 6710 [Lon. CS/5-6844]. Ashkenazy.
(M) **(*) CBS 61886/*40-*. Fou Ts'ong.
**(*) Nimbus 2133. Ronald Smith.
(B) ** CfP CFP/*TC-CFP* 4392. Hobson.

Études, Op. 10/1–12; Op. 25/1–12; 3 Nouvelles Études.
* Nimbus Dig. 2136. Sasaki.

Études, Opp. 10 and 25; Waltzes Nos. 1–19.
(M) **(*) DG Priv. 2721 208 (2). Vásáry.

Pollini's electrifying account is masterly. He won the Warsaw Chopin Prize in 1959 when he was only eighteen and his playing of the Polish master has not declined in the meantime. These must be given a strong recommendation in spite of the recording, which, though good, is not in the demonstration class.

Ashkenazy's Decca issue completely supersedes his earlier record on Melodiya imports or *Chant du Monde*. Playing of total mastery and excellently recorded, this can safely be recommended alongside Pollini's, and the choice left to individual taste. Both are superb. There are good (if not outstanding) cassettes of both performances. They are comparatively early transfers and although the piano tone is clear there is a touch of hardness on both. The Decca is preferable.

Fou Ts'ong is at his best here and gives an impressive demonstration of his fine musicianship and expressive powers. Indeed, many individual studies compare well with the very finest available on record, though no easy equation emerges from comparisons. His insights are no less penetrating than Vásáry's, and his powerful technique is not in question either. He is not as well recorded as Ashkenazy (and the cassette is rather clattery in the upper range). Moreover CBS have omitted to provide scrolls between each of the studies, surely a mistake in so competitive a market. Impressive pianism and no mean artistry, but not a first choice.

Vásáry's performances have been in and out of the catalogue in various packages and formats and at many price levels. On each appearance their attractions seem stronger: Vásáry is a poetic artist and his keyboard prowess is second to none. There is elegance in the *Waltzes*, brilliance in the *Études* when required, and fine intelligence and taste throughout. The recording still sounds remarkably fresh, and admirers of this artist need not hesitate.

Ronald Smith is a reliable and often poetic artist whose formidable technique and fine musicianship have earned him an enviable reputation. He proves an admirable guide through these *Études* and though he may not be as consistently imaginative as Ashkenazy or Vásáry, his version can hold its own alongside the best – and he is accorded sound that is both lifelike and natural.

Ian Hobson, winner of the 1981 Leeds Piano Competition, and finalist in many competitions before that, is a formidable virtuoso. The incisiveness and dexterity of his playing in these ever-demanding studies is never in doubt, yet Chopin really requires more affection than Hobson allows here, more lyrical warmth. The *G flat Study* here is an iron butterfly. Only when he learns to relax in the recording studio will his full artistry emerge. On both disc and cassette he is very well recorded, and this is certainly worth its bargain price.

Ken Sasaki brings sensitivity to the *Études* and his playing is often accomplished. He is alone in offering the *Trois nouvelles études* which come off nicely. However, by the side of many of his rivals in the catalogue, the personality seems a little pale, though his technique and musicianship are good.

Impromptu in A flat, Op. 29; Largo in E flat, Op. posth.; Mazurkas: Op. 30/1–4; Op. 33/1–4; Nocturnes: Op. 32: Nos. 1 in B; 2 in A flat; in C min., Op. posth.; Scherzo in B flat min., Op. 31; Variation No. 6 in E (from Hexameron); Waltz in F, Op. 34/3.
*** Decca Dig. **410 122-2**; 410 122-1/*4*. Ashkenazy.

Volume Eight in Ashkenazy's continuing historical series is the first to be issued on compact disc (apart from the separate anthology of 'favourite' items – see below). It is well up to the high standard of the series, both in sensibility and recording, with a splendid chrome tape, every bit the equal of the LP. The opening *Impromptu* is thrown off with a marvellous unaffected insouciance and the programme – which is concerned with music written in 1836–8 – includes a memorably serene account of the *Sylphides Nocturne*, Op. 32/2. The playing is full of mercurial contrasts, the *B flat minor Scherzo* a fine example of Ashkenazy's current style combining bold drama with subtlety of inner feeling. The virtually unknown *Largo* is a rather solemn piece, but fits splendidly into a recital that is as well planned as it is expertly played. The variety of nuance within the eight *Mazurkas* included gives special pleasure.

Mazurkas Nos. 1–51.
*** RCA SB 6702 (Nos. 1–17); SB 6703 (Nos. 18–33); SB 6704 (Nos. 34–51) [LSC 6177 (3)]. Rubinstein.

The *Mazurkas* contain some of Chopin's most characteristic music. That they are often ignored by virtuoso pianists simply reflects the fact that as a rule they are less tricky technically, and concert pianists prefer to show off. Yet, as Rubinstein continually demonstrates, they contain some wonderfully pianistic ideas, none the worse for being simply expressed. At the one end you have certain *Mazurkas* which are first cousins to Chopin's *Polonaises* and at the other end some that might almost be *Nocturnes*, while a lot in the middle could almost as readily have been included with the *Waltzes*. All are delightful, even if there is no need to linger very long over some of them. Rubinstein could never play in a dull way to save his life, and in his hands these fifty-one pieces are endlessly fascinating, though on occasion in such unpretentious music one would welcome a completely straight approach. By American standards of piano tone the recorded sound is very good.

Mazurkas: in C; in F, Op. 68/1 and 3; in D; Nocturnes: in B flat min.; in C min.; in B, Op. 9/1–3; in C min.; Polonaises: in F min., Op. 71/3; in G flat, Op. posth.; Souvenir de Paganini; Variations in D for piano duet; Waltzes: in B min., Op. 69/2; in D flat, Op. 70/3; in E; in E min., Op. posth.
*** Decca Dig. SXDL/*KSXDC* 7584 [Lon. LDR/5- 71084]. Ashkenazy.

The opus numbers are misleading since for the uninitiated they convey the impression that these *Mazurkas* and the *Polonaises* are later than they are. In fact, this record concentrates on the year 1829, though the *D major Variations*, in which Ashkenazy is joined by his son, are a bit earlier. The three *Op. 9 Nocturnes* are the centrepiece and musically the most substantial pieces to which Ashkenazy adds the *C minor Nocturne* of 1837. Ashkenazy could hardly be more persuasive and brings elegance to all these miniatures. Nor is there any need to grumble about the excellence of the Decca recording. This is proving an invaluable series. The chrome cassette matches the disc closely, full in timbre and clear, without edge.

Nocturnes Nos. 1–19; 20 and 21, Op. posth.
*** RCA SB 6731-2/*RK 11553* and *43130* [LSC 7050 (2)] – Nos. 1–19 only. Rubinstein.
*** DG Dig. 2741/*3382* 012 [id.]. Barenboim.
*** Ph. 6747 485/*7699 088* [id.]. Arrau.
(M) **(*) CBS 61827/8/*40*-. Fou Ts'ong.
(M) **(*) DG Priv. 2726 070 (2) [136 486/7]. Vásáry.

The Rubinstein set of *Nocturnes* makes a firm recommendation. The piano tone has an acceptably full quality and Rubinstein's magical sense of nuance and the fascinating inevitability of his rubato immediately capture the listener's imagination. Rubinstein is a magician in matters of colour, and again and again throughout these two discs (available separately) there are moments of sheer perfection, where the timing of a phrase exactly catches the mood and atmosphere of the composer's inspiration. The recording is the best Rubinstein has ever had for his solo records. The cassettes have been recently remastered and are now fully acceptable.

Barenboim's playing is of exceptional eloquence, and he is superbly recorded (the chrome tapes outstanding alongside the discs). These are intense, poetic and thoughtful readings, the phrasing beautifully moulded, following rather in the mid-European tradition. In this Barenboim has something in common with Arrau, whose approach clearly reflects his boyhood training in Germany, creating tonal warmth coupled with inner tensions of the kind one expects in Beethoven. In the *Nocturnes* it can be apt to have an element of seriousness, and this too is a very compelling cycle, given rich, refined recording on both disc and cassette.

Fou Ts'ong sometimes reminds one of Solomon – and there can surely be no higher tribute. He is at his very best in the gentle poetic pieces; in the more robust *Nocturnes* his rubato is less subtle, the style not so relaxed. But this is undoubtedly distinguished, and with good recording (the cassettes too are among CBS's best transfers) it is competitive at medium price. But Rubinstein's RCA set of *Nocturnes* remains in a class of its own.

From Vásáry, playing of character and insight by a pianist whose flexibility in moulding a Chopin phrase to find its kernel of poetry is always apparent. Why then the reservation? It is partly because sometimes the approach seems *too* positive, the relaxation within the melodic line *too* calculated. This impression is at least partly caused by the character of the recorded image. In technical terms this cannot be faulted; it is clear, bright, a little dry perhaps, but beautifully focused. But even in the softest music there is no conveyed sense of liquidity such as Askenase found in his mono set made many years ago for the same company.

Polonaises Nos. 1–7.
*** DG 2530/*3300* 659 [id.]. Pollini.

Polonaises Nos. 1–6.
**(*) RCA SB 6640 [(d) in LSC 7037]. Rubinstein.

Pollini offers playing of outstanding mastery as well as a subtle poetry. He recorded a couple of the *Polonaises* on an HMV recital discussed on p. 288, but this wider selection is even more spellbinding. It easily leads the field and is well recorded. Unfortunately the cassette is disappointingly shallow.

Artur Rubinstein has recorded these pieces more than once before, but his last attempt – recorded in Carnegie Hall – was as freshly individual as ever. Master pianist that he was, he seems actually to be rethinking and recreating each piece, even the hackneyed *'Military'* and *A flat* works, at the very moment of performance. Other performances may bring out different facets of the pieces, but none is likely to outshine Rubinstein's in easy majesty and natural sense of spontaneous phrasing. Despite Carnegie Hall, the recording quality remains rather hard.

24 Preludes, Op. 28; Preludes Nos. 25, Op. 45; 26, Op. posth.
*** DG 2530/*3300* 550 [id.] (Nos. 1–24 only). Pollini.
*** CBS 76422/*40-* [M 33507]. Perahia.
(B) *** Con. CC/*CCT* 7511 [DG 2530 231]. Eschenbach.
(M) **(*) Ph. Seq. 6527/*7311* 091 [6500 622/*7300 335*]. Arrau.

24 Preludes; Ballade No. 2; Waltz in A flat, Op. 34.
*** Decca SXL/*KSXC* 6877 [Lon. CS/*5-*7101]. Ashkenazy.

We are eminently well-served in this repertoire, and as is so often the case, choice will be a matter of personal predilection. It goes without saying that all these pianists are masters of the keyboard, but some are artists of such strong personality that criticism is altogether silenced. Such is the case with Maurizio Pollini, whose reading evinces an effortless and complete mastery. While listening to him, one has difficulty in imagining that there can be any alternative interpretation. He has impeccable taste in handling rubato, the firmest sense of line and form, and no trace of excess sentiment. His recording is a good one, though the sound is not quite as natural or as fresh as the balance Decca provide for Ashkenazy. Even so, one would be tempted to make Pollini first choice, were one to possess only one version.

Murray Perahia brings a remarkable freshness to the *Preludes*. There are no routine expressive gestures; everything radiates a spontaneity tempered with impeccable control. In deed, he inflects certain phrases (in the *A flat Prelude*, for example) with a subtlety and poetic feeling second to none. Unfortunately the CBS recording does not do full justice to him (though it is a great improvement on his record of the *Sonatas* or the Mendelssohn *Concertos*) but in spite of that handicap, this record is in the very first flight. He is an artist of genuine vision. Pollini's cassette is clearly transferred but a trifle dry; Perahia's CBS tape, for some curious reason, creates rather more body and bloom for the piano timbre than the disc, without too much loss of range.

Ashkenazy's set of the *Preludes* forms part of his chronological surveys. All the music in this issue was published in 1838–9; the Op. 38 *Ballade* and the *Waltz*, which was written in 1835 but not published until three years later, precede the *Preludes*. Ashkenazy gives a dramatic and powerful reading that takes its place alongside those of Perahia and Pollini.

Reissued at bargain price, Eschenbach's set is very competitive. He is beautifully recorded; the tone is warm, clear and resonant, completely natural, and the cassette is successful too, slightly fuller if with a marginally restricted upper range. The performances are characteristically musical and perceptive, thoughtful, with the bravura (which is never in doubt) never aggressively extrovert. Occasionally there is a hint of under-characterization, which brings a slightly unidiomatic quality, but as a set this gives much pleasure.

The Arrau set is much admired, and he certainly receives an opulent, full-bodied recording, on disc and tape alike, which does justice to his subtle nuances of tone. Every prelude bears the imprint of a strong personality, to which not all listeners respond. Arrau can sometimes sound a shade calculated (his rubato seeming arbitrary and contrived), but there is little evidence of this here. His *Preludes* appear to spring from an inner conviction, even if the outward results will not be universally liked.

Scherzi Nos. 1 in B min., Op. 20; in B flat min., Op. 31; 3 in C sharp min., Op. 39; 4 in E, Op. 54.

(M) *** HMV SXLP/*TC-SXLP* 30510. Sviatoslav Richter.

**(*) RCA SB 2095 [LSC 2368]. Rubinstein.

Scherzi Nos. 1–4; Barcarolle, Op. 60; Prelude in C sharp min., Op. 45.

*** Decca SXL 6334 [Lon. CS/5- 6562]. Ashkenazy.

Chopin's *Scherzi* are a long way from the original derivation of the genre as essentially light-hearted and humorous, and Rubinstein's immensely powerful readings play up the strength of the writing in a highly cogent way. The RCA recording is clear and reasonably faithful, though it needs plenty of bass boost to take off the dryness. This might be first choice were it not for the existence of the superb Ashkenazy disc offering dazzling playing of the highest order and first-rate Decca sound. Moreover the two substantial bonuses are played equally beautifully.

Electrifying playing from Richter. He is at his most imaginative in No. 3, but throughout there is characteristic flair. The recording is a little dry but not shallow, and the cassette transfer is excellent.

Piano sonata No. 1 in C min., Op. 4; Contredanse in G flat; Funeral march in C min., Op. 72/2; Mazurkas: in B flat; in G; in A min., Op. 68/2; Nocturne in E min., Op. 72/1; Polonaise in B flat, Op. 71/2; Rondo in C, Op. 73; Waltzes: in E flat; in A flat, Op. posth.

*** Decca SXL/*KSXC* 6911 [Lon. CS 7135]. Ashkenazy.

This record does not, as might at first sight be thought, depart from the chronological plan of Ashkenazy's series. Despite their late opus numbers these *Mazurkas* and other pieces all date from 1827–9, though many of them did not appear in print until after Chopin's death. The *C minor Sonata*, Op. 4, is the rarity here: it comes from 1827 and, apart from Magaloff's complete edition on Philips, this is its only available recording at present. It is not deeply characteristic and is of greater interest to students of Chopin's style and budding pianists than to the wider musical public. Ashkenazy makes out a more persuasive case than anyone who has recorded it so far, but the distance Chopin covered between this and the two concertos is really quite amazing. There are some marvellous pieces among the shorter works on the second side, notably the *A minor Mazurka*, Op. 68/2, and the *E minor Nocturne*, Op. 72/1.

Piano sonata No. 2 in B flat min. (*Funeral march*), *Op. 35; Mazurkas: in C sharp min.; E min.; B; A flat, Op. 41/1–4; Polonaises: in A; C min., Op. 40/1 and 2; Scherzo No. 3 in C sharp min., Op. 39.*
*** Decca SXL/*KSXC* 6995 [Lon. CS/5-7235]. Ashkenazy.

This disc brings us the Op. 40 *Polonaises* (the *C minor* was finished on Mallorca) and the *C sharp minor Scherzo*, which Chopin began there. The *Mazurkas* of Op. 41 all come from the same period (1838–9), the year after he began the *Sonata*. This covers the years 1837 to 1839 when the *Sonata* was finished. These are performances of no mean stature, and Ashkenazy's account of the *Sonata* is no less dazzling than his live recording of 1972 and in some respects surpasses it. Indeed the first movement in particular seems more concentrated in feeling and the finale is very exciting indeed. In this repertoire one cannot speak of the finest performance, for this is terrain that has been conquered by Rachmaninov, Horowitz, Rubinstein, Perahia and others, but it would be surprising if this account does not (like the finest of its rivals) enjoy classic status, and it is certainly the best-recorded with very vivid sound. The cassette is wide-ranging but with a touch of hardness right at the top, but the bass end of the spectrum is admirable.

Piano sonatas Nos. 2; 3 in B min., Op. 58.
*** RCA SB 2151 [LSC 3194]. Rubinstein.
*** CBS 76242/*40*- [M/*MT* 32780]. Perahia.
(M) ** DG Priv. 2535/*3335* 230. Vásáry.
(M) ** CBS 61149/*40*-. Fou Ts'ong.
*(*) Nimbus 2109. Perlemuter.

Piano sonata No. 2; Études, Op. 10/8 in F; 10 in A flat; Op. 25/6 in G sharp min.; Nocturne in E flat, Op. 55/2; Scherzo No. 3, Op. 39.
*** DG 2531/*3301* 346 [id.]. Pogorelich.

Piano sonata No. 2; Mazurka in A flat, Op. 59/2; Nocturnes: in F; F sharp, Op. 15/1 and 2; Grande valse brillante, Op. 18.
*** Decca SXL/*KSXC* 6575 [Lon. CS/5-6794]. Ashkenazy.

Piano sonata No. 3; Andante spianato et grande polonaise brillante, Op. 22; Introduction and Rondo in E flat, Op. 16.
**(*) Chan. Dig. ABRD/*ABTD* 1040. Artymiw.

Piano sonata No. 3; Berceuse, Op. 57; Mazurkas, Op. 59/1–5; Nocturnes: in F min.; in E flat, Op. 55/1–2.
*** Decca SXL/*KSXC* 6810 [Lon. CS/5-7030]. Ashkenazy.

Piano sonata No. 3; Polonaises Nos. 3 in A; 4 in C min., Op. 40/1–2; 6 in A flat, Op. 53.
(M) *** DG Sig. 2543/*3343* 530 [2531 099 PSI]. Gilels.

Ashkenazy's 1972 recording of the *Second Sonata* was made during a live recital at Essex University, and the concert was also filmed. Decca made sure that the sound suffered no loss from the circumstances; indeed the quality is outstandingly natural: the piano has splendid resonance and realism. The opening (and closing) applause is an irritant, but in all other respects this record earns the highest praise. The performance of the *Sonata* is of the highest distinction, of great power and eloquence, yet with the music's poetry fully realized – the playing of the middle section of the slow movement is exquisite. The rest of the programme has a comparable spontaneity, and if the final *Presto* of the *Sonata* is not absolutely immaculate, who will cavil, with music-making of this quality. There is an outstanding cassette too.

Of the records coupling both *Sonatas*, Rubinstein's remains hard to surpass. His strength is balanced by a poetic feeling that springs directly from the music, and the control of rubato brings many moments of magic, with wonderful examples in the second subject of the first movement and later in the central section of the *Funeral march*. The sound is richer and less brittle than some of Rubinstein's records.

Murray Perahia seems naturally attuned to working in the recording studio. Like his first record of Schumann, this one shows a spontaneous imagination at work, questing onwards. The technique is remarkable even by today's standards, but it is so natural to the player that he never uses it for mere display, and always there is an underlying sense of structural purpose. The dry, unrushed account of the finale of the *B flat minor Sonata* is typical of Perahia's freshness, and the only pity is that the recording of the piano is rather clattery and close. The cassette is not distinguished either.

Gilels's account of the *B minor Sonata* is thoughtful and ruminative, seen through a powerful mind and wholly individual fingers, and there are some highly personal touches, for example the gentle undulating accompaniment, like quietly tolling bells, caressing the second group of the first movement. There is a beautifully pensive and delicately coloured slow movement; the first movement is expansive and warmly lyrical, and there is not a bar that does not set one thinking anew about this music. An altogether haunting reading and an obligatory acquisition even if it does not prompt one to discard Lipatti, Perahia or Rubinstein. The three *Polonaises* are superb; they have majesty, grandeur and poetry. A rather special record altogether. The chrome cassette is of first-class quality, natural, full in timbre and with good range and presence.

Ivo Pogorelich is the Yugoslav pianist who leapt to prominence during the 1980 Warsaw Chopin Competition. Martha Argerich was so incensed when he was eliminated before the final round that she resigned from the jury in protest. The attendant publicity has led to far greater exposure for Pogorelich than for the winner, Thai Son Dang from Vietnam. It is obvious that Pogorelich possesses an outsize personality and a keen awareness of colour. He is a commanding pianist of undoubted charisma, and his playing has temperament and fire in abundance. There are many wilful touches here and some agogic mannerisms that will not have universal appeal. All the same, these are performances to be reckoned with. The balance is close and probably does not do full justice to the quality of his pianissimo tone – which, even as it is, sounds remarkable. The cassette transfer is first-class, well balanced and clear.

The Decca issue continues Ashkenazy's distinguished series with a memorable performance of the *B minor Sonata* (some might not like the accelerando treatment of the finale, but it is undoubtedly exciting), set within a beautifully arranged programme. The *Berceuse* is played very gently, but the *Mazurkas* bring a splendid element of contrast. Ashkenazy's flexible, poetic phrasing is always a joy. The recording is well up to the high standard set by this series, on disc and tape alike.

Both sonatas fare admirably in Vásáry's hands. The performances are unaffected, beautifully shaped and controlled with a masterly sense of rubato. Very natural and highly accomplished; moreover they are given good recorded sound, on disc and cassette alike, which stands the passage of time extremely well (these accounts originally appeared in the mid-1960s). At the same time, Vásáry does not bring those very special qualities of individuality that mark the accounts of Ashkenazy, Perahia and Rubinstein, though he gives great satisfaction nonetheless.

Though not a first choice for this coupling, Fou Ts'ong is perceptive and brilliant in both sonatas. His sensitivity is always in evidence, and there is poetry when required. The recorded quality is acceptable though not distinguished.

Despite Perlemuter's great reputation, his coupling of the sonatas does not survive comparison with such poetic readings as Ashkenazy's and Perahia's. The piano sound is not particularly satisfactory, with clangorous climaxes and unappealing colour, and the playing lacks the finish and command of more youthful rivals.

The rarity on Artymiw's record is the *Introduction and Rondo in E flat*, written in 1832, a piece which inspires Miss Artymiw to the widest range of expressiveness from introspection to explosive brilliance. Her performance of the better-known *Grande polonaise* is more contained, but fresh and attractive. The *Sonata* has a hint of caution too, but erupts superbly in the finale. First-rate recording on both disc and tape, although the cassette balance is over-bright on top.

Waltzes Nos. 1–14.
*** DG 2530/*3300* 965 [id.]. Zimerman.
*** RCA SB 6600/*RK 11705* [LSC 2726/*RK 1071*]. Rubinstein.
*** Ph. **400 025-2**; 9500 739/*7300 824* [id.]. Arrau.
(M) ** Decca SPA/*KCSP* 486 [Lon. STS 15305]. Katin.
(M) ** DG Priv. 2535/*3335* 267 [id.]. Vásáry.
(B) ** CfP CFP/*TC-CFP* 414417-1/*4*. (Nos. 1–19) Fowke.
(M) (***) World mono SH 383. Cortot.
*(*) Ph. Dig. 6514/*7337* 280 [id.] (Nos. 1–19). Kocsis.

Very distinguished playing from the Polish pianist Krystian Zimerman, who won the 1975 Warsaw competition at the age of eighteen. He is in the same line as Pollini and Argerich (who also record for DG), and his account of the *Waltzes* is uncommonly mature. The playing has a spontaneity and polish that have prompted comparison with Rubinstein and Lipatti – and rightly so. There is a sparkle and finesse that are established in the opening bars of the *E flat Waltz* and that inform everything on the record. Yet while there is every evidence of buoyant virtuosity and youthful brilliance, there is no want of perception and poetic insight. This is very fine indeed and is well recorded. This is arguably the finest version of the *Waltzes* to have appeared since Lipatti's, for the Rubinstein is let down by shallow recording. The cassette transfer is truthful but made at a low level. Detail is good, but there is some loss of presence.

Rubinstein's approach has a chiselled perfection that suggests finely cut and polished diamonds, and here the tonal quality of the recording, which is crystal-clear, hard and brilliant, emphasizes the metaphor. The rubato is subtle and the phrasing most beautiful, yet a fractional lack of warmth prevents the intimacy of approach from making absolute contact with the listener. In many ways this is a very fine record indeed, but it should be heard before purchase. The cassette is not recommended.

Arrau produces his own specially rich, rounded tone-colours and is accorded beautiful sound by the Philips engineers. These are performances of elegance and finesse, though there are, as always, moments when the great pianist invests detail with a heavier significance than some listeners may feel is justified. But these are readings of real personality, and however the individual collector may respond, they are searching and considered. The tape quality is bold and full but lacks a little sparkle at the top compared with the disc. The compact disc is very fine indeed, and there is virtually no appreciable background noise, even though it has been made from an analogue master.

Peter Katin plays the *Waltzes* not in numerical order, as is customary, but in chronological order, which seems more sensible. He is very well recorded. Having said this, one must confess to slight disappointment. The playing is thoughtful, even affectionate, and certainly assured; yet the vivid waltzes do not always sparkle as they might. Even so, this is musical playing and not without poetry, and the cassette transfer of Katin's performances is outstanding – extremely secure and natural.

Vásáry's tempi are fast and his manner sometimes seems unnecessarily brisk. He is more persuasive in the relaxed, lyrical pieces, and elsewhere there is the occasional flash of poetry, but for the most part the performances, although not lacking style, have less individuality, and they seldom charm the ear. The recording is crisp and clean, but the piano quality is rather dry.

From Philip Fowke polished, elegant, meticulously accurate playing, nicely nuanced and not without sparkle, but curiously cool and uninvolving. There is much to admire here but the playing sounds too calculated. The recording is excellent.

Cortot's classic accounts of the *Waltzes* have been out of circulation for so long that newcomers to them will not fail to respond to their freshness and individuality, even if not everything Cortot does is to modern taste. He is extraordinarily vital and fiery, impulsive, poetic and totally compelling. Recorded in 1934, the performances have transferred well to LP, even if the sound is limited in range and colour. Sparkling playing of this order, highly personal and far from perfect, is in a special category; no Chopin lover should be without this set even if it involves duplication.

Zoltán Kocsis is full of fire and temperament but just a little too concerned to dazzle us with his superb technical prowess. Many of these are breathlessly fast and rushed, though there is no want of poetry in some of them. He includes five of the posthumous waltzes omitted by Lipatti, Rubinstein and Zimerman. Kocsis is vividly, albeit too closely, recorded but his playing is too eccentric and rushed to displace Zimerman.

Readers are reminded that Lipatti's famous set is still available on HMV HLM 7075 although the equivalent cassette recently available as an import from Europe (2C 251 00167) is not recommended. It is non-Dolby and the sound is totally unacceptable. The LP, however, is remarkably truthful in timbre and focus.

Miscellaneous recitals

Albumblatt in E, B. 151; Allegro de concert in A, Op. 46; Cantabile in B flat, B. 34; Contredanse in G flat, B. 17; Funeral march in C min., Op. 72/2; Largo in E flat, B. 109; Mazurka in D, B. 4; Nocturnes: in C min., B. 108; in E flat, Op. 9/2; Rondo in C, B. 26.
** Pearl SHE 544. Lear.

A sensibly planned recital of off-beat Chopin played with evident dedication and capably recorded. The *Allegro de concert* (1841) was a reworking of material Chopin had intended for his third concerto; most of the other pieces here waited for publication until after Chopin's death. If none of them is a masterpiece, all are worth having on record. Angela Lear is a gifted artist, though perhaps lacking the spontaneity and authority of more established Chopin interpreters.

Andante spianato et grande polonaise brillante, Op. 22; Étude in F, Op. 10/8; Mazurkas: in G min.; in C; in B flat min., Op. 24/1–2 and 4; Preludes, Op. 28, Nos. 17 in A flat; 18 in F min.; Scherzo No. 4 in E, Op. 54; Waltz in A flat, Op. 34/1.
(M) *(**) DG Sig. 2543/*3343* 519 [2530 826]. Zimerman.

A remarkably promising début. This first recital leaves no doubts as to the astonishing security of Zimerman's technique (there are some breathtaking passages in the *E major Scherzo* and the *Andante spianato*) nor the individual quality of his artistic personality. Here is an artist to watch. He survives a cruelly close balance in a dry acoustic which is why this disc, made by Polskie Nagrania, cannot be recommended without some reservation. But the performances are another matter.

'Classics': (i) *Ballades Nos. 1 in G min., Op. 23;* (ii) *3 in A flat, Op. 47;* (iii) *Études Nos. 5 in G flat; 12 in C min., Op. 10/5 and 10; 13 in A flat; 21 in G flat, Op. 25/1 and 9;* (iv) *Fantaisie-impromptu, Op. 66;* (i) *Mazurkas Nos. 5 in B flat, Op. 7/1; 23 in D, Op. 33/2;* (v) *Nocturnes Nos. 10 in A flat, Op. 32/2; 15 in F min., Op. 55/1;* (i) *Polonaises Nos. 3 in A (Military), Op. 40/1; 6 in A flat, Op. 53;* (iv) *Prelude No. 15 in D flat, Op. 28/15;* (ii) *Scherzos Nos. 2 in B flat min., Op. 31; 3 in C sharp min., Op. 39; Waltzes Nos. 2 in A flat, Op. 34/1;* (i) *6 in D flat; 7 in C sharp min., Op. 64/1–2; 11 in G flat, Op. 70/1.*
(M) *** HMV *TC2-COS 54254.* (i) Malcuzynski; (ii) Adni; (iii) Kersenbaum; (iv) Ogdon; (v) Lympany.

A strikingly well-recorded double-length chrome tape offering distinguished performances (the contribution from Malcuzynski is notable) and a well-planned programme. There are plenty of favourites here.

'Popular Chopin': Ballade No. 1 in G min., Op. 23; Études Nos. 3 in E, Op. 10/3; 12 in C min. (Revolutionary), Op. 10/12; Fantaisie-impromptu in C sharp min., Op. 66; Mazurkas Nos. 5 in B flat, Op. 7/1; 23 in D, Op. 33/2; Nocturnes Nos. 2 in E flat, Op. 9/2; 5 in C sharp, Op. 15/2; Polonaises Nos. 3 in A, Op. 40/1; 6 in E flat, Op. 53; Preludes Nos. 7 in A, Op. 28/7; 15 in D flat (Raindrop), Op. 28/15; Waltzes Nos. 6 in D flat (Minute); 7 in C sharp min., Op. 64/1–2.
(M) ** HMV HQS/*TC-HQS* 1189. Ogdon.

This is playing of strong character, but it is a little uneven in penetrating the core of the music. Highlights include the two *Polonaises*, which open the disc boldly, and the *Ballade*, which provides a melting, romantic conclusion. The *Nocturnes* too are successful, the rubato personal but convincing. The *Mazurkas* seem less sure in style, and in the *Fantaisie-impromptu*, although the slow middle theme is beautiful, there is some flurry in the outer sections. But taken as a whole, this recital is successful, even if the title of the disc suggests a more out-and-out popular selection than Ogdon provides. The cassette transfer is well managed.

Ballade No. 1 in G min., Op. 23; Fantaisie in F min., Op. 49; Nocturnes: in F sharp, Op. 15/2; in D flat, Op. 27/2; in E min., Op. posth. 72/1; Scherzo No. 2 in B flat min., Op. 31.
*(*) HMV Dig. ASD/*TC-ASD* 4333. Egorov.

Egorov, sensitive, temperamental, an elusive defector from the Soviet Union, here gives flashes of the artistry which has given him such a reputation, particularly in the United States. Only in the *Nocturnes* does his vision bring consistently satisfying performances. Excellent piano sound on disc, but the iron-oxide tape is undistinguished, lacking range and bloom.

Ballade No. 1 in G min., Op. 23; Mazurkas Nos. 19 in B min., 20 in D flat, Op. 30/2–3; 22 in G sharp min., 25 in B min., Op. 33/1 and 4; 34 in C, Op. 56/2; 43 in G min., 45 in A min., Op. 67/2 and 4; 46 in C; 47 in A min., 49 in F min., Op. 68/1–2 and 4; Prelude No. 25 in C sharp min., Op. 45; Scherzo No. 2 in B flat min., Op. 31.
**(*) DG 2530 236/*3300 349* [id.]. Michelangeli.

Although this recital somehow does not quite add up as a whole, the performances are highly distinguished. Michelangeli's individuality comes out especially in the *Ballade*, a very free rhapsodic performance, which nevertheless holds together by the very compulsion of the playing. Michelangeli's special brand of poetry is again felt in the *Mazurkas*, which show a wide range of mood and dynamic; and the *Scherzo* is extremely brilliant yet without any suggestion of superficiality. The piano tone is real and lifelike, and there is a good cassette.

Ballade No. 3 in A flat, Op. 47; Barcarolle in F sharp, Op. 60; Berceuse in D flat, Op. 57; Fantaisie-impromptu, Op. 66; Impromptu No. 1 in A flat, Op. 29; Scherzo No. 3 in C sharp min., Op. 39; Piano sonata No. 2 in B flat min. (Funeral march), Op. 35.
(B) **(*) Con. CC/*CCT* 7543. Kempff.

This exceedingly generous sampler of Kempff's individuality in Chopin makes a fine bargain. Kempff is not at his best in music that calls for striking bravura, like the *Scherzo*, or the finale of the *Sonata*, but his special quality of poetry infuses the overall performance of Op. 35 with great romantic warmth. Kempff's shading of phrases, even if the rubato is slightly mannered, also illuminates pieces like the *Barcarolle* and *Berceuse*, while the *Ballade* and *Fantaisie-impromptu* are full of personality. The recording is bold and clear, a little variable between items. On cassette the timbre is a little plummy, although this is less noticeable on side two.

'Favourite Chopin': Ballade No. 3 in A flat, Op. 47; Barcarolle in F sharp, Op. 60; Études, Op. 10, Nos. 3 in E (Tristesse); 5 in G flat (Black keys); 12 in C min. (Revolutionary); Op. 25, No. 11 in A min. (Winter wind); Nocturne in F min., Op. 55/1; Polonaise in A, Op. 40/1; Preludes: in D flat (Raindrop), Op. 28/15; in C sharp min., Op. 45; Waltzes: in D flat; C sharp min., Op. 64/1 and 2.
*** Decca **410 180-2** [id.]. Ashkenazy.

Digitally remastered from recordings made between 1975 and 1982, the sound here is slightly variable, but has striking vividness and presence. The upper range is less soft-grained than on the original LPs, with the treble brightly lit and often producing an edge on top in fortissimos, notably in the *Revolutionary study* and the *Polonaise*, while the *Black keys study* is somewhat clattery. The background silence serves to enhance this effect. Yet the middle range is warm and the bass firm and resonant. As can be seen, the selection is generous (nearly an hour of music) and popular. Ashkenazy is shown at his most commanding, though perhaps the inclusion of more *Nocturnes* would have given a better-balanced picture of his special sensibilities in this repertoire.

Ballade No. 3 in A flat, Op. 45; Études, Op. 10: Nos. 1 in C; 12 in C min. (*Revolutionary*)*; Polonaise* (*Fantaisie*) *in A flat, Op. 61.*

(M) **(*) DG Priv. 2535/*3335* 495. Sviatoslav Richter – DEBUSSY: *Estampes* etc.***

Richter's Chopin recital (recorded at a public concert) opens with a wonderfully poetic account of the *Polonaise fantaisie*, played with complete spontaneity and freshness. The *Étude in C major* which follows has rather too many accents, and the passage-work is not especially clear, but the *Revolutionary study* is full of fervour (although there are some background noises), and the *Ballade* has a convincing individuality. The recording is rather dry. The cassette is transferred at an unnecessarily modest level and the piano is given limited presence.

'Favourite Chopin': Ballade No. 3 in A flat, Op. 47; Études: in G flat, Op. 10/5; in A flat, Op. 25/1; in G flat, Op. 25/9; Nocturnes Nos. 10 in A flat, Op. 32/2; 15 in F min., Op. 55/1; Polonaise No. 6 in A flat, Op. 53; Preludes, Op. 28, Nos. 6 in B min.; 20 in C min.; Scherzo No. 3 in C sharp min., Op. 39; Waltzes Nos. 1 in E flat (*Grande valse brillante*)*, Op. 18; 11 in G flat, Op. 70/1.*

(M) *** EMI Em. EMX/*TC-EMX* 41 2045-1/*4*. Adni.

This record was made in 1971 to provide a brilliant début record for a young and talented artist who was only nineteen at the date of the recording. His sensibility in this repertoire is striking, and his musicianship is matched by the kind of effortless technique that is essential to give Chopin's music its essential line and flow. From the glitter and brilliance of the opening *Grande valse brillante* to the evocative yet expansive reading of the famous *'Sylphides' Nocturne in A flat major*, the tonal shading is matched by the spontaneity of the rubato. The whole of the first side of the disc is beautifully balanced to make a miniature recital, working towards a superb account of the *Scherzo in C sharp minor*. This is one of the freshest and most enjoyable Chopin collections available at any price, and it is given most natural recorded sound, with sparkle and sonority in equal measure. Cassette and disc are fairly closely matched, though the level of the tape drops on side two (most noticeably in the closing *Polonaise*).

'Favourites': (i) *Ballade No. 4, Op. 52;* (ii) *Barcarolle in F sharp, Op. 60;* (iii) *Boléro in C, Op. 19;* (i) *Étude in C min.* (*Revolutionary*)*, Op. 10/12;* (iv) *Mazurkas Nos. 5, Op. 7/1; 47, Op. 68/2; Polonaise No. 6, Op. 53;* (v) *Preludes, Op. 28, Nos. 3 in G; 5 in D;* (vi) *Waltzes Nos. 1, Op. 18* (*Grande valse brillante*)*; 7, Op. 64/2.*

(B) **(*) Con. CC/*CCT* 7513. (i) Sviatoslav Richter; (ii) Argerich; (iii) von Karolyi; (iv) Vásáry; (v) Anda; (vi) Askenase.

The title 'Favourites' stretches the word a little, but with such a glittering array of talent this recital cannot fail to be rewarding. Even the least interesting player here, Julian von Karolyi, is at his best in the little-known *Boléro*, not one of Chopin's most revealing essays. But many of the others are favourites, and the excitement of Richter's impetuous *Revolutionary study* and the more controlled heroism of Vásáry's *Polonaise in A flat major* contrast well with the style of Askenase's *Waltzes* (bold playing this), and the effortless brilliance of Anda's *Études*. Richter's *Ballade No. 4* is a personal reading but always interesting; Vásáry's *Mazurkas* are in the best tradition of Chopin playing. All are well recorded, and the cassette matches the disc fairly closely.

'Favourite pieces': (i) *Étude in E, Op. 10/3; Fantaisie-impromptu, Op. 66;* (ii) *Mazurkas Nos. 5, Op. 27/1;* (iii) *23, Op. 33/2;* (iv) *Nocturnes, Op. 9/2;* (ii) *Op. 55/1; Polonaises Nos. 3, Op. 40/1;* (v) *6, Op. 53;* (iv) *Prelude in D flat, Op. 28/15;* (vi) *Waltzes Nos. 1, Op. 18; 6, 7, Op. 64/1–2; 11, Op. 70/1.*

(M) **(*) Decca Viva VIV/*KVIC* 13. (i) Davis; (ii) Vered; (iii) Magaloff; (iv) Cooper; (v) Katchen; (vi) Katin.

Although with so many sources the recording quality tends to vary somewhat between items, the performances are generally good and often excellent. Ilana Vered's opening *Polonaise* is arresting, as is Katchen's, which closes side one. Peter Katin's *Waltzes* are stylish, and Joseph Cooper plays the *Raindrop prelude*, Op. 28/15, and the *E flat Nocturne* memorably, The recital is well composed and the sound is always reliable, the cassette sometimes slightly less rounded in timbre than the disc, but never shallow.

Cilea, Francesco (1866–1950)

Adriana Lecouvreur (complete).
**(*) CBS 79310 (3) [M3 34588]. Scotto, Domingo, Obraztsova, Milnes, Amb. Op. Ch., Philh. O, Levine.
**(*) Decca SET 221/3. Tebaldi, Simionato, Del Monaco, Fioravanti, St Cecilia, Rome Ac. Ch. and O, Capuana.

This is a curious but attractive opera with one pervading Grand Tune that should alone ensure its survival. It is the story of a great actress caught up in international intrigue, and in the manner of the veristic school we are given a chance to observe her for a moment or two in her roles before she deals with her own life-drama. Renata Scotto gives a vibrant, volatile, dramatically strong account of the title role, not as electrifying as Maria Callas would have been (to judge by her recordings of the two big arias) but vividly convincing as a great actress. The tendency of her voice to spread on top is exaggerated by the closeness of balance of the voices, but her control of legato and a beautiful line amply compensate. Domingo, Milnes and Obraztsova make a strong supporting team, not always idiomatic but always relishing the melodrama, while Levine draws committed playing from the Philharmonia. The Decca set with Tebaldi, which served its purpose for many years, is not quite superseded, though Tebaldi's consistently rich singing misses the delicacy as well as the flamboyance of Adriana's character. With Tebaldi both *Io sono l'umile ancella* and *Poveri fiori* are beautiful but little more. But then this is an opera which relies very largely on its vocal line for its effect. I only wish del Monaco was as reliable as Tebaldi, but as always we have some coarse moments amid the fine plangent top notes. Simionato is a little more variable than usual, but a tower of strength nonetheless. The recording is outstanding in every way, rich, brilliant and atmospheric, and the album contains excellent notes and translation by Peggie Cochrane.

Cimarosa, Domenico (1749–1801)

Double flute concerto in G.
(M) ** Decca Ser. SA/*KSC* 8. Aurèle and Christiane Nicolet, Stuttgart CO, Münchinger – C. P. E. BACH: *Flute concerto.***

Although not momentous music, Cimarosa's concerto for two flutes has undeniable charm, and its gay final rondo is quite memorable. The only drawback is the composer's emphasis on florid writing with the two solo instruments playing consistently in thirds and sixths. The performance here is warmly gracious, with a good accompaniment and excellent sound on disc and cassette alike.

Oboe concerto in C min. (arr. Benjamin).
(B) *** PRT GSGC/*ZCGC* 2003. Rothwell, Pro Arte O, Barbirolli – ALBINONI and MARCELLO: *Concertos.****
(M) *** DG Priv. 2535/*3335* 417 [139152]. Holliger, Bamberg SO, Maag – BELLINI, DONIZETTI, SALIERI: *Concertos.****

This enchanting concerto was arranged by Arthur Benjamin from four single-movement keyboard sonatas. It sounds in no way manufactured and is one of the finest concertante works available for the oboe. The concerto is given a quite ideal performance and recording by Evelyn Rothwell and her husband. The pastoral opening theme is phrased exquisitely, and after the gentle allegro which follows, the beautiful flowing Siciliana is played with a wonderful combination of affection and style. The gently rollicking finale is again caught to perfection, with Sir John sensitive to his wife's mood in every bar. The recording is excellently judged in matters of balance and tone. This is perhaps the most successful of all the six oboe concertos recorded by this memorable partnership. The tape is clear and well focused.

Holliger brings out its classical spirit and is wholly persuasive, though his approach is slightly less resilient than the version by Lady Barbirolli. The DG recording is first-class (with an immaculate matching cassette), and the three couplings are equally desirable.

Requiem (rev. Negri).
(M) *** Ph. 9502/*7313* 005 [id.]. Ameling, Finnilä, Van Vrooman, Widmer, Montreux Festival Ch., Lausanne CO, Negri.

Cimarosa's *Requiem*, an impressive, even formidable work, puts an unexpected slant on the composer of the brilliant comic opera with which his name is most usually associated. The choral writing, whether in big contrapuntal numbers or in more homophonic passages with solo interpolations, is most assured, and it is a pity that the choral singing here is slightly blurred by rather reverberant recording, and not more incisive in effect. Vittorio Negri secures excellent playing from the Lausanne orchestra, best known for its contributions to Haydn opera recordings under Dorati. The tape transfer is exceptionally successful, one of Philips's very best cassettes, with the choral sound full and rich and almost better focused than on the disc.

Clarke, Rebecca (1886–1979)

(i) *Piano trio;* (ii) Songs: *The aspidistra; Cherry blossom wand; The donkey; Eight o'clock; God made a tree; June twilight; The seal man; Shy one; Tiger tiger.*
*** British Music Soc. Dig. *BMS 404*. (i) Alley, Ovens, Ives; (ii) Trew, Alley.

Even more than the Supraphon record of the *Viola sonata* this cassette, published by the British Music Society, confirms the quality and individuality of Rebecca Clarke's music. The *Piano trio* is a major addition to the repertoire, a work of striking lyric power, with its restless opening movement, hauntingly atmospheric *Andante* – with absorbed influences from Debussy and Ravel – and the vigorous, jocular finale which also transforms material from the first movement. The songs are hardly less rewarding, the highly imaginative piano accompaniments again hinting at French impressionism. The delightfully romantic *Shy one* was once in the repertoire of Gervase Elwes, but most remarkable are the settings of Masefield's *Seal man* and Housman's *Eight o'clock*, while for diversity there is the wry waltz pastiche of *The aspidistra* and the vibrantly passionate *Tiger tiger*. Performances are thoroughly committed and sensitive with Graham Trew's baritone admirably suited to the special colour of the vocal line. The real-time cassette offers a natural sound balance, although the recording is rather reverberant.

Viola sonata.
(M) *** Sup. 1111 2694. Kodousek, Novotná – BRITTEN: *Lachrymae*; ECCLES: *Sonata*.***

Most readers will be astonished on examining the sleeve to learn that this *Sonata* is 'one of the best works ever written for the viola' – high praise indeed for a musician who is hardly a household name. In the early years of the century Rebecca Clarke was a well-established violist, a pupil of Stanford, and an obviously accomplished composer. In the 1940s she married the pianist James Friskin, a Bach interpreter of real quality. Her *Sonata*, written in 1919, occupies the whole of the second side of the disc and is a fine piece, fluent, well argued, finely constructed and in idiom not unrelated to the world of Bax, Bloch and Ireland. Josef Kodousek and Kveta Novotná deserve gratitude for rediscovering this rewarding piece, which is new to the gramophone and is superbly served here.

Clementi, Muzio (1752–1832)

Symphonies Nos. 1 in C; 2 in D; 3 in G (Great National Symphony); 4 in D.
*** Erato STU 71174 (2). Philh. O, Scimone.

Clementi, publisher as well as composer, tragically failed to put most of his symphonic output into print, and it has been left to modern scholars to unearth and in many cases reconstruct the works which were being performed around 1800, some of them prompted by Haydn's visits to London. All four works here, made available thanks to the researches of Pietro Spada, amply explain Clementi's high reputation in his lifetime as a composer for the orchestra, not just the piano. The most immediately striking is the *Great National Symphony*, with *God Save the King* ingeniously worked into the third movement so that its presence does not emerge until near the end. Scimone's performances with the Philharmonia are both lively and sympathetic, and the recording is excellent.

Piano sonatas: in F, Op. 33/2; in D, Op. 40/3; in G min. (Didone abbandonata), Op. 50/3. Monferrinas, Op. 49: Nos. 3 in E; 4 in C; 12 in C.
**(*) Hyp. A 66057. McCabe.

A useful reminder of Clementi's stature. Apart from Horowitz's commanding record of 1954, there has been scant representation of Clementi's sonata output in the catalogue. The music is inventive and resourceful and he is far from the 'mere mechanicus' that Mozart found. Indeed there are many prophetic touches in his work and the slow movement of *Didone abbandonata*, when taken out of context, could well deceive one into believing that it was much later. John McCabe is as always an intelligent guide to this repertoire and the quality of the sound is fresh and lifelike, though the acoustic is a shade dry.

Clérambault, Louis-Nicolas (1676–1749)

Harpsichord suites: in C; in C min.
(M) *** Argo ZK 64. Gilbert – LA GUERRE: *Suite*.***

The two suites recorded here represent only a fraction of Clérambault's output for the harpsichord, but this is all that survives. Both suites were published during his lifetime in 1702 or 1704. They have splendidly improvisatory preludes rather in the style of Louis Couperin, and are notated without barlines. Although not as distinctive or original as Clérambault's organ music, the suites have a genuine vein of lyricism, not inappropriate in a composer of so much vocal music, and they are most persuasively and authoritatively played by Kenneth Gilbert on a period instrument, a 1747 harpsichord of Sebastian Garnier.

Coates, Eric (1886–1958)

By the Sleepy Lagoon. The Dambusters: march. From Meadow to Mayfair: suite (complete). *London suite: Knightsbridge march. Music Everywhere.* (i) *Saxo-rhapsody. Summer Days suite: At the dance. The Three Elizabeths suite: Elizabeth of Glamis. Wood nymphs.*
** Columbia Studio 2 TWO 226. Royal Liv. PO, Groves, (i) with Brymer.

The Studio Two brashness takes some of the geniality out of the *Knightsbridge march* (which opens the disc), and the choice of the complete *From Meadow to Mayfair* is curious: it is not one of the composer's strongest suites. The most striking work here is the *Saxo-rhapsody*. It is played with considerable subtlety by Jack Brymer, and Groves accompanies skilfully. The piece is thematically repetitive but has both character and atmosphere. *Elizabeth of Glamis*, the central movement of the *Three Elizabeths suite*, does not expand as it might. It is surprising that the first movement was not included too, as this was familiar as the introductory music for the BBC TV *Forsyte Saga*. On the whole, Groves proves – with his obvious affection – a good conductor of this music, and although the collection is valuable, one laments that it was not recorded in ordinary EMI sound.

Calling all Workers march; The Jester at the Wedding: suite; The Merrymakers: overture; Miniature suite; The Three Elizabeths: suite.
(M) *** HMV Green. ESD 7005. CBSO, Kilbey.

The reissue of the finest collection of Eric Coates's music in the present catalogues on HMV Greensleeve is most welcome. The Studio Two edge has all but disappeared in the remastering, and the quality now is more natural. Indeed most of the collection offers very good sound, only *The Three Elizabeths* having slightly less sparkle and body than the rest of the programme. Reginald Kilbey proves himself the ideal Coates conductor, with a real flair for catching the vitality of Coates's leaping allegro figurations. His shaping of the secondary theme of the lovely slow movement of the *Three Elizabeths suite* has an affectionate grace. Equally the *Scène de bal*, with its evocation of porcelain china dancing figures, is done with point and style. The marches are alive and vigorous, and the first movement of the *Three Elizabeths* is sustained with a consistent throbbing forward momentum, in spite of the fact that the recording's lack of middle frequencies here gives less internal support than intended by the composer.

Four Ways suite: Northwards; Eastwards. London suite. Three Elizabeths suite.
(M) **(*) Mercury SRI 75109. L. Pops O, Fennell.

Polished, spirited and sympathetic performances of two of Coates's best-known suites, including the most popular march of all, *Knightsbridge*. The novelty is the inclusion of the engaging excerpts from the *Four Ways suite*, played with great rhythmic character. Fennell's pacing throughout is well judged and he never pushes too hard. The slow movement of the *Three Elizabeths* is nicely expressive but suffers (as does the rest of the programme to a greater or lesser extent) from the close, clear recording, which seeks brilliance and detail rather than warmth and atmosphere.

Coleridge-Taylor, Samuel
(1875–1912)

(i) *Hiawatha's wedding feast;* (ii) *Petite suite de concert.*
(M) *** HMV Green. ESD/*TC-ESD* 7161 [Ara. 8005/*9005*]. (i) Lewis, Royal Choral Soc., Philh. O, Sargent; (ii) Philh. O, Weldon.

In its day, *Hiawatha's wedding feast* blew a fresh breeze through a turgid British Victorian choral tradition, and freshness is exactly the quality of this splendid performance from Sir Malcolm. The music throughout is delightfully melodious and extremely well written for the voices. The somewhat over-heavy orchestration, which one notices at a live performance, is happily toned down by the recording balance, which is nigh perfect. Indeed this is a most spectacular record from a technical point of view and a demonstration of how much a fine choir benefits from the ambience around it. Everything about this disc is a success, including of course Richard Lewis's stylish performance of *Onaway! Awake, Beloved!* For the Greensleeves reissue EMI have generously added a bonus in George Weldon's polished Philharmonia recording of the *Petite suite de concert*, a salon pastiche of great charm. The second movement (*Demande et response*) with its delicate string melody was once a popular 'hit' in long-gone Palm Court days. The cassette is transferred at a disappointingly low level and much of the sparkle is taken from the choral sound.

Conus, Julius (1869–1942)

Violin concerto in E min.
*** HMV ASD/*TCC-ASD* 4206 [Ang. DS/*4XS* 37770]. Perlman, Pittsburgh SO, Previn – KORNGOLD: *Concerto.****

Julius Conus, of French extraction from a family of musicians, wrote his *Violin concerto* in Moscow in 1896–7, a ripe romantic piece in one continuous movement with few memorable ideas but with luscious violin writing. It was a favourite of Heifetz's (like the Korngold work on the reverse) and needs a powerful, persuasive advocate to sound anything more than trivial. Perlman, as in Korngold, shows his supreme mastery in giving the piece new intensity, helped by fine playing from Previn and the Pittsburgh Orchestra. Excellent, rich recording but with the violin very close. The cassette is rather fierce on top.

Cooke, Arnold (born 1906)

Clarinet concerto.
*** Hyp. A 66031. King, N. W. CO of Seattle, Francis – JACOB: *Mini concerto*; RAWSTHORNE: *Concerto.****

Unfairly, Arnold Cooke has for most of his career been saddled with the label 'pupil of Hindemith', which may be true enough, but which gives little indication of his individuality. His music does contain an element of Hindemithian formalism, carefully crafted, but the slow movement of this concerto soars well beyond. Thea King makes a passionate advocate, brilliantly accompanied by the Seattle orchestra in excellent sound.

Symphony No. 3 in D; Jabez and the Devil (ballet): *suite.*
*** Lyr. SRCS 78. LPO, Braithwaite.

Arnold Cooke, like his teacher, Hindemith, is doomed perhaps to remain an unfashionable composer, but a record like this demonstrates formidably his ability to write a well-made, highly enjoyable symphony, which deserves more than the occasional airing. It may not break new ground, but on record it can provide just the sort of occasional refreshment that eludes many listeners on records of more advanced music. There is something of Hindemith remaining in the style, but far more of Cooke himself, confident and positive in theme and argument. The ballet from which the suite is taken was written for the Royal Ballet in 1961, a collection of atmospheric pieces. Performances and recording are excellent.

Coperario, John (*c.* 1575–1626)

Consort music: *Fantasia; Two Fantasias – Almonds – Ayrs; Fantasia à 3; Fantasia à 4; Fantasia à 5 chiu puo miravi.* (i) *Songs of Mourning: To the most sacred King James; To the most sacred Queen Anne; To the high and mighty Prince Charles; To the most princely and virtuous the Lady Elizabeth; To the most illustrious and mighty Frederick V, Count Palatine of the Rhine; To the most disconsolate Great Britain; To the world.*
*** O-L DSLO 511. Cons. of Musicke, Rooley, (i) with Hill, Rooley, Jones.

Coperario or Coprario revised his name after a visit to Italy in 1604 (he was born John Cooper). His influence on the English repertoire for viols has been compared to that of Thomas Morley on the English madrigal. His own pieces for viols are contrapuntal but purer and freer than so many of the *In nomines* of the Elizabethan period, and many of them are quite impassioned, particularly the five-part *Fantasia Chiu puo miravi* included in this anthology. The first side brings us the *Songs of Mourning*, written on the death of James I's eldest son, Henry, Prince of Wales, to poems by Campion, richly expressive pieces that are sung superbly by Martyn Hill and colleagues, while the second side is given over to instrumental music. It is well worth investigating this often beautiful music, here eloquently played and truthfully recorded, much of it for the first time. This is well up to the high standards of the Florilegium label, not least in the elegance of its presentation. Strongly recommended.

Consort music: *Fantasias Nos. 1–3, 5, 8; 2 Almains; 2 Galliards. Funeral Teares* (cycle of 7 songs).
*** O-L DSLO 576. Kirkby, York Skinner, Cons. of Musicke, Rooley.

The *Funeral Teares* of 1606 can be thought of as the first English song cycle, and its tone of elegiac intensity makes it a quite affecting experience. The music is darkly passionate and sensitively performed here, as are the *Fantasias* and other instrumental pieces. A valuable addition to the growing representation of this hitherto underrated master – and excellently recorded into the bargain.

Copland, Aaron (born 1900)

Appalachian spring (ballet): full original version for small orch.
(M) *** CBS 61894/*40*- [M/*MT* 32736]. Columbia CO, composer.

Appalachian spring (complete ballet); *Music for movies* (suite).
**(*) Argo ZRG 935 [id.]. L. Sinf., Howarth.

Copland turned his *Appalachian spring* ballet for Martha Graham into an orchestral suite which rightly has become one of his most popular works; but the full original version, with its sparer, more cutting instrumentation, has more bite. This recording under the composer also includes a passage omitted from the full orchestral score, a substantial sequence leading up to the final fortissimo appearance of the celebrated Shaker hymn *Simple gifts*. Copland draws alert, refreshing performances from his chosen players, and they are very well recorded, making an outstanding mid-price issue. The cassette – one of CBS's very best – is remarkably full and vivid.

The Argo version by the London Sinfonietta under Elgar Howarth has the advantage of a splendid modern recording and an attractively appropriate coupling. The ballet (32′ 47″) is complete on one side, yet the sound loses nothing in amplitude and has an almost digital clarity. The tingling rhythmic bite of the strings is balanced by tenderly expressive qualities in the score's lyrical pages. This has not quite the character of the composer's own version but remains very enjoyable.

The *Music for movies* was drawn together by the composer from his film scores for *The City*, *Of Mice and Men* (both 1939) and *Our Town* (1940). The evocative opening picture of the New England countryside occupies the same musical world as the ballet, and the jaunty third piece, *Sunday traffic*, has a marked choreographic feeling. Again fine playing and first-rate recording.

Appalachian spring: ballet suite.
*** DG Dig. 2532/*3302* 083 [id.]. LAPO, Bernstein – BARBER: *Adagio*; BERNSTEIN: *Candide overture*; SCHUMAN: *American festival overture*.***

(i) *Appalachian spring suite;* (ii) *Billy the Kid: Celebration;* (i) *El Salón México;* (iii) *Fanfare for the common man;* (ii) *Rodeo: Hoe Down.*
(M) *** CBS 61431/*40*- [MS 7521]. (i) NYPO, Bernstein; (ii) LSO, composer; (iii) Phd. O, Ormandy.

Appalachian spring suite; Danzón Cubano; El Salón México; Fanfare for the common man.
*** CBS 60139/*40*- [MY/*MYT* 37257]. NYPO, Bernstein.

Appalachian spring suite; Fanfare for the common man; (i) *Lincoln portrait.*
**(*) CBS 72872 [Col. M 30649]. LSO, composer, (i) with Henry Fonda.

Appalachian spring suite; Fanfare for the common man; Rodeo: 4 Dance episodes.
(*) Telarc **CD 80078; DG 10078 [id.]. Atlanta SO, Lane.

Bernstein's newest recording of the concert

version of *Appalachian spring* has wonderful spontaneity and ardour. It was recorded at a live performance and the conductor communicates his love of the score in a strong, yet richly lyrical reading. Some might feel that, carried away by the occasion, he pushes the climax of the variations on the haunting Shaker theme, *Simple gifts*, too hard, but the compulsion of the music-making is obvious. The recording is close but not lacking atmosphere both on disc and the demonstration-standard chrome tape. With outstanding couplings, this is a very attractive issue.

There are two permutations from the outstanding Bernstein/NYPO recordings of the 1960s (plus a double-length tape issue – see below). Either of them will give satisfaction, for the orchestral playing has marvellous spirit and the recording is extremely vivid in the CBS manner.

There is an innocence, a fresh purity about Copland's London reading of *Appalachian spring* which is most appealing. His earlier version with the Boston Symphony Orchestra had moments of greater resonance, but with cleaner recording quality and beautiful hushed string playing this is preferable. The coupling does not help. The *Fanfare for the common man* is the more effective for being slightly underplayed, but with narration that sounds too stagey the *Lincoln portrait* is unconvincing. For non-Americans Copland ought to devise a version without narration.

The Telarc coupling is given recording of demonstration quality, naturally balanced and with glowing ambient warmth and vivid woodwind colouring. Lane's account of *Appalachian spring*, without missing the score's lyrical qualities, has an attractive feeling of the ballet theatre about it, with the strings lightly rhythmic. *Rodeo* too is not as bitingly dramatic and incisive as Bernstein's version (see below), but is more amiable and atmospheric. The recording is even more vivid on the compact disc and the silent background is a great boon. However, the snag is the extremely forward balance of the bass drum and tam tam at the opening of the *Fanfare for the common man.* The sheer force and amplitude of that opening simultaneous crash is unnerving. The level of transfer is extremely high, and apart from making the listener jump (to say the least), if the volume control is set too high, one fears for the safety of the loudspeaker cones!

Appalachian spring: suite; Billy the Kid: suite; Danzón Cubano; Fanfare for the common man (from *Symphony No. 3*)*; Rodeo: 4 Dance episodes; El Salón México.*
(M) *** CBS *40-79020*. NYPO, Bernstein.

This excellent double-length tape gathers together Bernstein's vintage recordings of Copland's most popular works, and it was a good idea to feature the famous *Fanfare* by using an extract from the *Third Symphony*. The playing of the New York orchestra, on peak form, is superb and the music-making is full of electricity. The sound is slightly less sharply defined at the top than the LP originals, but that is not an aural disadvantage, for there is no lack of atmosphere. The only drawback is the documentation which consists solely of a list of titles on the front of the box.

Billy the Kid; Rodeo: 4 Dance episodes.
*** CBS 72888 [M 30114]. LSO, composer.
(M) *** CBS 60114/*40*- [MY/*MYT* 36727]. NYPO, Bernstein.

Copland and the LSO have, over the years of their recording sessions together, built up a splendid rapport, and it would be hard to find any rival version that nudged Copland's dance rhythms so seductively. In these same two pieces Bernstein may be more thrustfully extrovert – it is arguable that the intense, extended structure of *Billy the Kid* hangs together better with him – but Copland himself is unrivalled in implying emotion even in apparently lighthearted genre dances, tears and laughter often very close. The playing and recording are outstanding. A coupling to recommend warmly to anyone wanting to sample this composer at his most approachable.

Both these scores are right up Bernstein's street, and his performances are in no way inferior to the composer's own. With marvellous playing from the New York Philharmonic, rhythmically pungent and immaculate in ensemble, everything glitters and glows spontaneously. Bernstein finds a depth of beauty too in the quiet lyrical music; he is clearly totally identified with every bar, and this readily communicates itself to the listener. The recording is forward and brilliant, but does not lack ambient atmosphere. It has been remastered and sounds fuller than in the original premium-priced issue. The cassette is lively and full-bodied.

(i) *Clarinet concerto;* (ii) *Fanfare for the common man;* (iii) *Piano concerto.*
(M) *** CBS 61837 [(d) MS 6497 and 6698]. (i) Goodman, Columbia SO, composer; (ii) LSO, composer; (iii) composer, NYPO, Bernstein.

Piano concerto.
(*) Chan. ABR/*ABT* 1061. Lin, Melbourne SO, John Hopkins – BRITTEN: *Piano concerto.*(*)

This mid-price collection recorded by the composer both as pianist and conductor makes a welcome addition to CBS's 'Meet the Composer' series, designed to celebrate Copland's eightieth birthday. The recordings vary in quality, and Copland's playing in the *Piano concerto* lacks something in virtuoso flair, but few will be disappointed. It is good too to have Benny Goodman in a work he himself inspired.

Gillian Lin is undoubtedly successful in the Copland *Concerto*, bringing out the jazz element in this syncopated music. Copland uses that easily imitable idiom far more imaginatively than most of his American colleagues – which helps to explain the work's continuing success – and one would hardly appreciate from the idiom alone how this is a work (written in 1926) which represents the composer before he had attained full maturity. As a performance Copland's own recording with Leonard Bernstein is clearly preferable, but if you seek the Britten coupling, this makes an excellent recommendation in full modern stereo. The cassette transfer is made at a lower level than the Britten coupling, and has slightly less immediacy. But it still sounds well.

Dance symphony; Short symphony (*No. 2*).
(M) *** CBS 61997 [MS 7223]. LSO, composer.

Dance symphony; El Salón México; Fanfare for the common man; Rodeo (ballet)*: 4 Dance episodes.*
**(*) Decca Dig. SXDL/*KSXDC* 7547 [Lon. LDR/5- 71047]. Detroit SO, Dorati.

The *Dance symphony* dates from 1929, and its companion from only a few years later. Both are short, full of originality and energy and tautly constructed. They are rewarding scores, though the listener approaching them for the first time may feel that the influence of Stravinsky has not yet been fully assimilated. The composer's performances are extremely telling and the playing of the LSO could scarcely be bettered, even by an American orchestra. The CBS recording has warmth and brilliance as well as richness of detail and a more natural perspective than is often the case in records from this source. On a cassette the sound is bright and slightly astringent.

There is a bright, extrovert brilliance about Dorati's attractive collection of Copland works, chosen for their immediate, cheerful, wide-open-spaces qualities. The playing demonstrates very clearly that orchestral virtuosity in the United States extends to orchestras other than the big five, and the digital recording has a clarity and impact that suit the music. The only reservation is that, rather surprisingly, Dorati's treatment of jazzy syncopations – an essential element in Copland of this vintage – is very literal, lacking the lift we think of as idiomatic.

Fanfare for the common man.
(M) *** Decca SPA/*KCSP* 525. LAPO, Mehta – GERSHWIN: *American in Paris,* etc.***

The use of Copland's *Fanfare* on television has made it specially popular, and the dramatic presentation here should satisfy all tastes. The opening on the drums is highly spectacular, and the brass has splendid sonority too in this vivid recording, equally effective on disc and tape. With its attractive couplings this is a highly recommendable issue on all counts.

Film scores: (i) *Down a Country Lane; John Henry; Letter from Home;* (ii) *Music for movies; The Red Pony.*

(M) *** CBS 61672/*40*- [M 33586]. (i) LSO; (ii) New Philh. O; both cond. composer.

This collection of the lighter Copland on CBS's mid-price label is most attractive, with dedicated performances brightly recorded. The *Red Pony* suite is the major item, a collection of vividly atmospheric genre pieces from a highly successful film score, the most haunting being *Walk to the Bunkhouse*. The other pieces are also taken from music originally written for films, of which the simplicity of *Letter from Home* is most affecting in a typical Copland way. There is a good cassette.

An Outdoor overture; Our Town; 2 Pieces for string orchestra; Quiet City.

(M) *** CBS 61728/*40*- [MS 7375]. LSO, composer.

Our Town is particularly evocative and touching in its simplicity: the music comes from a score to Thornton Wilder's play of the same name. Written in 1940, it is one of Copland's most endearing shorter compositions and, like its companions here, shows his talents at their freshest. The *Two Pieces for strings* are much earlier, dating from the 1920s and originally designed for string quartet. Both are powerfully wrought, and *Quiet City*, which also originated in incidental music, is another rewarding piece. Its evocative tapestry features cor anglais and trumpet soloists, and the playing here is first-class. Although the balance is not always ideal the recording throughout has genuine body and warmth of tone, and the performances under the composer's own baton are predictably expert. This is one of the finest of Copland's own records in the CBS series. The cassette transfer is wide-ranging and lively.

Quiet City.

*** Argo ZRG/*KZRC* 845 [id.]. ASMF, Marriner – BARBER: *Adagio*; COWELL: *Hymn*; CRESTON: *Rumor;* IVES: *Symphony No. 3.****

A most poetic and evocative account of Copland's *Quiet City*. It is better recorded even than Copland's own, and the playing of both trumpet and cor anglais soloists is of the highest order. Superb recording and valuable couplings make this a most attractive proposition. The sound on the cassette too is outstanding.

Symphony No. 3.

(M) *** CBS 61869/*40* [M 35113]. Philh. O, composer.

(M) **(*) CBS 61681 [(d) MS 6954]. NYPO, Bernstein – HARRIS: *Symphony No. 3.* **(*)

Copland and the LSO recorded his *Third Symphony* for Everest in the early days of stereo. The newer version has more gravitas, a fine recording of great breadth and atmosphere, and splendid Philharmonia playing, especially from the woodwind soloists. By the side of Bernstein's vibrant account with the NYPO the composer's approach seems comparatively mellow, even gentle at times (as in the scherzo, with its almost oriental delicacy, where Bernstein draws links with Prokofiev and Shostakovich). But Copland's natural authority is commanding and the work's freshness of inspiration communicates anew, especially in the eloquent slow movement. Any listener who responds to the famous *Fanfare for the common man* will be delighted to find it in use here as a launching pad for the finale: the way it steals in is sheer magic. Apart from one or two explosive drum entries, the cassette matches the disc closely, and the work is highly enjoyable in its tape format.

Piano music: *Down a Country Lane; In Evening Air; Midsummer nocturne; Night Thoughts (Homage to Ives); Passacaglia; 4 Piano blues; Piano fantasy; Piano sonata; Piano variations; Scherzo humoristique; The Cat and the Mouse; Sunday Afternoon music; The Young Pioneers.*

*** CBS [M2 35901]. Smit.

The sound quality here may not be ideal – the piano is recorded in a rather small acoustic – but this is nonetheless an important and valuable set. It contains all of Copland's piano music right from the earliest pre-Boulanger days down to his most recent work, *Night Thoughts*, composed in 1972 as a tribute to Ives. The two most important works, the *Sonata* (1941) and the *Fantasy* (1957), occupy a side each, and neither is otherwise currently available in stereo: indeed none of the Copland piano music is! Leo Smit has been closely associated with Copland's music over the years (the first of the *Four Piano blues* and the *Midsummer nocturne* of 1947, which here receives its first recording, are both dedicated to him), and he recorded the *Sonata* in the days of 78s. It would be difficult to find anyone who is more inside the idiom and whose command of nervous energy so well matches the needs of this vital music. Authoritative, stimulating, vivid performances. This recording has been withdrawn in the UK.

(i) *Old American songs, Sets 1 and 2.* (ii) *12 Poems of Emily Dickinson.*
(M) **(*) CBS 61993/*40*- [(d) MS 6497 and M 30375]. (i) Warfield, Columbia SO, composer; (ii) Addison, composer.

Sentimental, witty, and attractive after their many guises, the *Old American songs* rightly form one of the most popular groups in Copland's vocal output. William Warfield sings them with great warmth and affection, bringing genuine American style to support a vigorous voice and a real talent for this kind of repertoire. Needless to say, Copland's direction of the orchestra is a delight from start to finish. Anybody wishing to become painlessly acquainted with modern American vocal music could hardly find a better introduction. In the settings of Emily Dickinson it is good to hear Copland accompanying at the piano, but the recording is coarse and close and Adele Addison is a soprano who may bring out American folk associations but whose timbre is often shrill as recorded. This quality is slightly toned down in the cassette transfer, which remains admirably vivid in the *Old American songs.*

Corelli, Arcangelo (1653–1713)

Concerti grossi, Op. 6/1–12.
*** Argo ZRG 773/5 [id.]. ASMF, Marriner.
(M) *** HM 1C 065 99613 (Nos. 1–4); 1C 065 1997281 (Nos. 5–8); 1C 065 99803 (Nos. 9–12). La Petite Bande, Kuijken.
** Erato Dig. NUM 750163 (3). Sol. Ven.
** Chan. Dig. DBRD/*DBRT* 3002 (2). Cantilena, Shepherd.

Concerti grossi, Op. 6/6, 7, 8 (Christmas) and 12.
*** Argo ZRG 828 (from above set, directed Marriner).

Corelli's masterly Op. 6 concertos are rich in melodic invention and harmonic resource, and one wonders why they have been neglected for so long at a time when much lesser music of this period has been duplicated on record. The Argo set has been prepared with evident thought and care, and if one must cavil it is only at two small points: some fussy continuo playing here and there, and a certain want of breadth and nobility of feeling in some of the slow movements. These are small points, however, when weighed alongside the vitality and intelligence of these performances, expertly played as ever by the Academy, and beautifully recorded.

The individual disc, making the *Christmas concerto* available separately, is most welcome.

La Petite Bande offers a useful alternative to the Academy of St Martin-in-the-Fields' recording on Argo, and in some respects this may be regarded as superior. Authentic instruments are used, but to excellent effect; the textures are more transparent as a result, and the playing is always expressive and musical. The recordings are made in a highly sympathetic acoustic, that of the Cedernsaal at Schloss Kirchheim, and are splendidly lifelike. These performances convey more of the nobility and grandeur of Corelli than the Argo set.

I Solisti Veneti offer more polished accounts of the set than Cantilena on Chandos and are well enough recorded by the Erato engineers. They bring a robust vitality to some of the quicker movements but are heavy-handed on occasion. Generally speaking, they offer no real challenge to the Academy, if you want modern instruments, or to La Petite Bande in the concertos they have recorded on period instruments.

Although digitally recorded, with an excellent cassette equivalent, the Cantilena performances are not as polished as those by the ASMF, nor do they have the authentic feeling and nobility of the playing by La Petite Bande. The approach is genial; slow movements are sometimes rather lazy-sounding, while the livelier music lacks the pointed rhythmic resilience of the Argo set.

Concerto grosso Op. 6/8 in G min. (*Christmas*).
(M) ** EMI Em. EMX/*TC-EMX* 2037 [Sera. S/*4XG* 60271]. Toulouse CO, Auriacombe – ALBINONI: *Adagio;* MOZART: *Serenade No. 13;* PACHELBEL: *Canon.***

The Toulouse performance is part of a popular baroque anthology and is the most memorable performance on the disc. Indeed the playing is fresh and nicely expressive with good sound to match. However, the couplings are somewhat less distinguished. The cassette matches the disc fairly closely.

Oboe concerto (arr. Barbirolli).
(B) *** PRT GSGC/*ZCGC* 2007. Rothwell, Hallé O, Barbirolli – HAYDN: *Concerto* ** (*); PERGOLESI: *Concerto.****

Barbirolli's concerto is cunningly arranged from a trio sonata, and in its new form it makes one of the most enchanting works in the oboe repertoire. The performance here is treasurable. The opening, with its beautiful Handelian theme, is shaped with perfect dignity, and the gracious, stately allegro that follows has a touch of gossamer from the soloist. The finale is no less delectable, and the clean, clear recording projects the music admirably. The cassette is less secure in texture than the disc, especially at pianissimo level.

12 Violin sonatas, Op. 5.
**(*) EMI 1C 151 03637/8. Menuhin, Malcolm, Donnington.
(M) * Ph. 6768 128(2) [id.]. Grumiaux, Castagnone.

Corelli's Op. 5 *Sonatas* appeared in 1700 and exerted a powerful influence on later works in this genre, including those by Handel. They show his lyrical and inventive powers to good advantage and *No. 12 in D minor* is the most widely known, thanks to its use of the familiar *La Follia.* Menuhin and George Malcolm give sympathetic accounts of them, taking cognizance of recent scholarship without allowing it to inhibit natural musical expression, and their playing conveys something of the grandeur of Corelli's melodic inspiration.

Arthur Grumiaux and Riccardo Castagnone are eminently well recorded on the Philips Living Baroque label but their approach could not be further removed from that of Melkus and Huguette Dreyfus on DG Archive (currently out of the catalogue). Both they and Menuhin have ample continuo support, while Grumiaux has no cello continuo at all. Moreover he plays in a more nineteenth-century fashion than we are accustomed to nowadays with a fairly wide vibrato at times. There is a blandness about his set which diminishes the strength of its appeal.

Corrette, Michel (1709–95)

6 Organ concertos, Op. 26.
(M) *** Ph. 9502/*7313* 068. Houbart, Thomas CO.

These lively and amiable concertos from a minor eighteenth-century French composer are here given admirably spirited and buoyant performances, splendidly recorded. The orchestral detail is well revealed and the solo playing of François-Henri Houbart projects strongly. Michel Corrette's invention has genuine spontaneity and this makes an enjoyable collection to dip into. The sound on tape is just as clean and vivid as the disc.

Coste, Napoleon (1806–83)

(i) *March and Scherzo, Op. 33; Le Montagnard, Op. 34. Adagio and Minuet, Op. 50; Andante and Polonaise (Souvenirs de Jura), Op. 44; Rondo, Op. 40; La Source du Lyson, Op. 47.*
*** Chan. ABR/*ABT* 1031. Wynberg (guitar), (i) with Anderson (oboe).

Napoleon Coste, who was the son of a French army officer – hence the Christian name – made his career in Paris, where he studied under Sor. He was reputedly an admirer of Berlioz, but his own music, although attractive and often atmospheric in feeling, displays little of the quirky originality of that master. Of the solo guitar music, the fantasy *La Source du Lyson* is attractively picturesque, its second movement a pleasing *Andante* in pastoral style. The two works for oboe and guitar are even more engaging, ingenuous but effectively laid out. Here the creamy tone of the oboist, John Anderson, is persuasive, and Simon Wynberg makes the most of the solo pieces, recorded in a suitably warm acoustic. The recording is of high quality, with little to choose between disc and cassette.

Couperin, François (1668–1733)

Harpsichord suites, Book 1, Ordres 1–5.
(M) *** HM HM 351/4 [id.]. Gilbert.

Harpsichord suites, Book 2, Ordres 6–12; L'Art de toucher le clavecin, Preludes 1–8; Allemande.
(M) *** HM HM 355/8 [id.]. Gilbert.

Harpsichord suites, Book 3, Ordres 13–19. (i) *3rd Concert Royal; 2nd Concert Royal: Echoes.*
(M) *** HM HM 359/62 [id.]. Gilbert, (i) with Lyman-Silbiger.

Harpsichord suites, Book 4, Ordres 20–27.
(M) *** HM HM 363/6 [id.]. Gilbert.

The Canadian scholar Kenneth Gilbert has edited the complete keyboard works of Couperin, and his recording of them is made on an exact copy of an instrument by Henry Hemsch (1750) made by Hubbard in Boston. It is slightly below modern pitch and tuned to unequal temperament, which Couperin is known to have preferred. Kenneth Gilbert's performances are scrupulous in matters of registration, following what is known of eighteenth-century practice in France. Changes of registration within a piece are rare, but it must not be thought that his playing is in any way cautious or austere. There is no want of expressive range throughout the series and Professor Gilbert plays with authority and taste – and, more to the point, artistry. He is also well served by the engineers. In the later records, Books 2, 3 and 4, a different recording venue is used: the first Book (Ordres 1–5) was recorded in Montreal and the others in the Abbey of St-Benoît-du-Lac, which produces a slightly richer sonority. Readers should note that the sound throughout the series is of excellent quality and altogether on a par with the performances. It is impossible to dwell on the individual felicities of each Ordre. As with the *48*, there is little to be gained in making recommendations to start with any particular disc; the important thing is to start somewhere. (Perhaps the *Huitième Ordre*, containing the famous *Pasacaille*, might make a good beginning, though Professor Gilbert does not play it with the panache of the late Thurston Dart.) Once started, the listener will want to explore this rewarding world more fully, and there is no doubt that Kenneth Gilbert is an eminently authoritative guide.

Pièces de clavecin, Book 1: La Ténébreuse. Book 2: Les Moissonneurs; Les Baricades mistérieuses; Le Moucheron; Passacaille; L'Etincelante. Book 3; Le Rossignol en amour; Le Carillon de Cythère; L'Amour au berceau; Musète de Taverni; Les Petits Moulins à vent; Sœur Monique; Le Tic-toc-choc. Book 4: Les Tricoteuses.
*** Mer. E 77012. Woolley.

This is a useful introduction to Couperin's keyboard music, assembling some of his most popular and accessible pieces. Robert Woolley is a young and persuasive harpsichordist; he understands the period conventions thoroughly and also conveys a sense of pleasure in what he is doing. He is recorded at a rather high level but otherwise there is little to fault here, except the somewhat haphazard tonal sequence.

Pièces de clavecin (Harpsichord suites): Book 2: Ordres 8 and 11; Book 3: Ordres 13 and 15.
(M) ** Ph. 6770 013 (2). Puyana.

When they first appeared just over ten years ago, this pair of discs faced formidable competition from Kenneth Gilbert's scholarly exploration of the complete Couperin keyboard music on RCA. This has now migrated to the Harmonia Mundi label and is very much the set to go for. Rafael Puyana is a brilliant exponent of Couperin and has an impressive instrument at his disposal, a Ruckers which embodies certain modifications of Taskin. There are some splendidly played things which outweigh the odd inconsistency (he sometimes plays a figure with *notes inégales*, only to play them completely differently later) but rather brisk tempi do at times prove irksome and the sound, which is forward, underlines the brilliance rather than the poetry of the conception.

Pièces de clavecin: Book 2: Les Moissonneurs; Les baricades mistérieuses; Les bergeries; La bavolet-flotant; La Triomphante: Fanfare. Les graces naturelles; La zénobie. Book 3: Le carillon de Cithére; L'evaporée; La Distraite; La Superbe, ou La Forqueray; Sœur Monique; Le tic-toc-choc, ou les Maillotins; L'artiste. Book 4: Les tambourins; La Petite Pince-sans-rire; Les tours de passe-passe; La Montflambert; La pantomime; Saillie.
(M) *** HM HMB 340/*40*. Gilbert.

This selection from Kenneth Gilbert's complete recording is inscribed 'for my friends' and Gilbert has included also some quotations from the composer's thoughts. Couperin tells us: 'the titles relate to ideas that have occurred to me, and I shall be forgiven if I do not account for them'; and 'the harpsichord is a complete instrument by virtue of its range, and I shall always be grateful to those who by consummate skill, supported by good taste, are able to render this instrument, which can neither swell nor diminish its sounds, capable of expression'; and again 'I would much rather be moved than be astonished'. The programme is admirably chosen and the expert performances would surely have delighted the composer (who was very particular about ornamentation). The recording too is first-class on disc and tape alike.

Trois Leçons de ténèbres.
(M) *** HM HM 210 [id.]. Deller, Todd, Perulli, Chapuis.

Trois Leçons de ténèbres; Motet pour le jour de Pâques.
*** O-L DSLO 536 [id.]. Nelson, Kirkby, Ryan, Hogwood.

The *Trois Leçons de ténèbres* were written for performance on Good Friday and were the only ecclesiastical music Couperin published during his lifetime. Unlike Bach's cantatas, Couperin's settings had female voices in mind, and he could barely have hoped for more ethereal timbres than those of Judith Nelson and Emma Kirkby. Purity and restraint rather than warmth and humanity are the keynote of these performances, but few are likely to complain of the results. The recordings are admirably vivid, and the Easter motet is an additional attraction.

Deller's account of the *Trois Leçons* is less authentic, since this music, written for a convent, did not envisage performance by male voices. In every other respect, however, it has a wonderful authenticity of feeling and a blend of scholarship and artistry that gives it a special claim on the attention of collectors. Though less pure than its Oiseau-Lyre rival, Deller's has greater insight and no less spirituality. Both approaches are very different; some may be swayed by the presence of a fill-up in Hogwood's recording, but, except for those who do not respond to Deller's art, this carries stronger persuasive powers.

Messe propre pour les couvents des religieux et religieuses; Messe solonnelle à l'usage des paroisses.
*** Ph. 6768 346 (2). Koopman (organ of St Jacques/St Christophe, Houdan, France).

Like his predecessors (Marie-Claire Alain on Erato, Lionel Rogg on HMV and Gillian Weir on Argo – all deleted as far as the UK is concerned), Ton Koopman gives us these pieces without the plainsong framework in which they were intended to be heard. Unlike any of his colleagues, he does use an instrument of Couperin's time by Louis-Alexandre Clicquot dating from 1734, a year after the composer's death. (Miss Weir used a modern Swiss instrument, Marie-Claire Alain a Clicquot from the end of the century at Poitiers and Rogg a Silbermann at Marmoutier). Koopman moreover confines himself to the registration indicated by Couperin and plays with a consistently sustained feeling for style. It goes without saying that, divorced from the plainsong setting and listened to as a long organ recital, there is a certain amount of aural fatigue to be borne. Yet there is no doubting the flair and good taste of this artist, and the only reservation one might have concerns the rather close scrutiny to which the instrument is subjected; the obvious gain in detail and presence does involve a loss in atmosphere. Nonetheless, this is to be recommended.

Couperin, Louis (1626–61)

Harpsichord suites: in A min.; in C; in F; Pavane in F sharp min.
*** HM 1 C 065 99871. Leonhardt.

Gustav Leonhardt duplicates some of the repertoire recorded by Alan Curtis (DG Arc. 2533 325, now deleted) and pays his rival the compliment of using his edition. Whereas Curtis used an undated instrument from the seventeenth century, probably French and recently restored to excellent condition, Leonhardt plays a copy by Skowroneck of a 1680 French instrument. The sound is altogether more vivid and appealing, and the quality of the recording is completely natural and lifelike. Louis Couperin's music is not always as rich in character or invention as that of his nephew, and it needs playing of this order to show it to best advantage. Leonhardt's playing has such subtlety and panache that he makes the most of the grandeur and refinement of this music, to whose sensibility he seems wholly attuned. This is the best introduction to Louis Couperin's music now before the public.

Cowell, Henry (1897–1965)

Hymn and fuguing tune No. 10 for oboe and strings.
*** Argo ZRG/*KZRC* 845 [id.]. Nicklin, ASMF, Marriner – BARBER: *Adagio*; COPLAND: *Quiet City*; CRESTON: *Rumor*; IVES: *Symphony No. 3.****

Henry Cowell attracted a good deal of attention in the 1920s with his inconoclastic piano music (it was he who invented 'tone clusters') and he was a prolific symphonist. He also wrote a pioneering study of Ives. This likeable *Hymn and fuguing tune* is well worth having and is expertly played and recorded here. The cassette is of Argo's best quality.

Creston, Paul (born 1906)

A Rumor.
*** Argo ZRG/*KZRC* 845 [id.]. ASMF, Marriner – BARBER: *Adagio*; COPLAND: *Quiet City*; COWELL: *Hymn*; IVES: *Symphony No. 3.****

At one time Creston was represented in the catalogue by his *Second* and *Third Symphonies*, and his current neglect seems unjust. *A Rumor* is a thoroughly witty and engaging piece and is played here with plenty of character by the Academy under Neville Marriner.

It completes a thoroughly rewarding and approachable disc of twentieth-century American music that deserves the widest currency. The cassette is of demonstration quality.

Crumb, George (born 1926)

Ancient Voices of Children (song cycle).
*** None. H 71255 [id.]. De Gaetani, Dash, Contemporary Chamber Ens., Weisberg.

Crumb, like many other composers today, whether in America or in Europe, uses weird effects on conventional instruments ('preparing' piano, harp and mandolin in various unexpected ways) as well as using unconventional percussion instruments such as a toy piano. The wonder is that this setting of extracts from Lorca's poems shows genuine imagination. Whatever the means, the words are enhanced, and this brilliant performance gives one all the dynamism needed if one is to surmount the difficulties of such music.

Music for a Summer Evening (*Makrokosmos III*).
** None. H 71311 [id.]. Kalish, Freeman, DesRoches, Fitz.

Music for a Summer Evening is the third of Crumb's *Makrokosmos* cycle; the first is his *Fantasy* for solo piano (see below). On this particular summer evening we are taken for a quick flight in space. There are five 'movements' before one does in fact return to base. It is all faithfully and brilliantly done here.

Makrokosmos, Vol. 1 (*Fantasy pieces for amplified piano*).
** None. H 71293 [id.]. Burge.

The player of *Makrokosmos* needs not only to be a skilled pianist, but his technique must stretch to the various 'other' effects indicated and include an ability to whistle too. Mr Burge (if indeed it is always he) meets all these demands with aplomb. Each of the twelve pieces is named after one of the signs of the Zodiac and each also has an association with a person born under the appropriate sign (shades of Elgar's *Enigma variations*). The variety of styles here certainly suggests great diversity in the characters of the composer (he is *Scorpio*), his associates and the creative artists he admires (Schoenberg, Debussy *et al.*). The invention here is lively in its very unconventional way, and the recording has plenty of projection.

Crusell, Bernhard (1775–1838)

Clarinet concertos Nos. 1 in E flat, Op. 1; 3 in E flat, Op. 11.
*** Hyp. A/*KA* 66055. King, LSO, Francis.

Crusell, born in Finland in 1775 but working in Stockholm most of his career, was himself a clarinettist. Most of the works, which on record and in the concert hall have latterly been infiltrating the repertory, include that instrument, and these two delightful concertos are among the most impressive. The echoes are of Mozart, Weber and Rossini with a hint of Beethoven, and though the writing is demanding for the soloist, Crusell generally avoided cadenzas. Thea King with her beautiful liquid tone makes an outstanding soloist, well accompanied by Francis and the LSO. The recording is full and atmospheric. The cassette is first-class, vivid and wide-ranging to match the disc.

Clarinet quartets Nos. 1 in E flat, Op. 2; 2 in C min., Op. 4; 3 in D, Op. 7.
*** Hyp. A/*KA* 66077. King, Allegri Qt (members).

These are captivatingly sunny works given superb performances, vivacious and warmly sympathetic. Thea King's tone is positively luscious, as recorded, and the sound is generally excellent with a splendid high-level cassette transfer in the demonstration class.

Czerny, Carl (1791–1857)

Études (ballet, arr. Riisager).
(M) ** HMV Green. ESD/*TC-ESD* 7149. L. Fest. Ballet O, Kern – HELSTED: *Napoli.**(*)

The ballet, arranged from Czerny's *Études*, is skilfully scored (on the whole) and has one or two engaging moments. But for the most part this is instantly forgettable music, although it is vivaciously played and vividly recorded on disc and cassette alike.

Dandrieu, Jean-François (1681–1738)

Premier Livre de pièces d'orgue: Pièces in A. min. and G min.
(M) *** Argo ZK 84. Weir (organs of St Leonhard, Basle, and St Maximin, Thionville).

Dandrieu was a younger contemporary of Couperin le Grand and, like him, came from a musical family. He spent most of his life as organist at Saint Merry in Paris and at the Royal Chapel. The *First Book of Organ Pieces*, published in 1739, a year after his death, contains a number of suites, two of which are recorded here, consisting of an offertory, several other short movements and a series of couplets which comprise the organ's contribution to the Magnificat. The music is more than just historically interesting; the invention is full of character and resource. Gillian Weir plays each suite on a different instrument, both of them recorded in a lively acoustic, and her interpretations are marked by authority and taste. The engineers provide first-class sound, and the readers interested in this repertory (and even those who are not) should investigate this thoroughly satisfying issue.

Danyel, John (*c.* 1565–*c.* 1630)

Lute songs (1606): *Coy Daphne fled; Thou pretty bird; Me whose desires are still abroad; Like as the lute delights; Dost thou withdraw thy grace; Why canst thou not; Stay, cruel, stay; Time, cruel time; Grief keep within; Drop not, mine eyes; Have all our passions; Let not Cloris think; Can doleful notes; No, let chromatic tunes; Uncertain tunes; Eyes, look no more; If I could shut the gate; I die whenas I do not see; What delight can they enjoy; Now the earth, the skies, the air.*
*** O-L DSLO 563. Cons. of Musicke, Rooley.

These unpretentious examples of the art of the Elizabethan lutenist John Danyel (virtually all of his songs that have survived) are performed with typical style and polish by the members of the Consort of Musicke. Specially fine is *Like as the lute delights*, with the words 'a wailing descant on the sweetest ground' ingeniously illustrated in music. The recording is first-rate.

Daquin, Louis-Claude (1694–1772)

12 Noëls for organ.
*** Erato STU/*MCE* 71118. Alain (organ of St Théodorit d'Uzes, Cathedral).

Daquin's twelve Christmas chorales are attractively diverse in invention from the buoyant imitation of *Le Noël en duo*, to the piquant colouring of *Noël sur les flutes* and the lively closing *Noël Suisse*. Each of the twelve has its own individual character and the melodic appeal is striking, particularly in the later pieces. Marie-Claire Alain registers them imaginatively and plays with spirit and obvious enjoyment. The organ is admirably chosen and the recording excellent on disc and tape alike.

Debussy, Claude (1862–1918)

Berceuse héroïque; La Boîte à joujoux; Children's Corner suite; (i) *Danse sacrée et danse profane;* (ii) *Fantasy for piano and orchestra; Images; Jeux; Khamma; Marche écossaise; La Mer; Nocturnes; Petite suite; Prélude à l'après-midi d'un faune; Printemps;* (iii) *Rhapsody for clarinet;* (iv) *Rhapsody for saxophone; Le Roi Lear; Tarantelle styrienne.*

(M) *** HMV SLS 893 (5) [Ang. S 37064/8]. O Nat. de l'ORTF, Martinon, with (i) Jamet, (ii) Ciccolini, (iii) Dangain, (iv) Londeix.

Debussy's orchestral output can be comfortably fitted on to four records: this set fills out the ten sides with the *Fantasy* for piano and orchestra, *La Boîte à joujoux*, which is scored by André Caplet, *Khamma*, which is scored by Koechlin, Caplet's scoring of *Children's Corner* and Henri Büsser's of the *Petite suite*. Even so, the orchestral interludes to *Le Martyre de Saint Sébastien*, in whose scoring Caplet also had a hand, are omitted. We are given the rarely heard music to *Le Roi Lear* and the *Rhapsodies*. Martinon gets some extremely fine playing from the ORTF Orchestra, and these performances can in general hold their own with almost any in the catalogue. The *Nuages* is perhaps too slow and could be more atmospheric. *Jeux* could, one feels, breathe a little more freely, though in some ways it is to be preferred to Boulez's almost clinical account. Certainly this *La Mer* is highly competitive: only Karajan and Ormandy are better. *La Boîte à joujoux* is not so delicately articulated or quite so atmospheric as was Ansermet's, though there is no doubt that this is the better orchestral playing. The recording throughout is quite superb, with great atmosphere and space though without any loss of presence or detail. This set will give great pleasure, and at its permanent bargain price is highly competitive.

La Boîte à joujoux (orch. Caplet); *6 Épigraphes antiques* (orch. Ansermet); *Sarabande* (orch. Ravel).

**(*) Erato STU/*MCE* 71458 [id.]. Basle SO, Jordan.

Debussy's delightful ballet score about adventures in a children's box of toys has an entirely miniature flavour. Although the work was completed by the composer in 1913, five years before his death, he only sketched the orchestration, which was completed later by André Caplet. Ansermet's own recording for Decca (currently out of the catalogue) had a pellucid vividness, not quite matched by the Basle account, but Armin Jordan is the only alternative. The other version by the French Radio Orchestra under the late Jean Martinon is the best of all, but is not available except as part of a 5-record set. The present issue is serviceable, though not really distinguished by playing of the very first order. But it is well recorded, the performance is eminently respectable and thoroughly idiomatic and the coupling most attractive. Ansermet's orchestration of the *Six Épigraphes antiques* is highly effective and, in the absence of his own version, this is most welcome, as is Jordan's sympathetic account of Ravel's arrangement of the Sarabande from *Pour le piano*. In the absence of competition this is a well worthwhile record, even if this is not the Philharmonia under Giulini! The cassette is transferred at a rather low level on side one (which contains the two shorter works) but the level rises on side two with a striking increase in vividness for the ballet, although the resonance prevents absolute sharpness of focus.

(i) *Danses sacrée et profane. Images; Jeux; Marche écossaise; La Mer; Nocturnes; Prélude à l'après-midi d'un faune.* (ii) *Rhapsody for clarinet and orchestra.*

(M) *** Ph. 6768 284 (3) [PSI id.]. Concg. Ch. and O, Haitink, with (i) Badings, (ii) Pieterson.

Outstanding performances and recording. The *Images* and *Jeux* are about the best now available, and all the other performances on these three records are among the very finest now before the public. Immaculate surfaces and clean, revealing, well-balanced recording make this a most desirable set.

Danses sacrée et profane.

** Chan. ABR/*ABT* 1060 [id.]. Loney, Sydney SO, Otterloo – RAVEL: *Introduction* *and allegro***; MARTIN: *Petite symphonie concertante.***(*)

(i) *Danses sacrée et profane. 2 Arabesques; Rêverie; Suite bergamasque* (arr. for harp).
HMV ASD/*TCC-ASD* 186673-1/*4* [Ang. DS/*4XS* 37339]. Allen, (i) LACO, Schwarz – RAVEL: *Introduction and allegro*, etc.(*)

The harp is larger than life in the Chandos recording, which derives from the Australian Broadcasting Commission, but the performance is a fine one with plenty of atmosphere, and though not to be preferred to Haitink on Philips is well worth considering if the coupling appeals to you. The cassette is of good quality and naturally balanced – the resonance does not cloud the image.

No complaints about the HMV *Danses sacrée et profane* either on grounds of performance or recording but the value of the disc by the side of its rivals will be the coupling, which is obviously designed to display the skills of the harpist, Nancy Allen. Not that her arrangements of the *Suite bergamasque* and the Ravel pieces are not felicitous, but that most collectors will prefer to have them in the form their composers intended. Clear and well-defined sound on disc and cassette alike.

(i) *Danses sacrée et profane; La Mer; Nocturnes; Prélude à l'après-midi d'un faune; Rêverie* (arr. Smith)*; Suite bergamasque: Clair de lune* (arr. Caillet).
(M) **(*) CBS *40-79023*. Phd. O, Ormandy; (i) with M. Costello.

A double-length cassette to show the Philadelphia Orchestra at the height of its powers during the Ormandy regime. The sound is remarkably good, with a slight smoothing at the top to mellow the bright lighting from which CBS recordings of this orchestra have often suffered. Detail remains quite clear and the music-making is vividly projected. The overall impression is languorous, the *Nocturnes* especially atmospheric and *La Mer* evocative, though the last movement, the *Dialogue of the wind and the waves*, is as exciting as anyone could want, with superb unselfconscious bravura from all departments of the orchestra. With ninety minutes' music offered, this is excellent value and the arrangements at the end of the concert make attractive *bonnes-bouches*: they are beautifully played and warmly recorded. The documentation, however, is a disgrace, with just a list of titles on the front of the hinged plastic box.

(i) *Fantasy for piano and orchestra;* (ii) *Rhapsody for clarinet and orchesta;* (iii) *Rhapsody for saxophone and orchestra.*
*** Erato STU/*MCE* 71400. Monte Carlo Op. O, Jordan, with (i) Queffélec, (ii) Morf, (iii) Delangle.

Not a well-filled but certainly a well-played and excellently recorded disc. The *Rhapsodies* for saxophone and clarinet respectively are underrated, though they have rarely been absent from the catalogue (even in pre-war days, when Piero Coppola recorded them). Here they receive eloquent performances, as also does the *Fantasy for piano and orchestra.* Not a strong work this, but in Anne Queffélec's hands it makes a good impression. There is an excellent cassette, full, clear and atmospheric, matching the disc closely.

Images; (i) *Danses sacrée et profane.*
*** Ph. 9500 509/*7300 669* [id.]. Concg. O, Haitink, (i) with Badings.

Images; Prélude à l'après-midi d'un faune.
C *** HMV Dig. **CDC 747001-2**; ASD/-*TCC-ASD* 3804 [Ang. DS/*4ZS* 37674]. LSO, Previn.
(M) *** DG Priv. 2535/*3335* 370 [2530 145]. Boston SO, Tilson Thomas.
*(*) DG Dig. 2532/*3302* 058 [id.]. O de Paris, Barenboim.

Previn's account of *Images* was the first EMI digital record to appear, and understandably it was also included in the first release of HMV compact discs. Detail emerges more clearly than in any of its rivals, yet there is no highlighting and no interference in the natural perspective one would expect to encounter in reality. Every colour and sonority, however subtle, registers, and so vivid is the picture that there seems no intermediary between the musicians and the listener. Such is the clarity that this factor outweighs such reservations as one might have (it won both the *Gramophone* awards for the best sound and the best orchestral record of 1979). There is much to admire in Previn's performance too. Dynamic nuances are carefully observed; there is much felicitous wind playing and no want of intelligent and musical phrasing. By the side of some of Previn's rivals there does seem to be a want of atmosphere in *Gigues*, which comes over much more magically in Tilson Thomas's record. Nor is that last ounce of concentration and electricity that is the hallmark of a great performance present in the other movements, particularly *Rondes de printemps*. Previn himself has given us more atmospheric accounts of the *Prélude à l'après-midi d'un faune* than this, though none is more vividly captured by the engineers. The chrome cassette is hardly less demonstration-worthy than the disc, with the widest range, a natural balance and vivid detail. The CD confirms the triumphant technical success, with the silent background enhancing the tangibility and refinement of the orchestral texture.

Michael Tilson Thomas offers the same coupling as Previn, though the technical success of the EMI record has somewhat overshadowed rival achievements. Tilson Thomas's record was made in the early 1970s and does not match the digital recording in terms of clarity, depth and range. It has two strong advantages, however. First, it is better played and far more atmospheric; it conveys the flavour of *Gigues* and the languor of the middle movement of *Ibéria* far more convincingly than most of its rivals, and the playing is fresher and more committed too. Secondly, this is a mid-price issue. Moreover, the recording, though it must yield to the EMI, or for that matter to the Philips, is very good indeed. It is truthfully balanced, there is plenty of presence and body, and no want of detail. This is in every way a splendid record, and the tape is also impressive. The transfer level is modest, but detail is good and the recording's atmosphere is well caught.

Haitink's reading of *Images* is second to none in its firmness of grip and fidelity to the score. His *Gigues* is scrupulously prepared and beautifully played by the wonderful Dutch orchestra: the sonorities are delicate and the dynamic shadings sensitively observed, though there could be even more atmosphere both here and in *Les parfums de la nuit*. The superlative quality of the orchestral playing is matched by recording of a high order, scarcely less impressive in its range and body than the digital recording EMI have provided for Previn. The fill-up differs: Haitink gives us an attractive account of the beguiling *Dances sacrée et profane*, with elegant playing from the harpist Vera Badings, who is excellently balanced. An impressive, indeed distinguished record. The tape is more opaque than the disc in *Images* (though still impressive); the quality in the *Danses*, however, is admirably fresh.

Barenboim secures a good response from the Orchestre de Paris and there are many felicitous touches. However, there is nothing very special here: the performances of both works remain serviceable rather than distinguished and there is ultimately a lack of real profile. This team have given us some atmospheric Debussy in the past, including a fine account of *La demoiselle élue*, but this record curiously disappoints. There is quite a good chrome cassette, though the transfer level is low, especially on side two.

Images; Le Martyre de Saint Sébastien (symphonic fragments).

(M) *** Ph. Seq. 6527/*7311* 185. LSO, Monteux.

The restoration of Monteux's classic coupling to the catalogue is most welcome, and it makes a splendid addition to the Debussy discography, particularly as the new pressing has fine immediacy and detail. Indeed one would hardly suspect that the recording dates from the mid-1960s, for the woodwind colouring is translucent and there is a fine sheen of sensuousness to the string tone (especially in *Les parfums de la nuit*). Monteux's performance of the *Images* was notable for its freshness and impetus (although this is achieved by the electricity of the playing rather than fast tempi). There is a vivid yet refined feeling for colour which is carried through into the orchestral sections from *Le Martyre* (in its fuller form a cantata written to a text by D'Annunzio). The delicacy of texture of Debussy's exquisite scoring is marvellously balanced by Monteux and he never lets the music become static. The cassette is of good quality, but a higher transfer level would have brought more sharply defined detail.

Images: Ibéria. La Mer; Prélude à l'après-midi d'un faune.
(M) *** Mercury SRI 75053. [id.]. Detroit SO, Paray.

Paray's collection, dating from the beginning of the 1960s, gave us the first successful stereo recording of *La Mer*. The balance is slightly recessed with a convincing concert-hall ambience, which gives plenty of atmosphere to Paray's hazily sentient reading of the *Prélude à l'après-midi d'un faune* and his glitteringly evocative account of *Ibéria*. The finale of *La Mer* is notable for some fine pianissimo playing to match the vividly expansive climaxes. At lower mid-price, this remains very competitive, although Karajan's version of *La Mer* is even finer (see below).

Jeux; La Mer; Prélude à l'après-midi d'un faune.
** CBS 60144/*40*- [MY/*MYT* 37261]. New Philh. O, Boulez.

Jeux; (i) *Nocturnes.*
C *** Ph. **400 023-2**; 9500 674/*7300 769* [id.]. Concg. O, Haitink, (i) with women's ch. of Coll. Mus.

However overstocked the catalogue may be, there must always be a place for performances and recording of the quality of the Philips issue. The playing of the Concertgebouw Orchestra is of the highest order, and Haitink's *Jeux* far surpasses any recent rivals. Indeed it even matches such historic accounts as those of Cluytens and the Paris Conservatoire Orchestra and de Sabata's pioneering set of 78s. His reading is wonderfully expansive and sensitive to atmosphere, and *Jeux* undoubtedly scores over Boulez's much (and rightly) admired version from the more measured tempo and pensive approach that Haitink chooses. Competition is even stiffer in the *Nocturnes*, but this great orchestra and conductor hold their own. The cruel vocal line in *Sirènes* taxes the women of the Collegium Musicum Amstelodamense, but few versions, even those of Abbado and Giulini, are quite so beguiling and seductive as Haitink's. Add to this an equally admirable recorded quality, with transparent textures, splendidly defined detail and truthful perspective – in short demonstration sound – and the result is very distinguished indeed. So is the handsome presentation, which reproduces Whistler's *Nocturne in Blue and Silver* to striking effect. In its ordinary LP format this received a twin *Gramophone* award, for the best orchestral and best engineered record of 1980. It is, of course, an analogue recording but has been digitally remastered for its compact disc issue which brings just a little greater sense of concert-hall presence, with the bass also somewhat better defined. The very opening of *Nuages* and the middle section of *Fêtes* are examples where the focus is that bit sharper. The quality on cassette is richly atmospheric too, but there is a slight loss of range at the top compared with the LP, and this is more striking if the comparison is made with the compact disc.

Boulez has won critical accolades for his concert performances of *La Mer* and *Jeux*, but there seems little to excite undue enthusiasm here. True, he secures some first-class playing from the New Philharmonia, and no one would deny that *Jeux* is persuasively given. However, the playing lacks atmosphere and the last degree of poetry, and were Boulez's name left off the record label, one doubts whether the performances would have aroused anything like the enthusiasm they did in the press. *La Mer* is not remotely comparable with the Karajan on DG, and is not superior to most rival accounts listed. Much the same applies to the *Prélude à l'après-midi d'un faune*. The cassette transfer is vivid but unrefined (the upper woodwind partials are discoloured).

La Mer.
*** DG 2531/*3301* 264 [id.]. LAPO, Giulini – RAVEL: *Ma Mère l'Oye; Rapsodie.****
(M) *** Decca Jub. JB/*KJBC* 136. LSO, Stokowski – BERLIOZ: *Dance*; RAVEL: *Daphnis suite No. 2.****
(B) ** PRT GSGC/*ZCGC* 2011. Hallé O, Barbirolli – RAVEL: *Daphnis* etc.**
*(*) Decca SXL 6905 [Lon. CS/5- 7129]. Cleveland O, Maazel – SCRIABIN: *Poème de l'extase.**(*)

La Mer; Marche écossaise; Prélude à l'après-midi d'un faune; (i) *Rhapsody for clarinet and orchestra.*

*** Ph. 9500 359/*7300 586* [id.]. Concg. O, Haitink, (i) with Pieterson.

La Mer; (i) *Nocturnes.*

*** Ph. Dig. 6514/*7337* 260 [id.]. Boston SO, Sir Colin Davis, (i) with Tanglewood Fest. Ch.

(M) **(*) HMV SXLP/*TC-SXLP* 30146. Philh. O, Giulini, (i) with Ch.

(M) ** EMI Em. EMX/*TC-EMX* 2027. O de Paris, Barbirolli, (i) with female ch.

(M) *(*) Decca VIV/*KVIC* 56 [Lon. STS/*5*- 15585]. Cleveland O, Maazel; (i) with Cleveland Ladies' Ch.

La Mer; Prélude à l'après-midi d'un faune.

(M) *** DG Acc. 2542/*3342* 116 [(d) 138 923/*923 075*]. Berlin PO, Karajan – RAVEL: *Boléro.****

** HMV ASD/*TC-ASD* 3431 [Ang. S/*4XS* 37438]. Berlin PO, Karajan – RAVEL: *Boléro.****

** Decca SXL/*KSXC* 6813 [Lon. CS/*5*-7033]. Chicago SO, Solti – RAVEL: *Boléro.***

La Mer; Prélude à l'après-midi d'un faune; Printemps.

(M) **(*) DG Sig. 410 834-1/*4*. O de Paris, Barenboim.

Even after nearly two decades Karajan's DG account of *La Mer* is very much in a class of its own. So strong is its evocative power that one almost feels one can see and smell the ocean. It enshrines the spirit of the work as effectively as it observes its letter, and the sumptuous playing of the Berlin orchestra, for all its virtuosity and beauty of sound, is totally self-effacing. The performance of the *Prélude à l'après-midi d'un faune* is no less outstanding, the cool perfection of the opening flute solo matched by ravishing string playing in the central section. These performances are now recoupled with *Boléro* instead of the magical version of the second suite from *Daphnis et Chloé*, no doubt to compete with the newer EMI remake. However, this would still lead the field even if it were at full price! The cassette transfer is of outstanding quality, matching the disc closely, although there is a degree of background hiss noticeable at pianissimo levels.

Giulini's DG version of *La Mer* is also very fine. During his tenure at Los Angeles he has produced a sound from the orchestra that is infinitely more cultured; the string texture is both richer and finer-textured, and the wind blend is altogether more homogeneous. There is much excitement here as well as poetry. The way in which Giulini shapes the hushed D flat passage towards the end of *Dialogue du vent et de la mer* is quite magical, and a model of the sensitivity that does not draw attention to itself. The sound is fully acceptable, though perhaps the balance is not quite natural. This does not displace the DG Karajan or entirely banish memories of Giulini's earlier Philharmonia set, but it is highly competitive and those wanting this particular coupling on disc need not hesitate. The cassette is disappointing; the transfer level is low and pianissimo detail is not sharply focused, while the climaxes lack range at the top.

Sir Colin Davis's *La Mer* is a great success too. The waters that this reading evokes are colder and greyer than Giulini's, and there is always the sense of tremendous power used with restraint. One critic was reminded of Sibelius here and Sir Colin does grasp the essentials of both. The set of *Nocturnes* is also very fine. Some will be surprised at Sir Colin's measured approach to *Sirènes*, but it is a convincing one, and marvellously sustained in both feeling and atmosphere. *Nuages* is hardly less concentrated in poetic feeling and, like Giulini's HMV version, slow and ethereal. This is a very different view of *Nocturnes* from that of Haitink and the Concertgebouw Orchestra (see above), but it is no less valid and sumptuously played and recorded. Inevitably in this repertoire choice will be, to some extent, dictated by coupling. The very good sound of the disc is not matched by the chrome cassette which, as so often with Philips, is transferred at too low a level and suffers from lack of range and presence.

Stokowski's version of *La Mer* was originally recorded using Decca's Phase 4 techniques to most brilliant effect. Some ears will find the balance artificial, but the effect is breathtaking in its vividness and impact, with a first-class cassette offered alongside this

Jubilee reissue, which has very slightly more body than the disc, without loss of detail. The performance has surprisingly slow basic tempi, even for Stokowski. But the playing has a wonderful intensity, with marvellously moulded sound. Like Ansermet and Karajan, Stokowski adds the extra brass parts in the last movement, which are authentic although excised from the printed score. This is among the finest performances of *La Mer* available and with a rich version of the *Second suite* from *Daphnis et Chloé* as the main coupling, it is highly recommendable at medium price.

Giulini's earlier account of *La Mer* is very distinguished, and it is given the benefit of excellent EMI recording. It would be difficult to fault this reading, and at its highly competitive price this disc should come near to the top of the recommended list. The Philharmonia are in splendid form. Under Giulini the *Nocturnes* are played with great delicacy of feeling and refinement of detail. *Nuages* is perhaps a little too dreamy but nonetheless full of atmosphere. *Sirènes* is all too wanting in a sense of movement: it is slow to the point of sluggishness. However, it is beautifully recorded and preferable in some ways to many of its rivals. There is a good, if not outstandingly refined cassette.

Haitink's reading of *La Mer* is much closer to Karajan's tempo in his 1965 recording than in his more recent EMI version. Both conductors pay close attention to dynamic gradations and both secure playing of great sensitivity and virtuosity from their respective orchestras. *De l'aube à midi sur la mer* has real atmosphere in Haitink's hands. The *Jeux de vagues* is no less fresh; the *Dialogue du vent et de la mer* is both fast and exciting. An interesting point is that the brief fanfares that Debussy removed eight bars before Fig. 60 are restored (as they were by Ansermet), but Haitink gives them to horns. (Karajan, who omitted them in the DG version, restores them in his HMV record, but on trumpets.) The *Prélude à l'après-midi d'un faune* and the undervalued *Clarinet rhapsody* are atmospherically played too, though the former is more languorous in Karajan's hands. The Philips recording is truthful, natural, with beautiful perspective and realistic colour, a marvellously refined sound. The cassette is not quite so impressive; the upper range is less telling and refined.

The Signature reissue shows Barenboim's way with Debussy in its best light. The sound is first-rate. The *Prélude* has a digital source, and its languorous feeling is undoubtedly telling, even if there is some lack of vitality. However, *Printemps* is one of his finest recordings. Barenboim succeeds in balancing intensity with atmospheric feeling, and the result is very persuasive. Both this and the account of *La Mer* are highly individual in their control of tempo, but there is great electricity. *Jeux de vagues* in *La Mer* reaches a superb climax and the finale is no less exciting. The recording is spacious and well balanced with good definition and range, and this generally registers well on the tape, in spite of the low level of transfer.

Karajan's 1978 re-recording of *La Mer* for HMV may not have the supreme refinement of his earlier version – partly a question of the warmer, vaguer recording – but it has a comparable concentration, with the structure persuasively and inevitably built. At the very opening of the work the extremes of dynamic and tempo may seem exaggerated, and at times there is a suggestion of the pursuit of beauty of sound for its own sake, but there is never any doubt about the brilliance and virtuosity of the Berlin orchestra. The *Prélude* has an appropriate languor and poetry, and there is a persuasive warmth about this performance, beautifully moulded; but again the earlier version distilled greater atmosphere and magic. The new recording is well engineered, although the cassette is not quite the equal of the disc.

Barbirolli's Eminence reissue offers sympathetic direction of both scores and he shows a strong feeling for atmosphere. But there is a lack of inner tension about the playing, and the recordings, though they have plenty of body, need just a little more clarity of detail. The cassette has less range at the top than the disc and the focus is blunted further (the chorus in *Sirènes* notably so). In the bargain basement Barbirolli's much earlier version of *La Mer* might well be considered a better representation of this conductor's special feeling for Debussy's music. It is again an atmospheric performance, but has more grip than the later Paris version, and becomes increasingly exciting in its closing section. The recording still sounds acceptable, vivid if somewhat restricted. The cassette matches the disc fairly closely.

Whether or not influenced by the character of the Ravel coupling, Solti treats the evocative Debussy works as virtuoso showpieces. That works very well in the two fast movements of *La Mer* (helped by brightly analytical recording), but much of the poetry is lost in the opening movement, not to mention *L'Après-midi*. Like the disc, the cassette sound is brightly lit, verging on fierceness.

The Cleveland Orchestra plays magnificently enough for Maazel, but his *La Mer* is neither as atmospheric nor as imaginative as the best of its rivals. The analytical recording, though well-lit and finely detailed (the cassette as vivid as the disc), does not redeem matters. The Viva recoupling is sensible and economically priced and the performance of the *Nocturnes* is more successful than *La Mer*. But the analytical balance does not help: the wind are by no means distant enough at the opening of *Nuages*, and although Maazel is far from insensitive to matters of dynamic nuance, there are inconsistencies in the observance of some of the *pianissimo* or *ppp* markings. The viola tone at Fig. 6 in *Nuages* sounds overnourished. Yet these remain superbly disciplined performances and Maazel's reading of the *Nocturnes* has more grip than Giulini's.

La Mer; Petite suite; Prélude à l'après-midi d'un faune; Suite bergamasque; Clair de lune; Tarantelle styrienne.
(M)** Decca SPA/*KCSP* 231. SRO, Ansermet.

This anthology, issued at medium price, is an excellent way of sampling Ansermet's individual and often rewarding approach to the music of Debussy. It includes the second of his three LP versions of *La Mer*, which was made in 1957. Yet the sound is not too dated, and the performance is direct and unmannered. The *Petite suite*, heard in Büsser's charming orchestration, is more controversial: some ears find the phrasing charmless and the weakness of intonation distracting. The other fill-ups are attractively played and, given the price tag, the record makes an eminently worthwhile bargain. There is a fair equivalent cassette. The transfers of some of the music seem to have been more successful than others (this was an early Decca tape issue).

Nocturnes: (Nuages; Fêtes; Sirènes).
(M) *** DG Sig. 2543/*3343* 521. New England Conservatory Ch., Boston SO, Abbado – RAVEL: *Daphnis suite No. 2; Pavane.****

Abbado's 1970 DG recording of the *Nocturnes* still sounds extremely well and remains one of the finest in the catalogue, comparable with Davis and Giulini. If the couplings are suitable this remains highly competitive at mid-price. He shows fastidious care for detail without ever succumbing to preciosity and has a keen feeling for atmosphere without ever losing sight of the music's structure. The playing of the Boston orchestra is immensely polished but not glossy, and there is a naturalness about this performance that also distinguishes the recording. Here the balance is good, dynamics are allowed to register without artificial boosting, and the tone quality is firm. The acoustic may be a little too reverberant for some tastes but most people will find this a rewarding issue in every way. The chrome cassette is of DG's best quality; the chorus in *Sirènes* is beautifully caught, and this issue is equally recommendable in both formats.

Prélude à l'après-midi d'un faune.
(M) ** EMI Em. EMX/*TC-EMX* 2008. Philh. O, Maazel – MUSSORGSKY: *Pictures.***

A fine but not really memorable performance, although the Philharmonia playing is first-class, and the sound well balanced on both disc and cassette.

Rhapsody for clarinet and orchestra.
(M) * Sup. 1110 3187. Zahradnik, Czech PO, Vajnar – FALLA: *Harpsichord concerto*; MARTIN: *Petite symphonie concertante.**

Rhapsody for clarinet and orchestra; Rhapsody for saxophone and orchestra.
(M) ** CBS 60341. Drucker, Raschner,

NYPO, Bernstein – HONEGGER: *Pacific 231* etc.**

The scoring of the *Première rapsodie* for clarinet was by the composer, but the work for saxophone was arranged by Roger Ducasse and the piece not first performed until 1919, a year after the composer's death. Each begins atmospherically and exploits the virtuosic nature of the solo instrument later. Both soloists in the New York recording are first-class and Bernstein accompanies sympathetically. The sound is very bright and forward in the CBS manner. The couplings are worthwhile, but also suffer from a too-close recorded balance; otherwise this is a distinguished issue.

On Supraphon, Bohuslav Zahradnik is no match for Stanley Drucker and his vibrato is a shade obtrusive. The Supraphon disc also offers repertoire of unusual interest.

CHAMBER MUSIC

Cello sonata; Petite pièce for clarinet and piano; Première Rapsodie for clarinet and piano; Sonata for flute, viola and harp: Violin sonata: Syrinx for solo flute.
*** Chan. ABR/*ABT* 1036. Athena Ens.

This set scores over rival versions in being more generously filled. In addition to the three late sonatas and *Syrinx*, we are given the two clarinet pieces (the *Rapsodie* is better-known in its orchestral form). The most ethereal of these pieces is the *Sonata for flute, viola and harp*, whose other-worldly quality is beautifully conveyed here; indeed this version can hold its own with the best in the catalogue. In the case of the other sonatas there are strong competitors (Kyung-Wha Chung and Lupu in the *Violin sonata*, Rostropovich with Britten in the *Cello sonata*). The works for wind are especially successful in the cassette version, which sounds admirably fresh; the string pieces are slightly less immediate.

(i) *Cello sonata in D min.;* (ii; iii) *Sonata for flute, viola and harp;* (iv) *Violin sonata in G min.;* (ii) *Syrinx.*
(M) *** Ph. 6503/*7303* 062. (i) Gendron, Françaix; (ii) Bourdin; (iii) Lequien, Challan; (iv) Grumiaux, Hajdu.

Cello sonata; Sonata for flute, viola and harp; Violin sonata.
(M) **(*) DG Priv. 2535/*3335* 455 [2530 049]. Boston Symphony Chamber Players.

During the early years of the First World War Debussy planned to compose a set of six sonatas for various combinations of instruments but unfortunately died before he could complete the project. However, the three that he did write are all masterpieces, particularly the exquisite *Sonata for flute, viola and harp.* It is a logical idea to assemble them on one disc and though the performances do not wholly dislodge others from one's affections, Rostropovich's account of the *Cello sonata* or the Chung version on Decca of the *Violin sonata*, they are very nearly as fine. Gendron's version of the *Cello sonata* is most eloquent and is splendidly recorded. Both in the quality of the performances and the recording this is to be preferred to its only rival (the Boston Symphony Ensemble on DG) and readers are strongly recommended to acquire it. The Philips cassette, though not transferred at the very highest level, is admirably clear and natural.

The Boston musicians (who include Joseph Silverstein as violinist and Michael Tilson Thomas as an elegant pianist) do not disappoint in any of these beautiful pieces, but the reverberation of the Boston acoustic is less well chosen than that where the Philips collection was recorded, and the resonance slightly clouds the textural subtleties, especially in the *Trio*. Nevertheless this remains quite competitive (even though it offers one item less) and, if the Philips disc were to disappear, could be a good alternative choice. The cassette transfer is excellent, atmospheric, without loss of definition.

Cello sonata in D min.
(M) *** Decca Jub. 410 168-1/*4* [Lon. JL/*5*-41068]. Rostropovich, Britten – BRITTEN: *Sonata;* SCHUMANN: *Fünf Stücke.****
*** ASV ALH/*ZCALH* 911. Lloyd Webber, Seow – RACHMANINOV: *Cello sonata* etc.***

Cello sonata; Minstrels; La plus que lente (both arr. Maisky).
*** HMV Dig. ASD 4334. Maisky, Argerich – FRANCK: *Cello sonata.****

Like Debussy's other late chamber works, this is a concentrated piece, quirkily original, not least in the central *Serenade*, with its sharp pizzicatos imitating the guitar. Lloyd Webber and his fine partner are as persuasive in Debussy as in Rachmaninov, and they are beautifully recorded. However, the classic version by Rostropovich and Britten, now restored to the catalogue at mid-price on Jubilee, has a clarity and point which suits the music perfectly. The recording is first-class, and if the couplings are suitable this holds its place as first choice.

Mischa Maisky brings such ravishing warmth of tone and finesse of colour to the *Sonata* that one is almost inclined to forgive him the bizarre coupling he has chosen. His recording has greater presence than that of Lloyd Webber and Yitkin Seow, though they offer a more interesting programme including the Rachmaninov *Sonata* and two short rarities. The most logical coupling of all is doubtless that of Gendron and Jean Françaix on Philips. Taken on its merits, the Maisky and Argerich recording is as good as any, but Debussians will probably want something other than the Franck.

String quartet in G min.
❀ *** DG 2531/*3301* 203 [id.]. Melos Qt – RAVEL: *Quartet.**** ❀
(M) *** EMI Em. Dig. EMX/*TC-EMX* 41 2048-1/*4*. Chilingirian Qt – RAVEL: *Quartet.****
*** Ph. LY 835 361 [id.]. Italian Qt – RAVEL: *Quartet.****
(M) * Argo ZK/*KZKC* 46. Aeolian Qt – RAVEL: *Quartet.**
* Ph. Dig. 6514/*7337* 387 [id.]. Orlando Qt – RAVEL: *Quartet.***

The Melos Quartet of Stuttgart is a much admired ensemble whose reputation can only be enhanced by this outstanding coupling. The playing of the quartet is distinguished by perfect intonation and ensemble, scrupulous accuracy in the observance of dynamic markings, a natural sense of flow and great tonal beauty. It would be difficult to imagine a finer account of the Debussy than this; and though the Italian Quartet recording on Philips has long been a yardstick against which newcomers are measured, the Melos have the advantage of excellent recorded sound, wider in range and sonority than the Philips; the balance is neither too forward nor too reticent, and is truthful in matters of perspective as well as of timbre. The cassette too is most successful, with only a hint of fierceness in the upper range at climaxes, which is easily smoothed.

At mid-price the Chilingirian coupling is in every way competitive. They give a thoroughly committed account of both the Debussy and Ravel *Quartets* with well-judged tempi and very musical phrasing. The scherzo of the Debussy is vital and spirited and there is no want of poetry in the slow movement. The recording has plenty of body and presence and has the benefit of a warm acoustic. This newcomer can certainly hold its own both artistically and so far as the quality of the sound is concerned. A very strong contender and second only to the Melos of Stuttgart.

It need hardly be said that the playing of the Italian Quartet is also outstanding. Perfectly judged ensemble, weight and tone make this a most satisfying alternative choice, and the recording engineers have produced a vivid and truthful sound-picture, with plenty of impact.

Neither the Debussy nor the Ravel quartets receive the subtlety and polish that they require from the Aeolian Quartet. Given the strength of the opposition, this issue is a non-starter.

The Orlando Quartet is a superlative ensemble and throw themselves into this work with complete dedication. They have a wide dynamic range, yet rarely does one feel that any detail is exaggerated and their tonal blend is magnificent. However, obtrusive editing rules this record virtually out of court: seven bars after Fig. 1 comes a sudden drop in pitch, where it is clear that a different 'take' has been used, and later on (6 bars before 5) there is another discernible pitch change. The playing itself is so characterful throughout and so vividly recorded that one would want to report that these discrepancies are of no moment, but alas they are. The cassette transfer is satisfactory.

Violin sonata in G min.
❀ *** Decca SXL/*KSXC* 6944 [Lon. CS 7171]. Kyung-Wha Chung, Lupu – FRANCK: *Sonata.* *** ❀

Kyung-Wha Chung and Radu Lupu are superbly balanced and most truthfully recorded. This is arguably the best account of the Debussy *Sonata* since the late David Oistrakh's Philips record of the mid-1960s with Frida Bauer. The only snag, perhaps, is that this is a rather short side at a little over fourteen minutes: the Franck is accommodated on the other side, so there would have been room for another substantial piece. Kyung-Wha Chung plays with marvellous character and penetration, and her partnership with Radu Lupu could hardly be more fruitful. Nothing is pushed to extremes, and everything is in perfect perspective, as far as both the playing and the recording are concerned. The cassette is of demonstration quality.

PIANO MUSIC

2 Arabesques; Ballade slave; Berceuse héroïque; Children's Corner; Danse; Danse bohémienne; D'un cahier d'esquisses; Estampes; 12 Études; Hommage à Haydn; Images, Books 1 and 2; L'Isle joyeuse; Masques; Mazurka; Nocturne; Le Petite Nègre; La plus que lente; Pour le piano; Préludes, Books 1 and 2; Rêverie; Suite bergamasque; Valse romantique.
(M) *(*) Ph. 6770/*7650* 036. Haas.

Werner Haas enjoyed an enviable reputation as an interpreter of French music and his marvellously sensitive account of Debussy music for two pianos (*En blanc et noir* and the *Six Epigraphes antiques* etc.) with Noël Lee (Ph. 6500 173) is sorely missed from the current catalogue. Although there are fine things in his survey of the (virtually) complete Debussy piano music – and it goes without saying that it never falls below a certain standard – the set falls short of ultimate distinction. The playing is rarely routine, but at the same time it does not achieve a consistently sustained level of inspiration to recommend as a complete survey. When these appear individually, his Book 2 of *Préludes* and many of the pieces from its companion will be worth having. Those collecting Pascal Rogé's set will not, however, need to regret their choice. The sound on disc is very good indeed and the cassette transfers, though not always at a high enough level, are often realistic.

2 Arabesques; Ballade; Children's Corner; Danse bohémienne; Hommage à Joseph Haydn; Mazurka; Nocturne; Le Petit Nègre; Tarantelle styrienne; Valse romantique.
(M) ** Saga 5480. Rev.

Children's Corner is the best-known item here and the most substantial. Livia Rev plays it well enough, though without quite the elegance we find in Pascal Rogé's more expensive record (see below). That is coupled with Book 1 of the *Préludes*, while Miss Rev has various odds and ends which the collector intent on having everything will want but which is not always essential Debussy.

2 Arabesques; Berceuse héroïque; Children's Corner; Estampes; Études Nos. 7, 8, 10, 11 and 12; Images (1905; 1907); L'Isle joyeuse; Masques; La plus que lente; Pour le piano; Préludes, Books 1–2; Rêverie; Suite bergamasque.
* EMI 2C 191 11651/4. François.

There is some spirited playing from Samson François whose collection is less complete than that of Werner Haas. The piano is well enough recorded, but François is not consistently sensitive nor does he always observe the dynamic nuances so important in this repertoire. Robust rather than refined, and no match for such younger French artists as Collard, Beroff and Rogé.

2 Arabesques; Danse bohémienne; Estampes; Mazurka; Pour le piano; Rêverie; Suite bergamasque.
*** Decca SXL/*KSXC* 6855. Rogé.

An excellent performance of the *Suite*

bergamasque, with crisp, well-articulated playing in the *Passepied* and genuine poetry in the famous *Clair de lune*. *Pour le piano* is no less effective, and only in *La soirée dans Grenade* does one feel that perhaps a shade more atmosphere would not be out of place. But this is a minor quibble, and there is much to admire here: Rogé is both vital and sensitive, and his intelligence and fine technique are always in evidence. The sound is superbly well defined on both LP and cassette. The disc is a shade more open at the top (this is where the difference really shows) but otherwise there is very little to choose between them. The quality is eminently secure and firm and the bottom end of the piano reproduces in a most lifelike fashion. If this is not quite as distinguished as Michelangeli's Debussy (DG 2530 196/*3300 226*), it is nonetheless very beautiful playing.

2 Arabesques; L'Isle joyeuse; Masques; La plus que lente; Pour le piano; Suite bergamasque; Tarantelle styrienne.
(M) *** DG Priv. 2535 158 [139 458]. Vásáry.

This is distinguished playing, and the disc is well planned so that side one includes the earlier works written between 1888 and 1890 and side two shows the composer's developing style, although it is a pity that the most mature item, *La plus que lente* (1910), receives the least convincing performance. Here Vásáry's rubato sounds slightly unspontaneous. He is at his very best, however, in the opening *Suite bergamasque*, and *Clair de lune* is beautifully played, as is the more famous of the *Arabesques*. In all, this is a satisfying recital, and DG's clear piano image suits it well.

Berceuse héroïque; D'un cahier d'esquisses; Études, Books 1 and 2; Morceau de concours No. 6.
(M) *** Saga 5475. Rev.

The *Études* are not so generously represented in the catalogue as the *Préludes* or the *Images*. Livia Rev is imaginative, and her playing has considerable poetic feeling as well as great technical accomplishment. This is a worthy successor to her earlier Debussy records, and at mid-price it can be confidently recommended.

Children's Corner; Images, Sets 1 and 2.
*** DG 2530 196/*3300 226* [id.]. Michelangeli.

Michelangeli's record is outstanding here. It is a magical and beautifully recorded disc. Michelangeli has made few records, but this is one of his best. It is also among the most distinguished Debussy playing in the catalogue. The cassette transfer is of good quality, the timbre slightly mellower than the LP.

Children's Corner; Préludes, Book 1 (complete).
*** Decca SXL/*KSXC* 6928. Rogé.

Pascal Rogé brings genuine poetic feeling and refinement of keyboard colour to the first book of the *Préludes*. He communicates atmosphere and character in no small measure and has much greater warmth than Michelangeli. In addition to the good Decca recording, there is a fill-up, which neither Michelangeli nor Arrau offers. Rogé plays *Children's Corner* with neat elegance. A very impressive disc and arguably the best buy in this repertoire – at least among modern records. The cassette transfer, made at a high level, offers beautiful quality, like the disc, but the warm resonance of the sound sometimes softens the transients in the *Préludes*, although (as the *Golliwogg's cakewalk* readily shows) this is less noticeable in *Children's Corner*.

Danse; D'un cahier d'esquisses; Images, Sets 1 and 2; L'Isle joyeuse; Masques.
*** Decca SXL/*KSXC* 6957. Rogé.

Pascal Rogé produces consistently beautiful tone, and this recital gives great pleasure on that score. His playing is distinguished by keen intelligence and sympathy, as well as a subtle command of colour, and moreover he is supported by recording quality of real excellence. There are occasional moments when one feels the need for more dramatic projection (in the earlier part of *L'Isle joyeuse* he tends to understate a little) and the *Hommage à Rameau* movement calls for more concentration (one feels that it needs to be held together just a shade more tautly). But there is so much to enjoy here and such accomplished pianism and finesse that any individual qualifications are unlikely to disturb even the most discriminating listener. Strongly recommended. The cassette quality is first-class, although (perhaps because of the transfer level, modest for Decca) the treble has marginally less range than on the disc.

En blanc et noir.
*** Ph. 9500 434/*7300 644*. Argerich, Bishop-Kovacevich – BARTÓK: *Sonata*; MOZART: *Andante.****

An intensely vital and imaginative account of one of Debussy's most neglected yet rewarding scores. *En blanc et noir* comes from the last years of his life and is full of unexpected touches. This is the finest account yet to have appeared on record and certainly the best recorded. On tape, however, the low transfer level has brought less sharp definition than on disc, although the quality is pleasing.

Estampes; Images, Sets 1 and 2.
*** Ph. 9500/*7300* 965 [id.]. Arrau.

Arrau has been consistently underrated as a Debussy interpreter, though some records he made for American Columbia in the 1950s should have alerted one to his stature. Good though his accounts of the two Books of *Préludes* are, this is arguably even finer. Indeed, it is one of his very best records and combines sensitivity and atmosphere with a warmth that somehow eludes Michelangeli in his much (and rightly) admired Debussy records. Arrau is superbly recorded too and cannot be too highly recommended. There is little appreciable difference in sound between the disc and the excellent cassette.

Estampes; Images, Sets 1 and 2; Préludes Books 1 and 2.
(M) ❀ *** HMV mono RLS 752 (2). Gieseking.
*** Ph. 6768 357 (3). Arrau.

In his day Walter Gieseking was something of a legend as a Debussy interpreter, and these superb transfers testify to his magic. The performances derive from LPs that appeared in the mid-1950s and not his earlier coarse-groove 78s, some of which are even more inspired than the remakes. The later versions are fine enough in all conscience and possess the advantage of splendid sound, which in these impeccable transfers often conveys the illusion and richness of sonority of modern stereo. Gieseking penetrates the atmosphere of the *Préludes* more deeply than almost any other artist, though there are individual pieces where Michelangeli or Richter may be as successful in one detail or another. In addition to the *Préludes*, this compilation offers the *Estampes* and both sets of *Images*; all in all, superb value!

The Philips compilation offers all of Arrau's Debussy made in recent years. Its merits have been detailed at some length under the individual issues. Playing of rare distinction, and beautifully recorded too.

Estampes; Préludes, Book 1: Voiles; Le Vent dans la plaine; Les Collines d'Anacapri.
(M) *** DG Priv. 2535/*3335* 495. Sviatoslav Richter – CHOPIN: *Ballade No. 3* etc.**(*)

Richter's recital offers wonderful Debussy playing, subtly characterized, the spontaneity of a live performance entirely compensating for the few audience noises. The recording itself is on the dry side, but there is no lack of brilliance, witness the glittering close of *Les Collines d'Anacapri*. The record is inexpensive, yet offers masterly performances: try the magical *Jardins sous la pluie* or the gentle exoticism of *Pagodes*. The cassette is faithful, the level slightly higher than the Chopin coupling, but still modest, although the focus is not impaired.

Préludes, Book 1 (see also under *Children's Corner*).
*** Ph. 9500 676/*7300 771* [id.]. Arrau.
**(*) DG 2531/*3301* 200 [id.]. Michelangeli.

Préludes, Book 2.
*** Ph. 9500 747/*7300 832* [id.]. Arrau.
(M) *** Saga 5442. Rev.

Arrau is an impressive Debussy interpreter and his account of Book 1 makes one regret that he has not recorded more of this composer. True, the *Danseuses de Delphes* are perhaps a little too stately; generally speaking, Arrau's tempi are unhurried, but that is no bad thing. There are some beautifully coloured details and a fine sense of atmosphere. This has not the glacial perfection of Michelangeli, but it has more warmth of appeal. The recording is richly defined and has plenty of bloom; the quality in both disc and cassette formats is extremely impressive.

It goes without saying that Michelangeli's account reveals the highest pianistic distinction. It is in many ways a wholly compelling and masterful reading of these miniature tone poems, with hardly a note or dynamic out of place, and it can be confidently recommended. Yet it remains for the most part remote and cool; authoritative playing that is somehow wanting in mystery and humanity. Clean, detailed recording; the tape transfer is natural and secure in timbre.

Arrau's account of Book 2 is an invaluable record – to be treasured alongside the classic accounts of Gieseking and Casadesus. At first Arrau's approach in *Brouillards* and *Feuilles mortes* seems a bit too leisurely, but these pieces gain in atmosphere at this speed. It is difficult to imagine a more penetrating or revealing account of *Canopes*, whose otherworldly melancholy is fully conveyed. Not everything is equally successful: *Les fées sont d'exquises danseuses* and *Feux d'artifice* would have sounded a shade lighter and more effortlessly wrought a few years ago. The Philips recording is extremely impressive – really vivid and lifelike – and there is no appreciable difference between the disc and the cassette, which is strikingly rich in colour with a natural bass resonance yet no loss of range at the top.

Livia Rev is a highly sensitive and accomplished artist whose Debussy series must be accounted an uncommon success. Her account of Book 2 of the *Préludes* has stiff competition but holds its own against all comers in terms of sensibility and atmosphere. Her keyboard mastery is beyond question and she is a fine colourist. She receives a very good recording, with admirably smooth surfaces, and she has, of course, the advantage of being on a medium-priced label.

VOCAL MUSIC

Song cycles: *Ariettes oubliées; 3 Ballades de François Villon; 3 Chansons de Bilitis; 2 Chansons de France; 4 Chansons de jeunesse; Fêtes galantes 1 and 2; 5 Poèmes de Charles Baudelaire; 3 Poèmes de Stéphane Mallarmé; Le Promenoir des deux amants; 4 Proses lyriques.* Mélodies: *Aimons-nous et dormons; Les Angélus; Beau soir; La Belle au bois dormant; Les Cloches; Dans le jardin; En sourdine; L'Échelonnement des haies; Fleur des blés; Jane; Mandoline; La Mer est plus belle; Noël des enfants; Nuit d'étoiles; Paysage sentimental; Romance; Rondeau; Rondel chinois; Voici que le printemps; Zéphyr.*

**(*) EMI 2C 165 16371/4. Ameling, Command, Mesplé, Von Stade, Souzay; Baldwin.

This box collects Debussy's vocal output on to eight sides, and it is an obvious convenience to have all sixty songs in one place. Debussy's songs are probably less revealing than his piano music; were they his only music to survive, our picture of him would be less complete than if we had only his keyboard or his orchestral music. All the same, the greatest of these songs, such as the *Chansons de Bilitis* and the *Fêtes galantes*, are indeed inspired and are in no sense diminished by the less interesting earlier ones. It is inevitable in an enterprise of this scale that not all the performances are of equal accomplishment. The unifying factor throughout is Dalton Baldwin; he provides polished accompaniments, though there are, it is true, more poetic Debussians. Gérard Souzay's Villon songs are one of the triumphs of the set, as are the *Chansons de Bilitis* of Michèle Command. It must be said that Mady Mesplé is not the most persuasive advocate for the less inspired earlier songs. But, though not an unqualified success, this is still a useful set in repertoire which is not over-represented at present, and it would be curmudgeonly not to give it a warm welcome.

(i) *3 Ballades de François Villon;* (ii) *La Damoiselle élue;* (iii) *Invocation;* (iv) *Salut printemps.*

**(*) DG 2531 263 [id.]. (i) Fischer-Dieskau; (ii) Hendricks, Taillon; (iii) Pezzino; (iv) Vallancien; Ch. and O de Paris, Barenboim.

Although this record gives shorter measure than we expect on a full-price label, it does at least offer some Debussy rarities. The *Villon Ballades* are seldom heard in their orchestral form, and the *Invocation* and *Salut printemps* are very early pieces, written when Debussy was twenty or so, and entered for the Prix de Rome. The fugue subject of the *Salut printemps* was provided by Gounod and Debussy's piece earned the disapproval of the jury. Neither this nor its successor, the *Invocation*, is first-class Debussy, but both are well worth having on record. Also welcome is *La Damoiselle élue*; Barbara Hendricks sings with great sensitivity and beauty, and Barenboim draws playing of genuine atmosphere from the Orchestre de Paris. There are problems of intonation with the chorus but, that apart, this is an intelligently planned and rewarding issue, well recorded too.

La damoiselle élue.
C *** Ph. Dig. **410 043-2**; 6514/*7337* 199 [id.]. Ameling, Taylor, women's voices of San Francisco Symphony Ch., San Francisco SO, De Waart – DUPARC: *Songs;* RAVEL: *Shéhérazade.**** C

The purity of Elly Ameling's voice makes for a ravishingly beautiful account of Debussy's early cantata. Other versions have either been more sensuous or more brightly focused, but the gentleness of this is certainly apt for such a pre-Raphaelite vision. Radiant recording to match which is enhanced by the compact disc. This has a remarkable translucent richness of texture, with the chorus slightly distanced yet naturally focused. The chrome cassette offers generally faithful sound, but does not begin to match the compact disc, which is an outstanding demonstration of the advantages of the new medium.

Fêtes galantes 1 and 2; Le Promenoir des deux amants (complete). *Beau soir; Chevaux de bois; Les Cloches; De soir; L'Échelonnement des haies; Green; Jet d'eau; Mandoline; La Mer; Pour ce que plaisance; Le Son du cor; Le Temps a laissiè son manteau.*
(M) *** DG 2543 813. Souzay, Baldwin.

Souzay is in his element in this programme, and he sings exquisitely. One can hardly imagine such a collection being better presented, and as the accompaniments are intuitively sympathetic and the recording has striking immediacy, this can be recommended without reservation.

5 Poèmes de Baudelaire; 3 Poèmes de Stéphane Mallarmé. Mélodies: *Les Angélus; Dans le jardin; L'Échelonnement des haies; Fleur des blés; Mandoline; Nuit d'étoiles; L'Ombre des arbres; Romance; Le Son du cor s'afflige.*
**(*) Nimbus 2127. Cuénod, Isepp.

Debussy song recitals are not so thick on the ground that we can afford to neglect any newcomer, and this issue is rather remarkable, since few singers these days record at the age of seventy-five. Older readers may recall that the tenor Hugues Cuénod took part in Nadia Boulanger's famous pre-war records of Monteverdi madrigals, and he had for long taken character parts in opera, such as the Astrologer in *Le Coq d'or.* Of course the voice has lost its bloom and there are vocal deficiencies; but these are few and the characterization of the songs could hardly be bettered, nor could the enunciation – or the piano playing. So, while allowances must perforce be made, there is much here to invite admiration, and the recording is fully acceptable too.

Pelléas et Mélisande (complete).
❀ *** HMV SLS/*TC-SLS* 5172 (3) [Ang. SZX 3885]. Stilwell, Von Stade, Van Dam, Raimondi, Ch. of German Op., Berlin, Berlin PO, Karajan.
*** Erato STU 71296 (3). Tappy, Yakar, Huttenlocher, Loup, Taillon, Monte Carlo Op. Ch. and O, Jordan.
**(*) CBS [M3 30119]. Shirley, Söderström, McIntyre, Ward, Minton, Ch. and O of ROHCG, Boulez.
** Decca SET 277/9 [Lon. OSA 1379]. Maurane, Spoorenberg, London, Hoeckman, Veasey, Ch. of Grand Theatre, Geneva, SRO, Ansermet.

Karajan promised that this would be his finest achievement on record, and he was not far wrong. It is a performance that sets Debussy's masterpiece as a natural successor to Wagner's *Tristan* rather than its antithesis. To that extent the interpretation is controversial, for this is essentially a rich and passionate performance with the orchestral tapestry at the centre and the singers providing a verbal obbligato. Debussy after all rests a high proportion of his argument on the many interludes between scenes; paradoxically, the result of this approach is more not less dramatic, for Karajan's concentration carries one in total involvement through a story that can seem inconsequential. The playing of the Berlin Philharmonic is both polished and deeply committed, and the cast comes near the ideal, with Frederica von Stade a tenderly affecting heroine and Richard Stilwell a youthful, upstanding hero set against the dark incisive Golaud of Van Dam. The recording is outstandingly rich and atmospheric on disc and cassette alike.

Armin Jordan's sensitive and idiomatic version on Erato provides an excellent alternative for those who find Karajan's treatment too large-scale. At its centre is the finely focused Golaud of Huttenlocher, fresh and expressive, well contrasted with the tenor of Eric Tappy, a brighter-toned singer than is usual for Pelléas, a role generally taken by a *bariton marin*. Rachel Yakar's vocal acting as Mélisande is first-rate, and though neither the playing nor the recording matches that given to Karajan, the whole performance is most convincing.

Boulez's sharply dramatic view of Debussy's atmospheric score made a strong impact at Covent Garden, and this complete recording vividly recaptures the intense excitement of that experience. This is a performance which will probably not please the dedicated Francophile – for one thing there is not a single French-born singer in the cast – but it rescues Debussy from the languid half-tone approach which for too long has been accepted as authentic. Boulez's attitude may initially stem from a searching analysis of the musical structure – Debussy anticipating today's avant-garde in so many ways – but the dramatic element has become sharper-focused too, for he sees the characters as flesh and blood, no mere wayward shadows. He is loyally supported by a strong cast. The singing is not always very idiomatic, but it has the musical and dramatic momentum which stems from sustained experience on the stage. In almost every way this has the tension of a live performance. The recording – made in EMI's Abbey Road studio – does not allow a true pianissimo, but is still aptly vivid, although the balance is not very natural. This set has been withdrawn in the UK.

Debussy's great opera is nothing if not atmospheric, and the gain from having superlative stereo recording is enormous. But Ansermet as in so many of his Debussy recordings is curiously literal, and rarely does the beauty of sound bring with it that evocative frisson that the composer surely intended. It is largely a question of tension, and Ansermet's direction tends to be in a low key. Maurane's Pelléas is excellent, and Spoorenberg has a simple charm without ever seeming quite at home in the part. George London's Golaud is coarse and ill-defined, but that is perhaps right with so unpleasant a character.

Delalande, Michel-Richard

(1657–1726)

3 Leçons de ténèbres.
*** Erato STU 71147. Etcheverry, Charbonnier, Boulay.

A very different Lalande appears here from the one we know from the more celebrated *Sinfonies pour les soupers du roi.* These are for the relatively austere combination of voice and continuo favoured in France at this time and perhaps best-known from their use by Couperin and Charpentier. Lalande brings a distinctive personal stamp to his settings and is no less a master of the arioso style than his contemporaries; indeed in melodic richness some of this is even finer than the Couperin version. And the continuo realization was spontaneous and not prepared in every detail beforehand; it sounds fresh and immediate without having the fussiness that often marks continuo realizations. Micaëla Etcheverry is an excellent soloist, and the artists are eminently well balanced and recorded.

De Profundis (*Psalm 129*); *Regina coeli.*
(M) ** Erato Pres. EPR 15510. Selig, Chamonin, Mallabrera, Corazza, Mars, Caillat Ch., Paillard CO, Caillat.

Delalande's setting of Psalm 129 is a most moving and impressive piece. There is real depth here and the performance is committed and eloquent. It dates from 1962 and the recording is not quite as fresh or spacious as the best of that period. However, the sound is more than acceptable and the performance on modern instruments is indeed pleasing. It is good to hear a warm string sound after the rawness of baroque instruments and to note good wind intonation. The *Regina coeli* is rather less striking though still worthwhile. Something of a find, all the same: a disc that will reward the curiosity of the collector.

Delibes, Léo (1836–91)

Coppélia (complete).
*** HMV SLS/*TC-SLS* 5091 (2) [Ang. SB/*4X2S* 3843]. Paris Op. O, Mari.
(M) *** Decca Jub. DJB/*KDJBC* 2002 (2). SRO, Bonynge.
(B) **(*) Decca DPA 581/2. SRO, Ansermet.
(M) ** Mercury SRI/*MRI* 77004 (2) [id.]. Minneapolis SO, Dorati.
** Ph. 6769 035/*7699 126* (2) [id.]. Rotterdam PO, Zinman.

The HMV set of *Coppélia* under Jean-Baptiste Mari is in every way worthy of Delibes's masterpiece. The elegant and sensitive orchestral playing conjures up a marvellous theatrical atmosphere, and the stage scene is readily re-created in the mind's eye. Mari uses ballet tempi throughout, yet there is never any loss of momentum, and the long-breathed string phrasing is a source of continual pleasure. The telling musical characterization, from the robust peasantry to the delicately pointed *Dance of the Automatons*, is vividly memorable. The superb sound, balanced most musically and within a perfectly chosen acoustic, recommends this as one of the finest ballet recordings ever made.

Now reissued on Jubilee with matching chrome tapes, the Bonynge set sounds freshly minted. He secures a high degree of polish from the Swiss orchestra, with sparkling string and wind textures and sonority and bite from the brass. There is nothing to choose in recorded quality between disc and cassette, and at Jubilee price this is fully competitive. Ansermet's older set – now effectively offered at bargain-price – has a classic character of its own, but the playing is much less refined. Yet Ansermet's authoritative hand is always apparent, and his power of evocation (especially in the first scenes of Act II) makes some delightful effects. The *Dance of the Automatons* sparkles like a musical-box, and the passage where Swanhilda pretends to be Coppélia coming to life and dances her stiff little waltz is pointed with loving care. The *Divertissement* is brilliantly played. One must accept the French quality of the woodwind, but the recording is very good, and this set will give much pleasure. The cassette transfer (KDPC-2 7045) is poorly managed and is not recommended.

Dorati's recording from the early stereo era still sounds well, though it is not as rich as the modern versions. It has a wide dynamic range, and needs a high setting of the controls for maximum impact. The orchestral playing is good, with neatly pointed strings and nicely turned woodwind phrasing (although the oboe is small-toned and somewhat reedy). This has undoubted merits, but it is not preferable to Ansermet and costs more.

David Zinman's performance of *Coppélia* is beautifully played and smoothly recorded. It has no want of vigour or refinement, but it lacks the character of Jean-Baptiste Mari's outstanding set with the Paris Opera Orchestra. The Philips tape transfer is made at a very low level, with a consequent loss of immediacy and range compared with the discs. Fortunately the HMV tapes have been remastered and now make a satisfactory alternative to the LPs.

Coppélia: suite.
(M) *** DG Priv. 2535/*3335* 189 [136 257]. Berlin PO, Karajan – CHOPIN: *Les Sylphides.****

Coppélia: highlights; *Sylvia:* suite.
(M) *** Decca SPA 314. SRO, Ansermet.

Coppélia: highlights; *Sylvia:* highlights.
**(*) [Lon. JL/5-41071]. SRO, or New Philh. O, Bonynge.

Karajan secures some wonderfully elegant playing from the Berlin Philharmonic Orchestra, and his lightness of touch is delightful. The *Valse de la Poupée* is beautifully pointed and the variations which follow have a suave panache which is captivating. The *Czárdás* is played very slowly and heavily, and its curiously studied tempo may spoil the disc for some. The recording is even better than on the reverse and can be made to sound very impressive. The cassette also offers sparkling quality.

An excellent selection from Ansermet's *Coppélia* is balanced by an equally vivacious suite from *Sylvia* (originally part of a concert disc that did not stay in the catalogue very long). With sound that seldom even hints at the age of the originals, this is a first-rate bargain. There are just a couple of moments where an over-effusive bass drum seems to muddy the texture slightly in tutti, but these are not serious.

Bonynge's selection (available in the USA only) from *Sylvia* is particularly enjoyable. He mixes a couple of unfamiliar items in with the usual suite and is served with most beautiful playing by the New Philharmonia. The *Coppélia* selection is less imaginative. Most of the music is taken from Act I and too little comes from the two succeeding acts. The absence of the *Automatons* number is regrettable (that was not omitted even in the very first extensive selection from this ballet on 78 r.p.m. discs, conducted by Constant Lambert). But despite these reservations, this is still very enjoyable with its vivid Decca recording.

Le Roi s'amuse: ballet music.
(M) *** HMV SXLP 30260. RPO, Beecham – BIZET: *Symphony*; BERLIOZ: *Troyens:* excerpts.***

Delibes's ballet music for *Le Roi s'amuse* is not an independent work, but was written for a revival of Victor Hugo's play in 1882. The music has an element of pastiche and its grace and elegance are superbly realized under Beecham's baton. Indeed the orchestral playing is a constant source of delight. The recording is very good too. This is a delightful compilation.

Sylvia (complete).
(M) *** Mercury SRI/*MRI* 77005 (2) [id.]. LSO, Fistoulari.

The ballet *Sylvia* appeared five years after *Coppélia* and was first produced at the Paris Opéra in 1875. While confirming the success of the earlier work, *Sylvia* has never displaced it in the affections of the public, and understandably so. It is an attractive score with some memorable tunes, but to be honest nearly all of these are contained in the suite, and in the full score we hear them more than once. But if the work is not as consistently inspired as *Coppélia*, it contains some delightful music and characteristically felicitous scoring.

Fistoulari was one of the great ballet conductors of the post-war era and his splendid Mercury recording from the beginning of the 1960s remains fully recommendable, especially at medium-price. The conductor shows his deep affection for the ballet in every bar: his sense of delicacy and his feeling for the specially French elegance of the woodwind writing are displayed again and again through all four sides. The LSO play superbly for him, the woodwind ensemble is outstanding and the solo playing most beautiful. The principal horn, in particular, offers a relaxed limpidity of phrasing that is strikingly lovely, and he has much to play. Mercury's recording is superior in almost every way to that given to Dorati in *Coppélia*. Obviously the London acoustic was very well judged and the luminous quality of the pianissimos is matched by the expansive, exciting climaxes. The muted strings sound especially well. A highly recommendable set.

OPERA

Lakmé (opera): complete.
*** Decca SET 387/9 [Lon. OSA 1391]. Sutherland, Berbié, Vanzo, Bacquier, Monte Carlo Op. Ch. and O, Bonynge.

Lakmé is a strange work, not at all the piece one would expect, knowing simply the famous *Bell song* with its clattering coloratura at the end. Predictably enough it has, at the beginning, its measure of orientalism, but quickly we have comedy introduced in the shape of Britons abroad, and Delibes presents it with wit and charm. This performance (with Monica Sinclair a gloriously outrageous Governess) seizes its opportunities with both hands, while the more serious passages are sung with a regard for beautiful vocal line that should convert anyone. Of course, as so often, Sutherland swallows her consonants, but the beauty of the singing with its ravishing ease and purity up to the highest register is what matters, and she has opposite her one of the most pleasing and intelligent of French tenors, Alain Vanzo. Excellent contributions from the others too, spirited conducting and brilliant, atmospheric recording. Highly recommended.

Delius, Frederick (1862–1934)

Air and dance; Fennimore and Gerda: Intermezzo; Hassan: Intermezzo and Serenade; Koanga: La Calinda; On Hearing the First Cuckoo in Spring; A Song before Sunrise; Summer Night on the River; A Village Romeo and Juliet: The Walk to the Paradise Garden.
*** Argo ZRG/*KZRC* 875. [id.]. ASMF, Marriner.

No grumbles here: these are lovely performances, warm, tender and eloquent. They are played superbly and recorded in a splendid acoustic. The recording is beautifully balanced – the distant cuckoo is highly evocative – though with a relatively small band of strings the sound inevitably has less body than with a full orchestral group. The cassette transfer is first-class. No collector need hesitate.

2 Aquarelles (arr. Fenby); *Fennimore and Gerda: Intermezzo* (arr. Beecham); *Hassan: Intermezzo and Serenade* (arr. Beecham); *Irmelin: Prelude; Late Swallows* (arr. Fenby); *On Hearing the First Cuckoo in Spring; A Song before Sunrise; Summer Night on the River.*
(M) *** Chan. CBR/*CBT* 1017. Bournemouth Sinf., Del Mar.

There are few finer interpreters of Delius today than Del Mar, once a protégé of Beecham, and this nicely balanced collection of miniatures is among the most broadly recommendable of Delius collections available. The performances are just as warm and atmospheric as Barbirolli's in his HMV collection (see below) which overlaps this one, and if anything have a stronger sense of line. Warm, modern recording to match. This record was originally issued at full price by RCA and the Chandos medium-price reissue has been digitally remastered, with a matching chrome tape, in the demonstration class.

Brigg Fair; Fennimore and Gerda: Intermezzo; A Song before Sunrise; Marche-caprice; On Hearing the First Cuckoo in Spring; Summer Night on the River; Sleigh Ride.
❀ *** HMV ASD 357 [Sera. S/*4XG* 60185]. RPO, Beecham.

Beecham's collection is a unique and treasurable memorial of his art. His finespun magic with Delius's orchestral textures is apparent from the delicate opening bars of *Brigg Fair*, and the string playing in *On Hearing the First Cuckoo* and more especially *Summer Night on the River* is ravishing yet never too indulgent. The recording was one of the finest Beecham was given in stereo and still sounds beautiful.

Brigg Fair; Fennimore and Gerda: Intermezzo; Florida suite; Irmelin: Prelude; Marche-caprice; On Hearing the First Cuckoo in Spring; Sleigh ride; Summer Evening; Summer Night on the River.
(M) ; *** HMV *TCC2-POR 154601-9*. RPO, Beecham.

To the contents of ASD 357, above, this double-length tape adds the *Florida suite* (see below) and two other pieces, no less valuable, which are not otherwise available. The sound on the cassette is very beautiful, smooth, refined and full, yet well detailed. With freedom from background disturbance, short of a compact disc, this is an ideal way to listen to Delius, and this issue fully deserves to share our Rosette given to the LP as above.

Brigg Fair; Eventyr; In a Summer Garden; A Song of Summer.
(B) *** CfP Dig. CFP/*TC-CFP* 40373. Hallé O, Handley.

Although the tempi are sometimes controversial, Handley is an understanding and exciting Delian, and these pieces are beautifully played. The digital recording is superb, matching clarity of definition with ambient lustre and rich colouring, on disc and cassette alike. A splendid bargain in every way.

Cello concerto.
*** RCA RS/*RK* 9010. Lloyd Webber, Philh. O, Handley – HOLST: *Invocation*; VAUGHAN WILLIAMS: *Fantasia*.***

Lloyd Webber is inside the idiom and plays the concerto – not one of Delius's strongest works perhaps though it was the composer's own favourite among his four concertos – with total conviction. Its lyricism is beguiling enough but the concerto proceeds in wayward fashion and the soloist must play every note as if he believes in it ardently – and this Lloyd Webber and his partners do. Though he does not produce a big sound in the concert hall, the RCA balance is ideal and conveys an almost chamber-like quality at times with great warmth and clarity. One of the strengths of this version, apart from its technical excellence, is the interest of the coupling, which brings a first recording of Holst's *Invocation*. There is an equally recommendable chrome cassette, the sound fresh yet atmospheric to match the disc closely.

Violin concerto; (i) *Double concerto for violin, cello and orchestra.*
**(*) HMV ASD 3343. Menuhin, RPO, Meredith Davies, (i) with Tortelier.

Both these concertos refute in their superbly balanced one-movement structures the idea that Delius had no grasp of musical logic. Deryck Cooke published an intensive analysis of the *Violin concerto* showing the inter-relationship of almost every bar, and the same can readily be done for the even more neglected *Double concerto*. They make the ideal Delius coupling, and it is good to have the works presented by two master musicians in warm, wide-ranging recordings. As a performance the more successful is the *Double concerto*, where Tortelier's example was plainly a challenge to Menuhin. Theirs is a somewhat lighter view of the work than that of the soloists in the earlier Pye version (currently unavailable) and there Norman Del Mar drew more richly expressive playing from the RPO than Meredith Davies does. But the four-square power of the work is never in doubt here. In the *Violin concerto* Menuhin does not always produce his sweetest tone, but he gives a heartfelt performance, and the radiant beauty of the writing above the stave is wonderfully caught.

Dance rhapsody No. 2; Florida suite; Over the Hills and Far Away.
(M) *** HMV SXLP/*TC-SXLP* 30415. [Ang. Sera. S 60212]. RPO, Beecham.

The *Florida suite*, Delius's first orchestral work, is lightweight, but strong in melodic appeal and orchestral colour. The tune we know as *La Calinda* appears in the first movement. Elsewhere the Negro influences absorbed by Delius even suggest a Dvořákian flavour. The writing is untypical of the mature Delius rather in the same way as the *Karelia* suite is of Sibelius. With the *Second Dance rhapsody* and the somewhat episodic *Over the Hills* this makes a fine medium-priced anthology, and the recording sounds astonishingly undated. The tape matches the disc closely; the quality is both vivid and transparent. An indispensable reissue.

(i) *Dance rhapsody No. 1; Eventyr; Paris, the song of a great city;* (ii) *Song of summer*; (iii) *Cynara*; (iv) *Sea drift.*
(M) *** HMV *TCC2-POR 54295*. (i) Royal Liv. PO, (ii) RPO; Groves with (iii) Shirley-Quirk; (iv) Noble, Royal Liv. PO Ch.

For any conductor attempting to interpret

Delius today the first thing is to try to forget the ghost of Sir Thomas Beecham and to produce spontaneous-sounding performances that may or may not correspond to his. Groves does just this in the magnificent picture in sound *Paris*, as well as the shorter works. The tempi are less extreme than Beecham's, but refreshingly persuasive. *Cynara* (1907) is a setting of Dowson. John Shirley-Quirk does the solo part impressively (it was the poor solo singing that so badly let down Beecham's mono LP of this work) and the performance of this work is very fine, falling not far short of Beecham's standard though lacking his sense of magic. *Sea drift* is by comparison disappointingly matter-of-fact, failing to convey the surge of inspiration that so exactly matches the evocative colours of Walt Whitman's poem about the seagull, a solitary guest from Alabama. However, taken as a whole this 'Portrait of the artist' double-length chrome cassette certainly shows Groves as a persuasive Delian, and none of the performances are otherwise available. The sound is generally excellent.

Fennimore and Gerda: Intermezzo; Irmelin: Prelude; Koanga: La Calinda (arr. Fenby)*; On Hearing the First Cuckoo in Spring; Sleigh Ride; A Song before Sunrise; Summer Night on the River; A Village Romeo and Juliet: The Walk to the Paradise Garden* (arr. Beecham).
(B) *** CfP CFP/*TC-CFP* 40304. LPO, Handley.

All Delius conductors are haunted by the ghost of Beecham, whose close identification with the composer has deterred challenging batons. While his readings are still an indispensable cornerstone for any library, it is good to welcome more up-to-date recordings. Here Vernon Handley covers much the same ground as Neville Marriner (see above), but he includes the *Irmelin Prelude* for good measure, and this issue has a considerable price advantage over the Argo. Some collectors may find Handley's *Walk to the Paradise Garden* a little overheated in sentiment; but, generally speaking, this is a successful anthology, with expansive and imaginative phrasing, and the LPO responds with some fine wind playing. The quality of the recorded sound is admirable; the acoustic is appropriately warm and open, while the engineers succeed in meeting the diverse claims of tonal homogeneity and clarity of texture. At times the wind seem a trifle too close, but there need be no serious reservation on technical grounds. The tape transfer is as successful as the disc, clear in detail with plenty of warmth and body.

Fennimore and Gerda: Intermezzo; Irmelin: Prelude; On Hearing the First Cuckoo in Spring; The Walk to the Paradise Garden (*A Village Romeo and Juliet*).
(B) ** PRT GSGC/*ZCGC* 2055. Hallé O, Barbirolli – *Idyll.***

Barbirolli offers here four of Delius's most characteristically beautiful pieces of orchestral tone-painting. They are lovingly played, the Hallé responding well. The recording is good throughout, and these are among the most evocative Delius performances in the catalogue. The disc is excellent value at the price asked. The cassette is well managed and has full sound and a pleasing balance: it is quite the equal of the LP.

In a Summer Garden; Koanga: La Calinda (dance)*; Late Swallows* (arr. Fenby)*; On Hearing the First Cuckoo in Spring; A Song before Sunrise; Summer Night on the River; Hassan* (incidental music): *Intermezzo;* (i) *Serenade.*
*** HMV ASD/*TC-ASD* 2477 [Ang. S/*4XS* 36588]. Hallé O, Barbirolli, (i) with Tear.

Atmospheric and loving performances of these colourful scores. Sir John shows an admirable feeling for the sense of light Delius conjures up and for the luxuriance of texture his music possesses. At times he dwells a little too affectionately over details and one wishes for the music to move on, but for the most part reservations on this score are few. The recording is admirably rich and detailed, but there are times when one could wish for a slightly more backward woodwind balance. The cassette transfer has been beautifully managed, one of EMI's best early cassettes.

Irmelin: Prelude; A Song of Summer; The Walk to the Paradise Garden (A Village Romeo and Juliet).
(M) *** HMV Green. ESD/*TC-ESD* 7092 [Ang. S 36415]. LSO, Barbirolli – BAX: *Tintagel*; IRELAND: *London overture*.***

These are richly romantic rather than delicately subtle performances: Sir John does not provide the limpid evanescent textures for which Beecham was famous. The music is most persuasive not when it is in repose but rather when Barbirolli can bring his almost Italianate romanticism to Delius's passionate arching string phrases. Lovely playing throughout, and first-rate sound. The tape transfer too is of outstanding quality, clear in detail, yet with plenty of warmth and bloom.

CHAMBER AND INSTRUMENTAL MUSIC

(i; ii) *Cello sonata*; (iii) *Preludes Nos. 1–3; Zum Carnival – Polka.* (ii) Extract from *Delius as I knew him* (narration).
(M) *** Uni. Dig. DKP 9021 (i) Lloyd Webber, (ii) Fenby; (iii) Parkin – BOULANGER: *Collection*.***

The *Cello sonata* dates from the fruitful period of the First World War, when Delius wrote a sequence of richly lyrical and imaginative works – concertos as well as sonatas – in what ostensibly were conventional forms but which in fact he moulded to his own very personal expression. Lloyd Webber is a warmly persuasive advocate, understandingly accompanied by the composer's amanuensis, who introduces the Delius items with a personal reminiscence. Eric Parkin also breathes Delian air naturally. The *Preludes* are typical miniatures, the *Polka* an oddity. Atmospheric recording set in a natural acoustic.

String quartet.
*** O-L DSLO 47 [Lon. CS 7238]. Fitzwilliam Qt – SIBELIUS: *Quartet*.***

The Delius quartet is rarely heard either in the concert hall or on record (a Pye disc made by the Fidelio Quartet in the early 1970s did not survive very long). The Fitzwilliam Quartet make out a more convincing case for this score than any other we have had and they play with evident affection and commitment. Ensemble and intonation are excellent; phrases are carefully matched and rhythms vitally articulated. Undoubtedly the best (and best-known) movement is more familiar in Eric Fenby's arrangement for strings (*Late Swallows*), but it sounds eloquent in these young players' hands. The recording too is excellent.

Violin sonatas Nos. 1–3.
(M) *** Uni. UNS 258. Holmes, Fenby.

Eric Fenby with the help of Ralph Holmes has often given deeply illuminating as well as witty lectures on his years as Delius's amanuensis. These sonatas, particularly the last, which we owe entirely to Fenby's ability to transcribe the blind and paralysed composer's inspirations, form an important part of his theme. On the Unicorn disc we have a historic and moving set of all three sonatas – among the finest of all Delius's chamber works – which amply confirms the high claims made by Fenby for their cogency of argument. Though Fenby as pianist may not be a virtuoso, the persuasiveness of his playing and that of Ralph Holmes make this one of the most treasurable of Delius records. Fenby himself contributes a spoken introduction. First-class recording.

VOCAL AND CHORAL MUSIC

(i) *Appalachia. Brigg Fair.*
(M) *** HMV Green. ESD 7099. Hallé O, Barbirolli, (i) with Jenkins, Amb. S.

The reissue on HMV Greensleeve of Barbirolli's account of *Appalachia* is most welcome. Beecham's famous LP was marred by an unconvincing soloist but in every other respect was totally magical. Barbirolli dwells a little too lovingly on detail to suit all tastes, but for the most part he gives an admirably atmospheric reading that conveys, with the help of a richly detailed recording, the exotic and vivid colouring of Delius's score. The performance of *Brigg Fair* is no less evocative.

Appalachia; Sea Drift.
*** Argo ZRG/*KZRC* 934 [id.]. Shirley-Quirk, LSO Ch., RPO, Hickox.

This exceptionally generous coupling brings fresh and dedicated performances under Richard Hickox, urgent in their expressiveness rather than lingering. John Shirley-Quirk sings with characteristic sensitivity, and the chorus – trained by Hickox – is outstanding. The long sides do not prevent the recording from being fresh and clean. The cassette transfer is vivid but the choral focus is less refined than on disc.

2 Aquarelles. (i) *Caprice and elegy. Fantastic dance; Irmelin: Prelude; Koanga: La Calinda; A Song of Summer.* (ii) *Cynara.* (ii; iii) *Idyll.* (iv) *A Late Lark.* (v) *Songs of Farewell.*
(M) ❀ *** Uni. Dig. DKP/*RT* 9008/9. Fenby, with (i) Lloyd Webber; (ii) Allen; (iii) Lott; (iv) Rolfe Johnson; (v) Amb. S., RPO.

Eric Fenby, the musician without whom these works of Delius's last period would literally not exist, draws loving, dedicated performances from the RPO, and the digital recording is outstandingly fine. *A Song of Summer* is the finest of the works which Fenby took down from the dictation of the blind, paralysed and irascible composer, but the *Songs of Farewell* (to words of Whitman) and the love scene entitled *Idyll*, rescued from an abortive opera project, are most beautiful too, with Felicity Lott and Thomas Allen especially impressive in the *Idyll.* These major works, like such trifles as the *Fantastic dance* (dedicated to Fenby), were based on earlier sketches, while other items here were arranged by Fenby with the composer's approval. The *Irmelin Prelude*, for example, took material from the opera at a time when it seemed it would never receive a full performance. Christopher Palmer's notes on the pieces are deeply sympathetic as well as informative, making this two-disc issue essential for anyone interested in Delius. The cassettes are presented in a box and are of demonstration quality. Although they use iron-oxide stock they are 'real time' which means what it says, that they are transferred at normal playing speed. The quality is wonderfully refined, indeed in many ways the cassette balance is preferable to the discs, with the smooth upper range giving a particularly natural choral focus and (without any loss of detail) putting a most agreeable bloom on the orchestra. Highly recommended.

Idyll (*Once I passed through a populous city*).
(B) ** PRT GSGC/*ZCGC* 2055. Fischer, Walters, Hallé O, Barbirolli – *Orchestral collection.***

For his *Idyll*, completed in 1932, Delius drew on music from an opera, *Margot-la-Rouge* (see below), written at the turn of the century. To introduce the work the gently rapturous prelude is transplanted complete. The words which follow are from Walt Whitman and they form a duologue between baritone and soprano. The work is rather patchy – the setting of the opening words is not very imaginative – but as the passion of the lovers reaches its climax, the quality of the music deepens. Sir John makes a fine climax and it is a pity that Sylvia Fischer's voice is inclined to become squally when pressed. Jess Walters is rather more reliable, and both singers are thoroughly professional, but although there is considerable poignancy in the blissful closing pages, neither voice is in essence tonally beautiful enough for such limpid music. The recording is good and there is an excellent cassette; this vintage reissue is well worth trying, in spite of its limitations.

A Mass of Life.
*** HMV SLS 958 (2). Harper, Watts, Tear, Luxon, LPO Ch. and LPO, Groves.

There are few moments in Delius quite so exhilarating as the opening of his *Mass of Life*, and though the inspiration does not remain on quite the same level of white heat throughout the work, it still stands as one of his masterpieces. That passionate invocation to the Will (to words of Nietzsche taken from *Also sprach Zarathustra*) is followed by a sequence of poetic visions, superbly illustrated by Delius. Groves inspires his performers to a magnificent account, fully worthy of the work. It is good to have this music in such fine modern stereo, though curiously the very mistiness of some passages in Beecham's old mono set made the results more evocative still.

OPERA

The Magic Fountain.
*** BBC BBC 2001 (2) [Ara. 8121-2L/*9121-2L*]. Mitchinson, Pring, Welsby, Anglas, Thomas, BBC Singers, BBC Concert O, Del Mar.

This BBC recording is taken direct from the world première performance given on Radio 3 in November 1977. In this passionately committed reading under Del Mar, *The Magic Fountain* emerges as arguably the most consistently inspired of the Delius operas. Writing in the 1890s, Delius was influenced in his plot by *Tristan*: the heroine's hatred of the hero – a Spanish nobleman searching for the Fountain of Eternal Youth – turns to passionate love. The pity is that Delius's dramatic sense let him down. There is much beautiful atmospheric writing – particularly for the chorus – and although none of these soloists is perfect and the sound effects are sometimes intrusive, this is a most valuable and enjoyable set, cleanly recorded.

Margot La Rouge (complete).
*** BBC REGL 458 [Ara. 8134L/*9134L*]. McDonall, Woollam, Donelly, Andrew, Jackson, Wicks, BBC Concert O, Del Mar.

That Delius of all composers opted to write an opera using a Grand Guignol melodramatic story may seem odd, until you discover that he was simply abiding by the rules of an Italian competition he entered. He rejected the piece, but in the last years of his life with Eric Fenby rearranged some of the love music to words by Walt Whitman and so produced the *Idyll*. The full score of the opera was subsequently mislaid but using a piano score made by Ravel (the story gets odder) Fenby reconstructed the whole piece, and that was given its world première on BBC Radio 3 in October 1981. Thanks to the Delius Trust, that performance was put on this commercial disc. With warmly committed, highly atmospheric playing under Del Mar and with a strong if not ideally characterful cast, it makes an important addition to the Delius canon. The theatrical action music is effective but unoriginal. The real Delius lies in the love music alone. Beautifully balanced recording.

Destouches, André (1672–1749)

Première Suite des éléments (ballet music).
*** O-L DSLO 562 [id.]. AcAM, Hogwood – REBEL: *Les Éléments.****

A few years before Rebel composed his highly original ballet on *The Elements*, André Destouches, even better-connected as a court composer, wrote this ballet on the same theme. The result is less original but still well worth hearing, especially in this refreshing performance on original instruments.

Dickinson, Peter (born 1934)

Meditation on Murder in the Cathedral; Paraphrase 1; Study in pianissimo; Toccata.
*** Hyp. Dig. A 66061. Bate (organ of St James' Church, Muswell Hill) – BERKELEY: *Fantasia* etc.***

Peter Dickinson, former pupil of Berkeley, here matches the work of his master with organ works splendidly designed to bring out the spectacular qualities of the king of instruments, particularly one as richly resonant as that of St James', Muswell Hill. The impact of these pieces is enhanced by the degree of restraint in the writing – the titles alone bear witness to that – and Jennifer Bate gives performances as ideal as could be imagined.

Dittersdorf, Karl von (1739–99)

Harp concerto in A (arr. Pilley).
*** Argo ZRG/*KZRC* 930 [id.]. Robles, ASMF, Iona Brown – BOIELDIEU and HANDEL: *Concertos.****

Dittersdorf's *Harp concerto* is a transcription of an unfinished keyboard concerto with additional wind parts. It is an elegant piece, not quite as memorable as the Boieldieu coupling but very pleasing when played with such style. The recording too is from Argo's topmost drawer. There is no perceptible difference between disc and cassette; both are of demonstration quality.

Dodgson, Stephen (born 1924)

(i) *Guitar concerto No. 1.* (i; ii) *Duo concertante for harpsichord and guitar. Partita No. 1 for guitar.*

(M) **(*) CBS 61841/*40*- [MS 7063]. Williams, with (i) ECO, Groves; (ii) Puyana.

Stephen Dodgson is a civilized composer whose invention is matched by good taste and fine craftsmanship. John Williams is an eloquent and authoritative exponent and the *Concerto* could hardly hope for a more persuasive performance. Much the same goes for the companion pieces; the rewarding and resourceful *Duo concertante* is splendidly played. The recording, while not in the very first flight, is still very good indeed, and readers need not hesitate on this count. The cassette transfers are of CBS's best quality, losing comparatively little compared with the disc. In the *Concerto* the orchestra is given an attractive sense of space.

Guitar concerto No. 2.
(*) CBS 76634/*40*- [M 35172]. Williams, ECO, Groves – ARNOLD: *Serenade*; CASTELNUOVO-TEDESCO: *Concerto.*(*)*

This concerto was written in 1972 expressly for John Williams, who has consistently championed the music of Stephen Dodgson. It is a work of both charm and substance; the ideas hold the listener, the textures are varied and imaginative, and the sound world is fresh and luminous. This performance is expert and although the sound picture is not perfectly natural (the guitar is closely observed and looms too large in the aural canvas) few will object. The overall timbre is faithful and orchestral detail is vivid and in good perspective. More bloom and expansiveness in the top register, and it would rate three stars. But this is a rewarding work and an authoritative performance.

Dohnányi, Ernst von (1877–1960)

Piano concerto No. 1 in E min., Op. 3.
**(*) PRT GSGC/*ZCGC* 2052 [Gene. 1022]. Vazsonyi, New Philh. O, Pritchard.

A committed and fiery account by Vazsonyi of an early and very Brahmsian concerto by Dohnányi. Vazsonyi is a Dohnányi pupil as well as his biographer, and he commands a very considerable technique. Both the orchestral accompaniment and the Pye recording are excellent, and those interested in this underrated Hungarian master's output will find this useful. It is unashamedly derivative, but no worse for that. The cassette is obviously an early transfer which has not been remastered and the sound is boomy and middle- and bass-orientated.

Variations on a nursery tune (for piano and orchestra), *Op. 25*.
*** HMV ASD/*TC-ASD* 3197 [Ang. S 37178]. Ortiz, New Philh. O, Koizumi – RACHMANINOV: *Rhapsody*.***
*** Decca Ace SDD 428 [Lon. STS/5-15406]. Katchen, LPO, Boult – RACHMANINOV: *Rhapsody*.***

(i) *Variations on a nursery tune; Ruralia Hungarica* (suite), *Op. 32b*.
*** Hung. SLPX 12149. Budapest SO, Lehel, (i) with Lantos.

Since the mid-1950s, two different Decca records featuring Julius Katchen and Sir Adrian Boult have had a special niche in the catalogue with their coupling of Dohnányi and Rachmaninov. Here they are challenged by the superb HMV disc by Cristina Ortiz in partnership with the young Japanese conductor Kazuhiro Koizumi. They are helped by a recording of demonstration quality, but the performance itself is equally memorable. Dohnányi's score is characterized with feeling and wit; every point is made with telling skill, from the melodrama of the opening and the innocent piano entry through to the beautifully managed coda. The music-making has flair, humour, spontaneity and conveyed enjoyment, and the coupling is first-class too. The equivalent cassette also offers outstanding quality and is demonstration-worthy in its own right.

The Katchen/Boult disc, now at medium price, holds its own with a performance that is both perceptive and spontaneous, and by any ordinary standards the Decca recording is first-rate.

Although recordings of the *Nursery variations* are legion, the *Ruralia Hungarica* suite is something of a rarity. Much of Dohnányi's music is often thought of as Brahmsian, and it is true that he is by no means as national in outlook as either Bartók or Kodály. Yet *Ruralia Hungarica*, though a cultivated score, still has an element of peasant earthiness. There is, too, in its five movements wide variety of mood and it rises to considerable eloquence. György Lehel and the Budapest orchestra successfully convey its exuberance and poetry, and the pianist in the *Variations*, István Lantos, is characterful as well as brilliant. The recorded sound is truthful and well balanced.

Serenade in C, Op. 10.
(*) CBS [M/*MT* 35152]. Perlman, Zukerman, Harrell – BEETHOVEN: *Serenade*.(*)

This is an expressive and inventive piece with a particularly beautiful slow movement. The present issue resembles its pioneering record by Heifetz, Primrose and Feuerman in two respects: the brilliance and mastery of the playing and the dryness of the recording! It is not otherwise available, however, and as a performance it is difficult to imagine it being bettered. It has been deleted in the UK.

Donizetti, Gaetano (1797–1848)

Cor anglais concerto in G.
(M) *** DG Priv. 2535/*3335* 417 [139 152]. Holliger, Bamberg SO, Maag – BELLINI, CIMAROSA, SALIERI: *Concertos*.***

Holliger changes from oboe to cor anglais for Donizetti's attractive concerto, yet plays as stylishly and nimbly as ever. This is an outstanding collection, equally desirable on disc and tape.

Ballet music from: *L'Assedio di Calais; Don Sébastien; La Favorita; Les Martyres*.
*** Ph. 9500 673/*7300 768* [id.]. Philh. O, Almeida.

Music from the baroque period has given us dozens of records which are validly used for aural wallpaper. This ballet music from four of the operas which were presented in Paris provides a nineteenth-century equivalent, sparkling, refreshing dances of no great originality, delivered here with great zest and resilience and excellently recorded. The cassette does not quite match the disc in sparkle, but the balance is good and the effect lively. If only Philips had used a bit more level, this would have been an outstanding tape.

Overtures: Don Pasquale; Linda di Chamounix; Maria di Rohan; Marin Faliero; Les Martyres.
*** Erato STU/*MCE* 71211. Monte Carlo Op. O, Scimone.

These sprightly performances of overtures which in a generalized way could be fitted to almost any kind of opera make up an attractive and entertaining collection, lightness and energy presented without involvement. The recording is bright to match the performances. The cassette is quite well balanced but noticeably lacks sparkle on top, although side two is slightly better than side one.

String quartet No. 13 in A.
*** CRD CRD 1066/*CRDC 4066*. Alberni Qt – PUCCINI: *Crisantemi*; VERDI: *Quartet*.***

This, the thirteenth of nearly twenty quartets which Donizetti wrote in his early twenties, is an endearing work with a scherzo echoing that in Beethoven's *Eroica* and with many twists of argument that are attractively unpredictable. It is well coupled here with other works for string quartet by Italian opera composers, all in strong, committed performances and well recorded. The cassette transfer has plenty of character with good body and detail, although the treble is brighter and has more edge than in the couplings.

Miserere in D min.
(M) **(*) Hung. SLPX 12147. Pászthy, Bende, Slovak Philharmonic Ch., and O, Maklári.

Written at the age of twenty-three when Donizetti had just completed his studies, this *Miserere* presents a setting of Psalm 51 (Vulgate 50) which happily and fluently keeps straying into a secular style more appropriate for opera, with jollity always ready to take over from penitence. The soprano, for example, has an aria with sweet violin solo and pizzicato bass which asks for salvation from bloodshed; but at least in the outer movements the composer presents a properly grave face, with the finale sporting a fully-fledged fugue. It is an agreeable curiosity, here given a committed performance helped by well-balanced recording.

Requiem.
(M) ** Decca Ace SDD 566. Cortez, Pavarotti, Bruson, Washington, O e Coro Ente Lirico Arena di Verona, Fackler.

There are passages in this *Requiem* which may well have influenced Verdi when he came to write his masterpiece. Generally Donizetti's inspiration is short-winded, and it is not helped here by limited performance and recording and generally indifferent singing and playing. Pavarotti is the obvious star, singing flamboyantly in his big solo, *Ingemisco*.

OPERA

Anna Bolena (complete).
**(*) Decca SET 446/9. Suliotis, Horne, Alexander, Ghiaurov, V. State Op. Ch. and O, Varviso.

This Decca recording is far more complete than any stage performance is likely to be and it gives a fine idea of an opera which represents the composer in his most exuberant early flight (date 1830). Suliotis makes a formidable heroine and often produces Callas-like overtones. But with such dramatic command it is sad to report vocal carelessness that sometimes verges on the painful. The rest of the cast is more reliable, Marilyn Horne notable as Giovanna, Ghiaurov a rich-toned if rather unimaginative Henry VIII. Varviso conducts strongly and the Decca recording is characteristically vivid.

Il Campanello (complete).
*** CBS Dig. 38450/*40*- [Pro Arte 125]. Baltsa, Dara, Casoni, Romero, Gaifa, V. State Op. Ch., VSO, Bertini.

A modern recording of this sparkling one-Act piece on something like the same story which Donizetti developed later in *Don Pas-*

quale is very welcome. The principals all catch a nice balance between musical precision and playing for laughs, generally preferring to rely on vocal acting. Enzo Dara as the Apothecary, Don Annibale, and Angelo Romero as the wag, Enrico, are delightful in their patter duet, and Agnes Baltsa is a formidable but sparkling Serafina. Gary Bertini is a sympathetic conductor who paces things well, and the secco recitatives – taking up rather a large proportion of the disc – are well accompanied on the fortepiano. Generally well-balanced recording.

Don Pasquale (complete).
*** HMV Dig. SLS/*TC-SLS* 143436-3/5. Bruscantini, Freni, Nucci, Winbergh, Amb. Op. Ch., Philh. O, Muti.
**(*) Decca SET 280/1 [Lon. OSA 1260]. Corena, Sciutti, Oncina, Krause, V. State Op. Ch. and O, Kertesz.

Muti's is an outstanding set of Donizetti's most brilliant comic opera. With sparkle and spring on the one hand and easily flexible lyricism on the other, this is a delectably idiomatic-sounding reading, one which consistently captures the fun of the piece. It helps that three of the four principals are Italians. Freni is a natural in the role of Norina, both sweet and bright-eyed in characterization, excellent in coloratura. The buffo baritones, the veteran Bruscantini as Pasquale and the darker-toned Leo Nucci as Dr Malatesta, steer a nice course between vocal comedy and purely musical values. They sound exhilarated, not stressed, by Mutti's challenging speeds for the patter numbers. On the lyrical side, Muti is helped by the beautifully poised and shaded singing of Gösta Winbergh, honey-toned and stylish as Ernesto. Responsive and polished playing from the Philharmonia and excellent studio sound, with matching tapes which lose only a little of the upper range.

Kertesz may have been Hungarian and the use of the Vienna State Opera Chorus and Orchestra may bring some moments which suggest operetta rather than Italian opera, but the important thing is that jollity is conveyed all the time. This is done partly by allowing the characters to laugh a great deal and make jolly noises. Occasionally the effects may seem coarse if separated out of context but, heard as a whole, there is no doubt that this performance succeeds remarkably well. One can even forget that the standard of florid singing today is hardly what it was. Corena is an attractive buffo even if his voice is not focused well enough to sing semi-quavers accurately. Juan Oncina as always on record sounds rather strained, but the tenor part is very small, and Graziella Sciutti is charming from beginning to end, bright-toned and vivacious and remarkably agile in the most difficult passages. The recording is excellent.

L'Elisir d'amore (complete).
*** Decca SET 503-5/*K 154 K32* [Lon. OSA 13101]. Sutherland, Pavarotti, Cossa, Malas, Amb. S., ECO, Bonynge.
*** CBS 79210 (2) [M3 34585]. Cotrubas, Domingo, Evans, Wixell, ROHCG Ch. and O, Pritchard.

L'Elisir d'amore: highlights.
*** Decca SET 564 [Lon. OS 26343]. (from above set cond. Bonynge).

Joan Sutherland's comic talents in a Donizetti role came out delectably in her performances on stage and on record of *La Fille du régiment*. Here she repeats that success in the less rumbustious, more delicate part of Adina. Malibran, the first interpreter of the role, was furious that the part was not bigger, and got her husband to write an extra aria. Richard Bonynge found a copy of the piano score, had it orchestrated, and included it here. Quite apart from that, the text of this frothy piece is unusually complete, and in the key role of Nemorino Luciano Pavarotti proves ideal, vividly portraying the wounded innocent. Spiro Malas is a superb Dulcamara, while Dominic Cossa is a younger-sounding Belcore, more of a genuine lover than usual. Bonynge points the skipping rhythms delectably, and the recording is sparkling to match. The highlights disc reflects the complete set's qualities admirably.

Geared to a successful Covent Garden production, this CBS issue presents a strong and enjoyable performance, well sung and well characterized. Delight centres very much on the delectable Adina of Ileana Cotrubas. Quite apart from the delicacy of her singing, she presents a sparkling, flirtatious character to underline the point of the whole story. Placido Domingo by contrast is more a conventional hero and less the world's fool that Nemorino should be. It is a large voice for the role, and *Una furtiva lagrima* is not pure enough in its legato; but otherwise his singing is stylish and vigorous. Sir Geraint Evans gives a vivid characterization as Dr Dulcamara, though the microphone sometimes brings out roughness of tone, and Ingvar Wixell is an upstanding Belcore. Bright, nicely balanced recording and effective stereo staging.

La Favorita (complete).
**(*) Decca D 96 D 3/*K96 K33* (3) [Lon. OSA/5- 13113]. Pavarotti, Cossotto, Bacquier, Ghiaurov, Cotrubas, Ch. and O of Teatro Comunale, Bologna, Bonynge.

No opera of Donizetti shows more clearly than *La Favorita* just how deeply he influenced the development of Verdi. Almost every scene brings anticipations not just of early Verdi but of the middle operas and even of such mature masterpieces as *Don Carlos* and *La Forza del destino. La Favorita* may not have so many headily memorable tunes as the finest Donizetti operas, but red-blooded drama provides ample compensation. Set in Spain in the early fourteenth century, the story revolves round the predicament of Fernando – strongly and imaginatively sung here by Pavarotti – torn between religious devotion and love for the beautiful Leonora, who (unknown to him) is the mistress of the king.

This recording made in Bologna is not ideal – showing signs that the sessions were not easy – but the colour and vigour of the writing are never in doubt. The mezzo role of the heroine is taken by Fiorenza Cossotto, formidably powerful if not quite at her finest, while Ileana Cotrubas comparably is imaginative as her confidant Ines, but not quite at her peak. Bacquier and Ghiaurov make up a team which should have been even better, but which will still give much satisfaction. Bright Decca recording, again not quite out of the top drawer. The cassette transfer is generally well managed.

La Fille du régiment (complete).
*** Decca SET 372/3*K 23 K 22* [Lon. OSA/5- 1273]. Sutherland, Pavarotti, Sinclair, Malas, Coates, ROHCG Ch. and O, Bonynge.

This is a fizzing performance of a delightful Donizetti romp that can be confidently recommended for both comedy and fine singing. It was with this cast that the piece was revived at Covent Garden, and Sutherland immediately showed how naturally she takes to the role of tomboy. Marie is a *vivandière* in the army of Napoleon, and the jolly, almost Gilbertian, plot involves her translation back to a noble background from which as an infant she was lost. This original French version favoured by Richard Bonynge is fuller than the Italian revision, and with a cast that at the time of the recording sessions was also appearing in the theatre the performance could hardly achieve higher spirits with keener assurance. Sutherland is in turn brilliantly comic and pathetically affecting, and no better sampler of the whole set need be suggested than part of the last side, where Marie is reunited with her army friends (including the hero). Pavarotti makes an engaging hero, Monica Sinclair a formidable Countess, and even if the French accents are often suspect it is a small price to pay for such a brilliant, happy opera set. The tape transfer is of Decca's highest quality, bright and sparkling yet offering both warmth and bloom: a demonstration set. The libretto is clearly printed and easy to read.

Linda di Chamounix: Ah! tardai troppo . . . O luce di quest' anima. Lucia di Lammermoor: Ancor non giunse! . . . Regnava nel silenzio; Mad scene (complete).
(M) ❀ *** Decca Jub. JB/*KJBC* 97 [Lon. OS/5- 25111]. Sutherland, Paris Conservatoire O, Santi – VERDI: *Arias.****

No rave notice could really exaggerate the quality of this singing, and in many ways the first recording made by Joan Sutherland of the *Lucia* Mad scene has not been surpassed by either of her complete recordings of the opera (1961 and 1971). In fact this issue must be set on a pedestal as one of the finest and most dramatically thrilling displays of coloratura ever recorded. It is not just that Sutherland shows here a Tetrazzini-like perfection, but that she makes these stylized tunes and florid passages into something intensely moving. The youthful freshness of the voice is extremely appealing, and the tonal beauty is often quite magical. With its atmospheric stereo recording this remains one of the gramophone's great recital discs, and the newly transferred Jubilee cassette matches the disc very closely in vividness and range.

Lucia di Lammermoor (complete).

*** Decca SET 528-30/*K2 L22* [Lon. OSA/5- 13103]. Sutherland, Pavarotti, Milnes, ROHCG Ch. and O, Bonynge.

(M) *** Decca Ace GOS 663/5. Sutherland, Cioni, Merrill, Siepi, St Cecilia Ac., Rome, Ch. and O, Pritchard.

**(*) Ph. 6703 080/*7699 056* (3) [id.]. Caballé, Carreras, Sardinero, Ahnsjö, Ramey, Amb. S., New Philh. O, Lopez-Cobós.

(M) **(*) HMV SLS/*TC-SLS* 5166 [Ang. SBX/*4X2S* 3601]. Callas, Tagliavini, Cappuccilli, Ladysz, Philh. Ch. and O, Serafin.

(M) (***) HMV mono SLS/*TC-SLS* 5056 (2). Callas, Di Stefano, Gobbi, Maggio Musicale Fiorentino, Serafin.

It was hardly surprising that Decca re-recorded Sutherland in the role with which she is inseparably associated. Though some of the girlish freshness of voice which marked the 1961 recording disappeared in the 1971 set, the detailed understanding was intensified, and the mooning manner, which in 1961 was just emerging, counteracted. Really there is no one today to outshine Sutherland in this opera; and rightly for this recording she insisted on doing the whole of the Mad scene in a single session, making sure it was consistent from beginning to end. Power is there as well as delicacy, and the rest of the cast is first-rate. Pavarotti, through much of the opera not so sensitive as he can be, proves magnificent in his final scene. The recording quality is superb, though choral interjections are not always forward enough. In this set, unlike the earlier one, the text is absolutely complete. There is a first-class cassette transfer.

The earlier Sutherland version, conducted by John Pritchard, remains an attractive proposition in Decca's mid-price Grand Opera Series. Though in 1961 consonants were being smoothed over, the voice is obviously that of a younger singer, and dramatically the performance was closer to Sutherland's famous stage appearance of that time, full of fresh innocence. Though the text is not quite so full as in the later version, a fascinating supplement is provided in an aria (from *Rosmonda d'Inghilterra*) which for many years was used as a replacement for the big Act I aria *Regnava nel silenzio*. The recording remains very fresh and atmospheric, though not everyone will like the prominent crowd noises. Sutherland's coloratura virtuosity remains breathtaking, and the cast is a strong one, with Pritchard a most understanding conductor.

The idea behind the set with Caballé is fascinating, a return to what the conductor, Jesus Lopez-Cobós, believes is Donizetti's original concept, an opera for a dramatic soprano, not a light coloratura. Compared with the text we know, transpositions paradoxically are for the most part upwards (made possible when no stratospheric coloratura additions are needed); but Cobós's direction hardly compensates for the lack of brilliance, and, José Carreras apart, the singing, even that of Caballé, is not especially persuasive. Good, refined recording.

Maria Callas's flashing-eyed interpretation of the role of Lucia remains unique, though in her second recording (SLS/*TC-SLS* 5166) the voice has its edgy and unsteady moments to mar enjoyment. One instance is at the end of the Act I duet with Edgardo, where Callas on the final phrase moves sharpwards and Tagliavini – here past his best – flatwards. Serafin's conducting is a model of perception, and the stereo recording is fair for its period. The cassette transfer is admirable, with a fresh, lively overall sound balance and only the occasional peaking on the diva's fortissimo high notes. The score has the cuts which used to be conventional in the theatre.

The earlier mono set, which dates from 1954, is given an effective remastering, which brings out the solo voices well, although the acoustic is confined and the choral sound less well focused. It was Callas who, some years before Sutherland, emerged as the Lucia of our time and established this as a vividly dramatic role, not just an excuse for pretty coloratura. Here, needless to say, is not the portrait of a sweet girl, wronged and wilting, but a formidably tragic characterization. The diva is vocally better controlled than in her later stereo set (indeed some of the coloratura is excitingly brilliant in its own right) and there are memorable if not always perfectly stylish contributions from Di Stefano and Gobbi. As in the later set, the text has the usual stage cuts, but Callas's irresistible musical imagination, her ability to turn a well-known phrase with unforgettable inflections, supremely justifies the preservation of a historic recording. The cassettes are less successful than the discs in making the most of the restricted sound.

Lucia di Lammermoor: highlights.
*** Decca SET/*KCET* 559 [Lon. OS 26332]. (from above set, cond. Bonynge).

Those who already have Joan Sutherland's 1961 version may not wish to invest in another complete performance by her, even as tempting as the 1971 recording. For them this selection of items should be ideal; it contains the Fountain scene, the sextet, the Mad scene and the great tenor aria in the last scene. Superb recording quality, and a very good cassette.

Highlights are also available from the Callas stereo set on an EMI import (1C 061/*261* 0772).

Lucrezia Borgia (complete).
*** Decca D 93 D 3/*K 93 K 32* (3) [Lon. OSA/*5*- 13129]. Sutherland, Aragall, Horne, Wixell, London Op. Voices, Nat. PO, Bonynge.

In preparation for her formidable appearances as Lucrezia at Covent Garden and elsewhere, Dame Joan Sutherland made this vivid and dramatic recording with a first-rate cast. In this opera Bonynge believes in underlining the contrasts, bringing out the anticipations of Verdi – as in the funeral chant and bell tolling in the last act, which provided something of a model for the *Miserere* in *Il Trovatore*.

Sutherland is in her element. In one or two places she falls into the old swooning style, but as in the theatre her singing is masterly not only in its technical assurance but in its power and conviction, which make the impossible story of poisoner-heroine moving and even sympathetic. Aragall sings stylishly too, and though Wixell's timbre is hardly Italianate he is a commanding Alfonso. Marilyn Horne in the breeches role of Orsini is impressive in the brilliant *Brindisi* of the last act, but earlier she has moments of unsteadiness. The recording is full and brilliant on disc and tape alike. The layout on tape is superior, with sides tailored to the ends of each Act. Thanks to researches by Richard Bonynge, the set also includes extra material for the tenor, including an aria newly discovered, *T'amo qual dama un angelo*.

Maria de Rudenz (complete).
*(**) CBS [M/*MT* 3.36948]. Ricciarelli, Nucci, Cupido, Ch. and O of Teatro La Fenice, Inbal.

William Ashbrook in his detailed study of Donizetti was dismissive of this opera: 'It is difficult to believe that *Maria di Rudenz* will ever see the stage again', he said. Undeterred, the Fenice Theatre in Venice put on a new production, and CBS recorded it live. The sound is rough and the performance very variable, with a principal tenor who for all his heroic tone sings under the note. What matters is that number after number is proved to be Donizetti of the very highest quality, written two years after *Lucia di Lammermoor*. He may fill in with choruses of mourning that are absurdly jolly, but the material is far more memorable than many an opera of this vintage, and some of the arias vie with anything Donizetti ever wrote. There is also a magnificent ensemble at the end of Act I, where the crazed heroine, believed dead, emerges at the wedding ceremony of her rival and puts an end to it. The absurdity of the story (a variation on *La Nonne sanglante*, cheerfully gruesome) is hardly a bar to enjoyment on record, and the performances of Katia Ricciarelli and Leo Nucci in the two principal roles (the baritone here more important than the tenor) provide the necessary focus. For all its imperfection (which includes loud contributions from prompter and audience alike), this recording of a long-lost melodrama is well worth investigating. This set has been withdrawn in the UK.

Maria Stuarda (complete).
*** Decca D2 D 3/*K2 A33* [Lon. OSA/*5-13117*]. Sutherland, Tourangeau, Pavarotti, Ch. and O of Teatro Communale, Bologna, Bonynge.

Among the fictional versions of English history which attracted Italian opera composers of the last century, Donizetti's opera on the conflict of Elizabeth I and Mary Queen of Scots stands out as one of the most tellingly dramatic. The confrontation between the two Queens is so brilliantly effective, one regrets that history did not actually manage such a meeting between the royal cousins. In presenting the opera on record, Richard Bonynge and the Decca producers have vividly captured the feeling of a stage performance. Unusually for Decca, the text is slightly cut, but only the extreme purist will be worried. The contrast between the full soprano Maria and the dark mezzo Elisabetta is underlined by some transpositions, with Tourangeau emerging as a powerful villainess in this slanted version of the story. Pavarotti turns Leicester into a passionate Italian lover, not at all an Elizabethan gentleman. As for Sutherland, she is at her most fully dramatic too, and the great moment when she flings the insult *Vil bastarda* at her cousin brings a superb snarl. In the lovely prayer before the Queen's execution with its glorious melody, Sutherland is richly forthright but does not quite efface memories of Janet Baker's 1973 stage performances at the Coliseum (involving different transpositions). Otherwise, Sutherland remains the most commanding of Donizetti sopranos, and Richard Bonynge directs an urgent account of an unfailingly enjoyable opera. Bright, full recording and a vivid cassette transfer.

Mary Stuart (complete in English).
**(*) HMV Dig. SLS/*TCC-SLS* 5277 (3) [Ang. OSCX 3927]. Baker, Plowright, Rendall, Opie, Tomlinson, English Nat. Op. Ch. and O, Mackerras.

Mary Stuart was one of the English National Opera Company's outstanding successes in 1973, when it first appeared with Dame Janet Baker in the name part. It was the choice of opera at the ENO when nine years later Dame Janet decided to retire from the opera stage, and happily HMV took the opportunity to make live recordings of a series of performances at the Coliseum.

Though far from ideal, the result is strong and memorable with Dame Janet herself rising nobly to the demands of the role, snorting fire superbly in her condemnation of Elizabeth as a royal bastard, and above all making the closing scenes before Mary's execution deeply moving with the canary-fancying associations of Donizetti totally forgotten. Her performance is splendidly matched by that of Rosalind Plowright, though the closeness of the recording of the singers makes the voice rather hard. The singing of the rest of the cast is less distinguished, with chorus ensemble often disappointingly ragged, a point shown up by the recording balance. The acoustic has the listener almost on stage with the orchestra relatively distant. It is a valuable and historic set, but the Decca version with Sutherland gives a fuller idea of the work's power. The cassette transfer is admirable, avoiding vocal peaking, yet providing excellent fullness and presence. The libretto is clearly printed too, in a decent-sized type-face.

Arias: *Don Sébastien: Deserto in terra. Il Duca d'Alba: Inosservato, penetrava . . . Angelo casto e bel. La Favorita: Spirto gentil. Lucia di Lammermoor: Tomba degli avi miei . . . Fra poco a me.*
*** Decca SXL/*KSXC* 6377 [Lon. OS/*5-26087*]. Pavarotti, V. Op. O, Downes – VERDI: *Arias.****

This recital record was one of the first to alert the world to the emergence of a new star among tenors. The beauty and purity of the voice in every register are marvellously caught, and if at this early stage in his career Pavarotti seems at times just a little cautious, there are no distracting mannerisms or vulgarities to mar enjoyment. Recording very true and vivid on disc and cassette alike.

Arias: *L'Elisir d'amore: Prendi, per me sei libero. La Figlia del reggimento: Convien partir. Lucrezia Borgia: Tranquillo ei posa! . . . Com'è bello!*

** HMV ASD/*TC-ASD* 3984. Callas, Paris Conservatoire O, Rescigno – ROSSINI: *Arias*.*(*)

This is a fair example of the latter-day Callas (the recording dates from the mid-1960s), never very sweet-toned yet demonstrating the usual Callas fire. But the singing does not show her at her most imaginative, and there are few phrases that stick in the memory by their sheer individuality. Indeed there are patches approaching dullness, and that is not Donizetti's fault. Good, bright recording, and a vivid tape transfer with few hints of strain at peaks.

Dowland, John (1563–1626)

Consort music: *Alman a 2; Can she excuse galliard; Captain Piper's pavan and galliard; Dowland's first galliard; Fortune my foe; Frog galliard; Katherine Darcie's galliard; Lachrimae antiquae novae pavan and galliard; Lachrimae pavan; Lady, if you so spite me; La Mia Barbara pavan and galliard; Mistress Nichol's alman; Mistress Nichol's alman a 2; Mistress Nichol's alman a 5; M. John Langton's pavan and galliard; Pavan a 4; Round battell galliard; Susanna fair galliard; Tarleton's jigge; Volta a 4; Were every thought an eye.*

*** O-L DSLO 533 [id.]. Cons. of Musicke, Rooley.

It is by no means certain that all the music recorded here is authentic Dowland, but this anthology does serve to remind us how widely his music was admired and arranged during his lifetime. Three of the *Pavans* and *Galliards* come from Thomas Simpson's *Opusculum* (1610) and two of the *Pavans* are direct recompositions of Dowland's *Lachrimae*. Four of the settings are from Morley's *Consort Lessons*, and there are five pieces from the Cambridge MS. that are performed most attractively here. Marvellous playing comes in the pieces from Simpson's *Taffel-consort* (1621). The recording maintains the high standard of this Oiseau-Lyre series, although the forward balance brings a comparatively limited dynamic range. In all other respects the sound is first-class, and the tape transfer offers quality sophisticated in detail and timbre.

Consort music: *Captain Digorie Piper, his pavan and galliard; Fortune my foe; Lachrimae; Lady Hunsdon's almain; Lord Souch's galliard; Mistress Winter's jump; The shoemaker's wife (a toy); Sir George Whitehead's almain; Sir Henry Guildford's almain; Sir Henry Umpton's funeral; Sir John Smith's almain; Sir Thomas Collier's galliard; Suzanna.*

*** Hyp. Dig. A 66010. Extempore String Ens.

The Extempore Ensemble's technique of improvising and elaborating in Elizabethan consort music is aptly exploited here in an attractively varied selection of pieces by Dowland. Performers in turn are each allowed what the jazz musician would recognize as a 'break', and on record, as in concert, the result sounds the more spontaneous. Excellent recording.

Lachrimae.

*** HM 20328. Schola Cantorum Basiliensis, Wenzinger.

*** O-L DSLO 517 [id.]. Cons. of Musicke, Rooley.

Wenzinger's version of the *Lachrimae* is not of recent provenance (it dates from 1962), but the performances are wonderfully expressive and deeply musical. It is this profound musicianship that outweighs all other considerations and prompts one to prefer this issue, at long last available domestically, to any of its rivals. Rooley's version has the merit of clarity and authenticity (not that Wenzinger's group is lacking in either), but this version has the benefit of superbly eloquent playing from first-class instrumentalists, and the recorded sound is warm and rich. To be recommended alongside the Rooley but in some ways to be preferred.

The *Lachrimae* are played with splendid taste and feeling by the Consort of Musicke under Anthony Rooley. Two baroque violins are used in the dances other than *Lachrimae*; otherwise viols are employed. The recording is worthy of these excellent and sensitive performances. This completely supersedes the Dart recording from the late 1950s.

Complete lute music (divided into 5 separate recitals).
*** O-L D 187 D 5 (5). Bailes, Lindberg, North, Rooley, Wilson.

This impressive five-record survey of Dowland's lute music is entrusted to more than one player and contains a number of surprises. Though Dowland is best-known for his melancholy – *semper dolens* etc. – he has far greater range than the popular imagination would give him credit for. Of particular note are some of the fantasias on Jakob Lindberg's record; their chromatic boldness and fantasy place them among the greatest music for this instrument. Taken in large doses some of the dances and genre pieces do not make the best effect, but if they are heard in judicious musical context, their expressive power is without peer at this time. Both Christopher Wilson and Anthony Bailes play very freely and expressively (some may feel they could do with a tauter sense of rhythm), but they and their colleagues give performances that are dedicated and highly accomplished. The notes in this set are worth mentioning for they are authoritative and helpful. The only reservation concerns the balance of the recordings, which is slightly too close to avoid fingerboard noises and the odd sniff and grunt. With suitable adjustment of the controls this can be made fully acceptable, and such a tiny reservation should not deter readers from investigating a veritable treasure trove.

Lute music: *Captain Digorie Piper's galliard; 2 Fancies* (*Nos. 5 and 73*)*; Farewell; Forlorn hope fancy; Galliard to Lachrimae; Mr Langton's galliard; My Lord Chamberlain, his galliard; My Lord Willoughby's welcome home; Piper's pavan; Resolution; Sir John Souche's galliard.*
*** RCA RL/*RK* 11491. Bream.

An impeccably played recital, as might be expected from this fine artist. Bream captures the dolorous colouring of Dowland's galliards with uncanny insight, and the music is full of atmosphere. The recording is well nigh perfect. It needs to be reproduced at a relatively low level, but then the illusion is complete. The tape transfer is immaculate and the background is silent.

'Miscellany': Come again; Earl of Essex galliard; Galliard; If my complaints; 2 Lachrimae; Lachrimae Doolande; Lady Rich galliard; Lord Chamberlayne his galliard; Lord Willoughbie's welcome home; Pavan Lachrymae; Pipers pavan; Solus cum sola pavan; Sorrow, stay.
*** O-L DSLO 556. Cons. of Musicke, Rooley.

This is an anthology of arrangements of Dowland's music, presented not as second-best (as we today think of arrangements) but as a genuine illumination, a heightening of the original inspiration. Particularly attractive are the items for two or more lutes. As ever, Rooley draws most stylish playing from the Consort, and the recording is exemplary.

Keyboard transcriptions by Dowland of music by others: ANON.: *Can she excuse; Dowland's almayne; Frog's galliard; Pavion solus cum sola.* BYRD: *Pavana lachrymae.* FARNABY: *Lachrimae pavan.* MORLEY: *Pavana and Galliard.* PEERSON and BULL: *Piper's pavan and Galliard.* SIEFERT: *Paduana* (*La mia Barbara*). SCHILDT: *Paduana lachrymae.* WILBYE: *The frogge.*
*** O-L DSLO 552 [id.]. Tilney.

This interesting anthology is less 'transcriptions for the keyboard of Dowland' but rather pieces composed 'after' Dowland. The Byrd is closest to a transcription, while the Melchior Schildt is almost a recomposition. In any event these performances are elegant and have plenty of body, and the recording, if cut at a high level, is faithful and vivid.

VOCAL MUSIC

First Book of Songes (1597): *1, Unquiet thoughts; 2, Whoever thinks or hopes; 3, My*

thoughts are wing'd with hopes; 4, If my complaints; 5, Can she excuse my wrongs; 6, Now, O now I needs must part; 7, Dear, if you change; 8, Burst forth my tears; 9, Go crystal tears; 10, Think'st thou then; 11, Come away, come sweet love; 12, Rest awhile; 13, Sleep wayward thoughts; 14, All ye who love or fortune; 15, Wilt thou unkind; 16, Would my conceit; 17, Come again; 18, His golden locks; 19, Awake, sweet love; 20, Come, heavy sleep; 21, Away with these self-loving lads.
*** O-L DSLO 508/9 [id.]. Cons. of Musicke, Rooley.

This is the first in a series that will embrace Dowland's entire output, and if the rest is done with the sympathy and distinction that marks the present double-album, collectors will have every reason to be delighted. Rooley and the Consort of Musicke he directs have recorded all the contents of the *First Book of Songes* of 1597 in the order in which they are published, varying the accompaniment between viols, lute with bass viol, voices and viols, and even voices alone. There is hardly any need to stress the beauties of the music itself, which is eminently well served by this stylish ensemble and beautifully recorded.

Second Booke of Songes (1600): *I saw my lady weep; Flow my tears; Sorrow, stay; Die not before thy day; Mourn, day is with darkness fled; Time's eldest son; Then sit thee down; When others say Venite; Praise blindness eyes; O sweet words; If floods of tears; Fine knacks for ladies; Now cease my wond'ring eyes; Come, ye heavy states of night; White as lilies was her face; Woeful heart; A shepherd in a shade; Faction that ever dwells; Shall I sue; Toss not my soul; Clear or cloudy; Humour say what mak'st thou here.*
**(*) O-L DSLO 528/9 [id.]. Cons. of Musicke, Rooley.

The *Second Booke* contains many of Dowland's best-known songs, such as *Fine knacks for ladies, I saw my lady weep* and *Flow my tears*. Incidentally, the latter are performed on lute and two voices, the bass line being sung by David Thomas; this is quite authentic, though many listeners will retain an affection for its solo treatment. The solo songs are given with great restraint (sometimes perhaps rather too great) and good musical judgement, while the consort pieces receive expressive treatment. Emma Kirkby gives an excellent account of *Come, ye heavy states of night* and *Clear or cloudy*. Perhaps it is invidious to single her out, as the standard of performance throughout is distinguished. Refined intelligence is shown throughout by all taking part. This will inevitably be the most sought-after of the *Bookes of Songs* since it contains so many of Dowland's finest and most inspired pieces. The recording is of the highest quality.

Third Booke of Songes (1603); *Farewell too fair; Time stands still; Behold a wonder here; Daphne was not so chaste; Me, me and none but me; When Phoebus first did Daphne love; Say, Love, if ever thou didst find; Flow not so fast, ye fountains; What if I never speed; Love stood amazed; Lend your ears to my sorrow; By a fountain where I lay; O, what hath overwrought; Farewell unkind; Weep you no more, sad fountains; Fie on this feigning; I must complain; It was a time when silly bees; The lowest trees; What poor astronomers; Come when I call.*
**(*) O-L DSLO 531/2 [id.]. Cons. of Musicke, Rooley.

Although there are certain details with which to quarrel – a general air of sobriety and an excessive restraint in colouring words – there is a great deal of pleasure to be derived from this project. The performers show dedication and accomplishment, and in all cases they are expertly served by the engineers. David Thomas gives an excellent account of himself in *What poor astronomers they are*, and Emma Kirkby's voice is a delight too. The whole set is well worth investigation and an impressive achievement; the instrumental support is of high quality, as is the presentation. Apart from a certain reluctance to characterize, this set commands admiration.

A Pilgrimes Solace (*Fourth Booke of Songes*): *Disdain me still; Stay, sweet, awhile; To ask for all thy love; Love, those beams that breed; Shall I strive with words to move; Were every thought an eye; Stay, time, awhile thy flying; Tell me, true love; Go, nightly cares; From*

silent night; Lasso vita mia; In this trembling shadow; If that a sinner's sighs; Thou mighty God; When David's life; When the poor cripple; Where sin sore wounding; My heart and tongue were twins; Up, merry mates; Welcome, black night; Cease these false sports.
**(*) O-L DSLO 585/6 [id.]. Cons. of Musicke, Rooley.

A Pilgrimes Solace, Dowland's *Fourth Booke of Songes*, appeared when he was fifty. In its Preface he dwells on the decline of his fortunes in life and love, and of the remorseless advance of age. In a collection pervaded by melancholy, variety has been achieved here by using contrasts of texture: some of the songs are performed in consort, others are given to different singers. Emma Kirkby sings with great purity and beauty of tone, though she is not always as warm or poignant as the verse and music would warrant. However, hers is a most beautiful voice, and the set also offers some perceptive singing from Martyn Hill. Anthony Rooley's playing is accomplished and so is his direction of the proceedings. The eloquence of this music comes over.

Ayres and Lute-lessons: *Prelude and Galliard; All ye whom love; Away with these self-loving lads; Come again sweet love; Come heavy sleep; Go christall teares; If my complaints; My thoughts are winged; Rest awhile;* (Lute) *Semper Dowland, semper dolens. A shepherd in a shade; Sweet stay awhile; Tell me, true love; What if I never speede; When Phoebus first did Daphne love; Wilt thou unkind.*
(M) **(*) HM HM 1076/*40*-. Deller Consort, Mark Deller; Spencer.

Dowland's ayres were also designed for use by a consort of singers as well as solo singer and lute, and it is good to hear them in this form. The record draws on the *First Booke* of 1597 and those of 1600, 1603 and 1612, as well as two of the Lute Lessons excellently played by Robert Spencer. The performances are exemplary though some might be worried by the tendency to over-colour certain words but, for the most part, these give consistent pleasure. The disc suffers from traces of pre-echo, but the cassette transfer has admirable clarity and presence.

Ayres and Lute-lessons: *Can she excuse* (galliard); *Come away, come away sweet love; Fortune my foe; Flow my tears; Frog galliard; Galliard; Lady Laiton's almain; Lasso, vita mia; Me, me and none but me; Mistress White's thing; The Round battle galliard; The shoemaker's wife; Sorrow stay; Weep you no more, sad fountain; What if I never speede; Wilt thou, unkind, thus reave me of my heart?*
(M) *** HM HMB 244/*40*. Deller, Spencer, Consort of 6.

An admirably planned recital. Deller is in excellent voice (songs like *Come away sweet love* and *Sorrow stay* suit his special timbre and style especially well) and variety is provided by interweaving his solos with lute pieces and music for the Elizabethan consort of six instruments (two viols, flute, lute, cittern and bandora). The recording is naturally balanced on both disc and tape (although our copy of the tape had some disfiguring pitch fluctations).

Ayres and Lute-lessons: *Captain Candish's galliard; Lady Laiton's almain; Preludium and Lachrimae pavan; Semper Dowland, Semper dolens; Musical Banquet: Lady, if you so spite me. A Pilgrim's Solace: Shall I strive?; Tell me true love.* (i) *First Booke of Songes: Awake, sweet love; Can she excuse?; Come again!; Go crystal tears. Second Booke of Songes: Fine knacks for ladies; Shall I sue?; Sorrow, stay. Third Booke of Songes: Flow not so fast; Me, me and none but me; What if I never speed?; When Phoebus first did Daphne love.*
(M) *** Saga 5449. Spencer, (i) with J. Bowman.

This record contains songs from all three *Bookes* as well as some lute solos played in exemplary fashion by Robert Spencer. In many respects this makes an admirable introduction to Dowland's art, since it includes such justly popular pieces as *Fine knacks for ladies, Come again! sweet love doth now invite* and *Sorrow, stay*. Moreover they are sung with wonderful artistry by James Bowman, who brings sensitivity and intelligence to each song, and characterizes them far more powerfully than do his colleagues in the *Complete Works* project on the Oiseau-Lyre Florilegium label.

There is no lack of contrast, and each phrase is floated with imagination. The recording is excellent too, and the price is very reasonable. By the side of this issue, many of the songs on the Florilegium set seem inhibited.

Henry Noell Lamentations: Lord, turn not away; Lord, in thy wrath; Lord, consider my distress; O Lord of whom I do depend; Where Righteousness does say; Lord, to thee I make my moan; Lord, hear my prayer. Psalmes: All people that on earth do dwell (2 versions); *Behold and have regard; Lord, to thee I make my moan; My Soul praise the Lord; A prayer for the Queen's most excellent Majesty; Put me not to rebuke, O Lord. Sacred songs: An heart that's broken; I shame at my unworthiness; Sorrow, come.*
*** O-L DSLO 551 [id.]. Cons. of Musicke, Rooley.

In his comprehensive survey of Dowland's music for Oiseau-Lyre, Anthony Rooley here presents a superb collection of motets and sacred songs, an invaluable counterpart of the better-known secular works, instrumental and vocal. The recording, as ever from this source, is first-rate.

Dowland, Robert (*c.* 1585–1641)

Collection: *'A musicall banquet'* (1610): HOLBORNE: *My heavy sprite.* MARTIN: *Change thy mind.* HALES: *O eyes, leave off your weeping.* ANON.: *Go, my flock; O dear life.* PASSAV: *Amor su arco desarmado; Sta notte mi sognava; Vuestros ojos tienen d'Amor; O bella più.* BATCHELAR: *To plead my faith.* TESSIER: *In a grove most rich of shade.* DOWLAND, John: *Far from triumphing court; Lady, if you spite me; In darkness let me dwell.* GUEDRON: *Si le parler; Ce penser qui; Vous que le bonheur rappelle.* MEGLI: *Si di farmi morire.* CACCINI: *Dovrò dunque morire; Amarilli mia bella.*
*(*) O-L DSLO 555. [id.]. Cons. of Musicke, Rooley.

Robert Dowland, the great lutenist's son, compiled and published but did not compose this 'musicall banquet'. The composers range from his celebrated father to lesser-known masters such as Holborne and Tessier or more familiar ones such as Caccini. The anthology is dedicated to Sir Robert Sidney and, as in many similar instances, is scarcely intended for continuous performance. Indeed the songs do not possess a particularly wide emotional range, and readers tempted by this music will find it best to take three or four songs at a time rather than a whole side. Not all the performances are equally satisfying; problems of intonation arise in some of them and may well pose difficulties for listeners. The recordings are faithful enough and the music is not otherwise recorded (apart from Dowland's pieces); but the issue does not inspire great enthusiasm.

Drigo, Riccardo (1846–1930)

Le Corsaire: Pas de deux and variations (arr. Lanchbery).
(M) *(*) HMV Green. ESD/*TC-ESD* 7148. L. Fest. Ballet O, Kern – BELLINI: *Night shadows;* HELSTED: *La Fête des Fleurs à Genzano.***

The Drigo *Pas de deux* is vulgarly spectacular in Lanchbery's opulent orchestration, but it is not a piece one would want to hear often in spite of committed playing and recording. Essentially for balletomanes.

Dring, Madeleine (1923–77)

5 Betjeman songs; Dedications: To daffodils; To the virgins; To the willow tree; To music; To Phillis. Melisande, the far away princess;

My proper Bess. 4 night songs; 3 Shakespeare songs.
*** Mer. E 77050. Tear, Ledger.

Madeleine Dring was the wife of Roger Lord, one of London's most distinguished orchestral players, for many years principal oboe of the LSO. This wide-ranging collection of her songs, most of them easily lyrical but written with professional finesse, makes an attractive recital. Even the Shakespeare settings of words much used for songs have freshness, and John Betjeman fires her to some of the most delightful items, notably the Blues for *Song of a Nightclub proprietress*, which both Tear and Ledger relish memorably. Sensitive performances and first-rate recording.

Dufay, Guillaume (*c.* 1400–1474)

Complete secular music.
*** O-L D 237 D 6 (6). [id. PSI]. Medieval Ens. of L., dir. Peter and Timothy Davies; Kite (organ and clavichord).

The collector with special interests in this period will naturally acquire this handsomely produced and lovingly performed set, but the non-specialist might well be deterred by the sheer scale of the enterprise: ninety-six songs are quite a lot. There is no alternative collection and apart from the late David Munrow's records and those of the Munich Capella Antiqua, this repertoire is not generously served. What will surprise those who dip into these discs is the range, beauty and accessibility of this music. There is nothing really specialized about this art save for the conventions within which the sensibility works. The texts that Peter and Timothy Davies use are those established by Heinrich Besseler, and where the songs survive only with a fragmentary poem, they give the music in purely instrumental form. The documentation is thorough and the performances have great commitment and sympathy to commend them. The actual sound quality is of the first order, and readers who investigate the contents of this collection will be rewarded with much delight.

Secular music: *Adieu ces bon vins de Lannoys; La belle se siet au piet; Ce moys de may soyons; Dona i ardenti ray; Les douleurs; Entre les plus plaines danoy; Entre vous, gentils amoureux; He, compaignons, resvelons nous; Helas, et quant vous veray?; J'atendray tant qu'il vous playra; J'ay grant; J'ay mis mon cuer; Je me complains piteusement; Je n'ai doubté fors que des envieux; Je vous pri; Lamentatio sanctae matris; Ma belle dame souveraine; Mille bonjours; Par le regard de vos beaux yeux; Portugaler; Puisque celle qui me tient en prison; Resvelons nous; Se le face ay pale; Trop lonc temps ai esté en desplaisir.*
*** O-L DSLO 611. (from above recording, directed Peter and Timothy Davies).

For those collectors intimidated by the daunting prospect of acquiring all ninety-six of Dufay's songs, the present issue will be welcome. It offers no fewer than two dozen, only two of which are longer than four minutes. Nine of the pieces here survive with fragmentary texts and are played on instruments – and very well too. The effect of the later and longer songs can be quite striking and this aspect of Dufay is unrepresented here. However, the range is wide and there is no want of variety. The documentation and presentation are exemplary.

Missa ecce ancilla Domini. Chansons: *Anima mea liquefacta est; Je me complains; Navre je suy.* Motets: *Ave regina coelorum; Ecclesie militantis; Gloria resurrexit dominus.*
(M) *** None. H 71367 [id.]. Pomerium Musices, Blachly.

Dufay's *Missa ecce ancilla Domini* is one of his greatest works. Recent scholarship suggests that this Mass was conceived for the Cambrai Cathedral Choir and would have been performed without instrumental support.

Alexander Blachly uses ten singers in his account of the Mass, which tallies with recent research. There is no instrumental support whatever and the version Blachly records has the advantage of great textural accuracy. His edition returns to the manuscript sources. Much of the writing is austere (some of it only two-part), but its effect is of grave and compelling beauty.

Dukas, Paul (1865–1935)

L'Apprenti sorcier (*The Sorcerer's apprentice*).
(M) *** Chan. CBR/*CBT* 1003. SNO, Gibson – ROSSINI: *La Boutique fantasque;* SAINT-SAËNS: *Danse macabre.****
(M) *** Decca SPA 175. SRO, Ansermet (with Concert: '*Danse macabre*'***).
(M) *** Decca Jub. JB/*KJBC* 36 [Lon. CS 6367]. SRO, Ansermet – HONEGGER: *Pacific 231*; RAVEL: *Boléro* etc.***

L'Apprenti sorcier; La Péri (with *Fanfare*); *Polyeucte: overture.*
*** Ph. [9500 533/*7300 677*]. Rotterdam PO, Zinman.

L'Apprenti sorcier; Symphony in C.
** Decca SXL 6770. LPO, Weller.

Gibson is given the advantage of brilliant modern recording (althought the cassette has marginally less sparkle than the disc). His basic tempo is convincing and he secures excellent playing from the Scottish National Orchestra. The performance is straightforward rather than imaginatively evocative, but there is fine momentum and zest. Moreover the couplings in this medium-priced reissue are attractive, especially the splendid account of *La Boutique fantasque*.

Ansermet's performance is more relaxed, yet it has a cumulative effect: one has a feeling of real calamity before the magician hurriedly returns to put right the mischief his apprentice has wrought. There is atmosphere here, but the recording (though the Jubilee issue is equally impressive on disc or tape) has less brilliance than the Chandos version.

Those who cherish rosy memories of the pre-war set of *La Péri* by Philippe Gaubert and the Paris Conservatoire Orchestra will not be disappointed by this newcomer, which is every bit as haunting and atmospheric. In fact David Zinman and the Rotterdam Philharmonic give us what is arguably the finest account of Dukas's colourful score ever to have been put on record. Here is a conductor acutely sensitive to the most delicate colourings and the hushed atmosphere of this evocative score, and he captures its fairy-tale spirit better than any of his rivals. This account is better-played than Ansermet's from the late 1950s and more magical than the now deleted Boulez version, and it is certainly better recorded. The engineers have given us a natural balance with wide-ranging dynamics and a truthful perspective. *L'Apprenti sorcier* receives an effective performance, as does the less interesting *Polyeucte overture*. The cassette is one of Philips' best, although in *La Péri* textures are more refined in detail on the disc. (This record is withdrawn in the UK.)

Elgar with a French accent would be a fair description of Dukas's youthfully urgent symphony, written when he had turned thirty but was still just finding his feet as a composer. The link is César Franck, who indirectly influenced Elgar and provided a direct model for Dukas.

Though Weller's performance is not very affectionate, the incisiveness of the playing and the brilliance of the recording (in which the thickness of Dukas's orchestration is cleverly concealed) make it worth considering. *The Sorcerer's apprentice* is also played rather literally, although the performance is not without brilliance and a sense of the dramatic.

Piano Sonata in E flat min.; La Plainte au loin du Faune (*pour Le tombeau de Claude Debussy*)*; Prélude élégiaque* (*on a theme of Haydn*).
** EMI 2C 069 16288. Duchable.

Dukas wrote very little during his long life and this record by François Duchable contains three of his four piano works. The *Sonata* is not new to the catalgue (Ogdon recorded it in a box called 'Pianistic Philosophies' in the mid-1970s, and there was another version by Françoise Thinet) but Duchable has the measure of the challenge – and it is a powerful and symphonic score. It dates from the turn of the century and is densely textured and highly individual. Duchable also offers the late *Prélude élégiaque* of 1920 and the later tribute to Debussy written for *La Revue Musicale* in 1920. An interesting disc, but let down by a rather shallow and unsympathetic recording.

Ariane et Barbe-bleue (opera) complete.
*** Erato Dig. NUM 750693 (3). Ciesinski, Bacquier, Paunova, Schauer, Blanzat, Chamonin, Command, Fr. R. Ch. and O, Jordan.

Ariane et Barbe-bleue is a rarity and this is its first appearance on records. It is rich in invention and atmosphere, as one would expect from the composer of *La Péri* and *L'Apprenti sorcier*, and its vivid colours should ensure its wide appeal. Dukas was enormously self-critical and consigned an earlier opera, *Horn and Rimenhild*, to oblivion, along with much other music. *Ariane* is, like Debussy's *Pelléas*, to a Maeterlinck text but there is none of the half-lights and the dream-like atmosphere of the latter. The performance derives from a French Radio production and is with one exception well cast; its direction under the baton of Armin Jordan is sensitive and often powerful. The recording is eminently acceptable and the five sides of the set come for the price of four. There are exceptionally good notes by Harry Halbreich, and in addition to a line-by-line libretto, the booklet reproduces an article by Dukas himself from 1910 and a tribute to the work by Messiaen, reproduced from a 1936 issue of *La Revue Musicale*. This is a most enterprising and valuable issue and is strongly recommended.

Duparc, Henri (1848–1933)

Mélodies: *Au pays où se fait la guerre; L'Invitation au voyage; Le Manoire de Rosemonde; Phidylé; La Vie antérieure.*
❀ *** HMV ASD/*TC-ASD* 3455 [Ang. S 37401]. Baker, LSO, Previn – CHAUSSON: *Poème de l'amour*. *** ❀

Duparc, most sparing of composers, actually dared to orchestrate some of the handful of songs he wrote in his early career. Purist lovers of French mélodie will no doubt prefer the original piano accompaniments, but this record will triumphantly prove to non-specialists that the extra richness and colour of the orchestral version add to the depth and intensity of these exceptionally sensitive word-settings, especially in the greatest of them all, *Phidylé*. But as Baker and Previn present them, each one of these songs is a jewelled miniature of breathtaking beauty, and the clear, ripe, beautifully balanced recording is fully worthy of the performances. The cassette is marginally less clear than the disc, but the sound remains gloriously atmospheric.

Mélodies: *Chanson triste; Élégie; Extase; L'Invitation au voyage; Lamento; Le Manoir de Rosemonde; Phidylé; Sérénade Florentine; Soupir; Testament; La Vague et la cloche; La Vie antérieure.*
(M) *** EMI 2C 063 11678. Souzay, Baldwin.

A pity that Duparc's output for the voice can be accommodated on one record. One would give a lot for some more. As it is, the songs could find no more eloquent interpreter than Gérard Souzay, who also recorded them some twenty years ago for Philips. These performances are equally fine, and every bit as well recorded. A superlative record in every way.

Chanson triste; Extase; Phidylé; Testament.
*** Pearl SHE 524. Ian Partridge, Jennifer Partridge – FAURÉ: *Songs*.***

These four Duparc songs, including the most moving of all, *Phidylé*, make a splendid supplement to Ian Partridge's collection of Fauré songs. This is singing of supreme distinction, beautiful in every phrase, and the accompaniment by the singer's sister matches his imagination. Fair recording.

Chanson triste; L'Invitation au voyage.
C *** Ph. Dig. **410 043-2**; 6514/*7337* 199 [id.]. Ameling, San Francisco SO, De Waart – DEBUSSY: *La damoiselle élue*; RAVEL: *Shéhérazade*.*** C

L'Invitation au voyage gains from being orchestrated, with Ameling's pure and lovely voice warmly supported. *Chanson triste* is beautifully sung too, but it sounds slightly overblown with orchestral rather than piano accompaniment. An apt, unusual coupling for the two bigger works, beautifully recorded. There is a good chrome cassette, but it is the splendid compact disc that shows these performances off to best advantage: it is wonderfully atmospheric, with a natural balance for the voice and a beguilingly rich orchestral texture.

Dupré, Marcel (1886–1971)

Preludes and fugues, Nos. 1–3.
** Mercury SRI 75088 [id.]. Composer (organ of St Sulpice, Paris) – MESSIAEN: *Le Banquet céleste* etc.***

Dupré's writing is within the tradition shared by Vierne and Widor, but is what might be described as well wrought and the invention is not memorable. Played by the composer on an organ of his own choice, and very well recorded, its claims to be definitive are impossible to resist. But the Messiaen coupling is much more interesting music.

Duruflé, Maurice (born 1902)

Organ suite, Op. 5.
(*) Abbey LPB 792. Cleobury – FRANCK: *Grande pièce symphonique*.(*)

Now in his early eighties, Maurice Duruflé remains one of the least flamboyant and prolific of composers. He has published barely more than a dozen works in his lifetime, the best-known of which is his *Requiem*. The *Suite*, Op. 5, dates from the early 1930s and is a pleasing, atmospheric piece, fastidious in its layout and always dignified. Stephen Cleobury gives a fine account of the work, and the organ of Westminster Abbey is musically recorded; the dynamic range is wide, and the resonance of the Abbey and the discreet balance militate a little against the greatest clarity in the final *Toccata*. Yet on good equipment this will yield more than acceptable results, and since recordings of this fine music have never been legion, this is worth investigation.

Messe cum jubilo, Op. 11.
*** Argo ZRG 938. Roberts, Richard Hickox Singers, Hickox; Ross – LANGLAIS: *Mass*.**(*)

Duruflé's *Mass* is a rather serene if pale work, full of subtle, muted colourings and reflective in spirit. Not strongly distinctive but nonetheless rewarding, particularly in such capable hands as those of the Richard Hickox Singers and Alistair Ross (organ). Well-defined detail and good balance make this a more attractive proposition than the Langlais coupling.

Requiem, Op. 9.
**(*) Argo Dig. ZRDL/*KZRDC* 1009 [id.]. Palmer, Shirley-Quirk, Boys of Westminster Cath. Ch., LSO Ch., LSO, Hickox.

Requiem; Danse lente, Op. 6/2.
*** CBS 76633 [M 34547]. Te Kanawa, Nimsgern, Amb. S., Desborough School Ch., New Philh. O, Andrew Davis.

(i; ii) *Requiem;* (ii) *Prelude et fugue sur le nom d'Alain.*
*** Argo ZRZ 787 [id.]. (i) St John's College Ch., Camb., Guest; (ii) Cleobury (organ).

(i) *Requiem*. Motets on Gregorian chants: *Tantum ergo; Tu es Petrus.*
*** HMV Dig. ASD/*TCC-ASD* 4086 [Ang. DS 37813]. King's College Ch., Ledger, (i) with Baker, Roberts; Butt (organ).

Those who have sometimes regretted that the lovely Fauré *Requiem* remains unique in the output of that master of delicate inspiration should investigate this comparably evocative *Requiem* of Duruflé. The composer wrote it in 1947, overtly basing its layout and even the cut of its themes on the Fauré masterpiece. The result is far more than just an imitation, for (as it seems in innocence) Duruflé's inspiration is passionately committed. Andrew Davis directs a warm and atmospheric reading, using the full orchestral version with its richer colourings. Kiri Te Kanawa sings radiantly in the *Pie Jésu*, and the darkness of Siegmund Nimsgern's voice is well caught. In such a performance Duruflé establishes his claims for individuality even in the face of Fauré's comparable setting. The fill-up is welcome too, and the recording is excellent, nicely atmospheric.

Philip Ledger's version of the *Requiem* uses organ rather than orchestral accompaniment. (Duruflé made two orchestral versions of the score – Andrew Davis opts for the richer of the two.) Yet such is the clarity of the recording and the sense of atmosphere engendered by the performance (and enhanced by the acoustic) that one scarcely misses the additional dimension of colour that the orchestra provides. The singing is splendid, and the grave beauty and emotional restraint of Duruflé's music splendidly conveyed. Many will prefer this version to the Davis, the absence of the orchestra notwithstanding, as it is so beautifully recorded. The chrome cassette, however, transferred at only a modest level, has disappointingly poor definition, especially at the opening.

The earlier Argo account, recorded at St John's, uses trebles as soloists instead of women singers, even in the solo of *Pie Jésu* – exactly parallel to Fauré's setting of those words, which was indeed first sung by a treble. The alternative organ version is again used here, not so warmly colourful as the orchestral version, but very beautiful nonetheless. The organ piece, another sensitive example of Duruflé's withdrawn genius, makes an apt coupling. The recording is vividly atmospheric.

On the more recent Argo digital issue Hickox tempers the richness of the orchestral version by using boys' voices in the choir. He relishes the extra drama of orchestral accompaniment with biting brass at the few moments of high climax, though he does not always provide as luminous a texture as Andrew Davis on CBS. Felicity Palmer and John Shirley-Quirk sing with deep feeling and fine imagination, if not always with ideally pure tone. The recording has a pleasantly ecclesiastical ambience, which adds to the ethereal purity of the trebles. The stereo spread is very wide. There is an impressive chrome cassette, full and atmospheric and generally well focused.

Dušek, František Xaver (1731–99)

Piano concertos: in D; E flat.
(M) ** Sup. 1110 2850. Novotný, Pardubice State CO, Pešek.

As a glance at his dates will show, this Dušek is not the one with whom we are more familiar, Jan Ladislav Dusik or Dussek (1760–1812). He was in fact a friend of the Mozarts, and it was while staying with him in Prague that Mozart finished *Don Giovanni*. Apart from his importance as a teacher, Dušek played a role in the evolution of the keyboard concerto. These pieces are slight but have charm, and the slow movements are of particular interest on account of their being of much greater length than was customary. The performances are alert and responsive, and the recorded sound is very decent without being in the top flight.

Dvořák, Antonin (1841–1904)

Overtures: Carnaval, Op. 92; In Nature's Realm, Op. 91; My Home, Op. 62; Othello, Op. 93.
(M) ** Sup. 1110 2968. Czech PO, Neumann.

A welcome and useful anthology, bringing the three overtures of 1891–2 together with the earlier *My Home* of 1882. The Czech Philharmonic Orchestra are obviously on familiar territory and the wind playing in particular is very fine. Neumann's readings, however, while fresh and musical, lack something in flair. The Supraphon recording is bright but somewhat dry in the bass. Kertesz's version of *Carnaval* – see below – catches its exuberant holiday spirit with greater exhilaration.

Carnaval overture, Op. 92; The Golden Spinning Wheel, Op. 109; Scherzo capriccioso, Op. 109.

(M) *** Decca Jub. JB/*KJBC* 109. LSO, Kertesz.

For their Jubilee reissue, Decca have recoupled Kertesz's Dvořák series recorded with the LSO. This group, coupling *The Golden Spinning Wheel*, with its evocative horn calls, to outstanding versions of *Carnaval* and the *Scherzo capriccioso*, is most attractive. First-class LSO playing and vivid recording from a vintage Decca period. On cassette the transfer of *Carnaval* is slightly disappointing, the level down and the transients lacking crispness, but the other works sound well, especially *The Golden Spinning Wheel* which is strikingly vivid and rich.

Carnaval overture; Slavonic dances, Op. 46/1 and 3; Op. 72/2 and 7.

(M) ** CBS 60103/*40*- [MY/*MYT* 36716]. Cleveland O, Szell – SMETANA: *Vltava* etc.**

Superb playing from the Cleveland Orchestra and brilliantly zestful readings from Szell. The recording is very bright and forward in the CBS manner; if it had been richer this would have been a three-star issue, for the players readily convey their enjoyment of the music.

Cello concerto in B min., Op. 104.

*** DG 139 044/*923 098* [id.]. Rostropovich, Berlin PO, Karajan – TCHAIKOVSKY: *Rococo variations.****

(M) *** DG 2725/*3374* 107 (2). Rostropovich (as above with concertos by BOCCHERINI; SCHUMANN; VIVALDI – see Concerts.***).

(M) *** HMV SXLP/*TC-SXLP* 30176 [Sera. S/*4XG* 60136]. Rostropovich, RPO, Boult.

(M) *** DG Priv. 2535/*3335* 106 [id.]. Fournier, Berlin PO, Szell.

(B) *** CfP CFP/*TC-CFP* 41 4468-1/*4*. Robert Cohen, LPO, Macal – TCHAIKOVSKY: *Rococo variations.****

(*) Decca Dig. **410 144-2; SXDL/*KSXDC* 7608 [Lon. LDR/*5*- 71108]. Harrell, Philh. O, Ashkenazy – BRUCH: *Kol Nidrei.***(*)

(B) *(**) RCA VICS/*VK* 2002 [AGL1/*AGK1* 3878]. Piatigorsky, Boston SO, Munch.

*(*) HMV ASD/*TC-ASD* 3452 [Ang. S/*4XS* 37457]. Rostropovich, LPO, Giulini – SAINT-SAËNS: *Concerto No. 1.***

(B) *(*) Con. CC/*CCT* 7585 [Mercury 75045]. Starker, LSO, Dorati – BRUCH: *Kol Nidrei.**(*)

Cello concerto; Rondo in G min., Op. 94; Waldesruhe (Silent woods), Op. 68 (both for cello and orchestra).

(M) *** Ph. Seq. 6527/*7311* 186 [6570/*7310* 112]. Gendron, LPO, Haitink.

Cello concerto; Silent woods, Op. 68.

**(*) HMV ASD/*TC-ASD* 3652. Tortelier, LSO, Previn.

The larger-than-life musical personality of Rostropovich tends to dominate recordings of Dvořák's *Cello concerto*. His DG version is available coupled in two different ways, and his earlier account on HMV with Boult remains competitive, although the most recent partnership with Giulini produced disappointing results. Certainly the collaboration of Rostropovich and Karajan makes a superb version, warm as well as refined in reflection of the finest qualities in each of the two principals. If Rostropovich can sometimes sound self-indulgent in this most romantic of cello concertos, the degree of control provided by the conductor gives a firm yet supple base, and there have been few recorded accounts so deeply satisfying. The result is unashamedly romantic, with many moments of dalliance, but the concentration is never in doubt. Splendid playing by the Berliners, beautifully refined recording, and a bonus (not to be taken for granted with this concerto) in the shape of Tchaikovsky's glorious variations.

The cassette has recently been remastered and sounds well.

Rostropovich's earlier version (also now in the medium price-range) was recorded with Boult in the late 1950s and still sounds amazingly fresh and vital. No one would guess its age. The balance is superbly judged and the timbre truthful; the texture sounds open and vivid, so there need be no reservations in recommending this classic account, particularly at its new price. It competes very strongly with any of the available alternatives and will be preferred by many to them all. The cassette is strikingly successful: the orchestra has plenty of life and the cello timbre is warmly resonant yet clear.

If Gendron's performance, also reissued at medium price, is a little less larger-than-life than Rostropovich's, it is nonetheless well worth considering as an alternative. It is unidiosyncratic, marvellously fresh and lyrical, and has the advantage of impeccable orchestral support from the LPO under Haitink. There is a real spontaneity about this playing, and its warmth is splendidly captured by the Philips engineers, who produce first-class sound. There are two engaging fill-ups. There is a very good cassette.

Fournier's reading has a sweep of conception and richness of tone and phrasing which carry along the melodic lines with exactly the mixture of nobility and tension that the work demands. Fournier can relax and beguile the ear in the lyrical passages, and yet catch up the listener in his exuberance in the exciting finale. The phrasing in the slow movement is ravishing, and the interpretation as a whole balances beautifully. DG's recording is rich, forward and vivid, with a broad, warm tone for the soloist. This is yet another highly recommendable disc, and for those who prefer a straightforwardly romantic reading of this concerto it could prove first choice, irrespective of price. The cassette, however, is slightly fierce and not too well focused, with 'buzzy' cello timbre.

Robert Cohen was only twenty when he recorded the Dvořák *Concerto*, but his is anything but an immature reading, strong and forthright, very secure technically, with poetry never impaired by his preference for keeping steady speeds. The result is most satisfying, helped by comparably incisive and outstanding accompaniment from the Czech conductor Zdenek Macal. With first-rate modern recording and a generous coupling, it makes an excellent choice irrespective of price, and as a bargain issue it is outstanding. The cassette matches the disc very closely indeed; if anything, the cassette gives the cello slightly more body.

Lynn Harrell's newest recording of the Dvořák *Concerto* for Decca is a little disappointing and does not match his earlier RCA version, with the LSO under James Levine, at present out of the catalogue. The RCA collaboration proved powerful and sympathetic, with richly satisfying accounts of the first and second movements, culminating in a reading of the finale which proved the most distinctive of all. Here again the finale is the most successful, but generally the performance, though still impressive in its strength and detail, lacks the spontaneous power and incisiveness of the RCA account. The Decca digital sound is richly vivid (though forwardly balanced) and the compact disc is especially fine. There is a good chrome cassette.

Piatigorsky's performance has undoubted presence and fervour; he is at his finest here, and Munch provides a powerful and vivid accompaniment. But with a forward balance and a fierce recording – partly caused by the acoustic throwback of the Boston auditorium – this cannot be recommended very enthusiastically, even at bargain price.

The richness of Tortelier's reading has long been appreciated on record, and his 1978 recording with Previn has a satisfying centrality, not as passionately romantic as Rostropovich, not as urgent as Harrell on RCA, but with the tenderness as well as the power of the work held in perfect equilibrium. What is less perfect is the balance of the recording, favouring the cellist a little too much, though the fullness, weight and warmth of the EMI sound are impressive, with the strongly rhythmic playing of the LSO well caught. The cassette transfer catches the reverberant recording admirably, with richly resonant tone for the soloist.

Rostropovich's newest version (with Giulini) is his least successful on record. He makes heavy weather of most of the *Concerto*, and his unrelieved emotional intensity is matched by Giulini, who focuses attention on beauty of detail rather than structural cohesion. But of course there are many beauties that compel admiration, and the engineering is impressive.

Starker's performance has a Mercury source. It lacks romantic intensity (although Dorati certainly sets the scene with a passionate opening tutti). The soloist is not helped by a recording balance which slightly exaggerates the upper partials of the cello timbre at the expense of the overall body of sound.

Piano concerto in G min., Op. 33.

*** HMV ASD/*TC-ASD* 3371 [Ang. S 37329]. Sviatoslav Richter, Bav. State O, Carlos Kleiber.

(M) ** Sup. 1110 2373. Kvapil, Brno State PO, Jílek.

Dvořák's *Piano concerto* comes from a vintage period which also saw the completion of the *F major Symphony*. Richter plays the solo part in its original form (and not the more pianistically 'effective' revision), and his judgement is triumphantly vindicated. This is the most persuasive and masterly account of the *Concerto* ever committed to disc; its ideas emerge with an engaging freshness and warmth, while the greater simplicity of Dvořák's own keyboard writing proves in Richter's hands to be the more telling and profound. Never has the slow movement sounded so moving as it does here. Carlos Kleiber secures excellent results from the Bavarian orchestra, and the recording, though not in the demonstration class, has clarity and good definition to commend it. A most impressive record, which one hopes will restore the work to greater public favour. The cassette was originally transferred at too high a level, with resulting coarseness and distortion. It is likely to have been remastered by the time we are in print.

Radoslav Kvapil is an admired interpreter of Dvořák and has recorded all his piano music. He lacks the poetic insight of Richter, and the orchestral playing under František Jílek is no match for Kleiber's; nor is the recording so finely detailed. There are good things here, but it is very much a second choice.

Violin concerto in A min., Op. 53; Romance for violin and orchestra, Op. 11.

*** Ph. 9500 406/*7300 614* [id.]. Accardo, Concg. O, Sir Colin Davis.

*** HMV ASD 3120 [Ang. S/*4XS* 37069]. Perlman, LPO, Barenboim.

(M) *** Sup. 1410 2423. Suk, Czech PO, Neumann.

Accardo's is a noble performance and he is given splendid support by the Concertgebouw Orchestra under Sir Colin Davis. With such superb versions as Suk's and Perlman's on the market, any newcomer must have special claims. To begin with, the Philips recording is by far the most detailed and has greater body than its rivals. Secondly, the performance is finely characterized, with the distinguished soloist making the most but never too much of the rhetoric and poetry. Accardo is slightly too forward, perhaps, but, this small reservation apart, his version deserves unqualified praise. The slow movement is inward and the finale has a splendid singing quality, even if the Suk version has slightly more sparkle and spring in this movement. There is beautiful playing from all concerned in the *Romance* too. The cassette offers pleasingly full sound, but the upper range does not match that of the disc.

Admirers of Perlman can safely invest in his version. In warmth and virtuosity he matches Accardo and he is accorded a fine and clear recording, even if the Philips sound is marginally superior. This is a distinguished record and Perlman's account of the *Romance* is no less successful.

Suk recorded the same coupling in 1961, but this newer Supraphon recording is an improvement on the earlier disc. It is fresher and clearer, and although the balance places the soloist well forward, orchestral detail comes through. As before, Suk's performance is lyrical in the simplest possible way, and its eloquent innocence is endearing. The *Romance* is also played with skill and affection. At medium price this Supraphon issue is fully competitive.

Czech suite in D, Op. 36.

(M) ** Ph. Seq. 6527/*7311* 129 [id.]. ECO, Mackerras – VOŘÍŠEK: *Symphony*.**

Czech suite, Op. 39; Nocturne for strings in B, Op. 40; Polka for Prague students in B flat,

Op. 53a; Polonaise in E flat; Prague waltzes.
*** Decca Dig. SXDL/*KSXDC* 7522 [Lon. LDR/5- 71024]. Detroit SO, Dorati.

A collection of Dvořák rarities exhilaratingly performed and brilliantly recorded. The *Czech suite* can sometimes outstay its welcome, but certainly not here. The other items too have the brightness and freshness that mark out the Dvořák *Slavonic dances*, especially the *Polka* and *Polonaise*. The most charming piece of all is the set of *Waltzes* written for balls in Prague – Viennese music with a Czech accent – while the lovely *Nocturne* with its subtle drone bass makes an apt filler. The recording has an attractive warmth and bloom to balance its brightness, and this is as impressive on cassette as it is on disc, although on the tape there is a momentary excess of bass resonance in the *Polonaise*.

Mackerras gives a fresh, lively performance of the *Czech suite* and the Philips recording is naturally balanced. For those fancying the attractive Voříšek *Symphony* as coupling, this could be a good medium-priced choice. The cassette is of Philips' best quality, full and clear.

Legends, Op. 59.
(M) *** Sup. 110 1393. Brno State PO, Pinkas.

Now that Leppard's Philips record has gone, Dvořákians will find this well-recorded Supraphon issue an indispensable alternative. The warmth and colour of this delightful music is fully brought out, the lyrical character of the writing caught with the special idiomatic quality that Czech performers can bring to Dvořák.

Scherzo capriccioso; Slavonic rhapsody No. 3, Op. 45/3.
*** HMV SLS 5151 (2) [Ang. SB 3870]. Dresden State O, Berglund – SMETANA: *Má Vlast.****

Berglund's *Scherzo capriccioso* is warmly engaging, not the most brilliantly exciting version on record – for that one must turn to Kertesz on Jubilee coupled with *Carnaval* and *The Golden spinning wheel*, see above – but with plenty of impetus and a lilting second subject. The *Slavonic rhapsody* is superbly done, and the recording is first-class.

Serenade for strings in E, Op. 22.
*** Ph. 9500 105 [id.]. ECO, Leppard – TCHAIKOVSKY: *String serenade.****
*** DG Dig. **400 038-2**; 2532/*3302* 012 [id.]. Berlin PO, Karajan – TCHAIKOVSKY: *String serenade.**** C
(*) Argo ZRG/*KZRC* 848 [id.]. ASMF, Marriner – TCHAIKOVSKY: *String serenade.**
(*) Argo ZRG/*KZRC* 670 (as above, cond. Marriner) – GRIEG: *Holberg suite.**
(*) ASV Dig. DCA/*ZCDCA* 505. O of St John's, Lubbock – TCHAIKOVSKY: *String serenade.*(*)

(i) *Serenade for strings;* (ii) *Serenade for wind in D min., Op. 44.*
C *** Ph. **400 020-2**; 6514/*7337* 145 [id.]. ASMF, Marriner.
(M) **(*) Sup. 50760. (i) Czech PO, Vlach; (ii) Prague Chamber Harmony, Turnovsky.
(M) ** EMI Em. Dig. EMX/*TC-EMX* 2013. (i) ECO, Mackerras; (ii) ECO (without conductor).

Serenade for wind, Op. 44.
(M) *** Ph. Seq. 412 004-1/*4*. Neth. Wind Ens., De Waart – GOUNOD: *Petite symphonie;* SCHUBERT: *Octet, D. 72.* ***
(M) *** Decca Jub. JB/*KJBC* 87. LSO (members), Kertesz – BRAHMS: *Serenade No. 2.****
*** CRD CRD 1110/*CRDC 4110*. Nash Ens. – KROMMER: *Octet-Partita.****
(B) ** PRT GSGC/*ZCGC* 2037. Hallé O (members), Barbirolli – GOUNOD: *Petite symphonie.***

There is a wide choice here and readers must think carefully about couplings. Leppard's outstanding analogue version of the *String serenade* remains highly desirable, but Karajan's similar Berlin Philharmonic coupling is very fine too, and his performance of the Tchaikovsky *Serenade* is perhaps the most beautifully played ever committed to disc, with the DG compact disc of demonstration quality. (Marriner's vintage early Argo recording of the Tchaikovsky *Serenade* is also available in a mid-priced Jubilee reissue, more appropriately coupled with the *Souvenir de Florence*.)

An obvious primary recommendation would therefore seem to lie with Marriner's newest (Philips) version of the Dvořák *String serenade* which is aptly joined with the lesser-known, but equally delightful, wind piece. This latest issue is also far preferable as a performance to his Argo account. Earlier mannerisms (as at the start) are eliminated, with speeds ideally chosen and with wonderfully refined yet spontaneous-sounding and resilient playing. The *Wind serenade* on the reverse is just as stylish and beautifully sprung, and the recording is outstandingly vivid. With a gloriously rich and firm bass, the compact disc brings the best sound of all, for there the brightness of the treble is nicely balanced against the ample lower register. The *Wind serenade* has an uncanny sense of immediacy, set against a rather drier acoustic. The chrome tape is full but lacks range in the work for strings; Op. 44 is livelier.

On Leppard's Philips disc the English Chamber Orchestra is given superb analogue recording, wide in range and natural in timbre. Leppard's approach is direct, even robust, perhaps not quite as refined as Marriner, but missing that overtly expressive quality which at the very opening of the Argo discs verges on indulgence. The tempi of the allegros have a strong momentum, but Leppard's natural flexibility prevents the brisk manner from losing its resilience. The finale is wonderfully bright and invigorating.

Karajan's digital version is given a recording of striking finesse and detail. The brilliance of the LP is slightly tempered on the compact disc, which is transferred at a marginally lower level than the Tchaikovsky coupling. The recording has plenty of atmosphere and a very wide dynamic range, plus a slight tendency for the image to recede a little at pianissimo level. Karajan's approach is warmly affectionate in the opening movement and there is greater expressive weight than with Leppard, with the colouring darker. Yet the playing is both sympathetic and very polished; though the focus is slightly more diffuse and less firm in the bass than the Tchaikovsky coupling (which earns a technical accolade), many will feel that the softer delineation suits the music. The chrome cassette too is of DG's best quality, matching the compact disc quite closely.

As can be seen above, Marriner's Argo version is offered in a choice of couplings. The sound is agreeably rich-textured and some ears might find that this combination of almost velvety timbres with Marriner's somewhat indulgent manner, particularly in the first movement, is not entirely attuned to the innocent simplicity of Dvořák's invention. But with such beguiling playing the performance is undoubtedly engaging, and the alternative couplings are superbly done. Both Argo cassettes are of first-class quality.

It was Lubbock and the Orchestra of St John's who provided the digital debut for the Dvořák *Serenade*. The strings are given striking presence and focus here, although the sound is very brightly lit in the treble (the cassette matches the disc closely in this respect), and the resonance of middle and bass frequencies is less telling than in (for instance) Leppard's analogue recording. Lubbock gives a strongly characterized performance, with an athletic scherzo and brilliant finale contrasting well with the work's lyrical elements. Those who enjoy crystal-clear sound may find this worth investigating; others will feel that Karajan makes a better digital choice for this coupling, for the Berlin Philharmonic playing is peerless.

The Czech performances repeat a coupling Supraphon made famous as an early mono LP. Then Talich gave a magical account of the *String serenade* and it was coupled to a wonderfully earthy performance of the companion work for wind by a group of professors from the Prague Conservatoire. As so often happens on the gramophone, this remake does not quite match that earlier success. Czech chamber-music playing is justly renowned, but Josef Vlach does not find the incandescence that illuminated the Talich performance; and the wind group, although it has attractive moments of lightness and humour, has not quite the earthy grace those professors found. But having said this, the present pairing is still most enjoyable. It is full and clear as a recording, and the playing in the *String serenade* has an easy, unforced way with it that suits Dvořák's ingenuous mood. The middle movements are especially warm and beautiful.

The Eminence issue offers sound that is

exceptionally clear in both works, although the strings in Op. 22 have a degree of 'digital edge' that some ears may find slightly aggressive. The cassette tempers this slightly, and as otherwise disc and tape are closely matched some will prefer the latter. Mackerras is surprisingly direct in the *String serenade* and his seemingly deliberate lack of charm is exaggerated by the sound. The *Wind serenade* is played without a conductor and the result is agreeably crisp and sparkling, with vivid recording. At mid-price this makes quite a good recommendation.

In the *Wind serenade* the playing of the Netherlands Ensemble admirably blends spontaneity and discipline. It is not easy to imagine a more refreshing performance and the recording is vividly truthful.

Kertesz too gives a delightful performance of the enchanting *Wind serenade*, which is accorded splendid treatment by the Decca engineers. The cassette transfer has a full, lively quality, although the resonance tends to spread the focus somewhat in the slow movement.

The Nash Ensemble can hold their own with the competition in the *D minor Serenade*, and their special claim tends to be the coupling, a Krommer rarity that is well worth hearing. The CRD version of the Dvořák is very well recorded (the chrome cassette is the best available of this work) and the playing is very fine indeed, robust yet sensitive to colour, and admirably spirited.

Sir John Barbirolli directs a performance of persuasive charm, and his affection is answered with good playing. Originally this issue suffered from pre-echo and other cutting faults, but recent pressings seem to have cured these defects. A good bargain recommendation. The cassette however is insecure and poorly focused.

Slavonic dances Nos. 1–16, Opp. 46/1–8; 72/1–8.

(M) **(*) CBS 60263/*40*- [Odys. Y2-33524/ *YT 34626/7*]. Cleveland O, Szell.

(M) ** Sup. 1110 2981/2 [PRO 2020]. Czech PO, Košler.

Slavonic dances Nos. 1–16; My Home overture, Op. 62; Scherzo capriccioso, Op. 66.

(M) *** DG Priv. 2726 122 (2) [2530 466 and 593]. Bav. RSO, Kubelik.

Slavonic dances Nos. 1, 3–9.

(M) ** Ph. Seq. 6527/*7311* 032. Minneapolis SO, Dorati – BRAHMS: *Hungarian dances.****

Slavonic dances Nos. 1, 3, 7, 10, 16.

(M) **(*) DG Sig. 2543/*3343* 509 [(d.) 138 080]. Berlin PO, Karajan – SMETANA: *Vltava* etc.**(*)

Slavonic dances Nos. 1, 3, 8, 9–*10*.

(M) *** Decca VIV/*KVIC* 18 [Lon. STS 15009]. VPO, Reiner – BRAHMS: *Hungarian dances.****

(M) *** Decca SPA 202 [Lon. STS 15409]. Israel PO, Kertesz – SMETANA: *Vltava* etc.***

Slavonic dances Nos. 1, 5, 6, 8, 9, 10.

(M) *** Decca Jub. 411 725-1/*4*. LSO, Boskovsky – BRAHMS: *Hungarian dances.****

Slavonic dances Nos. 3 and 10.

*** HMV ASD/*TC-ASD* 3312. Cleveland O, Szell – BRAHMS: *Double concerto.****

Dvořák's sixteen *Slavonic dances* are not easy to fit on two LP sides (with dividing bands) without some loss of amplitude or range in the recording. DG have solved this problem (but relatively expensively) by using two full discs with fillers. For those who want the best regardless of cost, this pair of medium-priced LPs makes a first-class recommendation for the complete set, with polished, sparkling orchestral playing splendidly recorded. The extra items are very well done too.

However, many may prefer the alternative CBS disc under Szell. Even though the recording is harder in outline and not ideally transparent, with careful use of the controls it can be made to sound well. And Szell provides a really first-rate set, with brilliant and often virtuoso playing, witness the confidence of the strings, and the superbly moulded rubato of the reprise of the main theme in Op. 72/2. This is an orchestra glorying in its own virtuosity in the most musical way, and Dvořák's texture glows with life. Szell's rubato, here as throughout, is most skilfully managed, and the bright Cleveland sound suits his extrovert approach. Perhaps in some of the gentler moments a touch more intimacy would have added an extra degree of charm, but for the most part these performances are very satisfying. There is no appreciable difference in sound between the disc and the excellent chrome tape. In the USA, Szell's recording is spread over two discs and cassettes.

The Czech Philharmonic Orchestra have a special feeling for this repertoire, and provide touches of phrasing and colour that are not always found in other versions. However, the recording, though good, has not quite the brilliance and range of Kubelik's set and there are no fillers. Košler's direction is alert and sympathetic, but Kubelik sparkles even more.

Of the shorter collections, Boskovsky's Decca issue with the LSO makes an easy first choice, with vivacious performances matched by really first-class recording. Boskovsky's degree of flexibility is such as to make the music sound freshly-minted without overdoing the rubato.

Kertesz's disc too is first-rate value. The Israel orchestra is not one of the world's finest, but here the playing is irresistible in its gaiety and vivacious colouring. The furiants go with the wind, but Kertesz maintains the underlying lyricism of the music. The recording is marginally over-reverberant and may need a slight treble control, but is otherwise not too dated.

Reiner's way with Dvořák's dance music is indulgent but has plenty of sparkle, and the Vienna Philharmonic are clearly enjoying themselves. The sound of this reissue hardly dates at all, and any reservations about the conductor's idiosyncrasies are soon forgotten in the pleasure of listening to such colourful music so vivaciously presented. The cassette matches the disc closely.

Virtuoso performances from Karajan, which remain stylish because of the superbly polished playing. The recording is rather overbrilliant, but can be tamed. Disc and chrome tape are closely matched.

Dorati's performances are vivid and sparkling, but the Minneapolis recording has an early Mercury source and though it does not lack brilliance, it is not as full-bodied as the excellent Brahms coupling. There is a good equivalent cassette.

Szell's HMV performances are brilliant and polished, yet have no lack of warmth. They make an excellent fill-up for one of the finest available performances of Brahms's *Double concerto.*

SYMPHONIES

Symphonies Nos. 1–9.
(M) *** Decca D6 D7(7) [Vox SVBX 5137/9]. LSO, Kertesz.
(M) **(*) DG 2740 237(9). Berlin PO, Kubelik.
(M) ** Ph. 6770 045. LSO, Rowicki.

Kertesz's idiomatic and exciting performances of the symphonies are here coupled economically together in an album of seven records, a magnificent memorial to a conductor who died sadly young.

The Kubelik set originally appeared in the early 1970s as part of DG's Symphony edition. It has much to recommend it: first and foremost, the glorious playing of the Berlin Philharmonic and the natural warmth that Kubelik brings to his music-making. He sounds less convinced by the earlier symphonies than Kertesz and in No. 3, for example, he sounds almost routine by comparison with the pioneering stereo performance of Vaclav Smetáček. Indeed, taken overall, the Kertesz is the more vital and invigorating set, but in the later symphonies, Kubelik is very impressive indeed and in spite of some idiosyncratic but not unidiomatic touches, he achieves glowing performances of Nos. 6–9, all of which are of three-star quality. The recordings are all good though they are not quite as fresh and transparent as the quality Decca achieved for Kertesz or Philips for Rowicki. At mid-price, however, this is still a most desirable set.

Rowicki's Dvořák cycle was rather overshadowed when it first appeared on separate records by the Kertesz series with the same orchestra. Heard as a whole in this mid-price box, Rowicki's readings present a consistent and fairly satisfying view of Dvořák, slightly understating the expressiveness of slow movements and often in fast movements adding a touch of fierceness. The opening of No. 6, for example, with the syncopated accompaniment very clearly defined, sounds unusually fresh and individual, even if one would not always want to hear it interpreted in that way. The recording is pleasantly refined, excellent for its mid-1960s vintage.

Symphony No. 1 in C min. (The Bells of Zlonice), Op. 3.
(M) *** Decca Jub. JB/*KJBC* 110 [(d) in SVBX 5137]. LSO, Kertesz.
(M) *** Sup. 1110 2877. Czech PO, Neumann.

This symphony, written early in 1865, was lost for over half a century, and even when the score turned up in Germany in the possession of a namesake of the composer (no relation) it had to wait years for performance, and was not published until 1961. But Dvořák remembered it when on the fly-leaf of the score of the *New World* he made a complete list of his symphonies. Clearly, had he kept hold of the score he would have made revisions. Though the piece took him only five weeks to write, it is the longest of all his symphonies – over fifty-four minutes in the Kertesz performance – and the fluency is not always matched by the memorability of the material. But it still has much attractive writing in it, and no one should miss it who has enjoyed the other early Dvořák symphonies. Zlonice was the place where Dvořák served his musical (and butcher's) apprenticeship, but the music is not intended to convey a programme. The LSO under Kertesz play excellently and give us the complete score without any of the cuts introduced into the earlier LP on Supraphon under Václav Neumann. The Decca recording has splendid body and presence; the cassette transfer is admirably lively and vivid, with a striking upper range, although it is a little dry in the bass.

In his newest recording Neumann does not observe Dvořák's first movement exposition repeat, but that is not necessarily a disadvantage, for the material contains much repetitive rhetoric. In general Neumann's account has more forward thrust than Kertesz's and the Czech playing shows greater expressive fervour, especially telling in the finale. The Supraphon sound is brighter than the Decca, with slightly more vivid inner detail; it also has a fiercer upper range. But the performance is undoubtedly first-class; the Czech musicians are undoubtedly very much at home in the music and their commitment is strongly communicated. The score is played complete.

Symphony No. 2 in B flat, Op. 4.
(M) *** Decca Jub. JB/*KJBC* 111 [(d) in SVBX 5137]. LSO, Kertesz.

Dvořák wrote his *Second Symphony* in 1865 within months of his *First*, but then he left it on the shelf for a full fifteen years before submitting it to a thorough revision. The original 260 pages of score were contracted to 212, and though this left the finale in an oddly unbalanced state, it is suprising that Dvořák's publisher, Simrock, refused to take the work when it was submitted to him along with Symphonies Nos. 3 and 4. Admittedly the ideas are not so strongly Dvořákian as they might be, and some movements tend to outstay their welcome, but anyone who has ever been charmed by Dvořák's wide-eyed genius will find much to enjoy, notably in the highly engaging ideas of the first movement. One oddity – and weakness – is that each movement has a slow introduction, a case of the composer 'clearing his throat' before launching out. As in his other Dvořák performances, Kertesz takes a crisp, fresh, straightforward approach to the music, and the recording is first-rate. Thus this symphony is admirably served in every way, and the scherzo has all the authentic, idiomatic flavour one could possibly want. The recording has the finest qualities of the Decca set. The high-level cassette transfer is first-class, full and lively and matching the disc fairly closely.

Symphony No. 3 in E flat, Op. 10; Symphonic variations, Op. 78.
(M) *** Decca Jub. JB/*KJBC* 112 [(d) in SVBX 5137]. LSO, Kertesz.

This was the first of Dvořák's symphonies to show the full exuberance of his genius. When he wrote it in 1873 – eight years after the first two – he was very much under the influence of Wagner, but nowhere do the Wagnerian ideas really conceal the essential Dvořák. Even the unashamed crib from *Lohengrin* in the middle section (D flat major) of the slow movement has a Dvořákian freshness, particularly here, as Kertesz adopts a fastish speed – faster than the score would strictly allow – and deliberately lightens the texture. This very long slow movement is in any case the weakest of the three, but the outer movements are both delightful and need no apology whatever. The very opening of the symphony with its 6/8 rhythm and rising-scale motifs can hardly miss, and the dotted rhythms of the second subject are equally engaging. For its Jubilee reissue the symphony has been generously recoupled with the *Symphonic variations*, a splendid work, with Brahmsian derivations but always showing the Czech composer's freshness of spirit, which Kertesz readily demonstrates. The playing of the LSO is consistently alert and polished, and the Decca recording is bright and vivid on disc and cassette alike.

Symphony No. 4 in D min., Op. 13; In Nature's Realm overture, Op. 91.
(M) *** Decca Jub. JB/*KJBC* 113. LSO, Kertesz.

Compared with the exuberant symphonies which flank it on either side in the Dvořák canon, this is a disappointment. The opening theme – a fanfare-like idea – is not so characterful as one expects, but then the second subject soars aloft in triple time. The slow movement begins with so close a crib from the *Pilgrims' Music* in *Tannhäuser* one wonders how Dvořák had the face to write it, but the variations which follow are attractive, and the scherzo has a delightful lolloping theme, which unfortunately gives way to a horribly blatant march trio with far too many cymbal crashes in it. The finale, despite rhythmic monotony, has at least one highly characteristic and attractive episode. And, whatever the shortcomings of the work, there is much that is memorable. Kertesz gives a good dramatic performance, and receives excellent recording quality. Compared with the disc the cassette has a slight loss of focus in tutti, caused by the resonance.

Symphony No. 5 in F (originally Op. 24 (1875); published as Op. 76)*; Hussite overture, Op. 67.*
(M) *** Decca Jub. JB/*KJBC* 114 [(d) Lon. CS 6511]. LSO, Kertesz.
(M) **(*) Sup. 110 1333. Czech PO, Neumann.

Even more than most Dvořák, the *Fifth Symphony* is a work to make one share, if only for a moment, in the happy emotions of a saint, and what could be more welcome in modern, nerve-racked life? The feeling of joy is here expressed so intensely that it provokes tears rather than laughter, and it is hard to understand why this marvellous work has been neglected for so long. It used to be called the *Pastoral*, but although it shares Beethoven's key and uses the flute a great deal (a Dvořákian characteristic) the nickname is not specially apt. What initially strikes one are the echoes of Wagner – forest murmurs (Bohemian ones) in the opening pages, a direct lift from *Siegfried's Rhine Journey* in the second theme and so on – but by the time he wrote the work, 1875, Dvořák's individuality as a musician was well established, and the composer's signature is in effect written on every bar. The slow movement is as beautiful as any in the symphonies, the scherzo is a gloriously bouncing piece with themes squandered generously, and the finale, though long, is intensely original in structure and argument. Kertesz's performance is straight and dramatic, with tempi very well chosen to allow for infectious rhythmic pointing. The new Jubilee coupling is the *Hussite overture*, patriotic in inspiration and including themes based on the Hussite hymn and St Wenceslas plainchant. Excellent Decca recording throughout, with the first-class cassette making a very close match with the disc.

As in their recording of the *First Symphony*, the Czechs show a more positive ardour than the playing of the LSO. With Kertesz the symphony is made to fit into an overall European tradition and at times evokes associations with Glazounov. The Czechs make the music very much their own, and the playing has striking thrust and individuality of character. The woodwind in the scherzo is a delight. The Supraphon sound is brighter than the Decca, not always to advantage, although detail is that bit clearer.

Symphony No. 6 in D, Op. 60; My Home overture, Op. 62.
(M) *** Decca Jub. JB/*KJBC* 115. LSO, Kertesz.
** CBS Dig. 36708 [id.]. Philh. O, Andrew Davis.

If the three immediately preceding Dvořák symphonies reflect the influence of Wagner, this one just as clearly reflects that of Brahms, and particularly of Brahms's *Second Symphony*. Not only the shape of themes but the actual layout of the first movement has strong affinities with the Brahmsian model, but Kertesz's performance effectively underlines the individuality of the writing as well. This is a marvellous work that with the *Fifth* and *Seventh* forms the backbone of the Dvořák cycle, and that is hardly an idea we should have been likely to advance before Kertesz gave us fresh insight into these vividly inspired works. His reading is fresh, literal and dramatic in his characteristic Dvořák manner, and his tempi are eminently well-chosen. The *My Home overture* was written as an expression of patriotic Czech sentiment at a time when, under the thumb of the Austrians, the Czechs were turning to music as an important safety-valve. The themes are taken from Czech folk music (one of them will be recognized from the Czech national anthem). The excellent recording is well up to the high standard of the series, with little to choose between disc and cassette.

Andrew Davis gives a strong and fresh performance which yet lacks a little in idiomatic warmth. It is a pity that he omits the exposition repeat in the first movement. The recording is warm and well-balanced, but at full-price this does not compete with the Decca issue, which also offers an extra work.

Symphony No. 7 in D min., Op. 70.
*** Ph. 9500 132/*7300 535* [id.]. Concg. O, Sir Colin Davis.
(M) *** Sup. Dig. 1110 3139. Czech PO, Neumann.

Symphony No. 7; Legends, Op. 59/4, 6, and 7.
(B) ** PRT GSGC/*ZCGC* 2057. Hallé O, Barbirolli.

Symphony No. 7; The Noonday Witch, Op. 108.
(M) *** Decca Jub. JB/*KJBC* 116 [(d) in SVBX 5139]. LSO, Kertesz.

The delightful *Seventh* is surprisingly under-represented in the current catalogue. With Paita's outstanding version currently unobtainable, and Monteux's famous early Decca account still not reissued, choice is relatively restricted. Fortunately Sir Colin Davis's Philips recording with its bracing rhythmic flow is refreshingly direct and has a good matching tape, both brilliant and full. The typically refined Philips recording (one or two odd balances apart) matches Davis's clean, urgent approach. In the scherzo, with its attractive cross rhythms he marks the sforzandos more sharply than usual, keeping rhythms very exact. There is a toughness and fierceness in the outer movements, but there is resilience too; and the slow movement brings the most distinctive performance of all, less sweet than usual, almost Brucknerian in its hushed nobility and sharply terraced contrasts.

Neumann in his later digital version remains a straight, direct interpreter of Dvořák rather than an affectionate one, but the rhythmic style is lighter, and more pointed. At mid-price with good recording it is a first-rate choice although, unlike Kertesz, there is no coupling.

Kertesz's version of the *D minor Symphony* was one of the first to be recorded in his LSO series, following soon after his extremely successful version of the *Eighth*. However, whereas that performance has striking extrovert brilliance, the approach to the *Seventh* is essentially relaxed. The tension is well maintained, but the voltage is lower, and the climaxes do not catch fire with quite the same vividness as in the rest of the cycle. Even so, with warm orchestral playing there is much to give pleasure, and there is a burst of energy in the finale. For the Jubilee reissue, Decca have added Kertesz's colourful and atmospheric portrayal of *The Noonday Witch* (the traditional ogress threatened to erring children by distraught mothers). With excellent sound this is certainly attractive at medium price, and the cassette transfer is of Decca's best quality, both full and lively. The symphonic poem – which opens the proceedings, with the first movement of the symphony following – has striking colour and warmth.

Barbirolli makes a fair recommendation in the bargain range. The first movement has a fine lyrical exhilaration; the slow movement has stature and warmth, and the scherzo individuality. The finale gathers momentum to become highly exciting. The snag is the recording, which tends to be gritty in the treble, with not enough weight for the upper strings, and rather light and dead in the bass. However, with flexible controls an acceptable sound can be obtained. The *Legends* are better recorded and make an attractive bonus. The cassette offers bright, clear sound in the symphony but the range is restricted on top in the *Legends*, though still agreeable.

Symphony No. 8 in G, Op. 88.
*** Ph. 9500 317/*7300 611* [id.]. Concg. O, Sir Colin Davis.
*** Ph. Dig. 6514 050/*7337 050* [id.]. Minnesota SO, Marriner.
(M) *** Decca Jub. JB/*KJBC* 71. VPO, Karajan – TCHAIKOVSKY: *Romeo and Juliet.****
*** DG Priv. 2535/*3335* 397. Berlin PO, Kubelik.
(M) ** Ph. Seq. 6527/*7311* 199. LSO, Rowicki.
** DG Dig. 2532/*3302* 034 [id.]. VPO, Maazel.

Symphony No. 8; Carnaval overture.
** ASV ALH/*ZCALH* 912. Hallé O, Loughran.

Symphony No. 8; Scherzo capriccioso.
(B) **(*) PRT GSGC/*ZCGC* 2056. Hallé O, Barbirolli.
*(*) HMV ASD/*TC-ASD* 4058 [Ang. SZ 37719]. LPO, Rostropovich.

Symphony No. 8; The Water Goblin, Op. 107.
(M) *** Decca Jub. JB/*KJBC* 117 [(d) Lon. STS 15526]. LSO, Kertesz.

With the appearance of a number of new recordings and the reissue of some very successful older ones, the choice for Dvořák's *G major Symphony* is wide and varied. For those seeking a new recording of the highest quality and prepared to pay premium price even though no coupling is offered, the outstanding Philips issue played by the Amsterdam Concertgebouw Orchestra under Sir Colin Davis must receive the strongest advocacy. The reading has Davis's characteristic directness, and the performance balances an engaging zestful exuberance in the outer movements with a beautifully played and eloquent *Adagio* and a lightly pointed scherzo. Here the Amsterdam strings have a delightful lyrical freshness in the trio, and there is a spontaneous burst of sheer high spirits in the coda. The recorded sound is excellent in every way on both disc and tape (in the latter a slight bass cut improves the balance).

In the re-shuffling of Kertesz's Dvořák series for the Jubilee reissues, the particularly apt pairing with the *Scherzo capriccioso* has been abandoned in favour of Dvořák's folktale setting about a malevolent *Water Goblin*. Kertesz's reading of the *G major Symphony* has long been famous for its freshly spontaneous excitement, with well-judged tempi throughout and an affectionately expressive account of the slow movement. The sound balance is forward and brightly lit, but is notable also for the warmth of the middle and lower strings. The performance of the symphonic poem too is highly evocative and atmospherically and vividly recorded. The cassette offers demonstration quality in the symphony, admirably fresh and vivid; in the symphonic poem the focus is slightly less clean.

Marriner's is a performance which more than any presents the smiling side of Dvořák. In principle one might object to the very relaxed espressivo manner in the first movement, but Marriner is so persuasive that the joy and felicity are irresistible. The slow movement is both genial and elegant, and the third has a delectable Viennese lilt. The finale very much breathes the air of the *Slavonic dances*, with fine rhythmic bite and no pomposity whatever. On this showing Marriner and the Minnesota orchestra have built up a superb rapport. The refinement of the playing goes with fresh, clean-cut digital sound, finely balanced. Unfortunately the chrome cassette is slightly bass-heavy and the upper range lacks range and brilliance.

The other Jubilee issue, from Karajan and the Vienna Philharmonic, is also generously recoupled with an excellent 1961 recording of Tchaikovsky's *Romeo and Juliet*. Karajan's performance has the merit of superb orchestral playing, with the Vienna strings at their creamiest. There are moments of self-indulgence in the scherzo, but for the most part this is a most winning performance, blending polish and spontaneity in almost equal measure. The orchestra sound as if they are enjoying this symphony – and so do we. The recording too still sounds wonderfully fresh and finely detailed. The cassette matches the disc closely, though fractionally drier in the bass.

Kubelik's Privilege reissue also still holds its place at the top of the list. Kubelik's recording is hardly less brilliant than Kertesz's Decca, yet the balance is slightly more distanced, so that the orchestral perspective is highly convincing. The performance is outstandingly fine. Without personal idiosyncrasy (except for a modest touch of indulgence for the string theme in the trio of the scherzo) this is a vibrant reading, very faithful to the composer's intentions, with the personality of the orchestra coming through strongly. The cassette transfer too is outstanding, one of DG's best, with fresh, vivid upper strings, plenty of bloom on the orchestra and excellent detail.

Barbirolli's performance of this symphony was one of his best Pye records. The reading has immense vitality and forward impetus, the kind of spontaneous excitement that is rare in the recording studio, and yet the whole performance is imbued with a delightful, unforced lyricism. Only in the third movement does Sir John miscalculate. When the strings take over the main tune of the trio he indulges in a heavy vibrato and fruity portamento which the Philadelphia Orchestra's strings might have brought off but the Hallé cannot. But this is a small blot on an otherwise remarkably good performance. The recording can be made to sound well, and the *Scherzo capriccioso*, if not on the level of the symphony, is warm and exciting. The cassette sounds vivid and lively on side one, but at the turn-over the upper range is restricted and the finale and the *Scherzo capriccioso* lack bite and brilliance.

Loughran's Hallé recording is not very competitive at full-price, in spite of an enjoyably lively bonus in the *Carnaval overture*. The recording has little presence and certainly does not flatter the orchestra, its balance contributing a degree of reticence to the proceedings. Yet the playing is fresh (especially the woodwind) and Loughran's reading is musical and direct, if not very individual.

Rowicki's reading, too, is sympathetic and without personal idiosyncrasy. Indeed the performance is rather anonymous in character, although it is well played and given a naturally balanced recording of good Philips vintage. But with Karajan and Kertesz available in the same price range (each offering a substantial coupling) this Sequenza issue is hardly competitive. There is a first-class cassette transfer.

Maazel's is a fierce performance, lacking the glow of warmth one associates with this work. Despite excellent, incisive playing the hardness of the reading is underlined by the recording balance, which favours a bright treble against a rather light bass. Though the trumpet fanfare heralding the start of the finale is wonderfully vivid, the sound lacks something in body.

Rostropovich shares with Barbirolli Kertesz's old coupling of the *G major Symphony* and *Scherzo capriccioso*, but with slow tempi and a consciously espressivo manner the performance of the symphony refuses to catch fire, and in the slow movement Rostropovich sounds too studied and unspontaneous. The *Scherzo capriccioso* is far more incisive and energetic, but here, as in the symphony, the recording balance favours the treble and there is a marked absence of bass. The sound on cassette is also rather fierce and dry, although the *Scherzo capriccioso* is fuller in body than the symphony.

Symphony No. 9 in E min. (*From the New World*), *Op. 95*.

(M) *** DG Priv. 2535/*3335* 473 [2530 415]. Berlin PO, Kubelik.

*** Ph. 9500 511/*7300 671* [id.]. Concg. O, Sir Colin Davis.

*** HMV ASD/*TC-ASD* 3407 [Ang. S/*4XS* 37437]. Berlin PO, Karajan – SMETANA: *Vltava*.***

*** DG 138 922/*923 008* [id.]. Berlin PO, Karajan.

(M) *** HMV SXLP/*TC-SXLP* 100491-1/*4*. Berlin PO, Karajan – SMETANA: *Vltava*.***

C *** Decca Dig. **400 047-2**; SXDL/*KSXDC* 7510 [Lon. LDR/*5*-10011]. VPO, Kondrashin.

(B) *** CfP CFP/*TC-CFP* 4382. LPO, Macal.

(B) *** RCA VICS/*VK* 2038. New Philh. O, Stokowski.

(M) *** CBS 60150/*40*-. Cleveland. O, Szell.
(M) *** Decca SPA/*KCSP* 87 [Lon. STS/*5*-15101]. VPO, Kertesz.
**(*) DG 2530/*3300* 881 [id.]. Chicago SO, Giulini.
(*) Decca Dig. **410 116-2; 410 116-1/*4* [id.]. Chicago SO, Solti.
**(*) Telarc Dig. DG 10053 [id.]. St Louis SO, Slatkin.
** Nimbus 45 r.p.m. 45 45202. LPO, Bátiz.

Symphony No. 9; Carnaval overture.
(M) **(*) HMV SXLP/*TC-SXLP* 30163 [Sera. S/*4XGS* 60045]. Philh. O, Giulini.
(*) DG Dig. **410 032-2; 2532/*3302* 079 [id.]. VPO, Maazel.
(M) ** Decca VIV/*KVIC* 41 [Lon. CS/*5*-6980]. LAPO, Mehta.

Symphony No. 9; Othello overture.
(M) *** Decca Jub. JB/*KJBC* 118 [Lon. JL/*5*- 41022]. LSO, Kertesz.

In our last edition we gave a lukewarm reception to Kondrashin's digital recording of the *New World Symphony*, commenting favourably on the excellent sound of the Decca LP and cassette, but finding the performance genial rather than dramatic. The effect of the compact disc calls for a reassessment. Its impact is quite remarkable and no previous recording of the symphony can match its vividness. Recorded in the Sofiensaal, the range of the sound is matched by its depth. The upper strings are brilliant, yet have body and sheen; the bass is rich and firmly defined, the woodwind is luminously clear, and the brass combines sonority with bite, with the characteristic timbre of the Vienna trumpets unmistakable. The ambient effect of the hall prevents a clinical effect, yet every detail of Dvořák's orchestration is revealed, within a highly convincing perspective. Other performances of the first movement (exposition repeat included) may show a higher level of tension, but there is a natural spontaneity here and certainly no lack of excitement. In the *Largo* the Berlin Philharmonic play even more beautifully for Karajan (whichever version is chosen), but with Kondrashin the cor anglais solo is easy and songful, and there is an appealing simplicity in the way the music unfolds. But it is the finale that makes this version especially satisfying, with the wide dynamic range bringing dramatic projection to climaxes, and the refinement and transparency of the orchestral texture uncovering the composer's ingenious reworking of ideas recalled from earlier movements. There are few better or more enjoyable demonstrations of the potential of the digital compact disc than this.

For those interested in a normal LP or cassette choice is wide, for the *New World* has been an exceptionally successful work in the recording studio. There are three outstanding accounts from Karajan and the Berlin Philharmonic which must be seriously considered, for the Berlin Philharmonic playing is peerless, but the reissue of Kertesz's 1967 LSO recording on Decca Jubilee must stand with Kubelik at the head of the list. Both have the advantage of economy and Kertesz undoubtedly offers one of the finest performances ever committed to record, with a most exciting first movement (exposition repeat included) and a *Largo* bringing playing of hushed intensity to make one hear the music with new ears. Tempi in the last two movements are perfectly judged, and the recording quality remains outstanding on disc and cassette alike.

Kubelik's marvellously fresh account with the Berlin Philharmonic, recorded in the early 1970s, is certainly among the very finest. The hushed opening immediately creates a tension which is to be sustained throughout, and the approach to the gentle second subject of the first movement underlines the refinement which is the hallmark of the reading. The slow movement has a compelling lyrical beauty, with playing of great radiance from the orchestra. With a scherzo of striking character and a finale of great urgency – the forward impulse magically slackened as the composer is allowed dreamily to recall his earlier themes – the playing throughout is of the first rank. The recording is well up to the standard of Kubelik's DG Dvořák series, firm, smoothly blended and clear. There is a slight lack of resonance in the bass, but at medium price this has strong claims to be at the very top of a distinguished list. There is a first-class cassette.

Among the newer versions, that by Sir Colin Davis and the Concertgebouw Orchestra stands high in general esteem. It is completely free from egotistic eccentricity. The music is allowed to unfold in the most natural way, its drama vividly projected, and with beautiful orchestral playing throughout and really outstanding recording (rich and full-blooded, clearly detailed yet with a natural bloom on the whole orchestra), this is very engaging. For some listeners Davis's very directness may have its drawbacks. The cor anglais solo in the slow movement has an appealing simplicity, yet the effect is not very resilient, and later, when the horns echo the theme at the end of the opening section, the impression is positive rather than seductively nostalgic. The cassette transfer is one of Philips's very best, the level higher than usual, balancing clarity with weight and richness.

A splendid alternative choice is provided by Karajan's 1977 recording for HMV, which has the advantage of a generous coupling, a highly successful account of *Vltava*. Karajan's view of the symphony is more romantic than Davis's, but it is refined too, and has an unselfconscious warmth. It may not have quite the polish that marked Karajan's earlier reading for DG, but the result is robust and spontaneous-sounding, with the cor anglais solo of the *Largo* very fresh at a fractionally more flowing tempo than in the earlier version. The EMI sound is warmly atmospheric rather than analytical. Originally the cassette transfer was not entirely successful, lacking in refinement, but it is likely to have been remastered by the time we are in print.

Karajan's 1964 DG version has held its place in the catalogue for two decades and it is obviously due for relegation to the mid-priced Accolade label. When it does, it may be for some listeners the most rewarding of the three Karajan recordings, with its remarkable freshness. The accent here is on lyricism, and in spite of the exciting build-up of power in the first movement it is the lovingly phrased second subject group that remains in the memory. In the great *Largo*, Karajan achieves a kind of detached repose which lets the music speak for itself, and in the scherzo the rustic qualities in the second strain of the first section as well as the trio are evoked gently to captivating effect. The finale begins boldly and conveys a feeling of sheer high spirits; then in the marvellous lyrical reflective passage (just before the music sweeps away tremendously in its final burst of passion) the conductor relaxes and invites the listener to revel with him in the sheer beauty of the writing. DG's recording still sounds extremely well, although the cassette (which also includes the First *Slavonic dance*, Op. 46/1) needs remastering, for the sound is brighter on side two than side one.

Karajan's 1958 HMV version of the symphony was thought sufficiently competitive for it to be reissued at full price in 1973. Now at its cheaper price on HMV Concert Classics, it still remains so, and must be numbered among the best. The balance is most musically judged and the perspective natural, for it comes from the vintage years of stereo, and the performance is a thrilling one.

Macal's is an outstanding performance, fresh, sparkling and incisively dramatic, beautifuly played and brilliantly recorded in excellent digital sound. Even making no allowance for price, it stands at or near the top of a long list. Macal as a Czech takes a fresh and unsentimental view with speeds far steadier than usual in the first movement. Yet with idiomatic insights there is no feeling of brutality or rigidity, with the beauty of the slow movement purified, the scherzo crisp and energetic set against pastoral freshness in the episodes and the finale, again strong and direct, bringing a ravishing clarinet solo. There is an excellent cassette.

Stokowski's New Philharmonia recording for RCA was originally issued coupled with his 78 r.p.m. version of 1927. Now it is available separately at bargain price. That comparison proved highly instructive, however, for, as an interpretation as well as technically, the new version is the one to admire. In every way it reveals more intensely the maestro's genius for moulding phrases and tempi, for pointing the drama of such music as this. There are one or two Stokowskian idiosynrasies – trumpet trills at the end of the first movement, for example – and almost every repeat is omitted, but as a historic document of a great musician in his nineties it provides a warming experience. Sharp stereo separation and particularly vivid reproduction of timpani and brass. There is a chrome tape.

Szell's Cleveland recording was made in 1959 when his orchestra was at its peak. The reading combines vitality, marvellous orchestral discipline and expressive resilience. The *Largo* offers refinement and a sense of repose;

the scherzo has splendid rhythmic bite and the finale is exhilarating. The recording is not expansive, but is certainly vivid. The cassette – without loss of brightness – has a rather more full-bodied bass response than the disc.

Kertesz's earlier Vienna performance remains available at lower middle price. One might cavil at the unnaturally forward balance of the timpani in the introduction, but in all other respects the sound on disc (the tape tends to be coarse at climaxes) remains full-blooded and brilliant. The performance is agreeably fresh, not without its occasional idiosyncrasy – the gentle treatment of the first movement's second subject is less convincingly prepared than in Kertesz's later LSO disc, and there is a sudden quickening of tempo after its reprise at the end. There is plenty of excitement, and the Vienna Philharmonic play the *Largo* most beautifully.

Giulini recorded the *New World* for HMV when the old Philharmonia was at its peak. The result has a refinement, coupled with a degree of detachment, which for some will make it an ideal reading. This is emotion observed from outside rather than experienced direct, and the result, with its beautiful moulding of phrase, is very refreshing. For a general recommendation this may well be too cool a reading, but with vivid recording quality, excellent for its period, this clearly has a place in the catalogue. The cassette has been remastered and now matches the disc closely. The tape offers also a surprise bonus of Bizet's *Jeux d'enfants*, which makes it even more recommendable than the equivalent disc. Both LP and cassette include a sparkling account of *Carnaval.*

Solti's is a characteristically fierce reading, somewhat larger than life, recorded with rather aggressive brilliance, impressive but not too sympathetic. There is an excellent chrome cassette, but the CD, vivid though it is, does not match Kondrashin's version in beauty of texture and refinement of detail.

As in his Philharmonia version of the early 1960s, Giulini on DG takes a sympathetic but slightly detached view of the *New World*, and the high polish of the Chicago orchestra's playing ensures that this recording is most enjoyable. But by the highest standards – and that includes the earlier Giulini account – the new performance is slightly over-refined and lacking in spontaneity, with the last two movements biting less sharply than before. Fine full recording, if at a somewhat low level; the cassette matches the disc fairly closely, but has slightly more projection and bite on the second side.

Maazel's is a high-powered and superbly played reading, incisive to the point of fierceness (like his reading of No. 8) but with moments of affection, most strikingly in the poised and pure account of the slow movement. On compact disc the aggressive sound of Maazel's DG recording (lacking bloom on high violins in fast movements) cannot compare with Kondrashin's far warmer sound with the same orchestra on Decca, though here too the benefits of the new medium with its absence of background are considerable. The chrome cassette, however, transferred at only a modest level, is comparatively mellow with much less sharply defined detail.

The St Louis Symphony plays for Slatkin with polish and refinement, the cor anglais solo of the slow movement is so velvety it hardly sounds like a reed instrument at all. One or two mannerisms apart, the reading is enjoyably direct, and the recording, though not one of Telarc's most spectacular digital offerings, brings out the sweetness of the strings even in the gentlest pianissimos.

Bátiz directs a measured reading with speeds maintained more steadily than usual. The recording, transferred at 45 r.p.m., is of exceptional range. The opening has great hi-fi impact, and the acoustic is warm as well as brilliant, though the string sound is less sharply focused than that of the wind. The playing of the LPO is not ideally crisp.

Mehta's is a brilliant extrovert reading, crisply disciplined and recorded massively to match; it misses most of Dvořák's subtler shadings, lacking grace and charm. The transfer offers brilliant full-blooded sound, and there is a first-class cassette. In its direct, rather earthy way this account certainly communicates, when the sound is so good.

(i) *Symphony No. 9* (*New World*)*;* (ii) *Scherzo capriccioso, Op. 66;* (iii) *Serenade for strings in E, Op. 22.*

(B) *** DG Walkman *413 147-4.* (i) Berlin PO; (ii) Bav. RSO; (iii) ECO; Kubelik.

This bargain-priced (tape-only) reissue is self-recommending, costing less than the Privilege reissue of the *Symphony* alone. Kubelik's version of the *New World* is outstanding in every way – see above – and the accounts of the *Scherzo capriccioso* and *String serenade* have a comparable freshness. The *Scherzó* is attractively spirited and colourful, while the account of the *Serenade* is beautifully lyrical, yet strong in impulse. The playing of the ECO here is attractively polished as well as resilient. The recording is brightly lit and, like the *Symphony*, somewhat dry in the bass, but the chrome-tape transfers are of DG's finest quality. The *Symphony* is offered without a break.

CHAMBER AND INSTRUMENTAL MUSIC

Bagatelles (for 2 violins, cello and harmonium), *Op. 46*.
(M) *** Ph. 6570/*7310* 918. Berlin PO Octet (members) – BRAHMS: *Clarinet quintet*.***

Dvořák wrote his *Bagatelles* for two violins, cello and harmonium for performance at the house of a critic who possessed no other keyboard instrument. They present a charming solution to a technical problem which Dvořák seems to solve with characteristic artlessness. They are not great music, but have enough haunting moments to make an unusual attractive coupling for a fine account of Brahms's *Clarinet quintet*. The recording is of Philips' finest quality, full, clear and naturally balanced. The cassette transfer is good too, though not quite as vivid as the coupled Brahms *Quintet*.

Ballad in D min., Op. 15; Humoresque in G, Op. 101/7; Mazurek in E min., Op. 49; Nocturne in B, Op. 40; Romantic pieces, Op. 75; Slavonic dance No. 2, Op. 46/2 (all for violin and piano); *Violin sonata in F, Op. 57; Violin sonatina in G, Op. 100*.
(M) ** Sup. 111 1311/2. Suk, Holeček.

Idiomatic performances, as one would expect from the composer's grandson and his accomplished partner. The *Sonata* and the *Sonatina* are both delightful pieces, which these artists have recorded before. The sound quality stands in the way of an unqualified recommendation, but the music will more than reward perseverance.

Piano quartets Nos. 1 in D, Op. 23; 2 in E flat, Op. 87.
(M) *** Ph. 6570/*7310* 886. Beaux Arts Trio with Trampler.

These are delightfully inventive works and will give enormous pleasure to all music lovers. The playing here is as fresh and spontaneous as the music itself, and given first-class engineering, with smooth, well-defined and admirably blended tone quality, the record is self-recommending. There is a pleasing cassette, although the transfer level is only modest and the upper range is less telling than the resonant bass.

Piano quintet in A, Op. 81.
(M) *** Decca Ace SDD 270 [Lon. STS 15525]. Curzon, VPO Qt – SCHUBERT: *Quartettsatz*.**

(i) *Piano quintet in A. String quintet in E flat, Op. 97*.
(M) *** Ph. 6570/*7310* 571. Berlin Philharmonic Octet (members), (i) with Bishop-Kovacevich.

Curzon's recording with members of the Vienna Philharmonic dates from 1963, but the recording was one of Decca's finest and the newest transfer has lost none of the original richness and glow. It is a wonderfully warm and lyrical performance, among the most beautiful and satisfying of all chamber-music records.

It is surprising that the two masterly quintets on the Philips disc have not been recorded more often. Paired generously together at mid-price – each work lasts over half an hour – they make a superb coupling. The Berlin players have a consistent freshness, an easy warmth which never develops into sentimentality. In that they are splendidly matched in the *Piano quintet* by Stephen Bishop-Kovacevich, whose clarity of articulation is a marvel. The recording is not as weighty as it might be, lacking a little in bass, but it is still satisfyingly balanced. The cassette is first-class, fresh, full and wide-ranging.

Piano trios Nos. 1 in B flat, Op. 21; 2 in G min., Op. 26; 3 in F min., Op. 65; 4 in E min. (Dumky), Op. 90.

(M) *** Ph. 6703 015 (3) [id.]. Beaux Arts Trio.

(M) *** Sup. 1411 2621/3. Suk Trio.

Piano trios Nos. 1–4; 4 Romantic pieces (for violin and piano), *Op. 78; Romance in G min.* (for cello and piano), *Op. 94.*

**(*) CRD CRD 1086/8/*CRDC 4086/8.* Cohen Trio.

The Beaux Arts versions of the trios come from the early 1970s but sound amazingly fresh and sparkling. The *F minor*, arguably the most magnificent and certainly the most concentrated of the four, is played with great eloquence and vitality; the splendours of the *Dumky* are detailed below under the individual mid-price disc. The recording is splendidly vivid and truthful.

The Suk Trio bring a special authority to this music (after all, Josef Suk can trace his ancestry back to the composer himself), and their readings have the benefit of concentration and intellectual grip. They hold the architecture of each movement together most impressively, and they also have the advantage of very good recorded sound. Perhaps the Beaux Arts Trio score in their wonderful pianist, Menahem Pressler, who brings such sensitivity and imagination to his part; Jan Panenka is very good, but not quite so inspired. But honours are very evenly divided, and both these sets are at medium price.

The Cohen is a family trio, so opportunities for rehearsal should be unlimited! Their set also adds Opp. 78 and 94, which the two rival accounts do not include, but the price is higher. The playing is always thoroughly musical, though not quite as masterly as that of the Beaux Arts. The recording is very good, and collectors are unlikely to find much here to disappoint them. The cassettes are each available separately and offer faithful transfers, although one notices slightly greater presence on the second sides of CRDC 4086 and 7 than the first. On CRDC 4088, which couples the *Dumky trio* with Opp. 75 and 94, the level is higher and this cassette is demonstrably more vivid.

Piano trio No. 3 in F min., Op. 65.

(M) *(**) CBS 60264/*40*- [M 33447]. Heifetz, Piatigorsky, Pennario – STRAVINSKY: *Suite Italienne*; GLIÈRE: *Duo*; HALVORSEN: *Passacaglia.****

It is a pity that the balance is so artificial, for there is some marvellous playing here and the performance has great lyrical ardour and excellent detail. The scherzo is especially fine. But Heifetz is placed forward and the microphone puts an edge on his tone (the finale has some very shrill moments) while Piatigorsky's timbre is dry. The piano is in the background, but has fair body. With adjustments to the controls there is a good deal to admire, but it is the couplings that make this famous record worth seeking out, for all its technical faults.

Piano trio No. 4 (Dumky).

(M) *** Ph. 6833 231 [(d) 802 918]. Beaux Arts Trio – HAYDN: *Piano trio No. 25.****

(M) *** Sup. 111 1089. Páleníček, Czech Trio – NOVÁK: *Trio.****

*** Pearl SHE 553. Beaux Arts Trio – MENDELSSOHN: *Piano trio No. 1.****

On its first appearance the Beaux Arts' Philips performance of the *Dumky trio* occupied two sides, which made it an expensive proposition at full price. Now it has the advantage of a fill-up as well as a reduction in cost. The performance has great sparkle and freshness and the quality of the recording is altogether exemplary, vivid and lifelike and with marvellously silent surfaces. This is arguably the best buy now at any price.

On Supraphon the Czechs play with enormous commitment. Moreover they are well recorded. Those who fancy the interesting Novak *Trio quasi una ballata* instead of Haydn will find this account is satisfying too.

We associate the Beaux Arts Trio with Philips and therefore wonder whether we are dreaming when their names are clearly printed in black and white on the Pearl label. They have recorded both the *Dumky* and the Mendelssohn trio for Philips, and there is not a great deal to choose between these performances; perhaps surprisingly, there is also little difference in recorded quality. So the question of couplings and, of course, the cost – the Pearl disc is at full price – can be left to the reader to decide.

String quartets Nos. 1–14; Quartettsatz; Quartet in F: Fragment; Cypresses; 2 Waltzes, Op. 54.
(M) *** DG 2740 177 (12). Prague Qt.

Dvořák's *Quartets* span the whole of his creative life: the *First, in A Major*, Op. 2, comes from 1862 thus preceding the *First* and *Second symphonies* by three years, while the last, *in G Major*, Op. 106, comes two years after the last of his symphonies, (*From the New World*). They contain surprises: *No. 3 in D* (1869–70) spills over on to a third side, and takes the best part of seventy minutes. Both this and *No. 2 in B flat* and *No. 4 in E Minor*, written at the same period, survive by chance since Dvořák had determined on their destruction. However, he thought well enough of part of the *E Minor* to turn it into the *Notturno for strings*, Op. 40. The beauties of the mature quartets from the *D Minor*, Op. 34 (actually the *Ninth*), are well known, though, astonishingly enough, only the *F Major*, Op. 96, has achieved popularity on the gramophone. Recordings of such masterpieces as Opp. 105 and 106 are still thin on the ground. The Prague Quartet put us all the more in their debt with this ambitious venture which in addition to the string quartets themselves goes on to include the *Fragment* of a *Quartet in F Major* from 1881, an *Andante* movement from 1873, the *Cypresses* (1887) and the two *Waltzes* of Op. 54 from 1880. The performances are eminently serviceable and often very fine indeed, and the recording is perfectly satisfactory too. An important set for all libraries.

String quartets Nos. 11 in C, Op. 61; 12 in F (American), Op. 96.
*** Cal. CAL 1617/*4617* [id.]. Talich Qt.
(M) **(*) Decca Ace SDD 565. Gabrieli Qt.

The *C major Quartet* has little of the spontaneity that distinguishes the *Violin concerto* or the *Sixth Symphony* of the previous year and it is less endearing than its immediate predecessors (Opp. 34 and 51). The late Alec Robertson spoke of its scherzo as 'inhibited' and added, 'For the *C major Quartet*, one can have admiration but not love'.

The Talich Quartet are completely at home in this repertoire and their performance of the *American Quartet* is wonderfully warm and persuasive. The lesser-known C Major work is given a no less distinguished performance and the recording has admirable body and a natural ambience. The cassette too is first-class, a high-level transfer which is full and wide-ranging without being edgy.

The Gabrielis also make out a good case for the *C major Quartet* and they are well recorded too. Theirs is a more lyrical reading than that of the Prague City Quartet in the complete DG set. The coupling is the more familiar *F Major*, of which this is their second recording. It is an eminently sound performance without achieving the distinction of the Orlando or the Quartetto Italiano. Those who have their earlier disc coupling Opp. 51 and 105 will not be disappointed, and the sound is fully acceptable.

String quartet No. 12 in F (American), Op. 96.
*** Ph. 9500/*7300* 995 [id.]. Orlando Qt – MENDELSSOHN: *Quartet No. 1.****
(M) *** Ph. 6503/*7303* 108 [id.]. Italian Qt – BORODIN: *Quartet No. 2.****

The Orlando Quartet were new to the catalogue when this Philips issue appeared, and the sleeve-note of both disc and cassette concentrates on the artists rather than the music, which is familiar enough. They are based in Holland and have won wide acclaim for their concert appearances. The Dvořák is played with finely balanced and well-blended tone, excellent musical judgement and great sensitivity. Indeed this ranks among the very best versions of the quartet currently available and can stand comparison with the classic account by the Italian Quartet. The recording is completely natural and lifelike; the cassette transfer is admirable, wide-ranging, fresh and clean.

The earlier Philips recording by the Italian Quartet, coupled with Borodin, holds its place in the catalogue. It is predictably fine and splendidly engineered on disc and tape. A bargain.

String quintet in G, Op. 77; Waltzes, Op. 54/1 and 4.
* None. Dig. D 79012. Augmented Sequola Qt.

Although the *G major Quintet* has been recorded by both Czech and Viennese forces, neither is currently in the catalogue. The interest of the present issue is that it restores the *Nocturne*, omitted from the 1888 Simrock edition but republished in the Collected Edition. Thus, the present issue lets us hear the work as it was presented at the very first performance in 1876. The playing of the Sequola Quartet and Julius Levine (double-bass) is not in the first flight and intonation sometimes poses a problem, nor is the sound particularly distinguished. In the absence of rival versions – and because of the *Nocturne*, which is a beautiful movement – this issue will have an appeal, but it would have been greater had the opportunity been used to retake certain passages.

PIANO MUSIC

3 Album leaves; Eclogues; Impromptu in G; Pieces, Op. 52.
(M) **(*) Sup. 111 1395. Kvapil.

Berceuse in G; Capriccio in G min.; Dumka and Furiant, Op. 12; Humoresque in F sharp; Impromptu in D min.; 7 Mazurkas, Op. 56.
(M) **(*) Sup. 111 1179. Kvapil.

Dumka, Op. 35; 2 Furiants, Op. 42; 2 Minuets, Op. 28; Scottish dances, Op. 41; Theme and variations, Op. 36.
(M) **(*) Sup. 111 0862. Kvapil.

Humoresques Nos. 1–8, Op. 101; Suite in A, Op. 98.
(M) **(*) Sup. 111 0865. Kvapil.

Poetic pictures, Op. 85, Nos. 1–13.
(M) **(*) Sup. 111 0566. Kvapil.

Silhouettes, Op. 8; Waltzes, Op. 54.
(M) **(*) Sup. 111 0820. Kvapil.

Dvořák's piano music is not as widely known as his chamber music; nor is it as good. The composer was a formidable sight-reader and a highly musical but not a great pianist. Many of the works recorded in Kvapil's survey are pleasing rather than memorable. The *Silhouettes* will give pleasure to those who know the first two symphonies, for they use some of the same thematic material.

Kvapil's account of the *Silhouettes* is coupled with the delightful *Waltzes*, Op. 54. This is the record with which to start, for it can hardly fail to delight the true Dvořákian. The *A major Suite* is delightful too and readers not intending to collect the whole series will probably find that 111 0820 and 111 0865 will give them a fair taste of Dvořák's output in this medium at a very reasonable cost. Others of course will want the lot; Dvořák is rarely less than endearing, though the inspiration in some of the shorter pieces is distinctly variable. Kvapil is a faithful guide through this terrain and the recordings are eminently acceptable.

The Op. 56 *Mazurkas* are highly melodious and appealing, and are of good vintage, being written in the same year as the great *D major Symphony*. Kvapil plays with real musical feeling and fine rhythm, and the disc only misses three stars on account of the recording, which, though very good, needs just a little wider range to be distinguished.

Slavonic dances Nos. 1–16, Opp. 46 and 72.
*** DG 2531/*3301* 349 [id.]. Alfons and Aloys Kontarsky.

Characteristically crisp and clean performances by the Kontarsky brothers of some of the most delectable piano duets ever written. More than they usually do, these pianists here allow themselves the necessary rubato, conveying affection and joy along with their freshness. Excellent recording and a splendid high-level cassette transfer, matching the disc closely.

VOCAL AND CHORAL MUSIC

Biblical songs, Op. 99, Nos. 1–5; Mass in D, Op. 86; Psalm 149, Op. 79; Te Deum, Op. 103.
(M) ** Sup. 112 0981/2. Soloists, Czech Philharmonic Ch., Prague SO, Smetáček.

A useful compilation. The *Te Deum*, a delightful work (not otherwise available), is full of a Haydnesque joy in life and a charming rusticity. This is music that glows from the page. The *D major Mass* is of course available in its original form (chorus and organ) on Preston's admirable Argo record: it is here recorded in the orchestral version on which Dvořák's publishers insisted. There are no alternative versions of this or of *Psalm 149*, and although the acoustic is a little over-resonant, the set must be recommended. It also includes the first five of the *Biblical songs*, which Soukupová recorded complete.

4 Folksongs, Op. 73; Gipsy songs, Op. 55.
*** Mer. E 77042. Walker, Vignoles – BRAHMS: *Mädchenlieder* etc.***

Songs my mother taught me is the one everyone knows from the *Four Folksongs* (here sung in Czech). The others too, and the *Gipsy songs*, are beautifully suited to Sarah Walker's vibrant personality. An attractive coupling for the exactly comparable Brahms songs, with excellent accompaniment from Roger Vignoles and very good recording.

Mass in D, Op. 86.
*** Argo ZRG 781 [id.]. Christ Church Cath. Ch., Oxford, Preston.

The *D major Mass* is also available in the two-disc Supraphon set (see above). It is good, but does not match the fine performance and recording that we have here from Oxford. The *Mass* was originally scored for small forces, and this version presents it in its original form. It was finished in 1887, a year or two before the *G major Symphony*, and though not a major work by any means, it has many delights to offer. In such a beautifully shaped reading, and with such impeccable recording, it is self-recommending.

Moravian duets, Op. 32.
(M) (***) HMV mono HLM/7267. Schwarzkopf, Seefried, Moore – MONTEVERDI: *Duets;* CARISSIMI: *Duets.*(***)

The partnership of Schwarzkopf and Seefried in their early prime is irresistible. The *Moravian duets*, sung in German, have a wonderful Slavonic zest. The mono recording is limited but well-balanced.

Requiem, Op. 89.
*** Decca SET 416/7 [Lon. OSA 1281]. Lorengar, Komlossy, Ilosfalvy, Krause, Amb. S., LSO, Kertesz.
**(*) Erato STU/*MCE* 71430 (2). Zylis-Gara, Toczyska, Dvorsky, Moroz, Fr. R. Ch. and O, Jordan.

The *Requiem* reflects the impact of the English musical world of the day on Dvořák and has a good deal of relatively conventional writing in it. However, no Dvořák work is wholly conventional, and given such fervent advocacy the work cannot fail to make its maximum effect. Kertesz conducts with a total commitment to the score and secures from both singers and orchestra an alert and sensitive response. Pilar Lorengar's vibrato is at times a trifle disturbing but it is the only solo performance that is likely to occasion any reserve. The recording matches the performance: it has a splendid weight and sonority and a lifelike balance. The recording certainly outclasses the DG which was available at one time, and readers who are attracted by the work can rest assured that any new version will have to be very good indeed to equal this.

Jordan's Erato version appeared over ten years after the outstanding Kertesz on Decca, but it fails to match its predecessor. The performance is weakly characterized by comparison, less sharply contrasted in its moods, less idiomatic. Only Zylis-Gara, more incisive than Pilar Lorengar on Decca, might be counted preferable. Even the recording shows little or no improvement, generally less well balanced. The cassette packaging is flimsy, an inadequate slimline format with poor documentation. The sound is not of Erato's best with side two of each tape offering a sharper focus than side one.

The Spectre's Bride (cantata), *Op. 69.*
(M) ** Sup. 50381/2. Tikalová, Blachut, Mráz, Czech Singers Ch., Czech PO, Krombholc.

For *The Spectre's Bride*, a cantata commissioned for the Birmingham Festival, Dvořák chose a typical nineteenth-century subject, a folk legend of a man risen from the grave to claim his promised bride. Dvořák was not really the composer to write horror music on a large scale, but with a red-blooded performance in Czech (so avoiding the Victorian infelicities of the English text) there is much to enjoy. Blachut at the time of the recording was at his peak, but it is a pity that a more youthful voice was not chosen for the heroine: Tikalová is heavy and wobbly. Variable recording.

Stabat Mater, Op. 58.
*** DG 2707 099 (2) [id.]. Mathis, Reynolds, Ochman, Shirley-Quirk, Bav. R. Ch., and SO, Kubelik.
**(*) Sup. Dig. 1112 3561/2. Beňačková, Wenkel, Dvořský, Rootering, Czech PO Ch. and O, Sawallisch.

Dvořák's devout Catholicism led him to treat this tragic religious theme with an open innocence that avoids the sentimentality of other works which made their mark (as this one did) in Victorian England. Characteristically four of the ten movements are based on major keys, and though a setting of a relatively short poem which stretches to eighty minutes entails much repetition of words, this idiomatic DG performance, warmly recorded and with fine solo and choral singing and responsive playing, holds the attention from first to last.

With Czech singers and players but a non-Czech conductor, the opposite of the DG casting, the Supraphon set provides a useful contrast. Sawallisch takes a far straighter approach than Kubelik, made the fresher and more immediate by the clarity of a digital recording. Both are highly recommendable, each with excellent solo singing, but this is a work which benefits from a persuasive approach such as Kubelik adopts. The singing of the Bavarian chorus is also a degree more refined than that of the Czechs. Among the soloists Beňačková sings seraphically in the opening movement and the only serious cause for hesitation is the contralto, Ortrun Wenkel, whose vibrato is wider than is desirable. But Sawallisch has certainly caught the spirit of this piece.

OPERA

Dmitrij: excerpts.
(M) ** Sup. 1116 3040. Pribyl, Beňačkova-Cápová, Dvořákova, Randová, Zítek, Svorc, Prague R. Ch., and SO, Stych.

Dmitrij occupied Dvořák during the early 1880s, at the time of the *D major Symphony*, and was first staged in Prague in 1882, only to be revised the following year – and then overhauled yet again in 1897 well after his return from America and his last visit to London. The present issue presents highlights from the work which was based on the Dmitrij of *Boris Godunov* who enters Moscow in triumph at the end of Mussorgsky's opera. There are scenes from four of the five Acts well sung and passably recorded, and it is a useful addition to the growing representation of Dvořák's opera on record.

The Jacobin (opera).
**(*) Sup. SUP 2481/3 [Pro. PAC/*P4C* 3000]. Blachut, Machotková, Zitek, Přibyl, Tuček, Prusa, Kantilena Children's Ch., Kuhn Ch., Brno State PO, Pinkas.

The Jacobin dates from the most contented period of Dvořák's life, and though the background to the piece is one of revolt and political turmoil, he was more interested in individuals, so that this is more a village comedy than a tract for the times. Václav Zitek sings the heroic part of the Jacobin himself with incisive strength, but the role which one remembers is that of the old musician, Benda, charmingly portrayed here by the veteran tenor Benno Blachut. Vilem Přibyl is less dominant than usual in the other tenor role of Jiři, one of a first-rate team. The conducting of Jiři Pinkas could be more positive, but the richness and variety of inspiration in a muddled but warmly satisfying opera come out most persuasively, helped by very acceptable recording.

Kate and the Devil (opera).
(M) **(*) Sup. 1116 3181/3. Barová, Novák, Ježil, Šulcová, Brno Janáček Op. Ch. and O, Pinkas.

This delightful fairy-tale opera about the girl who literally makes life hell for the devil who abducts her has more in common with Smetana and *The Bartered Bride* than with Wagner, whose techniques Dvořák – writing in 1899, towards the end of his career – was here consciously using. The jolly folk atmosphere of the opening is established in peasant choruses with the tenor hero (a shepherd) slightly tipsy. The devil appears in the guise of a handsome gamekeeper, and in his wooing brings obvious Wagnerian references. It is charmingly effective to have the supernatural represented in more chromatic music and to have a distant imitation of Wagner's Nibelheim music for the scene in hell in Act II. Kate naturally wins in her contest with the devil. Here the mezzo-soprano Anna Barová makes a formidable Kate, with Milos Ježil a sharply projected, Slavonic-sounding tenor as the shepherd and Richard Novák comparably Slavonic as the devil who makes a mistake. Pinkas directs a lively performance with his Brno forces. The recording is bright to the point of edginess, but can easily be tamed.

Eccles, Henry (1670–*c.* 1742)

Viola sonata in G min. (arr. Klengel).
(M) *** Sup. 1111 2694, Kodousek, Novotná – BRITTEN: *Lachrymae*; CLARKE: *Sonata.****

The interest of this record lies in the Britten and Rebecca Clarke works. The Eccles is not particularly individual, but it has dignity and makes an appealing makeweight in this eloquent performance.

Elgar, Edward (1857–1934)

Adieu (arr. Geehl). *Beau Brummel: Minuet. Sospiri, Op. 70. The Spanish Lady: Burlesco. The Starlight Express: Waltz. Sursum corda, Op. 11.*
(M) *** Chan. CBR/*CBT* 1004. Bournemouth Sinf., Hurst – VAUGHAN WILLIAMS: *Collection.****

A collection of delightful Elgar rarities. Most unexpected is the *Sursum corda* for organ, brass, strings and timpani (no woodwind), an occasional piece written for a royal visit to Worcester in 1894, which has real nobilmente depth. The *Burlesco*, a fragment from the unfinished Elgar opera, is delightfully done, and each one of these items has its charms. Well coupled with rare Vaughan Williams, warmly performed and atmospherically recorded.

3 Bavarian dances, Op. 27. Caractacus, Op. 35: Woodland interludes. Chanson de matin; Chanson de nuit, Op. 15/1 and 2. Contrasts, Op. 10/3. Dream children, Op. 43. Falstaff, Op. 68: 2 Interludes. Salut d'amour. Sérénade lyrique. (i) *Soliloquy for oboe* (orch. Jacob).
(M) *** Chan. CBR/*CBT* 1016. Bournemouth Sinf., Del Mar, (i) with Goossens.

The real treasure in this superb collection of Elgar miniatures is the *Soliloquy* which Elgar wrote right at the end of his life for Leon Goossens. It was the only movement completed of a projected suite, a wayward improvisatory piece which yet has a character of its own. Here the dedicatee plays it with his long-recognizable tone colour and feeling for phrase in an orchestration by Gordon Jacob. Most of the other pieces are well known, but they come up with new warmth and commitment in splendid performances under Del Mar. The (originally RCA) recording is of high quality, full and vivid, and it has now been digitally remastered with a chrome cassette of good quality.

3 Bavarian dances, Op. 27; Chanson de matin; Chanson de nuit, Op. 15/1 and 2; The Wand of Youth suites Nos. 1 and 2, Op. 1a and b. (see also below).
*** HMV ASD 2356. LPO, Boult.

Sir Adrian's performances of the *Wand of Youth* suites catch both the innocence and the intimacy of this very personal music. The fragile charm of the delicate scoring is well realized and there is plenty of schoolboy gusto for the rollicking *Wild Bear* (only playfully wild, of course). The orchestral playing is first-rate and carries through the conductor's obvious affection to the listener. The excellent recording is only just short of EMI's highest standard; occasionally there might have been more inner transparency, and the reverberation has not been perfectly calculated to prevent the roisterous scoring for *Wild Bear* becoming a fraction noisy. The string tone, however, is very beautiful. It is a pity that, instead of the admittedly attractive salon pieces, we were not given a full version of the *Bavarian dances*, with chorus.

'The miniature Elgar': Bavarian dance No. 2. Beau Brummel: Minuet. Chanson de matin. Dream Children, Op. 43/1 and 2. Nursery suite. The Serious Doll. The Starlight Express: (i) *Organ Grinder's songs: My Old Tunes; To the Children. The Wand of Youth suites:* excerpts: *Serenade; Sun dance; The Tame Bear.*
(M) *** HMV Green. ESD/*TC-ESD* 7068. RPO, Collingwood, (i) with Harvey.

Inspired by the BBC TV *Monitor* film on Elgar's life, this wholly delightful anthology collects together some of the composer's most attractive contributions in the lighter field, including several of those fragile and nostalgic little portraits which give the *Nursery* and *Wand of Youth* suites their special character. Frederick Harvey joins the orchestra for two *Organ Grinder's songs* written as incidental music for *The Starlight Express.* These are splendidly alive, with as much interest in the orchestra as in the stirringly melodic vocal line. Throughout this very well recorded collection the orchestral playing under Lawrence Collingwood is especially sympathetic, and the programme as a whole has been cleverly planned to make a highly enjoyable concert in itself. The cassette transfer is immaculate, first-class in every way.

Caractacus, Op. 35: Triumphal march. Carillon, Op. 75. Dream Children, Op. 43/1 and 2. Elegy for strings, Op. 58. Grania and Diarmid, Op. 42: Funeral march. The Light of Life, Op. 29: Meditation. Polonia, Op. 76. Funeral march (Chopin, orch. Elgar).
**(*) HMV ASD 3050. LPO, Boult.

The main interest here is provided by two pieces Elgar wrote at the beginning of the First World War as a gesture to help refugees from Belgium and Poland. The *Carillon*, written for 'gallant little Belgium', is rather effective and one can imagine its success at the time; the *Polonia* has character too, and both show the composer's flair for flag-waving orchestral sounds. The rest of the programme, although it displays a good sprinkling of Elgarian fingerprints, is uneven in quality and does not seem to fire Sir Adrian to his more persuasive advocacy. Even the *Dream Children* seem on the cool side, although some will undoubtedly like the restraint which Boult provides. The orchestration of Chopin's *Funeral march* is moderately effective. Excellent recording throughout.

Caractacus: Triumphal march; Carillon, Op. 75; Cockaigne overture, Op. 40; Dream Children, Op. 43/1 and 2; Froissart overture, Op. 19; In the South: overture, Op. 50.
(M) *** HMV Green. ESD/*TC-ESD* 7167. LPO, Boult.

This mid-priced Greensleeve reissue combines the three concert overtures (originally available at full price with the *Overture in D minor* arranged from Handel) and adds some extra items from ASD 3050 (see above). Boult's unique insight into the problems of Elgar interpretation is characteristically illustrated in the overtures. Though other Elgarians – Barbirolli for instance – may be more ripely romantic, Boult with his incisiveness is both dramatic and noble. The recording – not quite consistent between pieces – still sounds full and atmospheric, but the cassette, though clear, has not quite the upper range of the disc.

Caractacus: Triumphal march. Coronation march, Op. 65; Crown of India suite, Op. 66; Grania and Diarmid, Op. 42: Funeral march. Imperial march, Op. 32; The Light of Life, Op. 29: Meditation. Nursery suite; Severn suite, Op. 87.
(M) *** HMV *TCC2-POR 154590–9*. Royal Liv. PO, Groves.

It is good to have these performances by Sir Charles Groves – recorded while he was principal conductor of the Royal Liverpool Philharmonic Orchestra – restored to the catalogue. This is all music that he understands warmly, and the results give much pleasure. One does not have to be an imperialist to enjoy any of the occasional pieces, and it is interesting to find the patriotic music coming up fresher than the little interlude from *The Light of Life*, beautiful as that is. The *Triumphal march* from *Caractacus* makes one want to try the complete recording of this major cantata (see below). It is played with fine swagger. Both the *Nursery suite* (written for the Princesses Elizabeth and Margaret Rose) and the orchestral version of the *Severn suite* (written for a brass band contest) come from Elgar's very last period when his inspiration came in flashes rather than as a sustained searchlight. The completely neglected *Funeral march* was written in 1901 for a play by W. B. Yeats and George Moore. It is a splendid piece. The collection is gathered together on a double-length chrome tape of high quality, with recording that is rich, vivid and has plenty of bite on the brass in the marches, though side two is transferred at a higher level than side one. The cassette is poorly documented, offering no information about the music except titles and the performing cast.

'The lighter Elgar': Carissima. Contrasts, Op. 10/3. May song. Mazurka, Op. 10/1. Mina. Minuet, Op. 21. (i) *Romance for bassoon and orchestra. Rosemary* (*That's for remembrance*). *Sérénade lyrique. Sérénade mauresque, Op. 10/2. Sevillana, Op. 7.*
(M) *** HMV Green. ESD 7009. Northern Sinf. O, Marriner, (i) with Chapman.

The best of Elgar's light music has a gentle delicacy of texture, and as often as not a touch of melancholy, which is irresistible to nearly all Elgarians. Not everything here is on the very highest level of invention, but all the music is pleasing and a good deal of it is delightful for its tender moods and restrained scoring, favouring flute, bassoon, and the clarinet in middle or lower register. A boisterous piece like *Sevillana* may be rather conventional, but it has Elgar's characteristic exuberance, which represents the other side of the coin. The most distinguished item here is the rhapsodic *Romance for bassoon and orchestra*, but the whole programme offers quiet enjoyment and is just the thing for the late evening. It is played with style and affection by the Northern Sinfonia under Neville Marriner, and HMV have provided that warm, glowing orchestral sound that is their special province for Elgar's music. There is an outstanding cassette too: TC-ESD 7009.

Cockaigne overture (see also above); *Crown of India suite, Op. 66; Pomp and circumstance marches Nos. 1–5, Op. 39.*
(M) **(*) Chan. CBR/*CBT* 1012. SNO, Gibson.

Overtures: Cockaigne; Froissart; In the South. Overture in D min. (arr. from Handel: *Chandos anthem No. 2*).
*** Chan. **CHAN 8309**; ABRD/*ABTD* 1077 [id.]. SNO, Gibson.

Cockaigne overture; Pomp and circumstance marches Nos. 1–5. National anthem (arrangement).
*** Decca SXL/*KSXC* 6848 [Lon. CS/5-7072]. LPO, Solti.

(i) *Cockaigne overture;* (ii) *Introduction and allegro for strings, Op. 47;* (i) *Variations on an original theme* (*Enigma*), *Op. 47.*
(M) ❀ *** HMV Green. ESD/*TC-ESD* 7169. (i) Philh. O, (ii) London Sinf. and Allegri Qt; Barbirolli.

Elgar's picture of London in *Cockaigne* is of course an Edwardian one, but little of the scenery has changed; the military bands and the Salvation Army are still there, and if the lovers in the park today are more uninhibited, they should not be disappointed with Barbirolli's warmth in their music. Indeed, Barbirolli, himself a Londoner, paints a memorably vivid picture. H M V's splendid recording does Elgar's richly painted canvas real justice, and the whole piece moves forward with a sweep worthy of the greatest city in the world. Barbirolli's reading of the *Enigma variations* is no less satisfying. It has both richness and warmth, and is superbly played and recorded, and especially in the variations where the strings are given their head, the music could have no more eloquent advocate. To make this mid-priced Greensleeve reissue absolutely irresistible, E M I have made room for Barbirolli's inspired performance of the *Introduction and allegro for strings*, recorded with the London Sinfonia and Allegri Quartet. Here Barbirolli's passionate lyricism, plus exceptionally fine string playing, provides a quite outstanding and definitive version of Elgar's masterly string work. The E M I stereo is fully worthy of the playing, the string timbre characteristic of vintage analogue sound of the very highest quality. The cassette too is excellent, robust and well detailed, matching the disc closely.

Sir Alexander Gibson's Chandos collection is given a brilliantly truthful digital recording. The Scottish orchestra makes a vividly cohesive sound, although the strings are just a little lacking in richness of timbre. The picture of London is full of bustle and pageantry, with bold brass and flashing percussion, and the closing pages have striking impact. *In the South* does not lack impetus (although it does not quite match Silvestri – see below) and Gibson's directness serves *Froissart* and the Handel arrangement equally well. There is a touch of digital edge on the L P sound; as the chrome tape tempers this a little, while remaining of demonstration liveliness, many will prefer tape to disc. On both the bass response is firm. The C D is very impressive, the treble smoother and the overall effect extremely vivid with greater tangibility and body to the sound.

Gibson's earlier S N O reissue (from 1978) remains competitive at mid-price, especially for those interested in the *Crown of India suite*. Here again Gibson directs vigorously sympathetic performances of an attractive programme, well recorded. *Cockaigne* is attractively spirited, and although the Scottish orchestra misses something of the music's opulence, this is undoubtedly enjoyable. The *Pomp and Circumstance marches* are taken at a spanking pace, but with no lack of swagger, and there is a strong feeling of pageantry too. The music has great forward thrust, and the recording acoustic is suitably reverberant.

Solti's view of the marches is refined, with sharp pointing in the outer sections, spaciousness in the great melodies. The result is richly satisfying. *Cockaigne* too is sharply dramatic, and the recording quality gives a bloom to all the performances which few Elgarians will resist. The cassette transfer is first-class, with thrilling impact and weight. This performance of *Cockaigne* is also available coupled with the *Enigma variations* – see below.

Cello concerto in E min., Op. 85.

❀ *** H M V ASD/*TC-ASD* 655 [(d) Ang. S 36338]. Du Pré, LSO, Barbirolli – *Sea pictures.**** ❀

*** Decca SXL/*KSXC* 6965 [Lon. CS/*5*-7195]. Harrell, Cleveland O, Maazel – TCHAIKOVSKY: *Rococo variations* etc.***

(M) ** DG Priv. 2535/*3335* 201 [id.]. Fournier, Berlin PO, Wallenstein – BLOCH: *Schelomo.***

*(*) Chan. Dig. ABRD/*ABTD* 1007 [id.]. Kirshbaum, SNO, Gibson – WALTON: *Concerto.***

Cello concerto; Cockaigne overture; Introduction and allegro for strings.

**(*) Ph. Dig. 6514/*7337* 316 [id.]. Schiff, Dresden State O, Marriner.

Cello concerto; Elegy for strings; In the South.

(B) *** CfP CFP/*TC-CFP* 40342. Robert Cohen, LPO, Del Mar.

Cello concerto; Introduction and allegro for strings; Serenade for strings in E min., Op. 20.

*** HMV ASD/*TC-ASD* 2906. Tortelier, LPO Boult.

(i) *Cello concerto;* (ii) *Variations on an original theme* (*Enigma*).

*** CBS 76529/*40* [M/*MT* 34530]. (i) Du Pré, Phd. O, (ii) LPO; both cond. Barenboim.

(B) ** PRT GSGC/*ZCGC* 2017. Navarra, Hallé O, Barbirolli.

It was in the Elgar *Cello concerto* that Jacqueline du Pré first won world recognition, and the HMV recording gives a wonderful idea of how so young a girl captured such attention and even persuaded the Americans to listen enraptured to Elgar. Du Pré is essentially a spontaneous artist. No two performances by her are exactly alike, and wisely Barbirolli at the recording sessions encouraged her above all to express emotion through the notes. The style is freely rhapsodic. The tempi, long-breathed in first and third movements, are allowed still more elbow-room when du Pré's expressiveness requires it, and in the slow movement, brief and concentrated, her 'inner' intensity conveys a depth of expressiveness rarely achieved by any cellist on record. Brilliant virtuoso playing too in scherzo and finale. There is a good cassette.

Jacqueline du Pré's second recording of the Elgar *Cello concerto* was taken from live performances in Philadelphia in November 1970, and whatever the slight blemishes (questionable balances, some coughing) this is a superb picture of an artist in full flight. Here on CBS you have the romantic view of Elgar at its most compelling, and though some Elgarians will fairly enough prefer more restraint in this autumnal work, the mastery of du Pré lies not just in her total commitment from phrase to phrase but in the feeling for the whole. More than in any other account on record, even her own with Barbirolli, this one sets sights on the moment in the Epilogue where the slow-movement theme returns, the work's innermost sanctuary of repose. In the finale, at a cracking basic tempo, the ensemble is not flawless, but all through the Philadelphia Orchestra plays with commanding virtuosity, and Daniel Barenboim is the most understanding of accompanists.

Barenboim's view of *Enigma* is full of fantasy. Its most distinctive point is its concern for the miniature element. Without belittling the delicate variations, Barenboim both makes them sparkle and gives them emotional point, while the big variations have full weight, and the finale brings extra fierceness at a fast tempo. A fine coupling, beautifully recorded. The original issue of the cassette had unacceptable sound quality, with very limited range. However, current copies are on chrome tape, although the recording has not been remastered. The sound is quite vivid, but *piano* detail is less sharply defined than on the LP.

Lynn Harrell's outstanding account of the Elgar *Cello concerto* with the Cleveland Orchestra is the first to challenge the du Pré versions for HMV and CBS. With eloquent support from Maazel and the orchestra (the woodwind plays with appealing delicacy), the reading, deeply felt, balances a gentle nostalgia with extrovert brilliance. The slow movement is tenderly spacious, the scherzo bursts with exuberance, and after a passionate opening the finale is memorable for the poignantly expressive reprise of the melody from the *Adagio*, one of Elgar's greatest inspirations. The recording of the orchestra is brightly lit in the American way; the solo cello is rich and firmly focused, a little larger than life but convincingly balanced. The cassette matches the disc closely: it is slightly smoother on top, mellowing the sheen on the orchestral strings.

The Classics for Pleasure disc is an outstanding bargain. Robert Cohen's performance is strong and intense, with steady tempi, the colouring more positive, less autumnal than usual, relating the work more closely to the *Second Symphony*. Yet there is no lack of inner feeling. The ethereal half-tones at the close of the first movement are matched by the gently elegiac poignancy of the *Adagio*. Del Mar's accompaniment is wholly sympathetic, underlining the soloist's approach. He also directs an exciting account of *In the South* (recorded in a single take), not quite as exhilarating as Silvestri's famous performance (HMV ESD 7013) but certainly spontaneous in effect. The *Elegy* makes an eloquent bonus. The recording is wide-ranging and brilliant but shows Cohen's tone as bright and well-focused rather than especially resonant in the bass. The cassette matches the disc, with slightly less edge at the top, rather more body.

Tortelier gives a noble and restrained performance which will appeal to those who feel that Jacqueline du Pré wears her heart a little too much on her sleeve in this work, marvellous though her playing is. Boult accompanies with splendid tact and on the reverse side gives committed and finely recorded accounts of the *Introduction and allegro* and the *Serenade for strings*. The recording has breadth and range, detail is well defined and vivid, and the balance admirably judged. The cassette transfer is of good quality, full and rich, if lacking bite in the treble. But the overall balance is good, especially in the concerto.

On Philips the richness and resonance of sound from the Dresden orchestra, the strings above all, go with warmly flexible readings from Marriner. It would be hard to find more passionate playing of Elgar from any other non-British orchestra, and this imaginatively detailed version of *Cockaigne*, and the more direct account of the *Introduction and allegro* are ripely enjoyable, both superbly rehearsed. In the *Concerto* the performance is not quite so idiomatic, but Schiff gives a warm, thoughtful account, at his most successful in the lovely slow movement and the slow epilogue, both played with soft, sweet tone. Other readings may convey more of the structural cohesion but with the Elgar coupling this lyrical view has its place. The sound is superb to match the orchestra's richness. The elegiac atmosphere at the opening of the *Concerto* is especially persuasive. The chrome cassette, as so often with Philips, is disappointing, lacking the range and refinement at the top of the LP, although the *Concerto* sounds better than the other two works.

Fournier's account has both fervour and conviction, but unfortunately he suffers from a close microphone balance, and the result (besides reducing the dynamic contrast of the solo playing) obscures some of the orchestral detail. Even so this is a moving and eloquent account that might well be thought competitive if the coupling is suitable. The cassette transfer is faithful.

Navarra's is a strong and firm view, and with his control of phrasing and his wide range of tone colour, the performance culminates in a most moving account of the Epilogue. Only the scherzo falls short – slower than usual and not completely assured – but Navarra manages the virtuoso passages of the finale with reliable intonation. Barbirolli's view of *Enigma* as ever is rich and red-blooded, not as polished as his later HMV, but enjoyable. The sound remains agreeable, limited in range, but not thin, and there is a good cassette.

Kirshbaum, a fine cellist, is disappointing here. At the very start the great double-stopped chords are anything but commanding, not helped by recessed recording, and the whole performance sounds tentative rather than expressing spontaneity. Originally issued as an analogue disc, this is now displaced by a digital version, which is crisper in outline but cannot cure the balance.

Violin concerto in B min., Op. 61.

❀ *** CBS 76528/*40*- [M 34517]. Zukerman, LPO, Barenboim.

*** Decca SXL/*KSXC* 6842 [Lon. CS/*5*-7064]. Kyung-Wha Chung, LPO, Solti.

(M) *** HMV SXLP/*TC-SXLP* 290000-1/*4*. Menuhin, New Philh. O, Boult.

(*) DG Dig. **413 312-2; 2532/*3302* 035 [id.]. Perlman, Chicago SO, Barenboim.

Zukerman, coming fresh to the Elgar *Violin concerto* (the most difficult concerto he had ever attempted, so he said), was inspired to give a reading which gloriously combines the virtuoso swagger of a Heifetz with the tender, heartfelt warmth of the young Menuhin, plus much of individual responsiveness. In the first movement, with the command and the warmth superbly established, Zukerman gives a breathtaking account of the third theme, hushed and inner as though in personal meditation. The slow movement is altogether simpler, rather less involved, while the finale in its many sections is masterfully held together, brilliant but never breathless in the main *Allegro* and culminating in a deeply felt rendering of the long accompanied cadenza, freely expansive yet concentrated. With rich recording (the violin a shade on the close side) this represents the version of a masterpiece that many Elgarians have been waiting for over decades. When first issued, the CBS cassette offered very restricted sound, though side two was brighter than side one. A new copy sampled as we go to press has not improved matters: now side two has even less range at the top than side one, and the poorly defined orchestral image is unacceptable. Perhaps in due course this will be issued on chrome stock, as has the companion recording of the *Cello concerto* – see above.

Kyung-Wha Chung's is an intense and deeply committed reading which rises to great heights in the heartfelt account of the slow movement – made the more affecting by its vein of melancholy – and the wide-ranging performance of the finale. At the start of that third movement Chung at a fast tempo finds a rare element of fantasy, a mercurial quality, and the great accompanied cadenza is commandingly done, ending on an achingly beautiful phrase from the third subject of the first movement. The first movement itself brings much beautiful playing too, but there are one or two tiny flaws of intonation, and here Solti's accompaniment does not have quite so firm a grasp. But as an illuminating alternative to the Zukerman performance, this will be refreshing for any Elgarian. The brilliant Decca recording, giving first-class results on disc, sounds rather edgy in its cassette format.

It was an invidious task for Menuhin to try to remake what is one of the most famous gramophone recordings ever. It was in 1932 that young Master Menuhin played the solo part in this work with the composer himself conducting, and it took over thirty years for Menuhin to be persuaded back to do it again. The recording which resulted has now attained something of a vintage quality. Boult directs the performance with a passionate thrust in the outer movements and the warmest Elgarian understanding in the beautiful slow movement. If the poise of the violin's first entry and the sweetness of tone in the elegiac *Andante* are not quite what they were in Menuhin's first recording, the finale – longer than the other two movements and the most difficult to keep together – is stronger and more confident than it was. The long-breathed musings of the violin in the unaccompanied cadenza have a wonderful intensity, and Boult produces a superb burst of energy in the work's closing pages. The recording is warmly atmospheric and vivid on both disc and the excellent tape, and this medium-priced reissue now has documentary as well as musical value to set alongside Menuhin's mono version, recorded with the composer, and still available, successfully transferred to LP (HLM 7107).

Perlman's ease in tackling one of the most challenging violin concertos ever written brings a very enjoyable performance, though he misses some of the darker, more intense elements in Elgar's inspiration. The solo instrument is forwardly balanced and the recording is bright and vivid rather than rich (especially on cassette), lacking some of the amplitude one expects in the Elgar orchestral sound.

Early post-war (mono) recordings: *Dream children; Falstaff, Op. 68; Overtures: Froissart; In the South; Nursery suite; Pomp and circumstance marches Nos. 1–5; Symphony No. 1 in A flat, Op. 55; Variations on an original theme (Enigma); Wand of youth suite No. 1.*

(M) (***) HMV mono RLS/*TC-RLS* 7716 (3). LPO, Boult.

This set, intended as a birthday tribute to Sir Adrian Boult, arrived not long after his death at the age of ninety-four. It brings memorable accounts of the *First Symphony*, from 1949, and *Falstaff* from the following year (a more characterful account than the version he recorded with the same orchestra in the early 1970s), as well as his 1955 versions of *In the South* and *Froissart*. His authority in this repertoire is effortlessly asserted and these performances, whether of large-scale works or the charming miniatures of the *Nursery suite*, have a directness of utterance and a freshness that is disarming. The transfers have immediacy and clarity, and there has been no attempt to turn them into phoney stereo. The cassettes are cleanly transferred and match the discs fairly closely. There is plenty of range and the *Nursery suite*, the *Enigma variations* and *Falstaff* are particularly successful.

(i) *Elegy for strings, Op. 58; Froissart overture, Op. 19; Pomp and circumstance marches, Op. 39, Nos.* (ii) *1 in D;* (i) *2 in A min.; 3 in C min.;* (ii) *4 in G;* (i) *5 in C;* (i) *Sospiri, Op. 70.*

(M) *** HMV SXLP/*TC-SXLP* 30456. (i) New Philh. O; (ii) Philh. O; cond. Barbirolli.

The five *Pomp and circumstance marches* make a very good suite, with plenty of contrast in Nos. 2 and 3 to offset the Edwardian bombast of 1 and 4. The splendid nobilmente of No. 5 closes the set in rousing fashion. Barbirolli is obviously determined not to overdo the patriotism, and the studio recording suits this fresh approach. The sound is brilliant, but one notices that the recording of the string pieces offers more warmth in the middle range. The *Elegy* shows Barbirolli at his gentle best; *Sospiri* is contrastingly passionate, and the collection concludes with the early overture

Froissart. Here the orchestral links with Brahms are strong, but the fingerprints of the Elgar to emerge later are everywhere, and if the piece is loose in structure it has a striking main theme. The cassette equivalent of this issue has been remastered and sounds lively and vivid. *Froissart* is marginally less full-blooded than the other items.

Elegy for strings, Op. 58; Introduction and allegro for strings, Op. 47; Serenade for strings in E min., Op. 20; Sospiri, Op. 70; The Spanish Lady; suite (ed. Young).

**(*) Argo ZRG/*KZRC* 573. ASMF, Marriner.

At first hearing Marriner's interpretations of these Elgar works sound strangely unidiomatic. They grow on one – even the somewhat stiff manner of the *Introduction and allegro* – and the subtlety and strength of Marriner's unique band of string players are never in doubt. The disc is valuable for Elgarians in including the brief snippets arranged by Percy Young from Elgar's unfinished opera *The Spanish Lady*, but musically they have little substance. But what musical riches in all the rest – reflection of the composer's lifelong understanding of string tone. Indeed Marriner's version of the *Serenade*, wonderfully fresh and resilient, demonstrates this especially well. There is an excellent cassette, matching the disc closely.

Falstaff, Op. 68; In the South, Op. 50.

** Decca SXL/*KSXC* 6963 [Lon. CS 7193]. LPO, Solti.

With Vernon Handley's recording on CfP now withdrawn, *Falstaff* is poorly represented in the present catalogue with Boult's mono version only available in a box – see above. The tensions of Solti and Elgar can be invigorating, and in these performances of two of the more problematic Elgar works there is much that is very exciting. But with Decca recording in which the brilliance is not matched by weight or body (as is essential in Elgar), the results are too nervy and unrelaxed, particularly in *Falstaff*. The playing is excellent. There is no appreciable difference in sound between disc and cassette.

Introduction and allegro for strings, Op. 47 (see also under *Cockaigne; Cello concerto; Elegy*).

*** Decca SXL 6405 [Lon. CS 6618]. ECO, Britten (with Concert of English music ***).

(B) **(*) RCA VICS/*VK* 2001 [AGL1/*AGK1* 3790]. Boston SO, Munch – BARBER: *Adagio*; TCHAIKOVSKY: *Serenade*.**(*)

Introduction and allegro for strings; Serenade for strings.

*** HMV ASD 521. Sinf. of L., Allegri Qt, Barbirolli – VAUGHAN WILLIAMS: *Tallis fantasia* etc.*** ❀

Introduction and allegro for strings; Serenade for strings; Variations on an original theme (*Enigma*).

(M) **(*) EMI Em. Dig. EMX/*TC-EMX* 412011-1/*4*. LPO, Handley.

Introduction and allegro for strings; Variations on an original theme (*Enigma*).

(B) ** CfP CFP/*TC-CFP* 40022. LPO, Boult.

Barbirolli's outstanding versions of both Elgar's string works are here ideally coupled with an inspirational performance of Vaughan Williams's *Tallis fantasia*. This is a superb disc in every way, but no doubt the *Serenade* and the Vaughan Williams works will shortly appear recoupled at mid-price.

Like Neville Marriner's account of the *Introduction and allegro* (see above), Britten's is not idiomatic, but then as a fellow creator he provides a slant that is interesting for its own sake, and in any case secures the richest, most committed playing from the ECO strings. Characteristically Britten marks out the geography of the work more clearly than usual, but departs from his generally brisk manner for a gloriously romantic interpretation of the 'Welsh' tune. One would like to have heard him conducting one of the symphonies. A valuable item in an outstanding disc superbly recorded.

Boult's earliest stereo account of the *Enigma variations* is enjoyable enough if seeming a little undercharacterized. This is partly caused by the recording, which is vivid and clear but lacking in richness and atmosphere. Even so, if the coupling is suitable this is quite a good bargain, for the performance of the *Introduction and allegro*, athletic and strong rather than indulgent, is very successful.

Vernon Handley's generously full Eminence collection is given brilliantly wide-ranging digital sound (although the cassette has a more restricted treble response). The readings are in the Boult tradition and very well played. But Handley's strong personal identification with the music brings a consciously moulded style that tends to rob the *Enigma variations* of its forward impulse. The Elgarian ebb and flow of tension and dynamics are continually underlined in a highly expressive manner and although he uncovers much imaginative detail, there is a consequent loss of spontaneity. The performances of the string works are more direct although the *Larghetto* of the *Serenade* is also somewhat indulgent. Comparison with Barbirolli and Boult is not in Handley's favour, although his performances are full of insights.

A striking performance from Munch, individual in that his tempo for the big *Sul G* unison tune must be the slowest on record. But otherwise the reading has plenty of vitality, and the recording is full, with only a touch of the characteristic Boston harshness found in recordings from the early stereo era. The chrome cassette is first-rate.

In the South (*Alassio*) (concert overture), *Op. 50.*

(M) *** HMV Green. ESD 7013. Bournemouth SO, Silvestri – VAUGHAN WILLIAMS: *Tallis fantasia* etc.***

A really stunning performance of *In the South*, given one of EMI's most spectacular recordings. Silvestri knits the work's structure together more convincingly than one would have believed possible, and the strong forward momentum does not prevent the Italian sunshine (seen through English eyes) bringing a Mediterranean glow to the gentler, atmospheric pages of the score. But it is the virile opening and closing sections which Silvestri makes especially compelling, and at the same time he shows the music's parallel with the style of Richard Strauss. It was not a coincidence that the composer of *Don Juan* found an affinity with the bursting melodic fervour which was a dominant part of Elgar's musical personality, and which is so exhilarating here. The Bournemouth orchestra offers playing of a virtuoso order and the same absolute commitment which distinguishes Silvestri's direction.

King Arthur: suite; (i) *The Starlight Express, Op. 78: suite.*

(M) ** Chan. CBR/*CBT* 1001. Bournemouth Sinf., Hurst, (i) with Glover, Lawrenson.

The *King Arthur suite* is put together from incidental music that Elgar wrote in 1923 – well after his creative urge had fallen away – for a pageant-like play by Laurence Binyon. Though not great at all, it is full of surging, enjoyable ideas and makes an interesting novelty on record. *The Starlight Express suite* is similarly taken from music Elgar wrote in the First World War for a children's play, very much from the same world as the *Wand of Youth suites*, with a song or two included. Though the singers here are not ideal interpreters, the enthusiasm of Hurst and the Sinfonietta is well conveyed, particularly in the *King Arthur suite.* The recording is atmospheric if rather over-reverberant. The cassette transfer is acceptable but lacks range (most noticeably in *King Arthur*). The solo voices are naturally caught.

Nursery suite; Wand of Youth suites Nos. 1 and 2, Op. 1a and 1b.

*** Chan. Dig. **CHAN 8318**; ABRD/*ABTD* 1079. Ulster O, Bryden Thomson.

An admirable coupling. The Ulster Orchestra plays most beautifully and the ambience of the recording is well suited to the music's moments of gentle nostalgia. Although Boult's performances of the more robust items from the *Wand of Youth* bring marginally more exuberance, the playing in Ulster is attractively spirited and in the gentle pieces (the *Sun dance, Fairy pipers* and *Slumber dance*) which show the composer at his most magically evocative, the music-making engagingly combines refinement and warmth. The *Nursery suite* is strikingly well characterized and with first-class digital sound this is highly recommendable. On the otherwise excellent chrome cassette the upper strings are made to sound marginally thinner than on LP.

Pomp and circumstance marches, Op. 39/1–5; Empire march (1924); *Imperial march, Op. 32.*
*** HMV ASD/*TC-ASD* 3388 [Ang. S/*4XS* 37436]. LPO, Boult – WALTON: *Marches.****

Boult's approach to the *Pomp and circumstance marches* is brisk and direct, with an almost no-nonsense manner in places. There is not a hint of vulgarity, and the freshness is most attractive, though it is a pity he omits the repeats in the Dvořák-like No. 2. The *Empire march*, written for the opening of the 1924 Wembley Exhibition, had not been recorded again since then. It is hardly a great discovery, but makes a good makeweight for the more characteristic pieces. Warm, immediate and resplendent recording; the cassette is not as sharply focused as the disc.

Pomp and circumstance marches Nos. 1–5, Op. 39; Variations on an original theme (*Enigma*).
(M) *** DG Priv. 2535/*3335* 217. RPO, Del Mar.
**(*) CBS 37755/*40*- [id.]. Philh. O, Andrew Davis.
(M) ** Decca SPA/*KCSP* 536. LSO, Monteux or Bliss.

In the *Enigma variations* Del Mar comes closer than any other conductor to the responsive rubato style of Elgar himself, who directed an unforgettable performance on record in 1926. Like the composer, Del Mar uses the fluctuations to point the emotional message of the work with wonderful power and spontaneity, and the RPO plays superbly. Recorded in Guildford Cathedral with plentiful reverberation, this version has the advantage of a splendid contribution from the organ at the end. The five *Pomp and circumstance marches* on the reverse are given Prom-style performances full of flair and urgency, although some might feel that the chosen speeds are a trifle fast and Del Mar's approach not relaxed enough to bring out the nobilmente. The reverberant sound here adds something of an aggressive edge to the music-making. Even so, at medium price this is a very competitive issue. The cassette transfer is of high quality, minimizing the edge in the *Marches* without robbing them of bite and offering splendid sound in the *Variations.*

Andrew Davis's CBS version was his second stereo version of *Enigma* (the first was for Lyrita – coupled with *Falstaff* – and is now withdrawn), and brought a remarkable development in the interpretation with the slow variations far more expansive than before. Fast variations remain crisp and incisive, and the playing of the Philharmonia, beautifully recorded, is splendid. Yet for many this reading will feel a little too plain, lacking idiosyncrasy, not quite idiomatic. The marches come off very well. There is a brilliant chrome cassette, clear and clean and naturally balanced.

Monteux's reading is as fresh as ever. Here it is recoupled with Bliss's account of the *Marches*, where rumbustious vigour is leavened with a proper touch of nobilmente. Both recordings have been remastered and now show their age (they were made more than twenty years ago), with thin upper strings. The cassette tends to emphasize this more than the disc.

Serenade for strings in E min., Op. 20 (see also above under *Cello concerto; Elegy; Introduction and allegro*).
** ASV Dig. DCA/*ZCDCA* 518. ASMF, Marriner – TIPPETT: *Fantasia concertante* **; VAUGHAN WILLIAMS: *Lark ascending* etc.**(*)
(M) ** HMV SXLP 30126. Philh. O, Sargent – HOLST: *Beni Mora* etc.; WARLOCK: *Capriol suite.***
** Abbey ABY 810. Scottish Bar. Ens., Friedman – BRITTEN: *Simple symphony;* WARLOCK: *Capriol suite;* WILLIAMSON: *English lyrics.***(*)

Neville Marriner's recording of the *Serenade*, for ASV, offers well-defined and cleanly focused sound indeed; perhaps it is just a little too 'present' and forward, though not unreasonably so. The performance adds nothing to his earlier recording on Argo, made in the late 1960s, which generates greater atmosphere (see above). Choice will doubtless be governed by the coupling required. The cassette transfer is well managed, but does not match the quality afforded on Argo.

Sargent's couplings are enterprising, and his reading of the *Serenade* is well recorded and characteristically well made. But it has not the individuality of Barbirolli's (coupled with the *Introduction and allegro*) or Marriner's (coupled with the *Elegy* etc.).

The Scottish Baroque Ensemble give an alert if not especially elegant performance of Elgar's delightful *Serenade*, not as polished as some, but brightly recorded and interestingly coupled.

The Starlight Express (incidental music), *Op. 78.*

(M) *** HMV Green. ESDW/*TC2-ESDW* 711. Masterton, Hammond Stroud, LPO, Handley.

The Starlight Express was a children's play, adapted from a novel by Algernon Blackwood, which in 1916 its promoters hoped would prove a successor to Barrie's *Peter Pan*. Though the play failed to attract a comparable following, Elgar himself at the time recorded a whole sequence of numbers from it. Even that failed to keep the music alive, and it has been left to latter-day Elgarians to revive a score which reveals the composer at his most charming. On record in this dedicated reconstruction with even the linking fragments included (but without the spoken dialogue) one is conscious of an element of repetition, but the ear is continually beguiled and the key sequences suggest that this procedure would have won the composer's approval. Some of the words reflect the coy manner of the original libretto, but much of the orchestral music has that nostalgically luminous quality that Elgarians will instantly recognize. Both soloists are excellent, and the LPO plays with warmth and sympathy. The 1976 recording is excellent, and the glowing quality of the cassette transfer (the music all on a single double-length tape) makes this an ideal way to dip into a delightful score and discover Vernon Handley already emerging as a distinguished Elgarian.

Symphonies Nos. 1 and 2.

*** ASV ALHB 201 (2). Hallé O, Loughran.

Loughran directs deeply sympathetic performances of both symphonies, beautifully played, with the refinement of pianissimo from the Hallé strings more remarkable than from this orchestra in the past. Loughran, in the Boult tradition, takes a direct view, less overtly expressive or emotional than Handley on CfP, for example, so that, though the result may be less exciting, it has a reflective quality that is very satisfying too. The slow movement of No. 1 makes a culmination, with the third theme ravishingly beautiful in its tenderness. In No. 2 Loughran's feeling for climax is unerring, but his relatively slow tempi in the last two movements bring a slight lack of intensity, with the chains of sequential phrases sounding too unpointed, rhythmically heavier than they need be. Splendid recording, with the timpani vividly caught, but with a general distancing that matches the degree of reserve in the performances.

Symphony No. 1 in A flat, Op. 55.

(B) *** CfP CFP/*TC-CFP* 40331. LPO, Handley.

*** Decca SXL/*KSXC* 6569 [Lon. CS 6789]. LPO, Solti.

*** HMV ASD/*TC-ASD* 3330. LPO, Boult.

*** HMV Dig. ASD/*TC-ASD* 107794-1/*4*. Philh. O, Haitink.

*** ASV ALH/*ZCALH* 907. Hallé O, Loughran.

(M) ** HMV SXLP 30268. Philh. O, Barbirolli.

(B) ** PRT GSGC/*ZCGC* 2010. Hallé O, Barbirolli.

(B) ** RCA VICS 2010. SNO, Gibson.

No work of Elgar's more completely captures the atmosphere of uninhibited opulence which his generation of composers was the last to enjoy. Elgar, unlike composers after him, did not have to apologize for writing a symphony nearly an hour long, nor for writing tunes of a warmth and memorability that are strikingly his.

Vernon Handley directs a beautifully paced

performance of Elgar's *First*. The LPO has recorded this symphony many times before, but never with more poise and refinement than here, and the Elgar sound is gloriously captured, particularly the brass. Not surprisingly Handley, a former pupil of Sir Adrian Boult, takes a direct view. As in his fine recording of *Falstaff* (currently deleted), there is sometimes a hint of restraint which then opens up, with power in reserve. It is in the slow movement, more spacious and lovingly expressive than Sir Adrian allows, that Handley scores above all. Even making no allowance for price, this is outstanding among current versions. The cassette transfer too is first-class, remarkable in its wide amplitude and range.

Before Solti recorded the *First* he made a searching study of Elgar's own 78 recording, and the modifications of detailed markings implicit in that are reproduced here, not with a sense of calculation but with very much the same rich, committed qualities that mark out the Elgar performance. Solti even more than in Mahler seems freed from emotional inhibition, with every climax superbly thrust home and the hushed intensity of the glorious slow movement captured on record as never before. The recording is of demonstration quality, rich but refined too, and rightly Decca ensured that the important link between the second and third movements comes in mid-side, even though that makes for a very long second side. A superlative disc in every way, and a very good cassette too.

If Solti, following the composer, underlines the passionate dedication of the *First Symphony*, Boult on HMV more clearly presents it as a close counterpart of the *Second*, with hints of reflective nostalgia amid the triumph. Until this final version, made when Sir Adrian was eighty-seven, his recordings of the *First* had been among his less riveting Elgar performances. But the HMV disc, recorded with an opulence to outshine even the Decca sound for Solti, contains a radiantly beautiful performance, less thrustful than Solti's, with speeds less extreme in both directions: richly spaced in the first movement, swaggering in the syncopated march-rhythms of the scherzo and similarly bouncing in the Brahmsian rhythms of the finale. Most clearly distinctive is the lovely slow movement, presented as a seamless flow of melody, faster, less 'inner' than with Solti and above all glowing with untroubled sweetness. This HMV disc now completely supersedes Boult's earlier (now deleted) Lyrita version, made with the same orchestra. The HMV cassette transfer is rich and full-blooded. Although the level is quite high it nevertheless needs a high-volume replay to bring out the full detail and impact. It can be made to sound very well indeed.

With consistently slow tempi – far slower than Boult or Barbirolli used to adopt – Haitink's is a spacious reading, which in its measured way takes a straight and thoughtful look at Elgar's score. The result is hardly idiomatic, but with superb playing from the Philharmonia under Haitink's concentrated direction, it is profound and moving, elegiacally glowing with genuine Elgarian warmth. Splendid digital sound to match and a fine cassette which, though not transferred at the highest level, offers the most beautiful sound to match the disc, with detail undiminished.

Loughran's performance, direct and understanding, is also very fine with a memorably beautiful slow movement. The recording is first-class, naturally balanced, but vivid. There is an element of reserve here, but the performance makes a strong impression. The cassette is well managed, but has less bite and range at the top than the disc.

Barbirolli's HMV reissue still sounds very well. However, Barbirolli's tempi are controversial; apart from the very slow speed for the slow movement, there is a hint of heaviness in the first movement too, where after the march introduction the music should surge along.

Compared with Barbirolli's Philharmonia version, the Hallé account has its moments of roughness in the playing (the strings are by no means so smooth), but the first movement is far more vigorous. Barbirolli's faster tempo means that the expansively unfolding argument carries through more convincingly, whereas on HMV he does not avoid a feeling of dragging. The slow movement too is more affectionately done in this earlier version. The snag is that the (1957) recording quality is far less vivid. The cassette is full-bodied and clear, but not very wide-ranging at the top.

Gibson draws a direct, intelligent performance from the Scottish National Orchestra, but he lacks the urgency and commitment of the finest readings on record. On Victrola he competes directly with Handley's fine CfP issue, which is preferable not only as a performance but also as a recording. The RCA disc has less body, and Gibson's view of Elgar is rather literal, starting with a matter-of-fact view of the motto march-theme.

Symphony No. 2 in E flat, Op. 63.

(B) ❀ *** CfP CFP/*TC-CFP* 40350. LPO, Handley.

*** HMV ASD/TC-*ASD* 3330 [Ang. S 37218]. LPO, Boult.

*** Decca SXL 6723 [Lon. CS 6941]. LPO, Solti.

**(*) ASV ALH/*ZCALH* 906 [None. 71406]. Hallé O, Loughran.

(M) ** HMV SXLP/*TC-SXLP* 30287. Hallé O, Barbirolli.

(B) ** PRT GSGC/*ZCGC* 2016. LPO, Boult.

Handley's is the most satisfying modern version of a work which has latterly been much recorded. It is broadly in the Boult mould, never forcing the pace (as Elgar himself did, and, following him, Solti) but equally adopting tempi such as Sir Adrian preferred at the height of his career, rather more urgent, less elegiac. What Handley conveys superbly is the sense of Elgarian ebb and flow, building climaxes like a master, and drawing excellent, spontaneous-sounding playing from the orchestra which more than any other has specialized in performing this symphony. The sound is warmly atmospheric, and vividly conveys the added organ part in the bass just at the climax of the finale (eight bars after Fig. 165 in the score), which Elgar himself suggested 'if available': a tummy-wobbling effect. This would be a first choice at full price, and as a bargain there are few records to match it. The cassette is every bit the equal of the disc and in many ways preferable. It has slightly more warmth and body without loss of upper range.

For his fifth recording of the *Second Symphony* Sir Adrian Boult, incomparable Elgarian, drew from the LPO the most richly satisfying performance of all. Over the years Sir Adrian's view of the glorious nobility of the first movement had mellowed a degree. The tempo is a shade slower than before (and much slower than Solti's or the composer's own in the great leaping 12/8 theme), but the pointing of climaxes is unrivalled. With Boult more than anyone else the architecture is clearly and strongly established, with tempo changes less exaggerated than usual. The peak comes in the great *Funeral march*, where the concentration of the performance is irresistible. The LPO strings play gloriously, with the great swooping violin phrases at the climaxes inspiring a frisson as in a live performance. The scherzo has lightness and delicacy, with Boult very little slower than Solti but giving more room to breathe. In the finale, firm and strong, Boult cleverly conceals the repetitiveness of the main theme, and gives a radiant account of the lovely epilogue. With superb, opulent recording, this is a version to convert new listeners to a love of Elgar. The tape transfer too is admirably rich, yet with good detail, one of EMI's best cassettes.

Solti's incandescent performance is modelled closely on Elgar's own surprisingly clipped and urgent reading, but benefits from virtuoso playing by the LPO and superbly balanced sound. Fast tempi bring searing concentration and an account of the finale that for once presents a true climax. This is a fitting companion to Solti's magnificent account of No. 1.

Even more than in his recording of No. 1 Loughran's *Second* has an element of emotional reticence. He chooses a steady pacing for the last two movements and the finale has less exuberance than with Handley. This is still a performance of considerable character, but it is in the last resort less involving than are either Boult or Solti. The recording is excellent, well balanced and spacious. The sound on cassette is good, but although there is body and impact, the relative lack of upper range reduces the bite.

Barbirolli's version was originally issued as a two-disc set, coupled with *Falstaff*. The mid-priced reissue fits the performance on to two sides without striking loss of amplitude (the cassette, although lively, lacks ripeness in the middle range). Barbirolli's interpretation is a very personal one, deeply felt, but with the pace of the music often excessively varied, sometimes coarsening effects which Elgar's score specifies very precisely and weakening the structure of the finale.

Boult's bargain version on PRT, recorded in 1963, presents a nobler, more dedicated performance, and the sound, though dated, has come up surprisingly well in the latest dubbing. The performance is glorious, and at the price many Elgarians will accept the less than ideal recording. On cassette, side two has a brighter, more sharply defined upper range than side one.

Variations on an original theme (Enigma), Op. 36 (see also above under *Cockaigne; Cello concerto; Introduction and allegro; Pomp and circumstance marches*).

*** HMV ASD/*TC-ASD* 2750 [Ang. S/*4XS* 36799]. LPO, Boult – VAUGHAN WILLIAMS: *English folk songs suite* etc.**(*)

(M) *** Decca SPA/*KCSP* 121. LSO, Monteux – BRAHMS: *Variations.****

(M) *** Decca Jub. JB/*KJBC* 106. LAPO, Mehta – MUSSORGSKY: *Pictures.***(*)

*** HMV ASD/*TC-ASD* 3857 [Ang. SZ/*4ZS* 37627]. LSO, Previn – VAUGHAN WILLIAMS: *Tallis fantasia; Wasps.****

(M) ** HMV SXLP/*TC-SXLP* 20007 [Sera. S/*4XG* 60173]. Philh. O, Sargent – VAUGHAN WILLIAMS: *Tallis fantasia.***

(i) *Enigma variations;* (ii) *Cockaigne overture.*

**(*) Decca SXL 6795 [(d) Lon. CS 6954]. (i) Chicago SO; (ii) LPO; Solti.

Enigma variations; Crown of India: March of the Mogul Emperors; Pomp and circumstance marches Nos. 1 and 2.

*(*) DG Dig. 2532/*3302* 067 [id.]. BBC SO, Bernstein.

Elgar's best-loved work is available in an almost infinite variety of couplings, but first choice lies with Barbirolli's magnificently red-blooded reading coupled with the *Cockaigne* and the *Introduction and allegro* (see above) or with Boult's version which has a wonderfully direct spontaneity, with each variation growing naturally and seamlessly out of the music that has gone before. The performance has warmth and nobility too and it is marvellously captured in a vintage analogue recording. *Nimrod* in particular glows in beauty, superbly sustained. Perhaps the finale lacks the fire that Barbirolli gave it, but the richness of texture, detailed but finely moulded, has rarely if ever been so magnificently captured on record before. The cassette transfer (originally non-Dolby) is an early one, and the sound, though now given the Dolby treatment, still tends to be bass-orientated.

Monteux's reading too remains highly distinctive, and in its original format (it is also available re-coupled with *Pomp and circumstance* – see above) the disc still sounds well, though the cassette was never one of Decca's best and is marginally less refined. There is a marvellous freshness about Monteux's approach – what a remarkably versatile musician he was – and the music is obviously deeply felt. He secures a real pianissimo at the beginning of *Nimrod*, the playing hardly above a whisper, yet the tension electric. Slowly the great tune is built up in elegiac fashion, and the superb climax is the more effective in consequence. Differences from traditional tempi elsewhere are marginal, and add to rather than detract from one's enjoyment.

Mehta, born and brought up in India, has evidently not rejected all sympathy for the British Raj and its associations. Certainly he is a strong and sensitive interpreter of Elgar, if this highly enjoyable account is anything to go by. There are no special revelations, although the transition from the spacious climax of *Nimrod* to a delightfully graceful *Dorabella* is particularly felicitous. The vintage Decca recording, with the organ entering spectacularly in the finale, is outstanding, and the cassette is excellent too, every bit as vivid and only marginally less rich.

Previn uniquely but imaginatively couples Elgar's most popular orchestral work with what are probably the two most popular pieces of Vaughan Williams. This *Enigma* is not entirely idiomatic, but it is refreshingly spontaneous. The points which may initially strike the Elgarian as unusual, particularly on the question of speed fluctuation, result from a literal reading of the score, the proverbial 'new look'. In some ways it is a similar reading to that of Monteux with the same orchestra, strong and consistent, noble rather than passionate. The recording is impressively ample, and the cassette transfer is comparably full-blooded.

With Solti the variations become a dazzling showpiece. Though the charm of the work is given short measure, the structure emerges the more sharply with the fast variations taken at breakneck speed and with the Chicago orchestra challenged to supreme virtuosity. The disappointment is *Nimrod*, where from a basic tempo faster than usual Solti allows himself to get faster and faster still, in a style that misses the feeling of nobilmente. Solti's view of *Cockaigne* is similarly one of extremes, but here, with the LPO, recorded more richly and just as brilliantly, there is more sparkle, a mercurial element.

Sargent's recording is impressive in sonority (if not always in clarity) and the closing pages with their organ bass are very exciting. Sargent's performance is a traditional one and makes much of the nobilmente character of the score. With its well-chosen coupling this is good value. The cassette has been remastered and now matches the disc closely.

Bernstein's is quite the most perverse reading of *Enigma* ever recorded, and not all listeners will respond to its outrageous self-indulgence, not least in *Nimrod* which is dragged out to almost unimaginable lengths. Though wilful, Bernstein is always passionate, and with good playing and recording he may attract those who want to hear a fresh view, or who enjoyed the television programme made at the time of the recording. Best of all are the fill-ups, bold and swaggering. There is a first-class chrome cassette, wide-ranging, full and brilliant.

CHAMBER MUSIC

Allegretto on a theme of five notes; Bizarrerie, Op. 13/2; La Capricieuse, Op. 17; Chanson de matin; Chanson de nuit, Op. 15/1 and 2; Gavotte; Une idylle, Op. 4/1; Mot d'amour, Op. 13/1; Offertoire; Pastourelle, Op. 4/2; Reminiscences; Romance, Op. 1; Salut d'amour, Op. 12; Sospiri, Op. 70; Virelai, Op. 4/3.
*** Pearl SHE 523. Georgiadis, Parry.

John Georgiadis, brilliant leader of the LSO, shows his flair as a soloist in this collection, which includes virtually all of Elgar's music for violin and piano except the *Sonata*. These are trifles with few pretensions, mainly early works, yet such is Elgar's natural imagination, his feeling for the violin (his own instrument) and Georgiadis's expressiveness that this recital brings the fullest variety. Strong, close-up recording.

(i–ii) *Piano quintet in A min.*, Op. 84; (iii) *String quartet in E min., Op. 83;* (iv) *Violin sonata in E min., Op. 82;* (i) (Piano) *Adieu; Concert allegro, Op. 41; Serenade; Sonatina.*
**(*) HMV SLS 5084 (2). (i) Ogdon; (ii) Allegri Qt; (iii) Music Group of London Qt; (iv) Bean, Parkhouse.

Elgar turned to chamber music towards the end of the First World War at a time of personal disillusion which also produced the elegiac *Cello concerto*. The *Piano quintet* is the most ambitious of his three chamber works, and though there are moments when Elgar's instrumentation brings unwanted Palm Court associations, the slow movement is among his greatest, and every bar is distinctive and memorable. John Ogdon and the Allegri Quartet give a strong performance which misses some of the deeper, warmer emotions in the music but which still gives considerable satisfaction. The *Concert allegro* is a valuable oddity, resurrected by Ogdon (the music was long thought to be lost) and splendidly played, and the shorter pieces too bring some charming ideas, even if they reveal Elgar's obvious limitations when writing for the keyboard. Originally issued as a single disc, these recordings now appear in a reasonably-priced box with a second disc including the *String quartet* and the *Violin sonata*, both superbly recorded. There is an autumnal quality about this music, and it responds to ripe treatment such as Hugh Bean and David Parkhouse bring to the *Sonata*. The *Quartet* is well done too, and this performance is generally preferable to the Claremont performance on Nonesuch (see below), even if the last degree of understanding is missing.

String quartet in E min., Op. 83.
(M) **(*) None. H 71140 [id.]. Claremont Qt – SIBELIUS: *Quartet*.**(*)

Of the three chamber works which Elgar wrote at the end of his career the *String quartet* shows the clearest mastery. On the face of it the mood is one of restraint. Elgar makes no grand gestures, gives no echo of late Beethoven, yet the intimacy of expression brings intensity of its own. On the surface some of the ideas may have kinship with Elgar's salon pieces, yet their refinement belongs to an utterly different world, and even Elgar rarely wrote a slow movement so beautiful as the middle movement here. English performances, when one hears them, tend to underline the gentleness, yet an American group coming to Elgar fresh takes an entirely different view, and though the result may upset the Elgarian traditionalists there is no denying that, in the outer movements at least, the inner strength of the work is reinforced. The slow movement unfortunately is not hushed enough: like so many American players the Claremont Quartet is reluctant to give anything less than a mezzo piano. Unless the Sibelius coupling is particularly wanted, the HMV box (see above) is a better investment.

Violin sonata in E min., Op. 82.
(*) HMV ASD 3820. Y. and H. Menuhin – VAUGHAN WILLIAMS: *Sonata.*(*)

The Menuhins present a large-scale view of this sonata, the least ambitious of Elgar's three late chamber works but one which still brings echoes of the *Violin concerto*. Unfortunately, though slow speeds bring their moments of insight and revelation at the hands of a Menuhin, the result overall is too heavy, and is marred too by imperfect intonation. The recording is first-rate.

VOCAL AND CHORAL MUSIC

Angelus; Ave Maria; Fear not, O land; Give unto the Lord (Psalm 29)*; Go, song of mine; Great is the Lord* (Psalm 48)*; I sing the birth; O harken thou; O salutaris hostia; They are at rest.*
*** Abbey ABY 822. Worcester Cath. Ch., Hunt; Trepte; Hill (organ).

Framed by two very grand Psalm settings (designed for Westminster Abbey and St Paul's Cathedral respectively) this admirable selection of Elgar church music covers an area seriously neglected on record. The Worcester Cathedral Choir, faithfully and atmospherically recorded (but not in a washy cathedral acoustic), sings with fine fresh tone. Grandeur is given to the Psalms (both settings from the high peak of Elgar's maturity) and tenderness to the shorter pieces, of which *Go, song of mine* (not strictly religious) is the finest.

The Apostles, Op. 49 (with talk: *The Apostles and The Kingdom* by Michael Kennedy; read by Sir Adrian Boult).
*** HMV SLS 976 (3). Armstrong, Watts, Tear, Luxon, Grant, Carol Case, Downe House School Ch., LPO Ch., LPO, Boult.

Sir Adrian Boult at eighty-five directed one of his most inspired recordings, an account of Elgar's long-neglected oratorio (the first of a projected trilogy; *The Kingdom* was the second) which must warm the heart of any Elgarian. That the work failed earlier to make the impact it deserves stands as a condemnation of fashion. It may not have quite such memorable melodies as *Gerontius* or *The Kingdom*, but many of the numbers, like the setting of the Beatitudes, *By the Wayside*, show Elgar at his most inspired, and the characters of Mary Magdalene and Judas are unexpectedly rounded and sympathetic. Generally fine singing – notably from Sheila Armstrong and Helen Watts – and a recording as rich and faithful as anyone could want.

Ave verum corpus; Ecce sacerdos magnus; Great is the Lord (Psalm 48).
** Abbey LPB 813. Leeds Parish Church Ch., Lindley; Corfield (organ) – LISZT: *Via crucis.***

The *Ave verum corpus* is an early work, and so is *Ecce sacerdos magnus* (the latter is not otherwise available). *Psalm 48*, a later work, is rather more impressive; the early pieces do not wholly escape the charge of sounding sanctimonious, and they do not really show the master at his most inspired. Good choral singing and a decent accompaniment from the organist, Tom Corfield.

Caractacus, Op. 35.
*** HMV SLS 998 (2). Armstrong, Tear, Glossop, Rayner Cook, King, Stuart, Liv. Philharmonic Ch., Royal Liv. PO, Groves.

Caractacus, based on the story of the ancient British hero pardoned by the Emperor Claudius, dropped out of the regular repertory long ago, forgotten except for the rousing *Triumphal march* and some notorious lines about the nations standing to 'hymn the praise of Britain like brothers hand in hand'. In fact only a tiny proportion of the piece is at all jingoistic, and such passages as the duet between Caractacus's daughter and her lover are as tenderly beautiful as anything Elgar wrote before *Enigma*. This is a fine performance which with ripe recording brings out all the Elgarian atmosphere (even if it does not manage a clear projection of the words); but it partly explains the neglect. The dramatic interest is limited, and the melodies are generally not as memorable as they might be. But *Caractacus* gives a rich insight into the happy Elgar early in his career, a composer still limited but delightfully approachable.

Coronation ode, Op. 44; National anthem (arr. Elgar).
*** HMV ASD 3345. Lott, Hodgson, Morton, Roberts, Camb. University Music Soc., King's College Ch., New Philh. O, Band of Royal Military School of Music, Ledger – PARRY: *I was glad.****

(i) *Coronation ode, Op. 44; The Spirit of England, Op. 80.*
(M) **(*) Chan. CBR/*CBT* 1013. Cahill, SNO Ch. and O, Gibson; (i) with Anne Collins, Rolfe Johnson, Howell.

Elgar's *Coronation ode* is far more than a jingoistic occasional piece, though it was indeed the work which first featured *Land of Hope and Glory*. The most tender moment of all is reserved for the first faint flickerings of that second national anthem, introduced gently on the harp to clarinet accompaniment. All told, the work contains much Elgarian treasure, and Ledger is superb in capturing the necessary swagger and panache, flouting all thought of potentially bad taste. With recording of demonstration quality – among the finest ever made in King's College Chapel – and with extra brass bands, it presents a glorious experience. Excellent singing and playing, though the male soloists do not quite match their female colleagues.

Gibson directs a stirring and forthright reading of the *Coronation ode*, helped by excellent soloists; but it cannot match the HMV account in urgency, and the actual execution is less polished. Nonetheless it presents a valuable addition to the catalogue, *The Spirit of England*, a wartime cantata to words by Laurence Binyon. The final setting of *For the fallen* rises well above the level of occasional music, at times even foreshadowing Britten's *War requiem*. Clean, reliable recording, here digitally remastered, and a first-class tape.

Part songs: *Credo in E min.; Death on the hills; Evening scene; Good morrow; How calmly the evening; Lo! Christ the Lord is born; Love; O happy eyes; O mightiest of the mighty; Serenade; To her beneath whose steadfast star; Weary wind of the west; Windlass song.*
** Mer. E 77040. Philharmonic Chamber Ch., Temple; Beniston (organ).

Though the atmosphere is rather like that of the daily service on BBC Radio, Elgarians will welcome this collection of rarities, not least the minor-key setting of the *Credo*, which has remained unpublished. The rest span the whole of Elgar's composing career up to 1924. Performances are clear and tasteful and are atmospherically recorded.

The Dream of Gerontius, Op. 38.
❀ *** HMV SLS/*TC-SLS* 987(2). Watts, Gedda, Lloyd, Alldis Ch., New Philh. O, Boult.
**(*) Decca SET 525/6. Minton, Pears, Shirley-Quirk, LSO Ch., King's College Ch., LSO, Britten.
**(*) CRD CRD 1026/7. Hodgson, Tear, Luxon, SNO Ch. and O, Gibson
**(*) HMV SLS 770(2). Baker, Lewis, Borg, Hallé and Sheffield Philharmonic Ch., Amb. S., Hallé O, Barbirolli.

Boult provided here the performance of *The Dream of Gerontius* for which Elgarians had waited since the advent of stereo recording. Listening to this wonderful set one feels that this is the culmination of a long history of partial or complete recordings of this great masterpiece which stretches far back into the days of acoustic 78 r.p.m. discs. Here Boult's total dedication is matched by a sense both of wonder and of drama. The spiritual feeling is intense, but the human qualities of the narrative are fully realized, and the glorious closing pages are so beautiful that Elgar's vision is made to become one of the most unforgettable moments in all musical literature. Boult's unexpected choice of Gedda in the role of Gerontius brings a new dimension to this characterization, which is perfectly matched by Helen Watts as the Angel. The dialogues between the two have a natural spontaneity as Gerontius's questions and doubts find a response which is at once gently understanding and nobly authoritative. It is a fascinating vocal partnership, and it is matched by the commanding manner which Robert Lloyd finds for both his roles. The orchestral playing is always responsive and often, like the choral singing, very beautiful. The lovely wind playing at the opening of Part 2 is matched by the luminosity of tone of the choral pianissimos, while the dramatic passages bring splendid incisiveness and bold assurance from the singers. The recording is truly first-class, of genuine demonstration quality.

There were problems with the early issue of this work on cassette, but it has now been satisfactorily remastered and the full body and dynamic range of the sound restored. The focus is softer-grained than the discs, but the quality is still impressive.

Britten may seem an unlikely interpreter of Elgar, and he was persuaded to interpret *The Dream of Gerontius* as a result of hearing Peter Pears singing in it under Sir Adrian Boult. He first conducted the work at the Aldeburgh Festival, later recording it (also in the Maltings), and the pity is that a different chorus was imported. For whatever reason, the LSO Chorus is well below its finest form, the sound not nearly so powerful as it can and should be. Nonetheless the dedication of Britten's reading, the sense of fresh creation, is most moving. Pears (not always in his finest voice) is an involving Gerontius, while John Shirley-Quirk and Yvonne Minton are excellent too, even if Minton can hardly match Janet Baker in spiritual concentration. Atmospheric recording, generally helped by the lively Maltings acoustic.

Gibson's performance cannot really compete with Boult, or indeed Britten. It is impressively spontaneous and very dramatic, as is immediately apparent in the strong contrasts of dynamic in the *Prelude*. When in his opening section Gerontius (Robert Tear) describes 'this strange innermost abandonment, this emptying out of each constituent', the orchestral response sends a shiver down the spine. The same sense of drama attends the demons (who are forthright rather than sinister); and the moment when the soul of Gerontius goes to meet his maker is positively apocalyptic. The male soloists match Gibson's urgency, although there is no lack of repose in the dialogue between the Angel (sensitively portrayed by Alfreda Hodgson) and Gerontius at the opening of Part 2. But Gibson does not manage to create the sense of unearthly stillness and quiet beauty that is so moving in Boult's marvellous performance. Equally the accelerando to the close of the *Praise to the Holiest* section is not as intuitively calculated as in Britten's version (which uncannily matches the composer's own performance, which Britten could not have heard, as it was not published when he made his Decca set). The closing pages with Gibson are sensitively done but are without the magical feeling of blissful infinity that Boult conjures up. The CRD recording is generally excellent. It has almost too wide a dynamic range: a volume setting where the gentler music is absolutely clear is overwhelming at a fortissimo. But at a concert this account would bring down the house, and rightly so.

Those who do not look for a spiritual experience from *Gerontius* will not be disappointed with Sir John's red-blooded and dramatic reading. Janet Baker, especially, sings superbly – even if her style is purposely operatic, following Sir John's conception – and Richard Lewis is also good. Kim Borg makes a disappointing priest. His rather colourless account of the music is not helped by his lack of command of the diction of the English language, and the blurred consonants prevent forthright delivery. The *Go forth* chorus is splendid, however, and so is the music of the demons, helped by the stereo recording. Elsewhere, and especially in the dialogue between the soul of Gerontius and the Angel, and in the closing pages, Boult evokes a much greater feeling of spirituality and repose.

From the Bavarian Highlands, Op. 27.
*** HMV ASD/*TC-ASD* 4061. Bournemouth Ch. and SO, Del Mar – VAUGHAN WILLIAMS: *In Windsor Forest.****

The three *Bavarian dances* for orchestra, which Elgar extracted from this suite of part songs, are well known, but not the original choral work, which is as effective as it is enjoyable. Here, although the recording is agreeably rich and full-bodied, balances are not always ideal, with the choral descant in the *Lullaby* third movement outweighing the orchestral detail. However, the performances are infectiously spirited, conveying warmth as well as vigour. The cassette is rather less clean in focus than the disc, but still sounds well.

The Kingdom, Op. 51.
*** HMV SLS 939 (2). Price, Minton, Young, Shirley-Quirk, LPO Ch., LPO, Boult.

Boult was devoted to this noble oratorio, openly preferring it even to *Gerontius*, and his dedication emerges clearly throughout a glorious performance which should help to establish a splendid work at last in the repertory. It has often been suggested that it is too static, but the Pentecost scene is intensely dramatic, and the richness of musical inspiration in the rest prevents any feeling of stagnation, certainly in a performance as inspired as this. The melody which Elgar wrote to represent the Holy Spirit is one of the noblest that even he created, and the soprano aria *The sun goeth down* (beautifully sung by Margaret Price) leads to a deeply affecting climax. The other soloists too sing splendidly, and the only reservation concerns the chorus, which is not quite so disciplined as it might be and sounds a little too backward for some of the massive effects which cap the power of the work. Excellent recording otherwise.

The Light of Life, Op. 29.
*** HMV ASD/*TC-ASD* 3952. Marshall, Watts, Leggate, Shirley-Quirk, Royal Liv. Ch. and PO, Groves.

The Light of Life was one of the works immediately preceding the great leap forward which Elgar made with *Enigma* in 1899. This compact oratorio – telling the story of Jesus giving sight to the blind man – has many foretastes of *The Dream of Gerontius*, but with an uninspired libretto, the overall flavour has something of updated Mendelssohn rather than pure Elgar. The fine opening prelude, *Meditation*, is the only passage that is at all well known, but that includes some of the finest, most memorable motifs. The tenor aria for the blind man is almost operatic in its intensity, but the attempt to dramatize the incident is so naïve that the modern listener may well remain unconvinced. Otherwise there is a fine baritone aria for Jesus, *I am the good shepherd*, and much else to delight the committed Elgarian. Sir Charles Groves's understanding performance features four first-rate soloists and strongly involving, if not always flawless, playing and singing from the Liverpool orchestra and choir. The recording is warm and atmospheric in EMI's recognizable Elgar manner. The cassette transfer is good, but made at rather a modest level for EMI, especially on side two, where the choral climaxes have a reduced sharpness of focus and the soloists less presence.

The Music Makers, Op. 69.
(*) HMV ASD 2311 [Van. 71225]. Baker, LPO Ch., LPO, Boult – PARRY: *Blest Pair of Sirens.*

Elgar's long-neglected cantata sets the Shaughnessy poem of the same name. It was a mature work, written soon after the *Symphonies* and *Violin concerto*, and is full of warm, attractive writing for both voices and orchestra. But it is some measure of the musical material that the passages which stand out are those where Elgar used themes from his earlier works. If only the whole piece lived up to the uninhibited choral setting of the *Nimrod* variation from *Enigma*, it would be another Elgar masterpiece. As it is there are enough moments of rich expansiveness to make it essential for any Elgarian to hear, particularly in so understanding a performance as this. Janet Baker sings with dedicated mastery, though unfortunately her example is not always matched by the comparatively dull-sounding choir.

The Music Makers, Op: 69; 3 Bavarian dances, Op. 27; Chanson de matin; Chanson de nuit, Op. 15/1–2; The Wand of Youth suites Nos. 1–2, Op. 1a–1b.
(M) **(*) HMV *TCC2-POR* 54291. (from above recordings, cond. Boult).

It was a happy idea to include *The Music Makers* in EMI's *'Portrait of the Artist'* series and place it complete on one side of an extended-length chrome tape. The sound is good, only losing a little of the upper range (the chorus has rather more bite on disc). But to couple this with much slighter music, however attractively performed, is more controversial. The orchestral quality is bright and clear. The cassette includes no information whatsoever about the music, except titles and details of performers.

Songs: *Pleading; The river; The torch; 3 Songs, Op. 59.*
*** HMV ASD 3896. Tear, CBSO, Handley – BUTTERWORTH: *Love Blows as the Wind****; VAUGHAN WILLIAMS: *On Wenlock Edge.***(*)

At his most creative period in the early years of the century Elgar planned another song cycle to follow *Sea Pictures*, but he completed only three of the songs, his Op. 59. The other three songs here are even more individual, a fine coupling for the Vaughan Williams. Incisive and characterful performances from Tear, and good recording, warm and atmospheric.

Sea Pictures (song cycle), *Op. 37.*
❀ *** HMV ASD/*TC-ASD* 655. Baker, LSO, Barbirolli – *Cello concerto.****❀
*** HMV ASD 2721 [Ang. S 36796]. Baker (as above) – MAHLER: *Rückert Lieder.****

(i) *Sea Pictures. Pomp and circumstance marches, Op. 39/1–5.*
*** CfP CFP/*TC-CFP* 40363. LPO, Handley, (i) with Greevy.

Sea Pictures hardly matches the mature inspiration of the *Cello concerto* with which it is coupled on HMV, but it is heartwarming here nonetheless. Like du Pré, Dame Janet Baker is an artist who has the power to convey on record the vividness of a live performance. With the help of Barbirolli she makes the cycle far more convincing than it usually seems, with words that are often trite clothed in music that seems to transform them. Warm recording. The cassette transfer is of good quality, only marginally less refined then the LP.

Although the original coupling with the *Cello concerto* is particularly apt, the alternative will especially please Janet Baker's admirers, for some of her finest recorded art is here.

Bernadette Greevy – in glorious voice – gives the performance of her recording career in an inspired partnership with Vernon Handley, whose accompaniments are no less memorable, with the LPO players finding a wonderful rapport with the voice. The singer's imaginative illumination of the words is a constant source of delight and her tenderness in the *Sea slumber song* and the delightfully idyllic *In haven* contrasts with the splendour of the big central and final songs, where Handley revels in the music's surging momentum. Here he uses a telling ad lib organ part to underline the climaxes of each final stanza. The recording balance is ideal, the voice rich and clear against an orchestral background shimmering with atmospheric detail. The coupled *Marches* are exhilaratingly brilliant, and if Nos. 2 and (especially) 3 strike some ears as too vigorously paced, comparison with the composer's own tempi reveals an authentic precedent. Certainly the popular *First* and *Fourth* have an attractive gutsy grandiloquence. The recording is again excellent. The cassette matches the disc closely, but the *Sea Pictures* is slightly less refined on top (although the difference is marginal).

Enesco, Georges (1881–1955)

Roumanian rhapsody No. 1.
C **(*) RCA Dig. **RCD 14439** [id.]. Dallas SO, Mata (with Concert).**(*) C

Roumanian rhapsodies Nos. 1 and 2.
(M) **(*) Mercury SRI/*MRI* 75018 [id.]. LSO, Dorati – LISZT: *Hungarian rhapsodies Nos. 2 and 3.***(*)

For the general musical public Georges Enesco seems fated to remain a one-work composer like Paul Dukas with his *Sorcerer's apprentice*. Enesco's chimerical *First Roumanian rhapsody* combines a string of glowing folk-derived melodies with glittering scoring to make it the finest genre piece of its kind in laminating eastern gypsy influences under a bourgeois orchestral veneer. The Dallas performance, with the help of superbly lustrous digital sound, brings out all the colour and much of the sparkle, although Mata does not quite find the flair and exhilaration in the closing pages which distinguish the Dorati and Previn (see Concerts) versions. But the RCA compact disc is truly demonstration-worthy in its natural vividness.

Dorati offers the *Second Rhapsody* too, which is a much less interesting piece, and his coupling with Liszt, though appropriate, offers rather short measure. Yet the Mercury sound, from the early 1960s, is well up to the standards of the house, and the LSO playing is admirably spirited. There is an excellent cassette, though not transferred at the very highest level and presented without musical notes.

Falla, Manuel de (1876–1946)

Harpsichord concerto.
(M) * Sup. 1110 3187. Růžičková, Cech, Chvapil, Dlouhy, Vik, Novosad – DEBUSSY: *Rhapsody No. 1*; MARTIN: *Petite symphonie concertante.**

(i) *Harpsichord concerto;* (ii) *Psyché;* (ii; iii) *Master Peter's puppet show* (*El retablo de Maese Pedro*).
*** Argo ZRG 921. (i) Constable, (ii) Jennifer Smith, (iii) Oliver, Knapp; L. Sinf., Rattle.
(M) *** Erato ERA/*MCE* 9241. (i) Veyron-Lacroix, (ii) Higueras-Aragon, (iii) Cabrera, Bermudez; Instrumental Ens., Dutoit.

Simon Rattle and the London Sinfonietta have exactly the same coupling as Dutoit on Erato. There is little to choose between them: the orchestral response in the Argo version is every bit as incisive, alive and characterful as Dutoit's, and the Argo singers – particularly Jennifer Smith as the boy – are if anything even better. John Constable is an admirable interpreter of the *Concerto*, though his instrument is more reticently balanced than Robert Veyron-Lacroix, who also recorded it in the early days of stereo as well as for Dutoit. Those who want the greater presence of a more forward harpsichord should choose the Erato, where Veyron-Lacroix plays with elegance and panache, but there is no doubting the truth and subtlety of the Argo balance, or the excellence of the performance. *Psyché*, also common to both discs, is a setting of words by Jean Aubry for voice and a small instrumental grouping of the size used in the *Harpsichord concerto*. Though honours are pretty evenly divided here, Rattle's Argo disc has a marginal lead over its distinguished rival.

The Czech performance on Supraphon is not as naturally balanced as John Constable on Argo or as idiomatic in feeling as Robert Veyron-Lacroix. Zuzana Růžičková is a shade inflexible and the close balance is not in her favour.

El amor brujo (*Love, the Magician;* ballet): complete.
(M) *** Decca Jub. JB 50. Mistral, New Philh. O, Frühbeck de Burgos – GRANADOS: *Goyescas*; RAVEL: *Alborada* etc.***

El amor brujo; The Three-cornered Hat (ballet): complete.
C ❀ *** Decca Dig. **410 008-2**; SXDL/*KSXDC* 7560 [Lon. LDR/*5*- 71060]. Boky, Tourangeau, Montreal SO, Dutoit.

El amor brujo: Ritual fire dance (only)*; The Three-cornered Hat* (ballet): complete.

*** Ph. Dig. **411 046-2**; 6514/*7337* 281 [id.]. Von Stade, Pittsburgh SO, Previn.

The Three-cornered Hat (complete).
(M) *** DG Sig. 410 844-1/*4*. Berganza, Boston SO, Ozawa – RAVEL: *Rapsodie espagnole*.**

The Three-cornered Hat (complete); *La vida breve: Interlude and dance.*
(B) **(*) Con. CC/*CCT* 7560. Berganza, SRO, Ansermet.

The Three-cornered Hat: Suites Nos. 1 and 2.
*** HMV Dig. ASD/*TCC-ASD* 3902 [Ang. DS/*4XS* 37742]. Phd. O, Muti – CHABRIER: *España*; RAVEL: *Rapsodie*.***
(*) Decca SXL 6956. LAPO, Lopez-Cobos – CHABRIER: *España*; RIMSKY-KORSAKOV: *Capriccio*.

Dutoit provides the ideal and very generous coupling of Falla's two popular and colourful ballets, each complete with vocal parts. Few more atmospheric records have ever been made, and particularly in the compact-disc version the very opening, the mezzo-soprano slightly distanced, with castanets, cries of '*Olé!*' and insistent timpani, is immediately involving. Performances are not just colourful and brilliantly played, they have an idiomatic feeling in their degree of flexibility over phrasing and rhythm. The ideal instance comes in the tango-like seven-in-a-bar rhythms of the *Pantomime* section of *El amor brujo* which is lusciously seductive. The sound is among the most vivid ever in whatever format, but compact disc easily takes priority in its tangibility.

Previn's crisp and refreshing view of *The Three-cornered Hat* provides a strong contrast with the sensuously beautiful Dutoit version. In its clarity and sharpness of rhythm it underlines the point that this Diaghilev ballet followed in the line of Stravinsky's. The difference of approach is brought out at the very start, when von Stade's mezzo is presented very close, not distanced at all. Next to the Decca issue, the Philips fill-up is ungenerous, only a single item from *El amor brujo* instead of the whole ballet. Excellently clean-cut recording, although the relatively low-level chrome cassette has not quite the sparkle of the LP.

Ozawa's complete recording of *The Three-cornered Hat* is one of the best versions on the market and at medium-price it remains competitive, even though the coupled Ravel *Rapsodie* is at a lower voltage. Berganza was also the soloist in Ansermet's recording, but the quality of the orchestral playing in the Boston version is superior to that of the Suisse Romande, while the vivid DG recording brings plenty of colour and presence without distorting perspectives, though Berganza is not located off-stage as directed. If the choral opening sounds somewhat self-conscious on DG, the introductory *'Olés'* on the Frühbeck de Burgos/Los Angeles HMV version (see below) are no more convincing. The DG cassette is transferred on chrome stock and is of good quality.

Frühbeck de Burgos provides us with a recommendable mid-priced version of *El amor brujo*. His superbly graduated crescendo after the spiky opening is immediately compelling, and the control of atmosphere in the quieter music is masterly. Equally the *Ritual fire dance* is blazingly brilliant. Nati Mistral has the vibrant open-throated production of the real flamenco singer. Brilliant sound, a trifle light in the bass, but offering luminous textures in the quieter sections. The cassette transfer, made at a high level, is admirably vivid.

In *The Three-cornered Hat* the Suisse Romande Orchestra play with vigour and spirit for Ansermet: even the occasional roughness of detail seems appropriate and there is no lack of vividness. Berganza is a characterful soloist. Vintage Decca sound from the 1960s with good range and clarity of definition so that this makes an excellent bargain recommendation. The coupling is not generous but has plenty of character.

Muti's reading of the colourful suites is characteristically thrustful, lacking just a little in rhythmic subtlety but making up for that in bite. They incorporate the greater part of the ballet, with *The Corregidor*, *The Miller's Wife* and *The Grapes* sections complete. The recording, typically reverberant, is among the finest yet from Philadelphia. The chrome-cassette transfer is remarkably brilliant, the resonant acoustic having no detrimental effect on the inner detail.

Helped by an extremely vivid recording (the

opening timpani are arresting) and understanding conducting from Jesus Lopez-Cobos, with nicely managed rhythmic inflections, the Decca version is undoubtedly enjoyable, as the orchestral playing is lively, though not absolutely first-class. But Muti's Philadelphia coupling is outstanding in every way and the glittering digital sound is even more spectacular.

Nights in the gardens of Spain.

(M) *** HMV Green. ESD 143648-1/*4*. Soriano, Paris Conservatoire O, Frühbeck de Burgos – RODRIGO: *Concierto de Aranjuez.***(*)

C *** Decca Dig. **410 289-2**; 410 289-1/*4* [id.]. De Larrocha, LPO, Frühbeck de Burgos – TURINA: *Rapsodia Sinfónica.****** (with ALBÉNIZ: *Rapsodia española* ***).

(B) **(*) DG Walkman *413 156-4*. Margrit Weber, Bav. RSO, Kubelik – RODRIGO: *Concierto serenata* etc.**

Falla's masterly evocation of the beautiful gardens of the Generalife in the Alhambra of Granada, and the Sierra de Córdoba, was conceived for solo piano but, in its final format, the piano assumes a concertante role within the orchestral tapestry. The balance of Soriano's fine HMV version recognizes this, with vivid orchestral presence and detail and the piano placed slightly backward, yet with the soloist able to dominate when necessary. The performance has a magical atmosphere, yet great vitality too, and moves forward spontaneously, with Frühbeck de Burgos relishing the fine-spun colouristic effects, yet never losing a sense of momentum. The vintage 1963 recording is first-class on both disc and tape. The coupling may be a drawback for some collectors who would do well to consider the alternative double-length-tape issue in HMV's *'Portrait of the Artist'* series – see below.

Alicia de Larrocha has recorded the work before for Decca, but her newest version – made in Walthamstow Town Hall – has the advantage of superb digital sound, rich and lustrous, with refined detail. The piano image, although admirably tangible and truthful in timbre, is well forward, yet this allows the listener to relish the freshness and brilliance of the soloist's articulation in the work's latter sections. Miss Larrocha's playing has undoubted poetry and in the first movement there is a thoughtful improvisatory quality which catches the evocative feeling of the shimmering Andalusian night. The following two movements are more volatile, but the performance has less of a forward sweep than Frühbeck de Burgos's earlier account with Soriano. The closing pages, consciously moulded, are given a valedictory feeling. The beauty of the sound adds much to the effect of the playing.

The DG recording is exceptionally vivid with the performers going all out to bring the utmost grip and excitement to the score. With Margrit Weber giving a brilliant account of the solo part, particularly in the latter movements, the effect is both sparkling and exhilarating. A little of the fragrant atmosphere is lost, particularly in the opening section (where both De Larrocha and Soriano are gentler), but the performance, with its strong sense of drama, is certainly not without evocative qualities. This generously full Walkman cassette is in the main devoted to the music of Rodrigo, and the three coupled recordings are of mixed appeal, but those wanting Rodrigo's *Concierto serenata* for harp (not otherwise currently available) should not be disappointed in the Falla.

(i; ii) *Nights in the gardens of Spain;* (ii) *El amor brujo: Ritual fire dance.* (iii; iv) *The Three-cornered Hat* (ballet): complete; (iii; v) *La Vida breve:* excerpts.

(M) *** HMV *TCC2-POR 154591-9*. (i) Soriano, (ii) Paris Conservatoire O, (iii) Los Angeles, (iv) Philh. O, (v) Higuero, Moreno, Ch., Nat. O of Spain; all cond. Frühbeck de Burgos.

An outstanding double-length chrome tape collection, let down only by the (total) lack of provision of back-up documentation. It seems perverse to include a fascinating selection of excerpts from *La Vida breve* and offer no information whatsoever about the scenario. Soriano gives a first-class account of the solo part in *Nights in the gardens of Spain* and Frühbeck de Burgos accompanies with a natural feeling for the subtleties of Falla's scoring.

Apart from the opening *'Olés'* (which were recorded separately and dubbed on), the performance of the complete *Three-cornered Hat* is highly recommendable, combining warmth with high spirits. Victoria de los Angeles does not sound quite earthy enough, but she sings splendidly and the sound is consistently vivid. In the attractive *Vida breve* excerpts there is demonstration presence.

PIANO MUSIC

Cuetro piezas españolas; Fantasia Baetica; El amor brujo: suite; The Three-Cornered Hat: 3 dances.

*** Decca SXL 6683 [Lon. CS 6881]. De Larrocha.

This welcome and attractive issue fills an admirable place in the catalogue. It assembles the main piano music of Falla on two sides in exemplary performances and good recordings.

Master Peter's puppet show: see *Harpsichord concerto*, above.

Fasch, Johann (1688–1758)

Trumpet concerto in D; Sinfonias: in A; in G.

** Erato STU/*MCE* 70468 [FRL1/*FRK1* 5468]. André, Paillard CO, Paillard – PACHELBEL: *Canon; Suites.***

Fasch's *Trumpet concerto* is a short, unambitious work, and it is not really surprising that it is seldom played. The works for strings are equally unadventurous. Maurice André provides superior playing, with a gleaming tone and polished articulation, and the string group play with fair warmth in the *Suites*. The recording is pleasant and clear.

Fauré, Gabriel (1845–1924)

Ballade for piano and orchestra, Op. 19; Berceuse for violin and orchestra, Op. 16; Caligula, Op. 52; Les Djinns (orchestral version), *Op. 12; Élégie for cello and orchestra, Op. 24; Fantaisie for piano and orchestra, Op. 111; Masques et bergamasques* (complete), *Op. 112; Pavane, Op. 50; Pelléas et Mélisande* (incidental music), *Op. 80; Pénélope: Prélude; Shylock, Op. 57.*

*** HMV SLS 5219 (3). Collard, Yan-Pascal and Paul Tortelier, Von Stade, Gedda, Bourbon Vocal Ens., Toulouse Capitole O, Plasson.

Although Fauré's most deeply characteristic thoughts are intimate rather than public, and his most natural outlets are the mélodie, chamber music and the piano, this set of his orchestral music nonetheless contains much that is highly rewarding. It includes the delightful *Masques et bergamasques* and the *Pelléas et Mélisande* and *Shylock* music as well as such rarities as *Les Djinns* and *Caligula*. The Orchestre du Capitole de Toulouse may lack the finesse and bloom of the leading Parisian orchestras, but Michel Plasson gets an alert and spirited response and is blessed with very decent orchestral sound. He shows a genuine feeling for the Fauréan sensibility, and the fine-spun lyricism of the *Nocturne* from *Shylock* is well conveyed. The two works for piano and orchestra are particularly valuable; Jean-Philippe Collard gives a really distinguished account of both the early *Ballade* and the seldom-heard *Fantaisie*, Op. 111. This is a lovely set in every way, though the piano sound is a trifle hard (not the playing, of course); but it can be tamed with some treble cut. This collection contains many delights and cannot be too warmly recommended.

Caligula, Op. 52; Les Djinns, Op. 12; Masques et bergamasques, Op. 112; Pavane, Op. 50; Pelléas et Mélisande, Op. 80; Pénélope: Prélude; Shylock, Op. 57.

(M) *** HMV *TCC2-POR 154596-9*. (from above set, cond. Plasson).

By omitting the concertante works, EMI have been able to transfer the rest of Michel Plasson's Fauré anthology on to one double-length XDR ferric tape, which copes well with the warm resonance of the recording. Indeed the sound is consistently beautiful, catching voices as well as orchestra quite naturally and only losing a little of the upper range although, with a slight drop in level, definition in the choral writing is slightly less clear on side two. Nevertheless this is highly rewarding music, and tape collectors should find this a worthwhile investment.

(i) *Ballade for piano and orchestra, Op. 19; Masques et bergamasques, Op. 112; Pavane, Op. 50; Pelléas et Mélisande, Op. 80: suite.*
**(*) Erato STU/*MCE* 71495. (i) Hubeau; Lausanne CO, Jordan.

The affecting simplicity and gentleness of the *Ballade* are worlds apart from the usual display piece for piano and orchestra and account for its relative neglect. Both Ogdon and the alternative mid-price version by Marie-Françoise Bucquet have now disappeared and the only current UK alternative is by Jean-Philippe Collard which comes as part of a three-record set and is not available separately at present. Although Jean Hubeau is not quite as aristocratic or poetic as Collard, his is a fine version and meets a real need. Moreover, the remainder of the programme is very decently played and recorded and can hold its own with most of the competition from the Plasson box.

Dolly (suite), Op. 56 (orch. Rabaud).
*** ASV Dig. DCA/*ZCDCA* 515. ASMF, Marriner (with Concert of French music***).

Part of an attractively arranged anthology called *'The French connection'*, Fauré's *Dolly suite* has plenty of charm here, if not quite the finesse and magic of the old Beecham set. The sound is excellent, if a little lacking in ambient feeling, and there is a good (iron-oxide) cassette which loses only a little of the upper range.

Dolly (suite), Op. 56; Masques et bergamasques, Op. 112; Pelléas et Mélisande, Op. 80: suite.
**(*) EMI 2C 069 10584. O de Paris, Baudo.

Serge Baudo's 1969 record with the Orchestre de Paris enjoyed a brief lease of life in the domestic UK catalogue and is now available as an import. The *Pelléas* is dignified and the Prelude given with great feeling. The string playing is most eloquent and the recording has plenty of warmth. Fauré is the least assertive of composers; his originality is none the less profound for that. It is as if he possesses the quiet confidence in his own claims that he never feels the necessity to assert them. Tempi are well judged and though not as well recorded as the most recent Marriner anthology on Argo (see below), the playing is the more idiomatic and felt.

Fantaisie for flute and orchestra (arr. Galway).
*** RCA RL/*RK* 25109 [ARL 1/*ARK 1* 3777]. Galway, RPO, Dutoit – CHAMINADE: *Concertino*; IBERT: *Concerto*; POULENC: *Sonata.****

James Galway's arrangement of a *Fantaisie for flute and piano* that Fauré composed in the late 1890s makes an appealing fill-up to an enterprising collection of concertante flute works impeccably played and finely recorded. There are two genuine flute concertos here (Ibert and Chaminade) and two arrangements, this and Lennox Berkeley's expert orchestration of Poulenc's *Flute sonata.* A fine disc and a well-transferred tape that will give great pleasure.

(i) *Fantaisie for flute and orchestra, Op. 79* (orch. Aubert); *Masques et bergamasques, Op. 112; Pavane, Op. 50; Pelléas et Mélisande: suite, Op. 80.*
** Argo Dig. **410 552-2**; ZRDL/*KZRDC* 1003 [id.]. (i) Bennett, ASMF, Marriner.

This ASMF Fauré recital scores over its rivals in having excellent sound; detail is well defined and there is excellent body. There is a first-class matching chrome cassette, but the recording is most impressive of all on the compact-disc version. Were the performances in quite the same league, this would be an indispensable issue for all lovers of the French composer. Not that the playing is second-rate or routine, and William Bennett is most sensitive in the *Fantaisie*, but there could be greater freshness and charm. (Put the wonderful Prelude to *Pelléas* alongside that of Serge Baudo on a similar Fauré anthology made in the late 1960s and the magic of the French version is immediately apparent (see above).)

Fantaisie for piano and orchestra, Op. 111.
*** Decca SXL 6680 [Lon. CS 6878]. De Larrocha, LPO, Frühbeck de Burgos – RAVEL: *Piano concertos.****

The Fauré *Fantaisie* is a late work which has been neglected by the gramophone. Grant Johannesen recorded it some years ago, but this is at present deleted. Alicia de Larrocha's fine recording is the only current version available separately, and its presence as a fill-up makes her Ravel *Concertos*, the main items on the record, well worth considering. An aristocratic work of great distinction, the *Fantaisie* is to late Fauré what the *Ballade* is to his earlier period.

Pavane, Op. 50 (arr. Gerhardt).
(M) *** RCA Gold GL/*GK* 25451 [AGL1/*AGK1* 4948]. Nat. PO, Gerhardt – RAVEL: *Introduction and allegro; Le tombeau;* SATIE: *Gymnopédies.****

The *Pavane* (with William Bennett the flute soloist) is beautifully played and recorded under Gerhardt and forms an engaging bonus for a first-class coupling of music by Satie and Ravel. Chrome tape and disc are closely matched.

Pelléas et Mélisande (incidental music), *Op. 80.*
*** Ph. 6769 045 (2) [id.]. Gomez, Rotterdam PO, Zinman – SCHOENBERG and SIBELIUS: *Pelléas.***(*)

To couple together three different orchestral works inspired by Maeterlinck's drama seems a good idea, although not everyone who responds to Fauré and Sibelius will be drawn to the more inflated symphonic poem of Schoenberg (which is also less effective here as a recorded performance). However, Fauré's incidental music is beautifully played, and to make the selection complete Jill Gomez gives a delightful account of the song *The three blind daughters*, not previously recorded. David Zinman's refined approach suits Fauré admirably, and there is a pervasive tenderness and delicacy (the *Sicilienne* is memorable). The recording too is naturally balanced and of high quality.

CHAMBER MUSIC

(i) *Andante in B flat, Op. 28; Berceuse in D, Op. 16;* (ii) *Cello sonatas Nos. 1 in D min., Op. 109; 2 in G min., Op. 117; Élégie in C min., Op. 24;* (iii) *Fantaisie in C, Op. 79; Morceau de concours in F;* (i) *Morceau de lecture à vue in A;* (ii) *Papillon in A, Op. 77;* (iv) *Piano quartets Nos. 1 in C min., Op. 15; 2 in G min., Op. 45; Piano quintets Nos. 1 in D min., Op. 89; 2 in C min., Op. 115; Piano trio in D min., Op. 120;* (ii) *Romance in A, Op. 69; Serenade, Op. 98; Sicilienne, Op. 78;* (iv) *String quartet in E min., Op. 121;* (i) *Violin sonatas Nos. 1 in A, Op. 13; 2 in E min., Op. 108.*
*** EMI 2C 165 16331/6. Collard, with (i) Dumay, (ii) Lodéon, (iii) Debost, (iv) Parrenin Qt.

In 1971 Erato issued a five-record set of the complete chamber music of Fauré – Tortelier playing the *Cello sonatas*, Jean Hubeau the pianist throughout, Raymond Gallois-Montbrun the violinist, and the Via Nova Quartet – a set that has done excellent service and whose value is enhanced by the perceptive notes of Harry Halbreich. This new EMI survey is even more comprehensive in that it also includes some of the smaller pieces such as Opp. 16, 24, 28, 69, 77–79 and 98, and so runs to an extra record. It has the advantage of a more imaginative pianist in Jean-Philippe Collard as well as other gifted French artists of the younger generation, such as Augustin Dumay and Frédéric Lodéon. Normally there are disadvantages in this kind of compilation, but they are minimized here because so much of this rewarding and civilized music is not widely duplicated in the catalogue. True, there are excellent accounts of the *Violin sonatas* from the Grumiaux/Crossley and Amoyal/Queffélec partnerships and a fine set of the *Cello sonatas* from Ingloi and Benson on CRD. Generally speaking, however, there are no strong rivals in the bigger works such as the *Piano quartets*, and neither of the *Quintets* is available separately. The attractions of the compilation are also enhanced by the generally admirable standard of performance and recording. There are masterpieces hidden away in this set, such as the *String quartet in E minor*, Fauré's last utterance, and it will yield enormous rewards.

Cello sonatas Nos. 1 in D min., Op. 109; 2 in G min., Op. 117; Élégie, Op. 24; Sicilienne, Op. 78.
**(*) CRD CRD 1016. Igloi, Benson.

Noble performances from the late Thomas Igloi and Clifford Benson that do full justice to these elusive and rewarding Fauré sonatas. Emile Vuillermoz's remark that Fauré 'concealed his harmonic learning where another composer would have advertised it' applies to all his music but particularly these late sonatas. Here is a master who never parades his artistry but leaves one to discover it oneself. His music will always elude those in search of quick returns and has corresponding rewards for those prepared to look below its surface. Ingloi plays with fervour and eloquence within the restrained expressive limits of the music and the recording is clear, if not one of CRD's finest in terms of ambient effect.

Piano trio in D min., Op. 120; (i) *La Bonne Chanson, Op. 61.*
*** CRD CRD 1089/*CRDC 4089.* Nash Ens., (i) with Sarah Walker.

The characterful warmth and vibrancy of Sarah Walker's voice, not to mention her positive artistry, come out strongly in this beautiful reading of Fauré's early settings of Verlaine, music both tender and ardent. The passion of the inspiration is underlined by the use of a long-neglected version of the cycle in which the composer expanded the accompaniment by adding string quartet and double-bass to the original piano. Members of the Nash Ensemble give dedicated performances both of that and of the late and rarefied *Piano trio*, capturing both the elegance and the restrained concentration. The atmospheric recording is well up to CRD's high standard in chamber music; on cassette there is a hint of edge on the voice in *La Bonne Chanson*, and in the *Piano trio* the resonance brings an inner focus that is slightly less sharp than on disc.

Violin sonatas Nos. 1 in A, Op. 13; 2 in E min., Op. 108.
❀ *** Ph. 9500 534 [id.]. Grumiaux, Crossley.
*** Erato STU/*MCE* 71195. Amoyal, Queffélec.

Violin sonata No. 2.
** Sup. 1111 3165. Suk, Hála – RESPIGHI: *Sonata.***

Four decades separate the two Fauré sonatas and they make a perfect coupling. The *First* is a richly melodious piece which, strangely enough, precedes the César Franck sonata by a dozen or so years, while the *E minor* was written in the same year as Debussy's (1917). They are immensely refined and rewarding pieces, with strange stylistic affinities and disparities: the second movement of the *E minor* actually uses a theme intended for a symphony that Fauré had discarded more than thirty years earlier. Although they have been coupled before (by Barbizet and Ferras, and Gallois-Montbrun and Hubeau), they have never been so beautifully played or recorded as on the Philips issue. Indeed, this is a model of its kind: there is perfect rapport between the two artists, and both seem totally dedicated to and captivated by Fauré's muse. Moreover, they are accorded recorded quality that is little short of superb. The two artists sound as if they are in the living room; the acoustic is warm, lively and well-balanced. The *Second* is not so readily accessible as the *First* and it is difficult to imagine more persuasive advocacy than this. Unfortunately Fauré is not and never will be a popular composer and it is doubtful whether this record will survive the lifetime of this *Guide*, so do not hesitate.

Pierre Amoyal and Anne Queffélec are hardly less successful in this coupling than Grumiaux and Crossley, but though their performance is just as impassioned (perhaps more so) and no less authoritative, it falls short of the distinction of the Grumiaux. Amoyal plays with great purity of tone and is the equal of Grumiaux in the *First Sonata* but less convincing in the more elusive half-lights of the *E minor*. Queffélec is a splendid player and the result of their partnership is undoubtedly satisfying, as well as being well-recorded. In the absence of the Grumiaux/Crossley disc, this would be a strong first choice. The Erato recordings alone have a cassette equivalent and it is a good one, transferred at a high level, with excellent range and immediacy.

Josef Suk and Josef Hála have a less logical coupling than either Amoyal or Grumiaux, the only link being that the Fauré and Respighi sonatas were composed at the same time (1916–17). The Suk is a more leisurely and expansive reading than either of its main rivals but the recording is not so vivid or well-focused as the Philips, which has plenty of space round the instruments, but at the same time has the more 'present' image.

PIANO MUSIC

Barcarolles Nos. 1–13.
**(*) EMI 2C 069 11328. Collard.

The *Barcarolles* span the best part of Fauré's life, the first (Op. 26) coming from 1883 and the last (Op. 116) from 1921, and contain some of his most haunting inspiration. Jean-Philippe Collard has the qualities of reticence yet ardour, subtlety and poetic feeling to penetrate their world, and it is hard to think of any artist temperamentally more attuned to these pieces, which cast quite a spell on the listener. He has exceptional beauty and refinement of tone at all dynamic levels, and the only regret we have is that full justice is not done to it by the French engineers. He is fairly closely balanced in a less than ample acoustic, and while too much should not be made of this reservation, playing of this order deserves the very best.

Barcarolles Nos. 1 and 6; Impromptu No. 3 in A flat, Op. 34; Nocturnes Nos. 1 in E flat min.; 3 in A flat, Op. 33/1 and 3; 4 in E flat, Op. 36; 6 in D flat, Op. 63; 13 in B min., Op. 119; Romances sans paroles, Op. 17/3.
(M) *** Saga 5385. Ferber.

Albert Ferber, a grossly underrated English artist, has recorded a selection of pieces here on an inexpensive Saga disc that will prove invaluable to the impecunious collector. Not only is it artistically worthwhile, it also happens to be technically good. This is a real find.

Barcarolle No. 2, Op. 41; 8 Short pieces, Op. 34; Nos. 1, Capriccio; 2, Improvisation; 5, Adagietto. 9 Preludes, Op. 103; Theme and variations, Op. 73.
(M) *** Saga 5466. Ferber.

Fauré's piano music is grievously neglected both in the concert hall and on the gramophone. Neither of the complete surveys, by Evelyne Crochet and (briefly available on Erato) by Jean Doyen, was wholly satisfactory, and it is good to report that this issue is a signal success. Albert Ferber is a sensitive player who penetrates far more deeply into Fauré's often elusive world than almost any of his rivals past or present on record. This disc is particularly valuable in making available the *Nine Preludes*, Op. 103, composed in 1909–10. These well repay the repeated attention the gramophone affords, for they are not immediately accessible, yet are deeply rewarding. The *Theme and variations*, popular with students, is given a well-characterized and finely considered reading too, and there are some welcome smaller pieces. What a fine pianist Albert Ferber is: imaginative, poetic and content to let the music speak for itself. He is well-recorded, and at such a modest price this is surely a record not to be missed.

Dolly (suite), Op. 56.
* DG 2531/*3301* 389 [id.]. Kontarsky Duo – BIZET: *Jeux d'enfants*; MILHAUD: *Scaramouche*.*

There is precious little charm here and the dryish acoustic and close balance do not commend this record. It is business-like and highly polished but unpersuasive. Disc and chrome tape are closely matched.

Impromptus Nos. 1–5; Préludes, Op. 103.
**(*) EMI 2C 069 73058. Collard.

The first three of the *Impromptus* come from 1883 while the last two come from 1906 and 1910 respectively, in which last year Fauré embarked on his set of *Neuf Préludes*. Despite the long interruption, the *Impromptus* sound well as a complete set – as for that matter do the *Préludes*, with whose intimate world Jean-Philippe Collard is wholly attuned. Collard is indeed the foremost interpreter of this composer now before the public, and there are no finer versions to be had. The quality of the recorded sound is not in the first flight – at least in the case of the *Impromptus*, but readers are urged to investigate this disc for the sake of its musical rewards.

Nocturnes (complete); *Pièces brèves, Op. 84.*
**(*) CRD CRD 1106-7/*CRDC 4106-7*. Crossley.

Nocturnes (complete); *Theme and variations, Op. 74.*
*** EMI 2C 069 12575/6. Collard.

This is glorious music which ranges from the gently reflective to the profoundly searching. The *Nocturnes* are thirteen in number, composed over the best part of half a century: the first was sketched at the time of the *First Violin sonata* (1875–6), and the last dates from 1921. They offer a glimpse of Fauré's art at its most inward and subtle; and they take a greater hold of the listener at each hearing, the quiet-spoken reticence proving more eloquent than one would ever suspect at first. Immensely civilized yet never aloof, this music offers balm to the soul. There have been a few complete recordings before but none so wholly identified with the Fauréan sensibility as Jean-Philippe Collard's. His account of the *Theme and variations* is no less masterly, combining the utmost tonal refinement and sensitivity with striking keyboard authority. The recording, which dates from 1974, is good, though it has not the bloom and freshness of the very finest piano records.

Paul Crossley has great feeling for this repertoire and penetrates its elusive world. It is good news indeed that he is to record the complete Fauré piano music for CRD, for he has a great deal to say about it. The recording is rather closely balanced, albeit in an ample acoustic, but the result tends to emphasize a percussive element that one does not normally encounter in this artist's playing. The beautifully inward *F sharp minor Nocturne*, Op. 104, No. 1, almost loses the intimate private quality of which Crossley speaks in his excellent notes, and it is not the only one to do so. There is much understanding and finesse and the *Pièces brèves* are a valuable fill-up, but Collard is better served and plays magically. Tape collectors may well decide that the Crossley recordings are worth investigating, as the chrome transfers are first-class, accurately mirroring the discs. Collard is available on LP only.

VOCAL AND CHORAL MUSIC

Mélodies: *Adieu; Après un rêve; Barcarolle; Chanson d'amour; Clair de lune; En prière; Nell; Poème d'un jour; Le secret.*
*** Pearl SHE 524. Ian Partridge, Jennifer Partridge – DUPARC: *Mélodies.****

Not many collections of Fauré songs recorded in recent years can match this one for its radiant beauty and tenderly subtle expression. Poised evenness of legato goes with a range of tone colour which transforms even the best-known of these songs, making them seem fresh and new. So *Après un rêve*, *Chanson d'amour* and *Clair de lune* find Partridge singing like the master of miniature that he is, a classic artist in every way, and superbly supported by his sister as accompanist. Fair recording.

Mélodies: *Après un rêve; Arpège; Au bord de l'eau; Au cimetière; L'Aurore; Les berceaux; Clair de lune; Dans la forêt de Septembre; Dans les ruines d'une abbaye; En sourdine; La fée aux chansons; Lydia; Mandoline; Notre amour; Le papillon et la fleur; Prison; Rêve d'amour; Roses d'Ispahan.*

*** HMV ASD/*TCC-ASD* 4183 [Ang. DS/*4XDS* 37893]. Von Stade, Collard.

Frederika von Stade is a deeply persuasive interpreter of French mélodie and there are few, if any, more sympathetic collections of Fauré songs on record than this. The selection is a delight, ranging as it does from the most popular (*Après un rêve*, *Clair de lune*) to relative rarities. It is good to have Fauré's simple and delicate setting of *Mandoline* (an early song) better known in Debussy's setting. Collard makes an understanding and idiomatic accompanist. Excellent recording.

Requiem, Op. 48.
(B) *** CfP CFP/*TC-CFP* 40234 [Ang. S. 35974]. Los Angeles, Fischer-Dieskau, Brasseur Ch., Paris Conservatoire O, Cluytens.
** Erato STU/*MCE* 70735. Clement, Huttenlocher, St Pierre-aux-Leins de Bulle Ch., Berne SO, Corbóz.
(M) *(*) Decca SPA/*KCSP* 504. Danco, Souzay, L'Union Chorale de la Tour de Peilz, SRO, Ansermet.

Requiem; Cantique de Jean Racine, Op. 11.
*** Argo ZRG/*KZRC* 841. Bond, Luxon, St John's College Ch., ASMF, Guest; Cleobury (organ).
*** HMV ASD/*TC-ASD* 3501. Burrowes, Rayner Cook, CBSO Ch. and O, Frémaux.

(i) *Requiem;* (ii) *Messe basse.*
**(*) HMV Dig. ASD/*TCC-ASD* 4234 [Ang. DS/*4XDS* 37918]. (i) Auger, Luxon; (ii) Smy; King's College, Camb., Ch., ECO, Ledger; Butt (organ).

Requiem; Pavane, Op. 50.
*** CBS 76734/*40-* [M 35153]. Popp, Nimsgern, Amb. S., Philh. O, Andrew Davis.
(M) *** HMV SXLP/*TC-SXLP* 102568-1/*4* [Ang. S/*4XS* 37077]. Armstrong, Fischer-Dieskau, Edinburgh Fest. Ch., O de Paris, Barenboim; Puig-Roget (organ).
*** HMV ASD/*TC-ASD* 2358 [Sera. SZ/*4XG* 60096]. Chilcott, Carol Case, King's College Ch., Camb., New Philh. O, Willcocks.

The directness and clarity of Andrew Davis's reading go with a concentrated, dedicated manner and a masterly control of texture to bring out the purity and beauty of Fauré's orchestration to the full. Moreover the fresh vigour of the choral singing achieves an admirable balance between ecstasy and restraint in this most elusive of requiem settings. The style of the phrasing is not so openly expressive as in some other versions, but that is in character with the intimacy of the reading, culminating in a wonderfully measured and intense account of the final *In Paradisum.* Lucia Popp is both rich and pure, and Siegmund Nimsgern (if less memorable) is refined in tone and detailed in his pointing. The recording, made in a church, matches the intimate manner, and the cassette transfer is one of the finest we have heard from CBS.

However, the Los Angeles/Fischer-Dieskau version made under the late André Cluytens in the early 1960s is available at bargain price, and its claims on the collector's pocket are almost irresistible. It has always been a good-sounding version, with great expressive eloquence in its favour, even if the choir is not as fine as St John's. The transfer to tape is of excellent quality, with plenty of atmosphere and good detail.

George Guest's performance is on a smaller scale than the CfP version. The excellence of both is not in question, but in these matters tastes differ, although undoubtedly the St John's set has a magic that works from the opening bars onwards. The Argo recording is wide-ranging and exceptionally truthful, but the smaller scale of the conception may not enjoy universal appeal.

Barenboim too has the advantage of first-class sound (rich and full-bodied) on disc and cassette alike and at medium-price this is well worth considering. His choir is freshly responsive throughout and there is splendidly pure solo singing from Sheila Armstrong. Fischer-Dieskau is more dramatic perhaps under Barenboim, if not always quite as mellifluous as on the Cluytens CfP version. Certainly the *Pié Jesu* comes off more successfully than in the Cluytens, where Los Angeles is a little strained, though the spirituality of her contribution is not in question.

The earlier King's College version under Willcocks, like the St John's on Argo, and the Erato version, all use treble soloists. The King's performance is certainly eloquent, but should be sampled by collectors; admirers of the composer may think its Anglican accents unidiomatic, but the treble soloist is far purer in tone than his opposite number from St John's and many may feel that the King's performance is the finer of the two. Its cassette has been remastered and offers excellent quality to match the disc closely.

Frémaux's HMV version is attractively atmospheric, the recording comparatively recessed. Frémaux has a moulded style which does not spill over in too much expressiveness, and there is a natural warmth about this performance that is highly persuasive. Norma Burrowes sings beautifully; her innocent style is most engaging. On tape the backward balance means that the focus is not as clear as on the CBS version.

Ledger presents the *Requiem* on a small scale with unusual restraint. The digital recording allows many details of scoring to come through that are normally hazed over. The singing is refreshingly direct, but anyone who warms to the touch of sensuousness in the work, its Gallic quality, may well be disappointed. It is not nearly so beautiful a performance as the earlier one from King's Choir under Sir David Willcocks. The *Messe basse*, also sweetly melodic, makes an unusual and apt coupling. The sound on the chrome tape is atmospheric if a little misty.

Corbóz offers no filler at all, and at full price his Erato disc seems uncompetitive. The conductor's measured tempi do not always avoid the feeling of sluggishness, and the choral sound is not always very clear. However, the choir sings well enough, and the treble soloist is notably fresh-sounding.

Ansermet's version is technically immaculate, but its clarity serves only to emphasize the rather thin-toned contribution of the chorus. The solo singing is still good (even if Danco is no match for Victoria de los Angeles in sheer spiritual beauty), and this may be considered fair value for money at its price. However, the Classics for Pleasure version with Los Angeles and Fischer-Dieskau under Cluytens remains a clear first choice in the bargain range.

Pénélope (opera; complete).

*** Erato STU 71386 (3) [id.]. Norman, Taillon, Vanzo, Huttenlocher, Van Dam, La Forge Vocal Ens., Monte Carlo PO, Dutoit.

Pénélope, Fauré's only opera, is a rarity in the theatre and seldom surfaces on the radio. A concert performance mounted by the French Radio in the mid-1950s, with Régine Crespin in good voice and no less a conductor than Inghelbrecht in charge, has recently appeared in a mono recording, but this Erato issue is the first commercial stereo set. The work itself is often haunting, nearly always noble and rarely uncompelling. Though it is overtly Wagnerian in its adoption of leitmotiv, it seldom sounds in the least Wagnerian, and as it was written in the years immediately before the First World War, it has all the harmonic subtlety and refinement of late Fauré. The title role is eloquently sung by Jessye Norman, a beautifully characterized performance, and the singing throughout is first-class. Charles Dutoit secures good ensemble and committed playing from his orchestra, and the only possible criticism would be one or two inconsistencies of balance. The work takes not much more than two hours and could have been accommodated on two records. But such are the musical rewards of this glorious work that readers will not begrudge the price of this set, which moreover has the advantage of an admirable essay by the French Fauré expert, Jean-Michel Nectoux, as well as the usual libretto.

Ferneyhough, Brian (born 1943)

Transit.

*** Decca HEAD 18. Hardy, Hurst, Harrison, Hall, Etheridge, Earle, L. Sinf., Howarth.

The complex and thorny textures of Brian Ferneyhough do not make easy listening, but for the unprejudiced ear there is no doubt of the concentration and depth of feeling in this ambitious work (with Heraclitus and Paracelsus among its sources of inspiration), which leads to a genuinely visionary climax. The impact of the music – strong enough to set the listener searching behind the expressionistic gestures to the inner logic – is greatly enhanced by the singers of the London Sinfonietta, under the dedicated direction of Elgar Howarth; the craggy lines, varied vibrato and glissando effects hold no terrors for them. Excellent recording.

Fibich, Zdeněk (1850–1900)

Symphony No. 2 in E. flat, Op. 38.
(M) ** Sup. 410 2165. Brno State PO, Waldhans.

All three of the mature symphonies that Fibich composed during his later years have been recorded at one time or another. The *Second* is the most often played, and though its melodic inspiration is not as fresh or spontaneous as that of Dvořák and Smetana, it has considerable appeal. Fibich's phrase structures tend to be four-square, and the music proceeds at times in a somewhat predictable way, but it is nonetheless congenial and, at its best, as in the scherzo, it is stirring and colourful. The Brno orchestra under Jiři Waldhans give a straightforward performance, though the balance does not flatter the tone of the first desks. Indeed the recording is somewhat opaque, and tutti could be more cleanly defined. In some respects the earlier recording under Karel Sejna had more inner vitality, but this newcomer has more sense of space.

Symphony No. 3 in E min., Op. 53.
(M) *** Sup. 1110 3038. Brno State PO, Bělohlávek.

Fibich composed his first symphony when he was only fourteen and followed it with a second two years later, when he was a student at Leipzig. However, he excluded both from his list of works and his two best-known symphonies (*No. 2 in E flat* and the present work) both date from the last decade of his life: indeed, the *Third* was written only two years before his death. An earlier record of it is no longer in circulation but this newcomer is hardly less persuasive. The invention is fresher than that of its predecessor and the scherzo with its catchy syncopations has great charm. Fibich suffers from a certain squareness but this symphony is less vulnerable on this score and should win his music friends.

(i) *Piano quintet in D* (for violin, clarinet, horn, cello and piano), *Op. 42; Piano trio in F min.*
(M) **(*) Sup. 111 1617. Fibich Trio, (i) with Dlouhý, Tylšar.

The *Trio* was written during his twenties, in 1872, while the *Quintet* dates from the last decade of Fibich's life. His music is often stolid but has distinct charm, and the *Quintet* is a far from negligible piece that will well reward the reader with an interest in music off the beaten track. The performances are fine, but the recording is somewhat wanting in presence and refinement.

Šárka (opera; complete).
(M) *** Sup. 1416 2781/3. Děpoltová, Přibyl, Randová, Zítek, Brno Janáček Op. Ch. and State PO, Štych.

Some of Fibich's invention is prosaic and predictable, but there is much that is both endearing and fresh too. *Šárka* is his sixth opera and was composed in 1896–7, during the last years of his short life. In addition to the nationalist element, there is a strong awareness of Wagner too. Although it has never caught on outside Czechoslovakia, it has been recorded before (by the Prague National Opera under Chalabala), but this new version has the advantage of far superior recording and an atmospheric and committed performance. Fibich, though a composer of the second order, is nonetheless far from unrewarding, and there are some colourful and melodically appealing episodes here, even if the quality of the inspiration is not consistent. The music is not as ardent and captivating as Novák's *The Storm* nor as searching as the *Asrael symphony* of Suk (to name two lesser-known Czech pieces neglected on record), but readers will still find it worth investigation.

Field, John (1782–1837)

Piano concertos Nos. 1 in E flat; 2 in A flat; 3 in E flat; 4 in E flat; 5 in C; 6 in C; 7 in C min.
**(*) Claddagh CSM/*4CSM* 55/8 [Fidelio 55/58]. O'Connor, New Irish CO, Furst.

John Field, during his years in St Petersburg, wrote this enormous series of piano concertos for his own concerts. One can imagine that he must have been a great personality as a piano virtuoso, for though the material is often slight and usually exploited at excessive length, the result certainly has charm. It is a set to dip into rather than to play consecutively, with inspiration very uneven. In some ways he never surpassed the bright, brief *Concerto No. 1*, written when he was still in his teens before his ideas had grown grand. No. 5 has the intriguing title *'L'incendie par l'Orage'* and includes a dramatic (if vapid) storm sequence. The committed performances do all that can be done to make a case for these long-neglected works, and are generally well recorded. We have not heard the cassettes.

Nocturnes Nos. 1–19.
* Claddagh CSM/*4CSM* 50/51. McSwiney.

We badly need a satisfactory set of the Field *Nocturnes.* Veronica McSwiney is very well recorded on disc (although the cassettes are badly engineered, with 'wow' and poor focus). But she shows little feeling for the delicacy of Field's inspiration, her manner is stiff and deliberate. There is a Turnabout set available in the USA [TV 34349/50] played by Mary Louise Boehm who chooses a classical rather than a romantic style. She is to be preferred on most counts, although the Turnabout recording is clear rather than luminous. Alas, the excellent Gemini set by Rucky van Mill has disappeared. She found a remarkable affinity between certain of Field's *Nocturnes* and the more famous works of Chopin (linking Chopin's Op. 9, *No. 2 in E flat* with Field's *No. 9* in the same key and Chopin's *Berceuse* with Field's *No. 6*), yet there is no direct evidence that Chopin ever heard any of Field's music.

Piano sonatas, Op. 1/1–3; in B, H.17; Rondo in E (Midi), H.13.
**(*) Concert Artist/Fidelio *FED-TC 004*. Challis.

As in the *Concertos* the musical material of the *Sonatas* is slight and often conventional. But it is not without charm and, sometimes, melodically catchy, as in the finale of the *C minor Sonata*, Op. 1/3. Philip Challis, a pianist of undoubted sensibility, has the measure of this writing and he plays with an attractive simplicity, yet is by no means unimaginative. He is especially good in the best-known piece, the engaging *Midi Rondo*, which is thrown off with considerable flair yet elegantly articulated. He is well recorded on this real-time cassette. There is at present no equivalent disc.

Finzi, Gerald (1901–56)

Cello concerto, Op. 40.
*** Lyr. SRCS 112. Ma, RPO, Handley.

Completed right at the end of Finzi's life, before his premature death at the age of fifty-five, the *Cello concerto* is one of the most ambitious as well as the most searching of all his works, notably in the long first movement, which pointed towards important stylistic developments that were to remain unfulfilled. The central slow movement has Elgarian nobility but also a poignancy that is typical of Finzi. The rondo finale is less concentrated than the other two movements, but completes a work which should certainly be in the repertory alongside the Elgar and Walton concertos. Yo Yo Ma is one of the outstanding cellists of his generation, and though he does not always convey the full power of Finzi's vision, he responds most sensitively, helped by first-rate playing from the RPO under Handley and recording of Lyrita's usual excellence.

Clarinet concerto, Op. 31.
*** Hyp. A/*KA* 66001. King, Philh. O, Francis – STANFORD: *Concerto.****

(i) *Clarinet concerto;* (ii) *Eclogue for piano and strings, Op. 10; Grand fantasia and toccata, Op. 38.*
**(*) Lyr. SRCS 92. New Philh. O, Handley, with (i) Denman, (ii) Katin.

Finzi's *Clarinet concerto*, composed in 1948, is one of his finest works. If it lacks the contemplative qualities of the ambitious *Cello concerto*, its more extrovert character is no less compelling. The expressive intensity of the slow movement communicates immediately, and the joyous pastoral lyricism of the finale has a sharp memorability. On the Hyperion label, Thea King (pupil of the dedicatee of the concerto, Frederick Thurston, who gave the first performance and advised the composer during composition) gives a definitive performance, strong and clean-cut. Her characterful timbre, using little or no vibrato, is highly telling against a resonant (marginally too resonant) orchestral backcloth. The accompaniment of the Philharmonia under Alun Francis is sympathetic, bringing out the amiability of the finale in fine contrast to the eloquent *Adagio*. Even though the orchestral recording lacks sharpness of internal focus, there is a vivid overall projection. The cassette transfer is of demonstration quality, virtually identical with the LP. With Stanford's even rarer concerto this makes a most attractive issue.

The two works for piano and orchestra included on the Lyrita disc both date from the late 1920s and show a different side to Finzi's personality; they are less searching and individual than the *Clarinet concerto*, but they make an interesting coupling. John Denman gives an eloquent account of the work for clarinet, and the two earlier pieces are well served by Peter Katin and the orchestra under Vernon Handley. The Lyrita recording has clarity and definition to commend it and is flawless.

The Fall of the Leaf (*Elegy for orchestra*), *Op. 20.* (i) *Introit for small orchestra and solo violin. Love's Labour's Lost* (*suite*), *Op. 28; 3 Soliloquies for small orchestra; Nocturne* (*New Year music*), *Op. 7; Prelude for string orchestra, Op. 25; Romance for string orchestra, Op. 11; A Severn rhapsody, Op. 3.*
*** Lyr. SRCS 84. LPO, Boult, (i) with Friend.

This collection of shorter orchestral works has some charming miniatures, the music reflecting the wistful, often death-obsessed side of Finzi's character: thus in the *Nocturne* the New Year brings regret rather than celebration. The pure beauty of the *Introit* (surviving movement from a violin concerto whose outer movements were withdrawn) and the easy Englishness of the *Severn rhapsody* are equally characteristic, implying more than they seem to. Boult's affectionate performances are superbly recorded, and Rodney Friend is an understanding soloist in the concerto movement.

VOCAL MUSIC

Dies natalis; For St Cecilia.
**(*) Argo ZRG 896 [id.]. Langridge, LSO Ch., LSO, Hickox.

Dies natalis is one of Finzi's most sensitive, deeply felt works, using contemplative texts on the theme of Christ's nativity by the seventeenth-century writer Thomas Traherne. Finzi's profound response to the words inspires five intensely beautiful songs; only the central *Rapture*, subtitled *Danza*, provides vigorous contrast to the mood of contemplation. The cantata commissioned for the annual St Cecilia's Day celebration in 1947 is an altogether more external work, but even there Finzi was able to respond individually to the text specially written by his contemporary Edmund Blunden. The performances in their contrasted moods are both strong and convincing, though an earlier version of *Dies natalis* (now deleted) with the late Wilfred Brown was even more searching. The Argo recording is excellent.

Earth and Air and Rain (song cycle to words by Hardy).
*** Argo ZRG 838 [id., PSI]. Luxon, Willison – BUTTERWORTH: *Shropshire Lad* etc.***

These songs are sensitive and characteristically fastidious. Finzi's personality is slight but distinctive, although there is sometimes a flavour of Vaughan Williams in the music. They make a splendid coupling for the outstanding performances of Butterworth on the same disc. Fine recording.

(i) *Farewell to Arms, Op. 9;* (ii) *In Terra Pax;* (iii) *Let Us Garlands Bring, Op. 18;* (i) *2 Sonnets by John Milton, Op. 12.*
*** Lyr. SRCS 93. (i) Partridge; (ii) John Alldis Ch.; (iii) Carol Case; New Philh. O, Handley.

Very few composers, even those with the deepest insights into English lyric poetry, have been able to put great sonnets into a fitting musical setting. Finzi – who actually turned Wordsworth's *Intimations of Immortality* into a successful choral work – here sets highly compressed Milton sonnets in a way that genuinely intensifies the words, reflecting the composer's own intimations of death at the time of composition. They are beautifully sung by Ian Partridge, who is also the soloist in the introduction and aria *Farewell to Arms. In terra pax* is a Christmas cantata in miniature, charming in Finzi's most relaxed folk-based style; *Let Us Garlands Bring* has John Carol Case as soloist in five Shakespeare lyrics, delicate and individual. A valuable collection which helps to fill in the complex personality of a minor composer who is still underappreciated. Excellent recording.

Intimations of Immortality (ode), *Op. 29.*
*** Lyr. SRCS 75. Partridge, Guildford Philharmonic Ch. and O, Handley.

Finzi has generally been regarded as a miniaturist, but in this, his most ambitious work, as well as in the large-scale *Cello concerto* (now recorded by Yo Yo Ma), he showed what mastery he had over larger forms. Anyone prepared to accept the validity of setting the Wordsworth poem in the first place (and the daring of seeking to illustrate so centrally self-sufficient a work of literature cannot be exaggerated) is almost certain to respond to the patent sincerity of the music, which is in the richest English choral tradition. It is here performed with a passionate sense of involvement. In this the beauty and intensity of Ian Partridge's singing are a key factor, and equally the choral singing is richly committed, while the Guildford Philharmonic is challenged to playing that would not disgrace a much more famous orchestra. Those who respond to the choral works of Vaughan Williams, for example, should certainly investigate. Excellent recording.

Flotow, Friedrich (1812–83)

Martha (complete).
*** Eurodisc 25422 (3)/*ZC 500217.* Popp, Soffel, Jerusalem, Nimsgern, Ridderbusch, Bav. R. Ch. and O, Wallberg.
**(*) EMI 1C 197 30241/3. Rothenberger, Fassbaender, Gedda, Prey, Weller, Bav. State Op. Ch. and O, Heger.

Martha is a charming opera that should be much better known in England than it is. The delicacy of its story, set in and around Richmond in the reign of Queen Anne, allows for moments of broader humour which are not so far distant from the world of Gilbert and Sullivan, and there are always the established favourite numbers to look forward to, culminating in the often repeated but still exquisite *Letzte Rose – The last rose of summer.*

The Eurodisc cast is as near perfect as could be imagined. Lucia Popp is a splendid Lady Harriet, the voice rich and full (her *Letzte Rose* is radiant) yet riding the ensembles with jewelled accuracy. Doris Soffel is no less characterful as Nancy, and Siegfried Jerusalem is in his element as the hero, Lionel, singing ardently throughout. Not only is his famous *Ach! so fromme* a superb highlight; the *Gute Nacht* sequence which becomes the *Mitternacht notturno* is glorious, a quartet to equal almost any rival in operatic magic. Siegmund Nimsgern is an excellent Lord Tristan, and Karl Ridderbusch matches his genial gusto, singing Plunkett's *Porter-Lied* with weight as well as brio. Wallberg's direction is marvellously spirited, and the opera gathers pace as it proceeds; the first-act finale is taken at a fizzing tempo, and the drama and passion of Acts III and IV bring genuine grandeur. The Bavarian Radio Chorus sings with joyous precision and the orchestral playing sparkles. With first-class recording, full and vivid, this is highly recommended. The cassettes are very lively too, and even without a libretto it is a marvellously entertaining set, with the soaring choral finale leaving any romantically inclined listener in a state of satisfied exhilaration.

The Electrola recording (once available in the UK on HMV SLS 944) is not ideal, but captures the right atmosphere and still gives pleasure. Curiously, the veteran conductor Robert Heger, for all the delicacy of his pointing, sometimes chooses slow tempi, and Gedda as Lionel is a little stiff; but otherwise there is a stylishness and a jollity all round, with Rothenberger in clear, fresh voice as the heroine and Brigitte Fassbaender excellent as Nancy. Prey, agreeably expressive in a light-toned way, makes a youthful-sounding Plunkett. Minimal cuts and bright, atmospheric recording.

Foerster, Josef (1859–1951)

Cyrano de Bergerac (*suite*), *Op. 55.*
(M) **(*) Sup. 1110 2456. Czech PO, Smetáček.

Josef Bohuslav Foerster was a highly respected figure in Czech musical life during his long career. He died in Prague at the age of ninety-one. Though his music bears the same national stamp as Dvořák, Smetana and Janáček, his years in Hamburg and Vienna (where he was a friend of Mahler) lend his music a more cosmopolitan flavour. His *Fourth Symphony* (1905) has an Elgarian nobility, and its scherzo, which shows a delightful fecundity of invention, was recorded by both Kubelik and Smetáček. *Cyrano de Bergerac*, which bears an adjacent opus number to the symphony, caused something of a stir in the first decade of this century, and like the symphony it is the product of a refined and cultivated musical mind. There is a warm lyrical feel to the music which mingles Strauss and other post-romantic influences with Czech nationalism. As is the case with the symphony, the best movements are the first two; there is less concentration and more self-indulgence in the later movements. The playing of the Czech Philharmonic is alert and vital, but the recording is acceptable rather than distinguished; the climaxes tend to be a little opaque, and the overall image could be more finely detailed. Nonetheless this is a record that will give pleasure.

Foss, Lukas (born 1922)

Baroque variations (*1, On a Handel Larghetto; 2, On a Scarlatti Sonata; 3, On a Bach Prelude, Phorion*).
(M) ** None. H 71202 [id.]. Buffalo PO, composer – CAGE: *Concerto.***

The Webernization of three baroque models: Lukas Foss describes the three sections as not so much variations as 'dreams', and with the original pieces providing virtually all the notes, in however skeletal form, the results are nothing less than charming. The specialist can delve into the detailed musical logic, the non-specialist can simply enjoy the dreamlike experience of tuning into music as though from another room, or even another world.

Foulds, John (1880–1939)

String quartets Nos. 9 (Quartetto intimo), Op. 89; 10 (Quartetto geniale), Op. 97. Aquarelles, Op. 32.
❀ *** Pearl SHE 564 [id.]. Endellion Qt.

This superb first recording by the Endellion Quartet, one of the outstanding groups of its generation, brings an exciting rediscovery. John Foulds, born in Manchester, was early recognized for his serious work, not least by Hans Richter, conductor of the Hallé, but he later came to be known best for his light music. Then, withdrawing to India in the 1930s, he continued the impressive series of string quartets he had begun in his youth. The *Quartetto intimo*, written in 1931, is a powerful five-movement work in a distinctive idiom more advanced than that of Fould's British contemporaries, with echoes of Scriabin and Bartók. Also on the disc is the one surviving movement of his tenth and last quartet, a dedicated hymn-like piece, as well as three slighter pieces from earlier. Passionate performances and excellent recording.

Françaix, Jean (born 1912)

(i) *Piano concerto;* (ii) *Rhapsody for viola and small orchestra;* (iii) *Suite for violin and orchestra.*
(M) **(*) [Turn. TV 34552]. R. Lux. O, composer, with (i) Paillard-Françaix; (ii) Koch; (iii) Lautenbacher.

This useful disc fills a significant gap in the American catalogue. The music of Jean Françaix is unaccountably neglected; at its best, as in the delightful *Concertino* for piano and orchestra or the ballet *La Dame dans la lune*, it has an irrepressible charm and high spirits. The *Piano concerto*, which occupies the first side here, dates from 1936; the night-club exuberance in its first movement and its general air of carefree gaiety at times recall Milhaud, though the scoring is lighter than in many of the latter's works. It has the authority of the composer's direction and his daughter's advocacy at the keyboard; Françaix recorded it himself in the days of 78s, with Nadia Boulanger conducting, but this performance naturally is better recorded and it has more charm. The second side is occupied by the early *Suite for violin and orchestra* (1932) and a post-war viola *Rhapsody* (mislabelled on the actual record as for violin instead of viola). There is a nice mixture of whimsy and a certain wistful melancholy throughout these pieces. The performances are good, though the orchestral playing could have a little more finish. The sound is reasonably well-balanced and has greater dynamic range than is sometimes encountered on this label. A rewarding and recommendable issue, not currently available in the UK, but we hope Conifer may include it with their imports on this label.

Divertissement for oboe, clarinet and bassoon; Divertissement for bassoon and string quintet.
(M) **(*) HMV Green. ESD/*TC-ESD* 102021-1/*4*. Melos Ens. – POULENC: *Trio*; RAVEL: *Introduction and allegro*.***

Unfortunately neither of the two *Divertissements* on this record shows Françaix at his most inventive, though both pieces are pleasant. Recordings and performances are of high quality. The clearly defined cassette is in the demonstration class.

Franck, César (1822–90)

Symphonic poems: *Le Chasseur maudit; Psyché;* (i) *Nocturne* (orch. Ropartz).
(M) **(*) DG 2543 821 [id.]. O de Paris, Barenboim, (i) with Ludwig.

In *Psyché* Barenboim limits himself to the purely orchestral passages of this extended work, leaving room on side two for the exciting *Le Chasseur maudit* and a relatively brief song orchestrated by Guy Ropartz. Barenboim draws rich, refined playing from the Paris orchestra, a little sleepy at times in *Psyché* but superbly energetic in Franck's graphic portrayal of the accursed huntsman, helped there by brighter, clearer recording.

Symphonic variations for piano and orchestra.
(M) *** Decca Jub. JB/*KJBC* 104 [Lon. STS/*5*- 15407]. Curzon, LSO, Boult – GRIEG: *Concerto*; LITOLFF: *Scherzo*.***
(*) Decca SXL 6599 [Lon. CS 6818]. De Larrocha, LPO, Frühbeck de Burgos – KHACHATURIAN: *Concerto*.

Symphonic variations; Symphony in D.
**(*) Decca SXL 6823 [Lon. CS/*5*- 7044]. Rogé, Cleveland O, Maazel.
**CBS 61356 [(d) Odys. Y 32174]. Casadesus, Phd. O, Ormandy.

Curzon's Decca performance of the *Symphonic variations* has stood the test of time. It is an engagingly fresh reading, without idiosyncrasy, and can be recommended unreservedly, particularly as the couplings are equally brilliantly done. The recording is beautifully clear and vivid; disc and cassette are very closely matched, and there is certainly no loss of quality or range on tape.

The Spanish interpreters, Alicia de Larrocha and Frühbeck de Burgos, give a reading that more than usual brings out the French delicacy of the variations. Good recording quality: an unexpected coupling for a variable account of the Khachaturian *Concerto*.

It is curious that the coupling with the *Symphony* has not been used more often. Decca's issue vies with the much older CBS disc which cannot compete in terms of recorded sound, but in other respects holds its own well enough. The orchestral playing on the Decca disc is crisp and polished and the performances are exciting but a lack of lyrical tenderness robs the *Symphony* of some of its more appealing qualities. The rich melody of the second subject finds Maazel introducing tenutos, which in so clipped and precise a performance seem obtrusive. Maazel's earlier account on Privilege (now deleted) was more moving and impressive. In the *Variations* Pascal Rogé shows himself particularly sensitive to dynamic shadings and reveals a fine blend of intelligence and technique, even if his playing is a trifle reticent at times. Brilliant recording.

On CBS Casadesus gives an agreeable performance of the *Symphonic variations* but is let down somewhat by the piano sound, which is rather shallow. Ormandy's account of the *Symphony* is bold and powerful, and the recording has plenty of impact without being glossy. Nevertheless some ears find that this music-making has a certain streamlined quality, although it has plenty of character too. The record is a fair bargain.

Symphony in D min.
(M) *** HMV SXLP/*TC-SXLP* 30256. Fr. Nat. RO, Beecham.
(*) DG Dig. **400 070-2; 2532/*3302* 050 [id.]. O Nat. de France, Bernstein – SAINT-SAËNS: *Rouet d'Omphale*.***
** Ph. 9500 605/*7300 727* [id.]. Concg. O, De Waart.
** Ph. Dig. 6514/*7337* 119 [id.]. Bav. RSO, Kondrashin.
(M) *(*) DG Sig. 410 833-1/*4*. O de Paris, Barenboim (with Berlioz: *Le carnaval Romain overture*, and Saint-Saëns: *Danse macabre* ***).

Symphony in D min.; Le Chasseur maudit.
**(*) HMV Dig. ASD/*TCC-ASD* 4175 [Ang. DS/*4XS* 37889]. Phd. O, Muti.

With Karajan's EMI version deleted and Monteux's famous RCA performance still not reissued in the UK (it is available in the USA on ATL 1 4156) César Franck's *D minor Symphony* is not generously represented at present. DG have also inexplicably withdrawn Maazel's splendid Privilege account, so first choice remains with Beecham's 1962 recording which in its Concert Classics reissue sounds both robust and clear. With Beecham the sheer gusto of the outer movements is exhilarating, and even though Sir Thomas's treatment of the second subject of the first movement is somewhat indulgent, the interpretation remains highly convincing. There are expressive mannerisms in the slow movement too, but Beecham conjures eloquent playing from the orchestra and maintains a high level of tension. Beecham's magnetism is compelling, and this version – however idiosyncratic – will be first choice for all those who admire his special feeling for French music. The HMV tape transfer is lively if a little fierce.

Bernstein conducts a warmly expressive performance, which thanks in part to a live recording carries complete conviction in its flexible spontaneity. It has its moments of vulgarity, but that is part of the work. Next to Beecham the very opening may sound sticky, and the central *Allegretto* is unusually slow and drawn out, while the return of the *Allegretto* in the finale brings a vulgar slowing, but the reservations are of little importance next to the glowing positive qualities of the performance. The recording is vivid and opulent, but with the brass apt to sound strident. The compact-disc version brings out the qualities the more positively and is specially valuable for its absence of background in the *Allegretto* and the expanses of the slow introduction. The chrome cassette is clear, very brilliant – the treble needs a little taming.

Muti's is a strongly committed but unsentimental reading marred by rather opaque recording which makes the Philadelphia violins sound unnaturally distant and thin. The cor anglais solo in the *Allegretto* is most beautiful, and the finale is specially refreshing in its directness. The fill-up is apt and welcome, a vividly dramatic symphonic poem strongly presented. As in the symphony, heavily scored passages are not ideally clear. The chrome cassette, however, is one of EMI's best, wide-ranging and robust in timbre, at least the equal of the disc.

Edo de Waart's performance is well-prepared and has undoubted romantic feeling, and the Concertgebouw Orchestra plays beautifully, especially in the slow movement. However, this version lacks the charisma of Beecham's (though it is much better recorded). The cassette matches the excellent recorded quality of the disc, vivid and well-balanced.

Kondrashin's digital recording was made at a live performance, but unlike Bernstein's it sounds relatively unspontaneous in its modifications of tempi, with the outer movements distractingly fast in their basic speeds. The sound is refined, but this is very short measure for a full disc. The low-level chrome tape does not match the disc in immediacy, though side two is rather more sharply detailed than side one.

Barenboim's account is rather disappointing. He adopts a surprisingly plodding main tempo, the first subject lacking bite, with the strings sounding thin and unconvincing. There are places too where the reading is self-indulgent, though in a generally fine account of the slow movement the cor anglais solo is disappointingly wooden. The new couplings are very successful, with the Berlioz overture exciting and the orchestra on its toes. *Danse macabre* comes off well, too, with the recording even more flattering than for the *Symphony*. The chrome cassette is well managed.

CHAMBER MUSIC

Piano quintet in F minor.
(M) **(*) Decca Ace SDD 277. Curzon, VPO Qt.

Not as seductive a performance as some will want in a work that can sound very luscious indeed. But for repeated playing there is a strong case for not letting the emotion spill over, and Curzon and the Vienna Philharmonic Quartet are sensitive and firm at the same time. Curzon's playing is particularly fine. The recording sounds appropriately full-blooded. It has a rather ample bass, which wants cutting back a little for an ideal balance. One might criticize the lack of inner clarity, but the rich, homogeneous texture happens to suit the music rather well.

String quartet in D.
*** O-L DSLO 46 [id., PSI]. Fitzwilliam Qt.

Franck's *Quartet*, highly ambitious in its scale, its almost orchestral textures and its complex use of cyclic form, always seems on the point of bursting the seams of the intimate genre of the string quartet. Yet as a very late inspiration it contains some of the composer's most profound, most compelling thought, and this magnificent performance by the Fitzwilliam Quartet, superbly triumphing over the technical challenge with totally dedicated, passionately convincing playing, completely silences any reservations. In every sense this is a work which seeks to take up the challenge presented by late Beethoven in a way that few nineteenth-century composers attempted, not even Brahms. Richly recorded, with the thick textures nicely balanced, this is one of the finest chamber records of the 1980s.

Violin sonata in A.

❀ *** Decca SXL/*KSXC* 6944 [Lon. CS 7171]. Kyung-Wha Chung, Lupu – DEBUSSY: *Sonata.* *** ❀

*** DG 2531/*3301* 330 [id.]. Danczowska, Zimerman – SZYMANOWSKI: *Myths* etc.***

*** Decca SXL/*KSXC* 6408 [Lon. CS 6628]. Perlman, Ashkenazy – BRAHMS: *Horn trio.****

(*) Ph. 6503/*7303* 111 [9500 568]. Grumiaux, Sebök – GRIEG: *Sonata.**

*HMV SLS/*TCC-SLS* 143443-3/9 (2). Mutter, Weissenberg – BRAHMS: *Sonatas 1–3.**

Kyung-Wha Chung and Radu Lupu give a superb account, full of a natural and not overprojected eloquence and most beautifully recorded. The slow movement has marvellous repose and the other movements have a natural exuberance and sense of line that carry the listener with them. The quality of the recorded sound is very distinguished indeed, completely natural in perspective and thoroughly lifelike in timbre and colour. The Franck is, incidentally, accommodated on one side: as the Debussy is so short, readers might well imagine it was split over two. The cassette also offers demonstration quality and is the equal of the disc. Among recent versions this undoubtedly stands out.

Kaja Danczowska was a pupil of Eugenia Uminska and the late David Oistrakh, and on the evidence of this record she is an artist to reckon with. Her account of the Franck is distinguished by a fine sense of line and great sweetness of tone, and she is superbly partnered by Krystian Zimerman. Indeed, in terms of dramatic fire and strength of line, this version can hold its own alongside the finest, and it is perhaps marginally better-balanced than the Kyung-Wha Chung and Radu Lupu recording, where the violinist is slightly backward. This issue also has a particularly interesting coupling and would be worth acquiring on that score alone. The cassette transfer is first-class, both atmospheric and with good range and clarity. Strongly recommended.

Those preferring the coupling with Brahms's *Horn trio* (and it is a very fine performance) can invest in the older Decca recording by Perlman and Ashkenazy with confidence. The first movement catches the listener by the ears with its forward impulse, and the whole performance has the kind of spontaneity which is too rare in recordings. The passionate commitment of the playing in no way swamps the work's lyrical flow. The cassette transfer is of good quality (the Franck is more pleasing than the Brahms coupling), but the level is low and by Decca standards this tape is rather disappointing.

There is such plentiful competition in the Franck *Sonata*, though not in the Grieg, which is the coupling on the Philips disc, that one wonders whether a further version, even from so distinguished an artist as Arthur Grumiaux, is worthwhile. Yet his account, if less fresh than Kyung-Wha Chung's, has nobility and warmth to commend it. He is slightly let down by his partner, who is not as imaginative as Lupu or Zimerman in the more poetic moments, including the hushed opening bars. And, while Grumiaux's purity of line is to be admired throughout, his playing is not quite as inspired as we remember from his earlier record, made in the 1960s with István Hajdu. The balance very slightly favours the violin, but the overall sound is thoroughly lifelike in the best tradition of the house. There is a good cassette.

Mutter is fluent and often powerful, but her partner is wanting in imagination and sensitivity. He does not begin to compare with such artists as Zimerman (DG) or Lupu (Decca) or, indeed, many pianists considered unworthy of making records. The recording is very good indeed on both disc and tape, but this cannot be recommended on artistic grounds.

Cello sonata in A (trans. of *Violin sonata*).

*** HMV Dig. ASD 4334. Maisky, Argerich – DEBUSSY: *Cello sonata* etc.***

(*) CRD CRD 1091/*CRDC 4091*. Robert Cohen, Vignoles – GRIEG: *Cello sonata.*(*)

Misha Maisky is a remarkably fine artist and it seems strange that his choice for a first record with EMI should have alighted on the Franck which sounds so much more effective in its original form. When such glorious works as the Fauré sonatas, the Barber Op. 6, the Prokofiev, the *Second Sonata* of Miaskovsky, and even the Rachmaninov are relatively neglected or unrecorded altogether, it seems odd to turn to this transcription. However, for those who want it, there is no doubting Misha Maisky's eloquence, his range of colour and beauty of tone, nor the sensitivity of Argerich's accompaniment. Good recording too!

Cohen gives a firm and strong rendering of the Franck *Sonata* in its cello version, lacking a little in fantasy in the outer movements but splendidly incisive and dashing in the second-movement *Allegro*. The Grieg coupling is attractive and apt, but the recording is more limited than one expects from CRD, a little shallow. The high-level cassette transfer is impressively close to the disc in balance and range.

Flute sonata in A (trans. of *Violin sonata*).
*** RCA LRL1 5095/*RK 25029*. Galway, Argerich – PROKOFIEV: *Flute sonata*.***

Although the prospect of hearing the Franck *Violin sonata* arranged for flute may strike you as unappealing, the fact is that the actual experience strangely belies expectation, thanks to the expert advocacy of these artists. Of course, in the scherzo the flute cannot match the character and bite of the violin, but elsewhere it is surprising how well this music responds to James Galway's transcription and his sweet-toned virtuosity. Argerich is absolutely superb here, and the recording is truthful in quality and wide-ranging. The balance is just a trifle close but is thoroughly musical and, played at a slightly lower-level setting than usual, it yields a sound that is pleasingly fresh and well-defined. An outstanding record, and a first-class cassette too.

Prelude, chorale and fugue.
(B) *** CfP CFP/*TC-CFP* 40380. D'Ascoli – LISZT: *Sonata* etc.***

Bernard d'Ascoli, prizewinner in the 1981 Leeds Piano Competition, here gives a beautifully balanced performance of a work which needs persuasion. On the one hand he brings out the Bachian associations – not least in the final fugue which has a Kempff-like clarity – but also the romantic side as in the relentless build-up of the chorale. The sound is a little dry but faithful. With the Liszt coupling, an outstanding bargain. There is no appreciable difference between disc and tape.

ORGAN MUSIC

3 Chorales (*in E; B min.; A min.*); *Interlude symphonique de Rédemption; 3 Pièces* (*Fantaisie in A; Cantabile; Pièce héroïque*); *6 Pièces* (*Fantaisie No. 1 in C, Op. 16; Grande pièce symphonique, Op. 17; Prélude, fugue et variation, Op. 18; Pastorale, Op. 19; Prière, Op. 20; Final, Op. 21*).
*** Erato STU 71035/7 (without *Interlude*). Alain (organ of St-François-de-Sales, Lyons).
*** DG Dig. 2741 024 (3) (without *Interlude*). Rübsam (organ of Orléans Cathedral).
**(*) O-L D 165 D 3 (3) [id.]. Steed (organs of Bath Abbey, Holy Rude, Stirling).

These three sets of records include all of Franck's most important works for the organ: the *Six Pieces* written between 1860 and 1862 (Opp. 16–21), the *Three Pieces* of 1878 and the *Three Chorales* of 1890, written in the last year of the composer's life. Marie-Claire Alain uses a Cavaillé-Coll that is virtually unaltered since it was built in 1879. The Cavaillé-Coll instruments are as closely related to Franck's muse as, say, Peter Pears' voice was to Britten's, and in this respect Marie-Claire Alain enjoys a distinct advantage over her rival on Oiseau-Lyre. And it is not only the instrument which makes the Erato issue so distinguished; the sympathy which this player brings to the music and the authority of the results give it a special claim on the allegiance of collectors. The quality of sound achieved by the engineers is very good.

Wolfgang Rübsam, like Marie-Claire Alain on Erato, also uses a Cavaillé-Coll, at the Cathedral of Saint-Croix, Orléans, and he has moreover the advantage of a digital recording. Unlike Steed, who must regretfully be relegated to the second division, Rübsam takes his time and allows the music to unfold at a natural and unforced pace. In this respect he proves a most idiomatic guide and the playing has the feel of the period. The *Chorales* are particularly good though the earlier music comes off well too. The recorded sound gives no grounds for complaint and the set can be recommended alongside, though not in preference to, the Erato.

Graham Steed makes the music sound highly effective at the organ of Bath Abbey; his fill-up on side six is devoted to a transcription by Marcel Dupré of the orchestral interlude from *Rédemption*, recorded on the organ of the Holy Rude, Stirling. Steed has devoted a lifetime of study to these works and plays with evident authority, though some may feel that he moves the music on a little too much in the *Chorales*, where phrases could afford to breathe more expansively. Textures, however, are always clear and beautifully focused, and the recording, engineered by the late Michael Smythe, offers most impressive detail and a vivid sense of presence.

Cantabile; Fantaisie in A; Pièce héroïque; 8 Pieces from 'L'Organiste'.
(M) *** Saga 5390. Cochereau (organ of Notre Dame, Paris).

This is excellent value. The performances of the *Cantabile* and *Fantaisie* have far more life and momentum than usual, and the *Pièce héroïque* is suitably massive. The eight miniatures from *L'Organiste* are charming – an adjective one did not expect to apply to Franck's organ music. The recording does not blur and is easy to reproduce, but does not disappoint in the *Pièce héroïque*.

Cantabile; Grande pièce symphonique; Pastorale; Pièce héroïque.
*** Cal. CAL 1920/*4920* [id.]. Isoir.

An outstanding collection, very well recorded, with an excellent cassette. The Cavaillé-Coll organ of Luçon is admirably suited to this repertoire and André Isoir's performances with their improvisatory character could hardly be bettered. The *Grande pièce symphonique* is especially successful, and the *Pièce héroïque* is also strikingly spontaneous. (No supporting notes are provided with the tape.)

Chorales Nos. 1–2.
(*) ASV ALH 918. Grier (organ of Christ Church, Oxford) – MESSIAEN: *Messe.*(*)

Francis Grier plays the new Rieger organ of Christ Church Cathedral, Oxford. The acoustic is dryish and the closely balanced recording obviously aims at the hi-fi demonstration room, for its clarity is stunning and, on occasion, not wholly convincing. Francis Grier is a fine player, of that there is no doubt, and of its kind this is a superb record. Those who want more sense of the acoustic ambience should look to the Rübsam, Steed and Marie-Claire Alain sets (and one recalls the old Germani set of the *Chorales* made at Selby Abbey in the 1960s which had superb range and presence, and which still sounds good). For those who like this rather clinical study of the organ textures, this record will be a rewarding experience.

Fantaisie in A; Grande pièce symphonique, Op. 17; Pastorale, Op. 19/4.
(M) **(*) Mercury SRI 75059 [id.]. Dupré (organ of Saint-Sulpice, Paris).

When this collection was issued in the early 1960s it was the first in stereo to use an authentic Cavaillé-Coll organ. The recording still sounds impressive and the touch of harshness on the climaxes may well have been intended by Dupré to give bite in the upper range. He obviously has a natural feeling for this repertoire, and the performance of the *Grande pièce symphonique* (far more like a genuine organ symphony than any of Widor's works in this genre) has striking grip. But elsewhere the tension is rather relaxed, especially in the *Pastorale* which is made to sound uneventful.

Grande pièce symphonique, Op. 17.
(*) Abbey LPB 792. Cleobury (Westminster Abbey organ) – DURUFLÉ: *Suite.*(*)

Stephen Cleobury's account of this powerful work succeeds in evoking its sense of mystical fervour, though here the somewhat distant balance diminishes the impact of the piece a little. The actual sound is admirable, no attempt being made to compress the wide dynamic range of the instrument, and the attraction of the disc is enhanced by the interest of the coupling.

Frederick II (The Great) of Prussia (1712–86)

Flute concertos Nos. 1 in G; 2 in G; 4 in D.
(M) *** Ph. 9502/*7313* 058 [id.]. Redel, Munich Pro Arte O.

Though not so lively as the symphonies also recorded by Redel and the Munich Orchestra, these flute concertos (three out of the four that Frederick is known to have written) are elegant and stylish in their conservative way, pointedly melodic but with limited harmonic interest. In first-rate performances and recording, they make up an excellent mid-price issue. The cassette is first-class, the sound excellent in every way.

Symphonies Nos. 1 in G; 2 in G; 3 in D; 4 in A.
(M) *** Ph. 9502/*7313* 057 [id.]. Mun. Pro Arte O, Redel.

Whether or not Frederick the Great wrote all these symphonies they are most lively and attractive pieces, here vigorously played and well recorded on an excellent mid-price issue. No. 3 is the most ambitious and generally the most successful, Italianate and galant rather than Germanic, using wind as well as strings. The other three are for strings alone, unpretentious but attractive examples of the baroque with one or two most distinctive movements, like the *Andante* of the *Symphony No. 1*. The cassette transfer is admirable, clear and transparent and wide-ranging.

Frescobaldi, Girolamo (1583–1643)

Il Primo Libro di Toccate (1615–1637): excerpts. Il Secondo Libro di Toccate (1637): excerpts.
*** O-L D260 D 2 (2) [id.]. Hogwood (harpsichord, virginal).

This pair of discs covers about a third of the two books of *Toccatas and Partitas*, the first disc offering us two *Toccatas*, a set of variations on the *Follia* and various other pieces, while the second brings four *Toccatas* from the 1637 book and a number of other pieces, *Canzone*, *Gagliarde* and so on. Between them, the two discs cover music suitable for the harpsichord or spinet from all periods of Frescobaldi's career, save only for the last years. Christopher Hogwood uses four instruments, all of which are reproduced on the handsome cover: three are from the last half of the seventeenth century, while there is an early Venetian spinet of 1540 for the *Aria detta Balletto*. Frescobaldi's music is unfailingly interesting and its expressive freedom often takes the listener by surprise. Christopher Hogwood has both the artistic flair and the feeling for style to do it justice, and the clarity and presence of the recording are really beyond praise.

Gabrieli, Andrea (*c.* 1510–1586)

Aria della battaglia a 8; Ricercar del duodecimo tuono a 4.
** Decca Dig. SXDL/*KSXDC* 7581. Philip Jones Brass Ens., Jones – GABRIELI, G.: *Collection*.***

The *Aria della battaglia* is a rambling piece lasting over ten minutes, too long to retain the listener's interest. The *Ricercar* is altogether more concise (2′17″), an effective little piece of brass 'chamber music'. Both are very well played on modern brass instruments and the recording is clear and nicely resonant, with little to choose between disc and chrome tape.

Gabrieli, Giovanni (1557–1612)

Canzonas Nos. 1, 4, 7–8; Sonatas Nos. 13, 19 and 21; Sacrae symphoniae: Canzonas 2–3 and 13.
**(*) DG 2533 406. L. Cornett and Sackbut Ens., Parrott.

Using authentic instruments, Andrew Parrott and the London Cornett and Sackbut Ensemble present stylish performances of a well-chosen collection of Gabrieli's instrumental pieces, not as dramatic or incisive as some we have heard on modern brass instruments but beautifully recorded in spacious stereo. Best-known is the magnificent *Sonata pian' e forte.*

Canzona a 6; 2 Canzonas a 8; Canzon per sonar a 4; Canzon primi toni a 8; Canzon septimi toni a 8; Canzon, La Spiritata a 4; Canzon vigesimaottava a 8; Canzon vigesimasettima a 8; Sonata a 3; Sonata pian' e forte a 8.
** Decca Dig. SXDL/*KSXDC* 7581. Philip Jones Brass Ens., Jones – GABRIELI, A.: *Aria della battaglia* etc.**

The music is played immaculately on modern brass instruments, skilfully balanced and recorded in an acoustic which gives a nice resonant bloom, good detail and excellent antiphony. Yet the result is essentially bland; there is a lack of colour contrast here. While 'original' instruments are not essential for the effective performance of these pieces, the absence of any evocative atmosphere means that each side of this record (or tape, for they are almost indistinguishable) tends to outstay its welcome.

Canzon primi toni; Canzon quarti toni; Canzon septimi toni; Canzon septimi toni No. 2; Canzon noni toni; Canzon duodecimi toni; Canzon a 12; Canzon a 12 in echo; Canzoni per sonare Nos. 2; 27; 28; Sonata octavi toni; Sonata pian' e forte.
(M) **(*) CBS 60265/*40-* [MS 7209]. Cleveland, Philadelphia and Chicago Brass Ensembles, Kazdin.

This collection dates from 1968 when Andrew Kazdin of CBS took an opportunity to assemble the brass players of the Cleveland, Chicago and Philadelphia orchestras for this Gabrieli programme. Some might feel the results anachronistic, for with the balance fairly close, the ear is very conscious that these are modern brass players. Yet the expert, polished playing is attractively resplendent and there is a proper sense of spectacle with the use of two and sometimes three groups. Not taken all at once, this is enjoyable, with the chrome tape equally impressive technically alongside the disc.

'Venetian festival music': Canzon septimi toni a 8 (for brass); *Angelus ad pastores; Buccinate in Neomenia tuba; Hodie Christus natus est; Hodie completi sunt; O domine Jesu Christe; O magnum mysterium; Omnes gentes, plaudite manibus.*
(M) *** EMI Em. EMX/*TC-EMX* 2032. King's College, Camb., Ch., Camb. University Musical Soc., Bach Ch., Wilbraham Brass Soloists, Willcocks – SCHEIDT: *In dulci jubilo;* SCHÜTZ: *Psalm 150.****

Originally issued in quadraphonic sound, the ordinary stereo remains very impressive, with the richness of brass and choral textures resonantly magnificent. The performances are splendid, of striking spaciousness, power and dignity. The reverberant acoustic has transferred remarkably well to tape where the focus is very close to that on the disc. At Eminence price this is a bargain.

Symphoniae sacrae II (1615): *Buccinate in neomania* (*a 19*)*; In ecclesiis* (*a 14*)*; Jubilate Deo* (*a 10*)*; Magnificat a 14; Magnificat a 17; Misericordia* [*a 12*]*; Quem vidistis pastores* (*a 14*)*; Surrexit Christus* (*a 11*)*; Suscipe* (*a 12*).
**(*) O-L DSLO 537. Taverner Ch., L. Cornett and Sackbut Ens., Parrott.

As principal composer of ceremonial music at St Mark's, Venice, the younger Gabrieli had to write all kinds of appropriate church music, and this fine collection contains some of the pieces of his later years, when – relying on instrumentalists rather than choristers – he came to include elaborate accompaniments for cornetts and sackbuts. Here, for example, six sackbuts accompany the six-part setting of *Suscipe*, with glowing results; and although after modern brass these more authentic instruments may seem on the gentle side, with Gabrielian panoply underplayed, the singing and playing are most stylish and are helped by first-rate recording.

Gade, Niels (1817–90)

Symphony No. 8 in B min., Op. 47; (i) *Spring fantasia.*
**(*) Danish Music Anthology DMA 046. Danish R. SO, Frandsen, (i) with soloists, Møller (piano).

The symphony was Gade's last and dates from 1871–2 when he was in his mid-fifties. Though the debt to Mendelssohn remains, this is a stronger work than many of its companions and is well able to sustain interest. It is cultured and well crafted, even if one must admit that it is ultimately deficient in thematic vitality. There are charming moments in the *Spring fantasia* (*Forårs-Fantasi*) on the reverse, written for his fiancée, the daughter of the composer J. P. E. Hartmann. This is a cantata for four soloists and orchestra, and includes an extensive and brilliant part for the piano. It radiates genuine happiness and has some of the charm that distinguishes *Elverhøj*, once available on Turnabout and soon to be re-recorded. The performances are both good, though the choral work fares better than the symphony, and the recording is eminently satisfactory without having the transparency and presence of the best modern recordings.

Violin sonatas: Nos. 1 in A, Op. 6; 3 in B flat, Op. 59.
** Danish Music Anthology DMA 035. Kontra, Jedlickova.

These two sonatas come from opposite ends of Gade's career, the first from 1842, the same year as the *First Symphony*, and the third from 1885 when the composer was nearing his seventieth year. There is very little evidence of stylistic growth here except for the hint of Brahms in the first movement of No. 3. Anton Kontra and Bohumila Jedlickova give fluent performances and the recording is satisfactory, but it is as difficult to work up as much enthusiasm for these sonatas as it is for the even later *String quartet in D major*, Op. 63 on Turnabout.

Gay, John (1685–1732)

The Beggar's Opera (arr. Bonynge and Gamley).
*** Decca Dig. D 252 D 2/*K 252 K 22* (2) [Lon. LDR/5- 72008]. Kanawa, Sutherland, Dean, Marks, Lansbury, Resnik, Rolfe Johnson, L. Voices, Nat. PO, Bonynge.

This entertaining new version of *The Beggar's Opera* creates the atmosphere of a stage musical. The spoken prologue comes before the overture (rather in the way some films complete the opening sequence before the main titles appear). With Warren Mitchell and Michael Hordern immediately taking the stage, the listener's attention is caught before the music begins. The musical arrangements are free – including an unashamedly jazzy sequence in Act II, complete with saxophones – but the basic musical material is of vintage quality and responds readily to a modern treatment which is always sparkling and often imaginative. The casting is imaginative too. With Alfred Marks and Angela Lansbury as Mr and Mrs Peacham a touch of humour is assured, and if James Morris is not an entirely convincing Macheath, he sings nicely, and Joan Sutherland makes a spirited Lucy. The rest of the participants show themselves equally at home with singing and speaking, an essential if the piece is to spring fully to life. Kiri Te Kanawa as Polly undoubtedly steals the show, as well she should, for it is a peach of a part. She sings deliciously and her delivery of the dialogue is hardly less memorable. The whole show is done with gusto, and the digital recording is splendid, as spacious as it is clear. The chrome tapes too are admirably vivid, although the extensive libretto/booklet is much less attractive in its reduction for the tape box than the LP original.

Geminiani, Francesco (1687–1772)

6 Concerti grossi, Op. 3.
*** O-L DSLO 526 [id.]. AcAM, Schröder; Hogwood.

Some of these concertos have been available in various anthologies, but this is the first complete set for some years, and it reveals the vigour and freshness of Geminiani's invention to admirable effect. Though Burney hailed Op. 3 as establishing Geminiani's character and placing him at the head of all the masters then living, it must be conceded that they are less inspired than Handel or the best of Vivaldi, though still melodious and resourceful. They are given performances of genuine quality by the Academy of Ancient Music under their Dutch leader, and readers normally resistant to the cult of authentic instruments can be reassured that there is no lack of vigour, body and breadth in these performances. They are also extremely well recorded.

12 Concerti grossi, Op. 5.
*** Ph. 6768 179/*7699 156* (2). Michelucci, I Musici.

The music on which Geminiani based his Op. 5 is drawn from the splendid *Sonatas* of Corelli *for violin and continuo* which have the same opus number. In 1726 when the Geminiani set was published in London (where Geminiani lived until he moved to Dublin in 1733) Corelli's works were very popular. Their skilful adaptation to concerto grosso form features a viola in the solo group as well as violins and cello. The basic musical material is unaltered in any harmonic or thematic sense, but textures are filled out and greater variety of colour is provided. The result is entirely successful. The music balances serenity and a noble expressive feeling in slow movements, with vigorously spontaneous allegros. The performances by I Musici are admirable in all respects, spirited and responsive, polished, yet never bland. The recording is first-class, too, both on disc and tape where the robust transfers are wide-ranging, full and clearly detailed. Highly recommended: there is some very rewarding music here.

6 Concerti grossi, Op. 7.
**(*) ASV ALH/*ZCALH* 927. ASMF, Iona Brown.

The six *Concertos* of Op. 7 are the last of his three sets and date from 1746. They are fertile in ideas and encompass a wide range of styles, contrasting the French and Italian, and enriching the texture with two viola parts. These are compelling pieces and greatly enrich his representation on record. The performances have plenty of life and imagination, but the acoustic ambience is not spacious enough and the texture is not as transparent or as well ventilated as one could wish. The music is, however, very rewarding indeed. The cassette sound is agreeably full and vivid, and indeed is in some ways preferable to the disc, but the upper range is more restricted, and the harpsichord continuo is slightly muffled.

The Enchanted Forest (*La Foresta incantata*) (ballet).
(*) None. H 71151 [id.]. Milan Angelicum O, Newell Jenkins – LOCATELLI: *Il Pianto d'Arianna.*(*)

The Enchanted Forest was first given in Paris in 1754, and charmingly reflects the taste of what was musically a transitional period. The performance is well pointed and the recording admirably balanced.

6 Cello sonatas, Op. 5.
**(*) O-L DSLO 513 [id.]. Pleeth, Hogwood, Webb.

Geminiani's six *Sonatas*, Op. 5, appeared first in Paris in 1746, and in London the following year. The present recording is based on the London edition and, as is the practice in the Florilegium series, uses a replica of an eighteenth-century cello and bow and a 1766 Kirckman harpsichord. The admirable players do their best to reproduce contemporary performance practice, though the absence of vibrato (and the prominence of the cello continuo) tends to tire the ear. The music is often rewarding and imaginative, while the recording is in the high traditions of this series.

Gerhard, Roberto (1896–1970)

The Plague.
**(*) Decca HEAD 6 [id.]. McCowen (narrator), Washington Nat. SO and Ch., Dorati.

Gerhard, whose originality blossomed with the years, was inspired by a sinister passage from Camus which he fashioned into this melodrama – 'melodrama' in the strict sense of a work for speaker and orchestra. The impact is immediate if hardly ingratiating in any way, but closer acquaintance allows one to appreciate the purely musical strength of argument. Dorati's performance with Washington forces is strong and committed if not ideally atmospheric. The discrepancy between McCowen's English accent and the American accents of the chorus may be distracting for some. A powerful work, well recorded.

Gershwin, George (1898–1937)

(i) *An American in Paris; Piano concerto in F; Cuban overture; I Got Rhythm: variations; Porgy and Bess: Symphonic picture* (arr. Robert Russell Bennett); *Rhapsody in blue;* (ii) *Second Rhapsody. 3 Piano Preludes.* (iii) Songs: *Aren't you kind of glad we did; Bidin' my time; He loves and she loves; I've got a crush on you; Looking for a boy; The man I love.*
(M) *** Ph. 6747 062 (3). (i) Haas, Monte Carlo Op. O, De Waart or (ii) Inbal; (iii) Sarah Vaughan, Hal Mooney and O.

This splendid mid-priced box assembles some excellent performances of Gershwin's music from the early 1970s with Werner Haas a fine soloist and Edo de Waart achieving vivid and warmly attractive performances with the Monte Carlo orchestra. The recording has a natural balance and appealing body and warmth, even though there is some lack of sheer brilliance at the top. The playing has plenty of vigour and rhythmic vitality, and atmosphere too. The *Concerto* is particularly successful (its lyrical moments have a quality of nostalgic melancholy which is very attractive), and the big blues melody in *An American in Paris* is glamorously relaxed. There is a cultured, European flavour about the music-making that does not detract from its vitality, and indeed the performance of the *Porgy and Bess Symphonic picture* is superb, each melody given its own individuality and the sumptuous acoustic bringing evocative qualities as well as sonic splendour. This is every bit the match of Previn's HMV version (see below) and is less self-consciously brilliant. The last disc, with the *Second Rhapsody*, is of a more recent provenance and the sound increases its brilliance and range. The songs are slow and romantic, and are splendidly sung with a vibrant, smoky timbre by Sarah Vaughan to Hal Mooney's silky accompaniments. Miss Vaughan sounds a little like Cleo Laine with an extra half-octave at the bottom of the voice.

(i; ii) *An American in Paris;* (iii; iv) *Piano concerto in F;* (v; ii) *Overtures: Funny Face; Girl*

Crazy; Let 'Em Eat Cake; Of Thee I Sing; Oh, Kay; Strike Up the Band; (iv) *Porgy and Bess: Symphonic picture* (arr. Bennett); (vi; ii) *Rhapsody in blue.*

(M) **(*) CBS 79329/*40*- (3). (i) NYPO, (ii) Tilson Thomas, (iii) Entremont, (iv) Phd. O, Ormandy, (v) Buffalo PO, (vi) composer (recorded from piano rolls), Columbia Jazz Band.

This collection is distinguished by including the composer's famous piano-roll recording of *Rhapsody in blue*, to which the accompaniment by the Columbia Jazz Band was added many years afterwards. The fast tempi adopted by Gershwin (who at the time of his recording had no need to consider the problems of an instrumental accompaniment) may raise a few eyebrows – some have suggested an untruthful reproduction of the original piano roll – but he was obviously enjoying himself. The result is audaciously extrovert and certainly exhilarating, if at times a little breathless. Tilson Thomas also directs *An American in Paris*, plus an exuberant collection of Broadway overtures (see below). Ormandy conducts the other two items and Philippe Entremont joins him in the *Concerto*, which is well played, the Philadelphia Orchestra being especially persuasive in the slow movement. But the recordings are not of recent provenance; the concerto suffers from twangy piano timbre, and both here and in the *Porgy and Bess Symphonic picture* the upper strings are excessively bright and unrefined in texture. The sound on cassette is smoother, but in the concerto the bass drum brings other problems, resulting in the occasional textural hiatus. However, generally the tapes are fully acceptable, the *Rhapsody*, *American in Paris* and (especially) the overtures all sound well.

An American in Paris; (i) *Piano concerto in F; Porgy and Bess: Symphonic picture* (arr. Bennett); (i) *Rhapsody in blue.*

(**) CBS *40-79024*. (i) Entremont; Phd. O, Ormandy.

Besides being without proper documentation, this cassette includes an unacceptable break in the middle of the *Rhapsody in blue*. Such an action, taken with the object of saving a few feet of tape, is obviously dictated by the commercial approach with which CBS have produced this double-length cassette series. The original recordings were rather edgy on disc and this has been smoothed here to a considerable extent, but in its place there is some uncomfortable bass drum resonance in the first movement of the *Concerto*. Otherwise the sound is quite good, and Ormandy's imaginative approach to the symphonic picture from *Porgy and Bess* (with superb orchestral playing throughout) makes this piece sound uncommonly fresh, especially the atmospheric opening section. The famous blues tune in *An American in Paris* is played with a cultured lyrical warmth that is most pleasing and there are many individual touches in the accompaniments to the *Concerto* and the *Rhapsody*. Entremont plays well enough, but it is Ormandy's direction that is memorable here.

An American in Paris; Piano concerto in F; Rhapsody in blue.

(B) *** CfP Dig. CFP/*TC-CFP* 41 4413-1/*4*. Blumenthal, ECO, Bedford.

**(*) HMV ASD/*TC-ASD* 2754 [Ang. SF/*4XS* 36810]. Previn (piano and cond.), LSO.

An American in Paris; Cuban overture; Porgy and Bess: Symphonic picture (arr. Bennett).

** RCA Dig. **RCD 14551**; RL 14149 [ATC1/*ATK1* 4149]. Dallas SO, Mata.

(i) *An American in Paris;* (ii) *Cuban overture;* (i; iii) *Rhapsody in blue;* (iv) *I got rhythm: variations.*

(M) ** Decca VIV/*KVIC* 29 [Lon. STS 15571]. (i) L. Fest. O, Stanley Black; (ii) Cleveland O, Maazel; (iii) Black, LSO; (iv) Parkhouse, L. Fest. Ens., Herrmann.

An American in Paris; Rhapsody in blue.

(M) ❀ *** CBS 60135/*40*- [MY/*MYT* 37242]. Bernstein (piano and cond.), NYPO or Columbia SO.

*** CBS 76509/*40*- [M/*MT* 34205]. NYPO; composer (piano; from 1925 piano roll), Columbia Jazz Band; both cond. Tilson Thomas.

(M) *** Decca SPA/*KCSP* 525. LAPO, Mehta; Katchen, LSO, Kertesz – COPLAND: *Fanfare*.***

(*) Telarc Dig. DG **CD 80058; 10058 [id.]. List, Cincinnati SO, Kunzel.

Rhapsody in blue; Prelude (for piano) *No. 2.*
(*) DG Dig. **410 025-2; 2532/*3302* 082 [id.]. Bernstein (piano and cond.), LAPO – BERNSTEIN: *West Side Story: Symphonic dances.****

The 1976 CBS recording of the *Rhapsody in blue*, using the composer's 1925 piano roll and re-creating the original instrumentation (as scored by Ferde Grofé for Paul Whiteman's orchestral jazz band) is uniquely exhilarating. Michael Tilson Thomas and his Columbia Jazz Band fit their accompaniment to the composer's prerecorded piano solo with remarkable flair, and whether or not the reproduction of the roll is accurate in the matter of the actual recorded tempo, the spontaneity of the occasion is unquestionable. Speeds are sometimes disconcertingly fast, but the music-making certainly has what (in retrospect) seems an irresistible flavour of the 1920s, the rhythms exhilaratingly rooty-tooty. As coupling Tilson Thomas provides a first-class performance of *An American in Paris* with the New York Philharmonic Orchestra, where the episodic nature of the music is drawn together in a most satisfying way. The recording is brilliant and the cassette – slightly more mellow than the disc – is one of CBS's best.

Those who seek an uncontroversial presentation can turn to Bernstein's mid-priced CBS reissue. This record, dating from 1960, set the standard by which all subsequent versions of the *Rhapsody* and *An American in Paris* have been judged. It still sounds astonishingly well as a recording, the *Rhapsody* in particular, with better piano tone than CBS often give us in the 1980s. Bernstein's approach is exceptionally flexible but completely spontaneous. It is a masterly account in every way, with broader tempi than in the composer's performance, but quixotic in mood, rhythmically subtle and creating a great surge of human warmth at the entry of the big central tune. The performance of *American in Paris* is vividly characterized, brash and episodic, an unashamed American view, with the great blues tune marvellously phrased as only an American orchestra can do it. The recording here is not so rich but certainly brilliant. There is something really special about this record. There is a good cassette too.

At bargain price and with first-rate recording Daniel Blumenthal, American prizewinner in the Leeds Piano Competition, gives performances of the two concertante pieces which convincingly combine Ravelian delicacy of articulation with genuine feeling for the jazz-based idiom. The syncopations are often naughtily pointed, to delightful effect, and Bedford and the ECO, unlikely accompanists as they may be, give warm and understanding support. *An American in Paris* is warmly done too but with less panache, the episodic nature of the piece undisguised. But for those wanting a cultured flavour in this music, this can be strongly recommended. The cassette has slightly less sparkle than the disc, but is quite well balanced.

The coupling of Mehta's splendidly alive account of *An American in Paris* with the European-style version of the *Rhapsody in blue* from Katchen and Kertesz also makes a bargain in Decca's lower mid-price range. Katchen made this recording not long before he died, but listening to the vivid, exciting playing no one would suspect that his health was anything other than robust. Although the performance is cultured and lacking something in idiomatic feeling, it is spontaneous and enjoyable. The sound is excellent on disc and cassette alike.

Previn's HMV disc might seem an obvious investment for those wanting Gershwin's three key orchestral and concertante works, but is in the last resort disappointing. The HMV recording, although warm and atmospheric, lacks sparkle, notably in the *Rhapsody* and *American in Paris* which have been squeezed on to one side. The sound is, of course, very pleasing and it suits the mellow Previn approach. This is essentially a European one, with an overlay of smooth sophistication. Listen to the way the famous tune in the *Rhapsody* comes over, and compare it with any of the other versions to see the way the character of the melody has lost its transatlantic feeling. Previn's sophistication is more effective in the *Concerto*, a fine performance by any standards, and here the recording has more bite. The cassette was originally issued in non-Dolby form, but has now been successfully remastered.

Eugene List has also recorded the *Rhapsody*

in blue for Turnabout. Then he used the original scoring; on Telarc he is accompanied by a full symphony orchestra and very sumptuously recorded indeed in a glowingly resonant acoustic. Some of the work's rhythmically abrasive qualities are submerged, but the pianist does not lose the skittish character of the work's scherzando section. The rich sound is ideal for those who like to wallow in the melodic richness of *An American in Paris*. The great blues tune certainly sounds expansive and there is no real lack of vitality, although in both works the hi-fi-conscious engineers have provided rather too much bass drum (a characteristic of Telarc records).

Stanley Black's performances of the *Rhapsody* and *An American in Paris* were originally recorded in Phase 4 and the sound is brilliant to the point of brashness. The performances show a real feeling for the music's style, although *An American in Paris* is not held together with any special skill. The addition of Maazel's lively Cleveland version of the *Cuban overture* and the agreeable *'I got rhythm' Variations* may attract some collectors to this mid-priced issue and the sound is certainly vivid, the cassette slightly less refined than the LP.

Mata's performances are recorded in sumptuous digital sound and the compact disc offers gorgeously rich textures. But the conductor is not completely at home in this repertoire and the playing tends to lack vitality. The *Porgy and Bess symphonic picture* is the most successful piece here but Dorati's CD is even finer.

In his most recent recording for DG, Bernstein rather goes over the top with his jazzing of the solos in Gershwin. The encore too brings seductively swung rhythms, one of the three solo piano *Preludes*. Such rhythmic freedom was clearly the result of a live rather than a studio performance. The big melody in *Rhapsody in blue* is rather too heavily pointed for comfort (almost in the style of his reading of Elgar's *Nimrod*), but the effect of live recording is compelling. There is an excellent chrome cassette, but the immediacy of the occasion is most compellingly projected on the compact disc.

Cuban overture. (i) *Second Rhapsody* (arr. McBride). *Porgy and Bess: Symphonic picture* (arr. Bennett).

*** HMV Dig. **CDC 747021-2**; ASD/*TC-ASD* 3982 [Ang. DS 37773]. LSO, Previn, (i) with Ortiz.

Gershwin's *Cuban overture* is too long for its material, but the music has genuine vitality. Here Previn plays it with such gusto, and the digital recording is so infectiously brilliant, that one's reservations are almost swept aside. Similarly the *Second Rhapsody* cannot compare with the *Rhapsody in blue* for melodic appeal (Gershwin, like Hollywood, was not good at sequels); but this performance is very persuasive. The highlight here is of course the brilliant arrangement by Robert Russell Bennett of themes from *Porgy and Bess*, which has established a separate identity of its own. At the opening one fears the performance is going to be too self-conscious (although one can understand Previn revelling in the gorgeous LSO playing – *Summertime* is ravishing). But the music soon takes wing and again the ear revels in the glittering sonics. The chrome tape is every bit as demonstration-worthy as the disc.

Broadway overtures: Funny Face; Girl Crazy; Let 'Em Eat Cake; Of Thee I Sing; Oh, Kay; Strike Up the Band.

*** CBS 76632/*40*- [Col. M/*MT* 34221]. Buffalo PO, Tilson Thomas.

The Broadway overtures are given expert and idiomatic performances by Michael Tilson Thomas and the Buffalo orchestra. After the success of his first Gershwin record, one would expect no less from this brilliant conductor. The recording is well detailed, with good stereo definition and wide range. Balance and perspective are perfectly truthful and the strings reproduce cleanly and smoothly at the top of the aural spectrum. A first-class issue that will give wide pleasure, whether on disc or on the cassette, which is excellently transferred (at the highest level).

Porgy and Bess: Symphonic picture (arr. Bennett).

C *** Decca Dig. **410 110-2**; 410 110-1/*4* [id.]. Detroit SO, Dorati – GROFÉ: *Grand Canyon suite*.*** C

Robert Russell Bennett's famous arrangement of Gershwin melodies has been recorded many times, but never so beautifully as on this Decca digital version from Detroit. The performance is totally memorable, the opening evocatively nostalgic, and each one of these wonderful tunes is phrased with a warmly affectionate feeling for its character, yet never vulgarized. The sound is quite superb and on compact disc the strings have a ravishing, lustrous radiance that stems from the refinement of the playing itself, captured with remarkable naturalness.

Orchestral arrangements of songs

Bidin' my time; But not for me; Embraceable you; Fascinating rhythm; I got rhythm; Liza (all the clouds'll roll away); Love is sweeping the country; Love walked in; The man I love; Oh, lady be good; Someone to watch over me; 'S wonderful.
(M) **(*) Mercury SRI 75127 [id.]. O, Fennell.

Sophisticated arrangements played with taste and understanding. Although the Mercury sound is a little studio-ish in acoustic, it has plenty of colour and is less glossy in effect than the Kostelanetz collection. Without the words, such a collection tends to become wallpaper music, but it is very good of its kind. Frederick Fennell has obvious affection for this repertoire.

Damsel in Distress: A foggy day. Funny Face: 'S wonderful. Girl Crazy: medley. *Lady, be Good; The man I love; Fascinating rhythm. Love walked In. Of Thee I Sing: Wintergreen for President. Oh, Kay; Someone to watch over me. Porgy and Bess:* medley. *Shall We Dance: Promenade. Strike Up the Band.*
** CBS 61449/*40*-. Kostelanetz and his O.

Though the performances are rather high-powered, and the glossy recording is brilliant to the point of fierceness (the cassette reflecting the disc in this respect), there is no denying that Kostelanetz's orchestra is first-class and that he understands the demands of an orchestral approach to songs without words. The excerpts from *Porgy and Bess* provide an attractive atmospheric interlude while *Strike up the band* has a uniquely transatlantic exuberance. But turn down the treble before you start.

PIANO MUSIC

Piano concerto in F; Rhapsody in blue (versions for 2 pianos).
**(*) Ph. 9500/*7300* 917 [id.]. Katia and Marielle Labèque.

Both the *Rhapsody in blue* and the *Concerto* were originally sketched out on four staves, and the *Rhapsody* and two movements of the *Concerto* were first performed on two pianos. Katia and Marielle Labèque are a highly accomplished duo actively interested in jazz, and they play with flawless ensemble and superb attack. These are sparkling accounts and are vividly recorded. The cassette is of excellent quality, matching the disc quite closely. Anyone with an interest in this repertoire should consider this issue, although both works undoubtedly lose a good deal of colour without the orchestral contrast.

Rhapsody in blue (solo piano version); *3 Preludes;* Songs: *Do it again; I got rhythm; I'll build a stairway to paradise; Liza; The man I love; Nobody but you; Oh, lady be good; Somebody loves me; Swanee; Sweet and low-down; 'S wonderful; That certain feeling; Who cares.*
(M) ** CBS 60311/*40*- [M/*MT* 34221]. Watts.

Only the keenest Gershwin collector is likely to want the solo piano version of the *Rhapsody in blue*, even though André Watts's performance is thoughtful as well as brilliant. However, the songs are ever attractive, even without the vocals, and these assured if sometimes wilful performances have plenty of life. The recording is somewhat hard in the American manner. The cassette is closely matched to the disc on side one; rather mellower on side two.

Impromptu in 2 keys; Jazzbo Brown blues (from *Porgy and Bess*); *Merry Andrew; Promenade; Preludes 1–3; Three quarter blues; 2*

Waltzes in C. Arrangements of songs: *Clap yo' hands; Do it again; Do, do, do; Fascinating rhythm; I got rhythm; I'll build a stairway to paradise; Liza; The man I love; My one and only; Nobody but you; Oh, Lady be good; Somebody loves me; Strike up the band; Swanee; Sweet and low-down; 'S wonderful; That certain feeling; Who cares.* (With DONALDSON W.: *Rialto ripples.*)
**(*) EMI EMD/*TC-EMD* 5538. Bennett.

Richard Rodney Bennett turns a composer's ear on Gershwin's piano music, including the composer's own arrangements of some of his most famous songs, and perhaps that is why the performances are not always fully idiomatic. Their rhythmic vigour is underpinned by considerable expressive conviction, yet the melodic exhilaration does not always come over, although there are undoubted insights. But such a comprehensive collection is welcome, especially as the recording – made in a resonant acoustic – is first-class, with an excellent wide-ranging cassette to match the disc.

VOCAL MUSIC

Songs: *But not for me; Embraceable you; I got rhythm; The man I love; Nice work if you can get it; Our love is here to stay; They can't take that away from me. Blue Monday: Has anyone seen Joe. Porgy and Bess: Summertime; I loves you, Porgy.*
**(*) Ph. 9500/*7300* 987 [id.]. Hendricks, Katia and Marielle Labèque.

An obvious follow-up to the Labèque duo's LP of the *Concerto* and *Rhapsody in blue.* Here they are joined by Barbara Hendricks, an impressively gifted coloured singer who studied at the Juilliard School of Music and played Clara in Maazel's set of *Porgy and Bess.* She is at her finest in the operatic numbers (*I loves you, Porgy* is particularly eloquent), and the warm beauty of the voice gives much pleasure throughout the programme. The performances of the songs are lushly cultured, often indulgently slow (even the faster numbers lack something in vitality), and create a sophisticated Hollywoodian image of late-evening cocktails and cigarette smoke, low-cut silky dresses and dinner jackets. The piano arrangements are elaborate; the playing is elegantly zestful, not out of style, but giving the presentation a European veneer that is in its way very beguiling. The sound is first-class and the stereo layout most realistic, with an excellent cassette equivalent.

But not for me (medley); *Nice work if you can get it* (medley). Songs: *Do it again; Fascinating rhythm; A foggy day; I've got a crush on you; The man I love; My man's gone now; Sweet and low-down. Porgy and Bess: Overture and medley.*
*** CBS 73650/*40*- [M/*MT* 34205]. Sarah Vaughan and Trio; LAPO, Tilson Thomas.

This is live recording at its most impressive. The sound itself is vivid and the intercommunication between Miss Vaughan and her audience brings performances of consistently high voltage (*Fascinating rhythm* and *Strike up the band* are a *tour de force*). One can readily forgive the beat in the voice and the occasional strident moment. The accompaniments are worthy of the occasion with the orchestra under Tilson Thomas exciting in its own right. Often – as in *Porgy and Bess* – one gets just snippets of the songs, but the programme is much more generous than the above listing would indicate, the medleys including many favourites. With any reservations about the soloist, not always at her best vocally, this remains a compelling musical experience on both disc and the lively chrome tape which matches it closely.

OPERA

(i) *Blue Monday* (chamber opera). (ii; iii) *Let 'Em Eat Cake:* choral scenes. (iv; v) Songs: *By Strauss; In the Mandarin's Chinese garden.* (iii; v; vi) Madrigals: *The jolly tar and the maid; Sing of spring.*
(M) *** [Turn. TV 34638]. (i) Andrews, Mason, Richardson, Bogdan, Meyer; (ii) Bogdan, Magdamo; (iii) Gregg Smith Singers; (iv) Lees; (v) Cybriwsky (piano); (vi) Aks, Meyer.

Two years before he wrote *Rhapsody in blue* Gershwin completed *Blue Monday*, his first sustained composition. As part of a revue it was a failure, but Paul Whiteman was impressed enough to commission the *Rhapsody*. This performance, using a reduced orchestration (Gershwin never did one himself), brings out the tangy jazz-influenced flavour well, and the other rarities on the disc are well worth hearing, including the satirical choral scenes from *Let 'Em Eat Cake*; all are given clean and fresh performances and recording to match.

Porgy and Bess (complete).

*** Decca SET 609-11/*K 3 Q28* [Lon. OSA/*5*- 13116]. White, Mitchell, Boatwright, Quivar, Hendricks, Clemmons, Thompson, Cleveland Ch., Children's Ch., Cleveland O, Maazel.

*** [RCA ARL3/*ARK3* 2109]. Ray Albert, Dale, Andrew Smith, Shakesnider, Marschall, Children's Ch., Houston Grand Op. Ch. and O, DeMain.

If anyone was ever in doubt whether Gershwin in *Porgy and Bess* had really written an opera as opposed to a jumped-up musical, this superb recording with Cleveland forces conducted by Maazel establishes the work's formidable status beyond question. For one thing Maazel includes the complete text, which was in fact cut even before the first stage presentation. Some half-hour of virtually unknown music, including many highly evocative passages and some striking choruses, reinforces the consistency of Gershwin's inspiration. It is not just a question of the big numbers presenting some of the most memorable melodies of the twentieth century, but of a grand dramatic design which triumphs superbly over the almost impossible conjunction of conventions – of opera and the American musical.

With a cast that makes up an excellent team, there is no attempt to glamorize characters who are far from conventional, and the story is the more moving for that, with moments potentially embarrassing ('I's the only woman Porgy ever had,' says Bess to Crown in Act II) given genuine dramatic force à la Puccini. The vigour and colour are irresistible, and the recording is one of the most vivid that even Decca has produced. Willard White is a magnificent Porgy, dark of tone, while Leona Mitchell's vibrant Bess has a moving streak of vulnerability, and François Clemmons as Sportin' Life achieves the near-impossible by actually singing the role and making one forget Cab Calloway. But it is above all Maazel's triumph, a tremendous first complete recording with dazzling playing from the Cleveland Orchestra. There is an excellent cassette set, only marginally less brilliant than the discs.

The distinction is readily drawn between Maazel's Cleveland performance and John DeMain's equally complete and authoritative account on RCA. Where Maazel easily and naturally demonstrates the operatic qualities of Gershwin's masterpiece, DeMain – with a cast which had a riotous success with the piece on Broadway and elsewhere in the United States – presents a performance clearly in the tradition of the Broadway musical. There is much to be said for both views, and it is worth noting that American listeners tend to prefer the less operatic manner of the RCA set. The casts are equally impressive vocally, with the RCA singers a degree more characterful. Donnie Ray Albert, as Porgy, uses his bass-like resonance impressively, though not everyone will like the suspicion of hamming, which works less well in a recording than on stage. That underlining of expressiveness is a characteristic of the performance, so that the climax of the key duet, *Bess, you is my woman now*, has a less natural, more stagey manner, producing, for some ears, less of a frisson than the more delicate Cleveland version. For others the more robust Houston approach has a degree of dramatic immediacy, associated with the tradition of the American popular theatre, which is irresistible. This basic contrast will decide most listeners' approach, and although the RCA recording has not quite the Decca richness it is strikingly vivid and alive. The RCA tape transfer is not quite so sophisticated as the Decca, but it matches the records in presence, giving fine projection of the solo voices, although the chorus is sometimes less well focused.

Porgy and Bess: excerpts.

**(*) RCA Gold GL/*GK* 13654 [AGL 1 3654]. Price, Warfield, Boatwright, Bubbles, RCA Victor Ch. and O, Henderson.

This studio compilation, which was recorded in the mid-1960s, a decade before the complete versions appeared, uses a cast of the finest opera-house singers, rather than those trained in the American Musical tradition, to underline the clear claims of *Porgy and Bess* to be regarded as a work in the mainstream of opera. Both Price and Warfield sing magnificently and the supporting group is given lively direction by Skitch Henderson. One may miss favourite touches – the style is direct and full-blooded – but the impact of such committed singing is undeniable. The cassette transfer emphasizes the treble, and both voices and orchestra sound thin and fierce.

Gesualdo, Carlo (*c.* 1560–1613)

Motets: *Ave dulcissima Maria; Dolcissima mia vita; Ecco morirò dunque; Hei mihi, Domine; Moro lasso al mio duolo; O vos omnes.*
(B) ** Con. CC/*CCT* 7572. Monteverdi Ch. (with instrumental accompaniment), Gardiner – MONTEVERDI: *Motets.***

Here are convincing and fluent performances of six Gesualdo pieces, music that is full of character even when it is not wholly convincing. The singers have excellent ensemble and intonation and are well recorded, though they tend to leave nothing to the listener's imagination. An interesting recital nonetheless, and worth exploring in this bargain-priced reissue.

Madrigals: *Dolcissima mia vita; Ecco morirò dunque; Hai, già mi discoloro; Io tacerò; Itene o miei sospiri; Ivan dunque, o crudele; Moro lasso al mio duolo. Sacrae cantiones: Ave, dulcissima Maria; Ave Regina coelorum; Hei mihi, Domine; O crux benedicta; O vos omnes.*
(M) ** HM HMB 203/*40*. Deller Cons., Deller.

A useful rather than distinguished anthology. Half the record is devoted to madrigals and the other to Gesualdo's *Sacrae cantiones* of 1603. They are all sung with considerable feeling for the expressive content of the words, but intonation is not always impeccable in one or two of the madrigals. The recording dates from 1967 and is truthfully balanced, and there is a good cassette.

Responsoria: Animam meam dilectam tradidi in manus iniquorum; Omnes amici mei dereliquerunt me et praevalerunt insidiantes mihi; Tamquam ad latronem existis cum glaudiis et fustibus comprehendere me; Tenebrae factae sunt; Velum templi scissum est; Vinea mea electa, ego te plantavi.
(M) *** HM HMA 230. Deller Cons., Deller.

Responsoria: Feria quinta; Responsoria et alia ad officium; Hebdomadae Sanctae Spectantiae.
(M) *** HM HMA 220. Deller Cons., Deller.

The *Responses* for Holy Week of 1611 are as remarkable and passionately expressive as any of Gesualdo's madrigals, and in depth of feeling they can be compared only with the finest music of the age. The idiom is less overtly chromatic than in the madrigals, yet dissonance is used whenever it can heighten an expressive effect, and one has the same awareness of words that fires Gesualdo's responses in the madrigals. The invention is often unpredictable and nearly always highly original. Now that his sacred music is beginning to attract more attention, it is clear that he poured great feeling into this medium. The Deller Consort bring to this music much the same approach that distinguishes their handling of the madrigal literature. The colouring of the words is a high priority yet it never oversteps the bounds of good taste to become precious or over-expressive. The consort blends excellently, and intonation is excellent.

Gibbons, Orlando (1583–1625)

2 Fantasias a 3: Fantasia a 4; In nomine a 5; Anthems: *Almighty and everlasting God; O Lord I lift my heart; O Lord increase my faith; Oh, my love how comely; This is the record of John; Thus angels sung. The Cries of London.* Madrigals: *The silver swan; What is our life.*
(M) *** DG Arc. Priv. 2547/*3347* 081. Deller Cons.; Schola Cantorum Basiliensis.

Organ fantasia; Fantasia for double organ; Voluntary. Anthems and verse anthems: *Almighty and everlasting God; Hosanna to the Son of David; Lift up your heads; O Thou the central orbe; See, see the word is incarnate; This is the record of John.* Canticles: *Short service: Magnificat and Nunc dimittis. Second service: Magnificat and Nunc dimittis.* Hymns and songs of the church: *Come kiss with me those lips of thine; Now shall the praises of the Lord be sung; A song of joy unto the Lord.*
*** ASV Dig. DCA/*ZCDCA* 514. King's College, Camb., Ch., Ledger; Butt (organ); L. Early Music Group.

On ASV a splendid introduction to the music of this marvellous composer. It overlaps in one or two instances the Argo version made in the late 1950s with David Willcocks, Thurston Dart and the same choir (which is no longer available), but the clarity and presence of the 1982 recording will in any case win over most collectors. The performances are generally most convincing and totally attuned to that vein of poetic feeling in which Gibbons's art is rich. The singing is wonderfully alive and only in the hymns does one feel that the choir invest too much sophistication in their presentation. *This is the record of John* turns up in another anthology from the 1950s now reissued on DG Archive, which also includes a couple of madrigals (*What is our life* and *The silver swan* with the Deller Consort) and four *Fantasias* (with the viol consort of the Schola Cantorum Basiliensis). It is very early stereo but sounds astonishingly good and is a useful complement to the present issue. There is an iron-oxide cassette of good quality, though slightly less refined than the sound on the ASV disc, while the DG Archive recording is also available in cassette format which, because of the forward balance, is admirably clear and especially vivid in *The cries of London*, presented robustly.

Fantasia a 6; In nomine a 5; Pavan. Madrigals: *Ah, dear heart!; Dainty fine bird; The silver swan; What is our life.* Sacred music: *Behold thou hast made my days; Great king of Gods; O Lord in Thy wrath; Prayer to Hezekiah; The secret sins; Song of Moses.*
(M) ** HM HMA 219/*40* [id.]. Deller Cons., Jaye Cons. of Viols, Deller.

Deller's approach to this music is respectful, and the music's expressive serenity is at the heart of the performances, rather than any sense of drama. The singing is beautifully blended but the slow pacing of the sacred music coupled to its homophonic style does not lend itself to variety. The Jaye Consort play the instrumental pieces with comparable sobriety. Taken sectionally, there is much here to ravish the ear, but as a whole this collection lacks vitality. The sound is excellent, on disc and tape alike.

Keyboard music: *2 Almans; Alman: The King's jewel; Coranto; A Fancy; 2 Fantasias; Fantasia of 4 parts; 4 Galliards; Ground; Italian ground; Lincoln's Inn masque; 2 Pavans; Pavan: Lord Salisbury; Prelude; The Queen's Command; Verse.*
*** O-L DSLO 515. Hogwood (cabinet organ; Italian spinet; harpsichord).

An admirable anthology of Gibbons's keyboard music, as well played and recorded as any of this period. Christopher Hogwood uses three instruments: a Bernard Smith chamber organ from 1643, an Italian spinet of about 1590 and a Ruckers harpsichord. His choice of Gibbons's music tends towards the more thoughtful rather than the outward-looking pieces, but variety is obtained by the contrasting tone-colours of the instruments. The spinet tends to sound a little thin and uneven in the treble, but there is no need for any reservations about either the quality of the music, the performance, or the recording, which does full justice to the character of each instrument. An invaluable addition to the repertoire.

Hymns and songs of the church Nos. 1, 3, 4, 5, 9, 13, 18, 20, 22, 24, 31, 47, 67. Hosanna to the Son of David; I am the resurrection; Lord we beseech thee; O clap your hands; O Lord in thy wrath; Praise the Lord, O my soul; See, see the word is incarnate.
❀ *** Cal. CAL 1611/*4611* [id.]. Clerkes of Oxenford, Wulstan.

A thrilling collection, whether heard on the splendidly recorded disc or the no less excellent cassette. Like the companion Tallis recordings by the same group, this is outstanding in its field, bringing the music tinglingly to life and balancing authority with expressive intensity. The opening *Praise the Lord* has extremely testing writing for two solo trebles which is sung with aplomb; *Lord we beseech thee* has an affecting dark melancholy, while the joyously lively polyphony of *O clap your hands* makes yet another contrast. The closing *Hosanna to the Son of David* has an apotheosis-like eloquence and power, while the simpler hymns are presented with a care for detail and dynamic contrast which brings them fully to life in the manner of Bach chorales. The acoustic is ideal, providing resonance without clouding. A superb issue in every way.

Madrigals and motets: *Ah, dear heart; Dainty fine bird; Fair is the rose; Fair ladies that to love; Farewell, all joys; How art thou thralled: I feign not friendship; I see ambition never pleased; I tremble not at noise of war; I weigh not fortune's frown; Lais now old; 'Mongst thousands good; Nay let me weep; Ne'er let the sun; Now each flowery bank of May; O that the learned poets; The silver swan; Trust not too much fair youth; What is our life; Yet if that age.*
*** O-L DSLO 512. Cons. of Musicke, Rooley.

Gibbons left only one book of madrigalian pieces, and the Consort of Musicke here presents it complete. Performances are eminently thoughtful, half the pieces are sung *and* played with viols, and sensitive attention is paid to phrasing and colour. The diction of the singers is not always first-class, though the director is at some pains to avoid obtrusive or explosive consonants. It would be curmudgeonly to dwell on minor criticisms in so worthy and enjoyable an enterprise, for the set, expertly recorded and beautifully produced, is a most welcome addition to Gibbons's representation on record.

Gilles, Jean (1669–1705)

Requiem (with *Carillon* by Corrette).
*** DG Arc. 2533 461. Rodde, Nirouet, Hill, Studer, Kooy, Ghent Coll. Vocale, Col. Mus. Ant., Herreweghe.
(M) ** Erato Pres. EPR/*MCE* 15515. Simon, Meurant, Hamel, Depraz, Caillard Ch., Paillard CO, Paillard.

Like his English contemporary Purcell, the Provençal Jean Gilles died sadly young. This *Requiem*, which for many years was a favourite work in France, was rejected by the two families who originally commissioned it, so Gilles decreed that it should be used for his own funeral, when it was conducted by Campra. The rhythmic and harmonic vigour (with plentiful false relations to add tang) is well caught in this Archive performance on original instruments. First-rate recording.

Paillard's recording was made in 1956 but sounds remarkably fresh for the period, and readers need have few fears on this score. This performance uses modern instruments and is recorded in the warm and spacious acoustic of St Eustache in Paris, and those who are allergic to the nasal sound of baroque violins may well find this a useful alternative to the Archive issue. Of course, the greater transparency and detail of the latter make it a clear first choice.

Ginastera, Alberto (1916–83)

Harp concerto (revised 1968).
*** DG 2543 806 [id.]. Zabaleta, L'ORTF O, Paris, Martinon – SAINT-SAËNS: *Morceau de concert*; TAILLEFERRE: *Concertino*.***

This concerto is the most substantial work in an outstanding triptych of twentieth-century concertante pieces for harp and orchestra. The Argentine composer Alberto Ginastera wrote it in 1956 for Zabaleta; it was subsequently revised before the present recording, which may be taken as definitive. The piece has remarkable magnetism, particularly the evocative and atmospheric slow movement in which Martinon and Zabaleta generate considerable electricity. The opening ostinato and the robustly energetic finale, with its popular feeling, make an effective frame. With admirable recording, vivid yet refined in ambience and detail, this is surprisingly memorable.

Giordano, Umberto (1867–1948)

Andrea Chénier (complete).
*** RCA [ARL3/*ARK3* 2046]. Domingo, Scotto, Milnes, Alldis Ch., Nat. PO, Levine.
(M) **(*) Decca GOS 600/1 [Lon. OSA 1303]. Tebaldi, Del Monaco, Bastianini, Ch. and O of St Cecilia Ac., Rome, Gavazzeni.
(M) **(*) HMV SLS/*TC-SLS* 143653-3/*5* (2). Corelli, Sereni, Stella, Rome Op. Ch. and O, Santini.

Levine's RCA set is not available in the UK at the time of going to press, but for American readers it will make an obvious first choice. Levine has rarely if ever displayed his powers as an urgent and dramatic opera conductor more potently than on this splendid set, in almost every way a reading that will be hard to better. Giordano always runs the risk – not least in this opera with its obvious parallels with *Tosca* – of being thought of in the shadow of Puccini, but this red-blooded score can, as here, be searingly effective with its defiant poet hero – a splendid role for Domingo at his most heroic – and the former servant, later revolutionary leader, Gérard, a character who genuinely develops from Act to Act, a point well appreciated by Milnes. Scotto was here near the beginning of the intensive spell of recording which compensated for the record companies' neglect earlier, and though a few top notes spread uncomfortably, it is one of her most eloquent and beautiful performances on record. The bright recording intensifies the dramatic thrust of playing and singing. The cassettes are vivid and generally well focused.

The reissued Decca set dates from 1960. Apart perhaps from *La Forza del destino*, it is the most desirable of the Tebaldi/del Monaco sets. The blood and thunder of the story, with the threat of the guillotine hanging over, suits both singers admirably, and Gianandrea Gavazzeni is at his best. It is a work that thrives on 'give-it-all-you've-got' technique, and Tebaldi and del Monaco certainly oblige. Sample the final duet if you have any doubts. But finer still than the soprano and tenor is Bastianini as Gérard. His finely focused voice is beautifully caught and he conveys vividly the conflicts in the man's character. The full-priced stereo version was originally issued on six sides. Now the stereo version is accommodated on four sides in this reissue, without loss of vividness or atmosphere.

The glory of the HMV version, also now made available on two mid-price discs instead of three full-price, is the Chénier of Corelli, one of his most satisfying performances on record with heroic tone gloriously exploited. The other singing is less distinguished. Though Stella was never sweeter of voice than here, she hardly matches such rivals as Tebaldi. The 1960s recording still sounds well, though no better than the even earlier Decca. There are excellent matching cassettes, catching the full bloom on voices and orchestra alike, although transfer levels are variable between sides.

Fedora (opera): complete.
**(*) Decca SET 435/6. Olivero, Del Monaco, Gobbi, Monte Carlo Op. Ch. and O, Gardelli.

Puccini was unique among his Italian contemporaries in sustaining his operatic reputation over a long series of works. Giordano, like Leoncavallo, Mascagni and others, failed to live up to early success, and with Giordano it is significant that this opera, like his most famous one, *Andrea Chénier*, dates from the earliest part of his career. He went on to marry the rich daughter of a hotelier, and prosperity was no doubt the bogey of invention. *Fedora* will always be remembered for one brief aria, the hero's *Amor ti vieta*, but, as this highly enjoyable recording confirms, there is much else that is memorable in the score, even if nothing quite approaches that. The piece is adapted from a Sardou melodrama designed for Sarah Bernhardt (parallel with *Tosca*), with an absurd plot involving a passionate volte-face when the heroine's hatred of the hero (her wicked brother's murderer) suddenly turns to love. Meaty stuff which brings some splendid singing from Magda Olivero and (more intermittently) from del Monaco and Gobbi in a light comedy part. Fine atmospheric recording. Well worth trying by anyone with a hankering after *verismo*.

Giuliani, Mauro (1781–1828)

Guitar concerto No. 1 in A, Op. 30.
(M) *** RCA Gold GL/*GK* 13883 [AGL 1/*AGK 1* 3883]. Bream, Melos Ens. – ARNOLD: *Concerto.****
*** CBS 79334 (3) [M3X 31508]. Williams, ECO (with *Concertos* by Castelnuovo-Tedesco, Rodrigo. Villa-Lobos and Vivaldi).

Guitar concertos Nos. 1; 3 in F, Op. 70.
*** HMV Dig. ASD/*TC-ASD* 143558-1/*4* [Ang. DS/*4XS* 37967]. Angel Romero, ECO, Leppard.

Giuliani's innocent concerto is uncommonly well played by Julian Bream, and the recording (dating originally from 1961) still sounds well. This issue also has the advantage of a very attractive coupling, Malcolm Arnold's *Guitar concerto*, one of his best works and certainly his wittiest. The cassette quality produces a somewhat spiky upper range in the orchestra.

John Williams's account, too, is elegantly turned and he is well recorded and given considerable immediacy and presence by the CBS balance. It has been withdrawn in its single-disc format but remains available in an attractive box (with the ECO conducted either by Daniel Barenboim or Sir Charles Groves) which includes distinguished accounts of the Rodrigo *Concierto de Aranjuez* and *Fantasia para un gentilhombre*, the *Concerto* of Castelnuovo-Tedesco and a comprehensive version of the Villa-Lobos, plus two concertos of Vivaldi (RV. 93 and RV. 158), played with predictable liveliness and artistry. The balance often places the soloist too far forward but the sound is generally good.

However, many will feel that the digital HMV coupling is the most sensible of all. Moreover Leppard also provides accompaniments which match sparkle with elegance and in Op. 30 he restores some hundred bars representing the first movement's development section (about a third of the total length!). Angel Romero is not always such a positive soloist as Pepe or John Williams (or indeed Julian Bream, whose RCA version coupled with Malcolm Arnold's delightful *Guitar concerto* is especially enjoyable). But he plays the slow movement very engagingly, and he is on top form in the *F major Concerto*, which is almost a mirror-image of the *A major*, equally innocent and charming, and no less tuneful (even if the Sicilian theme and variations which make up the slow movement are perhaps a trifle long). This was originally written for the Terz guitar, which is tuned a minor third higher than the standard instrument. Angel Romero plays it on a normal guitar with the pitch raised. The HMV recording is first-class and there is no appreciable difference in sound between LP and tape, even though the *Second Concerto* is transferred at a higher level than the *First*.

Sonata for violin and guitar.
*** CBS 76525/*40*- [M/*MT* 34508]. Perlman, Williams – PAGANINI: *Cantabile* etc.***

Giuliani's *Sonata* is amiable enough but hardly substantial fare; but it is played with such artistry here that it appears better music than it is. The recording is in need of more ambience, but sound is invariably a matter of taste, and there is no reason to withhold a strong recommendation. The cassette is of good quality.

Variations on a theme by Handel, Op. 107.
*** CBS 73745/*40*-. Williams – PAGANINI: *Terzetto* etc.***

The *Variations* are on the theme known as *The Harmonious Blacksmith.* Their construction is guileless but agreeable, and they are expertly played and well recorded here. This is only a very small part of a collection mostly devoted to music of Paganini.

Glazounov, Alexander
(1865–1936)

Birthday Offering (ballet, arr. Irving).
(M) *** HMV Green. ESD 7080. RPO, Irving – LECOCQ: *Mam'zelle Angot.***(*)

The ballet *Birthday Offering* was arranged by Robert Irving for the silver jubilee of the Sadler's Wells Ballet in 1956. The music derives from a number of Glazounov's works, particularly *The Seasons*, *Ruses d'amour*, *Scènes de ballet* and the *Concert waltz No. 1.* It is tuneful and nicely varied in mood and is all thoroughly engaging when played with such wit and polish. The recording dates from 1959, and that shows a little in the upper strings, but otherwise the sound is full and vivid.

Violin concerto in A min., Op. 82.
*** Erato STU/*MCE* 71164. Amoyal, RPO, Scimone – BRUCH: *Concerto No. 1.***(*)

Glazounov was an exact contemporary of Sibelius and composed his concerto at about the same time as did the Finnish master. Pierre Amoyal plays it quite superbly, and his reading must be accounted (after Heifetz) the best now before the public. He has the measure of Glazounov's sweetly effortless lyricism and aristocratic poise, and both in terms of purity of line and generosity of feeling he scores a real success. The soloist is slightly too forward but this does not diminish the strength of this record's attractions. The cassette transfer is of good quality, well focused and full. In the USA Heifetz's incomparable account is available separately, coupled with the Mozart *Sinfonia concertante* [LSC 2734], whereas in the UK it can only be obtained in a boxed set of six records (RL 00720 – see Concerts). As a performance it's a knock-out!

The Seasons (ballet), *Op. 67; Concert waltzes Nos. 1 in D, Op. 57; 2 in F, Op. 51.*
*** HMV ASD 3601 [Ang. S/*4XS* 37509]. Philh. O, Svetlanov.

The Seasons is an early work, first performed at St Petersburg in 1900, the choreography being by the famous Petipa. With colourful orchestration, a generous sprinkling of distinctive melody and, at the opening of *Autumn*, one of the most virile and memorable tunes Glazounov ever penned, the ballet surely deserves to return to the repertoire. Svetlanov's account is most beautifully played and recorded. His approach is engagingly affectionate; he caresses the lyrical melodies persuasively, so that if the big tune of the *Bacchanale* has slightly less thrust than usual it fits readily into the overall conception. The richly glowing HMV recording is outstanding in every way.

PIANO MUSIC

Barcarolle and Novelette, Op. 22; 3 Études, Op. 31; Prelude and fugue, Op. 62; Prelude, caprice-impromptu and gavotte, Op. 49; Variations on a Finnish folksong, Op. 72.
*** Pearl SHE 548. Howard (piano).

A useful companion disc to the two sonatas

that Leslie Howard has recorded for this same company. The music can all be found in the first volume of the complete edition; nearly all of it is of interest and none is otherwise available in modern recordings. The most substantial piece is the *Variations on a Finnish folk-song* (the same theme that crops up in Glazounov's orchestral *Finnish fantasy*, Op. 88). Howard projects all these pieces with admirable character and undoubted fluency. He does not possess the refined sensibility of a Gilels or Richter, but he has the benefit of strength, intelligence and sound musical judgement. He is admirably recorded.

Piano sonatas Nos. 1 in B flat min., Op. 74; 2 in E min., Op. 75; Grand concert waltz in E flat, Op. 41.
**(*) Pearl SHE 538 [id.]. Howard.

Both of Glazounov's piano sonatas date from 1901 and neither is otherwise available. Though not as distinctively personal as Rachmaninov's, which are a few years later, nor as impressively wrought as Balakirev's superb essay in this form, the Glazounov sonatas are well worth investigating, particularly in performances as committed and as well-recorded as these. Leslie Howard is a devoted champion of neglected composers and his fine technique and fluent fingers make out a strong case for both pieces, and for the slighter concert waltz that serves as fill-up. Howard does not always make the most of the poetry here and is not always consistent in observing dynamic nuances, but there is more to praise than to criticize. Admirers of Glazounov's art should investigate this issue.

Glière, Reinhold (1875–1956)

Symphony No. 3 in B min. (Ilya Murometz), Op. 42.
(M) *** Uni. Dig. PCM/*UKC* 500/1. RPO, Farberman.

Glière's massive programme symphony manages to stretch thin material extraordinarily far, but those who respond to the composer's open, colourful style will be delighted that Farberman, unlike his predecessors in stereo, has recorded the score absolutely complete. His conducting cannot be described as volatile, and he is never led into introducing urgent stringendos to add to the passion of a climax, but his very patience, helped by superb recording, makes for very compelling results. Enterprisingly Unicorn got in ahead of even the major companies (except Decca) in bringing out one of the first digital recordings, and though the long finale is marginally less clean in its textures, the sound from first to last has natural balance and warmth. If at the start of the main allegro of the first movement of the RPO cellos and basses have limited resonance, that is clearly a reflection of how the players actually sounded in the hall. The cassette transfer is acceptable, well balanced with no obvious congestion. But compared to the discs the upper range is restricted; the violins lack freshness at the top, and the big climax of the last movement does not match the LP sound in its feeling of spectacle.

Duo for violin and cello.
(M) *** CBS 60264/*40*- [M 33447]. Heifetz, Piatigorsky – DVOŘÁK: *Piano trio No. 3**(**); HALVORSEN: *Passacaglia*; STRAVINSKY: *Suite Italienne.****

Glière's *Duo* is a miniature lasting only 2′17″. It is elegiac in quality. But the playing here is so marvellous that this performance alone is worth the price of the disc. The piece is placed as an interlude between Stravinsky's *Suite Italienne* and the Halvorsen *Passacaglia on a theme of Handel*. The recording is forward but truthful.

Glinka, Michail (1804–57)

Ivan Susanin (A Life for the Tsar): complete.
(***) EMI mono 2C 163 73011/3. Christoff, Stich-Randall, Gedda, Ch. and LOP, Markevitch.

*(**) HMV SLS 165112-3 (3). Nesterenko, Rudenko, Shcherbakov, Sinyavskaya, Bolshoi Theatre Ch. and O, Ermler.

Ivan Susanin – formerly entitled *A Life for the Tsar* before the Soviets became touchy – was the first of the two operas which Glinka completed, marking the birth of genuinely Russian opera. Ermler conducts a lively, idiomatic reading blessed with superb singing from Nesterenko, but the text has been seriously cut, presumably following Bolshoi stage practice. It is particularly sad, when the tenor, Shcherbakov, is a fine artist with a bright, clear voice, that his big aria in Act IV with its phenomenal high notes is omitted. The women are less impressive, though Sinyavskaya's is a distinctive Slavonic contralto, warm and pleasing if not at all convincing in the role of a boy. Bela Rudenko is shrill and wobbly in the role of heroine. The recording though full in range is a little dry.

On balance, in spite of 1950s mono recording, the earlier version under Igor Markevitch – which can still be bought as an EMI import to Britain – remains preferable, with a far finer Antonida in Teresa Stich-Randall and excellent singing from Boris Christoff and Nicolai Gedda. The Yugoslav Chorus rivals that of the Bolshoi.

Gluck, Christoph (1714–87)

Don Juan (ballet): complete.
*** Erato STU 71449. E. Bar. Soloists, Eliot Gardiner.
(M) *** Decca Ser. 410 133-1. ASMF, Marriner.

Although he drew on some of the music for the French version of *Orfeo*, and three numbers turn up in *Iphigénie en Aulide*, *Don Juan* never preserved the popularity it enjoyed during the 1760s and 1770s. (Even Boccherini paraphrased some of it in his *La Casa del Diavolo* symphony.) Like the operas, it was a 'reform' work, intended to confront the audience with real human emotions on the stage. There is a certain lack of tonal variety that presents problems when the music is heard on its own, divorced from the stage spectacle. However, the invention is of high quality and, given the dramatic fire of this excellent performance by the English Baroque Soloists under John Eliot Gardiner playing on original instruments, it makes a strong effect.

Although Marriner's version on Decca is altogether delightful and has great lightness of touch to commend it, there is a cleaner dramatic profile in the Erato version which makes one understand why this music was so revolutionary in its day. Marriner does not sound in the least bland but he does produce a more mellifluous sonority which John Eliot Gardiner does not strive for. The Erato recording is very good indeed, well balanced and in an agreeably warm acoustic with good presence and detail.

Marriner's version is also very well recorded, and now has the advantage of economy. The playing is altogether excellent and captures the lightness of touch as well as the dramatic intensity of the score.

OPERA

Alceste (complete).
(M) ** Decca GOS 574/6. Flagstad, Jobin, Young, Hemsley, Geraint Jones Singers and O, Jones.

This originally appeared in 1957 on four mono LPs, but the stereo is genuine and considering its age remarkably good. *Alceste* is a magnificent work, and this performance is notable for Kirsten Flagstad's noble queen. She is not always in perfect sympathy with the style, and her intonation is a trifle suspect at times, but this is of small account given her star quality. The rest of the cast is perfectly acceptable, even if Raoul Jobin's Admetus is not absolutely ideal. Geraint Jones directs the chorus and orchestra to good effect: tempi are well judged and though the performance is not thrilling (it wants the last ounce of polish) it is still worth having. Jones does the Italian version of the work, and even though the quality of recorded sound is not in the first flight, the set is valuable when Gluck's representation in the catalogue is so meagre.

Armide (complete).
*** HMV SLS/*TC-SLS* 107751-3/5 (3). Palmer, Rolfe Johnson, Herincx, Finnie, Burgess, Slorach, Windmuller, Richard Hickox Singers, City of L. Sinf., Hickox.

Anyone who thinks of Gluck's operas as objects of static beauty should hear this vital, highly dramatic work, performed here with aptly joyous vigour. The studio recording followed live performances at the 1982 Spitalfields Festival, when Wolf-Siegfried Wagner devised a striking and inventive production which matched the lively conducting of Richard Hickox, here making his first complete opera recording.

That stage experience – albeit in the limited area of Christ Church, Spitalfields – has given this whole performance a magnetic compulsion. Now that we are so much more familiar with opera seria, the real revolution that the operas of Gluck represented comes out vividly in such a piece as this, with duets and ensembles as well as arias fused into the structure far more flexibly than in previous opera. The character of the sorceress, Armide, Princess of Damascus, dominates the whole opera. Felicity Palmer in her finest achievement on record gives a performance of fire-eating intensity, searingly dramatic but musically commanding too. Hers is not a beautiful voice but a strongly characterful one, and it has never been more appealingly caught on record before. Though not all the voices are distinguished, the solo singing is consistently responsive and stylish, with outstanding contributions from Anthony Rolfe Johnson as Renaud, Sally Burgess as one of Armide's attendants and Linda Finnie in the allegorical role of Hate. The chorus and orchestra add consistently to the involvement. The five compact and eventful Acts fit neatly on to the six sides, the first four each complete on a side, the Fifth (with its ballet) taking two. The recorded sound is both clear and atmospheric, set in an ideal acoustic, with little to choose between the sound of discs and cassettes. Perhaps the upper range is slightly softer-grained on tape, but the difference is of no consequence.

Orfeo ed Euridice (complete).
*** Erato Dig. NUM 750423 (3) [id.]. Baker, Speiser, Gale, Glyndebourne Ch., LPO, Leppard.
**(*) Decca SET 443/4 [Lon. OSA 1285]. Horne, Lorengar, Donath, ROHCG Ch. and O, Solti.
** HMV Dig. SLS/*TCC-SLS* 5255 [Ang. DS2X 3922]. Baltsa, Marshall, Gruberova, Amb. Op. Ch., Philh. O, Muti.
(M) ** DG Priv. 2726 043 (2). Fischer-Dieskau, Janowitz, Moser, Munich Bach Ch. and O, Karl Richter.
*(*) Ph. Metronome Dig. 0180 088 (3) [id., PSI]. Hoffmann, Conwell, Bergius, Tolz Ch., Cologne Ch. and PO, Panzer.

The Erato version, directly based on the Glyndebourne production in which Dame Janet Baker made her very last stage appearance in opera, was recorded immediately after the run of live performances. That brought the advantage of the sort of dramatic commitment and spontaneity of a live performance allied to studio precision.

Leppard, abetted by the producer, Sir Peter Hall, aimed in the theatre to contrast the bitingly passionate quality in the score against the severely classical frame. Often credited with being a romanticiser of the eighteenth century, Leppard in fact presents the score with freshness and power, indeed toughness. Nowhere is that clearer than in the great scene leading up to the aria, *Che farò*, where Dame Janet commandingly conveys the genuine bitterness and anger of Orpheus at Eurydice's death. That most famous of Gluck arias comes over fresh and clear with no sentimentality whatever, and conversely the display aria which brings Act I to a close has passion and expressiveness even in the most elaborate coloratura. Elisabeth Speiser as Eurydice and Elizabeth Gale as Amor are both disappointing but, as in the theatre, the result is a complete and moving experience centring round a great performance from Dame Janet. The recording is bright to the point of edginess, but otherwise clear and well-balanced. As in the theatre, the complete ballet-postlude is included, delightful celebration music.

The surprise of the Decca set is the conducting of Georg Solti, which combines his characteristic brilliance and dramatic bite with a feeling for eighteenth-century idiom which is most impressive. Where often in this opera the progress of the drama can be forgotten, here the experience is riveting, the more so when Solti and Horne opt to conclude Act I, not as the Gluck score prescribes, but with a brilliant display aria, *Addio, o miei sospiri*, taken from the contemporary opera *Tancredi* by Ferdinando Bertoni. That may sound like cavalier treatment for Gluck, but stylistically in every way Solti justifies not only that course but his whole interpretation, which combines drama with delicacy. Marilyn Horne makes a formidably strong Orfeo, not so deeply imaginative as Dame Janet Baker, but wonderfully strong and secure with fine control of tone. Pilar Lorengar sings sweetly, but is not always steady, while Helen Donath is charming in the role of Amor. Recording quality is outstandingly fine.

Muti chose to record the relatively severe 1762 version, which eliminates some much-loved passages added later, but then opted for a most unstylish approach, sleek and smooth but full of romantic exaggerations. The pity is that the trio of principals is one of the strongest on record. Sadly, even Agnes Baltsa cannot make *Che farò* sound stylish, when the speed is so leaden. The recording is warm and rounded. This is the only set available on cassettes and the sound is generally first-class, although on our copy there was some insecurity of texture on side two (noticeable in the *Dance of the Blessed Spirits*).

Though the singing is stylish and there is much to enjoy on the DG Privilege set, the very fact that a baritone is featured in the main role, singing a part written for alto (or tenor in the Paris version), means that this recording is not a serious contender. But Fischer-Dieskau's extra expressiveness and his response to word meanings bring sure rewards, and the rest of the cast supports him well, so admirers of this artist will find this worth exploring.

The Philips Metronome digital set is a special import and unlikely to be available for long. Having a Heldentenor in the role of Orfeo is an oddity, for Panzer's set uses not the French version with tenor but the Italian version in transposition. Though Peter Hoffmann has his effective heroic moments, the result is heavy and unstylish, thanks also to the lumpish conducting of Heinz Panzer.

Arias: *Alceste: Divinités du Styx. Armide: Le perfide Renaud. Iphigénie en Aulide: Vous essayez . . . Par la crainte; Adieu, conservez dans votre âme. Iphigénie en Tauride: Non, cet affreux devoir. Orfeo ed Euridice: Che puro ciel; Che farò senza Euridice. Paride ed Elena: Spiagge amate; Oh, del mio dolce ardor; Le belle immagini; Di te scordarmi. La Rencontre imprévue: Bel inconnu; Je cherche à vous faire.*
*** Ph. 9502/*7313* 112. Baker, ECO, Leppard.

Helped by alert and sensitive accompaniments from Raymond Leppard and the ECO, Janet Baker's singing of Gluck is a revelation, completely undermining any idea of something square or dull in his inspiration. The most famous arias bring unconventional readings – *Divinités du Styx* deliberately less commanding, more thoughtful than usual – but the rarities are what inspire Dame Janet most keenly: the four arias from *Paride ed Elena*, for example, are vividly contrasted in their sharply compact form. Outstandingly beautiful recording, and the tape quality is first-class, transferred at a high level.

Goehr, Alexander (born 1932)

Metamorphosis/Dance, Op. 36; (i) *Romanza for cello and orchestra, Op. 24.*
(M) *** Uni. Dig. DKP 9017. (i) Welsh; Royal Liv. PO, Atherton.

Goehr wrote the *Romanza*, one of his most lyrical works, with Jacqueline du Pré in mind. Moray Welsh plays warmly and stylishly, but it is a pity that the dedicatee never recorded this piece, which in its serial argument still requires persuasiveness, with its rhapsodic layout of *Aria* incorporating scherzo and cadenza. *Metamorphosis dance* was inspired by the Circe episode in the *Odyssey*, a sequence of elaborate variations full of strong rhythmic interest. Not for nothing did the composer describe the piece as an 'imaginary ballet', though he would have done better to choose a less daunting title. Excellent performances and recording.

Goldmark, Karl (1830–1915)

Violin concerto No. 1 in A min., Op. 28.
(*) HMV ASD/*TC-ASD* 3408 [Ang. S/*4XS* 37445]. Perlman, Pittsburgh SO, Previn – SARASATE: *Zigeunerweisen.*

Like the *Rustic Wedding symphony* this, the first of Goldmark's two violin concertos, maintains a peripheral position in the catalogue. It is a pleasing and warm-hearted concerto in the romantic tradition that deserves to be better known. It could not be more beautifully played than by Itzhak Perlman, whose effortless virtuosity and lyrical poise even challenge Milstein's aristocratic record of the late 1950s (now deleted). The latter was better balanced, for the EMI engineers have placed Perlman very much in the foreground – so much so that orchestral detail does not always register as it should. The sound quality is fresher in the newer recording, and Previn accompanies sympathetically. This is very charming and likeable music, and Perlman plays it most winningly. The cassette transfer matches the disc fairly closely, though the climaxes could reproduce more smoothly.

Rustic Wedding symphony, Op. 26.
*** [Ang. SZ/*4ZS* 37662]. Pittsburgh SO, Previn.
** Decca Dig. SXDL/*KSXDC* 7528 [Lon. LDR 71030]. LAPO, Lopez-Cobos.

The *Rustic Wedding symphony* was one of the three colourful works – the others being the *Violin concerto No. 1* and the opera *The Queen of Sheba* – which appeared in quick succession in the mid-1870s and which together have alone sustained Goldmark's reputation to the present day. 'Clear-cut and faultless', Brahms called this large but consciously unpretentious programme symphony, wittily echoing what Schumann had once said to Brahms himself, that 'it sprang into being, a finished thing, like Minerva from the head of Jupiter'. The opening movement brings not a sonata-form structure but a simple set of variations with one or two pre-echoes of Mahler in *Wunderhorn* mood, and though there are no neurotic tensions whatever, with a tale of a peasant wedding simply told, it seems likely that Mahler learnt something from the piece. Previn relishes the contrasts, the rhythmic drive and the innocent lyricism, drawing excellent playing from the Pittsburgh orchestra, as he did accompanying Perlman in the *Violin concerto No. 1.* Warm, red-blooded recording to match. The cassette offers similarly attractive sound, rich, glowing and atmospheric. Highly recommended, but, alas, deleted in the UK.

Lopez-Cobos directs a refreshing and attractive reading. The generally fast tempi detract from the charm of the piece – Previn's version is altogether more colourful and persuasive – but with wide-ranging digital sound, which presents the Los Angeles orchestra untypically at a distance, it is a fair recommendation. The cassette transfer is admirable, crisp and clear to match the disc closely.

Die Königin von Saba (opera).
(M) **(*) Hung. SLPX/*MK* 12179/82. Nagy, Gregor, Kincses, Jerusalem, Miller, Takács, Hungarian State Op. Ch. and O, Fischer.

Goldmark's most successful works came within a relatively short span in his career, of which this long opera is the most ambitious product. With the Queen of Sheba representing evil and the lovely Sulamit representing good, its theme links directly with that of Wagner's *Tannhäuser*, but in style Goldmark rather recalls Mendelssohn and Gounod, with a touch of Meyerbeer. In the tenor role of Asad, Siegfried Jerusalem gives a magnificent performance, not least in his aria *Magische Töne*. Klára Takács is dramatic and characterful as the Queen of Sheba, but on top the voice is often raw. Sándor Nagy is an impressive Solomon, and Adam Fischer, one of the talented family of conductors, draws lively performances from everyone. The recording is very acceptable.

Goossens, Eugene (1893–1962)

Symphony No. 1, Op. 58.
(M) *** Uni. KP 8000. Adelaide SO, Measham.

Between the wars Eugene Goossens was thought of as a composer of considerable talent: two of his operas were produced at Covent Garden and works like *Kaleidoscope* kept his name alive among pianists. The *First Symphony* was written in 1940 and it is appropriate that an Australian orchestra should record it, since Goossens spent many years there as conductor of the ABC Sydney Symphony Orchestra. The idiom is wholly accessible, and readers who enjoy the symphonies of Bax should investigate this well-constructed and finely paced score, which has variety both of colour and of substance. David Measham gets very impressive results from the Adelaide orchestra, and the warm acoustic, which is alive and spacious, helps the well-detailed and vivid recording. Strongly recommended.

Gould, Morton (born 1913)

Spirituals for string choir and orchestra; Foster Gallery.
** Crystal Clear CCS 7005 [id.]. LPO, composer.

A modern recording of Gould's *Spirituals* is most welcome, particularly one so rich and spacious and naturally balanced. But the composer's performance is disappointing. The elegiac quality of the slow movement, *Sermon*, is expressively caught, and the strident percussive effects of *Protest* are extremely telling; but there is a disappointing lack of wit in the miniature scherzo, *A little bit of sin*, with its sly humour and quotation of *Shortnin' bread.* The *Foster Gallery* derives its material from Stephen Foster melodies, but apart from a delicate appearance of *Jeannie with the light brown hair* it is surprisingly unmemorable.

Gounod, Charles (1818–93)

Petite symphonie in B flat (for wind).
(M) *** Ph. Seq. 412 004-1/*4*. Neth. Wind Ens., De Waart – DVOŘÁK: *Serenade;* SCHUBERT: *Octet, D.72.* ***
(M) *** Sup. 1411 2844. Coll. Mus. Pragense – D'INDY: *Chanson et danses*; GOUVY: *Suite gauloise.****
(B) ** PRT GSGC/*ZCGC* 2037. Hallé O (members), Barbirolli – DVOŘÁK: *Wind serenade.***

Gounod's *Petite symphonie* is wonderfully fresh, witty and civilized and its charm is irresistible in the crisp and vital Netherlands performance, given the realism of the Philips recording.

The Collegium Musicum Pragense are hardly less accomplished than the Netherlands Wind Ensemble who recorded this some years earlier, though tastes inevitably differ in these matters: the Czech flautist has a wider vibrato and the clarinets a slightly watery tone. However, there can be no doubts as to the excellence and spirit of the playing of this group or the vivid if forward recording. What a charming piece it is!

Barbirolli's account from the 1960s still sounds well (though the cassette does not match the disc, lacking range at the top). The performance has plenty of character, yet a suitably light touch; and Barbirolli's affection is obvious. The Hallé players are in fine form.

Messe solennelleà Sainte Cécile.
** HMV SXLP 30206 [Ang. S/*4XS* 36214].

Lorengar, Hoppe, Crass, René Duclos Ch., Paris Conservatoire O, Hartemann.

One welcomes back to the catalogue Jean-Claude Hartemann's performance of this highly attractive Victorian piece. The *Credo* is the thing to sample first – a rollicking setting with more than a hint of a Beatles tune. Gounod, having invented a good tune, has no inhibitions about using it, and whatever the rhythm of the words he brings it back whenever he wants, ending with a very secular-sounding augmentation almost in Hollywood style. If that is the most vulgar movement of this Mass it is also the most enjoyable. The rest is agreeable without being terribly memorable, but it should serve to show that Gounod's other works besides *Faust* are well worth the occasional airing. This Paris performance is capable without being very distinguished. The recording is only fair, but at medium price the disc is well worth exploring.

OPERA

Faust (complete).

(M) **(*) HMV SLS 816 (4) [Ang. SDL 3622]. Los Angeles, Gedda, Blanc, Christoff, Paris Nat. Op. Ch. and O, Cluytens.

** HMV SLS/*TC-SLS* 5170 (4) [Ang. SZDX/*4Z4X* 3868]. Freni, Domingo, Allen, Ghiaurov, Paris Op. Ch. and O, Prêtre.

** Decca SET 327-30/*K 127 K 43* [Lon. OSA/ 5- 1433]. Sutherland, Corelli, Massard, Ghiaurov, Amb. S., Highgate School Ch., LSO, Bonynge.

*(*) Erato STU 71031 (4). Caballé, Aragall, Plishka, Huttenlocher, Ch. of Op. du Rhin, Strassbourg PO, Lombard.

Faust has not been a particularly lucky opera on record and the vintage (1960) HMV set still holds its place fairly securely at the top of the list. This was in fact a re-make of an earlier mono set, and the contributions of de los Angeles, Gedda and Christoff have all, if anything, improved. The seductiveness of Los Angeles's singing is a dream and, as she has twice shown before on record, the agility required in the *Jewel song* holds no terrors for her. It is a pity that the recording hardens the natural tone-colour slightly. Christoff is magnificently Mephistophelian. The dark rich bass voice with all its many subtle facets of tone colour is a superb vehicle for the part, at once musical and dramatic. Gedda, though showing some signs of strain, sings intelligently, and among the other soloists Ernest Blanc has a pleasing, firm voice, which he uses to make Valentin into a sympathetic character. Cluytens's approach is competent but somewhat workaday. He rarely offers that extra spring which adds so much to Gounod's score in sheer charm, and he shows a tendency to over-drive in the more dramatic passages. The recording is good but not exceptional, atmospheric in choral and offstage passages, and on the whole well balanced, although at times some of the soloists are oddly placed on the stereo stage.

Even in French music Prêtre is an unpersuasive conductor. His four principals are all fine singers, aptly chosen for their roles, but without magic from the conductor they only fitfully produce their best singing, and too often the results are lumpy and unidiomatic. When Freni sings *Ah, je ris* at the beginning of the *Jewel song*, laughter is nowhere near. Domingo is less stylish than he usually is in French music; Ghiaurov is less rich and resonant than he was in the Bonynge set of 1967; and only Thomas Allen gives a performance which matches the best on the Cluytens set. The recording is full and warm, and the cassette transfer captures the resonance with only marginal loss of crispness. The layout, with each Act complete on a cassette side and side six given to the ballet music, is admirable.

Decca provide a performance of *Faust* with only one Frenchman in the cast (Robert Massard as Valentin). In the event it is not surprising if the flavour is only intermittently authentic. Richard Bonynge's conducting is fresh and stylish – the most consistently successful contribution – but much of the singing, including Sutherland's, falls short. It goes without saying that the heroine produces some exquisite sounds, but too often she indulges in her 'mooning' style, so that *Le Roi de Thule* provokes unclean attack all through, and ends with a really disagreeable last phrase on *Et doucement*. Corelli's faults are more than those of style, and his French is excruciating.

Ghiaurov too hardly sounds at home in the music. But when Gounod's aim is clear, then all the singers' efforts click into place, and the final trio is wonderfully rousing. A memorable contribution from Monica Sinclair as Martha. The text is more complete than that of any previous recording, and the recording quality is outstanding. On tape the opera is laid out on three cassettes, with each of the five Acts complete on one side except Act III which (transferred, incidentally, at a slightly lower level than the rest of the opera) splits over two. The libretto booklet has been handsomely reduced; however, the side analysis remains unaltered to follow the discs and not the tapes! The transfer is vivid, with the choral scenes well focused, but there is a degree of fierceness in the treble, most striking in the outer Acts.

The Erato version is disappointing, not one of Lombard's successes as an opera conductor. The unatmospheric recording and singing either unstylish or dull do not help. Caballé is the chief offender, plainly seeing herself as a prima donna whose vagaries and self-indulgences have to be wooed. Aragall produces some beautiful sounds, but he does not seem completely happy in French, and Paul Plishka lacks flair and devilry as Mephistopheles. The Cluytens set with Los Angeles, Gedda, Blanc and Christoff remains the most attractive available version.

Faust: highlights.
** Decca SET 431 (from above set, cond. Bonynge).

On the Decca disc Bonynge's achievement is beyond question. If not exactly in the Beecham class in his handling of this lovely score, he at least treats it with rare delicacy and sympathy, and arguably provides the strongest constituent in a set that contains irritating disappointments. Excellent recording. There is a highlights disc taken from the Los Angeles/Gedda/Christoff/Cluytens set available as a special EMI import (2C 059 43184).

Faust: ballet music.
** Decca Jub. JB/*KJBC* 12 [Lon. JL/5-41029]. ROHCGO, Solti – OFFENBACH: *Gaîté Parisienne.***

Bright, intense playing under Solti. There is some lack of poise and elegance, but the music-making certainly has sparkle and excitement and the sound is vivid. The transfer to tape is admirably lively.

Faust: Ballet music and Waltz.
** Ph. Dig. 6514/*7337* 070 [id.]. Rotterdam PO, Zinman – CHOPIN: *Les Sylphides.**(*)

The *Faust ballet music* springs more readily to life in Zinman's recording than its Chopin coupling and the playing is often nicely turned. The *Waltz* is taken very fast. This is not really distinguished, although the sound is good on both disc and chrome tape.

Mireille (complete).
*** EMI 2C 167/*297* 73021/3 [Ang. SZCX 3905]. Freni, Vanzo, Rhodes, Van Dam, Bacquier, Toulouse Capitole Ch. and O, Plasson.

Based on an improbable rustic epic in Provençal – a subject which had Gounod temporarily taking up residence in Provence – *Mireille* is nicely divided between scenes of country innocence (cue for airy tunes and skipping rhythms that to British ears suggest Sullivan) and high sentimental drama, including an excursion à la *Freischütz* into the supernatural when the villain is borne off by a phantom boatman. Gounod as ever is most memorable when he is not aiming too high, and one regrets that the freshness of the opening scenes has to give way to the heavy sentiment, which on the heroine's death at the end grows oppressive. Nonetheless, in so strong and committed a performance as Plasson's, with attractive and generally stylish singing, it makes a very welcome rarity. Vanzo, Bacquier and Van Dam are all in excellent form, and though Freni does not always sound comfortable in French, it is an appealing performance. It is a pity that in the interests of authenticity this recording of the original text excludes the most famous number, the coloratura *Waltz song*.

Roméo et Juliet: highlights.
(M) *(*) HMV SXLP/*TC-SXLP* 30304.

Carteri, Gedda, Paris Op. O, Lombard – BIZET: *Pêcheurs de perles*: highlights.*(*)

Gounod's Shakespeare opera is so poorly represented on record that any items are welcome, but these selections (including the *Waltz song* from Act II, *Nuit d'hyménée* from Act IV, and the Act V tomb scene) are not very stylish, with even Gedda less impressive than usual. The recording is satisfactory on both disc and cassette.

Gouvy, Louis-Théodore
(1819–98)

Suite gauloise.
(M) *** Sup. 1411 2844. Coll. Mus. Pragense – D'INDY: *Chanson et danses;* GOUNOD: *Petite symphonie.****

Louis-Théodore Gouvy was a German composer of French parentage who abandoned law for music early in his career and though he never held any official appointments went on to write seven symphonies, five string quartets, an opera, *Le Cid*, and a variety of works in the traditional forms rather than the tone poems and programme works that were in favour. This piece is fresh and charming and makes no pretensions to significance. It is not strongly individual but always well crafted and extremely well played, even if the wide vibrato of the clarinet may worry some listeners.

Grainger, Percy (1882–1961)

(i) *Blithe bells;* (ii) *Children's march; Over the hills and far away;* (ii; iii) *Colonial song;* (iv) *Country gardens; Handel in the Strand;* (ii) *Harvest hymn;* (v) *In a Nutshell (suite);* (iv) *Irish tune from County Derry; Mock morris; Molly on the shore; Shepherd's hey;* (i) *We were dreamers;* (ii) *Youthful suite* (piano): (vi) *Lincolnshire posy (suite);* (vii) *Knight and shepherd's daughter; Walking tune.* Arr. of Gershwin: *The man I love.*
(M) *** HMV SLS/*TC-SLS* 5249 (2). (i) Adelaide SO; (ii) Sydney SO; both cond. Hopkins; (iii) with Berridge, Parker; (iv) Light Music SO, Dunn; (v) E. Sinf., Dilkes; (vi) Howard and Stanhope; (vii) Adni.

The orchestral highlights here are provided by vivid recordings of six of Grainger's most famous miniatures (including *Country gardens, Handel in the Strand, Mock morris* and *Shepherd's hey*) by the Light Music Society Symphony Orchestra under Sir Vivian Dunn. The sound is forwardly balanced (it was originally a hi-fi-orientated Studio 2 issue) but the performances are polished and particularly spontaneous. The English Sinfonia play persuasively in the little-known *In a Nutshell suite* (with its piano obbligato) and the *Pastoral* is memorable. But otherwise the composer's inspiration, here and in the *Youthful suite*, is uneven. The style of the writing has affinities with both Eric Coates and Edward German. Leslie Howard and David Stanhope give a positive if somewhat unyielding account of the two-piano version of a *A Lincolnshire Posy,* and they are not helped by the somewhat over-resonant recording (otherwise truthful). Daniel Adni's three contributions are delightful, especially the Gershwin arrangement. The playing of the Adelaide and Sydney orchestras has plenty of character (one is glad to welcome the wordless vocal duet included in the *Colonial song*) and in general this is a thoroughly worthwhile anthology. The cassettes, transferred at a high level, match the discs fairly closely, although occasionally the reverberation brings a slight loss of refinement of focus.

Children's march; Colonial song; Country gardens; Handel in the Strand; Immovable Do; Irish tune from County Derry; Mock morris; Molly on the shore; My Robin is to the greenwood gone; Shepherd's hey; Spoon River.
(M) ** Mercury SRI/*MRI* 75102 [id.]. Eastman Rochester Pops O, Fennell.

Lively and sympathetic performances from

Fennell, and a nicely balanced programme. But the Mercury sound (from the beginning of the 1960s) is slightly abrasive, with pithy strings, almost giving an impression of baroque period instruments. The *Londonderry air* sounds the very opposite of sumptuous. The recording does not lack ambience, but some allowances will have to be made for the close positioning of the microphones.

Irish tune from County Derry; Lincolnshire posy; Molly on the shore; Shepherd's hey.
*** ASV ALH/*ZCALH* 913. L. Wind O, Wick – MILHAUD and POULENC: *Suites françaises.****

First-class playing and vivid recording, with the additional attraction of delightful couplings, make this highly recommendable. The Grainger pieces come off excellently, and the sound could hardly be better balanced. This is in the demonstration class, and the cassette is splendidly managed too.

Lincolnshire posy; Shepherd's hey.
*** Telarc Dig. DG 10050 [id.]. Cleveland Symphonic Winds, Fennell – ARNAUD: *Fanfares;* VAUGHAN WILLIAMS: *English folksongs suite* etc.***

Grainger scored *Shepherd's hey* for wind band as a result of his experience as a recruited musician in the US Army during the First World War. The six-movement *Lincolnshire posy* was written in New York in 1937. It is the highlight of this impressive compilation, played with marvellous bravura and understanding. The climax of *Rufford Park poachers* is splendidly made, and the nice wit of *The brisk young sailor*, which follows, offers a perfect foil. The recording has superb clarity and a real feeling of spectacle. A demonstration disc indeed, the pressing absolutely clean and surfaces immaculate.

VOCAL MUSIC

Duke of Marlborough fanfare; Lisbon; My Robin is to the greenwood gone; Shepherd's hey; Piano duet: *Let's dance gay in green meadow;* Vocal and choral: *Bold William Taylor; I'm seventeen come Sunday; Lord Maxwell's goodnight; The lost lady found; The pretty maid milkin' her cow; Scotch strathspey and reel; Shallow Brown; The sprig of thyme; There was a pig went out to dig; Willow willow.*
*** Decca SXL 6410. Pears, Shirley-Quirk, Amb. S., ECO, Britten; Britten and Tunnard (pianos).

This is an altogether delightful anthology, beautifully played and recorded by these distinguished artists. Grainger's talent was a smaller one than his more fervent advocates would have us believe, but his imagination in the art of arranging folk-song was prodigious. The *Willow song* is a touching and indeed haunting piece and shows the quality of Grainger's harmonic resource. The opening fanfare too is strikingly original and so is *Shallow Brown*. Indeed each of the items here, with one or two exceptions, is obstinately memorable, and the recording is an extremely good one.

Granados, Enrique (1867–1916)

Goyescas: Intermezzo.
(M) *** Decca Jub. JB 50. New Philh. O, Frühbeck de Burgos – FALLA: *El amor brujo*; RAVEL: *Alborada* etc.***

A lusciously brilliant performance, superbly recorded by Decca. The cassette transfer is also first-class.

Spanish dance, Op. 37/5: Andaluza.
(M) ** Decca SPA/*KCSP* 551. LSO, Gamba – RAVEL: *Boléro* etc.; SARASATE: *Carmen fantasy.***

Granados's most famous melody is here vividly performed and recorded (on disc and tape alike), but this is only a bonus item for a coupling of two of Ansermet's Ravel performances and Ricci's super-brilliant account of the Sarasate.

(i) *Piano quintet in G min. A la Cubana, Op. 36; Aparición; Cartas de Amor – valses intimos, Op. 44; Danza característica. Escenas poéticas* (2nd series).
*** CRD CRD 1035. Rajna (piano), (i) with Alberni Qt.

The *Piano quintet* is a compact work, neat and unpretentious, in three attractive movements, including a charming lyrical *Allegretto* and a vigorous finale where the piano is most prominent. Among the piano music here, the evocative pieces in the *Escenas poéticas II* are the most valuable, but even the more conventional colour-pieces which make up the rest of the disc are well worth hearing in such perceptive readings as Thomas Rajna's. The CRD recording is first-rate.

PIANO MUSIC

A la pradera; Barcarola, Op. 46; Bocetos; Cuentos de la Juventud, Op. 1; Mazurka, Op. 2; Mosque y Árabe; Sardana; Los soldados de cartón.
*** CRD CRD 1036/*CRDC 4036*. Rajna.

Allegro de concierto; Capricho español, Op. 39; Carezza vals, Op. 38; 2 Impromptus; Oriental; Rapsodia aragonesa; Valses poéticos.
*** CRD CRD 1023. Rajna.

Escenas románticas; Seis piezas sobre cantos populares españoles; Danza lenta.
*** CRD CRD 1022. Rajna.

6 Estudios expresivos; Estudio, Op. posth.; Impromptu, Op. 39; 2 Marches militaires; Marche militaire; Paisaje, Op. 35; Pequeña suite (*In the garden of Elisenda*).
*** CRD CRD 1037/*CRDC 4037*. Rajna.

Not all of Granados's works are as inventive as the *Goyescas*, but though this music is of uneven quality, Thomas Rajna plays it with great sympathy and flair. He is moreover accorded an excellent balance by the engineers; the piano reproduces most comfortably and cleanly in a warm acoustic. Apart from the *Danzas españolas* (see below) some of the finest music is to be found in the *Escenas románticas* and in the other pieces on CRD 1022/3. The later volumes, however, excellently played and recorded, should nonetheless be acquired, and not merely for the sake of completeness. The *Seis Estudios* serve to point the formative influences in Granados's style – Schumann and, to a lesser extent, Fauré – while the other pieces, including the *Marches militaires* (in which Rajna superimposes the second piano part), are unfailingly pleasing. Obviously not essential Granados but certainly recommended for the enthusiast. The cassettes are of CRD's usual excellent quality, matching the discs closely.

Danzas españolas, Op. 37.
*** Decca SXL/*KSXC* 6980 [Lon. CS/5-7209]. De Larrocha.
*** CRD CRD 1021. Rajna.

In this repertoire Alicia de Larrocha enjoys special authority and this fine Decca recording supersedes her earlier account on Erato/RCA. She has an aristocratic poise to which it is difficult not to respond and plays with great flair and temperament. There have been other fine accounts but this is undoubtedly the most desirable and best-recorded version in circulation. The cassette, too, is one of Decca's best, clear and wide-ranging, yet full and naturally coloured in the middle range.

Rajna's performances are first-class and the CRD recording is of high quality, and those collecting his complete series will not be disappointed here.

Goyescas (complete).
*** Decca **411 958-2**; SXL 6785 [Lon. CS/5-7009]. De Larrocha.

Goyescas; Escenas poéticas; Libro de horas.
** CRD CRD 1001 2/*CRDC* 4001 2. Rajna.

The Decca recording is most distinguished. Alicia de Larrocha brings special insights and sympathy to the *Goyescas*; her playing has the crisp articulation and rhythmic vitality that these pieces call for, and the overall impression could hardly be more idiomatic in flavour. These performances displace the alternative listing (Rajna on CRD), not least for the excellence of the recorded sound. It is remarkably firm and secure.

Thomas Rajna's interpretations, however,

are clear and persuasive; in his hands the music sounds greater than one expects. The fill-ups, more immediately charming, less ambitious, are valuable too. One soon gets used to the off-centre balance of the piano. The cassettes are excellently transferred, the sound full and clear. The Decca cassette has, however, been withdrawn in the UK.

Grechaninov, Alexander

(1864–1956)

The Lane (5 children's songs), *Op. 89*.
*** Decca SXL 6900 [Lon. OS 26579]. Söderström, Ashkenazy – MUSSORGSKY: *Nursery;* PROKOFIEV: *Ugly Duckling*.***

Grechaninov, much influenced by Mussorgsky, wrote these songs in 1920, and though they are far less original and intense than the Mussorgsky cycle on the reverse, they make an admirable fill-up for a superb record, vividly performed and recorded.

Gregorian chant

First Christmas Mass.
(M) *** DG Priv. 2535/*3335* 345. Benedictine Monks' Ch. of St Martin's Abbey, Beuron, Pfaff.

Third Christmas Mass.
(M) *** DG Arc. Priv. 2547/*3347* 001. Ch. of St Martin's, Beuron, Pfaff.

Easter Sunday Mass.
(M) *** DG Arc. Priv. 2547/*3347* 016. Ch. of St Martin's, Beuron, Pfaff.

The German tradition of plainsong combines dedication with careful preparation. It is different in style and timbre from the choirs of Italy and France, but not less eloquent. These three recordings made in the spacious acoustic of the Abbey at Beuron demonstrate the skill and devotion of the choir's director, Father Maurus Pfaff. The recording, from the early 1960s, is first-class, and the tape transfers are strikingly vivid (though on 3347 016 there is at times a hint that the level is fractionally too high). This is music especially suited for cassettes, with their freedom from background disturbances.

Requiem Mass.
*** DG Arc. Priv. 2547/*3347* 028. Ch. of St Martin's, Beuron, Pfaff.

The liturgy for the *Missa pro defunctis* dates back to the earliest days of the Christian church. Besides its use at funerals, this *Requiem Mass* (which assumed its present form in the Middle Ages) is celebrated in the church calendar on All Souls Day (2 November). The music is understandably sombre, and its simplicity makes a powerful effect, especially in a performance such as is given here under Father Pfaff. The recording – as in the rest of the Beuron series – is of high quality, with sonorous choral tone, a clear focus, and a convincing ambience. The cassette transfer is outstandingly well managed, and the tape, like the disc, is provided with admirable notes and a full translation.

OTHER COLLECTIONS

Antiphons; Gospel tone; Hymns; Responsories; Laudes seu Acclamationes; Gradual: Flores apparuerunt; Alleluia; Communions; Antiphon: Montes Gilboe; Ave verum; Antiphonal Psalmody; Mariam antiphons.
(M) *** Decca Ser. SA/*KSC* 22. Carmelite Priory Ch., London, McCarthy.

Planned by the late Alec Robertson, who also provided a fascinating sleeve-note describing the music's ecclesiastic and spiritual background, this beautifully sung and excellently recorded anthology is the finest possible introduction to plainsong. Extra variety of tone is provided by the use of female voices as well as male. But care is taken to see that the ladies do not introduce an unwanted romantic element, and their vibrato-less vocal line is admirably pure in character. Edgar Fleet acts as cantor, and John McCarthy directs the singing with dedication and authority. The excellent cassette is in the demonstration class.

Einsiedeln Codex: First Mass for Christmas; Mass for Epiphany; Mass for Easter Sunday; Mass for Ascension Day.
*** DG Arc. 2533 131 [id.]. Ch. of Maria Einsiedeln Monastery, Bannwart.

This disc offers a fascinating glimpse into other traditions of performing the Roman liturgy. The production is well up to the high standards of the Archive series, but, at the price asked, of interest to the specialist rather than the ordinary collector.

Ancient Spanish chants: *Dominus regnavit; Vide domine; Laudate dominum; Ecclesiam sanctam catholicam; Nomina offerentium; Pacem meam; Introibo ad altare; Sanctus; Vere sanctus; Credo; Pater noster; Gustate et videte; Kyrie; Gloria; Offerte domino; Sanctus; Agnus Dei; Statuit Dominus; Lamentatio Jeremiae.*
*** DG Arc. 2533 163 [id.]. Santo Domingo de Silos Abbey Ch., Cuesta.

Like the companion Archive anthologies centred on Christmas and Easter, this record is of the highest quality, imaginatively extending our knowledge of Gregorian tradition in different parts of Europe.

Grétry, André (1741–1813)

Zémir et Azor (complete).
**(*) EMI 2C 167 12881/2 [Ara. 8060-2L/*9060-2L*]. Mesplé, Bufkens, Louis, Orliac, Simonka, Belgian R. and TV Ch. and CO, Doneux.

Written in 1771, Grétry's *Zémir et Azor* is an attractive example of pre-revolutionary opéra comique in France, a charming adaptation of the *Beauty and the Beast* fable. Though the recording is absurdly over-reverberant and the orchestral playing could be more precise, this is a generally lively and stylish performance with Roland Bufkens fresh and firm in the high tenor role of the hero. Mady Mesplé as Zémir sometimes indulges in ugly portamento, but this is a sweeter and truer performance than most she has recorded.

Grieg, Edvard (1843–1907)

Piano concerto in A min., Op. 16.
*** Ph. 6500 166/*7300 113* [id.]. Bishop-Kovacevich, BBC SO, Sir Colin Davis – SCHUMANN: *Concerto.****
(M) *** Decca Jub. JB/*KJBC* 104 (Lon. STS/*5-* 15407]. Curzon, LPO, Fjeldstad – FRANCK: *Symphonic variations*; LITOLFF: *Scherzo.****
(M) *** EMI Em. EMX/*TC-EMX* 2002. Solomon, Philh. O, Menges – SCHUMANN: *Concerto.****
(*) Decca SXL/*KSXC* 6624 [Lon. CS 6840]. Lupu, LSO, Previn – SCHUMANN: *Concerto.*(*)*
(M) **(*) CBS 60266/*40-* [Odys. Y/*YT* 30668]. Fleisher, Cleveland O, Szell – SCHUMANN: *Concerto.***(*)*
(M) **(*) CBS 61040/*40-*[M/*MT* 31801]. Entremont, Phd. O, Ormandy – RACHMANINOV: *Rhapsody.* **(*)
(B) **(*) Con. CC/*CCT* 7506. Katchen, Israel PO, Kertesz – SCHUMANN: *Concerto.* **(*)
*(*) DG Dig. 2532/*3302* 043 [id.]. Zimerman, Berlin PO, Karajan – SCHUMANN: *Concerto.***
*(*) Ph. 9500/*7300* 891 [id.]. Arrau, Boston SO, Sir Colin Davis – SCHUMANN: *Concerto.* *(*)
*HMV ASD/*TC-ASD* 3133 [Ang. S/*4XS* 36899]. Sviatoslav Richter, Monte Carlo Op. O, Matacic – SCHUMANN: *Concerto.**(*)

Stephen Bishop-Kovacevich and Colin Davis, having already proved how fruitful is their recording collaboration in the music of Beethoven, next turned to two of the great romantic concertos where they show an equal freshness and imagination. Whether in the clarity of virtuoso fingerwork or the shading of half-tone, Bishop-Kovacevich is among the most illuminating of the many great pianists who have recorded the Grieg *Concerto*. This is Grieg presented with bravura and refinement, the spontaneity of the music-making bringing a sparkle throughout. With excellent recording this is highly recommendable among the many discs of this coupling. On tape, however, the low-level transfer brings a limited upper range and reveals comparatively little orchestral detail, although the sound is pleasant and the piano timbre reasonably truthful. There is hiss too.

The sensitivity of Curzon in the recording studio is never in doubt, and the Jubilee compilation has been a favourite disc and cassette over a long period. The recording hardly shows its age and the coupling includes one of the finest versions of the Franck *Symphonic variations* to have appeared throughout the LP era. Curzon's approach to the Grieg is wonderfully poetic, and this is a performance with strength and power as well as freshness and lyrical tenderness. The sound on disc and cassette is virtually identical; indeed the tape offers demonstration quality in all respects.

Current pressings of Solomon's performance provide greatly improved quality compared with the original full-priced issue. The mellow piano tone is matched by a truthful orchestral picture, and the overall balance is excellent. Solomon's poetic lyricism has a special appeal in this work, and although the orchestral contribution is sound rather than inspired, there is some sensitive string playing in the *Adagio*. This is an outstanding coupling at medium-price, with disc and tape very closely matched.

Radu Lupu is given a bold, brightly lit recording (one of Decca's very best, in fact) and his performance is enjoyable. There is both warmth and poetry in the slow movement; the hushed opening is particularly telling. There is a hint of calculation at the coda of the first movement, but the performance – if without quite the individuality of Solomon's – does not lack spontaneity, and the orchestral contribution under Previn is a strong one. The Schumann coupling, however, is rather less attractive. The cassette transfer is in the demonstration class, strikingly fresh and immediate.

Fleisher is an outstanding artist and his recordings are too little known in Europe. His performances here of both the Grieg and Schumann concertos rank with the finest, combining strength with poetry in a satisfying balance. The Cleveland Orchestra gives a very positive accompaniment under Szell who communicates his affection for the Grieg with deeply expressive playing in the *Adagio*. There is plenty of sparkle in the outer movements.

Entremont's is a fresh, vital account and, if the Rachmaninov coupling is suitable, readers will find this too is a compulsive performance, with Ormandy as well as Entremont on top form. The sound has a vintage CBS forward balance.

Katchen's performance, reissued at bargain price on Contour, is strong and commanding, a touch of wilfulness tempered by a natural flexibility and a feeling for the work's poetry. Kertesz provides plenty of life in the accompaniment, and the recording is vivid and powerful in Decca's more spectacular manner. Some ears find that the sound here has a reverberant twang, and the effect is certainly somewhat high-powered. The cassette, with its slightly reduced upper range, is effectively mellower, but neither on disc or tape does this issue displace Solomon.

Zimerman and Karajan do not seem the ideal partnership either. There are, of course, many things to admire from this remarkable young pianist, but neither concerto on this record conveys the sense that these artists are enjoying themselves very much, and there is a certain want of freshness. Judged by the standards he has set himself, Zimerman is not so illuminating or, indeed, quite so sensitive as one would expect in this most gentle and poetic of scores. The recording is admirably full and brilliant, with a chrome cassette in the demonstration class.

Arrau too is well recorded (although on tape the sound benefits from a reduction of bass), but this concerto does not seem to suit his temperament. The playing, while thoroughly musical, is curiously lacking in vitality, its romanticism reflective, even studied, and there is a serious lack of spontaneity and fire.

Richter's performance, recorded in Monte Carlo, is disappointingly wilful, with the soloist drawing out many passages self-indulgently. With indifferent sound, this is not a competitive version.

(i) *Piano concerto in A min;* (ii) *Peer Gynt: suite No. 1, Op. 46.*
(M) ** Decca SPA/*KCSP* 170. (i) Katin, LPO, Sir Colin Davis; (ii) LSO, Fjeldstad – LITOLFF: *Scherzo.***

(i) *Piano concerto in A min.; Peer Gynt:* excerpts.
(B) *(*) CfP CFP/*TC-CFP* 160. Katin, LPO, Pritchard.

Peter Katin's earlier Decca performance is fresh and completely unhackneyed. Katin seemed to have reacted deliberately against the frequently made criticism that his performances are lightweight: there is no question of the comment applying here. If anything he seems loath to colour his playing with half-tones. The outer movements are the most successful, with Davis's brisk and masterly conducting adding to the feeling of a new work. The slow movement does not relax quite enough, but there is the compensation that this is utterly unsentimental. With Fjeldstad's fine account of the *First Peer Gynt suite* (extracted from his Jubilee disc), besides the original coupling of the Litolff *Scherzo*, this issue must be counted a keen competitor for its very positive qualities. The recording is excellent and there is a good cassette equivalent.

The later recording on CfP is also fresh enough, but this performance of the *Concerto* is somehow unmemorable, and the *Peer Gynt* music (*Suite No. 1* without the *Death of Aase*; plus the *Arab dance* and *Solveig's song*) seems equally matter-of-fact. The sound is good on disc and cassette alike.

2 Elegiac melodies, Op. 34; Holberg suite, Op. 40; 2 Norwegian melodies (*In the style of a folksong; Cowkeeper's tune and Country dance*), *Op. 63; Peer Gynt: Death of Aase; Sigurd Jorsalfar* (suite), *Op. 56; Homage march.*
** Decca SXL 6766. Nat. PO, Boskovsky.

Though Willi Boskovsky presents an attractive Grieg programme and the recording is both rich and brilliant, the actual performances are undistinguished, lacking the point and refinement one expects of this orchestra, formed largely for recording. Boskovsky's rhythmic flair is less apparent here than in his home repertory.

2 Elegiac melodies, Op. 34; Norwegian melodies, Op. 63, No. 2; Cowkeeper's tune and Country dance; Wedding Day at Troldhaugen, Op. 65/6.
(M) *** Decca SPA/*KCSP* 91 [Lon. STS 15159]. L. Proms O, Mackerras – SIBELIUS: *Finlandia* etc.***

Mackerras offers here a most pleasant selection of Grieg miniatures played with sympathy and taste. The *Cowkeeper's tune and Country dance* (which end one side of the disc) are particularly enjoyable, the gentle eloquence of the opening delightfully offset by the rustic pizzicatos of the dance. The *Elegiac melodies* too are played most beautifully, although the recording here is bright and clear rather than especially rich. Mackerras has arranged the programme to intersperse the Grieg items with some lesser-known but attractive music of Sibelius. This enjoyable lightweight disc is a good deal more than the sum of its component parts. Highly recommended. There is a good cassette too.

2 Elegiac melodies, Op. 34; Peer Gynt suite No. 1, Op. 46; Symphonic dances Nos. 1–4, Op. 64.
(B) *(*) PRT GSGC/*ZCGC* 2004. Hallé O, Barbirolli.

The new transfer of Barbirolli's collection cannot disguise the dated sound, with not much body to the strings and small-scale woodwind imagery. Even so, the *Peer Gynt suite* emerges with stronger character here than on some better-recorded discs. The *Elegiac melodies* offer better string tone than one might expect and are played with considerable feeling, but the highlight of the collection is the fine performance of the *Symphonic dances*, where the recording is at its best. Sir John brings out all their drama and colour, and the orchestral wind soloists make an often memorable contribution. The tape matches the disc fairly closely, though side two is livelier than side one and may need a little smoothing.

Holberg suite, Op. 40; Lyric suite, Op. 54; 4 Norwegian dances, Op. 35; Old Norwegian Romance with variations, Op. 51; Peer Gynt: suites Nos. 1 and 2; Symphonic dances, Op. 64.
(M) ** Ph. 6725/*7655* 033 (3) [id.]. ECO; Philh. O, Leppard.

This collection is somehow less than the sum of its parts. Leppard's Grieg is refined, but at times lacking in vitality. There are better versions of the *Holberg suite*, and the *Peer Gynt* incidental music is rather underdramatized. On disc the sound is naturally balanced, but not always as vivid as it might be. Chrome tape has been used for the cassettes, but, as so often with Philips, the ear senses that sharper detail could have been obtained at a higher level. By far the most successful items are the *Old Norwegian Romance* and *Symphonic dances* – recorded digitally – and these are available separately (see below).

Holberg suite, Op. 40.
*** DG Dig. **400 034-2**; 2532/*3302* 031 [id.]. Berlin PO, Karajan – MOZART: *Serenade No. 13*; PROKOFIEV: *Symphony No. 1.****
*** Argo ZRG/*KZRC* 670 [id.]. ASMF, Marriner – DVOŘÁK: *Serenade for strings.**(*)*

Holberg suite; Lyric suite, Op. 54; Sigurd Jorsalfar suite, Op. 56.
** Ph. 9500 748/*7300 833* [id.]. ECO, Leppard.

Karajan's performance of the *Holberg suite* is the finest available. The playing has a wonderful lightness and delicacy, with cultured phrasing not robbing the music of its immediacy. There are many subtleties of colour and texture revealed here by the clear yet sumptuous digital sound. The cassette transfer is very successful, but it is the compact disc which presents this recording in the best light of all, with striking presence and detail.

If not perhaps quite as fresh as Karajan's, Marriner's richly lyrical account is still very enjoyable. The *Air* has a pleasing graciousness and the final *Rigaudon* plenty of sparkle. The first-class analogue sound on disc has a matching tape of Argo's best quality.

Leppard includes the delightful *Lyric suite*, which is under-represented in the catalogue. It is the finest of the performances in his collection, freshly played and warmly recorded. The *Holberg suite*, however, is made to sound rather bland. *Sigurd Jorsalfar* is reasonably vivid but not memorable. The recording is naturally balanced with the cassette matching the disc fairly closely.

(i) *Holberg suite, Op. 40;* (ii) *Norwegian melodies, Op. 63, No. 2: Cowkeeper's tune and Country dance;* (iii) *Peer Gynt* (incidental music): *Suite No. 1, Op. 46; Suite No. 2, Op. 55; Solveig's song; Sigurd Jorsalfar* (suite), *Op. 56.*
(M) **(*) Decca SPA/*KCSP* 421. (i) Stuttgart CO, Münchinger; (ii) L. Proms O, Mackerras; (iii) LSO, Fjeldstad.

Fjeldstad's *Peer Gynt* items (taken from his fuller selection) are distinguished by freshly refined playing and very good recording that seldom betrays its age. The climax of *In the Hall of the Mountain King* is superb, and *Solveig's song* is phrased with disarming eloquence. The *Sigurd Jorsalfar suite* is equally fine, beautifully played and finely recorded. After this Münchinger's *Holberg suite* seems a trifle dour, though it is well played, and the recording is thinner here in the matter of string texture. However, the *Cowkeeper's tune* is richly done and the *Country dance* makes an infectious close to the concert. Here the sound is first-rate. The cassette transfer is of high quality (slightly brighter than the LP), but it has a curious patch of insecure texture (not pitch) in *Solveig's song*.

Old Norwegian Romance with variations, Op. 51; 4 Symphonic dances, Op. 64.
*** HMV Dig. ASD/*TCC-ASD* 4170. Bournemouth SO, Berglund.
*** Ph. Dig. 6514/*7337* 203 [id.]. Philh. O, Leppard.

A useful coupling which brings a choice of recordings of the slight but engaging *Old Norwegian Romance with variations*. Both records are very enjoyable. The HMV sound is brighter, slightly sharper in focus, and Berglund's performances are more volatile to match. Leppard's phrasing is the more subtle and he secures beautifully refined playing from the Philharmonia strings, which is especially enjoyable in the *Variations*; however, Berglund's greater sense of drama is telling in the *Symphonic dances*, and his more moulded shaping of the lovely oboe solo in No. 2 gives a personal imprint to the performance. Leppard is less assertive and his approach brings a pastoral feeling to the music, to contrast with Berglund's folksy atmosphere. The HMV cassette is virtually identical with the disc; the Philips tape is closely matched too, but with marginally less range at the top.

Symphony in C min.
*** Decca Dig. SXDL/*KSXDC* 7537 [Lon. LDR 71037]. Bergen SO, Anderson.

Symphony in C min.; In Autumn (concert overture), *Op. 11.*
*** BIS LP 200. Gothenburg SO, Kamu.

The *Symphony* is a student work written while Grieg was living in Denmark and completed before he was twenty-one. The two inner movements were published in a piano-duet reduction in 1869 as his Op. 14, but Grieg forbade performances of the work after hearing Svendsen's *First Symphony* in 1867, and the score was bequeathed to Bergen Public Library on the understanding that it was never to be performed. Rumour has it that a copy was illicitly made and the score performed in the USSR. In any event the Bergen Harmonien played the work in 1865 for the first time under Grieg. It is now recorded in excellent digital sound. The piece takes just over thirty-seven minutes, and those expecting characteristic Grieg will be disappointed: it sounds like the work of any highly talented Leipzig student of the day, only one figure on the oboe towards the end of the second group of the first movement betraying signs of things to come. There are endearing moments but much of the material is uninspired. The scherzo is distinctly second-rate; the corresponding movement of Svendsen's *First* is in a wholly different league, sparkling, inventive and captivating. But although much of Grieg's symphony is pretty unmemorable, it is good to hear for ourselves the kind of music he composed in his youth, and the first movement is arguably as well put together as the first movement of the Op. 7 *Piano sonata*. In some ways the finale is the most confident of the four movements, though its seams are clearly visible. The ideas are fresher than in the inner movements and though it is no masterpiece, it is uncommonly assured for a youth of twenty, and well laid out for the orchestra. The Decca recording is truthfully balanced, with good perspective and colour, and detail reproduces with fine definition. Like the disc, the excellent cassette has a wide range, plus an attractive ambient warmth.

Okko Kamu's version is hardly less persuasive. Phrases breathe very naturally and details are sensitively shaped: take, for example, the way in which he prepares for the second group of the first movement as well as the generosity of feeling that marks the theme itself. The orchestral playing is arguably finer than that of the Bergen orchestra and the greater detail and presence of the Decca digital recording is counterbalanced by the excellence of the Gothenburg acoustic and the naturalness of the balance. It was recorded at a live concert and those put off by such things should note that audience noises between the second and third movements and the applause afterwards have not been edited out. Kamu also gives us the overture *I Høst* (*In Autumn*), and very well played it is too. The Decca version is digital and undoubtedly wider in range, and this will no doubt sway some readers; but Kamu produces most musical results and his version is no also-ran.

Cello sonata in A, Op. 36.
(*) CRD CRD 1091/*CRDC 4091*. Robert Cohen, Vignoles – FRANCK: *Cello sonata.*(*)

With his clean, incisive style Cohen gives a strong performance of the rarely heard Grieg *Sonata*, sensitively accompanied by Roger Vignoles. In the folk element Cohen might have adopted a more persuasive style, bringing out the charm of the music more; but certainly he sustains the sonata structures well. The last movement is one of Grieg's most expansive.

The recording lacks a little in range at both ends, but presents the cello very convincingly. The cassette transfer is of CRD's usual high quality.

Violin sonatas Nos. 1 in F, Op. 8; 2 in G, Op. 13; 3 in C min., Op. 45.
(M) **(*) Sup. 1111 3164. Brož, Vrána.

Violin sonata No. 3 in C min., Op. 45.
(M)*** Ph. 6503/*7303* 111 [9500 568]. Grumiaux, Sebök – FRANCK: *Sonata.***(*)

The first two *Sonatas* are early: the *First* comes from 1865, a year later than the *Symphony*, and brought him the acclaim of both Liszt and Gade, while the *Second*, written two years later, is more national in feeling and makes allusion to the traditional fiddle techniques of Norway in the ornamentation and double-stopping, and its finale is a *springdans*. The *Third*, which Gade had urged him to make 'less Norwegian', is much later, dating from 1887, a year later than the Brahms *A major Sonata*, Op. 100, and the Franck. It is better held together, though Grieg was never completely at ease in the larger forms and never returned to sonata design after this work. The Supraphon issue is, at present, the only disc to couple all three (at least in the UK) and Zdeněk Brož and Jan Vrána play them very well indeed. They do not displace Grumiaux and György Sebök in the *C minor* and are not as well recorded as they are, but, given the attractions of the coupling and a perfectly acceptable though not distinguished recording, this can be recommended.

In the *C minor Sonata* Grumiaux plays with his usual blend of warmth and nobility and is given good support by György Sebök, even though memories of his earlier accompanist, István Hajdu (and other pianists we have heard in this piece), are not obliterated. Lifelike recording.

Piano works (complete).
** BIS LP 104/117. Eva Knardahl.

The BIS label have entrusted the complete output of Grieg to the Norwegian pianist, Eva Knardahl, who gives eminently acceptable and idiomatic accounts of this now neglected repertoire. She is very well recorded, too, and though her imagination and sensitivity are surpassed by others (both on record and off), the performances are a reliable enough guide to this music and both the standard of recording and presentation are high.

Lyric pieces: Op. 12/1; Op. 38/1; Op. 43/1–2; Op. 47/2–4; Op. 54/4–5; Op. 57/6; Op. 62/4 and 6; Op. 68/2, 3 and 5; Op. 71/1, 3 and 6–7.
(M) *** DG Acc. 2542/*3342* 142 [2530 476]. Gilels.

A generous selection of Grieg's *Lyric pieces*, from the well-known *Papillon*, Op. 43/1, to the less often heard and highly poetic set Op. 71, written at the turn of the century. This excellently recorded survey is an admirable alternative to Daniel Adni's (deleted) complete box, but the playing is of a different order. Good though Mr Adni was, with Gilels we are in the presence of a great keyboard master whose characterization and control of colour and articulation are wholly remarkable. An altogether outstanding record in every way, and the cassette too offers first-class quality. At medium price this is irresistible.

Piano sonata in E min., Op. 7.
(M) * CBS 60290/*40*-. Gould – BIZET: *Nocturne; Variations.***

Piano sonata in E min., Op. 7; Lyric pieces, Opp. 12 and 43.
*** Ph. Dig. 6514/*7337* 115 [id.]. Kocsis.

The brilliant young Hungarian pianist gives a strongly characterized performance of the Grieg *Sonata* and is more persuasive than any of his rivals have been on record. It is an early and not wholly convincing piece, in which the seams are clearly audible. Kocsis is hardly less admirable in the two books of *Lyric pieces* on the reverse, though he is not totally free from affectation. Gilels's inspired anthology still remains in a class of its own. The chrome cassette is first-class and closely matches the LP in presence.

Glenn Gould's view of the *Sonata* is a little too eccentric to be recommendable even though there are perceptive things in it. He takes the opening *Allegro moderato* at a very slow speed (at least to start with), and adds two minutes to Zoltán Kocsis's timing (6′, as opposed to 4′26″). The recording is not in the first flight and there is the usual crooning from the artist. The unusual coupling makes this worth considering all the same, for the Bizet pieces are not otherwise available. Chrome cassette and LP are virtually identical in sound.

VOCAL MUSIC

Landkjenning (cantata), *Op. 31.*
** Swedish Soc. SLT 33146. Ekborg, Lidstam Ch., Swedish RO, Westerberg – LARSSON: *Lyric suite* etc.**

Landkjenning (*Recognition of Land*): cantata, *Op. 31.* (i) *Olav Trygvason* (operatic fragments), *Op. 50: Scenes 1–3.*
*** Uni. RHS/*UKC* 364. Hansli, Oslo Philharmonic Ch., LSO, Dreier, (i) with Carlsen, Hanssen.

Grieg was at the height of his fame when these excerpts from *Olav Trygvason* first saw the light of day in 1888. Olav was the Norwegian King from A.D. 995 to 1000 who converted his pagan countrymen to Christianity, and these three scenes scored a great success at their first performance. But neither they nor *Landkjenning*, an earlier cantata that portrays the Norwegian King sighting land as he returns from his travels to claim the throne, is vintage Grieg, though as always there are some appealing ideas, particularly in the third scene of *Olav*. The cantata was originally written for organ and scored some years later. The Norwegian soloists and chorus respond in exemplary fashion to Per Dreier, who also produces sensitive and idiomatic playing from the LSO. The recording is equally clean and well focused on disc and tape, and readers with a special interest in this eternally fresh composer need not hesitate.

The performance on the Swedish Society issue is also a good one, but this record is principally of interest for its Larsson coupling.

Peer Gynt (incidental music), *Op. 23* (complete).
(M) ❀ *** Uni. RHS/*UKC* 361/2. Carlsen, Hanssen, Bjørkøy, Hansli, Oslo Philharmonic Ch., LSO, Dreier.

Grieg's incidental music to *Peer Gynt* is far more extensive than the familiar suites. The score used at the first performance of the play with his music in Oslo in 1876 survives in the Norwegian Music Archives, and the Royal Library in Copenhagen possesses the revised version Grieg prepared for the 1886 production. This recording includes thirty-two numbers in all, including Robert Henriques's scoring of the *Three Norwegian dances* used in the 1886 production in Copenhagen. The score, whether familiar or unfamiliar, continues to astonish by its freshness and inexhaustibility. At once time Ibsen had wanted Grieg to replace Act IV with a tone-poem describing Peer's wanderings over the globe. Grieg himself found many of these suggestions unmanageable and even went so far as to describe the famous *Hall of the Mountain King* in a letter to Ibsen thus: 'I have written something for the hall of the Troll king which smacks so much of cow-dung, ultra-Norwegianism and self-satisfaction that I literally cannot bear to listen to it.'

Hearing the complete score brings many delightful surprises and serves as a reminder that there is much more to Grieg than the 'sweetmeats filled with snow' of Debussy's image. There are occasional reminders even of Berlioz (*The thief and the receiver* is an instance in point, and *Scene on the upturned boat* could easily have come from Liszt). The scoring is often delicate and imaginative, while the two folk dances in the First Act are immensely characterful and far removed from the familiar sweetness associated with Grieg. The playing and singing here are of a high order and though memories of Beecham are not banished in the familiar music, it must be said that the Norwegian conductor Per Dreier achieves very spirited results from his soloists, the Oslo Philharmonic Chorus and our own LSO, with some especially beautiful playing from the woodwind. The recording is generally first-class with a natural perspective between soloists, chorus and orchestra. There is no want of presence and range, though it could do with greater richness in the middle bass. This is perennially fresh and delightful music, and this issue will almost double the amount of music most people know from *Peer Gynt*. The cassettes are splendidly managed, the sound always clear and well balanced and often reaching demonstration quality.

Peer Gynt: extended excerpts.

(M) *** HMV SXLP/*TC-SXLP* 30423 [Ang. RL/*4RL* 32026]. Hollweg, Beecham Ch. Soc., RPO, Beecham.

(M) *** EMI Em. EMX/*TC-EMX* 41 2049-1/*4* [Ang. S/*4XS* 36531]. Armstrong, Amb. S., Hallé O, Barbirolli.

**(*) Decca SXL 6901. RPO, Weller.

(*) HMV Dig. **CDC 747003-2; ASD/*TCC-ASD* 143440-1/*4* [Ang. DS/*4XDS* 37968]. Popp, Amb. S., ASMF, Marriner.

(*) Ph. Dig. **411 038-2; 6514/*7337* 378 [id.]. Ameling, San Francisco SO, De Waart.

(M) ** Ph. Seq. 6527/*7311* 086. Stolte, Leipzig GO, Neumann.

All the single-disc compilations from *Peer Gynt* rest under the shadow of Beecham's, which is not ideal as a recording (the choral contribution lacks polish and is rather fiercely recorded), but which offers moments of magical delicacy in the orchestral playing. Beecham showed a very special feeling for this score, and to hear *Morning*, the gently textured *Anitra's dance*, or the eloquent portrayal of the *Death of Aase* under his baton is a uniquely rewarding experience. Ilse Hollweg too is an excellent soloist. The orchestral recording shows its age in fortissimos, where there is a lack of weight in the upper strings, but this fault is minimized by the cassette transfer, which has a slightly smoother treble response than the disc. It is otherwise vivid and well detailed.

Barbirolli's record dates from 1969 and was originally recorded in EMI's hi-fi-conscious Studio Two system. But the sound is ripely resonant and not in the least dated (the cassette has less sparkle on top but otherwise matches the disc closely). If Beecham achieved a greater subtlety in some of this music, Barbirolli (at his finest) is at least equally impressive, and has memorable vocal contributions from the fresh-voiced Sheila Armstrong and the Ambrosian Singers. This is excellent value at mid-price.

Weller's is a purely orchestral collection, very positively characterized and showing the RPO in excellent form. The Decca recording is of demonstration quality.

No disrespect is intended in calling Neville Marriner's account of *Peer Gynt* serviceable, for the performance and recording are of good quality, the acoustic is pleasant and the sound agreeably fresh. No grumbles here, then, save for the fact that Lucia Popp sings in German – but then so does Ilse Hollweg for Beecham. At the same time, this is not a performance that attains real distinction or character and in spite of the excellence of the engineering, it does not displace Beecham or Barbirolli. The cassette matches the disc closely. The compact disc is freshly detailed and glowing but the music-making does not really lift off here.

De Waart directs a warmly sympathetic reading of the *Peer Gynt* music, less sharply focused than the rival Marriner version on HMV. It brings an advantage in that Ameling, a fine soloist, sings in Norwegian, where Popp uses German. The *Wedding march* is not included, but the brief unaccompanied choral piece, *Song of the church-goers*, is. Otherwise the selection follows the now accepted expanded grouping of movements. Warm, full, not specially brilliant recording.

Neumann's Leipzig version omits the *Prelude* and the *Dance of the Mountain King's daughter*, but it is at medium price (as, of course, is Beecham), and the playing is warm and attractive, and there is a fine soloist in Adele Stolte. The recording is pleasingly reverberant and (with a small bass cut) sounds especially well in its tape format, where there is more body given to the upper strings.

Peer Gynt: suites Nos. 1, Op. 46; 2, Op. 55.

*** DG Dig. **410 026-2**; 2532/*3302* 068 [id.]. Berlin PO, Karajan – SIBELIUS: *Pelléas et Mélisande.****

(M) ** CBS 60105/*40*- [MY/*MYT* 36718]. NYPO, Bernstein – SIBELIUS: *Finlandia* etc.**

Peer Gynt: suites Nos. 1–2; Prelude; Dance of the Mountain King's daughter.

(M) *** Decca Jub. JB/*KJBC* 141 [Lon. STS/*5-* 15040]. LSO, Fjeldstad.

Peer Gynt: suites Nos. 1–2; 4 Norwegian dances, Op. 35.
**(*) Ph. 9500 106/*7300 513* [id.]. ECO, Leppard.

Peer Gynt: suites Nos. 1–2; Sigurd Jorsalfar (suite), Op. 56.
*** DG 2530 243/*3300 314* [id.]. Berlin PO, Karajan.

Peer Gynt: suites Nos. 1–2; 4 Symphonic dances, Op. 64.
(M) *** HMV SXLP 30105. Philh. O, Susskind.

Peer Gynt: suites Nos. 1–2. Songs: *From Monte Pincio; Ich liebe dich; Lauf der Welt; The Princess; The swan.*
**(*) CBS 76527 [M 34531]. Söderström, New Philh. O, Andrew Davis.

Grieg's perennially fresh score is marvellously played in Karajan's latest recording, though there are small differences between this and his earlier DG version with the same orchestra: Anitra danced with greater allure though no less elegance in 1973 and there was greater simplicity and repose in *Aase's Death.* The expressive portamenti in the latter may not be to all tastes but the silkiness of the Berlin strings disarms criticism. The new recording is one of the best to have emerged from the Berlin Philharmonic and the compact disc is particularly striking for its combination of presence, body and detail. Karajan's earlier analogue record remains available, with a good matching cassette. The highly expressive performances were played with superlative skill and polish and most listeners will be lost in admiration for the orchestral playing. The coupling is different and any reader preferring *Sigurd Jorsalfar* will not be disappointed.

In its original form Fjeldstad's record was one of the really outstanding early Decca stereo LPs, and its reissue on Jubilee makes an attractive purchase in the medium price-range. The LSO is very sensitive, and the tender string playing in *Solveig's song* is quite lovely. The conductor begins *In the Hall of the Mountain King* rather slowly but builds up a blaze of excitement at the end and quite justifies his conception. The chrome cassette matches the disc very closely on side one; on side two the cassette quality is somewhat brighter than the LP.

Susskind's performances of the *Peer Gynt suites* are beautifully played and spaciously recorded. Both *Morning* and *Solveig's song* offer lovely strings and melting playing. At the very beginning of the *Arab dance* the bass drum is only just audible, but this is the only miscalculation in an outstanding set of performances. The recording is somewhat less full in the *Symphonic dances* but still vivid, and Susskind's performances are very well characterized. He finds plenty of colour in Nos. 2 and 3 and the contrasts in No. 4 are made with the subtlety only possible with an orchestra of the calibre of the Philharmonia.

Leppard's disc is beautifully recorded, the sound at once rich and sparkling. The music-making is fresh and has an air of thoughtfulness which will appeal to many, especially as the orchestral playing is so good. However, there is occasionally just a hint of a lack of vitality: *In the Hall of the Mountain King*, for instance, opens slowly and atmospherically, then does not build up quite the head of steam one expects. The *Four Norwegian dances* are splendidly done, with playing of vigour and showing a fine sense of colour. The cassette transfer is good but not quite so refined in texture as the LP.

With Andrew Davis's CBS record bright, immediate recording goes with freshly thought performances of some of Grieg's most familiar music. A special attraction is the singing of Elisabeth Söderström, not only in *Solveig's song* but in the orchestral songs (some of them with Davis's instrumentation), which make a delightful and original fill-up.

The slightly mannered performance of *Anitra's dance* and the touch of melodrama in the *Second Suite* add individuality to Bernstein's performances, which are very well played and brilliantly recorded in CBS's brightly lit manner. The string tone in *Morning* lacks bloom in consequence, but the *Arab dance* is strikingly exotic.

Peer Gynt: suite No. 1; suite No. 2: Ingrid's lament; Arab dance.
(*) Telarc Dig. **CD 80048; DG 10048 [id.]. St Louis SO, Slatkin – BIZET: *Carmen suites.***(*)

Peer Gynt: suite No. 1; suite No. 2: Ingrid's lament; Solveig's song.

(M) *** Decca Jub. JB/*KJBC* 16. VPO, Karajan – TCHAIKOVSKY: *Nutcracker suite.****

Peer Gynt: suite No. 1; suite No. 2: Solveig's song.

(B) *** Con. CC/*CCT* 7570 [SPA/5-21142]. Boston Pops O, Fiedler – TCHAIKOVSKY: *Nutcracker suite.****

(i) *Peer Gynt suite No. 1;* (ii) *Sigurd Jorsalfar: Homage march. Wedding day at Troldhaugen, Op. 65/6.*

(M) * DG Priv. 2535/*3335* 635 [id.]. (i) Bamberg SO, Richard Kraus; (ii) Nordmark SO, Steiner – SIBELIUS: *Finlandia* etc.***

The Telarc digital recording is impressively vivid and clear. The over-resonant bass drum which muddies the fortissimos of the coupled incidental music from Bizet's *Carmen* is less troublesome here (although the climax of *In the Hall of the Mountain King* is not absolutely clean). The orchestral playing is good (*Morning* is not so evocative as in the finest versions) but the overall balance is natural. *Anitra's dance* is played by the first desks of the strings, which gives an intimate, chamber-scale presentation that is not ineffective.

Karajan's selection offers excellent sound. There is occasionally a faint buzz in the upper string tone, but otherwise the rich, clear recording is outstanding. The readings are broad in style, less individual perhaps than Fjeldstad's or Beecham's in their complete sets, but not lacking in freshness. *Solveig's song* is particularly beautiful. An excellent cassette is available.

Fiedler's performance is direct, alive and spontaneous. It is recorded with exceptional life and vividness and is very enjoyable indeed. There are more tender accounts of *Solveig's song* available, but that is the only reservation, and the Tchaikovsky coupling is equally good. The cassette faithfully reflects the disc. A good bargain recommendation.

Richard Kraus's Bamberg version of the *First Peer Gynt suite* is well characterized, but the recording dates from 1959 and the lack of body to the upper strings is a serious drawback (it is even thinner on tape than on disc), although the recording is otherwise effectively balanced. The other performances under Steiner are less appealing, and the 1965 sound is no more beguiling. The coupling – Sibelius performances by the Berlin Philharmonic under Karajan – is of high quality.

COLLECTIONS

'Favourite composer': (i) *Piano concerto in A min.;* (ii) *Holberg suite;* (iii; iv) *Lyric suite;* (iii; v) *Peer Gynt: suites Nos. 1–2; Prelude; Dance of the Mountain King's daughter; Sigurd Jorsalfar* (suite).

(B) *** Decca DPA 567/8. (i) Katchen, Israel PO, Kertesz; (ii) Stuttgart CO, Münchinger; (iii) LSO; (iv) Black; (v) Fjeldstad.

Most of these performances are discussed above under their original couplings. They make an outstanding anthology. The only item below the remarkably high overall standard is Münchinger's rather unsmiling account of the *Holberg suite*. But this can be forgiven when the discs are generously full and the *Peer Gynt* and *Lyric suites* are so successful; indeed Stanley Black's performance of the latter work is one of the more memorable items.

A somewhat similar collection is available on an HMV double-length cassette (*TC2-COS 54255*) but the selection is more bitty and as the major complete performance is John Ogdon's disappointing version of the *Piano concerto*, this cannot be recommended with any enthusiasm.

Grofé, Ferde (1892–1972)

Grand Canyon suite.

C *** Decca Dig. **410 110-2**; 410 110-1/*4* [id.]. Detroit SO, Dorati – GERSHWIN: *Porgy and Bess.**** C

(M) *(*) CBS 61266 [(d) M/*MT* 30446]. Phd. O, Ormandy – ALFVEN: *Swedish rhapsody*.(**)

(i) *Grand Canyon suite;* (ii) *Mississippi suite.*

**(*) HMV Dig. ASD/*TC-ASD* 165484-1/*4*. RPO, Bátiz.
(M) ** CBS 60146/*40*- [(d) M/*MT* 31824]. NYPO, (i) Bernstein; (ii) Kostelanetz.

Dorati has the advantage of superlative Decca recording, very much in the demonstration class, with stereoscopically vivid detail. Yet the performance combines subtlety with spectacle and on compact disc the naturalness of the orchestral sound-picture adds to the sense of spaciousness and tangibility. With its outstanding coupling this version is very much in a class of its own.

Bátiz's HMV record makes a good alternative choice for those preferring the *Mississippi suite* as coupling. The RPO is committed and sensitive in both works, and while the feeling of triviality remains in the Mississippi music, Bátiz's characterization is strong and the playing spirited. The HMV sound is as vivid as anyone could want, but the effect is brasher than with Dorati – some might feel appropriately so in such picaresque music. There is a very good tape.

Grofé's technicolor picture of the *Grand Canyon* is painted with relish by the Philadelphia Orchestra. They manage the storm with the utmost sense of spectacle, and play *On the trail* with idiomatic wit. The recording is on a big scale but is unfortunately rather harsh.

The sound of the NYPO disc is more acceptable (though hardly worthy of this spectacular piece). Clearly Bernstein has much affection for the music and *On the trail* is nicely done. The overall effect is vivid, but with good detail. Kostelanetz directs the *Mississippi suite*, a much slighter score, with little to remain in the memory. The cassette is not recommended: its upper range is impossibly shrill.

Groven, Eivind (1901–77)

Draumkvaedet; Hjalarljod: overture.
**(*) Ph. Dig. 6529 139. Carlsen, Bjørkøy, Hansli, Brighton Fest. Ch., RPO, Dreier.

Eivind Groven belongs to the same generation of Norwegian composers as Harald Saeverud and Sparre Olsen and his idiom is strongly diatonic and nationalist. Indeed, Groven is more thoroughly steeped in the folksong and hardangar music of Telemark in Western Norway than any of his contemporaries; for many years he was the Norwegian Radio's consultant on folk music. *Draumkvaedet*, which he set in 1962, is a folk ballad from the Telemark district which tells how its hero, Olav Åsteson, visits the spirit world during the course of a long and deep sleep. If you find Grieg and Nielsen congenial, you will feel at home in this piece, as the English forces involved in this recording evidently do. The folk naïvistic style is as distinctive as is that of Saeverud and the music has undoubted directness of appeal. Were it less prolix, it could enjoy wide popularity outside Norway, for the best passages have great charm. The performance, some small lapses of vocal finesse apart, is sympathetic and the recording well balanced. The overture is not particularly distinguished or interesting, but there is enough good music in the main work to reward the listener.

Guastavino, Carlos (born 1912)

Las Presencias No. 6 (Jeromita Linares) for guitar quintet.
*** CBS Dig. 36671/*41*-. Williams, L. Qt – BOCCHERINI: *Quintets.****

Carlos Guastavino studied at the Buenos Aires conservatoire and later in London. He is best known, it would seem, for his vocal music, which reflects something of the character of his native Argentina. *Las Presencias No. 6* takes just over thirteen minutes and is conventional both in language and in layout, eminently unmemorable and really quite empty. The three stars are for the performance and a vivid (if somewhat forward) recording. The high-level chrome tape is full-bodied and clear.

Guilmant, Alexandre (1837–1911)

Allegro in F sharp min.; Elevation in A flat; March on a theme of Handel; Sonata No. 1 in D min.; Wedding march.
*(*) Abbey LPB 794. Jackson (York Minster organ).

Guilmant is not generously represented on record at present, though he was a key figure in French organ music during his lifetime and one of the founders of the Schola Cantorum. The *Organ sonata* is arguably his best work and certainly has greater interest than the other pieces on this record. The problems of York Minster are considerable, for the period of reverberation is long, yet the engineers have achieved no mean degree of clarity here. There is plenty of atmosphere, but the texture becomes clouded in the lower register. There is nothing spectacular about this music or the playing or the recorded sound, but there is still pleasure to be had for those with an interest in this repertoire, even if the York instrument is not wholly suited to the Gallic style.

Gurney, Ivor (1890–1937)

Ludlow and Teme (song cycle).
*** Hyp. A 66013. Hill, Johnson, Coull Qt – VAUGHAN WILLIAMS: *On Wenlock Edge.****

Gurney's setting of Housman poems uses exactly the same forces as the Vaughan Williams cycle, making the perfect coupling. Gurney, poet as well as composer, is tender and lyrical here, giving hints of tragic overtones by inference merely, himself unhinged by his experiences in the First World War. Martyn Hill with his clear-cut tenor gives understanding performances, admirably accompanied by Graham Johnson and the Coull Quartet. The recording is nicely atmospheric.

Hadley, Patrick (1899–1973)

(i) *One Morning in Spring* (rhapsody for small orch.); (ii) *The Trees So High* (symphonic ballad).
*** Lyr. SRCS 106. (i) LPO, Boult; (ii) Allen, Guildford Philharmonic Ch., New Philh. O, Handley.

For most of his working career Patrick Hadley was the archetypal Cambridge composer, seduced by the charms of life as a senior member of the university from writing the music he plainly had in him. *The Trees So High*, described as a symphonic ballad, is a wide-ranging choral work taking the folksong of that name as its base. The idiom is broadly in the Vaughan Williams school but spiced with invention eclectically drawn from later composers. Thomas Allen makes an outstanding soloist, and Vernon Handley draws persuasive singing and playing from his large forces. The fill-up is a short piece written for the seventieth birthday of Vaughan Williams, charming in its lack of pretension. Both works are beautifully recorded.

Hahn, Reynaldo (1875–1947)

Songs: *À Chloris; L'Air; L'Automne; 7 Chansons Grises; La chère blessuré; D'une prison; L'enamourée; Les étoiles; Fêtes galantes; Les fontaines; L'Incrédule; Infidélité; Offrande; Quand je fus pris au pavillon; Si mes vers avaient des ailes; Tyndaris.*
*** Hyp. A/*KA* 66045. Hill, Johnson.

Hahn's was a miniature genius, and though it is not recommended to try and sample all the musical marshmallows in this present collection at a single sitting, the delights are many, the charm great. It is partly that swift or brisk songs are so few, and the classical pastiches of *Chloris* and *Quand je fus pris au pavillon* come as quite a refreshment. The sad thing is that Hahn never quite matched the supreme inspiration of his most famous song, *Si mes vers avaient des ailes*, written when he was in his early teens. Hill – ideally accompanied by Johnson – modifies his very English-sounding tenor to give delicate stylish performances, well recorded. There is a touch of pallor about this singing, but in general it suits the music.

Halvorsen, Johann (1864–1935)

Passacaglia on a theme of Handel.
(M) *** CBS 60264/*40*- [M 33447]. Heifetz, Piatigorsky – DVOŘÁK: *Piano trio No. 3* *(**); GLIÈRE: *Duo*; STRAVINSKY: *Suite Italienne*.***

The theme is taken from the *Harpsichord suite No. 7 in G minor* and the variations give an unashamed opportunity for bravura, although the music is quite attractively worked out. Stunning playing from Heifetz and Piatigorsky (Heifetz recorded the piece in the early 1940s with William Primrose, but this version is quite its equal). The recording is forward but acceptable; it is the playing that counts and its controlled virtuosity is remarkable.

Handel, George Frideric (1685–1759)

Ballet music from *Alcina* (including *Overture* and *Dream music*); *Ariodante* (including *Overture*); *Il Pastor Fido:* Hunting scene.
(M) *** Argo ZK/*KZKC* 68. ASMF, Marriner.

One of Sir Thomas Beecham's hobbies was exploring the lesser-known music of Handel to find items for his ballet suites. Here we have a generous selection using Handel's original scoring. The music from *Alcina* is particularly diverse in invention, and all is played with grace and marvellous rhythmic point by Marriner and his splendid orchestral group. The recording is of superlative quality, and the cassette transfer is admirable, offering warmth as well as Argo's characteristic bright clarity.

Concerto grosso in C (Alexander's Feast); Concerti a due cori in B flat and F; 3 Oboe concertos; Music for the Royal Fireworks; Overtures in D and B flat; Sonata a 5 in B flat for violin, oboe and strings; Sonata in G min. for oboe and strings; Water music (suites Nos. 1–3).
(M) *** Ph. 6725/*7655* 037. Nicklin, Davis, ASMF, Marriner.

A self-recommending set featuring many of the more recent Handel recordings made by the St Martin's Academy under Marriner. Stylish playing and first-rate sound. Most of the discs are reviewed separately below. The newer version of the *Fireworks music* is an elegant, concert-hall performance rather than one designed for a grand occasion in the open air. Perhaps most attractive of all are the shorter works, notably the solo *Oboe concertos*, beautifully played by Celia Nicklin (and digitally recorded). The cassettes are of good quality, fairly close to the discs in range and immediacy.

Concerto grosso in C (Alexander's Feast); Concerto a due cori No. 2 in F; Music for the Royal Fireworks.
(M) ** DG Arc. Priv. 2547/*3347* 006. Cappella Coloniensis or Schola Cantorum Basiliensis, Wenzinger.

These recordings were made in the early days of stereo, but the sound is not very dated and Wenzinger's performances are alert and stylish. The account of the *Fireworks music* has a splendid feeling for the open-air style of the writing, with crisp buoyant rhythms. The use of original instruments gives a suitably robust effect (together with less than perfect intonation). The cassette quality is less refined than the disc, especially in the *Concerto a due cori*, and the *Alexander's Feast Concerto grosso* is rather lacking in body and bloom.

Concerti grossi, Op. 3/1–6.
*** Ph. Dig. 6514/*7337* 114 [id.]. ASMF, Marriner.
(M) *** Ph. 9502/*7313* 006. ECO, Leppard.
(M) *** Decca Ser. 411 715–1/*4*. ASMF, Marriner.
(M) **(*) ASV ACM/*ZCACM* 2004. Northern Sinf., Malcolm.
** Erato STU 71367. E. Bar. Soloists, Gardiner.

Concerti grossi, Op. 3/1–6; Oboe concerto No. 3 in G min.
** Tel. EX6.35545 (2). VCM, Harnoncourt.

In Marriner's latest version with the Academy tempi tend to be a little brisk but the results are inspiriting and enjoyable. The playing is of the usual high standard that we take for granted from this ensemble and the wind playing particularly distinguished. The continuo is divided between organ and harpsichord, though the latter is reticently balanced. Otherwise the recording is altogether excellent, clean and well-detailed with an agreeable ambience. This is certainly among the best now before the public and if one regrets the absence of real grandeur and breadth, which earlier versions such as the Mainz Chamber Orchestra under Günther Kehr found, or the flair which Thurston Dart brought to the harpsichord in his earlier recordings, there is much more to admire than to cavil at. The cassette is hardly less vivid and fresh than the disc, though the upper range is slightly lacking in bite.

Lively, fresh performances too from Leppard on Philips and very good sound on both disc and cassette. Leppard includes oboes and bassoons and secures excellent playing all round. At times one wonders if he isn't just a shade too elegant, as if he were playing Arne, but these are fleeting thoughts, and in general this set ranks among the very best versions of Op. 3.

Marriner's earlier Argo set remains fully competitive (it is also available at medium price coupled with Op. 6 – see below) for musical scholarship and, what is even more to the point, for musical expressiveness and spontaneity. The ASMF was in peak form when this recording was made.

George Malcolm's performances are spirited and stylish and not lacking polish. The recording is vivid, but the forward balance of the oboes makes them sound rather larger than life and tends to reduce the dynamic range, although the contrasts of light and shade within the strings are effective. Rhythms are sometimes jogging rather than sprightly, but this is enjoyable music-making, and the vivid cassette transfer has striking life and detail.

There is some very lively playing from the English Baroque Soloists under John Eliot Gardner, who give the Op. 3 concertos with no want of style. However, there is a lack of finish in one or two places, and some poor intonation in No. 2 in B flat. There are, of course, many good things here – not least an admirably balanced and fresh-sounding recording – but this issue cannot be regarded as a first choice.

Harnoncourt's version of Op. 3 is presented here very uneconomically, even if it includes the alternative version of the *F major Concerto* (No. 4b). It is spread over 3½ sides with the *Oboe concerto* as (agreeable) make-weight. Tempi are on the whole relaxed, but the reason for the presentation is nothing to do with the pacing, but because each side only contains about twenty minutes of music. The performances are enjoyable in their easy-going way, the colouring of the baroque oboes distinctly attractive and the string sound unaggressive. Indeed the sound is very good, but this cannot compete in a market crowded with excellence.

Concerti grossi, Op. 3/1–6; Op. 6/1–12.
(M) *** Decca SDDB 294/7 [(d) Lon. 2309]. ASMF, Marriner; Dart (harpsichord), Andrew Davis (organ).

Like the fine set of Bach orchestral suites, this integral recording of the Handel *Concerti grossi* makes a permanent memorial of the partnership formed by the inspired scholarship of Thurston Dart and the interpretative skill and musicianship of Neville Marriner and his superb ensemble. Great care went into preparing the scores which are the basis of these recordings. A double continuo of both organ and harpsichord is judiciously used to vary textural colour and weight. Flutes and oboes are employed as Handel intended in Op.

3, and in Op. 6 the optional oboe parts indicated by the composer are used in concertos 1, 2, 5 and 6. The final concerto of Op. 3 features the organ as a solo instrument, which very much conjures up the composer's spirit hovering in the background. Incidentally Thurston Dart makes the point that the warm and beautiful acoustic used in the recording is different from the dry theatre ambience Handel would have expected. The recording engineers show they have understood the tonal subtleties involved in this change by their careful balance of the chamber organ. With the greater degree of reverberation (and indeed the richer sound possible from the techniques of modern string playing) there is less need to add tonal body to the main orchestral group. 'Marvellous music', comments Dart in his notes, and how right he is! With such superlative playing Op. 3 emerges as gloriously extrovert, enjoyable music, and Op. 6 as one of the great masterpieces of the Baroque period. This set has a breadth and beauty of texture which those versions using 'original instruments' show less readily.

12 Concerti grossi, Op. 6.
**(*) HM 1C 153 99645/7. Coll. Aur., Maier.
**(*) DG Arc. Dig. 2742/*3383* 002 (3) [id.]. E. Concert, Pinnock.
** Tel. Dig. GX6.35603 (3). VCM, Harnoncourt.

Concerti grossi, Op. 6/1–4.
(*) DG Arc. Dig. **410 897-2; 410 897-1/*4*. E. Concert, Pinnock.

Concerti grossi, Op. 6/5–8.
**(*) DG Arc. Dig. 410 898-1/*4*. E. Concert, Pinnock.

Concerti grossi, Op. 6/9–12.
**(*) DG Arc. Dig. 410 899-1/*4*. E. Concert, Pinnock.

Concerti grossi, Op. 6/1, 2, 4, 6, 8 and 11.
(M) ** DG Priv. 2726 068 (2). Berlin PO, Karajan.

(i) *Concerti grossi, Op. 6/3–4 and 8.* (ii) *Music for the Royal Fireworks.*
(M) ** DG Priv. 2535/*3335* 269. Berlin PO, (i) Karajan, (ii) Kubelik.

In Handel's Op. 6, as in their Bach recordings, the Collegium Aureum, led by Franzjosef Maier, use original instruments; but the effect is tempered by the warmth of the acoustic. There is no acid-like astringency here, and phrasing in slow movements is warmly expressive and unsqueezed. Baroque oboes and bassoons are featured in Nos. 1, 2, 5 and 6 to add weight and colour within the string texture, rather than hinting at a solo role. They are fairly well submerged by the resonance. Throughout, tempi are uncontroversial and generally well-judged, though the basic approach is mellow, with the famous melody in No. 12 sounding as gracious as anyone could wish. The effect is thus slightly old-fashioned, but very agreeably so. The solo playing is first-class. The recorded sound is beautiful, natural in timbre and detail (allowing for the reverberation). The dedication and musicianship of the performances are never in doubt and if there is less imagination here than in the Marriner/Dart versions (and at times one might detect a hint of blandness), nevertheless the breadth and variety of Handel's inspiration is consistently caught, and as a whole the set gives great satisfaction.

In his pursuit of authentic performance on original instruments Pinnock finds a fair compromise between severe principle and sweetened practice. This set of Handel's most ambitious series of concertos, like Pinnock's set of Bach's *Brandenburgs*, adopts positive speeds which on the one hand give exhilaration and thrust to the fast movements (notably in the fugal writing) and provide an expressive feeling to slow movements. For all its 'authenticity', this is never unresponsive music-making, with fine solo playing set against an attractively atmospheric acoustic. Ornamentation is often elaborate but never at the expense of line. Yet these are performances to admire and to sample but hardly to warm to. If listened through, the sharp-edged sound eventually tends to tire the ear and there is little sense of grandeur and few hints of tonally expansive beauty. It is difficult to believe that Handel's generation did not expect greater richness of texture in works of this kind. The chrome cassettes are every bit the equal of the discs, with striking range and detail. Pinnock's set is also available on three separate discs and tapes, with the first four *Concerti* also on compact disc.

While the ASMF set under Marriner

(see above) offers a more generally acceptable compromise between scholarship and tradition, Karajan's recordings tend to reach towards the other extreme of putting an anachronistic veneer on the music's expressive qualities. Moreover with only three concertos to a disc, DG's format is not very economical, even at Privilege price. Karajan directs from the harpsichord, but with a reverberant acoustic and the use of a fairly large string group the overall balance does not always suggest a truly Handelian texture. But the ear is easily persuaded by such superb playing. Karajan obviously cares about the music, and if he is sometimes indulgent, he does not miss the nobility of the writing, or the feeling of contrast. If in other respects the full baroque spirit is sometimes a little submerged, there is still much to enjoy, and the recording is only slightly dated. Kubelik also uses a full orchestra for the *Fireworks music* and there is some predictably fine playing. The sound, however, is not ideally transparent. The quality on tape is acceptable but not outstanding because of the low transfer level.

As the beginning of the *First Concerto* demonstrates, Harnoncourt's version is eccentrically individual. After the rhythmically gruff opening flourish, the texture immediately lightens and the following allegro is fast and nimble. It is a performance of brutal contrasts, yet with the playing of the solo group often lingeringly expressive. Harnoncourt's insistence on continual dynamic change between phrases and often within a phrase gives the music a curiously restless feeling, with the emphatic fortissimos sometimes inelegantly heavy. There is much beautiful playing too, and the wonderfully refined recording, with its depth and natural detail, is certainly the finest this work has yet received. This makes the overcharacterization the more frustrating, so that No. 5, one of the most inspired of the set, loses much of its humanity and repose and the famous melody of No. 12, fast and jaunty, is almost unrecognizable, while its forceful reprise reaches the point of ugliness. Vitality there is here in plenty (and the sound of the 'original' stringed instruments is much more congenial than in the DG Archive set), but in the last resort Harnoncourt's wilfulness misses the breadth and vision of Handel's instrumental masterpiece.

Concerti a due cori Nos. 1 in B flat; 2–3 in F.
(M) **(*) Ph. 9502/*7313* 021. ECO, Leppard.

The *Concerti a due cori* were almost certainly written for performance with the three patriotic oratorios (No. 1 with *Joshua*, 2 with *Alexander Balus* and 3 with *Judas Maccabaeus*). Leppard gives very stylish accounts of them and there is some marvellous wind-playing. At times one feels the need for a greater sense of space or majesty, but the alertness and brilliance of the playing are always a source of pleasure. At medium price this issue is competitive. The cassette transfer, however, is made at an unexpectedly high level, which brings a degree of congestion from the horns in the two *F major Concerti.*

Harp concerto, Op. 4/6.
*** Argo ZRG/*KZRC* 930 [id.]. Robles, ASMF, Iona Brown – BOIELDIEU and DITTERSDORF: *Concertos.****

Handel's Op. 4/6 is well-known in both organ and harp versions. Marisa Robles makes an unforgettable case for the latter by creating the most delightful textures, yet never letting the work sound insubstantial. She is well served by the excellent Argo recording and the stylish and beautifully balanced accompaniment from the ASMF under Iona Brown. The cassette transfer is splendidly fresh and clean, retaining the luminous texture of the outstanding disc. This collection as a whole makes perfect late-evening listening.

Concerto for 2 lutes in B flat, Op. 4/6.
(*) RCA RL/*RK* 11180 [ARL 1/*ARK 1* 1180]. Bream, Spencer, Monteverdi O, Gardiner – KOHAUT and VIVALDI: *Concertos.*(*)

Here the ever-engaging Op. 4/6 appears in Thurston Dart's reconstruction for lute and harp, which Bream has further adjusted and elaborated, using a chitarrone for the slow-movement continuo. The performance is a fine one (Bream plays both solo parts), but it suffers from an unnatural recording balance, with the soloists placed forwardly so that their dynamic range approaches that of the orchestra, with very little contrast. The cassette transfer, made at the highest level, is extremely vivid.

Oboe concertos Nos. 1–2 in B flat; 3 in G min.
(M) *** HMV SXLP/*TC-SXLP* 30294. Goossens, Bath Fest. CO, Menuhin – BACH and VIVALDI: *Concertos.****

This is the star item in an attractive collection of baroque concertos recorded in the early 1960s. Leon Goossens is in ravishing form, and although his recorded image is not as forward as usual, this integration into the string texture, in the nature of a concerto grosso, in no way diminishes the projection of his personality. Menuhin accompanies sympathetically and the recording does not sound its age. The tape transfer is smooth and realistic.

(i) *Oboe concertos Nos. 1–3; Variation of No. 2; Solomon: Arrival of the Queen of Sheba. Berenice: overture.*
(M) **(*) Argo ZK 2 [ZRG 5442]. (i) Lord; ASMF, Marriner.

This is an attractively planned disc, beautifully played, and recorded with the richness of timbre Argo characteristically provide for music of this period. If the overall style could have had a touch more vivacity (the famous *Arrival of the Queen of Sheba*, for instance, lacks bite in the tuttis) this collection would have been really memorable. The *Berenice overture* is best-known for its famous minuet tune, but it is all attractive, and the *Oboe concertos* have a similar immediate appeal, their style predominantly lyrical.

Oboe concertos Nos. 1–3; Sonata in G min. for oboe and strings; Sonata a 5 in B flat; Overture in B flat; Hornpipe in D.
*** Ph. Dig. 6514/*7337* 385 [id.]. Nicklin, ASMF, Iona Brown.

This comes from the Academy of St Martin-in-the-Fields box (see above) and makes a welcome separate issue. All the music is appealing and particularly the *Oboe concertos*, with Celia Nicklin a first-class soloist. The recording is clear, but its somewhat ample textures will not appeal to the 'original instrument' lobby. There is a very good matching chrome tape.

Organ concertos Nos. 1–6, Op. 4/1–6; 7 in F (*Cuckoo and the nightingale*)*; 8 in A; 9* (from *Concerto grosso, Op. 6/10*)*; 10* (from *Concerto grosso, Op. 6/1*)*; 11* (from *Concerto grosso, Op. 6/5*)*; 12* (from *Concerto grosso, Op. 6/6*) (all Set 2); *13–18, Op. 7/1–6; 19 in D min.; 20 in F.*
*** Erato STU 71097 (4). Alain (organ of Collegiate Church), Paillard CO, Paillard.

Organ concertos Nos. 1–8; 13–20; Il trionfo del tempo e del disinganno; Sonata.
(M) **(*) Argo D3 D4 (4) [id.]. Malcolm (organs of Merton College, Oxford; St John's, Islington; St Mary's, Rotherhithe; or harpsichord), ASMF, Marriner.

Organ concertos Nos. 1–4.
**(*) Argo ZRG/*KZRC* 939. (from above set, with Preston).

Organ concertos Nos. 2; 4; 7 (*Cuckoo and the nightingale*)*; 16.*
**(*) Argo ZRG/*KZRC* 888 [id.]. (from above).

Organ concertos Nos. 5–6; 13–14.
**(*) Argo ZRG/*KZRC* 940. (from above).

Organ concertos Nos. 7–8; 19–20.
**(*) Argo ZRG/*KZRC* 942. (from above).

Organ concertos Nos. 7; 16–18.
(M) *** Ph. 9502/*7313* 022. Chorzempa, Concerto Amsterdam, Schröder.

Organ concertos Nos. 8; 19–20.
(M) *** Ph. 9502/*7313* 007. Chorzempa, Concerto Amsterdam, Schröder.

Organ concertos Nos. 15–18.
**(*) Argo ZRG/*KZRC* 941. (from above).

A French view of Handel might be expected to provide a new look, and in fact the Erato set is a highly successful venture on almost every count: the playing has breadth and an appropriate feeling of grandeur at times, as well as the expected elegance. The Op. 7 set is particularly successful. The solo playing is consistently alert and imaginative; the dance movements are delightful. Op. 7/1, after an impressively regal opening, has an enchanting closing *Bourrée*, while in No. 3 of the same set the contrasts of colour between soloist and ripieno in the fugal *Spiritoso* third movement are matched by the rhythmic grace of the minuet. The *Andante larghetto e staccato* of Op. 7/5 is a set of Handelian variations over an ostinato bass, and this brings some characterfully rhythmic articulation from the soloist, and the elegance of the closing *Gavotte* is no less striking. Among the four concertos without opus numbers, *The Cuckoo and the nightingale* can surely never have been more winningly registered on disc, and its *Siciliano* slow movement is most graciously played. The *A major Concerto* is an arrangement of a *Concerto grosso* (Op. 6/11); the finale specializes in echoes which are realized stereophonically by the antiphonal use of two manuals. Marie-Claire Alain's creative contribution is unfailingly stylish and inventive, and it seems almost churlish to mention the slight reservation that the first four concertos of the Op. 4 set, although still enjoyable, seem to have marginally less life and spontaneity than the rest. On the other hand the registration at the opening of Op. 4/6 (also well-known in transcribed versions) is memorable. Taken as a whole, this set would seem to be a clear first choice in this repertoire.

In the matter of ornamentation and interpolations Malcolm is both imaginative and stylishly impeccable. He plays two of the concertos on the harpsichord (Op. 4/3, and Op. 7/6) and here is given a comparatively distant balance, the harpsichord in proper scale with the orchestra. The organ registrations he produces are often softer-grained than those of Chorzempa, and their piquancy is a source of great charm (in Op. 4/4, for instance). With lithe, resilient orchestral textures, noticeably lightweight in Op. 4, slightly more ambitious in Op. 7, the feeling of delicacy is often to the fore, even an element of fantasy (Op. 4/6), so refined and subtly shaded are the sounds that reach the listener's ears. But (and especially if listening to the works as a set) sometimes the ear craves a more robust effect. This point could be exaggerated, but occasionally one feels that the element of sophistication asserts itself too readily. The recorded sound is superb, with the most beautiful orchestral textures, and the balance between organ and accompaniment perfectly judged. As can be seen these recordings have now been reissued (at full price!) in a breakdown of five separate records, with duplication of the more popular works. There are cassettes too, and they are bright and wide-ranging to match the LPs closely.

Chorzempa uses a Dutch organ and the Concerto Amsterdam play on period instruments. Even so, the overall effect is undoubtedly more robust than that achieved by the Argo recordings. Yet this added weight does not imply less incisiveness and there is plenty of vitality here. It is in the slow movements that Chorzempa is marginally less imaginative. Nevertheless the two Philips reissues from his integral set give much pleasure, with fine recording on disc matched by cassettes which are in the demonstration class.

Overtures: *Admeto; Alcina; Esther; Lotario; Orlando; Ottone; Partenope; Poro.*
(M) *** Ph. 9502/*7313* 079 [id.]. ECO, Leppard.

Characteristically elegant performances from Leppard, richly recorded. The orchestral playing is gracious and polished, and the acoustic adds the necessary weight to Leppard's conceptions. There is some fine music here and at medium-price this disc is worth exploring by everyone. The cassette too is of excellent quality, full and lively.

Music for the Royal Fireworks (original wind scoring).
C *** Telarc Dig. **CD 80038**; DG 10038 [id.]. Cleveland Symphonic Winds, Fennell – HOLST: *Military band suites.**** C ❀

Music for the Royal Fireworks (original wind score); *Concerto a due cori No. 2 in F.*
(B) *** PRT GSGC/*ZCGC* 2013. Pro Arte O, Mackerras.

(i) *Music for the Royal Fireworks* (original wind score); (ii) *Water music:* excerpts. *Concerto in F.*
(M) **(*) HMV Green. ESD/*TC-ESD* 143613-1/*4*. (i) LSO; (ii) Prague CO; Mackerras.

(i) *Music for the Royal Fireworks*; (ii) *2 Arias for oboes, horns, and bassoons*; *Flute sonata in A* (*Chrysander No. 17*).
*** O-L DSLO/*KDSLC* 548. (i) AcAM, Hogwood; (ii) Stephen Preston, Pleeth, Hogwood.

Music for the Royal Fireworks; (i) *Oboe concertos Nos. 1–3.*
** Decca Dig. SXDL/*KSXDC* 7549 [Lon. LDR/*5*- 71049]. SCO, Münchinger, (i) with Koch.

Music for the Royal Fireworks; (i) *Oboe concerto in G min.; Acis and Galatea: Sinfonia; Alexander's Feast: Overture.*
** ASV Dig. DCA/*ZCDCA* 521. Scottish CO, Gibson; (i) with Miller.

Music for the Royal Fireworks; Water music: suites Nos. 1–3 (complete).
*** Argo ZRG/*KZRC* 697 [id.]. ASMF, Marriner.

Music for the Royal Fireworks; Water music: extended suite.
(M) *** Ph. Seq. 6527/*7311* 047. ECO, Leppard.

Music for the Royal Fireworks; Water music: suite in F.
*** O-L Dig. **400 059-2**; DSLC/*KDSLC* 595 [id.]. AcAM, Hogwood.

Music for the Royal Fireworks: suite; Water music: suite (arr. Harty and Szell); *The Faithful Shepherd: Minuet* (ed. Beecham); *Xerxes: Largo* (arr. Reinhardt).
(M) *** Decca SPA/*KCSP* 120 [Lon. CS/*5-6236*]. LSO, Szell.

Music for the Royal Fireworks: suite; Water music: suite (both arr. Harty); *Overture in D min.* (arr. Elgar).
(*) Ph. Dig. **411 047; 6514/*7337* 366 [id.]. Pittsburgh SO, Previn.

Music for the Royal Fireworks; Water music: suite (arr. Stokowski).
(B) * RCA VICS/*VK* 2034 [AGL1/*AGK 1* 2704]. RCA Victor SO, Stokowski.

For collectors wanting a coupling of the *Royal Fireworks* and *Water music* in first-class performances, but not insisting on the original score in the former, nor on the use of baroque instruments in the latter, the 1972 Argo issue by the Academy of St Martin-in-the-Fields remains an obvious choice. Marriner directs a sparkling account of the complete *Water music*. All the well-loved movements we once knew only in the Harty suite come out refreshed, and the rest is similarly stylish. Scholars may argue that textures are inaccurate, but for most listeners the sounds which reach the ears have a welcome freedom from acerbity. It is a substantial advantage that the disc and cassette (for the transfer is very successful) – unlike any of its rivals – also include the complete *Fireworks music*. There Marriner's interpretation is more obviously controversial, for he deliberately avoids a weighty manner, even at the magisterial opening of the overture. In this Leppard – see below – who manages to combine point with a sense of ceremony is preferable. But with full, resonant recording, Marriner's generous coupling makes sound sense.

The other vintage recording of this repertoire is the outstanding bargain disc (now supplemented with an excellent cassette) of the *Fireworks music*, which Charles Mackerras made on the night of the 200th anniversary of Handel's death during the hours when virtually all of London's oboists and a sufficient number of brass players would be free. Here is the original as Handel scored it for twenty-four oboes, twelve bassoons and contra-bassoons, nine horns, nine trumpets, side-drums and three pairs of kettle-drums. The result is a tour de force, and the recording sounds as fresh now as on the night when it was made. The spontaneity of the playing is exhilarating and the sonorities rich and exciting. It is coupled to an attractive *Double concerto*, where strings are added.

Mackerras has since re-recorded the same score for HMV and the impact of this later performance is vividly and powerfully caught by more modern recording. But the earlier version is not displaced. It has a remarkable sense of occasion, while Mackerras's Greensleeve coupling of an extended suite from the *Water music*, with the Prague Chamber Orchestra, has a heavyweight quality in the string tone (hardly a question of recording) which weighs the music down too often and prevents it from sparkling. The sound is rich and vivid, but there are several finer versions. This record includes also the *Concerto in F* – the source of some of the material in the *Fireworks*.

Those seeking a spectacular modern digital version of the original score of the *Fireworks music* can turn to the Telarc record, made in 1978 in Severance Hall, Cleveland, Ohio. On that occasion that famous American maestro of wind-band music, Frederick Fennell, gathered together the wind and brass from the Cleveland Orchestra and recorded a new performance to demonstrate spectacularly what fine playing and digital sound could do for Handel's open-air score. Not all the sound is massive, of course; there is some refreshingly sprightly articulation in the *Bourrée*. But in the *Overture*, *La Réjouissance* and the closing section of the *Minuet*, the effect is remarkable. The record also includes an inflated account of Bach's *Fantasia in G*, but that is not an asset. The performance of the Handel represents one of the first great classic successes of digital recording, and the reading itself has genuine grandeur. The overall sound balance tends to favour the brass (and the drums), but few will grumble when the result is so overwhelming as it is on the marvellous compact disc. There are few better demonstration records of this new medium, for the sharpness of focus is matched by the presence and amplitude of the sound image.

Those hooked on the astringencies of the 'true' baroque sound can readily turn to the Academy of Ancient Music on Oiseau-Lyre, whose coupling with a suite in F, extracted from his complete version of the *Water music*, is also available on an impressive compact disc. This makes a vivid impact (if not giving such an impression of grandeur and spectacle as Fennell's Telarc alternative). The added clarity does also emphasize some faults in balance. Nevertheless Hogwood's version of the *Fireworks* music is as good as any at present before the public and has lively rhythms and keen articulation. He gives a vivid impression of the score, even if no attempt is made to reproduce the forces heard in 1749. Those, however, who have collected his excellent account of the *Water music* will prefer the original Oiseau-Lyre issue (DSLO 548). This offers, instead of the *Water music*, a more enterprising coupling of an agreeable *Flute sonata* (not positively identified as by Handel, but given persuasive advocacy by Stephen Preston) plus two delightful *Arias for wind*. The first, based on an excerpt from *Teseo*, is especially winning, but both are most welcome on disc. The cassette is not recommended. The resonance creates a degree of blurring in the treble which approaches congestion.

On the mid-price Philips Sequenza label Leppard's is an outstanding coupling. The resonance of the sound in the *Fireworks music* matches the broad and spectacular reading, while the substantial extract from Leppard's complete *Water music* recording has comparable flair, combining rhythmic resilience with an apt feeling for ceremony. The sound is excellent (the cassette full and lively too, if marginally less sharp in focus than the disc), and this is good value.

Many readers will have a nostalgic feeling for the Handel–Harty suites from which earlier generations got to know these two marvellous scores. George Szell and the LSO offer a highly recommendable coupling of them on a Decca lower-mid-priced issue with Handel's *Largo* and the *Minuet* from Beecham's *Faithful Shepherd suite* thrown in for good measure. The orchestral playing throughout this disc is quite outstanding, and the strings are wonderfully expressive in the slower pieces. The horns excel, and the crisp new Decca re-transfer makes for a good bargain. The cassette is vivid too, although not quite as clean as the disc.

From Previn old-fashioned readings of the Harty arrangements, comfortable and well-stuffed. Where Szell's vitality gives these period-piece orchestrations a new lease of life, Previn's way is indulgently amiable. So the *Water music Air* is taken slowly and expressively. Quick movements are crisp in the Previn manner, but overall mellowness – even in the brilliant Elgar arrangement with its elaborate percussion – is emphasized by the warm Pittsburgh recording. The chrome tape is transferred at quite a high level, but is generally less refined.

Münchinger's well-played version of the *Royal Fireworks music* is recorded in very clear and well-focused sound, perhaps a little chilly at the top end of the spectrum, and suffering one curious shift of perspective in the *Overture* when, at the end of the *Grave* section, the trumpets suddenly appear to recede, and another at the beginning of the *Bourrée* when strings and wind seem too distant. In the three *Oboe concertos*, Lothar Koch produces a glorious, creamy sound and embellishes freely. The orchestral playing seems rather cool by comparison. The chrome cassette is in the demonstration class, with the *Oboe concertos* sounding especially beautiful.

Alexander Gibson and the Scottish Chamber Orchestra are accorded a more consistent perspective than Münchinger, though the texture is more transparent in the Decca. However, the ASV recording has a better-defined bass and there is no lack of brilliance. The performance is thoroughly straightforward, fairly consistent in matters of double-dotting and generally stylish, but does not offer a serious challenge to the top recommendations. Sound, reliable playing without attaining real distinction – but thoroughly musical and enjoyable. Whereas Münchinger offers three *Oboe concertos*, Gibson gives us only one, finely played by Robin Miller, who does not ornament the line quite so excessively as Lothar Koch and who produces great purity of tone. Gibson gives solid support and no more than routine accounts of the remaining pieces. There is a good cassette, but with a less vivid upper range than the disc.

By any possible standards of baroque scholarship Stokowski's record with its souped-up spectacular orchestrations is hopelessly unauthentic. Yet it is easy to feel a sneaking admiration for the sheer personality of his presentation. His warmth is obvious in the lyrical music, and even with the use of organ-inspired swell effects as well as the echo devices in the phrasing, there are moments when the listener can be seduced in spite of himself. The recording has some coarseness in fortissimo, which appears to stem from the master tape, but it sounds opulent at mezzo-forte. There are genuine moments of grandeur in the *Fireworks music*, and at the end (reasonably enough, but only Stokowski would dare to do it) fireworks effects and enthusiastic crowd noises are introduced momentarily, laminated to the closing tutti. One cannot but smile at the effective ingenuousness of such an interpolation. A collector's item, and an attractive reminder of a great musician who made his own rules.

(i) *Royal Fireworks music; Water music* (both complete)*;* (ii) *Harp concerto, Op. 4/6;* (iii) *Messiah: Sinfonia.*

(B) ** DG Walkman *413 148-4*. (i) Berlin PO, Kubelik; (ii) Zabaleta, Kuentz CO, Kuentz; (iii) LPO, Karl Richter.

Kubelik's full-orchestral version of the complete *Water music* is freshly remastered here, and combines a sense of grandeur with liveliness. It is splendidly played, as is the *Fireworks music*, where the focus of the sound is slightly less clean. Zabaleta's approach to the *Harp concerto* is a trifle cool but eminently musical and the sound balance is excellent. At bargain-price this Walkman tape is certainly good value; the only other coupling of the two major works is Marriner's and that is still at full price.

Royal Fireworks music; Water music: suite in F (both arr. Howarth); *The Harmonious blacksmith* (arr. Dodgson). *Berenice: Minuet. Occasional oratorio: March. Solomon: Arrival of the Queen of Sheba. Xerxes: Largo* (arr. Archibald or Hazell).

*** Decca Dig. **411 903-2**; SXDL/*KSXDC* 7564. Philip Jones Brass Ens., Howarth.

This is a fun concert played with true baroque spirit, combining polish with bravura and spectacularly recorded. The *Arrival of the Queen of Sheba* initially needs a mental adjustment, but is disconcertingly vivid in its very different costume while *The Harmonious blacksmith* stands at his anvil in similar bold relief. In the *Berenice Minuet* and the famous *Largo*, the sentiment of the bandstand is handsomely avoided, though the playing is warmly expressive, but it is the fast pieces with their intricately exhilarating detail that catch the ear. The chrome cassette matches the disc in brilliance and clarity on side one, but in the resplendent account of the *Fireworks music* the LP handles the wide dynamic range more comfortably.

Water music: suites Nos. 1–3 (complete).

*** DG Arc. Dig. **410 525-2**; 410 525-1/*4* [id.]. E. Concert, Pinnock.

*** O-L DSLO/*KDSLC* 543 [id.]. AcAM, Hogwood.

*** ASV Dig. DCA/*ZCDCA* 520. ECO, Malcolm.

*** Ph. 9500 691/*7300 779* [id.]. ASMF, Marriner.

(M) *** Ph. 9502/*7313* 096 [6500 047/*7300 060*]. ECO, Leppard.

*** Delos Dig. DMS 3010 [id.]. LACO, Schwarz.

(M) *** EMI Em. EMX/*TC-EMX* 412047-1/*4* [Ang. S/*4XS* 36173]. Bath Fest. O, Menuhin.

**(*) Decca Dig. SXDL/*KSXDC* 7550. SCO, Münchinger.

(M) ** DG Priv. 2535/*3335* 137 [138799]. Berlin PO, Kubelik.

(B) ** PRT GSGC/*ZCGC* 2001. LPO, Boult.

(B) *(*) CfP CFP/*TC-CFP* 40092. Virtuosi of E., Davison.

For those wanting a performance of the *Water music* featuring original instruments, choice lies between the Academy of Ancient Music and the English Concert under Pinnock. While the former is very attractive in its own special way, Pinnock's version on DG Archive will be even more enticing for many. Speeds are consistently well chosen and are generally less controversial. One test is the famous *Air*, which is briskly treated by Hogwood, but here remains an engagingly gentle piece. The recording is beautifully balanced, clear but with bloom on the sound on disc and chrome cassette alike, although on tape when the brass enters on side two the refinement of the transfer slips a little. On compact disc the freshness and immediacy of the sound create a striking sense of presence and tangibility.

The Academy of Ancient Music has made many records for Oiseau-Lyre but few more immediately appealing than this account of music familiar in less 'authentic' renderings. Though it may come as a surprise to hear the well-known *Air* taken so fast – like a minuet – the sparkle and airiness of the invention have rarely been so endearingly caught on record. The unusual timbres of original instruments are here consistently attractive, with vibratoless string tone never squeezed too painfully. It was with this work that the Academy made its Prom début in the summer of 1978, and the joy of that occasion is matched by this performance, in which scholarship and imagination are convincingly joined. The cassette transfer is lively but rather astringent in the treble. The upper partials could be cleaner, and the trumpets in the third suite are not free from discoloration.

Those whose taste does not extend to thin baroque string textures should be well satisfied with Malcolm's splendid new digital recording for ASV. The playing is first-class, articulation is deft and detail is admirable. Decoration is nicely judged, and if the approach is lightweight, the alertness of the music-making combined with the full, vivid sound makes a strong impact. There is a sense of delight in the music which makes this version especially appealing. This is a strong recommendation for those who have the *Fireworks music* coupled with other music. The iron-oxide tape transfer is made at a high level, but the sound, though full and clear, loses something of the upper range of the disc.

The Philips version of the *Water music* brings Neville Marriner's second complete recording, and characteristically he has taken the trouble to correct several tiny textual points wrongly read before. The playing too is even finer, helped by full-ranging, refined recording. For anyone wanting a version using modern instruments this is highly recommendable, although one cannot forget that the Argo issue – (ZRG/*KZRC* 697) which still sounds extremely well – offers the *Fireworks music* too. The Philips cassette is of excellent, natural quality but does not sparkle at the top like the Argo tape.

For anyone wanting the *Water music* alone, a medium-priced issue is undoubtedly attractive, and Raymond Leppard and the ECO give elegant, beautifully turned and stylish performances of all three suites, with well-judged and truthful recording. Moreover the equivalent cassette, transferred at a high level, offers virtually demonstration quality, fresh, vivid and clean, with no problems from the brass entry in the third suite.

The Los Angeles performance under Gerard Schwarz is hardly less enjoyable, its character more athletic, with playing that is both polished and sprightly, less warmly elegant than Leppard. It has an attractive freshness of spirit, yet is without the abrasiveness of Hogwood's early instrumental timbres. In the second movement of the first suite the oboe soloist takes an extra degree of rhythmic freedom, yet still plays very stylishly. The sound is first-class; the horns are crisp and in the D major suite, which is placed second, the trumpets are bright and gleaming. The clear detail does not prevent an overall ambient warmth. However, this record is very much more expensive than its companions.

Menuhin uses a fairly recent edition prepared by Neville Boyling. His approach is genial and he secures excellent playing from his Bath Festival group. There is an attractive alertness about the music-making and, although the sound is not as recent as Leppard's comparable Philips issue, it is still very good. The cassette is slightly richer than the LP, and loses only a little at the top, but our copy produced some momentary slipping of refinement in the upper partials of wind and brass at the opening of side two.

Münchinger's Stuttgart recording is a compromise between authenticity and German tradition. He uses recorders most effectively, and the balance, helped by Decca's very clear and transparent recording, is often attractively lightweight. Yet occasionally tempi seem a shade on the slow side. Nevertheless there is much to enjoy here, not least the sound (which is very good indeed on cassette), but other versions are more consistently buoyant (even though Münchinger is by no means dull).

Kubelik uses the full Berlin Philharmonic Orchestra, and the playing is predictably fine, but Kubelik's manner is sometimes unresilient. The recording has been freshened but, understandably, sounds rather thick in texture to ears that have sampled the Academy of Ancient Music. Even so this is enjoyable in its way, and there is a well-managed cassette.

Boult's is a good bargain version, fresh and intelligent, with relatively little ornamentation. The recording, dating from the mid-1950s, comes up brightly. By the side of this Davison's *Water music* seems comparatively dull, for all its purposeful authenticity of style.

Water music (suite, arr. Harty).
*** Chan. DBR/*DBT* 2001 (2). Ulster O, Thomson – HARTY: *Violin concerto* etc.***
(M) *** Chan. CBR/*CBT* 1005. (as above) – HARTY: *John Field suite* etc.***

It was Sir Hamilton Harty's famous suite that introduced many listeners to Handel's *Water music*. It has fallen out of favour in recent years, though it still retains a foothold in the catalogue. Bryden Thomson gives a good account of it, but frankly the main interest here is the couplings. The two-disc set offers a substantial Harty work in the form of the *Violin concerto* (not on the medium-priced separate issue) and some lighter music from his pen, all well recorded. The tape transfer is vivid and well balanced, but the upper range is restricted compared with the LP version.

CHAMBER MUSIC

Flute sonatas: in E min., Op. 1a/1b; in G, Op. 1/5; in B min., Op. 1/9; Halle sonatas Nos. 1–3; Trio sonatas: in G; B min., Op. 2/1b; in F, Op. 2/4; Concerto a quattro in D min.
** CRD CRD 1073-4/*CRDC 4073-4* [id.]. L'École d'Orphée.

Flute sonatas, Op. 1a/1b; in D; Halle sonatas Nos. 1–3.
*** Ph. Dig. 6514/*7337* 096. Bennett, Kraemer, Vigay.

Recorder sonatas, Op. 1/2, 4, 7 and 11.
*** HMV Dig. ASD/*TCC-ASD* 146683-1/*4* [Ang. DS/*4XS* 37983]. Linde, Hogwood, Ros.

Recorder sonatas, Op. 1/2, 4, 7, 11; in B flat; in D min.
*** Tel. DX 6.35359 (2). Brüggen, Bylsma, Leonhardt – TELEMANN: *Essercizii musici.****

Halle Trio sonatas (for 2 oboes and continuo), Nos. 1–6.
*** Ph. 9500/*7300* 766 [id.]. Holliger, Bourgue, Sax, Jaccottet.

Trio sonatas, Op. 2/1a; 2; 3; 5–9.
**(*) CRD CRD 1075-6/*CRDC 4075-6*. L'École d'Orphée.

The first pair of CRD records and cassettes is very well recorded (although the tape transfer tends to emphasize the abrasive timbre of the baroque violin). It includes seven sonatas for flute (three are the so-called *'Halle' sonatas* published in 1730 and thought to be the product of Handel's youth) as well as for flute (Stephen Preston), recorder (Philip Pickett), oboe (David Reichenberg), strings and continuo, and is announced as the first in a comprehensive survey of Handel's instrumental chamber music. The question of the authenticity and provenance of some of the music here is too complicated to be gone into in these pages, but is clearly set out in Basil Lam's notes. The recordings are cut at a high level but the overall sound is well defined and clean. The balance places the listener rather too close to the players at times, though the acoustic setting is warm. The playing itself is always spirited and intelligent, though the violin in the *Concerto a quattro* and the *G major Trio sonata* (vibrato-less and with the usual bulges) is razor-edged and most unpleasing.

William Bennett's record includes the three *'Halle' sonatas* and two others: one from the

Op. 1 set and the other a more recent discovery from a Brussels manuscript. Modern instruments are used but there is an excellent sense of period style and accurate intonation. Nicholas Kraemer and Denis Vigay provide admirable support and the Philips recording is very clean indeed and well balanced. Collectors who must have 'authentic' instruments will want the CRD set, but this comprises two records and is not ideal in all respects, though Stephen Preston produces some beguiling sounds; but even they will find much to admire in these performances, both in terms of style and execution, and it must carry a strong recommendation. The cassette is of high quality too.

The Telefunken recordings all come from the mid-1960s. Frans Brüggen is at his most effortless and inspired in the Handel, where he seems wholly untroubled by such considerations as taking breath! His sense of style matches his technical command, and the recording is fresh and immediate.

While Brüggen's set is on two records, the HMV Linde issue collects the four *Sonatas* from Op. 1 on a single disc with an excellent matching tape. There need be no hesitation here, for the playing is imaginative and fresh, and the recording first-class, very truthful and lifelike. In fact these artists will be very hard to beat.

Although no autograph survives for the *'Halle' Trio sonatas*, the flute player Weidemann copied them while in London and Handel acknowledged them as having been written while he was studying with Zachow. Holliger and his team give scrupulous and imaginative performances, beautifully balanced and elegant in every way. They are extremely well recorded and should appeal to all lovers of this period save those who feel strongly that baroque instruments are essential for this music. Certainly this music sounds as well on oboes as it does on flutes.

The eight *Trio sonatas* recorded by L'École d'Orphée in their second CRD set comprise four from the Op. 2 set published by Walsh in 1732, an alternative version of another sonata of Op. 2 (namely *No. 1 in C minor* which appears in its B minor form for flute, violin and continuo in the previous volume, CRD 1073-4) and the three so-called *'Dresden' sonatas*, which Chrysander first published in the Händel-Gesellschaft edition in 1879. Only one of them is totally authentic, though whoever composed the remaining two was no mean figure, and indeed a sequential passage in the opening movement of the *G minor* (No. 8 in the Chrysander edition) is echoed in the *Organ concerto*, Op. 7, No. 5. There are many musical riches here and no wanting of accomplishment in the performances. The two violins in use, one by Mariani of 1650 and another 'Anon. after Stainer *c.* 1740', have markedly different tone quality; and though the playing is brilliant when required, it could with advantage be more full-blooded. Readers unresponsive to the baroque violin may find their pleasure diminished by the raw, vinegary timbre of the violins here, but those for whom this presents no problems will find much to admire. The recording tends to place the harpsichord at a disadvantage but this does not seriously impair the production, which has excellent notes from Anthony Hicks. The chrome cassettes are admirably truthful and wide-ranging, although just a little smoothing of the treble might be useful.

Violin sonatas, Op. 1/1, 3, 10, 12–13 and 15.
(M) *(*) Ph. 9502 023 [id.]. Grumiaux, Veyron-Lacroix.

Violin sonatas, Op. 1/3, 6, 10, 12–15; Fantasia in A; Sonata in D min.
**(*) Ph. 6769 022 (2). Iona Brown, Vigay, Kraemer.

Some will find it a relief to turn to the modern violin after the Gilette-like strains of the baroque variety. Iona Brown plays with vigour and spirit, and there is a welcome robustness and vitality about these performances. At times, even in the well-known *D major*, one feels the need for greater warmth and spaciousness. There are touches of the routine here and there but, nonetheless, the set is likely to give much pleasure overall and it is well recorded in the best Philips tradition.

The Grumiaux/Veyron-Lacroix performances are less readily recommendable. The slow movements are rather romanticized, which is not wholly unwelcome, but in the outer movements both Grumiaux and his partner do not sound wholly committed. Well played and recorded though it is, this issue raises little real enthusiasm.

KEYBOARD MUSIC

Chaconne in G, HWV 435; Harpsichord suites: in B flat, HWV 434; in D min., HWV 436; in E min., HWV 438; in G, HWV 441.
*** DG Arc. Dig. 410 656-1/*4* [id.]. Pinnock (harpsichord).

Trevor Pinnock has real panache and he plays this repertoire as to the manner born. This issue has been widely praised and rightly, for there is flair here and imagination too.

Fantasia in C; Lesson in B flat; Prelude and allegro in A min.; Sonata in G min.; Sonatina in G min.; Suites Nos. 5 in E; 8 in G.
** None. Dig. D/*D4* 79037. Kipnis (harpsichord).

Igor Kipnis's record is called 'The Virtuoso Handel' and gives ample evidence of his formidable powers of display. He uses an instrument from the workshop of Rutkowski and Robinette in New York which the sleeve tells us is 'patterned on but not a copy of' the largest Haas instruments of the mid-eighteenth century. The sound is rather big and larger than life, even when the disc is reproduced at a lower listening level. There are moments when the exuberance and virtuosity might strike some as just a shade excessive. He is undoubtedly a brilliant player and the recording has clarity and presence. In one sense a somewhat more distant balance might have lent greater enchantment. The *Lesson in B flat* includes the famous *Aria con variazioni* which Brahms was to use in his Op. 24 and the finale of the *Suite in E* is the set of variations (*The Harmonious Blacksmith*). Ornamentation is liberally applied throughout the recital.

Harpsichord suites Nos. (i) *1 in A;* (ii) *2 in F; 3 in D min.;* (i) *4 in E min.;* (ii) *5 in E;* (i) *6 in F sharp min.; 7 in G min.;* (ii) *8 in F min.; 9 in G min.;* (i) *10 in D min.; 11 in D min.;* (ii) *12 in E min.;* (i) *13 in B;* (ii) *14 in G;* (i) *15 in D min.;* (ii) *16 in G min.*
*** HMV SLS 5234 (4). (i) Gavrilov; (ii) Sviatoslav Richter (piano).

Harpsichord suites Nos. 1–8.
(M) *** HM HM 447/8. Gilbert (harpsichord).

This four-record set of the Handel suites derives from the 1979 Touraine Festival and was recorded at the Château de Marcilly-sur-Maulne, which has a sympathetic and warm acoustic. It is a joy to hear this repertoire on the piano with its variety of tone colour when the playing is of this order. Occasionally the tempi are a shade extreme in the slower movements (some of Gavrilov's *Sarabandes* are funereal), but the sheer refinement and finesse of their playing is a joy in itself. For too long, pianists have felt intimidated by the Early Music lobby and have refrained from trespassing on this territory. Although Bach on the piano has remained a current phenomenon, thanks to Kempff, Glen Gould and Rosalyn Tureck, this is the first Handel record to speak of, for more than two decades, and the only regret one has is that HMV have not chosen to make the discs available separately. The piano sound is altogether natural and the audience noise mostly unobtrusive.

Those understandably preferring the harpsichord to the piano will find Gilbert's recordings of the first eight *Suites* make an admirable alternative. Gilbert is a scholar as well as a distinguished player. He uses a copy of a Taskin harpsichord by Bedard. Gilbert observes most first-half repeats but not the second, and he is as imaginative in the handling of decoration and ornamentation as one would expect. If one were to quibble, it would be merely that some grandeur, some larger-than-life vitality, is missing; but so much else is there that there is no case for qualifying the recommendation. The recording is much better balanced and more natural than recent rivals.

VOCAL AND CHORAL MUSIC

Acis and Galatea (masque).
*** Argo ZRG 886/7/*K 114 K 22* (2) [id.]. Gomez, Tear, Langridge, Luxon, Ch. and ASMF, Marriner.
*** DG Arc. 2708 038 [id./*3375 004*].

Burrowes, Rolfe Johnson, Hill, Elliot, White, E. Bar. Soloists, Gardiner.

The refinement and rhythmic lift of the Academy's playing under Marriner make for a lively and highly engaging performance of *Acis and Galatea*, marked by characterful solo singing from a strong team. The choruses are sung by a vocal quartet (not the same singers) and with warmly atmospheric recording the result is a sparkling entertainment. Robert Tear's tone is not always ideally mellifluous (for instance in *Love in her eyes sits playing*), but like the others he has a good feeling for Handel style, and the sweetness of Jill Gomez's contribution is a delight. The cassette transfer, made at a characteristically high level, has plenty of range and detail, capturing the resonant acoustic faithfully and placing soloists and chorus in realistic perspective.

Some of John Eliot Gardiner's tempi are idiosyncratic (some too fast, some too slow), but the scale of performance, using original instruments, is beautifully judged to simulate domestic conditions such as they might have been in the first performance for the Duke of Chandos, with the vocal soloists banding together for the choruses. The acoustic is far drier than in the Argo version, and the soloists are less characterful, though more consistently sweet of tone. The authentic sounds of the English Baroque Soloists are finely controlled so as not to offend unprepared ears too blatantly, and those who prefer vibrato-less string tone for music of this period should certainly select this. The DG cassettes are only available in the USA. The transfer is made at a somewhat lower level than the Argo, producing an extra smoothness in the treble, although there is no lack of life to the voices. The orchestra, in particular, has splendid presence and detail.

Alceste (overture and incidental music).
*** O-L DSLO 581 [id., PSI]. Nelson, Kirkby, Cable, Elliot, Thomas, AcAM, Hogwood.

Commissioned to write incidental music for a play by Smollett (something to associate with Purcell, not Handel), the composer was stopped in his tracks with the abandonment of the whole project. Nonetheless there is much to enjoy here, not just solo items but also some simple tuneful choruses, all introduced by an impressive dramatic overture in D minor. Hogwood draws lively performances from his usual team and as ever is very well recorded.

L'Allegro, il penseroso, il moderato.
*** Erato STU/*MCE* 71325 (2). Kwella, McLaughlin, Jennifer Smith, Ginn, Davies, Hill, Varcoe, Monteverdi Ch., E. Bar. Soloists, Gardiner.

Taking Milton as his starting point, Handel illustrated in music the contrasts of mood and character between the cheerful and the thoughtful. Then, prompted by his librettist, Charles Jennens, he added compromise in *Il moderato*, the moderate man. The final chorus may fall a little short of the rest (Jennens's words cannot have provided much inspiration), but otherwise the sequence of brief numbers is a delight, particularly in a performance as exhilarating as this, with excellent soloists, choir and orchestra. The recording is first-rate.

Anthem for the Foundling Hospital; Ode for the birthday of Queen Anne.
*** O-L DSLO/*KDSLC* 541. Nelson, Kirkby, Minty, Bowman, Hill, Thomas, Ch. of Christ Church Cath., Oxford, AcAM, Preston.

Two splendid examples of Handel's occasional music make an excellent coupling, superbly performed and recorded. The *Ode* is an early work, written soon after Handel arrived in England. It has its Italianate attractions, but it is the much later *Foundling Hospital Anthem* on the reverse which is much the more memorable, not just because it concludes with an alternative version of the *Hallelujah chorus* (sounding delightfully fresh on this scale with the Christ Church Choir) but because the other borrowed numbers are superb too. An extra tang is given by the accompaniment on original instruments. The tape transfer is of excellent quality, with plenty of bloom as well as clarity and a very good choral focus, considering the degree of resonance.

Beato in ver; Langue geme (duets). *Parti, l'idolo mio; Sento la che ristretto* (cantatas); *Tanti strali* (duet).
*** HM HM 1004. Nelson, Jacobs, Kuijken, Christe, Junghanel.

Beato in ver was written in 1741, late in Handel's career, but the other items all come from his early years in Italy, charming and refreshing inspirations hardly at all known, all of them here beautifully sung by the poised and pure Judith Nelson and the distinctive-toned counter-tenor, René Jacobs. First-rate recording.

(i) *Cecilia vogi un sguardo* (cantata); *Silete venti* (motet).
*** DG Arc. Dig. 2534 004. Jennifer Smith, Elwes, E. Concert, Pinnock.

These two fine cantatas come from a later period than most of Handel's Italian-language works in this genre. Both reveal him at his most effervescent, a quality superbly caught in these performances with excellent singing and playing, most strikingly from Jennifer Smith whose coloratura has never been more brilliantly displayed on record. Excellent recording.

Chandos anthems: In the Lord Put I my Trust; I Will Magnify Thee.
*** Argo ZRG 766 [id.]. Friend, Langridge, King's College Ch., ASMF, Willcocks.

Here are two of Handel's anthems (these are Nos. 2 and 5) written for the Duke of Chandos, attractive for their freshness of inspiration, their economical vocal writing for small forces producing agreeably resilient textures. The choral singing here is well up to King's standard, and the solo contributions have plenty of character; Philip Langridge is notable for his eloquence and simplicity of approach. With characteristically fine Argo recording, in the best King's tradition, this can be enthusiastically recommended.

Coronation anthems: (*1, Zadok the Priest; 2, The King shall rejoice; 3, My heart is inditing; 4, Let Thy hand be strengthened*).
*** DG Arc. Dig. **410 030-2**; 2534/*3311* 005 [id.]. Westminster Abbey Ch., E. Concert, Preston; Pinnock (organ).
**(*) HMV Dig. ASD/*TCC-ASD* 143445-1/*4* [Ang. DS/*4XDS* 37969]. King's College Ch., ECO, Ledger.
**(*) Argo ZRG/*KZRC* 5369 [id.]. King's College Ch., ECO, Willcocks.
*(*) ASV ACM/*ZCACM* 2041. Huddersfield Choral Soc., Northern Sinf., Pritchard; Rhodes (organ).

It is thrilling on the Archive disc after the lightness and clarity of the introduction to *Zadok the Priest*, to have the choir enter with such bite and power, most strikingly of all in the compact-disc version which underlines the freshness and immediacy. Though the Westminster Abbey Choir is not large, the recording gives ample sense of power, and the use of original instruments gives plenty of character to the accompaniments. An exhilarating version. Cassette collectors will find the chrome-tape transfer is of first-class DG quality.

With ample reverberation adding to the grandeur, Ledger (using what by name are the same forces as his predecessor, Sir David Willcocks, on his Argo record) directs a reading which favours measured speeds. Though the choir is small – like those on most rival versions – the recording balance, in excellent digital sound, has the voices standing out clearly to reinforce the weight of the reading. This is a valid alternative to Simon Preston's with the Westminster Abbey Choir on DG Archive, for though it is not nearly so exciting, it presents modern string sound rather than the edginess of original instruments. On tape the choral focus is not quite as sharp as on disc, although this is more noticeable on side two than side one where *Zadok the Priest* projects well.

On Argo, fine performances, brilliantly recorded, except in the matter of balance, and that is a problem inherent in the choral singing itself. This is stylish enough, but the kind of sound the choir makes is rather too light-textured for these large-scale ceremonial pieces. The result is that the orchestra tends to overwhelm the vocal sound, even though the engineering minimizes this as much as possible. However, even with reservations this is a sensible collection, extremely well recorded, and there is a great deal to enjoy. There is a good cassette.

For those who prefer the idea of these anthems sung by a big choir the ASV version makes a fair alternative with John Pritchard drawing a crisp and direct performance from his forces. The snag is that the choral sound is not bright or forward enough, but otherwise the recording is good.

Dettingen Te Deum; Dettingen anthem.

*** DG Arc. Dig. **410 647-2**; 410 647-1/*4* [id.]. Westminster Abbey Ch., E. Concert, Preston.

Dettingen Te Deum.

** Cal. CAL 1688/*4688* [id.]. Knibbs, Hill, Stafford, Peter, George, Ch. and O of Paris Sorbonne, Grimbert.

The *Dettingen Te Deum* was written to celebrate a famous victory during the War of the Austrian Succession. It is splendidly typical work and continually reminds the listener of *Messiah*, written the previous year. Arias and choruses alike are full of attractive invention and one has the suspicion that Handel is knowingly capitalizing on the familiarity of his oratorio in almost plagiarizing himself. But for the listener the result is highly rewarding, particularly as the florid baroque scoring, with liberal use of trumpets, gives so much pleasure in itself. The Calliope recording apparently uses the original score, and the orchestral playing is spirited. The choral contribution is impressive too, but the soloists are adequate and no more. Even so, with an obvious sense of enjoyment conveyed by Jacques Grimbert and his forces overall this readily communicates. The recording is resonant but generally clear, the tape not quite as cleanly focused as the disc, but fully acceptable.

However, this earlier version is now completely superseded by Preston's new Archive performance, with original instruments, from the English Concert. It makes an ideal recommendation with its splendid singing, crisp but strong (Stephen Varcoe does the two brief airs beautifully), excellent recording and a generous, apt coupling. This setting of *The King shall rejoice* should not be confused with the *Coronation anthem* of that name. It is less inspired, but has a magnificent double fugue for finale.

Dixit Dominus; Zadok the Priest.

*** Erato STU/*MCE* 71055. Palmer, Marshall, Brett, Messana, Morton, Thomson, Wilson-Johnson, Monteverdi Ch. and O, Gardiner.

Dixit Dominus.

(M) ** HMV SXLP/*TC-SXLP* 30444 [Ang. S 36331]. Zylis-Gara, Baker, Lane, Tear, Shirley-Quirk, King's College Ch., ECO, Willcocks.

Handel's *Dixit Dominus* dates from 1707 and was completed during his prolonged stay in Italy from 1706 to 1710. It divides into eight sections, and the setting, while showing signs of Handel's mature style in embryo, reflects also the baroque tradition of contrasts between small and large groups. The writing is extremely florid and requires bravura from soloists and chorus alike. John Eliot Gardiner catches all its brilliance and directs an exhilarating performance marked by strongly accented, sharply incisive singing from the choir and outstanding solo contributions. In high contrast with the dramatic choruses the duet for two sopranos, *De torrente*, here beautifully sung by Felicity Palmer and Margaret Marshall, is languorously expressive but stylishly so. Other soloists match that, and the recording is first-rate. The cassette quality is good on side one, although ultimately lacking upper range; but the sound is brighter and much more extended on side two.

The performance on HMV is also alive and spirited, but one senses that the security that comes with complete familiarity is not always present. The intonation of the soloists is not above reproach, and the trio *Dominus a dextris*, which comes at the beginning of side two, is not very comfortable. The chorus seems not completely happy with the virtuoso running passages a little later; Sir David Willcocks might have achieved more security had he been content with a slightly slower pace. There is vigour and enthusiasm here but not always the last degree of finesse. The recording is atmospheric, but the focus is not absolutely sharp. The cassette matches the disc closely.

Funeral anthem for Queen Caroline: The Ways of Zion Do Mourn.

*** Erato STU/*MCE* 71173. Burrowes, Brett, Hill, Varcoe, Monteverdi Ch. and O, Gardiner.

Queen Caroline – whom Handel had known earlier as a princess in Hanover – was the most cultivated of the royal family of the Georges, and when she died in 1737 he was inspired to write a superb cantata in an overture and eleven numbers. He later used the material for the first Acts of *Israel in Egypt*. Gardiner directs a performance which brings out the high contrasts implicit in the music, making the piece energetic rather than elegiac. Excellent work from soloists, chorus and orchestra alike, all very well recorded.

Israel in Egypt.
*** Argo ZRG 817/8 [id.]. Gale, Watson, Bowman, Partridge, McDonnell, Watt, Christ Church Cath. Ch., Oxford, ECO, Preston.
**(*) Erato STU/*MCE* 71245 (2). Knibbs, Clarkson, Elliot, Varcoe, Monteverdi Ch. and O, Gardiner.

Simon Preston, using a small choir with boy trebles and an authentically sized orchestra, directs a performance of this great, dramatic oratorio which is beautifully in scale. He starts with the *Cuckoo and the Nightingale organ concerto* – a procedure sanctioned by Handel himself at the first performance – and though inevitably the big plague choruses lack the weight which a larger choir gives them, the vigour and resilience are ample compensation, so that the text is illustrated with extra immediacy. Though Elizabeth Gale is not so firm a soprano as Heather Harper on the deleted Archive issue, the band of soloists is an impressive one, and the ECO is in splendid form. The recording is warmly atmospheric, more realistically balanced if not always so clear as the rival Archive one.

Israel in Egypt has been lucky on record. Gardiner's fine version with its bitingly dramatic and incisive choral singing follows on the versions of Mackerras (with chamber orchestra but large choir, now deleted in the UK) and Simon Preston (with boy trebles in the authentically sized choir). On choir alone the Gardiner is probably the finest of the three, but unlike the other versions the soloists here come from the choir itself, and though they sing well they rarely match in imagination the star singers of the other two sets. Nonetheless the vigour and concentration of the performance are formidably convincing, helped by excellent recording. The cassette layout uses two tapes but opens the second part of the oratorio near the end of side two, negating any advantage. The slim presentation is flimsy and there are no notes. Moreover the choral sound is thick and approaches the point of no return on side two, with congestion brought by too high a transfer level. This is not recommendable.

Jephtha.
*** Argo D 181 D 4/*K 181 K 43* (4) [id.]. Rolfe Johnson, Margaret Marshall, Hodgson, Esswood, Keyte, Kirkby, Ch. and ASMF, Marriner.

Jephtha, the last oratorio that Handel completed, is a strange and not always very moral tale. With the threat of blindness on him the composer was forced to break off from writing for several months, but that threat seems only to have added to the urgency of inspiration, and Marriner's performance, helped by the bright tones of boy trebles in the choruses, is refreshing from first to last, well sprung but direct in style. The soloists are excellent, with Emma Kirkby nicely distanced in the role of the Angel, her clean vibrato-less voice made the more ethereal. It is a very long oratorio, but in this performance it hardly seems so, with such beautiful numbers as Jephtha's *Waft her, angels* given a finely poised performance by Rolfe Johnson. The recording is first-rate, and the cassette transfer has a fine sparkle, with lively presence and detail.

Judas Maccabaeus.
*** DG 2723 050/*3376 011* (3) [id.]. Palmer, Baker, Esswood, Davies, Shirley-Quirk, Keyte, Wandsworth School Ch., ECO, Mackerras.

Judas Maccabaeus may have a lopsided story, with a high proportion of the finest music given to the anonymous soprano and contralto roles, Israelitish Woman (Felicity Palmer) and Israelitish Man (Dame Janet

Baker), but the sequence of Handelian gems is irresistible, the more so in a performance as sparkling as this one under Sir Charles Mackerras. Unlike many versions, particularly those which in scholarly fashion attempt to restore Handel's original proportions, this holds together with no let-up of intensity, and though not everyone will approve of the use of boys' voices in the choir (inevitably the tone and intonation are not flawless) it gives an extra bite of character. Hearing even so hackneyed a number as *See, the conquering hero* in its true scale is a delightful surprise. The orchestral group and continuo sound splendidly crisp, and when the trumpets come in at *Sound an alarm* the impact is considerable, just as it must have been for the original Handelian audience. Though some may regret the passing of the old-style fruity singing in the great tenor and bass arias, Ryland Davies and John Shirley-Quirk are most stylish, while both Felicity Palmer and Dame Janet crown the whole set with glorious singing, not least in a delectable sequence on the subject of liberty towards the end of Act I. The recording quality is outstanding, ideally fresh, vivid and clear, and the tape transfer too is of demonstration quality, indistinguishable from the discs.

Lucrezia (cantata); Arias: *Ariodante: Dopo notte; Atalanta: Care selve; Hercules: Where shall I fly?; Joshua: O had I Jubal's lyre; Rodelinda: Dove sei, amato bene?; Xerxes: Ombra mai fù* (*Largo*).

(M) *** Ph. 9502/*7313* 097. Baker, ECO, Leppard.

Even among Janet Baker's records this Handel recital marks a special contribution, ranging as it does from the pure gravity of *Ombra mai fù* to the passionate commitment and supreme coloratura virtuosity in *Dopo notte* from *Ariodante*. Leppard gives sparkling support, and the whole is recorded with natural and refined balance. An outstanding disc, and a very good cassette.

Psalms: *Laudate Pueri in D; Nisi Dominus; Salve Regina*.

(M) **(*) HM HM/*40-* 1054. Deller Cons., King's Musick, Mark Deller.

These psalm settings come from early in Handel's career, when he was still working in Italy. Though *Nisi Dominus* ends with a conventional fugue of the kind which marks out later Handel, there is a lightness characteristic of the period, well brought out in these fresh and urgent performances, brightly if rather aggressively recorded. The cassette, while still lively and natural, is smoother on top than the disc.

Messiah (complete).

C *** Ph. Dig. **411 041-2**; 6769/*7654* 107 (3) [id.]. Marshall, Robbin, Rolfe Johnson, Brett, Hale, Quirke, Monteverdi Ch., E. Bar. Soloists, Eliot Gardiner.

(M) *** HMV SLS/*TC-SLS* 774 (3) [Ang. SCL 3705]. Harwood, Baker, Esswood, Tear, Herinx, Amb. S., ECO, Mackerras.

*** Ph. 6703 001/*7699 009* (3) [id.]. Harper, Watts, Wakefield, Shirley-Quirk, LSO Ch., LSO, Sir Colin Davis.

*** O-L **411 858-2**; D189 D3/*K 189 K33* [id.]. Nelson, Kirkby, Watkinson, Elliot, Thomas, Christ Church Cath. Ch., Oxford, AcAM, Hogwood.

*** Erato STU 70921/*MCE 70962* (3) [RCA CRL3 1426]. Palmer, Watts, Ryland Davies, Shirley-Quirk, ECO Ch., ECO, Leppard.

*** HMV SLS 845 (3). Trebles, Bowman, Tear, Luxon, King's College Ch., ASMF, Willcocks.

**(*) Decca D18 D3/*K 18 K 32* (3) [id.]. Ameling, Reynolds, Langridge, Howell, Ch. and ASMF, Marriner.

The newest digital recording of *Messiah* directed by John Eliot Gardiner, the first to be issued complete on compact discs, takes the freshening process started by Sir Colin Davis and Sir Charles Mackerras in the mid-1960s a stage further. The momentum set off by these two famous recordings was continued by Marriner and Hogwood, both of whom attempted to re-create specific early performances and leave behind forever the Victorian tradition of massive choral forces, exemplified by the Royal Choral Society and the famous Huddersfield Choir, directed in their halcyon years by Sir Malcolm Sargent.

However, Gardiner's approach is not re-creative but essentially practical, with variants from the expected text rather the exception. Thus the duet version of *He shall feed his flock* and the *Pastoral symphony* (with squeezed accents from the strings preventing the line from sounding too mellifluous) are both included. He chooses bright-toned sopranos instead of boy trebles for the chorus, on the grounds that a mature adult approach is essential. Conversely he uses, very affectingly, a solo treble to sing *There were shepherds abiding*. Speeds are usually even faster and lighter than Hogwood's (or even Davis's) and the rhythmic buoyancy in the choruses is very striking. *For unto us a child is born* is a delightful example, and *Let us break their bonds asunder* is exhilaratingly fast. Sometimes one might feel he goes too far, as in the clipped rhythms of *Who is the King of glory*, while the lightness of touch at the very opening of *Hallelujah* is a little disconcerting, even though the singing becomes more robust as the chorus proceeds. There is drama and boldness too. *Why do the nations* and *The trumpet shall sound* (both sung with great authority) have seldom come over more strongly. Perhaps most dramatic of all is the moment when after a deceptively sedate opening, the *Amen chorus* suddenly bursts into full flood after the brief and gentle melisma from the violins, helped by the wide dynamic range of the recording. The soloists are all first-class with the soprano Margaret Marshall finest of all, especially in *I know that my Redeemer liveth* (tastefully decorated). There are times when one craves for more expansive qualities; and the baroque string sound, though not as aggressively thin as it is under Hogwood, still can give cause for doubts. Yet there are some wonderful highlights, not least Margaret Marshall's angelic version of *Rejoice greatly*, skipping along in compound time, so that one can forgive *He shall purify* sounding as if the chorus are taking the purification on themselves. The set is admirably presented on three discs and cassettes with each of the three parts complete on two sides. Unfortunately the chrome cassettes are transferred at an almost unbelievably low level, so, though the sound is good, there is inevitable background hiss. The CD layout follows the discs, with most items individually cued. The sound is outstandingly beautiful, fresh and natural, with much of the edge lifted from the baroque violins, so that while the bite remains there is beauty of texture too. Solo voices sound remarkably tangible and the choral sound is wonderfully refined.

Earlier versions are by no means outclassed by this new look and there will be many who will resist the baroque strings and prefer a more robust choral sound, as on the splendid HMV version under Mackerras. When this was first issued, only a month or two after the Davis set, it seemed to come into direct competition, to its disadvantage. But relistening confirms that the Mackerras view can give equal pleasure. The choruses on HMV have not the same vitality as on Philips, but they have a compensating body and richness. Indeed there is much to commend the Ambrosian/ECO set, not least the modest price. One could well argue that Basil Lam's edition of the score goes deeper than Davis's in pursuing the authentic approach, but for the layman the main difference will be that, more than Davis, Mackerras adopts Handel's generally forgotten alternative versions. So the soprano aria *Rejoice greatly* is given in its optional 12/8 version, with compound time adding a skip to the rhythm. A male alto is also included among the soloists, and he is given some of the bass arias as well as some of the regular alto passages. Among the soloists Dame Janet Baker is outstanding. Her intense, slow account of *He was despised* – with decorations on the reprise – is sung with profound feeling. Good recording, rather warmer and less bright than the rival Philips. Like Davis, Mackerras includes all the numbers traditionally omitted. On tape the HMV set is particularly successful, with warm vocal tone and the richness of the recorded ambience well transferred.

The earlier Philips recording has not lost its impact. Initially the traditionalist may be worried by the very fast speeds Davis tends to adopt for choruses, but a fine professional body (unnamed) copes with every technical difficulty with ease. The chorus is always fresh, the texture beautifully clear and, thanks to Davis, the rhythmic bounce of such choruses as *For unto us* is really infectious. Even *Hallelujah* loses little and gains much from being performed by an authentic-sized chorus, and the bite of the recorded sound more than makes amends at every point for lack of 'Huddersfield-style' massiveness. Excellent singing from all four soloists, particularly Helen Watts, who following early precedent is given *For He is like a refiner's fire* to sing instead of the bass, and produces a glorious chest register. With Davis's briskness there is everything to be said for the inclusion of all the numbers traditionally omitted. On cassette the focus of the upper partials in both orchestra and chorus has a hint of 'tizz' which has come from the master tape. It can be filtered out but robs the quality of some of its freshness.

Christopher Hogwood in aiming at recreating an authentic version – based meticulously on material from the Foundling Hospital, reproducing a performance of 1754 – has managed to have the best of both worlds, punctilious but consistently vigorous and refreshing, never falling into dull routine. The boy trebles of Christ Church are superb, and though the soloists cannot match the tonal beauty of the finest of their rivals on other sets, the consistency of the whole conception makes for most satisfying results. As to the text, it generally follows what we are used to, but there are such oddities as *But who may abide* transposed for a soprano and a shortened version of the *Pastoral symphony*. The recording is superb, clear and free to match the performance, and the cassette transfer is exceptionally successful, virtually indistinguishable from the discs.

Raymond Leppard presents a fine, enjoyable account which avoids the extremes of his principal rivals. His tempi, unlike Davis's, are never exaggeratedly fast, and his ornamentation is less fancy than Mackerras's on HMV. The nearest to eccentricity is Leppard's tempo for *The trumpet shall sound*, very fast indeed, like Davis's with the same baritone; and *All we like sheep*, preceded by a delightful flourish from the organ, is even jauntier than Davis's account. Leppard has the same contralto, Helen Watts, as well as the same bass, and if anything they are both in even finer form. Felicity Palmer is fresher-toned than she sometimes is on record, while Ryland Davies sings brightly and cleanly. The chorus is admirably clear and precise. A slight snag is the inconsistency of recording quality, generally very good but slightly variable between numbers.

The cassette set is on two individual cassettes in normal plastic boxes, with the oratorio's sections sensibly divided. The transfer level is not especially high and while the sound is good and natural, the upper range is not as bright as on the discs, until side four when a rise in level brings a sharper focus.

Often as *Messiah* has been recorded, there seems plenty of room in the market for new versions, particularly ones which show a new and illuminating view of the work. Willcocks's recording has been described as the 'all-male *Messiah*', for a counter-tenor takes over the contralto solos, and the full complement of the trebles of King's College Choir sings the soprano solos, even the florid ones like *Rejoice greatly*, and the result is enchanting. The whole approach is light and airy, with some delightful continuo playing and splendid contributions from the St Martin's Academy as well as the famous choir. Vivid atmospheric recording against the King's acoustic. A gimmicky version, perhaps, but one that few will resist.

The idea behind Neville Marriner's attractive version was to present *Messiah* as nearly as possible in the text followed in its first London performance in 1743. So the refiner's fire of the contralto has no rushing to it, for that graphic passage was introduced later in Handel's revisions, and as in the Mackerras version on HMV, the skipping 12/8 version of *Rejoice greatly* is followed instead of the usual one. The losses are as great as the gains, but the result has unusual unity, thanks also to Marriner's direction. His tempi in fast choruses can hardly be counted as authentic in any way, for with a small professional chorus he has gone even further than Davis in lightening them, and has thus made possible speeds that almost pass belief. Purist doubts tend to be dissipated by the overall sense of fantasy, and though Anna Reynolds's contralto is not ideally suited to recording, it is otherwise an excellent band of soloists, and in any case Miss Reynolds sings *He was despised* most movingly on a thread of sound. Vivid recording, with a tape transfer of demonstration quality.

Messiah: highlights.
*** O-L **400 086-2**; DSLO/*KDSLC* 592 [id.].
(from above set, cond. Hogwood).

(M) *** Ph. Seq. 6527/*7311* 118. (from above set, cond. Davis).
*** Argo ZRG/*KZRC* 879 [id.]. (from above set, cond. Marriner).
(M) ** Decca Jub. JB/*KJBC* 80. Sutherland, Bumbry, McKellar, Ward, LSO Ch., LSO, Boult.
*(*) CfP CFP/*TC-CFP* 40020 [Sera. S/*4XG* 60220]. Morison, Thomas, Lewis, Huddersfield Ch. Soc., Royal Liv. PO, Sargent.

Messiah: choruses.
*** O-L DSLO/*KDSLC* 613 [id.]. (from above set, cond. Hogwood).
**(*) HMV CSD 3778. (from above set, cond. Willcocks).

Messiah: (i) *Behold the Lamb of God;* (ii) *He was despised;* (i) *Surely he hath borne; And with his stripes; All we like sheep.*
(M) *** Decca SPA/*KCSP* 588. (i) Ch., LSO; (ii) Ferrier, LPO; Boult – BACH: *Passion* excerpts.***

The digitally remastered compact disc of highlights from the Hogwood set is particularly successful. There is just a little blurring at the top caused by the resonance, but soloists and chorus alike (and of course the sharp-edged strings) are vividly projected against a virtually silent background. It is a fine sampler for the 'new' if not the 'newest look' *Messiah.* Indeed listeners may immediately judge their reactions from the opening *Comfort ye* with its florid decorations. The solo singing is always fresh, David Thomas's *The trumpet shall sound* giving a robust reminder of an enduring style of presentation of this justly famous item. The recording is excellent; the cassette transfer is not quite as clean as the disc in reproducing the chorus.

The other discs represent the qualities of the sets from which they are taken, though, unfortunately, the cassette of the Davis selection is disappointingly lacking in bite, and the choral sound is flabby.

A highlights disc or tape is probably the best way to sample the Marriner performance, with its fresh sound and splendid solo and choral singing. The selection is generous. The same comment might apply to Boult's 1961 version, where Sutherland alone pays any attention to the question of whether or not to use ornamentation in the repeats of the *da capo* arias. One of the most enjoyable components of this set is the choral singing, and so it was a happy idea to extract choruses from this version to frame Kathleen Ferrier's famous account of *He was despised*, which is appropriately coupled to Passion music of Bach. The sound is excellent, with no perceptible difference between disc and tape.

Many will undoubtedly want a sampler of Sir Malcolm Sargent's traditional account of *Messiah.* This contains some fine solo singing, notably from Elsie Morison and Richard Lewis, but the choruses are disappointing, heavy in style and recorded in a curiously muffled way which cannot entirely be the fault of the singing itself. Moreover the tape transfer is not a success, with fuzzy choral sound.

For those seeking choruses alone (and one wonders what Handel would have thought of the idea of listening to choruses without the contrasting arias, taking away any thought of narrative line) there is a choice between King's College and the newer, lighter Hogwood style. There is some lack of robustness in both but, heard in isolation, the Hogwood versions certainly make a vivid impact. There is a good Oiseau-Lyre cassette, although on tape the choral focus is slightly less sharp than on disc.

Cantatas: *Nell'Africane selve; Nella stagion che, dio viole e rose.* Duets: *Quel fior che all'alba ride; No, di voi non vo' fidarmi; Tacete, ohimè, tacete!* Trio: *Se tu non lasci amore.*
*** O-L DSLO 580. Kirkby, Nelson, Thomas; Hogwood, Sheppard.

The most ear-catching items among these Italian cantatas are those which Handel later drew on in *Messiah* for such numbers as *His yoke is easy, For unto us a child is born* and *All we like sheep.* Emma Kirkby and Judith Nelson sing them brilliantly; and one of the less striking pieces yet presents an amazing virtuoso display from the bass, David Thomas, who is required to cope with an enormous range of three octaves. In the fast movements Hogwood favours breathtaking speeds (in every sense), yet the result is exciting, not too hectic, and the recording is outstanding.

Ode for St Cecilia's Day.
*** ASV DCA/*ZCDCA* 512. Gomez, Tear, King's College Ch., ECO, Ledger.
(M) **(*) Decca Ser. SA/*KSC* 9 [Argo ZRG 563]. Cantelo, Partridge, King's College Ch., ASMF, Willcocks.

An outstanding new version of Handel's splendid *Ode for St Cecilia's Day* from Ledger. With superb soloists – Jill Gomez radiantly beautiful and Robert Tear dramatically riveting in his call to arms, *The trumpet's loud clangour* – this delightful music emerges with an admirable combination of freshness and weight. Ledger uses an all-male chorus, and the style of the performance is totally convincing without being self-consciously authentic. The recording is first-rate, rich, vivid and clear; the cassette is very good too, if not quite so sharp in its upper focus. Highly recommended.

The earlier Argo version also sounds bright and lively in the medium-priced Serenata reissue. This is a performance we have perhaps underrated in previous editions of this *Guide*: April Cantelo is not as beguiling as Jill Gomez on ASV, but she sings sensitively and accurately, and although Ian Partridge is less vibrant than Robert Tear in *The trumpet's loud clangour*, it is still a highlight of the Serenata performance. Willcocks is less energetic at the opening than Ledger, but his closing chorus (*As from the power of sacred lays*) is faster and brighter, and some may prefer this approach. Certainly elsewhere the choral singing is incisive, but generally the ASV version has more imaginative detail, and the sound is richer. However, the crisp Argo recording has transferred exceptionally well to cassette, where the focus is admirably sharp throughout.

La Resurrezione.
*** O-L D 256 D 3/*K 256 K 33* [id.]. Kirkby, Kwella, Watkinson, Partridge, Thomas, AcAM, Hogwood.

In 1708, halfway through his four-year stay in Italy, the young Handel wrote this refreshingly dramatic oratorio. With opera as such prohibited in Rome it served as a kind of substitute, and though it does not have the great choral music which is so much the central element of later Handel oratorios, it is a fine and many-faceted piece. Hogwood directs a clean-cut vigorous performance with an excellent cast of singers highly skilled in authentic performance of baroque music. Emma Kirkby is at her most brilliant in the coloratura for the Angel, Patrizia Kwella sings movingly as Mary Magdalene and Carolyn Watkinson as Cleophas adopts an almost counter-tenor-like tone. Ian Partridge's tenor has a heady lightness as St John, and though David Thomas's Lucifer could have more weight, he too sings stylishly. Excellent recording and a very good cassette transfer, well balanced and natural in all respects, with an attractive ambient bloom.

Samson.
*** Erato STU 71240 (4). Baker, Watts, Tear, Luxon, Shirley-Quirk, Burrowes, Lott, L. Voices, ECO, Leppard.

Leppard directs a highly dramatic account of Handel's most dramatic oratorio, one which translates very happily to the stage; its culmination, the exultant aria, *Let the bright seraphim*, is here beautifully sung by Felicity Lott, but for long was associated with Joan Sutherland at Covent Garden. The moment when the orchestra interrupts a soloist in mid-sentence to indicate the collapse of the temple is more vividly dramatic than anything in a Handel opera, and Leppard handles that and much else with total conviction. Robert Tear as Samson produces his most heroic tones – rather too aggressively so in *Total eclipse* – and the rest of the cast could hardly be more distinguished. Dame Janet Baker – not by nature a seductress in the Dalila sense – yet sings with a lightness totally apt for such an aria as *With plaintive notes*, and the others are in excellent voice. The recording is outstanding, atmospheric and well balanced.

Saul (complete).
*** DG Arc. 2722 008 [2710 014]. Armstrong, Price, Bowman, Ryland Davies, English, Dean, McIntyre, Leeds Fest. Ch., ECO, Mackerras.

Few Handel choral works have been recorded with such consistent imagination as this fine performance conducted by Mackerras. With an excellent complement of soloists he steers an exhilarating course in a work that naturally needs to be presented with authenticity but equally needs to have dramatic edge. His scholarship is worn lightly, and the result is powerful on one hand, moving on another, sparkling on yet another. The contrast of timbre between Armstrong and Price, for example, is beautifully exploited, and Donald McIntyre as Saul, Ryland Davies as Jonathan, and James Bowman as a countertenor David are all outstanding, while the chorus willingly contributes to the drama. An outstanding set, beautifully recorded.

The Triumph of time and truth.
*** Hyp. A 66071/2 [id.]. Fisher, Kirkby, Brett, Partridge, Varcoe, L. Handel Ch. and O, Darlow.

This is officially Handel's very last oratorio, dating from 1757, an allegory on the subject suggested by the title. Almost all the material in fact dates from much earlier, much of it from an Italian treatment of the same subject which Handel wrote for Rome in 1707.

Darlow's performance with the London Handel Choir and Orchestra using original instruments has an attractive bluffness. This is broader and rougher than the authentic recordings by John Eliot Gardiner which are now such a feature of the Handel repertory, but it is hardly less enjoyable. The soloists all seem to have been chosen for the clarity of their pitching – Emma Kirkby, Gillian Fisher, Charles Brett and Stephen Varcoe, with the honey-toned Ian Partridge singing even more beautifully than the others, but with a timbre too pure quite to characterize 'Pleasure'. Good atmospheric recording, though the chorus is a little distant.

Utrecht Te Deum and Jubilate.
*** O-L DSLO/*KDSLC* 582 [id., PSI]. Nelson, Kirkby, Brett, Elliot, Covey-Crump, Thomas, Ch. of Christ Church Cath., Oxford, AcAM, Preston.

Utrecht Te Deum and Jubilate; Zadok the Priest.
(M) **(*) DG Arc. Priv. 2547/*3347* 022. Wolf, Watts, Wilfred Brown, Hemsley, Geraint Jones Ch. and O, Jones.

Handel wrote the Utrecht pieces just before coming to London, intending them as a sample of his work. Using authentic instruments and an all-male choir with boy trebles, Preston directs a performance which is not just scholarly but characteristically alert and vigorous, particularly impressive in the superb *Gloria* with its massive eight-part chords. With a team of soloists regularly associated with the Academy of Ancient Music, the disc can confidently be recommended; the cassette too is well managed, if marginally less refined at the top. However, the rival version of Geraint Jones, reissued on a mid-price Archive issue, has many points in its favour, particularly for those who resist a performance on original instruments. At a cheaper price it contains an extra item, *Zadok the Priest.* Although this dates from the earliest days of stereo, the recording is well balanced and clean. Small resources are used to great effect (the *Coronation anthem* is not as overwhelming as some like it to be) and with excellent soloists the result is vivid and lively, the choral focus marginally sharper on disc than on tape.

OPERA AND THEATRE MUSIC

The Alchymist (incidental music); *Comus* (incidental music). *Universal passion: I like the am'rous youth. The Way of the world: Love's but the frailty of the mind. The What d'ye call it: Twas when the seas were roaring.*
*** O-L DSLO 598. Kwella, Cable, Thomas, AcAM, Hogwood.

This collection of Handel's theatre music contains some delightful rarities. The *Comus* music was discovered only recently, and though some of it was later used in the *Occasional oratorio*, it makes a refreshing item, intended as it was as an epilogue for a performance of Milton's masque. Performances by the Academy under Hogwood have all the freshness and vigour one associates with his earlier series of Purcell theatre music.

Alcina (complete).
(M) ** Decca Ace GOS 509/11 [Lon. OSA 1361]. Sutherland, Berganza, Sinclair, Alva, Sciutti, Freni, Flagello, LSO, Bonynge.

This represents the extreme point of what can be described as Sutherland's dreamy, droopy period. The fast arias are stupendous. The conductor, Sutherland's husband Richard Bonynge, does not spare her at all, and in the brilliant Act I finale he really does rush her too fast, the result dazzling rather than musically satisfying. But anything slow and reflective, whether in recitative or aria, has Sutherland mooning about the notes, with no consonants audible at all and practically every vowel reduced to 'aw'. It is all most beautiful, of course, but she could have done so much better. Of the others, Berganza is completely charming in the castrato part of Ruggiero, even if she does not manage trills very well. Monica Sinclair shows everyone up with the strength and forthrightness of all her singing. Both Graziella Sciutti and Mirella Freni are delicate and clear in the two smaller parts of Morgana and Oberto. Richard Bonynge is very good indeed, drawing crisp, vigorous playing from the London Symphony Orchestra. Only in those rushed showpiece arias for his wife does he sound too inflexible. The recording is well up to Decca's vintage standard of the early 1960s and at Ace of Diamonds price this is well worth trying for the music alone.

Ariodante (complete).
*** Ph. 6769 025/*7699 112* (4) [id.]. Baker, Mathis, Burrowes, Bowman, Rendell, Oliver, Ramey, L. Voices, ECO, Leppard.

Set improbably in medieval Scotland, Handel's *Ariodante* has a story far more direct and telling in simple emotional terms than most of his operas, even though the conflict between characters does not emerge until well into the Second Act. The libretto inspired Handel – who had just lost some of his finest singers to a rival opera company – to write an amazing sequence of memorable and intensely inventive arias and duets, with not a single weak link in the chain, a point superbly conveyed in this colourful, urgent performance under Raymond Leppard.

The castrato role of Ariodante is a challenge even for Dame Janet Baker, who responds with singing of enormous expressive range, from the dark agonized moments of the C minor aria early in Act III to the brilliance of the most spectacular of the three display arias later in the Act. Dame Janet's duets with Edith Mathis as Princess Ginevra, destined to marry Prince Ariodante, are enchanting too, and there is not a single weak member of the cast, though James Bowman as Duke Polinesso is not so precise as usual, with words often unclear. Though this long work is given uncut, it is perhaps the most riveting Handel opera recording available, helped by the consistently resilient playing of the English Chamber Orchestra and the refined, beautifully balanced recording, equally impressive on disc and cassette.

Giulio Cesare: arias.
(M) **(*) Decca Ace SDD 574. Sutherland, Horne, Sinclair, New SO, Bonynge.

With the items dotted in no particular order, this selection at medium price hardly represents a 'potted version' but is welcome for much brilliant and beautiful singing. In 1964 Sutherland's coloratura was magnificent, and though in the slow music she too readily adopts a swooning manner her six arias are most impressive. Equally welcome items include Cornelia's beautiful lament sung by Marilyn Horne and a stunning display from Monica Sinclair in Ptolemy's aria, spanning in range a full three octaves. Good reverberant recording.

In the USA there is a fairly complete recording of the opera available with Norman Treigle, Beverly Sills, Maureen Forrester, Beverly Wolff and Spiro Malas, based on a New York stage production. While not all the problems are solved it has the life of a performance that has existed in its own right (rather than being created in the studio). The conductor Julius Rudel's approach is intelligent and this gives considerable enjoyment, although the singing of the name part by a baritone (while effective on stage) means that the music does not lie exactly right for the voice: [RCA LSC 6182].

Hercules (complete).
*** DG Arc. Dig. 2742/*3383* 004 (2). Tomlinson, Sarah Walker, Rolfe Johnson, Jennifer Smith, Denley, Savidge, Monteverdi Ch., E. Bar. Soloists, Eliot Gardiner.

Though the English libretto has its unintentional humour (the jealous Dejanira tells her husband Hercules to *'Resign thy club'*, meaning his knobkerrie not the Athenaeum), this is a great opera. Gardiner's generally brisk performance using authentic forces may at times lack Handelian grandeur in the big choruses, but it superbly conveys the vigour of the writing, its natural drama. Writing in English, Handel concentrated on direct and involving human emotions more than he generally did when setting classical subjects in Italian. Numbers are compact and memorable, and the fire of this performance is typified by the singing of Sarah Walker as Dejanira in her finest recording yet. John Tomlinson makes an excellent, dark-toned Hercules with florid passages well defined except for very occasional sliding. Youthful voices consistently help in the clarity of the attack – Jennifer Smith as Iole, Catherine Denley as Lichas, Anthony Rolfe Johnson as Hyllus and Peter Savidge as the Priest of Jupiter. Refined playing and outstanding recording quality with a fresh, clear chrome-cassette equivalent. The chorus loses just a little of its sharpness of focus, but overall the sound has fine immediacy and detail.

Partenope (complete).
*** HM 1C 153 99853/4 [Pro Arte P4C 4000]. Laki, Jacobs, York, Skinner, Varcoe, Müller-Molinari, Hill, La Petite Bande, Kuijken.

By the time he wrote *Partenope* in 1730 Handel was having to cut his cloth in opera production rather more modestly than earlier in his career. This opera in its limited scale has few heroic overtones, yet a performance as fresh and alert as this amply demonstrates that the result can be even more involving. One problem for Handel was that his company at the time could call on only one each of soprano, tenor and bass, but with an excellent team of counter-tenors and contralto this performance makes light of that limitation. With the exception of René Jacobs, rather too mannered for Handel, the team of soloists is outstanding, with Krisztina Laki and Helga Müller-Molinari welcome newcomers. Though ornamentation is sparse, the direction of Sigiswald Kuijken is consistently invigorating, and the recording is excellent.

Rinaldo (complete).
*** [CBS M3 34592]. Watkinson, Cotrubas, Scovotti, Esswood, Brett, Cold, Gr. Écurie, Malgoire.

The vigour of Malgoire's direction of an opera which plainly for him is very much alive, no museum piece, will attract many who normally steer clear of Handel opera, particularly in performances like this which use authentic instruments. The elaborate decorations on *da capo* arias are imaginatively done, but most effectively the famous *Cara sposa* is left without ornamentation, sung beautifully by the contralto Rinaldo, Carolyn Watkinson. The finest singing comes from Ileana Cotrubas, but under Malgoire the whole team is convincing. The bright but spacious recording adds to the vigour, and the magic sounds associated with the sorceress Armida, such as the arrival of her airborne chariot, are well conveyed. Needless to say, the story about the crusader Rinaldo hardly matters at all, but Handel's invention is a delight. This set is no longer available in the UK.

Semele (complete).
*** Erato STU 714453 (3) [id.]. Burrowes, Kwella, Friday, Della Jones, Denley, Rolfe Johnson, Lloyd, Penrose, Thomas, Monteverdi Ch., E. Bar. Soloists, Eliot Gardiner.

With English words *Semele* stands equivocally between the genres of opera and oratorio, though the Covent Garden production of 1982 showed how viable it is on stage. John Eliot Gardiner's lively performance using original instruments appeared at very much the same time as that staging, and in its brisk, well-sprung manner equally demonstrated the dramatic vigour of the piece alongside its unfailing musical inspiration. This is far from being the stiffly formal piece which Victorian manners may have made it appear. The cast is first-rate with Norma Burrowes outstanding in the name part of the god-obsessed heroine anxious to become immortal herself – a satire on George II's ambitious mistress, Lady Yarmouth. Della Jones is splendidly characterful as the jealous Juno and Anthony Rolfe Johnson gives a lyrical rather than a heroic performance as Jupiter with *Where'er you walk* most beautifully done. Ornamentation is generally executed most stylishly, and Gardiner magnetizes the whole ensemble, singers and players alike. Excellent recording.

Serse (*Xerxes;* complete).
**(*) [CBS M3 36941 (3)]. Watkinson, Esswood, Wenkel, Hendricks, Rodde, Cold, Studer, Bridier Vocal Ens., Gr. Écurie, Malgoire.

Malgoire's vigorous, often abrasive style in baroque music makes for a lively, convincing performance of one of Handel's richest operas, helped by a fine complement of solo singers. Carolyn Watkinson may not be the most characterful of singers in the high castrato role of Xerxes himself, but it is good to have the elaborate roulades so accurately sung. The celebrated *Ombra mai fù* is most beautiful. Paul Esswood is similarly reliable in the role of Arsamene (originally taken by a woman) and the counter-tenor tone is pure and true. Barbara Hendricks and Anne-Marie Rodde are both outstanding in smaller roles, and the comic episodes (most unexpected in Handel) are excellently done, Malgoire's generally heavy rhythmic pulse here paying dividends. There are detailed stylistic points one might criticize in his rendering (for example, the squeeze effects on sustained string notes), but the vitality of the performance is never in doubt, and the recording, somewhat close, is vivid too. Like the recording of *Rinaldo*, by the same forces, this set has been withdrawn in the UK.

VOCAL COLLECTIONS

Arias: (i) *Acis and Galatea: I rage, I melt, I burn . . . O ruddier than the cherry.* (ii) *Alexander's Feast: Revenge, Timotheus cries.* (iii) *Atalanta: Care selve.* (ii) *Judas Maccabaeus: I feel the Deity within . . . Arm, arm, ye brave;* (iv) *Father of heaven;* (v) *My arms . . . Sound an alarm.* (vi) *Messiah: I know that my Redeemer liveth.* (v) *Ptolemy: Silent worship.* (vii) *Radamisto: Gods all powerful.* (v) *Semele: Where'er you walk.*
(M) *** Decca SPA/*KCSP* 566. (i) Brannigan; (ii) Forbes Robinson; (iii) Greevy; (iv) Ferrier; (v) McKellar; (vi) Armstrong; (vii) Flagstad.

Enticingly titled *'Where'er you walk'* this is an outstandingly successful popular anthology. Kenneth McKellar's warmly lyrical voice is heard at its most appealing in the title song and in the equally memorable *Silent worship*. Owen Brannigan's inimitably genial *O ruddier than the cherry* is unforgettable, and Forbes Robinson, another distinguished Handelian, makes several fine contributions. Kathleen Ferrier and Bernadette Greevy have comparable nobility of line, matched by the eloquence of Sheila Armstrong's *I know that my Redeemer liveth.* The only comparative disappointment is Flagstad's 1957 recording of *Gods all powerful*, where the voice is not always fully in control. The recording is vivid throughout, and the high-level tape transfer matches the disc closely.

Arias: *Acis and Galatea: Love in her eyes sits playing. Jephtha: Waft her, angels. Judas Maccabaeus: How vain is man; Sound an alarm. Messiah: Comfort ye; Ev'ry valley. Ptolemy: Silent worship* (*Did you not hear my lady?*). *Semele: Where'er you walk. Xerxes: Ombra mai fù* (*Largo*).
(B) ** Con. CC/*CCT* 7559. McKellar, ROHCG O, Boult.

Kenneth McKellar sings in fair style, his words are clear, and Boult's accompaniment is most sympathetic and, like the voice, beautifully recorded. Handel's melisma needs a perfectly managed breath control if it is to fall into its natural shape, and here and there one senses that McKellar has not calculated the music's line perceptively. There is a suggestion, if not of strain, that the voice is being taxed to its limit at the end of a long phrase. However, one can exaggerate this: there is a great deal to enjoy here and much beautiful tone.

Arias: *Agrippina: Pur ritorno a rimirarvi. Alexander's feast: Revenge, Timotheus cries. Belshazzar: Oh memory still bitter . . . Oppress'd with never-ceasing grief. Berenice: Si tra i ceppi. Ottone: Con gelosi sospetti . . . Doppo l'orrore. Samson: Honour and arms. Saul: To him ten thousands; With rage I shall burn. Serse: Frondi tenere e belle . . . Ombra mai fù* (*Largo*). *Solomon: Prais'd be the Lord . . . When the sun o'er yonder hills. Susanna: Down my old cheeks . . . Peace, crown'd with roses.*
(M) **(*) DG Acc. 2542/*3342* 187 [2530 979]. Fischer-Dieskau, Munich CO, Stadlmair.

Opening with an arresting performance of *Revenge, Timotheus cries* from *Alexander's Feast*, this collection nevertheless emphasizes the lyricism of these excerpts rather than the drama. Fischer-Dieskau is forwardly balanced and his voice is most naturally caught, although the orchestra, within the resonant acoustic, gives a pleasing impression rather than a vividly detailed one. The cassette is well managed, although the transfer level is modest (especially on side one).

Arias: *Judas Maccabaeus: Father of Heaven. Messiah: He was despised; O thou that tellest. Samson: Return, O God of hosts.*
(M) *** Decca SPA/*KCSP* 531. Ferrier, LPO, Boult – BACH: *Arias.****

The reissue of Kathleen Ferrier's outstanding recital of Bach and Handel arias, where the new stereo-recorded accompaniment was lovingly superimposed over the old mono orchestral contribution, is most welcome. The transfer to tape has also been well done; the voice is naturally caught.

'Great choruses': Coronation anthem: Zadok the Priest. Israel in Egypt: He spake the word; He gave them hailstones. Jephtha: When his loud voice. Judas Maccabaeus: See the conquering hero comes. Messiah: Hallelujah; For unto us a child is born; Worthy is the Lamb; Amen. Saul: Gird on thy sword. Solomon: May no rash intruder.
(M) *** Decca SPA/*KCSP* 567. Handel Op. Soc. Ch. and O, Farncombe.

A most enjoyable concert, freshly sung and vividly recorded. It opens with an attractively buoyant account of *Hallelujah*, and there is an unexpected refinement in *For unto us a child is born*. Of the lesser-known choruses, *May no rash intruder* from *Solomon* with its evocative pastoral scene is particularly successful. The small orchestral group and indeed the excellent amateur choral singing readily make up in spontaneity for any lack of polish. The recording, originally made in Phase Four, is forward but has depth as well as impact, and the tape transfer is outstandingly successful, approaching demonstration quality in its vividness and clarity.

Opera arias: *Agrippina: Bel piacere. Orlando: Fammi combattere. Partenope: Funbondo spira il vento. Rinaldo: Or la tromba; Cara sposa; Venti turbini; Cor ingrato; Lascio ch'io piango mia cruda sorta. Serse: Frondi tenere; Ombra mai fù.*
**(*) Erato NUM/*MCE* 75047. Horne, Sol. Ven., Scimone.

Horne gives virtuoso performances of a wide-ranging collection of Handel arias. The flexibility of her voice in scales and trills and ornaments of every kind remains formidable, and the power is extraordinary down to the tangy chest register. The voice is spotlit against a reverberant acoustic. Purists may question some of the ornamentation, but voice-fanciers will not worry. There is a first-class chrome cassette.

OTHER COLLECTIONS

Concerti grossi in B flat, Opp. 3/1 and 6/7. Oboe concerto No. 3 in G min. Organ concerto No. 7 in F (*The Cuckoo and the Nightingale*). *Music for the Royal Fireworks. Water music* (complete). *Alcina: Dream music. Berenice: Overture. Il Pastor fido: Hunting scene. Solomon: Arrival of the Queen of Sheba.* (Vocal) *Acis and Galatea: I rage, I melt, I burn . . . O ruddier than the cherry. Jephtha: Scenes of horror; Waft her, angels. Messiah: Hallelujah.*

Ode for St Cecilia's day: The trumpet's loud clangour. (Opera) *Alcina: Verdi prati. Ezio: Se un ball'ardire.*

(M) *** Argo D 242 D 3 (3)/*K 242 K 33*. ASMF, Marriner, with Lord, Malcolm; Luxon, Hodgson, ASMF Ch.; Partridge, King's College Ch.; Greevy, Forbes Robinson.

This engaging anthology should especially suit a small collection and invite further exploration. The *Fireworks* and *Water music* are complete, and no better versions are available. The selection of oratorio and opera excerpts on the final side is particularly enjoyable. Performances and recording are characteristically reliable, and the cassettes match the discs very closely (losing a very slight degree of refinement in the *Fireworks music*). At medium price this is thoroughly recommendable.

'The glory of Handel': (i; ii) *Concerto grosso in B min., Op. 6/6: Musette.* (i; iii) *Royal Fireworks music: Overture.* (iv) *Saul: Dead march.* (i; iii) *Water music: Overture; Hornpipe.* (v) *Harpsichord suite No. 5 in E min.: Air and variations* (*Harmonious Blacksmith*). (iv; vi) *Judas Maccabaeus: See the conquering hero comes.* (vii) *Messiah: Hallelujah chorus; I know that my Redeemer liveth.*

(M) ** DG Priv. 2535/*3335* 247. (i) Berlin PO; (ii) Karajan; (iii) Kubelik; (iv) ECO, Mackerras; (v) Stadelmann; (vi) Wandsworth School Ch.; (vii) Donath, John Alldis Ch., LPO, Karl Richter.

A well-balanced collection on this DG Privilege issue, showing not just the German way with Handel but the British view too. The selection is well made, and the generally excellent performances are matched by good recording, although on cassette the choral focus is marginally less sharp than on disc.

'The world of Handel': (i; ii) *Music for the Royal Fireworks: Overture. Water music: Air; Hornpipe. Solomon: Arrival of the Queen of Sheba.* (iii) *Coronation anthem: Zadok the Priest. Judas Maccabaeus: See the conquering hero comes. Messiah:* (iv) *He was despised;* (v) *Hallelujah chorus.* (*vi*) *Samson: Let the bright Seraphim.* (i; vii) *Acis and Galatea: I rage . . . O ruddier than the cherry.* (i; viii) *Rodelinda: Dove sei* (*Art thou troubled*). (ix) *Xerxes: Ombra mai fù* (*Largo*).

(M) *** Decca SPA/*KCSP* 448. (i) ASMF; (ii) Marriner; (iii) Handel Op. Soc. Ch. and O, Farncombe; (iv) Ferrier; (v) LSO Ch., LSO, Boult; (vi) Sutherland; (vii) Forbes Robinson; (viii) Greevy; (ix) McKellar.

These are excellent performances and the recording is consistently good too. The selection is well-made and there is a matching cassette.

Hanson, Howard (1896–1981)

Symphonies Nos. 1 in E min. (*Nordic*)*; 3.*

(M) *** Mercury SRI/*MRI* 75112 [id.]. Eastman-Rochester O, composer.

We are lucky to have the Hanson symphonies made available, as the Mercury stereo catalogue is re-released here. The *First* is a sombre, powerful work. Hanson was of Swedish descent and his music has a strong individuality of idiom and colour. The *Third* is a more extrovert piece with an exultant finale that most listeners will respond to. Hanson's invention is always interesting, and his harmonic language is in no way difficult. This is highly accessible music and it is played with authority and very well recorded. The cassette transfer is fully acceptable even if it is without back-up documentation. The sound is clear, a little lacking in body compared with the disc. It needs a high-level playback to make the best effect.

Symphony No. 2 (*Romantic*)*, Op. 30;* (i) *Lament for Beowulf.*

(M) *** Mercury SRI/*MRI* 75007 [id.]. Eastman-Rochester O, (i) Eastman School of Music Ch.; composer.

Hanson's *Second Symphony* was written in 1930 for the fiftieth-anniversary season of the Boston Symphony Orchestra. It is subtitled

Romantic and is warmly appealing and melodically memorable, especially when played with such ardour and recorded with such warmth. (Incidentally, the music was used as a background score for a famous recent science-fiction film called *The Alien.*) The coupling is a cantata which makes an immediate impression, but is in fact a much more conventional piece. It is very well sung here. The cassette is welcome, even though it is supplied without notes. The transfer of the *Symphony* is successful, but the choral work lacks body and focus compared with the LP.

Symphony No. 4.
(M) *** Mercury SRI 75107 [id.]. Eastman-Rochester O, composer – PISTON: *Symphony No. 3.****

Hanson wrote his *Fourth Symphony* in 1943 as an orchestral requiem for his father. The titles of the four movements show that it draws its inspiration from the church liturgy: *Kyrie eleison*, *Requiescat*, *Dies irae* and *Lux aeterna.* Even at a first hearing it is impossible not to be impressed by this powerful work, cyclic in thematic construction, compressed (it plays for only twenty minutes), but with clearly defined movements, the first agitated and impassioned, the second eloquently expressive, the scherzo full of energy and fire, and the finale reaching a moving apotheosis. The performance under the composer's direction is deeply committed, and though the Mercury recording is not ideally expansive, it is clear and vivid, and communicates instantly.

Harris, Roy (1898–1979)

Concerto for piano and strings; Cimarron (symphonic overture); *West Point symphony* (for band).
** Varese VC 81100 [id.]. J. Harris, International String Congress O, UCLA Wind Ens.; Westbrook or composer.

The important work here is the *Concerto*, which is an arrangement of the *Piano quintet* of 1937. Roy Harris was a dominant figure in American music in the 1930s and 1940s, but his wider reputation rests almost exclusively on the *Third* and *Seventh Symphonies* – and this quintet-cum-concerto. Harris made a number of alterations in the score before recording the concerto version in 1960. It was given in Puerto Rico, and unfortunately the sound quality is wanting in transparency, and the piano itself sounds in poor condition. The composer's widow is certainly not able to secure the sensitive results that distinguished her earlier recording of it in its chamber form. The band symphony precedes the *Seventh.* It is a well-wrought piece that bears Harris's distinctive stamp, without perhaps having the freshness of his greatest work. However, this and *Cimarron* are still worth investigating, and both the performances and recordings are vital and bright.

Symphony No. 3 in one movement.
(M) **(*) CBS 61681. NYPO, Bernstein – COPLAND: *Symphony No. 3.***(*)

Roy Harris's *Third Symphony* is arguably the greatest American symphony yet to be written (with Piston's *Fourth* as a strong runner-up). Bernstein's performance with the New York Philharmonic is superbly committed, and he makes the most of the powerful eloquence of this tautly constructed and organically conceived work. He may not pack the punch of Koussevitzky's old 1942 discs that pioneered this symphony on the record scene, but he does not fall far short of it and he is much better recorded. Since this is coupled with the Copland *Third* (which originally took two sides) and itself occupied a whole side on its initial appearance, there is some loss of level and range (hence the qualification on its third star). However, this is an indispensable record for all collectors.

(i) *Piano quintet. String quartet No. 3* (*4 Preludes and fugues*).
** Varese VC 81123 [id.]. Blair Qt, (i) with J. Harris.

'Arguably the greatest single chamber work

by any American composer', says the front cover of the record about the *Piano quintet*, and it is a claim that is well vindicated. Written in 1937 as a wedding present for Harris's wife Johana, who is the soloist here, this is powerful stuff, very much in the spirit of the *Third Symphony* (1938), with the same sense of span and feeling for line. It is a noble piece and among Roy Harris's finest works. So too is the *Third Quartet*, which dates from 1939, the year which saw the first performance of the *Third Symphony*. It is in the form of four preludes and fugues and is both learned (as befits a work premiered for an international convention of musicologists) and satisfying, sinuous and sinewy. This is a masterful work which repays study. The Blair Quartet play well though one would welcome a wider dynamic range and a more flattering recorded sound. The *Piano quintet* is not as well recorded as one could wish (the piano seems diffuse and a shade unreal), but the performance is authoritative enough.

Harty, Hamilton (1879–1941)

A Comedy overture; (i) *Piano concerto in B min.;* (ii) *Violin concerto;* (ii) *In Ireland* (*fantasy*); *Irish symphony; Variations on a Dublin air; With the wild geese;* (iv) *The Children of Lir; Ode to a nightingale.*
*** Chan. Dig. DBRD/*DBTD* 4002 (4). (i) Binns, (ii) Holmes, (iii) Fleming, Kelly, (iv) Harper; Ulster O, Thomson.

Sir Hamilton Harty is better remembered as an interpreter than as a composer; conducting gradually made such inroads into his life that he spent less time composing later in his career. But his music has individuality and charm. When played (and sung) with such sympathy and expertise as in this splendid Chandos box, which collects together four records and cassettes discussed individually below, criticism is disarmed by gratitude that such agreeable repertoire should be made accessible. The recordings are consistently first-class on disc and chrome tape alike.

(i) *Piano concerto in B min.;* (ii) *In Ireland* (*Fantasy for flute, harp and orchestra*); *With the wild geese.*
❀ *** Chan. Dig. ABRD/*ABTD* 1084 [id.]. (i) Binns; (ii) Fleming, Kelly; Ulster O, Thomson.

This is the most engaging of the records issued so far in this enterprising series which is uncovering the art of a minor but rewarding talent. The *Piano concerto*, written in 1922, has strong Rachmaninovian influences (there are indelible associations with that composer's *Second Concerto* in both slow movement and finale). But the melodic freshness remains individual and in this highly sympathetic performance the work's magnetism increases with familiarity, in spite of moments of rhetoric. The *In Ireland fantasy* is full of delightful Irish melodic whimsy, especially appealing when the playing is so winning. Melodrama enters the scene in the symphonic poem, *With the wild geese*, but its Irishry asserts itself immediately in the opening theme. Again a splendid performance and demonstration-standard digital sound, both on disc and on the excellent chrome tape, where a slightly lower transfer level in the *Concerto* softens the edge on the upper strings very appropriately.

(i) *Violin concerto. A John Field suite; Londonderry air; Variations on a Dublin air.*
*** Chan. DBR/*DBT* 2001 (2). Ulster O, Thomson, (i) with Holmes – HANDEL: *Water music suite.****

(i) *Violin concerto. Variations on a Dublin air.*
*** Chan. ABR/*ABT* 1044 [id.]. (as above).

A John Field suite.
(M) *** HMV Green. ESD/*TC-ESD* 7100. E. Sinfonia, Dilkes – *Concert* (*English music*).***

A John Field suite; Londonderry air.
(M) *** Chan. CBR/*CBT* 1005. Ulster O (as above) – HANDEL: *Water music suite.****

The *Violin concerto* is an early work and comes from 1908; it was written for Szigeti, who gave the first performance. Though it has no strongly individual idiom, the invention is fresh and often touched with genuine poetry. Ralph Holmes gives a thoroughly committed account of the solo part and is well supported by an augmented Ulster Orchestra under Bryden Thomson. The other music in the Chandos collection is less impressive though thoroughly enjoyable, and readers who imagine that the orchestral playing will be indifferent (this is the début record of a provincial orchestra) will be pleasantly surprised. These are accomplished and well-recorded performances – and it is good to hear Harty's attractive arrangement of the John Field pieces again after so long an absence from the catalogue. The recording is excellent; the tape transfers are well balanced but lack the last degree of range and sparkle in the treble. As can be seen the collection has also been split up into separate issues, the second at medium price. However, those wanting the engaging *John Field suite* may prefer the excellent Dilkes version within an anthology of music by Bax, Bridge and Butterworth (see the Concerts section below).

An Irish symphony; A Comedy overture.
*** Chan. Dig. **CHAN 8314**; ABRD/*ABTD* 1027 [id.]. Ulster O, Thomson.

The *Irish symphony* dates from 1904 and arose from a competition for a suite or symphony based on traditional Irish airs, inspired by the first Dublin performance of Dvořák's *New World symphony*, 'founded upon negro melodies'! Harty's symphony won great acclaim for its excellent scoring and good craftsmanship. He revised it twice, and though it lays no claim to being a work of exceptional individuality, it is an attractive and well-wrought piece of light music. The scherzo is particularly engaging. It is extremely well played by the Ulster Orchestra under Bryden Thomson and the overture is also successful and enjoyable. The recording is absolutely first-class in every respect. The cassette is marginally less wide-ranging than the disc, but still yields excellent results.

The Children of Lir; Ode to a nightingale.
*** Chan. Dig. ABRD/*ABTD* 1051 [id.]. Harper, Ulster O, Thomson.

These two fine works span the full breadth of Harty's composing career. His setting of Keats's *Ode to a nightingale* written in 1907 reflects a time when a British (or Irish) composer could tackle boldly a grand setting of a poetic masterpiece almost too familiar. It says much for Harty's inspiration that the result is so richly convincing, a piece written for his future wife, the soprano, Agnes Nicholls. The other work, directly Irish in its inspiration, evocative in an almost Sibelian way, dates from 1939 and uses the soprano in wordless melisma, here beautifully sung by Heather Harper. The performances are excellent, warmly committed and superbly recorded. The cassette transfer of the symphonic poem on side one is made at only a modest level and lacks something in immediacy; the *Ode* is more effectively managed with a good vocal presence and natural balance.

Haslam, David (born 1940)

Juanita, the Spanish lobster.
** CRD CRD 1032/*CRDC 4032*. Morris, Northern Sinf., composer – PROKOFIEV: *Peter and the Wolf.****

Johnny Morris's tale of how Juanita, the Spanish lobster, gets caught and rescued in the nick of time has more narrative detail than story-line. It is supported by a colourful and undoubtedly tuneful score by David Haslam, but the music is not really distinguished enough for re-hearing by way of a recording, although it is not without charm. The narrator is given some songs to provide variety within the spoken text, and they have something of an *Alice in Wonderland* flavour. Johnny Morris's personality is well projected by an excellent recording, and the performance is first-rate. The cassette matches the disc closely.

Haydn, Josef (1732–1809)

Cello concertos in C and D, Hob VIIb/1–2.
*** O-L Dig. DSDL/*KDSDC* 711 [id.]. Coin, AcAM, Hogwood.
**(*) HMV ASD 3255 [Ang. S/*4XS* 37193]. Rostropovich, ASMF, Marriner.
**(*) CBS 76978/*40*- [M/*MT* 36674]. Yo Yo Ma, ECO, Garcia.
**(*) HMV Dig. ASD/*TCC-ASD* 4157. Tortelier, Wurttemberg CO, Faerber.
** HMV Dig. ASD/*TCC-ASD* 4286 [Ang. DS/*4XDS* 37843]. Harrell, ASMF, Marriner.

(i) *Cello concerto in C;* (ii) *Horn concertos Nos. 1–2 in D.*
(M) *** Decca Jub. JB/*KJBC* 121 [(d) Lon. 6419]. (i) Rostropovich, ECO, Britten; (ii) Tuckwell, ASMF, Marriner.

Cello concerto in D.
(M) *** Ph. Seq. 6527/*7311* 124. Gendron, LPO, Casals – BOCCHERINI: *Cello concerto.****
(M) ** Uni. UNS 207. Tortelier, London CO – C. P. E. BACH: *Concerto.***

The discovery of Haydn's early *C major Cello concerto* in Prague in the early 1960s provided a marvellous addition to the limited cello repertory. For some this concerto is even more attractive than the well-known D major work that for a time was fathered on Anton Kraft instead of Haydn. Although usually coupled together, currently the best way to acquire these concertos is by choosing the two separate medium-priced issues, on Decca Jubilee and Philips Sequenza, respectively. Rostropovich's earlier performance of the *C major Concerto* is undoubtedly romantic, and some may feel he takes too many liberties in the slow movement. But tempi are well judged and, with marvellously sympathetic conducting from Britten, Rostropovich's expressiveness and beauty of tone colour are bewitching. The 1964 Decca recording is of vintage quality and the cassette transfer is in the demonstration class. The coupling of first-class versions (originally issued on Argo – see below) of the *Horn concertos*, by Tuckwell in peak form, is self-recommending.

In the *D major Concerto* Gendron is right on form, and the stylishness of his phrasing, coupled to complete security of intonation, make for an admirable performance of this attractive concerto, especially when one bears in mind that the coupling is the authentic original version of Boccherini's *Concerto*. Pablo Casals's sympathetic handling of the orchestral contribution plays no little part in making this record the success that it undoubtedly is. The cassette is well managed, full and clear.

For those wanting the two concertos paired together, the young French soloist, Christophe Coin, provides a ready answer. He is a superb soloist and, provided the listener has no reservations about the use of original instruments, Hogwood's accompaniments are equally impressive. The style is not aggressively abrasive, but gives extra clarity and point to the music, not least in the breathtakingly brilliant account of the finale of the *C major Concerto*. Certainly no fresher or more vital performance of these two works has been put on disc, although Coin's own cadenzas – undoubtedly stylish – are on the long side. Excellent sound, although the focus is slightly cleaner on disc than the matching chrome tape.

Rostropovich's earlier recording of the *C major Concerto* with Britten was brilliant enough, but at even faster speeds in the outer movements his virtuosity in the HMV performance is even more astonishing. With warmer, more modern and intimate recording some may prefer this account, especially as it is aptly coupled with the *D major Concerto*; but quite apart from the extra haste (which brings its moments of breathless phrasing), Rostropovich's style has acquired a degree of self-indulgence in the warmth of expressiveness.

Yo Yo Ma provides an attractive alternative to Rostropovich's recording of the two Haydn concertos, both of them works of the sharpest imagination. His approach is more restrained in expression, not so lovingly moulded in the lyrical slow movements, a degree more detached. The result is not so compellingly individual, but many will prefer directness in music firmly belonging to the classical eighteenth century. Apart from one or two odd points of balance, the recording is clean and full.

Tortelier gives a warmly expressive performance of the two concertos, more relaxed than some rivals, and is sympathetically, if not always immaculately, accompanied by the Württemberg Chamber Orchestra. Clear yet warm digital sound to match and a chrome cassette of excellent quality with the solo instrument clearly focused.

Harrell at least as much as Rostropovich seeks to turn these elegant eighteenth-century concertos into big virtuoso pieces. The result is strong and impressive, helped by beautifully played accompaniments, but rather fails to hang together, when touches of over-romantic expressiveness intrude. Cadenzas are distractingly and unstylishly long. Very full digital recording, though balance favours the soloist. The cassette is transferred on iron-oxide stock and the upper focus is less sharp than on disc, although the balance overall is satisfactory.

Tortelier's earlier Unicorn performance is a good but not a memorable one. There is some lack of momentum and spontaneity in the first movement, although the slow movement is nicely done and the finale has plenty of life. The accompaniments, directed by the soloist, are good, and the recording is fair, with presence but no special lustre.

Horn concertos Nos. 1–2; Acide e Galatea: Overture; 6 German dances.

*** Argo ZRG 5498 [id.]. Tuckwell, ASMF, Marriner.

Haydn's *Horn concerto No. 1* is a fine work, worthy to stand alongside the four Mozart concertos. It is technically more difficult than any of these, especially as played by Barry Tuckwell with a profusion of ornaments and trills. These help to lighten the basically rather square main theme of the opening movement, the soloist adding asides, witty or decorative. The finale is in the 'hunting' style of the period. But the highlight of the work is the *Adagio*, a beautifully shaped cantilena for the soloist. The *Second Concerto* is less memorable. It has an attractive first movement with a basic dotted rhythm; the slow movement, not unlike that of the *First Concerto* in style, has a touch of melancholy to its mood, but seems a trifle over-long. The authorship of this work is not proved.

Tuckwell has recorded these works twice, first for Argo in 1966 and again for HMV (now deleted). The Argo versions are also available, more economically, on a Decca Jubilee reissue attractively coupled with Rostropovich in the *C major Cello concerto* – see above. They have the advantage of particularly stylish accompaniments from Marriner and the ASMF with detail beautifully pointed. The recording too is from a vintage Argo period. The fill-ups on the full-priced disc, above, are slight, but the playing in the *Dances* and *Overture* is a wonderful example of sheer style, yet readily conveys the players' enjoyment of this innocent but rewarding music.

(i) *Horn concerto No. 1 in D;* (ii) *Organ concerto No. 1 in C;* (iii) *Trumpet concerto in E flat.*

(M) *** Decca VIV/*KVIC* 12 [Lon. STS/5-15446]. ASMF, Marriner, with (i) Tuckwell, (ii) Preston, (iii) Stringer.

An appropriate budget-priced realignment of familiar performances, generally well recorded on disc (though the cassette focus of the solo instruments is less agreeable). Tuckwell plays the *Horn concerto* superbly, particularly the beautiful *Adagio*. The *Organ concerto* is not one of Haydn's most memorable works, but Simon Preston and Marriner are persuasive: the registration is vivid and the accompaniment spirited. Alan Stringer favours a forthright open timbre for the *Trumpet concerto*, but he plays the famous slow movement graciously and the orchestral playing has striking elegance and finesse. Good value on disc, but the tape needs remastering.

KEYBOARD CONCERTOS

3 Keyboard concertos, Hob XVIII/F2; 3 and 11; 3 Keyboard concertinos, Hob XIV/11 and 12; Hob XVIII/4; (i) *Double concerto for violin and keyboard in F, Hob XVIII/6. 9 Divertimenti, Hob XIV/1; C2; 3; 4; 7; 8; 9; 11 and 13.*

*** Ph. 6725 011 (4) [id.]. Koopman (harpsichord), (i) Huggett; Amsterdam Bar. O or Amsterdam Mus. Ant.

This set complements the pair of discs Ton Koopman made on the organ of St Bartholomew at Beek-Ubbergen near Nijmegen (see below). Here Koopman presents all the remaining concertos, save for those listed in the Hoboken catalogue which are no longer thought to be authentic Haydn. They include eleven small concertos from the 1760s called either *Divertimenti* or *Concertini*, which are of little real substance and they make undemanding listening. There are also four longer concertos including the famous *D major* and the *Double concerto for violin, keyboard and strings*, Hob XVIII/6 (also included in Accardo's set of the violin concertos). As sound, these recordings could hardly be bettered: the balance is finely judged and the acoustic warm. Detail registers perfectly but the listener is not placed too close to the performers, and surfaces are impeccably silent. The performances themselves are highly accomplished, though occasionally Koopman could allow the music to unfold at a more leisurely pace. No reservations, however, need diminish the recommendation, save for the warning that this is not the best Haydn.

Piano concerto in D, H.XVIII/2.
*** Decca SXL/*KSXC* 6952 [Lon. CS 7180/5-]. De Larrocha, L. Sinf., Zinman – BACH: *Concerto No. 5*; MOZART: *Concerto No. 12.****

With clean, crisp articulation, Alicia de Larrocha obviously seeks to evoke the fortepiano. The outer movements are strongly characterized, and the crisp rhythmic snap of the 'gypsy' finale is a joy. David Zinman's accompaniment is excellent and the scale of the recording is highly effective, the resonance giving breadth to the orchestral group. The cassette transfer is of high quality, a fraction over-bright. But whether heard on LP or tape, this is a very rewarding coupling.

Keyboard concertos: in D; in F; in G, H.XVIII/2–3 and 9.
**(*) Erato STU 70989. Jaccottet (harpsichord), Lausanne Instrumental Ens., Corbóz.

Although the *D major Concerto* comes off much better on the piano, it is effectively played here by Christiane Jaccottet on the harpsichord. She is forwardly balanced, but that is inevitable given the realities of the instrument, and few would find it unacceptable. The *G major Concerto* is less successful, but the other works are so persuasive in the hands of these Swiss artists that collectors are unlikely to be disappointed by this issue. None of these pieces is essential Haydn, but of the recordings now on the market this is the one that shows them in the best light. The sound is extremely good.

Oboe concerto in C.
(B) **(*) PRT GSGC/*ZCGC* 2007. Rothwell, Hallé O, Barbirolli – CORELLI and PERGOLESI: *Concertos.****

Of the three concertos on this delectable disc the Haydn, because of its very positive classicism, suits Miss Rothwell's style marginally less well than the other two. But Sir John's strong opening has all the classical verve anyone could want, and in the first movement his wife's delicacy makes a delicious foil for the masculine orchestral sound; in particular the phrasing of the second subject is enchanting. The slow movement too is well brought off, and it is only in the finale that, for all the pleasure of the feminine tessitura, others have shown that a stronger style is even more effective. But the rest of this collection is treasurable and, taken as it is, the performance offers much pleasure in its own way. The 1958 recording is resonant and full, though on cassette pianissimo passages are not always texturally completely secure.

Organ concertos, H.XVIII/1, 2, 5, 7, 8 and 10.
*** Ph. 6769 065 (2) [id.]. Koopman, Amsterdam Bar. O.

3 Organ concertos in C, H.XVIII/1, 5 and 10.
*** Erato STU/*MCE* 70998. Alain, Bournemouth Sinf., Guschlbauer.

Ton Koopman has chosen the organ of St Bartholomew at Beek-Ubbergen near Nijmegen which is reproduced to vivid effect in this excellently engineered pair of discs. The sonorities blend perfectly with those of the Amsterdam Baroque Orchestra and the performances have great personality and spirit. This is not great music but, played like this, it affords much stimulus and pleasure.

Marie-Claire Alain offers the three best-known *C major Concertos*. They are agreeably lively and inventive and the baroque orchestration with trumpets adds plenty of extra colour. It is difficult to imagine them being presented more effectively than they are on this Erato issue. Marie-Claire Alain's registration is admirable and both solo playing and accompaniments are alert and sparkling. The sound is fresh and there is a bright matching cassette.

Trumpet concerto in E flat.
(M) ** Uni. RHS 337. Lang, Northern Sinf., Seaman – HUMMEL and NERUDA: *Concertos.***

(i) *Trumpet concerto in E flat; L'incontro improvviso: overture; Sinfonia concertante in B flat* (for oboe, bassoon, violin, cello and orchestra).
*** Erato STU/*MCE* 70652 [id.]. (i) André; Bamberg SO, Guschlbauer.

William Lang, like Alan Stringer (see above – coupled with horn and oboe concertos), favours a forthright, open tone although Lang also has a broadness of production that shows his brass-band background – there are hints of the cornet here. No doubt such a sound is nearer the primitive instrument Haydn would have known. Maurice André's crisp articulation is more sophisticated: this is trumpeting of the highest order. Moreover he uses a first-class cadenza in the first movement to show his mettle, and the finale has a similar sparkling bravura. In the *Andante* André's warmly flexible line and creamy colouring are irresistible. Unfortunately his accompanying orchestra is none too clearly caught by the resonant sound of the Erato recording, and the Unicorn disc scores here with its clean orchestral image.

But what gives the Erato disc a very special appeal is the splendid double coupling. The three-part Italian overture for *L'incontro improvviso* with its Turkish percussion parts reminds one of Mozart's *Il Seraglio*. This is splendidly played and well recorded, as is the vivacious account of the *Sinfonia concertante*, with warm, sparkling solo playing and a most gracious slow movement. This makes a most attractive collection.

Violin concerto in C, H.VIIa/1.
(M) *** Ph. 6527/*7311* 120. Grumiaux, ECO, Leppard – BACH: *Violin concertos.****
** CBS Dig. 37796 [id.]. Lin, Minnesota O, Marriner – VIEUXTEMPS: *Concerto No. 5.***

Violin concertos: in C; in A; in G, H.VIIa/1, 3 and 4; Double concerto for violin and harpsichord in F, H.XVIII/6; Sinfonia concertante in B flat, H.I/105.
*** Ph. 6769/*7643* 059 (3) [id.]. Accardo, Canino, Black, Sheen, Schiff, ECO.

The three *Violin concertos* are all early; the *C major*, written for Tomasini, is probably the best. The other two have only come into the limelight since the war. In the *G major*, Accardo follows the critical edition rather than the Melk autograph published by the Haydn-Mozart Presse, and omits the two horns listed in the Breitkopf 1771 catalogue. Not that this is of any great importance, for although Accardo plays with great elegance and charm, it would be idle to pretend that this is great music. The same goes for the *Double concerto for violin and harpsichord*, which is of relatively slender musical interest. The *Sinfonia concertante* is of course a totally different affair, and the playing here splendidly relaxed and musical. The soloists are a shade forward perhaps, but the quality is life-like, with impeccable surfaces on the discs. The cassette transfers too are admirably faithful. The second tape, containing the *Violin concertos*, offers demonstration quality.

In Grumiaux's sensitive hands Haydn's slight but engaging *C major Concerto* is made to sound like a minor masterpiece. The *Adagio* has a serenade-like quality and Grumiaux's playing has a gentle innocence that captures its spirit perfectly. The buoyant finale makes a fine contrast, lightweight and sparkling.

With first-class recording – dating from 1964 but sounding as fresh as the day it was made – this is highly recommendable, with an excellent cassette to match the disc.

Cho-Liang Lin is a Taiwanese-born player of formidable technical prowess and flair. His style is perhaps less suited to the Haydn than Accardo, Grumiaux and others who have recorded this, for his playing is just a bit too high-powered. This is an artist-orientated record related to this brilliant young player's capability and designed to show him to good advantage, for the coupling has little appeal to the collector not following his career. The sound is well-lit but not over-bright and the balance musically judged, even if the soloist is a shade too big.

SYMPHONIES

Symphonies Nos. 1–19.
(M)⊛*** Decca HDNA 1/6 [Lon. STS 15310/15]. Philh. Hungarica, Dorati.

Antal Dorati's complete set of Haydn symphonies is one of the gramophone's finest achievements, in many ways an achievement for the 1970s that can be justly compared to the first complete stereo recording of Wagner's *Ring* cycle made by the same record company a decade earlier. Our rosette is awarded to the complete series.

Though Haydn's earliest symphonies make such a long list, there is not an immature one among them. By his own calculation he did not start writing symphonies until he was twenty-five. The urgent crescendo which opens *Symphony No. 1* at once establishes the voltage of inspiration, and from then on there is no suspicion of a power failure. These works – antedated by one or two works that are later in the Breitkopf numbering – came from the early Esterházy period, 1759–63, and show the young, formidably gifted composer working at full stretch, above all in the relatively well-known trilogy of symphonies, *Le Matin*, *Le Midi* and *Le Soir*, with their marvellous solos for members of the Esterházy orchestra. Dorati left these symphonies until well on in his great recording project, and the combination of exhilaration and stylishness is irresistible. Excellent recording.

Symphonies Nos. 1 in D; 2 in C; 4, 10 and 15 in D; 18 in G; 37 in C.
(M) *** Saga HAYDN 1 (3). L'Estro Armonico, Solomons.

It is well known that the generally accepted numbering of Haydn's symphonies contains many anomalies. The composer himself stated very clearly which was No. 1, but a dramatic discovery after the Second World War – original parts for the first twenty-five symphonies, which had lain hidden in a castle library in Hungary – indicated the order of those at least. Derek Solomons directs a band of authentic-music specialists (the membership overlapping with other groups in London) in performances that are alert and refreshing. The smallness of the string band and the intimacy of the acoustic are apt, adding to the bite of the performances, nicely sprung and with non-vibrato strings rarely if ever squeezing too painfully. What emerges from this sequence – as in Dorati's conventional cycle from his much larger-scaled readings – is that from the start Haydn's symphonic writing was fully mature and strongly imaginative.

Symphonies Nos. 3 in G; 5 in A; 11 in E flat; 27 in G; 32 in C; 33 in C; in B flat (Morzin symphonies).
(M) *** Saga HAYDN 2 (3). L'Estro Armonico, Solomons.

The second instalment of this series of early Haydn symphonies recorded in chronological order with authentically intimate forces is as successful as the first. In terms of musical vitality Dorati is more compelling in these works, but the rivalry is hardly direct. As before, L'Estro Armonico uses original instruments and vibrato-less string sound very convincingly, and generally sweetly, well caught by the excellent recording.

Symphonies Nos. 6 in D (Le Matin); 7 in C (Le Midi); 8 in G (Le Soir).
*** Ph. Dig. **411 441-2**; 6514/*7337* 076 [id.]. ASMF, Marriner.

Although Marriner and the Academy can at times seem bland, this performance of the three symphonies Haydn composed not long after taking up his appointment at the Esterházy court in 1761 has plenty of character. This has been a popular coupling over the years, but the Marriner set is probably the best we have had for some time: it is generally fresher and more polished than the rival set from the Prague Chamber Orchestra and Bernhard Klee (now deleted). The cassette transfer is pleasing, but – as so often with Philips – its upper range is less sharp than on the LP.

Symphonies Nos. 20–35.
(M) *** Decca HDNB 7/12 [Lon. STS 15257/62]. Philh. Hungarica, Dorati.

Because of the idiosyncrasies of the Breitkopf numbering, this sequence of symphonies includes one work later than the rest, *Lamentatione*, a transitional symphony leading into the dark, intense manner of Haydn's middle period. It gives marvellous perspective to the rest, all of them fascinating and many of them masterly. What an amazing sound Haydn creates, for instance, by using two cors anglais in the opening chorale of the *Philosopher*, almost like an anticipation of *Zauberflöte*. But even the early festive symphonies, like Nos. 32 and 33, both in C major with trumpets and timpani, have their individual marks of inspiration, for example in the C minor slow movement of No. 33. As in the rest of the cycle, Dorati's performances, helped by vivid recording, have you listening on from one symphony to another, compulsively following the composer's career.

Symphonies Nos. 22 in E flat (Philosopher); 43 in E flat (Mercury); 44 in E min. (Trauersymphonie); 48 in C (Maria Theresia); 49 in F min. (La Passione); 55 in E flat (Schoolmaster); 59 in A (Fire); 85 in B flat (La Reine); 94 in G (Surprise); 96 in D (Miracle); 100 in G (Military); 103 in E flat (Drum Roll).
(M) *** Ph. 6768 003 (6). ASMF, Marriner.

This set is superbly recorded and splendidly played, and readers wanting this compilation of named symphonies need not hesitate. The orchestral playing is more polished and urbane than in rival accounts by Dorati and others, though ultimately there is an earthier quality in the music than Marriner perceives. But despite the hint of blandness, these are satisfying performances that will give much pleasure.

Symphonies Nos. 22 in E flat (Philosopher); 48 in C (Maria Theresia).
(M) **(*) Ph. Seq. 6527/*7311* 096. ECO, Leppard.

This reissue is a re-coupling. These are warm, gracious performances, more notable for their elegant playing than for any special degree of sparkle. In No. 22 Leppard responds to Haydn's 'walking style' in the opening *Adagio* with clear phrasing and crisp, even accents, but he brings out the unusual colouring, featuring cor anglais. In the *Maria Theresia symphony* trumpets are used rather than alto horns, so that those familiar with the Dorati performances will register surprise. However, in every musical aspect these are both fine performances and the remastered recording sounds admirably fresh, with a matching cassette offering splendid life and range.

Symphonies Nos. 22 in E flat (Philosopher); 55 in E flat (Schoolmaster).
**(*) Ph. 9500 198 [id.]. ASMF, Marriner.

Very good performances, excellently recorded. The *Philosopher* comes off very well and, generally speaking, is to be preferred to Bernhard Klee's neat, well-trimmed account with the Prague Chamber Orchestra (now deleted). The *Schoolmaster* too is nicely characterized and has greater charm than in Dorati's version on Decca. There is a hint of blandness in the second movement, but the performance as a whole undoubtedly gives pleasure. The recording has freshness and refinement of detail, good perspective and a warm but not over-reverberant acoustic.

Symphonies Nos. 31 in D (Horn-signal); 45 in F sharp min. (Farewell); 73 in D (Hunt); 82 in C (The Bear); 83 in G min. (The Hen); 92 in G (Oxford); 101 in D (Clock); 104 in D (London).
(M) **(*) Ph. 6768 066 (4). ASMF, Marriner.

Generally speaking, this set is distinguished by lively, musicianly playing that cannot fail to give satisfaction, even though none of these performances can be numbered among Marriner's best. He has set himself high standards, and though there is much to admire in each of these performances, all fall short of real distinction, just as, at the same time, they rise above the mere routine.

Symphonies Nos. 31 in D (Horn-signal); 73 in D (Hunt).
** Ph. 9500 518/*7300 674* [id.]. ASMF, Marriner.

A logical pairing that has a certain wit. The performances are musicianly and well shaped, but a little faceless. Even on a second hearing the *Horn-signal* gave relatively little pleasure, though it would be difficult to fault the players. Excellent recording; the cassette transfer, made at a characteristically modest level, produces smooth natural sound, without quite the upper range of the LP.

Symphonies Nos. 35 in B flat; 38 in C (Echo); 39 in G min.; 49 in F min. (La Passione); 58 in F; 59 in A (Fire).
**(*) CBS D3 37861/*40-* [I3M/*I3T* 37861]. L'Estro Armonico, Solomons.

Like Derek Solomons's earlier recordings of fourteen of Haydn's very first *Morzin symphonies* for Saga, this set from 1766–8 is recorded in chronological order. The style (using original instruments and a small band) is fresh and lively, though ensemble is not always immaculate and not everyone will like the 'squeeze' style of slow movements with vibrato virtually eliminated. On their intimate scale these make an attractive alternative, well recorded, to the Dorati series on Decca. The chrome cassettes are slightly disappointing, having a restricted upper range compared with the discs (because of the resonance).

Symphonies Nos. 36–48.
(M) *** Decca HDNC 13/18 [Lon. STS 15249/54]. Philh. Hungarica, Dorati.

Despite the numbering, this set of symphonies arguably includes the very first work of all, No. 37 in C, revealing – as H. C. Robbins Landon points out in his absorbing commentary – 'impeccable craftsmanship and enormous energy'. The 3/8 finale is exhilarating, but then all of these works as played by Dorati and the Philharmonia Hungarica reflect the composer's unquenchable genius. This particular sequence brings the frontier in Dorati's interpretations between using and not using harpsichord continuo. He switches over in the middle of No. 40 – not illogically when the finale is a fugue in which continuo would only be muddling. The last three named symphonies make a superb trio of works, leading into the searing intensity of Haydn's so-called *Sturm und Drang* period. Unfailingly lively performances and first-rate recording.

Symphonies Nos. 44 in E min. (Trauer-symphonie); 49 in F min. (La Passione).
*** Ph. 9500 199 [id.]. ASMF, Marriner.

Superlative playing from Marriner and the Academy: even among their many fine Haydn couplings this stands out. The wonderfully expressive string phrasing of the opening *Adagio* of No. 49 is superbly contrasted with the genial and buoyant rhythms of the second-movement *Allegro*. There is some excellent horn-playing in both works, almost self-effacing in its delicacy. But perhaps the highlight of this splendid coupling is the tender way Marriner shapes the radiantly elegiac slow movement of No. 44, which Haydn is reported to have chosen for performance at his funeral (hence the title). A discreet harpsichord continuo is used in both symphonies. The contrast between repose and restless vitality which is at the heart of both these works is the hallmark of the performances, which are recorded with characteristic Philips naturalness and glow.

Symphonies Nos. 45 in F sharp min. (Farewell); 101 in D (Clock).
*** Ph. 9500 520/*7300 676* [id.]. ASMF, Marriner.

Very satisfactory accounts of the *Farewell* and the *Clock*, vital and intelligent. The Philips engineers produce outstanding quality, and the playing of the Academy is very spruce and clean. Marriner has slightly more finesse than Dorati but not quite so much character and earthiness; however, the honours are pretty evenly divided. The tape transfers are made at a moderate level, and a slight bass cut improves the balance. Then there is good detail and no lack of life at the top.

Symphonies Nos. 46 in B; 47 in G.
*** DG 2531/*3301* 324 [id.]. ECO, Barenboim.

Sweet-toned, cultured and vital performances of two of the so-called *Sturm und Drang* symphonies. No. 46 could perhaps with advantage be more severe than Barenboim makes it, but generally speaking there is no cause here to withhold a three-star recommendation, for both playing and recording are of the highest quality. The cassette transfer is smooth and pleasing; the sound is very slightly bland in the slow movements.

Symphonies Nos. 49–56.
(M) *** Decca HDND 19/22 [Lon. STS 15127/30]. Philh. Hungarica, Dorati.

These eight symphonies show Haydn in the full flight of his *Sturm und Drang* period – tense, exhilarating works full of anguished minor-key arguments that belie the old idea of jolly 'Papa' Haydn working patiently for his princely master. The emotional basis of these works points forward very clearly to the romantic movement which within decades was to overtake music. Indeed the literary movement which gives the appellation *Sturm und Drang* itself marks the stirring of romanticism. To hear a sequence of eight such works as this is to experience their historical impact in the way that Prince Esterházy and his court must have done. The impact is the more powerful because of the splendid notes written by Professor Robbins Landon, whose comments are fascinating at every level, whether for the specialist or for the beginner. Such works as *La Passione* are already reasonably well-known, but the others are no less compelling, and in vigorous, committed performances by Dorati and his orchestra of Hungarian exiles it is impossible to be bored for a moment. The recording is outstandingly vivid.

Symphonies Nos. 57–64.
(M) *** Decca HDNE 23/6 [Lon. STS 15131/4]. Philh. Hungarica, Dorati.

It may help that three of these middle-period symphonies have nicknames. All in major keys, they represent the comparatively extrovert period immediately after Haydn had worked out the bitterest tensions of the *Sturm und Drang* period. As in the other albums, Professor Robbins Landon's notes provide an ideal preparation for listening with a historical ear, and even his tendency to underestimate the merits of the lesser-known works makes one enjoy them the more out of defiance for his authority. Even if these are not quite so interesting as the surrounding works, they maintain an amazing standard of invention, with such movements as the *Adagio* and 6/8 finale of No. 61 endlessly fascinating. The only serious flaw in Dorati's interpretations – and it is something to note in a few of the symphonies in other albums too – is his tendency to take minuets rather slowly. In many of them Haydn had already moved halfway towards a scherzo. With amazing consistency the Philharmonia Hungarica maintains its alertness, never giving the suspicion of merely running through the music. Excellent recording to match the rest of this outstanding series.

Symphonies Nos. 60 in C (Il Distratto); 63 in C (La Roxelane).
*** Ph. Dig. 6514/*7337* 113 [id.]. ASMF, Marriner.

Both symphonies derive from the theatrical entertainments presented at Esterháza in the mid-1770s. The first movement of No. 60 served as the overture to Jean-François Regnard's *Il Distrait* and the remaining five were interspersed in the five Acts. No. 63 has a more complex background: it derives from incidental music to *Soliman II* or the *Three Sultanas of Charles-Simon Favart*, for whose first movement Haydn drew on the overture to his opera, *Il mondo della luna*. He used an earlier minuet and trio and then added a set of variations called *'La Roxelane'* after the heroine of the play. Haydn put it into its definitive form as late as 1779, adding a new minuet and finale. Marriner gives us the first version of the work as reconstituted by H. C. Robbins Landon with trumpets and timpani restored. (Dorati recorded the definitive version in his complete cycle and the present version in a two-disc set of Appendices.) The performances here are eminently lively and highly polished, though in *Il Distratto* Dorati has the greater sense of theatre. By and large, however, the orchestral playing of the Academy is more finished and the recording is well balanced and finely detailed. The chrome cassette is disappointing and lacking in range at the top end of the spectrum.

Symphonies Nos. 65–72.
(M) *** Decca HDNF 27/30 [Lon. STS 15135/8]. Philh. Hungarica, Dorati.

This was the first album of symphonies to be issued in Decca's integral series, and with works that had previously been not just neglected but absurdly underrated, the dynamic tone of the whole project was at once brought home. This was not the first time that a complete series of Haydn symphonies was planned – the late Max Goberman in New York had started one – but with superb notes by Professor Robbins Landon the attractions of the Dorati cycle at once set a new standard. One was forced to take one's bearings in a comparatively uncharted sector of the Haydn globe, and the result was exhilarating. Even Robbins Landon underestimates the mastery of these symphonies from the period after Haydn had worked *Sturm und Drang* tensions out of his system but before he expanded into the international world of music-making with the *Paris* and *London symphonies*. With the exception of an occasional movement (No. 69/II or No. 70/III) this music is riveting, and even where the actual material is conventional, as in the theatrical first movement of No. 69 (nicknamed '*Laudon*' after a field marshal), the treatment is sparkling, with many surprising turns. The recording matches the vividness of the playing.

Symphonies Nos. 73–81.
(M) *** Decca HDNG 31/4 [Lon. STS 15182/5]. Philh. Hungarica, Dorati.

This collection, unlike the previous albums in Dorati's series, contains works written more or less consecutively over a compact period of just over four years. Robbins Landon emphasizes that these are much more courtly works than their *Sturm und Drang* predecessors, and that Haydn was regarding the symphony at this time as a side concern, being mainly concerned with opera. Even so, what will strike the non-specialist listener is that whatever the courtly manners of the expositions (and even there moods vary, particularly in the two minor-key symphonies) the development sections give a flashing reminder of Haydn's tensest manner. Kaleidoscopic sequences of minor keys whirl the argument in unexpected directions. On this showing, even when he was not really trying, Haydn was incapable of being boring, and some of these works are in every way remarkable in their forward-looking reminders, often of Mozart's most visionary works. At the time Haydn had just made contact with Mozart, and though the direct similarities can only be accidental on chronological evidence, the influence is already clear. The performances achieve an amazing degree of intensity, with alertness maintained throughout.

Symphonies Nos. 82–7 (*Paris*)*; 88–91; Sinfonia concertante in B flat.*
(M) *** Decca HDNH 35/40 [Lon. STS 15229/34]. Philh. Hungarica, Dorati.

Dorati's versions almost always outshine their direct rivals in sparkling performances, vividly recorded. Not just the set of six *Paris symphonies* (Nos. 82–7), with which this album begins, but the other Paris-based works too are given fresh, stylish performances by Dorati and his indefatigable band of Hungarian exiles. Even the least-known of the Paris set, No. 84, has a first movement of the most delicate fantasy, and No. 89 is rounded off with an extraordinarily witty movement that looks straight forward to the fun of Johann Strauss's polkas, with a delicious *portamento* in each reprise down to the main theme.

Symphonies Nos. 82–7 (*Paris symphonies*).
**(*) Ph. 6725/*7655* 012 (3). ASMF, Marriner.

** DG Dig. 2741/*3382* 005 (3). Berlin PO, Karajan.
** DG Dig. 2532/*3302* 037 (*Nos. 82; 87*); 2532/*3302* 038 (*Nos. 84; 85*); 2532/*3302* 039 (*Nos. 83; 86*) (from above, cond. Karajan).

From Marriner spirited and well-played accounts of the *Paris symphonies*, distinguished by excellent ensemble and keen articulation. Nos. 86 and 87 are digital recordings, the remainder being analogue. They have a certain charm that eluded the Karajan set, which is also superbly played and recorded but somewhat wanting in grace and courtliness. It is possible to imagine performances of greater character and personality than these (in the slow movements in particular, there is a certain blandness) but, generally speaking, they are very lively and musical and a good alternative to the Dorati set. In the cassette format, 86 and 87 are on chrome tape and the remainder on iron oxide, which on some machines produce an excessive bass resonance.

Karajan's set is big-band Haydn with a vengeance; but of course the orchestra of the *Concert de la Loge Olympique* for which Haydn wrote these symphonies was a large band, consisting of forty violins and no fewer than ten double-basses. It goes without saying that the quality of the orchestral playing is superb, and Karajan is meticulous in observing repeats and in his attention to detail. There is no trace of self-indulgence or mannerisms. However, these are rather heavy-handed accounts, closer to Imperial Berlin than Paris; generally speaking, the slow movements are kept moving and the minuets are very slow indeed, full of pomp and majesty – and, at times, too grand. In spite of the clean if slightly cool digital recordings, which have splendid presence, these performances are too charmless and wanting in grace to be wholeheartedly recommended. There is no appreciable difference in quality between discs and cassettes.

Symphonies Nos. 83 in G min. (*La Poule*); *85 in B flat* (*La Reine*).
(B) ** PRT GSGC/*ZCGC* 2024. SW German PO, Von Pitamic.

Keenly rhythmic playing here by a relatively small group. Some might feel the manner a little stiff at times, but the articulation is polished and not without elegance. With bright, lively (1970) recording, on disc and cassette alike (the second side of the tape needs a degree of taming) this music-making projects very positively.

Symphonies Nos. 86 in D; 98 in B flat.
*** Ph. 9500 678/*7300 773* [id.]. Concg. O, Colin Davis.

Superbly alive and refined playing from the Concertgebouw Orchestra and Sir Colin Davis. This Haydn series is one of the most distinguished things Davis has given us in recent years, and its blend of brilliance and sensitivity, wit and humanity gives these issues a special claim on the collector. There is no trace of routine in these performances and no failure of imagination. The recordings are first-class, and one is tempted to say that although both these symphonies have had outstanding performances on record (in the case of No. 86 one thinks of the pre-war Bruno Walter and for No. 98 there are Beecham and Jochum), these are second to none and arguably finer. The tape transfer is one of Philips's best, offering warm, rich sound with excellent bloom. The strings are fresh, and only the last degree of upper range is missing in comparison with the disc.

Symphonies Nos. 87 in A; 103 in E flat (*Drum Roll*).
*** Ph. 9500 303/*7300 589* [id.]. Concg. O, Sir Colin Davis.
*** CRD CRD 1100/*CRDC 4100* [id.]. Bournemouth Sinf., Ronald Thomas.

No one sampling these Davis performances will be in any doubt as to the distinction of the playing and the stature of the readings. Marriner's account of the *Drum Roll* coupled with No. 100 (the *Military*) is superbly recorded and played with consummate musicianship, and might well be preferred by those who resist the big-band approach to Haydn. But Sir Colin Davis's account seems of an altogether higher order of sensitivity and imagination, almost in the Beecham tradition. Phrasing is the soul of music-making, and

Davis inspires the great Dutch orchestra to playing that exhibits delicacy and vitality and phrasing that breathes naturally. The cassette is marginally less fresh and wide-ranging than the disc, but there is little to choose between them.

Thomas and the Bournemouth Sinfonietta also have a winning way with Haydn, and like the companion disc of No. 88 and No. 104, this coupling of one *Paris symphony* and one *London symphony* provides an exhilarating combination of chamber scale and richness of tone, with rhythms beautifully pointed. The recording is outstanding, warm and vivid. No. 103 starts with the drumroll of the title played at a commanding fortissimo, as suggested in H. C. Robbins Landon's Breitkopf edition. The chrome tape is lively to the point of fierceness and the treble needs cutting well back.

Symphonies Nos. 88 in G; 104 in D (*London*).
*** CRD CRD 1070/*CRDC* 4070. Bournemouth Sinf., Ronald Thomas.

A much-admired record which has received wide acclaim both for the quality of the performances and for the sound. Although the orchestra is smaller than the Concertgebouw or LPO, the playing has great freshness and vitality; indeed it is the urgency of musical feeling that Ronald Thomas conveys which makes up for the last ounce of finesse. They are uncommonly dramatic in the slow movement of No. 88 and bring great zest and eloquence to the rest of the symphony too. In No. 104 they are not always as perceptive as Sir Colin Davis, but this brightly recorded coupling can be recommended alongside his version. The cassette is vividly transferred and matches the disc closely.

Symphony No. 90 in C.
** Abbey ABY 733. L. Moz. Players, Blech – MOZART: *Symphony No. 35.***

Blech and the London Mozart Players made a breakthrough in performance of Mozart and Haydn in the 1950s, and though they have not quite kept up with their younger rivals, it is good to have them represented once again on record in this repertory. The woodwind players are specially impressive. The recording is acceptable but not ideally clear.

Symphonies Nos. 91 in E flat; 92 in G (*Oxford*).
*** Ph. Dig. 410 390-1/*4* [id.]. Concg. O, Sir Colin Davis.

It is good to see that the success of their set of *London symphonies* has prompted Philips to continue with more Haydn with the Concertgebouw Orchestra under Colin Davis. The *Oxford* and its immediate predecessor in the canon, No. 91 in E flat, are given performances that are refreshingly crisp and full of musical life. It would be a sad day if Haydn were only to be heard on period instruments, for the sheer joy, vitality and, above all, sanity that these performances radiate is inspiriting and heart-warming. Excellent recorded sound, though the quality is less transparent on tape and detail is not so sharply focused.

Symphonies Nos. 93–104 (*London*).
❀ *** Ph. Dig. 6725/*7655* 010 (6/*4*). Concg. O, Sir Colin Davis.
(M) *** Decca HDNJ 41-6/*K89 K64* (4) [Lon. STS 15319/24]. Philh. Hungarica, Dorati.
*** DG Dig. 2741/*3382* 015 (6). Berlin PO, Karajan.

This Philips set collects the performances we have listed separately. In short, this is likely to remain unsurpassed and is to the 1980s what Beecham's set was to the 1960s and Jochum's to the 1970s. It is a clear first recommendation in which one can have every confidence. The actual sound, too, is first-class though the cassettes are less conveniently laid out than the rival Karajan set on DG, which offers a symphony per side. This spreads the twelve symphonies over four cassettes, thus involving starting in the middle of a side in some instances. However, the transfers are very good indeed with plenty of range and body.

Dorati and the Philharmonia Hungarica, working in comparative isolation in Marl in West Germany, carried through their monumental project of recording the complete Haydn symphonies with not a suspicion of routine. These final masterpieces are performed with a glowing sense of commitment, and Dorati, no doubt taking his cue from the editor, H. C. Robbins Landon, generally chooses rather relaxed tempi for the first movements – as in No. 93, which is just as deliciously lilting as in Szell's masterly version. In slow movements his tempi are on the fast side, but only in No. 94, the *Surprise*, is the result really controversial. Though an extra desk of strings has been added to each section, the results are authentically in scale, with individual solos emerging unforcedly against the glowing acoustic, and with intimacy comes extra dramatic force in sforzandos. A magnificent conclusion to a magnificent project. On tape the sound is highly sophisticated in its detail and bloom. The body of the recording is matched by its transparency, which only slips a fraction momentarily in the 'military' sections of No. 100. The only snag is the ham-fisted presentation, which apportions three symphonies to each cassette, so that in each case the middle symphony is split between the two sides. The booklet too could have used a larger type-face to advantage.

There is much in the Berlin set with Karajan that commands admiration. Like the Davis on Philips, it is big-band Haydn – but what a band! Generally speaking, Karajan seems more responsive to these symphonies than to the *Paris* set and there is evidence of tenderness in some of the slow movements, witness the close of No. 98 in B flat. At times the Berlin Philharmonic do not sound fully involved in this music and many of the minuets are wanting in the sparkle and humour that distinguished Sir Thomas's version that dominated the 1960s. But there is no want of breadth and dignity, and the sound of the Berlin Philharmonic is in itself a joy. The set (we gather) has enjoyed the imprimatur of no less an authority than H. C. Robbins Landon, and there is no doubt as to its distinction. But it inspires admiration rather than affection.

For cassette collectors its claims may be stronger than the Davis, for the layout is more practical – and the presentation more handsome. Moreover, the sound is wide-ranging and clean with plenty of body and warmth while there is no lack of bite and brilliance. These are some of DG's best transfers.

Quite surprisingly, although withdrawn in the UK, Beecham's Royal Philharmonic performances of Nos. 93–8 plus No. 40 are available in the USA on the enterprising Arabesque label [LP: 8035/cassette: *9035*]. The playing has an inner life and vitality that puts this music-making in a class of its own. The old Breitkopf texts are used.

Symphonies Nos. 93 in D; 94 in G (*Surprise*).
*** Ph. Dig. 6514/*7337* 192 [id.]. Concg. O, Sir Colin Davis.
(M) *** CBS 60148/*40-*. Cleveland O, Szell.
**(*) DG Dig. 410 649-1/*4* [id.]. Berlin PO, Karajan.

Finely paced and splendidly recorded in clean but warm digital sound, these Davis performances top the present lists. They have something of the spirit of Beecham about them, and the playing of the Amsterdam Concertgebouw Orchestra cannot be faulted in any department. The chrome cassette is first-class too, proving that Philips can do it if they try.

Szell's performances too are outstandingly brilliant. The perfection of detail, the buoyancy of the playing (Szell's minuets have a greater rhythmic spring than Bernstein's), the precision all add up to music-making of striking character and memorability. And this is not cold playing: there are many little touches from Szell to show that his perfectionist approach is a dedicated and affectionate one. But the recording is very brightly lit, the violin tone in the tuttis conveys a hint of aggressiveness, and the slightly dry, close CBS sound emphasizes this. The tape is mellower.

In the Berlin coupling under Karajan, the playing is of a high order, a joy in itself (though ensemble is not always impeccable). First movement exposition repeats are observed and there is plenty of breadth and dignity, though in both symphonies the overall impression is a little serious and unsmiling. The finale of No. 93 lacks the sparkle and humour of Beecham. Davis and the Concertgebouw Orchestra are preferable but among newer versions this is still a thoroughly recommendable alternative. The sound is first-class, though on the cassette the balance is rather orientated towards the middle and bass.

Symphonies Nos. 94 in G (Surprise); 96 in D (Miracle).
*** Ph. 9500 348 [id./*7300 594*]. ASMF, Marriner.

Another fine issue in the Academy series of Haydn symphonies. The freshness of the playing is matched by the natural warmth of the recordings. There is most delightful woodwind detail in No. 96 (the oboe solo in the trio of the minuet is a joy) and the genially resilient rhythms in the first movements are matched by the lightness of the finale. No. 94 has a particularly fine performance of the variations which form the slow movement (the 'surprise' itself most effective). The recording is well up to Philips's high standard.

Symphonies Nos. 94 in G (Surprise); 101 in D (Clock).
*** DG 2530 628 [id.]. LPO, Jochum.
(M) *** Decca SPA/*KCSP* 494. Philh. Hungarica, Dorati.
(*) DG Dig. **410 869-2 [id.]. Berlin PO, Karajan.
(M) **(*) CBS 60267/*40*- [M/*MT* 32101]. NYPO, Bernstein.
(B) ** Con. CC/*CCT* 7552 [DG 138 782/*923 033*]. Berlin PO, Karl Richter.

Jochum's performances derive from the complete set of *London symphonies* DG released here in 1973, the *Surprise* having appeared the previous year as a trailer. Marvellously fresh, crisp accounts of both symphonies, and well recorded.

In Decca's cheapest price-range, the coupling of Dorati's versions of the *Surprise* and the *Clock* makes an attractive sampler for his whole series, though, as mentioned above, the *Surprise* with its brisk slow movement is one of his more controversial readings. There is a first-class cassette transfer.

Karajan's recoupling of two popular named symphonies is on compact disc only. The performances are discussed above and below; their emphasis is on breadth rather than geniality and charm, though No. 94 is not without humour. The sound made by the Berliners is always impressive, and there is a gain here (if only marginal) in firmness and transparency.

Bernstein's performances have plenty of character, with fine playing from the NYPO, alert in the allegros and with expressive phrasing in slow movements. Only the minuets are inclined to sound too heavy. The sound is vivid and spacious but the bright upper range has an element of harshness. There is little to choose between LP and chrome tape.

Karl Richter's approach is rather sober, but he secures excellent playing from the Berlin Philharmonic, with fine woodwind detail. The overall effect is straitlaced, but the recording is full and clear (the cassette slightly less transparent than the disc).

Symphonies Nos. 94 in G (Surprise); 103 in E flat (Drum Roll).
** HM 1C 065 99873. Coll. Aur., Maier.

The Collegium Aureum is a conductorless orchestra that uses authentic period instruments and is led from the front desk by Franzjosef Maier. The recording is made in the resonant acoustic of Schloss Kirchheim, so that readers fearing the worst (thin, vinegary string tone reminiscent of a school band) can be reassured. In fact the Collegium Aureum do not sound out-of-tune or inhibited, and are closer to the conventional orchestra than many other groups such as the Academy of Ancient Music. Dynamics tend to be more constricted than is either usual or desirable, but the performances are musicianly enough, even if they lack the stamp of personality. But rival accounts have far more character and are textually correct too.

Symphonies Nos. 94 in G (Surprise); 104 in D (London).
(B) **(*) CfP CFP/*TC-CFP* 4400 [Ang. SZ 37575]. Pittsburgh SO, Previn.

In a coupling of what are arguably Haydn's two most popular symphonies, Previn conducts lively performances, very well played and recorded. The only reservations are over the slow movements, which sound just a little perfunctory, lacking in poise. However, reissued at bargain price this makes very good sense and there is a first-class cassette, matching the disc in all but the last degree of upper range.

Symphonies Nos. 95 in C min.; 96 in D (Miracle).
** DG Dig. 410 867-1/*4* [id.]. Berlin PO, Karajan.

In Karajan's hands, No. 95 in C minor is slower than most on record, taken at four-in-the-bar as opposed to the alla breve of Davis, Jochum and Reiner. The latter is ideally paced if you take the view that the marking is *allegro moderato* and not merely *allegro*. One becomes reconciled to Karajan only because of the beauty of the playing and the dignity and breadth of the conception. After this majestic view of the movement, there is insufficient contrast in character with the next movement. The minuet is far too slow, any gain in grandeur being offset by a loss of momentum. No. 96 is another matter and, though the conception is spacious, tempi do not seem excessively slow. Davis is definitely to be preferred in No. 95.

Symphonies Nos. 95 in C min; 97 in C.
*** Ph. Dig. 6514/*7337* 074 [id.]. Concg. O, Sir Colin Davis.

These are performances of real power and unfailing style. Throughout this series the playing of the Concertgebouw Orchestra has been beyond praise and Colin Davis's direction is authoritative. The festive No. 97 in C is a worthy successor to Beecham's recordings of this work. The cassette needs a high-level playback to sound its best.

Symphonies Nos. 95 in C min.; 101 in D (Clock).
(B) *** RCA VICS/*VK* 2007 [AGL 1 1275]. SO, Reiner.

No. 95 is unlikely ever to be as popular as the *Clock symphony*, yet it is a splendid work, with a fine, graciously melodic slow movement and an agile cello melody to catch the ear in the trio of the minuet. It is beautifully played here and makes an outstanding coupling for a highly individual account of the *Clock*. Some may resist Reiner's slow tempo for the *Andante*, but the playing itself is most beguiling. It was one of his last recordings made within two months of his death. A pick-up orchestra is used, but among the players were several members of his Chicago orchestra who had travelled east to work with their old maestro. At bargain price and with a splendid chrome cassette (there is no appreciable difference in sound between disc and tape) this is most attractive. The mid-1960s recording sounds admirably fresh.

Symphonies Nos. 96 in D (Miracle); 100 in G (Military).
(M) ** Decca VIV/*KVIC* 23. VPO, Münchinger.

These recordings date from 1957 and 1961 respectively, but even in the earlier (No. 96), the sound remains both fresh and full, although a slight bass cut is useful. Münchinger is not perhaps the most imaginative of Haydn conductors but the playing of the VPO is first-class and there is no stiffness in the phrasing, and wind solos have plenty of colour. The spirited finale of No. 96 is particularly sprightly.

Symphonies Nos. 96 in D (Miracle); 101 in D (Clock).
** Decca Dig. SXDL/*KSXDC* 7544. LPO, Solti.

Solti gives brilliant performances, rather too taut to convey much of Haydn's charm. With wide-ranging digital sound to match, they can be recommended for demonstration rather than for relaxed listening. The cassette uses chrome tape and has the same brilliant qualities as the disc.

Symphonies Nos. 100 in G (Military); 103 in E flat (Drum Roll).
**(*) Ph. 9500 255 [id./*7300 543*]. ASMF, Marriner.

These are fine performances, with beautifully sprung rhythms and excellent detail. The atmosphere at the opening of the *Drum Roll* is wonderfully caught, and the first movement's second subject shows the fine pointing and lightness of touch which distinguish the music-making throughout. The recording is sophisticated in balance and natural in timbre. In both symphonies Davis evinces slightly more personality, although there is not a great deal to choose between them in terms of orchestral execution.

Symphonies Nos. 100 in G (Military); 104 in D (London).
*** Ph. 9500 510/*7300 670*. Concg. O, Colin Davis.
(M) *** DG Priv. 2535 347/*3335 347* [2530 525]. LPO, Jochum.

Sir Colin Davis's coupling has genuine stature and can be recommended without reservation of any kind. It has better claims than any current rivals; the performances have breadth and dignity, yet are full of sparkle and character. The playing of the Concertgebouw Orchestra is as sensitive as it is brilliant, and Davis is unfailingly penetrating. The performances also benefit from excellent recorded sound, with fine clarity and definition. There is warmth and humanity here, and in either work collectors need look no further. The cassette, however, is disappointing, the sound opaque and bass-heavy, with congestion in the percussion effects of the *Military symphony*.

Jochum secures some fine playing from the LPO and is well recorded; but in spite of many felicitous touches, both his performances yield to Davis and the Concertgebouw in terms of sensitivity and refinement. The playing of the LPO in the finale of No. 100 is very good indeed, and at medium price this record deserves to do well. But the Davis is worth the extra money. Jochum's cassette transfer, however, is much better managed by the DG engineers than the Philips tape. There are no problems with the percussion in the *Military symphony*, and there is both detail and warmth.

Symphonies Nos. 101 in D (Clock); 102 in B flat.
*** Ph. 9500 679/*7300 774*. Concg. O, Colin Davis.
*** DG Dig. 410 868-1/*4* [id.]. Berlin PO, Karajan.

Sir Colin Davis's set of late Haydn symphonies strikes the most sympathetic resonances: it has the eloquence and strength of Jochum with the finesse of Beecham. It is big-band Haydn and of its kind very impressive. There is superb playing from the Concertgebouw, and the recording is excellent. The cassette is of demonstration quality, one of Philips's finest, with striking range as well as body and richness. The orchestral detail comes through splendidly.

Under Karajan tempi are broad and unhurried, yet there is no lack of forward movement, and the Berliners do not disappoint in the slow movement of the *B flat Symphony* which is given with great eloquence. The minuets in both are stately and majestic and retain their dance character, which was not the case in No. 95. These can be recommended alongside Sir Colin Davis.

Symphonies Nos. 102 in B flat; 103 in E flat (Drum Roll).
** Decca Dig. SXDL/*KSXDC* 7570 [Lon. LDR/*5*- 71070]. LPO, Solti.

The beauty and refinement of the playing of the LPO under Solti are admirable, but the tensions – with even the lovely *Adagio* of No. 102 failing quite to relax – speak of the twentieth rather than the eighteenth century. Excellent recording. The chrome cassette is extremely lively and wide-ranging, but it makes the strings sound thin and glossy above the stave, particularly in No. 103 on side two.

Symphonies Nos. 103 in E flat (Drum Roll); 104 in D (London).
(M) *** HMV SXLP/*TC-SXLP* 30257. RPO, Beecham.
*** DG Dig. **410 517-2**; 410 517-1/*4* [id.]. Berlin PO, Karajan.
(M) *** Decca VIV/*KVIC* 55. VPO, Karajan.

Beecham's coupling is self-recommending. Haydn's last two symphonies have rarely, if ever, sounded so captivating and sparkling as they do here. Beecham does not use authentic texts – he was a law unto himself in such matters – but the spirit of Haydn is superbly caught, whether in the affectionately measured (but never mannered) slow movements or in the exhilarating rhythmic spring of the outer movements. The recording is warmly attractive, and the cassette transfer is admirably managed.

In Karajan's recent (digital) Berlin coupling the first movement of No. 104 has impressive power and dignity with altogether splendid string playing from the Berlin Philharmonic. As in his earlier Vienna account, Karajan observes the exposition repeat and refrains from any interpretative self-indulgence. The Minuet and Trio is even marginally faster than the earlier record or that of Davis. Recording quality is rich-toned and full-bodied with very good presence and is worth the additional outlay. Disc and cassette are virtually identical. Overall there is more spontaneity from Davis and the Concertgebouw (who are differently coupled) but there is an undeniable breadth and grandeur here, as well as magnificent orchestral playing.

Karajan's Decca performances were recorded at the beginning of the 1960s, but the recording still sounds extremely vivid (the cassette is remarkably lively) and this Viva reissue remains competitive. No. 103 is a polished, well-made account. There is some lack of warmth and humanity in the reading, although the tempi are sensible and the recording balance is good. The reading of No. 104 is more direct, with plenty of earthy vigour in the outer movements and a beautifully shaped slow movement. In both symphonies the alert and responsive playing of the VPO gives much pleasure.

Symphony No. 104 in D (*London*).
(M) *** DG Sig. 2543/*3343* 531. LPO, Jochum – MOZART: *Symphony No. 41.****

Jochum's is among the most musically satisfying accounts of Haydn's *London symphony* in the catalogue. It is very well recorded with fresh timbre and with wide range. The chrome-cassette transfer is also very well managed. If the coupling with an equally outstanding version of Mozart's *Jupiter symphony* is suitable, this could be a prime recommendation.

Symphonies Nos. A in B flat; B in B flat; 22 in E flat (*Philosopher*) (second version); *53 in D* (*L'Impériale*): 3 finales; *63 in C* (*La Roxelane*) (second version); *103 in E flat* (*Drum Roll*): original finale.
(M) *** Decca HDNK 47/8 [Lon. STS 15316/7]. Philh. Hungarica, Dorati.

It is a measure of Dorati's dedication to Haydn's scholarship – helped by the editor of the scores and commentator for the series, H. C. Robbins Landon – that he included this supplementary album of alternative movements in his complete Haydn series. So far from proving a merely academic exercise, the result might almost be regarded as a sampler for the series, with examples of Haydn's work at every period, culminating in the magnificent, somewhat more expanded version of the finale of the *Drum Roll*. Symphonies Nos. A and B were not included in the original numerical list simply because they were originally thought not to be symphonies at all, while the other alternative movements – some of them probably not by Haydn – come from different editions of his work published through Europe. It gives a vivid idea of the working conditions of the music world in Haydn's time. Exhilarating performances, superb recording.

CHAMBER MUSIC

Baryton trios Nos. 63–4, 82, 87–8, 107, 110.
(M) *** HMV HQS 1424. Esterházy Baryton Trio.

Prince Nikolaus Esterházy was an enthusiastic baryton player and Haydn composed some 126 trios for his noble patron. The baryton is a kind of large viola d'amore, with six or seven bowed strings and up to twenty-two sympathetic strings which can be plucked. It produces a beguiling sound and blends splendidly with the viola and cello. Most of the recordings of this repertoire which proliferated around the time that our last edition went to print have disappeared from the catalogue, but the above mid-priced HMV disc remains as a sampler. The playing is expert and lively. Although Haydn did not pour his finest inspiration into this medium, there are some good moments in all these trios. The recording is excellent.

Octets with baryton, Hob. X:2, 5 and 6.
*** DG Arc. 2533 465. Mun. Baryton Trio and soloists.

For those who have found the baryton trios which have appeared in recent years of less than pressing interest, these persuasive and refined performances will prove a welcome surprise. The invention is fresh and at times, particularly in the slow movements, quite searching, and the recording does full justice to the subtle colourings of this music. They make ideal late-night listening and although one could not claim that they represent Haydn at his most consistently elevating, they are musically most satisfying.

Flute trios, Hob IV, Nos. 1 in C; 2 in G; 3 in G; 4 in G (London). Divertimentos. Hob IV, Nos. 7 in G; 11 in D.
*** CBS Dig. 37786/*40*- [id.]. Rampal, Stern, Rostropovich.

Eminently winning performances of some charming if minor pieces of Haydn's London years, as well as some earlier *Divertimenti*. These players convey a sense of enjoyment and pleasure, and the recording is perfectly acceptable. The disc enjoys a slight superiority over the cassette, but the latter is still admirably fresh and clean.

Guitar quartet in E, Op. 2/2.
(M) *** CBS 61842/*40*- [(d) Col. MS 7163]. Williams, Loveday, Aronowitz, Fleming – STRAUBE: *Sonatas*.**(*)

This recording originally appeared in 1968 coupled with a Paganini *Terzetto*. John Williams's arrangement of the quartet draws on both the lute transcription and the original, and the compromise is a successful one. This is a beguiling performance, more appealing than the string quartet itself. The new coupling, however, is not an improvement on the old. The cassette transfer is full and clear, with plenty of range.

Piano trios (complete).
❀ *** Ph. 6768 077 (14). Beaux Arts Trio.

Most of the performances in this set have been noticed individually in earlier volumes of the *Penguin Stereo Record Guide*. This is a remarkable and invaluable collection which is unlikely to be challenged, let alone surpassed. It is not often possible to hail one set of records as a 'classic' in quite the way that Schnabel's Beethoven sonatas can be so described. All too few performances attain that level of artistic insight, and such is the sheer proliferation of material that records have a greater struggle for attention. Yet this set can be described in those terms, for the playing of the Beaux Arts Trio is of the very highest musical distinction. The contribution of the pianist, Menahem Pressler, is little short of inspired, and the recorded sound is astonishingly lifelike. The performances follow the Critical Edition of H. C. Robbins Landon, whose indefatigable researches have increased the number of trios we know in the standard edition from thirty-one to forty-three. This is the kind of inflation one welcomes! Most collectors will find something new in this box, and its riches will stand us in good stead for many decades. Here is music that is sane and intelligent, balm to the soul in a troubled world.

Piano trios, Hob XV, Nos. 24-31 (complete).
(M) *** Ph. 6768/*7656* 361 (2). Beaux Arts Trio.

Taken from the box discussed above, this admirable compilation of the last eight *Piano trios* will suit those not able to invest in the complete set. They are all splendid works. No. 25 with its *Gypsy rondos* is the most famous, but each has a character of its own, showing the mature Haydn working at full stretch (they are contemporary with the *London symphonies*). The playing here is peerless and the recording truthful and refined, with excellent cassettes to match the discs, even if the transfer level is unadventurous.

Piano trio No. 25 in G.
(M) *** Ph. 6833 231. Beaux Arts Trio – DVOŘÁK: *Piano trio No. 4*.***

A delightful performance and splendid recording make the appealing *Trio No. 25* a desirable fill-up for Dvořák's *Dumky trio*. The latter is arguably the best version on the market.

String quartets: in E flat, Op. O; Nos. 1–4 and 6, Op. 1/1–4 and 6; 7–8; 10 and 12, Op. 2/1–2, 4 and 6.
(M) **(*) Argo HDNM 52/6 [Lon. STS 15328/32]. Aeolian Qt.

The early quartets of Haydn have not quite the unquenchable flow of original ideas that the early symphonies have, but they make easy and enjoyable listening, even if some of them outstay their welcome. Even the Aeolians cannot quite sustain our interest, when the quartets of Opp. 1 and 2 all have five movements with two minuets and trios in each. It is not always an advantage that the Aeolians are wedded to observing repeats. Nonetheless, on their own relatively unpretentious level these are charming works, and Emanuel Hurwitz, the leader of the quartet, readily takes his chances in such a quartet as Op. 2/1, which includes stylish cadenzas. Good, atmospheric recording, with none of the disadvantages of the sound quality in the set of quartets Opp. 71 and 74.

String quartets Nos. 13–18, Op. 3/1–6; 50–56 (The Seven last words of Jesus Christ), Op. 51/1–7.
(M) *** Argo HDNV 82/4 [Lon. STS 15459/61]. Aeolian Qt (with Pears).

Though Haydn authorities claim that the Op. 3 quartets are by Romanus Hofstetter, not Haydn, it was wise of the Aeolian Quartet to include them in the collected edition, if only because the *Andante cantabile* of Op. 3/2 is so very popular, the so-called *Serenade* with its lovely melody of muted violin with pizzicato accompaniment. There are other treasures here, but the real reason for having this box is the magnificent quartet version of the *Seven Last Words*, here avoiding any risk of monotony from so many *Adagios* in succession by inserting poetry readings between movements. The texts are beautifully chosen and read by Sir Peter Pears. Excellent atmospheric recording.

String quartets Nos. 17 in F (Serenade), Op. 3/5; 38 in E flat (Joke), Op. 33/2; 76 in D min. (Fifths), Op. 76/2.
(M) *** Decca Ace SDD 285 [Lon. CS 6385]. Janáček Qt.

The performances here are strong and dedicated, and careful to sense that the style of Haydn is not that of either Beethoven or Mozart. The music itself is highly agreeable; whether or not Haydn did not write that delicious tune which forms the slow movement of the *Serenade quartet* seems irrelevant; it is an attractive little work and makes a good foil for the really splendid music of its companions. The recording is outstanding, even by Decca's standards, and it is quite possible to imagine that the Janáček Quartet are recessed in a small concert chamber at the end of one's living room. Highly recommended.

String quartets Nos. 17 in F (Serenade), Op. 3/5; 67 in D (Lark), Op. 64/5; 76 in D min. (Fifths), Op. 76/2.
(M) *** Ph. 6570/*7310* 577. Italian Qt.

At first these performances strike one as slightly undercharacterized, but on closer acquaintance they reveal qualities of insight that had escaped one. The first movement of the *Lark* is a bit too measured in feeling and could do with more sparkle, but the performance of the *Serenade quartet* is as fine as any available. The *D minor Quartet* is admirably poised and classical in feeling; this rivals if not outclasses the performance by the Janáček Quartet (Decca SDD 285 [Lon. CS 6385]). The recording is most musically balanced and emerges freshly in this Musica da Camera reissue. The cassette transfer is first-class.

String quartets Nos. 19–24, Op. 9/1–6; 25–30, Op. 17/1–6.
(M) *** Argo HDNQ 61/6 [Lon. STS 15337/42]. Aeolian Qt.

Though few of these early works are consistently inspired from beginning to end (the G major, No. 29, is a marvellous exception), they all contain their moments of magic and every one of them has a superb finale, showing the young Haydn at full stretch. At this period in his career at the Palace of Esterháza Haydn was experimenting in every direction, and though the first movements here are not all as inventive as one might hope, they generally match the equivalent symphonies of the period in sharpness of inspiration. Even at this period Haydn had developed his quartet-writing beyond the stage of giving all the interesting writing to the first violin. The Aeolian Quartet, having settled into their task of recording the complete cycle, play with consistent freshness and imagination, and are well recorded.

String quartets Nos. 31–36, Op. 20/1–6; 63–68, Op. 64/1–6.
(M) **(*) Argo HDNT 70/75 [Lon. STS 15447/52]. Aeolian Qt.

This set offers the Opp. 20 and 64 quartets in decent, eminently well-prepared and musical accounts that match those in the rest of the excellent Aeolian cycle.

String quartets Nos. 34 in D; 35 in F min., Op. 20/4–5.
*** DG 2531/*3301* 380 [id.]. Tokyo Qt.

This is highly accomplished playing and the tonal blend of the Tokyo Quartet could hardly be improved upon. Tempi are well judged and there is more repose in the slow movements than in their Op. 76 set for CBS. In terms of aural luxuriance, they are unlikely to be surpassed, though they do not wholly efface memories of the old Schneider set from the early days of LP. There is a finesse and elegance here which is impressive, though some of the innocence of Haydn's invention eludes them. The recording is of the highest quality and the high-level transfer in the cassette has striking range and immediacy.

String quartets Nos. 37–42, Op. 33/1–6; 43 in D min., Op. 42; 44–49, Op. 50/1–6.
(M) *** Argo HDNU 76/81 [Lon. STS 15453/8]. Aeolian Qt.

'Written in a new and special way', said Haydn of his six Op. 33 quartets. Tovey described them as 'the lightest in all Haydn's mature comedies', for by the time he wrote them in 1781, many years after the Op. 20 group, he was learning from the young Mozart. Mozart returned the compliment in the six masterpieces he dedicated to Haydn, and in turn Haydn responded with his Op. 50 group, cogent in their monothematic sonata form. The Aeolian Quartet came to these marvellous works later on in their complete cycle, but the players' perception and energy are if anything keener than ever. Not all their tempi are beyond question, but the wonder is how consistently enjoyable their playing is. Warm, well-balanced recording.

String quartets Nos. 44 in B flat; 45 in C, Op. 50/1–2.
(M) *** DG Priv. 2535/*3335* 464. Tokyo Qt.

Not since the Schneider Quartet in the 1950s, or perhaps even the pre-war 78s of the Pro Arte, have the quartets of Op. 50 been better served on record. The Tokyo Quartet play with impeccable style and a refreshing and invigorating vitality. They are admirably unaffected but phrase with real imagination. DG give them well-defined and excellently balanced recording and the usual impeccable surfaces. This is an outstanding issue, strongly recommended. The cassette transfers are immaculate, although Op. 50/1 would have benefited from a slightly higher level to match its companion. Even so the sound is fresh and clean.

String quartets Nos. 50–56 (The Seven Last Words), Op. 51; 57–9, Op. 54; 60–62, Op. 55; 63–8, Op. 64; 69–71, Op. 71; 72–4, Op. 74; 75–80, Op. 76; 81–2, Op. 77; in D min., Op. 103.
(B) **(*) DG 2740 250 (14). Amadeus Qt.

These fourteen records collect the last twenty-seven Haydn quartets plus the *Seven Last Words*, in recordings made by the Amadeus over the last eighteen years. Most of them are from the 1970s, and there will be few quarrels with the quality of the sound. Apart from the Aeolian Quartet, no other ensemble has offered all this repertoire in recent years, though older collectors will doubtless still cherish the Schneider and even the pre-war Pro Arte versions of some of them. The Amadeus do not always penetrate the depths of Haydn's slow movements, and Norbert Brainin's vibrato is not to all tastes, but reservations about individual movements should not temper admiration for the undertaking as a whole. Individually these performances may be surpassed by such ensembles as the Orlando, Italian and Tokyo quartets, but it would be curmudgeonly not to extend a warm welcome to this bargain-price reissue.

String quartets Nos. 50–56 (The Seven Last Words of our Saviour on the cross), Op. 51.
**(*) Ph. Dig. 6514/*7337* 153 [id.]. Kremer, Rabus, Causse, Iwasaki.

The Aeolian Quartet version (HDNV 82) intersperses readings by Peter Pears between each of the movements which enhances the impact of this work. This Philips account presents the seven movements without a break, as have all the preceding versions. Musically this does not displace the Aeolian, as either a performance or a recording, but it is a useful addition to the catalogue, as no single-disc alternative is currently in the lists and it is the only version available on tape. Good recording and an excellent matching chrome cassette.

String quartets Nos. 57–9, Op. 54/1–3; 60–2, Op. 55/1–3 (Tost Quartets).
(M) **(*) Argo HDNS 67/9 [Lon. STS 15346/8]. Aeolian Qt.

Choice here resides between the Aeolian and the Amadeus (see above), though the latter's larger format comprises fourteen discs. The Aeolians offer plainer readings, free from expressive idiosyncrasy, with some occasional want of the last ounce of polish.

String quartets Nos. 57 in G; 58 in C, Op. 54/1–2.
*** Ph. 9500/*7300* 996 [id.]. Orlando Qt.

The Orlando Quartet is based in Holland and can boast four different nationalities among its members (Hungarian, Austrian, Rumanian and German). Their Haydn enhances their reputation: this is alert, sensitive and refined playing, scrupulous in its recognition of dynamic nuance (yet without ever being too self-conscious, as the Alban Berg Quartet have become) and superb in its accuracy of ensemble and tonal blend. These are marvellously fresh performances and cannot be too strongly recommended. The *C major Quartet*, with its unusual *Adagio* finale, is a particularly fine work. The cassette matches the disc closely in lively naturalness.

String quartets Nos. 69–71, Op. 71/1–3; 72–74, Op. 74/1–3.
(M) ** Argo HDNL 49/51 [Lon. STS 15325/7]. Aeolian Qt.

This was the first album to be issued of the complete quartet cycle by the Aeolians, using a new edition prepared by H. C. Robbins Landon and Reginald Barrett-Ayres. Though the performances of these works, which have been unjustifiably neglected on record, are vigorously enjoyable, the recording quality masks their merit. In this first album – but not in the succeeding ones – the engineers gave the four players a degree of 'helpful' reverberation which made them sound like a string orchestra.

String quartets Nos. 69 in B flat; 70 in D, Op. 71/1–2.
*** Hyp. A 66065. Salomon Qt.

The Salomon Quartet use period instruments (or, in the case of the viola, a modern copy of a 1690 Stradivarius) and play without vibrato. Those who fear that the results will sound excessively nasal can be reassured: the texture is transparent, the sound admirably blended and the playing thoroughly vital and committed. These performances have real spirit and panache without any of the inhibited quality that afflicts some Early Music ensembles. Most musical – and splendidly recorded too.

String quartets Nos. 74 in G minor (Rider), Op. 74/3; 77 in C major (Emperor), Op. 76/3.

*** Tel. AS 6.41302 [641302]. Alban Berg Qt.

A quite superb disc in every way, with playing of wonderful resilience and sparkle. The famous slow movement of the *Emperor quartet* has never before been played on record with such warmth and eloquence, and the slow movement of No. 74 is even more beautiful. Indeed the performance of this quartet is masterly. The bright, clear sound matches the resilience of the playing, and this is one of the most rewarding of all Haydn quartet couplings.

String quartets Nos. 75–80, Op. 76/1–6.
**(*) CBS 79339 (3) [M3/*M T3* 35897]. Tokyo Qt.
(M) **(*) Hung. SLPX 1205/7. Tátrai Qt.

After their prize-winning Bartók cycle and their magnificent Haydn Op. 20, the appearance of this complete Op. 76 aroused the highest expectations. The Tokyo Quartet offer superb playing and an immaculate tonal blend, and they are unfailingly intelligent. Yet at the same time, it is a pity that they do not relax a little more and allow the music to unfold at greater leisure, for they do not convey the humanity and charm that distinguishes the classic Tátrai set of the 1960s. They are not as well served by the engineers as they were by DG and the sound is wanting in bloom; but at the same time, until the Quartetto Italiano or the Orlando go on to complete the set, anyone wanting the Erdödy quartets should consider these.

The Tátrai Op. 76 is also a desirable set, beautifully played, with remarkably good stereo for a Hungarian import label. The playing is serious but dedicated; the *Adagios* are played as real adagios and most expressively sustained, and the finales are notable for their high spirits as well as the virtuosity of the playing. Only sometimes in the opening movements does the playing seem too lightweight, and in the *Emperor* the variations on the famous tune are not very imaginatively done.

String quartets Nos. 75–80, Op. 76/1–6; 81–2, Op. 77/1–2; 83 in B flat, Op. 103.
(M) *** Argo HDNP 57/60 [Lon. STS 15333/6]. Aeolian Qt.

Continuing their series of the complete quartets the Aeolians give eminently straightforward and unmannered accounts of Opp. 76 and 77 and the two-movement Op. 103 quartet. This is one of the most successful of their albums, and the excellence of the annotations enhances the value of the box.

String quartet No. 76 in D min. (Fifths), Op. 76/2.
(*) DG 410 652-1/*4* [id.]. Amadeus Qt – BEETHOVEN: *Quartet No. 9.*(*)

The Amadeus account coupled with the *C major Rasumovsky* comes from a public concert given at the Wigmore Hall in January 1983 to mark their thirty-fifth anniversary. Hence tuning and applause are included and the performance has the feel of a living musical experience. It is not to be preferred to the long-serving but impressive Quartetto Italiano version on Philips – or, for that matter, the Janáček on Decca – but admirers of this distinguished ensemble may well want to consider its claims. Good recorded sound.

String quartet No. 77 in C (Emperor), Op. 76/3.
*** Ph. 9500 662 [id./*7300 762*]. Italian Qt – MOZART: *Quartet No. 17.***(*)
(M) *** DG Acc. 2452/*3342* 122. Amadeus Qt – MOZART: *Quartet No. 17.****
(*) DG Dig. **410 866-2; 410 866-1/*4* [id.]. Amadeus Qt – MOZART: *Quartet No. 17.***(*)

The Italian version of the *Emperor* is already available in a more sensible coupling (Haydn's Op. 76/4 – see below), but Philips have now coupled this relatively recent performance with the B flat Mozart, K. 458, recorded in the mid-1960s, without reducing it to medium price. Both are noble performances, and they are extremely well recorded; but the more competitive Amadeus, now on the mid-price DG Accolade label, may tempt some readers. The Amadeus version of the *Emperor* was always one of their best records from the mid-1960s, and it has breadth and warmth. The over-sweet vibrato of Norbert Brainin is less obtrusive here than in many other Amadeus records of this period. Though the Italians are more spacious and have greater nobility (and more modern recording), the excellent Mozart coupling and the competitive price are in the Amadeus's favour. The high-level cassette transfer makes this one of the most attractive string quartet couplings available on tape.

Although the recording is obviously more modern, the newest version of the *Emperor* from the Amadeus is not an improvement on the old. The playing is expert, but there is an element of routine here, and the overall impression is a lack of communicative warmth. The recording has great presence on the compact disc but also has a touch of edginess; it sounds smoothest on the excellent chrome cassette.

String quartets Nos. 77 in C major (*Emperor*); *78 in B flat major* (*Sunrise*), *Op. 76/3–4*.
*** Ph. 9500 157/*7300 523* [id.]. Italian Qt.
(M) **(*) Argo ZK 16. Aeolian Qt.

The Italian performances are beautifully shaped, keenly alert and marvellously recorded. By their side the Aeolians' playing is less refined, but these also are most enjoyable accounts. The slow movement of the *Emperor* is played in rather a measured fashion but with considerable eloquence, and the fresh, crisp articulation in the first movement of Op. 76/4 is very attractive. In short, while the Italians remain first choice, this is an admirable medium-priced alternative, and the cassette transfer offers demonstration quality throughout. However, the Philips cassette – issued after the disc – is of this company's best, full-bodied and live.

String quartets Nos. 78 in B flat (*Sunrise*); *80 in E flat, Op. 76/4 and 6*.
C *** Ph. Dig. **410 053-2**; 6514/*7337* 204 [id.]. Orlando Qt.

One of the best Haydn quartet records currently available. The playing has eloquence, vitality and warmth; there is a keen sense of rhythm and phrases breathe with refreshing naturalness. Philips have given this fine ensemble first-rate recorded sound and the record can be recommended with enthusiasm and so can the chrome cassette. This coupling also has the distinction of being the first Haydn chamber music to be issued on compact disc. The naturalness is enhanced; there is a striking body and realism to the sound image, especially in Op. 74, No. 6 which is very slightly smoother on top than its companion. What a wonderful work it is!

Piano sonatas Nos. 36 in C min. (*H.XVI/20*); *44 in E flat* (*H.XVI/49*).
*** Ph. 9500 774/*7300 862* [id.]. Brendel.

If all Haydn sonata performances were of this quality, they would be more firmly entrenched in the catalogue. This is playing of real distinction, aristocratic without being aloof and concentrated without being too intense. Everything is cleanly articulated and finely characterized. Brendel observes all the repeats, and he is accorded lifelike and vivid recording. The cassette is particularly fine.

Piano sonatas Nos. 58 in C (*H.XVI/48*); *60 in C* (*H.XVI/50*); *61 in D* (*H.XVI/51*).
C *** Ph. Dig. **411 045-2**; 6514/*7337* 317 [id.]. Brendel.

Brendel plays magnetically in these three mature and original works. He uses crisp, bright articulation which keeps the piano sound in scale, but in such movements as the opening *Andante con espressione* of No. 58(48) he conveys a Beethovenian intensity without overweighting the music with emotion. Rightly in the large-scale *allegro* of No. 60 Brendel takes repeats of both halves. The piano sound is among the most vivid ever, uncannily real-sounding on compact disc with its silent background. The chrome cassette is transferred at quite a high level and is of good quality, but the upper range is less open than on either of the disc versions.

VOCAL MUSIC

The Creation (*Die Schöpfung*): complete (in German).

(M) *** DG 410 951-1/*4* (2). Janowitz, Ludwig, Wunderlich, Krenn, Fischer-Dieskau, Berry, V. Singverein, Berlin PO, Karajan.

*** Ph. 6769 047/*7699 154* [id.]. Mathis, Fischer-Dieskau, Baldin, Ch., ASMF, Marriner.

(M) *** Decca Jub. 410 270-1/*4* (2). Ameling, Spoorenberg, Krenn, Krause, Fairhurst, V. State Op. Ch., VPO, Münchinger.

**(*) Decca D50 D2/*K50 K22* (2) [Lon. OSA/*5-* 12108]. Popp, Hollweg, Dose, Luxon, Moll, Brighton Fest. Ch., RPO, Dorati.

(*) DG Dig. **410 718-2; 2741/*3382* 017 (2). Mathis, Araiza, Van Dam, V. Singverein, VPO, Karajan.

**(*) Decca Dig. D 262 D 2/*K 262 K 22* (2) [Lon. LDR/*5-* 72011]. Burrowes, Greenberg, Wohlers, Morris, Nimsgern, Chicago Ch. and SO, Solti.

** Erato Dig. NUM/*MCE* 750202 (2). Marshall, Branisteanu, Tappy, Huttenlocher, Rydl, SRO Ch., Lausanne Pro Arte Ch., Lausanne CO, Jordan.

** HM 1C 157 99944/5. Auger, Sima, Schreier, Berry, Herrman, Arnold Schoenberg Ch., Coll. Aur., Kuhn.

The Creation is a lucky work on record, and Karajan produces one of his most rapt choral performances. His concentration on refinement and polish might in principle seem out of place in a work which tells of religious faith in the directest terms. In fact the result is outstanding. The combination of the Berlin Philharmonic at its most intense and the great Viennese choir makes for a performance that is not only polished but warm and dramatically strong too. The soloists are an extraordinarily fine team, more consistent in quality than those on any rival version. This was one of the last recordings made by the incomparable Fritz Wunderlich, and fortunately his magnificent contribution extended to all the arias, leaving Werner Krenn to fill in the gaps of recitative left unrecorded. The recording quality has a warm glow of atmosphere round it. Though Marriner's set has more modern recording, Karajan's is clearly the safest recommendation, on disc and tape.

Marriner's version makes an excellent choice if you fancy the work on a relatively intimate scale. With generally fast tempi Marriner draws consistently lithe and resilient playing and singing from his St Martin's team. There is no lack of weight in the result. The great cry of *Licht* on a fortissimo C major chord when God creates light is overwhelming. You might even count Dietrich Fischer-Dieskau in the baritone role as too weighty, recorded rather close, but his inflection of every word is intensely revealing. The soprano is Edith Mathis, very sweet of tone if not always quite so steady as some of her rivals on record, with *Nun beut die Flur* (*With verdure clad*) very light and pretty. The one notable snag is that Aldo Baldin's tenor is not well focused by the microphones. Otherwise the recording is first-rate; so are the cassettes, which in spite of a modest transfer level offer sound that is both robust and clear.

A fine performance from Münchinger that stands well even in competition with Karajan. Münchinger has rarely conducted with such electric tension on record, and some no doubt will prefer his more direct, squarer style in comparison with the highly polished Karajan. His soloists nearly match those of the Karajan set (the sopranos not quite so beautiful as Janowitz). Fine recording in Decca's best Vienna tradition. The very high level of the tape transfer brings rough choral sound.

Dorati, as one would expect, directs a lively and well-sprung account, but neither in crispness of ensemble nor in detailed imagination does it match its finest rivals. It is partly the fault of the recording that the chorus sounds less well defined than it ought, and though the soloists make a good team, their singing is rarely distinguished. This joyful performance would be acceptable if the Marriner or the Karajan version were not available, but as it is it falls short. The Decca cassettes, however, are exceptionally successful; technically this is among the most enjoyable *Creations* in tape format.

Karajan's later recording is taken from a live performance given at the Salzburg Festival in 1982. Not surprisingly it cannot match the perfection of the earlier one either in musical ensemble or in recording balance, but there are many compensations, for there is greater warmth in the later version. For example the *'flexible tiger'* (*der gelenkige Tiger*) bounces along more engagingly in Uriel's recitative with Van Dam's bass firm and beautiful, and the choruses brim with joy at speeds generally a degree more relaxed. Edith Mathis cannot match her predecessor, Gundula Janowitz, in ethereal purity, but she gives a sweeter-toned performance than she did for Marriner on Philips, though the close balancing of voices is hardly flattering to any of the soloists. The sense of presence is what matters, and this is a fine memento of a powerful, glowing occasion, caught in wide-ranging digital sound. The chrome cassettes too are strikingly vivid, with the choral focus sharper in the second and third parts of the work. The compact discs offer a tangible presence but also give more emphasis to the faults of balance. The choral focus too is less than ideal.

Solti is predictably fierce in some of the big choruses (*Die Himmel erzählen*, for example), but this generally presents a relatively genial view, helped by outstanding choral singing and vivid digital sound. Norma Burrowes is fresh, bright in her girlish tone, but much of the other solo singing is variable with James Morris's baritone taking unkindly to the microphone. The admirable chrome cassettes are of Decca's best quality.

The glory of Jordan's version, recorded with the Lausanne Choir, is the singing of Margaret Marshall in the first two parts with *Nun beut die Flur* sounding radiant at a very slow speed. There is much else to commend, though Kurt Rydl is a gruff bass soloist, and for all its discipline the chorus's words are unclear. On balance this cannot quite match the finest versions, despite cleanly balanced sound.

Kuhn's version, like Karajan's of 1982, was recorded at a public performance, but there the similarity ends. Using the excellent Collegium Aureum, it is a performance on an intimate scale with original instruments. Speeds are often brisk, textures clear, but rhythms are sometimes stiff or unrelenting. Like Marriner, Kuhn has a piano (or fortepiano) in the recitatives. Outstanding among the soloists is the soprano in the first two parts, Arleen Auger, with Walter Berry a characterful bass. The recording is very good and the cassettes capture the resonant acoustic and wide dynamic range satisfactorily.

The Creation (complete; in English).
**(*) HMV SLS/*TC-SLS* 971 (2) [Ara. 8039-2/*9039-2*]. Harper, Tear, Shirley-Quirk, King's College Ch., ASMF, Willcocks.

There are special reasons for breaking the general rule of the recording world today and presenting this oratorio in an English version. Quite apart from the fact that it is based on Milton, the idea was first presented to Haydn in the form of an English libretto provided by the impresario Salomon. Baron Gottfried van Swieten prepared not only a German version but an English one too, which was later modified in the score published in England. David Willcocks captures something of the spirit which made the King's version of *Messiah* so captivating, and it is good to have 'the flexible tiger' and 'the nimble stag' so vividly portrayed. Though Heather Harper is not always quite as steady or sweet-toned as usual, this is a first-rate team of soloists, and the choral singing and the playing of the Academy could hardly be more stylish. Warm reverberant recording in the King's manner. The iron-oxide cassettes are disappointing; the transfer level is not especially high, and the King's acoustic tends to blunt the upper range of the sound, especially in the choruses, while the balance is somewhat bass-heavy. The layout does not attempt to tailor each part of the work to a separate cassette.

Lieder; English songs and folksong settings (complete).
*** Ph. 6769 064 (3). Ameling, Demus.

'The unknown Haydn', says an essay accompanying this delightful set, but with Elly Ameling projecting these simple but often touching songs to perfection, that is hardly true any more. The celebrated ones like *The Sailor's Song* (with its improbable refrain of 'hurly-burly') and *My mother bids me bind my hair* are well matched by dozens of others almost equally charming, some with clear anticipations of nineteenth-century Lieder. The collection ends with the *Emperor's hymn*, first the Austrian and later the German national anthem: with Ameling, even that is made moving in its simplicity. Joerg Demus is a brightly sympathetic accompanist, and the recording is first-rate.

Folk-song arrangements: *Barbara Allen; Blue bonnets; The glancing of her apron; Green grow the rushes; Jockie and Sandy; Lizae Baillie; Marg'ret's ghost; O can ye sew cushions; Up in the morning early; Will ye go to Flanders?*
(*) HM 1C 069 99940. Griffett, Maier, Mandalka, Tracey – BEETHOVEN: *Folk-songs.**

Haydn's folk-song settings – many of them written like Beethoven's for George Thomson – are relatively simple in their accompaniments, but Haydn like Beethoven did put his own stamp on familiar melodies, if only by giving them a formal frame. Sadly in this selection the high tessitura of the very first item, *The glancing of her apron*, finds Griffett at his most hooty with suspect intonation on top. Otherwise his bright, fresh manner and immaculate diction are ideal, and the accompaniment on original instruments sounds undistractingly authentic. Excellent, well-balanced recording. One song, *Marg'ret's Ghost*, comes with no fewer than seventeen verses.

Masses Nos. (i) *1 in F major* (*Missa brevis*); (ii) *4 in G major* (*Missa Sancti Nicolai*).
*** O-L DSLO/*KDSLC* 538. Nelson, Ch. of Christ Church Cath., Oxford, AcAM, Preston, with (i) Kirkby; (ii) Minty, Covey-Crump, Thomas.

Haydn wrote the early *Missa brevis* when he was seventeen. The setting is engagingly unpretentious; some of its sections last for under two minutes and none takes more than three and a half. The two soprano soloists here match their voices admirably and the effect is delightful. The *Missa Sancti Nicolai* dates from 1772 but has a comparable freshness of inspiration. The unconventional time-signature of the *Kyrie* established the composer's individuality, and the deeply expressive central section of the *Credo* is matched by the characterful opening of the *Sanctus* and the touch of melancholy in the *Agnus Dei*. This performance is first-rate in every way, beautifully sung, with spontaneity in every bar, and a highly characterful accompaniment. The recording is first-class, the cassette only marginally less clearly focused than the disc (because of the reverberation).

Mass No. 2 in E flat (*Missa in honorem Beatissimae Virginis Mariae*).
**(*) O-L DSLO 563 [id.]. Nelson, Watkinson, Hill, Thomas, Ch. of Christ Church Cath., AcAM, Preston.

In this early Mass Haydn followed the rococo conventions of his time, dutifully giving weight to the *Gloria* and *Credo* in culminating fugues but generally adopting a style featuring Italianate melody, which to modern ears inevitably sounds operatic. This first Haydn essay from Preston and his distinguished choir was not quite so crisp or enlivening as most of their records with the Academy of Ancient Music; but with fine, atmospheric recording it is well worth investigating. One intriguing point in the Mass is Haydn's use of a pair of cors anglais, which add a touch of darkness to the scoring. The recording is excellent; there are some delightful sounds here.

Mass No. 3 in C (*Missa Cellensis*); *Missa rorate coeli desuper: Gloria.*
*** O-L DSLO 583/4 [id., PSI]. Nelson, Cable, Hill, Thomas, Ch. of Christ Church Cath., AcAM, Preston.

The *Missa Cellensis* (also known as the *Missa Sanctae Caeciliae*) is Haydn's longest setting of the liturgy; the *Gloria* alone (in seven cantata-like movements) lasts nearly half an hour. By contrast the *Gloria* of the little *Missa rorate coeli desuper* is only nine bars long, and with the words all jumbled together it lasts well under a minute. That miniature setting was written by Haydn when he was still a choirboy in Vienna, and it may well be his earliest surviving work. Not everything is perfunctory, for the *Agnus Dei* has a touching gravity. Nonetheless this two-disc set is chiefly valuable for presenting yet another unknown work of Haydn full of vigorous inspiration, with a setting of the *Benedictus* which is darker than one would expect from Haydn. Preston directs an excellent performance with fine contributions from choir and soloists, set against a warmly reverberant acoustic.

Masses Nos. 5 in B flat (Little organ Mass); 6 in C (Missa Cellensis): Mariazeller Mass. Mechanical organ pieces Nos. 3, 6–8.

*** Argo ZRG 867 [id.]. Jennifer Smith, Watts, Tear, Luxon, St John's College Ch., ASMF, Guest; Scott (organ).

The *Little organ Mass* dates from 1775 and fares better here than in the earlier version under Münchinger. There is some fine invention in this piece, though it is not by any means the equal of the *Mariazeller Mass* of 1782, which H. C. Robbins Landon called 'the most perfect large-scale work Haydn achieved' in this particular period. The singing is of excellent quality, and so too is the orchestral playing. Excellent recording and good balance make this a desirable issue for all Haydn lovers.

Mass No. 7 in C (Missa in tempore belli; Paukenmesse).

*** Argo ZRG 643 [id.]. Cantelo, Watts, Tear, McDaniel, St John's College Ch., ASMF, Guest – M. HAYDN: *Salve regina*.***

(M) ** DG Priv. 2535/*3335* 442. Morison, Thomas, Witsch, Kohn, Bav. R. Ch. and O, Kubelik.

The final offering in Argo's series of Haydn's magnificent late Masses is well up to the standard set previously. With the St John's College Choir George Guest provides a clean, brightly recorded account with good soloists, although Heather Harper (in the earlier HMV recording from King's College, now deleted) was markedly sweeter-toned than April Cantelo here. That said, the Argo performance is every bit the equal of the earlier one, and it offers a splendid fill-up in the beautiful *Salve regina* by Haydn's brother Michael.

The DG version under Kubelik is not as fine as the Argo disc, but the mixed team of soloists works well, and Kubelik's dramatic yet lyrical approach brings direct and forthright music-making, but does not miss the colour and atmosphere in which this score abounds. With a spacious recording which still sounds well this is fair value at Privilege price. The cassette is of excellent quality, a close match with the LP.

Mass No. 8 in B flat (Heiligmesse): Missa Sancti Bernardi von Offida.

*** Argo ZRG 542 [id.]. Cantelo, Minty, Partridge, Keyte, St John's College Ch., ASMF, Guest.

The *Heiligmesse* is one of the most human and direct in its appeal of all Haydn's Masses. Its combination of symphonic means and simple vocal style underlines its effectiveness. Haydn started writing this Mass in the first year after his return from London, at about the time he wrote the *Paukenmesse*, but it was not completed until later, and was finally dedicated to the memory of St Bernard of Offida, newly canonized by Pope Pius VI barely a century after his death. The name *Heiligmesse* derives from the church song on which Haydn based the *Sanctus*. Among the special points of interest in the work are the slow introduction to the *Kyrie*, very like the introductions to Haydn's late symphonies, and the subdued *Agnus Dei* in the (for the time) extraordinary key of B flat minor. Like the other records in this series this is superlatively engineered and splendidly performed. The solo singing is good if not always equally distinguished, and the choral response is excellent. Along with the *Harmoniemesse*, this is among the most successful of the Argo series.

Mass No. 9 in D minor (Nelson Mass); Missa in angustiis.

*** Argo ZRG/*KZRC* 5325 [id.]. Stahlman, Watts, Wilfred Brown, Krause, King's College Ch., LSO, Willcocks.

Haydn's *Nelson Mass* is a tremendous work and clearly among his greatest music. Its impact in this splendid performance and recording is breathtaking. The solo singing is uniformly good, Sylvia Stahlman negotiating her florid music with great skill; and David Willcocks maintains quite remarkable tension throughout. The recording manages the many exciting and very loud climaxes without any difficulty and transfers the King's acoustic with complete success on disc and tape alike.

Mass No. 10 in B flat (Theresienmesse).
*** Argo ZRG 5500 [id.]. Spoorenberg, Greevy, Mitchinson, Krause, St John's College Ch., ASMF, Guest.

The *Theresa Mass* followed on a year after the *Nelson Mass*, the best known of the six magnificent settings of the Mass which Haydn wrote for his patron, Prince Esterházy, after his return from London. It may be less famous, but the inspiration is hardly less memorable, and Haydn's balancing of chorus against soloists, contrapuntal writing set against chordal passages, was never more masterly than here. George Guest injects tremendous vigour into the music (as in the *Harmoniemesse* there is a 'military' conclusion in the *Dona nobis pacem*), and the St John's Choir shows itself a ready match for the more famous choir at King's College. Good solo singing and brilliant, vivid recording.

Mass No. 11 in B flat (Schöpfungsmesse).
*** Argo ZRG 598 [id.]. Cantelo, Watts, Tear, Forbes Robinson, St John's College Ch., ASMF, Guest.

The *Schöpfungsmesse* or *Creation Mass* was the last but one of the magnificent series that Haydn wrote yearly in his retirement for his patron, Prince Esterházy. George Guest draws from his own St John's College Choir and an excellent band of professionals a fresh, direct performance to match the others of his highly successful series. Argo started recording these masses with the other great Cambridge choir, at King's College, but after the *Nelson Mass* Argo moved down the road to St John's. Excellent solo singing, notably from Robert Tear in the lovely *Incarnatus est*. Clear, forward recording.

Mass No. 12 in B flat (Harmoniemesse).
*** Argo ZRG 515 [id.]. Spoorenberg, Watts, Young, Rouleau, St John's College Ch., ASMF, Guest.

The *Harmoniemesse* was the last of the six Masses, all of them masterpieces, that Haydn, wrote after his return from London. In 1802, when he wrote it, the Esterházy orchestra was at its most expansive, and Haydn typically took advantage of the extra wind instruments available. He was already over seventy when he started writing it, but the freshness and originality of the writing are as striking as anything in the earlier works. In particular the last section of the Mass brings a wonderfully memorable passage, when from a gentle setting of the *Agnus Dei* Haydn bursts out with fanfares into a vigorous, even aggressive *Dona nobis pacem*. The performance matches the fine quality of George Guest's other recordings with the St John's Choir and Academy of St Martin's. The quartet of soloists is strong, with Helen Watts in particular singing magnificently. The recording is brilliantly real even by Argo standards.

Il ritorno di Tobia (oratorio).
*** Decca D 216 D 4 [Lon. OSA/5- 1445]. Hendricks, Zoghby, Della Jones, Langridge, Luxon, Brighton Fest. Ch., RPO, Dorati.

Haydn's first commission from Vienna, written while he was still at Esterháza, is by modern standards a great stranded whale of a piece, full of marvellous material but absurdly long for concert conditions. Based on a subject from the Apocrypha, the story of Tobias and the Angel, it has a libretto which undermines dramatic interest, but on record this objection largely disappears and Haydn's inspiration can at last be appreciated once more. This is the equivalent in oratorio terms of *opera seria*, and though the arias are very long they generally avoid *da capo* form. Most invigorating are the coloratura arias for the Archangel Gabriel (here the dazzling Barbara Hendricks) and the arias for the other soprano, Sara (the radiant Linda Zoghby), which include a lovely meditation, accompanied unexpectedly by antiphonies between oboes and cors anglais in pairs. The other soloists do not quite match the sopranos. but the Brighton Festival Chorus is lively and fresh-toned; and except in the rather heavy recitatives Dorati springs the rhythms beautifully, with the five magnificent choruses acting as cornerstones for the whole expansive structure. The recording is both brilliant and atmospheric.

The Seasons (in German).
*** Ph. Dig. **411 428-2**; 6769/*7654* 068 (3) [id.]. Mathis, Jerusalem, Fischer-Dieskau, Ch. and ASMF, Marriner.
**(*) Decca D 88 D 3/*K 88 K 32* (3) [Lon. OSA/*5*- 13128]. Cotrubas, Krenn, Sotin, Brighton Fest. Ch., RPO, Dorati.

Neville Marriner followed up the success of his resilient recording of *The Creation* with this superbly joyful performance of Haydn's last oratorio, effervescent with the optimism of old age. Edith Mathis and Dietrich Fischer-Dieskau are as stylish and characterful as one would expect, pointing the words as narrative. The tenor too is magnificent: Siegfried Jerusalem is both heroic of timbre and yet delicate enough for Haydn's most elegant and genial passages. The chorus and orchestra, of authentic size, add to the freshness. The recording, made in St John's, Smith Square, is warmly reverberant without losing detail. Highly recommended. The chrome cassette transfer has been made at a low level, and while the soloists sound fresh the chorus is less sharply focused than on disc.

Dorati brings to the work an innocent dedication, at times pointing to a folk-like inspiration, which is most compelling. This is not always so polished an account as others available, but with excellent solo singing and bright chorus work it is just as enjoyable. The choruses of peasants in Part 3, for instance, are strikingly robust, with accented rhythms to give a boisterous jollity. Textually there is the important advantage that, with the encouragement of H. C. Robbins Landon (who provides the excellent album notes), Dorati has restored the original version, notably the cuts in the introductions to *Autumn* and *Winter*, the latter with some wonderfully adventurous harmonies. The gains are marginal but important, and the recording quality is of outstanding vividness, though the chorus might have been more sharply focused. The orchestral detail is well realized; the pictorial effects towards the end of Part 2 are highly effective. The performance as a whole is splendidly animated. With Dorati this is above all a happy work, a point made all the more telling by the immediacy of the sound, equally impressive on disc and tape.

The Seasons (in English).
(M) *** Ph. 6770/*7650* 035 (3) [id.]. Harper, Davies, Shirley-Quirk, BBC Ch., BBC Ch. Soc., BBC SO, Sir Colin Davis.

Like Marriner (see above), Sir Colin Davis directs a tinglingly fresh performance of Haydn's mellow last oratorio, and choice can safely be left to a preference for the original German text or an excellent English translation. In this work – based with flamboyant freedom on a German translation of James Thomson's English poem – there is more than usual reason for using a translation, and the excellent soloists and chorus attempt with fair success to get the words over clearly. Although the tape transfer seems to be at an unnecessarily low level, the cassettes produce bright fresh sound and a little treble cut is possible to minimize hiss. The choral sound is full and clear and the performance overall makes a good impact.

Stabat Mater; Salve Regina.
*** Argo ZRG 917/8. Auger, Hodgson, Rolfe Johnson, Howell, L. Chamber Ch., Argo CO, Heltay.

Stabat Mater.
**(*) Erato Dig. NUM/*MCE* 72025. Armstrong, Murray, Hill, Huttenlocher, Lausanne Vocal Ens. and CO, Corbóz.

Haydn's *Stabat Mater*, one of his first major masterpieces, showing him at full stretch, was written in his early years at Esterháza. Scored for strings with oboes, the work is far bigger in aim than that scale might suggest, and some of the choruses include harmonic progressions which in their emotional overtones suggest music of a much later period. On record as in the concert hall the work is scandalously neglected, and it is good that Heltay's reading conveys its essential greatness, helped by admirable soloists and atmospheric recording. The *Salve Regina*, another early work, comparable in its depth of feeling, is here given with full chorus, although solo voices were orginally intended; the weight of the piece is better conveyed in this way.

On Erato the thirteen movements of the *Stabat Mater* – most of them slow – are squeezed neatly on to two sides merely, thanks in part to speeds brisker than usual. With an excellent quartet of soloists, fine choral singing of the kind we have come to expect of the Lausanne Choir, and first-rate recording, it makes a most recommendable issue, even if the Argo version on two discs brings a more devotional manner. Those wanting a cassette version will find the Erato transfer is of excellent quality, coping with the resonance with very little loss of refinement in the upper range.

OPERA

Armida (complete).
*** Ph. 6769 021 (3) [id.]. Norman, Ahnsjö, Burrowes, Ramey, Leggate, Lausanne CO, Dorati.

Armida, considered in Haydn's time to be his finest opera, was the last he produced at Esterháza and the one most frequently performed there. It is a piece in which virtually nothing happens. Rinaldo, a crusader seduced away from crusading by the sorceress Armida, heavily disguised as a goody, takes three Acts to decide to cut down the myrtle tree which will undermine Armida's wicked power. But, more than most works in this stilted form, *Armida* presents a psychological drama, with the myrtle tree the most obvious of symbols. On record it makes fair entertainment, with splendid singing from Jessye Norman, even if she hardly sounds malevolent. Claes Ahnsjö as the indecisive Rinaldo does better than most tenors coping with the enormous range. The whole team of soloists is one of the most consistent in Dorati's Haydn opera series, with Norma Burrowes particularly sweet as Zelmira. As well as some advanced passages, *Armida* also has the advantage that there is relatively little secco recitative. The recording quality is outstanding.

Armida: excerpts; *La vera costanza:* excerpts.
(M) *** Ph. 6529/*7339* 060 [id.]. Norman, Ahnsjö, Lausanne CO, Dorati.

Arias and duets with Jessye Norman, taken from two of Philips's Haydn opera series, make an attractive compilation, an appetizer for the complete sets. The voice is superbly captured in fine recording on both LP and cassette with Claes Ahnsjö impressive also in two duets. Lively and sympathetic conducting from Dorati.

La fedeltà premiata (complete).
*** Ph. 6707 028 (4) [id.]. Cotrubas, Von Stade, Valentini, Alva, Landy, Titus, Mazzieri, Swiss R. Ch., Lausanne CO, Dorati.

The operatic mastery of Mozart has always dogged the reputation of Haydn in this field, but this first of Philips's series of Haydn operas could hardly be more promising. *La fedeltà premiata* may have a preposterous plot, but this sparkling performance suggests that in all the complications of who was in love with whom, Haydn was sending up classical conventions with tongue firmly in cheek, almost like eighteenth-century G. and S. That at least would tie in with the concept of court entertainment at Esterháza, designed for particular singers and players performing before a select and familiar group of patrons. We can only guess what private jokes were involved, but above all in the extended finales to the first and second Acts one finds Haydn as opera composer setting a dramatic and musical pattern not so far different from Mozart at his peak.

Antal Dorati, having made such a success of his Haydn symphony cycle, here launched on another series with equal effervescence, helped by another excellent Haydn-sized orchestra and a first-rate cast. The proud Amaranta is superbly taken by the American mezzo Frederica von Stade, while Haydn's unconventional allocation of voices brings a fine baritone, Alan Titus, to match her as the extravagant hero; but the sweetest and most tender singing comes from Ileana Cotrubas as the fickle nymph Nerina. The recording is superb – intimate but with plenty of atmosphere.

L'Incontro improvviso (complete).
*** Ph. 6769 040 (3) [id.]. Zoghby, Marshall, Della Jones, Ahnsjö, Trimarchi, Luxon, Prescott, Lausanne CO, Dorati.

In eighteenth-century Vienna the abduction

opera involving moorish enslavement and torture became quite a cult – strange masochistic taste when Turkish invasions were not that distant. The greatest example is Mozart's *Entführung*, but this example of the genre from Haydn, a light entertainment for Prince Esterházy's private theatre, is well worthy of comparison with its very similar story. In forty-seven generally brief numbers, but with finales of almost Mozartian complexity, it may lack depth of characterization (Haydn was using a libretto set by Gluck) but the result is musically delightful. The most heavenly number of all is a trio for the three sopranos in Act I, *Mi sembra un sogno*, which with its high-flown legato phrases keeps reminding one of *Soave sia el vento* in *Così fan tutte*. The tenor's trumpeting arias are beautifully crisp and the vigorous canzonettas for the two buffo basses include a nonsense song or two. Benjamin Luxon and Domenico Trimarchi are delectable in those roles. Claes Ahnsjö is at his finest, resorting understandably to falsetto for one impossible top E flat; the role of heroine is superbly taken by Linda Zoghby, and she is well supported by Margaret Marshall and Della Jones. The secco recitatives are rather heavy, as ever contradicting Dorati's generally well-sprung style in Haydn. The recording conveys a most convincing theatre atmosphere.

L'Infedeltà delusa (complete).
** Hung. SLPX 11832/4. Kalmár, Pászthy, Rozsos, Fülöp, Gregor, Liszt CO, Frigyes Sándor.

L'Infedeltà delusa (complete). Arias from: *Acide e Galatea; Ifigenia in Tauride; I finti eredi; La Circe.*
*** Ph. 6769 061 (3) [id.]. Mathis, Hendricks, Ahnsjö, Baldin, Devlin, Lausanne CO, Dorati.

This was the last of the admirable Philips series of Haydn operas, recorded with Antal Dorati and the Lausanne Chamber Orchestra, providing an important nucleus of the operas written for performance at Esterháza. This one, a simple rustic comedy, may not be the most imaginative dramatically, but by the standards of the time it is a compact piece, punctuated by some sharply memorable arias such as a laughing song for the hero Nencio (the admirable Claes Ahnsjö) and a song of ailments for the spirited heroine, Vespina (Edith Mathis lively and fresh). Vespina is first cousin to Despina in *Così fan tutte*, and there is a splendid Mozartian anticipation when in the finale of Act I she slaps Nencio's face, Susanna-style. Dorati draws vigorous, resilient performances from everyone (not least the delightful Barbara Hendricks), and the final side devoted to arias and ensembles that Haydn devised for other men's operas adds to the attractions, ending with an amazing eating-and-drinking trio. Splendid and full-bodied recording.

The Hungaroton version is quite a strong contender even in the face of Dorati's fine Philips recording of this delightful piece. Sándor's approach is a degree more relaxed, and though the vocal quality is not so consistent, it is plain that the singers have performed this music on stage together, and a sense of involvement comes over. The recording is good but cannot match the excellence of the Philips, and there is no fill-up.

L'Isola disabitata (complete).
*** Ph. 6700 119 (2) [id.]. Lerer, Zoghby, Alva, Bruson, Lausanne CO, Dorati.

By eighteenth-century standards *L'Isola disabitata* (*The Uninhabited Island*) is an extremely compact opera, and were it not for the preponderance of accompanied recitative over set numbers it would be an ideal one to recommend to the modern listener. As it is, many passages reflect the *Sturm und Drang* manner of the middle-period Haydn, urgently dramatic with tremolos freely used. But in Act I it is only after twenty minutes that the first aria appears, a delightful piece for the heroine with a hint of *Che farò* in Gluck's *Orfeo*. Vocally it is the second soprano here, Linda Zoghby, who takes first honours, though the baritone, Renato Bruson, is splendid too. The piece ends with a fine quartet of reconciliation, only the eighth number in the whole piece. The direction of recitatives is unfortunately not Dorati's strong point – here as elsewhere in the series rather too heavy – but with excellent recording this makes a fascinating issue.

Il Mondo della luna (complete).
*** Ph. 6769 003 (4) [id./*7699 078*]. Auger, Mathis, Von Stade, Valentini Terrani, Alva, Rolfe Johnson, Trimarchi, Swiss R. Ch., Lausanne CO, Dorati.

Il Mondo della luna (*The World on the Moon*) is better known (by name at least) than the other Haydn operas that the Philips series has progressively disinterred. Written for an Esterházy marriage, it uses the plot of a naïve but engaging Goldoni comedy as its basis. A bogus astronomer (played by Luigi Alva) hoodwinks the inevitable rich old man (Domenico Trimarchi sparkling and stylish in comic vocal acting) into believing he has been transported to the moon. All this is in aid of getting the rich man's lovelorn daughter married to the hero of her choice, and though by the standards of the time the plot is simple it takes a long time in the resolving. Much of the most charming music comes in the brief instrumental interludes, and most of the arias are correspondingly short. That leaves much space on these records devoted to secco recitative, and as on his earlier Haydn opera issues, Dorati proves a surprisingly heavy and sluggish harpsichord continuo player. Nonetheless, with splendid contributions from the three principal women singers, this is another Haydn set which richly deserves investigation by anyone devoted to opera of the period. Excellent, finely balanced recording.

Orlando paladino (complete).
*** Ph. 6707 029 (4) [id.]. Auger, Ameling, Killebrew, Shirley, Ahnsjö, Luxon, Trimarchi, Mazzieri, Lausanne CO, Dorati.

One might well infer from this delightful send-up of a classical story in opera that Haydn in his pieces for Esterháza was producing sophisticated charades for a very closed circle. Though long for its subject, this is among the most delightful of all, turning the legend of Roland and his exploits as medieval champion into something not far from farce. Roland's madness (*Orlando furioso*) becomes the amiable dottiness of a Disney giant with a club, and there are plenty of touches of parody: the bass arias of the King of Barbary suggest mock-Handel and Charon's aria (after Orlando is whisked down to hell) brings a charming exaggeration of Gluck's manner. Above all the Leporello-like servant figure, Pasquale, is given a series of numbers which match and even outshine Mozart, including a hilarious duet when, bowled over by love, he can only utter monosyllables, cue for marvellous buffo singing from Domenico Trimarchi. The singing team is strong, with Arleen Auger as the heroine outstandingly sweet and pure. George Shirley as Orlando snarls too much in recitative, but it is an aptly heroic performance, and Elly Ameling and Gwendolyn Killebrew in subsidiary roles are both excellent. The recitatives here, though long, are rather less heavily done than on some other Dorati sets, and the recording is first-rate.

Lo Speziale (complete recording of surviving music).
** Hung. SLPX 11926/7. Fülöp, Istvan, Kalmár, Kincses, Liszt CO, Lehel.

Lo Speziale (*The Apothecary*), written for the inauguration of the opera house at the new palace of Esterháza, is a conventional buffo piece based on Goldoni. Though Haydn had had little or no experience of the stage, he produced individual numbers which are brilliantly successful, notably when two bogus notaries falsify a marriage contract as it is being dictated. It gained currency in Germany in the present century in a garbled edition, but here Lehel seeks to return to the original, and directs a lively if not always polished performance. The four young-sounding soloists (Fülöp rather too young for the role of Apothecary) are fresh-toned, singing agreeably if with little distinction. Fair recording.

La vera costanza (opera): complete.
*** Ph. 6703 077 (3) [id.]. Norman, Donath, Ahnsjö, Ganzarolli, Trimarchi, Lovaas, Rolfe Johnson, Lausanne CO, Dorati.

Written, like most of Haydn's operas, for private performance at Esterháza, *La vera costanza* keeps an elegantly urbane tone of voice illustrating what is on the face of it a preposterous story of a shipwreck and a secret marriage. But like Mozart's *Figaro* the piece has serious undertones, if only because the proletarian characters are the ones who consistently inspire sympathy, while the aristocrats come in for something not far short of ridicule. The individual numbers may be shorter-winded than in Mozart, but Haydn's sharpness of invention never lets one down, and the big finales to each of the first two Acts are fizzingly impressive, pointing clearly forward to *Figaro*. Overall the opera is nicely compact.

In every way except one this is a delectable performance. The conducting of Dorati sparkles, Jessye Norman is superb as the virtuous fisher-girl, Rosina, secretly married to Count Enrico, while the others make up an excellent team, well cast in often difficult roles designed for the special talents of individual singers at Esterháza. The snag is the continuo playing of Dorati himself, heavy and clangorous, holding up the lively singing of the secco recitatives. Apart from some discrepancy of balance between the voices and a touch of dryness in the acoustic, the recorded sound is excellent.

Arias: *Acide e Galatea: Tergi i vezzosi rai. Il Disertore: Un cor si tenero. La Scuola di gelosi: Dice benissimo. La vera costanza: Spann' deine lange Ohren.*
(M) *** Decca Jub. JB 100. Fischer-Dieskau, V. Haydn O, Peters – MOZART: *Arias*.**(*)

'Haydn and Mozart rarities', the disc says, and very delightful they prove, even if Haydn gets much less attention, with comparatively lightweight and simple pieces. Fischer-Dieskau is as thoughtfully stylish as ever, though it is a pity that he did not take more advice about the inclusion of appoggiaturas. Yet this is a most enjoyable recital and well worth investigating at Jubilee price. The recording is excellent.

COLLECTION

'Music for England': Symphony No. 94 (Surprise), arr. for flute, string quartet and piano; *Piano trio in A, H.XV/18; String quartet No. 71 in E flat, Op. 71/3; London trios Nos. 2 and 3, H.IV/2-3; Country dance; English canzonetta; Mermaid's song; Pastoral song; 6 Scottish songs; Lord Cathcart's welcome home.*
(M) *** O-L D 263 D 2/*K 263 K 22* [id., PSI]. Nelson, Elliott, AcAM, Hogwood.

This is a charming collection, originally compiled for the Folio Society, but making an excellent regular issue too. With the *Surprise Symphony* given in this chamber arrangement, it gives a vivid idea of the sort of music-making which Haydn's visits to London inspired. Judith Nelson and Paul Elliott sing stylishly in the vocal items, and the Academy's performances on original instruments have all their usual freshness and clarity. Clear recording to match on both LP and tape.

Haydn, Michael (1737–1806)

Salve regina.
*** Argo ZRG 634 [id.]. St John's College Ch., Guest – J. HAYDN: *Mass No. 7*.***

This lovely unaccompanied motet makes an unexpected and welcome fill-up for the fine Argo version of the *Paukenmesse*.

Hebden, John (18th century)

6 Concertos for strings (ed. Wood).
(*) Chan. Dig. **CHAN 8339; ABRD/*ABTD* 1082 [id.]. Cantilena, Shepherd.

Little is known about John Hebden except that he was a Yorkshire composer who also played the cello and bassoon. These concertos are his only known works, apart from some flute sonatas. Although they are slightly uneven, at best the invention is impressive. The concertos usually feature two solo violins and are well constructed to offer plenty of contrast. The performances here are accomplished, without the last degree of polish, but full of vitality. The recording is clear and well balanced; the chrome tape is wide-ranging but has a touch of edginess on top.

Hedges, Anthony (born 1931)

Scenes from the Humber, Op. 80; Kingston sketches, Op. 36; (i) *A Humberside cantata (Bridge for the living), Op. 62.*
*** Mer. E. 77047. (i) Adrian Thompson, Hull Ch. Union; Humberside Sinf., composer.

Sponsored by Humberside Leisure Services, this record may primarily reflect a local event, the opening of the Humber Bridge in 1981, but the professionalism of Hedges' writing deserves a wider hearing. As Reader in music at Hull University, he divides his activity between academic work and composition 'almost exclusively to commission.'

There is an unashamed flavour of film music both in the *Scenes from the Humber* and the brief collection of genre pieces making up the *Kingston sketches.* Walton is very much there, and something of Vaughan Williams, Delius even, but the sheer skill of the writing is what matters. The *Cantata* with words expressly written by Philip Larkin is more ambitious, but equally need not frighten anyone. Adrian Thompson is the clear-toned tenor. Excellent recording except that the chorus is backwardly balanced.

Helsted, Edvard (1816–1900)

La Fête des Fleurs à Genzano: Pas de deux et variations (with Paulli).
(M) ** HMV Green. ESD/*TC-ESD* 7148. L. Fest. Ballet O, Kern – BELLINI: *Night shadow***; DRIGO: *Le Corsaire.**(*)

Two Danish composers apparently collaborated to produce this quite engaging if ingenuous set of variations on an agreeable if not quite memorable theme. Playing and recording (with disc and tape sounding very similar) are excellent.

Napoli: suite dansante (with Paulli).
(M) *(*) HMV Green. ESD/*TC-ESD* 7149. L. Fest. Ballet O, Kern – CZERNY: *Études.***

The musical content of *Napoli* is negligible: there is rhythm and colour certainly, but nothing to capture the imagination. The reverberant recording is effective on disc, but somewhat coarsened by the high-level cassette transfer.

Hely-Hutchinson, Victor (1901–47)

A Carol symphony.
(M) ** HMV Green. ESD/*TC-ESD* 7021. Pro Arte O, Rose – VAUGHAN WILLIAMS: *Fantasia; Carols.***

Hely-Hutchinson's *Carol symphony* dates from the late 1920s, when it was still fashionable to regard the 'symphony' as an appropriate formal design for even a light-hearted piece. The snag is that carols, if they are good ones, are outstanding little works of art in their own right and don't admit improvement by 'symphonic' treatment. All you can do with them is to alter their orchestral dress, their harmony (which is seldom an improvement) or, as Constant Lambert observed about the symphonic treatment of folk-songs, play them again louder. Hely-Hutchinson does all these things and in the slow movement introduces Mahlerian harmonies for the *Coventry carol.* But he also creates a deliciously imaginative effect where the solo harp embroiders *Nowell,* even if the climax which follows goes on too long. The first movement too could do with judicious cuts; the scherzo is quite effective and in the finale the composer gathers all the strands together very engagingly; but without a Beecham at the helm the work as a whole tends to outstay its welcome. The performance is sensitive and competent, but Guildford Cathedral was not the proper venue for a piece of this intimate nature. The cassette transfer is disappointingly lacking in body (with 'tizzy' strings).

Henze, Hans Werner (born 1926)

(i) *Compases para preguntas ensimismadas* (music for viola and 22 players); (ii) *Violin concerto No. 2* (for solo violin, tape voices and 33 instrumentalists, using Hans Magnus Enzensberger's poem: *Homage à Gödel*).
*** Decca HEAD 5 [id.]. (i) Fukai, (ii) Langbein; both with L. Sinf., composer.

Compases is a gentle work, with the solo instrument supported by a shimmering orchestral texture, a piece that can easily seem flat and uneventful until you have a chance to hear it repeatedly on record. Of the *Violin concerto No. 2* Henze said that it is 'very nearly a stage piece but not quite', and with a poem by Enzensberger sung and recited during its course, the drama of the music is strongly presented, with the violin as the prime actor. Excellent performances and vivid recording.

Voices.
*** Decca HEAD 19/20. Walker, Sperry, L. Sinf., composer.

Voices outshines most of the other products of Henze's revolutionary fervour in the sharpness of detailed imagination. He sets a sequence of twenty-two texts in English, Spanish, German and Italian, using a wide variety of styles to match the variety of revolutionary protest which they contain. It matters little that echoes of Shostakovich rub shoulders with echoes of Weill along with unashamed lyricism of a kind that the composer has rarely allowed himself. The virtuosity of the writing is matched by the brilliance of the performance, designed as a whole evening of entertainment, here crisply caught on record, with the London Sinfonietta at its most inspired.

Hérold, Ferdinand (1791–1833)

La Fille mal gardée (ballet, arr. Lanchbery): extended excerpts.
❀*** HMV Dig. ASD/*TC-ASD* 10770–1/4. Royal Liv. PO, Wordsworth.
*** Decca SXL/*KSXC* 2313. ROHCG O, Lanchbery.

The ballet *La Fille mal gardée* dates originally from 1789 and has had a long and chequered history. The tale is a simple one of thwarted rustic love which comes right in the end, and the original score was made up from folk melodies and 'pop' songs of the time. Since 1789 it has been revised and rewritten by Hérold (1828), Hertel (1864) and Feldt (1937). The present score, commissioned by Frederick Ashton for the Royal Ballet revival, was prepared and exceedingly skilfully scored by John Lanchbery, who drew in the main on Hérold's version. However, Lanchbery also interpolates a single Hertel number, a gorgeously vulgar *Clog Dance* for Simone (who as a character is one of the ancestors of our pantomime Dame). Hérold's score also included tunes from Rossini's *Barber of Seville* and *Cenerentola*, together with a Donizetti selection (mainly from *L'Elisir d'amore*). That the ballet is therefore a complete hotch-potch does not prevent it from being marvellously entertaining. The music is popular in appeal but, being French, is witty too, and of course it is tuneful from beginning to end.

The ballet has been well served until now by John Lanchbery's own version which was first issued in 1962. Its success is confirmed by the fact that it has stayed in the catalogue at full price for over twenty years, backed up by a generally excellent cassette. Playing and recording are of high quality. But it is completely outclassed by this new HMV issue, spectacularly recorded in digital sound that is both glittering and sumptuous, and naturally balanced within an ideal acoustic. Pianissimos are as refined as climaxes are expansive. Yet it is the playing of the Royal Liverpool Philharmonic Orchestra – kept up on their toes from the first note to the last – that one remembers most of all. It combines delicacy with elegance, wit with humour (and not only in the famous *Clog dance*) and above all it has an exhilarating, life-enhancing exuberance. Barry Wordsworth's choice of tempi is admirable and he never secures polish at the expense of spontaneity: this performance alternately sparkles and beguiles the ear in the most ravishing way. Unfortunately the cassette does not match the LP in range, and it is without the delicious transparency of texture that makes the gentler pages sound so luminous on disc.

Herrmann, Bernard (1911–75)

North by Northwest (film score).
**(*) Uni. Dig. DKP 9000 [id.]. L. Studio SO, Laurie Johnson.

Although inventive and scored with Herrmann's usual feeling for atmosphere, this selection of incidental music is a bit thin. It has a distinctly attractive romantic strain, but much of the rest is unmemorable away from the visual images, which it seldom recalls. The playing is excellent and the digital recording is of high quality.

Vertigo (film score).
*** Mercury SRI/*MRI* 75117. Sinf. of L., Muir Matthieson.

This is a much more interesting score than the incidental music Herrmann provided for *North by Northwest*; it is highly evocative and scored with great skill. Even so one wonders if it will stand up to repetition away from the visual imagery. The recording, however, is of demonstration quality, extraordinarily vivid and atmospheric. The cassette is less spectacular, if full-bodied and clear. But it has no accompanying descriptive notes and does not even name the orchestra.

Hildegard of Bingen (1098–1179)

Hymns and sequences: *Ave generosa; Columba aspexit; O Ecclesia; O Euchari; O Ierusalem; O ignis spiritus; O presul vere civitatis; O virdissima virga.*
*** Hyp. **CDA 66039**; A/*KA* 66039. Gothic Voices, Muskett, White, Page.

Abbess Hildegard of Bingen was one of the great mystics of her age and both Popes Gregory IX and Innocent IV proposed her canonization. From 1141 onwards she was Abbess of the Benedictine Order at Disibodenberg near Bingen, twenty-five miles south-west of Mainz. She was naturalist, playwright, poetess as well as composer, and corresponded with many of the leading figures of the age, popes, emperors, kings, archbishops and so on. Her series of visions, *Scivias*, occupied her for the best part of a decade (1141–51), and this record draws on her collection of music and poetry, the *Symphonia armonie celestium revelationum* – 'the symphony of the harmony of celestial revelations'. These hymns and sequences, most expertly performed and recorded, have excited much acclaim – and rightly so. A lovely record: the cassette is of the highest quality, too, with good range and presence. The LP won the *Gramophone Early Music Award* for 1983.

Hindemith, Paul (1895–1963)

(i) *Concert music for piano, brass and harps, Op. 49. Concert music for strings and brass, Op. 50; Morning music for brass.*
*** Argo Dig. ZRDL 1000. Philip Jones Ens., Howarth, (i) with Crossley.

When he wrote these pieces in 1930 and 1931, Hindemith was at the peak of his powers, practising his *Gebrauchsmusik* as a practical musician but finding individual inspiration in the specific challenge of strange groupings of instruments as well as specific commissions. The *Concert music for Strings and Brass*, a powerful and inventive piece, is the more immediately attractive of the two big works, but thanks to the inspired playing of Paul Crossley, the poetry as well as the severe logic of the Op. 49 work comes over compellingly. The *Morgenmusik* for brass alone is a brief but worthwhile makeweight. The digital recording is outstanding, the perfect foil for the Ensemble's unfailing virtuosity.

Mathis der Maler (symphony).
(M) *** HMV SXLP/*TC-SXLP* 30536 [Ang. S 35949]. Berlin PO, Karajan – BARTÓK: *Music for strings, percussion and celesta.***(*)
(M) **(*) Uni. RHS/*UKC* 312 [None. 71307]. LSO, Horenstein – R. STRAUSS: *Death and transfiguration.***

Karajan's 1960 account of the *Mathis symphony* is beautifully spacious and among the very finest versions of the work ever made. Karajan succeeds in producing a more refined and transparent texture than we are accustomed to, and both dynamic nuances and details of phrasing are attentively followed without creating a sense of beautification. The first two movements in particular are fresh and atmospheric, and the opening of the finale is wonderfully dramatic. The recording is atmospheric too, but rather wanting in body. It is not the equal of Karajan's EMI recordings made much earlier in London with the Philharmonia. However, the performance is so fine – and certainly the best on the market at the time of writing – that the recommendation must be unqualified. The cassette transfer is strikingly vivid.

Horenstein's account was the last record he made, and has the merit of breadth and weight. Although the coupling is not a welcome one (there are at least four stunning accounts of *Death and transfiguration* that eclipse Horenstein's version), Horenstein's admirers will probably want this issue nonetheless. The tape transfer is first-class, the sound brilliant and clear.

5 Pieces for strings, Op. 44.
*** Argo ZRG 763 [id.]. ASMF, Marriner – SCHOENBERG: *Verklaerte Nacht;* WEBERN: *5 Movements.****

With finely etched playing in precise ensemble, Marriner and the Academy transform the Hindemith *Pieces* from exercises to works of genuine imagination. This is an unexpected but worthwhile coupling for Schoenberg and Webern, with excellent recording.

Symphonic metamorphosis on themes by Weber.
*** Decca SXL 6398. LSO; Abbado – JANÁČEK: *Sinfonietta.****
(*) Telarc Dig. DG 10056/7 [id.]. Atlanta SO, Shaw – ORFF: *Carmina Burana.*(*)

It is a relief to find a conductor content, like Abbado, to follow the composer's own dynamic markings and who does not succumb to the temptation to score interpretative points at the music's expense. The stopped notes on the horns at the beginning of the finale, for example, are marked piano and are played here so that they add a barely perceptible touch of colour to the texture. The Decca engineers balance this so musically that the effect is preserved. This admittedly unimportant touch is symptomatic of the subtlety of Abbado's approach in a performance that in every respect is of the highest quality.

Robert Shaw treats Hindemith's colourful variations almost neoclassically. His is a sharp, incisive performance that misses some of the bounce and charm, but makes a fair fill-up for a three-sided version of *Carmina Burana*. The recording here is not quite of the demonstration quality given to the Orff.

Symphonic metamorphosis on themes by Weber; Symphony in E flat.
(M) ** CBS 60288/*40-*. NYPO, Bernstein.

Although Hindemith's representation in the current catalogue is marginally better than it was some years ago, there is no alternative listing of this fine *Symphony* now that Sir Adrian's more dignified account is no longer in print, and admirers of this composer will want to snap this up in spite of the rather brash account of the first movement and less than ideal recording. It is pleasing to see that this also appears in cassette form where Hindemith's listings are pretty sparse. At its modest price, this can be recommended, for the 1940 *Symphony* is a most eloquent piece. The performance of the Weberian *Symphonic metamorphosis* is also a vital one. The chrome cassette is bright and brilliant but slightly shallow in the *Symphony*, fuller and better balanced in the *Symphonic metamorphosis*.

Kammermusiken: Nos. 1 for small orchestra, Op. 24/1; 2 for piano and 12 solo instruments; 3 for cello and 10 solo instruments; 4 for violin and chamber orchestra; 5 for viola and chamber orchestra, Op. 36/1–4; 6 for viola d'amore and chamber orchestra; 7, Organ concerto, Op. 46/1–2.

*** HM 1C 165 99 721/3. Ensemble 13, Baden-Baden, Reichert.

These chamber concertos for various instruments are from a vintage period and are full of rewarding invention both in terms of musical ideas and novel textures. Here we have music that is highly original and much lighter in touch than the name Hindemith would lead many collectors to expect. It is marvellously recorded, too, and will yield quite unexpected pleasures to those enterprising enough to invest in it. The performances are all highly accomplished and imaginative.

Kleine Kammermusik, Op. 24/2.

*** Uni. RHS 366. Danish Wind Quintet – MILHAUD: *Cheminée du Roi René* *(*); NIELSEN: *Quintet.***

Alert and sensitive playing here from the Danish Wind Quintet, who are far more imaginative and responsive in the *Kleine Kammermusik* than in their native Nielsen. Dynamic nuances are scrupulously observed here, whereas in the latter they are not. Good recording of engaging music.

When Lilacs last in the dooryard bloom'd (Requiem).

(M) *** DG 2543 825 [id.]. Burmeister, Leib, Berlin R. Ch. and SO, Koch.

This was one of the most ambitious works that Hindemith wrote in his later years. Using a German translation (by the composer himself) of Walt Whitman, it may have little relationship with a requiem and little in it is dramatic, but it contains many beautiful ideas, notably in the choral writing. The close of the work is particularly fine. This is a first-rate performance, recorded originally in 1966, but sounding well in this mid-price reissue.

OPERA

Cardillac (complete).

(M) *** DG 2721 246 (2) [id.]. Fischer-Dieskau, Kirschstein, Grobe, Kohn, Cologne R. Ch. and SO, Keilberth.

Taken from a live radio performance, this is a valuable issue of an important modern opera that shows Hindemith at his most vigorous. In this story of a Parisian goldsmith who resorts to murder to save his own creations, he uses academic forms such as fugue and passacaglia with Bachian overtones in the idiom but with striking dramatic effect. Fischer-Dieskau as the goldsmith has a part which tests even his artistry, and though the other soloists are variable in quality the conducting of Keilberth holds the music strongly together. This is the original 1926 version of the score, fresher and more effective than Hindemith's later revision.

Mathis der Maler (opera; complete).

*** EMI 1C 165 03515/7 [Ang. SZCX 3869 (3)]. Fischer-Dieskau, Feldhoff, King, Schmidt, Meven, Cochran, Malta, Grobe, Wagemann, Bav. R. Ch. and SO, Kubelik.

There is little doubt that the opera *Mathis der Maler* is Hindemith's masterpiece. The fine symphony which he extracted from it gives only a partial idea of its quality, for here Hindemith's theorizing went with a deep involvement with the subject. There is no mistaking that behind the characteristic gruffness of manner there is not just urgency but warmth. Fischer-Dieskau proves the ideal interpreter of the central role, the painter Mathias Grünewald, who in the troubled Germany of the sixteenth century joins the cause of the rebellious peasants – a subject with a very clear relevance to the times when the piece was written, during the rise of the Nazis. Other fine contributions come from James King as the Archbishop, Donald Grobe as the Cardinal, Alexander Malta as the army commandant and Manfred Schmidt as the Cardinal's adviser. The women principals are less happily chosen: Rose Wagemann as Ursula is rather squally. But with splendid playing and singing from Bavarian Radio forces under Kubelik, it is a highly enjoyable as well as an important set.

Hoddinott, Alun (born 1929)

(i) *Nocturnes and cadenza for cello and orchestra; Overture: Jack Straw;* (ii) *Sinfonia Fidei.*
*** Uni. Dig. RHD 401 [id.]. (i) Welsh; (ii) Gomez, Burrows, Philh. Ch., Philh. O, Groves.

Sinfonia Fidei, written in 1977, is one of the most impressive of Hoddinott's later works, purposeful and dramatic in argument, returning to a rather more conservative harmonic idiom than that contained in his purely serial music. The economy of the piece has one following the argument with relative ease. By comparison, the *Nocturnes and cadenzas* present a more withdrawn face, not helped by an idea which rather limits the quota of fast music. Moray Welsh is a fine cello soloist, and Sir Charles Groves draws excellent playing from the Philharmonia, not least in the brief *Overture, Jack Straw*. First-rate recording.

Symphony No. 2, Op. 20; Variants for orchestra.
**(*) Oriel ORM 1003. LSO, Del Mar.

Alun Hoddinott is a serialist who refuses to be channelled into formalism, and uses twelve-note technique as a spur rather than a crutch. This symphony dates from 1962 and still retains an allegiance to tonal centres; *Variants*, written four years later, is more ingenious in formal layout (in modern terms just as much a symphony), with six movements that are 'a double set of variants running out of parallel'. The orchestration too is here more individual, and the main point that brings a reservation is that too high a proportion of the music in both works is slow and solemn. Hoddinott should let his vivid sense of humour have freer rein, even in his most serious utterances. Fine direction from Del Mar; good recording.

Welsh dances, Op. 15.
*** Oriel ORM 1001. RPO, Groves – JONES: *The Country beyond the stars;* WILLIAMS: *Penillion.****

Hoddinott's *Welsh dances* are the equivalent of Malcolm Arnold's sets of orchestral dances, just as colourful and unpretentious – surprising pieces, perhaps, from a serialist composer, but welcome ones. An attractive supplement to a nicely planned disc, featuring excellent performances and recording.

Hoffmann, Johann (1776–1822)

Mandolin concerto in D.
(M) ** Turn. TV/*KC* 334003 [TV 34003]. Kunschak, V. Pro Musica O, Hladky – HUMMEL: *Mandolin concerto.***

This work is of considerably less musical interest than the Hummel concerto on the other side, but the playing of Elfriede Kunschak is lively enough. By no means a masterpiece, but of interest to mandolin enthusiasts.

Hoffmeister, Franz (1754–1812)

Flute concerto No. 6 in D.
(M) ** ASV ACM/*ZCACM* 2020 [None. 71388]. Dingfelder, ECO, Mackerras – C. P. E. BACH: *Flute concerto.***

Franz Hoffmeister, a Viennese music publisher, is best remembered for his association with Mozart's K.499 *String quartet*. His *Concerto* is a well-made, elegant piece, if not a memorable one. The performance here is sprightly and polished and Mackerras's accompaniment has plenty of spirit. The sound is first-class and the high-level cassette matches the disc very closely.

Holborne, Anthony (died 1602)

Cradle pavane and galliard (*The woods so wild*); *Countess of Pembroke's paradise; Holborne's almain* (suite); *Muy linda; Nowell's galliard; 2 Pavans and galliards; Quadro pavan and galliard. Suite: Galliard: Heres paternus; Heigh ho holiday; The wanton.*
*** Mer. E 77027. Extempore String Ens., Weigland.

The Extempore String Ensemble attempts to live up to its name by playing spontaneously even in the recording studio. This Holborne disc does not have quite the expressive abandon which made the group's earlier record of consort music by different composers so compelling, but it presents an illuminating musical portrait of a long-neglected but fascinating Elizabethan, a key figure in spheres other than music. First-rate recording.

Pavanes and galliards (1599): *Almayne; As it fell on a holie eve; Ecce quam bonum; The funerals; 3 Galliards; Heigh ho holiday; Heres paternus; The Honiesuckle; Image of melancholy; Infernum; Muy linda; Paradizo; Pavan; Pavana ploravit; The sighes; Sic semper soleo.*
*** O-L DSLO 569 [id.]. Guildhall Waits, Cons. of Musicke, Trevor Jones or Rooley.

Holborne's *Pavanes and galliards* were published in 1599 and comprise sixty-five five-part dances, of which seventeen are included on this record. The music is very appealing indeed, and though it could easily sound unvaried, the planners of the record have achieved satisfactory results by contrasting the Guildhall Waits (cornetts and sackbutts) with the strings of the Consort of Musicke. The cornetts and sackbutts sound a shade inhibited at times and, generally speaking, a little more abandon would not have come amiss in what is a lively anthology. The recording is cut at a high level but does not give trouble to pick-ups that are tracking properly. If there is end-of-side distortion (as stated in one or two reviews) you can be sure that it is not the fault of the record if the copy corresponds to the ones we have tried.

Holbrooke, Josef (1878–1958)

The Birds of Rhiannon, Op. 87.
*** Lyr. SRCS 103. LPO, Handley – ROOTHAM: *Symphony No. 1.****

A recording of remarkable clarity, definition and depth. *The Birds of Rhiannon* is a shortish piece, lasting about fifteen minutes and drawing on Holbrooke's operatic trilogy on Welsh legends that occupied him from 1912 to 1920. Arthur Hutchings suggests that *The Birds of Rhiannon* may well bear much the same relationship to the operas as the *Siegfried idyll* does to the *Ring*. The piece ends with bird song, as does the opera *Bronwen*, when the seven heroes are so beguiled by the magical sounds that they remain at Harlech for seven years. The level of inspiration of Holbrooke's piece does not quite rise to the theme, and it would be idle to pretend that it is a masterpiece. The playing of the LPO under Handley is excellent, as also in the rather more interesting coupling.

Holloway, Robin (born 1943)

(i) *Romanza for violin and small orchestra, Op. 31;* (ii) *Sea-surface full of clouds, Op. 28.*
*** Chan. Dig. ABRD/*ABTD* 1056 [id.]. (i) Gruenberg; (ii) Walmsley-Clark, Cable, Brett, Hill, Hickox Singers, City of L. Sinf., Hickox.

Robin Holloway is one of the most imaginative British composers of his generation, and the two works recorded here show him at his most accessible. *Sea-surface full of clouds*, composed in 1974–5, is a setting of Wallace Stevens and runs to nearly thirty-eight minutes, all comfortably accommodated on one side. The textures radiate a world that is related in feeling to Delius, Szymanowski, Nicholas Maw and Berg, yet the atmosphere is quite personal. The *Romanza* of 1976 is a much shorter piece but hardly less eloquent: moments of gentle lyricism are broken up by contrasting vigorous sections. The overall atmosphere of the work is quite haunting. Erich Gruenberg is a persuasive soloist and Richard Hickox draws altogether excellent results from the assembled forces. The recording, made in St Giles Church, Cripplegate, is in every way admirable with good balance and perspective. A worthwhile issue. On both disc and the high-level chrome tape.

Holmboe, Vagn (born 1909)

Cello concerto, Op. 120.
*** BIS LP 78. Bengtsson, Danish R. SO, Ferencsik (with Koppel: *Cello concerto****).

The recording derives from the first performance in 1975 and differs a little from the London Prom performance in 1979 when the final pages were slightly extended. In some ways this original version seems more convincing. Right from the outset, one is aware that this is a distinctive sound world and though the thematic ideas (with two exceptions) do not linger in the memory, the whole atmosphere remains long after the music is over. The textures are pale and luminous like the northern light, and the web of sound is splendidly transparent. It is played with eloquence and feeling by Erling Bløndal Bengtsson and the recording is beautifully natural. Moreover it has a most interesting coupling, an attractive concerto by another Dane.

Symphony No. 10, Op. 105.
*** Cap. CAP 1116. Gothenberg SO, Ehrling – NYSTROEM: *Sinfonia breve.****

The Danish composer Holmboe possesses a powerful and inquiring mind; his music betrays a strong sense of purpose and establishes a sound world that is immediately identifiable. The *Tenth* of his eleven symphonies was written for Sixten Ehrling and the Detroit Orchestra, and dates from 1971. It is music of vision and individuality whose language will strike a responsive chord in any admirer of Nielsen, though Holmboe's music does not resemble that of his great countryman. It is well played and recorded and should not be overlooked by any collector with an interest in the Scandinavian symphonic tradition.

Collectors may like to know that the *Seventh Symphony*, one of Holmboe's best works, has also been recorded by the Danish Radio Symphony Orchestra under John Frandsen (DMA 018). A concentrated and compelling work, with a mixed programme on the back, and decently played and recorded (but not more). The same label has also put out some of his motets from the *Liber canticorum* sung by the Young Academic Choir of Copenhagen under Niels Møller (DMA 028), grave and serene music, elevated in spirit and substance.

String quartets: Nos. 15, Op. 135; 16, Op. 146.
*** Danish Mus. Ant. DMA 048. Copenhagen Qt.

The string quartets occupy as central a place in Holmboe's output as do his eleven symphonies, and they contain some of his most deeply characteristic and searching thought. It is a measure of the importance he attaches to the medium that he waited until his fortieth year before ascribing a number to a quartet (the *First* of 1949 was in fact his ninth work in the genre). The first three were available in the UK in the early 1950s and Turnabout/ Vox issued the *Eighth* in 1970. All, except 13 and 14, have been recorded by the Copenhagen Quartet, and the two coupled here date from 1977 and 1981 respectively. No. 15 is a powerfully argued piece, its ideas fresh and astringent, and can be numbered among the very finest of the cycle (1, 3, 7, 8, 10, 14). They are splendidly played and well recorded. This is rewarding music.

Holst, Gustav (1874–1934)

(i) *Beni Mora (oriental suite), Op. 29/1;* (ii) *St Paul's suite, Op. 29/2.*
(M) ** HMV SXLP 30126. (i) BBC SO; (ii) RPO; Sargent – ELGAR: *Serenade*; WARLOCK: *Capriol suite.***

Beni Mora, an attractively exotic piece that shows Holst's flair for orchestration vividly, is well played here, while Sir Malcolm Sargent's account of the *St Paul's suite* is accomplished, full of verve and character with good recording.

(i) *Beni Mora (suite);* (ii) *Brook Green suite.*
(M) *** HMV Green. ESD/*TC-ESD* 290022-1/*4*. (i) from above, cond. Sargent; (ii) ECO, Bedford – *Choral hymns from the Rig Veda* etc.***

These performances are a generous makeweight for a valuable collection of short vocal works – see below.

Brook Green suite (for strings); *A Somerset rhapsody.*
*** HMV ASD/*TC-ASD* 3953. Bournemouth Sinf., Del Mar – VAUGHAN WILLIAMS: *The Wasps.****

Like the *St Paul's suite*, this *Brook Green suite* was originally written for the St Paul's School for Girls, where Holst was in charge of music. It emerged as far more than an exercise for students, as this dedicated performance demonstrates, very strikingly in the vigorous final dance. The *Somerset rhapsody*, one of Holst's most evocative pieces, is here most persuasively played, helped by recording of demonstration quality. Indeed this record with its delightful Vaughan Williams coupling is more than the sum of its parts, and the cassette is equally recommendable, offering warmly atmospheric textures, the resonance captured most naturally.

Brook Green suite for strings; Nocturne for strings; St Paul's suite, Op. 29/2; (i) *Fugal concerto for flute, oboe and strings, Op. 40/2;* (ii) *Lyric movement for viola and small orchestra.*
**(*) Lyr. SRCS 34. ECO, Imogen Holst, with (i) Bennett; Graeme; (ii) Aronowitz.

An enterprising anthology, excellently played and recorded. The familiar *St Paul's suite* ought to be as popular as any work in the string repertoire, and apart from this splendid work, the record offers the pensive and searching *Lyric movement for viola and small orchestra*, one of the most beautiful of Holst's later pieces. Its addition to the catalogue is most welcome and Cecil Aronowitz gives the most convincing and persuasive account of it. The *Fugal concerto* is much less taking. It seems little more than an academic study, with none of the character or inspiration of the *Lyric movement*. But the latter is so outstanding that the record is worth getting for its sake.

(i) *Egdon Heath, Op. 47; The Perfect Fool: ballet suite, Op. 39;* (ii) *Choral fantasia, Op. 51;* (iii) *Hymn of Jesus, Op. 37.*
(M) *** HMV Green. ESD/*TC-ESD* 178304–1/*4*. (i) LSO, Previn; (ii) Baker, Partridge, Purcell Singers, ECO, Imogen Holst; (iii) St Paul's Cath. Ch., LSO Ch., LPO, Groves.

(i) *Egdon Heath, Op. 47; The Perfect Fool: ballet suite, Op. 39;* (ii) *Hymn of Jesus, Op. 37.*

(M) *** Decca Jub. JB/*KJBC* 49. (i) LPO; (ii) BBC SO and Ch.; Boult.

Fine performances and vintage recording on the Decca Jubilee disc, with a brilliant and colourful account of *The Perfect Fool* ballet music, and Boult bringing out the bleak, sombre evocation of *Egdon Heath*. The sound is equally good on disc and tape (the latter being one of Decca's best transfers). However, the account of the *Hymn of Jesus*, although dramatic and atmospheric, is perhaps not quite so penetrating as Groves on HMV. Sir Charles Groves brings great sympathy and conviction to this beautiful and moving score, whose visionary quality has never paled. He is given a recording of great clarity and presence. Moreover the HMV collection includes also the *Choral fantasia*, a setting of words written by Robert Bridges in commemoration of Purcell. It is not an easy work to grasp but it is well worth getting to know and, with Dame Janet Baker once again showing her supreme quality as a recording artist, the performance could hardly be more persuasive, owing much to the inspired direction of the composer's daughter. Previn gives a darkly intense performance of *Egdon Heath*, illuminatingly different from Boult's coolly detached one. The rip-roaring ballet music from *The Perfect Fool* presents a colourful contrast. Both are given vivid recording of EMI's best quality.

Hammersmith (*Prelude and scherzo*), *Op. 52.*
(M) *** Mercury SRI/*MRI* 75028 [id.]. Eastman Wind Ens., Fennell – JACOB: *William Byrd suite;* WALTON: *Crown Imperial.****

Frederick Fennell established his reputation as a leading exponent of wind band music in the mono era. The present stereo recording, from the early 1960s, shows him still in a class of his own in this repertoire. Holst insisted that *Hammersmith* is not programme music, yet admitted that the nearby continuously flowing Thames was part of his inspiration. Certainly the result is one of his most immediately appealing and memorable works, with an indelible principal theme and wonderful atmospheric feeling. Fennell's account is definitive, both structurally impressive and highly evocative, and the playing of the Eastman wind group commands great admiration. The recording is first-class and there is an excellent cassette (though it is without accompanying descriptive notes). The Gordon Jacob coupling may be anachronistic but it is wonderfully life-enhancing. A highly recommendable issue to supplement the Telarc disc of the *Military band suites* – see below.

Hammersmith: Prelude and scherzo, Op. 32; Military band suites Nos. 1 in E flat; 2 in F, Op. 28.
*** ASV ACA/*ZCACA* 1002. L. Wind Soloists, Wick – VAUGHAN WILLIAMS: *English folksongs suite* etc.***

Military band suites Nos. 1–2.
C❀*** Telarc Dig. **CD 80038**; DG 10038 [id.]. Cleveland Symphonic Winds, Fennell – HANDEL: *Royal Fireworks music.**** C

Holst's two *Military band suites* contain some magnificent music – much underrated because of the medium – and they have been lucky on records. Frederick Fennell's famous Mercury recording, made at the beginning of the 1960s, is remembered nostalgically by many collectors and was a landmark in its day. His new versions have more gravitas though not less *joie de vivre*. They are magnificent, and the recording is truly superb – digital technique used in a quite overwhelmingly exciting way. Perhaps there is too much bass drum, but no one is going to grumble when the result is so telling. The *Chaconne* of the *First Suite* makes a quite marvellous effect here. The playing of the Cleveland wind group is of the highest quality, smoothly blended and full in slow movements, vigorous and alert and with strongly rhythmic articulation in fast ones. To be reproduced properly, the compact disc version needs amplifier and speakers that can easily handle the wide amplitude and range of the sound; then the result offers a most remarkable demonstration of spectacular sound reproduction, that should convince even the most hardened sceptic of the full possibilities of this new format.

The recording by the London Wind Soloists (a group drawn from the LSO) is enjoyable in quite a different way. The performances are altogether more lightweight, but they have great spontaneity. The music's lyrical feeling is displayed more readily: the *March* from the *Second Suite* is resilient; the *Fantasia on the Dargason* has unmistakable sparkle and *Hammersmith* too has an attractive rhythmic freshness. The recording is altogether less massive than the Telarc disc, but still very good indeed, and with worthwhile couplings this is well worth investigating as an attractively different approach. The cassette is just a little disappointing, good but with only a modest transfer level; the transients are less sharp than on the disc.

Invocation for cello and orchestra, Op. 19/2.
*** RCA Dig. RS/*RK* 9010. Lloyd Webber, Philh. O, Handley – DELIUS: *Concerto;* VAUGHAN WILLIAMS: *Folk songs fantasia.****

Holst's *Invocation for cello and orchestra* comes from 1911 and pre-dates *The Planets*. Indeed, in her book on her father, Imogen Holst spoke of it as 'trying out some of the ideas for the texture of Venus'. It is a highly attractive and lyrical piece well worth reviving, and a valuable addition to the growing Holst discography. Both the performance and recording are of admirable quality with little to choose between LP and the excellent chrome tape. Strongly recommended.

The Lure, H.149; The Morning of the year: Dances, H.184 (ed. I. Holst; Matthews); (i) *The Mystic trumpeter, H.71.*
*** Lyr. SRCS 128. (i) Armstrong; LSO, Atherton.

It is good that Lyrita is turning its attention to rare Holst. *The Mystic trumpeter* comes from 1904 though it was revised eight years later, and is a setting of Whitman. There are some striking things in it and, both in its harmonic language and metrical freedom, it looks forward to things to come. Sheila Armstrong gives an impressive account of this rarity and is given sympathetic support from Atherton and the LSO. *The Lure* is a later work, composed in 1921 but never performed in Holst's lifetime. Indeed, he withdrew this ballet from his list of works and, though it is not top-drawer Holst, it is well worth hearing and, like the Dances from *The Morning of the year*, written in the mid-1920s at the behest of the BBC (it was the very first work to be commissioned by the Music Department), has many characteristic touches. The playing is very good indeed and the recording is in the best tradition of the house.

The Planets (suite), Op. 32.
*** DG Dig. **400 028-2**; 2532/*3302* 019 [id.]. Berlin PO and Ch., Karajan.
*** HMV ASD/*TC-ASD* 3649. LPO, Mitchell Ch., Boult.
(M) *** Decca Jub. JB/*KJBC* 30 [Lon. JL/*5-41005*]. VPO and V. State Op. Ch., Karajan.
*** Decca SET/*KCET* 628 [Lon. CS/5-7110]. LPO and Ch., Solti.
*** HMV ASD/*TC-ASD* 3002 [Ang. S/*4XS* 36991]. LSO, Amb. S., Previn.
(M) *** HMV Green. ESD/*TC-ESD* 7135 [Ang. S/*4XS* 36420]. New Philh. O, Amb. S., Boult.
*** Chan. Dig. **CHAN 8302**; ABRD/*ABTD* 1010 [id.]. SNO and Ch., Gibson.
(M) *** RCA GL/*GK* 13885 [AGL1/*AGK1* 3885]. Phd. O, Mendelssohn Club Ch., Ormandy.
*** DG Priv. 2535/*3335* 485 [2530 102]. Boston SO and Ch., Steinberg.
**(*) HMV Dig. ASD/*TCC-ASD* 4047 [Ang. DS/*4XS* 37817]. Philh. O, Amb. Ch., Rattle.
(*) CBS Dig. **CD; 37249/*40-* [id.]. O Nat. de France and Ch., Maazel.
**(*) Decca VIV/*KVIC* 21 [Lon. CS/*5-6734*]. LAPO, with Master Chorale, Mehta.
(M) **(*) EMI Em. EMX/*TC-EMX* 2003. BBC SO and Ch., Sargent.
(M) **(*) CBS 60125/*40-* [MY/*MYT* 37226]. NYPO and Ch., Bernstein.
(B) ** CfP CFP/*TC-CFP* 40243. Hallé O and Ch., Loughran.
(B) * Con. CC/*CCT* 7518. LPO and Ch., Herrmann.

It is perhaps not surprising, when one surveys the long and successful list of recordings above, that *The Planets* should be the first work to receive the accolade of three different compact disc issues, when at the same time not all the Beethoven Symphonies are yet available in this new medium. It would, however, have amazed Holst, who (as recently as 1915) found considerable difficulty in getting his work before the public in the first place. As it so happens, the compact disc of Karajan's performance is just a little disappointing. The sound is vividly wide-ranging, of course. Indeed the dynamic range is something to be marvelled at, and the opening of *Mars* has remarkable bite, while the marvellously sustained pianissimo playing of the Berlin Philharmonic – as in *Venus*, and the closing pages of *Saturn* and *Venus* – is the more telling against a background of silence. But the 'digital edge' on the treble detracts from the overall beauty of the orchestral sound in fortissimos, and *Jupiter* ideally needs a riper body of tone. The bass is less resonant than in some digital recordings from this source, so that the organ pedals at the end of *Saturn* come through more positively in the old (Eminence) Sargent recording from the earliest days of stereo. But one should not make too much of this. Both the ordinary LP and chrome cassette are very impressive indeed, and it would be perverse to suggest that the compact disc does not add to the impact and refinement of detail. Moreover it is a thrilling performance that makes one hear Holst's brilliant suite with new ears. With the Berlin Philharmonic at peak form, Karajan improves even on the performance he recorded two decades earlier with the Vienna Philharmonic, modifying his reading to make it more idiomatic; for example in *Jupiter* the syncopated opening now erupts with joy and the big melody has a natural flow and nobility to make one long to hear Karajan conducting Elgar. *Venus* has sensuous string phrasing, *Mercury* and *Uranus* have beautiful springing in the triplet rhythms, and the climax of that last movement brings an amazing glissando on the organ, made clear by the thirty-two-channel recording.

It was Sir Adrian Boult who, over sixty years ago, first 'made *The Planets* shine', as the composer put it, and in his ninetieth year he recorded it for the last time. It sets the seal on a magnificent Indian summer in the recording studio, a performance at once intense and beautifully played, spacious and dramatic, rapt and pointed. If the opening of *Mars* – noticeably slower than in Boult's previous recordings – suggests a slackening, the opposite proves true: that movement gains greater weight at a slower tempo. *Mercury* has lift and clarity, not just rushing brilliance, and it is striking that in Holst's syncopations – as in the introduction to *Jupiter* – Boult allows himself a jaunty, even jazzy freedom which adds an infectious sparkle. The great melody of *Jupiter* is calculatedly less resonant and more flowing than previously but is more moving, and *Uranus* as well as *Jupiter* has its measure of jollity, with the lolloping 6/8 rhythms delectably pointed. The spacious slow movements are finely poised and the recording is of demonstration quality, gloriously full and opulent, with the tape measuring up well to the disc.

Still very competitive indeed – especially for those who value the rather more blurred and (some would say) natural outlines of first-rate analogue sound – is Karajan's earlier version which, even though it is (amazingly) over twenty years old, is still very impressive with its richly atmospheric Decca sound. Now reissued on Jubilee this easily leads the mid-price field and indeed remains near the top of the list on most counts. It was here we first heard Karajan's transformation of a work we had tended to think of as essentially English into an international score. There are many individual touches, from the whining Wagnerian tubas of *Mars*, the *Venus* representing ardour rather than mysticism, the gossamer textures of *Mercury* and the strongly characterized *Saturn* and *Uranus*, with splendid playing from the Vienna brass. The cassette like the disc is technically first-class.

The Decca recording for Solti's Chicago version is also extraordinarily fine. With *Mars* opening with a brilliant cutting edge and at the fastest possible tempo, Solti's version could not be more contrasted with Boult's newest recording, which arrived simultaneously. Solti's pacing is exhilarating to the point of fierceness in the vigorous movements, and undoubtedly his direct manner is refreshing, the rhythms clipped and precise, sometimes at the expense of resilience. His directness in *Jupiter* (with the trumpets coming through splendidly) is certainly riveting, the big tune taken literally rather than affectionately. In *Saturn* the spareness of texture is finely sustained; here the tempo is slow, the detail precise, while in *Neptune* the coolness is even more striking when the pianissimos are achieved with such a high degree of tension. The recording has remarkable clarity and detail, and Solti's clear-headed intensity undoubtedly brings refreshing new insights to this multi-faceted score, even if some will prefer a more atmospheric viewpoint. The recording gives the orchestra great presence. The cassette is very impressive, clearly detailed yet with plenty of atmosphere and striking weight and sonority in the bass.

Previn's too is an outstandingly attractive version. The recording is of demonstration quality, exceptionally clear and vivid, with many of Holst's subtleties of orchestral detail telling with greater point than on many other discs. The performance is basically traditional, yet has an appealing freshness. The recording acoustic, however, is a trifle dry. The cassette, transferred at a high level, has moments of roughness at climaxes.

Boult's earlier New Philharmonia performance is brilliantly literal and it is given an equally clear and brilliant HMV recording. Those who find Karajan too wayward in style should be well satisfied. Boult's *Venus* is without the sensual undertones of Karajan's reading, and the beginning of the big string tune in *Jupiter* is a splendid moment of truly British orchestral tone. Yet as a whole this reading seems less imaginative than Karajan's or Previn's. The recording has been remastered, with disc and cassette sounding very similar, although one notices, on the tape especially, that although there is plenty of sparkle on top, the middle range is less expansive than in Boult's newer LPO version, which remains a clear first choice.

Gibson's version with the Scottish National Orchestra had the distinction of being the first set of *The Planets* to be recorded digitally. The reading is characteristically direct and certainly well played. Other versions have more individuality and are more involving, but there is no doubt that the Chandos recording has fine bite and presence (slightly too much so in *Neptune*, with the chorus too positive and unethereal) and excellent detail, although even on the compact disc there are moments when one would have expected a greater degree of transparency. The compact disc format has a marginal element of fierceness in *Mars* but gains at the lower dynamic levels from the absence of any kind of background interference. With this vivid sound, the impact of such a colourful score is enhanced, but undoubtedly there will be other compact discs which will give a richer overall sound (notably in *Jupiter*) and more delicacy of texture in *Venus* and *Neptune*. The cassette is well managed but is less wide-ranging in the treble.

Ormandy's version of *The Planets* was one of the finest records he made in the last few years before he retired as the principal conductor of the Philadelphia Orchestra. The playing has great electricity, and it is a pity that the recording is so fiercely brilliant (the orchestra does not sound like this in the flesh). Even so, this is a highly compelling reading, and the sound gives added edge to the ferocity of *Mars*, balanced by an eloquently peaceful *Venus* with rapt, translucent textures. Ormandy, like Bernstein, paces the central tune of *Jupiter* slowly and deliberately. (This seems almost to be an American tradition; transatlantic performances of Vaughan Williams's arrangement of *Greensleeves* show a similar gravity.) The performance is at its finest in *Uranus* (with crisply vigorous brass articulation) and the restrained melancholy of *Saturn*, deeply felt and somehow personal in its communication. *Neptune* too is beautifully tapered off at the close. The recording sounds much the same on disc and cassette and its super-brilliance responds quite well to the controls, without loss of the undoubtedly vivid detail.

In the DG American performance Steinberg draws sumptuous playing from the Boston Symphony, and he is helped by reverberant recording that makes this a feast of sound. Anyone who wants to wallow in the opulence and colour of this extrovert work will certainly be delighted, the more so, one suspects, when Steinberg departs in certain respects from British convention. *Mars* in particular is intensely exciting. At his fast tempo he may get to his fortissimos a little early, but rarely has the piece sounded so menacing on record. The testing point for most will no doubt be *Jupiter*, and there Steinberg the excellent Elgarian comes to the fore, giving a wonderful nobilmente swagger. The cassette transfer is made at a high level and the sound matches the disc in its richly vivid qualities. The resonance brings just a hint of clouding at times, but there is extra transient bite on side two. This is a rewardingly individual account and there are associations here with Richard Strauss as well as Elgar.

For Simon Rattle, HMV's digital recording provides wonderfully atmospheric sound at the very opening (the col legno tapping at the start of *Mars*) and the very close of *Neptune* (the fading chords in endless alternation from the offstage women's chorus). The quality in *Venus* and *Mercury* is also very beautiful, warmly translucent. Otherwise it is not so distinctive a version as one might have expected from this leading young conductor; it is sensibly paced but neither so polished nor so bitingly committed as Karajan, Previn or Boult or, for that matter, Ormandy, who is at his finest on his Philadelphia record. The HMV chrome cassette matches the disc with impressive faithfulness; disappointingly, in *Jupiter* the Kingsway Hall resonance on both disc and cassette takes the edge of brilliance from the sound.

Maazel's crisply disciplined performance set against CBS's uncharacteristically diffused recording makes for an attractive reading, and though *Mars* is taken very slowly indeed, *Saturn* ends with a marked sense of happy release (strange response), and *Uranus* sounds spiky in a Stravinskian way. At the end of *Jupiter*, Maazel uses a military drum instead of the expected tambourine. The compact disc format impressively clarifies the texture against the reverberant acoustic, but this version cannot compare with the DG or Chandos compact discs.

When it was first issued in 1971, the Los Angeles Decca recording set a new standard for sonic splendour in a work which has since the 78 days put the recording engineers on their mettle. The power and impact of *Mars* are still impressive; the strings in *Venus* are richly sensuous; and the brass and timpani in *Uranus* have superb body and bite. In short this is vintage Decca analogue sound (though the remastered cassette is a little disappointing, not quite as refined as the LP in the upper range). But one has a few reservations about the performance which has not the individuality of those of Karajan, Boult, Previn or even Steinberg. Yet in the lower-medium price-range this remains quite competitive.

The EMI engineers have freshened the quality of Sargent's early stereo recording, especially on side two, where *Uranus* has splendid clarity and bite, and the organ pedals come through well in *Saturn*. Sargent's performance is full of character, with a sombre *Saturn* and the central tune in *Jupiter* given special dignity. The tape transfer is admirably clear and vivid.

Bernstein, like Ormandy, suffers from a characteristically over-brilliant transatlantic sound balance, and is also rather dry in the bass. Like Ormandy's, the performance is charismatic, with moments of striking individuality. The choral singing in *Neptune* is most refined and the closing diminuendo very beautiful. The tape, which has a more limited range, softens the lighting of Holst's vivid score (some may think too much).

Loughran, whose recorded performances with the Hallé Orchestra have consistently conveyed alertness and spontaneity, is not at his best here. He finds plenty of atmosphere in Holst's score, but the music-making is relatively pedestrian, even though the playing itself is often very fine. The compensating factor is the recording which is ripely vivid and marvellously refined in detail, with plenty of bite, on disc and tape alike.

It is curious that Contour should have chosen the (originally Phase Four) Herrmann set of *The Planets* instead of reissuing the excellent Bournemouth performance under George Hurst. With unconventionally slow tempi Herrmann's is the only recorded version to have almost no virtues at all except good orchestral playing. Even the possibilities of an artificially close balance fail to make it project vividly, and the cassette is even less impressive than the disc. At budget price the versions by Sargent, Mehta and Loughran are far preferable.

(i) *The Planets; Egdon Heath; The Perfect Fool: suite.*

(M) **(*) HMV *TCC2-POR 54290.* LSO, Previn, (i) with Amb. S. – BUTTERWORTH: *The Banks of green willow;* VAUGHAN WILLIAMS: *Fantasia on Greensleeves.***(*)

It may suit some tape collectors to have available a performance of *The Planets* with the music heard uninterrupted on one side, as on a compact disc. But the advantage in a work which is a series of independent sound-pictures is less obvious than with a large-scale symphony, and the couplings (though attractive) are rather piecemeal. The sound is very good, though marginally less sharp at the top than the equivalent discs. All three performances are discussed above, and many will feel that the alternative Greensleeve tape which includes *Egdon Heath* and *The Perfect Fool* is a better investment, unless Previn's version of *The Planets* is especially required.

(i) *Choral hymns from the Rig Veda, Op. 26/4 (Second group); Festival Te Deum; Ode to Death, Op. 38;* (ii) *Psalm 86*.
(M) *** HMV Green. ESD/*TC-ESD* 290022-1/4. (i) LSO Ch., Choristers of St Paul's Cath., LPO, Groves; (ii) Partridge, Purcell Singers, ECO, Imogen Holst.

Like *Hymn of Jesus*, the short *Festival Te Deum* comes from 1919 but takes only a little over four minutes and is an 'occasional' piece, less original than the *Hymn*. The *Ode to Death* is from the same period, written in memory of Holst's friends killed in the 1914–18 war. A setting of Whitman, it must be accounted one of Holst's most inspired and haunting scores, comparable in quality with the *Choral fantasia*, and it is eloquently performed here. Its neglect is unaccountable; this is its first recording. The second group of *Rig Veda hymns* are less of a revelation: they were written in the immediate wake of Holst's Algerian visit of 1909, which also produced *Beni Mora*. These are on familiar Holstian lines, though they make considerable demands on the singers. The setting of *Psalm 86* with its expressive tenor part sung beautifully by Ian Partridge is also included in this generous compilation (alongside two orchestral works). The recording is outstanding and the success of this performance owes much to the inspired direction of the composer's daughter.

OPERA

At the Boar's Head (complete).
*** HMV ASD/*TC-ASD* 4387. Langridge, Palmer, Ross, Tomlinson, Royal Liv. PO, Atherton.

Holst's formula for his Falstaff opera is an attractive one. Finding that Shakespeare's lines went naturally to dances and tunes from Playford's collection, he used that material on a libretto drawn entirely from the relevant scenes of *Henry IV, Parts One and Two*. The result is busy-sounding in its emphasis on chattering comedy, and dramatically it is questionable. But on record the charm and colour and originality of the piece come over well, starting with an improbable drunken opening, when without accompaniment Bardolph starts in what for a moment sounds like sing-speech. Plainly a piece which has never been successful on stage, yet deserved a recording. With some fine singing and first-rate playing this issue serves admirably with its excellent digital sound. The cassette is well managed.

(i) *Savitri* (chamber opera), *Op. 25;* (complete); (ii) *Choral hymns from the Rig Veda (3rd group) Op. 26/3*.
(M) *** Argo ZK 98 [id., PSI]. Baker, Tear, Hemsley, Purcell Singers, ECO, Imogen Holst; (ii) Purcell Singers (sopranos and altos), Ellis.

(i) *Savitri* (complete); (ii) *Dream city* (song cycle, orch. Matthews).
**(*) Hyp. Dig. A 66099. (i) Langridge, Varcoe, Kwella, Hickox Singers; (ii) Palmer; City of L. Sinf., Hickox.

There are few chamber operas so beautifully scaled as Holst's *Savitri*. The simple story is taken from a Sanskrit source – Savitri, a woodcutter's wife, cleverly outwits Death, who has come to take her husband – and Holst with beautiful feeling for atmosphere sets it in the most restrained way. With light texture and many slow tempi, it is a work which can fall apart in an uncommitted performance, but the interpreters here could hardly be more imaginative, and Janet Baker in particular produces some of her most intense and expressive singing. There is no mistaking that the piece is one of Holst's most perfectly conceived works. Aptly the *Rig-Veda hymns* which make the fill-up are also from a Sanskrit source, and the composer himself suggested that the last of them could, if necessary, be used as a prelude to *Savitri*. The opening *Hymn to the Dawn* brings echoes of *Neptune* from *The Planets*, and the fast and rhythmically fascinating *Hymn to the Waters* is even more attractive. Beautifully atmospheric recording to match intense and sensitive performances.

The Hyperion version of this raptly beautiful chamber opera makes an excellent alternative to Imogen Holst's earlier recording with Dame Janet Baker, bringing the positive advantage not just of fine digital recording but of completeness on a single side. Felicity Palmer is more earthy, more vulnerable as Savitri, her grainy mezzo well caught. Philip Langridge and Stephen Varcoe both sing sensitively with fresh, clear tone, though their timbres are rather similar. Hickox is a thoughtful conductor both in the opera and in the orchestral song-cycle arranged by Colin Matthews (with Imogen Holst's approval) from Holst's settings of Humbert Wolfe poems. Patrizia Kwella's soprano at times catches the microphone rather shrilly.

Honegger, Arthur (1892–1955)

Cello concerto (in one movement).
(M) ** Sup. 110 0604. Sádlo, Czech PO, Neumann – SHOSTAKOVITCH: *Concerto No. 1.*

Honegger's *Cello concerto* is attractively lyrical, a work with the occasional exotic overtone, and in its unpretentions way well worth knowing. It makes a good coupling for the magnificent Shostakovich *Concerto*. Acceptable recording.

Piano concertino.
(M) ** Sup. 1410 2705. Krajný, Prague CO, Macura – POULENC: *Aubade***(*); ROUSSEL: *Piano concerto.***

Honegger's engaging and fresh *Concertino* is not otherwise available at present, but Boris Krajný's version misses something of the sparkle and dash of its first section. Nonetheless, the performance is eminently serviceable.

Concerto da camera.
** None. Dig. D/*D1* 79018 [id.]. Shostac, Vogel, LA CO, Schwarz – R. STRAUSS: *Duet concertino.***

Honegger's *Concerto da camera* for flute, cor anglais and strings comes from 1949. It is a work of immediate charm and strong appeal, and is as civilized and atmospheric as the *Fourth Symphony*. Good though not distinguished playing and recording.

Pacific 231.
(M) *** Decca Jub. JB/*KJBC* 36 [Lon. CS 6367]. SRO, Ansermet – DUKAS: *L'Apprenti sorcier;* RAVEL: *Boléro; La Valse.****

The polyphonic climax of Honegger's orchestral portrayal of a railway locomotive needs reasonable clarity of recording to achieve its maximum impact. The reverberation is perhaps not quite perfectly judged here, but the power of the mighty engine is marvellously conveyed and its surging lyricism too, while the grinding tension of the final braking gives this mechanical monster an almost human personality. The cassette matches the disc closely.

Pacific 231; Pastorale d'été; Rugby (3 Symphonic movements).
** CBS 60341/*40-*. NYPO, Bernstein – DEBUSSY: *Rhapsodies.***

These three works of Honegger (all dating from the 1920s) make an acceptable triptych, with the *Pastorale d'été* as a peaceful centrepiece to offset the athletic stridency of the other two literally descriptive pieces. They sound dated now, partly because the somewhat clinical – though spectacular – recording emphasizes the clarity of the music at the expense of its atmosphere. Bernstein, too, misses some of the underlying lyricism of *Pacific 231* which Ansermet brings out so well in his account. Still this record is very sensibly coupled and with such clear (if slightly harsh) sound admirers of Honegger should find this a useful issue. This is a case where the cassette is clearly preferable to the LP, for the upper range is softened somewhat and the music sounds more agreeably atmospheric.

Symphonies Nos. 1; 2 for strings and trumpet; 3 (Liturgique); 4 (Deliciae basiliensis); 5 (Di tre re). Chant de joie; Pacific 231; Pastorale d'été.
(M) *** Sup. 110 1741/3. Czech PO, Baudo.

Symphonies Nos. 1–5; Pacific 231.
** EMI 2C 167 16327/9. Toulouse Capitole O, Plasson.

Honegger's symphonies are currently much underrated, and their scant representation in the concert hall scarcely reflects their artistic standing. The *First* was commissioned by Koussevitzky for the fiftieth anniversary of the Boston Symphony (along with Stravinsky's *Symphony of psalms*, Prokofiev's *Fourth Symphony* and Roussel's *Third*). The *Second* is a probing, intense wartime composition that reflects something of the anguish Honegger felt during the German occupation. The Czech Philharmonic recording of this coupled with the *Third Symphony* (*Liturgique*), which dates from the end of the war, was made in the early 1960s. The performances are totally committed but the sound is very reverberant and could do with more body. The *Fourth Symphony*, composed for Paul Sacher, makes use of Swiss folk material. It is perhaps the most underrated of them all, for its delights grow fresher every time one hears it, and its melodic charm is irresistible. Underneath its pastoral, smiling surface, there is a gentle vein of nostalgia and melancholy, particularly in the slow movement. The finale is sparkling and full of high spirits, though even this ends on a bitter-sweet note. The *Fifth* is a powerful work, inventive, concentrated and vital, very well played too, though again the recording is a little pale. Generally speaking, the Czech versions of the symphonies and the three pieces coupled with the *Fifth Symphony* give such pleasure that reservations can be set aside. This is a most rewarding set.

Michel Plasson has the advantage of more modern recording: his set was made in the late 1970s whereas Baudo's cycle dates from the previous decade. However, the performances do not have the same panache and virtuosity that the Czech orchestra brings to this music. The scherzo of the *Fifth Symphony*, for example, sounds very tame by the side of the Czech version, though the sound quality is richer and more transparent. One other point: in the *Symphony for strings* (the *Second*) the trumpet for which Honegger called to strengthen the chorale, but which he did not regard as mandatory, is omitted.

Symphony No. 2 (for strings and trumpet); (i) *A Christmas cantata.*
(M) ** Decca Ace SDD 189. SRO, Ansermet, (i) with Mollet, R. Lausanne Ch. and Children's Ch.

Ansermet's performance of the *Second Symphony* is vigorous and spirited, and it is well recorded. The Berlin version under Karajan (see below) is, of course, in a class of its own. The *Christmas cantata* dates from 1953; much of it was written in hospital during a painful illness which led to the composer's early death a couple of years later. It is an effective and often moving work which is enjoying increasing popularity. The performance is committed, and though problems of intonation crop up from time to time, they do not detract from the overall pleasure this disc gives.

Symphonies Nos. 2 and 3.
(M) ❀ *** DG 2543 805 [id.]. Berlin PO, Karajan.

On its first appearance we greeted this as a first recommendation in both works and as 'an altogether marvellous record'. There is no reason to modify this view: it is arguably the finest version of any Honegger works ever put on record. The playing of the Berlin strings in the wartime *Second Symphony* is superb, sumptuous in tone and refined in texture. The *Third Symphony* (*Liturgique*) has never sounded more brilliant or poetic and the coda is quite magical. The quality of the recorded sound is in the highest bracket and with the welcome reduction of price, this is an indispensable issue.

La danse des morts.
**(*) Cal. CAL 1855. Collart, Seghers, Piquemal, Davy, De Lassus Vocal Ens., Douai Youth O, Vachey.

La danse des morts is something of a rarity and has not been recorded since Münch's prewar 78s with Jean-Louis Barrault as speaker and Charles Panzera, no less, as baritone (available coupled with his pioneering set of the *Symphony No. 2* on EMI 2C 061-10901). Like *Jeanne d'Arc au bûcher*, which also dates from 1938, *La danse des morts* is based on a Claudel text. It is an exciting work and though it does not have the immediate appeal of either *King David* or *Jeanne d'Arc*, it has no lack of substance. The baritone lament, not so memorably sung here as it was by Panzera, is a powerful piece and there is a generally high level of inspiration throughout. Henri Vachey directs his youthful forces with great skill and there need be no fears on either artistic or technical grounds. The work only takes just over half an hour so that the disc is short measure, but that is the only major complaint one can make.

Jeanne d'Arc au bûcher (complete).
*** Sup. 1121 651/2. Chateau, Rodde, Brachet, Proenza, Jankovsky, Loup, Kühn Children's Ch., Czech PO and Ch., Baudo.

The ear-catching effects and mixture of styles in this brilliant and dramatic oratorio have tended to draw attention away from its musical strength. So plainsong and folksong on the one hand go with the ondes martenot on the other. Such a performance as this under the direction of Baudo, a Honegger specialist who has also recorded the symphonies, presents the piece at its most impressive, helped by outstanding choral singing, first-rate playing and a most touching rendering of the role of the Saint from Nelly Borgeaud, with her youthful speaking voice. The recording is most atmospheric, with apt reverberation.

Le Roi David.
(B) **(*) Decca DPA 593/4 [(d) Lon. STS 15155/6]. Audel (nar.), Danco, De Montmollin, Martin, Hamel, SRO and Ch., Ansermet – MARTIN: *In terra pax.****

Le Roi David is better described as a dramatic mosaic rather than a symphonic psalm. It was for many years Honegger's best-known work (with the sole exception of *Pacific 231*), largely on account of its pageantry and atmosphere. This Decca recording, made under the authoritative guidance of Ernest Ansermet, dates from the mid-1950s and originally appeared in mono only. The sound lacks the range and body of the most modern recordings, but it wears its age lightly and, given the enormous interest and invention this score offers, and the interest of its coupling, readers need not hesitate to invest in it. Judged by the highest standards, the orchestral playing is a little wanting in finish, but there is now no alternative at any price, and no collector is likely to be dissatisfied with the distinguished cast, or this richly inventive tapestry of sound. A thoroughly rewarding set.

Howells, Herbert (1892–1983)

Hymnus Paradisi.
(M) *** HMV Green. ESD/*TC-ESD* 102066-1/*4*. Harper, Tear, Bach Ch., King's Coll. Ch., New Philh. O, Willcocks.

Howells is one of the most respected English composers of the older generation, though his music has made little real headway in the concert hall. *Hymnus Paradisi* is a dignified and beautifully wrought work but, more important, it is both moving and powerful. Howells is not the most original of English composers but on the strength of this he is surely among the most civilized and disciplined. The performance is an eloquent one and the recording exemplary. The relatively low level of the transfer and the resonance of the acoustic mean that on tape the choral focus is much less sharp than on the disc, though the sound is pleasing.

Requiem.
*** Hyp. A 66076 [id.]. Corydon Singers, Best – VAUGHAN WILLIAMS: *Mass*; *Te Deum.****

Howells's *Requiem* was composed in the immediate aftermath of his son's death, and some of its material was reworked in the *Hymnus Paradisi.* In some ways this piece, which he released for publication only three years before his death, is more concentrated and direct than the *Hymnus*, its language shorn of any artifice. This is a most moving piece and one of the crowns of English church music. The Corydon Singers sing with conviction and eloquence, and the recording, made in a spacious acoustic, serves them and the composer well.

Hummel, Johann (1778–1837)

Mandolin concerto in G.
(M) ** Turn. TV/*KC* 334003 [TV 34003]. Edith Bauer-Slais, V. Pro Musica O, Hladky – HOFFMANN: *Mandolin concerto.**
*

Mandolin enthusiasts will be glad to have this coupling; others might find the limitation of tone-colour a drawback, although Hummel exploits the instrument's possibilities skilfully. The invention is attractive if not memorable. The soloist here makes the most of the work, and the accompaniment is sound.

Trumpet concerto in E flat.
(M) *** Decca Ser. 410 134-1/*4*. Wilbraham, ASMF, Marriner (in Concert***).
(M) ** Uni. RHS 337. Lang, Northern Sinf. O, Seaman – HAYDN and NERUDA: *Trumpet concertos.***

John Wilbraham's account of Hummel's engaging *Concerto* is among the finest ever recorded. He plays the slow movement elegantly, while the finale sparkles irresistibly. This is part of an excellent and generous collection of trumpet concertos admirably accompanied by Marriner and his St Martin's Academy in their vintage period with Argo. The Decca sound too is excellent, although the cassette is not quite as well focused as the LP.

William Lang's brass-band background comes more noticeably to the fore in Hummel's *Trumpet concerto* than in either of his two couplings. His tone is strikingly bold and open, with cornet-colouring often prevalent. He is a strong and not unstylish player, but one feels Hummel's *Concerto* needs a rather more elegant approach. However, in other respects the Unicorn issue cannot be faulted, with clean accompaniments and excellent recording.

Grand military septet in C, Op. 114.
*** CRD CRD 1090/*CRDC 4090.* Nash Ens. – KREUTZER: *Septet.****

Hummel's *Military septet* is not really as grand as its name implies. It features a trumpet, certainly, but that only makes a major contribution in the third movement, although in the first its fanfare-like interjections do bring in a somewhat refined reminder of the work's title. The invention throughout is ingenuous but attractive, particularly in such a delightfully spontaneous account as is provided by the Nash Ensemble. There is sparkle and warmth, and the playing itself has beguiling elegance. The recording is superb (with a demonstration-worthy cassette to mirror the disc), and the balance of the trumpet part (very nicely played by James Watson) is most felicitous. Highly recommended, especially in view of the apt coupling.

Septet in D min., Op. 74.
*** CRD CRD 1044/*CRDC 4044.* Nash Ens. – BERWALD: *Septet.****

An enchanting and inventive work with a virtuoso piano part, expertly dispatched here by Clifford Benson. The *Septet* is full of vitality, and its scherzo in particular has enormous charm and individuality. A fine performance and excellent recording make this a desirable issue, particularly in view of the enterprising coupling, which is not otherwise available. The cassette too is up to the usual high standard of CRD chamber-music tapes: the sound has warmth and bloom, with good detail.

Humperdinck, Engelbert
(1854–1921)

Hänsel und Gretel (complete).

(M) *** HMV SLS 5145 (2). Schwarzkopf, Grümmer, Metternich, Ilosvay, Schürhoff, Felbermayer, Children's Ch., Philh. O, Karajan.

*** CBS 79217/*40*- (2) [Col. M2-35898]. Cotrubas, Von Stade, Ludwig, Nimsgern, Te Kanawa, Söderström, Cologne Op. Children's Ch., Cologne Gürzenich O, Pritchard.

**(*) Decca D 131 D 2 (2) [Lon. OSA 12112]. Fassbaender, Popp, Berry, Hamari, Schlemm, Burrowes, Gruberova, V. Boys' Ch., VPO, Solti.

Karajan's classic 1950s set of Humperdinck's children's opera, with Schwarzkopf and Grümmer peerless in the name parts, is enchanting; this was an instance where everything in the recording went right. The original mono LP set was already extremely atmospheric – the cuckoos in the wood, for example – but the stereo transcription adds an irresistible further bloom without losing the inner focus. One notices that the main image stays fairly centrally situated between the speakers, but in all other respects the sound has more clarity and warmth than rival recordings made in the 1970s. There is much to delight here; the smaller parts are beautifully done and Else Schürhoff's Witch is memorable.

Beautifully cast, the Pritchard version from CBS is the first in genuine stereo to challenge the vintage Karajan set. Cotrubas – sometimes a little grainy as recorded – and Von Stade both give charming characterizations, and the supporting cast is exceptionally strong, with Söderström an unexpected but refreshing and illuminating choice as the Witch. Pritchard draws idiomatic playing from the Gürzenich Orchestra, and though the recording has not the sharply focused brilliance of Solti's Decca sound, it is pleasingly atmospheric. Moreover the CBS tape transfer is most effective, with voices and orchestra very well balanced.

Solti with the Vienna Philharmonic directs a strong, spectacular version, emphasizing the Wagnerian associations of the score. It is well sung – both principals are engaging – but just a little short on charm. The solo singing is not so steady in tone as on the EMI set, and the lack of geniality in the atmosphere is a drawback in a work of this nature. Needless to say, Solti does the *Witch's ride* excitingly, and the VPO are throughout encouraged to play with consistent fervour. Edita Gruberova is an excellent Dew Fairy and Walter Berry is first-rate as Peter. Anny Schlemm's Witch is a very strong characterization indeed, and there are some imaginative touches of stereo production associated with *Hocus pocus* and her other moments of magic. The recording is admirably vivid, but its sense of spectacle does not erase one's memory of the Karajan version.

Hansel and Gretel (complete, in English).

(B) *** CfP CFPD/*TC-CFPD* 414432-3/*5* (2). Kern, Neville, Hunter, Herinx, Howard, Sadler's Wells Ch. and O, Bernardi.

At bargain-price this first full-length opera-recording by the old Sadler's Wells Company (latterly the English National) is welcome back to the catalogue. The vitality and warmth of Mario Bernardi's conducting carries one over any slight shortcomings in the singing, and the playing is rich and full-bodied. Margaret Neville makes a freshly girlish Gretel, and Patricia Kern's voice blends well, though it is on the heavy side. Diction is admirable – a vital point in one of the rare recordings of opera in English – and though the recording is somewhat larger than life, it is admirably atmospheric. Generally this set – for English-speaking listeners – is among the most enjoyable of those available, and it certainly sounds well, with no appreciable difference between disc and tape.

Hänsel und Gretel: favourite scenes.
**(*) Decca SET 633 (from above set, cond. Solti).

The Decca set of excerpts includes the overture, the *Witch's ride*, *Dream pantomime*, gingerbread house scene and finale. It reflects admirably the vivid qualities of the complete set and the slightly dry brilliance of the Decca recording.

Königskinder (complete).
*** EMI 1C 157 30698/700 [Ara. 8061-3L/*9061-3L*]. Prey, Donath, Ridderbusch, Bar. R. Ch., Mun. RO Wallberg.

The success of *Hänsel und Gretel* has completely overshadowed this second fairy-tale opera of Humperdinck, which contains much fine music, notably in the love duets (for the goose-girl who tragically falls in love with a prince), the fiddler's songs and the preludes to the three acts. Humperdinck had expanded his incidental music to a play to make this opera, which was given its première in New York in 1910. In an entertainment for children the sadness and cruelty of a typical German fairy-tale, not to mention the heavy vein of moralizing, are a serious disadvantage, but in a recording as fine as this it is a piece well worth investigation. Both the conducting and the singing of the principals are most persuasive.

Hurlstone, William (1876–1906)

(i) *Piano concerto in D. Fantasie-variations on a Swedish air.*
*** Lyr. SRCS 100. LPO, Braithwaite, (i) with Parkin.

Hurlstone's was a tragic career. He was a prodigy as a composer and as a pianist, but ill-health and poverty prevented him from developing those talents, and he died at the age of thirty. Neither of these works has the formal strength of some of his chamber music (Lyrita have just recorded the *Piano quartet* of 1898), but they are both distinctive, the *Concerto* the more positive, the *Variations* the more quirkily individual. Good performances and recording.

Hvoslef, Ketil (born 1939)

(i) *Concerto for double-bass and orchestra;* (ii) *Trio for soprano, contralto and piano;* (iii) *Octet for flutes.*
*** Ph. 6529 041. (i) Kerr, LPO, Dreier; (ii) Taranger, Zlatanou, Smebye; (iii) Ens. Dreier.

Ketil Hvoslef is the son of Harald Saeverud but adopted his mother's maiden name to avoid confusion in his native Norway. There are some moments in his *Concerto* where one recognizes that he is his father's son, but for the most part, however, he is very much his own man. Indeed, he is a composer of real imagination and resource, with a keenly developed feeling for sonority. The *Octet for flutes* of 1978 is a highly original piece: the ensemble is made up of eight identical instruments, not a combination of different types of flutes. If you imagine that the ear tires of this tone colour, you should try this unfailingly inventive piece; it is something of a *tour de force*. Hvoslef is a composer bursting with ideas and he possesses a mind of keen intelligence and rich fantasy. The *Trio* is diverting and often amusing, and the only reservation one might have is that the *Concerto* is a shade overlong. Excellent performances and sound quality: a most stimulating record.

Ibert, Jacques (1890–1962)

Flute concerto.
*** RCA RL/*RK* 25109 [ARL 1/*ARK 1* 3777]. Galway, RPO, Dutoit – CHAMINADE: *Concertino*; FAURÉ: *Fantaisie*; POULENC: *Sonata*.***

Ibert's high-spirited and inventive concerto deserves the widest currency; it is full of charm and lyrical appeal, particularly when it is as well performed as it is here by James Galway and the RPO under Charles Dutoit. Moreover it has the distinct advantage of highly attractive couplings. There is no alternative in the catalogue, but it will be difficult to supersede this version, which enjoys a clear, spacious recording on disc, and has been skilfully transferred to tape.

Divertissement.
*** ASV Dig. DCA/*ZCDCA* 517. ASMF, Marriner (with Concert of French music.***)

Ibert's *Divertissement* is derived from incidental music to *Un chapeau de paille d'Italie* and its raciness and high spirits come across well here, with bright sound and excellent playing. This is part of a concert of French music entitled *The French connection* discussed in our Concerts section. The cassette is only transferred on iron-oxide stock, but it still sounds quite vivid.

d'India, Sigismondo
(*c.* 1582–*c.* 1630)

Duets, laments and madrigals: *Amico, hai vinto; Ancidetemi pur, dogliosi affani; Chi nudrisce tua speme; Giunto a la tomba; Langue al vostro languir; O leggiadr' occhi; Quella vermiglia rosa; Son gli accenti che ascolto; Torna il sereno Zefiro.*

(M) ** HM HM 1011. Concerto Vocale.

Sigismondo d'India was among the vanguard of the new movement founded by Monteverdi at the beginning of the seventeenth century, and his laments show him a considerable master of expressive resource. He is highly responsive to the emotions of the poetry, and the harmonies and the unpredictable lines make this music fascinating. The performances are authoritative, though there are moments of slightly self-conscious rubato that hold up the flow. The recording could be more spacious and warmer, but in spite of that qualification this is thoroughly recommendable.

Madrigals for 5 voices: Book No. 8 (complete).
*** O-L Dig. DSDL 707 [id.]. Cons. of Musicke, Rooley.

Like Monteverdi, Sigismondo d'India continued to cultivate the polyphonic style alongside the *stile nuovo* and wrote no fewer than eight books of madrigals. For twelve years from 1611 onwards, he worked at Turin as director of music to the Duke of Savoy and it was for this court that the bulk of his secular music was written. His eighth and last book was, however, written for the court at Modena in 1624. John Whenham's note reminds us that the Modenese court continued the tradition of virtuoso ensemble music begun by Ferrara during the 1580s where 'there was an ensemble of singers with extremely agile voices who practised complex concerted ornamentation and cultivated a theatrical manner of delivery, employing gradations of tempo and dynamics, different forms of vocal attack and even facial expressions and movements of the hands to underline the emotions of the music they sang'. Small wonder, then, that the eighth book has a dramatic cycle of five madrigals to a text from the fourth Act of *Il pastor fido* which would obviously show off the dramatic skills of the singers. Nevertheless, there is also a variety of styles and one or two moments which make one wonder whether Sigismondo d'India was not a composer of much greater stature than one has hitherto supposed. This is a most welcome record and the Consort of Musicke, with Emma Kirkby making her presence felt, make out a most persuasive case for this music. They are splendidly recorded; an additional attraction of this issue is the fact that no duplication is involved with the Harmonia Mundi issue listed above.

d'Indy, Vincent (1851–1931)

Chanson et danses, Op. 50.
(M) *** Sup. 1411 2844. Coll. Mus. Pragense – GOUNOD: *Petite symphonie*; GOUVY: *Suite gauloise*.***

Vincent d'Indy's two-part divertimento for winds dates from 1898, and still has Wagnerian touches (there are echoes of the *Siegfried Idyll* at one point in the opening movement). It is an appealing work of much stronger personality than the Gouvy *Suite*; its melodic ideas have character, and the writing for wind is always expert. There is no other version and the work is well worth having for the sake of its opening movement.

Concerto for piano, flute, cello and strings, Op. 89; Karadec (incidental music), *Op. 34; Suite dans le style ancien for 2 flutes, trumpet and string quartet, Op. 24.*
** Erato STU/*MCE* 71423. Rampal, Pierlot, Duchable, Lodéon, Paillard CO, Paillard.

The *Concerto for piano, flute, cello and strings* is d'Indy's very last symphonic work and dates from 1926, while the other two pieces are earlier: the *Suite* comes from 1886 and the incidental music to André Alexandre's play, *Karadec*, was written four years later. All are new to the gramophone and fill in our picture of this underrated composer, though none of it is essential d'Indy. There are moments in *Karadec* that remind one of the d'Indy of *Fervaal* of which we need a recording, but the *Concerto* is a kind of *septième Brandenbourgeois*, well wrought and resourceful without being really compelling. The performances are lively and are well recorded, but collectors who know and admire *Jour d'été à la montagne* or *La Forêt enchantée* and the *Second symphony* will find this musically disappointing. There is a good cassette.

La Forêt enchantée, Op. 8; Jour d'été à la montagne, Op. 61; Tableaux de voyage, Op. 36.
*** EMI 2C 069 16301 [(d)Ara. 8097-2/*9097-2*]. Loire PO, Dervaux.

The most substantial work on this record is *Jour d'été à la montagne*, composed just after Debussy's *La Mer*, and inspired by the beauties of the Vivarais region of central France, where d'Indy was born. He was a devoted Wagnerian, but that influence is more completely assimilated in this triptych than in, say, *Fervaal* or the early tone poem *La Forêt enchantée* with which it is coupled. The latter is all the same a finely wrought and highly imaginative piece, reminiscent of the best tone poems of Liszt and Franck, yet distinctively individual too. The make-weight is a delightful suite, *Tableaux de voyage*, originally written for piano. This is a most enjoyable collection that reveals d'Indy as a far richer and more rewarding composer than most people give him credit for, and the performances are in no sense second-rate, even though the Orchestre Philharmonique des Pays de Loire is hardly of international standing. The sound too is absolutely first-class. The sleeve (and *Grove*) describes *La Forêt enchantée* as Op. 8, but the annotator refers to it throughout as Op. 7. This is a distinguished and likeable release, well worth acquiring.

Symphony No. 2 in B flat, Op. 57.
*** EMI 2C 069 73100. Toulouse Capitole O, Plasson.

The *Second Symphony* (1902–3) is as impressive as it is neglected. Indeed, this is its first recording since the Monteux set with the San Francisco Symphony in 1942 – at least as far as the UK is concerned. Although its cyclic organization betrays its Franckophilia, there is intellectual vigour, charm (as in the modal folk-like *Modéré* of the third movement) and nobility in the arching lines of the fugue in the finale. Michel Plasson proves a sympathetic and committed advocate and his orchestra, though not in the luxury bracket, responds with enthusiasm and sensitivity to his direction. The recording, too, is very acceptable indeed, spacious and warm without quite being in the demonstration bracket. Those who complain about the repeated duplication of the Franck *Symphony* should investigate this fine example which must be numbered among this composer's most powerful works.

Ireland, John (1879–1962)

Concertino pastorale.
(M) **(*) Uni. UNS 260. Westminster Cath. String O, Mawby – L. BERKELEY: *Antiphon*; M. BERKELEY: *Meditations.***(*)

The *Concertino pastorale*, written for the Boyd Neel Orchestra in 1939, is a gently persuasive piece, rather long for its unambitious material but always attractive. It is an important addition to the limited range of Ireland's music on record, and is here well coupled.

Piano concerto in E flat.
(*) Lyr. SRCS 36. Parkin, LPO, Boult – *These Things Shall Be.*(*)

John Ireland's only *Piano concerto* is worthy to rank with the finest twentieth-century works in this form. It has distinctive melodic inspiration throughout all three movements, and its poetic lyricism, if not forward-looking, is in the ageless tradition of the greatest English music. The work's potentialities are fully realized in this sensitive performance by Eric Parkin, and there is some obviously dedicated playing by the LPO under Boult. The recording is outstanding technically, and it is a great pity that the reverberant acoustic rather blows up the textures of the music – piano and orchestra alike – detracting from the intimacy of the presentation.

A London overture.
(M) *** HMV Green. ESD/*TC-ESD* 7092 [Ang. S 36415]. LSO, Barbirolli – BAX: *Tintagel*; DELIUS: *Collection.****

One of Ireland's most immediately attractive works, and Barbirolli's performance of it is a great success. The main theme (rhythmically conjuring up the bus conductor's call 'Piccadilly') is made obstinately memorable, and the warm romanticism of the middle section is perfectly judged. The recording sounds remarkably fresh and vivid in this excellent Greensleeve reissue, the cassette as crisp and full as the disc.

The Overlanders: suite (arr. Mackerras).
*** Uni. KP 8001. W. Australian SO, Measham – VAUGHAN WILLIAMS: *On Wenlock Edge.***(*)

The Overlanders is not the best of Ireland, but it is as persuasively presented here as it was by Sir Adrian Boult on a deleted Lyrita disc, where the couplings (other Ireland works) were perhaps less appealing than the Vaughan Williams offered by Unicorn Kanchana. The sound here is admirably vivid.

Cello sonata.
(*) ASV ACA/*ZCACA* 1001. Lloyd Webber, McCabe – BRIDGE: *Elegy*; BRITTEN: *Suite.**

The *Cello sonata* is among Ireland's most richly inspired works, a broad-spanning piece in which ambitious, darkly intense outer movements frame one of his most beautiful slow movements. Julian Lloyd Webber, who has long been a passionate advocate of the work, here conveys its full expressive power. The piano is placed at a distance, but perhaps that is apt for a work in which the cello should be presented in full strength. The cassette matches the disc fairly closely, though the resonance means that the focus is marginally less sharp.

Phantasy trio in A min.; Piano trios Nos. 2 and 3 in E.
*** Lyr. SRCS 98. Neaman, Lloyd Webber, Parkin.

The *Phantasy trio* and the *Second Trio in E major* are accommodated on the first side. The former, an early piece dating from 1908, is not particularly individual; its companion has more substance, and the *Andante* section has a splendid sense of desolation. The finest of the three is the last, which began life as a trio for clarinet, violin and piano in 1913 but was totally rewritten in 1938. This has much greater imaginative vitality and a transparency of texture that calls to mind Ireland's great admiration for the Ravel *Trio*. Few pianists understand Ireland's piano writing better than Eric Parkin does, and he and his partners give an eloquent account of all three pieces. They are excellently recorded.

PIANO MUSIC

Ballade; Greenways (*3 Lyric pieces*); *Month's Mind; 2 Pieces* (*February's Child; Aubade*); *Sarnia; Sonatina.*
*** Lyr. SRCS 89. Parkin.

Ireland was arguably at his most natural when writing for the piano. He seems fully to have understood the instrument, and he poured into it some of his finest invention. *Sarnia*, subtitled *An island sequence*, is certainly among his best pieces; it was inspired by the Channel Islands, whose atmosphere Ireland evoked in many other works, including *The Forgotten Rite*. Eric Parkin plays all these pieces with complete sympathy and subtlety. Indeed, it is difficult to imagine his performances being surpassed, for he brings a command of colour and a temperamental affinity to this music. The recording is excellent.

Piano music: *Decorations; London pieces; Merry Andrew; 4 Preludes; Prelude in E flat; Rhapsody; The Towing Path.*
*** Lyr. SRCS 87. Parkin.

This was the first stereo anthology to be made by one of the composer's pupils, Eric Parkin. His sympathy with the music is in no doubt and his technique is no less impressive. Some of Ireland's finest music is in the piano repertoire, and here the *Decorations* and *London pieces* are alone worth the price of the disc, which is excellently recorded.

Piano sonata; The Darkened valley; Equinox; On a birthday morning; 2 Pieces (*For Remembrance; Amberley wild brooks*); *2 Pieces* (*April; Bergomask*); *Summer Evening.*
*** Lyr. SRCS 88. Parkin.

Ireland made a distinctive and distinguished contribution to the language of twentieth-century piano music, and his *Sonata* is rightly admired as being among his finest compositions. It has a directness yet subtlety of appeal that seem as fresh today as when it was first committed to paper. Eric Parkin is an authoritative and sympathetic advocate of Ireland's always personal idiom, and both in the *Sonata* itself and in the shorter pieces on this record his playing carries the ring of real conviction. He also enjoys the benefit of good modern recording.

VOCAL MUSIC

3 Arthur Symons songs; 3 Thomas Hardy songs. Songs: *Bed in summer; Earth's call; East Riding; Heart's desire; The Land of Lost Content; Love is a sickness; Mother and child; My true love hath my heart; Remember; Hawthorne time; Sacred flame; Three Ravens; The Trellis; What art thou thinking?*
**(*) Lyr. SRCS 118. Hodgson, Mitchinson, Rowlands.

Earth's call is the most ambitious of these songs – almost a dramatic scena – but most of them reflect the tinge of melancholy that was an essential part of Ireland's temperament, subtle miniatures which sensitively follow the cadences of English lyric poetry. These thoughtful performances (with the piano balanced rather backwardly) make an excellent companion to the earlier Lyrita issues covering the baritone songs that make up the rest of Ireland's contribution to the genre.

Songs: *3 Housman settings* (*We'll to the woods no more; In boyhood; Spring will not wait – piano solo*); *Marigold* (*Youth's spring-tribute; Penumbra; Spleen*); *5 poems by Thomas Hardy* (*Beckon to me; In my sage moments; It was what you bore with you, woman; The tragedy of the moment; Dear, think not*); *Songs of a*

Wayfarer (*Memory; When daffodils begin to peer; English May; I was not sorrowful*); *3 Songs* (*Love and friendship; Friendship in misfortune; The one hope*); *Songs: Hope the Hornblower; Sea fever; When the lights go rolling round the sky.*
*** Lyr. SRCS 65. Luxon, Rowlands.

Ireland's songs as well as his warmly characterful piano music deserve better of performers today, and this first instalment of a complete collection of the songs is highly attractive, even if Luxon's voice is not always ideally smooth. The first side contains songs written when Ireland was in early maturity, before the First World War, and though the ever-popular *Sea fever* may still strike most indelibly, the others too have the vigorous memorability of youthful inspiration. Ireland became more melancholy with age, but the second side too contains a whole sequence of beautiful, sensitive songs. Excellent recording.

2 songs (*Tryst: During music*); *5 Sixteenth-century songs; 6 songs sacred and profane; Songs: Bells of San Marie; Blow out you bugles; Great things; If there were dreams to sell; If we must part; I have twelve oxen; The journey; Merry month of May; Santa Chiara; Spring sorrow; Tutto è sciolto; Vagabond; When I am dead.*
*** Lyr. SRCS 66. Luxon, Rowlands.

This instalment of Lyrita's admirable series of songs by John Ireland, has fewer famous songs (*I have twelve oxen* is an exception), but like the first it presents Ireland as a central contributor to an English genre which has yet to be fully appreciated. The finest songs here deserve to be bracketed with German Lieder and French mélodie (the setting of Symons's *Santa Chiara*, for example), and Luxon's understanding performances, splendidly accompanied, should attract not only listeners but new performers. Excellent recording.

These Things Shall Be (for baritone solo, chorus and orchestra).
(*) Lyr. SRCS 36. Carol Case, LPO Ch., LPO, Boult – *Piano concerto*.(*)

John Ireland chose exactly the right moment to write *These Things Shall Be* (1936–7). The words, taken from *A Vista* by John Addington Symonds, are optimistic in an almost unbelievably naïve way, but during the war when things were not going well, this direct life-assertive faith in a possible Utopian state of human relationships suited the need of public mood and morale exactly. One can remember Prom performances of great power and eloquence, and certainly the music, with its mixture of Elgarian *nobilmente* and Waltonian declamation (without the dissonant bite of *Belshazzar's Feast*), is very effective and easy to enjoy. This recorded performance has less thrust and conviction than those far-off wartime accounts, but it is well sung and played, and if you turn up the volume – for the recording is very good indeed – a good deal of the impact of the writing comes over. The music itself is melodic, spacious in phrase and very readily enjoyable at its face value.

Isaac, Heinrich (*c.* 1450–1517)

Chansons, Frottole and Lieder: *Ain frewlich wesen; Donna di dentro; Es het ein Baur; Et je boi d'autant; Et qui la dira; Fille vous avez; Fortuna desperata; Greiner, zancker; Helas que devra; Hora e di maggio; Der Hund; Insbruck; J'ay pris amours; Je ne me puis vivre; La martinella; Maudit soit; Mich wundert hart; Mon père m'a donne mari; La morra; Ne più bella; O venus bant; Par ung jour; Le Serviteur; Un dì lieto giamai; Wann ich des morgens; Zwischen berg.*
*** O-L 410 107-1 [id.]. Medieval Ens. of L., Peter and Timothy Davies.

This record can claim to be the first to be devoted to the secular songs of Isaac which number eighty in all, more than a quarter of which are on this record. What will surprise those who investigate it is the sheer diversity and range of the music recorded here. These excellent singers and players cover his contribution to the chanson, frottole and Lieder, and the presentation and notes are up to the high standards of the series. New and unusual repertoire that well rewards investigation. Superb recording too.

Ives, Charles (1874–1954)

Symphony No. 2.
*** CBS Dig. 37300/*40*- [id.]. Concg. O, Tilson Thomas.

Although Ives's *Second Symphony* dates from the turn of the century (it occupied him from 1897 until 1902), it had to wait half a century for its first performance under Leonard Bernstein in 1951. Bernstein recorded it some years later, using a copy of Ives's pencil score that the composer preferred to the slightly revised ink score that he had once sent to Walter Damrosch. This new issue uses the critical edition prepared by Malcolm Goldstein and based on new material that came to light after Ives's death in 1954. It is its first recording and very good it is too. The *Symphony* is still firmly rooted in the European tradition but already makes sorties into Americana, with its quotations from *Turkey in the straw* and a favourite hymn, *When I survey the wondrous cross*, and either quotes or alludes to Beethoven and Brahms as well as the prelude to *Tristan*. Michael Tilson Thomas secures finely cultured playing from the Concertgebouw Orchestra and his is undoubtedly the best recorded version, even if the CBS engineers do not quite produce the richness and range that their Decca colleagues secure in the Haitink Shostakovich cycle. There is a good chrome cassette though the second side has rather more warmth than the first.

Symphony No. 3 (The Camp meeting).
*** Argo ZRG/*KZRC* 845 [id.]. ASMF, Marriner – BARBER: *Adagio*; COPLAND: *Quiet city*; COWELL: *Hymn*; CRESTON: *Rumor*.***

(i) *Symphony No. 3; Central Park in the dark;* (ii) *Decoration Day;* (iii) *The Unanswered question.*
(M) *** CBS 60268/*40*- [MS 6843]. NYPO, (i) Bernstein; (ii) Ozawa; (iii) Peress (supervised, Bernstein).

Symphony No. 3; Three Places in New England.
(M) **(*) Mercury SRI 75035 [id.]. Eastman Rochester O, Hanson.

On CBS an indispensable collection for anyone attracted to the strange, wild music of Charles Ives. The *Symphony* is (for Ives) rather mild and even unambitious, being adapted from quartet movements and organ voluntaries written earlier. But it gets one in the right frame for the three intensely individual pieces on the reverse, which like the pieces which make up *Three Places in New England* can be regarded as a brilliant collection of evening sounds, evocative yet bewildering. Their musical complexity demands two quite separate conductors, and that is why Ozawa and Peress directed the piece under Bernstein's supervision. *Decoration day* is a hilarious example of Ives's feeling for colour and humour – a mournful procession to the cemetery to honour the war-dead, followed by loud junketing on the return. *The Unanswered question* is probably the most purely beautiful music Ives ever wrote, with muted strings (curiously representing silence) set against a trumpet representing the problem of existence. No need to worry about Ives's philosophy when the results are so naturally moving. The CBS recording from the mid-1960s still sounds well (with LP and chrome tape virtually indistinguishable) and the playing of the New York Philharmonic under various direction is of high quality.

Ives's quixotic genius is at its most individual in the *Three Places in New England.* Written between 1903 and 1914 this music is still able to shock the ear, especially the second movement, *Putnam's Camp, Redding, Connecticut*, with its phantasmagoric orchestral fantasy-images inspired by a child's dream at a site connected with the American War of Independence. The outer movements too are highly original and searingly atmospheric. The work is most understandingly presented here under Howard Hanson, but the recording is rather close and studio-bound (the bass drum too insistent). Similarly the *Third Symphony* is not ideal as sound; the quality is full-bodied but forward and lacking dynamic contrast, although again the performance is thoroughly sympathetic. This is a very worthwhile reissue, reasonably priced.

Those wanting the *Third Symphony* alone will find Marriner's account is first-rate in every way. It is more faithfully recorded than Bernstein's version, and has no less sense of conviction. Moreover it comes in an anthology that is of unusual interest and merit. Both disc and cassette offer sound in the demonstration class.

Jacob, Gordon (1895–1984)

Mini concerto for clarinet and string orchestra.
*** Hyp. A 66031. King, N.W. CO of Seattle, Francis – COOKE: *Clarinet concerto*; RAWSTHORNE: *Concerto.****

Gordon Jacob, in his eighties, responded to an earlier recording of his music by Thea King by writing this *Miniature concerto* for her, totally charming in its compactness with not a note too many. The slow movement in particular is a gem. Thea King is the most persuasive of dedicatees, splendidly accompanied by the orchestra from Seattle and treated to first-rate sound.

5 Pieces.
*** Argo ZRG 856 [id.]. Reilly (harmonica), ASMF, Marriner – MOODY: *Little suite;* TAUSKY: *Concertino;* VAUGHAN WILLIAMS: *Romance.****

The *Five Pieces* are delightful, and the invention is of a consistently high standard; the *Cradle song* and *Threnody* are particularly charming. The scoring is extremely felicitous, and with such beautiful playing and recording this is a rewarding collection.

William Byrd suite.
(M) *** Mercury SRI/*MRI* 75028 [id.]. Eastman Wind Ens., Fennell – HOLST: *Hammersmith;* WALTON: *Crown Imperial.****

Gordon Jacob's arrangement of the music of Byrd is audaciously anachronistic, but sounds marvellous when played with such flair under that supreme maestro of the wind band, Frederick Fennell. The closing number, *The Bells*, is a *tour de force*. A highly entertaining collection with an excellent matching cassette. The tape is let down, however, by the absence of any documentation about the music.

Clarinet quintet.
*** Hyp. A 66011. King, Aeolian Qt – SOMERVELL: *Quintet.****

Gordon Jacob wrote his fine *Clarinet quintet*, an ambitious work lasting over half an hour, in 1942 for Frederick Thurston, one of the great clarinettists of his time who represented a more severe style of tone and technique than has become accepted more recently. Thea King, Thurston's widow and former pupil, plays with deep understanding, and is strongly matched by the Aeolian Quartet. Good recording.

Janáček, Leoš (1854–1928)

The Ballad of Blaník; The Fiddler's child; Jealousy: Overture; Lachian Dances.
(M) *(*) Sup. 1110 2840. Brno PO, Jílek.

Although Janáček did not publish the *Lachian Dances* as a suite of six pieces until 1925, they were all composed much earlier and were clearly influenced by the example of Dvořák's *Slavonic Dances. The Fiddler's child* is far more representative, an affecting and poignant miniature tone-poem from 1912, and the *Ballad of Blaník* is post-war. František Jílek gets a workmanlike response from the Brno orchestra, though he is not as well recorded in the *Lachian Dances* as were François Huybrechts and the LPO on Decca, nor does he secure such poetic results as did Břetislav

Bakala or Jiří Waldhans who both recorded it with the same orchestra. Neither the recording nor the performances are outstanding, but there is at present no alternative version and both later pieces are well worth having.

(i) *Idyll for strings;* (ii) *Mládí for wind sextet.*
**(*) None. Dig. D/*D4* 79033. (i) LACO, Schwarz; (ii) LA Wind Ens.

Mládí (Youth) is a work of Janáček's old age and the *Idyll* for strings a product of his youth. The latter, written in 1878 when he was in his early twenties, springs from the tradition of Dvořák though its thematic material lacks the spontaneity and freshness of that master. It is very persuasively played by the Los Angeles Chamber Orchestra under Gerard Schwarz who are sensitive to dynamic nuances and shape phrases with imagination. The sound is very lifelike and clean. *Mládí* occupies the whole of the second side which at just under 17 minutes is short measure. The wind players of the Los Angeles orchestra play marvellously and with altogether superb ensemble and blend. They show sensitivity, too, in the *Andante sostenuto* (particularly from fig. 6 onwards), though they are not quite as poignant and expressive as are the players in the London Sinfonietta box on Decca (see below) who enjoy the advantage of a more natural and distant balance. The Los Angeles team are placed very forward, though the acoustic is warm and the detail remarkably clean.

Sinfonietta.
*** Decca SXL 6398. LSO, Abbado – HINDEMITH: *Symphonic metamorphoses.****

Sinfonietta; Preludes: The House of the Dead; Jenůfa; Kátya Kabanová; The Makropoulos affair.
(B) **(*) PRT GSGC/*ZCGC* 2018. Pro Arte O, Mackerras.

Sinfonietta; Taras Bulba (rhapsody).
*** Decca Dig. **410 138-2**; SXDL/*KSXDC* 7519 [Lon. LDR/*5*- 71021]. VPO, Mackerras.
*** HMV Dig. ASD/*TC-ASD* 143522-1/*4* [Ang. DS/*4XS* 37999]. Philh. O, Rattle.
(M) *** HMV SXLP 30420 [Ang. S 36045]. Chicago SO, Ozawa, or RPO, Kubelik.
(M) ** Sup. 50380 [Quint. PMC/*P4C* 7184]. Czech PO, Ančerl.

Mackerras's coupling comes as a superb supplement to his Janáček opera recordings with the Vienna Philharmonic. The massed brass of the *Sinfonietta* has tremendous bite and brilliance as well as characteristic Viennese ripeness, thanks to a spectacular digital recording. *Taras Bulba* too is given more weight and body than is usual, the often savage dance rhythms presented with great energy. The cassette has comparable brilliance and range, although on some machines the upper range is fierce and needs taming. The compact disc thrillingly combines tangibility and presence with atmosphere and increases the sense of a natural perspective.

Simon Rattle hardly puts a foot wrong in this coupling and he has the benefit of splendid recording too. Detail is well defined, there is good perspective and a spacious acoustic yet no want of presence. The *Sinfonietta* has a resplendent fervour that almost (but not quite) matches that of Mackerras. *Taras Bulba* is given with the utmost feeling and naturalness, and the Philharmonia Orchestra (and in particular the brass) respond with enthusiasm. It does not displace the Mackerras version, which is spectacularly recorded and perhaps just that bit more authoritative, but is an eminently recommendable alternative. Where Mackerras, helped by the more aggressively brilliant Decca sound, brings out the sharp originality of this music, Rattle with his extra degree of expressiveness finds more delicacy, even tenderness, presenting a more romantic view. The luminous HMV recording contributes, but there is no lack of bite in the brass chorales of the *Symphony*, even if the cassette is softer-edged than the disc.

Kubelik's account of *Taras Bulba* dates from the late 1950s, though it is difficult to credit that, so vivid and full-blooded is the quality. His later version made with the Bavarian Radio Orchestra is a little more refined but not less vital. This offers excellent value for money, particularly with Ozawa's brilliant account of the *Sinfonietta* on the reverse. In the mid-price range this is a highly competitive coupling, though one cannot deny the claims of Mackerras's recording, which is both authoritative and technically superb.

Abbado gives a splendid account of the *Sinfonietta* and evokes a highly sympathetic response from the LSO. One of the strengths of this conductor is his acute sensitivity to dynamic nuances and his care for detail, which never seems to degenerate into pedantry or excessive fastidiousness. This is thoroughly alive and fresh playing, and the Decca engineers have given him a superb balance in which the subtlest of colours is allowed to register without artificial boosting. The coupling too is first-class.

Mackerras's early Pye disc dates from 1960 and in its day was a companion issue to his famous version of Handel's *Fireworks music*. The sonority of the brass has a similar feeling of spectacle, and it is amazing how well this record sounds today. The performance is vivid and sympathetic, and the coupling of four operatic preludes (at a time when the music was little known outside Janáček's homeland) was an imaginative choice. They are strongly characterized too; though, compared with the most recent Janáček recordings there is a lack of refinement here, this PRT reissue is still a bargain, and there is a good tape as well. Ančerl's record sounds its age and will perhaps now gracefully retire. His *Taras Bulba* has vitality, but the recording lacks impact and there is far more detail and colour in the Pye recording of the *Sinfonietta*.

Suite for string orchestra.

*** Argo ZRG 792 [id.]. LACO, Marriner – R. STRAUSS: *Capriccio: Introduction***(*); SUK: *Serenade.****

Marriner's first record with his new Los Angeles group was made in England during the orchestra's 1974 tour. The recording site was St John's, Smith Square (where many successful Argo discs have been made), and the recording is characteristically ripe. The *Suite for strings* is an early and not entirely mature piece, but when played as committedly as it is here, its attractions are readily perceived, and it does not want character.

CHAMBER MUSIC

(i; ii) *Capriccio for piano and 7 instruments; Concertino for piano and 6 instruments;* (iii; i) *Dumka for violin and piano;* (ii) *Mládí for wind sextet;* (iv; i) *Presto for cello and piano;* (iii; i) *Romance for violin and piano;* (v) *String quartets Nos. 1 and 2;* (iv; i) *A Tale for cello and piano;* (iii; i) *Violin sonata (for violin and piano)*. (Piano) (i) *In the Mist; On an Overgrown Path; Recollection; Piano sonata; Theme and variations.* (vi; ii) *Rikadia for chamber choir and 10 instruments.*

(M) *** Decca D 223 D 5 (5). (i) Crossley; (ii) L. Sinf. (members), Atherton; (iii) Sillito; (iv) Van Kampen; (v) Gabrieli Qt; (vi) L. Sinf. Ch.

This five-record box offers the essential Janáček in absolutely first-class performances and recordings. The performances of the string quartets, which are discussed below, are the equal of any rivals. Paul Crossley is the impressive soloist in the *Capriccio* and the *Concertino*, performances that can be put alongside those of Firkusný – and no praise can be higher. This account of *Mládí* is to be preferred to the version by the Vienna Wind Soloists; the work's youthful sparkle comes across to excellent effect here. Crossley's survey of the piano music is both poetic and perceptive, and his mastery of keyboard colour and feeling for atmosphere is everywhere evident, while the sound that the engineers have achieved is very truthful and satisfying. The set brings a number of rarities to the catalogue too, the *Violin sonata* (which Suk and Panenka have also recorded) and the *Rikadia* for chamber choir and ten instruments. A distinguished set.

Capriccio for piano and 7 instruments; Concertino for piano and 6 instruments; (Piano) *On an overgrown path I and II; In the mist; Piano sonata; Zdenka Variations.*

(M) *** DG Priv. 2721 251 (2). Firkusný; members of Bav. R. SO, Kubelik.

An eminently recommendable set, particularly at mid-price, and preferable to the same package recorded by Josef Páleníček and members of the Czech Philharmonic on Supraphon 1111481–2, good though that is. Firkusný played to Janáček as a small boy and has long been regarded as the most authoritative exponent of the piano music. These performances of the *Capriccio* and *Concertino* are of high quality and are thoroughly idiomatic, as one would expect with Kubelik at the helm. They come with the complete solo piano music which is played with characteristic sensitivity and perception. All the same, in returning to these performances which date from the early 1970s, one or two movements from *On an overgrown path* and *In the mist* seemed less poignant and poetic than his broadcast and concert performances that one remembers, and in some movements Crossley is arguably even more searching. That apart, this is nonetheless a most impressive set and the recording is very good indeed.

String quartets Nos. 1 (*Kreutzer sonata*); *2* (*Intimate pages*).
(M) *** Decca Ace SDD 527 [Lon. STS 15432]. Gabrieli Qt.
(M) *** EMI Em. EMX/*TC-EMX* 41 2046-1/*4*. Medici Qt.

Janáček's two string quartets come from his last years and are among his most deeply individual and profoundly impassioned utterances. The Gabrieli Quartet have the measure of this highly original music and give just as idiomatic an account of these masterpieces as did the Janáček Quartet in the 1960s. They have the advantage of a finely focused and beautifully balanced recording which has maximum clarity and blend as well as considerable warmth.

The Medici too give a thoroughly impassioned and imaginative account of both quartets, and are no less inside the music than the Gabrielis. Indeed honours are so evenly divided in places that it is difficult to say which is to be preferred. The Gabrielis have slightly greater polish and fervour, and their recording is better focused; the Medici are more understanding, less biting, and are rather more spread between the two speakers. But even though this newer EMI issue does not displace the Gabrieli, it deserves a strong recommendation. There is no appreciable difference in sound between the LP and the excellent chrome tape.

PIANO MUSIC

On an overgrown path (*Sets I and II*); *Theme and variations* (*Zdenka*).
(M) **(*) Sup. 1111 2976. Klánský.

On an overgrown path – excerpts; Piano sonata; In the mist.
*** None. Dig. D/*D4* 79041. Moravec.

The best thing in Moravec's recital is *In the mist*, which is most poetic. He is expansive, inward-looking and rhapsodic, conveying the sense of nostalgia and regret as effectively as anyone on record. He produces a hardly less successful account of the *Sonata*, thoughtful yet having the measure of the dramatic rhetoric. The smaller pieces from the first book of *On an overgrown path* are done with great feeling and gentleness. This is a lovely record and the only complaint one can have is that it gives short measure: the *Sonata* and *In the mist* are about a quarter of an hour each and the three pieces from *On an overgrown path* run to 10 minutes. The recording balances the piano rather too closely but the sound is still very good indeed.

Heard immediately after the Moravec on Nonesuch, Ivan Klánský's Supraphon recording sounds a bit shallow. There is nothing shallow about his playing, however, which has strength and personality. He has a good feeling for mood even if one has heard more affecting and poetic accounts of some of the *Overgrown path* pieces. He uses the 1979 Critical Edition, as indeed does Yitkin Seow on Camerata (for readers in the Far East and the USA). He offers the ten numbers of the first book of the *Overgrown path*, the *Sonata* and *In the mist* and in the former he penetrates the gentle melancholy of some of these pieces as memorably as any of his rivals.

Amarus (lyric cantata).
(M) ** Sup. 1121678. Gubauerová, Zahradníček, Tuček, Czech PO Ch., Ostrava Janáček PO, Trhlík – SUK: *Under the Apple Tree.***

Janáček's *Amarus*, though not a fully mature piece, has many facets of the familiar personality and some striking invention in the course of its thirty-odd minutes. It is a setting of a poem by Jaroslav Vrchlický that must have struck a responsive chord in a composer whose own upbringing had been entrusted to a monastery. The hero of the poem is a monk who pines for life and love, and prays for deliverance from his earthly lot. It is scored for three soloists, mixed chorus and orchestra, and was first performed in 1900 under Janáček's own baton. The performance is committed enough, with some sensitive and responsive orchestral playing and some fine choral singing. The tenor is unsympathetic, however, and the recording could do with more opulence. Apart from the slightly *can belto* singer, this is a useful contribution to the Janáček discography.

Male choruses: *Ach vojna* (*The soldier's lot*); *Ceská legie* (*Czech Legion*); *Coz ta nase bríza* (*Our birch tree*); *Kantor Halfar* (*Schoolmaster Halfar*); *Klekánica* (*The evening witch*); *Marycka Magdonova; Potulý sílenec* (*The wandering madman*); *Rozlouceni* (*Leave-taking*); *Sedmesát tisíc* (*Seventy-thousand*).
(M) **(*) Sup. 112 0878. Moravian Teachers' Ch., Tucapský.

This is marvellous stuff. Janáček was a master of this medium and the Moravian Teachers' Choir was closely associated with him throughout his mature life. *The evening witch* was especially written for them after he first heard them in 1904. The singing has great eloquence and the music has both passion and inspiration to commend it. Strongly recommended, even though the recording is not ideally refined.

The Diary of one who disappeared.
(M) **(*) Sup. 1112 2414. Márová, Přibyl, Kühn Female Ch., Páleniček.
(M) ** DG 2543 820 [id.]. Haefliger, Griffel Female Ch., Kubelik.

Janáček's narrative song cycle is based on the diaries of an unknown son of a peasant who disappeared from a Wallachian village. He left behind him verses in which he avowed his love for a gipsy girl by whom he had had a child and for whose sake he left home. The burden of the narrative is given to the tenor, but the voice of the beloved is also heard in some of the poems, and there are female voices behind the scenes in parts IX and X. It is left to the piano to provide the dramatic background of the story and to evoke atmosphere.

This Czech version was made in 1978. The tenor is an impassioned singer, but the voice could do with greater variety of colour and timbre. Libuše Márová and the female choir give a good account of themselves and are well enough recorded. Josef Páleniček is a capable pianist but he lacks perhaps the last ounce of imagination in his treatment of the quieter passages of this demanding part. However, there is much more to admire here than to cavil at.

Haefliger is a splendid soloist, as his earlier version for Philips showed, but even he cannot make German lyrics fit the phrases in the way that only Czech words can. But this is still recommendable in a different way from the Czech version, less earthy, more sophisticated, but strongly felt.

Choral cantatas: *The eternal Gospel; Lord have mercy; Our Father; There upon the mountain.*
(M) *(*) Sup. 50680. Wysoczanská, Mrázová, Blachut, Svejda, Jedlicka, Czech Philharmonic Ch., Prague SO, Pinkas or Veselka.

These are not important Janáček compositions but they are more than welcome as additions to the catalogue. *The eternal Gospel* and *Our Father* are the major pieces here; the other two are short. Some of the inspiration is noble and ardent, but readers should not expect any of these works to equal the Janáček of the *Glagolitic Mass.* The performances are well-shaped and spirited, but the recordings are satisfactory rather than excellent. There is a certain pallor about the sound quality that suggests they originate from the early 1960s.

Glagolitic Mass.
*** HMV Dig. ASD/*TCC-ASD* 4066 [Ang. DS/*4XS* 37847]. Palmer, Gunson, Mitchinson, King, CBSO and Ch., Rattle.

(M) *** Decca Jub. 411 726-1/*4*. Kubiak, Collins, Tear, Schone, Brighton Fest. Ch., RPO, Kempe.

(M) **(*) Sup. 50519. Domaninská, Soukupová, Blachut, Haken, Czech. Philharmonic Ch. and O, Ančerl.

(M) ** Sup. 1112 2698 [Pro Arte PMC/*P4C* 1060]. Beňačkova-Cápová, Randová, Přibyl, Kopčák, Czech. Philharmonic Ch., Brno State PO, Jílek.

Written when Janáček was over seventy, this is one of his most important and most exciting works, full of those strikingly fresh uses of sound that make his music so distinctive. The opening instrumental movement has much in common with the opening fanfare of the *Sinfonietta*, and all the other movements reveal an original approach to the church service. The text is taken from native Croatian variations of the Latin text, and Janáček himself said that he had village services in mind when he wrote the work. Not that this complex and often advanced music could be performed in any ordinary village church, but its vitality bespeaks a folk inspiration. Rattle's performance is strong and vividly dramatic, with the Birmingham performers lending themselves to Slavonic fervour. This is the finest version yet.

The Decca recording is also an extremely good one, Kempe's reading is broader, and the Brighton chorus sings impressively. The playing of the Royal Philharmonic too is wonderfully committed and vivid, and there is first-rate solo singing, with Teresa Kubiak particularly impressive. This makes a good alternative to Rattle, although it does not have the snapping authenticity of Ančerl's much-admired version. This earlier Czech performance remains a classic account and the recording is atmospheric, if not as clear and vivid as the Decca or HMV. The later version under Jílek is very good too, with much fervour and excitement to commend it. The recording is rather more refined than the earlier Supraphon and it is only when one hears the brilliant new HMV recording (with its excellent chrome-tape equivalent) that one appreciates the greater sophistication of Western digital recording.

OPERA

The Cunning little Vixen.

*** Decca Dig. D257 D2/*K257 K22* (2) [Lon. LDR/*5*- 72010]. Popp, Randová, Jedlická, V. State Op. Ch., Bratislava Children's Ch., VPO, Mackerras.

Mackerras's thrusting, red-blooded reading is spectacularly supported by a digital recording of outstanding demonstration quality on LP and chrome tape alike. His determination to make the piece more than quaint is helped by the Viennese warmth of the playing. That Janáček deliberately added the death of the vixen to the original story points very much in the direction of such a strong, purposeful approach. The inspired choice of Lucia Popp as the vixen provides charm in exactly the right measure, a Czech-born singer who delights in the fascinating complexity of the vixen's character: sparkling and coquettish, spiteful as well as passionate. The supporting cast is first-rate too.

The excursions of Mr Brouček (complete).

(M) *** Sup. 1116 3291/3. Přibyl, Jonášová, Marsík, Novák, Marková, Tuček, Souček, Krejčik, Márová, Olejníčnek, Hanuš, Czech Philharmonic Ch. and O, Jílek.

Unlike the previous Supraphon recording of this most bizarre of Janáček's operas, this one is done complete. Previously with Vaclav Neumann, cuts were made in such passages as the religious discussion in the second part. Though Janáček seems to have intended it as a biting satire, this performance comes over more gently, with real charm, thanks partly to the warmly understanding conducting of František Jílek but also to the characterization of the bumbling central character, Mr Brouček (literally, Mr Beetle). Vilem Přibyl makes him an amiable, much-put-upon figure as he makes his excursions backwards in time to the Middle Ages and to the moon. The big team of singers (doubling up roles in the different parts) is first-rate with Vladimir Krejčik outstanding in no fewer than seven roles. The recording is warm and atmospheric, sorting out the many complex strands in the vocal writing. The orchestra is placed a little behind.

Fate (complete).
(M) **(*) Sup. 1116 2011/2. Přibyl, Hajóssyová, Palivcová, Krejčik, Ch. and O of Brno State Th. Op., Jílek.

Semi-autobiographical and including scenes at a spa and at a music academy, *Fate* (*Osud*) is a strange work. It took the composer four years to complete after he had written his first operatic masterpiece, *Jenůfa*. Though the story is quirky in the way one associates with Janáček's later operas, he was aiming at a wide popular appeal, and there are a few nods in the direction of Puccini. In the context of the rest of Janáček's work – now increasingly recognized as a unique *oeuvre* – *Fate* has an important though secondary place among the operas. A performance as strong and well-recorded as this is very welcome, and it can be warmly recommended to the converted.

From the House of the Dead (complete).
❀ *** Decca Dig. D 224 D 2/*K 224 K 22* (2) [Lon. LDR 10036]. Zahradniček, Zídek, Janska, Zítek, V. State Op. Ch., VPO, Mackerras.

With fine digital recording adding to the glory of the highly distinctive instrumentation, the Decca recording of Janáček's last opera outshines even the earlier recordings in this Mackerras series. By rights this piece based on Dostoyevsky should in operatic form be intolerably depressing. In effect, as this magnificent performance amply demonstrates, the mosaic of sharp response, with sudden hysterical joy punctuating even the darkest, most bitter emotions, is consistently uplifting. Apart from one exception the cast is superb, with a range of important Czech singers giving sharply characterized vignettes. The exception is the raw Slavonic singing of the one woman in the cast, Jaroslav Janska as the boy Aljeja, but even that fails to undermine the intensity of the innocent relationship with the central figure, which provides an emotional anchor for the whole piece. The cassette production is characteristic of Decca's usual high standard, although the transfer level is not as high as on some Decca sets, so that the transients are slightly sharper on disc. Even so the sound is extraordinarily vivid.

Jenůfa (complete).
❀ *** Decca Dig. D276 D3 (3)/*K276 K32* (2) [Lon. LDR/5- 73009]. Söderström, Ochman, Dvorský, Randová, Popp, V. State Op. Ch., VPO, Mackerras.
(M) ** Sup. 1116 2751/2. Beňačková, Krejčik, Kniplová, Přibyl, Pokamá, Brno Janáček Op. Ch. and O, Jílek.

This is the warmest and most lyrical of Janáček's operas, and it inspires a performance from Mackerras and his team which is both deeply sympathetic and strongly dramatic. After Mackerras's previous Janáček sets it was natural to choose Elisabeth Söderström for the name part. Mature as she is, she creates a touching portrait of the girl caught in a family tragedy. Where this set scores substantially over previous ones is in the security and firmness of the voices with no Slavonic wobblers. The two rival tenors, Peter Dvorský and Wieslav Ochman as the half-brothers Steva and Laca, are both superb; but dominating the whole drama is the Kostelnitchka of Eva Randová. For the first time on record one can register the beauty as well as the power of the writing for this equivocal central figure. Some may resist the idea that she should be made so sympathetic, but particularly on record the drama is made stronger and more involving. The chrome cassette layout on two tapes is preferable to the discs and the sound matches the LPs very closely indeed. A set in the demonstration class, whichever medium is chosen.

This Supraphon version of *Jenůfa* lacks the concentration of Mackerras's Janáček performance for Decca, but the performance is fresh, sharp and enjoyable. A strong cast is headed by two veteran singers, Vilém Přibyl as Laca and Nadejda Kniplová as the Kostelnitchka; their singing is most assured but their voices are often raw for the gramophone. So too with most of the singers in the smaller parts, though the role of Jenůfa has gone to a fine, creamy-toned soprano with no hint of Slavonic wobble, Gabriela Beňačková. As Steva, the tenor Vladimir Krejčík confirms the excellent impression he made in the Decca set of *The Makropoulos Affair*.

Kátya Kabanová (complete).
*** Decca D 51 D 2/*K 51 K 22* (2) [Lon. OSA/5- 12109]. Söderström, Jedlička,

Dvorský, Márová, Kniplová, Svehla, V. State Op. Ch., VPO, Mackerras.

An altogether superb issue on all counts. Sir Charles Mackerras draws playing of great eloquence from the Vienna Philharmonic. *Kátya Kabanová* is based on Ostrovsky's play *The Storm*, which has inspired other operas as well as Tchaikovsky's overture, and was Janáček's first stage work after the First World War. (It is worth adding that this was the first recording of a Janáček opera ever made outside Czechoslovakia.) Elisabeth Söderström dominates the cast as the tragic heroine and gives a performance of great insight and sensitivity; she touches the listener far more deeply than did her predecessor on Supraphon, and is supported by Mackerras with an imaginative grip and flair that outstrip his Czech colleagues. The plot (very briefly) centres on Kátya, a person of unusual goodness whose marriage is loveless, and her husband, who is dominated by his mother. Her infatuation with Boris (Peter Dvorský), her subsequent confession of adultery and her ultimate suicide are pictured with music of the most powerful and atmospheric kind. The other soloists are all Czech and their characterizations suitably authentic. But it is the superb orchestral playing and the inspired performance of Söderström that make this set so memorable. The recording has a realism and truthfulness that do full justice to Janáček's marvellous score. The difference between disc and cassette is minimal.

The Makropoulos Affair (*Věc Makropulos;* complete).
*** Decca D 144 D 2/*K 144 K 22* (2) [Lon. OSA/*5-* 12116]. Söderström, Dvorský, Zítek, Jedlička, Krejčík, Blachut, V. State Op. Ch., VPO, Mackerras.

Mackerras and his superb team provide a thrilling new perspective on an opera which is far more than the bizarre dramatic exercise it once seemed, with its weird heroine preserved by magic elixir well past her 300th birthday. In most performances the character of the still-beautiful Emilia seems mean past any sympathy, but here the radiant Elisabeth Söderström sees it rather differently, presenting from the first a streak of vulnerability. She is not simply malevolent: irritable and impatient rather, no longer an obsessive monster. Framed by richly colourful singing and playing, Söderström amply justifies that view, and Peter Dvorský is superbly fresh and ardent as Gregor. The recording, like the others in the series, is of demonstration quality, the cassettes only marginally less sharp in focus than the discs.

Janequin, Clément (*c.* 1485–1558)

Chansons: *A ce joly moys; Assouvy suis; L'aveugle dieu qui partout vole; Le chant des oyseaux; Le chant du rossignol; Hellas, mon Dieu, ton ire; Herbes et fleurs; Il estoit une fillette; J'atens le temps; Las on peult juger; M'amye a eu de Dieu; Ma peine n'est pas grande; M'y levay par ung matin; O doulx regard; O mal d'aymer; Or sus vous dormés trop* (*L'alouette*)*; Quand contrement verras; Quelqu'un me disoit l'aultre jour; Toutes les nuictz; Ung jour Colin.*
*** HM HM/*40.* 1099. Clément Janequin Ens.

This record offers twenty-one Janequin pieces which give an excellent picture of his range and variety, for although the onomatopoeic *Chant des oyseaux* (1528) and the *Chant de l'alouette* (1537) are well admired for their wit and resource, there is another side to Janequin, as witnessed by *O doulx regard* (1548), a moving chanson of unrequited love. It must also be said that these performances far surpass the previous anthology from Charles Ravier and the Ensemble Polyphonique de France (now deleted). The four singers (counter-tenor, tenor, baritone and bass) are most impressive both in their ability to blend with each other and their unfailing sense of style – and, one might add, virtuosity! The lutenist, too, is of similar quality. The documentation is thorough and helpful and the recording quality, though a trifle synthetic (it was made in one of the studios of the *Maison de la Radio* in Paris), is very vivid. The cassette is of Harmonia Mundi's finest quality, strikingly vivid and clear.

Jenkins, John (1592–1678)

Consort music: *Almain No. 9 in D; Fancy-air sett No. 6 in G min.; Fantasy in D min.; Lady Katherine Audley's Bells; A New Year's Gift to T.C.; Pavan in G min.; Suite in D min. (Divisions); Suite of 3-part ayres in C (Nos. 53–5); 4-part ayre No. 51.*
*** Mer. E. 77020. Ars Nova, Holman.

The career of John Jenkins – who died at the age of eighty-six – spanned virtually the whole period between the two English giants, Byrd and Purcell. The *New Grove* suggests that in the mid-seventeenth century his consort music was the mainstay of the repertory; and so it deserved to be, if this fine collection is anything to go by. On record Jenkins has been shockingly neglected, but these first-rate performances, well recorded, should do much to rectify that.

Consort music: *Ayre (No. 31); Corant (No. 44); Fancy-air set No. 4 in C; Fantasias Nos. 3 in G min.; 6 in F; 8 in A min.; 12 in D; Fantasy suites Nos. 1 in G min.; 17 in E min.; Galliard (No. 24) in D; In nomine (No. 1) in G min.; Newark siege (No. 23); Pavans Nos. 2 in G min.; 51; Sarabande (52).*
*** O-L DSLO 600. Cons. of Musicke, Trevor Jones.

It is difficult to understand the long neglect Jenkins has suffered on the gramophone. Apart from the Meridian disc listed above, there has been little sign of interest since the Oxford Chamber Players directed by Raymond Clauson devoted a complete disc to him in the late 1950s on Argo. True, Faber Music published a handsome edition by Dr Andrew Ashbee of the *Consort Music in Five Parts* in the early 1970s which forms the basis for these recordings. This music is not only original, it has eloquence and depth, and should not be thought of as the preserve of specialists. The Consort of Musicke under the direction of Trevor Jones play it with dedication and communicate its freshness and lyricism. Jenkins has been called 'the supreme composer of music for viols' and there is no doubt that he has a distinctive voice. Readers who are not normally drawn to this repertoire should seek this record out, for it will give them unexpected rewards. The recorded sound is excellent.

Jones, Daniel (born 1912)

Symphony No. 4 (In memory of Dylan Thomas); Symphony No. 7.
*** Oriel ORM 1002. RPO, Groves.

There is no doubt listening to these two symphonies that Daniel Jones is a genuine symphonic thinker, capable of arguing in long, coherently related paragraphs. The *Fourth Symphony*, written in memory of Dylan Thomas, is powerful in atmosphere and the *Seventh* too is strong in feeling and organically conceived. Unfortunately here there is a want of real musical personality: one does not immediately feel that the composer has created a world that is instantly recognizable as his own and his own alone! All the same, these are well worth hearing and, given such fine playing and recording, can be strongly recommended.

Symphony No. 6.
(M) *** Oriel ORM 1004. RPO, Groves – MATHIAS: *Symphony No. 1.***(*)

Daniel Jones is a much underrated composer whose symphonies are strikingly coherent and impressively argued. The *Sixth Symphony* is eclectic in style, but strong in personality, and the cogency of the argument (all six movements use the same basic material) is matched by an ability to communicate emotional experience. The main 'first movement' *Agitato*, the following

Sostenuto, and the scherzo, if somewhat conventional in material, are striking in their projection of the composer's personality. The symphony is splendidly played, and both conductor and orchestra show their commitment. The recording too has plenty of body and colour.

Symphonies Nos. 8–9; Dance fantasy.
*** BBC REGL 359 [Ara. 8081/*9081*]. BBC Welsh SO, Thomson.

Daniel Jones's music has genuine integrity and power: he possesses the qualities of a real symphonist, a sense of movement and a feeling for growth. The two symphonies recorded here are both finely crafted and tersely argued. Purposeful music, very well played by the BBC Welsh Orchestra under Bryden Thomson and truthfully recorded. A valuable issue, well worth investigating.

3 String quartets (1975; 1978; 1980).
*** Chan. Dig. ABRD/*ABTD* 1043. Delmé Qt.

Although Daniel Jones's symphonies have been well served by the gramophone, his chamber music has not. An Argo record brought us his *Ninth Quartet*, written in the late 1950s, together with the *Sonata for three kettledrums*. In recent years the composer has stopped numbering his quartets, merely assigning them dates, and the three recorded here sustain the favourable impression aroused by earlier works. All three are distinguished by seriousness of purpose and fine craftsmanship. Yet for the most part, this is more than just expertly fashioned music: it consistently places matter before manner and there are rarely any superfluous gestures. He is an unflamboyant composer who deserves to be more widely known, and all three works are of substance. They are played with dedication by the Delmé Quartet and excellently recorded, too. The cassette is wide-ranging and reproduces admirably.

The Country beyond the Stars.
*** Oriel ORM 1001. Ch., RPO, Groves – HODDINOTT: *Welsh dances*; WILLIAMS: *Penillion.****

Daniel Jones's cantata is designed to suit the traditional qualities of Welsh choirs, warm, relaxed writing, easy on the ear. The five choral movements are settings of the Breconshire poet Henry Vaughan, and are divided by a purely orchestral third movement, *Joyful Visitors*. Fine performance and recording.

Joplin, Scott (1868–1917)

'The Redback Book': *The Cascades; The Chrysanthemum; The Easy Winners; The Entertainer* (2 versions); *Maple Leaf rag; Ragtime dance; Sugar Cane; Sunflower slow drag* (2 versions).
(M) **(*) EMI ESD/*TC-ESD* 7175 [Ang. S/*4XS* 36060]. New England Conservatory Ragtime Ens., Schuller; Romanul (piano).

Scott Joplin wrote fifty-one piano rags (some in conjunction with other composers) and it is not clear how much hand he had in the orchestral arrangements, probably little. Joplin's talent was narrow in range but strong in personality, so that almost any of his compositions is instantly recognizable, not only by the fairly rigid rhythmic straitjacket, but also by its melodic and harmonic individuality. 'The Redback Book' was a New Orleans nickname for a collection of simple orchestrations (using up to fifteen instruments) and all the rags included here, except *Sugar cane*, come from this source, no doubt adapted by Günther Schuller. His group gives authentic and convincing performances, easygoing but with plenty of projection and no lack of spontaneity. The recording is atmospheric and perhaps a shade lacking in bite, with disc and cassette closely matched.

Elite syncopations (ballet).
**(*) CRD CRD 1029. Gammon (piano), members of the Royal Ballet O.

These are authentic arrangements, many of them by Günther Schuller, and they are played with a fine sense of style. Most of the favourite rags are included (though not *The Entertainer*), plus some novelties, and the orchestrations are nicely varied, with the solo piano often left to play alone. The recording is really first-class (on disc and tape alike) and Joplin fans will find this very enjoyable, although some might feel the playing is *too* sophisticated.

Rags (arr. Perlman): *Bethena; The Easy Winners; Elite syncopations; The Entertainer; Magnetic rag; Pineapple rag; Ragtime dance; Solace; The strenuous life; Sugar cane rag.*
*** HMV ASD/*TC-ASD* 3075 [Ang. S/*4XS* 37113]. Perlman, Previn.

Perlman and Previn letting their hair down present a winning combination in a whole sequence of Joplin's most naggingly haunting rags. This is very much Previn's country, and his rhythmic zest infects his brilliant partner. Different copies of the cassette have yielded different quality, not always satisfactory: this is a tape to try before purchase.

Arrangements: *Bethena; The Cascades; The Chrysanthemum; Cleopha march and two-step; Combination march; Elite syncopations; The Entertainer; The Favorite; Great crush collision march; Harmony Club waltz; Maple Leaf rag; Original rags; Ragtime dance.*
*** CBS 73685/*40*- [FM/*FMT* 37818]. Rampal, Ritter, Manne, Johnson.

Jean-Pierre Rampal's Joplin collection has an engagingly light touch. His programme is generous and varied and there is a stylish backing provided by John Ritter (piano or harpsichord), Shelly Manne (drums), plus Tommy Johnson's nicely balanced tuba. The music-making is elegant in a very French way, though the rhythmic feeling is authentic. The pacing tends to be brisk, which helps the impression of delicacy of feeling. The whole programme is agreeably spontaneous and very well recorded, both on disc and on a matching chrome tape.

Piano collections

Complete works for piano: Rags; Marches; Waltzes. *Improvisations on 12 famous rags. School of Ragtime: 6 exercises* (Joplin's text read by Eubie Blake).
(M) *** RCA [CRL 5 1106 (5)]. Hyman.

Although extravagantly presented, this is by far the most distinguished issue in the Joplin discography. Apart from its obvious attraction of completeness, it cannot be faulted on either style or arrangement. The *Rags* are played in chronological order; then come the *Marches* and *Two-steps*; and finally the *Waltzes*. As an appendix the ninety-two-year-old Eubie Blake reads Joplin's own short course on how to play rags, with brief illustrations. The instructions, intended for the amateur, are simplistic, but that adds to their charm, and Eubie Blake's enunciation has a special character; he knew Joplin and heard him play. To round off the set, Dick Hyman makes a dozen improvisations in the spirit of James P. Johnson, Fats Waller and other Harlem artists. These do not have the distinction of, say, an Oscar Peterson, but they are pleasing, and throughout the body of the anthology Hyman's playing is first-rate. His rhythmic flexibility, nimble touch, and sensibility in matters of light and shade mean that music that can easily sound stereotyped remains fresh and spontaneous-sounding throughout. The recording is faithful if not sonorous, but the piano image (not too heavy, but not shallow either) seems right for the music. Unfortunately this set has been withdrawn in the UK.

Bethena; Elite syncopations; Eugenia; Leola; Paragon rag; Pineapple rag; Rose leaf rag; Solace (*A Mexican serenade*).
**(*) None. H/*N5* 71264 [id.]. Rifkin.

The Cascades; The Chrysanthemum; Country Club; The Nonpareil; Original rags; Stoptime rag; Sugar Cane; Weeping Willow.
**(*) None. H/*N5* 71305 [id.]. Rifkin.

The Entertainer; Euphonic sounds; Fig Leaf rag; Gladiolus rag; Magnetic rag; Maple Leaf rag; Ragtime dance; Scott Joplin's new rag.
**(*) None. H/*N5* 71248 [id.]. Rifkin.

Rags (as listed above on H/*N5* 71248 and 71264).
**(*) None. HB 73026 (2). Rifkin.

Joshua Rifkin is the pianist whose name has been indelibly associated with the current Scott Joplin cult, originally stimulated by the soundtrack background music of the very successful film *The Sting*. His relaxed, cool style, rhythms not too exact, and more than a hint of monochrome in the tone colour, is distinctive. Perhaps the playing is a trifle too studied – a little more obvious joy in the music would be attractive – but there is no doubt that this playing has style. However, if it is taken a whole record at a time the danger of monotony is real, when the basic approach is comparatively rigid. The recording is excellent, slightly more mellow on the first album (H 71248), to match the playing itself. The cassette transfers are faithful.

Rags: *The Entertainer; Easy winners; Gladiolus; Heliotrope bouquet; Magnetic rag; Maple Leaf rag; Paragon rag; Pineapple rag; Solace – A Mexican serenade.*
*** HMV Dig. EMD/*TCC-EMD* 5534 [Ang. DS/*4ZS* 37331]. Rifkin.

In his newest EMI selection Rifkin plays with the same articulate rhythms and deliberate manner as before (on Nonesuch). Some may feel that he sounds too calculatedly uninvolved, yet his steady tempi are what the composer himself advocated. The playing is alive, and it certainly has style; and the programme includes the obvious favourites. The digital recording is very good indeed, and the piano image has striking body and presence both on disc and on the excellent chrome tape.

Binks' waltz; Cleopha march and two step; Easy winners; Elite syncopations; Maple Leaf rag; Original rags; Peacherine rag; Pineapple rag; Strenuous life; Sunflower slow drag.
(M) ** CBS 60269/*40-*. Biggs (pedal harpsichord).

Of all the permutations on the Joplin repertoire this collection by the late E. Power Biggs, recorded with great verve on the pedal harpsichord, is the most original. But, as the sleeve note points out, the actual sound is not so far removed from that of a honky-tonk piano. Biggs is clearly enjoying himself and the closely balanced recording projects admirably. Not to be taken all at once, but no one could fault the rhythmic style, and the playing is undoubtedly infectious. The chrome cassette is faithful although side two, at a higher level, brings additional presence.

Treemonisha (opera; arr. and orch. Schuller): complete.
**(*) DG [2707 083 (2)]. Balthrop, Allen, Rayam, White, Houston Grand Op. Ch. and O, Schuller.

The tragic story of Scott Joplin's life hinges on his desire to flee from composing the rags which gave him a degree of fame, and to write a full-blown opera. In the end, having completed the score of *Treemonisha*, he managed to sponsor a single performance in an obscure hall in Harlem in 1915, only to be faced with a total flop. He died two years later. Over half a century after, with Joplin's rags suddenly the rage once more, Günther Schuller orchestrated and edited the surviving piano score, and the result was presented on stage in Houston and New York. This well-rehearsed performance on record stems from that live production, and something of a live occasion is conveyed. The deliciously ingenuous score will not appeal to all tastes, with its mixture of choral rags, barber's shop quartets, bits of diluted Gilbert and Sullivan, Lehár and Gershwin and much that is outrageously corny, but – to some ears – irresistibly so. The story (with libretto by Joplin himself) tells of a black girl who fights with all too ready success against the primitive superstitions of her race. For this to have bitten as it should, one would need a far sharper portrayal of evil. Thus the work has the ethos of the Musical rather than the opera house. But (with the exception of some unlovable singing from Betty Allen as Monisha) the performance and recording are first-class and many will find themselves warming to the spontaneity of Joplin's invention. The set is currently only available in the USA.

Josephs, Wilfred (born 1927)

Symphony No. 5 (Pastoral), Op. 75; Variations on a theme of Beethoven, Op. 68.
*** Uni. Dig. DKP 9026. Adelaide SO, Measham.

Josephs, best known as one of the most successful writers of television signature-tunes as well as of film music, is colourful, inventive and immediately communicative in his more serious works. The *Symphony* is here the more ambitious piece, relying rather too much on slow sobriety but with beautiful orchestral sounds. The *Beethoven variations* are ingenious and fascinating, contrasting two versions of the same theme, used both in the *Septet* and in the little *Piano sonata*, Op. 49, No. 2. Cleverly Josephs has the orchestra imitating the sound of a piano. Excellent performances under Measham and first-rate recording.

Josquin des Prés (*c.* 1450–1521)

Absalom, fili mi; Ave Maria gratia plena; De profundis clamavi; Veni sanctus spiritus (motets). Chansons: *La déploration de la mort de Johannes Ockeghem (Nymphes de Bois); El grillo; En l'ombre d'ung buissonet au matinet; In te domine speravi, per trovar pietà; Je me complains; Je ne me puis tenir d'aimer; Mille regretz; Petite camusette; Scaramella fa la galla (Loyset Compère); Scaramella va alla guerra.*
❀ *** HMV ASD/*TC-ASD* 143573-1/*4* [Ang. S 38040]. Hilliard Ens., Hillier.

Josquin is ill-served in the catalogue at present so that any addition is most welcome. However, this issue must have a particularly warm reception since these beautiful motets are given with a restrained eloquence and fine musicianship that are most persuasive. The chansons are comparably characterful and engaging. The forces involved are small, but there is clarity and a fine blend here as well as real musical feeling. Although memories of Jeremy Noble's Josquin anthology from the late 1960s are not eclipsed, this is an absolutely first-class issue and is excellently recorded too, with little to choose between disc and the first-class XDR tape.

Missa Pange lingua.
(*) Mer. 45 r.p.m. E 77052. St John's College Ch., Camb., Guest; Lucas (with TITELOUZE: *3 verses.*(*))

Missa pange lingua; Motets: *Descendi in hortum meum; Nymphes des bois; Recordare, virgo mater; Ut Phoebi radiis; Vive le Roy.*
** HM HM 5119/*40*. Boston Camerata, Cohen.

Josquin's *Missa Pange lingua* is one of the greatest works of the Renaissance (it was first published in 1539, almost two decades after the composer's death) and is among the most frequently recorded too. The Boston Camerata preface the Mass with the Gregorian hymn, *Pange Lingua Gloriosi* on which Josquin draws, and fill up the second side with five motets including the glorious *Descendi in hortum meum* and the famous lament on the death of Ockeghem. Joel Cohen makes discreet use of instrumental support in the Mass and two of the motets. The singers are more forwardly balanced and fewer in number than the rival version from St John's College, Cambridge, and women's voices are used. A more attractive acoustic setting would have greatly enhanced the appeal of this disc, though this is not to say that the sound on this issue is anything other than acceptable. There is an excellent cassette too.

While the Boston Camerata find room for some Josquin motets, Meridian break up the continuity of the Mass by offering three verses on the Gregorian hymn by Titelouze, prefacing the Mass with the first, placing the second between the *Credo* and the *Sanctus*, and finishing with the last. Like the Bostonians, they also include the Gregorian hymn itself. The Choir of St John's College, Cambridge, produce a wider range of tone than the Boston Camerata, who take a very different but wholly legitimate chamber-like view of the texture. The acoustic of the Chapel does help enormously in giving the boys' voices an appealing aural halo and their great familiarity with sixteenth-century music and the Renaissance repertoire, which is their daily fare, tells. The sound is finely blended and the singers phrase as if they care about this music. The organist in the Titelouze pieces is Adrian Lucas who plays them very well, and the 45 r.p.m. recording is good without being really outstanding.

Joubert, John (born 1927)

Dance suite, Op. 21; Piano sonatas Nos. 1, Op. 24; 2, Op. 71.
*** Pearl SHE 520. McCabe (piano).

John McCabe, a formidable recording artist, as his (deleted) Haydn series showed, proves an equally powerful advocate for the neglected music of John Joubert. The two strongly conceived *Sonatas* – the second, dating from 1971, is a particularly powerful work – are coupled with the five contrasted movements of the *Dance suite*, not as relaxed a work as one might expect from the title. Good recording.

Kabalevsky, Dmitri (born 1904)

Cello concerto No. 1 in G min.
*** CBS Dig. 37840/*40*- [id.]. Yo Yo Ma, Phd. O, Ormandy – SHOSTAKOVICH: *Cello concerto No. 1.****

Both of Kabalevsky's cello concertos have been recorded before, though neither with such persuasive force as Yo Yo Ma brings to the *First*. This is an amiable piece to which great depth of feeling is quite alien. It opens very much in the manner of Prokofiev and Myaskovsky, and is well crafted and pleasing. The excellence of the performance is matched by a fine recording and both the cassette and the disc are equally distinguished.

Symphony No. 2, Op. 19.
(M) **(*) Uni. RHS 346. New Philh. O, Measham – MIASKOVSKY: *Symphony No. 21.****

Kabalevsky's *Second Symphony* enjoyed some popularity in the 1940s and is high-spirited, well crafted and far from unappealing. It has not the substance or depth of Miaskovsky with which it is coupled, but is nonetheless worth having as an example of the 'official' Soviet symphony. David Measham secures excellent results from the New Philharmonia, and although the sound is just a little wanting in transparency the overall picture is truthfully in focus, and the surface is exemplary.

Kálmán, Emmerich (1882–1953)

Grafin Mariza (operetta): complete.
**(*) EMI 1C 15729068/9 [Ara. 8057-2/*9057-2*]. Rothenberger, Gedda, Mijakovic, Moser, Brokmeier, Boehm, Bavarian State Op. Ch., Graunke O, Mattes.

Here Kálmán's operetta is given a full-blooded opera-house treatment, with fine singing and richly resonant sound, but with the lightness and sparkle of the original not always fully captured. There are splendid moments, of course, the ensembles are spirited and the duets come off especially well. But for the lyrical music Willi Mattes sometimes overdoes the kitsch and the effect becomes languorous. Spread over two discs with dialogue included, the score is almost complete, although for some unaccountable reason the chorus *Wir singen dir* is omitted. English notes are included but no libretto.

Countess Maritza: highlights (in English).
*** That's Entertainment CDTER TER/*ZCTER* 1051. Hill-Smith, Remedios, Barber, Livingstone, Tudor Davies, Moyle, New Sadler's Wells Op. Ch. and O, Wordsworth.

The label, 'That's Entertainment', has brought out an enterprising series of recordings of stage musicals. Here it adds a recording based on the New Sadler's Wells production (in English) of Kálmán's operetta. Voices are fresh, playing and conducting are lively, and the recording excellent. Much recommended for those who prefer their operetta in English.

Ketèlbey, Albert (1875–1959)

'Appy 'Ampstead; Bells across the meadow; In a Chinese temple garden; In a monastery garden; In a Persian market; In the mystic land of Egypt; The Phantom melody; The Sanctuary of the heart; Wedgwood blue.
(M)*(*) Decca SPA 187. New SO of London, Sharples.

The medium-price earlier record is well played and recorded but lacks flair. The chorus is rather unimpressive; the bell across the meadow is obviously the same one that calls the monks in from their garden and it is too loud and too near anyway. There is no imagination here and no feeling of good humour either.

Bank holiday; Bells across the meadow; The clock and the Dresden figures; Dance of the merry mascots; In a Chinese temple garden; In a monastery garden; In a Persian market; In the mystic land of Egypt; Sanctuary of the heart; With honour crowned.
(*) Ph. Dig. **400 011-2; 6514/*7337* 152 [id.]. Reeves, Dale, Amb. Ch., L. Prom. O, Faris.

It is appropriate that Ketèlbey, whose music has found a secure place in the gramophone catalogue since the earliest days of recording, should be represented among the first compact disc issues. The enterprise is in proper scale, the effect not too overblown and the contributions of Michael Reeves, Laurence Dale and the Ambrosian Chorus are tasteful. The recording too is excellent, best on the compact disc, the chrome cassette agreeable, but not matching the other media in sparkle at the top. But the performances while enjoyable do not equal those under Lanchbery on HMV – see below – which is the best Ketèlbey collection available, by a considerable margin.

Bells across the meadow; Chal Romano (Gypsy lad); The Clock and the Dresden figures; In a Chinese temple garden; In a monastery garden; In a Persian market; In the moonlight; In the mystic land of Egypt; Sanctuary of the heart.
*** HMV ASD/*TC-ASD* 3542 [Ang. S/*4XS* 37483]. Midgley, Temperley, Amb. S., Pearson (piano), Philh. O, Lanchbery.

A splendid collection in every way. John Lanchbery plainly has a very soft spot for Ketèlbey's tuneful music (and there are some very good tunes here), and he uses every possible resource to ensure that when the composer demands spectacle he gets it. *In the mystic land of Egypt*, for instance, uses soloist and chorus in canon in the principal tune (and very fetching too). *The Clock and the Dresden figures* is deliciously done, with Leslie Pearson playing the concertante piano part in scintillating fashion. Perhaps in the *Monastery garden* the distant monks are a shade too realistically distant, but in *Sanctuary of the heart* there is no mistaking that the heart is worn firmly on the sleeve. The orchestral playing throughout is not only polished but warm-hearted – the middle section of *Bells across the meadow*, which has a delightful melodic contour, is played most tenderly and loses any hint of vulgarity. Yet when vulgarity is called for it is not shirked – only it's a stylish kind of vulgarity! The *Chal Romano* has an unexpectedly vigorous melodic impulse, reminding the listener of Eric Coates. The recording is excellent, full and brilliant. The cassette is marginally less refined than the disc but still good.

Khachaturian, Aram (1903–78)

Piano concerto in D flat.
(B) *** PRT GSGC/*ZCGC* 2065. Katz, LPO, Boult – PROKOFIEV: *Piano concerto No. 1.****
** Decca SXL 6599 [Lon. CS 6818]. De Larrocha, LPO, Frühbeck de Burgos – FRANCK: *Symphonic variations.***(*)

Mindru Katz gives a really gripping performance of this colourful work. It is the breadth of his playing that is so impressive; the bravura (and there is plenty of opportunity for it in the outer movements) does not turn the work into a mere display of pianistic fireworks, but is used to add strength and shape to the overall structure. Yet there is plenty of sparkle too, and the slow movement – complete with the original flexatone, played perhaps somewhat hesitantly – is highly expressive. The recording of both piano and orchestra is really first-class. It dates from the very beginning of the 1960s, but is a fine example of early stereo techniques at their most impressive. The cassette has somewhat less upper range than the disc but is fully acceptable.

The *Piano concerto* is not as strong a work as the *Violin concerto*; its first movement can sound rambling. But in the hands of a Spanish pianist and a Spanish conductor the slow movement sounds evocatively like Falla, and the finale too is infectiously jaunty. Not so the opening movement which is disappointingly slack in rhythm at a dangerously slow tempo. First-rate recording.

With Ricci's Decca account withdrawn, the *Violin concerto* is currently not represented in the British catalogues, although in the USA versions are available by both Ricci and David Oistrakh and, intriguingly, a transcription for flute played by Rampal. It is the composer's best work, outside the ballet theatre, and deserves a new recording.

Gayaneh (ballet): highlights.
(M) *** RCA Gold GL/*GK* 25449. Nat. PO, Tjeknavorian.

These generous excerpts come from Tjeknavorian's definitive recording of Khachaturian's original 1942 version of *Gayaneh.* The composer later reworked the score to fit a new scenario (as the earlier narrative with its ingenuous wartime moral tone had become embarrassing to the Soviets). The fresh inspiration of the original is often vulgarized in the later version – it is a case of all loss and no gain. However, this splendid disc (with a matching chrome tape, if anything better balanced than the LP) provides an admirable representation of the composer's first thoughts. Like the underrated *Violin concerto*, the melodic and harmonic colouring has a strongly Armenian flavour, and the scoring continues the oriental tradition established by Glinka. Numbers like the *Dance of the Young Kurds, Lullaby, Lezghinka* and the *Dance of the Rose maidens* readily demonstrate the quality of Khachaturian's invention, while here the famous *Sabre dance* comes off splendidly. Indeed, throughout, the excellence of the orchestral playing, under a conductor uniquely fitted by his Armenian birth to direct the proceedings, is full of sparkle, colour and high spirits.

Gayaneh: excerpts; *Spartacus* (ballet): excerpts.
*** Decca SXL/*KSXC* 6000 [Lon. CS 6322]. VPO, composer.
**(*) HMV ASD/*TC-ASD* 3347 (Ang. S 37411]. LSO, composer.

The Decca recording dates from 1963, the HMV from over a decade later. The latter is immensely spectacular and recorded (with quadraphonic sound in mind) in a very resonant acoustic. Thus the *Spartacus* excerpts (in particular the *Adagio of Spartacus and Phrygia* with its *Onedin Line* associations) sound very sumptuous indeed and certainly match the Hollywoodian epic qualities of the Bolshoi production. On the other hand, the reverberation sometimes sounds excessive in *Gayaneh* and the opening *Lezghinka*, for instance, loses some of its clarity and bite. The HMV cassette is muddied by the resonance even more than the disc. In many ways the Decca record – from a vintage period – sounds fresher and this too has a spectacular ambience. If this is reissued at mid-price it will be even more competitive.

Gayaneh: suite; Masquerade: suite; Spartacus: suite.
(M) **(*) Decca VIV/*KVIC* 54 [Lon. SPA/5-21184]. LSO, Black.

(i) *Gayaneh: suite;* (ii) *Masquerade: suite; Spartacus: Adagio.* (iii) *2 Armenian dances.*
(M) ** Ph. Seq. 6527/*7311* 187. (i) LSO, Dorati; (ii) Monte Carlo Op. O, Van Remoortel; (iii) Eastman-Rochester O, Fennell.

Masquerade: suite; Spartacus: suite; Russian fantasy.
**(*) RCA RS/*RSK* 6038. LSO, Tjeknavorian.

Tjeknavorian is a naturally sympathetic interpreter of Khachaturian's music and he secures passionate and vivid playing from the LSO. The recording is very reverberant and gives a rather noisy effect to tuttis, but in other respects projects the music well.

However, the mid-priced Decca disc is fully competitive; the sound is characteristically colourful and rather better focused in tuttis (it has a Phase Four source which means a forward balance for wind soloists, but this is not a drawback here). The cassette matches the disc closely, although the upper strings sound less rich. Stanley Black understands the spirit of this music and the LSO playing is consistently alive and colourful.

Needless to say, Dorati too is first-class in *Gayaneh* (and he offers three extra items), but the Monte Carlo performances, though agreeable, are less strongly characterized (and not as well played). The two *Armenian dances* offered as a bonus are not memorable; neither is the *Russian fantasy* on RCA. The Philips cassette is effectively transferred at quite a high level.

Kielland, Olav (born 1901)

(i) *Symphony No. 1, Op. 3;* (ii) *String quartet, Op. 22.*
*** Ph. 6529 039. (i) LPO, composer; (ii) Hindar Qt.

An invigorating, bracing symphony in the Nordic tradition with a distinctive Norwegian feel to it. Anyone who likes Nielsen or, say, the Stenhammar *Second Symphony*, will find himself completely at home in the idiom. Olav Kielland studied conducting with Weingartner and was for many years conductor of the Oslo Philharmonic, before retiring to the Telemark district of Norway where he composes. This symphony dates from 1935, and its invention is fresh and vigorous; there is a strong feeling for dramatic contrast, and an expert handling of the orchestra. The eighty-year-old conductor certainly got excellent results from the LPO, and at no time does the work outstay its welcome. One is gripped from start to finish, and left longing to hear the other three symphonies he has written. Perhaps they are disappointing, for the *Quartet* with which it is coupled and which dates from the early 1960s lacks its bold, confident profile. To be fair, it is not very well played by the Hindar Quartet, whereas the LPO obviously enjoy the symphony. First-class recording, natural and realistic.

Knussen, Oliver (born 1952)

Symphony No. 3; Ophelia dances, Book 1.
*** Uni. Dig. RHD 400. Philh. O or L. Sinf., Tilson Thomas – BAINBRIDGE: *Viola concerto.****

Oliver Knussen first attracted attention with his *Symphony No. 1*, written when he was only sixteen and first performed by the LSO with the boy composer conducting (in place of an indisposed Istvan Kertesz). He studied with John Lambert and Günther Schuller. His *Third Symphony* was finished in 1979 and dedicated to Michael Tilson Thomas, who conducted its first performance at a Prom the same year. The idiom is accessible; its sound world is distinctive and reflects an alive, vivid imagination. The language itself seems to have grown from Messiaen – and even perhaps Britten and Henze – yet its accents are personal. It is a short fifteen-minute piece in one movement, and it is superbly performed and recorded. The *Ophelia dances* played by the London Sinfonietta which make up the side are from 1975; they are related to the symphony and are no less inventive and rewarding.

Kodály, Zoltán (1882–1967)

Concerto for orchestra; Summer evening.
(M) *(*) DG 2543 809 [id.]. Budapest PO, composer.

Kodály's *Concerto for orchestra* is a slight, lyrical work which was commissioned in 1939 for the fiftieth anniversary of the Chicago Symphony Orchestra. It does not set out to rival the Bartók *Concerto*, but in its own way it is attractive and easy to listen to. *Summer night*, a rhapsodic piece, dates from ten years earlier. It is always interesting to hear a composer conduct his own works, but here the reins are slackly held and the total effect is not helped by a recording which is atmospheric and recessed rather than seeking immediacy of impact. Ormandy has recorded this piece for CBS and his performance has more fervour and intensity but, unfortunately, suffers from fierce recording. No doubt Dorati's Decca version will return to the catalogue shortly.

Dances of Galánta; Dances of Marosszék; Háry János: suite.
(M) **(*) CBS 60270/*40*-. Phd. O, Ormandy.

Dances of Galánta; Háry János: suite; Variations on a Hungarian folk-song (*Peacock*).
(M) *** Decca Jub. JB/*KJBC* 138. Philh. Hungarica, Dorati.

Dances of Galánta; Háry János: suite; (i) Arias: *Poor I am still; Once I had a brood of chicks.*
(M) *** Decca Jub. JB/*KJBC* 55. LSO, Kertesz; (i) with Szönyi.

Háry János: suite.
(M) *** CBS 61193 [MS 7408]. Cleveland O, Szell – PROKOFIEV: *Lieutenant Kijé*.***

When Dorati and the Philharmonia Hungarica finished their monumental task of recording Haydn's symphonies complete, they turned to the music of their compatriot, Kodály. Though, of course, the string section is augmented, there is the same sense of commitment here as in the performances of Haydn. The performances of the *Galánta dances* and the familiar *Háry János* suite are first-class, and the *Peacock variations* – luxuriantly extended, highly enjoyable, and deserving of greater popularity – are equally fine. The recording is in the demonstration class on both disc and the outstandingly vivid cassette.

Kertesz's readings too are superbly played and he has the advantage of hardly less impressive Decca recording from the vintage mid-1960s. The balance of the cimbalom is expertly managed, and throughout the music-making has superb élan. The two arias are short measure (compared with the offerings of Dorati and Ormandy) but they are attractive, and Miss Szönyi sings with such character that her Slavonic wobbles can be forgiven. Again the Decca cassette is an example of the highest standard of the art of tape transfer: the quality is strikingly rich and vivid throughout.

Those wanting the more traditional triptych of the *János suite* plus the two sets of dances can turn to Ormandy who plays these famous scores with thrilling panache. The Philadelphia Orchestra is in superb form. It is a pity that the balance is so close, reducing the dynamic range and producing a giant-sized cimbalom in *Háry János*. However, it is easy to forgive the faults of balance when everything is so vivid and the playing so zestful. The chrome cassette matches the disc in brilliance and has no lack of body and range.

Szell – Budapest born – is also in his element in the *János suite*. Superb Cleveland polish matches the vitality of the playing, with a humorous sparkle in Kodály's first two movements, and the mock pomposity of the Napoleon episode wittily dramatized. The full romantic sweep of the *Song* and *Intermezzo* comes over too, with deliciously pointed woodwind in the trio of the latter. The recording is CBS sound at its most glittering. Some might feel that its excess in the upper register verges on crudeness, but the recording itself is dramatically right; the engineers certainly capture the exhilaration of the playing in this way, and with a little tonal control a sparkling, reasonably lustrous sound emerges, if you don't mind the too-forward cimbalom.

(Unaccompanied) *Cello sonata, Op. 8.*
*(*) Nimbus 2117. Hocks – BRIDGE: *Sonata.***

(Unaccompanied) *Cello sonata, Op. 8;* (i) *Duo for violin and violoncello, Op. 7.*
(M) *** Saga 5386. Starker; (i) with Eidus.

The *Duo* is a fine work and it is marvellously played by Eidus and Starker. The recording is not new but is genuine and well-defined stereo. The coupling is Starker's first recording of the *Solo cello sonata*; no one has ever surpassed it on record and its virtuosity and intensity are as striking as ever. It is not in genuine stereo but that is of small account, for this is one of the classics of the gramophone.

Christian Hocks is a young cellist of mixed German and Russian parentage, who has studied with Fournier and Navarra. He plays the Kodály *Sonata* with fervour and commitment, but the recording lets things down. The acoustic is very resonant, and full justice is not quite done to this artist's tone, which sounds coarser than in the Bridge *Sonata* on the other side. An imaginative and enterprising coupling nonetheless, and it deserves support. Though it is not the equal of the Starker performance or that of Frans Helmersen (briefly available on BIS and coupled with a Bach suite), Hocks plays with an ardour that is refreshing.

(i) *Missa brevis;* (ii) *Psalmus Hungaricus.*
(M) *** Decca Jub. JB/*KJBC* 122. (i) Gale, Le Sage, Francis, Hodgson, Caley, Rippon; Broadbent (organ), Heltay; (ii) Kozma, Brighton Fest. Ch., Wandsworth School Ch.; LSO, Kertesz.

Psalmus Hungaricus is Kodály's most vital choral work and this Decca version comes as close to an ideal performance as one is likely to get. Kertesz's energy takes one compellingly through all the straight homophonic writing, which in a lesser performance can diminish the work's stature. Here, with a chorus trained by another Hungarian musician the results are electrifying, and the recording is outstandingly brilliant too (on both disc and tape). The light tenor tone of Lajos Kozma is not ideal for the solo part, but again the authentic Hungarian touch helps.

Laszlo Heltay – the trainer of the Brighton chorus – takes over the direction of the *Missa brevis* and injects his excellent choristers with an authentic zest. The *Missa brevis* is literally a short setting of the Mass, not one which omits the *Credo*. It is an unassuming piece but highly effective with such fine soloists, understanding accompaniments and excellent Kingsway Hall sound.

Koechlin, Charles (1867–1950)

(i) *Ballade for piano and orchestra; Seven stars symphony (suite), Op. 12.*
*** HMV Dig. ASD 173139-1/*4* [Ang. DS/*4XS* 37940]. (i) Rigutto; Monte Carlo PO, Myrat.

The 'stars' of the *Symphony* are terrestrial not galactic, Fairbanks and Marlene Dietrich rather than Betelgeuse and Sirius. Koechlin is an interesting figure whose output ran to more than 350 works. In some quarters he has been spoken of as a French Charles Ives, though so glib a comparison does not do justice to his singular individuality of mind. There is never any want of finesse and his imagination is richly stocked, yet there is a sense in which his works contain the raw material of a work of art rather than achieve artistic fulfilment. The *Seven stars symphony* is not, strictly speaking, a symphony but rather a suite of sketches evoking the great personalities of the cinema in the 1920s and '30s, and it is coupled here with an earlier work written for the pianist Henriette Fauré. Koechlin's music lacks the concentration and distinction of Magnard or the perfection of Roussel and, ultimately, offers less real nourishment, yet he is a stimulating figure and, given the keen advocacy of these artists and the excellence of the sound, this enterprising issue well rewards investigation. There is an impressive cassette.

Kohaut, Carl (Joseph) (1736–93)

Lute concerto in F.
(*) RCA RL/*RK* 11180 [ARL 1/*ARK 1* 1180]. Bream, Monteverdi O, Gardiner – HANDEL and VIVALDI: *Concertos.*(*)

Kohaut, a Bohemian composer, was himself a lutenist, and this is a well-made little work, *galant* in style and with an attractively simple *arioso* forming the slow movement. The performance is excellent and the recording good except for the jumbo-sized solo instrument created by the unnaturally forward balance. The cassette matches the LP closely.

Kokkonen, Joonas (born 1921)

Symphony No. 3.
**(*) Finlandia FA 311. Finnish RSO, Berglund (with Sibelius: *Tapiola* **).

Kokkonen is the finest Finnish symphonist of his generation and his music has a distinctive profile. This symphony previously available on Decca has a genuine sense of forward flow and an arresting musical argument. The texture is clear and the musical language thoroughly approachable, even though it has uncompromising integrity. The BIS label has put out its immediate neighbours in recordings deriving from Finnish Radio performances, No. 2 (1961) being conducted by Okko Kamu and No. 4 (1971) by Leif Segerstam, and it is well worth investigating (BIS LP189). They are both imaginative pieces and the *Fourth* is arguably his most impressive work to date, with an economy, sense of line and a feeling of inevitability that carry the listener with it. Persuasive playing and excellent recording too.

The Conifer lists also include the *Cello concerto* (1969) written for and played by Arto Noras, a master cellist, with the Helsinki Philharmonic Orchestra under Paul Freeman (FA310) and coupled with the Haydn *C major Concerto*. The Kokkonen is immediately accessible and has some of the harmonic flavouring and pale melancholy of Frank Martin. Some may find the concerto insufficiently astringent and he does work the main idea of the *Adagio* to death, but there is undoubted resource here as evidenced in the scherzo, and the music is deeply felt. The recording is very good indeed and well balanced too.

Koppel, Herman (born 1932)

Cello concerto, Op. 56.
*** BIS LP 78. Bløndal Bengtsson, Danish RSO, Schmidt – HOLMBOE: *Cello concerto.****

Older collectors may recall Koppel's records of Nielsen's piano music from the 1950s, but as a composer he has made little headway outside Denmark. The *Cello concerto* dates from 1952 and was written for the then 20-year-old Erling Bløndal Bengtsson. It is a most imaginative piece – the opening almost calls to mind the Tippett of *Midsummer Marriage* and is positively luminous. The language is quite accessible, the ideas often appealing though obstinately unmemorable, and at moments the texture is surprisingly lush, though the main theme of the finale is a little Stravinskian. This interesting and attractive work does not have quite the depth of the Holmboe with which it is coupled, but it leaves one impatient to explore his other works which include seven symphonies and five piano concertos. It is beautifully played too, and the recording made at a live concert is first-class.

Korngold, Erich (1897–1957)

Violin concerto in D, Op. 35.
*** HMV ASD/*TCC-ASD* 4206 [Ang. DS/ *4XS* 37770]. Perlman, Pittsburgh SO, Previn – CONUS: *Concerto*.***

Korngold's film scores have largely disappeared from the UK catalogue, although American readers are better served and the British may be able to obtain some of them as special imports. The *Symphony* has gone too (for the moment) on both sides of the Atlantic – which is a great pity as Kempe's Munich recording is first-class and his performance could hardly be more persuasive. We are left with the *Violin concerto* which largely draws its material from the film scores. It was written for Huberman, but was a favourite of Heifetz's. He gave the first performance, and one would have thought that his recording would remain forever the supreme interpretation. It has to be played as if it is a masterpiece and with consummate virtuosity if it is to carry conviction. Perlman, dashing and romantic, with more of a sense of fun than the older maestro, gives such a superlative account, and though he is placed too close to the microphone (which brings a sharp-edged quality to the cassette transfer) the recording overall is rich and vivid, with Previn and the Pittsburgh Orchestra warmly committed in their accompaniment. Although it is pure kitsch, there is something endearing about this piece and it deserves a place in the catalogue, if only to remind us of the calibre of this famous Hollywood musician. It is also marvellous violin music. Heifetz's version (coupled with the Max Bruch) is available as an RCA import from Conifer (26.41236).

Die tote Stadt (opera): complete.
*** RCA Conifer RL 01199 (3) [ARL 3 1199]. Neblett, Kollo, Luxon, Prey, Bav. R.Ch., Tolz Ch., Mun. R.O, Leinsdorf.

Before he moved to Hollywood to begin his career as a film composer and provide scores for the swashbuckling films of Errol Flynn, Erich Korngold had earlier in Germany been a brilliant prodigy of a composer. At the age of twenty-three he had his opera, *Die tote Stadt*, presented in simultaneous world premières in Hamburg and Cologne, some feat! The fantasy story of a bereaved husband meeting a girl exactly like his newly dead wife ventures into dream worlds. The setting might have been sick and morbid but for Korngold's youthfully exuberant score. Many echoes include obvious cribbing from Puccini and Strauss, who similarly knew how to manoeuvre excitingly near cliff-edges of vulgarity. *Die tote Stadt* may not be a great opera, but in a performance like this, superbly recorded, it is one to revel in on the gramophone. René Kollo is powerful if occasionally coarse of tone, Carol Neblett sings sweetly in the equivocal roles of the wife's apparition and the newcomer. Hermann Prey, Benjamin Luxon and Rose Wagemann make up an impressive cast.

Violanta (complete).
**(*) CBS 79229 (2) [Col. M2 35909]. Marton, Berry, Jerusalem, Stoklassa, Laubenthal, Hess, Bav. R. Ch., Mun. R. O, Janowski.

Korngold was perhaps the most remarkable composer-prodigy of this century; he wrote this opera at the age of seventeen. It was given its first triumphant performance under Bruno Walter, and even Ernest Newman seriously compared Korngold to Mozart. The story of the piece is a sort of compressed version of *Tristan*, but there is more of Lehár and Puccini in the idiom than of Wagner. Though luscious of texture and immensely assured, the writing lets one down in an absence of really memorable melody, but with a fine red-blooded performance – the remarkable Siegfried Jerusalem showing enormous promise as the hero – it makes a fascinating addition to the recorded repertory. The Hungarian Eva Marton, not always beautiful of tone, combines power and accuracy in the key role of the heroine, suddenly floating high pianissimos with unexpected purity. The recording is warm if unsubtle.

Kozeluch, Leopold (1747–1818)

Symphonies: in F; in G min.
(M) ** Sup. 110 2078. Prague SO, Hlaváček.

Kozeluch was a Bohemian contemporary of Haydn and Mozart, though he outlived them both. His music is far from negligible, and both these symphonies, written in 1787, after Haydn's *Paris symphonies*, are well constructed and – up to a point – inventive. Yet his melodic inspiration lacks the humanity and richness of his great contemporaries, and though the slow movements have a certain dignity, they seem by the side of Haydn to be going through the motions rather than achieving any real depth. The performances are lively enough and the recording perfectly acceptable.

Kraus, Joseph Martin (1756–92)

Keyboard sonatas Nos. 1 in E; 2 in E flat.
*** Cap. CAP 1173. Negro (harpsichord).

Joseph Martin Kraus was German-born but settled in Sweden, becoming kapellmeister at the Royal Theatre. He has a Gluck-like breadth and an inquiring mind that suggests *Sturm und Drang* Haydn or C. P. E. Bach. The two sonatas recorded here on period instruments (one a Swedish instrument by Johan Söderberg and the other a south German instrument, both in the Stockholm Museum) are of more than just historical interest, and they are played with quite exceptional insight and sensibility by Lucia Negro. The sonatas come from 1785 and 1787, and are worthy to be compared only with the very finest examples of their kind by Haydn and C.P.E. Bach. Excellent recording. This is well worth the attention of a wide public.

Kreisler, Fritz (1875–1972)

Andantino in the style of Martini; Allegretto in the style of Boccherini; Caprice viennoise, Op. 2; Chanson Louis XIII and Pavane in the style of Couperin; La Gitana; Liebesfreud; Liebeslied; Recitativo and scherzo capriccio, Op. 6; Rondino on a theme of Beethoven; Schön Rosmarin; Tambourin chinois, Op. 3. Arrangements: Albéniz: *Tango.* Dvořák: *Slavonic dance No. 3 in G.* Falla: *La Vida breve: Danse espagnole.*
*** HMV ASD 3258 [Ang. S/*4XS* 37171]. Perlman, Saunders.

Perlman is on sparkling form in these *morceaux de concert* of Fritz Kreisler, and the recording is of the highest quality. If the invention is lightweight it is never trivial, and much of this music is very entertaining, as it was meant to be. (For his second anthology (ASD 3346) Perlman concentrated on transcriptions and arrangements, and that recital is listed in the Collections section below.)

Caprice viennoise, Op. 2; La Gitana; Liebesfreud; Liebeslied; Polichinelle; La Précieuse; Recitativo and scherzo-caprice, Op. 6; Rondo on a theme of Beethoven; Syncopation; Tambourin chinois; Zigeuner (Capriccio). Arrangements: Albéniz: *Tango.* Weber: *Larghetto.* Wieniawski: *Caprice in E flat.* Dvořák: *Slavonic dance No. 10 in E min.* Glazounov: *Sérénade espagnole.* Granados: *Danse espagnole.*
*** DG 2531/*3301* 305 [id.]. Mintz, Benson.

One can understand why DG chose to introduce Shlomo Mintz with this Kreisler programme, alongside his coupling of the Bruch and Mendelssohn concertos. He plays with a disarmingly easy style and absolute technical command to bring out the music's warmth as well as its sparkle. Try *La Gitana* to sample the playing at its most genially glittering. A very attractive programme, given first-class recording and a refined cassette equivalent (perhaps a little lacking in level for maximum impact).

Kreutzer, Conradin (1780–1849)

Septet in E flat, Op. 62.
*** CRD CRD 1090/*CRDC 4090*. Nash Ens. – HUMMEL: *Military septet.****

Kreutzer's *Septet* is a delightful work, and it is given a thoroughly engaging performance here by the Nash Ensemble, whose playing is as lyrically elegant as it is full of refined detail. The care of the players over the use of dynamic graduation is matched by the warmth of their phrasing. The Hummel coupling too is most apt, as both works date from the same period (around 1830). The recording is first-class in every way and beautifully balanced, with a demonstration-worthy cassette to match the disc.

Krommer, Franz (František) (1759–1831)

(i) *Clarinet concerto in E flat, Op. 36;* (ii) *Oboe concerto in F, Op. 37.*
**(*) EMI 1C 065 03429. Prague CO, Vajnar, with (i) Zahradnik, (ii) Mihule.

A fluent composer rather than a profound one, the Moravian Franz Krommer (or František Kramár) bridges the classic and romantic eras, and this record has a foot in both camps. The *Oboe concerto* belongs firmly to the eighteenth century; the *Clarinet concerto* is of a more romantic sensibility. The performances are expert, and the recording, though a little lacking in warmth, has exemplary clarity. Pleasant music which is well worth investigation.

Symphony in D, Op. 40.
(M) *** Sup. 1110 2809. Prague CO, Vajnar – MAŠEK: *Symphony.***

This *Symphony in D major* dates from 1803 and is the second of nine, and is scored for a much larger band than the Mašek with which it is coupled. It is a work of much greater substance and power too, and inhabits a world quite different from that of the wind partitas and *Harmonien* that Supraphon have issued in the past. Indeed, there is a Beethovenian feel to this work and, as Antonin Myslik says in his sleeve-note, the work is 'marked by the troubled atmosphere of war events and by the influence of new streams of thought from the time of the French Revolution'. This is a very interesting piece and though the playing of the Prague orchestra under František Vajnar is a shade stiff and one could imagine more persuasive advocacy, this is still highly recommendable.

(i) *Bassoon quartet in E flat, Op. 46* (for bassoon, 2 violas and cello); (ii) *Oboe quartets Nos. 1 in C; 2 in F* (for oboe, violin, viola and cello).
(M) *** Sup. 1111 2824. Suk Qt (members), with (i) Seidl; (ii) Mihule.

The *Bassoon quartet* is a delight; it has warmth, individuality and a fund of good invention. The unusual combination of instruments produces a rich-bodied texture, and the playing of Jiri Seidl is sensitive both in its dynamic range and in its variety of colour. This *Quartet* makes thoroughly civilized listening; it dates from 1804, later than the two *Oboe quartets*, which are elegantly played and often witty (the finale of the F major even has a Haydnesque false ending). The recording has more body and colour than many from this source, and though it is a trifle on the close side, the timbre is natural and there is plenty of range. A thoroughly enjoyable record – and the *Bassoon quartet* is really something of a discovery.

Clarinet quartet in D, Op. 82.
*** O-L DSLO 553. Hacker, Music Party – WEBER: *Clarinet quintet.****

Krommer's *Clarinet quartet* is a pleasing and accomplished work written at much the same time as its Weber coupling. Alan Hacker plays a clarinet in A from 1825 and the quartet (led by Duncan Druce) use period instruments. The strings play without vibrato and there is an inevitable loss of warmth. The clarinet is played with sensitivity and skill, and the recording is alive and splendidly balanced.

Octet-Partita in E flat, Op. 79.
*** CRD CRD 1110/*CRDC 4110*. Nash Ens. – DVOŘÁK: *Serenade, Op. 44*.***

The Nash Ensemble give an excellent and lively account of this attractive Krommer piece. It is not great music, but it is highly agreeable and the Nash readily demonstrate its charm in a direct way for which the bright recording is admirably suited.

Kuhnau, Johann (1660–1722)

Der Gerechte kommt um (motet).
*** O-L DSLO/*KDSLC* 572. Ch. of Christ Church Cath., AcAM, Preston – BACH: *Magnificat*.***

Kuhnau was Bach's predecessor in Leipzig. He wrote this charming motet with a Latin text; it was later arranged in a German version, and there are signs of Bach's hand in it. The piece makes an excellent makeweight to a fine version of the *Magnificat*.

La Guerre, Elisabeth de (1659–1729)

Harpsichord suite in D min.
(M) *** Argo ZK 64. Gilbert – CLÉRAMBAULT: *Suites*.***

Elisabeth Jacquet de la Guerre is one of the earliest women of music, though it would be going too far to describe her as the Ethel Smyth of Versailles. Louis XIV took great delight in her playing, and she appeared at court when she was hardly fifteen, drawing much praise alike for improvisation and for compositions. Titon de Tillet wrote in *Le Parnasse François* (1732): 'A person of her sex has never before had such great gifts for composition and for amazing performance upon the harpsichord and the organ'. There are three volumes of cantatas, trio sonatas and even a full-scale opera, *Céphale et Procris*, in five Acts from her pen. These pieces comprising the *D minor Suite* are full of personality (there is striking use of major/minor contrasts) and there is much delicacy and refinement. Kenneth Gilbert plays with obvious relish and authority and is beautifully recorded on a 1747 harpsichord of Sebastian Garnier.

Lalo, Édouard (1823–92)

Cello concerto in D min.
❀ *** CBS Dig. 35848 [id.]. Ma, O Nat. de France, Maazel – SAINT-SAËNS: *Concerto No. 1*. *** ❀

Cello concerto in D min.
*** RCA RL/*RK* 25420 [RCA ARL 1/*ARK 1* 4665]. Lloyd Webber, LPO, Lopez-Cobos – RODRIGO: *Concierto como un divertimento*.***

Yo Yo Ma is an artist who eschews overstatement, and his account of the Lalo *Concerto* must rank as the finest now available. It has great sensitivity, beauty of tone and expressive feeling to commend it, and indeed it makes the work seem better than in fact it is. Moreover Maazel and the Orchestre National de France give magnificent support, matching the sensitivity of the soloist. The quality of the recorded sound is first-class, beautifully balanced and spacious, yet with detail well in focus.

No complaints about Julian Lloyd Webber's account of the Lalo *Concerto*. It is played with style and feeling. The performance does not quite match that of Yo Yo Ma on CBS, which also has a finer recording, although the RCA is perfectly satisfactory, if less rich. But many may choose the attractive Rodrigo coupling, one of that composer's most endearing recent works.

Namouna (ballet): *Rhapsodies Nos. 1 and 2; Cigarette waltz. Rapsodie norvégienne.*
(M) **(*) DG 2543 803 [id.]. Paris ORTF O, Martinon.

There is much engaging music in *Namouna*, a ballet score greatly admired by Debussy and dating from 1882. The first movement opens with an unashamed Wagnerian crib from *Das Rheingold*, but elsewhere Lalo's music is more individual. He is at his finest in the gentler atmospheric writing: the *Sérénade*, the *Valse de la cigarette*, and the enchanting Beechamesque lollipop, *La Sieste*. These are all memorable and nicely played. The *Pas des cymbales* is admirably crisp, although in the louder sections of the score the recording is inclined to fierceness, making the music sound noisier than necessary. Jean Martinon is a sympathetic exponent throughout, and he also gives us the attractively tuneful *Rapsodie norvégienne* in its adapted version for orchestra alone (1879). (The original, composed a year earlier, featured a concertante violin.)

Scherzo for orchestra.
(M) *** HMV Green. ESD 7048. O de Paris, Jacquillat – MESSAGER: *Deux pigeons;* PIERNÉ: *Marche* etc.***

Lalo's *Scherzo for orchestra* is a first-rate piece which enhances this splendid collection of French music. The compilation also includes Berlioz's arrangement of *La Marseillaise* (all verses included) for soloists, choirs and orchestra. Like everything else on the disc, this is presented with flair and excellently recorded.

Symphonie espagnole, Op. 21.
*** DG Dig. **400 032-2**; 2532/*3302* 011 [id.]. Perlman, O de Paris, Barenboim – BERLIOZ: *Romance.****
(B) *** CfP CFP/*TC-CFP* 40364. Menuhin, Philh. O, Goossens – SAINT-SAËNS: *Havanaise* etc.***
*** Decca Dig. **411 952-2**; SXDL/*KSXDC* 7527 [Lon. LDR/*5*- 71029]. Kyung-Wha Chung, Montreal SO, Dutoit – SAINT-SAËNS: *Concerto No. 1.****

Lalo's brilliant five-movement distillation of Spanish sunshine is well served here. While the compact-disc version of Perlman's newest DG digital recording shows no marked improvement on the LP (if anything it emphasizes the degree of digital edge), the sound remains both vivid and refined. The very opening sets the style of the reading, with a strongly articulated orchestral introduction from Barenboim that combines rhythmic buoyancy with expressive flair. The lyrical material is handled with great sympathy, and the richness and colour of Perlman's tone are never more telling than in the slow movement, which opens tenderly but develops a compelling expressive ripeness. The scintillating brilliance of the scherzo is matched by the dancing sparkle of the finale. The recording is extremely lively – the chrome cassette matching the disc closely – and the forward balance of the soloist in no way obscures orchestral detail and impact.

Menuhin's recording, now reissued at bargain price on Classics for Pleasure, remains very competitive indeed. It dates from the earliest days of stereo, and its extreme brightness brings a touch of fierceness to the upper range. However, with a treble cut and bass increase it can produce excellent results. The cassette is a shade less brightly lit than the disc and may be found preferable. It is a glittering performance, and the clean sound, with excellent woodwind detail, is especially effective in the delectable finale. Menuhin is on top form throughout and the warm spontaneity of his playing is matched by his feeling for the music's rhythmic character. The way he shapes the sinuous secondary theme of the first movement is wonderfully engaging. The accompaniment too is excellent, with the orchestra on its toes throughout. The Saint-Saëns couplings are superbly played.

Kyung-Wha Chung has the advantage of a first-class Decca digital recording (the cassette matching the disc closely), with a highly effective, natural balance. Hers is an athletic, incisive account, at its most individual in the captivatingly lightweight finale, with an element almost of fantasy. For some ears the lack of sumptuousness of style as well as timbre may be a drawback; Miss Chung does not have quite the panache of Perlman. But Charles Dutoit's accompaniment is first-class and the orchestral characterization is strong throughout.

Lambert, Constant (1905–51)

(i) *Piano concerto* (for piano and 9 players); *Elegiac blues; Elegy.*

(M) *** HMV Green. ESD/*TC-ESD* 7164. Bennett (i) with E. Sinf., Dilkes (with Bliss: *The Rout Trot;* Walton: *Façade: Old Sir Faulk;* Goossens: *Folk-tune;* Williams, Gerard: *Valsette brut; Raquette extra sec****).

Lambert's *Concerto for piano and nine solo instruments* presents a clever marriage between neo-classical and jazz conventions. Unsympathetically or slackly performed it can seem very dry indeed, but here Richard Rodney Bennett makes the music sparkle with wit, pointing the rhythms with fractional hesitations and underlinings that bring it to life. The sleight-of-hand pay-off endings to each movement are delectably done. The coupling could hardly be more apt, a collection of short pieces by Lambert and others with direct debts to jazz. The key item is Lambert's own *Elegiac blues,* which Bennett presents rather slowly and expressively. The *Elegy,* more ambitious in scale, is less sharply inspired, but every item here has its point, with Bliss's piece like a cross between Scott Joplin and Grainger's *Country Gardens*; and Walton's *Old Sir Faulk* shines out as the finest example of all in this tiny but delightful genre. Good bright recording on disc, but on tape the combination of the resonance and a high transfer level slightly blurs the focus of the solo piano items, although the *Concerto* sounds bold and clear.

Pomona; Romeo and Juliet (ballets).

*** Lyr. SRCS 110. ECO, Del Mar.

The sparky invention of the extraordinarily precocious Lambert is well represented in these two ballet scores (he wrote most of *Romeo and Juliet* before he was twenty). In these crisp, unpretentious dances the brilliant young man showed how cleverly he could pick up tricks from those fashionable in Paris at the time, Stravinsky, Milhaud and others. It is not surprising that Diaghilev appreciated Lambert's talent enough to put on *Romeo* – though scandal followed the first production, with the composer forcibly prevented from recovering his score. Del Mar directs bright and persuasive performances, well recorded.

Trois pièces nègres.

** Auracle AUC 1001. Lawson, Scott – BERNERS: *Fantaisie* etc.** (with Lane: *Badinages***).

Lambert's *Trois pièces nègres pour les touches blancs* were written in 1949 when the composer was visiting Palermo for a festival of the International Society of Contemporary Music. Indeed, it was its president, Edward Clark, who commissioned them. They are slight and pleasing, much in the spirit of Satie, and are played with real character by Christopher Scott and Peter Lawson, though the acoustic ambience is not really spacious enough and the listener feels just a shade too close to the piano. The side is completed by *Badinages* by Philip Lane who has championed Berners' cause in recent years. He wrote these pieces while he was waiting to take his O-levels and describes them as an affectionate tribute to the French school active in the first half of the century and, in particular, Poulenc and Milhaud. As an Opus 1, they are quite accomplished and excite curiosity as to his subsequent development.

The Rio Grande.

(*) HMV ASD 2990. Ortiz, Temperley, L. Madrigal Singers, LSO, Previn – WALTON: *Symphony No. 2* etc.*

The Rio Grande is one of the most evocative works of the 1920s, with its colourful and genial jazz references in a setting of Sacheverell Sitwell's exotic poem. Though Cristina Ortiz is not quite idiomatic in her playing of the central piano solo, Previn directs a strong and enjoyable performance, superbly recorded. Lambert, one of the real characters of British music, may not have been a great composer, but this is his masterpiece.

Lanchbery, John (born 1923)

Tales of Beatrix Potter (ballet arranged from popular tunes of the Victorian era).
*** HMV CSD 3690. ROHCG O, Lanchbery.

Here is a companion score for John Lanchbery's arrangement of *La Fille mal gardée*. The music is not as distinguished melodically as the compilation of Hérold tunes, but the colourful and witty orchestration is a source of delight and this is top-drawer EMI sound, as the opening bars readily show. The composer-arranger used Victorian tunes (including some by Sullivan) of the period of the Beatrix Potter stories and they are so skilfully linked that one would think the score was 'composed' as original music. The sleeve-presentation is very attractive.

Langgaard, Rued (1893–1952)

Symphony No. 6 (*Det Himmelrivende*); (i) *Music of the Spheres* (*Sfaerernes*).
** Danish DMA 064. Danish R. SO, Frandsen; (i) with Guillaume R. Ch.

Rued Langgaard was something of an outsider in Danish music and has been compared with such figures as Ives and Havergal Brian. Although his roots were firmly in the nineteenth century, his musical language is not wholly consistent (one of his later symphonies sounds almost Schumannesque). For much of his career he struggled to gain recognition as an organist and was eventually appointed to Ribe cathedral in 1940. His music is not highly personal but, at the same time, it must be admitted that the two works recorded here are quite unlike anything else: indeed, the *Music of the Spheres* has a manic intensity which is compelling and on occasion quite disturbing. The *Symphony* comes from 1920 and derives its title (*The storming of the heavens*) from St Paul ('Then Jesus used force and drove the storming armies of evil under the canopy of heaven'). At times the work seems ungainly and inexpert, but there are glimpses of real vision. *Music of the Spheres* (1918–20) lay neglected after its first performance until the 1960s, when a shortened version of it was recorded by the Stockholm Philharmonic under Blomstedt (HMV CSDS 1087). In this Danish performance recorded in 1980, it is given in its entirety: it is a quite extraordinary piece and it is not easy to convey the impression it creates. The sonorities are 'advanced' for the period and include tone-clusters and a piano struck directly on the strings, and skilful use is made of scraps of simple tunes that are repeated to almost hypnotic effect. Indeed, it is almost surrealistic in vision and its colouring (the dynamics are almost a whisper) quite remarkable. The scoring is for two orchestras, one off-stage with a soprano soloist. This provides an excellent introduction to Langgaard's music: there are other records of organ music and a piano sonata from 1928 played by Noël Lee on the Fona label but this is the most interesting (if perplexing) to have come our way. The recordings, made at live concerts, are acceptable rather than distinguished, and the performances are reasonably persuasive though the Danish Radio Orchestra's strings sound a bit thin.

Langlais, Jean (born 1907)

Mass: Salve Regina.
(*) Argo ZRG 938. Richard Hickox Singers, Philip Jones Brass Ens., Hickox – DURUFLÉ: *Messe.**

The Langlais Mass *Salve Regina,* which dates from 1949, is pure pastiche, but good clean fun all the same. It is scored for three choirs, two organs and two brass ensembles and would make an excellent score for a TV production set in Renaissance France. Both performance and sound are good, but the Duruflé Mass is more worthy to be taken seriously.

Larsson, Lars-Erik (born 1908)

God in disguise (Förklädd Gud): Lyric suite, Op. 24.
*** EMI 4E 061 35149. Ligendza, Wixell, Von Sydow, Swedish R. Ch. and SO, Westerberg – RANGSTRÖM: *Songs.****
Swedish Soc. SLT 33146. Söderström, Saedén, Ekborg, Lidstam Ch., Swedish RSO, Westerberg (with Grieg: *Landkjenning*).

Larsson's *God in disguise* (1939) was the outcome of a commission from Swedish Radio whose staff the then young composer had just joined, and was the result of collaboration with the poet, Hjalmar Gullberg. During this period, broadcasting stations cultivated a kind of programme that has since fallen out of fashion, a literary-cum-musical entertainment in which poetry and song were mingled. In some measure Larsson's suite has dated, but there is much charm and a naïvistic simplicity that is endearing. The prelude is pure Nielsen (and none the worse for that) and the pastoral chorus that follows is appealing. Catarina Ligendza and Ingvar Wixell are the soloists in the 1973 EMI record which is beautifully recorded. The Swedish poems may diminish the attractions of this work for some listeners but they are short – and beautifully spoken. The earlier recording is of special interest to admirers of Elisabeth Söderström who was still in her twenties and in wonderful voice when she made this disc. Few would believe that it dates from 1956, so fresh is the sound. Only in the climaxes does it begin to show its age. This is a good performance too, and offers a fill-up in the form of Grieg's *Landkjenning* about which the sleeve is completely reticent.

Pastoral suite.
** Blue. BELL 101. Örero SO, Nilson (with: Söderman: *The Maid of Orleans*; Lundquist: *Violin concerto***).

Pastoral suite; A Winter's tale (incidental music): *suite.*
*** EMI 7C 061 53598. Stockholm PO, Björlin (with Berwald: Tone poems***).

Larsson's most popular work is the *Pastoral suite,* which was paired in the early days of LP with Dag Wirén's *Serenade.* Like *God in disguise,* it is actually the product of his work in the Swedish Radio and derives from incidental music. It is in any event light and captivating, extremely well played by the Stockholm Philharmonic and Ulf Björlin and excellently recorded. The coupling is derived from the set of Berwald orchestral works Björlin recorded with the RPO in the mid-1970s and includes two of the tone poems, as well as the charming suite from Larsson's incidental music to *A Winter's tale.*

The rival account is very well played. The recording acoustic is not as expansive, however, and though the strings sound well blended the wind are rather too prominent. The conducting is sensitive, and so too is much of the playing. The couplings, Söderman's *The Maid of Orleans* overture and a neo-romantic (and quite effective) *Violin concerto* by Torbjörn Lundquist, with Karel Šneberger as soloist, might sway some collectors in its favour, but the dry acoustic weighs against this issue.

Lassus, Orlandus (*c*. 1530–1594)

Le Lagrime de San Pietro a 7.
*** O-L DSDL 706. Kirkby, Tubb, Nichols, Cass, Cornwell, King, Wistreich, Cons. of Musicke, Rooley.

Le Lagrime de San Pietro (*The Tears of St Peter*) is a late work, a setting of twenty verses by the poet, Luigi Transillo (1510–68), a Neapolitan best known for his lyrical love-sonnets, and there is a final motet in which Christ speaks directly from the Cross for which Lassus himself possibly provided the text. Like much Renaissance music, it can be performed by a vocal consort or a choir, with or without instruments. The work is rich in variety of expressive means: Howard Mayer Brown calls it a work 'of almost Baroque religious fervour', and much of its eloquence is communicated by these artists. The performance is given one voice to a part and its impact might perhaps have been heightened if the artists had permitted themselves an even wider tone colour. The absence of vibrato produces a whiteness of tone that eventually tires the ear even though there is every sensitivity to the words and great clarity of texture. Instruments are used in the closing motet but otherwise much is made of the madrigalian character of this work, which was not so effectively conveyed in the Hungaraton version by the Chamber Choir of the Liszt Academy. There are, of course, many legitimate approaches to this work and this admirably recorded and well-annotated disc will surely give much satisfaction.

Missa Pro defunctis a 4.
** Hyp. Dig. A 66066. Pro Cantione Antiqua, Mark Brown.

The Pro Cantione Antiqua sing this four-part *Requiem* one voice to a part and the gain in clarity of texture is offset by a loss of grandeur and majesty. The singers are impressive for all that, and the *Requiem* is interspersed with plainchant from the Office for the Dead. The recording, made in the warm acoustic of St John's Church, Hackney, places the singers rather close to the listener, which again helps clarity but reduces the sense of mystery. The four singers blend well and intonation is generally true.

Missa super Bell' Amfitrit' altera; Psalmus poenitentialis VII.
❀ *** Decca Ser. SA/*KSC* 18. Christ Church Cath. Ch., Oxford; Preston.

This splendid record is doubly welcome in this Decca Serenata medium-price reissue and it can be recommended wholeheartedly. The trebles are firm in line, strong in tone, and the choir produces marvellously blended tone-quality. The acoustic is warm and atmospheric (the performances were recorded in Merton College, Oxford) and the texture is thus heard to best advantage. The performances have an admirable vitality and plenty of expressive range, though there is not the slightest trace of self-indulgence or excessive fervour. The *Mass* comes from about 1585 and is Venetian in style, scored for double choir each comprising SATB. Simon Preston secures magical results, and the recording is one of the finest choral records of the mid-1970s, rich in detail and firmly focused in sound. The cassette transfer too is first-class, the sound full, vibrant and wide-ranging.

Music for Holy Week and Easter Sunday.
*** Hyp. Dig. A 66051/2. Pro Cantione Antiqua, Turner.

These performances by the Pro Cantione Antiqua under Bruno Turner are more likely to persuade listeners that Lassus is a great composer than previous anthologies devoted to the *Lamentations*. The singing is expressive and vital with none of the white, vibrato-less tone that is currently in fashion among Early Music groups. Each side of the two records is devoted to one of the days of Holy Week from Maundy Thursday onwards, and the music is not only elevating but is also given the benefit of admirably warm recording which combines the merits of clarity and homogeneity.

Madrigals: *Al dolce suon'; Ben convenne; Bestia curvafia pulices; Ove d'alta montagna;*

Praesidium sara; Spent'è d'amor. Motets: *Beati pauperes – Beati pacifici; Da pacem, Domine; Domine, quando veneris; Gloria patri et filio.* Chansons: *Lucescit jam o socii; Voir est beaucoup.*
** Tel. Dig. AZ 6 42632. Alsfelder Vocal Ens., Helbich.

Expertly directed performances, with good intonation and tonal blend. Wolfgang Helbich does not vary the forces involved here, however; everything is done with full chorus, whereas many of the items would have benefited from greater variety of vocal texture. Thus the overall impact of this issue is less than the sum of the parts.

Lawes, William (1602–45)

Setts for one violin: Nos. 3 in A min.; 8 in D; Setts for two violins: Nos. 2 in G; 3 in A min.; 8 in D; Sett No. 1 in G min. for two division viols and organ.
*** O-L DSLO 564. Cons. of Musicke, Rooley.

William Lawes, the younger of the two composer brothers, the one who died fighting for Charles I at the siege of Chester, was also the more prolific. These *Setts* (or suites) represent some of the works with viols accompanied by keyboard (here a chamber organ) as opposed to the consort music. Here too Lawes shows his mastery of contrapuntal writing, and though the bulging technique of the players here may at first be hard for the modern ear to appreciate, this selection is invaluable for bringing to life a long-neglected figure. Performances and recording are first-rate.

Setts for three lyra viols: Nos. 1 in D min.; 7 in A min.; 8 in C; Fantazia; Saraband.
*** O-L DSLO 573. Cons. of Musicke, Rooley.

These *Setts* include in their extended sequences of movements some that are as ambitious as any consort music of the period – for example, the sarabande in the first *Sett*, the superb contrapuntal *Fantazia,* and the pavan at the start of the *Eighth Sett.* With authentic performing practice (in other words, no vibrato) the modern ear may resist hearing more than one work at a time, and the three lyra viols hardly sound sweet in multiple stopping; but Rooley directs performances that it would be hard to beat, and the recording is excellent.

Viol consort music: *Setts Nos. 2 in A min.; 3 in C min.; 3 in F; 4 in B flat.*
*** O-L DSLO 560. Cons. of Musicke, Rooley.

These viol pieces show William Lawes more as a thoughtful, inward-looking composer rather than as precursor of the early baroque style. Particularly in the fantasies and the slower movements of these *Setts,* we find him as chromatic and bold as Jenkins. The example of his master Coperario and the chromaticism of the Italian madrigalists were a spur to his imagination, and the results are of unfailing interest harmonically and full of bold and original touches. The Consort of Musicke plays with authority and virtuosity, and the recording is made in a sympathetic acoustic. A really outstanding record in every way.

Dialogues, psalms and elegies: *The cats as other creatures doe; Cease, O cease, ye jolly shepherds; Charon, O Charon; Charon, O gentle Charon, let me wooe thee; Come heavy heart; How like a widow; Musicke, the master of arts is dead; Orpheus, O Orpheus; Psalm 22; Tis not, boy; When death.* (Also includes: Jenkins: *Why is this shade of night?*; H. Lawes: *Psalm 22.*)
*** O-L DSLO 574. Cons. of Musicke, Rooley.

William Lawes was an inventive composer whose diversity and resource are well conveyed in this selection, which ranges from the elegiac to the comic. Good performances from the Consort of Musicke under Anthony Rooley.

Lebrun, Ludwig (1752–90)

Oboe concertos: Nos 1 in D min.: 2 in G min.; 3 in C; 4 in B flat; 5 in C; 6 in F.
*** DG Arc. Dig. 2742 005 (2). Holliger, Camerata Bern, Füri.

Lebrun, a contemporary of Mozart, joined the Mannheim orchestra as oboist in the mid-1760s and soon rose to fame as one of the great virtuosi of the age. After 1778 he toured widely and his links with the Mannheim court weakened. He is more than an interesting historical figure, or a note-spinner, like so many of his contemporaries. While these concertos do not have the depth of Haydn or Mozart, they are compositions of substance and imagination and well worth committing to disc. The playing of Heinz Holliger and the Camerata Bern under Thomas Füri could hardly be more persuasive. A really well worthwhile discovery.

Leclair, Jean-Marie (1697–1765)

6 Concertos, Op. 7; 6 Concertos, Op. 10.
*** Erato STU 71093 (3). Jarry, Larde, Paillard CO, Paillard.

The twelve concertos recorded here make up Leclair's complete orchestral output. Op. 7 was composed in 1737 and Op. 10 in 1743–4; generally speaking, they are underrated, and their merits are considerable, although one cannot include among them a strongly individual lyrical power. But they are fresh, well-constructed, and often highly expressive, even if the ideas are not in themselves memorable. These performances by the violinist Gérard Jarry and flautist Christian Larde are of exemplary style and virtuosity. There is nothing here that is wanting in stylistic sense or musical verve. The notes by Harry Halbreich are particularly thorough and helpful, and the recordings first-class.

Lecocq, Alexandre (1832–1918)

Mam'zelle Angot (ballet)*: suite* (arr. Jacob).
(M) **(*) HMV Green. ESD 7080. RPO, Irving – GLAZOUNOV: *Birthday Offering.****

La Fille de Madame Angot was a highly successful operetta of the 1870s. The ballet, which dates from 1943, follows the story of the operetta but also includes music from other works by Lecocq. The score is wittily arranged by Gordon Jacob in the manner of Constant Lambert's *Les Patineurs* (Meyerbeer). The spirits of both Adam and Offenbach occasionally hover in the background. The music is stylishly played and brightly recorded, although the age of the original issue (1959) shows in a lack of overall opulence. But this remains an attractive coupling, and the music is delightful.

LeFanu, Nicola (born 1947)

(i) *But stars remaining;* (i, ii) *The same day dawns for soprano and five players;* (ii; iii) *Deva for cello and seven players.*
*** Chan. ABR/*ABT* 1017. (i) Manning; (ii) Nash Ens.; (iii) Van Kampen.

But stars remaining, a setting of Day Lewis for unaccompanied soprano, is beautifully sung by the formidably talented Jane Manning. More ambitious is *The Same Day Dawns,* a sequence of settings of oriental poems in different languages; LeFanu uses an ensemble of five players to provide a spare and free commentary on the vocal line. More beautiful than either is *Deva,* where the cello soloist is similarly the focus of a rather larger ensemble. Excellent performances and recording, the cassette admirably vivid and atmospheric to match the disc closely.

Lehár, Franz (1870–1948)

Waltzes: *Eva; Gold and silver; Gypsy love. The Count of Luxembourg: Luxembourg. Giuditta: Where the lark sings. The Merry widow: Ballsirenen.*

(*) HMV Dig. **CDC 747020-2; ASD/*TC-ASD* 143540-1/*4* [Ang. DS/*4XS* 38025]. Johann Strauss O of Vienna, Boskovsky.

Gold and silver was Lehár's waltz masterpiece; the others are his arrangements, using melodies from the operettas. They are ravishingly tuneful; given such warmly affectionate performances and a recording which is both sumptuous and has sparkling detail, this is easy to enjoy. Lehár's scoring is often imaginative, but in the last resort one misses the voices. The XDR cassette is of good quality though the balance emphasizes the bass, and while the upper range is quite lively it is not quite as fresh as the disc, with the resonance blunting some of the very highest frequencies. The CD is first-class in every way.

The Count of Luxembourg (highlights, in English).

*** That's Entertainment TER/*ZCTER* 1050. Hill-Smith, Jenkins, Tierney, Nicoll, Richard, New Sadler's Wells Op. Ch. and O, Wordsworth.

Like its companion disc of selections from Kálmán's *Countess Maritza*, this record from That's Entertainment presents lively and fresh performances from the cast of the New Sadler's Wells Opera production. Particularly in the general absence of records of operetta in English, this is very welcome. Bright digital sound.

The Land of Smiles (*Das Land des Lächelns;* complete in German).

*** HMV Dig. SLS 5274 [Ara. 8055-2/*9055-2*]. Jerusalem, Donath, Lindner, Finke, Hirte, Bav. R. Ch., Mun. RO, Boskovsky.

The Land of Smiles is a strange piece, a revamped version of an operetta, *The Yellow Jacket*, which was a failure in 1923. In 1929 its mixture of Eastern and Western values (with the principal tenor a Chinese prince) proved a great success, thanks in good measure to the tailoring of that central role to the needs of Richard Tauber, who promptly made the song *Dein ist mein ganzes Herz* an enormously popular signature-tune of his own. Siegfried Jerusalem, who plays Sou-Chong here, has nothing like the same charm as Tauber, but it is a strong and sympathetic reading, lacking only a vein of implied tragedy, the wistfulness behind the smile. Helen Donath sings sweetly as his beloved Lisa, and the whole ensemble is admirably controlled in a colourful performance, warmly recorded, by Willi Boskovsky.

The Merry Widow (*Die lustige Witwe;* complete in German).

❀ *** HMV SLS 823 (2) [Ang. SBL 3630]. Schwarzkopf, Gedda, Waechter, Steffek, Knapp, Equiluz, Philh. Ch. and O, Matacic.

Matacic provides a magical set, guaranteed to send shivers of delight through any listener with its vivid sense of atmosphere and superb musicianship. It is one of Walter Legge's masterpieces as a recording manager. He had directed the earlier *Merry Widow* set, also with his wife Elisabeth Schwarzkopf as Hanna, and realized how difficult it would be to outshine it. But outshine it he did, creating a sense of theatre that is almost without rival in gramophone literature. If the Decca approach to opera has always been to conceive it in terms of a new medium, Legge went to the opposite view and produced something that is almost more theatrical than the theatre itself. No other opera record more vividly conveys the feeling of expectancy before the curtain rises than the preludes to each Act here.

The Merry Widow (in an English version by Bonynge): highlights.

** Decca SET/*KCET* 629 [Lon. OSA/*5-1172*]. Sutherland, Krenn, Resnik, Ewer, Nat. PO, Bonynge.

Although not everyone will take to Sutherland's Widow, this is generally an attractive English version. The exuberantly breezy overture (arranged by Douglas Gamley) sets the mood of the proceedings, and the slightly brash recording (the sheen on the strings sounding artificially bright) is determinedly effervescent. The chorus sings with great zest and the ensembles are infectious. The whole of the closing part of the disc – the finale of Act II; Njegus's aria (nicely done by Graeme Ewer); the introduction of the girls from Maxims and the famous Waltz duet – is certainly vivacious; the Parisian atmosphere is a trifle overdone, but enjoyably so. Earlier, Sutherland's *Vilja* loses out on charm because of her wide vibrato, but the Waltz duet with Krenn is engaging. There is little difference between disc and tape.

'The world of Lehár'; (i) *Giuditta: Meine Lippen, sie küssen.* (i; ii) *Der Graf von Luxemburg: Sind sie von sinnen . . . Lieber Freund . . .* Waltz: *Bist du's lachendes Glück.* (iii; iv) *Das Land des Lächelns: Dein ist mein ganzes Herz; Wer hat die Liebe uns ins Herz gesenkt.* (i; v) *Die lustige Witwe: Dance; Vilja;* Waltz: *Lippen Schweigen;* Finale: *Ja, das Studium der Weiber ist schwer.* (iv) *Paganini: Gern hab' ich die Frau'n geküsst.* (iii) *Schön ist die Welt: Ich bin verliebt.* (i; ii) *Der Zarewitsch: Wolgalied: Allein wieder allein! Kosende Wellen;* Finale. (i) *Zigeunerliebe: Hör ich Cymbalklänge.*

(M) *** Decca SPA/*KCSP* 517. (i–iv) V. Volksoper Ch. and O, various conductors; (i) Gueden; (ii) Kmentt; (iii) Holm; (iv) Krenn; (v) Grunden, V. State Op. Ch. and O, Stolz.

An excellent anthology, the best collection of Lehár's music on a single disc or tape. The compiler has drawn heavily on a stylish operetta duet recital of Renate Holm and Werner Krenn (his opening *Dein ist mein ganzes Herz* is splendid) and also on Hilde Gueden's vintage recordings from the late 1950s and early 1960s. Highlights include the delicious *Ich bin verliebt* (Renate Holm) from *Schön ist die Welt* and Hilde Gueden's enchanting waltz song from *Giuditta, Meine Lippen, sie küssen so heiss.* The excerpt from *Der Zarewitsch* has a splendidly atmospheric gipsy accompaniment. On side two there are some lively items from Decca's 1958 (long ago deleted) *Merry Widow.* The recordings come up surprisingly well, and the tape transfers are generally vivid.

Lehmann, Liza (1862–1918)

In a Persian garden (song cycle).

*** Argo ZK 87 [id., PSI]. Harwood, Greevy, Langridge, Forbes Robinson; Constable.

In the early years of this century, this exotic song-cycle had all too much success, but the reaction of undue neglect was quite unjust. It is a charming sequence of songs, soaringly melodic (as one would expect of a composer who had been a concert singer) and with elegant piano accompaniments. Though balance is not ideal (the bass soloist too far forward) this is an admirable, highly enjoyable performance, with Philip Langridge splendid in *Ah moon of my delight.*

Leigh, Walter (1905–42)

Agincourt overture.

*** Lyr. SRCS 95. New Philh. O, Braithwaite – *Concert* (*Overtures*).***

The overture forms part of an ingenious Lyrita collection using a variety of orchestras and conductors. It is well worth investigating.

Leoncavallo, Ruggiero (1858–1919)

I Pagliacci (complete).

(M) *** DG 413 275-1/*4* (3/*2*). Carlyle, Bergonzi, Benelli, Taddei, Panerai, La Scala Milan Ch. and O, Karajan – MASCAGNI: *Cavalleria Rusticana.****

(*) HMV SLS 5187 (3) [Ang. SZCX/*4Z3X* 3895]. Scotto, Carreras, Nurmela, Amb. Op. Ch., Philh. O, Muti – MASCAGNI: *Cavalleria Rusticana.*(*)

** Decca D 83 D 3/*K 83 K 32* (3) [Lon. D 13125]. Freni, Pavarotti, Wixell, L. Voices, Finchley Children's Group, Nat. PO, Patané – MASCAGNI: *Cavalleria Rusticana.***(*)

I Pagliacci: complete. Arias: *La Bohème: Ed ora, conoscetela; Musette svarie sulla bocca; Non parlate così; Io non ho; Scuoti o vento. Zazà: Mamma, io non l'ho avuta mai; Zazà, piccola zingara. Chatterton: Non saria meglio.*
*** RCA [LSC 7090 (2)]. Caballé, Domingo, Milnes, Alldis Ch., LSO, Santi.

The Italian opera traditionalists may jib at Karajan's treatment of Leoncavallo's melodrama – and for that matter its companion piece. He does nothing less than refine them, with long-breathed, expansive tempi and the minimum exaggeration. One would expect such a process to take the guts out of the drama, but with Karajan – as in *Carmen, Tosca, Aida,* etc. – the result is superb. One is made to hear the beauty of the music first and foremost, and that somehow makes one understand the drama more. Passions are no longer torn to tatters, Italian-style – and Karajan's choice of soloists was clearly aimed to help that – but the passions are still there, and rarely if ever on record has the Scala Orchestra played with such beautiful feeling for tone colour. Bergonzi is among the most sensitive of Italian tenors of heroic quality, and it is good to have Joan Carlyle doing a major operatic role on record, touching if often rather cool. Taddei is magnificently strong, and Benelli and Panerai could hardly be bettered in the roles of Beppe and Silvio. The recording is good but needs to be reproduced at a high volume level if it is to have full immediacy. This applies to the cassettes as well as the discs. However, in either format this mid-priced reissue is by any standards a bargain.

For those who do not want the obvious coupling with *Cavalleria Rusticana,* the RCA set (currently not available in the UK) is a first-rate recommendation, with fine singing from all three principals, vivid playing and recording, and one or two extra passages not normally performed – as in the Nedda–Silvio duet. Milnes is superb in the Prologue, and though Caballé does not always suggest a young girl this is technically the most beautiful account of the role of Nedda available on record. The fill-up of six rare Leoncavallo arias sung by the three principals is particularly attractive.

Under Muti's urgent direction both *Cav.* and *Pag.* represent the music of violence. In both he has sought to use the original text, which in *Pag.* is often surprisingly different, with many top notes eliminated and Tonio instead of Canio delivering (singing, not speaking) the final *La commedia è finita.* Muti's approach represents the opposite of Karajan's smoothness, and the coarse rendering of the *Prologue* in *Pag.* by the rich-toned Kari Nurmela is disappointing. Scotto's Nedda goes raw above the stave (more so than her Santuzza on the RCA *Cav.*), but the edge is in keeping with Muti's approach with its generally brisk speeds. Carreras seems happier here than in *Cav.,* but it is the conductor and the fresh look he brings which will prompt a personal choice here. The sound is extremely vivid.

Pavarotti links the latest Decca recordings of *Cav.* and *Pag.,* both of them beefy performances, very well recorded. In *Pag.,* Pavarotti gives a committed performance, though in both operas he seems reluctant to sing anything but loud. Voices are recorded rather close, which exaggerates this fault, and Freni is not helped by the balance either, not as sweet as she usually is. Wixell as Tonio is somewhat out of character, giving a Lieder-style performance, full of detail. The cassettes match the discs closely in vividness and clarity.

I Pagliacci: highlights.
(M) *** DG Priv. 2535/*3335* 199 [136 281]. (from above set, cond. Karajan) – MASCAGNI: *Cavalleria Rusticana:* highlights.***
** Decca SXL/*KSXC* 6986. (from above set, cond. Patané) – MASCAGNI: *Cavalleria Rusticana:* highlights.**(*)

Choice here is plain. Karajan is at mid-price and makes an obvious 'best buy' on both disc and cassette. The Decca selection is more generous than usual, and vividly recorded in both formats. It is welcome enough, even if the performances are flawed. In the USA a selection is also available from the Muti set [Ang. S/*4XS* 37884].

Ligeti, György (born 1923)

Aventures; Chamber concerto for 13 instruments; Nouvelles aventures; Ramifications.
*** DG 410 651-1. Ens. Intercontemporain, Boulez.

This presents a useful supplement to the Decca record below, and admirers of this composer's cloud-sound textures can safely investigate. In the two purely instrumental pieces (the *Concerto* and *Ramifications*) the specific notes matter less than the washes of colour. The two other pieces with voices are thinner still in argument, bringing copious menagerie noises, squeaks, grunts and howls, most musically interpreted (as far as is humanly possible) by the long-suffering Mary Thomas, Jane Manning and William Pearson. Excellent recording.

Chamber concerto for 13 instrumentalists; (i) *Double concerto for flute, oboe and orchestra; Melodien for orchestra.*
*** Decca HEAD 12. L. Sinf., Atherton, (i) with Nicolet, Holliger.

The *Chamber concerto* comes from 1969–70 and the two other works followed in the early 1970s. Ligeti, now in his sixties, has developed, over the past decade or so, a technique of micro-polyphony that produces strongly atmospheric and distinctive textures, well exemplified in the works recorded here. The *Double concerto* makes great play with micro-intervals, not exact quarter-tones but deviations. The resulting sonorities will not always please but should consistently interest or even exasperate the unprejudiced listener. Ligeti is not generously represented in the catalogue at present but this disc, which is superbly recorded, serves him well. The distinguished soloists and the London Sinfonietta give accomplished accounts of these complex scores.

(i) *String quartet No. 2;* (ii) (Organ) *Etude No. 1; Volumina;* (iii) *Lux aeterna.*
(M) *** DG 2543 818 [id.]. (i) La Salle Qt; (ii) Zacher (organ); (iii) N. German R. Ch., Franz.

In the memorable sequence of works used as incidental music in the *Space Odyssey, 2001*, these choral pieces of Ligeti took an honoured place, fascinating the unlikeliest listeners with their evocative clouds of sound. They are well worth hearing more seriously on record, and are splendidly coupled with an equally striking and individual instrumental work, the *String quartet No. 2*, in which the avant-garde effects seem pointful and illuminating in an ear-teasing way, not at all outlandish. Excellent recording.

Lilburn, Douglas (born 1915)

(i) *Aotearoa overture;* (ii) *Divertimento for strings;* (iii) *Symphony No. 2 in C.*
**(*) Jerusalem ATD 8203. (i) New Zealand SO, Hopkins; (ii) New Zealand BC Schola Musicum, Ashley Heenan; (iii) New Zealand SO, Heenan.

Douglas Lilburn is the doyen of New Zealand composers whose *Third Symphony* (1961) was briefly available on records in the early 1970s. It was, incidentally, coupled with the *Aotearoa* overture, which reappears here; the overture derives its title from the Maori name for New Zealand and is an early work dating from 1940, when he was in his mid-twenties. Lilburn is no iconoclast but possesses a genuine feeling for form and it is this, together with his sympathy for nature, which draws his muse into the Sibelian orbit. What impresses one in the first movement of the symphony is the fine control of pace. True, it has derivative touches and the thematic material, particularly in the second movement, is not always distinguished. It is an eminently worthwhile work all the same, and has a keen integrity that wins over the listener. It is very well played though the orchestra is obviously not in the luxury class. The recording could have greater warmth, but there is no want of clarity and presence.

Lindblad, Adolf (1801–78)

Symphony No. 1 in C: Overture, Frondörerna.
❀*** Cap. CAP 1197. Stockholm PO, Kamu.

Lindblad is commonly thought of as 'the Father of Swedish song' and some of his attractive songs have been recorded by Söderström on Decca. He also composed two symphonies, the first of which was first heard in 1832. As befits a friend of Mendelssohn, the work has strong overtones of Beethoven and is scored with uncommon lightness. It would make an attractive alternative to the Weber symphonies as early-morning listening. It is fresh and delightful without being profoundly original. It is played with great charm by the Stockholm orchestra under Okko Kamu, who obviously enjoyed making its acquaintance. It is quite beautifully recorded with a natural balance and plenty of space round the instruments. The work is quite long – nearly forty minutes – and the fill-up is an overture to *Frondörerna* (*The Rebels*), the opera in which Jenny Lind made her debut at the age of fifteen. There is a handsome 20-page booklet with copious musical and pictorial illustrations as well. Most attractive.

Liszt, Franz (1811–86)

Ce qu'on entend sur la montagne (*Bergsymphonie*). (i) *Dante symphony. Festklänge; Hunnenschlacht; Die Ideale; Orpheus; Les Préludes; Tasso; Von der Wiege bis zum Grabe* (symphonic poems).
*** HMV SLS 5235 (4). Leipzig GO, Masur, with (i) Leipzig Thomanerchor.

(i) *A Faust Symphony. 2 Episodes from Lenau's Faust* (*Mephisto waltz No. 1; Der nächtliche Zug*)*; Hamlet; Héroïde funèbre; Hungaria; Mazeppa; Mephisto waltz No. 2; Prometheus.*
*** HMV SLS 5236 (4). Leipzig GO, Masur, with (i) Leipzig R. Ch. Male Voices.

Apart from *Les Préludes*, the splendid *Mazeppa*, and to a lesser extent *Tasso*, Liszt's symphonic poems enjoy a fairly limited popularity if successive record catalogues are anything to go by, and even Liszt's most fervent champions are sparing in their praises of all but a handful of them. Some of the earlier pieces, such as *Ce qu'on entend sur la montagne* and *Festklänge*, suffer not only from formal weakness but also from a lack of interesting melodic invention. But elsewhere, in *Hamlet*, the *Héroïde funèbre* and *Prometheus* for example, there is a lot to admire. *Hamlet* has great dramatic intensity, particularly in the hands of Kurt Masur, who is a vivid and sympathetic exponent throughout. *Die nächtliche Zug*, the first of the *Two Episodes from Lenau's Faust*, strikes the listener immediately with its intent, brooding atmosphere. These performances – and, whatever one may think of it, this music – cast a strong spell, and with rare exceptions Masur proves as persuasive an advocate as any on record. It is the rich sonority of the lower strings, the dark, perfectly blended woodwind tone and the fine internal balance of the Leipzig Gewandhaus Orchestra that holds the listener throughout – for in the weaker pieces Liszt needs all the help the interpreters can give him.

Only in *Orpheus* does Masur let us down. He breezes through it at record speed and misses the endearing gentleness that Beecham brought to it in the early 1960s. In the two symphonies, which are allotted one to a box, Masur is impressive, though even in the *Gretchen* movement of the *Faust symphony* he moves things on, albeit not unacceptably, and there is no want of either delicacy or ardour. Masur's *Faust symphony* can certainly hold its own against all comers, and the *Dante symphony* has one current rival. The recordings are well balanced and refined, perhaps not as transparent as the finest 1982 Decca or Philips recordings, but still very good indeed. Liszt's influence was enormous in his lifetime – on Wagner, the Russians, the French – and listening to these records one realizes that the personality has lost none of its magnetism even in a field that he was slow to conquer.

(i) *Piano concertos Nos. 1–2. Années de pèlerinage, 1st year, G. 160: Vallée d'Obermann; 2nd year, G. 161: Sonetti 104, 123 del Petrarca; Après une lecture du Dante; 3rd year, G. 163: Les jeux d'eaux à la Villa d'Este. Ballade No. 2, G. 171; 6 Chants polonais (Chopin), G. 480; Concert paraphrases of Verdi* (complete); *Etudes de concert, G. 144/5; Etudes d'exécution transcendante, G. 139. Harmonies poétiques et religieuses, G. 173: Bénédiction de Dieu dans la solitude; Funérailles. Sonata in B min., G. 178; Valse oubliée No. 1, G. 215.*
(M) *** Ph. 6768 355 (7). Arrau, (i) LSO, Sir Colin Davis.

(i) *Piano concertos Nos. 1–2. 2 Concert studies, G. 145; Concert paraphrases of Verdi, G. 431–436 and 438; 3 Etudes de concert, G. 144; 12 Etudes d'exécution transcendante, G. 139; Harmonies poétiques et religieuses: Bénédiction de Dieu dans la solitude, G. 173/3; Piano sonata in B min., G. 178.*
(M) *** Ph. 6725 013 (5). Arrau (i) with LSO, Sir Colin Davis.

Claudio Arrau's recent Liszt recordings come in two alternative forms: a five-record set comprising the concertos (with Colin Davis and the LSO), the *Transcendental studies* made in the late 1970s, both of which are discussed as individual issues, as well as one disc devoted to the Verdi paraphrases (including *Rigoletto*, *Ernani*, *Trovatore*, *I Lombardi*, *Aïda*, *Don Carlos* and *Simon Boccanegra*) and his classic account of the *Sonata*; and a seven-record set which adds *Dante sonata*, *Funérailles*, the six Chopin transcriptions discussed under Philips 6514 273, and a 1970 record of *Vallée d'Obermann*, the *Ballade No. 2*, the *Sonetti* 104 and 123 of Petrarch.

Excellent though it is, there seems no case for recommending the smaller set when the larger one is available, and one can only imagine that the latter will supersede the former. Those who have consulted the individual reviews over the years will know that these are performances of some stature and no mean distinction, and the recordings are first-rate in all cases.

Piano concerto No. 1 in E flat, G. 124.
*** HMV Dig. ASD/*TCC-ASD* 4307 [Ang. DS/*4XS* 38004]. Ousset, CBSO, Rattle – SAINT-SAËNS: *Piano concerto No. 2.****
(M) *** DG Sig. 2543/*3343* 503 [(d) 139 383/*923 083*]. Argerich, LSO, Abbado – TCHAIKOVSKY: *Piano concerto No. 1.****

Piano concertos Nos. 1; 2 in A, G. 125.
*** DG 2530/*3300* 770 [id.]. Berman, VSO, Giulini.
*** Ph. 9500 780/*7300 854* [id.]. Arrau, LSO, Sir Colin Davis.
(M) *** Decca VIV/*KVIC* 11 [Lon. STS/*5*-15562]. Ivan Davis, RPO, Downes.
*(*) Ph. Dig. 6514/*7337* 200 [id.]. Dichter, Pittsburgh SO, Previn.

Piano concertos Nos. 1–2; Totentanz, G. 126.
*** Ph. 6500 374/*7300 229* [id.]. Brendel, LPO, Haitink.

Piano concertos Nos. 1–2; Liebestraum No. 3 in A flat, G. 541; Mephisto waltz No. 1, G. 514.
(B) **(*) CfP CFP/*TC-CFP* 4402 [(d) Ang. RL/*4RL* 32046]. Ohlsson, New Philh. O, Atzmon.

Brendel's Philips record from the early 1970s holds its place at the top of the list. This offers a valuable extra work and well-nigh flawless recording: the sound is beautifully balanced and produces the most truthful and well-detailed quality throughout the spectrum. The performances are as poetic as they are brilliant, and those who doubt the musical substance of No. 2 will find their reservations melt away. There is an excellent cassette transfer, bold and clear, which lacks only the last degree of glitter (the triangle in the scherzo of the *First Concerto* is somewhat reticent).

Lazar Berman has the advantage of Giulini's sensitive and masterly accompaniment with the Vienna Symphony, and even if you feel that these scores hold no surprises for you, try to hear his record. Berman's playing is consistently poetic and he illuminates detail in a way that has the power to touch the listener. Some of his rapt, quiet tone would probably not register without the tactful assistance of the DG engineers, who enable all the detail to 'tell', but the balance is most musical and well-judged. A very thoughtful account of No. 1 and a poetic reading of the *A major* make this a most desirable record. Giulini keeps a strong grip on the proceedings and secures an excellent response from his players. These performances do not eclipse Brendel's, but they are among the best currently available. The cassette is of high quality.

Claudio Arrau made a stunning record of the *E flat Concerto* with Ormandy and the Philadelphia Orchestra in the 1950s, and this newer account, made in his mid-seventies, is scarcely less fine. Even though some of the youthful abandon is tamed, Arrau's virtuosity is transcendental. There is a greater breadth in No. 1 here than in the earlier version, and there are many thoughtful touches throughout. This artist's Indian summer shows no loss of fire, and he brings plenty of panache to the *A major Concerto*. This does not displace Brendel or Berman, but takes its place beside them. First-class sound, although the cassette transfer lacks something in upper range (the triangle is almost inaudible in its famous solo passage in No. 1).

Ivan Davis shows a genuine feeling for both concertos, revealing their poetry as well as their flamboyance. He is admirably accompanied by the RPO under Edward Downes, and the recording is, in its way, in the demonstration class. Originally made in Decca's Phase Four, it has vivid spotlighting of orchestral soloists, not quite natural but effective enough when the piano too is forwardly balanced and boldly recorded. There is little to choose between disc and cassette, and this reissue is excellent value in the lower-mid-price range.

American readers should not forget Pennario whose coupling with the LSO under Leibowitz has been reissued on a Victrola cassette [*ALK1 4491*] as we go to press. These are sparkling and immensely enjoyable accounts, perhaps not penetrating too far beneath the surface of the music, but striking for their easy virtuosity and extrovert spontaneity.

In the UK Garrick Ohlsson's EMI coupling has been reissued on CfP with two generous fillers, one on each side to follow as encore pieces after the *Concertos*. The account of the *Mephisto waltz* is dazzling, with wide dynamic variation, although Ohlsson misses some of the sense of fantasy which marks out the greatest Liszt performances on record. The concerto performances are ripe and full-blooded, fearlessly presenting the music at its most dramatic and again underlining the contrasts of dynamic. Atzmon equally shows himself as a Lisztian with a concern for detail, and the *Second Concerto* is especially strongly characterized. If in the blaring march rhythms of the finale he does not avoid vulgarity, the zest and energy of the playing communicates strongly, and the *Liebestraume* which follows makes a warmly romantic contrast. The recording is resonant but of excellent quality (mid-1970s vintage) and there is no appreciable difference between disc and cassette.

As they have recorded Arrau, Brendel and Richter (now withdrawn) in the Liszt concertos, it is odd that Philips should have cast yet another of their pianists in this repertoire. Misha Dichter is an impressive player but there is nothing very special about his accounts of the Liszt; though, to be fair, the orchestral support from the Pittsburgh orchestra under Previn is relatively ordinary too. The digital recording has plenty of presence but, as so often, the piano looms too large. However, the chrome tape, transferred at a low level, brings more recessed imagery, although No. 2 has more presence than No. 1.

Turning to recordings of the *First Concerto*, Ousset's is a magical performance, sparklingly individual, full of spontaneity. The scherzando movement and the final *Allegro marziale* have wit and humour with Ousset making light of technical difficulties. Rattle equally draws exciting and warmly expressive playing from the CBSO and the recording is first-rate, save for the forward balance of the soloist, who seems to be in a slightly different acoustic. The iron-oxide cassette is strikingly vivid, full and clear.

A clear, direct, sometimes even fastidious approach to the *First Concerto* from Martha Argerich. She plays the *Larghetto* meltingly, and there is an excellent partnership between pianist and conductor. Both are agreed to minimize the work's flamboyance without reducing the voltage. This is very much a performance to live with and many should find it exactly to their taste, even if Liszt himself might have found it a trifle sophisticated. Now reissued on DG's mid-priced Signature label with a brilliant chrome-tape equivalent (slightly dry in the bass), the coupling with one of the finest available versions of the Tchaikovsky *B flat minor Concerto* makes for a stronger recommendation than the original full-priced issue (which remains available in the USA, coupled with the Chopin No. 1).

Concerto in the Hungarian style (orch. Tchaikovsky); *Hungarian fantasia for piano and orchestra, G. 123;* (with Schubert: *Wanderer fantasia, D. 760,* arr. by Liszt for piano and orchestra).
**(*) HMV Dig. ASD/*TCC-ASD* 4258 [Ang. DS/*4XS* 37888]. Katsaris, Phd. O, Ormandy.

Katsaris plays with flair and brilliance a concoction that claims to be a long-lost work of Liszt. The story is that a favourite pupil, Sophie Menter, asked the composer for a work she could play on a tour of Russia, but he gave her only a piano version without orchestration. She persuaded Tchaikovsky to orchestrate it, which he certainly did (see the *New Grove*), but she claimed the piece as her own, when he was so antipathetic to Liszt. It is a banal piece, full of the most paltry (if brilliant) variations and corny melodies. The *Hungarian fantasia* seems a masterpiece next to it, for it needs persuasiveness such as Katsaris and Ormandy display to make it palatable. The recording presents the piano twangily but it is wide-ranging, on disc and chrome tape alike.

Dante Symphony, G. 109.
**(*) Decca Dig. SXDL/*KSXDC* 7542. Collège Voltaire Ch., Ch. de Genève, SRO, Lopez-Cobos.

Lopez-Cobos's version comes with Liszt's alternative conclusion, a sudden loud outburst full of hallelujahs from the trebles after the usual *ppp* ending. It is most effective, crowning a performance which is more remarkable for its refinement of sound and balance than for its dramatic thrust. The playing of the Suisse Romande Orchestra could be much more brilliant, but the recording, with woodwind kept in place, not highlighted, is admirable. The cassette too is first-class with an excellent choral focus.

(i) *Dante Symphony; Mephisto waltz No. 2; Les Préludes; Tasso lamento e trionfo.*
(M) **(*) HMV *TCC2-POR 54292.* (i) Arndt, St Thomas's Ch., Leipzig; Leipzig Gewandhaus O, Masur.

This double-length iron-oxide tape, in EMI's 'Portrait of the artist' series, offers a selection from Masur's distinguished Liszt recordings (see above) with the *Dante symphony* complete on one side, without a break. The sound is full-bodied, perhaps lacking a little in sparkle on top, but well detailed and convincingly balanced.

Fantasia on themes from Beethoven's The Ruins of Athens, G. 122; Wanderer fantasia on Schubert's Wanderer fantasy, G. 366; Polonaise brillante on Weber's Polacca brillante in E, G. 367.
**(*) Turn. [TV 34708]. Rose, Philh. Hungarica, Kapp.

Jerome Rose plays with fine dash and is especially good in the *Beethoven Fantasia.* The accompaniments under Richard Kapp are commendably alert, and the Turnabout recording is bold and full, better-balanced than is usual on this label. An enjoyable and useful collection that fills an important gap in the American catalogue. It is not at the moment available in the UK.

A Faust symphony, G. 108.
*** DG 2707 100 (2) [id.]. Riegel, Tanglewood Fest. Ch., Boston SO, Bernstein – BOITO: *Mefistofele: Prologue.***
* Ph. Dig. 6769/*7654* 089. Kozma, Concg. Ch. and O, Dorati – BERLIOZ: *Damnation de Faust* excerpts; WAGNER: *Faust overture.***

(i) *A Faust symphony; Les Préludes.*
*** HMV Dig. SLS/*TC-SLS* 143570-3/5 (2) [DSB/*4X2S* 3928]. (i) Winbergh, Westminster Ch. College Male Ch., Phd. O, Muti.

Muti's version of Liszt's *Faust Symphony*, coupled with a suitably exuberant account of *Les Préludes*, offers a fairly clear first choice in this repertoire. As an ardent Tchaikovskian, Muti shows a natural sympathy for a piece which can readily seem overlong, and he finds obvious affinities in the music with the style of the Russian master. Some might feel that he is too overtly melodramatic in the finale, yet his pacing of the first movement is admirable, finding tenderness as well as red-blooded excitement. In the *Gretchen* movement he conjures the most delicately atmospheric playing from the orchestra and throughout he is helped by the ambience of the Old Met. in Philadelphia which seems especially suitable for this score. The digital recording is brilliant yet full-bodied, and without glare (although *Les Préludes*, not inappropriately, is made to sound slightly brasher). The XDR cassettes match the discs very closely, though the LPs have slightly more energy in the highest frequencies, which gives a greater dynamic bite in fortissimos.

Bernstein recorded this symphony in the mid-1960s, but his newer version, made in Boston, is both more sensitive and more brilliant. It was the first modern recording to offer a serious challenge to Beecham's classic account made in the late 1950s, deleted in the UK but not the USA [Ang. Ser. S 6017]. The *Gretchen* movement is most beautifully played here, with finely delineated detail and refined texture. The tenor soloist in the finale is excellent, and the Boston orchestra produce some exciting and atmospheric playing. The recording too is extremely fine.

The excellence of the playing of the Concertgebouw Orchestra is not in question in the Philips set, recorded at public performances in 1982, but there is very little dramatic characterization here. The middle movement is very slow indeed and Dorati shows little of the firmness of grip one associates with him in his best records. Although the fill-ups fare better, no one will be buying two records just for the one side. This set does not present serious (or, indeed, any) competition to the Bernstein, Muti, or Masur sets. The chrome tapes are generally satisfactory and reproduce good quality but the recording itself is not the finest Philips have produced in the Concertgebouw.

Symphonic poems: *Festklänge, G. 101; Les Préludes, G. 97; Prometheus, G. 99.*
*** Decca SXL 6863 [Lon. C 5/5- 7084]. LPO, Solti.

Solti is just the conductor for Liszt's symphonic poems: he finds the right kind of intensity so that *Les Préludes* is exciting, without vulgarity, yet does not lose its flamboyant character. The closing pages are superbly rousing, but are not without dignity. There is plenty of drama in *Prometheus* and some beautifully refined orchestral playing in *Festklänge*, yet the tension is strongly held. The recording has superb life and colour, and the cassette transfer (only available in the USA) is one of Decca's best.

Hungarian rhapsodies for orchestra Nos. 2–3, G. 359.
(M) **(*) Mercury SRI/*MRI* 75018 [id.]. LSO, Dorati – ENESCO: *Roumanian rhapsodies Nos. 1 and 2.* **(*)

Hungarian rhapsodies Nos. (i) *2 and* (ii) *4, G. 359.* (iii) *Les Préludes, G. 97.*
(M) *** DG Priv. 2335/*3335* 628. (i) Bamberg SO, Richard Kraus; (ii) Berlin PO, Karajan; (iii) Berlin RSO, Fricsay – BRAHMS: *Hungarian dances.* **(*)

Dorati's is undoubtedly the finest set of orchestral *Hungarian rhapsodies*. He brings out the gipsy flavour, and with lively playing from the LSO there is both polish and sparkle, but the music does not become urbane. The use of the cimbalom within the orchestra brings an authentic extra colouring. The Mercury recording is characteristically vivid if a little thin on top. The tape transfer is first-class. However, this reissue offers rather short measure.

Richard Kraus's account of Liszt's most famous *Hungarian rhapsody* has both sparkle and panache, while Karajan shows characteristic flair in No. 4, with its quixotic changes of mood and colour. But what makes the DG collection doubly attractive is the inclusion of Fricsay's superb *Les Préludes*. Fricsay had the right temperament for this fine piece, and his performance has enormous conviction and an extremely vivid recording. Indeed the sound throughout is excellent on disc and cassette alike.

Symphonic poems: Orpheus, G. 98; Les Préludes, G. 97; Tasso, lamento e trionfo, G. 96.
(M) **(*) Ph. Seq. 6527/*7311* 201 [id.]. LPO, Haitink.

The music of *Les Préludes* and *Tasso* creates its scenic backgrounds and unfolds its narrative with bold strokes of the brush. Haitink's approach is more refined than usual, and his way with *Les Préludes* may appeal to some for whom a more full-blooded performance seems too blatant. His performance is not without conviction and spontaneity. In *Orpheus* the refinement of the playing is more obviously appropriate, but *Tasso* is effective too, providing one does not look for the brightest primary colours. The recording has been successfully freshened and has far more life than the original full-priced issue. The cassette too is well managed, although the transfer level is not especially high.

(i) *Les Préludes;* (ii) *Mazeppa, G. 100.*
(M) **(*) Decca VIV/*KVIC* 37 [Lon. STS/5-15589]. (i) VPO; (ii) LAPO, Mehta – TCHAIKOVSKY: *Marche slave;* WAGNER: *Die Meistersinger.***

Mehta gives exciting and theatrically robust performances of both works that communicate strongly. With excellent, committed playing from both orchestras and brilliant recording (the cassette extremely vivid to match the disc) this is also good value at lower-mid-price. *Mazeppa* is an underrated piece; it has some of Liszt's most spectacular and imaginative orchestral effects.

Totentanz, G. 126.
*** EMI 4E 063 34284. Solyom, Mun. PO, Westerberg – STENHAMMAR: *Piano concerto No. 2.****

A superb account of the *Totentanz* from Janos Solyom, whose brilliance and virtuosity are second to none. He is well supported by Westerberg and the Munich Philharmonic Orchestra and excellently recorded. For Liszt collectors, however, Brendel will remain first choice, since he offers superb performances of the two concertos as well as a dazzling *Totentanz*. Solyom's record has a Stenhammar rarity.

PIANO MUSIC

Années de pèlerinage, 2nd Year, G. 161: Après une lecture du Dante (Dante sonata); 6 Chants polonais (Chopin), G. 480; Harmonies poétiques et religieuses, G. 173: Funérailles.
C *** Ph. Dig. **411 055-2**; 6514/*7337* 273 [id.]. Arrau.

This is very distinguished playing, and astonishing for an artist approaching his eightieth birthday. The *Dante sonata* is wonderfully commanding: it has a magisterial grandeur; and *Funérailles* is hardly less impressive. The transcriptions of Chopin songs are done with great charm and subtlety too. The recording quality is totally realistic and splendidly focused – among the best recordings of the instrument we have had in the last year or so. The compact disc makes near-perfection by adding a reliably silent background.

Années de pèlerinage, 2nd year, G.161: Sposalizio: Il penseroso; Canzonetta del Salvator Rosa; Sonetti del Petrarca Nos. 47, 104, 123; Après une lecture du Dante.
*** Ph. 6500 420 [id.]. Brendel.
** Decca SXL 6968. Rogé.

Superlative playing and recording from Philips. This was among the finest Liszt recitals to have appeared in the 1970s; not only is the playing highly poetic and brilliant, but the recording presents some of the most realistic piano quality.

Pascal Rogé made his debut on Decca with the Liszt *Sonata* when he was only eighteen and it goes without saying that his disc of the second book of the *Années de pèlerinage* is never less than highly accomplished and often much more. He is a poetic artist, but his performance is not as consistently sustained in its concentration of feeling as his rivals on record. He is well recorded and commands many insights but, taken overall, this does not add up to a first recommendation.

Années de pèlerinage, 2nd year, G.616; 3 Sonetti del Petrarca (Nos. 47, 104, 125); Consolations Nos. 1–5, G.172; Liebesträume Nos. 1–3, G.541.
*** DG 2531/*3301* 318 [id.]. Barenboim.

The Liszt *Consolations* are not otherwise available at present and Barenboim proves an ideal advocate. His playing has an unaffected simplicity that is impressive, and throughout this compilation there is a welcome understatement and naturalness. The quality of the recorded sound is excellent and does full justice to the lyricism of these interpretations. The cassette matches the disc closely, though the transfer level is not especially high.

Concert paraphrases of Schubert Lieder: *Auf dem Wasser zu singen; Aufenthalt; Erlkönig; Die Forelle; Horch, horch die Lerch; Lebe wohl!; Der Lindenbaum; Lob der Tränen; Der Müller und der Bach; Die Post; Das Wandern; Wohin.*
*** Decca Dig. SXDL/*KSXDC* 7569. Bolet.

Superb virtuosity from Bolet in these display arrangements of Schubert. He is not just a wizard but a feeling musician, though here he sometimes misses a feeling of fun. First-rate recording on disc and chrome tape alike.

Concert paraphrases of Schubert Lieder: *Der Doppelgänger, G.560; Erlkönig, G.558/4; Die Forelle, G.563/6; Der Lindenbaum, G.561/7; Des Mädchens Klage, G.563/2; Morgenständchen, G.558/9; Der Müller und der Bach, G.565/2; Rastlose Liebe, G.558/10; Das Sterbeglöcklein, G.563/3; Die Taubenpost, G.560/13.*
**(*) Mer. E/*KE* 77019. Bingham.

It is good to have John Bingham's fresh and distinctive talents recognized on record, though this first major recording from him does not quite convey the full intensity one witnesses in recital. This is an admirable choice from the fifty-eight transcriptions that Liszt made of Schubert songs, and Bingham is most persuasive in producing singing tone as well as pianistic sparkle. The piano tone is good if a little rough at climaxes. The cassette, transferred at only a moderate level, offers a piano image that is smooth and altogether softer-grained.

Concert paraphrases of Wagner: *Lohengrin: Elsa's bridal procession* (arr. Liszt); *Die Meistersinger: Prelude* (arr. Kocsis); *Parsifal: Festive march; Tristan: Liebestod* (arr. Liszt); *Prelude* (arr. Kocsis).
*** Ph. 9500/*7300* 970 [id.]. Kocsis.

Fine playing and splendid recording though it must be admitted that piano transcriptions of Wagner do not enjoy universal appeal. Zoltán Kocsis is an eloquent player as always, and proves an effective transcriber also. He is given a most natural and truthful balance, and in this respect, his anthology scores over the Barenboim on DG. The chrome cassette is first-class and of demonstration standard, with fine amplitude and natural focus.

Concert paraphrases of Wagner: *Der fliegende Holländer: Spinning chorus; Ballade. Lohengrin: Elsa's dream and Lohengrin's rebuke. Rienzi: Fantasia on themes from Rienzi. Tannhäuser: Entry of the guests. Tristan: Isolde's Liebestod.*
** DG Dig. 2532/*3302* 100 [id.]. Barenboim.

Barenboim's recital overlaps with Kocsis's in offering the *Liebestod* from *Tristan*, but in every other respect the discs are complementary. Liszt transcribed four passages from *Lohengrin* and their choice does not coincide. The sound is not as realistic or natural as Philips provide for Kocsis. Barenboim lacks the youthful ardour of the young Hungarian and his response to the *Flying Dutchman* episodes is (by his standards at any rate) relatively routine, though there are many good things too, notably the *Liebestod* itself and the excerpts from *Lohengrin*. The excellent chrome cassette, transferred at a high level, matches the disc closely.

3 Concert studies, G.144; 2 Concert studies, G.145; Concert paraphrase: *Réminiscences de Don Juan* (Mozart), *G.418.*
*** O-L DSLO 41 [id.]. Bolet.

Jorge Bolet is still seriously under-represented in the catalogues, and this Liszt offering is among his finest records yet, particularly valuable for the *Don Giovanni* paraphrase, a piece which itself is neglected on record. Bolet may convey even keener electricity in the concert hall, but here the combination of virtuoso precision and seeming spontaneity is most compelling. The recording captures his wide range of timbre very well.

Harmonies poétiques et religieuses, G.173; excerpts (*3, Bénédiction de Dieu dans la solitude; 4, Pensées des morts*)*; Prelude and fugue on the name BACH, G.260; Variations on Bach's 'Weinen, Klagen, Sorgen, Zagen', G.673.*
*** Ph. 9500 286/*7300 565* [id.]. Brendel.

The *Prelude and Fugue on the name BACH* and the *Variations on 'Weinen, Klagen, Sorgen, Zagen'* are better known in their organ version but sound no less impressive on the piano, particularly when they are played so masterfully as by Brendel. This is a magnificent recital, and the recording is wide-ranging and realistic. The sound quality of the cassette yields little if anything to that of the disc, which is high praise indeed.

Hungarian rhapsodies, G.244, Nos. 2 in C sharp min.; 5 in E min. (*Héroïde élégiaque*)*; 9 in E flat* (*Carnival in Pest*)*; 14 in F min.; 15 in A min.* (*Rákóczy march*)*; 19 in D min.*
(M) *** DG Priv. 2535/*3335* 420 [2530 441]. Szidon.

Roberto Szidon offers Liszt playing of the highest order, and recording quality to match. Szidon won acclaim some years ago with his début record (Prokofiev *Sixth Sonata*, Scriabin No. 4 and Rachmaninov No. 2), and his set of the complete *Hungarian rhapsodies* more than fulfilled the promise shown in his very first record. He has flair and panache, genuine keyboard command and, when required, great delicacy of tone. All six pieces here are of high musical quality, and the playing readily demonstrates Szidon's finely judged rubato, boldness of line, and sure sense of style. The recording is first-class on both disc and cassette.

2 Legends, G.175; La lugubre gondola, Nos. 1 and 2, G.200; Piano sonata in B min., G.178.
C*** Ph. Dig. **410 040-2**; 6514/*7337* 147 [id.]. Brendel.

Piano sonata.
(M) **(*) Saga 5460. Wilde – SCHUMANN: *Fantasia.***(*)

Piano sonata; Ballades Nos. 1–2, G.170–1.
**(*) Chan. Dig. ABRD/*ABTD* 1042 [id.]. Gillespie.

Piano sonata; Concert studies, G.145, Nos. 1 (*Waldesrauschen*)*; 2* (*Gnomenreigen*)*; Harmonies poétiques et religieuses: Bénédiction de Dieu dans la solitude, G.173/3.*
**(*) Ph. 6500 043 [id.]. Arrau.

Piano sonata; Concert study No. 3 (*La Leggierezza*)*, G.144.*
(B) *** CfP CFP/*TC-CFP* 40380. D'Ascoli – FRANCK: *Prelude, chorale and fugue.****

Piano sonata; Grand galop chromatique, G.219; Liebesträume Nos. 1–3, G.541; Valse impromptu, G.213.
*** Decca Dig. 410 115-1/*4*. Bolet.

Brendel's latest account of the *Sonata* has received wide acclaim, and critics of *Gramophone* magazine voted it *the* piano record of 1983. It is certainly a more subtle and concentrated account than his earlier version made in the mid-1960s – brilliant though that was – and must be numbered among the very best now before the public. There is a wider range of colour and tonal nuance, and yet the undoubted firmness of grip does not seem achieved at any expense in spontaneity. There have been many outstanding versions of this work in the past but this certainly ranks with them, among other reasons because of the striking excellence of the engineering, for it is amazingly well-recorded. In its cassette format, the sound is hardly less vivid and matches the quality of the LP in almost every respect. On compact disc, the presence of the recording is enhanced by the absence of any intrusive noise, yet there is a feeling of ambience; although the balance is close the effect is very realistic, with piano tone which combines warmth and body with an upper range that can glitter (as in the *Legends*) without any sense of artifice.

The power, imagination and concentration of Bolet are superbly brought out in his fine account of the *Sonata*. With the famous *Liebestraum* (as well as its two companions) also most beautifully done, not to mention the amazing *Grand galop*, this is one of the most widely appealing of Bolet's outstanding Liszt series. Excellent recording. The chrome cassette too is first-class.

Arrau's performance of the *Sonata* has a characteristic eloquence and power. Its style, however, is somewhat deliberate, even pontifical, but admirers of this pianist should not be disappointed. About the rest of the recital there are no reservations whatsoever: the *Bénédiction* is exceptionally imaginative and rewarding, and the bravura in *Gnomenreigen* is riveting. The recording is resonant and full-blooded and makes a considerable impact.

Bernard d'Ascoli displays classical qualities in his refreshing and intense reading of this most romantic of sonatas. It is the sort of interpretation that one might have expected Wilhelm Kempff to give, with articulation of pearly clarity, wonderfully singing legato in the big melodies and an emphasis on control and concentration rather than thrusting urgency. It is not the most exciting reading, but a most satisfying one, well coupled with a delicate account of *La Leggierezza* and the neglected Franck work. An outstanding bargain with dry but faithful recording. There is no appreciable difference between LP and cassette.

David Wilde's account of the *Sonata* is impressive. He possesses technique in abundance and is completely inside this music. A dazzling performance that deserves a high place in any recommended list even though the quality of the recorded sound is not in the very first flight. There is a certain shallowness at times, particularly at the top end of the register, but, given playing of such flair and the relatively modest price, this does not matter too much.

Rhondda Gillespie, in a clear-cut reading of this formidable sonata, is refreshingly imaginative. Even in the highest-powered company it stands up well, and with excellent recording it has the advantage of an unusual and apt coupling, the *Four Ballades* written in the years before and after the sonata. *Ballade No. 2* is among the finest of Liszt's shorter pieces, and Miss Gillespie admirably spans its breadth of emotion. She is very well recorded but the chrome tape – which has good range and presence – is unnaturally bright on top, giving a clangorous quality to the treble.

Weihnachtsbaum (*Christmas Tree*) *suite, G.186.*
** Chan. ABR/*ABT* 1006. Gillespie.

The *Christmas Tree suite* is a charming rarity which deserved a recording, and though the sound on this Chandos issue is disappointing, Rhondda Gillespie plays with obvious dedication.

MISCELLANEOUS COLLECTIONS

Années de pèlerinage, 1st year, G.160: Vallée d'Obermann; 2nd year, G.161: Sonetti del Petrarca Nos. 104, 123; 3rd year, G.163: Les jeux d'eaux à la Villa d'Este; Ballade No. 2 in B min., G.171; Valse oubliée No. 1, G.215.
*** Ph. SAL 3783 [802 906]. Arrau.

Arrau is extremely well recorded, the piano tone has depth as well as brilliance, and the effect is highly satisfying. The performances have remarkable eloquence and power. There is bravura in the *Ballade*, while the *Petrarch sonnets* (like the other items from *Années de pèlerinage*) have a finely calculated atmosphere and most subtle colouring. Sometimes on records Arrau's intellectual powers have been apparent at the expense of musical spontaneity, but that is not the case here: the playing throughout is remarkably alive and gripping. A most distinguished issue.

Années de pèlerinage, 2nd year, G.161: Sonetti del Petrarca Nos. 47, 104 and 123; Supplement, Venezia e Napoli: Gondoliera, G.162; Consolation No. 3, G.172; Études de concert, G.144, No. 3 in D flat. Impromptu, G.191; Liebestraum No. 3, G.541.
*** CRD CRD 1108/*CRDC 4108*. Crossley.

Very fine performances of wide range and keen sensitivity from Paul Crossley who has the measure of this repertoire. He is on the whole well recorded though the piano is at times too closely observed so that the sound is more percussive than one encounters from this artist in the flesh. However, for all that this is a most persuasive recital.

Années de pèlerinage: 2nd year, G.161: Sonetto 123 del Petrarca; Après une lecture du Dante. 3rd Year, G.163: Les jeux d'eaux à la Villa d'Este. Harmonies poétiques et religieuses, G.173: Bénédiction de Dieu dans la solitude.
(M) *** Ph. Seq. 6527/*7311* 132. Brendel.

This recital assembled from several full-priced records makes a tempting mid-priced sampler of Brendel's very special feeling for Liszt's music and, indeed, Philips's penchant for recording him with the most natural effect.

Années de pèlerinage, 3rd year, G.163: Nos. 2, Aux cyprès de la Villa d'Este; 4, Jeux d'eaux à la Villa d'Este; 5, Sunt lachrymae rerum. Csárdás macabre, G.224. Mosonyi's Funeral Procession, G.194. Schlaflos, Frage, und Antwort, G.203. Unstern, G.208. Valse oubliée No. 1, G.215. Schlummerlied.
*** Ph. 9500 775/*7300 863* [id.]. Brendel.

There is something stark and bitter about some of these late pieces, and Brendel's playing is distinguished by a concentration and subtlety of nuance that are wholly convincing. This is a most distinguished issue, and an obligatory acquisition for all lovers of Liszt. The sound is first-class and if the cassette has fractionally less range at the top it is still extraordinarily fine. If the richly resonant bass is cut back just a little, the balance is first-class.

Concert paraphrase on Verdi's Rigoletto, G.434; Études d'exécution transcendante d'après Paganini: La Campanella, G.140/6. Harmonies poétiques et religieuses: Funérailles, G.173/7. Hungarian rhapsody No. 12, G.244; Liebestraum No. 3, G.541/3. Mephisto waltz No. 1, G.514.
C *** Decca Dig. **410 257-2**; SXDL/*KSXDC* 7596 [LDR/5- 71096]. Bolet.

Bolet's is a superb collection of Liszt items, the first of a projected series. The playing is magnetic, not just because of virtuosity thrown off with ease (as here in the *Rigoletto paraphrase*) but because of an element of joy conveyed, even in the demoniac vigour of *Mephisto Waltz No. 1*. The relentless thrust of *Funérailles* is beautifully contrasted against the honeyed warmth of the famous *Liebestraum No. 3* and the sparkle of *La Campanella*. Even with the most hackneyed pieces, Bolet – superbly recorded – conveys complete freshness. Chrome tape and LP sound very much the same. The compact disc is thrillingly realistic in its spectacular sense of presence. A real demonstration disc!

ORGAN MUSIC

Fantasia and fugue on 'Ad nos, ad salutarem undam'; Prelude and fugue on the name BACH, G.260; Variations on Bach's 'Weinen, Klagen, Sorgen, Zagen', G.673.
(M) *** ASV ACM 2008. Bate (Royal Albert Hall organ).

Jennifer Bate gives superb performances of these Liszt warhorses. The clarity and inciveness of her playing go with a fine sense of line and structure; and even making no allowance for the Royal Albert Hall's acoustic problems the recording captures an admirable combination of definition and atmosphere.

VOCAL MUSIC

Lieder: *Der Alpenjäger; Anfangs wollt ich fast verzagen; Angiolin dal biondo crin; Blume und Duft; Comment, disaient-ils: Die drei Zigeuner; Du bist wie eine Blume; Der du von dem Himmel bist; Enfant, si j'étais roi; Ein Fichtenbaum steht einsam; Es muss ein Wunderbares sein; Es rauschen die Winde; Der Fischerknabe; Gastibelza; Gestorben war ich; Der Hirt; Hohe Liebe; Ich möchte hingehn; Ihr Glocken von Marling; Im Rhein, im schönen Strome; In Liebeslust; J'ai perdu ma force; Kling leise, mein Lied; Lasst mich ruhen; Die Lorelei; Morgens steh' ich auf und frage; Oh! Quand je dors; O Lieb, so lang; Petrarch sonnets Nos. 1–3; Schwebe, schwebe blaues Auge; S'il est un*

charmant gazon; Die stille Wasserrose; Des Tages laute Stimmen schweigen; La tombe et la rose; Der traurige Mönch; Über allen Gipfeln ist Ruh; Die Vätergruft; Vergiftet sind meine Lieder; Le vieux vagabond; Wer nie sein Brot; Wieder möcht' ich dir; Wie singt die Lerche schon.
*** DG 2740 254 (4) [id.]. Fischer-Dieskau, Barenboim.

As in a number of other fields Liszt has been severely under-appreciated as a song-composer. This collection of forty-three songs plus an accompanied declamation should do much to right the balance. Fischer-Dieskau, so far from making such an enormous project sound routine, actually seems to gather inspiration and intensity with the concentration; for example, the most famous of the songs, the *Petrarch sonnets*, are here even more inspired than in his previous performances. The sheer originality of thought and the ease of the lyricism – not least in *O Lieb*, which everyone knows as the famous piano solo, *Liebestraum No. 3* – are a regular delight, and Barenboim's accompaniments could hardly be more understanding, though Liszt presented surprisingly few virtuoso challenges to the pianist. The recording is excellent.

Lieder: *Du bist wie eine Blume; Der du von dem Himmel bist; Die drei Zigeuner; Es war ein König in Thule; Die Fischerstochter; Freudvoll und leidvol; Im Rhein, im schönen Strome; Die Lorelei; S'il est un charmant gazon; Über allen Gipfeln ist Ruh; Vätergruft; Das Veilchen.*
*** HMV ASD/*TC-ASD* 3906. Baker, Parsons.

Dame Janet Baker's selection of songs – starting with the most ambitious and one of the most beautiful, *Die Lorelei*.– brings out the wide range of Liszt in this medium. His style is transformed when setting a French text, giving Parisian lightness in response to Hugo's words, while his setting of the *King of Thule* from Goethe's *Faust* leaps away from reflectiveness in illustrating the verses. The glowing warmth of Janet Baker's singing is well matched by Geoffrey Parsons's keenly sensitive accompaniment. The recording is first-rate, even fuller on cassette than on disc.

Lieder: *Die drei Zigeuner; Enfant, si j'étais roi; Es muss ein Wunderbares sein; Es war ein König in Thule; Kling leise, mein Lied; Die Lorelei; Ne brany menya moy drug; Vergiftet sind meine Lieder.*
*** Decca SXL 6964. Sass, Schiff – BARTÓK: *5 Songs.****

The vibrant Sylvia Sass and the inspirational Andras Schiff give dedicated performances of eight Liszt songs. The occasional rawness in Sass's voice seems apt in performances which bring out the Hungarian flavours, and which with often weighty underlining convey operatic overtones. Next to Dame Janet Baker in some of the songs Sass sounds extrovert, if splendidly full of temperament. The recording is outstandingly clear.

Hungarian Coronation Mass, G.11.
(M) ** DG 2543 802 [id.]. Szecsödy, Tiszay, Simándi, Faragó, Ch. and O of Coronation Church, Budapest, Ferencsik.

A great deal of Liszt's music, even the worthwhile compositions, still remains almost unknown, and this 1961 recording of the *Coronation Mass* makes therefore a welcome return to the catalogue. Ferencsik has his forces well under control, and the choir and orchestra make an impressive and exciting burst of sound when occasion demands. None of the four soloists is well known outside Budapest, and to be honest none of them counts as a really great voice, but they sing with admirable enthusiasm and contribute a good deal, musically, to the overall impression. Parts of the work are original almost to the point of being prophetic, and its construction is challenging enough to excite interest in those concerned with the development of liturgical music in the romantic era.

Via crucis.
** Abbey LPB 813. Connolly, Holmes, Wheeler, Leeds Parish Church Ch., Lindley; Jackson (organ) – ELGAR: *Ave verum* etc.**

A stately, unaffected performance from Leeds, wanting only in the bite and emotional fervour that Hungarian artists would and have brought to it. The sound is musically balanced, and readers wanting this interesting and underrated score need not hesitate.

Litolff, Henri (1818–91)

Concerto symphonique No. 4, Op. 102: Scherzo.
(M) *** Decca Jub. JB/*KJCB* 104. Curzon, LPO, Boult – GRIEG: *Concerto*; FRANCK: *Symphonic variations.****
(M) *** Decca Jub. JB/*KJBC* 29. Curzon (as above) – TCHAIKOVSKY: *Concerto No. 1.***(*)
(B) *** CfP CFP/*TC-CFP* 115. Katin, LPO, Pritchard – TCHAIKOVSKY: *Piano concerto No. 1.* *(*)
(M) ** Decca SPA/*KCSP* 170. Katin, LPO, Sir Colin Davis – GRIEG: *Concerto; Peer Gynt suite No.1.***

Curzon's performance is available either in its original combination with Franck and Grieg or coupled with his 1960 recording of the Tchaikovsky *B flat minor Concerto.* Curzon provides all the sparkle Litolff's infectious *Scherzo* requires, and this is a delightful makeweight, whichever coupling is chosen. The fine qualities of the original sound, freshness and clarity, remain equally impressive on both disc and cassette; there is no appreciable difference between the two.

On Classics for Pleasure too a scintillating performance, brilliantly recorded; if only the concerto which forms the coupling had the same kind of panache this disc would be a world-beater. The cassette transfer too is of demonstration quality.

On Decca SPA the *Scherzo* is rattled off at hair-raising speed. One might prefer something more infectiously gay, but Katin and Davis still manage something of a skipping lilt, and as a fill-up for an excellent Grieg coupling it is welcome enough. Like the coupling it is very well recorded, as is the tape.

Lloyd, George (born 1913)

Symphony No. 5.
*** Lyr. SRCS 124. Philh. O, Downes.

George Lloyd wrote his *Fifth Symphony* in the immediate aftermath of a depression and nervous breakdown so serious that its recurrence subsequently prevented him from composing for many years. On the surface you would never know that such life-and-death emotions were afflicting the composer, but heard with an understanding ear this symphony is all the more poignantly moving, when seemingly happy and carefree ideas plainly do hide strong emotions. It is in five movements, and the *Pastorale* first movement typifies the deceptive happiness of the piece. The slow movements – a *Corale* which comes second and a *Lamento* which is fourth – more directly speak of dark emotions, but paradoxically Lloyd is the more involving when he is less explicitly weighty. Excellent performances and recording.

Symphony No. 8.
*** Lyr. SRCS 113. Philh. O, Downes.

After his severe depression and nervous breakdown, Lloyd for many years gave up composing entirely, earning his living instead as a mushroom farmer, only gradually turning back to composition. The *Eighth Symphony* – the first to be heard in public – is a product of that long recuperative period, and in the openness of the inspiration it both belies earlier depression (passionately English, rather like Strauss translated) and testifies to the success of composition as therapy. The writing has its English awkwardnesses, and the three movements are arguably too long for the material, but the flavour will certainly attract those with a taste for the English Renaissance. Excellent performance and recording.

Lloyd Webber, Andrew
(born 1948)

Variations.
**(*) MCA MCF/*TC-MCF* 2824. Julian Lloyd Webber, Airey, Argent, Hiseman, Mole, More, Thompson, composer.

This fascinating hybrid work inhabits the world of 'pop' music of the late 1970s yet draws inspiration from the classical mainstream of variations on Paganini's ubiquitous theme, which has inspired so many diverse compositions over the past century and a half. Andrew Lloyd Webber's piece began life as a comparatively short twenty-minute work, composed with his brother's brilliant cello-playing very much in mind. It was then expanded to the format here recorded, lasting about half an hour, and has since been blown up to even greater proportions. The vulgarity of the ambience of its 'pop' sections will exasperate many listeners, yet its sheer vitality cannot be ignored and the lyrical variations, featuring the flute and solo cello, are genuinely memorable. The recording is good, if inflated; the cassette is acceptable but does not match the disc in range and transient sharpness.

Tell me on a Sunday (song cycle).
*** Polydor POLD/*POLDC* 5031. Webb, LPO, Rabinowitz.

This inspired song cycle by Andrew Lloyd Webber with splendid lyrics by Don Black chronicles a disastrous series of love affairs of an English girl living in America. The theme of the songs is both nostalgic and life-enhancing, for the heroine gradually comes to terms with her failures and it is she who makes the final break. The music itself is totally memorable. One thinks of the lovely curving contour of *It's not the end of the world*, the steamy *Sheldon Bloom*, the witty tunefulness of *Capped teeth and Caesar salad*, with its repeated pay-off line 'Have a nice day', the sparklingly happy *I'm very you* (the lyrics of these songs continually recalling Cole Porter) and above all the haunting title melody. The communication throughout is of a kind one despairs of finding in so much of today's 'serious' music, and the marvellous performance by Marti Webb (for whom the cycle was written) cannot be too highly praised. She is splendidly accompanied by Harry Rabinowitz and members of the LPO, and there is much fine solo playing. The recording is first-class on disc and tape alike, and the only small snag is that the opening number, *Take that look off your face*, was stridently heated up to secure its entry into the charts as a hit single.

The success of both the above works persuaded Lloyd Webber to join them together for a stage show called *Song and dance*, which proved a riveting theatrical experience. The performances of the music, further altered and extended for live presentation, are available together on a double-album (or extended-length tape), with Marti Webb still the soloist and Rabinowitz in charge (PODV/*PODVC* 4) although, for unexplained reasons, *I'm very you, you're very me* – one of the best songs – is not included on the cassette. But in any case this cannot compare with the original recordings. The further extension of the *Variations* is not an advantage and while *Tell me on a Sunday* includes a delectable additional number, the 'live' recording, with audience reactions, detracts considerably from the appeal of the song cycle, and tends to coarsen the performance.

Locatelli, Pietro (1695–1764)

Concerti grossi, Op. 1/8, 11 and 12.
(M) **(*) Ph. 9502/*7313* 069. I Musici.

Locatelli's Op. 1 is much indebted to Corelli but none the worse for that, and the three concertos recorded here are far from routine examples of the genre. Indeed the *F minor* is possessed of real expressive grandeur. The performances date from the early days of stereo but wear their years lightly. The harpsichord is somewhat reticent but the balance is otherwise good and I Musici play with genuine feeling.

Il Pianto d'Arianna, Op. 7/6.
(*) None. H 71151 [id.]. Biffoli, Milan Angelicum O, Jenkins – GEMINIANI: *The Enchanted Forest.*(*)

Locatelli's concertante piece for violin and orchestra makes an attractive fill-up for the unusual Geminiani ballet. It is in the form of an operatic scena, with recitative leading to elegiac slow movements and a brilliant allegro before a final slow movement resolving the tension. Well performed and recorded.

12 Flute sonatas, Op. 2.
*** O-L DSLO 578/9. Preston (with McGegan in No. 12), Pleeth, Hogwood.

Apart from the concertos the twelve *Flute sonatas* are perhaps the most important collection among Locatelli's works. Published in 1732, they take a traditional line in their use of binary form, but the amiable freshness of the writing is most persuasive in fine authentic performances like these. No. 12 here includes the optional rendering of the *Largo* as a canon, with Nicholas McGegan taking the second flute part. The recording is excellent.

Locke, Matthew (1630–77)

Music for His Majesty's sackbutts and cornetts; Canon in 6 parts; Pavan in 6 parts; A plaine song given by Mr William Brode of Hawford; Saraband in 4 parts; Harpsichord suite No. 4. Songs: The despondent lover's song; A dialogue between Thersis and Dorinda; Lucinda, winke or vaile those eyes; My lodging it is in the cold ground; Orpheus with his lute; A pastoral; To a lady singing to herself by the Thames' side; Urania to Parthenissa; When Phyllis watched her harmless sheep; Wrong not your lovely eyes.
*** EMI 1C 069 46404. Kwella, Rogers, Bailes, Tilney, L. Cornett and Sackbutt Ens.

This is an excellent issue in Electrola's (German EMI) admirable Reflexe series, aimed as a rival to DG's Archive series of authentic performances. This collection of songs and instrumental pieces by the long-lived Carolingian composer is well chosen and beautifully performed, notably an extended dialogue between two pastoral characters, Thersis and Dorinda. Locke on this showing was inventive with his titles as well as his music, for instance: *To a lady singing to herself by the Thames' side* and *Lucinda, winke or vaile those eyes*, both for tenor. Nigel Rogers' voice is a little dry-sounding, but Patrizia Kwella's is most beautifully caught, both singing most tastefully. Excellent recording.

(i) *The Tempest* (incidental music written in collaboration with Pelham Humfrey, Pietro Reggio, John Bannister, James Hart); (ii) *Music for His Majesty's sackbutts and cornetts.*
*** O-L DSLO 507. (i) Nelson, Hill, Thomas, soloists, AcAM, Hogwood; (ii) Michael Laird Cornett and Sackbutt Ens.

1977 was the tercentenary of Matthew Locke's death, and this record of the *Tempest* music, the work by which he was known in his lifetime and for a century afterwards, was a worthy tribute. The performance could not be bettered, and the balance of the recording is judged with taste and discretion. Every detail is firmly in focus, and every singer and instrument is life-size and life-like. The performance of the *Music for His Majesty's sackbutts and cornetts* is no less impressive. It is difficult to fault this record on any count.

Loewe, Carl (1796–1869)

Ballads: *Archibald Douglas; Edward; Erlkönig; Herr Oluff; Hinkende Jamben; Kleiner Haushalt; Meeresleuchten; Der Mohrenfürst auf der Messe; Der Schätzgraber; Süsses Begrabnis; Tom der Reimer.*
*** DG 2531 376 [id.]. Fischer-Dieskau, Demus.

In an ideal selection of some of Loewe's most memorable songs and ballads Fischer-Dieskau, admirably accompanied by Joerg Demus, gives performances which have the commitment and intensity of spontaneous expression, while remaining flawlessly controlled and strongly thought through. This alternative setting of the *Erlking* is in its way as dramatic as Schubert's if less subtle musically, and the story-telling in other songs too is so graphic that even a non-German-speaker will have little need to refer to the English translations. Excellent sound.

Lortzing, Albert (1801–51)

Der Waffenschmied (complete).
*** EMI 1C 153 28930/1. Prey, Böhme, Litz, Unger, Bav. Op. Ch. and O, Lehan.

Question: which opera besides *Trovatore* includes an anvil chorus? The answer is this charming comic piece, *Der Waffenschmied, (The Armourer)*, written in 1846, one of Lortzing's later operas. With its background of a medieval craft and its dramatic layout, it clearly anticipates *Der Meistersinger*, though the manner could hardly be less weighty. The music is consistently jolly rather than soulful. Typical are the Polacca aria for the hero, Georg, *Man wird ja einmal geboren*, and an aria for the heroine, Marie, later in the Act which is very nearly a polka. Singing is good rather than outstanding with Kurt Böhme at his steadiest, characterfully rotund as the master armourer, Hans Stadinger. Gerhard Unger is also in fresh, clear voice, though the women are rather less sweet on the ear. The recording, made in 1964, still sounds vivid, with the sound stage well defined.

Der Wildschütz (operetta): complete.
*** DG 2740 271 (3). Mathis, Soffel, Schreier, Hornik, Von Ottenthal, Sotin, Resick, Suss, Berlin R. Ch., Berlin State O, Klee.
**(*) EMI 1C 149 28534/6. Rothenberger, Litz, Wunderlich, Vordemfelde, Ollendorf, Schadle, Ehrengut, Bav. State Op. Ch. and O, Heger.

Der Wildschütz (*The Poacher*), written in 1848, year of revolutions, is the least revolutionary of comic operas, a rustic piece that aims merely to charm and delight in an idiom that echoes Mendelssohn and Weber rather than any more advanced composer. Dramatically it may be slow-moving (with the spoken German dialogue not always a blessing on record), but in this glowing, beautifully sung, played and produced performance under Bernhard Klee you can readily understand why it has never been out of the operatic repertory in Germany and remains a firm favourite. The tangle of plot is improbable, a storm in a rustic teapot, but the characters are sharply and endearingly delineated, and the entertainment must be strongly recommended to opera-lovers wanting something different. The ensembles are a special delight, and it is to the credit of a cast without a weak link that it also makes an excellent team. Excellent, atmospheric recording.

The EMI/Electrola set dating from 1963 is most enjoyable too, though the performance sparkles less, and the recording is more limited. It is still well worth considering (despite the lack of an English translation of the libretto) for the singing of the late Fritz Wunderlich in the role of the hero, even finer than Peter Schreier on DG.

Zar und Zimmermann (complete).
*** EMI 1C 183 29302/4. Prey, Schreier, Köth, Burmeister, Gedda, Frick, Taschler, Vogel, Leipzig R.Ch., Dresden State Op. O, Heger.

Robert Heger was over eighty when in 1966 he made this ripe and sparkling recording of Lortzing's delightful comic opera about Peter the Great's incognito visit (as a carpenter) to Holland to study shipbuilding. The tenor hero is also a Russian visitor and is also called Peter, which causes much confusion both diplomatically and in the love story. Problems are not helped when the heroine's guardian uncle, the local mayor, is a pompous ass, a superb comic role magnificently taken here by Gottlob Frick. The rest of the cast is near ideal, and though Erika Köth as Marie has some shrill moments, she characterizes the young girl very convincingly. The warm acoustic lends a glow to the sound, which remains very vivid. As an Electrola import from Germany, the libretto is in German only, with no more than a summary of the plot in English.

Luigini, Alexandre (1850–1906)

Ballet Egyptien: suite, Op. 12.
(M) *** HMV Green. ESD/*TC-ESD* 7115. RPO, Fistoulari – MEYERBEER: *Les Patineurs***; PONCHIELLI: *Dance of the Hours***(*); TCHAIKOVSKY: *Nutcracker suite.***

Luigini's amiable and tuneful *Ballet Egyptien* suite was for many years regarded as salon music, and there is some doggerel about 'Dame Ella Wheeler Wilcox' which neatly fits the famous opening rhythm. However, the music is highly engaging, especially when played as stylishly as it is here under that master conductor of ballet, Anatole Fistoulari. The recording is lively, a little dry: the cassette is slightly softer-grained than the disc and preferable.

Lully, Jean-Baptiste (1632–87)

Pièces de symphonie (suite of music from operas: *Acis et Galathée; Amadis; Atys; Béllérophon; Persée; Phaeton; Thésée*).
(M) *** Decca Ser. SA 27. ECO, Leppard.

Here is another of Raymond Leppard's enjoyably stylish selections from the high noon of classical French opera. The playing is first-rate, and the excellent recording presents the music in the best possible light. This is not for those who insist on original instruments, but for the non-specialist collector who will find much attractive music here.

Le Bourgeois Gentilhomme (incidental music; complete).
(M) *** HM HM 20320/1. Nimsgern, Jungmann, Schortemeier, Jacobs, Tölz Ch., La Petite Bande, Leonhardt.

Entertainment rather than musical value: in itself Lully's score offers no great musical rewards. The melodic invention is unmemorable and harmonies are neither original nor interesting; but if the music taken on its own is thin stuff, the effect of the entertainment as a whole is quite another matter. This performance puts Lully's music into the correct perspective of the stage, and with such sprightly and spirited performers as well as such good recording, these discs can hardly fail to give pleasure. The orchestral contribution under the direction of Gustav Leonhardt is distinguished by a splendid sense of the French style.

(i) *Dies Irae;* (ii) *Miserere mei Deus.*
**(*) Erato STU/*MCE* 70940. (i) Jennifer Smith, Devos; (ii) Alliot-Lugaz, Bufkens; (i; ii) Vandersteene, Bessac, Huttenlocher, Valence Vocal Ens., Paillard O, Paillard.

Lully's *Miserere* is a work of great eloquence. Like the *Dies Irae*, it is written for double choir, and the antiphonal dialogue between the two groups is a vital part of Lully's musical architecture. Its realization was not possible on the famous and distinguished Oiseau-Lyre recording directed by Anthony Lewis, who tried to simulate a dialogue effect by means of a subtle control of light and shade. Paillard makes no attempt to divide his forces and does much the same thing, relying mainly on the contrast with the solo group. Both performances here are suitably restrained and dignified, but the *Dies Irae*, a noble piece encapsulating a mood of dark melancholy, makes the strongest impression here, with a notably dedicated contribution from the soloists. The effect has a striking elegiac beauty. The sudden choral interjections at a faster pace are convincingly managed. The orchestra accompanies expressively, and the overall balance is good. Paillard does not offer the last word on the *Miserere*, but the record is worth having for the *Dies Irae* alone. The cassette is very successful, rich and refined, with good range.

Te Deum.
*** Erato STU/*MCE* 70927. Jennifer Smith, Bessac, Vandersteene, Devos, Huttenlocher, Valence 'A Cœur Joi' Vocal Ens., Paillard O, Paillard.

The *Te Deum* and the *Miserere* are probably Lully's best-known sacred pieces. The setting of the *Te Deum* dates from 1677 and is a work of genuine splendour and breadth rather than the general-purpose pomp favoured by Lully and his followers. The work makes effective use of the contrast between soloists, chorus and orchestra, and Jean-François Paillard and his forces give a thoroughly committed and eloquent account of the piece. Recording is eminently satisfactory; it is cut at a fairly high level, but reproduces cleanly. Incidentally, it was while conducting this work that Lully vigorously brought down on his right foot the heavy stick that served to mark the beat: gangrene ultimately set in and he died a couple of months later!

Alceste (opera): complete.
** CBS [M3-34580 (3)]. Palmer, Nigoghossian, Rhodde, Brewer, Elwes, Van Egmond, Vento, Maigat, La Grande Écurie et la Chambre du Roy, Malgoire.

CBS have put us in their debt by making this opera available. The revival of interest in Couperin and Rameau has been welcome and should extend to Lully. This is the first of his operas to be recorded complete and dates from 1674, two years after his first tragédie en musique, set to Quinault. All in all, it would be idle to pretend that the music is as fully rewarding or as lyrically convincing as Rameau, but despite some occasional longueurs, this is undoubtedly a set to have. Malgoire always brings vitality to whatever he does, and in spite of the rough edges there is a sense of dramatic continuity that in the end proves compelling. The reader must not expect opera of the calibre of Handel or Rameau nor should he shrink from the odd imperfections of ensemble (and intonation). But these are of small account in the balance sheet, and gratitude to M. Malgoire and his colleagues far outweighs the odd reservation one may have about the chorus. The forward balance may worry some (more than it did us), but the recording on the whole is as satisfactory as the performance is spirited. This set has been withdrawn in the UK.

Armide (complete).
*** Erato STU 715302 (2) [id.]. Yakar, Vandersteene, Borst, Gari, De Reyghere, Cold, De Mey, Studer, Chapelle Royal Voc. and Instrumental Ens., Herreweghe.

Using the same libretto which a hundred years later was to provide Gluck with some of his finest operatic inspirations (see under Gluck for an outstanding recording), Lully equally, according to his period, transcended stiff conventions. Under Herreweghe, using original instruments, this is a lively and refreshing account of what in this discreetly tailored text becomes a relatively fast-moving work, once its symbolic prologue is over. Outstanding singing, both stylish and rich-toned, from Rachel Yakar and first-rate contributions from the others too, helped by well-balanced recording.

Lutoslawski, Witold (born 1913)

(i) *Cello concerto. Concerto for orchestra; Jeux vénitiens; Livre; Mi-Parti; Musique funèbre; Postlude No. 1; Preludes and fugue for thirteen solo strings; Symphonic variations; Symphonies Nos. 1–2.* (ii) *5 Lieder for soprano and orchestra.* (iii) *Paroles tissées.* (iv) *3 Poèmes d'Henri Michaux.*
*** EMI 1C 165 03231/6. Polish Nat. RSO or Polish CO, composer with (i) Jablonski; (ii) Lukomska; (iii) Devos; (iv) Krakau Polish R. Ch., Michniewski.

Unbelievably Lutoslawski is a senior figure in contemporary music, past his seventieth birthday. This six-record set is a kind of 'retrospective', collecting most of his major orchestral pieces right from the early and wholly beguiling *Symphonic variations,* with their Szymanowskian palette and luminosity, to works like the *Second Symphony* (1966–7) and the *Preludes and fugue* (1972) which consolidate the new language he formed after his change of style in the mid-1950s. Lutoslawski has not been neglected on record, and individual performances of such works as the *Concerto for orchestra,* the *Paroles tissées* by its dedicatee, Peter Pears, the *Musique funèbre* and the *Cello concerto,* which Rostropovich recorded with the composer himself, have long been in circulation. Readers who have missed these but want to explore Lutoslawski's work in greater depth could not do better than to turn to this box. The performances and recordings are of a high standard and show this imaginative composer's sound world to good advantage. Given so large a package, it would be idle to dwell on individual works at any length. Obviously this set is for collectors already committed to the cause, but others too will find many rewarding pieces to justify the considerable outlay.

Mi-Parti.
(M) *** Sup. 1410 2734. Prague RSO, Kasprzyk – BAIRD: *Elegeia*; PENDERECKI: *Anaklasis* etc.***

Mi-Parti is a relatively recent work, dating from 1976. To explain its title, the composer describes it as *composée de deux parties égales mais différentes* ('music composed of two equal but different parts'), though it must be said that the haunting atmosphere of the quieter lyrical section, with its luminous Szymanowskian colourings, exerts the stronger appeal. *Mi-Parti* is also available under the composer's own baton (see above), but this performance is thoroughly committed and will be welcomed by those who do not want to invest in the complete EMI box. The recording is perfectly acceptable and the interest of the coupling enhances the attractions of the disc.

Variations on a theme of Paganini.
*** Ph. Dig. **411 034-2**; 6514/*7337* 369 [id.]. Argerich, Freire – RACHMANINOV: *Suite No. 2;* RAVEL: *La valse.****

Lutoslawski's *Variations* for piano duo date from 1941 and are exhilarating and played with great virtuosity by Martha Argerich and Nelson Freire. The recording is very realistic and natural on disc and tape alike. The compact disc makes more obvious the rather reverberant acoustic of the recording location.

Paroles tissées.
*** Decca HEAD 3 [id.]. Pears, L. Sinf., composer – BEDFORD: *Tentacles of the Dark Nebula;* BERKELEY: *4 Ronsard sonnets.***(*)

Lutoslawski, like the other two composers represented on this disc, has written with fine understanding of Peter Pears' special qualities. The texts are from poems of Jean-François Chabrun, with haunting imagery recurring in a manner mirrored exactly by Lutoslawski's finely textured, sharply conceived writing. Performance and recording are ideal.

MacCunn, Hamish (1868–1916)

Overture: Land of the Mountain and the Flood.
(B) *** CfP CFP/*TC-CFP* 40320. Hallé O, Handford (with Concert of *'Encores'* ***).

MacCunn's descriptive overture is no masterpiece, but it is attractively atmospheric and effectively constructed. It makes a more than agreeable Scottish contribution to this CfP collection of shorter orchestral works, including Barber's *Adagio for strings*, Copland's *Fanfare for the common man* and Satie's *Gymnopédies.* The performance is admirably spirited; at bargain price, with good recording on both LP and cassette, this is well worth considering, now that Gibson's version has been withdrawn.

MacDowell, Edward (1861–1908)

(i) *Piano concerto No. 2 in D minor, Op. 23; Suite No. 2 (Indian), Op. 48.*
**Turn. [TV 34535]. Westphalian SO, Landau, (i) with Eugene List.

Although List plays brilliantly, the performance of the *Concerto,* with its shallow recording, lacks the refinement of Szidon's DG account (now deleted). But the *Indian suite* is another matter. It is based on genuine folk melodies of the Iroquois, Chippewa, Iowa and Kiowa tribes, and what memorable tunes they are. MacDowell gives them a civilized gloss, but their vitality remains unimpaired. The performance is sympathetic and the recording is better on this side of the disc. At the price this is well worth investigating by American readers – it is currently not available in the UK.

Suite for large orchestra, Op. 42; Suite No. 2 (Indian), Op. 48.
(M) *(*) Mercury SRI 75026 [id.]. Eastman-Rochester O, Hanson.

MacDowell is best known for his miniature, *To a wild rose.* The suite – although it too has evocative titles – is more ambitious, but fails to make a really memorable impression, except of conscientious musical craftsmanship. The *Indian suite,* using ethnic melodies unselfconsciously, is very different, its high point being a *Dirge,* an eloquent melisma based on an Indian lament. Both performances are of high quality, as one would expect from this source, but the recording of the *Indian suite* is a 'stereo transcription' from a mono source, and the sound is not entirely convincing. American readers would do better with the Turnabout alternative, listed above. (NB: Clive Lythgoe's persuasive account of the *Woodland sketches* – the source of *To a wild rose* – is still listed in Schwann as being available in the USA as a Polygram special import. It is coupled with an equally impressive performance of MacDowell's ambitious *Piano sonata No. 2 (Eroica),* a musical evocation of the Arthurian legend on a really large scale. The Philips recording is excellent [9500 095].)

Machaut, Guillaume (1300–77)

Un lay de consolation; Le lay de la fonteinne.
*** O-L DSLO Dig. DSDL 705. Medieval Ens. of L., Peter and Timothy Davies.

Machaut was the leading poet and composer of his age and though he made an important contribution to the ballade and rondeau, this record serves as a reminder that his *lais* were hardly less innovatory and forward-looking. The *lai* emerged at the end of the twelfth century and differs from the rondeau and ballade in that it has many stanzas: indeed, all but two of the nineteen *lais* of Machaut have twelve stanzas, including the two recorded here. In *Le lay de la fonteinne,* written during the period 1349–63, each of the even-numbered stanzas is a canon in three parts at the unison. *Un lay de consolation* is a work of the last decade of Machaut's life and survives only as a monophonic piece. However, the American scholar Richard Hoppin discovered that the two halves of each stanza fit to produce two-part polyphony, and it is performed like this, the second part being assigned to instruments. *Le lay de la fonteinne* is the longer of the two lasting nearly half an hour and is sung by three singers, only one of whom has the text in the canonic sections; the others vocalize. Music of specialist appeal but of an undoubted beauty. The recording and presentation are altogether exemplary.

Messe de Nostre Dame.
**(*) HMV ASD/*TC-ASD* 143576-1/4 [Ang. S 38044]. Taverner Ch. and Cons., Parrott.

Andrew Parrott's version of this great work sets it in the context of a plainsong liturgy, thus greatly enhancing its effect. The (deleted) Grayson Burgess version used no instruments and interspersed organ music between the Mass sections. This HMV issue is splendidly recorded on both disc and cassette, and there are many beauties too, some of them obscured by Parrott's decision to transpose the work down a fourth, thus darkening its texture, which reduces internal clarity.

Maconchy, Elizabeth (born 1907)

(i) *Serenata concertante for violin and orchestra; Symphony for double string orchestra.*
*** Lyr. SRCS 116. Parikian, LSO, Handley.

These two ambitious works both testify to the strength and seriousness of Elizabeth Maconchy's imagination. The *Symphony* in four sharply contrasted movements is very much in the tradition of British string music with a flavour not too distant from Tippett's *Concerto for double string orchestra.* It ends with a beautiful and moving slow *Passacaglia.* The *Serenata concertante* – a violin concerto in all but name – is grittier and less lyrical, at least until you come to the slow third movement, which builds up in simple lyricism to a grinding climax of a sharpness like that of Walton's *First Symphony.* Handley directs superb, committed performances, vividly recorded.

Maderna, Bruno (1920–73)

Aura; Biogramma; Quadrivium.
*** DG 2531 272 [id.]. N. German RSO, Sinopoli.

This record usefully brings together three of Bruno Maderna's key works, among the last he wrote before his untimely death when still in his early fifties. Earliest is *Quadrivium,* for four orchestral groups, each with percussion, a work designed 'to entertain and to interest, not to shock the bourgeois'. In 1972 came *Aura* and *Biogramma*; the former won the composer (posthumously) the city of Bonn's Beethoven prize. Excellent recording for dedicated performances.

Magnard, Alberic (1865–1914)

Symphony No. 4 in C sharp min., Op. 21; Chant funèbre, Op. 9.
*** EMI PM 173184-1/*4*. Toulouse Capitole O, Plasson.

The *Fourth Symphony* dates from 1913, the year before the composer's death, and is a welcome addition to the catalogue. It has an impressive intellectual power. Like his countryman Guy-Ropartz, with whom he is often paired, Magnard is grievously neglected even in his home country and, as is the case with the *Third Symphony*, his music is well crafted and there is no shortage of ideas. For all the appearance of academicism there is a quiet and distinctive personality here and dignity too. The fill-up, the *Chant funèbre*, is an earlier work that has a vein of genuine eloquence. The Toulouse Capitole Orchestra under Michel Plasson play this music as if they believe in every note, as indeed they should, and the recording is sonorous and well defined. This is the first of his works to appear on cassette.

Mahler, Gustav (1860–1911)

Symphony No. 1 in D (Titan).
*** Decca SXL 6113 [Lon. CS 6401]. LSO, Solti.
(M) *** Decca VIV/*KVIC* 57. RPO, Leinsdorf.
(M) *** DG Priv. 2535/*3335* 172 [id.]. Bav. RSO, Kubelik.
(M) *** Uni. RHS/*UKC* 301. LSO, Horenstein.
*** RCA [ARL1/*ARK1* 0894]. LSO, Levine.
(M) *** HMV SXLP/*TC-SXLP* 30548 [Ang. RL/*4RL* 32037]. Chicago SO, Giulini.
(*) DG Dig. **400 033-2; 2532/*3302* 020 [id.]. Chicago SO, Abbado.

(M) **(*) CBS 60128/*40*- [MY/*MYT* 37235]. Col. SO, Walter.
(M) **(*) Ph. Seq. 6527/*7311* 062 [6500 342/ *7300 397*]. Concg. O, Haitink.
**(*) HMV ASD/*TC-ASD* 3541 [Ang. S/ *4XS* 37508]. LPO, Tennstedt.
(B) ** RCA VICS/*VK* 2007 [ALK1 4983]. Boston SO, Leinsdorf.

Symphony No. 1 in D (original 1893 version, including *Blumine*).
(B) ** PRT GSGC/*ZCGC* 2045. Philh. O, Morris.

Among the top half-dozen or so listed recordings it is very difficult to suggest a clear first recommendation. Each represents conductor and orchestra on top form, recorded in vintage analogue sound, and several of the finest versions are economically priced (it seems likely that Solti's Decca account will be reissued on Jubilee during the lifetime of this book). Final choice will therefore be personal and subjective. The London Symphony Orchestra play Mahler's *First* like no other orchestra. They catch the magical writing at the opening with a singular evocative quality, at least partly related to the peculiarly characteristic blend of wind timbres. Solti gives the orchestra its full head and coaxes some magnificent playing from the brass in the finale and throughout wonderfully warm string tone. His tendency to drive hard is only felt in the second movement, which is pressed a little too much, although he relaxes beautifully in the central section. Specially memorable is the poignancy of the introduction of the *Frère Jacques* theme in the slow movement, and the exultant brilliance of the closing pages.

Taking sound quality as well as interpretation into account, Leinsdorf's Decca version might be considered best buy in the budget price-range. Although Leinsdorf may not be as poetic as Kubelik, his is a strong and colourful version, finely controlled and built with sustained concentration. The recording, with brass well forward, is one of the best made in Decca's Phase Four system. The transfer to tape is among the cleanest available of this symphony.

Kubelik gives an intensively poetic reading. He is here at his finest in Mahler, and though, as in later symphonies, he is sometimes tempted to choose a tempo on the fast side, the result here could hardly be more glowing. The rubato in the slow funeral march is most subtly handled. In its Privilege reissue the sound is a little dry in the bass (but still excellent); the cassette, however, has a tendency to be over-bright.

Unicorn had the laudable aim of securing a modern recording of Horenstein in Mahler's *First*, and the result has a freshness and concentration which put it in a special category among the many rival accounts. Solti, Leinsdorf and Kubelik provide a sharper experience, more immediately exciting in virtuosity; but with measured tempi and a manner which conceals much art, Horenstein links the work more clearly with later Mahler symphonies. Fine recording, though the timpani is balanced rather too close. The cassette transfer is admirably done.

Like Solti and Horenstein, James Levine has the LSO for this symphony, and arguably he draws from it the most exciting playing of all. It is a reading of high contrasts, with extremes of tempo and dynamic brought out with total conviction. In that emphasis on drama Levine presents a complete contrast to Horenstein, but the result is just as convincing. Excellent, brilliant recording. (This record has been withdrawn in the UK.)

Giulini's account with the Chicago Symphony Orchestra has been remastered and the recording freshened without loss of bloom, with a matching cassette that is first-class in every way. It is an outstanding version; the conductor's transparent honesty prevents any feeling of excessive sophistication, and he never whips up excitement synthetically, for his tempi are generally on the slow side, like those of Horenstein.

Abbado directs a pure and superbly refined reading, consistently well paced and recorded in excellent digital sound. By rights it should be an easy first choice, and yet he misses some of the natural tension of a performance that communicates as in a live concert. In the *Wunderhorn* inspirations of the first two movements the music too rarely smiles. The funeral march of the slow movement is wonderfully hushed, more spontaneous-sounding than the rest. Even with those reservations it stands fairly high on a long list. The chrome tape accommodates the wide dynamic range impressively, but the opening pianissimo is heard to finest effect on the excellent compact disc. The absolute silence, however, does serve to emphasize the lack of electricity during this sequence.

To have a modern stereo recording of a characteristic Bruno Walter Mahler performance on medium-priced label will seem to most a bargain too good to miss. The sound is good, and the opening movement, with especially fine horn-playing, has rarely been performed on disc with more atmosphere. The finale is less successful; here Walter's broad treatment lets the tension sag, and the closing pages of the work have not the apotheosis-like concentration that the music needs.

When Philips gathered together Haitink's recordings of Mahler symphonies, they took the trouble to make a new version of No. 1; and not only is it far more refined as a recording, the reading is if anything even more thoughtfully idiomatic than before in Haitink's unexaggerated Mahler style. Reissued now on Sequenza, this makes a good medium-price recommendation for those finding Leinsdorf too extrovert. The cassette transfer is of good quality, with a brighter upper range than many Philips cassettes, if not as clean as the disc.

Tennstedt's manner in Mahler is somewhat severe, with textures fresh and neat and the style of phrasing generally less moulded than we have come to expect. This concentration on precision and directness means that when the conductor does indulge in rubato or speed-changes it does not sound quite consistent and comes as a surprise, as in the big string melody of the finale. Most Mahlerians will prefer a more felt performance than this, but for some it could be a good choice; its rich warm recording is first-class and has transferred surprisingly well to cassette, considering the resonance and the wide amplitude of the sound.

Leinsdorf's Boston version competes with his own later mid-priced RPO version, more idiomatic and better-recorded. The only advantage of the Boston version is that it includes the exposition repeat. The 1963 recording is none too clear. The chrome tape matches the disc closely.

Wyn Morris, like Ormandy on his RCA disc (now deleted), adds to the usual four movements of Mahler's *First Symphony* the recently unveiled movement *Blumine* that came second in the composer's original scheme. Morris goes further than Ormandy in adopting in the other four movements the original scoring instead of Mahler's revision. The result is a curiosity well worth investigating. If with less polish than in the best rival versions, the playing has both warmth and spontaneity and the recording is fully acceptable, with a surprisingly good cassette. An interesting bargain.

Symphony No. 2 in C min. (*Resurrection*).

*** DG 2707 094 (2)/*3370 015* [id.]. Neblett, Horne, Chicago SO Ch. and O, Abbado.

(M) *** HMV SLS 802/*TCC2-POR 54293* [Ang. S 3634]. Schwarzkopf, Rössl-Majdan, Philh. Ch. and O, Klemperer.

*** Decca Dig. **410 202-2**; D 229 D 2/*K 229 K 22* [Lon. LDR/*5*- 72006]. Buchanan, Zakai, Chicago SO Ch. and O, Solti.

(M) *** Decca Jub. DJB/*KDJBC* 2001 (2). Harper, Watts, LSO Ch., LSO, Solti.

(M) *** CBS 61282/3 [Odys. Y2-32681]. Cundari, Forrester, Westminster Ch., NYPO, Walter.

**(*) HMV Dig. SLS/*TCC-SLS* 5243 (2/*1*) [Ang. DS/*4X2S* 3916]. Mathis, Soffel, LPO Ch., LPO, Tennstedt.

(M) *(**) CBS [M2/*M2T* 32681]. Armstrong, Baker, Edinburgh Fest. Ch., LSO, Bernstein.

(M) ** DG Priv. 2726/*3372* 062 [id.]. Mathis, Procter, Bav. R. Ch. and SO, Kubelik.

(B) ** DG Walkman *413 149-4*. (from above recording, cond. Kubelik).

(M) (**) Decca mono D 264 D 2/*K 264 K 22* (2). Ferrier, Vincent, Concg. Ch. and O, Klemperer.

If on occasion Abbado has seemed to be a little too controlled on record, his collaboration with the Chicago orchestra in this, which was his first recording of a Mahler symphony, combines almost miraculous precision with electrifying urgency. The total conviction of the performance establishes itself in the very first bars, weighty yet marvellously precise on detail, with dotted rhythms sharply brought out. It proves a performance of extremes, with variations of tempo more confidently marked than is common but with concentration so intense there is no hint of self-indulgence. The delicacy of the Chicago orchestra in the second and third movements is as remarkable as its precision – the second movement is relatively fast, like an elegant minuet – while the great contrasts of the later movements prove a challenge not only to the performers but to the DG engineers, who produce sound of superlative quality – even if the actual range of dynamic may prove a problem to those anxious not to annoy the neighbours. Generally the singing is as splendid as the playing, but if there is even a minor disappointment, it lies in the closing pages. Other versions – such as Klemperer's or Solti's – there convey a more overwhelming emotional involvement, the triumph of Judgement Day itself, whereas Abbado keeps his sharpness of focus to the very end. The tape transfer is impressive, maintaining the very wide dynamic range with only a degree of hiss in the quietest moments, but accommodating the climaxes without strain.

Klemperer on HMV gives one of his most compelling performances on record, bringing out the music's ruggedness. The first movement, taken at a fairly fast tempo, is intense and earth-shaking, and that is surely as it should be in a work which culminates in a representation of Judgement Day itself. Though in the last movement some of Klemperer's speeds are designedly slow he conveys supremely well the mood of transcendent heavenly happiness in the culminating passage, with chorus and soloists themselves singing like angels. The Last Trump brings a shudder of excitement to make one forget any prejudice against such literal representation. The less grand middle movements too have their simple charm under Klemperer, and the recording is among EMI's best. The cassette, issued quite separately in EMI's 'Portrait of the Artist' series, puts the symphony on one double-length tape. The transfer is successful but ideally might have been made at a slightly higher level; the pianissimo choral detail is less sharp here than with Solti. The discs have been impressively remastered and the recording can still hold its own against most competition.

In digital sound of extraordinary power Solti re-recorded with the Chicago orchestra this symphony which with the LSO was one of the finest achievements of his earlier Mahler series. Differences of interpretation are on points of detail merely, with a lighter, more elegant rendering of the minuet-rhythms of the second movement. Though the digital recording is not always so well balanced as the earlier analogue (Isobel Buchanan and Mira Zakai are too close, for example) the weight of fortissimo in the final hymn, not to mention the Judgement Day brass, are breathtaking. Interpretatively too the outer movements are as fiercely intense as before, but it is only in the concluding passage of the last movement that Solti really outshines the DG performance of Abbado with the same orchestra, a reading that is more affectionate in all five movements without ever sounding mannered, featuring playing just as brilliant. The Decca cassettes are first-class, sparklingly clear, full and wide-ranging. The compact discs with their extra precision make the brilliant sound of the Chicago orchestra even more immediate. In the last movement the first cellist's groan before his solo – made more evident on CD – may worry some listeners.

Solti's earlier recording (1966) has been reissued on Jubilee and it remains a demonstration of the outstanding results Decca were securing with analogue techniques at that time. In the slow *Ländler* of the second movement Solti brings superb refinement of detail and a precise control of dynamic, and again in the third movement he concentrates with hushed intensity on precise control of dynamic and atmosphere and the natural ambience of the recording is particularly striking here (on both LP and chrome tapes, for there is no appreciable difference between them). Helen Watts is wonderfully expressive in the chorale, conveying real 'inner' feeling, while the choral focus has a rapt intensity that is the more telling when the recording perspectives are so believable.

Like Walter's other Mahler recordings, the CBS reissue remains a classic of the gramophone. In the first movement there is restraint and in the second a gracefulness which provide a strong contrast with a conductor like Klemperer. The recording, one of the last Walter made in New York, is remarkably good for its period, and for those who warm to Walter's Mahler this will be an indispensable set.

Tennstedt's is a dedicated performance, not quite as well played as the finest, conveying

Mahlerian certainties in the light of day, underplaying neurotic tensions. The recording is excellent and the work is conveniently fitted on a single chrome tape, also of EMI's highest quality.

Bernstein made a memorable television film concurrently with recording this symphony in Ely Cathedral. The CBS set with the LSO is valuable in recalling that idiosyncratic performance with its superb contributions from the two soloists, not to mention the chorus and orchestra, but the recording is far too badly balanced for the discs to be recommended generally.

Kubelik's comparatively refined approach is enjoyable enough and he is certainly well recorded. But there is not enough thrust, and the performance fails to give any kind of monumental impression. The cassette transfer is one of DG's best, clear and vivid with an excellent choral focus. Kubelik's recording has additionally been issued at what amounts to bargain price on a Walkman cassette, with the recording sounding strikingly vivid on chrome tape.

It is fascinating to eavesdrop on Klemperer's live performance recorded from Dutch radio on 12 July 1951 towards the end of Kathleen Ferrier's brief career. The mono sound is limited but reasonably clear. What is disappointing is the lack of the very quality one looks for in a live performance, the drive and thrust which are often difficult to recapture in the studio. Only in the final movement and its vision of heaven does the magic quality at last emerge at full intensity, but even there the later Philharmonia studio performance gives a more complete idea of Klemperer's genius, and elsewhere there is no question of the superiority of the studio account, one of the conductor's strongest statements. The soloists are wonderfully characterful, Vincent as well as Ferrier. These are the two who appeared in the first performance of Britten's *Spring symphony* and here provide the best justification for hearing the set. The cassette transfer is clear and clean.

Symphony No. 3 in D min.

*** DG Dig. 2741/*3382* 010 (2) [id.]. Norman, V. State Op. Ch., V. Boys' Ch., VPO, Abbado.

*** HMV Dig. SLS/*TC-SLS* 5195 (2) [Ang. DS/*4Z 2S* 3902]. Wenkel, Southend Boys' Ch., ladies of LPO Ch., LPO, Tennstedt.

(M) *** Uni. RHS 302/3. Procter, Wandsworth School Ch., Amb. S., LSO, Horenstein.

*** RCA [ARL2/*CRK2* 1757 (2)]. Horne, Ellyn Children's Ch., Chicago SO Ch. and O, Levine.

(M) **(*) CBS 77206 (2) [M2S 675]. Lipton, Schola Cantorum Ch., Boys' Ch., NYPO, Bernstein.

**(*) Decca Dig. D 281 D 2/*K 281 K 22* (2) [Lon. LDR/*5*-72014]. Dernesch, Glen Ellyn Children's Ch., Chicago SO Ch. and O, Solti.

**(*) Decca D 117 D 2/*K 117 K 22* (2) [Lon. CSA 2249]. Forrester, LAPO Ch. and O, Mehta.

(M) ** DG Priv. 2726 063 (2). Thomas, Bav. R. Women's Ch., Tolz Ch., Bav. R. SO, Kubelik.

*(*) Decca SET 385/6 [Lon. CSA 2223]. Watts, Wandsworth School Boys' Ch., Amb. Ch., LSO, Solti.

With sound of spectacular range, Abbado's performance is sharply defined and deeply dedicated. The range of expression, the often wild mixture of elements in this work, is conveyed with extraordinary intensity, not least in the fine contributions of Jessye Norman and the two choirs. The chrome cassette transfer is not made at the highest level and while the sound is generally very good, the pianissimos (the famous posthorn solos, for instance) lose a degree of projection and the background noise becomes apparent.

Tennstedt too gives an eloquent reading, spaciousness underlined with measured tempi. With Ortrun Wenkel a fine soloist and the Southend boys adding lusty freshness to the bell music in the fifth movement, the HMV performance with its noble finale is very impressive, and it is splendidly recorded on both disc and cassette. On tape the quality only slips slightly at the choral entry, where the focus is marginally less sharp than on disc.

More than the earlier issues of Mahler, Nielsen and Simpson in Unicorn's excellent series of records with Horenstein, this account of the Mahler *Third* shows the conductor at his most intensely committed. The manner is still very consistent in its simple dedication to the authority of the score, its rejection of romantic indulgence, but with an extra intensity the result has the sort of frisson-making quality one knew from live Horenstein performances. Above all the restraint of the finale is intensely compelling. Though the strings are rather backwardly balanced and the timpani are too prominent, the recording quality is both beautiful and brilliant. Fine vocal contributions from Norma Procter, the Ambrosian Singers and the Wandsworth School Boys' Choir.

James Levine directs a superbly rhythmic account of the *Third Symphony,* less severe than that of Horenstein, with splendidly judged tempi which allow extra swagger (most important in the first movement), more lilt and more sense of atmosphere. The choral contributions too are outstandingly fine. In the radiant finale Levine's tempo is daringly slow, but he sustains it superbly, though in that movement the recording has some congestion at climaxes. Otherwise the sound is nicely rounded, with the posthorn beautifully balanced in the third movement. (This set is currently not available in the UK.)

Bernstein's reading of the *Third,* one of the first to be recorded in his Mahler cycle, remains one of the most satisfying, strong and passionate with few of the stylistic exaggerations that sometimes overlay his interpretations. His style in the final slow movement is more heavily expressive than Horenstein's, but some will prefer a more extrovert way. The recording copes well with the heavy textures, though next to the finest versions it is somewhat coarse. At mid-price this makes an excellent recommendation.

In Solti's earlier series of Mahler recordings for Decca with the LSO the *Third Symphony* brought disappointment, notably in the brassy and extrovert account of the last movement. That movement in his Chicago version is transformed, hushed and intense, deeply concentrated, building up superbly even though the hastening is a shade excessive towards the end. The other movements have brilliance, freshness and clarity with Helga Dernesch a fine if rather detached soloist. Solti remains a bold Mahler interpreter, missing some of the *Wunderhorn* fun. The virtuoso playing of the Chicago orchestra is brilliantly caught by the wide-ranging recording, though the posthorn of the third movement is placed unatmospherically close. The chrome cassettes offer strikingly beautiful sound, refined, rich and clear. The focus is perhaps marginally less sharp than the LPs, but there is little in it. The transfer level is not quite as high as usual from Decca.

Mehta in his years in Los Angeles rarely recorded a performance so authentically Viennese as this Decca account of Mahler's *Third.* The crisp spring of the first movement leads to a fruitily Viennese view of the second and a carefree account of the third in which the *Wunderhorn* overtones come out vigorously. The singing is excellent, and the sharpness of focus of the reading as a whole is impressive, underlined by brilliant and rather too close recording. (On the strikingly vivid and clear tape version the posthorn solos seem much too near.) Yet the performance leaves a feeling of aggressiveness which detracts from the warmer side of the reading.

There is a practical advantage in Kubelik's version: the first movement is squeezed without a break on to the first side, but this is bought at the expense of tempo. As in the later Mahler symphonies Kubelik is tempted to lighten the music with rushed speeds, and when there are such fine rival versions, his can only be commended to those who want his cycle complete.

Solti's LSO set is a disappointing reading, with not even the merit of good discipline. To compare these same players under Solti and under Horenstein is most illuminating, particularly in the finale, where for Solti there is no half tone.

Symphony No. 4 in G.

*** DG 2531/*3301* 205 [id.]. Mathis, Berlin PO, Karajan.

*** HMV ASD/*TC-ASD* 3783 [Ang. SZ 37576]. Ameling, Pittsburgh SO, Previn.

(M) *** CBS 60124/*40-* [MY/*MYT* 37225]. Raskin, Cleveland O, Szell.

*** RCA [ARL1/*ARK1* 0895]. Blegen, Chicago SO, Levine.

*** HMV ASD/*TCC-ASD* 4344 [Ang. DS/*4XS* 37954]. Popp, LPO, Tennstedt.

*** Ph. Dig. 6514/*7337* 201 [id.]. Price, San Francisco SO, De Waart.

**(*) DG Priv. 2535/*3335* 119 [id.]. Morison, Bav. R. SO, Kubelik.

**(*) Decca Dig. SXDL/*KSXDC* 7501 [Lon.

LDR 1004/*5*-]. Hendricks, Israel PO, Mehta.
**(*) Chan. Dig. ABRD/*ABTD* 1025. Margaret Marshall, SNO, Gibson.
** DG 2530/*3300* 966 [id.]. Von Stade, VPO, Abbado.
(M) ** Ph. Seq. 6527/*7311* 203 [id.]. Ameling, Concg. O, Haitink.
** Pearl SHE 552. Harper, Berlin R. SO, Maazel.

With playing of incomparable refinement – no feeling of rusticity here – Karajan directs a performance of compelling poise and purity, not least in the slow movement, with its pulse very steady indeed, most remarkably at the very end. Karajan's view of the finale is gentle, wistful, almost ruminative, with the final stanzas very slow and legato, beautifully so when Edith Mathis's poised singing of the solo is finely matched. Not that this quest for refinement means in any way that joy has been lost in the performance, and with glowing sound it is a worthy companion to Karajan's other Mahler recordings. The cassette is of demonstration quality; the sound is full, natural and transparent and carries the widest dynamic range without a trace of congestion.

Previn recorded this symphony immediately before taking the Pittsburgh orchestra on a European tour, where they proved – as on this record – what an outstanding band they have become. Previn starts the first movement slower than usual, underlining the marked speed-changes very clearly, and the second movement is unusually light and gentle. But it is the spaciousness of the slow movement, at a very measured pace, that provides total fulfilment, followed by a light and playful account of the finale, with Ameling both sweet-toned and characterful. The recording has outstanding depth and range. The cassette transfer is vivid and full, and undoubtedly wide-ranging, but it has marginally less bloom than the LP.

Szell's recording sounds somewhat dated now, although it was good for its day (1967) and the performance is undoubtedly a great one, one of his finest achievements on record. His approach is cool, but the music blossoms, partly because of the marvellous attention to detail but more positively because of the committed and radiantly luminous orchestral playing. The central climax of the slow movement has superb exuberance and the closing pages have rarely sounded so beautiful on record. In the finale Szell found the ideal soprano to match his conception: Judith Raskin sings without artifice, and her voice has an open colouring like a child's. An outstanding choice in the medium-price range.

James Levine, a thoughtful yet warmly committed Mahlerian, mature beyond his years, draws a superlative performance from the Chicago orchestra, one which stands comparison with the finest versions, bringing out not just the charm but the deeper emotions too. The subtlety of his control of tempo, so vital in Mahler, is superbly demonstrated, and though he may not quite match the nobility of Szell in the great slow movement, he has the advantage of more brilliant, modern recording. Blegen makes a fresh, attractive soloist. (This version is not available in the UK.)

Tennstedt conducts a strong, spacious reading which yet conveys an innocence entirely in keeping with this most endearing of the Mahler symphonies. He makes the argument seamless in his easy transitions of speed, yet he never deliberately adopts a coaxing, charming manner, and in that he is followed most beautifully by Lucia Popp, the pure-toned soloist in the finale. The peak of the work as Tennstedt presents it lies in the long slow movement, here taken very slowly and intensely. The recording is among EMI's finest, full and well-balanced, and there is a good, though not outstanding, cassette.

De Waart's is an attractively lightweight reading, full of sparkle and charm, crowned by an outstandingly beautiful solo from Margaret Price in the finale. The fine playing of the San Francisco orchestra is matched by the clear and beautifully co-ordinated recording. The chrome tape is acceptable, but has less sparkle and clarity than the disc. The transfer level is only modest.

The Bavarian orchestra phrase beautifully, and their playing has great vitality. With generally faster tempi than is common, the effect is light and luminous, with a charming, boyish account of the final song from Elsie Morison. Recommended to those collecting Kubelik in Mahler, but it is not so generally recommendable as Szell. There is an outstanding cassette version.

Fresh and spontaneous-sounding, with an apt hint of rusticity, Mehta's reading with the Israel orchestra has excellent digital sound, cleanly defined if rather forward, so that individual players can occasionally be picked out in the string sections. The slow movement is unusually expansive, finely concentrated, and though Mehta occasionally indulges in an exaggerated espressivo, it is a performance which holds together in its amiability, not least in the finale, where Barbara Hendricks brings a hint of boyishness to the solo. The cassette transfer has very striking clarity, with luminous woodwind quality, although the sharpness of the detail tends to emphasize the slightly febrile timbre of the Israeli upper strings.

Gibson secures some delightfully fresh and stylish playing from his Scottish orchestra. His is a characteristically unmannered reading, slightly wanting in drama but not in tenderness. The finale, however, lacks some of the repose essential in this child-song, with Margaret Marshall sounding a little tense. The digital recording conveys the breadth and clarity of the sound impressively without lacking ambient bloom, and the cassette transfer is first-class.

After his superb performance of the Mahler *Second* with the Chicago orchestra, Abbado's record of the *Fourth* is disappointing, above all in the self-consciously expressive reading of the slow movement. There is much beauty of detail, but the Vienna Philharmonic has played and has been recorded better than this.

Haitink's version is predictably well played and recorded, but the performance is rather sober and lacking in imaginative detail and fire. The cassette transfer is of good quality, fresh and pleasing, but this remains rather disappointing.

Maazel's account with the Berlin Radio Orchestra appeared first on Concert Hall, but on Pearl remains at full price. It is a clean-cut, forthright reading, brightly recorded and well played except that the slow movement, taken at a relatively fast tempo, sounds a little unsettled, failing to convey its emotional warmth. The song-finale too sounds unspontaneous, despite some beautiful singing from Heather Harper.

Symphony No. 5 in C sharp min.

❀ *** HMV SLS/*TC-SLS* 785 (2). New Philh. O, Barbirolli – *5 Rückert Lieder*.*** ❀

*** DG 2707 081/*3370 006* (2) [id.]. Berlin PO, Karajan – *Kindertotenlieder*.***

(*) Decca SET 471-2/*KCET2 7001* [CSA/5- 2228]. Chicago SO, Solti – *Des Knaben Wunderhorn*.(*)

(*) DG 2707 128/*3370 040* (2) [id.]. Chicago SO, Abbado – *5 Rückert Lieder*.*

** CBS [M2S-698]. NYPO, Bernstein – *Kindertotenlieder*.**

(M) ** DG Sig. 2543/*3343* 535 [id.]. Bav. R. SO, Kubelik.

Symphony No. 5; Symphony No. 10 in F sharp: Adagio.

*** HMV SLS/*TC-SLS* 5169 (2) [Ang. SZ 3883]. LPO, Tennstedt.

**(*) RCA [ARL 2/*ARK 2* 2905]. Phd. O, Levine.

**(*) Ph. 6700 048/*7505 069* (2) [id.]. Concg. O, Haitink.

** Decca SXL 6806/7 [Lon. CS/5- 2248]. LAPO, Mehta.

Barbirolli's recording of Mahler's *Fifth* provides a unique experience. On any count it is one of the greatest, most warmly affecting performances he ever committed to record, and it brings on the fourth side a performance of the *5 Rückert Lieder* with Janet Baker as soloist that achieves a degree of poetic intensity rarely heard on record, even from these superlative artists. The *Fifth* saw Barbirolli as ever an expansive Mahlerian, yet far more than in his recording of the *Sixth* (made a year earlier) his concentration convinces one that his tempi are right. Though the very opening may lose something in sheer dramatic bite there is always a sense of power in reserve, and when the main funeral march emerges there is a frisson such as one would experience in the concert hall but rarely on record. A classic performance, given a gloriously ripe recording. Very good cassettes too.

Karajan's characteristic emphasis on polish and refinement goes with sharpness of focus. His is at once the most beautiful as well as the most intense version available, starting with an account of the first movement which brings more biting funeral-march rhythms than any rival. Resplendent recording, rich and refined, to match the radiant playing of the Berlin Philharmonic. Christa Ludwig's warm singing in *Kindertotenlieder* marks out a valuable fill-up. The cassette version is of excellent quality.

Rather like Barbirolli, Tennstedt takes a ripe and measured view of this symphony, and though his account of the lovely *Adagietto* lacks the full tenderness of Barbirolli's (starting with an intrusive balance for the harp), this is an outstanding performance, thoughtful on the one hand, warm and expressive on the other. The first movement of the *Tenth Symphony* makes an acceptable fill-up; the recording, not quite as detailed as in Tennstedt's later digital Mahler recordings with the LPO, is warm and full to match the performance. The cassettes, however, are rather patchy, not as cleanly focused as the best EMI transfers. (The older Barbirolli set is preferable.)

Apart from a self-consciously slow account of the celebrated *Adagietto,* Levine directs a deeply perceptive and compelling performance, one which brings out the glories of the Philadelphia Orchestra. The other movements are beautifully paced, and the fourth side brings a wonderfully luminous account of the first movement of the *Tenth Symphony*.

Those who resist Barbirolli's expansiveness and Karajan's refinement will probably find the ideal alternative in Haitink's fresh and direct reading, with finely judged tempi, unexaggerated observance of Mahler's markings, and refined playing from the Concertgebouw. The famous *Adagietto* is relatively cool, but its beauty is as intense as ever. Good, well-balanced Philips recording, and a first-class cassette.

The opening *Funeral march* sets the tone of Solti's reading. At a tempo faster than usual, it is wistful rather than deeply tragic, even though the dynamic contrasts are superbly pointed, and the string tone could hardly be more resonant. In the pivotal *Adagietto* too Solti secures intensely beautiful playing, but the result lacks the 'inner' quality one finds so abundantly in Barbirolli's interpretation. Gloriously rich if slightly over-reverberant recording, and the cassette transfer is characteristically brilliant.

Abbado's readings of Mahler with the Chicago orchestra are always refined but they are not consistently convincing. Unlike the superb account of No. 2, this version of No. 5 lacks something in spontaneity. The *Adagietto,* for example, is hardly at all slower than with Karajan but the phrasing by comparison sounds self-conscious. Nonetheless it is a polished reading, with first-rate digital sound, which can be recommended to those collecting Abbado's Mahler series. The cassette transfer has an impressively wide range and matches the discs closely; it is a pity that on the first tape the opening trumpet solo is discoloured for a few bars, but this may not apply to later batches. The *Rückert Lieder* – beautifully sung by Hanna Schwarz – offer demonstration quality in both media.

The highlight of Bernstein's performance is in the *Adagietto* for strings and harp, which has a heady beauty so delicate one holds one's breath. Elsewhere Bernstein's care for detail means that he never seems quite to plumb the depth of Mahler's inspiration. The first movement, for example, seems too careful, for all the virtuosity of the playing. (This set is not available in the UK.)

Kubelik in the opening *Funeral march* is gentle rather than tragic, and his relative lightness of manner, coupled with refined textures, misses the epic quality of the work. Nor does he succeed in disguising the patchwork structure of the last movement. However, the reissue of this version on a single medium-priced record puts it in the bargain range. The sound is bright and clear, slightly lacking in depth and with a rather dry bass. There is virtually no difference in quality between disc and chrome tape.

Brilliant as the recording is of Mehta's Los Angeles version, and the playing too, it misses the natural warmth of expression that the same conductor found in his reading of No. 2 with the Vienna Philharmonic. Most impressive is the virtuoso scherzo, but in their different ways the opening *Funeral march* and the beautiful *Adagietto* both lack the inner quality which is essential if the faster movements are to be aptly framed. The brilliance of the finale is exaggerated by Mehta's very fast tempo, missing the *Wunderhorn* overtones of this most optimistic of Mahler's conclusions. The cassette transfer is cleanly focused, one of Decca's best.

Symphonies No. 5; 6 in A min.

** CBS Dig. D-3 37875/*40*- (3) [id.]. VPO, Maazel.

Maazel's coupling of the *Fifth* and *Sixth* brings superb playing from the Vienna Philharmonic. His is a direct, unexaggerated approach, refreshing and clear but, particularly in slow movements, he misses the depth and emotional intensity which is an essential element in Mahler. Bright, full recording.

Symphony No. 6 in A min.
*** DG 2707 106/*3370 026* (2) [id.]. Berlin PO, Karajan.
*** HMV Dig. SLS/*TC-SLS* 143574-3/*5* [Ang. DSB/*4X2S* 3945]. LPO, Tennstedt.
*** Decca SET 469/70 [Lon. CSA 2227]. Chicago SO, Solti – *Lieder eines fahrenden Gesellen.****
(B) **(*) CfP CFP/*TC-CFP* 414424-3/*5*. New Philh. O, Barbirolli.
**(*) DG 2707 117/*3370 031* (2) [id.]. Chicago SO, Abbado.
**(*) Ph. 6700 034 (2). Concg. O, Haitink.
(M) **(*) DG Priv. 2726 065. Bav. RSO, Kubelik – *4 Rückert Lieder.****

Symphony No. 6 (revised by Erwin Ratz); *Gustav Mahler remembered:* reminiscences by Mahler's daughter, Anna Mahler, associates and musicians who played under his baton.
(M) *** CBS 77215 (2) [(d) Col. M3S-776]. NYPO, Bernstein.

Symphony No. 6 (*also includes Jascha Horenstein reminiscing with Alan Blyth*).
(M) *** Uni. RHS 320/1. Stockholm PO, Horenstein.

With superlative playing from the Berlin Philharmonic, Karajan's reading of the *Sixth* is a revelation, above all in the slow movement, which here becomes far more than a lyrical interlude. With this *Andante moderato* made to flower in poignant melancholy and with a simpler lyrical style than Karajan usually adopts, it emerges as one of the greatest of Mahler's slow movements. The whole balance of the symphony is altered. Though the outer movements firmly stamp this as the darkest of the Mahler symphonies, their sharp focus in Karajan's reading – with contrasts of light and shade heightened – makes them both compelling and refreshing. Significantly, in his care for tonal colouring Karajan brings out a number of overtones related to Wagner's *Ring*. The superb DG recording, with its wide dynamics, adds enormously to the impact. It is given a characteristically sophisticated cassette transfer, although on tape the bass response is a little dry.

Tennstedt's reading is characteristically strong, finding more warmth than usual even in this dark symphony. So the third movement *Andante* is open and songlike, almost Schubertian in its sweetness, though there is never any question of Tennstedt taking a sentimental view of Mahler. His expressiveness tends towards conveying joy rather than Mahlerian neurosis, and that for some may make this too comfortable a reading. Karajan has more power and bite; his scale is bigger and bolder, the Berlin playing more brilliant. Naturally Tennstedt in his digital recording gains from extra range in the recording of the famous hammer-blows of fate in the finale. The sound is warm and rich, if not as detailed as some from this source.

Solti draws stunning playing from the Chicago orchestra. This was his first recording with them after he took up his new post as principal conductor, and, as he said himself, it represented a love-affair at first sight. The electric excitement of the playing confirms this and with brilliant, immediate but atmospheric recording, Solti's rather extrovert approach to Mahler is here at its most impressive. His fast tempi may mean that he misses some of the deeper emotions, but with an outstandingly successful performance of the *Wayfaring Lad* cycle on the fourth side (Yvonne Minton a splendid soloist) this is a very convincing and attractive set.

Leonard Bernstein's account of the *Sixth* stands out even among the other fine Mahler recordings he has made. One can argue that his tempi are inclined to be too fast – particularly in the first movement, which no longer sounds like a funeral march – but here, even more than usual, the searing intensity of a live Bernstein performance comes over, and the experience puts any rival version in the shade. The recording is one of CBS's finest, despite the usual close-up sound. The fourth side includes an interesting collection of personal reminiscences of the composer.

Though a studio performance more polished than this live one from the Stockholm Philharmonic would have been even more welcome, there is a firm place for Horenstein's version on Unicorn. At a more measured tempo than most recording conductors (though not so measured as Barbirolli), Horenstein finds extra weight in the first movement, a sober reading that holds together with wonderful concentration. Not that Horenstein's view of Mahler lacks flexibility, and the slow movement brings the most persuasive rubato. The finale brings another broad, noble reading, though it involves an unfortunate side-break. Horenstein's reminiscences take up the second half of side four. Considering that this is a live performance, the recording is amazingly faithful.

Barbirolli's account – reissued on CfP at bargain price – dates from 1968. It was originally issued coupled with his even finer account of No. 9. The performance of No. 6 is characteristically expansive, but in places – particularly the long first movement – the tension is allowed to drop. Nevertheless with vintage sound (the cassettes match the discs closely, lacking only a little in transient bite) this is thoroughly worthwhile, especially bearing in mind its modest cost.

Abbado's reading of No. 6 comes somewhere between his radiant account of No. 2 and the too contained rendering he gave of No. 4, all with the Chicago orchestra. Though the playing is superlative, Abbado cannot quite match the incandescence of Karajan on the same label in the first movement, starting at a lower level of tension; but in the third movement he matches Karajan in his measured view, and the finale is drawn tautly together. It is a performance to win admiration rather than move one deeply. The cassette transfer is sophisticated, although the modest transfer level brings some image recession at pianissimo levels, notably in the first movement. Each movement is complete on one side.

Haitink, like Bernstein and Solti, takes a fast tempo for the first movement, but the performance is marked by refinement rather than fire, helped by well-balanced Philips recording. The whole performance reflects Haitink's thoughtful, unsensational approach to the composer, a characteristically satisfying reading.

Kubelik in one of his most successful Mahler recordings directs a performance both refined and searching. Without ever coarsening the result he allows himself generous ritardandi between sections, though ultimately the fineness of control gives a hint of reserve. The 1969 sound remains very acceptable and the coupling - from five years earlier - restores to the catalogue a valuable Fischer-Dieskau performance, four of the five *Rückert Lieder*.

Symphony No. 7 in E min.

*** Decca SET 518/9 [Lon. CSA 2231]. Chicago SO, Solti.

*** Ph. 6700 036 (2) [id.]. Concg. O, Haitink.

*** HMV Dig. SLS/*TC-SLS* 5238 (2) [Ang. DS/*4X2S* 3908]. LPO, Tennstedt.

**(*) RCA [ATC2-4245 (2)]. Chicago SO, Levine.

(*) Ph. Dig. **410 398-2; 410 398-1/*4* [id.]. Concg. O, Haitink.

(M) **(*) DG Priv. 2726 066 (2). Bav. R. SO, Kubelik – *Kindertotenlieder*.***

The sound of Solti's Decca issue is glorious, even riper and more brilliant than that of his two earlier Chicago recordings of Mahler and much clearer. In interpretation this is as successful as his fine account of No. 6, extrovert in display but full of dark implications. The tempi tend to be challengingly fast – at the very opening, for example, and in the scherzo (where Solti is mercurial) and the finale (where his energy carries shock waves in its trail). The second *Nachtmusik* is enchantingly seductive, and throughout the orchestra plays superlatively well. On balance this is even finer than the Haitink version.

Haitink gives a finely wrought, intensely convincing reading. It is less idiosyncratic than the versions of his more flamboyant rivals, but for many this will prove more satisfying for repeated listening, when the drama is clear-headed rather than darkly intense. With Haitink one can see forward more clearly to the sublimities of the *Ninth Symphony*, where his approach to Mahler is so completely at home. The tempo for the most delectable movement of this work, the second *Nachtmusik*, is on the fast side, but Haitink's pointing is still persuasive. The recording is one of Philips' finest.

Tennstedt is predictably spacious in his approach to Mahler's least recorded symphony. The first movement's architectural span is given the kind of expansive structural unity that one associates with Klemperer; but the concentration of the LPO playing under Tennstedt brings more success here than Klemperer found in his disappointing New Philharmonia version. In the central movements Tennstedt is not so imaginative as Solti but he is again at his most impressive in the finale, showing his directness and strength and with vigorous support from the LPO players, who are on top form throughout the symphony. The HMV digital recording is characteristically clear in detail. The cassette equivalent is ideally laid out on a single chrome tape (presented in a box), with the first two movements on side one and the remainder on side two. The quality is beautifully clear and detailed, yet expands weightily in the finale.

With a broad, warmly expressive account of the first movement and a riotously extrovert one of the finale, Levine's reading has many of the fine qualities of his other Mahler recordings but, with recording balances odd at times and some rhythmic self-indulgence, it cannot match the finest. At present this set is not available in the UK.

Beauty is the keynote of Haitink's newer, digitally recorded version of this most problematic of the Mahler symphonies. The superb playing of the Concertgebouw Orchestra is richly and spaciously caught but, with spacious speeds to match, tensions have tended to ease since Haitink's earlier account. The vision of darkness is softened a degree. The chrome cassettes are refined and clear but – as usual with Philips – transferred at a modest level.

Now coupled with Fischer-Dieskau's version of the *Kindertotenlieder*, Kubelik's *Seventh* is attractively introduced to the medium-priced range. Kubelik is at his most impressive in what can be described as Mahler's *Knaben Wunderhorn* manner. The start of the second movement has an open-air innocence, but conversely Kubelik produces no sense of nocturnal mystery in the second *Nachtmusik*. The outer movements are characteristically refined and resilient, but something of Mahler's strength is missing. Fine recording.

Symphony No. 8 in E flat (*Symphony of 1000*).
❀ *** Decca SET 534-5/*KCET2 7006* [Lon. OSA/*5* 1295]. Harper, Popp, Minton, Watts, Kollo, Shirley-Quirk, Talvela, V. Boys' Ch., V. State Op. Ch. and Singverein, Chicago SO, Solti.

*(**) CBS [M2S-751 (2)]. Spoorenberg, Jones, Reynolds, Procter, Mitchinson, Ruzdjak, McIntyre, Leeds Fest. Ch., Orpington Junior Singers, Highgate School Boys Ch., Finchley Children's Music Group, LSO, Bernstein.

** Ph. Dig. **410 607-2**; 6769/*7654* 069 (2) [id.]. Robinson, Blegen, Quivar, Riegel, Luxon, Howell, Tanglewood Fest. Ch., Boston Boys' Ch. and SO, Ozawa.

** DG Priv. 2726/*3372* 053 (2). Arroyo, Spoorenberg, Hamari, Procter, Grobe, Fischer-Dieskau, Crass, Bav. R., N. and W. German R. Choirs, Regensburg Cath. Ch., Bav. R. SO, Kubelik.

** Ph. 6700 049 (2) [id.]. Cotrubas, Harper, Van Bork, Finnila, Dieleman, Cochran, Prey, Sotin, Amsterdam Choirs, Concg. O, Haitink.

Solti's is a classic recording. Challenged by the tightest possible recording schedule, the American orchestra and European singers responded to Solti at his most inspired with a performance that vividly captures the atmosphere of a great occasion – essential in this of all works. There is nothing cautious about the surging dynamism of the first movement, the electrifying hymn, *Veni Creator spiritus*; and the long second movement setting the final scene of Goethe's *Faust* proceeds through its contrasted sections with unrelenting intensity. The hushed prelude in Solti's hands is sharp-edged in pianissimo, not at all comforting, while the magnificent recording copes superbly with every strand of texture and the fullest range of dynamic – spectacularly so in the great final crescendo to the words *Alles vergängliche*. A triumph for everyone concerned, and the quality of the cassette transfer is little short of astonishing.

Bernstein recorded Mahler's epic *Symphony of a Thousand* at Walthamstow Town Hall in the days immediately following a hazard-ridden live performance at the Royal Albert Hall, in which emergency measures had to be taken to reinforce the choral strength. You would hardly know that from this fine recorded performance, though the hazards still left their mark. One of them was entirely to the good, the last-minute inclusion of John Mitchinson among the soloists following his predecessor's indisposition. The Orpington Junior Singers too did valiant work in taking on more than their share of the children's choir music. In the final recorded account the Leeds Festival Chorus is strongly stiffened with professional choristers, and the result is splendidly incisive. The unfortunate point, undermining much of the superb achievement in the performance, is the closeness of sound and resulting lack of atmosphere in the recording quality. This of all symphonies requires spacious reverberant sound, and here one seems to be among the very performers.

Though the Philips digital recording is very good indeed, Ozawa's Boston reading of the *Symphony of a Thousand* rather lacks the weight and intensity of its finest rivals. It is a performance which has one thinking back to earlier Mahler of *Wunderhorn* vintage rather than accepting the epic scale. There is much beautiful singing and playing, recorded in a mellow acoustic, but this work needs more sense of occasion. On CD the refinement and beauty of the recording are particularly striking in the work's closing section.

Even in this massive symphony Kubelik concentrates on refinement, and the recording engineers faithfully match him. The result is crisp and clear but largely unexciting, giving little idea of a live occasion. Generally good solo singing. There is an excellent cassette transfer, even if the level is not especially high.

Haitink's reading, characteristically thoughtful, lacks the electricity needed in this work, and the solo singing is very variable, while the recording lacks the expansive atmosphere one wants in such massive music.

Symphony No. 9 in D min.

*** Ph. 6700 021 (2) [id.]. Concg. O, Haitink.

*** DG Dig. **410 726-2** (2) [id.]. Berlin PO, Karajan.

*** DG 2707 125/*3370 038* (2) [id.]. Berlin PO, Karajan.

*** HMV SLS/*TC-SLS* 5188 [Ang. SZB/*4Z2S* 3899]. LPO, Tennstedt.

(B) *** CfP CFP/*TC-CFP* 414426-3/*5*. Berlin PO, Barbirolli.

(M) *** HMV SXDW 3021 (2). New Philh. O, Klemperer.

(M) *** CBS 61369/70 [(d) Odys. Y2-30308]. Col. SO, Walter – *Lieder eines fahrenden Gesellen*.**

(M) **(*) Decca Jub. 410 264-1/*4* (2) [Lon. CSA 2220]. LSO, Solti.

(*) Decca Dig. **410 012-2; D 274 D 2/*K 274 K 22*. Chicago SO, Solti.

(M) **(*) DG Priv. 2726 067 (2). Bav. R. SO, Kubelik – WOLF: *Penthesilea*.**(*)

** DG 2707 097/*3370 018* [id.]. Chicago SO, Giulini.

** RCA [ARL2/*ARK2* 3641]. Phd. O, Levine.

Haitink is at his very finest in Mahler's *Ninth*, and the last movement, with its slow expanses of melody, reveals a unique concentration. Unlike almost all other conductors he maintains his intensely slow tempo from beginning to end. This is a great performance, beautifully recorded, and with the earlier movements superbly performed – the first movement a little restrained, the second pointed at exactly the right speed, and the third gloriously extrovert and brilliant – this will be for most Mahlerians a first recommendation.

Karajan's two recordings both transcend his earlier Mahler. In the 1980 analogue version it is the combination of richness and concentration in the outer movements that makes for a reading of the deepest intensity, while the middle two movements bring point and humour as well as refinement and polish. In the finale Karajan is not just noble and stoic; he finds the bite of passion as well, sharply set against stillness and repose. The recording is rich and spacious with cassettes only marginally less well focused than the discs. Yet within two years Karajan went on to re-record the work even more compulsively at live performances in Berlin and it is this newer version which appears on CD. The major difference is that there is a new, glowing optimism in the finale, rejecting any Mahlerian death-wish, making it a supreme achievement. Despite the problems of live recording, the sound is bright and full, if somewhat close

Tennstedt directs a performance of warmth and distinction, underlining nobility rather than any neurotic tension, so that the outer movements, spaciously drawn, have architectural grandeur. The second movement is gently done, and the third, crisp and alert, lacks just a little in adrenalin. The playing is excellent and the recording rich. The cassette issue (on one double-length tape, but supplied in a box) is vivid and well detailed, although the upper range is a trifle over-bright and needs smoothing.

Barbirolli's version from 1964 – now reissued at bargain price – is also one of the finest accounts of the *Ninth* ever recorded. Barbirolli greatly impressed the Berliners with his Mahler performances live, and this recording reflects the players' warmth of response. He opted to record the slow and intense finale before the rest, and the beauty of the playing makes it a fitting culmination. The other movements are strong and alert too, and the sound remains full and atmospheric. The cassette transfer is successful also, only a fraction less refined at the top than the discs.

Klemperer's performance is one of stoic nobility. He recorded it in 1967 after a serious illness, and his refusal to languish pays tribute to his physical and spiritual defiance. Characteristically he insisted on a relatively close balance, with woodwind well forward against warm, full string tone, and the physical power is underlined. The sublimity of the finale comes out the more intensely when overt expressiveness, as here, is held in check, with deep emotion implied rather than made explicit. In the second movement the rustic humour is beautifully pointed, and even the comparative heaviness of the third movement has its justification in bringing out Mahler's parody of academic forms. On the mid-price Concert Classics label it is doubly welcome as one of the very finest of Klemperer's later recordings.

Walter's performance – recorded during his Indian summer in retirement in California – lacks mystery at the very start, but through the long first movement Walter unerringly builds up a consistent structure, controlling tempo more closely than most rivals, preferring a steady approach. The middle two movements similarly are sharply focused rather than genial, and the finale, lacking hushed pianissimos, is tough and stoically strong. A fine performance, not at all the reading one would have predicted from Walter. Mildred Miller's somewhat unimaginative reading of the *Wayfaring Lad* cycle makes an acceptable fill-up on this mid-price reissue.

Solti's 1967 version of Mahler's *Ninth* was an outstandingly successful example of Decca's vintage analogue techniques. The sound is superb, with a fantastic range of dynamic combined with fine detail and a natural perspective. It is a brilliant, dramatic reading, but one which finally falls just a little short of being a great performance in its extrovert approach to the spiritual beauty of the finale. In the middle two movements it would be hard to match Solti for the point and precision of the playing. The tempo for the second movement *Ländler* may be slow, but with such pointing the slowness is amply justified – quite apart from following Mahler's marking. The third movement is given the most brilliant account ever; but in the outer movements one feels that Solti is not penetrating deeply enough. He allows Mahler's passionate utterances to emerge too readily. He makes Mahler wear his heart on his sleeve, and although there may be justifications for that, it leaves out something we have come to expect. The matching cassette version is now on chrome tape.

Clear and certain from the very first hushed murmur of the opening movement, Solti in his newest Chicago version – in forward and full digital sound – presents the power of the piece in total conviction. What he lacks in the outer movements is a sense of mystery, and he is short of charm too in the central movements, which should present a necessary contrast. His earlier LSO reading was much warmer and more spontaneous-sounding, with recording balanced more naturally, outstanding for its time. The compact disc version – in a neat two-box hinged package – brings considerable advantage in the absence of background, but with the sound so cleanly focused there is even less feeling of mystery and the lateral spread of sound seems a fraction narrower. The range is formidable. The chrome cassettes are brilliant and clear. Though the sound is treble-orientated, it is very spectacular and free.

Kubelik's restraint in the first movement means that the performance remains on a relatively low pitch of intensity. Though the result is in every way beautiful, it is only in the serenity of the finale that Kubelik achieves the sublimity to equal his finest rivals on record. But with an unusual and unexpected coupling it makes an interesting alternative among mid-price versions, and the recording is still very acceptable.

Giulini's version lacks the very quality one expects of him, dedication. He sets tempi that are a shade too measured for a sense of impetus to assert itself. The orchestral playing and the recording are of the highest quality, although the sound itself, unexpectedly glamorized, does not help in conveying hushed concentration.

After some of his other Mahler recordings Levine's account of the *Ninth* is disappointing. Not only is the sound thin and poorly defined; the slow tempi for the outer movements sound self-conscious, particularly in the finale. Nonetheless there is much fine playing.

Symphony No. 10 in F sharp (*Unfinished;* revised performing edition by Deryck Cooke).
*** HMV Dig. SLS/*TC-SLS* 5206 (2) [Ang. DS 3909]. Bournemouth SO, Rattle.
**(*) RCA Dig. [CTC 2/*CTK 2* 3726]. Phd. O, Levine.

With digital recording of demonstration quality on both disc and tape, Simon Rattle's vivid and compelling reading of the Cooke performing edition has one more than ever convinced that a remarkable revelation of Mahler's intentions was achieved in this painstaking reconstruction. To Cooke's final thoughts Rattle has added one or two detailed amendments, and the finale in particular, starting with its cataclysmic hammer-blows and growling tuba line, is a deeply moving experience, ending not in neurotic resignation but in open optimism. In the middle movements, too, Rattle, youthfully dynamic, has fresh revelations to make. The Bournemouth orchestra plays with dedication, marred only by the occasional lack of fullness in the strings. On cassette the work is admirably laid out on a single double-length tape.

Levine's planned complete Mahler symphony cycle will be the first to include the full five-movement version of the *Tenth Symphony*. The performance typically reveals Levine as a thoughtful and searching Mahlerian; the spacious account of the first movement is splendid, with refined Philadelphia string tone, but the recording, digital or not, does not always do justice to the high violins, which lack something in bloom, not least in the epilogue to the finale. The sound lacks a little in bass too. Although the playing is more polished than that of the Bournemouth orchestra on the rival HMV version, Levine as a rule is less intense, relaxing well in the jolly second movement, for example, but not quite conveying the same range of emotion as the work develops.

LIEDER AND SONG CYCLES

Kindertotenlieder.
(M) *** DG Priv. 2726 066 (2). Fischer-Dieskau, Berlin PO, Boehm – *Symphony No. 7.***(*)*
*** DG 2707 081/*3370 006* (2) [id.]. Ludwig, Berlin PO, Karajan – *Symphony No. 5.****
** CBS [M2S-698]. Tourel, NYPO, Bernstein – *Symphony No. 5.***

(i) *Kindertotenlieder; Lieder eines fahrenden Gesellen;* (ii) *5 Rückert Lieder.*
*** HMV ASD/*TC-ASD* 4409 [(d) Ang. S 36465]. Baker, (i) Hallé O; (ii) New Phil. O, Barbirolli.

Dame Janet Baker's collaboration with Barbirolli represents the affectionate approach to Mahler at its warmest. The Hallé strings are not quite so fine as the New Philharmonia (in the *Rückert Lieder* – see also below), but this generous recoupling brings results that are still intensely beautiful, full of breathtaking moments. The spontaneous feeling of soloist and conductor for this music comes over as in a live performance, and though a baritone like Fischer-Dieskau can give a stronger idea of these appealing cycles, this brings out the tenderness to a unique degree. The remastering has freshened the sound and there is an excellent tape.

Fisher-Dieskau's account of the *Kindertotenlieder* is now only available coupled with Kubelik's performance of Mahler's *Seventh Symphony*. It is a superb performance. The recording is atmospheric, with the singer placed backwardly, but as there is much to enjoy in the orchestra, this balance is highly effective. Karl Boehm's accompaniment is full of imaginative detail.

Ludwig's singing is characterful too, if not so magical as Baker's. It is the distinction and refinement of playing and conducting which stand out above all.

Jeannie Tourel is in excellent voice, but this version will only be of interest to American readers requiring Bernstein's account of the *Fifth Symphony*.

(i) *Kindertotenlieder;* (ii) *Lieder eines fahrenden Gesellen;* (iii) Lieder: Frühlingsmorgen; Hans und Grete; Liebst du um Schönheit; Des Knaben Wunderhorn: Ich ging mit Lust durch einen grünen Wald; Der Schildwache Nachtlied; Wer hat dies Liedlein.

(M) **(*) HMV SXLP/*TC-SXLP* 143652-1/*4*. Ludwig, Philh. O, (i) Vandernoot; (ii) Boult; (iii) Moore (piano).

A valuable and attractive compilation of Ludwig's EMI recordings of Mahler, made when her voice was in its early prime and at its richest, whether in the orchestral items or the songs with piano. Other versions may find a deeper response to the words, but the freshness of the singing here gives much pleasure.

(i; ii; iii) *Kindertotenlieder*; (iv; v; vi; iii) *Des Knaben Wunderhorn*; (vii) *Lieder eines fahrenden Gesellen; Rückert Lieder: Ich bin der Welt; Abhanden gekommen;* (iv; viii; ii; iii) *Das Lied von der Erde*.

**(*) CBS 79355 (3) [M3X 37892]. (i) Baker; (ii) Israel PO; (iii) Bernstein; (iv) Ludwig; (v) Berry; (vi) NYPO; (vii) Von Stade, LPO, Andrew Davis; (viii) Kollo.

Years after Janet Baker made her unforgettable recording of *Kindertotenlieder* with Barbirolli (see above), she gave a sequence of performances in Israel with Bernstein conducting, and this recording was made at the time. The contrasts are fascinating, with the performance under Barbirolli generally more tender and beautiful, the one under Bernstein tougher and darker. The closeness of the CBS recording sometimes exaggerates a slight beat in Dame Janet's voice, never there before, but it is a gloriously involving performance. In the fifth song the storm music is wonderfully sharp and biting with the cradle-song resolution beautifully poised and steady.

The performance of *Des Knaben Wunderhorn* has a comparable vividness. It is arguable that orchestral Lieder need a more dramatic approach than comparable Lieder with piano, and there is a strong case for Bernstein's rich and robust account of these endlessly fascinating songs. Full-blooded recording quality to match the performance.

The recording of the *Lieder eines fahrenden Gesellen* by Frederica von Stade is discussed below. The disappointment of this box is the Israel recording of *Das Lied von der Erde*. Bernstein, Ludwig and Kollo had all earlier appeared in other versions of this work, but the conjunction of the three did not produce extra illumination; rather the reverse. The recording, idiosyncratically balanced and put together from a series of live performances, hardly rivals the best available.

Das klagende Lied (published version).

** Ph. 6500 587 [id.]. Harper, Procter, Hollweg, Netherlands R. Ch., Concg. O, Haitink.

The published version of *Das klagende Lied* is not complete, but the first section of the work, which Mahler jettisoned on its revision, was not destroyed and there is a complete recording by Boulez with Söderström, Lear, Hoffman, Burrows, Haefliger, Nienstedt and the London Symphony Orchestra and Chorus. This is still available in the USA [CBS M2-30061], and we must hope it will be reissued in the UK.

For those who remain content with the two regularly published sections, Haitink's reading must suffice. It is not ideal, lacking urgency and a sense of imaginative imagery, but the recording remains wonderfully refined – it was a demonstration record in its day (1974).

Des Knaben Wunderhorn.

*** HMV ASD/*TC-ASD* 100098-1/*4*. [Ang. S 36547]. Schwarzkopf, Fischer-Dieskau, LSO, Szell.

*** Ph. 9500 316/*7300 572* [id.]. Norman, Shirley-Quirk, Concg. O, Haitink.

In his last years Szell on his visits to Europe made a number of records which reflect a warmth and tenderness in his nature not often revealed in his work in Cleveland. This is one of that superlative group of records, with the most refined control of pianissimo in the orchestra matching the tonal subtleties of the two incomparable soloists. Wit and dramatic point as well as delicacy mark these widely contrasted songs, and the device of using two voices in some of them is apt and effective. There is more polish and style here than in the (now deleted) earlier version with Janet Baker and Geraint Evans, though in some songs that is not surpassed, and the EMI recording quality here is no finer. It has been freshened in this new pressing. The cassette transfer is first-rate, admirably vivid, with fine presence and range as the very opening immediately demonstrates.

Haitink's Philips version is less sharply characterful, but – as usual with this conductor – with such keenly imagined songs, the results are still refined and satisfying. With the help of superb recording – as impressive in the cassette version as on disc – the singing of both Jessye Norman and John Shirley-Quirk brings out the purely musical imagination of Mahler at his finest, while Haitink draws superbly clean and polished playing from his own Concertgebouw Orchestra.

Des Knaben Wunderhorn: excerpts (*Das irdische Leben; Verlor'ne Müh; Wo die schönen Trompeten blasen; Rheinlegendchen*).
(*) Decca SET 471-2/*KCET2 7001* [Lon. CSA/*5*- 2228]. Minton, Chicago SO, Solti – *Symphony No. 5*.(*)

Yvonne Minton, a singer whom Solti encouraged enormously in her career at Covent Garden, makes a splendid soloist in these colourful songs from *Des Knaben Wunderhorn*. A pity that as a fill-up they make rather short measure. Fine recording, as in the symphony, and a brilliant cassette transfer.

Lieder eines fahrenden Gesellen.
*** Decca SET 469/70 [Lon. CSA 2227]. Minton, Chicago SO, Solti – *Symphony No. 6*.***
(M) ** CBS 61369/70 [(d) Odys. Y2-30308]. Miller, Col. SO, Walter – *Symphony No. 9*.***

No one quite rivals Fischer-Dieskau in these songs for his range and beauty of tone, conveying the heartache of the young traveller. His famous mono recording with Furtwängler (coupled with the *Kindertotenlieder* under Kempe) is still available as an EMI import (1 C 063 00898) and so, at the moment of going to press, is his later stereo version with Kubelik, coupled with the *Fifth Symphony* (DG Priv. 2726 064). However, as the latter has now been reissued more economically on a single disc, no doubt the Privilege set will disappear.

Yvonne Minton's performance of the *Wayfaring Lad* cycle is also outstandingly successful and very well recorded too. Mildred Miller's account is less imaginative, but has the advantage of medium price and an outstanding coupling.

Lieder eines fahrenden Gesellen; Lieder und Gesänge (*aus der Jugendzeit*); *Im Lenz; Winterlied.*
❀ *** Hyp. A/*KA* 66100 [id.]. Baker, Parsons.

Dame Janet presents a superb collection of Mahler's early songs with piano, including two written in 1880 and never recorded before, *Im Lenz* and *Winterlied*; also the piano version of the *Wayfaring Lad* songs in a text prepared by Colin Matthews from Mahler's final thoughts, as contained in the orchestral version. The performances are radiant and deeply understanding from both singer and pianist, well caught in atmospheric recording. A heartwarming record.

Lieder eines fahrenden Gesellen; 5 Rückert Lieder; Des Knaben Wunderhorn: excerpts (*Rheinlegendchen; Wer hat dies Liedlein erdacht*).
**(*) CBS 76828/*40*- [Col. M/*MT* 35863]. Von Stade, LPO, Andrew Davis.

Von Stade, normally so assured and stylish, has moments of ungainliness in the taxing *Rückert Lieder,* the legato line not always even. However, both there and, more strikingly, in the highly enjoyable account of the *Wayfaring Lad* cycle, there is a hint of youthful ardour which contrasts with most other recorded performances. If the playing seems at times to lack refinement, it is partly the fault of close recording; but the cassette is one of CBS's best, with rich sound and a striking bloom on the voice.

Das Lied von der Erde.

*** Ph. 6500 831/*7300 362* [id.]. Baker, King, Concg. O, Haitink.

*** DG 2531/*3301* 379 [id.]. Ludwig, Kollo, Berlin PO, Karajan.

*** [Lon. OS/*5*- 26292]. Minton, Kollo, Chicago SO, Solti.

*** HMV SAN 179 [(d) Ang. S 3704]. Ludwig, Wunderlich, New Philh. O and Philh. O, Klemperer.

(M) **(*) Decca Jub. JB/*KJBC* 13 [Lon. OS/*5*- 26005]. King, Fischer-Dieskau, VPO, Bernstein.

** Ph. Dig. 6514/*7337* 112 [id.]. Norman, Vickers, LSO, Sir Colin Davis.

We were taken to task by many readers for the omission of *Das Lied* from our 1982 supplementary edition, as there had been no new recording during the five-year coverage of that book (1977–82). Perhaps this was understandable with Dame Janet Baker's outstanding version dominating the field. Indeed the combination of this most deeply committed of Mahler singers with Haitink, the most thoughtfully dedicated of Mahler conductors, produces radiantly beautiful and moving results, helped by superbly refined and atmospheric recording. If usually these songs reflect a degree of oriental reticence, Dame Janet more clearly relates them to Mahler's other great orchestral songs, so complete is the sense of involvement, with the conductor matching his soloist's mood. The concentration over the long final *Abschied* has never been surpassed on record (almost all of it was recorded in a single take). Haitink impressively opens the cycle with an account of the first tenor song which subtly confirms its symphonic shape, less free in tempo than usual but presenting unusually strong contrasts between the main stanzas and the tender refrain, *Dunkel ist das Leben.* James King cannot match his solo partner, often failing to find fantasy, but his singing is intelligent and more sympathetic than it was on the Bernstein Decca set. The balance with the tenor is admirably realistic, but Dame Janet's voice is brought a shade closer. There is an outstanding cassette version, notable for its warmth and atmosphere, with the voices most naturally caught.

If Haitink presents *Das Lied* as a great symphonic masterpiece (Mahler himself called it a symphony, but for superstitious reasons failed to number it), Karajan presents it as the most seductive sequence of atmospheric songs. It may seem strange that so central a conductor generally avoided Mahler until late in his career, but the result here is everything one could have hoped for, combining Karajan's characteristic refinement and polish with a deep sense of melancholy. The balancing of textures, the weaving of separate strands into a gorgeously transparent tapestry, has never been so flawlessly achieved on record as here, and though some may want more bite in their Mahler sound, Karajan's way of presenting Mahler's orchestration in the subtlest tones rather than in full colours is arguably more apt. In any case what matters is that here, along with his characteristic refinement, Karajan conveys the ebb and flow of tension as in a live performance. He is helped enormously by the soloists, both of whom have recorded this work several times, but never more richly than here. Originally issued as a two-record set, the recording has been successfully remastered on to two sides, with sound quality which cocoons the listener atmospherically, on both disc and the excellent cassette.

In sheer beauty of sound and precision of texture, few versions match Solti's with the Chicago orchestra, helped by brilliant but refined recording. As an interpretation it may lose something in mystery from this very precision, but the concentration of Solti in a consciously less romantic style than Bernstein adopts is highly compelling, above all in the final *Abschied,* slower than usual and bringing in the final section an unusually close observance of Mahler's pianissimo markings. Minton exactly matches Solti's style, consistently at her most perceptive and sensitive, while Kollo presents Heldentenor strength combined with sensitivity. The recording has no need to give the tenor an unnaturally close balance, and the result is the more exciting. The tape transfer is outstandingly brilliant and clear, if perhaps not quite as atmospheric as the Haitink/Philips issue. (This recording has been currently withdrawn from the British Decca catalogue, but remains available in the USA.)

Klemperer's way with Mahler is at its most individual in *Das Lied von der Erde,* and that will enthral some as it must infuriate others. True, there is less case for Klemperer nobility in so evocative oriental-inspired a piece as *Das Lied* than there is in the symphonies, but if the ear is open, Klemperer's preference for slow tempi and his refusal to languish reveal qualities far removed from the heaviness his detractors criticize. With slower speeds the three tenor songs seem initially to lose some of their sparkle and humour, but thanks to superb, expressive singing by the late Fritz Wunderlich – one of the most memorable examples of his artistry on record – and thanks to pointing of rhythm by Klemperer himself, subtle but always clear, the comparative slowness will hardly worry anyone intent on hearing the music afresh as Klemperer intends. As for the mezzo songs, Christa Ludwig sings them with a remarkable depth of expressiveness. In particular the final *Abschied* has the intensity of a great occasion. Excellent recording (1967 vintage) apart from forward woodwind balance.

It is a pity that the great merits of the Bernstein and Klemperer sets of this greatest of orchestral song cycles cannot be married together. The Decca engineers gave Bernstein a ravishing recording aura in which the sound of the Vienna Philharmonic is magically beautiful, and all through his tempi are less wilful than Klemperer's, suiting the music more naturally. So the tenor songs sparkle as they should, and though the final *Abschied,* taken at a very slow tempo indeed, puts extra strain on everyone, Bernstein's intensity carries the performance through. Doubts do arise over the soloists. James King is a strong-voiced tenor, but compared with Wunderlich his phrasing and word-pointing sound comparatively stiff. Fischer-Dieskau is as sensitive as ever, but it is doubtful whether even he can match the finest contralto in the role, for one needs a lightening of tone in the even-numbered songs rather than – as here – a darkening. Nor can a baritone voice give quite such precision to the notes, which Mahler's rounded melodies clearly need. The cassette is vivid and clear, but less rich and atmospheric, with a rather dry bass.

Davis rarely if ever recorded Mahler before his London reading of *Das Lied von der Erde*. Despite beautifully refined playing, the result is stiff and unpersuasive, lacking in tension. Vickers strains uncomfortably in the first song, gritty of tone, with no attempt at a pianissimo for *Dunkel ist das Leben*. Jessye Norman as ever is magnificent, deeply and naturally expressive, quite the finest element in the reading. Full and refined recording with a matching tape (although the transfer level is low).

5 Rückert Lieder (*Blicke mir nicht in die Lieder; Ich atmet' einen linden Duft; Um Mitternacht; Liebst du um Schönheit; Ich bin der Welt abhanden gekommen*).

❀ *** HMV SLS/*TC-SLS* 785 (2). Baker, New Philh. O, Barbirolli – *Symphony No. 5.**** ❀

*** HMV ASD 2721 [Ang. S 36796]. Baker (as above) – ELGAR: *Sea pictures.****

(M) *** DG Priv. 2726 065 (2) (Nos. 1–3; 5 only). Fischer-Dieskau, Berlin PO, Boehm – *Symphony No. 6.***(*)

*** DG 2707 128/*3370 040* (2) [id.]. Schwarz, Chicago SO, Abbado – *Symphony No. 5.***(*)

Few more lovely Mahler records have ever been made than this collection of the *Five Rückert Lieder* used as a fill-up for Barbirolli's ripe and expansive account of the *Fifth Symphony*. The range of tone colour used by Dame Janet Baker in these subtly contrasted songs is ravishing, and it is matched by dedicated playing from the New Philharmonia. No Mahlerian should miss hearing this. The recording is one of the finest ever produced by EMI. For those who, for whatever reason, do not want the symphony, the alternative coupling with Elgar's *Sea Pictures* is equally recommendable.

The missing song in the Fischer-Dieskau recording is *Liebst du um Schönheit*. He sings the others superbly and Karl Boehm's accompaniment is a model in its loving care of detail and shading of orchestral timbre to match and blend with the vocal line.

Hanna Schwarz, too, sings most beautifully and her recording is in the demonstration class.

Malvezzi, Cristofano (1547–99)

La Pellegrina (Intermedi for Medici Wedding – with settings also by: Archeli; Marenzio; Caccini; Bardi; Peri; Cavalieri).
** HMV SLS/*TC-SLS* 130114-3/*9*. Stockholm Chamber Ch., Linde Cons., Linde.

For the wedding of Ferdinando de Medici and Christine of Lorraine in 1589, a group of composers was asked to provide music for the dramatic entertainment, *La Pellegrina;* the result brought the world of music very close to the realm of opera, just about to be invented. Historically important and full of musical interest, this issue is yet disappointing as a performance, partly because of a failure to lighten textures and partly (a related point) because of the far too reverberant acoustic which obscures much detail, choral and instrumental. The result is heavy where it should be sparkling. The boxed cassette issue offers one double-length chrome cassette of good quality, though side two, at a higher level, has greater presence than side one.

Manzoni, Giacomo (born 1932)

Masse: Omaggio a Edgard Varèse.
*** DG Dig. 2532 023 [id./*3302 023*]. Pollini, Berlin PO, Sinopoli – SCHOENBERG: Chamber symphony.***

Manzoni might be broadly classed as a follower of Luigi Nono, a teacher and critic as well as a composer. *Masse* has nothing to do with church liturgy, but refers to measures or quantities, and in its tribute to Varèse follows up a scientific-based mode of thought which proves surprisingly dramatic and colourful. Only the piano solo has much in the way of melodic interest, and Pollini exploits it all he can, not least in the elaborate cadenza-like passages. Sinopoli too in his first major recording already revealed the feeling for texture and dynamic which has since made his conducting so memorable.

Marcello, Alessandro (1669–1750)

6 Oboe concertos (*La Cetra*).
*** DG Arc. 2533 462 [id.]. Holliger, Pellerin, Camerata Bern, Füri.

Alessandro, the brother of the better-known composer Benedetto Marcello, was an accomplished practitioner of the other arts, notably painting, engraving and poetry. The six concertos of *La Cetra* are concertante exercises rather than concertos in the accepted sense of the word, and reveal a pleasing mixture of originality and convention. At times there is a certain want of expertise (as in the *E minor Concerto,* the second of the set) and a reliance on relatively routine gestures, but elsewhere one is surprised by a genuinely alive and refreshing individuality. These performances are vital and keen (occasionally almost aggressively bright) but full of style and character, and the recording is very faithful.

Oboe concerto in C minor (arr. Bonelli).
(B) *** PRT GSGC/*ZCGC* 2003. Rothwell, Pro Arte O, Barbirolli – ALBINONI and CIMAROSA: *Concertos.****

Sir John's subtlety in matters of light and shade within an orchestral phrase brings the music immediately alive and at the same time prevents the rather jolly opening tune from sounding square. There is a beautiful *Adagio* and a gay finale, both showing the soloist on top form, and the well-balanced recording adds to one's pleasure. The cassette is clear and well focused.

Marcello, Benedetto (1686–1739)

6 Cello sonatas.
*** O-L DSLO 546. Pleeth, Webb, Hogwood.

Marcello came from an old patrician family and spent much of his life in public affairs. He was a member of the Council of Forty in his native Venice for some fourteen years and ended his career as Papal Chamberlain at Brescia. If he described himself as 'Dilettante di contrappunto', the fact remains that his music is far from wanting in craftsmanship and polish. The six sonatas for cello and continuo probably appeared in Venice between 1712 and 1717; an English edition comes from 1732. They may lack the emotional scale of the finest baroque music, but they are nonetheless the work of a cultured musician. The melodic ideas are not without appeal and, though the music lacks depth, given such persuasive performances and excellent recording as this, it will undoubtedly give pleasure to connoisseurs of the period. Anthony Pleeth does not try to make this music more searching than it is, and plays with keen musicianship and intelligence. The six sonatas are best heard separately rather than at one sitting.

Marenzio, Luca (1553–99)

La Pellegrina (Intermedi for Medici Wedding) – see under MALVEZZI.

Madrigals: *Come inanti de l'alba; Crudele, acerba; Del cibo onde il signor; Giunta a la tomba; Rimanti inpace; Sola angioletta; Strider faceva; Tirsi morir volea; Venuta era; Vezzosi augelli.*
*** HM HM 1065/*40* . Concerto Vocale.

Luca Marenzio enjoyed an enormous reputation during his lifetime, particularly in England into which his madrigals were introduced by *Musica transalpina.* He served in Poland at the court of Sigismund III and at the Papal Chapel – and also corresponded with Dowland. His output includes some four hundred madrigals and this record gives an altogether admirable picture of his breadth and range. There are poignant and expressive pieces such as *Crudele, acerba* from the last year of his life (1599) which is harmonically daring, and lighter pastoral madrigals such as *Strider faceva,* which this excellent group of singers, occasionally supported by theorbo and lute, project to striking effect. Excellent singing and recording serve to make this a most desirable issue.

Marias, Marin (1656–1728)

La Gamme en forme de petit opéra; Sonata à la marésienne.
*** HM 1105/*40*. L. Bar.

This is something of a curiosity. Published in 1723, *La Gamme* is a string of short character-pieces for violin, viole de gambe and harpsichord that takes its inspiration from the ascending and descending figures of the scale. Although it is *en forme de petit opéra,* its layout is totally instrumental and the varied pieces and dramatic shifts of character doubtless inspire the title. It plays without a break of any kind – unlike, say, the sets of character-pieces one encounters in the Couperin *Ordres,* and its continuity is enlivened by much variety of invention and resource. The *Sonata à la marésienne* is less unusual in character but it, too, has variety and character. The London Baroque is an excellent group, and they are well recorded too.

Marini, Biagio (died 1665)

Sinfonias for strings Nos. 2 and 5; Sonatas for strings Nos. 1–4; Balletto primo (Gagliarda prima; Corrente nona). (i) *Le Lagrime d'Erminia* (1623).
*** O-L DSLO 570. Cons. of Musicke, Rooley or Trevor Jones, (i) with Kirkby and Rogers.

Marini was a younger contemporary of Monteverdi, his life spanning the first half of the seventeenth century. The prize discoveries here are the string sonatas, lively and imaginative; the other instrumental items too are far from routine. The songs are less interesting, but with fresh, characterful singing from Emma Kirkby and Nigel Rogers, they help to fill out the picture of an interesting historical figure long neglected. Performances and recording are typical of the excellent Florilegium series.

Martin, Frank (1890–1974)

Petite symphonie concertante.
(*) Chan. ABR/*ABT* 1060 [id.]. Sydney SO, Otterloo – DEBUSSY: *Danses;* RAVEL: *Introduction and allegro.*
(M) * Sup. 1110 3187. Kodadová, Růžičková, Páliniček, Czech PO, Vajnar – DEBUSSY: *Rhapsody No. 1;* FALLA: *Harpsichord concerto.**

Frank Martin's *Petite symphonie concertante* is arguably his masterpiece, and its highly resourceful contrast of sonorities makes it particularly appealing. It is a searching, inventive and often profound work, though inevitably it causes problems of balance between the three concertante instruments and the double strings. These were solved in its pioneering mono record under Ansermet (Decca LXT 2631), but they seem to have eluded recording engineers fairly consistently in the stereo era. The soloists are a bit forward in this Chandos version, but not unreasonably so, and the performance is atmospheric and committed, capturing much of the work's subtle contrasts and pale colouring. The strings of the Sydney Symphony Orchestra are a little wanting in bloom but this is, *faute de mieux,* the best version currently available and the work is as haunting as it is masterly. There is a successful cassette transfer, lacking only the last degree of upper range.

The Supraphon record also places the soloists rather too close and they loom larger than life in the aural picture. Vajnar adopts a very slow tempo and there is an initial gain in breadth. This is offset, however, by a certain want of impetus and he is slower than the metronome markings in places. He takes four minutes longer than van Otterloo or the dedicatee, Paul Sacher, who recorded it in the 1970s on the Swiss Composers' label (CTS42).

In terra pax (oratorio).
(B) *** Decca DPA 593/4. Buckel, Höffgen, Haefliger, Mollet, Stämpfli, SRO and Ch., Ansermet – HONEGGER: *Le Roi David.***(*)

Frank Martin's beautiful score was commissioned by the Swiss Radio in preparation for the announcement of the end of the 1939–45 war, and it was first performed by Ansermet. Originally this score occupied a whole disc but here it has been accommodated without appreciable loss of quality on a side and a half. Martin's music has an appropriate eloquence and spirituality, and he is admirably served by these fine soloists. The score falls into four short sections, all with biblical texts, and its sincerity and sense of compassion leave a strong impression. Coupled to Honegger's atmospheric pageant *Le Roi David* in an almost equally fine performance, this is an outstanding bargain. The recording, from the mid-1960s, is of high quality.

6 Monologues from Jedermann (Everyman); 3 Fragments from the opera, The Tempest (Der Sturm).
(M) *** DG 2543 819. Fischer-Dieskau, Berlin PO, composer.

Frank Martin's setting of von Hofmannsthal's *Jedermann* was completed during the war, but not orchestrated until 1949, and it made a deep impression at one of the early Edinburgh Festivals. His opera on Shakespeare's *The Tempest* was written in 1956, but so far has failed to establish itself fully, despite sensitive atmospheric writing with the recognizable fingerprints that have made such works as the *Petite symphonie concertante* popular. These performances could hardly be bettered with the composer directing and Fischer-Dieskau displaying all his usual interpretative insight. The recording is very good.

Martinů, Bohuslav (1890–1959)

Comedy on the Bridge: suite. Mirandolina: Saltarello. The Suburban Theatre: suite (arr. Řiha). *Les Trois Souhaits: Le départ* (intermezzo).
(M) *** Sup. 1110 1620. Brno State PO, Jílek.

The first side is occupied by a suite from Act I of *The Suburban Theatre* (1935–6) arranged by Milos Řiha, which is highly attractive and will appeal to Martinů's growing band of admirers. Like the suite from *Comedy on the Bridge,* which Martinů himself arranged, the music has directness and melodic appeal. *Mirandolina* is a light comedy based on Goldoni, dating from the mid-1950s. Perhaps the most interesting of the works here is the intermezzo from *Les Trois Souhaits* (1928–9). None of this music shows Martinů at his most substantial, but it is well played and tolerably well recorded, albeit in a reverberant acoustic.

(i) *Concertino for piano trio and small orchestra;* (ii) *Sinfonietta giocosa for piano and small orchestra.*
(M) *** Sup. 4102 198. Panenka, Czech PO, cond. (i) Neumann (with Suk, Chuchro), (ii) Košler.

The *Sinfonietta giocosa* is one of Martinů's most engaging scores, remarkably high-spirited and carefree given the fact that at the time he was fleeing from the Nazis and living in great privation. The work bubbles over with wit, good humour and an infectious love of life. It is frankly neoclassical in outlook, its opening having something of the gait of a concerto grosso theme. All the tunes sparkle, and if we were living in a just world the score would enjoy the widest popularity. The *Concertino for piano trio and orchestra* is not quite top-drawer Martinů, but it is thoroughly attractive. It is an earlier work, dating from the 1930s, and its melodic inspiration is fresh, without being as memorable as that of its companion on this disc. The performances are lively and keen, and the recording has plenty of presence and clarity of detail, even if the upper strings have a certain edge that needs to be tamed. Strongly recommended all the same.

(i) *Cello concerto No. 1;* (ii) *Double concerto for violin, piano and orchestra.*
(M) *** Sup. 110 1348. Czech PO, Košler, with (i) Chuchro; (ii) Grumliková, Kolar.

A welcome coupling of two works that have much in common. In each the outer movements have strong elements of concerto grosso style, and in fact the *First Cello concerto* (an early work, dating from 1930) was originally planned as a concerto grosso using a small wind group and strings. Martinů had second thoughts about it and rescored it twice more to produce the final version recorded here. Like the *Double concerto* the work has an eloquent and highly rewarding slow movement. If anything the *Concerto for violin and piano* is an even finer piece. Of the same vintage as the *Sixth Symphony* (1953), it shows the composer at his most engaging. The first movement is fresh and vital and the slow movement is very beautiful indeed. The performances are spirited, and although the recording is reverberant it does not detract from the great pleasure to be had from this disc.

Cello concerto No. 2.
(M) *(*) Sup. 50883. Večtomov, Prague SO, Košler.

This is an ambitious work and has a fine

opening sweep that the rest of the first movement fails to live up to. The slow movement also begins more promisingly than it continues, and the toccata-like finale is empty. The soloist makes the most of the material and plays with enthusiasm, but the orchestral contribution seems less spontaneous. Typical reverberant Supraphon sound.

(i) *Concerto for double string orchestra, piano and timpani;* (ii) *3 Frescoes* (*Les Fresques de Piero della Francesca*).
(M) **(*) Sup. 50109. Czech PO, (i) Sejna, (ii) Ančerl.

The Supraphon recording dates from the early 1960s, though this new pressing is cut at a slightly lower level than the original. The *Double concerto,* written for Paul Sacher and the Basle Chamber Orchestra in 1938, at about the same time as Bartók wrote his *Music for strings, percussion and celesta* for the same artists, is arguably Martinů's masterpiece and this performance has an enormous sweep and energy. The coupling has the *Frescoes of Piero della Francesca* glowingly played and recorded. They are much later than the *Concerto,* belonging to the winter of 1954/5. There is a marked difference in style between the two for even when Martinů is concerned with the battle scenes of the *Frescoes* he depicts his own emotional reactions, and does not write descriptively. Martinů, like Bartók, relaxed stylistically towards the end of his life, possibly in the hope of reaching a wider public, but his creative ability and colouristic skill were hardly diminished. This music has a strong appeal; the slow movement is particularly atmospheric.

Harpsichord concerto (for harpsichord and small orchestra).
(M) ** Sup. 50926. Ružičková, Prague Chamber Soloists, Sanderling – POULENC: *Concerto.**(*)

The *Harpsichord concerto* (1935) is a characteristically vital work, with a strong underlying vein of lyricism to balance the abounding energy. The performance by Ružičková is spirited, and she is fortunate in having her instrument recorded with good presence and clarity.

Oboe concerto.
(M) *** Sup. 50486. Hanták, Brno State PO, Turnovsky – R. STRAUSS: *Oboe concerto.***

Martinů's *Concerto* is a splendid addition to the modern repertory for the oboe. While the writing is not so florid as that in the Richard Strauss *Concerto* on the reverse, it still needs considerable flexibility of technique on the part of the soloist if the work's essential lyricism is to flow through the decoration. The basic quality of the music is high-spirited and confident. The recording is somewhat close, but otherwise good. Recommended.

Violin concertos Nos. 1 and 2.
(M) *** Sup. 410 1535 [PRO 1065]. Suk, Czech PO, Neumann.

The *Second Concerto* is the one written for Mischa Elman, and an earlier recording of it is available on this same label coupled with the *Piano concerto No. 3.* It is a serene, lovely work to whose lyricism Suk's art is so naturally attuned. Strangely enough, it appeared at the height of the war in 1943. No. 1 was written a decade earlier for Samuel Dushkin, for whom Stravinsky wrote his concerto. It is full of motoric rhythms and the neoclassical habits of speech current at the time: a stimulating piece, distinguished by Martinů's fine craftsmanship and resourceful technique. The recordings are very good, though not in the Decca or EMI demonstration class. Nevertheless three stars for the interest value of this repertoire.

(i; ii) *Jazz suite;* (iii) *La Revue de cuisine;* (ii) *Who is the most powerful in the world – Shimmy foxtrot;* (iv) *Sextet for piano and wind;* (i) (Piano) *Trois Esquisses;* (v; ii) (Choral) *Le Jazz.*
(M) **(*) Sup. 110 1014. (i) Jílek; (ii) Prague SO, Vostrák; (iii) Instrumental Ens.; (iv) Panenka, Prague Wind Quintet; (v) Pánek Singers.

This record presents a useful compilation of Martinů's jazz-inspired compositions from the 1920s. They are moderately entertaining, and readers interested in the development of the great Czech composer will want to investigate this aspect of his personality. On the whole, however, the disc will enjoy limited appeal and none of the music, even if it offers amusing moments as in *La Revue de cuisine,* is in any way substantial.

(i) *Sinfonietta La Jolla; Toccata e due canzoni.*
(M) *** Sup. 110 1619. Prague CO, (i) with Hnat.

These two delightful works come from the immediate post-war years. The *Toccata e due canzoni* was written for Paul Sacher and the *Sinfonietta* for the Music Society of the small Californian town of La Jolla. The *Sinfonietta* is unfailingly inventive and refreshing and should exert a strong appeal for Martinů's growing number of admirers. The *Toccata e due canzoni* was originally intended to be in the form of a concerto grosso, but the two 'light, gay, very simple chansons' Martinů had planned turned into something more substantial. The first of the canzoni is an inward-looking piece, darker in feeling than its companions, and almost recalling the *Concerto for double string orchestra, piano and timpani,* written for Sacher in the late 1930s. Both performance and recording are excellent. This attractive music has immediate appeal but also offers enduring musical rewards.

Spalíček (ballet): *Suites Nos. 1 and 2.*
(M) ** Sup. 110 1129. Brno State PO, Waldhans.

A lively inventive score that will delight admirers of this composer. It was written in the early 1930s but revised and expanded in Paris in 1940. No one listening to it would guess that it was finally put into shape during a period of anxiety and uncertainty, for it is relentlessly extrovert and cheerful in mood. *The Dance of the Maids of Honour* from the second suite is highly memorable and is difficult to dislodge from one's mind. There are other attractive ideas too; but at the same time it must be conceded that there is also a good deal of routine Martinů optimism.

The performance is a fine one, though it is recorded in a somewhat reverberant studio.

Symphonies Nos. 1–6; Inventions.
(M) *** Sup. 1410 3071/4. Czech PO, Neumann.

These performances are also still available separately – see below.

Symphony No. 1; Inventions.
(M) *** Sup. 1410 2166 [PRO 1006]. Czech PO, Neumann.

The *First Symphony* dates from 1942, the year after Martinů arrived in the United States, and, like so much good music of the period, it was written in response to a commission from Koussevitzky. Virgil Thomson's panegyric has been much quoted (but rightly so): 'The shining sounds of it sing as well as shine . . . Personal indeed is the delicate but vigorous rhythmic animation, the singing (rather than dynamic) syncopation that permeates the whole work.' The 'singing syncopation' has indeed something of the quality of Hopkins's 'sprung' rhythm, and lends this music a forward thrust and subtlety that are exhilarating. The three *Inventions* are earlier, dating from 1934, and are highly imaginative and appealing. In every way this is a welcome addition to the growing Martinů discography. The performance is excellent and the recording fully acceptable.

Symphonies Nos. 2; 6 (Fantaisies symphoniques).
(M) *** Sup. 1410 2096. Czech PO, Neumann.

Martinů's first five symphonies followed each other at annual intervals. The *Second* (1943) is the most relaxed of the six; its ideas are unforced, its mood easy-going and bucolic. Much of it is exhilarating, particularly the delightful finale, and it has much charm in its pastoral slow movement. The *Sixth* is much later and was introduced to the gramophone by Charles Munch and the Boston Symphony, to whom the work is dedicated. For some time Martinů was doubtful about its symphonic status; he subtitled it *Fantaisies symphoniques* and even briefly asked for it not to be included in his numbered symphonies. The vivid colouring and exotic textures (the opening sounds for all the world like a cloud of Amazonian insects) must for him have outweighed the effect made by the musical cogency and sweep of the score. Václav Neumann's performance has an impressive spaciousness, though there could be more urgency and fire in places. The Czech orchestra plays splendidly, but the recording, made in the somewhat resonant House of Artists in Prague, could perhaps be more sharply focused. Yet detail, even if lacking the last ounce of presence, has been kept in truthful perspective. No reservations should qualify the recommendation this disc must have; and those who do not know the Martinů symphonies should start here.

Symphonies Nos. 3–5.
(M) *** Sup. 1410 2771/2. Czech PO, Neumann.

The *Third* is in some ways the weightiest of Martinů's wartime symphonies; it is without doubt the most concentrated and powerful of the cycle, with the possible exception of the *Sixth*. It has too something of the dark purposefulness and vision of the *Double concerto*; the middle movement has great intensity of feeling and real depth. Neumann gives an authoritative reading, with well-shaped phrasing, and his conception is more spacious than was Sejna's in his post-war set. The first two movements of the *Fourth Symphony* (1945) serve as a fill-up; the remainder spill over to the next record, and the *Fifth* likewise bestrides the end of one side and goes over to the fourth – not an ideal arrangement, perhaps. (There is still enough first-rate Martinů to serve as fill-up material if each symphony had been more tidily accommodated on one disc.) The *Fifth* is a marvellous piece whose closing pages radiate an almost incandescent quality and a life-enhancing power quite out of tune with the bleak post-war years that gave it birth. The *Fourth* is perhaps the most immediately attractive and appealing of all six, and though Neumann's performances do not in every respect displace previous accounts by Ančerl, Turnovský and others, they are eminently recommendable in spite of the reverberance of the acoustic.

CHAMBER AND INSTRUMENTAL MUSIC

3 Impromptus for violin and piano; Nonet; Piano sextet (for Piano and wind instruments); *Violin sonata in D min.*
(M) ** Sup. Panton 110 282. Tomášek, Ružička, Czech Nonet (members).

Despite the interest of the repertoire they offer, many Panton records do not rate an entry on account of their shoddy pressings and noisy surfaces. This disc, however, is fully up to standard though the recording is not distinguished. All the works come from the 1920s; the earliest is the *Nonet* (1924–5) the first two movements of which were lost, and the latest is the *Sextet* of 1929. The *Three Impromptus* are relatively 'routine' Martinů, nicely played though they are, but the *Sextet* is quite irresistible, full of Gallic charm and wit, making entertaining use of jazz elements and showing the influence of *Les Six*. It is altogether delightful and will give wide pleasure. The *Nonet* is of substance, too, and the value of the disc is further enhanced by an early *Violin sonata* (1926; the first numbered sonata comes three years later). The performances are most musical and expert. The engineers judge the balance well, but the overall sound image wants the presence and range of a first-class Western recording to do it justice. Nevertheless, do not miss this disc.

(i) *Madrigal sonata.* Piano music: (ii) *Butterflies and Birds of Paradise;* (iii) *3 Czech dances; Les Ritournelles.*
(M) ** Sup. Panton 110 446. (i) Dostlova, Motulkova, Kramska; (ii) Krajný; (iii) Holena.

The *Butterflies and Birds of Paradise* dates from 1920 and reflects the influence of Debussy. The other two piano pieces, the *Czech dances* and the 1932 *Ritournelles,* come from Martinů's Paris years; the latter has genuine depth. The *Madrigal sonata* for flute, violin and piano, a two-movement work dating from the war years, is diverting and inventive without being really memorable. All the same this is welcome – recommendable though not indispensable Martinů. Good performances and decent recording.

Nonet; Trio in F for flute, cello and piano; La Revue de cuisine.
*** Hyp. A66084. Dartington Ens.

A delightful record. Only one of these pieces is otherwise available (though Schwann lists an alternative account of the *Trio* with a Ned Rorem work on the back), and all of them receive first-class performances and superb recording. The sound has space, warmth, perspective and definition. *La Revue de cuisine* is very much of its decade and the *Charleston* is most engaging, even if not all the others are Martinů at his most characteristic or inventive. The *Trio,* written after a bout of depression in 1944, is as fresh and inventive as his very best work and is deliciously played, and its *Andante* deserves to be singled out for special mention: it is a most beautiful movement. The *Nonet,* for string trio plus double-bass, flute, clarinet, oboe, horn and bassoon, was finished five months before his death and is as life-enhancing as the *Sinfonietta giocosa* of 1940, also composed when he was in penury and danger. An indispensable issue for lovers of Martinů's music.

Piano trio No. 3 in C; Bergerettes.
(M) **(*) Sup. 50698. Foerster Trio.

Martinů's five *Bergerettes* for piano trio make enchanting listening. They have the melodic and rhythmic spontaneity of Dvořák's *Slavonic dances* and the scoring for piano trio gives them an even greater bite and freshness than if they were conceived for orchestra. The spirited performances here are ideal and the recording quality matches the vivacious playing. The *Third Piano trio* is slightly less successful. Its kernel is in the pungent *Andante*. The outer movements follow Martinů's *moto perpetuo* manner, the strong rhythmic impetus not covering the underlying lyricism. Here the playing is alive but the recording not quite so clear as in the *Bergerettes.* But this remains a valuable disc and one not to be missed by those who have already discovered the immediacy of the composer's style.

String quartet No. 1 (French).
(M) *** Sup. 1111 3018. Panocha Qt.

The first of Martinů's seven string quartets comes from the early 1920s and is a long work, heavily indebted, as its title might lead one to presume, to the world of Ravel and Debussy. Indeed it scarcely reveals a glimpse of the Martinů we know, and yet, if it is an exercise in the French idiom, it certainly succeeds in conveying Gallic charm, and admirers of the composer will not begrudge the outlay. This is its first recording. The Panocha Quartet is an excellent ensemble and they are well recorded; the sleeve is particularly attractive, too!

String quartets Nos 4; 6.
*** Sup. 1111 2845. Panocha Qt.

Neither quartet is new to the catalogue. No. 4 was composed in 1937 and has been recorded by the Smetana Quartet, while its companion on this disc comes from 1946 and was coupled with the Roussel. Neither performance was as winning as these new accounts by the Panocha. If you are looking for the fertility of invention that marks the best of Martinů's orchestral music, you are going to be disappointed. But the first movement of the *Sixth* is a powerful and disturbing piece, and is alone worth the price of the record. There is a sense of scale and a vision that raises it well above its companion – or No. 7, for that matter – and the only reservation one has is that it is not balanced by a slow movement of comparable weight and substance. Well worth investigating. Good recording.

String quartets Nos. 5; 7 (Concerto da camera).
*** Sup. 1111 2675. Panocha Qt.

Of the two, the *Fifth* is the more substantial piece. It dates from the same year as the *Double concerto for two string orchestras and timpani* (1938) to which it is close in spirit, particularly in the two inner movements. It is not as powerful or searching as the *Concerto* but it is arguably the finest of the cycle. No. 7, subtitled *Concerto de camera,* comes from 1947 and is written in the wake of the *Fifth Symphony*. It is fluent, well-crafted and nicely fashioned, but its *joie de vivre* does not quite ring true. There is none of the spontaneity and freshness of the *Sinfonietta giocosa* or the *Fourth Symphony*. These two quartets have been coupled together before, but this new version completely displaces its predecessor and is also superior to its Panton rival played by the much (and rightly) admired Talich Quartet (8116 0025) which is not quite as well recorded.

Borová: Czech dances Nos. 1–7; Études and polkas, Books 1–3 (complete).
(M) *(*) Sup. 111 1104. Hála.

These are lively and engaging pieces. Martinů composed the *Études and Polkas* in America during the war years; many of them are delightful and all of them are short. They are not particularly varied in style or mood and one only wants to hear one book at a time, but they are inventive and highly characteristic pieces. The *Czech dances* are much earlier but no less rewarding. Josef Hála plays intelligently, but he is not well served by the engineers and the disc must be given a qualified recommendation on that account. The piano tone is badly focused: it is fuzzy and glassy, and the acoustic is reverberant. This does seriously impair pleasure and calls for some tolerance.

VOCAL MUSIC

Cantatas on words by Miroslav Bureš: Dandelion romance; The Legend of the smoke from the potato-tops; Mikeš from the mountains; The opening of the wells.
(M) *** Sup. 1112 3631–2. Soloists, Kühn Children's Ch. various instrumentalists, Czech Philharmonic Ch., Veselka.

All four cantatas date from the last four years of his life, indeed *Mikeš from the mountains* was only finished a few months before Martinů's death in 1959. *The romance of the dandelions* is for soprano and an unaccompanied mixed chorus, but all the others have instrumental support of various kinds. The four cantatas are all settings of words by Miloslav Bureš and they radiate a freshness of experience mingled with keen nostalgia. Martinů never returned to his native land after the war, hence the vividness of these folk-poetic visions. The recordings are not of recent provenance but they are still very good and, for the most part (excepting the spoken narration in *The opening of the wells*), enchanting.

The Epic of Gilgamesh.
(M) *** Sup. 1121 808. Machotková, Zahradniček, Zitek, Prusa, Brousek, Czech PO Ch., Prague SO, Belohlavek.

The Epic of Gilgamesh is one of Martinů's finest achievements. It belongs to his last years and touches greater depths than almost any other of his later works, with the possible exception of *The Prophecy of Isaiah. Gilgamesh* predates the Homeric epic by at least 1,500 years, and Martinů's oratorio draws one into this remote world with astonishing power. The second and third parts of the oratorio centre on the themes of death and immortality, and it is here that some of the most imaginative and mysterious music is to be found. Part 2 recounts the death of Enkidu and Gilgamesh's grief, his plea to the gods to restore Enkidu and his search for immortality; the third part records his failure to learn its secrets. But it is not only these sections that inspire music of great atmosphere and mystery; the whole work has a concentration of vision and feeling, and an imaginative resource which shows that this legend triggered off particularly sympathetic resonances in the composer. The performance is responsive and spacious (tempi are leisurely), though not enough is made of the drama. When Gilgamesh is granted a vision of the underworld and Enkidu rises to answer his questions with the simple words 'I saw', the atmosphere could be more chilling and haunting: it is a superb moment. The Czech narration is a small element and need not deter anyone. *Gilgamesh* is an inspiring and rewarding work, not to be missed by Martinů's admirers.

The Prophecy of Isaiah (cantata).
(M) *(*) Sup. 50778. Tattermuschová, Mrázová, Berman, Czech PO Ch. and O, Ančerl – STRAVINSKY: *Symphony of Psalms*.*(*)

This cantata, a setting of words from Isaiah, was the last work that Martinů completed, and, perhaps in anticipation of approaching death, the style is sparer and darker than we expect of this composer. The choral writing is powerful, and though some of the soloists have troublesome Slavonic wobbles, the performance is vivid and dramatic. This is not immediately attractive music, despite the easiness of the idiom, but it is an important extension of our knowledge of a composer not yet given his due. Excellent recording quality.

OPERA

The Greek Passion (sung in English).
❀ *** Sup. Dig. 1116 3611/2 [id.]. Mitchinson, Field, Tomlinson, Joll, Moses, Davies, Cullis, Savory, Kuhn Children's Ch., Czech PO Ch., Brno State PO, Mackerras.

Written with much mental pain in the years just before Martinů died in 1959, this opera was the work he regarded as his musical testament. Based on a novel by Nikos Kazantzakis (author of *Zorba the Greek*), it tells in an innocent, direct way of a village where a Passion play is to be presented, and the individuals – tragically, as it proves – take on qualities of the New Testament figures they represent. At the very opening there is a hymn-like prelude of diatonic simplicity, and what makes the work so moving – giving occasional overtones of Janáček, Mussorgsky and Britten – is Martinů's ability to simplify his message both musically and dramatically. On stage the degree of gaucheness might be hard to present effectively, but on record it is quite different. This superb recording was made by a cast which had been giving stage performances for the Welsh National Opera; the singing is not just committed but accomplished too. The Czechs were happy to record the opera (digitally, using Japanese equipment) in what in effect is the original language of Martinů's libretto, English. Virtually every word is crystal-clear and the directness of the communication to the listener is riveting, particularly as the choral perspectives are so tellingly and realistically managed. The combination of British soloists with excellent Czech choirs and players is entirely fruitful. As a Czech specialist Mackerras makes an ideal advocate, and the recorded sound is both brilliant and highly atmospheric. In its simple, direct way *The Greek Passion* makes a most moving experience, and this set is strongly recommended; it is a major achievement to rank alongside Mackerras's splendid Janáček opera recordings for Decca.

Julietta (complete).
(M) *** Sup. 50611/3. Tauberová, Zídek and cast of Prague Nat. Th. production, Prague Nat. Th. Ch. and O, Krombholc.

Julietta is a key work in Martinů's output and highly esteemed by all the authorities on the composer. It dates from the 1930s and is based on Georges Neveux's play *La Clé des songes*. The opera has no plot in the proper sense of the word, for the play balances on the fine edge of reality and illusion, so that all reality seems to be fiction, and fiction assumes the guise of reality. Suffice it to say that the opera drew from Martinů inspiration of the highest quality: the score is full of variety, both of texture and of colour, the music is unfailingly inventive and imaginative, with a strong and at times luminous atmosphere. This magical work will more than repay study, particularly in so idiomatic and beautifully recorded a performance.

Mascagni, Pietro (1863–1945)

L'Amico Fritz (complete)
(M) *** [Ang. SBL/*4X2X* 3737 (2)]. Pavarotti, Freni, Sardinero, ROHCG Ch. and O, Gavazzeni.

The haunting *Cherry duet* from this opera whets the appetite for more, and it is good to hear so rare and charming a piece, one that is not likely to enter the repertory of our British opera houses. Even so, enthusiasm has to be tempered a little, because no other number in the opera approaches the famous duet in its memorability. The libretto too is delicate to the point of feebleness. This performance could be more refined, though Freni and

Pavarotti are most attractive artists and this was recorded in 1969 when they were both at their freshest. The Covent Garden Orchestra responds loyally; the recording is warm and atmospheric, and it has transferred very successfully to tape. While the dramatic conception is at the opposite end of the scale from *Cavalleria Rusticana*, one is easily beguiled by the music's charm, and the Puccinian influences are by no means a disadvantage. This set is currently not available in the UK.

Cavalleria Rusticana (complete).

*** RCA RL/*RK* 13091 [CRL1/*CRK1* 3091]. Scotto, Domingo, Elvira, Isola Jones, Amb. Op. Ch., Nat. PO, Levine.

(M) *** DG 413 275-1/*4* (3/*2*). Cossotto, Bergonzi, Guelfi, Ch. and O of La Scala, Milan, Karajan – LEONCAVALLO: *I Pagliacci.****

(*) HMV SLS 5187 (3) [Ang. SZCX /*4Z3X* 3895]. Caballé, Carreras, Manuguerra, Varnay, Amb. Op. Ch., Philh. O, Muti – LEONCAVALLO: *I Pagliacci.*(*)*

(*) Decca D 83 D 3/*K 83 K 32* (3) [Lon. D 13125]. Varady, Pavarotti, Cappuccilli, Gonzales, L. Op. Ch., Nat. PO, Gavazzeni – LEONCAVALLO: *I Pagliacci.*

There is far more than its compact format on a single disc (libretto included) or tape to recommend the RCA version. On balance in performance it stands as the best current recommendation, with Domingo giving a heroic account of the role of Turiddù, full of defiance. Scotto, strongly characterful too, though not always perfectly steady on top, gives one of her finest performances of recent years, and James Levine directs with a splendid sense of pacing, by no means faster than his rivals (except the leisurely Karajan), and drawing red-blooded playing from the National Philharmonic. The recording is very good (particularly remembering the long sides), and the cassette transfer is first-class, one of RCA's very best.

Karajan's direction of the other half of the inevitable partnership matches that of *Pagliacci.* He pays Mascagni the tribute of taking his markings literally, so that well-worn melodies come out with new purity and freshness, and the singers have been chosen to match that. Cossotto quite as much as Bergonzi keeps a pure, firm line that is all too rare in this much-abused music. Together they show that much of the vulgarity lies in interpretations rather than in Mascagni's inspiration. Not that there is any lack of dramatic bite (except marginally, because of the recording balance in some of the chorus work). Good recording but at rather a low level. The cassette transfer (an early one) is made at a higher level than usual for DG and gives excellent results. Now reissued at mid-price, this is a genuine bargain.

There are fewer unexpected textual points in the HMV *Cav.* than in *Pag.,* but Muti's approach is comparably biting and violent, brushing away the idea that this is a sentimental score, though running the risk of making it vulgar. The result is certainly refreshing, with Caballé – pushed faster than usual even in her big moments – collaborating warmly. So *Voi lo sapete* is geared from the start to the final cry of *Io son dannata,* and she manages a fine snarl on *A te la mala Pasqua.* Carreras does not sound quite so much at home, though the rest of the cast is memorable, including the resonant Manuguerra as Alfio and the veteran Astrid Varnay as Mamma Lucia, wobble as she does. The recording is forward and vivid.

With Pavarotti loud and unsubtle as Turiddù – though the tone is often most beautiful – it is left to Julia Varady as Santuzza to give the Decca version under Gavazzeni its distinction. Though her tone is not heavyweight, the impression of youth is most affecting; the sharpness of pain in *Voi lo sapete* is beautifully conveyed, and the whole performance is warm and authentic. Cappuccilli's Alfio is too noble to be convincing, and as in the companion *Pag.* the main claim to attention lies in the brilliant forward recording, equally impressive on disc and tape.

Cavalleria Rusticana: highlights.

(M) *** DG Priv. 2535/*3335* 199 (from above set, cond. Karajan) – LEONCAVALLO: *I Pagliacci: highlights.****

(*) Decca SXL/*KSXC* 6986 (from above set, cond. Gavazzeni) – LEONCAVALLO: *I Pagliacci: highlights.*

Karajan's disc, at mid-price, is the obvious choice here and the cassette is as vivid as the disc. The Decca excerpts from *Cavalleria Rusticana* include *Santuzza's prayer* and *Voi lo sapete,* very welcome because Julia Varady is the most individual member of the cast in the complete set. The selections from both operas are rather more generous than usual, and the recording is excellent. The cassette transfer too is extremely vivid. In the USA there is a selection available from the Muti set [Ang. S/*4XS* 37884].

Mašek, Vincenc (1755–1831)

Symphony in Dis.
(M) ** Sup. 1110 2809. Prague CO, Vajnar – KROMMER: *Symphony.****

Václav Vincenc Mašek was born the year before Mozart and was a notable keyboard player, making successful tours to Germany, Holland and Denmark before becoming director of the St Nicholas Choir at Malá Strana in Prague. His output includes several operas, *Traveller through the East Indies* and *The Mirror Knight,* as well as many wind partitas and serenades. This *Sinfonia in Dis* (D sharp) probably comes from the beginning of the 1780s and is fresh in character, though its ideas and their development are simple to the point of naïvety. The '*Dis*' of the title is contemporary usage for E flat, the *Eroica Symphony* being so described on its first appearance. Despite the thinness of texture and invention, this is quite an attractive and likeable piece which the Prague Chamber Orchestra under František Vajnar play with evident affection. Good recording quality.

Massenet, Jules (1842–1912)

(i) *La Cigale* (divertissement-ballet; complete) *Valse très lente.*
*** Decca SXL 6932 [Lon CS 7163]. Nat. PO, Bonynge, (i) with Hartle, L. Voices.

A late work written with Massenet's characteristic finesse, *Cigale* was totally neglected until Richard Bonynge revived it in this recording. The ballet tells, in somewhat sentimental terms, the story of the La Fontaine fable about the grasshopper and the ant. The melodic invention does not match Massenet's finest, but the score is charming and colourful, and it is brightly played and sung and brilliantly recorded.

Scènes pittoresques; Le Cid; ballet music *La Vierge: The Last Sleep of the Virgin.*
(M) *** HMV Green. ESD/*TC-ESD* 7040 [Klavier 522]. CBSO, Frémaux.

Frémaux's record was originally issued in full quadraphonic form in a Studio Two pressing, and the reissue is one of the most impressive compatible quadraphonic records. The muted strings in *The Last Sleep of the Virgin* are quite beautiful. This was a favourite piece of Sir Thomas Beecham's, and Frémaux plays it lovingly. But in the spectacular recording of the *Cid* ballet music the sonic splendour is remarkable. The sound is vivid and rich, and the performances both of the ballet music and of the charming *Scènes pittoresques* are highly effective. The *Aubade* in the ballet suite is a demonstration item. In spite of the resonance, the cassette transfer too is highly successful.

Scènes alsaciennes; Scènes dramatiques; Scènes de féerie; Scènes pittoresques; Don Quichotte: Interludes; La Vierge: The last sleep of the Virgin.
** Erato STU 71208 (2)/*MCE 71209/10.* Monte Carlo Op. O, Eliot Gardiner.

The Erato box gathers together four out of Massenet's seven orchestral suites, plus a few encores, including one of Sir Thomas Beecham's favourites, *The last sleep of the Virgin.* In fact this is all music that would respond to the Beecham touch. John Eliot Gardiner secures quite impressively characterized performances; he finds suitable gravitas and breadth in the *Scènes dramatiques,* and the *Scènes pittoresques* are bright and fresh, the horns tolling the Angelus with resonant impact. But the Monte Carlo orchestra produces a rather thin-bodied tutti, and though the full, atmospheric recording minimizes this effect, the ear remains conscious that the playing lacks the last degree of polish and elegance. The sound is limited in range and colour alongside Frémaux's HMV coupling. The tape layout is on two separate cassettes (the first includes *Scènes dramatiques, Scènes de féerie,* and *Le dernier sommeil*) and the sound is ample to the point of being bass-heavy, with a lack of compensating sparkle on top. However, an acceptable balance can be obtained with a bass cut.

OPERA

Cendrillon (complete).
**(*) CBS 79323 (3) [Col. M3 35194]. Von Stade, Gedda, Berbié, Bastin, Amb. Op. Ch., Philh. O, Rudel.

Julius Rudel directs a sparkling, winning performance of Massenet's Cinderella opera, less a pantomime than a fairy story in which the magic element (direct from Perrault) is vital. The Fairy Godmother is a sparkling coloratura (here the bright-toned Ruth Welting) and Cendrillon a soprano in a lower register. Von Stade gives a characteristically strong and imaginative performance, untroubled by what for her is high tessitura. The pity is that the role of the prince, originally written for soprano, is here taken by a tenor, Gedda, whose voice is no longer fresh-toned. Jules Bastin sings most stylishly as Pandolfe and the others make up a well-chosen team. The recording is more spacious than many from this source.

Le Cid (opera): complete.
** CBS 79300 (3) [Col. M3 34211]. Bumbry, Domingo, Bergquist, Plishka, Gardner, Camp Chorale, NY Op. O, Queler.

This recording of *Le Cid* is taken from a live performance directed by Miss Eve Queler in New York, and inevitably suffers in comparison with well-produced studio recordings. The recording quality is boxy, the performance very variable (only with the entry of Placido Domingo in Scene 2 does the occasion get going), and the French accents are often comically bad. Even so the attractions of Massenet's often beautiful score survive all the shortcomings. As an opera this tale of conflict between love and duty, based distantly on Corneille, is strikingly different from most in the Massenet canon, and makes a valuable addition to the list on record. Domingo, not always as stylish as he might be, is in heroic voice, and Grace Bumbry as the proud heroine responds splendidly. The popular ballet music is given a sparkling performance.

Le Cid: ballet music; *Ariane: Lamento d'Ariane.*
*** Decca SXL/*KSXC* 6812 [Lon. CS/5-7032]. Nat. PO, Bonynge – MEYERBEER: *Les Patineurs.****

Decca have, over the years, made a house speciality of recording the ballet music from *Le Cid* and coupling it with Constant Lambert's arrangement of Meyerbeer. Bonynge's new version is the finest ever, with the most seductive orchestral playing, superbly recorded. The sumptuous richness of the sound is in no way inflated and every minute of this disc is of demonstration quality. The cassette is fine too, only marginally less free and wide-ranging than the superlative disc. Bonynge's bonus item, the *Lament* from *Ariane,* is pleasing but not distinctive.

Esclarmonde (opera): complete.
*** Decca SET 612/4 [Lon. OSA 13118]. Sutherland, Aragall, Tourangeau, Davies, Grant, Alldis Ch., Nat. PO, Bonynge.

Massenet was straying down the road to Bayreuth, said his contemporaries, when *Esclarmonde* appeared in 1889. Certainly the libretto, based on a medieval romance involving song-contests and necromancy, has more than its share of Wagnerian echoes, with a number of situations directly imitated. The scoring too is heavier than one expects from Massenet. The actual idiom brings only distant Wagnerian echoes, though with its more ambitious tone of voice it is not always typical of its composer, and on record the spectacular scene-setting has the visual imagination working overtime. Verdi is another composer who keeps coming to mind; Berlioz too; and there are signs that Puccini, as late as *Turandot*, was influenced by this opera revolving round an isolated princess-heroine.

The central role calls for an almost impossible combination of qualities, written as it was for Sybil Sanderson, the rich American singer for whom Massenet later wrote *Thaïs*. In our generation Joan Sutherland is the obvious diva to compass the demands of great range, great power and brilliant coloratura, and her performance in its way is as powerful as it was in Puccini's last opera. Aragall proves an excellent tenor, sweet of tone and intelligent, and the other parts, all of them relatively small, are well taken too. Richard Bonynge draws passionate singing and playing from chorus and orchestra, and the recording is rich and spectacular to match the story.

Manon (complete).
**(*) HMV SLS/*TC-SLS* 173141-3/*5* (3) [Ang. DSX/*4X3X* 3946]. Cotrubas, Kraus, Quilico, Van Dam, Ch. and O of Capitole, Toulouse, Plasson.

Though it does not efface memories of the classic version conducted by Pierre Monteux for HMV (with Victoria de los Angeles a captivating heroine), Plasson's set recorded in Toulouse presents a stylish performance well characterized and well sung. Cotrubas is a charming Manon, more tender and vulnerable than Los Angeles on the earlier set but not so golden-toned and with a more limited development of character from the girlish chatterbox to the dying victim. Alfredo Kraus betrays some signs of age, but this is a finely detailed, subtle reading with none of the blemishes which marred his *Werther* performance for HMV. Louis Quilico has a delightfully light touch as Lescaut, and Van Dam is a superb Comte Des Grieux. The warm reverberation of the Toulouse studio is well controlled to give bloom to the voices, and though Plasson is rougher with the score than Monteux, his feeling for French idiom is good. Discs and XDR cassettes sound almost identical.

La Navarraise (opera): complete.
*** CBS [M 33506]. Popp, Vanzo, Souzay, Sénéchal, Sardinero, Meloni, Amb. Op. Ch., LSO, Almeida.
***RCA [AGL1/*AGK1* 3793]. Horne, Domingo, Milnes, Zaccaria, Bacquier, Davies, Amb. Op. Ch., LSO, Lewis.

La Navarraise, a compact 'lyric episode' lasting barely forty minutes, finds Massenet challenging the *verismo* school and succeeding convincingly. The flavour is of a cross between *Carmen* and *Cavalleria Rusticana* with a touch of *Il Tabarro*. To earn her dowry before marrying her beloved, the intrepid heroine penetrates the enemy lines in the Carlist wars and for money assassinates the Royalist general's direct adversary. By a misunderstanding the hero follows her and is mortally wounded. In despair the heroine promptly goes mad – a great deal of story for so short a piece. It says much for Massenet's dramatic powers that he makes the result as convincing as he does, and the score is full of splendid atmospheric effects. It was produced in the same year as *Thaïs* (1894), with a première at Covent Garden. Massenet originally had a heavyweight Carmen voice in mind, but here Lucia Popp, best-known for her coloratura, is both moving and stylish, making the scalp tingle in the final mad scene. Alain Vanzo, long neglected on record, is impressive as the hero, singing sensitively and idiomatically. The rest of the cast sings well too, and Antonio de Almeida, apart from one or two passages where he presses on too hard, is warmly sympathetic in his conducting. Excellent atmospheric recording.

The RCA version, which had the misfortune to appear five months after the CBS (the most unlikely of duplications), presents another fine, red-blooded performance. On paper the cast looks more star-studded, but in practice these soloists are a degree less stylish. Marilyn Horne would seem an apter choice for the role of heroine with her heavy Carmen voice, but the upper register is not as firm as it was. Domingo as the hero has richer tone than Vanzo, but sings less characterfully. It is swings and roundabouts at every level, with the RCA performance a degree grander but the CBS more sharply dramatic. No one is likely to be seriously disappointed with either, and the opera is ideally suited to the gramophone. Neither recording is currently available in the UK.

Le Roi de Lahore (complete).

*** Decca D 210 D 3/*K 210 K 33* (3) [Lon. LDR 10025]. Sutherland, Tourangeau, Lima, Milnes, Morris, Ghiaurov, L. Voices, Nat. PO, Bonynge.

With a libretto that sets high melodrama against an exotic background – even introducing the supernatural with an Act set in the paradise of Indra – *Le Roi de Lahore* was Massenet's first opera for the big stage of L'Opéra in Paris and marked a turning-point in his career. The characters may be stock figures out of a fairy tale, but in the vigour of his treatment Massenet makes the result red-blooded in an Italianate way. This vivid performance under Bonynge includes passages added for Italy, notably a superb set-piece aria which challenges Sutherland to some of her finest singing. Massenet's idea of the exotic extends to a saxophone waltz (here made deliciously Parisian), but generally the score reflects the eager robustness of a young composer stretching his wings for the first time. Sutherland may not be a natural for the role of innocent young priestess, but she makes it a magnificent vehicle with its lyric, dramatic and coloratura demands. Luis Lima as the King is sometimes strained by the high tessitura, but it is a ringing tenor, clean of attack. Sherrill Milnes as the heroine's wicked uncle sounds even more Italianate, rolling his 'r's' ferociously; but high melodrama is apt, and with digital recording of demonstration quality, rich and rounded, this shameless example of operatic hokum could not be more persuasively presented. The cassettes are as demonstration-worthy as the discs.

Werther (complete).

*** Ph. 6769/*7654* 051 (3). Carreras, Von Stade, Allen, Buchanan, Lloyd, Children's Ch., O of ROHCG, Colin Davis.

**(*) DG 2709 091/*3371 048* (3) [id.]. Domingo, Obraztsova, Auger, Grundheber, Moll, Col. Children's Ch. and R. SO, Chailly.

** HMV SLS 5183 (3) [Ang. SZX/*4Z3X* 3894]. Kraus, Troyanos, Manuguerra, Barbaux, Ch. and LPO, Plasson.

Sir Colin Davis has rarely directed a more sensitive or more warmly expressive performance on record than his account of *Werther*. The magic of sound hits the listener from the opening prelude onwards, and the refined recording, coupled with a superbly cast performance based on a stage production at Covent Garden, makes for consistent compulsion. Frederica von Stade makes an enchanting Charlotte, outshining all current rivals on record, both strong and tender, conveying the understanding but vulnerable character of Goethe's heroine. Carreras may not be quite so clearly superior to all rivals, but, like his compatriot Placido Domingo on the DG set (marred by an inadequate Charlotte), he uses a naturally beautiful voice freshly and sensitively. Others in the cast, such as Thomas Allen as Charlotte's husband Albert and Isobel Buchanan as Sophie, her sister, are excellent too. This is one of the finest of recent sets of French opera. The tape transfer uses two cassettes as against three discs, but no attempt is made to tailor the first two Acts so that each is complete on a single side. The transfer level is (as usual with Philips) comparatively low, but as chrome tape has been used there is only minor loss of definition, and the sound has a pleasing naturalness and bloom. However the typeface of the libretto is minuscule.

With a recording that gives a beautiful bloom to the sound of the Cologne orchestra, down to the subtlest whisper from pianissimo strings, the DG version stands at an advantage over its HMV rival, particularly as Chailly proves a sharply characterful conductor, one who knows how to thrust home an important climax as well as how to create evocative textures, varying tensions positively. Placido Domingo in the name part sings with sweetness and purity as well as strength, coping superbly with the legato line of the aria *Pourquoi me réveiller*. Elena Obraztsova is richer and firmer than she usually is on record, but it is a generalized portrait, particularly beside the charming Sophie of Arleen Auger. The others make up a very convincing team. The DG cassette transfer is very successful, matching the discs closely.

It is sad that Alfredo Kraus, one of the most stylish of tenors as a rule, came to record *Werther* so late in his career. Listen to this account of *Pourquoi me réveiller,* and the effortful underlining, with its chopping of the melodic line, is almost unrecognizable as his work. Elsewhere the strained tone is less distracting, and his feeling for words is generally most illuminating. Troyanos makes a volatile Charlotte, but the voice as recorded is grainy. Manuguerra produces rich tone as the Bailiff, but the engineers have not been kind to the LPO strings, which sound rather thin, particularly when compared with those on the DG set. Plasson is a stylish conductor but at times fails to present the full power of the piece.

Mathias, William (born 1934)

Symphony No. 1, Op. 31.
(M) **(*) Oriel ORM 1004. RPO, Groves – JONES: *Symphony No. 6.****

Mathias is of a different generation from his compatriot Daniel Jones, whose *Sixth Symphony* forms the coupling on this valuable record of contemporary Welsh music. Mathias's *First Symphony* was commissioned for the 1966 Llandaff Festival. The music is more aggressive, less comfortable than Jones's idiom. The work has a tonal basis, but relies a good deal on rhythmical elements (in the scherzo with a Stravinskian flavour) and colouristic devices. The writing in the outer movements has plenty of energy and forward momentum, but for all its driving force does not stay in the memory in the same way as the more conventional structure by Daniel Jones on the reverse. Nevertheless with such a committed and well-played performance this is well worth having.

Maunder, John (1858–1920)

Olivet to Calvary (cantata).
(M) **(*) HMV ESD 7051. Mitchinson, Harvey, Guildford Cath. Ch., Barry Rose; Moorse (organ).

It is easy to be patronizing about music like this. Its melodic and harmonic flavour will for many tastes seem too highly coloured and sugary for the subject, but provided one accepts the conventions of style in which it is composed the music is effective and often moving. The performance has an attractive simplicity and genuine eloquence. Just occasionally the soloists overdo the drama in their enunciation, but for the most part they are sensitive to the text and the obvious dedication of the music. Frederick Harvey is particularly moving at the actual moment of Christ's death: in a passage that, insensitively handled, could be positively embarrassing, he creates a magical, hushed intensity. The choir sing beautifully, and in the gentler, lyrical writing (the semi-chorus *O Thou whose sweet compassion*, for example) sentimentality is skilfully avoided. The HMV recording is first-class in every way.

Maw, Nicholas (born 1935)

Life studies Nos. 1–8.
*** Argo ZRG 899 [id.]. ASMF, Marriner.

Life studies for fifteen solo strings makes a formidable addition to the line of great string works by British composers. On one level the eight movements present virtuoso exercises in texture and sonority; but with their broad range of expression in Maw's uninhibited style their impact is above all emotional, particularly in so strong a performance as this. The passionate unison melody of the eighth movement makes a superb culmination. The recording is excellent.

(i) *La vita nuova* (for soprano and chamber ens.); (ii) *The Voice of Love.*
*** Chan. ABR/*ABT* 1037. (i) Christie, Nash Ens.; (ii) Walker, Vignoles.

These two song cycles represent Maw's work at different periods of his career, yet both give warm evidence of his exceptional sensitivity towards the voice. To words specially written by the poet Peter Porter, *The Voice of Love* tells of the love affair of a seventeenth-century authoress, surrounding romantic emotion with colour and point in a rather Britten-like way. Sarah Walker, accompanied by the pianist Roger Vignoles, characterizes superbly. Nan Christie in the more recent cycle – setting Italian Renaissance love-lyrics – is less sweetly caught; but here too the natural expressiveness of Maw's writing comes over most persuasively, helped by first-rate recording. The tape transfer is also excellent; there is little to choose between disc and cassette.

Maxwell Davies, Peter
(born 1934)

(i) *Antechrist;* (i; ii) *From Stone to Thorn;* (i; iii) *L'Homme armé;* (iv) *Hymnos.*
*** O-L DSLO 2. (i) Fires of L., composer; (ii) Mary Thomas; (iii) Vanessa Redgrave (speaker); (iv) Hacker, Pruslin.

Much of Maxwell Davies's creative energy has been projected towards writing works for the two overlapping groups which he formed and directs, first the Pierrot Players and later the Fires of London. These are four characteristic works regularly given at their concerts, starting with *Antechrist,* a sort of exuberant overture. *L'Homme armé,* a more extended but comparable work, similarly working on a medieval motif, is also most approachable, while the other two works, thornier in argument, directly display the formidable talents of – among others – the soprano Mary Thomas and the clarinettist Alan Hacker. A valuable disc, well recorded.

Ave Maris Stella; (i) *Tenebrae super Gesualdo.*
*** Uni. KP 8002. Fires of L., composer, (i) with Walker (guitar), Thomas (sop.).

These two elegiac pieces – dating from 1975 and 1972 respectively – find Maxwell Davies at his most severe and demanding. Based on the chant of that name, *Ave Maris Stella* is yet more than a ritual, conveying inner tensions in its sharp contrasts. The *Tenebrae,* less complex in their textures but equally extended, are also deeply felt. The composer's concentration is reflected in the performances of both works under his direction; both are beautifully recorded.

Eight songs for a mad king.
(M) *** Uni. UNS 261. Eastman (reciter), Fires of L., composer.

There are many levels of imagination at work in this extraordinary, unforgettable piece, probably the most successful example of music-theatre that Davies has written. It is at once a re-creation of George III's madness, the reciter/singer taking the role of the king with nerve-jangling realism; at once an extraordinary example of new expression in sing-speech, with vocal harmonics and double-notes produced as part of the king's raving; at once a dramatic fantasy with flute, clarinet, violin and cello representing birds in cages, the birds the king tried to teach; at once a musical fantasy on tunes played by a mechanical organ that the king actually possessed and which survives today. It is harrowing in its surrealism, its playing on the hidden nerve, but the power of inspiration, superbly interpreted here and splendidly recorded, is undeniable.

Mayer, John (born 1930)

(i) *Flute concerto* (*Mandada ki raga sangeet*); (ii) *Sri Krishna* (for flute, piano; harpsichord and tanpura).
❀ *** RCA Dig. RL/*RK* 25389. Galway, (i) LPO, Iwaki; (ii) Mayer; Moll.

Musical collusions between the cultures of East and West can easily become collisions, but this admirable example of the music of John Mayer is a highly diverting exception. Mayer was born in Calcutta and studied within both the Indian and Western traditions of classical music. The result is an easy symbiosis of styles, leaning rather more towards the West in the final melodic and harmonic patterns, but drawing on Indian idioms and folklore most persuasively. *Sri Krishna* is a wholly engaging suite of seven miniatures where the solo flute is given sparing accompaniments from piano, tanpura and harpsichord. In the *Concerto* the accompaniment is comparably discreet in mixing instrumental colours from both the composer's geographical sources. The result has some affinity with Rodrigo's Spanish evocations in the lightness of Mayer's touch, and the spiciness of the rhythmic and harmonic effects. It goes without saying that Galway's playing is masterly; it also has striking spontaneity. The accompaniments are first-class too, and the digital sound is clear, luminous and well balanced. The chrome tape matches the disc closely. Highly recommended.

McPhee, Colin (1901–64)

Tabuh-Tabuhan (Toccata for orchestra).
(*) Mercury SRI 75116 [id.]. Eastman Rochester O, Hanson – SCHULLER: *7 Studies on themes of Paul Klee**; BLOCH: *Sinfonia breve.***(*)

McPhee's *Tabuh-Tabuhan* is inspired by the Balinese Gamelan orchestra. The piece is in three movements: *Ostinatos, Nocturne* and *Finale*, and in the first there is rather too much repetition of phrases not memorable in themselves. Indeed, in general the melodic content is sparse, although there is no lack of rhythmic vitality. The performance is first-class, and the results are certainly exotic and the recording of vintage Mercury quality. The main interest of this disc is Schuller's ingenious set of *Studies on themes of Paul Klee*.

Medtner, Nikolai (1880–1951)

Dithyramb, Op. 10/2; Elegy, Op. 59/2; Skazki (Fairy tales): No. 1 (1915); in E min., Op. 14/2; in G, Op. 9/3; in D min. (Ophelia's song); in C sharp min., Op. 35/4. Forgotten melodies, 2nd Cycle, No. 1: Meditation. Primavera, Op. 39/3; 3 Hymns in praise of toil, Op. 49; Piano sonata in E min. (The Night Wind), Op. 25/2; Sonata Triad, Op. 11/1–3.
*** CRD CRD 1038/9. Milne.

Medtner remains lamentably neglected in the recital room and in the catalogues. His art is as subtle and elusive as that of, say, Fauré, whose piano music has also never found the wider public favour it deserves. Far from being the Russian Brahms or Rachmaninov-without-the-tunes, Medtner is very much his own man. He shows an aristocratic disdain of the obvious, a feeling for balance and proportion, and a quiet harmonic refinement that offer consistent rewards. This two-record set of piano music by Hamish Milne forms an admirable introduction to his art. Milne wisely avoids the *G minor Sonata*, Op. 22, and the *Reminiscenza*, Op. 38 (which Gilels recorded in the 1960s), and concentrates on music new to the catalogue. The most substantial piece in this set is the *E minor Sonata* (*The Night Wind*), which should dispel any doubts as to Medtner's capacity to sustain an argument on the grandest scale; it is a one-movement sonata taking the best part of half an hour. Milne also includes the less ambitious single-movement sonatas, Op. 11, which are finely concentrated, elegantly fashioned works. There is hardly a weak piece in this set, and Milne is a poetic advocate whose technical prowess is matched by first-rate artistry. The recording too is very truthful and vivid.

4 Skazki, Op. 26; Sonata-Ballade in F sharp, Op. 27; Sonata minacciosa in F min. (Sonata orageuse), Op. 53/2.
*** Pearl SHE 535. Binns.

The *Sonata-Ballade* comes from 1913 and was recorded by the composer himself on 78s towards the end of his life. It is an eloquent and often subtle statement whose feeling is nonetheless potent for being restrained. The *Four Fairy tales* are full of fantasy, and the *Sonata minacciosa*, a later work dating from the 1930s, is also a find. Malcolm Binns is more than equal to the demands these pieces make, and his artistry is faithfully served by the engineers.

Mendelssohn, Felix (1809–47)

Piano concertos Nos. 1 in G min., Op. 25; 2 in D min., Op. 40.

*** CBS 76376/*40*- [M 33207]. Perahia, ASMF, Marriner.

(M) *** DG Priv. 2535/*3335* 416. Gheorghiu, Leipzig RSO, Kegel.

*** Decca Dig. SXDL/*KSXDC* 7623 [Lon. LDR/*5*- 71123]. Schiff, Bav. RSO, Dutoit.

*(*) Erato Dig. NUM/*MCE* 75028. Duchable, Paris O Ens., Wallez.

Mendelssohn's two *Piano concertos* are not in the class of the famous *Violin concerto in E minor*, but when played with discernment they are agreeably entertaining. Perahia's playing catches the Mendelssohnian spirit with admirable perception. There is sensibility and sparkle, the slow movements are shaped most beautifully and obviously the partnership with Marriner is very successful, for the Academy give a most sensitive backing. The recording is fair. The CBS cassette was originally muffled and had a very limited range, but no doubt it has been remastered by now to match this company's current standard.

Valentin Gheorghiu is well known in his native Rumania and made an impressive record of the Liszt *Sonata* on HMV in the days of mono LP. These performances originally appeared as part of a Mendelssohn–Schubert package and were never issued separately on a full-price DG record. Gheorghiu's playing has both sensitivity and strength, and his readings make a characterful alternative to the imaginative and thoroughly idiomatic account by Murray Perahia on CBS. However, Gheorghiu is better recorded, and though his playing does not quite match Perahia's delicacy of feeling, this must be accounted a highly competitive issue. The clean cassette transfer matches the disc closely.

If Perahia's CBS recording is not ideal as sound, neither, in a very different way, is Decca's. The timbre is fresher and more natural (and in this respect an improvement on the CBS) but the balance is not entirely satisfactory, for not only does it place the soloist too far forward so that the hammers are audible, but the middle and bass of the instrument seem nearer than the top end. Andras Schiff plays marvellously, with great delicacy and fluency: his virtuosity is effortless and never pursued for the sake of personal display. There is plenty of poetic feeling, too, though he does not bring quite such tenderness and meaning to some details (such as the second group of the first movement of the *D minor Concerto*) as does Perahia, nor is there quite the sense of sweep and panache that distinguishes both Valentin Gheorghiu and Perahia, particularly in the *G minor Concerto.* However, the Schiff is still excellent and deserves a three-star recommendation too. There is an excellent chrome tape.

The French pianist, François-René Duchable, is no match for Gheorghiu, let alone Perahia, in these concertos. He is brilliant but relatively unpoetic, an impression that is hardly helped by the balance which places the piano too forward and as a result masks some of the orchestral detail. Steely-fingered and charmless. The chrome tape matches the disc closely.

Violin concerto in D min., Op. posth.; Violin concerto in E min., Op. 64.

**(*) HMV ASD 2809 [Ang. RL/*4RL* 32102]. Menuhin, LSO, Frühbeck de Burgos.

Mendelssohn's early *D minor Violin concerto* was completed when he was thirteen, after he had written the first five *Symphonies for strings*. As a structure it is amazingly accomplished, but only the finale has memorable themes. Menuhin plays it with obvious devotion. In the famous *E minor Concerto* his performance has its moments of roughness but it has a magic too – at the appearance of the first movement's second subject and in the slow movement. The HMV recording is clear rather than especially rich.

Violin concerto in E min., Op. 64.

*** HMV ASD/*TC-ASD* 2926 [Ang. S/*4XS* 36963]. Perlman, LSO, Previn – BRUCH: *Concerto No. 1.****

*** Decca Dig. **410 011-2**; SXDL/*KSXDC* 7558 [Lon. LDR/*5* 71058]. Kyung-Wha Chung, Montreal SO, Dutoit – TCHAIKOVSKY: *Concerto.****

*** DG Dig. **400 031-2**; 2532/*3302* 016 [id.]. Mutter, Berlin PO, Karajan – BRUCH: *Concerto No. 1.****

*** CRD 1069/*CRDC 4069*. Ronald Thomas, Bournemouth Sinf. – BEETHOVEN: *Romances*; SCHUBERT: *Konzertstück.****

*** HMV ASD/*TC-ASD* 334. Menuhin, Philh. O, Kurtz – BRUCH: *Concerto No. 1.****

(M) *** Decca VIV/*KVIC* 4. Ricci, Netherlands RO, Fournet – TCHAIKOVSKY: *Concerto.****

(M) *** Decca SPA/*KCSP* 88 [Lon. STS 15402]. Ricci, LSO, Gamba – BRUCH: *Concerto No. 1.****

(***) RCA Conifer 26.35038 (2) [VCS 7058]. Heifetz, Boston SO, Munch – BRAHMS *(**) and TCHAIKOVSKY: *Concertos* (***).

(*) DG 2531/*3301* 304 [id.]. Mintz, Chicago SO, Abbado – BRUCH: *Concerto No. 1.* *

(M) **(*) CBS 60111/*40-* [MY/*MYT* 36724]. Stern. Phd. O, Ormandy – TCHAIKOVSKY: *Concerto.***(*)

(*) CBS 72768 [MS 7313]. Zukerman, NYPO, Bernstein – TCHAIKOVSKY: *Concerto.*(*)

(B) ** CfP CFP/*TC-CFP* 40374. Milstein, Philh. O, Barzin – BRUCH: *Concerto No. 1.***

(M) ** DG Priv. 2535/*3335* 294 [id.]. Uck Kim, Bamberg SO, Kamu – BRUCH: *Concerto No.1.**(*)

*(*) Ph. 9500 321/*7300 583* [id.]. Szeryng, Concg. O, Haitink – TCHAIKOVSKY: *Concerto.**(*)

(M) * Ph. Seq. 6527/*7311* 061 [Quin. 7194]. Szeryng, LSO, Dorati – SCHUMANN: *Concerto.**

The Mendelssohn *E minor Concerto* is another work which is splendidly served by the gramophone. Perlman gives a performance as full of flair as any available, and he is superbly matched by the LSO under Previn, always an illuminating interpreter of this composer. With ripe recording quality, this stands as one of the first recommendations for a deservedly much-recorded work. The cassette has been remastered (originally it had a restricted dynamic range). It sounds well now, although there is a slight loss of sharpness of detail.

Chung favours speeds faster than usual in all three movements, and the result is sparkling and happy with the lovely slow movement fresh and songful, not at all sentimental. With warmly sympathetic accompaniment from Dutoit and the Montreal orchestra, amply recorded, the result is one of Chung's happiest records. Some may find the helter-skelter of the finale a little too breathless, but the exhilaration of a tight challenge superbly taken is very hard to resist. This is almost the reading that Heifetz might have recorded with speeds similarly fast but manner far sweeter and more relaxed. The Tchaikovsky coupling is generous. On cassette the sound is of high quality, but the focus of the solo instrument benefits from a slight treble cut. The compact disc version emphasizes the closeness of the soloist, but with its clarity and tangibility of atmosphere, the result is very real.

Here even more than in her Bruch coupling, the freshness of Anne-Sophie Mutter's approach communicates vividly to the listener, creating the feeling of hearing the work anew. Her gentleness and radiant simplicity in the *Andante* are very appealing, and the closing pages have real magic, with Karajan catching the mood and scale in his accompaniment. Similarly the second subject of the first movement has great charm, and the light, sparkling finale (again with the orchestral balance superbly managed) is a delight. There is a greater spontaneity here than in Mintz's slightly riper version, and the recording is most realistically balanced on both disc and tape. The sound on compact disc is refined, but emphasizes the rather artificial microphone set-up. Mutter is given a small-scale image, projected forward from the orchestral backcloth, but the orchestral layout itself does not have the luminous detail of the Decca recording, with the wind tending to congeal slightly when playing together.

Ronald Thomas's, too, is in many ways the opposite of a dashing virtuoso approach, yet his apt, unforced choice of speeds, his glowing purity of intonation and the fine co-ordination with the orchestra he regularly leads (an amazing achievement in this often complex, fast-flowing music) put this among the most satisfying versions available. It is intensely refreshing from first to last, and is helped by excellent recording on disc and cassette alike.

Menuhin's recording is not new, but it has withstood the test of time. The restrained warmth of his phrasing of the famous principal melody of the slow movement has long been a hallmark of Menuhin's reading, and the finale has plenty of sparkle. Efrem Kurtz accompanies ably. The cassette was originally issued in non-Dolby format, but this has now been corrected and the sound is now bright – the soloist forward and dominating the texture – and clearly detailed, yet the solo violin timbre is not edgy.

Ricci's Viva reissue was originally recorded in Phase Four. The performance is even finer than his successful earlier version with Gamba. The balance places him well forward and reveals plenty of orchestral detail by the close microphoning of the woodwind. In the finale the listener's pleasure is enhanced by Fournet's precision in matching the solo line with the accompaniment, which adds considerable extra sparkle. The slow movement has a disarming simple eloquence, and the reading as a whole is undoubtedly distinguished. The vivid recording is admirably transferred to the cassette, though the tape has a marginally less dramatic dynamic range.

Ricci's earlier performance is clean and sympathetic, and technically brilliant. There is perhaps some lack of repose and depth of feeling in the slow movement, but Ricci is far from being one of the virtuosi who ride roughshod over a work. Gamba too conducts with vigour and sympathy. For those who need a cheaper stereo recording, and who particularly want the fine Bruch coupling, this is a good recommendation, with an excellent cassette version too.

As one might expect, Heifetz gives a fabulous performance, but one which will probably infuriate almost as many listeners as it enthrals. His speeds are consistently fast. Some will consider that the slow movement, for example, is rattled through, but when Heifetz's flexible phrasing sounds so inevitable and easy it is hard not to be convinced. The recording is clear but hard and lacks atmosphere.

Mintz's version is powerfully conceived, less reticent than Mutter, less spontaneous than Perlman. It is not quite the equal of the Bruch coupling, although Abbado gives fine support. The tape is more opaque than the disc.

Stern's performance with the Philadelphia Orchestra was made at a peak period in his recording career. It has great bravura, culminating in a marvellously surging account of the finale. The slow movement too is played with great eloquence and feeling. but when pianissimos are non-existent – partly, but not entirely, the fault of the close recording balance – the poetic element is diminished. It remains a stirring account, and the recording is vivid if not refined, with a good cassette.

Zukerman gives a sweet-toned but never cloying account. His playing is impeccable from the technical point of view and the support he receives from Bernstein and the New York orchestra is thoroughly sympathetic. An extremely fine performance, and one which would be a match for almost any, were it not for the recording, which is not as naturally balanced or as rich in tone as one would like. The cassette transfer is of good quality, clear and vivid.

Milstein is not at his most fervently lyrical or totally committed in his 1961 version of the Mendelssohn. There is some patchy intonation at one point in the first movement, but that is not enough in itself to cause more than a passing raised eyebrow. There is a certain quality of detachment here, and for all its fine musicianship (there is some good orchestral playing) this is not as memorable or characterful as the best versions in this highly competitive field. But it is good value at Classics for Pleasure price. There is little to choose between disc and tape; the cassette is very slightly smoother on top.

The Privilege performance by Yong Uck Kim is genuinely touching, with an unforced eloquence that carries conviction. Unfortunately the soloist is handicapped by less than first-class orchestral support, and as a whole the coupling does not challenge the finest of its rivals. However, this is a rewarding performance which was underrated on its first appearance; those who investigate it may well feel that the rewards of Yong's playing outweigh the drawback of the orchestral support. The recording is eminently satisfactory.

Szeryng's full-priced account with Haitink is sensitive and lyrical, but it has no specially individual qualities, either from the soloist or in the accompaniment. The earlier Sequenza version with Dorati has a recording balance which does not do Szeryng justice, and this is not one of his best records, with a dull coupling.

(i) *Violin concerto in E min., Op. 64;* (ii) *Symphony No. 4 in A* (*Italian*), *Op. 90;* (iii) *A Midsummer Night's Dream: Overture and incidental music.*

(B) *** DG Walkman *413 150-4*. (i) Milstein, VPO, Abbado; (ii) Berlin PO, Maazel; (iii) Mathis, Boese, Bav. RSO with Ch., Kubelik.

This attractive compilation is one of the outstanding bargains in DG's Walkman series of double-length chrome tapes aimed at collectors with miniaturized personal cassette reproducers. Milstein's 1973 account of the *Violin concerto* is highly distinguished. With excellent recording and balance this is worthy to rank with the best, and it is greatly enhanced by the sensitivity of Abbado's accompaniment. Maazel's *Italian* offers a fast, hard-driven but joyous and beautifully articulated performance of the first movement and equal clarity and point in the vivacious finale. The central movements are well sustained and altogether this is highly enjoyable, the recording resonantly full-timbred. Kubelik's fairly complete version of the incidental music for *A Midsummer Night's Dream* is no less enjoyable (see below) and the sound is first-class here too.

Overtures: Calm Sea and Prosperous Voyage, Op. 27; Fair Melusina, Op. 32; The Hebrides (*Fingal's Cave*), *Op. 26; A Midsummer Night's Dream, Op. 21; Ruy Blas, Op. 95.*

(M) ** DG Priv. 2535/*3335* 460. LSO, Chmura.

Gabriel Chmura is clearly a talent to watch. He has won both the Cantelli and the Karajan competitions and is still only in his thirties. He is obviously on guard against the impetuosity of youth, and these performances tend towards the other extreme: he errs on the side of excessive caution in *The Hebrides*, where his tempo is a bit too measured. This could have more lightness of touch, and *Ruy Blas* too needs more zest if it is to be really exciting. Yet he pays scrupulous attention to detail and is plainly both conscientious in his approach and deeply musical. The orchestral playing is obviously well prepared and has real finish, while the recording is clean, well focused and bright without being over-lit. The cassette transfer is well balanced, but a lower level on side two (*Midsummer Night's Dream* and *Calm Sea*) brings a loss of range and immediacy.

Symphonies for string orchestra, Nos. 2 in D; 3 in E min.; 5 in B flat; 6 in E flat.

(M) *** HMV Green. ESD 7123. Polish CO, Maksymiuk.

Digitally recorded on a mid-price label, this collection of the boy Mendelssohn's early *String symphonies* (written when he was only twelve) is most invigorating. These earlier symphonies of the series of twelve may look to various models from Bach to Beethoven, but the boy keeps showing his individuality and, however imitative the style, the vitality of the invention still bursts through. The slow movement of the *Symphony No. 2*, for example, is a Bachian meditation that in its simple beauty matches later Mendelssohn. The Polish strings are set in a lively acoustic, giving exceptionally rich sound.

Symphonies for string orchestra, Nos. 6 in E flat; 7 in D min.; 10 in B min.

**(*) HM 1C 065 99823 [PRO 1007]. Ens. 13 Baden Baden, Reichert.

Drawn from members of the South-West German Radio Orchestra, this ensemble plays as stylishly here as in its more customary twentieth-century repertoire. Tempi are at times eccentrically fast in what after all are easy-going boyhood inspirations, but this selection is most welcome.

Symphonies Nos. 1–5 (complete).
*** DG 2740 128/*3371 020* [id.]. Berlin PO, Karajan (with soloists and chorus in *No. 2*).

Karajan's distinguished box from 1975 still dominates the catalogue. There are some reservations to be made about the *Reformation symphony*, but the set as a whole remains a thoroughly worthwhile recommendation. The *Scottish symphony* is a particularly remarkable account and the *Italian* shows the Berlin Philharmonic in sparkling form, as does the early *C minor* work. The soloists in the *Hymn of praise* (No. 2) are a good team, rather than showing any memorable individuality, but the choral singing is very fine and the recording is excellent, as it is throughout. The tape box was an early DG transfer and originally showed transfer faults, including one or two moments of coarseness caused by the relatively high level. However, this is likely to have been corrected by now.

Symphonies Nos. 1; 4 in A (Italian), Op. 90.
** Ph. 9500 708/*7300 803* [id.]. LPO, Haitink.

(i) *Symphonies Nos. 2;* (ii) *3 in A min. (Scottish), Op. 56.*
*** Ph. 6769 042/*7699 128* [id.]. (i) Price, Burgess, Jerusalem, LPO, and Ch.; (ii) LSO; both cond. Chailly.

Mendelssohn's *Hymn of Praise* was once a favourite work with Victorian choral societies, who often forgot to include the first three purely instrumental movements. Latterly it has been unduly neglected, because it so manifestly falls short of its great model, Beethoven's *Ninth Symphony*. The *C minor Symphony*, on the other hand, is anything but pretentious; with its delightful scherzo it is another example of Mendelssohn's electrically precocious genius.

One clear advantage of the Chailly version of *Hymn of Praise* lies in its outstanding trio of soloists, with Margaret Price soaring radiantly in *Lobe den Herrn, meine Seele* and the women of the London Philharmonic Choir matching her. Siegfried Jerusalem also sings gloriously, with tone both bright and sweet, not least in the duet with Price. The recording is exceptionally realistic and beautifully balanced, so that Chailly's fresh and unaffected interpretation has its maximum impact, helped by fine playing and choral singing from London Philharmonic sources. With the London Symphony Orchestra Chailly gives a comparably enjoyable performance of the *Scottish symphony*, though the distancing of the sound in a rather reverberant acoustic takes some of the bite away.

The *Italian symphony* really needs more sparkle than Haitink brings to it in his LPO version. It is always fresh and honest, but magic never quite develops, though some may be attracted by the unusual – but very apt – coupling of the early *Symphony No. 1*. The recording is fair but not one of Philips' clearest; the high-level cassette transfer is excellent.

Symphony No. 3 in A min. (Scottish), Op. 56; Athalia: Overture and War march of the Priests.
**(*) Decca SXL 6954 [Lon. CS/*5-* 7184]. VPO, Dohnányi.

Symphony No. 3; Overture: Calm Sea and Prosperous Voyage.
*** Ph. 9500 535/*7300 678* [id.]. LPO, Haitink.

Symphony No. 3; Fair Melusina overture.
**(*) CBS Dig. 37282/*40-* [id.]. Bav. RSO, Andrew Davis.

Symphony No. 3; Overture: The Hebrides (Fingal's Cave).
*** DG 2530 126/*3300 181* [id.]. Berlin PO, Karajan.
(M) *** Decca SPA/*KCSP* 503 [Lon. STS/*5-* 15091]. LSO, Maag.
(B) *** CfP/*TC-CFP* 40270. SNO, Gibson.
**(*) DG 2531/*3301* 256 [id.]. Israel PO, Bernstein.

Symphonies Nos. 3; 4 (Italian).
(M) *** Decca Jub. JB/*KJBC* 103. LSO, Abbado.
(M) *** ASV ACM/*ZCACM* 2012. O of St John's, Lubbock.
(*) Argo **411 931-2; ZRG/*KZRC* 926 [id.]. ASMF, Marriner.

Haitink's Philips recording of the *Scottish symphony* has gloriously beautiful sound, the upper strings glowingly fresh and woodwind rich and luminous. Yet the sumptuous body of tone of the full orchestra does not bring clouded detail. Haitink sets a fast pace in the opening movement yet loses nothing of the music's lyrical power. There is a feeling of symphonic breadth too (helped by the resonant fullness of the recording), in spite of the omission of the exposition repeat. In the other three movements the warmth and glow of the Philips recording are always telling, especially at the opening of the scherzo, and for the dancing violins in the finale. The final peroration sounds magnificent. The evocation of the overture is similarly persuasive. The Philips cassette is slightly less sumptuous than the disc, but the sound is full, fresh and wide-ranging – one of Philips' very best tapes.

Karajan's account is very fine indeed, although it is surely due for reissue on Accolade as the sound, though bright and clear, lacks the last degree of bloom on top. The performance contains some slight eccentricities of tempo: the opening of the symphony is rather measured, while the closing pages of the finale are taken with exuberant brilliance. But the orchestral playing is superb – the pianissimo articulation of the strings is a pleasure in itself – and the conductor's warmth and direct eloquence, with no fussiness, is irresistible. The scherzo is marvellously done and becomes a highlight, while there is no doubt that Karajan's final coda has splendid buoyancy and power. With a characterful account of *Fingal's Cave* as coupling, this remains highly recommendable. There is a good cassette.

Under Maag too the *Scottish symphony* is played most beautifully, and its pastoral character, occasioned by Mendelssohn's considerable use of the strings throughout, is amplified by a recording of great warmth. The opening string cantilena is poised and very gracious and thus sets the mood for what is to follow. The stereo is excellent. One small complaint: Maag is too ponderous in the final *Maestoso*, but there is a compensating breadth and the effect is almost Klempererian. The remastered sound quality is first-class, disguising the age of the original recording, with bright, natural strings and glowing woodwind detail. LP and cassette are closely matched. *Fingal's Cave* is no less successful, and this remains one of the most satisfying accounts of this evocative overture in the catalogue.

Dohnányi's record has also been much praised, particularly and justifiably for its superb recording, among the finest the *Scottish symphony* has received (though the timpani are too prominent). The cassette transfer too is outstandingly successful. The performance is fresh and alert and the recording helps to underline the stormy quality that Dohnányi aptly finds in the first movement, though in other movements this is a less characterful reading than the best rivals. Not all the woodwind playing is elegant, and the welcome fill-up, a march once deservedly popular, is given a square performance.

In the bargain range the CfP version, appropriately recorded in Scotland, is very competitive. Gibson and his orchestra are on top form and they play the piece with warmth and eloquence. The string phrasing is strikingly fresh, and among the wind soloists the clarinets distinguish themselves (as also in the overture). The reading is agreeably relaxed and its presentation is helped by the rich glowing recording, with its full body and natural perspective. The (high-level) tape transfer has marginally less range and transparency than the disc but is still very good.

The CBS digital recording is of high quality and Andrew Davis's reading is freshly straightforward, supported by excellent playing from the Bavarian Radio Orchestra. But the score's pianissimo markings are much less strikingly contrasted here than with Karajan, and this is not just a matter of the forward balance. The scherzo is very successful (helped by the transparent detail of the sound) and the slow movement is memorable, nicely paced and beautifully shaped. The finale is alert and zestful. Davis's coupling is attractive and well done too; but, all in all, both the Haitink and Karajan versions are more characterful in their different ways. The high-level CBS chrome tape matches the disc very closely.

Bernstein and the Israel orchestra, recorded live in Munich, give a loving performance whose expansive tempi run the risk of overloading Mendelssohn's fresh inspiration with heavy expressiveness, making the slow introduction and the slow movement sound almost Mahlerian. The rhythmic lift of the scherzo and finale make amends, and throughout the performance a feeling of spontaneity helps one to accept the exaggerations; but it is not a version to recommend for repeated listening. The recording is well balanced and the coupling apt if ungenerous. The cassette is well managed, fresh, rich and clear.

While Haitink, Karajan and Maag all have much in their favour, Abbado has the advantage of a highly competitive coupling, now offered at medium price, and first-rate Decca recording, 1968 vintage, warm, lively and very well balanced, notwithstanding the length of the sides. The cassette is very good too, although on tape in the *Third symphony* there is slight loss of sharpness in the detail because of the attractively resonant ambience. Abbado's *Scottish* is beautifully played, each phrase sensitively moulded, and the LSO responds to his direction with the greatest delicacy of feeling, while the *Italian symphony* has a comparable lightness of touch matched with lyrical warmth.

With a chamber-sized string section, Lubbock offers a refreshingly direct performance of the *Scottish symphony*, presenting Mendelssohn's refined textures with delightful lightness and clarity. The tempo for the first-movement allegro is very brisk indeed (the reading could not be further removed from Haitink's in its approach), but there is no sense of hurry and the effect is almost Mozartian. The other movements are a little lacking in individuality, but the performance as a whole is most enjoyable. The *Italian symphony* has extremely vivacious outer movements (room was found to include the first-movement exposition repeat) and a nicely paced, engagingly delicate *Andante*. The recording is bright and clean, with no lack of bloom (the cassette and disc a close match), and the balance brings out the extra woodwind detail that naturally emerges from a performance with reduced strings. The playing may be a shade less polished than with Abbado or Marriner, but it is attractively spirited.

In Marriner's Argo performance the *Adagio* of the *Scottish* is so spacious (arguably too much so, since the middle section grows heavy) that the finale has to be put on side two. This means that the *Italian* has to be given without the exposition repeat and the twenty-bar lead-back. The performances are stylish and well sprung but have no more individuality than Lubbock's. Again the use of a smaller-scaled ensemble brings a crisper, more transparent effect than usual. The recording is excellent, although the cassette has a less cleanly focused upper range than the disc; Lubbock's ASV tape is much brighter and cleaner.

Symphony No. 4 in A (Italian), Op. 90.
C *** DG Dig. **410 862-2**; 410 862-1/*4* [id.]. Philh. O, Sinopoli – SCHUBERT: *Symphony No. 8.*** C ❀
(M) *** Decca VIV/*KVIC* 33. LSO, Abbado – SCHUBERT: *Symphony No. 8.***
(*) HMV Dig. ASD/*TCC-ASD* 3963 [Ang. DS/*4ZS* 37760]. Berlin PO, Tennstedt – SCHUMANN: *Symphony No. 4.*(*)

Symphony No. 4; Overtures: Calm Sea and Prosperous Voyage; The Hebrides.
*** Decca Dig. SXDL/*KSXDC* 7500 [Lon. LDR 10003/*5*-]. VPO, Dohnányi.

Symphony No. 4; Overtures: The Hebrides; A Midsummer Night's Dream; Ruy Blas.
*** HMV ASD/*TC-ASD* 3763 [Ang. SZ 37614]. LSO, Previn.

Symphony No. 4; A Midsummer Night's Dream: Overture, Op. 21; Scherzo; Nocturne; Intermezzo; Wedding march, Op. 61.
(M) **(*) CBS 60147/*40*-. Cleveland O, Szell.

Previn's HMV version of the *Italian symphony* comes in what is in effect an ideal Mendelssohn coupling (perfect for recommending to anyone who just wants a single disc to represent the composer), his best-loved symphony matched against the three most popular overtures. Previn, always an inspired Mendelssohnian, gives exuberant performances. In the symphony he has modified the tempo of the *Pilgrims' march* very slightly from his earlier RCA reading, making it more clearly a slow movement, while the third movement has a cleaner culmination on the reprise. The outer movements as before are urgent without sounding at all breathless, and are finely sprung; the recording balance has the strings a little less forward than they might be, but the fullness of sound is impressive. The cassette too is first-class, rich and vivid and only fractionally less refined than the disc.

Sinopoli's great gift is to illuminate almost every phrase afresh. His speeds tend to be extreme – fast in the first movement, but with diamond-bright detail, and on the slow side in the remaining three. Only in the heavily inflected account of the third movement is the result at all mannered, but with superb playing from the Philharmonia and excellent Kingsway Hall recording, this rapt performance is most compelling. Like the disc, the chrome cassette is first-class, but for refinement of detail, especially at lower dynamic levels, the compact disc is among the most impressive digital recordings to have come from DG. Interestingly, the engineers achieve here a brighter lighting for the upper strings than is usual in this venue.

Abbado's highly persuasive account, beautifully recorded, with an extremely lively cassette, is discussed above, where it is more attractively coupled.

Dohnányi, in one of the first digital recordings to be issued, gives a characteristically refreshing account of the *Italian symphony*, never pushed too hard, even though the *Saltarello* is taken exhilaratingly fast. It is a pity that – unlike many of the finest versions (Previn's, Leppard's and Abbado's) – this omits the exposition repeat in the first movement, so one misses the extended lead-back passage. No doubt it was decided that for so important a digital issue wide groove-spacing was essential, and the two overtures on the reverse bring sound even more impressive, with the whispered opening of *Meerestille* particularly evocative. *The Hebrides* is taken rather slowly and romantically.

Tennstedt's account of the *Italian* is vividly articulated and obviously felt. He is not quite as spontaneous as Bernstein and the Israel Philharmonic (see below), though the quality of the Berliners' playing is finer. The digital sound has admirable body and clarity to recommend it (the chrome cassette is first-class too), and this is certainly a version to be considered.

Szell and his mid-1960s Cleveland Orchestra are heard in bravura form in their Mendelssohn coupling. This was the first stereo recording to include the first movement's exposition repeat. Szell's approach is dramatic and often exhilarating, but, as Klemperer and others have proved, the work's gaiety and sunlight can be readily captured with more relaxed tempi. Yet the precision of the playing is remarkable and there is never any hint of scurrying. About the *Midsummer Night's Dream* excerpts there can be no reservations. This was a work over which Szell lavished much loving care – see his Sequenza version with the Concertgebouw Orchestra below – and the orchestra is in superb form. The tension is high and the articulation in the *Overture*, the sparkling scherzo and the Intermezzo is marvellous. The *Nocturne*, too, comes off well, the solo horn cool but sensitive. The sound is bright and forward, but attractively vivid on both disc and tape alike.

Symphonies Nos. 4 (Italian); 5 in D min. (Reformation), Op. 107.

(M) *** Erato EPR/*MCE* 15533. ECO, Leppard.

*** DG 2531/*3301* 097 [id.]. Israel PO, Bernstein.

(M) **(*) DG Sig. 2543/*3343* 511 [2530 416/*3300 418*]. Berlin PO, Karajan.

Leppard directs joyful performances of both symphonies. Consistently he shows how infectiously he can lift rhythms, so that the first movement of the *Italian* has exhilaration with no feeling of rush. The relatively small string section of the ECO may sound a little thin in the third movement of the *Italian*, but the *Saltarello* finale brings superbly clean articulation of triplets. In the *Reformation* the scale of the performance, coupled with Leppard's rhythmic flair, helps to lighten a work that can sometimes seem too heavy for its material. The *Allegro con fuoco* gets its fire not from high speed but from crisp precision; the scherzo too is beautifully lilting, and the *Allegro maestoso* of the finale firmly replaces pomposity with joy. The recording is airily atmospheric to match.

Bernstein's performances of both symphonies are also sparkling and persuasive, never falling into the rather exaggerated expressiveness which in places mars the companion account of the *Scottish symphony*. As with that work, the recordings were made at live concerts, and though the speeds are often challengingly fast, they never fail to convey the exhilaration of the occasion. In the *Reformation symphony* Bernstein encourages the flute to give a meditative account of the chorale *Ein feste Burg*, but he makes it a revelation, not a distraction. The recording is convincingly atmospheric without being ideally clear. The cassette transfer lacks the last degree of refinement, with a tendency for the bass to boom a little in the *Italian* and a touch of roughness in the finale of the *Reformation*.

It goes without saying that the playing of the Berlin Philharmonic for Karajan is outstandingly fine, but good though the performances are, they are just a shade wanting in spontaneity and sparkle The *Reformation symphony* is most beautifully shaped and finely phrased, though rhythms in the first movement are perhaps a little too heavily accented, with the result that there is a certain lack of forward movement. The chrome cassette is vivid and wide-ranging, but rather dry in the bass. Side one (*No. 4*) is transferred at a high level which brings a degree of fierceness to the upper strings. The tape sounds best played with chrome equalization (whereas most chrome tapes are intended to be played with the setting for 'normal' iron-oxide stock).

CHAMBER AND INSTRUMENTAL MUSIC

Cello sonatas Nos. 1 in B flat, Op. 45; 2 in D, Op. 58.
** Ph. 9500 953. Bijlsma, Hoogland (fortepiano).

Anner Bijlsma plays a gut-stringed Pressenda cello from Turin and Stanley Hoogland a Broadwood, both from the mid-1830s. The *Sonatas* date from 1838 and 1843 respectively; the former is 'a very pleasant and equable work', to quote Philip Radcliffe, and the latter 'rises higher and sinks lower' than its predecessor. The first movement has a certain affinity with the *Italian symphony*. The outer movements of both sonatas are facile but the slow movements have genuine eloquence. The keyboard instrument is somewhat clattery but the forward balance does not help in this respect. A good but not indispensable record, though at present there is no alternative version on modern instruments available in the UK, although in the USA the partnership of Lynn Harrell and James Levine brings a reading of genuine distinction of the *Second D major Sonata* offering most beautiful playing, every detail showing alike the artistry and imagination of both artists. They are well recorded too and the coupling, Schubert's *Arpeggione sonata*, is equally fine [RCA AGL1/*AGK1* 4903].

Octet (for strings) in E flat, Op. 20.
(M) *** Ph. 6570/*7310* 884. I Musici – SPOHR: *Octet.***(*)
*** Argo ZRG 569 [id.]. ASMF – BOCCHERINI: *Quintet, Op. 37/7.****
** DG Dig. 2532/*3302* 077 [id.]. Berlin PO (members) – BRUCH: *Septet.****
*(*) Decca Dig. SXDL/*KSXDC* 7506 [Lon. LDR 10009]. Israel PO, Mehta.

Octet; String symphonies Nos. 10 and 12.
(M) *** Ph. Seq. 6527/*7311* 076. I Musici.

Octet; (i) *Piano sextet in D, Op. 110.*
(M) *** Decca Jub. JB/*KJBC* 138. Vienna Octet (members); (i) with Panhoffer.

Octet; String quintet No. 2 in B flat, Op. 87.
*** Ph. 9500 616/*7300 825* [id.]. ASMF Chamber Ens.

The Academy's earlier Argo record of the *Octet*, with a Boccherini quintet as a fill-up, dates from the late 1960s, and, good though it was in almost every way, this newcomer is an improvement. The playing has greater sparkle and polish; the recorded sound is also superior; and it has the advantage of an altogether excellent coupling. Whereas on the earlier disc the *Octet* split over to the second side, here it can be played without a break and room is left for an important work of Mendelssohn's later life, the *Second Quintet*. This is an underrated piece, and it too receives an elegant and poetic performance that will give much satisfaction and is unlikely to be surpassed for a long time.

The I Musici version of the *Octet* is also one of the finest available, smooth in contour but with a fine balance between vitality and warmth. The *String symphonies* are obviously smaller in scale than on the alternative full orchestral versions, but they are beautifully played. The recording is excellent and the tape transfer smooth and quite lively. The I Musici performance is also offered in an alternative coupling with Spohr's *Octet*.

The Vienna version of the *Octet* is highly competitive and is happily accommodated on one side without any loss of quality. Indeed the recorded sound is excellent. The new coupling is the *Piano sextet* which, despite its high opus number, is a work of the composer's youth, written when he was only fifteen. Like much of his music of that time, it has an engaging immediacy and remarkable sureness of technique. The performance here is of a very high standard, with a recording to match. On tape the high-level transfer gives striking immediacy to the *Sextet*, but the effect in the *Octet* – at a lower level – is mellow and there is less presence.

The digital record from members of the Berlin Philharmonic celebrates the fact that both featured composers were child prodigies: Mendelssohn was sixteen when he composed the *Octet*, but Bruch's *Septet* appeared when the composer was a mere eleven! Indeed, it is the novelty of the coupling, with the Bruch not otherwise available, which will attract the collector. The *Octet* is well enough played though something of this score's magic is lost: the marvellous scherzo could sound fresher, but the rather clinical and close balance may to some extent be held responsible. Chrome tape and disc sound virtually identical.

Mehta's account using a full complement of orchestral strings is brilliantly and clearly recorded, but the effect is glossy. The cassette is sweeter and smoother on top than the LP and is generally preferable. The playing itself emphasizes vitality at the expense of warmth.

Piano quartet No. 3 in B min. Op. 3; Piano sextet in D, Op. 110.
(M) *** Ph. 6570/*7310* 921. Haas, Berlin PO Octet (members).

Mendelssohn began writing the *Piano quartet* in the same year as the *Piano sextet* (1824), but the work was not complete until a year later. It is dedicated to Goethe and shows even greater maturity in both mood and structure, with a spacious first movement deeper in content than the *Sextet*. The *Adagio* is essentially a song without words, and the last two movements are impetuously spirited. The Philips performances are first-class in every way, sensitive and spontaneous, and the recording is natural in timbre and balance on both disc and the excellent tape. Highly recommendable, especially to those who already have a recording of the *Octet*.

Piano trio No. 1 in D min., Op. 49.
*** HMV ASD/*TC-ASD* 3894. Kyung-Wha Chung, Tortelier, Previn – SCHUMANN: *Trio No. 1.****
*** Pearl SHE 553. Beaux Arts Trio – DVOŘÁK: *Trio No. 4.****

Piano trios Nos. 1; 2 in C min., Op. 66.
(M) **(*) Ph. 6570/*7310* 885. Beaux Arts Trio.
*** Erato STU 71025. Queffélec, Amoyal, Lodéon.

Mendelssohn's *D minor Trio* is one of his most richly inspired chamber works, challenging the sharply contrasted musical personalities of Chung, Tortelier and Previn to provide a fascinating interplay. If anyone leads, it is Previn, whose agility is remarkable in fast passage-work; but above all the emotional drive of a piece which can easily seem sentimental comes out magnificently in this exceptional matching of talent. The recording is excellent; on cassette the sound is full, but not quite so clear and refined as on the disc.

The Beaux Arts Trio offer an obvious and sensible coupling on Philips. Their playing is always splendidly alive and musical, and they are vividly recorded (the sound on cassette is not as lively as the disc). The playing in the *D minor Trio* is not quite in the same category as the Chung/Tortelier/Previn version, which shows greater drive and warmth, but nonetheless at medium price it is extremely acceptable and the coupling is a valuable one, even if the acoustic is somewhat cramped.

On Erato the excellent partnership of Anne Queffélec, Pierre Amoyal and Frédéric Lodéon provides expert, spontaneous and characterful performances with refreshing sparkle and zest. The recording too is first-class, well detailed and with plenty of presence. It has slightly more body than the Beaux Arts version (made in the late 1960s), and the playing is by no means inferior either. However, while the Philips version, with its considerable price advantage, is still available the

Erato disc is likely to remain marginally second choice.

On Pearl the Beaux Arts offer a further alternative choice for those only requiring the *D minor Trio*. The two performances are of equal attractiveness and there is very little to choose between the Philips and Pearl recording quality. Of course the Pearl disc is premium-priced but it includes an excellent account of the *Dumky Trio* which many readers may want to have.

String quartets: Nos. 1 in E flat, Op. 12; 2 in A min., Op. 13; 3–5, Op. 44/1–3; 6 in F min., Op. 80; 4 Movements, Op. 81.
** DG 2740 267 (4) [id.]. Melos Qt.

Mendelssohn's string quartets are not well served on record and the majority are at present unavailable except in this set by the Melos Quartet of Stuttgart. His first quartet was written as early as 1823, a year before the *C minor Symphony* (No. 1), but was probably not intended for publication, and the last was finished only a few months before his death. The present set has the merit of completeness and also has the advantage of good engineering. However, the performances succumb to the temptation to play far too quickly: the first movement of the *A minor* loses all charm as a result, and they undercharacterize many of the ideas, giving an overall impression of blandness. They do not observe exposition repeats in the first movements of Op. 44. There is more to these quartets than this brilliant ensemble finds but, in the absence of any alternatives, this set is acceptable enough.

String quartet No. 1 in E flat, Op. 12.
*** Ph. 9500/*7300* 995 [id.]. Orlando Qt – DVOŘÁK: *Quartet No. 12.****

String quartet No. 2 in A minor, Op. 13.
*** CRD CRD 1017. Alberni Qt – SCHUMANN: *Quartet No. 3.****

The delightful *E flat Quartet* was composed when Mendelssohn was twenty, and the *A minor* (1827), despite the later opus number, precedes it by two years. Both are strong works, though the scherzo of Op. 12 has a close affinity with Cherubini's quartet in the same key, written in the previous decade, Mendelssohn's inspiration is fresh and spirited.

The Orlando Quartet, a superb ensemble, has been widely acclaimed for its concert appearances – small wonder, if they are as accomplished and sensitive as this account of the *E flat Quartet*, which is among the very best ever put on record. It is played with lightness of touch, delicacy of feeling and excellent ensemble. The recording is totally natural and lifelike, and the cassette transfer is of Philips' best quality, matching the disc closely.

The Alberni players too are thoroughly at home in the *A minor* work, which shows such extraordinary originality in its teenage composer, with its fully mature slow movement and its highly individual *Allegretto* and scherzo. It is a warm, understanding performance, well recorded and with an excellent coupling.

String quintets Nos. 1 in A, Op. 18; 2 in B flat, Op. 87.
(M) *** Decca Ace SDD 562. V. Philharmonic Quintet.

The two *Quintets* come from either extreme of Mendelssohn's career. The first was composed when he was a youth of seventeen, only a year after the *Octet* – to which, it must be admitted, it is inferior. The second dates from 1845, two years before his death, and is the more rewarding of the two. The Vienna Philharmonic Quintet give performances of great suavity and finesse, though at times they do not observe the finer dynamic nuances. The logical coupling and the excellent recording are as strong a factor in this issue's favour as its medium price. However, there is no doubt that the Academy of St Martin-in-the-Fields bring a shade more imagination and feeling to the Op. 87 *Quintet*; their performance is coupled with the *Octet* (see above).

Violin sonata in F min., Op. 4.
*** O-L DSLO 571 [id.]. Schröder, Hogwood – SCHUBERT: *Sonata, D. 574.****

As its opus number indicates, the Mendelssohn *Violin sonata* is an early piece, written when he was a boy of fourteen. It is not the most memorable of his early works, though it has many endearing moments and is here most persuasively presented on period instruments: Jaap Schröder plays a Stradivarius of 1709 and Christopher Hogwood a fortepiano of the mid-1820s. Beautifully alive and natural recording.

PIANO MUSIC

Fantasia in F sharp min. (*'Sonata écossaise'*), *Op. 28; 3 Fantaisies du caprices, Op. 16; Rondo capriccioso in E, Op. 14; Sonata in E, Op. 6.*
*** Chan. Dig. ABRD/*ABTD* 1081 [id.]. Artymiw.

The *Sonata* was written when Mendelssohn was seventeen, the year he conceived the *Octet* and the *Midsummer Night's Dream overture.* It does not have the magic of either of these masterpieces, but the second movement is attractively characteristic and the work as a whole shows extraordinary sureness of structural technique. Lydia Artymiw is highly persuasive here as she is in the other works, which are by no means inconsequential. The *Fantasia* is a considerable piece and the three movements which make up Op. 16 are delightful, as is the more famous *Rondo capriccioso*, which sparkles. This is an altogether excellent disc, very well recorded on disc and chrome tape alike.

Scherzo from A Midsummer Night's Dream, Op. 61 (trans. Rachmaninov).
*** Hyp. A 66009. Shelley – RACHMANINOV: *Variations* etc.***

Rachmaninov's transcription was one of the composer-virtuoso's favourite party pieces, and Howard Shelley, with fabulously clear articulation and delectably sprung rhythms, gives a performance of which Rachmaninov himself would not have been ashamed. This is a delightful makeweight for an outstanding disc of Rachmaninov variations.

Songs without Words Nos. 1–48; Albumblatt in E min., Op. 117; Kinderstücke, Op. 72; 2 Klavierstücke.
*** DG 2740 104 (3) [2709 052]. Barenboim.

Barenboim is the ideal pianist for what have come to be regarded (for the most part wrongly) as faded Victorian trifles. Whether in the earlier, technically more difficult pieces or in the later simple inspirations, Barenboim conveys perfectly the sense of a composer relaxing. He himself seems to be discovering the music afresh, regularly turning phrases with the imagination of a great artist, relishing the jewelled passage-work of many of the pieces in superb, easy virtuosity. With fine recording quality this is a set to charm any listener.

Songs without Words, Book 1, Nos. 1, 5, 6 (*Venetian gondola song*); *Book 2, Nos. 9, 10, 12* (*Venetian gondola song*); *Book 3, Nos. 14, 15, 17; Book 4, Nos. 20, 21; Book 5, Nos. 23, 29* (*Venetian gondola song*), *30* (*Spring song*); *Book 6, Nos. 32, 34* (*Spinning song*), *35, 36; Book 7, Nos. 39, 42; Book 8, Nos. 43, 46, 48.*
*** DG 2531 260 [id.]. Barenboim.

An admirable selection from Barenboim's fine complete set of the *Songs without Words* (2740 104), which is still available. The playing is fresh and imaginative, and the recording maintains the excellent quality of the original.

Songs without Words Nos. 1, 3, 6, 7, 10, 12, 14, 17, 18, 20, 25, 26, 29, 30, 32, 34, 43, 45, 47.
(M) *(*) HMV Green. ESD/*TC-ESD* 7113. Adni.

Adni's selection is at medium price, but it is seriously lacking in charm. The recording is excellent on disc and cassette alike, but Barenboim's full-priced DG disc is far more rewarding.

6 Organ sonatas, Op. 65; 3 Preludes and fugues, Op. 37.
(M) **(*) O-L SOL 350/1. Fisher (organ of Chester Cath.).

Mendelssohn's *Organ sonatas* were commissioned by an English publisher (Coventry and Holland), so it seems slightly unreasonable to reflect that the registrations Roger Fisher conjures from his instrument at Chester sound too bland. Fisher obviously has the measure of the music and can produce bursts of power when called for, as in the exciting closing pages of the finale of Sonata No. 4. He is at his best in the *Preludes and fugues*. But the reverberation tends slightly to blur the articulation in fast passages (this is not the fault of the admirably truthful recording), and the lack of bite and piquancy of colour gives an impression of sympathetic scholarship rather than persuading the listener that these works offer the best of Mendelssohn.

VOCAL MUSIC

Lieder: *Auf Flügeln des Gesanges; Der Blemenkranz; Der Blumenstrauss; Es weiss und rat es doch Keiner; Frage; Frühlingsglaube; Herbstlied; Hexenlied; Ich hör ein Vöglein; Im Grünen; Morgengruss; Nachtlied; Neue Liebe; Reiselied; Scheidend; Die Steme schau'n in stiller Nacht.*
*** HMV ASD/*TC-ASD* 4070. Baker; Parsons.

Mendelssohn's songs, often dismissed as trivial ballads, bring repeated revelations from Dame Janet with Geoffrey Parsons a comparably perceptive accompanist. Whether in the airy beauty of the most famous of the songs, *Auf Flügeln des Gesanges* (*On wings of song*), the golden happiness of *Morgengruss*, the darkness of *Reiselied* or the expressive narrative of *Hexenlied*, Dame Janet sings not just with rare intensity and acute sense of detail, but with an unexpected heightening of expression in tone-colours beautifully contrasted. Mendelssohn's songs, she clearly tells us, are not just tuneful, they can communicate with the resonances of Schubert Lieder. Well-balanced recording. The cassette is disappointing, lacking in upper range on side one, though side two is better, if still with a middle emphasis.

Lieder: *Auf Flügeln des Gesanges; Bei der Wiege; Das erste Veilchen; Frühlingslied; Gruss; Hexenlied; Im Herbst; Der Liebende schreibt; Lieblingsplätzchen; Das Mädchens Klage; Der Mond; Nachtlied; Neue Liebe; Romanze* (Op. 8/10)*; Suleika* (*2 songs, Op. 34/4 and Op. 57/3*)*; Tröstung.*
**(*) CBS Dig. 36678 [id.]. Ameling, Jansen.

Though many of the songs overlap, Ameling's Mendelssohn collection makes a refreshing and nicely contrasted supplement to the revelatory record of Dame Janet Baker. The sweetness and purity of the voice go well with Mendelssohn's simple lyricism. The lighter songs have consistent charm. Her serious manner for the Goethe (including two *Suleika songs*) finds her a little self-conscious in expressiveness, though the results are always beautiful. Good recording.

Elijah (oratorio), *Op. 70.*
*** HMV SLS/*TC-SLS* 935 (3/2) [Ang. S 3738]. Woolf, Gwyneth Jones, Baker, Gedda, Fischer-Dieskau, Wandsworth School Boys' Ch., New Philh. Ch. and O, Frühbeck de Burgos.
** CBS 79353 (3) (in German). Auger, Schreckenbach, Tear, Nimsgern, Gächinger Kantorei, Stuttgart R SO, Rilling.

It is some years since Mendelssohn's *Elijah* was the public's firm second favourite among choral works in Britain after Handel's *Messiah*. The time has now come when we can appreciate once more its fine dramatic directness, which, with the Baal choruses as centrepiece, makes this oratorio far more vivid in its story-telling than many an opera. Frühbeck proves an excellent Mendelssohnian, neither a callous driver nor a romantic meanderer. The choice of Fischer-Dieskau to take the part of the prophet is more controversial. His pointing of English words is not always idiomatic, but his sense of drama is infallible and goes well with a Mendelssohnian new look. Gwyneth Jones and Nicolai Gedda similarly provide mixed enjoyment, but the splendid work of the chorus and above all the gorgeous singing of Janet Baker, dominant whether in hushed intensity or commanding fortissimo, make this a memorable and enjoyable set. The cassette transfer is recent, issued not long before we went to press. There are two tapes with the layout rearranged so that each part is complete on two sides. The sound is splendid: solo voices and chorus are equally vivid with climaxes strikingly well focused, especially on side four where the level rises for the work's closing section.

There is room for a performance of *Elijah*

in German, when Mendelssohn composed from a German text. The first performance (in Birmingham) was in English of course, and England has tended to appropriate the piece. This live recording from Stuttgart is hardly the answer, generally a rather dull performance with variable singing. Best among the soloists is the pure-toned Arleen Auger, and Robert Tear is as reliable as ever but hardly inspired. Nimsgern as Elijah himself sounds uninvolved, and Gabriele Schreckenbach is disappointingly monochrome. In every way the Frühbeck de Burgos Philharmonia performance is preferable.

(i) *Das erste Walpurgisnacht* (*cantata*), *Op. 60;* (ii) *Infelice* (concert aria), *Op. 94.*

**(*) EMI 1C 065 02487. (i) Burmeister, Buchner, Lorenz, Leipzig R. Ch.; (ii) Moser; with Leipzig GO, Masur.

As a boy, Mendelssohn became a favourite visitor of the poet Goethe, and later he repaid the affection in this setting of an early and rather odd Goethe poem about Druids and their conflict with early Christians, seen – perhaps unexpectedly – from the point of view of the Druids. It is not great music, but especially in the big tarantella-like chorus for the Druids it is lively and enjoyable, particularly as played and sung here by Leipzig forces. The concert aria is more conventional but a worthwhile fill-up. Good atmospheric recording. There is an alternative account of the main work available in the USA, under Ormandy [RCA ARL1/*ARL1* 3460]. It is a straightforward and well-conceived performance, but it has less natural flair than this EMI version.

A Midsummer Night's Dream: Overture, Op. 21; Incidental music, Op. 61 (1, Scherzo; 2, Melodrama; 2a, Fairy march; 3, You spotted snakes; 4, Melodrama; 5, Intermezzo; 6, Melodrama; 7, Nocturne; 8, Melodrama; 9, Wedding march; 10, Melodrama; 10a, Funeral march; 11, Dance of the clowns; 12, Melodrama; 13, Finale).

*** HMV ASD/*TC-ASD* 3377 [Ang. S/*4XS* 37268] (complete). Watson, Wallis, Finchley Children's Music Group, LSO, Previn.

*** Erato STU/*MCE* 71090 (complete). Gale, Murray, LPO and Ch., Leppard.

*** Ph. Dig. **411 106-2**; 411 106-1/*4* [id.] (omitting Nos. 2, 4, 6, 8, 12). Auger, Murray, Amb. S., Philh. O, Marriner.

(M) *** DG Priv. 2535/*3335* 393 [138959] (omitting Nos. 2, 4, 6, 8, 10, 12). Mathis, Boese, Bav. R. Ch. and O, Kubelik.

(M) **(*) HMV SXLP/*TC-SXLP* 30196 [Ang. S 35881] (omitting Nos. 2, 4, 6, 8, 10, 12). Harper, Baker, Ch., Philh. O, Klemperer.

(M) **(*) Decca Jub. JB/*KJBC* 72 (complete). Bork, Hodgson, Amb. S., New Philh. O, Frühbeck de Burgos.

Previn offers a wonderfully refreshing account of the complete score; the veiled pianissimo of the violins at the beginning of the overture and the delicious woodwind detail in the *Scherzo* certainly bring Mendelssohn's fairies into the orchestra. Even the little melodramas which come between the main items sound spontaneous here, and the contribution of the soloists and chorus is first-class. The *Nocturne* (taken slowly) is serenely romantic and the *Wedding march* resplendent. The recording is naturally balanced and has much refinement of detail. There is a good cassette.

Like Previn's version, Leppard's includes even the tiny fragments between scenes, not just the main items. Musically they may be of slight value, but they help to intensify the atmosphere of this most imaginative of incidental music. Leppard like Previn gives the music sparkle and resilience, taking the *Nocturne* with its horn solo more persuasively at a flowing tempo, though the *Wedding march* is here relatively heavy. There is also a case for preferring Leppard's use of a women's choir instead of children's voices (as in the Previn), though the extra bite and edge of young voices in *You spotted snakes* makes the Previn refreshing and individual. Leppard's account of the lovely epilogue to the overture, later reproduced in the finale after the concluding chorus, is particularly beautiful. The Erato recording is admirably refined.

For those preferring the score without the inconsequential melodramas, Marriner could be an excellent choice. The *Overture*, taken briskly, has the lightest possible touch, with the most delicate articulation from the strings; the *Scherzo* too is engagingly infectious in its gentle bustle, while there is a complementary sense of joy and sparkle from soloists and chorus alike. The *Nocturne* is rather broadly romantic, yet the *Wedding march* sounds resplendent when the quality is so vivid. There is a short cut at the end of the *Intermezzo* but, this apart, the Philips recording, warm as well as refined in detail, has much to recommend it. There is a good chrome tape, but we have not been able to hear the compact disc.

Among reissues, that by the Bavarian Radio Orchestra takes pride of place. The playing and recording (equally clear and clean on disc and cassette, yet not lacking atmosphere) are both strikingly fresh. Even with the advantage of economy, however, this does not displace Previn where the performance, like Leppard's, has extra imagination and sparkle (the *Nocturne*, too, is more romantic); but at medium price the DG version is still very attractive.

Klemperer's recording (which dates from 1961) also sounds remarkably fresh in this new transfer. The record was made when the Philharmonia was at its peak and the orchestral playing is superb, the wind solos so nimble that even the *Scherzo*, taken slower than usual, has a light touch. The contribution of soloists and chorus is first-class and the disc has the advantage of including Nos. 2a and 10a. There is an excellent cassette: the quality is remarkably fresh and transparent, yet there is no lack of body.

The reissue at medium price of the Frühbeck de Burgos version is also attractive; the sound, though reverberant, is beautiful on disc and tape alike, with a striking bloom overall. The orchestral playing is very fine, and although the overture is not quite so evocative as under Leppard and Previn, this is the only mid-priced issue to present the score complete.

A Midsummer Night's Dream: Overture, Op. 21; Scherzo; Nocturne; Wedding march, Op. 61.

(M) *** Ph. Seq. 6527/*7311* 056. Concg. O, Szell – SCHUBERT: *Rosamunde.****

Superlative playing from the Concertgebouw Orchestra under Szell. He seldom recorded in Europe, but when he did the results were always impressive. Here the lightness and clean articulation of the violins in the overture are a delight; the wonderfully nimble wind playing in the *Scherzo* is no less engaging, and there is a fine horn solo in the *Nocturne*. The recording has been freshened for this reissue and sounds admirably clear, without loss of bloom. Szell's Schubert performances are equally rewarding, and there is no better version of this attractive coupling. The cassette transfer is good.

Paulus, Op. 36.

*** EMI 1C 157 30701/3. Donath, Schwarz, Hollweg, Fischer-Dieskau, Boys' Ch., Dusseldorf Musikverein and SO, Frühbeck de Burgos.

Paulus, or in English *St Paul*, was for long notorious as one of the most sanctimonious of Victorian oratorios. This sympathetic performance under the conductor who helped us review our ideas on *Elijah* – see above – gives the lie to that, a piece full of ideas well worthy of the composer of the *Italian symphony*. Like *Elijah* ten years later, *Paulus* – completed in 1836 – was Mendelssohn's substitute for opera. In youthful zest it erupts in great Handelian choruses, and a Bachian style of storytelling is neatly updated in its choral interjections and chorales with the soprano joining the traditional tenor in the narration. What reduces the dramatic effectiveness of *Paulus* is that Mendelssohn, ever the optimist, comes to his happy resolution in the plot far too quickly with too little struggle involved.

This performance glows with life. Fischer-Dieskau takes the name part (as he did for *Elijah*), leading an excellent team of soloists with admirable support from the Dusseldorf Choir and Orchestra. The recording is warmly atmospheric.

Psalms Nos. 42; Wie die Hirsch schreit (*As pants the hart*), *Op. 42; 95: Kommt, lasst uns anbeten* (*Come, let us worship*), *Op. 46.*

*** Erato STU/*MCE* 71101. Baumann, Silva, Blaser, Lisbon Gulbenkian Foundation Ch. and O, Corboz.

Choral works like these may characteristically glide over the problems of religious faith in an easy and sweet setting of texts (Psalm 42 begins with what is suspiciously close to a waltz); but in fine performances they are still worth hearing. The best inspirations in each of these cantatas point directly back to Mendelssohn's great model, J. S. Bach. Recording is full and atmospheric. The cassette transfer is well managed and the sound is fresh and lively.

Psalms Nos. 98: Singet dem Herrn ein neues Lied, Op. 91; 115; Nicht unserm Namen, Herr, Op. 31. Lauda Sion, Op. 73.
*** Erato STU/*MCE* 71223. Brunner, Ihara, Ramirez, Huttenlocher, Lisbon Gulbenkian Foundation Ch. and O, Corbóz.

The two psalm settings inspire Mendelssohn to some of his most effectively Bach-like writing. The text of Psalm 98 inspired Bach too, and though austerity periodically turns into sweetness, both pieces are most welcome in performances as fresh and alert as these. *Lauda Sion* is less varied in its expression, a persistent hymn of praise. The cassette transfer is acceptable, though the resonance tends to cloud the sound and the chorus is rather mushy in quality.

Die beiden Pädagogen.
*** HM 1C 065 45416. Laki, Fuchs, Dallapozza, Fischer-Dieskau, Bavarian R. Ch., Mun. R. O, Wallberg.

This little *Singspiel* about the quarrels of pedagogues – a subject on which the young Mendelssohn had personal experience – makes a charming entertainment, an amazing piece of work for a twelve-year-old. Tongue in cheek, he uses academic devices like fugue with the assurance of a master, never making the joke too heavy. The ensemble in which rival pedagogues argue their different ideas of education and shout their allegiance with cries of *Pestalozzi* and *Basedow* is hilarious. Fischer-Dieskau is only one of the excellent soloists in this superbly produced recording, a sparkling performance to match the boy Mendelssohn's inspiration.

Die Heimkehr aus der Fremde.
*** EMI 1C 065 30741. Donath, Schreier, Fischer-Dieskau, Bavarian R. Ch., Mun. R. O, Wallberg.

The German title conceals what we generally know in English-speaking countries (from the overture at least) as *Son and Stranger*. That inspired piece, much admired by Richard Strauss among others, leads to a *Singspiel* which was written with charm and tenderness for the silver wedding of the composer's parents, being presented to them (aptly, since the title means *The Return from Abroad*) on his return from a lengthy stay in England. Apart from the overture, one of the arias was once also well-known in its English translation, *I am a rover*. In the drama it is sung by a disagreeable grocer – a splendid vehicle here for Fischer-Dieskau. Although the plot is predictable, with troubles for the returning soldier finally being solved, the piece is enchanting in a performance such as this, at once effervescent and touching, and helped by excellent recording.

Menotti, Gian-Carlo

(born 1911)

Amahl and the Night Visitors (opera for television): complete.
(M) **(*) RCA [LSC 2762]. Yaghjian, King, McCollum, Cross, Paterson, Ch. and O, Grossman.

Menotti's television opera for Christmas may not stand the test of time as comparable Britten works for children do. Its musical inspiration is altogether more ephemeral, but with a sure-fire – if blatantly sentimental – plot, it certainly has a magic of its own, and a stereo version which brings out the highly atmospheric qualities – the arrival of the Wise Men and so on – is most welcome. This performance was based on the NBC presentation in 1963, and is attractively direct, with few of the distracting exaggerations of characterization that marred the earlier mono version. The voices may sometimes sound a little pale, but the atmosphere of a home entertainment (preferable to something sophisticatedly professional) is attractively maintained. This record is not currently available in the UK.

Messager, André (1853–1929)

Les Deux Pigeons (ballet): suite; *Isoline* (ballet): suite.
(M) *** HMV Green. ESD 7048. O de Paris, Jacquillat – LALO: *Scherzo*; PIERNÉ: *Marche* etc.***

What an enchanting score is Messager's *Two Pigeons* ballet; and there is some lovely music in *Isoline* too. Part of a wholly recommendable concert of French music, this can be welcomed with the utmost enthusiasm. The recording is most successful, offering plenty of warmth and colour as well as sparkle.

Messiaen, Olivier (born 1908)

L'Ascension; Hymne; Les offrandes oubliées.
*** Erato STU 70673. French R. and TV PO, Constant.

This record briefly appeared here in the latter half of the 1970s and its return to currency should be welcomed. The works are all early: *Les offrandes oubliées* was composed when Messiaen was only twenty-two and is astonishingly powerful in atmosphere, as for that matter are the *Hymne* (1932) and the more ambitious *L'Ascension* (1933). These are all moving works, static in feeling but highly personal in flavour, and would make an excellent introduction for those who normally resist this composer. Marius Constant and the Orchestre Philharmonique de Radio France provide a most persuasive entry into Messiaen's sound-world and they are admirably served by the engineers. An altogether excellent issue.

Les couleurs de la cité céleste; Et exspecto resurrectionem mortuorum.
**(*) Erato STU 70302 [CBS MS 7356]. Loriod, Strasbourg Instrumental and Percussion Group, Boulez.

This record originally appeared in the UK on CBS and dates from 1966. It still sounds impressive, however; readers fascinated by the extraordinary sonorities Messiaen draws from these forces (woodwind, brass and metallic percussion in the case of *Et exspecto*, and piano, wind and percussion in its companion) will find much to engross them. *Et exspecto* withstands the test of the years and exerts a hypnotic grip over the listener for much of the time with its curiously inert yet strongly atmospheric world. Both works date from the early 1960s and *Et exspecto* draws liberally on bird-song, ranging from Brazil to New Zealand, as a source of inspiration.

Réveil des oiseaux (*The Awakening of the Birds*); *Oiseaux exotiques* (*Exotic Birds*); *La Bouscarle* (from *Catalogue d'oiseaux*).
(M) *** Sup. 50749 [Can. 31002]. Loriod, Czech PO, Neumann.

All three scores here are associated with Messiaen's beloved birdsong. There is no question of Messiaen's imaginative flair, and the music is vivid, varied and colourful to match the plumage of the creatures which provided the composer's inspiration. With the dedicated Yvonne Loriod as soloist and the composer himself supervising the recording sessions, this is an authentic and important issue.

Turangalîla symphony.
*** HMV SLS/*TC-SLS* 5117 (2) [Ang. S 3853]. Béroff (piano), Loriod (ondes martenot), LSO, Previn.

Messiaen's *Turangalîla symphony* was written at a time (1946–8) when – Shostakovich notwithstanding – the symphonic tradition seemed at its lowest ebb. Yet is is unquestionably a masterpiece: an uneven masterpiece perhaps, but a work of great magnetism and imaginative power. Its characteristic mysticism is balanced by its strongly communicative nature – even at a first hearing it evokes a direct and immediate response in its audience. Messiaen's conception is on an epic scale, to embrace almost the totality of human experience. This is immediately implied in the Sanskrit title, a complex word suggesting the interplay of life forces, creation and dissolution, but which is also divisible: *Turanga* is Time and also implies rhythmic movement; *Lîla* is Love, and with a strong inspiration from the Tristan and Isolde legend Messiaen's love music dominates his conception of human existence. The actual love sequences feature the ondes martenot with its 'velvety glissandi'. This fascinating texture is a truly twentieth-century sound, and at times it has an unearthly quality suggesting Man looking out into a universe which is almost his to grasp. The piano obbligato is also a strong feature of the score, and the balance here is skilfully managed so that it is integrated within the orchestral tapestry yet provides a dominating decorative influence. The spirit of Debussy hovers over the piano writing, while the Stravinsky of *Le Sacre* is clearly an influence elsewhere. But this is by no means an eclectic work; it is wholly original and its themes (with their element of vulgarity as well as mysticism) are undoubtedly haunting.

The essence of the symphony is more readily captured in the concert hall than in the recording studio, but Previn's vividly direct approach, helped by recording of spectacular amplitude and dynamic range, certainly creates tingling electricity from the first bar to the last. Perhaps the music's atmospheric qualities are marginally less well captured here than in Ozawa's earlier RCA set (now long deleted), which was softer-grained. Previn is at his very best in the work's more robust moments, for instance the jazzy fifth movement, and he catches the wit at the beginning of *Chant d'amour 2*. The idyllic *Garden of the sleep of love* is both serene and poetically sensuous, and the mysterious opening of the third movement is highly evocative. The apotheosis of the love theme in the closing pages is jubilant and life-enhancing. The bright, vivid detail of the recording is also captured extraordinarily well on tape, which on an A/B comparison with the discs reveals fractionally more sharpness of detail, but, correspondingly, marginally less depth. However, the differences are minimal.

Quatuor pour la fin du temps.
*** DG 2531 093 [id.]. Yordanoff, Tetard, Desurment, Barenboim.
*** Ph. 9500 725 [id.]. Beths, Pieterson, Bylsma, De Leeuw.

Barenboim and his colleagues recorded the *Quatuor pour la fin du temps* in the presence of the composer. Messiaen's visionary and often inspired piece was composed during his days in a Silesian prison camp. Among his fellow-prisoners were a violinist, clarinettist and cellist, who with the composer at the piano made its creation possible. Barenboim is a strong personality who carries much of this performance in his hands, and inspires his colleagues with his own commitment to the music. The performance is certainly better recorded than any of its rivals so far, and readers wanting to invest in this strange and often haunting work need have no doubts as to its excellence.

The Dutch team are also given good recording. Indeed their account has the merit of outstanding team-work, and Reinbert de Leeuw has a keen sense of atmosphere, though he does not dominate the proceedings. There is some superbly eloquent playing from George Pieterson and Anner Bylsma too. Honours are pretty evenly divided between this and the DG record, and choice can be safely left to personal taste and availability.

PIANO MUSIC

4 Études (complete); *Préludes* (complete).
*** EMI 2C 069 16229. Béroff.

This record was made to mark the occasion of Messiaen's seventieth birthday and was not issued in the UK, nor is it currently listed in Schwann. The *Préludes* are early, dating from 1929, while the *Quatre Études* come from 1949–50. They are interesting pieces, atmospheric and inventive, and though Béroff is not recorded with quite the same distinction as in his set of the *Vingt regards* (there is some hardness at times above forte), the sound is still extremely fine and he plays very brilliantly indeed.

Vingt regards sur l'Enfant-Jésus.
*** EMI 2C 181 11117/8. Béroff.

This first appeared in the early 1970s when

it had considerable competition to contend with, including John Ogdon's Argo set and Thomas Rajna's Saga version (both now withdrawn). Even at that time we found Béroff the most inspired of all, creating the illusion of spontaneous re-creation. Time has not dimmed its appeal and, even were the catalogue full of rival accounts, this would still be difficult to beat. Even for listeners not wholly attuned to Messiaen's sensibility and language, this can be strongly recommended –and it might even make converts to this original master. Clean, well-focused sound.

ORGAN MUSIC

L'Apparition de l'église eternelle; L'Ascension; Diptyque.
*** Uni. Dig. DKP 9015. Bate (organ of St Pierre de Beauvais Cath.).

L'Ascension takes up the first side of this collection, four movements specifically inspired by selected texts. *L'Apparition* builds commandingly to a central climax, then recedes. *Diptyque* is an early work, dedicated to Messiaen's teachers, Dukas and Dupré, already recognizably his style. Jennifer Bate plays this often slow-moving music with hypnotic concentration and is superbly recorded. An excellent introduction to Messiaen's organ music.

Le Banquet céleste; Messe de la Pentecôte; Verset pour la fête de la dédicace.
*** Uni. Dig. DKP 9018. Bate (organ of Beauvais Cath.).

This (fourth) volume of Jennifer Bate's Messiaen series brings more superb performances and rich, atmospheric sound from the ideally chosen organ of Beauvais Cathedral. *Le Banquet céleste* is among the earliest of Messiaen's works to have been published and among the best known, already an intense comment on the religious experience which has inspired all of Messiaen's organ music. The *Mass* brings together most tellingly the three principal elements of Messiaen's style – plainsong, birdsong and his own rich brand of harmony – in a particularly satisfying combination.

Le Banquet céleste. La Nativité du Seigneur: Les bergers.
(M) *** Mercury SRI 75088 [id.]. Dupré (organ of St Sulpice, Paris) – DUPRÉ: *Preludes and fugues.***

Fine performances, well recorded. Marcel Dupré is particularly good with *Les bergers* and the music resonates hauntingly in the memory afterwards. The coupling of Dupré's own music is less interesting.

Messe de la Pentecôte.
(*) ASV ALH 918. Grier (organ of Christ Church Cath., Oxford) – FRANCK: *Chorales.*(*)

This is a demonstration record of quite remarkable realism. Oddly enough, the acoustic is relatively dry, which must be quite an achievement in this environment; at times, the aural impact is almost too spectacular and Messiaen is made to sound as if he has composed an electronic work. The *Messe de la Pentecôte* dates from 1950 and is an organ Mass almost in the tradition of Tournemire, though the material draws on wider sources including Greek and Hindu rhythms and birdsong. The Rieger organ which was installed in Christ Church, Oxford, in 1979 is said to be among the finest in the country and speaks with immediate clarity – and in this recording not without some degree of fierceness. The more spacious acoustic of the Beauvais organ used by Jennifer Bate may well be preferred by some collectors, but there is no question that the present instrument is a splendid beast.

La Nativité du Seigneur.
❀ *** Uni. Dig. DKP 9005. Bate (organ of Beauvais Cath.).

'C'est vraiment parfait!' said Messiaen after hearing this superb record of one of his most extended, most moving and most variedly beautiful works. The nine movements are each hypnotically compelling in their atmospheric commentaries on the Nativity story, never more so than when played by so naturally understanding an artist as Jennifer Bate on an ideally toned instrument. The recording is of demonstration quality.

VOCAL MUSIC

Chants de terre et de ciel; Harawi (Chants d'amour et de la mort); Poèmes pour Mi; Trois Mélodies.
**(*) EMI 2C 167 16226/8. Command, Petit.

These three records offer Messiaen's complete vocal output in performances of considerable power and authority. The early songs (the *Trois Mélodies* of 1930 and the two sets from the mid-1930s, *Poèmes pour Mi* and *Chants de terre et de ciel*) are given with great sensitivity and eloquence, even if the voice sometimes seems too big for these settings. *Harawi* dates from the post-war years; the title is a Peruvian-Indian word meaning a love song leading to the lovers' death. It forms part of the *Tristan*-inspired pieces which engaged Messiaen in the late 1940s and also include the *Turangalîla symphony* and the *Cinq Rechants*. The performances were presumably recorded over a longish period and there is some inconsistency in balance, the piano varying in prominence from the reticent to the forward. So far Michèle Command is the only French artist to have given us a comprehensive survey of Messiaen, and collectors with an interest in this key figure in post-war French music can invest in this set with confidence.

La Transfiguration de Notre Seigneur Jésus-Christ.
*** Decca HEAD 1/2. Sylvester, Aquino, Westminster Symphonic Ch., Loriod, Instrumental soloists, Washington Nat. SO, Dorati.

This massive work of fourteen movements – divided into two parallel septenaries – seems to sum up the whole achievement of Messiaen. It was written for the Gulbenkian Festival in 1969 (having taken nearly four years to complete), and though the unconverted may feel it has its longueurs, no one can doubt the dedication of the composer, his ability beyond almost any contemporary to convey through music his personal religious exaltation. Dorati magnificently holds together the unwieldy structures, and though such an evocative work ideally ought to be heard against a more reverberant acoustic, the brilliance and immediacy of the recording are most impressive.

Meyerbeer, Giacomo
(1791–1864)

Les Patineurs (ballet suite, orch. Lambert).
*** Decca SXL/*KSXC* 6812 [Lon. CS/5-7032]. Nat. PO, Bonynge – MASSENET: *Le Cid ballet* etc.***
(M) ** HMV Green. ESD/*TC-ESD* 7115 [(d) Ang. S 35833]. Philh. O, Mackerras – LUIGINI: *Ballet Egyptien* ***; PONCHIELLI: *Dance of the Hours* **(*); TCHAIKOVSKY: *Nutcracker suite*.**

Les Patineurs was arranged by Constant Lambert using excerpts from two of Meyerbeer's operas, *Le Prophète* and *L'Étoile du Nord*. Bonynge's approach is warm and comparatively easy-going. The recording too with its ample bass line adds to the expansive quality, but with such polished orchestral playing and obvious dedication from Bonynge, this version is extremely beguiling. There is a fine matching cassette.

Sir Charles Mackerras's approach is characteristically alert and lively, and there is plenty of vivacity in his Greensleeve version. However, the 1960 recording, though vivid, is rather dry, both on disc and on tape.

Les Huguenots (opera) complete.
*** Decca SET 460/3 [Lon. OSA 1437]. Sutherland, Tourangeau, Vrenios, Ghiuselev, Bacquier, Arroyo, Cossa, Amb. Op. Ch., New Philh. O, Bonynge.

The revival of Meyerbeer's once-popular opera of epic length provided an exceptional challenge for Richard Bonynge. He prepared for this recording with a concert performance in the Royal Albert Hall, and in both instances his own passionate belief in the music was amply evident. It is good too to have Sutherland augmenting the enticing sample of the role of the Queen which she gave in *The art of the prima donna*. The result is predictably impressive, though once or twice there are signs of a 'beat' in the voice, previously unheard on Sutherland records. But the rest of the cast is uneven, and in an unusually episodic opera, with passages that are musically less than inspired (Meyerbeer's melodic inspiration was often very square), that brings disappointments. Gabriel Bacquier and Nicola Ghiuselev are fine in their roles, and though Martina Arroyo is below her best as Valentine the star quality is unmistakable. The tenor Anastasios Vrenios can easily be criticized in the role of Raoul in that this is too small a voice for a heroic part, but very few other tenors and certainly not those who have been applauded in stage performances can cope with the extraordinarily high tessitura and florid diversions. Vrenios sings the notes, which is more than almost any rival could. Fine recording to make this ambitious project well worth investigating by lovers of French opera.

Miaskovsky, Nicolai (1881–1950)

Symphony No. 21, Op. 51.
*** Uni. RHS 346. New Philh. O, Measham – KABALEVSKY: *Symphony No. 2.***(*)

The *Twenty-first* is Miaskovsky's most recorded symphony and arguably his finest. David Measham has the measure of Miaskovsky's blend of melancholy and nostalgia, and in both the contemplative opening and the poetic closing pages he does this score full justice. Though it is conservative in idiom, this symphony stands the test of time remarkably well, and Miaskovsky's elegiac musings ring far truer than many more overtly 'modern' scores of the early 1940s. The timbre of the various instruments reproduces truthfully and the recording is fully acceptable, though it is a little wanting in transparency and range at the top.

Milford, Robin (1903–59)

(i) *Elegiac meditation, Op. 83. Elegy for James Scott, Duke of Monmouth and Buccleugh, Op. 50; Fishing by moonlight, Op. 96a;* (ii) *Suite in D min. for oboe and strings, Op. 8;* (iii) *A Prophet in the Land* (oratorio), *Op. 21: Whither, O whither. Songs: Love on my heart; Tolerance.*
** Hyp. A 66048. (i) Wellington; (ii) Rothwell, Southern Pro Arte O, Finzi; (iii) Milford; Benson.

Robin Milford, son of a successful publisher, was a prolific composer of songs and instrumental pieces in an easy English pastoral manner. His songs at their finest have sunshine in them, yet behind the musical happiness lay a depressive personality, and that is reflected here in some of the instrumental pieces. These may not be powerful inspirations, but they are consistently sensitive, particularly in direct response to English verse. It is sad that the performances here are not polished enough to present the music at its most convincing, but lovers of this brand of pure Englishry should still investigate.

Milhaud, Darius (1892–1974)

Le Bœuf sur le toit (ballet); *La Création du monde* (ballet); *Saudades do Brazil Nos. 7-9 and 11.*
**(*) HMV ASD 3444 [Ang. S/*4XS* 37442]. O Nat. de France, Bernstein.

Milhaud was essentially a Mediterranean composer whose scores radiate a sunny, relaxed charm that is irresistible. The *Saudades do Brazil* come from the period when he served as Claudel's secretary in Rio de Janeiro, while the two ballet scores come from the 1920s. As one would expect, Bernstein finds this repertoire thoroughly congenial, though his performance of *La Création du* monde disappoints slightly: the French orchestra do not respond with the verve and virtuosity that the Boston orchestra gave Munch in the RCA recording (now deleted). Nor does *Le Bœuf sur le toit* have quite the sparkle and infectious gaiety that the music ideally demands. This is not to deny that these are good performances and well worth acquiring, particularly as the recordings are well balanced and vividly detailed.

Le carnaval d'Aix.
*** DG 2543 807 [id.]. Helffer, Monte Carlo Op. O, Frémaux – ROUSSEL: *Bacchus et Ariane, suite No. 2***(*); SATIE: *Parade.***

Milhaud's delicious score has an abundance of ideas and is rich in colour and atmosphere. Its relaxed Mediterranean charm is neatly conveyed by Claude Helffer and the Monte Carlo orchestra under Louis Frémaux. Why is it that this tuneful, scatty and exhilarating score is so neglected on record? It derives from the music to the ballet, *Salade* (1924), which Milhaud rearranged for a concert tour he made of the United States three years later. Although it is twenty years old, the recording still sounds very good indeed and the performance is to be preferred to the one available some years ago under the composer's own direction with Carl Seeman as soloist.

Les quatres saisons (*The Four seasons*): (i) *Concertino de printemps, Op. 135;* (ii) *Concertino d'été, Op. 311;* (iii) *Concertino d'automne, Op. 309;* (iv) *Concertino d'hiver, Op. 327.*
(M) *** Ph. Seq. 6527/*7311* 221. (i) Goldberg; (ii) Wallfisch; (iii) Joy, Bonneau; (iv) Suzan; Lamoureux Concerts Ens., composer.

The *Concertino de printemps* has an infectious gaiety and is engagingly played by Szymon Goldberg. What captivating music this is with its gamin charm and easy-going fluency. The other three concertos are not quite as memorable, but they are still rewarding and inventive and well worth having, particularly in such persuasive and authoritative hands. Milhaud is irresistible and these performances have the merit of good recorded sound.

Suite française.
*** ASV ALH/*ZCALH* 913. L. Wind O, Wick – GRAINGER: *Irish tune* etc.; POULENC: *Suite française.****

The *Suite française* is an enchanting piece, full of Mediterranean colour and an earthy vitality. It would be difficult to imagine a more idiomatic or spirited performance than this one, which has excellent balance and blend. Vivid recording. This is an extraordinarily appealing work and ought to be far more popular than it is. There is a first-class cassette.

Music for wind: *La Cheminée du Roi René, Op. 105; Divertissement en trois parties, Op. 399b; Pastorale, Op. 47; 2 Sketches, Op. 227b; Suite d'après Corrette, Op. 161b.*
**(*) Chan. ABR/*ABT* 1012 [id.]. Athena Ens., McNicol.

La Cheminée du Roi René.
*(*) Uni. RHS 366. Danish Wind Quintet – HINDEMITH: *Kleine Kammermusik* ***; NIELSEN: *Quintet.***

Two of these pieces were derived from film music: *La Cheminée du Roi René* is based on a score Milhaud wrote to *Cavalcade d'Amour*, set in the fifteenth century; and the *Divertissement* draws on material composed for a film on the life of Gauguin. The *Suite d'après Corrette* features music written for a Paris production of *Romeo and Juliet*, using themes by the eighteenth-century French master, Michel Corrette. Though none of this is first-class Milhaud, it is still full of pleasing and attractive ideas, and the general air of easy-going life-loving enjoyment is well conveyed by the alert playing of the Athena Ensemble. One's only quarrel with this issue is the somewhat close balance, which picks up the mechanism of the various keys, and does less than justice to the artists' pianissimo tone. However, this can be remedied a little by a lower level setting, and there is far too much to enjoy here to inhibit a recommendation. The cassette transfer is excellent, matching the disc closely.

The Unicorn recording also suffers from a limited dynamic range; but, more seriously, there is also a lack of the kind of charm and sparkle that might persuade doubters.

PIANO MUSIC

(i) *L'automne, Op. 115;* (i; ii) *Le bal martiniquais, Op. 249;* (i–iv) *Paris, Op. 284;* (ii) *Le printemps, Opp. 26 and 66;* (i; ii) *Scaramouche, Op. 165b.*
*** EMI 2C 069/*2C 269* 12076. (i) Noël Lee; (ii) Ivaldi; (iii) Béroff; (iv) Collard.

A sunny record of some charming music for one, two and four pianos. *Scaramouche* is the best-known piece and is extremely well played by Christian Ivaldi and Noël Lee, and is much to be preferred to the Kontarskys' record on DG. The earliest piece is *Le printemps,* which comes from 1919–20 and is beguilingly played by Ivaldi. Milhaud spoke in his last BBC broadcast of his 'happy life' and this exuberant, carefree quality comes over beautifully in such pieces as *Le bal martiniquais*, written during the last war and engagingly played by Ivaldi and Noël Lee, and the post-war *Paris*, Op. 284, for four pianos. The recordings, made in 1971, are fresh and lively (and much more natural than the DG *Scaramouche*) and collectors will find much pleasure here.

Scaramouche (suite).
* DG 2531/*3301* 389 [id.] Kontarsky Duo – BIZET: *Jeux d'enfants;* FAURÉ: *Dolly.**

This fine duo dispatches *Scaramouche* with undoubted efficiency; but charm, so essential an ingredient in this repertoire, is in short supply. The recording is close and the acoustic dryish. There is little to choose between disc and chrome tape.

3 Rag-Caprices; Saudades do Brazil; Spring.
(M) **(*) None. H 71316 [id.]. Bolcom.

William Bolcom is a persuasive advocate of this delightful music. He was a Milhaud pupil for a number of years and proves an effective guide round the various districts of Rio de Janeiro epitomized in the *Saudades do Brazil* (Milhaud was stationed in the Brazilian capital during the First World War and came to love it). Although the *Saudades* have been available in their orchestral guise, they have not been recorded for the piano for some time, and the *Rag-Caprices* and *Spring* are not otherwise available. All in all, a valuable disc.

Millöcker, Karl (1842–99)

Der Bettelstudent (complete).
*** EMI 1C 157 30162/3. Streich, Holm, Litz, Prey, Unger, Bav. R. Ch., Graunke SO, Allers.

With a first-rate cast and excellent teamwork (the charming trio at the beginning of the third Act is a good example) the EMI set offers a consistently vivacious account of *Der Bettelstudent*. The plot, with its extraordinary mixture of Polish patriotism, mistaken identities and the triumph of true love, is supported by an attractively lyrical score, which is admirably presented and well recorded here. It is a pity that the libretto booklet, although it gives a synopsis of the story-line in English, does not provide a translation; but there is only a comparatively small amount of linking dialogue.

Gasparone (complete recording).
**(*) EMI Dig. 1C 157 46571/2. Rothenberger, Brokmeier, Wewel, Prey, Finka, Fuchs, Bav. State Op. Ch., Mun. R. O, Wallberg.

Millöcker wrote his operetta *Gasparone* immediately after his most famous piece, *Der Bettelstudent*. It contains a fund of tunes, but this recording is not of the original work. In 1931 it was radically recomposed by Ernst Steffan with extra material added, and with the flavour of nineteenth-century operetta diluted in favour of the twentieth-century musical. It makes an agreeable entertainment in a performance which draws out the expressive warmth of Millöcker's melodies to the full. Anneliese Rothenberger is not at her sweetest as the heroine. Hermann Prey sings with bravura, but could be more tender. Clear digital recording.

Minkus, Leon (1826–1917)

La Bayadere: The Kingdom of the Shades. Paquita: Pas de dix.
** HMV Dig. ASD/*TC-ASD* 183425-1/*4*. Sydney SO, Lanchbery.

This music comes from the world of *Giselle. Paquita* dates from 1846, five years after *Giselle* had its first performance. It is agreeable enough, with one quite stirring romantic tune, and much pretty orchestration (some of it contributed by Lanchbery, who also admits to varying both harmony and melodic line). If this is pretty thin stuff, it is masterly compared with *La Bayadere,* where the interest is primarily historical. The excerpt depicts an hallucination which on stage gives the excuse for two dozen ballerinas to come out of the darkness down an invisible ramp, apparently a *coup de théâtre* of its time (1877). After the entrance comes a grand divertissement. The opening draws an appropriately sombre texture from the orchestra, but the clouds swiftly draw back and all is sweetness and light, with music that is singularly ingenuous and vapid. It is well played and vividly and colourfully recorded, though the XDR tape is disappointing, somewhat thick in the bass and with less space and air round the sound on top.

Moeran, Ernest J. (1894–1950)

(i) *Cello concerto. Overture for a masque; Rhapsody No. 2 in E.*
** Lyr. SRCS 43. LPO, Boult, (i) with Coetmore (cello).

Peers Coetmore, widow of E. J. Moeran, is the dedicatee of the *Cello concerto,* a fine lyrical work written as a wedding present in 1945, the year of their marriage. One cannot miss the intensity of feeling in her playing. This is a deeply felt offering to a long-neglected composer, but the solo playing falls short of the virtuoso standard that one demands on record. One has to listen with a sympathetic ear. No such reservations about the colourful *Rhapsody* (an early work dating from 1924) and the jolly *Overture,* written in wartime to lighten the blackout. Boult is an intensely sympathetic conductor, and the recording quality matches Lyrita's excellent standards.

Rhapsody in F sharp for piano and orchestra.
*** Lyr. SRCS 91. McCabe (piano), New Philh. O, Braithwaite – BRIDGE: *Phantasm.****

Moeran's *Rhapsody in F sharp* is fresh and spontaneous, as one would expect from this underrated composer. His art offers directness of utterance and a disarming sincerity, and he is well served by John McCabe and the New Philharmonia under Nicholas Braithwaite. The excellent recording, which is truthfully balanced and well detailed, and the interesting coupling, a Bridge rarity, make this a most desirable issue.

Symphony in G min.
❀ *** Lyr. SRCS 70. New Philh. O, Boult.

Moeran's superb *Symphony in G minor* was written between 1934 and 1937. It is in the best English tradition of symphonic writing and worthy to rank with the symphonies of Vaughan Williams and Walton, with which it has much in common. But for all the echoes of these composers (and Holst and Butterworth too) it has a strong individual voice. There is no question of the quality of the invention throughout the lyrical sweep of the first two movements, and in the rhythmically extrovert and genial scherzo. If the structure and atmosphere of the finale are unmistakably Sibelian – there is a striking passage very like the climax in *Tapiola* – it makes a cogent and satisfying close to a very rewarding work.

Sir Adrian Boult directs a radiant performance, spacious and opulent in sound. Characteristically he refuses to push too hard too soon, but the ebb and flow of tension are superbly controlled to build the most powerful possible climaxes. Rarely, even in Vaughan Williams, has Boult adopted so overtly expressive a style, and the recording quality, refined and clear, allows the widest dynamic range down to the gentlest pianissimo for the hushed, intense opening of the slow movement.

Monteverdi, Claudio

(1567–1643)

MADRIGALS

Madrigals for 5 voices, Book 3 (complete).
(M) **(*) Ph. 9502 008 [id.]. Armstrong, Eathorne, Watson, Hodgson, Collins, English, Partridge, Dean, Keyte; Leppard.

Monteverdi's *Third Book of Madrigals*, dating from 1592, was the one where the sharpness of his originality began to make itself felt to the full – not just musically but in his serious treatment of subjects, breaking away from formality. Outstanding among the soloists here is Ian Partridge, but too much of the rest lacks the bite which generally marks Leppard's performances of Monteverdi. The result is a little too smooth, though the quality of the music itself and its rarity are enough to make this a most attractive issue, particularly at medium price; and it is very well recorded.

Ah dolente partita; Al lume delle stelle; Amor, che deggio far; Chiome d'oro; Damigella tutta bella; Dolci miei sospiri; Eccomi pronta ai baci; La piaga ch'ho nel core; Lamento della ninfa; Non vedro mai le stelle; O come sei gentile; Sfogava con le stelle; Si ch'io vorrei morire.
(M) *** Argo ZK 66. Purcell Cons., Grayston Burgess.

Ever since Nadia Boulanger made her historic recording of Monteverdi madrigals in the late 1930s, the Nymph's Lament, *Lamento della ninfa*, has been a favourite, and here again it stands at the centre of the collection. With Eileen Poulter as soloist, this is a less personal reading than Boulanger's, but at a slower tempo and with a purer-toned soprano this is if anything even more beautiful. *Chiome d'oro* is another which coincides with the original Boulanger collection, here more authentically allotted to two sopranos instead of Boulanger's tenors (one of them the incomparable Hugues Cuénod) and not nearly so witty. But the wonder is that these performances stand comparison so well with that classic example. This is cleaner and straighter in style than Raymond Leppard's Contour collection (see below), and it is a wonderful record for anyone simply wanting to sample the irresistible glories of this great musical revolutionary. It is beautifully recorded.

Madrigals: *Addio Florida bella; Ahi com'a un vago sol; E così a poco a poco torno farfalla; Era l'anima mia; Luci serene e chiare; Mentre vaga Angioletta ogn' anima; Ninfa che scalza il piede; O mio bene, a mia vita; O Mirtillo, Mirtill'anima mia; Se pur destina; Taci, Armelin deh taci; T'amo mia vita; Troppo ben può questo tiranno amore.*
*** HM HM/*40* 1084. Concerto Vocale.

A highly attractive collection of generally neglected items briskly and stylishly performed. The most celebrated of the singers is the male alto, René Jacobs, a fine director as well as soloist. With continuo accompaniment – the common factor in this set, in which no *a cappella* madrigals are included – the contrasting of vocal timbres is superbly achieved. Excellent recording.

Duets: *Ardo e scoprir; Baci cari; Dialogo di ninfa e pastore; Io son vezzoseta pastorella.*
(M) (***) HMV mono HLM 7267. Schwarzkopf, Seefried, Moore – DVOŘÁK: *Moravian duets;* CARISSIMI: *Duets.*(***)

Monteverdi with piano accompaniment was normal enough when these duets were recorded in the mid-1950s. The unauthentic approach will hardly deter lovers of fine, characterful singing from two favourite sopranos in their early prime. A delectable and unexpected coupling in limited but reasonably balanced mono sound.

Ardo e scoprir; Di far sempre giore; Io mi son Giovinetta; Lasciatemi morire; Maladetto sia l'aspetto; Non è di gentil core; Questi vaghi

concenti; Sfogava con le stelle; Si dolce è il tormento; Tirsi e Clori; Vorrei baciarti.
*** Erato STU 70849. Lausanne Vocal and Chamber Ens., Corboz.

Bel pastor; Eccomi pronta al baci; Ecco mormorar l'onde; Hor che'l ciel e la terra; Lamento della ninfa; La mia Turca; Ohimè ch'io cado; Perchè fuggi; Presso un fiume tranquillo; Si ch'io vorrei morire.
*** Erato STU 70848. Lausanne Vocal and Chamber Ens., Corboz.

Now that Leppard's set of Books 8–10 of the madrigals has disappeared from the Philips lists, these anthologies from Lausanne and Michel Corboz are to be welcomed. The singing and playing of this group is everywhere accomplished, and these familiar madrigals are given without excessive sophistication and with admirable feeling. Good recording quality enhances the strength of the recommendation.

Bel pastor; Della bellezza le dovute lodi; Dolci miei sospiri; Fugge il verno; Gira il nemico insidioso; Lamento della ninfa; Lidia spina del mio core; Non così; Ohimè ch'io cado; O Rosetta; La pastorella; Si dolce è il tormento.
(B) *** Con. CC/*CCT* 7534. Wolf, Tear, English, Keyte, ECO, Leppard.

This was the first of Raymond Leppard's madrigal anthologies, dating from the mid-1960s, and at bargain price it still makes a splendid introduction to this wonderful repertoire. Not since Nadia Boulanger made her first, historic recording of Monteverdi madrigals in Paris in the 1930s (imagine it, a piano continuo!) had the most sensuously beautiful of the works in this form, *Lamento della ninfa*, been recorded with such feeling. For that item alone the record would be worth the price, for with wonderfully clear recording and imaginative direction by Leppard, its beauty is irresistible. Some who know the Boulanger version may feel it is taken too slowly, but that only prolongs the ecstasy. Not only this but all the other items here are most welcome. The singing is fresh, and in its new bargain-priced format this collection cannot be too highly recommended. The casette is nearly as lively as the disc.

Madrigali erotici: Chiome d'oro; Come dolce hoggi l'auretta; Con che soavità; Mentre vaga Angioletta; Ogni amante è guerrier; Ohimè dov'è il mio ben; Parlo, miser'o taccio; S'el vostro cor, madonna; Tempro la cetra; Vorrei baciarti.
*** O-L Dig. DSLO/*KDSLC* 703. Kirkby, Nelson, Holden, Elliott, King, Wistreich, Thomas, Cons. of Musicke, Rooley.

The majority of the madrigals on this record come from the Seventh Book of 1619, very much a watershed in Monteverdi's output. They are in many instances for virtuoso singers and make a break with the past in that they call for instrumental accompaniment. They are very well sung by this group who, as usual, eschew the vibrato that lends colour to their tone, and some ears may well tire of the somewhat white sound that results. Words are well projected and clear and there is no want of vitality. (Listening to *Chiome d'oro* and *Ohimè dov'è il mio ben* serves as a reminder that the gloriously vital and life-loving (mono) accounts by Nadia Boulanger have now been reissued – Hyperion Helios H88004 – and should not be missed.) The present issue is very well recorded and presented, and collectors need not hesitate to investigate it. The chrome tape too is first-class, naturally balanced and clear, clean and open in the upper range.

Ballets and madrigals: *Hor ch'el ciel e la terra; Io mi son giovinetta; O rossignuol; Piagn'e sospira; Si ch'io vorrei morire; Tirsi e Clori; Zefiro torna.*
(M) *** HM HMA 209/*40*. Deller Cons., Coll. Aur., Deller.

With admirable contributions from the Collegium Aureum, the Deller Consort present a beautifully chosen selection of ballets and madrigals, including some of the most memorable. Deller was not always well served on record, but this recording from late in his career is among his most successful with its excellent, bright sound on disc and tape alike.

COURT AND CHURCH MUSIC

Adoramuste; Cantate Domino; Domine ne in furore; Era l'anima mia; Ohimè se tanto amate; Zefiro torna.
(B) ** Con. CC/*CCT* 7572. Monteverdi Ch. Gardiner – GESUALDO: *Motets.***

These performances are marked by excellent singing, with firm tone and intonation, but there is an element of interpretative exaggeration that is not wholly in style. Dynamics and tempi are rather extreme, but still there is no lack of life here, and the excellent recording will undoubtedly tempt many collectors, especially at bargain price.

Ab aeterno ordinata sum; Confitebor tibi, Domine (3 settings)*; Deus tuorum militum sors et corona; Iste confessor Domini sacratus; Laudate Dominum, O omnes gentes; La Maddalena: Prologue: Su le penne de venti. Nisi Dominus aedificaverit domum.*
❀ *** Hyp. Dig. **CDA 66021**; A/*KA* 66021. Kirkby, Partridge, Thomas, Parley of Instruments.

There are few records of Monteverdi's solo vocal music as persuasive as this. The three totally contrasted settings of *Confitebor tibi* (Psalm 110) reveal an extraordinary range of expression, each one drawing out different aspects of word-meaning. Even the brief trio *Deus tuorum militum* has a haunting memorability – it could become to Monteverdi what *Jesu, joy of man's desiring* is to Bach – and the performances are outstanding, with the edge on Emma Kirkby's voice attractively presented in an aptly reverberant acoustic. The accompaniment makes a persuasive case for authentic performance on original instruments. The cassette (issued some time after the disc had become something of a best-seller in its field) gives the performers a natural presence, and is very well balanced.

Sacred concertos: *Audi caelum; Beatus vir; Exsulta filia; Gloria in excelsis Deo; Laudate Dominum, O omnes gentes; Salve Regina.*
** DG Arc. 2533 137 [id.]. Dorow, Nordin, Rogers, Partridge, Keyte, Hessenbruch; Hamburg Monteverdi Ch. Instrumental Ens., Jürgens.

A finely recorded and well-performed set of sacred concertos from the *Selva morale e spirituale*. Perhaps there is some evidence of fussiness in the continuo support, and the instrumental accompaniment is editorial. However, given such good singing and recording, the disc can be recommended.

Audi caelum; Exsulta filia; Salve Regina. Madrigals: *Mentre vaga Angioletta; Ninfa che scalza il piede; O mio bene; Se vittoria si belle; Zefiro torna.*
(M) *(*) DG Arc. Priv. 2547/*3347* 041. Rogers, Partridge, Keyte, Tilney.

The sacred works come from the disc above and are generally well done, especially the *Salve Regina*, but the madrigals are much less successful. Tempi tend to be a shade too fast and there is little sense of poetic feeling. The recording is rather forward, which does not help. *Zefiro torna* is absurdly quick. There is an excellent cassette.

Laudate pueri; Mass in 4 parts (1640); *Mass in 4 parts* (1651); *Ut queant laxis.*
(M) **(*) Argo ZK 15 [id., PSI]. Turner, Odom, Birts, Bishop, Keen, St John's College Ch., ASMF, Guest.

There is a finer version of the 1640 *Mass* on a Serenata disc conducted by George Malcolm (see below). But this is well sung, and the other items include much fine music that is well worth having. At medium price this is worth investigating; the recording is excellent.

Magnificat à 6 voci; Messa à 4 voci.
(M) *** Decca Ser. SA/*KSC* 14. Carmelite Priory Ch., London, Malcolm; Mawby (organ).

The *Magnificat* is part of the collection of pieces more familiar as the *Vespers*. Like the four-part *Mass* of 1640, it shows Monteverdi's genius at its most spontaneous. The performances here have great character, the opening of the *Magnificat* has a remarkable feeling of radiance and throughout the singing, like the recording, is of the highest quality. So too is the cassette transfer, full and splendidly focused to match the disc closely.

Selva morale e spirituale: *Beatus vir a 6; Confitebor tibi; Deus tuorum militum a 3; Dixit Dominus a 8; Domine a 3; Jubilet tota civitas; Laudate dominum a 5; Laudate pueri a 5; Magnificat a 8; Salve Regina a 3.*

**(*) HMV Dig. ASD/*TC-ASD* 143539-1/*4* [Ang. S/*4XS* 38030]. Kirkby, Rogers, Covey-Crump, Thomas, Taverner Cons. Ch. and Players, Parrott.

There is some good singing from Emma Kirkby and Nigel Rogers, and the recorded sound is very good indeed. The performances really need more breadth and grandeur and there is at times a somewhat bloodless quality about some of the pieces, but there is enough to admire, such as the attractive account of *Salve Regina* and the opening *Dixit Dominus*, to make it well worth considering. XDR cassette and LP are virtually identical in sound, both offering the highest quality.

Selva morale e spirituale: *Confitebor secondo; Gloria a 7; Laudate dominum a 5; 2nd Magnificat; Salve Regina.*

**(*) Erato STU 70387. Staempfli, Perrin, Dufour, Loup, Lausanne Vocal and Instrumental Ens., Corboz.

Selva morale e spirituale: *Currite populi; Laetatus sum a 5; Laudate pueri dominum; Leataniae della Beata Vergine; Nisi dominus; O beata viae.*

**(*) Erato STU 70386. Staempfli, Schwarz, Huttenlocher, Loup, Lausanne Vocal and Instrumental Ens., Corboz.

This pair of Erato records comes from 1968 and uses modern instruments. The sound is ample, the acoustic warm and the overall effect is pleasing. The *Laetatus sum* uses the same basic material as the madrigal, *Chiome d'oro*. Generally speaking, these performances do justice to both the gentleness and the majesty of this music, and though style in performing practice has changed, these accounts stand the test of time.

Vespro della Beata Vergine (*Vespers*).

*** Decca SET 593/4. Gomez, Palmer, Bowman, Tear, Langridge, Shirley-Quirk, Rippon, Monteverdi Ch. and O, Salisbury Cath. Boys' Ch., Jones Brass Ens., Munrow Recorder Cons., Gardiner.

**(*) Tel. DX6. 35045 (2) [635045]. Hansmann, Jacobeit, Rogers, Van t'Hoff, Van Egmond, Villisech, V. Boys' Ch. soloists, Hamburg Monteverdi Ch., VCM, Plainsong Schola of Mun. Capella Antiqua, Jürgens.

** HMV SLS 5064 (2) [Ang. S 3837]. Ameling, Burrowes, Brett, Rolfe Johnson, Tear, Hill, Knapp, Noble, King's Coll. Ch., Early Music Cons., Ledger.

Vespro della Beata Vergine (*Vespers*)*; Magnificat; Missa in illo tempore.*

*** DG Arc. 2723 043/*3376 010* (3) [2710 017]. Esswood, Kevin Smith, Partridge, Elwes, Thomas, Keyte, Instrumental Soloists, Regensburg Cath. Ch., Schneidt.

Vespro della Beata Vergine; Magnificat.

(M) *** DG Arc. Priv. 2727/*3377* 018 (2). (from above set, cond. Schneidt).

Schneidt's is the most dedicated and beautiful performance of Monteverdi's choral masterpiece yet put on record. With male voices alone – soloists as well as choir – and a small authentic band of instrumentalists (the cornetti squealing delightfully), its intimacy is set against a gloriously free church acoustic, which yet allows clarity. The Regensburg Choir uses young voices, and the tenor and bass singing is not always as incisive as it might be, but the rest is superbly sensitive, not just the bright-sounding trebles but the superb team of soloists, all of them from Britain. In live performance it may not be possible for two male altos to take the solo parts in *Pulchra es,* but here Paul Esswood and Kevin Smith sing radiantly, while Ian Partridge in *Nigra sum* excels even his standards of expressiveness and beautiful tone-colour. Not the least attraction is that DG also includes the alternative and scarcely less elaborate setting of the *Magnificat,* as well as the superb *Missa in illo tempore*. With cassettes matching the discs closely, this set is highly recommendable in either format. However, to tempt collectors even further, DG have now made a two-record medium-priced issue which includes both settings of the *Magnificat* and omits only the original coupling of the *Missa in illo tempore*. This makes a bargain, by any standards, and should tempt readers who might not normally explore this repertoire.

'The grand quasi-theatrical design of this spectacular work has always seemed compelling to me,' says John Eliot Gardiner, and his fine set presents the music very much in that light. Modern instruments are used and women's voices, but Gardiner's rhythms are so resilient the result is more exhilarating as well as grander. The whole span of the thirteen movements sweeps you forward with a sense of complete unity. Singing and playing are exemplary, and the recording is one of Decca's most vividly atmospheric.

The Jürgens set is scholarly yet not without warmth. The liturgical sequence is respected and authentic instruments are used. The continuo tends to be somewhat lightweight, but there is a sure sense of style. Some might feel that the approach could be less smooth, more dramatic, but the beautifully judged aural perspective of the Telefunken recording helps to give atmosphere and a feeling of space.

On paper it may seem that the King's performance presents an excellent midway course between Gardiner's large-scale dramatic performance, using full forces, and Schneidt's reflective, intimate one, using male voices and authentic accompaniment; but in practice there are disappointments. The tempi are often disturbingly fast and lacking in the rhythmic exuberance which makes the rival versions so compelling. The solo singing is good, and the recording quality predictably atmospheric, but there is a perfunctory element which prevents this glorious music from flowering quite as it should.

OPERA AND OPERA-BALLET

Il Ballo delle ingrate; Il Combattimento di Tancredi e Clorinda (opera-ballets).

(M) *** Ph. 9502/*7313* 098. Harper, Watson, Howells, Alva, Wakefield, Dean, Amb. S., ECO, Leppard.

Monteverdi's mastery in these earliest examples of opera is readily brought out in finely sung performances from Volume 8 of the madrigal collection, the complete recording of which is now, alas, deleted. The famous dramatic narrative of *Tancredi and Clorinda* is matched here by the eloquence of the opera-ballet which tells of the 'ungrateful' ladies who were condemned to the domain of Pluto, not indeed for profligacy but for their lack of ardour. The poignant climax to this remarkably expressive work comes with the final beautiful aria, sung by a 'lost spirit' who stays behind to plead the cause of her companions. The recording is first-class to match the music-making; the cassette too is of high quality, smooth yet naturally focused and vivid.

Il Combattimento di Tancredi e Clorinda. L'Arianna: Lasciatemi morire (Ariadne's lament). *Lamento d'Olimpia.* (With Farina: *Sonata in G min.*)

*** DG Arc. 2533 460 [id.]. Kwella, Watkinson, Rogers, Thomas, Col. Mus. Ant., Goebel.

Il Combattimento di Tancredi e Clorinda. Madrigals: *Altri canti di Marte; Amorosa pupilletta; Batto qui pianse ergasto; Chiome d'oro; Due bell'occhi; Et e pur dunque vero.*

** Erato STU/*MCE* 71228. Hardy, Huttenlocher, Brodard, Vocal Ens., Drottningholm Bar. Ens., Corboz.

Under Reinhard Goebel the Cologne Musica Antiqua using original instruments has built up a formidable reputation on record, and these tasteful performances of a masterly set of Monteverdi pieces, well coupled with the sonata by Monteverdi's contemporary Carlo Farina, are most welcome. Carolyn Watkinson's singing of the two laments is finely controlled, and after initial uncertainty positively dramatic. Excellent recording.

Using baroque instruments, Corboz directs a light, crisp and clear reading of Monteverdi's dramatic narrative. It is a refreshing performance well recorded, but cannot quite match the even finer version (also using original instruments) from the Cologne Musica Antiqua on DG Archiv. Performances of the madrigals are more variable, not always avoiding dullness. Good clear sound. There is an excellent equivalent cassette vividly transferred at a high level.

L'Incoronazione di Poppea (complete).

**(*) Tel. HD6. 35247 (5) [635247]. Donath, Söderström, Berberian, Esswood, Luccardi,

Hansmann, Langridge, VCM, Harnoncourt.

L'Incoronazione di Poppea (abridged).
(M) *** HMV SLS/*TC-SLS* 5248 (2) [Ang. Sera. SIB 6073]. Laszlo, Bible, Lewis, Dominguez, Marimpietri, Cava, Alberti, Cuénod, Glyndebourne Fest. Ch., RPO, Pritchard.

When it was first issued in the mid-1960s, the abridged version of the Glyndebourne production of *L'Incoronazione di Poppea* was an important milestone in the history of Monteverdi on records. It was the first of his operas to be recorded in stereo (apart from a Vox set which could not measure up to it in standards of performance) and it was the first to show a real feeling for style, as opposed to the more academic manifestations including plentiful use of old and supposedly authentic instruments. Raymond Leppard, who edited this version, makes use of two harpsichords, two organs, two cellos, lute, guitar and harp for the continuo group – a most generous array of instruments which serve to colour the score in the best baroque manner. John Pritchard coaxes from the Royal Philharmonic Orchestra a truly Monteverdian sound, and the Glyndebourne chorus makes brief but significant contributions, notably in the scene of Seneca's farewell. Carlo Cava, as Seneca, suggests the character of the noble and revered philosopher and statesman, and his excellent low register never loses its flexibility. Frances Bible, as Ottavia, and Walter Alberti, as Ottone, portray the cast-off wife and lover with admirable skill. Vocally superior to these are Lydia Marimpietri, whose Drusilla is a marvel of characterization, and Orelia Dominguez, who plays the difficult and exacting role of Poppea's nurse and confidant. Hugues Cuénod's short scene with Nero could hardly be bettered as a musical picture of inebriation, hiccups and all. The stars of the piece, Richard Lewis and Magda Laszlo, are on top of their form, and their final love duet comes as a magnificent end to a great opera to which stereo has lent added enchantment.

Harnoncourt's recording of *L'Incoronazione di Poppea* has the dual advantages of being both complete and authentic. There are features of any performance of this great work which are bound to be conjectural, and here scholars may argue about the instrumentation used or the ornamentation (which matches it in elaboration). But there is no question that the dramatic power of the music comes across. Helen Donath is commanding as Poppea, and she is extremely well supported by Paul Esswood as Ottone and Cathy Berberian, whose characterization of Ottavia is an imaginative one. Donath's singing has not the richness and dignity that Janet Baker gives to this role, but she brings the character fully to life. Elisabeth Söderström has the almost impossible task of creating a heroic image in the role of Nero, written for a high castrato, but her performance is excellent, even if she fails wholly to submerge her femininity. Harnoncourt brings plenty of vitality to the performance as a whole, and his instrumental group provides beautiful if arguably over-decorative accompaniments.

Orfeo (opera): complete.
*** DG Arc. 2723 018 (3) [2710 015]. Rogers, Petrescu, Reynolds, Bowman, Elwes, Partridge, Dean, Malta, Hamburg Monteverdi Ch., Instrumental Ens., Jürgens.
** Tel. FK 6.35020 (3) [3635020]. Kozma, Hansmann, Katanosaka, Berberian, Rogers, Equiluz, Van Egmond, Villisech, Mun. Capella Antiqua, VCM, Harnoncourt.

In a lively, atmospheric performance like Jürgens's, Monteverdi's score emerges as amazingly modern, an innovatory work that reveals its total originality still. In the massive aria in which Orfeo pleads with Charon, Nigel Rogers treats the florid writing not as a technical obstacle race but as a test of expressiveness, giving the character extra depth. His fine virtuoso performance is matched by the singing of such artists as James Bowman and Ian Partridge. Alexander Malta as Charon and Stafford Dean as Pluto are wonderfully dark and firm in bass tone, while Emilia Petrescu as Euridice and Anna Reynolds as Silvia equally combine stylishness with expressive strength. The chorus and orchestra are outstanding. The recording – in total contrast with the Telefunken version – has an ample acoustic, simulating a performance in a nobleman's hall. The sound of the plucked instruments is especially beguiling.

Harnoncourt's speciality in the endless search for authenticity is the use of ancient instruments, and the Ritornello of the Prologue here might almost be by Stravinsky, so sharply do the sounds cut. Otherwise Harnoncourt is an altogether more severe Monteverdian than Jürgens. In compensation the simple, straightforward dedication of this performance is most affecting, and the solo singing, if not generally very characterful, is clean and stylish. One exception to the general rule on characterfulness comes in the singing of Cathy Berberian as the Messenger. She is strikingly successful, and though slightly different in style from the others, she sings as part of the team. Excellent restrained recording.

Il Ritorno d'Ulisse in patria (arr. Leppard; complete).
*** CBS 79332 (3) [Col. M3 35910]. Von Stade, Stilwell, Power, Lewis, Parker, Murray, Bryson, Glyndebourne Ch., LPO, Leppard.

Scholars may argue about the lush sounds which Leppard draws from his forces – especially here in Henry Wood Hall, very different from the dry Glyndebourne acoustic where these same artists were appearing at the time of the sessions – but no one will miss the depth of feeling behind this performance. The role of the faithful Penelope is superbly taken here by Von Stade, one of her very finest performances on record, while Richard Stilwell gives a noble account of Ulisse's music. Some may prefer a more detached view of an early-seventeenth-century opera, but the freshness and life, the immediacy and involvement of the drama set this apart among recordings of Monteverdi operas; for Leppard both as conductor and editor holds together what can easily seem a very long opera, here expertly tailored for a modern audience. With lavish and exotic continuo, the strings of the LPO have rarely sounded sweeter. The voices are balanced rather close but not objectionably so.

Moody, James (born 1925)

Little suite.
*** Argo ZRG 856 [id.]. Reilly (harmonica), ASMF, Marriner – JACOB: *5 pieces;* TAUSKY: *Concertino;* VAUGHAN WILLIAMS: *Romance.****

James Moody's *Little suite* consists of five miniatures, beautifully written and expertly scored. Their diversity of mood and colour gives great pleasure, especially when they are so immaculately played and recorded.

Moore, Douglas (1893–1969)

The Ballad of Baby Doe (opera): complete.
**(*) DG [2709 061 (3)]. Sills, Cassel, Bible, Hecht, NY City Op. Ch. and O, Buckley.

Douglas Moore's opera is an oddity. It is based on the life of Mrs Horace Tabor, widow of a silver-mine tycoon who lost all his money. Loyal to the last, she lived into the 1930s and finally froze to death over the derelict mine. Earlier her life was more glamorous, and this easy-going setting of a colourful story has its attractions, even if the actual idiom is rarely very original and the melodies are not quite memorable enough. This recording was made in 1958 at the time the New York City Opera presented the work (two years after the première in Central City, Colorado), and vocally its interest lies mainly in the contribution of the young Beverly Sills, who has some beautiful moments of singing in her upper register. Most of the rest of the singing is undistinguished, though the direction is alert and the illusion of live performance strong. Dated but acceptable recording. (This is not available in the UK.)

Morley, Thomas (1557–1603)

Ballets, Madrigals, Pavanes: *About the maypole new; Arise, awake; Barlowe; Frog galliard; Hard by a crystal fountain; Ho! who comes here; Love took his bow and arrow; Now is the month of Maying; O mistress mine; Pavane; You that wont to my pipes*. Sacred music: *Agnus Dei; Galliard to the Sacred End; I call with my whole heart; Let my complaint come before Thee; Nolo mortem peccatoris; O amica mea; Out of the deep; Sacred End pavane*.
(M) *** HM HMU 241. Deller Cons., Deller Instrumental Ens., Munrow.

It was shrewd of Alfred Deller to go to David Munrow and his then newly formed Early Music Consort to accompany this record of Morley's music, one of the few specifically devoted to that Italianate Elizabethan. This anthology, well recorded, provides not just a beautifully contrasted programme but one which, like a concert, ends with the finest item of all, the *Sacred End pavane*. Deller, long neglected by the British record companies, here showed that his band of singers was as lively as ever.

Ayres and Madrigals: *Absence, hear thou my protestation; Arise, awake; Besides a fountain; Deep lamenting; Fire and lightening; Hard by a crystal fountain; Hark! Alleluia; In every place; Mistress mine; No, no, Nigella; O grief ev'n on the bud; Phyllis I fain would die now; Singing alone; Sleep slumb'ring eyes: Stay heart, run not so fast; With my love*.
*** O-L Dig. DSDL 708. Cons. of Musicke, Rooley.

Morley is generally thought of as a lesser figure than his contemporaries, even though he was the pioneering English madrigalist. This record should do something to modify the picture of him, for although the lighter canzonetti and balletti based on Italian models (and in particular Gastoldi) are in evidence, there are more searching and thoughtful pieces. *Deep lamenting, grief betraying* is one such piece and there are others that make one feel that the range of his musical personality has not been adequately reflected before. This is an interesting recital and has the benefit of well-projected performances and good recorded sound.

Mozart, Leopold (1719–87)

Cassation in G (includes *Toy symphony*, attrib. Haydn).
** DG 2531/*3301* 275. ECO, Barenboim – PROKOFIEV: *Peter*.**(*)

This *Cassation* seems an insubstantial coupling for *Peter and the Wolf*, even though it is well enough played and recorded. There is an alternative version of the *Toy symphony* on ASV ACM/*ZCACM* 2033: see below under Poulenc's *Babar*.

Mozart, Wolfgang (1756–91)

Adagio and fugue in C min., K.546; 3 Divertimenti for strings, K.136/8; Serenade No. 13 in G (Eine kleine Nachtmusik), K.525.
**(*) Abbey ABY 809. Scottish Bar. Ens., Friedman.

No complaints about the Scottish Baroque Ensemble, who give alert performances on this record. Their attack is clean and their ensemble good, and the playing has sensitivity without ever showing too much sophistication. They are quite well recorded, and though the performances do not displace Boskovsky or Marriner (see below), and do not quite match them in elegance, they are thoroughly recommendable all the same.

Adagio and fugue in C min., K.546; Divertimento No. 1 for strings in D, K.136; Serenades

Nos. 6 (Serenata notturna), K.239; 13 in G (Eine kleine Nachtmusik), K.525.
(M) ** Ph. Seq. 6527/*7311* 189. I Musici.

The performances here are very relaxed (the central movements of K.525 especially so, and this group's later account of the *Night music* – see below – is fresher and more spontaneous). The *Adagio and fugue* lacks cumulative tension and the *Serenata notturna* is played steadily – it is serviceable rather than sparkling. But the *String Divertimento* is attractively done, and generally the breadth of the sound and the warmth of the playing carry the day. The high-level cassette transfer is very successful, although the opening of the *Serenata notturna* is slightly less sharp in focus than the rest of the programme.

Cassations Nos. 1 in G, K.63; 2 in B flat, K.99.
(M) *** Decca Jub. JB 66. V. Moz. Ens., Boskovsky.

The delightful *First Cassation* has two enchanting slow movements. The first is a delicate *Andante* (nicely atmospheric here), which is reminiscent of *Così fan tutte* in its mood and colour; the second introduces a cantilena for solo violin. K.99 is almost equally attractive. Boskovsky's performances are excellent in every way. The playing is marvellously alive and stylish, investing these comparatively lightweight works with considerable stature. The recording is flawless.

(i) *Bassoon concerto in B flat, K.191;* (ii) *Clarinet concerto in A, K.622.*
*** DG 2530 411/*3300 383* [id.]. (i) Zeman; (ii) Prinz, VPO, Boehm.

(i) *Bassoon concerto;* (ii) *Clarinet concerto;* (iii) *Adagio and rondo for glass harmonica, K.617.*
(M) ** DG Priv. 2535/*3335* 188. (i) Allard, LOP, Markevitch; (ii) Leister, Berlin PO, Kubelik; (iii) Zabaleta, Kuentz CO.

(i) *Bassoon concerto;* (ii) *Clarinet concerto;* (iii) *Andante for flute and orchestra in C, K.315.*
*** Ph. 6500 378/*7300 301* [id.]. (i) Chapman; (ii) Brymer; (iii) Claude Monteux, ASMF, Marriner.

(i) *Bassoon concerto;* (ii) *Clarinet concerto. March in D, K.249; Thamos, King of Egypt, K.345: Entr'acte No. 2.*
(M) *** HMV SXLP/*TC-SXLP* 30246 [(d) Sera. S 60193]. (i) Brooke; (ii) Brymer, RPO, Beecham.

The recording of the *Clarinet concerto* on Philips is the third that Jack Brymer has made. In some ways it is the best, for he plays with deepened insight and feeling. Only in the balance of the recording must we enter a reservation: Brymer plays a jumbo clarinet and is thus out of proportion to the excellent Academy. However, the recording is otherwise realistic and eminently truthful in timbre, and the performance is altogether outstanding. Although Michael Chapman too is rather prominently positioned in relation to the orchestra, his recording of the *Bassoon concerto* is eminently recommendable. He plays with great spirit and verve, and is stylishly supported. Indeed, in some respects this is to be preferred to almost any of its rivals, though Zeman and Boehm are better balanced.

The early HMV coupling of the *Bassoon* and *Clarinet concertos* is one of Beecham's most beguiling recordings. Both his soloists play with great character and beauty, and the affectionate accompaniment is wonderfully gracious. The recording in no way sounds its age, and current copies of the cassette match the disc closely. The bonuses are a pair of most welcome 'lollipops'.

Zeman gives a highly competitive account of the *Bassoon concerto,* a distinguished performance by any standards. Prinz's account of the *Clarinet concerto* too is beautifully turned; both deserve a position of honour in the field. The recording is truthful and well balanced, and the cassette transfer is faithful too.

On the Privilege issue Karl Leister gives a thoughtfully sensitive and musical performance of the *Clarinet concerto,* but with his gentle, introvert style and lack of a forceful personality the effect is rather too self-effacing. However, Kubelik's attention to detail and gracious phrasing mean that the orchestral contribution gives special pleasure. The recording is excellent. When one turns over for the *Bassoon concerto* the orchestral quality is thinner. But Maurice Allard plays a characterful bassoon; his timbre is attractively woody (it suggests a French instrument, certainly) and his reading shows imagination and humour. The transcription of Mozart's *Adagio and rondo,* K.617, for harp with flute, oboe, viola and cello, is most engaging; it is beautifully played and recorded. The tape transfers are well managed throughout.

Clarinet concerto in A, K.622.
(M) **(*) Uni. UNS 239. McCaw, New Philh. O, Leppard – NIELSEN: *Concerto.***(*)
(*) Mer. E 77022. King, ECO, Francis – SPOHR: *Concerto No. 4.**

(i) *Clarinet concerto;* (ii) *Flute and harp concerto in C, K.299.*
(M) *** Decca VIV/*KVIC* 25 [Lon. STS 15071]. (i) Prinz; (ii) Tripp, Jellinek; VPO, Münchinger.

(i) *Clarinet concerto;* (ii) *Sinfonia concertante for violin and viola in E flat, K.364.*
(M) **(*) Decca Jub. JB/*KJBC* 48. (i) De Peyer, LSO, Maag; (ii) I. and D. Oistrakh, Moscow PO, Kondrashin.

The Decca coupling under Münchinger has stood the test of time (it was recently available on SPA/*KCSP* 495) and in this new mid-priced Viva pressing the recording is smooth, rich, nicely reverberant yet well defined. The cassette too is first-class, every bit the equal of the disc. The balance between soloists and orchestra is finely calculated and the performances are admirable. Refinement and beauty of tone and phrase are a hallmark throughout, and Münchinger provides most sensitive accompaniments. Highly recommended.

Gervase de Peyer's performance of the *Clarinet concerto* is as fine as any available, fluent and lively, with masterly phrasing in the slow movement and a vivacious finale. It was a happy idea to recouple it on Jubilee with the Oistrakhs' version of the *Sinfonia concertante.* This performance also offers distinguished solo playing and is notable for its relaxed manner. Everything is shaped most musically, but sometimes the listener might feel that the performers, in their care for detail, are less involved with the music itself. However, the outer movements have plenty of vitality, and the sound is good, the cassette tending to show up the date of the original recording of the *Sinfonia concertante* (1964) more strikingly than the disc.

John McCaw's tone production is well suited to Mozart and his playing gives pleasure. The accompaniment under Leppard is beautifully made and the recording is clear and immediate. McCaw's approach is comparatively leisurely and the performance as a whole has no special individuality, but if the imaginative coupling is attractive, this is certainly recommendable.

Thea King, who earlier recorded an outstandingly sensitive account of the *Clarinet quintet* for Saga, sounds a degree less assured in the *Concerto.* Where the *Quintet* brought deeply expressive playing in the meditative slow movement, there is less sense of repose here, and the strength of the performance lies in its brightness, its rhythmic qualities, notably in the finale. The recording is generally well balanced, and this version can be considered by anyone who fancies the coupling.

(i) *Clarinet concerto;* (ii) *Clarinet quintet in A, K.581.*
(M) **(*) CBS 60273/*40-* [(d) MY/*MYT* 37810]. (i) (Marcellus, Cleveland O, Szell; (ii) Wright, Schneider Ens.

An attractive coupling on CBS that might have been used more often. Both performances are highly musical and cultured and Szell's accompaniment in the *Concerto* is very polished. The effect is leisurely and slightly suave, but still warmly enjoyable. Tempi in the *Quintet* are not conventional either, with the *Larghetto* elegant but not lingering. The finale is particularly felicitous with a nicely pointed style from the string group led by Alexander Schneider. But soloists are first-rate, although neither displays great individuality. The sound balance is forward but pleasing, both on disc and on the excellent matching chrome tape.

Flute concertos Nos. 1 in G; 2 in D, K.313/4.
(B) *** Pick. SHM 3010. Galway, New Irish Chamber Ens., Prieur.
*** Argo ZRG 910 [id.]. Bennett, ECO, Malcolm.

Flute concertos Nos. 1–2; Andante in C for flute and orchestra, K.315.

*** RCA LRLI 5109/*RK 11732* [ARL1/*ARK1* 2159]. Galway, Lucerne Fest. O, Baumgartner.
**(*) Erato STU 71144 [RCA AGL/*AGK1* 4290]. Rampal, Jerusalem Music Centre CO, Stern.

To have modern recordings of Mozart's two *Flute concertos* played by James Galway available in the cheapest price-range is bounty indeed. Moreover the accompaniments, ably directed by André Prieur, are polished and stylish, and the recording (although it gives a rather small sound to the violins) is excellent, clear and with good balance and perspective. It might be argued that Galway's vibrato is not entirely suited to these eighteenth-century works, and that his cadenzas too are slightly anachronistic. But the star quality of his playing disarms criticism. The slow movement of the *First Concerto* is beautifully paced; the timbre and phrasing have exquisite delicacy, and the pointed articulation in the finale (nicely matched by the orchestra) is a delight. In No. 2 Galway again floats the melodic line of the first movement with gossamer lightness, and after another enchanting slow movement the finale sparkles joyously, with the orchestra once more on top form.

William Bennett gives a beautiful account of the concertos, among the finest to have appeared in recent years. Every phrase is shaped with both taste and affection, and the playing of the ECO under George Malcolm is fresh and vital. The recording is clean, well detailed and with enough resonance to lend bloom to the sound.

Galway's performances on RCA can be recommended with no reservations whatsoever; and without modifying one's admiration for both Zöller and Adeney, he becomes an obvious choice in this coupling. This playing has spontaneity, virtuosity, charm and refinement, and Galway is well supported by the Lucerne orchestra. He is well recorded into the bargain. However, while his earlier versions remain available on Pickwick it would seem perverse to recommend the RCA issue which costs twice as much, even if it does offer a bonus in the way of the *Andante*, K.315.

Jean-Pierre Rampal gives a performance of the highest distinction, as one would expect from an artist of his stature. His is playing of vital imagination, and his record also has the advantage of including the *Andante*. The orchestral contribution is not perhaps of the same order of sensitivity, though it is perfectly acceptable. Rampal is too closely balanced in relation to the orchestra, but in other respects the sound is very good.

Flute concerto No. 1 in G, K.313; Andante in C, K.315; (i) *Flute and harp concerto in C, K.299.*

(M) *** Ph. Seq. 6527/*7311* 148. Claude Monteux; (i) Ellis; ASMF, Marriner.

(i) *Flute concerto No. 1 in G, K.313;* (ii) *Flute and harp concerto in C* (see also above).

(M) **(*) DG 2535/*3335* 477. (i) Linde, Mun. CO, Stadlmair; (ii) Zöller, Zabaleta, Berlin PO, Märzendorfer.
**(*) HMV ASD 2993 [(d) in Ang. SC 3783 (3)]. (i) Blau; (ii) Galway, Helmis; Berlin PO, Karajan.

(i) *Flute concerto No. 1;* (ii) *Oboe concerto in C, K.314.*

(M) **(*) DG Arc. Priv. 2547/*3347* 015 [id.]. (i) Linde; (ii) Holliger; Mun. CO, Stadlmair.

Exquisite playing on the Sequenza reissue from all concerned. The only reservation is that the solo instruments sound larger than life as balanced. In every other respect this disc is highly recommendable. The tape is well managed too, though in the gentle *Andante* one reflects that a slightly higher transfer level should have been possible. Nevertheless definition remains good.

There are no strictures about the Zöller/Zabaleta account of the *Flute and harp concerto*. The flautist is a most sensitive player, and his phrasing is a constant source of pleasure, while Zabaleta's sense of line knits the overall texture of this solo-duet most convincingly. Märzendorfer conducts with both warmth and lightness; the outer movements have an attractive rhythmic buoyancy. The recording is clear and clean, if not as rich as we would expect today. The cassette transfer is not wholly successful, with the tuttis of the *Flute and harp concerto* less refined than on disc. The solo concerto - see below - offers no problems.

Despite the superb artistry of James Galway and Fritz Helmis and the refined and highly polished response of the Berlin Philharmonic, this well recorded performance does not wholly escape the blandness that afflicts Karajan's set of the wind concertos. Of course there are many details to enjoy and admire, and the HMV engineers produce a warm, well-detailed sound picture. Andreas Blau's account of the *Flute concerto* too is impeccably played and superbly accompanied, but it has less freshness and sparkle than its competitors.

Impeccably played and neatly recorded, Linde's performance of the *Flute concerto* has a hint of rhythmic stiffness in the outer movements. The highlight is the slow movement, where the playing is beautifully poised, and the melody breathes in exactly the right way. Holliger's account of the *Oboe concerto* is, needless to say, first-class, his tone appealing and his style and technique serving the music's grace and elegance. But Stadlmair's accompaniment is crisply straightforward rather than especially imaginative, and though this makes a good medium-priced coupling (with a faithful cassette alternative) Holliger's later, full-priced Philips version, coupled with Richard Strauss's *Concerto* (6500 174/*7300 119*), is more masterly, more refined.

Readers should also be reminded that Claude Monteux's sunny performance of the flute version of this concerto (K.314) is available on a bargain-priced Contour reissue (CC/*CCT* 7504). It is part of a concert also including music of Bach and Gluck (see the Concerts section below).

(i) *Flute and harp concerto in C, K.299. Flute concerto in G, K.622G* (arrangement of *Clarinet concerto,* ed. Galway).

**(*) RCA RL/*RK* 25181 [ARL1/*ARK1* 3353]. Galway, LSO, Mata, (i) with Robles.

The *Flute and harp concerto* has seldom sounded so lively in a recording as it does here, with an engaging element of fantasy in the music-making, a radiant slow movement, and an irrepressibly spirited finale. Marisa Robles makes a characterful match for the ubiquitous Galway. The balance of the soloists is forward, but not unrealistically so. The *Flute concerto* arranged from Mozart's masterpiece for clarinet is more controversial; the key of G major as well as Galway's silvery flute timbre make for even lighter results than one might have anticipated. The scintillating finale is especially successful. The recording is admirably bright and clear, the cassette slightly less refined than the disc.

(i) *Flute and harp concerto; Sinfonia concertante for wind in E flat, K.297b* (see also above and below).

**(*) Ph. 6500 380 [id.]. (i) Claude Monteux, Ellis; ASMF, Marriner.

The performances here are delightful, but Osian Ellis and Claude Monteux play on jumbo-sized instruments and the flautist's intake of breath is all too audible. Karlheinz Zöller and Nicanor Zabaleta (see above) are much better balanced, and their performance is also a distinguished one; however, they use Reinecke's cadenza, which may not be to all tastes, and the splendid wind *Sinfonia concertante* gives this Philips disc a strong advantage. Marriner's account of this latter work is also handicapped by larger-than-life soloists, but the performance is so songful and elegant that it carries all before it.

Harpsichord concerto, K.107, No. 1 in D.

*** CRD CRD 1011 [id.]. Pinnock (harpsichord), E. Concert – C.P.E. BACH: *Concertos.****

In the early 1770s the teenage Mozart turned three sonatas by J. C. Bach into keyboard concertos, adding accompaniments and ritornellos as well as cadenzas. The first of the group, stylishly performed on original instruments, makes an excellent coupling for the fine C. P. E. Bach concerto on the reverse of the CRD disc.

Horn concertos Nos. 1 in D, K.412; 2–4 in E flat, K.417, 447, 495.

*** Tel. AW6.41272/*CX 4 41277* [641272]. Baumann (natural hand-horn), VCM, Harnoncourt.

(B) *** CfP CFP/*TC-CFP* 148. James Brown, Virtuosi of L., Davison.

Horn concertos Nos. 1–4; Concerto No. 5 (fragment).

(M) *** Decca Jub. JB/*KJBC* 70 [JL/5-41015]. Tuckwell, LSO, Maag.

Horn concertos Nos. 1–4; Concerto No. 5 (fragment); Concert rondo in E flat, K.371.

(M) *** HMV Green. ESD 102225-1/*4* [Ang. S/*4XS* 36840]. Tuckwell, ASMF, Marriner.

Horn concertos Nos. 1–4; Concert rondo.

*** EMI Em. EMX/*TC-EMX* 2004. Civil, RPO, Kempe.

All recordings of the Mozart *Horn concertos* stand to be judged by the set recorded by Dennis Brain in mono and now available in a highly successful stereo transcription (HMV ASD/*TC-ASD* 1140). Boyd Neel once said that Brain, besides being a superb horn player, was also the finest Mozartian of his generation. Certainly his accounts of these marvellous concertos have a unique combination of poetry and exuberance of spirit. Barry Tuckwell was the first 'natural successor' to the Brain mantle. His easy technique, smooth, warm tone and obvious musicianship command attention and give immediate pleasure. His actual tone is broader than that of Brain and he spreads his phrases widely. His HMV disc conveniently and economically collects together all Mozart's concertante music for horn and orchestra. The *Fragment in E major* ends where Mozart left it at bar 91. It provides a somewhat inconclusive close to side one, rather after the manner of some performances of Bach's *Art of fugue*. Throughout, the playing is vigorous, rich in phrase, with beautifully managed accompaniments. The recording too is warm and the quality does not appear to suffer from cramming a good deal of music on to each side. This is very enjoyable, but the approach is straightforward, rather than providing special moments of magic or new illumination of the three more famous concertos. Indeed, Tuckwell's robust style here seems to suit No. 1 best of all. There is a good tape, although the horn timbre tends to spread in the resonant acoustic.

Tuckwell's earlier Decca recording of the four *Horn concertos*, plus the fragment from *No. 5 in E major* (which again ends where Mozart left it at bar 91) continues to stand up against almost all competition. The solo playing is vigorous, spontaneous, and lyrically exuberant. Peter Maag's accompaniments are admirably crisp and nicely scaled, giving the soloist buoyant support. The recording is excellent on disc and tape alike, and the Jubilee reissue is also attractively priced.

Alan Civil has recorded the concertos three times and, of the three sets, his earliest, originally made in 1967 for World Record Club, is the finest. This is a really lovely disc. Civil plays with a simple eloquence, a warm velvety tone, and a flawless technique. He never forces his personality in front of that of the composer, yet his sensitivity is present in every bar. So flexible is his phrasing and so inherently musical his line that he can indulge in gentle contrasts of light and shade, and touches of rubato, with the listener only being aware that the music is unfolding in the most spontaneous way. Civil has not perhaps the exuberance of spirit of Dennis Brain, but in every other way he is a worthy successor. Kempe accompanies attentively and with great affection; one can almost sense him beaming down on his talented soloist as they share the delights of the slow movement of No. 2, which is beautifully managed, or the gay vivacity of the famous finale of No. 4. Civil includes also a lively yet quite imaginative performance of the *Concert rondo*, the orchestral part of which he has completed and edited himself. The recording is of vintage EMI quality, full and naturally balanced in this Eminence reissue. There is a good cassette, though the upper range of the disc is noticeably more extended.

The other outstanding version is on Telefunken. We are not convinced that the playing of 'original instruments' always demonstrates their full expressive potential and in the case of the french horn it would seem perverse to use a valveless instrument, when a narrow-bore modern horn (of the kind used by Dennis Brain in his earliest recordings – see our Concerts section below) can sound the same, yet produce uniformity of timbre and stay in tune throughout its compass. Yet Hermann Baumann successfully uses the original hand-horn, without valves, for which the concertos were written, and the result is a *tour de force* of technical skill, not achieved at the expense of musical literacy and expressive content. Inevitably this implies at least some alteration in timbre, as certain notes have to be 'stopped', with the hand in the bell of the instrument, if they are to be in tune. But Herr Baumann is not in the least intimidated by this problem: he plays throughout with consummate tonal smoothness and a totally relaxed manner. He only lets the listener hear the stopped effect when he decides that the tonal change can be put to good artistic effect, as for instance in the rondo of No. 2 or his own cadenza for No. 3. Here also he uses horn chords (where several notes are produced simultaneously by resonating the instrument's harmonics), but as a complement to the music rather than as a gimmick. The slow movement of No. 3 has one of Mozart's richest melodies and its touch of chromaticism is managed with superb flexibility and smoothness, so that one can only wonder at Baumann's artistry and skill. In short these are remarkably satisfying performances, by any standards. Baumann's execution in the gay rondos is a delight and his tone is particularly characterful. It is splendid to have such a successful representation of the horn technique that Mozart would have recognized, and which indeed all nineteenth-century composers would have expected.

On Classics for Pleasure, James Brown's performances have plenty of life and spirit and are enjoyably spontaneous. Arthur Davison's contribution is a major one. Using a small group of genuine Mozartian dimensions, he achieves crisply sprung accompaniments and he is always attentive to the soloist's style. This is straightforward and musical. The cassette version is of good quality.

(i) *Horn concerto No. 4, K.495;* (ii) *Piano concerto No. 21 in C, K.467;* (iii) *Serenade No. 13 (Eine kleine Nachtmusik), K. 525.*
(M) **(*) HMV *TC-IDL 510.* (i) Tuckwell, ASMF, Marriner; (ii) Annie Fischer, Philh. O, Sawallisch; (iii) Philh. O, Kempe.

This tape-only compilation, otherwise very attractive, is let down a little by Kempe's account of *Eine kleine Nachtmusik*, which, though elegantly phrased and given a warm, clear recording, has a flaccid minuet and shows a similar lack of sparkle in the finale. The *Horn concerto* shows Tuckwell in first-class form, and Annie Fischer's silken touch in the K.467 *Piano concerto* (which has a distinguished accompaniment from the Philharmonia under Sawallisch) makes delightful listening, particularly as the recording matches the playing in its refinement of timbre and detail.

Oboe concerto in C, K.314.
*** Ph. 6500 174/*7300 119* [id.]. Holliger, New Philh. O, De Waart – R. STRAUSS: *Oboe concerto.****

Holliger's reputation goes from strength to strength. This is his second version of Mozart's charming *Oboe concerto*, and it is even more masterly, more refined than the DG one made in Munich (see above). The coupling is imaginative, the most delectable of twentieth-century oboe concertos. The cassette transfer is of excellent quality, if, more than the disc, it reveals the age of the recording (1972).

PIANO CONCERTOS AND RONDOS

Piano concertos Nos. 1–6, 8, 9, 11–27 (complete); *Concert rondo* (for piano and orchestra) *No. 1 in D, K.382.*
(B) *** HMV SLS 5031 (12). Barenboim, ECO.

Piano concertos Nos. 1–6; 8, 9; 11–16; 22; Concert rondo in D, K.382.
(M) **(*) HMV *TC C-SLS* 5292 (4). Barenboim, ECO.

Piano concertos Nos. 17–21; 23–27.
(M) **(*) HMV *TCC-SLS* 5293 (4). Barenboim, ECO.

Piano concertos Nos. 1–6, 8, 9, 11–27.
(B) *** DG 2720 030 (12) [id.]. Anda, Camerata Ac. of the Salz. Mozarteum.

The sense of spontaneity in Barenboim's performances of Mozart concertos, his message that this is music hot off the inspiration-line, is hard to resist, even though it occasionally leads to idiosyncrasies. On balance, fast movements are faster than usual, slow movements slower, but that view has powerful backing and any inconsistencies or romantic touches seem merely incidental to the forward drive. These are as nearly live performances as one could hope for on record, and the playing of the English Chamber Orchestra, on the whole warmly and fully recorded, is splendidly geared to the approach of an artist with whom the players have worked regularly. Certainly the most invigorating complete cycle of the Mozart concertos yet issued.

Barenboim's set is also available on chrome tape, with generally first-class transfers, fresh and wide-ranging with plenty of bloom on the piano timbre. Some transfer levels, however, vary considerably and once or twice seem fractionally too high, notably Nos. 8 and (especially) 13 in box one and Nos. 18 and 20 in box two. In the latter case the refinement slips a little, with the upper partials fractionally discoloured. The sound in No. 22 is a trifle opaque, while the *First concerto* is not quite as fresh-sounding as some of the others. The layout puts many of the early concertos two to a side, and in box two, K.414 in A and K. 449 in E flat are split between sides.

Anda's performances are beautifully poised and have excellent feeling for style. The recordings do not quite match those of Barenboim in clarity or definition, but they are well balanced and give consistent enjoyment. The set is extremely competitively priced.

Piano concertos Nos. 5 in D, K.175; 9 in E flat, K.271.
(M) *** HMV SXLP/*TC-SXLP* 30418. Barenboim, ECO.

Barenboim's recording of K.175 is delightful and played with great spirit. Some may find that his version of K.271 displays too great awareness of refinements of tone and dynamics that are strictly speaking anachronistic. Faced with such masterly pianism, however, and such alert and musical direction, few are likely to grumble. The most serious reservation concerns the minuet of the last movement, which is far too measured. On balance, Ashkenazy's sparkling account on Decca (coupled with No. 8, K.246) is still the finest in the current catalogue and it is better recorded; but those who want the Barenboim coupling can rest assured that this is a distinguished record. The tape transfer is not one of EMI's best; a bass cut improves the sound balance, but inner detail is not ideally clean.

Piano concertos Nos. 5 in D, K.175; 25 in C, K.503.
*** CBS Dig. 37267/*40-* [id.]. Perahia, ECO.

Murray Perahia never loses sight of the space and grandeur of the *C major*, K.503, and, like Bishop-Kovacevich on Philips and Brendel (particularly in his Vox recording from the 1960s), has the measure of its strength and scale as well as tenderness. Perahia invests the landscape with delicate and subtle colourings and there is a sparkle and poetry that is unfailingly affecting. The sheer refinement of keyboard sound is a joy in itself and never narcissistic; at only one point – the F major section of the finale (bar 163 onwards) – does the listener wonder whether Perahia and the wind players of the ECO caress the melodic line in a way that almost steps outside the sensibility of the period. A wonderful performance, however, and coupled with an account of the *D major*, K.175, which has an innocence and freshness that is completely persuasive. The recording is good without being as distinguished as the performance. The high-level chrome cassette is impressively wide-ranging and clear, although the treble is slightly less refined than the disc.

Piano concertos Nos. 6 in B flat, K.238; 20 in D min., K.466.
**(*) Decca SXL 6353 [Lon. CS/*5-* 6579]. Ashkenazy, LSO, Schmidt-Isserstedt.

An eloquent performance of a charming work, beautifully accompanied, and a worthy companion to Ashkenazy's other discs of Mozart concertos. Unfortunately the great *D minor Concerto* is too well regulated in emotional temperature and is a little lacking in spontaneity and sparkle. The recording is excellent.

Piano concertos Nos. 8 in C, K.246; 9 in E flat, K.271; Concert rondo (for piano and orchestra), *No. 2 in A, K.386.*

❀ *** Decca SXL 6259 [Lon. CS/*5*- 6501]. Ashkenazy, LSO, Kertesz.

Magnificent performances and recording. Ashkenazy has the requisite sparkle, humanity and command of keyboard tone, and his readings can only be called inspired. The *C major Concerto* is under-represented in the catalogue, but with playing of this order further duplication is rendered unnecessary. Ashkenazy is well supported by the LSO under Kertesz, and the recording is superb.

Piano concertos Nos. 8 in C, K.246; 22 in E flat, K.482.
*** CBS 76966/*40*- [*M*/*MT* 35869]. Perahia, ECO.

Murray Perahia's version of the great *E flat Concerto* is second to none. He has the measure of its scale, and yet every phrase is lovingly shaped too. Perahia is an artist who blends unusual qualities of spirit with wonderful sensuousness; not only does he draw magical sounds from the keyboard, he also inspires the wind players of the ECO, who invest the serenade-like episodes in the slow movement with great eloquence. This is a reading of real stature. It is well recorded, though there is not quite the range and depth that distinguished Perahia's slightly earlier coupling of K.414 and K.595. The early *C major Concerto* is unfailingly fresh and elegant in his hands. The cassette, on chrome tape, is of good quality.

Piano concertos Nos. 9 in E flat, K.271; 11 in F, K.413; 14 in E flat, K.449; 20 in D min., K.466; 21 in C, K.467; 24 in C min., K.491.
❀ *** CBS 79317/*40*- (3). Perahia, ECO.

These are among the most distinguished Mozart performances in the catalogue. They are not unblemished (there is some less than perfect intonation from the wind in K.271 and K.466), but Perahia offers playing of a consistent excellence and distinction. He has the power to draw from the keyboard a variety of timbre that few of his rivals can begin to approach. In K.413 and K.466 the recording does justice to the quality and range of colour that he commands, and elsewhere the sound is eminently satisfactory. These are searching and poetic performances that only gain by repetition, and the reservations mentioned in some of the individual reviews melt away as one gets to know these beautiful readings more closely. Perahia's blend of sensuousness and spirituality is very special. This set earns a rosette in its disc format, and the cassette transfers are among the best to come from CBS. They are slightly variable in level, and the orchestral quality is not always as rich and detailed as on disc (the upper strings noticeably lack bloom in K.271); but the piano timbre is consistently natural.

Piano concertos Nos. 9 in E flat, K.271; 11 in F, K.413.
*** DG Arc. Dig. **410 905-2**; 410 905-1/*4* [id.]. Bilson, E. Bar. Soloists, Eliot Gardiner.

Bilson's coupling is the first of a projected complete series of the Mozart keyboard concertos, featuring original instruments and including a copy of Mozart's own concert piano. Bilson may have made his reputation as an academic but here he shows himself a lively and imaginative artist, well matched by the ever-effervescent and alert Gardiner. The recording on both disc and tape catches superbly the lightness and clarity of the textures, with the fortepiano sound not too twangy and with wind balances often revelatory. The darkness of the C minor slow movement of K.271 is eerily caught. The lightness of keyboard action encourages Bilson to choose fast allegros but never at the expense of Mozart. The sound on compact disc is particularly fine in its extra realism and immediacy.

Piano concertos Nos. 9 in E flat, K.271; 17 in G, K.453.
** DG Dig. 2532/*3302* 060 [id.]. Serkin, LSO, Abbado.

Serkin has a powerful musical mind but his magisterial reputation should not obscure the fact that his playing is not so supple and refined as it once was. The second group of the first movement of the *G major Concerto*, K453, is ungainly in presentation and there are other inelegances that diminish pleasure. There are no quarrels with the sound, however, which is very vivid and clear both in the disc and cassette format.

Piano concertos Nos. 9 in E flat, K.271; 21 in C, K.467.
*** CBS 76584 [M/*MT* 35462]. Perahia, ECO.

Perahia's reading of K.271 is wonderfully refreshing, delicate, with diamond-bright articulation, urgently youthful in its resilience. In the C minor slow movement, beautifully poised, Perahia finds gravity without weighing the music down. The famous *C major Concerto* is given a more variable, though still highly imaginative, performance. If the first movement is given charm rather than strength, it is the opposite with the slow movement and finale. Faithful, well-balanced recording. The cassette is less impressive than the disc, with the orchestral quality somewhat amorphous. K.467 is also available coupled with No. 20 in D minor, K.466 – see below.

Piano concerto No. 9, K.271; (i) *Double concerto in E flat, K.365.*
*** Ph. 9500 408/*7300 616* [id.]. Brendel, ASMF, Marriner, (i) with Cooper.

Alfred Brendel gives us a finely proportioned and cleanly articulated account of the *Jeunehomme concerto*, with a ravishing performance of the slow movement. The finale has great sparkle and finesse, and the recording has exemplary clarity. In the eight-record box in which this first appeared it occupied two sides, but Philips have sensibly accommodated it on one here. The other side gives us a spirited version of the *Double piano concerto*, in which Brendel is joined by Imogen Cooper. This is an alert and finely recorded performance, but it does not quite efface memories of the DG recording with Gilels *et fille* under Karl Boehm, which has slightly more repose. Yet there is no ground for complaint about anything on this issue, and the cassette transfer is of excellent quality: the *Double concerto* is strikingly full and vivid.

Piano concertos Nos. 11, K.413; 20 in D min., K.466.
*** CBS 76651/*40*- [M/*MT* 35134]. Perahia, ECO.

This is the most impressive of Perahia's Mozart concerto records so far. He plays both works with abundant artistry and imagination and is well served by the CBS engineers. These are finely integrated readings: the solo entry in the first movement of K.413 could hardly emerge more organically from the texture, and in the slow movement he is more withdrawn, more private than many of his colleagues. Here he is at the other end of the spectrum from Barenboim, whose reading is more outgoing and life-loving. Perahia brings less dramatic fire to K.466 than some of his colleagues, but there is a strong case for this; too many artists view the work from the vantage-point of *Don Giovanni* rather than seeing it in terms of its own unique sensibility. None of the disturbing undercurrents goes unnoted, but at the same time the spiritual dimensions remain within the period: not the only way of looking at this work but a most convincing one. The cassette is not as wide-ranging as the disc but is satisfactorily balanced.

Piano concerto No. 12 in A, K.414.
*** Decca SXL/*KSXC* 6952 [Lon. CS/*5*-7180]. De Larrocha, L. Sinf., Zinman – BACH: *Concerto No. 5*; HAYDN: *Concerto in D.****

An outstanding account of the *A major Concerto* from Alicia de Larrocha and David Zinman, who form a splendid partnership. The opening movement is graciously phrased yet has an engaging momentum and resilience. The slow movement is beautifully played and the finale is full of rhythmic character and sparkle. Excellent recording too, with no appreciable difference between cassette and disc. If the couplings are suitable this can be recommended highly.

Piano concertos Nos. 12 in A, K.414; 13 in C, K.415.
C *** Decca Dig. **410 214-2**; SXDL/*KSXDC* 7556 [Lon. LDR/*5*- 71056]. Ashkenazy, Philh. O.

Vladimir Ashkenazy's account of K.414 and 415 must be numbered among the most successful of his cycle. The *A major* is well served on record with splendid versions from De Larrocha and Perahia, both of which will give pleasure. Ashkenazy's account admirably combines expressive feeling with sparkle and conveys real enjoyment: he is moreover fortunate in having the benefit of well-defined and transparent recording, superior to that given Perahia. The *C major* has equally strong claims and readers collecting the Ashkenazy survey will not be disappointed. The compact disc is particularly impressive. The piano is forwardly balanced, but the naturalness of timbre and the bloom on the overall sound picture are such as to confound criticism. The slow movement of K.414 is given memorable depth when the quality is so beautiful and the ambience so attractive.

Piano concertos Nos. 12 in A, K.414; 20 in D min., K.466.
*(*) DG Dig. **400 068-2**; 2532/*3302* 053 [id.]. Serkin, LSO, Abbado.

Serkin made some distinguished Mozart concerto records way back in the days of shellac, and has now embarked on a new cycle at nearly eighty years of age. It would be a pleasure to report on the *A major* with enthusiasm, but Serkin's playing is far from elegant and, though there are flashes of authority, the ends of phrases are not beautifully turned. This offers no real challenge to De Larrocha, Ashkenazy and Perahia in K.414 or Brendel, Perahia and Bishop-Kovacevich in the *D minor*, K.466. The recording is clean and vivid, both in its LP and cassette format, and those who are prepared to bear with the prosaic pianism for the sake of the musical insights that do emerge will have no quarrels with this issue technically. The compact disc offers the usual advantages.

Piano concertos Nos. 12 in A, K.414; 21 in C, K.467.
(M) **(*) Decca Jub. JB/*KJBC* 124 [Lon. CS 6894]. Lupu, ECO, Segal.

There is much that is beautiful here, including really lovely sounds from the orchestra, and hushed playing from Radu Lupu in the slow movements of both concertos. The music-making has life and sensibility, and both performances are very enjoyable. Even if No. 12 is not quite as sparkling as Alicia de Larrocha's account, and there are even finer full-priced versions of K.467, this is excellent value in the Jubilee price-range. The high-level chrome cassette is of first-class quality.

Piano concertos Nos. 12, K.414; 27 in B flat, K.595.
*** CBS 76731/*40*- [M/*MT* 35828]. Perahia, ECO.

Murray Perahia has the capacity to make the piano breathe and to persuade the listener that the sound he produces is almost independent of any physical agent. Yet this spiritual dimension harmonizes with a flesh-and-blood intensity and strongly classical instincts. Both these performances have great sparkle and a sense of naturalness and rightness: listening to the finale of K.414, one feels it could not be taken at any other speed or phrased in any other way. In K.595 Perahia produces some wonderfully soft colourings and a luminous texture, yet at the same time he avoids underlining too strongly the sense of valediction that inevitably haunts this magical score. There is a sublime simplicity to the slow movement in these artists' hands – for the ECO too seem as inspired as the soloist-director. The CBS sound is excellent, fresh-toned and well balanced. The cassette has less upper range than the disc, but with a bass cut the sound balance is pleasing, and there is no muffling of the strings.

Piano concertos Nos. 13 in C, K.415; 14 in E flat, K.449.
*** Ph. 9500 565/*7300 714* [id.]. Brendel, ASMF, Marriner.

The *E flat Concerto*, K.499, is distinguished by beautifully clean and alive passage-work, and there is superb control and poise. The main ideas are well shaped without being overcharacterized. Tempi are wisely chosen and perfectly related, though the finale is a little less playful than Perahia's. Indeed, with Brendel one views the landscape with all the clarity of high noon, every detail sharply in focus, while with Perahia there are many pastel colourings and all the sparkle and freshness of early morning. In the *C major Concerto* there is no want of surface elegance yet it is never allowed to obscure the music's depths or to attract attention to itself. A refreshingly classical reading without a trace of self-indulgence; indeed in the second group of the first movement Brendel might have allowed himself something of the beguiling eloquence that Barenboim brought to this idea. However, these are most distinguished performances and beautifully recorded too, on disc and tape alike.

Piano concertos Nos. 14 in E flat, K. 449; 17 in G, K.453.
(M) ** CBS 60275/*40*-. Serkin, Columbia SO, Schneider.

Serkin made an altogether magical account of the *E flat Concerto*, K449, with the Busch Chamber Players (HMV DB3690-92) before the war and memories of this remain unsullied. The present account, though not quite as special, is well worth hearing; the *G major Concerto*, though at times dour by comparison with Edwin Fischer, Barenboim, Perahia and others, is still to be preferred to his recent version with Claudio Abbado. Acceptable but not outstanding recording.

Piano concertos Nos. 14 in E flat, K.449; 24 in C min., K.491.
*** CBS 76481/*40*- [M/*MT* 34219]. Perahia, ECO.

Very distinguished playing from Perahia. K.449 is an immensely civilized reading and full of grace. This artist has the power to make each phrase sound freshly experienced and vibrant, though greater robustness might not be out of place. All the same, this is one of the best accounts of the concerto to have appeared recently. The slow movement of the *C Minor* is exquisitely played, and Perahia's control of keyboard colour and his sensitivity in matters of tonal nuance excite unstinted admiration. He also conducts and secures excellent results and responsive phrasing (though less than impeccable wind intonation in one place) from the ECO. His is an inward reading, not so full of the dramatic intensity of some rivals, but enormously rewarding. He is better served by the engineers than in any of his earlier records, but the cassette version offers poorer internal definition of the orchestra, although the piano timbre is fully acceptable.

Piano concerto No. 15 in B flat, K.450; Symphony No. 36 in C (Linz), K.425.
(M) **(*) Decca Jub. JB/*KJBC* 95 [Lon. JL/*5*- 41025]. Bernstein, VPO.

Such a record as this claims Leonard Bernstein as a European at heart. In the performance of the *Linz symphony* one may keep recognizing the characteristic Bernstein touches that we know from his New York performances – the glowing violin lyricism in the slow introduction, the bristling manner of the *Allegro* – but somehow a carefree quality is there too, such as one finds only rarely in his American records. In addition the recording quality provided by the Decca engineers, not to mention the comparatively small forces used, gives a transparency to the sound of a kind one may hear from Bernstein in the concert hall but rarely on record. The concerto, even more than the symphony, conveys the feeling of a conductor enjoying himself on holiday. Bernstein's piano playing may not be as poised in every detail as that of full-time virtuoso pianists, but every note communicates vividly. So much so that in the slow movement he even manages to make his dual tempo convincing – faster for the tuttis than for the more romantic solos. The finale is taken surprisingly slowly, but Bernstein brings it off. Some may resist his individuality but it is only too easy to come under the spell of this engagingly spontaneous music-making, especially as the sound is first-rate on both disc and cassette.

Piano concertos Nos. 15 in B flat, K.450; 16 in D, K.451.
❀ *** CBS Dig. 37824/*40*- [id.]. Perahia, ECO.
*** Decca **411 612-2**; SXL/*KSXC* 7010 [Lon. CS/*5*- 7254]. Ashkenazy, Philh. O.

These two concertos, written for subscription concerts in March 1774, make an apt and attractive coupling. Perahia's are superbly imaginative readings, full of seemingly spontaneous touches and turns of phrase very personal to him, which yet never sound mannered. This is as near to live music-making as a record can approach. Perahia's version of the *B flat Concerto* has all the sparkle, grace and intelligence one would expect to encounter from this artist; both these performances uphold the special claims this cycle has of being to the 1980s what Edwin Fischer's Mozart concerto records were to the 1930s – that is to say, very special indeed. The recording is absolutely first-rate, intimate yet realistic and not dry, with the players continuously grouped round the pianist. Trumpets and timpani in K.451 come out the more sharply. There is a refined chrome-cassette transfer.

Needless to say, Ashkenazy's performances too show characteristic sensibility. He takes a more direct view, yet there are many imaginative touches: both slow movements are played very beautifully yet without a trace of narcissism, and the finales sparkle. There is some splendid wind playing from the Philharmonia and the result is consistently clean and refreshing, but rather less individual than Perahia. The Decca sound is first-rate – with a cassette in the demonstration class – but suggests a bigger scale, with the Kingsway Hall acoustic adding reverberation.

Piano concertos Nos. 15 in B flat K.450; 21 in C, K.467.
*** Ph. Dig. **400 018-2**; 6514/*7337* 148 [id.]. Brendel, ASMF, Marriner.

Brendel is fine in K.450 and hardly less so in its companion. The outer movements of K.467 are brisk, but tempo is not in itself a problem. Each detail of a phrase is meticulously articulated, every staccato and slur carefully observed in an almost didactic fashion. The finale sounds over-rehearsed, for some of the joy and high spirits are sacrificed in the sense of momentum. However, it is curmudgeonly to dwell on reservations when there is so much to delight in these performances. The playing is very distinguished indeed, and so, too, is the recording. In the compact disc form the sound is more 'present' though the LP has excellent range and detail, too. The cassette is of good quality though, by comparison with the disc, it is less transparent.

Piano concertos Nos. 17 in G, K.453; 18 in B flat, K.456.
*** CBS Dig. 36686/*40*- [id.]. Perahia, ECO.

Perahia's cycle goes from strength to strength, and his account of the *G major Concerto* must rank among the very finest now before the public. It has all the sparkle, grace and finesse that one expects from him, and like its companion offers a thoroughly integrated view of the score. He has established a rapport with his players that recalls Edwin Fischer or Adolf Busch. An indispensable issue for Mozartians even if they already have other versions of these concertos. Good sound, clean yet not in any way lacking in warmth, and the chrome cassette offers a first-class transfer.

Piano concertos Nos. 17, K.453; 21 in C, K.467.
*** Decca **411 947-2**; SXL/*KSXC* 6881. [Lon. CS/*5*-7104]. Ashkenazy, Philh. O.

Vladimir Ashkenazy's first Mozart concerto records made a great impression in the 1960s, and this coupling is in every way a worthy successor. Both performances are directed from the keyboard, and combine a refreshing spontaneity with an overall sense of proportion and balance. There is a fine sense of movement and yet nothing is hurried; detail is finely characterized, but nothing is fussy. Moreover the recording is clear and lucid, with the balance between soloist and orchestra finely judged. The cassette transfer is made at the very highest level, and although the sound is rich, very full and has striking range, there is just a hint of the refinement slipping marginally in tuttis.

Piano concertos Nos. 18 in B flat, K. 456; 27 in B flat, K. 595.
*** Ph. 6500 948 [id.]. Brendel, ASMF, Marriner.

These are enchanting performances, most

beautifully recorded. There is immaculate and supremely intelligent playing in both concertos from Brendel and the Academy of St Martin-in-the-Fields. The slow movement of K.595 has not quite the breadth of Gilels, which remains in a class of its own. However, those collecting Brendel's cycle will need no prompting to add these splendid performances. Everything is deeply thought out, but retains its spontaneity.

Piano concertos Nos. 19 in F, K.459; 20 in D min., K.466.
(M) *** CBS 60129/*40*- [MY/*MYT* 37236]. Serkin, Columbia SO, Szell.

A superb coupling of two of Mozart's greatest concertos in performances that match the music's greatness. There is no charm in Serkin's approach to Mozart, and in his essential seriousness he is supported by Szell. But the subtle refinement of the orchestra goes hand in hand with the natural spontaneous mastery of Serkin, who for all his failure to ingratiate himself with the listener grips the attention infallibly. In the searchingly romantic *D minor Concerto* Serkin aptly uses the Beethoven cadenzas (no Mozart ones survive). The *F major Concerto*, equally strong in the contrapuntal complexities of the finale, has Mozart's own cadenzas. Among Mozart concerto records there is no finer bargain in the catalogue. The cassette is vivid and full on side one, but the high level on side two coarsens the orchestral focus in fortissimos.

Piano concertos Nos. 19 in F, K.459; 22 in E flat, K.482.
*** Decca Dig. **410 140-2**; SXDL/*KSXDC* 7566 [Lon. 71066/*5*-]. De Larrocha, VSO, Segal.

Whereas Richter's K.482 (see below) spills over to a second side, the Decca engineers accommodate it on one, as have DG for Kempff and CBS for Perahia. De Larrocha can hold her own against most of her rivals both in terms of scale and sensitivity, though her K.482 is neither as completely integrated nor as touching as the Perahia which has particularly eloquent playing from the ECO wind. She is on good form, too, in the *F Major* and the Decca recording is beautifully transparent and clear, as well as being warmly resonant which increases the tinge of romantic feeling in these performances. The sound on compact disc is particularly natural, with the upper range smooth yet well defined. Although the ear is slightly drawn to the forward balance of the woodwind, the piano image is most believable, the treble pellucid with no edge. The chrome cassette too is first-class; even by comparison with the compact disc it loses little in refinement and range on top. Again the piano timbre is most impressive.

Piano concertos Nos. 19 in F, K.459; 23 in A, K.488.
*** DG 2530/*3300* 716 [id.]. Pollini, VPO, Boehm.
*** Ph. 6500 283 [id.]. Brendel, ASMF, Marriner.

The DG is a very distinguished record. Pollini is sparkling in the *F Major*, and in the *A Major* has a superbly poised, vibrant sense of line. Every phrase here seems to speak, and he is given excellent support from Boehm and the Vienna orchestra. There is no sense of haste in the outer movements; everything is admirably paced. Good, well-detailed and finely balanced recording make this one of the finest Mozart concerto records DG have given us. Among the K.488s, this must be ranked very highly. The transfer to cassette is immaculate.

With Brendel the first movement of K.459 is played at a slightly quicker tempo than usual, but the performance sparkles throughout, and the playing of the Academy of St Martin-in-the-Fields could hardly be improved upon. The slow movement is quite magical, and the finale again has great zest and brilliance. Brendel's account of K.488, too, is among the best in the catalogue. It is more spontaneous in feeling than Curzon's (masterly though that is), in better taste than Barenboim's (he indulges in some marvellously sensuous but out-of-style phrasing and rushes the finale), and is impeccably played. The decoration of the solo part in the slow movement is never obtrusive, always in style, and the playing exhibits throughout a sensibility that is at one with the composer's world.

The recording is a fine one, with truthful balance and wide range.

Piano concertos Nos. 19 in F, K.459; 24 in C min., K.491.
*** Decca SXL/*KSXC* 6947 (Lon. CS/*5-7174*]. Ashkenazy, Philh. O.

Ashkenazy's account of the *C minor Concerto* is a strong one, and must be numbered among the very finest now on the market. He has the measure of the work's breadth and emotional power, and his playing, while showing all the elegance and poise one could desire, never detracts from the coherence of the whole. His is a balanced view of the first movement which avoids investing it with excessive intensity yet never loses impact. He is every bit as sensitive as his most formidable rivals (Barenboim and Perahia) in the middle movement and highly characterful in the finale. The *F major Concerto* also comes off effectively; it is subtle and sparkling. Clean, well-focused recording and an orchestral response that does almost as much credit to the pianist as his solo contribution. The cassette transfers are of Decca's highest quality: the *C minor Concerto* sounds particularly beautiful.

Piano concertos Nos. 19 in F, K.459; 25 in C, K.503.
*(*) DG Dig. **410 989-2**; 410 989-1/*4* [id.]. Serkin, LSO, Abbado.

If Serkin's 1984 Mozart was as good as the pre-war vintage – or, for that matter, some of the recordings he made at Marlboro in the 1960s – this would be a most valuable coupling. There is much to admire including a clear and well-focused recording, but he is no match for the current competition and the insights this distinguished Mozartian brings to these concertos do not compensate for the ungainly passage work and other infelicities.

Piano concertos Nos. 20–27.
(M) **(*) DG 2740 138 (4) [id.]. Anda, Camerata Ac. of Salz. Mozarteum.

Anda's set of Mozart concertos stands the test of time very well. He is unfussy and thoroughly musical. This package of the last eight concertos appeared at the time of his death and can be confidently recommended to those wanting sane and reliable accounts of this repertoire. The recordings still sound fresh.

Piano concertos Nos. 20 in D min., K.466; 21 in C, K.467.
*** CBS 74082/*40-*. Perahia, ECO.

The Perahia is a recoupling of two already familiar performances: K.466 originally appeared in harness with the *F major*, K.413, and K.467 with the *Jeunehomme*, K.271, during 1977–8. They are discussed in greater detail in their original couplings. These readings are second to none and better than most. The original coupling of K.467 is now withdrawn in the UK.

Piano concertos Nos. 20–21; 24 in C min., K.491.
(M) *(*) HMV *TCC2-POR* 54277. Barenboim, ECO.

Barenboim's account of *No. 20 in D minor*, K.466, is among his finest Mozart recordings, and *No. 22*, K.467, is also highly accomplished (both are otherwise coupled on disc). The *C minor*, K.491, is at present only available in LP format within his boxed set, and is rather more controversial. The very first entry of the piano shows to what degree Barenboim wants to make it a romantic work. His conviction is unfailing, but some may find the first two movements too heavy for their taste, while the finale is compensatingly fast and hectic. The layout of the three works on one extended-length cassette has the advantage of economy, but little else. The sound is generally good, although there is some loss of refinement in K.466 in the upper range of the orchestral tuttis; moreover there is an irritating side-break after the first movement of K.467.

Piano concertos Nos. 20 in D min., K.466; 23 in A, K.488.
*** HMV ASD/*TC-ASD* 2318. Barenboim, ECO.
**(*) Ph. 9500 570/*7300 703* [id.]. Bishop-Kovacevich, LSO, Colin Davis.

An enchanting record from Barenboim. This was the first of his Mozart concerto series with the ECO, and his playing has all the sparkle and sensitivity one could ask for. There are times when his delicacy of fingerwork comes close to preciosity, as at the end of the opening of the theme in the slow movement of the *A major*, but it never goes over the edge. The orchestral accompaniment is admirably alive, and one's only serious reservation concerns the somewhat fast tempi he adopts in the finales. The stereo sound is spacious and truthful and the whole production is a distinguished one. The tape too is of good quality.

There is a clarity and directness about the combination of Bishop-Kovacevich and Sir Colin Davis in Mozart concertos which is always refreshing. If their coupling of the *D minor* and the *A major* lacks the magic of the earlier coupling of the two *C major Concertos* from the same artists, it is largely that the playing of the LSO is less polished, the strings often edgy. Nonetheless the minor-key seriousness of the outer movements of K.466 and the F sharp minor *Adagio* of K.488 comes out superbly. It is a token of the pianist's command that without any expressive exaggeration the K.488 slow movement conveys such depth and intensity. The recording is bright and clear, although the definition at the top is slightly less sharp on tape than on disc.

Piano concertos Nos. 20 in D min., K.466; 24 in C min., K.491.

*** Ph. 6500 533 [id.]. Brendel, ASMF, Marriner.

Brendel's account of the *D minor* originally appeared as a sampler for his Philips set, coupled with K.488. The two minor concertos are superbly played and recorded, though perhaps they miss the last ounce of tragic intensity. Curzon has the greater character in the *C minor*, and with Serkin's CBS account of the *D minor* available at mid-price, one is reminded of the intense competition. However, there is nothing to inhibit a three-star recommendation.

Piano concertos Nos. 20 in D min., K. 466; 27 in B flat, K.595.

X DELETED NOV/DEC 1989

❀ *** Decca SXL/*KSXC* 7007. Curzon, ECO, Britten.

In September 1970 Sir Clifford Curzon went to the Maltings at Snape, and there with Benjamin Britten and the ECO recorded these two concertos. K.595, the last concerto of all, was always the Mozart work with which he was specially associated; and not surprisingly – when he was the most painfully self-critical and distrusting of recording artists – he wanted to do it again. Just before he died in September 1982, sessions had been organized to make such a recording (as they had on previous occasions), but anyone hearing this magical record, full of the glow and natural expressiveness which always went with Britten's conducting of Mozart, will recognize both performances as uniquely individual and illuminating, with Curzon at his very finest. The record was kept from issue till after Sir Clifford's death, but still sounds rich and beautiful, with the tape matching the disc, if a little soft-grained in the treble.

Piano concertos Nos. 21 in C, K.467; 22 in E flat, K.482.

*** DG 2531/*3301* 372 [id.]. Kempff, Bav. RSO, Klee.

(M) *** HMV SXLP 30124. Annie Fischer, Philh. O, Sawallisch.

(M) **(*) DG Priv. 2535/*3335* 317. Anda, Camerata Ac. of Salz. Mozarteum.

Kempff in his mid-eighties still produced magical playing in this demanding coupling. Speeds in outer movements tend to be relaxed, with central *Andantes* on the fast side, but if anyone has the idea that Kempff's Mozart is too dainty, then the answer comes very clearly in his first entry in K.467. In K.482 the *Figaro* kinship in the first movement is made delightfully clear, while the 6/8 finale has a bucolic flavour, and the C minor slow movement, at a flowing speed, brings a bite to the tragedy with the wind-band episodes calling to mind the great *Serenade*, K.388. Excellent, full recording though the piano is balanced close. The cassette matches the disc and is lively and well focused.

Annie Fischer's coupling was very highly regarded when it first appeared in 1959 (mono only) on CX 1630. The general style of performance of Mozart concertos in recent years has tended to become more robust, but even so Miss Fischer's gentle, limpid touch, with its frequent use of half-tones, gives a great deal of pleasure. The slow movements of both concertos are beautifully done, and the pianist's intimate manner is often shared by the Philharmonia's wind soloists, who offer playing of polish and delicacy. Sawallisch's contribution too is considerable, and his firm directing hand ensures that neither performance becomes effete. These are essentially small-scale readings, and the refined approach does reduce the opportunities for displaying sparkle and wit. But the coupling is convenient and Miss Fischer's silken touch is highly persuasive. The recording is nicely balanced, full in tone, and does not sound too dated, and this makes an excellent medium-priced recommendation.

Géza Anda's account of the *E flat major Concerto,* K.482, has previously occupied a side and a half, so that there is some loss of level in this new but competitive transfer. There are compelling accounts of this concerto from Brendel and Perahia at the top end of the catalogue, but Anda's is one of the most impressive of his cycle. Even though the strings do not sound as fresh as they did, this version is still able to hold its own and in this coupling with Anda's poetic account of the *C major Concerto*, K.467, it can surely be said to offer very good value. In the *E flat Concerto*, moreover, Anda's cadenzas are thoroughly idiomatic and appropriate – which is more than can be said for Annie Fischer's famous recording, good though that is (she uses cadenzas by Busoni). Thoroughly recommendable in both disc and cassette format.

Piano concertos Nos. 21 in C, K.467; 23 in A, K.488.

(M) *** HM 22477. Demus, Coll. Aur., Maier.

(B) **(*) Con. CC/*CCT* 7505. Vered, LPO, Segal.

** DG Dig. **410 068-2**; 2532/*3302* 095 [id.]. Serkin, LSO, Abbado.

In one sense the Harmonia Mundi performances have no competitors, because Joerg Demus is the only artist to have used a period instrument in these concertos. Those whose hearts sink at the prospect of Mozart concertos on the fortepiano should nonetheless try this issue: it is generally very well played and the special colour and timbre of the instrument are in their way quite haunting. The fortepiano is unlikely to drive out the modern grand as the harpsichord displaced Bach on the piano, but it is revealing to hear Mozart concertos on the scale on which they were conceived. Good recording.

Ilana Vered plays with the spontaneity of youth, phrasing most persuasively. In K.488 she takes a dangerously slow tempo for the central *Adagio* and does not avoid heaviness, but that is an exception. Close-up recording, originally Decca Phase Four, and generally well balanced and full. At bargain price, this is good value on disc but not on tape, where the transfer has a boomy bass and limited upper range, especially in K.467.

It is sad that Serkin had to leave it until his eighties to attempt a full series of the Mozart concertos. Though his thoughtfulness as an artist is often clear, his playing is distressingly prosaic with no dynamic less than mezzo forte, scrappy passage-work and uneven scales. Refined accompaniment from Abbado and the LSO, but even there the styles clash. There are stronger and more sensitive accounts of both concertos, though few that are better recorded. The compact disc is of first-class quality, even if it reveals some of the soloist's vocal additions, and both LP and cassette formats are realistic.

Piano concertos Nos. (i) *21 in C, K.467;* (ii) *24 in C min., K.491.*

(M) **(*) CBS 60276/*40*-. (i) Lhevinne, Juilliard O, Morel; (ii) Gould, CBC SO, Susskind.

An interesting and rewarding coupling from the CBS archives. The vivid vintage recording comes from the beginning of the 1960s. The balance is close, but the sound is fresh and the piano timbres convincing. The style of the two performances is fascinatingly different. The *C Major* brings an essentially classical ambience, with crisply stylish solo playing from Rosina

Lhevinne. The *Andante* is beautifully done, and outer movements are keenly alert. The mood of the *C Minor* is altogether more romantic, yet Glenn Gould's contribution is uneccentric (apart from the appreciative crooning noises which were a basic part of his presentation). His imaginative colouring in the *Larghetto* is matched by the warmly expressive orchestral contribution. In the outer movements, which are strongly characterized, the CBC orchestra phrases elegantly, with delightful detail emerging from the woodwind. Both performances here are highly spontaneous and give pleasure, and at mid-price this disc is competitive. The chrome cassette offers first-class quality every bit the equal of the disc.

Piano concertos Nos. 21 in C, K.467; 25 in C, K.503

❀ *** Ph. 6500 431 [id.]. Bishop-Kovacevich, LSO, Sir Colin Davis.

This is still among the most searching and satisfying records of Mozart piano concertos available. The partnership of Bishop-Kovacevich and Davis almost invariably produces inspired performances, and here their equal dedication to Mozart, their balancing of strength and charm, drama and tenderness, make for performances which retain their sense of spontaneity but which plainly result from deep thought. Never has the famous slow movement of K.467 sounded so ethereally beautiful on record as here, with superb LSO string tone, and the weight of both these great C major works is formidably conveyed. The recording (dating from 1974) is beautifully balanced and refined.

Piano concertos Nos. 21 in C, K.467; 26 in D (Coronation), K.537.

(M) ** Ph. Seq. 6527/*7311* 147 [id.]. Haebler, LSO, Rowicki.

The first movement of Ingrid Haebler's K.467 is a little straitlaced, without the breadth and dignity that some artists have brought to it or the urgency that one has from some others. Neither soloist nor conductor can wholly escape the charge of prettifying the music. Haebler plays her own cadenzas – and very good they are – but in the heavenly slow movement she is not as imaginative as Annie Fischer. (Alas, Miss Fischer uses Busoni's somewhat inappropriate cadenzas.) Rowicki's direction is on the whole excellent. The coupling of the *Coronation concerto* is not to be confused with the earlier version Haebler made with Sir Colin Davis and the same orchestra. Her account of the first movement is direct and dignified, but in the main theme of the slow movement she exaggerates staccato markings and even plays the top A of the theme staccato, which seems to trivialize it. (Her earlier version – now deleted – was more judiciously pedalled.) Despite the excellent balance and fresh sound quality, warm and refined on disc and tape alike, this is not a strong recommendation for either work.

Piano concertos Nos. 21 in C, K.467; 27 in B flat, K.595.

(M) *** DG Sig. 2543/*3343* 508. Gulda, VPO, Abbado.

**(*) HMV ASD/*TC-ASD* 2465. Barenboim, ECO.

This DG performance of K.467 was first issued at about the same time as a TV programme showing Gulda and Abbado rehearsing and playing together. On television Gulda used a Bösendorfer piano (which he has favoured previously in the recording studio), and one suspects that this instrument was used here. The piano timbre is clean, crisp and clear. The quality of its tone colour is admirably suited to these readings which show an element of classical restraint in the soloist, yet at the same time have no overall lack of warmth. In short, the partnership of Abbado and Gulda works better than the not dissimilar combination of this conductor with Rudolf Serkin on the same label. The introduction to the *C major Concerto* is especially striking and the orchestral wind-playing is delightful. The famous slow-movement melody is simply phrased; there is elegance but not excess romanticism, and the gay finale makes a perfect foil. In the valedictory *B flat Concerto* Gulda disciplines his responses splendidly, though there is no want of finesse or feeling. Abbado again provides appropriately sensitive and well-shaped accompaniment with the Vienna

Philharmonic on top form. Excellent recording with a chrome tape virtually indistinguishable from the disc.

There need be no reservations about Barenboim's account of K.467, which is accomplished in every way. His version of K.595 will be more controversial. He indulges in great refinements of touch, and his reading of the slow movement in particular is overtly romantic. Anda (not now available separately) was more successful in obtaining the right perspective and holding the balance between detail and structure. A good cassette is available.

(i) *Piano concerto No. 21 in C, K.467. Serenade No. 13 in G (Eine kleine Nachtmusik), K.525.*
(B) **(*) CfP CFP/*TC-CFP* 40009. (i) Lympany; Virtuosi of L., Davison.

Although this issue is obviously inspired by the *Elvira Madigan* film, the performance is in no way over-romanticized. It is of authentic Mozartian proportions, neat, small in scale, but with plenty of character. The account of *Eine kleine Nachtmusik* is first-rate. It is robust yet elegant, not polished to the final degree but crisply articulated, with a beautifully judged *Romanze*, spontaneous and graceful. The recording is clear and vivid to suit the performances. On the excellent cassette there is a delightful bonus, a first-class performance of the *Oboe quartet* from Ian Wilson and the Gabrieli Quartet. The recording is fresh and refined throughout.

Piano concerto No. 22 in E flat, K.482; Concert rondos Nos. 1 in D, K.382; 2 in A, K.386.
*** Ph. 9500 145 [id./*7300 121*]. Brendel, ASMF, Marriner.
*** Decca SXL/*KSXC* 6982 (without *Rondo No. 2*). Ashkenazy, Philh. O.

A very distinguished account of the *E flat Concerto* from Brendel and the Academy, beautifully recorded by the Philips engineers. Brendel's earlier account with Paul Angerer, like his K.503, enjoyed a well-deserved celebrity in its day, but the newer version has more sparkle and greater depth and is infinitely better recorded. Brendel's first movement has breadth and grandeur as well as sensitivity, while the slow movement has great poetry. There have been some impressive accounts of this concerto in recent years but it is fair to say that there is none finer than this, nor any that is more beautifully recorded. The two *Concert rondos* – the first (K.382) is the Viennese alternative to the *Salzburg concerto* (K.175) – are no less elegantly performed.

Ashkenazy's account of the *E flat Concerto* also belongs at the top of the list. He has the measure of its strength and enjoys the advantage of rich and finely detailed recorded sound; in this he is better served than either Brendel or Perahia. Both of them give performances of the greatest distinction, but Ashkenazy is scarcely less thoughtful or lyrical. He evidently does not use the *Neue Mozartausgabe* edition, as he leaves out two bars in the first movement, but that is hardly likely to weigh heavily in the balance for most collectors. This is thoroughly recommendable and nicely recorded too; the cassette matches the disc closely, but the resonance has brought a very slight loss of refinement at the top in the orchestral tuttis. The piano is most naturally caught.

(i) *Piano concerto No. 22 in E flat, K.482; Symphony No. 24 in B flat, K.182.*
** HMV ASD/*TCC-ASD* 143528-1/*4* [Ang. DS/*4XS* 37740]. (i) Sviatoslav Richter; Philh. O, Muti.

Sviatoslav Richter has given us comparatively little Mozart on record and only one concerto (the *D Minor*, K.466). He plays with all the poise and authority one would expect, but for all the elegance of his pianism, there is a curiously aloof quality and a detachment that makes his performance, which is admirably recorded, ultimately uninvolving. One admires and indeed relishes numerous pianistic felicities, but one is never drawn into or consumed by the performance as a whole. One point of interest is that Richter plays cadenzas by Benjamin Britten; however, taken overall this is not a first choice among the available recordings of this concerto. Muti draws lively enough playing from the Philharmonia Orchestra both here and in the coupled *Symphony*, though it is well drilled rather than sparkling. The cassette is vivid and clear, matching the disc closely.

Piano concertos Nos. 23 in A, K.488; 24 in C min., K.491.

(M) *** DG Priv. 2535/*3335* 204 [id.]. Kempff, Bamberg SO, Leitner.

**(*) Decca SXL 6354. Curzon, LSO, Kertesz.

(B) **(*) CfP CFP/*TC-CFP* 4404. Hobson, ECO, Gibson.

Kempff's is a quite outstanding coupling of two of Mozart's greatest concertos. The sunny mood of the outer movements of the *A major Concerto* is perfectly contrasted here with the darker colouring of the *Adagio* (a wonderfully expressive performance), and the sombre yet dramatic atmosphere of the opening of the C minor work is perceptively caught by Leitner, who provides distinguished accompaniments to both works. The poetry of Kempff's playing is a constant joy, and with excellent recording this remains very highly recommendable. The cassette transfer is an early one and was originally too bright in the treble. Current copies may well show an improvement.

Curzon's account of these two concertos is immaculate and no connoisseur of the piano will fail to derive pleasure and instruction from them. Curzon has the advantage of sensitive support both from Kertesz and from the Decca engineers, and only the absence of the last ounce of sparkle and spontaneity prevents this from being strongly recommended. Kempff's DG record remains preferable.

Hobson gives clean, generally refreshing performances remarkably free of mannerism. His base as a pianist may – as usual with a virtuoso prizewinner – be in the romantic repertory, but on this showing he is a stylish Mozartian, if a somewhat reticent one. That extends to his clear and tasteful cadenza for K.491. Speeds are unexceptionable, the accompaniment admirable and the sound first-rate. An excellent bargain with a very good cassette equivalent, clear and vivid, yet retaining the recording's full bloom.

Piano concertos Nos. 23 in A, K.488; 27 in B flat, K.595.

*** Decca Dig. **400 087-2**; SXDL/*KSXDC* 7530 [Lon. LDR/*5-* 71007]. Ashkenazy, Philh. O.

Ashkenazy is on his finest form in both concertos and gets excellent results from both the keyboard and the Philharmonia Orchestra. His *A Major* is beautifully judged, alive and fresh, yet warm – one of the most satisfying accounts yet recorded. No quarrels either with the *B flat* which is as finely characterized as one would expect. The recording focuses closely on the piano, but nonetheless no orchestral detail is masked and the overall impression is very lifelike, particularly in the excellent compact-disc format. Along with Brendel, Perahia and Gilels, this is one of the best versions of the *B flat*. The quality on the chrome cassette is superb, luminous, rich and clear with completely natural piano timbre. The CD is also very fine, but there is a slight edge on the strings, and in many ways the cassette remains marginally preferable in its sound balance.

Piano concerto No. 25 in C, K.503.

(M) *** CBS 60149/*40-*. Fleisher, Cleveland O, Szell – BEETHOVEN: *Concerto No. 4.****

Fleisher and Szell achieve a memorable partnership in this 1959 recording. The kernel of the performance is the beautiful slow movement, classically serene. Szell's accompaniment matches the soloist in poise, and the music is given a Beethovenian depth, while the outer movements, briskly paced, have splendid vitality. Fleisher shapes the first movement's second subject most engagingly and is wonderfully nimble in the finale, and Szell's orchestral detail is a constant source of pleasure. The sound is very acceptable, with a lively cassette to match the disc fairly closely. With its outstanding coupling this is very highly recommendable.

Piano concerto No. 25, K.503; Concert rondo No. 1 in D, K.382.

(M) *** Ph. Seq. 6527/*7311* 085 [id.]. Brendel, ASMF, Marriner.

This is a more elegant and finished account of the *C major Concerto* than Brendel's Turnabout version made in the early 1960s with Angerer. Yet that had fine concentration and a sense of pace which compelled admiration, even though the orchestral playing and the quality of the recorded sound were not top-drawer. However, there is the same keen intelligence here, and the Academy of St Martin-in-the-Fields under Marriner is alert and supportive, while the recording has ample bloom and finesse. The cassette is warm and agreeable, but the focus is not particularly sharp.

Piano concerto No. 27 in B flat, K.595; (i) *Double piano concerto in E flat, K.365.*
❀ *** DG 2530 456/*3300 406* [id.]. Gilels, VPO, Boehm, (i) with Elena Gilels.

Gilels playing Mozart is in a class of his own. His is supremely lyrical playing that evinces all the classical virtues. No detail is allowed to detract from the picture as a whole; the pace is totally unhurried and superbly controlled. There is no point-making by means of agogic distortion or sudden rapt pianissimo; all the points are made by means of articulation and tone and each phrase is marvellously alive. The slow-movement theme, for example, is played with a simplicity that is not arch as it is in some performances; nor is it over-refined in tone, and the result gives added depth and spirituality. This is playing of the highest order of artistic integrity and poetic insight, while Boehm and the Vienna Philharmonic provide excellent support. The performance of the marvellous *Double concerto* is no less enjoyable. Its mood is rather more serious than the Brendel/Klien version (now deleted), but this is not to suggest that the music's sunny qualities are not brought out, and the interplay of phrasing between the two soloists is beautifully conveyed by the recording without exaggerated separation. The quality both on disc and on tape is first-class, and this is certainly one of the very finest Mozart piano concerto couplings in the catalogue.

Double piano concerto in E flat, K.365; (i) *Triple piano concerto in F, K.242.*
**(*) HMV Dig. ASD/*TCC-ASD* 4257 [Ang. DS/*4XS* 37903]. Eschenbach, Frantz, (i) Helmut Schmidt; LPO, Eschenbach.
** Decca SXL 6716 [Lon. CS 6937]. Ashkenazy, Barenboim, (i) Fou Ts'ong; ECO, Barenboim.

Eschenbach's version of the *Double concerto* which he directs from the keyboard is the only one to include the clarinets, trumpets and timpani published in the orchestral material by Breitkopf & Härtel in 1881. These instruments were added for the Vienna performance of 1781, but there is some doubt as to their authenticity. Both Eschenbach and Frantz are lively and persuasive in the concerto, though comparison with the Gilels version on DG, coupled with K.595, is not to their advantage: that is a glorious record. In the *Triple concerto* the third pianist is Helmut Schmidt, at the time of the record Chancellor of West Germany, who makes a creditable showing. The digital recording is very good indeed but the coupling does not displace the Gilels in K.365. The chrome cassette is first-class, with a high-level transfer for the *Triple concerto* producing demonstration quality. However, both label and notes incorrectly suggest that this work comes on side one, whereas the *E flat Concerto* comes first.

Barenboim, who recorded all the other Mozart piano concertos for HMV, insisted on playing the *Double* and *Triple concertos* with his friend Vladimir Ashkenazy, a contracted Decca artist. In the end Decca won the argument, and after a highly successful television programme about these artists rehearsing and playing the *Double concerto,* it was expected that the record would be a winner. Not so. It finds both artists self-conscious in the *Double concerto,* particularly in the slow movement, which is taken very slowly. There is slackness too in the *Triple concerto.*

VIOLIN CONCERTOS

Adagio in E (*for violin and orchestra*), *K.261; Violin concertos Nos. 1–5;* (i) *Concertone, K.190. Rondos* (*for violin and orchestra*) *Nos. 1–2, K.269 and K.373;* (ii) *Sinfonia concertante in E flat, K.364.*
(M) **(*) Ph. 6747 376 (4). Szeryng, New Philh. O, Gibson, with (i) Poulet, (ii) Giuranna.
(M) ** HMV SLS/*TC-SLS* 828 (4). [Ang. SD 3789]. D. Oistrakh (violin or viola), Berlin PO, with (i; ii) I. Oistrakh.

Adagio in E, K.261; Violin concertos Nos. 1–7; 2 Rondos.

** Decca D239 D4 (4). Fujikawa, RPO, Weller.

Violin concertos Nos. 1–5; (i) *Sinfonia concertante in E flat, K.365.*
(M) *** Ph. 6768 365 (3) [id./*7505 003*]. Grumiaux, LSO, Sir Colin Davis, (i) with Pelliccia.

Grumiaux's accounts of the Mozart *Violin concertos* come from the early 1960s and are among the most beautifully played in the catalogue at any price. The orchestral accompaniments have sparkle and vitality, and Grumiaux's contribution has splendid poise and purity of tone. There are many delights here, for the music-making has warmth as well as refinement, and the recording sounds remarkably good, with clean, fresh string tone and well-defined bass. The *Sinfonia concertante* is outstanding. Grumiaux and Pelliccia give a most expressive performance, but one completely free from any thought of over-romanticizing Mozart. The phrasing in the slow movement is wonderfully flexible, and as a whole the playing is very enjoyable indeed.

Szeryng's set which originally appeared in 1971 was restored to the catalogue as part of the Philips Complete Mozart Edition and also offers excellent value. Szeryng plays with great purity of style and musical insight (although some find his approach a shade cool), and the orchestral support is well shaped and responsive. For the most part these recorded performances give pleasure, particularly the *Sinfonia concertante*, in which Szeryng is splendidly partnered with the violist, Bruno Giuranna. Recordings too are musically balanced and truthful in timbre.

Oistrakh is predictably strong and positive as a Mozartian, and he is well accompanied by the Berlin Philharmonic; but there are too many touches of unwanted heaviness to make this an ideal cycle. Needless to say, the performances have their fine moments. The slow movements of the *G major* (K.216) and *D major* (K.218) *Concertos* are memorably expressive and the *Rondo concertante* (K.269) played with real sparkle. On the other hand the *Sinfonia concertante* is disappointingly unimaginative, and the *Concertone* too is given a pedestrian reading. The recordings are consistently lively with the soloist balanced well forward. The cassette transfer level is high and although there are occasional patches where the refinement of orchestral texture slips (usually caused by the horns) the sound is generally bright and clear.

Mayumi Fujikawa is an impressive artist, as listeners to her broadcasts will know, and there is every evidence of musicianship and imagination. Particularly to be admired are her accounts of the *B flat Concerto* (K.207) and the *Adagio* of the *G major* (K.216), which reinforce the positive impression she makes. One hopes that these performances will appear individually in the fullness of time though, as a complete set, it would be difficult to prefer it to the Grumiaux which has now resurfaced on Philips and which omits the spurious later concertos. Davis is unfailingly vital and responsive, and although the Decca recording is lively and more full-bodied, there is a more aristocratic feel to the Philips set.

Violin concertos Nos. 1 in B flat, K.207; 5 in A (Turkish), K.219.
*** Argo Dig. ZRDL/*KZRDC* 1014. Iona Brown, ASMF, Marriner.

This is a worthy successor to Iona Brown's earlier record coupling the *G major*, K.216, and *D major*, K.218 (see below). The playing has a freshness and vigour that is winning, and both soloist and the Academy convey a sense of pleasure in what they are doing; they are beautifully recorded. There is not enough space between movements, which is an irritant. Iona Brown's playing does not suffer from excessive vibrato and yet is admirably coloured. Not everyone responds to her tone which does not cultivate mellifluousness or beauty for its own sake, but these performances have an engaging liveliness. The chrome cassette is wide-ranging and clear, but has just a hint of edginess on top.

Violin concertos Nos. 2 in D, K.211; 3 in G, K.216.
(M) **(*) DG Priv. 2535/*3335* 443 [id.]. Schneiderhan, Berlin PO.

(i) *Violin concerto No. 3;* (ii) *Sinfonia concertante in E flat, K.364.*
(B) ** Con. CC/*CCT* 7586. (i) Schneiderhan

(as above); (ii) Brandis, Cappone, Berlin PO, Boehm.

Schneiderhan recorded the five *Violin concertos* with the Berlin Philharmonic at the end of the 1960s. He plays with effortless mastery and a strong sense of classical proportion. The Berlin Orchestra accompany well for him, though there is a slightly unsmiling quality at times. The pairing of the two concertos is preferable to the coupling with the *Sinfonia concertante*, let down ultimately by the slow movement, which is just a touch too brisk and prosaic; the finale is also a little unyielding. The soloists have excellent style and are perfect in all matters of phrasing, intonation and so on, but the reading is just a shade lacking in personality by comparison with the most formidable accounts in the catalogue. There is little to choose in sound quality between tape and disc on either issue, though the slightly more forward balance for the soloist in K.216 brings a noticeably sharper edge to the sound in the cassette format.

Violin concertos Nos. 2 in D, K.211; 4 in D, K.218.
*** HMV Dig. **CDC 747011-2**; ASD/*TCC-ASD* 4185 [Ang. DS/*4XS* 37904]. Mutter, Philh. O, Muti.

Anne-Sophie Mutter follows up her famous record of the *G Major*, K.216, and *A Major*, K.219, with Karajan on DG – see below – with the two D major concertos on HMV and a different orchestra and conductor. The results are hardly less successful. She is given very sensitive support from the Philharmonia under Muti. Her playing combines purity and classical feeling, delicacy and incisiveness, and is admirably expressive. Its freshness too is most appealing and she is a strong contender in a very competitive field. The HMV recording is very good indeed, outstanding on CD.

Violin concerto No. 3 in G, K.216.
(M) **(*) Decca Ser. SA/*KSC* 23. Loveday, ASMF, Marriner – VIOTTI: *Concerto No. 3*.*(*)

An intimate reading of the *G major Concerto* by Loveday recorded within the resonant ambience of St John's, Smith Square. There is no lack of Mozartian stylishness and the sound is fresh on disc and tape alike. But the coupling is a curious choice.

Violin concertos Nos. 3 in G, K.216; 4 in D, K.218
*** Argo ZRG/*KZRC* 880 [id.]. Iona Brown, ASMF, Marriner.
*** CRD CRD 1041/*CRDC 4041*. Thomas, New L. Soloists Ens.

Iona Brown gives a particularly successful account of these two concertos and is well able to hold her own with the most celebrated rivals. There is a spring-like freshness about the outer movements of the *G major* and a sultry Mediterranean warmth in the middle movement. Beautifully integrated performances, with recording to match. The cassette transfer is crisp and clean, of Argo's best quality.

Choice between this and the alternative coupling from CRD is by no means straightforward. Ronald Thomas has a warm, clear tone and plays very sensitively, with no romantic overtones yet plenty of feeling. His approach is extremely stylish. The accompaniments are alert and sparkling, crisply small-scale (a continuo is used in the orchestra) and strictly in period. One of the pleasures of the coupling is the gracious phrasing by soloist and orchestra alike of both slow movements. The spirited finales provide excellent contrast. Besides directing the orchestra, Thomas plays his own admirable cadenzas. The balance is undoubtedly realistic and the sound excellent on both disc and tape.

Violin concertos Nos. 3, K.216; 5 in A (Turkish), K.219.
*** DG 2531/*3301* 049 [id.]. Mutter, Berlin PO, Karajan.
(M) *** HMV SXLP/*TC-SXLP* 30449 [Ang. RL/*4RL* 32000]. Menuhin, Bath Fest. CO.
(*) DG Dig. **410 020-2; 2532/*3302* 080 [id.]. Perlman, VPO, Levine.

Extraordinarily mature and accomplished playing from Anne-Sophie Mutter, who was a mere fourteen years of age when this recording was made. Her playing has polish but artistry too, and it has remarkable freshness. It goes without saying that she receives the most superb orchestral support from the Berlin Philharmonic and Karajan. With a well-balanced and finely detailed modern recording this is an eminently recommendable issue; but in the cassette transfer the forward placing of the soloist means that, although the timbre and detail of the violin are admirably clear (if very bright), the recessed orchestral detail is less clean, notably in the finale of No. 5.

Menuhin's versions, recorded at the beginning of the 1960s, have an attractively intimate air. The orchestra is authentic in scale and the clear, lively recording is excellently detailed (the cassette is very bright, and side one needs some treble cut). Menuhin is in good form and finds characteristic warmth in the slow movements. However, he uses his own cadenzas, and some may feel that they are not entirely Mozartian. But this is the only reservation; the music-making has both charisma and spontaneity.

With the violin balanced rather close, Perlman treats these two most popular of the Mozart violin concertos rather more as virtuoso showpieces than is common. For some the tone will be too sweet for Mozart, and though with sympathetic accompaniment these are both enjoyable performances, they have not quite the natural felicity that marks Perlman's finest work on record. Full digital recording which brings out the idiosyncrasy of the balance. This is equally noticeable on the lively chrome cassette and even more so on the compact disc, where one hears also that the woodwind is somewhat reticent. On CD the sound is strikingly clear and clean, but there is just a touch of digital edge on top.

Violin concertos Nos. 4, K.218; 5 (Turkish), K.219.

*** Nimbus Dig. **NIM 5009**; 2140. Shumsky, Scottish CO, Pascal Tortelier.

(M) *** Ph. Seq. 6527/*7311* 049. Grumiaux, LSO, Sir Colin Davis.

**(*) Erato STU 71207. Amoyal, Lausanne CO, Jordan.

Shumsky's performances with the Scottish Chamber Orchestra have the advantage of being totally unaffected, natural and full of character. He seems to have an excellent rapport with Yan Pascal Tortelier who secures a very alive and thoroughly musical response from the Scottish Chamber Orchestra. They do not produce as sumptuous or as beautiful a sound as do the Vienna Philharmonic for Levine on Perlman's DG record of Nos. 3 and 5, yet the results are every bit as enjoyable, because the players themselves convey enthusiasm and pleasure. The recording is nicely balanced.

Grumiaux's series of Mozart concerto recordings with Davis is admirable, with a fine sense of classical poise and purity and crisp, clean accompaniments. The sound is not as rich as its Erato competitor, but at mid-price the Philips disc is very good value.

Warm, strongly felt and beautifully turned performances from Amoyal, well if not distinctively accompanied. The recording is resonant and full; the forward balance of the soloist, however, makes him seem rather larger than life-size.

Violin concertos Nos. 4 and 6 in D, K.218 and 271a.

(M) *** HMV SXLP/*TC-SXLP* 30454. Menuhin, Bath Fest. O.

Menuhin's performance of K.218 is well knit and lively, with his Bath Festival Orchestra at their sympathetic best. The first movement sounds dignified yet sufficiently ebullient, thanks to a nice choice of tempo, and the seraphic melody of the slow movement has seldom floated more gracefully and effortlessly than it does here. In the finale everyone is alert and extrovert. K.271a is almost certainly spurious, but if accepted by the listener simply as a late-eighteenth-century concerto of better than average quality it can be enjoyed for its own sake rather than as a work that might or might not be Mozart's. Menuhin makes the very most of its qualities. The recording is rather bright and sharply focused, but responds to the controls. The cassette transfer is admirably clean and clear.

(i) *Concertone in C, K.190;* (ii) *Sinfonia concertante in E flat, K.364.*

(M) **(*) Decca Ser. SA/*KSC* 17 [Lon. STS/ *5*- 15563]. (i) Iona Brown, Kaine; (ii) Loveday, Shingles; ASMF, Marriner.

With the ample acoustic of St John's, Smith Square, to help, this account of the early *Concertone* is amiable and charming, with a fastish tempo for the central *Andantino grazioso*. The contribution of the soloists is very capable and a special mention is required for the oboist, Tess Miller, whose playing is exquisite. The performance of the *Sinfonia concertante for violin and viola in E flat*, with two other regular members of the Academy as soloists, also goes for elegance rather than any stronger Mozartian qualities. Rival versions may make the outer movements sound more searingly inspired and the slow movement here is wistfully refined rather than tragic, but there is a clear case for this approach.

4 Contredanses, K.267; Contredanse in G (Les filles malicieuses), K.610; 2 Marches in D, K.290 and 445; Minuets: in E flat, K.122; in D and G, K.164/3–4; 5 Minuets, K.461; 2 Minuets with a Contredanse, K.463; Overture and 3 Contredanses, K.106.

(M) *** Saga 5478. Angerer Ens., Angerer.

Paul Angerer directs a talented group of solo strings in stylish performances of an appetizing group of Mozart dances. The sound is a little forward, but the more involving for that. With Boskovsky's famous Decca set encompassing Mozart's complete marches and dances currently out of the catalogue, this Saga disc is more than welcome.

3 Divertimenti for strings, K.136/8; Serenade No. 6 in D (Serenata notturna), K.239.

(M) *** Decca Ser. SA/*KSC* 1. ASMF, Marriner.

The reissue of Marriner's set of *String Divertimenti* on Decca's mid-priced Serenata label tends to sweep the board. The playing is marvellous, and Marriner's choice of tempi is equally apt. The same warm stylishness distinguishes the *Serenata notturna*, where timpani are added to the strings. The Argo recording, rich in texture and detail, sounds admirably fresh here, and the cassette transfer is splendid too. The sparkle of this music-making is irresistible.

(i) *Divertimenti for strings Nos. 1 in D, K.136; 3 in F, K.138; Serenades Nos. 6 (Serenata notturna);* (ii) *13 (Eine kleine Nachtmusik);* (iii) *Sinfonia concertante in E flat, K.297b.*

(B) **(*) DG Walkman *413 152-4*. (i) Berlin PO, Karajan; (ii) VPO, Boehm; (iii) Berlin PO, Boehm.

Karajan's performances of the two *String Divertimenti* and the *Serenata notturna* are beautifully played and as such they prompt the liveliest admiration. At the same time there is a predictably suave elegance that seems to militate against spontaneity. Cultured and effortless readings, beautifully recorded and well balanced, they somehow leave one untouched. There is too much legato and not always a balancing sparkle. Boehm's contribution to this generous bargain-priced Walkman tape is another matter. His 1976 VPO version of Mozart's *Night music* is among the finest available, polished and spacious, with a neat, lightly pointed finale. The account of the *Sinfonia concertante* is of superlative quality, sounding amazingly idiomatic and well blended, with the balance between soloists and orchestra nicely managed. This is altogether refreshing. The chrome-tape transfers are first-class, except in *Eine kleine Nachtmusik* where the upper range lacks the last degree of freshness, although the quality remains full and clear in detail.

Divertimento No. 1 for strings in D, K.136; Serenades Nos. 5 in D, K.204; 6 in D (Serenata notturna), K.239.

(M) *** Decca Jub. JB/*KJBC* 88. V. Moz. Ens., Boskovsky.

This is a new recording in Decca's series of *Divertimenti* and *Serenades* by Boskovsky and the Vienna Mozart Ensemble which began way back in the 1960s. The *Serenata notturna* receives a sparkling and delightful performance, as good as any ever made, and the fine *D major Serenade* is elegantly done. (The only rival, by Edo de Waart and the Dresden State Orchestra, is in the ten-record set of the *Serenades* in the Philips Complete Mozart

Edition.) The performance has a smiling, captivating quality that should win this piece many admirers. A first-rate record in every respect; the cassette too is excellent, the sound clear and transparent, yet with plenty of body and warmth.

Divertimento No. 1 for strings in D, K.136; Serenades Nos. 6 (Serenata notturna), K. 239; 13 (Eine kleine Nachtmusik), K. 525.
(M) **(*) HMV Dig. Green. ESD/*TC-ESD* 7157. Polish CO, Maksymiuk.

Characteristically Maksymiuk with his talented Polish band chooses unusually fast speeds for these favourite pieces. It works exceptionally well with the early *Divertimento*, a so-called *'Salzburg symphony'*, refreshingly so with *Eine kleine Nachtmusik*, but rather less sympathetically with the *Serenata*, gentler in its manners. The balance in that piece between the solo quartet and the rest is not ideal, reducing the necessary contrast. Otherwise bright clear digital recording.

Divertimento No. 1 for strings in D, K.136; Symphony in F, K.19a; Symphony No. 29 in A, K.201.
*** O-L DSLO/*KDSLC* 608. AcAM, Schröder.

This is both a sampler and a supplement to the Academy's great enterprise of recording the Mozart symphonies complete in the most authentic way possible. The supplement is the little *Divertimento* (or string symphony) which is not in the main series. Also the even earlier work, the *London Symphony*, K.19a, discovered as recently as 1980, is known previously only through an incipit in a catalogue. Both show the boy Mozart at his most vigorous, and are well coupled with the performance of his greatest 'early' symphony taken from the complete set, all with every possible repeat observed. As ever, the astringent sound of authentic instruments is reproduced with splendid clarity. The chrome cassette too is clear and full, perhaps a shade thinner on top than the LP.

Divertimento No. 2 for strings in B flat, K.137; Divertimento No. 15 in B flat, K.287.
(M) *** Decca Jub. JB/*KJBC 90*. V. Moz. Ens., Boskovsky.

The K.287 *Divertimento* occupies the larger part of this record and is given a performance that has both charm and elegance. Like the *F major Divertimento*, K.247, this piece was intended for solo instruments (and was so recorded by the Vienna Octet on Decca Ace of Diamonds). Here even the solo line at the beginning of the fourth movement is done by several players, though the cadenza at the end is not. In any event, there is nothing here that lets down the high standard achieved by the Boskovsky series, both in terms of playing and recording. The *B flat Divertimento*, K.137, provides a short fill-up. As on disc, the quality of sound on tape is superb, with splendid life and bloom and excellent detail.

Divertimento No. 3 for strings in F, K.138; Divertimento No. 10 in F, K.247; Serenade No. 8 in D for four orchestras, K.286.
(M) *** Decca Jub. JB/*KJBC* 89. V. Moz. Ens., Boskovsky.

Like the *Divertimenti in B flat*, K.287, and *D major*, K.334, the *F major*, K.247, is for solo instruments and sounds much better in that form. However, if one is to have it in orchestral dress, none could be more elegant than this. Boskovsky draws playing of great finesse from the Vienna Mozart Ensemble, and few collectors will want to grumble at the results. The *Serenade for four orchestras* gains immeasurably from stereo and comes off beautifully in this new recording. (Many of the Decca Jubilee issues of the *Serenades* and *Divertimenti* derive from the series of superb recordings Boskovsky made in the late 1960s, but this one is quite new.) The tape transfer is strikingly rich and spacious, one of Decca's finest cassettes, with a wide amplitude and plenty of range.

German dances, K.509/1–6; K.571/1–6; K.600/1–6; K.602/1–4; K.605/1–3; 3 Marches in D, K.189 and K.335/1–2.
**(*) Ph. 6514/*7337* 207 [id.]. ASMF, Marriner.

Mozart wrote these dances in his capacity as Royal and Imperial Chamber Musician in Vienna, to which he was appointed in December 1787 (and was paid less than half as much as his predecessor, Gluck). They are hardly among his greatest music but contain much attractive invention and some individual touches like the use of the hurdy-gurdy in K.602, while in K.600/5 there is a 'canary' trio. The *Sleigh ride* of K.605 is justly famous. The performances here are spirited and nicely turned, but perhaps a shade heavy in rhythmic feeling at times, although the reverberant acoustic contributes to this effect. The playing itself is admirably warm and suitably elegant. The set of dances, K.571, are especially enjoyable and the closing number has a suitably neat coda. Excellent sound, both on disc and the lively chrome tape.

A Musical Joke, K.522; Serenade No. 1 in D, K.100.

(M) *** Decca Jub. JB/*KJBC* 51. V. Moz. Ens., Boskovsky.

With playing of such elegance and sparkle, and recording well up to the high standard of this Decca series, it is not surprising that Boskovsky and his Viennese group provide yet another highly delectable coupling. They even succeed with a piece like the *Musical Joke*, making it appear as an almost unqualified masterpiece.

A Musical Joke, K.522; Serenade No. 13 in G (Eine kleine Nachtmusik), K.525.

*** DG Dig. **400 065-2**; Analogue 2531/*3301* 253 [id.]. Augmented Amadeus Qt.

Eine kleine Nachtmusik has rarely sounded so refreshing and exhilarating as here; the finale in particular is delectably resilient. The musical clowning in the *Musical Joke*, which can so often seem heavy and unfunny, is here given charm. The horn players, Gerd Seifert and Manfred Klier, are from the Berlin Philharmonic. The recording is first-rate, although on the cassette the horns create slight problems of focus in the *Musical Joke* when they are playing loudly. The compact disc has revealed a digital master recording, alongside the analogue version used for LP and cassette.

Overtures: La Clemenza di Tito; Così fan tutte; Don Giovanni; Die Entführung aus dem Serail; Idomeneo; Lucio Silla; Le Nozze di Figaro; Der Schauspieldirektor; Die Zauberflöte.

*** HMV Dig. **CDC 747014-2**; ASD/*TCC-ASD* 4101 [Ang. DS/*4XS* 37879]. ASMF, Marriner.

*** Ph. 9500/*7300* 882 [id.]. LPO, Haitink.

Marriner's collection is strongly characterized, emphasizing the spirit of the opera house, offering plenty of drama in *Don Giovanni* and *Idomeneo* and a sense of spectacle with the percussion effects in *Die Entführung*. *Così fan tutte* and *Figaro* bring a lighter touch, but throughout the ASMF playing is characteristically spirited and stylish, with the string detail nicely clean and polished. The digital recording is bright and bold, giving the upper strings a brilliant sheen. Chrome cassette and disc are closely matched. The CD, however, softens the focus and the sound is more natural.

Some will undoubtedly prefer Haitink's performances, recorded within a warmer, more spacious ambience, emphasizing the weight and giving suitable *gravitas* to the introductions for *Don Giovanni* and *Die Zauberflöte*. The acoustic suits *Le Nozze di Figaro* less well, but the warmth and richness of the sound always give pleasure. Haitink lavishes special care on the less well-known pieces, *Der Schauspieldirektor, La Clemenza di Tito* and *Lucio Silla*, which the LPO strings play with elegance and sparkle, while the woodwind shine in *Così fan tutte*. Most enjoyable, but not for those who favour the more astringent approach to Mozart of the Academy of Ancient Music. The cassette transfer is well balanced but lacks the last degree of upper range.

Overtures: *La Clemenza di Tito; Così fan tutte; Don Giovanni; Die Entführung aus dem Serail; Le Nozze di Figaro; Der Schauspieldirektor; Die Zauberflöte.*

(M) **(*) ASV ACM 2035. O of St John's, Lubbock.

Lubbock's collection is more intimate in scale than any of his competitors. It is well played and recorded and, if the performances lack a little in sparkle, they emerge freshly and clearly with their use of relatively few strings. Good value at medium price, with concert endings included.

Overtures: *Così fan tutte; Don Giovanni; Die Entführung aus dem Serail; Le Nozze di Figaro; Der Schauspieldirektor; Die Zauberflöte. Symphony No. 32 in G, K.318.*
(M) **(*) DG Priv. 2535/*3335* 229 [id.]. Various orchestras, Boehm.

These performances are nearly all taken from Boehm's complete opera sets, which sometimes means that, without the concert ending, the music cuts off disconcertingly. On the credit side the performances are of very high quality, with plenty of life and sparkle, and the recording (if varying a little in character between items) is generally excellent. The inclusion of the little *G major Symphony* (itself structured in the three-part style of an Italian overture) was a happy idea. There is a lively cassette transfer, although this tends to have an over-bright treble response on the second side; nevertheless the sound can be rebalanced satisfactorily.

Serenades Nos. 3 in D, K.185; 13 in G (Eine kleine Nachtmusik), K.525.
(M) *** Decca Jub. JB/*KJBC* 19. V. Moz. Ens., Boskovsky.

After their success with the Mozart *Dances* and *Marches*, Boskovsky and the Vienna Mozart Ensemble turned their attention to the *Serenades* and the *Divertimenti*, which bring no less persuasive results and recording which is consistently out of Decca's top drawer. JB 19 is notable for offering what is in many ways the freshest account of *Eine kleine Nachtmusik* on disc, and the *Serenade* is managed with comparable sparkle. There is a beautiful cassette transfer of these performances, offering demonstration quality throughout. In the *Night music* the illusion that this modest, perfectly sized, admirably balanced string group is playing at the end of one's room is very real.

Serenades Nos. 6 in D (Serenata notturna), K.239; 13 (Eine kleine Nachtmusik), K.525; (i) *Sinfonia concertante in E flat, K.364.*
(M) **(*) DG Priv. 2535/*3335* 492 [id.]. Berlin PO, Boehm; (i) with Brandis, Cappone.

Boehm's performance of *Eine kleine Nachtmusik* dates from 1958 but the recording wears its years lightly and sounds comparable with K.239 which is much more recent (1971). The performance of Mozart's *Night music* is very enjoyable, gracious, stylishly phrased with a gentle finale. If the *Sinfonia concertante* really requires more individual solo playing (especially in the slow movement) than Messrs Brandis and Cappone provide, the strong directing personality of the conductor keeps the music alive throughout and the sound is full and notably well balanced. The cassette is successful too.

Serenades Nos. 6 (Serenata notturna), K.239; 13 (Eine kleine Nachtmusik) K.525; Symphony No. 29 in A, K.201.
**(*) CRD 1040/*CRDC 4040*. New L. Soloists Ens., Thomas.

A pleasingly gracious account of *Eine kleine Nachtmusik* is matched by an equally elegant *Serenata notturna*. The symphony is given an alert, genial performance of considerable character. The music-making is authentic in scale, but it seems stretching the point a little to use a harpsichord continuo in *Eine kleine Nachtmusik*. The sound is spaciously resonant, but on tape the levels vary between sides and the *Night music* is not as vividly projected as the symphony.

Serenades Nos. 7 in D (Haffner), K.250; 9 in D (Posthorn), K.320; 2 Marches in D, K.335/1–2.
(M) *** Ph. 6770 043 (2). Dresden State O, De Waart.

We are well served with separate issues of the *Haffner* and *Posthorn* serenades, with Boskovsky's admirable accounts available separately on Decca's mid-priced Jubilee label (see below). Though not quite so well recorded, Edo de Waart's Dresden version of the *Haffner* is perhaps the only one that can be mentioned in the same breath. It has rhythmic poise and delightful spontaneity and warmth; moreover the same artists' account of the *Posthorn serenade* is in some ways preferable even to Boskovsky's, though the recorded sound is not as fresh. The Dresden orchestra displays superb musicianship and the effect reminds one a little of some of Bruno Walter's pre-war Mozart records. With sparkling playing and very well disciplined, the reading also uses the marches that Christa Landon includes in her edition of the score, which preface and round off the performance. This set is well worth considering alongside Boskovsky.

Serenade No. 7 in D (Haffner), K.250.
(M) *** Decca Jub. JB/*KJBC* 31 [Lon. STS 15414]. V. Moz. Ens., Boskovsky.

Boskovsky's version of the *Haffner serenade* is marvellously alive, full of sparkle and elegance, with admirable phrasing and feeling for detail. The recording too is outstanding, fresh and vivid, although the cassette is a little dry and lacking in bloom (it benefits from a treble cut and balancing bass lift).

Serenade No. 9 in D (Posthorn), K.320.
(M) *** Decca Jub. JB/*KJBC* 34 [Lon. STS 15415]. V. Moz. Ens., Boskovsky.
***HM 1C 065 99697. Coll. Aur., Maier.

Serenade No. 9 (Posthorn), K.320; 2 Marches, K.320a.
** CfP CFP/*TC-CFP* 4464-1/*4*. LPO, Schönzeler.

The Jubilee issue upholds the fine tradition set by the Decca series. Boskovsky's performance, with its natural musicality and sense of sparkle, has the advantage of superb Decca recording and is recommendable in every way. The cassette transfer is a little dry in the matter of string tone compared with the disc, but there is plenty of bloom on the wind and detail is crisp and clean.

Aficionados should also not overlook the Collegium Aureum version, recorded in the warm acoustic of Schloss Kirchheim. The playing is sensitive and vital, and never sounds pedantic. About twenty-five instrumentalists take part, playing period instruments or copies, and the inevitable problems of intonation are altogether minimal. The tempo of the two concertante movements is a little leisurely, but on the whole the playing is so musical that this seems of little account. This is one of the most successful of the Collegium Aureum's records.

Framed by two associated *Marches*, intended as entry and exit music, Schönzeler's account of the *Posthorn serenade* is spirited, with clean string phrasing and stylish wind solos, notably from oboe and flute. The recording is bright and clear and well balanced, if a little dry. There is a lack of charm here, although everything is alert and vivid.

Serenades Nos. 9 in D (Posthorn), K.320; 13 in G (Eine kleine Nachtmusik), K.525.
*** DG Dig. **410 085-2**; 2532/*3302* 098 [id.]. VPO, Levine.

James Levine is a fine Mozartian and his account of the *Posthorn serenade* is among the very best now available. It has more sparkle than the deleted Boehm account on DG and ranks alongside Boskovsky and the splendid Philips version from De Waart. Tempi are well judged and the Vienna Philharmonic play with real distinction for him and are given excellent recording too. It is a pity that the coupling is yet another *Eine kleine Nachtmusik*, but there are no quarrels with the performance. Choice will depend on the collector's individual requirements but there is no doubting the excellence of each. On cassette the DG digital recording certainly sounds bright and clear, though there is a touch of edginess on the upper strings, most noticeable on side one. The compact disc, too, has a sharpness of outline which suggests that microphones were slightly too close to the musicians, though there is no lack of ambience.

Serenades Nos. 10 in B flat, K.361; 11 in E flat, K.375; 12 in C min., K.388.
(M) *** Ph. 6770 047 (2). Neth. Wind Ens., De Waart.
(M) *** HMV SXDW 3050 (2). L. Wind Quintet and Ens., or New Philh. Wind Ens., Klemperer.

The Dutch players offer performances that are marvellously fresh and alive. They are admirably sensitive both in feeling for line and in phrasing but never linger too lovingly over detail. This is both refreshing and satisfying and, apart from the sheer quality of the playing, the discs are enhanced by the presence and sonority of the recording, which is beautifully balanced and combines rich homogeneity of timbre with crispness of focus. The performance of the famous *B flat major Serenade* for thirteen wind instruments does not erase memories of the outstanding Barenboim version (which has the advantage of being available separately: see below), but anyone investing in the Philips box will find its qualities are very special indeed. The pressings are immaculate.

Admirers of Klemperer will find the alternative HMV double-album no less worthwhile in gathering together this great conductor's memorable performances of Mozart's great wind masterpieces. Though tempi tend to be on the slow side, the rhythmic control and fine ensemble make for performances which despite their magisterial weight are bright and refreshing, not heavy. They are far from being conventional readings but as the expression of a great Mozart interpreter they are endlessly illuminating. The mid-1960s recording still sounds first-rate.

Serenade No. 10 in B flat for 13 wind instruments, K.361.

*** HMV ASD/*TC-ASD* 3426 [Ang. S/*4XG* 60377]. ECO, Barenboim.

(M) **(*) Decca Ace SDD 579. V. Wind Soloists.

**(*) DG Dig. 2532/*3302* 089 [id.]. Berlin PO (members).

** Argo ZRG 919. L. Sinf., Atherton.

The Barenboim ECO reading is undoubtedly the most stylish of recent years. It is most distinguished and only the old Furtwängler Vienna account (mono) matches it in terms of warmth and humanity. Here we have expertly blended wind tone, free from the traces of self-indulgence that occasionally mar Barenboim's music-making. Tempi are a little on the brisk side (especially in the first movement) but none the worse for that when the playing itself is so resilient, and the quality of the recorded sound is beautifully focused, with no want of body and definition. The cassette too reproduces extremely well, and there is little to choose between the quality in either format.

The freshness of the new Vienna recording is also very striking. The sound is of demonstration quality, wonderfully vivid and clear yet with a natural overall blend. The alert, strongly characterized allegros are attractively buoyant here, and there is much delightful colouring. If in the *Adagio* and *Romanze* the playing is a shade literal and overall the performance does not quite have the incandescence of Barenboim's version, at medium price this remains well worth considering.

The newest DG digital recording is more controversial. Some ears find the balance too analytical, although it is only fair to say that the sound is robust as well as clearly detailed, and this applies equally to disc and the excellence chrome tape. The playing of the Berlin Philharmonic wind is in its way impeccable but curiously bland. There is none of the feeling of fresh discovery here and many moments when the dead hand of routine seems to touch their music-making. This is not the case in the glorious variation movement but, otherwise, the performance is wanting in real personality.

The London Sinfonietta's reading lacks fire. The results are not mannered, as in their companion record of K.375 and K.388, and the slow movements here are naturally expressive; but there are finer versions available. Unlike Barenboim this group does not use the latest amended edition of the score. The recording is nicely balanced.

Serenades Nos. 11 in E flat, K.375; 12 in C min., K.388.

** Argo ZRG 911. L. Sinf., Pay.

This coupling is disappointing, lacking the alertness and bite one expects of the London Sinfonietta and with expressive mannerisms sounding intrusive. The recording is first-class.

Serenades Nos. 11, K.375; 13 in G (Eine kleine Nachtmusik), K.525.

*(*) O-L DSLO 549. Music Party.

The *Serenade,* K.375, which we know as a wind octet, was originally conceived for wind sextet with pairs of clarinets, horns and bassoons but no oboes. The Music Party gives a performance on original instruments with plenty of spirit, but collectors are warned that the tone is often raw. Textually one difference between this and the octet version is that repeats are included in both halves of the first movement (neither of which the Music Party observes). The account of *Eine kleine Nachtmusik*, also on original instruments, is an even less persuasive example of authentic performance; quite apart from intonation problems without the help of vibrato, the tempi tend to be deliberate and the repeats many.

Serenade No. 13 in G (Eine kleine Nachtmusik), K.525.

C *** Ph. Dig. **410 606-2**; 6514/*7337* 370 [id.]. I Musici (with concert of Baroque music.***).

*** DG Dig. **400 034-2**; 2532/*3302* 031 [id.]. Berlin PO, Karajan – GRIEG: *Holberg suite*; PROKOFIEV: *Symphony No. 1.****

(M) ** EMI Em. EMX/*TC-EMX* 2037 [Sera. S/*4XG* 60271]. Toulouse CO, Auriacombe – ALBINONI: *Adagio*; CORELLI: *Christmas concerto*; PACHELBEL: *Canon.***

Recordings of Mozart's celebrated *Night music* are legion, coupled in various ways, but Boskovsky's should not be forgotten, an exceptionally successful mid-priced version, paired with the *Serenade No. 3 in D*, K.185 – see above. It was Karajan who gave the work its digital début in an early compact disc entitled 'Digital concert'. Apart from a self-conscious and somewhat ponderous minuet, it is a very fine performance, the playing beautifully cultured, with finely shaped phrasing and well-sprung rhythms. The digital sound, however, though well detailed and not without bloom, is a little sharp-edged and the CD shows this more readily than the disc or the excellent chrome tape.

First choice undoubtedly rests with the new version from I Musici who play the music with rare freshness, giving the listener the impression of hearing the work for the first time. The playing is consistently alert and sparkling, with the *Romanze* particularly engaging. There is no better version than this and the recording is beautifully balanced, on both LP and the first-class high-level chrome tape. Obviously the CD brings a degree more refinement and presence, but this is in the demonstration class in all formats.

On Eminence the Toulouse performance is cleanly played but rather square. The recording dates from 1968 but sounds full and bright, with disc and cassette fairly closely matched, the latter smoother and slightly less wide-ranging.

Sinfonia concertante in E flat for oboe, clarinet, horn, bassoon and orchestra, K.297b; (i) *Sinfonia concertante in E flat for violin, viola and orchestra, K.364.*

**(*) Erato STU/*MCE* 71370. (i) Amoyal, Causse; Lausanne CO, Jordan.

** HM 1C 065 99801. (i) Maier, Graf; Coll. Aur., Maier.

It is perhaps surprising that there are not more examples of this coupling. The Erato issue is certainly successful with good recording and lively accompaniments with the Lausanne Chamber Orchestra, both spirited and expressive. In K.364 Pierre Amoyal is a strong stylish soloist and he is well partnered by Gerard Causse, who matches him in body of timbre, and whose phrasing is only marginally less flexible. In the *Andante* their combined personalities dominate the music-making and the finale is infectiously buoyant. The wind soloists in the coupled K.297b play well together, if without the last degree of refinement in the slow movement, but again Jordan directs with understanding and the finale is highly engaging. The cassette has been transferred at a high level and is attractively vivid, if with a slightly less clean focus in tuttis.

The Collegium Aureum version features original instruments. In K.297b, with a forward balance for the wind soloists (which reduces dynamic contrast) the effect is robust with some lack of refinement in the *Andante* – early instruments can at times sound a little clumsy. There is compensation in the finale, however, which has engaging colour and geniality. Franzjosef Maier and Heinz-Otto Graf make a favourable impression in K.364 and, although their contribution is not especially individual, the slow movement is expressively phrased and the finale spirited. Here the resonant sound counteracts any sharpness of timbre and gives breadth to the accompanying group.

Sinfonia concertante in E flat for violin, viola and orchestra, K.364.
❀ *** DG Dig. 2741/*3382* 026 (2) [id.]. Perlman, Zukerman, Israel PO, Mehta – BACH: *Double concerto*; VIVALDI: *Four seasons* etc.***

This fine DG version of Mozart's *Sinfonia concertante* was recorded at the Huberman Festival in Tel Aviv in December 1982. It is an outstanding example of 'live' recording with the music-making caught on the wing. The rapport between Perlman and Zukerman is remarkable, and the contrast of timbres equally striking, with Zukerman's viola sounding firm and rich. The performance has great expressive eloquence and reaches its peak at the climax of the *Andante*, with Mehta's accompaniment memorably poetic in the closing bars. The finale is high-spirited and sparkling. The sound balance is excellent and the recording altogether most truthful on disc and chrome tape alike, with the acoustic of the Mann Auditorium captured in a surprisingly flattering way.

SYMPHONIES

Symphonies Nos. 1–41 (complete).
(M) **(*) DG 2740 109 (8) (Nos. 1–24); 2740 110 (7) (Nos. 25–41). Berlin PO, Boehm.

The two DG boxes of Mozart symphonies under Boehm are ultimately let down by a certain stiffness and want of sparkle. Of course, the orchestral playing from the Berlin Philharmonic is a joy in itself; phrasing is immaculate and ensemble beautifully disciplined. Boehm's seriousness is not without a compensating dignity and eloquence. The second set (Symphonies Nos. 25–41) has been issued in cassette form (*3378 066*; six tapes in a very compact album). The quality is superb, and the format is ideal for exploring the middle and late symphonies at leisure.

In the USA, the early Mozart symphonies up to and including No. 34, and those numbered after No. 41 are available in four 3-disc Vox boxes [SVBX 5118/20] in admirable performances by the Mainz Chamber Orchestra directed by Günter Kehr. These recordings date from the 1960s, but in many respects can compete with later rivals in showing a real Mozartian spirit. The earliest symphonies, in particular, have a spontaneity and vitality that make them preferable to the Boehm set on DG. Gunter Kehr draws stylish and vital playing from his Mainz orchestra, which is well recorded: the sound is fresh and well detailed. The second box [SVBX 5119] is especially recommendable, and American readers will find full details of the contents in Schwann.

Symphonies Nos. 1, 4–6, 7a, 8–20, 42–7, 55; in C, K.208/102; in D, K.45, 111/120, 141a and 196/121; in G.
(M) *** Ph. 6769 054 (8). ASMF, Marriner.

Marriner's survey has a splendid Mozartian vitality and seems to combine the best qualities of both Boehm and Kehr (see above). The Academy play with great style, warmth and polish, while the Philips engineers respond with alive and vivid recording. These are altogether delightful records and can be strongly recommended.

Symphonies Nos. 1 in E flat, K.16; 4 in D, K.19; in F, K.19a; 5 in B flat, K.22; in D, K.32; 11 in D, K.73q; 13 in F, K.112; 44 in D, K.73e; 45 in D, K.73n; 46 in C, K.111; in D, K.111a; 47 in D, K.73m.
*** O-L D 167 D 3/*K 167 K 33* [id.]. AcAM, Schröder; Hogwood.

This Volume 1 of the Academy's monumental series of the complete Mozart symphonies authentically performed gathers together the works which the boy Mozart wrote on his foreign tours in England, Italy and the Netherlands. The earliest pieces here are the three London symphonies written in Chelsea in 1764, when Mozart was only 8½, obviously influenced by J. C. Bach, then an arbiter of musical fashion in London. K.19a was only recently rediscovered. A little later come two symphonies written for The Hague, but most of the works – taking two of the three discs –

were written for Italy, including the overture to the opera, *Mitridate*, written for Milan in 1770. With vigour and resilience in outer movements and no lack of charm in slow movements, this is among the most successful of an important and historic series, superbly recorded. Excellent cassettes, the sound vivid, clean and wide-ranging; the reverberation offers very little clouding. Throughout the series, the performances are directed by Jaap Schröder, with Christopher Hogwood contributing the continuo from the harpsichord.

Symphonies Nos. 6 in F, K.43; 7 in D, K.45; 8 in D, K.48; 40 in G min., K.550 (2nd version); *in F, K.42a; in B flat, K.45b; in D, K.46a* (*K.51*); *in G* (*New Lambacher*); *in B flat, K.74g* (*K.216*); *in G, K.425a* (*K.444*).
*** O-L D 173 D 3/*K 173 K 33* (3) [id.]. AcA M, Schröder; Hogwood.

This final volume (as issued) of the Academy's monumental series is crowned by the clarinet version of No. 40 (the original version with oboe is in Volume 6) and also by the *Symphony* 'No. 37', in fact the work of Michael Haydn but with a slow introduction by Mozart, a fine piece aptly included. The other works are early pieces, some of them doubtfully by Mozart, but the depth and perception of the scholarship behind the series are superbly demonstrated not only in the performances but (as in all the volumes) by the detailed and illuminating annotations of the American Mozart scholar, Neal Zaslaw, who acted as musicological adviser throughout. Performances fresh, clear and alert as in the rest of the series. Brilliant recording to match. The cassettes too are of good quality, but the upper range needs taming.

Symphonies Nos. 9 in C, K.73; 14 in A, K.114; 15 in G, K.124; 16 in C, K.128; 17 in G, K.129; in C, K.35; in D, K.38; in D, K.62a/K.100; (*42*) *in F, K.75; in G, K.75b/K.110.*
*** O-L D 168 D 3/*K 168 K 33* (3). AcA M, Schröder; Hogwood.

The fourth volume to appear in the Academy of Ancient Music series deals with the earliest Salzburg symphonies (those that Mozart composed before 1770 were written in London). The work in D, K.62a, is also known and played as the *Serenade No. 1*, K.100, which Boskovsy has recorded very stylishly. His approach reveals much more expressive warmth, for it is vitality and sharpness of articulation which dominate the reading here. In the later symphonies textures are sometimes thinned ever further by the use of solo strings in sections of the music, which produces the feeling of a chamber ensemble, and seems a questionable practice. However, Schröder and his group are nothing if not consistent, and those collecting this series can be assured that this volume is as vigorous and dedicated as the others. The recording too is lively, although the acoustic at times seems somewhat over-resonant, especially in the earlier works. This brings problems for the tape transfer, where with a high level (probably too high) there are moments of roughness and a recurring degree of congestion in tuttis.

Symphonies Nos. 18 in F, K.130; in D, K.141a; 19 in E flat, K.132; 20 in D, K.133; 21 in A, K.134; in D, K.135; 26 in E flat, K.161a; 27 in G, K.161b; 22 in C, K.162; 23 in D, K.162b; 24 in B flat, K.173dA.
*** O-L D 169 D 3/*K 169 K 33* (3) [id.]. AcA M, Schröder; Hogwood.

This was the first box of the Academy of Ancient Music's issued complete recording of Mozart symphonies using authentic texts and original instruments; and very invigorating it proved. The series, meticulously planned under the guidance of the American Mozart scholar Neal Zaslaw, aims to reproduce as closely as possible the conditions of the first performances. It includes not just the symphonies in the regular numbered series but works which might have been compiled as symphonies (the overture to *Lucio Silla*, for example), and the variety of scale as well as of expression makes it a very refreshing collection, particularly as the style of performance, with its non-vibrato tang, is so bright and clean, sharply picking out detail of texture rather than moulding the sound together. The recording is excellent, and the sophisticated tape transfer catches the wide amplitude of the sound without loss of range and focus.

Symphonies Nos. 22–41.
(M) *** Ph. 6769 043 (8) [id.]. ASMF, Marriner.

Marriner, following up the success of his splendid volume of the early symphonies, here presents the later works in comparably stylish, well-recorded performances. Perhaps when he reaches the *Jupiter* he fails quite to capture the full weight of Mozart's argument (exposition repeat not observed in the finale); but the wonder is that so many of the symphonies have been performed with no hint of routine. Nos. 35 and 40 were recorded (in original instrumentation) in 1970, but they marry well with the refined sounds of the recordings from the late 1970s.

Symphonies Nos. 25 in G min., K.183; 28 in C, K.200; 29 in A, K.201.
** ASV ALH/*ZCALH* 937. Northern Sinf., Myung-Whun Chung.

The Northern Sinfonia respond well to Myung-Whun Chung who secures neat, lively and sensitive playing from them. There could be more fire and dramatic tension, perhaps, but there is no doubt that this conductor is an intelligent and often perceptive artist. Good, well-balanced recording. Not first recommendations by any manner of means but enjoyable performances all the same and good value for anyone for whom the coupling is suitable. The iron-oxide tape is full and bright, but internal detail is marginally less refined than on disc, though the sound is warm and natural.

Symphonies Nos. 25 in G min., K.183; 28 in C, K.200; 29 in A, K.201; 30 in D, K.202; in D, K.203, 204 and 196/121.
*** O-L D 170 D 3/*K 170 K 33* (3) [id.]. AcAM, Schröder; Hogwood.

With this second batch of Salzburg works the Academy of Ancient Music come to symphonies that have long been established in the regular modern repertory. It is a revelation to find that a symphony such as the *G minor* (No. 25) is not a 'little *G minor*' at all, for with repeats all observed (even those in the minuet the second time round), it acquires extra weight; and in so lively and fresh a performance as this the extra length from repetition proves invigorating, never tedious. The *A major* – another 'big' symphony – also has a new incisiveness and clarity, without losing anything in rhythmic bounce; so too with the less well-known works. Though it is confusing not to have the regular numbers appended – particularly when the series is so liberally supplied with rarities – the notes by Neal Zaslaw add enormously to the excitement of new discovery. As in the other volumes, the recording is superb, and the cassettes match the discs closely. Sometimes the string timbre seems slightly drier on tape than on disc, and there is just a hint of overloading from the horns in the finale of No. 29; but the resonance does not cloud over the detail as it sometimes can on cassette.

Symphonies Nos. 25 in G min., K.183; 29 in A, K.201
*** Decca SXL 6879. ECO, Britten.
(M) *** Decca Ser. 411 717-1. ASMF, Marriner.

Several years before his untimely death Benjamin Britten recorded these exhilarating performances of the two greatest of Mozart's early symphonies. Inexplicably the record remained unissued, finally providing a superb codicil to Britten's recording career. It is striking that in many movements his tempi and even his approach are very close to those of Neville Marriner on his excellent Argo disc (now on Decca's mid-priced label); but it is Britten's genius along with his crisp articulation and sprung rhythms to provide the occasional touch of pure individual magic. Britten's slow movements provide a clear contrast, rather weightier than Marriner's, particularly in the little *G minor*, where Britten, with a slower speed and more expressive phrasing, underlines the elegiac quality of the music. Rich, well-balanced recording and a first-class cassette transfer.

Marriner's Argo coupling from the early 1970s has now been reissued on Serenata. The performances have splendid life and polish. The pointing of the phrases of the little *G minor* is done with a superb sense of style and the scale of No. 29 is broad and forward-looking. The recording may be too reverberant for some tastes but the disc can be warmly recommended at mid-price to all Mozartians.

Symphonies Nos. 25 and 40 in G min., K.183; 550.
*(*) Tel. Dig. **ZK8**; AZ6/*CX4* 42935 [642935]. Concg. O, Harnoncourt.

Harnoncourt secures fine playing from the Concertgebouw, but his coupling of the two G minor symphonies (in itself not a good plan) is only variably successful with some extreme speeds (as in the very brisk slow movement of No. 40) and an unsettled mood overall, hardly Mozartian. There is a brilliant chrome tape.

Symphonies Nos. 26 in E flat, K.184; 31 in D (Paris), K.297; 38 in D (Prague), K.504.
(M) **(*) DG Acc. 2542/*3342* 127. Berlin PO, Boehm.

This is a recoupling. Symphonies Nos. 26 and 31 come from the mid-1960s, but the *Prague* is much earlier and the upper strings are recorded with less body and bloom. The performances, however, are alert and sensitive. The playing is first-class, as one would expect, and show Boehm on his best Mozartian form. The sound is lively and well balanced on disc and cassette alike.

Symphonies Nos. 28 in C, K.200; 41 in C (Jupiter), K.551.
*** Ph. Dig. 6514/*7337* 206 [id.]. Dresden State O, Sir Colin Davis.

Just as the *G minor Symphony* (No. 40) has a 'little' precursor (No. 25), so the less familiar No. 28 makes a logical companion for the *Jupiter*, but whereas single-disc LPs of No. 25 have been relatively abundant, Colin Davis's version with the Staatskapelle Dresden has the field to itself. Not that it need fear competition, for this is a sparkling and delightful version that surpasses his 1963 account for Oiseau-Lyre in almost every respect. Davis has recorded the *Jupiter* more than once, and this newcomer is all that one would expect: alert, sensitive, perceptive and played with vitality and finesse by the Dresden orchestra. Philips also provide very good recording and few are likely to be disappointed with this LP on either artistic or technical grounds. The chrome cassette, however, is bass heavy and, in No. 28, inner detail is noticeably less well defined than on the disc.

Symphonies Nos. 29 in A, K.201; 33 in B flat, K.319.
(M) **(*) DG Priv. 2535/*3335* 155. Berlin PO, Karajan.

A sparkling account of the *A major Symphony* from Karajan, but one which may be a trifle too smooth for some tastes. The orchestral playing is, of course, superlative, and the DG sound is warm and full. Much the same comments apply to the *B flat Symphony*. There is a very good cassette transfer. The recording dates from 1966.

Symphonies Nos. 29; 35 (Haffner); 38 (Prague); 39–41 (Jupiter), Masonic funeral music.
(M) **(*) DG 2740 268 (3). VPO, Boehm.

In these days of performances on original instruments Boehm's unashamedly nineteenth-century approach may at times seem heavy, particularly when he consistently favours allegros on the slow side, even in the first movement of No. 40. These were in fact recorded much later than Boehm's complete set of the Mozart symphonies made with the Berlin Philharmonic, and though they are even weightier they have a relaxedness and a glowing resonance which make them more endearing, mature products of octogenarian wisdom. They may sometimes lack the drive of other performances, but they remain most compelling, not least in the spacious accounts of the slow movements. The *Masonic funeral music* makes a worthwhile filler. Good, warm DG recording.

Symphonies Nos. 29; 39 in E flat, K.543.
*** Ph. Dig. 6514/*7337* 205 [id.]. Dresden State O, Sir Colin Davis.

Vital and imaginative playing from the Staatskapelle Dresden under Colin Davis, finely paced and beautifully balanced. Arguably the finest account of the *E flat Symphony* currently on the market – at least since the days of Beecham and Walter. Davis's earlier account of No. 29 in A was in some ways slightly fresher, but this is still magnificent. The recording, made in collaboration with VEB of East Germany, is in the best traditions of Philips.

Symphonies Nos. 29; 41 (Jupiter).
(B) *(*) PRT GSGC/*ZCGC* 2032 or 2054. Hallé O, Barbirolli.

Barbirolli's reading of the *Jupiter*, like Barenboim's, highlights the finale, which is played incisively and with some weight. Before that the approach is very mellow, with an Italianate warmth in the *Andante cantabile* and the minuet rhythmic but relaxed, its main theme floating gracefully over the accompanying chords. No. 29 is warm but rather slack, with the minuet lacking vigour. The recording is agreeable but not refined; on tape side two (which includes the finale of the *Jupiter*) is brighter than side one. This issue appears to be available under two separate catalogue numbers. It is not one of Barbirolli's best records.

Symphonies Nos. 31 in D (Paris), K.297; 33 in B flat, K.319; Andante K.297.
(*) Tel. Dig. **ZK8; AZ6/*CX4* 42817 [642817]. Concg. O, Harnoncourt.

Harnoncourt, when he stops conducting an orchestra of original instruments, may still favour speeds rather slower than usual, but the manner is relatively romantic in its expressiveness. This is the most successful of his Mozart records with the Concertgebouw, with beautiful, cleanly articulated playing. The alternative slow movements are given for the *Paris*, the second one much lighter in weight. In No. 33, Harnoncourt overdoes his slowness in the *Andante*, but adds to the breadth of the finale by giving the repeats of both halves. Very good recording. There is a vivid chrome cassette, although it makes the orchestral upper range sound rather dry. On compact disc the strings are given a very tangible presence, woodwind is somewhat more forward than under live concert-hall conditions, yet the bright vividness and realism of the sound are most impressive.

Symphonies Nos. 31 in D (Paris), K.297; 34 in C, K.338; 39 in E flat, K.543; 40 in G min., K.550.
(M) *** HMV *TCC2-POR 154598-9*. ECO, Barenboim.

This is the second, as issued, of Barenboim's groupings of Mozart symphonies, taken from recordings made in the late 1960s. The first is discussed below. Both make distinguished and useful additions to HMV's *'Portrait of the artist'* tape series. There are no disc equivalents. Here the *Paris symphony* is given an outstanding performance, the contrasts of mood in the first movement underlined and the finale taken at a hectic tempo that would have sounded breathless with players any less brilliant than the modest-sized ECO. No. 34 (a later recording, dating from 1972) also has a vivacious finale and the playing is equally impressive with its consistently imaginative phrasing. Barenboim's approach to No. 39 is warmer, marginally more expressive than Colin Davis's, and some may well prefer it for just these qualities. The responsive phrasing from the strings, both here and in the *G minor Symphony*, is matched by wind playing in which the colour is well brought out. The performances are thoughtful, yet spacious, alive and exciting too. The scale is right, and the warm, smooth recording, perhaps a little lacking in ultimate range at the top, is generally well balanced (only in the *Paris* does the bass resonance become a fraction too insistent at times).

Symphonies Nos. 31 in D (Paris) (2 versions)*; 35 in D (Haffner), K.385* (2nd version)*; 38 in D (Prague), K.504; 39 in E flat, K.543; 40 in G min., K.550* (1st version)*; 41 in C (Jupiter).*
*** O-L Dig. D.172 D.4/*K.172 K.43* (4/3) [id.]. AcAM, Schröder; Hogwood.

The last and greatest of Mozart symphonies fare well in the Academy's collected edition, for performances on original instruments bring sharpness and intensity to compensate for any lack of weight or resonance expected by modern ears. Outer movements are consistently refreshing and incisive, and though the lack of expressive freedom typical of slow movements in this series may be disappointing to some, the relative lightness comes to seem apt, even in the *Prague* and *Jupiter*. Only the slow movement of No. 40 disappoints in its rather prosaic manner. The *Paris symphony* is given two complete performances with alternative slow movements, both using more strings than the rest, as witnessed by the first Paris performances. Excellent recording, as in the whole series. The chrome-tape transfer is extremely vivid and does not lack fullness, but the upper range of the violin timbre is emphasized and made to sound thin and wiry.

Symphonies Nos. 31 in D (Paris); 35 in D (Haffner); 40 in G min., K.550; 41 in C (Jupiter).
(B) *** DG Walkman *413 151-4*. Berlin PO, Boehm.

These recordings date from between 1960 and 1966 and are all available otherwise coupled – see above and below. This bargain-priced Walkman cassette offers uncommonly good value, for the performances are authoritative and the recorded sound has come up freshly in these new chrome-tape transfers. Not for those hooked on the Academy of Ancient Music, but Boehm's big-band Mozart remains stylish in its own special way.

Symphonies Nos. 31 in D (Paris), K.297; 40 in G min., K.550.
*** O-L **410 197-2**; DSLO/*KDSLC* 716. AcAM, Schröder; Hogwood.

A fine sampler from the complete Mozart symphony set by the Academy with original instruments at their freshest and brightest in crisp, clear interpretations with all possible repeats observed. The clarity and bite are made the cleaner and more immediate on compact disc. The chrome cassette too is of Decca's finest quality.

Symphonies Nos. 32 in G, K.318; 33 in B flat, K.319; 34 in C, K.338; 35 in D (Haffner), K.385; 36 in C (Linz), K.425; in C, K.213c/208; in D, K.248b/250 and 320.
*** O-L D 171 D 4/*K 171 K 44* (4) [id.]. AcAM, Schröder; Hogwood.

This volume of the Academy of Ancient Music's collected edition of Mozart symphonies includes the works that Mozart wrote between 1775 and 1783, not just those in the regularly numbered series (Nos. 32 to 36) but two other symphonies extracted from large-scale serenades (the *Haffner serenade* and the *Posthorn serenade*) as well as a short Italian-style *Sinfonia* taken from the overture to *Il Re pastore*. As before, using authentic performance style with all repeats observed, the readings are always fresh and illuminating, the speeds often brisk but never rushed, though some will prefer a more relaxed, less metrical style in slow movements. The recordings – with Hogwood's harpsichord presented clearly against the full ensemble – strings 9.8.4.3.2 – are superbly faithful to the aim of re-creating the sounds Mozart originally heard. The cassette transfer offers the finest tape quality in this series so far; the sound is full and resonant and has a striking life and upper range. Only on the last side is there a hint of stridency in the upper strings; otherwise this is demonstration-worthy.

Symphonies Nos. 32, K.318; 35 in D (Haffner), K.385; 36 in C (Linz), K.425; 38 in D (Prague), K.504; 39 in E flat, K.543; 40 in G min., K.550; 41 in C (Jupiter), K.551.
*** DG 2740 189/*3371 038* (3) [id.]. Berlin PO, Karajan.

It is difficult to conceive of better big-band Mozart than these beautifully played and vitally alert readings. There are details about which some may have reservations: the minuet and trio of the *Linz* may seem too slow, and the opening of the *G minor*, which is a shade faster than in Karajan's Vienna performance, may not be quite dark enough for some tastes. In general, however, these are such finely proportioned readings, so exquisitely paced and shaped, that it is hard to see how they could be surpassed. As recordings they are well balanced, alive and yet smooth. Either as a complete set or as individual issues (listed below), these hold their own with the best; and the cassette transfers are altogether excellent.

Symphonies Nos. 32, K.318; 35 (Haffner); 36 (Linz).
*** DG 2531/*3301* 136 [id.]. Berlin PO, Karajan.
(M) **(*) DG Acc. 2542/*3342* 119. Berlin PO, Boehm.

Boehm's 1967 recording of the *Linz* is one of his finest Mozart performances, balancing vitality with warmth, and the vivacious account of the 'Italian overture', K.318, is no less attractive. The *Haffner* dates from 1960, and the recording has just a hint of stridency in the upper string timbre (though this is smoothed slightly in the cassette transfer). The performance is a good one, though less imaginative than the other two. The recorded sound is generally good, slightly warmer and fuller on cassette than on disc.

Symphonies Nos. 32, K.318; 35 (Haffner); 36 (Linz); 41 (Jupiter).
(M) *** HMV *TCC2-POR 54298*. ECO, Barenboim.

These Barenboim recordings were made towards the end of the 1960s and are not available in disc form. This extended-length ferric tape is of high quality, the sound full, clear and well balanced. Barenboim is at his finest in Mozart's last and longest symphony where he rightly focuses attention on the finale. He observes the second-half repeat as well as the first, to give Mozart's complex fugal design a majesty comparable only with Beethoven, and that at a brisk, swashbuckling tempo. The rest of the symphony is interpreted with equal compulsion. The *Haffner* is also strongly vigorous, the first movement bold almost to the point of brusqueness. In the *Prague*, Barenboim obviously intends the full weight of the imposing introduction to be felt. When the allegro arrives it is gracious and alive and the impetus is nicely judged. The finale too is light-hearted and gay, to make a foil with the rather serious-minded *Andante*. The account of Mozart's *'Italian overture' symphony* is straightforward and spirited. With an authentic-sized orchestra, playing very stylishly on modern instruments, this makes an attractive compilation.

Symphonies Nos. 34 in C, K.338; 35 in D (Haffner), K.385.
(*) Tel. Dig. **ZK8; AZ6/*CX4* 42703. Concg. O, Harnoncourt.

With bright, clear digital recording – quite different from the sound which Philips engineers get from this orchestra – the Harnoncourt coupling provides refreshing, directly dramatic performances of these two symphonies, marked by unforced tempi. Charm is rather missing, and the coupling provides rather short measure; but the immediacy of sound is what compels attention. On compact disc, although the sound picture is vividly clear, there is a dryness in tuttis which borders on harshness. This is much less attractive than the companion CD coupling *Symphonies 31* and *33*.

Symphony No. 35 in D major (Haffner), K.385.
** Abbey ABY 733. L. Moz. Players, Blech – HAYDN: *Symphony No. 90.***

Compare this Mozart sound with one of the early LPs (mono) that Blech made with his then pioneering chamber orchestra, and it is amazing, allowing for the development of recording technique, that the sound is so consistent. This is not as polished a performance as the best in the catalogue, but it will please the many devotees of Blech and the London Mozart Players.

Symphonies Nos. 35, (Haffner); 36 in C (Linz).
*** O-L DSLO/*KDSLC* 602. AcAM., Schröder; Hogwood.
** HM 1C 065 99903. Coll. Aur., Maier.

This *Haffner* is the earlier version extracted from the *Serenade* and finds the Academy in very good form. At times in the slow movements one feels the absence of warmth, but for the most part these performances are lively and imaginative and can be recommended to all who want an authentic-instrument version of these symphonies. The cassette is lively on top, but the resonant bass brings slight clouding in fortissimos.

Maier's performances belong to a now apparently almost outdated way of re-creating the 'original' sound of Mozart's time, for though early instruments are used, timbres are much more like a modern group than those of the Academy of Ancient Music. Yet the direction here is thoroughly musical and tempi are well judged. The recording is full-bodied and has good detail.

Symphonies Nos. 36 in C (Linz), K.425; 38 in D (Prague), K.504.
(M) *** DG Sig. 410 840-1/*4*. Berlin PO, Karajan.

It is good to see Karajan's fine performances at mid-price, thus bringing them within reach of a wider public. There are one or two things about which one might quibble (the broadening of tempo at bar 71 in the first movement of the *Linz*) but, generally speaking, the playing is so superlative and the sense of pace so well judged that one surrenders to the sheer quality of this music-making. The recording is as cultured as the performances themselves and collectors wanting this coupling from these artists need not hesitate. The chrome tape is not one of DG's best, though very acceptable. No. 38 sounds rather sharper in focus than No. 36 because of the higher transfer level on side two, but the resonant sound is somewhat cleaner on disc, in both works.

Symphony No. 38 in D (Prague), K.504.
** Tel. Dig. AZ6/*CX4* 42805 [642805]. Concg. O, Harnoncourt.

Even allowing for the demonstration excellence of the recording – the chrome tape matching the disc in clarity and body of tone – and the finely played, stylish performance, it is difficult to imagine that anyone would be willing to accept a single Mozart symphony spread over two sides of one LP or cassette. Harnoncourt plays every possible repeat (there is over thirty-seven minutes of Mozart here) and secures playing of fine spontaneity and polish that is a pleasure to listen to, but even so this issue is difficult to take seriously in today's highly competitive market place.

Symphonies Nos. 38 (Prague); 39 in E flat, K.543; 40 in G min., K.550; 41 in C (Jupiter), K.551.
(M) **(*) DG Acc. 2725/*3374* 104. Berlin PO, Boehm.

This mid-price two-disc folder neatly couples the last four symphonies from Boehm's complete series recorded in Berlin in the 1960s. With generally slowish tempi there is an attractive honesty and strength about them. The weight of sound from a relatively large band is not obtrusive, and though they may be a little short on charm and some of the finales lack sparkle, there is a comfortable quality of inevitablity here, perpetuating a long Mozart tradition. The recordings still sound very well, although on cassette the lively upper range needs cutting back a little.

Symphonies Nos. 38 (Prague); 39 in E flat.
*** O-L Dig. **410 233-2**; 410 233-1/*4*. AcAM, Schröder.
*** DG 2531/*3301* 137 [id.]. Berlin PO, Karajan.
(M) **(*) HM 20370. Coll. Aur., Maier.
**(*) Decca Dig. SXDL/*KSXDC* 7588 [Lon. LDR/*5*- 71088]. Chicago SO, Solti.

Two splendid samples from the complete set of Mozart symphonies recorded on original instruments. The weight and scale of the *Prague* are the more keenly apparent in such a performance as this with all repeats observed, even if Hogwood's and Schröder's determination not to overload slow movements with anachronistic expressiveness will disappoint some. Excellent, finely scaled recording, although the chrome cassette is a minor disaster, with coarse sound in both works, in spite of a modest level of transfer. We have not heard the compact disc.

Karajan's record is strongly recommendable (see the entry for his set above). This is big-band Mozart, but the effect remains resilient as well as strong and the Berlin Philharmonic playing is superb. The recording sounds equally impressive on disc or tape.

Under Maier, the performance of No. 39 is particularly successful, with the early clarinets making a piquant contribution to the minuet. Spirited playing in the outer movements and an expressive but not over-romanticized *Andante* make this an account to remember. The *Prague* is good too, and though interpretatively it may seem a little cautious it is good to hear 'original' string instruments producing a timbre that has body as well as edge. The recording is resonant but nicely detailed and gives the ensemble agreeable weight and good detail.

It would be easy to underestimate Solti's performances, for the Decca digital sound brings an excessively bright sheen to the upper strings. The recording sounds best on the chrome tape, where the richness and detail are retained and the treble is smoother. Solti's approach is in no way glossy, indeed there is a sense of serious purpose here, notably in the first movement of No. 39, while both slow movements are beautifully played, the phrasing supple and sensitive. The vigour of the opening movement of the *Prague* is exhilarating and the finales of both works are alert and sparkling. On the whole the *E flat Symphony* (No. 39) is the more memorable. Even if the minuet sounds a bit heavy, the *Andante* shows Solti and his orchestra at their finest. But this could hardly be further removed from the ambience of the Academy of Ancient Music.

Symphonies No. 39 in E flat; 40 in G min.
(M) **(*) HMV SXLP/*TC-SXLP* 30527. Berlin PO, Karajan.

Karajan offers us big-band Mozart – but what a band! Tempi are sensible and entirely free from egocentric touches. Karajan's views about both symphonies have remained consistent over the years and there is the same high regard for detail and beauty and refinement of tone. The only reservation might be the tempo for the *Andante* of No. 39, somewhat faster than listeners brought up on Beecham or Bruno Walter might like. To some ears the first movement of No. 39 might seem overgroomed, but its breadth and sense of stature command admiration. The sound is slightly more opaque than in Karajan's more recent DG set, but it is still very good indeed. On tape the quality is rather dry and harsh.

Symphonies Nos. 39; 41 (Jupiter).
*** Ph. Dig. **410 046-2** [id.]. Dresden State O, Sir Colin Davis.

In their normal LP/cassette formats, these performances are otherwise coupled, No. 39 is with No. 29 and the *Jupiter* with No. 28. The performances are discussed above. Philips deemed the present pairing more commercial for the compact disc, which can be recommended with all enthusiasm.

Symphony No. 40, K.550; Serenade No. 6 in D (Serenata notturna).
(M) *** Decca Jub. JB/*KJBC* 107. ECO, Britten.

Symphony No. 40, K.550; Serenade No. 13 in G (Eine kleine Nachtmusik).
(B) **(*) Con. CC/*CCT* 7507. VPO, Kertesz.
(M) *(*) CBS 60274/*40-*. Marlboro Fest. O, Casals.

Britten takes *all* repeats (the slow movement here is longer than that of the *Eroica*); but there are a composer's insights and he is almost totally convincing. The *Serenade* is enchanting. With the rich Maltings sound to give added breadth to the symphony, and at Jubilee price, this is well worth trying. The cassette is outstandingly full and wide-ranging in the *Symphony*; the *Serenade* has rather less body and refinement.

Kertesz underlines the richness of the music of the *G minor Symphony*, tempi on the slow side (except in the finale), with dramatic underlining of dynamic contrasts. The orchestral playing is first-class and with a warmly elegant account of *Eine kleine Nachtmusik* this is attractive at bargain price, especially as the recording is of vintage Decca quality, full and clear. The cassette transfer lacks range, especially in the symphony.

Recorded at the Marlboro Festivals of 1967/8 in Vermont, the music-making on the CBS issue has the spirit of a live occasion, and Casals communicates his own affinity with the music in various grunts and noises of exhortation or appreciation. The performances are characterful rather than refined (the mood of the first movement of the *G minor Symphony* is nicely judged), but the playing is alert and expressive and with acceptable recording this coupling may attract admirers of the great cellist, even though there are finer versions of both works readily available.

Symphonies Nos. 40–41 (Jupiter).
*** DG 2530/*3300* 780 [id.]. VPO, Boehm.

*** DG 2531/*3301* 138 [id.]. Berlin PO, Karajan.
(B) *** CfP CFP/*TC-CFP* 40253. LPO, Mackerras.
(M) **(*) Decca VIV/*KVIC* 6 [Lon. STS/*5-15540*]. VPO, Karajan.
(M) ** Decca Jub. JB/*KJBC* 8 [Lon. JL/*5-41008*]. New Philh. O, Giulini.
*(*) DG 2531/*3301* 273 [id.]. LSO, Abbado.
*(*) RCA Dig. **RCD 14413** [ARC1/*ARK1* 4413]. Chicago SO, Levine.

Boehm recorded this same coupling earlier with the Berlin Philharmonic as part of his complete Mozart cycle, but his Vienna versions, as well as being more vividly and immediately recorded, also present more alert, more spontaneous-sounding performances, with the octogenarian conductor sounding more youthful than before. Boehm takes a relatively measured view of the outer movements of No. 40, but the resilience of the playing rivets the attention and avoids any sort of squareness. Excellent recommendations for both symphonies, though in No. 41 the single-sided format prevents the observance of exposition repeats which many count desirable in Mozart's most massive symphony. There is a very good cassette transfer.

Some ears find the DG Karajan recordings, made in Berlin in 1979, rather streamlined, and the opening of the *G minor Symphony* is here not as subtle in colour and feeling as in some versions. But the orchestra plays superbly and the *Jupiter* has weight and power as well as surface elegance. The sound is wholly admirable on disc and cassette alike.

This coupling is extremely well provided for in the bargain and medium-price ranges. Mackerras directs excellent clean-cut performances which stand comparison with any at whatever price. He observes exposition repeats in the outer movements of the *G minor*, but not in the *Jupiter* (uncomfortably long for a single side), which is a pity in so majestic a work. Some may prefer a more affectionate style in slow movements, but at half the price of the Boehm or Karajan DG discs and with clean modern recording, this is an outstanding bargain. The cassette originally had a restricted dynamic range but has now been satisfactorily remastered.

Karajan's earlier Vienna recordings, dating from the early 1960s, remain good value in the medium price-range. In the *G minor* every detail is beautifully in place, each phrase nicely shaped and in perspective. The exposition repeat in the first movement is observed, though the chords linking it to the development are prominent at a slightly higher level and the balance thereafter appears to be closer. Beautifully articulate and suave, this performance has a genuine dramatic power, even though one feels that it all moves within carefully regulated emotional limits. Karajan does tend to beautify detail without adding corresponding stature. The reading of the *Jupiter* is a strong one, one of the best things Karajan did in his short period in the Decca studios. The performance is direct and has breadth as well as warmth. The orchestral playing is excellent, and with first-rate sound this is certainly enjoyable, although there is no exposition repeat in the first movement. There is no appreciable difference in sound between disc and cassette.

The Decca Jubilee reissue was Giulini's first recording for Decca with the New Philharmonia. They play well for him and the recording is warm and detailed, of Decca's finest quality. However, the performances, although they offer beautifully polished playing, are curiously lacking in vitality, neither classically poised nor romantically charged. The tape transfer is exceptionally successful, the quality splendidly fresh, clean, brightly lit yet without any suggestion of glare.

Abbado directs generally immaculate but curiously faceless performances of Mozart's last symphonies. The *Jupiter* is marginally more convincing, but there are far better versions of this coupling.

Levine's performances are available in the UK on compact disc only, and they cannot be recommended with any enthusiasm. The *G minor* is matter-of-fact and wanting in real warmth and while the *Jupiter* is more than routine, it is less than distinguished, given the reputation of the orchestra and the musicianship and insight of this conductor. The recording, made in the Medinah Temple, Chicago, has no want of clarity and presence, but its claims cannot be pressed over rival performances, for instance Colin Davis or Jochum in the *Jupiter*.

Symphony No. 41 (Jupiter), K.551.
(M) *** DG Sig. 2543/*3343* 531 [(d) 2530 357]. Boston SO, Jochum – HAYDN: *Symphony No. 104.****
(M) *** HMV SXLP/*TC-SXLP* 30443 [Sera. S 60367]. RPO, Beecham – SCHUBERT: *Symphony No. 6.****
** Tel. Dig. AZ6/*CX4* 42846 [642846]. Concg. O, Harnoncourt.

Symphony No. 41; Rondo, K.373.
(M) *** HM 20323. Coll. Aur., Maier (violin).

Jochum's 1974 version of Mozart's *Jupiter symphony* is one of the most satisfying accounts of the work ever recorded. The sound balance is exceptionally successful, full and atmospheric. If anything, the sound is even firmer in outline on chrome tape than it is on LP, with the Boston acoustic presenting no problems of inner clarity. The performance is strong and spacious, classical in feeling, yet admirably expressive, superbly backed by splendid playing from the Boston orchestra. If the coupling is suitable (and it is no less distinguished), this record is unbeatable at mid-price.

Characteristically Beecham makes the *Jupiter* an elegant work rather than a magisterial one, and the minuet is a classic example of Beechamesque nuance, inimitably shaped at a slowish tempo. The outer movements are crisp and immediate, the slow movement gracious. Already this has become a period performance. The 1950s recording sounds well enough and its slightly dry quality has transferred very successfully to cassette.

Maier directs (from the leader's desk) a refined and sensitive performance of the *Jupiter* using original instruments, and with wide groove-spacing the sound is outstandingly vivid. This may miss some of the full power of the finest versions, but unless you insist on the original flat pitch, it is an admirable example of authentic performance, not so abrasive as those by the Academy of Ancient Music. However, with only the (well played) *Rondo* for violin and orchestra, K.373, for coupling this seems a very uneconomical way of acquiring the symphony, even at mid-price.

Harnoncourt, early advocate of authentic performance on original instruments, turns into a much more romantic animal in Mozart with a modern orchestra. The result here, in spite of superb playing, is on the heavy side with speeds slower than usual. A strong reading but not a consistently illuminating one, very well recorded. While all repeats are included, however, this is poor value spread over two sides at premium price. There is an excellently balanced chrome cassette of the highest quality.

CHAMBER AND INSTRUMENTAL MUSIC

Adagio and rondo in C. min., K.617 (for glass harmonica etc.); *Oboe quartet in F, K.370; Oboe quintet in C min., K.406* (arr. of *Serenade No. 12, K.388*).
(M) *** Ph. 6503/*7303* 113. Hoffmann (glass harmonica), Holliger, Nicolet, Krebbers, Schouten, Munk-Gerö, Decross.

With such a distinguished roster it is not surprising that these performances are first-class. Moreover they are beautifully recorded. Holliger's bright clear timbre dominates the strings without too forward a balance. The curiosity is Mozart's own arrangement of his *Wind serenade*, K.388, which some might feel sounds best in its original format. However, the playing here is undoubtedly persuasive, and of course the account of the *Oboe quartet* is peerless. Finally and certainly not least is the work for glass harmonica played on Bruno Hoffmann's set of drinking glasses (with moistened fingers). It is an unforgettably piquant sound and the result is delightful (the piece does not outstay its welcome).

Clarinet quintet in A, K.581.
*** DG Dig. 410 670-1/*4* [id.]. Meyer, Berlin Philharmonic Qt – WEBER: *Introduction, theme and variations.****
(M) **(*) HMV HQS 1395 [(d) Ang. S 36241]. De Peyer, Melos Ens. – WEBER: *Clarinet quintet.***(*)*

(*i*) *Clarinet quintet;* (ii) *Clarinet trio in E flat, K.498.*
(M) ** Ph. 6570/*7310* 573 [6500 073]. Brymer; (i) Allegri Qt; (ii) Bishop-Kovacevich, Ireland.
(M) *(*) Decca Ace SDD 558. Schmidl, New V. Octet (members); (ii) with Medjimorec.

(i) *Clarinet quintet; Divertimento in D, K.136.*
(M) *** Saga 5291. (i) Thea King; Aeolian Qt.

Clarinet quintet; Horn quintet in E flat, K.407; Oboe quartet in F, K.370.
*** Ph. 9500 772/*7300 848* [id.]. Pay, Black, Timothy Brown, ASMF Chamber Ens.

(i) *Clarinet quintet;* (ii) *Oboe quartet in F, K.370.*
(B) *** CfP CFP/*TC-CFP* 40377. (i) Andrew Marriner; (ii) Hunt; Chilingirian Qt.
*** DG 2530/*3300* 720 [id.]. (i) De Peyer, (ii) Koch; Amadeus Qt.
(M) **(*) DG Priv. 2535/*3335* 287. (i) Leister; (ii) Koch; Berlin PO Soloists.

(i) *Clarinet quintet;* (ii) *Piano and wind quintet in E flat, K.452.*
(B) ** Con. CC/*CCT* 7544. (i) Alfred Boskovsky; (ii) Panhoffer; Vienna Octet (members).

(i) *Clarinet quintet; String quartet No. 3 in G, K.156.*
*** Cal. CAL 1628/*4628*. Zahradnik; Talich Qt.

Mozart's *Clarinet quintet* is understandably the most popular and most frequently recorded of all his chamber works, and it is very well represented in all price ranges. Its digital debut is provided by Sabine Meyer, the young clarinetist whose appointment to the Berlin Philharmonic occasioned the open rift between Karajan and the orchestra that clouded their long relationship in early 1983. Judging from this account of the Mozart, she is a most gifted player whose artistry is of a high order. She produces a full, rich and well-focused tone that is a delight to the ear, and she phrases with great musicianship and sensitivity. The performance is one of the best in the catalogue and is well recorded. The balance is well judged if (in the present DG fashion) placing the listener rather forward. However, the effect is eminently realistic and there is no qualification on technical grounds to stand in the way of a three-star recommendation. On the outstanding compact disc, which is issued by Denon in the USA **[38C37-7038]**, the sound is remarkably refined and natural, although, of course, the forward balance remains. The only drawback to Ms Meyer's version is the coupling, which though agreeable is neither very substantial nor generous.

Taking everything into account, the 'best buy' for this work would seem to be the bargain-priced CfP version recorded in 1981 by the young Andrew Marriner – son of Neville – whose persuasive account is in the front rank, quite irrespective of price. It is coupled with an equally fine performance of the delightful *Oboe quartet* by Gordon Hunt, another young musician and principal oboe with the Philharmonia at the time of the recording. Marriner's playing in the *Quintet* is wonderfully flexible. It reaches its apex in the radiantly beautiful reading of the slow movement, although the finale is also engagingly characterized. The *Oboe quartet* is delectable too, with Hunt a highly musical and technically accomplished soloist. The Chilingirian players contribute most sympathetically to both works and the performances are much more generous in repeats than the competing DG Amadeus coupling. The CfP issue was recorded in the Wigmore Hall and the sound balance is most believable, with no appreciable difference between disc and tape.

The Amadeus coupling, of course, is splendid. Gervase de Peyer gives a warm, smiling account of the *Clarinet quintet*, with a sunny opening movement, a gently expressive *Larghetto* and a delightfully genial finale. The performance is matched by the refinement of Koch in the *Oboe quartet*. With creamy tone and wonderfully stylish phrasing he is superb. The Amadeus accompany with sensibility, and the recording is flawless. So is the cassette transfer, a demonstration tape. The recording dates from 1977, and is still at full price.

Antony Pay is a mellifluous and sensitive artist, and the account of the *Clarinet quintet* by the Academy of St Martin-in-the-Fields players must also be numbered among the strongest now on the market. Contours are beautifully shaped, and the performers convey a strong sense of enjoyment. Neil Black's playing in the *Oboe quartet* is distinguished, and again the whole performance radiates pleasure. This issue gives excellent value in also including the *Horn quintet* in a well-projected and lively account with Timothy Brown. Both full-priced DG records offer only a single piece as coupling: here we have another major work besides – and all three are beautifully finished and musically alive performances, while the recording is truthful and naturally balanced. On cassette the sound is pleasingly warm and mellow, yet does not lack range and detail.

Thea King is a fine Mozartian. She plays the *Quintet* in a classical manner, but with great refinement in matters of tonal shading, and her phrasing is most beautiful. There is, it is true, a touch of coolness in the first two movements, but the music still glows, and Miss King's articulation in the third-movement solos and in the delightfully pointed finale is a joy to hear. The closing pages of the work are especially beautiful. This is all helped by excellent support from the Aeolian Quartet and one of the best recordings we have had from Saga. The filler is bright and breezy, with very fast tempi for the outer movements and a graceful, if matter-of-fact account of the *Andante*.

Czech wind-playing has a well-deserved reputation for individuality and character and Bohuslav Zahradnik's account of Mozart's famous *Quintet* on Calliope does not disappoint. He plays with striking imagination, his timbre is most attractive and his articulation and phrasing combine to provide the most engaging effect. There is an essentially genial quality about this performance: the minuet is particularly memorable and the improvisatory quality of the middle section of the finale is balanced by a disarming delicacy – from the Talich players as well as the soloist – at the reprise of the jaunty main theme. The coupling is slight, the early three-movement *String quartet in G* (very nicely played), but this remains one of the most rewarding of all recorded versions of the *Quintet*. Unfortunately the cassette is very highly modulated, to the point of minor discoloration in the upper partials of the clarinet, most noticeable in the blissful account of the slow movement.

The Privilege reissue offers fine playing but a somewhat suave atmosphere in the central movements of the *Clarinet quintet*. Karl Leister, the clarinettist, does not emerge as a strong individual personality, but he plays most musically and this performance undoubtedly gives pleasure. Lothar Koch shows a sweetly pointed timbre and a most sensitive feeling for the style of the *Oboe quartet*, though this is not quite so distinguished as his later Amadeus version. The recording is very good and the tape transfers are of excellent quality; the *Clarinet quintet* is especially vivid, the level unusually high for DG.

Gervase de Peyer's earlier recording of the *Clarinet quintet* for HMV has not quite the vitality of his newer DG version (coupled to the *Oboe quartet*), but its limpid warmth is very attractive. Now recoupled to the Weber *Quintet* this makes an attractive medium-price reissue. The sound is clear and refined, with no lack of bloom.

Brymer's interpretation of the *Quintet* is warm and leisurely. In some ways Brymer follows the famous Bavier recording from Decca's early mono LP days in choosing slow tempi throughout. He is nearly as successful as Bavier in sustaining them, although in the finale the forward flow of the music is reduced to a near-crawl. In the *Trio* the piano is backwardly balanced and Stephen Bishop's contribution makes less than its proper effect. But otherwise the recorded sound is beautiful, on disc and tape alike.

Boskovsky's account of the *Clarinet quintet* is gracious and intimate, a little lacking in individuality, but enjoyable in its unforced way. The closing pages of the work are given with a real Viennese lilt. The recording is warm and sympathetic. The account of the *Piano and wind quintet* might best be described as sturdy. Not all the subtleties of Mozart's part-writing are fully revealed, and the playing is rather earth-bound. The recording is a fairly old one but sounds remarkably fresh, although the stereo has not a great deal of inner separation when the group are all playing together. This is quite good value in the bargain price-range.

It is difficult to fault the playing in the Viennese performances by Peter Schmidl and members of the New Vienna Octet, but both in the *Clarinet quintet* and in the *Trio* the overall effect is of blandness. Cassette and disc are closely matched in quality.

Divertimento in E flat for string trio, K.563.

(M) *** Ph. 6570/*7310* 572. Grumiaux, Janzer, Szabo.

*** CBS 76381 [M 33266]. Stern, Zukerman, Rose.

Divertimento, K.563; Duo in B flat, K.424.

(M) ** Decca Ace SDD 577. Küchl, Staar, Bartolomey.

Grumiaux has long been remarkable even among the most outstanding virtuosi of the day for his purity of intonation, and here he is joined by two players with a similarly refined and classical style. They may only be an ad hoc group, but their unanimity is most striking, and Grumiaux's individual artistry gives the interpretation an extra point. The hushed opening of the first-movement development – a visionary passage – is played with a magically intense half-tone, and the lilt of the finale is infectious from the very first bar. The title *Divertimento* is of course a monumental misnomer, for this is one of the richest of Mozart's last-period chamber works, far too rarely heard in the concert hall. The recording is exceptionally vivid, but refined too, on disc and also on the excellent cassette.

This is certainly a masterpiece that can stand characterful treatment, and the trio of famous virtuosi brings a more individually characterized performance, if one that does not have quite the same unified concentration as the Philips version. Stern, Zukerman and Rose prefer slower tempi for slow movements, and though the recording is rather close, there is good atmosphere and separation, with hushed playing accurately conveyed.

Though well recorded, Rainer Küchl, Josef Staar and Franz Bartolomey (two of whom are members of the Konzertverein or formerly Küchl Quartet) do not offer a strong challenge to the Grumiaux Trio on Philips, except that they do have the advantage of a fill-up, the *Duo in B flat for violin and viola, K.424*. There are many good things in their account of the *Divertimento* and some charm but, by comparison with Grumiaux, they seem hurried, and both in the opening movement and the fourth, they press on too much.

Flute quartets Nos. 1 in D, K.285; 2 in G, K.285a; 3 in C, K.285b; 4 in A, K.298.

*** Ph. 6500 034 [id.]. Bennett, Grumiaux Trio.

There seems general agreement about the merits of the William Bennett–Grumiaux Trio accounts of the *Flute quartets*. They are, to put it in a nutshell, exquisitely played and recorded and are in every way finer than other versions which have appeared and disappeared over the years. The freshness of both playing and recording gives very great pleasure.

(i) *Horn quintet, K.407. A Musical Joke, K.522; Serenade No. 13 in G* (*Eine kleine Nachtmusik*), *K.525.*

(M) ** Ph. 6503/*7303* 066. Berlin PO Octet, (i) with Klier.

A modestly priced and well-recorded set of performances which appeared in various couplings in the late 1960s. The *Horn quintet* is admirably played, and *Eine kleine Nachtmusik* is also given with some spirit and genuine refinement. Good, albeit not outstanding performances, with excellent sound. But the *Musical Joke* needs a more imaginative performance than it receives here, and it rather weakens the attractions of this issue. The tape transfer has been remastered and now sounds fresh, vivid and clean, with the horn well focused in the *Quintet*. There is a degree of edge on the string timbre in the *Night music*.

Piano quartets Nos. 1 in G min., K.478; 2 in E flat, K.493.

*** Decca SXL 6989 [Lon. CS 7220]. Previn, Musikverein Qt.

**(*) DG 2531/*3301* 368 [id.]. Klien, Amadeus Qt.

**(*) RCA [ARL1/*ARK1* 2676]. Rubinstein, Guarneri Qt.

** CBS 60277/*40-* [MS 6683]. Horszowski, Budapest Qt.

Previn's sparkling playing gives these parallel masterpieces – especially the *G minor* – a refreshing spontaneity. Though the tuning of the Musikverein Quartet is not as sweet as that of the Amadeus on DG, this Decca coupling is preferable for the extra vitality.

The DG performances, with a straighter, less individual pianist, are well played and very well recorded (with disc and tape very closely matched). But in sheer electricity the performance of No. 2 markedly outshines that of No. 1, which sounds less spontaneous.

The pity is that Rubinstein's bright and invigorating playing with members of the Guarneri Quartet has its brightness and forwardness exaggerated in the recording. This is not so much a tasteful rendering of two of Mozart's most delectable chamber works as a mercurial re-creation at the hands of a pianist who is nothing if not an individualist. Details matter less than the overall sweep of spontaneous expression. The liveliness of Rubinstein even in his eighties enjoying himself with fellow-musicians is ample reason for hearing this coupling. However, this is a pleasure denied at present to British readers as the record has been withdrawn in the UK.

The Horszowski/Budapest versions are alive and polished, the recording forward but well integrated. The sound is (agreeably) smoother on top on the chrome tape (though side two has added bass resonance). However, there is a lack of a smiling quality to these performances. The musicians convey their respect more readily than a feeling of relaxed enjoyment.

Piano trios Nos. 1 in B flat, K.254; 2 in G, K.496; 3 in B flat, K.502; 4 in E, K.542; 5 in C, K.548; 6 in G, K.564.
(M) ❀ *** Ph. 6768 032/*7650 017* (2). Beaux Arts Trio.

Although these performances were recorded in the late 1960s, they still sound amazingly vivid and wonderfully fresh. Even if there were an alternative version – and at present this is the only contender – the Beaux Arts would be difficult to beat either artistically or in terms of recording. This set sounds exceptionally well in its tape format, which is beautifully transferred, the quality fresh and clear and perfectly balanced.

Piano and wind quintet in E flat, K.452.
*** Decca SXL 6252. Ashkenazy, L. Wind Soloists – BEETHOVEN: *Quintet.****
*** CRD CRD 1067/*CRDC 4067*. Nash Ens. – BEETHOVEN: *Quintet.****
(M) *(*) Ph. 6570/*7310* 881. Haebler, Bamberg Wind Qt – BEETHOVEN: *Quintet.**(*)

Ashkenazy's performance is in a class of its own, polished, urbane, yet marvellously spirited. The balance and sound quality are of the highest rank.

Vital and fresh playing makes the Nash Ensemble's version of the Mozart *Quintet* most desirable. Mozart thought this one of his best works, yet its representation in the catalogue is relatively slender. This version, which offers some good playing from the pianist Ian Brown, does not displace the Ashkenazy account, but it is worthy to stand alongside it. It has the advantage of an excellent cassette transfer, the quality vivid and clear.

Ingrid Haebler is characteristically stylish, but the wind-playing in Bamberg does not take flight, and the performance as a whole is straightforward rather than imaginative. The recording is naturally balanced on both disc and tape.

String quartets and quintets

String quartets Nos. 1–23; Adagio and fugue in C min., K.546; Divertimenti for strings Nos. 1–3, K.136–8.
(M) *** Ph. 6747 097 (9). Italian Qt.

This playing is absolutely first-class, everything perfectly matched, with beautifully homogeneous tone, spontaneous yet polished phrasing, in a recording of considerable naturalness and realism. The set of the six *Haydn Quartets* is outstanding, and the complete set makes an outstanding investment, particularly as it is so competitively priced.

String quartets Nos. 14–19 (Haydn Quartets).
*** CRD CRD 1062-4/*CRDC* 4062-4 [Bach HM 80/2]. Chilingirian Qt.
**(*) DG 2740 249 (3) [id.]. Melos Qt.
*O-L D 220 D 3 (3). Esterházy Qt.

String quartets Nos. 14–23.
(M) ** DG 2720 055 (5) [id.]. Amadeus Qt.

String quartets Nos. 14 in G, K.387; 18 in A, K.464.
(M) *** Ph. 6503/*7303* 067. Italian Qt.

String quartets Nos. 15 in D min., K.421; 19 in C (Dissonance), K.465.
(M) *** Ph. 6570/*7310* 888. Italian Qt.

String quartets Nos. 16 in E flat, K.428; 17 in B flat (Hunt), K.458.
(M) *** Ph. 6570/*7310* 922. Italian Qt.

The set of six quartets dedicated to Haydn contains a high proportion of Mozart's finest works in the genre, music which uncharacteristically he took (for him) a long time to complete, writing without the compulsion of a commission. The Chilingirian Quartet plays with unforced freshness and vitality, avoiding expressive mannerism but always conveying the impression of spontaneity, helped by the warm and vivid recording. International rivals in these works may at times provide more poise and polish but none outshines the Chilingirians in direct conviction, and their matching of tone and intonation is second to none. Unlike most quartets they never sound superficial in the elegant but profound slow movements. The equivalent cassettes are each packaged separately and offer demonstration quality, every bit the equal of the discs in presence and natural clarity.

The recordings by the Italian Quartet date from 1967 and over previous editions have carried an unqualified recommendation as being the finest available. Now reissued on three separate discs, they remain highly competitive at mid-price, even if, in these new pressings, the recording does begin to sound its age, producing a hint of edginess on top, especially on 6570 888 and 6503 067. The excellently transferred cassettes match the discs closely, and in all other respects the sound is still very good, well balanced and refined in detail. The playing is in impeccable style throughout, stylish, unfailingly perceptive and most musical.

Taken by and large the Melos Quartet set offers performances which are soundly conceived and finely executed. There are disappointments, but the playing is unmannered, thoughtful and usually vital, and the recording is first-class. However, this repertoire is dominated by the recordings by the Chilingirians and Italian Quartet, both of which remain preferable.

The DG album offers us the 'Ten Celebrated Quartets'. The Amadeus play with great polish and fluency, though their style in Mozart is not to everyone's taste. But they have a devoted following, and the set can be warmly recommended to their admirers.

The Esterházy use period instruments and impose the restraint of no vibrato. The gain in textural clarity is offset by a loss of warmth and richness of feeling. This is particularly evident in slow movements. The severity of the approach is at first striking but soon appears inhibited and self-conscious, and though the playing itself is of the highest order of accomplishment, it does not bring us close to Mozart, well recorded though it is.

String quartet No. 17 (Hunt), K.458.
(M) *** DG Acc. 2542/*3342* 122 [2543/*3343* 502]. Amadeus Qt – HAYDN: *Quartet No. 77.****
(*) Ph. 9500 662 [id./*7300 762*]. Italian Qt – HAYDN: *Quartet No. 77.**
(*) DG Dig. **410 866-2; 410 866-1/*4* [id.]. Amadeus Qt – HAYDN: *Quartet No. 77.***(*)*

The Amadeus, recorded in the mid-1960s, will have the edge on the Italians for some listeners. Their performance is slightly more characterized, and though there are some touches that will not have universal appeal (in the slow movement, for example, these artists do not always allow the music to speak for itself), it is, generally speaking, a most satisfying version – and well recorded too, on disc and cassette alike.

The Italian Quartet gives a fine and unaffected account of the *Hunt*. Some may feel that it is a shade under-characterized in places, and it is certainly over-priced, even though it is coupled with a modern recording of the *Emperor*. The cassette transfer, made at a high level, is first-class in every way.

In their repeat of a famous coupling, the new Amadeus performance is less attractive than the earlier version from the 1960s. There is a distinct absence of charm. The new compact disc has striking presence, but the quality of the recording is not ideally smooth; it sounds most impressive on the chrome cassette.

String quartets Nos. 19 (Dissonance); 20 in D (Hoffmeister), K.499.
(M) *** Decca Ace SDD 561. Gabrieli Qt.

The Gabrieli Quartet's recording of the *Dissonance* comes from the same label as the version by the Musikverein group (now deleted); and even had an adjacent catalogue number, though it is at least differently coupled. The Gabrielis are also first-class (if not quite as brilliant or as superbly integrated as the Musikverein) and give expressive and eloquent performances of both the *Dissonance* and the *Hoffmeister*. They are a little too robust perhaps in the trio section of K.465 but for the most part their playing is of a high order.

String quartets Nos. 20 (Hoffmeister), K.499; 21 in D, K.575; 22 in B flat, K.589; 23 in F, K.590 (Prussian Nos. 1–3).
(M) *** Ph. 6770 042 (2) [id.]. Italian Qt.

Philips have reissued the Italian Quartet's versions of the last four Mozart quartets as a double-record set at medium price. The performances originally appeared in the early 1970s and were rightly hailed at the time as among the very finest. We still hold the view stated in the first edition of the *Penguin Stereo Record Guide* that in terms of musical distinction these superbly shaped and balanced performances are unlikely to be surpassed for a very long time, and they certainly hold a special place in the Mozart discography. The recordings still sound remarkably lifelike and are in no way inferior to more recent rivals.

String quintets Nos. 1–6.
(M) *** Ph. 6747 107 (3). Grumiaux Trio with Gerecz, Lesueur.
(M) ** DG 2740 122 (3). Amadeus Qt with Aronowitz.

No reservations about the Grumiaux ensemble's survey of the *String quintets*: immensely civilized and admirably conceived readings that moreover have the advantage of refined and truthful recording. Throughout the set the vitality and sensitivity of this team are striking, and in general this eclipses all other recent accounts. The Amadeus is a distinguished team and their set will give pleasure to their admirers. But in terms of both interpretation and recorded sound, the Grumiaux is fresher and purer in utterance.

String quintets Nos. 2 in C min., K. 406; 6 in E flat, K.614.
(M) **(*) Sup. 1111 3159. Smetana Qt with Suk.

The *C Minor*, K.406, is of course an arrangement of the *Serenade for wind octet*, K.388, which Mozart made in 1787 and the *E flat*, K.614, is his last important chamber work, written in the year of his death. The Smetana Quartet and Josef Suk give extremely fine accounts of both works, though they do not quite have the same lightness of touch of the Grumiaux set (see above). They are accorded very realistic sound and the disc, a co-production with Nippon Columbia, Tokyo, can be warmly recommended, though not in preference to Grumiaux.

String quintets Nos. 3; 4 in G min., K.516.
(M) *** Ph. 6570/*7310* 574. Grumiaux Ens.
* O-L DSLO 610. Esterházy Qt with Wim Ten Have.

These performances by the Grumiaux team sweep the board. They have the advantage of first-class recording on both disc and cassette.

The Esterházy play on period intruments and eschew vibrato and other expressive devices. To modern listeners K.515 will sound in B major and K.516 in F sharp minor, which some will find disturbing. The playing is of a high order in terms of intonation and ensemble but the restraints these accomplished players impose on themselves diminish the scale and range of Mozart's world. The slow movements are pale and inhibited. The recording is very good indeed but these performances are not for us.

String quintet No. 4 in G min., K.516.
(M) * Argo ZK/*KZKC* 35. Aeolian Qt (augmented).

A most disappointing performance of Mozart's most famous string quintet. The playing is expressive, with some sensitive detail, but there is a lack of finesse and certainly no hint of magic.

String quintets Nos. 5 in D, K.593; 6 in E flat, K.614.
(M) *** Ph. 6503/*7303* 112. Grumiaux Ens.

A further outstanding issue from the Grumiaux set, given refined sound, on both disc and tape, to match performances of remarkable sensibility. The *E flat Quintet* is especially fine.

Violin sonatas Nos. 17 in C, K.296; 18 in G, K.301; 19 in E flat, K.302; 20 in C, K.303; 22 in A, K.305.
**(*) ASV ALH/*ZCALH* 930. Shumsky, Balsam.

Shumsky and Balsam are recorded in a rather dry acoustic which makes for clarity (and, though dry, the sound is not unpleasing). The performances are eminently vital and articulate, with neat eloquent phrasing from the violinist and neat-fingered piano support. Balsam's playing is stylish if monochrome (he does not offer so wide a range of dynamic gradations as did Lupu or Haskil – both now deleted – and it is his contribution that strikes one as the less imaginative. The balance is good and the cassette transfer is admirably fresh and clear.

Violin sonatas Nos. 18–21, K.301–4.
*** DG Dig. **410 896-2**; 410 896-1/*4* [id.]. Perlman, Barenboim.

Some very distinguished playing here from Perlman and Barenboim, with fine teamwork and alert and vital phrasing. The recording, too, is extremely lifelike on both disc and chrome tape (it will perhaps be too forward for some tastes) but it is amazingly clean and vivid, particularly in its compact-disc form.

Violin sonatas Nos. 25 in F, K.377; 30 in C, K.403; 34 in A, K.526.
** Ph. Dig. 6514 244 [id.]. Lubotsky, Boris Berman.

Boris Berman is an extremely fine player, in his thirties, who – reasonably enough in this repertoire – is billed first on the sleeve and is also given greater prominence by the engineers. These artists do not, incidentally, play the Stadler conclusion of the *Allegretto* movement of the *C major Sonata* but break off after the first twenty bars, where Mozart's autograph ends. The playing is very musical and highly finished but at times a little unsmiling. The Philips recording is first-class as usual in this repertoire.

Piano duets

Adagio and allegro, K.594; Andante and variations, K.501; Fantasia in F min., K.608; Duo-Sonatas: in C, K.19d; in B flat, K.358; in D, K.381; in D, K.448; in F, K.497; in C, K.521.
(M) *** DG 2740 258 (3). Eschenbach, Frantz.

We thought well of these performances when they first appeared and they stand up to the test of time. (They were made between 1972 and 1975.) Eschenbach and Frantz play with exemplary ensemble and fine sensitivity, and though finer performances of individual pieces may have come one's way in the concert hall or the radio, the standard maintained by these artists still remains higher than any of their recent rivals on record. The recordings are clean and well balanced, if occasionally a shade dry.

Andante and variations, K.501.
*** Ph. 9500 434/*7300 644* [id.]. Argerich, Bishop-Kovacevich – BARTÓK: *Sonata*; DEBUSSY: *En blanc et noir.****

The charming *Andante and variations* is here taken at a rather brisker tempo than usual, but the playing of this duo is unfailingly sensitive and vital. The companion works by Bartók and Debussy are unlikely to be surpassed either artistically or as recordings. The cassette does not match the disc in range, though the Mozart suffers less from the low-level transfer than the two couplings.

Solo piano music

Adagio in B min., K.540; Allegro in G min., K.312; Minuet in D, K.355; Sonata in F, K.533/494; Variations on a Dutch song, K.24.
**(*) Mer. E 77023. Ward.

David Ward provides an unusual and attractive collection of pieces, including the

Variations on a Dutch song written when Mozart was a boy of ten. That is one of the shorter pieces on side two. Side one is devoted to the least-heard of the late sonatas, which Ward characteristically plays with fine clarity and directness. If the readings are just a little lacking in character, it is good to hear a pianist distinguishing himself with playing that is so naturally thoughtful and purposeful. The recording is a little light in bass but not inappropriately so.

Fantasias: in C min., K.475; in D. min., K.397; Piano sonatas Nos. 8 in A min., K.310; 11 in A, K.331.
(M) *** DG Priv. 2535/*3335* 168. Kempff.

Kempff's disarming simplicity of style hides great art. This is a wonderful record, in a class of its own and not to be missed on any account. The performance of the mature *Fantasy*, K.475, is surely one of the most beautiful pieces of Mozart-playing on record. The recording is good, and there is an excellent cassette too.

Rondos: in D, K.485; in A min., K.511.
*** None. Dig. H 71377 [id.]. Bilson (fortepiano) – BEETHOVEN: *Sonatas Nos. 13 and 14.****

Malcolm Bilson uses a modern copy of the Walter which Mozart owned. He plays with sensitivity and imagination as well as scholarship. Tastes differ in these matters and some will want the *A minor Rondo* very marginally slower, but few will find much to quarrel with in either piece, and the recording is most lifelike.

Piano sonatas Nos. 1–17; Fantasia in C min., K.475.
(M) *** Decca D 222 D 6 (6). Schiff.

Andras Schiff is a first-class artist whose fingerwork and sense of colour excite admiration. He takes a rather more romantic view of Mozart than Christoph Eschenbach, who was the last to give us a comprehensive survey (on DG), and he is slightly prone to self-indulgence in the handling of some phrases. This is a fine achievement all the same, and splendidly recorded. Taking the excellent sound balance into account, this set can be recommended as probably the most satisfying way of acquiring this repertoire.

Collectors in Scandinavia will need no reminder than Hans Leygraf's cycle on the Swedish Radio label has strong claims too. His account of the *C minor Sonata* and the *Fantasia* (SRLP 1391-92) has real style and distinction; poised, classical and patrician are the adjectives that spring to mind, and the recording is good too.

Piano sonatas Nos. 2 in F, K.280; 3 in B flat, K.281; 9 in D, K.311; 10 in C, K.330.
❀ *** DG 2531/*3301* 052 [id.]. Zimerman.

Marvellous playing. Krystian Zimerman makes no pretence of playing a fortepiano, using a wide range of tonal shading and phrases delicately echoed in the baroque manner. Yet the playing is essentially robust, and the slow movements of K.311 and K.330 are performed with great eloquence, without ever taking the music outside the period of its natural sensibility. The recording is flawless, absolutely natural in balance, and the cassette also offers superbly realistic piano-tone, rich, clear in detail, and perfectly focused.

Piano sonatas Nos. 4 in E flat, K.282; 8 in A min., K.310.
*** Decca SXL 6951 [Lon. CS 7179]. De Larrocha – BEETHOVEN: *Bagatelles.****

Alicia de Larrocha plays the early *E flat Sonata* simply, yet with an attractive balance between warmth and poise. She is at her finest in the A minor work, with its memorable slow movement, which she plays beautifully. The Decca recording is first-class and if the Beethoven coupling is suitable, this can be recommended.

Piano sonatas Nos. 8 in A min., K.310; 17 in D, K.576; Rondo in A min., K.511.
*** Decca SXL 6439 [Lon. CS 6659]. Ashkenazy.

Immaculate playing. Ashkenazy shows his

usual impeccable judgement and taste, and this Mozart recital must be numbered among the finest of his earlier records. The recording is first-class. No serious collector should overlook this release.

Piano sonatas Nos. 11 in A, K.331; 13 in B flat, K.333; Adagio in B min., K.540.
*** Ph. 9500 025 [id.]. Brendel.

Very distinguished playing indeed. One is tempted to suggest that the reader adds this to his collection even at the cost of duplication, so thoughtful and illuminating are Brendel's insights. This will uncover new areas of feeling in these sonatas and (not to be forgotten) the *B minor Adagio*. Superbly realistic piano sound.

Piano sonatas Nos. 13 in B flat, K.333; 14 in C min., K.457; 15 in C, K.545; Fantasia in C min., K.475.
*** Decca SXL 6997 [Lon. CS 7240]. Schiff.

This record affords an opportunity for collectors to sample Schiff's cycle for themselves. He is an imaginative and sensitive player, sometimes prone to caress a phrase rather too lovingly, but this is a fault in the right direction. There is more than an hour's music here and it is beautifully recorded. Particularly impressive are the *C minor Fantasy* and *Sonata*.

VOCAL AND CHORAL MUSIC

Lieder: *Abendempfindung; Als Luise die Briefe ihres Ungetreuen Liebhabers verbrannte; An die Einsamkeit; An die Freundschaft; An die Hoffnung; Dans un bois solitaire; Eine kleine deutsche Kantate; Gesellenreise; Die grossmütige Gelassenheit; Die kleine Spinnerin; Das Lied der Trennung; Oiseaux, si tous les ans; Ridente la calma; Sehnsucht nach dem Frühling; Das Veilchen; Der Zauberer; Die Zufriedenheit.*
(M) *(**) Saga 5441. Gomez, Constable.

Jill Gomez sings a delightful selection of Mozart songs very charmingly, and she is well accompanied by John Constable. On the Saga bargain label, that should be recommendation enough, as the recording is fresh and well balanced. Early pressings of this disc suffered from bad pre-echo. This has now been cured by lowering the level of modulation. However, the *Little German cantata* which closes the recital (and is one of the major pieces) is still cut too high and there is peaking on the voice at fortissimos.

Adoramus te, K.Anh.109/3; Ave verum corpus, K.618; De profundis clamavi, K.93; Ergo, interest, an quis; God is our refuge, K.20; Justum deduxit Dominus, K.93d; Kyrie (for 5 sopranos), *K.73k; Regina coeli, K.74d.*
** Abbey LPB 773. Gomez, St Bartholomew's Ch., Morris; St Bartholomew's Hospital Ch. Soc., Anderson; Sinfonia of St Bartholomew; Brockless (organ).

There are rarities here: the *Regina coeli*, K.108/74d, is one, and quite a number of the others are not available in alternative versions. Jill Gomez sings with her usual accomplishment and warmth, while the forces assembled here produce musical and pleasing results. The sound is acceptable. (The proceeds of the disc go to cancer research.)

Alma Dei creatoris, K.277/272a; Dixit et Magnificat, K.193/186a; Kyrie, K.341; Litaniae Lauretanae de BMV (2 versions, *K.109/74e; K.195/186d*)*; Litaniae de venerabili altaris sacramento* (2 versions, *K.125; K.243*)*; Misericordias Domini, K.222/205a; Regina coeli* (2 versions, *K.127; K.276/321b*)*; Sancta Maria, Mater Dei, K.273; Te Deum, K.141/66b; Venite populi, K.260/248a; Vesperae solennes de Domenica, K.321.*
(M) *** Ph. 6725 015 (4). Soloists, Leipzig R. Ch. and SO, Kegel.

This collection of Mozart's early choral music contains many exhilarating inspirations, even if in many of the works there is little if any evidence of devotional intensity. Mozart always seems to have regarded his religious music as an offshoot of his secular, and one simply has to accept it on that level. The Leipzig Radio Chorus is one of the finest professional choirs in Europe, and here under Kegel with often brisk allegros the electricity of the inspiration is irresistible, though paradoxically the two maturest and most ambitious works here, K.243 and K.321, bring marginally less compelling performances. Excellent recording, bright and atmospheric.

Ave verum corpus, K.618; Exsultate jubilate, K.165; Kyrie in D minor, K.341; Vesperae solennes de confessore in C, K.339.
*** Ph. 6500 271/*7300 173* [id.]. Te Kanawa, Bainbridge, Ryland Davies, Howell, LSO Chorus, LSO, Sir Colin Davis.

This disc could hardly present a more delightful collection of Mozart choral music, ranging from the early soprano cantata *Exsultate jubilate*, with its famous setting of *Alleluia*, to the equally popular *Ave verum*. Kiri Te Kanawa is the brilliant soloist in the cantata, and her radiant account of the lovely *Laudate Dominum* is one of the highspots of the *Solemn vespers*. That work, with its dramatic choruses, is among Mozart's most inspired of his Salzburg period, and here it is given a fine responsive performance. Good, reverberant recording. The cassette transfer is truthful, although the level is low.

Concert arias (complete).
*** DG 2740 281 (5). Popp, Gruberová, Mathis, Sukis, Schwarz, Araiza, Ahnsjö, Berry, Lloyd, Salzburg Moz. O, Hager.

Concert arias for soprano.
*** Decca D 251 D5 (5). Te Kanawa, Gruberová, Laki, Hobarth, Berganza; VCO, György Fischer; or LSO, Pritchard.

On DG, ten generously filled sides contain no fewer than 44 concert arias, ranging from *Va del furor portata*, K.21, written in London in 1765, to *Per questa bella mano*, K.612, of 1791, both for baritone. The chronological arrangement is by far the most convenient for finding items, and the documentation is admirable. The singers make a splendid team, as stylish a group as might be assembled today, and Hager directs pointed accompaniments, lifting rhythms, clarifying textures. He himself plays the piano in Edith Mathis's vehement yet well-controlled account of the most taxing of the arias, *Ch'io mi scordi di te*. Specially beautiful are the contributions of Lucia Popp, but all the singers are in excellent voice. Unlike the rival Decca set – which on ten sides covers only the soprano arias in a less convenient order – this one does not include Mozart's own alternative arias to his operas. Considering the length of sides, the sound is remarkably fine and realistic.

With rich, spacious recording, the Decca set covering Mozart's complete concert arias for soprano provides an attractive alternative to the complete DG set. Each of the five records features a different soprano, which means that the order of items is arbitrary; but, unlike the rival set, this one does include such items as alternative arias for Susanna in Figaro, *Un moto di gioia* (sung by Edita Gruberová) and *Al desio di chi t'adora* (sung by Teresa Berganza). Fischer's conducting is lively and responsive but is sometimes lacking in detail. Berganza's account of *Ch'io mi scordi di te* is taken from much earlier sessions with John Pritchard and the LSO, though that earlier recording hardly lets down the excellent general quality.

Concert arias: *A Berenice . . . Sol nascente, K.70. Andromeda: Ah, lo previdi! . . . Ah, t'invola . . . Deh, non varcar. Artaserse: Oh, temerario Arbace! . . . Per quel paterno amplesso; Per pietà, bell'idol mio. Il burbero di buon core: Chi sa, chi sa, qual sia. Didone abbandonata: Basta vincesti . . . Ah, non lasciarmi, no. Nehmt meinen Dank, ihr holden Gönner, K.383. Olimpiade: Alcandro, lo confesso . . . Non so d'onde viene.*
*** DG 410 961-1/*4* [id.]. Popp, Salzburg Moz. O, Hager.

Lucia Popp's contribution was a highlight of the DG box of concert arias and it makes a splendid separate issue. She is especially impressive in the most ambitious scena, *Ah, lo previdi!* (which is over thirteen minutes long) but perhaps most beautiful of all is *Per pietà, bell'idol mio*. There is a winning combination of charm and lyrical intensity throughout this collection. The recording is excellent with a good tape.

Concert arias: *Ah, lo previdi . . . Ah, t'invola, K.272; Bella mia fiamma . . . Resta oh cara, K.528; Chi sa, K.582; Nehmt meinen Dank, ihr*

holden Gönner, K.383; Non più . . . Non temer, K.490; Oh temerario Arbace! . . . Per quel paterno amplesso, K.79/K.73d; Vado, ma dove, K.583.
*** Decca **411 713-2**; SXL/*KSXC* 6999 [Lon. OS 26661]. Te Kanawa, VCO, György Fischer.

Kiri Te Kanawa's contribution to Decca's set of Mozart's concert arias for soprano makes a beautiful and often brilliant separate issue. Items range from one of the very earliest arias, *Oh temerario Arbace*, already memorably lyrical, to the late *Vado, ma dove*, here sung for its beauty rather than for its drama. Atmospheric, wide-ranging recording. The cassette is lively and wide-ranging too, although there is a touch of edge on the voice.

Concert arias: *Alceste: Popoli di Tessaglia . . . Io non chiedo, eterni Dei. Artaserse: Fra cento affanni. Il curio indiscreto. No, che non sei capace; Vorrei spiegarvi, oh Dio'. Demofoonte: Non curo l'affetto; Ma che vi fece, o stelle . . . Sperai vicino il lido. L'eroe cinese: Ah se in ciel, benigne stelle. Zemira: Mia speranza adorata! . . . Ah non sai qual pena sia.*
*** DG 410 960-1/*4* [id.]. Gruberová, Salzburg Moz. O, Hager.

The extraordinary agility of Edita Gruberová's singing is what impresses the listener most in her disc, taken from the DG box. The half-octave above top C holds no problems for her, and intonation is astonishingly secure under pressure. Her vocal skill is at its most spectacular in *Popoli di Tessaglia!* near the end of side one, but the latter part of the recital also contains much to impress. The music itself gives more opportunity for display than charm, although *Vorrei spiegarvi* (while not less technically demanding) offers an engaging duet with a solo oboe, very nicely brought off. The sound is brilliant, the voice forward; the iron-oxide tape copes with minimal hints of peaking.

Concert arias: *Arsace: Ombra felice! . . . Io ti lascio. Artaserse: Conservati fedele. Demofoonte: Misero me! . . . Misero pargoletto; Se ardire e speranza. Idomeneo: Ch'io mi scordi di te? . . . Non temer, amato bene. Le Nozze di Figaro: Giunse alfin . . . Al desio di chi t'adora.*
*** Decca SXL/*KSXC* 7001. Berganza, VCO, Fischer; LSO, Pritchard; Parsons (piano).

Berganza's contributions to the Decca set of Mozart concert arias make a varied and attractive recital. They cover not just the concert arias for mezzo soprano but the most demanding soprano aria of all, *Ch'io mi scordi di te*, recorded (with Pritchard and the LSO) a decade earlier than the rest. Full, bright recording and an excellent cassette, although the focus of the piano is slightly less sharp than the accompanying orchestra.

Arias: *Artaserse: Per pietà, bell' idol mio. Il barbiere di Siviglia: Schon lacht der holde Frühling. Demofoonte: Se tutti i mali miei. Didone abbandonata: Basta, vincesti . . . Ah non lasciarmi no. Ezio: Misera, dove son! . . . Ah! non son io che parlo. I due baroni di Rocca Azzurra: Alma grande e nobil core. Le Nozze di Dorina: Voi avete un cor fedele. Le Nozze di Figaro: Un moto di gioia. Sismano nel Mogol: Se tutti i mali miei.*
*** Decca SXL/*KSXC* 7000 [Lon. OSA/*5*-26662]. Gruberová, VCO, Fischer.

This is a separate reissue of the second disc of Decca's box of concert arias for soprano, and brings brilliant and charming performances from Gruberová, full of sparkle and character, and superbly articulated. Warm, vivid recording. The cassette transfer is vivid and wide-ranging, but there is a slight edge on the voice at times.

Concert arias: *Al desio di chi t'adora, K.577; Bella mia fiamma, K.528; Ch'io mi scordi di te, K.505; Nehmt meinen Dank, K.383; Non più tutto ascoltai, K.490; Vado, ma dove, K.583; Vorrei spiegarvi, K.418.*
*** RCA Gold GL/*GK* 12124. Price, LPO, Lockhart.

There are not many finer performances of Mozart concert arias than Margaret Price's. This beautiful record confirmed her status as one of the most accomplished of Mozart sopranos today, and though occasionally she squeezes the tone in a way that once regularly marked her singing, this is in general a superb achievement, both tenderly expressive and commandingly brilliant, with splendid attack on top notes. Such a collection of some of the finest of all the soprano concert arias is most welcome. Good, bright recording. The first-class chrome cassette, although not transferred at the highest level, is admirably natural and clear.

Concert arias: *Ah se in ciel, K.538; Mia speranza adorate . . . Ah, non sai, K.416; Nehmt meinen Dank, K.383; No, che non sei capace, K.419; Popoli di Tessaglia! . . . Io non chiedo eterni Dei, K.316/300b; Vado, ma dove, K.583; Vorrei spiegarvi, K.418.*
(M) *** DG Priv. 2535/*3335* 465. Streich, Bav. RSO, Mackerras.

Though her voice is not really large enough for the more dramatic items, Rita Streich gives delightful performances of this attractive collection of Mozart concert arias. The agility in this often florid music is amazing, and though the performances date from 1959 the sound remains relatively fresh. The cassette transfer is disappointing, emphasizing the age of the recording, with a tendency to peakiness in the voice and without lustre in the orchestral accompaniment.

Concert arias: *Alma grande e nobil core, K.578; Ch'io mi scordi di te, K.505; Nehmt meinen Dank, K.383; Vado, ma dove, K.583.*
*** HMV ASD 2493 [Ang. S 36643]. Schwarzkopf, LSO, Szell; Brendel – R. STRAUSS: *Lieder.****

To have an artist as potent as Alfred Brendel doing the piano obbligato in *Ch'io mi scordi di te* may give some idea of the sumptuousness of the presentation of this disc, and it is reflected by superb performances from Schwarzkopf and Szell. Their finesse and refinement are a joy to the ear, and even if some of the florid singing finds Schwarzkopf taxed rather hard (a pity she did not record them at the time when she sang Fiordiligi in *Così fan tutte* so commandingly), the Mozartian stylishness is still as compelling as ever. Fine recording – a lovely coupling for the lusciously beautiful Strauss songs on the reverse.

Litaniae lauretanae in D, K.195; Mass No. 16 in C (Coronation), K.137.
*** Argo ZRG 677. Cotrubas, Watts, Tear, Shirley-Quirk, Schola Cantorum of Oxford, ASMF, Marriner.

This fine coupling of two of Mozart's most appealing early choral works can be strongly recommended. The solo work is outstandingly good (notably the singing of the soprano, Ileana Cotrubas), and the Academy provides the most sensitive, stylish accompaniment, beautifully recorded.

Masonic music: *Masonic funeral music* (*Maurerische Trauermusik*), *K.477; Die ihr des unermesslichen Weltalls Schöpfer ehrt* (cantata), *K.619; Die ihr einen neuem Grade, K.468; Dir, Seele des Weltalls* (cantata), *K.429; Ihr unsere neuen Leiter* (song), *K.484; Lasst uns mit geschlungnen Händen, K.623a; Laut verkünde unsere Freude, K.623; O heiliges Band* (song), *K.148; Sehen, wie dem starren Forscherange, K.471; Zerfliesset heut', geliebte Brüder, K.483.*
(M) *** Decca Ser. SA 25. Krenn, Krause, Edinburgh Fest. Ch., LSO, Kertesz.

This Decca issue contains the more important of Mozart's Masonic music. A fuller selection is available on two Turnabout discs in the USA. However, the Decca recording is beautiful and the performances here are more polished and sophisticated. The highlights are Kertesz's strongly dramatic account of the *Masonic funeral music* and the two lively songs for chorus which begin side two, *Zerfliesset heut'* and *Ihr unsere neuen Leiter*, which are sung with warm humanity. Indeed the choral contribution is most distinguished throughout; the tenor, Werner Krenn, who dominates much of the other music, is lyrical rather than especially robust in manner. Occasionally one feels a sturdier approach would have been more effective.

Mass No. 4 in C min., K.139.
**(*) HM 1C 065 99910. Hennig, Harten, Elwes, Varcoe, Hanover Boys' Ch., Coll. Aur., Hennig.

Mozart was a boy of twelve when he

composed this Mass and conducted its first performance at the official opening of a new church for an orphanage in Vienna in the presence of the Empress. He may well have had the advantage of parental 'guidance' in this piece, for it is of considerable maturity. Unlike the Leipzig performance under Kegel on Philips, this makes use of authentic instruments and boys' voices, and there is spirited playing from the Collegium Aureum directed by Heinz Hennig. Whoever wrote the *Agnus Dei* or, for that matter, the very opening, the music is worth hearing and the performance of both the boys and the English singers is good and the recording warm but unspectacular.

Mass No. 12 in C (Spaur), K.258; Vesperae solennes de confessore, K.339 (see also above).
*** Argo ZRG/*KZRC* 924. Palmer, Cable, Langridge, Roberts, St John's College Ch., Wren O, Guest.

The *Spaur Mass* is not among Mozart's most inspired, but in a vigorous performance like this, with trombones justifiably doubling some of the choral lines, it is most enjoyable. The coupling is a masterpiece, and though this does not always match the version by Sir Colin Davis, for example – Felicity Palmer is a less poised soloist than Kiri Te Kanawa – this has the advantage of authenticity in the use of boys in the chorus. The recording is warmly atmospheric and the cassette transfer first-class, bright and lively with no loss of choral focus; indeed the treble may need a little softening.

Mass No. 16 in C (Coronation), K.317.
(*) DG 2530/*3300* 704 [id.]. Tomowa-Sintow, Baltsa, Krenn, Van Dam, V. Singverein, Berlin PO, Karajan – BRUCKNER: *Te Deum.**

If the Bruckner coupling is attractive, then Karajan's version offers a great deal to enjoy. It is a dramatic reading, lacking something perhaps in rhythmic resilience, but with excellent solo singing as well as a sharply defined contribution from the chorus. There is no lack of strength, and the score's lyrical elements are sensitively managed. Unfortunately the cassette suffers from recession of image in the music's gentler pages and is a trifle fierce otherwise.

Mass No. 18 in C min. (Great), K.427.
*** DG Dig. **400 067-2**; 2532/*3302* 028 [id.]. Hendricks, Perry, Schreier, Luxon, V. Singverein, Berlin PO, Karajan.
*** HMV ASD 2959 [Sera. S/*4XG* 60257]. Cotrubas, Te Kanawa, Krenn, Sotin, Alldis Ch., New Philh. O, Leppard.
** Ph. 9500 680/*7300 775* [id.]. Marshall, Palmer, Rolfe Johnson, Howell, Ch. and ASMF, Marriner.
*(*) Erato STU/*MCE* 71100. Masterson, Baumann, Klietmann, Brodard, Lisbon, Gulbenkian Foundation Ch. and O, Corbóz.

Karajan gives Handelian splendour to this greatest of Mozart's choral works, and though the scale is large, the beauty and intensity are hard to resist, for this, unlike much of Karajan's Mozart, is strongly rhythmic, not smoothed over. Solo singing is first-rate, particularly that of Barbara Hendricks, the dreamy beauty of her voice ravishingly caught. Though woodwind is rather backward, the sound is both rich and vivid, and the compact disc is even more impressively realistic, though, as the opening shows, the internal balance is not always completely consistent. On CD the thirteen movements are all separately banded. The chrome tape is of good quality but not as clear in detail as some of DG's digital issues, though side two is slightly sharper in focus than side one.

Raymond Leppard uses the Robbins Landon edition, rejecting the accretions which were formerly used to turn this incomplete torso of a work into a full setting of the liturgy. He uses a modest-sized professional choir and his manner is relatively affectionate, which many will prefer, even in this dark work. The sopranos are the light-givers here, and the partnership of Ileana Cotrubas and Kiri Te Kanawa is radiantly beautiful. Fine, atmospheric recording, more naturally balanced than Karajan's digital version.

Neville Marriner secures a good response from his artists, though this performance falls short of being really inspired. Marriner's is a well-thought-out and conscientious reading, and there is some fine singing. His account does not quite communicate the sense of stature this music calls for, but he is not helped by less than transparent recorded sound on disc and tape alike. A serviceable rather than distinguished issue, then, which does not challenge existing recommendations.

There is some good singing in the Lisbon performance directed by Michel Corbóz, particularly from the two sopranos, and the overall conception is sound in every way. But the gramophone is a cruel taskmaster and good though this might seem at a public performance, it falls short of those qualities that would compel one to return to it time and again. The recording is serviceable but not distinguished. Again no challenge to either the Karajan or Leppard versions.

Requiem mass (*No. 19*) *in D min., K.626.*

*** Ph. Dig. **411 420-2**; 6514/*7337* 320 [id.]. Margaret Price, Schmidt, Araiza, Adam, Leipzig R. Ch., Dresden State O, Schreier.

*** DG 2530/*3300* 705 [id.]. Tomowa-Sintow, Baltsa, Krenn, Van Dam, V. Singverein, Berlin PO, Karajan.

(B) **(*) CfP CFP/*TC-CFP* 4399. Mathis, Bumbry, Shirley, Rintzler, New Philh. Ch. and O, Frühbeck de Burgos.

**(*) HMV ASD/*TC-ASD* 3723 [Ang. SZ 37600]. Donath, Ludwig, Tear, Lloyd, Philh. Ch. and O, Giulini.

(M) **(*) Ph. Seq. 6527/*7311* 152. Donath, Minton, Ryland Davies, Nienstedt, Alldis Ch., BBC SO, Sir Colin Davis.

(M) **(*) Decca SPA/*KCSP* 476. Ameling, Horne, Benelli, Franc, V. State Op. Ch., VPO, Kertesz.

** Argo ZRG/*KZRC* 876 [id.]. Cotrubas, Watts, Tear, Shirley-Quirk, Ch. and ASMF, Marriner.

(M) ** DG Priv. 2535/*3335* 257. Lipp, Rössl-Majdan, Dermota, Berry, V. Singverein, Berlin PO, Karajan.

*(*) Tel. Dig. **ZK8**; AZ6/*CX4* 42756 [642756]. Yakar, Wenkel, Equiluz, Holl, V. State Op. Ch., VCM, Harnoncourt.

Peter Schreier's is a forthright reading of Mozart's valedictory choral work, bringing strong dramatic contrasts and marked by superb choral singing and a consistently elegant and finely balanced accompaniment. The recording is exceptionally well balanced and the orchestral detail emerges with natural clarity. The singing of Margaret Price in the soprano part is finer than any yet heard on record, and the others make a first-rate team, if individually more variable. Only in the *Kyrie* and the final *Cum sanctis tuis* does the German habit of using the intrusive aitch intrude. Altogether this is the most satisfying version currently available. It sounds well on the chrome tape too (where the focus does not cloud), but best of all on the compact disc where the refinement of detail is even more striking.

Unlike his earlier recording (now available on Privilege), Karajan's 1976 version is outstandingly fine, deeply committed. The toughness of Karajan's approach is established from the start with incisive playing and clean-focused singing from the chorus, not too large and set a little behind. The fine quartet of soloists too is beautifully blended, and through everything – whatever the creative source, Süssmayr or Mozart – the conductor superbly establishes a sense of unity. The reading has its moments of romantic expressiveness, but nothing is smoothed over, and with superbly vivid recording such a passage as the *Dies irae* has exceptional freshness and intensity. The cassette generally matches the spaciousness of the disc, although the choral quality is marginally less refined.

The glory of Frühbeck's HMV reissue is the singing of the New Philharmonia Chorus, and with the choral music very much the centre of interest, that gives it an edge over Sir Colin Davis's version on Philips. This is unashamedly big-scale Mozart, and that is perhaps apt for a work that has less need for apology than was once thought. (Research suggests that Süssmayr's contribution was smaller than was once believed, and certainly the aesthetic test is clear: very little indeed falls below what one would expect of a Mozart masterpiece, and much is of supreme greatness.) Frühbeck does not have a very subtle Mozart style, and on detail some of his rivals outshine him; for instance, Davis's *Recordare* is much more relaxed and refined. But as an interpretation it stands well in the middle of the road, not too romantic, not too frigidly classic, and quite apart from the choral singing – recorded with beautiful balance and richness – the soloists are all first-rate. The cassette transfer does not give the chorus as much bite as on disc, but otherwise it is effective in capturing the spaciousness and immediacy of the disc.

Giulini directs a large-scale performance which brings out both Mozartian lyricism and Mozartian drama, and anyone who fancies what by today's standards is an unauthentic approach may consider this version. The choir is in excellent incisive form, and the soloists are a first-rate quartet. As one would expect, what Giulini's insight conveys is the rapt quality of such passages as the end of the *Tuba mirum* and the *Benedictus*. The recording is warm rather than brilliant; the cassette is well balanced but slightly opaque.

Davis with a smaller choir gives a more intimate performance than is common, and with his natural sense of style he finds much beauty of detail. In principle the performance should have given the sort of 'new look' to the Mozart *Requiem* that was such a striking success in Handel's *Messiah*, but Davis does not provide the same sort of 'bite' that in performances on this scale should compensate for sheer massiveness of tone. The BBC Symphony Orchestra is in good form and the soloists – although varying in quality – keep up a laudably high standard. Anyone wanting a version on this authentic scale need not hesitate, but this is plainly not the definitive version. The recording is good but neither as sweet nor as crystal-clear as it might be. The tape transfer is well made, the choral sound lacking crispness but with a natural overall balance.

Kertesz takes a large-scale view of Mozart's last work, but unfortunately he cannot rely on a really first-rate chorus. Much of the choral singing here is rather wild and smudgy, enthusiastic but not stylish enough for Mozart, and the impression is made worse by the forward balance of the singers against the orchestra. Kertesz goes further than usual towards a romantic view of the work, and though the recording has the usual Decca brilliance, it does not quite match that of Karajan's DG disc. The cassette transfer, however, is admirably clear and crisp.

Marriner, who can usually be relied on to produce vigorous and sympathetic performances on record, generates less electricity than usual in the *Requiem*. It is interesting to have a version which uses the Beyer Edition and a text which aims at removing the faults of Süssmayr's completion, amending points in the harmony and instrumentation; but few will register any significant differences except in such points as the extension of the *Osanna*. Solo singing is good, but the chorus could be more alert. Excellent, atmospheric recording and a first-class cassette transfer, the chorus sounding clean and incisive.

Karajan's earlier, 1962 reading, now reissued on Privilege, took a suave view of the work. The chief objection to this version is that detail tends to be sacrificed in favour of warmth and atmosphere. The solo quartet are wonderfully blended, a rare occurrence in this work above all, and though the chorus lacks firmness of line they are helped out by the spirited playing of the Berlin Philharmonic. The sound is good on disc, acceptable on cassette. But Karajan's newer full-priced version is well worth the extra cost.

Harnoncourt's distinctive view of Mozart – heavier than you would expect from one so wedded to authenticity – is here negated by the washiness of the recording of voices. The chorus might have been performing in a swimming bath, and though ambience adds some glamour to the solo voices, a good team, it is disconcertingly inconsistent to have an orchestra of original instruments in all its clarity set against vocal sound so vague. Disc and chrome tape are much the same. The compact disc only serves to emphasize the flabbiness of the choral focus.

Thamos, King of Egypt (incidental music), *K.345*.

**(*) DG 2537 060 [id.]. Latschbacher, Kania, Salamonsberger, Holl, Salz. Chamber Ch., Mozarteum O, Hager.

(*) Tel. Dig. **ZK 8; AZ6/*CX4* 42702 [642702]. Perry, Mühle, Van Alterna, Thomaschke, Van der Kemp, Netherlands Chamber Ch., Concg. O, Harnoncourt.

Hager's enjoyable series of Mozart recordings provides a generally well-sung and well-played account of Mozart's inspired incidental music to Tobias Gebler's heroic drama, much of it looking forward to *Zauberflöte*. Though the result is less vigorous than the rival disc from Harnoncourt, solo singing is generally preferable and the recording on a more apt, less expansive scale.

Harnoncourt directs a spirited account of the *Thamos* incidental music, now thought to date from rather later than originally estimated and here made to seem strong and mature in incisive, sharply articulated performances. Playing is excellent, and though chorus and soloists are rather backwardly placed in a reverberant acoustic, the singing is enjoyable too. The chrome cassette is admirably clear in focus but rather dry.

OPERA

Apollo et Hyacinthus (complete).

*** DG 2707 129 (2) [id.]. Mathis, Wulkopf, Auger, Schwarz, Salz. Chamber Ch., Mozarteum O, Hager.

This school opera was written when Mozart was eleven, with all but two of the parts taken by schoolchildren. The style of the writing and vocalization is rather simpler than in other dramatic works of the boy Mozart, but the inspiration is still remarkable, astonishingly mature. Specially delightful is the eighth of the nine numbers, a duet between the heroine, Melia, and her father after her brother, Hyacinthus, has died. The accompaniment of muted violins with pizzicato second violins and bass with divided violas is magical. The performance here is stylish and very well sung though, as so often in early Mozart, recitatives seem far too long. Excellent, clear and well-balanced recording.

La Clemenza di Tito (complete).

*** Ph. 6703 079/*7699 038* (3) [id.]. Baker, Minton, Burrows, Von Stade, Popp, Lloyd, ROHCG Ch. and O, Sir Colin Davis.

It was a revelation, even to dedicated Mozartians, to find in the 1970s Covent Garden production that *La Clemenza di Tito* had so much to offer. Sir Colin Davis's superb set, among the finest of his many Mozart recordings, sums up the achievement of the stage production and adds still more, for, above all, the performance of Dame Janet Baker in the key role of Vitellia has deepened and intensified. Not only is her singing formidably brilliant, with every roulade and exposed leap flawlessly attacked; she actually makes one believe in the emotional development of an impossible character, one who develops from villainy to virtue with the scantiest preparation. Whereas earlier Dame Janet found the evil hard to convey on stage, here the venom as well as the transformation are commandingly convincing. The two other mezzo-sopranos, Minton as Sesto and Von Stade in the small role of Annio, are superb too, while Stuart Burrows has rarely if ever sung so stylishly on a recording as here; he makes the forgiving emperor a rounded and sympathetic character, not just a bore. The recitatives add to the compulsion of the drama – here they are far more than mere formal links – while Davis's swaggering manner in the pageant music heightens the genuine feeling conveyed in much of the rest, transforming what used to be dismissed as a dry *opera seria*. Excellent recording, which loses a little in brightness and immediacy in cassette form because of the relatively low level of the Philips transfer.

Così fan tutte (complete).

(M) ❀ *** HMV SLS/*TC-SLS* 5028 (3/*2*) [Ang. S 3631]. Schwarzkopf, Ludwig, Steffek, Kraus, Taddei, Berry, Philh. Ch. and O, Boehm.

(M) (***) HMV mono RLS/*TC-RLS* 7709 (3/*2*). Schwarzkopf, Otto, Merriman, Simoneau, Panerai, Bruscantini, Philh. Ch. and O, Karajan.

*** Ph. 6707 025/*7699 055* (4/*2*) [id.]. Caballé, Baker, Cotrubas, Gedda, Ganzarolli, Van Allan, ROHCG Ch. and O, Sir Colin Davis.

*** HMV Dig. SLS/*TC-SLS* 143516-3/*5* (3) [Ang. DSCX/*4X3X* 3940]. Marshall, Battle, Baltsa, Araiza, Morris, Van Dam, V. State Op. Ch., VPO, Muti.

**(*) Erato STU 71110 (3). Te Kanawa, Stratas, Von Stade, Rendall, Huttenlocher, Bastin, Strasbourg PO, Lombard.

** DG 2740 206/*3371 019* (3) [id.]. Janowitz,

Fassbaender, Schreier, Prey, Panerai, V. State Op. Ch., VPO, Boehm.
*(*) Decca D 56 D 4 (4) [Lon. OSA 1442]. Lorengar, Berganza, Berbié, Ryland Davies, Krause, Bacquier, ROHCG Ch., LPO, Solti.

Unlike Davis's set (and for that matter Solti's) Boehm's HMV presents a discreetly tailored text, with cuts in the long recitatives and two brief cuts in the finales. But once that is said (and there is a case for not regarding it as a disadvantage), there is everything in favour of this classic set, which presents Boehm at his most genially perceptive and with glorious solo singing, headed by the incomparable Fiordiligi of Schwarzkopf and the equally moving Dorabella of Ludwig. With sound that remains sparklingly atmospheric, vividly creating the illusion of a stage performance and production that remains a superb memento of Walter Legge's artistic finesse, it would stand any comparison at full price. In this reissue it offers a bargain without parallel. Listen to Schwarzkopf's commanding account of *Come scoglio*, more perfect in detail than any since, and you are not likely to hesitate. The cassette transfer is generally good, but it fails to cope with the recording's extremes of dynamic securely: the distant effects are too distant and there is some peaking in the voices at fortissimos. The layout on two tapes is ideal.

Karajan's Philharmonia recording of *Così* from the mid-1950s is a classic, arguably his finest ever Mozart recording. Though the mono sound is limited, the brilliance and sparkle of the performance are irresistible with ensembles given a precision never surpassed, and with ravishingly beautiful singing from Schwarzkopf and Nan Merriman, not least in the heavenly account of their little trio with Alfonso, *O soave sia il vento*, with Bruscantini in his prime. The men too are admirable, with Simoneau sweeter-toned than any direct rival. Like the Boehm set (and the Davis) the tape layout with one Act complete on each of four sides is preferable to the discs. The transfer is fresh and clear, if at rather a low level.

Colin Davis has rarely if ever made a more captivating record than his magical set of *Così fan tutte*. His energy and sparkle are here set against inspired and characterful singing from the three women soloists, with Montserrat Caballé and Janet Baker proving a winning partnership, each one challenging and abetting the other all the time. Cotrubas equally is a vivid Despina, never merely arch. The men too make a strong team. Though Gedda has moments of rough tone, his account of *Un aura amorosa* is honeyed and delicate, and though Ganzarolli falls short in one of his prominent arias, it is a spirited, incisive performance, while Richard van Allan here naturally assumes the status of an international recording artist with flair and imagination. Sparkling recitative (complete) and recording which has you riveted by the play of the action. The transfer to tape sometimes has a distinctly edgy quality (noticeable on the male voices immediately after the overture). The female voices are less affected by this, and with a treble cut the sound can be smoothed. But although it has good presence the recording (on tape) has not as much body as the EMI Boehm set.

Muti's recording of *Così fan tutte* was planned and executed by EMI producers and engineers in an incredibly short time, when in the summer of 1982 it was decided at a few days' notice to take advantage of the success of the Salzburg Festival production. It was possible to record only three of the live performances, and one of those had a different tenor. When Michael Hampe's production was elaborate, with plenty of stage movement, the job of the engineers was formidable, and in effect the third of three performances was the one which provided almost all the finished recording.

The result is vivid, vigorous and often very beautiful. Ensemble is not always flawless, but this is far more polished than Boehm's eightieth-birthday performance, also recorded live (for DG) at the Kleines Festspielhaus. Muti's vigour is infectiously captured, and also his ability to relax into necessary tenderness. Though purists will prefer the extra precision of a studio performance – Boehm's Philharmonia set or Karajan's stand out – this newer EMI version with its vividly if oddly balanced digital sound gives an irresistible flavour of the theatre and the sparkle of Mozartian comedy.

Margaret Marshall, formidable in *Come scoglio*, sounds sweeter here than she did in the theatre, and Agnes Baltsa is a superb Dorabella. Francisco Araiza has few rivals today as Ferrando, though the tone is sometimes dry, while José van Dam is an incisive Alfonso, younger-sounding than usual. Kathleen Battle is an engaging Despina, James Morris a stylish if rather gruff-sounding Guglielmo. The cassettes are disappointing. The layout is on six instead of the more usual four sides, and while the sound is pleasing it lacks the range and immediacy of the discs, and there is little sense of the sharp clarity of detail one expects from a digital source, although the voices are natural and have plenty of bloom. The libretto is clearly printed in bold type.

Alain Lombard's sextet of young soloists together make up a team that rivals almost any. Outstanding is Kiri Te Kanawa, rich and creamy of tone, commanding in *Come scoglio* and tenderly affecting in *Per pietà*. Frederica von Stade's Dorabella is almost as distinguished, with fine detail and imaginative phrasing. David Rendall is a fresh-toned tenor, and the others too give firm, clean performances. Lombard is not the most perceptive of Mozartians, and some of the tempi are on the slow side; but for any who follow the singers in question this set is very desirable indeed, and it is well recorded.

Boehm's third recording makes a delightful memento. It was recorded live during the Salzburg Festival performance on the conductor's eightieth birthday, and though the zest and sparkle of the occasion come over delightfully, with as splendid a cast as you could gather, the ensemble is not quite crisp enough to sustain repeated listening. Quite apart from occasional mishaps (remarkably few) the balance favours the voices, with stage noises made the more prominent. There is certainly a place for this set, but hardly in competition with Boehm's glorious HMV version. The DG cassette transfer is lively, with good presence.

Solti's set will please those who want high voltage at all costs even in this most genial of Mozartian comedies. There is little relaxation and little charm, which underlines the shortcomings of the singing cast, notably of Pilar Lorengar, whose grainy voice is not well treated by the microphone, and who here in places conveys uncertainty. It is a pity that the crackling wit of Solti's Covent Garden performances was not more magically captured on record. Brilliant recording.

Così fan tutte: highlights.

(M) *** HMV SXLP/*TC-SXLP* 30457 [Ang. S 36167]. (from above set, cond. Boehm).

It is impossible to assemble on a single disc or cassette all the many delectable highlights of the Boehm recording of *Così*, and it seems almost perverse to recommend the HMV selection (even though it contains much to give great pleasure) when the complete set is so reasonably priced. However, the sound certainly maintains the quality of the original, and the cassette transfer is crisp and clean.

Don Giovanni (complete).

❀ *** HMV SLS/*TC-SLS* 5083 (3/*2*) [Ang. S 3605]. Waechter, Schwarzkopf, Sutherland, Sciutti, Alva, Taddei, Philh. Ch. and O, Giulini.

*** Ph. 6707 022/*7699 054* (4/*2*) [id.]. Wixell, Arroyo, Te Kanawa, Freni, Burrows, Ganzarolli, ROHCG Ch. and O, Sir Colin Davis.

(M) *** Decca Ace GOS 604/6 [Lon. OSA 1401]. Siepi, Gueden, Della Casa, Danco, Dermota, Corena, V. State Op. Ch., VPO, Krips.

**(*) CBS 79321/*40-* (3) [M3 35192]. Raimondi, Moser, Te Kanawa, Berganza, Riegel, Van Dam, Paris Op. Ch. and O, Maazel.

(M) **(*) HMV SLS 143462-3/*9* (3/*2*). Ghiaurov, Watson, Freni, Ludwig, Gedda, Berry, New Philh. Ch. and O, Klemperer.

** Decca D 162 D 4/*K 162 K 42* (4/*2*) [Lon. OSA/*5-* 1444]. Weikl, Sass, Price, Popp, Bacquier, Burrows, Moll, LPO and Ch., Solti.

(M) * Sup. 1116 2531/3. Zitek, Děpoltová, Hajóssyová, Jonášová, Kocián, Berman, Prague CO and Ch., Pešek.

The return of the classic Giulini HMV set to the catalogue brought out vividly just what had been lacking in rival versions. Not only is the singing cast more consistent than any other; the direction of Giulini and the playing of the vintage Philharmonia Orchestra give this performance an athletic vigour which carries all before it. The whole production owes much to the work of Walter Legge, uncredited in the original issue but the prime mover behind this and so many other Philharmonia issues. Legge's wife, Elisabeth Schwarzkopf, as Elvira, emerges as a dominant figure to give a distinctive but totally apt slant to this endlessly invigorating drama. No wilting sufferer this, but the most formidable of women, who flies at the Don with such cries as *Perfido mostro!* unforgettably sung. The young Sutherland may be relatively reticent as Anna, but with such technical ease and consistent beauty of tone, she makes a superb foil. Taddei is a delightful Leporello, and each member of the cast – including the young Cappuccilli as Masetto – combines fine singing with keen dramatic sense. Recitatives are scintillating, and only the occasional exaggerated snarl from the Don of Eberhard Waechter mars the superb vocal standards. Even that goes well with his fresh and youthful portrait of the central character. The reissue sounds excellent, bright and well balanced, and the cassette transfer is generally very successful and ideally laid out on two tapes.

The final test of a recording of this most searching of operas is whether it adds up to more than the sum of its parts. Colin Davis's certainly does, with a singing cast that has fewer shortcomings than almost any other on disc and much positive strength. For once one can listen untroubled by vocal blemishes. Martina Arroyo controls her massive dramatic voice more completely than one would think possible, and she is strongly and imaginatively contrasted with the sweetly expressive Elvira of Kiri Te Kanawa and the sparkling Zerlina of Freni. As in the Davis *Figaro*, Ingvar Wixell and Wladimiro Ganzarolli make a formidable master/servant team with excellent vocal acting, while Stuart Burrows sings gloriously as Don Ottavio, and Richard van Allan is a characterful Masetto. Davis draws a fresh and immediate performance from his team, riveting from beginning to end, and the recording, though not as clear as it might be, is refined in the recognizable Philips manner. The cassette transfer is not always as sharply focused as is desirable, and sometimes lacks the last degree of body and richness. However, the level is quite high, and there is no lack of presence and atmosphere. The opera is well laid out on two cassettes with one Act complete on each, but the libretto offers extremely fine print that will seem elusive to all but the youngest eyes.

Krips's recording of this most challenging opera has kept its place as a mid-priced version which is consistently satisfying, with a cast of all-round quality headed by the dark-toned Don of Cesare Siepi. The women are not ideal, but they form an excellent team, never overfaced by the music, generally characterful, and with timbres well contrasted. To balance Siepi's darkness, the Leporello of Corena is even more saturnine, and their dramatic teamwork is brought to a superb climax in the final scene – quite the finest spine-tingling performance of that scene ever recorded. The 1955 recording – genuine stereo – still sounds remarkably well.

Whatever the inhibitions and influences of preparing his CBS recording as a soundtrack for the Losey film of *Don Giovanni*, Lorin Maazel directs a strong and urgent performance, generally very well sung. An obvious strength is the line-up of three unusually firm-toned basses: José van Dam a saturnine Leporello, not comic but with much finely detailed expression; Malcolm King a darkly intense Masetto, and Ruggero Raimondi a heroic Giovanni, not always attacking notes cleanly but on balance one of the very finest on record in this role. Among the women Kiri Te Kanawa is outstanding, a radiant Elvira; Teresa Berganza as a mezzo Zerlina generally copes well with the high tessitura; and though Edda Moser starts with some fearsome squawks at her first entry, the dramatic scale is certainly impressive and she rises to the challenge of the big arias. Unfortunately the recording, made in a Paris church, has the voices close against background reverberation. Considering this, the cassettes are well enough focused, although on tape the orchestral sound is thin in the overture.

The lumbering tempo of Leporello's opening music will alert the listener to the predictable Klemperer approach, and some may at that point dismiss his performance as 'too heavy'; but the issue is far more complex than that. Most of the slow tempi which Klemperer regularly adopts, far from flagging, add a welcome spaciousness to the music, for they must be set against the unusually brisk and dramatic interpretation of the recitatives between numbers. Added to that, Ghiaurov as the Don and Berry as Leporello make a marvellously characterful pair. If the glory of Giulini's Philharmonia performance is the dominance of the female cast – originally planned for Klemperer to conduct – this one restores the balance to the men, and with Klemperer's help they make the dramatic experience a strong masculine one. Nor is the ironic humour forgotten with Berry and Ghiaurov about, and the Klemperer spaciousness allows them extra time for pointing. Among the women Ludwig is a strong and convincing Elvira, Freni a sweet-toned but rather unsmiling Zerlina; only Claire Watson seriously disappoints, with obvious nervousness marring the big climax of *Non mi dir*. It is a serious blemish, but with the usual reservations, for those not allergic to the Klemperer approach, this stands as a good recommendation – at the very least a commanding experience. There is a generally excellent tape transfer (properly tailored to fit a pair of cassettes), with sound full and vivid, the upper range both lively and refined, and only an occasional hint of peaking on vocal fortissimos.

Solti directs a crisp, incisive performance, with generally fast tempi and very well-directed recitatives. If it shows no special signs of affection, it contains one glorious performance in Margaret Price's Anna, pure in tone and line but powerfully dramatic too, always beautiful. Next to her Sylvia Sass as a somewhat gusty Elvira sounds rather miscast, characterful as her singing is. The two baritones, Bernd Weikl and Gabriel Bacquier, are clearly contrasted as Giovanni and Leporello respectively, though the microphone is not kind to either. The recording is brilliant in its realistic clarity on disc and tape alike (the pair of cassettes offer the ideal presentation).

It is good to find Czech Supraphon undertaking a major Mozart opera recording, for aptly enough this Prague performance uses the original Prague version of the score with fine playing from the Prague Chamber Orchestra. Sadly not one of the soloists is up to international standards. Not only do Slavonic wobbles predominate, the sense of style is uncertain and characterization and production weak. The recording is nicely atmospheric.

Don Giovanni: highlights.
*** CBS 73888/*40*- [Col. M/*MT* 35859]. (from above set, cond. Maazel).
(M) *** HMV SXLP/*TC-SXLP* 30300 [Ang. S 35642]. (from above set, cond. Giulini).

The CBS highlights disc from the Maazel version, containing an hour of music, presents a far more coherent idea of the opera's shape than any other, completing each side with a substantial slice of each finale. Choice of individual items is very good, though many will regret that Kiri Te Kanawa has – apart from her contribution to the finales – only one of her arias, *Mi tradi*. As in the complete set the recording is flawed, because of an over-reverberant acoustic, but again the cassette is well balanced (there is a slight lack of upper range, but it is not too serious); and undoubtedly this issue matches value with genuine enjoyment.

On performance grounds alone, although it is much less generous in content, first choice would be the mid-price HMV issue, which makes an excellent sampler of the outstanding set under Giulini. Not surprisingly it concentrates on Sutherland as Anna and Schwarzkopf as Elvira, and the Don and Leporello get rather short measure. But Sciutti's charming Zerlina is also given fair due, and with the recording sounding well, it can be recommended to those who already own a different complete set. The sound is excellent on disc and cassette alike.

Arrangements for wind: *Don Giovanni: Overture* and excerpts (arr. Triebensee).
**(*) Chan. ABR/*ABT* 1015. Athena Ens.

The Athena Ensemble give a thoroughly delightful account of the *Don Giovanni* arrangements, with plenty of spirit and no want of sensitivity. They are crisply and brightly recorded, just a shade too close for some tastes, with the result that the odd click of a key mechanism can be heard.

Die Entführung aus dem Serail (complete).
*** DG 2740 203 (3) [2709 051]. Auger, Grist, Schreier, Neukirch, Moll, Leipzig R. Ch., Dresden State O, Boehm – *Der Schauspieldirektor*.***
** Ph. 6769 026/*7699 111* [id.]. Eda-Pierre, Burrowes, Burrows, Tear, Lloyd, Jurgens, Alldis Ch., ASMF, Sir Colin Davis.

Boehm's is a delectable performance, superbly cast and warmly recorded, providing at last an adequate successor to the inspired but flawed Beecham version (now deleted). Arleen Auger proves the most accomplished singer on record of the role of Constanze, girlish and fresh, yet rich, tender and dramatic by turns, with brilliant, almost flawless coloratura. The others too are outstandingly good, notably Kurt Moll whose powerful, finely focused bass makes him a superb Osmin, one who relishes the comedy too. Boehm with East German forces finds a natural, unforced Mozartian expression which carries the listener along in glowing ease. Good if rather reverberant recording.

Sir Colin Davis, using a smaller orchestra, the St Martin's Academy, than he usually has in his Mozart opera recordings, produces a fresh and direct account, well but not outstandingly sung. There are no performances here which have one remembering individuality of phrase, and even so characterful a singer as Robert Tear does not sound quite mellifluous enough in the role of Pedrillo, while Robert Lloyd as Osmin is outshone by a number of his rivals, especially the incomparable Gottlob Frick in the deleted Beecham set. Crisp as the ensembles are, Davis's reading rather lacks the lightness and sparkle, the feeling of comedy before our eyes, which makes the Boehm version on DG such a delight from beginning to end. The Philips set justifies its three discs by including five alternative arias and duets. The recording is clear and refined on disc, but the low-level tape transfer robs the orchestra of transient crispness (as can be heard immediately in the Turkish music of the overture). The solo voices are naturally caught.

Idomeneo (complete).
*** DG 2740 19/*3371 043* (4/*3*) [id.]. Ochman, Mathis, Schreier, Varady, Winkler, Leipzig R. Ch., Dresden State O, Boehm.
**(*) Tel. GX 6/*MU4* 35547 (3) [id.]. Hollweg, Schmidt, Yakar, Palmer, Zürich Op. O, Harnoncourt.

Textually Karl Boehm's version of *Idomeneo* gives grounds for regrets. The score is snipped about in the interests of a staged production, and, like previous recordings, it opts for a tenor in the role of Idamante. But once that is said, this is an enormously successful and richly enjoyable set, completing Boehm's incomparable series of Mozart's operatic masterpieces with a version of this *opera seria* which as a dramatic experience outshines all previous ones. Boehm's conducting is a delight, often spacious but never heavy in the wrong way, with lightened textures and sprung rhythms which have one relishing Mozartian felicities as never before. Even where the tempi are unconventional, as in the hectic speed for the final chorus, Boehm conveys fresh delight, and his singing cast is generally the best ever recorded. As Idomeneo, Wieslaw Ochman, with tenor tone often too tight, is a relatively dull dog, but the other principals are generally excellent. Peter Schreier as Idamante too might have sounded more consistently sweet, but the imagination is irresistible. Edith Mathis is at her most beguiling as Ilia, but it is Julia Varady as Elettra who gives the most compelling performance of all, sharply incisive in her dramatic outbursts but at the same time precise and pure-toned, a Mozartian stylist through and through. Hermann Winkler as Arbace is squarely Germanic, and it is a pity that the secco recitatives are heavily done; but whatever incidental reservations have to be made this is a superbly compelling set which leaves one in no doubt of the work's status as a masterpiece. The recording is first-class on disc and cassette alike.

Using a text very close to that of the Munich première of Mozart's great *opera seria*, and with the role of Idamante given to a soprano instead of being transposed down to tenor register, Harnoncourt presents a distinctive and refreshing view, one which in principle is preferable to general modern practice. The vocal cast is good, with Hollweg a clear-toned, strong Idomeneo, and no weak link. Felicity

Palmer finds the necessary contrasts of expression as Elettra. Exaggerated by aggressive digital recording (though the chrome cassettes, without loss of range and presence, are smoother than the discs), the voices are sometimes given an unpleasant edge, and the sharp articulation of the recitatives is initially disconcerting. It is surprising that in an account which aims at authenticity appoggiature are so rarely used. This is hardly a performance to warm to, but it is refreshing and alive.

Le Nozze di Figaro (complete).

*** Decca Dig. **410 150-2**; D267 D4/*K267 K42* (4/2) [Lon. LDR/5- 74001]. Te Kanawa, Popp, Von Stade, Ramey, Allen, Moll, LPO and Ch., Solti.

(M) *** HMV SLS/*TC-SLS* 5152 (3/2) [Ang. S 3608]. Schwarzkopf, Moffo, Cossotto, Taddei, Waechter, Philh. Ch. and O, Giulini.

*** Ph. 6707 014/*7699 053* (4/2) [id.]. Freni, Norman, Minton, Ganzarolli, Wixell, Grant, Tear, BBC Ch. and SO, Sir Colin Davis.

*** DG 2740 204/*3371 005* [2711 007/id.]. Janowitz, Mathis, Troyanos, Fischer-Dieskau, Prey, Lagger, German Op. Ch. and O, Boehm.

(M) *** Decca Ace GOS 585-7/❀ *K 79 K 32* (2). [Lon. OSA/5- 1402]. Gueden, Danco, Della Casa, Dickie, Poell, Corena, Siepi, V. State Op. Ch., VPO, Erich Kleiber.

** Decca D 132 D 4/*K 132 K 42* [Lon. OSA/5- 1443]. Cotrubas, Tomowa-Sintow, Von Stade, Van Dam, Krause, V. State Op. Ch., VPO, Karajan.

It is important not to judge Solti's effervescent new version of *Figaro* by a first reaction to the overture. It is one of the fastest on record (matching Karajan in the 'egg-timer' race). Elsewhere Solti opts for a fair proportion of extreme speeds, slow as well as fast, but they rarely if ever intrude on the quintessential happiness of the entertainment.

Rejecting the idea of a bass Figaro, Solti has chosen in Samuel Ramey a firm-toned baritone, a virile figure. He is less a comedian than a lover, superbly matched to the most enchanting of Susannas today, Lucia Popp, who gives a sparkling and radiant performance to match the Pamina she sang in Haitink's recording of *Zauberflöte*. The Count of Thomas Allen is magnificent too, tough in tone and characterization but always beautiful on the ear. Kurt Moll as Dr Bartolo sings an unforgettable *La vendetta* with triplets very fast and agile 'on the breath', while Robert Tear far outshines his own achievement as the Basilio of Colin Davis's amiable recording. Frederica von Stade, as in the Karajan set, is a most attractive Cherubino, even if *Voi che sapete* is too slow; but crowning all is the Countess of Kiri Te Kanawa, challenged by Solti's spacious tempi in the two big arias, but producing ravishing tone, flawless phrasing and elegant ornamentation throughout. With superb, vivid recording this now makes an excellent first choice for a much-recorded opera. The brilliantly transferred chrome cassettes offer the ideal layout with one Act complete on each of four sides.

Giulini's set with its star-studded cast, unavailable for some years, is now reissued at medium price in an excellent transfer on to six sides instead of eight. If Giulini misses some of the fun of the comedy, his is a beautifully paced, consistently stylish reading which provides an admirable frame for the extraordinary team of soloists. Taddei with his dark baritone may be an odd choice as Figaro, but he amply justifies it, and the trio of women singers has rarely if ever been matched, with Schwarzkopf the most patrician of Countesses and Moffo at her freshest and sweetest. The cassette transfer is clear and clean but just a little lacking in warmth.

Colin Davis produces one of the most enjoyable of modern versions of this much-recorded opera. In particular his pacing of the recitatives has a sparkle that directly reflects experience in the opera house, and his tempi generally are beautifully chosen to make their dramatic points. Vocally the cast is exceptionally consistent. Mirella Freni (Susanna) is the least satisfying, but these are all steady voices which take to recording well, and it is good to have so ravishingly beautiful a voice as Jessye Norman's for the Countess. The Figaro of Wladimiro Ganzarolli and the Count of Ingvar Wixell project with exceptional clarity and vigour, and there is fine singing too from Yvonne Minton as Cherubino, Clifford Grant as Bartolo and Robert

Tear as Basilio. The recording, though not so clean as EMI's for Giulini (it has more reverberation than many will like for this opera), is commendably atmospheric. The cassettes too are well managed with no lack of presence for the voices, and the same layout as the other major sets, with Acts tailored to the four sides.

Boehm's earlier version of *Figaro* was once available on the cheap Fontana Special label, but unlike that sprightly performance this newer one gives a complete text, with Marcellina's and Basilio's Act IV arias included. This is among the most consistently assured performances available. The women all sing most beautifully, with Janowitz's Countess, Mathis's Susanna and Troyanos's Cherubino all ravishing the ear in contrasted ways. Prey is an intelligent if not very jolly-sounding Figaro, and Fischer-Dieskau gives his dark, sharply defined reading of the Count's role. All told, a great success, with fine playing and recording, though at about half the price Kleiber presents a version with at least as many merits. Boehm's set is available in a good cassette version, although the transfer level is not very high.

Kleiber's famous set was one of Decca's Mozart bicentenary recordings of the mid-1950s. It remains an outstanding bargain at mid-price, an attractively strong performance with much fine singing. Few if any sets have since matched its constant stylishness. Gueden's Susanna might be criticized but her golden tones are certainly characterful, while Danco and Della Casa are both at their finest. A dark-toned Figaro in Siepi brings added contrast and if the pace of the recitatives is rather slow, this is not inconsistent within the context of Kleiber's overall approach. The recording still sounds remarkably well on disc but is best heard in its tape format. It was one of the early triumphs of the cassette catalogue and when originally issued gave us the first opportunity of experiencing Kleiber's masterly reading with each Act uninterrupted. Heard in this way the onward flow of the performance is very compulsive (especially the miraculous Act II) and the warm, honeyed sound of the remastered recording gives constant pleasure. This is an indispensable version, in spite of more recent accounts.

With Karajan the speed and smoothness of the overture establish the character of the whole performance. Too much is passed over with a deftness which quickly makes the result bland, despite superb singing and playing. Only Frederica von Stade as Cherubino establishes the sort of individuality of expression that is the very stuff of operatic drama; she alone emerges as a rounded character. With a bloom on the sound (equally striking on both disc and cassette) the performance is a joy to the ear but is likely to leave any Mozartian unsatisfied.

Le Nozze di Figaro: highlights.

(M) *** Decca SPA 514. Della Casa, Peters, Elias, London, Tozzi, V. State Op. Ch., VPO, Leinsdorf.

(M) **(*) HMV SXLP/*TC-SXLP* 30303 [Ang. S 35640]. (from above set, cond. Giulini).

** Decca SXL/*KSXC* 6987. (from above set, cond. Karajan).

The excellent and thoroughly enjoyable Decca sampler reminds us of the many qualities of Leinsdorf's *Figaro* recording. The selection is generous (52 minutes); it is subtitled 'Scenes and arias', and thus makes no attempt to provide a potted opera, which is impossible with a work so teeming with highlights. It rightly concentrates on the contributions of the ladies, who stand out in a generally good cast, Roberta Peters a sparkling Susanna, and Lisa della Casa characteristically fine as the Countess. Their famous *Letter duet* (*Cosa mi narri?*) shows how delightfully the voices match, and the beauty of Della Casa's *Porgi amor* and *Dove sono* are complemented by Susanna's charming *Deh vieni*, while Rosalind Elias as Cherubino provides a no less memorable *Voi che sapete*. But there are fourteen numbers here and they give an excellent sampler of the fresh, alert qualities of the performance as a whole. The recording is vivid and lively. It dates from 1960 and only shows its age slightly in the timbre of the upper strings.

In the selection from the Giulini recording, which is not particularly generous, arias have been preferred to ensembles. That brings many splendid performances, including Figaro's three arias (intensely sung by Taddei) and the Countess's two (given with rare poise by Schwarzkopf), but it seems a pity that the overture was included instead of one or other of the ensembles. The recording is clear and bright, although in the cassette transfer there is a noticeable lack of warmth in the orchestral balance.

Though overall Karajan's reading, with its wilful speeds, is too slick for so fizzing a comedy as *Figaro*, such polish and refinement deserve to be sampled – notably Frederica von Stade's Cherubino. This selection, beautifully recorded, does the job admirably.

Der Schauspieldirektor (*The Impresario;* opera): complete.

*** DG 2740 203 (3) [2709 051]. Grist, Auger, Schreier, Moll, Dresden State O, Boehm – *Die Entführung*.***

This performance of *Der Schauspieldirektor* is without dialogue, so that it fits on to a single side. Reri Grist's bravura as Madame Herz is impressive, and Arleen Auger – the attractive Constanze in the *Entführung* coupling – is again pleasingly fresh and stylish here. The tenor and bass make only minor contributions, but Boehm's guiding hand keeps the music alive from the first bar to the last.

Zaïde (complete).

**(*) HM SO 55832H (2). Blegen, Hollweg, Schone, Moser, Holl, Salz. Mozarteum O, Hager.

Zaïde, written between 1779 and 1780 and never quite completed, was a trial run for *Entführung* based on a comparable story of love, duty, escape and forgiveness in the seraglio. It has nothing like the same sharpness of focus dramatically, which may perhaps account for Mozart's failure to complete the piece when within sight of the end. For whatever reason, he left it minus an overture and a finale, but it is simple enough for both to be supplied from other sources, as is done here: the *Symphony No. 32* makes an apt enough overture, and a *March* (K.335, No. 1) rounds things off quickly and neatly. Much of the music is superb, and melodramas at the beginning of each Act are strikingly effective and original, with the speaking voice of the tenor in the first heard over darkly dramatic writing in D minor. Zaïde's arias in both Acts are magnificent: the radiantly lyrical *Ruhe sanft* is hauntingly memorable, and the dramatic *Tiger aria* is like Constanze's *Martern aller Arten* but briefer and more passionate.

Leopold Hager adds this attractive piece to his fresh and enjoyable Mozart opera series in a performance generally well sung and warmly recorded. It does not quite match the earlier Philips set under Bernhard Klee either in playing or singing. The Sultan of the earlier version, Werner Hollweg, here becomes the hero, Gomatz, free-toned and stylish if hardly passionate. Judith Blegen makes an appealing Zaïde, though the voice could be steadier. Robert Holl is a fine, dark-toned Osmin.

Die Zauberflöte (complete).

*** HMV Dig. SLS/*TCC-SLS* 5223 (3). Popp, Gruberová, Lindner, Jerusalem, Brendel, Bracht, Zednik, Bav. R. Ch. and SO, Haitink.

*** DG Dig. **410 967-2**; 2741/*3382* 001 (3) [id.]. Mathis, Ott, Perry, Araiza, Hornik, Van Dam, German Op. Ch., Berlin PO, Karajan.

*** HMV SLS 912 (3) [Ang. S 3651]. Janowitz, Putz, Popp, Gedda, Berry, Frick, Schwarzkopf, Ludwig, Höffgen, Philh. Ch. and O, Klemperer.

**(*) DG 2709 017/*3371 002* (3) [id.]. Lear, Peters, Otto, Wunderlich, Fischer-Dieskau, Hotter, Crass, Berlin RIAS Chamber Ch., Berlin PO, Boehm.

(***) HMV mono RLS/*TC-RLS* 143465-3/*9* (3) [Turn. THS 65078/80]. Lemnitz, Berger, Roswaenge, Hüsch, Strienz, Berlin PO and Ch., Beecham.

**(*) Decca SET 479-81/*K2 A4* [Lon. OSA/5- 1397]. Lorengar, Deutekom, Burrows, Fischer-Dieskau, Prey, Talvela, V. State Op. Ch., VPO, Solti.

** RCA RL 03728 (4) [CTC4 4124]. Donat, Cotrubas, Kales, Tappy, Talvela, Boesch, V. State Op. Ch., VPO, Levine.

Haitink in his first ever opera recording directs a rich and spacious account of *Zauberflöte*, superbly recorded in spectacularly wide-ranging digital sound. There is a sterling honesty in Haitink's approach to every number. With speeds generally a shade slower than usual, the point of the playing and the consistent quality of the singing present this as a Mozart masterpiece that is weighty as well as sparkling. The dialogue – not too much of it, nicely produced and with sound effects adding to the vividness – frames a presentation that has been carefully thought through. Popp makes the most tenderly affecting of Paminas (as she did in the Salzburg production) and Gruberová has never sounded more spontaneous in her brilliance than here as Queen of the Night: she is both agile and powerful. Jerusalem makes an outstanding Tamino, both heroic and sweetly Mozartian; and though neither Wolfgang Brendel as Papageno nor Bracht as Sarastro is as characterful as their finest rivals, their personalities project strongly and the youthful freshness of their singing is most attractive. The Bavarian chorus too is splendid, and the recording's perspectives featuring the chorus are extraordinarily effective, particularly in the superb Act I finale. The chrome cassettes are no less outstanding technically than the discs, offering sound of remarkable range, body and presence. Some readers will certainly prefer Karajan's more urgent, more volatile Berlin version, but the gravitas of Haitink's approach does not miss the work's elements of drama and charm, though nothing is trivialized.

Zauberflöte has also inspired Karajan to one of his freshest, most rhythmic Mozart performances, spontaneous-sounding to the point where vigour is preferred to immaculate precision in ensembles. The digital recording is not always perfectly balanced, but the sound is outstandingly fresh and clear, on disc and chrome cassettes alike. There are numbers where the tempi are dangerously slow (Tamino's *Dies Bildnis*, both of Sarastro's arias and Pamina's *Ach, ich fühl's*), but Karajan's concentration helps him to avoid mannerism completely. The choice of soloists may seem idiosyncratic, and in principle one would want a darker-toned Sarastro than José van Dam, but the clarity of focus and the fine control, not to mention the slow tempi, give the necessary weight to his arias. Francisco Araiza and Gottfried Hornik make impressive contributions, both concealing any inexperience. Karin Ott has a relatively weighty voice for the Queen of the Night, but in his tempi Karajan is most considerate to her; and the Pamina of Edith Mathis has many beautiful moments, her word-pointing always intelligent.

Klemperer's conducting of *The Magic Flute* at Covent Garden was disappointing, but here he is inspired, making the dramatic music sound more like Beethoven in its monumental strength. But he does not miss the humour and point of the Papageno passages, and to a surprising degree he gets the best of both worlds. The cast is outstanding – look at the distinction of the Three Ladies alone – and curiously it is the most generally reliable of all the singers, Gottlob Frick as Sarastro, who comes nearest to letting the side down. Lucia Popp is in excellent form, and Gundula Janowitz sings Pamina's part with a creamy beauty that is just breathtaking. Nicolai Gedda too is most tasteful as Tamino and Walter Berry is a firm-voiced Papageno. The recording was made in the summer of 1964 at a time when Philharmonia fortunes were not at their happiest, but from the results you would never know that. It is a pity the dialogue is not included, but on that point Klemperer was insistent, and the set is after all his triumph.

One of the glories of Boehm's DG set is the singing of Fritz Wunderlich as Tamino, a wonderful memorial to a singer much missed. Passages that normally seem merely incidental come alive thanks to his beautiful intense singing. Fischer-Dieskau, with characteristic word-pointing, makes a sparkling Papageno on record (he is too big of frame, he says, to do the role on stage) and Franz Crass is a satisfyingly straightforward Sarastro. The team of women is well below this standard – Lear taxed cruelly in *Ach, ich fühl's*, Peters shrill in the upper register (although the effect is exciting), and the Three Ladies do not blend well – but the direction of Boehm is superb, light and lyrical, but weighty where necessary to make a glowing, compelling experience. Fine recording. The cassette transfer was originally issued in non-Dolby form, but subsequently remastered, although the quality remains rather uneven. The level is not especially high, yet in the female vocal climaxes there is occasionally a hint of peaking.

Beecham's recording, made in November 1937, was the first ever of *Zauberflöte* complete, and the first complete opera recording undertaken by Walter Legge as producer.

Beecham's conducting is magical, and one at least of the solo performances has never been surpassed, that of Gerhard Hüsch as Papageno. The rest is vocally variable, though Lemnitz is a radiant Pamina for all but a few isolated passages. Roswaenge has his strained moments as Tamino, heroic as the voice is, and neither Berger as Queen of the Night nor Strienz as Sarastro matches up to the best of later rivals. But, well transferred, it makes a fascinating, genuinely historic set, with sound still amazingly clear and well-balanced. The cassettes are clean and well-focused, giving the voices bloom, although the orchestra sounds thin. The libretto reduction is clear.

If one is looking for Mozartian charm in this most monumental of Mozart's operas, then plainly Solti's reading must be rejected. It is tough, strong and brilliant, and it is arguable that in this opera those are the required qualities above all; but even so the absence of charm has a cumulative effect. The drama may be consistently vital, but ultimately the full variety of Mozart's inspiration is not achieved. On the male side the cast is very strong indeed, with Stuart Burrows assuming his international mantle easily with stylish and rich-toned singing. Martti Talvela and Fischer-Dieskau as Sarastro and the Speaker respectively provide a stronger contrast than usual, each superb in his way, and Hermann Prey rounds out the character of Papageno with intelligent pointing of words. The cast of women is less consistent. Pilar Lorengar's Pamina is sweetly attractive as long as your ear is not worried by her obtrusive vibrato while Cristina Deutekom's Queen of the Night is technically impressive, though marred by a curious warbling quality in the coloratura, almost like an intrusive 'w' where you sometimes have the intrusive 'h'. The Three Ladies make a strong team (Yvonne Minton in the middle), and it was a good idea to give the parts of the Three Boys to genuine trebles. Superb recording quality, and sumptuously illustrated libretto. The cassettes too are well-managed.

RCA's project to record the memorable Salzburg Festival production of this opera was an admirable one, but only a German-speaker will want as much dialogue as is given here – spreading the opera on to eight instead of the usual six sides. Christian Boesch – an enchanting Papageno in the Felsenreitschule – is more an actor than a singer, and two of the singers who latterly made the production a delight – Lucia Popp as Pamina and Edita Gruberová as Queen of the Night – are on the Haitink HMV version, not this. Levine is not at his most sparkling, and neither is the recording.

Die Zauberflöte: highlights.

*** HMV Dig. **CDC7 47008-2**. (from above recording, cond. Haitink).

*** DG 2532/*3302* 004 [id.]. (from above set, cond. Karajan).

(M) *** HMV Green. ESD/*TC-ESD* 100326-1/*4* [Ang. S/*4XS* 36315]. (from above set, cond. Klemperer).

(M) **(*) Decca VIV/*KVIC* 50. Gueden, Lipp, Loose, Simoneau, Berry, Boehm, V. State Op. Ch., VPO, Boehm.

** RCA Dig. **RCD 14621.** (from above recording, cond. Levine).

Haitink's selection has at present no LP or cassette equivalents, but the compact disc has all the virtues of the new system, giving an added sense of presence and atmosphere. The selection is well made to include many favourites with the Papageno/Papagena music well represented to make a contrast with the lyrical arias and the drama of the Queen of the Night.

This selection from the Karajan set concentrates on the major arias, and very impressive it is. The buoyancy as well as the spaciousness of Karajan's reading come over well, helped by the bright digital recording. The cassette transfer is not made at the highest level but retains the immediacy and range of the complete set.

The selection from the Klemperer set is well balanced and fairly generous, although it is a pity it does not include the passage most characteristic of Klemperer with the Armed Men. However, it does include the ensemble *Hm, hm, hm* between Papageno, Tamino and the Three Ladies, with Schwarzkopf, Ludwig and Höffgen at their very finest. The chief glory of the set vocally is the singing of the women; Gedda's Tamino and Frick's Sarastro are by comparison disappointing. But this makes a good sampler of a performance which, while distinctly massive, manages to find sparkle and humour too. The resonant sound has produced some problems in the tape transfer with a somewhat bass-orientated balance.

The Decca selection comes from Boehm's flawed 1956 Vienna recording and his personality dominates the proceedings. The selection is not very generous (about 23 minutes on each side) but successfully concentrates on the stronger members of the cast, notably Wilma Lipp's impressively agile Queen of the Night, Leopold Simoneau's sensitive Tamino and Walter Berry's delightful Papageno; indeed quite a lot of the Papagena/Papageno music is included, and with Boehm's smiling accompaniments it is highly enjoyable. The recording still sounds remarkably good, and the cassette is first-class, losing nothing on the LP quality.

The RCA highlights compact disc is generous in offering fifteen excerpts and has a certain charm in detailing each in a lurid English translation; thus the Queen of the Night's second aria (*Die Hölle Rache*) is given as 'The vengeance of Hell boils in my heart'. It is splendidly sung. Zdzislawa Donat's contribution is one of the few outstanding performances here, alongside Cotrubas's Pamina – her aria *Ach, ich fühl's* is equally fine. Neither artist is named on the insert leaflet; however, this does provide a synopsis of 'The Plot'. There is nothing special about the CD sound, apart from the background silence. Nonetheless the dialogue which weighs down the complete set is omitted here.

MISCELLANEOUS VOCAL RECITALS

Arias: *Ch'io mi scordi di te, K.505. Exsultate, jubilate, K.165: Alleluia. Vorrei spiegarvi, K.418. Le Nozze di Figaro: Porgi amor; Voi che sapete; Dove sono; Deh vieni, non tardar. Il re pastore: L'amerò, sarò costante. Die Zauberflöte: Ach, ich fühl's.*

**(*) Decca SXL/*KSXC* 6933 [Lon. 26613]. Sutherland, Nat. PO, Bonynge.

It is a pity that this Mozart recital was not recorded earlier, for by 1980 when it was issued Sutherland's voice, as recorded, had acquired a beat that in this precise, classical writing was obtrusive; and her habit of attacking first notes of phrases from below was damaging too. The coloratura remains a delight, with *Alleluia* one of the highspots of the recital. *Ach, ich fühl's* brings the purest singing here, a fair reminder of one of the first roles which at Covent Garden in the 1950s first alerted perceptive opera-lovers to the arrival of a major star. The recording is of good Kingsway Hall vintage.

Arias: *Così dunque tradisci . . . Aspri rimorsi atroci, K.432. Un bacio di mano, K.541. Mentre ti lascio, K.513. Ein deutsches Kriegslied, K.539: Ich möchte wohl der Kaiser sein. La finta giardiniera: Nach der welschen Art. Le Nozze di Figaro: Hai già vinta la causa; Vedrò mentr'io sospiro. Warnung, K.433; Männer suchen stehts zu naschen.*

(M) **(*) Decca Jub. JB 100. Fischer-Dieskau, V. Haydn O, Peters – HAYDN: *Arias.****

The Mozart rarities on this disc are more numerous and more interesting than the Haydn items, and it is particularly fascinating to hear the Count's aria from *Figaro* in a version with a high vocal line which the composer arranged for performances in 1789. There is also a beautiful aria from two years earlier, *Mentre ti lascio*, which reveals Mozart's inspiration at its keenest. The other items too bring their delights. Fischer-Dieskau sings most intelligently, if with some pointing of word and phrase that is not quite in character with the music. The sound is first-class, the cassette matching the disc closely.

Arias: *La Clemenza di Tito: Ecco il punto . . . Non più di fiori; Parto, parto. Don Giovanni: Vedrai carino. Le Nozze di Figaro: Non so più; Voi che sapete.*

*** Ph. 9500 098/*7300 511* [id.]. Von Stade, Rotterdam PO, de Waart – ROSSINI: *Arias.****

Frederika von Stade was first heard in Britain as a uniquely compelling Cherubino, and the Mozart side of her 1977 recital begins splendidly with the page's two arias, followed by an equally charming account of Zerlina's aria. She shows rather less imagination in the arias from *La Clemenza di Tito*. Excellent recording.

Arias: *La Clemenza di Tito: Non più di fiori vaghe catene. Così fan tutte: Come scoglio. Don Giovanni: In quali eccessi . . . Mi tradi quell'alma ingrata. Crudele? non mi dir bell' idol mio. Die Entführung aus dem Serail: Welcher Kummer . . . Traurigkeit ward mir zum Lose. Idomeneo: Solitudini amiche . . . Zeffiretti lusinghieri. Le Nozze di Figaro: Voi che sapete; Giunse al fin il momento . . . Deh vieni; Porgi amor. Il re pastore: L'amerò, sarò costante.*
** HMV Dig. **CDC 747019-2**; ASD 146787-1/*4* [Ang. DS/*4XS* 38023]. Popp, Mun. RO, Slatkin.

Lucia Popp was perhaps mistaken at this stage in her career to have attempted to assume such a wide variety of Mozartian roles within a single recital. She is an enchanting Susanna – *Deh vieni* is the highlight of the disc – but while her portrayal of Cherubino (*Voi che sapete*) is fresh and light, her characterization of the Countess (*Porgi amor*) lacks maturity of feeling. The *Don Giovanni* excerpts although impressive both musically and technically are made to sound almost like concert arias, and *Come scoglio* lacks fire. The recording is generally flattering except at moments in the highest vocal range, and the XDR cassette is well managed.

Arias: *La Clemenza di Tito: S'altro che lagrime. Così fan tutte: Ei parte . . . Sen . . . Per pieta. La finta giardiniera: Crudeli fermate . . . Ah dal pianto. Idomeneo: Se il padre perdei. Lucio Silla: Pupille amate. Il re pastore: L'amerò sarò costante. Zaïde: Ruhe sanft, mein holdes Leben. Die Zauberflöte: Ach ich fühl's es ist verschwunden.*
*** Ph. Dig. 6514/*7337* 319 [id.]. Te Kanawa, LSO, Sir Colin Davis.

Kiri Te Kanawa's is one of the loveliest collections of Mozart arias on record with the voice at its most ravishing and pure. One might object that Dame Kiri concentrates on soulful arias, ignoring more vigorous ones, but with stylish accompaniment and clear, atmospheric recording, beauty dominates all.

Arias: *Così fan tutte: Un' aura amorosa; Ah lo veggio; In qual fiero contrasto. Don Giovanni: Il mio tesoro; Dalla sua pace. Die Entführung aus dem Serail: Hier soll ich denn sehen; Wenn der Freude Tränen fliessen; O wie angstlich, o wie feurig; Ich baue ganz auf deine Stärke. Idomeneo: Fuor del mar. Die Zauberflöte: Dies Bildnis; Wie stark ist nicht dein Zauberton.*
(M) **(*) Decca 410 143-1/*4*. Burrows, LPO or LSO, Pritchard.

This is a reissue of a Oiseau-Lyre record dating from 1976. It fills an obvious gap in the catalogue for there is no comparable collection of Mozart's tenor arias. Stuart Burrows was in peak form when the recordings were made and the voice has a golden warmth of timbre which is most appealing. The phrasing is eminently musical too and if characterization is less individual, admirers of this fine artist should not be disappointed. The accompaniments are well made and the recording equally flattering on disc or the excellent matching cassette.

Arias, duets and trios: (i) *La Clemenza di Tito: Ah perdonna al primo affetto; S'alto che lagrime.* (i; ii) *Così fan tutte: Soave sia il vento.* (ii) *Don Giovanni: Là ci darem la mano; Batti, batti; Vedrai carino;* (iii) *Per queste tue manina. Le Nozze di Figaro:* (ii; iv) *Cosa sento! Tosto andate;* (ii) *Crudell! perchè finora; Giunse alfin . . . Deh vieni. Il re pastore: L'amerò sarò costante. Zaïde: Ruhe sanft.* (ii) *Die Zauberflöte: Bei mannern.*
(M) *** Decca Grandi Voci GRV 23. Popp with (i) Fassbaender; (ii) Krause; (iii) Bacquier; (iv) Krenn.

With many of these items taken from Decca's two-disc 'Mozart Festival' issue (SET 548-9, long deleted) conducted by Istvan Kertesz, the sweetness, brightness and charm of Popp's singing even in the early years of her career are superbly demonstrated. Though more recently she may have intensified her characterizations, there are few more attractively varied Mozart soprano recitals. Excellent recording for its period.

COLLECTIONS

(i) *Violin concerto No. 3 in G, K.216. Serenades Nos. 6 in D (Serenata notturna), K.239; 13 in G (Eine kleine Nachtmusik), K.525.* (i; ii) *Sinfonia concertante for violin and viola, K.364. Symphonies Nos. 25 in G min.; 29 in A. Exsultate, jubilate. Litaniae lauretanae: Sancta Maria. Coronation Mass: Agnus Dei.*
(M) **(*) Argo D 243 D 3/*K 243 K 33* (3). Soloists, Ch. and ASMF, Marriner, with (i) Loveday, (ii) Shingles.

This anthology, centred on recordings by the St Martin-in-the-Fields Academy, is attractive if rather arbitrary. Alan Loveday's intimate reading of the *Violin concerto* is balanced with an account of the *Sinfonia concertante* that goes for elegance rather than any stronger Mozartian qualities, the slow movement gently refined. But *Eine kleine Nachtmusik* is outstandingly successful, fresh and unaffected, and the two symphonies have splendid life and polish. The pointing of the phrases of the 'little *G minor*' is done with a superb sense of style, and the scale of No. 29 is broad and forward-looking, with an exuberant finale. The recording tends to be reverberant, though not unattractively so. The vocal items are welcome and enjoyable, acting merely as a sampler of this side of Mozart's output. The cassettes are for the most part very successful, although the resonance in the last movement of No. 29 causes a momentary problem at the climax.

'Classics': (i) *Horn concerto No. 4 in E flat, K.495;* (ii; iii) *Piano concerto No. 21 in C, K.467;* (iii; iv) *Serenade No. 13 (Eine kleine Nachtmusik); Così fan tutte: Overture;* (v; vi) *Soave sia il vento;* (v) *Come scoglio. Don Giovanni:* (vii; viii) *La ci darem;* (vii) *Batti, batti. Le nozze di Figaro:* (ix) *Non più, andrai.* (iii; iv) *Die Zauberflöte: Overture.*
(M) **(*) HMV *TC2-COS 54256.* (i) Tuckwell, ASMF, Marriner; (ii) Annie Fischer; Sawallisch; (iii) Philh. O, (iv) Sir Colin Davis; (v) Schwarzkopf; (vi) Ludwig, Berry; (vii) Sciutti; (viii) Waechter; (ix) Taddei.

The artists' roster on this extended-length tape is impressive and there is nothing to disappoint here except the actual recorded sound which, though lively, tends to emphasize the age of the originals, most of which date back to the very beginning of the 1960s. The arias and duets are very enjoyable although the transfer of *Come scoglio* brings some peaky top notes. Otherwise the sound is bright and clean.

'The world of Mozart': (i) *Clarinet concerto:* 2nd movt; (ii) *Horn concerto No. 4 in E flat, K.495:* finale; (iii) *Piano concerto No. 20 in D min., K.466:* 2nd movt; (iv) *German dance, K.605/3; Sleighride; Serenade No. 13 (Eine kleine Nachtmusik), K.525:* 1st movt; (v) *Symphony No. 40 in G min., K.550:* 1st movt; (vi) *Piano sonata No. 11 in A, K.331: Rondo alla Turca;* (Vocal) (vii) *Ave verum corpus, K.618;* (viii) *Exsultate, jubilate, K.165: Alleluia;* (ix) *Così fan tutte: Soave sia il vento* (trio); (x) *Don Giovanni: Deh vieni alla finestra* (serenade); (xi) *Le Nozze di Figaro: Voi che sapete;* (xii) *Die Zauberflöte: Der Vogelfanger.*
(M) *** Decca SPA/*KCSP* 251. (i) De Peyer; (ii) Tuckwell; both with LSO, Maag; (iii) Katchen; Stuttgart CO, Münchinger; (iv) V. Moz. Ens., Boskovsky; (v) New Philh. O, Giulini; (vi) Backhaus; (vii) Ch. of St John's College, Camb.; (viii) Spoorenberg; (ix) Popp, Fassbaender, Krause, V. Op. O, Kertesz; (x) Bacquier; (xi) Berganza; (xii) Geraint Evans.

A really outstanding collection, brilliantly compiled so that each excerpt makes the right kind of contrast with what has gone before. The performances are all of high quality and this should tempt many to explore further, while for the confirmed Mozartian it makes a glorious concert of favourites. Highly recommended on disc or tape.

Muffat, Georg (*c.* 1645–1704)

Florilegium secundum: suites Nos. 1–4.
**(*) O-L DSLO 591. Ac AM, Hogwood.

Georg Muffat was born in Megève, Savoy, and baptized in 1653 which many books of reference give as his date of birth. He is of Scottish ancestry (Moffat) and though he studied in Paris during the 1660s and then near Strasburg, where he was briefly organist, he thought of himself as German and spent the better part of his career in Salzburg and Augsburg. When he was in Italy in the 1680s he came into contact with Corelli whose concerti grossi made a great impression on him. The *Florilegium secundum* is a much later work than the *Armonico tributo* (listed below) and was published in 1698 at Passau where he served at the court of the bishop. It is a set of eight orchestral suites, the first four of which are recorded here. They are formally more adventurous than the dance movements of such contemporaries as Fischer and Schmelzer, though not all of them are of equal interest. The performances are on period instruments and those unresponsive to the razor-edged strings will find these performances unpleasing. The playing is often a bit heavy-handed too, but those wanting this set have no current alternative and the recording is really very good indeed.

Armonico tributo.
*** Hyp. A 66032. Parley of Instruments, Goodman.

The five sonatas of *Armonico tributo* were published in Salzburg in 1682 and are for two violins, two violas and continuo, though Muffat defined them as 'chamber works suitable for few or many instruments', and they are performed here one to a part, but with a more elaborate continuo group including violone, theorbo, harpsichords and organ. In these sonatas Muffat explored some of the possibilities of the concerto principle, when he later arranged them in his concerti grossi, and the Parley of Instruments under Roy Goodman and Peter Holman follow the indications in the score indicating tutti and solo passages contrasting a smaller group (two violins, cello and continuo) with a larger (the solo group plus violas, bass and continuo). The invention is rich and the writing often distinguished. The performances, too, are very persuasive and stylish. An excellent introduction to this composer whose first published work this was.

Mundy, William (*c.* 1529–*c.* 1591)

Vox Patris caelestis.
(B) *** CfP CFP/*TC-CFP* 40339 [Ang. RL/*4RL* 32122]. Tallis Scholars, Phillips – ALLEGRI: *Miserere****; PALESTRINA: *Missa Papae Marcelli.***(*)

Mundy's *Vox Patris caelestis* was written during the short reign of Queen Mary (1553–8). While it is almost exactly contemporary with Palestrina's *Missa Papae Marcelli*, its florid, passionate polyphony is very different from that of the Italian composer. This is emphasized by Peter Phillips's eloquent performance, which presses the music onwards to reach an exultant climax in the closing stanza with the words '*Veni, veni, veni, caelesti gloria coronaberis*'. The work is structured in nine sections in groups of three, the last of each group being climactic and featuring the whole choir, with solo embroidery. Yet the music flows continuously, like a great river, and the complex vocal writing creates the most spectacular effects, with the trebles soaring up and shining out over the underlying cantilena. The imaginative force of the writing is never in doubt, and the Tallis Scholars give an account which balances linear clarity with considerable power. The recording is first-class and the reverberant acoustic adds bloom and richness without blurring the detail. The sound on disc and cassette is virtually identical.

Mussorgsky, Modest (1839–81)

The Capture of Kars (march). *St John's Night on the Bare Mountain. Scherzo in B flat. Khovantschina: Prelude to Act I;* (i) *Introduction to Act IV. The Destruction of Sennacherib.* (i; ii) *Joshua.* (i) *Oedipus in Athens: Temple chorus. Salammbô: Priestesses' chorus.*
*** RCA [ARL 1/*ARK 1* 3988]. LSO, Abbado, with (i) LSO Ch., (ii) Zehava Gal.

To commemorate the centenary of Mussorgsky's death Abbado and the LSO came up with this attractive and revealing anthology of shorter pieces. Some of the orchestral items are well enough known, but it is good to have so vital an account of the original version of *Night on the Bare Mountain*, different in all but its basic material from the Rimsky-Korsakov arrangement. Best of all are the four choral pieces; even when they are early and untypical (*Oedipus in Athens*, for example) they are immediately attractive, and they include such evocative pieces as the *Chorus of Priestesses* (intoning over a pedal bass) from a projected opera on Flaubert's novel. The chorus is rather recessed, but not inappropriately so, and the orchestra is given refined recording. The high-level cassette transfer is one of RCA's best, and it is a pity that this valuable issue has, for the moment, been withdrawn in the UK.

Night on the Bare Mountain; Khovantschina: Prelude; Dance of the Persian slaves.
(M) *** Decca SPA 257. Berlin PO, Solti (with *Concert****).

Night on the Bare Mountain appears in a great many concert discs. The performance (and recording) by Solti is among the very best, and the performance of the beautiful *Khovantschina* prelude is the finest in the present catalogue. This disc is called *The world of Russia* and is discussed in our Concerts section below.

Night on the Bare Mountain (arr. Rimsky-Korsakov); *Pictures at an Exhibition* (orch. Ravel).
C *** Telarc Dig. **CD 80042**; DG 10042 [id.]. Cleveland O, Maazel.
(B) *** DG Walkman *413 153-4*. Boston Pops O, Fiedler; Chicago SO, Giulini – TCHAIKOVSKY: *1812* etc.**(*)
(M) ** CBS 60113/*40-* [Col. MY 36726]. NYPO, Bernstein.
*(*) Ph. Dig. 9500 744/*7300 829* [id.]. Concg. O, Colin Davis.

All current versions of this coupling rest under the shadow of the magnificently recorded Telarc disc, one of the first great successes of the early digital era. The quality of the recording is apparent at the very opening of *Night on the Bare Mountain* in the richly sonorous presentation of the deep brass and the sparkling yet unexaggerated percussion. With the Cleveland Orchestra on top form the *Pictures* are strongly characterized; this may not be the subtlest reading available, but each of Mussorgsky's cameos comes vividly to life. The opening trumpets are more robust than in the Philadelphia version (see below), and *The old castle* is particularly evocative. The chattering children in the Tuileries are matched in presence by the delightfully pointed portrayal of the cheeping chicks, and if the ox-wagon (*Bydlo*) develops a climax potent enough to suggest a juggernaut, the similarly sumptuous brass in the *Catacombs* sequence cannot be counted as in any way overdramatized. After a vibrantly rhythmic *Baba-Yaga*, strong in fantastic menace, the closing *Great Gate of Kiev* is overwhelmingly spacious in conception, and quite riveting as sheer sound. On compact disc the background silence enhances the realism, although detail is not so sharply outlined as in the fine Abbado alternative – see below. With the Cleveland set the ear is conscious of the warm, glowing ambience of Severance Hall, although often individual wind solos have a luminous realism. The record's producer, Robert Woods, and the sound engineer, Jack Renner, continue their love affair with the bass drum, which is occasionally allowed to dominate the orchestral texture. But it is the richness and amplitude of the brass which make the work's final climax unforgettable. The programme notes provided with the CD are fully adequate, but a simple list of titles would have been useful; moreover the *Pictures* are not separately banded. However, within the technical information supplied is the laudable claim that 'it is Telarc's philosophy to employ additional microphones *only* when the size of the performing forces is greater than can be accommodated appropriately by the basic three'. This recording impressively bears out the success of Telarc's refusal to embrace close multi-microphone techniques, much beloved in Europe at present, and often producing the most unnatural effects.

Giulini's Chicago recording of Mussorgsky's *Pictures* is also available on Signature, coupled with Prokofiev's *Classical symphony* (see below), but is here paired with an excitingly volatile account of *Night on the Bare Mountain* directed by Fiedler. Both sound well on this bargain-priced Walkman tape, generously coupled with Tchaikovsky.

The New York Philharmonic is on top form for Bernstein's performance of the *Pictures*, with crisp ensemble and vivid solo playing, so that the conductor can relax, yet each of Mussorgsky's pictures is strongly characterized. The recording is spacious, but its rather fierce upper range becomes more apparent when one turns over for *The Great Gate of Kiev* (presented very grandly) and the *Night on the Bare Mountain*.

This first digital recording from Philips was technically a disappointment. The recording, refined enough, lacked body and immediacy, and the performance too is strangely short on brilliance. The speeds are often on the slow side, which makes the music fragile and undercharacterized rather than weighty. A performance like this sounds like a run-through, and though some may like the total absence of vulgarity in the *Night on the Bare Mountain*, it too sounds disappointingly tame. The cassette transfer is bass-heavy, and detail is muffled.

Pictures at an Exhibition (orch. Ravel).
*** DG Dig. **410 033-2**; 2532/*3302* 057 [id.]. LSO, Abbado – RAVEL: *La valse*.**(*)
*** HMV ASD/*TC-ASD* 3645 [Ang. S/*4XS* 37539]. Phd. O, Muti – STRAVINSKY: *Firebird suite*.***
*** DG 139 010/*923 018* [id.]. Berlin PO, Karajan – RAVEL: *Boléro*.***
*** DG Sig. 410 838-1/*4* [2530/*3300* 783]. Chicago SO, Giulini – PROKOFIEV: *Symphony No. 1*.***
*** Decca Dig. **400 051-2**; SXDL/*KSXDC* 7520 [Lon. LDR/*5*- 10040]. Chicago SO, Solti – RAVEL: *Tombeau de Couperin*.**
(B) *** RCA VICS/*VK* 2042 [ATL1/*ATK1* 4268]. Chicago SO, Reiner.
(M) **(*) Decca Jub. JB/*KJBC* 106 [(d) Lon. J/*5*- 41012]. LAPO, Mehta – ELGAR: *Enigma variations*.***
(B) **(*) CfP CFP/*TC-CFP* 40319. LPO, Pritchard – PROKOFIEV: *Symphony No. 1*.*(*)
(M) ** EMI Em. EMX/*TC-EMX* 2008. Philh. O, Maazel – DEBUSSY: *Prélude à l'après-midi d'un faune*.**

Pictures at an Exhibition. Khovantschina, Act IV: Entr'acte and Dance of the Persian slaves.
(M) *** HMV SXLP/*TC-SXLP* 30445 [(d) Ang. S 35430]. Philh. O, Karajan – BORODIN: *Polovtsian dances*.***

Abbado's takes a straighter, more direct view of Mussorgsky's fanciful series of pictures than usual, less consciously expressive, relying above all on instrumental virtuosity and the dazzling tonal contrasts of Ravel's orchestration. He is helped by the translucent and naturally balanced digital recording, equally impressive on disc and chrome tape. Indeed the sound is superb, making great impact at climaxes yet also extremely refined, as in the delicate portrayal of the unhatched chicks. Abbado's speeds tend to be extreme, with both this and *Tuileries* taken very fast and light, while *Bydlo* (the Polish ox-cart) and *The Great Gate of Kiev* are slow and weighty. Both readily demonstrate the recording's wide dynamic range. The fullness and clarity are especially impressive in the compact disc version, which although not as sumptuous as the famous Telarc disc, is among the finest of DG's issues in the new format. The digital effect is brilliant and sharply defined, but not as aggressive in the way that the Decca sound is for Solti's Chicago version.

Muti's reading is second to none. Any comparison is only with the finest previous versions (Toscanini, Koussevitzky, Karajan), and given the excellence of its recorded sound, it more than holds its own. Moreover it is one of the first records to do justice to the Philadelphia sound (although the balance is forward and perhaps not all listeners will respond to the brass timbres at the opening). But it is a far richer and more full-blooded quality than we have been used to in recent years from this source. The lower strings in *Samuel Goldenberg and Schmuyle* have extraordinary body and presence, and *Baba-Yaga* has an unsurpassed virtuosity and attack as well as being of demonstration standard as a recording. The richly glowing colours, the sheer homogeneity of the strings and the perfection of ensemble are a consistent source of admiration. The coupling is no less thrilling. The focus on the cassette is marginally less clean than the disc, but remains impressive.

Karajan's DG version dates from the mid-1960s, yet as both performance and recording it still holds its own. As with many of Karajan's finest records one has the feeling here that he has re-thought the score. One fascinating feature of his reading is that the *Promenades* are often slower than usual, suggesting that the 'visitor to the exhibition' is taking a more leisurely stroll between the exhibits. It is the remarkable sophistication of the orchestral playing that makes this issue so distinctive. The brass in particular are superb, and especially so in the famous *Catacombs* sequence, where the aural sonority has a unique majesty. The lightly pointed tuba-playing in *The hut on fowl's legs* is a delicious example of the subtlety of this performance, which is again shown in the restraint of *The old castle.* A splendid disc in every way. The tape transfer is strikingly successful, and the range and clarity of the sound are impressive, especially in the final climax.

Karajan's Philharmonia recording dates from the earliest days of stereo, yet here also the quality of the sound is astonishing, another tribute to the immense skill of Walter Legge and his early Philharmonia recording team. There is extraordinary clarity and projection, and it is matched by the brilliantly polished detail of the orchestral playing – the vintage Philharmonia offering breathtaking standards of ensemble and bite. The characterization of each picture is outstandingly vivid, and *The Great Gate of Kiev* is a frisson-creating climax of great splendour. The main work is framed by the two excerpts from *Khovantschina*, which are played most seductively, and the Borodin *Polovtsian dances* are hardly less riveting. This is not to be missed, even if purchased as a second version. The cassette transfer is first-class, full-bodied, clear and clean, without a trace of distortion at climaxes.

It is fascinating that Giulini's equally successful account should use the Chicago orchestra, thus repeating Reiner's success of the early days of stereo. The modern recording, however, is noticeably more refined and detailed, with brilliant percussive effects (a superb bass drum in *The hut on fowl's legs*). With superlative orchestral playing and strong characterization this is highly recommendable, and the tape transfer is generally of excellent quality.

Solti's performance is fiercely brilliant rather than atmospheric or evocative. He treats Ravel's orchestration as a virtuoso challenge, and with larger-than-life digital recording it undoubtedly has demonstration qualities. The cassette is one of Decca's very finest, matching the disc closely, but softening the edge of the sound picture very slightly without losing detail. It is no less demonstration-worthy than the disc, and many might feel that its focus is more natural. But whether heard on disc or tape this is a listening experience that tingles with energy and electricity. The Ravel fill-up makes an original coupling, although here the brilliantly forward sound balance is less appropriate. On CD the orchestral clarity is given an almost X-ray precision, and the transparency of texture, given the forward balance, provides quite startling clarity.

Reiner's famous RCA version is another demonstration of vintage stereo recording at its most impressive, using simple microphone techniques to achieve a natural balance. The record was originally issued in the UK in 1959 a few months after Karajan's Philharmonia account. The RCA sound-balance is more atmospheric than the EMI recording, if less sharply focused. But Reiner's approach is evocative to match and *The old castle*, the lumbering ox-wagon, and the superb brass-playing in the *Catacombs* sequence are all memorable. The final climax of *The Great Gate of Kiev* is massively effective. The chrome cassette is brilliant to the point of fierceness and the disc is much preferable.

Mehta's version also has vintage (Decca) sound – from the early 1970s – and a very attractive and generous coupling. Thus it becomes more than the sum of its parts though it is not as imaginative as Reiner, nor as vivid (or as finely played) as Karajan's mid-priced HMV competitor. Both disc and cassette have impressive range and body of sound.

The Classics for Pleasure issue offers at bargain price a brilliant account from the

LPO under Pritchard, in which the personality of the orchestra comes over strongly, the players obviously enjoying themselves and their own virtuosity. The very clear, dry recording makes every detail of the orchestration glitter, even if it lacks atmosphere, and the conductor's characterization of each picture is equally positive. The building of the *Great Gate of Kiev* finale is vividly exciting. This recording has been remastered and recoupled, and its sharpness of detail is now even more striking, both on disc and on tape (which approaches demonstration standard). Unfortunately the Prokofiev coupling has less attractive sound.

Maazel's Eminence issue is well recorded, though in the finale the sound is less expansive than in other versions. The Philharmonia playing is, of course, first-class, but the characterization here is effective rather than sharply memorable. The cassette matches the disc, if without quite the same brilliance in the treble.

Pictures at an Exhibition (orch. Ashkenazy).
** Decca Dig. 410 121-1/*4*. Philh. O, Ashkenazy – BORODIN: *Polovtsian dances.****

Ashkenazy's score cannot match Ravel's in subtlety of detail; it concentrates on broad washes of orchestral sound – helped by the richness of the Kingsway Hall acoustic – so that climaxes are massive rather than electrifying. The character of the pictures is not very individual, either, although Ashkenazy undoubtedly finds plenty of Russian feeling in the music itself. The recording is opulent rather than glittering, on disc and chrome tape alike. A disappointment, even though Ashkenazy corrects a number of textual errors inherent in Ravel's version, which have never been put right, until now.

Pictures at an Exhibition (arr. Stokowski).
(M) (**) Decca VIV/*KVIC* 26 [Lon. STS/*5 15558*]. New Philh. O, Stokowski – TCHAIKOVSKY: *1812*.(**)

Stokowski's own orchestration of Mussorgsky's *Pictures* is not notable for its subtlety, but is certainly not lacking in flamboyance. The originally Phase Four recording provides an exaggerated immediacy, with everything right on top of the listener. The inner tension seems continually stretched to fever point – the ox-wagon trundles past at an unnerving pace – and spectacle, rather than individuality of characterization, is the keynote. The New Philharmonia players are obviously stretched by the high voltage, but the listener also is left breathless at the end.

Pictures at an Exhibition (arr. for brass ensemble by Elgar Howarth).
*** Argo ZRG 885 [id.]. Jones Brass Ens., Howarth.

There is no reason why Mussorgsky's famous piano work should not be transcribed for brass as effectively as for a full symphony orchestra, and Elgar Howarth's inspired arrangement fully justifies the experiment. There is never any feeling of limited colour; indeed the pictures of the unhatched chicks and the market place at Limoges have great pictorial vividness, and the evocation of the dead has an almost cinematic element of fantasy. *The Great Gate of Kiev* is as thrilling here as in any orchestral recording, and elsewhere the deep brass effects are superbly sonorous. This version has already acquired 'collector' status as a demonstration record.

Pictures at an Exhibition (original piano version).
(M) *** DG Sig. 2543/*3343* 526 [id.]. Berman – PROKOFIEV: *Romeo and Juliet.****
*** Decca Dig. SXDL/*KSXDC* 7624 [Lon. LDR/*5*- 71124]. Ashkenazy (with: BORODIN: *Scherzo*. TCHAIKOVSKY: *Dumka, Op. 59*. LIADOV: *The music box, Op. 32*. TANEYEV: *Prelude and fugue, Op. 29* ***).
(*) Decca SXL/*KSXC* 6840 [(d) Lon. CS/*5*- 6559]. Ashkenazy – TCHAIKOVSKY: *Piano concerto No. 1.**
(*) HMV Dig. ASD/*TCC-ASD* 4281. Ousset – RAVEL: *Gaspard de la nuit.**
(B) ** Con. CC/*CCT* 7516 [DG 2535/*3335* 272]. Firkusny – RACHMANINOV: *Preludes.****

Lazar Berman opens his account of the original piano version of the *Pictures* with an uncompromisingly fast pacing of the *Prome-*

nade. One can picture him striding round the exhibition brusquely, hands behind his back, only stopping to admire those pictures which take his fancy. The ox-wagon (*Bydlo*) certainly does, and undoubtedly *Catacombs* and *Cum mortuis* make a very direct communication, for the playing here has arresting power and atmosphere. On the other hand the *Ballet of the unhatched chicks* finds him more concerned with articulation (the playing is superb) than evocation. *The Great Gate of Kiev* makes a riveting (if not overwhelming) climax, and with splendid sound this is undoubtedly the most compelling account of the work to have been recorded in recent years. For the Signature reissue, DG have remastered the recording and it is now complete on one side without loss of quality. The new coupling is more generous too and superbly played. Our copy of the chrome tape matched the disc very closely in all respects.

Ashkenazy's digital account of the *Pictures at an Exhibition* does not differ in its broad essentials from his earlier recording. The newer disc has the greater clarity and also the benefit of an enterprising coupling. The Taneyev *Prelude and fugue* is well worth having and Liadov's *The music box* is enchantingly played. The chrome cassette is spectacularly wide-ranging and clear, though a little hard on top.

Ashkenazy's earlier analogue version is distinguished by poetic feeling, but lacks something of the extrovert flair with which pianists like Richter or Berman can make one forget all about the orchestral transcription. Decca have recoupled this with the Tchaikovsky *B flat minor Piano concerto* and have taken the opportunity to improve the sound still further. If the coupling is attractive, this cannot be faulted on technical grounds.

The French pianist Cécile Ousset gives a commanding account of the *Pictures* and is responsive to their changing moods and colours. Hers is a big-boned and powerful reading, recorded in realistic sound on both disc and tape and can be recommended alongside the best. She is perhaps not quite as aristocratic as Ashkenazy and not to be preferred to Lazar Berman's newly reissued DG version which makes one forget the absence of the orchestra.

At bargain price Firkusny's version deserves to be considered. The playing is spontaneous, and the music sounds fresh and well characterized, even if there is some lack of extrovert bravura at the end. The piano tone on tape is firm and realistic; the cassette has marginally less range than the disc but is fully acceptable.

Pictures at an Exhibition (arr. for organ by Wills).
(M) ** Hyp. Dig. A/*KA* 66006. Wills (organ of Ely Cath.).

Arthur Wills's registration is effective enough, if showing no especial creative flair, and the performance too is competent rather than inspired. The problem is the articulation of the quick music: the children playing in the Tuileries, the chicks, and *Baba-Yaga* all lack the sharpness of attack that the piano (or orchestral instruments) can readily provide. *Bydlo*, the Polish ox-wagon, comes off splendidly, and *The Great Gate of Kiev* is massive, if not overwhelming. The recording is spectacularly realistic, and the disc has been advocated for demonstration by some hi-fi magazines. The cassette transfer too is impressively free from congestion.

The Nursery (song cycle).
*** Decca SXL 6900 [Lon. OS 26579]. Söderström, Ashkenazy – GRECHANINOV: *Lane*; PROKOFIEV: *Ugly Duckling*.***

Elisabeth Söderström's series of song recordings with Vladimir Ashkenazy has mainly concentrated on Rachmaninov, but here she chooses an illuminating group of pieces about children, which, with thrillingly imaginative accompaniment, are characterized with vivid intensity. The Mussorgsky cycle has one registering the different voices – nurse or child – with extraordinary immediacy. There are few records of Russian song as refreshing and exciting as this. The recording of both voice and piano is outstanding.

Song cycles: *The Nursery; Sunless*. Songs: *Gathering mushrooms; Gopak: The magpie; The orphan; Where are you, little star?*
(M) **(*) Saga 5357. Slobodskaya, Newton.

It is sad that so positive an artist as Oda Slobodskaya did not record much more. This is a welcome sample, even though the voice is not caught at its best, and the recording is limited. But her interpretations of Mussorgsky are unique and characterful, and on a budget label they are well worth investigating.

Songs and Dances of Death (song cycle). *Song of the Flea*.
*** Decca SXL 6974. Talvela, Gothoni – RACHMANINOV: *Songs*.**(*)

Martti Talvela's magnificent bass is superbly caught in brilliant Decca sound to make his account of Mussorgsky's dark, intense cycle vividly immediate and involving. A singer with an operatic background gains enormously here, and there has not been a finer version since Boris Christoff's many years ago. Gothoni's imaginative accompaniment is not nearly so well caught, but it is the voice which compels attention.

Boris Godunov (ed. Rimsky-Korsakov; complete).
*** Decca SET 514–7/*K 81 K 43* (4/*3*) [Lon. OSA 1439]. Ghiaurov, Vishnevskaya, Maslennikov, Spiess, Talvela, Kelemen, V. Boys' Ch., Sofia R. Ch., V. State Op. Ch., VPO, Karajan.

The Decca set comes nearer than previous recordings to conveying the rugged greatness of Mussorgsky's masterpiece, partly because of the superb control of Karajan, partly because of the recording quality, more vivid than that of earlier versions. If Ghiaurov in the title role lacks some of the dramatic intensity of Christoff on the two HMV sets, he is more accurate in singing the notes rather than indulging in evocative sing-speech. Not everyone will like the baritonal tinge which results, but ultimately this is exceedingly satisfying for repeated hearings. Karajan – as in his Salzburg performances, on which this is based – has opted for the Rimsky-Korsakov version, which will disappoint those who would prefer the darker, earthier original version, but which matches Karajan's qualities. Only the Coronation scene lacks something of the weight and momentum one ideally wants. For the rest the chorus is finely intense. The only serious disappointment vocally is the Marina of Vishnevskaya, too squally for Western ears. The tape set is satisfactorily tailored to fit three cassettes against four discs and the layout is generally preferable. It is technically outstanding and the depth, clarity and resonance of the big choral scenes of the Prologue and Act IV are remarkable.

Boris Godunov (original version): highlights.
**(*) HMV ESD/*TC-ESD* 143617-1/*4*. Talvela, Haugland, Gedda, Kinasz, Mróz, Paprocki, Krakow Polish R. Ch. and Nat. SO, Semkow.

This generous selection of items comes from the first ever complete recording of Mussorgsky's original score, sparer, darker and tougher than the usual more highly coloured Rimsky-Korsakov version. The Polish performance lacks something in bite – with the recording a little diffused – but with Martti Talvela as a very musical, if not deeply moving Boris and with a strong supporting cast, it is a valuable issue. As can be heard in the opening Coronation scene, the cassette transfer is not a success, with muddy, confused choral sound and a generally poor focus at climaxes.

Boris Godunov (arr. Rimsky-Korsakov): highlights.
(M) **(*) HMV SXLP/*TC-SXLP* 30547. Christoff, Lanigen, Ouzousov, Lear, Alexieva, Sofia Nat. Op. Ch., Paris Conservatoire O, Cluytens.

Although Cluytens' EMI stereo recording – available complete in the USA [Ang. S 3633 (4)] – did not match Christoff's earlier mono set in intensity, it is good to have a generous representation, at mid-price, of Christoff's famous assumption of the title role. He is well partnered by the beautiful non-Slavonic Marina of Evelyn Lear, and though the Sofia Chorus is far from ideal, this collection (which includes the Coronation scene, Pimen's monologue, Varlaam's song, Boris's monologue, the Clock scene, Love duet, Pimen's monologue and the death of Boris) is well worth its modest cost. The remastered recording sounds vivid both on disc and the excellent tape, with Christoff's resonant bass superbly caught.

Salammbô (arr. Pesko).
** CBS [M2-36932]. Schemchuk, Seleznev, Stone, Surjan, Arena, Italian R. and TV Ch. and SO, Pesko.

The chorus of Libyan warriors here brings a sudden reminder that Mussorgsky raided such early works as this when he came to write his masterpiece, *Boris Godunov*: the high priest in the Carthaginian temple with chorus presents the great melody which later became Boris's Act II monologue. Mussorgsky was in his early twenties when he attempted to turn Flaubert's exotic novel into an opera and sketched out some five scenes, mostly in piano score merely. Zoltan Pesko, the conductor here, has completed these to produce a sort of cantata. Indifferently recorded at a live concert presented by Italian Radio, it can be recommended to anyone curious about a composer too often unable to carry his strokes of genius to real fulfilment. This recording has been withdrawn in the UK.

Neruda, Jan (1708–*c.* 1780)

Trumpet concerto in E flat.
(M) ** Uni. RHS/*UKC* 337. Lang, Northern Sinf. O, Seaman – HAYDN and HUMMEL: *Trumpet concertos.***

The concerto by the Czech composer Jan Neruda is flexible of line and exploits the possibilities of its solo instrument in a conventional way, without producing music that is in any way memorable. William Lang's bold style with its open tone gives the music plenty of character and the recording is excellent. There is an acceptable cassette, though the LP has more range at the top.

Nielsen, Carl (1865–1931)

Andante Lamentoso (At the bier of a young child); Bohemian-Danish folk tune; Helios overture, Op. 17; An imaginary trip to the Faroe Islands; Pan and Syrinx, Op. 49; Saga-Drøm, Op. 39; Symphonic rhapsody.
(M) *** HMV Green. ESD/*TC-ESD* 143447-1/*4*. Danish RSO, Blomstedt.

While Nielsen's symphonies have been well represented in the catalogues over the last two or three decades, his shorter orchestral works have not been so well served. This is the first LP to collect them all, from the early *Symphonic rhapsody* of 1889, intended for a symphony, through to the late *Rhapsodic overture, An imaginary trip to the Faroes* of 1927, in eminently sound and idiomatic performances by the Danish Radio Symphony Orchestra under Herbert Blomstedt. At mid-price this is an invaluable offering. The recording is excellent, and the sound on cassette admirably refined (especially the upper strings) and detail is vivid.

Clarinet concerto, Op. 57.
(M) **(*) Uni. UNS 239. McCaw, New Philh. O, Leppard – MOZART: *Clarinet concerto.***(*)

A fine performance from John McCaw, direct but not lacking atmosphere. Perhaps the element of mystery and the musing improvisatory quality of the music are not entirely caught here, but the excellent accompaniment and clear recording certainly offer a very positive reproduction of Nielsen's score.

Symphony No. 1 in G min., Op. 7.
(M) **(*) Uni. KPM 7001/*UKC 7130* (with *Symphony No. 3*). LSO, Schmidt.

Nielsen's *First Symphony* is a delight. Its seams may be clearly visible but its musical ideas have such warmth, freshness and imagination that any doubts are instantly banished. Nielsen rightly retained a strong affection for it.

Ole Schmidt is a Nielsen conductor of vital instinct, but he is by no means so self-effacing as such distinguished predecessors as Thomas Jensen and Erik Tuxen, who recorded this composer in the 1950s. The *First* was composed while Nielsen was still a member of the Royal Orchestra, and its youthful freshness is not enhanced by a number of agogic distortions that Schmidt makes in the inner movements. The recording is not, perhaps, ideally balanced, but it is still good. On cassette the work is offered complete on one side, backed by the *Third Symphony*. The quality is full, clear and vivid.

Symphony No. 2 (The Four Temperaments), Op. 16.
(M) *** Uni. KPM 7002/*UKC 7250* (with *Symphony No. 5*). LSO, Schmidt.

Symphony No. 2 (The Four Temperaments); Aladdin suite, Op. 34.
*** BIS **CD 247**; LP/*MC* 247. Gothenburg SO, Myung-Whun Chung.

The *Second* is one of Nielsen's most appealing scores, and Ole Schmidt's account with the LSO is among the best to have been recorded since Thomas Jensen's pioneering 78s. He characterizes each of the four temperaments enshrined in the work to excellent effect, and every detail comes to life. The brass could perhaps have been more discreetly balanced in relation to the wind and strings; but this small reservation should not deter collectors. The cassette version is complete on a single side, coupled with the *Fifth Symphony*. The transfer is lively and the sound vivid, though slightly over-bright on top.

Myung-Whun Chung has a real feeling for this repertoire and his account of the *Second Symphony* is also very fine, in some ways even more impressive than Ole Schmidt's version. The Gothenburg Symphony Orchestra is not quite as fine an orchestra as the LSO, but proves an enthusiastic and responsive body of players; Chung, who studied with Sixten Ehrling at the Juilliard, does not put a foot wrong. The recording in all three formats is impressive too (the chrome cassette is excellent) and can be recommended with enthusiasm. There is no current alternative version of the *Aladdin* music. The Gothenburg orchestra plan to record all of Nielsen's output – as well as the complete Sibelius and a complete Stenhammar – and if the rest of the symphonies are as good, this will be a very distinguished set.

Symphony No. 3 (Sinfonia espansiva), Op. 27.
(M) **(*) Uni. KPM 7003/*UKC 7130* (with *Symphony No. 1*). Gomez, Rayner Cook, LSO, Schmidt.
** Uni. Kanchana KP/*UKC* 8006. Rehling, Hansen, Danish RSO, Ahronovich.

The *Sinfonia espansiva* is given a good performance under Schmidt, even if it falls short of the highest distinction. The first movement is a little wanting in momentum, but, generally speaking, tempi are well judged and there is evidence of sensitivity and breadth. Memories of earlier Danish performances of the 1950s from Erik Tuxen and John Frandsen are not wholly banished, but there is no serious reason to withhold a recommendation. The recording is not as refined or as transparent as the best modern engineering can produce but it is fully acceptable. On cassette the symphony is coupled with the *First Symphony*. The transfer is well managed, though a high-level playback is needed.

Ahronovich's *Espansiva* was recorded at a public concert in 1981. Its strength lies in the quality of sound Ahronovich secures from the strings who play with a lyrical intensity that does them credit and are responsive to his demands throughout the dynamic range. The wind, too, are finely blended and, throughout the orchestra, ensemble, tonal blend and balance are much to be admired. The Danish orchestra has this music in their bones but they produce a finer sonority for Ahronovich than they did for Blomstedt in his complete set. (His *Espansiva* is due for reissue in the lifetime of the present book and is coupled with the *Flute concerto*.) The weakness of Ahronovich's performance is the excessive care that he lavishes on the ends of phrases with some loss of momentum: *poco rit* becomes, more often than not, *molto rit*. There are gear-changes too that would prove irksome on repetition. Schmidt is to be preferred, even if he is at times more prosaic.

Symphony No. 4 (Inextinguishable), Op. 29.
*** DG Dig. **413 313-2**; 2532/*3302* 029 [id.]. Berlin PO, Karajan.
(M) *** Uni. KPM 7004/*UKC 7460* (with *Symphony No. 6*). LSO, Schmidt.
(B) ** PRT GSGC/*ZCGC* 2031. Hallé O, Barbirolli.

By far the best performance of Nielsen's *Fourth* ever recorded comes from Karajan. The orchestral playing is altogether incomparable and there is both vision and majesty in the reading. The strings play with passionate intensity at the opening of the third movement, and there is a thrilling sense of commitment throughout. The wind playing sounds a little over-civilized by comparison with the pioneering record from Launy Grøndahl and the Danish State Radio Orchestra, made in the early 1950s, but what exquisitely blended, subtle playing this is. It is excellently recorded, too. The sound on cassette is bright and vivid but rather light in the bass.

Schmidt gives a vital and invigorating account of the *Fourth Symphony* that captures its spirit as completely as any on record. Only a minor reservation has to be made: the wind are a little recessed, though the balance between them and the strings is well judged; but the brass are in a closer perspective and this is occasionally disturbing. On cassette the coupling is with the *Sixth*; the sound is very brilliant and needs a little taming.

At bargain price Barbirolli's version, despite the less than distinguished recording (equally shallow on both LP and tape, but quite acceptable), might be considered. Sir John secures some felicitous playing, notably in the *Poco allegretto* and *Poco adagio*. In the USA, Markevich's Turnabout version [TV 34050] is the best buy in the lower-price range. Markevich has genuine fire and a real feeling for Nielsen, and he secures a fine response from the Royal Danish Orchestra. Unfortunately the level of the disc is cut rather low.

Symphonies Nos. 4 (Inextinguishable), Op. 29; 5, Op. 50; Helios overture, Op. 17; Saga-drøm, Op. 39.
(M) **(*) HMV *TCC2-POR 154593-9*. Danish RSO, Blomstedt.

Tape collectors should find this double-length 'Portrait of the Artist' cassette worth acquiring. Each symphony is complete on one side with one of the two shorter works as a filler. The sound is full and brilliant. Blomstedt's version of the *Fourth* is excellent with some fine wind playing from the Danish orchestra. In the *Fifth* Berglund is to be preferred (see below), but with two major works offered for the price of one, this is good value.

Symphony No. 5, Op. 50.
(M) *** EMI Em. EMX/*TC-EMX* 2033. Bournemouth SO, Berglund.
(M) *** Uni. KPM/*UKC* 7250 (with *Symphony No. 2*). LSO, Schmidt.

Nielsen's *Fifth* is well served by both these records. Berglund's version is probably the better buy, both in terms of performance and recording. Berglund is sometimes unimaginative on disc, but here he gives of his very best. The recording is very fine; it has wide range and atmosphere. The sound on cassette is acceptable, but does not match the disc in upper range, and climaxes seem less expansive in consequence.

Ole Schmidt's account is also first-class. He brings freshness and authenticity of feeling to this music, and the LSO respond positively to his direction. Minor reservations about balance apart, this is a well-recorded and highly recommendable version. The cassette transfer too is impressive; there is plenty of bite and impact at climaxes yet no congestion and beautifully refined string pianissimos.

Symphony No. 6 (Sinfonia semplice).
(M) *** Uni. KPM 7006/*UKC 7460* (with *Symphony No. 4*). LSO, Schmidt.

Nielsen's *Sinfonia semplice* is one of his strangest and most haunting utterances. The first and third movements in particular must rank among his most remarkable and visionary achievements. As with No. 5, Ole Schmidt scores a resounding success here, and his version is closer to the spirit and the letter of this work than any of the previous rivals. Much the same reservations apply to the recorded sound as we have noted in the companion discs, but they are not serious enough to inhibit a strong recommendation. The cassette version (coupled with the *Fourth*) needs a little smoothing on top but is vivid and clear.

CHAMBER MUSIC

Canto serioso; Fantasias for oboe and piano, Op. 2; The Mother (incidental music), *Op. 41; Serenata in vano; Wind quintet, Op. 43.*
** Chan. ABR/*ABT* 1003. Athena Ens.

A most useful record which collects Nielsen's output for wind instruments in chamber form. The Athena Ensemble give a thoroughly lively account of the *Wind quintet*; they earn gratitude for observing the exposition repeat in the first movement but none for ignoring some of the dynamic markings! The ostinato figure at letter D in the first movement is marked *pp* but does not really sound it here, though the close balance does not help matters. The balance is rather more disturbing in the *Serenata in vano*, where the clarinet is in your lap, and similar points could be made about the other pieces. But none of them is otherwise available and all are beautiful; they are also very well played. The cassette transfer is of good quality, smooth and refined.

String quartets: Nos. 1 in F min., Op. 5; 2 in G min., Op. 13; 3 in E flat, Op. 14; 4 in F, Op. 44.
*** RCA Conifer RL40252 (2). Kontra Qt.

Nielsen's quartets are all comparatively early, the last dating from 1906, the year that saw the production of *Maskarade*. The first numbered quartet, which was eventually published as Op. 13, comes from 1888, the same year as the quintet and the *Little suite*, Op. 1, though it is by no means as original as the latter. Another and more individual work came two years later in 1890, but it is not until the *E flat* and *F major Quartets* that one can speak of real masterpieces. It is astonishing that no major international quartet has championed them either in the concert hall or on record. The Kontra Quartet give an impassioned and totally committed account of all four; their tonal blend is excellent, their ensemble good and they possess a wide dynamic range. At times they project almost too much, and in the chorale movement of No. 4 they could have allowed the music to speak for itself a little more. The earlier Turnabout/Vox accounts with the Copenhagen Quartet were more relaxed, but the Kontras do not compare unfavourably to them in other respects and are better recorded. They are also to be preferred to their DG rivals, never issued in the UK, made by the Carl Nielsen Quartet whose technical address is not fully the equal of the Kontra. (They couple Opp. 5 and 14 on DG 2531 135 and Opp. 13 and 44 on DG 2530 920 and are recommendable, but not in preference to the RCA set.)

Wind quintet, Op. 43.
** Uni. RHS 366. Danish Wind Quintet – HINDEMITH: *Kleine Kammermusik* ***; MILHAUD: *Cheminée du Roi René*.*(*)

Well recorded though they are, the Danish Wind Quintet do not play with quite the same sensitivity as their namesakes who made the pioneering set of this work. There are felicitous touches, of course, but dynamic inconsistencies – the absence of really soft playing – and a certain want of poetry diminish the impact of this performance. It would be wrong to place too much weight on its shortcomings, for we are not well served at present (the Melos version is deleted); but this remains a stop-gap that falls short of the ideal.

Maskarade (opera; complete).
(M) *** Uni. RHS 350/2. Hansen, Plesner, Landy, Johansen, Sørensen, Bastian, Brodersen, Haugland, Danish R. Ch. and SO, Frandsen.

Maskarade is new to the gramophone: only the overture and a handful of interludes have been recorded before. It is Nielsen's second and last opera and must be accounted a triumphant success in this recording. The libretto derives from Holberg's comedy of 1724, which Nielsen himself shaped into operatic form with the literary historian Vilhelm Andersen as collaborator. The plot is straightforward and simple, and to recount it would do scant justice to the charm and interest of the opera. *Maskarade* is a buoyant, high-spirited score full of strophic songs and choruses, making considerable use of dance and dance rhythms, and having the unmistakable lightness of the *buffo* opera. It is excellently proportioned: no Act outstays its welcome, one is always left wanting more, and the scoring is light and transparent. The performance here is delightful and is distinguished by generally good singing and alert orchestral support. The sound is well focused and the singers well blended; even if they are a trifle forward in relation to the orchestra, this is in no way obtrusive. Above all, the sound is musical, the images well-located and firm. There are none of the awkward edits that disfigured *Saul and David*, and the sound is altogether more vivid.

Maskarade: highlights.
(M) *** Uni. RHM/*UKC* 100 (from above recording, cond. Frandsen).

A delightful anthology of highlights from Nielsen's opera for those reluctant to invest in the whole work. This will give a good picture of the work as a whole, and the only reservation one might have in recommending it is that, having acquired it, few will be able to resist the temptation to invest in the complete opera. The sparkling tape is of demonstration quality, matching the disc in every way.

Saul and David (opera): complete (in English).
(M) **(*) Uni. RHS 343/5. Christoff, Young, Söderström, Hartmann, Langdon, Borg, Alldis Ch., Danish R. Ch. and SO, Horenstein (supplementary retakes cond. Joel Lazar).

Saul and David is the first of Nielsen's two operas and is from the same period as the *Second Symphony*. This performance emanates from a broadcast organized by the EBU in 1972 and leaves no doubt as to the opera's quality. The firm melodic line, the individual fresh vein of chromaticism and the resourceful harmonies, the sense of forward movement: all these will be familiar to those who know their early Nielsen. The high quality of the choral writing is evident right from the beginning: Nielsen's writing for chorus is of striking beauty and originality. It is on Saul that the opera mainly centres: his is the classic tragic story of the downfall of a great man through some flaw of character, and it is for him that Nielsen mobilizes our deepest interest and sympathy. Christoff brings power and nobility to the role, though there are times when pressure results in some obtrusive vibrato. The other distinguished soloists, particularly Söderström as Michael and Alexander Young as David, give well-characterized accounts of their roles, and we are not likely to get as conscientious and noble a reading of the score as that given us by the late Jascha Horenstein. The Danish Radio Orchestra responds sensitively to all the demands he makes on them. The recording is good rather than distinguished, and there are some awkward edits. But these should on no account put readers off getting this glorious opera, which will give enormous pleasure.

Nono, Luigi (born 1924)

A floresta è jovem e cheja de vida (1965/6) for soprano, voices, clarinet, copper plates and magnetic tape; . . . sofferte onde serene . . . (1976) for piano and magnetic tape.
*** DG 2531 004 [id.]. Poli, Pollini, Bove, Vicini, Troni, William Smith, cond. Canino.

sofferte onde serene represents Nono's direct response to the playing of Pollini, his sympathy and admiration heightened by family bereavements suffered by composer and pianist. The concentration of the performance helps one to make light of the difficulty of idiom. The other work has a frankly political purpose, containing as it does a setting of words by an Angolan guerrilla and an appeal against the war in Vietnam. For full appreciation it plainly requires a degree of political involvement matching that of the composer, but the vitality of the writing is not in doubt, with shouting and gasping of texts set against regular singing. Performances and recording here are excellent.

Novák, Vítězslav (1870–1949)

Tone poems: *About the Eternal Longing, Op. 33; In the Tatras, Op. 26.*
(M) ** Sup. 50747. Czech PO, Sejna.

Novák was a pupil of Dvořák, and his best work, *The Storm* (see below), is warm-hearted, richly generous music which shows perhaps the influence of Strauss, Debussy and Janáček. *In the Tatras* is an opulent Straussian tone-poem, though Novák speaks with distinctive accents. Both works here are persuasively played, though the recordings are reverberant and a little pale.

De profundis (tone poem), *Op. 67.*
(M) **(*) Sup. 50476. Brno State PO, Vogel – SUK: *War triptych.***(*)

De profundis is a wartime work, written in 1941 during the last decade of the composer's life. It is noble and dignified, well argued and obviously deeply felt. This fine performance should win many friends for the piece; it also has the merit of excellent recording.

Marysa overture; Slovak suite.
(M) *** Sup. 110 0648. Brno State PO, Sejna.

What a heavenly score the *Slovak suite* is! *Two in love*, its fourth movement, could well become as widely popular as any piece of music you care to think of. Much of the score is as appealing as Dvořák; and although the *Marysa overture* is not quite as delightfully inventive it is still a welcome bonus. Sejna does not play with quite the open-hearted geniality that marked Talich's LP of the 1950s, but he is better recorded and there need be no reservations on grounds of quality.

Trio quasi una ballata, Op. 27.
(M) *** Sup. 111 1089. Czech Trio, Páleníček (piano) – DVOŘÁK: *Piano trio No. 4.****

Novák's finest music has a nobility that recalls his master, Dvořák, as well as his freshness, with something too of the richness and the dignity of Elgar and Strauss. The *Trio quasi una ballata* is an intense, rather emotional piece, and here is given an impassioned performance.

The Storm, Op. 42; Ranoša, Op. 19/1.
(M) *** Sup. 1112 3231/2. Soloists, Czech Ch. and PO, Košler.

The Storm is arguably Novák's finest composition and this is its first stereo recording. It was briefly available in mono in a fine performance by Jaroslav Krombholc, and this newcomer is long overdue. It is a work of great beauty and imagination, scored with consummate mastery and showing a lyrical gift of a high order. It has warmth and genuine individuality; the idiom owes something to Richard Strauss as well as the Czech tradition, and there is an impressive command of both melody and structure. This is noble, moving and powerful music – very different from, say, Janáček but recognizably from the same part of the world and equally fresh. This is a fine recording and performance, though the sound is just a shade wanting in real depth. *Ranoša* is a miniature cantata for chorus and orchestra based on a Moravian folk poem. It is a straightforward, attractive piece and makes a good fill-up for the major work. Strongly recommended.

Nystroem, Gösta (1890–1966)

Sinfonia breve.
*** Cap. CAP 1116. Gothenburg SO, Ehrling – HOLMBOE: *Symphony No. 10.****

Gösta Nystroem studied painting and music as a young man, and spent his formative years in Paris. His music shows something of the influence of Honegger, and though it is deficient in melodic vitality, he is able to project a certain atmosphere. The *Sinfonia breve* comes from the period 1929–31, thus preceding by a few years his finest work, the *Sinfonia espressiva*, which enjoyed a brief vogue in this country after the war. It is well played and recorded here, though it must be conceded that the main attraction of this disc is the Holmboe symphony, a most powerful and cogently argued work.

Ockeghem, Johannes

(*c*. 1410–1497)

30 Chansons (complete secular music).
*** O-L D 254 D 3 (3) [id.]. London Medieval Ens., Peter and Timothy Davies.

Ockeghem was not a prolific master: apart from the chansons collected here, there are eleven masses, a requiem and a number of motets. This set of records includes all the chansons attributed to him in fifteenth-century manuscripts, including twenty-two of whose authenticity there is no doubt. He is generally thought to be the most outstanding composer of chanson after Dufay and there is no doubt as to the elegance and refinement of many of the pieces recorded here, nor can there be much about their diversity and range. The accompanying essay and texts of the songs is most helpful in going through this rewarding set. The performances are intelligent and sensitive and the use of instrumental support imaginative. At times the ear tires of the somewhat white timbre of the voices but there is no doubting the accomplishment of these artists, or the excellence of the recording.

Offenbach, Jacques (1819–80)

Gaîté parisienne (ballet, arr. Rosenthal).
*** Ph. Dig. **411 039-2**; 6514/*7337* 367 [id.]. Pittsburgh SO, Previn.
(*) Decca Dig. **411 708-2; 411 708-1/*4*. Montreal SO, Dutoit (with GOUNOD: *Faust: ballet music***(*)).
(M) ** HMV Green. ESD/*TC-ESD* 7152 (*Suite*); [(d) Ang. S/*4XS* 37209]. Monte Carlo Op. O, Rosenthal – ROSSINI: *La Boutique fantasque*.**(*)
(M) ** Decca Jub. JB/*KJBC* 12 [Lon. JL/*5*-41029]. ROHCG O, Solti – GOUNOD: *Faust: ballet*.**
(M) *(*) Decca VIV/*KVIC* 60. New Philh. O, Munch.

Previn's digital recording sweeps the board. He realizes that tempi can remain relaxed, and the music's natural high spirits will still bubble to the surface. The orchestral playing is both spirited and elegant, with Previn obviously relishing the score's delightful detail. The rhythmic spring is captivating, as is the gentle lilt in the *Barcarolle*, Ländler and Waltz movements (from *La Belle Hélène*, for instance). The fizzing effervescence does not prevent a minor sense of *gravitas* when necessary and this is mirrored by the Philips sound balance which has substance as well as atmosphere and brilliance. Perhaps the tuba thumbing away in the bass is a shade too present, but it increases one's desire to smile through this engagingly happy music. The chrome cassette tends to be bass-orientated, but with adjustment of the controls can be made to produce good results. The CD is splendid.

Dutoit has the advantage of sound that is brighter and has rather more projection than Previn's Philips disc, though the acoustic is resonant and detail is no clearer. But the recording is undoubtedly out of Decca's top drawer. He opens the music racily and there are many admirable touches, yet as the ballet proceeds there is a hint of blandness in the lyrical moments, and the *Barcarolle* is somewhat disappointing. Some might like the extra feeling of breadth Dutoit generates, but Previn catches the spirit of the score more naturally. The Decca record has the advantage of including also the *Faust* ballet music, warmly and elegantly played, but here also Dutoit's touch is a shade heavy. The feeling in both works is redolent of the concert hall rather than the ballet theatre. There is an excellent chrome cassette, but we have not sampled the compact disc.

After this, all the other versions are also-rans. Rosenthal's own account is only heard in a selection on the Greensleeve record (in the USA the full ballet is offered), but the reading is not strong on sparkle, though the bright recording brings good projection and the orchestral playing is lively.

Solti drives the music hard and misses its essential geniality. But his orchestra give a virtuoso performance and their bravura is certainly infectious, even if sometimes a little breathless. The reverberant sound is both brilliant and sumptuous and there is a first-class matching cassette.

Munch's Decca Viva disc is a reissue of a recording originally made in Phase Four. The balance is very forward and while the new pressing has clarified the detail it also increases the feeling of aggressiveness, for the music is hard-driven and there is a complete absence of charm.

Overtures: *Barbe-Bleue; La Belle Hélène; Les deux Aveugles; La Fille du tambour-major; La Grande Duchesse de Gérolstein; Orphée aux enfers* (*Orpheus in the Underworld*); *La Périchole; La Vie parisienne.*
*** Ph. Dig. 6514/*7337* 098 [id.]. Philh. O, Marriner.

Where Karajan in his Offenbach collection – see below – tended to use inflated versions of these operetta overtures by hands other than the composer's, Marriner prefers something nearer to the original scale, even though *Orpheus*, *Belle Hélène* and *La Périchole* are not originals. This music suits the sprightly, rhythmic style of Marriner splendidly, and the Philharmonia responds with polished playing, very well recorded. The chrome cassette is less lively than the LP.

Overtures: *La Belle Hélène; Bluebeard; La Grande-Duchesse de Gérolstein; Orpheus in the Underworld; Vert-vert. Barcarolle* from *Contes d'Hoffmann.*
(*) DG Dig. **400 044-2; 2532/*3302* 006 [id.]. Berlin PO, Karajan.

Other hands besides Offenbach's helped to shape his overtures. Most are on a pot-pourri basis, but the tunes and scoring are so engagingly witty as to confound criticism. *La Belle Hélène*, by Haensch, is well constructed, and the delightful waltz tune is given a reprise before the end. Karajan's performances racily evoke the theatre pit, and the brilliance is extrovert almost to the point of fierceness. But the Berlin playing is very polished and with so much to entice the ear this cannot fail to be entertaining. The demonstration item is *Vert-vert*, which is irresistibly tuneful and vivacious. The digital recording is extremely vivid and there is no appreciable difference between disc and cassette: both have plenty of range and immediacy. The compact disc emphasizes the dryness of the orchestral sound, and the effect is rather clinical with the strings lacking bloom. This is disappointing.

Le Papillon (ballet-pantomime): complete.
*** Decca SXL 6588 [Lon. CS 6812]. LSO, Bonynge.

Le Papillon is Offenbach's only full-length ballet and it dates from 1860. The quality of the invention is high, the music sparkles from beginning to end, and in such a sympathetic performance, vividly recorded, it cannot fail to give pleasure. Highly recommended to all lovers of ballet and Offenbach.

Cello duos, Op. 54: Suites Nos. 1 and 2.
*** HM HM/*40* 1043. Pidoux, Peclard.

This Harmonia Mundi issue is an unexpected and delightful surprise. Offenbach was himself a very accomplished cellist, and these two works are bristling with bravura, but tuneful too and imaginatively laid out to exploit the tonal possibilities of such a duo. The two works offer plenty of contrast and Offenbach's natural wit is especially apparent in the *First Suite in E major*. The performances here are excellent and so is the recording.

Les Contes d'Hoffmann (*The Tales of Hoffmann*): complete.
❀ *** Decca SET 545-7/*K 109 K 32* (2) [Lon. OSA/*5*-13106]. Sutherland, Domingo, Tourangeau, Bacquier, R. Suisse Romande and Lausanne Pro Arte Ch., SRO, Bonynge.

** EMI 1C 157 00045/7 [Ang. S 3667]. Schwarzkopf, Los Angeles, D'Angelo, Gedda, Fauré, Benoit, Ghiuselev, London, Blanc, Laffage, Geay, Duclos Ch., Paris Conservatoire O, Cluytens.

Joan Sutherland gives a virtuoso performance in four heroine roles here, not only as Olympia, Giulietta and Antonia but as Stella in the Epilogue, which in this version – very close to that prepared by Tom Hammond for the English National Opera – is given greater weight by the inclusion of the ensemble previously inserted into the Venice scene as a septet, a magnificent climax. Bonynge opts for spoken dialogue, and puts the Antonia scene last, as being the more substantial. His direction is unfailingly sympathetic, while Sutherland is impressive in each role, notably as the doll Olympia and in the pathos of the Antonia scene. As Giulietta she hardly sounds like a *femme fatale*, but still produces beautiful singing. Domingo gives one of his finest performances on record, and so does Gabriel Bacquier. Superb atmospheric recording quality, on disc and tape alike. It is a memorable set, in every way, much more than the sum of its parts.

Several bad mistakes in the casting prevent the alternative EMI set from being the rare delight it should have been. It has some marvellous moments, and the whole of the *Barcarolle* scene with Schwarzkopf is a delight, but the very distinction of the cast-list makes one annoyed that the result is not better. In particular André Cluytens surprisingly proved quite the wrong conductor for this sparkling music, for he has little idea of caressing the music (as Beecham for example did so ravishingly) and rarely fails to push on regardless. Gianna d'Angelo's Olympia is pretty but shallow, George London's Coppelius and Dr Miracle unpleasantly gruff-toned and, most disappointing of all, Victoria de los Angeles is sadly out of voice, with the upper register regularly turning sour on her. But with such artists even below their best there are characterful moments which take the listener along well enough. Cluytens in his ruthlessness has a certain demonic energy which has its dramatic side. The recording lacks the sort of brilliance one would expect, but is atmospheric enough.

Les Contes d'Hoffmann: highlights.
*** Decca SET/*KCET* 569 [Lon. OS/5-26369]. (from above recording, cond. Bonynge).
** HMV SXLP/*TC-SXLP* 30538 [Ang. S 36413]. (from above recording, cond. Cluytens).

The Decca highlights disc is outstandingly generous. One of the finest compilations of its kind from any opera, it gives a superbly managed distillation of nearly all the finest items, and it is edited most skilfully. The cassette version is of demonstration quality.

With the complete Cluytens set of this opera performed with varying success, a selection may be the answer for the collector unable to resist the casting. Most of the best moments are here, including the Schwarzkopf/Gedda duet from the Venetian scene, not to mention the famous *Barcarolle* and the brilliant *Septet*. De los Angeles and London again provide the vocal disappointments. The cassette is vividly transferred, if a trifle fierce.

Les Contes d'Hoffmann: excerpts.
(M) *** Decca GRV/*KGRC* 22. Domingo, Sutherland. (from above set, cond. Bonynge) – BIZET: *Carmen*: excerpts.***

It was understandable that Decca should combine these highly successful excerpts (including the *Kleinzach ballade* and the duet, *C'est une chanson d'amour*) with scenes from *Carmen* for Domingo's 'Grandi voci' representation. The singing is first-class and the sound out of Decca's top drawer. On tape the upper range needs a little smoothing.

La Grande Duchesse de Gérolstein (complete).
(M) *** CBS 79207 (2) [M2- 34576]. Crespin, Mesplé, Vanzo, Massard, Ch., O of Capitole, Toulouse, Plasson.

Enter the Grand Duchess to inspect her troops (*Oh how I love the military men*) and there before her, a humble private, is simple Fritz, whom she promptly promotes in a series of rapid moves to be commander in chief of the Gérolstein army. Though the story later has a black streak, when the Grand Duchess herself grows tired of a favourite who persists in not understanding her designs, it is an irresistible formula. Régine Crespin gives a great performance, the grandest of grand ladies with a twinkle in her eye. Michel Plasson directs a scintillating account with an excellent cast, in which Alain Vanzo as Fritz and Robert Massard as General Boum stand out. The spoken dialogue is brilliantly acted and produced too, to make this a delectable set.

(i) *Mesdames de la Halle*. (ii) *Monsieur Choufleuri*. (iii) *Pomme d'Api* (complete recordings).
*** HMV Dig. SLS/*TC-SLS* 173174-3/5 (3). (i–iii) Mesplé, Lafont; (i; ii) Burles, Trempont, Hamel; (i; iii) Pezzino; Laforge Ch. Ens., Monte Carlo PO, Rosenthal.

All three of these sparkling one-Act operettas make delightful listening, idiomatically performed under Manuel Rosenthal. *Pomme d'Api* has the usual triangle between an old man, his nephew and the girl they both fancy. *Monsieur Choufleuri* involves a party scene with imitations of grand opera, while *Mesdames de la Halle* is a knockabout farce with three characters in drag, set in the Parisian fruit-market. The proportion of French spoken dialogue may be rather high for repeated listenings, but the zest of the many musical numbers is well worth investigating. Mady Mesplé is less shrill of tone than she has sometimes been, hardening only on top. Like the other principals she has the right style. Outstanding among the others is the baritone, Jean-Philippe Lafont. Warm, atmospheric recording, with discs and tapes sounding virtually identical.

Orphée aux enfers (*Orpheus in the Underworld;* 1874 version).
*** HMV SLS 5175 (3) [Ang. SZX/*4Z3X* 3886]. Sénéchal, Mesplé, Rhodes Burles, Berbié, Petits Chanteurs à la Croix Potencée, Toulouse Capitole Ch. and O, Plasson.

Plasson recorded his fizzing performance – the first complete set in French for thirty years – in time for the Offenbach centenary. He used the far fuller four-Act text of 1874 instead of the two-Act version of 1858, so adding such delectable rarities as the sparkling *Rondo* of Mercury and the *Policemen's chorus*. Mady Mesplé as usual has her shrill moments, but the rest of the cast is excellent, and Plasson's pacing of the score is exemplary. The recording is warmly atmospheric and the leavening of music with spoken dialogue just enough.

Orpheus in the Underworld: abridged version (in English).
**(*) HMV CSD/*TC-CSD* 1316. Bronhill, Shilling, Miller, Weaving, Steele, Nisbett, Thurlow, Crofoot, Sadler's Wells Op. Ch. and O, Faris.

With a single reservation only, this is an enchanting disc. Without visual help the recording manages to convey the high spirits and genuine gaiety of the piece, plus – and this is an achievement for a non-Parisian company – the sense of French poise and precision. June Bronhill in the *Concerto duet* is infectiously provocative about her poor suitor's music. One's only complaint is that Alan Crofoot's King of the Boeotians is needlessly cruel vocally. The sound is full and brilliant, with plenty of atmosphere, and there is no doubt that this issue is very successful. The cassette transfer sparkles. There is just a hint of peaking on one or two female high notes, but this is not too serious.

La Périchole (complete).
**(*) HMV Dig. SLS/*TCC-SLS* 5276 (2) [Ang. DSBX/*4X2X* 3923]. Berganza, Carreras, Bacquier, Sénéchal, Trempont, Delange, Toulouse Capitole Ch. and O, Plasson.

A good modern recording of this delightful piece was badly needed, and in many ways this fills the bill admirably, for though the sound (as usual in Toulouse) is over-reverberant, the ensemble work is excellent, with diction surprisingly clear against warm orchestral sound. The incidental roles are superbly taken, but it is odd that Spaniards were chosen for the two principal roles. José Carreras uses his always lovely tenor to fine effect but is often unidiomatic, while Teresa Berganza – who should have made the central character into a vibrant figure, as Régine Crespin used to – is surprisingly heavy and unsparkling.

La Vie parisienne (complete).
*** HMV SLS 5076 (2). Crespin, Mesplé, Masson, Sénéchal, Ch. and O of Capitole, Toulouse, Plasson.

Hardly less effervescent than the parallel version of *La Grande Duchesse*, also conducted by Michel Plasson for CBS, *La Vie parisienne* is a scintillating example of Offenbach's work, an inconsequential farce around the heady days of the International Exhibition in Paris. Though the HMV recording is not quite so consistent as the CBS one of *The Grand Duchess*, the performance and presentation sparkle every bit as brilliantly, with the spoken dialogue for once a special attraction. Régine Crespin in a smaller role is just as commanding, and though the cast lacks the excellent Vanzo and Massard, the style is captivatingly authentic.

'The world of Offenbach': Overtures: (i; ii) *La Belle Hélène;* (iii; iv) *La Fille du tambour-major;* (i; ii) *Orpheus in the Underworld.* (iii; iv) *Le Papillon: Valse des rayons. Les Contes d'Hoffmann:* (v; i; iv) *Ballad of Kleinzach;* (vi; i; iv) *Doll's song;* (vi; vii; i; iv) *Barcarolle. La Grande Duchesse de Gérolstein:* (viii; i; ix) *Piff-paff-puff;* (x–xii) *Portez armes . . . J'aime les militaires. La Périchole:* (x; i; xii) *Air de lettre; Ah! quel dîner.*
(M) *** Decca SPA/*KCSP* 512. (i) SRO; (ii) Ansermet; (iii) LSO; (iv) Bonynge; (v) Domingo; (vi) Sutherland; (vii) Tourangeau; (viii) Corena; (ix) Walker; (x) Crespin; (xi) V. Volksoper O; (xii) Lombard.

A characteristically felicitous Decca anthology, as generous as it is wide-ranging. The performances can hardly be faulted; Ansermet and Bonynge offer much character in the overtures, and the vocal numbers – which come from a wide variety of sources – are no less colourful. The recording throughout is immensely vivid on disc and tape alike. Ansermet incidentally takes the final *Can-can* of the *Orpheus overture* (which closes the concert) slower than usual, but invests it with such rhythmic vigour that the music sounds freshly minted.

Ohana, Maurice (born 1914)

(i) *Mass;* (ii) *Lys de madrigaux.*
*** Erato STU 71482. (i) Garcisanz, Schaer, Etchebarne, Ens., French R. Ch., Riebel; (ii) Instrumental Ens., French R. Ch., Riebel.

Maurice Ohana is a Gibraltar-born composer of Moroccan descent who lives in Paris. His *Guitar concerto* (1950–57), subtitled *Tres Gráficos*, was recorded some years ago by Narciso Yepes (DG 2530 585) and is a highly imaginative piece, and his setting of Lorca's *Lament for the death of Sanchez Mejas* enjoyed a *succès d'estime* in the early 1950s. The *Mass* comes from 1977 and is a thoughtful, static, mystical piece, contemporary in idiom yet far from inaccessible and often highly atmospheric. In the *Lily of madrigals* of 1976 there are many touches of fantasy, and some of the choral and instrumental effects almost suggest the fierce light of the south and the heat haze of North Africa. Many readers will find this interesting and rewarding, and the performances are as expert as is the French Radio engineering.

Orff, Carl (1895–1982)

Carmina Burana (cantata).
*** HMV ASD/*TC-ASD* 3117 [Ang. S/*4XS* 37117]. Armstrong, English, Allen, St Clement Danes Grammar School Boys' Ch., LSO Ch., LSO, Previn.
*** HMV ASD/*TC-ASD* 3900 [Ang. SZ/*4ZS* 37666]. Auger, Summers, Van Kesteren, Southend Boys' Ch., Philh. Ch. and O, Muti.
(M) *** HMV Green. ESD/*TC-ESD* 7177

[Ang. S/*4XS* 36333]. Popp, Unger, Wolansky, Noble, New Philh. Ch., Wandsworth School Boys' Ch., New Philh. O, Frühbeck de Burgos.

*** DG 139 362/*923 062* [id.]. Janowitz, Stolze, Fischer-Dieskau, Schöneberger Boys' Ch., German Op. Ch., Berlin PO, Jochum.

(B) *** DG Walkman *413 160-4*. (as above, cond. Jochum) – STRAVINSKY: *Rite of spring*.**(*)

(M) **(*) RCA VICS/*VK* 2026 [AGL1/*AGK1* 4082]. Mandac, Kolk, Milnes, Children's Ch., New England Conservatory Ch., Boston SO, Ozawa.

(*) Telarc Dig. **CD 80056; DG 10056/7 [id.]. Blegen, W. Brown, Hagegard, Atlanta Ch. and SO, Shaw – HINDEMITH: *Symphonic metamorphoses*.**(*)

(*) RCA Dig. **RCD 14550; RL 13925 ATC1/*ATK1* 3925. Hendricks, Adler, Hagegard, Boys of St Paul's Cath., LSO Ch., LSO, Mata.

(B) **(*) PRT GSGC/*ZCGC* 2000. Hartman, Brunner, Knoll, Salz. Mozarteum Ch. and O, Prestel.

**(*) Ph. 9500 040/*7300 444* [id.]. Casapietra, Heistermann, Stryczek, Dresden Boys' Ch., Leipzig R. Ch. and SO, Kegel.

** Decca Jub. JB/*KJBC* 78 [Lon. JL/*4-41006*]. Burrows, Devos, Shirley-Quirk, Southend Boys' Ch., Brighton Fest. Ch., RPO, Dorati.

** DG Priv. 2535/*3335* 275 [id.]. Vulpius, Rotzsch, Rehm, Hübenthal, Children's Ch., Leipzig R. Ch. and SO, Kegel.

** CfP CFP/*TC-CFP* 4381. Armstrong, Rayner Cook, Hall, Manchester Grammar School Boys' Ch., Hallé Ch. and O, Handford.

HMV have seemingly almost secured a monopoly on recommendations for Orff's most colourful work. Previn's version, richly recorded with a closely matching cassette, is strong on humour and rhythmic point. The chorus sings vigorously, the men often using an aptly rough tone, but they do not quite match the superb precision of Frühbeck's and Jochum's choirs. The main point of contrast between Previn and these two fine rivals lies in the resilience of rhythms, finely sprung, which brings out a strain not just of humour but of real wit. This is a performance which swaggers along and makes you smile. The recording captures the antiphonal effects brilliantly, better even in the orchestra than in the chorus. Among the soloists Thomas Allen's contribution is one of the glories of the music-making, and in their lesser roles the soprano and tenor are equally stylish.

Partly because of recording which dramatically brings out the fullest weight of bass (timpani and bass drum most spectacular at the opening) Muti's is a reading which underlines the dramatic contrasts, both of dynamic and tempo. So the nagging ostinatos are as a rule pressed on at breakneck speed, and the result, if at times a little breathless, is always exhilarating. The soloists are first-rate; Arleen Auger is wonderfully reposeful in *In trutina* and Jonathan Summers in his first major recording characterizes well. The Philharmonia Chorus is not quite at its most polished, but the Southend Boys are outstandingly fine. This is a performance which may lose something in wit and jollity but is as full of excitement as any available. On cassette the choral sound is satisfyingly full-blooded but the wide dynamic range has brought serious recession of image when the soloists are singing quietly.

Frühbeck de Burgos gives the kind of performance of *Carmina Burana* which is ideal for gramophone listening. Where Ozawa favours a straightforward approach, with plenty of impact in the climaxes, it is in the more lyrical pages that Burgos scores with his much greater imagination and obvious affection. This is not to suggest that the Philharmonia account has any lack of vitality. Indeed the sheer gusto of the singing is the more remarkable when one considers the precision from both singers and orchestra alike. The brass too bring out the rhythmic pungency, which is such a dominating feature of the work, with splendid life and point. Lucia Popp's soprano solo *Amor volat* is really ravishing, and Gerhard Unger, the tenor, brings a Lieder-like sensitivity to his lovely singing of his very florid solo in the tavern scene. To complete the picture the HMV stereo is wide in dynamic range; while being as vivid as anyone could want in the climaxes, it also brings out the gentler colourings that Burgos coaxes so luminously from singers and orchestra alike. The cassette is marginally over-modulated and the focus coarsens at climaxes.

The DG production under Jochum is also highly distinguished, and some might well acquire it for Fischer-Dieskau's contribution. His singing is refined but not too much so, and his first solo, *Omnia Sol temperat*, and later *Dies, nox et omnia* are both very beautiful, with the kind of tonal shading that a great Lieder singer can bring. Perhaps *Estuans interius* needs a heavier voice, but Fischer-Dieskau is suitably gruff in the Abbot's song – so much so that for the moment the voice is unrecognizable. Gerhard Stolze too is very stylish in his falsetto *Song of the roasted swan*. The soprano, Gundula Janowitz, finds a quiet dignity for her contribution and this is finely done. But she is no match for Lucia Popp in *Amor volat*, where her upper register is less creamy. The chorus are best when the music blazes, and the closing scene is moulded by Jochum with a wonderful control, almost Klemperian in its restrained power. The snag is that in the quieter music the choral contribution is less immediate. The recording is wide in dynamic range, and the spacious acoustic (with plenty of detail coming through nonetheless) means that when the singing is gentle it is in danger of losing impact, and there is not a compensating increase of tension in the performance. The cassette matches the disc closely, although the level rises on side two, bringing more edge to the chorus.

Jochum's recording is also available on a bargain-priced Walkman cassette. It is admirably transferred on to chrome stock and in this format it sounds first-class. The Stravinsky coupling is rather less successful because of a resonant acoustic, but this remains very good value.

A strong, incisive performance from Seiji Ozawa. The clarity of the recording emphasizes the bold simplicity of the score, rather than dwelling on its subtlety of colour. The solo singers too are characterful rather than showing great beauty of tone, although there is no lack of understanding of the music's line. But of its kind this is an effective account, and the blaze of inspiration of Orff's masterpiece comes over with spontaneity. The high-level chrome cassette gives a vibrant edge to the choral sound. There is plenty of body and range, though in one or two fortissimos the bass is somewhat explosive.

Spreading *Carmina Burana* on to three sides instead of the usual two makes for wide groove spacing, and Telarc characteristically present exceptionally full and brilliant sound, though hardly more so than the analogue sound given to Muti on HMV. Like Muti, Robert Shaw – who was for some years Toscanini's choir-master – prefers speeds on the fast side, though his manner is more metrical. In *The Court of Love* one wants more persuasive treatment, though the choral singing – recorded rather close in analytical sound – is superb. The soloists are good, but the Atlanta boys cannot quite match their rivals on most European versions. The compact disc issue is on two sides only, but the recorded sound is unflattering to the soloists – notably the baritone, Hakan Hagegard – although the choral and orchestral sound is certainly spectacular. (The CD of course omits the Hindemith coupling.)

Mata's is a volatile performance, not as metrical in its rhythms as most, which at times means that the LSO Chorus is not as precise in ensemble as it is for Previn. The choristers of St Paul's Cathedral sing with perfect purity, perhaps not boyish enough, and though the soloists are first-rate (with John Adler coping splendidly, in high refined tones, with the roast swan episode), the recording – digital but lacking a little in bass – does not put a very persuasive bloom on their voices. However this is corrected in the compact disc which has fine warmth of atmosphere and no lack in the lower range. Pianissimo choral detail is not sharply defined, but in all other respects the sound is superb and the background silence adds a great deal, especially when the tension is not as consistently high as in some versions.

On bargain label there is an excellent case for Kurt Prestel's version. This is amiably earthy and direct, in a reading which favours rather slow speeds but does not lose forward momentum. By the standards of more expensive versions the imprecisions of ensemble may irritate some ears, but there is a vitality about the performance that suits Orff's prose well. The cassette matches the disc closely with fine sparkle and edge, though one or two climaxes are slightly explosive (notably on side one).

On Philips, Herbert Kegel secures very fine

singing from the superb Leipzig choir, but the lightness of his touch produces some lack of tension in places, in spite of the variety of colour he finds in Orff's score. The very opening of the work, for instance, lacks the last degree of exuberance, and there is certainly a lack of electricity in the closing section of *Cours d'amours*. The soloists make a good team, and project well, notably the tenor, Horst Heistermann. The recording is of the highest quality, both natural and vivid, and the tape is technically among the most impressive available of this work.

Dorati's Jubilee version was originally recorded in Phase Four. It is a beefy, vibrant account with good singing and playing. Despite some eccentric speeds, Dorati shows a fine rhythmic sense, but the performance cannot quite match the best available. Moreover the high-level recording has hints of overmodulation at peaks, noticeable both on disc and on cassette (which is otherwise successfully transferred).

On his earlier DG recording, reissued on Privilege, Kegel directs a literal, largely unpointed reading which conveys little of the fun of the extrovert numbers or the tenderness of the first spring chorus. The ensemble of the magnificent Leipzig choir is superb, sounding relatively small in a very clean acoustic. The recording is nicely balanced and immediate in its disc format, but the tape is rather opaque and lacking bite and range.

The CfP version is a modern recording, notable for its excellent soloists, with Sheila Armstrong coming close to matching her supremely lovely performance for Previn. The men of the Hallé Choir provide some rough singing at times, but the women are much better, and the performance gathers energy and incisiveness as it proceeds, although there is some fall-off in tension at the very end. With recording both atmospheric and refined (and the cassette fairly close to the disc), this might be considered, although on LP Frühbeck's version at mid-price is well worth the extra outlay.

Catulli Carmina (cantata).
(M) *** DG Priv. 2535/*3335* 403 [id.]. Auger, Ochman, German Op. Ch., four pianos and percussion, Jochum.

Though in sheer memorability it cannot match *Carmina Burana*, Orff's sequel (using much the same formula) has its nagging attractions. For anyone hypnotized by the earlier and more popular work, *Catulli Carmina* is the Orff piece to recommend next. Jochum's version is as fine as any available. His chorus sings with sharp rhythmic point, and if imagination is called for in such music, Jochum matches flexibility with a spark of humour in control of mechanistic rhythms. His soloists are individual and sweet-toned. In this Privilege reissue the recording is outstanding, although on side two the evocative pianissimo section is a shade over-recessed. There is no appreciable difference between disc and cassette; both need to be played at a high level for maximum impact.

Die Klüge (opera-cantata).
** Ph. 6769 094 (2). Falewick, Buchner, Stryczek, Lorenz, Suss, Leipzig RSO, Kegel.

(i) *Die Klüge;* (ii) *Der Mond.*
*** EMI 1C 137 43291/3 [(d) Ara. 8021]. (i) Schwarzkopf, Corder, Frick, Witer, Kusche, Prey, Neidlinger; (i; ii) Christ, Kuen; (ii) Schmitt-Walter, Graml, Hotter, Peter, Rosner, Holloway (speaker), Children's Ch., Philh. Ch. and O, Sawallisch.

Orff's two fairy-tale opera-cantatas were never more persuasively performed than in Sawallisch's superb readings with the Philharmonia Orchestra. With both reissued in coupling on six sides instead of eight, they make an attractive package, particularly when the 1950s sound is still impressive, highly atmospheric and beautifully balanced. Schwarzkopf and Frick are superb in *Die Klüge*, but it is *Der Mond*, the earlier of the two pieces (1937–8 as against 1941–2), which is the more sharply memorable, in its allegory less superficial than it might seem. The composer helped to supervise both recordings.

Kegel is an incisive, sharply rhythmic choral conductor (and trainer), but with a lack-lustre group of soloists, his version of the fairy-tale opera-cantata, *Die Klüge*, lacks magic, particularly in contrast with the classic recording with Schwarzkopf, Frick and Prey made in the 1950s. Orff's writing for voices may be limited in its lyricism, but it still benefits from fine singing and great artistry. The Philips sound is first-rate.

Pachelbel, Johann (1653–1706)

Canon in D.
(M) ** EMI Em. EMX/*TC-EMX* 2037 [Sera. S/*4XG* 60271]. Toulouse CO, Auriacombe – ALBINONI: *Adagio*; CORELLI: *Christmas concerto*; MOZART: *Serenade: Eine kleine Nachtmusik*.**

Canon; Suites for strings: in G; No. 6 in B flat.
** Erato STU/*MCE* 70468 [RCA FRL1/*FRK1* 5468]. Paillard CO, Paillard – FASCH: *Trumpet concerto* etc.**

Pachelbel's *Canon* is justly famous, indelible in its simplicity. There are many versions of it. Münchinger's is as good as any (Decca SA/*KSC* 20 [Lon. JL/*5*- 41007]) in a Concert of Baroque Music by the Stuttgart Chamber Orchestra. Or there is a more opulent account, superbly managed by Karajan and his Berlin Philharmonic Orchestra in another Concert called 'Adagio' (DG 2530 237/*3300 317*). For those needing the more abrasive effect of original instruments, it is available within a collection by the Academy of Ancient Music with CD optional (**410 179-2**; DSDL/*KDSLC* 709). Almost as if in response, Karajan has re-recorded the piece digitally, the sound richly refined, the mood stately and somewhat sombre, with the *Gigue* following to offer a little light relief (**410 309-2**; 410 309-1/*4*), in yet another baroque collection.

Auriacombe's is a rather solemn version, the detail failing to add any feeling of exuberance. The sound is satisfactory on both disc and tape and the couplings are appropriate, though not distinctive.

The *Canon* is played on this Erato record with a steady, yet controlled increase of tension which produces an impression of stature in what is a comparatively small-scale structure. The invention in the two *Suites* is not on this level, but they are agreeable works, and the performances here are quite nicely judged. The sound is pleasing on both disc and cassette, although on the latter the upper range is more restricted.

Aria Sebaldina; Ciacona in F min.; Fantasia in G min.; Fugues: in D; in D min.; Magnificat quinti toni; Magnificat sexti toni (4 settings); *Der Tag, der ist so freudenreich; Toccatas: in C min.; in E min.; Vom Himmel hoch; Wenn wir in höchsten Nöten sein.*
*** Argo Dig. ZRDL 1015. Hurford (organ of Knox Grammar School Chapel).

Pachelbel was essentially a small-time composer. The nature of his music is well understood by Peter Hurford who has chosen his organ perceptively and whose registration is a model of discernment and taste. The two most ambitious pieces are the *Aria Sebaldina* and the *Ciacona* (both in F minor). The Chaconne is simply structured and both sets of variations, though somewhat ingenuous, are not without charm. Pachelbel's miniaturism is readily demonstrated elsewhere, notably in the neat little *Fugue in D major* (which lasts just 1′58″). The two *Toccatas* are attractively florid and very nicely registered, as is the delightfully piquant 'extemporization' on *Vom Himmel hoch*. But most memorable are the five brief *Magnificat* versets, intended as organ interludes within the canticle sung at Vespers on Saturday afternoons. These are very engaging and two of them anticipate Bach's *Fugue à la gigue*. With such sympathetic playing, balancing momentum with repose, and outstandingly natural (unaggressive) digital recording, this is an ideal record for late evening.

Paganini, Niccolò (1782–1840)

Violin concertos Nos. 1–6.
*** DG 2740 121 (5). Accardo, LPO, Dutoit.

Paganini's concertos can all too often seem sensationally boring, and it is a tribute to the virtuosity and artistry of Salvatore Accardo that they reveal so much musical interest in his hands. Accardo has a formidable technique, marvellously true intonation and impeccable good taste and style, and it is a blend of all these that makes these performances so satisfying and enjoyable. He is moreover beautifully accompanied by the LPO and Charles Dutoit, and the recording is exemplary.

Violin concerto No. 1 in D, Op. 6.
❀ *** HMV ASD 2782 [Ang. S/*4XS* 36836]. Perlman, RPO, Foster – SARASATE: *Carmen fantasy.**** ❀

Violin concerto No. 1; 24 Caprices, Op. 1.
(M) *** HMV SLS 832 (2). Perlman (as above) – SARASATE: *Carmen fantasy.****

Itzhak Perlman demonstrates a fabulously clean and assured technique. His execution of the fiendish upper harmonics in which Paganini delighted is almost uniquely smooth, and with the help of the EMI engineers, who have placed the microphone in exactly the right place, he produces a gleamingly rich tone, free from all scratchiness. The orchestra is splendidly recorded and balanced too, and Lawrence Foster matches the soloist's warmth with an alive and buoyant orchestral accompaniment. Provided one does not feel strongly about Perlman's traditional cuts, there has been no better record of the *D major Concerto*, and when it is played with this kind of panache the effect is most entertaining. The *Caprices* are done with equal virtuosity, and the Sarasate *Carmen fantasy* offered as a bonus is quite stunning. The alternative issue (without the *Caprices*) will for most collectors be irresistible – the finest of all available discs of Paganini's music.

Violin concertos Nos. 1; 2 in B min., Op. 7.
(M) *** DG Priv. 2535/*3335* 207 [id.]. Ashkenasi, VSO, Esser.
** HMV SXLP/*TC-SXLP* 100194-1/*4*. Menuhin, RPO, Erede.

With Shmuel Ashkenasi the many technical difficulties are surmounted in an easy, confident style. The accompaniment too is nicely made, and the slightly dry recording focuses everything exactly, with the soloist spotlighted in the foreground. Some might feel a lack of flamboyance, but most will sense Ashkenasi's natural sympathy. The close microphone may seem to some ears to be too close in some of the fiendish high tessitura, but the bravura displayed by the soloist generally, and especially in the *La Campanella* finale of No. 2, shows how completely he is in control, and this is one of the highlights of a good medium-priced coupling. There is an excellent cassette which tends to smooth the solo violin's higher partials agreeably and which is fresh and well balanced.

Menuhin's performances have plenty of attack, although the accompaniments have rather less life and fire. But characterful though these readings are – and Menuhin can be very rewarding in the lyrical music – one feels that fiery bravura is not really Menuhin's *métier*, and his timbre sometimes sounds undernourished in the stratospheric reaches of the solo part (especially on the cassette, which is very bright and clear).

Violin concertos Nos. 1; 3 in E; 4 in D min.
(M) **(*) Ph. 6725 029 (2). Szeryng, LSO, Gibson.

Paganini's *Fourth Concerto* only reappeared in 1954 and subsequently his family made available the parts of the *Third*; and, with a great deal of publicity, Szeryng gave its first posthumous performance and made the present recording. His performance is technically dazzling. The first movement, however, is not of great musical interest, and the work's main claims rest in the *Adagio* with its brief aria-like format, eloquent in shape and marked by the composer *Cantabile spianato*. The *Fourth Concerto* has some attractive music in it, once the boring tutti at the beginning is over. The simple melodies over ticking pizzicato accompaniments are most attractive; the slow movement (F sharp minor contrasting interestingly with D minor) is not too heavily tragic, and the finale brings a bolero complete with tambourine. Szeryng's performances show his accustomed brilliance and mastery. No. 1 is somewhat cut (as is customary) and in all three concertos Gibson is a sympathetic accompanist. The recording balance places Szeryng too far forward, but the quality is still good, although No. 4 sounds a bit thin on top.

Violin and guitar: *Cantabile; Centone di sonate No. 1 in A; Sonata in E min., Op. 3/6; Sonata concertata in A.*
*** CBS 76525/*40*- [M/*MT* 34508]. Perlman, Williams – GIULIANI: *Sonata.****

Superb playing from both Perlman and John Williams ensures the listener's attention throughout this slight but very agreeable music. With a good balance, the music-making here gives much pleasure, and this is generally a distinguished disc. The cassette transfer too is of good quality.

24 Caprices, Op. 1.
(M) *** DG Sig. 2543/*3343* 523. Accardo.
*** HMV ASD 3384 [Ang. S/*4XS* 36860]. Perlman.
*** DG Dig. 2532/*3302* 042 [id.]. Mintz.

These two dozen *Caprices* probably represent the peak of violinistic difficulty, even though more than a century has gone by since their composition, and many new works continue to exploit the extraordinary range of effects possible on one four-stringed instrument.

Accardo's set originally appeared on two discs with every repeat observed. Such is his purity of tone and sense of style that he succeeds in making the most routine and empty of phrases sound a noble utterance. Indeed he invests these *Caprices* with an eloquence far beyond the sheer display they offer. His set now resurfaces shorn of repeats and at mid-price, and so enjoys an even stronger advantage over its rivals.

Perlman's playing too is flawless, wonderfully assured and polished, yet not lacking imaginative feeling. He is extremely well recorded, but so too is Accardo, who has a price advantage.

Shlomo Mintz is often dazzling, as are most of the violinists who have recorded these astonishing pieces. There are many breathtaking things to admire and plenty of colour and life in the set as a whole. He is recorded with admirable clarity and definition in good digital sound though the overall effect is not as warm as Perlman's HMV record, which is if anything more dazzling. There are times (*No. 17 in E flat* is an example) when one could wish that he had not been in quite so much of a hurry, for the characterization would gain as a result. On the other hand, others such as the *F major, No. 22*, could hardly be improved upon.

(i) *Terzetto for violin, cello and guitar. Caprice No. 24, Op. 1/24; Sonata in A* (arr. Williams).
*** CBS 73745/*40*-. Williams, with (i) Loveday, Fleming – GIULIANI: *Variations.****

The *Terzetto* is a small-scale but very charming work, and it is beautifully played here. John Williams is also in excellent form in the makeweights, the *Sonata* and *Caprice*, both originally for violin. The CBS recording is of high quality though forwardly balanced.

Palestrina, Giovanni da
(*c.* 1525–1594)

Alma Redemptoris Mater (antiphon)*; Missa Papae Marcelli; Peccantem me quotidie* (motet)*; Stabat Mater.*
(M) **(*) ASV ACM 2009. L. Pro Cantione Antiqua, Turner.

In this record of well-known masterpieces Bruno Turner uses small forces, and the gain in clarity is at the expense of a certain radiance of texture. The acoustic is clear and precise. Yet it should be emphasized that these are most beautiful performances of all four pieces, offering both intelligence and sensitivity in the handling of each line. Rather forward recorded balance enhances clarity of texture. This is not the only way of performing Palestrina, but it is nonetheless impressive.

Antiphon – Assumpta est Maria; Missa – Assumpta est Maria; Missa brevis.
*** Argo ZRG 690 [id.]. Hunt, Tudhope, St John's College, Camb., Ch., Guest.

The *Assumpta est Maria* Mass is one of Palestrina's most sublime works, and its return to the catalogue, coupled with the four-part *Missa brevis*, is more than welcome, particularly when the performances are as persuasive as here. Some may find them a little lacking in Latin fervour: the trebles sound distinctly Anglican, but, this reservation apart, this is fine singing by any standards and is splendidly recorded. It was a good idea to include the Antiphon on which this Mass is based.

Exsultate Deo; Hymnus in adventu Dei; Jesu Rex admirabilis (hymn); *Magnificat VI toni; Tua Jesu dilectio; Veni sponsa Christi* (antiphon; mass and motet).
(M) *** Argo ZK 69. St John's College Ch., Guest.

Dignified performances, well recorded, of some fine Palestrina works. Although these performances are firmly in the Anglican tradition and lack some of the fervour one would find on the Continent, they have great purity of tone and beauty of phrasing. Moreover the acoustic has atmosphere, yet detail is not lost.

Hodie Beata Virgo; Litaniae de Beata Virgine Maria in 8 parts; Magnificat in 8 parts (*Primi Toni*); *Senex puerum portabat; Stabat Mater.*
(M) *** Argo ZK/*KZKC* 4. King's College Ch., Willcocks.

This is an exceptionally fine collection. The flowing melodic lines and serene beauty which are the unique features of Palestrina's music are apparent throughout this programme, and there is no question about the dedication and accomplishment of the performance. Argo's recording is no less successful and this record may be highly recommended, especially in this medium-priced reissue. The cassette is of generally fine quality.

Ave Maria Mass in 6 parts.
*** HMV ASD/*TCC-ASD* 3955. King's College Ch., Ledger.

Palestrina wrote two *Ave Maria* Masses, neither of which was published in his lifetime: this did not appear in the original book of six-part Masses of 1594 but was included two years later. The merit of this recording, apart from the excellence of the singing of the King's College Choir under Philip Ledger, is the inclusion of the plainchant of the Introit, Gradual and so on, that lends perspective to this Mass. The chant is sung with impressive restraint and sense of space, and the acoustic of the College is heard to good advantage. Yet although this is superbly atmospheric as both a recording and performance, there is splendid clarity of texture too. An indispensable issue for admirers of this period and this choir with an excellent tape equivalent, the focus unblurred.

Missa Nigra sum.
** Gimmell 1585-03/*T.* Tallis Scholars, Phillips. (with Lhéritier: *Nigra sum* (motet); Silva: *Nigra sum* (motet); Victoria: *Nigra sum* (motet); *Plainsong: Nigra sum*).

The Palestrina Mass is not otherwise available and is a work of much beauty based on the Jean Lhéritier motet *Nigra sum* ('I am black but comely'). The Tallis Scholars blend excellently and use women's rather than boys' voices. In addition to the motet by Lhéritier, a pupil of Josquin, which Palestrina parodies, the record includes two other motets on the same text, one by Andreas de Silva or Silvanus, a relatively little-known Flemish singer and composer who sang in the papal chapel in Rome and later went to Mantua. The most sensuous of the settings is Victoria's. The performances are accurate and committed though one would welcome a greater range of dynamics, particularly at the end of a melodic line. Cadences are often treated just like the middle of a phrase and the effect is at times jarring. However, the acoustic of Merton College, Oxford, gives the sound a most appealing aura and the chrome cassette is in the demonstration class.

Missa Papae Marcelli.
(B) **(*) CfP CFP/*TC-CFP* 40339 [Ang. RL/*4RL* 32122]. Tallis Scholars, Phillips – ALLEGRI: *Miserere*; MUNDY: *Vox Patris caelestis.****

Missa Papae Marcelli; Missa brevis.
(M) ** HMV HQS 1237 [Sera. S 60187]. King's College Ch., Willcocks.

Palestrina's *Missa Papae Marcelli* has a famous historical reputation for its influence on decisions made at the Council of Trent. The Catholic hierarchy had become concerned that the elaborate counterpoint of much church music, and the interpolation of non-liturgical texts, was obscuring the ritual purpose of the Mass itself. Palestrina's work, with its syllabic style and clear text, supposedly demonstrated that great music need not cover the religious message and so influenced the decision not to ban polyphony altogether. If the story is apocryphal, there is no doubt that Palestrina's settings satisfied the authorities, while the quality of his music, and the memorability of the *Missa Papae Marcelli* in particular, are equally certain. With its apparent simplicity of line and serene beauty which disguises an underlying fervour, it is not a work which lends itself readily to performers with an Anglican background. This account by the Tallis Scholars is certainly the finest at present available on record, catching the music's cool dignity and much of its expressive richness. The singing has purity of tone, a refined control of dynamics and beauty of phrasing. It is splendidly recorded within the admirably reverberant acoustic of Merton College, Oxford. The cassette transfer too is of the highest quality, and in this music freedom from extraneous background noises is essential.

From King's College smooth, limpid performances, well recorded. The singing style is direct and unmannered, but although the control of dynamic is impressive, the inner mystery of the music is not readily conveyed.

Missa Tu es Petrus. Motets: *Ave Maria; Quam pulchri sunt; Tu es Petrus.*
*(*) HM 1C 065 99685. Tölz Boys' Ch., Schmidt-Gaden.

There is no lack of life here in the six-part Mass, but pleasure is somewhat diminished by the less than secure intonation of the boys. For all the keenness of musical intention, this does not really merit a strong recommendation, and the same applies to the rest of the collection.

Panufnik, Andrzej (born 1914)

(i) *Autumn music. Heroic overture.* (i) *Nocturne. Tragic overture.*
(M) *** Uni. RHS 306. LSO, Horenstein, (i) with Peebles.

A collection of four works by the Polish composer Panufnik, who fled from Warsaw in the early 1950s and settled in Britain. The two overtures are early pieces and of relatively little musical interest, but the other works are worth hearing, though they may strike some listeners as musically uneventful. Indeed they are static mood pieces that perhaps too readily fall back on repetition and ostinati, but the opening of the *Nocturne* is really very beautiful indeed and there is a refined feeling for texture and a sensitive imagination at work here. The LSO under Horenstein play with conviction and they are beautifully recorded. If Panufnik employed a wider range of musical devices and had a more robust inventive resource, he would be a very considerable composer indeed.

Concerto festivo; (i) *Concerto for timpani, percussion and strings. Katyń epitaph; Landscape.*
*** Uni. Dig. DKP 9016. LSO, composer, (i) with Goedicke and Frye.

Andrzej Panufnik's music is invariably approachable, finely crafted and fastidiously scored. This superbly recorded disc gives a good example of his feeling for atmosphere and colour; the textures are always transparent and clean, and there is an alert and refined sensibility. Perhaps the only criticism one could make is of a certain motivic economy that borders dangerously on paucity. The *Katyń epitaph* is powerfully eloquent and, oddly enough, is reminiscent at one point of the atmosphere of the last pages of Britten's *A Time There Was*, though the Panufnik was written some years earlier. The LSO play well for the composer himself; the recording is excellently balanced and in the demonstration class. The best of this music is deeply felt.

Sinfonia rustica (*Symphony No. 1*); *Sinfonia sacra* (*Symphony No. 3*).
(M) **(*) Uni. UNS 257. Monte Carlo Op. O, composer.

The *Sinfonia rustica* was the work which first attracted attention to Panufnik shortly after the war. It is the more individual of the two works recorded here and has plenty of character, though its invention is less symphonic than in the style of a sinfonietta. The performances of both works under the composer's baton are alert and spirited, though the Monte Carlo orchestra is not in the first flight. The recording, made by EMI, is excellent: the stereo is very much in the demonstration class.

Sinfonia di sfere (*Symphony No. 5*); *Sinfonia mistica* (*Symphony No. 6*).
*** Decca HEAD 22. LSO, Atherton.

Both these works date from the late 1970s and exploit Panufnik's increasing preoccupation with geometrical forms as his source of musical inspiration. The *Sinfonia di sfere*, his fifth symphony, consists of three movements in ternary form representing a journey through three concentric spheres. The *Sinfonia mistica*, his sixth symphony, takes the number six as its root in a single movement of six sections, with each parameter dominated by that division into sixths. Though the cerebration of the scheme sometimes has one questioning the intensity of emotion conveyed, the idiom is not difficult, and the structural firmness adds very plainly to the immediate sense of conviction in each sharp contrast as it develops. Excellent performances and recording.

Symphony No. 8 (*Sinfonia votiva*).
*** Hyp. Dig. A 66050 [id.]. Boston SO, Ozawa – SESSIONS: *Concerto for orchestra*.***

Like most of Panufnik's major works the *Sinfonia votiva* – written, like the Sessions *Concerto* on the reverse, for the 1981 centenary of the Boston orchestra – has a strongly formalistic structure, but its message is primarily emotional. It marks the response of the composer not only to the miraculous icon of the Black Madonna in his native Poland but to the tragedy of current events in that country. It begins with an extended slow movement which is then daringly balanced against a briskly contrasted finale. Though Panufnik's melodic writing may as a rule reflect the formalism of his thought rather than tap a vein of natural lyricism, the result is most impressive, particularly in a performance as fine as Ozawa's, a good coupling for the thorny Sessions work, equally well recorded.

(i) *Thames Pageant. Invocations for Peace*.
(M) *** Uni. UNS 264. King's House School Ch., Thames Youth Ens., Stuckley, (i) with Amis.

Thames Pageant, a choral suite written for children to perform, ends riotously with a musical representation of the Oxford and Cambridge boat race (with John Amis the commentator). There is an engaging directness too about the earlier movements, which include a march representing Julius Caesar and a nicely pointed portrait of Alexander Pope. Inevitably the performance has its rough edges, but the spirit is what matters. The *Invocation* is in a sparer style, with trebles accompanied by brass and bells. The recording is commendably clear.

Parry, Hubert (1848–1918)

Symphony No. 5 in B min.; Symphonic variations; Elegy to Johannes Brahms.
*** HMV ASD 3725. LPO, Boult.

This was the last record made by Sir Adrian Boult, whose recording career was longer than that of any important rival. The *Fifth Symphony*, the last that Parry wrote, is broadly Brahmsian in style but with the four movements linked in a Lisztian cyclic manner; the slow movement is particularly beautiful.

Equally impressive is the *Elegy*, not merely an occasional piece but a full-scale symphonic movement which builds to a powerful climax. The sharply inventive *Symphonic variations* – also recorded by Boult for an earlier Lyrita disc – complete the Parry portrait. Recording and performances are exemplary, a fitting coda to Sir Adrian's recording career.

Shulbrede tunes Nos. 1–2 and 4–7; Theme and 19 variations.
** Pearl SHE 546. Parry – STANFORD: *3 Rhapsodies.***

Parry's *Theme and variations* dates from 1885 and is fashioned with predictable expertise. It is not music of great personality or character, but nor is it without merit. The *Shulbrede tunes* are short, rather Schumannesque vignettes, written just before the First World War and portraying family members and life at his daughter's house. John Parry plays with commitment and makes out a good case for these neglected pieces.

Blest Pair of Sirens.
** HMV ASD 2311. LPO Ch., LPO, Boult – ELGAR: *The Music Makers.***(*)

As a fill-up to Elgar's rarely heard cantata it is good to welcome so enjoyably professional a motet as Parry's *Blest Pair of Sirens.* Much of the once-popular music by Parry and his contemporaries is unacceptably inflated, but certainly not this. The performance by the London Philharmonic Choir should be more incisive, but it still conveys much of the right atmosphere.

I was glad (from Psalm 122).
*** HMV ASD 3345. Camb. University Music Soc., King's College Ch., Camb., New Philh. O, Ledger – ELGAR: *Coronation ode* etc.***

This expansive version of Parry's most popular church anthem makes an excellent coupling for Elgar's magnificent *Ode*. Splendid recording too.

Ode on the Nativity.
*** Lyr. SRCS 125. Cahill, Bach Ch., Royal College of Music Ch., LPO, Willcocks – VAUGHAN WILLIAMS: *Sons of Light.****

Parry's *Ode* is an elaborate, often highly contrapuntal setting of a poem of William Dunbar. Each of the six stanzas ends with the Latin line, *Et nobis Puer natus est*, which each time inspires Parry to a moment of dedicated intensity. The thematic material may not be as memorable as in some of Parry's finest works (it was written in 1912, only five years before his death) but in a performance as committed as this, beautifully recorded, it makes a welcome rarity on record.

Payne, Anthony (born 1936)

(i) *Phoenix Mass;* (ii) *Paean;* (iii) *The World's Winter.*
*** BBC REH 297. (i) BBC Singers, Jones Brass Ens., Poole; (ii) Bradshaw; (iii) Manning, Nash Ens., Friend.

Payne's music, thoughtful and closely argued, is well represented by these three works. *The World's Winter*, a setting for soprano and instrumental ensemble of two poems by Tennyson, uses Payne's personal brand of numerical serialism. The *Mass* relies on more complex textures, but in its contrasts of expression is just as communicative. The piano piece *Paean*, written for Susan Bradshaw, makes an apt fill-up. The BBC recordings are very acceptable, though the *Mass* is a little too reverberant for full clarity.

Peeters, Flor (born 1903)

Missa festiva, Op. 62.
*** Argo ZRG 883 [id.]. St John's College Ch., Guest – POULENC: *Exultate Deo* etc.***

The Belgian composer and organist Flor Peeters is now past his eightieth year and his output includes eight Masses and more than two hundred organ works, some of which are available on specialist labels. The *Missa festiva* is a highly accomplished work, more severe than the Poulenc pieces with which it is coupled but no less inventive and dignified. The relative unfamiliarity of this composer should not deter readers from investigating this Mass, which is well balanced and cleanly recorded.

Penderecki, Krzysztof (born 1933)

Anaklasis for strings and percussion; The Awakening of Jacob.
(M) *** Sup. 1410 2734. Prague RSO, Kasprzyk – BAIRD: *Elegeia*; LUTOSLAWSKI: *Mi-Parti*.***

The two Penderecki works complete each side: *The Awakening of Jacob* follows the *Mi-Parti* on side one, and *Anaklasis*, an inventive piece for strings and percussion, comes after the *Elegeia*. Neither is longer than about six minutes, and both hold the listener. *Anaklasis* is the earlier piece, dating from 1959–60; its companion comes from 1974. With fine, committed performances and good sound this makes a thoroughly worthwhile anthology.

Violin concerto.
*** CBS 76739 [M 35150]. Stern, Minnesota SO, Skrowaczewski.

This concerto, written for Isaac Stern in 1977, marked Penderecki's return to a more conservative idiom. Even so, his fingerprints are clearly identifiable, and the compression of thematic material, combined with spare, clean textures, makes for memorable results. The single movement, which lasts almost forty minutes, contains within it the traces of a funeral march, a scherzo and a meditative adagio. The performance here is passionately committed, with Stern at his most inspired, and the recording is splendidly detailed.

St Luke Passion.
*** HM 1C 157 99660/1. Woytowicz, Hiolski, Ladysz, Bartsch (speaker), Tölz Boys' Ch., Col. R. Ch. and SO, Czyz.

The *St Luke Passion*, written between 1963 and 1965, is the key work in Penderecki's career, the one which firmly launched him as an international figure. Taking a broadly Bachian view of setting the Passion, Penderecki with great virtuosity uses an enormously wide spectrum of choral and orchestral effects. The result is powerfully dramatic in a way which communicates directly to audiences unused to hearing advanced music. That drama is splendidly conveyed in this recording under the direction of the conductor who has specialized in Penderecki's music. Ensemble and solo singing are admirable, and so is the recording.

Pergolesi, Giovanni (1710–36)

Concerti armonici (attrib.) – see WASSENAER.

Flute concertos Nos. 1 in G; 2 in D.
*** Decca SA/*KSC* 13 [Lon. STS/5- 15561]. Rampal, Stuttgart CO, Münchinger – BACH: *Suite No. 2*.**(*)

These *Flute concertos* (originally coupled with Münchinger's set of *Concerti armonici*) offer invention of a high order and they are played delightfully by Rampal. Münchinger accompanies flexibly and there is no hint of sentimentality. Excellent sound on disc and tape alike.

Oboe concerto (arr. Barbirolli).
(B) *** PRT GSGC/*ZCGC* 2007. Rothwell, Hallé O, Barbirolli – CORELLI: *Concerto* ***; HAYDN: *Concerto* **(*).

Miss Rothwell's neat, feminine style suits this work to perfection. This is a Barbirolli arrangement using tunes from sonatas, a song and the *Stabat Mater*; but the whole is so felicitously put together that no one could guess it was not conceived in this form. The predominant mood is pastoral, with a slow opening leading to a gracious *Allegro* with an *Andantino* intervening before the gentle finale. The performance characterizes the music perfectly. The sound on disc is full and quite well balanced, but the tape transfer is insecure at pianissimo level.

Violin concerto con più stromenti; Concerto a cinque in F; Sonata in B flat for violin and strings.
(M) **(*) Ph. 6768 163/*7699 146* (2) [id.]. Carmirelli, I Musici – WASSENAER: *Concerti armonici.***(*)

Whether or not these two concertos are by Pergolesi or another hand (as are the coupled *Concerti armonici*) seems uncertain. They are attractive if rather conventional works given characteristically committed performances with plenty of Italianate warmth in slow movements, and pleasing vigour in the fast ones. The expressive qualities sometimes bring a hint of languor, and the recording helps this impression with its resonance and ample textures, both on disc and the high-quality iron-oxide cassettes (which benefit from a bass cut, but are not deficient on top).

Magnificat.
(*) Argo ZRG 505 [id.]. Vaughan, Baker, Partridge, Keyte, King's College Ch., ASMF, Willcocks – VIVALDI: *Gloria.*(*)

This Pergolesi *Magnificat* – doubtfully attributed, like so much that goes under this composer's name – is a comparatively pale piece to go with the great Vivaldi *Gloria*. But King's Choir gives a beautiful performance, and the recording matches it in intensity of atmosphere.

Miserere No. 2 in C min.
*** Argo ZRG 915. Wolfe, James, Covey-Crump, Stuart, Magdalen College Ch., Wren O, Rose.

Pergolesi's *Miserere* was long listed under doubtful or spurious works, but modern opinion seems to favour its probable authenticity. In his sleeve-note, Dr Rose argues its similarity to the *Stabat Mater*, where there are striking parallels in melodic lines, motifs and harmonic progressions. Whatever the case, this work is both ambitious and moving. It consists of fifteen numbers, seven solo arias, two trios and six choruses. The singers are all of quality, particularly Richard Stuart, and Bernard Rose secures expressive and persuasive results from the Magdalen College Choir and the Wren Orchestra. The recording, made in Magdalen College Chapel, Oxford, is warm and atmospheric.

Stabat Mater (revised Soresina).
(M) *(*) Ph. 9502/*7313* 100. Lear, Ludwig, Berlin RIAS Chamber Ch., Berlin RO, Maazel.

Stabat Mater; Concertino armonico No. 2 in G.
** Argo ZRG/*KZRC* 913 [id.]. Palmer, Hodgson, St John's College Ch., Argo CO, Guest.

Stabat Mater; Salve Regina in C min.
**(*) Erato STU/*MCE* 71179. Cotrubas, Valentini Terrani, Sol. Ven., Scimone.

Well-coupled with a rare *Salve Regina*, the Scimone version of the *Stabat Mater* makes an excellent choice. It is a performance which brings out the devotional side of the work, even in music which has many secular, even theatrical overtones. Though the portamento style of both soloists is at times distracting, the voices are sweet and blend well, and the playing of I Solisti Veneti is admirable, though the recording is not ideally clear. The cassette transfer – full and vivid – is made at a high level and there is some hint of strain on the soprano's fortissimo high notes.

George Guest directs a sensible, unaffected performance that misses much of the music's variety, and neither soloists nor choir are at their liveliest. The fill-up is attractive, and far more resiliently performed. Good recording, and an excellent cassette transfer, the richly expansive acoustic caught without problems.

On Philips an unashamedly romantic performance of Pergolesi's most famous choral work. Evelyn Lear and Christa Ludwig could hardly be bettered when it comes to expressive musicianship and beauty of tone, but those who have concern for authenticity of style will be disturbed by the weight of emotion the performers try to wring out of fundamentally simple music. In this Maazel must of course take most of the blame. It is music that can so easily sound sentimental, and though opinions will obviously differ here, Maazel does not seem to appreciate the dangers he runs. Good playing and recording. The cassette is only transferred at a modest level, though the sound is quite clear.

La Serva padrona (complete).
(M) **(*) HM 20343/*30.343*. Bonifaccio, Nimsgern, Coll. Aur., Maier.
(M) **(*) Ph. 9502/*7313* 065 [id.]. Bustamente, Capecchi, ECO, Ros-Marba.

Maier directs an admirably lively performance of a comic opera which can easily seem over-long. Though the soprano has her moments of shrillness she takes the role of the servant very characterfully, and Nimsgern, stepping out of his usual repertory, proves admirable in the buffo role of Uberto, never resorting to unmusical exaggerations of character. The recording is first-rate, though it dates from 1970. It is a pity that no libretto is provided, let alone an English translation. There is an excellent cassette.

The principal merits of the Philips version (originally issued on the Pye Ensayo label) are the stylish playing of the ECO under Ros-Marba, the traditional buffo singing of Capecchi, very well-timed if not always perfectly vocalized, and the stage production which in its atmospheric sound perspectives has one vividly imagining the stage scene. Carmen Bustamente makes a rather cool Serpina, as a character far less sharply portrayed than her master. The cassette transfer is first-class, catching the full perspectives, yet with excellent projection of the soloists.

Perugia, Matteo da (died 1418)

Belle sans per (virelai); *Dame d'honour* (rondeau); *Dame que j'aym; Dame souvrayne* (virelais); *Gia de rete d'amour* (ballata); *Helas merci* (rondeau); *Ne me chaut* (virelai); *Pour bel accueil* (rondeau); *Pres du soleil; Se je me plaing* (ballades); *Seta que, zorno mai* (ballata); *Trover ne puis* (rondeau).
*** O-L DSLO 577. L. Medieval Ens., P. and T. Davies.

Matteo da Perugia was the first *maestro di cappella* of Milan Cathedral and one of the leading figures of the period between Machaut and Dufay. His songs, which number two dozen in all, constitute the largest surviving secular output by any composer of that period (the beginning of the fifteenth century). Although he was presumably from Perugia, his secular music is predominantly French in style, and all but two of the songs on this disc are to French texts. Yet although this period is relatively unexplored on record, this disc is by no means just for specialists. It is thoroughly accessible and enjoyable, and the performances are of a high level of accomplishment throughout. So, too, is the recording, which does credit to all concerned. This is an issue that would give great pleasure to many readers who do not realize its potential.

Peterson-Berger, Wilhelm
(1867–1942)

Symphony No. 2 in E flat (Sunnanfärd).
*** EMI 7C 061 35455. Swedish RSO, Westerberg.

Peterson-Berger is remembered in his native Sweden for his smaller instrumental pieces in folk idiom and as a lively critic of Shavian stamp. He composed five symphonies, however, the second, subtitled *'Journey to the Sun'*, dating from the first decade of the present century. It is not in the same league as Stenhammar's *Second Symphony*, nor is it as assured as those of Atterberg. Yet for all its naïvistic touches and moments of inelegance, there is something worthwhile here. It opens promisingly, and the reflective dreamlike episode in the second movement is altogether haunting, though taken as a whole it lacks cohesion and concentration. Yet it strikes more sympathetic resonances than Alfvén or Rangström. Not a well-argued symphony, perhaps: the three stars are for the excellent performance and recorded sound.

Pettersson, Allan (1911–80)

Violin concerto No. 2.
*** Cap. CAP 1200. Haendel, Swedish RSO, Blomstedt.

The Swedish composer Allan Pettersson suffered neglect in his native country during the 1950s and enjoyed a subsequent popular vogue in the last decade or so of his life. His musical language is predominantly diatonic and direct in utterance, though some of his gestures are strongly Mahlerian in character and not wholly free from self-pity and self-indulgence. It is the kind of music that excites the allegiance of some and the impatience of others. His *Second Violin concerto* is no exception. Like many of his symphonies (there are thirteen in all) it is long; its one movement takes the best part of an hour, and it wears its heart very much on its sleeve, as does so much of his music. Admiration for Pettersson's work is tempered by the note of self-pity that he strikes and by its sheer garrulity. As always with this composer, there are moments of eloquence when one is touched, and Ida Haendel, for whom the work was written, braves its difficulties gallantly. The three stars are for the performance and the recording.

Pfitzner, Hans (1869–1949)

Symphony in C.
(M) **(*) DG 2543 817 [id.]. *Berlin PO, Leitner* † WAGNER: *Symphony.***(*)

Pfitzner wrote his *Symphony in C* early in the Second World War, when he was already seventy. It was almost as an escapist exercise, and might be compared with the late neoclassical works of Richard Strauss, though it lacks their sharpness of invention. It is an attractive, undemanding piece, an interesting curiosity to make an unusual makeweight for the early Wagner symphony. The 1959 recording barely shows its age.

Pierné, Gabriel (1863–1937)

Les Cathédrales: No. 1, Prélude. Images, Op. 49. Paysages franciscains, Op. 43.
*** EMI 2C 069 16302. Loire PO, Dervaux.

Gabriel Pierné was a leading figure in French musical life during the years of Debussy and Ravel. The music recorded here is urbane, civilized and charming, and should make him many friends, particularly in view of the persuasive accounts of these scores given by Pierre Dervaux and the Orchestre Philharmonique des Pays de Loire. The first side is occupied by *Images*, a late work composed in 1935, only two years before Pierné's death. It derives from a divertissement of a pastoral character which shows not only Pierné's virtuosity as an orchestrator but his subtlety as a composer. The score is full of touches of pastiche – a reference to Dukas's *La Péri* in the opening, an allusion to Debussy's *Gigues* and so on – and there is also a set of pieces in which he developed two of the numbers of his *Divertissement* under the title *Viennoise et Cortège blues*! The *Paysages franciscains* (1920) on the reverse side betrays the composer's love of Italy, and was inspired by a Danish writer, Johannes Joergensen (1866–1956), much influenced by French symbolism and Catholic culture. The *Prélude* to *Les Cathédrales* (1915) is an evocation of the desolation caused by war. Rewarding music in the best French tradition and extremely well played and recorded. Pierné ought to be a popular composer.

Cydalise et le chèvre-pied (ballet): *suite; Ramuntcho overture.*
*** EMI 2C 069 14140. Paris Op. O, Mari.

Everyone will recognize the opening of *Cydalise et le chèvre-pied*, for as the *Entry of the Little Fauns* it enjoyed great popularity in the 1940s and '50s. Indeed its fame has helped to keep Pierné's name alive and led to the current resurgence of interest in him in France. The whole ballet dates from 1919 and was first produced in 1923. The ideas are fresh, often modal, beautifully fashioned though ultimately not really distinguished. Nonetheless, this is music that deserves the widest circulation, and even the *Ramuntcho overture*, an earlier piece dating from 1907 and based on popular Basque themes, has vitality and charm. The Paris Opéra Orchestra responds with enthusiasm to this music and Jean Baptiste Mari secures excellent results. The recording is bright and well-detailed, and the presentation in a gate-folder sleeve is exceptionally informative; the cover, Zuccarelli's *Bacchanale*, is most attractive.

Marche des petits soldats de plomb.
(M) *** HMV Green. ESD 7048. O de Paris, Jacquillat – LALO: *Scherzo*; MESSAGER: *Deux Pigeons* etc.***

Pierné's *March of the little lead soldiers* sounds deliciously piquant here, and with attractive couplings and excellent recording, this is a delightful disc on all counts.

Piston, Walter (1894–1976)

The Incredible Flutist (ballet): *suite.*
(M) **(*) Mercury SRI 75050. Eastman-Rochester SO, Hanson – CHADWICK: *Symphonic sketches.***

Walter Piston's ballet *The Incredible Flutist* comes from 1938 and is one of the most refreshing and imaginative of all American scores. It deserves to be heard as often as *Appalachian Spring* for it has the same fertility and resource. Its ideas are instantly memorable and yet their charms remain durable. It was composed some years after his studies with Nadia Boulanger in Paris and the very opening is distinctively Gallic in atmosphere. It is a highly attractive score that deserves the widest popularity and it is a pity that it is encumbered with a well-made but uninspired work by Chadwick. The performance is spirited but the recording is a little glassy. (This ballet would suit Bernstein and we must hope that he will one day record it: he was briefly a pupil of Piston during the 1940s.)

Symphony No. 3.
(M) *** Mercury SRI 75107 [id.]. Eastman-Rochester O, Hanson – HANSON: *Symphony No. 4.****

Piston's *Third Symphony* is a more ambitious canvas than its Hanson coupling (thirty-four minutes against twenty). It was commissioned by the Koussevitzky Music Foundation and completed in 1947. The music, which has no stated programmatic implications, is nevertheless deeply subjective, often sombre in mood, with a searching quality in the first and third movements and an abrasively biting scherzo. The finale is positive and vigorous, and the work stands out among twentieth-century American symphonies.

Hanson's performance is eloquent and committed and although the Mercury sound is not ideally expansive, it is not without body and has good detail.

Play of Daniel (medieval)

The Play of Daniel (liturgical drama).
*** O-L DSLO 612. Cantione Antiqua, Landini Cons., Mark Brown.

The Play of Daniel first became widely known thanks to the re-creation by the American Noah Greenberg; his dramatic view of a medieval miracle play made an understandably strong impact on record. This version under Mark Brown is much more austere and far more authentic. There is a simplicity and restraint in both the performance and the treatment which with such sensitive, felt singing and playing is most affecting. The recording is excellent.

Ponce, Manuel (1882–1948)

Concierto del sur (for guitar and orchestra).
(M) **(*) HMV Green. ESD/*TC-ESD* 165105-1/*4*. Moreno, Mexican State SO, Bátiz – CHÁVEZ: *Zarabanda****; SOLER: *Sonatas.***

Ponce's *Concerto* was composed, towards the end of his life, for Segovia who recorded it in the 1950s. It does not possess either the dark intensity or imaginative resource of the *'Folia de España'* variations and fugue, nor is it as memorable or attractive as the Rodrigo *Concierto de Aranjuez*. Alfonso Moreno does not quite command the poise and finesse that John Williams brought to this piece (whose version is now deleted) and there are some obtrusive fingerboard noises, but he does have plenty of temperament and is given the advantage of clear digital recording, albeit too closely balanced. The Mexican orchestra, though not in the front rank, plays with some enthusiasm, and the Chávez on the reverse side is quite memorable. The cassette transfer is first-class.

Hace ocho meses; Marchita el alma; 3 Mexican folksongs; La Valse; Variations on 'Folia de España' and fugue; Yo adoro a mi madre.
❀ *** CBS 76730/*40*- [M 35820]. Williams.

Aficionados will welcome John Williams's record devoted to the music of Manuel Ponce, and those not normally drawn to the guitar repertoire should investigate it. The *Variations on 'Folia de España'* are subtle and haunting, and their surface charm often conceals a vein of richer, darker feeling. The writing is resourceful and imaginative (perhaps it is least successful when Ponce attempts imitative textures), and there is a refined harmonic awareness in some of the more reflective variations. The second side is given over to smaller pieces, all of which are played with consummate mastery. The CBS engineers have produced sound that is more natural and lifelike than has often been the case with this artist, and though the balance is far from distant, there is no distortion of perspective and no feeling that the instrument is larger than life; adjustment of the level enables one to set the image further back, should one so desire. The sound is admirably clean and finely detailed yet at the same time warm. The cassette too is excellent.

Sonatina meridional; Suite in A; Variations on 'Folia de España' and fugue.
** Mer. E 77041. Artzt.

Alice Artzt has formidable competition in the *Folia* variations, notably from John Williams on CBS. She makes an impressive showing, though neither in terms of poetry nor concentration of mood does she displace Williams in *La Folia*. The recording is very good indeed and her technique is impressive.

Ponchielli, Amilcare (1834–86)

La Gioconda (complete).

*** Decca Dig. D 232 D 3/*K 232 K 33* (3) [Lon. LDR/5- 73005]. Caballé, Baltsa, Pavarotti, Milnes, Hodgson, L. Op. Ch., Nat. PO, Bartoletti.

*** Decca SET 364/6 [Lon. OSA 1388]. Tebaldi, Horne, Bergonzi, Merrill, Ch. and O of St Cecilia Ac., Rome, Gardelli.

(M) *** HMV SLS/*TC-SLS* 5176 (3) [Ang. S 6031]. Callas, Cossotto, Ferraro, Vinco, Cappuccilli, Companeez, Ch. and O of La Scala, Milan, Votto.

The colourfully atmospheric melodrama of this opera gives the Decca engineers the chance to produce a digital blockbuster, one of the most vivid opera recordings yet made by this process. The casting could hardly be bettered, with Caballé just a little overstressed in the title role but producing glorious sounds. Pavarotti, for long immaculate in the aria *Cielo e mar*, here expands into the complete role with equally impressive control and heroic tone. Commanding performances too from Milnes as Barnaba, Ghiaurov as Alvise and Baltsa as Laura, firm and intense all three. Bartoletti proves a vigorous and understanding conductor, presenting the blood and thunder with total commitment but finding the right charm in the most famous passage, the *Dance of the hours*. The chrome cassettes match the discs closely (there is very little loss of focus, in spite of the resonance), but the smaller libretto supplied with the tape box is much less attractive to read.

Tebaldi's complete *Gioconda*, made when many were mourning the end of her recording career, is one of her most impressive performances ever put on record. She had never taken the role on the stage, and asked for advice beforehand on what other singers to study. Tactfully her adviser suggested the Milanov version, but when later he visited her, he found her absorbed studying with rapt attention the Callas version. 'Why didn't you tell me Maria's was the best?' she asked. It is doubtful now whether Maria's does remain the best, for (apart from the new Caballé version) Tebaldi conveys an astonishing depth of dramatic feeling and though the actual voice quality is not so even as it used to be, the actual musical interest of the performance is far more intense than one would have expected from earlier Tebaldi performances. Though Callas does of course remain unique, no one who has ever been won over by Tebaldi should miss hearing this set,which has a fine supporting cast – Bergonzi, Horne and Merrill all very good, if a little too comfortable-sounding – and has first-class recording quality.

In the title role in Ponchielli's highly melodramatic opera, Maria Callas gave one of her most vibrant, most compelling, most totally inspired performances on record, with vocal flaws very much subdued. The challenge she presented to those around her is reflected in the soloists – Cossotto and Cappuccilli both at the very beginning of distinguished careers – as well as the distinctive tenor Ferraro and the conductor Votto, who has never done anything finer on record. The recording still sounds well, though it dates from 1960. The cassette transfer is exceptionally successful, the solo voices vibrant and the choral detail clear, with an atmospheric perspective; the break between sides one and two is ill-chosen, but Acts III and IV are each given a cassette side.

La Gioconda: Dance of the hours.

(M) **(*) HMV Green. ESD/*TC-ESD* 7115. Philh. O, Mackerras – LUIGINI: *Ballet Égyptien* ***; MEYERBEER: *Les Patineurs* **; TCHAIKOVSKY: *Nutcracker suite.* **

Walt Disney's *Fantasia* gave the short ballet sequence from Ponchielli's opera worldwide popularity, and interestingly it was the only piece in the film that Stokowski extended to fit the animated narrative (much of the other music had to be truncated). Here is the original in a vivacious performance under Sir Charles

Mackerras, with the Philharmonia in brilliant form. The bright 1960 recording is not without bloom but is slightly lacking in body. There is little appreciable difference between disc and tape.

Poulenc, Francis (1889–1963)

Aubade (for piano and 18 instruments).
(M) **(*) Sup. 1410 2705. Krajný, Prague CO – HONEGGER: *Concertino***; ROUSSEL: *Piano concerto*.**

The *Aubade* shows Poulenc at his most Stravinskian and wittily self-conscious, and Krajný and the Prague Chamber Orchestra capture its spirit admirably. Indeed, this is as good a performance as any past accounts, though the reverberant acoustic presents problems to the engineers. But the sound is far from unattractive, and this disc is also welcome for its couplings.

(i) *Aubade* (*Concerto choréographique*); (ii) *Concert champêtre for harpsichord and orchestra;* (iii) *Double piano concerto in D min.*
(M) *** HMV Green. ESD/*TC-ESD* 7165. (i) Tacchino; (ii) Van de Wiele; (iii) composer and Fevrier; Paris Conservatoire O, Prêtre.

At medium price this is self-recommending. The composer may only have been an amateur pianist, but his interpretation (with partner) of his own skittish *Double concerto* is infectiously jolly. One could never mistake the tone of voice intended. In the imitation pastoral concerto which forms the principal coupling Prêtre is not ideally flexible, but the finale has the right high spirits. The *Aubade* is an exhilarating work of great charm. It dates from the late 1920s and is a send-up of Mozart, Stravinsky, etc. The performance is admirably pointed and fresh and the recording quality, from the mid-1960s, is excellent. There is a good high-level cassette transfer.

Babar le petit éléphant (orch. Françaix).
(M) ** HMV Green. ESD 7020. Ustinov, Paris Conservatoire O, Prêtre – SAINT-SAËNS: *Carnival*.***

Babar: original version (also includes L. MOZART: *Toy symphony*; MOZART: *3 German dances, K.605**(*).
(M) ** ASV ACM/*ZCACM* 2033. Rippon, Parkhouse.

Poulenc's *Babar*, an entertainment for children, was originally written for narrator and piano and is most effective in this form. The music is unambitious but has a gentle charm, notably in the expressions of unforced melancholy when things are not turning out quite as Babar expected. The orchestration, by Françaix, is nicely judged, and is played quite persuasively under Prêtre, with Ustinov providing a characteristically avuncular narration.

In the ASV recording of the original, David Parkhouse makes the very most of the piano part, playing with commitment and character. Angela Rippon, however, seems not always at home in the narrative and does not readily find a balance between the melodrama (there are two moments of sudden death) and the more congenial events. But her direct, friendly style certainly communicates to younger listeners. The recording is excellent (the cassette, the most suitable medium for children, is admirably clear and faithful). The fill-ups, played by the Orchestra of St John's under John Lubbock, are not memorable: the *Toy symphony* is rather lacking in vitality.

(i) *Les Biches* (ballet; complete). *L'Éventail de Jeanne: Pastourelle. La Guirlande de Campra: Matelot provençale. Variations sur le nom de Marguerite Long: Bucolique.*
❀ *** HMV Dig. ASD/*TCC-ASD* 4067 [DS/*4XS* 37848]. Philh. O, Prêtre, (i) with Amb. S.

Georges Prêtre recorded *Les Biches* in the 1960s but not in its complete form or with the choral additions that Poulenc made optional when he came to rework the score. The title is untranslatable: it means 'female deer' and is also a term of endearment. Noel Goodwin's sleeve-note defines the *biches* as 'young girls on the verge of adventure in an atmosphere of wantonness; which you would sense if you are corrupted, but which an innocent would not be conscious of'. The music is a delight, and so too are the captivating fill-ups here: a gravely touching tribute to Marguerite Long, which comes close to the Satie of the *Gymnopédies*, and the charming *Pastourelle* from *L'Éventail de Jeanne*. High-spirited, fresh, elegant playing and sumptuous recorded sound enhance the claims of this issue. The strings have wonderful freshness and bloom, and there is no lack of presence. The chrome cassette too is of outstanding quality, matching the disc in its tonal richness and brilliance. The chorus is beautifully focused.

(i) *Les Biches* (ballet suite)*;* (ii) *Concerto for organ, strings and timpani;* (iii) *Deux Marches et un intermède; Les Mariés de la Tour Eiffel; La Baigneuse de Trouville; Discours du Général; Sinfonietta; Suite française d'après Claude Gervaise.*

(M) *** HMV *TCC2-POR 54289*. (i) Paris Conservatoire O; (ii) Duruflé, French Nat. RO; (iii) O de Paris; Prêtre.

HMV have surely done Georges Prêtre proud in this tape-only issue in their 'Portrait of the Artist' series, one of the most imaginatively programmed of any double-length cassette of its kind. All the music is attractive; the little-known *Sinfonietta* has much in common with Prokofiev's *Classical symphony*, while the scoring of the *Suite française* is attractively quirky. All the performances are good ones, notably the *Organ concerto*. The ambience for *Les Biches* is somewhat over-resonant, but throughout the tape transfer is of high quality and this compilation is not to be missed, even if it means duplicating the ballet suite with Prêtre's later complete version of *Les Biches*.

Concert champêtre for harpsichord and orchestra.

(M) *(*) Sup. 50926. Ružičková, Czech PO, Sanderling – MARTINŮ: *Harpsichord concerto.***

Although not as fine as the Erato or HMV performances (see below), this Supraphon account is a lively one and it is a pity that the heavily reverberant recording damps down some of the wit and charming point of Poulenc's elegant score.

(i) *Concert champêtre;* (ii) *Concerto in G min. for organ, strings and timpani.*

*** Erato STU 70637 [id.]. ORTF O, Martinon, with (i) Veyron-Lacroix, (ii) Alain.

*** HMV ASD/*TC-ASD* 3489 [Ang. S/*4XS* 37441]. Preston, LSO, Prcvin.

(M) *** Decca Jub. 410 172-1/*4* [Argo ZRG 878]. Malcolm, ASMF, Iona Brown.

The splendid *Concert champêtre* written for Landowska is most stylishly played by Robert Veyron-Lacroix and the ORTF Orchestra under the late Jean Martinon. The Erato disc is well balanced, with the harpsichord occupying a realistic amount of space in relation to the orchestra. Nor need Marie-Claire Alain's record of the *Organ concerto* fear comparison with Preston's (see below), and those who require this coupling need not hesitate for one moment. The performances are exhilarating, the recording admirably natural, and the music delightful.

On HMV each of the recordings is realistically balanced, and Simon Preston, who plays the solo parts in both concertos (the first artist to have done so in the recording studio), produces readings of great fluency and authority. Previn, too, has a genuine feeling for the music, though in the finale of the *Concert champêtre* there are odd moments when the phrasing might be more characterful. But there need be no real reservations here; the playing is always musical, often sparkling, and the recording is first-class, setting new standards. On cassette the *Concert champêtre* is beautifully managed, with everything natural and in perspective, but the *Organ concerto* is less refined, with a degree of coarseness at fortissimo levels.

George Malcolm follows Simon Preston's example in playing both concertos and does so with considerable success. The engineers have not succumbed to the temptation of making the harpsichord sound larger than life in the *Concert champêtre* – indeed, for some tastes they may have gone too far in the other direction. (Aimée van der Wiele's first stereo LP struck perhaps the right compromise.)

George Malcolm rather rushes things in the finale, but in every other respect his is an exemplary account that can well be recommended alongside the Preston. The playing of the Academy of St Martin-in-the-Fields is splendidly crisp and vital, both here and in the *Organ concerto*. The sound on both disc and cassette is first-class, although there are moments in the tape version of the *organ Concerto* when the focus slips. The Jubilee reissue has the advantage of economy, and for many this will make it first choice.

(i) *Concerto in G min. for organ, strings and timpani;* (ii) *Gloria.*
*** HMV ASD 2835 [Ang. S 35953]. ORTF O, Prêtre, with (i) Duruflé, (ii) Carteri, and Ch.

The *Gloria*, one of Poulenc's last works, has an arresting theatrical quality as well as many touching moments. Poulenc could move from Stravinskian high spirits to a much deeper vein of feeling with astonishing sureness of touch. Carteri is a rather glacial soloist, but the performance in every other respect is exemplary and – since it was recorded in the presence of the composer – presumably authoritative. The *Organ concerto* is a splendid piece and receives a spirited performance from Duruflé and the ORTF Orchestra. The recording has admirable presence and definition. Strongly recommended.

Piano concerto in C sharp min.
(*) HMV Dig. ASD/*TC-ASD* 107785-1/*4*. Ousset, Bournemouth SO, Barshai – PROKOFIEV: *Piano concerto No. 3.*(*)

(i) *Piano concerto;* (ii) *Gloria.*
*** HMV ASD 3299 [Ang. S 37246]. CBSO, Frémaux; with (i) Ortiz; (ii) Burrowes, CBSO Ch.

Cristina Ortiz gives an alert and stylish account of this disarming work and is given splendid support from Louis Frémaux with the Birmingham orchestra. His account of the *Gloria* competes with Prêtre's superb version (see above), a reading that has great fervour and electricity. Frémaux secures excellent results too, and the recording is spectacular.

Ousset gives a good performance of the *Concerto*, but she has not quite the same charm or character as Cristina Ortiz, nor has Barshai quite the same lightness of touch that her conductor (Louis Frémaux) brought to this delicious score. The recording is extremely good and is in the demonstration bracket, with disc and cassette sounding virtually identical.

Suite française.
*** ASV ALH/*ZCALH* 913. L. Wind O, Wick – GRAINGER: *Irish tune* etc.; MILHAUD: *Suite française.****

This engaging suite is based on themes by the sixteenth-century composer Claude Gervaise, which Poulenc scored for a small ensemble of wind instruments for a production of a play of Édouard Bourdet called *La Reine Margot*. They are dance pieces which Poulenc has freely transcribed and which come up very freshly in these artists' hands. Excellent recording and couplings. Thoroughly recommendable. The cassette, like the disc, is in the demonstration league.

Sonata for clarinet and bassoon; Trio for oboe, bassoon and piano.
(M) *** HMV Green. ESD/*TC-ESD* 102021-1/*4*. Melos Ens. – RAVEL: *Introduction and allegro* ***; FRANÇAIX: *Divertissements.***(*)

Both these Poulenc pieces are delightful, particularly the delicious *Trio for oboe, bassoon and piano*, which has an admirably dry wit and unfailing inventiveness. The record is worth having for this alone, and the playing is above reproach. Excellent recording, with the cassette in the demonstration class.

Sonata for flute and orchestra (orch. Berkeley).
*** RCA RL/*RK* 25109 [ARL 1/*ARK 1* 3777]. Galway, RPO, Dutoit – CHAMINADE: *Concertino*; FAURÉ: *Fantaisie*; IBERT: *Concerto.****

Poulenc's *Flute sonata*, composed in the mid-1950s towards the end of his life, deserves to be widely popular, so beguiling is its delightful opening theme. Yet so far it remains relatively neglected in the British catalogue (though not in the American one) and this is the only version currently available. Let us hope that Sir Lennox Berkeley's delightful arrangement and James Galway's persuasive advocacy will bring it to a larger public. The performance is elegant and polished and the orchestration highly successful. The recording is admirably spacious and well detailed and the tape transfer is clear and clean.

PIANO MUSIC

L'Album des Six: Valse. L'Éventail de Jeanne: Pastourelle. 3 Mouvements perpétuels; 8 Nocturnes; 3 Novelettes; Presto in B flat; Suite française d'après Claude Gervaise.
** EMI 2C 069/*269* 73134. Tacchino.

The *Suite française* is the piano transcription of dances by the sixteenth-century French composer, Claude Gervaise, which are recorded in their orchestral form by Georges Prêtre. These are delightful and are crisply played by this excellent artist. Slight though much of the other music is, some of it is curiously haunting and one finds pieces like the *C minor Nocturne*, illustrating a passage from a novel by Julian Green, obstinately memorable. Many of the pieces have a delicately observed period flavour as well as Poulenc's sophisticated harmonic sense. The recording dates from the late 1960s but wears its years well. There is a good cassette, though the quality is a little lacking in warmth.

Suite française (d'après Claude Gervaise); Intermezzi Nos. 1–3; Pièce brève sur le nom d'Albert Roussel; Les soirées de Nazelles; Theme and variations; Valse-Improvisation sur le nom de Bach; Villageoises (Petites pièces enfantines).
** EMI Dig. 2C 069/*269* 73101. Tacchino.

This second Tacchino recital is digitally recorded and the sound is rather dry. The two major works included are both sets of variations. *Les soirées de Nazelles* was written between 1930 and 1936. Each piece is given a sobriquet and the descriptive mood here is slightly more serious than in the *Thème varié*, with its eleven brief miniatures – also titled – alternately lyrical and drole. The six *Villageoises* (1933) are witty and brittle, with a general feeling of pastiche. The *Polka* even includes a whiff of Handel's *Harmonious Blacksmith*. The three *Intermezzi* are agreeably romantic, while the *Pièce brève* and *Valse-Improvisation* are obviously intended as encores. The latter was written for Horowitz and features a continuous accelerando, which Tacchino brings off with only moderate flair. The rest of the programme is strongly characterized, at times perhaps a shade too strongly, but the piano timbre does not help. Worth exploring, just the same. There is a good cassette.

VOCAL MUSIC

Ave verum corpus; Exultate Deo; Laudes de Saint-Antoine de Padoue; (i) *Litanies à la Vierge Noire; Quatre motets pour le temps de Noël; Quatre Motets pour le temps de pénitence; Salve Regina.*
*** EMI 2C 069/*269* 73030. Groupe Vocal de France, Alldis; (i) with Alain.

An outstanding collection. This is music that ideally needs French voices and John Alldis has trained his French group splendidly so that they combine precision and fervour with a natural feeling for the words. The soaring *Ave verum* is matched by the exhilaration of the *Exultate Deo* and the originality of the *Litanies* with its stabbing bursts of organ tone. The *Salve Regina* is very fine too, and the four *Christmas motets* which close the concert have the right extrovert joyfulness and sense of wonder. The recording is made within an ecclesiastical ambience, yet definition is admirable. The high-level cassette is generally first-class too.

(i; ii) *Le Bal masqué (cantate profane); Le Bestiare (ou Cortège d'Orphée);* (iii) *Gloria;* (iv) *Quatre motets pour le temps de penitence;* (ii; iv; v) *Stabat mater.*
(M) ** HMV *TCC2-POR 154597-9.* (i' Benoît; Maryse Charpentier (piano); (ii) Paris Conservatoire O; (iii) Carteri, Fr. Nat. R. TV Ch. and O; (iv) René Duclos Ch.; (v) Crespin; all cond. Prêtre.

A thoroughly worthwhile tape-only anthology, let down by inadequate documentation (only music titles and performers' names are indicated) and the use of iron-oxide instead of chrome tape, plus variable transfer levels. The choral sound in the *Stabat mater* on side one is mushy and untransparent and the recording, transferred at a low level, has generally poor definition. The *Motets* which follow are rather more effectively projected and *Le Bestiare*, admirably presented by Jean-Christophe Benoît, has more presence. Side two with an outstanding version of the *Gloria* – recorded in the presence of the composer – is more vivid; and the forward balance of *La Bal masqué* with its witty accompaniment, offering an obvious musical similarity to Ravel's *L'Enfant et les sortilèges*, comes off best of all in terms of clarity and liveliness.

Christmas motets (*O magnum mysterium; Quam vidistis pastores dicite; Videntes stellam; Hodie Christus natus est*); *Easter motets* (*Timor et tremor; Vinea mea electa; Tenebrae factae sunt; Tristis est anima*).
*** Argo ZRG 720. Christ Church Cath. Ch., Oxford, L. Sinf., Preston – STRAVINSKY: *Mass.****

These motets are of great beauty and simplicity. Simon Preston's account of them with the Christ Church Cathedral Choir could hardly be improved on, and the Argo engineers produce mellifluous and rich quality.

Exultate Deo; Mass in G; Salve Regina.
*** Argo ZRG 883 [id.]. Bond, St John's College Ch., Guest; Scott (organ) – PEETERS: *Missa festiva.****

The Choir of St John's College, Cambridge, offers the pre-war *Mass in G major* with two motets, finely wrought pieces, in performances of great finish. There is little to choose between this version of the *Mass* and that of the Uppsala forces on Erato (see below). The more logical coupling on Erato is likely to exert the stronger appeal on collectors, though the Flor Peeters Mass is excellent. The St John's College forces cope with the delicacy and sweetness of Poulenc's chromatic harmony, and the recorded sound is eminently realistic and truthful.

Figure humaine (cantata)*; Mass in G; Quatre petites prières de Saint-François d'Assise.*
*** Erato STU 70924 [id.]. Mellnäs, Sunnegärdh, Uppsala Academic Chamber Ch., Kfum Chamber Ch., Stenlund.

Figure humaine is a wartime work written during the occupation to words of Paul Éluard. It is perhaps Poulenc's most substantial and deeply felt work in this medium, and these Swedish forces convey its eloquence to good effect. The pre-war *Mass in G major* is less intense but contains a moving soprano solo, which is beautifully done here. The four male-voice settings are post-war and are effectively projected by these fine Uppsala singers. A strongly recommended disc, which offers atmospheric sound.

La fraîcheur et le feu (*1–7*)*; Tu vois le feu du soir.*
(M) **(*) HMV SXLP/*TC-SXLP* 30556. Norman, Gage – SCHUBERT: *Lieder* ***; WAGNER: *Wesendonk Lieder.***(*)

The Poulenc songs – brightly done, if with less point than she would have achieved later – make a charming filler to Jessye Norman's early recital record of Schubert and Wagner, well recorded.

Gloria (see also above under *Organ concerto*).
*** CBS 76670 [M/*MT* 34551]. Blegen, Westminster Ch., NYPO, Bernstein – STRAVINSKY: *Symphony of Psalms.****
(*) Argo Dig. ZRDL/*KZRDC* 1010 [id.]. Greenberg, Lausanne Pro Arte Ch., SRO, Lopez-Cobos – BIZET: *Te Deum.*(*)

The *Gloria* is one of Poulenc's last compositions and among his most successful. Bernstein perhaps underlines the Stravinskian springs of its inspiration and produces a vividly etched and clean-textured account which makes excellent sense in every way and is free from excessive sentiment. Judith Blegen is an appealing soloist, and the recording, though not the last word in refinement, is really very clear, well detailed and spacious. With its outstanding Stravinsky coupling this is a very attractive issue.

Very good recording on Argo and a useful alternative to the versions by Frémaux and Bernstein, though it does not displace them. Lopez-Cobos also underlines the Stravinskian elements in the score and has the advantage of excellent sound, clean and well detailed without being too analytical. His coupling is an early Bizet curiosity rather than the more substantial offerings that his two rivals give us. The pioneering version by Prêtre still sounds impressive and has a certain authenticity of feeling that Lopez-Cobos does not wholly capture. However, his is undoubtedly the better recording and, in its cassette format, detail is vivid and well in focus. Perhaps the choral tone is less refined in the cassette transfer than on the disc, but in most other respects there is little to choose between them.

Mélodies (complete recording).
*** EMI 2C 165 16231/5. Ameling, Gedda, Parker, Sénéchal, Souzay; Baldwin.

The art songs of Poulenc, here collected in strongly characterized performances, present a developing portrait of the composer. Starting in the 1920s with brilliant squibs of inspiration typical of Paris at that period (as in settings of Apollinaire), he grew in stature in the 1930s, and from then on the expression became consistently deeper and more intense, if with some loss of lyrical invention. Though Pierre Bernac was the singer with whom Poulenc was most regularly associated, it is not just songs for baritone that here provide delight. Those sung by the soprano, Elly Ameling, are among the most charming in their freshness. The tenor songs are well divided between the characterful Sénéchal and the lyrical Gedda. Soûzay has most of the baritone songs, but more seductively beautiful is the singing of William Parker. Dalton Baldwin makes a superb, consistently imaginative accompanist. Recordings (1974–7) are first-rate.

Praetorius, Michael (1571–1621)

Dances from Terpsichore (Suite de ballets; Suite de voltes). (i) Motets: *Eulogodia Sionia: Resonet in laudibus; Musicae Sionae: Allein Gott in der Höh sei Ehr; Aus tiefer Not schrei ich zu dir; Christus der uns selig macht; Gott der Vater wohn uns bei; Polyhymnia Caduceatrix: Erhalt uns, Herr, bei deinem Wort.*
*** HMV CSD 3761 [Ang. S/*4XS* 37091]. Early Music Cons. of L., Munrow, (i) with Boys of the Cath. and Abbey Church of St Alban.

Terpsichore is a huge collection of some three hundred dance tunes used by the French-court dance bands of Henry IV. They were enthusiastically assembled by the German composer Michael Praetorius, who also harmonized them and arranged them in four to six parts. Moreover he left plenty of advice as to their manner of performance, although he would not have expected any set instrumentation – this would depend on the availability of musicians. Any selection is therefore as arbitrary in the choice of items as it is conjectural in the matter of their orchestration. David Munrow's instrumentation is imaginatively done (the third item, a *Bourrée* played by four racketts – a cross between a shawm and comb and paper in sound – is fascinating), but the playing itself sometimes seems too refined in manner. But one must not exaggerate this. This collection is still a delightful one and the motets on side two remind one very much of Giovanni Gabrieli. The record is splendidly documented (with an eight-page insert leaflet, record-sleeve size) and most atmospherically recorded.

Premru, Raymond (born 1934)

Music from Harter Fell.
*** Argo ZRG 906 [id.]. Jones Brass Ens. – ARNOLD: *Symphony* **(*); SALZEDO: *Capriccio.***

Raymond Premru is one of the trombonists in this ensemble, and his *Music from Harter Fell* is expertly laid out for three trumpets and three trombones. The invention is fresh and the style adventurous, and though it is slow to take wing, there is genuine inspiration and vision here. The playing and recording are both superb.

Previn, André (born 1929)

A Different Kind of Blues (*Look at him go; Little face; Who reads reviews; Night thoughts; A different kind of blues; Chocolate apricot; The five of us; Make up your mind*).
*** HMV Dig. ASD/*TCC-ASD* 3965 [Ang. DS 37780]. Perlman, Previn, Manne, Hall, Mitchell.

Perlman, unlike his colleagues here, is no jazz musician, and he had to have the 'improvisations' written out for him; but the challenge of this project, with Previn's colourful and appealing pieces dividing sharply between brilliant and sweet, is very clear from first to last. There are not many better examples of 'middle-of-the-road' records, and the haunting *Chocolate apricot* could become a classic. No information is given on which critic gave rise to *Who reads reviews*. The digital recording is immediate and vivid, and the chrome cassette matches the disc closely.

It's a Breeze (*It's a breeze; Rain in my head; Catgut your tongue; It's about time; Bowing and scraping; A tune for Heather; Quiet diddling; The red bar*).
*** EMI Dig. EMD/*TCC-EMD* 5537. Perlman, Previn, Manne, Hall, Mitchell.

This second instalment of Previn's jazz pieces written for Perlman is if anything even more persuasive than the first, recorded at Heinz Hall, Pittsburgh, as a relaxed supplement to more serious sessions. Such sweet numbers as *A tune for Heather* are particularly attractive, with a tingle of Walton. The digital recording presents balances that are closer to those preferred in pop than to those one would expect in a semi-classical issue, but the sound is very vivid. The chrome cassette is marginally less refined on top than the disc.

Prokofiev, Serge (1891–1953)

American overture, Op. 42; Lieutenant Kijé (*suite*), *Op. 60; Love of Three Oranges* (opera)*: suite.*
*** CBS 76987/*40*- [M/*MT* 36683]. LAPO, Tilson Thomas.

Michael Tilson Thomas's performance of *Lieutenant Kijé* is intensely nostalgic, presenting the music almost as if in a dream sequence, bringing a pervading elegiac feeling to the opening and closing pages and in the delightfully played *Romance*. The *Troika* and wedding sequence make a robust contrast. The recording is unusually atmospheric for CBS, with a recessed balance, yet detail remains clear (on disc and the excellent chrome tape alike). The characterization of the *Love of Three Oranges suite* could hardly be more different, full of venom in the witch's music, with a brilliant edge on strings and brass alike. The Love scene here is perhaps a trifle cool, but the famous *March* is vigorously exuberant. The *American overture* was written in 1926 for the opening of a New York music emporium. It is a busy but rather empty piece.

American overture; The Prodigal Son (ballet), *Op. 46.*
*** HMV ASD 4164 [Vox C 9036]. Moscow RSO, Rozhdestvensky.

The Prodigal Son has long been absent from the catalogue in its original form. (Much of the material is familiar from its reincarnation, the *Fourth Symphony* – and the seventh of its ten movements was transcribed for the piano as the *Étude*, Op. 52, No. 3.) The melodic invention is unflagging and the harmonic spicing is as fresh and appealing as ever. Rozhdestvensky secures responsive playing from the Moscow Radio Symphony Orchestra, though the last ounce of polish and finesse is wanting. Yet it is a great improvement on the old Ansermet set from the 1960s, which was not complete anyway. If you like the better-known ballets, this is well worth investigating, particularly as there is no current alternative. The *American overture* is highly original in scoring (two pianos, two harps, celeste, five woodwind, two trumpets, trombone and three double-basses, one of which was later changed for a cello, plus percussion). The recording though not in the top flight is very good indeed and readers should not overlook this interesting and rewarding issue.

Chout (*The Buffoon;* ballet)*: suite, Op. 21; Romeo and Juliet* (ballet)*: suite, Op. 64.*
(M) *** Decca Jub. JB/*KJBC* 56 [Lon. STS 15477]. LSO, Abbado.

It is difficult to see why a well-selected suite from *Chout* should not be as popular as any of Prokofiev's other ballet scores. It is marvellously inventive music which shows Prokofiev's harmonic resource at its most engaging. Abbado's version with the LSO offers a generous part of the score, including some of the loosely written connecting tissue, and Abbado reveals a sensitive ear for balance of texture. The excerpts from *Romeo and Juliet* are well chosen: they include some of the most delightful numbers that are normally omitted from the suites, such as the *Dance with mandolins*, the *Aubade* and so on. The *Dance of the girls* is very sensuous but too slow, far slower than Prokofiev's own 78s. But despite a slight want of intensity and fire, there is an admirable delicacy and lightness of touch that are most captivating. The recording is a model of its kind, with a beautifully balanced perspective and no lack of stereo presence. The cassette transfer too is of Decca's top quality, splendidly vivid and detailed. Highly recommended.

Cinderella (ballet; complete), *Op. 87.*
*** HMV Dig. SLS/*TC-SLS* 143595-3/*5* (2) [Ang. DSB/*4X2S* 3944]. LSO, Previn.
*** Decca Dig. 410 162-1/*4* (2) [Lon. LH2 410 162-1/*4*]. Cleveland O, Ashkenazy.

Prokofiev's enchanting score has been neglected in recent years and no complete version has appeared since Rozhdestvensky's HMV Melodiya set with Moscow Radio forces made in the mid-1960s. Now two new sets have appeared, both by artists who are completely inside the Prokofiev idiom. Honours are very evenly divided between the two: they both occupy two records and they are very well played; if one is not readily to hand, one can safely invest in the other without fear of disappointment. Some dances come off better in one version rather than the other, and there is a fair element of swings and roundabouts in assessing them. Detail is more closely scrutinized by the Decca engineers who produce a bright, vivid image, while the EMI engineers have the more spacious acoustic within which to work and yet lose no detail. The playing of the LSO for Previn is extremely alert and beautifully characterized, the wind playing is particularly fine, and there is a good sense of theatre. The HMV cassettes match the discs very closely.

Ashkenazy gets excellent results from the Cleveland Orchestra and his account displaces the old Rozhdestvensky in terms of the quality of the orchestral response. There are many imaginative touches in this score – as magical, indeed, as the story itself – and the level of invention is astonishingly high. The Decca team give wonderful definition to the orchestral detail, though it must be said that the HMV has the greater warmth and the richer acoustic ambience. Where a choice must be made, the EMI version scores on this very count and, perhaps, in the grace and delicacy of the orchestral playing in some of the more lightly scored dances, and indeed the more homogeneous sound one finds in climaxes. The Decca tape transfer is on chrome stock, but with only a modest transfer level possible because of the Kingsway Hall resonance; the sound, though beautifully refined in detail, does not have more range and presence than Previn's HMV XDR set.

Cinderella: excerpts; (ii) *Romeo and Juliet* (ballet), *Op. 64:* excerpts.
(M) *** HMV Green. ESD/*TC-ESD* 7151 [(d) Sera. S 60340]. (i) RPO, Irving; (ii) Philh. O, Kurtz.
(M) *(*) Decca SPA/*KCSP* 226 [(d) Lon. STS 15481]. SRO, Ansermet.

A very generous selection from both ballets is included on the Greensleeve reissue. Kurtz's *Romeo and Juliet* comes from the mid-1960s, but Irving's performances are from 1958, yet no one could guess the dates of either from the sound here, which is quite admirable in its definition and body. The cassette too is in the demonstration class, splendidly vivid and clear. Irving secures very fine playing from the RPO, crisply rhythmic and sympathetic. In *Romeo and Juliet*, Kurtz's performances are slightly lacking in dramatic tension in the longer movements, although the shorter dances come off superbly. But what beautifully shaped phrasing the Philharmonia give us and what full timbre. Given the outstanding quality of the recording, this is most competitive.

Ansermet's excerpts are taken from a two-disc album providing extended selections from both ballets, which Ansermet recorded in 1962. The one-disc condensed version is fair value for money, as Ansermet's Prokofiev is nearly always characterful. But the orchestral playing is less than distinguished, and Ansermet's directing hand seems less assured than usual in matters of style. The recording is vivid but at the loudest moments it is not as open and free from congestion as the best recordings from this source. The cassette transfer is only fair and this is outclassed by the HMV disc, above, which is in the same price range.

(i–iii) *Piano concertos Nos. 1–5;* (ii; iv) *In Autumn* (*Autumnal*), *Op. 8; Symphony No. 1 in D* (*Classical*), *Op. 25;* (i; v) *Overture on Hebrew themes, Op. 34.*
(M) *** Decca 15BB 218-20/*K3 H14* [Lon. CSA/*5-* 2314]. (i) Ashkenazy (piano); (ii) LSO; (iii) Previn; (iv) cond. Ashkenazy; (v) Puddy, Gabrieli Qt.

Piano concertos Nos. 1, 4 and 5.
*** EMI 2C 069 02795. Béroff, Leipzig GO, Masur.

Piano concertos Nos. 2–3.
*** EMI 2C 069 02764. Béroff, Leipzig GO, Masur.

Honours are more evenly divided between Ashkenazy and Béroff than one might expect. Not that Ashkenazy's staggering virtuosity is challenged by the young Frenchman, though he too plays masterfully; rather that both versions prove amazingly satisfying on closer acquaintance. For some the bottom-heavy balance of the Decca recording and the prominence given to the soloist will be a drawback, though the actual orchestral quality is beautifully transparent. The balance in the EMI version is better, and though the overall sound picture is not wholly natural, the timbre of the piano is more sympathetically captured. Béroff is a pianist of genuine insight where Prokofiev is concerned, and Masur gives him excellent support. He is free from some of the agogic mannerisms that distinguish Ashkenazy (in the first movement of No. 2 and the slow movement of No. 3) and he has great poetry. Ashkenazy has marvellous panache, of course, and Previn is a sensitive accompanist throughout. To be frank, both sets give almost equal pleasure in their different ways. The cassette transfer of the Decca set is of outstanding quality, and because the bass is rather less ample the sound balance is generally better than on the discs.

Piano concerto No. 1 in D flat, Op. 10.
(B) *** PRT GSGC/*ZCGC* 2065. Katz, LPO, Boult – KHACHATURIAN: *Piano concerto.****

(i) *Piano concerto No. 1 in D flat, Op. 10. Romeo and Juliet: Scene and dance of the young girls* (arr. for piano by composer).
*** HMV ASD 3571 [Ang. S/*4XS* 37486]. Gavrilov, (i) with LSO, Rattle – RAVEL: *Concerto for left hand; Pavane.****

A dazzling account of the *First Concerto*

from the young Soviet pianist Andrei Gavrilov, who replaced Richter at Salzburg in 1975 and has astonished audiences wherever he has appeared. This version is second to none for virtuosity or for sensitivity: it is no exaggeration to say that this exhilarating account is the equal of any we have ever heard and superior to most. Apart from its brilliance, this performance scores on all other fronts too; Simon Rattle provides an excellent orchestral support and the EMI engineers offer vivid recording. An outstanding issue. On tape, as the opening tutti shows, the reverberation causes some blurring in the orchestral focus, but the piano quality is excellent and the general detail of the recording is good in all but the most expansive fortissimos.

A sparkling performance from Katz, the bravura very apparent. The piano tone is bold and clear, but the balance is excellent. The orchestral playing is good if not as polished as that of the soloist. Overall the effect is of sophisticated brilliance, which is very effective in making the most of the music without introducing artificiality. This is most enjoyable, and as the coupling is outstanding this makes a highly recommendable bargain disc, particularly as the recording is so good. The cassette is well managed too, although the disc has more range at the top.

(i) *Piano concertos Nos. 1; 2 in G min., Op. 16;* (ii) *Overture on Hebrew themes for clarinet, string quartet and piano, Op. 34.*
*** Decca SXL/*KSXC* 6767 [Lon. CS/*5*-7062]. Ashkenazy, (i) LSO, Previn, (ii) Puddy, Gabrieli Qt.

Ashkenazy is a commanding soloist in both concertos, and his virtuosity in the *First* is quite dazzling. He is curiously wayward in the opening of the *Second*, where he indulges in excessive rubato, but there is no question that this is a masterly performance. The piano is very forwardly placed and is bottom-heavy, as recorded here. The accompaniments are splendidly idiomatic and, apart from the reticent balance, the string tone is beautifully fresh in quality. Orchestral quality is also bottom-heavy. However, none of this should inhibit readers from acquiring these most distinguished performances. The cassette transfer is extremely brilliant and very well balanced, although the quality in the *Overture* is smoother and rather less well defined.

Piano concerto No. 3 in C, Op. 26.
*** DG Acc. 2542/*3342* 149 [139 349]. Argerich, Berlin PO, Abbado – RAVEL: *Concerto in G.****
(*) HMV Dig. ASD/*TC-ASD* 107785-1/*4*. Ousset, Bournemouth SO, Barshai – POULENC: *Concerto.*(*)
*(**) Chan. ABR/*ABT* 1054. Judd, Moscow PO, Lazarev – TCHAIKOVSKY: *Piano concerto No. 1.**(**)

(i) *Piano concerto No. 3;* (ii) *In Autumn, Op. 8; Symphony No. 1 in D* (*Classical*), *Op. 25.*
**(*) Decca SXL/*KSXC* 6768 [(d) Lon. CS/*5*- 6964]. (i) Ashkenazy, LSO, Previn; (ii) cond. Ashkenazy.

Martha Argerich made her outstanding coupling of the Prokofiev and Ravel concertos in 1968, while still in her twenties, and this record helped to establish her international reputation as one of the most vital and positive of women pianists. There is nothing ladylike about the playing, but it displays countless indications of feminine perception and subtlety. The Prokofiev *C major Concerto*, once regarded as tough music, here receives a sensuous performance, and Abbado's direction underlines that from the very first, with a warmly romantic account of the ethereal opening phrases on the high violins. When it comes to the second subject the lightness of Argerich's pointing has a delightfully infectious quality, and surprisingly a likeness emerges with the Ravel *G major Concerto* (given on the reverse), which was written more than a decade later. This is a much more individual performance of the Prokofiev than almost any other available and brings its own special insights. The recording remains excellent and the cassette transfer too is first-class, matching the disc closely. A highly recommendable mid-priced reissue.

From Decca this is the least attractive of the three discs from the Prokofiev concerto box. Ashkenazy's account of the *Third Concerto* is keen-edged and crisply articulated, and he is sympathetically supported by Previn and the LSO. One's reservation concerns the slow movement: Ashkenazy's entry immediately after the theme is uncharacteristically mannered. Good, though slightly bottom-heavy, recording. But competition is stiff here, and Argerich is to be preferred. The early *In Autumn* is eminently worth having if you missed it in the *Symphonies* box; and the *Classical symphony* receives a neat and well-turned reading. This sounds especially well on the equivalent cassette.

Cécile Ousset has the advantage of superb recording – indeed, the sound is of demonstration standard on both disc and cassette – but the performance, expert though it is, wants the dash and sparkle that such artists as Argerich and Béroff brought to their recordings. Tempi are just that bit slower than Prokofiev's own, in his pioneering recording, and Barshai's direction sounds slightly sluggish.

Recorded live when the late Terence Judd was competing in the 1978 Moscow Tchaikovsky Competition, his urgent and dynamic account of the Prokofiev makes up in impulse and conviction what it lacks in refinement. The recording favours the piano. Like the Tchaikovsky performance on the reverse, this is a valuable and compelling reminder of a talent tragically cut off. Limited sound with an acceptable cassette.

Piano concertos Nos. 4 in B flat for left hand, Op. 53; 5 in G, Op. 55.
*** Decca SXL 6769 [(d) Lon. CS/*5*- 6964]. Ashkenazy, LSO, Previn.

Ashkenazy gives an admirable account of No. 5; every detail of phrasing and articulation is well thought out, and yet there is no want of spontaneity or any hint of calculation. Richter is wittier and more glittering in the second movement, where Ashkenazy adopts the more measured tempo. In No. 4 he is no less authoritative, though his choice of tempo at figure 51 is puzzling. As in the companion discs, the accompaniment is sensitively played, though the recording has a fair amount of bass resonance.

(i) *Piano concerto No. 5; Piano sonata No. 8 in B flat, Op. 84; Visions fugitives, Op. 22, Nos. 3, 6, 9.*
(M) *** DG 2543 812. Richter (i) with Warsaw PO, Rowicki.

Richter's account of the *Fifth Piano concerto* is a classic. It first appeared in 1960 as a fill-up to the Mozart *D minor*, and in its most recent incarnation it was coupled with Monique Haas's performance of the Ravel *G major*. The present transfer is just that bit cleaner and richer than the 1975 version when the treble was a little enhanced. In any event it cannot be too strongly recommended to all admirers of Richter, Prokofiev and great piano playing. Richter lingers a little over this and that detail in the *Eighth Sonata*, but all the same it is a wonderful performance. The recording is rather lower in level than is ideal but the surfaces are absolutely impeccable.

Violin concertos Nos. 1 in D, Op. 19; 2 in G min., Op. 63.
C *** DG Dig. **410 524-2**; 410 521-1/*4* [id.]. Mintz, Chicago SO, Abbado.
*** HMV Dig. **CDC 747025-2**; ASD/*TCC-ASD* 4098 [Ang. DS/*4XS* 37800]. Perlman, BBC SO, Rozhdestvensky.
*** Decca SXL/*KSXC* 6773 [Lon. CS 6997]. Kyung-Wha Chung, LSO, Previn.
*** Erato STU 70866. Amoyal, Strasbourg PO, Lombard.
**(*) CBS Dig. 37802 [id.]. Stern, NYPO, Mehta.
**(*) Decca Dig. SXDL 7579 [Lon. 411 704-1/*4*]]. Belkin, LPO, Kondrashin or Barshai.
(M) **(*) CBS 61796/*40*-. Stern, Phd. O, Ormandy.

Violin concerto No. 2.
(M) *** Ph. Seq. 6527/*7311* 041 [Quin. 7150]. Szeryng, LSO, Rozhdestvensky – SIBELIUS: *Concerto.***(*)

Prokofiev's two *Violin concertos* are eminently well served in the present catalogue. Mintz's performances are as fine as any; he phrases with imagination and individuality – the opening of the *G minor* is memorably poetic – and if he does not display quite the overwhelming sense of authority of Perlman, there is an attractive combination of freshness and lyrical finesse. He has the advantage of Abbado's sensitive and finely judged accompaniments. Abbado has a special feeling for

Prokofiev's sound-world and here there is much subtlety of colour and dynamic nuance, yet the music's vitality is undiminished. In short this partnership casts the strongest spell on the listener and, with recording which is both refined and full, and a more realistic – if still somewhat forward – balance for the soloist, this record and the excellent equivalent tape must receive the strongest advocacy. The compact disc is in the demonstration league, one of the most impressive to come from DG, adding to the presence and range of the sound-picture without overemphasis.

Perlman's performances bring virtuosity of such strength and command that one is reminded of the supremacy of Heifetz. Though the HMV sound has warmth and plenty of bloom, the balance of the soloist is unnaturally close which has the effect of obscuring important melodic ideas in the orchestra behind mere passagework from the soloist, as in the second subject of the *First Concerto*'s finale. Nevertheless in their slightly detached way these performances are impossible to resist: one is left in no doubt that both works are among the finest violin concertos written this century. Apart from the balance, the recording is very fine, with a matching cassette of demonstration quality. Even so, many will opt for the alternative Decca coupling where Kyung-Wha Chung gives performances to emphasize the gloriously lyrical quality of these concertos, with playing that is both warm and strong, tender and full of fantasy. Not since David Oistrakh's mono recordings of the 1950s has the full range of expression in these works been so richly brought out on record, thanks to the deeply understanding accompaniment from Previn and the LSO. The lovely melody which opens the slow movement of No. 2 – almost Bellinian, as has often been said – finds Chung playing with an inner, hushed quality, as though the emotion is too deep to be uttered out loud, and the ravishing modulation from E flat to B a page or so later brings an ecstatic *frisson*. The recording is gloriously full, with the soloist naturally balanced. Unfortunately on tape the Decca recording is too brightly lit, giving a very aggressive edge to the solo violin tone, and there is an absence of bloom on the orchestra.

Pierre Amoyal is not a virtuoso in the same sense as Heifetz or Stern but he is profoundly musical and has an excellent technique. The *First Concerto* has an effortless eloquence that is moving, and the first movement unfolds with an unforced and unhurried quality that is all the more telling for its lack of ostentation. The Strasbourg orchestra under Alain Lombard are most sensitive in the *First* and are recorded in a warm, open acoustic. The balance between soloist and orchestra is life-like and natural. No. 2 is not so imaginative a reading but again there is no attempt to glamorize detail or draw attention away from the music to the interpreters. A most enjoyable record.

In his digital recordings, made in New York, Stern's are warmly and boldly extrovert readings, a degree freer in expression and more spontaneous-sounding than his 1965 versions recorded in Philadelphia. Again the balance favours the soloist, though the digital recording preserves a sense of natural presence in the sound. Stern may here lack the depth of poetry of Chung and the fearless brilliance of Perlman, but were these versions absent, he would make an excellent alternative.

Belkin's readings, warmly expressive, naturally responsive as they are (with the half-tone opening of the slow movement of No. 2 outstandingly beautiful), are less positive in their characterization than the finest available. Nonetheless the vividness of the digital recordings makes them most attractive, fuller and better-balanced than Perlman's HMV.

In his earlier Philadelphia coupling with Ormandy, Stern is hardly less extrovert in his romanticism, holding little back; these remain confident and ripely perceptive performances, revelling in and bringing out the full lyricism of these fine concertos. Stern's warmly expressive approach is matched by Ormandy, who provides an orchestral texture well suited to the soloist's needs. However, the forward balance and the consequent lack of a really hushed quality precludes the element of mystery. Even so, at medium price, this disc remains competitive. The CBS sound is extremely vivid and the playing often makes a dazzling impact. The cassette matches the disc fairly closely, with only marginal loss of refinement (more noticeable in No. 2). Stern's later New York recording is not available on tape in the UK.

Szeryng's account of the *Second Concerto* is in every way first-class. Perhaps it has less powerful projection than Stern's version, but Szeryng finds a greater degree of tenderness and he is more poetic in the slow movement. Rozhdestvensky accompanies sensitively and the overall impression is eloquent and committed. The balance of the Philips recording is admirable; the sound has warmth as well as presence. The cassette transfer is one of Philips' best, matching the disc closely.

Lieutenant Kijé (incidental music for a film)*: suite, Op. 60.*

*** HMV ASD 3029 [Ang. RL/*4RL* 32105]. LSO, Previn – SHOSTAKOVICH: *Symphony No. 6.****

(M) *** CBS Classics 61193 [MS 7408]. Cleveland O, Szell – KODÁLY: *Háry János suite.****

Lieutenant Kijé is given a colourful, swaggering performance by Previn and the LSO, an excellent fill-up for their fine account of Shostakovich's *Sixth Symphony*. Szell, even more than in the *Háry János* coupling, is on his highest form. Seldom on record has the *Lieutenant Kijé* music been projected with such drama and substance, and Szell is wonderfully warm in the *Romance* without a suggestion of sentimentality. The recording, like the coupling, is aggressively close but it can be tamed, and there is no doubt about the projection of the music.

Lieutenant Kijé: suite; Love of Three Oranges (opera)*: suite; Symphony No. 1 in D* (*Classical*)*, Op. 25.*

**(*) Ph. 9500/*7300* 903 [id.]. LSO, Marriner.

** HMV Dig. ASD/*TCC-ASD* 4414 [Ang. DS/*4XS* 37960]. LPO, Bátiz.

On Philips good playing and recording; if you want this particular coupling, there is little here to disappoint. Individually these pieces are available in other versions that are as good as (if not superior to) this compilation, but these are lively performances in well-ventilated sound.

As sound, the HMV record is altogether superb with startling clarity and body, particularly in the *Scène infernale* of *Love of Three Oranges*. Throughout the range, this is extremely impressive and should be in much demand in demonstration showrooms. (The same holds for the chrome cassette which is of excellent quality too.) There is much to admire in the performances, though throughout all three works one feels the need for a stronger grip from the conductor and more alert responses from the players. By comparison with Michael Tilson Thomas and the Los Angeles Orchestra in *Love of Three Oranges* or Previn and the LSO in *Kijé*, this sounds undistinguished and it is only the superb recording that at first persuades one otherwise.

Lieutenant Kijé (suite); *Romeo and Juliet:* excerpts; *Symphony No. 1 in D* (*Classical*)*;* (i) *Alexander Nevsky* (cantata)*, Op. 78.*

(M) *** HMV *TCC2-POR 54278.* LSO, Previn, (i) with Reynolds, LSO Ch.

EMI could hardly have chosen better to represent Previn in their 'Portrait of the Artist' double-length tape series. The performances of the *Kijé suite* and the *Classical symphony* are among the finest available and are discussed under their original couplings. *Alexander Nevsky* is currently not available in the UK in disc format (it is issued in the USA, however, on [Ang. RL/*4RL* 32081]) and here it is presented without a break on one side of the cassette. All the weight, bite and colour of the score are captured and though the timbre of the singers' voices may not suggest Russians, they cope very confidently with the Russian text, and Previn's dynamic manner ensures that the great *Battle on the ice* scene is powerfully effective. Anna Reynolds sings the lovely lament for the dead most affectingly. The transfers are very sophisticated throughout, the sound vivid with excellent range and a good choral focus.

Lieutenant Kijé: suite, Op. 60; Scythian suite, Op. 20.

*** DG 2530 967 [id.]. Chicago SO, Abbado.

This offers a fine account of *Lieutenant Kijé* coupled with what is probably the best version of the *Scythian suite* to have appeared for many years. Previn has slightly more character in his version of *Kijé*, but Abbado gets wonderfully clean playing from the Chicago orchestra and he is accorded excellent engineering. The *Scythian suite* has drive and fire: in the finale – and even in the second movement – Abbado could bring greater savagery and brilliance than he does, but given the power that the Chicago orchestra do bring to this score, and the refined colouring that Abbado achieves in the atmospheric *Night* movement, there need be no real reservation in recommending this.

Love of 3 Oranges: suite; Scythian suite.
(*) Mercury SRI 75030 [id.]. LSO, Dorati – BARTÓK: *Miraculous Mandarin: suite.*

Dorati's performances are sympathetic and strongly characterized and the LPO playing is first-class. Dorati finds warmth as well as pungency in the *Scythian suite*, and though his version is not as distinguished as Abbado's, and the reverberant acoustic does blunt the transients a little, this remains a satisfying coupling at mid-price. It is difficult to believe that this record is over twenty years old, for the sound has richness as well as immediacy.

Peter and the Wolf, Op. 67.
(M) *** Decca VIV/*KVIC* 40. Richardson, LSO, Sargent – BRITTEN: *Young person's guide to the orchestra***; R. STRAUSS: *Till Eulenspiegel.****
(M) *** HMV Green. ESD/*TC-ESD* 7114 [Sera. S/*4XG* 60172]. Flanders, Philh. O, Kurtz – BRITTEN: *Young person's guide*; SAINT-SAËNS: *Carnival.****
*** HMV ASD/*TC-ASD* 2935 [Ang. S/*4XS* 36962]. Farrow, LSO, Previn – BRITTEN: *Young person's guide.****
(M) *** ASV ACM/*ZCACM* 2005. Rippon, RPO, Hughes – SAINT-SAËNS: *Carnival.****
*** CRD CRD 1032/*CRDC 4032*. Morris, Northern Sinf., Haslam – HASLAM: *Juanita.***
(B) *** Con. CC/*CCT* 7519 [Lon. STS/*5*-15592]. Connery, RPO, Dorati – BRITTEN: *Young person's guide.***(*)
(*) RCA RL/*RK* 12743 [ARL 1/*ARK 1* 2743]. Bowie, Phd. O, Ormandy – BRITTEN: *Young person's guide.*
(*) DG 2531/*3301* 275 [id.]. Du Pré, ECO, Barenboim – L. MOZART: *Cassation.*
(B) ** CfP CFP/*TC-CFP* 185. Richard Baker, New Philh. O, Leppard – BRITTEN: *Young person's guide.***
(M) * CBS 60152/*40*-. Bernstein with NYPO – SAINT-SAËNS: *Carnival.**

Of the many fine versions of *Peter and the Wolf*, Sir Ralph Richardson's vivid narration remains top favourite; it is still available coupled to an excellent version of the *Classical symphony* – see below – but has now been reissued at lower-mid-price on Viva, sounding admirably fresh, on disc and tape alike, and generously recoupled to Dorati's lively account of the *Young person's guide to the orchestra* and Fritz Reiner's highly distinguished version of *Till Eulenspiegel*.

However, another reissue from HMV on their similarly-priced Greensleeve label is equally attractive in offering the excellent 1959 Michael Flanders recording of *Peter* together with Saint-Saëns's *Carnival of the Animals*, plus an even more characterful account, under Sir Charles Groves, of Britten's *Young person's guide to the orchestra*. Michael Flanders adds a touch or two of his own to the introduction and narration, and, as might be expected, he brings the action splendidly alive. The pace of the accompaniment under Kurt is attractively vibrant, and the Philharmonia are first-rate. The recording is crisply vivid on disc and cassette alike.

Mia Farrow treats *Peter and the Wolf* as a bedtime story, admirably unmannered and direct. Almost certainly the best version for younger children, and the recording quality is the finest yet given to this colourful fable. It is an advantage too having the narrator in the same acoustic as the orchestra, which under Previn's direction produces playing both rich and jaunty, with some superb solo work. The cassette transfer offers warm, pleasing sound, with only slight clouding of orchestral detail by the reverberation; the voice is clear and well projected.

Angela Rippon narrates with charm yet is never in the least coy; indeed she is thoroughly involved in the tale and thus involves the listener too. The accompaniment is equally spirited, with excellent orchestral playing, and the recording is splendidly clear, yet not lacking atmosphere. Anyone attracted to this coupling will find it a first-class investment. The cassette matches the disc closely.

Johnny Morris provides a completely new and extended text. The narration continues with the music far more than in the standard version, the characterizations are filled out and the narrator becomes more integrated with the story. For instance Grandfather wears slippers and they go 'Sl-ip, sl-op' beautifully to Prokofiev's music. At the very end it is suggested that the tale does not end happily ever after for everyone; the Wolf is now in the zoo and the Duck (in spite of the ghostly 'Quack') is almost certain not to see the light of day again. It is all very vivid and convincing, and although obviously aimed at younger children it is never arch. The wind players add to the effect of the new version by superb musical characterization, and they are beautifully recorded; the cassette is excellent, like the disc. It is a pity that the coupling is less recommendable, for undoubtedly this 'new-look' *Peter and the Wolf* is a great success.

Sean Connery uses a modern revision of the narrative by Gabrielle Hilton. This exchanges economy of words for a certain colloquial friendliness and invites the narrator to participate more than usual in the narrative. Sean Connery does this very well. His relaxed style, the vocal colour like brown sugar, is certainly attractive from the very beginning (if you can accept such extensions as a 'dumb duck' and a pussy-cat who is 'smooth, but greedy and vain') and when the tale reaches its climax he joins in the fray most enthusiastically. Dorati supports him well and the pace of the orchestral contribution quickens appropriately (in tension rather than tempo). The recording, originally Phase Four, is clear, brilliant and colourful, the spotlight well used. Children of all ages who have no preconceived notions about the words of the narrative will enjoy this. Both sides start attractively with the orchestra tuning-up noise, and here the introductory matter is entirely fresh and informal. The cassette transfer is acceptable but not as crisply focused as the disc (though this may not apply in the USA).

David Bowie's narration has undoubted presence and individuality. He makes a few additions to the text, and colours his voice effectively for the different characters. He has the face to say 'Are you sitting comfortably?' before he begins, and on the whole the narration seems aimed at a younger age-group. The manner is direct and slightly dead-pan, but definitely attractive. Ormandy accompanies imaginatively, and the orchestral players enter fully into the spirit of the tale. The recording is generally excellent (David Bowie's voice is very close, but admirably real), although at times the cassette transfer has slight blurring caused by the reverberation. However, with so many versions available at less than full price this issue seems expensive.

Jacqueline du Pré's is a leisurely and intimate account, like a bedtime story. That is not to suggest she is uninvolved, but with her husband pacing the accompaniment in similar mood, the story unfolds without a great deal of excitement, although the narrative line is not without individuality and colour. Yet after the moral of the tale has been rather nicely pointed, the orchestral postlude fails to reflect Peter's self-congratulatory high spirits. The coupling too is in no way memorable. Excellent sound on both LP and cassette.

Richard Baker, balanced well forward in a different acoustic from the orchestra, provides an extra introductory paragraph which might become tedious on repetition. But he enters into the spirit of the story well enough and is only occasionally coy. Leppard provides an excellent account of the orchestral score and the recording is vivid. But in the last resort one's reaction to this record depends on how one takes to the narration, and there will be mixed views on this. The disc is excellent value, and so is the cassette.

Bernstein introduces *Peter and the Wolf* with a kind of quiz about the characters. The effect is patronizing and certainly unattractive for repeated listening, though the story itself is quite well told and the orchestral playing is excellent. The coupling, for rather similar reasons, cannot be recommended.

(i) *Peter and the Wolf, Op. 67. Symphony No. 1 in D (Classical), Op. 25.*

(B) *** Decca SPA 90 [Lon. STS/5- 15114]. LSO, Sargent, (i) with Richardson.

Sir Ralph Richardson's account is superbly recorded in the very best Decca manner, rich and colourful. Sir Malcolm's direction of the orchestral contribution shows his professionalism at its very best, with very finely prepared orchestral playing, and many imaginative little touches of detail brought to one's attention, yet with the forward momentum of the action perfectly sustained. Sir Ralph brings an actor's feeling for words to the narrative. He dwells lovingly on their sound as well as their meaning, and this preoccupation with the manner in which the story is told matches Sargent's feeling exactly. There are some delicious moments when that sonorous voice delights in its own coloration, none more taking than Grandfather's very reasonable moral: 'and if Peter had not caught the wolf ... what then?' But of course he did, and in this account it was surely inevitable. The *Symphony* too is superbly played and recorded. All the tempi, except perhaps the finale, are slow, but Sir Malcolm's self-assurance carries its own spontaneity, and this is one of the richest gramophone offerings he gave us. There is a good cassette too.

Romeo and Juliet (ballet), *Op. 64:* complete.
*** HMV SLS/*TCC-SLS* 864 (3) [Ang. SC/*4X3S* 3802]. LSO, Previn.
*** Decca SXL 6620-2/*K 20 K 32* (3/*2*) [Lon. CSA/*5*- 2312]. Cleveland O, Maazel.
(M) **(*) HMV SLS/*TC-SLS* 165093-3/*9*. Bolshoi Theatre O, Zuraitis.

Almost simultaneously in 1973 two outstanding versions appeared of Prokofiev's complete *Romeo and Juliet* ballet, strongly contrasted to provide a clear choice on grounds of interpretation and recording. Previn and the LSO made their recording in conjunction with live performances at the Royal Festival Hall, and the result reflects the humour and warmth which went with those live occasions. Previn's pointing of rhythm is consciously seductive, whether in fast jaunty numbers or the soaring lyricism of the love music. The recording quality is warm and immediate to match. Maazel by contrast will please those who believe that this score should above all be bitingly incisive. The rhythms are more consciously metrical, the tempi generally faster, and the precision of ensemble of the Cleveland Orchestra is little short of miraculous. The recording is one of Decca's most spectacular, searingly detailed but atmospheric too; and there is a superb tape set transferred from this recording, truly of demonstration quality. The HMV tape set, issued quite recently, is comparatively disappointing. The quality is generally good, though not as wide-ranging as the discs, but the big Act III climax brings hints of congestion.

Though Zuraitis's version takes only two discs instead of three, he includes an important supplement in addition to the usual complete ballet score. Having studied the original manuscript material, he adds three movements finally omitted in the ballet, the *Nurse and Mercutio* (using familiar material), a sharply grotesque *Moorish dance* and a so-called *Letter scene* which provides a sketch for what eight years later became the scherzo of the *Fifth Symphony*. Zuraitis has scored this last with reference to the symphony. The performance generally may lack something in rhythmic flair and orchestral refinement compared with those of Previn and Maazel, but in its direct way it is warm and committed, with digital sound of colour and power, not always perfectly balanced. The chrome cassettes match the discs closely, and are well laid out, with Acts tailored to side-ends.

Romeo and Juliet: Suites Nos. 1–2, Op. 64a/b.
(*) DG Dig. **410 519-2; 2532/*3302* 087 [id.]. Nat. SO of Washington, Rostropovich.
*(*) HMV Dig. **CDC 747004-2**; ASD/*TCC-ASD* 4068 [Ang. DS/*4XS* 37776]. Phd. O, Muti.

Rostropovich gives a carefully prepared account, thoroughly attentive to details of dynamic markings and phrasing, but symphonic rather than balletic in approach. At no time does the listener feel tempted to spring into dance. Nonetheless the effect is atmospheric in a non-theatrical way, and to some ears the feeling of listening almost to an extended tone-poem is most rewarding, though to others the effect of Rostropovich's approach is ponderous at times. To be fair, some movements give no cause for complaint. Friar Lawrence is even enhanced by the slower tempo, and the *Dance* (No. 4 of the *Second*

Suite) has no want of momentum or lightness of touch. The recording is clean with sharply focused detail (even on cassette, where the wide dynamic range has brought only a modest transfer level); and it makes a thrilling impact on the compact disc which is far more successful than Muti's, where the glossily brilliant sound tends to weary the ear.

Muti gives us the *First Suite* as published, and then in the *Second* he omits the *Dance* that forms the fourth number and the penultimate *Dance of the girls with lilies*. There is very impressive virtuoso playing from the Philadelphia Orchestra, and a full-blooded digital recording. There are some magical moments such as the opening of the *Romeo and Juliet* movement of the *First Suite* but, for the most part, the performance is overdriven. Had Muti relaxed a little, the gain in atmosphere and charm would have been enormous. Other versions bring one closer to the heart of this wonderful score; Muti leaves us admiring but unmoved. The chrome cassette is wide in range though there is a degree of glassiness on the strings, but the sound is in every other respect brilliantly clear. On CD the sharpness of detail and the 'digital edge' on the upper strings in fortissimo increase the feeling of aggressiveness.

Romeo and Juliet, Op. 64: excerpts.
*** Decca SXL 6668 [Lon. CS 6865]. Cleveland O, Maazel.
*** [Ang. S/*4XS* 37020]. LSO, Previn.
(M) *** CBS 60279/*40-* [Odys. Y/*YT* 60038]. NYPO, Mitropoulos.
(M) **(*) Ph. Seq. 6527/*7311* 153 [id.]. Rotterdam PO, De Waart.

The Decca and EMI discs predictably reflect the qualities of the complete sets from which they come. Previn's selection is entitled *Scenes and dances* and seems chosen fairly arbitrarily on the 'highlights' basis. The Decca selection has been chosen to follow through the action of each of the three Acts and, besides giving a bird's-eye picture of the complete work, it shows marvellously the diversity of Prokofiev's inspiration. The EMI/Angel LP has been withdrawn in the UK, but the Decca compilation makes an obvious first choice for those not wanting the complete ballet.

Mitropoulos's splendid record comes from 1958 but, considering its date, the recording is remarkably good; it is very brightly lit, but responds to the controls. The playing of the NYPO is electrifying; Prokofiev's score can seldom have received more passionate advocacy, yet there are gentle moments too, for Mitropoulos can be tender as well as pungent. Even though the drama of the narrative is thrillingly projected, there is no feeling of aggressiveness as with Muti.

Edo de Waart secures fine playing from his Rotterdam orchestra and the result is impressive with refined Philips sound on disc (the cassette – with a low transfer level – is more diffuse). He only includes eleven numbers, taken from the two suites, but this is fair value at mid-price.

Romeo and Juliet, Op. 64: Suite No. 1: excerpts.
(M) *** DG Priv. 2535/*3335* 422 [2530 308/*3300 284*]. San Francisco SO, Ozawa – BERLIOZ: *Roméo et Juliette: Love scene*; TCHAIKOVSKY: *Romeo and Juliet*.***

The Prokofiev items make an attractive contrast to the other two very romantic evocations of Shakespeare on the same theme. Ozawa draws from his 'other' orchestra warmly committed playing, helped by rich recording quality. There is no appreciable difference between disc and cassette.

Romeo and Juliet: excerpts; *Symphony No. 1 in D* (*Classical*), *Op. 25.*
*(*) Decca Dig. **410 200-2**; SXDL/*KSXDC* 7587. Chicago SO, Solti.

Solti compiles a selection of his own from *Romeo and Juliet*. He is wholly unmannered and secures a brilliant response from the Chicago orchestra. The outer movements of the *Symphony* could do with more spontaneity and sparkle. The slow movement, however, has an occasional moment of charm. As far as the sound is concerned there is spectacular presence and impact, a wide dynamic range and maximum detail. Alas, there is little distance to lend enchantment and many collectors will find everything fiercely overlit. Neither work comes anywhere near the top of the recommended lists.

(i) *Summer Day* (children's suite for small orchestra), *Op. 65a;* (ii) *A Winter Camp-fire* (suite), *Op. 122.*

(M) *** Sup. 50773. (i) Prague CO (without conductor); (ii) Prague RSO and Children's Ch., Klima.

A wholly delightful and unexpected coupling which will give great pleasure to all those who love *Peter and the Wolf*. The *Summer Day* suite has seven short characteristic movements of great charm. Each sets the other off: the opening *Morning*, lazily atmospheric, is contrasted with *Tag*, which shows the composer at his wittiest, and is played and recorded with irresistible crispness; then comes a beguilingly gentle miniature waltz, and so on. The alert playing of the Prague Chamber Orchestra is a joy. Side two offers a work obviously primarily aimed at boys, with its opening and closing patrol and an enchanting central chorus round the camp-fire, infectiously sung here. The music is presented with great affection; the recording is excellent throughout.

Symphony No. 1 in D (*Classical*), *Op. 25* (see also above).

(M) *** Decca Jub. 410 167-1/*4* [Lon. JL/*5*-41065]. ASMF, Marriner – BIZET: *Symphony*.***

*** DG Dig. **400 034-2**; 2532/*3302* 031 [id.]. Berlin PO, Karajan – GRIEG: *Holberg suite*; MOZART: *Eine kleine Nachtmusik*.***

*** DG Sig. 410 838-1/*4* [2530/*3300* 783]. Chicago SO, Giulini – MUSSORGSKY: *Pictures*.***

(B) *(*) CfP CFP/*TC-CFP* 40319. LPO, Davison – MUSSORGSKY: *Pictures*.**(*)

Marriner's famous recording has been reissued at mid-price on Jubilee and sounds marvellously fresh. Marriner's tempi are comparatively relaxed, but the ASMF are in sparkling form and play beautifully in the slow movement. Detail is deliciously pointed (the bassoon solo in the first movement is a joy) and the finale is vivacious, with a touch of elegance rather than irrepressibly fast. The sound has a fine bloom and there is a splendid cassette. It is transferred at the highest level and is in the demonstration class.

Karajan's performance is predictably brilliant, the playing beautifully polished, with grace and eloquence distinguishing the slow movement. The outer movements are wanting in charm alongside Marriner. The recording is bright and clearly detailed, though the balance is not quite natural. The compact disc has something of a 'digital edge' on the upper strings, but the ambience is attractive.

A refined and spacious account from Giulini, the tempo of the first movement rather measured but not lacking momentum, the slow movement ethereally beautiful, and the finale comparatively easy-going and gracious. Only in the *Gavotte* is the ensemble marginally less than immaculate. With first-class recording to match, this is an attractively different view of the symphony. There is an excellent cassette.

An artificially bright sound-balance detracts from Davison's modern LPO recording. The brightness here is even less appropriate because the performance is basically genial and relaxed. But when the piccolo joins the violins the shrillness is piercing, and the sound is much the same on both disc and cassette.

Symphony No. 1; Lieutenant Kijé: Troika; Love of Three Oranges: March.

(M) ** CBS 60112/*40*- [MY/*MYT* 36725]. NYPO, Bernstein – BIZET: *Symphony*.**(*)

In the first two movements Bernstein's homage to the *Classical symphony*'s eighteenth-century ancestry produces a slightly self-conscious stiffness of manner, but even so the bassoon manages a gentle smile in his solo and the poise of the strings in the slow movement's upper cantilena is superb. The finale is exhilarating, yet played with admirable precision. The original bonus (Dukas's *L'Apprenti sorcier*) has been replaced with two of Prokofiev's most famous lollipops, brilliantly played. The sound is very bright but not harsh.

Symphonies Nos. 1 (Classical); 3 in C min., Op. 44.
**(*) Decca SXL 6469 [Lon. CS 6679]. LSO, Abbado.

Abbado's account of the *Classical symphony* is fresh and beautifully played. It is one of the best-recorded versions, but the reading has not quite the sparkle that was offered by Kurtz (now alas deleted). In the *Third Symphony* Abbado penetrates the atmosphere and mystery of the highly imaginative inner movements most successfully. These inner movements exert quite a powerful spell and their impact is all the greater for Abbado's total lack of exaggeration. The other movements are not quite as impressive: Rozhdestvensky had slightly more bite and momentum, but his version is no longer available. The Abbado issue scores in the opulence and presence of the recording, which is in the demonstration class. It has great range, clarity of detail, and body of sound.

Symphonies Nos. 1 and 7.
*** [Ang. S/*4XS* 37523]. LSO, Previn.

In both symphonies (a popular coupling since the earliest days of LP) Previn is highly successful. He produces much inner vitality and warmth, and the EMI engineers provide a strikingly realistic and integrated sound. The *Classical symphony* is more successful here than in Previn's earlier version on RCA (now deleted); it is genuinely sunlit and vivacious, and the ripe recording is entirely appropriate. Previn is obviously persuaded of the merits of the underrated and often beguiling *Seventh Symphony*. The sound on tape is not quite as crisply focused as on disc (the percussive transients are less sharp), but the quality remains rich and vivid. This coupling has been withdrawn in the UK.

Symphonies Nos. 1 (Classical); 7 in C sharp min., Op. 131; Love of Three Oranges: suite.
(M) *** HMV SXLP/*TC-SXLP* 30437. Philh. O, Malko.

Malko's performances were recorded in 1955, and the accounts of the two symphonies were the first stereo EMI ever made. (They did not appear at the time.) All the performances are quite excellent, and the *Seventh Symphony*, of which Malko conducted the UK première, is freshly conceived and finely shaped. What is so stunning is the range and refinement of the recording. The engineers have now accommodated the *Seventh Symphony* on one side without any loss of immediacy, and the excellence of the balance and the body of the sound are remarkable. No less satisfying is the *suite* from *Love of Three Oranges*, an additional bonus making this outstanding value. The reverberation brings minor problems in the cassette transfer, notably in the *Love of Three Oranges*, which lacks sharpness of focus. There is a touch of harshness in the *Seventh Symphony*.

Symphony No. 2 in D, Op. 40; Love of Three Oranges: suite.
*** Decca SXL 6945. LPO, Weller.

The *Second* is undoubtedly the most dissonant and violent of the Prokofiev symphonies. Its first movement more than vindicates the composer's avowed intention of writing a work 'made of iron and steel'. Indeed it leaves the impression of being an interminably sustained fortissimo – relieved from time to time by a forte. In sheer density of sound Prokofiev never surpassed it. Formally the work is modelled on Beethoven's Op. 111 and is in two movements, the second being a theme and variations. One or two of the variations may be overscored, but the movement as a whole is full of fantasy and invention. At times in his cycle of the symphonies for Decca, Walter Weller has shown a certain want of bite and concentration, but he gives an altogether impressive account of this problematic score, and he draws from the LPO playing of great refinement and finesse. The second variation of the second movement is rushed, but otherwise this is a remarkably fine performance. So, too, is that of the fill-up. The recording is of demonstration standard.

Symphony No. 5 in B flat, Op. 100.
** CBS Dig. **CD 35877** [35877/*HMT*]. Israel PO, Bernstein.

With Previn's version now withdrawn, Prokofiev's *Fifth Symphony* is currently represented only by Bernstein's compact disc in the British catalogue (although in the USA there is a wide choice, including Previn, Karajan, Martinon and Szell).

Bernstein's digital version, edited from live performances, is disappointing. He overloads Prokofiev's free-flowing melodies with romantic expressiveness in a way which undermines the natural freshness of the inspiration. Bernstein is superb at building climaxes, but there is too much heaviness of the wrong kind. The recording is bass-heavy to exaggerate that fault.

CHAMBER AND INSTRUMENTAL MUSIC

Cello sonata in C, Op. 119.
*** Chan. Dig. **CHAN 8340**; ABRD/*ABTD* 1072 [id.]. Turovsky, Edlina – SHOSTAKOVICH: *Sonata.****

Yuli Turovsky and Luba Edlina are both members of the Borodin Trio and are eloquent advocates of this *Sonata*, which is a late work dating from 1949 not currently available in any alternative form. Rostropovich and Richter recorded it in the days of mono LP, but its subsequent appearances on record have been few. A finely wrought and rewarding score, it deserves greater popularity, and this excellent performance and recording should make it new friends. The chrome cassette has fine presence, but the high-level transfer brings a rather dry timbre to the cello's upper range.

String quartets Nos. 1, Op. 50; 2, Op. 92.
(M) *** Ph. 6503/*7303* 114. Novák Qt.

Prokofiev's *First Quarter* dates from the 1930s while the *Second*, a more brilliantly constructed and characterful work, comes from the war years. The *Second* is a particularly striking work and though the Novák Quartet play it with genuine feeling, those who can recall the Hollywood Quartet version on an early Capitol mono LP will find it wanting in the last ounce of bite and virtuosity. However, at medium price this reissue is thoroughly worthwhile; it is well balanced and sonorous with a very good equivalent cassette.

Flute sonata in D, Op. 94.
*** RCA LRL 1 5095/*RK 25029*. Galway, Argerich – FRANCK: *Flute Sonata.****

Prokoviev's *Flute sonata* (1943) is one of his sunniest and most serene wartime compositions. It is difficult to imagine a more delightful performance than this one with its combination of effortless virtuosity and spontaneity of feeling; every detail falls naturally into place. The recording is most sympathetic and there is a good tape.

Violin sonata No. 1 in F min., Op. 80.
(B) ** PRT GSGC/*ZCGC* 2053. Duo Landolfi – SZYMANOWSKI: *Violin sonata.***

Violin sonatas Nos. 1; 2 in D, Op. 94a.
(B) *** RCA VICS/*VK* 2008 [AGL 1/*AGK 1* 3912]. Perlman, Ashkenazy.

Both of the *Violin sonatas* date from the years immediately after Prokofiev returned to the Soviet Union. The *F minor Sonata* is one of his very finest works, and the *D major*, originally written for the flute and sometimes heard in that form, has a winning charm and melodiousness. Both works are masterly and rewarding, and Perlman and Ashkenazy play them superbly. The recording is well balanced, slightly dry in timbre, but otherwise truthful.

The performance of the *F minor Sonata* by the Duo Landolfi (Mary Nemet and Roxane Wruple) is well worthy of attention. The playing may be less polished than with Perlman and Ashkenazy, but it shows Prokofievian understanding and is thoroughly committed while the recording is fully satisfactory, with the sound on cassette matching the disc quite closely.

Romeo and Juliet: suite.
(M) *** DG Sig. 2543/*3343* 526 [id.]. *Berman* † MUSSORGSKY: *Pictures.****

Prokofiev made these piano transcriptions of the *Romeo and Juliet* music before the Bolshoi ballet itself was staged, and played them in public in 1937. Berman characterizes each piece to excellent effect and is well served by the engineers, who produce clean and well-focused tone. The cassette too is first-class, natural and clear to match the disc closely.

Piano sonata No. 6 in A, Op. 82.
❀ *** DG Dig. **413 363-2**; 2532/*3302* 093 [id.]. Pogorelich – RAVEL: *Gaspard de la nuit.****❀
** HMV Dig. ASD/*TCC-ASD* 4321 [Ang. DS/*4XS* 38010]. Donohoe – RACHMANINOV: *Étude tableau, Op. 33/3*; STRAVINSKY: *Petrushka.***

Pogorelich's performance of the *Sixth Sonata* is quite simply dazzling; indeed, it is by far the best version of it ever put on record and arguably the finest performance of a Prokofiev sonata since Horowitz's hair-raising account of the *Seventh.* It is certainly Pogorelich's most brilliant record so far and can be recommended with the utmost enthusiasm. There is a faithful chrome cassette, though the transfer level is not especially high.

By its side, Peter Donohoe's account seems quite ordinary, though, to be fair, it is a perfectly good one – and is very faithfully recorded. His instrument is not quite the equal of the piano used for the DG recording and some octaves produce a twang not present in the latter. Good tempi and a genuine feel for this composer, and were the Pogorelich not so exceptional, this would be perfectly recommendable. The cassette is impressively natural in timbre, wide-ranging and clear.

Piano sonata No. 7 in B flat, Op. 83.
*** DG 2530 255/*3300 458* [id.]. Pollini – STRAVINSKY: *Three movements from Petrushka.**** ❀

This is a great performance, one of the finest Prokofiev performances committed to disc, well in the Horowitz or Richter category. So too is the coupling, the *Three movements from Petrushka.* Good recording.

Alexander Nevsky (cantata), *Op. 78.*
*** DG 2531/*3301* 202 [id.]. Obraztsova, LSO Ch., LSO, Abbado.
**(*) Decca Dig. 410 164-1/*4* [id.]. Arkhipova, Cleveland Ch. and O, Chailly.

With playing and singing of great refinement as well as of great power and intensity, Abbado's performance is one of the finest he has ever recorded with the LSO. One might argue that a rougher style is needed in what was originally film music, but the seriousness underlying the work is hardly in doubt when it culminates in so deeply moving a tragic inspiration as the lament after the battle (here beautifully sung by Obraztsova) and when the battle itself is so fine an example of orchestral virtuosity. The chorus is as incisive as the orchestra, and the recording is exceptionally brilliant to match. The cassette transfer is most successful, refined in its warmth, detail and atmosphere yet creating the fullest spectacle in the *Battle on the ice.* A folded booklet provides notes and a translation; indeed the presentation is a model of its kind.

Chailly has the advantage of superb Decca digital sound, and its richness adds to the emotional weight of the opening sections. The *Battle on the ice* is characteristically impulsive, although it is not as incisive as Abbado's version; but with Irina Arkhipova touchingly expressive in her elegiac aria, Chailly finds an effective exuberance in the work's closing pages. The full-blooded recording is equally impressive in its chrome-tape format.

The Ugly Duckling, Op. 18.
*** Decca SXL 6900 [Lon. OS 26579]. Söderström, Ashkenazy – GRECHANINOV: *Lane*; MUSSORGSKY: *Nursery.****

Prokofiev's extended song-narrative on the Hans Andersen story makes a vivid item in Elisabeth Söderström's splendid collection of Russian songs about children, sharp in its focus thanks not just to the singer but to the pianist too. The recording is excellent.

Puccini, Giacomo (1858–1924)

Capriccio sinfonico; Crisantemi; Minuets Nos. 1–5; Preludio sinfonico; Edgar: Preludes, Acts I and III. Manon Lescaut: Intermezzo, Act III. Le Villi: Prelude; La Tregenda (Act II).
C *** Decca Dig. **410 007-2**; SXDL/*KSXDC* 7607 [Lon. LDR/*5*-71107]. Berlin RSO, Chailly.

In a highly attractive collection of Puccinian juvenilia and rarities, Chailly draws opulent and atmospheric playing from the Berlin Radio Symphony Orchestra, helped by outstandingly rich and full recording. The compact disc version is of demonstration quality, and the chrome cassette too is admirably fresh and clear. The *Capriccio sinfonico* of 1876 brings the first characteristically Puccinian idea in what later became the opening Bohemian motif of *La Bohème*. There are other identifiable fingerprints here, even if the big melodies suggest Mascagni rather than full-blown Puccini. *Crisantemi* (with the original string quartet scoring expanded for full string orchestra) provided material for *Manon Lescaut* as did the three little *Minuets*, pastiche eighteenth-century music.

Crisantemi for string quartet.
*** CRD CRD 1066/*CRDC 4066*. Alberni Qt – DONIZETTI: *Quartet No. 13*; VERDI: *Quartet*.***

Puccini's brief essay in writing for string quartet dates from the late 1880s; three years later he used the main themes in his first fully successful opera, *Manon Lescaut*. It is given a warm, finely controlled performance by the Alberni Quartet and makes a valuable makeweight for the two full-scale quartets by fellow opera-composers. The cassette transfer is of demonstration quality, admirably vivid and clear.

Messa di gloria.
**(*) Ph. 9500 009. Lövaas, Hollweg, McDaniel, West German R. Ch., Frankfurt RSO, Inbal.
**(*) Erato STU/*MCE* 70890 [id.]. Johns, Huttenlocher, Lisbon Gulbenkian Foundation Ch. and SO, Corboz.

Puccini's *Messa di gloria*, completed when he was twenty, rebuts any idea that this composer was a late developer. Very much under the influence of Verdi (hearing *Aïda* was a strongly formative experience), Puccini still showed his positive character as a composer, writing bold melodies with just a hint here and there of individual fingerprints, and using the orchestra with astonishing maturity. The different parts were written at different times and even for different purposes; but with the exception of an oversweet rendering of *Agnus Dei* (later used in *Manon Lescaut*) the work stands well together. Best of all is the ambitious and strong setting of the *Gloria*, the longest section and the earliest written. It has a cheeky recurring march theme which may be doubtfully apt for church but is richly enjoyable. The section ends with a formidable fugue echoing Beethoven's *Missa solemnis*, no less. The Philips version has the advantage of cleaner, better-balanced recording with slightly more stylish soloists, and Inbal's directness is nicely refreshing. Corboz's account is more affectionate, and has splendid choral singing, but the recording is disturbingly reverberant. However, the Erato cassette handles the resonance surprisingly well and there is no serious blurring of focus.

La Bohème (complete).
(M) ❀ *** HMV SLS/*TC-SLS* 896 (2) [Sera. SIB/*4X2G* 6099]. Los Angeles, Bjoerling, Merrill, Reardon, Tozzi, Amara, RCA Victor Ch. and O, Columbia Boychoir, Beecham.
*** Decca SET 565-6/*K2 B5* [Lon. OSA/*5-1299*]. Freni, Pavarotti, Panerai, Ghiaurov, Harwood, German Op. Ch., Berlin PO, Karajan.
**(*) RCA [ARL 2/*ARK 2* 0371 (2)]. Caballé, Domingo, Milnes, Sardinero, Raimondi, Blegen, Alldis Ch., Wandsworth School Boys' Ch., LPO, Solti.
**(*) Decca D5 D2/*K5 K22* (2) [Lon. JL/*5-42002*]. Tebaldi, Bergonzi, Bastianini, Siepi, Corena, D'Angelo, St Cecilia Ac. Ch. and O, Rome, Serafin.
(M) **(*) HMV *TCC2-POR 1545 999* [Ang. SBL 3643]. Freni, Gedda, Adani, Sereni, Rome Op. Ch. and O, Schippers.
(M) **(*) HMV SLS/*TC-SLS* 5059 (2). Callas, Di Stefano, Moffo, Panerai, Zaccaria, Ch. and O of La Scala, Milan, Votto.
** HMV SLS 5192 (2) [Ang. SZBX/*4Z2X* 3900]. Scotto, Kraus, Milnes, Neblett, Plishka, Manuguerra, Trinity Boys' Ch., Amb. Op. Ch., Nat. PO, Levine.
** Ph. 6769 031 (2)/*7699 116* [id.]. Ricciarelli, Carreras, Wixell, Putnam, Hagegard, ROHCG Ch. and O, Colin Davis.

Beecham recorded his classic interpretation of *Bohème* in 1956 in sessions in New York that were arranged at the last minute. It was a gamble getting it completed, but the result was incandescent, a unique performance with two favourite singers, Victoria de los Angeles and Jussi Bjoerling, challenged to their utmost in loving, expansive singing. It was always rumoured that three of the four Acts had been recorded in stereo, and though this reissue claims only that this is 'transcription stereo' it sounds remarkably like the real thing, with the voices made more vivid. The tape version too has plenty of life, if perhaps rather less bloom than the LPs. With such a performance one hardly notices the recording, but those who want the very finest modern stereo can turn readily to Karajan.

Karajan too takes a characteristically spacious view of *Bohème*, but there is an electric intensity which holds the whole score together as in a live performance – a reflection no doubt of the speed with which the recording was made, long takes the rule. Karajan unerringly points the climaxes with full force, highlighting them against prevailing pianissimos. Pavarotti is an inspired Rodolfo, with comic flair and expressive passion, while Freni is just as seductive a Mimi as she was in the Schippers set ten years earlier. Elizabeth Harwood is a charming Musetta, even if her voice is not so sharply contrasted with Freni's as it might be. Fine singing throughout the set. The reverberant Berlin acoustic is glowing and brilliant in superb Decca recording, and the tape transfer generally offers vividly sumptuous quality.

The glory of Solti's set of *Bohème* is the singing of Montserrat Caballé as Mimi, an intensely characterful and imaginative reading which makes you listen with new intensity to every phrase, the voice at its most radiant. Domingo is unfortunately not at his most inspired. *Che gelida manina* is relatively coarse, though here as elsewhere he produces glorious heroic tone, and never falls into vulgarity. The rest of the team is strong, but Solti's tense interpretation of a work he had never conducted in the opera house does not quite let the full sparkle of the music have its place or the full warmth of romanticism. Good recording, not quite as detailed as Decca's for Karajan. (This is currently not available in the UK.)

The earlier Decca set with Tebaldi and Bergonzi was technically an outstanding recording in its day. Vocally the performance achieves a consistently high standard, Tebaldi as Mimi the most affecting: she offers some superbly controlled singing, but the individuality of the heroine is not so indelibly conveyed as with Los Angeles, Freni or Caballé. Carlo Bergonzi is a fine Rodolfo; Bastianini and Siepi are both superb as Marcello and Colline, and even the small parts of Benoit and Alcindoro (as usual taken by a single artist) have the benefit of Corena's magnificent voice. The veteran Serafin was more vital here than on some of his recordings. The tape transfer is very lively.

HMV have reissued the Schippers 1964 *Bohème* on a single extended-length tape. The use of iron-oxide stock, even with the XDR monitoring system, means that the upper range is not quite as sharply focused as on the discs (which are still available in the USA), but the resonant acoustic is attractive and there is no lack of vividness. The presentation includes a plot summary instead of a libretto, but with the four Acts pairing neatly between the two sides (with only two seconds difference in their combined timing) the layout is convenient and this is a bargain. Freni's characterization of Mimi is so enchanting that it is worth ignoring some of the less perfect elements. The engineers placed Freni rather close to the microphone, which makes it hard for her to sound tentative in her first scene, but the beauty of the voice is what one remembers, and from there to the end her performance is conceived as a whole, leading to a supremely moving account of the death scene. Nicolai Gedda's Rodolfo is not rounded in the traditional Italian way but there is never any doubt about his ability to project a really grand manner of his own. Thomas Schippers's conducting starts as though this is going to be a hard-driven, unrelenting performance, but quickly after the horse-play he shows his genuinely Italianate sense of pause, giving the singers plenty of time to breathe and allowing the music to expand.

Callas, flashing-eyed and formidable, may seem even less suited to the role of Mimi than to that of Butterfly, but characteristically her insights make for a vibrantly involving performance. The set is worth getting for Act III alone, where the predicament of Mimi has never been more heart-rendingly conveyed in the recording studio. Though Giuseppe di Stefano is not the subtlest of Rodolfos, he is in excellent voice here, and Moffo and Panerai make a strong partnership as the second pair of lovers. Votto occasionally coarsens Puccini's score – as in the crude crescendo in the closing bars of Act III – but he directs with energy. The stereo transcription captures the voices well and the tape transfer is of very high quality. The comparatively restricted dynamic range means that the singers appear to be 'front stage', but there is no lack of light and shade in Act II. The orchestra sounds full and warm, and the voices are clearly and vividly caught.

On the newest HMV set, conducted by James Levine, Alfredo Kraus's relatively light tenor sets the pattern at the very start for a performance that is strong on comedy. One registers the exchanges more sharply than usual on record, and though Kraus (no longer so sweet of timbre as he was) tends to overpoint in the big arias, it is a stylish performance. Scotto – who first recorded the role of Mimi for DG in 1962 – is not flatteringly recorded here, for the rawness and unevenness which affect her voice at the top of the stave are distracting, marring an affectionate portrait. Milnes makes a powerful Marcello and Neblett a strong Musetta, a natural Minnie in *Fanciulla* transformed into a soubrette. Levine, brilliant in the comic writing of Acts I and IV, sounds less at home in the big melodies. The recording has wide range but lacks a little in stage atmosphere.

As in *Tosca*, Sir Colin Davis here takes a direct view of Puccini, presenting the score very straight, with no exaggerations. The result is refreshing but rather lacks wit and sparkle; pauses and hesitations are curtailed. Ricciarelli's is the finest performance vocally, and Davis allows her more freedom than the others. *Sì, mi chiamano Mimì* is full of fine detail and most affecting. Carreras gives a good generalized performance, wanting in detail and in intensity and rather failing to rise to the big moments. Wixell makes an unidiomatic Marcello, rather lacking in fun, and Robert Lloyd's bass sounds lightweight as Colline. Ashley Putnam makes a charming Musetta, and the recording quality is typically refined. The cassette transfer is acceptable but less sharply focused than the discs.

La Bohème: highlights.
*** Decca SET/*KCET* 579 [Lon. OS/*5*-26399]. (from above set, cond. Karajan).
(M) **(*) Decca Jub. JB/*KJBC* 11. (from above set, cond. Serafin).
(M) ** HMV Green. ESD/*TC-ESD* 7023 (from above set, cond. Beecham).

It is a pity to cut anything from so taut a score as *Bohème*, but those who need a single LP instead of two will find the selection from the Karajan set ideal. For collectors who want a reminder of Tebaldi with Bergonzi in *Bohème*, the Decca Jubilee selection is well chosen; the recording reflects the qualities of the complete set, with a degree of thinness in the upper register of the orchestra needing a careful balance of the controls. The overall sound, however, has plenty of resonance and warmth. The Beecham selection is clumsily edited. The very opening (*Al quartiere Latin*) begins in mid-air, and the excerpts from Act II are faded in and out very ineptly. The quality of the tape transfer is unrefined, but there are good cassettes of both the Decca selections.

Edgar (complete).
** CBS 79213 (2) [M2 34584]. Scotto, Bergonzi, Sardinero, Killebrew, NY Schola Cantorum and Op. O, Queler.

'What is wanted is a subject which palpitates with life and is believable', wrote Puccini after one performance of *Edgar*, his second opera, a work which, as we can see now, took him in the wrong direction, away from realism towards this medieval fantasy in which the knightly hero has to choose between the loves of the symbolically named Fidelia and Tigrana (a Carmen figure without the sparkle). The motivation was made even less convincing by the cutting which Puccini carried out in later editions; but, as this recording makes plain, there is much to enjoy. The melodies are not quite vintage Puccini, but Scotto as Fidelia, Killebrew as Tigrana, and Bergonzi as Edgar give them compelling warmth. Eve Queler proves a variably convincing conductor, with

Act III in need of more rehearsal. But this set, edited from live performances at Carnegie Hall and commendably well-recorded, makes a welcome stop-gap.

La Fanciulla del West (*The Girl of the Golden West;* complete).

(M) ❀ *** DG 413 285-1/*4* (3/*2*. Neblett, Domingo, Milnes, Howell, ROHCG Ch. and O, Mehta.

(M) **(*) Decca GOS 594/6 [Lon. OSA 1306]. Tebaldi, Del Monaco, MacNeil, Tozzi, St Cecilia Ac. Ch. and O, Rome, Capuana.

Like *Madama Butterfly*, *'The Girl'*, as Puccini called it in his correspondence, was based on a play by the American David Belasco. The composer wrote the work with all his usual care for detailed planning, both of libretto and of music. In idiom the music marks the halfway stage between *Butterfly* and *Turandot*, and the first audience must have been astonished at the opening of an Italian opera dependent on the whole-tone scale in a way Debussy would have recognized as akin to his own practice. Nevertheless it produces an effect wildly un-Debussian and entirely Puccinian. DG took the opportunity of recording the opera when Covent Garden was staging a spectacular production in 1977. With one exception the cast remained the same as in the theatre and, as so often in such associated projects, the cohesion of the performance in the recording is enormously intensified. The result is magnificent, underlining the point that – whatever doubts may remain over the subject, with its weeping goldminers – Puccini's score is masterly, culminating in a happy ending which brings one of the most telling emotional coups that he ever achieved.

Mehta's manner – as he makes clear at the very start – is on the brisk side, not just in the cakewalk rhythms but even in refusing to let the first great melody, the nostalgic *Che faranno i viecchi miei*, linger into sentimentality. Mehta's tautness then consistently makes up for intrinsic dramatic weaknesses (as, for example, the delayed entries of both heroine and hero in the first Act). Sherrill Milnes as Jack Rance was the newcomer to the cast for the recording, and he makes the villain into far more than a small-town Scarpia, giving nobility and understanding to the first-Act *arioso*. Domingo, as in the theatre, sings heroically, disappointing only in his reluctance to produce soft tone in the great aria *Ch'ella mi creda*. The rest of the Covent Garden team is excellent, not least Gwynne Howell as the minstrel who sings *Che faranno i viecchi miei*; but the crowning glory of a masterly set is the singing of Carol Neblett as the Girl of the Golden West herself, gloriously rich and true and with formidable attack on the exposed high notes. Rich atmospheric recording to match, essential in an opera full of evocative offstage effects. These very distant effects have only fractionally less sharpness of focus on tape than on disc, and this medium-priced reissue is a bargain, whichever format is chosen.

The earlier Decca set – a classic recording in its day – remains worthwhile in the medium-price range. Tebaldi gives one of her most warm-hearted and understanding performances on record, and Mario del Monaco displays the wonderfully heroic quality of his voice to great – if sometimes tiring – effect. Cornell MacNeil as the villain, Sheriff Rance, sings with great precision and attack, but unfortunately has not a villainous-sounding voice to convey the character fully. Jake Wallace's entry and the song *Che faranno i viecchi miei* is one of the highspots of the recording, with Tozzi singing beautifully and the Decca engineers providing brilliant stereo atmosphere. Indeed the sound is astonishingly effective when one realizes that it dates from 1958.

Gianni Schicchi (complete).

*** CBS [M 34534]. Cotrubas, Gobbi, Domingo, Amb. Op. Ch., LSO, Maazel.

The combination of Maazel and Gobbi in this most scintillating of Puccini's scores is irresistible. Gobbi's earlier version on HMV, recorded in the 1950s, was marred by hazy recording, where the latest CBS sound gives a splendidly sharp focus over the stereo spectrum – vital in this busy comedy with its crowd scenes and stage movement. As for Gobbi, one would never know that a couple of decades had passed, for the voice in this role is gloriously firm and well projected. Only the ironic *Addio Firenze* passage with its *legato* and high tessitura shows a hint of strain. Otherwise Gobbi gives a classic performance, aided by the finest team of singers yet recorded in this work. Placido Domingo, treated as a star, yet justifies his inclusion with a swaggering performance of his big aria. Cotrubas is slightly below her best form as Lauretta, just a little fluttery, but still sings very sweetly. Maazel draws the brilliant score together superbly, bringing out its structural strength as well as its superb dramatic timing. This record has been withdrawn in the UK although the boxed set of *Il Trittico* remains available – see below.

Madama Butterfly (complete).

❀ *** Decca SET 584-6/*K2 A1* [Lon. OSA/*5-13110*]. Freni, Pavarotti, Ludwig, Kerns, V. State Op. Ch., VPO, Karajan.

(M) *** HMV SLS/*TC-SLS* 100081-3/*9* [Ang. SCL/*4X3X* 3702]. Scotto, Bergonzi, Di Stasio, Panerai, Rome Op. Ch. and O, Barbirolli.

*** CBS 79313/*40-* (3) [M3 35181]. Scotto, Domingo, Knight, Wixell, Amb. Op. Ch., Philh. O, Maazel.

(M) **(*) Decca D4 D3 (3) [Lon. 411634-1]. Tebaldi, Bergonzi, Cossotto, Sordello, St Cecilia Ac. Ch. and O, Rome, Serafin.

(M) **(*) [Ang. S/*4X3S* 3604]. Los Angeles, Bjoerling, Pirazzini, Sereni, Rome Op. Ch. and O, Santini.

(M) *(**) HMV SLS/*TC-SLS* 5015 (3). Callas, Gedda, Borriello, Danieli, Ch. and O of La Scala, Milan, Karajan.

Karajan inspires singers and orchestra to a radiant performance, which brings out all the beauty and intensity of Puccini's score, sweet but not sentimental, powerfully dramatic but not vulgar. He pays the composer the compliment of presenting each climax with precise dynamics, fortissimos surprisingly rare but those few presented with cracking impact. Freni is an enchanting Butterfly, consistently growing in stature from the young girl to the victim of tragedy, sweeter of voice than any rival on record. Pavarotti is an intensely imaginative Pinkerton, actually inspiring understanding for this thoughtless character, while Christa Ludwig is a splendid Suzuki. The recording is one of Decca's most resplendent, with the Vienna strings producing glowing tone. There is a superb cassette version too.

Sir John Barbirolli had some apprehensions before going to Rome to make his first major recording of a complete opera, but at the very first session he established his mastery. The result is a performance in which against all the rules the conductor emerges as the central hero, not through ruthlessness but sheer love. Players and singers perform consistently with a dedication and intensity rare in opera recordings made in Italy, and the whole score – orchestrated with masterly finesse – glows more freshly than ever. One has only to hear such a passage as the nostalgic duet between Pinkerton and Sharpless in the first scene to realize how Barbirolli reinforces the work of the singers, draws them out to their finest. There is hardly a weak link in the cast. Bergonzi's Pinkerton and Panerai's Sharpless are both much more sensitively and beautifully sung than one expects these days; Anna di Stasio's Suzuki is more than adequate, and Renata Scotto's Butterfly has a subtlety and perceptiveness in its characterization that more than make up for any shortcoming in the basic beauty of tone colour. It is on any count a highly individual voice, used here with great intelligence to point the drama up to its tragic climax. The set has been successfully remastered for its mid-price reissue and the sound freshened. The cassettes are impressively wide-ranging and vivid, the quality vibrant and full. The tape layout over four sides is ideal, and the libretto has been clearly reduced.

Eleven years after her recording with Barbirolli, Renata Scotto recorded this role again with Maazel, and the years brought nothing but benefit. The voice – always inclined to spread a little on top at climaxes – had acquired extra richness and was recorded with a warmer tonal bloom. In perception too Scotto's singing is far deeper, most strikingly in Butterfly's *Un bel dì*, where the narrative leads to special intensity on the words *Chiamerà Butterfly dalla lontana*. Maazel is warmly expressive without losing his architectural sense; he has not quite the imaginative individuality of a Karajan or a Barbirolli, but this is both powerful and unsentimental, with a fine feeling for Puccini's subtle orchestration. Other contributors are incidental, even Placido Domingo, who sings heroically as Pinkerton but arguably makes him too genuine a character for such a cad. Wixell's voice is not ideally rounded as Sharpless, but he sings most sensitively, and Gillian Knight makes an expressive Suzuki. Among the others Malcolm King as the Bonze is outstanding in a good team. The recording is rich and warm without having the bloom of Karajan's Decca set, and the voices are balanced relatively, though not uncomfortably, close. The cassette transfer, however, while clear and immediate, is disappointingly lacking in warmth and cannot compare with the discs.

The reissue of one of Decca's earliest stereo opera sets, one which survived in the catalogue at full price for no less than seventeen years, presents an alternative mid-price version. Though Tebaldi was never the most deft of Butterflies dramatically (she never actually sang the role on stage before recording it), her singing is consistently rich and beautiful, breathtakingly so in such a passage as where in Act I she tells Pinkerton she has changed her religion. Serafin like Karajan and Barbirolli prefers expansive tempi and refined textures, though the drama bites less sharply. The recording is dated now, yet amazingly fine for its age, though the balance keeps the voices rather distant.

In the late 1950s and early 1960s Victoria de los Angeles was incomparable in the role of Butterfly, and her 1960 recording displays her art at its most endearing, her range of golden tone-colour lovingly exploited, with the voice well recorded for the period, though rather close. Opposite her Jussi Bjoerling was making one of his very last recordings, and though he shows few special insights, he produces a flow of rich tone to compare with that of the heroine. Mario Sereni is a full-voiced Sharpless, but Miriam Pirazzini a disappointingly wobbly Suzuki, while Santini is a reliable, generally rather square and unimaginative conductor who rarely gets in the way. With recording quality very acceptable this is another excellent mid-priced recommendation. There is a tiny accidental cut at the start of the suicide aria, eliminating three of the heroine's cries of *Tu!* This set has been withdrawn in the UK.

The idea of the flashing-eyed Maria Callas playing the role of the fifteen-year-old Butterfly may not sound convincing, and certainly this performance will not satisfy those who insist that Puccini's heroine is a totally sweet and innocent character. But Callas's view, aided by superbly imaginative and spacious conducting from Karajan, gives extra dimension to the Puccinian little woman, and with some keenly intelligent singing too from Gedda as Pinkerton (a less caddish and more thoughtful character than usual) this is a set which has a special compulsion. The mono recording has been given a useful face-lift in this stereo transcription. On tape there is a more noticeable lack of range than on disc, and the choral climaxes lack definition.

Madama Butterfly: highlights.

*** Decca SET/*KCET* 605 [Lon. OS/*5*-26455]. (from above set, cond. Karajan).

(M) **(*) HMV SXLP/*TC-SXLP* 30306 [Ang. S/*4XS* 35821]. (from above set, cond. Santini).

(M) **(*) Decca Jub. JB/*KJBC* 32 [Lon. 25084/*5*-]. Tebaldi, Bergonzi, Cossotto, Ch. and O of St Cecilia Ac., Serafin.

The obvious first choice for a highlights tape from *Butterfly* (if the purchase of the complete set is impossible) is the generous selection (it includes the *Humming chorus*, omitted from the Jubilee issue) from Karajan's outstanding version. The recording is quite as rich and naturally managed as the complete set from which it comes, offering first-class Decca quality throughout on both LP and cassette.

The well-chosen selection from the warmly compelling HMV set is most welcome. For a generation Los Angeles was the most tenderly affecting of Butterflies, golden-toned; and Bjoerling plainly enjoyed this late trip to the recording studio. The recording is good for its late-1950s vintage, although there are a couple of uncomfortably quick cut-offs at the end of excerpts. The cassette transfer is lively, though the voices show a touch of harshness at climaxes.

There are many fine moments too in Tebaldi's performance, even if here she rarely shows the creative insight of characterization that Freni and Scotto bring to the part. Yet vocally this recording was one of Tebaldi's finest achievements. Few sopranos can float a soft note with such apparent ease, and her rich creamy tone is often all-enveloping in its beauty. The recording is vivid on both disc and tape, though its age is betrayed by the sound of the upper strings.

Manon Lescaut (complete).

**(*) HMV SLS 962 (2) [Ang. S/*4X2X* 3782]. Caballé, Domingo, Sardinero, Mangin, Tear, Amb. Op. Ch., New Philh. O, Bartoletti.

(M) **(*) Decca Ace GOS 607/8 [Lon. OSA 1317]. Tebaldi, Del Monaco, Corena, Ch. and O of St Cecilia Ac., Rome, Molinari-Pradelli.

(M) (***) HMV mono RLS 737. Callas, Di Stefano, Fioravanti, Ch. and O of La Scala, Milan, Serafin.

Manon Lescaut, Puccini's first great success, has been neglected unjustly in the opera house. Fortunately on record its great merits come out vividly, whether in the richly inspired first Act, with its intricate interweaving of music and drama into a kind of massive rondo form, whether in the superb scene at the end of Act III, where Manon and the prostitutes board the ship for America, whether in the heroine's agonized death scene, which on the stage is too static to be effective, but which on record can be most moving.

Caballé makes a sympathetic Manon, particularly in that last scene, where her translation from flirtatious girl to tragic heroine is complete. Placido Domingo sings strongly and sensitively, and the rest of the cast is consistently good. Bartoletti is not quite as understanding a conductor as he might be, overforcing in places, and the recording is not always ideally clear. But in general this makes a good first choice.

The Decca set with Tebaldi, dating from the mid-1950s, is by no means outclassed by the more recent version. The recording still sounds very well, with good detail, and the direction of Molinari-Pradelli is warm and intense. While Tebaldi is not quite the little woman of Puccini's dreams, she still produces a flow of gorgeous, rich tone. Only the coarseness of Mario del Monaco as Des Grieux mars the set, but this is exciting, red-blooded singing and he does not overwhelm Tebaldi in the duet sequences.

The early La Scala mono set partnering Callas and Di Stefano has even more individuality and dramatic power. It is typical of Callas that she turns the final scene – which usually seems an excrescence, a mere epilogue after the real drama – into the most compelling part of the opera. Serafin, who could be a lethargic recording conductor, is here electrifying, and Di Stefano too is inspired to one of his finest complete opera recordings. The cast list even includes the young Fiorenza Cossotto, impressive as the singer in the Act II madrigal. The recording – still in mono, not stereo transcription – minimizes the original boxiness and gives good detail.

La Rondine (complete).

*** CBS Dig. D2 37852/*40-D2* [id.]. Te Kanawa, Domingo, Nicolesco, Rendall, Nucci, Watson, Knight, Amb. Op. Ch., LSO, Maazel.

La Rondine was a product of the First World War, and though in subject nothing could be less grim than this frothy tale told in Viennese operetta-style, the background to its composition and production may have had their effect. It has never caught on, and a recording like this will almost certainly surprise anyone at the mastery of the piece, with a captivating string of catchy numbers. The story is based on a watered-down *Traviata* situation, culminating not in tragedy but in a sad-sweet in-between ending such as the Viennese (for whom it was written) loved. It is not just a question of Puccini taking Viennese waltzes as model but all kinds of other suitable dances such as tangos, foxtrots and two-steps. Not aggressively at all, for as with so much that this most eclectic of composers 'cribbed', he commandeered them completely, to make the result utterly Puccinian. If there is a fault, it lies in the inability of the story to move the listener with any depth of feeling, but a recording does at least allow one to appreciate each tiny development with greater ease than in the theatre.

Maazel's is a strong, positive reading crowned by a superb, radiant Magda in Dame

Kiri Te Kanawa, mature yet glamorous. From the stratospheric phrases in *Il sogno di Doretta* which are headily beautiful, her performance has one spellbound. Domingo, by age too mature for the role of young hero, yet scales his voice down most effectively in the first two Acts, expanding in heroic warmth only in the final scene of dénouement. Sadly the second pair are far less convincing, when the voices of both Mariana Nicolesco and David Rendall take ill to the microphone. Others in the team are excellent, and though Maazel launches the very opening too aggressively, the rest is most sympathetically done, with fine playing from the LSO. Excellent atmospheric recording.

Suor Angelica (complete).
*** CBS [M34505]. Scotto, Horne, Cotrubas, Desborough School Ch., Amb. Op. Ch., New Philh. O, Maazel.
**(*) Decca SET 627 [Lon. OSA/5- 1173]. Sutherland, Ludwig, Collins, London Op. Ch., Finchley Children's Music Group, Nat. PO, Bonynge.
(*) Hung. Dig. **HCD; SLPD *TC-SLPD* 12490 [id.]. Tokody, Poka, Barlay, Takacs, Hungarian State Op. Ch. and O, Gardelli.

Although Maazel insists on a relatively straight approach, with little feeling of the atmosphere of a convent, his is the strongest version on record, with fine singing and playing helped by vivid, immediate recording. Sound effects (such as Sister Osmina's bad-tempered slamming of her door) are generally omitted, but the purely musical strength of the score, far sharper and more controlled than is commonly realized, comes out the more forcibly. Maazel is superb at building the sequence of climactic moments, each one subtly graduated, so that there is no question of the score seeming sentimental or the heroine's fate leaving one unmoved. Scotto is in commanding form, and so is Marilyn Horne as the formidable Zia Principessa, while it is good to have so fine a singer as Ileana Cotrubas in the relatively small role of Sister Genoveva. (NB: This record is withdrawn in the UK although the complete *Il Trittico* remains available.)

Puccini's atmospheric picture of a convent is superbly captured on Decca, with sound of spectacular depth. Bonynge's direction is most persuasive, and Dame Joan Sutherland rises superbly to the big dramatic demands of the final scenes. With Sutherland, Angelica is in no sense a 'little woman' or even an inexperienced girl, but a formidable match for the implacable Zia Principessa, here superbly taken by Christa Ludwig, detailed and unexaggerated in her characterization. The supporting cast is outstanding, and the pity is that Sutherland did not record the piece rather earlier, before the beat developed in her voice. The first off-stage entry and opening scene catch it rather distractingly.

Gardelli conducts a beautifully paced reading, marked by effective characterization from the Hungarian cast (suggesting stage experience) and vivid, lifelike digital sound. Ilona Tokody makes an attractively girlish-sounding Angelica, but above the stave her voice is shrill. The Zia Principessa of Eszter Poka is breathy and wobbly and not even formidable, the one unconvincing characterization.

Il Tabarro (complete).
** CBS [M 34570]. Scotto, Domingo, Wixell, Amb. Op. Ch., Nat. PO, Maazel.

Maazel takes a characteristically direct view of Puccini's evocative score, concentrating less on atmospheric effects (in which it abounds) than on musical cogency. The result may initially be a shade disconcerting, but need not deter anyone who wants to hear Scotto and Domingo in this music; both of them are very powerful, even if Domingo's voice is less flatteringly recorded (rather close) than in his RCA set under Leinsdorf, now deleted. The snag is Wixell's portrait of the cuckolded bargemaster, thoughtful and intelligent, full of detail, but lacking the tragic bite and earthiness essential if the murder is to carry conviction. The supporting singers are a good team, and the recording is bright and forward. Like the other individual operas which make up *Il Trittico*, this CBS version is not available in the UK separately, only in the boxed set – see below.

Tosca (complete).

(M) ❀ (***) HMV SLS/*TC-SLS* 825 (2). Callas, Di Stefano, Gobbi, Calabrese, Ch. and O of La Scala, Milan, De Sabata.

(M) *** Decca 5BB 123-4/*K 59 K 22* [Lon. OSA/*5*-1284]. Price, Di Stefano, Taddei, V. State Op. Ch., VPO, Karajan.

*** DG 2707 121/*3370 033* (2) [id.]. Ricciarelli, Carreras, Raimondi, Corena, German Op. Ch., Berlin PO, Karajan.

(M) *** RCA Gold GL 20105 (2) [ARL 2/*ARK 2* 0105]. Price, Domingo, Milnes, John Alldis Ch., Wandsworth School Boys' Ch., New Philh. O, Mehta.

**(*) HMV Dig. SLS/*TCC-SLS* 5213 (2) [Ang. DSBX/*4X2X* 3919]. Scotto, Domingo, Bruson, Amb. Op. Ch., St Clement Danes School Boys' Ch., Philh. O, Levine.

*(**) HMV SLS 917 (2) [Ang. SBL 3655]. Callas, Bergonzi, Gobbi, Paris Op. Ch., Paris Conservatoire O, Prêtre.

** Decca D 134 D 2/*K 134 K 22* (2) [Lon. 12113/*5*-]. Freni, Pavarotti, Milnes, Wandsworth School Boys' Ch., L. Op. Ch., Nat. PO, Rescigno.

(M) *(*) Decca Ace GOS 612/3. Tebaldi, Del Monaco, London, Ch. and O of St Cecilia Ac., Rome, Molinari-Pradelli.

There has never been a finer recorded performance of *Tosca* than Callas's first, with Victor de Sabata conducting and Tito Gobbi as Scarpia. One mentions the prima donna first because in this of all roles she was able to identify totally with the heroine, and turn her into a great tragic figure, not merely the cipher of Sardou's original melodrama. Gobbi too makes the unbelievably villainous police chief into a genuinely three-dimensional character, and Di Stefano as the hero, Cavaradossi, was at his finest. The conducting of De Sabata is spaciously lyrical as well as sharply dramatic, and though the recording (originally mono, here stereo transcription) is obviously limited, it is superbly balanced in Walter Legge's fine production. The cassette transfer too is very successful, vivid and atmospheric. In both media the ear can easily forget the mono source.

Karajan deserves equal credit with the principal singers for the vital, imaginative performance recorded by Decca in Vienna. Some idea of its quality may be gained from the passage at the end of Act I, just before Scarpia's *Te Deum*. Karajan takes a speed far slower than usual, but there is an intensity which both takes one vividly to the Church of San Andrea and builds the necessary tension for depicting Scarpia's villainy. Taddei himself has a marvellously wide range of tone colour, and though he cannot quite match the Gobbi snarl, he has almost every other weapon in his armoury. Leontyne Price is at the peak of her form and Di Stefano sings most sensitively. The sound of the Vienna orchestra is enthralling – both more refined and richer than usual in a Puccini opera – and the recording is splendidly vivid in this current transfer, both on disc and tape.

Karajan's alternative superbly unified reading for DG presents *Tosca* as very grand opera indeed, melodrama at its most searingly powerful. For Karajan the police chief, Scarpia, seems to be the central character, and his unexpected choice of singer, a full bass, Raimondi, helps to show why, for this is no small-time villain but a man who in full confidence has a vein of nobility in him – as in the *Te Deum* at the end of Act I or the closing passage of the big solo addressed to Tosca, *Già mi dicon venal*. Detailed illumination of words is most powerful, and Karajan's coaching is evident too in the contribution of Katia Ricciarelli – another singer who had not taken the role on stage before the recording. She is not the most individual of Toscas but the beauty of singing is consistent, with *Vissi d'arte* outstanding at a very slow tempo indeed. Carreras is also subjected to slow Karajan tempi in his big arias, and though the recording brings out an unevenness in the voice (this is not as sweet a sound as in the performance he recorded with Colin Davis for Philips), it is still a powerful, stylish one. The recording is rich and full, with the stage picture clearly established and the glorious orchestral textures beautifully caught. The difference between discs and tapes is only marginal (the discs are fractionally sharper in focus).

Leontyne Price made her RCA recording of *Tosca* ten years after her 1963 Decca set. The interpretation remained remarkably consistent, a shade tougher in the chest register – the great entry in Act III is a magnificent moment – a little more clipped of phrase. That last modification may reflect the relative manners of the two conductors, Karajan on Decca more individual in his refined expressiveness, Mehta on RCA more thrustful. On balance, taking Price alone, the preference is for the earlier set, which still sounds splendidly vivid on disc or cassette. But Mehta has even more modern recording (no more refined than the earlier one) and his set boasts a spectacular cast, with the team of Domingo and Milnes at its most impressive. At medium price this reissue is very competitive.

With extreme speeds, both fast and slow, and fine playing from the Philharmonia Orchestra, Levine directs a red-blooded performance which underlines the melodrama. Domingo here reinforces his claim to be the finest Cavaradossi today, while the clean-cut, incisive singing of Renato Bruson presents a powerful if rather young-sounding Scarpia. Renata Scotto's voice is in many ways ideally suited to the role of Tosca, certainly in its timbre and colouring; but as caught on record the upper register is often squally, though not so distressingly so as in some other recent records. The digital recording is full and forward.

EMI chose a tigress for their Tosca. This Callas set is exciting and disappointing in roughly predictable proportions. There are very few points of improvement on the old mono set with Callas in the title role and De Sabata conducting far more imaginatively than Prêtre here. And when it comes to vocal reliability the comparison with the old is just as damaging as an impartial observer might predict. Gobbi is magnificent still, but no more effective than he was in that old Columbia set, and Bergonzi's Cavaradossi, intelligent and attractive, is belittled by the recording balance in his disfavour.

The action of the drama is superbly caught in the vividly recorded Decca version under Nicola Rescigno. The three principals were originally lined up for a Karajan recording on Decca, but plans turned in other directions. Pavarotti is a bright-eyed Cavaradossi, but it is only in Act III that the voice acquires its full magic. As Tosca, Freni sounds rather taxed, so that even *Vissi d'arte* produces her stressed tone rather than even, lyrical sound. Milnes as Scarpia gives a fresh, direct performance, with words finely enunciated, a fine characterization. The big snag is Rescigno's conducting, for his control of rubato sounds forced and unspontaneous, strange from an Italian conductor. The Decca cassettes offer demonstration quality: the projection of voices and orchestra is superbly vivid, with the *Te Deum* scene memorable in its amplitude and impact.

In the Ace of Diamonds set, well recorded, Tebaldi is splendidly dramatic and it is a great pity that the other two principals do not match her.

Tosca: highlights.
*** DG 2537/*3306* 058 [id.]. (from above set, cond. Karajan).
** Decca SXL/*KSXC* 6984. (from above set, cond. Rescigno).

The breadth of Karajan's direction is well represented in the selection of longer excerpts – for example the opening of Act I up to the end of the love duet and Act III from *E lucevan le stelle* to the end of the opera. There is also Tosca's *Vissi d'arte*, but Scarpia's music is under-represented (the torture scene of Act II plus the duet with Tosca). That is a pity when Raimondi made such a distinctive Scarpia with his dark bass timbre. Bright vivid sound despite long sides.

Though the selection of items is good, the highlights disc from the Rescigno set brings an undistinguished performance. Rescigno makes an oddly undynamic conductor who regularly lets the music stagnate. Pavarotti is in fine voice but rarely shades his tone below mezzo forte. Freni sounds strained at times, but Milnes produces glorious sounds as Scarpia. Fine full recording.

Il Trittico: (i) *Il Tabarro;* (ii) *Suor Angelica;* (iii) *Gianni Schicchi.*
**(*) CBS 79312 (3) [Col. M3 35912]. Maazel, (i; ii) Scotto, (i; iii) Domingo, (i) Wixell, Sénéchal, (ii) Horne, (ii; iii) Cotrubas, (iii) Gobbi, Amb. Op. Ch., (ii) Desborough School Ch., (i; ii) Nat. PO, (iii) LSO.

Hearing Maazel's performances of the three *Trittico* operas together underlines his consistency. *Il Tabarro* may most seriously lack atmosphere, but his directness is certainly refreshing, and in the other two operas it results in powerful readings; the opening of *Gianni Schicchi*, for example, has a sharp, almost Stravinskian bite. In the first two operas, Scotto's performances have a commanding dominance, presenting her at her finest. In *Gianni Schicchi* the veteran Tito Gobbi gives an amazing performance, in almost every way as fine as his HMV recording of twenty years earlier – and in some ways this is even more compelling. The generally close recording has a pleasantly full range.

Turandot (complete).

*** Decca SET 561-3/*K 2 A 2* (3/2) [Lon. OSA/*5*- 13108]. Sutherland, Pavarotti, Caballé, Pears, Ghiaurov, Alldis Ch., Wandsworth School Boys' Ch., LPO, Mehta.

*** DG Dig. **410 096-2**; 2741/*3382* 013 (3) [id.]. Ricciarelli, Domingo, Hendricks, Raimondi, V. State Op. Ch., V. Boys' Ch., VPO, Karajan.

*** HMV SLS 921 (3) [Ang. SCL/*4X3X* 3671]. Nilsson, Corelli, Scotto, Mercuriali, Rome Op. Ch. and O, Molinari-Pradelli.

** RCA Conifer 26.35116 (3) [AGL3/*AGK3* 3970]. Nilsson, Bjoerling, Tebaldi, Tozzi, Rome Op. Ch. and O, Leinsdorf.

(M) *(*) Decca Ace GOS 622/4. Borkh, Del Monaco, Tebaldi, Ch. and O of St Cecilia Ac., Rome, Erede.

The role of Turandot, the icy princess, is not one that you would expect to be in Joan Sutherland's repertory, but here on record she gives an intensely revealing and appealing interpretation, making the character far more human and sympathetic than ever before. This is a character, armoured and unyielding in *In questa reggia*, whose final capitulation to love is a natural development, not an incomprehensible switch. Sutherland's singing is strong and beautiful, while Pavarotti gives a performance equally imaginative, beautiful in sound, strong on detail. To set Caballé against Sutherland was a daring idea, and it works superbly well; Pears as the Emperor is another imaginative choice. Mehta directs a gloriously rich and dramatic performance, superlatively recorded, and on tape too the sound is richly atmospheric and deals with the moments of spectacle without strain.

Karajan takes a characteristically spacious view of Puccini's last opera. His tempi are regularly slower than those in rival versions, yet his concentration is irresistible and he relishes the exotic colourings of the sound, just as he puts an unusual slant on the vocal colouring as well as the dramatic balance by his distinctive casting of the two contrasted heroines. Both the Liù of Barbara Hendricks and the Turandot of Katia Ricciarelli are more sensuously feminine than is usual. Hendricks with her seductively golden tone is almost a sex-kitten, and one wonders how Calaf could ever have overlooked her. This is very different from the usual picture of a chaste slave-girl. Ricciarelli is a far more vulnerable figure than one expects of the icy princess, and the very fact that the part strains her beyond reasonable vocal limits adds to the dramatic point, even if it subtracts from the musical joys. By contrast Placido Domingo is vocally superb, a commanding prince, and the rest of the cast presents star names even in small roles. The sound is full and brilliant if at times rather close in the manner of DG engineers working in the Berlin Philharmonic. Ensemble is not always quite as flawless as one expects of Karajan with Berlin forces, though significantly the challenge of the manifestly less inspired completion of Alfano has him working at white heat. Admirably laid out on three cassettes – one to each Act – the chrome-tape set offers DG's finest quality, clear, with natural perspectives (witness the opening of Act III) and the widest dynamic range. The climaxes have great impact. Even finer are the compact discs which bring added presence, although not all ears will find the balance completely satisfactory.

The HMV set brings Nilsson's second assumption on record of the role of Puccini's formidable princess. As an interpretation it is very similar to the earlier RCA performance, but its impact is far more immediate, thanks to the conducting of Molinari-Pradelli – much warmer than Leinsdorf's for RCA – and thanks to the more forward if less refined recording quality. The climax of *In questa reggia* is far more telling when the conductor pushes forward beforehand with a natural – if unexaggerated – *stringendo*. There are many similar effects to notice. Corelli may not be the most sensitive prince in the world –

Bjoerling is far better on detail – but the voice is in glorious condition. Scotto's Liù is very beautiful, more in character than Tebaldi's on RCA.

There Nilsson is certainly an icy princess. She has power and attack, even if some of her top notes are too hard to be acceptable even from the Princess Turandot. Tebaldi as Liù is warmer and more sympathetic than she was in the earlier Decca set and Bjoerling is a splendid Calaf. This was one of his last recordings, but he was as clear-voiced and youthful-sounding as ever. The rest of the cast matches this standard, but Leinsdorf's conducting is chilly. The recording is brilliant but, like the performance, rather lacking in warmth.

The early Decca recording still has glitter and brilliance. Yet the performance lacks atmosphere and sheer vitality; nor does the singing match that on the other sets.

Turandot: highlights.
*** Decca SET/*KCET* 573 [Lon. OS/5-26377). (from above set, cond. Mehta).
(M) *** HMV Green. ESD/*TC-ESD* 100382-/*4* [Ang. S/*4XS* 36537]. (from above recording, cond. Molinari-Pradelli).
**(*) DG 410 645-1/*4*. (from above set, cond. Karajan).

A very generous and shrewdly chosen collection of excerpts from the glorious Decca set of *Turandot. Nessun dorma*, with Pavarotti at his finest, is here given a closing cadence for neatness. Outstanding recording, and a very good cassette.

Nilsson's portrait of the icy princess is memorable and this mid-priced HMV reissue offers an admirable selection from the opera, including as it does not only the major part of Turandot's music in Act II but also the important arias of both Calaf and Liù. The recording still sounds vivid.

Karajan's is also a generous and intelligently planned collection of excerpts from his complete set, including not just the principal arias but a choral sequence from Act I and roughly half the Alfano completion. The selection rather highlights the idiosyncrasy of Karajan's casting with the shortcomings of Ricciarelli's overstressed performance the more obtrusive. Bright and bold recording, lacking a little in spaciousness.

Le Villi: complete.
*** CBS 76890 [Col. M/*MT* 36669]. Scotto, Domingo, Nucci, Gobbi, Amb. Op. Ch., Nat. PO, Maazel.
*(*) Chan. ABR/*ABT* 1019 [id.]. Richardson, Parker, Christiansen, Adelaide Fes. Chorale, Corinthian Singers, Fredman.

Maazel directs a performance so commanding, with singing of outstanding quality, that one can at last assess Puccini's first opera on quite a new level. Its weaknesses have always been the feeble, oversimplified story and the cardboard characterization. With such concentration, and with musical qualities emphasized, the weaknesses are minimized, and the result is richly enjoyable. Puccini's melodies may be less distinctive here than they later became, but one can readily appreciate the impact they had on early audiences, not to mention Puccini's publisher-to-be, Giulio Ricordi. Scotto's voice tends to spread a little at the top of the stave, but like Domingo she gives a powerful performance, and Leo Nucci as the hero's father avoids false histrionics. A delightful bonus is Tito Gobbi's contribution reciting the verses which link the scenes; he is as characterful a reciter as he is a singer. The recording is one of CBS's best.

The Chandos version cannot compare with the CBS, though John Culshaw's production brings with it sound even clearer and more brilliant. The conducting is persuasive but at times languid, and the spoken verses between the scenes are omitted. None of the soloists, as recorded, is of full international standard. The cassette transfer is vividly full-blooded, although the overall range is not as refined as the disc and on side two of the review copy there were patches of discoloration in the woodwind. A folded libretto is provided which does not fit inside the cassette case.

Arias: *La Bohème: Sì, mi chiamano Mimì; Donde lieta uscì. Gianni Schicchi: O mio babbino caro. Madama Butterfly: Un bel dì; Con onor muore. Manon Lescaut: In quelle trine morbide; Sola, perduta. Suor Angelica: Senza Mamma. Turandot: Signore, ascolta!; In questa reggia; Tu che di gel sei cinta.*

(***) HMV mono ALP/*TC-ALP* 3799. Callas, Philh. O, Serafin.

This collection of Puccini arias – recorded in mono when Callas was at her peak – brings a classic example of her art. Even when her concept of a Puccinian 'little woman' has eyes controversially flashing and fierce, the results are unforgettable, never for a moment relaxing on the easy course, always finding new revelation, whether as Turandot or Liù, as Manon, Mimì or Butterfly. Well-balanced recording, and a strikingly successful tape transfer, the voice vividly projected and with plenty of depth and detail in the orchestra.

Arias: *La Bohème: Sì, mi chiamano Mimì; Donde lieta uscì. La Fanciulla del West: Laggiù nel Soledad. Gianni Schicchi: O mio babbino caro. Madama Butterfly: Un bel dì; Con onor muore. Manon Lescaut: In quelle trine morbide; Sola, perduta. La Rondine: Sogno di Doretta. Suor Angelica: Senza Mamma. Tosca: Vissi d'arte. Turandot: Signore, ascolta!; In questa reggia; Tu che di gel sei cinta.*
(M) *** Decca GRV 3 [Lon. OSA 26448]. Tebaldi.

It was understandable that Decca should choose a Puccini recital to represent Tebaldi in their *Grandi voci* series, for in this repertoire her glorious voice with its creamy richness of tone is consistently telling. Hearing a series of arias like this (recorded between 1958 and 1965, mostly taken from complete sets, and very well edited) reminds the listener that characterization was not her strong point. The assumption of both soprano roles in *Turandot* brings primarily a contrast of drama and lyricism, although she identifies most readily with Liù, as she does with Manon and Mimì, producing ravishing phrases and engaging the listener's sympathy with her natural warmth. She was never finer on record than in *Butterfly*, and *Con onor muore* makes a powerful impact. The sound is consistently vivid and generally kind to the voice itself.

Arias: *La Bohème:* (i) *Che gelida manina;* (ii) *Sì, mi chiamano Mimì;* (iii) *Musetta's waltz song.* (iv) *La Fanciulla del West: Ch'ella mi creda.* (v) *Gianni Schicchi: O mio babbino caro. Madama Butterfly: Un bel dì.* (i) *Manon Lescaut: Donna non vidi mai.* (vi) *Tosca: Recondita armonia;* (vii) *Vissi d'arte;* (vi) *E lucevan le stelle. Turandot:* (viii) *In questa reggia;* (ix) *Nessun dorma.*
(M) **(*) Decca SPA/*KCSP* 574. (i) Bergonzi, (ii) Chiara, (iii) Zeani, (iv) Bjoerling, (v) Weathers, (vi) Di Stefano, (vii) Cerquetti, (viii) Tebaldi, (ix) Prevedi.

Highlights here are Felicia Weathers's contributions (a vibrant *One fine day* and a characterful *Oh my beloved father*) and Maria Chiara's ravishing *Sì, mi chiamano Mimì*. Bergonzi's *Che gelida manina* is very effective too; otherwise this is a stock anthology, and neither Jussi Bjoerling nor Tebaldi are heard at their very best. The recording is characteristically vivid on both disc and cassette.

Arias: *La Bohème: Quando m'en vo' soletta. Gianni Schicchi: O mio babbino caro. Madama Butterfly: Un bel dì. Manon Lescaut: In quelle trine morbide. La Rondine: Chi il bel sogno. Tosca: Vissi d'arte. Le Villi: Se come voi.*
*** CBS Dig. 37298/*40*- [id.]. Te Kanawa, LPO, Pritchard – VERDI: Arias.***

The creamy beauty of Kiri Te Kanawa's voice is ideally suited to these seven lyrical arias – including rarities like the little waltz-like song from *Le Villi*. Expressive sweetness is more remarkable than characterization, but in such music, well recorded, who could want more? The chrome tape is transferred at a low level which leaves the voice sounding pure and natural but does not afford a great deal of presence to the orchestra.

Arias: *La Bohème; Sì, mi chiamano Mimì; Donde lieta uscì. Gianni Schicchi: O mio babbino caro. Madama Butterfly: Un bel dì; Tu, tu piccolo Iddio. Manon Lescaut: In quelle trine morbide; Sola, perduta, abbandonata. La Rondine: Chi il bel sogno di Doretta. Tosca: Vissi d'arte. Turandot: Signore, ascolta!; Tu che di gel sei cinta. Le Villi: Se come voi piccina.*
*** HMV SXLP/*TC-SXLP* 30562 [Ang. S/*4XS* 36711]. Caballé, LSO, Mackerras.

Montserrat Caballé uses her rich, beautiful voice to glide over these great Puccinian melodies. The effect is ravishing, with lovely recorded sound to match the approach. This is one of the loveliest of all operatic recital discs and the comparative lack of sparkle is compensated by the sheer beauty of the voice. The cassette transfer is extremely successful, vivid yet retaining the full vocal bloom.

Arias and duets: *La Bohème: Sì, mi chiamano Mimì; Addio Che! Vai? . . . Donde lieta uscì. Madama Butterfly: Bimba, bimba, non piangere.*

(M) **(*) Ph. 6527/*7311* 161 [id.]. Ricciarelli, Carreras; cond. Sir Colin Davis or Gardelli – VERDI: Arias.***

In Sir Colin Davis's recording of *La Bohème* Ricciarelli was the outstanding soloist, and Mimì's two big arias are welcome items in this recital, as is the Act I duet from *Butterfly* (with Carreras) taken from an earlier collection. The cassette transfer is quite full and vivid.

Arias and duets: *La Bohème: Che gelida manina . . . Sì, mi chiamano Mimì; O soave fanciulla; La commedia è stupenda . . . Quando men vo. La Fanciulla del West: Ch'ella mi creda. Gianni Schicchi: O mio babbino caro. Madama Butterfly: Bimba dagli occhi* (Love duet)*; Un bel dì; Humming chorus. Manon Lescaut: In quelle trine morbide; O sarò le più bella! . . . Tu, tu amore?. Tosca: Sante ampolle! . . . Recondita armonia; Tre sbirri . . . Te Deum; Vissi d'arte; E lucevan le stelle. Turandot: Signore, ascolta! . . . Non piangere, Liù . . . Ah! per l'ultima volta; In questa reggia; Nessun dorma!; Tu che di gel sei cinta.*

(M) ** Decca 410 217-4. Tebaldi, Bergonzi, Bastianini, Siepi, Cesari, D'Angelo, Corena, Del Monaco, London, Borkh, Zaccaria, Ch. and O of St Cecilia Ac., Rome, Serafin, Gardelli, Molinari-Pradelli or Erede.

This double-length tape (providing ninety minutes of music) generally follows the layout of the previous issue in Decca's two-disc 'Favourite Composer' series, drawing on this company's first generation of Puccini stereo recordings. It is especially valuable in seeking a major contribution from Tebaldi, one of the richest voices of our time, or any other time. She is partnered with varying success, but the opening scenes from Serafin's 1958 *La Bohème* show her and Bergonzi at their finest. The rather thin upper range of the recording has been smoothed and in consequence there is some loss of bite, though the stereo imagery remains impressive. Of the other excerpts, *Tosca* is the least successful musically, with Mario del Monaco an unimpressive Cavaradossi; and *Turandot* (though recorded later in 1964) is also generally below Decca's usual high standard (though Tebaldi's portrayal of Liù is the exception). Side one tends to offer mostly romantic purple patches (made the more lush by the sound balance); side two has more dramatic contrast, but is much less successfully edited.

'The world of Puccini': (i; ii; iii) *La Bohème: Che gelida manina; Sì, mi chiamano Mimì; O soave fanciulla; In un coupe . . . O Mimì, tu più non torni.* (i; ii; iv) *Tosca: Te Deum; Vissi d'arte; E lucevan le stelle.* (i; ii) *Madama Butterfly: Love duet; Un bel dì; Humming chorus.* (i; v) *Turandot: Signore, ascolta!; Non piangere, Liù; Ah! per l'ultima volta!;* (vi) *Nessun dorma.*

(M) *** Decca SPA/*KCSP* 365. (i) Tebaldi; (ii) Bergonzi; (iii) Bastianini; (iv) London; (v) Del Monaco; (vi) Di Stefano, various orchestras and conductors.

This is a splendid anthology. It has been arranged with great skill so that we do not get a string of purple passages, yet many favourites are included. The scene from Act I of *La Bohème* has Tebaldi and Bergonzi on top form and also shows the fine atmospheric sound for which these recordings have been justly famous. After the *Love duet* and *Un bel dì* from *Butterfly* we are given the magical *Humming chorus*, and side two includes a scene from the early *Turandot* to show Tebaldi in ravishing voice as Liù. To finish the concert, Giuseppe di Stefano sings *Nessun dorma.* This is taken from a recital disc: a cunning idea, as Mario del Monaco's version from the complete set is considerably less stylish. Sometimes the age of the originals shows in the string tone, but for the most part the sound is as vivid as the performances. Highly recommended and very generous too. There is a very good cassette equivalent.

Punto, Giovanni (1748–1803)

Horn concertos Nos. 5 in F; 6 in E flat; 10 in F; 11 in E.
❀ *** HMV ASD 4008 [Ang. SZ 37781]. Tuckwell, ASMF, Marriner.

Giovanni Punto was a Bohemian, born a serf on the estate of Count Johann von Thun. In early youth he showed such a prodigious talent on the horn that the Count was willing to finance his studies in Prague, Dresden and Munich with the finest players of the day. Punto returned a great virtuoso in his own right, but after serving as a court musician for a period he became restless and escaped bondage (being unsuccessfully pursued by troops with orders to knock out his teeth when he was captured!). His reputation spread throughout Europe; Mozart composed his *Sinfonia concertante*, K.297b, with Punto in mind, and Beethoven wrote the *Horn sonata*, Op. 17, for him. This disc shows a successful and highly cultivated composer, and the four concertos recorded here are most engaging if eclectic in style. Interestingly they establish the three most effective keys in which the horn was to make its reputation as a solo instrument during the nineteenth century. The music itself is fluent and tuneful, demonstrating the tasteful elegance for which Punto's playing was famous. The finale of No. 5 bristles with bravura (Tuckwell here in his element) but, as in the florid minuet variations which form the finale of No. 11, the writing avoids empty note-spinning. No. 6 is a splendid work, Mozartian in feeling and line, with a fine, eloquent *Adagio* and a delightful rondo finale. The *Tenth* has a Hummelian opening movement, with an attractive dotted main theme (the playing of the ASMF under Marriner presents it with memorable grace) and a catchy finale that could readily become famous.

This record was issued to celebrate the fiftieth birthday of Barry Tuckwell, one of the great horn virtuosi of our own time, and it is fully worthy of the occasion. The solo playing is warmly eloquent and excitingly secure; the accompaniments are as stylish as they are sympathetic. The recording is of outstanding demonstration quality; the horn, understandably, is balanced a little forward, but there is splendid presence and life overall.

Purcell, Henry (1658–95)

Chacony in G min.; Fantasia in three parts on a ground in D; 5 Pavans; Trio sonata for violin, viola da gamba and organ.
*** O-L DSLO 514. AcAM, Hogwood – *Elegies.****

Fantasia (Chaconne) in three parts on a ground in D; Overtures in D min. and G min.; Pavans in A min. and B; Pavan of four parts in G min.; Sonata in A min.; Suite in G: Overture. Keyboard pieces: *Ground in D min.; New Ground in E min.; Sefauchi's farewell in D min.; Suite in D.*
(M) *** Tel. AQ6/*CQ4* 41222. Leonhardt Cons., Leonhardt.

The outstanding Leonhardt anthology, with harpsichord solos interpolated between the consort pieces to bring variety of texture, sounds as fresh today as when it was originally issued at the end of the 1960s. The Dutch ensemble gets right inside the spirit of Purcell's music, playing with taste and finesse. The *Fantasia on a ground* is a brilliant work exploiting the special sound of three violins over a repeated bass motive. The performances throughout balance expressive qualities with sparkle, and Leonhardt's interpretation of the harpsichord pieces leaves little to be desired. The stereo sound is full and lively, and the cassette offers demonstration quality in its crisp clarity.

The Academy of Ancient Music also offer first-class performances, with a slightly more abrasive style. On original instruments the sharpness of Purcell's inspiration comes over very compellingly, though the Academy tends to prefer tempi faster than one might expect. The *Chacony* is well-known, and the set of five *Pavans* also contains much splendid music. The full, bright recording captures the impact of the playing, as at the dramatic start of the four-part *Pavan in G minor* (also included in Leonhardt's collection).

15 Fantasias for viols.
*** DG Arc. 2533 366 [id.]. Ulsamer Collegium.
*** HMV ASD/*TC-ASD* 143631-1/4 [Ang. S/*4XS* 38079]. L. Baroque, Medlam.

The Purcell *Fantasias* are among the most searching and profound works in all music, and their neglect by the gramophone – and the public – is quite unaccountable. The Ulsamer Collegium do not shrink from investing them with an expressive eloquence that does not seem one whit out of place or out of period, and play with a warmth that is welcome.

The London Baroque are also a highly accomplished group and their intonation and blend are impeccable. However, the resonance of the acoustic in which this HMV recording was made may trouble some collectors, although we did not find the halo round the aural image unpleasing, and the cassette is also trasnferred very satisfactorily. At the same time it is possible to feel that in music so highly charged with feeling and so richly imbued with melancholy, the constraints exercised by these artists result in playing that at times is close to understatement. The rival Ulsamer Collegium play in a style nearer to our own day and nearer our own pitch.

A further and in many ways even finer set is available on the Amadeo label by the Concentus Musicus (AVRS 6206). Readers having the patience to seek out this imported disc will find that although they use period instruments they do so with greater inwardness and depth of feeling, penetrating and projecting the poignancy and introspection of these masterpieces to a greater effect than the London players.

Overtures: *Abdelazer; Bonduca; Dido and Aeneas; Distressed Innocence; The Fairy Queen; The Indian Queen; King Arthur; The Married Beau; The Old Bachelor; The Rival Sisters; Timon of Athens.*
**(*) Chan. ABR/*ABT* 1026 [id.]. Bournemouth Sinf., Thomas.

It was a good idea to collect Purcell overtures on a single disc, and Ronald Thomas directs lively performances, well recorded. His editing makes for varied repeats in some of the overtures, and the range of expression comes out well, not just a matter of extrovert energy but of heartfelt chromatic writing in adagios (as in *Bonduca*). The cassette offers uneven quality. Side one, which includes *Bonduca*, *The Fairy Queen*, *Dido and Aeneas*, *King Arthur* and *The Married Beau*, is transferred at a high level and offers the most vivid quality, with regal trumpets; on side two, the level drops and the sound becomes disappointingly recessed.

Abdelazer: orchestral suite; The Gordian Knot Untied: suite; The Old Bachelor: suite. Sonata in D, for trumpet and strings.
**(*) CBS Dig. 36707/*40*- [id.]. ECO, Leppard.

Those who like a rich orchestral tapestry in baroque music will be well satisfied with Leppard's collection of Purcell's theatre music, with its keenly resilient rhythms and nicely judged, expressive playing. The writing itself is consistently inventive and *Abdelazer* includes the tune – taken briskly here – which Britten made famous in his *Variations.* The forward balance and resonant acoustic produce attractively warm sound quality, but it may be too well-upholstered for those used to the Academy of Ancient Music: the harpsichord has had to be artificially balanced and it is only just audible in the quieter lyrical music. The chrome cassette, transferred at the highest level, has striking body and range, indeed on side one the bass is over-ample and needs cutting back.

10 Sonatas in 4 parts.
*** O-L DSLO 601. Mackintosh, Huggett, Coin, Hogwood.

It is odd that these ten *Sonatas*, surely the best of the period, should be relatively neglected both in the concert hall and on the gramophone. Hogwood's version is the only one currently available in the UK and is therefore self-recommending. However, were alternative versions available, it is doubtful whether they would displace this present disc. The playing is authoritative in style and feeling, and the recording is exemplary.

Harpsichord suites Nos. 1–8.
*** DG Arc. 2533 415 [id.]. Tilney (spinet).

Harpsichord suites Nos. 1–8. 2 Grounds in C min.; Lessons (suite)*; Musick's Handmaid, Part 2: 18 Pieces. 2 Trumpet tunes.* Airs: *Canary; Gavottes; Grounds; Hornpipe; Jig; Minuet; Prelude* (from *Suite No. 4*)*; Round.*
(M) *** Saga 5458/9. Woolley (harpsichord).

Robert Woolley is a young player, still in his mid-twenties. He plays copies of two eighteenth-century instruments by Benjamin Slade and his pupil Thomas Hitchcock, both of which sound well; they are not recorded at too deafening a level and produce crisp yet full-bodied sound. The playing itself is vital and far from unimaginative, and Woolley can hold his own against senior and better-known rivals. His two records include some music that is not otherwise available, which makes them even more competitive.

Colin Tilney, who uses a spinet dating from the end of the seventeenth century, is in excellent form. His record is full-price, but both sound and documentation are of high quality, and the playing is extremely fine. Choice between Tilney and Woolley rests on whether you want the additional pieces at the small extra outlay involved. Robert Woolley's playing is delightfully fresh.

Harpsichord suites Nos. 1 in G; 3 in G; 4 in A min.: Sarabande; 6 in D; A new ground. Songs: *An epithalamium; An evening hymn; Bonvica's song; Crown the altar; Here the deities approve; I attempt from love's sickness to fly; If music be the food of love* (first setting)*; Music for a while; Not all my torments; Sweeter than roses; What shall I do?; When first Amintas sued for a kiss.*
(M) *** Saga 5486. Kevin Smith; Aldwinckle.

Though the balance favours the voice, this is an attractive collection of items with songs contrasted against the *Harpsichord suites*. Many of Purcell's best-known songs are included, well suited to Kevin Smith's sweet, finely controlled counter-tenor.

MISCELLANEOUS VOCAL MUSIC

Songs: *Ah! cruel nymph, you give despair; Fly swift, ye hours; If music be the food of love* (3 versions)*; Love thou canst hear; Not all my torments; O fair Cedaria, hide those eyes; The sparrow and the gentle dove* (*Welcome song*). Theatre music: *Aurengzebe: I see she flies me. The Double Dealer: Cynthia frowns when'er I woo her. History of Diocletian: Let us dance, let us sing. King Arthur: Fairest isle. Oedipus: Music for a while. Pausanias: Sweeter than roses. Sophonisba: Beneath a poplar's shadow lay me.*
*** Hyp. A 66070. Esswood, Sonnleitner, Medlam.

Paul Esswood is quite simply superb in this valuable anthology which gives, among many other riches, all three versions of *If music be the food of love*. It would be difficult to flaw the quality of the balance or the naturalness of the vocal and instrumental timbres. Some Purcellians may be disturbed by the transpositions of various pieces (as much as a sixth in one instance), but Esswood sings with great sensitivity and artistry throughout.

Ayres: *Awake, awake, ye dead!* (*Hymn for Day of Judgement*). *Birthday ode for Queen Mary: Strike the Viol. Diocletian: Chaconne. Elegy on the death of Queen Mary. Evening hymn. The Fairy Queen: One charming night. How pleasant is this flowery plain* (ode). *If ever I more riches* (cantata)*: Here let my life. The Indian Queen: Why should men quarrel. King Arthur: Shepherd, shepherd, leave decoying. King Richard II: Retir'd from any mortal's sight. The Old Bachelor: Thus to a ripe consenting maid. There ne'er was so wretched a lover as I* (duet). *Timon of Athens: Hark how the songsters.*
(M) **(*) HM HMU 214. Deller Cons. and Ens., Deller.

Deller here put together what you might regard as a sampler of Purcell's vocal music, a varied collection which includes some of his most beautiful inspitarations,. Lovely performances and fair recording.

Benedicite omnia opera; Cantate domino; Deus misereatur; Funeral sentences: Man that is born of a woman; In the midst of life; Thou knowest, Lord. Jehova, quam multi sunt hostes mei; Magnificat (2 settings). *Nunc dimittis* (2 settings). Anthems: *Lord, how long wilt thou be angry; O God Thou art my God; O God Thou hast cast us out; O Lord God of hosts; O sing unto the Lord; Praise the Lord, O Jerusalem; Remember not, Lord, our offences; They that go down to the sea in ships. Te Deum and Jubilate in D.* Ode: *My heart is inditing.*
*** DG Arc. 2723 076 (3) [id.]. David Thomas, Christ Church Cath. Ch., Oxford, E. Concert, Preston.

Recorded in the Henry Wood Hall, London, this admirable collection of Purcell's church music, much of it not otherwise available, is self-recommending. Apart from David Thomas's fine contribution (in the verse anthems) the soloists come from the choir and very good they are too, especially the trebles. The performances are full of character, vigorous, yet with the widest range of colour and feeling, well projected in a recording which is both spacious and well detailed.

Benedicite; I Was Glad; Jehova, quam multi sunt hostes. Voluntary for double organ.
** Mer. E 77013. Ely Cath. Ch., Wills (organ) – BLOW: *Collection.***

Coupled with motets and voluntaries by Purcell's mentor Blow, these magnificent motets are given heartfelt performances under Arthur Wills, not as polished as some but very enjoyable. The *Organ voluntary* too (though it may not be by Purcell) is well worth having on disc.

Songs and airs: *Bess of Bedlam; The cares of lovers; Crown the altar; Dear pritty youth; Evening hymn; Hark! Hark!; I attempt from love's sickness to fly; If music be the food of love; Lovely, lovely Albina; Not all my torments; Olinda in the shades unseen; The Plaint; O, O let me weep; Sweeter than roses; Urge me no more; When first Amintas sued for a kiss; Ye gentle spirits of the air.*
*** O-L Dig. DSLO/*KDSLC* 713. Kirkby, Rooley, Hogwood.

The purity of Emma Kirkby's soprano – as delightful to some ears as it is disconcerting to others – suits this wide-ranging collection of Purcell songs splendidly, though you might argue for a bigger, warmer voice in the *Bess of Bedlam* song. The *Evening hymn* is radiantly done, and so are many of the less well-known airs which regularly bring new revelation. Excellent recording, if with the voice forward. The chrome cassette is superbly managed, the voice sounding every bit as fresh as on disc, and the accompaniments naturally balanced and clear.

Blow up the Trumpet (anthem); *Psalms Nos. 80, O Lord God of hosts; 89, My song shall be alway; 102, Hear my prayer;* (i) *106, O give thanks. O, Solitude* (arioso).
(M) *** HM HM/*40* 247 [id.]. Deller Cons., Deller, (i) with string ens.

As well as a group of fine anthems, vigorously sung by the Deller Consort, this excellent record has a valuable rarity in *O, Solitude*, a long arioso over ground bass set to a religious text. This inspires Deller to one of his finest performances on record, restrained but moving. The setting of *Psalm 89* too is a solo piece providing textural contrast. The recording is clear if a little hard.

Songs: *Come, let us drink; A health to the nut brown lass; If ever I more riches; I gave her cakes and I gave her ale; Laudate Ceciliam; The miller's daughter; Of all the instruments; Once, twice, thrice I Julia tried; Prithee ben't so sad and serious; Since time so kind to us does prove; Sir Walter enjoying his damsel; 'Tis women makes us love; Under this stone; Young John the gard'ner.*
(M) **(*) HM HM/*40* 242 [id.]. Deller Cons., Deller.

One side of this charming and stylish disc has a selection of Purcell's catches, some of them as lewd as rugby-club songs of today, others as refined as *Under this stone* – all of which the Deller Consort take in their stride.

The two final pieces are extended items; *If ever I more riches*, a setting of Cowley, has Not all my torments; O lead me to some peaceful gloom; The plaint; Retired from any some striking passages. The voices are not always perfectly caught, but the recording of the instruments is first-rate. The cassette is of good quality too.

Come, ye Sons of Art; Funeral music for Queen Mary (1695).
*** Erato STU/*MCE* 70911 [id.]. Lott, Brett, Williams, Allen, Monteverdi Ch. and O, Equale Brass Ens., Gardiner.

Come, ye Sons of Art, the most celebrated of Purcell's birthday odes for Queen Mary, is splendidly coupled here with the unforgettable funeral music he wrote on the death of the same monarch. With the Monteverdi Choir at its most incisive and understanding, the performances are exemplary, and the recording, though balanced in favour of the instruments, is clear and refined. Among the soloists Thomas Allen is outstanding, while the two counter-tenors give charming performance of the duet, *Sound the trumpet*. The *Funeral music* includes the well-known *Solemn march* for trumpets and drums, a *Canzona* and simple anthem given at the funeral, and two of Purcell's most magnificent anthems setting the *Funeral sentences*. There is a good cassette: the *Funeral music* on side two sounds especially impressive on tape, with sonorous brass and a good choral focus.

3 Elegies (*On the death of John Playford; On the death of Matthew Locke; On the death of Thomas Farmer*).
*** O-L DSLO 514. Hill, Keyte, AcAM, Hogwood – *Chacony* etc.***

The three *Elegies*, each written on the death of a friend and colleague, are particularly fine, and the performances here are first-rate, with eloquent soloists in Martyn Hill and Christopher Keyte.

Songs: *Evening hymn: Fairest isle; From rosy bow'rs; I attempt from love's sickness to fly; If music be the food of love; Music for a while; Not all my torments; O lead me to some peaceful gloom; The plaint; Retired from any mortal's sight; Since from my dear Astrea's sight; Sweeter than roses; Thrice happy lovers.*
(M) *** HM **CD 90**; HM/*40* 249 [id.]. Deller, Skeaping, Kuijken, Christie.

In one of his last records before his untimely death, Deller here collected solo items suitable for counter-tenor and gave characteristically expressive performances, his voice amazingly well-preserved, more distinctive than any successor. The recording is first-rate, with an excellent cassette.

(i) *Funeral music for Queen Mary*. Anthems and verse anthems: *Blessed are they that fear the Lord; Hear my prayer, O Lord; My beloved spake; Rejoice in the Lord always; Remember not, Lord, our offences.*
**(*) HMV ASD 3316 [Ang. S 37282]. Soloists, King's College Ch., Ledger, (i) with Philip Jones Brass Ens.

Funeral music for Queen Mary; Jubilate Deo in D; Te Deum in D.
**(*) Argo ZRG 724 [id.]. Bowman, Brett, Partridge, Forbes Robinson, St John's College Ch., Camb., ECO, Guest.

The *Funeral music for Queen Mary* consists of far more than the unforgettable *March* for lugubrious trombones (sackbuts) with punctuating timpani (later repeated without timpani), which still sounds so modern to our ears. In the event this brings the least effective performance on the Argo disc, not so bitingly tragic as it might be. The rest of the work is beautifully done, and so are the grand ceremonial settings of the *Te Deum* and *Jubilate*. The recording too is excellent.

Philip Ledger has the benefit of superbly expansive sound for his darkly memorable performance of the *March*, but the funeral anthems are here given less alert performances than on the rival St John's disc. However, the choice of three of Purcell's great verse anthems for coupling may well sway the balance. The soloists are from the choir.

Songs and dialogues: *Go tell Amynta; Hence fond deceiver; In all our Cinthia's shining sphere; In some kind dream; Lost is my quiet; Stript of their green; What a sad fate is mine; What can we poor females do; Why my poor Daphne, why complaining*. Theatre music: *Amphitryon: Fair Iris and her swain. Dioclesian: Tell me why. King Arthur: You say 'tis love; For love every creature is formed by his nature. The Old Bachelor: As Amoret and Thyrsis lay.*
*** Hyp. A 66056. Kirkby, Thomas, Rooley.

This further nicely planned Hyperion collection has one solo apiece for each of the singers, but otherwise consists of duets, five of them from dramatic works. Side one is the lighter in tone; side two brings contrasting gravity, but this is just the sort of inspired material of Purcell that unfairly has tended to be forgotten. These near-ideal performances, beautifully sung and sensitively accompanied on the lute, make a delightful record, helped by excellent sound.

In Guilty Night (*Saul and the Witch of Endor*); *Man that is Born of Woman* (*Funeral sentences*); *Te Deum and Jubilate in D.*
(M) **(*) HM HM/*40* 207. Deller Cons., Stour Music Fest. Ch. and O, Deller.

In Guilty Night is a remarkable dramatic scena depicting Saul's meeting with the Witch of Endor. The florid writing is admirably and often excitingly sung by Alfred Deller himself as the King and Honor Sheppard as the Witch. The *Te Deum and Jubilate* are among Purcell's last and most ambitious choral works; the *Funeral sentences* from early in his career are in some ways even finer in their polyphonic richness. The chorus here is not the most refined on record, but with sensitive direction this attractive collection is well worth hearing. The recording is fair. The cassette is fully acceptable if not ideally transparent.

Love's Goddess sure (*Ode for the birthday of Queen Mary*); *Ode on St Cecilia's Day* (*Welcome to all the pleasures*).
** HM HM/*40* 222 [id.]. Deller Cons., Stour Music Fest. CO, Deller.

These odes make an attractive coupling, two works which in spite of doggerel texts yet inspired Purcell to some striking and memorable ideas, as for example the duet for two counter-tenors, *Sweetness of nature*, in the *St Cecilia Ode*. The performances are not ideal, with rhythms a little heavy, and the recording is limited, though quite acceptable if you fancy this coupling. The sound is especially lively on the excellent cassette, one of Harmonia Mundi's best, full and well balanced.

My heart is inditing; O Sing unto the Lord; Te Deum and Jubilate in D.
*** DG Arc. 410 657-1/*4* [id.]. Christ Church Cath. Ch., Oxford, E. Concert, Preston.

This makes an attractive sampler from Simon Preston's three-disc box of Purcell choral music (see above), including his big setting of the morning service canticles and the coronation ode, *My heart is inditing*. Fine, spacious recording.

Ode on St Cecilia's Day (*Hail! bright Cecilia*).
*** Erato Dig. **ECD 88046**; NUM/*MCE* 75049. Jennifer Smith, Stafford, Gordon, Elliott, Varcoe, David Thomas, Monteverdi Ch., E. Bar. Soloists, Eliot Gardiner.
*** DG Arc. 2533 042 [id.]. Woolf, Esswood, Tatell, Young, Rippon, Shirley-Quirk, Tiffin Ch., Amb. S., ECO, Mackerras.

Gardiner's characteristic vigour and alertness in Purcell come out superbly in this delightful record of the 1692 *St Cecilia Ode* – not as well known as some of the other odes he wrote, but a masterpiece. Soloists and chorus are outstanding even by Gardiner's high standards, and the recording excellent. The chrome tape, however, is disappointing with the focus roughened every time the trumpets enter.

A splendid all-male performance of Purcell's joyous *Ode* on DG, with an exceptionally incisive and vigorous choral contribution matched by fine solo singing. The treble Simon Woolf later made a recital record to show his amazing technical and musical range, and he is ideally cast here. The recording is excellent, although the balance between soloists and tutti does not make much distinction in volume between the smaller and larger groups.

Anthems: *O Lord, rebuke me not; Praise the Lord, O Jerusalem; Praise the Lord, O my soul; Save me, O God; Why do the heathen.*
(M) **(*) HM HM 223. Deller Cons., Instrumental Ens., Deller.

Deller and his choir here give five verse anthems, products of Purcell's last years, two with organ accompaniment merely, three with strings and continuo also. Most striking is *Praise the Lord, O Jerusalem.* The singing here is fresh and alert if not always impeccably tuned, and the recording is atmospheric enough.

STAGE WORKS AND THEATRE MUSIC

Abdelazar: Overture; Suite. Distressed Innocence: Overture; Suite. The Gordian Knot Untied: Overture; Suite. The Married Beau: Overture; Suite.
*** O-L DSLO 504 [id.]. Joy Roberts, AcAM, Hogwood.

Most of the incidental music Purcell wrote for the theatre is relatively little heard. Taken in small doses it is highly attractive, particularly in these stylish and carefully prepared performances. These suites are of course compiled from scores not intended for continuous performance, but there is much invention that is fresh and original, even if there is not the variety and range one would expect from a work conceived as a whole. Splendid recording.

Amphitryon or The Two Sosias: Overture and suite; The Old Bachelor: Overture and suite; The Virtuous Wife or Good Luck at Last: Overture and suite.
*** O-L DSLO 550 [id.]. AcAM, Hogwood.

Purcell wrote some of his most attractive music for plays now long-forgotten, and the pieces revived here from three such Restoration entertainments make a delightful collection, refreshingly if abrasively played on original instruments. The overtures are the most extended of the pieces and the most valuable, but the slow numbers in particular are also very fine. The songs are sung very stylishly by Judith Nelson, Martyn Hill and Christopher Keyte, and the recording is excellent.

Bonduca: Overture and suite. Circe: suite. Sir Anthony Love: Overture and suite.
*** O-L DSLO 527 [id.]. Nelson, Lane, Lloyd, Bowman, Hill, Elliott, Byers, Bamber, Keyte, Taverner Ch., AcAM, Hogwood.

Purcell's theatre music, virtually buried along with the plays for which it was written, comes up with wonderful freshness in these performances using authentic instruments. As well as the charming dances and overtures, this disc contains songs and more extended scenas with soloists and chorus, which provide the meatiest items. Tastes may differ on style of baroque performances, but the vigour of Hogwood and his team is hard to resist. Excellent recording.

Dido and Aeneas (complete).
(M) ❀ *** O-L SOL 60047 [id.]. Baker, Clark, Sinclair, Herincx, St Anthony Singers, ECO, Anthony Lewis.
*** Decca SET/*KCET* 615 [Lon. OSA/*5*-1170]. Baker, Pears, Burrowes, Reynolds, L. Op. Ch., Aldeburgh Fest. Strings, Bedford.
*** Chan. Dig. **CHAN 8306**; ABRD/*ABTD* 1034 [id.]. Kirkby, Nelson, Thomas, Taverner Ch. and Players, Parrott.
(M) **(*) DG Arc. Priv. 2547/*3347* 032. Troyanos, Armstrong, Johnson, McDaniel, Hamburg Monteverdi Ch., N. German R. CO, Mackerras.
** Erato STU/*MCE* 71091. Troyanos, Stilwell, Johnson, ECO and Ch., Leppard.
(M) ** Ph. 9502/*7313* 116 [6500 131 PSI]. Veasey, Donath, Allen, Shirley-Quirk, Alldis Ch., ASMF, Davis.

It was Janet Baker's 1962 recording of *Dido*, for Oiseau-Lyre, that established her as a recording star in the front rank. It is a truly great performance. The radiant beauty of her voice is obvious enough, but here she goes beyond that to show what stylishness and insight she can command. The emotion is implied, as it should be in this music, not injected in great uncontrolled gusts. Listen to the contrast between the angry, majestic words to Aeneas, *Away, away!*, and the dark grief of the following *But death alas I cannot shun*, and note how Baker contrasts dramatic soprano tone colour with darkened contralto tone. Even subtler is the contrast between the opening phrase of *When I am laid in earth* and its repeat a few bars later: it is a model of graduated mezza voce. Then with the words *Remember me!* in a monotone she subdues the natural vibrato to produce a white tone of hushed, aching intensity. It will be surprising if a more deeply satisfying interpretation is recorded within the foreseeable future, and the rest of this production heightens the effect of Janet Baker's work. Anthony Lewis chooses fast speeds, but they challenge the English Chamber Orchestra (Thurston Dart a model continuo player) to produce the crispest, lightest playing, which never sounds rushed. The soloists and chorus give very good support. Herincx is a rather gruff Aeneas, and the only serious blemish is Monica Sinclair's Sorceress. She overcharacterizes in a way which is quite out of keeping with the rest of the production. Generally, by concentrating on musical values Lewis and his singers and instrumentalists make the clear, simple dramatic point of the opera all the more telling: it provides a most moving experience. Like most Oiseau-Lyre discs the record is beautifully engineered.

With many individual touches in sharp pointing and unexpected tempi that suggest earlier consultation with Benjamin Britten, the Decca version is the recording that Britten himself should have made. Steuart Bedford proves an admirable deputy, and the Britten/Holst edition, with its extra items completing Act II, is most effective. With Norma Burrowes a touchingly youthful Belinda, with Peter Pears using Lieder style in the unexpected role (for him) of Aeneas, with Anna Reynolds an admirable Sorceress and other star singers even in supporting roles, there is hardly a weak link, and the London Opera Chorus relishes the often unusual tempi.

As for Dame Janet Baker, here returning to the area of her earliest success in the recording studio, the portrait of Dido is even fuller and richer than before, with more daring tonal colouring and challengingly slow tempi for the two big arias. Some will still prefer the heartfelt spontaneity of the youthful performance on Oiseau-Lyre, but the range of expression on the newer version is unparalleled, and the rich modern recording quality adds to the vividness of the experience. The cassette transfer is generally of high quality, with plenty of presence to the voices and the atmosphere of the recording admirably caught.

Andrew Parrott's concept of a performance on original instruments has one immediately thinking back to the atmosphere of Josias Priest's school for young ladies where Purcell's masterpiece was first given. The voices enhance that impression, not least Emma Kirkby's fresh, bright soprano, here recorded without too much edge but still very young-sounding. It is more questionable to have a soprano singing the tenor role of the Sailor in Act III, but anyone who fancies the idea of an authentic performance need not hesitate. The compact disc is exceptionally refined, the sound well-focused, with analogue atmosphere, yet with detail enhanced. The tape transfer too is fresh and clean, retaining the recording's bloom. There is just the faintest hint of peaking on one or two of Miss Kirkby's high notes.

The other different versions of Purcell's compressed operatic masterpiece make for tantalizing comparisons. Sir Charles Mackerras gives perhaps the most satisfying direction, for as well as being scholarly it is very vital, with tempi varied more widely and – as he himself suggests – more authentically than usual. There is also the question of ornamentation, and as a whole Mackerras manages more skilfully than any of his rivals, with shakes, backfalls, forefalls, springers and so on, all placed authentically. Even so, his ideas for ornamenting Dido's two big arias are marginally less convincing than Anthony Lewis's on the Oiseau-Lyre disc, with many appoggiaturas and comparatively few turns and trills. He has the edge over Lewis in using Neville Boyling's edition based on the Tatton Park manuscript, and he adds brief extra items from suitable Purcellian sources to fill in the unset passages of the printed libretto. As to the singing, Tatiana Troyanos makes an imposing, gorgeous-toned Dido, and Sheila Armstrong as Belinda, Barry McDaniel as Aeneas, and Patricia Johnson all outshine the rival performances, but ultimately the Dido of Janet Baker is so moving it more than compensates for any relative shortcomings, and Thurston Dart's continuo-playing on the Oiseau-Lyre disc is much more imaginative than the Hamburg harpsichordist's. The DG cassette transfer is made at a rather modest level, and although the solo voices sound fresh and clear the choral focus is not as sharp as on the LP.

On the Erato disc Leppard directs a consistently well-sprung, well-played performance, as one would expect, but the overall impression is disappointing, largely because the climax of the opera fails to rise in intensity as it should. Tatiana Troyanos, stylish elsewhere, misses the tragic depth of the great lament of Dido, and without that focus the impact of the rest falls away. Having had a tenor Aeneas (Peter Pears) in Benjamin Britten's version, it is interesting here to have a baritone instead of a tenor (Richard Stilwell) singing the Sailor's song. The recording is excellent.

Davis's version is fresh and enjoyable but hardly inspired. It was a fascinating idea to have the same Dido here in Purcell as Davis chose for Berlioz's great opera on the same subject, and Veasey sings most reliably. But next to Baker and Troyanos she sounds a little stiff and unsympathetic. Good recording with an excellent matching cassette.

Don Quixote: Overture and incidental music.
*** O-L DSLO 534 [id.]. Kirkby, Nelson, Bowman, Hill, David Thomas, AcAM, Hogwood.

Purcell was one of the contributors of incidental music to the three plays which Thomas D'Urfey based on Cervantes's famous novel. The music was written at high speed, but, as this charming recording demonstrates, much of it was attractively lively and it richly deserves to be resurrected in such stylish and brightly recorded performances as these. This is one of the most successful of Hogwood's enjoyable series; there is some quite enchanting singing from both the soprano soloists, and the instrumental contribution has splendid bite. The quality of the recording is first-class.

The Double Dealer: Overture and suite. Henry II: In vain I strove. The Richmond Heiress: Behold the man. The Rival Sisters: Overture; 3 songs. Tyrannic Love: Ah! how sweet (duet and song).
*** O-L DSLO 561. Nelson, Kirkby, Hill, Thomas, AcAM, Hogwood.

This collection of music which Purcell wrote for a whole range of Restoration plays uncovers yet more charming examples of his spontaneous genius, with French-style overtures (pressed rather hard here), many dances and songs and a delightful duet from *The Richmond Heiress* representing a flirtation in music. Hogwood directs vigorous performances on original instruments, with bright-toned singing from the soloists, all superbly recorded.

The Fairy Queen (complete).
*** DG Arc. Dig. 2742 001 (3) [id.]. Harrhy, Jennifer Smith, Nelson, Priday, Penrose, Stafford, Evans, Hill, Varcoe, Thomas, Monteverdi Ch., E. Bar. Soloists, Eliot Gardiner.
*** Decca SET 499/500. Vyvyan, Bowman, Pears, Wells, Partridge, Shirley-Quirk, Brannigan, Burrowes, Amb. Op. Ch., ECO, Britten.

The Fairy Queen provides a classic example of a masterpiece made non-viable by changed conditions, which happily records can help to keep alive, a score which is crammed with the finest Purcellian inspiration. Gardiner's performance is a delight from beginning to end, for though authenticity and completeness reign, scholarship is worn lightly and the result is consistently exhilarating, with no longueurs whatever. The fresh-toned soloists are first-rate, while Gardiner's regular choir and orchestra excel themselves with Purcell's sense of fantasy brought out in each succeeding number. Performed like this, *The Fairy Queen* has an equivalent magic to *A Midsummer night's dream*, of which it usually seems so strange a distortion. Beautifully clear and well-balanced recording.

Britten's version from the early 1970s used a newly reshaped arrangement of the music by Britten himself, Imogen Holst and Peter Pears. The original collection of individual pieces is here grouped into four satisfying sections: *Oberon's Birthday*; *Night and Silence*; the *Sweet Passion*; and *Epithalamium*. This version was first heard at the Aldeburgh Festival in 1967, and here the authentic glow of a Maltings performance (1971 vintage) is beautifully conveyed in the playing, the singing and the recording. Philip Ledger's imaginative harpsichord continuo is placed too far to one side, but otherwise the sound can hardly be faulted. The cast is consistently satisfying, with Peter Pears and Jennifer Vyvyan surviving from the much earlier 'complete' mono version of Anthony Lewis on Oiseau-Lyre.

The Indian Queen (incidental music; complete).
(M) *** Decca Ser. 411 716-1 [SOL 294]. *Cantelo, Wilfred Brown, Tear, Keyte, St Anthony Singers, ECO, Mackerras.*
**(*) Erato STU/*MCE* 71275. Hardy, Fischer, Harris, Smith, Stafford, Hill, Elwes, Varcoe, Thomas, Monteverdi Ch., E. Bar. Soloists, Eliot Gardiner.

The Indian Queen; Timon of Athens (masque).
(M) **(*) HM HM 243 (2). Knibbs, Sheppard, Mark and Alfred Deller, Elliot, Bevan, Deller Singers, King's Musick, Deller.

The Indian Queen is one of the entertainments that fit into no modern category, a semi-opera. The impossible plot matters little, and Purcell's music contains many delights; indeed the score seems to get better as it proceeds. The Serenata version dates from 1966 and the recording, from a vintage era, remains first-rate. With stylish singing and superb direction and accompaniment (Raymond Leppard's harpsichord continuo-playing must be singled out), this is an invaluable issue. Charles Mackerras once again shows himself a strong, vivid as well as scholarly Purcellian. At medium price this record holds its place firmly at the top of the list.

The Erato disc is fully cast, and uses an authentic accompanying baroque instrumental group. The choral singing is especially fine, the close of the work movingly expressive. John Eliot Gardiner's choice of tempi is apt and the soloists are all good, although the men are more strongly characterful than the ladies. Yet the lyrical music comes off well. The advantage of having all the music on one record recommends this issue above Deller's set, although the performance has its own felicities. The recording is spacious and well balanced, though the cassette is disappointing, lacking the definition of the LP. Side two is better focused than side one.

Deller's group is at its liveliest and most characterful in both works. In *The Indian Queen*, *Ye twice ten hundred deities* is splendidly sung by Maurice Bevan; and the duet for male alto and tenor, *How happy are we* (with Deller himself joined by Paul Elliot), as well as the best-known item, the soprano's *I attempt from Love's sickness to fly* (Honor Sheppard), are equally enjoyable. The masque that Purcell wrote for Shakespeare's *Timon of Athens* makes a delightful supplement.

King Arthur (complete).
(M) ® *** O-L SOL 60008/9. Morison, Harper, Mary Thomas, Whitworth, Wilfred Brown, Galliver, Cameron, Anthony, Alan, Philomus. of L., St Anthony Singers, Lewis.
(M) **(*) HM HM 252/3 [id.]. Sheppard, Knibbs, Hardy, Alfred and Mark Deller, Elliot, Nixon, Maurice Bevan, Nigel Bevan, Deller Ch., King's Musick, Deller.

King Arthur contains some of Purcell's most memorable inspirations, not just his most famous song, *Fairest isle*, but a whole range of lively and atmospheric numbers. The score is incomplete and is a hunting-ground for musicological discussion.

This splendid 1959 performance and recording is fully worthy to stand alongside the companion Oiseau-Lyre set of *Dido and Aeneas*, although here the success of the interpretation does not centre on the contribution of one inspired artist, but rather on teamwork between a number of excellent singers and the stylish and sensitive overall direction of Anthony Lewis. Oiseau-Lyre's excellent stereo also plays a big part. This was an early set but one would never guess it from the warmth of the sound and indeed the sophistication with which the stereo is used for special effects. A very happy example is the chorus *This way, this way*, when the opposing spirits (good and wicked) make a joint effort to entice the King. Purcell's music is marvellously spontaneous and full of imaginative touches, like the famous freezing aria, which will surely send a shiver through the most warm-blooded listener. The story is easy to follow, for the libretto gives details of the action between the songs. The spoken dialogue is, sensibly, not included in the recording.

Deller's solutions to performing problems will satisfy almost everyone, and though the solo singing is not always polished, the performance has a refreshing vigour, and the recorded quality is good. However, while the marvellous Oiseau-Lyre version under Anthony Lewis is still available, Deller's set must take second place.

Excerpts from: *The Libertine; The Massacre of Paris; Oedipus; Theodosius. Overture in G min.*
*** O-L DSLO 590 [id.]. Kirkby, Nelson, Bowman, Hill, Thomas, AcAM, Hogwood.

The first side offers Purcell's earliest theatre music *Theodosius* (1680) and then the second brings *The Libertine* (1675), *The Massacre of Paris* (1689) and *Oedipus* (1679). There is much that is familiar (*Nymphs and Shepherds* comes from *The Libertine* and *Music for a while*, sung by James Bowman, derives from *Oedipus*) plus more that is both unfamiliar and new to the gramophone. Moreover, much of it is rich in invention and often remarkably beautiful. The performances and recording could not be improved upon.

The Tempest (incidental music).
*** Erato STU/*MCE* 71274. Jennifer Smith, Hardy, Hall, Elwes, Varcoe, David Thomas, Earle, Monteverdi Ch. and O, Eliot Gardiner.

Whether or not Purcell himself wrote this music for Shakespeare's last play (the scholarly arguments are still unresolved), Gardiner demonstrates how delightful it is, a masterly collection, in performances both polished and stylish and with excellent solo and choral singing. At least the overture is clearly Purcell's, and that sets the pattern for a very varied collection of numbers including three da capo arias and a full-length masque celebrating Neptune for Act V. The recording is full and atmospheric. The cassette, however, is transferred at marginally too high a level so that the strings sound fizzy and vocal sibilants are exaggerated.

Quilter, Roger (1877–1953)

7 Elizabethan lyrics, Op. 12; 3 Shakespeare songs, Op. 6; 5 Shakespeare songs, Op. 23; 4 Shakespeare songs, Op. 30; Songs: *Dream valley; Go, lovely rose; Love's philosophy; Now sleeps the crimson petal.*
** Pearl SHE 531. Johnston, Keyte, Ibbott or De Lisle (piano).

Roger Quilter wrote some of the most appealing of English songs in the early years of the century, unfailingly lyrical and sensitive. This record provides a delightful selection, and though the tenor's voice could be recorded more sweetly, and the baritone sometimes slides unstylishly, these feeling performances are most welcome.

Rachmaninov, Sergei (1873–1943)

Caprice bohémien, Op. 12; Symphonic dances, Op. 45.
(M) **(*) Ph. Seq. 6527/*7311* 125. LPO, De Waart.

The Philips recording is particularly refined here; textures are luminous, yet there is a consistently full and homogeneous body of sound, with musical perspectives finely judged. The *Caprice bohémien*, written in 1894, is attractive, but comparatively slight; the *Symphonic dances* are among Rachmaninov's finest orchestral pieces. They are well played and will undeniably give pleasure, even though the readings fall short of being totally idiomatic. De Waart (sympathetically but unwisely) confessed that he had not taken this latter work into his repertoire before recording it, and his reading does not sound so full-blooded as that of Ormandy which is currently only available in the USA [Odys. Y/*YT* 31246]. Indeed, as we go to press the *Caprice* is not otherwise available here so this issue is welcome. The tape transfer is well managed.

Piano concertos Nos. 1–4; Rhapsody on a theme of Paganini, Op. 43.
*** Decca SXLF 6565-7/*K 43 K 33* [Lon. CSA/5- 2311]. Ashkenazy, LSO, Previn.

Ashkenazy's recording of the Rachmaninov concertos and the *Rhapsody on a theme of Paganini* stands out as a major achievement. The individuality and imagination of the playing, and its poetic feeling, provide special rewards, and if sometimes one might ask for a more commanding style, Previn's accompaniments are sympathetic and perceptive to match Ashkenazy's sometimes withdrawn manner. The *Second Concerto* is an outstanding success, notable for perhaps the most beautiful performance of the slow movement currently on disc; the *Third* is more controversial in its waywardness, but undoubtedly has inspired moments, while the *Rhapsody* has received more brilliant, more boldly extrovert performances from other hands (notably Katchen's). Michelangeli's account of the *Fourth Concerto* is uniquely magical, but Ashkenazy is very fine too and more richly recorded. The Decca sound casts a warm glow over the music-making. Sometimes it is not ideally clear and sometimes one misses an element of glitter, but generally it matches the rhapsodic, musing lyricism of the performances admirably. The cassette box offers extremely sophisticated transfers.

Piano concertos Nos. 1 in F sharp min., Op. 1; 2 in C min., Op. 18.
*** Decca SXL/*KSXC* 6554 [Lon. CS/5-6774]. Ashkenazy, LSO, Previn.
(M) *(*) Decca SPA/*KCSP* 169 [Lon. STS 15225]. Katin, LPO or New SO, Boult or Sir Colin Davis.

In the opening movement of the *First Concerto* Ashkenazy's light, rhapsodic approach minimizes the drama: other accounts have provided more pointed music-making here, but the poetry of the slow movement and the sparkling lilt of the finale (the secondary lyrical theme played with just the right touch of restraint) are irresistible. Again in the *Second Concerto* it is the warm lyricism of the playing which is so compulsive. The opening tempo, like Richter's, is slow, but the tension is finely graduated towards the great climax, and the gentle, introspective mood of the *Adagio* is very beautiful indeed. The finale is broad and spacious rather than electrically exciting, but the scintillating, unforced bravura provides all the sparkle necessary. The recording is richly spacious, the piano tone slightly brighter in the *First Concerto*. The cassette transfer is of high quality.

Boult brings a sympathetic freshness to the *First Concerto*, and his conducting is matched by Katin's spirited playing. The pianist does not attempt a conventional bravura style, and some may be disappointed on this account, but in this shortest of Rachmaninov's concertos the added clarity and point given to so many passages more than make amends (if indeed amends need to be made). The orchestra responds well but does not always play with perfect precision. The stereo is excellent, with good definition and balance. Unfortunately the performance of the *Second Concerto* is underpowered. Katin takes the opening chords in a brisk, matter-of-fact way, and although the lyricism of the first movement is nicely managed, the performance as a whole is dull. The recording in No. 2 needs a reduction of bass and an increase of top, an unusual recipe for a Decca issue. Many will feel this fair value at the price for the *First Concerto* alone, but there are more vital bargain accounts of the *Second*. The cassette transfer is a good one.

Piano concertos Nos. 1; 4 in G min., Op. 40.
**(*) Ph. 6514/*7337* 377 [id.]. Kocsis, San Francisco SO, De Waart.

Warmly romantic performances on Philips, with sparkling detail from the soloist. Edo de Waart secures most responsive playing from the San Francisco orchestra and the atmospheric digital recording, the piano rich in timbre, gives much pleasure. There is some lack of bite at the opening of the *First Concerto* and in the finale of the *Fourth*, and these are not weighty or indeed thrustful readings. But the charisma of Kocsis's contribution brings both concertos fully alive while Rachmaninov's lyrical themes (as, for instance, in the finale of No. 1) are shaped most seductively by the San Francisco strings. The chrome tape tends to be middle- and bass-orientated.

Piano concerto No. 2 in C min.
(M) *** DG Sig. 2543/*3343* 538. Sviatoslav Richter, Warsaw PO, Wislocki – SCHUMANN: *Concerto.***(*)
(M) *** Mercury SRI/*MRI* 75032 [id.]. Janis, Minneapolis SO, Dorati – TCHAIKOVSKY: *Concerto No. 1.***
(M) *(**) Decca VIV/*KVIC* 16 [Lon. STS/5-15542). Vered, New Philh. O, Andrew Davis – TCHAIKOVSKY: *Concerto No. 1.***(*)
*(*) Decca SXL/*KSXC* 6978 [Lon. CS/5-7207]. De Larrocha, RPO, Dutoit – SCHUMANN: *Concerto.**(*)
(M) *(*) HMV SXLP/*TC-SXLP* 30552. Ogdon, Philh. O, Pritchard – TCHAIKOVSKY: *Concerto No. 1.***

Piano concerto No. 2; Études-tableaux, Op. 33/1, 2 and 5.
(M) ** Decca Jub. JB/*KJBC* 52 [Lon. JL/5-41001]. Ashkenazy, Moscow PO, Kondrashin.

(i) *Piano concerto No. 2. Preludes Nos. 3, 5–6, 8, 12–13.*
(M) *** DG Priv. 2535/*3335* 475 [138076/*923059*]. Sviatoslav Richter, (i) with Warsaw Nat. PO, Wislocki.

(i) *Piano concerto No. 2. Preludes Nos. 4, 7, 23.*
(M) **(*) EMI Em. EMX/*TC-EMX* 2042. Alexeev, RPO, Fedoseyev.

After two decades in the catalogue at full price, Richter's famous recording of Rachmaninov's Second Concerto has now reverted to DG's medium-price range. It is available on Privilege coupled with marvellous performances of six of the *Preludes*, or alternatively on Signature joined with the Schumann *Concerto*, which is marginally less recommendable. In considering a choice for the Rachmaninov, however, one must remember that Ashkenazy's later version, with Previn (see above), is generously coupled with the *First Concerto* and remains an outstanding recommendation, offering perhaps the most beautiful account of the slow movement ever recorded. There is also Tirimo's highly rewarding bargain-priced CfP disc, with digital sound and coupled with an equally fine version of the *Paganini rhapsody* – see below.

Richter has strong, even controversial ideas about speeds in this concerto. The long opening melody of the first movement is taken abnormally slowly, and it is only the sense of mastery which Richter conveys in every note which prevents one from complaining. One ends by admitting how convincing that speed can be in Richter's hands, but away from the magic one realizes that this is not quite the way Rachmaninov himself intended it. The slow movement too is spacious – with complete justification this time – and the opening of the finale lets the floodgates open the other way, for Richter chooses a hair-raisingly fast allegro, which has the Polish players scampering after him as fast as they are able. Richter does not, however, let himself be rushed in the great secondary melody, so this is a reading of vivid contrasts. Good recording of the piano, less firm of the orchestra, but an atmospheric acoustic adds bloom overall. The tape transfer has been remastered at a high level and is very successful, with good focus and detail and a bold, full piano image.

Byron Janis established himself at the beginning of the 1960s as a Rachmaninovian of distinction and made outstanding Mercury recordings of both the *Second* and *Third Concertos*. At that time Mercury were experimenting with 35-mm film instead of tape for their master recording and this has led to a greater level of background hiss alongside the higher fidelity and wider dynamic range. The account of the *Second Concerto* is splendidly full-blooded, and can rank alongside the finest. The playing is full of conviction and always sounds spontaneous. Janis has the full measure of the rising and falling of the emotional tension in the Rachmaninov melodic lines, while Dorati's shapely phrasing in the slow movement is magical, with the sustained tension of the coda especially impressive. The finale compares well with Richter for sheer brilliance. The recording brings an almost stereoscopic projection of the piano – it may seem too near for some ears, but never swamps the orchestra detail. There is an occasional buzz from the cellos and the upper strings have slightly edgy top (Philips tried to filter this out in a mid-1960s reissue with disastrous results), but this remains a vintage recording in every respect and though the Tchaikovsky performance with which it is joined is rather less successful, this is the best choice for those wanting this particular coupling of works. For once the (Philips) cassette transfer is made at an adequate level and there is virtually no difference in sound between disc and tape.

Ilana Vered is a naturally expressive interpreter of Rachmaninov, and the Decca Viva issue was the first to combine successful performances of the Rachmaninov *Second* and the Tchaikovsky concertos. The reading of the first movement reaches an impressive climax and the finale is undoubtedly exciting, but there is an element of languor in the slow movement which some may find overdone. However, the real drawback here is the recording balance, with an elephantine piano projected right into the room. The orchestra makes a fair impact, but the effect is artificial, even though it is certainly telling. There is no appreciable difference in quality between disc and tape.

Dimitri Alexeev won the 1975 Leeds Competition and this was his first concerto record, made in 1978. It is an enjoyable account, romantically flexible, with some lovely playing in the slow movement from soloist and orchestra alike. The finale is somewhat underpowered, but otherwise this version offers much to praise and the sound is first-class. The three *Preludes* chosen as a fill-up are also well characterized. The RPO under Vladimir Fedoseyev give good support in the *Concerto*, yet with Richter available in the same price-range and Tirimo's CfP disc even more economically priced, this is inevitably pushed fairly well down the list.

Ashkenazy's earlier recording with Kondrashin is a relaxed, lyrical reading which rises to the climaxes but is seldom as compelling as the best versions. The *Études-tableaux* make an attractive bonus and are, needless to say, very well played. The sound is generally excellent, although the massed string tone here is not as convincing as on Ashkenazy's later Decca recording, which is well worth the extra cost.

Alicia de Larrocha's partnership with Charles Dutoit produces unexpectedly disappointing results. The Rachmaninov performance is lethargic, the first-movement climax unconvincing. There is no lack of poetry in the slow movement, but in spite of first-class sound on disc and cassette alike, this reading fails to convince, and the Schumann coupling is only marginally more successful.

John Ogdon's 1962 performance is sensitive and introspective, but lacks impulse and romantic virility. The sound is good, on disc and tape alike, but this is not one of his best records.

(i) *Piano concerto No. 2 in C min.;* (ii) *Rhapsody on a theme of Paganini, Op. 43.*

(B) *** CfP Dig. CFP/*TC-CFP* 4383. Tirimo, Philh. O, Levi.

(M) *** Decca SPA/*KCSP* 505 [(d) STS/*5-*15086; 15046]. Katchen, (i) LSO, Solti; (ii) LPO, Boult.

**(*) HMV ASD/*TC-ASD* 2361 [Sera. S 60091/*4XS* 36982]. Anievas, New Philh. O, Atzmon.

(M) **(*) HMV Green. ESD/*TC-ESD* 7076 [Ang. S/*4XS* 37922]. Collard, Toulouse Capitole SO, Plasson.

(M) *(*) CBS 60109/*40-* [MY/*MYT* 36722]. Graffman, NYPO, Bernstein.

Concentrated and thoughtful, deeply expressive yet never self-indulgent, Tirimo is outstanding in both the *Concerto* and the *Rhapsody*, making this the most desirable version of this favourite coupling, irrespective of price. Speeds for the outer movements of the *Concerto* are on the fast side, yet Tirimo's feeling for natural rubato makes them sound natural, never breathless, while the sweetness and repose of the middle movement are exemplary. The digital recording is clear, brilliant and well-balanced. An outstanding bargain, with disc and cassette very close in sound quality.

Katchen gives a dramatic and exciting account of the *C minor Concerto* such as we would expect from this pianist. He had a fabulous technique, and generally in this recording that leads to the highest pitch of excitement; but there are a number of passages – notably the big climax as well as the coda of the first movement – where he plays almost too fast. Miraculously he gets round the notes somehow but the result inevitably seems breathless, however exciting it is. The stereo recording is in Decca's best manner and manages to be brilliant and well co-ordinated at the same time. The account of the *Rhapsody* with Boult is superbly shaped and is notable not only for its romantic flair and excitement but for the diversity and wit displayed in the earlier variations. There is no question of anti-climax after the eighteenth, for the forward impetus of the playing has tremendous power and excitement. The recording comes from a vintage Decca period and is bold and vividly coloured. The piano timbre is particularly firm and rich. The cassette transfer too is one of Decca's best, clear and full-bodied.

With splendidly rich recording Anievas's HMV disc makes an attractive coupling, and certainly these are rewarding performances. The first movement of the *Concerto* is the least convincing part of the performance, which is otherwise full-blooded and romantic; the *Rhapsody* is presented straightforwardly, and here the recording is particularly vivid to match the extrovert nature of the music-making. The famous eighteenth variation is passionately done, yet without creating a sense of anti-climax afterwards. The cassette – originally non-Dolby – has been remastered at a very high level and there is some roughness in the orchestral upper range at fortissimo levels. The tape, however, includes three Chopin *Études* not offered on the LP.

The partnership of Jean-Philippe Collard and Michel Plasson also brings performances of great intensity but less in the way of romantic delicacy. The slow movement of the *Concerto* is not wanting in lyrical ardour, but it misses the balancing sense of repose that is not lacking in the Katchen version. The opening of the finale has an almost explosive brilliance, to which it is impossible not to respond, yet ultimately this unrelenting vigour tends to overstate the case. The *Rhapsody* responds more readily to this degree of charismatic brilliance, with strong characterization throughout. The eighteenth variation is played with passionate fervour, and the work's closing pages undoubtedly have a cumulative excitement. The recording is super-brilliant and clear, the balance effective but not quite natural. The cassette transfer is first-class and tempers the very bright treble without losing detail.

The Graffman/Bernstein coupling is ultimately undistinguished. The *Concerto* performance is not convincing; the climax of the first movement is studied and unspontaneous. The *Rhapsody* is far more impressive, with striking bravura from Graffman, but here and in the *Concerto* the exaggerated forward balance of the piano negates any possibilities of dynamic contrast between orchestra and soloist. The sound too is lacking in warmth and bloom.

Piano concerto No. 3 in D min., Op. 30.

**(*) RCA [CRL1/*CRK1* 2633]. Horowitz, NYPO, Ormandy.

(M) *** Mercury SRI/*MRI* 75068 [id.]. Janis, LSO, Dorati.

(M) *** Decca Jub. JB/*KJBC* 53 [Lon. JL/*5*-41023]. Ashkenazy, LSO, Fistoulari.

**(*) Decca SXL/*KSXC* 6555 [Lon. CS/*5*-6775]. Ashkenazy, LSO, Previn.

(M) **(*) HMV Green. ESD 7032 [CBS M/*MT* 36685]. Gavrilov, USSR SO, Lazarev.

**(*) Decca Dig. SXDL/*KSXDC* 7609 [Lon. LDR/*5*- 71109]. Bolet, LSO, Fischer.

**(*) CBS [MY/*MYT* 37809]. Berman, LSO, Abbado.

(M) ** DG Priv. 2535/*3335* 493, Vásáry, LSO, Ahronovitch.

An ideal version of Rachmaninov's elusive *Third Concerto* has yet to appear. For many readers the possible first choice would be the splendid performance Byron Janis recorded with Dorati in the early 1960s for Mercury. The tempo and atmosphere of the first two movements are admirably caught; a gentle poetic feeling contrasts with bold surges of extrovert romanticism. As with the same artists' account of the *Second Concerto*, the playing is consistently imbued with spontaneity, its forward thrust passionately sympathetic, the ebb and flow of tension responding naturally to the Rachmaninovian melodic line. Dorati is very much an equal partner here and matches the brilliance of the soloist with a warmly romantic orchestral response; in the great closing climax of the finale the passion is built up – not too hurriedly – to the greatest possible climax. The recording is just a little unfocused on top, but the strings sound reasonably full and the piano timbre is firm and realistic. The acoustic and balance are convincing, and the sound has fine projection and impact. The cassette is good too, slightly smoother on top.

Ashkenazy's earlier account with Fistoulari is fresher in some ways and certainly more direct than his version with Previn. There is imaginative delicacy and poetry in the playing too, and the excellent sound (1963 vintage) is equally impressive on LP and tape. Ashkenazy's reading with Previn is more controversial. It has moments of undoubted insight and touches of sheer magic, but in the last analysis it remains not quite satisfying as a whole. The Kingsway Hall acoustic casts a warm, glowing haze over the sound.

Horowitz's version is listed first, but for many the sound quality will be unacceptable. It was recorded in Carnegie Hall in January 1978. Horowitz's legendary association with this work daunted even the composer himself, and certainly this new version is masterly. Inevitably, perhaps, with rosy memories of the famous 78 r.p.m. recording, there is a slight element of disappointment. Some of the old magic seems to be missing; this is partly due to the clear, clinical recorded sound. Every detail of the piano part is revealed, and the dryness of timbre is matched by the orchestral texture, which has little expansive richness. All the more credit to Ormandy for creating a genuinely expansive romanticism in the great slow movement. The outer movements have undoubted electricity, but it is the fascination of the detail that makes one want to return to this remarkable recorded document. Not quite all the playing is immaculate, and there is some rhythmic eccentricity in the finale; but for those who can accept the 'bare bones' of the recorded sound (if anything slightly smoother and warmer on cassette than on disc) this issue will be indispensable. At the moment it is withdrawn from RCA's UK catalogue.

Had the HMV Melodiya recording (issued on the Greensleeve label) been more transparent and refined in detail, the splendid performance by the young Russian virtuoso Andrei Gavrilov would have been first choice. The sound is perfectly acceptable, with bold piano tone; and certainly this is a memorable reading, strong and passionate, yet poetic too. Gavrilov uses the longer, more complex first-movement cadenza and plays it most excitingly; then he relaxes beautifully at the end to create a feeling of repose for the comparatively gentle beginning of the recapitulation. The slow movement is richly eloquent and the (uncut) finale offers a thrilling display of bravura, where Gavrilov's articulation is marvellously clear.

Bolet brings out the heroic side of this formidable concerto, and the recording of the piano – digitally bright to the point of clangorousness – underlines that. The clarity of articulation and bravura are breathtaking, but some of the work's romantic tenderness is lost, with the orchestra tending to sound aggressive.

For all the eloquence and authority of Lazar Berman's playing, his performance is in the last analysis disappointing. In spite of the English venue the recording is comparatively shallow; not only does the piano lack the richness of sonority one would like, but the orchestra, notably at the climax of the slow movement, also lacks body and depth. It is thus in the work's reflective moments (as at the end of the cadenza in the first movement) that Berman's playing is at its most appealing, although the undoubtedly exciting finale has great force and bravura. Abbado accompanies attentively but is let down by the thin-textured recorded sound. This record, also, is only available in the USA.

Vásáry uses the longer version of the first-movement cadenza, but with less spontaneity than Gavrilov. The slow movement is indulgent and lacks momentum. Vásáry's playing itself is clean, often gentle in style, but the conductor's extremes of tempi are less appealing. Taken as a whole, the performance is not without its poetry or excitement (especially in the finale), but in the last analysis its impetuosity of mood remains unsatisfying. The tape transfer is good, but not outstanding.

Piano concerto No. 4 in G min., Op. 40.
(M) ❀ *** HMV SXLP/*TC-SXLP* 30169 [Ang. S 35567]. Michelangeli, Philh. O, Gracis – RAVEL: *Piano concerto in G.****

As a performance this is one of the most brilliant piano records ever made. It puts the composer's own recorded performance quite in the shade and makes one wonder why the work has failed to achieve anything like the popularity of the earlier concertos. The fact that the slow movement has a theme which is a cross between *Three blind mice* and *Two lovely black eyes* – one reason given for its poor impact on the general public – in no way justifies neglect, for it is a very beautiful movement, set between two outer movements which have a brilliance that even Rachmaninov rarely achieved. Michelangeli's performance of the climax of the first movement has an agility coupled with sheer power which has one on the edge of one's seat. The recording does not quite match the superlative quality of the playing, but in the newest pressings it has been made to sound amazingly well, the piano tone clear and not hard. There is also an excellent cassette.

Piano concerto No. 4 in G min., Op. 40; Rhapsody on a theme of Paganini, Op. 43.
*** Decca SXL/*KSXC* 6556 [Lon. CS/5-6776]. Ashkenazy, LSO, Previn.

Ashkenazy's special quality of poetry, searchingly individual, is at its most illuminating in this coupling. The performance of the *Fourth Concerto* is the finest disc since Michelangeli's, and in the first movement the richness of the recording and its detail (the tuba making a striking contribution to the first movement) score points over the outstanding HMV record. The *Largo* is played with a disarming, simple eloquence and the finale is characteristically assured. The *Rhapsody* too is highly imaginative, not without sparkle or bravura, but with a wider range of feeling than one usually expects in this work. Yet there is no lack of ripeness in the famous eighteenth variation, and the closing variations too are very satisfying. There is a splendid cassette.

The Isle of the Dead, Op. 29; Symphonic dances, Op. 45.
*** Decca Dig. 410 124-1/*4* [id.]. Concg. O, Ashkenazy.

Ashkenazy's is a superb coupling, not just generous in length – with the *Symphonic dances* squeezed on to a single side – but rich and powerful in playing and interpretation. One here recognizes *The Isle of the Dead* as among the very finest of Rachmaninov's orchestral works, relentless in its ominous build-up, while at generally fast speeds the *Symphonic dances* have extra darkness and intensity too, suggesting no relaxation whatever at the end of Rachmaninov's career. The splendid recording, ample and brilliant on disc and chrome cassette alike, highlights both the passion and fine precision of the playing.

Rhapsody on a theme of Paganini, Op. 43.
*** HMV ASD/*TC-ASD* 3197 [Ang. S 37178]. Ortiz, New Philh. O, Koizumi – DOHNÁNYI: *Nursery variations.****
*** Decca Ace SDD 428 [Lon. STS/5-15406]. Katchen, LPO, Boult – DOHNÁNYI: *Nursery variations.****
(*) Ph. Dig. **410 052-2; 6514/*7337* 164 [id.]. Davidovich, Concg. O, Järvi – SAINT-SAËNS: *Concerto No. 2.****
(B) **(*) Con. CC/*CCT* 7594. Vered, LPO, Vonk – TCHAIKOVSKY: *Concerto No. 1.***(*)*
(M) **(*) CBS 61040/*40*- [M/*MT* 31801]. Entremont, Phd. O, Ormandy – GRIEG: *Concerto.***(*)*

Rachmaninov's *Rhapsody* dates from 1934 and thus belongs to the same period as the *Third Symphony*. In many ways it is the most satisfying work the composer wrote for piano and orchestra, its invention consistently inspired. The brilliantly vivid account by Ortiz and her Japanese partner now heads a distinguished list. The balance of the variations is beautifully calculated; there is sparkle and power, and the great romantic blossoming at No. 18 will surely disappoint no one. The recording is outstanding and the demonstration-worthy cassette can also be recommended.

The Katchen performance with Boult is superbly shaped and is notable not only for its romantic flair and excitement but for the diversity and wit displayed in the earlier variations. There is no question of anti-climax after the eighteenth, for the forward impetus of the playing has tremendous power and excitement.

Bella Davidovich is given the benefit of natural and vivid recorded sound with genuine warmth and space round the various instruments. She plays with fleet-fingered fluency and no want of either brilliance or poetry, and Neeme Järvi gives excellent support. This is a likeable performance, but the characterization is romantically relaxed and other versions show deeper insights. The compact disc offers richly atmospheric quality, with the Concertgebouw acoustic bringing an ambient glow and flattering the piano timbre. The chrome cassette is rather middle- and bass-orientated.

Ilana Vered is a sympathetic interpreter and, while showing no less romantic flair (the eighteenth variation is suitably expansive), her characterization is sharper than that of Miss Davidovich. The snag is the balance. Originally made in Phase Four, everything is microphone-manipulated and the larger-than-life piano is way out in front. The sound is ripe and full – with little to choose between disc and tape – and at bargain price, coupled to a very fine account of the Tchaikovsky concerto by Ivan Davis, this might well be considered.

A strongly directed performance from Ormandy, with Entremont rising excitingly to the challenge. Ormandy is one of the finest of all concerto conductors, and this work suits him admirably. The forward momentum becomes increasingly compulsive but does not prevent a full romantic blossoming, and the closing section of the work is a blaze of excitement. The recording is not naturally balanced, but is of good CBS quality, and if the Grieg coupling is suitable this is certainly recommendable.

Symphonic dances, Op. 45 (see also above under *Caprice bohémien* and *Isle of the Dead*). *Aleko: Intermezzo. Vocalise, Op. 34/14.*
(*) DG Dig. **410 894-2; 410 894-1/*4* [id.]. Berlin PO, Maazel.

Symphonic dances; Vocalise.
*** HMV Dig. ASD/*TC-ASD* 143611-1/*4* [Ang. DS/*4XS* 38019]. CBSO, Rattle.

With speeds slower than usual, Simon Rattle draws out the warmth behind Rachmaninov's last work, relating it more than usual to the composer's earlier, more lyrical style. The CBSO may lack the pinpoint brilliance of London or Berlin, but the expansive richness of the score as well as its wit are infectiously conveyed. A ripe account too of the *Vocalise*, set off by full-ranging recording made in the Maltings, Snape. The full resonance of the acoustic is well caught on the XDR tape and the sound has striking body and breadth. It is vivid too, although the upper range of Maazel's tape is more telling.

Maazel's is a crisp, light-textured reading of the *Symphonic dances*. Brilliance is there in plenty, but full warmth of lyricism is lacking, as it is too in the *Vocalise*. Bright, spacious recording, among the best made in the Philharmonie in Berlin. The chrome tape too is one of DG's finest, vivid and wide-ranging, yet with plenty of body. On compact disc the detail and focus of the sound are the more striking and the precision of ensemble is given added freshness and projection. But both Maazel and Rattle come into competition with Ashkenazy – see above – who offers an equally fine (if fascinatingly different) reading of the *Symphonic dances*, plus a much more substantial coupling.

Symphonies Nos. 1–3; The Isle of the Dead, Op. 29; The Rock, Op. 7.
(M) ** Ph. 6768 148 (3). Rotterdam PO, De Waart.

Symphonies Nos. 1–3; Aleko: Intermezzo and Dance.
(M) *** HMV SLS (3). LSO, Previn.

Previn's readings of Rachmaninov's *Second* and *Third Symphonies* have never been outshone, while his softer-grained view of the long *First Symphony* is also powerful, if not always sensuous or exciting. The 1970s recordings are all first-rate, the transfers of Nos. 1 and 3 made cleaner – though not warmer – than on their original issue by the elimination of SQ quadraphonic information. The two pieces from *Aleko* make an attractive if hardly generous fill-up for the *Third Symphony*.

Edo de Waart secures excellent results from the Rotterdam Philharmonic; these performances are all well shaped and proportioned, fresh in conception and refined in phrasing and sonority. What they lack, perhaps, is the all-pervasive melancholy and sense of rapture that lie at the core of Rachmaninov's sensibility. No complaints about the quality of the orchestral response at any point in this set; nor could one fault the excellence and truthfulness of the Philips recording.

Symphony No. 1 in D min., Op. 13.

*** Decca Dig. **411 657-2**; SXDL/*KSXDC* 7603 [Lon. LDR/*5-* 71031]. Concg. O, Ashkenazy.

**(*) HMV ASD/*TCC-ASD* 3137 [Ang. RL/*4RL* 32107]. LSO, Previn.

**(*) Decca Jub. JB/*KJBC* 91. SRO, Weller.

The *First Symphony* was a failure when it first appeared, and the composer suffered so keenly that he suppressed the work, which only came to light after his death. Its merits are now well-known, and high among them must be the sheer originality and lyrical power of the eloquent slow movement. The finale too, famous once as a television signature tune, has memorable ideas.

Ashkenazy's is an outstanding version, volatile and extreme in its tempi with the Concertgebouw players responding in total conviction. In the first movement the cellos and basses articulate their comments on the first theme with phenomenal clarity. This was the last of Ashkenazy's Rachmaninov symphony series to be recorded and it is the most convincing of all. The digital recording is most beautiful, for the sound is full, atmospheric and brilliant. It is superb on CD with nothing to choose between LP and chrome tape. Though the weight of the opening of the finale is magnificent, the relentless hammering rhythms are presented vividly in scale, where easily they can seem oppressive. The scherzo at a very fast speed has Mendelssohnian lightness, the flowing *Larghetto* is presented as a lyrical interlude.

Previn gives a forthright, clean-cut performance, beautifully played and very well recorded. It may lack some of the animal vitality that one recognizes in Russian performances (or for that matter Previn's own performances of the later Rachmaninov symphonies), but this is still an enjoyable account. The cassette has been remastered and the quality is a little uneven, with climaxes a little rough on side one, while side two needs a smoothing of the treble.

Weller's version is undoubtedly distinguished but suffers from the fact that the Suisse Romande Orchestra is unable to produce the body and richness of tone that the slow movement ideally demands. The performance has a fine feeling for the music's atmosphere (both inner movements show this readily). The recording is quite splendid; its range and impact tell in the outer movements and never more vividly than in the work's dramatic closing pages. The cassette transfer is of excellent quality, and the tape holds the climaxes of the finale with aplomb.

Symphony No. 2 in E min., Op. 27.

*** HMV ASD/*TCC-ASD* 2889 [Ang. S/*4XS* 36954]. LSO, Previn.

(M) *** Decca Jub. JB/*KJBC* 92. LPO, Weller.

*** Decca Dig. **400 081-2**; SXDL/*KSXDC* 7563 [Lon. LDR/*5-* 71063]. Concg. O, Ashkenazy.

**(*) DG Dig. 2532/*3302* 102 [id.]. Berlin PO, Maazel.

**(*) Chan. Dig. ABRD/*ABTD* 1021. SNO, Gibson.

(M) ** ASV ACM 2016. Philh. O, Ling Tung.

Previn's HMV record sweeps the board; it is one of the outstanding Rachmaninov records in the catalogue. The passionate intensity of this reading, with rich sweeps of string tone, is immensely satisfying, and although the performance is strongly romantic, the underlying feeling of melancholy is not glossed over. With splendid orchestral playing and vivid recording this is very highly recommended. The cassette is newly remastered, full-bodied and rich, yet clearer in detail than previous transfers.

Weller's performance is also a very fine one, and his Decca disc is undoubtedly competitive in its medium-price reissue, with an outstandingly rich, clear cassette to match the LP closely. Weller's reading is more restrained but genuinely symphonic in stature, with a dreamy, poetic quality in the slow movement. Here the LPO strings do not quite match those of the LSO under Previn in fervour, but the relative reserve of the playing is not unattractive for repeated hearings, and the Decca recording is superb, finer even than the HMV, with greater inner detail, achieved without loss of body and weight.

Ashkenazy began his Rachmaninov series with the Concertgebouw on this most popular of the symphonies, and though the result is most impressive, a performance of high contrasts, there are signs that the Dutch players had not fully adjusted to their guest conductor, notably in the *Adagio* third movement, where at a very slow speed the line is not always sustained, with the great clarinet solo sounding reedy and unrounded. The digital recording is full and brilliant but with a touch of edginess on the strings which becomes even more apparent on the compact disc, although it has a compensating depth and richness. Best of all, however, is the chrome tape, which retains the fullness and bloom, maintains excellent detail, yet softens the edge on top. It is very much in the demonstration class.

As with his account of the *Third Symphony*, Maazel's approach to the *E minor* is passionate and intense. From the brooding opening the allegro moves away swiftly (ignoring the composer's marking of moderato) and the powerful forward impulse generates considerable electricity. The scherzo is crisp and brilliant while the *Adagio*, with long-breathed phrasing, reaches a powerful climax, only to be capped in the exhilaratingly brilliant finale with an apotheosis of even greater fervour. The brightly lit digital recording (with disc and chrome tape closely matched) enhances the excitement, but in this work one ideally needs a warmer, more sumptuous sound balance.

Gibson and the Scottish National Orchestra have the advantage of an excellent digital recording, made in the Henry Wood Hall in Glasgow. The brass sounds are thrilling, but the slightly recessed balance of the strings is a drawback and there is not the body of tone demonstrated by both the HMV and Decca versions mentioned above. But this is a freshly spontaneous performance and overall the sound is admirably natural, even if it includes some strangely unrhythmic thuds at climaxes (apparently the conductor in his excitement stamping on the podium). The cassette transfer is clear and immediate, with crisply focused detail, but even more than on the LP the ear notices that the upper strings are not sumptuously rich in texture.

Ling Tung directs a warm and generally understanding reading, but neither the playing nor the recording matches up to the standards of other versions, with the Philharmonia violins somewhat backwardly balanced.

Symphony No. 3 in A min., Op. 44; Aleko (opera): *Intermezzo and Women's dance.*
*** HMV ASD/*TC-ASD* 3369 [Ang. S/*4XS* 37260]. LSO, Previn.

Symphony No. 3; The Isle of the Dead, Op. 29.
**(*) DG Dig. 2532/*3302* 065 [id.]. Berlin PO, Maazel.

Symphony No. 3; The Rock, Op. 7.
(M) *** Decca Jub. JB/*KJBC* 93. LPO, Weller.
(B) **(*) RCA VICS/*VK* 2028 [ALK1 4294]. LSO, Previn.

Symphony No. 3; Vocalise, Op. 34/14.
*** Desmar DSM 1007. Nat. PO, Stokowski.

Symphony No. 3; Youth Symphony (1891).
*** Decca Dig. **410 231-2**; SXDL/*KSXDC* 7531 [Lon. LDR/*5-* 71031]. Concg. O, Ashkenazy.

Previn's HMV record brings a stunning performance. There is much that is elusive in this highly original structure, and Previn conveys the purposefulness of the writing at every point, revelling in the richness but clarifying textures. The LSO has rarely displayed its virtuosity more brilliantly on record (reflecting the fact that the record was made immediately after a series of performances of the work in America), and the recording is ample to match. This is even finer than the excellent RCA version by the same forces: the differences may be summed up in the treatment of the glorious second-subject melody, where in this later version Previn's phrasing is less exaggerated but more deeply felt. Like the others in this series, the cassette has been remastered and now sounds both full-bodied and quite refined.

Ashkenazy's is a performance of extremes, volatile and passionate in a very Russian way. In the first movement the varying speeds are contrasted far more than usual, the allegros faster, the slow, lyrical passages (notably the great melody of the second subject) slower with copious rubato. The finale is fast and hectic to the point of wildness, but the Concertgebouw players respond superbly and the digital recording is full, rich and brilliant. The fragment of a projected symphony – with its first subject plainly indebted to Tchaikovsky's *Fourth* – was written when Rachmaninov was only nineteen. It is an enjoyable and unusual makeweight. Though some will prefer Previn's directness, Ashkenazy's reading is no less compulsive and the glorious sound is even more impressive on compact disc, while the chrome tape is outstanding, offering a beautiful overall bloom, refined detail and natural string timbre.

Weller's performance, too, is superbly recorded. There may be some slight sacrifice of detail to atmosphere, but the beautiful sound the orchestra consistently yields deserves this kind of richness and sense of space. The reading is an essentially lyrical one, showing great delicacy of feeling, notably in the preparation of the first movement's memorable second subject, but also in the sense of stillness that pervades the opening of the *Adagio* to make an absolute contrast with the scherzando middle section. The finale too responds to such spacious treatment, though its basic tempo has no lack of urgency. Weller's performance of *The Rock* is no less impressive, with a splendidly moulded climax. Like the disc, the cassette offers exceptionally sophisticated sound, rich, brilliant and detailed.

It was Stokowski who in 1936 in Philadelphia conducted the first performance of Rachmaninov's last symphony. Nearly forty years later in London he recorded it with Sydney Sax's fine team of selected orchestral players, and the result is rich and exciting. There are idiosyncrasies in plenty, not least a tempo for the finale that whirls one along in exhilarating danger; but with rather larger-than-life recording this is a glorious example of Stokowski's old-age energy, his ability to inspire players to a totally individual and riveting performance, not directly comparable with others. At the moment this Desmar disc is not available in the UK.

Maazel takes a highly distinctive view of both these Rachmaninov masterpieces. The symphony is unusally fierce and intense with refined, incisive playing spotlit by the digital recording. The result is sharper and tougher than one expects, less obviously romantic, with the great second-subject melody sounding detached and rather chilly. The finale is made to sound like a Walton comedy overture at the start, brilliant and exciting, but at the end it lacks joyful exuberance. *The Isle of the Dead* makes a generous fill-up. At a fast speed Maazel's view is less sombre and brooding than usual, but the climaxes are most powerful and the result is intensely compelling. There is an excellent chrome cassette, the transfer level quite high for DG, so that there is fullness and detail and transients are sparkling.

Previn's RCA account of the *Third* was made at the same time as his earlier version of the *Second* (now deleted). It does not show quite the firm grasp on overall shape that distinguishes his HMV record of the work, but the reading is very sympathetic and brilliantly played. The shaping of the second subject of the first movement is matched by the eloquence of the slow movement, and the bravura in the finale almost manages to make it sound completely convincing. Previn's account of *The Rock* is also an eloquent one, finely played. The recording too is first-class, with sparkle as well as richness, and at medium price this remains recommendable. The cassette is transferred at the highest level on chrome tape and, while the sound is exceptionally vivid, the bass tends to be explosive in some climaxes and there is some loss of refinement too.

Cello sonata in G min., Op. 19.
*(*) HMV ASD 2587. Tortelier, Ciccolini – CHOPIN: *Cello sonata.**(*)

Cello sonata; Prelude; Danse orientale, Op. 2/1–2.
*** ASV ALH/*ZCALH* 911. Lloyd Webber, Yitkin Seow – DEBUSSY: *Cello sonata.****

Rachmaninov's *Cello sonata*, one of the most ambitious written in this genre, was an inspiration of the period of the *Second Piano concerto* when he was cured of the deep depression that followed the failure of his *First Symphony*. Its exuberant flow of arresting and powerful ideas is splendidly caught by Julian Lloyd Webber and Yitkin Seow, and they are equally persuasive in the two brief works of Op. 2, written over a decade earlier. The recording is firm and immediate rather than atmospheric. The cassette focus is diffuse.

This work suits Tortelier better than its Chopin coupling; its passionate melodic lines are shaped with the right degree of nervous tension. But Ciccolini sounds here rather more like an accompanist than a full participant, although his playing is technically secure.

PIANO MUSIC

Études-tableaux, Op. 33; Piano sonata No. 2 in B flat min., Op. 36.
*** Decca SXL/*KSXC* 6996 [Lon. CS/*5*-7236]. Ashkenazy.

Ashkenazy returns to the original 1913 version of the *Sonata* in his fine Decca recording. In later years Rachmaninov wrote that he 'longed to revise it as I am not satisfied with the setting I gave it at that time', and in 1931 he carried out an extensive revision which not only involved many cuts but also the thinning-out of the texture with a view to greater clarity. Some feel that Rachmaninov's self-critical enthusiasm ran away with him and Horowitz restores a number of the incisions in his public performances recorded on RCA. Ashkenazy, however, performs a valuable service in putting the whole score before us and giving it with such virtuosity and feeling. His is a *tour de force* and the account he gives of the *Études-tableaux*, Op. 33, is hardly less impressive. The cassette is slightly disappointing, the quality somewhat amorphous compared with the disc.

Études-tableaux, Op. 39, Nos. 1–9; Preludes Nos. 1 in C sharp min., Op. 3/2; 21 in B min., Op. 32/10.
** CRD CRD 1003. Solyom.

The Hungarian pianist Janos Solyom is now resident in Sweden, where he recorded this recital. The playing is good, though not as impressive as Ashkenazy's or as imaginative. He is well but not outstandingly recorded; the acoustic does not give the sound much room to expand.

Études-tableaux, Op. 39, Nos. 1–9; Variations on a theme of Corelli, Op. 42.
*** Decca SXL 6604 [Lon. CS 6822]. Ashkenazy.

Superb performances from Ashkenazy make this the most desirable of Rachmaninov issues. The *Corelli variations* is a rarity and a very fine work. The recording is first-class.

24 Preludes (complete).
*** Decca 5 BB 221/2 [Lon. CSA 2241]. Ashkenazy.
(M) ** Uni. UNS 230/1. Katin.

24 Preludes; Preludes in D min. and F; Morceaux de fantaisie, Op. 3.
*** Hyp. A 66081/2. Shelley.

Considering his popularity and their quality, it is odd that Rachmaninov's *Preludes* have not been recorded complete more often. Ashkenazy's are in a class of their own both as performances and as recording. There is superb panache and flair about this playing.

Shelley is a compellingly individual interpreter of Rachmaninov. Each one of the preludes strikes an original chord in him. These are very different readings from those of Ashkenazy, and the famous *C sharp Minor* (one of the Opus 3 set of pieces here included in their entirety) is taken very slowly and portentously; but the intensity, well caught in full if reverberant recording, makes these readings an essential recommendation alongside those of the Russian pianist.

Katin too is splendidly recorded, and the bold, clear piano image itself lends a certain romantic splendour to these performances. Katin has the measure of the lyrical music and it is only in the pieces that make their full effect with sheer bravura that he is less than completely convincing.

Preludes Nos. 3 in B flat; 5 in D; 6 in G min.; 8 in C min., Op. 23/2, 4–5 and 7; 12 in C; 13 in B flat min., Op. 32/1–2.
(M) *** Con. CC/*CCT* 7516 [DG 2535/*3335* 272]. Sviatoslav Richter – MUSSORGSKY: *Pictures.***

Richter's marvellous performances make one hope that one day we shall have a complete set of the *Preludes* from him in stereo. The recording here is good; the cassette has rather less range than the disc but is fully acceptable.

Russian rhapsody; Symphonic dances, Op. 45.
*** Decca SXL/*KSXC* 6926 [Lon. CS/5-7159]. Ashkenazy, Previn.

The two-piano version of the *Symphonic dances* – Rachmaninov's last major work – was written not as an arrangement of the orchestral score but as a preparation for it. The ingenuity of his handling of a difficult medium produced a work which in pianistic detail as well as sharpness of argument is masterly. Ashkenazy and Previn are challenged to a dazzling performance, superbly recorded with bright, realistic piano sound. The coupling is an early work, musically rather naïve but well worth hearing in a performance as persuasive as this. The cassette, unusually for Decca, has not quite the upper range of the disc: the warmly resonant acoustic has accentuated the bass response.

Piano sonatas Nos. 1 in D min., Op. 28; 2 in B flat min., Op. 36 (revised 1931).
*** Hyp. A/*KA* 66047. Shelley.

Like John Ogdon before him, Howard Shelley chooses the 1931 version of the *Sonata* and couples it with the relatively little-known *D minor Sonata*, Op. 28, which comes from 1907 and was written between the *Second Symphony* and *The Isle of the Dead*. Shelley has plenty of sweep and grandeur and withstands comparison with the distinguished competition. He has something of the grand manner and an appealing freshness, ardour and, when required, tenderness. His is a valuable complement to the Ashkenazy and he is accorded an excellent balance by the engineers which places the piano firmly in focus. There is a first-class cassette.

Suites for 2 pianos, Nos. 1 (Fantasy), Op. 5; 2, Op. 17.
*** Decca SXL 6697 [Lon. CS 6893]. Ashkenazy, Previn.
*** DG 2531 345 [id.]. Güher and Süher Pekinel.

Suite No. 2, Op. 17.
*** Ph. Dig. **411 034-2**; 6514/*7337* 369 [id.]. Argerich, Freire – LUTOSLAWSKI: *Paganini variations*; RAVEL: *La valse.****

A delectable coupling of the two fine *Piano suites* on Decca, beautifully recorded. The colour and flair of Rachmaninov's writing are captured with wonderful imagination – reflection of a live performance by Ashkenazy and Previn at London's South Bank Summer Music in the summer of 1974.

Güher and Süher Pekinel are Turkish sisters who studied at the Juilliard School and also in West Germany. They are an accomplished duo and give sensitive and musicianly accounts of these delightful pieces, and they are admirably recorded. This can be recommended alongside but not in preference to the Ashkenazy/Previn recording of this same coupling, which has the benefit of warm, vivid sound quality.

Argerich and Freire give a dazzling virtuoso account of the *Suite*, rushing the waltzes off their feet (the movement is marked *presto* but they play it *prestissimo*). They are as fresh, idiomatic and thoughtful as their Decca rivals (Ashkenazy and Previn) and their performance is thoroughly exhilarating. They are well recorded and can be recommended alongside the Decca team who perhaps find more in the inner movements. The only drawback to the recording is the reverberation which seems a trifle excessive, even for an expansively romantic score, and this is even more striking on the excellent compact disc.

Symphonic dances, Op. 45 (see also above under *Russian rhapsody*).
** DG Dig. 410 616-1/4 [id.]. Argerich, Economou – TCHAIKOVSKY: *Nutcracker suite.***

Argerich and Economou play with great temperament and everything is marvellously alive and well thought-out. There is much sensitivity and a lively sense of enjoyment in evidence as well as (it goes without saying) great virtuosity. So there is from Ashkenazy and André Previn on Decca too, and they score in having much warmer, fresher and more open sound as well. The DG recording is perfectly acceptable – in fact, it is quite natural if a little dry – but nowhere near as realistic as the Decca. Disc and chrome cassette sound much the same.

Variations on a theme of Chopin, Op. 22; Variations on a theme of Corelli, Op. 42; Mélodie in E, Op. 3/3.
*** Hyp. A 66009. Shelley – MENDELSSOHN: *Scherzo.****

Rachmaninov's two big sets of variations for solo piano make an excellent coupling, and Howard Shelley gives dazzling, consistently compelling performances, full of virtuoso flair. The *Corelli variations* are the better-known set (see above), product of Rachmaninov's years in exile, sharply imagined but far less passionate than his earlier music. Strangely, the more expansive *Chopin variations* have been seriously neglected on record, but on any count they represent the composer at his most masterly, written as they were at the same rich period as the *Second Piano concerto*, the *Second Symphony* and the *Cello sonata*. The grouping of variations brings a kind of sonata balance, with the climax of the final section superbly built by Shelley, helped by first-rate piano sound.

VOCAL AND CHORAL MUSIC

Songs: *Again you leapt, my heart!; All at once I gladly owned; Beloved, let us fly; Brooding; C'était en avril; Christ is risen; Come, let us rest; Daisies; The heart's secret; How few the joys; I came to her; I shall tell you nothing; Like blossom dew-freshed to gladness; Morning; Oh stay, my love, forsake me not!; A prayer; Twilight has fallen; The water lily.* (i) *Two partings.* (Piano) *Daisies.*
*** Decca SXL 6869 [Lon. OS 26559]. Söderström, Ashkenazy, (i) with Shirley-Quirk.

This volume of Söderström and Ashkenazy's unique series contains fewer masterpieces (the highly characteristic *Brooding* is certainly one of them), but it presents rarities which make essential listening for those interested in the composer. Sonia's final speech in Chekhov's *Uncle Vanya* here becomes a song which nicely skirts sentimentality, and John Shirley-Quirk joins the soprano for the wry dialogue *Two partings*. Both singer and pianist are again intensely compelling in their inspired performances, and the recording is outstanding.

Songs: *All things depart; As fair as day in blaze of noon; By the gates of the holy dwelling; Do you remember the evening?; A flower fell; From St John's Gospel; Let me rest here alone; Love's flame; Night; O, do not grieve; Song of disappointment; The soul's concealment; 'Tis time; Thy pity I implore; Were you hiccoughing; When yesterday we met; With holy banner firmly held. Letter to Stanislavsky.* (Piano) *Lilacs.*
*** Decca SXL 6940 [Lon. OS 26615]. Söderström, Ashkenazy.

Filling in the gaps from the previous records in their outstanding series, Söderström and Ashkenazy here range over the wide span of Rachmaninov's career as well as his whole emotional range. So you find the richly intense *O, do not grieve* on the one hand, and on the other a comic skit on a drinking song, *Did you hiccough, Natasha?*; also a letter in music sent to Stanislavsky on the tenth anniversary of the Moscow Arts Theatre and the solo piano version of *Lilacs*. Model performances and recording.

Songs: *A-oo; Daisies; Dissonance; Dreams; The harvest of sorrow; How fair this spot; In my garden at night; The morn of life; The muse; Oh, never sing to me again; The Pied Piper; The storm; Vocalise; What wealth of rapture.*
*** Decca SXL 6718 [Lon. OS 26428]. Söderström, Ashkenazy.

This is a delectable record, with Söderström a fluent and radiant soloist inspired by her accompanist to performances of pure poetry. Many of the songs were obviously chosen for the complexity of the accompaniment – a challenge even to this most accomplished of Rachmaninov pianists – but there is the ease of inevitability in these performances. The songs are drawn mainly from Rachmaninov's last two collections, Op. 34 and Op. 38, written in the years just before the Russian Revolution. Like Russian Ravel, as one critic said on hearing this record. Excellent recording.

The Bells, Op. 35. Vocalise, Op. 34/14.
*** HMV ASD 3284 [Ang. S 37169]. Armstrong, LSO, Previn, (i) with Tear, Shirley-Quirk, LSO Ch.

In *The Bells*, as in Previn's equally fresh and direct account of another Russian choral work, Prokofiev's *Alexander Nevsky*, the LSO Chorus sings convincingly in the original language. The timbre may not be entirely Russian-sounding (cleaner and fresher in fact), but in what amounts to a choral symphony Previn's concentration on purely musical values as much as on evocation of atmosphere produces powerful results, particularly when the recording is of demonstration standard, rich and vivid. All the soloists are very good, and Sheila Armstrong, tenderly beautiful in the lovely second movement, depicting Poe's *Wedding Bells*, is more than a match for any rival.

Songs: *Christ is risen; A dream; The harvest of sorrow; How fair this spot; Night is mournful; Oh, never sing to me again; Oh stay, my love; When yesterday we met.*
(*) Decca SXL 6974. Talvela, Gothoni – MUSSORGSKY: *Songs and Dances of Death* etc.*

Talvela modifies his dark timbre, so apt for the Mussorgsky cycle, to suit the softer, gentler lines of these Rachmaninov songs, but as recorded – very vividly – the voice acquires a plaintive quality which is not quite pleasing. Nonetheless this is expressive and thoughtful singing, imaginatively accompanied, and the repertory is not so common that one can overlook this issue, particularly when it is so attractively coupled.

Song transcriptions: *Dreams; Floods of spring; In the silent night; The Little island; Midsummer eve; The Muse; O, cease thy singing; On the death of a linnet; Sorrow in springtime; To the children; Vocalise; Where beauty dwells* (trans. Wild).
** Dell'Arte DBS 7001. Earl Wild.

The piano sounds just a shade bottom-heavy but the recording is otherwise very pleasing with no want of ambience. The transcriptions are for the most part expert (Earl Wild heard Rachmaninov on numerous occasions) and, generally speaking, could not be bettered. The playing is just a shade wayward with not quite enough of the firm-centred quality that Rachmaninov calls for. Moreover, played at one sitting, there is not quite enough variety of mood to rivet the listener's attention.

Vespers, Op. 37.
*** HMV ASD 2973 [Quin. 2715]. RSFSR Ac. Russian Ch., Sveshnikov.
** Abbey Dig. ABY/*ABYC* 824. Scottish Philharmonic Singers, McCrorie.

Rachmaninov's *Vespers* (1915) must be counted among his most profound and fascinating works. The fifteen movements are superbly written and are as dark, deeply affecting and richly sonorous as any Orthodox Church music. The performances can only be called superlative, and it will be a long time before they are superseded. The basses in particular have incredible richness (at one point they sing a low B flat) and the recording is in an appropriately resonant acoustic. The recording is lively and has plenty of atmosphere, sometimes at the expense of detail, but no reservation should be put in the way of what is an outstanding record.

The Scottish singers also give a fine account of this haunting and passionate work and they sing with obvious feeling. But good as they are, this group cannot command the rich sonorities and black tone of Slavic choirs, and this cannot really compare with the Russian recording under Sveshnikov, even though the sound is first-class, with an outstanding matching chrome tape.

Raff, Joachim (1822–82)

Symphony No. 5 (Lenore).
(M) *** Uni. UNS 209. LPO, Herrmann.

The eleven symphonies of Joachim Raff have long been left in neglect, but Bernard Herrmann was an enthusiastic propagandist, and here thanks to the enterprise of Unicorn we have the chance to appreciate the colourful programmatic writing of what the surviving Raff enthusiasts often count the finest of the cycle. In some ways it is a very naïve work, based as it is on a high romantic ballad by the poet Bürger. A dead soldier lover calls for the girl he has left behind, and on a devil's ride he turns disconcertingly into a skeleton. The first two movements merely provide preparation for that dramatic development, and the third depicts the lovers' parting, with the main march heard first in crescendo and then diminuendo to represent the arrival and departure of a troop of the lover's regiment – a piece much beloved by the Victorians. A thoroughly enjoyable Mendelssohnian symphony, colourfully performed with clean and vivid recording and forward percussion.

Rameau, Jean Philippe (1683–1764)

Hippolyte et Aricie: orchestral suite.
(M) ❀ *** HM 1C 065 99837. La Petite Bande, Kuijken.

There were three productions of *Hippolyte et Aricie* during Rameau's lifetime, in 1733, 1742 and 1757, for which various instrumental additions were made. This record collects virtually all the orchestral music from the three, in performances so lively and winning that the disc is irresistible. Sigiswald Kuijken gets delightful results from his ensemble; the melodic invention is fresh and its orchestral presentation ingenious. In every way an outstanding release – and not least in the quality of the sound.

Le Temple de la gloire: suites 1 and 2.
(M) *** Decca Ser. SA/*KSC* 19. ECO, Leppard.

For those not insisting on the acerbities of original instruments this is a delightful record, and the first-class recording is fully worthy of the attractive music and the spirited, stylish playing. Rameau's scores have much character, and the *Air for the Demons* is especially evocative. Raymond Leppard too gives us here an object lesson on how to perform music of this period. His springy rhythms and, especially, his use of the continuo to colour the texture are most imaginative. This is a record not to be missed. The cassette is transferred at a high level and is generally of high quality, though the focus occasionally slips a little.

Pièces de clavecin (1724): excerpts. *Nouvelle suite de pièces de clavecin* (1728): excerpts. *5 Pièces de clavecin* (1741).
*** DG Arc. 410 648-1/*4* [id.]. Gilbert.

This record forms an admirable introduction to Rameau's keyboard output, now that the complete survey, from which this derives, has disappeared from circulation along with George Malcolm's Argo set. Archive have represented all three of the instruments used in the complete set: a Goujon (1749), another by Jean Henry Hemsch (1761), and a Dumont of 1697 restored by Taskin in the year of the French Revolution; and Gilbert plays with impressive artistry and taste. If you missed the complete set when it appeared in the late 1970s, don't miss this excellent anthology.

Pièces de clavecin: Suite (No. 1) in A minor; L'Agaçante; La Dauphine; L'Indiscrète; La Livri; La Pantomime; La Timide.
** CRD CRD 1020 [id.]. Pinnock.

For his second record of Rameau's harpsichord music (the first is listed below), Trevor Pinnock chose a more mellow instrument, making his stylish, crisply rhythmic performance even more attractive. The selection includes *La Dauphine*, the last keyboard piece that Rameau wrote, brilliantly performed. Excellent recording.

Harpsichord suites: in A min. (1728)*; in E min.* (1724).
** CRD CRD 1010 [id.]. Pinnock.

Excellent performances. Trevor Pinnock is restrained in the matter of ornamentation, but his direct manner is both eloquent and stylish. The harpsichord is of the French type and is well recorded.

Les Indes galantes: excerpts (harpsichord transcriptions).
*** HM HM/*40* 1028. Gilbert.

These transcriptions are Rameau's own, made some time after the success scored by his first opera-ballet, *Les Indes galantes*, in 1735. He grouped a number of items into four suites or '*concerts*', and these included not only dance numbers and orchestral pieces but arias as well. Kenneth Gilbert, playing a fine instrument in contemporary tuning, reveals these miniatures as the subtle and refined studies that they are. He could not be better served by the recording engineers. The cassette is transferred at a very high level indeed and, while the quality is excellent, the image tends to be right on top of the listener unless care is exercised with the controls.

Grand motets: *In convertendo; Quam dilecta laboravi.*
*** HM **CD 1078**; HM/*40* 1078 [id.]. Gari, Monnaliu, Ledroit, De Mey, Varcoe, Chapelle Royale Ch., Ghent Coll. Vocale, Herreweghe.

These two motets are among Rameau's finest works and come from the years preceding his first opera in 1733. The recordings are made in the Carmelite Church in Ghent which has a warm, reverberant acoustic and the Ghent Collegium vocale is stiffened by forces from La Chapelle Royale in Paris. They produce excellent results and the soloists are also very fine indeed. In his book on the composer Girdlestone speaks of *In convertendo* as Rameau's greatest piece of church music, and this record makes out the persuasive case for it. The instrumental ensemble includes several members of La Petite Bande and so its excellence can be almost taken for granted.

OPERA-BALLET AND OPERA

Anacréon (complete).
*** HM HM/*40* 1090 [id.]. Schirrer, Mellon, Feldman, Visse, Laplenie, Les Arts Florissants, Christie.

Rameau composed two works on the theme of the ancient Greek poet, Anacréon, famed for his devotion to Cupid and Bacchus! This is the second, originally designed as an *acte de ballet* to a libretto by P.-J. Bernard and composed in 1757. The music has charm even if it is not Rameau at his most inventive, and the performance is as authoritative and stylish as one would expect from William Christie's group. It is not essential Rameau, but readers with an interest in the period will want it – and it has moments of great appeal. The recording is admirable but in its cassette format, although the generally high level of transfer produces lively results, there are moments of peaking on solo voices.

Les Boréades (complete).
*** Erato STU/*MCE* 715343 (3). Jennifer Smith, Rodde, Langridge, Aler, Lafont, Monteverdi Ch., E. Bar. Soloists, Eliot Gardiner.

It was John Eliot Gardiner who in April 1975 conducted the first ever public performance of this last opera of Rameau, written when he had reached his eighties. The composer died during the rehearsals at the Paris Opéra, and the piece was never staged until in 1982 Gardiner presented it with the same cast as here at the Aix-en-Provence Festival with enormous success. Though the story – involving the followers of Boreas, the storm god – is highly artificial in a classical way, the music – involving many crisp and brief dances and arias – is as vital and alive as anything Rameau ever wrote, completely countering any idea of classical opera as static or boring. Gardiner directs an electrifying performance with generally first-rate singing, except that Jennifer Smith's upper register, in the central role of Alphise, Queen of Baltria, is not sweet. Chorus and orchestra are outstanding and the recording excellent (although side one of the otherwise very good chrome-tape transfer is overmodulated to the point of distortion). Bizarre copyright problems prevented a libretto from being included, which makes it hard to follow the complex plot.

Castor et Pollux (complete).
**(*) Erato Dig. NUM 750323 (3). Jeffes, Huttenlocher, Jennifer Smith, Buchan, Wallington, Parsons, E. Bach Fest. Singers and Bar. O, Farncombe.

Unlike Harnoncourt's (deleted) earlier recording for Telefunken, Farncombe – with a cast which gave this tragédie lyrique at Covent Garden and in Paris – uses the revised edition of 1754. The allegorical prologue is eliminated, and the rest made tauter and less expansive. The result is certainly more dramatic by today's standards, and though Farncombe – after a brisk and refreshing account of the overture – fails at times to spring rhythms brightly enough, this is an admirable set marked by some stylish singing, notably from Huttenlocher as Pollux, who was not in the stage performances. Excellently clear digital recording.

Dardanus (complete).
**(*) Erato STU 71416 (2) [id.]. Eda-Pierre, Von Stade, Gautier, Delvin, Soyer, Van Dam, Paris Op. Ch. and O, Leppard.

For the production at the Paris National Opéra, Leppard prepared a satisfying conflation of the very different versions of this important work (which Rameau revised): not just the 1739 score but the score for the 1744 revival, which involved radical rewriting of the last two Acts. Though the French chorus and orchestra here fail to perform with quite the rhythmic resilience that Leppard usually achieves on record, the results are refreshing and illuminating, helped by generally fine solo singing and first-rate recording. José van Dam as Ismenor copes superbly with the high tessitura, and Christiane Eda-Pierre is a radiant Venus. The story may be improbable (as usual), but Rameau was here inspired to some of his most compelling and imaginative writing.

Les Fêtes d'Hébé: 3rd Entrée: La Danse.
*** Erato STU/*MCE* 71089 [id.]. Gomez, Rodde, Orliac, Monteverdi Ch. and O, Eliot Gardiner.

Les Fêtes d'Hébé was first staged in 1739 in Paris, and was the fourth major work Rameau had composed for the lyric stage. It was his second in the opera-ballet genre, *Les Indes galantes* being the first. In its complete form, *Les Fêtes d'Hébé* consists of a prologue and three Acts dedicated to poetry, music and finally the dance. This last is a pastoral interspersed with dances in which Mercury courts the shepherdess Églé. Few people have done more in recent years for Rameau's music than John Eliot Gardiner, and this performance is distinguished by his great feeling for this composer and an alive sensitivity. He secures excellent playing and singing from his forces and is very well recorded too, with natural sound. The music itself is inventive and delightful; in short, a record not to be missed. The cassette lacks upper range and the sound is woolly and bass-orientated.

Hippolyte et Aricie (complete).
(M) **(*) Argo D 272 D 3. Shirley-Quirk, Baker, Tear, Hickey, St Anthony Singers, ECO, Lewis.

Rameau's operas do not deserve their neglect, as readers who have heard *Dardanus* or the present work will know. Although they have their longueurs, they reveal a vein of melodic invention of the highest order and a harmonic sophistication that more than compensate. Readers will find the quality of inspiration strikingly well sustained in this opera, which is a work whose impact deepens on closer acquaintance. Few scholars have greater authority in this area than Professor Lewis, though scholarship is not always a guarantee of an inspired performance. On this occasion, however, he secures playing of genuine liveliness and feeling, and the St Anthony Singers too show a more than adequate response. Of the soloists, both Janet Baker and John Shirley-Quirk give pleasure, though the rest of the cast is uneven and their French is not uniformly good. Angela Hickey does not always seem to be secure, but it is only fair to say that such reservations as one has are more than outweighed by gratitude at having the opera available at last. The recording has admirable clarity and detail.

Naïs (complete).
**(*) Erato STU 71439 (2) [id.]. Russell, Jennifer Smith, Mackay, Parsons, Caley, Caddy, Jackson, Ransome, Tomlinson, E. Bach Fest. Singers and Bar. O, McGegan.

Rameau's opera *Naïs* was commissioned by the Opéra to commemorate the Treaty of Aix-la-Chapelle and first appeared in 1749. It tells of Neptune's courtship of the water-nymph Naïs and is full of bold invention. The overture has some astonishing dissonances and syncopations, and the opening battle scenes in which the Heavens are stormed by the Titans and Giants are quite striking. The melodic invention later in the work is not perhaps as elevated or inspired as the very finest Rameau, but it is still of fair quality and at times is very beautiful indeed. The performance, based on the 1980 English Bach Festival production, is full of spirit and uses authentic period instruments to good effect. The work is not long, occupying only four sides, and its rewards are such as to counterbalance any reservations one might have as to imperfections in ensemble or the like. Admirers of Rameau will need no prompting to acquire this set; the unconverted should sample the opening, which will surely delight and surprise. Good, well-balanced sound.

Pigmalion (opera-ballet).
*** HM 1C 065 99914 [Pro. PAL/*PAG* 1082]. Elwes, Van Der Sluis, Vanhecke, Yakar, Paris Chapel Royal Ch., La Petite Bande, Leonhardt.

Leonhardt's account with La Petite Bande and a fine team of soloists is the first new version to appear for twenty years and it displaces the (deleted) Couraud. Leonhardt's direction is more leisurely and the textures more transparent, thanks to the excellent recording and also the lighter timbres of period instruments.

La Princesse de Navarre (incidental music).
*** Erato STU/*MCE* 71283. Hill-Smith, Harrhy, Chambers, Rees, Goldthorpe, Caddy, Wigmore, Savidge, E. Bach Fest. Singers and Bar. O, McGegan.

La Princesse de Navarre is a collection of dance movements, some of which Rameau used in other works, as well as interludes for the Voltaire *comédie*. The finest is a chaconne of some magnificence in which dancers and singers participate. This edition is the first to include all the music Rameau composed for the work. He made substantial revisions, probably more than once and possibly as late as 1763 when Voltaire added a new Prologue for a performance at Bordeaux. There is some altogether delightful music here and those who saw the Covent Garden staging in 1976 will need no reminders as to its quality. Of course, listening to 55 minutes of dances (even though some of them are choral) in close proximity is not the ideal way of enjoying Rameau, but the gramophone gives one the opportunity to pick and choose. Very good performances and an excellent recording too, although the cassette is transferred at marginally too high a level, which brings an edgy treble and over-resonant bass.

Rangström, Ture (1884–1947)

Symphony No. 1 in C sharp min. (*In memory of Strindberg*).
*** EMI 7C 061 35712. Swedish RO, Segerstam.

Ture Rangström was an almost exact contemporary of Arnold Bax or Ernest Bloch, though he did not possess the craftsmanship and orchestral expertise of either. His strength lies in his songs, which are among the finest in twentieth-century Swedish music. The first of his four symphonies, inspired by the death of Strindberg, is a lush, self-indulgent score in the post-national romantic idiom. It receives the most eloquent and persuasive advocacy from the Swedish Radio Orchestra under Leif Segerstam, though not even that can redeem the banality of some of its themes. First-class recording enhances the attractions of a disc introducing a composer who, for all his shortcomings, is well worth attention.

Symphony No. 3 in D flat (*Song under the stars*)*; Songs of King Erik; 2 Songs in the olden style.*
*(*) EMI 7C 061 35774. Hagegård, Halsingborg SO, Frandsen; Fürst.

The *Third Symphony* dates from 1929 and is pure kitsch. It is also indifferently performed here. But the disc is worth considering for the sake of Håkan Hagegård's golden voice in the *King Erik songs*. Rangström's scoring is occasionally inexpert but his invention is far better here than in the *Symphony*. All the songs are superbly sung, though the orchestra is less than first-class. A new record of the *Second Symphony* played by the ORF (Austrian Radio) Symphony Orchestra under Leif Segerstam (EMI Conifer 7C-061 35291) should be given a wide berth as it far surpasses the *Third* in banality and must be among the most appalling symphonies on record. However, the songs are another matter and well reward investigation.

Eighteen songs.
*** Cap. CAP1208. Hagegård, Scheja.

The Hagegård on this record is the tenor, Erland, and not his more celebrated cousin, Håkan. Nine of the songs on this disc have not been recorded before and nearly all are of high quality. *Pan* and *To anguish* are haunting and leave one in no doubt that Rangström was a miniaturist of real quality. Although Erland Hagegård's vibrato is on one or two occasions obtrusive, these are fine performances and are strongly characterized. His partner, Staffan Scheja, is excellent, too: he is a player who could sustain wider international exposure. Rangström as a *romans* composer (*romans* being the Swedish equivalent of Lieder or Mélodie) is a totally different proposition from the symphonist. Adventurous collectors attracted to Scandinavian music will find this collection well worth seeking out.

Three songs: *Vingar i natten; Vinden och trädet; Sköldmön.*
*** EMI Conifer 4E 061 035149. Ligendza, Swedish RSO, Westerberg – LARSSON: *A God in Disguise.****

Rangström's songs are really most beautiful and well worth taking the trouble to look for. There is none of the bombast and emptiness of the symphonies but a genuine lyrical gift and a fine sensibility. He has real feeling for language and sets words with complete directness and simplicity. Catarina Ligendza does the three chosen here excellently.

Ravel, Maurice (1875–1937)

Alborada del gracioso; Une Barque sur l'océan; Boléro; (i) *Piano concerto in G; Piano concerto for the left hand in D; Daphnis et Chloé* (complete)*; Ma Mère l'Oye* (complete)*; Menuet antique; Pavane pour une infante défunte; Rapsodie espagnole; Shéhérazade* (*Ouverture de Féerie*)*; Le Tombeau de Couperin;* (ii) *Tzigane. La Valse; Valses nobles et sentimentales.*
*** HMV SLS 5016 (5) [Ang. S/*4XS* 37147/51]. O de Paris, Martinon; with (i) Ciccolini; (ii) Perlman.

Martinon's performances are among the very best he has ever given us. His *Daphnis et Chloé* has an intoxicating atmosphere: its sense of ecstasy and Dionysian abandon are altogether captivating. The delicacy of colouring in the *Nocturne*, the naturalness with which each phrase unfolds, and the virtuosity of the Orchestre de Paris are a constant source of delight, as for that matter is the opulent and luminous recording. Even considering the outstanding new Dutoit version on Decca, this remains memorable. Like the *Daphnis*, *Ma Mère l'Oye* is exquisite, among the finest ever put on record (and again one does not forget the splendid new Previn compact disc). Some other works included here can be found in preferable versions below, notably the *Valses nobles et sentimentales* and *La Valse*, while Ciccolini's accounts of the piano concertos are acceptable but not the equal of the finest. Those not wanting the concertos might well consider the Haitink three-disc box below, but in most respects this is an outstanding set, and the recording is of EMI's finest quality, very lifelike and natural.

Alborada del gracioso; Boléro; Daphnis et Chloé: suites 1 and 2; Ma Mère l'Oye; Menuet antique; Pavane pour une infante défunte; Rapsodie espagnole; Le Tombeau de Couperin; La Valse; Valses nobles et sentimentales.
**(*) Ph. 6725 016 (3). Concg. O, Haitink.

An eminently recommendable compilation drawn from these artists' recordings made in the late 1970s. The performances are distinguished by instinctive good judgement and impeccable taste, and the orchestral playing has refinement and finish. The recordings are altogether first-class, with beautifully judged and natural perspective in the best Philips manner. The performances fall short in one respect: they fail to intoxicate and miss the heady, sensuous qualities of this music. Those wanting a collection without the concertos might well consider this, but note that the *Daphnis* comprises only the two suites, and one or two other smaller pieces included in the Martinon set are omitted.

Alborada del gracioso; Boléro; (i) *Daphnis et Chloé: Suite No. 2.*
** HMV Dig. ASD/*TCC-ASD* 4174 [Ang. DS/*4XS* 37885]. Phd. O and Ch., Muti.

Muti and the Philadelphians are at their finest in the extrovert, brilliant music of the *Danse générale* of *Daphnis* and the *Alborada*. *Daybreak*, with opening dawn music at the start of the *Daphnis suite*, is stickily sluggish, *Boléro* is slow and exaggeratedly expressive. The recording is full but not ideally spacious. The chrome cassette is vividly clear.

(i) *Alborada del gracioso;* (ii) *Boléro;* (i; iii) *Daphnis et Chloé: Suite No. 2;* (i) *La Valse.*
(M) **(*) CBS 60101/*40-* [MY/*MYT* 36714]. (i) NYPO; (ii) O Nat. de France; (iii) Schola Cantorum; Bernstein.

These are works at which Bernstein excels. He has recorded *Boléro* three times and here secures a first-class response from the French orchestra. The NYPO gives a glittering account of the *Alborada*, and *La Valse* has the expected panache. Only in the *Daphnis suite* (also superbly played, using the choral version of the score) is the ear left unsatisfied by the lack of sumptuousness in a recording which is elsewhere not without atmosphere, although brightly lit.

Alborada del gracioso; Boléro; Menuet antique; Rapsodie espagnole; Le Tombeau de Couperin.
(B) *** CfP CFP/*TC-CFP* 40375. Paris Conservatoire O, Cluytens.

In this Classics for Pleasure reissue Cluytens's highly regarded Ravel performances have been reshuffled, and this collection is exceptionally generous. Cluytens gives a brilliant account of the *Alborada*, and room has now been found for his excellent version of *Rapsodie espagnole*. In *Boléro* he maintains a consistent tempo: this is a vivid and unaffected account but in the last analysis not as exciting as some. *Le Tombeau de Couperin* is eminently stylish. With about an hour's music this is a bargain. The recording is atmospheric, and the cassette is only slightly less refined than the disc.

Alborada del gracioso; Boléro; Ma Mère l'Oye (complete ballet).
(M) ** DG Sig. 2543/*3343* 516. Boston SO, Ozawa.

Ozawa secures admirable orchestral playing here and the DG recording is first-class, with a beautifully clear matching cassette. Yet in the last resort the performances are wanting in the last degree of character. *Boléro* moves to its climax steadily in a curiously unmotivated way, while in *Ma Mère l'Oye* there is something really quite cool about the music-making that limits its appeal.

Alborada del gracioso; Boléro; Pavane pour une infante défunte; Rapsodie espagnole; La Valse.
(M) *** Mercury MRI/*SRI* 75033 [id.]. Detroit SO, Paray.

Paray's records of French music made in the early 1960s are distinguished in every respect. *Boléro* has a feeling of delicacy at the opening, yet it moves inexorably towards its expansive climax. *La Valse*, too, is impressively controlled, but it is the *Rapsodie* which is the highlight of the collection, with its languorously shimmering textures and sparkling *Feria*. It is followed by a glittering *Alborada* and a glowingly elegiac *Pavane*. The warm resonance of the Detroit hall compensates for a touch of glassiness in the upper range. The cassette is disappointing. Apart from a lack of proper documentation, the low transfer level pares down the upper range, especially on side two. The disc is excellent value.

Alborada del gracioso; Boléro; Pavane pour une infante défunte; La Valse.
(M) **(*) EMI Em. EMX/*TC-EMX* 2007 [Ang. S/*4XS* 36916]. New Philh. O, Maazel.

Maazel's are brilliant, extrovert performances of characteristic flair and intensity. The orchestral playing is first-class, the recording is spectacular, if slightly artificial, but its sharp-edged glitter is especially effective in the *Alborada del gracioso*. The *Pavane* is played very beautifully. Maazel is rhythmically mannered at the climaxes of both *La Valse* and *Boléro*. The former lacks something in refinement but the latter has plenty of panache and excitement. This is a successful issue of its kind. It was originally made in EMI's hi-fi conscious Studio Two system, and the forward balance leads to a seeming reduction of dynamic expansion in the cassette transfer of *Boléro*.

Alborada del gracioso; Boléro; Rapsodie espagnole.
(*) RCA Dig. **RCD 14438; RL 13686 [ARC1/*ARK1* 3686]. Dallas SO, Mata.

Mata has helped to build the Dallas orchestra into a splendid band, and it gives impressive performances of these virtuoso showpieces. There are more distinguished accounts of each work, but the coupling is certainly recommendable, helped by digital recording of great range. *Boléro* develops from a whisper of pianissimo at the start to a formidably loud climax, though the detailed balancing is not always consistent. The compact disc is impressive, but this cannot compare with Dutoit's even finer (and more generous) collection – see below.

Alborada del gracioso; Boléro; Rapsodie espagnole; La Valse.
C *** Decca **410 010-2**; SXDL/*KSXDC* 7559 [Lon. LDR/*5*- 71059]. Montreal SO, Dutoit.

Even if you possess alternative versions of the works on this record, you should consider this anthology, for it is a model of its kind. Not only is the playing of the Montreal orchestra under Charles Dutoit absolutely first-class and thoroughly atmospheric, but the recorded sound has a clarity, range and depth of perspective that is equally satisfying. This recording defines the state of the art and apart from the sumptuous music-making has impressive refinement and a most musically judged and natural balance. Outstanding on both LP and chrome tape, while the compact disc version has even greater immediacy and refinement of detail and texture.

Alborada del gracioso; Daphnis et Chloé: Suite No. 2; Pavane pour une infante défunte; Rapsodie espagnole; La Valse.
(M) ** Decca SPA 230. SRO, Ansermet.

Decca's collection, issued as part of 'The world of great classics' series, gives generous value. The *Daphnis suite* is not as well played or as sensuous as one might ideally ask (the latter being partly the fault of the clinical sound-balance of the recording), and the

Alborada is less vivid than with Paray. But Ansermet's coolness suits the *Pavane*, and the *Rapsodie* is quite effective. *La Valse*, always a piece Ansermet did well, is spectacular and atmospheric.

Alborada del gracioso; Pavane pour une infante défunte.

(M) *** Decca Jub. JB/*KJBC* 50 [Lon. STS 15358]. New Philh. O, Frühbeck de Burgos – FALLA: *El amor brujo;* GRANADOS: *Goyescas.****

Frühbeck de Burgos's *Alborada* is glitteringly brilliant, helped by one of Decca's best and most transparent recordings. The lovely *Pavane* is hardly less attractive, but this piece almost always seems to come off well in the recording studio. The cassette transfer is characteristically vivid and clear.

Alborada del gracioso; Rapsodie espagnole; Le Tombeau de Couperin; La Valse.

(M) *** [Ang. S/*4XS* 36939]. O de Paris, Karajan.

These are superb performances. The Orchestre de Paris responds splendidly to Karajan's sensuous approach to these scores, and only the saxophone-like quality of the french horns gives cause for complaint. The dynamic range is extremely wide and the acoustic somewhat too resonant. The atmospheric quality of these performances is not wholly free from a trace of self-consciousness, as if Karajan were admiring his own enormously subtle control of texture and colour. Still there is no doubt about the mastery of *La Valse*, which is extremely fine, or the *Rapsodie espagnole*, the best performance since Reiner's. The *Alborada* is a bit too slow (doubtless the reverberant acoustic prompted this). The cassette transfer too is very sophisticated. The resonance brings a degree of mistiness in pianissimo detail (noticeable at the opening of *La Valse*) and the upper range is marginally less refined, but the overall focus is impressive and the climaxes expand excitingly. An outstanding issue in every way. It has, unfortunately, been withdrawn in the UK.

Boléro.

(M) *** DG Acc. 2542/*3342* 116. Berlin PO, Karajan – DEBUSSY: *La Mer; Prélude.****

*** DG 139 010/*923 018* [id.]. as above – MUSSORGSKY: *Pictures.****

*** HMV ASD/*TC-ASD* 3431 [Ang. S/*4XS* 37438]. Berlin PO, Karajan – DEBUSSY: *La Mer; Prélude.***

** Decca SXL/*KSXC* 6813 [Lon. CS/*5-7033*]. Chicago SO, Solti – DEBUSSY: *La Mer; Prélude.***

(M) ** Decca Jub. JB/*KJBC* 133 [(d) Lon. CS 7132/5-]. LAPO, Mehta – R. STRAUSS: *Also sprach Zarathustra;* TCHAIKOVSKY: *Marche slave.***

Karajan's 1964 *Boléro* (also reissued here on DG Accolade) is marvellously controlled, hypnotic and gripping, with the Berlin Philharmonic at the top of its form. The sound is astonishingly good, though Karajan's re-make for EMI is even better in terms of presence. The EMI *La Mer*, however, is not so inspired as the performance with which this is coupled. Both cassettes are well managed, with only slight loss of crispness of focus at the pianissimo opening of *Boléro*.

Metrically rigorous, Solti builds up the nagging climax with superb relentlessness. Though it lacks seductive touches, the performance is beautifully poised and pointed. Brightly analytical recording, and a faithful cassette transfer giving the clearest sound of all three tapes listed here.

Mehta's performance, too, has plenty of adrenalin, though it is not subtle. It is well played and recorded, and generously coupled. The cassette transfer is robust and clear.

Boléro; (i) *Daphnis et Chloé: Suite No. 2; Menuet antique; La Valse.*

(M) *** CBS 60280/*40-*. NYPO, Boulez; (i) with Camerata Singers.

Boulez's way with Ravel achieves clarity, but never at the expense of atmosphere. Detail is beautifully observed, yet never seems coldly analytical. *Daphnis et Chloé* is particularly impressive; it has the essential ingredients, a sense of ecstasy, and an ability to transport the listener into the enchanted landscape the work inhabits. Perhaps *La Valse* is more magical in other hands (Paray's, for instance), but *Boléro* has a powerful climax and the *Menuet* makes a warmly elegant encore piece at the end. The recording is of vivid CBS vintage and there is a good chrome cassette, although here detail is less sharp at pianissimo levels (as at the very opening of *Boléro*).

Boléro; Daphnis et Chloé: Suite No. 2; Pavane pour une infante défunte.
*** HMV ASD/*TC-ASD* 3912 [Ang. SZ/*4ZS* 37670]. LSO, Previn.

Though an analogue recording, Previn's coupling of favourite Ravel pieces provides wonderfully rich, full and atmospheric sound for performances full of sparkle and flair. *Daphnis et Chloé* is sensuously beautiful (good augury for the complete recording of the ballet which Previn was scheduled to make within months), and *Boléro*, at a slow, very steady tempo rather like Karajan's, sounds splendidly relentless. The cassette quality too is outstandingly good, clear and full-bodied at the big climax of *Boléro*.

Boléro; Pavane pour une infante défunte; (i) *Daphnis et Chloé: Suite No. 2.*
*(*) Telarc Dig. **CD 80052**; DG 10052 [id.]. St Louis SO, Slatkin, (i) with Ch.

Slatkin directs capable performances of the Ravel showpieces, but they are lacking in rhythmic flair and the digital recording is, by Telarc standards, unspectacular, with a relatively limited range of dynamic.

Boléro; Daphnis et Chloé: Suite No. 2; Pavane pour une infante défunte; La Valse.
(*) DG Dig. **400 061-2; 2532/*3302* 041 [id.]. O de Paris, Barenboim.

At a slow speed *Boléro* brings fine balancing and smooth solos. The *Pavane* and *La Valse* too are both on the slow side, but the seductive phrasing makes them sound lusciously idiomatic. The *Daphnis suite* brings the most persuasive performance of all. The recorded sound is sumptuous to match, but it could have more air round it, qualities the more easily appreciable on compact disc. There is a good chrome cassette with side two sharper in focus than side one.

Boléro; Daphnis et Chloé: Suite No. 2; La Valse.
**(*) Erato STU/*MCE* 70930. Strasbourg PO, Lombard.

The acoustic here is resonant, perhaps a shade too much so for *Boléro*, but Alain Lombard builds his climax with an impressively steady increase of tension, and the orchestral soloists show individuality in the matter of colour. The orchestra is even finer in *Daphnis et Chloé*, playing with delicacy and restraint (the opening most evocative), with a superb contribution from the solo flautist. *La Valse* has splendid rhythmic vigour, and here the acoustic is exactly right: this is most exciting. The disc was originally issued at medium price for a limited period, and it is a pity the lower price was not made a permanent feature, which would have ensured that the collection remained competitive. The cassette transfer is vivid, the opening side-drum of *Boléro* is cleanly focused and the resonance does not spoil the impact of climaxes.

Boléro; Ma Mère l'Oye (ballet; complete); *La Valse.*
(M) **(*) Ph. Seq. 6527/*7311* 038 [6570/*7310* 092]. LSO, Monteux.

Monteux's complete version of *Ma Mère l'Oye* is a poetic, unforced reading, given a naturally balanced sound, though the recording is not as translucent as Paray's Mercury account. But at medium price this can be recommended on disc, even though Monteux's reading of *Boléro* has a slight quickening of tempo in the closing pages. The cassette has been remastered, and now matches the disc quite closely.

Boléro; Pavane pour une infante défunte; Le Tombeau de Couperin; La Valse.
** Ph. 9500 314/*7300 571* [id.]. Concg. O, Haitink.

Fine performances, distinguished by instinctive good judgement and taste. The orchestral playing has refinement and finish, and the engineers produce a sound to match; the perspective is truthful and the overall effect most pleasing. Yet Haitink's *La Valse* fails to enchant and captivate the listener as did Cluytens's recording, made in the early 1960s but sounding every bit as vivid as this (it was remarkable for its period); and there is not quite enough atmosphere in *Le Tombeau de Couperin*. The cassette is not as vivid as the disc.

Boléro; Pavane pour une infante défunte; La Valse.

(B) **(*) Con. CC/*CCT* 7521. RPO, Claude Monteux.

Claude Monteux, more familiar as a flautist, shows himself an able exponent of this repertoire, and the performances here are excellent, both polished and exciting. The recording has a Decca Phase Four source, and although basically well balanced it has vivid spotlighting of solos which will not be to all tastes. However, on disc this is undoubtedly excellent value at bargain price, but the cassette, with a compressed frequency and dynamic range, is not recommended.

Boléro; Rapsodie espagnole.

(M) ** Decca SPA/*KCSP* 551. SRO, Ansermet – GRANADOS: *Spanish dance*; SARASATE: *Carmen fantasy*.**

Boléro; La Valse.

(M) *** Decca Jub. JB/*KJBC* 36 [Lon. CS 6367]. SRO, Ansermet – DUKAS: *L'Apprenti sorcier*; HONEGGER: *Pacific 231*.***

Ansermet's Jubilee reissue offers outstanding performances, characteristically vivid, with excellent recording on both disc and tape and equally desirable couplings.

The SPA reissue replaces *La Valse* with a more than serviceable account of the *Rapsodie espagnole*. However, with Paray's version also available in the medium price-range (see above), this seems a much less attractive choice unless the other couplings are especially suitable. In the *Rapsodie* the upper strings sound rather smoother on tape than on disc.

Piano concerto in G.

(M) *** HMV SXLP/*TC–SXLP* 30169 [Ang. S 35567]. Michelangeli, Philh. O, Gracis – RACHMANINOV: *Concerto No. 4*.*** ❀

(M) *** CBS 60338/*40*-. Bernstein, NYPO – SHOSTAKOVICH: *Concerto No. 2*.***

*** DG Acc. 2542/*3342* 149 [139349]. Argerich, Berlin PO, Abbado – PROKOFIEV: *Concerto No. 3*.***

There are some exceptionally distinguished accounts of Ravel's *Concerto* on record, but the first choice is clear. It was daring of Michelangeli to couple this neoclassical, jazz-influenced work with the sunset-glow of Rachmaninov's No. 4. In the event he plays both with superlative brilliance which yet has great sympathy for the tender moments. He achieves exactly the right compromise between inflating the Ravel work and preventing it from seeming 'little'. The opening whipcrack could have been more biting, but the orchestra generally plays with great vigour. The recording shows the same characteristics as that of the Rachmaninov but is if anything warmer. The exquisite playing in the slow movement (surely one of the most melting of all recordings of piano and orchestra) makes up for any deficiencies of dimensional balance. The cassette has been remastered and is of the highest quality, clear, with bold piano timbre and excellent orchestral detail.

While not as brilliant pianistically as Michelangeli's incomparable interpretation, Bernstein's is a most beautiful performance, and with its equally enchanting coupling makes one of the most desirable of all records of twentieth-century concertos. It is astounding how in a modern concerto Bernstein performs the classical feat of conducting as well as playing the solo. One would never know from any lack of precision. As on the reverse the recording is well-defined; it is not new but was one of CBS's best. The cassette is clear and clean.

Argerich's half-tones and clear fingerwork give the *G major Concerto* unusual delicacy, but its urgent virility – with jazz an important element – comes over the more forcefully by contrast. Other performances may have caught the uninhibited brilliance in the finale more fearlessly, but in the first movement few other versions can match Argerich's playing. The compromise between coolness and expressiveness in the slow minuet of the middle movement is tantalizingly sensual. With fine recording and an admirable high-level cassette transfer, very close to the quality of the disc, this coupling is a first-rate recommendation.

Piano concerto in G; Piano concerto for the left hand in D.

❀ *** HMV ASD/*TC-ASD* 3845 [Ang. SZ 37730]. Collard, O Nat. de France, Maazel.

*** Decca SLX 6680 [Lon. CS/*5*- 6878]. De Larrocha, LPO, Foster – FAURÉ: *Fantaisie*.

*** Erato STU/*MCE* 70928. Queffélec, Strasbourg PO, Lombard.

(M) **(*) Ph. Seq. 6527/*7311* 209. Haas, Monte Carlo Op. O, Galliera.

(i) *Piano concerto in G; Piano concerto for the left hand. Une barque sur l'océan; L'éventail de Jeanne (Fanfare); Menuet antique.*

(*) Decca Dig. **410 230-2; SXDL/*KSXDC* 7592 [Lon. LDR/*5*- 71092]. (i) Rogé, Montreal SO, Dutoit.

Superbly vivid recording quality on HMV while Jean-Philippe Collard gives a meticulous, sparkling and refined account of the *G major Concerto* and a marvellously brilliant and poetic account of the *Left-hand Concerto*. He brings great *tendresse* to the more reflective moments and there is real delicacy of feeling throughout. Lorin Maazel gives thoroughly sympathetic support (anyone who knows his accounts of the Ravel operas will know how keenly attuned he is to this composer) and the Orchestre National play superbly. In the *Left-hand Concerto* Collard does not quite match the dash and swagger of Gavrilov's altogether dazzling account (see below), but he runs him pretty close. This is undoubtedly the best version of this coupling to have appeared for many years and will be difficult to surpass. The cassette transfer is of demonstration standard, extraordinarily vivid in projection with impressively crisp transients.

Pascal Rogé brings both delicacy and sparkle to the *G major Concerto* which he gives with his characteristic musical grace and fluency. He produces unfailing beauty of tone at every dynamic level, as indeed does Collard on HMV, who is more incisive in the outer movements. Rogé brings great poetry and tenderness to the slow movement but in the *Left-hand Concerto* he is a good deal less dynamic. There is a certain want of momentum here even though there is much to admire in the way of pianistic finesse – and charm! The Decca recording offers excellent performances of three short orchestral pieces as a makeweight which may tip the scales in its favour for some collectors.

Alicia de Larrocha too finds room for a substantial bonus, Fauré's *Fantaisie*. The performances of the two concertos are fine ones and, given Decca's first-class sound, this would seem a very good investment, if not a first choice.

Anne Queffélec should not be passed by. Her accounts of both concertos are thoughtful and imaginative. She is a thorough musician with a considerable technique and no mean sense of poetry. The excellent Strasbourg orchestra under Alain Lombard gives her admirable support, and the recording is well balanced and in a warm acoustic. It is a little too bottom-heavy to match the top recommendations. The cassette is well balanced but the resonance brings slight blurring of transients.

Werner Haas is a little strait-laced in this music, but the accompaniment adds to the authenticity of the performances, and with good recording this makes a good mid-priced recommendation of this obvious coupling. The musical impression is both refined and satisfying. Although the cassette is not transferred at the highest possible level, the sound is quite vivid and detail is good.

(i) *Piano concerto for the left hand. Pavane pour une infante défunte.*

*** HMV ASD 3571 [Ang. S/*4XS* 37486]. Gavrilov, (i) with LSO, Rattle – PROKOFIEV: *Concerto No. 1; Romeo and Juliet*.***

Gavrilov's recording of the *Left-hand Concerto* is altogether dazzling. He plays with effortless virtuosity, brilliance and, when required, great sensitivity. This is at least the equal of any of the classic accounts either on 78s or LP, and is magnificently recorded. The *Pavane* is also very distinguished; apart from the strangely impulsive closing bars, this too is beautiful playing. Gavrilov has superb dash and impeccable style.

(i) *Piano concerto in G. Pavane pour une infante défunte; Ma Mère l'Oye* (complete); *Le Tombeau de Couperin; Valses nobles et sentimentales.*
(M) **(*) HMV *TCC2-POR 154600-9*. O de Paris, Martinon; (i) with Ciccolini.

These recordings are all taken from Martinon's LP box – see above – and it is a pity that Ciccolini's version of the *Piano concerto* was included as it is in no way distinctive. The rest of the programme, however, affords much pleasure and the slightly softened focus of the transfer suits Martinon's ravishingly beautiful account of *Ma Mère l'Oye. Le Tombeau de Couperin*, too, is one of the finest versions available, the orchestral playing refined, and with plenty of bloom on the recording.

Daphnis et Chloé (ballet; complete).
C ❀ *** Decca Dig. **400 055-2**; SXDL/*KSXDC* 7526 [Lon. LDR/*5-71028*]. Montreal SO and Ch., Dutoit.
*** HMV Dig. ASD/*TCC-ASD* 4099 [Ang. S/*4XS* 37868]. LSO and Ch., Previn.
(M) *** Decca Jub. JB/*KJBC* 69 [Lon. STS 15090]. ROHCG Ch., LSO, Monteux.
(M) **(*) DG Priv. 2535/*3335* 484 [2530 563]. Boston SO, Tanglewood Fest. Ch., Ozawa.

The compact disc of the Dutoit Montreal *Daphnis et Chloé* immediately established itself as a demonstration disc *par excellence* of the new medium, bringing from the opening pianissimo a new dimension to sound recording. The sensation that a subtle veil is being withdrawn from the orchestral image persists throughout the performance which is sumptuously evocative, with Dutoit and his splendid orchestra creating the most ravishing textures. He adopts an idiomatic and flexible style, observing the minute indications of tempo change but making every slight variation sound totally spontaneous. The final *Danse générale* finds him adopting a dangerously fast tempo, but the Montreal players – combining French responsiveness with transatlantic polish – rise superbly to the challenge, with the choral punctuations at the end adding to the sense of frenzy. The digital recording is wonderfully luminous, with the chorus ideally balanced at an evocative half-distance, and the demonstration-worthy cassette matches the LP closely.

With rhythm more important than atmosphere, Previn directs a superbly vivid and very dramatic performance, an exciting alternative to the superlative Dutoit version, with equally spectacular sound on disc and chrome tape.

Monteux's version remains strongly recommendable at medium price. He conducted the first performance of *Daphnis et Chloé* in 1912, and it is a matter for gratitude that his poetic and subtly shaded reading should have been made available in such an outstanding recording. The performance was one of the finest things Monteux did for the gramophone, and the richly sensuous and atmospheric orchestral and choral sheen Decca have provided is fully worthy of such distinguished and memorable music-making. The cassette transfer is made at a relatively modest level.

Finely played and well recorded though it is, Ozawa's *Daphnis* has not the radiance or the magic of Dutoit, Monteux or Previn.

(i) *Daphnis et Chloé: Suites Nos. 1 and 2. Ma Mère l'Oye* (complete).
(M) *** Turn. [TV 34603/*CT 2131*]. Minnesota O, Skrowaczewski, (i) with St Olaf Ch.

The first *Daphnis suite* is absolutely magical in Skrowaczewski's hands, and in terms of sheer atmosphere and imaginative vitality these performances can well stand comparison with their most prestigious rivals. Though the Minnesota Orchestra is not so superlative an ensemble as the Amsterdam Concertgebouw Orchestra or the French Orchestre National, there is absolutely nothing second-rate about its playing, and the recording is beautifully balanced and wide-ranging. Skrowaczewski conveys every subtlety of texture and colour, and he shapes phrases not only with the good taste and fine musical judgement that Haitink gives us in his Philips records, but with a genuine feel for the sensuous, sumptuous qualities of these scores. His *Ma Mère l'Oye* is complete, like Monteux's and Previn's, and stands comparison with either. There are finer accounts of the second *Daphnis et Chloé suite* at full price (Karajan or Previn, for example), but this is still amazingly good. This disc is currently not available in the UK.

Daphnis et Chloé: Suite No. 2.
*** DG [138 923/*923 075*]. Berlin PO, Karajan – DEBUSSY: *La Mer*; *Prélude à l'après-midi d'un faune*.***
(M) *** Decca Jub. JB/*KJBC* 136. LSO Ch., LSO, Stokowski – DEBUSSY: *La Mer*; BERLIOZ: *Dance of the Sylphs*.***

Both these records offer vintage performances from great conductors, showing each in characteristic form. Karajan's account of the *Second Suite* is outstanding even among all others. It is one of the very best things he has ever done for the gramophone. He has the advantage of the Berlin Philharmonic Orchestra at their finest and it would be difficult to imagine better or more atmospheric playing, which is provided with a superb 1965 DG recording. The cassette transfer too is highly sophisticated. This coupling is currently not available in the UK but we hope it will soon be reissued on Signature.

Stokowski's Jubilee alternative comes from 1971, and was originally recorded using Decca's Phase Four system with impressive effect. The vivid detail, if anything, emerges more convincingly on cassette than on LP, as the tape seems to have slightly more body. Stokowski secures a glowing performance, with sumptuous playing from the LSO, but the Phase Four multi-channel technique is used to produce exactly the right disembodied, ethereal effect for the off-stage chorus. It is true that Phase Four highlights some of the woodwind bird noises excessively, but with the chorus the pervading presence is richly satisfying. Stokowski takes the choral parts from the complete ballet version of *Daphnis*, rather than the usual *Suite No. 2*. He adds a fortissimo chord at the very end, but after such an involving performance few will grudge him that.

Daphnis et Chloé: Suite No. 2; Ma Mère l'Oye: suite; Valses nobles et sentimentales.
(M) *** Mercury SRI/*MRI* 75066 [id.]. Detroit SO, Paray.

This compilation is made from two separate records recorded at the beginning of the 1960s in the flattering ambience of Detroit's Old Orchestral Hall. The sound is wonderfully luminous and rich, yet there is little loss of detail; indeed *Ma Mère l'Oye* compares favourably with Previn's much-praised compact disc version made some twenty years later. The performances are outstanding, showing Paray and his orchestra at their finest. In particular the *Valses nobles et sentimentales* is alluringly evanescent in texture and feeling. It is rhythmically free, with charismatic changes of tempo, the mood often magically gentle. The translucence of the recording gives much pleasure in itself, both here and in *Mother Goose*, beautifully played and gently evocative with its undercurrent of quiet ecstasy. Perhaps the sentience goes a shade too far in the *Daphnis suite*, yet this too is beguiling, and the *Danse générale* has no lack of energy and sparkle. It was a pity that Paray could not use a chorus, yet he achieves a ravishing effect without one. This record stands out among many distinguished issues on this remarkable label. The cassette is impressive too, losing only a little of the upper range. Detail is good. There are, however, no back-up notes about the music.

Daphnis et Chloé: Suite No. 2; Pavane pour une infante défunte.
(M) *** DG Sig. 2543/*3343* 521. Boston SO, New England Conservatory Ch., Abbado – DEBUSSY: *Nocturnes*.***

Abbado's performance of the suite is characteristically refined. His feeling for the music's atmosphere is matched by care for detail. The recording is natural yet vivid, and although the acoustic is resonant, there is no resulting inflation of tone and texture. This is a splendid coupling, and the disc is comparable with Karajan's. The chrome cassette matches the LP very closely, although the latter has fractionally more upper-range at the biggest climaxes (notably *Daybreak*), but there is little in it.

Daphnis et Chloé: Suite No. 2; La Valse.
(B) ** PRT GSGC/*ZCGC* 2011. Hallé O and Ch., Barbirolli – DEBUSSY: *La Mer.***

The Pye recording here (made in 1964) is much more immediate than on the reverse. In *Daphnis et Chloé* Sir John uses a choir as well as orchestra, and his shaping of the great yearning string tune is characteristically sensuous. Perhaps the *Danse générale* has sometimes exploded with greater abandon in a live performance, but this is still exciting. All in all, this disc represents a successful bargain. There is an excellent cassette, lively yet not lacking body.

Ma Mère l'Oye (complete ballet).
C *** Ph. Dig. **400 016-2**; 9500/*7300* 973 [id.]. Pittsburgh SO, Previn – SAINT-SAËNS: *Carnival of the Animals.****

In Previn's version of the complete *Mother Goose* ballet, played and recorded with consummate refinement, the quality of innocence shines out. The temptation for any conductor is to make the music exotically sensuous in too sophisticated a way, but Previn keeps a freshness apt for nursery music. The recording is superb, with the Philips engineers refusing to spotlight individual instruments but presenting a texture of luminous clarity. Those qualities come out the more impressively on compact disc. The chrome cassette sounds well too, but the disc versions have more refined detail.

Ma Mère l'Oye: suite.
(B) **(*) CfP CFP/*TC-CFP* 40086. SNO, Gibson – SAINT-SAËNS: *Carnival of the Animals*; BIZET: *Jeux d'enfants.****

Gibson is highly persuasive, shaping the music with obvious affection and a feeling for both the spirit and the texture of Ravel's beautiful score. The orchestral playing is excellent, the recording very good but wanting a little in atmosphere. But with its excellent couplings this is a fine bargain, equally attractive on disc or tape.

Ma Mère l'Oye: suite; Rapsodie espagnole.
*** DG 2531/*3301* 264 [id.]. LAPO, Giulini – DEBUSSY: *La Mer.****

The Giulini Los Angeles performance conveys much of the sultry atmosphere of the *Rapsodie espagnole*. Indeed some details, such as the sensuous string responses to the cor anglais tune in the *Feria*, have not been so tenderly caressed since the intoxicating Reiner version of the early 1960s. The *Ma Mère l'Oye suite* is beautifully done too, though it is not superior to Giulini's Philharmonia version; no one would guess that the recordings were separated by twenty years. The cassette transfer is disappointing, not matching the LP in range or detail.

Pavane pour une infante défunte; Le Tombeau de Couperin; (i) *Introduction and allegro for harp, flute, clarinet and strings.*
(M) *** RCA GL/*GK* 25451 [ARL1/*ARK1* 2783]. Nat. PO, Gerhardt, (i) with Watkins, Bennett, Kelly – FAURÉ: *Pavane*; SATIE: *Gymnopédies Nos. 1 and 3.****

Gerhardt secures performances of distinction from a first-class group of players. William Bennett (flute) and Tom Kelly (clarinet) make memorable contributions, and David Watkins's harp playing shows a wonderful feeling for atmosphere in the *Introduction and allegro*. *Le Tombeau de Couperin* is paced with great skill and in the first movement the lyrical flexibility of the oboist (David Theodore) is as impressive as is James Brown's horn solo in the *Pavane*. The recording is most naturally balanced and is equally enjoyable on disc and the excellent cassette. The couplings are no less recommendable and this is one of the most enticing available collections of twentieth-century French music.

Rapsodie espagnole.
*** HMV Dig. ASD/*TCC-ASD* 3902 [Ang. DS/*4XS* 37742]. Phd. O, Muti – CHABRIER: *España*; FALLA: *Three-cornered Hat.****
(M) ** DG Sig. 410 844-1/*4*. Boston SO, Ozawa – FALLA: *Three-cornered Hat.****

Muti directs a performance which is aptly refined in its textures and also strikingly vigorous in the sharp definition of the dance rhythms. The work here sounds more like Spanish music than French, so is well matched with the other items on the disc. The digital recording in the reverberant Philadelphia acoustic is first-rate, and the chrome cassette is excitingly vivid.

Ozawa's *Rapsodie* is superbly played but rather under-characterized, though it is excitingly recorded: the sound has plenty of glitter on disc and chrome tape alike. The *Feria* is especially vivid.

Le Tombeau de Couperin.
** Decca Dig. **400 051-2**; SXDL/*KSXDC* 7520 [Lon. LDR/*5*- 10040]. Chicago SO, Solti – MUSSORGSKY: *Pictures.****

Recorded with very different microphone placing from the main Mussorgsky work on the disc, *Le Tombeau de Couperin* in Solti's reading sounds hard and brilliant rather than classically elegant. The recording is partly to blame, with close-up sound reducing the sense of ambience (on both compact disc and LP). Nonetheless it makes an original coupling for the Ravel arrangement of Mussorgsky. The cassette transfer is softer-edged than the disc and the effect more atmospheric; many will prefer it.

Tzigane (for violin and orchestra).
*** Decca SXL/*KSXC* 6851 [Lon. CS/*5-7073*]. Kyung-Wha Chung, RPO, Dutoit – CHAUSSON: *Poème*; SAINT-SAËNS: *Havanaise* etc.***
*** HMV ASD 3125 [Ang. S/*4XS* 37118]. Perlman, O de Paris, Martinon – CHAUSSON: *Poème*; SAINT-SAËNS: *Havanaise*; *Introduction and rondo.****

With its seemingly improvisatory solo introduction, *Tzigane* is a work which demands an inspirational artist, and Kyung-Wha Chung is ideally cast, coupling this elusive piece with other concertante works too often neglected. Accompaniments and recordings are both excellent; the cassette needs a slight smoothing of the treble to sound its best.

Perlman's version of the *Tzigane* is also included in Martinon's five-disc anthology (see above). It is marvellously played and recorded, and this issue with its attractive couplings is also a winner.

La Valse.
(*) DG Dig. **410 033-2; 2532/*3302* 057 [id.]. LSO, Abbado – MUSSORGSKY: *Pictures.****

Though detail is not so needle-sharp for this Ravel fill-up as for the Mussorgsky–Ravel *Pictures* with which it is coupled, Abbado directs a fluent and incisive account, not quite ideally idiomatic and lilting in its dance rhythms, but with a thrilling surge of adrenalin in its closing pages. The digital recording is outstanding on LP and chrome tape alike, with the palm going to the compact disc, one of DG's best. The recording, however, has a shade too much resonance to be ideal, and this is even more obvious on the CD.

CHAMBER MUSIC

Introduction and allegro for harp, flute, clarinet and string quartet (see also above under *Pavane pour une infante défunte*).
(M) *** O-L SOL 60048. Melos Ens. – ROUSSEL: *Serenade* etc.***
(M) *** HMV Green. ESD/*TC-ESD* 102021-1/*4*. Melos, Ens. – FRANÇAIX: *Divertissements* **(*); POULENC: *Trio.* ***
** Chan. ABR/*ABT* 1060. Members of Sydney SO, Otterloo – DEBUSSY: *Danses***; MARTIN: *Petite symphonie.***(*)

(i) *Introduction and allegro. Ma Mère l'Oye: Pavane of the Sleeping Beauty; Laideronnette; Empress of the Pagodas* (arr. for harp).
(*) HMV ASD/*TC-ASD* 186673-1/*4* [Ang. DS/*4XS* 37339]. Nancy Allen (i) with Wilson, Shifrin, Tokyo Qt – DEBUSSY: *Danses sacrée* etc.

The beauty and subtlety of Ravel's sublime septet are marvellously realized by the earlier Melos account on Oiseau-Lyre, coupled to Roussel's almost equally delightful *Serenade* and music by Guy-Ropartz. The interpretation has great delicacy of feeling and is finely recorded. This is one of the most rewarding concerts of French music in the catalogue. The later HMV Melos Ensemble's account is also first-class, and the couplings are equally attractive. The cassette is in the demonstration class.

Nancy Allen and members of the Tokyo Quartet with David Shifrin and Ransom Wilson give a fine performance of the *Introduction and allegro*, very clearly recorded. It does not supersede the rival versions and certainly not the Melos, which brings great magic to this score, but it is very well done. The couplings diminish the attraction of this disc – basically a personality record centred on Nancy Allen, and one cannot imagine many collectors wanting these transcriptions. It would have been sensible for this accomplished artist to have concentrated on the not inconsiderable literature for the instrument by other French composers. There is an excellent cassette.

In the case of the Chandos account with members of the Sydney Symphony Orchestra, choice will be determined by the interest of the coupling. It is well played and recorded though it does not fully convey the ethereal quality of this music, perhaps because of the rather larger-than-life sound. Not a first choice but far from unacceptable. The cassette is smooth and well-balanced.

Piano trio in A min.

** HMV ASD 3729. De la Pau, Yan-Pascal and Paul Tortelier – SAINT-SAËNS: *Piano trio.****

Piano trio; Violin sonata in G; Violin sonata (1897).

*** EMI 2C 069 73024. Collard, Dumay, Lodéon.

(i) *Piano trio;* (ii) *Violin sonata in G; Tzigane.*

(M) **(*) Ph. 6570/*7310* 923 [6570/*7310* 177]. (i) Beaux Arts Trio; (ii) Grumiaux, Hajdu.

The three young French musicians, Augustin Dumay, Frédéric Lodéon and Jean-Philippe Collard, give as convincing an account of the *Trio* as any of their rivals. They are eminently well recorded, though perhaps not as vividly as the Tortelier group. The particular attraction of this performance is its combination of strength and repose, brilliance and *tendresse*. The value of the issue is enhanced by its couplings: a good account of the *Violin sonata* written in the mid-1920s along with the only recording of an early sonata in one movement dating from 1897. Though this is far from distinctive Ravel, it is nonetheless fastidiously crafted, elegant and poised. Dumay plays it and the *Sonata in G* excellently and is most sensitively partnered by Collard: a useful alternative to the Grumiaux version of the *G major Sonata*, though not perhaps as aristocratic.

The Beaux Arts give a predictably fine account of the *Trio*, and even though the recording is not of the most recent provenance – it dates from the 1960s – the sound is extremely good and the price a strong advantage. The only slight criticism would be an occasional want of charm on the part of Daniel Guilet, but that is a very small reservation. In the *Violin sonata in G*, Grumiaux's playing has great finesse and beauty of sound, and the recording is very natural too. The fill-up is the popular *Tzigane*, where both Grumiaux and his partner, István Hajdu, display appropriate panache. The cassette transfers are refined but are made at an unadventurously low level. Nevertheless the sound is naturally balanced and clean, lacking only the last ounce of immediacy. The disc sounds remarkably fresh.

Tortelier *père et fils* and Maria de la Pau enjoy the advantage of the most vivid recorded sound; the upper end of the piano is particularly clean and lifelike, and there is real presence here. It is a vital and thoroughly enjoyable performance (and has the advantage of an enterprising coupling) even if it does not displace earlier rivals. Maria de la Pau is an intelligent and agile pianist, but the softest dynamics do not always register, and, though too much should not be made of this small point, at the end of the first movement there is a lack of magic and sense of repose.

String quartet in F.

❀ *** DG 2531/*3301* 203 [id.]. Melos Qt – DEBUSSY: *Quartet.**** ❀

*** Ph. LY 835 361 [id.]. Italian Qt – DEBUSSY: *Quartet.****

(M) *** EMI Em. Dig. EMX/*TC-EMX* 41 2048-1/*4*. Chilingirian Qt – DEBUSSY: *Quartet.****

** Ph. Dig. **411 050-2**; 6514/*7337* 387 [id.]. Orlando Qt – DEBUSSY: *Quartet.**

For many years the Italian Quartet held pride of place in this coupling. Their playing is perfect in ensemble, attack and beauty of tone and their performance remains highly recommendable, one of the most satisfying chamber-music records in the catalogue. Yet the new Melos account is even finer, and this group brings artistry of the very highest order to this magical score. Their slow movement offers the most refined and integrated quartet sound; in terms of internal balance and blend it would be difficult to surpass it, and the reading has great poetry. In both the scherzo and finale the Melos players evince the highest virtuosity, and there is not the slightest trace of the prosaic phrasing that marred their Mozart *D minor Quartet*, K.421. They also have the advantage of superbly truthful recording. Highly imaginative playing touched with a complete identification with Ravel's sensibility. The cassette matches the disc closely, though there is a touch of fierceness in the treble which needs softening with the controls.

The Chilingirian recording has plenty of body and presence, and has the benefit of a warm acoustic. The players give a thoroughly committed account with well-judged tempi and very musical phrasing. The scherzo is vital and spirited, and there is no want of poetry in the slow movement. The Melos Quartet of Stuttgart undoubtedly bring a greater sense of magic to the slow movement and still remain unsurpassed. However, some collectors may be deterred by the extra outlay, and for them the Chilingirian can be strongly recommended.

The Orlando Quartet are wonderfully passionate and possess glorious tone and ensemble. They press the Ravel to greater expressive extremes than do the Melos Quartet of Stuttgart, and though they play with superb artistry and feeling, some will find the greater restraint of the Melos more telling, particularly in the slow movement. There is a sudden lurch in pitch in this movement due to ugly editing, though it is not quite so ruinous as is the case in the Debussy on the reverse side. There is an excellent cassette. However, the Melos and Quartetto Italiano remain unsurpassed.

PIANO MUSIC

À la manière de Borodin; À la manière de Chabrier. (i; ii) *Frontispiece. Gaspard de la Nuit; Jeux d'eau; Menuet antique; Menuet sur le nom de Haydn.* (i) *Ma Mère l'Oye. Miroirs; Pavane pour une infante défunte; Prélude; Sérénade grotesque.* (i) *Sites auriculaires. Sonatine; Le Tombeau de Couperin.* (i) *La Valse. Valses nobles et sentimentales.*
*** EMI 2C 167 73025/7. Collard, with (i) Béroff, (ii) Labèque.

Jean-Philippe Collard has already recorded outstanding performances of the Ravel concertos. His survey of the piano music is hardly less distinguished and is touched with much the same sensitivity. The three records include a version of *La Valse* for two pianos (with Michel Béroff) and the *Sites auriculaires*, which are not included in Pascal Rogé's survey. Collard has a strong sense of line and a keen rhythmic backbone. His *Valses nobles et sentimentales* are splendidly crisp, and his playing in *Gaspard de la Nuit* is finely characterized. He is recorded in a less flattering acoustic than was Rogé, whose set has great sensitivity and a sophisticated sense of keyboard colour. Put his *Le gibet* alongside Collard's, and the comparison is to his advantage which was not the case in the concert hall! Collard has undoubted style, however, and his set can be strongly recommended. The earlier editions of the *Penguin Stereo Record Guide* underrated the Rogé set: repeated hearing has revealed its strengths. Collard can be recommended alongside it, for he has a tautness and rhythmic strength that are appealing, as well as a fine sense of texture and tenderness.

À la manière de Borodin; À la manière de Chabrier; Prélude; Le Tombeau de Couperin; Valses nobles et sentimentales.
** Nimbus 2103. Perlemuter.

Gaspard de la Nuit; Jeux d'eau; Menuet antique; Pavane.
** Nimbus 2101. Perlemuter.

Menuet sur le nom de Haydn; Miroirs; Sonatine.
** Nimbus 2102. Perlemuter.

As a pupil of Ravel, Vlado Perlemuter enjoys some authority, but it would be idle to suggest that this survey, recorded in his seventies, is an unqualified success. The piano is somewhat distantly balanced and the resulting textures, though lifelike, could be cleaner and more strongly defined. The playing is natural enough and free from idiosyncrasy, but there is little real magic now. In recent years Perlemuter has become something of a vogue pianist in certain circles, but this set left a feeling of disappointment.

Gaspard de la Nuit.
❀ *** DG Dig. **413. 363-2**; 2532/*3302* 093 [id.]. Pogorelich – PROKOFIEV: *Sonata No. 6.**** ❀
*** Decca SXL 6215 [Lon. CS 6472]. Ashkenazy (with Recital ***).
*** HMV Dig. ASD/*TCC-ASD* 4281. Ousset – MUSSORGSKY: *Pictures.***(*)

Pogorelich's *Gaspard* is out of the ordinary. In *Le gibet*, there is the self-conscious striving after effect that mars his Schumann *Études symphoniques* and attention soon wanders from the ends to the means. We are made conscious of the pianist's refinement of tone and colour first, and Ravel's poetic vision afterwards. But for all that, this is piano playing of astonishing quality and, despite the touches of narcissism, this is a performance to relish. His control of colour and nuance in *Scarbo* is dazzling and its eruptive cascades of energy and dramatic fire have one sitting on the edge of one's seat. (Cécile Ousset's account is pretty incandescent, but sounds far less controlled than this DG version.) The coupling, Prokofiev's *Sixth Sonata*, is quite simply stunning.

Ashkenazy's account was recorded in 1966 and is part of a recital which includes music by Chopin and Debussy (see below in our Recitals section). The performance was the finest to be put on record since Gieseking's 78s and, with excellent recording, remains a distinguished alternative to Pogorelich.

Cécile Ousset's version of *Gaspard* was greeted with much acclaim on its first appearance and is very fine indeed. Her *Scarbo* is particularly dazzling with all the electricity of a live concert performance, even if by comparison with Pogorelich she sounds uncontrolled. She is better recorded than Jean-Philippe Collard, though he is the more poetic artist; but she does not displace him or Martha Argerich on DG – see below – nor Ashkenazy's Decca version from the mid-1960s. The HMV chrome cassette is of the highest quality, matching the disc very closely.

Gaspard de la Nuit; Sonatine; Valses nobles et sentimentales.
(M) *** DG Acc. 2542/*3342* 163 [2530 540]. Argerich.

Whatever one may think of her, Argerich has a strong artistic personality as well as very considerable virtuosity. Her *Gaspard de la Nuit* abounds in character and colour, even if certain touches may disturb the perspective. Her *Valses nobles* are most atmospheric and sensitive. These are telling performances, not likely to appeal to all tastes, but well worth hearing. The cassette is first-class, the piano timbre pellucid and clear.

Gaspard de la Nuit; Le Tombeau de Couperin.
(M) * HM HM/*40* 924. Helffer.

Claude Helffer is much admired as an interpreter of twentieth-century music, but *Gaspard de la Nuit* finds him in less than his most inspired form. Indeed, this is distinctly routine and *Le Tombeau de Couperin* hardly shows him at his best. There are finer accounts in the catalogue. On tape the quality is rather opaque with some excessive resonance in the bass.

La Valse.
*** Ph. Dig. **411 034-2**; 6514/*7337* 369 [id.]. Argerich, Freire – LUTOSLAWSKI: *Paganini variations*; RACHMANINOV: *Suite No. 2.****

The transcription is Ravel's own and was first heard in this form played by the composer himself and Alfredo Casella in Vienna in 1920. Indeed the first idea of such a work came as early as 1906. Though it is available in the complete Ravel set played by Jean-Philippe Collard (with Béroff as second pianist), this one is the only single issue of it. Brilliant, atmospheric playing and good recording.

VOCAL MUSIC

(i) *Chansons madécasses.* (ii) *Cinq Mélodies populaires grecques: Le réveil de la mariée; Tout gai!* (only); *Deux Mélodies hébraïques; Shéhérazade* (song cycle).
*** CBS 36665/*40*- [Col. IM/*HMT* 36665]. Von Stade, with (i) Dwyer, Eskind, Katz, (ii) Boston SO, Ozawa.

The distinctive timbre of Frederica von Stade's voice and her yearning expressiveness make for sensuous performances not just of *Shéhérazade* – here as evocatively beautiful as it has ever been on disc – but also of the often strikingly original songs which make up the apt coupling. In these, Ravel was writing unpredictably, and they need persuasive handling, which Ozawa and the Boston forces richly provide too. The digital recording is not of the most brilliant but is admirably atmospheric.

Shéhérazade (song cycle).
*** HMV ASD 2444 [Ang. S 36505]. Baker, New Philh. O, Barbirolli – BERLIOZ: *Nuits d'été*.***
C *** Ph. Dig. **410 043-2**; 6514/*7337* 199 [id.]. Ameling, San Francisco SO, De Waart – DEBUSSY: *La damoiselle élue*; DUPARC: *Songs*.*** C
(M) *** Decca Jub. JB/*KJBC* 15 [Lon. OS/*5*-25821]. Crespin, SRO, Ansermet – BERLIOZ: *Nuits d'été*.***
(*) Ph. 9500 783/*7300 857* [id.]. Norman, LSO, Sir Colin Davis – BERLIOZ: *Nuits d'été*.(*)

Janet Baker inspired Barbirolli to one of his most glowing performances in this atmospherically scored music. As in the Berlioz cycle on the reverse – given a peerless performance – Baker's range of tone and her natural sympathy for the French language make for heartwarming singing. Few records convey such natural intensity as this, and the recording is warm to match.

Elly Ameling has a voice of innocence, pure of tone. Yet when she sings Gershwin for example, she can colour it sensuously, and so it is here in Ravel's evocative song-cycle. Other versions may delve deeper into the exotic emotions behind the poems by 'Tristan Klingsor', but in its sweetness and beauty (enhanced by the orchestral playing and radiant recording) this has a place too, particularly when the coupling is apt and unusual. On the superb compact disc the effect is ravishing, the voice seemingly floating against a wonderfully luminous orchestral backcloth. Compact disc collectors may feel that this even takes precedence over the classic Baker version. There is also a good chrome cassette.

Crespin too finds a special sympathy for Ravel's magically sensuous writing, and she is superbly supported by Ansermet. As in the Berlioz coupling her style has distinct echoes of the opera house, but the sheer richness of the singer's tone does not prevent this fine artist from being able to achieve the delicate languor demanded by an exquisite song like *The enchanted flute*. Indeed her operatic sense of drama brings almost a sense of self-identification to the listener as the slave-girl sings to the distant sound of her lover's flute (while her master sleeps). The warm sheen of the glorious Decca recording spins a tonal web around the listener which is quite irresistible. Reissued at medium price, this is outstandingly attractive, and there is a fine tape version too.

Jessye Norman seems more at home in Ravel's song cycle than in the coupled account of the Berlioz, although she and Sir Colin Davis are languorous to the point of lethargy in *L'indifférent*. With the voice very forward, the balance is less than ideal, though otherwise the sound is rich and atmospheric. Ameling, Baker and Crespin, however, each have special qualities to offer which Miss Norman does not match. The Philips tape transfer is faithful, but made at a rather low level.

L'Enfant et les sortilèges.
*** HMV Dig. ASD/*TCC-ASD* 4167 [Ang. DS/*4XS* 37869]. Wyner, Auger, Berbié, Langridge, Bastin, Amb. S., LSO, Previn.
(M) **(*) Decca Ace SDD 168. Wend, Danco, Cuénod, Mollet, Geneva Motet Ch., SRO, Ansermet.

(i) *L'Enfant et les sortilèges;* (ii) *L'Heure espagnole* (operas; complete).
(M) **(*) DG Priv. 2726 076 (2). (i) Ogéas, Collard, Berbié, Gilma, RTF Ch. and O;

(ii) Berbié, Sénéchal, Giraudeau, Bacquier, Van Dam, Paris Op. O; cond. Maazel.

Given digital sound of demonstration quality (on both disc and tape), Previn's dramatic and highly spontaneous reading of *L'Enfant* brings out the refreshing charm of a neglected masterpiece. Helped by a strong, stylish team of soloists, this makes superb entertainment.

Maazel's recordings of the two Ravel one-Act operas were made in the early 1960s (*L'Enfant* in 1961, *L'Heure espagnole* four years later), and though the solo voices in the former are balanced too close, the sound is vivid and the performances are splendidly stylish. Neoclassical crispness of articulation goes with refined textures that convey the tender poetry of the one piece, the ripe humour of the other.

Incredibly, Ansermet's vintage account dates from 1955, though one would hardly guess from the lively stereo effects. This is generally a performance of high quality, with Hugues Cuénod, Pierre Mollet and Suzanne Danco all making distinguished contributions. The performance of Flore Wend in the central character of the Child is not ideally characterized, but Ansermet's direction shows this conductor at his most imaginative, achieving glittering colouristic effects from the orchestra and a wonderfully relaxed tension over the performance as a whole. The recording is not always too well balanced, but this is partly the conductor's fault: the biting comments of the orchestra are sometimes over-enthusiastic, to the detriment of the singers. However, admirers of Ansermet will still find this one of his most vivid discs: the *Cats' duet* on side two is memorable.

'The world of Ravel': (i) *Boléro;* (ii; iii; iv) *Piano concerto in G:* Finale; (iii; iv; v) *Daphnis et Chloé: Daybreak;* (iii; iv)*'Pavane pour une infante défunte; Rapsodie espagnole: Habanera;* (i) *La Valse;* (vi) *Introduction and allegro for harp, flute, clarinet and string quartet;* (vii; i) *Shéhérazade: La flûte enchantée.*

(M) **(*) Decca SPA 392. (i) SRO, Ansermet; (ii) Katchen; (iii) LSO; (iv) Monteux; (v) ROHCG Ch.; (vi) Melos Ens.; (vii) Crespin.

This ingenious Ravel anthology, cunningly assembled by Ray Crick, has two small drawbacks. It begins, understandably, with Monteux's gorgeous opening to *Daphnis et Chloé*, but because this is taken from a complete set and not a suite, it has to be faded. Also there is a slight miscalculation in including Katchen's brilliant account of the *Piano concerto* finale at the end of side one, immediately following the wonderful sense of stillness of the closing bars of the *Introduction and allegro*. Although the idea of complete contrast is good in theory, in practice this jars on the listener's sensibility. Having said that, one must add that the collection is a marvellous bargain, including as it does Ansermet's two best Ravel performances, *Boléro* and *La Valse*, Monteux's beautiful *Pavane*, the incomparable Melos account of the *Introduction and allegro*, and a reminder of Crespin's dramatic account of the song cycle *Shéhérazade*. The sound is of the highest class, although the end of *Boléro* (which comes at the close of a long side) is perhaps not quite as clean here as on some other discs (it is used on several).

Rawsthorne, Alan (1905–71)

Clarinet concerto.

*** Hyp. A 66031. King, N.W. CO of Seattle, Francis – COOKE: *Concerto*; JACOB: *Mini concerto.****

Though the *Clarinet concerto* is an early work of Rawsthorne's, it already establishes the authentic flavour of his writing with a certain gritty and angular quality masking the obvious depth of feeling behind. You feel he is about to unleash himself into a grand Waltonian melody, but he never actually does. That constraint yet makes for musical strength, the more obviously so in a performance as persuasive as this from soloist and orchestra alike. And even Rawsthorne relaxes in the brilliant finale. Excellent recording.

Divertimento for chamber orchestra.
*** Lyr. SRCS 111. ECO, Del Mar – BERKELEY and BRITTEN: *Sinfoniettas*; TIPPETT: *Divertimento.****

Brief as Rawsthorne's *Divertimento* is, its spare textures and bony argument give it genuine seriousness, most attractively in the songfulness of the central lullaby movement. A work that would usually get lost on LP here comes in an ideal coupling, splendidly performed and recorded.

Symphony No. 1; Symphonic studies.
*** Lyr. SRCS 90. LPO, Pritchard.

This is the first stereo recording of Rawsthorne's pre-war *Symphonic studies*, by general consent his most original and masterly composition, which well withstands the test of time. So, too, does the *Symphony No. 1* (1950), which is a much neglected piece – unjustly so. It is distinguished by impeccable craftsmanship and first-rate invention. The LPO under John Pritchard plays with evident enjoyment, and the recording has a fine sense of space and splendid detail. This is an outstanding issue in every way.

Street Corner: overture.
*** Lyr. SRCS 95. LPO, Pritchard – *Concert* (*Overtures*).***

The *Street Corner overture* is one of Rawsthorne's more familiar short pieces. The performance here is first-class and the recording excellent. It is part of a highly recommendable anthology discussed in the Concerts section below.

Rebel, Jean-Féry (1661–1747)

Les Éléments (ballet).
*** O-L DSLO 562 [id.]. AcAM, Hogwood – DESTOUCHES: *Suite.****

Rebel, a contemporary of Bach and Handel, was in his seventies when he wrote his ballet on the elements emerging out of Chaos, startling even twentieth-century listeners with the massive discord illustrating Chaos at the start. The sequence of dances, beautifully performed on original instruments by Hogwood's Academy, is consistently sharp and refreshing, helping to revive an undeservedly neglected name.

Reger, Max (1873–1916)

Variations and fugue on a theme by Telemann, Op. 134.
*** Decca SXL 6969 [Lon. CS 7197]. Bolet – BRAHMS: *Handel variations.****

Reger's *Telemann variations*, his last major work for solo piano, make a challenging and compelling coupling for Bolet's superb account of Brahms's Handel set. The virtuosity is phenomenal, not least in the fugue at the end which was once counted to be unplayable. Bolet breasts all difficulties with commanding strength. Anyone who generally finds Reger a dull, academic composer should hear this and discover how brightly imaginative he can be. First-rate recording.

Benedictus, Op. 59/2; Fantasia on a chorale 'Halleluja! Gott zu loben, bleib meine Seelenfreud', Op. 52/3; Fantasia and fugue on B.A.C.H., Op. 46; Toccata and fugue in D min./major, Op. 59/5–6.
*** Mer. E 77004. Sanger (organ of St Jude-on-the-Hill, London).

Reger, one of the most Germanic of composers, requires persuasive handling if he is not to sound lumpy and heavy, and that particularly applies to the organ music. David Sanger, using a moderate-sized, clean-textured instrument of fine quality, does wonders with these heavyweight works. With fine recorded sound this can be recommended to others besides organ enthusiasts.

Reich, Steve (born 1936)

Six Pianos; (i) *Music for mallet instruments, voices and organ.*
(M) (***) DG Priv. 2535/*3335* 463 [id.]. Chambers, Preiss, Hartenberger, Becker, Reich, Velez, with (i) Ferchen, Harms, Jarrett, LaBarbara, Clayton.

This disc might be entitled 'Stuck in a groove'. Both pieces exploit Reich's technique of endlessly repeating a very brief fragment which gradually gets transformed, almost imperceptibly, by different emphases being given to it. The result is mesmeric, though of very limited expressive value. No doubt the drug culture provides parallels. *Six Pianos* is the longer piece (no less than twenty-four minutes) and by its very texture more aggressive. With gentler marimbas the other side is far less wearing. The 1974 recording is by all reckonings faithful, though not as weighty as it might be. The cassette matches the disc closely. Frankly, this is music that some listeners will not be able to take seriously.

Reinecke, Carl (1824–1910)

(i) *Flute concerto in D, Op. 283;* (ii) *Flute sonata* (*Undine*), *Op. 167.*
**(*) RCA RL/*RK* 14034 [ATC1/*ATK1* 4034]. Galway, (i) LPO, Iwaki; (ii) Moll.

As can be seen from the opus number of the *Concerto*, Reinecke was a prolific composer (in all genres); he was also pianist, fiddler and teacher, and at one time conductor of the Leipzig Gewandhaus Orchestra. He has undoubted facility and some of the invention here is quite striking (as in the first movement of the *Sonata*). His writing, which has sudden florid bursts, makes an engaging vehicle for an artist of Galway's calibre, who is especially good in the finale of the Weberian *Concerto*. The drawback is that movements, though well wrought, tend to be a trifle long for the assembled ideas to sustain. Nevertheless Galway's advocacy is persuasive and the recording is bright and clear, though not glowing.

Respighi, Ottorino (1879–1936)

Ancient airs and dances: Suites Nos. 1–3.
(M) ❀ *** Mercury SRI/*MRI* 75009. Philh. Hungarica, Dorati.
*** Decca SXL 6846. LPO, Lopez-Cobos.

Dorati's famous and very distinguished Mercury recording of the 1960s has been in and out of the British catalogue over the years and now returns as an import, pressed in Holland, but using the original masters. The performance, one of the first recordings by this group of Hungarian expatriates based in Vienna, is of the utmost distinction. It combines brilliance with great sensitivity – the delicacy of articulation of the principal oboe is a special delight – to display a remarkable feeling for the colour and ambience of the Renaissance dances on which Respighi's three suites (the last for strings alone) are based. The refinement and warmth of the playing (and the sound) are very striking, particularly in the *Third Suite*, where the string textures are very beautiful. Dorati finds in this music a nobility and graciousness that make it obstinately memorable. Marriner's fresh and sunny account with the Los Angeles Chamber Orchestra is perhaps even more beautifully recorded (see below), but Dorati's version has very special claims on the collector, quite irrespective of its lower price. The cassette is first-class.

The Decca version by the LPO under Lopez-Cobos, however, is by no means an also-ran. It is superbly recorded, and the Kingsway Hall acoustic, with its characteristic warmth, gives the orchestra an enticing bloom. The Decca cassette matches the disc closely. The performance is not as elegant as Marriner's but it has striking intensity. The third movement of the *Second Suite* and the central movements of the *Third* demonstrate this readily. The LPO strings produce playing of considerable fervour, and there is plenty of sparkle in the lighter sections throughout.

(i) *Ancient airs and dances: Suites Nos. 1–3;* (ii) *The Birds; 3 Botticelli pictures.*
(M) *** HMV *TCC2-POR 54276.* (i) LA CO; (ii) ASMF, Marriner.

An admirable compilation chosen to represent Neville Marriner in HMV's 'Portrait of the Artist' double-length tape series. The account of the suite of dances is attractively light and gracious, offering an almost French elegance with attractively transparent textures. The performances of *The Birds* and the *Trittico Botticelliano* are no less delightful and beautifully recorded. The score for the *Botticelli pictures* is less well known and understandably so, for its inspiration is less assured but, with presentation of this standard, the music is certainly enjoyable. The chrome-tape transfer is of high quality, with the sound fresh and pleasing; *The Birds* and the *Botticelliano* are notably warm and refined, yet there is excellent detail.

The Birds (suite); *Brazilian impressions.*
(M) *** Mercury SRI 75023 [id.]. LSO, Dorati.

Respighi wrote his *Brazilian impressions* after spending a summer in Rio de Janeiro in 1927. The music is colourful and atmospheric and the triptych obviously recalls Debussy's *Ibéria.* The second impression sinisterly invokes the *Dies irae*, for it is named after Butantan, famous for its reptile institute where poisonous snakes are bred in vast numbers for the production of serum. Respighi's finale, *Canzone e danza*, does not match Debussy's festive morning scene, but is still highly evocative. Dorati's performance is vividly characterized, and it is coupled to a spirited account of *The Birds*, with its dance rhythms strongly projected and its pictorial piquancy well realized by the excellent LSO wind playing. The recording (from the beginning of the 1960s) is more forwardly balanced and makes a stronger impact than Kertesz's Decca version of *The Birds*, yet it has plenty of ambient warmth and does not sound dated. Recommended.

The Birds; The Fountains of Rome; The Pines of Rome (symphonic poems).
(M) *** Decca Jub. JB/*KJBC* 59. LSO, Kertesz.
(*) Ph. Dig. **411 419-2; 6514/*7337* 202 [id.]. San Francisco SO, De Waart.

The special attraction of Kertesz's disc is the inclusion of *The Birds*, an evocative and beautifully scored work, given a first-class performance and rich recording. In the two symphonic poems Kertesz is again at his finest. These are strongly characterized and deeply musical performances; the elements of spectacle (the turning on of the Triton fountain) and grandeur (the Trevi climax, with its evocation of Neptune's heavenly processional, are balanced by a magical sense of atmosphere in the central movements of *The Pines*, although in the finale of this work other performances find more excitement. The Decca engineers provide outstanding sound quality, the cassette matching the disc and handling the climaxes with aplomb. At medium price this is outstanding value.

De Waart conducts brilliant and sympathetic performances, but an unreal brilliance in the recording with unrealistic placing of instruments is underlined on the finest reproducers, not least in the compact disc version.

3 Botticelli pictures; (i) *Deità silvane;* (i; ii) *Lauda per la Natività del Signore.*
*** Argo ZRG 904 [id.]. L. Chamber Ch., Argo CO, Heltay, with (i) Tear, (ii) Gomez, Dickinson.

Here is a totally different side to Respighi from the familiar lush opulence of the Roman trilogy. This music is fastidiously scored for small forces, and the effect is of refinement and great skill in the handling of pastel colourings. The most familiar is the *Three*

Botticelli pictures (1927), a delicate and affecting piece well played by these artists, and already available on record. The two rarities are no less appealing. The *Lauda per la Natività del Signore* (1929) is a setting of words attributed to Jacopone da Todi, a Franciscan of the thirteenth century, and is ingeniously scored for two flutes, piccolo, oboe, cor anglais, two bassoons, piano (four hands) and triangle, while the voices are wonderfully handled. The *Deità silvane* (1917) was originally for soprano and piano but the composer scored it in 1926 for single wind, horn, percussion, harp and strings – to great effect. An enterprising and rewarding issue which reflects credit on all concerned and has the benefit of excellent sound too.

Brazilian impressions; Church windows (Vetrate di chiesa).
*** Chan. Dig. **CHAN 8317**; ABRD/*ABTD* 1098 [id.]. Philh. O, Simon.

Respighi's set of musical illustrations of church windows is not among his finest works (the second stained-glass portrait, representing St Michael, is the most memorable, with its extrovert colouring), but is well worth having when the recording is impressively spacious and colourful. Geoffrey Simon is sympathetic and he secures fine playing from the Philharmonia, though Dorati's version of the *Brazilian impressions* is not eclipsed. The spectacular digital recording and the useful coupling (which avoids duplication with Respighi's more famous works) will be an added incentive to collectors.

Feste romane.
(B) **(*) RCA VICS/*VK* 2006 [AGL 1/*AGK 1* 1276]. LAPO, Mehta – R. STRAUSS: *Don Juan.***(*)

This was one of Mehta's first recordings with the orchestra of which he became principal conductor in his twenties. Its flair for display in one of Respighi's most brilliant – if musically empty – showpieces is very striking. The recording is extremely bright and vivid, with an element of brittleness in the treble, common to both the disc and the excellent chrome cassette.

Feste romane; The Fountains of Rome; The Pines of Rome.
C *** Decca Dig. **410 145-2**; SXDL/*KSXDC* 7591 [Lon. LDR/*5-* 71091]. Montreal SO, Dutoit.

Dutoit as in other brilliant and colourful pieces draws committed playing from his fine Montreal orchestra. Where many interpreters concentrate entirely on brilliance, Dutoit finds a vein of expressiveness too, which – for example in the opening sequence of *The Pines of Rome* – conveys the fun of children playing at the Villa Borghese. There have been higher-powered, even more polished performances on record, but none more persuasive. The recorded sound is superlative, most of all on compact disc, where the organ pedal sound is stunning and where the format avoids the break in *Roman festivals* inevitable on LP. Cassette collectors too should be well satisfied, for the standard of tape transfer is remarkably fine.

Feste romane; The Pines of Rome.
*** Decca SXL 6822 [Lon. CS/*5-* 7043]. Cleveland O, Maazel.

Maazel's account of *Feste romane* (musically the least interesting of Respighi's three symphonic poems inspired by the capital city) is something of a revelation. The Decca recording is extremely sophisticated in its colour and detail, and Respighi's vividly evocative sound pictures are brought glitteringly to life. The orchestral playing shows matching virtuosity, and the final festival scene (*The night before Epiphany in the Piazza Navona*), with its gaudy clamour of trumpets and snatches of melody from the local organ-grinder, is given a kaleidoscopic imagery exactly as the composer intended. Elsewhere the superbly stylish playing has an almost baroque colouring, so wittily is it pointed. *The Pines of Rome* is given a strong, direct characterization, undoubtedly memorable, but without quite the subtlety or electricity of Karajan's version (see below). But the Decca recording throughout this disc (and especially in *Feste romane*) has a breathtaking, demonstration vividness, finer than many digital issues.

The Fountains of Rome; The Pines of Rome.
*** DG 2531/*3301* 055 [id.]. Berlin PO, Karajan.
(B) *** RCA VICS/*VK* 2040 [ATL1/*ATK1* 4040]. Chicago SO, Reiner.

Karajan is in his element in this music, and the playing of the Berlin Philharmonic is wonderfully refined. The evocation of atmosphere in the two middle sections of *The Pines of Rome* is unforgettable. A distanced and magically haunting trumpet solo is matched by the principal clarinet, who is hardly less poetic. This is all projected against a ravishingly sensuous background of string tone, and when the nightingale begins his song the effect is uncannily real. To set the scene of *The Pines of the Appian Way* Karajan creates a riveting pianissimo and slowly builds a climax of tremendous grandeur. In *The Fountains* the tension is rather less tautly held, but the pictorial imagery is hardly less telling when the playing is so beautiful. The Karajan cassette is of DG's highest quality, with only very fractionally less range than the LP.

Reiner's famous recording comes from the beginning of the 1960s. Here simple and highly effective microphone placing combines with the ambience of the Chicago auditorium to create an outstandingly natural recorded perspective. In *The Pines of the Appian Way* (which at its opening sounds quite sinister in Reiner's hands) there is an excess of bass resonance, but otherwise the sound is superbly balanced. The luminous orchestral playing has a rare element of rapture in both works, with the evocation of the sunset over the Villa Medici fountain hauntingly atmospheric. The nightingale singing in *The Pines of the Janiculum* is heard against a remarkably intense sustained pianissimo, and these performances have an unforgettable concentration and feeling for atmosphere. The chrome cassette is not recommended – it is over-modulated and sounds fierce and unrefined.

Rossiniana (suite arr. from piano pieces by Rossini: *Quelques riens pour album*).
(M) **(*) Decca Jub. JB/*KJBC* 79. RPO, Dorati – ROSSINI: *La Boutique fantasque.***(*)

It is perhaps curious that this work is usually catalogued under Respighi, whereas *La Boutique fantasque*, which Respighi also based on Rossini's music, is more often found under Rossini. *Rossiniana* is not so inspired a score as *La Boutique fantasque*, but it is beautifully played here and Dorati's affection is most persuasive. The recording is first-class. It has more atmosphere than in the coupling, although on cassette the difference is rather less striking than on disc.

Violin sonata in B min.
(M) ** Sup. 1111 3165. Suk, Hála – FAURÉ: *Sonata No. 2.***

Respighi's *Sonata* comes from the same period as the Fauré with which it is coupled. It is not of comparable stature or interest and has not been available on record for many years. Josef Suk and Josef Hála make out a good case for the work whose lyricism can often seem bland. The recording is perfectly acceptable though not outstanding.

Revueltas, Silvestre
(1899–1940)

Homage to Federico Garcia Lorca; Sensemayá.
(M) *** HMV Dig. Green. ESD/*TC-ESD* 7146 [Var. Sara. 704220]. Mexican State SO, Bátiz (with *Concert of Mexican music****).

Redes; Ocho por Radio.
(M) *** HMV Dig. Green. ESD/*TC-ESD* 270031-1/*4*. Mexican State SO, Bátiz (with *Music of Mexico, Volume 2* **(*)).

These vivid performances, given brilliant recording, are discussed below in the Concerts section.

Rimsky-Korsakov, Nikolas
(1844–1908)

Antar (Symphony No. 2), Op. 9; Russian Easter Festival overture, Op. 36.
** Ph. Dig. 9500/*7300* 971 [id.]. Rotterdam PO, Zinman.

Antar dates from 1869, some twenty years before *Scheherazade*, yet although its composer first called it a symphony (he had second thoughts later) it obviously anticipates the more famous work in style and shape, to say nothing of its similarly exotic atmosphere and sinuous melodic contours. Indeed the melodic content is strong in character. The motto theme is memorable, and the third-movement scherzo contains some of Rimsky-Korsakov's most attractive invention. The scoring too is full of felicitous touches.

Zinman makes the most of the central movements and there is some warmly beautiful playing from the Rotterdam orchestra. The recording is pleasingly rich and atmospheric (though the fairly low level of the chrome-tape transfer robs the cassette of the last degree of upper range) and if the performance lacks something in thrust and adrenalin it does not miss the music's colour and warmth. The overture has similar qualities: here a little more sheer zest would have been welcome.

Capriccio espagnol, Op. 34.
(B) *** RCA VICS/*VK* 2041 [AGL1/*AGK1* 4293]. RCA SO, Kondrashin – TCHAIKOVSKY: *Capriccio italien.****
** Decca SXL 6956. LAPO, Lopez-Cobos – CHABRIER: *España***; FALLA: *Three-cornered Hat.***(*)

Kondrashin's coupling from the early 1960s is not generous, but it easily makes up in quality for what it lacks in quantity. His performance has great flair and excitement with glittering colour and detail in the variations and the *Scena e canto gitano*. The orchestral bravura is exhilarating yet there is warmth too, and the resonant recording still sounds marvellous. There are no more satisfying performances available of either this or its equally compulsive Tchaikovsky coupling. The chrome tape is not recommended – it is over-modulated and climaxes sound fierce and coarse.

Lopez-Cobos is rather relaxed at the opening, and in the variations the Los Angeles string section is not ideally sumptuous (though the horns are splendid). The wind acquit themselves well in the cadenza section, and the closing *Fandango* really catches fire. The sound is characteristically vivid in the Decca manner.

Capriccio espagnol; Le Coq d'or: suite; Russian Easter Festival overture, Op. 36.
*** Decca SXL/*KSXC* 6966 [Lon. 7196]. Cleveland O, Maazel.

Maazel's famous early stereo recording of the *Capriccio espagnol* with the Berlin Philharmonic is not quite equalled in charisma and excitement by this new Cleveland version, but the other works included here come off splendidly. The performance of the *Russian Easter Festival overture* is full of imaginative touches, so that one has the sense of hearing the score for the first time. *Le Coq d'or* is gorgeously played and sumptuously recorded (the Queen of Shemakha's memorably sinuous theme is given a telling combination of delicacy and sensuous colour). Perhaps Maazel tends to indulge himself somewhat, luxuriating in the aural magic of Rimsky's scoring, but his warmth of affection communicates, and he creates a superb climax with *The marriage feast and lamentable end of King Dodon.* Even though the *Capriccio* is lacking in thrust, this is an indispensable collection, for the other two works have never been presented on record more enticingly. The Decca sound is of demonstration standard throughout, and the tape has only marginally less transient sparkle than the disc.

Capriccio espagnol; May night overture; Sadko, Op. 5; The Snow Maiden: suite.
** Ph. Dig. **411 446-2**; 6514/*7337* 306 [id.]. Rotterdam PO, Zinman; (i) with Alexander and Ch.

Zinman secures some quite lustrous playing from his Rotterdam orchestra in the *Capriccio*, and he finds both atmosphere and colour in *Sadko* and the *May night overture.*

But this is music that needs more than refined orchestral playing: there is a lack of charisma here, and the adrenalin only begins to run at the very end of the Spanish piece. In the *Danse des oiseaux* (from *The Snow Maiden*) there is an effective vocal contribution. The chrome tape only produces satisfactory results if played back at a very high level.

Capriccio espagnol; The Snow Maiden: Dance of the tumblers.
(M) ** CBS 60115/*40*- [MY/*MYT* 36728]. NYPO, Bernstein – TCHAIKOVSKY: *Capriccio italien* etc.**

Bernstein's CBS record favours a coupling familiar from the early days of LP, with bonus items as makeweight. The opening of the *Capriccio espagnol* is rather slow and positive, but later the New York orchestra is given plenty of opportunities to display its virtuosity, and the closing *Fandango* is very brilliant indeed. The *Dance of the tumblers* must be the fastest performance on record, and the effect is exhilarating, although here the tendency to fierceness in the recording's upper range is even more marked than earlier.

Le Coq d'or: suite.
(M) *** Mercury SRI 75016 [id.]. LSO, Dorati – BORODIN: *Prince Igor:* excerpts.**

A sumptuously colourful account of the richly-hued orchestral suite, given glowing recording by the Mercury engineers. As sound, the Borodin coupling is not quite so impressive, but this remains another vintage reissue from the Mercury catalogue of the early 1960s.

Le Coq d'or: suite; The Tale of Tsar Saltan: suite.
** Ph. Dig. **411 435-2**; 6514/*7337* 163 [id.]. Rotterdam PO, Zinman.

While new digital recordings of this repertoire are welcome and the Rotterdam orchestra plays with appealing freshness, Zinman's approach seems over-refined, and while there is no lack of colour, the sinuously sentient qualities of *Le Coq d'or* are minimized, and there is a lack of real sparkle elsewhere. The chrome tape, as usual with Philips, has less brilliance on top, but on CD the sound approaches demonstration standard.

Scheherazade (symphonic suite), *Op. 35.*
*** Ph. **400 021-2**; 9500 681/*7300 776* [id.]. Concg. O, Kondrashin.
*** Ph. 6500 410 [id.]. LPO, Haitink.
(B) *** CfP CFP/*TC-CFP* 40341. Philh. O, Kletzki – TCHAIKOVSKY: *Capriccio italien.***(*)
(M) *** Decca SPA/*KCSP* 89 [Lon. STS/*5*-15158]. LSO, Monteux.
*** HMV Dig. **CDC 747023-2**; ASD/*TCC-ASD* 4188 [Ang. DS/*4XS* 37851]. Phd. O, Muti.
(M) **(*) HMV SXLP/*TC-SXLP* 30253 [Ang. S/*4XS* 35505]. RPO, Beecham.
(B) **(*) Con. CC/*CCT* 7501 [Lon. STS 15126]. SRO, Ansermet.
**(*) Chalfont Dig. SDG 304 [id.]. LSO, Tjeknavorian.
**(*) Ph. Dig. 6514/*7337* 231 [id.]. VPO, Previn.
**(*) HMV Dig. ASD 4272 [Euro. 204009]. Moscow RSO, Fedoseyev.
(M) **(*) DG Priv. 2535/*3335* 474 [2530/*3300* 972]. Boston SO, Ozawa.
(B) **(*) DG Walkman *413 155-4*. (as above, cond. Ozawa) – STRAVINSKY: *Firebird suite;* KHACHATURIAN: *Gayaneh.***(*)

Scheherazade; Capriccio espagnol, Op. 34.
(*) Decca Dig. **410 253-2; 410 253-1/*4* [id.]. Montreal SO, Dutoit.

Scheherazade; Tsar Saltan: Flight of the bumble-bee; March.
(M) **(*) RCA Gold GL/*GK* 42703 [AGL 1/*AGK 1* 1330]. LSO, Previn.

Kondrashin's version with the Concertgebouw Orchestra has the advantage of marvellous recorded sound, combining richness and sparkle within exactly the right degree of resonance. Here the personality of Hermann Krebbers (the orchestra's concertmaster) very much enters the picture, and his gently seductive portrayal of Scheherazade's narrative creates a strong influence on the overall interpretation. His exquisite playing, especially at the opening and close of the work, is cleverly used by Kondrashin to make a foil to the expansively vibrant contribution of the orchestra as a whole. The first movement, after Krebbers' tranquil introduction, develops a striking architectural sweep; the second is vivid with colour, the third beguilingly gracious, while in the finale, without taking unusually fast tempi, Kondrashin creates an irresistible forward impulse leading to a huge climax at the moment of the shipwreck. It is significant that Philips chose this outstanding analogue recording for their excellent compact disc issue, rather than the Previn/VPO version which is digitally recorded. On CD one notices that inner detail is marginally less sharp than it would be with a digital recording, but the analogue glow and naturalness more than compensate, and the richness of texture is just right for the music. Unfortunately the cassette transfer, although well balanced, lacks the ultimate range and sparkle of the disc.

Haitink's LPO record dates from 1974 when it was the finest account of *Scheherazade* to appear for more than a decade. Compared with the Kondrashin, the recording shows its age just a little in the string timbre, but in all other respects it is exceptionally truthful in both sound and perspective. It is a relief to hear a solo violin sounding its natural size in relation to the orchestra as a whole. Yet Rodney Friend, who plays the solos subtly – like Krebbers with Kondrashin – dominates the performance, with his richly sinuous picture of Scheherazade herself as narrator of each episode. The playing of the LPO is both sensitive and alert, Haitink's interpretation wholly unaffected and totally fresh in impact.

Kletzki's famous recording of Rimsky-Korsakov's orchestral showpiece was a best-seller on HMV's Concert Classics label for over fifteen years. The recording has an attractively spacious acoustic, and the Philharmonia solo playing is superb, with highly distinguished violin solos from Hugh Bean. Kletzki's reading is broad in the first movement, and he makes the second glow and sparkle (the famous brass interchanges having the most vivid projection). The richness of the string playing in the third movement is matched by the exhilaration of the finale. The recording has been brightened in the new transfer and now sounds remarkably clear, though lacking something in sumptuousness, especially in the first movement. The second remains as demonstration-worthy as ever. The finale has rather more weight, but generally the sound balance is enhanced by a slight treble cut and comparable bass boost. As so often with CfP, there is minimal difference in sound between disc and cassette. The latter has fractionally less edge at the top but slightly more warmth.

Monteux is, if anything, even more vivid. The recording is at once brilliant and sparkling and full-blooded, the performance sensuous and exciting. The orchestral playing is perhaps not quite as polished as the Philharmonia's, but it has tremendous zest and spontaneity. This is a good alternative to Kletzki for those who put dramatic bite before tonal refinement. In the finale Monteux holds back the climax until the last minute and then unleashes the storm with devastating effect. The cassette version is first-class, technically.

Muti's reading is colourful and dramatic in a larger-than-life way that sweeps one along. The bravura has one remembering that this was the orchestra which in the days of Stokowski made this a party-piece. The great string theme of the slow movement has all the voluptuousness one expects of Philadelphia strings in one of the best of HMV's latterday Philadelphia recordings, more spacious than usual though not ideally balanced. There is a glare in the upper range to which not all ears will respond, even if the racy finale, with its exciting climax, carries all before it. The tape is transferred on iron-oxide stock at the highest level, and there is a slight loss of refinement, if not of impact.

Beecham's record was originally issued at full price at the same time as Kletzki's. It is a fine performance, notable for superlative wind playing and the solo violin contribution of Steven Staryk. Sir Thomas's reading has both glamour and panache, and if some other versions have more drama (especially in the first movement) there is a compensating elegance and warmth. The slight snag is the recording, which, on disc, lacks voluptuousness and is rather hard on top and light in the bass. The cassette has rather more breadth and body.

Ansermet's version (shorn of its original

Polovtsian dances coupling in this Contour bargain-priced reissue) was famous as a recording for its crystal clarity and vividness, rather than for any sensuous qualities. Thus the outer movements, with their undoubted sparkle, are the finest: the first is dramatic, and in the last the final climax makes a great impact. In Ansermet's hands the music's sinuous qualities are not missed and every bar of the score is alive. With a clean new master this is excellent value, though the cassette is not the equal of the disc.

Tjeknavorian's Chalfont digital record costs a great deal more than its competitors. Undoubtedly it is an arresting performance, and, with a notably clean pressing and extremely brilliant and detailed recording, its sharpness of detail will certainly appeal to some ears. The overall sound balance is bright rather than richly sumptuous, yet the bass response is strong and clear. Tjeknavorian paces the music briskly throughout; the first movement has a strong, passionate climax, and the slow movement has less repose than usual, sounding more elegant, less sensuous, its 6/8 rhythmic pattern readily apparent. The finale has a furious basic tempo, but the LSO players obviously revel in their virtuosity and the result is consistently exhilarating, with (for the most part) amazingly clear articulation. The climax has a brilliance to make the ears tingle, with a hint of fierceness in the recording itself.

Dutoit offers an exceptionally generous coupling and the long sides have no adverse effect on the recording which is characteristic of the Montreal acoustic, full and warm with luminous detail. There is an equally impressive chrome tape. But this is a relaxed, lyrical reading at speeds slower than usual. It is essentially an amiable view, lacking in virtuoso excitement. The *Capriccio espagnol* compensates to some extent for this shortcoming, again given a genial performance though not one lacking brilliance. On compact disc, in spite of the impressive Decca recording, first choice remains with Kondrashin.

Previn in his Vienna version opts for spacious speeds and a direct, unsentimental view of the fairy-tale suite. With his characteristic rhythmic flair and sumptuous playing from the Vienna Philharmonic, the result can be recommended to those wanting a more restrained reading than usual. Excellent, finely balanced sound on disc, but the chrome cassette lacks sparkle and the finale is bass-heavy.

The earlier Previn recording on RCA displays many of the same qualities as the later Vienna account. Tempi are expansive and Previn's view of the first three movements is unexpectedly cool, the very opposite of vulgar. With rhythmic pointing which is characteristically crisp the result grows attractive on repetition, while the finale brings one of the most dramatic and brilliant performances ever recorded of that showpiece. The fill-ups provide a charming makeweight, particularly the *Tsar Saltan march* with its reminders of Walton's *Henry V* and Vaughan Williams's *Wasps*. The recording is outstanding for its late-1960s vintage, making this an attractive mid-price issue. The tape transfer fully conveys the richness and warmth of the recording; it has some slight lack of range in the treble, but this is not serious.

The brilliant Russian digital recording projects the sound of the Moscow Radio Orchestra faithfully enough, with its rather febrile string timbre, braying brass and robust woodwind. The balance also favours the percussion, and in the finale the cymbals are almost overwhelming at times. There is no lack of adrenalin here, even the sinuous melody of the slow movement is kept moving; but though the overall effect is undoubtedly exciting and very Russian in feeling, elegance is almost entirely absent. The chrome cassette is brilliantly transferred, although the level drops on side two, taking some of the edge off the sound.

Ozawa's is an attractive performance, richly recorded. The first movement is strikingly spacious, building to a fine climax, and if the last degree of vitality is missing from the central movements the orchestral playing is warmly vivid. The finale is lively enough if not earthshaking in its excitement; but the reading as a whole has plenty of colour and atmosphere, and it is certainly enjoyable. The tape transfer is sophisticated.

Ozawa's version is also available on a Walkman cassette, making a bargain alternative if the couplings, Maazel's early stereo recording of the *Firebird suite* and Rozhdestvensky's *Gayaneh*, are suitable.

Mozart and Salieri (opera), *Op. 48* (complete in German).
(*) EMI 1C 065 46434. Schreier, Adam, Leipzig R. Ch., Dresden State O, Janowski.

In German instead of the original Russian, with no libretto and not even a synopsis provided, and with the part of Salieri taken by a singer whose voice is regularly forced into unsteadiness, this recording of Rimsky-Korsakov's sharp little Pushkin-based opera is barely even a stopgap. Peter Schreier in the role of Mozart, as well as the chorus and orchestra, provides some amends, all well recorded.

Robles, Marisa (born 1937)

Narnia suite.
*** ASV Dig. DCA/*ZCDCA* 513. Composer, Hyde-Smith, Robles Harp Ens.

This incidental music was commissioned for the integral recording of the C. S. Lewis *Narnia Chronicles.* Even though it consists entirely of a series of miniatures for harp, with the flute of Christopher Hyde-Smith used sparingly but to great effect, the music stands up well, away from the narrative. Its freshness and innocence are entirely in keeping with the wondrous world of princes and lords, fauns and dryads, talking animals and dwarfs, ruled over by High King Peter and Queen Susan under the ever-watchful eye of Aslan. Lewis never overdoes the Christian allegory; he is first and foremost a marvellous story-teller, and similarly Marisa Robles's music, with its indelible leitmotives for Narnia and Aslan, is memorable without being too insistent in characterization. The themes for *The Voyage of the Dawn Treader*, perhaps the most imaginative of all the tales, are particularly attractive. With the composer so admirably partnered, the music cannot fail to project, particularly as the digital recording is both lustrous and atmospheric as well as beautifully clear. The cassette too offers first-class quality. The actual *Chronicles* (including the incidental music) are available as follows: SWD/*ZCSWD* 351 (*The Magician's Nephew*); SWD/*ZCSWD* 352 (*The Lion, the Witch and the Wardrobe*); SWD/*ZCSWD* 353 (*The Horse and his Boy*); SWD/*ZCSWD* 354 (*Prince Caspian*); SWD/*ZCSWD* 355 (*The Voyage of the Dawn Treader*); SWD/*ZCSWD* 356 (*The Silver Chair*); SWD/*ZCSWD* 357 (*The Last Battle*). Michael Hordern proves an ideal narrator, colouring his voice with great skill to represent the multitude of characters, while his range of tone and expression is compellingly wide. Indeed his presentation is a *tour de force*, and the characters spring to vigorous life, not least the Sons of Adam and Daughters of Eve on whom the tales centre.

Rodrigo, Joaquín (born 1902)

A la busca del más allá; (i) *Concierto de Aranjuez; Zarabanda lejana, y Villancico.*
**(*) HMV Dig. ASD/*TCC-ASD* 4159 [Ang. DS/*4XS* 37876]. LSO, Bátiz; (i) with Moreno.

The *Zarabanda lejana* (Distant sarabande) was Rodrigo's first work for guitar (1926), written in homage to Luis Milan. He later orchestrated it and added the *Villancico* to make a binary structure, the first part nobly elegiac, the second a gay dance movement, with a touch of harmonic astringency, but having something of the atmosphere of a carol. The symphonic poem, *A la busca del más allá* (In search of the beyond) was written as recently as 1978 but, like all Rodrigo's music, its idiom is in no way avant-garde. It could easily be dismissed as film music without a film, yet it is evocatively and powerfully scored and makes a curiously indelible impression. Bátiz plays it with strong commitment, as he does the earlier piece, and the vividly brilliant, forwardly balanced digital sound produces a considerable impact. Unfortunately the performance of the ubiquitous *Concierto de Aranjuez*, although acceptable, is in no way outstanding, which reduces the attractions of this issue.

(i–iv) *Concierto Andaluz;* (i; iv) *Concierto de Aranjuez;* (i; ii; v) *Concierto madrigal;* (i; v) *Fantasia para un gentilhombre.*

(M) *** Ph. 6747 430 (2). (i) Angel Romero; (ii) Pepe Romero; (iii) Celedonio and Celin Romero; (iv) San Antonio SO, Alessandro; (v) ASMF, Marriner.

It was an excellent idea to gather these four first-class performances together in a medium-priced box. Rodrigo's music wears marvellously well: the melody is unpretentious yet obstinately memorable; the structures, though involving a good deal of repetition, show a natural craftsmanship. Some might feel that the first movement of the *Andaluzian concerto* is less imaginative than the composer's best music, but it has a hauntingly atmospheric slow movement, and the finale is typically felicitous and spirited. The other works are undoubtedly inspired. Both the *Concierto de Aranjuez* and the *Concierto madrigal* were written for the Romero family, and the performances here are definitive and beautifully recorded. Marriner's contributions to the latter work and the graciously noble *Fantasia para un gentilhombre* have real distinction, and the sound is superb. The pressings here are immaculately silent-surfaced.

(i) *Concierto Andaluz* (for four guitars and orchestra); (ii) *Concierto de Aranjuez.*

*** Ph. 9500 563/*7300 705* [id.]. ASMF, Marriner, with (i) Los Romeros; (ii) Pepe Romero.

Los Romeros and the Academy under Marriner make the very most of the *Concierto Andaluz*, with infectious life and spirit in the outer sections and plenty of romantic atmosphere in the slow movement. Pepe Romero's account of the *Concierto de Aranjuez* is second to none. The famous *Adagio* is memorable, with the opening and closing sections delicately rhapsodic, and a glamorous climax, bursting with Mediterranean feeling. The orchestral playing is a delight, more elegant and polished than in the earlier Philips version (see above), although both are very enjoyable. The recording is of demonstration quality on disc and tape alike (although on cassette there is a slight excess of bass in the finale of the *Concierto Andaluz*).

(i) *Concierto Andaluz;* (ii) *Concierto madrigal.*

*** Ph. **400 024-2** [id.]. (i) Los Romeros; (ii) P. and A. Romero, ASMF, Marriner.

Both these works are included in the two-disc collection of Rodrigo's guitar concertos – see above. This special recoupling for compact disc is entirely sensible, with the *Concierto de Aranjuez* already available on an outstanding Decca issue. The performances are memorable and the analogue recording is refined enough to lend itself to digital remastering.

(i) *Concierto Andaluz; Fantasia para un gentilhombre.*

(M) **(*) HMV Dig. Green. ESD/*TC-ESD* 7145 [Var. Sara. VCDM 1000150]. Ruiz, Mexico State SO, Bátiz; (i) with Moreno, Garibay, López.

This is a useful coupling as so often these works bring duplication for the collector who already has a favourite version of the *Concierto de Aranjuez* with which they are so often paired. The *Concierto Andaluz* has its weaknesses but remains engaging, if perhaps a trifle long for its material. Surprisingly the digital recording does not give a very impressive focus to the four soloists. However, orchestral detail is excellent in the *Fantasia* and Bátiz draws vivid sounds from his orchestra. The solo playing is excellent too. Chrome cassette and disc are closely matched, and this is certainly enjoyable.

Concierto de Aranjuez (for guitar and orchestra).

*** CBS 76369/*40-* [M/*MT* 33208]. Williams, ECO, Barenboim – VILLA-LOBOS: *Concerto.****

(B) *** Con. CC/*CCT* 7510 [(d) 2535/*3335* 170]. Behrend, Berlin PO, Peters – CASTELNUOVO-TEDESCO: *Concerto.****

(M) **(*) HMV Green. ESD/*TC-ESD* 143648-1/*4* [(d) Ang. S/*4XS* 36496]. Diaz, Professors of Spanish Nat. O, Frühbeck de Burgos – FALLA: *Nights in the gardens of Spain.****

(B) ** CfP CFP/*TC-CFP* 40012. Zaradin, L. Philomus. O, Barbier (with Recital**).

John Williams's newer analogue recording of the *Concierto de Aranjuez* with Barenboim is superior to his earlier version with Ormandy. The playing has marvellous point and spontaneity; the famous *Adagio* has rarely been played with this degree of poetic feeling. There is a hint of rhythmic over-emphasis in the articulation of the finale, but in general this performance is outstanding (although Behrend must also be considered). The balance is characteristically forward, but in all other respects the bright, detailed recording is highly attractive. The cassette has a lower frequency ceiling than the disc.

A first-rate bargain version of Rodrigo's famous *Guitar concerto* from Behrend, immensely alive and vivid both as a performance and for the bright-as-a-button recording. The cassette is only marginally less lively. This excellent performance was available at medium price (DG Privilege 135117 – now deleted) coupled to the *Concierto serenata* for harp; but the present coupling has undoubted charm and is no less effectively presented.

Diaz's recording was originally rather over-reverberant, but it has been remastered with a general improvement in the registration of detail, but at the expense of a touch of shrillness on the upper strings, mostly noticeable in the first movement. In the finale, the slight added edge is effective in emphasizing rhythmic point. The performance is quite distinctive, with the soloist giving the famous slow movement a hauntingly improvisatory feeling, while in the outer movements the Spanish professors ensure that the orchestral detail has plenty of personality.

Zaradin's performance is bright-eyed and straightforward, with a crisp, immediate recording. The orchestral outline is clear-cut in the somewhat dry manner favoured by John Boyden, who produced many of the early Classics for Pleasure original recordings. This is coupled with a recital of solo guitar pieces, discussed below in our Recitals section. Although the dynamic range of the recording of the concerto is limited by the close balance of the solo guitar, the recording conveys an attractive intimacy, and there is plenty of bloom on the sound on both disc and tape.

Concierto de Aranjuez; Fantasia para un gentilhombre.

C *** Decca Dig. **400 054-2**; SXDL/*KSXDC* 7525 [Lon. LDR/*5*- 71027]. Bonell, Montreal SO, Dutoit.
*** CBS Dig. IM/*IMT* 37848 [id.]. Williams, Philh. O, Frémaux.
(M) *** CBS 60104/*40*- [MY/*MYT* 36717]. Williams, Phd. O, Ormandy, or ECO, Barenboim.
**(*) Erato STU/*MCE* 71128. Santos, French Nat. Op. O, Scimone.
(M) ** DG Acc. 2542/*3342* 150 [139440/*3300 172*]. Yepes, Spanish R. and TV O, Alonso.
(M) *(*) Ph. Seq. 6527/*7311* 058 [6500 454]. Lagoya, Monte Carlo Op. O, Almeida.

The great success of the newest Decca issue is due not only to the exceptionally clear and well-balanced digital recording (as realistic and demonstration-worthy on cassette as on LP) and Bonell's imaginative and inspired account of the solo part, but equally to the strong characterization of the orchestral accompaniments by Charles Dutoit and his excellent Montreal orchestra. In the *Concierto* the series of vivid interjections by the orchestral wind soloists (cor anglais, bassoon and trumpet) is projected with the utmost personality and presence, and a feeling of freshness pervades every bar of the orchestral texture. Soloist and orchestra combine to give an outstandingly eloquent account of the famous slow movement, and the climax retains its clarity of texture as it does in no other version. The finale has irresistible sparkle. In the *Fantasia* the balance between warmly gracious lyricism and sprightly rhythmic resilience is no less engaging and here again the orchestral solo playing makes a strong impression. This is a clear first choice for this coupling, especially on compact disc, where the ambient warmth counters the bright upper range.

John Williams's newest version of the *Concierto* (his third) also has the advantage of fist-class digital recording. Indeed the CBS engineers are to be congratulated on the balance which is most believable, the soloist a little forward, but with the guitar image admirably related to the orchestra, where inner detail is impressively clear. The acoustic has agreeable atmospheric warmth, yet climaxes have brilliance without overemphasis. This is technically superior to both earlier versions (see above and below). The performance is even finer than Williams's previous analogue partnership with Barenboim (differently coupled). The slow movement is wonderfully atmospheric with the soloist's introspective yet inspirational mood anticipated and echoed by Frémaux who who secures most beautiful orchestral playing. The finale is light and sparkling with an element of fantasy and much delicacy of articulation in the accompaniment. The performance of the *Fantasia* is no less memorable. Its relaxed opening dialogue between soloist and orchestra is engagingly spontaneous and refined in feeling; later, when the music becomes more energetic, Frémaux brings out the Renaissance colours in the scoring most vividly. This is altogether a most winning coupling, not as extrovert as the Bonell/ Dutoit partnership, but no less distinguished.

John Williams's first recording of the *Concierto* with Ormandy is a red-blooded romantic reading, with the tension well held throughout. The recording is vivid and not lacking atmosphere, and the orchestral detail is telling, even though the soloist is balanced forwardly. The *Fantasia* too is impeccably played and thoroughly enjoyable, with Barenboim making the most of the vivid orchestral colouring. At medium price this is very competitive, and the cassette is bright and wide-ranging if fractionally less refined on top.

Santos's Erato recording is slightly more reverberant than the CBS version. This brings a sumptuously rich quality to the opening string melody in the *Fantasia*, but it means that in both works the inner orchestral detail is less sharply focused. Santos does not project a strongly individual personality (that again may be partly the effect of the acoustic) but he is very musical, and both performances are warmly sympathetic, with plenty of expressive feeling in the *Adagio* of the *Concierto*. However, this could not be recommended as a first choice in this coupling.

Yepes's 1970 DG version is disappointing. His much earlier identical coupling for Decca (now deleted) had the advantage of extremely lively accompaniments, directed by Argenta and Frühbeck de Burgos respectively, and vintage Decca sound. Alonso is much less imaginative, as is readily apparent in the *Concierto*'s outer movements (the finale is rhythmically stiff), and though Yepes is at his finest in the *Adagio* and plays nobly in the *Fantasia* (which is generally more successful), the dry DG recording does not help, although it ensures a clean and vivid cassette transfer.

Lagoya is a good player but he does not project strongly, except perhaps in the slow movement of the *Concierto*, which he plays with considerable feeling. The outer movements lack the sprightly momentum which distinguishes the best versions. The recording is fair, but the cassette is seriously lacking in range and sparkle at the top.

Concierto de Aranjuez; (i) *Concierto madrigal* (for two guitars).

**(*) DG 2531/*3301* 208 [id.]. Yepes, Philh. O, Navarro, (i) with Monden.

Yepes's 1980 version of the *Concierto de Aranjuez* is an improvement on his recording of a decade earlier (see above), mainly because of the superior accompaniment. But even here there is a lack of vitality in the outer movements, although the poetic element of the *Adagio* is well realized. The account of the *Concierto madrigal* (with Godelieve Monden the excellent second guitarist) is first-class; each of the twelve delightful miniatures which make up this engaging work springs vividly to life. The recording is excellent, with the cassette matching the disc very closely (indeed the *Concierto* has slightly more projection on tape). This is the only available record and cassette offering this coupling.

Concierto como un divertimento (for cello and orchestra).

*** RCA RL/*RK* 25420. Lloyd Webber, LPO, Lopez-Cobos – LALO: *Concerto.****

One suspects that Julian Lloyd Webber, in commissioning this new concerto, may not have known of the existence of the earlier *Concierto en modo galante* (written in 1949) now recorded by Robert Cohen – see below. If so, the gain is considerable, for the new work is delightful, and even more Spanish in feeling than the old. The style of writing is familiar, with a sinuously atmospheric *Adagio nostalgico* sandwiched between sparklingly inventive outer sections. The moto perpetuo finale has an engaging lyrical strain and the first movement, too, has a catchy main theme.

It is all characteristically friendly music and Lloyd Webber is obviously attuned to its spirit, and completely equal to its technical demands. The sound is clear and fresh on disc and vividly transferred to tape, though the upper range of the cassette is less refined than the LP.

(i) *Concierto de estío* (for violin); (ii) *Concierto en modo galante* (for cello).
*** HMV Dig. ASD/*TCC-ASD* 4198 [Ang. SD/*4XS* 37877]. LSO, Bátiz, with (i) Ara, (ii) Cohen.

The cello concerto dates from 1949 and the *Summer concerto* for violin ('conceived in the manner of Vivaldi') from 1943. We have waited a long time for these première stereo recordings, but HMV now makes amends with a really outstanding coupling. Agustín Léon Ara's account of the *Concierto de estío* catches its neoclassical spikiness admirably in the outer movements, and the central *Sicilienne* with its set of simple variations is most sympathetic. But it is the cello concerto that is the major addition to the repertoire, and it is given a masterly performance by Robert Cohen; he combines elegance of phrasing with warm beauty of timbre in the lovely secondary theme (*in tempo di minuetto galante*) of the first movement and the no less haunting melody which dominates the *Adagietto*. His spirited articulation of the opening ostinato idea and the lively *Zapateado* rondo finale is matched by Enrique Bátiz, who secures playing of fire and temperament from the LSO, all its members sounding as if they had just returned from a holiday in the Spanish sunshine. The digital recording is forward and at times brilliant to the point of fierceness, but it has excellent detail and an attractive ambient warmth, and the over-emphasis at the top is easily softened with the controls. The outstanding chrome tape is just as vivid but smoother on top.

(i) *Concierto madrigal; Musica para un jardin; Per la flor del Iliri blau.*
**(*) HMV Dig. ASD 165141-1/*4* [Ang. DS/*4XS* 37949]. (i) Moreno, Mariotti; LSO, Bátiz.

While a further recording of the engaging *Concierto madrigal* is welcome enough, the main interest here is the pair of symphonic poems. The *Musica para un jardin* is made up of four short berceuses, originally written for the piano and reaching their final orchestral form in 1957. Each piece is titled to evoke one of the four seasons, but the writing is delicately evocative rather than seeking robust programmatic implications. *Per la flor del Iliri blau* (For the flower of the blue lily) dates from 1934 and is based on a Valencian legend. It uses an actual poem for its scenario (given in translation on the sleeve) concerning the search of a prince for a rare flower with miraculous curative qualities, needed to aid his ailing father. He meets his death in ambush on the way home. The music has something in common with Smetana's famous cycle about his homeland, though Rodrigo is better in moments of gently atmospheric detail than in the melodrama. Both performances have considerable conviction and are finely played and vividly recorded (though the XDR tape is fractionally less wide-ranging at the top than the LP). The account of the *Concierto* is enjoyable, though not as fine as Marriner's with the Romeros.

Concierto pastoral (for flute and orchestra); *Fantasia para un gentilhombre* (arr. Galway for flute and orchestra).
*** RCA RL/*RK* 25193 [ARL 1/*ARK 1* 3416]. Galway, Philh. O, Mata.

The *Concierto pastoral* was composed for James Galway in 1978. Its spikily brilliant introduction is far from pastoral in feeling, but the mood of the work soon settles down. At first hearing, the material seems thinner than usual but Rodrigo's fragmented melodies and rhythmic ostinatos soon insinuate themselves into the listener's memory. The slow movement is especially effective, with a witty scherzando centrepiece framed by the *Adagio* outer sections. James Galway's performance is truly superlative, showing the utmost bravura and matching refinement. He is beautifully recorded (and the tape transfer is immaculately truthful), and the small accompanying chamber orchestra is well balanced. The arrangement of the *Fantasia* is a very free one, necessitating reorchestration, exchanging clarinet and horn instrumentation for the original scoring for trumpet and piccolo. The solo part too has been rewritten and even extended, apparently with the composer's blessing. The result is, to be honest, not an improvement on the original. But Galway is very persuasive, even if there is a persistent feeling of inflation.

(i) *Concierto serenata* (for harp and orchestra); (ii) *Concierto de Aranjuez; Fantasia para un gentilhombre.*

(B) ** DG Walkman *413 156-4*. (i) Zabaleta, Berlin RSO, Marzendorfer; (ii) Yepes, Spanish R. and TV O, Alonso – FALLA: *Nights in the gardens of Spain.***(*)

This is the only available version of the *Concierto serenata*, which has an unforgettable piquancy and charm in both its invention and its felicity of scoring. It is superbly recorded, with the delicate yet colourful orchestral palette tickling the ear in charming contrast to the beautifully focused timbre of the harp. The performance has great virtuosity and flair and (with the tape transfer in the demonstration class) still deserves the Rosette we awarded to the original LP issue (coupled with a different and much better version of the *Concierto de Aranjuez*). The present recordings of the *Guitar concerto* and the *Fantasia para un gentilhombre* are disappointingly lacking in sparkle. These two works have been recorded in a studio with an unattractively dry acoustic which seems to have damped the spontaneity out of the performances, except in the slow movement of the *Concierto* which seems indestructible. However, this inexpensive double-length tape is worth considering for the *Harp concerto* alone.

Bajando de la Meseta; Fandango; Junto al Generalife; 3 Petites pièces; Por los campos de España; En los trigales; Romance de Durandarte; Sonata a la española; Tiento antigua.

*** Ph. 9500/*7300* 915 [id.]. Pepe Romero.

An excellent anthology of Rodrigo's shorter works for solo guitar, distinguished by informative and articulate sleeve-notes from the composer himself. He tells us, for instance, that the Spanish subtitle for the *Sonata* has a certain irony, which Pepe Romero does not miss in his performance. Indeed he is strikingly responsive to the changing moods and colours of all these pieces, his rubato free but convincing and his evocation of atmosphere – as in the central section of *En los trigales* – telling. The closing *Romance de Durandarte* (originally written for the ballet *Pavana Real*) is particularly haunting. The Philips recording is close but realistic on disc and cassette alike.

Rootham, Cyril (1875–1938)

Symphony No. 1 in C min.

*** Lyr. SRCS 103. LPO, Handley – HOLBROOKE: *Birds of Rhiannon.****

Cyril Rootham, who was born in Bristol in 1875 and died the year before the outbreak of the Second World War, spent the bulk of his life at Cambridge, where his pupils included Arthur Bliss. The first of his two symphonies was composed in 1932 and leaves no doubt as to his expertise and powers of craftsmanship. Rootham was a serious and dedicated musician, though it must be said that his is not a distinctive voice in English music. His orchestration is very fine and it is reproduced by the engineers in sound of quite remarkable realism. Indeed, this is a demonstration record, with impressive clarity, definition and depth. Readers should investigate this record for themselves, for there is much to admire, even if few would claim that the symphony is a powerfully original work.

Rossini, Gioacchino (1792–1868)

La Boutique fantasque (ballet, arr. Respighi; complete).

❀ *** CBS Dig. 35842 [M/*HMT* 35842]. Toronto SO, Andrew Davis.

X DELETED NOV/DEC 1989.

C *** Decca Dig. **410 139-2**; SXDL/*KSXDC* 7549 [Lon. LDR/5-71039]. Nat. PO, Bonynge – BRITTEN: *Matinées; Soirées.****

(M) **(*) HMV Green. ESD/*TC-ESD* 7152 (slightly abridged). LSO, Gardelli – OFFENBACH: *Gaîté parisienne* **.

La Boutique fantasque: suite.

(M) *** Chan. CBR/*CBT* 1003. SNO, Gibson – DUKAS: *L'Apprenti sorcier*; SAINT-SAËNS: *Danse macabre.****

(M) **(*) Decca Jub. JB/*KJBC* 79. RPO, Dorati – RESPIGHI: *Rossiniana.***(*)

At last we are given an absolutely complete version of *La Boutique fantasque*, one of the great popular triumphs of Diaghilev's Ballets Russes. The new CBS digital recording is arrestingly brilliant, yet its surface sparkle is balanced by a glowing ambient warmth. Respighi's masterly scoring, glitteringly vivid and sumptuous, transmutes his relatively slight source material into a magical tapestry. In the sympathetic hands of Andrew Davis there is not a dull bar, for Respighi's linking passages (usually omitted) are marvellously crafted. The Toronto orchestra is in superb form, playing with matching bravura and affection: the gentler second half of the ballet is particularly beautiful. The recording has the widest dynamic range; the actual opening is a mere whisper and the first climax expands gloriously. A demonstration disc.

The Decca compact disc has even greater brilliance, and also registers remarkable inner detail. Against the silent background the opening bass pizzicatos nearly re-create the magic of Ansermet's famous early mono LP, and throughout the orchestral colours glitter and glow within the attractive resonance of Kingsway Hall, although the digital recording does also produce an edge on the treble. Bonynge goes for sparkle and momentum above all; Davis is more relaxed (as was Ansermet) but Bonynge's exuberance is certainly exhilarating when the sound is so spectacular. The LP is first-class too, but the chrome tape (like the CBS cassette) is transferred at a modest level to accommodate the very wide dynamic range, and its transients are more subdued. Whichever format is chosen, this issue is much more generous than the CBS; the Britten arrangements are highly engaging and the Decca record plays for over an hour.

Gardelli's performance was originally recorded complete, but was quickly withdrawn and is here reissued in a slightly abridged single-sided format, coupled with a generous selection from *Gaîté parisienne*. Gardelli's performance is both spirited and sympathetic, but the sound of the reissue has a very brilliant treble which needs taming, and there is less atmosphere than on the original disc. The cassette, however, offers warmer sound (on both sides), but here the upper range is somewhat short on sparkle. However, many will feel this is competitive at medium price; all the most important music is included.

For those content with the highlights, Gibson's Chandos reissue, with its excellent couplings, can be strongly recommended. Gibson's performance sounds for all the world as if he had been listening to Ansermet's famous record. Tempi are similar, and the opening is cunningly slow, with much of the magic that Ansermet found. The Scottish National Orchestra is on its toes, and the sound on disc is excellent. The cassette transfer would have been improved by a more ambitious level; as it is, the upper range lacks the last degree of glitter compared with the disc.

Dorati's performance has plenty of life and colour, but the recording acoustic is a little lacking in atmosphere: the very opening of *La Boutique fantasque* is made to sound rather dry and unevocative by the relative lack of ambient glow. However, it is easy to make too much of this. The vivacity and point of the orchestral playing are often exhilarating, and on cassette, where the sound is slightly richer than on the LP, the dryness is much less obvious.

Overtures: *Armida; Il Barbiere di Siviglia; Bianca e Faliero; La Cambiale di matrimonio; La Cenerentola; Demetrio e Polibio; Edipo a Colono; Edoardo e Cristina.* (i) *Ermione. La Gazza ladra; L'Inganno felice; L'Italiana in Algeri; Maometto II; Otello.* (i) *Ricciardo e Zoraide. La Scala di seta; Semiramide; Le Siège de Corinthe; Il Signor Bruschino; Tancredi; Il Turco in Italia; Torvaldo e Dorliska; Il Viaggio a Reims; William Tell. Sinfonia al conventello; Sinfonia di Bologna.*

(M) *** Ph. 6768 064/*7699 136* (4) [6500 878/*7300 368*; 9500 349/*7300 595*; 9500/*7300* 886-7]. ASMF, Marriner, (i) with Amb. S.

Marriner's four discs aim to collect Rossini's 'complete' overtures, but of course not everything is here. The early Neapolitan operas, with the exception of *Ricciardo e Zoraide* and *Ermione*, make do with a simple prelude, leading into the opening chorus. Sometimes Rossini uses the same overture for more than one opera, and there are extensive quotations of material from one to another. Even so, twenty-four overtures make a delightful package in such sparkling performances, which eruditely use original orchestrations. Rossini's earliest overture, *Demetrio e Polibio*, written when he was only fifteen (and later providing a theme for *Il Signor Bruschino*), is a charmer, and *Ermione* has offstage contributions from a male chorus. Clean, bright and atmospheric recording on disc; the cassettes are variable, often lacking transient sparkle on top.

Overtures: *L'assedio di Corinto; L'Italiana in Algeri; Maometto II; Otello; Semiramide.*
** Erato STU/*MCE* 71178. Philh. O, Scimone.

An interestingly off-beat collection from Scimone who secures excellent playing from the Philharmonia. The highlight is *Maometto II*, a delightful piece, presented with affection and style; but in the two most familiar overtures, *L'Italiana in Algeri* and *Semiramide*, the performances are a trifle staid; Beecham, for one, finds far more sparkle in the latter piece. The recording is good but the balance is rich rather than brilliant, especially on the cassette, which lacks brightness on top.

Overtures: *Il Barbiere di Siviglia; La Cenerentola; La Gazza ladra; L'Italiana in Algeri; Le Siège de Corinthe; Il Signor Bruschino.*
(M) ❀ *** DG Sig. 410 830-1/*4* [id.]. LSO, Abbado.

Brilliant, sparkling playing, with splendid discipline, vibrant rhythms and finely articulated phrasing – altogether invigorating and bracing. There is perhaps an absence of outright geniality here but these are superb performances and recorded with great fidelity, wide range and firm body. The cassette transfer is of outstanding quality, with a fine sparkle and bloom on the sound. Whether the disc or the tape is chosen, this remains one of the very finest collections of Rossini overtures in the present catalogue, for the wit is spiced with a touch of acerbity, and the flavour is of a vintage dry champagne which retains its bloom, yet has a subtlety all its own.

Overtures: *Il Barbiere di Siviglia; La Gazza ladra; La Scala di seta; Semiramide; William Tell.*
(M) *** Decca Jub. JB/*KJBC* 33 [Lon. JL/*5*-41027]. LSO, Gamba.

This is a very good collection. The performances are taut and exciting and the orchestral playing splendidly alive and polished, even at the very fast speeds sometimes chosen for the allegros. A strong disciplining force – not unlike Toscanini's style – is felt in every piece, and care in phrasing is noticeable at every turn. Particularly captivating is the string cantilena at the introduction of *The Barber of Seville*, which is phrased with a wonderful sense of line. Decca's recording is very good. The only quality perhaps missing is a touch of geniality. The tape transfer, made at a high level, tends to be somewhat fierce in the treble.

Overtures: *Il Barbiere di Siviglia; La Gazza ladra; La Scala di seta; Le Siège de Corinthe; Il Signor Bruschino; William Tell.*
(M) * Decca VIV/*KVIC* 52 [Lon. STS 15307]. New Philh. O, Gardelli.

A disappointingly mundane set of performances, surprising from such an experienced conductor. *La Scala di seta* has curious tempo changes that sound almost like unmatched tape-joins. Even the recording is below Decca's usual sparkling standard in this kind of music. The cassette, however, is strikingly rich and vivid, even if the forward balance reduces the dynamic contrast to some extent.

Overtures: *Il Barbiere di Siviglia; La Gazza ladra; William Tell.*

(M) *** DG Priv. 2535/*3335* 629. Berlin PO, Karajan – SUPPÉ: *Overtures.****

This Privilege selection is extracted from Karajan's full-priced disc (2530 144 – see below). The performances offer supreme polish and extrovert bravura. The recording is both lively and atmospheric on disc, but on tape the reverberation has produced roughness at climaxes, especially in *La Gazza ladra* and in the brilliant account of *William Tell.* Those favouring a coupling with some swaggering Suppé performances should choose the disc.

Overtures: *Il Barbiere di Siviglia; La Gazza ladra; L'Italiana in Algeri; La Scala di seta; Semiramide; Il Signor Bruschino; William Tell.*

(B) *** CfP CFP/*TC-CFP* 40379 [(d) Sera. S/*4XG* 60058 and 60138]. Philh. O, Giulini.

This CfP reissue combines performances from two different LPs (still available separately in the USA, one with the original Verdi coupling) and offers music-making which combines refinement of detail with sophisticated Philharmonia playing from this orchestra's peak period during the early 1960s. *La Scala di seta* has a ridiculously fast introduction, but *William Tell* has a natural flair. The recording is excellent and the cassette matches the disc very closely indeed.

Overtures: *Il Barbiere di Siviglia; La Gazza ladra; L'Italiana in Algeri; La Scala di seta; Semiramide; William Tell.*

*** DG 2530 144/*3300 186* [id.]. Berlin PO, Karajan.

(M) ** HMV SXLP/*TC-SXLP* 30203 [Ang. RL/*4RL* 32054]. Philh. O, Karajan.

On DG superbly made performances recorded in 1972. Karajan takes the main allegro of *La Scala di seta* very fast indeed, but the playing is beautifully light and assured, the oboist managing felicitous control of the phrasing without any suggestion of breathlessness. The oboe solo in *L'Italiana in Algeri* is played with similar poise and assurance. Of their kind these performances are beautifully shaped and the recording is first-class. The cassette transfer offers acceptable rather than outstanding sound, with a lack of refinement in places, caused by the resonance.

The reissue of Karajan's Philharmonia performances of the same set of overtures is much less attractive. The recording acoustic, somewhat over-resonant, does not produce very refined sound (notably in a piece like *La Scala di seta*), and the performances have bravura but little finesse, in spite of some excellent orchestral playing. The cassette originally had a grotesquely reduced dynamic range, but has now been remastered. It now produces a tendency to congestion at peaks on side one. Side two is transferred at a lower level and is acceptable.

Overtures: *La Cenerentola; La Scala di seta; Tancredi; William Tell. Il Barbiere di Siviglia: Una voce poco fa; Largo al factotum. La Danza.*

** Chan. Dig. BBRD/*BBTD* 1021. Black Dyke Mills Band, Parkes.

Admirably recorded in a suitably resonant acoustic, these performances demonstrate the excellence of the Black Dyke players. But inevitably there is much less finesse here than with orchestral versions (a cornet is a poor substitute for an oboe or strings in *La Scala di seta*) and the end effect is rather like a ballet dancer with clogs on. One wonders who will want *Una voce poco fa* with a brass soloist, although there is more sense of wit in John Clough's euphonium playing in *Largo al factotum.* The virtuosity in the closing section of *La Cenerentola* is impressive and of course the galop from *William Tell* comes off well too, but probably the most suitable piece for brass-band transcription is *La Danza.* The sound is of demonstration standard on disc and chrome tape alike.

Overtures: *La Gazza ladra; L'Italiana in Algeri; La Scala di seta; Il Signor Bruschino; Il Turco in Italia; Il Viaggio a Reims; William Tell.*

*** Decca Dig. **400 049-2**; SXDL/*KSXDC* 7534 [Lon. LDR/5- 71034]. Nat. PO, Chailly.

Decca's first compact disc of Rossini overtures gives much pleasure, and is undoubtedly among the finest of the first generation of recordings in this medium. The balance is truthful with the orchestral layout very believable. Each of the solo woodwind is naturally placed within the overall perspective, the violins have a clean focus, with pianissimo detail given uncanny presence. At times there is a degree of digital edge on tuttis, but the bustle from the cellos is particularly engaging. The background silence is especially telling when Rossini's scoring is so light and felicitous, while the overall bloom afforded by the Kingsway Hall acoustic completes the concert-hall effect. The solo playing is fully worthy of such clear presentation: the cellos at the opening of *William Tell* and the principal oboe and horn in *The Italian Girl* and *The Turk in Italy* (respectively) all demonstrate that this is an orchestra of London's finest musicians. The wind articulation in *La Scala di seta* is admirably clean, although the bow tapping at the opening of *Il Signor Bruschino* is rather lazy. Just occasionally elsewhere the ensemble slips when the conductor, Riccardo Chailly, lets the exhilaration of the moment triumph over absolute discipline and poise. But if you want precision and virtuosity alone, go to Karajan; under Chailly the spirit of the music-making conveys spontaneous enjoyment too, especially in *The Thieving Magpie* and the nicely paced account of *William Tell*. Incidentally *Il Viaggio a Reims* had no overture at its first performance, but one was put together later, drawing on the ballet music from *Le Siège de Corinthe*.

Sinfonia al conventello; Grand overture.
(*) None. Dig. D/*D4* 79023. LAPO, Schwarz – CHERUBINI: *Symphony*.(*)

These two overtures – the first one an early piece with a main theme later used in *Il Signor Bruschino* – are less sharply characterful than the famous opera overtures, but they have many of the same sparkling characteristics. Brilliantly played and vividly recorded in immediate digital sound, they make an unusual and apt coupling for the rare Cherubini *Symphony*.

String sonatas Nos. 1–6.
(M) *** Argo ZK 26/7. ASMF, Marriner – DONIZETTI: *String quartet No. 4*.***

String sonatas Nos. 1–6; Duet in D for cello and double bass; Une larme; Un mot à Paganini.
*** Ph. 6769 024 (2). Accardo, Gazeau, Meunier, Petrachi, Canino.

String sonatas Nos. 1–6; Overtures: La Cambiale di matrimonio; L'Inganno felice; La Scala di seta; Il Signor Bruschino.
(M) **(*) HMV Green. ESDW 717 (2) [Sera. S 60351 (Nos. 2–5)]. Polish CO, Maksymiuk.

String sonatas Nos. 1 in G; 3 in C; 5 in E flat; 6 in D.
*** Decca VIV/*KVIC* 49. ASMF, Marriner.

Unbelievably, the *String sonatas* were written when Rossini was only twelve, yet their invention is consistently on the highest level, bubbling over with humour and infectious spontaneity. The playing of the St Martin's group under Marriner is marvellously fresh and polished, the youthful high spirits of the writing presented with glowing affection and sparkle. The separate reissue on Viva offers four of the best sonatas. The recording has been remastered and the treble is more brightly lit than before, although the slight edge on the upper range is softened in the cassette version, which is in all other respects quite the equal of the disc.

On Philips these youthful pieces are given by single strings, and it would be difficult to imagine them being better done. The playing has an effortless virtuosity and elegance that are wholly captivating. All the rival accounts, including those of I Musici (at present deleted) and the Academy of St Martin-in-the-Fields, are for larger forces. But given such spontaneous playing and excellent recording, this set will be the first choice for many.

Maksymiuk with the Polish Chamber Orchestra consistently chooses challengingly fast speeds, and the playing is brilliant, though much of the fun is lost, notably in the overtures which come as a fill-up on side four of this mid-price double-folder. Marriner's readings with the Academy are both more refined and more stylish, but these virtuoso performances are still most enjoyable. Nos. 2, 3, 4 and 5 were recorded in analogue sound earlier than the rest, but no one will complain of the quality, which is excellent.

Giovanna d'Arco (cantata). Songs: *Adieux à la vie; Addio di Rossini; En medio a mis dolores; La passeggiata; La pastorella; Se il vuol la mulinara; L'ultima ricordo.*
**(*) CBS Dig. 37296 [id.]. Horne, Katz.

The coupling of the dramatic cantata on the theme of Joan of Arc and a sequence of Rossini songs works well, although Marilyn Horne treats the cantata more heavily than one wants in Rossini, even this piece. Hers are technically formidable performances, for even the monotone of *Adieux à la vie*, an amazing elegy on one note, demands vocal as well as interpretative assurance. Martin Katz characterizes each song well in his accompaniments, though the recording is hardly refined.

Messa di Gloria.
(M) *** Ph. Seq. 6527/*7311* 223 [6500 612]. Rinaldi, Gunson, Benelli, Mitchinson, Bastin, BBC Singers, ECO, Handt.

This fascinating and invigorating work was rescued from oblivion by the conductor of this record, himself a singer. It consists of appropriately ambitious but never heavy settings of the *Kyrie* and *Gloria*, products of Rossini's first full maturity at a time (1820) when he was otherwise totally occupied with writing operas. There are links between the tenor duet which starts the *Christe* and Mathilde's aria in *Guillaume Tell*, but the delight is that so much unknown Rossini contains so much new to charm us. The performance here is lively and well sung. Good atmospheric recording too, which has transferred excellently to cassette.

Petite Messe solennelle.
** Argo ZRG 893/4 [id.]. Marshall, Hodgson, Tear, King, London Chamber Ch.; Holford, Constable, Birch.
(M) *(*) Decca Ace SDD 567 (2). Freni, Valentini, Pavarotti, Raimondi, Ch. of La Scala, Milan, Gandolfi.

Rossini's *Petite Messe solennelle* must be the most genial contribution to the church liturgy in the history of music. The description *Petite* does not refer to size, for the piece is comparable in length to Verdi's *Requiem*; rather it is the composer's modest evaluation of the work's 'significance'. But what a spontaneous and infectious piece of writing it is, bubbling over with characteristic melodic, harmonic and rhythmic invention. The composer never overreaches himself. 'I was born for *opera buffa*, as well Thou knowest,' Rossini writes touchingly on the score. 'Little skill, a little heart, and that is all. So be Thou blessed and admit me to paradise.'

The Argo version must be regarded as a stopgap until the earlier Eurodisc recording under Sawallisch reappears. It was originally issued here on RCA. The recording on Argo is of the highest quality and has striking vividness and presence (the choral entry of the *Gloria* is arresting in its impact and realism), but the reading is much too literal and lacks geniality. Both Margaret Marshall and Alfreda Hodgson sing eloquently; there is some finely shaped and expressive choral singing, and good support from the two pianists, with John Birch on the harmonium; and the clean well-balanced sound is a constant source of pleasure. But the music-making does not fully catch the music's spirit and can give only limited satisfaction.

Gandolfi unfortunately takes a coarse view of a work which demands some refinement, letting his famous soloists have their head. Freni has some beautiful moments in the *Crucifixus* and *O salutaris*, but Pavarotti and Raimondi are both well below their best, and the chorus is fruity-sounding in the wrong way.

Stabat Mater.
(*) DG Dig. **410 034-2; 2532/*3302* 046 [id.]. Ricciarelli, Valentini-Terrani, Gonzalez, Raimondi, Philh. Ch. and O, Giulini.
**[*) Decca SXL 6534 [OS 26250]. Lorengar, Minton, Pavarotti, Sotin, LSO Ch. and O, Kertesz.
** HMV Dig. ASD/*TCC-ASD* 4256 [Ang. DS/*4XS* 37901]. Malfitano, Baltsa, Gambill, Howell, Ch. and O. of Maggio Musicale Fiorentino, Muti.

Rossini loses nothing of his natural jauntiness in setting a religious text, and generally conductors treat this music simply as an offshoot of Rossini opera. Giulini, however, takes a refined and dedicated view, one that lacks something in robust qualities. Some will feel that Rossini's broad, clean-cut tunes and strong rhythms should be presented more directly, but there is much here to enjoy in the singing of the chorus as well as of the soloists, though Ricciarelli is at times ungainly on top. This appeared simultaneously with Muti's Florence version for HMV, and it is a pity that the qualities of each could not be shared. The DG version has much the more refined and atmospheric recording, and it has transferred exceptionally well to chrome tape, which captures the wide dynamic range with striking sophistication and clarity of focus. But the compact disc is even more impressive, the sound richly atmospheric, the ambience adding a great deal to the choral sound and giving the listener a convincing concert-hall effect even though the balance of the soloists is well forward.

Kertesz was a refined and thoughtful musician and he too is given excellent sound. Like Giulini, he seems intent on avoiding any charges of vulgarity. This brings out an unexpected degree of beauty, notably in the fine choral singing, and even *Cujus anima* is given extra delicacy, with Pavarotti singing most beautifully and linking back to the main theme with a subtle half-tone. Some may understandably complain that Kertesz under-plays the work in removing the open-hearted vulgarity, but he certainly makes one enjoy the music afresh. Soprano, mezzo and bass may not have all the idiomatic Italian qualities, but their singing matches Kertesz's interpretation.

Muti's view of the *Stabat Mater* is a dramatic one, and it is sad that he did not record it with the Philharmonia (the orchestra for Giulini's DG version) or with the Vienna Philharmonic, with whom he gave a memorable reading at the 1983 Salzburg Festival. As it is, the Florence Festival forces are at times rough – notably the orchestra – and the singing at times unpolished, though the solo quartet is a fine one. Warm but rather unrefined recording, with a brilliant chrome tape to match the disc closely.

OPERA

Il Barbiere di Siviglia (complete).

*** Ph. Dig. **411 058-2**; 6769/*7654* 100 (3) [id.]. Baltsa, Allen, Araiza, Trimarchi, Lloyd, Amb. Op. Ch., ASMF, Marriner.

(M) *** HMV SLS/*TC-SLS* 853 (3) [Ang. SCL 3559]. Callas, Gobbi, Alva, Ollendorf, Philh. Ch. and O, Galliera.

(M) **(*) HMV SLS/*TC-SLS* 5165 (3). Los Angeles, Alva, Cava, Wallace, Bruscantini, Glyndebourne Fest. Ch., RPO, Gui.

**(*) DG 2709 041/*3371 003* (3) [id.]. Berganza, Prey, Alva, Montarsolo, Amb. Ch., LSO, Abbado.

**(*) Decca SET 285/7 [Lon. OSA 1381]. Berganza, Ausensi, Benelli, Corena, Ghiaurov, Rossini Ch. and O of Naples, Varviso.

*(*) [Ang. SCLX/*4X3X* 3761 (3)]. Sills, Gedda, Milnes, Capecchi, Raimondi, Alldis Ch., LSO, Levine.

*(*) CBS Dig. D3 37862/*40-3* [id.]. Horne, Nucci, Barbacini, Dara, Ramey, La Scala, Milan, Ch. and O, Chailly.

Marriner, conducting his first complete opera recording, finds a rare sense of fun. His characteristic polish and refinement – beautifully caught in the clear, finely balanced recording – never get in the way of urgent spontaneity, the sparkle of the moment. So for example in the big Act II quintet, when the wool is being pulled over Don Basilio's eyes, there is an ideal balance between musical precision and dramatic presentation. Thomas Allen as Figaro – far more than a buffo figure – and Agnes Baltsa as Rosina – tough and biting too – manage to characterize strongly, even when coping with florid divisions, and though Araiza allows himself too many intrusive aitches, he easily outshines latterday rivals, sounding heroic, not at all the small-scale tenorino, but never coarse either. Fine singing too from Robert Lloyd as Basilio. Though there is some reduction of range on top, the chrome-tape transfer is refined and of Philips's best quality. However, no attempt is made to lay out each Act on a single cassette. The libretto is clear, but in small print. On compact disc the theatrical feeling and sense of atmosphere are enhanced, with the placing of the singers strikingly clear. There is extensive cueing of individual numbers.

Gobbi and Callas were here at their most inspired, and with the recording quality nicely refurbished the HMV is an outstanding set, not absolutely complete in its text, but so crisp and sparkling it can be confidently recommended. Callas remains supreme as a minx-like Rosina, summing up the character superbly in *Una voce poco fa*. In the final ensemble, despite the usual reading of the score, Rosina's verse is rightly given premier place at the very end. The cassettes were issued in 1983 and are ideally tailored, with Act II complete on side four. The transfer is of EMI's highest quality, the sound vivid and clear, and the libretto is clearly printed.

Victoria de los Angeles is as charming a Rosina as you will ever find: no viper this one, as she claims in *Una voce poco fa*. Musically it is an unforceful performance – Rossini's brilliant *fioriture* done lovingly, with no sense of fear or danger – and that matches the gently rib-nudging humour of what is otherwise a recording of the Glyndebourne production of the early 1960s. It does not fizz as much as other Glyndebourne Rossini on record, but with elaborate stage direction in the stereo production and with a characterful line-up of soloists, it is an endearing performance, which in its line is unmatched. The recording still sounds well; the cassette transfer is generally first-class, indeed for the most part almost demonstration-worthy. The only small drawback is that the high transfer level has brought slight peaking on just one or two of Victoria de los Angeles's high fortissimos in her key arias. It is only a tiny blemish but a pity.

Abbado directs a clean and satisfying performance that lacks the last degree of sparkle. Berganza's interpretation of the role of Rosina remains very consistent with her earlier performance on Decca, but the Figaro here, Hermann Prey, is more reliable, and the playing and recording have an extra degree of polish. The text is not so complete as the Decca (omitting the tenor's Act II aria, for example). The cassettes have been remastered since their original issue, and the result is most successful, with plenty of sparkle and no loss of body. The layout, however, follows the discs.

Vocally the Decca set of the *Barber*, with Teresa Berganza as an agile Rosina, is reliable. It is also very well recorded, and Silvio Varviso secures electrifying effects in many of Rossini's high-spirited ensembles. There remain important reservations. Manuel Ausensi as Figaro himself is rather gruff both vocally and dramatically, though he was chosen specifically because of the authenticity of having a darker-toned voice than is usual in the part. Ugo Benelli is charming as the Count, a free-voiced 'tenorino', though he sounds nervous in his first aria. Corena's fine Dr Bartolo is already well-known from two earlier sets, and Ghiaurov sings with characteristic richness as Basilio. This version is textually not quite complete, but it contains much more than usual and it includes the often omitted Act II tenor aria which uses the *Non più mesta* theme from *La Cenerentola*.

Levine conducts vigorously in his Angel version, but neither the singing of Beverly Sills nor that of Nicolai Gedda can be recommended with any enthusiasm, the one unpleasing in tone for all its brilliance, the other seriously strained – a reminder, no more, of what Gedda's voice once was. Sherrill Milnes makes a strong, forthright Figaro, in every way the centre of attention here, and Ruggero Raimondi is a sonorous Basilio. Good recording. (This set has been withdrawn in the UK.)

Chailly's CBS version is a generally coarse and disappointing set, not helped by indifferent playing by the orchestra of La Scala. Marilyn Horne makes a formidable Rosina, the voice still agile if not so cleanly focused as once it was, but Paolo Barbacini is unacceptably rough as Almaviva. As Figaro, Leo Nucci is vocally inconsistent. All the singers are more impressive in ensembles than in solo items. The cassette layout follows the discs. The chrome-tape transfer is vivid and clear. The libretto is rather faintly printed.

La Cenerentola (complete).

** DG 2709 039 (3) [id.]. Berganza, Alva, Montarsolo, Capecchi, Scottish Op. Ch., LSO, Abbado.

La Cenerentola has not been lucky on records, and the DG set, although enjoyable, lacks the extrovert bravura and sparkle of an ideal performance. The atmosphere in places is almost of a concert version, with excellent balance between the participants, helped by the fine recording. The recitative in general has plenty of life, particularly when Dandini (Renato Capecchi) is involved. Berganza, agile in the coloratura, seems too mature, even matronly, for the fairy-tale role of Cinderella. Alva sings well enough but is somewhat self-conscious in the florid writing. Abbado, though hardly witty in his direction, inspires delicate playing throughout.

Elisabetta Regina d'Inghilterra (complete).
*** Ph. 6703 067 (3). Caballé, Carreras, Masterson, Creffield, Benelli, Jenkins, Amb. S., New Philh. O, Masini.

The first surprise in this lively operatic setting of the Elizabeth and Leicester story comes in the overture, which turns out to be the one which we know as belonging to *Il Barbiere di Siviglia*. It is one of a whole sequence of self-borrowings, which add zest to a generally delightful score. When Queen Elizabeth's big aria in Act II wanders into music which we know as the cabaletta to Rosina's *Una voce poco fa*, it may seem strange to have the formidable Tudor monarch associated with comedy, but in their different ways both ladies were certainly vipers. There are passages where Rossini's invention is not at its peak, and the libretto is typically unconvincing, but in a well-sprung performance like this, with beautiful playing from the LSO and some very fine singing, it is a set for any Rossinian to investigate. Of the two tenors José Carreras proves much the more stylish as Leicester, with Ugo Benelli, in the unusual role of a tenor-villain, singing less elegantly than he once did. Caballé produces some ravishing sounds, though she is not always electrifying. Lively conducting and splendid recording.

Guglielmo Tell (*William Tell*; complete).
*** Decca D 219 D 4/*K 219 K 44* [Lon. 1446/5-]. Pavarotti, Freni, Milnes, Ghiaurov, Amb. Op. Ch., Nat. PO, Chailly.

Rossini wrote his massive opera about William Tell in French, and the first really complete recording (under Gardelli on HMV) used that language. But Chailly and his team here put forward a strong case for preferring Italian, with its open vowels, in music which glows with Italianate lyricism. Chailly's is a forceful reading, particularly strong in the many ensembles, and superbly recorded. Milnes makes a heroic Tell, always firm, and though Pavarotti has his moments of coarseness he sings the role of Arnoldo with glowing tone. Ghiaurov too is in splendid voice, while subsidiary characters are almost all well taken, with such a fine singer as John Tomlinson, for example, finely resonant as Melchthal. The women singers too are impressive, with Mirella Freni as the heroine Matilde providing dramatic strength as well as sweetness. To fit this epic piece on to eight sides requires close-grooving, but the sound is superb, rich and atmospheric as well as brilliant. The cassette transfer is of outstandingly sophisticated quality; at times the choral sound might be fractionally more sharply focused on disc, but the vibrant projection of the soloists and the depth and atmosphere of the overall sound picture are consistently demonstration-worthy. The libretto/booklet too is admirably clear.

L'Italiana in Algeri (complete).
*** Decca SET 262/4 [Lon. OSA 1375]. Berganza, Corena, Alva, Panerai, Ch. and O of Maggio Musicale Fiorentino, Varviso.
*** Erato STU 71394 (3) [RCA ARL3/*ARK3* 3855]. Horne, Palacio, Ramey, Trimarchi, Battle, Zaccaria, Prague Ch., Sol. Ven., Scimone.

Choice between the Decca and Erato sets is by no means straightforward as each is first-class, and each has its own special merits. The Decca presentation, however, includes the usual fine documentation and a libretto, which one has come to expect from this source, and for most listeners this will tip the scales in its favour. This set appeared at about the same time as the Decca *Cenerentola* (now withdrawn) also with the chorus and orchestra of the Maggio Musicale Fiorentino. But there the similarities end, for where *Cenerentola* lacked the right Rossinian sparkle, this performance has it in abundance, and the music blossoms readily. Teresa Berganza makes an enchanting Italian girl, and the three principal men are all better – and certainly more characterful – than one has any right to expect in these days when florid singing is no longer cultivated (by men at least) in the way it should be. The recording is outstanding, and adds enormously to the sparkle of the whole presentation.

Scholarship as well as Rossinian zest have gone into Scimone's highly enjoyable version, beautifully played and recorded with as stylish a team of soloists as one can expect nowadays. The text is complete, the original orchestration has been restored (as in the comic duetting of piccolo and bassoon in the reprise in the overture) and alternative versions of certain arias are given as an appendix. Marilyn Horne makes a dazzling, positive Isabella, and Samuel Ramey is splendidly firm as Mustafa. Domenico Trimarchi is a delightful Taddeo and Ernesto Palacio an agile Lindoro, not coarse, though the recording does not always catch his tenor timbre well. Nonetheless the sound is generally very good indeed, and the only regret is that the booklet includes no English translation – a pity when there is more unfamiliar material here than usual.

Mosè in Egitto (complete).

*** Ph. Dig. 6769/*7654* 081 (3) [id.]. Raimondi, Anderson, Nimsgern, Palacio, Gal, Amb. Op. Ch., Philh. O, Scimone.

** Hung. SLPX 12290/2. Gregor, Sólyom, Nagy, Begányi, Hamari, Kalmár, Hungarian R. and TV Ch., Hungarian State Op. O, Gardelli.

For a century and more it was assumed that Rossini's later thoughts on the subject of a Moses opera – his expanded version for Paris – were the ones to be preferred. It is good that Scimone has taken scholarly advice and here, in a direct and understanding reading, presents the second and far preferable of the two Italian versions. So here the last and briefest of the three Acts is strongly expanded with a big ensemble based on Moses' prayer to make it almost a forerunner of another great chorus for the Children of Israel, *Va pensiero* from Verdi's *Nabucco*.

Other Verdian parallels come out, for some of the ceremonial writing suggests a much later Egyptian opera, *Aïda*, as well as a masterpiece written at that same period, the *Requiem*. Clearly Scimone justifies his claim that the 1819 version is dramatically more effective than both the earlier Italian one and the later Paris one. Among the soloists Raimondi relishes not only solemn moments like the great invocation in Act I and the soaring prayer of Act III but the rage aria in Act II, almost like Handel updated if with disconcerting foretastes of Dr Malatesta in Donizetti's *Don Pasquale*.

The writing for the soprano and tenor lovers (the latter the son of Pharaoh and in effect the villain of the piece) is relatively conventional, though the military flavour of their Act I cabaletta is refreshingly different. Ernesto Palacio and June Anderson make a strong pair, and the mezzo, Zehava Gal, is another welcome newcomer as Pharaoh's wife. Siegmund Nimsgern is a fine Pharaoh, Salvatore Fisichella an adequate Arone (Aaron). The recording is generally refined and well balanced. As usual with Philips, the chrome cassettes are not transferred at the highest level, with some loss of sharpness of focus in the chorus. The libretto is in very small print.

The Hungarian version of *Mosè*, using the Paris text of 1827 but translated back into Italian, has the merit of Gardelli's understanding conducting. Much of the singing is pleasing too, but when the far more vital 1819 text of *Mosè in Egitto* is available in the excellent Philips set, this is hardly competitive. Act II, Scene iii is omitted.

Otello (complete).

*** Ph. 6769 023 (3)/*7699 110* (2) [id.]. Carreras, Von Stade, Condò, Pastine, Fisichella, Ramey, Amb. S., Philh. O, Lopez-Cobos.

Quite apart from the fact that the libretto of Rossini's *Otello* bears remarkably little resemblance to Shakespeare – virtually none at all until the last Act – the layout of voices is odd. Not only is Otello a tenor role; so is Rodrigo (second in importance), and Iago too. It is some tribute to this performance, superbly recorded on both disc and cassette, and brightly and stylishly directed by Lopez-

Cobos, that the line-up of tenors is turned into an asset, with three nicely contrasted soloists. Carreras is here at his finest – most affecting in his recitative before the murder while Fisichella copes splendidly with the high tessitura of Rodrigo's role, and Pastine has a distinctive timbre to identify him as the villain. Frederica von Stade pours forth a glorious flow of beautiful tone, well-matched by Nucci Condò as Emilia. Samuel Ramey is excellent too in the bass role of Elmiro. *Otello* Rossini-style is an operatic curiosity, but this recording helps to explain why it so ensnared such a sensitive opera-lover as the novelist Stendhal.

Semiramide (opera): complete.
*** Decca SET 317/9 [Lon. OSA 1383]. Sutherland, Horne, Serge, Rouleau, Amb. Op. Ch., LSO, Bonynge.

Wagner once said of this opera that 'it exhibits all the faults by which Italian opera can be distinguished'; but taking the modern view, that is rather to its credit. The story is admittedly improbable, involving the love which almost all the male characters bear for the Princess Azema, a lady who rather curiously appears very little in the opera. Instead Rossini concentrates on the love of Queen Semiramide for the Prince Arsace (a mezzo-soprano role), and musically the result is a series of fine duets, superbly performed here by Sutherland and Horne. There are other numbers too – notably the big soprano aria, *Bel raggio* – that have survived the general neglect, but what a complete account brings out is the consistency of the drama, the music involving the listener even where the story falls short. Semiramide in Sutherland's interpretation is not so much a Lady Macbeth figure as a passionate, sympathetic woman, and with dramatic music predominating over languorous cantilena, one has her best, bright manner rather than her 'mooning' style. Horne is well contrasted, direct and masculine in style, and Spiro Malas makes a firm, clear contribution in a minor role. Rouleau and Serge are variable but more than adequate, and Bonynge once again confirms the high opinions of his alert, rhythmic control in opera recordings. Brilliant recording.

Duets from *Semiramide: Mitrane! . . . Serbami ognor si fido; No, non ti lascio . . . Eben . . . a te ferisci . . . Giorno d'orrore!*
*** Decca SET 456 [Lon. OS/5- 26168]. Sutherland, Horne, LSO, Bonynge – BELLINI: *Norma*: Duets.**(*)

Serbami ognor from the complete set of *Semiramide* provides one of the finest examples of duet-singing ever recorded. Even Sutherland and Horne have never surpassed this in their many collaborations. With a second *Semiramide* duet and two duets from *Norma* the disc is most attractive.

Le Siège de Corinthe (complete).
**(*) EMI 2C 167 02571/3 [Ang. SCLX 3819]. Sills, Verrett, Theyard, Diaz, Howell, Amb. Op. Ch., LSO, Schippers.

The Siege of Corinth, like other Rossini operas, had a chequered history. In its final form in French it was produced in Paris in 1826, a reworking of an earlier *opera seria*, *Maometto II*, given in Naples six years earlier. Thomas Schippers, the conductor here, first edited the score for a revival at La Scala, Milan, in 1969, and made this recording in preparation for another production at the Met in New York with virtually the same cast. The pity is that he encouraged the coloratura prowess of the prima donna, Beverly Sills, at the expense of Rossini's final thoughts, with display material drawn from the earlier version. Many Rossinians will no doubt remain untroubled by academic points, in gratitude that so much vigorously inspired music has been brought to the gramophone. The story of beleaguered Greeks besieged by the Turks in 1459 has stirring qualities, and some of the most striking passages are the patriotic choruses, recognizably Rossinian but not at all in his usual vein. Sills, as so often on record, is variable, brilliant in coloratura but rarely sweet of tone, and she is completely upstaged by Shirley Verrett, singing magnificently. Some strong singing too among the others, though not all the men are very deft with ornamentation. Good, warm recording.

Tancredi (complete).
** Arion ARN 338 010 (3) [Peters PLD 017/9]. Patricia Price, Francis, Stokes, Lewis, McDonnell, Jeffes, Ch. and O, Perras.

Written when Rossini was still only twenty-one, *Tancredi* – unbelievably, his ninth opera – was his first really serious one, a *melodramma eroico*, a tale of medieval chivalry in which the part of the hero, following the tradition of the *opera seria*, is a travesty role given to a mezzo-soprano. Here Patricia Price makes a firm-toned hero, a mezzo who can yet cope with a sudden top C; but neither she nor the other members of a largely British cast quite measures up to the fearsome technical demands of early Rossini with its elaborate *fioriture*. The orchestral playing is only just adequate, and with dry recording the set must be regarded as a stopgap only, valuable for illuminating a work that is full of superbly memorable ideas, not least the aria which at once made Rossini a star, *Di tanti palpiti*.

Il Turco in Italia (complete).
*** CBS Dig. D3 37859/*40-3* [id.]. Caballé, Palacio, Ramey, Dara, Nucci, Berbié, Barbacini, Amb. Op. Ch., Nat. PO, Chailly.

Il Turco in Italia (abridged).
(M) ** HMV SLS 5148 (2). Callas, Gedda, Rossi-Lemeni, Calabrese, Stabile, Ch. and O of La Scala, Milan, Gavazzeni.

Chailly's direction is lively in this complete version of a delightful opera previously known on record through a much-cut account featuring Maria Callas. Memories of the formidable and individual Callas may make Caballé's characterization of the heroine, young wife of the old Don Geronio, seem relatively pallid, but she sings well. Enzo Dara as Geronio, Samuel Ramey as the Turk and Leo Nucci as Geronio's friend, Prosdocimo, are all first-rate, and Ernesto Palacio copes well with the big challenging aria given to the heroine's servant, Narciso, and omitted from the Callas recording. Warm if not ideally refined sound. The big comic quintet of Act II makes an excellent sampler. The chrome cassettes are of demonstration quality, clear and vivid, with a fine bloom on the voices and the perspectives naturally caught. The libretto is well printed.

Callas was at her peak when she recorded this rare Rossini opera in the mid-1950s. As ever, there are lumpy moments vocally, but she gives a sharply characterful performance as the capricious Fiorilla, married to an elderly, jealous husband and bored with it. Nicola Rossi-Lemeni as the Turk of the title is characterful too, but not the firmest of singers, and it is left to Nicolai Gedda as the young lover and Franco Calabrese as the jealous husband to match Callas in stylishness. It is good too to have the veteran Mariano Stabile singing the role of the Poet in search of a plot. Walter Legge's production has plainly added to the sparkle, and the stereo transcription recording sounds well for its period. The tape transfer is smooth and quite well balanced: the sound reflects the limited range of the discs.

Arias: *Il Barbiere di Siviglia: Una voce poco fa. La Cenerentola: Nacqui all'affano. Otello: Assisa a'piè d'un salice.*
*** Ph. 9500 098/*7300 511* [id.]. Von Stade, Rotterdam PO, De Waart – MOZART: *Arias.****

Superbly sung, finely characterized, these performances of Rossini arias can hardly be faulted, whether it is Rosina's *Una voce poco fa* or the rare *Willow song and prayer* from Rossini's idiosyncratic version of *Otello*. Excellent recording.

Arias: *La Cenerentola: Nacqui all'affano. Guglielmo Tell: S'allontano alfin!; Selva opaca. Semiramide: Bel raggio lusinghier.*
*(*) HMV ASD/*TC-ASD* 3984. Callas, Paris Conservatoire O, Rescigno – DONIZETTI: *Arias.***

These recordings made in the mid-1960s show a degree of cautiousness that rarely marked Callas's earlier work. She was obviously very conscious of all the criticisms and did her utmost to avoid the worst blots. She generally succeeds, but there is something far less positive about the end result, and, more serious, the performances do not have that refinement of detail that at her peak lit up so many phrases and made them unforgettable. The recording is vivid; on cassette there are one or two moments of peaking on high fortissimos.

Roussel, Albert (1869–1937)

Bacchus et Ariane, Suite No. 2.
(M) **(*) DG 2543 807 [id.]. LOP, Markevitch – MILHAUD: *Carnaval d'Aix****; SATIE: *Parade.***

Markevitch secures good results from the Lamoureux orchestra in the second suite and the 1960 recording still sounds eminently satisfactory. Although he is at times short on poetry, the performance has dedication and the Parisian orchestra is completely at home in the idiom. At mid-price and given the attractions of the coupling, this deserves a strong recommendation.

Piano concerto, Op. 36.
(M) ** Sup. 1410 2705. Krajný, Prague CO, Macura – HONEGGER: *Concertino***; POULENC: *Aubade.***(*)

Roussel's textures are often congested and unrelieved in busier movements, and the somewhat reverberant acoustic of the House of Artists does not lend this score greater transparency. However, this is a reflective and intelligent performance which does more justice to the score than many earlier versions. At the time of writing there is no alternative recording of either the Roussel or the couplings.

Concerto for small orchestra, Op. 34; Symphony No. 2 in B flat, Op. 23.
**(*) EMI 26 069 73096. Colonne SO, Dervauz.

The *Second Symphony* is a powerful work dating from 1919–21 and marks a turning point in Roussel's career as does *Pour une fête de printemps* which had originally been intended to form part of the work. The *Symphony* is larger in scale than either of its successors and the conception is altogether more spacious and yet every bit as concentrated in mood. There are the same astringent harmonies and the same rhythmic vitality, yet the canvas is never overcrowded as it occasionally seems in the later symphonies. It is given a persuasive performance by the Colonne orchestra under Pierre Dervaux. The Orchestre National, who recorded it in the early 1970s under Jean Martinon, is the better orchestra and gives a more purposeful account of the work, coupling it more logically with *Pour une fête de printemps* (Erato STU 70569), but this is temporarily out of circulation. Dervaux offers another rarity, a neoclassical *Concerto for small orchestra* (1927), an inventive and original piece. The recording is absolutely first-class.

Symphonies Nos. 3 in G min., Op. 42; 4 in A, Op. 53.
**(*) Erato EPR/*MCE* 15546. LOP, Munch.

Roussel's *Third* and *Fourth Symphonies make an eminently satisfying coupling but, judging from deletion lists, it is one that seems to maintain only a tenuous hold on the catalogue. Munch's account with the Lamoureux orchestra dates from 1965 and had the benefit of infinitely better orchestral playing and greater commitment than its earlier rival* [*Ansermet and the Suisse Romande, made in the earliest days of stereo*]. *These are exhilarating performances, well worth paying money for, and although the recording is not as rich as the finest modern discs, it is perfectly acceptable. Although Munch's performances do not eclipse memories of Bernstein in No. 3 and Karajan in No. 4, until recently available in an excellent HMV transfer, they are marvellously exhilarating and powerful. The cassette is bright and clear, but the upper range is fierce and there is a lack of body.*

Serenade for flute, violin, viola, cello and harp, Op. 30.
(M) *** O-L SOL 60048. Melos Ens. – RAVEL: *Introduction and allegro* etc.***

The Melos version has held its place in the catalogue for more than two decades. It is an inspired account and beautifully engineered. It is part of a concert which includes an equally memorable account of Ravel's *Introduction and allegro.*

Serenade for flute, violin, viola, cello and harp, Op. 30; Trio for flute, viola and cello, Op. 40; Impromptu for harp, Op. 30.
*** H M H M A 735. Marie-Claire Jamet Quintet (members).

A welcome addition to the all-too-meagre Roussel discography. The inventive and charming *Serenade* is elegantly played, even if it does not efface memories of the Melos Ensemble version. The value of this issue lies in its including the only account of Roussel's powerful, original and beautifully-wrought *Trio for flute, viola and cello*, dating from 1929, not long before the *Third Symphony*. The performance is sensitive; Christian Lardé is particularly eloquent. Marie-Claire Jamet gives an elegant account of the *Impromptu for harp*, and the recording is eminently satisfactory. Self-recommending.

Rózsa, Miklós (born 1907)

Ben Hur (film score): extended excerpts.
*** Decca PFS 4394 [Lon. SPA 21166]. Nat. PO and Ch., composer.

Rózsa's score for *Ben Hur* is a potent mixture of orchestral spectacle and choral kitsch. There is an appealing lyrical theme for the love story, an exciting sequence for the galley slaves rowing into battle, and a stirring *Parade* for the famous chariot race. But towards the end the religiosity, with its lavish panoply of chorus and orchestra, overwhelms the listener in an ocean of sumptuous vulgarity. Certainly it is all presented here with great conviction, and the Decca Phase Four techniques create the maximum impact, with rich sonorities and a sparklingly brilliant upper range.

Piano sonata, Op. 20; Bagatelles, Op. 12; The Vintner's Daughter, Op. 23; Variations, Op. 9.
(M) *** Uni. UNS 259. Parkin.

The Hungarian Miklós Rózsa, well known for such scores as *Quo Vadis*, *Ben Hur* and other film spectaculars, is also a serious composer for the concert platform, and these accessible pieces show him to possess more than mere fluency. The *Sonata* is a powerful work of widely contrasting moods and well-integrated ideas. The piano writing is thoroughly idiomatic, and the playing of Eric Parkin is persuasive and commanding. Rózsa is not so deeply individual in his musical language as Bartók or Kodály, but he repays investigation nonetheless. Good recording.

Rubbra, Edmund (born 1901)

(i) *Soliloquy for cello and orchestra, Op. 57;* (ii) *Symphony No. 7 in C, Op. 88.*
*** Lyr. SRCS 119. (i) Saram, LSO, Handley; (ii) LPO, Boult.

The Rubbra *Seventh Symphony* originally appeared in harness with the *Tallis fantasia*, and its reappearance in this coupling may well attract collectors reluctant to duplicate the Vaughan Williams. The *Soliloquy*, a decade earlier than this *Symphony*, was written just before the *Fifth*. It has been described by Ronald Stevenson as 'a saraband, symphonically developed in flexible tempo . . . a meditation with flashes of interior drama', and its grave beauty exerts a strong appeal. Rohan de Saram plays with a restrained eloquence that is impressive, and he has excellent support from the LSO under Vernon Handley. The *Soliloquy* is placed after the *Symphony* on side two and takes about fifteen minutes. The *Symphony* itself is a considerable piece and Rubbra's admirers will surely be attracted to this new coupling. The recording is up to the high standards we expect from Lyrita.

Symphony No. 5 in B flat, Op. 63.
(*) Chan. ABR/*ABT* 1018 [id.]. Melbourne SO, Schönzeler – BLISS: *Checkmate.*(*)

Rubbra's *Fifth Symphony* is a noble work which grows naturally from the symphonic soil of Elgar and Sibelius. Although the Melbourne orchestra is not in the very first flight, they play this music for all they are worth, and the strings have a genuine intensity and lyrical fervour that compensate for the opaque effect of the octave doublings. The introduction is grander and more spacious here than in Barbirolli's pioneering record with the Hallé, made in the early 1950s, and the finale has splendid lightness of touch. More attention to refinement of nuance would have paid dividends in the slow movement, whose brooding melancholy does not quite emerge to full effect. Altogether, though, this is an imposing performance which reflects credit on all concerned. The recording is well balanced and lifelike; on tape its sonority comes over effectively, but the ear perceives that the upper range is rather restricted.

Symphonies Nos. 6, Op. 80; 8 (Hommage à Teilhard de Chardin), Op. 132.
*** Lyr. SRCS 127. Philh. O, Del Mar.

The *Sixth* is one of the most admired of Rubbra's symphonies and dates from 1953–4. It has much the same purity of spirit and directness of utterance that distinguish his very finest work, and its slow movement is arguably the most beautiful single movement in all of Rubbra's output: in tranquillity of spirit and serenity it almost recalls the *Missa in honorem Sancti Dominici* written five years earlier. As always in Rubbra there is a strong sense of linear continuity, of a melodic line that is supple yet unbroken. The *Eighth* (1968) pays tribute to Teilhard de Chardin and has something of the mystical intensity that finds its most visionary outlet in the *Ninth Symphony*. The clarity of its scoring reminds one that Rubbra was at one time a pupil of Holst. Norman Del Mar and the Philharmonia Orchestra play marvellously. Rubbra's music speaks with directness and without artifice and its sound world has never been better served by the engineers than it is here.

Piano music: *Introduction, aria and fugue, Op. 104; Introduction and fugue, Op. 19; 9 Little pieces, Op. 74; 8 Preludes, Op. 131; Prelude and fugue, Op. 69; 4 Studies, Op. 139.*
*** Phoenix DGS 1009. Moore.

Edmund Rubbra was a fine pianist, as older readers will recall, but his output for the instrument is so small that it can be accommodated on one record: half-a-dozen opus numbers in an *œuvre* comprising more than 150. Yet the music, quite apart from being well laid out for the piano, as one would expect, is far from uncharacteristic or insubstantial. Perhaps the most impressive of the pieces are the *Eight Preludes*, Op. 131, which are both inventive and atmospheric; but rewards are to be found in practically all this music. Edward Moore is a convinced and convincing advocate, and though he is not particularly well recorded, the sound is good enough to allow the interest of this issue to carry an unreserved recommendation.

Rubinstein, Anton (1829–94)

Piano sonatas Nos. 1 in F min., Op. 12; 3 in F, Op. 41.
*** Hyp. Dig. A 66017. Howard.

Leslie Howard is a fine virtuoso who has made a speciality of the music of Anton Rubinstein. One can hardly imagine more persuasive performances than these, though the actual invention is barely enough to sustain interest over ambitious spans. Rubinstein wrote these display works for himself to play in his recitals, and no doubt his personality helped to persuade early listeners. The digital recording is first-rate.

Ruggles, Carl (1876–1971)

(i) *Angels for brass* (two versions). (ii) *Evocations; Men; Men and Mountains; Organum; Portals* (for strings); *Sun-Treader*. (iii) *Evocations* (original piano version). (i; iv) *Exaltation for brass, chorus and organ*. (v) *Toys for voice and piano*. (vi) *Vox clamans in deserto* (for chamber orchestra and mezzo-soprano).
*** CBS 79225 (2) [Col. M2 34591]. (i) Brass Ens., Schwarz; (ii) Buffalo PO, Tilson Thomas; (iii) Kirkpatrick; (iv) Gregg Smith Singers; Raven; (v) Blegen, Tilson Thomas; (vi) Morgan, Speculum Musicae.

Carl Ruggles was in his way as striking an original among American composers as the more fêted Charles Ives. These two discs bring together all that he wrote, giving, with the help of dedicated performances, a complete portrait of a fascinating figure, whose experiments in atonality have a communicative directness to make them more essentially 'modern' than much more recent music. *Sun-Treader* is the biggest piece here, but every one of these often craggy items is important, with *Evocations* given in both its solo piano and orchestral form. With informative if idiosyncratic notes, this collection can be strongly recommended to any adventurous listener.

Rutter, John (born 1943)

The reluctant dragon; The wind in the willows.
**(*) Masterchord MCL/*MCK* 412. Richard Baker, King's Singers, City of L. Sinf., Hickox.

John Rutter is famous for his carols, but these settings of two famous Kenneth Grahame stories are no less tunefully communicative. They lie halfway between cantata and dramatized narrative and the musical style is characteristically eclectic. With Gilbert and Sullivan undertones and including songs simulating pop music of the 1940s (among other derivations), it is all highly agreeable if rather bland, notably a Rodgers-style ballad which sentimentalizes the end of the *Wind in the willows* episode, after Toad's escape from prison. All the music is expertly sung and played and blends well with the warmly involving narrative, splendidly done by Richard Baker. This will not suit children who are attuned to the more abrasive world of the disco, but in its way it is very successful, if somewhat complacently ingenuous. The recording is excellent; disc and tape are virtually indistinguishable.

Saint-Saëns, Camille (1835–1921)

Allegro appassionato for cello and orchestra, Op. 43; Caprice in D for violin and orchestra (arr. Ysaÿe); *Carnival of the animals: Le Cygne; Cello concerto No. 1 in A min., Op. 33; Wedding Cake* (*Caprice-valse*) *for piano and strings, Op. 76; Le Déluge: Prelude, Op. 45.*
**(*) HMV ASD 3058. Yan-Pascal Tortelier, De la Pau, Paul Tortelier, CBSO, Frémaux.

(i) *Allegro appassionato; Cello concerto No. 1; Le Cygne.*
(M) *** HMV Green. ESD/*TC-ESD* 107762-1/*4* [Ara. 8038/*9038*]. Tortelier (as above) – TCHAIKOVSKY: *Rococo variations* etc.***

Paul Tortelier gives an assured account of the *A minor Cello concerto*, but fails to make much of the busy but uninspired *Allegro appassionato*. Yan-Pascal Tortelier plays with charm in the *Caprice* and catches the *salon* element in the music without vulgarizing it. He plays with pleasing simplicity in the *Prelude* to the oratorio *Le Déluge*, which has a concertante part for the solo violin. The *Wedding Cake caprice* is also nicely done, even though Maria de la Pau does not reveal a strong personality. With *Le Cygne* (Paul Tortelier accompanied by a harp) thrown in as a bonus, this is quite an attractive anthology, well recorded. Part of it has been extracted and issued on Greensleeve, coupled with music by Tchaikovsky, and this generously filled mid-price issue is a good bargain, with very good sound on both disc and tape.

Carnival of the animals.

*** Ph. Dig. **400 016-2**; 9500/*7300* 973 [id.]. Villa, Jennings, Pittsburgh SO, Previn – RAVEL: *Ma Mère l'Oye.**** C.

(B) *** CfP CFP/*TC-CFP* 40086. Katin, Fowke, SNO, Gibson – RAVEL: *Ma Mère l'Oye***(*); BIZET: *Jeux d'enfants.****

(M) *** HMV Green. ESD/*TC-ESD* 7114. Hephzibah Menuhin, Simon, Philh. O, Kurtz – BRITTEN: *Young person's guide*; PROKOFIEV: *Peter.****

(M) *** ASV ACM/*ZCACM* 2005. Goldstone, Ian Brown, RPO, Hughes – PROKOFIEV: *Peter.****

(M) *** HMV Green. ESD 7020 [(d) Ang. S 36421]. Ciccolini, Weissenberg, Paris Conservatoire O, Prêtre – POULENC: *Babar.***

While in the bargain range the CfP version of Saint-Saëns's delightful zoological fantasy remains highly competitive for those not willing to go to a premium-priced issue, Previn's version makes a ready first choice, particularly when the coupling is outstanding and both are recorded in superbly rich and atmospheric sound. On some machines the bass resonance of the somewhat larger-than-life pianos may seem slightly excessive. That apart, the quality has remarkable bloom, particularly on the vivid compact disc. On chrome tape the bass overbalances the treble. The music is played with infectious rhythmic spring and great refinement. It is a mark of the finesse of this performance – which has plenty of bite and vigour as well as polish – that the great cello solo of *Le Cygne* is so naturally presented, with the engineers refusing to spotlight the soloist. The shading of half-tones in Anne Martindale Williams's exquisitely beautiful playing is made all the more tenderly affecting. Fine contributions too from the two pianists. The CD version brings out all these qualities even more strikingly.

On CfP the solo pianists, Peter Katin and Philip Fowke, enter fully into the spirit of the occasion, with Gibson directing the Scottish National Orchestra with affectionate, unforced humour. The couplings are attractive and, with excellent recording on disc and cassette alike, this is worth considering, irrespective of price.

However, HMV's Greensleeve reissue of Kurtz's splendid version from the end of the 1950s has even more generous couplings and offers some vintage solo contributions from members of the Philharmonia Orchestra. The recording too is first-class, although, curiously, the definition is poor for the double basses in their portrayal of *Tortoises*. Elsewhere orchestral detail is admirably firm and vivid, and *The Swan* is memorably serene. The two pianists are spirited, and Kurtz's direction is witty and attentive.

The two pianists on ASV play with point and style, and the accompaniment has both spirit and spontaneity. *The Swan* is perhaps a trifle self-effacing, but otherwise this is very enjoyable, the humour appreciated without being underlined. The recording is excellent, with the cassette matching the disc closely.

The Paris recording with Ciccolini and Weissenberg (who make a contribution of some distinction) offers a refreshingly brilliant account of Saint-Saëns's *jeu d'esprit*. It opens a little heavily, but the characterization is nicely managed, with some very good orchestral playing. This is thoroughly competitive, if the *Babar* coupling is attractive.

(i) *Carnival of the animals;* (ii) *Piano concertos Nos. 2 in G min., Op. 22; 4 in C min., Op. 44. 6 Études for the left hand only, Op. 135.*

(M) *** HMV *TCC2-POR 154595-9*. Ciccolini, with (i) Weissenberg and Prêtre (as above); (ii) O de Paris, Baudo.

Tape collectors should be more than satisfied with this generous compilation, which offers first-class sound. Ciccolini's performances of the two favourite *Concertos* are in every way distinguished; they combine elegance with spirit. No. 4 is especially fine. With the six *Études* thrown in as an attractive bonus (Saint-Saëns was a superb miniaturist) this is all most enjoyable.

(i) *Carnival of the animals;* (ii) *Cello concerto No. 1 in A min., Op. 33.*

(M) ** DG Priv. 2535/*3335* 491. (i) Kontarsky Duo, VPO, Boehm; (ii) Fournier, LAP, Martinon.

Marvellous playing from the Kontarskys and clean, rhythmic articulation from the orchestra in the *Carnival*. This is both stylish and spirited. The recording is good too, but it is thinner for the *Cello concerto*, recorded fifteen years earlier. Fournier brings his customary nobility and eloquence to this work and he is well supported by Martinon, but the dated sound is thrown into relief by the obviously more modern quality of the coupling. However, the cassette, which has rather less range than the disc, tends to smooth over the difference somewhat.

Carnival of the animals (trans. for brass and percussion by P. Reeve).

*(*) Decca Dig. 410 125-1/*4* [id.]. Jones Brass Ens. (with *Concert of French music* *(*)).

A promising idea which proves disappointingly coarse in its realization. The wit evaporates, and the solo horn is no substitute for the cello in portraying *The Swan*. The sound is first-class and the playing itself is technically brilliant.

Cello concerto No. 1 in A min., Op. 33.

❀*** CBS Dig. 35848 [Col. IM/*HMT* 35848]. Ma, O Nat. de France, Maazel – LALO: *Concerto.**** ❀

*** HMV ASD 2498 [Ang. S 36642]. Du Pré, New Philh. O, Barbirolli – SCHUMANN: *Concerto.****

*** Decca Dig. **410 019-2**; SXDL/*KSXDC* 7568 [Lon. LDR/*5*- 71068]. Harrell, Cleveland O, Marriner – SCHUMANN: *Concerto.****

** HMV ASD/*TC-ASD* 3452 [Ang. S/*4XS* 37457]. Rostropovich, LPO, Giulini – DVOŘÁK: *Concerto.**(*)

Yo Yo Ma's performance of the Saint-Saëns *Concerto* is distinguished by fine sensitivity and beautiful tone. As in the Lalo, one is tempted to speak of him being 'hypersensitive', so fine is his attention to light and shade; yet there is not a trace of posturing or affectation. The Orchestre National de France respond with playing of great refinement throughout. Superb recorded sound which reflects great credit on the engineers.

Jacqueline du Pré finds depth and a heroic quality in a work which is generally dismissed as merely elegant (Tovey used the diminutive term 'opusculum'). One is convinced by Du Pré that it is greater music than one ever suspected, and that is some achievement. The charming minuet movement is done with great delicacy. Coupled with a fine performance of the Schumann, well recorded, it makes an excellent disc.

Harrell's reading of the Saint-Saëns also makes light of any idea that he is always a small-scale composer. The opening is positively epic, and the rest of the performance is just as compelling with the minuet-like *Allegretto* crisply neoclassical. This coupling of Saint-Saëns and Schumann challenges comparison with the classic recording of Du Pré and Barenboim, even if in warmth and commitment it cannot quite match that model. Recording is outstanding, beautifully balanced, with the compact disc version particularly fine. The chrome cassette is slightly less refined at the top than the disc versions, but is otherwise full and vivid.

Rostropovich's performance serves as a filler for the Dvořák *Concerto* and is more successful than its coupling, though not as impressive as his earlier version (now deleted). There is less rhetorical intensity here than in the Dvořák, and the performance is warmly and atmospherically recorded, with a quite well-detailed cassette transfer.

Piano concertos Nos. 1–5; La Jeunesse d'Hercule, Op. 50.

*** Decca D 244 D 3/*K 244 K 33* (3). Rogé, Philh. O, LPO or RPO, Dutoit.

(i) *Piano concertos Nos. 1–5;* (ii) *Septet for trumpet, strings and piano, Op. 65.*

**(*) HMV SLS 802 (3) [Sera. SIC/*4X3G* 6081]. (i) Ciccolini, O de Paris, Baudo; (ii) Groupe Instrumental de Paris.

There may be little development of style between the first concerto, written when the composer was twenty-three, and the fifth, *The Egyptian*, written at Luxor when he was in his fifties; but this is first-rate gramophone material. Beethoven, Bach and Mendelssohn all get their due in the *First Concerto*. The *Second* and *Fourth* are already well known, but No. 5 is unexpectedly attractive, with oriental atmosphere tingeing the music rather than overwhelming it. The finale, in which Egyptian ideas are punctuated in turn by early honky-tonk and a big Tchaikovskian melody, is delightful. Only No. 3 falls short in its comparatively banal ideas, and even in that there is a hilarious finale which sounds like a Viennese operetta turned into a concerto.

Played as they are here, these concertos can exert a strong appeal: Pascal Rogé brings delicacy, virtuosity and sparkle to the piano part, and he receives expert support from the various London orchestras under Dutoit. Altogether delicious playing and excellent piano sound from Decca, who secure a most realistic balance. On the sixth side there is a rarity in the shape of *La Jeunesse d'Hercule*, Saint-Saëns's final tone-poem. In every respect, this set outclasses Aldo Ciccolini's survey of the early 1970s, good though that was. The cassettes sound splendid too, although the resonant acoustic, while creating an attractively rich and spacious effect, does bring a very marginal loss of focus, most noticeable at the evocative opening of the *Third Concerto*. Even so, tape collectors need not hesitate: this is still very sophisticated quality.

Ciccolini's performances are highly enjoyable and the *Septet* too shows the composer at his most vivid. But good though the EMI recording is, the Decca is outstanding and the Rogé set is an obvious first choice.

Piano concerto No. 2 in G min., Op. 22.
*** HMV Dig. ASD/*TCC-ASD* 4307 [Ang. DS/*4XS* 38004]. Ousset, CBSO, Rattle – LISZT: *Concerto No. 1.****
*** Ph. Dig. **410 052-2**; 6514/*7337* 164 [id.]. Davidovich, Concg. O, Järvi – RACHMANINOV: *Rhapsody on a theme of Paganini.***(*)

The most popular of Saint-Saëns's concertos has rarely received so winning a performance on record as Ousset's. The opening cadenza, so far from reflecting Bach-like qualities, is warm and urgent, genuinely romantic music, and the scherzo, spikier than usual, brings dazzlingly clear articulation. This performance consistently conveys the flair and contrasted tensions of a live recording, though it was made in the studio. The recording favours the soloist but is rich and lively. There is a good cassette, the sound full and vivid, although a relatively modest transfer level means that the upper range is not quite so brilliant as the disc.

Bella Davidovich also gives a most sympathetic account of the *G minor Concerto* and has the advantage of excellent orchestral support from the Concertgebouw Orchestra (Cécile Ousset is slightly let down by a flat oboe phrase after the orchestra's first entry). The recording is very natural and Davidovich draws more sympathetic tone quality from the instrument than Ousset even if she lacks the brilliance that the latter brings to the scherzo. This is warmly attractive music-making, but in the last resort it has less flair and life than Ousset's version, although on compact disc the richly atmospheric sound is very persuasive. The chrome tape, however, lacks something in sparkle at the top.

Piano concertos Nos. 2; 4 in C min., Op. 44.
*** Decca SXL/*KSXC* 7008. Rogé, RPO, Dutoit.
** Erato Dig. **ECD 88002**; STU/*MCE* 71460. Duchable, Strasbourg PO, Lombard.

The pairing of Saint-Saëns's two most attractive piano concertos in performances by Rogé as sparkling and elegant as these makes for a very enticing record indeed. The *Second* with an eclectic variety of style and a famous scherzo makes a good match for the *Fourth*, with its nicely varied chorale theme – among the composer's more memorable ideas. The music-making combines rhythmic vigour with a warm sensibility to give each work an unexpected feeling of stature without in any way minimizing its melodic charm. The digital recording is vivid and very well balanced, with a lively, wide-ranging cassette, not transferred at the highest level, but losing nothing in presence, body and range.

The Erato coupling is much less winning, even with the advantage of CD sophistication, and the recording lacks the luminous colouring of the Decca. The piano is forwardly balanced and Duchable's bold assertiveness in outer movements brings character of the wrong sort to music-making which at times sounds aggressive. There is little charm, and while the first movement of No. 2 is stronger than usual and the playing is never thoughtless or slipshod, this cannot compare with Rogé.

Violin concerto No. 1 in A, Op. 30.
*** Decca Dig. **411 952-2**; SXDL/*KSXDC* 7527 [Lon. LDR/*5* 71029). Kyung-Wha Chung, Montreal SO, Dutoit – LALO: *Symphonie espagnole.****

Saint-Saëns's *First Violin concerto* is a miniature, playing for only eleven and a half minutes. It was written for Sarasate, and if it seems somewhat insubstantial, Kyung-Wha Chung makes the most of the lyrical interludes and is fully equal to the energetic bravura of the outer sections. With a clear yet full-blooded digital recording and an excellent accompaniment from Charles Dutoit, this is persuasive. The cassette is of very good quality, matching the disc closely.

Violin concerto No. 3 in B min., Op. 61.
*** DG Dig. **410 526-2**; 410 526-1/*4* [id.]. Perlman, O de Paris, Barenboim – WIENIAWSKI: *Concerto No. 2.****
*** Decca SXL 6759 [Lon. CS/*5*- 6992]. Kyung-Wha Chung, LSO, Foster – VIEUXTEMPS: *Concerto No. 5.****

On DG Perlman achieves a fine partnership with his friend, Barenboim, who provides a highly sympathetic accompaniment in a performance that is both tender and strong. They join together in finding an elegiac quality in the *Andantino* while Perlman's verve and dash in the finale is dazzling. The forward balance is understandable in this work, but orchestral detail could at times be sharper. There is an excellent cassette.

Kyung-Wha Chung gives a characteristically passionate account of the finest of the Saint-Saëns concertos, so intense that even a sceptical listener will find it hard not to be convinced that this is a great work. Such music needs this kind of advocacy, and Miss Chung is splendidly backed up by the LSO under Foster. Rich, clear recording.

Danse macabre, Op. 40.
(M) *** Chan. CBR/*CBT* 1003. SNO, Gibson – DUKAS: *L'Apprenti sorcier;* ROSSINI: *Boutique fantasque.****

Gibson's performance is slightly lacking in panache, but it is vividly played and very well recorded (the cassette only marginally less brilliant than the disc). The couplings are both equally attractive.

Danse macabre; La Jeunesse d'Hercule, Op. 50; Marche héroïque, Op. 34; Phaéton, Op. 39; Le Rouet d'Omphale, Op. 31.
❀ *** Decca SXL/*KSXC* 6975 [Lon. CS 7204]. Philh. O, Dutoit.

Beautifully played performances, recorded in the Kingsway Hall with splendid atmosphere and colour. Charles Dutoit shows himself an admirably sensitive exponent of this repertoire, revelling in the composer's craftsmanship and revealing much delightful orchestral detail. *La Jeunesse d'Hercule* is the most ambitious piece, twice as long as its companions; its lyrical invention is both sensuous and elegant. The *Marche héroïque* is flamboyant but less memorable, and *Phaéton*, a favourite in the Victorian era, now sounds slightly dated. But the delightful *Omphale's Spinning Wheel* and the familiar *Danse macabre* show the composer at his most creatively imaginative. The slightly bizarre pictorial realization of the imagery of the *Danse macabre* by M. Jean Paul Veret makes a striking sleeve design. The cassette is of demonstration quality, quite the equal of the disc. On both LP and tape the various elements of the orchestra are ideally balanced and proportioned, and the sound is vivid, truthful and atmospheric, with wonderfully rich brass and light, feathery strings.

Havanaise, Op. 83; Introduction and rondo capriccioso, Op. 28.

*** HMV ASD 3125 [Ang. S/*4XS* 37118]. Perlman, O de Paris, Martinon – CHAUSSON: *Poème*; RAVEL: *Tzigane*.***
*** Decca SXL/*KSXC* 6851 [Lon. CS/*5*-7073]. Kyung-Wha Chung, RPO, Dutoit – CHAUSSON: *Poème*; RAVEL: *Tzigane*.***
(B) *** CfP CFP/*TC-CFP* 40364 [Sera. S/*4XG* 60370]. Menuhin, Philh. O, Goossens – LALO: *Symphonie espagnole*.***

Perlman plays these Saint-Saëns war-horses with splendid panache and virtuosity, and is admirably supported by the late Jean Martinon and the Orchestre de Paris. A natural concert-hall balance and rich, well-detailed sound make this a most welcome and desirable anthology.

On Decca the fireworks in two Saint-Saëns showpieces provide the necessary contrast for the more reflective works with which they are coupled. In both Kyung-Wha Chung shows rhythmic flair and a touch of the musical naughtiness that gives them their full charm. As in the other nicely matched pieces Dutoit accompanies most sympathetically, and the recording is excellent on disc and tape alike.

Menuhin was at the peak of his form when he recorded these superb performances at the end of the 1950s. The opening of the *Havanaise* is quite ravishing, and the shaping of the coda is no less seductive. Similarly he emphasizes the contrasts in Op. 28 by playing the *Introduction* with heart-warming beauty of tone and producing brilliant spiccato bravura at the end of the *Rondo capriccioso*. Goossens accompanies with considerable flair and the recording sounds freshly minted, the cassette marginally softer in outline than the disc.

Morceau de concert in G for harp and orchestra, Op. 154.

*** DG 2543 806 [id.]. Zabaleta, L'ORTF O, Paris, Martinon – GINASTERA: *Concerto*; TAILLEFERRE: *Concertino*.***

Saint-Saëns wrote his aptly named *Morceau de concert* when he was eighty-three. Its four miniature movements – the dainty scherzo only runs for 1′ 54″ – have a melodic structure which has much in common with the *Second Piano concerto*. But the work's charm rests on its delicacy of texture and the skill with which the accompaniment is tailored, so that it supports but never overwhelms the soloist. Yet the invention has characteristic facility and charm. The performance is wonderfully light and stylish and the recording excellent.

Le Rouet d'Omphale, Op. 31.

*** DG Dig. **400 070-2**; 2532/*3302* 050 [id.]. O Nat. de France, Bernstein – FRANCK: *Symphony*.**(*)

Saint-Saëns's delicate little tone-poem, beautifully done, makes an attractive if ungenerous coupling for the Franck *Symphony*. On compact disc, sounding even more transparent, it comes after the symphony, whereas on LP and cassette it acts as overture.

Symphony No. 3 in C min., Op. 78.

❀ *** ASV Dig. **CD**; DCA/*ZCDCA* 524. Rawsthorne, LPO, Bátiz.
*** DG 2530/*3300* 619 [id.]. Chicago SO, Barenboim.
(M) *** HMV Green. ESD 7038 [Kla. 526]. CBSO, Frémaux.
*** Chalfont Dig. SDG 312 [id.]. Rawsthorne, Royal Liv. PO, Tjeknavorian.
(M) *** Mercury SRI 75003 [id.]. Dupré, Detroit SO, Paray.
*** Decca Dig. **410 201-2**; SXDL/*KSXDC* 7590 [Lon. LDR/*5*- 71090]. Hurford, Montreal SO, Dutoit.
(M) *** RCA Gold GL/*GK* 14039. Boston SO, Munch.
*** Decca SXL 6482 [Lon. CS/*5*- 6680]. LAPO, Mehta.
(M) **(*) Decca VIV/*KVIC* 51. SRO, Ansermet.
(M) ** EMI Em. EMX/*TC-EMX* 41 2012-1/*4*. Parker-Smith, LPO, Baudo.
(M) ** CBS 60137/*40*-. NYPO, Bernstein.
*(*) Telarc Dig. **CD 80051**; DG 10051 [id.]. Phd. O, Ormandy.
* DG Dig. **400 063-2**; 2532/*3302* 045 [id.]. Cocherau, Berlin PO, Karajan.

(i) *Symphony No. 3;* (ii) *Danse macabre.*
(B) *** DG Walkman *413 423-4*. (i) Chicago SO (as above); (ii) O de Paris, Barenboim (with FRANCK: *Symphony**(*)).

(i) Symphony No. 3; (ii) *Danse macabre; Le Rouet d'Omphale.*
(M) *** HMV Green. ESD/*TC-ESD* 173191-

1/*4*. (i) French Nat. RO, Martinon; (ii) O de Paris, Dervaux.

Symphony No. 3; (i) *Wedding Cake* (*Caprice-valse*), *Op. 76*.
(M) ** Ph. Seq. 6527/*7311* 210. (i) Chorzempa, Rotterdam PO, De Waart.

The magnificent new ASV recording of this once neglected but now popular symphony sweeps the board, and is for the digital 1980s what Barenboim's mid-1970s version was for the previous decade. Under an inspirational Bátiz the orchestral playing is exhilarating in its energy and commitment, while the *Poco Adagio* balances a noble elegiac feeling with romantic warmth. The recording, made in Guildford Cathedral, brings an attractive overall bloom, yet registers detail naturally and vividly. After the vivacious scherzo the entry of the organ in the finale is a breathtaking moment, and the sense of spectacle persists, bringing an unforgettable weight and grandeur to the closing pages. The cassette is very successful too, matching the disc closely and losing only a fraction of the dynamic range.

Barenboim's is a superlative performance which glows with warmth from beginning to end. In the opening 6/8 section the galloping rhythms are irresistibly pointed, while the linked slow section has a poised stillness in its soaring lyricism which completely avoids any suspicion of sweetness or sentimentality. A brilliant account of the scherzo leads into a magnificent energetic conclusion, with the Chicago orchestra excelling itself in radiant playing in every section.

Barenboim's outstanding version is also available on a Walkman chrome tape which includes a fine account of *Danse macabre*. While the Franck *Symphony* used as coupling is much less recommendable, this remains a bargain, costing considerably less than the premium-priced LP and offering the Saint-Saëns work uninterrupted.

Martinon's Greensleeve reissue has the advantage (besides being economically priced) of two extra pieces, very well played by the Orchestre de Paris under Pierre Dervaux. *Omphale* acts as a delicate curtain-raiser for the *Symphony*, creating a suitably evocative mood, while the *Danse macabre* is a suitably extrovert encore, with its faintly abrasive violin solo at the opening making a nice foil for the preceding spectacle. Martinon's account of the *Symphony* is in every way distinguished, the first movement alert and sparkling, the *Poco Adagio* warmly romantic (with wonderfully rich recording), yet with a touch of nobility at the close. The organ entry in the finale is massively buoyant, but detail registers admirably, so that both here and in the vivacious scherzo the rippling piano figurations are clearer than usual. In fact the recording, with its attractive ambient glow, is almost ideally balanced and this record is very competitive. There is a good cassette, but the level drops on side two and the effect becomes more subdued than the disc.

Also in the mid-price bracket the richly enjoyable Birmingham version under Frémaux sounds splendidly opulent in this reissue. The performance is brilliantly played but warm-hearted too. The recording has excellent detail and the most vivid impact.

The new Chalfont digital recording, made in Liverpool Cathedral, is among the most sumptuous and spectacular so far, with an overwhelming climax at the close of the finale, organ pedals effectively underpinning the spacious orchestral tutti. Tjeknavorian's reading has plenty of energy in the first movement and the scherzo (which brings minor ensemble problems near the opening, caused by the resonant acoustic) and in the slow movement he balances repose and eloquence. The playing of the Liverpool orchestra is excellent and the reading as a whole is highly enjoyable, even if Tjeknavorian's pacing and interpretative control sound less natural and spontaneous than the Bátiz, Barenboim, Martinon and Frémaux versions.

Paray's distinguished version from the early 1960s is hardly less recommendable. Again the sound is richly resonant, but the excellent balance provides very good internal detail. After a glowing slow movement the scherzo has great energy and vivacity while the organ dominates the opening of the finale splendidly. At the work's close Paray's quickening is splendidly judged.

Dutoit brings his usual gifts of freshness and a natural sympathy to Saint-Saëns's attractive score. There is a ready spontaneity here. The recording is very bright with luminous detail, the strings given a thrilling brilliance above the stave. One notices a touch of digital edge, but there is a balancing weight. The reading effectively combines lyricism with passion. In the finale Hurford's entry in the famous chorale melody is more pointed, less massive than usual, although Dutoit generates a genial feeling of gusto to compensate. With its wide range (cassette and disc are closely matched) and bright lighting, this is a performance to leave one tingling after Dutoit's final burst of adrenalin. The compact disc shows no striking improvement on disc or tape, although the background silence is certainly telling.

Munch's Boston recording dates from 1960 (the same year as Paray's Detroit version) and it still sounds astonishingly well, another example of simple analogue techniques at their best. The performance is very exciting, moving forward in a single sweep of great intensity. The *Poco Adagio* section has an enveloping warmth and in the finale there is a thrilling contribution from the organist, Berj Zamkochian. There is just a hint of the acoustic throwback that marred some of RCA's early Boston stereo records, but generally this is a very invigorating and satisfying experience.

On Decca's earlier full-priced version the playing of the Los Angeles orchestra is first-class and Mehta draws a well-disciplined and exuberant response from all departments. The recording too is extremely fine, with good detail and a well-lit texture.

Ansermet's account dates from 1962. His is an essentially genial approach. Others find more bite in the first movement and scherzo, but none create a more sumptuous richness in the *Poco Adagio*, while there is plenty of weight in the finale too, even if the reading is more measured than with Munch or Paray. Yet such is Ansermet's charisma that even at this lower level of tension the performance remains rewarding, with vintage Decca sound hardly sounding dated.

Baudo on Eminence has the advantage of modern digital recording, refined in detail and with a very wide dynamic range (which has led to a particularly low-level cassette transfer). There is a hint of shrillness in the upper strings, but otherwise the quality is refined. The performance is more alert than Ansermet's, but somehow smaller in scale, although the organ entry in the finale is certainly grandiloquent. There is no lack of ardour here, but in the last resort this remains curiously unmemorable.

Bernstein's New York recording is reissued on CBS's 'Great Performances' logo. It is hardly that. The first movement is spacious, the *Poco Adagio* brings an elegiac delicacy and the finale has a proper impact. The recording is a little harsh, but the cassette transfer offers no problems.

Polished as the playing of the Rotterdam orchestra is, helped by refined Philips recording, the De Waart performance cannot compare in excitement with the finest accounts. Some may be swayed by the attractive fill-up, though after the organ glories at the end of the symphony few will want to go on at once to such relative triviality. There is a good matching cassette.

Ormandy's Telarc performance is curiously lacking in vitality. It is not helped by the recessed, over-resonant recording, in which the microphones place the organ in a forward, concerto-like position. Orchestral detail is poor and the piano contribution barely audible. In the finale the closing climax is effectively balanced, but elsewhere the performance makes little real impact. On CD the organ entry is impressive and some may like the overall sumptuousness.

Karajan's version is superbly played and obviously has its insights. But the recording is artificially balanced and the edginess of the sound turns into a fierce harshness in the finale when Pierre Cocherau opens up his big guns. Some equipment may respond more kindly to this than others, but this can hardly be recommended. The CD is a considerable sonic improvement on the LP, but the fierceness remains.

Piano trio in F, Op. 18.

*** HMV ASD 3729. De la Pau, Yan-Pascal and Paul Tortelier – RAVEL: *Piano trio.***

The *Piano trio* is an early work, written when Saint-Saëns was twenty-eight, before his disastrous marriage. He wrote it during a holiday in the Auvergne, and the invention is fresh and smiling. Here it has the advantage of superb recorded sound and a good, keenly alert performance. Though not a masterpiece, the *Trio* is well worth getting to know.

Messe à quatre voix, Op. 4.
**(*) Argo ZRG 889 [id.]. Colston, Rivaz, John Vickers, Owen, Harvey, Worcester Cath. Ch., Hunt; Massey (grand organ), Trepte (small organ).

Donald Hunt directs an enjoyable performance of an early rarity of Saint-Saëns. Written when he was only twenty-one, this *Mass* shows how well he had learnt his academic lessons, for at various points he uses with total freshness what at the time were archaic techniques, as in the beautiful *Agnus Dei* at the end. The organ writing is characteristically French, and though one finds few signs of deep feeling, the piece is well worth hearing. The soloists here are variable, but the choir is excellent and the recording atmospheric.

Samson et Dalila (opera; complete).
(M) *** DG 413 297-1/*4*(3/*2*). Obraztsova, Domingo, Bruson, Lloyd, Thau, Ch. and O. de Paris, Barenboim.

Barenboim proves as passionately dedicated as an interpreter of Saint-Saëns here as he did in the *Third Symphony*, sweeping away any Victorian cobwebs. It is important too that the choral passages, so vital in this work, are sung with this sort of freshness, and Domingo has rarely sounded happier in French music, the bite as well as the heroic richness of the voice well caught. Renato Bruson and Robert Lloyd are both admirable too, but sadly the key role of Dalila is given an unpersuasive, unsensuous performance by Obraztsove, with her vibrato often verging on a wobble. The recording is as ripe as the music deserves; the cassette transfer is very successful.

Salieri, Antonio (1750–1825)

Double concerto for oboe, flute and orchestra in C.
(M) *** DG Priv. 2535/*3335* 417 [139152]. Holliger, Nicolet, Bamberg SO, Maag – BELLINI, CIMAROSA, DONIZETTI: *Concertos.****

Heinz Holliger and Aurèle Nicolet make an expert partnership, and Salieri's *Double concerto* is a pleasant little work. All the couplings are first-class, as is the recording.

Sallinen, Aulis (born 1935)

(i) *Symphonies Nos. 1; 3;* (ii) *Chorali.*
*** BIS LP 41. Finnish RSO, (i) Kamu; (ii) Berglund.

Aulis Sallinen has won acclaim for his operas, *Ratsumies* (The Horseman) and *The Red Line*, both of which have been recorded in Finland. He is now in his late forties and the two symphonies recorded here are well worth the attention of the collector, more so than the operas. The *First* (1970) is a thoroughly accessible one-movement work, diatonic in idiom and inhabiting a sound-world that is quite haunting, even if one feels it is stronger in atmosphere than argument. The *Third* (1974–5) is a powerful and highly imaginative piece. True, it is too reliant on ostinati which create a feeling of expectation which is not always fulfilled, but there is a sure sense of stylistic identity and a genuine feeling for nature. At times one's thoughts stray to Sibelius's *Tempest* music from whose world the opening seems to spring, or to the landscape of Britten's East Anglia. There is a shorter piece, *Chorali* (conducted by Paavo Berglund) too. The engineering is as excellent as are the performances, and readers will find these two works both distinctive and rewarding.

Salzedo, Leonardo (born 1921)

Capriccio for brass quintet.
** Argo ZRG 906 [id.]. Jones Brass Ens. – ARNOLD: *Symphony* **(*); PREMRU: *Music.****

The playing and recording here are altogether magnificent, and it is only Leonard Salzedo's piece that falls short of the highest quality. His music is nothing if not accomplished: it is effectively laid out for a quintet of two trumpets, horn, trombone and tuba, and has considerable facility. It stretches the players and is an excellent showpiece, but its invention is not particularly distinguished or memorable.

Sarasate, Pablo (1844–1908)

Carmen fantasy, Op. 25.
❀ *** HMV ASD 2782 [Ang. S/*4XS* 36836]. Perlman, RPO, Foster – PAGANINI: *Concerto No. 1.**** ❀
*** HMV SLS 832 (2). Perlman (as above) – PAGANINI: *Concerto No. 1* and *Caprices.****
(M) ** Decca SPA/*KCSP* 551. Ricci, LSO, Gamba – GRANADOS: *Spanish dance*; RAVEL: *Boléro* etc.**

This is the filler for Perlman's account of Paganini's *First Violin concerto*, but what a gorgeous filler. Sarasate's *Fantasy* is a selection of the most popular tunes from *Carmen*, with little attempt made to stitch the seams between them. But played like this, with superb panache, luscious tone and glorious recording, the piece almost upstages the concerto with which it is coupled.

Ricci's account of Sarasate's *Carmen* potpourri has immense dash and virtuosity, but he is recorded very near the microphone and the resiny contact of bow on string is exaggerated. The cassette is marginally smoother than the disc.

Zigeunerweisen, Op. 20/1.
** HMV ASD/*TC-ASD* 3408 [Ang. S/*4XS* 37445]. Perlman, Pittsburgh SO, Previn – GOLDMARK: *Violin concerto No. 1.***(*)

Perlman's account of Sarasate's *Zigeunerweisen* is both virtuosic and idiomatic. The engineers have placed the distinguished soloist rather too close to the microphone, but he survives any amount of scrutiny, and in any event the results are in no way disturbing. This makes an attractive fill-up to Goldmark's charming concerto, and in spite of the spotlight on the soloist the orchestral sound is full-blooded. The cassette transfer is well managed.

(i) *8 Spanish dances: Malaguena; Habañera, Op. 21/1–2; Romanza andaluza; Jota navarra, Op. 22/1–2; Playera; Zapateado, Op. 23/1–2; Nos. 7–8, Op. 26/1–2.* (ii) *Navarra for two violins, Op. 22.*
*** O-L DSLO 22. Campoli, with (i) Ibbott, (ii) Blunt.

Campoli is in excellent form here, and with the art that disguises art he makes these dances sound effortless yet brilliant. The record contains the first four books of the *Spanish dances* and the *Navarra*, in which Campoli is joined by Belinda Blunt. Popular light music this may be, but it is all thoroughly enjoyable when the playing is of this quality. The recording, too, is very good indeed, and although at times it is a little close, this is never troubling.

Satie, Erik (1866–1925)

Gymnopédies Nos. 1 and 3.
(M) *** RCA Gold GL/*GK* 25451 [ARL1/*ARK1* 2783]. Nat. PO, Gerhardt – FAURÉ: *Pavane*; RAVEL: *Le Tombeau de Couperin* etc.***

Gerhardt's approach is languorously gentle. Satie's most famous *Gymnopédies* are played quite beautifully by the National Philharmonic with first-class recording to match, on disc and chrome tape alike. With equally desirable couplings this can be highly recommended.

Gymnopédies Nos. 1 and 3; Parade; Relâche (Parts 1 and 2).
(M) **(*) CBS 61992/*40-* [Col. M 30294]. RPO, Entremont.

Entremont presents the *Gymnopédies* sympathetically and brings plenty of bite and point to the other two scores, though he rather overdoes the humour in *Parade*. Still his *Relâche* is very good, and the recordings are fully acceptable both on disc and on the tape (which has the body of the LP but slightly less edge).

Monotones (ballet, arr. Lanchbery)*; Jack in the Box* (orch. Milhaud)*; Deux Préludes posthumes* (orch. Poulenc)*; Trois Morceaux en forme de poire* (orch. Désormière).
(M) *(*) HMV Green. ESD/*TC-ESD* 7069 [Ang. S 37580]. ROHCG O, Lanchbery.

The music for Sir Frederick Ashton's ballet *Monotones* is principally based on Satie's *Gnossiennes* and *Gymnopédies*. The music is fairly static, and although it is gracefully played there is a lack of momentum here: the best-known third *Gymnopédie* is extended by repetition and at Lanchbery's slow, stately pace almost outlasts its welcome. The arrival of the more lively *Jack in the Box* comes as a relief, but side two returns to the somewhat languid mood of the opening, and the two posthumous *Préludes* seem almost totally lacking in vitality. No doubt this issue will be sought after by balletomanes but it cannot be generally recommended with any enthusiasm. The recording is suitably atmospheric, although on tape the sound is not especially refined in detail, and *Jack in the Box* could do with more glitter.

(i) *Musique d'ameublement; Relâche* (*entr'acte*)*;* (ii) *Sonnerie pour réveiller le Roi des Singes;* (iii) *Vexations* (*extrait des Pages mystiques*).
** Erato STU/*MCE* 71336. (i) Ars Nova Ens., Constant; (ii) Thibaud, Jeannoutot; (iii) D'Alberto.

The *Entr'acte cinématographique, Relâche* was originally composed to serve as background music for a film of the composer's antics crawling on the façade of Notre Dame Cathedral. It has some outrageously repetitive sequences and the listener might be forgiven for thinking his pick-up has stuck in the groove. The *Musique d'ameublement* is also repetitive though amiable, while the fanfare for two trumpets is brief and pithy with some ingenious part-writing. The piano *Vexations* seems over-deliberate, at least as presented here. The orchestral music is played with understanding and spirit, but this is not a record one would regard as essential Satie. The recording is lively and there is a good cassette.

Parade.
(M) ** DG 2543 807 [id.]. Monte Carlo Op. O, Frémaux – MILHAUD: *Carnaval d'Aix****; ROUSSEL: *Bacchus et Ariane.***(*)

Parade was written for the Diaghilev company and reflects Satie's enthusiasm for the circus and its music. First comes a Chinese conjuror followed by an American silent-film star whose various escapades are illustrated by the sounds of pistol shots and a typewriter, and finally there is a pair of acrobats. Satie's surrealist score is well presented here though it must be admitted that Dorati's version with the LSO made in the 1960s had greater polish. However, this is a highly attractive coupling and deserves a strong recommendation.

PIANO MUSIC

Aperçus désagréables (for 4 hands); *Chapitres tournés en tous sens; Croquis et agaceries d'un gros bonhomme en bois; Enfantillages pittoresques; En habit de cheval* (for 4 hands)*; Gnossiennes Nos. 4, 5 and 6; Jack in the Box; Premier Menuet; Menus propos enfantins; Les Pantins dansent; Trois Nocturnes; Nocturnes Nos. 4 and 5; Peccadilles importunes; Petite ouverture à danser; Trois petites pièces montées; Poudre d'or; Prélude de la porte héroïque du ciel; Prélude en tapisserie; Trois Sarabandes; Sonatine bureaucratique; Sports et divertissements.*
(M) *** HMV Green. ESDW/*TC2-ESDW* 716. Ciccolini.

Avant-dernières Pensées; La Belle Excentrique (4 hands); *Descriptions automatiques; Embryons desséchés; Trois Gnossiennes; Trois Gymnopédies; Trois Morceaux en forme de poire; Passacaille; Préludes flasques* (*pour un chien*)*; Le Piège de Méduse; Véritables préludes flasques* (*pour un chien*).
*** HMV ASD/*TC-ASD* 2389. Ciccolini.

Although Satie's music is often overrated by his admirers, there is a desperate melancholy and a rich poetic feeling about much of this music which are altogether unique. The *Gymnopédies* or the famous *Morceaux en forme de poire* show such flashes of innocence and purity of inspiration that criticism is disarmed. Aldo Ciccolini is widely praised as a Satie interpreter, and he plays here with unaffected sympathy. Although the single-disc recital is admirably planned, the new compilation on Greensleeve is more ambitious and forms an excellent introduction to Satie's world. The recording is first-class on both, but the tape transfer of the ASD (slightly hard on top) is less successful than with the double-length medium-priced issue, which matches the LPs closely.

Avant-dernières pensées; Chapitres tournés en tous sens; Cinq Grimaces; Deux Rêveries nocturnes; Le Fils des étoiles; Gnossiennes Nos. 2–3; Je te veux – valse; Nocturnes Nos. 3 and 5; Les Pantins dansent; Pièces froides; Le Piège de Méduse; Première Pensée Rose et Croix; Prélude de la porte héroïque du ciel; Rêverie du pauvre; Trois Valses distinguées du précieux dégoûté; Valse-ballet.
(M) **(*) Saga 5472. McCabe.

This entertaining and attractive anthology is well played and recorded, and ranges from relatively neglected early works like the *Valse-ballet*, Satie's first published piano piece, dating from 1885, to the *Rêverie du pauvre* (1900) and the *Deux Rêveries nocturnes* (1911), published as late as 1968. This is all intelligently played, as one expects from this artist.

Avant-dernières pensées; Embryons desséchés; Gymnopédies Nos. 1–3; Gnossiennes Nos. 1–5; Nocturne No. 1; Sarabandes Nos. 1–3; Sonatine bureaucratique; Trois Valses distinguées du précieux dégoûté.
(M) ** CBS 61874 [M/*MT* 36694]. Varsano.

A good, cleanly focused but too closely balanced recording of the piano. Daniel Varsano has the measure of these pieces and plays admirably. Perhaps the first of the *Embryons desséchés* could have greater delicacy and wit, and there could be greater melancholy in the second of the *Gymnopédies*. The latter are spread out on the second side, the *Embryons desséchés* and *Sonatine bureaucratique* being sandwiched between them, and all five works in turn being placed between the fourth and fifth *Gnossiennes*. Likewise the first three *Gnossiennes* are distributed over the first side with other pieces interspersed. There are good things here, and it is a pity that the slightly dry sound and inelegant presentation (there are no notes) diminish the appeal of this issue.

Chapitres tournés en tous sens; Croquis et agaceries d'un gros bonhomme en bois; Gnossiennes Nos. 2 and 4; Trois Gymnopédies; Heures séculaires et instantanées; Nocturnes Nos. 2 and 4; Nouvelles pièces froides; Passacaille; Le Piège de Méduse; Prélude No. 2 (*Le Fils des étoiles*)*; Sonatine bureaucratique.*
(B) ** CfP CFP/*TC-CFP* 40329. Lawson.

Satie's deceptively simple piano writing poses problems for the interpreter; it has to be played with great sensitivity and subtlety if justice is to be done to its special qualities of melancholy and irony. Peter Lawson is very well recorded both on disc and on tape (there is little difference between them, except for the virtually silent background of the cassette). The recital opens with the famous *Gymnopédies*, played coolly but not ineffectively. The highlight is a perceptive and articulate characterization of *Le Piège de Méduse*, seven epigrammatic *morceaux de concert*, originally written as incidental music for a comedy in which Satie himself took the lead. Elsewhere Lawson's playing is fresh and clean but lacking in individuality. His way is quietly tasteful, and though he catches something of Satie's gentle and wayward poetry he is less successful in revealing the underlying sense of fantasy. There are more distinguished and memorable recordings available at full price; but the present issue is a good deal more than serviceable for those with a limited budget.

Danses gothiques; Fête donnée par des Chevaliers Normands en l'honneur d'une jeune demoiselle; Six Gnossiennes; Cinq Gymnopédies; Ogives; Petite Ouverture à danser; Pièces froides; Prélude d'Eginhard; Prélude de la porte

héroïque du ciel; Deux Préludes de Nazaréen; Prière; Trois Sarabandes; Trois Sonneries de la Rose Croix.
**(*) Ph. 6768 269 (3). De Leeuw.

This three-record set concentrates on Satie's earlier music and collects the bulk of his output from 1885 to 1900, much of it otherwise unobtainable. Reinbert de Leeuw is a sensitive player and thoroughly attuned to Satie's personality. He takes him at his word by playing many of the pieces *très lent*; indeed he overdoes this at times, though this impression may be caused by listening to too much at once. But if one occasionally feels the need for more movement (and on occasion greater dynamic nuance), these are still admirable performances, and they are beautifully recorded.

Embryons desséchés; 6 Gnossiennes; 3 Gymnopédies; Je te veux; Nocturne No. 4; Le Piccadilly; 4 Préludes flasques; Prélude en tapisserie; Sonatine bureaucratique; Vieux sequins et vieilles cuirasses.
*** Decca Dig. **410 220-2**; 410 220-1/*4*. Rogé.

Pascal Rogé gives Satie's music its compact disc debut in a fine recital which is splendidly caught by the microphone. Rogé has real feeling for this repertoire and conveys its bittersweet quality and its grave melancholy as well as he does its lighter qualities. He produces, as usual, consistent beauty of tone and this is well projected by the recording in all three formats.

Gnossiennes Nos. 1, 4 and 5; Trois Gymnopédies; Nocturne No. 1; Passacaille; Six Pièces (Désespoir agréable; Effronterie; Poésie; Prélude canin; Profondeur; Songe creux); Ragtime (from *Parade*, arr. Ourdine)*; Sarabandes Nos. 1 and 3; Sonatine bureaucratique; Sports et divertissements; Véritables préludes flasques; Vieux sequins et vieilles cuirasses.*
(M) ** Saga 5387. McCabe.

John McCabe's performances are cool, even deliberate, but they are not heavy, and his sympathy is never in doubt. He is quite well recorded.

Scarlatti, Alessandro
(1660–1725)

6 Concerti grossi.
*** Ph. 9500 603/*7300 725* [id.]. I Musici.

These noble and elevated works were first published by Benjamin Cooke in 1740, fifteen years after Scarlatti's death. Though far from radical in style, they have invention of quality to commend them; I Musici give performances of some eloquence and warmth, and great transparency. The latter is welcome in the fugal movements, which are numerous (eleven out of twenty-three). These very well-recorded performances are unlikely to be surpassed for a very long time. The cassette transfer is first-class, full, with plenty of life and detail.

12 Sinfonie di concerto grosso.
*** Ph. Dig. 6769 066(2). Bennett, Lenore Smith, Soustrot, Elhorst, I Musici.

All twelve pieces are elegantly and stylishly played. Eight are scored for flute and strings, and in No. 2 there is a trumpet as well, in No. 4 an oboe and in Nos. 1 and 5 a second flute. No complaints about the performances, which are lively and attractive and eminently well recorded. The harpsichord is a little reticent, but few will fail to derive pleasure from this set.

St Cecilia Mass.
*** Argo ZRG 903 [id.]. Harwood, Eathorne, Cable, Evans, Keyte, St John's College Ch., Wren O, Guest.

In this celebratory setting of the Mass, the most elaborate and expansive that Scarlatti wrote, he applied to church music the techniques he had already used in opera. This is far more florid in its style than Scarlatti's other Masses, and it receives from Guest a vigorous and fresh performance. The soloists cope with their difficult *fioriture* very confidently, and they match each other well. The recording is warmly atmospheric to set choir and orchestra nicely in place.

Scarlatti, Domenico
(1685–1757)

Keyboard sonatas (arr. for guitar), *Kk.159, 175, 208, 213, 380, 448.*
(*) CBS 73545/*40-* [M/*MT* 34198]. Williams – VILLA-LOBOS: *5 Preludes.**

Guitar arrangements of Scarlatti sonatas have their charms when played by an artist as imaginative as John Williams. The recording is faithful but rather close and somewhat larger than life. There is an excellent cassette transfer.

Keyboard sonatas, Kk. 28, 43, 69, 105, 133, 215, 259, 426, 460, 490, 517–18.
**(*) Hyp. A 66025. McCabe (piano).

John McCabe is a persuasive advocate for using the piano in Scarlatti sonatas. Inevitably the modern instrument brings romantic overtones, but McCabe has just the right rhythmic spring for this nicely chosen group, even if some of his speeds are controversial. Warm recording.

Keyboard sonatas, Kk. 46, 87, 99, 124, 201, 204a, 490–92, 513, 520–21.
*** CRD CRD 1068/*CRDC 4068*. Pinnock.

No need to say much about this: the playing is first-rate and the recording outstanding in its presence and clarity. There are few better anthologies of Scarlatti in the catalogue, and this has the advantage of including a half-dozen sonatas not otherwise available. The excellent cassette matches the disc closely.

Keyboard sonatas, Kk. 64, 87, 118, 146, 208, 213, 239, 278, 380, 429, 481, 517.
** Cal. CAL 1670. Södergren (piano).

The Swedish pianist, Inger Södergren, enjoys quite a following in Paris where she lives; this recital reveals her as an artist of considerable musicianship and sensitivity. The recording is made in a rather smaller studio than is desirable but the sound is not unsympathetic. This is not as distinguished a recital as that of Zacharias – see below – but it still gives pleasure even if the quicker sonatas could do with a shade more sparkle.

Keyboard sonatas, Kk. 111, 129, 142, 148–9, 160–61, 170, 176, 183–4, 199–200, 213–14, 225–6, 266–7, 274–6, 279–80, 283–4, 310–11, 322–5, 331–2, 335–6, 343–4, 352–3, 370–71, 376–7, 380–81, 424–5, 462–3, 474–5, 485–7, 503–4, 507–8, 514–15, 536–7, 540–41.
*(*) Erato ERA 9222 (4). Sgrizzi.

This box includes sixty-five sonatas, all of which bear witness to Luciano Sgrizzi's fine technique and vital musicianship. But four records is a lot to buy all at once, and in a number of the sonatas Sgrizzi's enthusiasm runs away with him and the performances are less keenly controlled than is ideal; and some of the rubato does not wholly convince. The sound is vivid and the harpsichord (by Anthony Sidey) reproduces well.

Keyboard sonatas, Kk. 118, 124, 208–9, 247, 436, 474–5, 516–17, 544.
(M) *** HMV Dig. ESD/*TCC-ESD* 7183. Zacharias (piano).

Most musical playing from Christian Zacharias who conveys the character of each of these pieces most effectively – how good it is to hear them on the piano when they are as well played and as truthfully recorded as they are here. A first-rate issue in every way.

Keyboard sonatas, Kk. 123–4, 147, 198, 326–7, 428–9, 454, 466–7.
*(*) O-L DSLO 567. Tilney.

Colin Tilney's recital is not an unqualified success, though the harpsichord on which he records is undoubtedly of interest: it is a Sodi of 1782 which is particularly warm and rich at the bass. Some of these pieces come off well, but others have a somewhat pedantic air and a stiffness out of key with Scarlatti's mercurial temperament. The sound is truthful enough and a number of these pieces are not obtainable elsewhere.

Scheidt, Samuel (1587–1654)

Tabulatura nova, Vol. 1: 12 Passamezzo variations.
(M) ❀ *** Argo ZK 65. Weir (organ of Clare College, Camb.) – BRUHNS: *Preludes.**** ❀

These *Variations* demonstrate Scheidt's mastery of variation technique, with imaginative invention throughout. Gillian Weir helps a great deal, not only by playing the music splendidly but by choosing registrations with great flair and a marvellous sense of colour. The piquancy of several of her combinations is unforgettably apt. She is superbly recorded, and this disc of pre-Bach German organ music is quite outstandingly attractive.

Cantiones sacrae a 8: In dulci jubilo.
(M) *** EMI Em. EMX/*TC-EMX* 2032. King's College Ch., Camb. University Music Soc., Bach Choir, Wilbraham Brass Soloists, Willcocks – GABRIELI: Collection; SCHUTZ: *Psalm 150.****

Scheidt's attractive setting of *In dulci jubilo* is an outstanding item in this fine collection. The recording seems particularly successful in this short piece, which is strong in personality and superbly sung and played. Disc and tape are fairly closely matched, though the brass detail is slightly clearer on disc.

Schmidt, Franz (1874–1939)

Symphony No. 4 in C.
*** Decca SXL 6544 [Lon. CS 6747]. VPO, Mehta.

The Schoenberg centenary overshadowed that of Franz Schmidt, whose noble *Fourth Symphony* is much loved in Vienna, as this performance so readily testifies. The work has the intensity of Mahler, without the hint of hysteria, and the breadth and spaciousness of Bruckner, though it is very different from either. It has the true breath of the symphonist (as Schoenberg said of Sibelius and Shostakovich) and a dignity that reminds one a little of Elgar. This is a deeply rewarding work, beautifully played and recorded.

Piano quintet, Op. 51.
(*) Accord **149528.** Bärtschi, Berne Qt.

Schmidt's *Piano quintet* was written between 1905 and 1908, but revised later and republished in 1919. It is conceived on the largest scale, sprawling out for a full 55 minutes, and its romantic atmosphere is permeated with *fin de siècle* decadence. Nonetheless it has its impressive moments, notably the opening of the slow movement which is quite haunting. It needs a better performance than this to be convincing. Though Werner Bärtschi is thoroughly at home in the piano part, the Berne Quartet sound uncomfortable, producing edgy timbre and suspect intonation, although the playing is committed, even passionate. The compact disc is only too clear, and this disc gives little pleasure.

Schnittke, Alfred (born 1934)

Violin sonata No. 1; Sonata in the olden style.
*** Chan. Dig. ABRD/*ABTD* 1089 [id.]. Dubinsky, Edlina – SHOSTAKOVICH: *Violin sonata.* ***

Schnittke is now fifty and has achieved prominence as one of the leading Soviet composers of the middle generation. In the early 1950s he composed a number of relatively conventional works including *Nagasaki* and *Songs of War and Peace*, but after steeping himself in the idiom of Shostakovich and Prokofiev, he became attracted to the more exploratory musical idiom of the Western avant-garde that built their foundations on the Second Viennese School. The *First Sonata* dates from 1963 when he was still in his late twenties and is a well-argued piece that seems to unify his awareness of the post-serial musical world with the tradition of Shostakovich. It is linked on this version with a pastiche dating from 1977 of less interest. Excellent playing from both artists and very good recording too. The chrome cassette matches the disc in presence and realism.

Violin sonata No. 2; Prelude (In memoriam Dmitri Shostakovich) for violin and tape.
*** Ph. 6514 102. Lubotsky, Edlina – SHOSTAKOVICH: *Violin sonata.****

Alfred Schnittke's *Second Sonata*, like its predecessor, was dedicated to Mark Lubotsky and was composed during the same year as the Shostakovich work with which it is coupled. One marvels at Lubotsky's virtuosity which is undaunted by any of the hurdles this music presents. The recording is of spectacular naturalness, not least impressive being the fact that one's attention is never consciously drawn to its excellence by overlit detail or striving after effect. Nothing dates more quickly than music that strives to be up-to-date; and Schnittke's *Sonata*, though no doubt a healthy enough response in the context of Soviet society, does exude an air of general-purpose modernity and contrivance. There are moments when a greater directness of utterance begins to surface, but for the most part its gestures seem disproportionate to the apparent emotional substance, and its difficulties both to the interpreter and to the listener are incommensurate with the comparatively modest musical rewards.

Schoeck, Othmar (1886–1957)

Élégie, Op. 36; 3 Hesse Lieder; 6 Eichendorff Lieder.
** Jecklin DISCO 0510/11. A. Loosli, CO, Hug; Grenacher (piano).

Nachhall, Op. 70; 12 Lenau Lieder; O du Land.
** Jecklin DISCO 0535. A. Loosli, Bern RCO, T. Loosli.

Der Postillon, Op. 18; 15 Lieder.
** Jecklin DISCO 0505. Haefliger, Wettinger Ch. and CO with Zürich Wind Ens., Grenacher; Grenacher (piano).

The Swiss composer Othmar Schoeck is more praised than played, but those who know his work testify to its rare qualities. He is arguably the finest song composer after Wolf (his only rival being the Finn, Yrjö Kilpinen), yet despite the advocacy of such an artist as Dietrich Fischer-Dieskau, who has made several records of his work, his cause has made little headway. Like his younger contemporary, Frank Martin, he creates a concentrated and powerful atmosphere, and he has a highly developed feeling for language. His early music shows the influence of Richard Strauss, but he soon developed an individual style, expressionist in feeling, assimilating the chromaticism of Berg into a language that is basically traditional yet thoroughly personal. He is a composer who stands aloof from the mainstream of the twentieth century, yet those who seek him out are rewarded with music that has both subtlety and substance. The records listed above give a fair sample of his large output of songs and (in the last record) choruses. The last disc dates from the late 1960s but no one with a serious interest in song should fail to explore this composer – the *Élégie*, settings of Lenau and Eichendorff, is a masterpiece. The performances are idiomatic and on the whole reasonably well recorded.

Schoenberg, Arnold (1874–1951)

Accompaniment to a cinematographic scene, Op. 34; 5 Pieces for orchestra, Op. 16; Variations for orchestra, Op. 31; (i) *A Survivor from Warsaw, Op. 46.*
*** CBS 76577 [M/*MT* 35882]. BBC SO, Boulez, with (i) Reich, BBC Singers.

Boulez's choice of four key works gives on a single disc a splendid conspectus of Schoenberg's achievement as a writer for orchestra.

This is a record which should win converts, for all these works communicate directly and immediately. Boulez's account of the thornily complex *Variations* may lack both the warmth and the polish of Karajan's celebrated version, but Boulez's earthiness is compelling too, unrelentingly forceful. The *Five Pieces for orchestra*, once regarded as difficult, now emerge as colourful and expressive, hardly more elusive than Debussy, while the *Film scene* is as atmospheric as one would expect, if not as emotionally involved as *A Survivor from Warsaw*, illustrating a tragic scene from the siege of that city in 1945, with a narrator telling the story and the chorus entering movingly to illustrate the defiance of the doomed Jews. Boulez's performances are strong and spontaneous-sounding, and are given large-scale, immediate recordings.

Chamber symphony No. 1, Op. 9.
*** DG Dig. 2532 023 [id.]. Berlin PO, Sinopoli – MANZONI: *Mass.****

A fine performance of Schoenberg's Op. 9 from Sinopoli. He links it positively back to the high romanticism of Richard Strauss, with the Berlin Philharmonic producing glorious sounds. Other versions may be more detailed but none richer or more full-blooded. Full recording to match. The coupling may be a deterrent for many, though of its kind it is a fine and colourful work.

(i) *Piano concerto in C, Op. 42;* (ii) *Violin concerto, Op. 36.*
(M) **(*) DG 2543 801. (i) Brendel; (ii) Zeitlin; Bav. RSO, Kubelik.

Schoenberg devotees tend to suggest that both these works, consciously echoing the world of the romantic concerto in twelve-note serial terms, present the most approachable road to appreciating the master. For some that may be so, particularly in performances as sympathetic as these, but, more than usual in these relatively late works, the thick textures favoured by Schoenberg obscure the focus of the argument rather than making it sweeter on the ear. Brendel – who made a recording for Vox very early in his career – remains a committed Schoenbergian, and Zeitlin is impressive too. Though even the DG engineers do not manage to clarify the thorny textures completely, the sound is good.

Pelleas und Melisande (symphonic poem), *Op. 5.*
(*) Ph. 6769 045 (2) [id.]. Rotterdam PO, Zinman – FAURÉ: *Pelléas**; SIBELIUS: *Pelléas.***(*)

In a useful anthology of music inspired by Maeterlinck's play, Zinman's reading of Schoenberg's somewhat inflated symphonic poem is strongly characterized and very well played. But the Rotterdam orchestra cannot match the opulence of Karajan's ravishing Berlin Philharmonic version (DG 2530 485), and the reverberant Philips recording is not always kind to Schoenberg's sometimes pungent scoring.

Pelleas und Melisande, Op. 5; Variations for orchestra, Op. 31; Verklaerte Nacht (orchestral version), *Op. 4.*
*** DG 2711014 (4) [id.]. Berlin PO, Karajan – BERG: *Lyric suite; 3 Pieces;* WEBERN: *Collection.****

It is a pity that Karajan in this superb four-disc collection of the orchestral music of the Second Viennese School omitted the key work of Schoenberg, the *Five Pieces*, Op. 16, especially now that the Dorati recording is deleted. Once that is said, these are superb performances, which present the emotional element at full power but give unequalled precision and refinement. *Pelleas und Melisande*, written at the same time as the Debussy opera but in ignorance of the rival project, is in its way a Strauss-like masterpiece, while the Op. 31 *Variations*, the most challenging of Schoenberg's orchestral works, here receives a reading which vividly conveys the ebb and flow of tension within the phrase and over the whole plan. Superb recording.

Variations for orchestra, Op. 31; Verklaerte Nacht, Op. 4.
*** DG 2530 627 [id.]. Berlin PO, Karajan.

Karajan's version of *Verklaerte Nacht* (from his four-disc set, see above) is incomparably the most sensitive and imaginative as well as the most beautifully played that has ever been on the market. A magical reading and beautifully recorded too. The *Variations for orchestra* are also made to sound far more atmospheric and sensuous than they have under less gifted hands. An outstanding disc.

Theme and variations, Op. 43b.

(M) ** CBS 60258/*40*-. Phd. O, Ormandy – BERG: *Lulu: suite;* WEBERN: *3 Pieces* etc. **

The arrangement recorded here is for full orchestra and not the wind-band version. The actual sound is full-bodied, and the Philadelphia Orchestra play with their usual consummate virtuosity and beauty of tone. This is not a wildly interesting piece, however, for all its expert craftsmanship and ingenuity. There is a good chrome tape, matching the disc fairly closely.

Variations, Op. 31.

** Decca SXL 7004 [(d) Lon. CS 6984]. Chicago SO, Solti – BRAHMS: *Variations on a theme of Haydn.***

Solti's reading of the challenging Schoenberg *Variations* is characteristically strong and forceful with the Chicago orchestra playing with virtuoso brilliance, but Karajan's recording has shown what extra depths this initially difficult music contains. The recording is hard.

Verklaerte Nacht, Op. 4.

(M) *** DG 2543/*3343* 510 [id.]. Berlin PO, Karajan – WAGNER: *Siegfried idyll.****

*** Decca Dig. **410 111-2**; 410 111-1/*4* [id.]. ECO, Ashkenazy – WAGNER: *Siegfried idyll.****

*** Argo ZRG 763 [id.]. ASMF, Marriner – HINDEMITH: *5 Pieces****; WEBERN: *5 Movements.***(*)

(*) CBS 76305 [M 35166]. NYPO, Boulez – BERG: *Lyric suite.*(*)

Karajan's classic performance (see above) is here reissued at medium price. The superlative playing of the Berlin orchestra puts this version in a class of its own and the Wagner coupling is no less fine. The recording is first-rate with disc and chrome tape sounding virtually identical.

Ashkenazy conducts an outstandingly warm and lyrical reading, one which brings out the melodic richness of this highly atmospheric work with passionate playing from the ECO. Full and brilliant recording. The compact disc brings an extra edge to the sound, not always quite comfortable on high violins.

Marriner manages to have the best of both worlds with the richness of orchestral texture and the clarity of the string-sextet version. His interpretation is relatively reticent until the culminating climaxes, when the final thrust is more powerful than with almost any rival. In a performance such as this, *Verklaerte Nacht* is sensuously beautiful. Superb atmospheric recording.

Boulez secures responsive playing from the strings of the New York Philharmonic and has the measure of Schoenberg's poetic essay. But this performance in no respect matches Karajan's superbly fashioned and sensitive account with the Berlin Philharmonic, and is not as richly recorded.

CHAMBER MUSIC

(i) *Chamber symphonies Nos. 1, Op. 9; 2, Op. 38; 3 Pieces (1910)*; (ii) *Erwartung, Op. 17;* (iii) *Die Gluckliche Hand;* (iv) *Die Jakobsleiter;* (v) *Lieder, Op. 22.*

*** CBS 79349 (3). (i) Ens. Intercontemporain; (ii) Martin; (ii) Nimsgern, BBC Ch.; (iv) 8 Soloists, BBC Ch.; (v) Minton; with BBC SO, Boulez.

This prize-winning collection gathers together some of the most memorable of Schoenberg's early works, including the ambitious oratorio, *Die Jakobsleiter* (Jacob's Ladder), the composition of which was interrupted by the composer's army service in the First World War. Only recently has it been completed and orchestrated from full sketches by Winfried Zillig, revealing an exceptionally powerful piece. The monodrama, *Erwartung*, contrasts well with the 'psychological pantomime', *Die Gluckliche Hand*, and to all the works, including the two warmly enjoyable *Chamber symphonies*, Boulez brings passion and commitment as well as sharp perception. Full, clear recording.

Chamber symphony No. 1, Op. 9; Verklaerte Nacht (for string sextet), *Op. 4*.
(M) *** Decca Ace SDD 519. Members of L. Sinf., Atherton.

Taken from the London Sinfonietta's superb set of Schoenberg chamber music (now deleted) these are outstanding performances. *Verklaerte Nacht* in its version for solo strings is richly passionate and atmospheric, and the *Chamber symphony* in an equally committed performance makes an ideal coupling. Excellent recording.

(i) *String quartet No. 2, Op. 10, with soprano;* (ii) *Verklaerte Nacht, Op. 4*.
(M) **(*) Ph. 6570/*7310* 576. New V. Qt, (i) with Lear, (ii) augmented.

At medium price this is a generous coupling of works which each last over half an hour. Though the matching of the New Vienna Quartet is not always flawless, these passionate performances will do much to persuade the unconverted that Schoenberg – at least early in his career – could be warmly sympathetic, not just in the post-Wagnerian *Verklaerte Nacht* but in the rather later *Second Quartet* too. Its last two movements (both slow) are intensified by the contribution of a soprano, here the admirable Evelyn Lear. First-rate recording and an excellent cassette, lively yet full-bodied.

String trio, Op. 45; Verklaerte Nacht, Op. 4.
*** None. Dig. D/*D4* 79028. Sante Fe Chamber Music Fest. Ens.

The Sante Fe performance is of the sextet version of *Verklaerte Nacht* and includes such players as Walter Trampler and Ralph Kirshbaum. It is a marvellously eloquent and beautifully recorded version, far more powerful and felt than the Vienna quartet and colleagues on Philips (see above). The performance of the less accessible *String trio* of 1946 is uncommonly persuasive and can be recommended to those who normally find Schoenberg rebarbative. It has wide dynamic range, great refinement and a compelling dramatic intensity. It, too, is splendidly recorded.

Gurre-Lieder.
*** CBS 78264 (2). Thomas, Napier, Minton, Nimsgern, Bowen, BBC Ch. Soc., Goldsmith's Ch. Union, LPO Ch., BBC SO, Boulez.
*** Ph. 6769 038/*7699 124* [id.]. McCracken, Norman, Troyanos, Arnold, Scown, Tanglewood Fest. Ch., Boston SO, Ozawa.

Boulez's warm, expressive style, using slow, luxuriating tempi, brings out the operatic quality behind Schoenberg's massive score. With Boulez the Wagnerian overtones are richly expressive, and though Marita Napier and Jess Thomas are not especially sweet on the ear, they show the big, heroic qualities which this score ideally demands, while Yvonne Minton is magnificent in the *Song of the Wood-dove*. Boulez builds that beautiful section to an ominous climax, which far outshines previous versions. In most ways this recording, with attractively vivid and atmospheric sound, combines the best features of earlier sets.

Ozawa directs a gloriously opulent reading of Schoenberg's *Gurre-Lieder*, one which relates it firmly to the nineteenth century rather than pointing forward to Schoenberg's own later works. The playing of the Boston Symphony has both warmth and polish and is set against a warm acoustic; among the soloists Jessye Norman gives a performance of radiant beauty, reminding one at times of Flagstad in the burnished glory of her tone colours. As the wood-dove Tatiana Troyanos sings most sensitively, though the vibrato is at times obtrusive, and James McCracken does better than most tenors at coping with a heroic vocal line without barking. Other versions have in some ways been more powerful – Boulez's, for one – but none is more sumptuously beautiful than this. The cassettes match the discs closely, encompassing the wide dynamic range without difficulty until the short but massive closing chorus, which lacks the open quality of the LP.

Gurre-Lieder: Song of the Wood-dove; Ode to Napoleon Bonaparte, Op. 41; Serenade, Op. 24.
*** CBS 74025 [M/*MT* 36735]. Norman, Shirley-Quirk, Ens. Incontemporain, Boulez.

The *Serenade* finds Schoenberg in rather crustily neoclassical mood. Even Boulez with his team (including John Shirley-Quirk) cannot bring out all the lightness the composer himself seems to have intended. With David Wilson-Johnson a characterfully ironic narrator the Byron-setting of the *Ode to Napoleon Bonaparte* is more warmly memorable, but best of all is the lovely *Song of the Wood-dove* in its chamber scoring, with Jessye Norman a radiant soloist, crowning her performance with a thrilling top B flat. Recording both warm and clear, if a little close.

(i) *Herzgewächse, Op. 20;* (ii) *Nachtwandler; Pierrot Lunaire, Op. 21. 3 Pieces for chamber orchestra; Ein Stelldichein.*
(M) *** Decca Ace SDD 520. Members of the L. Sinf., Atherton, with (i) Barton (ii) Thomas.

Compiled from the London Sinfonietta's splendid collection of Schoenberg chamber music, this record at medium price presents an ideal coupling for *Pierrot Lunaire*, here given an unusually sharp and incisive performance, full of atmosphere. The miniatures on side two are all fascinating, including *Ein Stelldichein*, intended as a sequel to *Verklaerte Nacht*; the three chamber pieces, which show Schoenberg very close to his pupil Webern; and *Herzgewächse*, a setting of Maeterlinck in German translation, which immediately preceded *Pierrot Lunaire*. First-rate recording.

Pierrot Lunaire, Op. 21.
*** None. H 71251 [id.]. DeGaetani, Contemporary Chamber Ens., Weisberg.
**(*) CBS 76720. Minton, Zukerman, Harrell, Debost, Pay, Barenboim, Boulez.

The New York performance on the Nonesuch mid-price label steers a splendidly confident course between all the many problematic points of interpretation. Jan DeGaetani is a superbly precise soloist, but there is no feeling whatever of pedantry in this performance which, more than most, allows a welcome degree of expressiveness while keeping a sharp focus.

Boulez's performance has a most distinguished group of instrumentalists, but the result lacks the expressive intensity one expects of this conductor in this music. With Yvonne Minton eschewing sing-speech, the vocal line is precisely pitched but with frequent recourse to half-tones. It is a most musical result but hardly conveys the cabaret associations which are important in this highly coloured melodramatic work. The recording is forward and clean, if lacking in bloom.

Schubert, Franz (1797–1828)

Konzertstück for violin and orchestra in D, D. 345.
*** CRD CRD 1069/*CRDC 4069*. Ronald Thomas, Bournemouth Sinf. – BEETHOVEN: *Romances;* MENDELSSOHN: *Concerto.****

The *Konzertstück* is hardly vintage Schubert, but Ronald Thomas's refreshing playing and direction make it well worth hearing along with the excellent Mendelssohn and Beethoven. The cassette transfer matches the first-class recording of the disc.

Overtures: Fierrabras, D.796; in the Italian style in C, D.591; Des Teufels Lustschloss, D.84.
(M) *** Decca Jub. JB/*KJBC* 76 [Lon. STS 15476]. VPO, Kertesz – *Symphony No. 8.****

These overtures provide an enterprising coupling for a first-rate account of the *Unfinished symphony. Des Teufels Lustschloss* is a juvenile work, and its bright-eyed freshness shows much in common with the music of the young Mendelssohn. *Fierrabras* is more melodramatic but lively in invention; and

Schubert's Rossini imitation nearly comes off here with such neat, sparkling playing. Excellent recording too on both disc and cassette.

Rosamunde: Overture, D.644; Ballet in G; Entr'acte in B flat, D.797.
(M) *** Ph. Seq. 6527/*7311* 056. Concg. O, Szell – MENDELSSOHN: *Midsummer Night's Dream.****

Those wanting the most famous numbers from *Rosamunde* with the traditional Mendelssohn coupling could hardly do better than this reissue, with recordings dating from the end of the 1960s and sounding admirably fresh here. The orchestral playing is first-class: the *Overture* has a striking resilient spring, and the *Ballet* and *Entr'acte* match polish with charm. Particularly engaging is the way Szell quickens the pace of the middle section of the *Entr'acte* so that the effect of the reprise of the famous principal melody is heightened. Recommended.

Symphonies Nos. 1–9. Rosamunde: Overture, D.644; incidental music, D.797.
**(*) DG 2740 127/*3378 082* (5). Berlin PO, Boehm.
**(*) HMV SLS/*TC-SLS* 5127 [Ang. SZCX/*4Z3X* 3862]. Berlin PO, Karajan.

Symphonies Nos. 1–9; 2 Overtures in the Italian style, D.590, D.591.
(M) ** Ph. 6747 491 [6770 015]. Dresden State O, Sawallisch.

With the deletion of the Kertesz set, choice now mainly lies between Boehm and Karajan; by the side of these performances Sawallisch's seems undercharacterized. Boehm has a somewhat unsmiling countenance here and there (especially by the side of Beecham in Nos. 3 and 5), but the playing of the Berlin Philharmonic is distinguished. Certainly the Berlin wind are a joy to listen to in most of these symphonies, and in Nos. 6, 8 and 9 Boehm is the very best of Schubertians. It is only in the early symphonies that he sometimes fails to capture the youthful sparkle of these delightful scores.

Here the point and elegance of the Berliners' playing under Karajan is more persuasive, yet the results are never mannered. One might criticize the reverberant acoustic for giving the impression of too large a band, one which rather lacks the brightness one associates with Schubert's songful writing; and the *Fourth Symphony*, the *Tragic*, finds Karajan less compelling. So does the *Great C major*, though this is a far less superficial reading than the one he recorded earlier for DG. The culmination of the set comes not in No. 9 but in the *Unfinished*, which with Berlin refinement at its most ethereal has an other-worldly quality, rapt and concentrated. Other versions convey more Schubertian freshness, but this set plainly earns a high place. The cassettes match the discs fairly closely, although in tuttis the upper range is not quite so clean.

Sawallisch gives refined, somewhat reticent readings of all the Schubert symphonies. He misses some of the fun in the early works and some of the weight of the later symphonies, but with polished playing from the Dresden orchestra it remains an enjoyable set, nowhere seriously disappointing. The recorded sound, of late-1960s vintage, is somewhat cautious, but Sawallisch's ability to compel attention on a pianissimo – so important when most of these symphonies begin with slow introductions – is most impressive, evidence of his unforced concentration and the beauty of the Dresden string section.

Symphonies Nos. 1 in D, D.82; 2 in B flat, D.125.
(M) ** Decca Jub. JB/*KJBC* 73 [Lon. STS 15473]. VPO, Kertesz.

Kertesz's performances are stylishly played and very well recorded on disc and cassette alike (the tape benefits from a slight treble cut). They also have the advantage of economy; but in the last analysis they lack sparkle.

Symphonies Nos. 1; 4 in C min. (Tragic), D.417.
*** Ph. Dig. 6514/*7337* 261 [id.]. ASMF, Marriner.

The style of Marriner and the Academy, their polish and point, is ideally suited to early Schubert. Even No. 4 is far less weighty than its subtitle suggests, and this performance captures the stirrings of romanticism (particularly in the outer movements) while keeping the results totally Schubertian in their lightness. Superb recording. The chrome tape is agreeable but rather bass-orientated.

Symphonies Nos. 2 in B flat, D.125; 6 in C, D.589.
*** Ph. Dig. 6514/*7337* 208 [id.]. ASMF, Marriner.

Marriner and the Academy gain over almost every rival in the lightness and clarity of articulation as well as the apt and refreshing choices of speed – particularly important in No. 6 which is a demanding work interpretatively. An outstanding issue like the others in Marriner's Schubert series, superbly recorded. The chrome cassette is generally pleasing, though it tends to be bass-heavy.

Symphonies Nos. 3 in D, D.200; 5 in B flat, D.485.
❀ *** HMV SXLP/*TC-SXLP* 30204. RPO, Beecham.
*** Ph. 6514/*7337* 149 [id.]. ASMF, Marriner.

Beecham's are magical performances in which every phrase breathes. There is no substitute for imaginative phrasing, and each line is shaped with affection and spirit. Sunny, smiling performances with beautifully alive rhythms and luminous textures. The recording is faithful in timbre, well-balanced and spacious. This is an indispensable record for all collections. The cassette transfer too is of excellent quality.

Stylish, fresh and beautifully sprung performances from Marriner and the Academy, superbly played and recorded. The classic Beecham coupling of the same two symphonies brought one or two extra touches of magic, but for charm and sparkle these performances are unsurpassed among modern versions. On the chrome cassette detail and focus are soft-grained; the disc is far preferable.

Symphonies Nos. 3; 6 in C, D.589.
(M) ** Decca Jub. JB/*KJBC* 74. VPO, Kertesz.

Good performances, though they lack the last ounce of character or distinction; the Vienna Philharmonic play well for Kertesz but not memorably. The recording is very good, with the cassette transfer lively if with slightly less bloom than the disc.

Symphonies Nos. 3; 8 in B min. (Unfinished), D.759.
**(*) DG 2531/*3301* 124 [id.]. VPO, Carlos Kleiber.

Carlos Kleiber is a refreshingly unpredictable conductor, but sometimes his imagination goes too far towards quirkiness, and that is certainly so in the slow movement of No. 3, which is rattled through jauntily at breakneck speed. The effect is bizarre even for an *Allegretto*, if quite charming. The minuet too becomes a full-blooded scherzo, and there is little rest in the outer movements. The *Unfinished* brings a more compelling performance, but there is unease in the first movement, where first and second subjects are not fully co-ordinated, the contrasts sounding a little forced. The recording brings out the brass sharply, and is of pleasantly wide range. On cassette the pianissimos of the *Unfinished* tend to recede a little; otherwise the transfer is of sophisticated quality and strikingly clear.

Symphonies Nos. 4 in C min. (Tragic); 5 in B flat.
*** Ph. Dig. **410 045-2** [id.]. ASMF, Marriner.
**(*) Decca Jub. JB/*KJBC* 75. VPO, Kertesz.

For the compact disc issue, the coupling is different from LP and cassette. The sound remains warm and luminous, but the refinement of the presentation against the silent background makes the ear realize that the balance is not quite ideal in the relationship of wind and strings and the recording is not as clearly defined internally as one might expect, with the overall focus less than sharp. Nevertheless this remains a highly desirable issue.

At mid-price the Kertesz Jubilee reissue remains good value. Apart from a few extreme tempi – a fast minuet in No. 4, a fast first movement and a slow start to the second in

No. 5 – this coupling offers attractive, stylish Schubert playing. Kertesz does not always find the smile in Schubert's writing, but the playing of the Vienna Philharmonic is beyond reproach and the recording exemplary. The remastered cassette transfer is first-class.

Symphonies Nos. 4; 8 (Unfinished).
** DG 2531/*3301* 047 [id.]. Chicago SO, Giulini.
** Erato **ECD 88008;** NUM/*MCE* 75063. Basle SO, Jordan.

Giulini's account of the *Tragic* is controversial in its choice of tempi. He makes heavy weather of the first-movement allegro (at roughly minim 92), adopting a speed which offers insufficient contrast with the *Andante*, and which impedes a proper sense of flow. In the second movement he applies the brakes just before the return of the main theme (bar 110) and passes some less than perfect intonation in the ensuing section. The scherzo is not remotely *vivace*, and the finale is only a little less pedestrian. The recording is full-blooded and the transfer to tape has good detail and range, although the bass needs cutting back somewhat. Giulini offers a deeply-felt reading of the *Unfinished* with much carefully considered detail. There are some magical things, such as the phrasing of the opening of the development of the first movement, but even so Giulini does not match here his earlier (1962) Philharmonia performance (now deleted).

Jordan's coupling is well played but the readings are in no way distinctive. The *Unfinished* lacks biting drama; neither does it have any special romantic feeling, while the *Tragic Symphony* is undercharacterized until the finale which suddenly springs to life. The recording is full and atmospheric but in no way special. A disappointing issue.

Symphonies Nos. 5; 8 (Unfinished).
**(*) DG 2531/*3301* 373 [id.]. VPO, Boehm.
(M) **(*) CBS 60034/*40-*. Columbia SO, or NYPO, Walter.
(M) ** EMI Em. EMX/*TC-EMX* 2031. Menuhin Fest. O, Menuhin.

Boehm's recordings of these two symphonies date from the very end of his career. In his eighties he preferred a tauter, more incisive view than he had given in his 1967 Berlin performances, weightier in the first movement of the *Unfinished* and the slow movement of No. 5. Both recordings are full and warm, No. 8 taken from a live performance given at the Hohenems Schubertiade. The cassette transfer is excellent, the full, resonant sound has good range and focus.

Bruno Walter brings special qualities of warmth and lyricism to the *Unfinished*. Affection, gentleness and humanity are the keynote of this performance; while the first movement of the *Fifth* is a shade too measured, there is much loving attention to detail in the *Andante*. The 1961 recording remains fully acceptable.

Menuhin proves a surprisingly direct Schubertian. His account of the *Unfinished* minimizes the romanticism, but though it may miss much of the magic of this unique work, it is refreshing to have so unsentimental a view, with dynamic shading beautifully controlled. At times one wants a little more relaxation, but even in No. 5 tempi are brisk (with the exception of the finale).

Symphony No. 6 in C, D.589.
(M) *** HMV SXLP/*TC-SXLP* 30443 [Sera. S.60367]. RPO, Beecham – MOZART: *Symphony No. 41.****

Few conductors have ever been as persuasive as Beecham in the 'little' *C major Symphony*. The rhythmic point and high spirits of the first movement and scherzo are irresistible, while the finale, taken rather more gently than usual, is delectably sprung. The 1950s recording still sounds well, and the coupling is most attractive. The cassette transfer is of excellent quality, the sound slightly dry but clear and clean and not lacking weight.

Symphony No. 8 in B min. (Unfinished).
C ❀ *** DG Dig. **410 862-2**; 410 862-1/*4* [id.]. Philh. O, Sinopoli – MENDELSSOHN: *Symphony No. 4.**** C
(M) *** DG Sig. 2543/*3343* 506. Berlin PO, Boehm – BEETHOVEN: *Symphony No. 5.***
(M) *** HMV SXLP 30513. Philh. O, Karajan – BRAHMS: *Symphony No. 2.****
(M) *** Decca Jub. JB/*KJBC* 76 [Lon. STS 15576]. VPO, Kertesz – *Overtures.* ***

(B) *** Con. CC/*CCT* 7503. VPO, Krips – BEETHOVEN: *Symphony No. 8.****

(M) **(*) CBS 60106/*40*- [MY/*MYT* 36719]. NYPO, Bernstein – BEETHOVEN: *Symphony No. 5.****

(M) ** Decca VIV/*KVIC* 33. VPO, Münchinger – MENDELSSOHN: *Symphony No. 4.* ***

* CBS Dig. **CD**; 36711/*40*- [id.]. VPO, Maazel – BEETHOVEN: *Symphony No. 5.*

Sinopoli here repeats a coupling made famous by Cantelli with the same orchestra (his World Records reissue, now withdrawn). Sinopoli secures the most ravishingly refined and beautiful playing; and the orchestral blend, particularly of the woodwind and horns, is magical. It is a deeply concentrated reading of the *Unfinished*, bringing out much unexpected detail with every phrase freshly turned in seamless spontaneity. The contrast, as Sinopoli sees it, is between the dark – yet never histrionic – tragedy of the first movement, relieved only partially by the lovely second subject, and the sunlight of the closing movement, giving an unforgettable, gentle radiance. The exposition repeat is observed, adding weight and substance. This takes its place among the recorded classics. The warmly atmospheric recording, made in Kingsway Hall, is equally impressive on LP and chrome tape; but on compact disc the opening pages of each movement are wonderfully telling with pianissimo orchestral tone projected against the silent background. The refinement of detail is matched by the drama inherent in the wide dynamic range. This is one of the finest CDs yet to come from DG.

Boehm conducts a glowing performance of the *Unfinished*, a splendid sampler of the Schubert cycle he recorded with the Berlin Philharmonic around 1960. The opening of the development in the first movement – always a key moment – gives the perfect example of Boehm magic, and the sound is still very acceptable.

Karajan's earlier *Unfinished* with the Philharmonia dates from the late 1950s. It is without any question a most beautiful account, and yet there is no attempt at beautification. The quality of the playing is remarkably fine and can hold its own against most of the mid-priced alternatives – and some of the full-price competition too. There is no doubt that this Karajan record belongs among the finest, and given the coupling (Brahms's *Second Symphony*) this must be accounted an outstanding bargain.

Kertesz's reading is one of the best of his Schubert cycle, spacious and unaffected and supported by fine orchestral playing. The recording is of the highest quality, with a wide dynamic range so that the woodwind solos in the second movement tend to sound a little distant. The pianissimo at the opening, however, immediately creates a degree of tension that is to be sustained throughout the performance. The cassette transfer is notably clear and vivid in Decca's best manner.

Krips recorded the *Unfinished* in the very early days of LP in a gentle, glowing performance, and here again he directs an unforced, wonderfully satisfying account, helped by excellent playing and recording. It may lack some of the bite which even this symphony should have, but anyone wanting this coupling will not be disappointed. The new Contour pressing sounds first-rate, but on cassette the sound lacks transparency and has an ill-defined bass.

Bernstein's is a highly dramatic account and an exciting one, with a great surge of energy in the first-movement development. Yet there is lyrical warmth too and at times a sense of mystery. The playing of the New York orchestra is first-class – the rich yet cleanly focused sound of the lower strings tells at the very opening – and this makes a memorable coupling for a fine version of Beethoven's *Fifth*. The recording is not strikingly lustrous but is fully acceptable. The cassette is one of CBS's best.

At the beginning of his reading of the *Unfinished* Münchinger achieves a degree of pianissimo rare on LP – cellos and basses barely audible – and the exposition is slow, steady and rather withdrawn. Then in the development Münchinger suddenly comes out into the open. The orchestral sound is brighter and freer: it is as though the climax is the real argument of the work and the business of the first and second subjects before and after is no more than a setting, for at the recapitulation we return to the withdrawn mood of the opening. The second movement is less idiosyncratic, thoughtful and again withdrawn. The recording's wide dynamic range does not mean that the sound is not robust, and the cassette too is vivid and wide-ranging.

It seems extraordinary that CBS should have chosen to issue Maazel's VPO account on compact disc. It was recorded during a Japanese concert tour and obviously conditions were not propitious for satisfactory results. The recording of the Beethoven coupling is little short of disastrous, thick and unclear; the *Unfinished* is slightly better but is neither invigoratingly dramatic nor lyrically warm-hearted. A non-starter.

Symphony No. 8 (Unfinished); Rosamunde: Overture (Die Zauberharfe, D.644); Ballet music Nos. 1 and 2; Entr'acte in B flat.

(*) Ph. Dig. **410 393-2; 410 393-1/*4* [id.]. Boston SO, Sir Colin Davis.

Symphony No. 8 (Unfinished); Rosamunde: Ballet music Nos. 1 and 2.

(B) **(*) DG Walkman *413 157-4*. Berlin PO, Boehm – SCHUMANN: *Symphony No. 1* etc.**(*)

Davis's is a strong, direct account of the *Unfinished*, the first movement taken briskly but beautifully played. The magic of the disc is concentrated on the second side where the refined, nicely sprung performances of the *Rosamunde* music are consistently refreshing. Warm Boston recording, made a degree clearer in the compact disc version, but sounding well on both LP and tape (where the transfer of the *Symphony* is made at quite a high level for Philips).

Boehm's warmly lyrical account of the *Unfinished* – see above – is coupled with Kubelik's Schumann on the bargain-priced Walkman tape. Only two items from *Rosamunde* are included and, with a fairly long stretch of blank tape at the side-end, one wonders why the *Overture* could not have been added. The sound is excellent.

Symphonies Nos. 8; 9 in C (Great), D.944; Rosamunde: Overture (Die Zauberharfe, D.644); Ballet music Nos. 1 and 2, D.797.

(M) *** DG Acc. 2725/*3374* 103 (2). Berlin PO, Boehm.

This mid-price folder gives an alternative format for the last two symphonies in Boehm's Berlin cycle of 1961. If you want this collection of Schubert works – with the *Rosamunde* items, recorded ten years later, filling the fourth side – it is highly recommendable; all of the performances are ripely persuasive in Boehm's very Austrian, at times almost rustic, style of Schubert interpretation. There are few accounts of the *Great C major* which glow so warmly as this. The *Unfinished* too is freshly radiant rather than brooding. The recordings of both vintages are very good, and the cassettes match the discs closely (although the transfer level is modest).

Symphony No. 9 in C (Great), D.944.

C *** Decca Dig. **400 082-2**; SXDL/*KSXDC* 7557 [Lon. LDR/*5*-71057]. VPO, Solti.

*** HMV ASD/*TC-ASD* 143662-1/*4* [Ang. DS/*4XS* 37898]. Berlin PO, Tennstedt.

*** DG 2531/*3301* 352 [id.]. Dresden State O, Boehm.

(M) *** Decca SPA 467 [Lon. STS 15140]. LSO, Krips.

*** Ph. 9500 097/*7300 510* [id.]. Concg. O, Haitink.

(M) *** EMI Em. EMX/*TC-EMX* 2010. Hallé O, Barbirolli.

(M) *** HMV SXLP/*TC-SXLP* 30558. LPO, Boult.

(B) *** Con. CC/*CCT* 7512 [Quin. 7100]. Bav. RSO, Jochum.

(M) *** Decca Jub. JB77 [Lon. STS 15505]. VPO, Kertesz.

(B) *** RCA VICS/*VK* 2036 [AGL1/*AGK1* 3789]. Boston SO, Steinberg.

(M) **(*) Ph. Seq. 6527/*7311* 156. Dresden State O, Sawallisch.

(M) **(*) CBS 60132/*40*- [*MY/MYT* 37239]. Cleveland O, Szell.

**(*) ASV ALH/*ZCALH* 905. Hallé O, Loughran.

*(*) Ph. 9500/*7300* 890 [id.]. Boston SO, Sir Colin Davis.

(M) * DG Priv. 2535/*3335* 290 [id.]. Berlin PO, Karajan.

Sir George Solti is not the first conductor one thinks of as a Schubertian, but the *Great C major symphony* prompted him to one of the happiest and most glowing of all his many records, an outstanding version beautifully paced and sprung in all four movements and superbly played and recorded. It has drama as well as lyrical feeling, but above all it has a natural sense of spontaneity and freshness, beautifully caught by the richly balanced recording, outstanding on both LP and chrome tape, but finest of all on compact disc. Here the slow movement, in particular, has wonderful refinement of detail so that one hears things even missed at a live performance, yet there is no sense that the added clarity is in any way unnatural. The silence which follows the central climax is breathtaking, and towards the end when the melody is decorated by pizzicatos running through the orchestra, the feeling of presence is uncanny. There are few of the first generation of CDs that show more readily the advantages of the new technology than this, at the same time confirming the Vienna Sofiensaal as an ideal recording location.

But Solti's splendid Decca disc does not have the digital field to itself, for many may find Tennstedt's HMV performance even more satisfying. It is an incandescent reading that brings home afresh how Schubert, even in this last and grandest of his symphonies, was still youthfully energetic. With superb playing from the Berlin orchestra in sound of a natural warmth, this is certainly among the very finest versions available. The recording may not be as transparent as Solti's Decca, but it is glowingly full and has excellent detail, with the XDR cassette losing little on the range and clarity of the disc. The slow introduction, subtle in its dynamic inflection, is kept nicely moving, fresh and well sprung, as is the main allegro, with a natural unexaggerated slowing bringing a sense of culmination in the coda. Tennstedt, however, goes against current fashion by not observing the exposition repeat. The slow movement is delectably pointed with the climax strong and unforced and with a gloriously warm cello melody following. The scherzo has rarely bounced its way so persuasively in Ländler fashion, while the finale is beautifully judged, with triplet textures lightened and rhythms unfailingly resilient.

Boehm's Dresden performance was recorded live in January 1979, and presented marvellous evidence of his continuing energy in his mid-eighties. If anything, this is a more volatile performance than the glowing one included in his cycle of the Schubert symphonies, with a marked relaxation for the second subject in the first movement and extreme slowing before the end. The slow movement is fastish, with dotted rhythms crisply pointed and a marked slowing for the cello theme after the great dissonant climax. The scherzo is sunny and lilting, the finale fierce and fast. It may not be quite so immaculate as the studio-recorded version, but it is equally a superb document of Boehm's mastery as a Schubertian, and the recording, though a little edgy on brass, has fine range. The tape is lively but slightly fierce on side two.

Josef Krips never made a finer record than this, and in the current reissue the sound is outstanding too, with a glowing bloom cast over the entire orchestra. The performance itself has a direct, unforced spontaneity which shows Krips's natural feeling for Schubertian lyricism at its most engaging. The playing is polished yet flexible, strong without ever sounding aggressive. In the final two movements Krips finds an airy exhilaration which makes one wonder how ever other conductors can keep the music earthbound as they do. The pointing of the trio in the scherzo is delectable, and the feathery lightness of the triplets in the finale makes one positively welcome every single one of its many repetitions. As a whole this reading represents the Viennese tradition at its very finest. A marvellous bargain.

Haitink's too is a fresh and beautiful performance, marked by superb playing from the Concertgebouw. The interpretative approach is generally direct, so that the end of the first movement brings fewer and less marked rallentandos than usual, with the result sounding natural and easy. The slow movement, more measured than usual, is lightened by superb rhythmic pointing, and the recording is both full and refined. The tape transfer is generally very successful.

Barbirolli's is a warm, lyrical reading, with the speeds perfectly chosen to solve all the notorious interpretative traps with the minimum of fuss. The Hallé playing may not be quite so polished as that of, say, the Concertgebouw on the Haitink version; but it is far more important that the Barbirollian magic is conveyed at its most intense. Barbirolli is completely consistent, and although, characteristically, he may always indulge in affectionate phrasing in detail, he is usually steady in maintaining tempi broadly throughout each movement. The second subject of the first movement, for example, brings no 'gear-change', but equally no sense of the music being forced; and again with the tempo changes at the end of the movement, Barbirolli's solution is very satisfying. The recording on disc is full and ample, but the high-level cassette transfer has brought some problems, with the sound not always refined and moments of coarseness in the finale.

A splendidly wise and magisterial account from the doyen of British conductors. There is none of the overstatement that some find in Barbirolli's account; indeed Sir Adrian's tendency to understate is evident in the slow movement, just as his feeling for the overall design is undiminished. The LPO respond with playing of high quality, and the EMI engineers have produced excellent results too. An eminently sound recommendation. The cassette is of excellent quality, full-bodied, with good upper range and clarity, even though the recording is resonant.

Jochum's recording dates from 1958, but one would hardly guess it from this splendidly vivid disc which though bright and detailed and with strong impact, has no lack of depth. The reading is immensely dramatic, with great vitality and unleisurely tempi that are varied flexibly with the ebb and flow of the music. The slow movement has less repose than usual (although there is no suggestion of hurry) and it has a climax of great power. The compelling thrust of the reading extends through the exhilarating scherzo to a finale which has an irresistible onward impulse. Jochum's use of light and shade is never more effective than here. The cassette transfer has not quite the range of the disc but it is acceptably lively.

Kertesz's disc is also in its way outstanding. It is remarkably well recorded, with a splendid overall warmth, yet plenty of bite and clarity. One is made conscious that the symphony is scored for trombones as well as horns, something that does not emerge clearly in some recordings. The performance is fresh, dramatic and often very exciting. Kertesz's springlike approach counteracts any feeling that each movement is just a shade too long.

Steinberg's Boston recording is also highly recommendable in the lower price-range. The reading is distinguished, superbly played, with many individual touches. The first movement is strong and spacious with an expansive coda, the central movements have an attractive lyrical flow, and there is impressive structural control of the finale, giving the close of the work a feeling of apotheosis. The Boston strings offer splendidly alert articulation here; and throughout, the woodwind – given an attractive forward balance – phrase warmly and elegantly; indeed there is a cultured feel to their playing. The sound is lively and full-bodied, and there is an excellent matching chrome cassette.

Sawallisch's reading, like his other recordings of the Schubert symphonies, is refreshingly direct. In this symphony some will find the result undercharacterized, but with refined playing from the Dresden orchestra and recording refined for its age it can be recommended at medium price. There is a good cassette, the sound is clear yet has warmth.

Szell's recording dates from 1959 and the sound is bright to the point of fierceness (the cassette is smoother than the disc and to be preferred). The performance is notable for the alertness and rhythmic energy of the playing rather than for any Schubertian glow. Yet there is no lack of resilience in the slow movement. The scherzo has great brio and leads naturally to the brilliant finale, which is a little lacking in weight, especially in the closing pages. Nonetheless the playing of the Cleveland Orchestra is first-class throughout and Szell's control of tempo in the first movement brings a convincing onward flow.

Loughran was the first conductor to record the *Great C major* with every single repeat observed. His reading is characteristically plain and direct, but its communication is helped by the lyrical warmth of the orchestral playing and the fullness of the recording. The reading has a leisurely feeling throughout, and such a performance may tend to outstay its welcome when the rhythms are not always quite resilient enough. Nevertheless this is a performance of distinct character. The cassette has a rather low transfer level, but the sound is pleasingly balanced, with an attractive overall bloom.

With rather bottom-heavy sound on disc (the cassette is better balanced), Sir Colin Davis's Boston version does not avoid dullness. From the slow introduction onwards Davis tends to prefer slow tempi which, with every single repeat observed, even in the finale, and a very straight approach to the notorious problems in the score (except for an over-expressive cello line after the climax of the slow movement), make the work outstay its welcome for once. The oboe in the slow movement sits under the note, but the ensemble of the Boston strings is superb.

Karajan's 1971 DG recording, reissued on Privilege, is an intense disappointment, with the ruggedness of the writing smoothed over to a degree surprising even from this conductor. The tempi are fast; but, as other conductors have shown, that does not necessarily mean that the work need be weakened. But Karajan skates over the endless beauties. There is no impression of glowing expansiveness; this is a tour of a chromium heaven.

Wanderer fantasia, D.760 (arr. for piano and orchestra by Liszt).

(*) HMV Dig. ASD/*TCC-ASD* 4258 [Ang. *DS/4XS* 3788]. Katsaris, Phd. O, Ormandy – LISZT: *Concerto in the Hungarian style* etc.(*)

The Liszt arrangement of Schubert's *Wanderer fantasia* is a splendid bravura piece, an admirable makeweight for Katsaris's Liszt coupling. His free and warm expressiveness is admirably matched by Ormandy. The recording is brilliant, the piano image sharply focused, on disc and chrome tape alike.

CHAMBER AND INSTRUMENTAL MUSIC

Arpeggione sonata, D.821 (arr. for cello).

*** HMV ASD 4075. Tortelier, De la Pau – BEETHOVEN: *Sonata No. 3.****

(*) Decca SXL 6426 [Lon. CS 6649]. Rostropovich, Britten – BRIDGE: *Sonata.**

** Nimbus 2111. Fleming, Parsons – BRAHMS: *Cello sonata No. 1.**(*)

Tortelier provides as unaffected a performance here as of its Beethoven companion. The piano playing may not be as imaginative as that of Benjamin Britten, the main rival at present, but Tortelier is less interested in making points than is Rostropovich. His is warm and delightfully fresh playing and the recording splendidly lifelike.

Rostropovich gives a curiously self-indulgent interpretation of Schubert's slight but amiable *Arpeggione sonata.* The playing of both artists is eloquent and it is beautifully recorded, but it will not be to all tastes. However, the record is particularly valuable for the sake of the Bridge *Sonata* on the other side.

Amaryllis Fleming uses an Amati of 1610 with five strings, much closer than the normal cello to the six-stringed arpeggione for which Schubert originally composed this sonata. She plays with strong feeling and an acute sense of line, though neither she nor her admirable partner ever steps over the bounds of expressive propriety. The *Adagio* is a bit on the slow side, but few will cavil at the musical perception and the quality of the phrasing here. Unfortunately the recording is less than first-class, though it is natural enough. The sound needs to be better focused and more expansive.

Octet in F, D.803.

*** Ph. 9500 400/*7300 613* [id.]. ASMF Chamber Ens.

(M) *** Decca Ace SDD 508 [Lon. STS/5-15436]. New V. Octet.

*** DG 2531/*3301* 278 [id.]. V. Chamber Ens.

(M) *** Ph. 6570/*7310* 887. Berlin Octet.

*(*) ASV ACA/*ZCACA* 1004. Music Group of L.

The Chamber Ensemble of the Academy of St Martin-in-the-Fields offer one of the very best versions of this endearing work. Everything is vital, yet polished and sensitive. The recording is beautifully balanced, and the performance has a warmth and freshness that justify the acclaim with which this issue was greeted. There is a high-level tape transfer of good quality, not quite as refined as the disc – there are hints at times that the level is fractionally too high.

The Vienna Chamber Ensemble do not overlap in personnel with the New Vienna Octet, though the performances have a similar polish and suavity. Mellifluous is the word for both performances, and those who adore the Viennese approach to this repertoire will find satisfaction in these elegant, highly finished accounts. The Vienna Chamber Ensemble produce a beautifully blended sound and are accorded excellent recording. There is so little difference between the two in quality of sound – the Decca is slightly brighter – or in the characterization of the playing that choice can be safely left to the reader. Given the price advantage enjoyed by the Decca, there seems no reason to prefer the DG newcomer. Those who find the Viennese approach too sweet should turn to the Philips medium-price disc by the Berlin Octet which is not the Berlin Philharmonic Octet's performance discussed in our first edition but a new recording by a different group, and a very good one too. The performance has an agreeable easygoing spontaneity, with some lovely relaxed playing in the slow movement and, after a perhaps slightly bland account of the minuet, a nicely prepared and resilient finale. The recording is resonant, but the balance and timbre of the instruments are very natural on disc and tape.

The Music Group of London get off to a rather sluggish start. There is some musical phrasing and some warmth in this performance, but it remains untouched by real distinction.

Octet for wind, D-72: Minuet and finale.
(M) *** Ph. Seq. 412 004-1/*4*. Neth. Wind Ens., De Waart – DVOŘÁK: *Serenade*; GOUNOD: *Petite symphonie.* ***

Two charming little miniatures from Schubert's youth, crisply and attractively played. An admirable fill-up to the delightful Gounod piece.

Octet in F; (i) *Piano quintet in A* (*Trout*), *D.667.*
(M) ** HMV *TCC2-POR 54281.* (i) Crowson, Melos Ens.

A very fine performance indeed of the *Octet* from the Melos group. The playing is fresh and spontaneous, yet polished, with excellent ensemble. The recording is well detailed and truthful. With the separate LP version deleted, this is now only available on a double-length tape, coupled with a less attractive version of the *Trout quintet*, mainly notable for a stunning account of the third movement, but less impressive in the other movements. Although the interpretation is sound and enjoyable, the discipline has not quite the pinpoint precision one ideally needs in a recording. Both recordings have transferred well; the quality is fresh and vivid, but the extended-length format has not been carried to its logical conclusion, and one must turn over after the first movement of the *Octet*.

Piano quintet in A (*Trout*), *D.667.*
*** Ph. **400 078-2**; 9500 442/*7300* 648 [id.]. Brendel, Cleveland Qt.
*** HMV Dig. **CDC 747009-2**; ASD/*TCC-ASD* 4032 [Ang. DS/*4XS* 37846]. Sviatoslav Richter, Borodin Qt.
(M) *** Decca Ace SDD/*KSDC* 185 [Lon. JL/*5*- 41019]. Curzon, V. Octet (members).
(M) *** Ph. 6570/*7310* 924. Haebler, Grumiaux, Janzer, Czako, Cazauran.
**(*) CBS 60127/*40*- [MY/*MYT* 37234]. Serkin, Laredo, Naegele, Parnas, Levine.
(M) ** HMV SXLP/*TC-SXLP* 30523 [Ang. RL/*4RL* 32112]. H. Menuhin, Amadeus Qt – BEETHOVEN: *Piano trio No. 4.***

Piano quintet (*Trout*); *Notturno in E flat, D.897.*
**(*) CRD CRD 1052/*CRDC* 4052. Nash Ens.

(i) *Piano quintet* (*Trout*); *String quartet No. 12* (*Quartettsatz*), *D.703.*
**(*) DG 2530/*3300* 646 [id.]. (i) Gilels; Amadeus Qt (augmented).

(i) *Piano quintet* (*Trout*); (ii) *Violin sonatina No. 2 in A min., D.385.*
(B) *(*) Con. CC/*CCT* 7525 [DG 2535/*3335* 332]. (i) Demus, Schubert Qt; (ii) Schneiderhan, Klien.

(i) *Piano quintet* (*Trout*); (ii) *Die Forelle.*
(M) *** Ph. Seq. 6527/*7311* 075. (i) Beaux Arts Trio, Rhodes, Hortnagel; (ii) Prey, Hokanson.

From the Beaux Arts Trio comes one of the most delightful and fresh *Trouts* now available. Every phrase is splendidly alive, there is no want of vitality and sensitivity, and a finely judged balance and truthful recording make it a most desirable version. The Sequenza reissue offers the small but happy bonus of the song itself, sung by Hermann Prey. On the cassette the focus of the upper strings is a little fluffy; otherwise the sound is good, with a firm piano image.

The Brendel/Cleveland performance may lack something in traditional Viennese charm, but it has a compensating vigour and impetus, and the work's many changes of mood are encompassed with freshness and subtlety. The second-movement *Andante* is radiantly played, and the immensely spirited scherzo has a most engagingly relaxed trio, with Brendel at his most persuasive. His special feeling for Schubert is apparent throughout: the deft pictorial imagery at the opening of the variations is delightful. The recording is well balanced and truthful on LP and tape alike, although on the cassette there is a hint of edginess in the upper strings. The compact disc is smooth and refined, but lacks something in upper range and sharpness of detail, and this cannot be the last word this new format has to offer on the *Trout*.

Richter dominates the HMV digital recording of the *Trout quintet*, not only in personality but in balance. Yet the performance has marvellous detail, with many felicities drawn to the attention that might have gone unnoticed in other accounts. The first movement is played very vibrantly indeed, and the second offers a complete contrast, gently lyrical. The variations have plenty of character, and taken as a whole this is very satisfying, even though other versions are better balanced and are stronger on Schubertian charm. The cassette, like the disc, gives striking presence to the piano, but adds just a hint of edginess to the strings, although this is more noticeable on side one. The CD emphasizes the somewhat artificial balance, but is certainly not lacking in projection. However, the upper string sound is thin and rather lacking substance.

The Decca Ace of Diamonds record offers a classic performance, with a distinguished account of the piano part from Clifford Curzon and splendidly stylish support from the Vienna players. Schubert's warm lyricism is caught with remarkable freshness, and the recording still sounds well. Some might find the brilliant scherzo a little too fierce to match the rest of the performance, but such vigorous playing introduces an element of contrast at the centre of the interpretation. There is a clear cassette transfer, but the tape tends to emphasize the age of the original (1958) more than the disc, with both ends of the spectrum not completely refined.

From Haebler a small-scale performance which is nonetheless very enjoyable. There is some admirably unassertive and deeply musical playing from Miss Haebler and from the incomparable Grumiaux, and it is this freshness and pleasure in music-making that render this account memorable. These artists do not try to make 'interpretative points' but are content to let the music speak for itself. The balance is not altogether perfect, but the quality of the recorded sound is good. The cassette is well transferred, smooth, full and natural; a slightly higher level would have brought even greater immediacy.

Also among the full-price *Trouts* that have claims for consideration is the DG issue including an excellent account of the *Quartettsatz*. In the main work there is a masterly contribution from Gilels, and the Amadeus play with considerable freshness. The recording is of good quality, but the cassette transfer lacks range and naturalness in the strings.

The Nash Ensemble version has spontaneity – indeed there is something of the quality of a live performance here – and the distinction of Clifford Benson's playing. There is a buoyant spirit and a freshness and vigour that are rewarding. Perhaps this does not match the Beaux Arts version in terms of imagination and flair, but it is still well worth considering. The account of the *Notturno* (a more intense piece than the title might suggest) is no less sympathetic. The recording is fully acceptable and well balanced; the cassette transfer lacks the last degree of range, but the sound is more refined on top than in many of the other tape versions and has good body and detail.

The Serkin performance is very distinguished, with some spontaneous if idiosyncratic playing from this master pianist. As a performance this is a strong favourite in the mid-price range, but the recommendation must be qualified, because the string tone is somewhat hard. The vivid, high-level cassette transfer brings an over-resonant bass, and on side one some lack of refinement in the treble.

The HMV version at medium price has a generous coupling in the shape of Beethoven's *Ghost trio*. The record is produced in tribute to the late Hephzibah Menuhin and the performance dates from 1960. The balance is not wholly ideal, though the recording wears its years lightly. There are moments of charm here and the performance will give much pleasure. Hephzibah Menuhin was an intelligent but not always subtle player, and repeats have been excised from this performance so as to accommodate an ample fill-up. This is not a disc that displaces the existing mid-price or newer recommendations. The cassette transfer is clear, but rather dry.

An agreeable performance on Contour, with Demus dominating, partly because the piano recording and balance are bold and forward and the string tone is thinner. There is – as befits the name of the string group – a real feeling for Schubert, and the performance has spontaneity. The first movement is especially arresting, and the *Theme and variations* are well shaped. The tape transfer, however, seems to emphasize the thinness of the strings, although the piano image is lifelike. The *Violin sonatina*, a most acceptable bonus, is well played and recorded.

(i) *Piano quintet (Trout); Impromptus Nos. 1–4, D.899; 2 Marches, D.819/2–3; 3 Marches militaires, D.733; Moments musicaux Nos. 1–6, D.780; Rondo in A, D.951; Sonata No. 17 in D, D.850.*
(M) (***) HMV mono RLS/*TC-RLS* 7713 (3). Schnabel; (i) Pro Arte Qt.

Older collectors will need no prompting to acquire Schnabel's Schubert. These recordings mostly date from the 1930s (the *Trout* quintet from 1935, the *D major Sonata* from 1939, and the *Moments musicaux*, which are marvellous, come from 1937): only the *Impromptus* are post-war (1950). It was thanks to Schnabel's pioneering work on their behalf that the sonatas became established in the concert repertoire after many decades of neglect. (EMI have also reissued the late sonatas in a second volume with other piano music – see below.) The recordings sound remarkably good for their period, save perhaps for the *Trout* which suffers from a dryish acoustic. There is a wisdom, naturalness and a depth of feeling here that transcend the odd pianistic inelegance and dated sound. The cassettes are admirably clear, but tend if anything to emphasize the dryness of the acoustic in the *Trout*. The *Sonata* is much more believable, and the *Impromptus* and *Moments musicaux* are fully acceptable.

Piano trio No. 1 in B flat, D.898.
(*) Chan. Dig. **CHAN 8308; ABRD/*ABTD* 1064 [id.]. Borodin Trio.

Piano trio No. 1 in B flat; Notturno in E flat, D.897.
(M) *** Sup. 1111 1896. Suk Trio.
(M) **(*) Ph. 6503/*7303* 069 [(d) 6770 001/*7650 015*]. Beaux Arts Trio.

There need be no reservations here. Josef Suk, Jan Panenka and Josef Chuchro give an account of the *Trio* that is alive, sensitive and joyful. The *Notturno*, which was in all probability the original slow movement, is given with the same attentiveness that marks the performance of the *Trio*. The quality of the recorded sound is excellent, and this is as good as if not better than any version currently on the market.

The Borodin Trio, too, gives a warm and characterful interpretation, more weighty and serious in overall tone than the Czech group, with natural expressiveness only occasionally overloaded with rubato. The impression is very much of a live performance, though in fact this is a studio recording marked by full and open sound. As the compact disc shows, the microphone balance is a little close, giving a slightly resiny focus to the strings. Otherwise there is fine presence and most realistic separation. This applies also to the chrome cassette, although here the upper range is slightly more abrasive.

The Beaux Arts performance has impeccable ensemble with the pianist, Manahem Pressler, always sharply imaginative, and the string playing sensitive in both line and phrase. The performance is perhaps on the lightweight side, although the slow movement has a disarming simplicity. The *Notturno*, eloquently played, makes an attractive bonus. The sound, from the late 1960s, is a little dated in the matter of upper string timbre, although this is more noticeable on the cassette (transferred successfully at quite a high level).

Piano trio No. 2 in E flat, D.929.
**(*) Chan. Dig. ABRD/*ABTD* 1045. Borodin Trio.
* EMI 2C 069 73067. Collard, Dumay, Lodéon.

The Borodin Trio gives a strong and understanding performance, generally preferring spacious tempi. The outer movements are made the more resilient, and only in the scherzo does the reading lack impetus. The speed for the slow movement is nicely chosen to allow a broad, steady pulse, and the full, atmospheric recording is excellent. The cassette is admirably clear and well balanced, though the sound seems drier in the treble than the disc.

The French team is rather dominated by the piano, but even if the balance were better it would be impossible to recommend this performance without qualification. The great French pianist adopts unacceptably brisk tempi in the outer movements even if he conveys charm in the others. There is some brilliant playing here, but these fine young players are not wholly attuned to this world.

String quartets Nos. 1–15.
**(*) DG 2740 123 (7) [id.]. Melos Qt of Stuttgart.

Apart from the Endres (in an old Vox box), no other quartet has tackled a complete Schubert cycle, and the Melos put us in their debt by so doing. The early quartets have an altogether disarming grace and innocence, and some of their ideas are most touching. The Melos are an impressive body whose accounts of this repertoire are unmannered and on the whole sympathetic. They are let down by recording quality that is less than distinguished, but there is no other reason for qualifying enthusiasm for this valuable release.

String quartets Nos. 7 in D, D.94; 13 in A min., D.804.
(M) **(*) Argo ZK 88. Allegri Qt.

The Allegri players give a very musical account of the *A minor Quartet*, less pensive perhaps than that of the Italian Quartet (see below) but eminently concentrated and coherent. They are well recorded too. They observe the exposition repeat in the first movement, and the quartet spreads on to the second side. The early *Quartet in D major* has an affecting charm that comes over well in their hands, and this issue is competitively priced, though for the *A minor Quartet* the Italians would be first choice.

String quartets Nos. 8 in B flat, D.112; 9 in G min., D.173.
(M) ** Argo ZK 96. Allegri Qt.

The Allegri give serviceable accounts of both of these delightful works whose representation on record is not so generous that one can afford to neglect any addition. Those who possess the Melos set may find these accounts less highly polished but, although they fall short of the highest distinction, Schubertians will find much to reward them and the playing has the merit of being natural and unaffected.

String quartets Nos. 9; 12 (Quartettsatz); 13; 14 (Death and the Maiden); 15.
(M) ** DG Priv. 2733 008 (3). Amadeus Qt.

Although there is some very fine playing in this set and the recording is generally excellent, the interpretations do not always have sufficient depth to be completely satisfying; nor do they always display a natural feeling for Schubert's very special lyrical impulse.

String quartets Nos. 9 in G min., D.173; 13 in A min., D.804.
*** Tel. AW 6.41882 [641882]. Alban Berg Qt.

Here the Alban Berg Quartet add to their laurels with more superb playing: finely integrated ensemble matched to genuine depth of feeling. The *A minor Quartet* has its slow movement based on Schubert's famous *Rosamunde* melody, and the eloquence of the playing here is gloriously natural and unforced. The *Andantino* of the *G minor* is also memorably done, and the crisp articulation in the finale is a joy. The recording is admirably balanced and truthful.

String quartets Nos. 10 in E flat, D.87; 13 in A min., D.804.
(M) *** Ph. 6503/*7303* 068 [9500 078 PSI]. Italian Qt.

The Italians get the *A minor Quartet* on to one side by omitting the exposition repeat in the first movement. The sound quality achieved is excellent, even though the side is not short. The slow movement is beautifully paced – though some may find it a bit too slow – and has an impressive command of feeling. These players' understanding of Schubert is reflected throughout, and the early *E flat Quartet* (the old Op. 125) also comes off beautifully. Altogether a lovely disc, arguably the best version of both quartets.

String quartet No. 12 in C min. (Quartettsatz), D.703.
*** CRD CRD 1034/*CRDC 4034*. Alberni Qt – BRAHMS: *String sextet No. 1*.***
(M) ** Decca Ace SDD 270 [Lon. STS 15525]. V. Philharmonic Qt – DVOŘÁK: *Piano quintet*.***

A fresh and agreeably warm account of this fine single-movement work, originally intended as part of a full string quartet but finally left by Schubert to stand on its own. The coupling with the Brahms *Sextet* is appropriate, for it was Brahms who in 1870 arranged for the first publication of the *Quartettsatz*. The recording is first-class, and the cassette transfer is of excellent quality; this can be highly recommended.

A rather mannered performance from the VPO Quartet, but it has a natural warmth to compensate for a certain lack of consistency in internal balance.

String quartets Nos. 12 (Quartettsatz); 14 (Death and the Maiden), D.810.
*** Ph. 9500 751 [id.]. Italian Qt.
(M) *** Ph. 6503/*7303* 115. Italian Qt.
(*) DG Dig. **410 024-2; 2532/*3302* 071 [id.]. Amadeus Qt.
** DG Priv. 2535/*3335* 314 [id.]. Amadeus Qt.
** DG 2530 533 [id.]. Melos Qt.

The Italian Quartet have made two recordings of this coupling, and both are currently available. The 1966 record (now reissued) was counted the finest available in its day, going much deeper than the Amadeus version. The slow movement is particularly impressive, showing a notable grip in the closing pages. Technically the playing throughout is quite remarkable. The sound of the reissue is first-class in every way, vivid and clear, with a matching cassette of Philips's best quality, transferred at a satisfactory level.

The full-priced 1981 successor is hardly less impressive, and has the advantage of more modern recording. The Italians again bring great concentration and poetic feeling to this wonderful score and they are free of the expressive point-making occasionally to be found in such rivals as the Melos Quartet of Stuttgart. Any newcomer will have to be very special to displace this.

The 1983 Amadeus version of *Death and the Maiden* offers much to admire. The performance has a powerful momentum and, though there is some rough playing from Brainin, there is relatively little sentimentality. The actual sound is not as pure as in their very first recording (reissued on RLS 767 – now deleted) when their blend was superb and the leader's vibrato unobtrusive. Good though it is, this does not displace the Italian Quartet. The compact disc brings impressive presence to the sound, but the balance seems a trifle close.

In their earlier recording on Privilege the Amadeus Quartet gives a wonderful impression of unity as regards the finer points of phrasing, for example at the very beginning of the variations in D.810. This is a worthwhile issue, even if this account of *Death and the Maiden* cannot match that of the Italians. The recording still sounds well, and the cassette transfer is smooth and pleasing.

The Melos Quartet's record comes from their complete set, which appeared in the mid-1970s. Highly accomplished and expertly played, both *Death and the Maiden* and its companion have many points of interest, even if there are some mannered touches. The recording, however, is a little hard and close and it inhibits a whole-hearted recommendation. Collectors in the Far East may care to note a version by the Vienna String Quartet, similarly coupled (on Camerata CMT 1066), superbly recorded in good digital sound and passionately committed and sensibly paced.

String quartets Nos. 13 in A min., D.804; 14 in D min. (Death and the Maiden), D.810; 15 in G, D.887.
**(*) Nimbus 2301/3. Chilingirian Qt.

The Chilingirian Quartet offer the three greatest Schubert quartets in a box, not available separately. They are fine players and can hold their own in the best company. A minor lapse of intonation in the *D minor* and another elsewhere are of no account, and the performances throughout are compelling. However, taken individually these records would not displace the Italian Quartet in this repertoire, nor are they as beautifully recorded.

String quartet No. 15 in G, D.887.
*** Ph. 9500 409/*7300 617* [id.]. Italian Qt.
*** HMV ASD 3882. Alban Berg Qt.
(M) *** Argo ZK 78. Allegri Qt.

Though the Italians are at full price and do not offer any makeweight, they are a strong front runner in this field. The conception is bold, the playing is distinguished by the highest standards of ensemble, intonation and blend, and the recording is extremely fine. The Italians take an extremely broad view of the first movement, and they shape the strong contrasts of tempo and mood into an impressively integrated whole. The playing is no less deeply felt elsewhere in the work, making this one of the most thought-provoking accounts of the quartet now before the public. The cassette transfer is first-class; there is little to choose between disc and tape.

In some ways the Alban Berg players are the most dramatic and technically accomplished of all in this marvellous work. Indeed they tend to over-dramatize: pianissimos are the barest whisper and ensemble has razor-edge precision. They are marvellously recorded, however, and beautifully balanced; but it is the sense of over-projection that somehow disturbs the innocence of some passages. They do not observe the exposition repeat in the first movement.

The Allegri are recorded in a somewhat resonant acoustic, but theirs is a far from negligible account. They observe the first-movement exposition repeat and are less given to extremes of tempo than are the Italians. The playing is both alive and sensitive, and as this is so modestly priced it could well appeal to those who find the Italians just a shade too self-conscious in their search for depth in the slow movement.

String quintet in C, D.956.
*** Decca Dig. SXDL/*KSXDC* 7571. Fitzwilliam Qt with Van Kampen.
*** HMV Dig. **CDC 747018-2**; ASD/*TC-ASD* 143529-1/*4* [Ang. DS/*4XS* 38009]. Alban Berg Qt with Schiff.
*** CRD 1018/*CRDC 4018* [id.]. Alberni Qt with Igloi.
(M) **(*) Saga 5266. Aeolian Qt with Schrecker.
**(*) DG 2530/*3300* 980 [id.]. Melos Qt with Rostropovich.
(M) ** Argo ZK 83. Allegri Qt with Welsh.
(M) * DG Acc. 2542/*3342* 139 [139105]. Amadeus Qt.

String quintet; String quartet No. 12 (Quartettsatz).
(B) ** Con. CC/*CCT* 7569. Weller Qt (augmented in *Quintet*).

The Fitzwilliam Quartet with Van Kampen give a reading exceptionally faithful to Schubert's markings, yet one which with freshness and seeming spontaneity conveys the work's masterly power and impulse too. They observe the exposition repeat in the first movement and play the second group with effortless elegance and lovely pianissimo tone. The melody is the more affecting in its simple tenderness when played here exactly as the composer intended. The reading overall is deeply thoughtful, never exaggerated in expressiveness, but naturally compelling. The great *Adagio* has a hushed intensity, played without affectation, and the last two movements are taken challengingly fast. Some might feel tempi are too brisk, yet the scherzo is the more exhilarating when played presto as marked, and the finale keeps its spring to the very end. Just occasionally in this performance the leader is not absolutely dead in the centre of the note, though intonation is never a serious problem at any time. The recording is superbly full and atmospheric and has remarkable presence, equally true on the splendid chrome cassette.

The Alban Berg do not observe the exposition repeat in the first movement but theirs is still a most satisfying account. They produce a wonderfully well-blended tone and give a strongly projected account of the whole work. They also have the advantage of excellent recording and, given the sheer polish and gorgeous sound that distinguishes their playing, this must rank alongside the Fitzwilliam version. The XDR cassette, however, is a little disappointing, not as refined in the upper range as the LP.

The Alberni Quartet with the late Thomas Igloi give a richly enjoyable performance, one which naturally conveys the give and take of ensemble playing. The record (rightly) won glowing opinions when imported into the United States, where till then this British group was unknown, and that may point a contrast with higher-powered but less intensely communicative readings. The concentration here justifies the exposition repeat in the long first movement, and though the Albernis do not match the hushed simplicity of the Fitzwilliam players in the sublime *Adagio*, theirs too conveys deep dedication. The last two movements receive spirited, unexaggerated performances. The recording is excellent, with a fine atmospheric bloom on it. There is a good cassette.

The Aeolian Quartet gives a strong, virile performance of what is arguably Schubert's greatest chamber work. Their style is direct, with no mannerisms whatever. It might seem bald were it not for the depth of concentration that the players convey in every bar. The finale, for example, is fresh and rustic-sounding, not because of pointing of the rhythm, but because of the very simplicity of utterance. In the slow movement the Aeolians daringly adopt the slowest possible *Adagio*, and the result might have seemed static but for the 'inner' tension which holds one breathless through hushed pianissimos of the most intense beauty. Never before on record, not even in Casals's old Prades version (mono), had the profundity of this music been so compellingly conveyed. The recording is not of the clearest, but quite acceptable, and at budget price no one is likely to complain.

Rostropovich plays as second cello in the Melos performance, and no doubt his influence from the centre of the string texture contributes to the eloquence of the famous *Adagio*, which like the performance as a whole is strongly, even dramatically characterized. The emphasis of the rhythmic articulation of the outer movements leaves no doubt as to the power of Schubert's writing, and while there is no lack of atmosphere in the opening and closing sections of the slow movement, the performance is in the last analysis less persuasive than the Fitzwilliam version with its greater emotional resilience and flexibility. The DG recording is live and immediate. On cassette the upper strings are sometimes a little husky in focus, but there is a good balance.

Very fine playing from the Weller Quartet on Contour (originally a Decca recording) though perhaps a trifle sweet and suave. The unpretentious account given by the Aeolians on Saga does not cost too much more and is undoubtedly more searching. The Weller performance, however, has a superior recording, and the *Quartettsatz* is an attractive filler.

The Allegri version has the merit of including the exposition repeat – making the first side exceedingly long – but generally, with intonation and ensemble not always immaculate, it cannot quite match the finest versions, sensitive as the playing is. The recording too has some odd balances.

Many find the playing of the Amadeus so refined and perfect in technique that this outweighs any reservations they harbour on points of interpretation. But not here. This performance of the *C major Quintet*, Schubert's sublimest utterance, is perfumed, mannered and superficial. The recording is good on disc and tape alike.

Violin sonata (Duo) in A, D.574; Fantaisie in C, D.934; Violin sonatinas Nos. 1 in D, D.384; 2 in A min., D.385; 3 in G min., D.408.
** Decca D 195 D 2 (2). Goldberg, Lupu.

Szymon Goldberg and Radu Lupu give us the complete violin and piano music (except for one small piece) in unaffected and well-recorded performances. Indeed Goldberg is vulnerable in that he almost under-characterizes the line: the *Fantasy* is just a shade wanting in freshness, and one could do with a greater variety of dynamic nuance and tonal colour. Yet the presence of Radu Lupu ensures that these performances give pleasure, and his playing has a vitality and inner life that are undoubtedly rewarding. In the *Duo* and the *Sonatinas*, however, the Grumiaux/ Crossley partnership (see below) is to be preferred.

Violin sonata (Duo), D.574.
*** O-L DSLO 571 [id.]. Schröder, Hogwood – MENDELSSOHN: *Violin sonata.****

The Schubert *Duo* is not otherwise available on period instruments and makes interesting listening, particularly in the sympathetic hands of these artists. Jaap Schröder uses a Stradivarius and Christopher Hogwood a piano from about 1825 by Georg Haschka, which he plays with exemplary skill and artistry. It does not produce the range of nuance and tonal subtlety of which the modern piano is capable, but its lightness of colour has its special charm. Jaap Schröder plays with characteristic authority and artistry, and both artists are beautifully recorded. Modern performances will enjoy the wider appeal – probably rightly – but this is undoubtedly a version to hear.

Violin sonata (Duo), D.574; Violin sonatinas Nos. 1–3, D.384-5, D.408.
*** Ph. 9500 394 [id.]. Grumiaux, Crossley.
(M) *** Ph. 6503/*7303* 116. Grumiaux, Veyron-Lacroix.

Violin sonatinas Nos. 1–3.
*** O-L DSLO 565 [id.]. Schröder, Hogwood.

These are lovely performances. Grumiaux has a supple sense of line and an aristocratic quality that communicates freshness and light, while his partner, Paul Crossley, is sensitive and imaginative, as one has come to expect. Rightly, they do not observe repeats, and they eschew any kind of egocentric interpretative point-making. The recording balance could scarcely be improved upon. Grumiaux recorded this coupling in the early 1970s with Robert Veyron-Lacroix, but this is even better.

The earlier set has now been reissued in Philips's mid-priced Musica da Camera series. The recording dates from 1972, and although the acoustic is resonant the balance is difficult to fault. The playing too is warm and fresh, and though Veyron-Lacroix does not emerge as quite so strong a personality as his partner, his response is admirably musical. There is an excellent equivalent cassette (the full-priced issue offers no tape equivalent), and this is altogether good value.

Those interested in hearing what this music sounded like in Schubert's own period should investigate the well-played Oiseau-Lyre disc. However, in these performances, the inclusion of repeats means there is not room for the *Duo* (the disc still plays for 44 minutes).

PIANO MUSIC

Fantasia in C (Wanderer), D.760.
*** DG 2530 473/*3300 504* [id.]. Pollini – *Sonata No. 16.****
*** Ph. 6500 285 [id.]. Brendel – *Sonata No. 21.****

Pollini's account is outstanding and, though he is not as well recorded as Brendel (and the tape too is not entirely satisfactory, rather hard-edged on top and lacking presence at pianissimo level), the playing shows remarkable insights.

Brendel's playing too is of a high order, and he is superbly recorded. This is coupled with what is perhaps Schubert's greatest *Sonata*, sometimes given a record to itself, or provided with only a small filler, so it is excellent value.

Impromptus Nos. 1–4, D.899; 5–8, D.935.
*** CBS 37291/*40-* [id.]. Perahia.
*** Ph. **411 040-2**; 9500 357/*7300 587*. Brendel.
*** Decca Dig. **411 711-2**; SXDL/*KSXDC* 7594. Lupu.
*** Hyp. A 66034. Ferber.

(M) *** Decca Ace SDD 563. Schiff.
**(*) DG Acc. 2542/*3342* 111 [139109]. Kempff.

Perahia's account of the *Impromptus* is very special indeed and hardly falls short of greatness. Directness of utterance and purity of spirit are of the essence here. As one critic has put it, Perahia's vision brings the impression of a tree opening out, whereas Brendel's suggests the moment of full bloom. The CBS recording is very good, truthful in timbre and sharper in focus than the Philips. Chrome cassette and LP are fairly closely matched.

Brendel's complete set of *Impromptus* on Philips was previously split into two separate groups (each coupled with other music of Schubert). Now they are joined and the result is truly magical. The recording is quite superb, rich with a glowing middle range and fine sonority. It is difficult to imagine finer Schubert playing than this; to find more eloquence, more profound musical insights, one has to go back to Edwin Fischer, and even here comparison is not always to Brendel's disadvantage. The cassette is no less recommendable than the disc, the focus a little softer. The compact disc has been digitally remastered but the piano image remains slightly diffuse.

Lupu's account of the *Impromptus* is of the same calibre as the Perahia and Brendel versions, and he is most beautifully recorded. Indeed in terms of natural sound this is the most believable image of the three. Lupu brings his own special insights to these pieces. Sometimes his rubato is almost Chopinesque in its delicacy, but the playing can also be robust and lyrically powerful. Perahia displays a fresher innocence; Brendel is more direct and wonderfully warm, but Lupu is compelling in his own way and these performances yield much that is memorable. His musing, poetic romanticism in the *G flat Impromptu* (D.899/3) is wonderfully telling, when the piano timbre is so ravishingly caught by the engineers. The cassette is superbly managed, quite the equal of the LP. Choice between the CBS, Philips and Decca versions is very difficult (we each have our own preferences) and the lack of a Rosette suggests that we might be inclined to award one to all three.

Albert Ferber is an underrated artist whose 78 r.p.m. set of Beethoven's *Les Adieux sonata* is still remembered and who has championed Fauré of late. His account of the *Impromptus* is effortless, musical and eloquent, and he is very truthfully recorded. Others may colour detail with more sophistication, but Ferber has a naturalness and an unaffected quality that are most appealing. This is a highly attractive version.

At medium price Andras Schiff's Ace of Diamonds set is also very competitive. The clarity and evenness of his articulation in the *E flat Impromptu* are a delight, the scales in triplets physically tickling the ear. His are refreshing, unmannered readings, superbly recorded (in Japan), which convey poetry in their songful openness. There are subtler readings on record, but none more engaging.

Predictably fine playing from Kempff, although here the magic comes more unevenly than usual. The D.899 set is beautifully done, and all the pieces are well characterized. DG's recording is faithful but a little dry in acoustic, so that the piano's middle register does not glow as perhaps it might. The cassette – transferred at rather a low level – matches the disc faithfully in this respect.

Impromptus Nos. 5–8, D.935.
(M) *** CBS 60282/*40*- [M 35178]. Serkin.

Serkin's performances may seem short measure, but the playing is distinguished and the recording, if slightly dry, is truthful; it sounds especially believable in its chrome cassette format. Serkin's manner is more severe than Brendel's, Lupu's or Perahia's, but the playing is searching and its individual insights bring comparable rewards. There is a sense of stature here, while the songful character of the writing is conveyed without a trace of sentimentality. The range of dynamic is matched by the pianist's sense of colour; the classical authority is balanced by the natural spontaneity of the music-making.

Impromptus Nos. 5–8, D.935; Impromptus (Klavierstücke), D.946, Nos. 1–3.
*** Ph. 6500 928/*7300 587* [id.]. Brendel.

It is difficult to imagine better Schubert playing than this. Brendel's earlier version of the *Klavierstücke* on Turnabout was searching enough, and one would hesitate to say that this goes even deeper; perhaps it does. In any event the recording is infinitely richer and has more presence.

Moments musicaux Nos. 1–6, D.780.
(M) *** Decca JB/*KJBC* 145 [Lon. STS 15483]. Curzon – *Piano sonata No. 17.****
(M) ** DG Sig. 2543/*3343* 525 [id.]. Barenboim – SCHUMANN: *Kinderscenen* etc.***

Moments musicaux Nos. 1–6, D.780; Impromptus (Klavierstücke), D.946, Nos. 1–3.
(M) *** Ph. Seq. 6527/*7311* 110. Brendel.

Both Curzon and Brendel on Philips give superb performances of the *Moments musicaux*. These readings are among the most poetic now in the catalogue, and the recording in both cases is exemplary. Brendel recorded the same coupling earlier for Turnabout, but this reissue offers marginally more natural sound. The three *Klavierstücke* are also welcome, but Curzon's coupling is far more substantial and equally well recorded, on disc and cassette alike.

In the *Moments musicaux* there is much to admire in Barenboim's performances. His mood is often thoughtful and intimate; at other times we are made a shade too aware of the interpreter's art, and there is an element of calculation that robs the impact of freshness. There are good things, of course, but this does not challenge Brendel or Curzon. The recording is excellent, and disc and chrome tape sound virtually identical.

Piano sonatas Nos. 14–21; Allegretto in C min., D.915; 11 Ecossaises, D.781; Fantasia in C (Wanderer), D.760; 16 German dances, D.783; Ungarische Melodie, D.817; Impromptus Nos. 1–4, D.899; Nos. 5–8, D.935; Impromptus (Klavierstücke), D.946, Nos. 1–3; 12 Ländler, D.790; Moments musicaux Nos. 1–6, D.780.
(M) *** Ph. 6747 175 (8). Brendel.

Though Brendel gives consistently concentrated performances of these late Schubert piano works, his approach to tempo is that of a romantic, for in the sonatas he freely indulges in tempo-changes, often making *accelerandi* to heighten climaxes. In a pianist of less formidable artistic integrity such manners might be distracting, but these performances are as powerful as any available on record, and the complete collection superbly confirms the expanding mastery of Schubert in his last years. Excellent, natural recording quality.

Piano sonatas Nos. 2 in C, D.279; 21 in B flat, D.960.
(M) *** DG Priv. 2535/*3335* 240 [id.]. Kempff.

It is a tribute to Kempff's artistry that with most relaxed tempi he conveys such consistent, compelling intensity in the *B flat major Sonata*. Hearing the opening one might feel that this is going to be a lightweight account of Schubert's greatest sonata, but in fact the long-breathed expansiveness is hypnotic, so that here quite as much as in the *Great C major Symphony* one is bound by the spell of heavenly length. Rightly Kempff repeats the first-movement exposition with the important nine bars of lead-back, and though the overall manner is less obviously dramatic than is common, the range of tone-colour is magical, with sharp terracing of dynamics to plot the geography of each movement. Though very much a personal utterance, this interpretation is no less great for that. It belongs to a tradition of pianism that has almost disappeared, and we must be eternally grateful that its expression has been so glowingly captured. The unfinished early *Sonata in C major* is given an appropriately direct performance. Here the recording is somewhat lacking in lustre, and there is a touch of hardness. Disc and tape are fairly closely matched.

Piano sonata No. 4 in A min., D.537.
** DG Dig. **400 043-2**; 2532/*3302* 017 [id.]. Michelangeli – BRAHMS: *Ballades.****

Michelangeli's Schubert is less convincing than the Brahms coupling. He rushes the opening theme and rarely allows the simple ideas of the first movement to speak for themselves. Elsewhere his playing, though aristocratic and marvellously poised, is not free from artifice, and the natural eloquence of Schubert eludes him. Splendid recording on both disc and chrome cassette, which approaches demonstration standard on the compact disc.

Piano sonatas Nos. 4 in A min., D.537; 13 in A, D.664.
** Ph. Dig. **410 605-2**; 6514/*7337* 282 [id.]. Brendel.

Brendel's account of the *A minor Sonata* sounds a little didactic: the gears are changed to prepare the way for the second group and this sounds unconvincing on the first hearing and more so on the repeat. He broadens, too, on the modulation to *F major* towards the end of the exposition, only to quicken the pulse in the development. The result is curiously inorganic and the *A major* is given with less simplicity and charm than one expects from this great artist. There are also some disruptive and studied agogic fluctuations which are not always convincing. Clear, well-focused recording, which sounds wonderfully natural in its compact-disc format.

Piano sonatas Nos. 9 in B, D.575; 11 in F min., D.625; 13 in A, D.664; 14 in A min., D.784. Impromptus, D.899/2 and 4; Moments musicaux, D.780/1, 3 and 6.
**(*) HMV Dig. SLS/*TCC-SLS* 5289 (2) [Vox C 9026]. S. Richter.

These performances derive from concerts given in Tokyo and, though the sound is on the dry side, it still does justice to Richter's veiled pianissimo tone as well as to his fortissimo. The two well-known sonatas in *A*, D.664, and *A minor*, D.784, were recorded in 1980 and the lesser-known *B major*, D.575, and the *F minor*, D.625, the following year. To the three movements of the latter, which Kempff recorded in his complete survey, he adds the *Adagio*, D.505, for which it was originally intended. In slow movements, generally, he tends to be a little self-communing and the playing elsewhere, though masterly and pure, does not always communicate charm.

Piano sonatas Nos. 13; 19–21; Allegretto in C min., D.915; 4 Impromptus, D.899.
(M) ** Ph. 6768 352 (4) [id.]. Arrau.

Claudio Arrau's Schubert will, of course, be wanted by his admirers but, for all its riches, it does not make an ideal introduction to the composer's late piano music. The recording of the *A major* is far from ideal and there are wayward touches in both the *C minor* and *B flat Sonatas* which will prove as irksome on repetition as they are disruptive on a first hearing.

Piano sonata No. 13 in A, D.664; 4 Impromptus, D.899.
** Ph. 9500 641/*7300 806* [id.]. Arrau.

Arrau conveys much of the pain that lies at the heart of this sonata (and of so much else in Schubert) but his is not an artless, innocent view of the sonata. His is a disturbing, perhaps over-subtle account and too highly personal for many tastes. The *Impromptus* are given with aristocratic refinement and the recordings are very fine both in tone and in timbre; the cassette matches the disc fairly closely.

Piano sonatas Nos. 13 in A, D.664; 14 in A min., D.784; Ungarische Melodie, D.817; 12 Waltzes, D.145.
❀ *** Decca SXL 6260 [Lon. CS 6500]. Ashkenazy.

A magnificent record in every respect. Ashkenazy is a great Schubertian who can realize the touching humanity of this giant's vision as well as his strength. There is an astonishing directness about these performances and a virility tempered by tenderness. This surpasses Ashkenazy's own high standards, and Decca have risen admirably to the occasion. The recording has splendid range and fidelity.

Piano sonata No. 16 in A min., D.845.
*** DG 2530 473/*3300 504* [id.]. Pollini – *Fantasia in C* (*Wanderer*).***

This is piano-playing of an altogether exceptional order. Pollini's account of the *A minor Sonata* is searching and profound. He is almost without rival in terms of sheer keyboard control, and his musical insight is of the same order. The piano sound as such could do with slightly more presence but, this apart, the recording is musically balanced and full of warmth. The cassette transfer offers a rather hard edge to the piano image.

Piano sonata No. 17 in D, D.850.
*** Decca Jub. JB/*KJBC* 145 [Lon. STS 15483]. Curzon – *Moments musicaux*.***

The passage to try first in the *Sonata* is the beginning of the last movement, an example of the Curzon magic at its most intense, for with a comparatively slow speed he gives the rhythm a gentle 'lift' which is most captivating. Some who know more forceful interpretations (Richter did a marvellous one) may find this too wayward, but Schubert surely thrives on some degree of coaxing. Curzon could hardly be more convincing – the spontaneous feeling of a live performance better captured than in many earlier discs. The Jubilee reissue is very generously coupled and the recording remains of Decca's finest analogue quality. The high-level cassette is bold and clear, matching the disc closely, perhaps a fraction harder-edged.

Piano sonata No. 18 in G, D.894.
*** Decca SXL 6602 [Lon. CS 6820]. Ashkenazy.

Ashkenazy's record of the *G major Sonata* is likely to be one of his most controversial. The first movement should be very leisurely indeed if it is to convey the self-communing as well as the sense of peace that lie at its heart. On first hearing Ashkenazy seems too slow by any standards: he robs it of its normal sense of movement. Further hearings prove much more convincing, largely because his reading is so totally felt and equally perceptive. He succeeds in making the piano sound exceptionally expressive and is given a recording that is unfailingly flattering. A most searching and poetic account.

Piano sonata No. 19 in C min., D.958; Moments musicaux Nos. 1–6, D.780.
*** Decca Dig. SXDL/*KSXDC* 7554. Lupu.

Schubert playing does not come very much better than this. Brendel's intense account of the sonata (no longer available separately), beautifully played and keenly dramatic, suffers from some disruptive agogic changes that would doubtless be more convincing in the recital room than when exposed to the repeated hearings one expects from a record, and Lupu's performance is innocent of this. Indeed his account has a simple eloquence that is most moving. Lupu's *Moments musicaux* are very fine indeed, though it is not possible to say that they are better than Brendel's or Curzon's, which are marvellous too. The Decca recording is very natural.

Piano sonatas Nos. 20 in A, D.959; 21 in B flat, D.960; (i) *Allegro in A min., D.947; Andantino varié in B min., D.823; Divertissement à la Hongroise in G min., D.818. 4 Impromptus, D.935; March in D, D.606.* (ii) *7 Lieder.*
(M) (***) HMV mono RLS/*TC-RLS* 143560-3/5 (3). Artur Schnabel; with (i) Karl Ulrich Schnabel; (ii) Therese Behr-Schnabel.

We owe the Schubert sonata revival to Schnabel, for only half a century ago these great works were a rarity in the concert hall. Schnabel's readings of the *A major* and *B flat Sonatas* may have been surpassed in pianistic terms by later artists such as Kempff, Curzon and Lupu, but, as a human and musical rather than pianistic document, these accounts from the late 1930s are in many respects unique. Schnabel is joined here to good effect by his son Karl Ulrich in the *Duos*, and his wife Therese is featured in a group of Lieder, although her contribution is more controversial. It is certainly not lacking character, if not always so strong on style and technique. The recorded sound is amazingly good (with excellent cassettes to match the discs closely). Readers should not expect the range of a modern recording but the timbre is unexpectedly full, especially in the late sonatas.

Piano sonata No. 20 in A, D.959.
* Ph. Dig. 6514/*7337* 368 [id.]. Arrau.

Arrau's thoughts on this sonata are far from unilluminating but the recording lets him down badly. The image is not in focus and the sound swims around the studio.

Piano sonata No. 21 in B flat, D.960.
*** Hyp. Dig. A 66004. Bishop-Kovacevich.
*** Ph. 6500 285 [id.]. Brendel – *Fantasy (Wanderer).****
** Ph. 9500/*7300* 928 [id.]. Arrau.

Piano sonata No. 21 in B flat; Impromptus, D.899/3 and 4; D.935/2.
❀ *** Decca Jub. JB/*KJBC* 140 [Lon. CS 6801]. Curzon.

Piano sonata No. 21 in B flat; Moment musical in A flat, D.780/6.
*** Decca Dig. SXDL/*KSXDC* 7567 [Lon. LDR/*5*- 71067]. De Larrocha.

In considering recordings of this sonata, Kempff's must not be forgotten, coupled to the early *C major Sonata*, D.279. It is a glowing and inspired performance, but it is not so well recorded as Curzon's, now reissued on Jubilee with more generous couplings.

Curzon's is perhaps now the finest account of the *B flat Sonata* in the catalogue. Tempi are finely judged, and everything is in fastidious taste. Detail is finely drawn but never emphasized at the expense of the architecture as a whole. It is beautifully recorded, and the piano sounds marvellously truthful in timbre. For the Jubilee reissue the coupling has been extended to include the three most memorable Schubert *Impromptus*, the playing no less distinguished. This is a truly magical disc and the cassette is equally recommendable.

Stephen Bishop-Kovacevich also gives one of the most eloquent accounts on record of this sublime sonata and one which is totally free of expressive point making. It is an account which totally reconciles the demands of truth and the attainment of beauty. The first-movement exposition repeat is observed. The recording reproduces the piano timbre with the same complete naturalness that Bishop-Kovacevich brings to the sonata itself.

Brendel's performance too is as impressive and full of insight as one would expect. He is not unduly wayward, for his recording has room for the *Wanderer fantasy* as well, and he is supported by quite outstanding Philips sound.

A fine performance too from Alicia de Larrocha, beautifully recorded on both LP and cassette. The heart of Miss Larrocha's reading lies in the slow movement, played respectively with great poetic feeling. Her poise and crisp articulation in the final two movements give much pleasure, but in the large span of the first movement she is less successful than Curzon and Kempff in finding the music's spiritual serenity.

Arrau's performance on Philips, though rich in insights, suffers from disruptive rubati which do not wear well on repetition – and, indeed, disturb on a first hearing. As always he produces distinctive, beautiful sonority and immaculate fingerwork, but this performance could not be a first recommendation. There is a good tape, though the level of transfer varies between sides.

VOCAL AND CHORAL MUSIC

'Lieder on Record 1898–1952' (anthology).
(M) (***) HMV RLS 766 (8). (Includes: Chaliapin, Fischer-Dieskau, Flagstad, Hotter, Kipnis, Lehmann, E. Schumann, Schwarzkopf, Seefried, Tauber).

Few collections of LP transfers of old 78 r.p.m. recordings have such fascinating scope as this collection of historic recordings of no fewer than sixty-four singers. Though interpretative mannerisms sometimes intrude, the modern listener must marvel at such clear and true voice production, not just from artists with names still famous (as listed above) but from dozens virtually forgotten. It is a special delight to compare strikingly different interpretations of individual songs. The collection closes aptly with a previously unpublished record (one of the many here) of Kirsten Flagstad at her most serene in *Über allen Gipfeln.*

Lieder: Volume 1 (Lieder composed from 1817 to 1828).
(M) *** DG 2720 006 (12). Fischer-Dieskau, Moore.

With over 200 songs on 24 sides, there would be danger of indigestion for even the most dedicated Schubertian were it not for the endless imagination of both these artists. In their Berlin recording sessions they adopted a special technique of study, rehearsal and recording most apt for such a project. The sense of spontaneity and new discovery is unfailing, since each take was in fact a performance. On a later occasion both artists might have taken a different view, but, used intelligently for sampling, this collection stands as a unique contribution to Lieder on record. The songs in this volume are presented broadly in chronological order, from *An die Musik* of 1817 onwards. Clean, well-balanced recording.

Lieder: Volume 2 (Lieder composed from 1811 to 1817).
(M) *** DG 2720 022 (13). Fischer-Dieskau, Moore.

Volume 2 of this great project presents an essential supplement to the collection of mature songs in the first volume. Already in 1811, as a boy in his early teens, Schubert was writing with astonishing originality, as is shown in the long Schiller setting, a *Funeral fantasy*, the very first item here, with its rough, clashing intervals of a second and amazing harmonic pointers to the future. Performances and recording are just as compelling as in Volume 1.

Lieder: *Abendbilder; An die Musik; An den Mond; Bertas Lied in der Nacht; Die Blumensprache; Erster Verlust; Frühlingssehnsucht; Der Knabe; Nachthymne; Schwestergruss; Sei mir gegrüsst; Die Sterne; Wiegenlied.*
C *** Ph. Dig. **410 037-2**; 6514/*7337* 298 [id.]. Ameling, Baldwin.

Elly Ameling's is a fresh and enchanting collection of Schubert songs starting with *An die Musik* and including other favourites like the *Cradle song* as well as lesser-known songs that admirably suit the lightness and sparkle of Ameling's voice. This was the first Lieder record to appear on compact disc, and it deserved our accolade, for the new medium with its absence of background enhances a recording already beautifully balanced. It gives astonishing sense of presence to the singer with the bright top of the voice perfectly caught and the piano unusually truthful. Some ears, however, may notice that the microphone is just a little close.

'Favourite songs': (i) *Abschied;* (ii) *An die Musik;* (iii) *An Sylvia;* (iv) *Du bist die Ruh;* (iii) *Erlkönig;* (v) *Die Forelle; Gretchen am Spinnrade;* (iv) *Heidenröslein;* (iii) *Im Abendrot;* (ii) *Der Musensohn;* (i) *Ständchen* (*Leise flehen*); (vi) *Ständchen* (*Zögernd leise*).
(M) ** Decca SPA/*KCSP* 524. (i) Krause, Gage; (ii) Ferrier, Spurr; (iii) Prey, Engel; (iv) Burrows, Constable; (v) Price, Lockhart; (vi) Watts, Elizabethan Singers, Halsey; Tunnard.

Certainly these are favourite songs, and the recital is enjoyable, with its vividly projected recording. One assumes that such a concert is aimed at the inexperienced listener, so it is useful to find the song-texts on the back of the sleeve. The performances are mixed in appeal. The opening items (*Die Forelle* and *Gretchen am Spinnrade*), sung by Margaret Price, are full of character, and Hermann Prey's group has plenty of atmosphere (especially *Im Abendrot*, with its beautiful pianissimo ending). Stuart Burrows's contributions are direct but not very subtle; on the other hand Tom Krause is on top form, and his *Abschied*, which ends side two, is most attractively sung. A good but not really outstanding anthology.

Secular vocal music: *Die Advocaten; An den Frühling; Andenken; Bardengesang; Bergknappenlied; Bootgesang; Coronach; Die Entfernten; Dessen Fahne Donnerstürme wallte; Das Dörfchen; Dreifach ist der Schritt der Zeit* (2 versions); *Ein jugendlicher Maienschwung; Die Eisiedelei; Erinnerungen; Ewige Liebe; Fischerlied; Flucht; Frisch atmet; Frühlingsgesang; Frühlingslied* (2 versions); *Geist der Liebe; Der Geistertanz; Gesang der Geister über den Wassern; Gold'ner Schein; Der Gondelfahrer; Gott in der Natur; Grab und Mond; Hier strecket; Hier umarmen sich; Hymnus an den heiligen Geist; Im gegenwärtigen Vergangenes; Jünglingswonne; Klage um Ali Bey; Lacrimosa son io* (2 versions); *Liebe; Liebe säuseln die Blätter; Lied im Freien; Lutzows wilde Jagd; Mailied* (3 versions); *Majestät'sche Sonnenrose; Mirjams Siegesgesang; Mondens chein; Der Morgenstern; Die Nacht; Nachtgesang im Walde; Nachthelle; Die Nachtigall; Nachtmusik; Naturgenuss; La Pastorella; Psalm 23; Psalm 92; Punschlied: Im Norden*

zu singen. Räuberlied; Ruhe; Ruhe, schönstes Glück der Erde; Schlachtgesang; Der Schnee zerrinnt; Sehnsucht; Selig durch die Liebe; Ständchen; Das stille Lied; Thronend auf erhabnem Sitz; Totengräberlied; Trinklied (4 versions); *Trinklied aus dem 16. Jahrhundert; Trinklied im Mai; Trinklied im Winter; Unendliche Freude* (2 versions); *Vorüber die stöhnende Klage; Wehmut; Wein und Liebe; Wer die steile Sternenbalm; Widerhall; Widerspruch; Willkommen, lieber schöner Mai; Zum Rundetanz; Zur guten Nacht; Die zwei Tugendwege.*
*** HMV SLS 5220 (5). Behrens, Fassbaender, Schreier, Fischer-Dieskau, Bav. R. Ch. and SO, Sawallisch.

This outstanding five-disc box, superbly performed and recorded, uncovers many rare treasures. Indeed, just looking through the list of contents must intrigue and entice any true Schubertian. Some of the bigger items, such as *Mirjams Siegesgesang* and *Nachtgesang im Walde*, both memorable pieces, have been recorded before, but much here is virtually unknown, including fragments from Schubert's workbench, drinking songs and the like, which were written for singing with friends round the table. However trivial the pieces, these dedicated, stylish performers produce magical results, and much of the content is far from trivial, showing the composer at his most imaginative. Highly recommended to any Schubertian eager for new discovery.

Goethe Lieder: *An den Mond I and II; Erlkönig; Der Fischer; Gesäng des Harfners I, II and III; Heidenröslein; Meeres Stille; Nachtgesang; Nähe des Geliebten; Rastlöse Liebe; Der Sänger; Schäfers Klagelied; Wanderers Nachtlied.*
*** DG 2530 229 [id.]. Fischer-Dieskau, Moore.

These fifteen settings of Goethe poems date from Schubert's earliest creative period up to the age of twenty, magically fresh inspirations ranging wide in mood and expression, and here performed with charm as well as deep insight. The *Songs of the Harper* are among the finest Schubert performances that even Fischer-Dieskau and Moore have given us. Fine recording.

Lieder: *An die Musik; An Sylvia; Auf dem Wasser zu singen; Du bist die Ruh; Die Forelle; Frühlingsglaube; Gretchen am Spinnrade; Heidenröslein; Die junge Nonne; Litanei; Der Musensohn; Nacht und Träume; Rastlose Lied; Der Tod und das Mädchen.*
*** HMV ASD/*TC-ASD* 4054. Baker, Parsons.

Take a poll of favourite Schubert songs, and a high proportion of these would be on the list. With a great singer treating each with loving, detailed care, the result is a charmer of a recital record. At the very start Dame Janet's strongly characterized reading of *Die Forelle* makes it a fun song, and similarly Parsons's naughty springing of the accompaniment of *An Sylvia* (echoed later by the singer) gives a twinkle to a song that can easily be treated too seriously. One also remembers the ravishing *subito piano* for the second stanza of *An die Musik* and the heart-felt expression of *Gretchen am Spinnrade*. The recording is of good EMI vintage, but does not quite catch the voice at its most rounded. The cassette is comfortably transferred, but there is some loss of projection and sharpness of focus.

Lieder: *An die Musik; An Sylvia; Auf dem Wasser zu singen; Ganymed; Gretchen am Spinnrade; Im Frühling; Die junge Nonne; Das Lied im Grünen; Der Musensohn; Nachtviolen; Nähe des Geliebten; Wehmut.*
❀ (**) HMV mono ALP/*TC-ALP* 3843. Schwarzkopf, E. Fischer.

At the very end of his career Edwin Fischer partnered Elisabeth Schwarzkopf near the beginning of hers, and the result was magical. The radiance of the voice, the control of line and tone (vibrato an important element, varied exquisitely) set this apart even among the finest Schubert recitals. The simplest of songs inspire intensely subtle expression from singer and pianist alike, and though Fischer's playing is not always perfectly tidy, he left few records so endearing as this. The mono sound has been beautifully refreshed, and the cassette transfer is clear and full.

Lieder: *An die Musik; An Sylvia; Erlkönig; Die Forelle; Ganymed; Heidenröslein; Im*

Abendrot; Der Musensohn. Die schöne Müllerin: Das Wandern. Schwanengesang: Abschied; Die Taubenpost. Der Tod und das Mädchen; Wanderers Nachtlied. Winterreise: Der Lindenbaum.
(M) *** Ph. Seq. 6527/*7311* 103. Souzay, Baldwin.

On a mid-priced label this is an outstanding recital showing Souzay's art at its most refined and communicative. The singing is unfailingly stylish and Dalton Baldwin provides understanding accompaniments, matching the singer's mood and line with natural sympathy. The sound is good and the selection very attractive. The cassette is in the demonstration class, beautifully balanced and vivid.

An die Musik; Ave Maria; Erlafsee; Die Forelle; Frühlingsglaube; Ganymed; Gretchen am Spinnrade. (i) *Der Hirt auf dem Felsen. Im Frühling; Der Jüngling und der Tod; Liebe schwärmt; Ständchen.*
(M) **(*) HMV HQS 1261. Ameling, Demus or Gage; (i) with Pieterson (clarinet).

This is in fact two recitals in one, as the songs were recorded in two groups (in 1970 and 1972). Quite apart from the fact that the recording is warmer and more kindly to the voice in the later recordings, the singing too shows greater maturity. The earlier songs are sung freshly and straightforwardly and give pleasure from their simple eloquence, but the later recordings, notably *Die Forelle*, *Der Jüngling und der Tod* and *Im Frühling*, are of a different calibre, showing much greater imagination, yet the voice as lovely as ever. *Der Hirt auf dem Felsen* is finely done; the contribution of the clarinettist, George Pieterson, is sensitive if without any special magic. At medium price this seems excellent value.

'A Schubert evening': An die Nachtigall; An die untergehende Sonne; Berthas Lied in der Nacht; Delphine; Ellen's songs from *The Lady of the Lake* (*Raste Krieger; Jäger, ruhe von der Jagd; Ave Maria*)*; Epistel an Hern Josef von Spaun; Gretchen am Spinnrade; Hin und wieder; Iphigenia; Die junge Nonne; Kennst du das Land; Liebe schwärmt; Das Mädchen; Das Mädchens Klage; Die Männer sind méchant; Mignon's songs Nos. 1, Heiss mich nicht reden; 2, So lasst mich scheinen; 3, Nur wer die Sehnsucht kennt; Schlummerlied; Schwestergruss; Suleika songs 1 and 2* (*Was bedeutet die Bewegung; Ach, um deine feuchten Schwingen*)*; Wiegenlied; Wiegenlied* (*Schlafe, schlafe*).
(M) *** HMV SLS 812 (2) [Sera. S 6083]. Baker, Moore.

Janet Baker ranges wide in an imaginative *Liederabend* of Schubert songs that includes a number of rarities. They range from the delectably comic *Epistel* to the ominous darkness of *Die junge Nonne*. The two cradle songs are irresistible, the Seidl setting even more haunting than the more famous one; and throughout the four sides Baker consistently displays the breadth of her emotional mastery and of her range of tone colour. With Gerald Moore (returning to the studio out of retirement) still at his finest, this is a rarely satisfying album. Only *Gretchen am Spinnrade* brings a performance which one feels Baker could have intensified on repetition. First-rate recording.

6 Antiphonen zur Palmweihe am Palmsonntag, D.696; Deutsche Messe, D.872; Kyries: in B Flat, D.45; in D min., D.31 and D.49; Mass in F, D.105; Mass No. 3 in B flat, D.324; Offertorium in B flat, D.963; Salve regina (2 settings): *in B flat, D.386; in F, D.379; Stabat Mater in G min., D.175; Tantum ergo* (2 settings): *in D, D.750 and E flat, D.962.*
*** HMV SLS 5254 (3). Donath, Fassbaender, Popp, Dallapozza, Schreier, Fischer-Dieskau, Bav. R. Ch. and SO, Sawallisch; E. Scholer (organ).

This is the first volume of a projected collection of Schubert church music, and consists almost entirely of rarities, many of them a delight. Even some of the shortest items – such as the six tiny *Antiphons*, allegedly written in half an hour – have magic and originality in them, and the early settings of the Mass bring superb lively inspirations, not to mention the separate *Kyries*. Plainer but still glowing with Schubertian joy is the so-called *Deutsche Messe* of much later, but with fine solo and choral singing (Lucia Popp a special delight), and with inspired conducting from

Sawallisch matched by rich, rounded recording, this is a set which has one thirsting for more.

'Favourite Lieder': Auf dem Wasser zu singen; Du bist die Ruh'; Der Erlkönig; Die Forelle; Heidenröslein; Der Jungling an der Quelle; Lachen und Weinen; Das Lied im Grünen; Litanei auf das Fest aller Seelen; Sei mir gegrüsst!; Seligkeit; Ständchen (2 versions); *Der Tod und das Mädchen; Der Wanderer.*
(M) *** HMV SXLP/*TC-SXLP* 30553. Fischer-Dieskau, Moore.

Most of this mid-price collection was recorded in the mid-1960s, with both artists at their very peak. It would be hard to devise a more delightful collection of Schubert favourites, and *Der Erlkönig* in particular has rarely been recorded with such intensity and élan. Recording still warm and well balanced, with a smooth, natural cassette equivalent.

Lieder: (i) *Auf der Strom. Gott im Frühling; Herbst;* (ii) *Der Hirt auf dem Felsen. Die Sommernacht; Vier Italienischen Lieder, D.638; Der Winterabend.*
**(*) CBS 76976. Ameling, Gage; (i) Deplus; (ii) Studebaker.

Though recorded with rather less natural and full sound, Ameling's CBS recital of Schubert brings performances just as sweetly and serenely magnetic as her Schubert collection on Philips. It also has the benefit of including longer songs like *Der Winterabend*, easily and spaciously done, and *The Shepherd on the rock* with Guy Deplus an admirable clarinettist. It is good also to have *Auf der Strom* with its memorable horn obbligato.

Lieder: *Auflösung; Der Einsame; Gesänge des Harfners; Gruppe aus dem Tartarus; Herbst; Hippolits Lied; Im Abendrot; Nachtstück; Nacht und Träume; Über Wildemann; Der Wanderer; Der Wanderer an den Mond.*
*** Ph. Dig. **411 421-2**; 6514/*7337* 384 [id.]. Fischer-Dieskau, Brendel.

The combination of Fischer-Dieskau and Brendel is particularly compelling in the dark or meditative songs which make up the majority of items here. A delicate song like *Der Einsame* loses something in lightness, but the intensity remains. A lifetime of experience in this repertoire brings a magical degree of communication from the great baritone, made the more immediate on compact disc, but the atmospheric recording, naturally balanced, sounds impressively realistic on LP and chrome cassette (transferred at a good level).

Lieder: *Auflösung; Dem Unendlichen; Der Winterabend.*
(M) *** HMV SXLP/*TC-SXLP* 30556. Norman, Gage – POULENC: *La Fraîcheur et le feu* etc.; WAGNER: *Wesendonk Lieder.***(*)

This Schubert group was taken from Jessye Norman's first record for EMI made in 1970 but never issued. The Schubert items, freshly and beautifully sung with natural presence, make a happy backing to the Wagner *Wesendonk Lieder* and some Poulenc. The voice is well caught in a recording still warm and fresh.

Auguste jam soelestium in G, D.488; Graduale in C, D.184; Kyrie in F, D.66; Magnificat in C, D.486; Masses Nos. 2 in G, D.167; 4 in C, D.452; 6 in E flat, D.950; Offertorium: Tres sunt, D.181; Tantum ergo (3 settings) *in C, D.460–1; D.739.*
*** HMV SLS 5278 (3). Donath, Popp, Fischer-Dieskau, Bav. R. Ch. and SO, Sawallisch.

This second volume of Schubert's church music is centred on three fine settings of the Mass, especially his masterpiece in this form, the *E flat Mass*. The third record brings smaller works, notably the *Magnificat*, in strongly characterized settings. Even the three settings of St Thomas Aquinas's *Tantum ergo* (all in C) have their charm. Though the chorus is not flawless in the *E flat Mass*, Sawallisch directs warmly understanding performances likely to give much pleasure. The recording is warm and atmospheric to match.

Deutsche Messe with Epilogue (The Lord's prayer), D.872; Hymn to the Holy Ghost, D.964; Psalms Nos. 23, D.706; 92, D.953; Salve Regina in F, D.379.
*** HMV ASD/*TCC-ASD* 4415. Fischer-Dieskau, Capella Bavariae, Bav. R. Ch. and SO (members), Sawallisch.

Though this does not contain the most imaginative and original music from the first volume of Sawallisch's collection of Schubert's choral music, it is a pleasing selection, easy and undemanding and superbly sung and recorded. Some of the items, such as the setting of Psalm 23, have piano accompaniment by Sawallisch. There is a good cassette, transferred on iron-oxide stock, but quite well focused.

Part-songs: *Das Dörfchen; Der Gondelfahrer; Grab und Mond; Im gegenwärtigen Vergangenes; Liebe; Lied im Freien; Mondenschein; Die Nacht; Nachthelle; Die Nachtigall; Nachtmusik; Ständchen; Trinklied aus dem 16. Jahrhundert; Wein und Liebe.*
*** Pearl SHE 549. Baccholian Singers, J. Partridge.

Atmospherically recorded, this is a delightful record, bringing together a sequence of rarities that have one imagining the Schubertiades which for long had to satisfy the young composer, otherwise starved of live performances of his music. Many of the items are relatively late, but most of them keep a sense of fun; much of this male-voice music is for friends drinking together. The Baccholian Singers give beautifully resilient, crisp performances, with their voices finely matched. Sometimes they sing unaccompanied; in other songs Jennifer Partridge admirably provides the piano accompaniment.

Lazarus (cantata), *D.689; Mass in G, D.167.*
*** Erato STU/*MCE* 71442 (2). Armstrong, Welting, Chamonin, Rolfe Johnson, Hill, Egel, Ch. and New Fr. R. PO, Guschlbauer.

Lazarus is a rarity both on the gramophone and in the concert hall. Schubert put the score on one side in February 1820 and never returned to it; perhaps he realized that it was too wanting in contrast and variety. About eighty minutes or so survive, and then the work comes to an abrupt ending in the middle of a soprano solo. Yet for all its uniformity of mood and pace, *Lazarus* is well worth having on record. Some of it is as touching as the finest Schubert and other sections are little short of inspired; there are some thoroughly characteristic harmonic colourings and some powerful writing for the trombones. Much of it is very fine indeed, though it would be idle to pretend that its inspiration is even or sustained. Nonetheless, no Schubertian will want to be without it, for the best of it is quite lovely. The singers and the French Radio forces are thoroughly persuasive and it would be difficult to fault Theodore Guschlbauer's direction or the warm quality of the sound achieved by the engineers. The *G major Mass*, an earlier piece, written when Schubert was only eighteen, has less depth and subtlety than the best of *Lazarus*. But there are some endearing moments, and the *Agnus Dei* is poignant. Again the performance and recording here are more than acceptable.

Lazarus, D.689; Mass No. 5 in A flat, D.678; Salve regina in D, D.223; Salve Regina in A, D.676; Salve Regina in C, D.811; Stabat Mater in D min., D.383; Totus in corde langueo in C, D.136.
*** HMV SLS 143607-3 (4). Popp, Donath, Fassbaender, Araiza, Tear, Fischer-Dieskau, Bav. R. Ch. and O, Sawallisch.

Another in Sawallisch's excellent series covering Schubert's choral music, this box is specially attractive in including two of the biggest works, the finest of the *Masses* (in A flat) and the religious drama, *Lazarus*. Unfortunately *Lazarus* – making up three of the eight sides – is no more dramatic than Schubert's operas, but it contains much delightful music. Also included are a number of settings of *Salve regina* and another major piece, his German setting of the *Stabat Mater* in Klopstock's reworking. The singing is outstanding, from chorus and soloists alike. Warm, well-balanced recording.

Magnificat, D.486; Offertorium, D.963; Stabat Mater, D.383.
**(*) Erato STU/*MCE* 71262. Armstrong, Schaer, Ramirez, Huttenlocher, Lausanne Vocal Ens. and O, Corbóz.

Schubert's setting of the *Stabat Mater* (in Klopstock's German translation) is a real rarity, and this well-sung performance (the chorus incisive both in counterpoint and in simple chordal writing) makes an excellent case for it. Philippe Huttenlocher has a sweet baritone, not quite dark enough for the solo *Sohn des Vaters*; the tenor, Alejandro Ramirez, gives a stylish performance of his very Bach-like aria. The other lesser pieces make a good coupling, also persuasively directed by Corbóz, though the recording is not as clear as it might be.

Mass No. 5 in A flat, D.678.
**(*) Argo ZRG 869 [id.]. Eathorne, Greevy, Evans, Keyte, St John's College Ch., ASMF, Guest.

This is not quite so successful a performance as George Guest's earlier version of Schubert's *E flat Mass*. The present work dates from 1822, though it was probably begun a few years earlier and was certainly revised later. It has many beauties, and in a fervently inspired reading can sound most impressive. This performance is faithful but just lacks the distinction that marked Guest's recordings of the Haydn Masses on this label; neither the singing nor the playing is in the least routine, but it lacks the personality that these musicians brought to the Haydn and the later Schubert. The recording is very fine, though not every strand of texture comes through. The cassette transfer is of good quality.

Mass No. 6 in E flat, D.950.
*** Argo ZRG 825 [id.]. Palmer, Watts, Bowen, Evans, Keyte, St John's College Ch., ASMF, Guest.

Having made vibrantly dramatic records of all of Haydn's late Masses, George Guest and the St John's Choir went on first to the Beethoven *C major Mass* (a direct successor) and then to this much-neglected work of Schubert. It may not have quite the electric originality of those other masterpieces, but in every way it is a richly rewarding work, product of the last year of Schubert's short life. The freshness of the singing here (the chorus far more important than the soloists) and the resilient playing of the Academy make this a delightful disc, superbly recorded.

Mass No. 7 in C, D.961; Gesang der Geister über den Wassern (Song of the Spirits over the Water), D.714; Eine kleine Trauermusik, D.79. Minuet and finale in D, D.72 (for wind).
**(*) Argo ZRG 916. Bryn-Julson, DeGaetani, Rolfe Johnson, King, Ch. and L. Sinf., Atherton.

Schubert was strangely trivial when setting this version of the Mass, not noticeably inspired by any of the detailed sentiments of the liturgy. But in a lively performance this last of the four early Masses has refreshment to offer. On the reverse, secular music brings more memorable inspiration, above all in Schubert's last setting of Goethe's *Song of the Spirits over the Water*, a magical piece. The mourning music is very early indeed, remarkable for its solemn brass writing. The recording is not ideally clear but nicely atmospheric.

Rosamunde: Overture (Die Zauberharfe, D.644); and incidental music, D.797.
(M) *** Ph. Seq. 6727/*7311* 211 [6570/*7310* 053]. Heynis, Netherlands R. Ch., Concg. O, Haitink.
(B) ** CfP CFP/*TC-CFP* 4396 [Pro. PAD 106]. Montgomery, St Hedwig's Cath. Ch., Berlin RSO, Kuhn.

Haitink shows the simple eloquence and musical sensitivity that he found also for his companion version of the incidental music for Mendelssohn's *A Midsummer Night's Dream* (currently awaiting reissue). The recording is a trifle resonant for scoring that was expressly (and skilfully) designed for the theatre-pit, but the tape transfer is well managed and the reverberation overhang is only really noticeable in the overture. Haitink does the third *Entr'acte* and the second *Ballet* quite beautifully, and Aafje Heynis is in fine voice as soloist in the lovely *Romance* (*The full moon shines on mountain peaks*). The chorus is excellent in the music for Spirits, Shepherds and Weberian

Huntsmen, although the focus lacks something in crispness here. For the most part the sound is clear and vivid, with disc and tape very closely matched.

Though lacking the charm and spring one ideally needs, Kuhn's fresh and direct reading of the *Rosamunde* music fully and warmly recorded in digital sound makes a fair bargain issue. Disc and cassette are closely matched.

Die schöne Mullerin (song cycle), *D.795*.
*** DG 2530 544 [id.]. Fischer-Dieskau, Moore.
*** Decca Jub. 411 729-1/*4*. Pears, Britten.
(B) *** CfP CFPD/*TC-CFPD* 41 4436-3/*5*. Ian and Jennifer Partridge – SCHUMANN: *Dichterliebe* etc. ***.
(B) ** Con. CC/*CCT* 7588 [2535/*3335* 133]. Wunderlich, Giesen.

Fischer-Dieskau has recorded this most approachable of the Schubert cycles many times, but this version, taken from the complete DG set of Schubert songs, is the finest of all, combining as it does his developed sense of drama, his mature feeling for detail and yet spontaneity too, helped by the searchingly sensitive accompaniments of Gerald Moore. Excellent recording.

Fischer-Dieskau may find more drama in the poems, and Gerald Moore matches his subtlety of inflection at every point; but Pears is imaginative too, if for once in rather gritty voice, and Britten brings a composer's insight to the accompaniments. The spontaneity and power of the DG account are striking and on balance Fischer-Dieskau provides more charm in this most sunny of song cycles; but the Pears/Britten partnership remains uniquely valuable.

Partridge's is an exceptionally fresh and urgent account. Rarely if ever on record has the dynamic quality of the cycle been so effectively conveyed, rising to an emotional climax at the end of the first half (complete on side one, unlike some other versions), with the song *Mein!*, expressing the poet's ill-founded joy, welling up infectiously. Partridge's subtle and beautiful range of tone is a constant delight, and he is most imaginatively accompanied by his sister Jennifer. Coupled with equally fine accounts of Schumann's *Dichterliebe* and the *Liederkreis*, Op. 39, this is an outstanding bargain issue that should win many new friends for Lieder. Discs and the excellent tapes sound virtually identical.

The late Fritz Wunderlich had one of the most headily beautiful voices among German tenors, and that alone makes his record worth hearing. But when he recorded it he had yet to develop as a Lieder singer, and for so subtle a cycle the reading lacks detail. Fair recording, with the high-level cassette slightly more vivid than the disc.

Song cycles: *Die schöne Müllerin, D.795; Schwanengesang, D.957; Die Winterreise, D.911*.
(M) *** DG 2720 059/*3371 029* (4). Fischer-Dieskau, Moore.
(M) *** HMV SLS 840 (3). Fischer-Dieskau, Moore.

Fischer-Dieskau and Moore had each recorded these great cycles of Schubert several times already before they embarked on this set as part of DG's Schubert song series. It was no mere repeat of earlier triumphs. If anything these performances – notably that of the greatest and darkest of the cycles, *Winterreise* – are even more searching than before, with Moore matching the hushed concentration of the singer in some of the most remarkable playing that even he has put on record. There is a superb cassette album, where the quality and balance are strikingly natural.

The HMV versions were recorded in the early 1960s, and represent the second wave of Fischer-Dieskau interpretations. Though the later DG set has greater thought and refinement, the direct power of expression here is superb too. Great performances which proclaim their greatness in every song, and good full recording which scarcely shows its age.

Schwanengesang (song collection), *D.957*.
(M) *** DG Acc. 2542/*3342* 144. Schreier, Olbertz.
*** DG 2531 383 [id.]. Fischer-Dieskau, Moore.
*** Ph. Dig. **411 051-2**; 6514/*7337* 383. Fischer-Dieskau, Brendel.

A tenor might not seem ideally suited to these often dark songs, but one has to remember that even the great song-cycle *Die Winterreise* was written with the tenor voice in mind, and Peter Schreier, as a keenly sensitive Lieder-singer, provides intensity and detail in place of weight. He is well accompanied and well recorded on an attractive mid-price reissue which comes with texts and translations. On cassette the quality is natural, but a lower transfer level on side one brings a slight recession of the piano image; on side two the recording approaches demonstration quality.

Taken from Volume 3 of the great Schubert series which they recorded, Fischer-Dieskau's and Gerald Moore's performances of these late songs – not conceived as a cycle by Schubert but well grouped together – are masterly. The singer may occasionally overemphasize individual words, but the magnetism, poetry and insight – matched by Moore's playing – have one consistently marvelling. The 1972 recording is still fresh.

Fischer-Dieskau's newest version offers deeply reflective performances both from the singer and from his equally imaginative piano partner. His voice is not as fresh as on the earlier DG set but, particularly with the clarity and immediacy of compact disc, this is a beautiful, compelling record. The chrome cassette is good too, though it offers slightly less presence (it is transferred at a rather lower level than the companion Fischer-Dieskau/Brendel digital compilation of miscellaneous Lieder – see above).

Winterreise (song cycle), *D.911.*

❀ *** Decca SET 270/1. Pears, Britten – SCHUMANN: *Dichterliebe.* ***

*** DG 2707 118 (2)/*3301 237* [id.]. Fischer-Dieskau, Barenboim.

** ASV ACA 1007. Tear, Ledger.

Die Winterreise. Lieder: *Frühlingslied; Jägers Liebeslied; Der Kreuzzug; Schiffers Scheidelied; Vor meiner Wiege; Das Weinen.*

(M) *** DG Priv. 2726 058 (2) [2707 028]. Fischer-Dieskau, Demus.

Schubert's darkest song-cycle was in fact originally written for high not low voice, and quite apart from the intensity and subtlety of the Pears/Britten version it gains enormously from being at the right pitch throughout. When the message of these poems is so gloomy, a dark voice tends to underline the sombre aspect too oppressively, where the lightness of a tenor is even more affecting. That is particularly so in those songs where the wandering poet in his despair observes triviality – as in the picture of the hurdy-gurdy man in the last song of all. What is so striking about the Pears performance is its intensity. One continually has the sense of a live performance, and next to it even Fischer-Dieskau's beautifully wrought singing sounds too easy. As for Britten he re-creates the music, sometimes with a fair freedom from Schubert's markings but always with scrupulous concern for the overall musical shaping and sense of atmosphere. The sprung rhythm of *Gefror'ne Tränen* is magical in creating the impression of frozen drops falling, and almost every song brings similar magic.

Fischer-Dieskau's fifth and latest recording of Schubert's greatest cycle, with the voice still in superb condition, is the most inspirational, prompted by Barenboim's spontaneous-sounding, almost improvisatory accompaniment. In expression this is freer than the earlier versions, and though some idiosyncratic details will not always please everyone, the sense of concentrated development is irresistible. The cycle is extravagantly spread over four sides, but the recording quality is excellent. On cassette the cycle is fitted on one double-length tape offered at normal price, an obvious bargain compared with the discs. The quality is very natural but a low transfer level on side one brings recession of the piano image; on side two the recording has slightly more presence.

There are those who regard Fischer-Dieskau's third recording of *Winterreise* as the finest of all, such is the peak of beauty and tonal expressiveness that the voice had achieved in the mid-1960s, and the poetic restraint of Demus's accompaniment. Certainly it makes an excellent recommendation in this medium-price Privilege reissue on three sides with six extra songs on the fourth side, none of them particularly well known. The recording still sounds well.

On two sides merely, it makes a fair bargain, but the version of Robert Tear and Philip Ledger is disappointing from two artists who might have been expected to follow in the inspired tradition of Pears and Britten. It is partly the dryness and lack of bloom in the recording – with the piano sounding like a cottage upright recorded too close – which underlines a degree of squareness in the slower songs. The vigorous songs go much better, but persuasiveness is undermined.

OPERA

Alfonso und Estrella (complete).
*** EMI 1C 157 30816/8 [Ang. SX 3878]. Schreier, Mathis, Prey, Adam, Fischer-Dieskau, Berlin R. Ch. and State Op. O, Suitner.

It is strange that Schubert, whose feeling for words in lyric poetry drew out emotions that have natural drama in them, had little or no feeling for the stage. Had his operas been produced, no doubt he would have learnt how to use music more positively; as it is, this tale of royal intrigue in medieval times goes its own sweet way without ever buttonholing the listener, as opera should. Once that is said, it contains a stream of delightful music, Schubert at his most open and refreshing, and under Suitner's direction it here receives a sparkling performance, excellently cast. Helen Donath makes a sweet heroine, and Peter Schreier sings radiantly, as if in an orchestrated *Schöne Müllerin.* The reconciliation duet between the hero's father and his usurper is most touching as sung by Fischer-Dieskau and Prey. The recording is richly atmospheric.

COLLECTIONS

'Schubertiade': Galop in G, D.735; 6 German dances, D.366; Impromptu in G Flat, D.899/3; Moment musical in A flat, D.780/2; Waltz in B, D.145/2. Lieder: *Abendstern* (i) *Auf dem Strom. Auflösung; Dass sie hier gewessen; Ellens Gesang, 1–3; Die Forelle; Frühlingsglaube; Heidenröslein;* (i) *Der Hirt auf dem Felsen. Im Frühling; Lachten und Weinen; Liebesbotschaft; Lob der Tranen; Nachtviolen; Seligkeit; Suleika 1 and 2.*
** HM HM 1023-4/*40*. Nelson; Demus; (i) Sollner; Prinz.

A simulation of one of Schubert's own domestic concerts is here recorded in a suitably intimate acoustic, well caught on disc and tape alike. Miss Nelson has a fresh treble-like lightness to her voice and her approach has a comparable degree of directness and lack of sensuous awareness. Her line is unforced and though the style is often comparatively unsubtle, certain songs, *Heidenröslein* for instance, respond well to her approach. Demus plays and accompanies attentively but the fortepiano lacks warmth of sonority and the *Impromptu* and *Moment musical* are without the kind of colour one is used to in recordings on a modern instrument. The clarinet and horn soloists are capable rather than memorable, and the overall recital lacks a conveyed sense of delight in the music.

'Classics': (i) *Marche militaire, D.733/1;* (ii) *Rosamunde: Entr'acte No. 3 in B flat. Symphony No. 8* (*Unfinished*). (iii) *Piano quintet* (*Trout*). (iv) *Impromptu in A flat, D.935/2;* (v) *Moment musical No. 3 in F min., D.780.* Lieder: (vi) *An die Musik; An Sylvia; Die Forelle;* (vii) *Ständchen.*
(M) **(*) HMV *TC2-COS 54259*. (i) Philh. O, Kurtz; (ii) RPO, Sargent; (iii) H. Menuhin, Amadeus Qt; (iv) Annie Fischer; (v) Arrau; (vi) Baker, Parsons; (vii) Fischer-Dieskau, Moore.

This HMV extended-length tape opens engagingly with a splendidly pointed account of the *Marche militaire* from Kurtz. It is an attractive anthology with Sargent at his best in the *Unfinished* and *Rosamunde*. The songs are well chosen, the performances distinguished, and the two piano pieces are equally enjoyable. The account of the *Trout*, however, although thoroughly musical is not as individual as some, and it is not helped by the rather dry recording acoustic. However, the tape transfers throughout are of excellent quality.

Schuller, Gunther (born 1925)

7 Studies on themes of Paul Klee.
(M) *** Mercury SRI 75116 [id.]. Minneapolis SO, Dorati – MCPHEE: *Tabuh-Tabuhan;* BLOCH: *Sinfonia breve.***(*)

Schuller's *Seven Studies* form a kind of modern 'Pictures at an exhibition', for Paul Klee was a visual artist. If the piece sounds academic, in fact the music is highly diverting, original in its response, and ingeniously scored. Titles like *Antique harmonies, Arab village* (with its weird evocation), *An eerie moment* and – not least – *The twittering machine* certainly spark off the composer to produce some imaginative ideas. The detail and range of the Mercury recording are first-class and if the couplings are less interesting musically, Dorati and his orchestra ensure that these miniatures are not easily forgotten.

Schuman, William (born 1910)

American festival overture.
*** DG Dig. **413 324-2**; 2532/*3302* 083 [id.]. LAPO, Bernstein – BARBER: *Adagio;* BERNSTEIN: *Candide: Overture;* COPLAND: *Appalachian spring.****

Schuman's overture is the least known of the four representative American works making up this attractive disc. It is rather like a Walton comedy overture with an American accent, and is played here with tremendous panache. Close, bright and full recording on both disc and cassette, which are closely matched. Highly recommended – this collection is more than the sum of its parts.

Schumann, Robert (1810–56)

Cello concerto in A min., Op. 33.
*** HMV ASD 2498 [Ang. S 36642]. Du Pré, New Philh. O, Barbirolli – SAINT-SAËNS: *Concerto No. 1.****
*** Decca Dig. **410 019-2**; SXDL/*KSXDC* 7568 [Lon. LDR/*5*- 71068]. Harrell, Cleveland O, Marriner – SAINT-SAËNS: *Concerto No. 1.****
(*) HMV ASD/*TC-ASD* 3728. Paul Tortelier, RPO, Yan-Pascal Tortelier – BOELLMANN: *Symphonic variations;* BRUCH: *Kol Nidrei.**

It took all of Jacqueline du Pré's youthful ardour to project this most difficult of cello concertos with the momentum needed, and she was ably assisted by Daniel Barenboim. Some will find this a wild performance, but anyone who has ever thrilled to du Pré's essentially spontaneous style will probably prefer this to more staid readings. The slow movement is particularly beautiful. The coupling is unexpected, but well worth having. Good recording.

The controversial point about Harrell's reading is that he expands the usual cadenza with a substantial sequence of his own. His is a big-scale reading, strong and sympathetic, made the more powerful by the superb accompaniment from the Cleveland Orchestra. The digital recording is outstandingly fine with the compact disc version presenting a vividly realistic sound spectrum. The chrome cassette, too, is impressively wide-ranging, though here the treble is marginally less refined in focus.

Tortelier's is a characteristically inspirational performance, at its most concentrated in the hushed rendering of the slow movement. The soloist's son matches the warmth of his father's playing in the accompaniment, and although this version is not the most distinguished available, it can be recommended to those who fancy the unexpected coupling. The cassette is acceptable, though it has not quite the upper range of the disc.

(i) *Cello concerto;* (ii) *Piano concerto in A min., Op. 54.*

(M) **(*) DG Priv. 2538 025/*3318 009* [(d) 2535/*3335* 112]. (i) Rostropovich, Leningrad PO, Rozhdestvensky; (ii) S. Richter, Warsaw PO, Rowicki.

Rostropovich's is a superbly made performance of the *Cello concerto*, introspective but at the same time outgoing, with a peerless technique at the command of a rare artistic imagination. In the USA this performance is coupled with the Tchaikovsky *Rococo variations*. In the UK it can also be found in a two-disc/two-cassette compilation including (besides these variations) concertos by Boccherini, Dvořák and Vivaldi (see Concerts – below). The coupling here with the *Piano concerto* would seem an obviously attractive one but Richter's performance of the *Piano concerto* is not so interesting as one would expect. Its opening speed is fast and the interpretation is in the main without idiosyncrasy, but only in the finale does one feel that vibrant quality in his playing which marks Richter out among even the greatest virtuosos. One suspects that the orchestra was partly to blame, and that its comparative sluggishness affected Richter's concentration. Not that the performance lacks style, but the intensity could be greater. The cassette transfers are of good rather than outstanding quality; the *Piano concerto* sounds rather dry; the *Cello concerto* has more warmth but is a little bass-orientated.

i) *Piano concerto;* ABEGG *Variations, Op. 1; Arabeske, Op. 18; Blumenstücke, Op. 19; Carnaval, Op. 9; Davidsbündlertänze, Op. 6; Études symphoniques, Op. 13; Fantasia in C, Op. 17; Fantasiestücke, Op. 12 and Op. 111; Faschingsschwank aus Wien, Op. 26; Humoresque in B Flat, Op. 20; Kinderszenen, Op. 15; Kreisleriana, Op. 16; Night visions, Op. 23; Noveletten, Op. 21; Papillons, Op. 2; 3 Romances, Op. 28; Sonatas Nos. 1 in F sharp min., Op. 11; 2 in G min., Op. 22* (also (i) GRIEG: *Piano concerto, Op. 16*)*(*)

(M) ** Ph. 6768 353 (10) [id.]. Arrau, (i) Concg. O, Dohnányi.

Arrau's Schumann derives mostly from the 1970s, though the *Carnaval* dates from 1967 and the *Concerto* is even earlier. Arrau's mood in this most romantic of all concertante works for piano and orchestra is serious almost to the point of gruffness. His weighty manner in the dialogues of the first movement is surely too unyielding, and the performance as a whole lacks any feeling of incandescence. In the solo piano music there are many beautiful things; the interpretations are deeply thought out and full of the individual touches one expects from this great pianist, but which are not to all tastes. However, this is a most valuable anthology that can be recommended to all admirers of this artist.

Piano concerto in A min., Op. 54.

*** Ph. 6500 166/*7300 113* [id.]. Bishop-Kovacevich, BBC SO, Sir Colin Davis – GRIEG: *Concerto.****

*** Ph. **412 251-2**; 950677/*7300 772* [id.]. Brendel, LSO, Abbado – WEBER: *Konzertstück.****

(M) *** EMI Em. EMX/*TC-EMX* 2002. Solomon, Philh. O, Menges – GRIEG: *Concerto.****

(M) **(*) CBS 60266/*40-* [Odys. Y/*YT* 30668]. Fleisher, Cleveland O, Szell – GRIEG: *Concerto.***(*)*

(*) Decca SXL/*KSXC* 6624 [Lon. CS 6840]. Lupu, LSO, Previn – GRIEG: *Concerto.*(*)*

(*) ASV ALH/*ZCALH* 931. Vásáry, Northern Sinf. – CHOPIN: *Concerto No. 2.*

(M) **(*) DG Sig. 2543/*3343* 538. S. Richter, Warsaw PO, Rowicki – RACHMANINOV: *Piano concerto No. 2.****

** DG Dig. 2532/*3302* 043 [id.]. Zimerman, Berlin PO, Karajan – GRIEG: *Concerto.**(*)*

(M) ** Decca VIV/*KVIC* 43. Backhaus, VPO, Wand – CHOPIN: *Concerto No. 2.****

(B) ** Con. CC/*CCT* 7506 [Lon. JL/*5*-41050). Katchen, Israel PO, Kertesz – GRIEG: *Concerto.* **(*)

*(*) Decca SXL/*KSXC* 6978 [Lon. CS/*5*-7207]. De Larrocha, RPO, Dutoit – RACHMANINOV: *Concerto No. 2.*(*)*

*(*) HMV ASD/*TC-ASD* 3133 [Ang. S/*4XS* 36899]. S. Richter, Monte Carlo Nat. Op. O, Matacic – GRIEG: *Concerto.**

*(*) Ph. 9500/*7300* 891 [id.]. Arrau, Boston SO, Sir Colin Davis – GRIEG: *Concerto*.*(*)

This much-recorded favourite concerto has proved less successful than some comparable works in the recording studio. The fusing together of its disparate masculine and feminine romantic elements has proved difficult even for the finest artists. Thus our primary recommendation continues to be with the successful symbiosis of Stephen Bishop-Kovacevich and Colin Davis who give an interpretation which is both fresh and poetic, unexaggerated but powerful in its directness and clarity. Bishop-Kovacevich more than most shows the link between the central introspective slow movement and the comparable movement of Beethoven's *Fourth Concerto*, and the spring-like element of the outer movements is finely presented by orchestra and soloist alike. Excellent recording. The cassette transfer while naturally balanced and smooth is disappointingly lacking in sparkle.

Of recent accounts Brendel's is easily the best. It is a thoroughly considered yet fresh-sounding performance, with meticulous regard to detail. There is some measure of coolness, perhaps, in the slow movement, but on the whole this is a most distinguished reading. The orchestral playing under Abbado is good, and the occasional lapse in ensemble noted by some reviewers on its first appearance is not likely to worry anyone. The recorded sound is up to the usual high standards of the house. The cassette offers rather less transparent sound than the disc. This does not efface memories of the fresh and poetic account by Bishop-Kovacevich and Sir Colin Davis but remains an attractive alternative, if the coupling is suitable.

Solomon's famous 1959 recording has been very successfully remastered and has pleasingly natural sound, with strikingly truthful piano timbre. Tape and disc are closely matched. The freshness of the performance gives much pleasure; Solomon plays very beautifully with the most delicate fingerwork, and both he and the principal clarinet caress lovingly their famous duet passage in the central section of the first movement. Menges, as in the Grieg, does not emerge as a strong musical personality, but he is always sympathetic and his comparative reticence does not seriously mar the performance, although in the slow movement the orchestral response is rather diffident. But there is much to give pleasure here, and at its new price the disc certainly remains competitive.

Fleisher's account with Szell is also distinguished, the reading combining strength and poetry in a most satisfying way, yet with a finale that sparkles. In the first movement Szell relaxes the tempo for the famous dialogues between the piano and the orchestral wind soloists, and the effect is beguilingly intimate. The orchestral recording is quite full, and if on disc the piano timbre is shallower than we would expect in a European recording, the chrome tape gives a rather warmer effect. On both, however, there is a curious added bass resonance that accompanies the piano fortissimos, although this will be more noticeable on some reproducers than others.

Lupu's performance with André Previn is also a fine one. The clean boldness of approach to the first movement is appealingly fresh, but the poetry is more unevenly apparent than with Solomon or Bishop-Kovacevich. The end of the slow movement is less magical than it might be and the finale, though brilliantly played, lacks the forward surge of the very finest accounts. The recording is first-class on disc and cassette alike.

Támás Vásáry directing from the keyboard gives a characteristically refined and yet strong account of the concerto, free from eccentricity and thoroughly straightforward. Poetic, likeable and decently recorded, this is recommendable for those wanting this coupling but, taken on its own merits, it does not displace Solomon or Bishop-Kovacevich. The recording is excellent and there is a good cassette.

Sviatoslav Richter usually finds special insights in the music of Schumann and for this Signature reissue his recording has been remastered and the focus is cleaner than originally, with the quality sounding virtually identical on disc and chrome tape. The solo contribution is not without freshness, but the first movement suffers from the relative inadequacy of the orchestral response – the solo wind playing in particular is undistinguished. The finale remains the most successful movement.

Zimerman gives a big-boned performance, bold rather than delicate. There is consummate pianism from this aristocrat of young artists, and Karajan draws fine playing from the Berlin orchestra. The sound is full and brilliant with the cassette lacking something in refinement and transparency. But there is an unyielding quality here in the place of a natural romantic spontaneity.

Backhaus's is a fascinatingly individual version, weighty, emphasizing the masculine character of the score, and not missing its classical inheritance. The orchestral contribution under Gunter Wand is matchingly strong. The *Intermezzo* is romantically full-blooded rather than meltingly delicate, and the finale combines assertive vigour with freshness. The 1963 recording now sounds its age a little but is not shallow, and the cassette is of Decca's finest quality, vivid and detailed, yet slightly smoother on top than the LP.

Katchen is given a clear, brilliant (perhaps slightly too brilliant) recording. This is essentially a virtuoso reading, but Katchen's wilfulness does not eschew romantic charm and there is a pervading freshness. The opening movement has a number of tempo changes and sounds more rhapsodical than usual. In the finale, which is basically very spirited, the fast main tempo hardly relaxes for the bumpy little second subject. The cassette is mellower than the disc, and although it has less range some will prefer it.

The reading by Alicia de Larrocha and Charles Dutoit is very relaxed indeed; it also has touches of wilfulness, as in the ritenuto before the recapitulation of the first movement. Poetry is certainly not absent: the exchanges between the piano and the clarinet are beautifully done, but the lack of overall vitality becomes enervating in the finale, where the approach is spacious, but the basic tempo too lazy to be convincing. The recording is first-class on disc and cassette alike.

Richter's later HMV reading of the Schumann, like that of the Grieg on the reverse, is extraordinarily wayward. Though with this composer Richter can hardly help bringing occasional illumination, this remains on the whole a disappointing version. The recording is excellent and the tape transfer is of good quality.

Arrau's re-recording of the *Concerto* in Boston with Sir Colin Davis produces a performance very similar to his earlier version with Dohnányi (see above); its romanticism curiously heavy, and the whole account lacking something in spontaneity and sparkle. The recording is refined and naturally balanced and there is a good tape.

(i) *Piano concerto; Concert allegro in A min., Op. 134;* (ii) *Introduction and allegro appassionato in G* (*Konzertstück*)*, Op. 92.*
*** Decca SXL/*KSXC* 6861 [Lon. CS 7082]. Ashkenazy, LSO, cond. (i) Segal, (ii) Ashkenazy.

Ashkenazy's reading of the *Concerto* has the aptest of couplings – and a generous one – in Schumann's two other works for piano and orchestra. In the *Concerto* Ashkenazy balances the demands of drama against poetry rather more in favour of the former than one might expect, but it is a refined reading as well as a powerful one, with the finale rather more spacious than is usual. The other two works receive bright, incisive performances, although musically the late *Concert allegro* cannot match its predecessors. The cassette transfer is brilliant but has some lack of bloom at the top in the *Concerto*; side two is warmer and smoother.

(i) *Piano concerto in A min.;* (ii) *Piano quintet in E flat, Op. 44.*
(M) ** CBS 60138/*40*- [MY/*MYT* 37256]. Serkin, (i) Phd. O, Ormandy; (ii) Budapest Qt.

Although this is not undistinguished music-making, the coupling hardly justifies inclusion under CBS's 'Great Performances' sobriquet and the recording is shallow. Nevertheless the partnership between Serkin and the Philadelphia under Ormandy works well in the *Concerto*, and there is both romantic feeling and sparkle. The *Quintet* does not lack either power or intensity (the slow movement is memorable) but suffers more than the *Concerto* from the sharp-edged treble and unnaturally close balance. The tape transfer has been made at too high a level, bringing discoloration in the *Concerto.*

Violin concerto in D min., Op. posth.
(*) HMV Dig. ASD/*TC-ASD* 143519-1/*4* [Ang. DS/*4XS* 37957]. Kremer, Philh. O, Muti – SIBELIUS: *Concerto.*
(M) * Ph. Seq. 6527/*7311* 061. Szeryng, LSO, Dorati – MENDELSSOHN: *Concerto in E min.**

The Schumann *Violin concerto* has had a generally bad press since it resurfaced in 1937. Kulenkampff and Menuhin were among its earliest champions. Its vein of introspection seems to suit Gidon Kremer who gives a generally sympathetic account of it and has very good support from the Philharmonia Orchestra under Riccardo Muti. It is not Schumann at his most consistently inspired, but there are good things in it including a memorable second subject and a characteristic slow movement. The recording is full-bodied, vivid and convincingly balanced, with disc and tape sounding virtually identical.

Szeryng's account is comparatively lifeless and does little to enhance the work's reputation. The recording is good on both disc and cassette, but with a similarly disappointing coupling, this is not one of this artist's more successful recording ventures.

(i) *Konzertstück in F for four horns and orchestra, Op. 86. Symphony No. 3 in E flat (Rhenish), Op. 97.*
**(*) HMV ASD/*TC-ASD* 3724 [Ang. SZ/*4XR* 37655]. Berlin PO, Tennstedt, (i) with Hauptmann, Klier, Kohler, Seifert.

The *Konzertstück*, with its brilliant horn writing, and the *Rhenish symphony*, with its whooping horn passages, make an excellent coupling, and these fine, ripe readings are welcome. The account of the symphony is firmly based on the strong symphonic structures of the outer movements, and the *Konzertstück* too is given an urgent performance. The recording is opulent on disc and cassette alike; the latter is well focused.

Symphonies Nos. 1–4; Manfred overture; Overture, Scherzo and Finale.
**(*) EMI 1C 149 02418/20 [Ara. 8102/*9102*]. Dresden State O, Sawallisch.

Symphonies Nos. 1–4; Overture, Scherzo and Finale.
*** DG 2740 129 (3) [2709 036]. Berlin PO, Karajan.

As we said in the earlier edition of the *Penguin Stereo Record Guide*, Karajan's set of the Schumann symphonies is undoubtedly the best. In the UK, choice is relatively restricted, but in the USA Schwann still lists (besides Sawallisch) sets by Barenboim, Levine and Szell, all of which have their individual merits; but Karajan's performances are beautifully shaped, with orchestral playing of the highest distinction. While Sawallisch's versions of Nos. 1 and 4 command the greatest admiration – see below – Karajan's accounts of Nos. 2 and 3 are among the most impressive ever committed to disc, combining poetic intensity with intellectual strength. The recording too has rich ambience and pleasing tone.

Sawallisch on EMI offers the *Manfred overture* as well as the *Overture, Scherzo and Finale*. The excellence of the Dresden State Orchestra can be taken for granted nowadays; it is surely second to none at the present time, and their records of Schumann's symphonies under Sawallisch are as deeply musical as they are carefully considered; the orchestral playing combines superb discipline with refreshing naturalness and spontaneity. Sawallisch catches all the varying moods of Schumann, and his direction has splendid vigour. Unfortunately the sound is less than ideal: the acoustic is reverberant and the upper strings have an unappealing edge. Yet Schumann's scoring does not suffer as much as it would from too analytical or detailed a recording. His symphonic argument is not conceived in terms of primary colours or clearly-etched lines, and the sound picture has the warmth so essential.

Symphony No. 1 in B flat (Spring), Op. 38; Manfred overture, Op. 115.
(B) **(*) DG Walkman *413 157-4*. Berlin PO, Kubelik – SCHUBERT: *Symphony No. 8* etc.**(*)

Kubelik's account of the *Spring symphony* dates from 1963 and the recording sounds well on this Walkman chrome tape. Both performances here have a sympathetic lyrical impulse and if the coupling is suitable this should not disappoint, for the price is very competitive.

Symphonies Nos. 1 in B flat (Spring), Op. 38; 2 in C, Op. 61.
(B) *(*) PRT GSGC/*ZCGC* 2040. LPO, Boult.

Boult's versions date from the late 1950s and the sound was never distinguished, with scrawny string timbre. But the performances are splendidly full-blooded and Boult's incisiveness compensates for the rough-shod quality of the orchestral playing so that the conceptions of both works, and No. 2 especially, have an integrity and directness that readily communicate to the listener. The cassette transfers are poor; No. 1 has insecure textures at pianissimo levels.

Symphonies Nos. 1 in B flat (Spring), Op. 38; 3 in E flat (Rhenish), Op. 97.
(M) *** DG Sig. 2543/*3343* 504 [id.]. Chicago SO, Barenboim.

Barenboim's record is a recoupling of two fine performances from his earlier complete set. Freshness and high spirits mark both performances, though there is no lack of Germanic weight either, from this German-orientated American orchestra. No. 3 is particularly impressive for the superb horn playing, and characteristically the Cologne Cathedral movement is taken slowly and heavily. The forward and opulent recording matches the interpretations. The chrome cassette is first-class, combining fullness with a lively upper range. This coupling represents the best features of Barenboim's cycle.

Symphonies Nos. 1; 4 in D min., Op. 120.
(M) *** HMV SXLP/*TC-SXLP* 30526. Dresden State O, Sawallisch.
(B) **(*) Con. CC/*CCT* 7532 [DG 2535/*3335* 116]. Berlin PO, Kubelik.

Sawallisch is a clear front runner in this coupling now that his issue is at medium price. These are distinguished performances, finely played, as one would expect from this great orchestra, and charged with great vitality and imagination. The recording, too, is really very good, the treble rather brightly lit but not excessively so. The cassette transfer is first-class: there is little appreciable difference between tape and disc – if anything the cassette makes a slightly mellower impression.

Kubelik's accounts are beautifully played and well recorded. They have not the drive of Sawallisch's versions, and this is especially noticeable in No. 4, but they are direct in manner and certainly enjoyable. The recording still sounds well, and at bargain price this is competitive. The sound on cassette is agreeably full but has less upper range than the disc.

Symphony No. 2 in C, Op. 61; Genoveva overture, Op. 81.
(B) **(*) Con. CC/*CCT* 7537, Berlin PO, Kubelik.
*(*) Decca SXL 6976 [Lon. CS/*5*- 7206]. VPO, Mehta.

This is one of the finest performances in the Kubelik set. It is beautifully played, eloquently shaped, and well recorded in a spacious acoustic. If the performance has less individuality than Karajan's with the same orchestra, it remains very enjoyable, and the *Genoveva overture* is a welcome novelty.

Mehta directs a totally un-Viennese performance of the *Second Symphony*, beautifully played but lacking in charm. Even Schumann's stronger qualities are diminished by Mehta's aggressive, baldly direct approach, in which the speeds – in principle well chosen – never sound quite right. Excellent recording.

Symphony No. 2; Manfred overture.
(*) DG Dig. **410 863-2; 410 863-1/*4* [id.]. VPO, Sinopoli.

Sinopoli's is a performance of extremes, consciously designed to reflect the composer's own mental torment. Even the lovely slow movement broods darkly rather than finding repose. The Vienna Philharmonic play with the necessary bite, with the recording providing some mellowness. There is a good chrome cassette.

Symphony No. 3 in E flat (Rhenish), Op. 97; Manfred overture, Op. 115.
*** DG Dig. **400 062-2**; 2532/*3302* 040 [id.]. LAPO, Giulini.
*** Ph. Dig. **411 104-2**; 411 104-1/*4* [id.]. Concg. O, Haitink.
(B) **(*) Con. CC/*CCT* 7538. Berlin PO, Kubelik.
** Decca Dig. SXDL/*KSXDC* 7555 [Lon. LDR/*5*- 71055]. VPO, Mehta.

Despite the aristocratic qualities that distinguish his performances and the spirituality that is in evidence, Giulini can often obtrude by the very intensity of his search for perfection and as a result, while the sound he produces is of great beauty, he does not always allow the music to unfold effortlessly. This *Rhenish* is, however, completely free of interpretative exaggeration and its sheer musical vitality and nobility of spirit are beautifully conveyed. The Los Angeles players produce a beautifully blended, warm and cultured sound that is a joy to listen to in itself. The recording is extremely fine, too, and reproduces well in its cassette format. This is among the best of recent versions and is particularly impressive in its compact-disc format where the focus is marginally sharper and detail clearer.

Haitink's is a characteristically strong and direct reading, beautifully played with outstandingly resonant and rich brass – most important in this of all the Schumann symphonies. Speeds are finely chosen with the slower movements nicely flowing. Good clean Concertgebouw sound, lacking a little in brilliance but allowing textures to be registered in detail. The high-level cassette does not quite achieve the inner definition of the LP and compact disc, but still sounds well.

In the *Rhenish symphony*, again Kubelik's straightforward, unmannered approach, coupled to a natural warmth, provides a musical and thoroughly enjoyable account. The overture too is apt and very well played, and the recording is up to the high standard of this series. The cassette is brighter than the disc (with thinner string timbre) on side one, but mellower on side two.

Zubin Mehta has the advantage of good Decca engineering on both disc and chrome cassette which helps to lessen the opaque impression of Schumann's scoring. He secures generally clean and well-disciplined playing from the Vienna Philharmonic, but ultimately the performance is wanting in real personality, and at no stage does it resonate in the mind once the disc is finished.

Symphonies Nos. 3 (Rhenish); 4 in D.
(M) **(*) Decca VIV/*KVIC* 46 [Lon. STS/*5*-15575]. VPO, Solti.
(B) ** PRT GSGC/*ZCGC* 2041. LPO, Boult.

This is a generous coupling of two symphonies which in Solti's hands glow with exuberance. Maybe it takes a great conductor to present this music with the intensity it deserves, making light of the problems of balance in the orchestration. Solti's sense of rhythm in Schumann is strikingly alert, so that the first movement of the *Rhenish* hoists one aloft on its soaring melodies, and the drama of the *Fourth Symphony* is given full force without ever falling into excessive tautness. There is still room to breathe. Though Karajan's Berlin Philharmonic performance of No. 3 is even finer, Solti's coupling is offered at what in effect is a very reasonable price. Good recording quality, but the remastering for the Viva reissue has brought a loss of ambient glow, and though the detail is cleaner the overall balance is less agreeable. The cassette, however, is of first-rate quality and, without loss of vividness and range, brings more body to the sound than the LP.

Much the same comments apply to Boult's recordings as to his companion coupling of the first two symphonies, except that the recording seems somewhat smoother. The orchestral playing is again poorly disciplined, but the performances have a life and character that rises above this – No. 4 especially – if the listener is not too critical in matters of ensemble. The cassette is acceptable, but the quality is restricted.

Symphony No. 4 in D min., Op. 120.
(*) HMV Dig. ASD/*TCC-ASD* 3963 [Ang. DS/*4ZS* 37760]. Berlin PO, Tennstedt – MENDELSSOHN: *Symphony No. 4*.(*)

Tennstedt gives a finely shaped account of this work, which is alive and vibrant in every bar, and the Berliners respond to his direction with keen sensitivity. Yet the overall impression is not entirely convincing. The *Romance* could be more expansive and ruminative, and the opening of the finale could have a shade more mystery and atmosphere. The recording is rich and full-bodied as well as brilliant, and there is a first-class chrome tape to match the disc closely. This is among the better versions of this symphony before the public, but it is not the whole story. For that one must turn to Sawallisch or Karajan.

CHAMBER MUSIC

(i) *Abendlied, Op. 85/12; Adagio and allegro in A flat, Op. 70; Fantasiestücke, Op. 73; 3 Romances, Op. 94* (all for oboe and piano). (Piano) *Fantasia in C, Op. 17; Fantasiestücke, Op. 12; Kinderscenen, Op. 15; Kreisleriana, Op. 16.*
*** Ph. 6725/*7655* 034 (3). Brendel (i) with Holliger.

A very distinguished set. The *Kreisleriana* are keenly intelligent and finely characterized, while the *Kinderscenen* is touched with real distinction. The *C major Fantasy* is new and, like the *Fantasiestücke*, is compelling, felt, ardent and imaginative – indeed these must rank among the best versions in recent years. On the third record Brendel is joined by Holliger who gives us not only the three *Romances*, Op. 94, written specifically for oboe, but transcribes the *Fantasiestücke*, Op. 73, for oboe d'amore and the *Adagio and allegro* too. He plays, as does Brendel, with the utmost artistry and the recordings are in the first rank.

Abendlied, Op. 85/12 (arr. Joachim); *Adagio and allegro in A flat, Op. 70; Fantasiestücke, Op. 73; 3 Romances, Op. 94; 5 Stücke im Volkston, Op. 102.*
*** Ph. 9500 740/*7300 847*. Holliger, Brendel.

On this delightful record Heinz Holliger gathers together pieces written in 1849, the most fruitful of composing years for Schumann. The three *Romances* are specifically for oboe, but Holliger – pointing out that Schumann never heard any of the pieces except on the violin – suggests that the others too are suitable for the oboe, since the composer himself gave different options. One misses something by not having a horn in the *Adagio and allegro*, a cello in the folk-style pieces, or a clarinet in the *Fantasiestücke* (the oboe d'amore is used here); but Holliger has never sounded more magical on record, and with superb recording and deeply imaginative accompaniment the result is an unexpected revelation. The cassette transfer is first-class, matching the disc closely.

Adagio and allegro in A flat, Op. 70.
*** DG 2531/*3301* 201 [id.]. Rostropovich, Argerich – CHOPIN: *Cello sonata* etc.***

The *Adagio and allegro* are normally given to the horn, but like other pieces from 1849 they can as well be played on the cello – or for that matter other instruments. Rostropovich is memorably expressive, making this an attractive coupling for the Chopin, very well recorded on disc and cassette alike.

Piano quartet in E flat, Op. 47; (i) *Piano quintet in E flat, Op. 44.*
*** Ph. 9500 065 [id.]. Beaux Arts Trio, Rhodes (viola), (i) with Bettelheim (violin).
**(*) CRD CRD 1024. Rajna (piano), members of the Alberni Qt.

The Beaux Arts Trio (with associates) gives splendid performances of both these fine chamber works, which in 1842 showed the composer branching out from his great year of song. The vitality of inspiration is consistently brought out, whether in the *Quintet* or the relatively neglected *Quartet*, and with that goes the Beaux Arts' characteristic concern for fine ensemble and refined textures. The recording has a beautifully judged atmosphere, giving a degree of romantic warmth.

Though not quite so flawlessly polished in their playing, Rajna and the Alberni give performances that are in their way as urgent and enjoyable as those on the Philips disc. The recording is brighter and crisper with less atmosphere, which gives an extra (and not unlikeable) edge to the performances.

Piano quintet in E flat, Op. 44.
*(*) DG 2531/*3301* 343 [id.]. Levine, LaSalle Qt – BRAHMS: *String quartet No. 3.**(*)

A rather hard-driven opening does not endear one to this version of the *Piano quintet*, although there is some sensitive playing from James Levine. It wants the spontaneity and freshness of the Beaux Arts team or the urgency and unforced eloquence of the alternative CRD version by Thomas Rajna and members of the Alberni Quartet. Both these issues – see above – are more appropriately coupled with the *Piano quartet*, Op. 47; the CRD tape is first-class in every way. The DG tape transfer is clear and clean, and whether on disc or cassette the sound has excellent presence.

Piano trio No. 1 in D min., Op. 63.
*** HMV ASD/*TC-ASD* 3894. Kyung-Wha Chung, Tortelier, Previn – MENDELSSOHN: *Trio No. 1.****

Schumann's *D minor Piano trio* makes an attractive and apt coupling for Mendelssohn's *Trio* in the same key. It is a more elusive work but in a performance as powerfully characterful as this – each individual constantly challenging the others – it emerges as a match for the other great Schumann chamber pieces with piano. As in the Mendelssohn, Previn's strongly rhythmic playing underpins the lyrical outpouring of the string players. The recording is first-rate, though the quality on the cassette is less transparent than the LP.

String quartets Nos. 1–3, Op. 41.
(M) *** Ph. 6703 029 (3) [id.]. Italian Qt – BRAHMS: *Quartets Nos. 1–3.****

String quartets Nos. 1 in A min.; 3 in A, Op. 41/1 and 3.
(M) *** Ph. 6503/*7303* 070. Italian Qt.

String quartet No. 2 in F, Op. 41/2.
(M) *** Ph. 6503/*7303* 061. Italian Qt – BRAHMS: *Quartet No. 3.****

The Italian Quartet give impressive and welcome accounts of the Schumann string quartets which have been seriously neglected by the recording companies. They are committed and persuasive advocates and are superbly recorded on both disc and tape (the cassette combining the *First* and *Third* is one of Philips's finest tape issues of chamber music). The earlier coupling with Brahms remains available, as we go to press, and is equally recommendable.

String quartet No. 3 in A, Op. 41/3.
*** CRD CRD 1017 [Bach HM 83]. Alberni Qt – MENDELSSOHN: *Quartet No. 2.****

This sympathetic performance of the *A major Quartet*, a searching, adventurous work, superbly crafted, is very welcome. More Schumann would have been preferable for coupling, but the youthful Mendelssohn *Quartet* equally deserves attention. Well-balanced recording.

Funf Stücke (5 Pieces) im Volkston (for cello and piano).
(M) *** Decca Jub. 410 168-1/*4*. Rostropovich, Britten – BRITTEN and DEBUSSY: *Sonatas.****

Though simpler than either the Britten or Debussy sonatas with which it is coupled this is just as elusive a work. Rostropovich and Britten show that the simplicity is not so square and solid as it might seem at first, and that in the hands of masters these *Five Pieces in folk style* have a rare charm, particularly the last, with its irregular rhythm. Excellent recording on both disc and cassette.

Violin sonatas Nos. 1 in A min., Op. 105; 2 in D min., Op. 121.
(M) *** HM HM/*40* 489. Oleg, Rault.

The *Violin sonatas* are products of Schumann's last years, composed at a period when he was fighting off insanity. Both are rewarding pieces and have been neglected by the gramophone since the Ferras/Barbizet DG recording from the mid-1960s. Raphael Oleg and Yves Rault are extremely young artists;

the former was not twenty when this record was made, and the latter was still on the right side of twenty-one. They play these pieces well and deserve plaudits for their enterprise in offering a coupling that well-established artists have shunned. Good recording too.

PIANO MUSIC

Arabeske in C, Op. 18; Kinderscenen, Op. 15.
(M) *** DG Sig. 2543/*3343* 525 [id.]. Barenboim – SCHUBERT: *Moments musicaux.***

Barenboim provides a sensitive, unmannered version of the *Scenes from childhood* and a thoroughly recommendable *Arabeske*. Good recording with no discernible difference between disc and chrome tape.

Carnaval, Op. 9; Faschingsschwank aus Wien, Op. 26.
* BBC REGL/*ZCF* 431. Michelangeli.

Michelangeli's accounts of *Carnaval* and *Faschingsschwank aus Wien* emanate from 1957 broadcasts and are inevitably in mono. There is impressive fire and impetuosity here and certain pieces (*Papillons* is one of them) that are rushed and others a shade mannered. But the playing is nonetheless exciting and has distinctive perceptions. The sound is acceptable. Barenboim's outstanding version of the same coupling is inexplicably deleted – containing perhaps the finest modern account of *Carnaval* – though still available in the USA [DG 2531 090]. We must hope it will soon be reissued on Signature.

Carnaval, Op. 9; Papillons, Op. 2; Toccata, Op. 7.
*** HMV Dig. ASD/*TCC-ASD* 4202 [Ang. DS/*4XS* 37850]. Egorov.

Yuri Egorov is full of temperament and offers many insights as well as superb pianism. His is among the finest versions of *Carnaval* and among the best recorded too, while his *Papillons* has a very great deal to commend it. Egorov does it with real imagination and much sensitivity, and though artistically his version is not superior to Murray Perahia's CBS account, the engineering is incomparably better. A strong contender in both works. The cassette has excellent presence and range although there is an element of clangour in fortissimos.

Davidsbündlertänze, Op. 6; Fantasiestücke, Op. 12.
*** CBS 73202 [M 32299]. Perahia.

Perahia has a magic touch, and his electric spontaneity is naturally caught in the studio. In works of Schumann which can splinter apart, this quality of concentration is enormously valuable, and the results could hardly be more powerfully convincing, despite rather coarse recording quality.

Davidsbündlertänze, Op. 6; Humoreske in B flat, Op. 20.
*** Chan. ABR/*ABT* 1029 [id.]. Artymiw.

Lydia Artymiw attracted attention at the 1978 Leeds Piano Competition as a player of temperament and personality. Her finely delineated accounts of the *Davidsbündlertänze* and the *Humoreske* can both hold their own with the best now on the market. In both works Artymiw shows her finesse as a Schumann interpreter, drawing together music which in its very structure presents problems. Never exaggerating, she conveys consistent intensity as in a live concert. She is perhaps not as touching in the *Davidsbündlertänze* as Murray Perahia (see above), but she has the advantage of better recording. Her cleanly articulated playing has true artistry to recommend it alongside the naturally balanced sound image, equally impressive on disc and cassette.

5 Études, Op. posth.; Études symphoniques, Op. 13.
** HMV Dig. ASD/*TC-ASD* 143627-1/*4* [Ang. DS/*4XS* 38075]. Sgouros – BRAHMS: *Paganini variations.***

As with the case of his Brahms *Paganini variations* with which this is coupled, Dmitris Sgouros's record of the *Symphonic studies* is more a record of a young keyboard lion (or lion cub) at fourteen, a memento of a remarkable phenomenon, than a serious contender in the catalogue. He is gifted but no match in musical wisdom for such artists as Perahia and Ashkenazy. The recording is bold and clear with fine presence, on disc and tape alike.

5 Études, Op. posth.; Études symphoniques, Op. 13; Papillons, Op. 2.
*** CBS 76635/*40*- [M/*MT* 34539]. Perahia.

Beautifully poetic accounts of all these works that can be strongly recommended. Murray Perahia has a special feeling for the *Symphonic studies* which is in evidence both on the concert platform and here, and he makes every expressive point in the most natural and unfussy way. He plays the additional five studies that Schumann omitted from the published score as an addendum rather than inserting them among the other studies as do Ashkenazy and Richter. The *Papillons* are unrivalled on record at present and are unlikely to be surpassed. The engineers give Perahia too close a balance to be ideal, but the sound has distinct clarity and with adjustment of the controls it yields a generally pleasing quality. The cassette is less distinguished, the quality at times somewhat opaque, at others rather hard on top.

Études symphoniques, Op. 13; Fantasia in C, Op. 17.
**(*) Decca SXL 6214 [Lon. CS 6471]. Ashkenazy.

Ashkenazy's playing is extremely fine: technically he is superb, and intellectually he obviously dominates the music. There are flashes of poetry and one or two really commanding moments where the sheer power of the pianism is most gripping. Ashkenazy includes all the studies, the original twelve and the five discovered later, which he inserts three-quarters of the way through the set. The recording is first-rate.

Études symphoniques; Toccata, Op. 7.
(*) DG Dig. **410 520-2; 2532/*3302* 036 [id.]. Pogorelich – BEETHOVEN: *Piano sonata No. 32.***(*)

Pogorelich opens his performance of the *Études symphoniques* with a self-conscious and studied presentation of the theme. This is pianism of the first order, but the listener's attention tends to be drawn from the music to the quality of the pianism. Yet this remains a performance to be reckoned with, even if it is not as fine as the fresh and ardent version by Murray Perahia. The recording is vivid and truthful, and has striking presence on compact disc. The chrome cassette is full, wide-ranging and well focused, but slightly dry in timbre.

Fantasia in C, Op. 17.
(M) **(*) Saga 5460. Wilde – LISZT: *Sonata.***(*)

David Wilde's account of the *C major Fantasy* is as powerful as the Liszt coupling. It is finely controlled and has splendid panache, and even though the recording falls short of the highest distinction, the playing ensures a high rating for this disc.

Fantasia in C, Op. 17; Fantasiestücke, Op. 12.
*** Ph. Dig. 6514/*7337* 283 [id.]. Brendel.

An outstanding new coupling from Brendel. As the very opening of the *Fantasiestücke* demonstrates, this is magically spontaneous playing, full of imaginative touches of colour, strong as well as poetic. The recording is very fine indeed with the chrome tape matching the disc closely and especially vivid in the *Fantasia*.

Fantasia in C, Op. 17; Piano sonata No. 1 in F sharp min., Op. 11.
*** DG 2530 379 [id.]. Pollini.

This is among the most distinguished Schumann records in the catalogue. The *Fantasia* is as fine as Richter's now deleted version, and Pollini's playing throughout has a command and authority on the one hand and deep poetic feeling on the other that instantly capture the listener spellbound. The recording is good but not outstanding.

Humoreske in B flat, Op. 20; Kreisleriana, Op. 16.
*(*) Decca SXL 6642 [Lon. CS 6859]. Ashkenazy.

One of Ashkenazy's least successful records. Not that his playing is a source of reproach; indeed its eloquence can be taken for granted. Unfortunately, though, the recording is too clangorous to give real pleasure: it is very reverberant and lacking in focus, though the ear can adjust to some extent.

Kinderscenen (*Scenes from Childhood*), *Op. 15; Kreisleriana, Op. 16.*
*** Ph. 9500/*7300* 964 [id.]. Brendel.
*(**) DG Dig. **410 653-2**; 410 653-1/*4* [id.]. Argerich.

Keenly intelligent and finely characterized playing from Brendel here. He is better recorded than most of his rivals, and though certain details may strike listeners as less spontaneous the overall impression is strong. The *Kinderscenen* is the finest for some years and is touched with real distinction. On cassette the sound has slightly less sharpness of focus than on disc, but remains very good.

There is no doubting the instinctive flair of Argerich's playing or her intuitive feeling for Schumann. However, she is let down by an unpleasingly close recording that somewhat diminishes pleasure, no less in compact-disc format than on LP and cassette.

Kinderscenen, Op. 15; Piano sonata No. 2 in G min., Op. 22.
(M) ** DG Acc. 2542/*3342* 155. Kempff.

Although nothing that Kempff does is without insights, neither of these is among his more compelling Schumann performances. The opening of *Kinderscenen* is cool; even the famous *Träumerei* sounds curiously literal, and it is only in the closing section of the work that the Kempff magic appears. The *Sonata* too, rather dryly recorded, is in no way memorable. The cassette transfer is faithful; the sound is warmer in *Kinderscenen.*

VOCAL AND CHORAL MUSIC

Lieder from Album für die Jugend, Op. 79: excerpts (14 songs). *Frauenliebe und Leben, Op. 42. Myrthen, Op. 25:* excerpts (8 songs). Lieder: *An den Mond; Die Blume der Ergebung; Die Fensterscheibe; Frühlingslied; Frühlingslust; Heiss mich nicht reden; Himmel und Erde; Die Karlenlegerin; Kennst du das Land; Die letzen Blumen starben; Liebeslied; Liebster deine worte stehlen; Mädchen-Schwermut; Mein Garten; Mond meiner Seele Liebling; Du nennst mich armes Mädchen; Die Nonne; Nur wer die Sehnsucht kennt; O ihr Herren; Reich mire die Hand; Röselein; Singet nicht in Trauertönen; So lasst mich scheinen; Die Soldatenbraut; Die Spinnerin; Stiller Vorwurf; Tief im Herzen trag'ich Pein; Das verlassene Mägdlein; Viel Glück zur Reisse; Volksliedchen; Der Zeisig.*
*** DG 2740 266 (3) [id.]. Mathis, Eschenbach.

This generous collection of songs for female voice brings consistently sensitive and imaginative singing from Mathis, well sustained by accompaniments from Eschenbach as sensitive as those he provided on other records for Dietrich Fischer-Dieskau. Mathis's performance of *Frauenliebe und Leben* (previously available separately) is fresh and delicately poised with girlish feelings portrayed, though inevitably she lacks a little in weight in the last song of bereavement. In other less well-known songs Mathis is equally perceptive, often transforming what seems a simple, even dull idea into something magical. First-rate recording.

Lieder from Album für die Jugend, Op. 79. Gedichte der Königin Maria Stuart, Op. 135. Myrthen Lieder, Op. 25: excerpts. *Abends am Strand; Die Kartenlegerin; Ständchen; Stille Tränen; Veratine Liebe.*
*** CRD CRD 1101/*CRDC* 4101 [id.]. Sarah Walker, Vignoles.

It is sad that so strong and characterful an artist as Sarah Walker has till now made so few records, but this Schumann collection is most cherishable, notably the five *Mary Stuart songs* which in their brooding darkness are among Schumann's most memorable. The voice is a little weighty for some of the lighter songs from the *Myrthen* collection, but with superb accompaniment and splendid recording this is an outstanding issue. The cassette, however, is disappointing, with the resonance blurring the upper range.

Liederalbum für die Jugend, Op. 79; Liederkreis, Op. 39.
*** Ph. 6769 037 (2) [id.]. Ameling, Demus.

The album of songs for the young contains many delightful inspirations, often so slight that in the world of significant Lieder-singing they are totally neglected. They are almost ideally suited to the light and sweet voice of Elly Ameling, and some of the most enchanting items of all come when with technical sleight-of-hand she is given the chance to sing duets with herself. The lightness of her voice is arguably less apt for the Op. 39 songs; there have been deeper readings on record, but by bringing out the vein of girlish freshness Ameling gives a special illumination. The accompaniment and recording are first-rate.

Dichterliebe (song cycle), *Op. 48.*
*** Decca SET 270/1. Pears, Britten – SCHUBERT: *Winterreise.**** ❀

Schumann's greatest song cycle coupled with Schubert's greatest: the combination is irresistible. On this fill-up Pears is not in quite such perfect voice, the vibrato occasionally gritty and obtrusive, but the imaginativeness of the whole interpretation is so compelling that that is merely a minor detail. In *Dichterliebe*, with its long piano postludes to many of the songs, the role of the accompanist is specially important, and Britten brings to the piano part an intense creative understanding unrivalled on any other version. Recording excellent.

Dichterliebe; Liederkreis, Op. 24.
(M) *** DG Acc. 2542/*3342* 156 [139 109]. Schreier, Shetler.

Often the market in Lieder recordings of the male voice seems to be so dominated by Dietrich Fischer-Dieskau that other artists must inevitably rest in the shadow of the great baritone. But here is a record of tenor Lieder-singing which, while fully reflecting the Fischer-Dieskau art and technique, yet shows the singer able to bring an added inspirational quality of his own to the songs. These performances have marvellous spontaneity and feeling – the impression is of being at a live recital. The contrasts of emotion behind the song sequence of *Dichterliebe* are strongly brought out, underlying tensions given an almost painful degree of poignancy. Similarly Schreier treats the Heine *Liederkreis* as a unified whole by giving it satisfying emotional shape. With the voice at its freshest the vocal quality combines tonal beauty with tenderness, while the colouring achieves consistent subtlety. The result involves the listener from the first song to the last. The recording is first-class, and the cassette too is of demonstration realism. Highly recommended to those new to this repertoire.

Dichterliebe; Liederkreis, Op. 39.
*** DG 2531 290 [id.]. Fischer-Dieskau, Eschenbach.
(B) *** CfP CFPD/*TC-CFPD* 41 4436-3/*5*. Ian and Jennifer Partridge – SCHUBERT: *Die schöne Müllerin.****

These two performances, taken from Fischer-Dieskau's boxes of Schumann Lieder, are most impressive when considered in detail against other versions of these much-recorded works. As his career has developed, so Fischer-Dieskau's readings have acquired a sharper edge, with the darkness and irony in some of these songs more specifically contrasted against the poetry and expressive warmth. The tone may not be so fresh as it once was, but Eschenbach's accompaniment is superb, consistently imaginative, and the recording is excellent: there are no finer versions of either cycle.

Ian and Jennifer Partridge recorded Schubert's *Die schöne Mullerin* first, with Ian showing himself a deeply sensitive Lieder singer, blessed with a radiantly beautiful light voice. He then went on to record both the *Dichterliebe* and the Op. 39 *Liederkreis* where thoughtfulness illuminates every line, helped, as in the Schubert, by superbly matched accompaniments. The recording is well balanced and equally truthful on LP and tape, and this bargain-priced two-disc set should win many newcomers over to much delightful and rewarding music, which still tends to be regarded by the general musical public as a 'specialist' area.

Frauenliebe und Leben, Op. 42.
*** Saga 5277. Baker, Isepp (with *Recital***(*)).

Janet Baker's range of expression in her earlier Saga recording of the Schumann cycle runs the whole gamut from a joyful golden tone-colour in the exhilaration of *Ich kann's nicht fassen* through an ecstatic half-tone in *Süsser Freund* (the fulfilment of the line *Du geliebter Mann* wonderfully conveyed) to the dead, vibrato-less tone of agony at the bereavement in the final song. The Saga recording is not perfect. The balance favours the piano, and the piano and voice tend to be separated to left and right, although newer pressings are better in this respect. (This is part of a Lieder recital discussed in our Recitals section – see below).

Frauenliebe und Leben; Liederkreis, Op. 39.
* Chan. ABR/*ABT* 1009. Lear, Vignoles.

Evelyn Lear's coupling is disappointing; the readings lack projection, and the voice sounds uncomfortable in the upper register and poorly recorded. The cassette transfer is faithful.

6 Gedichte und Requiem, Op. 90; 5 Lieder, Op. 40; Liederkreis, Op. 39.
**(*) CBS 76815 [M/*MT* 36668]. Pears, Perahia.

After Benjamin Britten's death Murray Perahia was the pianist who came to accompany Sir Peter Pears in his song recitals. Perahia may be of a totally different generation, but like Britten himself he is an inspirational pianist, able to snatch magic out of the air in Schumann's piano writing, not least in his important postludes. Unfortunately the rather close recording catches Pears's voice uncomfortably. At the very end of his singing career it had its measure of unevenness, which is exaggerated here; but the detailed perception and intensity in all these songs, matched by Perahia's playing, can be recommended to all admirers. The cassette is especially welcome with much of this repertoire not well served on tape. The sound is naturally balanced and loses only a slight degree of sharpness of focus.

Scenes from Goethe's Faust.
❀ *** Decca SET 567/8 [Lon. OSA 12100]. Harwood, Pears, Shirley-Quirk, Fischer-Dieskau, Aldeburgh Fest. Singers, Wandsworth School Ch., ECO, Britten.
**(*) EMI Dig. 1C 165 46435/6. Fischer-Dieskau, Mathis, Berry, Gedda, Daniels, Lövaas, Schwarz, Sharp, Gramatzki, Stamm, Düsseldorf Music Soc. Ch., Tölz Boys' Ch., Düsseldorf SO, Klee.

Britten made this superb recording of a major Schumann work, long neglected, in 1973, soon after a live performance at the Aldeburgh Festival. Though the reasons for neglect remain apparent – this episodic sequence of scenes is neither opera nor cantata – the power and imagination of much of the music, not least the delightful garden scene and the energetic setting of the final scene, are immensely satisfying. Britten inspired his orchestra and his fine cast of singers to vivid performances, which are here superlatively recorded against the warm Maltings acoustic.

Klee takes a sharply dramatic view of Schumann's strange collection of Goethe portraits and impressions, and with bright, atmospheric digital recording the score is made to seem less wayward than it can. The cast of singers is strong, but Fischer-Dieskau is here not as steady as he was in Britten's recording of ten years earlier. Nor – particularly in the final scene – does Klee have the imaginative insights that gave that recording such compelling magic.

Schurmann, Gerard (born 1928)

6 Studies of Francis Bacon for large orchestra; Variants for small orchestra.
*** Chan. ABR/*ABT* 1011 [id.]. BBC SO, composer.

Inspired by the fantastic, often violent or painful paintings of Francis Bacon, Schurmann here writes a virtuoso orchestral showpiece full of colourful effects. The vigour of the writing is admirably caught in this performance under the composer, as it is too in the often spiky writing of *Variants* for a rather smaller orchestra, set against passages of hushed beauty. First-rate recording and a good cassette.

Schütz, Heinrich (1585–1672)

Cantiones sacrae: Cantate Domino; O bone o dulcis; Sidcut Moses. 3 Passion motets: *Aspice, Pater; Nonne hic est; Reduc, domine deus meus. Jauchzet dem Herren. Magnificat. Stehe auf, meine Freundlin.*
**(*) Mer. E 77049. Rees, Bennet, Denis, Noble, L. Bach Soc. Ch. and Ens., Steinitz.

Steinitz has over many years built up a formidable reputation as a scholarly and perceptive Bach interpreter. Here he shows equal understanding of his remarkable predecessor, Schütz, in a well-chosen selection from the *Cantiones sacrae* as well as the magnificent polychoral *Magnificat*. These are not immaculate performances, but the conviction and concentration are never in doubt. Specially impressive is the fine setting of Psalm 100, *Jauchzet dem Herren*, with a small choir echoing the main body of singers. Good atmospheric recording.

Christmas oratorio (*Historia der Geburt Jesu Christi*).
(M) **(*) Decca Ser. SA 28 [Lon. STS/5-15602]. I. Partridge, soloists, Schütz Ch., Instrumental Ens., Jones Brass Ens., Norrington.

Norrington's Argo recording – reissued on Decca's Serenata label – is richly and vividly recorded, and offers some extremely fine singing from Ian Partridge as the Evangelist, while the Heinrich Schütz Choir phrases with great feeling and subtlety. Indeed some may feel that their singing is a little too self-consciously beautiful for music that is so pure in style. The instrumental accompaniment on modern instruments may also strike some listeners as too much of a good thing: the brass has more than a suspicion of heaviness at times. However, for all that, this version offers much to admire and the recording has great detail and sonority. In the USA there is a plainer version under Grischkat on Vox which has long held an honoured place in the catalogue [Turn TV 34088/*CT 2253*]. There are good if not outstanding soloists who work well together, and the contribution of the Swabian Choir is quite impressive. There is a simple eloquence about this account which is appealing, in spite of the comparative lack of sophistication.

German songs and madrigals: *Danklied; Die Erde trinkt für sich; Glück zu dem Helikon; Itzt blicken durch des Himmels Saal; Kläglicher Abschied; Lässt Salomon sein Bette nicht umgeben; Nachdem ich lag in meinem öden Bette; Ein Trauerlied; Tugend ist der beste Freund; Vier Hirtinnen, gleich jung, gleich schön; Wie wenn der Adler sich aus seiner Klippe schwingt.*
(M) *(*) Ph. 9502 062. Capella Lipsiensis, Knothe.

Schütz wrote little secular music, and after his return from Italy in 1613 became the composer of church and ceremonial music to various German courts. Although he was well able to compose in the style of the Italian madrigal, Schütz tends to be a good deal more sober and serious when setting German, and this group tend to be a little heavier than some of their Western counterparts. Decent, well-balanced recording.

(i) Madrigals: *Duncque addio, care selve; Io moro ecco ch'io moro; O dolcezze amarissime d'amore; O primavera gioventu de l'anno.* (ii) Cantatas: *Eile, mich Gott zu erretten; Lobe den Herren in seinem Heiligtum; O quam tu pulchra es; Veni de Libano.*

(B) ** Precision GSGC/*ZCGC* 2039. (i) Schutz Ch. of London, Norrington; (ii) Norrington; Hemsley, Goldsbrough Ens.

These madrigals are really more suitable for a much smaller choir (even a single voice to each part). However, these expressive performances are certainly alive and appealing, even though they achieve a broad emotional sweep rather than revealing any subtlety of detail. The cantatas, shared by Roger Norrington and Thomas Hemsley, are more uneven in style, though not unattractive. The recording (1969 vintage) is of good quality and the cassette matches the disc fairly closely, though sharper in focus on side two.

Italian Madrigals: Book 1 (*SWV 1–19*).
** Ph. 9502 061. Capella Lipsiensis, Knothe.

Schütz's first book of madrigals was the product of his studies with Giovanni Gabrieli, with whom he spent the period 1609–13. They exhibit the appropriate skill and expertise in madrigal technique and are well given by this Leipzig group who sing in a refreshingly old-fashioned style with vibrato and a certain expressive fervour. A lighter touch might have been in order, indeed, but the recording is useful as it fills in a gap in the catalogue.

Musikalische Exequien.
(M) *** Ph. 9502 025 [id.]. Dresden Kreuzchor, Mauersberger.

Schütz's *Mass for the dead* is one of his most austere and serious masterpieces. This performance eschews any of the compromises that are sometimes made – fleshing out the texture so as to make it correspond to Schütz's Venetian style. This is as austere as the music itself, and the forces involved (the continuo consists of a tenor viola da gamba, violine and organ) are eminently well balanced. The soloists include two fine boy trebles (Friedemann Jäckel and Andreas Göhler) and the tenor Peter Schreier. Good recorded sound (the disc comes from 1970), with excellent perspective. There is no alternative version at present in the catalogue, but this is thoroughly recommendable at this price.

Psalms of David, Nos. 115, 128, 136; Concerts: Lobe den Herren; Zion spricht; Motets: Die mit Tränen säen; Ist nicht Ephraim mein teurer Sohn.
(M) **(*) Ph. 9502 047. Soloists, Dresden Kreuzchor, Capella Fidicinia, Flämig.

The music is marvellous, the performances less so. The *Psalms of David* come from 1619, only a few years after Schütz had returned from Italy, and show the effect of his studies with Gabrieli. The magnificence and gravity of this music cannot fail to impress and move the listener; these performances are recorded in a suitable acoustic setting and the disc is admirably annotated. The singing, particularly of the boys, is less than first-class, but it is adequate to convey the majesty and nobility of this repertoire and is well recorded.

Psalm 150.
(M) *** EMI Em. EMX/*TC-EMX* 2032 [Sera S/*4XG* 60324]. King's College Ch., Camb. University Music Soc., Bach Choir, Wilbraham Brass Soloists, Willcocks – GABRIELI: *Collection*; SCHEIDT: *In dulci jubilo.****

Schütz's setting of Psalm 150 is for double choirs and soloists, each used in juxtaposition against the others, with built-in antiphony an essential part of the composer's conception. The majesty of Schütz's inspiration comes over vividly here, the closing *Alleluja* having remarkable weight and richness. The choral focus is not as clean as on the Argo King's records, but in all other respects this is superb. There is an admirably faithful tape transfer, which successfully catches the reverberant acoustic without further clouding.

St Matthew Passion.
(M) *** Decca Ser. SA/*KSC* 3. Pears, Shirley-Quirk, Luxon, Schütz Ch., Norrington.

Schütz's setting of the *St Matthew Passion* is an austere one. The story is told for the most part in a series of unaccompanied recitatives, eloquent but restrained in style. The drama is suddenly heightened at the choral entries, but these are comparatively few, and the work relies on the artistry of the soloists to project itself on the listener. The solo singing here is of a high order and the choral contribution fine enough to make one wish there was more of it. The closing chorus, *Glory be to Thee*, is more familiar than the rest of the work, for it is sometimes extracted to be sung on its own. The recording is excellent, and it is understandable that the original language is used. Even so, one feels the work would communicate more readily when sung in English. The cassette transfer is admirable, full yet clearly focused.

Scott, Cyril (1879–1970)

Piano concerto No. 1 in C.
*** Lyr. SRCS 81. Ogdon, LPO, Herrmann.

Cyril Scott's lush *First Piano concerto* dates from 1913–14, and its exotic, extravagant style undoubtedly belongs to that pre-war era. Those for whom Scott's name conjures memories of a piece called *Lotus Land* might feel that the atmosphere of this concerto is well expressed by that title. The colouring and orchestration are certainly exotic, even oriental: the celesta makes its mark in the 'serene twilight brooding' of the slow movement. But the first movement is broad-spanned and spacious and curiously memorable; and the finale, if it lacks momentum, is attractive in its indulgence. Neoclassical in mood, it is only marked *Allegro poco moderato*, and the pace slackens further in the middle for reminiscences of earlier material. This performance is very fine: somehow Ogdon and Herrmann make a coherent whole out of Scott's essentially rhapsodical piece, and the spontaneity and skill of the music-making seduce the listener into wanting to play the record again. This is ideal gramophone material, and the recording, as in virtually all Lyrita issues, is superb.

Piano concerto No. 2; Early one morning (poem for piano and orchestra).
**(*) Lyr. SRCS 82. Ogdon, LPO, Herrmann.

Admirers of Cyril Scott will be glad to have this coupling available, but the music itself is less readily recommendable to the non-specialist. The *Second Concerto* dates from Scott's later years, and although it has undoubted atmosphere, its shifting moods and rhapsodic chromaticism will not suit all tastes. Even the finale, marked *Energico*, quickly loses its momentum. The spirit of Delius is certainly evoked in this work, and it is even more apparent in the poem, *Early one morning*. Here the famous tune keeps setting off and then becoming fragmented in a vaguely unsatisfying way (although the orchestral sound itself is beautifully textured). But for all one's reservations, Scott's music has a haunting quality that makes one want to return to it. The composer is splendidly served by the performers here, who create a feeling of spontaneity even when the music itself eddies gently with comparatively little forward movement. The recording is quite excellent, of demonstration quality throughout.

Scriabin, Alexander (1872–1915)

Piano concerto in F sharp min., Op. 20; Prometheus – The poem of fire, Op. 60.
*** Decca SXL 6527 [Lon. CS 6732]. Ashkenazy, LPO, Maazel.

This is an admirable introduction to Scriabin's art and a very distinguished record in every respect. Ashkenazy plays the *Piano concerto* with great feeling and authority, and the Decca recording has both clarity and luminosity. Moreover Maazel accompanies most sympathetically throughout. *Prometheus* too is given a thoroughly poetic and committed reading by Maazel and the LPO, Ashkenazy coping with the virtuoso obbligato part with predictable distinction. Powerfully atmospheric and curiously hypnotic, the score reeks of Madame Blavatsky and Scriabin's wild mysticism, while abounding in the fanciful lines of *art nouveau*. Given such outstanding recording and performance, this makes a splendid starting point for any Scriabin collection. It was issued on 6 January 1972, the centenary of the composer's birth.

Poème de l'extase, Op. 54.
*(*) Decca SXL 6905 [Lon. CS/5-7129]. Cleveland O, Maazel – DEBUSSY: *La Mer*.*(*)

Maazel's account of Scriabin's heavily scented and erotic score is a shade too efficient to be really convincing. The playing is often brilliant, but others succeed in communicating the atmosphere of this music more effectively. The recording is superbly detailed and well-lit (on tape as well as disc), though the trumpets are somewhat forward and strident. But this will have to serve as a stopgap until Mehta's version with the Los Angeles Philharmonic Orchestra returns to the catalogue.

Symphonies Nos. 1 in E, Op. 26; 2 in C min., Op. 29; 3 in C min. (Le divin poème), Op. 43; Poème de l'extase, Op. 54; Prometheus, Op. 60.
*** Ph. 6769 041 (4) [id. PSI]. Soffel, Tenzi, Frankfurter Kantorei, W. Saschowa (piano), Frankfurt RSO, Inbal.

Yevgeny Svetlanov's box devoted to the Scriabin symphonies included the early *F sharp minor Piano concerto* and the *Rêverie*, but omitted *Prometheus*. In any event this Philips set has the field to itself, now that Svetlanov has succumbed to the deletions axe. The Frankfurt recordings are moreover a good deal smoother than the older set, and the playing of the Radio Orchestra under Eliahu Inbal is rather more refined, albeit less intoxicating than the Russian performances. The *Poème de l'extase* is not quite so voluptuous as it was in Abbado's hands (his record is now deleted), but it is still eminently persuasive, as is the performance of *Prometheus*. A valuable and recommendable set that deserves wide currency.

Piano sonatas Nos. 2 (Sonata-fantasy) in G sharp min., Op. 19; 7 in F sharp (White Mass), Op. 64; 10 in C, Op. 70; Deux Danses, Op. 73; Deux Poèmes, Op. 32; Quatre Morceaux, Op. 56.
*** Decca SXL 6868 [Lon. CS/5-7087]. Ashkenazy.

This issue fulfils the high expectations engendered by Ashkenazy's earlier Scriabin recital (see below). Ponti, Ogdon and Roberto Szidon have all given us complete Scriabin sonata cycles on disc, but none has matched Ashkenazy's commanding authority and sense of vision in this repertoire. Whether one likes this music or not, there is no questioning the demonic, possessed quality of the playing.

Piano sonatas Nos. 3 in F sharp min., Op. 23; 4 in F sharp, Op. 30; 5 in F sharp, Op. 53; 9 in F (Black Mass), Op. 68.
*** Decca SXL 6705 [Lon. CS/5-6920]. Ashkenazy.

Performances of the highest quality, superbly recorded. Of the four sonatas on this disc, three (Nos. 3, 5 and 9) have been recorded by Horowitz. Ashkenazy is hardly less magnificent, and readers interested in Scriabin's development could hardly find a more indispensable record.

Piano sonatas Nos. 7 in F sharp (White Mass), Op. 64; 8 in A, Op. 66; 9 in F (Black Mass), Op. 68; 10 in C, Op. 70.
(M) **(*) DG 2543 816. Szidon.

Roberto Szidon recorded all ten sonatas as well as the two early sonatas and the Op. 28 *Fantasy* in 1971, and this reissue on one record accommodates the last four, written in rapid succession between 1912 and 1913. The *Black Mass sonata* fares best and conveys real excitement. At mid-price this is an attractive reissue, though the Horowitz accounts of Nos. 9 and 10 are not to be overlooked (they are both listed in Schwann, but at the time of writing are out of the UK catalogues) and

Ashkenazy's series also has strong claims on the collector (he has recorded all of these save for No. 8). The DG recording is good but not ideal and the tone tends to harden just a little at climaxes.

Searle, Humphrey (born 1915)

(i) *Symphony No. 1, Op. 23;* (ii) *Symphony No. 2, Op. 33.*
*** Lyr. SRCS 72. LPO, (i) Boult, (ii) Krips.

Josef Krips in one of his last recording sessions conducted a superbly expressive performance of Searle's *Second Symphony*. Like its predecessor it follows the composer's characteristic brand of twelve-note serialism, but even more than the earlier work it shows Searle following the central English tradition. If Walton had ever written a serial symphony, it might sound very like this. The Boult performance of No. 1, also sponsored by the British Council, dates from the early 1960s, but still sounds excellent – a worthy match for the fine new recording of No. 2.

Sessions, Roger (born 1896)

Concerto for orchestra.
*** Hyp. Dig. A 66050 [id.]. Boston SO, Ozawa – PANUFNIK: *Symphony No. 8*.***

Sessions' *Concerto for orchestra*, completed when he was eighty-four, is a remarkable achievement for an octogenarian composer. The argument finds him at his thorniest and most uncompromising, with lyricism limited to fleeting fragments of melody, but the tapestry of sound presents its own logic with its contrasts of mood – the playful opening leading one on finally to a valedictory close – sharply defined. Ozawa makes a powerful advocate, helped by superb playing from the Boston orchestra. In its sound and production Hyperion matches in every way the efforts of major companies.

Shankar, Ravi (born 1920)

Sitar concerto.
**(*) HMV ASD 2752 [Ang. SFO/*4XS* 36806]. Shankar, LSO, Previn.

It would be easy to dismiss this concerto, since fairly evidently it is neither good Western music nor good Indian music. The idiom is sweet, arguably too sweet and unproblematic, but at least this is an attractive and painless conducted tour over the geographical layout of the Rága. It also prompts some brilliant music-making from Previn and the LSO, not to mention the composer himself, who launches into solos which he makes sound spontaneous in the authentic manner, however prepared they may actually be. In fact his playing has stiffened up compared with the original concert performance in January 1971. Provided one is not worried at having a forty-minute work with comparatively little meat in the way of good material, this provides a charming experience – ideal atmospheric background music. The recording is superb.

Sitar concerto No. 2; Rága Málá (*Garland of rágas*).
*** HMV Dig. ASD/*TCC-ASD* 4314 [Ang. DS/*4XS* 37920]. Shankar, LPO, Mehta.

If the *First Concerto* was found to taste, this second venture into combined Indian and Western musical territory will be found no less amenable. Whether or not so inflated a mixture of Eastern and Western music can be aesthetically viable, Ravi Shankar – whose personal magnetism beams out from every note of his sitar – is a persuasive advocate. With the LPO responding warmly to Mehta's direction and with brilliant, spacious sound, this is a colourful record which presents the music more effectively than would ever be possible in the concert hall. The exotic sounds are also splendidly caught on the chrome tape with its wide range and vivid colouring.

Rága Jogeshwari (*Alap; Jor; Gat I and II*).
*** DG 2531 280 [id.]. Composer, Rakha, Jiban, Widya.

Jogeshwari is a morning *rāg*. The note series itself is revealed only gradually; the ascending line is composed of larger intervals, the descending is partly diatonic and in part chromatic. At first the *rāg* is unfolded in the *Alap*, which is reflective and rhythmically free; the *Jor* which follows is metric yet still unaccompanied. Only on the second side of the record is Alla Rakha's virtuosity in evidence. Ravi Shankar is his usual masterly self and is eminently well recorded. There are helpful notes on the sleeve for the listener unversed in the procedures of Indian classical music.

Sheppard, John
(*c*. 1515–*c*. 1559/60)

Cantate Mass; Respond: Spiritus Sanctus.
*** Cal. CAL 1621 [id.]. Clerkes of Oxenford, Wulstan.

John Sheppard's claims to musical mastery have only recently come to be widely appreciated, and this fine record could hardly be better designed to show why this contemporary of Tallis deserves a place next to that long-acknowledged master. The *Cantate Mass*, sung here a third higher than the manuscript indicates, and involving the sopranos in formidable problems of tessitura, is among the most distinctive works of its time, presenting surprises in a way uncommon in civilized polyphonic writing. The textures are refreshingly clear, helped by the superb performances of the Clerkes of Oxenford. The five-part *Spiritus Sanctus* is less striking but makes an excellent coupling, equally well recorded.

The Western Wind mass; Verbum caro factum est (responsory).
*** ASV Dig. DCA 511 [Bach HM 85]. St John's College, Camb., Ch., Guest – TALLIS: *Antiphons and Mass.****

Sheppard's *Mass*, like Taverner's more famous one, is based on a famous tune of that name, and though the top voice tends to monopolize it, monotony is avoided by the amazing harmony implied in the daring part-writing. The performance here could be more sharply dramatic, but the originality of Sheppard (the outstanding composer of Mary Tudor's brief reign) needs no emphasis. Warmly atmospheric recording.

Shostakovich, Dmitri (1906–75)

Cello concerto No. 1 in E flat, Op. 107.
*** CBS Dig. 37840/*40*- [id.]. Yo Yo Ma, Phd. O, Ormandy – KABALEVSKY: *Cello concerto No. 1.****
*** HMV ASD 2924. Tortelier, Bournemouth SO, Berglund – WALTON: *Cello concerto.* ***
*** Chan. Dig. ABRD/*ABTD* 1085 [id.]. Wallfisch, ECO, Simon – BARBER: *Concerto.****
(M) ** Sup. 110 0604. Sádlo, Czech PO, Ančerl – HONEGGER: *Cello concerto.***

Rostropovich's pioneering record with Ormandy (now, incidentally, restored to circulation – see below) served to inhibit others entering the field. Milos Sádlo and Tortelier have recorded it during the last quarter of a century, but Yo Yo Ma on CBS now brings an ardent musical imagination to this score. He plays with an intensity that compels the listener and, as befits an artist who has been acclaimed as one of the greatest cellists now before the public, can hold his own with any competition, though the Philadelphia Orchestra play here at a slightly lower voltage than they did (also under Ormandy) a quarter of a century ago. The CBS recording has ample presence and warmth, with the balance slightly favouring the soloist, but very well judged overall. There is a sophisticated chrome-tape transfer, one of CBS's very best.

Some, however, may be more attracted to Wallfisch's Chandos alternative, coupled as it is with Barber's neglected yet perennially fresh score. Wallfisch handles the first movement splendidly though there is not quite the same sense of momentum as on the Rostropovich disc. However, this is a fine account with a very sensitive slow movement and thoughtful support from the ECO. The soloist is forward but by no means unacceptably so. A most welcome issue. The recording is in the demonstration class on disc and chrome tape alike, with striking pianissimo detail in the beautiful slow movement.

To have so strong a performance as the Supraphon is welcome on mid-price label. Sádlo is a fine artist for whom the technical difficulties of the solo part hold no terrors. One might almost feel that he copes with them too easily, but in every way this is a satisfying performance, well recorded and interestingly coupled.

(i) *Cello concerto No. 1 in E flat, Op. 107;* (ii) *Violin concerto No. 1 in A min., Op. 99.*
*** HMV ASD/*TC-ASD* 4046 [*Violin concerto* (d) Ang. S 36964]. (i) Tortelier, Bournemouth SO, Berglund; (ii) D. Oistrakh, New Philh. O, Maxim Shostakovich.

Tortelier's reading of the first of Shostakovich's two cello concertos is both tough and passionate. In sheer precision of bravura passages it does not always quite match the example of the dedicatee and first performer, Rostropovich, but in the urgency and attack of his playing Tortelier even outshines the Russian master, who made his recording before his interpretation really matured. Berglund and the Bournemouth orchestra provide colourful and committed accompaniment, and the recording is rich and vivid. David Oistrakh made three records of the *First Violin concerto*, which was written for him. The first, with Mitropoulos, had the most powerful atmosphere, and this latest version of the three does not dim memories of that. This is not so keenly characterized or so deeply experienced (in the mid-1950s the work was fresh), but it is only fair to add that it is a fine performance for all that. It also benefits from well-balanced and finely detailed EMI recording. Maxim Shostakovich does not display so firm a grip on proceedings as did Mitropoulos or Mravinsky, but the New Philharmonia plays with no want of commitment. This version is still highly recommendable. On cassette the resonant recordings lead to some slight loss of orchestral clarity, but both solo instruments are well focused.

(i) *Cello concerto No. 1;* (ii) *Symphony No. 1 in F, Op. 10.*
(M) *** CBS 60284/*40-* [(d) MS 6124; M 31307]. (i) Rostropovich, Phd. O, Ormandy; (ii) NYPO, Bernstein.

Within a few months of the first performance in Russia and within days of the first Western performance, Shostakovich himself attended the recording session in Philadelphia and gave his approval to the performance here recorded by Rostropovich and Ormandy. Rostropovich gives a uniquely authoritative reading, Ormandy and the Philadelphia Orchestra accompanying superbly, with a precision and warmth rare with new scores. The recording is clear and spacious, but the balance is far from natural. The soloist is far too prominent, and so, incongruously, is the glockenspiel at the end of the first movement. The coupling is a stunning performance of the *First Symphony*, with Bernstein (whom Shostakovich greatly admired as an interpreter of his music) drawing superb playing from the New York Philharmonic Orchestra, and an account of the last two movements that has never been surpassed on record in its combination of passion and desperate melancholy. The orchestral virtuosity in the first two movements is no less involving, and the listener is compelled to reflect on the extraordinary maturity of the composer's first essay in symphonic form. The recording too is vividly atmospheric and this is one of the most distinguished Shostakovich couplings in the catalogue. The chrome tape is equally vivid, with the upper range – to advantage – slightly softer-grained. However, in the *Symphony* the bass drum is made to sound somewhat explosive.

Piano concerto No. 1 in C min., for piano, trumpet and strings, Op. 35.
*** Argo ZRG 674 [id.]. Ogdon, Wilbraham, ASMF, Marriner – STRAVINSKY: *Capriccio.****

Piano concertos Nos. (i) *1, Op. 35;* (ii) *2 in F, Op. 101.*
*** CBS 73400 [(d) MS 6392]. NYPO, Bernstein, with (i) Previn, Vacciano; (ii) Bernstein (piano).
**(*) CBS 76822 [MS 6124]. List, Moscow R. and TV O, Maxim Shostakovich.

Piano concertos Nos. 1–2; 3 Fantastic dances, Op. 5.
**(*) HMV ASD 3081 [Ang. S 37109]. Ortiz, Bournemouth SO, Berglund.

Piano concertos Nos. 1–2; The Unforgettable year 1919, Op. 89: The Assault on beautiful Gorky (for piano and orchestra).
(B) *** CfP Dig. CFP/*TC-CFP* 41 4416-1/*4*. Alexeev, Philip Jones, ECO, Maksymiuk.

Alexeev is a clear first choice in both concertos, and his record would sweep the board even at full price. The digital recording is in every way excellent and scores over its rivals in clarity and presence. Artistically he has more personality than his rivals, and has the advantage of sensitive and idiomatic support from the ECO and Jerzy Maksymiuk. Alexeev does not always observe the composer's dynamic indications, but in nearly every other respect comes closest to both the spirit and the letter of the scores. (There are two small departures from the score in No. 1 but they are really too trivial to mention.) No. 1 is much more characterful than Ortiz and Berglund, and No. 2 is the best we have had since Bernstein's pioneering record, which still sounds uncommonly fresh (see below) and is an admirable second choice. There is a fill-up in the form of a miniature one-movement concerto from a film score called *The Unforgettable year 1919.* The sleeve calls it a kind of Soviet *Warsaw concerto* – without, one is tempted to add, the tune! However, given the quality of both the performance and the sound, this record should make new friends for the two concertos, particularly at such an attractive price. There is an admirably vivid cassette.

In the early summer of 1975 CBS and HMV simultaneously appreciated the need for a good coupling of the two Shostakovich *Piano concertos.* CBS shrewdly recoupled Bernstein's radiant account of No. 2 (see below) with Previn's equally striking reading of No. 1. Though these New York performances bring somewhat dated recording, both pianists have a way of turning a phrase to catch the imagination, and a fine balance is struck between Shostakovich's warmth and his rhythmic alertness.

Cristina Ortiz gives fresh and attractive performances of both concertos, a degree undercharacterized, but beautifully recorded and with a fine accompaniment from the Bournemouth orchestra. This music-making is not so individual as that on the CBS disc, but there is compensation in the superb EMI sound, and this disc offers a small bonus in the *3 Fantastic dances*, which are played with splendid character.

Eugene List plays the *First Concerto* with splendid dash and brilliance, underlining its brittle sonorities and brash swagger. He takes the finale of the *Second Concerto* very much up to speed, and throughout there is plenty of character and spirit. The strings of the Moscow Radio Orchestra are somewhat wanting in bloom and lustre, and in the slow movement of No. 1 the solo trumpet is not heard to best advantage; he is rather forwardly balanced, as is the rest of the orchestra. The sound on this CBS record is not quite as fresh and truthful as on Cristina Ortiz's less well characterized but freshly enjoyable version on HMV, but List has the advantage of the authority of Maxim Shostakovich's direction.

Those wanting the *First Concerto* alone can readily turn to John Ogdon's fine Argo coupling. As in the Stravinsky *Capriccio* Ogdon gives a clean, stylish performance, which compasses both the humour and the hints of romanticism in the *First Concerto.* He keeps a little more detached than his accompanists in the tender slow movement, and the trumpet-playing of John Wilbraham is masterly. In addition the recording quality is most vivid. The comparatively backward balance of the strings gives the work a chamber quality to match that of the work on the reverse, an unexpected but attractive coupling.

(i) *Piano concerto No. 1, Op. 35; Symphony No. 7 in C (Leningrad), Op. 60.*
(M) ** HMV *TCC2-POR 54297.* (i) Ortiz, Senior; Bournemouth SO, Berglund.

This is a sensible enough coupling for Paavo Berglund's representation in HMV's 'Portrait of the Artist' double-length tape series and these are both fine performances. However, the use of iron oxide instead of chrome tape has led to transfer problems. Both recordings are resonant and the full sharpness of focus is slightly blunted here. In the big climaxes of the symphony (and especially in that of the first movement where the side-drums should dominate the texture cleanly) the quality becomes slightly confused.

Piano concerto No. 2 in F, Op. 101.
(M) *** CBS 60338/*40*-. Bernstein, NYPO – RAVEL: *Concerto in G.****
(M) *** HMV SXLP/*TC-SXLP* 30514. Ogdon, RPO, Foster – BARTÓK: *Concerto No. 3.***(*)

This is a delightful concerto in every way, an unpretentious work which has all the qualities to become widely popular. Shostakovich had a wonderful deadpan way of making the most outrageously simple idea into vitally interesting music. Everything here is so memorable – the bright-eyed first subject, the sinuous second subject, the memorable tune of the slow movement, Rachmaninov distilled down to a single line of piano melody, and the captivating 7/8 rhythms of the finale. Bernstein's performance is first-rate, finer even than the composer's own recording (in the Russian catalogue). Where Shostakovich himself, in apparent impatience, rushes the speeds, Bernstein sounds more sympathetic and just as alive. Few piano concerto couplings of any period outshine this in attractiveness (one is thinking of the Ravel as well); and the recording, although an early one, still sounds full-blooded and reasonably atmospheric. The cassette transfer too is clear and vivid.

John Ogdon, at the height of his powers, also gives a splendidly idiomatic account of this concerto written originally for Shostakovich's son, Maxim. The playing is full of character, the outer movements striking for their wit and dash, and the beautiful slow movement richly romantic without being sentimentalized. The 1971 recording sounds as vivid as the day it was made. The cassette too offers demonstration quality. Although the coupling does not display quite the same degree of excellence, this medium-priced reissue is worth considering for the Shostakovich alone.

The Gadfly (film music): *Suite, Op. 97a.*
(B) *** CfP CFP/*TC-CFP* 41 4463-1/*4*. USSR Cinema SO, Emin Khachaturian.

Shostakovich wrote prolifically for the cinema, his finest score being for Kozintsev's *Hamlet* (1964). *The Gadfly* was made in 1955 and directed by Feinzimmer; and the score was turned into a twelve-movement suite, published in 1960 and recorded two years later. The music is at times quite pleasing but at others wholly uncharacteristic. It is for the most part unmemorable, but has been brought before the public quite recently by the use of a movement called *Romance* – ripely scored with concertante solo violin – as signature theme for a TV series, *Reilly, Ace of Spies*. The most haunting item, however, is a gentle passacaglia called *Introduction* (*into the dance*), while the *Interlude* and *Nocturne* (featuring a solo cello) are comparably appealing in their lyrical nostalgia. Throughout, both performers and engineers score full marks for a musically committed and pleasingly recorded issue (which has a Russian Melodiya source).

Symphonies Nos. 1 in F min., Op. 10; 9 in E flat, Op. 70.
*** Decca Dig. SXDL/*KSXDC* 7515 [Lon. LDR/*5*- 71017]. LPO, Haitink.

Haitink's reading of the brilliant *First Symphony* may lack something in youthful high spirits (the finale does not sound quirky enough in the strange alternation of moods), but it is a strong, well-played performance nonetheless, and it is coupled with a superb account of No. 9, a symphony that has long been written off as trivial. Without inflation Haitink gives it a serious purpose, both in the poignancy of the waltz-like second movement and in the equivocal emotions of the outer movements, which here are not just superficially jolly, as so easily they can seem. The recording is outstandingly clean and brilliant, with the cassette matching the disc closely.

Symphonies Nos. 2 (To October), Op. 14; 3 (The First of May), Op. 20.
*** Decca Dig. SXDL/*KSXDC* 7535 [Lon. LDR/*5-* 71035]. LPO Ch. and O, Haitink.

Shostakovich was still in his early twenties when he composed these symphonies, neither of which show him at his most inspired even if the opening of the *Second Symphony* enjoyed a certain avant-garde interest in its day. Admirable performances and excellently balanced sound with great presence and body. Those collecting Haitink's cycle need not hesitate. The cassette too is first-class.

Symphony No. 4 in C min., Op. 43.
**(*) Decca SXL/*KSXC* 6927 [Lon. CS/*5-* 7160]. LPO, Haitink.

If the *Fourth Symphony* usually seems overweight in its scoring, with the vehement brutality explaining why it remained on the shelf for so long, Haitink brings out an unexpected refinement in the piece, a rare transparency of texture. He is helped by recording of demonstration quality on both disc and tape. Detail is superbly caught; yet the earthiness and power, the demonic quality which can make this work so compelling, are underplayed. One admires without being fully involved.

Symphony No. 5 in D min., Op. 47.
C *** Decca Dig. **410 017-2**; SXDL/*KSXDC* 7551 [Lon. LDR/*5-* 71051]. Concg. O, Haitink.
*** CBS **CD**; 35854/*40-* [id.]. NYPO, Bernstein.
(M) *** RCA Gold GL/*GK* 42690. LSO, Previn.
(M) *** EMI Em. EMX/*TC-EMX* 2034. Bournemouth SO, Berglund.
(M) **(*) Sup. 50423. Czech PO, Ančerl.
(B) **(*) Con. CC/*CCT* 7593 [Lon. STS 15492]. SRO, Kertesz.
** DG Dig. **410 509-2**; 2532/*3302* 076 [id.]. Nat. SO of Washington, Rostropovich.
(M) ** CBS 60117/*40-* [MY/*MYT* 37218]. NYPO, Bernstein.
(M) *(*) HMV Green. ESD/*TC-ESD* 290054-1/*4* [Ang. S/*4XS* 37285]. Chicago SO, Previn.

Haitink is eminently straightforward and there are no disruptive changes in tempo. It comes as a breath of fresh air after the Rostropovich, and the playing of the Concertgebouw Orchestra and the contribution of the Decca engineers are beyond praise. There could perhaps be greater intensity of feeling in the slow movement, but, whatever small reservations one might have, it is at present a first recommendation artistically and way out ahead in terms of sheer sound. The compact disc is superb and makes the LP, itself a demonstration disc, sound like a carbon copy by comparison. The presence, range and body of the sound in both forms is impressive and the CD is one of the very best yet to appear. There is, however, an element of fierceness in the upper strings on the chrome tape.

Recorded in Tokyo in 1979, when Bernstein and the New York Philharmonic were on tour there, the CBS version is the weightiest on record, partly because of the interpretation but also because of the digital sound, which is particularly rich in bass. Unashamedly Bernstein treats the work as a romantic symphony. The very opening makes an impact rarely possible in the concert hall, and then exceptionally in the cool and beautiful second-subject melody Bernstein takes a slightly detached view, though as soon as that same melody comes up for development after the exposition, the result is altogether more warmly expressive. Yet the movement's central climax, with its emphasis on the deep brass, injects a powerful element of menace, and the coda communicates a strongly Russian melancholy, which is perhaps why the composer admired Bernstein above other American interpreters of his music. The *Allegretto* becomes a burlesque, but its Mahlerian roots are strongly conveyed. The slow movement is raptly beautiful (marvellously sustained pianissimo playing from the New York

Philharmonic strings), and the finale is brilliant and extrovert, with the first part dazzlingly fast and the conclusion one of unalloyed triumph, with no hint of irony. The chrome cassette is one of CBS's finest, carrying all the brilliance and weight of the disc. On CD the bass is made to sound even fuller and richer than the LP, and the slight distancing of the sound (compared with many CBS recordings) places the orchestra within a believable ambience. However, even so, this does not match the quality of Haitink's Decca CD.

Previn's RCA version with the LSO, which dates from the mid-1960s, is an altogether superlative account. The recording too was outstanding in all departments of the orchestra. The freshness and vitality of the reading and the first-class orchestral playing combine to produce a performance that is literal without lacking spontaneity. The kind of radiance that the strings achieve at the opening of the great slow movement is totally memorable; and throughout there is great intensity and eloquence. The buoyancy of the scherzo and the élan of the finale are highly exhilarating. Unfortunately the cassette transfer – although it generally sounds well – has a compressed dynamic range (the climax of the first movement is very much less telling here than on the disc).

Berglund's recording, reissued on EMI Eminence, dates from 1976, and the quality is superb, full-bodied, rich and atmospheric. The performance, however, seeks breadth and nobility rather than extrovert excitement, and although it has both atmosphere and eloquence some will find Berglund's approach too sober. However, it is splendidly played, and at mid-price it still has considerable appeal, on both disc and the good matching tape.

The kernel of Ančerl's performance on Supraphon is undoubtedly the *Largo*, and in this beautiful movement he secures some very fine playing from the Czech orchestra. His reading is warmly flexible and is especially moving in the closing pages. The first movement too is well-balanced. Ančerl takes the second-movement *Allegretto* fairly slowly, but vivid solo playing, especially from the horns, supports this account well. The finale too is broad, rather than frenetic, and if it loses a little out-and-out excitement, it gains in dignity. The Supraphon recording is one of this company's best, vivid as well as atmospheric.

Kertesz's reading is thoroughly musical but somewhat circumspect. Yet it is not uncommitted; and the clear yet vivid Decca sound adds much to the impact of the performance. Kertesz is especially good at the close of movements, and both the first and third end in a mood of radiant simplicity, although Previn finds more tension and colour in the climax of the *Largo*. The finale is taken steadily, but Kertesz provides a splendid burst of controlled exuberance for the coda. The sound is splendid in the bargain-priced Contour reissue, if anything even more vivid on tape than on disc.

Rostropovich's account is too idiosyncratic to be recommended without qualification. He secures a refined, cultured string-tone capable of searing intensity and strength, and all the sections of the orchestra play with excellent attack and ensemble. The opening is given with hushed *ppp* intensity (the marking is in fact *piano*) and all promises well until, as is so often the case with this great Russian musician, he disturbs the natural musical flow for the sake of expressive effect. The brakes are abruptly applied in the scherzo (at fig. 56) just before the horn figure is repeated, and he pulls other phrases around too. He wrings the last ounce of intensity out of the finale, which is undoubtedly imposing, but there is a hectoring quality too, which is distinctly unappealing. (It is like being lectured by Solzhenitsyn on the moral decline of the West.) The recording is good on the whole, even if it is a multi-mike, somewhat synthetic balance, and the CD will impress all who hear it as strikingly 'present'. It is only when the Decca CD is put alongside it that its limitations strike the listener. The cassette is wide-ranging and full-bodied, but slightly fierce on top.

Bernstein's earlier version comes from the beginning of the 1960s, and the reading displays plenty of emotional power and a driving force of great intensity. The New York players clearly feel the music the way Bernstein does, and the continual tension of the playing makes the very fast speed for the finale sound well in accord with the reading as a whole. The recording is very brightly lit, but the excess brilliance is somewhat tempered on the cassette which is full and clear.

Previn's second recording of the *Fifth*, made

in Chicago, does not match his earlier RCA version in intensity. His view of the work does not appear to have changed greatly in the intervening years, and although the playing of the Chicago orchestra is of the highest quality, there is little sense of freshness and urgency. The first movement is a good deal slower than usual, so much so that one feels the want of momentum. The scherzo is impressively played, but the slow movement is without a sense of forward movement and the climax, so impressive in the earlier version, lacks real urgency. The recorded sound is extremely impressive; it has been digitally remastered for this Greensleeve reissue.

Symphony No. 6 in B min., Op. 54.
*** HMV ASD 3029 [Ang. RL/*4RL* 32105]. LSO, Previn – PROKOFIEV: *Lieutenant Kijé.****

The opening slow movement of the *Sixth Symphony* is parallel to those of the *Fifth* and the *Eighth*, each among the composer's finest inspirations. Here Previn shows his deep understanding of Shostakovich in a powerfully drawn, unrelenting account of that massive structure, his slow tempo adding to the overall impact. After that the offhand wit of the central scherzo comes over the more delicately at a slower tempo than usual, leaving the hectic finale to hammer home the deceptively joyful conclusion to the argument. Even at the end Previn effectively avoids bombast in the exuberance of joy. Excellent recording.

Symphonies Nos. 6; 11 in G min. (1905), Op. 103.
*** HMV SLS 5177 (2). Bournemouth SO, Berglund.

Berglund gives new tragic depth to the *Sixth*, and with similar rugged concentration demonstrates the massive power of the *Eleventh*, a work which, with its programme based on the abortive 1905 uprising in Russia, usually seems far too thin in material. Shostakovich's pessimism in both works is underlined, with hardly a glimmer of hope allowed. In the *Sixth* the very measured tempo for the first movement, taken direct and with little *espressivo*, points the link with the comparable movement of the *Eighth Symphony*, and the remaining two movements are made ruthlessly bitter by not being sprung as dance movements, as is more usual. No Soviet optimism here. In the *Eleventh* too, even more daringly, Berglund lets the music speak for itself, keeping the long opening *Adagio* at a very steady, slow tread, made compelling by the hushed concentration of the Bournemouth playing. Superlative recording. Berglund's art has never been more powerfully conveyed on record.

Symphony No. 7 in C (Leningrad), Op. 60.
**(*) HMV SLS 897 (2). Bournemouth SO, Berglund.

Symphony No. 7 (Leningrad); Age of Gold: suite, Op. 22.
*** Decca Dig. D 213 D 2/*K 213 K 22* (2) [Lon. LDR/5- 10015]. LPO, Haitink.

With his characteristic refinement and avoidance of bombast Haitink might not seem an apt conductor for the most publicized of Shostakovich's wartime symphonies, but in effect he transforms it, bringing out the nobility of many passages. One sees that the long first-movement *ostinato* – now revealed as having quite different implications from the descriptive programme suggested by the Soviet propaganda machine in the war years – is almost an interlude in a work which otherwise in its deep seriousness challenges comparison with the other wartime symphony, the epic *Eighth*. The recording is of demonstration quality, and the fill-up, the joky *Age of Gold suite*, provides comparable brilliance. The cassette transfer is equally sophisticated, though the focus of the thundering side-drums slips just a little in the first-movement climax.

Berglund directs a doggedly powerful performance of a symphony of Shostakovich that has long been underestimated. Though Berglund is not always sensitive to the finer points of expressiveness, it is useful to have a good performance of what is often a noisy symphony, recorded with such rich, vivid sound.

Symphonies Nos. 7 (Leningrad); 9 in E flat, Op. 70.
(M) ** Sup. 110 1771/2. Czech PO, Neumann.

The Supraphon recording has far less presence and detail than the EMI for Berglund but Neumann has more poetry and the playing of the Czech Philharmonic is most responsive. Neumann's account of the *Ninth* is also a fine one and it is a pity that the less than vivid recording inhibits a three-star recommendation.

Symphony No. 8 in C min., Op. 64.
*** Decca Dig. **411 616-2**; SXDL/*KSXDC* 7621 [Lon. LDR/*5*- 71121]. Concg. O, Haitink.
*** HMV ASD 2917 [Ang. S 36980]. LSO, Previn.

The *Eighth Symphony*, written in response to the sufferings of the Russian people during the Second World War, is one of Shostakovich's most powerful and intense creations, starting with a slow movement almost half an hour long, which emerges as not only emotionally involving but cogent in symphonic terms too. The sharp unpredictability of the remaining movements, alternately cajoling and battering the listener, shows Shostakovich at his most inspired.

Haitink characteristically presents a strongly architectural reading of this war-inspired symphony, at times direct to the point of severity. After the massive and sustained slow movement which opens the work, Haitink allows no lightness or relief in the scherzo movements, and in his seriousness in the strangely lightweight finale (neither fast nor slow) he provides an unusually satisfying account of an equivocal, seemingly uncommitted movement. The playing of the Concertgebouw Orchestra is immaculate and the digital recording full, brilliant and clear on both disc and chrome cassette (though on tape the upper strings have marginally less body than on LP). The compact disc has the usual virtues of added presence and definition, although it is marginally less impressive than the companion CD of the *Fifth Symphony*.

Previn's HMV version remains fully recommendable, somewhat more charismatic in feeling, and with perhaps less *gravitas*, though not less emotional commitment. The London Symphony Orchestra is prompted by Previn to playing that is both intense and brilliant, while the recording is outstandingly rich and vivid, even making no allowance for the very long sides.

Symphony No. 10 in E min., Op. 93.
*** DG Dig. **413 361-2**; 2532/*3302* 030 [id.]. Berlin PO, Karajan.
*** HMV ASD/*TCC-ASD* 4405 [Ang. DS/*4XS* 37955]. LSO, Previn.
**(*) Decca SXL/*KSXC* 6838 [Lon. CS/*5*-7061]. LPO, Haitink.
(M) (***) CBS mono 61457. NYPO, Mitropoulos.

Already in his 1967 recording Karajan had shown that he had the measure of this symphony, and this newer version is if anything even finer. In the first movement he distils an atmosphere as concentrated as before, bleak and unremitting, while in the *Allegro* the Berlin Philharmonic leave no doubts as to their peerless virtuosity. Everything is marvellously shaped and proportioned. The *allegro* section of the finale is taken up to speed (176 crotchets to the minute), faster than Mitropoulos and much faster than most other rivals. The digital sound is altogether excellent, and this must now rank as a first recommendation. It has greater intensity and grip than Haitink (the LPO's playing is not quite in the same league), and though Mitropoulos's pioneering account is still to be treasured, this 1982 Berlin version is marvellously powerful and gripping. The cassette too is of demonstration quality; it has splendid range, body and detail.

Previn's is a strong and dramatic reading marked by a specially compelling account of the long first movement which steers an ideal course between expressive warmth and architectural strength. At marginally slower speeds than usual, Previn's rhythmic lift both in the scherzo and in the finale brings exhilarating results, less severe than such rivals as Haitink, but sparkling and swaggering instead. The digital recording is outstandingly full and firm. The cassette is transferred on iron-oxide stock and the transfer level is not especially high, yet even so the sound is impressively vivid.

As a recording Haitink's Decca version is in the demonstration class. It has impressive body, range and definition: the balance is very natural, yet every detail of Shostakovich's score registers, and the climaxes are astonishingly lifelike. Haitink really has the measure of the first movement, whose climaxes he paces with an admirable sense of architecture, and he secures sensitive and enthusiastic playing from the LPO both here and in the scherzo. In the third movement he adopts a slower tempo than usual, which would be acceptable if there were greater tension or concentration of mood. But here and in the slow introduction to the finale the sense of concentration falters, though this must not be allowed to detract from the overall integrity and eloquence that Haitink largely achieves. The sound quality from the cassette is hardly less impressive than that of the disc.

Mitropoulos's 1954 recording was the first made of Shostakovich's *Tenth.* It has all the freshness of new discovery, and the playing has tremendous intensity and power. While some allowances have to be made for the CBS mono recording, the communication of the music-making is riveting from the first bar to the last.

Symphony No. 12 in D min. (*The Year 1917*), *Op. 112; Overture on Russian and Kirghis folk themes, Op. 115.*

*** Decca Dig. SXDL/*KSXDC* 7577 [Lon. LDR/*5-* 71077]. Concg. O, Haitink.

The *Twelfth* is most strikingly recorded by the Decca team, even judged by the high standards of the house. Indeed the sheer quality of sound and the superb responsiveness and body of the Concertgebouw Orchestra might well seduce some listeners and make friends for a work that has so far found little favour. For while the finest of the symphonies have the epic, panoramic sweep of the great Russian novelists, the more 'public' works, among which the *Twelfth* must be numbered, come closer to the patriotic and more repetitive Eisenstein films. There is much of the composer's vision and grandeur but also his crudeness. The slow movement, however, has a marvellous sense of atmosphere which is well conveyed in this new performance – as it was, to be fair, in Mravinsky's pioneering account with the Leningrad Philharmonic. The control is masterly and the great Amsterdam orchestra play as if they believe every crotchet, though not even their eloquence can altogether rescue the finale. However, there is no doubt that this is the most successful version so far of No. 12 and it supersedes all its predecessors – and, moreover, offers a fill-up in the shape of the *Overture on Russian and Kirghis folk themes* from the same period. The chrome cassette is exceptionally wide-ranging and vivid, although, as with other tape issues in this Concertgebouw series, the upper range needs a little taming.

Symphony No. 13 in B flat min. (*Babi Yar*), *Op. 113.*

*** HMV ASD/*TC-ASD* 3911 [Ang. SZ 37661]. Petkov, LSO Ch., LSO, Previn.

*** Ph. Dig. 6514/*7337* 120 [id.]. Shirley-Quirk, Bav. R. Male Ch., and SO, Kondrashin.

This troubled work, inspired by often angry poems of Yevtushenko, is presented here at its most stark and direct. More usually the mood-painting of the poems is underlined, but Previn takes a relatively literal view of the sprung rhythms in the ironic second movement, *Humour*, and makes the picture of peasant women queueing for food in the snow less atmospheric than it sometimes is. The result is that this becomes a genuine symphony, not just an orchestral song-cycle. One might even relate the overall shape to that of the *Eighth Symphony*, starting with a bald slow movement punctuated by cliff-like dynamic contrasts and ending in wistfulness on a final *Allegretto*, *A Career*, with weaving flutes and gently lolloping pizzicato rhythms. Playing and recording are superb, among the very finest from this source. The cassette transfer is first-class, outstandingly clean and vivid.

Kondrashin gave the very first performance of the symphony, and an unofficial recording of it on the Everest label appeared in the West in the early 1960s. This is his third recording of it, and very impressive it is, too. The performance is every bit as concentrated in mood as Previn's and has real authenticity of feeling; and the recording, made at a public concert, is very fine even if it does not match the HMV in depth and range. This is a good alternative to the Previn though not quite displacing it as a first choice. The cassette is of good quality, though it has slightly less range than the LP.

Symphony No. 14, Op. 135.
*** Decca Dig. SXDL/*KSXDC* 7532 [Lon. LDR/5- 71032]. Varady, Fischer-Dieskau, Concg. O, Haitink.
*** CBS Dig. 74084/*40*- [M/*MT* 37270]. Kubiak, Bushkin, NYPO, Bernstein.

The *Fourteenth* is Shostakovich's most sombre and dark score, a setting of poems by Lorca, Apollinaire, Rilke, Brentano and Küchelbecker, all on the theme of death. It is similar in conception (though not in character) to Britten's *Nocturne* or *Spring symphony*, and is in fact dedicated to him. Earlier recordings under Barshai, Ormandy and Rostropovich have all been in Russian, but this version gives each poem in the original. This is a most powerful performance under Haitink, and it is impressively recorded. All but the Barshai have now disappeared from circulation, but in any case this fine reading would displace earlier recommendations. The outstanding recording is equally impressive on disc and the excellent chrome tape.

Leonard Bernstein's version of the *Fourteenth* with Teresa Kubiak and Isser Bushkin does not have the benefit of such excellent sound as its immediate predecessors (Rostropovich on HMV and Haitink on Decca) and is not so transparent or finely detailed. Yet taken in its own right, it is perfectly acceptable and the performance is both powerful and deeply felt without underlining expressive points to excess. Shostakovich's bleak ruminations on the theme of death exercise a compelling fascination even in those songs in which the quality of invention seems a little strained (as in *On watch*, the third of the Apollinaire settings). It casts its spell, for this is the sixth recording of the symphony in twice that many years (yet, though recordings are frequent, their life in the catalogue seems short). Bernstein gets good playing from the New Yorkers and there is a Mussorgskian atmosphere which inevitably eludes the polyglot version on Decca.

Symphony No. 15 in A, Op. 141.
❀ *** Decca SXL/*KSXC* 6096 [Lon. CS 7130]. LPO, Haitink.
(M) ** Sup. 1110 2967. Czech PO, Vajnar.

This was the second issue in Haitink's Shostakovich series and it brings a performance which is a revelation. Early readings of the composer's last symphony seemed to underline the quirky unpredictability of the work, with the collage of strange quotations – above all the *William Tell* galop, which keeps recurring in the first movement – seemingly joky rather than profound. Haitink by contrast makes the first movement sound genuinely symphonic, bitingly urgent. He underlines the purity of the bare lines of the second movement, and after the Wagner quotations which open the finale his slow tempo for the main lyrical theme gives it heartaching tenderness, not the usual easy triviality. The playing of the LPO is excellent, with refined tone and superb attack, and the recording is both analytical and atmospheric, as impressive on cassette as on disc. Although the textures are generally spare, the few heavy tuttis are difficult for the engineers, and Decca sound copes with them splendidly.

František Vajnar and the Czech Philharmonic on Supraphon give a good account of the work, but neither as a performance nor a recording does it match the Haitink on Decca. The sound is not quite as present or as vividly defined and the side-break comes before the end of the second movement, which may enhance the contrast between the second and third but naturally disrupts the continuity to little real purpose.

CHAMBER AND INSTRUMENTAL MUSIC

Cello sonata in D min., Op. 40.
*** Chan. Dig. ABRD/*ABTD* 1072 [id.]. Turovsky, Edlina – PROKOFIEV: *Sonata*.***

Yuli Turovsky and Luba Edlina play the *Cello sonata* with great panache and eloquence. At times, in the finale, they almost succumb to exaggeration in their handling of its humour – no understatement here. However, they are totally inside this music and the recording reproduces them truthfully. The record is also of particular value in restoring the Prokofiev *Sonata* to circulation after an absence of some years. The chrome cassette, made at the highest level, gives the artists great presence, but the balance gives slight exaggeration to the upper partials of the cello timbre.

Piano quintet in G min., Op. 57.
(*) CRD CRD 1051/*CRDC 4051* [id.]. Benson, Alberni Qt – BRITTEN: *String quartet No. 1.*(*)

Piano quintet, Op. 57; Piano trio No. 2 in E min., Op. 67.
(*) Chan. Dig. **CHAN 8342; ABRD/*ABTD* 1088 [id.]. Borodin Trio, Zweig, Horner.
**(*) ASV ALH 929. Music Group of L.

A vigorous and finely conceived account of the *Quintet* from Clifford Benson and the Alberni Quintet well recorded, with a first-class cassette equivalent – indeed, it is in the demonstration class.

The Chandos and ASV discs, however, bring together two of Shostakovich's most important chamber works. The Chandos version of the *Quintet* is bolder in character and more concentrated in feeling than either of the rival versions. There are one or two moments of vulnerable intonation but these are of little account, given the intensity of this playing. The Music Group of London show rather less panache but are still impressive, and in their hands the *Trio* is affectingly played. This is a particularly painful and anguished work dedicated to the memory of a close friend, Ivan Sollertinsky, who perished in a Nazi death camp in 1944, the year of its composition. Excellent balance and good recording quality make this ASV disc an attractive proposition, although on performance alone the Chandos issue remains first choice. Here the sound is vivid, though the microphones are rather close and there is too much reverberation round the piano. On the chrome tape the presence is no less striking, although the string focus is not absolutely clean.

String quartets Nos. 1–15.
❀ *** O-L D 188 D 7 (7). Fitzwilliam Qt.

String quartets Nos. 1–13.
(M) *** HMV SLS 879 (6). Borodin Qt.

Shostakovich concentrated on the symphony earlier in his career; the *First Quartet* was not written until 1938, a year after the *Fifth Symphony*, but into this medium he then poured some of his most private and inspired musical thinking. Here perhaps more than in the symphonies is the record of the real man. As is well known, the Fitzwilliam Quartet played to Shostakovich himself and gave the UK premières of his last three quartets, and they bring to the whole cycle complete and total dedication. They are splendid players and their accounts of these works have won wide acclaim and a number of awards, well deserved. They are given first-class recording too, with great presence and body; a rather forward balance is chosen but the results are wholly natural. There are minor criticisms, but they are too trivial to weigh in the balance, for this set is by any standards a formidable achievement.

The HMV set by the Borodin Quartet is also very fine. It is not quite complete, appearing before Nos. 14 and 15 had seen the light of day, but the performances and recordings are first-class. The set is modestly priced and immensely pleasurable, but it is inevitably superseded by the later and complete Fitzwilliam box.

String quartets Nos. 1 in C, Op. 49; 2 in A, Op. 68.
*** O-L DSLO 31 [id.]. Fitzwilliam Qt.

The *First Quartet* is a slight but charming work, fluent, sunny and lyrical. The *Second* is a wartime work, like the *Eighth Symphony* and the *Piano trio*, which immediately precede it. It is less appealing than its predecessor – understandably so – and less concentrated. The slow movement is problematic, and its recitative can easily seem to hang fire. The darker overtones of the waltz and the richness of the variation movement are well conveyed in this excellent performance. The recording has splendid presence and body.

String quartets Nos. 3, Op. 73; 11 in F min., Op. 112.
*** O-L DSLO 28 [id.]. Fitzwilliam Qt.

The *Third* is a five-movement work written

in the immediate wake of the *Ninth Symphony* (also in five movements) and completed in 1946. It is a powerful piece whose central *Allegro* movement almost foreshadows the scherzo of the *Tenth Symphony*. The Fitzwilliam players give a searching and thoughtful performance, with sensible tempi and total commitment. The quartet is split over two sides and prefaced on side one with the relatively lightweight *Eleventh Quartet* of 1966, a seven-movement piece of little more than a quarter of an hour's duration. This too is given an elegant performance, which can well hold its own with the Borodin Quartet's version once coupled with Maxim Shostakovich's account of the *Fifteenth Symphony*.

String quartets Nos. 4 in D, Op. 83; 12 in D flat, Op. 133.
*** O-L DSLO 23 [id.]. Fitzwilliam Qt.

These quartets come from widely different periods in Shostakovich's career: the *Fourth* was composed in 1949 in the immediate wake of the Zhdanov affair; the *Twelfth* was written in the late 1960s, a year before the *Fourteenth Symphony*. The *Fourth* is the most recorded (and possibly the most immediately attractive) of all the quartets, apart from No. 1. It is a measure of the Fitzwilliam players' achievement that they compare very favourably with competition past and present, and their account of the *Twelfth Quartet* is very impressive indeed. They pay scrupulous attention to dynamics, their tone is finely blended, and their intonation is admirably secure. The *Twelfth* is a profound and searching piece, and this account of it is powerful, often haunting.

String quartets Nos. 5 in B flat, Op. 92; 6 in G, Op. 107.
*** O-L DSLO 29 [id.]. Fitzwilliam Qt.

Two quartets from a vintage period. The *Fifth*, arguably the finest of the whole cycle, was composed immediately before the *Tenth Symphony*, and like the symphony it makes use of the autobiographical motivic fingerprint (DSCH). Its three movements have an emotional intensity that leaves no doubt that it meant a great deal to Shostakovich – as it obviously does to these young players. The *Sixth*, which immediately pre-dates the *Eleventh Symphony*, is a sunny and delightful work, finely proportioned and beautifully fluent. The Fitzwilliam Quartet gives strong, powerfully wrought performances, recorded with splendid presence.

String quartets Nos. 7 in F sharp min., Op. 108; 13 in B flat min., Op. 138; 14 in F sharp min., Op. 142.
*** O-L DSLO 9 [id.]. Fitzwilliam Qt.

This made an impressive début for this young English group, who demonstrate their spiritual affinity and keen sympathy with the Shostakovich quartets. They play with great feeling and aplomb, good ensemble and tonal blend, so that the minor lapses in intonation are of scant moment. They are given superbly realistic and well-defined recording.

String quartet No. 8 in C min., Op. 110.
(M) *** Decca Eclipse ECS 795 [Lon. STS 15046]. Borodin Qt – BORODIN: *Quartet No. 2.****

As the central motif of this fine quartet Shostakovich used a group of four notes derived, cipher-like, from his own name, and somewhat unpatriotically the cipher has a decided German bias. He takes his initial D, plus (in German notation) the first three notes of his surname (in German spelling) – E flat (or Es, as it is in German), C and B (or H, as it is in German). Hence the motif spells DSCH. All very involved, but in fact the motif is at least as fruitful as the famous one in the name BACH, and the argument throughout this impressive work is most intense. The fourth movement was inspired by memories of a German air-raid, with a high-pitched whine interrupted by crackling gunfire, but one does not have to know that fragment of programme to appreciate the immediacy of the music. The work concludes with a fine slow fugue on the DSCH motif. This performance is outstanding and the recording superb. With so attractive a coupling, at lower mid-price this makes an inviting point at which to begin exploring this part of Shostakovich's musical and personal world.

String quartets Nos. 8 in C min., Op. 110; 15 in E flat min., Op. 144.
*** O-L DSLO 11 [id.]. Fitzwilliam Qt.

The Fitzwilliam Quartet give a reading of the six-movement *Fifteenth Quartet* that has unusual sympathy and feeling, and these young players leave no doubts as to their musicianship and authority. The recording is among the most realistic string-quartet sounds on record; it is splendidly fresh and detailed, with a firmness and definition that are most impressive. The performance of No. 8 withstands comparison with the Borodins, and that of the elegiac No. 15 is equally moving and eloquent.

String quartets Nos. 9 in E flat, Op. 117; 10 in A flat, Op. 118.
*** O-L DSLO 30 [id.]. Fitzwilliam Qt.

The *Ninth* and *Tenth Quartets* both come from the same year (1964) and find Shostakovich at his most private and eloquent. The *Tenth*, in particular, is deeply powerful and intensely felt, and it ranks among the very finest of his works after the *Tenth Symphony*. These young English players exhibit the same sense of commitment and musicianship that has distinguished their whole cycle. Both quartets are superb and the players obviously have them in their blood. The forward balance of the recording secures body and presence, but as a result it tends to sacrifice real pianissimo tone, which imposes on the players a need to project pianissimi rather more than in fact they do. But this is only a small reservation and in no way dampens enthusiasm for this issue.

Violin sonata, Op. 134.
*** Ph. 6514 102. Lubotsky, Edlina – SCHNITTKE: *Sonata No. 2* etc.***
*** Chan. Dig. **CHAN 8343**; ABRD/*ABTD* 1089 [id.]. Dubinsky, Edlina – SCHNITTKE: *Sonata No. 1* etc.***

Shostakovich composed his *Sonata* for Oistrakh's sixtieth birthday, and since his pioneering record issued in the early 1970s there have been versions by Kremer and Gavrilov, also coupled with Schnittke and which succumbed (like the Oistrakh–Richter version) to rapid deletion. The two most recent versions are by Soviet artists Mark Lubotsky on Philips and Rostislav Dubinsky, who now live in the West and have a common pianist, Luba Edlina. One marvels at Lubotsky's virtuosity and the natural yet wonderfully vivid sound achieved. Unfortunately, the Shostakovich sonata is spread over two sides, the first movement being placed immediately after the Schnittke *Sonata* and thus the continuity achieved by its rivals is broken. The *Sonata* is a bitter and at times arid score, thought-provoking and, unusually in this composer, not totally convincing.

Rostislav Dubinsky's account is hardly less eloquent than that of his compatriot and can be recommended with equal warmth. The recording is excellent too, with vivid presence; though, if pressed to a choice, the refinement and naturalness of the Philips disc which places the artists just a shade further away gives it a certain advantage. The Chandos chrome tape, however, is clear and well focused and should provide a satisfying alternative in this medium.

Preludes and fugues Nos. 4 in E min.; 12 in G sharp min.; 14 in E flat min.; 15 in D flat; 17 in A flat; 23 in F, Op. 87.
(M) **(*) Ph. Seq. 6527/*7311* 224. S. Richter.

Shostakovich wrote twenty-four *Preludes and fugues*, one in each key. They are thus a modern equivalent of the Bach *48*, but they are far from cerebral pieces and are often dramatic and emotional. Their form too is by no means conventional. No. 15, for instance, has an ABA structure, with the most winning middle section, which Richter points beautifully. The present selection in fact has no unifying factor; these are presumably Richter's own favourites. He plays them superbly and even though the recording tends to be slightly hard, though not shallow, this reissue is very worthwhile. The cassette is every bit the equal of the LP. It is transferred at quite a high level, and the piano image is bold and (to advantage) slightly softer-edged at the top.

OPERA

Lady Macbeth of Mtsensk (opera; complete).
❀ *** HMV SLS 5157 (3) [Ang. SX 3866]. Vishnevskaya, Gedda, Krenn, Petkov, Meoz, Tear, Finnilä, Malta, Amb. Op. Ch., LPO, Rostropovich.

Rostropovich's recording proves with thrilling conviction that this first version of Shostakovich's greatest work for the stage is among the most original operas of the century. In text *Lady Macbeth* may not be radically different from the revised version, *Katerina Ismailova*, but it has an extra sharpness of focus that transforms what is much more than just a sordid love story involving three murders by the heroine. Here the brutality of the love affair between the rich merchant's wife and Sergei, the roving-eyed workman, has maximum punch, and Rostropovich, helped by superlative recording, gives a performance of breathtaking power. Vishnevskaya in her finest ever performance on record provides moments of great beauty alongside aptly coarser singing, and Gedda matches her well, totally idiomatic. As the sadistic father-in-law, Petkov is magnificent, particularly in his ghostly return, and there are fine contributions from Robert Tear, Werner Krenn, Birgit Finnilä and Alexander Malta.

Transcriptions: (i) *Tahiti trot* (arr. of *Tea for two*), *Op. 16*. (ii) D. Scarlatti: *2 Pieces, Op. 17*. (iii) Beethoven: *Mephistopheles' Song of the flea*. (iv) Strauss, Johann jr: *Vergnügungszug polka*. (v; vi) Rimsky-Korsakov: *I waited for you in the grotto*. Ressel: *Der armer Columbus: overture*. Shostakovich: (v) *Tale of the priest and his servant, Balda, Op. 36* (*suite*); *2 Fables, Op. 4;* (v; vii) *The dragonfly and the ant;* (iv; viii) *The ass and the nightingale*.
*** HMV ASD/*TC-ASD* 165033-1/4. (i) Leningrad PO; (ii) Wind Ens.; (iii) Nesterenko and Ens.; (iv) Moscow PO; (v) USSR SO; (vi) Abladerdyeva; (vii) Borisova; (viii) Moscow Conservatoire O; cond. Rozhdestvensky.

A highly diverting collector's item, this disc/cassette should be snapped up before it falls under the inevitable deletion axe. It is worth having for the whimsically ear-catching, if hardly idiomatic, transcription of *Tea for two* – completed in a single afternoon back in the 1920s before Russia was afraid of American influence – which readily captures first attention. What did Vincent Youmans, the original composer, think? The other transcriptions all have their point too, not least the orchestration for Yevgeni Nesterenko of Beethoven's *Song of the flea* with the Goethe poem translated (as for the Mussorgsky setting) into Russian. The bright imaginative suites from film scores make an excellent coupling, and the performances from different sources are lively and generally well recorded on both disc and tape.

Sibelius, Jean

(1865–1957)

Andante festivo for strings; Canzonette, Op. 62a; Dance intermezzo, Op. 45/2; The Dryad, Op. 45/1; Pan and Echo, Op. 53a; Romance in C, Op. 42; Spring song, Op. 16; Suite champêtre, Op. 98b; Suite mignonne, Op. 98a; Valse romantique, Op. 62b.
(M) *** HMV Green. ESD/*TC-ESD* 106227-1/4. Royal Liv. PO, Groves.

These chips from the master's workshop make up a delightful, undemanding disc, many of them reflecting the composer's desire to repeat the popular success of *Valse triste*. The playing is warmly expressive though ensemble is not immaculate. Warm recording to match in this mid-price reissue. The cassette too is very successful, the sound fresh as well as full. This collection, although lightweight, is more than the sum of its parts and will give much pleasure.

The Bard, Op. 64; En Saga, Op. 9; Finlandia, Op. 26; (i) *Humoreske No. 5 in E flat, Op. 89/3; Karelia suite, Op. 111: Intermezzo; Alla marcia. King Christian II suite, Op. 27; Kuolema, Op. 44: Valse triste; Scene with cranes. Legends, Op. 22: The Swan of Tuonela; Lem-*

minkaïnen's return. (ii) *Luonnotar, Op. 70; The Oceanides, Op. 73; Pohjola's daughter, Op. 49; Scènes historiques, Op. 25;* (i) *Serenade No. 2 in G min., Op. 69b; Spring song, Op. 16; Swan White (suite), Op. 54; Tapiola, Op. 112.*

(M) **(*) HMV SLS/*TC-SLS* 5269 (4). Bournemouth SO, Berglund (i) with Haendel; (ii) Valjakka.

This box of four discs brings together Berglund's Bournemouth recordings of shorter major Sibelius pieces. His direct approach generally goes with moderate speeds. You may find more urgently exciting accounts of *Tapiola* or more subtly persuasive ones of *En Saga*, and in the lighter pieces he may turn his back on mere charm, but all have an honest strength and compulsion, not least the captivating performance of the rare *Luonnotar* with the soprano solo sung idiomatically by Taru Valjakka. The recordings are warm and full, though those from Studio Two sources have some close-up balances.

The Bard, Op. 64; Karelia suite, Op. 11: Intermezzo; Alla marcia. King Christian II: suite, Op. 27; Scènes historiques, Suite No. 1, Op. 25; Spring song, Op. 16.

(M) *** HMV Green. ESD/*TC-ESD* 7160. Bournemouth SO, Berglund.

Berglund's performance of *The Bard* is very fine indeed. It has an appealingly direct eloquence and the orchestral playing is first-class. The *Karelia* items are good too, if not quite on this level, but the *King Christian II suite* again shows the conductor and his Bournemouth orchestra on top form – the string playing in the *Nocturne* and *Elégie* is very beautiful. With excellent sound this is a highly desirable anthology. The tape is vivid, although on side two (notably *Karelia*) climaxes are not as open as on the disc.

Violin concerto in D min., Op. 47.

*** HMV ASD/*TC-ASD* 3933 [Ang. SZ/*4ZS* 37663]. Perlman, Pittsburgh SO, Previn – SINDING: *Suite.****

*** Decca SXL/*KSXC* 6493. Kyung-Wha Chung, LSO, Previn – TCHAIKOVSKY: *Concerto.* ***

(M) **(*) Ph. Seq. 6527/*7311* 041 [Quin. 7150]. Szeryng, LSO, Rozhdestvensky – PROKOFIEV: *Concerto No. 2.****

(M) **(*) CBS 60287/*40-* [Odys. Y/*YT* 33522]. Francescatti, NYPO, Bernstein – WALTON: *Concerto.***

** HMV Dig. ASD/*TC-ASD* 143519-1/*4* [Ang. DS/*4XS* 37957). Kremer, Philh. O, Muti – SCHUMANN: *Concerto.***(*)

(M) ** CBS 60312 [(d) Odys. Y/*YT* 30489]. D. Oistrakh, Phd. O, Ormandy – TCHAIKOVSKY: *Concerto.***

Violin concerto; 6 Humoresques, Op. 87/1–2, Op. 89/1–4.

*** Ph. 9500 675/*7300 770* [id.]. Accardo, LSO, Sir Colin Davis.

Violin concerto; 2 Serenades, Op. 69/1–2; 2 Serious melodies, Op. 77/1–2.

**(*) Decca SXL/*KSXC* 6953 [Lon. 7181]. Belkin, Philh. O, Ashkenazy.

(i) *Violin concerto. Tapiola, Op. 112.*

**(*) DG Acc. 2542/*3342* 186. (i) Ferras; Berlin PO, Karajan.

Heifetz's dazzling account of the Sibelius *Concerto*, recorded in Chicago at the beginning of the 1960s, continues to be the yardstick by which all other versions are measured. It is only available in the UK within a box of 'Ten great violin concertos' (RL 00720 – see Concerts section below), but Schwann continues to list a separate American issue, coupled with the Prokofiev *Second* [on AGL1/*AGK1* 5241].

Itzhak Perlman first recorded this concerto in the mid-1960s with Leinsdorf and the Boston Symphony for RCA. Here he plays the work as a full-blooded virtuoso showpiece, and the Pittsburgh orchestra under André Previn support him to the last man. In the first movement his tempo is broader than that of Heifetz, and in the rest of the work he seems more expansive than he was in the earlier record (the new version takes 32′00″ and spills over to the second side, whereas his Boston performance took 29′15″ and fitted on one side). He is at his stunning best in the first cadenza and makes light of all the fiendish difficulties in which the solo part abounds. The balance places Perlman rather forward, but on both disc and cassette the sound is marvellously alive and thrilling. He takes a conventional view of the slow movement, underlining its passion (unlike Accardo, who is more inward-looking), and gives us an exhilarating finale.

The alternative recommendation on Decca is a most beautiful account of the work, poetic, brilliant and thoroughly idiomatic. Kyung-Wha Chung has impeccable style and an astonishing technique, and her feeling for the Sibelius *Concerto* is second to none. André Previn's accompanying cannot be too highly praised: it is poetic when required, restrained, full of controlled vitality and well-defined detail. The recording is superbly balanced and produces an unforced, truthful sound; and there is a good cassette too. This must be numbered among the finest versions of the work now available.

Salvatore Accardo brings a different perspective to bear on the whole work; the world of feeling he evokes is purer, its colours gentler and more subtle. His is a more broadly proportioned reading, though one never feels that tempi are too measured or that there is any want of momentum. Yet he conveys a greater sense of space and brings to the slow movement a quite special stillness and poetry, particularly in the closing bars. Sir Colin Davis fashions this movement in what seems to be complete harmony of spirit with his distinguished soloist, and the brass produce exactly the right kind of power and sonority. The finale is played with effortless brilliance by all concerned. On disc the recording is beautifully natural; the high-level tape transfer, however, is less refined on top, especially in the orchestral tuttis. Accardo also gives us the *Six Humoresques*, Opp. 87 and 89, and brings to them a fine sense of atmosphere and rapture. His readings have the full measure of their dreamy rhapsodizing and the 'white nights' and haunting landscape of the northern summer.

Boris Belkin is a powerful and sensitive player and brings a fiery temperament to the concerto. There are moments of exaggeration that might prove irritating, and although his playing has a Slavonic ardour and flamboyance, a boldness of attack and a spontaneity that are appealing, there are infelicities that do not improve on repetition: an ugly scoop at fig. 1 in the finale, and some less-than-true intonation in the sixths just after fig. 10 in the first movement. He inspires warm support from the Philharmonia under Vladimir Ashkenazy, and is very well recorded on disc and tape alike. But he resorts to an expressive distortion at the very beginning (playing *pp* instead of the *mf* marked) in aspiring to a rapt, other-worldly quality, then he suddenly exaggerates the earthiness of the G-string writing a couple of dozen bars later. However, the appeal of this issue is enhanced by the fill-ups, which are rarities: the *Two Serenades*, written just before the 1914–18 war, and the *Two Serious melodies*, Op. 77. These are marvellous works and are beautifully played here, with none of the zigeunerisms that mark the finale of the concerto. The two *Serenades* and the Op. 77 pieces are not otherwise available. The concerto, however, is not really as good as Kyung-Wha Chung's immaculate reading, as poetic as it is brilliant and thoroughly idiomatic.

From Szeryng, a spacious reading full of imaginative touches. Szeryng plays beautifully throughout and one's only quarrel is with his rather too measured tempo for the finale. Tovey spoke of this as 'a polonaise for polar bears', but it can hardly be said to suggest this here. Rozhdestvensky is a true Sibelian (if only someone would ask him to record a complete cycle), and the LSO play well for him. The recording has the usual Philips characteristics, a concert-hall balance, and a warm acoustic; in short it is excellent. The cassette too is one of Philips's best, with plenty of body and warmth and no constriction in the upper range. If the coupling is suitable this is a most competitive mid-priced version.

Francescatti's account is stunning in its immediacy and impact. With Bernstein fully matching the intensity of his soloist this is a performance impossible to forget. Francescatti's richness of tone is immediately evident in the opening theme and dominating the impassioned reading of the slow movement. Under such emotional stress the soloist's technique holds up with amazing security, and if this reading does not quite convey the noble assurance that Heifetz alone offers, the reading has understanding as well as power. The snag is the brightly lit recording with the solo violin well out in front, in a spotlight. The excess brilliance, however, is tempered on the excellent chrome cassette which is preferable to the disc. Francescatti's Walton coupling is no less memorable.

Ferras's performance is also a very good one. It has the advantage of being very well recorded; but, although Ferras begins the work with a winningly golden tone, when he is under stress at the end of the first movement and in the finale, his intonation and general security are no match for the superbly accurate Kyung-Wha Chung performance. But there is still much to enjoy and Ferras develops a rich, romantic tone for the main tune of the slow movement. The concerto has been recoupled for its Accolade reissue with Karajan's splendid version of *Tapiola* (see below, under *Finlandia*).

Kremer presents the *Concerto* essentially as a bravura showpiece and his is a vibrantly extrovert reading. While the recording balance places the soloist well forward, the orchestral texture has plenty of impact and good detail, and the fortissimo brass blaze out excitingly. There is undoubted poetry in the slow movement and throughout Muti gives his soloist splendid support. However, their version does not displace Perlman and Accardo, nor for that matter the Chung account which is beautifully subtle and warm. All three are more searching than Kremer and have more character, albeit in very different ways. Generally speaking, they all have more attractive couplings. The HMV XDR cassette matches the disc very closely.

A predictably good performance from David Oistrakh, but it fails to be fully competitive on grounds of recording quality, although for this reissue it is more generously coupled with an equally good version of the Tchaikovsky *Concerto*. (In the USA the original pairing with *The Swan of Tuonela* remains listed in Schwann.)

(i) *Violin concerto, Finlandia, Op. 26. Kuolema: Valse triste, Op. 44. Legend: The Swan of Tuonela, Op. 22/2. Symphonies Nos. 4–7. Tapiola, Op. 112.*
(B) *** DG 2740 255 (4). Berlin PO, Karajan, (i) with Ferras.

This box offers all the Sibelius recordings made by Karajan with the Berlin Philharmonic in the mid-1960s – at bargain price, so that there is a gain in purchasing them together rather than separately. An additional attraction is the Ferras account of the *Violin concerto* here coupled with the powerful version of *Tapiola* – originally this appeared with the *Fifth Symphony*. The strengths of the other performances are discussed below under the symphonies, but briefly the *Fourth*, *Fifth* and *Sixth* are among the very best performances on record, and the same goes for *Tapiola*. An outstanding bargain.

Finlandia; Karelia suite, Op. 11. Kuolema: Valse triste. Legends: Lemminkäinen's return, Op. 22/4; Pohjola's Daughter, Op. 49.
**(*) HMV ASD 2272 [Sera. S/*4XG* 60208]. Hallé O, Barbirolli.

Although the orchestral playing is not as polished as that of a virtuoso orchestra it is enthusiastic and has the advantage of excellent recording. *Pohjola's Daughter* is extremely impressive, spacious but no less exciting for all the slower tempi. A desirable introduction to Sibelius's smaller orchestral pieces, with admirable stereo definition.

Finlandia; King Christian II suite, Op. 27: Élégie; Musette. Kuolema: Valse triste. Pelléas et Mélisande, Op. 46: No. 8, Entr'acte.
(M) *** Decca SPA/*KCSP* 91 [Lon. STS 15159]. L. Proms O, Mackerras – GRIEG: *Collection.****

The performance of *Finlandia* is brashly exciting, but other versions make a greater impact with a more sonorous sound balance. In the rest of the pieces the sound is first-rate and the programme is sheer joy. The *Musette* from the *King Christian II suite* is enchanting, and the *Entr'acte* from *Pelléas* is almost equally delightful: both have the kind of vivid colouring which has made the *Karelia* suite so famous. The *Elegy* too is beautiful, and this attractive collection is well worth its modest cost in this clear new transfer. There is a good cassette too.

Finlandia. Kuolema: Valse triste. Legend: The Swan of Tuonela. Tapiola, Op. 112.
**(*) DG 139 019/*923 069* [id.]. Berlin PO, Karajan.

All these are familiar performances. *Valse triste* is played very slowly and in a somewhat mannered fashion. *Finlandia* is one of the finest performances available (tremendous orchestral tone from the Berliners), and the *Tapiola* is also impressive. It is a performance of great intensity and offers superlative playing. The recording too is excellent, but the disc offers short value for a full-priced record. There is a good cassette.

Finlandia; Kuolema: Valse triste; Legend: The Swan of Tuonela.
(M) *** DG Priv. 2535/*3335* 635 [id.]. Berlin PO, Karajan – GRIEG: *Peer Gynt* etc.*
(M) ** CBS 60105/*40*- [Col. MY/*MYT* 36718]. NYPO, Bernstein – GRIEG: *Peer Gynt.***

It is curious that instead of reissuing Karajan's vintage collection of Sibelius's short orchestral pieces, three only should here have been coupled with some much earlier Grieg recordings under other conductors, where the sound is rather thin and uninviting. The Sibelius items sound very well on both disc and cassette.

Bernstein's account of *Finlandia* is brilliant and exciting, but the recording sounds rather brash. *The Swan of Tuonela*, however, is beautifully played, with finesse as well as a fine sense of brooding atmosphere, and the recording here is quite spacious.

Finlandia. Kuolema: Valse triste; Legends: The Swan of Tuonela; Lemminkäinen's return. Tapiola.
**(*) HMV Dig. ASD/*TCC-ASD* 4186. Philh. O, Berglund.

Berglund's Philharmonia performances of this collection of favourite Sibelius pieces do not entirely supersede his earlier Bournemouth readings – included in his four-disc box – for not everyone will prefer the marginally slower speeds. The satisfying ruggedness remains, giving both more impact (as in *Tapiola*) and more refinement (as in *Valse triste* or the cor anglais solo of *The Swan of Tuonela*) by the new full-ranging digital recording. Because of the wide amplitude and resonance of the recording, the transfer level of the chrome cassette has been set very low to the point that the opening of *Valse triste* is almost inaudible. This apart, the sound is rich and quite vivid.

Finlandia; Legend: The Swan of Tuonela; En Saga, Op. 9; Tapiola.
*** HMV ASD/*TC-ASD* 3374 [Ang. S/*4XS* 37408]. Berlin PO, Karajan.

This almost duplicates Karajan's earlier DG Sibelius anthology, except that *En Saga* replaces *Valse triste*. This is Karajan's third recording of *Tapiola* but his first of *En Saga*, where he is a brisk story-teller, more concerned with narrative than atmosphere at the beginning; but the *lento assai* section and the coda are quite magical. *Finlandia* is superbly played and most realistically recorded. The *Tapiola* is broader and more expansive than the DG version, and at the storm section beginning at bar 513 the more spacious tempo is vindicated. The effect is altogether electrifying. The newer HMV recording is more forward and possesses great body and presence, so much so that some listeners may prefer the slightly more recessed yet atmospheric sound in the DG version. In any event, both are great performances and totally committed. There is an ugly blemish in bar 598, where some of the cellos play D sharp and others D natural. This should have been corrected. The cassette produces impressive results and has ample body and firmness.

Karelia: suite; Kuolema: Valse triste. Pohjola's Daughter, Op. 49; En Saga, Op. 9.
** Ph. 9500/*7300* 893 [id.]. Boston SO, Sir Colin Davis.

Beautifully refined and imaginative performances from the Boston orchestra, with a particularly distinguished account of *Pohjola's Daughter*; indeed, the latter ranks with the very finest performances ever recorded, though it is different from Koussevitzky's or Bernstein's. Sir Colin's maiden has real allure, Väinämöinen's struggles with his various tasks have never been more heroic. Unfortunately, the recording is (by Philips's standards) relatively wanting in clarity and detail (on both LP and cassette). Put Ashkenazy's *En Saga* alongside Sir Colin's, and one removes a gauze veil – and brightens the picture. A pity, for artistically this is first-rate.

The Oceanides, Op. 73; Pelléas et Mélisande, Op. 46: At the castle gate; A spring in the park; Pohjola's Daughter; En Saga; (i) *Luonnotar, Op. 70.*
**(*) HMV Green. ESD/*TC-ESD* 7159. Bournemouth SO, Berglund; (i) with Valjakka.

Berglund's account of *En Saga* is straightforward and unmannered and well recorded. The full, spacious recording creates a feeling of warmth in *The Oceanides* and moves its geography further south. *Pohjola's Daughter* is vivid as sound, but is a routine performance. The highlight of the collection is *Luonnotar*, where Berglund provides his eloquent soloist with genuinely imaginative orchestral support. The recording is full and vivid throughout – the famous *At the castle gate* makes a powerful impression. The cassette matches the disc in vividness, but is slightly less open at the top.

The Oceanides. Pelléas et Mélisande: suite. Tapiola.
❀ *** HMV SXLP 30197. RPO, Beecham.

The *Pelléas et Mélisande* performance is one of the classics of the gramophone. Never have Sibelius's textures sounded more luminous and magical. Beecham lavished enormous attention on details of phrasing, and the results have a special eloquence. Sibelius himself asked Beecham to record *The Oceanides*, the only one of his tone poems not directly related to Nordic mythology. This is his most poetic evocation of the sea, and this marvellous performance captures every nuance of the score. *Tapiola* has all the requisite brooding power and must be numbered among the very finest accounts committed to disc (with Kajanus, Koussevitzky and Karajan as alternatives), and the quality of these transfers (the performances date from the 1950s) completely belies their age.

Pelléas et Mélisande (incidental music): complete.
(*) Ph. 6769 045 (2) [id.]. Rotterdam PO, Zinman – FAURÉ: *Pelléas**; SCHOENBERG: *Pelleas.***(*)

The complete score is included here (including *At the seashore*) and the orchestral playing is of high quality. Zinman is undoubtedly sympathetic, but the music is just a shade undercharacterized. Nevertheless the couplings are pertinent (although not all lovers of Fauré and Sibelius are likely to respond to Schoenberg) and this is quite an attractive package.

Pelléas et Mélisande: suite.
*** DG Dig. **410 026-2**; 2532/*3302* 068 [id.]. Berlin PO, Karajan – GRIEG: *Peer Gynt suites 1 and 2.****

At last a version of Sibelius's subtle and atmospheric score that can compare with the classic Beecham version, originally dating from 1957. Indeed in certain movements, *By the spring in the park* and the *Pastorale*, it not only matches Sir Thomas but almost surpasses him. The *Pastorale* is altogether magical, and there is plenty of mystery in the third movement, *At the seashore*, omitted from the Beecham set. Although Horst Stein's fine Decca recording (see below) has vividly defined orchestral detail, the corporate response of the Suisse Romande does not begin to compare with the Berlin in sonority, ensemble and sensitivity. Some may find the opening movement, *At the castle gate*, a little too imposing, but the fervour and eloquence of the playing should win over most listeners. The recording, particularly on compact disc, is very striking indeed with greater clarity and presence. Although Beecham's record (see above) will remain indispensable for most Sibelians, the Karajan must now be a prime recommendation.

Pelléas et Mélisande, Op. 46; The Tempest (incidental music): *Prelude; Suite No. 1.*
*** Decca SXL 6912. SRO, Stein.

This record finds the Suisse Romande Orchestra in far better shape than it was in the late 1960s and early 1970s. Horst Stein secures a fine woodwind blend and a more firmly based and richer string sonority. Intonation may not be as impeccable as in the Concertgebouw – or our own Philharmonia – but it is very good. In *Pelléas et Mélisande* Horst Stein secures splendid results and (like Berglund, in his now deleted version, and Zinman) he includes *At the seashore*, intended to be played at the end of Act I and leading directly into *By the spring in the park*, which opens Act II. This is atmospheric, though without the magic of Beecham. *The Tempest* is impressive too, though we only get the *Prelude* and the *First Suite*. However, there is plenty of atmosphere, and even if *The Oaktree* is taken on the fast side, everything else is splendidly judged. The recording is of demonstration standard.

Symphonies Nos. 1–7; The Bard, Op. 64; En Saga, Op. 9; Scènes historiques, Op. 25; (i) *Kullervo, Op. 7.*
** HMV SLS/*TC-SLS* 5129 (7). Bournemouth SO, Berglund, (i) with Kostia, Viitanen, Helsinki University Ch.

Symphonies Nos. 1–7; Finlandia; Legend: The Swan of Tuonela; Tapiola.
*** Ph. 6709 011 (5) [id.]. Boston SO, Colin Davis.

The Davis set is impressive and arguably the finest of the collected editions – though Karajan's new cycle, which has yet to appear, will probably be a strong competitor. These versions of the *Third*, *Fourth* and *Sixth* are among the best – if not *the* best – before the public, and the remaining symphonies are all finely played and in general given excellent sound. Davis's feeling for Sibelius is usually matched by the orchestral response. Whatever individual reservations there may be, this is a cycle to be reckoned with, and the performances are more consistently vital and powerful than those of Berglund.

Berglund's is the only boxed set to include Sibelius's very first symphonic venture, *Kullervo*. This is an impressive five-movement piece on a Mahlerian scale: it precedes *En Saga* and contains some vividly imaginative choral writing. As for the symphonies themselves, the performances have their merits, but in almost every instance one can do better elsewhere. As recordings it would be difficult to improve on this set, and the orchestral playing is of high quality too. But judged by the highest standards, these conscientious and well-prepared versions remain just a shade too literal and earthbound to be recommended without qualification. The cassette transfers are clear and vivid. There is less warmth and richness of string timbre than on disc, and sometimes the upper range lacks something in bloom, but the choral focus in *Kullervo* is first-class, even clearer than on the LP version.

Symphony No. 1 in E min., Op. 39; Karelia suite.
*** HMV Dig. ASD/*TCC-ASD* 4097 [Ang. DS/*4XS* 37811]. Berlin PO, Karajan.
(M) *** Decca Jub. JB/*KJBC* 42. VPO, Maazel.

Symphony No. 1.
** BIS **CD 221**; LP 221. Gothenberg SO, Järvi.
(B) *(*) PRT GSGC/*ZCGC* 2058. Hallé O, Barbirolli.

Writing of Tchaikovsky, Sibelius once said 'There is much of that man in me', and it would be wrong to understate the Tchaikovskian legacy in the *First Symphony*. The slow movement is a spiritual relative of the *Pathétique symphony*, which was given in Helsinki in 1894 and 1897, even though it speaks with distinctly northern rather than Slavonic accents. Karajan does not view the early Sibelius through the eyes of the symphonist the composer was to become, but there is a sense of grandeur and vision here. In his early days Sibelius often bemoaned the fact that in Helsinki he could not enjoy the luxury of hearing a world-class orchestra, and one can only imagine how he would have thrilled to the opulence and virtuosity of the Berliners. Though one's admiration for the Maazel version is undimmed, there is an heroic dimension to Karajan's performance, that lends its claims to primary consideration a special weight. Good but not absolutely top-drawer recording. On tape the opening of *Karelia* on side one, transferred at only a modest level, is disappointingly subfusc, and the sound generally lacks sparkle; side two, containing most of the *Symphony* at a higher level, is brilliant, rich and expansive.

As a medium-priced alternative, Maazel's version leads the rest of the field. It has freshness and power to commend it, along with careful attention both to the letter and to the spirit of the score. The Vienna Philharmonic responds with enthusiasm and brilliance, and the Decca engineers produce splendid detail. The performance of the *Karelia suite* is first-rate. The cassette transfer is fairly sophisticated, but it seems not to have been remastered for its Jubilee reissue, and although the quality is full-blooded it lacks the crispness of detail of the others in this series.

No one would pretend that the Gothenburg Symphony ranks alongside the great orchestras that have recorded this symphony (Vienna, Berlin, Boston and the Philharmonia), but heaven forbid that this repertoire should be the sole preserve of the virtuoso orchestras. The Gothenburg strings are clean, well-focused in tone, lean and lithe; the wind are well-blended and the clarinet solo at the beginning is sensitively played, and there is an excellent sense of atmosphere. The first movement is finely shaped and preparation for the return of the first group in the restatement is handled with impressive power. The slow movement is restrained and all the more effective on this count and the symphony on the whole, one or two touches apart, is commendably straightforward. Neeme Järvi pulls back and is overemphatic at one bar after letter F in the finale. Better characterized than either Berglund or Gibson and very well recorded.

Barbirolli is impressively spacious in the first movement, while the melancholy of the *Andante* is affecting. However, the performance seems to lose its grip in the scherzo and the finale is disappointing, not helped by the lack of body of the Hallé string timbre, emphasized by the thin recording. The cassette transfer has a more restricted range and is bass-orientated.

Symphonies Nos. 1; 7 in C, Op. 105.

(M) **(*) HMV Green. ESD/*TC-ESD* 7095 [*No. 1* (d) Sera. S 60289]. Bournemouth SO, Berglund.

** Chan. Dig. **CHAN 8344**; ABRD/*ABTD* 1086 [id.]. SNO, Gibson.

This HMV medium-priced reissue is exceptionally generous, and the full sides have not impaired the splendidly vivid and realistic sound quality. The high-level cassette transfer also offers an impressively rich and well-detailed orchestral tapestry. Berglund's approach, rugged and steady, misses the last degree of intensity, but not the underlying nobility of Sibelius's inspiration. In the *Seventh* Berglund corrects a number of small mistakes that have crept into the Hansen score, mostly dynamic and expressive indications affecting tonal balance. As a result his performance is smoother in contour, and the warm, spacious acoustic serves to Latinize this starkest and most powerful of Sibelius's symphonies.

Sir Alexander Gibson has the advantage of excellent recording from Chandos and, in the case of the *First Symphony*, continuity. His earlier version with the Scottish National Orchestra took a whole record whereas this accommodates it (for the first time) on one side. There is an ugly edit at letter S in the first movement, where the pitch does not match, but neither this nor the patch of poor intonation in the slow movement (letter B) are as worrying as the general absence of tension and power. It has to be said that the SNO does not out-class its rivals on record and, discounting the luxury orchestras of Berlin, Vienna and Boston, the Bournemouth gives a more focused response, and the strings of the Gothenburg Orchestra on BIS produce a cleaner, finer-grained quality than those of the SNO. The *Seventh* which these artists recorded successfully in the 1960s is also deficient in electricity although in the closing pages of both symphonies Gibson draws the music together with an impressive breadth. The chrome cassette is very successful, both rich and clear, with a fine weight of string tone, especially in the *Seventh Symphony*.

Symphony No. 2 in D, Op. 43.

*** HMV Dig. ASD/*TC-ASD* 4060 [Ang. DS/*4ZS* 37816]. Berlin PO, Karajan.

(*) Decca Dig. **410 206-2; SXDL/*KSXDC* 7513 [Lon. LDR/*5*- 10014]. Philh. O, Ashkenazy.

(M) *** Decca Jub. JB 43 [Lon. JL/*5*- 41052]. VPO, Maazel.

(M) *** HMV SXLP 30414. Philh. O, Karajan.

(*) Chan. Dig. **CHAN 8303; ABRD/*ABTD* 1062 [id.]. SNO, Gibson.

(M) **(*) DG Priv. 2535/*3335* 458. Berlin PO, Kamu.

(B) **(*) Con. CC/*CCT* 7563 [Lon. STS 15098]. LSO, Monteux.
** CBS Dig. 37801 [id.]. Toronto SO, Andrew Davis.
(M) (***) Dell'Arte mono DA 9004. NBC SO, Stokowski.
(B) * PRT GSGC/*ZCGC* 2023. LPO, Pritchard.

(i) *Symphony No. 2;* (ii) *Finlandia.*
(M) *** Ph. Seq. 6527/*7311* 111 [(d) 6570/*7310* 054]. Concg. O, (i) Szell; (ii) Van Beinum.

Symphony No. 2; Legend: The Swan of Tuonela.
(M) **(*) EMI Em. EMX/*TC-EMX* 2006. Hallé O, Barbirolli.

The *Second Symphony* is exceptionally well represented on records, but the choice for a single version is essentially subjective. Not all listeners will warm to the grand (and measured) approach to the finale in Karajan's newest digital recording; Ashkenazy's performance also provokes a mixed response (as will be seen below), while Maazel's splendidly recorded Jubilee version will appeal to some more than others for its sumptuous Tchaikovskian romanticism.

Karajan's 1981 version with the Berlin Philharmonic is more spacious than his earlier reading with the Philharmonia. Tempi in all four movements are fractionally broader; nevertheless, the first movement is still a genuine *Allegretto* – much faster than with Maazel, Barbirolli or Ashkenazy – and basically in the brisker tradition of Kajanus, whose pioneering 1930 records were probably closer to Sibelius's intentions than most others. Throughout all four movements there is splendour and nobility here – and some glorious sounds from the Berlin strings and brass. The oboe theme in the trio section of the scherzo is most expressively moulded, and the finale is slower and grander than its rivals, though there is no loss of lyrical fervour. It is not as beautifully recorded as the Ashkenazy/Philharmonia account on Decca, but it is undoubtedly a performance of stature – and probably the finest of the full-price issues currently before the public. The chrome cassette transfer is faithful and wide-ranging but tends to emphasize the slightly lean orchestral textures, for the upper strings are given less amplitude and richness by EMI than on either of the Decca recordings.

We are divided in our response to the Ashkenazy version. There are no doubts about the quality of the recorded sound, which is superb. It is atmospheric, beautifully rounded in tone, and has splendid clarity, definition and depth. As for the performance, it is a passionate, volatile reading, in many ways a very Russian view of Sibelius, with Ashkenazy finding a clear affinity with the Tchaikovsky symphonies. At the very opening the quick, flexible treatment of the repeated crotchet motif is urgent, not weighty or ominous as it can be. Ashkenazy's control of tension and atmosphere makes for the illusion of live performance in the building of each climax, and the rich digital sound (recorded in the ideal acoustic of the Kingsway Hall) adds powerfully to that impression. Yet some listeners may find it more difficult to respond positively to this reading, and, like R.L., they may feel the performance is wanting in firmness of grip, especially in the slow movement, with the dramatic pauses lacking spontaneity and unanimity of response. The cassette matches the disc in richness and bloom, but the biggest climaxes seem marginally less expansive on tape. The compact disc is very impressive though not quite as fine as Ashkenazy's *Fourth Symphony*.

Maazel's account is more traditionally lush: it is sumptuously recorded and beautifully played by the Vienna Philharmonic, but his reading leans more to the romantic view of the work favoured by some virtuoso conductors. The Tchaikovskian inheritance is stressed, rather than the classical forebears. At medium price this issue is very competitive.

In its latest incarnation Szell's performance comes with a fill-up in the shape of *Finlandia*, excellently played by the Concertgebouw under Eduard van Beinum and recorded in the late 1950s. Szell's account of the *Second* still impresses by its lean tautness and grasp of architecture, though there is no want of feeling. It ranks among the best mid-price versions. It is not as richly recorded as Maazel's Jubilee version, but the quality is full and lively and makes an excellent impact.

Karajan's Philharmonia recording dates from 1960 and shows him very much at his best. It has dramatic intensity, a feeling for line and texture, and a grasp of the architecture. It is not in the least self-indulgent or excessively Italianate, and perhaps lacks the last ounce of spontaneity that marks the Barbirolli version. Yet it is freer, more expressively eloquent than Szell's version with the Concertgebouw. It goes without saying that it is extremely well, indeed superbly played, and the sound quality is remarkably vivid, rich and sonorous.

The *Second* is among the best of the Gibson cycle so far and scores, thanks to the impressive clarity and impact of the recording. Sir Alexander has been a long and doughty champion of Sibelius ever since the early 1960s and this version of the *Second* is honest and straightforward, free of bombast in the finale. Tempos are well judged and there is at no time any attempt to interpose the personality of the interpreter. The first movement is neither too taut nor too relaxed: it is well-shaped and feels right. The strings do not possess the weight or richness of sonority of the Berlin Philharmonic or the Philharmonia, and the performance as a whole does not displace the first recommendations. The cassette is first-rate, full, vivid and clean though side two (in the copy we sampled) is transferred at a lower level and needs a higher setting to make the maximum effect. The CD is impressive, one of the finest to come from Chandos. It is extremely vivid.

Okko Kamu secures highly polished and superbly refined playing from the Berlin Philharmonic; he indulges in some impulsive touches – the odd attention-seeking speed-up or slow-down – but these are not destructive. The recording here is first-class, both on disc and on cassette, bringing out the spacious sweep of the finale to great effect.

Barbirolli's reading with the Hallé Orchestra is also very well recorded and stresses the Slav ancestry and Italianate warmth of the work. Its fill-up is an additional attraction for the singing *Swan of Tuonela*; Barbirolli's vocalizations are clearly audible. The Eminence cassette matches the disc fairly closely, taming the rather bright treble a little. It is only marginally less refined in detail.

Monteux provides a first-rate bargain recommendation. The performance is thrilling, yet unmannered, the sound brightly lit, lacking the last degree of richness, but still excellently balanced. There is a matching tape. The alternative bargain issue from Pritchard dates from 1969. The sound is quite acceptable on both disc and tape, but the performance is not really distinguished, with the slow movement in particular failing to take wing, and the performance generally uninvolving.

A good, all-round performance from the Toronto orchestra under Andrew Davis. Speeds are sensible though the *Allegretto* could be a good deal faster (as was Kajanus's pioneering 1930 record which had the composer's imprimatur). The strings are richer-toned and better-tuned than those of the SNO, and the recording is well balanced and the perspective natural. However, in terms of musical personality there is nothing here to challenge Karajan, Szell and others in the catalogue.

The Stokowski account of the *Second Symphony* with the NBC Symphony Orchestra first appeared on HMV in the mid-1950s. By no stretch of the imagination can the first movement be called an *Allegretto* in his hands but there are marvellous things here all the same. The development has rarely sounded more mysterious and in the finale he makes the wind passage just after letter D sound exceptionally eloquent. The slow movement is passionate and intense and very different in its approach from Toscanini's, which was overdriven. The sound here has plenty of body and, given its age, is remarkably good. Here is a performance of real personality and character, well worth exploring.

Symphonies Nos. 3 in C, Op. 52; 5 in E flat, Op. 82.

(M) *** HMV Green. ESD/*TC-ESD* 7094. Bournemouth SO, Berglund.

Berglund's is a generous coupling, the more attractive at medium price. The *Fifth Symphony* is given a rugged, lustily exuberant performance, lacking a little in atmosphere and bite, with the slow movement a shade heavy, but with a superb build-up to the blazing coda of the finale. The *Third* emerges even more than usual as Sibelius's *Pastoral*, springy and genial in the first movement, freshly rustic in the slow movement, joyful and easy-going in the finale. The recording is remarkably opulent considering the length of sides. The cassette too, transferred at a high level, matches richness and body with excellent range and detail; moreover the brass has striking presence.

Symphonies No. 3; 6 in D min., Op. 104.
*** Ph. 9500 142. Boston SO, Sir Colin Davis.
(M) *(**) Decca Jub. JB/*KJBC* 44. VPO, Maazel.

Colin Davis's account of the *Third Symphony* triumphantly leads the field. He judges the tempi in all three movements to perfection; no conductor has more effectively captured the elusive spirit of the slow movement or the power of the finale. In this respect he surpasses even the authoritative Kajanus set of pre-war days. He is superbly recorded too. The *Sixth* is impressive, though not as poetic in feeling as Karajan's, even if the Boston recording is more vivid.

In the *Third Symphony* Maazel keeps a firm grip on the proceedings. He moulds phrases naturally and without affectation, and his build-up in the finale is most impressive. The slow movement is not quite poetic or reflective enough; he has little success in achieving the tranquillity and rapture (at fig. 6) that made Kajanus's set such a memorable experience. The *Sixth* is much less impressive than the *Third*; Maazel does not penetrate beneath the surface and seems to have little sympathy for this most elusive and refined of Sibelius's scores. It is a pity that this issue is only partly successful; on disc the recording is first-class, and apart from a short passage where the timpani cause a little muddle in the climax of the first movement of No. 3, the cassette transfer is sophisticated.

Symphony No. 4 in A min., Op. 63; Finlandia, Op. 26. (i) *Luonnotar, Op. 70.*
C *** Decca Dig. **400 056-2**; SXDL/*KSXDC* 7517 [Lon. LDR/*5*- 71019]. Philh. O, Ashkenazy, (i) with Söderström.

Ashkenazy achieves great concentration of feeling in the *Fourth.* The brightness of the Philharmonia violins and the cleanness of attack add to the impact of this baldest of the Sibelius symphonies, and Ashkenazy's terracing of dynamic contrasts is superbly caught in the outstanding digital recording. Like his other Sibelius readings this one has something of a dark Russian passion in it, but freshness always dominates over mere sensuousness, and as ever Ashkenazy conveys the spontaneity of live performance. There is splendid drama and intensity throughout, and this is a very impressive performance. The couplings add to the special attractions of this issue; *Finlandia* is made fresh again in a performance of passion and precision, and Elisabeth Söderström is on top form in *Luonnotar*, a symphonic poem with a voice (although some ears may find her wide vibrato and hard-edged tone not entirely sympathetic). The cassette offers impressively rich sound but has slightly less range at the top: the transients in *Finlandia* are less telling. The compact disc has most impact of all with the silent background adding to the dramatic impact of the performance and the dynamic contrasts even more telling. The close balancing of certain instruments is more noticeable, but the Kingsway Hall acoustic is demonstrated as ideal for this score, with the brass both biting and sonorous. The voice of Söderström in *Luonnotar* is given extra immediacy.

Symphony No. 4; Legend: The Swan of Tuonela, Op. 22/2.
(M) *** DG Acc. 2542/*3342* 128 [2535/*3335* 359]. Berlin PO, Karajan.

Karajan's Berlin account from 1965 gains in stature with every hearing. This music offers no false consolation, and like many great works of art has a serious, forbidding exterior that dispenses with any gesture towards the listener. No performance surpasses this in splendour of orchestral sound and magnificence of colour. At first, one feels that its very opulence is not a useful tool in uncovering the secrets of this strange world; instead of the well-modulated, rich tone of the Berlin strings one longs for the cold, disembodied sound that Beecham evoked in his famous performance in the 1930s. But over the years, this reading haunts one – and it is to the Karajan that one turns for certain qualities: perhaps most of all the music. It still sounds superb and the scherzo comes off more successfully than in the later HMV version. The tape transfer is made at a high level, and the richness and body of the orchestral texture are matched by the overall clarity. This is first-class.

Symphony No. 4; Tapiola, Op. 112.
(M) *** Decca Jub. JB/*KJBC* 45. VPO, Maazel.
**(*) HMV ASD/*TC-ASD* 3485 [Ang. S/*4XS* 37462]. Berlin PO, Karajan.

The *Fourth* is the most impressive of Maazel's Sibelius cycle. The orchestral tone is less richly upholstered than that of the Berlin Philharmonic in Karajan's HMV account, and Maazel brings to the music great concentration and power: the first movement is as cold and unremitting as one could wish, and throughout the work Maazel comes as close to the atmosphere and mystery of this music as almost anyone since Beecham. Apart from the slow movement, which could be a little more poetic, and one or two small points, there are no real reservations to be made. The recording here is superbly opulent and vivid. Maazel also gives a most impressive account of *Tapiola*. It is not so atmospheric as Karajan's at the outset, but it grows in power and impact as it proceeds. Maazel takes the famous storm section very slowly, and it gains immeasurably from this. The cassette transfer of Maazel's performances is of Decca's highest quality, with the most refined detail, the orchestral sound given splendid weight and atmosphere.

In some ways Karajan's re-recording of the *Fourth Symphony* for HMV must be counted controversial. He gives broadly spacious – and highly atmospheric – accounts of the first and third movements, a good deal slower than in his earlier DG version (see above). He conveys eloquently the otherworldly quality of the landscape in the third movement, even if in atmosphere the Davis account is more natural and intense. The first movement undoubtedly has great mystery and power. The recording is superb and the tape transfer is highly successful (one of HMV's best cassettes). Karajan's *Tapiola*, which is discussed above under its alternative coupling with *Finlandia* (ASD/*TC-ASD* 3374), is hardly less impressive, despite the error in bar 598.

Symphonies Nos. 4; 5 in E flat, Op. 82.
** Chan. Dig. ABRD/*ABTD* 1074. SNO, Gibson.

Chandos offer good value by coupling these two symphonies together, as did Ormandy and the Philadelphia way back in the mid-1950s. Moreover they provide a recording of impressive clarity and presence – disc and chrome cassette are closely matched, with the upper range only slightly less smooth on tape – which reflects great credit on the Chandos engineers, even if the results are not so immaculately blended as on Ashkenazy's Decca recordings, where every strand, though clearly audible, blends into a perfectly focused whole. The playing of the Scottish orchestra lacks something in refinement (there is for instance a moment of poor intonation from the cellos in the *Fourth*, and horn fluffs in the finale) but the impact and authenticity of these readings are not in doubt, even if there is some lack of tension and power.

Symphony No. 5 in E flat, Op. 82; Andante festivo; Karelia overture, Op. 10.
*(*) BIS **CD 222**; LP 222. Gothenburg SO, Järvi.

Symphony No. 5; Finlandia; Kuolema: Valse triste.
(M) *** DG Acc. 2542/*3342* 109. Berlin PO, Karajan.

Symphony No. 5; Night ride and sunrise, Op. 55.
C *** HMV Dig. **CDC 747006-2**; ASD/*TC-ASD* 4168 [Ang. DS/4XS 37883]. Philh. O, Rattle.

Symphony No. 5; En Saga.
*** HMV ASD/*TC-ASD* 3409 [Ang. S/*4XS* 37490]. Berlin PO, Karajan.
C *** Decca Dig. **410 016-2**; SXDL/*KSXDC* 7541 [Lon. LDR/*5-* 71041]. Philh. O, Ashkenazy.

Simon Rattle's record of the *Fifth Symphony* has collected numerous prizes in Europe and deserves them all. Right from the very outset one feels that he has found the *tempo giusto*. Ashkenazy conducting the same orchestra is just fractionally more measured, and that slight difference is enough to affect the sense of flow. Moreover, one notices that the woodwind are better blended in this version whereas in the Decca the clarinets slightly obtrude. Rattle is scrupulous in observing every dynamic nuance to the letter and, one might add, spirit. What is particularly impressive is the control of the transition between the first section and the scherzo element of the first movement where the listener is often made all too conscious of the changing of gears and releasing of levers. This relationship is ideally balanced and enables Rattle to convey detail in just the right perspective. There is a splendid sense of atmosphere in the development and a power unmatched in recent versions, save for the Karajan. The playing is superb and the recording to match. *Night ride* is very good but not quite as outstanding; however, this is undoubtedly an exceptional *Fifth*. The cassette quality is rather soft-grained, the upper range less open than the disc. The CD gains on the LP in range, depth and presence. It is strikingly natural and vivid, one of the best compact discs to come from EMI so far.

Karajan's DG version of the Sibelius *Fifth* is a great performance. We have tended to underrate it in the past, but the 1965 recording sounds even fresher and more vivid in this new Accolade transfer. The orchestral playing throughout is glorious, and the effect is spacious and atmospheric. Karajan finds an engrossing sense of mystery in the development section of the first movement, and there is jubilation in the finale. Karajan has now recorded this symphony four times (1952, 1960, 1965, 1978), but this third version strikes us as the most successful all round, though there are many impressive qualities in the others. At medium price and with a superb *Finlandia* and *Valse triste*, this is quite a bargain. The sound on cassette too is admirably full and clear.

The first movement of the symphony is broader and more spacious in Karajan's HMV version, and he achieves a remarkable sense of its power and majesty. His transition from the work's first section to the 'scherzo' is slightly more abrupt than in the 1965 recording, and the tempi generally in the work's first half are rather more extreme. The variety of tone-colour and above all the weight of sonority that the Berlin Philharmonic have at their command are astonishing, and the bassoon lament in the development section finds the Berlin strings reduced to the merest whisper. Both the slow movement and finale are glorious and have real vision, and the recording is excellent (as indeed it is in the 1965 DG version too). Some Sibelians are worried by the richness and sensuousness that Karajan brings to this score, but the sheer power and depth of this reading should convince. The performance of *En Saga*, which is discussed above under its alternative coupling with *Finlandia*, is no less compelling. The transfer to tape offers satisfying rich orchestral sound; although the detail of climaxes lacks the last degree of definition, the refinement does not slip.

Ashkenazy's performance is outstandingly well recorded, with fine, spacious and well-detailed digital sound. His reading is a thoroughly idiomatic one and disappoints only in terms of the balance of tempi between the two sections of the first movement. This is a fine rather than a great perfonnance. Ashkenazy's *En Saga* is the best version of that work now in the catalogue, and so, when one considers also the outstanding excellence of the recording, this issue will obviously have strong appeal. The chrome cassette is also very impressive, although in *En Saga* the bass is not so cleanly focused as on the disc. The compact disc must be listed among the best of Decca's earlier releases. The entry of the horns in the finale – perhaps the most impressive part of the performance – is especially telling, but overall the fullness of the sound is matched by its immediacy and warmth of atmosphere, with no trace of digital edginess, although the brass has bite as well as richness of sonority.

Neeme Järvi is broad and spacious in the first movement; indeed, he almost calls to mind the Tuxen account with the Danish Radio orchestra from the early days of LP. There is, however, insufficient sense of mystery in the development movement and the slow movement is a bit laboured. On the whole this is not to be preferred to the Bournemouth Orchestra and Berglund, and is certainly no match for Rattle or Karajan. At the same time, it is a useful issue in that it also includes the *Andante festivo* (1922), a broad dignified piece for strings (the only work that Sibelius himself recorded) and the *Karelia* overture, not otherwise available at the time of writing. The Gothenburg orchestra has the advantage of a superb acoustic: it has both warmth and clarity.

Symphonies Nos. 5; 7 in C, Op. 105.

(M) **(*) EMI Em. EMX/*TC-EMX* 41 2050-1/*4*. Hallé O, Barbirolli.

(M) **(*) Decca Jub. JB/*KJBC* 46. VPO, Maazel.

(M) ** HMV SXLP 30430 (*No.* 7 mono). Philh. O, Karajan.

The Eminence reissue offers one of Barbirolli's finest Sibelius records. In No. 5 Sir John draws playing of high quality from the Hallé Orchestra. Here they are obviously on top form and play with evident enthusiasm and conviction. Sir John takes an unhurried view of the first movement and one feels a certain lack of the requisite tension and mystery. In the first two movements he is less powerful than, say, Karajan, but the sparer, less opulent tone of the Hallé has a more authentic Nordic sound to commend it. Sir John's finale is admirably broad and extremely imposing. He takes 32′55″ overall, whereas Maazel rushes through in a mere 27′05″. A fine performance, not as compelling as Karajan's DG version but much more idiomatic than Maazel's. The *Seventh* does not match Maazel in breadth and majesty, but its feeling of power and sense of inevitability increases as the work proceeds. The EMI recording sounds slightly fuller on tape than on disc, with the upper range tamed a little, without losing the character of the sound.

Maazel's *Fifth Symphony* is terribly fast, though it sets out at the same tempo as Karajan's. His second movement is twice as fast as Karajan's versions; hence there is little sense of space or breadth – or for that matter mystery – in this performance. The *Seventh*, on the other hand, is marvellous: this is the greatest account of the work since Koussevitzky's 78 r.p.m. recording, and has a rugged, epic power that is truly thrilling. Indeed the closing pages are as fine as Koussevitzky's, and no praise could be higher. The recording is superlative, with an excellent cassette transfer of striking range and definition – well up to the high standard of this excellent Jubilee series.

Karajan's second account of the *Fifth Symphony* with the Philharmonia was recorded in 1960, while the *Seventh* comes from 1955 and is in mono. The actual sound quality in both is excellent and the playing of the Philharmonia is really distinguished. This version of the *Fifth* is not to be preferred to the 1965 Berlin recording but nonetheless runs it very close. In the *Seventh*, however, there is some loss of intensity. Karajan's tempi are broad and spacious and more measured in the faster sections than we are accustomed to. The C major idea (at the *allegro molto moderato* section just after fig. N) will be a shade too *dolce* for some tastes. The later Berlin reading is stronger in this respect though there are, of course, many good things here all the same.

Symphonies Nos. 6 in D min., Op. 104; 7 in C, Op. 105.

(M) *** DG Acc. 2542/*3342* 137 [139032]. Berlin PO, Karajan.

Despite a certain pallor in the recording of the *Sixth*, it is highly recommendable. Karajan gives a poetic and committed account of this elusive symphony, and his reading has stood the test of time very well. There is concentration here, and an ability to convey the pale sun of the Finnish summer landscape. The *Seventh* too comes off well, though Karajan's is a spacious view that misses the intensity and electricity of Koussevitzky's famous early recording in the quicker sections. However, this is a more powerful and convincing reading than Karajan's Philharmonia version from the 1950s. The cassette is of DG's top quality, matching the disc closely.

Symphony No. 7; Tapiola.

C *** Decca Dig. **411 935-2;** SXDL/-*KSXDC* 7580 [Lon. LDR/*5* 71080]. Philh. O, Ashkenazy.

Ashkenazy's warmly expressive view of Sibelius may diminish the sense of rugged strength in these two culminating works, but the *Seventh Symphony* in particular has rarely if ever been presented on record with such richness and weight, with a wonderful feeling of apotheosis in the closing pages, helped by digital recording outstanding even by the standards of Decca engineers working with the Philharmonia in Kingsway Hall. *Tapiola* – taken at a more measured pace than usual – also brings a performance which in its spontaneous expressiveness is the more compelling when one disregards preconceptions, a powerful reading beautifully played. The chrome cassette is one of Decca's finest, of demonstration standard throughout, with radiant strings and rich brass, and a glowing overall bloom which in no way blurs the internal detail. This is every bit the equal of the LP, although the compact disc is most impressive of all.

String quartet in D min. (Voces intimae), Op. 56.
*** O-L DSLO 47 [Lon. CS 7238]. Fitzwilliam Qt – DELIUS: *Quartet.****
(M) **(*) None. H 71140 [id.]. Claremont Qt – ELGAR: *Quartet.***(*)

Although there is an early quartet in B flat, Op. 4, and some other juvenilia, Sibelius composed only one mature quartet. The title *Voces intimae* refers to the three *ppp* chords of E minor in the slow movement which pinpoint the withdrawn, rapt quality of the piece. Since its pioneering recording by the Budapest Quartet in 1933 there have been a number of others; but none is in the same league as this record. These young players give a deeply felt and no less deeply considered account. In their hands the work becomes bigger in scale and more symphonic in feeling (Sibelius's diaries reveal dissatisfaction with one or two passages as quartet-writing). There is a wide range of sonority and a scrupulous regard for dynamic gradations. The opening is played very much *con amore*, but it is evident from the cello entry (bar 18) that this is going to be a big-boned account that declares its proximity to the *Fourth Symphony*. The generally measured tempo is justified in the sleeve-note by Alan George, the violist of the quartet, who bases their choice of tempi on metronome markings that the composer himself gave to the Griller Quartet. The 34′10″ the Fitzwilliam take has been splendidly accommodated by the Oiseau-Lyre engineers, for the recording is superb. This is a thought-provoking and impressive record which deserves the widest currency.

The Claremont Quartet give a finely poised account; the opening breathes naturally, and the inwardness and poetry in the slow movement are matched by a Lemminkäinen-like dash in the finale. This is a more conventional approach than the Fitzwilliam's, but it remains satisfying in its own way. The recording is good, but not as fine as the Oiseau-Lyre.

PIANO MUSIC

Kyllikki, Op. 41; Impromptus, Op. 5; Sonata, Op. 12; Finnish folksongs.
** BIS LP153. Tawaststjerna.

Sibelius's piano music is not otherwise represented on record now that Erwin Laszlo's RCA has disappeared and though much of it is uncharacteristic, there are many miniatures worth investigating, even apart from the celebrated Op. 67 *Sonatinas*. Erik Tawaststjerna, the son of the Finnish scholar, is an authoritative and perceptive advocate of this repertoire, and it is good news that he is recording the complete *oeuvre*. The second disc (BIS LP169) couples the Opp. 24 and 34, the latter much later than their opus number implies; the third (BIS LP195) offers Opp. 58 and 40, the former a much underrated set which has some rewarding and unusual numbers; and the fourth (BIS LP196) brings us to the *Sonatinas*, Op. 67, and two beautiful sets, Opp. 74 and 76. The recordings are not in the very first flight: the first, made in Nacka Aula, Sweden, does not give the sound enough room to expand, and the Op. 58 set is not really well focused.

CHORAL MUSIC

(i) *Kullervo symphony, Op. 7, Kuolema* (incidental music), *Op. 44; Scene with cranes, Swanwhite suite, Op. 54.*
*** HMV SLS 807 (2) [Ang. SB 3778]. Bournemouth SO, Berglund, (i) with Kostia, Viitanen, Helsinki University Male Voice Ch.

The *Kullervo symphony* is an ambitious five-movement work for two soloists, male-voice choir and orchestra, some seventy or so minutes long, which Sibelius wrote at the outset of his career in 1892. It brought him national fame and a commission from Kajanus that resulted in *En Saga*. After its first performance Sibelius withdrew the score and it was never performed in its entirety until 1958, a year after his death. It is revealed here as an impressive work, full of original touches, particularly in its thoroughly characteristic opening. Naturally there are immaturities: the slow movement is over-long and overtly Tchaikovskian. What impresses, however, is the powerful vocal writing, and the astonishing purity and dark, black tone of the Finnish choir. There are many exciting facets of Sibelius's early style to be found in this rewarding score, which is spectacularly well recorded. The fourth side offers some attractive rarities that enhance the value of this impressive set.

Sinding, Christian (1856–1941)

Suite, Op. 10.
*** HMV ASD/*TC-ASD* 3933 [Ang. SZ/*4ZS* 37663]. Perlman, Pittsburgh SO, Previn – SIBELIUS: *Concerto*.***

Heifetz recorded this dazzling piece in the 1950s, and it need only be said that Perlman's version is not inferior. Sinding's A minor *Suite* was originally composed in 1888 for violin and piano, and subsequently scored for double woodwind, two horns, strings and (in the finale) a harp. Its blend of archaism and fantasy sounds distinctively Scandinavian of the 1890s yet altogether fresh – and quite delightful. Such is the velocity of Perlman's first movement that one wonders whether the disc is playing at the right speed. Stunning virtuosity and excellent recording; the cassette too is brilliantly clear, its forward balance matching the disc.

Smetana, Bedřich (1824–84)

Symphonic poems: *Carnival in Prague; Haakon Jarl, Op. 16; Richard III, Op. 11; Wallenstein's Camp, Op. 14.*
(M) *** DG 2543 814 [id.]. Bav. RSO, Kubelik.

These symphonic poems can be recommended to those who are interested in the *Má Vlast* cycle. *Carnival in Prague* was written in 1883; the other three are much earlier works, dating from around 1860. The music is melodramatic, with a flavour of Dvořák if without that master's imaginative flair. The most spectacular is *Wallenstein's Camp* with its opportunities for offstage brass fanfares, very well managed here. This is very enjoyable in its ingenuous way, but perhaps the most distinguished piece here is *Haakon Jarl*, which has a strong vein of full-blooded romanticism. The playing is first-class throughout, the conductor's approach is fresh and committed, and the recording has excellent body and atmosphere.

Czech dances: *Furiant; The Little Hen; The Lancer; Obkročak; Skočná.* Polkas: *Louisa; Dahlia; From the Student's Life; The Country Woman; Bettina: To our Girls.*
(M) ** Sup. 110 1225. Brno State PO, Jilek.

The Czech dances were originally piano pieces and they have been orchestrated by other hands. This is all sparkling music, vividly played; the recording is clear but lacking something in bloom and atmosphere.

Festive symphony in E.
(M) *(*) Sup. 50875. Czech PO, Sejna.

Smetana's *Festive symphony* quotes from the Austrian national anthem (the tune by Haydn), and like many occasional pieces (it was composed for, but never played at, the wedding of the Emperor) it is not very distinguished music, apart from an attractive scherzo. This performance makes the most of it, but the recording is not one of Supraphon's best.

Má Vlast (complete).
*** HMV SLS 5151 (2) [Ang. SB 3870]. Dresden State O, Berglund – DVOŘÁK: *Scherzo capriccioso* etc.***
(M) **(*) DG Priv. 2726 111 (2) [2707 054]. Boston SO, Kubelik.
(M) ** Decca Jub. DJB/*KDJBC* 2004 (2). Israel PO, Weller.
(M) ** Sup. Dig. 1110 3431/2. Czech PO, Smetáček.

Paavo Berglund's complete *Má Vlast* with the Dresden Staatskapelle is undoubtedly the finest recording of this elusive cycle of symphonic poems to have appeared in stereo. Whereas so many recorded performances have done well by *Vltava* and *From Bohemia's Woods and Fields* and then fallen short on the other four pieces, it is in these less well-known works that Berglund is most impressive. Indeed if there is a criticism of this set it is that *Vltava*, although splendidly played, seems slightly undercharacterized alongside the other sections of the score. The opening *Vyšerad* is most beautifully played, full of lyrical evocation and atmosphere, while *Sárka* is arrestingly dramatic. *Tábor* and *Blaník* are played together and so often in previous accounts they have become engulfed in rhetoric: but not here. Berglund never lets the forceful rhythms hammer the listener into the ground, and the national feeling that is the basis of their inspiration here sounds surgingly jubilant. The closing pages of *Tábor* are beautifully managed, and the pastoral interlude in *Blaník* is engagingly lightweight, so that when the closing chorale appears it has a lilting step and conjures up memories of *The Bartered Bride* rather than bombastic militarism. The end of the work has a joyous release. Berglund does not shirk the melodrama, but he never lets it get the better of him. The Dresden orchestra plays magnificently and the recording is rich and full-blooded. The two Dvořák bonuses are no less engagingly played (the *Third Slavonic rhapsody* is delightfully fresh), and the recording is equally successful here.

Kubelik's DG performance is much more perceptive and penetrating than his earlier Decca set. He is careful to temper the bombast which too readily comes to the surface in this music (in *Tábor* and *Blaník* especially), and his skill with the inner balance of the orchestration brings much felicitous detail. The performances of the two unquestioned masterpieces of the cycle, *Vltava* and *From Bohemia's Woods and Fields*, are very well made, and the orchestral playing throughout is first-class. Just occasionally a touch more flair would have brought the orchestral colours out more vividly, but this lack of colour is partly caused by the DG sound, which, although brilliant and clear, rather lacks sumptuousness and warmth of texture. However, this has the advantage that the louder, brassy passages are not allowed to degenerate into noise.

Weller's Decca set is admirably recorded with nothing to choose in quality between LPs and matching chrome cassettes. But the opening *Vyšehrad* is curiously unevocative, and while Weller provides excellent detail in *Vltava* the Israel Philharmonic strings fail to captivate the ear in the glorious theme which spaciously represents the river. Weller is at his best in the later, more melodramatic pieces, and he secures generally good orchestral playing throughout. But in the mid-priced range, choice goes to Kubelik, even though the Decca sound is richer than the DG recording.

Smetáček's approach is broad and spacious, seeking to emphasize the music's epic qualities rather than finding sharpness of characterization. There is certainly an absence of melodrama and the closing pages of *Blaník* have a feeling of apotheosis. The orchestral playing is assured, and the resonant ambience is warmly attractive if not providing quite the vivid detail one expects with a digital recording. In the last resort this is not among the more memorable versions of Smetana's cycle.

Má Vlast: Vltava.
*** HMV ASD/*TC-ASD* 3407 [Ang. S/*4XS* 37437]. Berlin PO, Karajan – DVOŘÁK: *Symphony No. 9.****
(M) *** HMV SXLP/*TC-SXLP* 100491-1/*4* [Ang. S 35615]. Berlin PO, Karajan – DVOŘÁK: *Symphony No. 9.****

As a fill-up for an excellent version of Dvořák's *New World symphony* Karajan's account of Smetana's most popular piece is comparably warm and expressive, characteristically refined but richly spontaneous-sounding. The recording is warm to match rather than analytical. The lack of refinement of detail is more noticeable on cassette than on disc. This recording is, of course, at premium price, yet Karajan's 1958 version of the tone-poem is still one of the best around and comes up sounding remarkably fresh sonically. The balance is very musical and the perspective natural, for it comes from the vintage years of stereo, and it is also coupled to an excellent *New World.*

Má Vlast: Vltava. The Bartered Bride: Overture; Polka; Furiant.

(M) *** Decca SPA 202 [Lon. STS 15409]. Israel PO, Kertesz – DVOŘÁK: *Slavonic dances.****

Má Vlast: Vltava. The Bartered Bride: Polka; Furiant; Entry of the Comedians.

(*) DG Sig. 2543/*3343* 509 [id.]. Berlin PO, Karajan – DVOŘÁK: *Slavonic dances.*(*)

** CBS 60103/*40*- [MY/*MYT* 36716]. Cleveland O, Szell – DVOŘÁK: *Carnaval* and *Dances.***

With Kertesz these pieces are exceptionally vivid. The separate entries in the overture are beautifully positioned by the stereo, and the ambience makes the background rustle of all the strings weaving away at their fugato theme sound quite captivating. *Vltava* too is very brilliant, with fast tempi, yet not losing its picturesque qualities. The recording is perhaps overbright, but it glows in Decca's best fashion. It is also a shade over-reverberant but not seriously so. With its excellent coupling this is a bargain at medium price.

Karajan's excellent 1969 account of *Vltava* is coupled here with dances by both Smetana and Dvořák. The sound balance favours brilliance somewhat at the expense of warmth, with disc and chrome tape closely matched.

A strongly characterized version of *Vltava* from Szell and plenty of sparkle in the dances. The playing has flair, as well as polish, and if the bright, clear sound had been richer this would have earned the fullest recommendation.

Piano trio in G min., Op. 15.

(M) *** Ph. 6570/*7310* 920. Beaux Arts Trio – CHOPIN: *Piano trio.****

Smetana's *Piano trio* is a fine work, and given such powerful advocacy as that of the Beaux Arts Trio (and in particular their fine pianist, Menahem Pressler) and the superbly vivid and truthful Philips recording, there is nothing in the way of a strong recommendation. The Chopin is not a mature work but the coupling is still an attractive and logical one. There is an adequate cassette, but the transfer level is lower than it need be.

String quartets Nos. 1 in E min.; 2 in D min.

(M) *** Sup. 4112 130. Smetana Qt.

The personnel of the Smetana Quartet has remained the same for a quarter of a century, and their playing on the Supraphon disc is authoritative, idiomatic and fresh. The opening of the *Second Quartet* is especially convincing here, with scrupulously observed dynamic shading, and generally their approach is bold and committed. With good recording this is thoroughly recommendable.

Choruses: *The Dedication; Festive chorus; My Star; Our Song; The Peasant; The Prayer; The Renegade I and II; Song of the Sea; The Sunset; The Swallows Arrived; The Three Riders; Two Slogans.*

(M) ** Sup. 112 1143. Czech Philharmonic Ch., Veselka.

Apart from three short items, all these choruses are for male voices. The writing has plenty of vigour, and the singing here makes up in enthusiasm for what it lacks in refinement. The idiomatic quality of the Czech language brings a special colour to the music, and with translations provided this is an enjoyably spontaneous concert.

The Bartered Bride (complete, in Czech).

*** Sup. Dig. 1116 3511/3 [id.]. Beňácková, Dvorský, Novák, Kopp, Jonášová, Czech Philharmonic Ch. and O, Košler.

The digital Supraphon set under Košler admirably supplies the need for a first-rate Czech version of this delightful comic opera. The recording acoustic may be rather reverberant for comedy, but the orchestral sound is warm and the voices are given an attractive bloom, while the performance sparkles from beginning to end with folk rhythms crisply enunciated in an infectiously idiomatic way. The cast is strong, headed by the characterful Gabriela Beňácková as Mařenka and one of the finest of today's Czech tenors, Peter Dvorský, as Jeník. Miroslav Kopp in the role of the ineffective Vašek sings powerfully too. As Kecal the marriage-broker, Richard Novák is not always steady, but his swaggering characterization is most persuasive.

The Bartered Bride (complete, in German).
*** EMI 1C 149 30967/9. Lorengar, Wunderlich, Frick, Ch. and Bamberg SO, Kempe.

The Bartered Bride sung in German seems an unlikely candidate for a top recommendation, yet in the event this vivacious set is a remarkable success. This is an opera where the choruses form a basic platform on which the soloists can build their performances, and here they are sung with splendid lilt and gusto, Kempe's warm, guiding hand maintaining the lyrical flow perfectly. The discipline of the chorus and the lack of rigidity in the melodic line almost completely compensate for the absence of the idiomatic colouring that the Czech language can bring, and certainly the soloists here offer far more sophisticated singing than is likely from a Czech cast. Pilar Lorengar is most appealing as Mařenka and Fritz Wunderlich is on top form as Jeník. Gottlob Frick gives a strong, earthy characterization of Kecal, the marriage-broker. The whole production goes with a swing, and the high spirits do not drown the lyricism – Wunderlich and Lorengar see to that. The recording is bright and vivid, yet has plenty of depth. This is not an opera that calls for much 'production', but the entry of the comedians is particularly well managed.

For those buying the complete opera in Czech there is an admirable selection of highlights available (EMI 1C 061 29002).

The Kiss (complete).
(M) **(*) Sup. 1416 3341/3. Děpoltová, Vodička, Haken, Zítek, Márová, Brno Janáček Op. Ch. and O, Vajnar.

Though the tunes are rarely so memorable as those in *The Bartered Bride*, this comic opera – based on the most tenuous of plots with the heroine withholding a kiss from her beloved – has much the same fizz and charm. It receives a vigorous and colourful performance from the Brno company, generally well sung with Děpoltová a sweet and young-sounding heroine and Vodička a powerful tenor hero, strained only occasionally at the top. Slavonic wobbles are the exception happily, though Václav Zítek is a culprit, not helped by rather close – if vivid – recording of the voices. Orchestra and chorus are placed more distantly.

The English translation in the libretto is comprehensible despite some fractured English.

Libuse (complete).
(M) *(*) Sup. 50701/4. Subrtova, Kniplová, Bednár, Kroupa, Zídek, Prague Nat. Theatre Ch. and O, Krombholc.

Written for the opening of the National Theatre of Prague in 1881, this strongly nationalist piece (the plot is concerned with the Czech royal dynasty) has a limited appeal for the non-Czech listener. The characters are two-dimensional and the opera itself has little real dramatic development. The cast here is strong by Czech standards, but the recording is only fair. For the specialist rather than the ordinary opera-lover.

The Two Widows (complete).
(M) ** Sup. 1122 041/3. Sormová, Machotková, Zahradniček, Svehía, Horáček, Prague Nat. Th. Ch. and O, Jílek.

Rather cloudy recording mars what would otherwise be an endearingly bright and vigorous account of Smetana's country comedy about two widows. Though so Czech in its flavour, it was in fact drawn from a French source, and amid the rustic atmosphere there is something of Gallic sparkle. The two widows are here well contrasted, Sormová clear and agile if at times a little shrill, Machotková darker of tone but with an edge as well. The tenor Zahradniček is not so fresh-toned as the role of Ladislav really requires, but Jílek's direction is lyrical as well as energetic.

Soler, Antonio (1729–83)

3 Keyboard sonatas (orch. Halffter).
(M) ** HMV Green. ESD/*TC-ESD* 165105-1/4. Mexican State SO, Bátiz – PONCE: *Concierto***(*); CHAVEZ: *Zarabanda.****

Halffter made these transcriptions of Soler *Sonatas* in the early 1950s for the Mexican choreographer José Limon. Though amiable enough, they are not in themselves of great interest and few are likely to invest in this record for their sake. They are admirably played and well recorded (perhaps a bit too forward as far as balance is concerned), but the appeal of the record lies elsewhere. The cassette matches the disc closely.

Keyboard sonatas: in C min.; in C sharp min.; in D; in D min.; in D flat; in F sharp; Concerto in G; Fandango.
(M) **(*) Mercury SRI 75131. Puyana.

Rafael Puyana uses a modern harpsichord which features, alongside the damping 'harp' stop, a means of creating dynamic contrast without altering the timbre. He plays flamboyantly, with very free rubato, the articulation demonstrating the greatest bravura, not just in the sparkling passage-work but also in the subtle changes of colour and light and shade within phrases. This is not a recital for eighteenth-century purists, but Soler's music springs vividly to life, its melodic resource and its Spanish qualities emphasized equally. Try the opening *F sharp major Sonata* with its Catalonian folk influence, or the exciting *Fandango* which makes an evocative flamenco-style mid-side interlude and which, even more than the *Sonatas*, suggests affinities with the guitar. The recording is admirably faithful, but it is essential to cut the volume well back; the character of the instrument then emerges fully, with its bright treble and resonantly pungent lower registers.

Somervell, Arthur (1863–1937)

Clarinet quintet.
*** Hyp. A 66011. King, Aeolian Qt – JACOB: *Clarinet quintet.****

Sir Arthur Somervell, knighted by King George V for his work as a civil servant in charge of musical education, here shows what a skilful composer he was within his chosen Brahmsian idiom. This is just the sort of work (first performance 1919) which deserves resurrection on record when fashion no longer matters. The bubbling finale is a special delight, with Thea King and the Aeolian Quartet at their most persuasive, helped by very good recording.

Maud (song cycle).
*** Pearl SHE 527 [id.]. Carol Case, Ibbott – BUTTERWORTH: *A Shropshire Lad.***(*)

John Carol Case gives tenderly understanding performances of this long sequence of songs setting a poem of Tennyson much misrepresented (how can the very name Maud have any but comic associations?). Frustrated love draws sympathetic chimes from the composer, whose often difficult piano accompaniments (understandingly played by Daphne Ibbott) present an equal partnership. Good recording.

Sor, Fernando (1778–1839)

Étude in A, Op. 6/12; Fantaisie, Op. 7; Fantaisie elegiaque, Op. 59; Fantasia on 'Ye banks and braes', Op. 40; Sonata in C, Op. 15b.
*** Mer. E 77006. Artzt.

Alice Artzt is an outstandingly compelling guitarist, whose range of tone on a 1931 Hauser instrument is exceptionally beautiful. This collection of works by Sor – most of them rarities – gives an excellent idea why this composer, a Spanish contemporary of Beethoven, is regarded as the father of the modern guitar repertory. First-rate recording.

Sousa, John Philip (1854–1932)

Marches: Ancient and Honorable Artillery Company; Black Horse Troop; Golden Jubilee; Glory of the Yankee Navy; Gridiron Club; Kansas Wildcats; Manhattan Beach; National Game; New Mexico, Pride of the Wolverines; Rifle Regiment; Sesquicentennial Exposition march.
(M) **(*) Mercury SRI/*MRI* 75064 [id.]. Eastman Wind Ens., Fennell.

Expert playing and lively, vintage recording make this readily recommendable with the reservation that many of these marches are 'marching' marches rather than listening music: some of the invention here is unmemorable. One of the more striking items is the *Ancient and Honorable Artillery Company*, which incorporates *Auld lang syne* as its middle section. There is an excellent cassette.

Marches: Belle of Chicago; Black Horse Troop; The Crusader; El Capitan; The Fairest of the fair; The Gladiator ; High School Cadets; The Invincible Eagle; King Cotton; The Liberty Bell; Manhattan Beach; Semper fidelis; Stars and Stripes Forever; Washington Post.
*** HMV Dig. ASD/*TC-ASD* 165146-1/*4* [Ang. DS/*4XS* 38016]. HM Royal Marines Band, Hoskins.

The EMI digital recording is impressive with full sonority and sparkling transients (though the XDR tape is slightly less lively and has more bass-emphasis). The performances are admirably spirited and have plenty of character although the style is British with its self-conscious swagger, in the place of transatlantic exuberance. The programme is well chosen to include many favourites, with *The Stars and Stripes* presented with some sophistication as well as flair.

Marches: Bullets and Bayonets; The Gallant Seventh; High School Cadets; Invincible Eagle; Liberty Bell; Nobles of the Mystic Shrine; Our Flirtations; The Picadore; Riders for the Flag; Sabre and Spurs; Solid Men to the Front; Sound off.
(M) *** Mercury SRI/*MRI* 75047 [id.]. Eastman Wind Ens., Fennell.

One or two favourites here, but basically this is an adventurous collection, and the zest of the playing always carries the day. Again first-rate Mercury sound, although this is not a record to play all at once.

Marches: El Capitan; High School Cadets; The Invincible Eagle; King Cotton; Liberty Bell; Manhattan Beach; The Picadore; Semper fidelis; Stars and Stripes Forever; Washington Post.
(M) ** Decca SPA 404. Grenadier Guards Band, Harris.

These are fresh performances in the English manner, well played and alive. The sound is crisp and clear, and the cassette transfer is good too, with only a marginal loss of crispness in the transients.

Spohr, Ludwig (1784–1859)

Clarinet concerto No. 1 in C min., Op. 26.
(M) ** O-L SOL 60035 [id. PSI]. De Peyer, LSO, Sir Colin Davis – WEBER: *Clarinet concerto No. 2.***

Clearly modelled on Mozart's masterpiece, Spohr's *Concerto* primarily exploits the lyrical side of the clarinet. The main theme of the first movement, besides being of the kind that stays in the memory, is perfectly conceived for the instrument, and the *Adagio* – very much Mozart-patterned – is charming too. The finale is a captivating Spanish rondo. It chuckles its way along in sparkling fashion and then surprises the listener by ending gently. Gervase de Peyer is just the man for these suave melodic lines, and he is ably supported by Sir Colin Davis and the LSO. The stereo is well detailed and the recording convincing, except for a suspicion of stridency in the tuttis.

Clarinet concertos Nos. 1 in C min., Op. 26; 2 in E flat, Op. 57.
*** Argo ZRG 920 [id. PSI]. Pay, L. Sinf., Atherton.

Antony Pay and the London Sinfonietta give fluent, expert and thoroughly musical accounts of these concertos. The performances have the requisite lightness and wit, and do justice to the charm the concertos possess. The *Second* is perhaps not quite as memorable as the *First*, but still makes an enjoyable coupling. Good recording.

Clarinet concerto No. 4 in E min.
*** Mer. E 77022. King, ECO, Francis – MOZART: *Clarinet concerto.***(*)

Spohr's *Fourth Clarinet concerto* admirably illustrates his amiable and facile invention, above all in the *Rondo al espagnol* finale, a witty bolero which gives Thea King a splendid opportunity for display. So does the elaborate *Larghetto* slow movement, though there the performance sounds less spontaneous. Nonetheless, so stylish an account of so rare a work, well coupled with the Mozart and well recorded, is most welcome.

Violin concerto No. 8 in A min. (Gesangszene), Op. 47; Concertante in A flat for violin, harp and orchestra.
*** Erato STU/*MCE* 71318. Amoyal, Nordmann, Lausanne CO, Jordan.

Pierre Amoyal gives a fine-spun, lyrical yet intense account of the *Gesangszene concerto*, by far the best of those currently available – and the only one really worth listing. The *Concertante in A flat*, which Spohr wrote for his wife, the harpist Dorette Schneidler, makes an attractive fill-up. Amoyal is perhaps rather more forward than he would be if the balance were ideal, and tutti sound a little opaque; but there is no need to withhold a full three-star recommendation here. The *A minor Concerto* is one of Spohr's best-proportioned and most classically conceived works in spite of its innovatory features. The cassette matches the disc quite closely.

Nonet in F, Op. 31.
(M) **(*) Ph. 6570/*7310* 882. Berlin Philharmonic Octet (augmented) – WEBER: *Clarinet quintet.***

Spohr's invention is at its freshest here and his propensity for chromaticism is held in reasonable check. The Berlin performance is polished and beautifully balanced, though the approach is perhaps a shade too serious. Excellent sound, on disc and tape alike.

Nonet in F, Op. 31; Octet in E, Op. 32.
*** CRD CRD 1054/*CRDC 4054* [id.]. Nash Ens.

These works are both otherwise available in German performances, but not coupled together. They are inventive and charming pieces – and by no means mere note-spinning. They are very elegantly played here; the Nash Ensemble do not attempt to invest this music with more expressive feeling than it can bear. Quality throughout is natural and lifelike. This is civilized music, well worth having. The cassette is naturally balanced and agreeably smooth, lacking only the last fraction of upper range compared with the disc.

Octet, Op. 32.
(M) **(*) Ph. 6570/*7310* 884 [id.]. Berlin Philharmonic Octet – MENDELSSOHN: *Octet.* ***

The Berlin performance was originally issued spread over two sides; now it reappears coupled to an excellent account of Mendelssohn's *Octet* (by I Musici). The Berlin playing is polished and attentive to detail, but a trifle strait-laced. The sound is good on disc, but detail is less clear on the cassette, as the modest transfer level has reduced the sharpness of focus.

Piano and wind quintet in C min., Op. 52; Septet in A min., for flute, clarinet, horn, bassoon, violin, cello and piano, Op. 147.
*** CRD CRD 1099/*CRDC 4099* [id.]. Ian Brown, Nash Ens.

The Nash Ensemble has made a speciality of recording rarities from the early nineteenth century, neglected more for the difficulty of assembling a particular grouping of instruments than for any lack of musical merit. These two pieces are among Spohr's most delightful, both the sparkling *Quintet* and the more substantial but still charmingly light-hearted *Septet*. Ian Brown at the piano leads the ensemble with flair and vigour and the recording quality is outstandingly vivid on disc and tape alike, although side one of the cassette (the *Septet*) brings just a hint of roughness of focus at fortissimos.

Stainer, John (1840–1901)

The Crucifixion.
(M) *** Argo SPA 267. Lewis, Brannigan, St John's College, Camb., Ch., Guest; Runnett.

The music of Stainer's famous *Crucifixion* (written in 1887) is central to the tradition of nineteenth-century English oratorio and owes not a little to the Mendelssohn of *Elijah*. It is not melodically distinguished and includes such harmonic clichés as the cadence at the climax of *Fling wide the gates, the Saviour waits* (but one cannot be surprised at that, since the couplet is not the happiest choice of rhyme). There are five hymns in which the congregation is invited to join and these are included on the Argo record. Owen Brannigan is splendidly dramatic and his voice makes a good foil for Richard Lewis in the duets. The choral singing is first-class and so is the recording.

Stamitz, Johann (1717–57)

(i) *Clarinet concerto in B flat; Sinfonia pastorale in D, Op. 4/2; Symphonies: in D, Op. 3/2; in G.*
*** O-L DSLO 505 [id.]. AcAM, Hogwood; (i) with Hacker.

Burney spoke of Johann Stamitz as having 'pushed art further than anyone had done before him', and during his short life he made the Mannheim orchestra the finest in Europe. The *G major Symphony* is early; the *Sinfonia pastorale*, which quotes a Czech Christmas carol and includes descriptive effects such as a peal of bells and a peasant bagpipe drone, was published posthumously in the 1770s. The *Clarinet concerto* is no less delightful. (The horn parts are conjectural and there was at one time some doubt as to the work's authenticity. It was thought to be by Johann's son, Karl.) Alan Hacker plays it expertly on a period instrument and the orchestra also plays on authentic instruments, and at a lower pitch; A = 430 is used in this performance. Most stylish and accomplished playing from all concerned, beautifully recorded.

Stamitz, Karl (1745–1801)

Flute concertos: in A min.; in D.
(*) RCA RL/*RK* 25315 [ARL 1/*ARK 1* 3858]. Galway, New Irish CO, Prieur – C. P. E. BACH: *Sonata.**

The *G major Flute concerto* (not the same work as was recorded by Wanausek on Turnabout) is quite an ambitious piece, well wrought and with an expressive *Andante* and a genial rondo finale. The other concerto here is shorter and less individual. James Galway lends his charisma to both, and the accompaniments are admirably stylish; but this is not great music. The recording is good, the flute forward, the orchestra bright and clear if lacking the last degree of warmth. The cassette is vivid but needs a degree of taming, especially in the *D major Concerto* on side one.

Stanford, Charles (1852–1924)

Clarinet concerto in A min., Op. 80.
*** Hyp. A/*KA* 66001. King, Philh. O, Francis – FINZI: *Concerto.****

This Hyperion issue offers a particularly attractive coupling of a masterpiece by Gerald Finzi and this lighter but highly engaging work by Stanford. He wrote his *Clarinet concerto* for Richard Mühlfeld, the artist who inspired the late clarinet works of Brahms, but it remained unpublished for nearly a century and was totally neglected. In three linked sections it shows Stanford characteristically fastidious in developing his ideas; the clarinet repertory is not so rich that such a well-written piece should be neglected, particularly as the final section throws aside inhibition and presents more sharply memorable themes in a warm, late-romantic manner. Thea King's crisp-toned playing is most stylish, and the accompaniment thoroughly sympathetic. The recording is rather reverberant but otherwise attractively full and vivid; there is no appreciable difference in sound quality between disc and cassette.

Symphony No. 3 in F min. (*Irish*), *Op. 28.*
*** HMV ASD/*TC-ASD* 4221. Bournemouth Sinf., Del Mar.

This *Third* and most celebrated of the seven symphonies of Stanford is a rich and attractive work, none the worse for its obvious debts to Brahms. It was sheer bad luck that the *Irish symphony* appeared in 1887, only a year after Brahms's *Fourth*, for whether accidentally or not Stanford's slow movement has a close similarity in one of its themes to the main theme of Brahms's. The ideas are best when directly echoing Irish folk music, as in the middle two movements, a skippity jig of a scherzo and a glowing slow movement framed by harp cadenzas, while the finale gives an attractive forward glance to Stanford's pupils, Holst and Vaughan Williams. Norman Del Mar directs a performance as warm and ripe as the recording. The cassette is excellent, full, vivid and clear.

3 Rhapsodies for piano, Op. 92.
** Pearl SHE 546. Parry – PARRY: *Shulbrede tunes* etc.**

The *Three Rhapsodies* are as ambitious as they are neglected. They make considerable demands on the player, though only the *Francesca movement* rhapsody really justifies the effort. The *Beatrice portrait* (the work is inspired by Dante's *Inferno*) is pretty thin. The music dates from the first decade of the present century, and though it would be an exaggeration to hail it as important, there is no doubt that lovers of English music will find it of real interest.

A Fire of turn (song cycle), *Op. 139: excerpts.* Songs: *Heraclitus. An Irish idyll.* Irish songs and ballads: *Colonel Carey; A lament; Londonderry air; The ploughman's whistle; Trottin' to the fair; The zephyr's blast. The merry month of May. A Sheaf of songs from Leinster, Op. 140: A soft day. 3 Songs, Op. 175: A song of*

the bow; Drop me a flower; The winds of Bethlehem. Songs of Erin, Op. 76: The blackbird and the wren. Songs of Old Ireland: The confession; Jenny; My love's an arbutus; The willow tree.
** Hyp. A 66049. Griffet, Benson.

Trottin' to the fair and *A soft day* have always remained in the song-recitalist's repertoire, but many of the other songs are relatively little-known. This, the first of two Hyperion discs of Stanford, has the more immediately appealing items. Griffet's voice is not an easy one to record and, for all his intelligence and sensitivity, the colouring is rather thin and unvaried.

Magnificat and Nunc dimittis in A, Op. 12; Anthems: *For lo I raise up, Op. 145; Ye choirs of new Jerusalem, Op. 123; The Lord is my Shepherd; 3 Motets, Op. 38; Motets, Op. 135/1 and 3; Motet: O living will.*
**(*) Hyp. A/*KA* 66030. Worcester Cath. Ch., Hunt; Trepte (organ).

This characteristic collection of Stanford's church music brings uneven inspiration – with even some operetta overtones – but there are more than enough pieces which represent the Anglican tradition at its most compelling, even in easy-going performances like these. Mellow recording to match. The cassette is first-class in every way.

Songs of the sea, Op. 91; Songs of the Fleet, Op. 117.
**(*) HMV ASD/*TCC-ASD* 4401. Luxon, Bournemouth SO Ch. and O, Del Mar.

This is a very welcome coupling of Stanford at his most uninhibitedly vigorous. The four *Songs of the sea* are the more immediately memorable in their boisterous way (complete with male chorus), but the *Songs of the Fleet* (also setting Newbolt poems but with SATB chorus) make a pleasant sequel. Luxon's voice is caught a little grittily by the microphone and the chorus is on the dry side too, but Del Mar's understanding of the idiom (as in the *Irish Symphony*) makes for vigorous and enjoyable results. On cassette there is a vivid presence for the solo voice but the choral focus is less well defined.

Stanley, John (1712–86)

6 Organ concertos, Op. 10.
*** CRD CRD 1065/*CRDC 4065* [id.]. Gifford, Northern Sinfonia.

John Stanley published these six concertos in 1775, towards the end of his long career as organist and composer. He gave the option of playing the solo part on the harpsichord or fortepiano, but this is essentially organ music, and these bouncing, vigorous performances, well recorded as they are on the splendid organ of Hexham Abbey, present them most persuasively. No. 4, with its darkly energetic C minor, is particularly fine. The cassette is of first-class quality, matching the disc closely.

Steffani, Agostino (1654–1728)

Duets: *E perchè non m'uccidente; Già tu parti; Io voglio provar; Libertá! Libertá!; M'hai da piangere un di; No, no, non voglio se devo amare; Placidissime catene; Tu m'aspettasti al mare.*
*** DG Dig. Arc. 2534 008 [id.]. Mazzucato, Watkinson, Esswood, Elwes; Curtis, Moller.

Steffani was one of the leading Italian composers of the latter half of the seventeenth century and served various courts as both composer and diplomat; his output includes several operas and a quantity of sacred music (he was made a nominal bishop in 1708 but continued with his diplomatic career). He composed over eighty duets, most of which are relatively late. Five can be shown as having been composed in Brussels (1698–1700) where he was Hanoverian Ambassador. The eight duets recorded here are delightfully inventive and fresh and make a strong impression, thanks to the charm and expertise of these performances which are very persuasive indeed. They are well recorded too, and will repay with much pleasure the curiosity of readers who investigate them.

Steiner, Max (1888–1971)

Film scores: *Casablanca* (suite); *The Big Sleep: Love Theme; The Caine Mutiny: March; Key Largo* (suite); *Passage to Marseilles: Rescue at Sea; The Treasure of the Sierra Madre* (suite); *Virginia City* (excerpts). (Also includes: Waxman: *To Have and Have Not* (excerpts); *The Two Mrs Carrolls* (excerpts). Hollander: *Sabrina* (excerpts). Young: *The Left Hand of God: Love theme*. Rozsa: *Sahara: Main title sequence*.)
(M) ** RCA Gold GL/*GK* 43439 [AGL 1/*AGK 1* 3782]. Nat. PO, Gerhardt.

This collection concentrates on the key Humphrey Bogart movies and certainly shows Steiner's versatility. The changes of mood in the five brief sequences from *The Treasure of the Sierra Madre* are mirrored most imaginatively. However, the evocative piano solo so famous in *Casablanca* is not very successful here, although there is some touchingly romantic lyrical writing in the *Key Largo* sequence. Among the items by other composers the Waxman excerpts and the eloquent Victor Young melody written for *The Left Hand of God* stand out. But this is one of the least repeatable of Gerhardt's compilations. Performances and recordings are well up to standard; the cassette is not as refined as the disc at both ends of the spectrum in some of the biggest climaxes. It also omits the illustrated notes supplied within the LP sleeve.

Gone with the Wind: extended excerpts.
(M) *** RCA Gold GL/*GK* 43440 [ARL 1/*ARK 1* 0452]. Nat. PO, Gerhardt.

In 1939 Max Steiner wrote for *Gone with the Wind* the first really memorable romantic theme tune to be indelibly associated in the public mind with an epic movie. As introduced here in the title sequence, played with sweeping grandiloquence and sumptuously recorded, it cannot fail to involve the listener. It was imaginative of Steiner not to associate his most potent musical idea with one or more of the principal characters, but instead to centre it on Tara, the home of the heroine. Thus he could work it as a leitmotiv and have it return again and again through a complex score of some two and a half hours to remind the audience nostalgically that Tara represented permanence and continuity against a complex backcloth of changing human fortunes. It says something for the quality of Steiner's tune that its ability to haunt the memory remains after its many reappearances. The rest of the music is professionally tailored to the narrative line and makes agreeable listening, although the quality of the lyrical invention inevitably becomes more sentimental as the film nears its close. As ever, Charles Gerhardt is a splendid advocate and he secures fine playing and obvious involvement from his orchestra. The recording is both rich and brilliant, although there is less body of sound on the cassette than the LP. The cassette also omits the illustrated leaflet giving the film's background and synopsis.

Stenhammar, Wilhelm (1871–1927)

Piano concerto No. 2 in D min., Op. 23.
*** EMI 4E 063 32484. Solyom, Mun. PO, Westerberg – LISZT: *Totentanz*.***

Stenhammar was a pianist as well as a composer and conductor, and in his youth he was a formidable exponent of the Brahms *D minor Concerto*. Brahms can be discerned here and there in this concerto, though his is not the only influence; there are moments when one is reminded of Mendelssohn and, more particularly, Saint-Saëns. There is no want of brilliant keyboard writing, though the ballad-like figure that dominates the first movement is not one of Stenhammar's strongest ideas. There is also an excessive reliance on sequence that draws attention to itself, notably in the delightful scherzo. But if the concerto has less depth than the *Second Symphony*, there are moments of genuine individuality that shine through some of the conventional and less fresh invention. This performance is worth three stars, as is the recording. The work, however, is not as rewarding as the other Stenhammar works below.

Serenade for orchestra, Op. 31; (i) *Florez and Blanzeflor* (ballad), *Op. 3.*
❀ *** EMI 4E 061 35148. Swedish RSO, Westerberg, (i) with Wixell.

The *Serenade for orchestra*, written during the First World War, shows Stenhammar's invention and his mastery of orchestral resource at their very best. The newcomer to Stenhammar's music will find traces of Brahms and Reger in the Swedish composer as well as something of the gentleness of Fauré and the dignity of Elgar. His sensibility is distinctly northern, however, and his personality, though not immediately assertive, becomes more sympathetic and compelling as one comes to grips with his music. He was a man of the orchestra, and his experience shows in every bar of this work, and there is an exuberance about these ideas as well as a vein of poetry and fantasy. The *Romance* is a beautifully wrought movement, full of nostalgia and that gentle melancholy so characteristic of the Swedish sensibility. This performance is committed and eloquent; the Swedish Radio Symphony Orchestra is a very fine body. The recording is impressive, with much greater clarity and definition than in the old Kubelik record on DG. The fill-up is an early piece whose pages are crossed by the shadows of *Parsifal* and *Tristan*. It is beautifully sung by Wixell. This is the kind of record that deserves to reach a wide audience, who would surely respond if they only had the opportunity of making its acquaintance.

Symphony No. 1 in F.
*** BIS LP/*MC* 219 [id.]. Gothenburg SO, Järvi.

Stenhammar's *First Symphony* comes from 1902–3, and after its première in Stockholm there were plans for Hans Richter to conduct it with the Hallé Orchestra. Before this, however, the composer determined to revise it (he had just heard Sibelius's *Second Symphony* and had been bowled over by it), but never found time to do so. (In addition to his composition, he was much in demand as a pianist and conductor.) Had he done so, he would doubtless have reduced its length from the 54 minutes it takes, but might not have improved it. There are fleeting reminders of Brahms, of whom Stenhammar was an outstanding interpreter, and even of Berwald, whom he did much to champion. One is reminded of Bruckner in the breadth and nobility of the coda of the first movement, and in the charming *Allegro amabile* he even touches on the world of Elgar. But it is not so much the reminders of others that resonate in the mind as the emergence of the real Stenhammar that makes the appearance of this symphony so welcome. The horn writing is particularly original and imaginative – as, indeed, it is in the *Serenade*. For all its length, it at no time outstays its welcome. The performance is beautifully recorded, naturally balanced and very lifelike, and the playing totally committed. The cassette is also first-class.

Symphony No. 2 in G min., Op. 34.
*** Cap. CAP /*TC-CAP1* 1151. Stockholm PO, Westerberg.

Symphony No. 2; Overture, Excelsior!, Op. 13.
*** BIS **CD 251**; LP 251. Gothenburg SO, Järvi.

This is a marvellous symphony. It is an exact contemporary of Nielsen's *Fourth* and Sibelius's *Fifth* but resembles neither. It is direct in utterance; its ideas have splendid character and spirit; and there is a sense of forward movement, and the breadth and spaciousness of a symphonist with firm, secure roots. Stenhammar's classical sympathies lend his symphony strength; his feeling for nature gives it a distinctive sense of vision. Some of his music has a quality of reserve that masks his underlying warmth, but that is not the case here: the melodic invention is fresh and abundant, and the generosity of spirit it radiates is heart-warming. The Stockholm Philharmonic under Stig Westerberg play with conviction and eloquence; the strings have warmth and body, and they sing out as if they love playing this music. The wind are very fine too. The recording is vivid and full-blooded even by the digital standards of today: as sound, this record is absolutely first-class, and in terms of musical interest, its claims are scarcely less strong. The cassette transfer is generally well managed, although it needs a bass cut. But the upper range is not muffled.

The Gothenburg Symphony was Stenhammar's own orchestra and it was with them that he gave the first performance of this glorious symphony in 1915. Neeme Järvi takes an altogether brisker view of the first movement than Westerberg on Caprice (his overall timing is 42′37″ as opposed to the latter's 46′55″) but the playing is spirited and the recording very good indeed, though not quite as distinguished as on the Caprice rival. The special attraction of this issue, however, is the *Overture, Excelsior!*. This dates from 1896, the period of the *Second Quartet*, and it was first given by Nikisch and the Berlin Philharmonic, no less. It is an opulent but inventive score in the spirit of Strauss and Elgar and is played with enormous zest. In its LP form this makes a useful alternative to the Caprice disc, though it does not displace it. However, a compact-disc release is announced as this volume goes to press but not in time for us to sample it; and this, of course, has the field to itself.

String quartets Nos. 1 in C, Op. 2; 2 in C min., Op. 14; 3 in F, Op. 18; 4 in A min., Op. 25; 5 in C (Serenade), Op. 29; 6 in D min., Op. 35.
*** Cap. CAP 201-3/*TC-CAP 11201-3*. Fresk Qt; Copenhagen Qt; Gotland Qt.

Stenhammar was an active chamber musician as well as conductor and solo pianist, and it was his association with the Aulin Quartet which led to his interest in the quartet medium. The *First* (1894) shows him steeped in the chamber music of Beethoven and Brahms, though there is a brief reminder of the shadow of Grieg. It is a well-crafted work, its discourse civilized without being as yet personal. The *Second* is far more individual and one can detect the ardent voice of the real Stenhammar. By the *Third* and *Fourth*, arguably the greatest of the six, the influence of Brahms and Dvořák is fully assimilated and the composer thought highly enough of the latter to dedicate the work to Sibelius, who returned the compliment with his *Sixth Symphony*. The *Fourth* reflects that gentle melancholy which lies at the heart of Stenhammar's sensibility. The *Fifth* is the shortest, and Nielsen paid it the compliment of arranging it for full strings (and conducting it too). The *Sixth* comes from the war years when the composer was feeling 'worn out and deeply depressed' (as Dr Bo Wallner's copiously illustrated booklet, included with the set, tells us), though there is little evidence of this in the music. The Copenhagen Quartet play this marvellously, though the Frydén version (see below) takes a shade more time over the scherzo, allowing its ideas to be more distinctly articulated. Those who admire, say, the quartets of Nielsen, Suk and Fauré will feel at home with this beautifully produced set. Performances are generally excellent as indeed is the recording. Those wanting to sample the quartets singly can do so in the cassette format where they are coupled thus: Nos. 1 and 5 (Fresk); 2 and 6 (Copenhagen); 3 and 4 (Gotland). The sound quality is hardly less fine than in the disc versions. These quartets are the product of a cultivated mind and a refined sensibility. It takes a little time to get to know them well, but their reticence is well worth overcoming.

(i) *String quartet No. 6 in D min., Op. 35;* (ii) *Visor och Stämmingar, Op. 26.*
*** EMI 4E 053 35116. (i) Frydén Qt; (ii) Saeden, Ribera.

It is good to see that the last few years have brought a renaissance of interest in Stenhammar's music. This issue gives us the *Sixth* and last of the quartets, written in 1916 – a finely wrought piece, well worth investigating, but slow to yield its rewards, rather as is Fauré's late chamber music, yet profoundly satisfying when one has come to terms with it. *Visor och Stämmingar* (*Songs and Moods*) is earlier – from the period 1908–9 – and is inventive and often charming. It is beautifully sung by Erik Saeden and the recording, though not new (it was made in 1970), is perfectly acceptable. The *Quartet* recording is of later provenance and sounds excellent.

Stockhausen, Karlheinz
(born 1928)

Der Jahreslauf (concert version for 14 musicians, tape and sound projectionist).
*** DG 2531 358 [id.]. Ens. dir. composer.

This is one excerpt from Stockhausen's massive seven-day operatic cycle – part of the Tuesday episode from *Licht*. The first performance of this section was in Tokyo in 1977 using a Gagaku Ensemble with such instruments as zithers, lutes and shawms. This chamber version has instead harpsichord, guitar and three each of harmoniums, piccolos and soprano saxophones, plus percussion. Fascinating as the result is as sheer sound, it really needs visual help, but the bright, clear recording captures the events very effectively including short spoken passages (one demanding applause from the audience) and a surreal passage where a tape of Glenn Miller-like sounds is superimposed.

Sternklang (*Park music for 5 groups*).
*** DG 2707 123 (2) [id.]. Various artists dir. composer.

Sternklang, lasting over two hours, is designed as an extended ritual of meditation. Ideally the five groups of instruments are spread around an open-air setting, and a stereo recording can only approximate to what the composer intended towards 'sinking the individual into the cosmic whole, a preparation for beings from the stars and their arrival'. If that sounds pompous, Stockhausen does at least vary the mood more sharply than usual, with even some humour intended when perfect cadences are piled on each other in dance-like patterns. The virtuoso performance has the right tension and commitment, recorded as well as it can be in a conventional studio.

Donnerstag aus Licht.
*** DG 2740 272 (4) [id.]. Gambill, Meriweather, Holle, Ch., O, dir. composer.

One needs patience to appreciate so enormous a project as *Licht*, Stockhausen's seven-day operatic cycle. This Thursday episode, sharply eventful, has obvious concentration in its direct musical expression. The central character is the archangel, Michael, with the first Act devoted to his childhood, 'moon-eve' and examination, Act II to Michael's journey around the earth (with trumpet and orchestra), and Act III to Michael's return home representing finally Judgement Day and the end of time. The recording, made on different occasions mainly at live performances, is hardly a substitute for the full visual experience, but the originality of Stockhausen's aural imagination, not least in his use of voices, is brilliant and the sound is vivid.

Stradella, Allesandro (1644–82)

Sinfonia avanti in D (*Il Barcheggio*); *Sinfonia a tre in A min.; Sonata a quatro in D* (for 2 cornetts, 2 violins and continuo); *Sonata a otto viole con una tromba in D; Sonata di viole in D* (for 2 violins and lute).
(M) ** Ph. Dig. 9502/*7317* 074. Capella Clementina, Müller-Brühl.

A colourful figure, Stradella shares one distinction with Palestrina: his life inspired the composition of an opera – in his case by Flotow rather than Pfitzner. In his youth he was an accomplished musician (singer, violinist, harpsichordist, lutenist) as well as composer, and enjoyed the patronage of a number of noble families (he was himself of high birth). His patrons included Queen Christina of Sweden. He eloped with a pupil, the fiancée of a Venetian nobleman who hired assassins from whom he managed to escape, but a subsequent affair led to his murder at the age of thirty-seven. He is an important figure historically and played a significant role in the development of the concerto grosso. It must be said, however, that the thematic material of these (generally well-played) pieces is resolutely triadic and obstinately unmemorable, and the fact that every piece, save one, is in D major does not help to lend variety.

The recording is very good, but the cassette less so; indeed, it is only of acceptable quality.

Straube, Rudolf (1717–c. 1785)

Sonatas Nos. 1–3 for guitar and continuo.
(M) **(*) CBS 61842 [(d) M 31194]. Williams, Puyana – HAYDN: *Guitar quartet.****

This is routine stuff, eighteenth-century musical wallpaper, far from unpleasing but totally inconsequential. It is all expertly played and well (though forwardly) recorded. The cassette transfer is lively, but here even more than on the disc the resonant recording of the harpsichord is slightly tiresome.

Straus, Oscar (1870–1954)

Ein Walzertraum (*A Waltz Dream:* operetta; complete).
**(*) EMI 1C 157 29041/2. Rothenberger, Gedda, Fassbaender, Brokmeier, Anheisser, Moser, Bav. State Op. Ch., Graunke SO, Mattes.

Oscar Straus has no connection with the famous Strauss family; his more natural affinity is with Franz Lehár. They were born in the same month and year, and *A Waltz Dream* was specifically written to challenge the success of *The Merry Widow*. It is not its equal, of course, but the score is tuneful and vivacious, and although this recording contains more dialogue than is ideal (and no libretto is provided, only a synopsis of the plot), it remains good entertainment, especially with such a distinguished cast. The recording is lively, but the voices are very forward, so that some of the offstage effects are rather primitive and not well focused. There is a highlights disc available too (EMI 1C 061 28809).

Strauss, Franz (1822–1905)

Horn concerto in C min., Op. 8.
(M) ** Decca Jub. JB/*KJBC* 17. Tuckwell, LSO, Kertesz – R. STRAUSS: *Horn concertos.***(*)

This concerto by Franz Strauss, Richard's father, has its moments, but it shows a distressing tendency to fall into the style of the cornet air with variations. There are some bright ideas in the work too, of course, but nothing to stop the score being put back in the attic where it rightly belongs. The cassette transfer is clear and detailed in spite of a fair degree of resonance.

Strauss, Johann, Snr (1804–49)
Strauss, Johann, Jnr (1825–99)
Strauss, Josef (1827–70)
Strauss, Eduard (1835–1916)

(All music listed is by Johann Strauss Jnr unless otherwise stated)

Cinderella (*Äschenbrodel;* ballet, rev. and ed. Gamley; complete); *Ritter Pásmán* (ballet music).
**(*) Decca Dig. D 225 D 2/*K 225 K 22* (2) [Lon. LDR/*5*- 72005]. Nat. PO, Bonynge.

Strauss did not live to finish his only full-length ballet. Most of the first Act was completed, but the rest was pieced together and scored by Joseph Bayer. This version has been further revised and edited by Douglas Gamley. It would be nice to have discovered a hidden masterpiece, but this is not it (Mahler was so unimpressed that he even doubted the score's authenticity, though he revised that view later). Bonynge does his utmost to engage the listener and secures warm, elegant and sparkling playing. He is superbly recorded; both discs and cassettes offer demonstration quality. But as the *Ritter Pásmán* ballet suite, which is much more memorable, shows, *Cinderella* is inconsequential, though pleasing enough for background listening.

COLLECTIONS OF WALTZES, POLKAS, etc.

(Listed in alphabetical order under the name of the conductor and then in numerical order using the manufacturers' catalogue numbers.)

Annen polka, Op. 117; An der schönen blauen Donau (*Blue Danube*) *waltz, Op. 314; Geschichten aus dem Wiener Wald* (*Tales from the Vienna Woods*) *waltz, Op. 325;* Overtures: *Die Fledermaus; Der Zigeunerbaron; Pizzicato polka* (written with Josef Strauss). STRAUSS, Johann, Snr: *Radetzky march, Op. 228.*
(B) **(*) PRT GSGC/*ZCGC* 2008. Hallé O, Barbirolli.

These performances have a genuine Viennese lilt and are full of the warmth that comes from affectionate familiarity. Those who enjoyed Sir John's Manchester Viennese concerts will find that he managed to capture much of the spontaneity of those occasions in this well-planned concert. Each side begins with an overture, presented with great panache and vivacity, and after the march or polkas comes one of the two greatest waltzes. And the performance of the *Blue Danube* is stunning – there is no better on record. Highly recommended, in spite of dated recording (1958). The cassette matches the disc fairly closely, although the recording's lack of upper range is rather more noticeable on tape, especially on side one.

Waltzes: (i) *An der schönen Blauen Donau; Frühlingsstimmen* (*Voices of spring*)*;* (ii) *Geschichten aus dem Wiener Wald;* (i) *Kaiser* (*Emperor*)*; Künsterleben* (*Artist's life*)*;* (ii) *Rosen aus dem Süden* (*Roses from the South*)*; 1001 Nacht; Wein, Weib und Gesang* (*Wine, women and song*)*;* (i) *Wiener Blut* (*Vienna blood*)*;* (iii) STRAUSS, Josef: *Dorfschwalben aus Österreich* (*Austrian village swallows*).
(M) **(*) CBS *40-79026.* (i) NYPO, Bernstein; (ii) Phd. O, Ormandy; (iii) Cleveland O, Szell.

Ormandy is a superb Strauss conductor and his performances are as warm-blooded as they are exhilarating. The rubato is flexible, but never predictable in any stereotyped way; yet so firm is his rhythmic control that the Philadelphia Orchestra plays with wonderful unanimity, and the music-making retains its sparkle and spontaneity. In *Tales from the Vienna Woods* the zither is omitted, but the front desks take over its role with delicious effect. *Roses from the South* has an appealing sentient warmth, and *Wine, women and song* is agreeably spirited. Bernstein's way is more relaxed, but his performances too are highly distinctive with the New York Philharmonic obviously enjoying themselves. Szell contributes the single Josef Strauss number, complete with authentic bird-effects. The sound is good if a little variable; the Philadelphia recordings sound best with plenty of body and a positive bass. The documentation, as usual in this badly presented CBS tape-only series, lists only the titles, with the performance details in minuscule type, on the front of the box.

Polkas: *Banditen galop; Explosionen; Im Sturmschritt; Leichtes Blut; Unter Donner und Blitz* (*Thunder and lightning*). Waltzes: *Accelerationen*; *Lagunen*; *Morgenblätter* (*Morning papers*); *Schatz*. STRAUSS, Josef: *Feuerfest polka.*
**(*) HMV Dig. ASD/*TCC-ASD* 4041 [DS/*4XS* 37814]. Johann Strauss O of V., Boskovsky.

A genial digital supplement to the Boskovsky Strauss discography, without the electricity and sharply defined presence of his Decca series (see below). Boskovsky is especially good in the polkas, which have genuine exuberance; there is a hint of blandness in the waltzes, but the resonant warmth of the recording makes for enjoyable listening nonetheless. There is not a great deal of difference in sound between the disc and the chrome cassette.

Waltzes: *An der schönen blauen Donau; Frühlingsstimmen; Geschichten aus dem Wiener Wald; Kaiser; Künsterleben; Rosen aus dem Süden; Wiener Blut.*
*** HMV Dig. ASD/*TCC-ASD* 4178 [Ang. DS/*4XS* 37892]. Johann Strauss O of V., Boskovsky.

This is Boskovsky's most impressive Strauss collection since his Decca era. From the very opening of the *Blue Danube* the playing balances an evocative Viennese warmth with vigour and sparkle. Each performance is freshly minted, rhythmic nuances are flexibly stylish and the spontaneity is enjoyably obvious. The digital sound is full and vivid and agreeably rich – there is no digital edge on top, yet detail is realistic, within the resonant acoustic. The chrome tape needs a high-level playback, but then matches the disc closely. The spirit of the dance is strikingly present throughout this highly recommendable issue.

'Favourite waltzes': An der schönen blauen Donau; Du und Du; Frühlingsstimmen; Geschichten aus dem Wiener Wald; Kaiser; Künstlerleben; Rosen aus dem Süden; 1001 Nacht; Wein, Weib und Gesang; Wiener Blut; Wiener Bonbons.
(B) *** Decca DPA/*KDPC* 513/4. VPO, Boskovsky.

One might think that a succession of Strauss waltzes spread over two discs might produce a degree of listening monotony, but that is never the case here, such is the composer's resource in the matter of melody and orchestration. There are some splendid performances, and the transfer here is admirably smooth and vivid, with perhaps slightly less sparkle on the (very good) tapes than on LP.

'Favourite composer': Overtures: *Die Fledermaus; Der Zigeunerbaron. Egyptian march. Perpetuum mobile.* Polkas: *Auf der Jagd; Explosionen; Neue Pizzicato; Pizzicato* (with Josef); *Unter Donner und Blitz.* Waltzes: *An der schönen blauen Donau; Du und Du* (*Fledermaus waltz*); *Frühlingsstimmen; Geschichten aus dem Wiener Wald; Kaiser; Künstlerleben; Rosen aus dem Süden; 1001 Nacht; Wein, Weib und Gesang; Wiener Blut.*
(B) *** Decca DPA/*KDPC* 549/50. VPO, Boskovsky.

Following a sequence begun in the days of mono LPs with Clemens Krauss, Decca have over the years issued a series of incomparable stereo issues of the music of the Strauss family conducted with almost unfailing sparkle by Willi Boskovsky. The VPO have a tradition of New Year Strauss concerts, and it became a happy idea at Decca to link the new issues with the year's turn. This two-disc compilation, like the more extensive four-disc set below, uses material from the recordings made during the early 1960s, and with many favourites included it is a safe investment for those not objecting to a somewhat variable recorded quality, perhaps more noticeably uneven on the tape set than the discs.

'A Strauss Gala': Marches: *Egyptian; Napoleon; Persian.* Overtures: *Die Fledermaus; Der Zigeunerbaron. Perpetuum mobile.* Polkas: *Annen; Auf der Jagd; Banditen galop; Champagne; Eljen a Magyar; Explosionen; Leichtes Blut; Neue Pizzicato; Pizzicato* (with Josef); *Tritsch-Tratsch; Unter Donner und Blitz.* Waltzes: *Accelerationen; An der schönen blauen Donau; Frühlingsstimmen; Geschichten aus dem Wiener Wald; Kaiser; Künstlerleben; Morgenblätter; Rosen aus dem Süden; 1001 Nacht; Wein, Weib und Gesang; Wiener Blut; Wiener Bonbons; Wo die Zitronen blühn.* STRAUSS, Eduard: *Bahn frei polka galop.* STRAUSS, Johann, Snr: *Radetzky march.* STRAUSS, Josef: Polkas: *Eingesendet; Feuerfest; Jockey; Plappermäulchen.* Waltzes: *Mein Lebenslauf ist Lieb und Lust; Sphärenklänge.*
(B) *** Decca D 145 D 4/*K 145 K 44* (4). VPO, Boskovsky.

With Boskovsky making many of his newer recordings for HMV, Decca are taking the opportunity to reissue his earlier versions in a more economical format. This four-disc (and four-tape) compilation uses material from recordings made during the 1960s. It is remarkably comprehensive and very reasonably priced. The rearrangement of items is most successful, with a judicious selective order, so that polka and waltz alternate engagingly. The first group, opening with a particularly vivacious account of the *Die Fledermaus* overture, gets the set off to an excellent start, and there are generally very few disappointments among the performances. The inclusion of four polkas by Josef Strauss, together with two of his finest waltzes, is particularly welcome. The recording seldom sounds really dated and is often very good; the cassette transfers are remarkably consistent too, generally full, bright and well focused.

'New Year's Day concert in Vienna' (1979): Polkas: *Auf der Jagd; Bitte schön; Leichtes Blut; Pizzicato* (with Josef); *Tik-Tak*. Waltzes: *An der schönen blauen Donau; Bei uns z'Haus; Wein, Weib und Gesang*. STRAUSS, Johann, Snr: *Radetzky march; Loreley-Rhein-Klänge waltz*. STRAUSS, Eduard: *Ohne Bremse* (polka). STRAUSS, Josef: Polkas: *Die Emancipierte; Moulinet; Rudolfsheimer*. Waltz: *Sphärenklänge*. (Also includes Suppe: *Beautiful Galathea overture;* Ziehrer: *Hereinspaziert waltz*.)
*** Decca Dig. D 147 D 2/*KSXC2 7062* [Lon. LDR/5- 10001/2]. VPO, Boskovsky.

Polkas: *Auf der Jagd; Bitte schön; Leichtes Blut; Pizzicato* (with Josef)*; Tik-Tak;* Waltzes: *An der schönen blauen Donau; Bei uns z'Haus; Wein, Weib und Gesang*. STRAUSS, Johann Snr: *Radetzky march*. STRAUSS, Josef: *Moulinet polka: Sphärenklänge waltz*.
*** Decca Dig. **410 256-2** [id.]. (from above).

Decca chose to record Boskovsky's 1979 New Year's Day concert in Vienna as one of their very first digital issues, and this has remained a demonstration recording, notably in the *Radetzky march*, where with the audience participation included the presence of the sound is almost uncanny. But the clarity, immediacy and natural separation of detail are very striking throughout, although the upper strings of the Vienna Philharmonic at times seem to have their upper partials slightly exaggerated, so that there is some lack of bloom at the top. In all other respects the recording is first-class and the excellence applies to the cassette as well as the discs. One notices the naturalness of the sound immediately in the very well-focused audience applause at the opening, and the crispness of the side-drum is another striking feature, to say nothing of the freshness of the woodwind. The music-making itself gains much from the spontaneity of the occasion: its relaxed style is persuasive throughout, but one can feel the tension rising as the concert proceeds, and in the second half (and especially the encores) the electricity is very apparent. The performances are generally first-class and this is highly recommended, provided one can accept the applause and audience participation. The sound on disc and tape is almost identical.

The compact disc is not particularly generous and, while it conveys a sense of presence comparable to the LPs (notably in the *Radetzky march* which seems more tangible than ever), it tends to emphasize the comparative dryness of the recorded sound. Though the upper strings are smoother than on LP there is not the degree of ambient glow that Decca were to achieve in digital recordings made only a year or so after this.

Waltzes: *An der schönen blauen Donau; Geschichten aus dem Wiener Wald; Kaiser; Rosen aus dem Süden; Wein, Weib und Gesang; Wiener Blut*.
(M) ** HMV Green. ESD/*TC-ESD* 7025 [Ang. S/*4XS* 37070]. Johann Strauss O of V., Boskovsky.

Boskovsky's HMV analogue recordings were made in the early 1970s, and the quality is smoother than on the earliest of his Decca collections. However, the warm resonance of the sound does not provide a great deal of detail or sparkle, and although the playing is affectionate and idiomatic there is not the flair and spontaneity here that make Boskovsky's Decca series so distinctive. The cassette compares very favourably with the LP: there is very little difference, in fact.

'Family concert': Spanish march. Polkas: *Demolirer; Pizzicato* (with Josef). *Du und du (Fledermaus waltz)*. STRAUSS, Johann, Jnr, Josef, and Eduard: *Schützenquadrille*. STRAUSS, Eduard: *Bahn frei polka galop*. STRAUSS, Johann, Snr: *Radetzky march*. STRAUSS, Josef: *Brennende Liebe polka. Transaktionen waltz*.

(M) ** Decca Jub. JB/*KJBC* 28. VPO, Boskovsky.

In this further reshuffling of earlier Boskovsky/VPO material for Decca's Jubilee label there seems to be too great a proportion of music in duple or quadruple time; there are only two waltzes. But the collection is valuable for the inclusion of the *Schützenquadrille*, to which all three brothers contributed (it was written for a Viennese shooting contest in 1868). Of course the performances are lively and vivid and the recording good (though not so refined on tape as on disc); but unless these items are particularly wanted collectors will find many of Boskovsky's other issues more rewarding.

Overture and Entrance march: Der Zigeunerbaron. Polkas: *Im Krapfenwald'l; Tritsch-Tratsch; Vergnügungzug* (*Railway*). Waltzes: *Seid umschlungen Millionen; Wein, Weib und Gesang.* STRAUSS, Josef: *Aquarellen.*

**(*) Decca Jub JB/*KJBC* 130. VPO, Boskovsky.

From the first bars of the delectable performance of the *Gypsy Baron overture* the listener's ears prick up, not only at the superb style of the playing but also the sense of occasion conveyed in this New Year concert from 1966. The polkas go especially well; in the waltzes Boskovsky is very relaxed and affectionate. *Seid umschlungen Millionen* does not quite live up to the promise of its enticing opening, but *Wine, women and song* is one of Johann's very best, and *Aquarellen* is an attractive novelty. The recording is of vintage quality and its liveliness and bloom are well captured on the cassette, alongside the disc.

Egyptischer Marsch; Overture: Der Zigeunerbaron; Perpetuum mobile; Polkas: *Auf der Jagd; Pizzicato; Neue Pizzicato;* Waltzes: *An der schönen blauen Donau; Fledermaus; Frühlingsstimmen; Geschichten aus dem Wienerwald; Kaiser; Rosen aus dem Süden; 1001 Nacht; Wiener Blut.*

(B) *** Decca *KMC2 9001.* VPO, Boskovsky.

An irresistible ninety-minute tape from Decca's vintage period of Strauss recordings in Vienna at the end of the 1960s. The sound is remarkably vivid and the performances leap out from the speakers to grab the listener with lilting *joie de vivre*. The spontaneity of the playing is a joy throughout; many later Strauss recordings cannot match this for the combination of polish and sparkle. Highly recommended to brighten up any motorway journey.

'The Spirit of Vienna': Eine Nacht in Venedig overture. Polkas: *Champagne; Eljen a Magyar; Im Krapfenwald; Neue Pizzicato.* Waltzes: *An der schönen blauen Donau; Geschichten aus dem Wiener Wald; Kaiser; Künstlerleben; Rosen aus dem Süden; Wiener Blut; Wo die Zitronen blühn.*

(B) ** HMV *TC2-MOM 102.* Johann Strauss O of V., Boskovsky.

The Boskovsky recordings offered on this 'Miles of Music' double-length tape date from the early 1970s. The performances are genial and stylish; there is no lack of lilt in the phrasing, and the control of rubato is effective. Yet the playing is less memorable and individual than on Boskovsky's Decca VPO tape (see above). With warm, agreeably resonant recording, the effect in the car is pleasing, and this certainly makes entertaining and undistracting background entertainment for a long journey. At home the reproduction lacks something in brilliance and detail, but still sounds very acceptable.

'The world of Strauss', Vol. 1: An der schönen blauen Donau waltz; Auf der Jagd polka; Egyptian march; Frühlingsstimmen waltz; Geschichten aus dem Wiener Wald waltz; Perpetuum mobile; Pizzicato polka (with Josef); Waltzes: *Rosen aus dem Süden; 1001 Nacht; Wiener Blut.*

(M) *** Decca SPA/*KCSP* 10. VPO, Boskovsky.

Decca have been generous to offer so much, and although the disc is crammed full of good things, the recording quality does not suffer. Indeed in the *Pizzicato polka*, *Auf der Jagd* (watch out for the explosions), and several other items, this was top Decca sound (early 1960s vintage). Of the waltzes the *Blue Danube* is not so fetching as Barbirolli's, but *Tales from the Vienna Woods* is excellent, and both *Roses from the South* and *1001 Nights* are superb. An exhilarating collection. This LP got into the 'Top twenty' when it was first issued and deservedly so. The cassette equivalent was originally not Dolbyized, but we assume current copies will have been remastered.

'The World of Strauss', Vol. 2: Accelerationen waltz; Annen polka. Waltzes: *Kaiser; Künsterleben.* Polkas: *Leichtes Blut; Neue Pizzicato; Tritsch-Tratsch.* Overture: *Die Zigeunerbaron.* STRAUSS, Johann Snr: *Radetzky march.*
(M) ** Decca SPA/*KCSP* 73. VPO, Boskovsky or Knappertsbusch.

In Volume 2 Boskovsky shares the musical direction with Hans Knappertsbusch, who has earned a gramophone reputation for rather slow and sometimes lethargic tempi. But these performances (he conducts the *March*, all the polkas except the *New Pizzicato*, and the *Accelerations waltz*) are lively and committed. Boskovsky conducts the rest of the programme, and the recording for his items adds an extra richness. The playing throughout has the authentic Viennese lilt and this is an enjoyable concert, though not as fine as the first volume of the series. The cassette transfer is vivid, lacking only the last degree of refinement.

'The World of Strauss', Vol 3: Persian march; Die Fledermaus overture. Polkas: *Eljen a Magyar; Explosionen; Unter Donner und Blitz.* Waltzes: *Du und du; Liebeslieder; Morgenblätter; Wein, Weib und Gesang; Wiener Bonbons.*
(M) **(*) Decca SPA/*KCSP* 312. VPO, Boskovsky.

Most of these recordings date from the end of the 1950s, but the warm resonance of the recording provides a pleasing bloom, characteristic of this series, and only the string tone hints at the age of the originals. The *Fledermaus waltz* with its massed upper strings sounds a little spiky but yields to the controls. Boskovsky and his orchestra are on top form throughout, playing the waltzes with affection but without slackness. The overture opens the concert, and the march and polkas are interspersed to make a most attractive selection. The measure is generous and this is good value on disc. The cassette, however, is much less recommendable. The transfer has problems with the bass drum, and the sound is generally not ideally clear, though side one is better than side two.

'World of the Strauss family': Napoleon march; Champagne polka; Wo die Zitronen blühn waltz. STRAUSS, Johann, Jnr, Josef and Eduard: *Schützenquadrille.* STRAUSS, Johann, Snr: *Kaiser Franz Josef I Rettungs-Jubel march; Loreley-Rhein-Klänge waltz.* STRAUSS, Josef: Polkas: *Feuerfest; Jockey. Dorfschwalben aus Österreich waltz.*
(M) **(*) Decca SPA/*KCSP* 589. VPO, Boskovsky.

An agreeably lively family album, with characteristically vivid playing from the VPO and brilliant Decca sound. The three waltzes combine affection and sparkle, but elsewhere (as the *Napoleon march* demonstrates) the recording acoustic is sometimes very reverberant and this offers a degree of smudging on the cassette transfers.

Marches: *Persischer; Russischer. Perpetuum mobile.* Polkas: *Annen; Explosionen; Unter Donner und Blitz.* Waltzes: *Accellerationen;* (i) *An der schönen blauen Donau; Morgenblätter.* STRAUSS, Josef: Polka: *Feuerfest!* Waltzes: *Delirien; Sphärenklänge.*
C *** Decca **411 932-2** [id.]. VPO, Boskovsky; (i) with V. State Op. Ch.

Digitally remastered from recordings made in the 1970s (the earliest from 1971, the last 1976 – though the ear registers very little difference in quality) the results are astonishingly successful, and this makes an easy first choice for compact disc collectors in this repertoire. There is a glorious ambient warmth; the upper range gives the cymbals the right metallic sparkle, yet the strings are naturally clear and lustrous. Detail is refined and the analogue warmth and ambient bloom are most beguiling. The novelty here is the inclusion of the Vienna State Opera Chorus in the original choral version of the *Blue Danube*. These are not the original words (which caused a political storm at the time), but new lyrics introduced in 1890. The effect is rather more robust than the version for orchestra alone, but the performance has an infectious lilt with the singers conveying their enjoyment. The rest of the programme is up to the highest Boskovsky standard; the two Josef Strauss items are particularly successful, with the orchestra on top form. There is just about an hour of music here, the background is virtually silent, and the whole concert wonderfully spirited and life-enhancing.

Waltzes: *An der schönen blauen Donau; Frühlingsstimmen; Geschichten aus dem Wiener Wald; Künstlerleben; Wein, Weib und Gesang.*
(M) ** Decca VIV/*KVIC* 2 [Lon. STS 15545]. LPO, Dorati.

These are highly invigorating rather than romantic performances, supported by an extremely brilliant recording (originally made in Phase Four). Of its kind this is a good record, and those for whom the Viennese style is too droopy will not find a hint of slackness here. *Tales from the Vienna Woods* uses a zither, and the balance is never gimmicky. On cassette there is marginally less energy in the upper range in climaxes, and the effect is slightly smoother; however, Dorati's Hungarian liveliness still projects admirably.

Polkas: *Czech; Pizzicato* (with Josef). Waltzes: *Kaiser; Rosen aus dem Süden; Sängerlust; Wiener Blut; Wiener Bonbons.* STRAUSS, Johann, Snr: *Radetzky march.* STRAUSS, Josef: Polkas: *Feuerfest; Ohne Sorgen.*
(M) *** ASV ACM/*ZCACM* 2019. LSO, led Georgiadis (violin).

Among the new generation of Strauss recordings led in the authentic style by violinist-conductor, this collection from John Georgiadis, a brilliant virtuoso in his own right, is easily the most successful. The LSO is on top form, and the rhythmic feel of the playing combines lilt with polished liveliness. There is delicacy (the *Czech polka* is enchanting) and boisterousness, as in the irresistible anvil effects in the *Feuerfest polka.* The closing *Radetzky march* is as rousing as anyone could wish, while the waltzes combine vitality and charm. With first-class recording in a suitably resonant (but not over-reverberant) acoustic, this is highly recommendable, especially at medium price. The cassette transfer is slightly less sharply focused than the disc; side two seems to have more range than side one.

Waltzes: *An der schönen blauen Donau; Kaiser; Künstlerleben; Wein, Weib und Gesang.*
(B) **(*) CfP CFP/*TC-CFP* 165. LPO, Guschlbauer.

Theodor Guschlbauer readily conveys his affection in these Viennese-style performances, and he makes the London Philharmonic play almost as if they were Vienna-born. The shaping of the opening of each waltz is very nicely done, and the orchestra are obviously enjoying themselves, even though the tension is held on comparatively slack reins. The recording, made in a reverberant acoustic, has warmth and bloom, and the percussion comes over well. The cassette, however, is less successful in controlling the resonance than the disc: there is a degree of coarseness in *Wine, women and song.*

Polkas: *Eljen a Magyar; Pizzicato* (with Josef)*; Tritsch-Tratsch.* Waltzes: *Morgenblätter; 1001 Nacht; Wein, Weib und Gesang; Wo die Zitronen blüh'n. Indigo: Schulummerlied.* STRAUSS, Josef: *Feuerfest polka; Dorfschwalben aus Österreich.*
** Ph. Dig. 6514/*7337* 185 [id.]. V. Boys' Ch., Harrer.

Johann Strauss with fresh young voices and a piano duo instead of an orchestra. There is no lack of lilt, although sometimes there is the feeling of the school assembly hall. The rhythmic nuances are authentic, if sometimes rather overemphasized. Enjoyable in its way (though the upper range of the choir sometimes falters slightly under pressure). Everything sounds very well rehearsed but often the natural exuberance of the singers takes over. There is an excellent chrome cassette.

Overtures: *Die Fledermaus; Der Zigeunerbaron.* Polkas: *Annen; Tritsch-Tratsch.* Waltzes: *An der schönen blauen Donau; Kaiser.*
*(*) HMV ASD 3132 [Ang. S/*4XS* 37144]. Berlin PO, Karajan.

After the sumptuous *Die Fledermaus* overture, given rich, spacious (quadraphonic) recording, Karajan's newest Berlin Philharmonic collection is most disappointing. The *Annen polka* is stodgily phrased, and a similar heavy, mannered rubato takes most of the lilt out of the waltzes. The ample, resonant sound-picture does not help to provide resilience to the actual orchestra sound. There is a faithful cassette transfer. Readers will do far better with the admirable Decca Jubilee disc, below, where Karajan's art is demonstrated at its most beguiling in this repertoire.

Polkas: *Annen; Auf der Jagd. Geschichten aus dem Wiener Wald waltz.* Overtures: *Die Fledermaus; Der Zigeunerbaron.* STRAUSS, Josef: *Delirien waltz.*
(M) *** Decca Jub. JB/*KJBC* 68 [Lon. STS/*5* 15163]. VPO, Karajan.

Warmly recorded, presumably in the same hall where the Boskovsky records are made, this early stereo collection is distinguished. Karajan's touch with the *Gypsy Baron overture* is irresistible, and *Tales from the Vienna Woods* is really beautiful, one of the very finest recorded performances of this piece, with a perfectly judged zither solo. The polkas have the panache for which this conductor at his best is famous. Highly recommended: this is among the best popular Strauss collections available on disc. The cassette is a little disappointing; it is obviously made from an early master, and although the sound is lively there are hints of minor discoloration in the upper partials of the woodwind.

Die Fledermaus overture. Persischer Marsch. Polkas: *Eljen a Magyar; Leichtes Blut; Unter Donner und Blitz.* Waltzes: *Accelerationen; An der schönen blauen Donau; Künstlerleben.*
*** DG Dig. **400 026-2**; 2532/*3302* 025 [id.]. Berlin PO, Karajan.

A superbly played selection taken from Karajan's DG digital box (see below). The virility and flair of the waltzes (especially *Künstlerleben*) are matched by the exuberance of the polkas, and the *Fledermaus overture* sparkles so vividly it sounds like a new discovery. The sound is well matched on disc and chrome tape. The compact disc sounds slightly clinical in its added detail.

Der Zigeunerbaron overture. Polkas: *Annen; Auf der Jagd; Tritsch-Tratsch.* Waltzes: *Kaiser; Rosen aus dem Süden; Wein, Weib und Gesang.*
(*) DG Dig. **410 022-2; 2532/*3302* 026 [id.]. Berlin PO, Karajan.

This is less attractive than the first selection from Karajan's DG box. After a refined introduction, the *Emperor* does not achieve the zest of some of the other waltzes, and although the playing is not without elegance, the noble contour of the principal melody is less potent here than in some versions. The polkas go well, and the overture is a highlight. The digital sound is full and brilliant, and the chrome tape is of excellent quality. On compact disc, the wide dynamic range at the opening of the *Emperor* emphasizes the bright digital sheen on the upper strings. Detail is impressive, although ideally the recording could do with a little more warmth in the lower-middle range.

Napoleon march. Perpetuum mobile. Die Fledermaus: Quadrille. Waltzes: *Geschichten aus dem Wiener Wald; Wiener Blut.* STRAUSS, Johann, Snr: *Radetzky march.* STRAUSS, Josef: Waltzes: *Delirien; Sphärenklänge.*
*** DG Dig. **410 027-2**; 2532/*3302* 027 [id.]. Berlin PO, Karajan.

A splendid distillation from Karajan's Strauss box, with magically evocative openings to each of the four waltzes, and outstanding performances of *Sphärenklänge*, *Delirien* and (especially) *Wiener Blut*. *Perpetuum mobile* and the engaging *Fledermaus quadrille* make a piquant contrast as centrepieces of each side. The brilliant digital recording is equally impressive on disc and cassette. The compact disc, however, adds comparatively little, but emphasizes detail.

Polkas: *Annen; Tritsch-Tratsch; Unter Donner und Blitz.* Waltzes: *An der schönen blauen Donau; Geschichten aus dem Wiener Wald; Wiener Blut.*
(M) **(*) DG Acc. 2542/*3342* 143. Berlin PO, Karajan.

Karajan is usually consistent, and these

earlier DG Strauss recordings are basically very little different in conception from those in the later digital set. There is less vitality here, but the performances are beautifully played; the recording does not sound its age, and the cassette transfer too is of DG's best quality. Many will like a selection which includes both *The Blue Danube* and *Tales from the Vienna Woods* (the latter performance is only marginally less distinguished than the one in Karajan's Decca Jubilee concert). The polkas are lively and make a suitable contrast.

Overtures: *Die Fledermaus; Der Zigeunerbaron.*
(M) *** DG Sig. 2543/*3343* 533. Berlin PO, Karajan – SUPPÉ: *Overtures.***(*)

Impeccably vivacious performances from the Berlin Philharmonic under Karajan and a recording which combines ambient warmth with brilliance. The sound for the Suppé coupling is slightly less agreeable, however.

Overtures: *Die Fledermaus* (and *Quadrille*); *Der Zigeunerbaron. Musicalischer Scherz.* Marches: *Napoleon; Persian. Perpetuum mobile.* Polkas: *Annen; Auf der Jagd; Cagliostro in Wien; Eljen a Magyar; Leichtes Blut; Tritsch-Tratsch; Ungarische; Unter Donner und Blitz.* Waltzes: *Accelerationen; An der schönen blauen Donau; Geschichten aus dem Wiener Wald; Kaiser; Künstlerleben; Rosen aus dem Süden; Das Spitzentuch der Königin; Wein, Weib, und Gesang; Wiener Blut.* STRAUSS, Johann, Snr: *Radetzky march.* STRAUSS, Josef: Waltzes: *Delirien; Sphärenklänge.*
*** DG Dig. 2741/*3382* 003 (3) [id.]. Berlin PO, Karajan.

Karajan's new three-disc (or three-tape) set of music of the Strauss family is a major achievement. The digital recording is full and brilliant, and there is no great difference between discs and chrome tapes: the former have a fractionally cleaner focus, the latter a marginally softer image for the upper strings. The performances are splendid; the waltzes have a stirring virility, yet their evocative introductions have never been more effectively prepared. *Künstlerleben*, *Wiener Blut*, *Sphärenklänge* and *Delirien* are superbly done, and on *The Blue Danube* Karajan lavishes special care, opening atmospherically and building to a climax of striking lyrical power. Yet one section is cunningly repeated with an arresting drop to pianissimo – a device he also used in his earlier recording, now on Accolade (see above). The Berlin Philharmonic playing is glorious, with precise ensemble not interfering with the Viennese-style lilt, to underline the sheer beauty of the music. The two overtures are no less compelling; Karajan must have given them many times, but here they sound freshly minted, and the sheer vigour of the waltz introduction to *Die Fledermaus* is irresistible. The polkas, played with great zest and panache, are nicely placed between the waltzes to provide exhilarating contrast. Above all the set has a flowing spontaneity, and if you start at side one and play right through to the end, the music-making seems to become more spirited and involving as it proceeds.

Pizzicato polka (with Josef). Waltzes: *Accelerationen; An der schönen blauen Donau; Kaiser; Rosen aus dem Süden.*
(B) ** Con. CC/*CCT* 7522 [Lon. STS/*5* 15012]. VPO, Krips.

Krips's performances, with their gentle rhythmic emphasis, are attractively affectionate, and with the VPO in good form the result is bound to be enjoyable. The waltzes have spirit, and the *Pizzicato polka* comes off especially well (the recording here is strikingly live). This dates from the earliest days of stereo, but the acoustic is warm and the sound is surprisingly good. The cassette sounds richer than the disc but has a more restricted upper range.

'Viennese night': Egyptian march. Polkas: *Banditen; Im Krapfenwald'l; Pizzicato* (with Josef); Waltzes: *Geschichten aus dem Wienerwald; Morgenblätter; Rosen aus dem Süden; Der Zigeunerbaron: march.* STRAUSS, Eduard: *Bahn frei polka galop.* STRAUSS, Josef: *Eingesendet polka.*
(B) *(*) CfP CFP/*TC-CFP* 40256. Hallé O, Loughran.

A most disappointing record. The recording is curiously lacking in bloom and lustre, with poorly focused strings, and Loughran has obviously not inherited Barbirolli's mantle in this music, although he is better in the pieces not in waltz time.

'New Year in Vienna 1981': Ägyptischer Marsch; Einzugsmarsch. Polkas: *Explosionen; Leichtes Blut; Stürmisch in Lieb' und Tanz; Tritsch-Tratsch; Pizzicato* (with Josef). Waltzes: *Accelerationen; Frühlingsstimmen; Rosen aus dem Süden.* STRAUSS, Johann, Snr: *Seufzer Galop.* STRAUSS, Josef: Polkas: *Frauenherz; Ohne Sorgen. Transaktionen waltz.*
** DG Dig. 2532/*3302* 018. VPO, Maazel.

This record does not convey the electricity of Boskovsky's 1979 Decca digital concert (see above); indeed the audience response seems remarkably cool and well-behaved. Their presence is most felt in the *Pizzicato polka*, where one can sense the intercommunication as Maazel manipulates the rubato with obvious flair. He also gives a splendid account of *Transaktionen*, which has striking freshness and charm. For the rest these are well-played performances of no great memorability. The orchestra makes two rather self-conscious vocal contributions, and of course the playing itself is first-class. The digital sound is brilliant and clear, somewhat lacking in resonant warmth. Cassette and disc are closely matched.

'Happy New Year' (1982): Polkas: *Bitte schöne!; Electrophor; Vergnügungszug.* Waltzes: *Kaiser; Seid umschlungen Millionen.* STRAUSS, Eduard: *Mit Extrapost, polka.* STRAUSS, Josef: *Feuerfest polka; Delirien waltz.* STRAUSS, Johann Snr: *Cachucha galop; Radetzky march* (with Nicolai: *Overture: The merry wives of Windsor*).
**(*) DG Dig. 2532/*3302* 059. V. Boys' Ch., VPO, Maazel.

Maazel's 1982 recording is the most successful of his post-Boskovsky New Year concerts. The Vienna Philharmonic is on top form – the *Merry wives of Windsor overture* is beautifully played – and the Vienna Boys' Choir make a couple of vivacious contributions. They are forwardly placed and indeed the digital sound, while clear and vivid (both on disc and the excellent chrome tape), lacks something in reverberant warmth. Nevertheless the strings produce sumptuous tone for the opening of *Seid umschlungen Millionen*, which Maazel presents with obvious affection. Indeed, all three waltzes are persuasively shaped while the spirited polkas provide infectious contrast. The famous *Radetzky march* at the end, however, does not find here the sheer exuberance of Boskovsky's earlier digital Decca recording.

'Live in Vienna': Overture: *Waldmeister.* Polka: *Unter Donner und Blitz.* Waltz: *Morgenblätter.* STRAUSS, Josef: Polkas: *Die Emancipierte; Die Tanzende Muse.* Waltzes: *Aquarellen; Sphärenklänge* (*Music of the spheres*)*;* (with Lanner: *Hofball-Tänze*).
(M) *** DG Dig. 2560 099/*3309 061* [id.]. VPO, Maazel.

Presumably also drawn from Maazel's 1983 concert – see below – this digital mid-priced selection is something of a bargain, particularly as the repertoire offered is more adventurous than usual and includes a high proportion of music by Josef Strauss. The opening overture is not well-known either. It is a delightful piece and readily shows Maazel's affectionate response in its detail. The opening of the *Aquarellen waltz* brings an even greater delicacy of approach and the orchestra responds with telling pianissimo playing. Indeed throughout the programme the music-making is both lilting and sprightly with the exuberant Lanner piece making a fitting finale. The audience – applause apart – is not too intrusive. The recording is without the somewhat aggressive brightness of earlier issues in this series, and the excellent chrome tape matches the disc in its warmth and liveliness.

'Vienna bonbons' (New Year concert, 1983): Overtures: *Indigo und die vierdig Räuber; Eine Nacht in Venedig.* Polkas: *Eljen a Magyar; Freikugeln; Wiener bonbons.* Waltzes: *Geschichten aus dem Wiener Wald; Wo die Zitronen blüh'n.* STRAUSS, Josef: Polkas: *Aus der Ferne; Die Libelle; Vélocipède.*
** DG Dig. 410 516-1/*4*. VPO, Maazel.

After the noisy applause at the opening, the warmly recessed orchestral image is most welcome. The excess digital brightness which marred the sound of Maazel's earlier New Year concerts is here agreeably absent. The atmosphere is intimate and Maazel obviously seeks to beguile the ear rather than impress with energetic brilliance. But he goes to the opposite extreme, and both major waltzes are slack (although the indulgent opening piece, which gives the record its title, is rather more effective). The account of the *Night in Venice overture*, however, is noticeably self-conscious. In spite of the audience, the spontaneity of the occasion is only sporadically projected, although the orchestral playing is always assured. The cassette, like the LP, is smooth without loss of detail, and the strings are given an agreeable bloom.

Kaiser Franz Josef Marsch. Polkas: *Annen; Auf der Jagd; Fata Morgana; Tritsch-Tratsch*. Waltzes: *An der schönen blauen Donau; Kaiser; Morgenblätter; Wiener Bonbons*. STRAUSS, Johann, Snr: *Cachucha Galop*. STRAUSS, Josef: Polkas: *Moulinet; Ohne Sorgen*. *Aquarellen waltz*.
** Chan. Dig. ABRD/*ABTD* 1039 [id.]. Johann Strauss O, led Rothstein (violin).

Digital recording is not everything, and here it serves to emphasize the rather thin sound of the upper strings, although there is no lack of overall bloom. The playing is spirited and more infectious than Maazel's New Year digital concerts (see above); indeed the spontaneity of the music-making is the strongest feature of this collection.

Waltzes: *An der schönen blauen Donau; Geschichten aus dem Wiener Wald; Kaiser; Lagunen* (*Lagoon*)*; Rosen aus dem Süden; Wiener Blut*.
(M) ** EMI Em. EMX/*TC-EMX* 2038. VSO, Stolz.

These are relaxed, agreeable performances, understanding in style, but lacking brio. The recording is pleasingly warm with the cassette less lively than the disc, increasing the feeling of amiable blandness.

OPERETTA

Die Fledermaus (complete).
*** HMV SLS 964 (2) [Ang. SBLX/*4X2X* 3790]. Rothenberger, Holm, Gedda, Fischer-Dieskau, Berry, Fassbaender, V. State Op. Ch., VSO, Boskovsky.
**(*) Decca D 247 D 3/*K 247 K 32* (3/*2*) [Lon. OSA 1319] (Gala performance). Gueden, Koth, Kmentt, Waechter, Berry, Zampieri, Resnik, V. State Op. Ch., VPO, Karajan.
**(*) DG 2707 086/*3370 009* (2) [id.]. Varady, Popp, Kollo, Weikl, Prey, Rebroff, Bav. State Op. Ch. and O, Carlos Kleiber.

If the LP catalogue has never been infested with Fledermice, that is a recognition of the quality of earlier sets, first in mono and then notably Karajan's Decca version of 1960. The Boskovsky version, recorded with the Vienna *Symphoniker* instead of the Philharmonic, is more intimate than its predecessor, to provide a clear alternative. Though Boskovsky sometimes fails to lean into the seductive rhythms as much as he might, his is a refreshing account of a magic score. Rothenberger is a sweet, domestic-sounding Rosalinde, relaxed and sparkling, while among an excellent supporting cast the Orlofsky of Brigitte Fassbaender must be singled out as quite the finest on record, tough and firm. The entertainment has been excellently produced for records, with German dialogue inserted, though the ripe recording sometimes makes the voices jump between singing and speaking.

Karajan's set was originally issued – with much blazing of publicity trumpets – as a so-called 'Gala performance', with various artists from the Decca roster appearing to do their turn at the 'cabaret' included in the Orlofsky ball sequence. This was a famous tradition of performances of *Die Fledermaus* at the New York Met, in the early years of this century. Now Decca have digitally remastered this original version with remarkable effect. There are first-class chrome tapes too, and the sound (which unbelievably dates from 1960) is sparklingly clear on both LP and cassette, although the ambience now seems rather less natural and the applause in the party scene somewhat too vociferous.

The party pieces now have a vintage appeal and even Tebaldi's *Viljalied* (rather heavy in style) sets off nostalgia for an earlier era. There is a breathtaking display of coloratura from Joan Sutherland in *Il Bacio*, a Basque folk-song sung with delicious simplicity by Teresa

Berganza, and Leontyne Price is wonderfully at home in Gershwin's *Summertime*. But the most famous item is Simionato and Bastianini's *Anything you can do, I can do better*, sung with more punch than sophistication, but endearingly memorable, nearly a quarter of a century after it was recorded.

The performance of the opera itself has all the sparkle one could ask for. If anything, Karajan is even more brilliant than he was on the old Columbia mono issue, and the Decca recording is scintillating in its clarity. Where it does fall short, alas, is in the singing. Hilde Gueden is deliciously vivacious as Rosalinde, a beautifully projected interpretation, but vocally she is not perfect, and even her confidence has a drawback in showing how tentative Erika Köth is as Adèle, with her wavering vibrato. Indeed *Mein Herr Marquis* is well below the standard of the best recorded performances. Waldemar Kmentt has a tight, German-sounding tenor, and Giuseppe Zampieri as Alfred (a bright idea to have a genuine Italian for the part) is no more than adequate. The rest of the cast are very good, but even these few vocal shortcomings are enough to take some of the gilt off the gingerbread. It all depends on what you ask from *Fledermaus*; if it is gaiety and sparkle above everything, then with Karajan in control this is an excellent recommendation, and it certainly cannot be faulted on grounds of recording.

The glory of the DG set is the singing of the two principal women – Julia Varady and Lucia Popp magnificently characterful and stylish as mistress and servant – but much of the rest is controversial to say the least. Many will be delighted by the incisive style of Carlos Kleiber, deliberately rejecting many older conventions. Though he allows plenty of rhythmic flexibility, he is never easy-going, for in every rubato a first concern is for precision of ensemble; and that does not always allow the fun and sparkle of the score to emerge. But in its way the result is certainly refreshing, even electrically compelling, and the recording quality, both clear and atmospheric, is admirable. Hermann Prey makes a forthright Eisenstein, but René Kollo sounds lumberingly heavy as Alfred, and as for the falsetto Orlofsky of Ivan Rebroff, it has to be heard to be believed, unhealthily grotesque. For some ears this is so intrusive (as is the hearty German dialogue at times) as to make this set quite unacceptable for repeated listening. There is a first-class cassette transfer.

Die Fledermaus: highlights (in English).
(M) ** HMV Green. ESD/*TC-ESD* 7083. Studholme, Pollak, Elliot, Young, John Heddle Nash, Sadler's Wells Op., Tausky.

The Sadler's Wells Company often showed in the theatre that it was second to none in capturing Viennese gaiety, and on this record the whole production moves with great vigour. The chorus in particular has an incisiveness which will disappoint no one, but it must be admitted that the soloists, while always reliable, are not particularly memorable in their singing. Marion Studholme, for example, as Adèle sings with great flexibility, but there is a 'tweety' quality to her voice, as caught by the microphone, which prevents the final degree of enjoyment. Anna Pollak is the one serious disappointment. In the theatre this highly intelligent singer rarely failed to give dramatic as well as understanding performances, but here as Prince Orlofsky she sounds too old-womanly by far, and her attempts at vocal acting – effective in the theatre – sound over-mannered and only add to the womanliness. The recording is brilliant, with a clarity of definition and numerous directional effects which are most realistic. The cassette transfer is strikingly lively and vivid, with plenty of sparkle and projection. The high level brings hardly any peaking.

A Night in Venice (*Eine Nacht in Venedig*): complete.
(M) *** EMI 1C 149 03171/2. Schwarzkopf, Gedda, Kunz, Klein, Loose, Dönch, Philh. Ch. and O, Ackermann.

A Night in Venice was drastically revised by Erich Korngold many years after Strauss's death, and it is that version, further amended, which appears in this charming 'complete' recording, a superb example of Walter Legge's Philharmonia productions, honeyed and atmospheric. As a sampler try the jaunty little waltz duet in Act I between Schwarzkopf as the heroine, Annina, and the baritone Erich Kunz as Caramello, normally a tenor role. Nicolai Gedda as the Duke then appropriates the most famous waltz song of all, the *Gondola song*, but with such a frothy production purism would be out of place. The excellent stereo transcription preserves the balance of the mono original admirably. The price of this issue reflects the fact that the set is issued on three LP sides only. Highly recommended.

Der Zigeunerbaron (*The Gipsy Baron*): complete.
*** EMI 1C 149 03051/2. Schwarzkopf, Gedda, Prey, Kunz, Köth, Sinclair, Philh. Ch. and O, Ackermann.

The Gipsy Baron has had a poor showing in the recording studio, which is particularly surprising because there are relatively so few Strauss operettas, and by any standards this is outstanding. The plot (much praised in some quarters) is strangely offbeat, but the musical inspiration shows Strauss at his most effervescent, and this superb Philharmonia version from the mid-1950s has never been matched in its rich stylishness and polish. Schwarzkopf as the gipsy princess sings radiantly, not least in the heavenly Bullfinch duet (to the melody made famous by MGM as *One day when we were young*). Gedda, still youthful, sings with heady tone, and Erich Kunz as the rough pig-breeder gives a vintage echt-Viennese performance of the irresistible *Ja, das schreiben und das lesen*. The stereo transcription from excellent mono originals gives fresh and truthful sound, particularly in the voices.

Wiener Blut (complete).
*** EMI 1C 149 03180/1. Schwarzkopf, Gedda, Köth, Kunz, Loose, Donch, Philh. Ch. and O, Ackermann.
**(*) Eurodisc 88616 XDE (2) [72751]. Schock, Schramm, Gueden, Lipp, Kusche, Kunz, V. State Op. Ch. and SO, Stolz.
**(*) EMI 1C 157 30688/9. Rothenberger, Gedda, Holm, Hirte, Col. Op. Ch., Philh. Hungarica, Boskovsky.

To have Schwarzkopf at her most ravishing singing a waltz song based on the tune of *Morning Papers* is enough enticement for this superbly stylish performance of a piece which – with the composer a bored collaborator – was cobbled together from some of his finest ideas. The result may not be a great operetta, but in a recording it makes enchanting listening, with the waltz of the title made into the centrepiece. This Philharmonia version of the mid-1950s shows Walter Legge's flair as a producer at its most compelling, with Schwarzkopf matched by the regular team of Gedda and Kunz and with Emmy Loose and Erika Köth in the secondary soprano roles. The original mono recording was beautifully balanced, and the face-lift given here is most tactfully achieved in this extremely successful stereo transcription.

For those wanting a modern stereo set, the scintillating performance under the direction of Robert Stolz, with a first-rate singing cast headed by Rudolf Schock, Hilde Gueden and Erich Kunz, can be strongly recommended. Though the voices are balanced forward the production (with sound effects) is very atmospheric, making this Strauss confection – drawn from various earlier numbers with the blessing of the composer – a fizzing Viennese entertainment. Gueden sings charmingly, though hardly with the finesse of Schwarzkopf, whose performance in Walter Legge's medium-priced mono set of the mid-1950s is, of course, incomparable.

The alternative EMI set conducted by Willi Boskovsky also makes a delightful entertainment, the performance authentic with a strong singing cast. The recording is atmospherically reverberant, but there is no lack of sparkle. However, for some there will be too much German dialogue and they may prefer a disc of highlights (available on EMI 1C 061 30755).

Strauss, Richard (1864–1949)

An Alpine symphony, Op. 64.
*** HMV ASD 3173. Dresden State O, Kempe.
*** DG Dig. **400 039-2**; 2532/*3302* 015 [id.]. Berlin PO, Karajan.
*** HMV Dig. ASD/*TC-ASD* 143577-1/*4* [Ang. DS/*4XS* 38015]. Phd. O, Previn.
(M) *** Decca Jub. JB/*KJBC* 139 [Lon. CS/*5*- 6981]. LAPO, Mehta.

*** Decca SXL/*KSXC* 6959 [Lon. CS 7189]. Bav. RSO, Solti.

(M) *** RCA Gold GL/*GK* 42697. RPO, Kempe.

**(*) CBS Dig. 37292 [id.]. LPO, Andrew Davis.

The *Alpine symphony* has all the rhetoric, confidence and opulence of the great Strauss tone poems, but judged by the finest of them, its melodic invention is less fresh and its gestures sometimes ring a hollow note. But there is much to relish and enjoy when the performances are as good as these.

Kempe brings a glowing warmth and humanity to this score, and there is no doubt that in his hands it sounds the greater work. He moulds each phrase with more sensitivity and life, and though (as with Karajan) there is a strong sense of forward movement, there is also great expressive freedom and flexibility of phrase. The Dresden orchestra produces rich, cultured and vital tone quality. Kempe was a very great Strauss conductor, and this tells. The EMI recording (like Mehta's Decca) is an outstanding example of analogue techniques at their most impressive. It was originally made in quadraphony, but the stereo disc is hardly less fine.

Karajan's account is recorded digitally, but orchestral detail is less analytical than in Solti's Decca version. Indeed the latter is fresher and more transparent, and has not the slight edge to the upper strings that is a feature of the DG digital recording. But it would be wrong to give the impression that the DG sound is less than first-class and, as a performance, the Karajan is in the highest flight. It is wonderfully spacious, beautifully shaped and played with the utmost virtuosity. This is certainly one of the finest accounts now available, though Kempe's version has an equal breadth and majesty and no less atmosphere. The DG chrome cassette matches the disc closely, although side one has fractionally less sparkle at the top than side two. However, the edge noticeable on the disc is softened on tape. The compact disc increases the recording's presence and clarity and has a firmer, better-defined bass response.

Previn has the advantage of the superb Philadelphia Orchestra and a very good recording, the Old Met producing better sound in the hands of Christopher Parker and Suvi Raj Grubb than it has in some other recent Muti records. Indeed, as a recording it is arguably better than the Karajan on DG, though not as finely detailed or well lit as Solti on Decca nor as natural as Kempe who still reigns supreme. Previn immediately establishes the warm and amiable tone of his most sympathetic reading in the music representing the start of the climb. He is joyfully relaxed, where some conductors press on relentlessly as though in a marathon, and he makes this colourful description of a day's outing on the mountain into an individual experience full of colour and warmth rather than an epic event. Even at speeds often slower than usual, Previn's ability to spring a rhythm prevents a feeling of slackness, helped by the Philadelphia Orchestra in vintage form. But Previn's expansiveness may suggest to some ears that his account is wanting the firmness of grip and sense of purposeful forward movement of some versions, and the richly glowing orchestral tapestry (with disc and XDR tape sounding virtually identical) does produce a hint of blandness at times, though the echoing horns are superbly managed.

Those wanting a medium-priced version could hardly do better than turn to Mehta (though Kempe's earlier RCA recording should also be considered). Mehta's performance is among the best Strauss he has given us, and the vintage 1976 recording is outstandingly successful in combining range and richness with remarkable detail. It is not overlit, but the Decca engineers let every strand of the texture tell without losing sight of the overall perspective. The chrome tape too is in Decca's demonstration class, especially on side two.

The Bavarian Radio orchestra under Solti, recorded in the Herkulessaal in Munich, could hardly sound more opulent, with brass of incomparable richness. That warmth of sound and the superlative quality of recording tend to counterbalance the generally fast tempi. Many of them are in principle too fast, but with such sympathetic and committed playing in such a setting the results are warm rather than frenetic. The cassette matches the disc in depth and richness, although the LP has slightly more energy in the highest frequencies.

At medium price, Kempe's Gold Seal version makes an excellent alternative recommendation to Mehta, no less warm and committed than his later Dresden performance on HMV, and on balance a shade more spontaneous-sounding. The recording quality is very good for its mid-1960s vintage, but on cassette the relative lack of bass detracts from the fullness, and the treble lacks real sparkle too.

Andrew Davis's version is enjoyable in a clear-cut, refreshing way. The beauty of Strauss's orchestration – even at times a chamber quality within the huge orchestra – is well brought out, but the refusal to languish makes the result unevocative. The recording has plenty of detail but the treble is a little exaggerated.

An Alpine symphony: Ein Heldenleben.
(M) **(*) HMV *TCC-2 POR 54279*. Dresden State O, Kempe.

With no break in continuity in either work, this is one of the best-conceived issues in EMI's 'Portrait of the Artist' series and though, even using chrome stock, the reverberant acoustic has brought minor problems, with transients not absolutely clean, in all other respects this is a success. The richness of tone provided by this splendid orchestra is captured in all its sumptuousness and both performances are glowing with life, under one of the most distinguished Straussians of our time.

Also sprach Zarathustra; Death and Transfiguration; Don Juan; Don Quixote; Ein Heldenleben; Metamorphosen for 23 solo strings; Till Eulenspiegel; Salome: Dance of the Seven Veils.
(M) *** DG 2740 111 (5). Berlin PO, Karajan.

A fabulous collection. All these performances are of superlative quality and sumptuously recorded. *Ein Heldenleben* was recorded as long ago as 1959, but no one would suspect it was not made in the 1970s. Fournier's reading of the solo part in *Don Quixote* is arguably the finest on the market, and Karajan's earlier version of *Metamorphosen* led the field, until his newer digital recording appeared. This set is altogether in a class of its own and economically priced.

Also sprach Zarathustra, Op. 30.
❀*** DG 2530 402/*3300 375* [id.]. Berlin PO, Karajan.
C *** Ph. Dig. **400 072-2**; 6514/*7337* 221 [id.]. Boston SO, Ozawa.
(M) *** Ph. Seq. 6527/*7311* 212 [6500 624/*7300 280*]. Concg. O, Haitink.
(M) **(*) DG Priv. 2535/*3335* 494. Berlin PO, Boehm.
(*) CBS **CD 35888 [IM/*HMT* 35888]. NYPO, Mehta.
*(**) HMV ASD/*TCC-ASD* 3897 [Ang. DS 37744]. Phd. O, Ormandy.
(M) ** Decca Jub. JB/*KJBC* 133 [*JL*/5-41060]. LAPO, Mehta – RAVEL: *Boléro*; TCHAIKOVSKY: *Marche slave*.**
(M) (***) CBS 60136/*40*- [MY/*MYT* 37254]. Phd. O, Ormandy.

Sumptuous tone and virtuosity of the highest order make the DG Karajan an electrifying *Zarathustra*, arguably the best on the market. The engineers produce recorded sound of the greatest realism and warmth, wholly natural in its aural perspective and free from gimmickry. Karajan's earlier account, with the Vienna Philharmonic Orchestra, is also a fine one, famous for its spectacular recording of almost too wide a dynamic range. The playing is first-class and has considerable tonal opulence, but the newer DG version eclipses it in almost every way, though it remains a good recommendation in the medium-price range. Similarly the DG cassette outshines the Decca one (see below) with sumptuously rich sound and minimal transfer problems though climaxes are less refined than on disc.

In its compact disc version Ozawa's warmly persuasive version of *Zarathustra* became one of the first demonstration records for the new medium, when the depth and unforced firmness of the organ pedal sound leading on to an extraordinary crescendo over the spectacular introduction gave clear indication of its extra potential. The solo strings are balanced rather close, but otherwise this is a wonderfully warm and natural sound with both a natural bloom and fine inner clarity. Ozawa as a Strauss interpreter goes for seductive phrasing and warmth rather than high drama or nobility. The chrome cassette also offers an impressive sound balance, without a hint of distortion at the opening, but this has been achieved by using a very low transfer level with attendant hiss.

Those seeking a mid-priced version could do no better than turn to Haitink's account with the Concertgebouw Orchestra. It is no less impressively recorded than Karajan's on DG (with a very good cassette). This record was issued very much in the shadow of the Karajan, and if the strings of the Berlin Philharmonic have greater rapture and lyrical intensity, there is no want of ardour from the Concertgebouw players, and the reading has breadth and nobility.

Boehm's is also a distinguished performance, passionate and finely structured. But the 1958 recording is dated by its upper string timbre, though this is more noticeable on disc than on the (otherwise vivid) cassette.

Neither of the two earlier digital versions, under Mehta and Ormandy respectively, is completely satisfactory. Mehta's CBS account is predictably exciting and the recording is brilliantly clear and positive, with more tonal substance than the Ormandy HMV disc. There is some superbly eloquent horn playing, and the forceful thrust of Mehta's reading brings undoubted exhilaration at climaxes; the appearance of the midnight bell at the apotheosis of the *Tanzlied* makes a spectacular effect, and the closing *Nachtwanderlied* is tenderly played. But Karajan finds more mysticism in the score than Mehta, and the bright sheen on the New York strings is less telling than the Berlin string timbre in the 'Yearning' and 'Passion' sequences.

The very opening of the Ormandy disc is riveting in its clarity and impact, but elsewhere the massed Philadelphia strings are made to sound brittle by the crystalline brilliance of the lighting of the overall sound-picture. Yet in all this sharpness of focus Nietzsche's midnight bell tolls without impact, all but buried in the middle of the orchestra. The performance is not without fire and virtuosity, but the sound tires the ear, though the cassette is slightly smoother and fuller than the disc.

Both Mehta and Ormandy have recorded the work before. In the never-to-be-forgotten opening of Mehta's 1969 version for Decca – now reissued on Jubilee – he has the distinction of stretching those famous first pages longer than any rival. For many readers another point in favour will be the hi-fi brilliance of the recording quality. From the start this is plainly intended as a demonstration record, and as such it succeeds well; but there are other versions more understanding interpretatively. Mehta is a good Straussian, but he is a forceful rather than an affectionate one. The cassette transfer is appropriately robust, full-bodied and clear.

Ormandy's earlier version has tremendous grip and fervour. The power and virtuosity of the Philadelphia playing carries the music forward in a great sweep, so that the listener is taken by surprise at the sudden halt when the disc needs its turn-over. But the recording is impossibly overlit, the upper range almost uncontrollably shrill – one needs the treble cut back to about nine o'clock to achieve an acceptable balance. The cassette is smoother on top, but here the deep pedal note at the opening brings a degree of distortion and the sound is never refined (though in most respects it is preferable to the disc).

Also sprach Zarathustra; Don Juan, Op. 20.
*** DG Dig. **410 959-4**; 410 959-1/*4* [id.]. Berlin PO, Karajan.

Karajan's earlier DG version (see above) has long held sway and up to now would be a strong first recommendation, in spite of the excellence of many of its rivals. His 1984 version has, of course, the advantage of the new technology and, as far as the compact disc is concerned, can offer greater dynamic range and presence, particularly at the extreme bass and treble. As a performance this newcomer will be very hard to beat and, looking at it solely from the viewpoint of a CD collector, it could well be a first choice. The playing of the Berlin Philharmonic Orchestra is as glorious as ever; its virtuosity can be taken for granted along with its sumptuous tonal refinement, and in Strauss, of course, Karajan has no peer. As a recording it is very good indeed, though it does not offer the spectacular definition and transparency of detail of the Dorati CD version listed below. But the playing, it goes without saying, is in a totally different league. Of course, couplings also come into it and Dorati offers a rarity in the form of *Macbeth*, whereas both Ozawa and Mehta are handicapped by having no coupling at all. Karajan offers an exciting account of *Don Juan* and this performance is generally preferred to its current CD rivals (see below). To sum up, this new issue is a strong recommendation for CD collectors, while the chrome tape too is clearer and more refined than its analogue predecessor. But for LP collectors, Karajan's great 1974 record is not displaced. Put the CD alongside the LP, not of the present version but of Karajan's 1974 account, and you will be surprised to discover how well the latter holds up. In fact the upper strings have, if anything, slightly more bloom and glow in the earlier recording, though brass and lower strings are less clearly defined.

Also sprach Zarathustra; Don Juan, Op. 20; Till Eulenspiegel, Op. 28.
(M) *** Decca Jub. JB/*KJBC* 27 [Lon. JL/*5*-41017]. VPO, Karajan.

With superlative performances of Strauss's three most popular symphonic poems squeezed on to a single disc, the Jubilee issue is an outstanding bargain at medium price. In Strauss no one can quite match Karajan in the flair and point of his conducting, and these Vienna performances of the early 1960s make up in warmth what they may slightly lack in polish compared with Karajan's later Berlin versions for DG. The sound, though not as full as the DG recordings, is extremely good for its period. The cassette is generally satisfactory, although the spectacular opening is slightly more secure on the disc.

Also sprach Zarathustra; Macbeth, Op. 23.
**(*) DG Dig. 410 597-1/*4* [id.]. VPO, Maazel.
(*) Decca Dig. **410 146-2; SXDL/*KSXDC* 7613 [Lon. LDR/*5*- 71113]. Detroit SO, Dorati.

The main attraction of Maazel's *Zarathustra* resides in *Macbeth*, which is something of a rarity and not otherwise available. Not that his *Zarathustra* is in any way second-rate: he secures some glorious playing from the Vienna Philharmonic and the performance enjoys the advantage of continuity. The recorded sound, though well balanced, is not as analytical or finely detailed as the best of the current rivals on either LP or tape (both are at a relatively low level). *Macbeth* is an early work whose first version appeared in 1887 when Strauss was barely twenty-three; but Strauss revised it at the instigation of von Bülow, and it was completed in its definitive form after *Don Juan* – hence the later opus number. It is powerful and does not quite deserve the neglect it suffers in the concert hall. Kempe's 1973 record was freer and more imaginatively shaped than Maazel, and the DG recording is not superior to the older version. In its absence, however, this highly polished and superbly played account can be recommended, and only for those primarily interested in *Zarathustra* need there be any qualification.

There are no doubts as to the greater transparency and presence of the Decca recording which has wider range and more detail on both disc and tape. Yet it does not set out merely to produce a sonic spectacular: the sound is vivid and brilliant without being overlit. However, the Detroit orchestra is no match for the Vienna Philharmonic in terms of richness of sonority, homogeneity of tone and ensemble, and Maazel has the greater grip and keener vitality. Splendid though it sounds on its own, as soon as it is placed side by side with the DG version, Dorati's *Zarathustra* does not sound so firmly held together and *Macbeth* is not as well characterized. In *Zarathustra*, Karajan remains unsurpassed.

Also sprach Zarathustra; Till Eulenspiegel.
(B) **(*) Con. CC/*CCT* 7542. RPO, Henry Lewis.

Lewis gives a glowing, warm-hearted performance of *Also sprach Zarathustra*, not lacking excitement, and a broad-paced but nicely sprung performance of *Till Eulenspiegel*. The recordings, originally made for Decca's Phase Four label, have a boldly spectacular sound that makes plenty of impact. The cassette matches the disc fairly closely; it has slightly less brilliance at the top and is not quite so secure in the famous opening climax of *Also sprach Zarathustra*. A good bargain in the lowest price-range.

(i) *Burlesque in D min. for piano and orchestra;* (ii) *Violin concerto in D min., Op. 8.*
*** EMI 1C 063 02744. (i) Frager; (ii) Hoelscher, Dresden State O, Kempe.

These come from a distinguished box containing all Strauss's concertante works under Kempe, which has been withdrawn. The *Burlesque* is a comparative rarity on disc, a product of the composer's early twenties when his brilliance almost outshone his inventiveness. The *Violin concerto* is rarer still; an earlier recording was briefly available but it incorporated cuts, so Ulf Hoelscher's eloquent account is more than welcome. It has a delightfully lyrical first movement and a gay dance-like finale. With superb accompaniments from the Dresden orchestra and vivid recording this is well worth seeking out.

Capriccio (opera)*: Introduction* (arr. for string orchestra).
(*) Argo ZRG 792 [id.]. LACO, Marriner – JANÁČEK: *Suite*; SUK: *Serenade.**

A pity that on both discs the opening sextet to *Capriccio* is given to full strings, for it completely alters the intimate quality of this beautiful piece. Having said that, however, one must admit that it is easy to succumb to the eloquence of Marriner's account, which is superbly played and recorded.

Horn concertos Nos. 1 (Op. 11) and 2 in E flat.
(M) **(*) Decca Jub. JB/*KJBC* 17. Tuckwell, LSO, Kempe – F. STRAUSS: *Horn concerto.***
(M) ** Sup. 1110 2808. Bělohlávek, Prague SO, Tylšar.

Tuckwell does not usually disappoint, but here he does not get the style quite right. One can play the *First Concerto* as a successor to Mozart and it can be effective that way; but better to bring out the *Don Juan* boldness that is also inherent in the music, as Dennis Brain has demonstrated. Tuckwell falls between the two, and his manner and line are relatively unconvincing. He is at his best in the finale of the otherwise less memorable *Second Concerto*. The Decca recording is sumptuous, and on recording grounds alone is far superior to the HMV, while the Brain performances are only available within a boxed set – see under 'The Art of Dennis Brain' in our Recitals section below. On the Decca tape the orchestral sound is less richly expansive than on disc.

Jiri Bělohlávek is a fine player. He phrases musically, produces an agreeably rich timbre and articulates the finales of both these concertos with an attractively light touch. His romantic approach is persuasive, and the only drawback is that for some ears his use of vibrato, though subtly controlled, is at times intrusive, as in the bold central climax of the *Andante* of the *First Concerto*. The accompaniments are well made, and the integration of soloist and orchestra in No. 2 is striking. This is certainly enjoyable.

Oboe concerto in D.
(*) Ph. 6500 174/*7300 119* [id.]. Holliger, New Philh. O, De Waart – MOZART: *Concerto.**
** Sup. 50486. Hanták, Brno State PO, Vogel – MARTINŮ: *Concerto.****

Holliger is never less than masterly, and few oboists today could begin to match the assurance of this performance of one of Strauss's most glowing 'Indian summer' works. But there is a hint of efficiency at the expense of ripeness, an absence of sheer love for the music in its most absolute sense, which prevents this from being quite the ideal version one hoped for. The lack is comparatively small, and with a delightful coupling the disc can still be warmly recommended. There is an excellent cassette too. On both tape and disc the recording now sounds slightly dated.

In the Supraphon recording Hanták is placed right on top of the microphone, which gives a certain 'squawkiness' to the tone. The orchestra too is on the fierce side, although both these defects of balance are reasonably tameable on a flexible reproducer. The performance is vivid and forthright, not quite relaxed enough but no by means insensitive.

Death and Transfiguration, Op. 24.
*** DG 2530 368/*3300 421* [id.]. Berlin PO, Karajan – *4 Last Songs.***(*)
*** HMV ASD/*TCC-ASD* 4182 [Ang. DS/*4XS* 37887]. LPO, Tennstedt – *4 Last songs.****

(M) ** Uni. RHS/*UKC* 312. LSO, Horenstein – HINDEMITH: *Mathis der Maler*.**(*)

Karajan's superlative analogue version of *Death and Transfiguration* can still be regarded as a showpiece, even among Karajan's earlier set of Strauss recordings with the Berlin Philharmonic, although the sound is less sumptuous on tape than on disc. However, this is now available more suitably coupled alongside Karajan's newer digital recording – see below – and with a price advantage.

Tennstedt's is a direct yet impressively spacious performance, very well played and recorded, with a brilliant chrome tape to match; yet Karajan's version is finer still.

Horenstein's account is spacious and the recorded sound is vivid and has presence on both disc and tape. However, competition is stiff and Horenstein would not displace Karajan or indeed Tennstedt.

Death and Transfiguration; Don Juan; Metamorphosen for 23 solo strings; Till Eulenspiegel; Salome: Dance of the seven veils.

(M) **(*) HMV *TCC2-POR 54296*. Philh. O, Klemperer.

This double-length tape in EMI's 'Portrait of the Artist' series admirably assembles Klemperer's Richard Strauss recordings in convenient form at a reasonable price. In his hands it is the *Metamorphosen* and *Death and Transfiguration* that excite the greatest admiration. With Klemperer the work for strings has a ripeness that exactly fits Strauss's last essay for orchestra, while *Death and Transfiguration* is invested with a nobility too rarely heard in this work. Not everyone will respond to Klemperer's spacious treatment of the other works. His account of *Salome's dance* is splendidly sensuous, but the ennobled *Till* lacks something in boisterous high spirits and *Don Juan* is clearly seen as 'the idealist in search of perfect womanhood'. But with marvellous Philharmonia playing and a recording which still sounds strikingly sumptuous this collection is certainly not lacking in strength of characterization. The level of the tape transfers might have been higher (especially in *Metamorphosen* where the cello line is not always very clear) but generally detail is good, though on our copy there was some upper-range discoloration in *Don Juan*, suggesting the iron-oxide tape was reaching saturation point. However, this may well have been corrected in later batches.

Death and Transfiguration; Don Juan; Till Eulenspiegel.

*** Ph. Dig. 6514/*7337* 228 [id.]. Concg. O, Haitink.

(M) *** DG Sig. 410 839-1/*4*. Berlin PO, Karajan.

*** DG Dig. **410 518-2**; 2532/*3302* 099 [id.]. LSO, Abbado.

*** CBS Dig. **CD 35826** [IM/*IMT* 35826]. Cleveland O, Maazel.

*** Decca Dig. **400 085-2**; SXDL/*KSXDC* 7523 [Lon. LDR/*5*- 71025]. Detroit SO, Dorati.

*(**) CBS 60108/*40*- [MY/*MYT* 36721]. Cleveland O, Szell.

Among recent versions of this most popular coupling, Haitink's takes the palm. The Philips digital recording is less analytical than the sound pictures DG provide for Abbado or Decca for Dorati (which is exceptionally clear) but the ambient bloom of the Concertgebouw is admirably suited to Strauss's rich orchestral tapestries and detail is naturally defined. The performances are undoubtedly distinguished, superbly played, persuasively and subtly characterized. Even Karajan hardly displays more dash. He and the Berlin Philharmonic have a unique authority in this repertoire, but Haitink finds added nobility in *Death and Transfiguration*, while there is no lack of swagger in the characterizations of both the Don and Till. The easy brilliance of the orchestral playing is complemented by the natural spontaneity of Haitink's readings, seamless in the transition between narrative events, without loss of the music's picaresque or robust qualities. When the sound is so full and spacious as well as vivid (on the excellent chrome tape as well as the LP) this must receive the strongest recommendation.

Karajan's analogue recordings from the mid-1970s now resurface at mid-price and, even allowing for strides made in present-day digital recording, they are very competitive indeed. *Death and Transfiguration* has been superseded by Karajan's more recent version

– see below – but here *Don Juan* has a degree of rapture not surpassed in the digital re-make, and some might feel that the analogue recording of the Berlin Philharmonic's upper strings has marginally more ample richness and bloom. All three performances are winningly characterized and exhilarating in impulse, the orchestral playing in the highest class and the sound consistently vivid, with the excellent chrome-tape transfer matching the disc in almost every respect, although *Death and Transfiguration* is perhaps a little dry in the bass.

The performances under Claudio Abbado have plenty of dash and their brilliance is tempered with sensitivity. Some may feel that *Don Juan* veers too much towards the exuberant showpiece and vehicle for display, but both this and *Till Eulenspiegel* must be numbered among the best available. Abbado's *Death and Transfiguration* is scarcely less impressive than Karajan's and has a marvellously spacious opening. The strings produce some splendidly silky tone and there is much sensitive wind playing too. Karajan still reigns supreme in this work, but Abbado runs him very close and he is equally well recorded, though on the chrome tape *Don Juan* and *Till* present a rather recessed image, though *Death and Transfiguration* has more projection and brilliance.

Maazel repeats a coupling made famous by George Szell at the peak of his era with the Cleveland Orchestra, but Maazel's approach is entirely different. With superbly committed support from his players, he takes an extrovert view of *Death and Transfiguration*; the mortal struggle is frenzied enough, but there is comparatively little feeling of menace, and when the transformation comes, the opulent climax is endearingly rose-tinted. The portrayal of *Till* is warmly affectionate, but the reading is exhilaratingly paced and has excellent detail. *Don Juan* too is made totally sympathetic, with Maazel relishing every moment. In the famous love scene the oboe solo is glowingly sensuous, and the final climax is ecstatic, the tempo broadened when the strings rapturously take up the great horn tune. The CBS digital sound is sumptuous, richly glowing, but does not lack clarity, and the brass has telling bite and sonority. The chrome cassette too (transferred at a high level) has comparable body and brilliance, with a wide range. Only the compact disc version is available in the UK.

Dorati's Decca recording is also digital, and its internal clarity is striking. Dorati's approach to *Death and Transfiguration* is more austere than Maazel's; there is plenty of atmosphere, a certain dignity in the struggle and a sense of foreboding before the release at the end, where the climax has real splendour (and a magnificent breadth of sound). Dorati's view of *Don Juan* is heroic, the sensuality played down by the sound balance, brilliant rather than sumptuous. After a central love scene which is tenderly delicate, there is satiety and disillusion at the end. *Till* is essentially a picaresque portrait, not without humour and well paced, but a little lacking in affectionate involvement. In spite of a transfer level that is lower than usual from Decca, there is no appreciable difference in sound between disc and cassette. On CD the dazzling brilliance of detail and focus is even more telling.

Szell's version of *Death and Transfiguration* has tremendous electricity. The opening creates striking atmosphere, and the triumphant closing pages are the more telling for Szell's complete lack of indulgence. *Till* is irrepressibly cheeky, his characterization created from the most polished and vivid orchestral playing, so that every detail is crystal-clear. *Don Juan* is impetuously passionate in the thrustful urgency of his sexuality. Superb playing, the whole interpretation founded on a bedrock of virtuosity from this remarkable orchestra. The recording here is brilliant but rather dry. For those willing to accept the dated sound, this is a fine disc. The cassette has rather less range than the disc but sounds richer if less refined.

Death and Transfiguration; Don Juan; Till Eulenspiegel; Salome: Dance of the seven veils.
(M) *** HMV Green. ESD/*TC-ESD* 290053-1/*4*. Dresden State O, Kempe.

EMI have added the *Dance of the seven veils* to the more familiar compilation of the *Don*, *Till* and *Tod und Verklärung*, thus making this disc even more competitive. Kempe's versions are marvellously characterized and sumptuously recorded, and both his *Don* and *Till* could well be preferred to the Karajan – and the Dresden Staatskapelle is hardly less refined an instrument than the Berlin Philharmonic. A most competitive and attractive reissue. The cassette is absolutely first-class, just as rich and glowing as the LP, and with no appreciable loss in range and detail.

Death and Transfiguration; Metamorphosen for 23 solo strings.
❀ *** DG Dig. **410 892-2**; 2532/*3302* 074 [id.]. Berlin PO, Karajan.
(M) *** DG Acc. 2542/*3342* 164. Berlin PO, Karajan.

Karajan made the pioneering record of *Metamorphosen* with the Vienna Philharmonic in 1947 (available in an LP transfer on HMV RLS 7714) and brings a special authority to this valedictory work. His new digital account has even greater emotional urgency than the 1971 record he made with the Berlin Philharmonic and there is a marginally quicker pulse (in 1971 he took 27′ 30″ as opposed to 26′ 11″ in this 1983 version). The sound is fractionally more forward and cleaner (though some may find the richer ambience of the earlier analogue disc more appealing). The newer version, however, still sounds sumptuous and the account of *Death and Transfiguration* is quite electrifying. The recording balance is not so spectacular as Dorati's on Decca, nor so spacious as Tennstedt's on HMV (see above), but there is no lack of vividness and the playing of the Berliners is in itself thrilling. It would be difficult to improve on this coupling by the greatest Strauss conductor of the day. Nevertheless, with the earlier versions now economically re-coupled on Accolade, and given the competitive price of the reissue and its excellent analogue sound, this can still be strongly recommended to those with limited budgets. The Accolade tape is slightly less refined than the disc and benefits from a treble cut. However, the compact disc of the later recording is in a class of its own, bringing a marginally firmer image than the LP and greater range, while the background silence is especially telling in the *Metamorphosen.*

Don Juan, Op. 20.
(B) *** Con. CC/*CCT* 7528. VPO, Karajan – TCHAIKOVSKY: *Romeo and Juliet.****
(B) **(*) RCA VICS/*VK* 2006 [AGL 1/*AGK 1* 1276]. LAPO, Mehta – RESPIGHI: *Feste romane.***(*)*

Karajan's early Decca version of *Don Juan*, now reissued on Contour, is an outstanding bargain, for the performance is superbly played, and Karajan is as beguiling in the love music as he is exhilarating in the chase. The recording is excellent for its period (1961), and the Tchaikovsky coupling is equally exciting. The Contour cassette transfer lacks the lively upper range of the LP.

Extrovert brilliance is very much the principal quality of Mehta's version (one of the first records he made with the Los Angeles Philharmonic), but he relaxes expansively in the rich music of the love scene, drawing hushed and intense playing from the orchestra. With bright, atmospheric, but slightly brittle recording this might well be considered an alternative in the same price-range if the coupling is more suitable. The chrome tape mirrors the disc.

Don Quixote, Op. 35.
(M) *** DG Priv. 2535 195 [id./*3335 195*]. Fournier, Berlin PO, Karajan.

Fournier's partnership with Karajan is outstanding. His portrayal of the Don has no less nobility than previous rivals and he brings great subtlety and (when required) repose to the part. The finale and Don Quixote's death are very moving in Fournier's hands, while Karajan's handling of orchestral detail is quite splendid. Although Fournier is forwardly balanced, in every other respect the recording is of the highest quality and (given its price) this can be strongly recommended. At present both the Kempe recordings are withdrawn from the UK catalogue, although his fine Dresden version with Tortelier is still available in the USA: [Sera. S 60363].

Duet concertino for clarinet, bassoon, strings and harp.
** None. Dig. **79018-2**; D/*D1* 79018 [id.]. Shifrin, Munday, LACO, Schwarz – HONEGGER: *Concerto da camera.***

The Strauss work appeared within a year or two of the Honegger with which it is coupled, and so it is a late piece. It is very nicely played here though the performance does not obliterate memories of the Kempe version included in the Dresden Strauss complete-concertos box on HMV, which had greater warmth both as a performance and as sound. The present issue is a perfectly likeable account nonetheless.

Fanfare for Music Week in Vienna (1924)*; Fanfare for the Vienna Philharmonic; Feier Einzug der Ritter des Johanniterordens; Festmusik der Stadt Wien; Olympic hymn* (1936)*; Parade marches Nos. 1 and 2* (arr. Locke).
*** Chan. ABR/*ABT* 1002. Locke Brass Cons., Stobart.

Not all this music is of equal interest. The two *Parade marches*, which date from 1905, offer agreeable invention but were scored by others. On the other hand the *Festmusik* is a considerable piece in the grand manner, using antiphonal effects to acknowledge its baroque heritage, although this is not emphasized by the recording layout. Otherwise the sound is first-class, rich and sonorous and spacious in feeling. On tape a relatively low-level transfer has lost a fraction of the upper range, but the body and amplitude of sound remain impressive. An attractive if hardly essential collection.

Ein Heldenleben, Op. 40.
(M) *** Ph. Seq. 6527/*7311* 128 [id.]. Concg. O, Haitink.
(M) *** DG Priv. 2535 194 [id./*3335 194*]. Berlin PO, Karajan.
*** Ph. Dig. **400 073-2**; 6514/*7337* 222 [id.]. Boston SO, Ozawa.
(M) *** Decca Jub. JB 101. LAPO, Mehta.

Haitink's 1971 version of *Ein Heldenleben* is one of his finest records. He gives just the sort of performance, brilliant and swaggering but utterly without bombast, which will delight those who normally resist this rich and expansive work. With a direct and fresh manner that yet conveys consistent urgency, he gives a performance which makes even such fine rival versions as Mehta's or Karajan's sound a little superficial. In the culminating fulfilment theme, a gentle, lyrical 6/8, Haitink finds a raptness in restraint, a hint of agony within joy, that links the passage directly with the great Trio from *Der Rosenkavalier*. The Philips sound – freshened in this reissue – is admirably faithful, refined but full and brilliant too. The cassette is outstanding, one of Philips's best, matching the disc closely.

Karajan's 1959 *Heldenleben*, now reissued on Privilege, also sounds amazingly fresh; listening to this new transfer with its superb body and clarity of detail, one feels it still deserves a full three-star grading. It is a superb performance and at mid-price can be confidently purchased. Playing of great power and distinction from the Berlin Philharmonic and in the closing section an altogether becoming sensuousness and warmth.

Ozawa's view of *Heldenleben* is free-flowing, lyrical and remarkably unpompous. He consistently brings out the joy of the virtuoso writing, and though the playing of the Boston orchestra is not quite so immaculate as in the companion version of *Zarathustra*, the richness and transparency are just as seductive, superbly caught by the Philips engineers. The compact disc version adds significantly to the sense of presence and reality. The chrome cassette is full and clear, though not as wide-ranging on top. But there is attendant hiss, brought by the relatively low transfer level.

Mehta's is an extrovert and extremely exciting account to impress the Straussian weaned on the opening of *Also sprach Zarathustra*. It may miss some of the subtler qualities of a richly varied score, but its thrust is undeniable. It is superbly recorded.

Metamorphosen for 23 solo strings.
*** Argo ZRG 604 [id.]. ASMF, Marriner – WAGNER: *Siegfried idyll* etc.**(*)

Metamorphosen; Capriccio: Introduction.
(*) Erato STU/*MCE* 71333. Lausanne CO, Jordan – WAGNER: *Siegfried idyll.**

Marriner's version is not so strongly characterized as Karajan's, but it is finely played and recorded, and if the coupling is suitable this is recommendable.

Armin Jordan directs an impressively controlled account of *Metamorphosen*. The playing of the Lausanne Chamber Orchestra is excellent, though not quite as refined as in the ASMF version under Marriner, which has a similar coupling. The *Capriccio Introduction* is played by the full string section with considerable ardour. The sound is full-bodied and clear, and the coupling is attractive. The high-level cassette transfer is excellently managed, the sound is well focused and has plenty of body.

Till Eulenspiegel, Op. 28.
(M) *** Decca VIV/*KVIC* 40 [Lon. STS/5-15582]. VPO, Reiner – BRITTEN: *Young person's guide***; PROKOFIEV: *Peter.****

This is a famous vintage account of *Till.* The performance is superb, with the Vienna orchestra responding to this great Straussian in the manner born. The recording dates from 1959, yet in terms of presence and sonority it remains impressive. There is a vivid cassette.

CHAMBER MUSIC

Serenade for wind instruments, Op. 7; Sonatina No. 1 in F; Symphony for wind; Suite in B flat for 13 wind instruments, Op. 4.
(M) *** Ph. 6770 048 (2). Neth. Wind Ens., De Waart.

A highly attractive set of wind music spanning the whole of Strauss's creative career. The *Serenade* was composed while he was still at school, and its accomplished writing and easy melodic flow are immediately engaging. The *Symphony* is a late work, and is given a marvellously alert performance here. The *Sonatina*, also a late work, was written while Strauss was recovering from an illness, and is subtitled 'From an invalid's workshop'. It is a richly scored piece, as thoroughly effective as one would expect from this master of wind writing. (The scoring is for double wind, a C clarinet, a corno di bassetto, bass clarinet and double bassoon, and marvellously sonorous it is.) The *B flat Suite* was written in 1884 but not published until 1911. These delightful pieces are given beautifully characterized accounts here, and they are crisply and cleanly recorded.

VOCAL MUSIC

Lieder: *Das Bächlein; Das Rosenband; Meinem Kinde; Morgen; Ruhe, meine Seele; Wiegenlied; Winterweihe.*
*** HMV ASD 2493 [Ang. S 36643]. Schwarzkopf, LSO, Szell – MOZART: *Concert arias.****

These orchestrations (by the composer) of some of his best-loved Lieder are ravishing when sung by the greatest Strauss singer of recent years and accompanied by a master conductor who on his visits to Europe loved to relax. No one who has heard the earlier record of orchestrated songs (the coupling to the *Four Last songs* – see below) will doubt that this collaboration is a magical one, even if some of the velvet quality of that Berlin-made disc is missing here. The recording is beautifully refined to match the performances.

Lieder: *Liebeshymnus; Muttertändelei; Das Rosenband; Ruhe, meine Seele.*
(*) HMV ASD 3260 [Ang. RL/*4RL* 32017]. Baker, LPO, Boult – BRAHMS: *Alto rhapsody;* WAGNER: *Wesendonk Lieder.**

In Strauss Lieder with piano accompaniment Janet Baker has herself set supreme standards (HMV ASD 2431, now deleted), while in the orchestral arrangements Schwarzkopf's records have been in a class on their own. These are beautiful performances, as one would expect, but for once Dame Janet sounds a little effortful, less naturally spontaneous. Even so, as a fine fill-up for a delightful coupling, the songs make a welcome group. Excellent recording.

Four Last songs (*Vier letzte Lieder*).
*** HMV Dig. **CDC 747013-2**; ASD/*TCC-ASD* 4182 [Ang. DS/*4XS* 37887]. Popp, LPO, Tennstedt – *Death and Transfiguration.****
(*) DG 2530 368/*3300 421* [id.]. Janowitz, Berlin PO, Karajan – *Death and Transfiguration.**

Four Last songs; Lieder: *Befreit; Morgen; Muttertändelei; Ruhe, meine Seele; Wiegenlied; Zueignung.*

**(*) CBS 76794 [M/*MT* 35140]. Te Kanawa, LSO, Andrew Davis.

Four Last songs; Lieder: *Cäcilie; Meinem Kinde; Morgen; Ruhe, meine Seele; Wiegenlied; Zueignung.*
C ❀ *** Ph. Dig. **411 052-2**; 6514/*7337* 322 [id.]. Norman, Leipzig GO, Masur.

Four Last songs; Lieder: *Freundliche Vision; Die heiligen drei Könige; Muttertändelei; Waldseligkeit; Zueignung.*
❀ *** HMV ASD/*TC-ASD* 2888 [Ang. S 36347]. Schwarzkopf, Berlin RSO, Szell.

Strauss's publisher Ernest Roth says in the score of the *Four Last songs* that this was a farewell of 'serene confidence', and that is exactly the mood Jessye Norman conveys. The power of her singing reminds one that the first ever interpreter (with Furtwängler and the Philharmonia Orchestra at the Royal Albert Hall in May 1950) was Kirsten Flagstad. The start of the second stanza of the third song, *Beim Schlafengehen*, brings one of the most thrilling vocal crescendos on record, expanding from a half-tone to a gloriously rich and rounded forte. In concern for word detail Norman is outshone only by Schwarzkopf (unique in conveying the poignancy of old age) but in both the *Four Last songs* and the orchestral songs on the reverse, the stylistic as well as the vocal command is irresistible with *Cäcilie* given operatic strength. The radiance of the recording matches the interpretations, the more fully and immediately on compact disc.

It would be unthinkable if, in awarding a Rosette to Jessye Norman's beautiful new record, we withdrew the similar indication of esteem given in our first edition to Schwarzkopf's recording, for even she rarely if ever made a more radiantly beautiful record than this, and it is not surprising that it became one of EMI's classical best-sellers. Schwarzkopf's interpretation of the *Four Last songs* had long been known and loved in her old mono versions (see below), but if anything this is even more ravishingly expressive, with an 'inner' intensity adding to the depth of feeling as well as the beauty. Anyone who has ever fallen for Schwarzkopf must certainly hear this, and the Strauss Lieder with orchestral accompaniment on the reverse (all the orchestrations except *Zueignung* by Strauss himself) are just as captivating, ranging as they do from the playful song of the mother talking about her child to *Freundliche Vision* (somehow made more intimate by having orchestra instead of piano) and the group, that Strauss wrote for his mother, telling of the Three Kings. George Szell conducts and the Berlin Radio Orchestra play with the deepest sympathy and understanding for both the music and the singer. This is a desert-island record if ever there was one, and now there is a splendid matching tape for anyone who happens to be shipwrecked with a cassette player.

Lucia Popp, too, gives a ravishingly beautiful performance of the *Four Last songs*. With the voice given an ethereal glow, naturally balanced in a warmly atmospheric digital recording, the radiance of texture is paramount. This is an orchestral performance rather than a deeply illuminating Lieder performance, and that matches the coupling, the early tone poem on death which is quoted by the dying composer in the last of the songs. Tennstedt is a direct rather than a persuasive Straussian. The beauty of sound is unfailing, with a first-class matching chrome cassette. However, as the CD readily shows, the Philips recording for Jessye Norman has far more atmospheric warmth.

Kiri Te Kanawa gives an openhearted, warmly expressive reading of the *Four Last songs*. If she misses the sort of detail that Schwarzkopf uniquely brought, her commitment is never in doubt. Her tone is consistently beautiful, but might have seemed even more so if the voice had not been placed rather too close in relation to the orchestra. The orchestral arrangements of other songs make an excellent coupling (as a comparable selection does in the Schwarzkopf stereo version), and Andrew Davis directs most sympathetically if not with the sort of rapt dedication that Szell gave to Schwarzkopf.

Janowitz produces a beautiful flow of creamy soprano tone while leaving the music's deeper and subtler emotions underexposed. She is well recorded, but there are several finer versions of these songs.

(i) *Four Last songs.* (ii) *Arabella:* excerpts. (i) *Capriccio: closing scene.*
(M) (***) HMV mono RLS 751 (2). Schwarz-

kopf, Philh. O, cond. (i) Ackermann, (ii) Von Matačic, with Metternich, Gedda.

The separate mono recordings of Richard Strauss which Schwarzkopf made in the 1950s form a superb pendant to her two supreme complete opera recordings with Karajan, *Rosenkavalier* and *Ariadne auf Naxos*. Rarely if ever has the character of Arabella been conveyed so sparklingly yet with such tenderness as in these generous and well-chosen excerpts, helped by the fine singing of a baritone seldom heard on record, Josef Metternich, a magnificent Mandryka. The *Capriccio* last scene and the *Four Last songs* are a degree lighter than Schwarzkopf's later recordings, but just as detailed and searching, putting a different gloss on interpretations unlikely ever to be outshone. The transfers are first-rate.

Four Last songs. (i) *Capriccio: closing scene. Der Rosenkavalier, Act I: Da geht er hin.*
**(*) HMV Dig. ASD/*TCC-ASD* 4103. Söderström, Welsh Nat. Op. O, Armstrong; (i) with P. Joll.

Söderström, a deeply moving and beautiful Countess in the celebrated Glyndebourne production which was seen on television, here couples the ravishing final scene of that last opera with Strauss's very last work, as well as the *Marschallin's monologue* from *Rosenkavalier*. The digital sound is full and forward, and the closeness of balance does not always flatter Söderström's voice by exaggerating some unevenness of production. But the results are both moving and beautiful. The chrome tape is brilliant and detailed, yet lacks something in sumptuousness.

OPERA

Die ägyptische Helena (complete).
*** Decca D 176 D 3/*K 176 K 33* (3) [Lon. 13135]. Gwyneth Jones, Kastu, Hendricks, Willard White, Detroit SO, Dorati.

Last of the six operas in which Strauss collaborated with Hugo von Hofmannsthal, this grand classical extravaganza was initially designed as a vehicle for the glamorous soprano Maria Jeritza (famous above all for her provocative *Tosca*) and the tenor Richard Tauber. Hofmannsthal's device of mingling two Helen legends has an element of jokiness in it, but Ancient Greece, as so often with Strauss, prompted some heavyweight orchestral writing (echoes of *Elektra*), and Dorati, using the original Dresden version of the score, draws magnificent sounds from the Detroit orchestra, richly and forwardly recorded. The vocal sounds are less consistently pleasing. Gwyneth Jones has her squally moments as Helen, though it is a commmanding performance. Matti Kastu manages as well as any Heldentenor today in the role of Menelaus, strained at times but with a pleasing distinctive timbre. The others too are not always helped by the closeness, but with excellent documentation it is a richly enjoyable as well as a valuable set. The tape transfer is one of Decca's best, with full-bodied, sumptuous orchestral sound, splendidly achieved perspectives for the solo voices and chorus, and the most spectacular feeling of breadth for the powerful closing section of the work.

Arabella (complete).
*** HMV Dig. SLS 5224 (3) [Ang. DSCX 3917]. Varady, Fischer-Dieskau, Donath, Dallapozza, Schmidt, Berry, Bav. State Op. Ch. and O, Sawallisch.
(M) **(*) Decca Ace GOS 571/3 [id. PSI]. Della Casa, Gueden, London, Edelmann, Dermota, V. State Op. Ch., VPO, Solti.

It was high time that the magic of one of Strauss's sweetest inspirations was caught at full intensity on record. Fine as Sir Georg Solti's set was with Lisa della Casa, recorded in the late 1950s, this splendid digital recording is in every way superior, not just in sound but in the warmth and understanding of Sawallisch, the characterful tenderness of Julia Varady as the heroine, and Fischer-Dieskau's fine-detailed characterization of the gruff Mandryka, *der Richtige* ('Mr Right') according to the heroine's charmingly romantic view. Helen Donath too is charming as the younger sister, Zdenka, though the voice might be more sharply contrasted. If there are unappealing elements in an opera which would reach a happy ending far too quickly but for uncongenial twists of plot, this recording clothes them with an entirely Straussian glow of richness and charm. Highly recommended.

The Decca set is still available at medium-price, and remains persuasive. Della Casa soars above the stave with the creamiest, most beautiful sounds, and constantly charms one with her swiftly alternating moods of seriousness and gaiety. One moment one thinks of in particular is where in Act I she sees the stranger through her window, *der Richtige* ('Mr Right'), later to appear as Mandryka. Della Casa conveys wonderfully the pain and disappointment of frustrated young love as the man turns away and passes on. Perhaps Solti does not linger as he might over the waltz rhythms, and it may be Solti too who prevents Edelmann from making his first scene with Mandryka as genuinely humorous as it can be, with the Count's *Teschek, bedien'dich* as he goggles at Mandryka's generosity. Edelmann otherwise is superb, as fine a Count as he was an Ochs in the Karajan *Rosenkavalier*. Gueden too is ideally cast as Zdenka and if anything in Act I manages to steal our sympathies from Arabella, as a good Zdenka can. George London is on the ungainly side, but then Mandryka is a boorish fellow anyway. Dermota is a fine Matteo, and Mimi Coertse makes as much sense as anyone could of the ridiculously difficult part of Fiakermilli, the female yodeller. The stereo is most brilliant; one wishes that some of the effects could have been more realistic, such as the bells of Elemer's sleigh outside the hotel, but that is a tiny complaint.

Ariadne auf Naxos (complete).

(M) (***) HMV mono RLS 760 (3). Schwarzkopf, Schock, Streich, Donch, Seefried, Cuénod, Philh. O, Karajan.

**(*) [Lon. OSA 13131]. Leontyne Price, Gruberová, Kollo, Troyanos, Berry, Kunz, LPO, Solti.

In mono only and with a transfer that removes the fullness of bass, this classic reading of Strauss's most equivocal opera still surpasses any ever recorded in its power to captivate. Schwarzkopf makes the richest of Ariadnes, bringing an aching sense of tragedy to the great lament, while in the vignette of the prima donna in the Prologue she touches in a delectable caricature. Rita Streich's Zerbinetta is not just sparkling; she conveys total joy in her coloratura, and Irmgard Seefried as the Composer is in some ways the most moving of all, imprinting for ever her distinctive tones on the radiant solo *Musik ist eine heilige Kunst* ('Music is a holy art'). Rudolf Schock is a capable Heldentenor, and the rest of the cast includes some masterly performances in the small roles, such as the Harlequinade characters. Most magical of all is Karajan, here giving a performance that even he has rarely matched in its glowing ardour, with the Philharmonia Orchestra at its very peak.

Brilliance is the keynote of Solti's set of *Ariadne*. This extraordinary confection has so many elements that within its chosen limits this reading is most powerful and compelling, with brilliant playing and recording as well as some strong singing. What the performance is short of is charm and warmth. Everything is so brightly lit that much of the delicacy and tenderness of the writing tends to disappear. Nonetheless the concentration of Solti in Strauss is never in doubt, and though Leontyne Price has given more beautiful performances on record, she makes a strong central figure, memorably characterful. Tatiana Troyanos is affecting as the Composer, and Edita Gruberová establishes herself as the unrivalled Zerbinetta of her generation, though here she is less delicate than on stage. René Kollo similarly is the best Bacchus available, but not of all time. This set is not available in the UK.

Daphne (complete).

*** HMV Dig. SLS 143582-3 (2) [Ang. DSX/*4X2X* 3941]. Popp, Goldberg, Wenkel, Schreier, Bav. R. Ch. and SO, Haitink.

Strauss wrote this opera not long before the Second World War at a time when he was being almost universally accused of simply repeating himself. He turned several times to Greek classical sources, remembering the success of *Ariadne auf Naxos*, but in this delicately beautiful one-Act (100-minute) piece, he gave clear indication of what mastery was to come in his last 'classical' period of *Metamorphosen*, the *Oboe concerto* and the *Four Last songs*. On record this amiable telling of the story of the nymph Daphne wooed by Apollo and finally turned into a tree makes delightful entertainment. Haitink with his fine Bavarian forces takes a rather more restrained, spacious view of the piece than did Karl Boehm, the dedicatee, one of whose live performances in Vienna was recorded by DG (but is now withdrawn). There are many gains in a studio performance with beauty of balance so important in this score. The cast is a fine one with Popp an enchanting, girlish Daphne, Peter Schreier bringing Lieder-like feeling for detail to the role of Leukippos, and Reiner Goldberg producing heroic sounds as Apollo with little feeling of strain and with no coarseness. Kurt Moll is a fine Peneios. The recording is exceptionally rich yet refined too.

Elektra (complete).
*** Decca SET 354-5/*K 124 K 22* [Lon. OSA/5- 1269]. Nilsson, Collier, Resnik, Stolze, Krause, V. State Op. Ch., VPO, Solti.

The Decca set of *Elektra* was a *tour de force* of John Culshaw and his engineering team. Not everyone will approve of the superimposed sound-effects, but as in Wagner every one of them has justification in the score, and the end result is a magnificently vivid operatic experience created without the help of vision. Nilsson is almost incomparable in the part, with the hard side of Elektra's character brutally dominant. Only when – as in the recognition scene with Orestes – she tries to soften the naturally bright tone does she let out a suspect flat note or two. As a rule she is searingly accurate in approaching even the most formidable exposed top notes. One might draw a parallel with Solti's direction – sharply focused and brilliant in the savage music which predominates, but lacking the languorous warmth one really needs in the recognition scene if only for contrast. Those who remember Beecham's old 78 r.p.m. set of the final scene may not be completely won over by Solti, but we are not likely to get a finer complete *Elektra* for a long time. The tape transfer emphasizes the recording's brilliance. It is clinically clear, but lacks a balancing sumptuous quality. One needs a treble cut if the effect is not to become aggressive. The libretto is excellently done.

Elektra: Soliloquy; Recognition scene; Finale.
(B) *** RCA VICS/*VK* 2009. Borkh, Schoeffler, Yeend, Chicago SO, Reiner.

Inge Borkh never sang *Elektra* at the Met., but this record of excerpts made in the early days of stereo gives a tantalizing indication of what such a performance would have been like. With Borkh singing superbly in the title role alongside Paul Schoeffler and Francis Yeend, this is quite a collector's piece. Reiner provides a superbly telling accompaniment; the performances of the recognition scene and final duet are as ripely passionate as Beecham's old 78 excerpts and outstrip the complete versions. The balance by no means projects the singers at the expense of orchestral detail, and the recording, though dated, still sounds full and clear. The splendid chrome tape is if anything even more vivid than the disc.

Die Frau ohne Schatten (complete).
(M) ** Decca Ace GOS 554/7 [Rich. 64503]. Rysanek, Loose, Hopf, Terkal, Höngen, Böhme, V. State Op. Ch., VPO, Boehm.

It was a labour of love on the part of the Decca recording manager, Christopher Raeburn, that rescued this early stereo version of an opera – some would suggest Strauss's greatest – which is unlikely to be recorded again in the near future. For its mid-1950s period the sound is remarkably good, while Boehm's direction is masterly. Once one accepts the strange symbolism of Hofmannsthal's libretto, one can go on to appreciate the richness of Strauss's inspiration, a score utterly different from anything else he ever did, in many ways more ambitious. On any count this is a work that deserves the closest study, not just by Straussians but by those not normally attracted. The singing is variable, with a high proportion of wobblers among the soloists and Hans Hopf often producing coarse tone as the Emperor. But with stereo to help, the singing is still more than acceptable, and at mid-price on only four discs (the original mono took five) this is good value together with an excellently produced libretto.

Intermezzo (complete).
*** HMV SLS 5204 (3). Popp, Brammer, Fischer-Dieskau, Bav. RSO, Sawallisch.

What other composer but Strauss could turn an absurd little incident in his married life into an opera as enchanting as *Intermezzo*? He made no secret of the fact that the central character of Storch, the composer, was himself and the nagging but loving wife his own Pauline. That is very much the central role – the name Christine the flimsiest of disguises – involving a virtuoso performance which scarcely lets up for an instant. It was originally designed for the dominant and enchanting Lotte Lehmann, but I doubt if even she can have outshone the radiant Lucia Popp, for she brings out the charm of the character, which for all his incidental trials must have consistently captivated Strauss and provoked this strange piece of self-revelation. The piece inevitably is very wordy, but with this scintillating and emotionally powerful performance under Sawallisch, with fine recording and an excellent supporting cast, this set is as near ideal as could be, a superb achievement.

Der Rosenkavalier (complete).
❀ *** HMV SLS/*TC-SLS* 810 (4) [Ang. SDL 3563]. Schwarzkopf, Ludwig, Edelmann, Waechter, Stich-Randall, Philh. Ch. and O, Karajan.
*** Decca SET 418-21/*K3 N23* [Lon. OSA/5-1435]. Crespin, Minton, Wiener, Jungwirth, Donath, V. State Op. Ch., VPO, Solti.
**(*) CBS 77416 (4) [D4M 30652]. Ludwig, Gwyneth Jones, Berry, Gutstein, Popp, Vienna State Op. Ch., VPO, Bernstein.

From Karajan one of the greatest opera sets that Walter Legge ever produced, a classic performance with sound improved beyond recognition in the newest transfer. Schwarzkopf points her phrases, underlining the meaning of the words after the manner of a Lieder-singer, bringing out a character at once human and emotional, yet at the same time restrained and an object for admiration. She makes of the Marschallin more of a lover figure than a mother figure, and that is something which adds to the reality of the situation. Instead of the buxom prima donna we have a mature woman, still attractive, whom it would be quite understandable and sympathetic for the young Octavian to love. The moment in Act I when she tells Octavian how sometimes in the middle of the night she comes downstairs and stops all the clocks, so disturbed is she about the passage of time and the approach of old age, is particularly moving. With Schwarzkopf one feels that the singer is still young and attractive enough to feel this emotion as a pressing thing. She is matched by an Octavian in Christa Ludwig who has a rich mezzo but one which is neither fruity nor womanly, but steady and youthful-sounding. Teresa Stich-Randall too is wonderfully steady but her light soprano is exquisitely sweet, so that when in the presentation of the silver rose she sings the soaring phrase *Wie himmlische* one wants to use this same phrase ('How heavenly!') to describe her singing. In the final trio three such beautifully contrasted yet steady voices make a perfect match. Karajan here, as in the other emotional climaxes, chooses a speed rather slower than is customary. Some have objected, but when the result is vocally so secure and the playing of the Philharmonia Orchestra is so full-blooded the music can certainly take this treatment, and the emotional peak seems even higher than usual. These emotional climaxes are places where – as in Puccini – Strauss seems to intend his audience to weep, and Karajan plays up to this. Otto Edelmann's Ochs is rather coarser than the characterizations of some previous singers in the part, and he exaggerates the Viennese accent on such words as *Polizei*, *gut* and *herzel*; but vocally it is most commendable, for Edelmann really does sing on the notes and does not merely give the impression in sing-speech. The discs have been reprocessed from the original tapes to produce a sound of superb quality, even by the latest standards. There is also a fine version on tape. Those wanting a highlights disc can order an EMI special import: (1C 061 00720).

On two counts Solti scores over any other rival in this much-recorded opera. He opens out all the tiny cuts which over the years have been sanctioned in opera-house performances (often with the composer's blessing). In the second place the sound is sumptuously fine even by Decca standards, far finer than that of the later CBS set with Bernstein, also recorded in the Sofiensaal, with Decca engineers attending. Curiously enough, the Karajan set, beautifully refurbished for its HMV reissue, is a nearer rival in sound-quality, and the big question for most lovers of this opera will be the contrasting merits of the two Marshallins. Crespin is here at her finest on record, with tone well-focused; the slightly maternal maturity of her approach will for many appear ideal, but the range of expression, verbal and musical, in Schwarzkopf's interpretation stands unrivalled, one of the great performances of the gramophone. Manfred Jungwirth makes a firm, virile if not always imaginative Ochs, Yvonne Minton a finely projected Octavian and Helen Donath a sweet-toned Sophie. Solti's direction is fittingly honeyed, with tempi even slower than Karajan's in the climactic moments. The one serious disappointment is that the great concluding *Trio* does not quite lift one to the tear-laden height one ideally wants. The smoothly vivid richness has been well transferred to tape, and if the quality is marginally less open and sharply defined than on disc, the special effects and general detail are superior to the EMI production (although considering its age the latter measures up remarkably well).

Bernstein's account, though not so polished in orchestral playing or so consistently well sung as the rival versions of Karajan and Solti, has its place in commemorating a great theatrical occasion. The Viennese were swept off their feet – much to their surprise – by the magic of the American conductor. His direction of this opera at the Vienna State Opera was an almost unparalleled success, and this recorded version captures much of the ripeness, notably in the fine, mature Marschallin of Christa Ludwig, which plainly owes much to the example of Schwarzkopf (for whom, on the Karajan, Ludwig was the Octavian). Lucia Popp (as at Covent Garden) makes a charming Sophie, and Walter Berry a strong and expressive Ochs, less limited in the lower register than one might expect. But Gwyneth Jones's Octavian, despite the occasional halftone of exquisite beauty, has too many passages of raw tone to be very appealing, a bad blot on the set. Bernstein follows traditional cuts, where Solti records the score absolutely complete. Surprisingly when Decca engineers were responsible, the sound here is much more variable than on the Decca set, with a vulgarly close horn balance.

Der Rosenkavalier (abridged version).
(M) *** HMV mono RLS/*TC-RLS* 7704 (2). Lehmann, Schumann, Mayr, Olszewska, Ch. and VPO, Heger.

It is good to have a fresh transfer, immaculate in quality, of this classic recording of excerpts from *Rosenkavalier* made in 1934. LP versions have told us that this is not definitive, as we once may have thought, but Lehmann as the Marschallin and Schumann as Sophie remain uniquely characterful, and though 78 r.p.m. side-lengths brought some hastening from Heger, notably in the great trio of Act III, the passion of the performance still conveys a sense of new discovery, a rare Straussian magic. The cassette transfer is made on to one double-length tape (in a box) and the quality is admirably fresh and clear.

Der Rosenkavalier: excerpts (Act I: *Introduction; opening scene; Marschallin's monologue, Duet, closing scene;* Act II: *Presentation of the silver rose; Duet;* Act III: *Marschallin's meeting with Sophie; Trio and final duet*).
(M) *** Decca Jub. JB/*KJBC* 57. Crespin, Söderström, Gueden, Holecek, VPO, Varviso.

This was recorded in advance of Crespin's complete recording of the role of Marschallin under Solti. It is a much plainer performance than Schwarzkopf's (some may prefer it on that account) and the projection of character is less intense. But even so Crespin has rarely, if ever, made a better record, and she is beautifully supported by Söderström and Gueden. The selection is most generous and well-chosen, and the recording is first-class, from a vintage Decca period. The tape transfer too is of high quality and approaches demonstration standard on side two, where the level is considerably higher than on side one.

Salome (complete).
*** Decca SET 228-9/*K 111 K 22* [Lon. OSA/5- 1218]. Nilsson, Hoffman, Stolze, Kmentt, Waechter, VPO, Solti.

*** HMV SLS/*TC-SLS* 5139 (2) [Ang. SBLX/*4X2X* 3848]. Behrens, Bohm, Baltsa, Van Dam, VPO, Karajan.

This was the first Decca 'Sonicstage' production (strange jargon), with its remarkable combination of clarity and opulence: so often with Strauss recordings we have had to choose between brilliance, with details so clear they sound fussy, and rich, fruity sound that swallows up most of the inner parts. Here the orchestral balance brings out details never heard in the opera house, yet never getting the proportions wrong so that, say, a flute swamps the violins. The balance between voices and orchestra is just as precisely calculated. Some may complain that in the big climaxes the orchestra is too dominant, but what is remarkable is that even then the voice is clearly separated, an ideal solution. The technical trickery is on the whole discreet, and when it is not – as in the close-up effect at the end when Salome in delighted horror whispers 'I have kissed thy mouth, Jokanaan!' – it is very much in the interests of the drama, the sort of effect that any stage producer would include were it possible in the theatre. Nilsson is splendid. She is hard-edged as usual but on that account more convincingly wicked: the determination and depravity are latent in the girl's character from the start. In the final scene she rises to new heights, compelling one to accept and even enjoy the horror of it, while the uncleanness is conveyed more vividly than one can remember. One's spine tingles even as one squirms. Of this score Solti is a master. He has rarely sounded so abandoned in a recorded performance. The emotion swells up naturally even while the calculation of impact is most precise. Waechter makes a clear, young-sounding Jokanaan. Gerhard Stolze portrays the unbalance of Herod with frightening conviction, and Grace Hoffman does all she can in the comparatively ungrateful part of Herodias. The tape transfer is outstandingly successful, capturing the clarity and opulence of the recording with the widest dynamic range and an amazing feeling of spaciousness. The power of the opera's climax is given tremendous presence.

Recorded for EMI by Decca engineers in the Sofiensaal in Vienna, Karajan's sumptuously beautiful version faithfully recaptures the flair and splendour of the Salzburg product, which Karajan produced as well as conducted. It was daring of him when preparing both recording and stage production to choose for the role of heroine a singer then relatively unknown, but Hildegard Behrens is triumphantly successful, a singer who in the early scenes has one actively sympathizing with the girlish princess, and who keeps that sympathy and understanding to a stage where most sopranos have been transformed into raging harpies. The sensuous beauty of tone is ravishingly conveyed, but the recording – less analytical than the Decca set under Solti, also recorded in the Sofiensaal – is not always fair to her fine projection of sound, occasionally masking the voice. All the same the feeling of a live performance has been well captured, and the rest of the cast is of the finest Salzburg standard. In particular José van Dam makes a gloriously noble Jokanaan, and in the early scenes his offstage voice from the cistern at once commands attention, underlining the direct diatonic strength of his music in contrast to the exoticry representing Salome and the court. Karajan – as so often in Strauss – is at his most commanding and sympathetic, with the orchestra, more forward than some will like, playing rapturously. This is a performance which, so far from making one recoil from perverted horrors, has one revelling in sensuousness. The tape transfer is less well focused than the discs, producing a degree of congestion at climaxes.

Stravinsky, Igor (1882–1971)

Agon (ballet).
*** Argo ZRG 937 [id.]. L. Sinf., Atherton – BERG: *Chamber concerto*.***

Agon was written in the mid-1950s, when Stravinsky was beginning to turn his attention to what had once been anathema to him, serialism. There are already signs here of the developments in idiom which were to mark his last period, but in every bar the sharp, bright focus of the argument with its distinctive colourings is both memorable and immediately identifiable as the work of Stravinsky. Atherton directs a splendid performance, which without trying to soften any edges gives an emotional thrust to these formalized movements designed for an abstract ballet. As a coupling for the Berg *Chamber concerto* it is an unexpected but excellent choice, and the recording is very vivid indeed.

Complete ballets: *Apollon Musagète; Orpheus; The Rite of spring.*
*** CBS 79244 (2). Columbia SO, composer.

Stravinsky's own version of *The Rite* is required listening and for most collectors its purchase will be mandatory. It has real savagery and astonishing electricity, and in spite of the 1960 recording all the freshness of *The Rite* comes across. The disc includes his commentary, albeit spoken in a somewhat laboured fashion. *Apollo* and *Orpheus* come from 1965 and they, too, are indispensable.

Apollo (*Apollon Musagète;* ballet).
(M) *** DG Acc. 2542/*3342* 134 [2530 065]. Berlin PO, Karajan – BARTÓK: *Music for strings, percussion and celesta.***(*)

Apollo; Orpheus (ballet).
(M) *** ASV ACM/*ZCACM* 2025 [None. 71401]. O of St John's, Lubbock.

The ASV issue offers an ideal and generous coupling with refined performances and excellent recording. The delicacy of rhythmic pointing in *Apollo* gives special pleasure, and there is a first-rate solo violin contribution from Richard Deakin. This is one of Stravinsky's most appealing later scores, as readily accessible as the more famous ballets of his early years. The cassette transfer is smooth and natural and matches the disc closely.

Though Stravinsky tended to disparage Karajan's approach to his music as not being rugged enough, here is a work where Karajan's moulding of phrase and care for richness of string texture make for wonderful results. This neoclassical score is strong enough to stand such individual treatment, and the writing is consistently enhanced by the magnificent playing of the Berlin Philharmonic Orchestra. The recording is first-class on disc and cassette alike.

Apollo: complete; *Pulcinella* (ballet): *suite.*
(M) *** Decca Jub. 411 728-1/*4* [id.]. ASMF, Marriner.

This was one of the first records on which the St Martin's Academy, known for many years as an outstanding recording team in baroque music, spread its wings in the music of the twentieth century. The results are superb. It remains a demonstration disc, particularly the *Pulcinella* side, where the sharp separation of instruments (e.g. double-basses against trombones in the *Vivo*) makes for wonderful stereo, with the precision of the playing outshining that of almost all rival versions. The ethereal string-tones of *Apollo* (Stravinsky finally came to prefer the English to the French title) make an ideal coupling.

Capriccio for piano and orchestra.
*** Argo ZRG 674 [id.]. Ogdon, ASMF, Marriner – SHOSTAKOVICH: *Piano concerto No. 1.****

Thanks to the fine recording and the pointed playing of the St Martin's Academy the neoclassical quality of this charming work is beautifully underlined, while the soloist provides the contrasting element of sinewy toughness.

Circus polka; Concerto for strings in D; Symphony in C.
(M) *(*) DG 2543 810 [id.]. Berlin PO, Karajan.

These are extreme examples of Karajan's refined Stravinsky style. Though undeniably he brings elegance to these examples of Stravinsky's late neoclassicism, they lose their characteristic acerbity with lines smoothed over and rhythms weakened. Smooth, refined recording to match.

(i) *Circus polka.* (ii) *Dumbarton Oaks concerto in E flat.* (i) *4 Études for orchestra.* (ii) *Greeting prelude.* (i) *8 Instrumental miniatures for 15 players.* (i) *Suites 1 and 2 for small orchestra.*

(M) *** CBS 61839 [M 31729]. Members of (i) CBC SO, (ii) Columbia SO, cond. composer.

This medium-price reissue of some of Stravinsky's shorter and lighter pieces gives real point to CBS's 'Meet the Composer' series, underlining a sense of humour which came out more readily in the writings than in the music. Sharpest and most colourful are the two suites, but even the *Circus polka* for the Barnum and Bailey elephants and the *Greeting prelude* for Pierre Monteux (on *Happy birthday to you*) have the jewel of genius in them. The composer's own recordings, made when he was in his eighties, have not just unique historic interest but great vigour too, notably the delightful *Dumbarton Oaks concerto*, like a *Brandenburg* updated. The sound is bright but a little coarse.

(i) *Concerto for piano and wind;* (ii) *Violin concerto in D.*

(M) *** Ph. Seq. 6527/*7311* 160. (i) Bishop-Kovacevich, BBC SO (members), Sir Colin Davis; (ii) Grumiaux, Concg. O, Bour.

This recoupling is wholly admirable. In the *Concerto for piano and wind* Bishop-Kovacevich's manner is not simply aggressive, but recognizes that contrasts of delicacy are required. These are made without any hint of sentimentality. There is an espressivo quality in the slow movement which, miraculously, is achieved without any extra rhythmic freedom. It is a pity that the horns are placed rather backwardly, but generally the recording is attractively clean and forward. From Grumiaux comes a lithe and beautifully refined account of the *Violin concerto*. It is enormously vital, but its energy is controlled and the tone never becomes unduly aggressive or spiky. The recording too is faithful and reproduces smoothly; it preserves an excellent balance between soloist and orchestra. The cassette too is of good quality, with no lack of life in the upper range, although – as so often with Philips – the transfer level could have been higher.

Violin concerto in D.

*** Decca SXL/*KSXC* 6601 [Lon. CS 6819]. Kyung-Wha Chung, LSO, Previn – WALTON: *Concerto*.*** ❀

*** DG 2531/*3301* 110 [id.]. Perlman, Boston SO, Ozawa – BERG: *Concerto*.***

Kyung-Wha Chung is at her most incisive for the spikily swaggering outer movements, which with Previn's help are presented here in all their distinctiveness, tough and humorous at the same time. In the two movements labelled *Aria* Chung brings fantasy as well as lyricism, less overtly expressive than direct rivals but conveying instead an inner brooding quality. Excellent recording, and an outstandingly fine cassette.

Perlman's precision, remarkable in both concertos on this disc, underlines the neoclassical element in the outer movements of the Stravinsky. The two *Aria* movements are more deeply felt and expressive, presenting the work as a major twentieth-century concerto. The balance favours the soloist, but no one will miss the commitment of the Boston orchestra's playing, vividly recorded. The cassette transfer is first-rate, matching the disc closely. Kyung-Wha Chung's coupling is especially attractive; but if the Berg *Concerto* is wanted, Perlman's account of the Stravinsky can certainly be recommended.

Danses concertantes; Pulcinella (ballet): *suite.*

*** Chan. Dig. ABRD/*ABTD* 1065 [id.]. ECO, Gibson.

Gibson and the ECO are very well recorded on Chandos and give highly enjoyable accounts of both works. The *Pulcinella* suite does not quite eclipse the Marriner on Argo but it is still very lively, and the *Danses concertantes* scores even over the composer's own in terms of charm and geniality. The chrome cassette is vivid and extremely lively on top; indeed it may call for a little taming, in *Pulcinella* especially.

Ebony concerto; Dumbarton Oaks concerto in E flat; Concertino for string quartet; Double canon; Elégie for viola; Epitaphium; 8 Instrumental miniatures; 3 Pieces for clarinet.

*** DG 2531 278 [id.]. Intercontemporain Ens., Boulez.

The bright, close sound almost reminds one of the effect of some of the early Columbia records Stravinsky made before the war: the dry, spiky, black-and-white images of the early cinema. The playing of the Ensemble Intercontemporain is very brilliant indeed. There is much to enjoy in these performances which are spiced with the right kind of wit and keenness of edge, and even those who do not normally respond to Boulez's conducting will be pleasantly surprised with the results he obtains here.

Ballets: (i) *The Firebird* (complete); *Fireworks; Petrushka* (complete). (ii) *Suites Nos. 1 and 2.*
*** CBS 79243 (2). (i) Columbia SO, (ii) CBS SO, composer.

Another welcome pair of records which return some of Stravinsky's own performances, made in 1960–63, to circulation. Perhaps the least impressive is his *Firebird* which is somewhat wanting in poetry, but the rest are well worth having in one's Stravinsky collection and the sound is perfectly acceptable.

Ballets: *The Firebird: suite* (1919 score); *Jeu de cartes; Petrushka* (1911 score). (i) *Pulcinella. The Rite of Spring* (all complete).
(M) *** DG 2740 257 (4). LSO, Abbado, (i) with Berganza, Ryland Davies, Shirley-Quirk.

An attractive compilation of essential Stravinsky. The highlight is *Petrushka*, while both the *Firebird suite* and *Jeu de cartes* are given stunning performances of great vitality and sensitivity. The LSO play with superb virtuosity and spirit; moreover the DG recording is of demonstration standard. This coupling was awarded a rosette in a previous edition. There is a degree of detachment in Abbado's reading of *The Rite of Spring*.

Complete ballets: *The Firebird; Petrushka* (1947 score); *The Rite of spring*.
*** Ph. 6725/*7655* 017 (3). Concg. O, Sir Colin Davis.

On balance Sir Colin Davis's set of the three ballets with the Concertgebouw Orchestra makes the best of the packages currently on offer. Abbado does not give us the complete *Firebird* though his suite, coupled with *Jeu de cartes*, is very good, and in any event his version of *The Rite* is not given such natural recorded sound. All three ballets from Davis are in their own right strong contenders in single-disc form and are all three-star recommendations. The sound on cassette is full, lustrous and well-balanced, but there is some blurring of transients by the reverberation and climaxes are less clean than on LP. The transfer level is quite modest.

The Firebird (ballet): complete.
*** Ph. **400 074-2**; 9500/*7300* 742 [id.]. Concg. O, Sir Colin Davis.
*** Ph. 6500 483 [id./*7300 353* PSI]. LPO, Haitink.
C *** Decca Dig. **410 109-2**; 410 109-1/*4* [id.]. Detroit SO, Dorati.
(M) *** Mercury SRI 75058 [id.]. LSO, Dorati.
(M) *** HMV Green. ESD/*TC-ESD* 7147 [Ang. RL/*4RL* 32044]. O de Paris, Ozawa.
(B) *** Con. CC/*CCT* 7500. New Philh. O, Ansermet.
(*) HMV Dig. **CDC 747017-2; ASD/*TC-ASD* 143634-1/*4* [Ang. DS/*4XS* 38012]. Boston SO, Ozawa.
**(*) ASV ALH/*ZCALH* 924 [Musicmasters 20051]. RPO, Dorati.
**(*) Decca Dig. SXDL/*KSXDC* 7511 [Lon. LDR/*5*- 10012]. VPO, Dohnányi.

With superb analogue sound Sir Colin Davis directs a magically evocative account of the complete *Firebird* ballet, helped not just by the playing of the Concertgebouw Orchestra (the strings outstandingly fine) but by the ambience of the hall, which allows the finest detail yet gives a bloom to the sound, open and spacious, superbly co-ordinated. This is finer even than Haitink's splendid LPO version, and is probably the most satisfying account of the *Firebird* score ever committed to disc. The cassette is of good quality, but, as so often with Philips, the transfer level is unadventurous, and in some of the pianissimo passages the tape has not the sharpness of focus of the LP. The compact disc has been digitally remastered, which has sharpened up detail, somewhat at the expense of the magical analogue atmosphere. While there is more depth and bite, it is not all gain; and while the brass has greater presence, the high violins sound less natural. Background noise has been virtually eliminated.

No more refined performance of the complete *Firebird* has ever been put on record than Haitink's, and it is warmly recommended. The sheer savagery of *Kaschei's dance* may be a little muted, but the sharpness of attack and the clarity of detail make for a thrilling result, while the magic and poetry of the whole score are given a hypnotic beauty, with the LPO at its very finest. Recording of demonstration quality.

Dorati's Detroit version has the benefit of spectacular digital recording. The clarity and definition of dark, hushed passages is amazing with the contrabassoon finely focused, never sounding woolly or obscure, while string tremolos down to the merest whisper are uncannily precise. There is plenty of space round woodwind solos, and only the concertmaster's violin is spotlit. The performance is very precise too, and though Dorati's reading has changed little from his previous versions with London orchestras there is a degree more of caution. Individual solos are not so characterful and *Kaschei's dance* lacks just a degree in excitement, but overall this is both a strong and beautiful reading, even if the Mercury account is not entirely superseded. The somewhat literal quality of the Decca performance, lacking a degree of magic and intensity, is brought out the more on CD, though the vividness and impact of the sound are most impressive.

Dorati's electrifyingly dramatic 1960 recording remains a classic version. This reissue of the original Mercury disc sounds as fresh and vivid as the day it was made; the brilliant detail and enormous impact suggest a modern digital source rather than an analogue master tape made over twenty years ago. The stereo has remarkable atmosphere too, and the balance is superb. The performance sounds completely spontaneous, and the LSO wind-playing is most sensitive. At medium price this can still compete with the best of modern versions. Only the sound of the massed upper strings slightly hints at its age: the bite of the brass and the transient edge of the percussion are thrilling, especially in the finale.

Ozawa's earlier Greensleeve *Firebird* is of a luxurious and exotic plumage. On its first appearance in 1973, it was rapidly eclipsed by Haitink's, a pity since it had strong attractions – and still does! The sheer opulence and sumptuousness of the score strike one with renewed force; the sound is cleanly defined and has great warmth and body. True, in one or two pianissimo string passages (fig. 48 for example) there could be greater mystery and more tenderness but, for the most part, this is so well played and recorded that it holds its own with all available competition. Colin Davis is more refined and even better recorded, but that is at full price. The cassette is full and atmospheric, but the transfer level is not especially high and detail is less sharply defined than on LP.

Ansermet's New Philharmonia version makes a marvellous bargain on Contour in a strikingly clean pressing. It offers more polished playing than the performance Ansermet recorded earlier with his own Suisse Romande Orchestra, but generally the interpretations are amazingly consistent. At times one suspects that the new version is a degree slower, but on checking you find that the difference lies in the extra flexibility and polish of the London players. The recording is of vintage Decca quality and remains demonstration-worthy on disc, though not on cassette, where the bass is over-resonant at the opening and the upper range is restricted.

Ozawa's Boston version is more refined than his Paris record, also for HMV; but with the extra precision has come a degree of detachment, chill even. *Kaschei's dance* is less an orchestral showpiece than a delicate tapestry, relatively light and transparent, with dance rhythms well sprung and the bite of fortissimo reserved for sforzando chords. In the digital recording the brass lacks a little in body, and though the sound is not dry the acoustic is vague.

Dorati's ASV version with the RPO, using slightly faster tempi than those chosen by Ansermet or Haitink, is certainly dramatic and extremely vivid as a recording. However, the balance is rather close and relatively unatmospheric. The sound itself has superb bite and impact, and this may well appeal to those who like the Phase Four type of recording. It is exciting if lacking something in refinement. The cassette transfer is very successful but the ear is made aware that the forward balance has resulted in a reduction of dynamic contrast.

For a score as magical as *Firebird* a recording can actually be too clear, and the digital sound in Dohnányi's version tends to be too analytical, separating the threads in a way that prevents the music from making its full evocative effect. In any case the reading is on the chill side. The cassette matches the disc very closely indeed; if anything the tape quality is slightly more atmospheric and thus preferable.

The Firebird: suite (1919 version).

*** HMV ASD/*TC-ASD* 3645 [Ang. S/*4XS* 37539]. Phd. O, Muti – MUSSORGSKY: *Pictures*.***

(*) Telarc Dig. **CD 80039; DG 10039 [id.]. Atlanta SO, Shaw – BORODIN: *Prince Igor excerpts*.***

(B) **(*) DG Walkman *413 155-4*. Berlin R. O, Maazel – RIMSKY-KORSAKOV: *Scheherazade* **(*) (with KHACHATURIAN: *Gayaneh suite* **(*)).

Muti secures superb playing from the Philadelphia Orchestra here. There have been many excellent accounts of this score in recent years, from Abbado, Giulini and others, but in terms of magic and poetry this surpasses them all. The pianissimo tone Muti draws from the Philadelphia strings is ravishing. This is a wonderful coupling, and the transfer to tape is first-class; the difference in sound between disc and cassette is minimal.

The *Firebird suite* has been recorded by the finest orchestras in the world, and excellent as is the Atlanta Symphony, it would not claim to be of their number. Nevertheless Robert Shaw, the thoroughly musical conductor, achieves an atmospheric and vivid reading of Stravinsky's famous suite. The *Round dance of the princesses* is played very gently to maximize the shock of the entry of Kastchei. The very wide dynamic range of the digital recording achieves the most dramatic impact both here and in the closing pages of the finale. With its spectacular coupling this issue is designed to appeal to those wanting to show off their reproducer, and that it will certainly do. The surfaces too are completely silent and the pressing very clean. We have not heard the compact disc.

Maazel's reading of the *Firebird suite* has an enjoyable éclat and he has the advantage of the most beautiful woodwind playing; indeed the Berlin Radio Orchestra is consistently on top form. The recording dates from 1960 and tended to betray its age by the sound of the massed upper strings. However, in the present transfer the DG engineers have smoothed off the upper partials and in consequence the recording, although still impressive, has lost some of its bite. This applies to a lesser extent to Rozhdestvensky's version of the *Gayaneh* suite, which combines excitement with panache and includes all the best-known items. The *Sabre dance* is sensational, exploding into the room at the close of the *Firebird*.

The Firebird: suite (1919 score)*; Jeu de cartes* (ballet): complete.

*** DG 2530 537/*3300 483* [id.]. LSO, Abbado.

Stunning performances of great vitality and sensitivity. The LSO plays with superb virtuosity and spirit, and Abbado's feeling for atmosphere and colour is everywhere in evidence. Moreover the DG recording is of demonstration standard; it has plenty of detail, presence and impact, as well as an excellently judged musical perspective. This is one of the finest Stravinsky records in the catalogue, and the cassette is also outstanding.

The Firebird: suite (1919 score); *Petrushka:* complete (1947 score).

(M) *** CBS 60120/*40*- [MY/*MYT* 37221]. NYPO, Bernstein.

Bernstein's performance of *Petrushka* is one of the most involved and warm-hearted ever recorded. Even more than the composer himself, or Ansermet (whose sense of humour was pointedly stirred in this of all Stravinsky's music), Bernstein goes to the emotional heart of the score, without violating Stravinsky's expressed markings except in a couple of minor instances. The panoply of the fair music, the inbred hysteria of the puppet's rage, and above all the tragedy of his death are here conveyed with unrivalled intensity; and it adds to the compulsion of the performance to have it complete on one side (35 minutes), with splendidly vivid recording. *Firebird* is warmly done, if without quite the same superb precision. An outstanding disc at the price. The cassette is effectively vivid too, although side two (*Petrushka*) has a more restricted upper range than the LP.

The Firebird suite; The Rite of spring.
(M) (***) Dell'Arte mono DA 9005. Phd.O, Stokowski.

The Rite was recorded in sections, at various times during 1927–30 and sounded more vivid than its only rival at the time, Stravinsky's own with Parisian forces on Columbia. It still sounds pretty exciting even now and time has not dimmed its shock. The playing though vastly superior to the Stravinsky set is not impeccable though it is very good indeed, and most of the performance, including the *Danse sacrale*, is thrilling. According to the sleeve, there is some difference in the number of strings used in the various sessions, while there was also some variation in the level of surface noise from side to side of the 78 r.p.m. discs. However, for the most part this is surprisingly lively as pure sound and the transfer is expertly handled. *The Firebird* dates from 1927 – Stokowski recorded it in 1924 for the first time and again in the 1930s. This is not to be missed for the sake of *The Rite*.

Jeu de cartes; Orpheus (complete).
(M) **(*) Ph. Seq. 6527/*7311* 159 [id.]. LSO, Sir Colin Davis.

A splendidly alert performance of *Jeu de cartes* from Davis and the LSO who are completely inside the composer's idiom. The effect is spontaneous and the humour comes across more effectively here than in some earlier versions. *Orpheus* is a post-war ballet, written in 1947, and its smoothly classical lines mark something of a return to the manner of the late-1920s ballets, above all to *Apollo*. But the material is never quite so memorable or, for that matter, so varied, and even Colin Davis's excellent account does not entirely overcome an overall effect of greyness. The LSO playing, however, is excellent and the recording good, though on the cassette (transferred at only a modest level) there is some lack of bite in *Jeu de cartes* and a slight bass cut may be found useful to improve the balance.

Petrushka (ballet; 1911 score; complete).
*** DG Dig. **400 042-2**; 2532/*3302* 010 [id.]. LSO, Abbado.
(M) *** DG Priv. 2535/*3335* 419. LSO, Dutoit.
(M) ** Decca VIV/*KVIC* 42 [Lon. STS 15478]. New Philh. O, Leinsdorf.

Petrushka (1947 score; complete).
*** Decca Dig. SXDL/*KSXDC* 7521 [Lon. LDR/*5*- 71023]. Detroit SO, Dorati.
*** Ph. 9500 447/*7300 653* [id.]. Concg. O, Sir Colin Davis.
** HMV Dig. **CDC 747015-2**; ASD/*TCC-ASD* 4069 [Ang. DS/*4XS* 37822]. Phd. O, Muti.

Abbado's version of the 1911 *Petrushka* has the advantage of extremely fine digital sound, even though it is not quite as overwhelming sonically as Decca's for Dorati. The performance is strongly characterized, and the LSO play marvellously. Abbado combines refinement and a powerful sense of dramatic atmosphere (he is especially sympathetic in the central tableaux) with a kaleidoscopic brilliance. The recording has impressive range and colour, with the chrome tape very close to the disc. The compact disc, however, is slightly disappointing. It emphasizes the virtues of the LP by its clarity and silent background, but there is a degree of digital edge on the upper strings which is certainly not entirely natural.

Dorati's account of *Petrushka*, also digital, is based on the 1947 version, though at certain points Dorati reverts to the original 1911 scoring in accordance with his recollections of a conversation he had with Stravinsky himself. *Petrushka* has always been a vehicle for the virtuosity of recording engineers, right from the early days of LP, when Decca put the famous first Ansermet mono LP on to the market. Dorati's version creates a comparable digital landmark. The sound is breathtakingly vivid and clean, yet remains naturally balanced and transparent. The performance does not always have the refinement of Abbado's, but it is immensely dramatic and also very telling in the scene where the frustrated Petrushka is confined to his cell. Dorati is at his finest in the final tableau, bringing out the robust Russian earthiness of the dancing peasants. Abbado's account also has splendid physical exuberance here, but the projection of the Decca sound is even more striking. The Decca cassette is up to the highest standards of the house, extraordinarily vivid and clear to match the disc very closely indeed, even though, unlike the DG Abbado cassette, it uses ferric tape.

At medium price the DG Privilege version remains very competitive. It is brilliantly conducted by Charles Dutoit and is extremely vivid as a recording. Interestingly it was made almost impromptu: a planned opera recording fell through and sessions were hastily reallotted with little advance planning. The result is triumphantly spontaneous in its own right, with rhythms that are incisive yet beautifully buoyant, and a degree of expressiveness in the orchestral playing that subtly underlines the dramatic atmosphere, and is especially magical in the Third Tableau. The final section too is strongly coloured, so that the gentle closing pages make a touching contrast to the gaiety of the early part of the scene. The recording is rich and sparkling, the only fault of balance being the prominence of the concertante piano soloist, Tamás Vásáry, who (ably as he plays) is given a ridiculously out-of-proportion star billing. The tape transfer is extremely brilliant; it has plenty of bite and detail, but the treble needs cutting back or the upper strings sound shrill.

Sir Colin Davis's Philips version of the 1947 score combines brilliant and rich recording with a performance which to an exceptional degree makes a positive case for the 1947 score over the original. The recording has some curious and not always perfectly balanced spotlighting of instruments (most unexpected from Philips), but it reveals details of the rich texture that are normally obscured. From first to last Davis makes it clear that he regards this as fun music, drawing brilliantly precise playing from the Concertgebouw and rarely if ever forcing the pace, though always maintaining necessary excitement. The piano solo starts a little cautiously in the Russian dance, but that is an exception in an unusually positive reading. The cassette transfer is slightly soft-grained in the treble, and the tone of the upper strings is somewhat lacking in body compared with the rest of the orchestra; otherwise the quality is vivid.

Muti secures playing of stunning virtuosity from the Philadelphians; but if their response is breathtaking, his reading can best be described as breathless. There is unremitting drive here, with the *Danse russe* taken at breakneck speed and everything far too regimented. The recording has splendid impact and clarity, but there is too little tenderness and magic in this overdriven account. The chrome tape is comparably vivid. The compact disc is extremely brilliant, but though the sound has 'hi-fi' vividness the performance itself remains unsatisfying.

Leinsdorf's version was originally recorded in Phase Four. It is a brilliantly alive and dramatic reading, the interpretation always sympathetic and never forced, even if the New Philharmonia does not display the precision of ensemble of the finest versions. The disc has been recut for its Viva reissue and the effect is to brighten the treble to the point of glare, though detail is remarkable if the forward balance is acceptable. As often happens, the tape is smoother on top than the LP, without loss of vividness, and is greatly preferable (much less tiring on the ears).

The Rite of spring (complete).

(M) *** CBS 60285/*40-* [MS 6319]. Columbia SO, composer.

*** HMV ASD/*TC-ASD* 3807 [Ang. SZ/*4ZS* 37646]. Phd. O, Muti.

(M) *** CBS 60151/*40-* [MS 7293/*HM* 47293]. Cleveland O, Boulez.

*** DG 2530/*3300* 884 [id.]. Berlin PO, Karajan.

*** Decca Dig. **400 084-2**; SXDL/*KSXDC* 7548 [Lon. LDR/*5-* 71048]. Detroit SO, Dorati.

*** Ph. 9500 323/*7300 585* [id.]. Concg. O, Sir Colin Davis.

(M) *** Decca Jub. 410 169-1/*4* [Lon. CS/*5-* 6685]. Chicago SO, Solti.

*** DG 2530 635 [id.]. LSO, Abbado.

(*) Telarc Dig. **CD 80054; DG 10054 [id.]. Cleveland O, Maazel.

(B) **(*) DG Walkman *413 160-4*. Boston SO,

Tilson Thomas – ORFF: *Carmina Burana.****

(M) **(*) ASV ACM/*ZCACM* 2030. Nat. Youth O, Rattle.

(M) ** DG Acc. 2542/*3342* 165. Berlin PO, Karajan.

(M) ** Ph. Seq. 6527/*7311* 158. LSO, Sir Colin Davis.

(M) ** Decca VIV/*KVIC* 31 [Lon. STS/*5-15590*]. LPO, Leinsdorf.

** DG Dig. **410 508-2**; 2532/*3302* 075 [id.]. Israel PO, Bernstein.

*(*) HMV Dig. ASD 4271. Moscow RSO, Fedoseyev.

The Rite of spring; Fireworks.

(B) ** RCA VICS/*VK* 2021. Chicago SO, Ozawa.

The Rite of spring; (i) *The King of stars* (*Le Roi des étoiles*).

(M) **(*) DG Priv. 2535/*3335* 222 [id.]. Boston SO, Tilson Thomas; (i) with New England Male Conservatory Ch.

Among his recordings of his major ballet scores, Stravinsky's version of *The Rite* stands out. Its authority in matters of balance and detail brings a remarkable documentary value to this issue (for the CBS engineers obviously co-operated closely with the composer's wishes), and yet this is a mere bonus to a performance which in its vividness and sheer excitement leads all others. The feeling for atmosphere, plus a striking richness of colour in the lyrical passages, underpins the drama. The recording from the beginning of the 1960s still sounds remarkably satisfying and the cassette transfer is first-class. An indispensable issue; the only regret is that the composer's introductory talk about the work's historical background has been removed for this medium-priced reissue.

Among modern recordings there is a wide choice. In a Philadelphia line stretching back to Stokowski, Muti directs a performance of Stravinsky's barbaric masterpiece which is aggressively brutal yet presents the violence with red-blooded conviction. Muti generally favours speeds a shade faster than usual, and arguably the opening bassoon solo is not quite flexible enough, for metrical precision is a key element all through. There are signs that Muti has studied the last of Stravinsky's own recordings of *The Rite* (by far the most convincing of the three he made), and it is good to have the amendment to the horn part sanctioned in it in the *Sacrificial dance* (two bars before fig. 75). The recording, not always as analytically clear as some rivals, is gloriously full and dramatic, with brass and percussion exceptionally vividly caught. Like the disc, the tape has stunning body and impact: the timpani on side two are transferred without distortion and the effect is very exciting indeed.

Boulez's version dates from 1970, but the CBS engineers served him and the Cleveland Orchestra particularly well. The massive vividness of the sound matches the monolithic quality of the Boulez interpretation. Boulez developed his reading over the years, so that finally he came to this recorded view that tempi should generally be measured, approaching those of Stravinsky himself in his recorded version. Boulez is less lyrical than the composer, but compensates with a relentless rhythmic urgency. Many will feel that after Stravinsky's own version, which is not only uniquely authoritative but uniquely compelling too, this is the most completely recommendable account. If not quite as fine as Muti's digital version, the sound is thrilling, particularly in such moments as the brass contrasts in *Jeux des cités rivales*. The chrome tape matches the disc pretty closely, although once or twice on side one there is a moment of bass-drum resonance which is accommodated not quite comfortably.

Karajan's earlier recording of Stravinsky's masterpiece came in for much snide criticism from the composer, who described one passage as being a *'tempo di hoochie-koochie'*, and doubted whether Berlin Philharmonic traditions could encompass music from so different a discipline. In this more recent recording, tougher, more urgent, less mannered, Karajan goes a long way towards rebutting Stravinsky's complaints, and the result is superb, Karajan at his very finest, persuasive still but never obtrusively so, and above all powerfully dramatic. Outstanding recording quality. There is little to choose between tape and disc, and both are spectacular in their vividness and wide range.

However, in terms of recorded sound, Dorati's *Rite* with the Detroit orchestra scores over its rivals. This has stunning clarity and presence, exceptionally lifelike and vivid sound, and the denser textures emerge more cleanly than ever before. It is a very good performance too, almost but not quite in the same league as those of Karajan and Muti, generating plenty of excitement. The only let-down is the final *Sacrificial dance*, which needs greater abandon and higher voltage. The Detroit strings too are not as sumptuous as those of the Berlin and Amsterdam orchestras and sound distinctly undernourished in places. Yet too much should not be made of this. Although Dorati does not match the atmosphere of his finest rivals, the performance is so vivid that it belongs among the very best – and for those primarily concerned with recorded sound, it will probably be a first choice, especially in its compact disc format. The chrome cassette too is in the demonstration bracket.

Sir Colin Davis has his idiosyncrasies in this Stravinsky score (one of them is his strange hold-up on the last chord), but generally he takes an unusually direct view, and the result is strong, forthright and powerful. Some will prefer a more obviously involving reading, but with the opulent sound of the Concertgebouw Orchestra richly recorded the physical impact of this version is still irresistible. Its richness and body are well transferred to tape, but the cassette's upper range has less sparkle than the disc.

Solti's is a powerful, unrelenting account of Stravinsky's revolutionary score, with virtuoso playing from the Chicago orchestra and recording that demonstrates with breathtaking clarity the precision of inner detail. Some of the gentler half-tones of the score are presented rather glaringly, but this view of the work is magnificently consistent, showing Solti at his most tautly dramatic. The Decca cassette is of demonstration quality. It is extremely vivid and detailed, and highly spectacular too. At mid-price this is very competitive.

There is a degree of detachment in Abbado's reading with the LSO, which is arguably apt. In every way this is an outstanding reading, certain to excite the keenest admiration if not the warmest affection. Abbado even more than most rivals seems to have answered every problem on even the slightest point of detail. His observance of markings is meticulous, and an orchestra whose members have sometimes claimed they could play this score without a conductor (it has long been a favourite with the LSO) revels in the security given by the conductor's direction. The recording is breathtakingly brilliant, with a range of dynamic exceptionally wide even by latterday standards.

The sound on the Cleveland Orchestra version conducted by Lorin Maazel is pretty spectacular too. Indeed, it is superior in terms of balance to that of the Detroit version when the two CD versions are juxtaposed. However, there are a number of sensation-seeking effects such as excessive ritardandi in the *Rondes printanières* so as to exaggerate the trombone glissandi (fig. 53) which are vulgar. Compare, too, the opening of the second part in this version with that of Karajan or Davis and one is in a totally different world. Moreover the Maazel CD is overpriced, given the competition.

Michael Tilson Thomas's version of *The Rite of spring* has an important if brief makeweight in the rare motet of the same period – unperformed for several decades but here shown as an intensely imaginative, evocative choral work. The major offering is presented in a warmly expressive reading that misses some of the music's bite. The amply reverberant recording matches the approach. There is a very good cassette version too. The Tilson Thomas version is also available on a bargain-priced Walkman cassette, admirably transferred on to chrome tape. This has the advantage of continuity, while the Orff coupling, under Jochum, has the composer's imprimatur.

The performance of the National Youth Orchestra in this once-feared showpiece is not just 'good considering' but 'good' absolute; the youngsters under their young conductor produce warm and spontaneous playing. The conviction of the performance is the more evident because it was recorded in long takes, and the penalty of having a few imprecisions and errors is minimal. At medium price and with full and atmospheric sound this is well worth considering. The cassette transfer is excellent, matching the disc closely.

In their earlier recordings of *The Rite* the approaches of Colin Davis and Karajan could hardly be more contrasted. Davis is characteristically straightforward and thrusting; Karajan is smooth and civilized, yet not lacking in excitement. In this work the odds are heavily weighted in favour of the Davis approach, and whatever the incidental shortcomings – sometimes Davis misses out on detail – his full-bloodedness is to be preferred. Even so, the splendid Berlin playing for Karajan matches that conductor's approach, and it is certainly interesting to hear so sophisticated a performance, even though the absence of elemental strength is striking. The DG recording was technically outstanding in its day, and its very vivid projection counteracts a high degree of reverberation. The Philips recording for Davis is not super-brilliant but it is still very good. It sounds remarkably well in its cassette version, with the work's closing pages given a fine impact. The Accolade tape, however, has problems with the resonance, which robs the sound of absolute clarity, although the bite remains and there is no lack of body and atmosphere.

Leinsdorf directs a clean-cut, unspectacular account of Stravinsky's virtuoso score, and is well served by the LPO. The recording quality is balanced with typical Phase Four closeness. Nonetheless the bold colours may suit small machines particularly well, and the final *Danse sacrale* is very exciting. The cassette transfer is exceptionally successful, the vividness and impact as striking as the detail.

Stravinsky hailed Bernstein's earlier record of *The Rite* with the New York Philharmonic with an amazed 'Wow!' Now, a quarter of a century later, he has re-recorded the score with the Israel orchestra. Unfortunately the recording is made in a dry acoustic ambience (at the Mann Auditorium, Tel Aviv) and though there is no lack of clarity, there is a loss of atmosphere. Each strand in the texture is clearly audible and the dynamic perspective is perfectly judged, but the overall result sounds synthetic. The same criticism could be applied to the Dorati version on Decca but there is a much livelier acoustic in which to operate. In its CD format the clarity is quite stunning but the dryness of the acoustic even more striking. The strings of the Israel orchestra are not in the same league as those of the NYPO nor, for that matter, are some of the wind.

Ozawa's Chicago recording (with the *Fireworks* acting as a brief but highly effective curtain-raiser) offers a lightweight interpretation in the best sense. There is no serious lack of drama or – especially in the closing pages – excitement, but it is the spirit of the dance that pervades, although by bringing out the colour of the scoring Ozawa also demonstrates the work's affinities with *The Firebird*. The recording is resonant but vivid; the chrome cassette has rather more edge on the sound.

We have become so accustomed in the last three decades to highly polished accounts of *The Rite* from virtuoso orchestras that the score seems in danger of being robbed of its sense of shock; of being transformed into a display vehicle, a super-concerto for orchestra rather than an evocation of pagan Russia. *The Rite* has not enjoyed so long a performance history in the Soviet Union and so one turns to the Melodiya issue in the expectation of finding something of the freshness and even, perhaps, the sense of strain that one recalls from pioneering sets by the composer and Stokowski, as well as a spontaneity and intensity missing in some Western performances. However, in so competitive a field, Fedoseyev and the Moscow orchestra scarcely hold their own. True, the opening bassoon solo wails as if from the depths of the primeval past, but elsewhere there is less sense of atmosphere than one could hope for, and neither the wind nor brass produce a well-blended ensemble. The recording does not help either by placing some wind instruments nearer than others. There is little real excitement here, even if certain passages come off successfully.

The Soldier's Tale (*L'Histoire du soldat;* complete, in English).

(M) *** DG Priv. 2535 456 [2530 609]. Gielgud, Moody, Courtenay, Boston Chamber Players.

The Boston Chamber Players offer an eminently well-characterized and civilized reading, and they are superbly recorded, even if the spoken element, admirably produced by Douglas Cleverdon, does occupy the foreground when speech and music are mixed.

Symphony in E flat, Op. 1; Symphony in C; Symphony in 3 movements; Ode (*Elegiacal chant in 3 parts*).

*** Chan. Dig. **CHAN 8345/6**; DBRD/-*DBTD* 2004 (2). SNO, Gibson.

Even compared with the composer's own performances this collection by the Scottish National Orchestra – in excellent form – under Sir Alexander Gibson stands up well. The vividness of the digital recording makes up for any slight lack of sparkle, and while the *Symphonies for wind instruments* might have seemed a more obvious makeweight for the three major works, it is good to have the *Ode* in memory of Natalia Koussevitzky, which has an extrovert, rustic scherzo section framed by short elegies. The cassettes are of generally good quality but use iron-oxide stock and on side four (in the *Symphony in 3 movements*) the upper woodwind partials are not as clean as on LP. The accompanying leaflet, too, is poorly produced – but that is not unusual with tape sets.

Symphony in C; Symphony in 3 movements.
*** Decca Dig. SXDL/*KSXDC* 7543 [Lon. LDR/*5*- 71043]. SRO, Dutoit.
(M) **(*) Ph. Seq. 6527/*7311* 127 [id.]. LSO, Sir Colin Davis.

Although the Suisse Romande Orchestra is not in the very first rank, it is in much better shape than when it last recorded these symphonies in the 1960s for Ansermet; and the brilliant recording they now receive from the Decca team and the alert direction of Charles Dutoit make this a very winning coupling. These are both exhilarating pieces and Dutoit punches home their virile high spirits and clean-limbed athleticism. The sound is first-class, even if the woodwind may strike one at times as just a shade forward. No matter, this is a splendid issue and unlikely to be superseded for a while. The chrome tape is fresh and clear, though the transfer level could have been higher and brought more bite.

Davis's account of the *Symphony in C* is splendidly alert, well played and stimulating. The performance of the *Symphony in 3 movements* is also lively, but compared with Stravinsky's own it is over-tense. By taking very fast tempi which barely allow any lift to the rhythm, Davis ends by overplaying the music. The sound is good, though the cassette has a restricted upper range because of the low transfer level.

Symphony in C; (i) *Symphony of Psalms.*
*** CBS 72181 [MS 6548]. Columbia SO, composer, (i) with Toronto Fest. Singers.

Stravinsky never quite equalled the intensity of the pre-war 78 r.p.m. performance of the *Symphony of Psalms* he conducted with the Walter Straram Chorus and Orchestra. That had many more technical faults than this, and it is only fair to say that this later account still outshines many others by conductors such as Ančerl and Ansermet. It is just that with so vivid a work it is a shade disappointing to find Stravinsky as interpreter at less than maximum voltage. The *Symphony in C*, with its extraordinary, bleak ending, is splendidly done, and this is a valuable coupling.

CHAMBER AND INSTRUMENTAL MUSIC

Suite Italienne (arr. for violin and cello).
(M) *** CBS 60264/*40*- [M 33447]. Heifetz, Piatigorsky – DVOŘÁK: *Piano trio No. 3**(**); GLIÈRE: *Duo*; HALVORSEN: *Passacaglia.****

This is an arrangement of an arrangement, for the music is a further adaptation of Pergolesi (as in *Pulcinella*), and here it is heard in a version for violin and cello. The playing is a knock-out, of the kind that makes one realize why Heifetz was a legend in his own time. The blend of the two instruments is a miraculous amalgam and though the recording is much too forwardly balanced, it is fully acceptable.

(i) *Symphonies of wind instruments;* (ii) *3 Pieces for string quartet;* (iii) *3 Easy pieces: March. Rite of spring:* excerpts. (iv) *Les cinq doigts Nos. 1, 2 and 6; Ragtime; Studies, Op. 7/1 and 4.* (v; i) *3 Japanese lyrics;* (v; vi) *2 Poems of Balmont; 3 Little Songs: The Jackdaw. 4 Russian songs: The Drake. Mavra* (opera): *Parasha's aria.*
*** Chan. Dig. ABR/*ABT* 1048 [id.]. (i) Nash Ens., Rattle; (ii) Chilingirian Qt; (iii) Shasby and McMahon; (iv) Lumsden; (v) Manning; (vi) Rodney Bennett.

The performances are lively enough; but the purpose of the record, designed to accompany a course on the rise of modernism (1890–1920) and including five brief excerpts from *The Rite of spring* in piano duet form, renders its appeal limited. Nothing lasts more than about two minutes except, of course, the *Symphonies of wind instruments*. However, both the performances and recordings are very good. The cassette is in the demonstration class.

PIANO MUSIC

Circus polka; 4 Études, Op. 7; Piano rag music; Ragtime; Serenade in A major; Piano sonata; Tango.
(M) ** None. H 71212 [id.]. Lee.

Noël Lee misses the full range of tone needed in this angular piano music. He has nothing like the sharpness that the composer himself brought to the opening of the *Serenade*, and in gentler passages his touch is a degree too heavy. But there is still real spirit and understanding throughout the whole collection (which gathers together all of Stravinsky's music originally written for piano solo), and with good bright recording it is a valuable record, even making no allowance for price.

Concerto for 2 solo pianos; Petrushka (ballet): arr. for 2 pianos.
*** Ph. Dig. 410 301-1/*4* [id.]. Katia and Marielle Labèque.

Although there have been a number of memorable versions of the *Petrushka* transcription for one piano by Pollini, Gilels, Beroff and others, there is none of the version for two pianos (made by Victor Babin). It is marvellously exhilarating in the hands of the Labèque sisters and, like the *Concerto for two pianos* of 1935, sounds brilliant and lifelike in the acoustic of the Maltings at Snape. The latter work with its self-conscious neoclassicism is very much in sparkling monochrome, as opposed to the vivid, brittle, kaleidoscopic colours of the *Petrushka* arrangement. Marvellous playing and recording – though at barely a quarter of an hour on one side and just over eighteen minutes on the other, this is short measure. The chrome cassette is very satisfactory, the level not too low (though not perhaps as high as it could have been).

Three movements from Petrushka.
❀ *** DG 2530 225/*3300 458* [id.]. Pollini – PROKOFIEV: *Piano sonata No. 7.****
** HMV Dig. ASD/*TCC-ASD* 4321 [Ang. DS/*4XS* 38010]. Donohoe – PROKOFIEV: *Sonata No. 6* (with RACHMANINOV: *Étude tableau*, Op. 33/3**).

Staggering, electrifying playing from Pollini, creating the highest degree of excitement, and good recording put his disc in a class of its own.

Peter Donohoe gives a very good account of himself in the *Three movements from Petrushka* and is well enough recorded on both disc and tape. At the same time, it must be admitted that his version does not eclipse memories of the Gilels (recorded live in Prague in the early 1970s), nor does it constitute a challenge to the Pollini on DG.

VOCAL MUSIC

Songs: *Berceuses du chat; 4 Chants; Elegy for J.F.K.; 2 Geistliche Lieder* (from *Wolf's Spanish Lieder Book*)*; In memoriam Dylan Thomas; Pastorale; 3 Petites chansons; 2 poèmes de Paul Verlaine; 2 Poésies de Konstantin Balmont; 3 Poésies de la lyrique japonaise; Pribaoutki; 3 Songs from William Shakespeare; Tilimbom; Mavra: Chanson de Paracha.*
*** DG 2531 377 [id.]. Bryn-Julson, Murray, Tear, Shirley-Quirk, Intercontemporain Ens., Boulez.

Practically all of Stravinsky's songs are accommodated on this useful record, many of them not otherwise available. The early songs occupy more than a side: he wrote the bulk of his vocal output before or during the First World War, after which there is a long gap (1919–53) in which he abandoned the medium. (The *Chanson de Paracha* from *Mavra* was published as a separate song, but that is the sole exception.) The singing is very persuasive throughout and well characterized. The Verlaine songs are, oddly enough, given in Russian (Stravinsky originally set them in French), but Shirley-Quirk makes them sound very appealing nonetheless. The record also includes a 1968 transcription of two of Wolf's Spanish songs, his very last opus. Clean, well-focused sound.

(i) *Canticum sacrum. Symphony of Psalms.*
*** Argo ZRG 799 [id.]. Christ Church Cath. Ch., Oxford, Jones Ens., Preston, (i) with Morton, Creed.

It is fascinating to hear Stravinsky's rapt masterpiece in a performance with boys' voices, which the composer said he had in mind. The freshness of the choral sound, its ethereal clarity, make this a most moving performance, as though sung by an angel choir; and the *Canticum sacrum*, more taxing still in its serial austerity, brings another superb example of the artistry of these youngsters. There again Stravinsky's markings suggest that he may have had such a tone colour in mind, though in all normal circumstances it would seem near impossible to achieve it. The *Symphony* lacks some of the weight and bite of larger-scale performances, but with atmospheric, resonant sound this is a most beautiful record.

Mass.
*** Argo ZRG 720. Christ Church Cath. Ch., Oxford, L. Sinf., Preston – POULENC: *Christmas motets* etc.***

A finely classical reading of Stravinsky's austerely beautiful *Mass* for voices and instruments. Excellent recording.

(i) *Mass;* (ii) *Les Noces.*
*** DG 2530 880 [id.]. (i) Trinity Boys' Ch., E. Bach Fest. O; (i; ii) E. Bach Fest. Ch.; (ii) Mory, Parker, Mitchinson, Hudson; Argerich, Zimerman, Katsaris, Francesch (pianos), percussion; cond. Bernstein.

Bernstein directs characterful performances of both works, unexpectedly but imaginatively coupled. He reinforces the point that both the *Mass* and the much earlier ballet illustrating a folk wedding ceremony are intensely Russian in their inspiration. In the *Mass* the style is overtly expressive, with the boys of Trinity Choir responding freshly, but it is in *Les Noces* that Bernstein conveys an electricity and a dramatic urgency which at last on record give the work its rightful stature as one of Stravinsky's supreme masterpieces, totally original and even today unexpected, not least in its black-and-white instrumentation for four pianos and percussion. The star pianists here make a superb, imaginative team. Good atmospheric recording.

(i) *Les Noces;* (ii) *Ragtime for 11 instruments;* (iii) *Renard.*
(M) **(*) CBS 61975. (i) Barber, Copland, Foss, Sessions (pianos), soloists, Ch., Columbia Percussion Ens.; (ii) Koves (cimbalom), Columbia CO; (iii) Koves, Columbia Chamber Ens.; all cond. composer.

Stravinsky missed some of the barbaric bite of *Les Noces* when he came to record it in his eighties, and the translation into English hardly helps. But there remains a unique authority in this performance, not least with four such distinguished composers at the pianos, and the coupling of two lesser works of the same period, *Ragtime* and *Renard*, makes an attractive package. It is a pity that no text of *Renard* is given, and the recording is hardly refined, but these are issues of historic importance that should be permanently available and will give much pleasure.

(i) *Pulcinella* (complete). *Suites Nos. 1 and 2.*
*** HMV ASD 3604. Northern Sinf., Rattle; (i) with Jennifer Smith, Fryatt, King.
*** HMV Dig. ASD/*TCC-ASD* 4313 [Ang. DS/*4XS* 37899]. ASMF, Marriner; (i) with Kenny, Tear, Lloyd.

Simon Rattle, helped rather than hindered by a somewhat dry recording acoustic which gives the flavour of a small theatre, conveys far more than usual the links between this score and the much later neoclassical opera *The Rake's Progress*. As one hears this genial theatrical entertainment, Rattle might be directing it as an adjunct to *The Rake's Progress* at Glyndebourne. With lively colourful playing from the Northern Sinfonia (the solos strong and positive) and with first-rate contributions from the three soloists, all of them artists who deserve to record much more, the high spirits of this score come over superbly. The recording has a wide range and gives orchestra and voices alike the most vivid presence and detail. The two *Orchestral suites* are equally successful and make a valuable bonus.

Like Simon Rattle, Neville Marriner gives us the two *Suites* as a makeweight. If you have invested in the earlier account, there is no need to make the change to the later rival. However, the playing of the Academy of St Martin-in-the-Fields is very fine indeed, and they are accorded a natural balance with plenty of air round the instruments and no want of depth. The voices are a bit forward, but so they are in the Abbado set on DG, which is now only available in Abbado's boxed set. It is more brilliant and incisive, with the greater weight and sonority of a larger orchestra. Yet even if a harder-etched contour and a more vinegary bouquet are called for in this repertoire, Marriner's finely played record will give pleasure and can be confidently recommended. The iron-oxide cassette is smooth, warm and clear, though lacking a little in bite at the top.

Symphony of Psalms.

*** CBS 76670 [M/*MT* 34551]. E. Bach Fest. Ch., LSO, Bernstein – POULENC: *Gloria.****

** DG 2531/*3301* 048 [id.]. German Op. Ch., Berlin PO, Karajan – BACH: *Magnificat.***

(M) *(*) Sup. 50778. Czech PO Ch. and O, Ančerl – MARTINŮ: *Prophecy of Isaiah.**(*)

Bernstein's account of the *Symphony* ranks among the best, though his view of the work is not as austere and ascetic as the composer's own. Yet there is grandeur and a powerful sense of atmosphere as well as first-class singing and playing from the Bach Festival Chorus and the LSO. The recording, too, is distinguished by clarity and range. Though this is not an all-Stravinsky record it remains an indispensable item in the Stravinsky discography of recent years.

Even in Stravinsky Karajan keeps some of his characteristic smoothness – as the composer himself noted in waspish comments. This remains an unidiomatic version, the less recommendable because the coupling is disappointing, but the greatness of this masterpiece can stand the deviation, and the final *Alleluias* are most beautifully done. The cassette transfer is admirably faithful.

Ančerl's account of the *Symphony of Psalms* suffers from rhythmic heaviness in all three movements, for he fails to sustain his rather slow tempi, notably in the finale. The phrasing is not as flexible as it might be, but with more vivid and immediate choral recording than is usual from Supraphon the result still makes a fair coupling for the rare Martinů work on the reverse.

Oedipus Rex (opera-oratorio; complete).

**(*) Decca SET 616 [Lon. CS/*5*- 1168]. McCowen (narrator), Pears, Meyer, McIntyre, Dean, Ryland Davies, Luxon, John Alldis Ch., LPO, Solti.

(M) *(**) Sup. 50678. Desailly (narrator), Zídek, Soukupová, Barmann, Haken, Kroupa, Czech PO Ch. and O, Ančerl.

Solti's view of this highly stylized work is less sharp-edged than one would expect, and the dominant factor in the performance is not so much the conductor's direction as the heartfelt singing of Sir Peter Pears in the title role. It was he who sang the part in the composer's first LP recording twenty years earlier, and here the crispness and clarity of his delivery go with an ability to point the key moments of deep emotion with extraordinary intensity. The rest of the vocal team is good, if not outstanding, and the narrations (in English) of Alex McCowen are apt and undistracting. The recording is outstandingly full and brilliant.

With the Czech performance there is a degree of expressiveness in the phrasing that might not have pleased the composer himself, but when you have a group of virtuoso singers, the result is sharp and committed. Though the chorus is larger here, the precision of discipline is much more acute. The Czech soloists bring a Slavonic timbre which is not at all inappropriate in this work with its lingering traces of Russian influence, and the recording quality is very good. There remains one maddening technical flaw. The final two pizzicato notes at the very end of the opera have been snipped off the tape, and the piece is made to end with the gradual diminuendo on repeated triplets. The price may help to smooth any wound caused by that inadequacy.

The Rake's Progress (opera): complete.
*** CBS 77304 (3) [M3S-710]. Young, Raskin, Sarfaty, Reardon, Garrard, Sadler's Wells Ch., RPO, composer.

It was a splendid idea to get Stravinsky to come to London to record *The Rake's Progress* in a version which has elements of the Sadler's Wells production – which incidentally Stravinsky attended some time earlier. In particular the Rake of Alexander Young is a marvellous achievement, sweet-toned and accurate and well characterized. In the choice of the other principals too it is noticeable what store Stravinsky set by vocal precision; generally he seemed to like voices with little vibrato. Judith Raskin makes an appealing Anne Trulove, sweetly sung if not specially well projected dramatically. John Reardon too is remarkable more for vocal accuracy than for striking characterization, but Regina Sarfaty's Baba is marvellous on both counts, and her anger at being spurned just before the 'squelching' makes a superb moment. The Sadler's Wells Chorus sings with even greater drive under the composer than in the theatre, and the Royal Philharmonic (the only element from the earlier Glyndebourne production) plays with warmth and a fittingly Mozartian sense of style, to match Stravinsky's surprisingly lyrical approach to his own score. The recording is excellent, and few modern opera sets can be recommended more warmly: it is a work that grows in strength on the one hand and charm on the other with every hearing.

Suk, Josef (1874–1935)

(i) *A Fairy Tale* (suite), *Op. 16. Scherzo fantastique, Op. 25.*
(M) *** Sup. 1410 2699. Prague SO, Bělohlávek, (i) with Suk.

A Fairy Tale is drawn from the music Suk composed to Zeyer's dramatic tale *Radúz and Mahulena* (and is not to be confused with *A Summer Fairy Tale* of 1907–9, which bears a later opus number). The music shows Suk a master of colour and a highly imaginative and inventive composer, and serves as a reminder that his neglect in the concert hall and on the gramophone is our loss. There is no modern recording of *Asrael* or *Ripening*, and this issue is the first of *A Fairy Tale* since Zdeněk Mácal's of 1967. That too was coupled with the delightful *Scherzo fantastique*, which ought to be every bit as popular as the *Scherzo capriccioso* of Suk's father-in-law, Dvořák. The latter acclaimed *A Fairy Tale* as 'music from Heaven', and he might well have said the same of the *Scherzo*, which has a captivating tune that, once heard, is difficult to dislodge from one's mind. This vivid and warm music is splendidly played and recorded and can be strongly recommended. The violin solo, incidentally, is played by the composer's grandson – very beautifully, too.

(i) *Fantasy in G min. for violin and orchestra, Op. 24;* (ii) *Ballad for violin and orchestra, Op. 30; 4 Pieces for violin and piano, Op. 17.*
(M) ** Sup. 50777. Suk, with (i) Czech PO, Ančerl; (ii) Panenka.

We sorely need a first-class account of Suk's masterpiece, the *Asrael symphony*, a work of great depth and originality. Readers will get little idea of Suk's imaginative power from the three works collected on this disc, even if they make more than acceptable listening. The *Fantasy* is a brilliant piece, full of virtuosity, that relates to the traditional essays in violin wizardry as well as to the Czech national tradition. The work has music of characteristic fantasy, though the rhetorical brilliance tends to dominate. The orchestral accompaniment under Ančerl is no less staggering than Suk's playing, and most listeners will find the results refreshing and enjoyable even if they convey an inadequate picture of the composer's stature. The *Four Pieces*, Op. 17, are better known and very attractive, and the early

Ballad, if unmemorable, is by no means without interest. The recording of the orchestral side is a trifle reverberant and very bright, but the other side is altogether excellent.

Serenade for strings in E flat, Op. 6.
*** Argo ZRG 792 [id.]. LACO, Marriner – JANÁČEK: *Suite****; R. STRAUSS: *Capriccio: Introduction.***(*)

Suk's attractive *Serenade* ought to be better known. It is a work of considerable charm, but also has an underlying power and eloquence, as the superb account by Marriner and his Los Angeles orchestra fully reveals. The recorded sound is more brilliantly lit than we are used to in Marriner's Academy of St Martin-in-the-Fields discs, but it is of the highest quality and naturally balanced.

War triptych, Op. 35.
(M) **(*) Sup. 50476. Czech PO, Klima – NOVÁK: *De profundis.***(*)

Like the Novák *De profundis*, this is a noble and eloquent work, though it dates of course from the First rather than the Second World War. The performance has great conviction and is well recorded. Suk's music may show less personality than Janáček's or Martinů's, let alone his father-in-law Dvořák, but it has rich rewards for those who will take the trouble to investigate it.

(i) *Piano quartet in A min., Op. 1; String quartet No. 1 in B flat, Op. 11.*
(M) ** Sup. 1111 2974. (i) Stepan; Suk Qt.

The early *Piano quartet* is naturally derivative and much the same must be said of the *First Quartet* which the Smetana Quartet recorded way back in the 1960s. The mantle of his teacher and father-in-law, Dvořák, hangs discernibly on Suk's shoulders. However, the music is eminently pleasing and the slow movement of the *Piano quartet* is both engaging and touching. Good performances and acceptable, but not distinguished, recording.

Under the Apple Tree (cantata).
(M) ** Sup. 1121 678. Jelinková, Czech PO Ch., Ostrava Janáček PO, Trhlík – JANÁČEK: *Amarus.***

Under the Apple Tree is new to the catalogue and, like the Janáček coupling, comes from the turn of the century; it predates the *Asrael symphony*, the outpouring of grief on the deaths of Suk's father-in-law, Dvořák, and his wife, Otilia. This cantata may lack the depth of his later works, but it has some marvellous music in it. Not all the influences are fully digested: Dvořák and the Czech nationalists come to mind at the opening, Bruckner at the end, and there are moments of Lisztian-derived harmony that point towards Debussy in between. But Suk had a distinctive voice, even if in this work it was not yet fully developed. The performance is persuasive enough but the recording does not cope so well with the choral climaxes at the end of the side. However, this is well worth investigating.

Sullivan, Arthur (1842–1900)

Overtures: *The Gondoliers; HMS Pinafore; Iolanthe; The Mikado; Patience; The Yeomen of the Guard; Di Ballo.*
(M) **(*) HMV Green. ESD/*TC-ESD* 107754-1/*4*. Royal Liv. PO, Groves.

Groves is a naturally sympathetic conductor in this repertoire and these broadly spacious performances, although bringing the ambience of the concert hall rather than the theatre, are enjoyable in their affectionately lyrical way. The *Yeomen of the Guard* sets the mood of the music-making, with fairly leisurely pacing, and on side two the big fat bass-drum at the opening of *The Mikado* gives further emphasis to the relative gravitas of the approach. Excellent playing and full, resonant recording, with a good XDR tape to match the disc pretty closely.

Pineapple Poll (ballet music, arr. Mackerras).
(M) *** HMV Green. ESD/*TC-ESD* 7028 [Ara. 8016/*9016*]. RPO, Mackerras.
(B) ** PRT GSGC/*ZCGC* 2002. Pro Arte O, Hollingsworth.

Pineapple Poll; Overture: Di Ballo.
*** Decca Dig. SXDL 7619. Philh. O, Mackerras.

The new Decca digital recording of *Pineapple Poll* was made in the Kingsway Hall and its glowing ambience casts a pleasing bloom over the spirited and elegantly polished playing of the Philharmonia Orchestra. Mackerras conducts with great warmth and finds space for a delightful performance of *Di Ballo*, showing more delicacy of approach than Sir Charles Groves's otherwise admirable version – see above. The chrome cassette is first-class.

Mackerras's earlier record is not entirely superseded. Considered definitive in its day (1962), it is still striking for its sheer brio. The RPO is in excellent form and the HMV recording still sounds extremely well. At mid-price this remains competitive; the playing has a real feeling of the ballet theatre, even if the later version gains in breadth and atmosphere. There is a very good tape, only very marginally less refined than the disc.

Hollingsworth offers a lively reading supported on the whole by good orchestral playing, and the slightly brash recorded quality quite suits the ebullience of the score. The upper register is a trifle unclean but is easily smoothed out. A good bargain. The cassette has not quite the sparkle of the disc on side one, but side two is brighter and more vivid.

OPERAS

Cox and Box: complete.
*** Decca SKL 4138/40 [Lon. OSA 1323]. Styler, Riordan, Adams, New SO of L., Godfrey – *The Gondoliers.****

Cox and Box is a superb performance in every way. It is given a recording which without sacrificing clarity conveys with perfect balance the stage atmosphere. Those who feel that Sullivan's genius could operate solely with the catalyst of Gilbert's words will be surprised to find here that the music is almost as delightful as any written for Gilbert. *Cox and Box* has in fact words by F. C. Burnand and is based very closely on Maddison Morton's farce *Box and Cox*. It was written in 1867 and thus pre-dates the first Gilbert and Sullivan success, *Trial by Jury*, by eight years. One must notice the lively military song *Rataplan* – splendidly sung by Donald Adams, an ideal Bouncer – which was to set the style for many similar and later pieces with words by Gilbert, and also the captivating *Bacon 'Lullaby'*, so ravishingly sung by Joseph Riordan. Later on, in Box's recitative telling how he 'committed suicide', Sullivan makes one of his first and most impressive parodies of grand opera, which succeeds also in being effective in its own right.

The Gondoliers (complete, with dialogue).
*** Decca SKL 4138/40 [Lon. OSA 1323]. Reed, Skitch, Sandford, Round, Styler, Knight, Toye, Sansom, Wright, D'Oyly Carte Op. Ch., New SO of L., Godfrey – *Cox and Box.****
** Decca SKL 5277-8/*K 73 K 22* [OSA/*5*-12110] (with *Marmion overture*). Reed, Sandford, Reid, Rayner, Lilley, Metcalfe, Goss, Shovelton, Holland, D'Oyly Carte Op. Ch., RPO, Nash.

Even on musical grounds one would prefer the earlier Godfrey *Gondoliers* to the HMV performance under Sargent (see below). Certainly in that set there is some very fine singing, but this is offset by Sir Malcolm's often unaccountably slow tempi. Isidore Godfrey's conducting here is vividly alive and this is perhaps the best Gilbert and Sullivan he gave us on record, better even than the splendid *HMS Pinafore*. Decca provided a large and first-class orchestra and a spacious recording (generally better than the HMV sound). Perhaps during the opening scene one has the feeling of almost too much orchestra, the solo singers being a shade backward, but this is largely a question of getting the volume setting just right. The solo singing throughout is consistently good. Jeffrey Skitch and Jennifer Toye are a well-matched pair of lovers, and the two

Gondoliers and their wives are no less effective. Thomas Round sings *Take a pair of sparkling eyes* very well indeed. The ensemble singing is superbly balanced and always both lively and musical. The *Cachucha* is captivating and goes at a sparkling pace. Everywhere one can feel the conductor's guiding hand – an instance is the splendidly managed broadening of the orchestral ritornello which forms the closing bars of Act I. The dialogue is for the most part well spoken, and Kenneth Sandford, who is a rather light-voiced Don Alhambra, makes much of his spoken part as well as singing his songs with fine style. The fact that he is no match for Owen Brannigan on HMV is more a question of vocal timbre than poor singing or acting. John Reed is a suitably dry Duke of Plaza-Toro: he makes the part his own and is well partnered by Gillian Knight. All in all a considerable achievement.

The newer D'Oyly Carte set under Royston Nash manages to get the whole opera on to four sides even though it includes the dialogue. It is in fact the dialogue that will be the stumbling block for most listeners: the stylized speech of Casilda – her assumed impediment provides the consonant 'w' in place of every 'r', thus altering 'Barataria' to 'Bawatawia' – becomes irritating before the opera is over. The performance is generally fresh and lively, although in the overture Nash's rather heavy pointing of the gavotte immediately shows less rhythmic resilience than in Godfrey's classic account. The singing is generally good, and John Reed is on top form. The recording is clear, and especially lively in the tape version, but not as richly expansive as on the earlier set, which remains very much a first choice. The *Marmion overture*, inspired by Walter Scott's poem, makes an interesting if not indispensable bonus here.

The Gondoliers (complete, without dialogue).
(M) ** HMV SXDW/*TC2-SXDW* 3027 [Sera. SIB 6103]. Young, Lewis, Graham, Morison, Geraint Evans, Cameron, Marjorie Thomas, Brannigan, Glyndebourne Fest. Ch., Pro Arte O, Sargent.

One would have thought that, after *Yeomen*, *The Gondoliers* would be the most readily responsive of the popular operas to the full operatic treatment. However, Sargent's set, for all its virtues, is not a complete success, and strangely enough it is in the long opening scene, where one would have expected Sir Malcolm's forces to be completely captivating, that there is some lack of spontaneity. At the entrance of the Duke of Plaza-Toro things warm up considerably, and early on side two Owen Brannigan, as a perfectly cast Don Alhambra, sings a masterly *No possible doubt whatever*. From then onwards and throughout the rest of the opera there is much to delight the ear. Edna Graham's Casilda is charmingly small-voiced (by the same token Elsie Morison is a little heavy in her song at the beginning of side three). Sir Malcolm adopts some unaccountably slow tempi in places, especially for the *Cachucha*, but the small ensembles and unaccompanied singing are lovely. There is a great deal of musical pleasure to be had from this set, and, having the advantage of two discs against the earlier D'Oyly Carte's three, it is certainly competitive on grounds of price. There is a first-class cassette version (complete on two sides).

The Grand Duke (complete).
**(*) Decca SKL 5239-40/*K 17 K 22* [Lon. OSA/5- 12106]. Reed, Sandford, Ayldon, Goss, Holland, Meston, Reid, Rayner, D'Oyly Carte Op. Ch., RPO, Nash.

The Grand Duke was the fourteenth and last of the Savoy operas. In spite of a spectacular production and a brilliant first night on 7 March 1896, the work only played for 123 performances and then lapsed into relative oblivion, although it has been revived by amateur societies. The present recording came after a successful concert presentation in 1975, and the recorded performance, which has both polish and vigour, represents perhaps the ideal way to sample Sullivan's least-known major score. Less than first-rate Sullivan can still make rewarding listening, even though, compared with the sparkle and melodic inspiration of *HMS Pinafore*, the music shows a sad decline. Gilbert's libretto is impossibly complicated, but there are many felicities in the lyrics to reward the dedicated enthusiast. The recording is characteristically brilliant both on disc and in its tape version.

H M S Pinafore (complete, with dialogue).
⊛ *** Decca SKL 4081-2/*K 123 K 22* [Lon. OSA/*5*- 1209]. Reed, Skitch, Round, Adams, Hindmarsh, Wright, Knight, D'Oyly Carte Op. Ch., New S O of London, Godfrey.

There is a marvellous spontaneity about the invention in *Pinafore* and somehow the music has a genuine briney quality. The piece also contains Dick Deadeye, the strangest character in all the Savoy operas, who seems to have popped suddenly to the surface – in Freudian fashion – from Gilbert's subconscious, a more powerful figure than any of the matronly ladies at whom Gilbert liked to poke fun. It would be difficult to imagine a better-recorded performance of *Pinafore* than the earlier Decca. It is complete with dialogue, and here it is vital in establishing the character of Deadeye, since much of his part is spoken rather than sung. The dialogue is spoken extremely well, and Donald Adams is a totally memorable Deadeye and his larger-than-life personality underpins the whole piece. Among the others Jeffrey Skitch is a first-class Captain; Jean Hindmarsh is absolutely convincing as Josephine (it was a pity she stayed with the company for so short a time), and she sings with great charm. Thomas Round is equally good as Ralph Rackstraw. Little Buttercup could be slightly more colourful, but this is a small blemish, and among the minor parts George Cook is a most personable Bill Bobstay. The choral singing is excellent, the orchestral playing good and Isidore Godfrey conducts with marvellous spirit and lift. The recording has splendid atmosphere on disc and tape alike. A marvellous memento of a great theatrical tradition which is likely never to be quite the same again.

H M S Pinafore (complete, without dialogue).
(M) *** HMV SXDW/*TC-SXDW* 3034 (2) [Ang. SBL 3589]. George Baker, Cameron, Lewis, Brannigan, Morison, Sinclair, Glyndebourne Fest. Ch., Pro Arte O, Sargent – *Trial by Jury*.***

It is to Owen Brannigan's great credit that, little as he had to do here, without the dialogue, he conveyed the force of Deadeye's personality so strongly. For those who find the dialogue tedious in repetition this is a very happy set, offering some good solo singing and consistently lovely ensemble singing and chorus work. The whole of the final scene is musically quite ravishing, and throughout if Sir Malcolm fails to find quite all the wit in the music he is never less than lively. George Baker is of course splendid as Sir Joseph, and John Cameron, Richard Lewis and (especially) Monica Sinclair, as Buttercup, make much of their songs. Elsie Morison is rather disappointing; she spoils the end of her lovely song in Act I by singing sharp. However, she brings plenty of drama to her *Scena* in Act II. The male trio near the end of Act I is outstandingly well sung – full of brio and personality. The coupling with *Trial by Jury* makes this a fine bargain. The recording is bright and lively and does not lack atmosphere. For the cassette issue – unlike the rest of this series – two separate tapes are provided in a box. The transfer is of good quality, missing only the last touch of refinement.

Iolanthe (complete, with dialogue).
**(*) Decca SKL 5188-9/*K 2 C 35* [Lon. OSA/*5*- 12104]. Reed, Field, Merri, Holland, Williams, Sandford, Rayner, Ayldon, D'Oyly Carte Op. Ch., RPO, Nash.

Decca's first stereo recording of *Iolanthe* under Godfrey was produced with some panache, even introducing the Grenadier Guards Band into the *March of the Peers*. No doubt in due course this will be restored to the catalogue, for it is generally superior to the newer set. Nash was a good musical director, but Godfrey was inspired, over his thirty or so years with the company, to set standards of freshness in all he did that have never been matched. On two counts only does the new Decca *Iolanthe* improve on the old. John Reed's portrayal of the Lord Chancellor has understandably matured, and in the new set the character has a real vintage quality. The vocal inflections, squeaks and other speech mannerisms are a delight. Only in the *Nightmare song* does one feel that familiarity has bred too easy a manner, and with hardly any feeling of bravura (so fluently do the words trip out) some of the tension goes. The recording too offers a marginal gain in quality; notably the spoken words have more naturalness and realism, though there are a few moments when some emphasized sibilants are irritating. But as a whole the account has both charm and sparkle, and Nash's refined manner, immediately apparent in the overture, is a fair exchange for Godfrey's more robust high spirits. The new Queen of the Fairies has a splendidly ripe speaking voice, yet when she sings the tone is rather less attractive. Pamela Field as Phyllis manages her spoken dialogue with the two Earls in Act II very well indeed. John Ayldon's singing voice is rather throaty, and Michael Rayner as Strephon is very dark-toned. Kenneth Sandford shows a certain lack of resonance and authority in the *Sentry song*. On the earlier set he was in much better form. The choral singing is first-rate. Undoubtedly this newer recording will give pleasure, and on the extremely vivid tape transfer the dialogue springs to life with remarkable presence to give the whole performance added spontaneity.

Iolanthe (complete, without dialogue).
(M) **(*) HMV SXDW/*TC2-SXDW* 3047 (2). George Baker, Wallace, Cameron, Young, Brannigan, Sinclair, Morison, Glyndebourne Fest. Ch., Pro Arte O, Sargent.

There is much to praise in this HMV set, and EMI have refurbished the recording very successfully; it suits the studio-based performance and projects the music brightly without loss of inner warmth. The climax of Act I, the scene of the Queen of the Fairies' curse on members of both Houses of Parliament, shows most excitingly what can be achieved with the 'full operatic treatment': this is a dramatic moment indeed. George Baker too is very good as the Lord Chancellor; his voice is fuller and more baritonal than the dry monotone we are used to from John Reed, yet he provides an equally individual characterization. For some listeners John Cameron's dark timbre may not readily evoke an Arcadian Shepherd, although he sings stylishly. The Peers' chorus is not a highlight. It is treated lyrically, and the tenors are not very incisive; some might wish for a more robust effect here. Nevertheless there is much to enjoy. The two Earls and Private Willis are excellent, the famous *Nightmare song* is very well and clearly sung, and all of Act II (except perhaps Iolanthe's recitative and ballad near the end) goes very well. The famous *Trio* with the Lord Chancellor and the two Earls is a joy. The opening scene of Act I is effectively atmospheric, with Monica Sinclair a splendid Fairy Queen. The tape version is on a single double-length cassette, an ideal format, and the lively yet spacious effect of the discs is generally mirrored faithfully.

The Mikado (complete, without dialogue).
*** Decca SKL 5158-9/*K 22 K 22* [Lon. OSA/5- 12103]. Ayldon, Wright, Reed, Sandford, Masterson, Holland, D'Oyly Carte Op. Ch., RPO, Nash.
(M) *** HMV ESDW/*TC2-ESDW* 107718-3/9. Wakefield, Studholme, Holmes, Revill, Dowling, Allister, Sadler's Wells Ch. and O, Faris.
(M) ** HMV SXDW 3019/*TC2-EXE 1021* [Ang. SBL 3573]. Lewis, Evans, Wallace, Brannigan, Morison, Sinclair, Glyndebourne Fest. Ch., Pro Arte O, Sargent.

The D'Oyly Carte *Mikado* is a complete success in every way and shows the Savoy tradition at its most attractive. The Sadler's Wells recording, however, remains very competitive, and while traditionalists will undoubtedly go for Nash's account, others may find that the new look taken by Alexander Faris and his excellent cast is very rewarding. Not that there is any lack of freshness in the newer Decca recording. Indeed its effect is like a coat of bright new paint, and the G. and S. masterpiece emerges with a pristine sparkle. Musically this is by far the finest version the D'Oyly Carte company have ever put on disc. The choral singing is first-rate, with much refinement of detail. The glees, *Brightly dawns* and *See how the fates*, are robust in the D'Oyly Carte manner but more polished than usual. The words are exceptionally clear throughout without sizzling sibilants. This applies to an important early song in Act I, *Our great Mikado*, which contains the seeds of the plot and is sometimes delivered in a throaty, indistinct way. Not so here: every word is crystal clear. Of the principals, John Reed is a splendid Ko-Ko, a refined and individual characterization, and his famous *Little list* song has an enjoyable lightness of touch. Kenneth Sandford gives his customary vintage projection of Pooh Bah – a pity none of his dialogue has been included. Valerie Masterson is a charming Yum-Yum; *The sun whose rays* has rarely been sung with more feeling and charm, and it is followed by a virtuoso account of *Here's a how-de-do* which one longs to encore but cannot, because there is no dividing band. Colin Wright's vocal production has a slightly nasal quality, but one soon adjusts to it and his voice has the proper bright freshness of timbre for Nanki-Poo. John Ayldon's Mikado has not quite the satanic glitter of Donald Adams's classic version, but he provides a laugh of terrifying bravura. Katisha (Lyndsie Holland) is commanding, and her attempts to interrupt the chorus in the finale of Act I are superbly believable and dramatic. With excellent sound throughout (and an expert tape transfer), this is very enjoyable indeed.

But so is the Sadler's Wells set. It is traditional in the best sense, bringing also a humorous sparkle to the proceedings which gives a great delight. Clive Revill is a splendid Ko-Ko; his performance of *Tit willow* and his verse of *The flowers that bloom in the spring* (aided by a momentary touch of stereo gimmickry) have a charming individuality. John Heddle Nash is perhaps the best Pish-Tush we have ever had on record, and it is partly because of him that the *Chippy chopper* trio is so effective. The madrigal, *Brightly dawns*, is beautifully sung (more refined than in the D'Oyly Carte version), and the tale of the mythical execution of Nanki-Poo (*The criminal cried*) is a delight, so humorously is the story told by each of the three 'guilty' parties. Denis Dowling is a superb Pooh Bah, and Marion Studholme a charming Yum-Yum. She sings *The sun whose rays* with a delectable lightness of style. Katisha is first-rate in every way. The part is not hammed at all and she is often very dramatic. Listen to the venom she puts into the word 'bravado' in the Act I finale. Even the chorus scores a new point by their stylized singing of *Mi-ya-sa-ma*, which sounds superbly mock-Japanese. The one disappointment is John Holmes in the name part. He sings well but conveys little of the mock-satanic quality. But this is a small point in an otherwise magnificent set, excellently recorded, and available in a medium-priced reissue. It has a new overture arranged by Charles Mackerras. The tape is first-class, wide-ranging, full and clear, with one Act complete on each side, an ideal presentation.

The reissue of EMI's first stereo *Mikado*, under Sir Malcolm Sargent, makes an interesting comparison with the others. Certainly in this HMV set we have much sheer musicality – the grand-operatic style to the finales of both Acts, the trio about the 'death' of Nanki-Poo and the glee which follows: these are beautifully sung and played. But taken as a whole this is not as enjoyable as either the Sadler's Wells recording or the D'Oyly Carte set. There is less style, and the basic humour of the piece is only sporadically caught. Geraint Evans cannot hold a candle to John Reed or Clive Revill in the patter songs (nor in *Tit Willow*); Owen Brannigan certainly makes a brave show of the Mikado and is better than John Holmes. The star performance on HMV is Richard Lewis, who sings delightfully throughout. Monica Sinclair, however, has not the courage of her convictions when she exclaims *These arms shall thus enfold you*; but Elsie Morison sings nicely as Yum-Yum. The HMV sound has been enhanced in this remastering and there is a convenient single-tape version.

Patience (complete, with dialogue).

**(*) Decca SKL 4146-7/*K 76 K 22* [Lon. OSA 1217]. Sansom, Adams, Cartier, Potter, Reed, Sandford, Toye, D'Oyly Carte Op. Ch. and O, Godfrey.

The D'Oyly Carte *Patience* only really wakes up when the Dragoons come on stage, and this effect is accentuated in the Decca recording by the low-volume level of the ladies' opening dialogue (compared to the music). *Patience* has some charming music, to be sure, but the Act I finale is poor, and throughout one is led to feel that Sullivan is better with primary colours than pastel shades. Certainly *When I first put this uniform on* and *The soldiers of the Queen* are among the very best of all Sullivan's military numbers. Donald Adams is a worthy successor to Darrell Fancourt in these. Patience herself is well characterized by Mary Sansom, but her singing is less impressive. She is thoroughly professional, and excellent in the dialogue, but her songs lack style, although they are not without moments of charm. All the dialogue is here, and very important it is to the action. Unfortunately the poems are spoken with too much intensity, whereas they need throwing off if the barbs of the satire are to be lightly pointed as Gilbert intended. In all other respects both Bunthorne and Grosvenor are well played. Both chorus and orchestra have never sounded better, and Isidore Godfrey displays his usual skill with the accompaniments, which have a splendid bounce. The wide dynamic range of the recording (which is resplendent in the loud music) means that the quieter moments are prone to any surface noises there are about. However, there are no such problems on the tape set, which is very well managed.

Patience (complete, without dialogue).
(M) *** HMV SXDW/*TC2-SXDW* 3031 (2). Morison, Young, George Baker, Cameron, Marjorie Thomas, Sinclair, Harper, Harwood, Glyndebourne Fest. Ch., Pro Arte O, Sargent.

The HMV set of *Patience* was another of the great successes of the Sargent series, and it is in almost every way preferable to the Decca D'Oyly Carte version. Although there is no dialogue there is more business than is usual from HMV and a convincing theatrical atmosphere. The recording is vivid, with no lack of warmth, and the singing is consistently good. The opening scene is far more effective than with Decca and so is the Act I finale. The chorus is a strong feature throughout, and where the men and women sing different melodic lines the clarity of each is admirable. Elsie Morison's Patience, George Baker's Bunthorne and John Cameron's Grosvenor are all admirably characterized, while the military men are excellent too. The many concerted items continually beguile the ear and Sir Malcolm's accompaniments tell splendidly. All in all, this is the sort of production we anticipated when HMV first began their 'Glyndebourne' series, and it can be heartily recommended. The tape transfer (again conveniently on one double-length cassette) needs a strong treble reduction or the vocal consonants are given an unnatural sibilance and the strings sound thin.

The Pirates of Penzance (complete, with dialogue).
*** Decca SKL 4925-6/*K61 K22* [Lon. OSA 1277]. Reed, Adams, Potter, Masterson, Palmer, Brannigan, D'Oyly Carte Op. Ch., RPO, Godfrey.

Isidore Godfrey is helped by a more uniformly excellent cast than was present on the earlier Decca stereo recording, and now for the first time we are given all the dialogue too. The theatrical spontaneity is well maintained, and the spoken scenes with the Pirate King are particularly effective. Donald Adams has a great gift for Gilbertian inflection and some of his lines give as much pleasure as his splendidly characterized singing. Christine Palmer's Ruth is not quite so poised, but her singing is first-rate – her opening aria has never been better done. John Reed does not always show absolute poise in the patter songs, but this is a real characterization of the part and it grows on one. Valerie Masterson is an excellent Mabel, and if her voice is not creamy throughout its range, she controls it with great skill. Her duet with Frederick, *Leave me not to pine alone*, is enchanting, sung very gently. Godfrey has prepared us for it in the overture, and it is one of the highlights of the set. Godfrey's conducting is as affectionate as ever, more lyrical here, without losing the rhythmic buoyancy, and one can hear him revelling in the many touches of colour in the orchestration, which the Royal Philharmonic Orchestra present with great sophistication. But perhaps the greatest joy of the set is Owen Brannigan's Sergeant of Police, a part this artist was surely born to play. It is a marvellously humorous performance, yet the humour is never clumsy, and the famous *Policeman's song* is so fresh that it is almost like hearing it for the first time. The recording is superbly spacious and clear throughout, with a fine sense of atmosphere. The cassettes are also of excellent quality, with a notably high transfer level.

The Pirates of Penzance (complete, without dialogue).
(M) *** HMV SXDW/*TC2-SXDW* 3041 (2) [Sera. SIB 6102]. George Baker, Milligan, Cameron, Lewis, Brannigan, Morison, Glyndebourne Fest. Ch., Pro Arte O, Sargent.

This was one of the finest of Sir Malcolm Sargent's Gilbert and Sullivan sets. Besides a performance which is stylish as well as lively, conveying both the fun of the words and the charm of the music, the HMV recording has more atmosphere than usual in this series. Undoubtedly the star of the piece is George Baker; he is a splendid Major-General. Here is an excellent example of a fresh approach yielding real dividends, and Sargent's slower than usual tempo for his famous patter song means that the singer can relax and add both wit and polish to the words. As in the Decca D'Oyly Carte set, Owen Brannigan gives a rich portrayal of the Sergeant of the Police. The performance takes a little while to warm up: Sargent's accompaniment to the Pirate King's song is altogether too flaccid. Elsie Morison is a less than ideal Mabel: her opening cadenza of *Poor wandering one* is angular and overdramatic. However, elsewhere she is much more convincing, especially in the famous duet, *Leave me not to pine alone*. The choral contributions (the opening of Act II, for instance) are pleasingly refined, yet have no lack of vigour. *Hail poetry* is resplendent, while the choral finale is managed with poise and a balance which allows the inner parts to emerge pleasingly. The whole performance is in fact more than the sum of its parts. The recording has transferred smoothly and vividly to tape, and the reverberation has been successfully contained, so the focus is nearly always clean. A little treble cut may be useful, for the voices and chorus have plenty of presence. The single-tape format is doubly attractive here, as the two Acts are given a complete side each.

Princess Ida (complete, without dialogue).
*** Decca SKL 4708-9/*K 66 K 22* [Lon. OSA 1262]. Harwood, Sandford, Adams, Skitch, Reed, D'Oyly Carte Op. Ch., RPO, Sargent.

Sir Malcolm Sargent is completely at home here, and his broadly lyrical approach has much to offer in this 'grandest' of the Savoy operas. Elizabeth Harwood in the name part sings splendidly, and John Reed's irritably gruff portrayal of the irascible King Gama is memorable. He certainly is a properly 'disagreeable man'. The rest of the cast is no less strong, and with excellent teamwork from the company as a whole and a splendid recording, spacious and immediate, this has much to offer, even if Sullivan's invention is somewhat variable in quality. The cassette transfer is outstanding, one of Decca's best.

Ruddigore (complete, without dialogue).
(M) *** HMV SXDW/*TC2-SXDW* 3029 (2). George Baker, Lewis, Brannigan, Blackburn, Morison, Bowden, Sinclair, Glyndebourne Fest. Ch., Pro Arte O, Sargent.
**(*) Decca SKL 4504–5/*K 75 K 22* [Lon. OSA 1248]. Reed, Round, Sandford, Riley, Adams, Hindmarsh, Knight, Sansom, Allister, D'Oyly Carte Op. Ch., ROHCG O, Godfrey.

The HMV set has been most successfully remastered and offers first-class sound, the voices natural and well balanced with the orchestra, and much warmth and bloom on the recording. This matches Sargent's essentially lyrical approach and emphasizes the associations this lovely score so often finds with the music of Schubert. The performance is beautifully sung and the excellence is uniform. Perhaps George Baker sounds a little old in voice for Robin Oakapple, but he does the *Poor little man . . . poor little maid* duet in Act I with great charm and manages his 'character transformation' later in the opera splendidly. Pamela Bowden is a first-class Mad Margaret, and her short Donizettian scena is superbly done. Equally Richard Lewis is an admirably bumptious Richard. Perhaps, surprisingly, Owen Brannigan does not make quite as much of the *Ghosts' high noon* song as Donald Adams on the D'Oyly Carte set, but his delicious Act II duet with Mad Margaret has an irresistible gentility (and one can visualize their traditional little dance movements, so evocatively is this section managed). The drama of the score is well managed too: Sir Despard's Act I entry has real bravado (the words of the chorus here are wonderfully crisp), and later the scene in the picture gallery (given a touch of added resonance by the recording) is effectively sombre. Even the slightly prissy crowd effects in Act I seem to fall into place, giving an attractive feeling of stylization. A superb reissue, sounding splendid on disc and only marginally less refined on the first-class tape transfer, which has the advantage of providing the whole opera complete on a single cassette.

The Decca set is, after *The Sorcerer*, the least successful of all the D'Oyly Carte/Godfrey recordings. There are several instances of tempi that are fractionally too brisk (a fatal sign that a conductor is trying to brighten things up), and altogether a degree of charm is missing throughout. Savoyards will not be disappointed; here is the production they were used to, very well recorded, but in the Act II duet for the reformed Mad Margaret and Sir Despard the point is missed and this becomes another standard song. The omission of the dialogue is a mistake; the scene mentioned above is incomplete without the delightful spoken interchange about Basingstoke. Instead of the dialogue we have the original overture complete with the music for the original finale. The performance also includes the attractive duet *The battle's roar is over*, which is (for whatever reason) traditionally omitted. There is much to enjoy here. The principals are good (especially Gillian Knight and Donald Adams, whose *Ghosts' high noon* is a marvellous highlight), and the chorus and orchestra are excellent.

The Sorcerer (complete, without dialogue).
**(*) Decca SKL 4825/6. Reed, Adams, Palmer, Masterson, D'Oyly Carte Op. Ch., RPO, Godfrey.

John Reed's portrayal of the wizard himself is one of the finest of all his characterizations. Godfrey, however, with his robust, sparkling manner, seems at less than his usual inspired best in this recording, dating from 1967. The plot, with a love potion administered to the whole village by mistake, has considerable potential, but it drew from Sullivan a great deal of music in his fey pastoral vein, and not all of it comes fully to life. The performance wakes up marvellously at the entrance of John Wellington Wells, and his famous introductory aria is given a virtuoso performance here, while the spell-casting scene is equally compelling. The performance retains its buoyancy till the end of the Act, but is variable again in Act II until the final sequence of numbers, which go splendidly. There is notably fine singing from the chorus.

Utopia Ltd: complete. *Imperial march.*
**(*) Decca SKL 5225/6 [Lon. OSA/5-12105]. Field, Holland, Ayldon, Reed, Sandford, Ellison, Buchan, Conroy-Ward, D'Oyly Carte Op. Ch., RPO, Nash.

Utopia Ltd was first performed in 1893, ran for 245 performances and then remained unheard (except for amateur productions) until revived for the D'Oyly Carte centenary London season in 1974, which led to this recording. Its complete neglect is unaccountable; the piece stages well, and if the music is not as consistently fine as the best of the Savoy operas, it contains much that is memorable. Moreover Gilbert's libretto shows him at his most wittily ingenious, and the idea of a Utopian society *inevitably* modelled on British constitutional practice suggests Victorian self-confidence at its most engaging. Also the score offers a certain nostalgic quality in recalling earlier successes. Apart from a direct quote from *Pinafore* in the Act I finale, the military number of the First Light Guards has a strong flavour of *Patience*, and elsewhere *Iolanthe* is evoked.

Make way for the Wise Men, near the opening, immediately wins the listener's attention, and the whole opera is well worth having in such a lively and vigorous account. Royston Nash shows plenty of skill in the matter of musical characterization, and the solo singing is consistently assured. When Meston Reid as Captain Fitz-Battleaxe sings 'You see I can't do myself justice' in *Oh, Zara*, he is far from speaking the truth – this is a performance of considerable bravura. The ensembles are not always as immaculately disciplined as one is used to from the D'Oyly Carte, and *Eagle high* is disappointingly focused: the intonation here is less than secure. However, the sparkle and spontaneity of the performance as a whole are irresistible, with vivid recording and a first-class tape transfer, which has striking presence and clarity. As there is no overture as such, the recording uses Sullivan's *Imperial march*, written for the opening – by the Queen – of the Imperial Institute, five months before the première of the opera. It is an effective enough piece, but not a patch on the *March of the Peers* from *Iolanthe*.

Trial by Jury (complete).
(M) *** HMV SXDW/*TC-SXDW* 3034 (3) [Ara. 8052/*9052*]. George Baker, Cameron, Lewis, Brannigan, Morison, Sinclair, Glyndebourne Fest. Ch., Pro Arte O, Sargent – *HMS Pinafore*.***

An outstanding, thoroughly musical account, with a shade more 'production' than usual in the HMV series. The casting is excellent, and George Baker makes a fine judge. The recording is one of the best HMV have given us so far for G. and S.: it is clear, spacious and bright, and has some good but unexaggerated stereo effects. It is well transferred to tape, but it is a great pity that it could not have been given side four of this boxed tape set to itself. Not a great deal of tape has been saved by setting the beginning of the work clumsily just before the end of side three.

The Yeomen of the Guard (complete, without dialogue).
*** Decca SKL 4624-5/*K 60 K 22* [Lon. OSA 1258]. Hood, Harwood, Reed, Potter, Sandford, Adams, Knight, D'Oyly Carte Op. Ch., RPO, Sargent.
(M) *** HMV SXDW/*TC2-SXDW* 3033 (2). Thomas, Morison, Evans, Lewis, Brannigan, Carol Case, Sinclair, Glyndebourne Fest. Ch., Pro Arte O, Sargent.

Sir Malcolm Sargent recorded *The Yeomen of the Guard* in stereo twice very successfully. The later Decca set has the finer recording, but the solo singing in the HMV version is by no means outclassed by the Decca. Here Sir Malcolm's breadth of approach is at once apparent in the overture, and when the chorus enters (*Tower warders*) the feeling of opera rather than operetta is striking. Indeed one has seldom heard the choruses expand with such power, nor indeed has the orchestra (especially the brass) produced such a regal sound. As the work proceeds the essential lyricism of Sargent's reading begins to emerge more and more, and the ensemble singing is especially lovely. There is no lack of drama either, and indeed the only aspect of the work to be played down somewhat is the humorous side. The interjections of Jack and Wilfred in the Act I finale are obviously seen as part of the whole rather than a suggestion of the humour that somehow seems to intrude into the most serious of human situations. The pathos of the famous Jester's song in Act II is played up, and the only moment to raise a real smile is the duet which follows, *Tell a tale of cock and bull*. But with consistently fine singing throughout from all the principals (and especially Elizabeth Harwood as Elsie), this *Yeomen* is unreservedly a success with its brilliant and atmospheric Decca recording. The cassette transfer, too, has splendid presence and immediacy.

The singing on Sargent's HMV recording (which dates from 1960) is very persuasive. As on his more expensive Decca set, the trios and quartets with which this score abounds are most beautifully performed and skilfully balanced, and the ear is continually beguiled. Owen Brannigan's portrayal of Wilfred is splendidly larger than life and Monica Sinclair is a memorable Dame Carruthers. The finales to both Acts have striking breadth, and the delightfully sung trio of Elsie, Phoebe and the Dame in the finale of Act II is a good example of the many individual felicities of this set. *Strange adventure*, too, is most beautifully done. As in the Decca recording there is very little feeling of humour, but the music triumphs. The sound is excellent on disc. On cassette there is less absolute refinement at the highest levels, but this is only marginal; generally the voices have warmth and presence, and the music-making sounds vivid.

Excerpts from: *The Gondoliers; HMS Pinafore; Iolanthe; The Mikado; Patience; The Pirates of Penzance; Ruddigore; The Yeomen of the Guard*.

❀ *** HMV ASD/*TCC-ASD* 4392. Masterson, Tear, Bournemouth SO, Alwyn.

This is the most attractive Gilbert and Sullivan anthology in the present catalogue and perhaps the most engaging recital of its kind ever recorded. Quite apart from the excellence of the singing and the sparkling accompaniments so ably directed by Kenneth Alwyn, it is notable for the clever choice of material, with items from different operas engagingly juxtaposed instead of being gathered together in sequence. The singing itself is enchantingly fresh and spontaneous. Valerie Masterson's upper range is ravishingly fresh and free: witness the lovely close of *Refrain, audacious tar*, from *Pinafore*. Robert Tear's *A wandering minstrel* is wonderfully stylish, while in the duets the two artists consistently project their response to the words as well as the music – the final cadence of *Leave me not to pine alone* is very touching. The sound is bright and vivid on both disc and chrome tape, although a higher level of transfer might have been used to good effect on the latter.

'Favourites': from *The Gondoliers; HMS Pinafore; Iolanthe; The Mikado; Patience; The Pirates of Penzance; Ruddigore; Trial by Jury; The Yeomen of the Guard.*
(B) *** HMV *TC2-MOM 114*. (from above series, cond. Sargent).

This 'Miles of Music' selection includes excerpts from the nine most popular Savoy operas. It was a mistake to open with *The Mikado*, but the excerpts generally are unfailingly enjoyable, expecially the selections from *Patience*, *Iolanthe* and *Ruddigore*. There is a clumsy fade after George Baker's *Judge's song* from *Trial by Jury*, but for the most part the editing is well managed and the sound is first-class, vividly demonstrating EMI's transfer technology at its best. There is nearly an hour and a half of music here, equally suitable for car or home listening.

'Highlights' from *The Gondoliers; HMS Pinafore; Iolanthe; The Mikado; The Pirates of Penzance; The Yeomen of the Guard.*
(B) **(*) CfP CFP/*TC-CFP* 40238. (from above series, cond. Sargent).

An attractive selection of highlights, generously offering samples of six of Sir Malcolm Sargent's HMV recordings. There is some distinguished solo singing and if the atmosphere is sometimes a little cosy (the *Cachucha* from *The Gondoliers* sounds slower than ever, heard out of the context of the complete performance), there is a great deal to enjoy. The recording has transferred well, and there is a first-class cassette too.

'Gilbert and Sullivan spectacular': excerpts from *HMS Pinafore; The Mikado; The Pirates of Penzance; Ruddigore.*
(B) **(*) Con. CC/*CCT* 7508. Reed, Adams, Sandford, Masterson, soloists, D'Oyly Carte Opera Ch., RPO, Sargent.

Basically the recording is certainly spectacular, with a rich overall ambience and the soloists spotlighted well forward. The choral sound, however, is somewhat grainy. The conducting is musical and solid, without the wit of Isidore Godfrey, but genial in its way. The memorable items are *A wandering minstrel*, very nicely turned by Philip Potter, and Donald Adams's suberb versions of the Mikado's famous song (that laugh sounds even more horrifying than usual) and the *Policeman's song* from *Pirates* (which he did not usually sing). John Reed's contributions are very closely microphoned indeed and reveal a break in the voice occasionally. The reverberation produces a lack of clarity of focus on cassette, especially in the ensembles.

'The world of Gilbert and Sullivan': excerpts from *The Gondoliers; HMS Pinafore; The Mikado; Patience; Princess Ida.*
(M) *** Decca SPA/*KCSP* 28. D'Oyly Carte Op. Company, Godfrey or Sargent.

This is a brilliant anthology which is successful in picking not only some of the outstanding highlights from these operas but also from the records of them. With perhaps the single exception of the *Princess Ida* item, *For a month to dwell* (not showing Sir Malcolm Sargent in top form), everything is infectious and highly enjoyable. The other *Princess Ida* excerpt, *If you give me your attention*, is a favourite patter song, and John Reed does it well. The performances here are all from the Decca G. and S. complete sets, which are excellent technically, and indeed the disc opens with a stunning piece of atmospheric business before *I am the monarch of the seas* begins a trio of songs from *Pinafore*. The *Mikado* songs too (taken from the earlier, deleted D'Oyly Carte set) are cleverly chosen to show the cast at their most sparkling. *A wandering minstrel* (Thomas Round), *Three little maids* and *Tit willow* (Peter Pratt) are all excellent. *The Gondoliers* was perhaps the best thing Godfrey did, and all five excerpts are winners. Perhaps most striking of all are the *Patience* songs, with Donald Adams in splendid form in his *Catalogue song* and *When I first put this uniform on.* This is the best D'Oyly Carte anthology available and there is a good cassette equivalent.

'The world of Gilbert and Sullivan', Vol. 2: excerpts from *Iolanthe; The Pirates of Penzance; Ruddigore; The Yeomen of the Guard.*
(M) *** Decca SPA/*KCSP* 29. D'Oyly Carte Op. Company, Godfrey or Sargent.

This second disc is worth having for Donald Adams's classic performance of *When the night wind howls* from *Ruddigore*, which is superbly done. The record also includes *I know a youth*, with its Schubertian charm, and the patter trio *My eyes are fully open*, which is very successful. There is a nice selection from *Iolanthe*, ending with the vivacious final trio, and the *Pirates* excerpts are most enjoyable too. In the *Yeomen* section the chorus *Tower warders* comes before *When maiden loves*, but this seems sensible enough in this context. Good sound throughout, both on disc and on tape.

'The world of Gilbert and Sullivan', Vol. 3: excerpts from *The Gondoliers; Iolanthe; The Mikado; Patience; Ruddigore; The Sorcerer; Trial by Jury.*
(M) ** Decca SPS/*KCSP* 147. D'Oyly Carte Op. Company, Godfrey.

The third selection in this series is notable for a marvellous performance by John Reed of *My name is John Wellington Wells*, from *The Sorcerer*. This is one of Gilbert's very finest inspirations and the music points the words to perfection, but it comes from an otherwise comparatively unmemorable performance, as the companion duet, *Oh, I have wrought much evil with my spells*, readily shows. There are some good excerpts from *The Gondoliers* and *Patience*, and the selection is generous enough to merit recommendation even though one or two items have to be very quickly faded out at the end. In a selection of this kind, and with the whole range of operas to choose from, it ought to be possible to manage by only including pieces that extract easily from the master tape. There is again a good equivalent cassette.

Suppé, Franz von (1819–95)

Overtures: Beautiful Galathea; Boccaccio; Light Cavalry; Morning, Noon and Night in Vienna; Pique Dame; Poet and Peasant.
** Ph. 9500 399/*7300 612* [id.]. LPO, Marriner.

Marriner's collection is certainly well played (although the LPO violins do not show the virtuosity of the Berlin Philharmonic – the ensemble in *Light Cavalry*, for instance, is not as clean as it might be). Marriner is at his best in the overtures where elegance can add an attractive outer veneer to the music-making. Other versions of *Light Cavalry* are rhythmically more exhilarating, and the reprise of the fanfare theme in the coda is awkwardly managed. The opening of *Poet and Peasant* is so broad that it is almost sluggish. The warmly reverberant recording is agreeable enough on disc, but produces a smudged cassette transfer, with patches of uncomfortable congestion at climax.

Overtures: *Beautiful Galathea; Jolly robbers; Light Cavalry; Poet and Peasant.*
(M) **(*) DG Priv. 2543/*3343* 533 [2530 051]. Berlin PO, Karajan – J. STRAUSS: *Overtures.****

The sound had been remastered and rebalanced for this Privilege reissue; the added brilliance is slightly artificial, and the upper focus less clean, with the ambient richness of the original slightly dried out. The performances are marvellously played and have great panache, but the Privilege disc below has better sound.

Overtures: *Light Cavalry; Morning, Noon and Night in Vienna; Pique Dame; Poet and Peasant.*
(M) **(*) Decca SPA 374 [Lon. 411648-1/*4*]. VPO, Solti.

With only four items included (admittedly the most popular four) Solti's record, even at medium price, would be difficult to recommend were not both performances and recordings so brilliant. The recording has a wide dynamic range, too wide for the cello solos in *Morning, Noon and Night* and *Poet and Peasant*, where the instrument is backwardly balanced and sounds not unlike a viola. But if you like the old-fashioned, rather mellow type of Suppé performance, be warned, this is not the shop for that.

Overtures: Light Cavalry; Pique Dame; Poet and Peasant.
(M) *** DG Priv. 2535/*3335* 629 [id.]. Berlin PO, Karajan – ROSSINI: *Overtures.****

On disc this generous Privilege recoupling is a bargain, with Karajan's swaggeringly brilliant Suppé performances attractively coupled to Rossini. The resonant recording is highly effective. But on tape the reverberation brings problems: the opening fanfare of *Light Cavalry* blisters, and elsewhere climaxes are fierce and uncomfortable.

Szymanowski, Karol
(1882–1937)

(i; ii) *Concert overture, Op. 12; Symphony No. 2 in B flat, Op. 19;* (i; iii; iv) *Symphony No. 3 (Song of the Night), Op. 27;* (i; iii; v) *Symphony No. 4 (Sinfonia concertante for piano and orchestra);* (vi; vii) *Harnasie;* (vi; viii) *Mandragora.*
*** HMV SLS 5242 (3). (i) Polish R. Nat. SO, (ii) Kasprzyk; (iii) Semkow; (iv) with Ochman, Polish Krakow R. Ch.; (v) Paleczyny; (vi) Polish Krakow RSO, Wit; (vii) with Bachleda, and Ch.; (viii) Pustelak, Harazim, Lapinski.

This valuable and important set was issued in 1982 to mark the centenary of Szymanowski's birth. It includes all the symphonies (save for the *First*, which he left unfinished), the two ballets including his choral masterpiece, *Harnasie*, and the early *Concert* overture. These are the most atmospheric and sensitive performances currently on the market. Piotr Paleczyny is no mean artist and has all the finesse and imagination, as well as the requisite command of colour, that the *Symphonie concertante* calls for. The same goes for *The Song of the Night*, which though not so detailed and analytical a recording, has greater refinement and atmosphere. The last record brings *Mandragora*, a short ballet dating from 1920 and quite new to the gramophone, together with *Harnasie*. To be frank, *Mandragora* is not vintage Szymanowski: it is a slight, dryish piece, a harlequinade written for a production of *Le bourgeois gentilhomme*. *Harnasie* is another matter; it reflects Szymanowski's discovery of the folk music of the Tatras which surfaced first in the Op. 50 *Mazurkas* for piano. It calls for large forces including a full chorus and poses obvious practical production problems – as it is not much longer than the *Third Symphony*. As always there is the same sense of rapture, the soaring, ecstatic lines and the intoxicating exoticism that distinguish the mature Szymanowski, and it comes across even more effectively in this recording than in the earlier Rowicki account on Muza. An indispensable set for all who love this still underrated composer. Most natural recorded sound and committed performances too.

Violin concertos Nos. 1, Op. 35; 2, Op. 61
**(*) EMI 1C 065 03597. Kulka, Polish RSO, Maksymiuk.

These marvellous concertos have not been as well served on record as the Bartók or Prokofiev. The performances here are committed and highly finished; they convey much of the ecstasy, longing and sensuousness of these luminous scores. Both works are rich in atmosphere, full of the exotic colours and the sense of rapture that permeate Szymanowski's very finest scores. The acoustic is reverberant, and that adds to the overheated impression conveyed in the *Second*, which is powerfully played though it is not quite as refined in character here as in Szeryng's version made in the early 1970s. Kulka and Maksymiuk could perhaps have brought greater poignancy and longing to the *First Concerto*. The multi-mike balance produces vivid sound but the perspective is not completely natural, and the overall effect is one of glare. However, these performances are both persuasive enough to be recommendable.

Symphonies Nos. 2, Op. 19; (i) *3* (*Song of the Night*), *Op. 27.*
*** Decca Dig. SXDL/*KSXDC* 7524 [Lon. LDR/*5*- 71026]. Detroit SO, Dorati, (i) with Karczykowski, Jewell Chorale.

This is the first Western commercial record of either of these Szymanowski symphonies. *The Song of the Night* is one of his most beautiful scores, a setting made in the period 1914–16 of a poem by the great Persian Sufi mystic Djelaleddin Rumi. In recent years it has become fashionable to use a soprano rather than the tenor specified in the score (the composer apparently authorized performances without chorus, but the tenor was mandatory). The soprano has, of course, the ecstatic other-worldly quality that matches this score with its luminous textures, the heady, intoxicated – and intoxicating – atmosphere, the extraordinarily vivid colours and sense of rapture. Much of this is conveyed in the present performance, and the detail and opulence of the orchestral texture are revealingly captured by the digital recording. Rowicki brought an earthier, more sensual atmosphere to the score in his 1962 version, but Dorati's is the finer recording. The *Second* is not so rewarding a symphony as the *Third*. It dates from 1909–11 and is unusual formally: there are two movements, the second being a set of variations culminating in a fugue. The influences of Strauss and Scriabin are clearly audible and not altogether assimilated. But this is a most valuable issue. The cassette is of very good quality if not quite as sharply focused as the disc (especially in the choral symphony), although its slightly mellower upper range has its own appeal. There is no lack of vividness.

(i) *Symphony No. 4* (*Sinfonia concertante for piano and orchestra*), *Op. 60. 2 Études, Op. 4; 2 Mazurkas, Op. 50; 2 Preludes, Op. 1; Theme and variations in B flat min., Op. 3.*
** Uni. RHS 347. Blumenthal, (i) with Polish RSO, Kord.

The *Fourth Symphony* is a puzzling work, often haunting, though it is not altogether Szymanowski at his best. The opening idea is appealing, but as a whole the work lacks the richness of invention and distinctive profile of the two *Violin concertos*. The textures are unrelieved, and their density tends to diminish the impact of the work. Felicia Blumenthal is a persuasive exponent, though her performance is sound rather than inspired, and the playing of the Polish orchestra is committed. The second side gives us some of the earlier piano pieces, written at the turn of the century, and a couple of the Op. 50 *Mazurkas*.

Myths, Op. 30. Kurpian folk song; King Roger: Roxana's aria (both arr. Kochanski).
*** DG 2531/*3301* 330 [id.]. Danczowska, Zimerman – FRANCK: *Violin sonata.****

Apart from the EMI disc listed below, there is no alternative version of the *Myths* currently available, but it is difficult to imagine any other rivalling, let alone surpassing, this issue. The violinist, Kaja Danczowska, a pupil of Eugenia Uminksa and David Oistrakh, brings vision and poetry to the ecstatic, soaring lines of the *Fountain of Arethusa*. Her intonation is impeccable, and she has the measure of these other-worldly, intoxicating scores. There is a sense of rapture here that is totally persuasive, and Krystian Zimerman plays with a virtuosity and imagination that silence criticism. An indispensable issue, and very well recorded on both disc and cassette.

Myths, Op. 30; Romance, Op. 23; Paganini caprices, Op. 40; Notturno and tarantella, Op. 28.
* EMI Conifer 1C 067 46599. Hoelscher, Béroff.

This collects all of Szymanowski's music for violin and piano with the exception of the Op. 9 *Sonata* and the *Berceuse*, Op. 52, and so fills a useful gap in the catalogue. The masterpiece here is the *Myths*, and in this Hoelscher does not match the intensity and purity of tone of Kaja Danczowska, nor is Béroff's sensibility so completely attuned to Szymanowski as is Zimerman's. The latter have the advantage of much better balance than the two distinguished artists recorded here. In bar 74 of *The Fountain of Arethusa* the sound disappears briefly, giving the impression that someone has pressed the erase button by mistake. However, the rest of the recital is worth considering, but the balance tends to be too close and synthetic as far as the pianist is concerned.

Violin sonata in D min., Op. 9.
(B) ** PRT GSGC/*ZCGC* 2053. Duo Landolfi – PROKOFIEV: *Sonata No. 1.***

This is a useful stopgap, interestingly coupled, until a really outstanding version of this fine work appears. Mary Nemet and Roxanne Wruble are not quite as fluent here as in the Prokofiev, but they play with ardour and spirit and manage to solve most of the technical problems. They are well balanced and recorded, and there is an acceptable cassette.

Tailleferre, Germaine (1892-1983)

Concertino for harp and orchestra.
*** DG 2543 806 [id.]. Zabaleta, L'ORTF O, Paris, Martinon – GINASTERA: Concerto; SAINT-SAËNS: *Morceau de concert.****

Germaine Tailleferre's *Concertino* (dating from 1927) inhabits a different sound world from that of the Saint-Saëns piece with which it is coupled, with influences of Ravel, Poulenc and even Stravinsky peeping over the composer's shoulder. It is elegantly written and not without its own degree of urbanity, even if the lyrical element is more diffuse. The three movements have an attractive impetus, with the gay finale developing real exuberance. The performance is splendid, the solo part played with distinction and the accompaniment beautifully judged. The recording is first-class, and this outstanding triptych of twentieth-century works for harp and orchestra is more than the sum of its parts. Recommended.

Takemitsu, Toru (born 1930)

Corona (London version – for pianos, organ and harpsichord); *Far away; Piano distance; Undisturbed rest.*
*** Decca HEAD 4. Woodward (piano, organ, harpsichord); multiple recording techniques.

Roger Woodward sympathetically draws out a seductive range of keyboard colours in *Corona*, a work which seems to be more the performer's improvisation than a true creative product of the composer. The other music, in spite of its too easy reliance on texture, is still undeniably attractive if you are looking for music which doodles between Scriabin and the avant-garde. Excellent recording.

Tallis, Thomas (*c.* 1505–85)

Audivi vocem de Caelo; Honor virtus et potestas; O sacrum convivium; Salvator mundi; Sancte Deus.

*** CRD CRD 1072/*CRDC 4072* [Bach HM 78]. Ch. of New College, Oxford, Higginbottom – TAVERNER: *Western Wynde* etc.***

A welcome addition to Tallis's representation on record. The Choir of New College produces a clean and well-blended sound and, given the attractions of the valuable Taverner coupling, this disc should have a strong appeal for those interested in the period. The excellent chrome tape, transferred at the highest level, is vibrantly clear in focus.

Clarifica me, pater (3 organ settings); *Mass: Salve intermerata Virgo.*

*** ASV Dig. DCA 511. Shaw; St John's College, Camb., Ch., Guest – SHEPPARD: *Western Wind Mass* etc.***

The Tallis Mass is interspersed with his settings for organ of the Magnificat antiphon, *Clarifica me pater* from the Mulliner Book. The Mass is a parody mass drawing on a lengthy votive antiphon, *Salve intemerata virgo*, which he virtually 'cannibalized', incorporating all but two of the sixteen sections of the piece into the Mass. It uses five-part textures with extraordinary imagination. This is its first recording on LP and it is triumphantly successful. Guest directs a most beautiful performance, gentle in its expressiveness, yet deep and intense. Outstanding is the *Agnus Dei*. The recording is warmly atmospheric and well balanced.

Organ settings: *Clarifica me, pater; Fantasy; Iam lucis orto sidere.* Motets: *Audivi vocem; In ieiunio et fletu. Te Deum in 5 parts.*

(B) **(*) Con. CC/*CCT* 7591. White; St John's College, Camb., Ch., Guest – WEELKES: *Collection.***(*)

These are generally good performances though the Choir of St John's College are more impressive in the Motets than in the *Te Deum*. The three short organ voluntaries make an attractive mid-side interlude. The recording is excellent and the high-level tape is indistinguishable from the disc. This is enterprising repertoire for a bargain label and it deserves support.

Derelinquat impius; Ecce temptus idoneum. In ieiunio et fletu; In manus tuas; The Lamentations of Jeremiah the Prophet; O nata lux; Salvator mundi; Sancte Deus; Spem in alium (40-part motet); *Te lucis ante terminum* (2 settings); *Videte miraculum; Veni redemptor genitem. Organ Lesson.*

(M) *** Argo ZK 30/1. King's College Ch., Camb. University Musical Soc., Willcocks; Andrew Davis (organ).

This medium-priced set joins together two previously full-priced collections (originally ZRG 5436 and 5479). The King's College Choir are in their element in this music, for the most part written for Waltham Abbey and the Chapel Royal. The highlight of the first disc is the magnificent forty-part motet *Spem in alium*, in which the Cambridge University Musical Society joins forces with King's. But the simple hymn settings are no less impressive, and the performance of *The Lamentations of Jeremiah*, authentically using men's voices only, has the right element of restraint without being inexpressive. The two motets *Sanctus Deus* and *Videte miraculum* are for full choir and here the balance is less than ideal, giving too much prominence to the trebles. The recording throughout is distinguished, natural and atmospheric.

Ecce tempus idoneum; Gaude gloriosa Dei Mater; Hear the voice and prayer; If ye love me; Lamentations I; Loquebantur variis linguis; O nata lux; Spem in alium.

(B) ** CfP CFP/*TC-CFP* 41 4460-1/*4*. Clerkes of Oxenford, Wulstan.

A useful issue, since it gives us a bargain-label alternative to the King's version of *Spem in alium*. At the same time its value is diminished by the somewhat brisk tempi Dr Wulstan chooses, which leave the music wanting in its proper dignity. There is also some sense of strain among the women, though their tone is clean and well focused. Reservations notwithstanding, there are fine things on this disc and it can be recommended. The recording, made in Merton College Chapel, Oxford, is first-class, as the beautiful opening hymn, *O nata lux de lumine*, readily demonstrates. Disc and cassette sound virtually identical.

The Lamentations of Jeremiah. Mass: Puer natus est nobis; O nata lux; Salvator mundi; If ye love me (anthem).
*** HMV Dig. ASD/*TCC-ASD* 4285. King's College, Camb., Ch., Ledger.

The magnificent seven-part writing in the *Mass* (a work assembled in recent years from a variety of sources) contrasts well with the darkness of the two five-part *Lamentations*, probably Tallis's best-known works. The choir, beautifully recorded against an ample church acoustic (not necessarily King's Chapel itself), is at its very finest. Though these performances of the *Lamentations* are not so sharply defined in detail as those which Sir David Willcocks recorded earlier with the King's Choir, Ledger's approach – more direct in style, more varied in tempo – is more authentic. The chrome cassette is generally well focused and matches the disc fairly closely.

Mass: *Puer natus est.* Motets: *Salvator mundi; Suscipe quaeso domine.*
*** Cal. CAL 1623. Clerkes of Oxenford, Wulstan.

An outstanding record. The Mass is a reconstruction by David Wulstan and Sally Dunkley prompted by the researches and speculations of Joseph Kerman and Jeremy Noble. The details are too complex to be outlined here, but the results are so beautiful that readers should not miss this record. The Mass is among the finest Tallis and, for that matter, the finest music of the period, and it is performed with dedication and authority by these singers. There is no need to hesitate here: this is one of the most important recent issues of English music of this period and it is also one of the most successful artistically and technically.

Tárrega, Francisco (1852–1909)

Music for guitar: *Adelita; La Cartagenera; Columpio; Danza mora; Endecha; Estudio de velocidad; Estudio en forma de minuetto; Jota; Lagrima; La Mariposa; Minuetto; Oremus; Pavana; Preludio in G; Recuerdos de la Alhambra; Sueño.*
*** DG Dig. 410 655-1/*4*. Yepes.

Much of Tárrega's music is slight (though admirably crafted) but he was an important figure in the movement to restore the guitar to its rightful place as a solo instrument after the piano's popularity in the late nineteenth century had caused its temporary eclipse. Narciso Yepes presents these miniatures with disarming eloquence and obvious affection. His playing is consistently persuasive. The *Recuerdos de la Alhambra* remains the most memorable item, but much of the rest of the programme is very attractive in its gentle, unostentatious way, especially when played like this. The *Jota* – a set of variants – is quite a substantial piece. The recording is naturally balanced and has fine presence on disc and tape alike.

Tartini, Giuseppe (1692–1770)

Cello concerto in A.
(M) *** DG Sig. 2543/*3343* 517 [2530/*3300* 974]. Rostropovich, Zürich Coll. Mus.; Sacher – BOCCHERINI and VIVALDI: *Concertos.****
(M) ** DG Arc. Priv. 2547/*3347* 046. Mainardi, Lucerne Fest. Strings, Baumgartner – BOCCHERINI: *Concerto***; VIVALDI: *Concerto.***(*)

As with the other works in his collection, Rostropovich's view of Tartini's concerto is larger than life, but the eloquence of the playing disarms criticism, even when the cellist plays cadenzas of his own that are not exactly in period. The lively accompaniment is matched by bright, vivid recording, and this has transferred to chrome tape with plenty of presence.

Mainardi's performance is on a smaller scale, but he plays with warmth and colour and is clearly recorded, although the tonal balance favours the upper range of his instrument. Here the cassette is preferable to the disc, offering slightly more body of timbre and a smoother upper range.

(i) *Cello concerto in A*. (ii) *Violin concertos: in D min, for violin and strings, D.45; in D min. for violin, 2 horns and strings, D.21. Sonata in D for strings.*
*** Erato STU 70970. Sol. Ven., Scimone, with (i) Zannerini, (ii) Toso.

This collection was recorded in the mid-1970s but has only recently appeared here. Tartini's invention is at times almost romantic in character, and there are moments of vision that leave no doubt that he is underrated. The two *Violin concertos* are well worth investigation as is the *Cello concerto*, whose slow movement is quite striking. The playing is committed and persuasive, and the recording fully acceptable. A very worthwhile issue.

Violin concertos: in E min., D.56; in G, D.83.
(M)*** Ph. Dig. 9502/*7313*089. Accardo, ECO.

What a fine composer Tartini is! These two concertos follow the three-movement pattern of the period and date from the 1720s and 1730s, but have greater depth and range than one would expect. Accardo also includes the alternative slow movement for the *E minor*, D.56, and secures vital and eloquent playing from the ECO. The slow movements are particularly fine, songful and warm in feeling, and there is much nobility here. Excellent recording, with a chrome tape in the demonstration class. This is a bargain.

Violin sonatas: in A, Op. 1/1; in G. min., Op. 1/10; in F, Op. 1/12; in C; in A min., Op. 2/6–7; in G min. (*Devil's Trill*).
*** Erato STU 71023/4. Amoyal, Moses, Farina.

Violin sonatas: in A, Op. 1/3; in A min., Op. 1/5; in G min., Op. 1/10; in G min. (*Devil's Trill*).

(M) *** Ph. 9502 009. Michelucci, Walter, Sibinga.

Tartini's sonatas take their virtuosity for granted: there is none of the sheer display that his reputation as a great violinist and innovator would lead one to expect, yet they call for playing of the greatest technical finesse and musicianship. Spanning as he did both halves of the eighteenth century, Tartini possesses the lyrical purity of Corelli and Vivaldi with a forward-looking sensibility that is highly expressive. Pierre Amoyal plays them superbly; he makes no attempt to adapt his style to contemporary practice, but there is in a sense no need for him to do so. His playing has sweetness of tone and expressive eloquence to commend it, and though he is forwardly placed, the sound throughout is eminently acceptable. A most desirable pair of records.

Some of the sonatas in the Philips Michelucci collection overlap with Amoyal's Erato set, but this is on a single mid-price disc whereas its rival comprises two full-price records. Michelucci is a most beautiful player even if he sounds a shade bland by comparison with Amoyal. In its own right, however, this is a thoroughly enjoyable and often distinguished record, and Michelucci's partners have exemplary taste and musicianship. Excellent sound.

Tausky, Vilem (born 1910)

Concertino (for harmonica).
*** Argo ZRG 856 [id.]. Reilly, ASMF, Marriner – JACOB: *5 Pieces;* MOODY: *Little suite*; VAUGHAN WILLIAMS: *Romance*.***

Tausky's *Concertino* is an extremely well-made little work and it is beautifully played and recorded here. In the last analysis it is not really memorable, except for a theme in the first movement that recalls *Land of Hope and Glory* (in contour rather than substance).

Taverner, John (*c.* 1495–1545)

Christe Jesu pastor; Dum transisset sabbatum; Kyrie Le roy; Mater Christi; The Western Wynde (Mass).
(M) *** Argo 411 724-1/*4*. King's College Ch., Willcocks.

John Taverner's remarkable individuality is admirably shown by this excellent collection of early Tudor music. The *Western Wynde Mass* (so called because of its use of this secular tune as a constantly recurring ground) is a masterpiece of the highest order. It is hauntingly memorable. All the music here shows the composer's wide range of expressive power: the motets are also works of great beauty. With first-class performances from King's and one of Argo's most evocative recordings, this is an outstanding collection, though the newer version of the *Mass* under Higginbottom should also be considered – see below.

Mass in 4 parts: *The Western Wynde. Mater Christi.*
*** CRD CRD 1072/*CRDC 4072* [Bach HM 78]. Ch. of New College, Oxford, Higginbottom – TALLIS: *Audivi vocem* etc.***

This is the only version of Taverner's Mass to appear since the King's College, Cambridge, record of 1962. It is a worthy successor, and the acoustic is, if anything, superior to that of King's, producing results of greater clarity and definition. Higginbottom's choir sings with great feeling but with restraint and splendid control both of line and of ensemble. Although the King's version is not completely superseded, this newcomer is to be preferred. The cassette is in every way first-class, the choral sound vibrantly projected and admirably clear.

Missa Corona spinea; Votive antiphon: O Wilhelme Pastor Bone.
**(*) ASV Dig. DCA/*ZCDCA* 516. Christ Church Cath. Ch., Grier.

Francis Grier's pursuit of authenticity leads him to having his choir – as finely disciplined as it was under his predecessor, Simon Preston – singing this superb setting of the Mass a third higher than modern concert pitch. The result is a strain both on the boy trebles and on listeners' ears. A degree of abrasiveness nowadays seems a necessary ingredient of authentic performance, but greater ease in those high mellifluous lines would be more in character. The digital recording is admirably clear as well as atmospheric, and the high-level cassette transfer is fresh and vivid.

Tchaikovsky, Peter (1840–93)

Andante cantabile, Op. 11; Nocturne, Op. 19/4; Pezzo capriccioso, Op. 62 (1887 version); *2 Songs: Legend; Was I not a little blade of grass; Variations on a rococo theme, Op. 33* (1876 version).
*** Chan. Dig. **CHAN 8347**; ABRD/*ABTD* 1080 [id.]. Wallfisch, ECO, Simon.

This delightful record gathers together all of Tchaikovsky's music for cello and orchestra – including his arrangements of such items as the famous *Andante cantabile* and two songs. The major item is the original version of the *Rococo variations* with an extra variation and the earlier variations put in a more effective order, as Tchaikovsky wanted. The published version, radically different, was not sanctioned by him. Geoffrey Simon, following up the success of his record of the original version of the *Little Russian symphony*, draws lively and sympathetic playing from the ECO with Wallfisch a vital if not quite flawless soloist. Excellent recording with the clear, wide-ranging chrome-cassette transfer approaching demonstration standard on side one, but much softer-grained on side two, which rather suits the music.

Capriccio italien, Op. 45.
C *** RCA Dig. **RCD 14439.** Dallas SO, Mata (with Concert***).
(B) *** RCA VICS/*VK* 2041 [AGL1/*AGK1* 4293]. RCA SO, Kondrashin – RIMSKY-KORSAKOV: *Capriccio espagnol.****

(B) **(*) CfP CFP/*TC-CFP* 40341. Philh. O, Kletzki – RIMSKY-KORSAKOV: *Scheherazade.****

Tchaikovsky's *Capriccio italien* is given an extraordinarily successful compact disc debut on Mata's Dallas disc. The concert-hall effect of the recording is very impressive indeed with the opening fanfares as sonically riveting as the silences, when the reverberation dies away naturally. The performance is colourful and exciting, if not as outstanding as Kondrashin's, and the piece is issued within an attractive compilation of favourite orchestral showpieces – see our Concerts section below.

Kondrashin's RCA version is in a special class. It dates back to 1960 but the recording – demonstration-worthy in its day – still sounds stunningly vivid, with an analogue hall ambience to match that of Mata's compact disc. The performance has never been surpassed. It has great flair and excitement. The opening is alive in every bar and is a model of careful preparation, with the composer's dynamic markings meticulously observed. The pacing throughout is absolutely right and the closing section is highly exhilarating. The chrome tape, however, is not recommended: it is overmodulated and climaxes are fierce and coarse.

Kletzki's performance is very enjoyable. It offers superb Philharmonia playing and is well recorded (1960 vintage), making a good bonus for an outstanding version of *Scheherazade*. There is a good matching tape.

Capriccio italien; (i) *1812 Overture; Marche slave.*

(M) *** Decca SPA/*KCSP* 108 [Lon. STS/*5*-15221]. LSO, Alwyn; (i) with Band of Grenadier Guards.

** Decca SXL 6895 [Lon. CS/*5*- 7118]. Detroit SO, Dorati.

** DG Dig. **400 035**; 2532/*3302* 022 [id.]. Chicago SO, Barenboim.

Kenneth Alwyn's record dates from the very beginning of the stereo era. The story goes that Decca suddenly discovered they had no recording of *1812* to include in the first stereo release, and so sessions were hastily set up. As cannon were not available at such short notice, gunshots were used, with the tape slowed down to produce the right, deep resonance. Whether or not this story is apocryphal, the result was an outstandingly fine disc which gave Kenneth Alwyn his gramophone début. He shows a flair for Tchaikovsky rare in English conductors, and all three performances generate real intensity and excitement. The stereo – demonstration-worthy in its day – is still impressive, with a spectacular climax to *1812*. The cassette was an early issue and is not recommended. The end of *1812* is a mess, and there is a turnover break in the middle of the *Capriccio*, something Decca would not think of allowing today.

The Dorati issue marked the return of the Detroit orchestra to the international recording scene at the beginning of 1979. It is a somewhat brash début; Dorati was to go on to make more distinguished records than this. The somewhat aggressive brilliance may be partly contributed by the sound balance, which is obviously aimed at the hi-fi demonstration market, with an eruption of specifically American gunfire and bells at the end of *1812*. The performance of the *Capriccio* is not without elegance, but *Marche slave* seems excessively sombre until the change of mood at the coda, which is taken briskly. The music-making has plenty of confidence throughout and no lack of direct excitement, but in the last analysis it is unmemorable.

Barenboim gives a slinkily persuasive account of the *Capriccio*, but *1812* is disappointingly done and by Chicago standards poorly played. The chrome cassette matches the disc fairly closely, although the opening trumpet fanfare of *Capriccio italien* is not quite clean. The compact disc only confirms that the recording is not ideally balanced, with the end of *1812* sounding constricted, while the violin sound has a distinct digital edge. The *Capriccio* is more agreeable, but overall this is an acceptable rather than a memorable issue.

Capriccio italien; (i) *1812 Overture; Eugene Onegin: Polonaise.*

(M) *(*) EMI Em. EMX/*TC-EMX* 2005. Bournemouth SO, Silvestri; (i) with Band of H.M. Royal Marines.

This collection was originally recorded in EMI's hi-fi-conscious Studio Two system, and the recording is artificially brilliant to the point of shrillness, without compensating weight. Silvestri's performances are not without charisma, but his pacing is often unconvincing, especially in the *Capriccio*. The end of *1812*, with the introduction of the Marines Band, is certainly spectacular, but not satisfying. On our copy of the cassette the sound was compressed at climaxes, but this may have been corrected by the time we are in print.

Capriccio italien; Marche slave; Romeo and Juliet (fantasy overture); Mazeppa; Cossack dance.

(B) ** CfP Dig. CFP/*TC-CFP* 4405. Hallé O, Kamu.

Kamu's account of *Romeo and Juliet* is impressive. It is well paced and exciting with no lack of thrust, although there is a curious momentary broadening – it barely lasts a bar – at the climax of the love theme which some may find irritating on repetition. But the sombre opening and closing sections evoke a powerful and very Russian melancholy. The engaging *Gopak* from *Mazeppa* (famous in the 78 r.p.m. era) is also vivaciously done, and *Marche slave* moves to a resplendent climax, with plenty of detail on the way. The digital recording, made in the attractive ambience of the BBC's No. 7 Studio in Manchester, is clear and the string timbre is natural, with the Hallé playing well throughout. The snag to this record is the *Capriccio*, which is far too deliberate and conveys absolutely no sense of joy in music which was not taken too seriously by the composer, and designed as an entertaining display piece. Cassette and disc are closely matched.

Capriccio italien; Nutcracker suite; (i) *Andante cantabile for cello and string orchestra* (arr. Rostropovich from 2nd movt of *String quartet No. 1*).

❀ *** DG 2531/*3301* 112 [id.]. Berlin PO, Rostropovich (cond. and (i) cello).

An enchanting performance of the *Nutcracker suite*, quite the finest in the present catalogue, the characteristic dances played with engaging colour and charm. The *Sugar Plum Fairy* is introduced with ethereal delicacy, and the *Russian dance* has marvellous zip. The *Waltz of the Flowers* balances warmth and elegance with an exhilarating vigour. The *Capriccio italien* is highly successful too, and the vulgarity inherent in the principal theme (which Tchaikovsky thought was a folksong but which proved to be a local Italian 'pop' of the time) evaporates entirely, so decoratively elegant is the playing of the Berlin Philharmonic. There is a touch of rhythmic heaviness at the final climax, but otherwise this is first-rate. As an encore, Rostropovich indulges himself affectionately in a concertante arrangement of one of Tchaikovsky's loveliest melodies. The balance – all cello with a discreet orchestral backing – reflects his approach. The recording is spectacularly resonant, and the dynamic range extremely wide, with a rather low level of cut, meaning that this disc will be prone to any surface imperfections. But the pianissimos are very telling. The cassette transfer is first-class, encompassing the wide dynamic contrasts without problems.

Capriccio italien; Nutcracker suite; Eugene Onegin: Polonaise; Waltz.

(M) ** Ph. Seq. 6527/*7311* 079 [6500 766/*7300 332*]. LPO, Stokowski.

This reissue offers recordings made as recently as 1974, with resonant, full-blooded sound. But though nothing Stokowski did is without touches of magic, some fairly strong reservations must be expressed here. *Capriccio italien*, in spite of occasional nudges, has genuine panache, and the two *Eugene Onegin* dances have characteristic flair. But in the *Nutcracker* music (which he played so beautifully for Disney in *Fantasia*), after the introduction of a string tremolando at the opening of the *Dance of the Sugar Plum Fairy*, Stokowski indulges in very mannered phrasing; few will find this comfortable to live with. The reverberant sound brings some clouding of detail and a lack of transient sharpness to the cassette transfer.

Capriccio italien; Eugene Onegin: Polonaise; Waltz.

(M) ** CBS 60115/*40-* [Col. MY/*MYT* 36728]. NYPO, Bernstein – RIMSKY-KORSAKOV: *Capriccio espagnol.***

Bernstein is somewhat indulgent in the *Capriccio italien*, with freely fluctuating tempi, but the structure holds together, and the closing pages match splendour with weight. The New York orchestral playing is strikingly brilliant, both here and in the dances from *Eugene Onegin*, which are vigorously rhythmic. The sound is quite spacious but over-brilliant.

Capriccio italien; 1812 Overture; Mazeppa: Cossack dance.
** Telarc Dig. **CD 80041**; DG 10041 [id.]. Cincinnati SO, Kunzel.

Both the Telarc compact disc and LP give due warning that the cannon on this record dwarf the orchestra in *1812*. Indeed at the time of the sessions many nearby windows were shattered. So if you need a recording of cannon, plus *1812*, and your speakers can accommodate the dynamic range and amplitude, both impressively wide, then this issue is for you. In the *Capriccio* there are no cannon so the engineers substitute the bass drum, which is very prominent. The orchestral contribution throughout is lively but not memorable, and the playing simply does not generate enough adrenalin to compensate for the relative lack of projection of the orchestral tone. At the end of *1812* Tchaikovsky's carefully contrived climax, with its full-blooded scalic descent, seriously lacks weight. The most enjoyable item here is the lively *Cossack dance*.

Piano concerto No. 1 in B flat min., Op. 23.
*** DG 2530/*3300* 677 [id.]. Berman, Berlin PO, Karajan.
(*) CBS Dig. **CD 36660/*40-* [id.]. Gilels, NYPO, Mehta (with Bach: *Well-tempered Clavier: Prelude No. 10*, arr. Siloti ***).
(M) *** DG Sig. 2543/*3343* 503 [(d) 2535/*3335* 295]. Argerich, PO, Dutoit – LISZT: *Piano concerto No. 1.****
*** Ph. Dig. **411 047-2**; 6514/*7337* 118 [id.]. Argerich, Bav. RSO, Kondrashin.
*** Decca SXL/*KSXC* 6840 [(d) Lon. CS/*5-* 6360]. Ashkenazy, LSO, Maazel – MUSSORGSKY: *Pictures.***(*)
(B) **(*) Con. CC/*CCT* 7594. Ivan Davis, RPO, Lewis – RACHMANINOV: *Rhapsody on a theme of Paganini.***(*)
**(*) HMV ASD/*TC-ASD* 3818 [Ang. S 37679]. Gavrilov, Philh. O, Muti.
(M) **(*) CBS 60145/*40-* [MY/*MYT* 37263]. Graffman, Cleveland O, Szell (with Rachmaninov: *Preludes, Op. 23/5*; *Op. 32/8* and *12***(*)).
(M) **(*) Decca VIV/*KVIC* 16 [Lon. STS/*5-* 15542]. Vered, LSO, Kord – RACHMANINOV: *Concerto No. 2.**(**)
(M) **(*) Decca Jub. JB/*KJBC* 29 [(d) Lon. STS/*5-* 15471]. Curzon, VPO, Solti – LITOLFF: *Scherzo.****
*(**) Chan. ABR/*ABT* 1054 [id.]. Judd, Moscow PO, Lazarev – PROKOFIEV: *Piano concerto No. 3.**(**)
(M) ** Mercury SRI/*MRI* 75032 [id.]. Janis, LSO, Menges – RACHMANINOV: *Concerto No. 2.****
(M) ** HMV SXLP/*TC-SXLP* 30552 [(d) Ara. 8012/*9012*]. Ogdon, Philh. O, Barbirolli – RACHMANINOV: *Concerto No. 2.**(*)
(B) *(*) CfP CFP/*TC-CFP* 115. Katin, LPO, Pritchard – LITOLFF: *Scherzo.****

Even after the exaggerated fanfares of publicity which greeted the arrival of Lazar Berman in the West, this first of his concerto recordings outside the Soviet Union lived up to all expectations. It is interesting that credit for the incandescence of the performance must go almost as much to the conductor as to the pianist, and yet the conductor is Karajan, who has sometimes seemed too aloof as a concerto accompanist. Berman's character is firmly established in the massive chords of the introduction (though curiously he hustles the first group of all), and from there his revelling in dramatic contrast, whether of texture, tone colour, dynamic or tempo, makes this one of the most exciting readings ever put on record. It is not just a question of massive bravura but of extreme delicacy too, so that in the central scherzando of the slow movement it almost sounds as though Berman is merely breathing on the keyboard, hardly depressing the notes at all. The ripe playing of the Berlin Philharmonic backs up the individuality of Berman's reading, and the recording is massively brilliant to match. There is an excellent cassette transfer, which throws in Karajan's performance of the *Polonaise* from *Eugene Onegin* as a bonus.

Any Gilels record is an event, and this recording appears a quarter of a century after his first account with Fritz Reiner and the Chicago Symphony Orchestra. Gilels has an outsize musical personality and his is a performance of leonine calibre, with nobility and fire. There is no want of virtuosity – the double octaves leap off the vinyl – and there are the inward-looking qualities we associate with Gilels too. The performance was recorded live at Carnegie Hall, and the claims of Gilels's artistry have to be weighed against less than distinguished recorded sound and second-rate orchestral playing. The wind (bar 186) are not in tune and do not blend, and at no point does the orchestra respond as alertly or sensitively as it did in the days of Bernstein. The digital recording reproduces clean detail – the high-level tape transfer has striking range and brilliance, although the upper string timbre is rather crude – and the relationship between soloist and orchestra is well balanced. But the sound is not top-drawer. The compact disc offers very marginally greater refinement and the obvious advantage of background silence, but otherwise the difference between this and the LP is minimal. However, Gilels is Gilels, and the quality of his playing cannot be too highly praised. The Siloti arrangement of the Bach *Prelude* was his encore on the occasion of the recording, and it is affecting in its direct eloquence.

Argerich's DG version dates from 1971 and was originally issued (both at full price and on Privilege, which remains available in the USA) spread over two sides. Now for its Signature reissue it has been coupled with a highly individual account of the Liszt *No. 1*. The weight of the opening immediately sets the mood for a big, broad performance, with the kind of music-making where the personalities of both artists are complementary. The recording too is first-class, full-bodied, wide in dynamic range, and yet with a natural balance. Argerich's conception encompasses the widest range of tonal shading. In the finale she often produces a scherzando-like effect; then the orchestra thunders in with the Russian dance theme to create a real contrast. The quality of Dutoit's contribution to the music-making is never in doubt. The tempo of the first movement is comparatively measured, seeking power rather than surface excitement, and again when the build-up begins for the final statement of the great lyrical tune of the finale, the conductor creates his climax in deliberate, measured fashion. The slow movement is strikingly atmospheric, yet delicate, its romanticism lighthearted. A most satisfying account in every way. The chrome cassette is brilliant and wide-ranging, but the upper string timbre is clear rather than rich.

Argerich's Philips issue comes from a live performance given in October 1980, full of animal excitement with astonishingly fast speeds in the outer movements. The impetuous virtuosity is breathtaking, even if passagework is not always so cleanly articulated as in her superb studio performance for DG. That earlier version also brings more variety of tone, but you will not find more satisfying performances on record than either of these. The CD version clarifies and intensifies the already vivid sound. The chrome cassette, however, needs a bass cut and does not match the LP, let alone the CD in brilliance. The DG cassette of Argerich's earlier version is far preferable.

Originally issued spread uneconomically over two sides, Ashkenazy's version now occupies only one, and is coupled to Mussorgsky. The remastering is highly successful on both disc and cassette. The piano sounds splendidly bold and clear, while the orchestral balance is most realistic. Ashkenazy's essentially lyrical performance offers a genuine alternative to those of Gilels, Berman and Argerich. They remain more obvious first recommendations, but there are many who will enjoy Ashkenazy's thoughtfulness and his refusal to be stampeded by Tchaikovsky's passionate rhetoric. The biggest climaxes of the first movement are made to grow out of the music, instead of being part of a sweeping forward momentum, and the lyrical side of the writing associated with the beautiful second subject is distilled with obvious affection. In the *Andantino* too, Ashkenazy refuses to play flashily and thus uses the middle section as a contrasting episode to set in the boldest relief the return of the opening tune, which is played very beautifully. The finale is very fast and brilliant, yet the big tune is broadened at the end in a most convincing way.

The partnership of Ivan Davis and Henry Lewis is successful in providing a fresh look at Tchaikovsky's masterpiece. In spite of the strong opening, with plenty of weight from the strings, the first movement is without a thrustful forward momentum, but is spacious, pianist and conductor both relaxing to take in the movement's lyrical detail. The *Andantino* is played simply, and as in the first movement the element of contrast is strong. The restatement of the main theme is played very slowly and gently, the performers' affection clearly shown. The finale is comparatively lightweight but has genuine sparkle, and the closing pages have plenty of impact. The Decca sound is brilliant, clear and immediate, without any special exaggerations. The cassette and disc are closely matched. If the coupling is suitable, this is well worth considering.

Gavrilov is stunning in the finale of the concerto, which at a very fast tempo is scintillating from first to last. The prestissimo middle section of the slow movement too goes like quicksilver, equally displaying the vein of spontaneous imagination that we recognize in Gavrilov's other records. The element of daring, of naughtiness even, is not so convincing in the first movement, where contrasts of dynamic and tempo are so extreme they sound self-conscious. Nor is the recording one of EMI's best; the piano is close yet not well focused. The cassette, however, is extremely well managed, if anything cleaner than the disc, with no loss of body and impact.

Graffman's partnership with Szell produces a performance in which the electricity really crackles, with the spirit of Horowitz and Toscanini evoked in the finale, taken at a breathtaking pace. One senses Szell's personality strongly throughout, alongside that of his soloist. If the atmosphere may at times be too tense for some Tchaikovskians, the impact is undeniable, producing a splendid combination of power and breadth in the first movement, with lyrical contrast not forgotten, and an engaging delicacy for the outer sections of the *Andantino*. The snag is the recorded sound, with a crude upper edge on the orchestra. This is tamed a little on the cassette (which has slightly less range), and the piano timbre is given more body too. The well-played Rachmaninov *Preludes* make a fair coupling.

Ilana Vered, like Ivan Davis, offers an exceptionally generous coupling. The recording, originally Phase Four, is extremely brilliant. The larger-than-life sound (the piano very forward and real, so that one almost feels able to touch it) is immensely dramatic, and if the overall balance is not natural, one can forgive that when the immediacy is given to such exciting playing. Alongside the bravura, there are many imaginative touches from the soloist and a freshness in the orchestra which is similarly appealing. The refinement of piano tone at the opening and close of the slow movement, played with the utmost delicacy, gives much pleasure, and the finale has no lack of brilliance and power. The coupling is not quite so successful (and here the balance is even more exaggerated), but it undoubtedly increases the interest of this issue. The cassette transfer is of Decca's best quality, with little distinguishable difference between tape and disc.

Sir Clifford Curzon's 1969 recording has been freshly remastered and made to sound well (especially in the bold, full-blooded cassette transfer). Some faults of balance remain, and there are one or two obvious joins in the master tape. But Curzon matches thoughtfulness to unostentatious bravura, and the performance has fine zest and spontaneity. The coupling is not generous, but the performance is as scintillating as the recording, which is of demonstration quality.

Terence Judd contributed his powerful and urgent reading at the 1978 Tchaikovsky Piano Competition in Moscow, and though it has its moments of roughness and the recording is limited and badly balanced, the compulsion and urgency of the playing are hard to resist. This is hardly a competitive version for general listening, but with the Prokofiev equally magnetic, it is a splendid reminder of a fine pianist who died tragically young. The cassette is acceptable though the sound is rather constricted.

Byron Janis's is in many ways as dazzling a performance as his account of the coupled Rachmaninov *Second Concerto*. But where with the Rachmaninov there was always a feeling of urgency, here the partnership with Menges works less well than the symbiosis with Dorati, and the orchestra does not always match the bravura and impetuosity of the soloist. There is a lack of passion in the outer movements and the *Andantino* too is rather cool: it all sounds detached even, amid such dazzling display. The sound is generally excellent with tape and disc very closely matched.

The Ogdon/Barbirolli performance is highly musical, but the artists fail to set sparks off each other and the music-making is underpowered with the finale especially relaxed. The *Andantino* with its natural simplicity is the most successful movement. The recording still sounds vivid and full and there is a first-class tape.

Katin's Classics for Pleasure version is given a brilliant, modern recording (paid for by Wills' cigarettes, whose masthead is on the sleeve), and this is basically quite a strong, musical reading. But somewhere there is a lack of drama, and the absence of extrovert bravura from the soloist (especially in the middle section of the slow movement) produces an impression of facelessness. But no one could fault this bargain disc on grounds of taste, and it has an excellent filler. There is a good cassette.

Piano concertos Nos. 1; 3 in E flat, Op. 75.
(M) **(*) EMI Em. EMX/*TC-EMX* 2001. Gilels, New Philh. O, Maazel.
** Decca Dig. **410 112-2**; 410 112-1/*4* [id.]. Postnikova, VSO, Rozhdestvensky.

At medium-price this HMV reissue is worth investigating for the *Third Concerto* alone, a comparatively lightweight piece, but not lacking in memorable ideas. Gilels plays it with authority and freshness. The account of No. 1 is in many ways distinguished too and is much better recorded than Gilels's CBS version. It has a very fast opening, exhilarating in its way, but many Tchaikovskians will feel that this – one of his most famous melodies – needs a broader treatment. The performance as a whole has undoubted insights, but is in the last resort lightweight. The balance places the piano well forward; that said, the sound is first-class, although the cassette has noticeably less range at the top than the disc, especially on side two.

The collaboration of wife and husband in the Postnikova/Rozhdestvensky performances makes for very personal readings marked by spacious speeds. The very introduction is disconcertingly slow, and so is the basic tempo for the central *Andante*. There and in other places Postnikova's expressive fluctuations sound studied, but the clarity of articulation will for some make up for the lack of adrenalin. The long single movement of the *Third Concerto* too needs more consistently persuasive treatment, though the dactylic dance theme is delectably pointed. Close balance for the piano in a firm, clear recording.

(i) *Piano concerto No. 1;* (ii) *Concert fantasia in G, Op. 56.*
(M) *** Decca SPA/*KCSP* 168 [Lon. STS 15227]. Katin, with (i) LSO, Kundell; (ii) LPO, Boult.

The Decca recording of the *First Piano concerto* is bold and vivid, clear and immediate, and excellently balanced. The performance is equally alive and direct, the opening big tune taken fairly fast but with a fine sweep, the *Andantino* played very stylishly and the finale with plenty of bravura. Katin's Kempff-like clarity perfectly suits the *Concert fantasia*, with its *Nutcracker* overtones in the first movement. This two-movement piece is much less ambitious than the well-known concerto. Boult as well as Katin obviously relishes the delicacy of much of this music, and he induces his players to give a rhythmic spring which compensates completely for the occasional fault of ensemble. There is an overall freshness about the playing – in the full emotional passages as well as the rest – which should help to bring the piece the attention and popularity it deserves. The stereo is clear, the piano tone firm and bright. Altogether this is a most enjoyable record and a very happily planned coupling. There is a satisfactory cassette too.

(i) *Piano concerto No. 1;* (ii) *Violin concerto in D, Op.35;* (iii) *Serenade for strings: Waltz;* (iv) *Variations on a rococo theme, Op.33.*
(B) ❀ *** DG Walkman *413 161-4*. (i) Argerich, RPO, Dutoit; (ii) Milstein, VPO, Abbado; (iii) Berlin PO, Karajan; (iv) Rostropovich, Leningrad PO, Rozhdestvensky.

This extended-length (ninety-minute) chrome tape is the jewel in the crown of the first release in DG's Walkman series, always generous, but here exceptionally so, both in quality of performances and recording, as well as the amount of music offered. We award it a Rosette as the 'bargain of the year'. Argerich's account of the *B flat minor Piano concerto* is second to none; Milstein's (1973) performance of the *Violin concerto* is equally impressive, undoubtedly one of the finest available, while Abbado secures playing of genuine sensitivity and scale from the Vienna Philharmonic. Rostropovich's earlier (1961) version of the *Rococo variations* offers playing with just the right amount of jaunty elegance as regards the theme and the first few variations; and when the virtuoso fireworks are let off, they are brilliant, effortless and breathtaking in their éclat. Indeed Rostropovich needs no superlatives and his accompanist shows a mastery all his own. Karajan provides a stylishly polished account of one of Tchaikovsky's most memorable (and original) waltzes, here an elegant interlude between the *Variations* and the first movement of the *Piano concerto*. The only slight drawback is that the turnover then follows, before the *Andantino*. But it is difficult to see how this could have been avoided within the chosen format. The sound is first-class.

(i) *Piano concerto No. 1;* (ii) *Violin concerto in D, Op. 35.*
(M) *(*) Ph. Seq. 6527/*7311* 215. Rotterdam PO, De Waart, with (i) Orozco, (ii) Fujikawa.

Orozco's version of the *Piano concerto* is flamboyant enough, but in spite of the bravura, and although it is well recorded, this performance fails to be memorable. The prestissimo central section of the slow movement is certainly intended by the composer as an opportunity for the soloist to show his mettle, but the lack of refinement here is unattractive. Mayumi Fujikawa's account of the *Violin concerto* has a great deal more finesse, and in the slow movement her warmly lyrical phrasing gives much pleasure, particularly as the supporting woodwind detail is nicely played. But the first movement lacks impetus, and in spite of the attraction of the coupling this record is not such a bargain as it looks. The cassette transfers are made at a modest level, and the *Violin concerto* lacks vividness.

(i) *Piano concerto No. 1;* (ii) *Variations on a rococo theme for cello and orchestra, Op. 33.*
*** Decca SXL 6955. LAPO, Dutoit, with (i) Myung-Whun Chung, (ii) Myung-Wha Chung.

The brother and sister of Kyung-Wha Chung prove in this most attractive Tchaikovsky coupling that the family's musical inspiration extends to them too. Myung-Whun, nowadays equally well-known as a conductor, here shows why he won a piano prize at the Tchaikovsky Competition in Moscow. There is a hint of restraint, and the recording balances him naturally with the orchestra, not in front of it. It means that this is not a rip-roaring account, but rather a thoughtful and poetic one. Similarly the cellist Myung-Wha holds back until the later variations draw out her full expressiveness. Beautifully played and recorded, and a very apt coupling; it can be warmly recommended.

Piano concerto No. 2 in G, Op. 44.
*(*) Decca Dig. 410 113-1/*4*. Postnikova, VSO, Rozhdestvensky.

Piano concertos Nos. 2 in G, Op. 44 (with abridged Siloti version of *Andante*); *3 in E flat, Op. 75.*
(M) CBS 61990/*40*- [Col. MS 6755]. Graffman, Phd. O, Ormandy.

The Decca version uses the complete original score, but with slow speeds the performance hangs fire, and this can be no more than a stop-gap, in spite of vivid recording.

Graffman uses Tchaikovsky's original for the outer movements of the *Second Concerto* but reverts to Siloti's abridged version of the *Andante*, thus cutting about half the music. Perhaps it was a sensible decision, for the orchestral cello and violin soloists find little charm in the passages that remain. The outer movements are played strongly but aggressively, and there is no sense of geniality in the finale. The *Third Concerto* fares no better. The recording is excessively brilliant, with clattery piano timbre and a harsh, thin orchestral texture.

Violin concerto in D, Op. 35.

*** Decca Dig. **410 011-2**; SXDL/*KSXDC* 7558 [Lon. LDR/*5*- 71058]. Kyung-Wha Chung, Montreal SO, Dutoit – MENDELSSOHN: *Concerto.****

*** Decca SXL/*KSXC* 6493. Kyung-Wha Chung, LSO, Previn – SIBELIUS: *Concerto.****

(M) *** Decca VIV/*KVIC* 4. Ricci, Neth. RO, Fournet – MENDELSSOHN: *Concerto.****

(*) CBS 72768 [MS 7313]. Zukerman, LSO, Dorati – MENDELSSOHN: *Concerto.*(*)

(M) **(*) CBS 60111/*40*- [MY/*MYT* 36724]. Stern, Phd. O, Ormandy – MENDELSSOHN: *Concerto.***(*)

(***) RCA 26.35038 (2) [VCS 7058 (2)]. Heifetz, Chicago SO, Reiner – BRAHMS: *Concerto* *(**); MENDELSSOHN: *Concerto.*(***)

(M) ** CBS 60312 [Odys. Y/*YT* 33522]. D. Oistrakh, Phd. O, Ormandy – SIBELIUS: *Concerto.***

*(*) Ph. 9500 321/*7300 583* [id.]. Szeryng, Concg. O, Haitink – MENDELSSOHN: *Concerto.**(*)

(i) *Violin concerto. Capriccio italien.*

**(*) HMV Dig. ASD/*TCC-ASD* 4173 [Ang. DS/*4XS* 37847]. (i) Spivakov; Philh. O, Ozawa.

**(*) DG Acc. 2542/*3342* 162 [2543/*3343* 529]. Ferras, Berlin PO, Karajan.

Violin concerto; Sérénade mélancolique, Op. 26.

*** HMV ASD 3726 [Ang. SZ 37640]. Perlman, Phd. O, Ormandy.

** DG Dig. **400 027-2**; 2532/*3302* 001 [id.]. Kremer, Berlin PO, Maazel.

Violin concerto; Sérénade mélancolique; Valse-scherzo, Op. 34.

*** Erato STU/*MCE* 71452. Amoyal, Philh. O, Dutoit.

Chung's earlier recording of the Tchaikovsky *Concerto* with Previn conducting has remained one of the strongest recommendations for a much-recorded work ever since it was made, right at the beginning of her career. The remake with Dutoit is amazingly consistent. Though on the concert platform she is so volatile a performer, responding to the inspiration of the moment, she is a deeply thoughtful interpreter. So here as before she refuses to sentimentalize the central *Canzonetta*, choosing a flowing, easily songful speed. The result is the more tenderly affecting, though this time the violin is balanced more closely than before. The finale has, if anything, even more exhilaration, with technical problems commandingly overcome at a very fast speed. Like other recent versions this opens out the tiny cuts traditional in the finale. Excellent recording, warm and atmospheric. As in the Mendelssohn coupling the compact disc is even more vivid. There is a very good chrome cassette too, although here the treble needs a degree of smoothing – it is not quite as refined as the disc versions in the higher partials.

Those preferring the Sibelius coupling should be well satisfied with Chung's 1970 version of the Tchaikovsky which is still among the finest in the catalogue. Her technique is impeccable and her musicianship of the highest order, and Previn's accompanying is highly sympathetic and responsive. This has warmth, spontaneity and discipline, every detail is beautifully shaped and turned without a trace of sentimentality. The recording is well balanced and detail is clean, though the acoustic is warm. This is a very distinguished issue, and there is a good tape.

The expressive warmth of Perlman goes with a very bold orchestral texture from Ormandy and the Philadelphia Orchestra. The focus of sound is not quite so clean as this work ideally needs, and the coupling is less than generous, but anyone who follows Perlman – in so many ways the supreme violin virtuoso of our time – is not likely to be disappointed.

Ricci made an outstanding record of this concerto in the early days of mono LP. He then recorded it in stereo with rather less success, but his newer (originally Phase Four) recording with Fournet restores his reputation fully. The characteristic intense vibrato may not be to all tastes, but the ear readily submits to the compulsion and colour of the playing, which shows a rock-steady technique and a splendid lyrical feeling. Even though Ricci is very near the microphone, so secure is his left hand that the rich stream of tone is always securely based, and the larger-than-life image is attractive when the orchestral impact and detail are so vividly conveyed. The cassette transfer matches the disc closely, although the dynamic range is very slightly reduced.

Like Accardo before him (now deleted), Pierre Amoyal offers as his coupling all the other Tchaikovsky music for violin and orchestra though, unlike him, he makes the usual cuts in the *Concerto* itself. Even in a strongly competitive field, the Amoyal is highly recommendable. He plays with passionate commitment and his slow movement is particuarly beautiful, and he is sensitively accompanied too. Dutoit gets exciting results from the Philharmonia and they are extremely well recorded.

Zukerman's record is acceptable rather than outstanding as a recording but the performance is undoubtedly very fine, Zukerman's tone being clean and sweet. Perhaps his taste is not as refined as Kyung-Wha Chung's, but if this were as well engineered as the Decca, competition would be much closer than it is.

Stern was on peak form when he made his first stereo recording with Ormandy, and it is a powerfully lyrical reading, rich in timbre and technically immaculate. The playing has undoubted poetry but is not helped by the very close balance of the soloist, so that pianissimos consistently become mezzo fortes. The orchestral sound is vivid but lacks amplitude.

Spivakov takes a heavyweight view, rich and warm, helped by exceptionally full digital recording and a close balance of the violin. By contrast, with Ozawa directing a most persuasive performance by the Philharmonia, this is also a reading which brings out the almost Mozartian elegance of much of the writing, emphasizing the happiness of the inspiration. A joyful performance too from Ozawa of the colourful fill-up.

Consideration of the Ferras/Karajan performance must be affected by personal reactions to Ferras's characteristic tone, with its rather close vibrato in lyrical passages and tendency to emphasize the schmalz on the G string. One finds too that Ferras's playing tends to lack charm, but some may react differently, and this is a well-conceived reading, with Karajan shaping the work as a whole very convincingly. The recording is excellent, the brilliance emphasizing the style of the soloist. The fill-up is an exciting account of the *Capriccio italien*, the Berlin brass telling especially well.

Heifetz is recorded near the microphone and this emphasizes the powerful tension of his reading, but also provides the listener with some uncomfortable sounds as bow meets string in the many florid moments which this concerto offers. At the same time there is some gorgeous lyrical playing, and the slow movement marries passion and tenderness in ideal proportions. There is no question about the excitement of this performance or its technical assurance, but the snag is the orchestral recording, which is never more than fair, and distinctly rough in the louder tuttis.

The Oistrakh, needless to say, is an excellent performance, but whether the fault is of the American recording or not, Oistrakh's tone is thinner than usual. Such moments as the recapitulation of the second subject high among the ledger lines are beautifully done, but then in rather a similar interpretation with the same orchestra and conductor Isaac Stern is even more ravishing and his version (with only a ten-bar cut) is coupled with an equally memorable account of the Mendelssohn. Oistrakh's coupling is no less generous, and his admirers will find this too is a very good performance, though again let down somewhat by the recorded quality.

Kremer's was the first digital recording of the concerto and the first CD. This artist blends keen nervous energy with controlled lyrical feeling, and it goes without saying that his virtuosity is impressive. Self-regarding agogic distortions are few (bars 50–58 and the first-movement cadenza are instances), and there is no lack of warmth. Yet both here and in the *Sérénade mélancolique*, there is something missing. A great performance of this work refreshes the spirit and resonates in the mind. Here, although the recording, and the playing of the Berlin Philharmonic for Maazel, are undoubtedly excellent, there is not the humanity and perception of a special kind that are needed if a newcomer is to displace the superb versions already available.

Szeryng is sweetly lyrical, but he is not helped by Haitink, who provides a rather slack accompaniment. The relaxed manner of the performance of the first movement is in some ways like the Belkin version on Decca (now deleted), but that performance had strikingly more forward momentum and impulse. In the finale too Belkin showed a fire that Szeryng, although spirited, misses.

1812 Overture, Op. 49.

(M) **(*) DG Priv. 2538 142 [2536 298]. Don Cossack Ch., Berlin PO, Karajan – BEETHOVEN: *Wellington's victory.***

(M) (**) Decca VIV/*KVIC* 26 [Lon. STS/*5-15558*]. Ch., RPO, Grenadier Guards Band, Stokowski – MUSSORGSKY: *Pictures.*(**)

(M) *(*) Mercury SRI/*MRI* 75142. Minneapolis SO, Dorati – BEETHOVEN: *Battle symphony.**(*)

(B) (***) RCA VICS/*VK* 2035 [AGL1/*AGK1* 2700]. O, Gould – BEETHOVEN: *Wellington's victory.*

Karajan's version is also available differently coupled – see below. None of the alternatives is really recommendable. Gould's version is among the most exciting ever recorded, with adrenalin running very freely indeed in the orchestra. But the sound is inflated with moments of coarseness, and at the end the mêlée of gunshots and bells degenerates into cacophony. The Beethoven coupling is even more distorted.

Stokowski's *1812* is curiously slow and mannered. Its eccentricities include a sudden entry of the chorus, popping up from nowhere at the end to sing the Russian hymn amid a blaze of bells. The sound (originally Phase Four) is spectacularly forward but the reverberation at the close is rather messy.

The Dorati recording was famous for its pioneering use of real cannon, but the substance of the *Overture* itself produces a thin orchestral texture and when the cannonade and bells come in, the editing is hardly subtle. Certainly the final climax is spectacular and relatively clear, but this record is one of the few in this usually outstanding Mercury series to have been left behind by improvements in recording techniques.

1812 Overture; Marche slave, Op. 31.

*(*) CBS **CD 37252** [IM/*IMT* 37252]. V. State Op. Ch., VPO, Maazel – BEETHOVEN: *Wellington's victory.***(*)

Maazel's coupling is a rather good version of Beethoven's *Wellington's victory*. The recording is only available on compact disc in the UK. The performance of *1812* is in no way distinctive, with the chorus failing to add a frisson of excitement at the opening, as did the Mormon Tabernacle Choir in Ormandy's famous quadraphonic version. Moreover the CD adds little to one's enjoyment, serving only to emphasize the relative lack of ambient richness, with brass sharply defined and upper strings very brightly lit. The closing pages, with chorus, orchestra and cannon, certainly make a spectacle, but there is nothing really involving about the music-making itself. *Marche slave* is rather more successful, but there are other, better versions, not least Karajan's – see below.

1812 Overture; Marche slave; Romeo and Juliet.

*** HMV ASD/*TC-ASD* 2894 [Ang. S/*4XS* 36890]. LSO, Previn.

(B) **(*) DG Walkman *413 153-4*. (i) Boston Pops O, Fiedler; (ii) Berlin PO, Karajan; (iii) San Francisco SO, Ozawa – MUSSORGSKY: *Pictures* etc.***

(M) **(*) DG Sig. 2543/*3343* 532 [139 029/*923 045*]. Berlin PO, Karajan (with chorus).

(M) *(**) CBS 60110 [MY/*MYT* 36723]. NYPO, Bernstein.

(B) * Con. CC/*CCT* 7551. LSO, Ahronovitch.

Previn takes a clear-headed, totally unsentimental view of three of Tchaikovsky's most popular orchestral works. As a result the music emerges stronger in design (even *1812*) and no less exciting than usual. The recording quality is a little dry, concentrating on fidelity of sound and balance, but there is a hint of the studio rather than the concert hall in the overall ambience. However, of its kind this is satisfying. The cassette transfer, however, cannot really cope with the end of *1812*.

Fiedler's account of *1812* has plenty of adrenalin and is brilliantly recorded, with the effective display of pyrotechnics at the end adding spectacle without drowning the music. The direct manner of the performance does all Tchaikovsky asks, if with no special individuality. Nevertheless with Karajan's *Marche slave* and Ozawa's excellent *Romeo and Juliet* – see below – and first-class sound throughout, this Walkman chrome tape coupled with Mussorgsky is certainly good value.

Karajan's *1812* is also available coupled with Beethoven's *'Battle' symphony* – see above. The performance is very professional and quite exciting, with fine orchestral playing, but the chorus used to open the piece is not very sonorously recorded, and the closing pages have the cannon added in a calculated fashion rather than showing a touch of engineering flair. Karajan's interpretation of *Romeo and Juliet* is very effective here, with passion and dignity nicely blended. *Marche slave* too is presented with its full solemn character. It is a work that the Berlin orchestra do especially well, and the recording is splendid. Disc and tape sound virtually identical and the cassette has no problems with the closing pages of *1812*.

Bernstein's performances undoubtedly have charisma. There are one or two idiosyncrasies in *1812*, but the performance of *Romeo and Juliet* is thrillingly intense, while the coda of *Marche slave* has a similar projection of adrenalin. At the end of *1812* the fusillade is impressively spectacular, and the orchestral playing throughout is expert and totally committed. The snag is the recording, excessively brilliant, lacking sumptuousness in *1812* and harsh in the loud climaxes of *Romeo and Juliet*. Frankly this is not very congenial listening, for all the brilliance of the music-making itself.

Ahronovitch's performances are wilfully eccentric, and though the recording is lively and the record is cheap it cannot be recommended with any confidence.

(i) *1812 Overture; Romeo and Juliet.*

*** Ph. 9500/*7300* 892 [id.]. (i) Tanglewood Fest. Ch.; Boston SO, Sir Colin Davis.

(M) **(*) Decca Jub. JB/*KJBC* 96 [Lon. CS/*5*- 6670]. LAPO, Mehta.

Sir Colin Davis is not renowned as a Tchaikovskian, yet here he provides one of the most satisfying versions of *1812* ever recorded. Though he departs from the original score – with great effect – by including a chorus, it is musical values rather than any sense of gimmickry that make this version so successful. Men's voices alone are used to introduce softly the Russian hymn at the opening, with the ladies freshening the reprise. In the closing spectacle, the chorus soars above the bells and the effect is exhilarating. The music in between is splendidly played and satisfyingly alert. Without any special flamboyance the recording makes a fine impact throughout, as it does in the coupling, a slightly reserved performance of *Romeo and Juliet*, but one which in its minor degree of introversion does not miss the noble passion of the lovers nor the clash of swords in the feud sequences. A most rewarding disc. The tape is satisfactorily managed too, and the final climax of *1812* opens up very well. The transfer level is not high and *Romeo and Juliet* is bass-oriented, but responds to the controls.

Mehta's *1812* is spectacular and vivid, and moreover it is easy to reproduce. The performance itself, like that of *Romeo and Juliet*, is straightforward and exciting. Some other accounts of *Romeo* are more individual, but this one, which lets the music speak for itself, is certainly effective. The cassette transfer is acceptable in *Romeo and Juliet*, but the explosive climax of *1812* is uncomfortable.

(i) *1812 Overture; Serenade for strings.*

**(*) HMV Dig. ASD/*TCC-ASD* 3956 [Ang. DS/*4XS* 37777]. Phd. O, Muti.

An urgent, crisply articulated version of *1812*, concentrated in its excitement. The Philadelphia Orchestra takes the fast speed of the main allegro in its stride, with immaculate ensemble. Perhaps a sense of genial high spirits is missing, but, with a splendidly evocative sense of anticipation, the coda produces a spectacular closing climax which is accommodated as easily on the chrome tape as on the disc. The digital recording is a little fierce on top, and the ear notices this even more when the first movement of the *Serenade* begins on side one, after the end of the overture. Again in Tchaikovsky's string piece the articulation of the Philadelphia strings is very impressive, with freshness and resilience a feature of the *Waltz* and a strongly expressive *Elegy*. But other versions of the *Serenade*, notably Leppard's, are more smiling (see below).

Festival overture on the Danish national anthem, Op. 15. (i) *Hamlet: Overture and incidental music, Op. 67 bis. Mazeppa: Battle of Poltava and Cossack dance; Romeo and Juliet* (fantasy overture; 1869 version); *Serenade for Nikolai Rubinstein's saint's day.*
❀ *** Chan. Dig. **CD 8310/1**; DBRD/-*DBRT* 2003 [id.] (2). LSO, Simon, (i) with Janis Kelly, Hammond-Stroud.

The credit for the appearance of this enterprising set, indispensable for any true Tchaikovskian, lies with Edward Johnson, a keen enthusiast and Tchaikovsky expert. He spent many months trying to persuade one of the major recording companies to make an investment in this repertoire, and it was Chandos which finally responded, producing a resplendent digital recording fully worthy of the occasion. Tchaikovsky himself thought his *Danish Festival overture* superior to *1812*, and though one cannot agree with his judgement it is well worth hearing. The *Hamlet* incidental music is another matter. The overture is a shortened version of the *Hamlet Fantasy overture*, but much of the rest of the incidental music (which occupies two well-filled LP sides) is unknown, and the engaging *Funeral march* and the two poignant string elegies show the composer's inspiration at its most memorable. Ophelia's mad scene is partly sung and partly spoken, and Janis Kelly's performance is most sympathetic, while Derek Hammond-Stroud is suitably robust in the *Gravedigger's song*. The music from *Mazeppa* and the tribute to Rubinstein make engaging bonuses, but the highlight of the set is the 1869 version of *Romeo and Juliet*, very different from the final 1880 version we know so well. It may be less sophisticated in construction, but it uses its alternative ideas with confidence and flair. It is fascinating to hear the composer's early thoughts before he finalized a piece which was to become one of the most successful of all his works. The performances here under Geoffrey Simon are excitingly committed and spontaneous; the orchestral playing is nearly always first-rate, and the digital recording has spectacular resonance and depth to balance its brilliance. The cassette transfer is of the highest quality, matching the discs very closely. Edward Johnson provides the excellent notes and a translation of the vocal music, which is sung (as the original production of *Hamlet* was performed) in French. The compact discs are among Chandos's most impressive, with the strings in the *Hamlet* incidental music sounding attractively refined, although the forward balance of the vocal soloists is made more noticeable. Orchestral tuttis are given added weight and range.

Francesca da Rimini, Op. 32.
(B) ** Con. CC/*CCT* 7533. SRO, Varviso – BORODIN: *Symphony No. 2.***(*)

Varviso has the advantage of vintage Decca sound. The performance is well made, but the Suisse Romande Orchestra does not produce the kind of glowing colours in the middle section of the work that distinguished the (deleted) Rostropovich version. However, the inferno music is superbly managed by the recording, and its subtlety is revealed by the clever way the tam-tam is balanced, so that it adds its sombrely sinister warnings, as Tchaikovsky intended, and then at the end does not drown the orchestra in the final chords of the coda. The cassette transfer has a woolly bass and is not recommended.

Francesca da Rimini; Hamlet (fantasy overture), Op. 67a.
❀ *** Dell'Arte DA 9006 (45 r.p.m.). NY Stadium O, Stokowski.

Stokowski's famous Everest coupling – one of his greatest records – is here remastered by Bryan Crimp at 45 r.p.m., and emerges with the sound freshened and the pressing clean. Stokowski's performance of *Hamlet* is superb. He plays the central lyrical tune so convincingly that, if it has not quite the romantic panache of *Romeo and Juliet*, it has instead the proper sombre passion suitable to the altogether different atmosphere of Shakespeare's *Hamlet*. It is the dignity of the music and its close identification with the play that come over so strikingly. And, fascinatingly, Stokowski shows us how intensely Russian the music is: this is Shakespeare played in the vernacular of that great country, with its national feeling for epic drama; the funeral march at the end is extremely moving. *Francesca* is hardly less exciting. Surely the opening whirlwinds have seldom roared at such tornado speeds before, and the skilful way Stokowski builds up the climax out of the fragmentation of Tchaikovsky's score is thrilling indeed. The central section is played with the beguiling care for detail and balance for which this conductor was famous. When the great polyphonic climax comes, and the themes for the lovers' passion intertwine with music to suggest they are discovered, the tension is tremendous. The recording throughout is astonishingly vivid when one considers that it was made well over two decades ago: this is an outstanding reissue in every way.

Francesca da Rimini; Romeo and Juliet.
** DG 2531/*3301* 211 [id.]. Israel PO, Bernstein.
*(*) DG Dig. 2532/*3302* 069 [id.]. Chicago SO, Barenboim.
*(*) Ph. Dig. 9500 745/*7300* 830 [id.]. Concg. O, De Waart.

Rostropovich's outstanding LPO coupling of these two works was intensely individual and full of poetic feeling. His record has been withdrawn but *Romeo and Juliet* has now been reissued on Eminence, generously recoupled with the *Second Symphony*, and hopefully *Francesca* will also reappear during the lifetime of this book.

Bernstein's approach to *Francesca* certainly conveys the passion of the story, but the Israel Philharmonic is no match for the LPO in the idyllic central section; moreover Bernstein's pacing is idiosyncratic and unconvincing here. *Romeo and Juliet* is only moderately exciting, in spite of a brilliant sound balance. The cassette transfer has problems with the closing climax of *Francesca* and produces congestion.

Barenboim's record is disappointing. The recording has brilliant clarity and detail but lacks ambience. *Romeo and Juliet* is curiously lacking in ardour, and Barenboim's tempo is leaden, though there is a burst of excitement in the feud music. The middle section of *Francesca* yields some fine solo playing, notably from the clarinet, but the final climax is lacking in real tension.

The Philips digital recording for Edo de Waart has none of the clarity one usually associates with these new techniques; indeed the sound is muddy and bass-heavy. The performances are well played but not in any way distinctive. The cassette has almost no upper range at all.

Manfred symphony, Op. 58.
*** HMV Dig. ASD/*TCC-ASD* 4169 [Ang. DS/*4XS* 37752]. Phd. O, Muti.
*** Decca SXL/*KSXC* 6853 [Lon. CS/5-7075]. New Philh. O, Ashkenazy.
(M) *** EMI Em. EMX/*TC-EMX* 41 2060-1/*4*. LPO, Rostropovich.
*** Ph. 9500 778/*7300 853* [id.]. Concg. O, Haitink.
(M) (*) DG Priv. 2535/*3335* 476. LSO, Ahronovitch.

Undoubtedly Muti's thrilling new HMV recording (made in the Kingsway Hall) is in a special class – one of the most impressive EMI digital LPs yet issued. At the close of the first movement, Tchaikovsky's memorable climactic statement of the principal Manfred theme heard on the massed strings (*sul G*) brings a tremendous physical excitement, and when it is similarly reprised in the finale, capped with cymbals, the effect is electrifying. The weight of the sound emphasizes the epic style of Muti's reading, forceful and boldly dramatic throughout. Muti's scherzo has a quality of exhilarating bravura, rather than concentrating on delicacy; the lovely central melody is given a sense of joyous vigour. The *Andante*, after a refined opening, soon develops a passionate forward sweep; in the finale the amplitude and brilliant detail of the recording, combined with magnificent playing from the Philharmonia Orchestra, brings a massively compulsive projection of Tchaikovsky's bacchanale and a richly satisfying dénouement. The tape is thinner on top, and has less substance.

Under Ashkenazy the atmosphere and power of the opening movement are fully realized, and the scherzo has the most refined lyrical impulse, with wonderfully fresh string-playing and sparkling articulation in the outer sections. The *Andante* is even finer; indeed in Ashkenazy's hands it is revealed as one of Tchaikovsky's most successful symphonic slow movements, full of lyrical fervour when the playing shows such strength of feeling yet is completely without exaggeration. The reading culminates in a stunning account of the finale, Ashkenazy opting for a fast tempo and providing a tremendous forward momentum. The fugato section is especially incisive, and the work's closing pages are given a satisfying feeling of apotheosis. The recording is immensely full-blooded and brilliant, yet natural in perspective; the tape transfer is highly sophisticated, both rich and detailed, with splendid weight and impact. A comparison with the disc, however, shows that (as in Ashkenazy's version of the *Fifth Symphony*) the climaxes on cassette are marginally less richly expansive, although elsewhere the sound is almost identical.

By comparison with Ashkenazy, Rostropovich is weightier, more symphonic, yet the element of fantasy is not lost; the delightful chimerical detail of the scherzo inspires some marvellously polished LPO playing. Even more than Ashkenazy, Rostropovich catches the mood of brooding Byronic melancholy in the first movement, and the introduction of the lovely *Astarte* brings a moment of great poignancy, the rhythmic pulse tenderly volatile. Rostropovich's approach to the *Andante* is also more measured, the lyrical feeling intense to match the powerful mood of despair in the finale before the beginning of the fugato. Ashkenazy's greater vigour and momentum are more bitingly brilliant here, but at the close Rostropovich's weight and breadth are telling. The EMI recording is rich and full (slightly less immediate than the other symphonies in Rostropovich's complete cycle).

Haitink's account of *Manfred* is characteristically fresh and incisive. Where others bring out the rhapsodic expressiveness of a work which has close parallels with Berlioz's comparable Byronic *Harold in Italy*, Haitink more clearly relates it to the other symphonies. There is no want of urgency, but there is less spontaneous lyricism than under Ashkenazy and Rostropovich: in the passage depicting the vision of Astarte, Haitink misses some of the tenderness and sense of rapture, and the third movement is less passionate, more refined in line and texture. But there is genuine authority and grip, and the playing of the Concertgebouw is immaculate. The sound is superb, bringing out both the delicacy and the power of the piece. The cassette is well balanced, rich and full-bodied, but is slightly less brilliant at the top.

Ahronovitch is superbly recorded by DG, but his narcissistic ritenuto style, with constant agogic distortion of the rhythmic pulse, is totally unsatisfactory for repeated listening.

Marche slave, Op. 31.

(M) ** Decca VIV/*KVIC* 37 [Lon. STS/5-15589]. LAPO, Mehta – LISZT: *Les Préludes; Mazeppa***(*); WAGNER: *Meistersinger overture.***

A lively account of the Slavonic march from Mehta, very brilliantly recorded, with the cassette slightly tempering the upper range to advantage. The two Liszt symphonic poems are the main items of interest on this issue.

Ballets: *The Nutcracker; Sleeping Beauty; Swan Lake* (complete recordings).

(M) *** HMV Dig. SLS/*TCC-SLS* 5273 (8). Amb. S., Philh. O, Lanchbery.

Lanchbery's integral recordings of the three great Tchaikovsky ballets, made by EMI in conjunction with Du Maurier sponsorship, is a considerable achievement. The digital recording is first-class, wide-ranging, brilliant, substantial yet with excellent detail, and there are comparably excellent chrome cassettes. Technically this set is unbeaten in the present catalogue. The music is played with striking flair and polish, with the Philharmonia Orchestra on its toes. Lanchbery shows consistent care for detail and his approach combines a natural sympathy with strong theatrical feeling. The red livery of the presentation is very handsome, even if the association with cigarette packaging is undeniable.

The Nutcracker (ballet), *Op. 71* (complete).

*** HMV Dig. SLS/*TCC-SLS* 5270 (2) [Ang. DSG/*4X2S* 3933]. Amb. S., Philh. O, Lanchbery.

*** HMV SLS/*TC-SLS* 834 (2) [Ang. SB/*4X2S* 3788]. LSO, Previn.

(M) **(*) Decca Jub. 410 261-1/*4* [Lon. CSA/*5*- 2239]. Nat. PO, Bonynge.

Lanchbery's account of the *Nutcracker* may not be the most romantic on disc, but the performance has an attractive momentum and sweep. One has the feeling of being in the theatre with the narrative line strongly conveyed. The famous characteristic dances bring very polished solo contributions from the orchestra and the vitality of the music-making throughout is obvious. The recording is vivid, and the orchestral textures combine sparkle and bloom. The cassette issue is complete on a single chrome tape in a box, with the sound matching the LPs very closely.

The alternative HMV set is affectionately and sumptuously played by Previn and the LSO. The recording is warm and pleasing on side one, but immediately becomes more vivid and dramatic on side two when, after the end of the children's party, the magic begins to work. The *Transformation scene* is richly done, and the famous dances of Act II are played with much sophistication: indeed the orchestral playing throughout is of very high quality. This set can also be recommended most warmly. The cassette transfer is smooth, perhaps a little lacking in brilliance.

Bonynge's set is brilliantly recorded. In its tape format it is complete on a single chrome cassette, very closely matched to the discs. Bonynge's approach is sympathetic and he secures fine playing from the National Philharmonic recording group. In the opening scene the music-making seems somewhat literal and lacking atmosphere, but with the beginning of the magic as the Christmas tree expands, the playing catches fire and the *Transformation scene* is finely done. In the latter part of the ballet Bonynge is at his best, with fine passion in the Act II *Pas de deux* and plenty of colour in the characteristic dances. This is excellent value at mid-price.

The Nutcracker: highlights.
(M) *** Decca SPA/*KCSP* 357 [Lon. CS 6097]. SRO, Ansermet.

The Nutcracker: suite, Op. 71a; Suite No. 2.
*** Ph. 9500 697/*7300 788* [id.]. Concg. O (with chorus), Dorati.

Nutcracker suite.
(M) ** HMV Green. ESD/*TC-ESD* 7115. Philh. O, Malko – LUIGINI: *Ballet Egyptien****; MEYERBEER: *Les Patineurs***; PONCHIELLI: *Dance of the Hours.***(*)

Dorati offers a second suite to supplement Tchaikovsky's own selection. This is taken from his splendid Philips complete set (now deleted) and with refined playing and Dorati's warm attention to detail, this makes a clear first choice for a single-disc compilation. It was recorded in the ample acoustic of the Concertgebouw, and the resonance has brought a low-level tape transfer, which reduces the sparkle of the cassette sound.

Ansermet's disc of highlights comes from another famous complete set of the early stereo era which showed this conductor at his finest. The selection here is generous and includes the *Transformation scene*, which Ansermet did especially well. The newer transfer has lost just a little of the ambient bloom that distinguished the original, but still sounds full and vivid. There is a good cassette, though originally here the sound was brighter on side two than side one. This is likely to have been corrected by now.

Nicolai Malko's performance also dates from the earliest days of stereo, and the 1955 recording has surprising bloom and colour (it is richer than other items in this collection which were recorded more recently). The playing is polished and colourful; the characteristic dances are strikingly vivid. There is little to choose between disc and cassette.

Nutcracker suite, Op. 71a.
(M) *** Decca Jub. JB/*KJBC* 16 [(d) Lon. JL/*5*- 41021]. VPO, Karajan – GRIEG: *Peer Gynt.****
(B) *** Con. CC/*CCT* 7570 [Lon. SPA/*5*- 21142]. Boston Pops O, Fiedler – GRIEG: *Peer Gynt.****

Anyone who wants the coupling with *Peer Gynt* should be well satisfied with Karajan's disc. The readings are characteristically broad: the *Overture* is less miniature in effect than usual; the *Chinese dance* could be more piquant, and the Waltz could have a lighter touch, but these are mere carping criticisms.

This is typical Karajan conducting, with its usual panache, and the fine orchestral playing is matched by vivid recording of Decca's best quality. This is preferable to Karajan's earlier analogue Berlin Philharmonic version (see below). There is an excellent tape version.

Fiedler's performance has marvellous spirit and vigour. The vividly coloured recording helps to project the music-making, but the spontaneity and life of the playing itself are in no doubt. This was originally a Decca Phase Four recording and represented this system at its most impressive. The cassette transfer too is excellent. A bargain.

Nutcracker suite; Romeo and Juliet.
*** DG Dig. **410 873-2**; 410 873-1/*4*. Berlin PO, Karajan.
(*) Telarc Dig. **CD 80068; DG 10068. Cleveland O, Maazel.

Originally designed to accompany a picture biography of Karajan, this surprisingly rare Tchaikovsky coupling brings superbly played performances. The suite is delicate and detailed, yet perhaps lacks a little in charm, notably the *Arab dance* which, taken fairly briskly, loses something of its gentle sentience. The overture is both polished and dramatic, but Karajan draws out the climax of the love theme with spacious moulding, and there is marginally less spontaneity here than in his earlier recordings. The sound, characteristic of Berlin, is of high quality though the chrome cassette might usefully have been transferred at a higher level in the *Nutcracker suite*.

With vivid orchestral playing and bright, crisply focused recording within a natural ambience, Maazel's *Nutcracker suite* is enjoyably colourful. His manner is affectionate (especially in the warmly lilting *Waltz of the Flowers*), and the only idiosyncrasy is the sudden accelerando at the close of the *Russian dance*. *Romeo and Juliet* is given a spaciously romantic performance, reaching a climax of considerable passion. However, the almost overwhelming impact of the percussion in the undoubtedly exciting feud music is obviously designed for those who like to say 'Listen to that bass drum!' Others may feel that the balance is not exactly what one would experience in the concert hall.

Nutcracker suite; Romeo and Juliet; The Sleeping Beauty: suite, Op. 66; Swan Lake: suite, Op. 20.
(M) **(*) DG 2725/*3374* 105 (2). Berlin PO, Karajan.

This medium-price double album recouples recordings from the late 1960s and early 1970s. Karajan's DG version of *Romeo and Juliet* is very telling, with passion and dignity nicely blended. The *Nutcracker suite* is superbly played, but its piquancy of colour is slightly smoothed over. The *Sleeping Beauty* and *Swan Lake* suites show Karajan at his finest, with a high level of tension and playing that is imaginative as well as exciting. The recording is suitably brilliant, though the cassettes seem less sumptuous than the discs.

Nutcracker suite; Serenade for strings.
** Ph. Dig. 6514/*7337* 265 [id.]. ASMF, Marriner.

A good if not especially individual account of the *Nutcracker suite* is here coupled with a new version of the *Serenade* which is no match for Marriner's Decca account, recorded when the Academy was at an early peak (see below). By the side of this, the new performance, though well played, seems a routine affair. The recording is vivid and full-bodied.

Nutcracker: suite and No. 14a: Pas de deux; The Sleeping Beauty: suite.
(B) *** CfP CFP/*TC-CFP* 40369 [Ang. Sera. S/4XG 60176]. RPO, Boult.

Sir Adrian Boult did not make many Tchaikovsky records, but this coupling is highly successful. Originally made in EMI's hi-fi-conscious Studio Two system, the sound is very brilliant indeed, but there is an attractive hall ambience, and detail remains crystal-clear. The characteristic dances in the *Nutcracker* are especially vivid, and the addition of the great Act II *Pas de deux*, played with swirling passion, was a fine idea. The *Sleeping Beauty suite* is Boult's own selection and includes one or two attractive surprise items, but not all the familiar ones. The cassette transfer is of CfP's usual high quality; indeed there is little discernible difference between disc and tape. The latter is perhaps slightly softer-grained at the top, which is in no sense a disadvantage.

(i) *Nutcracker suite*. (ii) *The Sleeping Beauty: suite*. (iii) *Swan Lake: suite*.
(M) ** Ph. Seq. 6527/*7311* 065. (i) Minneapolis SO, Dorati; (ii) LSO, Fistoulari; (iii) LSO, Monteux.
(M) *(*) Decca SPA/*KCSP* 594. SRO, Ansermet.

Nutcracker suite; The Sleeping Beauty: excerpts; Swan Lake: suite.
*** HMV ASD/*TC-ASD* 3584. LSO, Previn.

The HMV issue offers the complete *Nutcracker suite*, the usual concert suite from *Swan Lake* and four items from *The Sleeping Beauty* (including the *Panorama*, which Previn floats magically). The performances show Previn's view of these works in the best light: the *Nutcracker suite* has glowing orchestral colours, well caught in the warmly vivid sound. The 'plushy' effect characteristic of the other complete sets is not minimized here by the recording balance, which is rich and full rather than especially brilliant. But this makes very congenial listening on either disc or cassette, which sound very much the same.

The Philips Sequenza issue draws on three different sources. The *Nutcracker suite* comes from Dorati's earlier complete set (so the *Dance of the Sugar Plum Fairy* has the extended ballet ending). The performance is alert and has no lack of sparkle. The sound has more freshness and range than in the previous incarnation of these excerpts (on Universo), but the upper strings lack body. The sound improves markedly for Monteux's excerpts from *Swan Lake*, which are characteristically vivid (one does not forget that he conducted for Diaghilev), and is really excellent for Fistoulari in the suite from *The Sleeping Beauty* (taken from one of his best records). This is a generous compilation and is certainly enjoyable; it sounds well on cassette too.

Ansermet's rather similar collection (drawn from his early stereo complete sets) is, surprisingly, spoiled by the sound, which is clear but lacks the warmth and sumptuousness of the originals. The music-making too is less impressive when items are reassembled like this than when heard in context, and the ear is made more aware of the inadequacies of some of the orchestral playing, especially by comparison with Previn's highly polished selections.

Nutcracker suite; Swan Lake: suite.
** Decca Dig. **410 551-2**; SXDL/*KSXDC* 7505 [Lon. LDR/*5*- 10008]. Israel PO, Mehta.

Here is a case where the compact disc is markedly superior to the LP recording of the same performances. The sound is fuller and much more refined and, in the *Nutcracker*, textures have more delicacy. The Mann Auditorium in Tel Aviv, where this record was made, does not usually provide a flattering ambience but on the CD it is caught most successfully. Climaxes swell up thrillingly and the brass is especially vivid. On LP the cellos sound rather buzzy at times and there is a curious bass-drum sound in *Swan Lake*. But even with the help of CD brilliance the performances are not distinctive enough to command a strong recommendation: there are better versions of both suites, which cost less than this.

Nutcracker suite; Swan Lake: extended suite.
(M) **(*) CBS 60131/*40*- [MY/*MYT* 37238]. NYPO, Bernstein.

These performances from the beginning of the 1960s find the NYPO on top form, during a vintage Bernstein period. The playing in the *Nutcracker suite* is civilized and polished, yet has plenty of sparkle, while the selection from *Swan Lake* is imaginative and unconventional, although in fact one of the more famous numbers (the *Dance of the Little Swans*) gives special pleasure for its piquancy. The recording is bright, thinner on top in *Swan Lake* but fully acceptable, with disc and tape sounding much the same.

Nutcracker suite: excerpts; Sleeping Beauty: excerpts; Swan Lake: suite.
(M) DG Sig. 410 846-1/*4*. Berlin PO, Rostropovich.

An ill-conceived issue which offers a truncated version of Rostropovich's splendid performance of the *Nutcracker suite* to make room for two purple patches from the *Sleeping Beauty*. The *Swan Lake* suite is left untouched. Performances and recording are first-rate. Displayed in a shop browser with all three titles blazoned in large letters on the front of the sleeve, this is likely to mislead any prospective purchaser.

Romeo and Juliet (fantasy overture).

*** HMV ASD/*TC-ASD* 3488 [Ang. RL/*4RL* 32047]. Philh. O, Muti – *Symphony No. 2.****

(M) *** EMI Em. EMX/*TC-EMX* 41 2062-1/*4*. LPO, Rostropovich – *Symphony No. 2.****

(M) *** DG Acc. 2542/*3342* 113 [(d) 2530 137]. Boston SO, Abbado – *Symphony No. 2.**(*)*

(M) *** DG Priv. 2535/*3335* 422 [2530 308/*3300 284*]. San Francisco SO, Ozawa – BERLIOZ: *Roméo et Juliette: Love scene*; PROKOFIEV: *Romeo and Juliet:* excerpts.***

(M) *** Decca Jub. JB/*KJBC* 71 [(d) Lon. JL/*5*- 41021]. VPO, Karajan – DVOŘÁK: *Symphony No. 8.****

(B) *** Con. CC/*CCT* 7528. Karajan (as above) – R. STRAUSS: *Don Juan.****

Muti's *Romeo and Juliet* is distinguished, one of the finest available, and full of imaginative touches. The opening has just the right degree of atmospheric restraint and immediately creates a sense of anticipation; the great romantic climax is noble in contour yet there is no lack of passion, while the main allegro is crisply and dramatically pointed. The repeated figure on the timpani at the coda is made to suggest a tolling bell, and the expressive woodwind playing which follows gently underlines the feeling of tragedy. The full, rich recording suits the interpretation admirably, and the cassette transfer has plenty of weight and generally good detail.

Like Rostropovich's accounts of the symphonies, his *Romeo and Juliet* is an intensely individual reading, with great concern for detail. The ebb and flow of tension has the spontaneity of a live performance and, although Rostropovich's pacing is as free as his moulding of the melodic lines, the listener is carried along by the expressive vitality of the orchestral playing. At the opening there are bold accents on the lower strings; later there is a compulsive accelerando before the final romantic climax, yet the love theme is introduced with the greatest tenderness. It is an epic approach, with a theatrical sense of drama. The recording is suitably resonant and spacious.

Abbado's too is a noble reading. At the first appearance of the love theme he shows considerable restraint, and there is great delicacy in the articulation of the secondary idea on muted strings. But the reprise brings a welling up of passion. The allegros have tremendous power and impact, and the coda – after a thunderous timpani roll – is wonderfully eloquent. A performance to live with: its spellbinding qualities increase with familiarity. The recording is splendid, very brilliant as well as full; there is no appreciable difference between cassette and disc.

In the DG collection of musical evocations of *Romeo and Juliet* it was inevitable that the Tchaikovsky fantasy overture should be included. This is a thoroughly worthwhile anthology and Ozawa draws from the San Francisco orchestra warmly committed playing, very well recorded on disc and cassette alike; this should not disappoint anyone who likes the idea of having three Romeos contrasted.

Karajan's account of the *Romeo and Juliet* overture is among the best of its period. It has dramatic fire and excitement and, when the music calls for it, tenderness. The recording is from the early 1960s and is not quite as rich as one would expect today. Yet this is well worth considering if you want a Dvořák *G major Symphony*. The cassette is less refined in tuttis than some Decca transfers. This performance is also available on the Contour bargain label in an excellent, clean pressing coupled with *Don Juan*. The Contour cassette (not made by Decca) is less wide-ranging than the disc though quite acceptable; but the LP is an obvious bargain.

Serenade for strings in C, Op. 48.

C *** DG Dig. **400 038-2**; 2532/*3302* 012 [id.]. Berlin PO, Karajan – DVOŘÁK: *Serenade.****

*** Ph. 9500 105 [id./*7300 532*]. ECO, Leppard – DVOŘÁK: *Serenade.****

*** Argo ZRG/*KZRC* 848 [id.]. ASMF, Marriner – DVOŘÁK: *Serenade.***(*)

(B) **(*) RCA VICS/*VK* 2001 [AGL 1/ *AGK 1* 3790]. Boston SO, Munch – BARBER: *Adagio*; ELGAR: *Introduction and allegro.***(*)

(*) ASV Dig. DCA/*ZCDCA* 505. O of St John's, Lubbock – DVOŘÁK: *Serenade.*(*)

A vigorously extrovert reading from Karajan, with taut, alert and superbly polished playing in the first movement, an elegant but slightly cool *Waltz*, a passionately intense *Elegy* and a bustling, immensely spirited finale. There is a lack of charm, but here the strikingly clear digital recording, with the strings very brightly lit above the stave, has its influence, for there is a lack of warmth in the middle range. The chrome tape, while retaining the inner clarity, is slightly richer and softer-grained on top. The compact disc, however, is one of the finest yet to come from DG. Although there is just a hint of digital edge on the violins, this is offset by the extension of the middle and lower range which is gloriously full and resonant, far superior to the LP. The refinement of inner detail is remarkable. Tchaikovsky often wrote antiphonally (when he was not using his strings in unison), and so clear is the definition that the effect almost becomes visual as ideas move back and forth within the string groupings.

Those seeking an analogue recording should be well satisfied with Leppard or Marriner (whose version is also available in an admirable alternative coupling – see below). Leppard is given some advantage in the richness and body of the Philips recording, slightly fuller than the Argo disc and tape (which matches it closely). However, Marriner's performance compensates with expressive phrasing, and the relative opulence of tone produced by the Academy is balanced by the imagination and freshness of the performance. Leppard's more direct manner does not inhibit him in the *Waltz* which is beautifully done.

A strong, full-blooded reading from Munch, with an elegant *Waltz* and an especially well-prepared finale. The conductor does not overplay his hand in the *Elegy*, and with playing from the Boston strings that is both committed and polished this is very involving. The early stereo recording sounds remarkably well, robust, yet well detailed and with plenty of colour and atmosphere. Disc and chrome cassette are virtually identical; if anything the tape has slightly more range than the disc, without loss of body. There is only a hint of the characteristic Boston ambient harshness. An excellent bargain.

Lubbock and the Orchestra of St John's, Smith Square, provided the digital début of Tchaikovsky's *Serenade*, and the sound here is if anything even more analytical than the DG recording. While one cannot complain that the timbre is untruthful, the listener is given the impression, almost, of being suspended near the first violins, with the middle resonances of violas and cellos less telling. Lubbock secures a strong, brisk first-movement allegro, but he relaxes very effectively at the end of the *Elegy* to bring a sense of repose, so that the lead into the finale is the more effective. The actual playing is of high quality, but does not quite match the Berlin Orchestra in polish. Nonetheless the performance communicates readily, and it certainly has vitality. The cassette matches the disc closely.

Serenade for strings; Souvenir de Florence, Op. 70 (orchestral version).

(M) ❀ *** Decca Jub. JB/*KJBC* 131. ASMF, Marriner.

Though Tchaikovsky asked for as big a body of strings as possible in his delectable *Serenade*, there is much to be said, in these days of increased string resonance and clever microphone placing, for having a modest band like the Academy of St Martin's. The insight of Marriner's 1969 performance, its glowing sense of joy combined with the finest pointing and precision of ensemble, put it in a class of its own. The unanimity of phrasing of the Academy's violins in the intense slow movement is breathtaking in its expressiveness, although here one does notice the lack of the sheer tonal weight that a bigger body of strings would afford. The coupling could hardly be more delightful, with the Academy tackling a work normally played by six solo strings and producing delectable results. The haunting second subject of the opening movement should certainly be sampled. The one snag is that to fit it on one side, the work has been subjected to some tactful cutting. Excellent, vividly atmospheric recording quality, with a cassette in the demonstration class.

The Sleeping Beauty (complete ballet), *Op. 66*.
❀ *** BBC BBC/*ZCBBC* 3001 (3) [Eurodisc 300575/*500575*]. BBC SO, Rozhdestvensky.
*** HMV Dig. SLS/*TCC-SLS* 5272 [Ang. DSC/*4X3S* 3932]. Philh. O, Lanchbery.
** Ph. 6769/*7699* 036 (3) [id.]. Concg. O, Dorati.

Rozhdestvensky's set was made as part of the BBC Symphony Orchestra's fiftieth anniversary celebrations and is fully worthy of the occasion. It is superb in every way, marvellously played and very well recorded in an excellent acoustic that is neither too dry nor too resonant for comfort (a problem with this particular score). There is occasional minor spotlighting of wind soloists, but who would cavil when all the solo playing is so outstanding – as indeed are the contributions of the strings and brass: the trumpet and horn fanfares are splendid. Rozhdestvensky uses the original Russian score, which is absolutely complete, even including music omitted from the ballet's première. There are those who hold that this is Tchaikovsky's greatest ballet score, finer even than *Swan Lake*; and these records do much to support that view. The work could not be entrusted to more caring or sensitive direction, and the ear is continually amazed by the consistent quality of Tchaikovsky's inspiration. Rozhdestvensky's loving attention to detail and his response to the textural colouring are matched by his feeling for the narrative drama, yet he never overplays his hand, so that the big moments of spectacle – the *Rose adagio*, for instance – have ardour without becoming emotionally aggressive. Tchaikovsky's continuously fertile imagination in matters of scoring is readily demonstrated, and the lighter characteristic dances sound as fresh as the day they were written. There is atmosphere too, and the magical *Sleep entr'acte* before the happy ending of the story is given a haunting sense of anticipation and fantasy. In disc form this is an outstanding achievement in every way. Unfortunately the Dolby treatment of the cassettes has been misjudged; the treble is unacceptably muffled unless the Dolby circuitry is switched out and a treble cut substituted, with its attendant hiss problem. The rosette is for the LP box only.

Lanchbery's Philharmonia recording is also highly recommendable, helped by splendid sound with the chrome tapes matching the discs closely – this is a first recommendation on cassette. The performance combines a gracious classical feeling with a theatrical sense of drama which is tellingly projected, yet never forced. Rozhdestvensky's account has an obviously more individual flavour, but Lanchbery too shows a fine concern for detail and the Philharmonia playing is first-class. The recording balance is slightly forward but the wide dynamic range is well judged, the brass has genuine splendour and the orchestral textures combine sparkle with bloom.

Dorati's is a vibrant and dramatic account, supported by firm, rich recording and splendid orchestral playing (especially in the last Act, which gives the orchestral wind soloists many chances to shine). Yet this is a score that – for all its melodic inspiration – can momentarily disengage the listener's attention; and here in spite of the drama this does happen. Everything is well characterized, but at times there is a lack of magic. The low-level cassette transfer can be made to sound well but is bass-heavy and lacks the range and sparkle at the top. Moreover the layout on two tapes instead of three discs is quite arbitrary and makes no attempt to tailor the Acts to fit the ends of sides.

Sleeping Beauty: highlights.
(M) **(*) Decca SPA/*KCSP* 358. SRO, Ansermet.

Taken from Ansermet's deleted complete set, this selection faithfully reflects its character. The *Prologue* and Act I excerpts are dramatic but rather cool. With the opening of side two and Act II, the music projects more vividly. The sound, from a vintage Decca era, remains very good though the tape transfer has more sparkle on side one than side two, which is mellower.

The Sleeping Beauty: excerpts; *Swan Lake: suite.*
(M) *** Decca VIV/*KVIC* 10 [Lon. 21008/5-]. New Philh. O, Stokowski.

Stokowski secures some electrifying playing from the New Philharmonia Orchestra. The recording (made originally in Decca's Phase Four system) is somewhat artificial in balance and very brilliant, but the conductor makes the very most of the sonic possibilities to project a generous selection of music in the most vivid way. The result makes an irresistible impact, and of its kind this is a classic issue, very much worth its relatively modest price. The cassette is lively too, but has a narrower range of dynamics.

Sleeping Beauty: suite; Swan Lake: suite.
*** DG 2531/*3301* 111 [id.]. Berlin PO, Rostropovich.
*** DG 2530 195/*3300 205* [id.]. Berlin PO, Karajan.
(M) **(*) Decca Jub. JB/*KJBC* 35 [Lon. JL/5- 41003]. VPO, Karajan.

Rostropovich provides here a highly distinguished companion disc for his DG coupling of the *Nutcracker suite* and *Capriccio italien.* Given superb recording, the performances combine Slavonic intensity with colour. The characteristic dances balance wit with delicacy: the whimsical portrait of the cats in *The Sleeping Beauty* is matched by the sprightly fledgling swans, while the glorious *Panorama* melody is floated over its gently rocking bass with magical delicacy. The recording expands spectacularly at climaxes, and elsewhere it attractively combines bloom with detail. The cassette matches the disc closely, having only marginally less upper range.

Of Karajan's recordings the DG is a clear first choice on disc, with superb playing from the Berlin Philharmonic Orchestra and plenty of charisma from Karajan, whose extrovert approach creates a high level of tension and electricity. The DG sound aims for brilliance rather than richness, but provides exciting projection. The tape, however, is overmodulated, and offers a degree of congestion, and problems with the bass drum.

The Decca recording, now reissued on Jubilee, dates from 1965. The sound is clear and brilliant, but although the performances are not without panache the Berlin orchestra produces more sumptuous textures. However, the cassette – bright and vivid – is more attractive than the disc, and is preferable to the DG tape.

Suites (for orchestra) *Nos. 1 in D min., Op. 43; 2 in C, Op. 53; 3 in G, Op. 55; 4 in G* (*Mozartiana*), *Op. 61.*
(M) **(*) Ph. 6768 035 (3) [Mercury 77008]. New Philh. O, Dorati.

Tchaikovsky's four *Orchestral suites* are directly descended from the dance suites of the baroque era. Nos. 1 and 3 are both as long as an average symphony, although their material is slighter. The invention is somewhat uneven, but each suite has its share of endearing inspiration. No. 4 draws on the music of Mozart, including the *Ave verum* and a set of piano variations which are given a tasteful orchestral dress. The weakest is No. 2, whose most striking movement is a *Scherzo burlesque* featuring the accordion as an ad lib soloist. The most famous is No. 3 with its familiar set of variations, often performed separately. Dorati's complete set first appeared at the end of the 1960s, and its return to the catalogue is welcome, for there is no serious competition (except in the case of the *Third Suite*). The performances are perceptive and generally well characterized. Dorati secures first-rate playing from the New Philharmonia, but the Philips recording now sounds just a little dated. However, this is good value at medium price, and the music itself is certainly worth investigating.

Suites Nos. 2 in C, Op. 53; 4 in G (*Mozartiana*), *Op. 61.*
**(*) CBS Dig. 36702 [Col. IM/*IMT* 36702]. Philh. O, Tilson Thomas.

Michael Tilson Thomas makes a very good case for Tchaikovsky's *Mozartiana suite*, finding both sparkle and elegance in the music and effectively balancing the personalities of both the composers represented. The Philharmonia playing is first-class, but the brilliant digital recording, though admirably clear, lacks ambient bloom. The bright, clean focus of the sound tends to emphasize the unevenness of the *Second Suite*, although the *Scherzo burlesque* with its accordions is effectively bustling and Tilson Thomas finds a wistful charm in the *Rêves d'enfant*; he directs the closing *Danse baroque* most stylishly.

Suite No. 3 in G, Op. 55.
*** CBS [M 35124]. LAPO, Tilson Thomas.

It is a great pity that this outstanding CBS record has been withdrawn in the UK. The performance of Tchaikovsky's *Third Suite* by Michael Tilson Thomas and the Los Angeles Philharmonic is in a class of its own; indeed it is one of the finest Tchaikovsky performances in the catalogue. So often the first three movements of this work are dwarfed by the finale, which undoubtedly contains the finest music, but here the conductor achieves a perfect balance. He opens and closes the first movement quite magically and takes its climax with just the right degree of romantic melodrama. The rhythmic character of the *Valse mélancolique* is deftly managed, and the crisp, gay scherzo is delightful, its middle section wittily and delicately pointed. At the opening of the fourth movement Tchaikovsky's fine melody is splendidly shaped, and the variations unfold with gripping spontaneity, their sheer diversity a constant joy. The closing *Polacca* is superbly prepared and Tilson Thomas ushers in the principal theme with a calculated ritenuto worthy of Sir Thomas Beecham. The trio has a swinging animation, and the piece closes with glorious vigour. The recording is vivid and well balanced, with fine detail. But it lacks something in bloom and warmth in the middle area of the orchestra, although it does not want brilliance.

Swan Lake (ballet), *Op. 20* (complete).
*** HMV SLS/*TCC-SLS* 5271 [Ang. DSC/*4X3S* 3931]. Philh. O, Lanchbery.
(M) **(*) Decca D 37 D 3/*K 37 K 33* (3) [Lon. OSA/*5*- 2315]. Nat. PO, Bonynge.
**(*) HMV SLS/*TC-SLS* 5070 (3) [Ang. SCLX/*4X3S* 3834]. Haendel, LSO, Previn.
**(*) DG 2709 099/*3371 051* (3) [id.]. Boston SO, Ozawa.

Tchaikovsky's score for *Swan Lake* is among his supreme masterpieces. It has a lyrical flow of inspired musical invention which runs uninterrupted for about two and a half hours. There is not a dull bar, and everywhere the felicity of the orchestration matches the quality of the invention. This is not surprising, for the composer told us that his ideas came to him (sometimes in the middle of the night, when he was forced to get up to write them down, so persistently did they demand his attention) complete with their harmony and orchestral dress.

With Fistoulari's account deleted, Lanchbery's new digital HMV set is a clear first choice. The orchestral playing is first-class, with polished, elegant string phrasing matched by felicitous wind solos. Lanchbery's rhythmic spring is a constant pleasure; everything is alert, and there is plenty of excitement at climaxes. Other conductors – notably Fistoulari – have made this score sound more romantically passionate, but there is no lack of emotional commitment here, even if Lanchbery seldom overwhelms the listener. The score's marvellous detail is revealed with long theatrical experience. The recording is splendid, the sound vivid and the perspectives realistic. Both discs and chrome tapes are very impressive, although on cassette the level drops in Act II with a slight loss of presence.

Bonynge's approach is essentially strong and vigorous, bringing out all the drama of the score if less of its charm. The forward impulse of the music-making is immediately striking, and Decca have matched the interpretation with a somewhat dry acoustic, producing leonine string tone and little feeling of sumptuousness. This is not to say that the richness of Tchaikovsky's scoring fails to tell, but the brightly lit sound picture provides robust detail in the place of glamour. The brass sounds too are open and vibrant, and the 'fairy castle' fanfares (side four) have here more of the atmosphere of a medieval tournament. The overall balance is well managed, although the violin solos sound rather larger than life. Perhaps they fail (like the performance as a whole) to distil all the romantic essence of this masterly score, but the commitment of the orchestral playing as a whole is never in doubt. There is consistent freshness here, and many of the spectacular moments are thrilling. Yet the lack of ripeness will be counted a drawback by some listeners. The transfer to tape is eminently successful. The quality has rather more warmth, yet there is little if any loss of detail and inner refinement. The effect is to make the score sound richer, more romantic, and the wide dynamic range of the recording is captured without difficulty.

Previn's set, like his recordings of the other Tchaikovsky ballets, offers extremely polished orchestral playing, with beautiful wind solos, helped by a warm, resonant recording which gives plenty of bloom to the overall sound picture. Miss Haendel's contribution is first-class, and there is much refined detail and no lack of drama when the music calls for it. And yet something is missing. One hesitates to use the adjective 'cosy', but there is nevertheless a feeling here of over-sumptuousness, helped by the indulgent textures of the recording. Many may find this exactly to their taste, but there is an inherent vitality about the Lanchbery set which is less apparent here. The HMV tape transfer is acceptable, but less refined than the discs, and the solo violin tone is given something of an edge by the brightness of the overall sound balance.

Ozawa's version omits the Act III *Pas de deux* but otherwise plays the complete original score as Tchaikovsky conceived it. His performance has not the verve of Lanchbery's HMV recording; the approach is more serious, less flexible. But the playing of the Boston orchestra is strikingly polished and sympathetic, and there are many impressive things here, with wind (and violin) solos that always give pleasure. The end result is a little faceless, in spite of a spectacular, wide-ranging recording, as vivid as it is powerful. On cassette (with a comparatively modest transfer level) the gentler moments lack something in presence, but the climaxes open up without distortion.

Swan Lake: highlights.

(B) *** CfP CFP/*TC-CFP* 40296. Menuhin, Philh. O, Kurtz.

**(*) DG 2531/*3301* 351 [id.]. (from above set, cond. Ozawa).

(M) ** Ph. Seq. 6527/*7311* 119 [6570/*7310* 187]. LSO, Monteux.

(B) ** Con. CC/*CCT* 7520. ROHCGO, Morel.

From Classics for Pleasure a splendid bargain compilation, with Menuhin present to play the violin solos. The Philharmonia are on top form and the woodwind acquit themselves with even more style than usual in Tchaikovsky's solos. The 1960 recording, originally HMV, matches the exuberance which Kurtz brings to the music's climaxes with the widest possible dynamic range and a sound balance that underpins surface brilliance with depth and atmosphere. The elegant Philharmonia string playing is beautifully caught. Menuhin finds a surprising amount to play here; besides the famous duet with the cello in the *Danse des cygnes*, which is beautifully done, he includes a ravishing account of the *Danse russe* as a postlude to the main selection. The cassette transfer (perhaps prudently) has a slightly more limited dynamic range, but otherwise sounds well; when it is heard away from the disc there is no really striking reduction of contrast.

The DG disc offers some fifty minutes from the complete Ozawa Boston set. The sophistication of both playing and recording is impressive, and the final climax expands magnificently; but overall this has less individuality than the Previn and Menuhin/Kurtz alternatives.

At medium price the Monteux selection might well be considered. The recording lacks the last degree of brilliance, but it is well balanced, and in the finale, which Monteux takes broadly and grandly, the weight of the sound makes a strong impact. The LSO playing is of good quality. The Sequenza reissue brings a new high-level tape transfer, with lively sound to match the disc closely.

The selection by Jean Morel and the Orchestra of the Royal Opera House, Covent Garden, was originally issued in the earliest days of stereo by RCA, although recorded by Decca. On Contour it emerges as a vivid and enjoyable disc with sound that is slightly dry but not too dated. The scale of the performance suggests the orchestral pit rather than the concert hall, but the intimacy of the *Waltz*, for instance, brings an added freshness. There is some very sensitive woodwind playing, especially by the oboe. With plenty of vitality throughout this is worth considering, though the Kurtz CfP version is even more attractive.

Symphonies Nos. 1–6.
*** DG 2740 219 (6)/*3378 084* (5). Berlin PO, Karajan.

Symphonies Nos. 1–6; Manfred symphony.
(M) *** Ph. 6768 267 (7). Concg. O, Haitink.

Symphonies Nos. 1–6; Manfred symphony; Romeo and Juliet (fantasy overture).
(M) *** HMV SLS 154530-3 (7). Philh. or New Philh. O, Muti.

Having recorded the last three Tchaikovsky symphonies three times over in little more than ten years, Karajan finally turned to the early symphonies; and there, displaying the same superlative refined qualities, he produced performances equally illuminating. It is typical that, though the opening *Allegro tranquillo* of the first movement of No. 1 is taken fast, there is no feeling of breathlessness, as there usually is: it is genuinely *tranquillo*, though the rhythmic bite of the syncopated passages, so important in these early symphonies, could hardly be sharper. The high polish may give a hint of the ballroom to some of the dance movements, with the folk element underplayed, but no finer set of symphonies has yet been recorded; it is commandingly consistent and vivid in sound, though (in the last three symphonies especially) it is not always richly resonant in the lower range. The tape transfers are of comparable sophistication. Because of the degree of dryness in the bass, the three later works are extremely clear and vivid. In the earlier symphonies the slight recession of the orchestral image (particularly in gentle woodwind solos) is a slight drawback. Nos. 1 and 4 are both complete on a single side each, back to back; all the others have a separate cassette. No. 5 includes the bonus of *Marche slave* (as on the separate issue), but this is not mentioned on the label or in the notes.

Haitink's complete Tchaikovsky cycle includes *Manfred* – and a very good *Manfred* it is too. Moreover the set is in the medium-price range, considerably cheaper than Karajan's. Haitink's readings are satisfyingly consistent and they have genuine symphonic strength. They are well-groomed and finely poised, and although they are only rarely incandescent and not all of them make the spine tingle, Haitink's avoidance of self-indulgence and overtly emotional responses is more than compensated for by his balance of concentration and freshness. Haitink's special advantage (alongside the superb playing of the Concertgebouw Orchestra) is the splendid Philips recording, rich, refined in detail and bringing nobility of sound to the later works especially.

Muti recorded this Tchaikovsky cycle over a period of six years, during which the New Philharmonia, thanks to its principal conductor, was restored not only to its original name but to its earlier quality. It is a measure of Muti's success that even the first-recorded of the series, *No. 1*, brings a refined, persuasive performance, though in virtuosity it cannot quite compare with the last-recorded, *Manfred*. Muti's view is generally brisk and dramatically direct, though never lacking in feeling. The EMI sound is reasonably consistent, full and rounded if at times a little close.

Symphony No. 1 in G min. (*Winter Daydreams*), *Op. 13.*
*** DG 2531/*3301* 284 [id.]. Berlin PO, Karajan.
(M) *** EMI Em. EMX/*TC-EMX* 41 2061-1/*4*. LPO, Rostropovich.
*** Ph. 9500 777/*7300 851* [id.]. Concg. O, Haitink.

Little more need be said about Karajan's marvellous performance of the *Winter Daydreams symphony*. It is not quite so richly recorded as Haitink's version, but in all other respects it is outstanding, almost certainly the finest performance of this work ever committed to disc. Karajan's approach is direct, yet his affection is obvious. The playing of the Berlin Philharmonic Orchestra is little short of miraculous, and because of Karajan's warmth the refinement of detail is never clinical. The fugato in the last movement is given classical strength (there is never any sign that Karajan sees the first three symphonies as immature), and the peroration has regality and splendour. The sound is excellent, brilliant and with a wide dynamic range. The cassette transfer is one of DG's best: there is little appreciable difference between tape and disc.

Rostropovich recorded his Tchaikovsky cycle concurrently with live performances at the Royal Festival Hall and though at certain points (as in some of the fugato development sections) the ensemble could be a shade crisper, the performances have not only passion and electricity but great charm and refinement too. The performance of the *First* is characteristically persuasive in its moulding of phrase and spring of rhythm, with speeds a degree more spacious than usual. The slow movement brings a glorious horn solo on the reprise, sensuous but unexaggerated, and the finale is exciting without sounding too rhetorical. The recording is admirably full and clear. At mid-price this is highly recommendable.

Haitink gives a most refreshing performance of Tchaikovsky's earliest sysmphony. Choice of speeds – very difficult in this work – always seems apt and natural, and it is typical of Haitink's flair for balance that the big horn solo which comes at the culmination of the slow movement has nothing of vulgarity in it. At the opening of this movement he is more atmospheric than Karajan, and is helped by the warm acoustic of the Concertgebouw. He does not find all the charm inherent in the scherzo, and at the close of the finale the rhetoric of the coda is negotiated with less than ideal aplomb (Karajan is more extrovert here, to good advantage); but overall this is very satisfying, and anyone following Haitink's series will not be disappointed. The cassette is of excellent quality, matching the disc closely.

Symphony No. 2 in C min. (*Little Russian*), *Op. 17* (original 1872 score).

*** Chan. Dig. **CHAN 8304**; ABRD/ *ABTD* 1071 [id.]. LSO, Simon.

This is the first recording of Tchaikovsky's original score of the *Little Russian symphony* and probably the first performance outside Russia. It was prompted (like the earlier Chandos set of rare Tchaikovsky – see above) by the enterprising enthusiasm of Edward Johnson, who provides an admirably exhaustive sleeve-note (included with the cassette also). Although the 1872 score gained considerable success at its early performances, it gave the composer immediate and serious doubts principally about the construction of the first movement and the length of the finale. Fortunately the work had only been published in piano-duet form, and so in 1879 Tchaikovsky retrieved the score and immediately set to work to rewrite the first movement. He left the *Andante* virtually unaltered, touched up the scoring of the scherzo, made minor excisions and added repeats, and made a huge cut of 150 bars (some two minutes of music) in the finale. He then destroyed the original. (The present performance has been possible because of the surviving orchestral parts.) There can be no question that Tchaikovsky was right. The reworked first movement is immensely superior to the first attempt and the finale – delightful though it is – seems quite long enough shorn of the extra bars. However, to hear the composer's first thoughts (as with the original version of *Romeo and Juliet*) is fascinating and this is an indispensable recording for all Tchaikovskians.

The original first movement begins and ends much like the familiar version with its andante horn theme based on the folksong, *Down by Mother Volga*, but the first subject of the exposition offers unfamiliar lyrical material. The working out is more self-consciously 'symphonic', and clearly there is more rhetoric than development. There are some exciting moments of course, but in the end one remains unconvinced. Geoffrey Simon secures a committed response from the LSO, there is some splendid string playing in the finale, and the brass is bitingly sonorous as recorded. Indeed the sound is first-class and the chrome tape is very impressive, too, in its range and impact. The compact disc is striking in its inner orchestral detail and freshness, and although the lower range is without the resonant richness of some CDs, the balance remains very good and the bass drum is telling without swamping the fortissimos.

Symphony No. 2 in C min. (*Little Russian*), *Op. 17*.

*** DG 2531/*3301* 285 [id.]. Berlin PO, Karajan.

(M) *** EMI Em. EMX/*TC-EMX* 41 2062-1/*4*. LPO, Rostropovich – *Romeo and Juliet*.***

*** HMV ASD/*TC-ASD* 3488 [Ang. RL/*4RL* 32047]. Philh. O, Muti – *Romeo and Juliet*.***

(M) **(*) DG Acc. 2543/*3342* 113. New Philh. O, Abbado – *Romeo and Juliet*.***

Karajan's performance of the *Little Russian symphony* is superbly played. Everything is in perfect scale; the tempo for the engaging *Andante* is very nicely judged, and the outer movements have plenty of drama and fire. The articulation in the finale is a joy, and the sound balance is excellent. The cassette is perhaps marginally less refined than the disc, but the difference is slight and the finale sounds especially well.

The first separate issue of Rostropovich's 1977 EMI recording with the LPO comes paired with an equally outstanding and individual performance of *Romeo and Juliet*. In the *Symphony* Rostropovich offers beautifully paced readings of all four movements, relaxed but rhythmically resilient, easily idiomatic. There is charm here as well as excitement and the LPO wind playing in the *Andantino* is most beguiling while the variations of the finale show a similar concern for colour and detail. The recording is full, vivid and spacious. At mid-price this leads the field for this particular coupling.

Muti's account is characteristically fresh. His warmth brings an agreeable geniality to the first movement, which does not lack excitement but is not too aggressively pointed. His *Andantino* takes Tchaikovsky's *marziale* rather literally, but its precise rhythmic beat has character without heaviness. Perhaps here, as in the finale, there is less than the full degree of charm, but the scherzo is vivacious and clean. In the finale Muti's degree of relaxed affection produces much colour, and the movement has strong character, even if the performance lacks a strong forward thrust of excitement. The recording is rich and full. The cassette transfer is successful until the finale, where the bass drum gives problems and the textures are muddied. On disc, however, coupled with a quite outstanding version of *Romeo and Juliet*, this is very competitive.

Abbado's first movement concentrates on refinement of detail and is a shade too deadpan. The *Andantino* is very nicely done and beautifully tapered off at the end, while the scherzo is admirably crisp and sparkling. The finale is quite superb, with splendid colour and thrust and a spectacular stroke on the gong before the exhilarating coda. Brilliant recording and an immaculate cassette transfer, capturing the percussive effects with aplomb.

Symphony No. 3 in D (*Polish*), *Op. 29*.

*** DG 2531/*3301* 286 [id.]. Berlin PO, Karajan.

(M) *** EMI Em. EMX/*TC-EMX* 41 2063-1/*4*. LPO, Rostropovich.

*** Ph. 9500 776/*7300 850* [id.]. Concg. O, Haitink.

(M) **(*) Decca Jub. JB 22. VPO, Maazel.

A clear first choice for Tchaikovsky's *Polish symphony* is difficult to determine. Karajan, Rostropovich and Haitink each have their own virtues. The playing of the Berlin orchestra is wonderfully polished and committed; Karajan's first movement is full of flair and in the central movements he is ever conscious of the variety of Tchaikovsky's colouring. He even finds an affinity with Brahms in the second movement, and yet the climax of the *Andante* is full of Tchaikovskian fervour. In the finale the articulation of the *Polacca* is both vigorous and joyful, and it brings a sense of symphonic strength, often lacking in other versions. The recording is bold, brilliant and clear, and the cassette transfer is strikingly successful, quite the equal of the LP.

At mid-price on EMI Eminence, Rostropovich's LPO account makes an outstanding bargain, with a swaggering first-movement allegro and affectionately detailed ballet overtones in the second. The central slow movement is given a songful beauty, and even the finale with its patriotic-sounding main theme avoids vulgarity, finding splendour and a sense of fulfilment. Excellent LPO playing, without quite the polish of the Berlin Philharmonic, but vividly bringing out the score's delectable colouring. The recording, full and spacious, is well up to the high standard of this series. This is in many ways the most attractive of Rostropovich's integral set.

Haitink's performance, beautifully played and warmly and resonantly recorded, has a disarmingly fresh directness of approach, bringing out the score's affinities with the ballet, which the composer saw no reason to be ashamed of. The slow movement is not as passionate as in some readings, but the delicacy of the scherzo is capped by a finale in which the rhetoric is minimized. Here the fugato has an attractive neoclassical feeling, and the peroration achieves remarkable dignity. Karajan is more symphonic, but throughout Haitink's version one senses that the Concertgebouw players are revelling in these consistently appealing textures. The cassette is most successful; transferred at a high level it seems almost to have greater range and brightness than the disc, an unusual occurrence for Philips.

Maazel's approach is direct and admirably fresh. The orchestral detail emerges with glowing colours, particularly as the Decca sound is so vivid. The outer movements have a fine thrust (the main theme, on the strings, of the first is articulated with infectious vigour). This is good value at mid-price.

Symphonies Nos. 4–6.

(M) *** DG Priv. 2726 040 (2) [2535/*3335* 235/7]. Leningrad PO, Mravinsky.

**(*) DG 2740 248 (3). LSO, Boehm.

Symphonies Nos. 4–6; Manfred symphony.

*** Decca D 249 D 4/*K 249 K 44* (4). Philh. O, Ashkenazy.

Had Ashkenazy started making his Tchaikovsky recordings in digital sound, no doubt Decca would have got him to record a complete cycle. This collection of three outstanding versions of the last symphonies is most attractive, and the inclusion of his superb, inspirational account of *Manfred* sets the seal on his achievement. The special quality which Ashkenazy conveys is spontaneity. The freshness of his approach, his natural feeling for lyricism on the one hand and drama on the other, is consistently compelling, even if at times the ensemble is not immaculate. Digital or not, the sound is outstanding.

The classic Mravinsky performances were discussed in an earlier edition when they were available on three Privilege records. They have now been transferred on to four sides without any loss of quality – and a considerable gain in economy. Strongly recommended, as was the two-record set of Mravinsky's earlier recordings of the *Fifth* and *Sixth* made in mono in the mid-1950s together with Sanderling's account of the *Fourth* (DG 2700 114). These were, if anything, even more exciting and sound marvellously vivid. Unfortunately they have been withdrawn as we go to press.

It was one of the more surprising developments in Boehm's career that his close association with the LSO led him to record Tchaikovsky. His readings were often idiosyncratic, translating Tchaikovsky's Russianness into the central European tradition. One might argue that they reveal more about Boehm than they do about Tchaikovsky, but with a conductor of such stature there is value in that. The recording – digital in No. 5 – is outstanding.

Symphony No. 4 in F min., Op. 36.

(M) ❀ *** DG Sig. 2543/*3343* 522 [2530 651]. VPO, Abbado.

(M) *** Ph. Seq. 6527/*7311* 191 [9500 622/*7300 738*]. Concg. O, Haitink.

*** DG 2530/*3300* 883 [id.]. Berlin PO, Karajan.

*** Decca SXL/*KSXC* 6919 [Lon. CS/*5-*7144]. Philh. O, Ashkenazy.

*** HMV ASD 3816 [Ang. S 37624]. Philh. O, Muti.

(B) *** Con. CC/*CCT* 7595 [6570/*7310* 163]. LSO, Markevitch.

(M) **(*) EMI Em. EMX/*TC-EMX* 41 2064-1/*4*. LPO, Rostropovich.

(*) Telarc Dig. **CD 80047; DG 10047 [id.]. Cleveland O, Maazel.

(M)**(*) DG 2542/*3342* 152. Berlin PO, Karajan.

Ph. Dig. **400 090-2; 9500/*7300* 972 [id.]. Pittsburgh SO, Previn.

(M) *(*) CBS 60153/*40-* [M/*MT* 33886]. NYPO, Bernstein.

(B) *(*) CfP Dig. 41 4414-1/*4*. LPO, Macal.

Abbado's recording of the *Fourth Symphony* on DG's mid-priced Signature label sweeps the board. From the riveting opening fanfare, the drama and weight of the reading are apparent. The beginning of the *Allegro*, with its very Russian melancholy, brings an elegiac quality of string tone, yet this swiftly erupts into a spontaneously passionate forte. The second subject is beautifully prepared and delicately phrased, the counter-melody graceful in the strings. Then comes a superbly graduated climax from the fragile piannissimo of magically rocking strings to the strong culmination where the horns blaze out with their big tune, à 4. The second movement is as near perfection as one could hope for, with its gentle oboe solo, and the contrasting vigour of the dotted secondary section in the strings, which takes flight gloriously. At the end of the movement the reprise of the main theme is deliciously decorated. The scherzo is witty, the trio superbly articulated by wind and brass alike, and the finale too has sparkle as well as power. Other performances (Szell's, for instance, now deleted) may have more weight, but not more of the spirit of the Russian peasant dance which was the source of Tchaikovsky's inspiration. Brilliant, extremely vivid sound makes this issue indispensable, whether on LP or the excellent equivalent chrome tape, which if anything is marginally fuller than the disc, without loss of range or detail.

Haitink's splendid Concertgebouw version is almost equally distinctive in its way. This too has been reissued at mid-price, the sound richer than that offered by the DG engineers for Abbado, and now accompanied by a first-class cassette which virtually matches the disc in brilliance and amplitude. Haitink steers a satisfying middle course in his approach to this charismatic symphony, and, supported by orchestral playing and sound of great power and refinement, his reading of all four movements makes an indelible impression. Compared with an earlier, somewhat under-characterized account that Haitink recorded with the same orchestra, this one has more rhythmic flair, with the different sections of the first movement beautifully drawn. Speeds are never hectic, but particularly in the finale the excitement of this version is second to none, with exceptionally wide groove-spacing allowing sound of outstanding range and richness.

Karajan's current version is undoubtedly more compelling than his previous recordings (one for DG and two for EMI). After a dramatically robust fanfare at the start of the first movement, the theme of the *Allegro* steals in silkily, and although its atmosphere has a tinge of melancholy, there is a hint of suaveness also. But any doubts are swept away by the vitality and drive of the performance as a whole, and the beauty of the wind playing at the opening and close of the slow movement can give nothing but pleasure. The finale has tremendous force to sweep the listener along, and the wide dynamic range of the recording makes the most dramatic effect. The tape transfer is extremely vivid, but there is some slight recession of the orchestral image in pianissimos.

Ashkenazy's opening fanfare has plenty of edge, and while his reading of the first movement is rhythmically straightforward, the nervous tension is held consistently, though the dynamic ebb and flow of climax and repose is handled in the most naturally spontaneous way. The two central movements combine ardour with delicacy and wit, and the ferociously brilliant finale confirms the Russian quality of the interpretation, projected by sound that matches weight with brilliance and yet is both luminous and sumptuous in Decca's best manner. The cassette has a comparable breadth and impact, even though in the finale there is a slightly ill-focused moment contributed by the bass drum.

With speeds on the brisk side in all four movements, Muti's is an urgent performance. The very opening of the symphony, with its fanfare motto, has no pomp whatever in it, for urgency reigns even there. With fine articulation from the Philharmonia players the fast speeds rarely if ever make for breathlessness, and though charm is not a quality one finds here, the directness is always refreshing, and the recording quality is both forward and rich. The high-level tape transfer is matchingly vivid and full-blooded, with only a fractional hint of strain at climaxes. The finale, as on disc, is highly spectacular.

Markevitch's version is as exciting as almost any available. It has a superbly thrusting first-movement *Allegro*, and although Markevitch allows himself a lilting degree of rubato in the rocking crescendo passage, it is the forward momentum of the performance that captures the listener. At the climax of the development Markevitch produces an exhilarating stringendo and then relaxes for the reprise of the second subject. The close of the movement, like the coda of the finale, brings the highest degree of tension and a real sense of triumph. The central movements are no less striking, with a vigorous dotted climax to the *Andantino* contrasting with the repose of the outer sections, and a fast scherzo where the duple rhythms of the woodwind trio are emphasized to bring out the peasant imagery. The recording is admirably full-blooded, and its spectacle and wide range have transferred to tape without any loss of impact and detail compared with the disc. A splendid bargain.

Rostropovich's reading of the outer movements is broadly spacious, and this gives the first movement a certain epic quality, particularly as the climaxes achieve the highest level of tension. Indeed the electricity of this performance is never in doubt. The slow movement is eloquent, with beautiful orchestral playing; the reprise of the main theme on the strings, deliciously decorated by the woodwind, is memorable. The scherzo is fast, with the balalaika effect well conveyed and a strongly characterized central section. The rich, full-blooded recording is up to the high standard of the series, and while the basic tempi of the outer movements may not suit all listeners, there is no doubt that the conductor's inspirational approach brings its own kind of spontaneity.

Maazel's Telarc Cleveland disc was one of the first digital records of any Tchaikovsky symphony and established a reputation for sound of spectacular depth and brilliance, within a natural overall balance. This is impressively borne out by the first big orchestral fortissimo chord at the end of the relatively mellow opening fanfare. The reading itself is unexpectedly low-powered, the first-movement *Allegro* lightly articulated so that the climaxes make a strong dramatic contrast, with the Cleveland brass providing a bright cutting edge. The slow movement, with a plaintive oboe solo, is distinctly appealing, but the finale seeks amplitude and breadth rather than extrovert excitement. Here the full, resonant recording makes the strongest possible impact. The compact disc is even more impressive in its amplitude and range.

Karajan's earlier DG recording from the late 1960s takes rather longer to generate its full tension in the opening movement. The slow movement makes amends and the central climax really takes wing, to be followed by a beautifully shaped closing section, Karajan here at his most effective. The scherzo goes well, but the central wind interlude is rather slow and heavy. The finale is superb, taken at a fantastic pace, and tremendously exciting in a purely physical way. The orchestral playing is unbelievably accurate at this tempo. The recording still sounds remarkably well, although there is a degree of fierceness at climaxes, less noticeable on cassette, which has slightly more body than the disc and a smoother upper range.

Previn's view is distinctive. His preference in Tchaikovsky is for directness and no mannerism, but with unusually slow speeds for the first three movements this produces little excitement and some lack of charm. The finale makes up for that with a very fast tempo, which is a formidable challenge for the Pittsburgh orchestra, here distinguishing itself with fine playing, well recorded. The chrome cassette, however, is transferred at a modest level and is in no way strikingly spectacular, even in the finale.

Bernstein's reading is highly self-indulgent, the first movement expansive but very mannered, and the pacing generally rather eccentric. There is fine playing here, but this account is essentially unconvincing.

Macal's digital CfP version, too, is disappointing, failing to repeat the success this conductor had with the same orchestra in Dvořák's *New World symphony*. After the fanfare the opening of the first movement fails to generate much tension, and later the rocking violin phrase with which Tchaikovsky builds the central climax is given a mannered tenuto which seems to have no discernible purpose. When the strings enter in the slow movement (after the oboe solo) their response is listless and the music drags. While the scherzo and finale go quite well, there is nothing distinctive here either. This cannot compare with Markevitch in the bargain range. He also may permit himself certain manipulations of the forward thrust, but still achieves an exhilarating spontaneity which eludes Macal. The CfP recording is bright and clear, but the upper strings lack something in bloom. The cassette, in contrast, has a restricted upper range and relatively little bite.

Symphony No. 5 in E min., Op. 64.
*** Decca SXL/*KSXC* 6884 [Lon. CS/*5*-7107]. Philh. O, Ashkenazy.
*** DG 2530/*3300* 699 [id.]. Berlin PO, Karajan.
*** HMV ASD/*TC-ASD* 3717 [Ang. S 37625]. Philh. O, Muti.
(M) *** CBS 60154/*40*- [Odys. Y/*YT* 30670]. Cleveland O, Szell.
(M) *** DG Sig. 410 831-1/*4*. LSO, Abbado.
(M) **(*) EMI Em. EMX/*TC-EMX* 41 2065-1/*4*. LPO, Rostropovich.
**(*) DG Dig. 2532/*3302* 005 [id.]. LSO, Boehm.
(M) **(*) DG Acc. 2542/*3342* 108 [2535/*3335* 318]. Berlin PO, Karajan.
(M) **(*) Decca VIV/*KVIC* 39 [Lon. STS/*5*-15559]. New Philh. O, Stokowski.
** Decca Dig. **410 232-2**; SXDL/*KSXDC* 7533 [Lon. LDR/*5*- 71033]. VPO, Chailly.
** Nimbus Dig. 45 r.p.m. 45203. LPO, Bátiz.
** CBS Dig. **CD 36700** [IM/*IMT* 36700]. Cleveland O, Maazel.

Ashkenazy made his major recording début on the rostrum with Tchaikovsky's *Fifth*, and at a stroke produced a richly enjoyable performance, as distinguished as any available and one which throws new light on a familiar masterpiece. The qualities of lyrical fervour and warmth that he brings to his reading have an unmistakable Russian fire. Tempi are admirably chosen throughout, and the forward flow of the music in all four movements is as natural as it is spontaneous. The second subject of the first movement blossoms with a most appealing romanticism; the slow movement too has an affecting warmth, the sense of repose in the opening and closing sections making an admirable framework for the passionate central climaxes. The *Waltz*, light and lilting, acts like an intermezzo between the second movement and the red-blooded finale with its gloriously rich string and brass tone. The recording is one of Decca's very best, brilliant and warm and with splendid detail and bloom; and on tape the sound is no less beautiful. But the sophistication of the transfer has been achieved by a very subtle reduction of the dynamic range, which means that the loudest climaxes do not expand quite so spectacularly as on the disc. For many this will be a ready first choice, but the Karajan version is the more physically exciting, though it is not nearly as richly recorded as the Decca. In his hands the climax of the slow movement is grippingly intense, though he shows considerable romantic feeling too with an elegiac preparation for the horn solo at the opening. The *Waltz* has plenty of character and in the finale Karajan drives hard, creating an electrifying forward thrust. However, the sound is sometimes too dry (the massed violins at the climax of the slow movement lack body) although the recording has great projection and impact. The cassette is virtually indistinguishable from the disc and as a bonus adds Karajan's fine performance of *Marche slave*.

Muti underlines the symphonic strength of the first movement rather than immediate excitement. The approach is direct and unmannered but with no stiffness of phrasing. The *Waltz* may lack a little in charm, and certain passages perhaps let the tension relax too far, but the slow movement is beautifully controlled, with the second theme genuinely *con nobilita* when the violins first play it, and passion kept in hand for the second half of the movement. As for the finale, it presents a sharp contrast with its fast tempo and controlled excitement. The recording is warm and full in the EMI manner; the cassette matches the disc closely.

Szell's CBS performance is also very fine, and the only drawback is the somewhat dated CBS recording. However, it has a resonant bass and with a treble cut-back the string tone, if not ideal in the matter of body and richness, can be made to produce satisfactory results. The performance is even finer than Szell's *Fourth* for Decca (now deleted). Its sense of romantic urgency is finely judged, with a splendid surge and momentum in the outer movements. The style of the horn soloist in the *Andante* may not suit every taste, but in all other respects the orchestral playing is first-rate. The third movement is beautifully done and the finale is most satisfying. The cassette has not the upper range of the disc but it tempers the upper strings satisfactorily, without too much loss of bite.

Abbado's version is relatively lightweight but freshly rewarding. The performance is both sophisticated and sparkling. There is lyrical intensity and the outer movements have plenty of vigour; the finale is genuinely exciting yet with no sense of rhetoric. There are more powerful accounts available but none more spontaneously volatile. The recording is strikingly well balanced; it has resonant richness as well as bright clarity. If not as distinctive as Abbado's *Fourth*, this remains highly recommendable as an alternative approach to a many-faceted romantic masterpiece.

Slow tempi predominate in Rostropovich's reading, and some may find his pacing too deliberate in the outer movements. Yet the playing is fully characterized, as the opening clarinet's *chalumeau* readily demonstrates, and even in the very broad statement of the finale's principal tune the eloquence of the music-making is in no doubt. The slow movement creates the highest degree of tension at its hushed opening; later the entries of the motto theme are suitably portentous, but lack the sheer drama of some other versions. The full-blooded richness of the recording and the fine playing of the LPO consistently sustain the conductor's approach, but the idiosyncrasies of the reading mean that the record must be approached with some caution.

Boehm's account of the *Fifth* is distinguished from his other two late Tchaikovsky recordings with the LSO by its relative lack of idiosyncrasy – this reading is straighter and more direct than Boehm's accounts of Nos. 4 and 6 – and by the fine digital sound. Boehm's refusal to press the music ahead from his very steady basic pace in the slow movement may on repetition seem a little heavy, but like the others in the series this presents Tchaikovsky very much from the point of view of the central European tradition, and for that distinctive view, commitedly presented, it is most welcome.

Karajan's earlier (1967) Berlin Philharmonic recording (now reissued on Accolade) is finely played and well conceived. It is more self-conscious than the later version, but the reading certainly does not lack excitement and the recording sounds remarkably fresh. There is very little difference in sound between disc and tape: the former has a slightly brighter string timbre; the cassette has greater body and richness and offers a fine account of *Marche slave* as an appreciable bonus.

Stokowski's disc offers, besides a fine performance, one of the most spectacular of currently available recordings. But his concern with tonal grandeur has its drawbacks. He tends to languish rather than press forward, and although the tension is well maintained the speeds for the main allegros of the first and last movements are considered rather than breathless, and there is some sacrifice of vitality in consequence. Yet with a flick of the wrist, as it were, Stokowski can create some fine blazes of excitement, as in the coda of the opening movement, or the climax of the *Andante cantabile*, or the closing moments of the symphony. The vivid impact of every department of the orchestra too makes each point of Tchaikovsky's imaginative orchestration. There are a few small cuts (four bars, twice, in the first movement, two bars in the introduction to the finale, and a longer cut later), but the most noticeable effect, for anyone without a score, is that Stokowski dispenses with the pause before the final coda. There is a brilliant tape transfer not lacking fullness, but the sound needs a little taming on side two.

Chailly's is a relatively lightweight and somewhat idiosyncratic reading which gives the impression of inexperience in this repertoire. There are some attractive things here, notably the exhilarating tempo for the finale, but the reading does not make a very convincing whole. The VPO playing is not always immaculate, and the horn solo in the slow movement is not really distinguished. Yet the lyrical momentum of the performance is certainly enjoyable, and the Decca digital recording, which has considerable richness and brilliance, is very attractive. The cassette, one of Decca's first chrome transfers, is first-rate in every way. The compact disc improves the focus without losing the bloom.

Bátiz, a brilliant conductor of exotic Spanish and Spanish-American music, takes a surprisingly direct, even understated view of this passionate symphony. The result is attractive and the sound – transferred at 45 r.p.m. – is full and brilliant, but there are subtler, more refined accounts.

Though the reading remains strong and direct, Maazel's Cleveland version is more inflated, more aggressive, less fresh-sounding than his earlier Vienna version for Decca (now deleted). Cleveland virtuosity is impressive, but with aggressive digital recording the result is cold. The sound on CD is unimpressive, with poorly focused strings. Chailly's Decca version has far superior sound.

Symphonies Nos. 5–6 (*Pathétique*).
(M) *** HMV *TCC2-POR 54284*. Philh. O, Muti.
(B) **(*) DG Walkman *413 429-4*. LSO, VPO, Abbado.

Muti's separate issues of these two symphonies are discussed above and below. This double-length chrome tape in EMI's 'Portrait of the Artist' series allows each work to be heard uninterrupted. The transfers are both first-class, the wide dynamic range admirably caught, with the sound throughout vivid and well detailed. The finale of the *Fifth* makes a superb impact and the *Pathétique* is much clearer here than in its separate tape issue.

The Walkman chrome cassette couples Abbado's lightweight but refreshingly individual accounts of Tchaikovsky's two most popular symphonies, which are discussed in greater detail under their individual Signature issues, each of which costs more than this bargain-priced pairing.

Symphony No. 6 in B min. (*Pathétique*), *Op. 74*.
*** Decca **411 615-2**; SXL/*KSXC* 6941 [Lon. CS/*5*- 7170]. Philh. O, Ashkenazy.
*** DG 2530/*3300* 774 [id.]. Berlin PO, Karajan.
(M) *** DG Acc. 2542/*3342* 154 [2535/*3335* 341]. Berlin PO, Karajan.
*** Ph. 9500/*7300* 739 [id.]. Concg. O, Haitink.
*** HMV ASD/*TC-ASD* 3901 [Ang. SZ 37626]. Philh. O, Muti.
(M) *** EMI Em. EMX/*TC-EMX* 41 2066-1/*4*. LPO, Rostropovich.
(B) *** CfP CFP/*TC-CFP* 41 4462-1/*4*. Philh. O, Kletzki.
(M) **(*) HMV SXLP/*TC-SXLP* 30534 [Ang. RL/*4RL* 32068]. Philh. O, Karajan.
(M) **(*) CBS 60155/*40*- [M/*MT* 31833]. Phd. O, Ormandy.
** DG Dig. **400 029-2**; 2532/*3302* 013 [id.]. LAPO, Giulini.
(M) ** DG Sig. 2543/*3342* 501 [2530 350]. VPO, Abbado.
** Nimbus Dig. 45 r.p.m. 45201. LPO, Bátiz.
(M) ** Decca VIV/*KVIC* 58. LAPO, Mehta.
(B) * Con. CC/*CCT* 7573. RPO, Kord.
(B) * ASV ABM/*ZCABM* 753. Royal Liv. PO, Handley.

After an arresting account of the sombre introduction, the urgency with which Ashkenazy and his Philharmonia players attack the *Allegro* of the first movement of the *Pathétique* belies the composer's *non troppo* marking. The directness and intensity of the music-making are supported by remarkably crisp articulation, producing an electrifying forward thrust. The emergence of the beautiful second subject offers the more striking contrast, with Ashkenazy's characteristic lyrical ardour bringing a natural warmth to the great melody. As in his other Tchaikovsky records this whole performance is pervaded with freshness and spontaneity, through the balletic 5/4 movement, with its essentially Russian quality of melancholy, and the vigorous march/scherzo, rhythmically buoyant and joyful rather than relentlessly high-powered, as under Karajan. The finale combines passion with tenderness, and the total absence of expressive hysteria brings a more poignant culmination than usual. With superb Decca Kingsway Hall sound, this is among the finest *Pathétiques* ever recorded. The Philharmonia is on peak form, and although the Berlin Philharmonic playing under Karajan is even more polished, the Decca version gains by its greater amplitude, warmth and colour, with the rich cassette transfer losing only a very little of the disc's sparkle at the top. The CD is digitally remastered, yet retains the analogue atmosphere while detail is clarified and intensified.

Karajan obviously has a special affinity with Tchaikovsky's *Pathétique symphony* (and – remembering Furtwängler's famous 78 r.p.m. set – so has the Berlin Philharmonic Orchestra). He has recorded it four times in stereo. For many the most recent (1977) version is the finest. With a brilliant recording of the widest dynamic range (though not an especially sumptuous lower resonance) the impact of Tchaikovsky's climaxes – notably those of the first and third movements – is tremendously powerful, the articulation of the Berlin players precise and strong. The climactic peaks are created with fierce bursts of tension, and the effect on the listener is almost overwhelming. In the 5/4 movement Karajan allows the middle section to increase the elegiac feeling, against a background of remorseless but distanced drum-beats, like a tolling bell. The finale has great passion and eloquence, with two gentle sforzandos at the very end to emphasize the finality of the closing phrase.

Turning back to Karajan's 1964 record (now reissued on Accolade), one finds a reading that is no less exciting but more consistent in its overall control of tension. For some ears this is the finest version of all, the steady tempo of the *Moderato mosso* in the first movement leading the ear on as the conductor builds towards the movement's climax with a steady emotional thrust. At the climactic point the deeply committed playing creates a quality of expressive fervour to send shivers down the spine, with a noble resolution from the Berlin brass. The sound has more bloom than in the later version (especially on cassette), and this brings a lighter, elegant quality to the 5/4 movement. The march/scherzo has an exhilaratingly consistent forward momentum, and with demonic playing from the Berlin orchestra, wonderfully sharp in ensemble, the aggressive force of the climaxes communicates the greatest physical excitement. Some listeners may find the effect too brutal, but Karajan's consistency is carried through to the passionate last movement, concluded, as in the later version, with those gentle stabbing chordal emphases. It is overall an engulfing experience, with no less impact on cassette than on disc.

Whether interpretatively or in execution, it would be hard to distinguish between Haitink's later reading here and his splendid earlier account. Their confident strength, natural expressiveness allied to a degree of restraint, make them both most satisfying for repeated listening on the gramophone. Where the second version gains is in the fullness and warmth of the recorded sound, which makes this a satisfying culmination for an outstanding series. On cassette the sound balance is impressively full and wide-ranging on side one, but on side two the level drops, the climax of the march/scherzo lacks brilliance, and the bass focus is not consistently clean.

Muti adopts characteristically fast tempi, yet the result is fresh and youthful, not over-hectic. The lyrical second subject, flowing faster than usual, has easy expressiveness without a hint of mannerism, and the 5/4 movement, also at a speed faster than usual, is most persuasive. The march for all its urgency never sounds brutal, and though the recording does not quite match the fine fullness which marks the others in Muti's series, it hardly detracts from a most refreshing reading. The cassette matches the disc's body and wide dynamics, but is not as clearly defined at pianissimo levels. The third-movement climax expands magnificently.

Of the Rostropovich readings of the three last Tchaikovsky symphonies the *Pathétique* can be recommended virtually without reservation. Like the others it is a personal view, but its eloquence is direct and its specially Russian lyric fervour is highly compelling. The outer movements have strength and nobility, and the finale balances passionate melancholy with restraint. The march/scherzo is perhaps less exhilarating than in some other versions, but it readily takes its place within the overall conception. The recording is splendidly full-blooded.

Kletzki's 1960 Philharmonia recording has consistently held its place near the top of the list and as a bargain version it is unbeatable. It has been remastered for this CfP reissue and the bloom has been restored to the strings; indeed the sound is remarkably good, vivid, well defined and impressively balanced. It is an outstanding performance which has stood the test of time. The first movement is impetuous but convincing. Kletzki's broadening of tempo at the reprise of the march is effective because the orchestral playing has a supporting power and breadth. This comes after a 5/4 movement which achieves a nicely balanced elegiac feeling. The deeply felt closing movement makes a powerful impact.

Karajan's first stereo recording of the *Pathétique* was made for EMI in 1959, with the Philharmonia Orchestra in splendid form and the Kingsway Hall providing the most congenial balance, astonishingly full for a record made nearly a quarter of a century ago. This adds a certain character to the orchestral sound, so that the 5/4 movement is noticeably glowing, with a relaxed lyricism. Broadly speaking this reading shows itself as a chrysalis for the later versions. It is less forceful – the second subject of the first movement is unmoulded and has a natural radiant freshness – and the first-movement climax has less fervour (though it is by no means uninvolving). The third movement is much more spaciously conceived, the scherzo skittishly pointed, the march climax grandiloquent rather then electrifying. The finale too is less remorseless in feeling, with surges of rubato at the first big climax and an elegiac close, the tension allowed to drain away without those stabbing emphases used on both the DG versions. The cassette transfer is strikingly vivid and clear, matching the disc in every way.

Ormandy's version dates from 1968. It is a performance of impressive dignity, full of imaginative touches. The 5/4 movement and the scherzo are particularly successful, and while the orchestra plays with considerable passion in the outer movements there is an element of restraint too which prevents any feeling of hysteria. The sound has a slight tendency to harshness, but has both weight and brilliance. Disc and tape sound very much the same.

Giulini's digital *Pathétique* is curiously lightweight, the mood set with the almost *scherzando* quality of the opening *Allegro*. The 5/4 movement is relatively unlilting, and though the march is impressive, it is no match for the Karajan or Ashkenazy versions. The finale does not lack eloquence, but Giulini's Philharmonia version of two decades earlier had more individuality than this. The digital recording is impressive if slightly dry, with little difference between disc and cassette. The compact disc tends to emphasize rather than disguise the recording's faults, and especially the close balance.

Abbado's account, like his performance of the *Fifth*, is also relatively lightweight. He provides a strong impulse throughout, and the second subject of the first movement sounds remarkably fresh, with radiant sounds from the strings. The climax, however, is slightly underpowered, and the finale too is restrained. The third movement is essentially a scherzo, the march-rhythms never becoming weighty and pontifical. This has many attractions for those who prefer a reading that is not too intense, and the slightly dry recording matches Abbado's conception, clean and clear in sound, rather than ripe.

Bátiz's reading – in very full-ranging digital sound transferred at 45 r.p.m. – is attractively fresh and direct with the great second subject melody the more telling for being understated and transitions just a little perfunctory. The brass is set rather too far forward in the third-movement march, but otherwise the sound is splendid.

Mehta's version comes from his complete set of 1978. The first movement is very successful, exciting, with a balancing tenderness for the second subject, but the 5/4 movement is entirely lacking in charm, driven on relentlessly. The scherzo is well paced and sparkling and the finale, direct rather than subtle, makes a strong impression. The recording is of high quality.

The recordings by Kord (Decca-sourced) and Handley also offer good sound, but the performances are routine ones and in a very competitive field these versions fail to register.

Variations on a rococo theme for cello and orchestra, Op. 33.

*** DG 139 044/*923 098* [id.]. Rostropovich, Berlin PO, Karajan – DVOŘÁK: *Concerto.****

(B) *** CfP CFP/*TC-CFP* 41 4468-1/*4*. Robert Cohen, LPO, Macal – DVOŘÁK: *Concerto.****

Variations on a rococo theme; Pezzo capriccioso, Op. 62.

(M) *** HMV Green. ESD/*TC-ESD* 107762-1/*4* [Ara. 8038/*9038*]. Tortelier, Northern Sinf., Yan Tortelier – SAINT-SAËNS: *Allegro apassionato* etc.***

*** Decca SXL/*KSXC* 6965 [Lon. CS/*5*-7195]. Harrell, Cleveland O, Maazel – ELGAR: *Concerto.****

No grumbles about Rostropovich's performance. He plays as if this were one of the greatest works for the cello, and he receives glowing support from Karajan and the Berlin Philharmonic. The *Rococo variations* is a delightful work, and it has never sounded finer than it does here. There is a good tape too.

A finely-wrought account from Tortelier *père*, accompanied by the Northern Sinfonia under Tortelier *fils*. This is very enjoyable (if perhaps not quite so distinguished as Rostropovich), and it is certainly recommendable if the Saint-Saëns coupling is suitable.

An excellent bargain version from Robert Cohen. He tends to avoid pronounced rubato, yet the result is warmly expressive as well as strong. First-class recording.

An assured, vividly characterized set of *Variations* from Lynn Harrell, with plenty of matching colour from the Cleveland woodwind. Harrell begins a little briskly, but there is no lack of poise here. Expressive feeling and sparkle are nicely matched, as shown by the elegant account of the *Andante* (Variation 6) which acts as an interlude before the exhilarating finale. The recording is bright and colourful, the cellist given a spotlight, but there is no lack of atmosphere and resonance. Some might prefer the cassette to the disc (it is slightly smoother on top).

CHAMBER MUSIC

Piano trio in A min., Op. 50.

**(*) HMV ASD 4036 [Ang. SZ 37678]. Ashkenazy, Perlman, Harrell.

**(*) Erato Dig. NUM 75036. Amoyal, Lodéon, Rogé.

** Chan. Dig. **CHAN 8348**; ABRD/*ABTD* 1049 [id.]. Borodin Trio.

Ashkenazy, Perlman and Harrell have regularly joined up to play this work at international recitals, so a recording was eagerly anticipated. Alas, the power and spontaneity of the concert hall are not consistently caught here. The dominating keyboard role of the first movement can so easily sound rhetorical rather than gripping and commanding; and this performance does not avoid that fault, though it is not without power. The *Variations* which form the second half of the work are much more successful, with engaging characterization and a good deal of electricity in the closing pages. The recording is forward, vivid and truthful, but a little more atmosphere is suitable for such an orchestrally conceived work. A very near miss.

Unlike the Borodin Trio, who make cuts, the French team give the *Trio* in its entirety. Theirs is an eloquent performance and finds Pierre Amoyal in impressive form. The same must be said of Pascal Rogé whose account of the piano part is hardly less brilliant and sensitive than that of Ashkenazy on HMV. The EMI recording is richer and has more space round the three instruments, but artistically the French team are not inferior.

The alternative version from Chandos is less distinguished. The clear digital recording serves to spotlight the string sounds, which are less polished and less rich than on the HMV record. The *Variations* have spontaneity and are not without charm, but the first movement is less convincing. The cassette transfer is lively, marginally less clean than the disc.

Nutcracker: suite (arr. for 2 pianos).

** DG Dig. 410 616-1/*4* [id.]. Argerich, Economou – RACHMANINOV: *Symphonic dances.***

Nicolas Economou is a Cypriot pianist and composer born in 1953 who now lives in Munich. His arrangement of the *Nutcracker suite* for two pianos works well though it does not banish memories of the transcription made by Mikhail Pletnyev, the 1978 Tchaikovsky Competition prizewinner, and recorded by him on HMV (now deleted) – dazzlingly brilliant and wonderfully imaginative playing that made one forget this music could ever exist in any other form. This is very good indeed but not quite so breathtaking – nor, for that matter, quite as well recorded. Nonetheless this playing is of a very high order and will give corresponding pleasure. There is a good chrome cassette, although the level of transfer is slightly lower than for the coupling.

The Seasons, Op. 37a.

(*) Chan. Dig. **CHAN 8349; ABRD/-*ABTD* 1070 [id.]. Artymiw.

Tchaikovsky's twelve *Seasons* (they would have better been called months) were written to a regular deadline for publication in the St Petersburg music magazine, *Nuvellist*. It is the gentler, lyrical pieces that are the most effective and Lydia Artymiw plays them thoughtfully and poetically. Elsewhere she sometimes has a tendency marginally to over-characterize the music, which is slight, but she also notices and brings out the orchestral feeling in fuller-sustained textures, and she is rhythmically alert and sparkling. The digital recording is truthful and the chrome tape too has excellent body and presence. A worthwhile issue.

VOCAL MUSIC

Songs: *Accept just once; Amid the din of the ball; As on hot ashes; As they kept saying 'Fool!'; Don Juan's Serenade; Don't leave me; Heroism; I bless you, forests; I never talked to her; The love of one dead; My genius; New Greek song; Not a sound; Oh if; On golden fields; A tear quivers.*
**(*) Ph. Dig. 6514/*7337* 116 [id.]. Fischer-Dieskau, Reimann.

Don Juan's Serenade is well-known, but too little of the rest of this impressive selection is. Fischer-Dieskau applies his German-based Lieder style to these often lightweight songs, and the result is compellingly intense if not always idiomatic. First-rate recording. There is a good cassette, though a higher transfer level would have brought more presence.

Songs: *Amid the din of the ball; Behind the window; Do not ask; Do not believe it, my friend; First tryst; If I'd only known; It was in the early spring; I was a little blade of grass; My guiding spirit; My little garden; Oh do sing that song; Rondel; Serenade; Take my heart away; To forget so soon; We sat together; Why did I dream of you; Zemfira's song.*
*** Decca Dig. SXDL 7606. Söderström, Ashkenazy.

This second record in the Söderström/Ashkenazy series brings many delights, including *Zemfira's song* – where a young girl repulses the attentions of an old man – and the spoken exchanges briefly present Ashkenazy as actor. *I was a little blade of grass* and *At the ball* are among Tchaikovsky's finest songs, but even the salon-type inspirations are enchanting as sung by this artist, with Ashkenazy an ever-imaginative partner. Excellent recording.

Songs: *As o'er the burning ashes; Aurore; Cradle song; The cuckoo; Deception; Does the day reign; Evening; The fearful minute; Les Larmes; Last night; Mezza notte; The nightingale; None but the lonely heart; Poème d'Octobre; Simple words; Spring; The sun has set; Why.*
*** Decca SXL 6972. Söderström, Ashkenazy.

Söderström and Ashkenazy in following up the success of their Rachmaninov song series began their Tchaikovsky collection with this attractive collection, centring round the most famous song of all, *None but the lonely heart*. Söderström sings that with touching simplicity. Her natural unforced artistry, her ability to turn a phrase with the sort of magic one also associates with Ashkenazy, is refreshing in the many rare items too. First-rate recording with a fine bloom on it.

Liturgy of St John Chrysostom, Op. 41.
** HM HM 138/*40*. Svetoslav Obretenov Ch., Rouskov.

Tchaikovsky was not a strongly religious man but he was sufficiently attracted to the Russian liturgy to write this short work in 1878, drawing on traditional material as well as adding his own touches. The music contrasts serene sonorities with bursts of fervour and its character is well realized here, although the singing is not very polished and not always secure in intonation. Yet, with the help of the acoustic of the Alexander Nevsky Basilica in Sofia, the effect remains impressive, although the cassette – transferred at a low level because of the reverberation – has not the immediacy of the disc.

Eugene Onegin (opera) complete.
*** Decca SET 596-8/*K 57 K 32* [Lon. OSA 13112]. Kubiak, Weikl, Burrows, Reynolds, Ghiaurov, Hamari, Senechel, Alldis Ch., ROHCG O, Solti.

In terms of recorded sound, the Decca/Solti version has remarkable transparency and detail. In addition to the superb sound, the orchestral playing is a delight. This set satisfies an important need. Solti, characteristically crisp in attack, has plainly warmed to the score, allowing his singers full rein in rallentando and rubato to a degree one might not have expected of him. The Tatiana of Teresa Kubiak is most moving – rather mature-sounding for the *ingénue* of Act I, but with her golden, vibrant voice rising to the final confrontation of Act III most impressively. The Onegin of Bernd Weikl may have too little variety of tone, but again this is firm singing that yet has authentic Slavonic tinges. Onegin becomes something like a first-person story-teller. The rest of the cast is excellent, with Stuart Burrows as Lensky giving one of his finest performances on record yet. Here for the first time the full range of musical expression in this most atmospheric of operas is superbly caught, with the Decca recording capturing every subtlety of sound – including the wonderful off-stage effects – with richness as well as brilliance. There is a degree of edginess in the tape transfer that needs smoothing, and the choral focus lacks something in refinement.

Telemann, Georg Philipp

(1681–1767)

Concerto in B flat for 2 flutes, 2 oboes and strings; Oboe concerto in E flat; Oboe d'amore concerto in D; Double concerto in E min. for recorder, flute and strings.

*** DG Arc. 2533/*3310* 454 [id.]. Aurèle and Christiane Nicolet, Holliger, Pellerin, Copley, Camerata Bern, Furi.

An entirely enchanting collection. Holliger produces the most winning timbre on the oboe d'amore, and there are some delightful sounds too in the *Concerto for two flutes and two oboes.* This is a first-class production in every way, and Telemann's invention is consistently amiable and lively. The excellent recording is also available on one of Archive's rare full-priced cassettes, which offers truly splendid quality, wonderfully warm and clear.

Concerto for flute, oboe d'amore and viola d'amore in E; Concerto polonois; Double concerto for recorder and flute in E min.; Triple trumpet concerto in D; Quadro in B flat.

*** O-L Dig. **411 949-2**; DSDL/*KDSDC* 701. Ac AM with soloists, Hogwood.

In the early years of the eighteenth century, Telemann had served as kapellmeister to Count Erdmann II of Promnitz at Sorau in Poland and the folk music he heard there made a great impression on him. 'An attentive observer could gather from these folk musicians enough ideas in eight days to last a lifetime,' he wrote; in three of the concertos recorded here, Polish ideas are to be found – indeed, one of the pieces is called *Concerto polonois.* As always Telemann has a refined ear for sonority and the musical discourse with which he diverts us is unfailingly intelligent and delightful. The performances are excellent and readers will not find cause for disappointment in either the recording or presentation. The chrome tape, however, is over-modulated and there is distortion at peaks.

Oboe concertos: in C min.; D; D min.; E min.; F min.

*** Ph. Dig. 6514/*7337* 232. Holliger, ASMF, Iona Brown.

The *C minor Concerto* with its astringent opening dissonance is the most familiar of the concertos on Holliger's record and the *E minor* has also been recorded before, but the remaining three are all new to the catalogue. Telemann was himself proficient on the oboe and wrote with particular imagination and poignancy for this instrument. The performances are all vital and sensitively shaped and a valuable addition to the Telemann discography. Well worth investigation. The high-level chrome tape is in the demonstration class.

Recorder concerto in G min.; Double concerto in A min. for recorder, viola da gamba and

strings; Double concerto in A for 2 violins in scordatura; Concertos for 4 violins: in C and D.
**(*) DG Arc. 2533 421 [id.]. Soloists, Col. Mus. Ant., Goebel.

These are chamber concertos rather than solo concertos such as we associate with Bach and Vivaldi. They are diverting and inventive without at any point touching great depths; like so much Telemann, they are pleasing without being memorable. They are eminently well served by these artists and nicely recorded too. Attractive but not indispensable.

Double concerto in F, for recorder, bassoon and strings; Double concerto in E min., for recorder, flute and strings; Suite in A min., for recorder and strings.
*** Ph. Dig. **410 041-2**; 6514/*7337* 165. Petri, Bennett, Thunemann, ASMF, Iona Brown.

The *E minor Concerto* for recorder, flute and strings is also included on the Academy of Ancient Music's anthology (DSDL 701) but is played on modern instruments on the Philips record. This is a delightful piece and is beautifully played, even though period instrument addicts will doubtless find William Bennett's tone a little fruity. The playing throughout is highly accomplished and the *Suite in A minor*, Telemann's only suite for treble recorder, comes off beautifully. Excellently played and recorded throughout, with a matching first-class cassette. The compact disc brings out the forward balance of the soloists in the *Double concerto* but the effect is not unattractive. The orchestral focus is not absolutely clean, though quite agreeable.

Double recorder concerto in A min.; Double concerto in E min. for recorder, flute and strings; Suite in A min. for recorder and strings.
(M) *** Sup. 1410 2849. Stivín, Válek, Klement, Prague CO, Munclinger.

This excellent Supraphon disc duplicates two of the works on the Telefunken issue below, but offers in place of the *Overture* an agreeable four-movement *Concerto for two recorders*. The Supraphon recording is more modern than the Telefunken, and the sound is impressively full and real, the warm resonance bringing bloom without clouding detail. The soloists are naturally balanced and are all excellent players. The performance of the famous *Suite in A minor* is alert and sparkling, with brisk tempi bringing lively articulation from Jiří Stivín, the splendid solo recorder player, as well as the accompanying group. The expressive movements are gracious and elegant without being over-romanticized. The attractive finale of the *Concerto for recorder and flute* is also memorable. A first-class collection.

Double concerto in E min. for recorder, flute and strings; Overture des nations anciens et modernes in G; Suite in A min. for recorder and strings.
(M) *** Tel. AQ6/*CQ4* 41342 [641039]. Brüggen, Vester, Amsterdam CO, Rieu.

These works show Telemann as an original and often inspired craftsman. His use of contrasting timbres in the *Double concerto* has considerable charm; the *Overture* is slighter but agreeably inventive, and the *Suite in A minor*, one of his best-known works, is worthy of Handel or Bach. Frans Brüggen and Frans Vester are expert soloists, and the accompaniments are crisp and stylish. The sound is excellent, and the cassette is of demonstration quality, with splendid body and presence.

(i) *Viola concerto in G; Don Quichotte suite; Overture in D for 2 oboes, 2 horns and strings.*
*** Argo ZRG/*KZRC* 836 [id.]. ASMF, Marriner; (i) with Shingles.

Anyone daunted by the sheer volume of Telemann's instrumental music could not do better than to investigate this splendid collection, which is superbly played and recorded. It presents a nicely varied group of works, not just the relatively well-known *Viola concerto* (with Stephen Shingles a stylish soloist) but the colourful and endearing *Don Quichotte suite*, a vivid example of early programme music, and the amazing *Overture in D*, written in 1765 when Telemann was well on in his eighties but still retained all his creative flair.

Each movement is intensely individual, and the work ends with a graceful carillon for oboes and pizzicato strings and a final rumbustious *Tintamare*. There is an excellent cassette of this issue.

Viola concerto in G; Suite in A min. for flute and strings; Tafelmusik, Production 2: *Triple violin concerto in F.*
(M) * Ph. 9502/*7313* 011 [id.]. Ghedin, Gazzelloni, Ayo, Apostoli, Colandrea, I Musici.

The *Triple concerto* comes from the second part of Telemann's *Tafelmusik* and is also available in the Archive version (see below). The *Viola concerto* is widely recorded, and so too is the *A minor Suite*. These performances are rather heavy-going and communicate little of the freshness of the music. Charmless – surprisingly so, considering the artists involved. Not recommended.

Trumpet concerto in D; Viola concerto in G; Triple violin concerto in F; Overture in C.
(M) *** Decca Ser. SA/*KSC* 30 [Lon. STS/5-15587]. Soloists, ASMF, Marriner.

Assembled from earlier full-priced recordings, this anthology is self-recommending at lower mid-price. Performances and recording are of high quality. The cassette transfer is particularly successful.

Overture in C (Hamburger Ebb und Fluth); Overture des nations anciens et modernes; Overture in C.
*** Argo ZRG/*KZRC* 837. ASMF, Marriner.

Here is another outstanding Argo record to match and supplement the companion disc including the *Viola concerto* and *Don Quichotte*. With string tone gloriously resonant, as rich and refined as any on record, this triptych of diverse Telemann suites is irresistible. The *Hamburg Ebb and Flow* has programmatic implications in the manner of Vivaldi, but the musical descriptions are never too literal and the titular associations with the figures of classical mythology serve only to inspire the composer's imagination. Similarly the *Ancient and Modern Nations* provide paired dances given colour by their contrasts of manner. If the Hamburg suite evokes the spirit of Handel, there are Bachian overtones too, and these extend to the dances in both the other suites. Certainly the C major work which has no title is no less distinguished in invention. Highly recommended both on disc and on tape, where the sound is slightly drier, but only marginally less refined.

Suite in A min.; Flute concertos in C and G.
**(*) RCA RL/*RK* 25204 [ARL 1/*ARK 1* 3488]. Galway, Zagreb Soloists.

Charismatic and completely musical playing from Galway, his fine-spun timbre bringing much colour to all this music, even if the feeling is slightly anachronistic. The Zagreb Soloists are well balanced with the soloist, but their contribution is competent rather than adventurous. The sound is good on both disc and cassette. This is for admirers of Galway rather than Telemann specialists; Frans Brüggen's version of the *Suite* (see above), played on the recorder, for which it was intended, is from an altogether different world and gives an equally impressive display of virtuosity.

Tafelmusik (complete).
(M) *** DG Arc. 2723 074 (6). Schola Cantorum Basiliensis, Wenzinger.
*** Tel. FX6 35298 (6). Brüggen, Concerto Amsterdam, Leonhardt.

Tafelmusik, Book II.
(M) *** Tel. DX6 35060 (2). Brüggen, Concerto Amsterdam, Leonhardt.

Tafelmusik, Book III.
(M) *** Tel. DX6 35064 (2). Concerto Amsterdam, Leonhardt.

The Telefunken set was made at the same time as the Wenzinger version on Archive, in the mid-1960s, and there is not a great deal to choose between them. The *Concerto for two horns* in the Third Book comes off better in the Telefunken set but elsewhere, the Wenzinger on Archive seems to score marginally. The attraction, if such it is, concerns the availability of the Books separately, two records at a time, for those who do not want to buy the work all at once. However, if this consideration does not worry you and you intend to acquire the whole work, the Wenzinger is the more convenient. The playing on the Telefunken set is very good indeed, however, and neither the performances nor the recordings will disappoint.

Tafelmusik: Double concerto in A for flute and violin; Double horn concerto in E flat; Triple violin concerto in F.
(M) ** Tel. AQ6/*CQ4* 41152. Concerto Amsterdam, Brüggen.
(M) ** DG Arc. 2547/*3347* 013. Schola Cantorum Basiliensis, Wenzinger.

This collection is planned to give contrast, but the selection of works does not show Wenzinger's group at its finest. The most attractive work is the *Concerto for flute and violin*, where the textures are fresh and luminous. The *Double horn concerto*, however (a florid but attractive piece), sounds unnecessarily clumsy here, while the approach to the *Triple violin concerto* seems a little severe. The recording sounds fresh and well balanced on disc and tape alike.

The Telefunken account of the *Double horn concerto*, with expert solo playing from Hermann Baumann and Adriaan van Woudenberg, is preferable to the version on Archive: it is no less authentic but the playing is much more polished. The performances have vitality throughout, though tonally the effect is more astringent, less elegant. The recording is fresh and bright on both disc and cassette.

Tafelmusik: Conclusions: in B flat; in D; in E min. Solo sonatas: in B min. for flute and continuo; in G min. for oboe and continuo; in A for violin and continuo.
(M) ** Tel. AQ6/*CQ4* 42557. Concerto Amsterdam, Brüggen.

This issue couples the short orchestral movements that end the three Productions of the *Tafelmusik* with the solo sonatas. There are distinguished soloists here and the playing has striking vitality, even if the music's expressive qualities are projected less strongly. The sound is bright and sharply focused in the Telefunken manner; on cassette there is an occasional hint of stridency.

Tafelmusik: Trio sonatas: in D; in E min.; in E flat.
(M) *** Tel. AQ6/*CQ4* 42700. Vester, Tromp, Mater, Schröder, Holtman, Pollard, Bylsma, Leonhardt.

This record collects the three trio sonatas from Telemann's *Tafelmusik* composed on the model of the Italian *sonata da chiesa*. The *E flat* from the First Book is still split over two sides, which is a pity since it is one of the best of all his trio sonatas. The performances are all exemplary and withstand the test of time remarkably well.

Essercizii musici: Sonatas in C and D min. Der getreue Music-Meister: Sonatas: in F; F min.; B flat and C.
*** Tel. DX 6.35359 (2). Brüggen, Bylsma, Leonhardt – HANDEL: *Recorder sonatas.****

The Telemann sonatas, like the Handel, are played with breathtaking virtuosity and a marvellous sense of style. The recording still sounds fresh. With the excellent coupling this is well worth investigating, especially for those who do not want the complete set of *Der getreue Music-Meister* (see below).

Fantasias for solo recorder: Nos. 4 in G min.; 6 in B flat; Methodical sonata in D, Op. 13/4; Partita No. 2 in G; Sonatas: in C and F; Trio sonata in B flat (all for recorder and continuo).
**(*) Ph. 9500/*7300* 941 [id.]. Michala Petri Trio.

Michala Petri is a young Danish virtuoso who attracted attention in her teens. Her trio consists of her mother, Hanne, at the harpsichord and her brother David, cello. Her playing is breathtaking in its virtuosity and range of colour, and the programme she offers is both varied and enjoyable. At times she is open to the charge of being a shade too unyielding in her approach – she needs to allow some of this music to breathe. However, this is superb playing in every other respect and is excellently recorded. The cassette transfer is admirable, fresh and clean.

Fantasias for unaccompanied violin, Nos. 1–12.
(M) *** Ph. 9502 010. Grumiaux.

Telemann's *12 Fantasias* for solo violin are a decade later than Bach's *Partitas* and *Sonatas*, and they are less ambitious and demanding. Yet there is much that is rewarding here, particularly given such artistry as Grumiaux's; Telemann's invention is fresh, though none of these short suites can claim depth.

Partitas for guitar duo: in A; in A (Polonaise); in D; in E.
** DG 2531/*3301* 350 [id.]. Yepes, Monden.

Telemann's *Guitar partitas*, like the Bach *Sonatas* and *Partitas* for unaccompanied violin and cello, are essentially groups of dance movements, usually including a brief introductory 'overture'. Frankly the inspiration is not scintillating; on the whole, the most memorable ideas come in the A major work subtitled *Polonaise*, but even here the invention is ingenuous. This is essentially wallpaper music. Yepes and Monden make a good team, but their presentation is rather square; they favour the alternation of *forte* and *mezzo forte* to provide variety within the melodic phrases. Perhaps it is not entirely their fault, for there is an excessive amount of moderately paced music here, but one feels there could have been more sparkle at times. An enterprising but disappointing contribution to Telemann's tercentenary, well recorded on disc and cassette alike.

Fantasias Nos. 1 in D; 5 in F; 8 in G min.; 9 in A; Overture No. 3 in F; Solo in C.
(M) *** Ph. 9502/*7313* 073. Koopman.

The four *Suites* come from a set published in 1733; the *Solo in C major*, despite its slight title, comes from a set of sonatas published a few years later under the title, *Essercizii musici*, and is the longest piece on the record. The invention is as fertile as it is fluent, and the Dutch harpsichordist, Ton Koopman, could hardly be more characterful or committed. He plays a copy of a Ruckers instrument, a little closely balanced perhaps, but still sounding very realistic and bright. Cassette and disc are closely matched.

VOCAL MUSIC

Funeral cantata: *Du aber, Daniel, gehe hin.*
(M) *** HM 21441. Ameling, McDaniel, Aachen Domchor, Coll. Aur., Pohl – BACH: *Cantata No. 106.****

Cantatas: *Du aber, Daniel, gehe hin; Ertrage nur das Joch der Mängel; Hochselige Blicke voll heiliger Wonne.*
(M) *** Ph. 9502 026. Soloists, Hamburg Monteverdi Ch., Hamburg Telemann-Gesellschaft, Jürgens.

Telemann's *Funeral cantata* dates from his years at Hamburg and is a work of striking expressive intensity and imagination. The text obviously touched a deeper vein of feeling than is often evident in this master, and both in musical resource and invention this is a work that can justify its presence in the company of Bach. There are some poignant harmonic progressions and a generous flow of melodic inspiration. The performers on Harmonia Mundi give an impressive account of the piece, and though the recording is in no way outstanding, it is well balanced in an appropriately generous acoustic. This is music that should be investigated even by readers normally resistant to Telemann's charms; it has real eloquence and some measure of depth.

The Philips record devotes itself entirely to Telemann cantatas, and those who already possess the Bach cantata offered by Harmonia Mundi will welcome this alternative which involves no duplication, brings two other charming Telemann works and is also less expensive. The performance too is very fine indeed; the soloists (Liselotte Rebmann and William Reimer) are less celebrated than those on the rival disc, they are nonetheless eminently satisfactory. Jürgen Jürgens is perhaps a little cool, but the performance as a whole has dignity and eloquence, and the recording is beautifully balanced. The two cantatas on the reverse derive from Telemann's *Der harmonische Gottesdienst* (1725) and are not otherwise available; Kurt Equiluz is excellent in *Ertrage nur das Joch der Mängel*. Whichever version is chosen, Telemann's *Funeral cantata* must be numbered among his most beautiful compositions and should not be overlooked.

Cantatas: (i) *Die Landlust;* (ii) *Der Schulmeister;* (i) *Von geliebten Augen brennen.*
*** HM 1C 065 99692. Coll. Aur., with (i) Speiser, (ii) Nimsgern, Stuttgart Hymnus Boys' Ch. (members)

Der Schulmeister is a diverting cantata about a schoolmaster teaching his class to sing, while its companions, *Die Landlust*, a lighter pastoral piece, and *Von geliebten Augen brennen*, a darker, more expressive work, are both inventive and worth exploring. Committed performances from both the soloists and the Collegium Aureum (who use period instruments) and a well-judged balance from the engineers make this a useful addition to the catalogue.

Magnificats: in C and D.
(M) **(*) Ph. 9502/*7313* 077. Giebel, Malaniuk, Altmeyer, Rehfuss, Reuter-Wold, Lausanne Ch., Mun. Pro Arte O, Redel.

These two settings of the *Magnificat* – one in Latin, one in German – make a fascinating contrast, the German work altogether gentler than the Latin setting. Telemann may not match Bach in sublimity of inspiration, but the vigour of his choral writing is always refreshing. Strong, well-tuned performances except for some unsteadiness from contralto and bass soloists. The 1960s recording still sounds well in this mid-price reissue and there is an excellent tape.

St Mark Passion.
(M) **(*) Ph. 6768 027 (2). Giebel, Malaniuk, Altmeyer, Rehfuss, Günter, Lausanne Youth Ch., Mun. Pro Arte O, Redel.

Telemann was as prolific in his vocal music as in his instrumental and orchestral works, and this setting of the *St Mark Passion* is one of many. It is an expressive piece, but only in places does the writing show real individuality. The performance, however, is an outstandingly good one, with fresh, intelligent solo singing and thoroughly committed and understanding direction from Kurt Redel. The recording dates from the mid-1960s and still sounds well; but four sides of this kind of music can be recommended only to the enthusiast.

St Matthew Passion.
(M) *(*) Ph. 6768 333 (2). Jurinac, Altmeyer, Lucerne Fest. Ch., Swiss Fest. O, Redel.

Telemann's setting of the *St Matthew Passion* has a certain historical interest because of the interpolations in the gospel story – after the death of Christ a soprano gets up and sings a cheerful little aria – but musically the impression is one of serene competence rather than great genius. This performance under Kurt Redel does nothing to redeem the general dullness of the score, although among the soloists Sena Jurinac is outstanding.

OPERA

Pimpinone (complete).
(M) *** Ph. 9502/*7313* 117. Roscher, Süss, Berlin State O, Koth.

This charming chamber opera anticipates *La serva padrona* and offers music of great tunefulness and vivacity. The opera has only two characters, no chorus whatever, and a small orchestra. Yet its music is as witty as its libretto, and from the very opening one can sense that Telemann is enjoying every moment of this absurd comedy about a serving maid (Vespetta) who battens on a wealthy but stupid gentleman (Pimpinone), eventually persuading him not only to marry her, but to give her the freedom of his purse and at the same time to do her bidding. The Philips singers do well and the playing too is of the highest order even if in matters of ornamentation one might have expected more decoration. But the overall impression is of freshness and the music is so delightful that it deserves the widest currency. The recording, too, has a naturalness and balance that is commendable. There is a first-class cassette.

Thomas, Ambroise (1811–96)

Hamlet (complete recording).
*** Decca Dig. 410 184-1/*4* (3/*2*) [id.]. Milnes, Sutherland, Morris, Winbergh, Conrad, Tomlinson, Ch. and O of Welsh Nat. Op., Bonynge.

One of the very finest of Sutherland's early recordings was of the famous Mad scene for Ophelia, and here after 24 years she still gives a triumphant display, tender and gentle as well as brilliant in coloratura, in that climactic scene of Act IV. Melba insisted that the opera should end at that point, but here Bonynge – who has conducted the piece in the Sydney Opera House but with a different soprano – provides a far better answer to the problems of Act V. He has devised a composite of Thomas's original happy ending (*'Vive Hamlet, notre roi!'* cries the chorus) and the suicide alternative which Thomas wrote for Covent Garden. It now follows Shakespeare reasonably enough – if with far too many survivors – and for the rest the opera is a surprisingly deft if inevitably superficial compression of Shakespeare, full of splendid theatrical effects. It has colour, atmosphere, soaring tunes and jolly dances presented in subtle and often original orchestration, with even a saxophone used to striking effect.

The weight of Shakespeare is missing, but this is more faithful to him than Gounod's *Faust* is to Goethe. *Être ou ne pas être* as a soliloquy may be dull, but Hamlet's swaggering drinking song greeting the players is most effective, quoted later in mad, Berlioz-like bursts at the climax of the Play scene, when Hamlet's ruse with Claudius has worked. Ophélie has priority vocally in brilliant and beautiful numbers, with Sutherland taking all challenges commandingly. The heroine's primacy is reinforced when the role of Hamlet is for baritone, here strongly taken if with some roughness by Sherrill Milnes. Outstanding among the others is Gösta Winbergh as Laerte (in French without the final 's'), heady and clear in the only major tenor role. John Tomlinson as the Ghost sings the necessary monotones resonantly, James Morris is a gruff Claudius and Barbara Conrad a fruity Gertrude. The compelling success of the whole performance of a long, complex opera is sealed by Bonynge's vigorous and sympathetic conducting of first-rate Welsh National Opera forces, brilliantly and warmly recorded on disc and chrome tape alike. The cassette layout, on four sides, is almost ideal.

Hamlet: ballet music.
*** Decca Dig. SXDL/*KSXDC* 7583. Nat. PO, Bonynge – CHOPIN: *Les Sylphides.***

Thomas's wittily extrovert ballet music for *Hamlet* may seem strangely inappropriate, coming as it does in the form of a fourth-Act divertissement, just before Ophelia's mad scene. However, played on its own, the gay, inventive writing gives much pleasure. It finds a stylish and sympathetic advocate here and the orchestral playing is crisply turned with freshness and sparkle the keynote. The bright digital sound suits the music-making and there is a lively chrome tape.

Mignon (opera; complete).
*** CBS [Col. M4 34590]. Horne, Welting, Vanzo, Zaccaria, Battedou, Meloni, Von Stade, Hudson, Amb. Op. Ch., Philh. O, Almeida.

It was admirably enterprising of CBS to record Thomas's once-popular adaptation of Goethe. As old record catalogues bear witness, it has many vocal plums, and here a very full account of the score is given, with virtually all the alternatives which the composer devised for productions after the first – not least one at Drury Lane in London where recitatives were used (as here) instead of spoken dialogue; an extra aria was given to the soubrette Philine, other arias were expanded and the role of Frédéric was given to a mezzo-soprano instead of a tenor. Frederica von Stade here is superb in that role, making one rather regret that she was not chosen as the heroine. Marilyn Horne sings with great character and flair, but she hardly sounds the frail figure of the ideal Mignon. Nonetheless, with Alain Vanzo a sensitive Wilhelm, Ruth Welting a charming Philine, and colourful conducting from Almeida, this is an essential set for lovers of French opera. The rest of the score may never match the plums in memorability, but it is all sweetly attractive. This set is deleted in the UK.

Thomson, Virgil (born 1896)

Film music: suites from: (i) *Autumn; The Plow that Broke the Plains; The River.*
*** [Ang. S 37300]. LACO, Marriner, (i) with Mason-Stockton (harp).

Virgil Thomson is probably best-known for his film score to Flaherty's *Louisiana Story* and his opera, *Four Saints in Three Acts*, as well as his criticism in the *New York Herald Tribune*. These pieces are often quite appealing, even if none of them is really first-rate. The *Autumn suite* has a cool yet distinctly American flavour, and many readers will find it highly attractive. The playing of the Los Angeles orchestra is altogether excellent, and the recording has admirable space and realism. This record has unfortunately been withdrawn in the UK.

(i) *Portraits; Sonata No. 4;* (ii) *Eight Portraits for violin alone;* (iii) *Family Portrait.*
*** None. Dig. D79024. (i) Jacobs (piano, harpsichord); (ii) Silverstein; (iii) American Brass Quintet.

The three stars are for the performers and the recording which merit praise. The late Paul Jacobs plays the keyboard pieces with evident care. The music itself is of scant interest and less distinction. All the pieces are mercifully short but in all but a few instances still outstay their welcome.

Four Saints in Three Acts (opera) complete.
**(*) None. Dig. D/*D B4* 79035 (2) [id.]. Allen, Matthews, Thompson, Dale, Quivar, Brown, Bradley, O of Our Time, Thome.

The paradoxical combination of Gertrude Stein's stream-of-unconsciousness libretto and Thomson's deliberately simple score (itself a paradox when Catholic mystics like St Ignatius and St Teresa are celebrated in Baptist/revivalist/Anglican music) delights many as much as it repels some. There is a childlike quality which is well caught in this performance, vigorously conducted by Joel Thome with a fair, if hardly distinguished, team of soloists. Bright digital recording.

Tiomkin, Dimitri (1894–1979)

Film scores: *Duel in the Sun: suite; Giant: Prelude; High Noon: suite; Night Passage: Follow the river; Red River: suite; Rio Bravo: suite.*
** Uni. Kanchana DKP 9002. Saker, McCarthy Singers, L. Studio SO, Johnson.

The choral theme of *Red River* is truly memorable, as of course is the music for *High Noon*, although the soloist here does not match the sound-track version (Tex Ritter), and the clear digital recording suggests that the chorus is a relatively small group. The short orchestral fantasia used to heighten the tension, called by the composer *The clock and showdown*, demonstrates impressive structural skill. Good performances, but not showing quite the flair of the RCA series under Gerhardt. The recording is brilliant and makes a powerful impact, but is not sumptuous.

Tippett, Michael (born 1905)

Concerto for double string orchestra; Fantasia concertante on a theme of Corelli; Little Music for strings.
*** Argo ZRG 680 [id.]. ASMF, Marriner.

Fantasia concertante on a theme of Corelli.
** ASV Dig. DCA/*ZCDCA* 518. ASMF, Marriner – ELGAR: *Serenade***; VAUGHAN WILLIAMS: *Tallis fantasia* etc.**(*)

The *Concerto for double string orchestra*, on any count one of the most beautiful of twentieth-century works for strings, here receives a performance more sumptuous and warm-hearted than any before on record. With utter commitment Marriner and his colleagues allow the jazz inflections of the outer movements to have their lightening effect on the rhythm, and in the heavenly slow movement the slowish tempo and hushed manner display the full romanticism of the music without ever slipping over the edge into sentimentality. The *Corelli fantasia*, a similarly sumptuous work but without quite the same lyrical felicity, and the *Little Music* provide an ideal coupling. The recording is outstanding.

The ASV digital recording of the *Fantasia* has great clarity and detail, but so does the earlier Argo account which has a more important coupling.

Triple concerto for violin, viola and cello.
*** Ph. Dig. 6514/*7337* 209 [id.]. Pauk, Imai, Kirshbaum, LSO, Sir Colin Davis.

This beautiful record, nominated Record of the Year in 1983 by the critics of *Gramophone* magazine, presents a near-ideal performance of one of Tippett's most beautiful later works. In 1979 when the *Concerto* was first heard – with this same conductor and soloists – the new, more exuberantly lyrical style represented an important development in Tippett's career.

Divertimento for chamber orchestra (*Sellinger's Round*).
*** Lyr. SRCS 111. ECO, Del Mar – BERKELEY and BRITTEN: *Sinfoniettas*; RAWSTHORNE: *Divertimento*.***

A series of variations on the English folk-dance tune by different hands led Tippett to develop his variation into this lively work, diverting exactly as a divertimento should be. Perfectly coupled, it comes in an excellent performance beautifully recorded.

(i) *Symphony No. 2;* (ii) *Sonata for 4 horns;* (iii) *The Weeping Babe.*
*** Argo ZRG 535 [id.]. (i) LSO, Sir Colin Davis; (ii) Tuckwell Horn Qt; (iii) Alldis Ch.

The *Second Symphony* is a superb work: it bears constant repetition and like Tippett's *Piano concerto* offers a wealth of interesting ideas to the listener. The composer began work on it in the mid-1950s and completed it in response to a commission from the BBC to mark the tenth anniversary of the Third Programme. When first one encounters it, the proliferation of ideas seems almost to undermine the sense of forward direction, and the detail attracts attention to itself before dissolving into another idea of almost equal interest. But closer acquaintance shows this to be misleading: the parts fit into an integrated and logical whole. The slow movement in particular has an atmosphere of striking imaginative quality: it explores the 'magical' side of Tippett's personality and deserves a place among his finest inspirations. The first movement opens with pounding C's, suggested to the composer when listening to some Vivaldi, and the music that flows from this has enormous vitality and complexity. The LSO under Colin Davis rise to the occasion and give a performance of great confidence and brilliance, and the sound-quality is quite superlative. Like the *Concerto for double string orchestra* and the *Piano concerto*, this is a must for all who care deeply about English music in general and Tippett in particular. *The Weeping Babe*, a setting of Edith Sitwell, is a wartime piece, of lyrical simplicity, and is excellently sung by the Alldis Choir. The *Sonata for four horns* is a brilliant virtuoso piece, whose hurdles the Barry Tuckwell Horn Quartet take in their stride. They complete an altogether outstanding disc.

Symphony No. 4; Suite for the birthday of Prince Charles.
*** Decca Dig. SXDL/*KSXDC* 7546 [Lon. LDR 71046]. Chicago SO, Solti.

This is a symphony where one should not be in a hurry to form judgements, for there are unsuspected rewards that are slow to surface. Readers put off by the often bewildering density of incident and apparently athematic character of Tippett's musical thinking (not to mention the heavy breathing effects which are used) should lower their resistance and lose no time in coming to terms with this important work. Some of its quieter sonorities spring from much the same soil that one glimpses in the sudden moments of repose in Henze's symphonies, moments of a poignant melancholy that resonate long after the tumult which surrounds them has subsided. There is a keenly focused atmosphere here, and each exploration of the landscape reveals new perspectives. The symphony is brilliantly played, and though there may be depths and a tenderness in the score yet to be uncovered, no praise can be too high for the achievement of these players under Sir Georg Solti or that of the Decca engineers, who produce sound of the utmost clarity and refinement. The *Suite for the birthday of Prince Charles* makes an agreeable fill-up even though it is not as substantial. The cassette transfer is extremely brilliant but has not quite the sharpness of focus of the disc. An indispensable issue for those who are concerned with contemporary music.

String quartets Nos. 1–3.
*** O-L DSLO 10 [id.]. Lindsay Qt.

The Oiseau-Lyre issue is an admirable record which usefully assembles Tippett's quartets on one disc, without any loss of quality. The performances carry the composer's imprimatur, and are faithfully recorded.

A Child of our Time (oratorio): complete.
**(*) Ph. 6500 985 [id.]. Norman, Baker, Cassilly, Shirley-Quirk, BBC Singers and Ch. Soc., BBC SO, Sir Colin Davis.

(i) *A Child of our time. The Midsummer marriage: Ritual dances Nos. 1–4.*
(B) **(*) Argo DPA 571/2. ROHCG O, Pritchard; (i) with Morison, Bowden, Lewis, Standen.

Davis's is a tough performance of the Tippett oratorio. His speeds tend to be on the fast side, both in the spirituals which here take the place which Bach gave to chorales and in the other numbers. Consistently he allows himself far less expressive freedom than John Pritchard on Argo (see below), and he misses the tenderness which makes the setting of *Steal Away* at the end of Part 1 so moving on the earlier version. He seems determined that there should be no suspicion of sentimentality in this commentary on a news story of the late 1930s. *A Child of our time*, says the title, and with Davis the time is not just the thirties or any period of comfortable nostalgia, but now. The performance of soloists and orchestra, not to mention the sharply defined recording quality, matches this approach. Though all sing well, the vocal quality of such a singer as Richard Cassilly is arguably too strenuous for such music.

In this new format the Pritchard version of *A Child of our time* is virtually the same price as the one-disc Philips version, and there is certainly a case for preferring it, despite the dated sound (fresh enough) and the less crisp ensemble. Pritchard's approach is more feeling and sympathetic, and this after all is music which speaks of deep emotion. Elsie Morison and Richard Lewis both sing most beautifully.

King Priam (opera; complete).
*** Decca D 246 D 3/*K 246 K 33* (3) [Lon. LDR 73006]. Bailey, Tear, Allen, Palmer, Minton, Langridge, Harper, L. Sinf. Ch., L. Sinf., Atherton.

When *King Priam* first appeared in 1962, the dry fragmentation of texture coupled with the choppy compression of the drama was disconcerting after the lyrical warmth of *The Midsummer Marriage*, particularly when a Homeric theme promised an epic approach.

In this superb performance under Atherton, with an outstanding cast and vivid, immediate recording, the power of the opera, offbeat as the treatment often is, both musical and dramatic, comes over from first to last. It is a superb demonstration of Tippett's single-mindedness as an opera composer, requiring the listener to think about attitudes afresh. Norman Bailey, thanks to his long association with Wagner, sounds agedly noble to perfection, Robert Tear is a shiningly heroic Achilles and Thomas Allen a commanding Hector, vocally immaculate, illuminating every word. 'The future of any twentieth-century opera depends quite a lot on recording,' says Tippett. On the showing of this recording, *King Priam* certainly deserves to succeed. The layout on three chrome cassettes matches the discs. The sound is vividly detailed but slightly less open at the top. A reduced-size booklet is provided, clearly printed but less attractive than the libretto offered with the LPs.

The Midsummer Marriage (opera): complete.
❀ *** Ph. 6703 027 (3). Remedios, Burrows, Carlyle, Harwood, Herincx, Watts, Ch. and O of ROHCG, Sir Colin Davis.

By almost every known rule of opera Tippett's great visionary work, created over a long period of self-searching, should not be an artistic success. That it does succeed triumphantly – if anything with even greater intensity on record than in the opera house – is a tribute above all to the exuberance of Tippett's inspiration, his determination to translate the glowing beauty of his vision into musical and dramatic terms. Any one moment from this 154-minute score should be enough to demonstrate the unquenchable urgency of his writing, his love of rich sounds. There are few operas of any period which use the chorus to such glorious effect, often in haunting off-stage passages, and with Colin Davis a burningly committed advocate and a cast that was inspired by live performances in the opera house, this is a set hard to resist even for those not normally fond of modern opera. The so-called 'difficulties' of the libretto, with its mystic philosophical references, fade when the sounds are so honeyed in texture and so consistently lyrical, while the story – for all its complications – preserves a clear sense of emotional involvement throughout. The singing is consistently fine, the playing magnificent, the recording outstandingly atmospheric.

The Midsummer Marriage: Ritual dances.
(M) *** Ph. Seq. 6527/*7311* 112 [id.]. Soloists, Ch. and O of ROHCG, Colin Davis – BRITTEN: *Peter Grimes: Sea interludes.****

The *Ritual dances* are here given not in the concert form that Tippett devised but in extracts from the complete recording of the opera, with choral contributions. This is most attractive, except that the last dance ends disconcertingly in mid-air before the final curtain. A first-rate medium-price coupling. The wide dynamic range of the recording brings a modestly levelled cassette transfer where the climaxes expand without distortion and the choral focus remains clear; however, the upper range is less refined and less far-reaching than the disc.

Tórroba, Federico (born 1891)

(i) *Concierto Iberico* (for 4 guitars); (ii) *Dialogos.*
**(*) Ph. 9500 749/*7300 834* [id.]. ASMF, Marriner, with (i) Los Romeros, (ii) Pepe Romero.

The *Concierto Iberico* is an amiable piece, effectively using its four guitars in concertante style. It was written in 1976, but its harmonic idiom is unadventurous. The *Dialogos* is an intimate solo concerto, also rather agreeable, written two years earlier for Segovia, who never performed it in public. Both works might be described as like Rodrigo but without the tunes. Pepe Romero is gentle and persuasive in the solo concerto, even though his material is slight, and Los Romeros give a committed and expert account of the companion piece. The recording offers beautiful sound and a natural balance on disc and tape alike.

Homenaje a la seguidilla.
*** HMV Dig. ASD 4171 [Ang. DS/*4XS 37880*]. Angel Romero, ECO, composer – CASTELNUOVO-TEDESCO: *Guitar concerto.****

Tórroba's *Homenaje* was written in 1962 but revised for a second première in 1975. It opens evocatively and, although the Spanish dance influences are strong, its moods are amiable and reflective rather than dashing, its colours pastel-shaded. The reflective *Andante* is gently memorable in this very fine performance, given a naturally balanced and ideally atmospheric recording. A worthwhile addition to the limited concertant repertoire for the guitar.

Aires de la Mancha; Madronos; Nocturno; Piezas caracteristicas; Sonatina; Suite Castellana.
(M) ** Saga 5462. Hill.

Tórroba wrote characterfully for the guitar, and these appealing pieces are likely to prove as popular as many more familiar. Eric Hill is a lively and sensitive player with a good technique. There is some uncertain tuning, but, this apart, the record can be enjoyed. The sound is clean and well focused.

Tosti, Francesco (1846–1916)

Songs: *L'alba sepàra della luce l'ombra; Aprile; 'A vucchella; Chanson de L'adieu; Goodbye; Ideale; Malia; Marechiare; Non t'amo; Segreto; La serenata; Sogno; L'ultima canzone; Vorrei morire.*
*** Ph. 9500 743/*7300 828* [id.]. Carreras, ECO, Muller.

Tosti (knighted by Queen Victoria for his services to music) had a gently charming lyric gift in songs like these, and it is good to have a tenor with such musical intelligence – not to mention such a fine, pure voice – tackling once-popular trifles like *Marechiare* and *Goodbye*. The arrangements are sweetly done, and the recording is excellent. The cassette, transferred at an unbelievably low level, has very little sparkle and cannot be recommended except where no disc playing equipment is available.

Tredici, David Del (born 1937)

Final Alice.
*** Decca Dig. SXDL 7516 [Lon. LDR 71018]. Hendricks, Chicago SO, Solti.

Improbably commissioned to celebrate the bicentennial of the United States in 1976, this instalment of Del Tredici's sequence of Lewis Carroll settings has much in it to fascinate the ear, particularly in a virtuoso performance like this. Familiar texts are neatly assembled, with the minimum of violence to the original, to present a dramatic cantata for just one voice and orchestra. Barbara Hendricks proves a characterful and urgent guide, a vibrant narrator as well as a fine singer. Solti and his superb orchestra plainly enjoy the fun from first to last: it is good to welcome an extended work which sustains its length without pomposity and with immediate warmth of communication. The recording is outstandingly brilliant.

Tubin, Eduard (1905–83)

Symphony No. 4 (Sinfonia lirica).
*** BIS LP 227 [id.]. Bergen SO, Järvi.

Here is something worth investigating. Eduard Tubin was an Estonian composer who fled to Sweden during the Soviet invasion in 1944 where he remained for the rest of his life. He wrote the *Fourth* of his ten symphonies in 1944, revising it during the last years of his life. The idiom is diatonic and accessible, the music well argued and expertly fashioned. The opening of the symphony has a Sibelian feel to it but, the closer one comes to this music, the more individual one realizes it is. It is obvious that the Bergen orchestra liked the piece for they respond to it with enthusiasm. Neeme Järvi is a persuasive advocate of the score and will, we hope, go on to record more of his countryman's work. (He has already recorded the *Sixth* for Melodiya and should do the elegiac and moving *Ninth*, the *Sinfonia semplice*.) The recording made at a live concert is very natural and the surfaces, as usual with BIS, are impeccable.

Turina, Joaquín (1882–1949)

Danzas fantásticas; La oración del torero; (i) *Canto a Sevilla.*
**(*) Decca Dig. 410 158-1/*4* [id.]. (i) Lorengar; SRO, Lopez-Cobos.

Lopez-Cobos secures sophisticated playing from the Suisse Romande Orchestra, and the *Danzas fantásticas* are given an unexpected subtlety of detail. The effect is altogether less brash than Bátiz's version, without loss of vividness. Of course the splendid Decca recording helps, colourful and brilliant yet refined. It sounds especially well in its cassette format. The *Canto a Sevilla* is a song cycle framed by an orchestral introduction and epilogue, with a central interlude. These are omitted here (even though the side runs for only about twenty minutes). Pilar Lorengar sings vibrantly, but her voice hardens under pressure and the pitch is not always perfectly focused. There is authentic feeling here and no lack of involvement, but not a great deal of charm.

Danzas fantásticas; (i) *Rapsodia sinfonica; Sinfonia Sevillana.*
**(*) HMV Dig. ASD/*TCC-ASD* 165007-1/*4* [Ang. DS/*4XS* 37950]. (i) Wibaut; LPO, Bátiz.

The three *Danzas fantásticas* are understandably better known than the other works included here. The *Sinfonia* is a programmatic triptych, with an attractive nocturnal slow movement. The scoring of the outer movements (as in the *Danzas*) is gaudy but effective. The *Rapsodia* is a pleasant but unmemorable piece for piano and orchestra. Bátiz is a sympathetic exponent of this repertoire and he persuades the LPO to bring out the Latin colours and atmosphere. The digital recording is vivid but a trifle brash in fortissimos. The chrome cassette is of EMI's best quality, spectacularly wide-ranging.

Rapsodia sinfónica, Op. 66.
*** Decca Dig. **410 289-2**; 410 289-1/*4* [id.]. De Larrocha, LPO, Frühbeck de Burgos – FALLA: *Nights in the gardens of Spain**** (also ALBÉNIZ: *Rapsodia****).

Turina's *Rapsodia sinfónica* has also been recorded by Wibaut and Bátiz (see above) but in the hands of Alicia de Larrocha it is played with such éclat that it becomes almost memorable and certainly thoroughly entertaining. The Falla coupling is poetic and atmospheric, while the delightfully chimerical Albéniz companion piece glitters most engagingly. Excellent, vivid sound out of Decca's top drawer.

Tye, Christopher (born *c.* 1500)

Euge Bone Mass in 6 parts.
*** HMV ASD/*TC-ASD* 4104. King's College Ch., Ledger – BYRD: *Mass in 5 parts.****

Christopher Tye's *Mass for six voices* is one of the glories of early Tudor music, amazingly rich and complex. This fine recording – attractively coupled with Byrd's masterpiece – is well balanced between clarity and atmosphere, and the quality of the singing is a fine tribute to Ledger's work with this unique choir. The chrome-tape transfer, made at a high level, is lively and clear, but marginally less refined than the Byrd coupling.

Western wind mass; Christ rising again from the dead; My trust, O Lord, in Thee is grounded; Omnes gentes plaudite manibus; Peccavimus cum patribus.
*** CRD 1105/*CRDC 4105*. New College, Oxford, Ch., Higginbottom.

As master of the choristers at Ely Cathedral in the troubled sixteenth century, Tye wrote for both the Latin and the English rite, keeping textures rather simpler for English, as this fine selection of his music demonstrates. Like Taverner and Sheppard, Tye wrote a Mass using the secular song *The Western Wynde* as basis, here effectively presented with solo voices singing where the texture grows sparer. Speeds are sometimes brisk but, with vividly atmospheric recording, these performances bring to life a figure generally known just from the history books. The admirable chrome cassette is very much in the demonstration class.

Valls, Francisco (1665–1747)

Mass: Scala Aretina.
*** CRD CRD 1071/*CRDC 4071* [id.]. Beattie, Hill, Long, Robson, Stafford, Fleet, Shelley, L. Oratory Ch., Thames CO, Hoban.

Valls, a contemporary of Bach and Handel, wrote this massively ceremonial setting of the Mass for use in Barcelona Cathedral, where for many years he was choirmaster. To academics in generations since then, the angularity of the writing for three choirs plus a limited orchestra (violins, cellos, trumpets and oboes with organ) may have seemed gauche, but we can now recognize an attractive earthiness. To our ears the breaking of rules merely makes the music sound modern. This fine performance, atmospherically recorded, is most welcome, restoring a totally neglected composer to his rightful place. The cassette is very well managed, although with forwardly balanced solcists there seems comparatively little dynamic contrast.

Varèse, Edgar (1885–1965)

Amériques; Arcana; Ionisation.
*** CBS 76520. NYPO, Boulez.

One might regard the block-like structures and timbres of these major works by Varèse as the equivalent of brutalistic architecture, but there is an intensity – particularly in performances as compelling as these – which makes the experiments in sound far more than pattern-making. *Amériques* is the most extended and ambitious of the three, a superb work in which sirens are given a genuinely artistic purpose. *Ionisation* for thirteen percussion players eliminates pitched sounds almost entirely, without seeming arid. An excellent issue, vividly recorded.

Arcana; Intégrales; Ionisation.
*** Decca SXL 6550. LAPO, LA Percussion Ens., Mehta.

Sumptuous presentation of three of Varèse's most characteristic works, an ideal disc for converting the unconvinced. Each work exploits unusual timbres and textures with a directness and freedom that suggest the work of the post-war avant-garde; yet the latest of these works, *Ionisation* for thirteen percussionists, dates from as long ago as 1931. The performances here have the easy expressiveness that comes from close and warm acquaintance by the players. The recording is brilliant to match.

Density (for flute); *Hyperprism; Intégrales; Ionisation; Octandre. Poème electronique* (for magnetic tape).
(M) *** CBS 60286/*40*- [(d) in MG 31078(2)]. Columbia SO, Craft.

This mid-price issue provides an admirable selection of Varèse's most strikingly original music for different combinations. Since the days when *Octandre* represented the last word in avant-garde outrage, it has become clear how strong and colourful Varèse's musical imagination is, original even when he is using electronic forces. Faithful recording, clear of texture. There is a very good chrome tape, vividly atmospheric if not quite matching the LP in transient bite.

Intégrales; Octandre; (i) *Ecuatorial;* (ii) *Offrandes.*
(M) *** None. H 71269 [id.]. Contemporary Chamber Ens., Weisberg, with (i) Paul, (ii) DeGaetani.

This useful collection of attractive and sharply distinctive works duplicates other Varèse discs, but it can be strongly recommended for the only available recording of *Ecuatorial*, a setting in Spanish with bass soloist of a Maya prayer, brightly colourful and sharp with heavy brass and percussion, organ, piano and ondes martenot. One is never in doubt that Varèse as a revolutionary had a mind of his own, and was as a rule decades ahead of his time. Good clear recording.

Vaughan Williams, Ralph
(1872–1958)

Concerto accademico for violin and orchestra in D min.
(M) *** Sup. 50959. Grumlikova, Prague SO, Maag – BRITTEN: *Violin concerto.****

Vaughan Williams's *Concerto accademico* is a delightful work, written in his most attractive pastoral vein. It dates from 1925, and the finale quotes from his opera *Hugh the Drover*. The Supraphon recording is of high quality and the performance is first-rate, Maag ensuring a sympathetic accompaniment. This is an imaginative coupling and the disc is well worth investigating at the modest price asked.

(i) *Concerto accademico;* (ii) *Tuba concerto in F min.; The England of Elizabeth: suite; The Wasps: Overture.*
(M) *** RCA Gold GL/*GK* 42953. LSO, Previn, with (i) Buswell; (ii) Fletcher.

When Previn's cycle of Vaughan Williams symphonies appeared in a collected edition, it was useful for the couplings to be issued separately. The two concertos are particularly valuable in these fine performances, and they are splendidly recorded on disc; but the cassette is not recommended. It has a shrill treble response and there is distortion too, especially in the *Tuba concerto*.

Concerto grosso for strings; (i) *Oboe concerto in A min.*
*** Argo ZRG/*KZRC* 881 [id.]. ASMF, Marriner, (i) with Nicklin – WARLOCK: *Capriol suite* etc.***

These two Vaughan Williams works, both under-appreciated, make an attractive coupling, well matched with Warlock's most popular work and the *Serenade* for his friend Delius. Celia Nicklin, first oboe of the Academy, gives a most persuasive account of the elusive *Oboe concerto*, while the rugged, easy manner of the *Concerto grosso*, written with amateurs in mind for two of the three groups of strings, is splendidly caught in this polished performance. Good wide-ranging recording and a lively, realistically balanced cassette.

(i; ii) *Oboe concerto in A min.;* (iii; iv) *Tuba concerto in F min.;* (ii; v) *The Lark Ascending.*
*** DG 2530 906 [id.]. (i) Black; (ii) ECO; (iii) Jacobs; (iv) Chicago SO; (v) Zukerman; cond. Barenboim.

Very good playing and recording of these three beautiful works. Zukerman's version of *The Lark Ascending* is full of pastoral rapture, and Barenboim secures sensitive pianissimo playing from the ECO. Arnold Jacobs gives a good account of himself in the *Tuba concerto*, though he is not quite as subtle as his rival John Fletcher on RCA. Neil Black's account of the *Oboe concerto*, not Vaughan Williams's strongest work, holds its own with current rivals, and the quality of sound accorded to all these performances is first-class. Though possibly not a first choice for any of the three works, it makes a very satisfying disc all the same.

English folksongs suite (arr. Gordon Jacob); *Fantasia on Greensleeves.*
(*) HMV ASD/*TC-ASD* 2750 [Ang. S/*4XS* 36799]. LSO, Boult – ELGAR: *Enigma variations.**

The *Folksongs suite* is not a very appropriate coupling for Boult's splendid account of *Enigma*, but this is delightful, unpretentious music, beautifully played and recorded. The cassette sounds agreeable, but the balance is bass-orientated and the *Folksongs suite* ideally needs more sparkle on top.

English folksongs suite; Toccata marziale.
*** Telarc Dig. DG 10050 [id.]. Cleveland Symphonic Winds, Fennell – ARNAUD: *Fanfares*; GRAINGER: *Lincolnshire Posy* etc.***
*** ASV ACA/*ZCACA* 1002 [None. 78002]. L. Wind O, Wick – HOLST: *Hammersmith* etc.***

The Telarc digital disc offers essentially robust performances, marvellously played and recorded. The contrasting central movement of the *Folksongs suite* is presented gently and with attractive delicacy of texture. Some might feel that the bass drum and cymbals are a trifle too insistent elsewhere, but the recording is so crisply spectacular (and the balance is not too forward) that it would be churlish to complain. The effect is certainly sparkling. The pressing itself is flawless.

On the analogue ASV alternative the pace is comparably zestful, and if the slow movement of the *Folksongs suite* might have been played more reflectively, the bounce of *Seventeen come Sunday* is irresistible. The *Toccata marziale*, written in 1924 for the British Empire Exhibition at Wembley, has plenty of flourish here. The sound is first-rate, if not quite so spectacular as the Telarc alternative, but the ASV cassette is a little disappointing. The relatively modest level has meant that transients (particularly the side-drum) are not ideally crisp.

English folksongs suite; Fantasia on Greensleeves; Fantasia on a theme of Thomas Tallis; Old King Cole (ballet for orchestra); *The Wasps: Overture.*
(B) ** PRT GSGC/*ZCGC* 2005. LPO, Boult.

Delving into its twenty-five-year-old store, PRT came up with two valuable Boult recordings that had never appeared before, a vigorous performance of *The Wasps Overture* and the delightful *Old King Cole* suite taken from a ballet of 1923, the only version in stereo. That with the other proved favourites makes an attractive bargain. The sound, obviously not modern, has been well cleaned up and, though restricted, is acceptably balanced. Disc and tape are closely matched, the bass on the LP somewhat cleaner.

Fantasia on Greensleeves.
(M) *** HMV *TCC2-POR 54290*. LSO, Previn – BUTTERWORTH: *Banks of Green Willow*; HOLST: *The Planets* etc.***

Fantasia on Greensleeves; Fantasia on a theme of Thomas Tallis.
⊛ *** HMV ASD 521 [Ang. S 36101]. Sinf. of L., Allegri Qt, Barbirolli – ELGAR: *Introduction and allegro; Serenade.****

The rich projection of the theme when it first appears in full, after the pizzicato introduction, sets the seal on Barbirolli's quite outstanding performance of the *Tallis fantasia*, one of the great masterpieces of all music. The wonderfully ethereal and magically quiet playing of the second orchestra is another very moving feature of this remarkable performance. HMV should be very proud both of the excellence of their stereo effect and of the warm realism of the string textures. The delightful *Greensleeves fantasia* makes a pleasing bonus.

Previn's excellent account of the *Greensleeves fantasia* is part of a double-length tape in HMV's 'Portrait of the Artist' series, of which the major contents are by Holst. The sound is first-rate.

Fantasia on Greensleeves; Fantasia on a theme of Thomas Tallis; Five Variants of Dives and Lazarus; (i) *The Lark ascending.*
*** Argo ZRG 696/*KZRC 15696* [id.]. ASMF, Marriner (i) with I. Brown.

Superbly balanced and refined performances of four favourite Vaughan Williams works, which with the help of sumptuous recorded sound here have great power and intensity. A richly rewarding record, and the excellent cassette offers three songs as a bonus. They are admirably sung by Robert Tear (*Linden Lea; Orpheus with his lute;* and *The Water mill*).

Fantasia on Sussex folk tunes for cello and orchestra.
*** RCA Dig. RS/*RK* 9010. Lloyd Webber, Philh. O, Handley – DELIUS: *Cello concerto*; HOLST: *Invocation.****

The *Fantasia on Sussex folk tunes* is new to the gramophone. It was composed for Casals, who gave its first performance in 1930 at a Royal Philharmonic Society concert, and comes from the same period as *Job* and the *Piano concerto.* The piece has lain neglected since its first performance, and it proves something of a discovery. This is a highly appealing work, most persuasively performed too by Lloyd Webber and the Philharmonia and Vernon Handley. The recording is first-class on both disc and tape.

Fantasia on a theme of Thomas Tallis.
❀ (M) *** HMV mono XLP/*TC-XLP* 60002. Philh. O, Karajan – BRITTEN: *Variations.****❀
(M) ** HMV SXLP/*TC-SXLP* 20007. Philh. O, Sargent – ELGAR: *Enigma variations.***

Karajan's version of the *Tallis fantasia* coupled with Britten's *Variations on a theme of Frank Bridge* is one of the outstanding records of the 1950s, sounding as fresh and sonorous today as it did then. Sonically it is little short of amazing, and artistically it is no less impressive. The playing of the Philharmonia strings for Karajan is altogether superlative, and the *Tallis fantasia* sounds both idiomatic and vivid, rather like a newly cleaned painting. Recordings of this work are legion, and stereo undoubtedly brings an added dimension, but this mono version ranks among the very best, from the early Boult set of 78s through such memorable accounts as that of Mitropoulos to the more recent versions from Barbirolli and Boult. The cassette of the Karajan performance is smooth and well balanced, not quite as open in sound as the spectacular coupling.

One could hardly fail to be moved by the tonal quality HMV provide in the Philharmonia recording, but Sir Malcolm's performance is disappointing. He was content simply to play the notes and there is little spiritual quality. The cassette had been remastered and is now quite the equal of the disc.

Fantasia on a theme of Thomas Tallis; Five Variants of Dives and Lazarus; Norfolk rhapsody No. 1; (i) *Towards the Unknown Region.*
*** HMV Dig. ASD/*TCC-ASD* 4089. CBSO, Del Mar, (i) with CBSO Ch.

Norman Del Mar's strong and deeply felt account of the *Tallis fantasia* is given a splendid digital recording, with the second orchestral group creating radiant textures. The direct approach, however, lacks something in mystery, and not all of the ethereal resonance of this haunting work is conveyed. Yet this remains an attractive record with its grouping of rarities, including the early cantata *Towards the Unknown Region* of 1907 to words of Walt

Whitman. Aptly the chorus is presented at an evocative distance. The chrome cassette matches the disc in breadth and clarity, with the big climax of the choral work splendidly caught.

Fantasia on a theme of Thomas Tallis; (i) *The Lark ascending.*
(*) ASV Dig. DCA/*ZCDCA* 518. (i) I. Brown, ASMF, Marriner – ELGAR: *String serenade;* TIPPETT: *Fantasia concertante.*

Iona Brown has recorded *The Lark ascending* before with Marriner and the ASMF (see above), but the present version is both eloquent and evocative and the great clarity of the recording makes it highly competitive. The *Tallis fantasia* is beautifully played too, but the effect here is relatively bland beside the earlier, Argo account. The acoustic is warm but not quite as expansive as the best of its rivals. But couplings are important with a record of this kind and neither shows these artists at their very best.

Fantasia on a theme of Thomas Tallis; The Wasps: Overture.
*** HMV ASD/*TC-ASD* 3857 [Ang. SZ/*4ZS* 37627]. LSO, Previn – ELGAR: *Enigma variations.****
(M) *** HMV Green. ESD 7013. Bournemouth SO, Silvestri – ELGAR: *In the South.****

Coupled with Elgar's most popular orchestral work, Previn's performances of the *Tallis fantasia* and the *Wasps overture* are warmly persuasive. The wasp-music buzzes with point and energy, while the *Fantasia,* after a restrained opening, builds up finally with great conviction into a blazing climax, with no inhibition over a stringendo. Warm, opulent recording to match; the cassette too is full-blooded and clear, although there is just a hint of roughness at the biggest climaxes.

Those wanting Silvestri's exhilaratingly memorable account of Elgar's *In the South* need not be deterred if they already have Barbirolli's account of the *Tallis fantasia.* This reading is quite different, more brilliant, less expansive, with remarkable tension in the opening and closing pages, and a touch of restraint in the handling of the second orchestra. But the central climax of the work is tremendously passionate, in a tighter, more direct way than Barbirolli. The playing is excellent, the recording only marginally less good. Silvestri's account of the *Wasps overture* makes the most of the brio, with crisp, fast tempi and the expansiveness of the great tune in the middle not allowed to interfere with the forward momentum. The vivacity of the playing and the vivid recording (only a trifle less good than *In the South*) make this very enjoyable indeed.

Hymn-tune preludes: Nos. 1, Eventide (arr. of Monk); *2, Dominus regit me* (arr. of Dykes); *The Poisoned Kiss: overture; The Running Set; Sea Songs: Quick march.*
(M) *** Chan. CBR/*CBT* 1004. Bournemouth Sinf., Hurst – ELGAR: *Adieu* etc.***

George Hurst directs no fewer than three first recordings on the Vaughan Williams side of a delightful collection of minor pieces. The overture to the opera *The Poisoned Kiss* is merely a potpourri, but it whets the appetite for a complete recording of a piece neglected simply because of its poor libretto. *The Running Set* is an exhilarating fantasy on jig rhythms, while the *March on sea songs,* with its bounding rhythms and surging melody in the trio, would make an ideal Prom item. Ripe performances and recording.

In the Fen Country. (i) *The Lark ascending. Norfolk rhapsody No. 1.* (ii) *Serenade to Music.*
*** HMV ASD 2847 [Ang. S/*4XS* 36902]. LPO, Boult, with (i) Bean; (ii) 16 vocal soloists.

An attractive coupling of four works that originally appeared as fill-ups to Boult versions of the symphonies, all beautifully performed and recorded.

Job (masque for dancing).
(M) ❀ *** EMI Em. EMX/*TC-EMX* 41 2056-1/*4*. LPO, Handley.
*** HMV ASD 2673 [Ang. S 36773]. LSO, Boult.

Job is undeniably one of Vaughan Williams's very greatest compositions. It shows his inspiration at its most deeply characteristic and at its most consistently noble. Boult is its dedicatee and this is his fourth recording of it. It is probably his most successful, and the LSO give of their very best throughout. The recording has exceptional range and truthfulness; indeed it is one of the finest of any analogue orchestral recordings.

However the new Eminence digital recording by the LPO, playing with inspired fervour under Vernon Handley – made in St Augustine's Church, London – offers sound of superlative quality, very much in the demonstration class. The breadth of dynamic range is used to enormous effect by Handley to increase the dramatic effect – the organ entry representing Satan enthroned in heaven has overwhelming impact and power – and one feels that had Diaghilev heard this record he would not have rejected Vaughan Williams's masterly score. The ravishingly luminous espressivo playing in the work's quieter lyrical pages is movingly beautiful, with the music's evocative feeling memorably captured. Even at full-price this record would be irresistible, one of Handley's major achievements in the recording studio. The cassette is also in the demonstration class.

Romance in D flat for harmonica, string orchestra and piano.
*** Argo ZRG 856 [id.]. Reilly, ASMF, Marriner – JACOB: *5 Pieces;* MOODY: *Little suite;* TAUSKY: *Concertino.****

Vaughan Williams's atmospheric *Romance,* if not one of his most inspired works, is still worth having on disc. But it is the Jacob and Moody works that make this anthology worth exploring.

Suite for viola and orchestra; (i) *Flos campi.*
(M) **(*) Chan. CBR/*CBT* 1019. Riddle, Bournemouth Sinf., Del Mar; (i) with Ch.

Originally issued in 1978 by RCA, this valuable coupling has been digitally remastered by Chandos with the choral sound enhanced. Neither work is over-familiar and the evocation of the Song of Solomon contained in *Flos campi* shows Vaughan Williams at his most rarefied and imaginative. The *Suite* is lightweight but engaging, unpretentious music to be enjoyed, with its charming *Carol* and quirky *Polka mélancolique.* Frederick Riddle is an eloquent soloist, even if the playing is not always technically immaculate, and Norman Del Mar directs sympathetically. On the otherwise good chrome tape the choral sound is a little misty.

Symphonies Nos. 1–9.
(B) *** RCA RL 43371 (7). Soloists, LSO Ch., LSO, Previn.

Symphonies Nos. 1–9; Norfolk rhapsody; The Wasps – overture.
(M) *** HMV SLS/*TC-SLS* 154708-3/9 (7). Soloists, LPO Ch., LPO, New Philh. O, Boult.

Previn recorded the Vaughan Williams symphonies over a five-year span from 1968 to 1972, and his achievement in this repertoire represented a peak in his recording career at that time. Here the nine symphonies minus the couplings have been neatly compressed on to seven discs. The most striking performances are those which were recorded last, Nos. 2, 3 and 5, for there Previn achieves an extra depth of understanding, an extra intensity, whether in the purity of pianissimo or the outpouring of emotional resolution. For the rest there is only one performance that can be counted at all disappointing, and that of the symphony one might have expected Previn to interpret best, the taut and dramatic *Fourth.* Even that is an impressive account, if less intense than the rest. Otherwise the great landscape of the whole cycle is presented with richness and detail in totally refreshing interpretations, brilliantly recorded.

Boult's late 1960s performances of the symphonies are wonderfully satisfying too, and many lovers of Vaughan Williams will prefer their superbly consistent view, patiently studied and broadly presented. If at times the playing is not so electrically urgent as with Previn, the maturity of Vaughan Williams's vision has never been more convincingly presented. The recording throughout is of the highest quality. The recordings have been effectively remastered and are now issued – like the Previn set – on seven discs, but including two attractive bonuses.

A Sea symphony (*No. 1*).
(M) *** HMV Green. ESD/*TC-ESD* 7104 [(d) Ang. S 3739]. Armstrong, Carol Case, LPO Ch., LPO, Boult.
(M) *** RCA Gold GL/*GK* 43576. Harper, Shirley-Quirk, LSO Ch., LSO, Previn.

Boult's is a warm, relaxed reading of Vaughan Williams's expansive symphony. If the ensemble is sometimes less perfect than one would like, the flow of the music consistently holds the listener, and this is matched by warmly atmospheric recorded sound. Boult, often thought of as a 'straight' interpreter, here demonstrates his affectionate style, drawing consistently expressive but never sentimental phrasing from his singers and players. John Carol Case's baritone does not sound well on disc with his rather plaintive tone colour, but his style is right, and Sheila Armstrong sings most beautifully. The set has been remastered and in this Greensleeve reissue it now fits comfortably on to two sides instead of three, without apparent loss of amplitude or clarity. The cassette, transferred at a high level to give the famous opening section plenty of impact, is fractionally less open than the disc but remains impressively full-bodied and clear.

Previn's is a fresh, youthful reading of a young composer's symphony. If his interpretation lacks some of the honeyed sweetness that Boult brings to music that he has known and loved for half a century and more, Previn's view provides a clearer focus. His nervous energy is obvious from the very start. He does not always relax as Boult does, even where, as in the slow movement, he takes a more measured tempo than the older conductor. In the scherzo Boult concentrates on urgency, the emotional surge of the music, even at the expense of precision of ensemble, where Previn is lighter and cleaner, holding more in reserve. The finale similarly is built up over a longer span, with less deliberate expressiveness. The culminating climax with Previn is not allowed to be swamped with choral tone, but has the brass and timpani still prominent. The *Epilogue* may not be so deliberately expressive but it is purer in its tenderness and exact control of dynamics. Even if Vaughan Williams devotees will disagree over the relative merits of the interpretations, Previn has clear advantages in his baritone soloist and his choir. The recording too is of excellent quality, with the vivid cassette transfer very slightly less refined than the disc. It benefits from a small treble reduction, which does not rob the choral focus of its sharpness and impact. The bass is lighter and cleaner than on Boult's HMV tape.

A London symphony (*No. 2*).
(M) *** RCA Gold GL/*GK* 43577. LSO, Previn.
*** HMV ASD 2740 [Ang. S/*4XS* 36838]. LPO, Boult.
(B) **(*) PRT GSGC/*ZCGC* 2035. Hallé O, Barbirolli.

A London symphony; Fantasia on a theme of Thomas Tallis.
(B) *** CfP CFP/*TC-CFP* 41 4411-1/*4*. LPO, Handley.

Previn underlines the greatness of this work as a symphony, not just a sequence of programmatic impressions. Though the actual sonorities are even more subtly and beautifully realized here than in rival versions, the architecture is equally convincingly presented, with the great climaxes of the first and last movements powerful and incisive. Most remarkable of all are the pianissimos, which here have new intensity, a quality of frisson as in a live performance. The LSO plays superbly and the recording, made in Kingsway Hall, is beautifully balanced and refined, coping perfectly with the widest possible dynamic range. The cassette transfer is successful, full and well detailed, and any slight loss of refinement in the upper range (it is very marginal) is more than compensated for by the freedom from intrusive background noises.

Boult's record of the *London symphony* is also given a superbly rich and spacious recording. The orchestral playing too is outstandingly fine. The reading itself is basically the same as on Boult's earlier Decca mono record, although the outer movements in the newer performance are more expansive, rather less taut. The central tranquillo episode of the first movement, for instance, is very relaxed, Boult indulging himself in the mood of nostalgic reverie. But here, as in the slow movements, the orchestra produces such lovely sounds, the playing obviously deeply committed, that criticism is disarmed. The scherzo is as light as thistledown, and the gentle melancholy which underlies the solemn pageantry of the finale is coloured with great subtlety.

Vernon Handley's performance on Classics for Pleasure is given a splendid modern recording of striking range. The subtlety of detail, especially at lower dynamic levels, means that many of the composer's orchestral effects are more telling here than in Barbirolli's 1959 bargain version, and the brilliant scherzo gains immeasurably from the sense of spectacle and wide dynamic contrasts. The performance is direct and undoubtedly effective. Tempi are well chosen; the slow movement has genuine poetry and its climax, like that of the finale (before the *Epilogue*), has eloquence. The orchestral playing is sensitive throughout (notably in the closing pages of the *Lento*). The reissue adds Handley's passionately persuasive account of the *Tallis fantasia*. With fine playing and good sound this record becomes a first-rate bargain. There is a good cassette matching the disc fairly closely.

Barbirolli's account of the *London symphony* dates from 1958 and was the finest of his Pye recordings of this period. It is an inspirational performance, entirely throwing off the fetters of the studio. The spontaneity of the music-making means that the reading gathers power as it proceeds, and the slow movement has great intensity and eloquence with the Hallé strings surpassing themselves. The recording is somewhat dated, but it has a wide dynamic range and plenty of atmosphere. It is still very competitive at bargain price and admirers of this great conductor should not miss it. The tape is less refined than the disc; side two is brighter than side one, but sounds a little fierce.

(i) *A London symphony;* (ii) *Symphony No. 5 in D.*

(M) *** HMV *TCC2-POR 54280*. (i) Hallé O; (ii) Philh. O, Barbirolli.

This is among the finest of HMV's enterprising 'Portrait of the Artist' tape-only series. Barbirolli was a great Vaughan Williams conductor, and his account of the *Fifth Symphony* is unforgettable, with the Philharmonia strings and brass making the most ravishing sounds. His HMV recording of the *London symphony* is more relaxed and expansive than his Pye version. In many places this yields greater authority to the interpretation, with the threads of the first movement drawn together at the end with striking breadth and majesty. The slow movement gains from the richer recording but has marginally less intensity than the earlier version. The scherzo is more controversial. It is taken relatively slowly, but the lack of boisterousness fits in with the overall interpretation. The powerful finale and finely graduated closing pages of the *Epilogue* make considerable amends and this remains an impressive account. In their tape format both works have the advantage of unbroken continuity and excellent transfers.

(i) *A Pastoral symphony* (*No. 3*); (ii) *Tuba concerto in F min.*

(M) *** RCA Gold GL/*GK* 43580 [LSC 3281]. LSO, Previn, with (i) Harper; (ii) Fletcher.

(i) *A Pastoral symphony* (*No. 3*); *In the Fen Country.*

*** HMV ASD/*TC-ASD* 2393 [Ang. S 36532]. New Philh. O, Boult (i) with Price.

One tends to think of Vaughan Williams's pastoral music as essentially synonymous with the English countryside, and it is something of a shock to discover that in fact the *Pastoral symphony* was sketched in Northern France while the composer was on active service in 1916, and the initial inspiration was a Corot-like landscape in the sunset. But the music remains English in essence, and its gentle rapture is not easily evoked.

Previn draws an outstandingly beautiful and refined performance from the LSO, the bare textures sounding austere but never thin, the few climaxes emerging at full force with purity undiminished. In the third movement the final coda – the only really fast music in the whole work – brings a magic tracery of pianissimo in this performance, lighter, faster and even clearer than in Boult's version. The recording adds to the beauty in its atmospheric distancing, not least in the trumpet cadenza of the second movement and the lovely melismas for the soprano soloist in the last movement. The high-level cassette transfer is vivid, but less refined in the upper range; this is most noticeable in the *Tuba concerto*, where the strings sound somewhat fierce.

Boult here is not entirely successful in controlling the tension of the short but elusive first movement, although it is beautifully played. The opening of the *Lento moderato*, however, is very fine, and its close is sustained with a perfect blend of restraint and intensity. After the jovial third movement, the orchestra is joined by Margaret Price, whose wordless contribution is blended into the texture most skilfully.

In the Fen Country follows on so naturally after the *Pastoral symphony* that it might be an extra movement. The middle section of the piece is perhaps on the whole less interesting, but the gentle rapture of the closing pages – beautifully sustained here – shows the composer weaving his most imaginative textures. The recording throughout is superb. For the most part the performance of the *Symphony* is very successful and certainly rewarding. The cassette is in the demonstration class and sounds very beautiful.

Symphony No. 4 in F min.; (i) *Concerto accademico for violin and orchestra in D min.*
(M) **(*) RCA Gold GL/*GK* 43581. LSO, Previn, (i) with Buswell.

Symphony No. 4; Norfolk rhapsody No. 1.
**(*) HMV ASD 2375 [Ang. S 36557]. New Philh. O, Boult.

Boult's was the first stereo recording of the *Fourth*, and although it would be possible to imagine a performance of greater fire and tenacity few will find much to disappoint them in this persuasive account. Sir Adrian procures orchestral playing of the highest quality from the New Philharmonia, and the slow movement, one of the composer's finest inspirations, is particularly successful. The recording, too, falls into the superlative category: it has body, clarity of detail and spaciousness. The performance does not obliterate memories of the composer's own recording, which Sir Adrian helped to prepare, and whose intensity and anguish had an immediacy that this does not quite capture. But it is very fine.

The *Norfolk rhapsody* (in spite of its number, there is no No. 2) is a lovely work and this, its first stereo recording, could not be bettered. It dates from the years immediately preceding the First World War, and despite its obvious indebtedness to the English folk-music tradition, it has great freshness and individuality and in its pensive moments a genuine delicacy of feeling. Boult evokes the most eloquent playing from the New Philharmonia, and the HMV engineers give us a well-focused, musically balanced and full-blooded sound.

Previn secures a fine performance of the *F minor Symphony*; only the somewhat ponderous tempo he adopts for the first movement lets it down. But on the whole this is a powerful reading, and it is vividly recorded. A good alternative to Boult's version, though not superior to it. The *Concerto* makes an attractive bonus. The sound on cassette is sharply defined and benefits from a slight treble cut; but it can be made to yield very good results.

Symphonies Nos. (i) *4;* (ii) *6 in E min.* (*original version*).
(M) (***) CBS 61432/*40*-. NYPO, (i) Mitropoulos; (ii) Stokowski.

Vaughan Williams's two apocalyptic symphonies make a satisfying coupling in historic New York recordings under highly characterful virtuoso conductors. The dim mono sound still allows one to appreciate the fire of Mitropoulos, in a reading approved by the composer himself, and the unsentimental thrust of Stokowski, disconcertingly fast in the slow movement and unpointed in the slow visionary finale.

Symphony No. 5 in D.
*** HMV ASD 2358 [Ang. S 36698]. LPO, Boult – *Serenade to music.***(*)
*** HMV ASD 2698 [(d) Ang. S 35952]. Philh. O, Barbirolli – *Fantasia on a theme of Tallis.****

Symphony No. 5; The Wasps: Overture.
(M) ❀ *** RCA Gold GL/*GK* 43578. LSO, Previn.
** HMV Dig. ASD/*TCC-ASD* 143441-1/*4*. RPO, Gibson.

If anyone has ever doubted the dedication of Previn as an interpreter of Vaughan Williams, this glowing disc will provide the clearest proof. In this most characteristic – and many would say greatest – of the Vaughan Williams symphonies Previn refuses to be lured into pastoral byways. His tempi may – rather surprisingly – be consistently on the slow side, but the purity of tone he draws from the LSO, the precise shading of dynamic and phrasing, and the sustaining of tension through the longest, most hushed passages produce results that will persuade many not normally convinced of the greatness of this music. In the first movement Previn builds the great climaxes of the second subject with much warmth, but he reserves for the climax of the slow movement his culminating thrust of emotion, a moment of visionary sublimity, after which the gentle urgency of the *Passacaglia* finale and the stillness of the *Epilogue* seem a perfect happy conclusion. It is some tribute to Previn's intensity that he can draw out the diminuendi at the ends of movements with such refinement and no sense of exaggeration. This is an outstanding performance, superbly recorded. The cassette transfer is made at the highest level (especially on side two) and has striking range. The sound is less refined in the treble than the disc and needs considerable control, but there is no lack of body and with care this can be made to yield impressive results.

Boult gives a loving performance of the *Fifth Symphony*, one which links it directly with the great opera *The Pilgrim's Progress*, from which (in its unfinished state) the composer drew much of the material. It is a gentler performance, easier, more flowing than Previn's, and some may prefer it for that reason, but the emotional involvement is a degree less intense, particularly in the slow movement.

The reissue of Barbirolli's performance is highly successful, and the recording sounds fresh and modern without loss of warmth. Barbirolli's reading shows rather more temperament than Boult's, and there are many wonderfully glowing moments. The string-playing is distinguished. With the generous coupling of the *Tallis fantasia*, one of the finest things Barbirolli did for the gramophone, this disc remains very competitive.

A full digital recording given to Gibson clarifies the often thick textures of this beautiful symphony, and the reading is attractively direct with a flowing *Moderato* first movement. But other versions get closer to the heart of the music with more refinement and more power at the climaxes. The chrome cassette is of good quality, vivid and clear, although it would have benefited from a higher transfer level. Hiss is not a real problem; nonetheless this is music where one needs a silent background if possible.

Symphony No. 6 in E min; (i) *The Lark ascending.*

**(*) HMV ASD 2329 [Ang. S 36469]. (i) Bean; New Philh. O, Boult.

There is an element of disappointment in discussing Boult's re-recording of the powerful *Sixth Symphony*; perhaps one expected too much. The performance is without the tension of the earlier mono recording Boult made for Decca, with the composer present. The sound of that record cannot of course compare with that of the newer version, but Boult's comparative mellowness here means that the reading is not as searching as the score demands. The strange finale is beautifully played, with a finely sustained pianissimo from wind and strings alike, but the atmosphere, if not without a sense of mystery, is somehow too complacent.

If one has some reservations about the performance of the symphony, one can find nothing but praise for this most beautiful account of *The Lark ascending*. Hugh Bean understands the spirit of the music perfectly; the lyricism of his tone and style is never over-indulgent, and the accompaniment is perfectly managed. The recording is fully worthy of the playing.

Symphonies Nos. 6; 8 in D min.

(M) **(*) RCA Gold GL/*GK* 43579. LSO, Previn.

Previn's is a sensible and generous coupling. The *Sixth Symphony*, with its moments of darkness and brutality contrasted against the warmth of the second subject or the hushed intensity of the final other-worldly slow movement, is a work for which Previn has a natural affinity. In the first three movements his performance is superbly dramatic, clear-headed and direct, with natural understanding. His account of the mystic final movement with its endless pianissimo is not, however, on the same level, for – whether or not the fault of the recording – the playing is not quite hushed enough, and the tempo is a little too fast. In its closely wrought contrapuntal texture this is a movement which may seem difficult to interpret, but which should be allowed to flow along on its own intensity. Boult here achieves a more vital sense of mystery, even though his account is not ideal. Previn's account of the *Eighth* brings no such reservations, with finely pointed playing, the most precise control of dynamic shading, and a delightfully Stravinskian account of the bouncing scherzo for woodwind alone. Excellent recording considering the length of sides, although the string tone is not always ideally expansive. The cassette transfer, made at a high level, is extremely bright, and the upper range needs some control if it is not to sound fierce. However, the recording has plenty of body and with an adjustment can give excellent results: the strings in the *Cavatina* of the *Eighth Symphony* and in the famous lyrical melody of the first movement of the *Sixth* have impressive breadth of timbre.

Sinfonia Antartica (*No. 7*).
*** HMV ASD 2631 [Ang. S 36763]. Burrowes, LPO Ch., LPO, Boult.
*** RCA Gold [GL/*GK* 43582]. Harper, Amb. S., LSO, Previn; Ralph Richardson (narrator).

The *Antartica* may be episodic but it is still a vital and dramatic symphony, deriving as it does from the score to the film *Scott of the Antarctic*. Sir Adrian gives a stirring account and is very well served by the EMI engineers. There is not really a great deal to choose between this and Previn's version as performances: both are convincing. Perhaps the EMI recording has slightly greater range and a more natural balance. The RCA recording, in its relatively distant balance, as well as Previn's interpretation concentrate on atmosphere rather than drama. The performance is sensitive and literal. Because of the recessed effect of the sound the picture of the ice fall (represented by an almost startling entry of the organ) has a good deal less impact here than on Boult's old Decca mono LP. But at medium price the RCA disc remains fully competitive, and the cassette transfer is highly successful, slightly sharper in focus than the disc, yet not lacking atmosphere.

Symphony No. 8 in D min.
(B) ** PRT GSGC/*ZCGC* 2059. Hallé O, Barbirolli – BAX: *Garden of Fand;* BUTTERWORTH: *Shropshire Lad.***

Barbirolli gave the première of Vaughan Williams's *Eighth* and was its dedicatee. It is a robust performance rather than a subtle one, but full of character and feeling; and it is joined to inspirational accounts of music of Bax and Butterworth only limited in appeal by the restricted (if fully acceptable) recording. The cassette is limited in range, like the disc, but well balanced.

Symphony No. 9 in D min.; The England of Elizabeth: suite.
(M) *** RCA Gold GL/*GK* 43583. LSO, Previn.

The *Ninth*, Vaughan Williams's last symphony, is one of his most consistently underrated works. It contains much noble and arresting invention and stimulates Previn to show a freshness and sense of poetry which prove particularly thought-provoking and rewarding. He secures smooth contours in the first movement and as a result of refined string playing he produces attractively transparent textures. The RCA recording is highly successful, and the string tone is expansive, well balanced in relation to the rest of the orchestra and free from the slight hint of hardness that sometimes disturbs this cycle. Listening to this reading reinforces the view that the critics of the day were unfairly harsh to this fine score. On the whole this version is finer than Boult's HMV account. The *England of Elizabeth suite* is a film score of no great musical interest but undoubtedly pleasant to listen to; both performance and recording are first-class. The high-level cassette is vivid and clear, but slightly less refined than the disc: in the symphony the resonance brings a hint of harshness at fortissimo level. But, as in the rest of the series, with control of the treble a full and lively balance can be obtained.

The Wasps (*Aristophanic suite*).
*** HMV ASD/*TC-ASD* 3953. Bournemouth Sinf., Del Mar – HOLST: *Brook Green suite* etc.***

The *Wasps overture* – here dashingly performed – is well enough known, but the other items in the suite are delightful too. Del Mar brings out the wit of the *March of the Kitchen Utensils* with his mock pomposity, and as in the Holst items the recording is outstanding. The cassette is first-rate too; both tape and disc offer sound of demonstration quality. Highly recommended.

6 Studies in English folksong for clarinet and piano.
*** Chan. Dig. ABRD/*ABTD* 1078 [id.]. Hilton, Swallow – BAX: *Sonata***; BLISS: *Quintet.****

These *Folksong Studies*, which Vaughan Williams published in arrangements for the viola and cello, come from the mid-1920s and are really very beautiful; they can be recommended even to those normally allergic to this kind of repertory. They are played with the utmost sensitivity by Janet Hilton and Keith Swallow. There is a first-class chrome cassette.

Violin sonata in A min.
(*) HMV ASD 3820. Y. and H. Menuhin – ELGAR: *Sonata.*(*)

The late Vaughan Williams *Sonata* is an unexpected piece for the Menuhins to record, and though in the first movement (as in the Elgar on the reverse) their tempo is controversially slow, giving the music unexpected weight, the whole performance makes a fine illumination of an elusive piece, not least from the pianist, who copes splendidly with the often awkward piano writing. The recording is first-rate.

PIANO MUSIC

Chorale and chorale prelude: Lord Jesus with us abide; Hymn tune prelude on Song 13 by Orlando Gibbons; The Lake in the mountains; Suite in G; 6 Teaching pieces.
**(*) Phoenix 45 r.p.m. DGS 1019. Jacobs.

Vaughan Williams was no pianist, but these fragments warmly reflect his career and sympathies, with the little teaching pieces for example reflecting his love of Bach. The most substantial piece, *The Lake in the mountains*, written in 1947, is taken from his music for the film *49th Parallel*, characteristically evocative. Perceptive playing and good recording, transferred at 45 r.p.m.

VOCAL AND CHORAL MUSIC

Choral music: *Benedicite; Dona nobis pacem; Fantasia on Christmas carols; Fantasia on the Old 100th; Flos campi; Hodie; Magnificat; Mass in G minor; 5 Mystical songs; An Oxford elegy; Sancta civitas; Serenade to Music: Towards the Unknown Region; 5 Tudor portraits; 5 Variants of Dives and Lazarus.*
(M) *** HMV SLS 5082 (7). Soloists (including Baker, Armstrong, Harper, Watts, Shirley-Quirk, Partridge, Lewis), var. choirs and orchestras, Boult, Willcocks or Meredith Davies.

Though devotees of Vaughan Williams will probably have collected some of these recordings in their separate issues, it was an attractive idea to issue this generous collection at a relatively modest price. All the performances can be recommended (most of them are three-star issues), and a number of them are no longer available separately, which makes this comprehensive issue even more valuable. The recordings are all of good EMI vintage.

Songs: *Blackmwore by the Stour; Idle tears; In the spring; Linden Lea; The splendour falls; Tears; The winter willow. 4 Poems by Fredegond Shove; 3 Poems by Walt Whitman; 4 Last songs.*
*** Phoenix DGS 1005. Savidge, Steptoe.

Linden Lea and *The Water mill* (to a poem by his niece, Fredegond Shove) are by far the most famous of the songs here, enchanting both of them; but the others present a beautiful cross-section of his whole career from the conventional but colourful setting of Tennyson's *The Splendour falls* through folk-style settings to some fine Whitman songs of the 1920s and the *Four Last songs* written to words by his wife, Ursula, when his inspiration grew rhapsodically free. Keen, intelligent performances from both baritone and pianist and good recording.

(i) *10 Blake songs.* (ii) *Songs of Travel.* Songs: *Linden Lea; Orpheus with his Lute; The Water Mill.*

(B) *** Con. CC/*CCT* 7577. Tear with (i) Black (oboe); (ii) Ledger.

Robert Tear cannot match the sheer beauty of Ian Partridge in his wonderfully sensitive account of the *Blake songs* (see below under *On Wenlock Edge*), but his rougher-grained voice brings out a different kind of expressiveness, helped by Neil Black's fine oboe-playing. The *Songs of Travel*, here presented complete with the five extra songs published later, make an excellent coupling, with Ledger a most perceptive accompanist. Excellent recording. A bargain.

Choral music: (i) *Bushes and briars; Down among the dead men;* (ii) *2 Elizabethan part-songs* (*Willow song; O mistress mine*)*;* (ii; iii) *Fantasia on Christmas carols;* (iv) *Lord, Thou hast been our refuge;* (v) *5 Mystical songs: Antiphon;* (iv; vi) *O clap your hands;* (vii) *O taste and see;* (ii) *3 Shakespeare songs;* (viii; ii) *The turtle dove;* (i) *Wassail song.*

(M) *** Argo ZK 34. (i) Elizabethan Singers, Halsey; (ii) King's College Ch., Willcocks; (iii) Alan, LSO; (iv) St John's College Ch., Guest; (v) St George's Chapel, Windsor, Ch., Campbell; (vi) L. Brass Players; (vii) St Michael's College, Tenbury, Ch., Nethsingha; (viii) Lindsay Heather.

The *Fantasia on Christmas carols*, one of the highlights here, and *O clap your hands* are also available in *The world of Vaughan Williams* (see below), but this collection concentrates entirely on vocal music. The selection has been well made to provide variety as well as showing the best side of the composer in this field. Performances and recording are both excellent.

5 English folksongs; Heart's music; Prayer to the Father in Heaven; The souls of the righteous; Te Deum in C; Valiant for truth; A Vision of Aeroplanes.

*** Abbey LPB 799. BBC Northern Singers, Wilkinson; Weir (organ).

The excellent BBC Northern Singers under their founder and conductor Stephen Wilkinson provide a most attractive programme of choral works, largely neglected. *A Vision of Aeroplanes* is improbably a setting of words from the Book of Ezekiel, an urgently imaginative piece as sung by such a choir, while the Bunyan setting, *Valiant for truth*, builds up to a superb close. Gillian Weir makes a powerful and stylish accompanist, and the recording is first-rate in its clean acoustic.

(i) *Fantasia on Christmas carols.* Arrangements: *And all in the morning; Wassail song.* (Also includes: trad. arr. Warlock: *Bethlehem down; Adam lay y-bounden.*)

(M) ** HMV Green. ESD/*TC-ESD* 7021. Guildford Cath. Ch., Pro Arte O, Rose, (i) with Barrow – HELY-HUTCHINSON: *Carol symphony.***

Vaughan Williams's joyful *Fantasia* is comparatively short. It was written for performance in 1912 in Hereford Cathedral, so the acoustic at Guildford is well chosen. The performance is suitably exuberant, and John Barrrow is an eloquent if not outstanding soloist. The rest of the side is made up with an attractive selection of traditional carols in arrangements either by Vaughan Williams or by Warlock. The recording is of good quality on disc, although on tape the sound is rather fierce.

(i) *Flos campi;* (ii) *5 Mystical songs;* (iii) *O clap your hands;* (iv) *5 Tudor portraits.*

HMV *TC C2-POR 54294.* (i) Aronowitz, Jacques O; (ii) Shirley-Quirk; (i; iii) King's College Ch.; (iii) ECO; (iv) Bainbridge, Carol Case, Bach Ch., New Philh. O, Willcocks.

A valuable issue in EMI's 'Portrait of the Artist' series, centred on Sir David Willcocks, let down by poor technology. The recordings needed chrome stock for adequate sound and the present iron-oxide transfers produce a fluffy choral focus and a limited upper range. Our copy was insecure in texture and had a number of drop-outs. The performances are admirable and the *Tudor portraits* are not otherwise available outside a seven-disc boxed set. We must hope later batches will be re-mastered.

In Windsor Forest (cantata).
*** HMV ASD/*TC-ASD* 4061. Fields, Bournemouth SO Ch. and O, Del Mar – ELGAR: *From the Bavarian Highlands*.***

The cantata *In Windsor Forest*, which Vaughan Williams adapted from his Falstaff opera, *Sir John in Love*, makes the perfect coupling for Elgar's suite of part-songs. The movements are not always exact transcriptions from the opera, for the composer re-thought and amplified certain passages. As in the Elgar, Del Mar directs warmly sympathetic performances, given excellent sound, warmly reverberant. On cassette the choral focus is not always quite clean at climaxes, though overall the sound is rich and well balanced.

(i) *Mass in G min.*; (i–iii) *5 Mystical songs* (*Rise, heart; I got me flowers; Love bade me welcome; The call; Antiphon*); (i–ii) *O clap your hands* (motet).
*** HMV ASD 2458 [Ang. S 36590]. (i) King's College Ch.; (ii) ECO; (iii) Shirley-Quirk, Willcocks.

Here with the finest band of trebles in the country Sir David Willcocks captures the beauty of Vaughan Williams's *Mass* more completely than any rival, helped by fine, atmospheric recording quality. This is a work which can on the one hand easily seem too tense and lose its magic, or on the other fall apart in a meandering style, and Willcocks admirably finds the middle course. In the *Five Mystical songs* to words by George Herbert, John Shirley-Quirk sings admirably. Considering the problems of balance the recording is very good.

Mass in G min.; Te Deum in C.
*** Hyp. A 66076. Corydon Singers, Best – HOWELLS: *Requiem*.***

The only current alternative version of Vaughan Williams's masterly *Mass in G minor* is fifteen years old (see above) and this newcomer is a worthy rival. It has the additional attraction of Herbert Howells's *Requiem*, a work of great depth and tranquillity of spirit. Matthew Best and the Corydon Singers give as committed an account as King's College Choir and, despite the spacious acoustic, there is admirable clarity of texture.

(i) *On Wenlock Edge* (song cycle from Housman's *A Shropshire Lad*); (ii) *10 Blake songs;* (iii) *The New Ghost; The Water Mill.*
(M) ❀ *** HMV HQS 1236 [(d) Ara. 8018/*9018*]. Ian Partridge, with (i) Music Group of L.; (ii) Craxton (oboe); (iii) Jennifer Partridge.

On Wenlock Edge (song cycle).
*** Hyp. A 66013. Hill, Coull Qt – GURNEY: *Ludlow and Teme*.***

On Wenlock Edge (orchestral version).
(*) HMV ASD 3896. Tear, CBSO, Handley – BUTTERWORTH: *Love Blows*; ELGAR: *Songs*.*
(*) Uni. Kanchana KP 8001. English, W. Australian SO, Measham – IRELAND: *The Overlanders*.*

The HMV mid-priced issue is an outstandingly beautiful record, with Ian Partridge's intense artistry and lovely individual tone-colour used with compelling success in Vaughan Williams songs both early and late. The Housman cycle has an accompaniment for piano and string quartet which can sound ungainly, but here, with playing from the Music Group of London which matches the soloist's sensitivity, the result is atmospheric and moving. The *Ten Blake songs* come from just before the composer's death, bald, direct settings that with the artistry of Partridge and Craxton are darkly moving. The tenor's sister accompanies with fine understanding in two favourite songs as a welcome extra. Warm, rounded recording.

Martyn Hill's voice records very cleanly,

and though he may have less beautiful colourings than some tenors, he gives a deeply understanding performance of the Vaughan Williams cycle, one which fully brings out word-meaning on the lines of German Lieder. *Is my team ploughing?* is made the more eerie when the Coull Quartet eliminates vibrato in the passages accompanying the words of the dead man. Well recorded, with a rare and apt coupling, it is an excellent issue. However, Ian Partridge's record with the Music Group of London (coupled with settings of Blake) is in a special class.

Vaughan Williams's own orchestration of the cycle, made in the early 1920s, has been strangely neglected. It lacks something of the apt ghostly quality of the version for piano and string quartet, but some will prefer the bigger scale. Tear sings sensitively, but with the voice balanced close the tone is not always sweet. Handley draws fine playing from the Birmingham orchestra, but this has less flair and imagination than the Unicorn version conducted by David Measham.

Gerald English is no less persuasive than Robert Tear in this repertoire, and the closer recorded balance helps him to convey greater dramatic intensity and ardour. Yet the sound, though forward, is never unacceptably so. Choice will doubtless depend on individual preference as far as couplings are concerned. The Ireland suite is not among that master's finest works.

Serenade to Music.
(*) HMV ASD 2538 [Ang. S 36698]. 16 vocal soloists, LPO, Boult – *Symphony No. 5.**

The *Serenade to Music*, written in honour of Sir Henry Wood, makes an ideal coupling for the *Fifth Symphony*, and it is good to have a performance which, following the original idea, uses solo singers, though these cannot, except in one or two instances, match the quality of the originals whose initials were placed in the score. The violin soloist disappointingly uses too sweet a style in his important part in the introduction. The recording matches the rest of the Boult cycle of the symphonies in its atmospheric warmth.

Songs of travel.
** Hyp. A 66037. Trew, Vignoles – BUTTERWORTH: *Songs.***(*)

Vaughan Williams's *Songs of travel* to words by Robert Louis Stevenson include three that have become very popular, *The Vagabond*, *Bright is the ring of words* and (most of all) *The Roadside fire*. The others, though not quite so memorable, are comparably sympathetic and here receive thoughtful performances, an excellent coupling for the rarer Butterworth settings on the reverse – which also include a setting of *The Roadside fire*. Trew's voice is rather dry, but he is very well accompanied, and the recording is truthful.

The Sons of Light.
*** Lyr. SRCS 125. Bach Ch., Royal College of Music Ch., LPO, Willcocks – PARRY: *Ode on the Nativity.****

Composed for the Schools Music Association in 1951 and given its first performance at the Royal Albert Hall by massed school choirs under Sir Adrian Boult, *The Sons of Light* has been unfairly neglected. Its three sections set words by Ursula Vaughan Williams, graphically and colourfully, starting with trumpet calls. Only marginally did the composer modify the tangy bluffness of his late idiom for young performers. In a strong and committed performance it makes a valuable coupling for the Parry rarity on the reverse. The recording is excellent.

OPERA

Hugh the Drover (complete).
**(*) HMV SLS 5162 (2). Tear, Armstrong, Watts, Lloyd, Rippon, Amb. Op. Ch., RPO, Groves.

Hugh the Drover is the most immediately appealing of the Vaughan Williams operas, the earliest of the full-length works. Described as a ballad opera and using folk-themes in full-throated lyricism, it has – as Michael Kennedy has said – at times an almost Puccinian warmth and expansiveness. That being so, it is a pity that Robert Tear was in such dry voice when he recorded the role of Hugh. That miscasting may not have been predictable, but it seriously detracts from the work's magic, and though Sir Charles Groves's conducting is thoroughly idiomatic, the result could have more emotional thrust. Nonetheless, with a very good supporting team and beautifully recorded, it is a most welcome issue.

The Pilgrim's progress (complete).
(M) *** HMV SLS/*TC-SLS* 143513-3/5 (2). Noble, Burrowes, Armstrong, Herincx, Carol Case, Shirley-Quirk, Keyte, LPO Ch., LPO, Boult.

This glowing performance under Boult should effectively ensure that this inspired opera, one of the composer's culminating lifeworks, is at last given its due. Though Vaughan Williams was right in insisting that it is not an oratorio (his word was a 'morality'), the choral writing frames it, sung here with heartfelt warmth by the London Philharmonic Choir. What comes out in a recorded performance is that, so far from being slow and undramatic, the score is crammed full of delectable ideas one after the other, and the drama of the mind – as in the book – supplements more conventional dramatic incident. John Noble gives a dedicated performance in the central role of Pilgrim, and the large supporting cast is consistently strong. Much of the material of Act I was also used in the *Fifth Symphony*, and like that masterpiece this opera stands at the heart of the composer's achievement. Vanity Fair may not sound evil here, but Vaughan Williams's own recoil is vividly expressed, and the jaunty passage of Mr and Mrs By-Ends brings the most delightful light relief. The fine 1972 recording has been remastered from three to two discs, and now there are outstanding chrome tapes as well. The tape transfer is first-class in every way with the chorus – so important in this work – well focused.

(i) *Riders to the sea* (complete). (i) Arrangements of folk songs: *An acre of land; Bushes and briars; Ca' the Yowes; Early in the spring; Greensleeves; John Dory; Loch Lomond; The seeds of love; The turtle dove; The unquiet grave; Ward the Pirate.*
*** HMV Green. ESD/*TC-ESD* 178299-1/4 [(d) Ang. S 36819]. (i) Burrowes, Price, Watts, Stevens, Luxon, Amb. S., Women's voices, O Nova, Meredith Davies; (ii) L. Madrigal Singers, Bishop.

Riders to the sea is a moving one-act opera, probably Vaughan Williams's most dramatically effective piece, with a consistently high level of inspiration. It is beautifully performed and recorded, though there is a bit too much of the wind machine. The new coupling is a selection of folksong arrangements taken from an admirable collection recorded by Christopher Bishop – one of EMI's recording managers – with a choir of hand-picked singers. There is nothing pretentious whatever about the settings; each is imaginative and never falls into mere routine. The singing of the London Madrigal Singers is admirably lithe and sensitive and this makes a first-rate and generous reissue with an excellent chrome tape to match the disc closely.

COLLECTION

'*The world of Vaughan Williams*': (i) *English folksongs suite;* (ii) *Fantasia on Greensleeves;* (ii; iii) *The Lark ascending;* (iv) *Prelude: Rhosymedre.* (v) *Fantasia on Christmas carols;* (vi) *O clap your hands;* (vii) *Songs: Linden Lea; Silent noon; The vagabond.*
(M) *** Decca SPA/*KCSP* 587. (i) Boston Pops O, Fiedler; (ii) ASMF, Marriner; (iii) Iona Brown; (iv) M. Nicholas (organ); (v) Alan, King's College Ch., LSO, Willcocks; (vi) St John's College Ch., Guest; (vii) Tear, Ledger.

Many collectors will feel that any single-disc summation of Vaughan Williams's art without the symphonies must include the great *Tallis fantasia.* However, this selection is undoubtedly well made as long as there is no objection to having songs with piano sandwiched between *Greensleeves* and *The Lark ascending*, heard in Iona Brown's elysian performance. The orchestral version of the *English folksongs suite* has less bite than the military band original but is brightly presented here. The lovely *Fantasia on Christmas carols* is especially welcome. The sound is excellent on disc and cassette alike.

Verdi, Giuseppe (1813–1901)

Overtures: *Aïda* (reconstructed and arr. Spada); *Aroldo; La Forza del destino; Luisa Miller; Nabucco; I Vespri siciliani.*
*** RCA Dig. **RCD**; RL/*RK* 31378. LSO, Abbado.

Abbado directs strong and brilliant performances of Verdi's most substantial overtures. The recording is brilliant and full, with resonant brass and a sparkling upper range on disc and cassette alike. The novelty is the introduction which Verdi originally wrote for the first Italian performance of *Aïda* and subsequently rejected. It is a considerably extended piece; in Spada's reconstruction one can see why the composer did not want in instrumental terms to anticipate effects far more telling in the full operatic setting, but heard independently it is most entertaining and deftly scored. The compact disc with its silent background brings extra magnetism to the pianissimos – especially the opening of *Aïda*, but also striking in *I Vespri siciliani.* However, the brightness of the upper range does produce a touch of shrillness on fortissimos.

Overtures and Preludes: *Aïda; Un Ballo in maschera; Il Corsaro; La Forza del destino; Luisa Miller; Macbeth; Nabucco; Rigoletto; La Traviata; I Vespri siciliani.*
*** DG 2531/*3301* 145 [id.]. Berlin PO, Karajan.

This is an excellent and generous selection from Karajan's complete set of preludes and overtures (2707 090/*3370 010* – now deleted) and can be strongly recommended. The playing has both panache and authority, and the recording is first-class on disc and tape; if anything the sound is fuller, though not less vivid, than in the original pressings.

Overtures and Preludes: *Aïda; La Forza del destino; Giovanna d'Arco; Luisa Miller; La Traviata; I Vespri siciliani. Macbeth: Ballet music.*
(M) ** Ph. Seq. 6527/*7311* 078 [id.]. New Philh. O, Markevitch.

A generous medium-priced collection, with four items to a side and strongly dramatic performances; *Giovanna d'Arco* and *I Vespri siciliani* are especially vivid. The *Aïda prelude* is beautifully played, and the *Traviata preludes* are well done too. The only reservation is about the recording balance. Verdi's brass writing is powerful enough without any help from the microphones, and here the strings tend to be overwhelmed at times. The middle strings in particular seem unable always to expand their tone, although when the whole section is playing together alone, the sound has plenty of lustre. On cassette the modest transfer level has reduced the sparkle at the top.

Overtures: *Aroldo; La Forza del destino; Giovanna d'Arco; Luisa Miller; Nabucco; Oberto: Conte de San Bonifacio; I Vespri siciliani.*
*** Decca Dig. **410 141-2**; SXDL/*KSXDC* 7595 [Lon. LDR/*5*- 71095]. Nat. PO, Chailly.

Chailly in his collection has the advantage of superb digital recording and a more generous list of overtures than his immediate rivals (except Karajan) with the four most obviously desirable – *Nabucco, I Vespri siciliani, Luisa Miller* and *Forza* – plus three rarities including the overture to his very first opera, *Oberto*, and the most substantial of the early ones, *Aroldo*. Crisp and incisive, Chailly draws vigorous and polished playing from the National Philharmonic. The chrome cassette is extremely brilliant and wide-ranging; some ears may need to tame the upper strings a little. The admirable compact disc clarifies the texture without loss of bloom.

String quartet in E min.
*** CRD CRD 1066/*CRDC 4066* [id.]. Alberni Qt – DONIZETTI: *Quartet No. 13;* PUCCINI: *Crisantemi.****

It is odd that Verdi, having written his *String quartet* as an exercise about the time he completed *Aïda*, should then have refused to let it be heard or published for many years. To us today its skill and finesse are what strike home; it is a unique work in Verdi's output, with a distinctive tone of voice and only one excursion into a recognizably vocal style – in the Neapolitan tune of the trio in the third movement. The Alberni Quartet's performance is strong and compelling, not as polished as the Amadeus version but in many ways the more effective for that; and it is most imaginatively and attractively coupled with the Puccini and Donizetti pieces. The excellent recording on disc is matched by one of CRD's best cassette transfers; it offers demonstration sound, full and with splendid detail and presence.

Requiem Mass.

*** HMV STS/*TC-SLS* 5185 (2) [Ang. SZ/*4Z2S* 3858]. Scotto, Baltsa, Luchetti, Nesterenko, Amb. Ch., Philh. O, Muti.

*** HMV SLS/*TC-SLS* 909 [Ang. SBL 3649]. Schwarzkopf, Ludwig, Gedda, Ghiaurov, Philh. Ch. and O, Giulini.

*** Decca **411 944-2**; SET 374-5/*K 85 K 22* [Lon. OSA/*5*- 1275]. Sutherland, Horne, Pavarotti, Talvela, V. State Op. Ch., VPO, Solti.

**(*) RCA [ARL2/*ARK2* 2476]. Price, Baker, Luchetti, Van Dam, Chicago Singers, Ch., and SO, Solti.

**(*) CBS 77231 (2). Arroyo, Veasey, Domingo, Raimondi, LSO Ch., LSO, Bernstein.

(M) **(*) Decca Jub. DJB/*KDJBC* 2003 (2) [Lon. JL/*5*- 42004]. L. Price, Elias, Bjoerling, Tozzi, V. Musikverein Ch., VPO, Reiner.

*(**) CBS Dig. D 2-36927 (2) [id.]. Caballé, Berini, Domingo, Plishka, Musica Sacra Ch., NYPO, Mehta.

(B) ** CfP CFPD/*TC-CFPD* 41 4428-3/*5* (2) [Ang. RL/*4RL* 3201]. Caballé, Cossotto, Vickers, Raimondi, New Philh. Ch. and O, Barbirolli.

(M) ** HMV SXDW/*TC2-SXDW* 3055 (2). Vartenissian, Cossotto, Fernando, Christoff, Rome Op. Ch. and O, Serafin.

*(*) DG 2707 120/*3370 032* (2) [id.]. Ricciarelli, Verrett, Domingo, Ghiaurov, Ch. and O of La Scala, Milan, Abbado.

(M) *(*) DG 413 215-1/*4* [2707 065/*3370 002*]. Freni, Ludwig, Cossutta, Ghiaurov, V. Singverein, Berlin PO, Karajan.

With spectacular sound – not always perfectly balanced but vividly wide in its tonal spectrum – the Muti performance has tremendous impact. Characteristically he prefers fast speeds, and in the *Dies irae* he rushes the singers dangerously, making the music breathless in excitement rather than grandly dramatic in its portrayal of the Day of Wrath. It is not surprising that Muti opted for a professional choir rather than the Philharmonia Chorus, and the engineers are able to give it fine impact. Unashamedly this is from first to last an operatic performance, with a passionately committed quartet of soloists, underpinned by Nesterenko in glorious voice, giving priestly authority to the *Confutatis*. Scotto is not always sweet at the top, but Baltsa is superb, and Luchetti, as on the Solti/RCA version, sings freshly. Generally speaking this Muti recording (which has a very successful tape equivalent, with a natural balance, excellent clarity and a striking absence of congestion in the spectacular *Dies irae*) must be counted first choice.

By its side Giulini's set is technically rather less satisfactory as a recording (and cannot be recommended in its cassette form). Yet Giulini's combination of refinement and elemental strength remains totally memorable. Such passages as the *Dies irae* are overwhelmingly exciting (though never merely frenetic), but the hushed tension of the chorus's whispers in the same movement and the warm lyricism of the solo singing are equally impressive. What Giulini proves is that refinement added to power can provide an even more intense experience than the traditional Italian approach. In this concept a fine English chorus and orchestra prove exactly right: better disciplined than their Italian counterparts, less severe than the Germans. The array of soloists could hardly be bettered. Schwarzkopf caresses each phrase, and the exactness of her voice matches the firm mezzo of Christa Ludwig in their difficult octave passages. Again with Ludwig you have to throw aside conventional Italian ideas of performance, but the result is undeniably more musical. Gedda is at his most reliable, and Ghiaurov with his really dark bass actually manages to sing the almost impossible *Mors stupebit* in tune without a suspicion of wobble.

Solti's Decca performance is not really a direct rival to any other, for with the wholehearted co-operation of the Decca engineers he has played up the dramatic side of the work at the expense of the spiritual. There is little or nothing reflective about this account, and those who criticize the work for being too operatic will find plenty of ammunition here. The team of soloists is a very strong one, though the matching of voices is not always ideal. It is a pity that the chorus is not nearly so incisive as the Philharmonia on the HMV set – a performance which conveys far more of the work's profundity than this. But if you want an extrovert performance with superlative recording you could hardly do better. The Decca cassettes are generally successful, but this was an early transfer and the *Dies irae* is not absolutely free from congestion, and elsewhere the choral peaks are not always as open as on disc. The soloists and orchestra are naturally caught.

Solti's alternative version on RCA (not currently available in the UK) has all the ingredients for success, with an unusually sensitive and pure-toned quartet of soloists – Luchetti perhaps not as characterful as the others, Price occasionally showing strain – and superb choral singing and orchestral playing. The pity is that the recording – so important in such a dramatic piece – seriously undermines the impact of the performance. Certainly in sound, and in other ways too, Solti's earlier Vienna version on Decca has more bite. But this set is well worth having for Dame Janet Baker's deeply sensitive singing. The cassettes – although slightly fierce on top – offer vivid sound, but the climaxes in the *Dies irae* are too explosive for comfort.

CBS opted to record the *Requiem* in the Royal Albert Hall. By rights the daring of that decision should have paid off, but with close-balancing of microphones and later processing of the tapes that did not allow a full, free atmosphere, the result is disappointing compared with other recent versions. Bernstein's interpretation remains marvellously persuasive in its drama, exaggerated at times maybe, but red-blooded in a way that is hard to resist. The quartet of soloists is particularly strong, making it all the more disappointing that the sound does not match the quality of performance.

Reiner's opening is very slow and atmospheric. He takes the music at something like half the speed of Toscanini, and shapes everything very carefully. Yet as the work proceeds the performance quickly sparks into life and there is some superb and memorable singing from a distinguished team of soloists. The recording is spectacular with a wide dynamic range. In its new Jubilee transfer it sounds remarkably fresh, even if the *Dies irae* is almost overwhelming. The cassette transfer too is sophisticated and loses very little refinement in the big fortissimos. On the whole this is the best buy in the lower price range, for the performance offers much to enjoy, with an excellent contribution from the chorus.

Mehta conducts his New York forces in a strong, well-paced reading, warmly sympathetic if with few touches of magic. The choir and orchestra are excellent and the soloists not only characterful but well matched. The snag is the recording, edgily digital with artificial microphone balance too obtrusive.

Barbirolli favoured slow tempi, as in his late recording of Verdi's *Otello* (shortly to be restored to the catalogue), but in the *Requiem* his concentration was not quite enough to sustain the necessary drama. At bargain price, the set is worth considering. It is an enjoyable, lyrical approach, but more is needed in this much-recorded work and, though the solo quartet is strong, Caballe is well below her finest form. The recording sounds well and the tape transfer is highly successful, notably so in the *Dies irae* and *Sanctus*.

Serafin's Rome set dates from the beginning of the 1960s. There are many beautiful moments in this performance, but at that time one could not expect the choral standard from an Italian opera-house chorus that we take for granted in this country. The solo singing, however, is very good indeed, Christoff is magnificent, and in such moments as the *Mors stupebit* the intensity of his quiet singing is spine-chilling. Cossotto too is outstanding. Her *Recordare* and her *Lacrymosa* are beautifully sung, and Fernandi scales his voice down for the *Ingemisco,* taken very slowly. Inevitably this is an operatic performance, and if Serafin is not particularly dynamic he is sensitive and sympathetic. The recording is not outstanding, with the chorus backwardly placed, but quite acceptable, as is the tape transfer, with the whole work accommodated on a single extended-length cassette.

Abbado's version was recorded at La Scala, Milan, when an opera project was abandoned at the last moment. So far from making the result operatic – as, for example, Muti's highly charged version is – it seems to have sapped tensions. It is a pity that so intense a Verdian did not have a more committed team of performers. The choral entry on *Te decet hymnus* gives an early indication of the slackness and lack of bite, and though the *Dies irae* is exactly in place (unlike Muti's hectic account) there is no excitement whatever, with the chorus sounding too small. The soloists too are often below their best, but, balances apart, the recording is first-rate. The cassette transfer is lively and avoids distortion in the *Dies irae*, although climaxes are rather dry and there is some recession of image at pianissimo levels.

Karajan smooths over the lines of Verdi's masterpiece with the help of a mellow Berlin acoustic. The result is undeniably beautiful, but it loses most of its dramatic bite. The tape transfer has been remastered on chrome tape for this mid-priced reissue and the sound matches the discs closely, with the climaxes caught without congestion.

Four Sacred pieces (*Ave Maria; Stabat Mater; Laudi alla Vergine; Te Deum*).
(M) *** HMV SXLP/*TC-SXLP* 30508 [Ang. S 36125]. Philh. Ch. and O, Giulini.
*** Decca SET 602 [Lon. OS/*5-* 26610]. Chicago Symphony Ch. and SO, Solti.
*** HMV Dig. ASD/*TC-ASD* 143572-1/*4*. Auger, Stockholm Chamber Ch., Berlin PO, Muti.

Verdi's *Four Sacred pieces* form his very last work – or, to be precise, group of works. There are echoes of the great *Requiem*, and many of the ideas have a genuine Verdian originality, but in general they mark a falling-off after the supreme achievement of the last two Shakespeare operas, *Otello* and *Falstaff*. All the same, in a performance as polished and dramatic as the superlative one by Giulini and the Philharmonia Orchestra and Chorus, the element of greatness is magnified, and any Verdi lover should make a point of hearing this disc, even though the recording is not ideally clear. The cassette is not recommended: it lacks range and refinement at both ends of the spectrum.

Solti's brand of dedication is one of brightness and tension. Many will prefer the more spiritual, more devotional manner of Giulini in this music, but, unlike Giulini, Solti never runs the risk of seeming mannered in his moulding. The Chicago Symphony Chorus cannot match the finest in Europe, but Solti draws finely shaded performances from his forces and the electricity is never in doubt. The climaxes in the *Stabat Mater* and *Te Deum* are thrilling, and their effect is enhanced by the bold, brilliant recording, equally impressive on disc and the splendid cassette, one of Decca's demonstration issues. This stands effectively between Giulini and the superbly sung version by the Stockholm Choir.

Muti directs a characteristically dramatic yet thoughtful reading of these late pieces, keenly attentive to Verdi's markings. The two big outward-going pieces, the *Te Deum* and *Stabat Mater*, suit him perfectly, and the incisiveness of the professional Swedish choir, freshly yet atmospherically recorded, is an asset. In the first and third pieces the performances are hushed and devotional without hint of sentimentality. The digital recording is full and bright. The iron-oxide cassette is less successful with the reverberation blurring the sound. Side two is bass-heavy.

OPERA

Aïda (complete).
❀ *** HMV SLS/*TC-SLS* 5205 (3) [Ang. SZCX/*4Z3X* 3888]. Freni, Carreras, Baltsa, Cappuccilli, Raimondi, Van Dam, V. State Op. Ch., VPO, Karajan.
*** Decca SXL 2167-9/*K 2 A 20* [Lon. OSA/*5-* 1313). Tebaldi, Bergonzi, Simionato, MacNeil, Van Mill, Corena, V. Singverein, VPO, Karajan.
*** Decca SET 427-9/*K 64 K 32* [Lon. OSA/*5-* 1393]. L. Price, Vickers, Gorr, Merrill, Tozzi, Rome Op. Ch. and O, Solti.

(*) DG Dig. **410 092-2; 2741/*3382* 014 (3) [id.]. Ricciarelli, Domingo, Obraztsova, Nucci, Raimondi, Ghiaurov, Ch. and O of La Scala, Milan, Abbado.

**(*) HMV SLS/*TC-SLS* 977 (3) [Ang. SCLX/*4X3X* 3815]. Caballé, Domingo, Cossotto, Cappuccilli, Ghiaurov, ROHCG Ch., New Philh. O, Muti.

**(*) RCA [LSC 6198/*ARK3 2541* (3)]. L. Price, Domingo, Bumbry, Milnes, Raimondi, Alldis Ch., LSO, Leinsdorf.

(M) (**) HMV SLS/*TC-SLS* 5108 (3). Callas, Tucker, Barbieri, Gobbi, Ch. and O of La Scala, Milan, Serafin.

Karajan's is a performance of *Aïda* that carries splendour and pageantry to the point of exaltation. At the very end of the Triumphal Scene, when the march resumes with brass bands, there is a lift, a surge of emotion, such as is captured only rarely on record. Plainly the success of the performance – more urgent if less poised than Karajan's earlier account – owes much to its being conceived in conjunction with a Salzburg Festival production. And for all the power of the pageantry, Karajan's fundamental approach is lyrical, the moulding of phrase warmly expressive from the prelude onwards. Arias are often taken at a slow speed, taxing the singers more, yet Karajan's controversial choice of soloists is amply justified. On record at least, there can be little question of Freni lacking power in a role normally given to a larger voice, and there is ample gain (as on stage) in the tender beauty of her singing. Carreras makes a fresh, sensitive Radames, Raimondi a darkly intense Ramphis and Van Dam a cleanly focused King, his relative lightness no drawback. Cappuccilli here gives a more detailed performance than he did for Muti on HMV, while Baltsa as Amneris crowns the whole performance with her fine, incisive singing. Vivid, wide-ranging recording of demonstration quality, equally thrilling, sonically, on disc and cassette, with superbly believable perspectives (notably in scene two of Act I and the first scene of Act IV).

The spectacular Decca set with Karajan and the Vienna Philharmonic long stood unrivalled as a stereo version of this most stereophonic of operas. This was one of those almost ideal gramophone performances: the more you hear it the more satisfying it becomes, largely because it lays stress all the time on the musical values, if necessary at the expense of the dramatic ones. In this Karajan is of course helped by having a Viennese orchestra, rather than an Italian one determined to do things in the 'traditional' manner. The chorus too is a very different thing from a normal Italian opera-house chorus, and the inner beauty of Verdi's choral writing at last manages to come out. But most important of all is the musicianship and musical teamwork of the soloists. Bergonzi in particular emerges here as a model among tenors, with a rare feeling for the shaping of phrases and attention to detail. Cornell MacNeil too is splendid. Tebaldi's interpretation of the part of Aïda is well known and much loved. Her creamy tone colour rides beautifully over the phrases (what a wonderful vehicle for sheer singing this opera is), and she too acquires a new depth of imagination. Too dominant a characterization would not have fitted Karajan's total conception, but at times Tebaldi is too selfless. Vocally there are flaws too; notably at the end of *O patria mia*, where Tebaldi finds the cruelly exposed top notes too taxing. Among the other soloists Arnold van Mill and Fernando Corena are both superb, and Simionato provides one of the very finest portrayals of Amneris we have ever had in a complete *Aïda*. The recording has long been famous for its technical bravura and flair. The control of atmosphere is phenomenal, changing as the scene changes, and some of the offstage effects are strikingly effective in their microscopic clarity at a distance. Helped by Karajan, the recording team have, at the other end of the dynamic scale, managed to bring an altogether new clarity to the big ensembles, never achieved at the expense of tonal opulence. But – and it is an important but – the dynamic range between loud and soft is almost too great, and for the quiet passages not to sound too distant, giving a 'back of the gallery' effect, the big climaxes must be played at a very high level, perhaps too high a level for small rooms. But this is a comparatively small niggle when the technical achievement was so outstanding. The cassette transfer has problems with the wide dynamic range of the recording, but the quality is good, if not as vivid as the discs.

The earlier Price version, recorded by Decca

in Rome, has been refurbished to fine effect, for it actually outshines the later Price version, recorded at Walthamstow ten years later, in sound as in performance. Price is an outstandingly assured Aïda, rich, accurate and imaginative, while Solti's direction is superbly dramatic, notably in the Nile Scene. Anyone wanting a more expansive, contemplative view still has the option of Karajan, but this second Decca set is more clearly red-blooded in its Verdian commitment. Merrill is a richly secure Amonasro, Rita Gorr a characterful Amneris, and Jon Vickers is splendidly heroic as Radames. First-rate sound, and the cassette transfer is outstandingly successful.

Fresh and intelligent, unexaggerated in its pacing, Abbado's version from La Scala lacks a little in excitement. It is stronger on the personal drama than on the ceremonial. Domingo gives a superb performance as Radames, not least in the Nile Scene, and the two bass roles are cast from strength in Raimondi and Ghiaurov. Leo Nucci makes a dramatic Amonasro, not always pure of line, while Elena Obraztsova produces too much curdled tone as Amneris, dramatic as she is. In many ways Ricciarelli is an appealing Aïda, but the voice grows impure above the stave, and floating legatos are marred. The digital recording – cleaner on compact disc than in other formats – fails to expand for the ceremonial, and voices are highlighted, but it is acceptably fresh. The chrome tapes are satisfactory, but the sound is less open than the Karajan HMV set and the big Act II choral scene sounds studio-bound and bass-heavy. The layout is improved on compact disc but the increased clarity serves only to emphasize the confined acoustic.

Caballé's portrait of the heroine is superb, full of detailed insight into the character and with countless examples of superlative singing. The set is worth having for her alone, and Cossotto makes a fine Amneris. Domingo produces glorious sound, but this is not one of his most imaginative recordings, while the Amonasro of Piero Cappuccilli is prosaic. So is much of Muti's direction – no swagger in the Triumphal Scene, unfeeling metrical rhythms in the Death Scene – and the recording, not quite boldly expansive enough, is a shade disappointing, not so vivid as the Decca sets of a decade and more earlier.

There is much to commend in Leontyne Price's 1971 recording of *Aïda*, and with a fine cast at less than full price it is a set worth considering. But it comes inevitably into direct comparison with Price's earlier set (still issued at full price) and by that standard it is a little disappointing. Price's voice is not so glowing as it was, and though there are moments where she shows added insight, it is the earlier performance which generates more electricity, has more dramatic urgency. Domingo makes a warm and stylish Radames, Milnes a strong if hardly electrifying Amonasro and Bumbry a superb imaginative Amneris. It is a pity that the recording, by the latest standards, does not capture the glamour of the score. Most of the earlier sets are more impressive in sound. (This is not currently available in the UK.)

The Nile Scene – focus of the central emotional conflict in a masterpiece which is only incidentally a pageant – has never been more powerful and characterfully performed on record as in the vintage La Scala set. Though Callas is hardly as sweet-toned as some will think essential for an Aïda, her detailed imagination is irresistible, and she is matched by Tito Gobbi at the very height of his powers. Tucker gives one of his very finest performances on record, and Barbieri is a commanding Amneris. The stereo transcription of the mono recording is outstandingly successful with the voices, which are vivid, full and immediate, and though the orchestral sound is limited, it is cleanly balanced. Discs and cassettes are closely matched.

Aïda: highlights.
*** HMV ASD/*TC-ASD* 3983. (from above set, cond. Karajan).
(M) *** Decca Jub. JB/*KJBC* 81. (from above set, cond. Solti).
**(*) DG Dig. 2532/*3302* 092. (from above set, cond. Abbado).

The highlights disc from Karajan's superb HMV set is most intelligently compiled. In the span of a single LP it is impossible to include all the favourite items, but this one enjoyably concentrates on Karajan's most successful moments. The Triumphal Scene, for example, has been skilfully edited to include both the opening and the close. Extremely vivid recording, with little to choose between disc and cassette.

On Jubilee Decca offer a generous mid-priced reminder of the excellence of Solti's 1962 set. Leontyne Price is an outstandingly assured Aïda, and Solti's direction is superbly dramatic. First-rate sound, even by today's standards, although the high-level cassette – otherwise extremely vivid – produces moments of peaking in Vickers's vibrant *Celeste Aïda*.

A generous, well-chosen selection from the variably sung Abbado set brings comparable qualities and flaws, in performance and recording. The chrome cassette, however, made at a high level, is certainly vivid.

Alzira (complete).
*** HM Orfeo SO 57832H (2) [id.]. Cotrubas, Araiza, Bruson, George, Bonilla, Bav. R. Ch., Munich R. O, Gardelli.

Of all the operas that Verdi wrote in his years slaving 'in the galleys', this was the one he most vigorously rejected, yet this fine, beautifully sung and superbly paced reading brings out the formidable merits of this very compact piece. It is the shortest of the Verdi operas, but its concision is on balance an advantage on record, intensifying the adaptation of Voltaire's story of Inca nobles defying the conformity of Christian conquerors. In musical inspiration it is indistinguishable from other typical 'galley' operas, with Verdian melodies less distinctive than they became later, but consistently pleasing. Gardelli is a master with early Verdi, and the cast is strong, helped by warm and well-balanced recording supervised by Munich radio engineers.

Aroldo (complete).
** CBS [M3X 35906]. Caballé, Cecchele, Lebherz, Pons, NY Oratorio Soc., Westchester Ch. Soc., NY Op. O, Queler.

Aroldo is Verdi's radical revision of his earlier, unsuccessful opera *Stiffelio*; he translated the story of a Protestant pastor with an unfaithful wife into this tale of a crusader returning from the Holy Land. Less compact than the original, it contains some splendid new material, such as a superb aria for the heroine, here beautifully sung by Caballé. The final scene too is quite new, for the dénouement is totally different. The storm chorus – with echoes of *Rigoletto* – is most memorable, but so are the rum-ti-tum choruses common to both versions. This recording of a concert performance in New York is lively, though the tenor is depressingly coarse. The recording is more faithful than others in the series. This set has been withdrawn in the UK.

Attila (complete).
*** Ph. 6700 056 (2) [id.]. Raimondi, Deutekom, Bergonzi, Milnes, Amb. S., Finchley Children's Music Group, RPO, Gardelli.

It is easy to criticize the music Verdi wrote during his 'years in the galleys', but a youthfully urgent work like this makes you marvel not at its musical unevenness but at the way Verdi consistently entertains you. The dramatic anticipations of *Macbeth*, with Attila himself far more than a simple villain, the musical anticipations of *Rigoletto*, the compression which on record if not on the stage becomes a positive merit – all these qualities, helped by a fine performance under Gardelli, make this an intensely enjoyable set. Deutekom, not the most sweet-toned of sopranos, has never sung better on record, and the rest of the cast is outstandingly good. First-rate recording.

Un Ballo in maschera (complete).
*** DG 2740 251/*3378 111* (3) [id.]. Ricciarelli, Domingo, Bruson, Obraztsova, Gruberova, Raimondi, Ch. and O of La Scala, Milan, Abbado.
*** HMV SLS/*TC-SLS* 984 (3) [Ang. SCLX 3762]. Arroyo, Grist, Cossotto, Domingo, Cappuccilli, ROHCG Ch., New Philh. O, Muti.
**(*) Ph. 6769 020/*7699 108* (3) [id.]. Caballé, Carreras, Wixell, Payne, Ghazarian, ROHCG Ch. and O, Sir Colin Davis.
** Decca SET 484-6 [Lon. OSA 1396]. Tebaldi, Donath, Resnik, Pavarotti, Milnes, Ch. and O of St Cecilia Ac., Rome, Bartoletti.

Abbado's is a powerful reading of *Ballo*, admirably paced and with a splendid feeling for the sparkle of comedy (so important in the rare mixture of this endlessly eventful piece), lacking just a little in the rhythmic elegance which Verdi specifically calls for in such passages as the haunting exit of the conspirators at the end of Act II. The cast is arguably the strongest assembled for this opera on record, with Ricciarelli at her very finest, darkly intense in her two big arias (taken very slowly), with raw tone kept to a minimum. Domingo is here sweeter of tone and more deft of characterization than he is in the Muti set of five years earlier, while Bruson as the wronged husband, Renato, sings magnificently, the vocal production splendidly firm. Obraztsova as Ulrica and Gruberova as Oscar are less consistently convincing, both a little heavy. The recording clearly separates the voices and instruments in different acoustics, which is distracting only initially and after that brings the drama closer. The DG cassette transfer is made at a rather low level and – as the opening scene demonstrates – detail at pianissimo level is less sharply defined than on disc. The voices, however, are freshly caught, and the recording's wide dynamic range is successfully encompassed without peaking.

On HMV the quintet of principals is also unusually strong, but it is the conductor who takes first honours in a warmly dramatic reading. His rhythmic resilience and consideration for the singers go with keen concentration, holding each Act together in a way he did not quite achieve in his earlier recording for HMV of *Aïda*. Arroyo, rich of voice, is not always imaginative in her big solos, and Domingo rarely produces a half-tone, though the recording balance may be partly to blame. The sound is opulent. The tape transfer is of good quality but has a rather narrow dynamic range.

Davis's version, based on the Covent Garden production, is particularly good in the way it brings out the ironic humour in Verdi's score. Caballé and Carreras match Davis's lightness, but the dramatic power is diminished. Despite fine recording, both the Abbado and the Muti sets are preferable. The Philips cassettes – with an unimaginative layout – are less attractive than the discs, less open at the top.

Tebaldi made her recording in the full maturity of her career. Much of her singing is very fine indeed, but there is no mistaking that her voice here is nowhere near as even as it once was. For the command of her performance this is a version well worth hearing and the supporting cast is strong, but in competition with Ricciarelli and Arroyo this can hardly be given preference, even though the Decca recording remains strikingly vivid.

Un ballo in maschera: highlights.
*** DG 2537/*3306* 059 [id.]. (from above set, cond. Abbado).

An excellent, well-chosen selection from the Abbado set, with good sound on both tape and disc.

La Battaglia di Legnano (complete).
*** Ph. 6700 120/*7699 081* (2) [id.]. Ricciarelli, Carreras, Manuguerra, Ghiuselev, Austrian R. Ch. and O, Gardelli.

First heard in January 1849, *La Battaglia di Legnano* is set against Italy's struggle in the face of Frederic Barbarossa's invasion. It is a compact, sharply conceived piece, made the more intense by the subject's obvious relationship with the situation in Verdi's own time. One weakness is that villainy is not effectively personalized, but the juxtaposition of the individual drama of supposed infidelity against a patriotic theme brings most effective musical contrasts. Gardelli directs a fine performance, helped by a strong cast of principals, with Carreras, Ricciarelli and Manuguerra all at their finest. Excellent recording; the cassette transfer is generally well managed, with good perspectives and plenty of bloom on voices and orchestra alike.

Il Corsaro (complete).
*** Ph. 6700 098 (2) [id.]. Norman, Caballé, Carreras, Grant, Mastromei, Noble, Amb. S., New Philh. O., Gardelli.

Verdi did not even bother to attend the first performance of *Il Corsaro* in Trieste in 1848, despite the inclusion in the cast of four of his favourite singers. It seemed as though his 'years in the galleys' had caught up with him in this, the thirteenth of his operas. By the time he had completed the score, Verdi had fallen out of love with his subject, an adaptation of Byron. Only latterly has the composer's own poor view of the piece, predictably parroted through the years, been revised in the light of closer study. The two-disc format points to one of the first merits of the piece, its compactness, and Piave's treatment of Byron is not nearly so clumsy as has been thought. Though the characterization is rudimentary, the contrast of the two heroines is effective, with Gulnara, the Pasha's slave, carrying conviction in the *coup de foudre* which has her promptly worshipping the Corsair, an early example of the Rudolph Valentino figure. The rival heroines are splendidly taken here, with Jessye Norman as the faithful wife, Medora, actually upstaging Montserrat Caballé as Gulnara. Likenesses in many of the numbers to some of the greatest passages in *Rigoletto, Trovatore* and *Traviata* give the opera vintage Verdian flavour, and the orchestration is often masterly. Gardelli, as in his previous Philips recordings of early Verdi, directs a vivid performance, with fine singing from the hero, portrayed by José Carreras. Gian-Piero Mastromei, not rich in tone, still rises to the challenge of the Pasha's music. Excellent recording.

Don Carlo (complete).

*** HMV SLS/*TC-SLS* 5154 (4) [Ang. SZDX/*4ZX4* 3875]. Freni, Carreras, Ghiaurov, Baltsa, Cappuccilli, German Op. Ch., Berlin PO, Karajan.

*** HMV SLS 956 (4) [Ang. SDL 3774]. Caballé, Verrett, Domingo, Milnes, Raimondi, Amb. Op. Ch., ROHCG O, Giulini.

*** Decca SET 305–8/*K 128 K 43* [Lon. OSA/*5-* 1432]. Tebaldi, Bumbry, Bergonzi, Fischer-Dieskau, Ghiaurov, Ch. and O of ROHCG, Solti.

As in the Salzburg Festival production on which this recording is based, Karajan opts firmly for the later four-Act version of the opera, merely opening out the cuts he adopted on stage. The results could hardly be more powerfully dramatic, one of his most involving opera performances, comparable with his vivid HMV *Aïda*. Though a recording can hardly convey the full grandeur of a stage peopled with many hundreds of singers, the Auto da fe Scene is here superb, while Karajan's characteristic choice of singers for refinement of voice rather than sheer size consistently pays off. Both Carreras and Freni are most moving, even if *Tu che la vanità* has its raw moments. Baltsa is a superlative Eboli and Cappuccilli an affecting Rodrigo, though neither Carreras nor Cappuccilli is at his finest in the famous oath duet. Raimondi and Ghiaurov as the Grand Inquisitor and Philip II provide the most powerful confrontation. Though many collectors will naturally resist the idea of the four-Act rather than the five-Act version on record, there is no doubt that this Karajan set is the most effective of the complete recordings, and it is very vivid as sound too, with discs and cassettes closely matched.

Giulini was the conductor who in the Covent Garden production of 1958 demonstrated in the opera house the supreme mastery of Verdi's score. Here he is conducting the same orchestra as Solti directed in the Decca version five years earlier, and predictably he is more flowing, more affectionate in his phrasing, while conveying the quiet dramatic intensity which made his direction so irresistible in the opera house. There is extra joy for example in the Auto da fe Scene as it is pointed by Giulini, and even when his singer is less effective than his Decca rival (as with the King Philip, Raimondi against Ghiaurov) the direction of Giulini amply compensates. Generally the new cast is a little stronger than the old, but each is admirably consistent. The only major vocal disappointment among the principals lies in Caballé's account of the big aria *Tu che la vanità* in the final Act. Like the Decca set this one uses the full five-Act text. The recording, not quite so pinpointed in brilliance, is even more warmly atmospheric.

The Decca version includes the important passages often excised, notably the Fontainebleau scene, and that may underline the one major deficiency of the set, that the dramatic temperature fails to rise as it should until the duet between Philip and Rodrigo at the end of Act II (Act I in the four-Act version). Till then Solti tends to be somewhat rigid, but once the right mood is established he does marvellously with his own Covent Garden forces, and the result in the Auto da fe Scene is very fine. Tebaldi too in this most exacting Verdian role warms up well, and gives a magnificent account of *Tu che la vanità*. Bumbry and Bergonzi both sing splendidly, and after some rather gritty singing early on, Fischer-Dieskau rises fittingly to Rodrigo's great death scene, sounding almost (but not quite) as moving as Gobbi in the old HMV set (mono). Ghiaurov as Philip is obviously not so dramatic as Christoff was on HMV, but the straighter approach brings a nobility, a sense of stoic pride, that is most compelling. The recording is of Decca's usual high standard, and though with such a marvellous array of talent one might feel the result should be still more overwhelming, there is no doubt that this version has a great deal to commend it. The set has been given a vibrant tape transfer, splendidly detailed (as the opening scene shows immediately) and strongly projected. The cassette layout is satisfactory and the libretto admirably bold and clear.

Don Carlo: highlights.
(M) *** HMV SXLP/*TC-SXLP* 30549 [Ang. S 36918]. (from above set, cond. Giulini).

This selection includes nothing from Act I and concentrates on three key numbers from Act IV with shorter excerpts from Acts II and III. The recording mirrors the complete set with disc and cassette sounding very much the same.

I due Foscari (complete).
*** Ph. 6700 105/*7699 057* (2). Ricciarelli, Carreras, Cappuccilli, Ramey, Austrian R. Ch. and SO, Gardelli.

As in so many of Verdi's most telling dramatic situations, it is the father–daughter relationship in *I due Foscari* which prompts some of the finest music, including superb duets. It had better be explained that the precise relationship between the Doge of Venice, Francesco Foscari, and the heroine, Lucrezia, is father and daughter-in-law, but the wonder is that with a very limiting plot – based loosely on one of Byron's undramatic dramas – Verdi overcomes the shortcoming that nothing changes much in the relationships from beginning to end, and that in any case the wicked are left unpunished while the good are brought low. Even so there are Verdian high spirits in plenty, which erupt in swinging cabalettas and much writing that anticipates operas as late as *Simon Boccanegra* (obvious enough in the Doge's music) and *La Forza del destino* (particularly in the orchestral motifs which act as labels for the principal characters).

The cast is first-rate, with Ricciarelli giving one of her finest performances in the recording studio to date and with Carreras singing tastefully as well as powerfully, not least in the prison aria, which even suggests that Verdi knew his *Fidelio*. Cappuccilli as the Doge brings out the likenesses with *Boccanegra*. The crispness of discipline among the Austrian Radio forces is admirable, but there is less sense of atmosphere than in the earlier London-made recordings in the series; otherwise good clean Philips recording. The cassette transfer too is admirably clean, and the sense of perspective is excellent: where there are distanced effects the clarity of focus is retained, although Miss Ricciarelli's voice (and to a lesser extent that of Carreras) tends to harden slightly when the recording is under pressure by strongly projected top notes.

Ernani (complete).
**(*) HMV Dig. SLS/*TC-SLS* 143584-3/*9* (3/*2*) [Ang. DSCX/*4X3X* 3942]. Domingo, Freni, Bruson, Ghiaurov, Ch. and O of La Scala, Milan, Muti.
** Hung. Dig. SLPD 12259/61 [id.]. Lamberti, Sass, Kovats, Miller, Takacs, Hungarian State Op. Ch. and O, Gardelli.

Ernani, the fifth of Verdi's operas, was the first to achieve international success. At this stage of his career Verdi was still allowing himself the occasional imitation of Rossini in a crescendo, or of Bellini in parallel thirds and sixths, but the control of tension is already masterly, and the ensembles even more than the arias give the authentic Verdian flavour. The great merit of Muti's set, recorded live at a series of performances at La Scala, is that the ensembles have an electricity rarely achieved in the studio. The results may not always be so precise and stage noises are often obtrusive with a background rustle of stage movement rarely absent for long, but the result is vivid and atmospheric. The singing, generally strong and characterful, is yet flawed. The strain of the role of Elvira for Mirella Freni is plain from the big opening aria, *Ernani involami*, onwards. Even in that aria there are cautious moments. Bruson is a superb Carlo, Ghiaurov a characterful Silva, but his voice now betrays signs of wear. Ernani himself, Placido Domingo, gives a commandingly heroic performance, but under pressure there are hints of tight tone such as he nowadays rarely produces in the studio. The recording inevitably has odd balances which will disturb some more than others. The XDR iron-oxide tapes are of quite good quality, but less wide-ranging at the top than the discs, though this is more noticeable in the final two Acts than at the beginning of the opera. The layout on four sides (against six on LP) is generally preferable.

Gardelli's conducting is most sympathetic and idiomatic in the Hungarian version, and like Muti's it is strong on ensembles. Sylvia Sass is a sharply characterful Elvira, Callas-like in places, and Lamberti a bold Ernani, but their vocal flaws prevent this from being a first choice. Capable rather than inspired or idiomatic singing from the rest. The digital recording is bright and well balanced.

Falstaff (complete).

(M) *** HMV SLS/*TC-SLS* 5211 (2) [Ang. SBL 3552]. Gobbi, Schwarzkopf, Alva, Panerai, Moffo, Merriman, Barbieri, Zaccaria, Philh. Ch. and O, Karajan.

*** DG Dig. **410 503-2**; 2741/*3382* 020 (3) [id.]. Bruson, Ricciarelli, Hendricks, Egerton, Terrani, Boozer, Los Angeles Master Ch., LAPO, Giulini.

(M) *** Decca 2 BB 104-6/*K110 K32* [Lon. OSA 1395]. Evans, Ligabue, Freni, Kraus, Elias, Simionato, RCA Italiana Op. Ch. and O, Solti.

*** CBS 77392 (3) [D3S-750]. Fischer-Dieskau, Ligabue, Panerai, Sciutti, Rössl-Majdan, Resnik, Oncina, V. State Op. Ch., VPO, Bernstein.

**(*) Ph. Dig. 6769/*7654* 060 (3). Taddei, Kabaivanska, Perry, Panerai, Ludwig, Araiza, V. State Op. Ch., VPO, Karajan.

In response to his newer digital recording of *Falstaff* on Philips, EMI reissued Karajan's 1957 HMV set, refreshing the sound, which loses nothing from its remastering on to two instead of three LPs (and cassettes). This earlier set presents not only the most pointed account orchestrally of Verdi's comic masterpiece (the Philharmonia Orchestra at its very peak) but the most sharply characterful cast ever gathered for a recording. If you relish the idea of Tito Gobbi as Falstaff (his many-coloured voice, not quite fat-sounding in humour, presents a sharper character than usual), then this is clearly the best choice, for the rest of the cast is a delight, with Schwarzkopf a tinglingly masterful Mistress Ford, Anna Moffo sweet as Nannetta and Rolando Panerai a formidable Ford. One reason why the whole performance hangs together so stylishly is the production of Walter Legge: this is a vintage example of his work. The cassette transfer is brilliantly clear and vivid and stands up remarkably well to direct comparison with the newer Philips tapes.

Recorded at a series of live performances in the Chandler Pavilion in Los Angeles, Giulini's reading brings the tensions and atmosphere of live performance with a precision normally achieved only in the studio. This was Giulini's first essay in live opera-conducting in fourteen years, and he treated the piece with a care for musical values which at times undermined the knockabout comic element. On record that is all to the good, for the clarity and beauty of the playing are superbly caught by the DG engineers, and though the parallel with Toscanini is an obvious one – also recorded at a live performance – Giulini is far more relaxed. Here the CD emphasizes the success of the engineers in the matter of balance, besides adding to the refinement of detail and the tangibility of the overall sound-picture.

The voices are given fine bloom but in a contrasted stage acoustic. Bruson, hardly a comic actor, is impressive on record for his fine incisive singing, giving tragic implications to the monologue at the start of Act III after Falstaff's dunking. The Ford of Leo Nucci, impressive in the theatre, is thinly caught, where the heavyweight quality of Ricciarelli as Alice comes over well, though in places one wants a purer sound. Barbara Hendricks is a charmer as Nannetta, but she hardly sounds fairy-like in her Act III aria. The full women's ensemble, though precise, is not always quite steady in tone, though the conviction of the whole performance puts it among the most desirable of modern readings.

The combination of Solti and Geraint Evans is irresistible. Their set, originally issued by RCA, comes up as sparkling as ever in this Decca reissue at a very modest price. There is an energy, a sense of fun, a sparkle that outshine rival versions, outstanding as they may be. Evans has never sounded better on record, and the rest of the cast admirably live up to his example. Solti drives hard, and almost any comparison with the ancient Toscanini set will show his shortcomings, but it is still an exciting and well-pointed performance, the rest of the cast well contrasted. The transfer to tape is clean and lively.

The CBS set is based on a production at the Vienna State Opera, and the fleetness of execution in hair-raisingly fast speeds suggests that Bernstein was intent on out-Toscanining Toscanini. The allegros may be consistently faster than Toscanini's, but they never sound rushed, and always Bernstein conveys a sense of fun, while in relaxed passages, helped by warm Viennese sensitivity, he allows a full rotundity of phrasing, at least as much so as any rival. It does not really matter, any more than it did in the Toscanini set, that the conductor is the hero rather than Falstaff himself. Fischer-Dieskau does wonders in pointing the humour. In his scene with Mistress Quickly arranging an assignation with Alice, he can inflect a simple *Ebben?* to make it intensely funny, but he finally suffers from having a voice one inevitably associates with baritonal solemnity, whether heroic or villainous. Just how noble Falstaff should seem is a matter for discussion. The others are first-rate – Panerai singing superbly as Ford, Ilva Ligabue (also the Alice of the Solti set), Regina Resnik as Mistress Quickly, and Graziella Sciutti and Juan Oncina as the young lovers. Excellent engineering by Decca.

Karajan's second recording of Verdi's last opera, made over twenty years later than his classic Philharmonia set, has lower standards of precision, but yet conveys a relaxed and genial atmosphere. With the exception of Kabaivanska, whose voice is not steady enough for the role of Alice, it is a good cast, with Ludwig fascinating as Mistress Quickly. Most amazing of all is Taddei's performance as Falstaff himself, full and characterful and vocally astonishing from a man in his sixties. The recording is not so beautifully balanced as the Philharmonia set, but the digital sound is faithful and wide-ranging, though the level of cut is on the low side. The chrome tapes are of the highest quality: the sound has striking range, depth and atmosphere.

La Forza del destino (complete).

*** RCA RL/*RK* 01864 (4) [ARL4 1864/*ARK3 2543*]. L. Price, Domingo, Milnes, Cossotto, Giaiotti, Bacquier, Alldis Ch., LSO, Levine.

(M) **(*) Decca Ace GOS 597-9 [Lon. OSA 1405]. Tebaldi, Del Monaco, Corena, Bastianini, Siepi, Ch. and O of St Cecilia Ac., Rome, Molinari-Pradelli.

James Levine, Music Director of the Met. in New York, directs a superb performance of an opera which can in less purposeful hands seem too episodic. The results are electrifying, and rarely if ever does Levine cut across the natural expressiveness of an outstanding cast. Leontyne Price recorded the role of Leonora in an earlier RCA version made in Rome in 1956, but the years have hardly touched her voice, and details of the reading have been refined. The roles of Don Alvaro and Don Carlo are ideally suited to the regular team of Placido Domingo and Sherrill Milnes, so that their confrontations are the cornerstones of the dramatic structure. Fiorenza Cossotto makes a formidable rather than a jolly Preziosilla, while on the male side the line-up of Bonaldo Giaiotti, Gabriel Bacquier, Kurt Moll and Michel Sénéchal is far stronger than on rival sets. The recording is not of RCA's brightest vintage, with the voices placed too close, but the sound is perfectly acceptable. The cassette transfer is very agreeable, although its dynamic range is more compressed than the discs, and the treble has less bite.

The Ace of Diamonds set, however, with Tebaldi on top form, offers formidable competition at its modest price, complete, yet now on three discs instead of the original four, with no loss in sound-quality; and the recording was outstanding for its time. Tebaldi, as always, makes some lovely sounds, and the *mezza voce* in the soaring theme (first heard in the overture) in *Madre, madre, pietosa Vergine* is exquisite. Mario del Monaco never really matches this. He sings straight through his part – often with the most heroic-sounding noises – with little attention to the finer points of shading that Verdi expects. That the whole performance does not add up to the sum of its parts is largely the fault of the conductor, Molinari-Pradelli. He is exciting enough in the proper places but his control of ensemble is a marked weakness. Fortunately this deficiency in the conducting is not nearly enough to mar enjoyment of the performance. The brilliance and atmosphere of the recording add much to the listener's pleasure.

La Forza del destino (slightly abridged).
(M) (***) HMV SLS/*TC-SLS* 5120 (3). Callas, Tucker, Rossi-Lemeni, Nicolai, Tagliabue, Capecchi, Clabassi, Ch. and O of La Scala, Milan, Serafin.

Callas was at her very peak when she took the role of Leonora in the Scala recording. Hers is an electrifying performance, providing a focus for an opera normally regarded as diffuse. Though there are classic examples of Callas's raw tone on top notes, they are insignificant next to the wealth of phrasing which sets a totally new and individual stamp on even the most familiar passages. The pity is that the stereo transcription process has (on tape as well as LP) taken away some of the brightness and edge of the recording as originally issued in mono; but in compensation one of the major cuts (at the opening of the final scene) has now been opened out. Apart from his tendency to disturb his phrasing with sobs, Richard Tucker sings superbly; but not even he and certainly none of the others – including the baritone Carlo Tagliabue, well past his prime – begin to rival the dominance of Callas. Serafin's direction is crisp, dramatic and well paced, again drawing the threads together, and the recording has plenty of atmosphere, which is retained in the tape transfer. The detail is remarkably good.

Un Giorno di regno (complete).
*** Ph. 6703 055 (3) [id.]. Cossotto, Norman, Carreras, Wixell, Sardinero, Ganzarolli, Amb. S., RPO, Gardelli.

This comic opera was Verdi's second work for the stage, and for almost 150 years it has been written off as a failure; but this superb, scintillating performance under Gardelli gives us a chance to make a complete reappraisal. It may not be the greatest comic opera of the period, but it clearly reveals the young Verdi as a potent rival even in this field to his immediate predecessors, Rossini and Donizetti. The Rossinian echoes are particularly infectious, though every number reveals that the young Verdi is more than an imitator, and there are striking passages which clearly give a foretaste of such numbers as the duet *Si vendetta* from *Rigoletto*. Despite the absurd plot (no sillier than is common) this is as light and frothy an entertainment as anyone could want. Excellent singing from a fine team, with Jessye Norman and José Carreras outstanding. Superb recording.

Giovanna d'Arco (complete).
**(*) EMI 2C 165 02378/80 [Ang. SCL 3791]. Caballé, Domingo, Milnes, Amb. Op. Ch., LSO, Levine.

This seventh of Verdi's operas, based very loosely indeed on Schiller's drama, is an archetype of the works which the master was writing during his 'years in the galleys'. 'Melodic generosity and youthful resilience' are the qualities singled out by Charles Osborne in his study of Verdi operas, and the score certainly confirms that. The pity is that James Levine, a youthful whirlwind, does not respond to the resilience more effectively. Though the ensemble is superb, he consistently presses too hard in fast music, with the rum-ti-tum hammered home. He is far more sympathetic in passages of 'melodic generosity', particularly when Caballé is singing. What had become a standard trio of principals for the 1970s gives far more than a routine performance. With fine recording there is much to enjoy, even when the plot – whittled down to Joan, her father (who betrays her) and the King – is so naïve.

I Lombardi (complete).
**(*) Ph. 6703 032 (3) [id.]. Deutekom, Domingo, Raimondi, Amb. S., RPO, Gardelli.

I Lombardi, first produced in 1843, followed *Nabucco*, which had appeared the year before, and it is good to have a stereo recording of so virile an early opera. If you are looking for sophisticated perfection this is not the opera to sample, but the directness of Verdi's inspiration is in no doubt. The many choruses bring an expected quota of rum-ti-tum, but they also look to the future in the most fascinating way, foreshadowing *Ballo in maschera* and *Macbeth*. In the arias *Otello* is anticipated, with Pagano's evil Credo and the heroine Giselda's *Salve Maria*. The work reaches its apotheosis in the famous *Trio*, well-known from the days of 78 r.p.m. recordings. By those standards Cristina Deutekom is not an ideal Verdi singer. Her tone is sometimes hard and the voice is not always perfectly in control, yet there are some glorious moments too, and the phrasing is often impressive. Domingo as Oronte is in superb voice, and the villain Pagano is well characterized by Raimondi. Among the supporting cast Stafford Dean and Clifford Grant must be mentioned, and Gardelli conducts dramatically. The recording is excellent, with plenty of atmosphere.

Luisa Miller (complete).
**(*) Decca SET 606-8/*K 2 L 25* (3/2) [Lon. OSA/5- 13114]. Caballé, Reynolds, Pavarotti, Milnes, Giaotti, Van Allan, L. Op. Ch., Nat. PO, Maag.
**(*) DG 2709 096/*3370 035* (3/2) [id.]. Ricciarelli, Obraztsova, Domingo, Bruson, Ch. and O of ROHCG, Maazel.

The Met. in New York had one of its most striking successes with this improbable opera (Montserrat Caballé in the name part), and though Verdi jogs along for much of the time, the big emotional moments prod him to characteristic heights of inspiration. Caballé, not as flawless vocally as one would expect (where is her trill?), yet gives a splendidly dramatic portrait of the heroine. Maag's conducting too underlines the light and shade, the atmospheric qualities of a score which, for all its imagination, can start sagging. Pavarotti's performance is comparable to Caballé's, full of detailed, seemingly spontaneous imagination, a creative interpreter, not just a beautiful singer of notes. Though Anna Reynolds cannot match Shirley Verrett on the old deleted RCA set, the Decca offering, brilliantly played and vividly recorded, has the balance of advantage. There is a first-class tape transfer.

Maazel directs a clean-cut, incisive performance based on the Covent Garden production. Its sharpness is somewhat exaggerated by the recording characteristic, which though at a relatively low level of cut gives an unpleasant edge for example to Ricciarelli in the title role. On balance the principals in the Maag set for Decca, recorded more atmospherically with a range if anything wider, are preferable, though Domingo here and Pavarotti in the Decca set are both superb. As conductor, Maag for Decca finds more delicacy than the rather literal, if always dramatic, Maazel. The DG cassette layout (like the Decca), using two tapes against three discs, is preferable and the slightly dry recording has transferred with admirable clarity and detail. The level is modest but there seems little, if any, loss of range. However, the Decca cassettes are outstanding, vibrantly clear without loss of atmosphere.

Macbeth (complete).
*** DG 2709 062/*3371 022* (3) [id.]. Cappuccilli, Verrett, Ghiaurov, Domingo, Ch. and O of La Scala, Milan, Abbado.
*** HMV SLS 992 (3) [Ang. SCLX/*4X3X* 3833]. Milnes, Cossotto, Raimondi, Carreras, Amb. Op. Ch., New Philh. O, Muti.
**(*) Decca SETB 510-2. Fischer-Dieskau, Suliotis, Pavarotti, Ghiaurov, Amb. Op. Ch., LPO, Gardelli.

In Abbado's scintillating performance the diamond precision of ensemble has one thinking of Toscanini. The conventional rum-ti-tum of witches' and murderers' choruses is transformed, becomes tense and electrifying, helped by the immediacy of sound. At times Abbado's tempi are unconventional, but with slow speeds he springs the rhythm so infectiously that the results are the more compelling. Based on the Giorgio Strehler production at La Scala, the whole performance gains from superb teamwork, for each of the principals is far more meticulous than is common about observing Verdi's detailed markings, above all those for pianissimo and sotto voce. Verrett, hardly powerful above the stave, yet makes a virtue out of necessity in floating glorious half-tones, and with so firm and characterful a voice she makes a highly individual, not at all conventional Lady Macbeth. As for Cappuccilli he has never sung with such fine range of tone and imagination on record as here, and José Carreras makes a real, sensitive character out of the small role of Macduff. Excellent, clean recording, and a natural, well-managed tape transfer.

Muti's version appeared within weeks of Abbado's, confirming that new standards were being set in this opera on record. Though Muti and his team do not quite match the supreme distinction of Abbado and his Scala forces, they provide a distinct and valid alternative that some will prefer. Quite apart from preference for individual singers – on which each collector will have his own views – there is the contrast of sound between the extremely sharp focus of the DG set and the more comfortable warmth of the EMI one, which conceals any slight shortcomings of ensemble compared with the superlative Scala standards. Both Milnes and Cossotto sing warmly, and are richly convincing in their relatively conventional views of their roles. The sixth side includes some valuable extra material from Verdi's first version of the opera; the death arioso for Macbeth is also included in the DG version (in its place in the last scene, not as an appendix).

It is now a matter of history that when, at the very last minute, Gobbi was prevented from attending the London recording sessions of *Macbeth*, Decca had the great good fortune to persuade Fischer-Dieskau to take part instead. The German baritone does not give a traditional performance in this great tragic role, for characteristically he points the words in full Lieder-style. Nor is he in his freshest voice, growing gritty in some climaxes; but it is still a marvellous, compelling performance which stands repeated hearing. Suliotis is – to put it kindly – a variable Lady Macbeth. In the first aria there are moments where Suliotis's voice runs completely out of control, but she still has imagination, and her 'voice of a she-devil' (Verdi's words) is arguably the precise sound needed. Certainly she settles down into giving a striking and individual performance, while Ghiaurov as Banquo and Pavarotti as Macduff sing with admirable poise. Gardelli and the LPO are treated to spectacularly vivid recording.

I Masnadieri (complete).

*** Ph. 6703 064 (3) [id.]. Caballé, Bergonzi, Raimondi, Cappuccilli, Amb. S., New Philh. O, Gardelli.

**(*) Decca D 273 D 3/*K273 K 32* (3/*2*) [Lon. LDR/*5*- 73008]. Sutherland, Bonisolli, Manuguerra, Ramey, Welsh Nat. Op. Ch. and O, Bonynge.

'We take this to be the worst opera which has been given in our time at Her Majesty's Theatre,' wrote the critic Henry Chorley after the first performance of this, the one opera which Verdi wrote for London. 'Verdi is finally rejected,' he said firmly. With Queen Victoria present at the première and the role of the heroine taken by the young Jenny Lind, the piece was an instant success, but not for long. As this excellent recording makes plain, its long neglect is totally undeserved, despite a libretto which is a bungled adaptation of a Schiller play. Few will seriously identify with the hero-turned-brigand who stabs his beloved rather than lead her into a life of shame, but on record flaws of motivation are of far less moment than on the stage. The melodies may only fitfully be out of Verdi's top drawer, but the musical structure and argument often look forward to a much later period in hints of *Forza*, *Don Carlo* and even *Otello*. With Gardelli as ever an urgently sympathetic Verdian and a team of four excellent principals, splendidly recorded, the set can be warmly recommended.

I Masnadieri, with four principal roles of equal importance, is not a prima donna's opera, but with Sutherland cast as Amalia it tends to become one. This is a weightier view than Caballé took in the earlier Philips recording, conveying more light and shade. The cabaletta for her great Act II aria brings a coloratura display with Sutherland still at her very peak. Bonisolli, though he sings with less refinement than Bergonzi on the rival set, has great flair as in his extra flourishes in the final ensemble of Act II. Manuguerra sings strongly too. He may not be as refined as his rival, Cappuccilli, but he sounds more darkly villainous. Ramey as Massimiliano sings with fine clarity, but the voice does not sound old enough for a father. The Welsh National Opera chorus sings with the lustiness of stage experience. The Decca recording is outstandingly full and brilliant, even if Kingsway Hall acoustic clouds some choral detail. On tape the layout on four sides with Acts tailored to side-ends is ideal, though the lightly printed libretto in the tape box is not. Tape one is drier in sound than tape two, but the sound throughout is wide-ranging.

Nabucco (complete).

*** DG Dig. **410 512-2**; 2741/*3382* 021 (3) [id.]. Cappuccilli, Dimitrova, Nesterenko, Domingo, Ch. and O of German Op., Berlin, Sinopoli.

*** Decca SET 298-300/*K 126 K 32* (2) [Lon. OSA/*5*- 1382]. Gobbi, Suliotis, Cava, Prevedi, V. State Op. Ch. and O, Gardelli.

**(*) HMV SLS 5132 (3) [Ang. SCLX/*4X3X* 3850]. Manuguerra, Scotto, Ghiaurov, Luchetti, Obraztsova, Amb. Op. Ch., Muti.

Sinopoli's first opera recording suggests in its freshness, its electricity and its crystal clarification the sort of insight that Toscanini must once have brought. Sinopoli makes Verdi sound less comfortable than traditional conductors, but he never lets the 'grand guitar' accompaniments of early Verdi churn along automatically. One keeps hearing details normally obscured. Even the thrill of the great chorus *Va, pensiero* is the greater when the melody first emerges at a hushed pianissimo, as marked, sounding almost offstage. Strict as he is, Sinopoli encourages his singers to relish the great melodies to the full. Dimitrova is superb in Abigaille's big Act II aria, noble in her evil, as is Cappuccilli as Nabucco, less intense than Gobbi was on Gardelli's classic set for Decca, but stylistically pure. The rest of the cast is strong too, including Domingo in a relatively small role and Nesterenko superb as the High Priest, Zaccaria. Bright and forward digital sound, less atmospheric than the 1966 Decca. The tape layout over four sides is sensible and the sound is vivid and full. Only in the big choruses does the upper range fall slightly short of the discs. This is more noticeable on the first tape than on the second, where the level rises slightly. The CD layout is also on four sides and increases the sense of vibrant presence and detail, while emphasizing the dramatic dynamic range.

In 1966 Decca set impressive standards in this first opera to show Verdi at full stretch. True, the choral contribution was less committed than one would ideally like in a work which contains a chorus unique in Verdi's output, *Va, pensiero*, but in every other way this is a masterly performance, with dramatically intense and deeply imaginative contributions from Tito Gobbi as Nabucco and Elena Suliotis as the evil Abigaille. Gobbi was already nearing the end of his full career, but even he rarely recorded a performance so full of sharply dramatic detail, while Suliotis made this the one totally satisfying performance of an all-too-brief recording career, wild in places but no more than is dramatically necessary. Though Carlo Cava as Zaccaria is not ideally rich of tone, it is a strong performance, and Gardelli, as in his later Verdi recordings for both Decca and Philips, showed what a master he is at pointing Verdian inspiration, whether in the individual phrase or over a whole scene, simply and naturally without ever forcing. The mid-1960s recording is brilliant and atmospheric, although the tape transfer (otherwise vividly detailed) needs a fair degree of control in the treble if the upper range is to sound completely natural. The layout is on two cassettes as against three discs.

When a decade later HMV attempted to rival the Decca set, the choice of Muti as conductor was promising, but in the event he failed to match Gardelli, either in detail or overall. The cast, as impressive as could be gathered at the time – with Manuguerra (an outstanding Scarpia in the Rostropovich *Tosca*) an imaginative choice as Nabucco –

failed nevertheless to equal the three-dimensional characterizations of the earlier team. Renata Scotto sang well but was far less inside the role than Suliotis; Manuguerra was strong and reliable but lacked the flair of Gobbi; and although Elena Obraztsova proved stronger vocally than Dora Carral as Fenena, the casting was inappropriate. Even the recording quality, firm and warm, failed to improve on the Decca.

Nabucco: highlights.
*** Decca SET 367. (from above set, cond. Gardelli).

Suliotis's impressive contribution is well represented on this highlights disc, and that alone will be enough to attract those who simply want a sampler of this first of Verdi's successes. Fine contributions too – if not quite so firm as of old – by Gobbi. Needless to say the great chorus *Va, pensiero* is given its place of honour. First-rate recording.

Otello (complete).
*** RCA RL/*RK* 02951 (3) [CRL 3/*CRK 3* 2951]. Domingo, Scotto, Milnes, Amb. Op. Ch., Boys' Ch., Nat. PO, Levine.
**(*) Decca D 102 D 3/*K 102 K 32* (3/*2*) [Lon. 13130]. Cossutta, M. Price, Bacquier, V. Boys' Ch., V. State Op. Ch., VPO, Solti.
** Decca D 55 D 3/*K 55 K 32* (3/*2*). Del Monaco, Tebaldi, Protti, V. State Op. Ch., V. Grisstadt Kindechor, VPO, Karajan.

Levine's is the most consistently involving version of *Otello*, with on balance the best cast, and it is superbly conducted as well as magnificently sung. Levine combines a Toscanini-like thrust with a Karajan-like sensuousness, pointing rhythms to heighten mood, as in the Act II confrontation between hero and heroine over Cassio. Domingo as Otello combines glorious heroic tone with lyrical tenderness. If anyone thought he would be overstrained, here is proof to the contrary: he himself has claimed that singing Otello has helped and benefited his voice. Scotto is not always sweet-toned in the upper register, and the big ensemble at the end of Act III brings obvious strain, but it is a deeply felt performance which culminates in a most beautiful account of the all-important Act IV solos, the *Willow song* and *Ave Maria*, most affecting. Milnes too is challenged by the role of Iago. His may not be a voice which readily conveys extremes of evil, but his view is far from conventional: this Iago is a handsome, virile creature beset by the biggest of chips on the shoulder. Recording could be fuller, but the balance between voices and orchestra is excellent. The cassette transfer is vivid and well balanced if without quite the range of the discs.

Although Solti recorded outstanding versions of *Aïda* and *Falstaff* in the 1960s, in later years he has neglected Verdi in his recording programme, so that the warmth and tenderness of his reading of *Otello* as well as its incisive sense of drama take one freshly by surprise. The recording is bright and atmospheric to match, which leaves the vocal contributions as a third and more debatable deciding point. Of the very finest quality is the singing of Margaret Price as Desdemona, a ravishing performance with the most beautiful and varied tonal quality allied to deep imagination. Carlo Cossutta as Otello is not so characterful a singer, but more than most rivals he sings with clear, incisive tone and obvious concern for musical qualities. Gabriel Bacquier gives a thoughtful, highly intelligent performance as Iago, but his relative weakness in the upper register brings obvious disappointment. The Decca recording, however, has a sense of spectacle (notably in the opening scene) and perspective which is particularly appealing, the whole production managed with characteristic flair. The Decca cassettes too are among this company's finest issues, the sound matching brilliance with warmth and bloom. Each Act is complete on one of the four cassette sides.

Decca's earlier set under Karajan is seriously flawed. Protti is admittedly not nearly so inadequate an Iago as one had expected. He is always reliable if never imaginative and never sinister – and that is a drawback in an opera whose plot hinges on Iago's machinations. Del Monaco is hardly a subtle Otello, although both he and Tebaldi give one of their finest gramophone performances. The Decca recording, masterminded by John Culshaw, is remarkable from the opening storm onwards, with a deliberate attempt to vary the stage perspective between scenes. There is also a most successful cassette issue, but in spite of Karajan's dramatic direction the set is outclassed by later versions.

Otello (complete; in English).
**(*) HMV Dig. SLS/*TC-SLS* 143605-3/*5*. Craig, Plowright, Howlett, Bottone, E. Nat. Op. Ch. and O, Elder.

That the ENO version, recorded live at the Coliseum in London under the direction of Mark Elder, comes on two instead of three discs is not just a commercial point in its favour but an artistic one too, when each of the four Acts is complete on one side. Those who seek records of opera in English need not hesitate, when almost every word of Andrew Porter's translation is audible, despite the very variable balances inevitable in recording a live stage production. Less acceptable is the level of stage noise, with the thud and rumble of wandering feet often intruding.

The result, flawed vocally as in the sound, is most enjoyable with dramatic tension building up compellingly. Charles Craig's Otello is most moving, with the character's inner pain vividly brought out, though top notes are fallible. Neil Howlett as Iago may not have the most distinctive baritone, but finely controlled vocal colouring adds to a deeply perceptive performance. Rosalind Plowright makes a superb Desdemona, singing with rich, dramatic weight but with poise and purity too. The Death scene reveals her at her finest, radiant of tone, with flawless attack. The recording is full and atmospheric and it has transferred well to tape (the opening spectacle impressively caught) which follows the discs in offering an ideal layout. The reduced libretto/booklet is admirably clearly printed.

Otello: highlights.
*** Decca SET 632. (from above set, cond. Solti).

A generous sampler of the Solti recording, including the *Willow song* and *Ave Maria* to show the beautifully sung and moving contribution of Margaret Price as Desdemona. The spectacle of the opening is impressively contained by the vividly brilliant recording.

Rigoletto (complete).
*** Decca SET 542-4/*K 2 A 3* (3) [Lon. OSA/5- 13105]. Milnes, Sutherland, Pavarotti, Talvela, Tourangeau, Amb. Op. Ch., LSO, Bonynge.
(M) **(*) RCA RL 42865 (2) [LSC 7027]. Merrill, Moffo, Kraus, Flagello, RCA Italiana Op. Ch. and O, Solti.
**(*) DG 2740 225/*3371 054* (*3*) [id.]. Cappuccilli, Cotrubas, Domingo, Obraztsova, Ghiaurov, Moll, Schwarz, V. State Op. Ch., VPO, Giulini.
(M) **(*) Ph. 6747 407/*7650 016* (2) [id.]. Capecchi, D'Angelo, Tucker, Sardi, Ch. and O of San Carlo Th. of Naples, Molinari-Pradelli.
(M) (***) HMV SLS/*TC-SLS* 5018 (3). Callas, Gobbi, Di Stefano, Zaccaria, Ch. and O of La Scala, Milan, Serafin (with recital by Callas: arias from Rossini: *Il Barbiere di Siviglia*; Meyerbeer: *Dinorah*; Delibes: *Lakmé*; Verdi: *I Vespri siciliani* (***)).

Just over ten years after her first recording of this opera Sutherland appeared in it again, and the set was far more than a dutiful remake. Richard Bonynge from the very start shows his feeling for the resilient rhythms, and the result is fresh and dramatic, underlining the revolutionary qualities in the score which nowadays we tend to ignore. Pavarotti too is an intensely characterful Duke: an unmistakable rogue but an unmistakable charmer too. Thanks to him and to Bonynge above all, the *Quartet* for once on a complete set becomes a genuine musical climax. Sutherland's voice has acquired a hint of a beat, but there is little of the mooning manner which disfigured her earlier assumption, and the result is glowingly beautiful as well as supremely assured technically. Milnes is a strong Rigoletto, vocally masterful and with good if hardly searching presentation of character. Urgently enjoyable, with good atmospheric recording, both on disc and on tape.

Robert Merrill sang Rigoletto in a very early RCA LP version of *Rigoletto*, but if anything this reissued set from the mid-1960s is even more impressive with its rich flow of tone and clean-styled musical strength. The Gilda of Anna Moffo is enchanting; Joan Sutherland, on her first Decca set (now deleted), may have been more dreamily beautiful, but aided by the rest of the production Moffo gives a firmer interpretation. Admittedly she is not always helped by Solti's conducting, for he seems determined to rush everyone on, and his beat is often too stiff for middle-period Verdi. But that is a comparatively small price to pay, for Solti's briskness brings the compensation that a complete performance, with only the barest 'statutory' cuts, is fitted on four sides with the breaks coming between Acts. The recording is very good for its period, if not quite so realistic as Sutherland's newest Decca, which remains first choice; but at medium price this can carry a strong recommendation.

Guilini, ever thoughtful for detail, directs a distinguished performance. Speeds tend to be slow, phrases are beautifully shaped, and, with fine playing from the Vienna Philharmonic, the dynamics are subtle rather than dramatic. The conductor seems determined to get away from any idea of *Rigoletto* as melodrama, but in doing that he misses the red-blooded theatricality of Verdi's concept, the basic essential. It may be consistent with Giulini's view but it further reduces the dramatic impact that Cappuccilli with his unsinister voice makes the hunchback a noble figure from first to last, while Domingo, ever intelligent, makes a reflective rather than an extrovert Duke. Cotrubas is a touching Gilda, but the close balance of her voice is not helpful, and the topmost register is not always comfortable. The recording, made in the Musikverein in Vienna, has the voices well to the fore, with much reverberation on the instruments behind. Although the cassette transfer level is not high – to accommodate the recording's wide dynamic range – the soloists are naturally caught and have good presence. Some orchestral detail at pianissimo levels is not as cleanly defined as it might be, but the sound overall is sophisticated, and the opening, with the recessed stage band, is given impressive perspective.

The Philips set with Capecchi, D'Angelo and Tucker dates from 1968 and was first issued in stereo on three super-bargain discs together costing only slightly more than one premium-priced LP at that time. The present reissue is at medium price, and the recording has been successfully retransferred on to four sides. (It includes all the traditional cuts.) The performance is not always polished but it is vigorously red-blooded, with a robust, yet not unstylish Duke from Tucker. D'Angelo's Gilda may have a touch of the soubrette at her first entry, but she soon settles down, and her beautifully sung *Caro nome* is a highlight. The star of the set is Renato Capecchi, whose portrayal of the name part is rivetingly dramatic. The recording is rather over-resonant but still fully acceptable at budget price. The cassettes have less edge on top than the discs – the transfer level is only modest – but the sound is not muffled. However, in the medium-price range this does not match the RCA Solti issue, also on two discs.

There has never been a more compelling performance of the title role in *Rigoletto* than that of Gobbi on his classic Scala set of the 1950s, originally mono, here given a generally effective stereo transcription. At every point, in almost every single phrase, Gobbi finds extra meaning in Verdi's vocal lines, with the widest range of tone-colour employed for expressive effect. Callas, though not naturally suited to the role of the wilting Gilda, is compellingly imaginative throughout, and Di Stefano gives one of his finer performances. The inclusion of some of Callas's best aria recordings of the late 1950s is most welcome. The tape transfer has more presence for the solo voices and chorus than in some other EMI transfers in this vintage series, but it is not without a degree of roughness at peaks. Gobbi's voice is very well caught, however. The cassette layout is on three sides, with the recital (less smoothly transferred) on side four.

Rigoletto (complete; in English).
*** HMV Dig. SLS/*TC-SLS* 270032-3/5 (2). Rawnsley, Field, Davies, Tomlinson, Rigby, E. Nat. Op. Ch. and O, Elder.

The flair of the original English National Opera production setting *Rigoletto* in the Little Italy area of New York in the 1950s and making the tenor a Mafia boss, the 'Duke', is superbly caught in the HMV version in English, economically squeezed on to two discs only. The intensity and fine pacing of the stage performances are splendidly caught in this studio recording thanks to Mark Elder's keenly rhythmic conducting, making this the most successful of the English National Opera Verdi sets. Outstanding vocally is the heady-toned Duke of Arthur Davies and though neither John Rawnsley as Rigoletto nor Helen Field as Gilda has a voice so naturally beautiful, they too sing both powerfully and stylishly. Excellent recording, clean, full and well balanced, unaffected by the exceptionally long sides. The cassettes are first-class too.

Rigoletto: highlights.
*** Decca SET/*KCET* 580 [Lon. OS 26401]. (from above set, cond. Bonynge).
**(*) DG 2537/*3306* 057 [id.]. (from above set, cond. Giulini).

On Decca an excellent selection from an outstanding set, although it was a pity that *Questa o quella* had to be given an edited fade. There is a good tape equivalent.

The highlights from the Giulini set represent tenor and soprano rather more effectively than Rigoletto himself. The variety of expression of Domingo's performance is well caught in his three arias as well as the quartet, and though the same reservations have to be made about Cotrubas's performance as in the complete set – largely a question of recording balance – it is good to have her two big arias as well as her duets with Rigoletto. The cassette transfer is fully acceptable but rather less vivid than the disc.

Simon Boccanegra (complete).
❀ *** DG 2740 169 [2709 071] [(3)/*3371 032* [*id*.]. Cappuccilli, Freni, Ghiaurov, Van Dam, Carreras, Ch. and O of La Scala, Milan, Abbado.

Abbado's recording of *Simon Boccanegra*, directly reflecting the superb production which the Scala company brought to London, is one of the most beautiful Verdi sets ever made. From this one can appreciate not just the vigour of the composer's imagination but the finesse of the colouring, instrumental as well as vocal. Under Abbado the playing of the orchestra is brilliantly incisive as well as refined, so that the drama is underlined by extra sharpness of focus. The cursing of Paolo after the great Council Chamber Scene makes the scalp prickle, with the chorus muttering in horror and the bass clarinet adding a sinister comment, here beautifully moulded. Cappuccilli, always intelligent, gives a far more intense and illuminating performance than the one he recorded for RCA earlier in his career. He may not match Gobbi in range of colour and detail, but he too gives focus to the performance, and Ghiaurov as Fiesco sings beautifully too, though again not so characterfully as Christoff on the deleted HMV set. Freni as Amelia sings with freshness and clarity, while Van Dam is an impressive Paolo. With electrically intense choral singing too, this is a set to put alongside Abbado's superb *Macbeth* with the same company. The cassettes – because of the modest transfer level –have not quite the sharpness of detail of the discs, but solo voices are naturally caught and the distant choral perspectives are convincing.

Stiffelio (complete).
*** Ph. 6769 039/*7699 127* (2) [id.]. Carreras, Sass, Manuguerra, Ganzarolli, V. ORF Ch. and SO, Gardelli.

Coming just before the great trio of masterpieces, *Rigoletto*, *Il Trovatore* and *La Traviata*, *Stiffelio* was a total failure at its first performance in 1850. It was too much to expect either the Italian censor or the public to accept a tale involving a Protestant pastor and his unfaithful wife. To make *Aroldo* six years later the score was in effect destroyed, and only through the discovery of two copyists' scores in the 1960s was a revival made possible. Though it lacks some of the beauties of *Aroldo*, *Stiffelio* is yet a sharper, more telling work, largely because of the originality of the relationships and the superb final scene when Stiffelio reads from the pulpit the parable of the woman taken in adultery. Gardelli directs a fresh performance, at times less lively than Queler's of *Aroldo* but with more consistent singing, notably from Carreras and Manuguerra. First-rate recording, although – as is so often the case with Philips – the low-level cassette transfer has less upper range and sparkle than the discs, as can be heard immediately in the overture.

La Traviata (complete).

*** Decca Dig. **410 154-2**; D 212 D 3 (3)/*K 212 K 32* (2) [Lon. LDR/*5*- 73002]. Sutherland, Pavarotti, Manuguerra, L. Op. Ch., Nat. PO, Bonynge.

**(*) HMV Dig. SLS/*TCC-SLS* 5240 (3) [Ang. DSCX/*4X3X* 3920]. Scotto, Kraus, Bruson, Amb. Op. Ch., Philh. O, Muti.

**(*) [Ang. SCL 3623]. Los Angeles, Del Monte, Sereni, Ch. and O of Rome Op., Serafin.

**(*) DG 2707 103/*3370 024* (2) [id.]. Cotrubas, Domingo, Milnes, Bav. State Op. Ch. and O, Carlos Kleiber.

(***) HMV mono RLS/*TC-RLS* 757 (2). Callas, Kraus, Sereni, Ch. and O of San Carlos Op., Lisbon, Ghione.

**(*) Decca SET 249-51 [Lon. JL/*5*- 42010]. Sutherland, Bergonzi, Merrill, Ch. and O of Maggio Musicale Fiorentino, Pritchard.

**(*) RCA [LSC 6180 (3)]. Caballé, Bergonzi, Milnes, RCA Italiana Op. Ch. and O, Prêtre.

**(*) [Ang. SCLX/*4X3X* 3780]. Sills, Gedda, Panerai, Alldis Ch., RPO, Ceccato.

(M) ** DG Priv. 2726 049/*3371 004* (2) [id.]. Scotto, Raimondi, Bastianini, Ch. and O of La Scala, Milan, Votto.

* WEA 25 0072-1/4. (soundtrack recording). Stratas, Domingo, MacNeil, Metropolitan Op. Ch. and O, Levine.

Sutherland's second recording of the role of Violetta has a breadth and exuberance beyond what she achieved in her earlier version of 1963 conducted by John Pritchard. This *Traviata* is dominated by the grand lady that Sutherland makes her. Some of the supremely tender moments of her earlier recording – *Ah dite alla giovine* in the Act II duet with Germont, for example – are more straightforward this time, but the mooning manner is dispelled, the words are clearer, and the richness and command of the singing put this among the very finest of Sutherland's later recordings. Pavarotti too, though he overemphasizes *Dei miei bollenti spiriti*, sings with splendid panache as Alfredo. Manuguerra as Germont lacks something in authority, but the firmness and clarity are splendid. Bonynge's conducting is finely sprung, the style direct, the speeds often spacious in lyrical music, generally undistracting. The digital recording is outstandingly vivid and beautifully balanced. The cassettes too offer Decca's best quality in the main, and the layout is ideal, with Acts tailored to side-ends. Surprisingly, however, there is some peaking on vocal climaxes, notably in *Ah fors'è lui*; and the libretto supplied with the cassettes is below this company's highest standard, with noticeably small print, especially in the notes. The difference between the sound on LP and CD is very marginal because of the resonant acoustic, but the layout is improved, with Acts and Scenes edited like the tapes. The CD booklet is a reduction and is not ideal.

Muti as a Verdi interpreter believes in clearing away performance traditions not sanctioned in the score. So cadential top notes and extra decorations are ruthlessly eliminated, and Muti with no concern for tradition insists on speeds, generally fast, for which he quotes the score as authority. So at the start of the Act I party music he is even faster than Toscanini, but the result is dazzling, and when he needs to give sympathetic support to his soloists, above all in the great Act II duet between Violetta and Germont, there is no lack of tenderness. It is an intensely compelling account using the complete text (like Bonynge and Prêtre) and it gains from having three Italian-based principals. Scotto and Kraus have long been among the most sensitive and perceptive interpreters of these roles, and so they are here, but with bright digital recording it is obvious that these voices are no longer young, with Scotto's soprano spreading above the stave and Kraus's tenor often sounding thin. Scotto gives a view of Violetta which even amid the gaiety of Act I points forward to tragedy with wonderful expansion in *Ah fors'è lui* on the phrase *Ah quell'amor*. Kraus takes *Dei miei bollenti spiriti* slowly but effectively so, with plenty of extra expression. Bruson makes a fine, forthright Germont, though it does not add to dramatic conviction that his is the youngest voice. Small parts are well taken and, though the recording is rather dry, the stage picture is vivid. The chrome cassettes are strikingly sophisticated, with the perspective in which voices and orchestra are placed more natural than usual, while everything is clear.

Even when Victoria de los Angeles made this EMI recording in the late 1950s the role of Violetta lay rather high for her voice. Nonetheless it drew from her much beautiful singing, not least in the coloratura display at the end of Act I, which, though it may lack easily ringing top notes, has delightful sparkle and flexibility. As to the characterization, Los Angeles was a far more sympathetically tender heroine than is common, and though neither the tenor nor the baritone begins to match her in artistry, their performances are both sympathetic and feeling, thanks in part to the masterly conducting of Serafin. All the traditional cuts are made, not just the second stanzas. The sound on both tape and disc is vivid and clear and seldom betrays the age of the recording. This set has been withdrawn in the UK.

For some, Cotrubas makes an ideal heroine in this opera, but what is disappointing in the DG recording is that the microphone-placing exaggerates technical flaws, so that not only is her breathing too often audible, her habit of separating coloratura with intrusive aitches is underlined, and the vibrato becomes too obvious at times. Such is her magic that some will forgive the faults, for her characterization combines both strength and vulnerability. But Carlos Kleiber's direction is equally controversial, with more than a hint of Toscanini-like rigidity in the party music, and an occasionally uncomfortable insistence on discipline. The characteristic contributions of Domingo and Milnes, both highly commendable, hardly alter the issue. The recording suggests over-reliance on multi-channel techniques. However, this has the advantage that the sound on disc and cassette is very closely matched, crisp and clear if artificially balanced.

Recorded at a live performance in March 1958, Callas's Lisbon-made version is uniquely valuable in spite of very rough sound. Here far more than in her earlier Cetra recording of this opera one can appreciate the intensity which made this one of her supreme roles, with exquisite detail conveying fleeting emotions even in such an obvious passage as the *Brindisi*. Kraus is a fresh, stylish Alfredo, Sereni a positive Germont, more characterful than in the HMV set with Los Angeles. For Callas admirers – who will not object to the occasional ugliness – it is an essential set. The cassettes, like the discs, reflect the boxy quality of the basic recording; intrusive audience noises and insecure balance are a drawback to concentration.

Opinions on Sutherland's earlier recording are sharply divided, and this characteristic performance from her will not win over her determined critics. It is true that her diction is poor, but it is also true that she has rarely sung with such deep feeling on record as in the final scene. The *Addio del passato* (both stanzas included and sung with an unexpected lilt) merely provides a beginning, for the duet with Bergonzi is most winning and the final death scene, *Se una pudica vergine*, is overwhelmingly beautiful. This is not a sparkling Violetta, true, but it is more perfect vocally than almost any other in a complete set. Bergonzi is an attractive Alfredo and Merrill an efficient Germont. Pritchard sometimes tends to hustle things along, with too little regard for shaping Verdian phrases, but the recording quality is outstandingly good.

Caballé too gives a wonderfully poised and pure account of Violetta's music, but this was one of her earlier complete opera sets, and she still had to learn how to project depth of emotion. Vocally, with such fine technicians as Bergonzi and Milnes as her colleagues, this set is consistently satisfying, but it does not add up as a dramatic experience. One is rarely moved, and that is partly the fault too of the conductor, Georges Prêtre, a degree too detached for Verdi. Good recording and an absolutely complete text (as also in the Sutherland versions). This set is deleted in the UK.

Beverly Sills makes an affecting Violetta, tenderly beautiful, with poised legato in *Dite alla giovine*, and producing much lovely singing elsewhere too. But when the voice is pressed, it grows shrill and unfocused. The character of an older woman knowing what suffering is to come remains firm, however, and with a fine Alfredo in Gedda, managing a genuine half-tone of delight at the start of *Dei miei bollenti spiriti*, this is a serious contender among current *Traviata* sets. Ceccato proves an alert and colourful director, and the Royal Philharmonic plays well for him, though the recording is almost too vividly realistic. Its reverberation brings home far too clearly the recording venue in a South London church. Panerai is a strong-voiced Germont, showing less imagination than one expects from him. Like the Sutherland and Caballé sets, this is complete down to the repetitions of cabalettas normally omitted entirely. This set is not available in the UK.

It is worth having the DG Privilege set just for the moving and deeply considered singing of Renata Scotto as Violetta, fresher in voice than in her later HMV set. In a role which has usually eluded the efforts of prima donnas on record, she gives one of the most complete portraits, and it is sad that the rest of the set is largely undistinguished, with even Bastianini roaring rather unfeelingly and the conductor giving routine direction. But on only two mid-price discs (usual stage cuts observed) this should not be dismissed. The tape transfer is clear and clean, a little dry but well projected. The layout is good, but there is no libretto, only a synopsis booklet.

Whatever the visual impact of the Zeffirelli film, the soundtrack recording is deeply disappointing. Domingo sings splendidly, but Teresa Stratas is shrill and embarrassingly ill-equipped for the coloratura of Act I. Neither the voices nor the pushful conducting of Levine can be properly appreciated with such poor sound.

La Traviata (complete; in English).
*** HMV SLS/*TC-SLS* 5216 (2). Masterson, Brecknock, Du Plessis, E. Nat. Op. Ch. and O, Mackerras.

The latterday economics of the gramophone have allowed few complete opera recordings in English, and this exceptional set, like the *Ring* cycle under Reginald Goodall, was recorded with the help of the Peter Moores Foundation. Unlike the *Ring* cycle, however, it is a studio performance, and it is beautifully balanced and refined in detail. Mackerras directs a vigorous, colourful reading which brings out the drama, and Valerie Masterson is at last given the chance on record she has so long deserved. The voice is beautifully – if not always very characterfully – caught, and John Brecknock makes a fine Alfredo, most effective in the final scene. Christian Du Plessis's baritone is less suitable for recording, but the conviction of the whole enterprise is infectious. Clear as most of the words are, it is a pity that no libretto is included, English or Italian; and be warned, Verdi in English has a way of sounding on record rather like Gilbert and Sullivan. The vivid cassettes match the discs closely.

La Traviata: highlights.
*** Decca Dig. **400 057-2**; SXDL/*KSXDC* 7562 [Lon. LDR/*5*- 71062]. (from above set with Sutherland, cond. Bonynge).
**(*) HMV SXLP/*TC-SXLP* 30305 [Ang. S/*4XS* 35822]. (from above set with Los Angeles, cond. Serafin).
**(*) DG 2537/*3306* 047 [2531/*3301* 170]. (from above set with Cotrubas, cond. Kleiber).

This Decca highlights disc was the first operatic issue on compact disc, and pointed forward to the extra immediacy possible with the new medium. One item is omitted compared with the LP – Germont's *Di Provenza* – but it remains an outstandingly generous selection at just on an hour of music, and CD irresistibly brings the sense of being face to face with the singers even while it brings out the forward balance of voices against orchestra. Pavarotti is less individual than Sutherland, but well-paced, and the whole selection brings highly enjoyable performances. There is a vivid chrome cassette, losing only a fraction of the focal clarity on top.

Victoria de los Angeles' voice was not ideally suited to the role of Violetta, but on record she was a unique charmer. This medium-price selection can be recommended to anyone who wants a sample rather than the complete set, though the tenor and baritone are safe rather than imaginative. Good 1950s recording, and an excellent cassette.

Though Cotrubas as Violetta is unflatteringly recorded, hers is certainly a performance, touching and intense, which deserves study, and this collection of highlights makes a convenient substitute for the complete set. It is valuable too for Carlos Kleiber's distinctive reading and the firm, musicianly contributions of Domingo and Milnes.

Il Trovatore (complete).
*** RCA [LSC 6194 (3)]. L. Price, Domingo, Milnes, Cossotto, Amb. Op. Ch., New Philh. O, Mehta.
**(*) Ph. Dig. 6769/*7654* 063 (3) [id.]. Ricciarelli, Carreras, Mazurok, Toczyska, ROHCG Ch. and O, Colin Davis.
(M) (***) HMV SLS/*TC-SLS* 869 (3). Callas, Di Stefano, Barbieri, Panerai, Ch. and O of La Scala, Milan, Karajan (with recital by Callas: arias from Boito: *Mefistofele*; Catalani: *La Wally*; Cilea: *Adriana Lecouvreur*; Giordano: *Andrea Chénier* (***)).
**(*) [Ang. SCLX/*4X3X* 3855 (3)]. L. Price, Bonisolli, Obraztsova, Cappuccilli, Raimondi, German Op. Ch., Berlin PO, Karajan.
** Decca D 82 D 3 (3)/*K 82 K 32* (2) [Lon. 13124/*5*-]. Sutherland, Pavarotti, Horne, Wixell, Ghiaurov, L. Op. Ch., Nat. PO, Bonynge.

Caruso once said of *Il Trovatore* that all it needs is 'the four greatest singers in the world'. Abounding as the opera does in great and memorable tunes, the orchestration is comparatively primitive, often like a kind of orchestral guitar. The support for the voices is a framework only, a dramatic framework, to be sure, but it covers up nothing. The singers alone have to create the necessary breadth and beauty of tone, and the proper dramatic projection. That is not to say the conductor is not important: red-blooded conducting is vital. This is why *Trovatore* is difficult to bring off in the opera house, and even more so on record. Of the earlier sets only the Callas/Karajan can match the RCA set in overall excellence. The soaring curve of Leontyne Price's rich vocal line (almost too ample for some ears) is immediately thrilling in her famous Act I aria, and it sets the style of the performance, full-blooded, the tension consistently held at the highest levels. The choral contribution is superb; the famous *Soldiers'* and *Anvil choruses* are marvellously fresh and dramatic. When *Di quella pira* comes, the orchestra opens with tremendous gusto and Domingo sings with a ringing, heroic quality worthy of Caruso himself. There are many dramatic felicities, and Sherill Milnes is in fine voice throughout, but perhaps the highlight of the set is the opening section of Act III, when Azucena finds her way to Conte di Luna's camp. The ensuing scene with Fiorenza Cossotto is vocally and dramatically quite electrifying. Unfortunately this set has been withdrawn in the UK and there is nothing to take its place.

Davis's is a refreshing and direct reading which in many ways is the antithesis of Karajan's Berlin version with its overblown sound. The refinement of the digital recording makes for a wide, clean separation but, with a low level of cut and backward placing of the orchestra, the result is rather wanting in dramatic impact. Even the *Anvil chorus* sounds rather clinical, and other important numbers too lack the necessary swagger. Ricciarelli's Leonora is most moving, conveying an element of vulnerability in the character. Carreras lacks the full confidence of a natural Manrico; he is less effective in the big extrovert moments, best in such inward numbers as *Ah si ben mio*. Toczyska's voice is presented rather grittily in the role of Azucena. Mazurok similarly is not flattered by the microphones. At least with clean, refined ensemble – helped by these performers' stage experience – this emerges as the opposite of a hackneyed opera. The chrome cassettes follow the disc layout and the sound well. Although the transfer level is low, the voices are naturally focused and do not lack presence.

The combination of Karajan and Callas is formidably impressive. There is toughness and dramatic determination in Callas's singing, whether in the coloratura or in the dramatic passages, and this gives the heroine an unsuspected depth of character which culminates in Callas's fine singing of an aria which used often to be cut entirely – *Tu vedrai che amore in terra*, here with its first stanza alone included. Barbieri is a magnificent Azucena, Panerai a strong, incisive Count, and Di Stefano at his finest as Manrico. Though the recording, originally mono, is limited, it is superbly balanced and surprisingly clear in inner detail. Unfortunately the cassette transfer is made at rather too high a level, and the sound is not always comfortable.

The new Karajan set with Leontyne Price promised much but proves disappointing, largely because of the thickness and strange balances of the recording, the product of multi-channel techniques exploited over-enthusiastically. So the introduction to Manrico's aria *Di quella pira* provides full-blooded orchestral sound, but then the orchestra fades down for the entry of the tenor, who in any case is in coarse voice. In other places he sings more sensitively, but at no point does this version match that of Mehta on RCA. If you must have Karajan, go for the stereo transcription reissue of the EMI set with Callas, which despite dated recording is clearer on detail than this modern offering.

Bonynge in most of his opera sets has been unfailingly urgent and rhythmic, but his account of *Il Trovatore* is at an altogether lower level of intensity, with elegance rather than dramatic power the dominant quality. Nor does the role of Leonora prove very apt for the present-day Sutherland; the coloratura passages are splendid, but a hint of unsteadiness is present in too much of the rest. Pavarotti for the most part sings superbly, but he falls short, for example, in the semi-quaver groups of *Di quella pira*, and, like Sutherland, Marilyn Horne as Azucena does not produce consistently firm tone. Wixell as the Count sings intelligently, but a richer tone is needed. Most recommendable in the set is the complete ballet music, more brilliantly recorded as well as better played than the rest. Discs and cassettes are closely matched.

Il Trovatore: highlights.
**(*) Decca SET/*KCET* 631. (from above set, cond. Bonynge).

The selection from Bonynge's Decca set is specially valuable as a reminder of Sutherland's Leonora. The size of the voice as well as its flexibility are splendidly caught, though a latterday beat afflicts the more sustained passages, and Bonynge does not conduct with his usual urgency. Pavarotti may be stretched by the role of Manrico, but he is nearly always magnificent. Horne is represented by her powerful *Stride la vampa*, Wixell by an undernourished *Il balen*. Excellent recording, with nothing to choose between disc and cassette versions.

I Vespri siciliani (complete).
**(*) RCA Conifer 26.35036 [ARL 4 0370 (4)]. Arroyo, Domingo, Milnes, Raimondi, Alldis Ch., New Philh. O, Levine.

This opera, epic in scale to please the Parisian audiences for whom it was written, is a transitional piece, following the firmly confident middle-period Verdi of *Rigoletto*, *Trovatore* and *Traviata*, but not quite achieving the dramatic intensity and musical richness of later operas. The work's great merit is not so much its grandeur as its searching portrayal of the father–son relationship between Monforte, the tyrannical governor of Sicily, and Arrigo, the son he has never known. Their Act II duet, using a melody well known from the overture, is nothing short of magnificent, with Domingo and Milnes at their very peak. The rest of the singing is good if rarely inspired, and though James Levine's direction is colourful and urgent, such a score needs more persuasiveness. Good recording.

COLLECTIONS

'Pavarotti premières': Aïda: overture. Attila: Oh dolore. I due Foscari: Si lo cento; (ii) *Dal più remoto esilio.* (ii) *Ernani: Odi il voto. Simon Boccanegra: Prelude. I Vespri siciliani: A toi que j'ai chérie.* (i) *Scene for two tenors and orchestra.*
**(*) CBS 74037/*40*- [M/*MT* 37228]. Pavarotti, La Scala O, Abbado; (i) A. Savastano; (ii) Morresi; Giacomotti.

This fascinating collection brings a series of alternative versions and additions generally forgotten, two orchestral, four vocal. The *Overture* to *Aïda* and the *Prelude* to *Boccanegra*, later cut, are both worth hearing, but the vocal items, splendidly sung by Pavarotti (with two head-voice top E flats in the *Due Foscari* item), are even more cherishable. The voice is presented in a different acoustic from that of the orchestra, and the strings sound unsubstantial. The very high-level chrome cassette brings some peaking at climaxes, but neither on tape nor disc is the sound very flattering.

Arias: *Aïda: Ritorna vincitor; Qui Radames verrà . . . O patria mia. Un Ballo in maschera: Ecco l'orrido campo . . . Ma dall'arido stelo divulsa; Morrò ma prima. Ernani: Surta la notte . . . Ernani, involami . . . Tutto sprezzo. Otello: Mi parea . . . Mi Madre avena . . . Ave Maria.*
**(*) Decca SXL/*KSXC* 6971 [Lon. OS 26660]. L. Price, Israel PO, Mehta.

Recorded in 1981, Leontyne Price's collection of arias presents her in a series of spinto roles specially suited to her, but in each instance earlier recordings show the voice in finer, fresher form. The cassette transfer is first-class, the voice free and clear.

Arias: *Un Ballo in maschera: Forse la soglia . . . Ma se m'è forza perderti. I due Foscari: Ah si, ch'io sento ancora . . . Dal più remoto esiglio. Luisa Miller: Oh! fede negar potessi . . . Quando le sere. Macbeth: O figli . . . Ah, la paterna mano.*
*** Decca SXL/*KSXC* 6377 [Lon. OS/*5*-26087]. Pavarotti, V. Op. O, Downes – DONIZETTI: *Arias.****

Like the Donizetti couplings Pavarotti's singing in this early recital shows a freshly exciting voice used without vulgarity, if sometimes with an element of reserve. The recording is excellent on disc and cassette alike.

Arias: *La Battaglia di Legnano: Voi lo diceste . . . Quante volte. I due Foscari: No . . . mi lasciate . . . Ah sì, conforto . . . La clemenza?. Il Trovatore: Che più t'arresti? . . . Tacea la notte . . . Ah! tu Partasti. Siam giunti . . . D'amor sull'ali rosee.*
(M) *** Ph. 6527/*7311* 161 [id.]. Ricciarelli; cond. Gardelli or Sir Colin Davis – PUCCINI: *Arias.***(*)

It was a good idea to collect some of the outstanding Verdi arias from the complete opera sets to which Ricciarelli has contributed, making this an unusual as well as an attractive selection, generally well-sung and recorded. The cassette transfer is quite vivid.

Arias: *Don Carlo: Ella giammai m'amo . . . Dormiro sol. Macbeth: Chi v'impose unirvi a noi . . . Come al ciel precipita. Nabucco: Gli arredi . . . Sperate, o figli!; Vieni o levita; Oh chi piange. Simon Boccanegra: A te l'estremo addio . . . Il lacerato spirito. I Vespri siciliani: O patria . . . O tu, Palermo.*
(M) *** Decca GRV6. Ghiaurov, Amb. S., LSO, Abbado.

Ghiaurov's superb collection of bass arias is here reissued in the mid-price Grandi Voci series with the advantage of Philip's aria from *Don Carlo* being added to the original selection. Mid-1960s recording, still first-rate.

'Heroines': Arias: *Don Carlos: Tu che le vanità. Ernani: Surta è la notte . . . Ernani! Ernani, involami. Macbeth: Nel dì della vittoria . . . Vieni, t'affretta; La luce langue; Una macchia è qui tuttora!* (Sleepwalking Scene). *Nabucco: Ben io t'invenni . . . Anch'io dischiuso un giorno.*
*** HMV ASD/*TC-ASD* 3817 [Ang. S 35763]. Callas, Philh. O, Rescigno.

Much of this is Callas at her very finest. Dismiss the top-note wobbles from mind, and the rest has one enthralled by the vividness of characterization as well as the musical imagination. It is sad that Callas did not record the role of Lady Macbeth complete. Here *La luce langue* is not so intense as the Act I aria and the Sleepwalking Scene, which are both unforgettable. Abigaille, Elvira and Elisabetta all come out as real figures, sharply individual. Finely balanced recording. The cassette transfer is vibrantly vivid, but at vocal peaks there are hints that the level might with advantage have been just a trifle lower.

Arias: *Don Carlo: Tu che le vanità. La Traviata: Ah fors è lui. Il Trovatore: Timor di me.*
*** CBS Dig. 37298/*40*- [id.]. Te Kanawa, LPO, Pritchard – PUCCINI: *Arias.****

The Verdi side of Kiri Te Kanawa's Verdi–Puccini recital brings three substantial items less obviously apt for the singer, but in each the singing is felt as well as beautiful. The coloratura of the *Traviata* and *Trovatore* items is admirably clean, and it is a special joy to hear Elisabetta's big aria from *Don Carlo* sung with such truth and precision. Good recording. The chrome tape is transferred at a low level. The voice sounds well, but the orchestra is recessed.

Arias: *Ernani: Surta è la notte; Ernani, involami. I Vespri siciliani: Mercè, dilette.*
(M) *** Decca Jub. JB/*KJBC* 97 [Lon. CS/*5*-25111]. Sutherland, Paris Conservatoire O, Santi – DONIZETTI: *Linda di Chamounix; Lucia: arias.* *** ❀

It is primarily for the Donizetti items that this magnificent recital is famous, but these two Verdi arias show a comparable level of memorability, with superb singing throughout. The cassette transfer has been remastered and now matches the disc closely.

Choruses from (i) *Aïda;* (ii) *I Lombardi; Macbeth; Nabucco; La Traviata; Il Trovatore.*
*** HMV ASD/*TC-ASD* 3979 [Ang. SZ/*4XS* 37795]. Philh. or New Philh. O, Muti, with (i) ROHCG Ch.; (ii) Amb. Op. Ch.

A red-blooded selection of choruses, some extracted from Muti's complete sets. The singing is both vibrant and atmospheric; the famous *Hebrew slaves' chorus* from *Nabucco* (*Va, pensiero*) is a highlight. The selection seems to emphasize Verdi's melodramatic qualities rather than the subtleties of his choral writing as in Abbado's deleted collection with the Chorus and Orchestra of La Scala, Milan (DG 2530 549/*3300 495*, awarded a rosette in the second edition of the *Penguin Stereo Record Guide*). But this programme is enjoyable for its spirit and colourful projection. The sound is appropriately ripe and brilliant; the focus on cassette is at times less sharp than on disc, but the sound has plenty of body and impact.

Choruses from *I due Foscari; Ernani; I Lombardi; Luisa Miller; Macbeth; Nabucco; Il Trovatore; I Vespri siciliani.*
**(*) HMV ASD/*TC-ASD* 3811. Welsh Nat. Op. Ch., Armstrong.

The Welsh National Opera made its initial reputation by the strength of its chorus work, and while these performances are not so refined as they might be they are for the most part vivid and lusty, with plenty of character and rhythmic feeling. The natural eloquence of the Welsh often surfaces in lyrical moments, but the famous *Va, pensiero* from *Nabucco*, although effective, is not as memorable as one might have expected. The witches in *Macbeth*, however, are rather quaintly characterized to provide a moment of light relief. Excellent recording, full and clear, and a good tape (especially impressive on side two, when the transfer level rises).

'The world of Verdi': Aïda: (i) *Se quel guerrier . . . Celeste Aïda. Don Carlo:* (i–ii) *Ascolta! le porte . . . Dio che nell' alma infondere. La Forza del destino:* (iii) *Overture. Luisa Miller:* (i) *Oh! fede negar potessi . . . Quando le sere. Nabucco:* (iv) *Va, pensiero. Otello:* (v) *Willow song. Rigoletto:* (vi) *La donna è mobile;* (v; vii) *Quartet: Bella figlia. La Traviata:* (viii) *Prelude to Act I;* (ii) *Di Provenza il mar. Il Trovatore:* (ix) *Vedi, le fosche;* (x) *Stride la vampa. I Vespri siciliani:* (xi) *Mercè, dilette.*
(M) ** Decca SPA 447. (i) Bergonzi; (ii) Fischer-Dieskau; (iii) St Cecilia O, Previtali; (iv) V. State Op. Ch. and O, Gardelli; (v) Sutherland; (vi) Pavarotti; (vii) Malagù, Cioni, MacNeil; (viii) German Op. O, Berlin, Maazel; (ix) Ch. and O of St Cecilia Ac., Rome, Franci; (x) Horne; (xi) Chiara.

Although acceptable, this is a comparatively disappointing selection. Side one, generously, has seven items on it, and this means a low level of cut, so that the opening *Forza overture* and the following *Chorus of Hebrew slaves* from *Nabucco* seem to lack impact and vibrancy. There are some very good things later, including Sutherland's *Willow Song*, Bergonzi's *Celeste Aïda*, and Maria Chiara's beautiful *Mercè, dilette*; but these serve to point the contrast with the *Traviata* and *Trovatore* excerpts, where the electricity is at a distinctly lower voltage.

Victoria, Tomas Luis de
(*c.* 1548–1611)

Ascendens Christus; Ave Maria; Estote fortes in bello; Gaudent in coelis; Hic vir despiciens mundum; Iste sanctus pro lege Dei; Veni, sponsa Christi. Litaniae de Beata Virgine; Magnificat primi toni; O Magnum mysterium; O quam gloriosum (Mass and motet); *Requiem Mass* (sex vocibus).
(M) **(*) Argo ZK 70/1 [id. PSI]. St John's College Ch., Guest.

This set draws together two separate issues by the St John's College Choir under George Guest, and while there are some reservations about the style of these performances, with so little of Victoria's music available in really distinguished versions this medium-priced reissue must be accorded a warm welcome. The motets can be numbered among the finest Victoria gave us, and the rest of the music too is of the highest quality. The St John's Choir sing well in tune, but their approach is often too 'Anglican' for this passionate Spanish music. The choirboys are sometimes flabby in tone (especially in the singing of the plainchant), while the men have big vibratos, and these two elements never really mix. But the motets fare much better than the *Requiem* and here the performances are often admirable in their way. The recording throughout is clear and well focused, and if one accepts the fact that English choirs lack the harsh lines drawn by the firmer-toned Spanish bodies, there is little to cavil at. This remains highly suitable for a collector who wants to sample the composer or his period.

Nigra sum (motet).
*** Gimmell 1585-03/*T*. Tallis Scholars, Phillips – PALESTRINA: *Missa Nigra sum.***

This is discussed under its coupling.

Vierne, Louis (1870–1937)

(Organ) *Symphony No. 1 in D min., Op. 14; Légende, Op. 31/13.*
*** Mer. E 77011. Sanger.

A pupil of Franck and Widor, Vierne was a commanding figure in the world of French organ music in his day. Since our last edition, there has been welcome evidence of greater interest in his work. David Sanger has embarked on a project to record all six organ symphonies, using as fill-ups some of the *Pièces libres,* Op. 31. Here, as in the companion volumes, he appears whole-heartedly identified with this repertoire, and readers unfamiliar with Vierne will find that Sanger leaves you sharing his evident enthusiasm for this music. He has recorded all his Meridian recitals – excellently balanced they are too – on the organ of the Italian Church of St Peter in Clerkenwell, London, an instrument well suited to the demands of this music. Vierne's style is often more harmonically sophisticated than the newcomer to this repertoire would suspect, and Sanger captures its quasi-improvisational yet thoughtful quality admirably. The *D minor Symphony* dates from the turn of the century and was dedicated to Guilmant. Its sense of power and its quiet originality make it well worth seeking out.

Symphony No. 2 in E min., Op. 20; Arabesque, Op. 31/15.
*** Mer. E 77021. Sanger.

The *Second Symphony* is a finely wrought piece, perhaps more concentrated than its predecessor and played with no less sympathy by David Sanger. It receives a recording of excellent depth and range.

Symphony No. 3 in F sharp min., Op. 28; Pièces en style libre, Op. 31: Prélude; Scherzetto; Le Carillon de Longpont; Berceuse.
*** Mer. E 77024. Sanger.

Symphony No. 3; Pièces, Op. 31: Cortège; Berceuse; Divertissement; Le Carillon de Longpont.
(M) ** Saga 5456. Wills.

In the *Third Symphony*, which is demanding both technically and musically, David Sanger again proves the equal of the challenge. Though this is generally not as dark a work as the wartime *Fourth,* it is distinguished by moments of genuine depth. There is no cause to complain of the sound quality, which maintains the high standards Meridian have set themselves.

Arthur Wills also couples the *Third Symphony* with some of the Op. 31 *Pièces*, playing them on the organ of Ely Cathedral to magnificent effect. He too is an eloquent exponent of this repertoire, but he is less well served by the engineers than his rival on Meridian; the sound is less refined and detail is less transparent than is ideal.

Symphony No. 5 in A min., Op. 47; Pièces en style libre, Op. 31: Préambule.
*** Mer. E 77048. Sanger.

David Sanger has genuine commitment to this repertoire and even though he is playing an instrument somewhat removed from the Cavaillé-Coll sound world, he succeeds in conveying an authentic feeling. He is completely at home in this music and has vivid recording to commend him.

Vieuxtemps, Henri (1820–81)

Violin concertos Nos. 4 in D min., Op. 31; 5 in A min., Op. 37.
*** HMV ASD 3555 [Ang. S/*4XS* 37484]. Perlman, O de Paris, Barenboim.

Vieuxtemps wrote six violin concertos, and it is surprising that so few violinists have attempted to resurrect more than the odd one. This coupling of the two best-known is not only apt; it presents superbly stylish readings, with Perlman both aristocratically pure of tone and intonation and passionate of expression. In his accompaniments Barenboim draws warmly romantic playing from the Paris Orchestra. Ripe recording to match.

Violin concerto No. 5 in A min., Op. 37.
*** Decca SXL 6759 [Lon. CS 6992]. Kyung-Wha Chung, LSO, Foster – SAINT-SAËNS: *Concerto No. 3.****
** CBS Dig. 37796. Lin, Minnesota O, Marriner – HAYDN: Concerto.**

Even more than the Saint-Saëns on the reverse, the Vieuxtemps concerto needs persuasive advocacy, and that is certainly what Kyung-Wha Chung provides, not just in her passionate commitment in the bravura sections but in the tender expressiveness of the slow movement, so much more compelling than the usual, more extrovert manner. Excellent recording.

Cho-Liang Lin is a Taiwanese-born player whose formidable technique is well able to meet the demands of this concerto. He plays it with flair and zest, and is well supported by Marriner and the Minnesota Orchestra. However, this disc is unlikely to appeal to the collector as much as Perlman's more logically coupled HMV version. It is an artist-oriented issue related to this brilliant player's capability and designed to show him to good advantage, for it is difficult to discern what appeal this coupling might have except for those following this young player's career. Good sound.

Villa-Lobos, Heitor (1887–1959)

Bachianas Brasileiras: No. 2 (includes *The Little Train of the Caipira);* (i) *No. 5* (for soprano and 8 cellos)*; No. 6* (for flute and bassoon)*; No. 9.*
**(*) HMV ASD 2994 [Ang. S/*4XS* 36979]. O de Paris, Capolongo, (i) with Mesplé.

A good selection of Villa-Lobos's most colourful (and most popular) works, vigorously directed and well recorded. Mady Mesplé's very French timbre does not ideally suit the lovely *Bachianas Brasileiras No. 5.*

Guitar concerto.
*** CBS 76369/*40*- [M/*MT* 33208]. Williams, ECO, Barenboim – RODRIGO: *Concierto de Aranjuez.****

The invention of this *Concerto* is rather thin, but John Williams's compulsive performance makes the very most of its finer points and especially the rhapsodic quality of the *Andantino*. The CBS recording is bright and fresh, the guitar recorded characteristically close. The coupling is among the finest available accounts of Rodrigo's famous *Concierto de Aranjuez*. The tape transfer, while lacking the last degree of upper range, offers greater freshness than in the Rodrigo coupling.

(i) *Guitar concerto. Étude in C sharp min.; 5 Preludes; Suite populaire brésilienne: Schottisch-Chôro.*
*** RCA RL/*RK* 43518 [AGL 1/*AGK 1* 4897]. Bream, (i) with LSO, Previn.

A highly distinguished account of the *Guitar concerto*, a work more striking for its atmosphere than for its actual invention. The rest of the programme also shows Bream in inspirational form; several of the *Preludes* are hauntingly memorable when the concentration of the playing is so readily communicated. The cassette transfer is of excellent quality, one of RCA's best, and it matches the disc closely.

Harmonica concerto.
*** Argo ZRG 905. Reilly, L. Sinf., Atherton – ARNOLD and BENJAMIN: *Concertos.****

Villa-Lobos wrote his concerto in 1955 for the American virtuoso John Sebastian. For a long time the score was lost until it was rescued from oblivion by Tommy Reilly, who plays it here. He finds a natural affinity for its rhapsodic pastoral moods, and the beautiful orchestral playing from the London Sinfonietta under David Atherton provides an understanding backcloth for the soloist. Perhaps the music lacks something in contrast, for even the finale has not the boisterous energy of the coupled works by Malcolm Arnold and Arthur Benjamin. But the performance here is persuasive and it is superbly recorded.

Études Nos. 1, 3, 5–8, 11, 12; Gavota-Chôro; Mazurka-Chôro; 5 Preludes; Schottisch-Chôro; Suite populaire brésilienne: Valsa-Chôro.
(M) ** Saga 5453. Hill.

An ambitious recital. Eric Hill is especially good in the *Five Preludes*: these performances are first-class. He makes less of a case for the short lightweight pieces, but brings out the full character and contrasts inherent in the *Études*. The guitar is balanced very forwardly, and its closeness to the microphone reduces the range of dynamic in writing which sometimes demands strongly marked crescendos and diminuendos as part of its structure. The close balance also emphasizes odd fingerboard noises.

5 Preludes for guitar.
*** CBS 73545/*40*- [M/*MT* 34198]. Williams – SCARLATTI: *Sonatas.***(*)

CBS provide excellent recording for John Williams's performance of the *Preludes*. Although he is closely balanced, his playing is of the highest order of mastery. A lower level-setting compensates for the close balance, and enables this artist's playing to register effectively. These are as perfect and as finely turned as any performances in the catalogue. There is a good cassette of this coupling.

Viotti, Giovanni (1755–1824)

Violin concerto No. 3 in A, G. 25.
*(*) Decca Ser. SA/*KSC* 23. Prencipe, Rossini O of Naples, Caracciolo – MOZART: *Concerto No. 3.***(*)

This is an inept coupling for a good performance of the Mozart *G major Concerto*, K. 216, played by different artists. The Viotti is a conventional sort of work though pleasant enough, and would need a stunning performance to make a strong impression. Here it receives only a competent one. The recording is good and there is a lively cassette.

Vivaldi, Antonio (1675–1741)

L'Estro armonico, Op. 3; La Stravaganza, Op. 4; The Four Seasons (from *The Trial between Harmony and Invention*), *Op. 8/1–4; La Cetra, Op. 9; Wind concertos, RV. 441, 443, 456, 498, 535, 539, 569, 574.*

(M) *** Argo D 101 D 10 (10) [id.]. Soloists, ASMF, Marriner or Iona Brown.

This admirable ten-disc set marks the outstanding achievement of the Academy of St Martin-in-the-Fields under Marriner and Iona Brown in the music of Vivaldi. Apart from an account of *The Four Seasons* which, after more than thirteen years in the catalogue and against the most formidable competition, remains at the top of the recommended list, the box adds a marvellous miscellany of diverse wind concertos, with distinguished soloists, offering playing that is consistently alert, finely articulated and free from over-emphasis. The major collections of violin concertos, *L'Estro armonico* and *La Stravaganza* (the latter given a rosette in our second edition), are rewarding not only for the solo playing and the ever resilient accompaniments but also for the highly imaginative continuo playing, using cello and bassoon as well as harpsichord and organ. *La Cetra,* directed by Iona Brown, is well up to the standard of the rest of the series. With outstanding recording this is perhaps the most distinguished Vivaldi compilation in the catalogue.

L'Estro armonico, Op. 3 (complete).

*** O-L D 245 D 2/*K 245 K 22* (2). Holloway, Huggett, Mackintosh, Wilcock, AcAM, Hogwood.

*** Argo ZRG 733-4/*K 119 K 22* (2) [id.]. Hogwood, Tilney, Spencer, ASMF, Marriner.

(M) **(*) DG 413 218-1/*4* (2) [2709 100/*3370 034* (3)]. Brandis, Spierer, Berlin PO (members).

(M) **(*) Ph. 6768/*7656* 307 (2) [id.]. Michelucci, Gallozzi, Cologni, Vicari, Colandrea, I Musici.

Even those who normally fight shy of 'authentic' performances of baroque music with their astringent timbres and purposive avoidance of romantic gestures will find it hard not to respond to the sparkling set of Vivaldi's Op. 3 from the Academy of Ancient Music directed by Christopher Hogwood. The captivating lightness of the solo playing and the crispness of articulation of the accompanying group bring music-making that combines joyful vitality with the authority of scholarship. Textures are always transparent, but there is no lack of body to the ripieno (even though there is only one instrument to each part). Hogwood's continuo is first-class, varying between harpsichord and organ, the latter used to add colour as well as substance. The balance is excellent, and the whole effect is exhilarating. While some listeners may need to adjust to the style of playing in slow movements, the underlying expressive feeling is never in doubt, and in the allegros the nimble flights of bravura from the four soloists are a constant delight. The recording is superb. Apart from the truthfulness of individual timbres there is a striking depth of acoustic, with the solo instruments given a backwards and forwards perspective as well as the expected antiphonal interplay. The overall effect is intimate yet spacious. The cassette transfer is of the Decca group's highest quality. The upper partials may be fractionally cleaner on disc, but the range, body and transparency of the sound on tape are very impressive, and with a slight reduction of treble the recording yields a demonstration standard.

Those who as yet have not been won over to the more abrasive sounds of 'original instruments' will find Marriner's set no less stylish. As so often, he directs the Academy in radiant and imaginative performances of baroque music and yet observes scholarly good manners. The delightful use of continuo – lute and organ as well as harpsichord – the sharing of solo honours, and the consistently resilient string-playing of the ensemble make for compelling listening. The recording is immaculate, and it is a positive advantage that the twelve concertos are fitted on to four sides, since Vivaldi in effect grouped them in four sets of three. The tape transfer is made at a very high level, and although it has striking presence and sophisticated detail, the upper range in tutti is marginally less sweet and refined than on disc, though the loss is not serious enough to prevent a firm recommendation.

The Berlin Philharmonic recording has been remastered from three on to two mid-priced discs and chrome tapes (the latter offered in a new-style miniature box packaging) and the sound is first-class in both formats. As might be expected, the playing of the Berlin Philharmonic and the soloists is superbly polished, with firm yet not heavy rhythms and with the slow-movement cantilenas expressively shaped. This is very much a German view of Vivaldi and, if the spirit of Telemann pops in here and there, the music-making is distinguished and certainly not without imaginative flair, though the continuo lacks creative importance. As we go to press, this is still listed in Schwann in its original three-disc premium-priced format.

The I Musici set comes from Philips' complete Vivaldi Edition. The recording dates from the early 1960s but still sounds very acceptable. The playing is reliable and fresh, and readers who acquire this mid-priced set are unlikely to be disappointed, though both Marriner and Hogwood are more imaginative. The Philips cassettes are of excellent quality, lively and clear.

L'Estro armonico: Concertos Nos. 1, 3–6 and 9.

(M) ** DG Arc. 2547/*3347* 012 [id.]. Soloists, Lucerne Fest. Strings, Baumgartner.

The Lucerne performances are well made and quite stylish (though not 'authentic', in spite of the label), with good solo playing. The impression is of sound team-work rather than extrovert manners. Good recording and generous measure at medium price. The tape is of excellent quality, clear and clean and with excellent body and range.

L'Estro armonico: Double violin concerto No. 8 in A min.

** CBS Dig. 37278/*40-* [id.]. Zukerman, Stern, St Paul CO, James – BACH: *Double concertos.***

This lovely *Double concerto* makes an apt coupling for the two Bach *Double concertos* on this record from Minnesota, but the same reservations have to be made about the excessive weight of bass, alongside comparable praise for the solo playing.

L'Estro armonico: Concerto No. 10 in B min. for 4 violins.

(M) *** HMV SXLP/*TC-SXLP* 30294 [Ang. S 36103]. Menuhin, Masters, Goren, Humphreys, Bath Fest. CO – BACH and HANDEL: *Concertos for violin and oboe.****

Menuhin's version of the *B minor Concerto* is part of an entertaining mixed concert of baroque concertos which he shares with Leon Goossens. The performance is striking and the sound is brighter and fresher than when this compilation first appeared in the early 1960s, and the cassette matches the disc closely.

L'Estro armonico, Op. 3; La Stravaganza, Op. 4.

(M) **(*) Ph. 6768 009 (5). Michelucci, Gallozzi, Ayo, Cotogni, Colandreo, I Musici.

The Vivaldi Edition, which Philips marketed in 1978 to mark the tercentenary of the composer's birth, drew on earlier performances familiar to collectors. Suffice it now to say that this is still one of the most economical and by no means the least musically satisfying ways of acquiring a basic Vivaldi collection. These are fresh and lively performances; melodies are finely drawn and there is little hint of the routine which occasionally surfaces in I Musici – and, for that matter, in Vivaldi himself. Where competition arises, this group often yields to the Academy of St Martin-in-the-Fields, who have crisper textures and convey greater enthusiasm, but here I Musici are a good choice and they are certainly recommendable to collectors of the series.

La Stravaganza (12 violin concertos), *Op. 4*: complete.
❀ *** Argo ZRG 800/1 [id.]. Kaine, Loveday, ASMF, Marriner; with Hogwood, Tilney (harpsichord and organ), Spencer, Rooley, Tyler (theorbos).
**(*) Erato STU 70955 (3). Toso, Rybin, I Sol. Ven., Scimone.

It has been held that, like *La Cetra, La Stravaganza* does not match the invention of *L'Estro armonico*, but if the quality of the earlier concertos of the set does not always show Vivaldi at his very best, from about halfway (from No. 6 onwards) one is constantly astonished at the music's vitality. Even earlier, in the finale of No. 3, or the poetic slow movement of No. 4, Vivaldi provides some marvellously imaginative music, but the later works have a consistency and show the composer at his most enticing. Marriner's performances make the music irresistible. The solo playing of Carmel Kaine and Alan Loveday is superb, and when the Academy's rhythms have such splendid buoyancy and lift it is easy enough to accept Marriner's preference for a relatively sweet style in the often heavenly slow movements. The recording is of the highest quality, and as usual the contribution of an imaginatively varied continuo (which includes cello and bassoon in addition to the instruments credited) adds much to the colour of Vivaldi's score. Very highly recommended.

Scimone directs energetic readings of the twelve concertos, very enjoyable in their way, with recording nicely balanced except for backward continuo. But Marriner's two-disc version, altogether more imaginative, is preferable.

6 Concertos, Op. 6; La Cetra, Op. 9.
(M) **(*) Ph. 6768 010 (4). Carmirelli, Ayo, Cotogni, I Musici.

La Cetra has been available before (it dates from the mid-1960s), and with Felix Ayo the principal soloist the playing is spirited, characterful and expressively rich. One drawback is that solo passages are given no continuo support, though there is an organ continuo for the ripieno sections. This is less individual than the ASMF set with Iona Brown (see below) but remains rewarding if the Op. 6 set is wanted. These concertos are not otherwise available and, while their invention is more uneven, their rarity may tempt some collectors. The performances, with Pina Carmirelli an excellent soloist, are polished, with well-judged tempi, if with no special imaginative flair. The sound is excellent.

12 Concertos, Op. 7; The Trial between Harmony and Invention, Op. 8 (complete).
(M) **(*) Ph. 6768 011 (5) [id.]. Accardo, Ayo, Holliger, I Musici.

The Op. 7 set is relatively unfamiliar and by no means unrewarding; indeed much of the invention is vital and appealing. The playing of Accardo and Holliger is altogether masterly, and they have fine rapport with their fellow-musicians in I Musici. The Op. 8 set is, of course, recorded in abundance, and Ayo's version of *The Four Seasons* is more than twenty years old (presumably the later recording was not available to the planners of this compilation on contractual grounds). It is a smooth rather than imaginative account, though the sound is still more than acceptable and the playing of Ayo himself is thoroughly polished. The ensemble is at times a shade heavy-handed in the remaining concertos of Op. 8, but there is still a great deal to enjoy in these performances, and though this would not necessarily be a first choice for Op. 8, the rewards of Op. 7 make a strong claim for this box.

The Trial between Harmony and Invention (*Il Cimento dell'armonia e dell'invenzione*), *Op. 8* (complete).
**(*) O-L Dig. D 279 D 2/*K 279 K 22* (2) [id.]. Bury, Hirons, Holloway, Huggett, Mackintosh, Piguet, AcAM, Hogwood.
**(*) CRD CRD 1025/*CRDC 4025* (Nos. 1–4; see also below); CRD 1048/9/*CRDC 4048* and *4049*, available separately (Nos. 5–10 and 11–12 plus *Flute concerto in D, RV.429*; *Cello concerto in B min., RV.424*). Standage, Preston, Pleeth, E. Concert, Pinnock.
**(*) Chan. DBR/*DBT* 3003 (3). Thomas, Digney, Bournemouth Sinf.

The first four concertos of Op. 8 are a set within a set, forming what is (understandably) Vivaldi's most popular work, *The Four Seasons*. Their imaginative power and their eloquence and tunefulness tend slightly to dwarf the remaining eight concertos, but there is some splendid music throughout the complete work, well worth exploring.

There is no want of zest in the Academy of Ancient Music's accounts of Op. 8. These are likeable and, generally speaking, well-prepared versions and differ from some rivals in choosing the oboe in two of the concertos, where Vivaldi has indicated an option. There are moments where more polish would not have come amiss (in the *G minor Concerto*, for example) and intonation is not above reproach either. However, admirers of the Academy will find much to enjoy here – as, indeed, will those who are not always in tune with period-instrument performances. In *The Four Seasons*, Pinnock is not displaced, however. The recordings are well up to standard on both disc and tape.

The CRD version of *The Four Seasons* is also an imaginative one and it features a baroque violin. As this first disc (and cassette) was issued separately in advance of the other two it is considered below with the other versions. The remaining two records of the set were then issued in a double sleeve, but the three cassettes are all individually packaged. Because six concertos are fitted on the second record and tape, the third is able to include two bonus concertos, of which the *Flute concerto* is particularly attractive. The performances throughout are alert and full of character, with eloquent slow movements. As on the Oiseau-Lyre set, there is a quality of astringency to the sound, which emphasizes the neat, scaled-down imagery. The acoustic is comparatively dry, and although here a chamber organ is used in the continuo to add extra touches of colour, there is little suggestion of fantasy or Mediterranean glow. Nevertheless these are undoubtedly distinguished performances, even if they are perhaps a little lacking in charm. The cassettes match the discs closely in quality.

The Bournemouth Sinfonietta set on Chandos is beautifully recorded and has much in its favour. The use of modern instruments does not preclude a keen sense of style, and the balance is convincing, with the continuo coming through not too insistently. The later concertos are particularly successful; Nos. 5 (*La Tempesta di mare*) and 6 (*Il Piacere*) are excellent, and there is some delectable oboe playing from John Digney in the final group. Allegros are alert without being rigid and slow movements are expressive, with musical phrasing and a fine sense of atmosphere. The drawback for most listeners will be the account of *The Four Seasons*, which is seen as part of the whole cycle rather than as individually dramatic. Ronald Thomas's approach emphasizes the music's breadth and lyricism rather than its colourful pictorialism, so that the shepherd's dog barks gently and the winds blow amiably, certainly never reaching gale force. In its way this is pleasing, but there remains an element of disappointment in the undercharacterization. The cassette transfer is very variable in level (the second side of *The Four Seasons* registers a big drop after side one), and the degree of immediacy and range varies accordingly.

The Four Seasons, Op. 8/1–4.

*** Argo ZRG/*KZRC* 654 [id.]. Loveday, ASMF, Marriner.

*** HMV ASD/*TC-ASD* 3293 [Ang. S/*4XS* 37053]. Perlman, LPO.

*** DG 2531/*3301* 287 [id.]. Kremer, LSO, Abbado.

*** DG Arc. Dig. **400 045-2**; 2534/*3311* 003 [id.]. Standage, E. Concert, Pinnock.

*** Ph. Dig. **410 001-2**; 6514/*7337* 275 [id.]. Carmirelli, I Musici.

(M) *** Decca Jub. JB/*KJBC* 63 [Lon. (d) JL/*5-* 41007]. Kulka, Stuttgart CO, Münchinger.

*** CRD CRD 1025/*CRDC* 4025 [id.]. Standage, E. Concert, Pinnock.

*** DG 2530 296/*3300 300* [id.]. Schwalbé, Berlin PO, Karajan.

**(*) Ph. 6500 017/*7300 312* [id.]. Michelucci, I Musici.

(M) **(*) Ph. 9502/*7313* 118. Ayo, Berlin CO, Negri.

**(*) CBS 60010/*40-* [M/*MT* 31798]. Zukerman, ECO.

**(*) Erato STU/*MCE* 70679 [id.]. Toso, Sol. Ven., Scimone.

(B) **(*) Con. CC/*CCT* 7527. Ferrari, Stuttgart Soloists, Couraud.
**(*) HMV Dig. ASD/*TCC-ASD* 3964 [Ang. DS/*4ZS* 37755]. Menuhin, Camerata Lysy, Gstaad, Lysy.
(M) **(*) Ph. Seq. 6527/*7311* 088. Ayo, I Musici.
(M) **(*) EMI Em. EMX/*TC-EMX* 2009. Jakowicz, Polish CO, Maksymiuk.
(B) **(*) CfP CFP/*TC-CFP* 40016. Sillito, Virtuosi of England, Davison.
** Delos Dig. DMS 3007 [id.]. Oliviera, LACO, Schwarz.
** Ph. 9500 717/*7300 809* [id.]. Iona Brown, ASMF.
(M) ** CBS 60342/*40*- [MS 6744]. Corigliano, NYPO, Bernstein.
(M) ** Decca SPA 201 [Lon. STS/*5*- 15403]. Krotzinger, Stuttgart CO, Münchinger.
(M) * Decca VIV/*KVIC* 3 [Lon. STS/*5*-15539]. Bean, New Philh. O, Stokowski.

(i) *The Four Seasons;* (ii) *L'Estro armonico: Concerto for 4 violins in B min., Op. 3/10.*
*** DG Dig. 2741/*3382* 026 (2) [id.]. (i) Stern, Zukerman, Mintz, Perlman; (ii) Stern, Gitlis, Haendel, Mintz; Israel PO, Mehta – BACH: *Double concerto*; MOZART: *Sinfonia concertante*.*** ❀

The Four Seasons; L'Estro armonico: Violin concerto in D min., Op. 3/11.
(M) **(*) DG Priv. 135024 [(d) 2535/*3335* 105]. Schneiderhan, Lucerne Fest. Strings, Baumgartner.

Vivaldi's *Four Seasons* is still a work much more frequently heard on records (and in the cinema and on TV) than in the concert hall. As can be seen above, it is the most often recorded of any piece of classical music. Its popularity is very much of our time. It was Münchinger's famous 1951 mono recording, with Rudolf Barchet and the Stuttgart Chamber Orchestra, that established its reputation in Britain, and it is good to see that a Münchinger record still holds its place in the Vivaldi 'top ten'. Yet it is Marriner's 1970 Academy of St Martin-in-the-Fields account with Alan Loveday – made during a vintage Argo recording period – that continues to dominate the many available versions. It has an element of fantasy that makes the music sound utterly new and is full of imaginative touches, with Simon Preston subtly varying the continuo between harpsichord and organ. The opulence of string tone may be too romantic for some, but there is no self-indulgence in the interpretation, no sentimentality, for the contrasts are made sharper and fresher, not smoothed over. The cassette is not quite as clean as the disc (especially on side two), but is still thoroughly recommendable alongside it.

For collectors seeking a second opinion there is plenty of choice. Those looking for an account of the solo role from an artist of international fame might turn to the HMV set from Itzhak Perlman. His finesse as a great violinist is evident from first to last. Though some will demand more reticence in baroque concertos, Perlman's imagination holds the sequence superbly together, and there are many passages of pure magic, as in the central *Adagio* of *Summer*. With an intimate acoustic, the sound is never inflated but in scale and sharply defined. The cassette transfer, however, is very bright, less refined than the disc.

In the DG version by Gidon Kremer with the LSO under Claudio Abbado, it is obvious from the first bar that Abbado is the dominating partner. This is an enormously vital account, with great contrasts of tempo and dynamic. The dramatization of Vivaldi's detailed pictorial effects has never been more vivid; the vigour of the dancing peasants is surpassed by the sheer fury and violence of the summer storms. Yet the delicacy of the gentle zephyrs is matched by the hazy somnolence of the beautiful *Adagio* of *Autumn*. After a freezingly evocative opening to *Winter*, Abbado creates a mandolin-like pizzicato effect in the slow movement (taken faster than the composer's marking) to simulate a rainshower. The finale opens delicately, but at the close the listener is almost blown away by the winter gales. Kremer matches Abbado's vigour with playing that combines sparkling bravura and suitably evocative expressive moments. Given the projection of a brilliantly lit recording, the impact of this version is considerable. Leslie Pearson's nimble continuo, alternating organ and harpsichord, sometimes gets buried, but drama rather than subtlety is the keynote of this arresting account. The cassette matches the disc closely, a little mellower, but the difference is marginal.

The most recent of the 'authentic' performances – the Archive version by Simon Standage with the English Concert directed from the harpsichord by Trevor Pinnock – has the advantage of using a newly discovered set of parts found in Manchester's Henry Watson Music Library, which has additionally brought the correction of minor textual errors in the Le Cène text in normal use. The Archive performance also (minimally) introduces a second soloist and is played on period instruments. The players create a relatively intimate sound, though their approach is certainly not without drama, while the solo contribution has impressive flair and bravura. The overall effect is essentially refined, treating the pictorial imagery with subtlety. The result is less voluptuous than with Marriner, less individual than with Perlman, less vibrant than the version under Abbado, but it finds a natural balance between vivid projection and atmospheric feeling. The digital recording is first-class on disc and chrome tape alike, while the compact disc offers the usual additional virtues of background silence, added clarity and refinement.

The recording made at the 1982 Huberman Festival in Tel Aviv takes the opportunity offered by a stellar gathering of fiddlers to give each of the four concertos to a different soloist. It makes one wonder why no record company has thought of doing this before. The result is an unqualified success, with each artist revelling in writing that offers equal opportunities for bravura and espressivo playing, plus a chance for the imagination to find a similar balance between the musical and pictorial aspects of Vivaldi's remarkable conception. The playing has striking freshness and spontaneity throughout, while in the *Quadruple Violin concerto* from *L'Estro armonico* an alternative foursome show integrated teamwork of a similar order. With outstanding recording quality (disc and tape are virtually identical) this is an example of 'live' music-making at its finest. The Bach and Mozart couplings are equally recommendable, so this is a set to be considered by those who already have alternative versions of some of this music. The audience is understandably quiet during the playing, although – reasonably enough – all four of the *Seasons* excite vociferous applause.

The new Philips digital recording is the third in stereo by I Musici and it is undoubtedly the finest of the three. Musical values as ever are paramount, but this time there is more vitality and the programmatic implications are more strikingly realized (indeed the bark of the shepherd's dog in *Spring* is singularly insistent). Yet Pina Carmirelli's expressive playing maintains the lyrical feeling and beauty of tone for which I Musici versions are remembered and combines it with attractively alert and nimble bravura in the allegros. The gentle breezes are as effectively caught as the summer storms, and the slow movement of *Autumn* (helped by especially atmospheric recording) makes an elegiac contrast. The opening of *Winter* is certainly chilly. The recording is outstandingly natural both on LP and the excellent chrome tape and most impressive of all on CD.

At medium price on Decca's Jubilee reissue, Konstanty Kulka gives a first-class solo performance, while Münchinger and the Stuttgart Chamber Orchestra, whose early LPs did so much to reawaken interest in Vivaldi, show that their stylish and lively manner is as compelling as ever, helped by vivid recording. Though this is brighter than many versions, it stands as one of the most satisfying. The cassette, like the disc, offers first-class sound; the transfer is fresh and transparent, the continuo and inner detail coming through clearly.

Simon Standage and the English Concert made an earlier 'authentic' version for CRD in 1976, six years before their DG Archiv record. Standage's baroque violin has a somewhat nasal character (especially noticeable on the wide-ranging chrome cassette) that not all will respond to, while the somewhat abrasive string textures heighten the sense of drama. The slow movement of *Autumn*, where the harpsichord plays simple arpeggios against the sustained strings, is most beautiful. But essentially this is a dramatic performance, strongly characterized. That is well illustrated by the *Adagio* of *Summer*, where the soloist is songfully poised while the bustling strings threaten the approaching storm which, when it arrives, has the fury of a tempest. This same vigour produces elsewhere tempi that verge on being too fast, but the vivacity is never in doubt and the dark colouring from the lower strings in tutti is another mark of the special character of this account. The cassette transfer is admirably vivid and clear.

Karajan's version is unexpectedly successful. Michel Schwalbé is a truly memorable soloist. His playing is neat, precise and wonderfully musical, with a touch of Italian sunshine in the tone. His sparkling playing is set against radiant Berlin Philharmonic string textures, and the engineers appear to have damped down the bass end of the audio spectrum to prevent too cushioned a sound. The tonal beauty of Karajan's conception is not achieved at the expense of vitality, and although the harpsichord hardly comes through, the overall scale is acceptable. Not a conventional account, then, but very rewarding of its kind. There is a good cassette.

I Musici must have played this work countless times and probably find it more difficult than most groups to bring freshness to each new recording. Here, Roberto Michelucci is a first-class soloist, displaying bursts of bravura in the outer movements but often musingly thoughtful in the slower ones. His expressiveness is finely judged, and the group are naturally balanced, with the harpsichord coming through in the right way, without exaggeration. The last degree of spontaneity is sometimes missing, but this is an enjoyable disc.

Schneiderhan's fine performance is also competitive at medium price, especially as, because of fast tempi, it is the only version that can make room for a bonus. The snag is the recorded quality, which is somewhat insubstantial and lacking in bass. Otherwise it is clean and clear. Surprisingly the bass returns in the bonus item (which indeed sounds a little plummy in tone), and then one is made aware of what was missing in the *Seasons*.

With a talented group from East Berlin, Felix Ayo secures playing of microscopic precision, and the string tone is sweet and resonant. It remains a solid middle-of-the-road version, marred only by one or two miscalculations, as in the very fast opening of *Winter* and occasional squeezed tone in lyrical slow movements. Warm recording, and a faithful cassette transfer.

Zukerman's performances come from his complete set (now deleted). The playing brings out all the drama, and although its expressive qualities are in no doubt and the slow movements offer thoughtful, often searching playing, this is not as imaginative as Marriner's disc. The cassette transfer is of fair quality.

The performance by Piero Toso and I Solisti Veneti is mercurial to say the least, with wide extremes of dynamic and tempo and unashamed rubato. The speed in the finale of *Spring* is a sustained example, but the impetuous burst of *molto vivace* in the coda of the first movement of *Autumn* is even more striking. The solo playing is matched by an imaginative accompaniment, and every minute of the performance is alive; but many will find this approach too eccentric. The recording is resonant, basically good, but occasionally a little gruff in the loudest tuttis.

The bargain-priced Ferrari reissue has a great deal to offer. Neither soloist nor orchestra plays with the last degree of polish, but there is striking commitment to the music throughout. Witness the short slow movement of *Autumn*, where the intensity is beautifully controlled, or indeed the vigour of any of the allegros, where the players' enjoyment is obvious. The music-making is helped by the excellent recording, smooth and warm yet vivid, giving Ferrari a gleaming tonal line, and enough detail for the orchestra without spotlighting any lack of precision. With such good sound and genuine stylistic sympathy this is certainly competitive. The cassette transfer is less wide-ranging than the disc but quite acceptable.

Menuhin's digital recording is designed as much to provide a framework for the youthful Camerata Lysy as for its illustrious soloist, whose rhythmic control is not always stable (notably in the opening movement of *Autumn*). Nevertheless this is a characterfully extrovert account, robust and exuberant rather than refined. The continuo is not significant, and while Menuhin's directness communicates readily, this cannot be given an unqualified recommendation because, in spite of the brilliant digital clarity, detail is not registered very subtly. The chrome cassette has a slightly mellower image than the disc but retains all its other qualities.

Felix Ayo's performance with I Musici dates from the beginning of the 1960s, but the warm, reverberant recording still sounds well.

This will be enjoyed by those for whom richness of sound is paramount, even at the cost of vitality. Felix Ayo produces lovely tone throughout and he plays as stylishly as ever.

The performance by Krysztof Jakowicz and the Polish Chamber Orchestra is characteristically bustling with vigour, with strong dynamic contrasts, and a similar balance between the fast, energetic allegros and the gentle sostenuto of the lyrical music. The solo playing offers arresting bravura but is sensitive too, so that the gentle breezes and summer languor are as readily communicated as the violent storms, and the icy briskness of what is plainly seen as a harsh winter. The recording is very bright – indeed, many will feel rather too brilliant – but this excess is tamed on the cassette which is otherwise clear and clean.

An enjoyable forthright performance from Arthur Davison and the Virtuosi of England, marked by assured violin-playing from Sillito. The soloist is balanced too far forward, which detracts from gentler expressiveness, but otherwise the sound is vivid and firm on both disc and tape.

The Delos recording by Elmar Oliveira and the excellent Los Angeles Chamber Orchestra under Gerard Schwarz made the digital début of *The Four Seasons* in 1980. The recording is extremely brilliant, the sharp spotlighting of the soloist bringing a degree of steeliness to his upper range. Tempi too are extremely brisk throughout: extrovert bravura is the keynote here rather than atmosphere. The recording balance ensures that the continuo comes through well. But – as the opening of *Winter* demonstrates – this is not an especially imaginative version, although the alert vivacity of the playing of soloist and orchestra alike is undoubtedly exhilarating, and slow movements are expressive and sympathetic.

The Academy of St Martin's earlier Argo recording under Neville Marriner, unauthentically sumptuous, had irresistible magic; but Iona Brown's version with the same band fails to repeat that. The mannered style, with exaggerated dynamic contrasts, suggests that she may have been attempting to do so, but not even in refinement of playing is this among the Academy's finest issues. The recording is rich, the cassette less cleanly detailed than the disc.

Bernstein chooses a wide range of tempi and thus the fast music is very fast (sometimes disconcertingly so) and the slower sections are played with great breadth. John Corigliano, the soloist, is fully up to the tempi chosen and imparts plenty of fire to the proceedings. The orchestral textures in some of the adagio passages are often of breathtaking beauty, although the reverberant texture diminishes any sense of authenticity of timbre. One cannot think that the virtuosity of Vivaldi's time was quite up to these allegros, but the whole effect is exhilarating without being brutal, and because the playing is so secure, it does not even sound rushed. Characteristically bright CBS sound.

Münchinger's first stereo recording with Krotzinger had lost the freshness of new discovery of his earlier mono set. This is a straightforward, rather Germanic account, somewhat phlegmatic in the familiar Münchinger way. The recording is good, though the treble is somewhat over-bright. Münchinger's more recent record with Kulka is a great improvement on this and well worth the extra money, on recording grounds alone.

Stokowski's version, originally recorded in Phase Four, with closely balanced sound, has a highly sensitive soloist, but the conductor's wilful unstylishness is endearingly wrong-headed. The mellowness of his approach – with sensuous warmth in *Spring* as well as *Summer* – irons out all Vivaldi's intended contrasts and there are curious ritenutos at the end of each allegro. The sound is over-resonant to the point of blurring most detail.

(i; ii) *The Four Seasons;* (iii) *Recorder concerto in C, RV.443;* (ii) *Double violin concerto in A (Echo), RV.552.*

(B) *** DG Walkman *413 142-4.* (i) Schneiderhan; (ii) Lucerne Fest. Strings, Baumgartner; (iii) Linde, Emil Seiler CO, Hofman (with: ALBINONI: *Adagio* (arr. Giazotto). CORELLI: *Concerto grosso in G min. (Christmas), Op. 6/8.* PACHELBEL: *Canon and Gigue in D* ***).

Schneiderhan's excellent version of *The Four Seasons* (see above) is offered here together with Vivaldi's ingenious *Echo concerto*, where the echo effects are not just confined to the soloists but feature the ripieno too; plus the engaging *Concerto for sopranino recorder*, RV.552. Then to make the concert doubly generous, this bargain-priced Walkman tape offers three other baroque favourites. Performances are of high quality throughout and the recording is consistently vivid, although there is a slight edge on the solo violin in *The Four Seasons*.

The Four Seasons, Op. 8/1–4 (arr. for flute and strings).
*** RCA RL/*RK* 25034 [LRL1/*LRK1* 2284]. Galway, I Solisti di Zagreb.

James Galway's transcription is thoroughly musical and so convincing that at times one is tempted to believe that the work was conceived in this form. The playing itself is marvellous, full of detail and imagination, and the recording is excellent, even if the flute is given a forward balance. The cassette transfer is comparatively unrefined.

Violin concertos, Op. 8, Nos. 5 in E flat (*La Tempesta di mare*), *RV. 253; 6 in C* (*Il Piacere*), *RV. 180; 10 in B flat* (*La Caccia*), *RV. 362; 11 in D, RV. 210; in C min.* (*Il Sospetto*), *RV. 199*.
*** HMV Dig. ASD/*TCC-ASD* 143442–1/*4*. Menuhin, Polish CO, Maksymiuk.

Menuhin's collection of five concertos – four of them with nicknames and particularly delightful – brings some of his freshest, most intense playing in recent years. Particularly in slow movements – notably that of *Il Piacere*, Pleasure – he shows afresh his unique insight in shaping a phrase. Fresh alert accompaniment and full digital recording. The sound on the chrome cassette is admirably wide-ranging and full.

La Cetra, Op. 9 (complete).
(M) *** Decca Jub. 411 851-1/*4* (2). Iona Brown, ASMF.

Iona Brown, for some years the leader of the St Martin's Academy, here acts as director in place of Neville Marriner. So resilient and imaginative are the results that one hardly detects any difference from the immaculate and stylish Vivaldi playing in earlier Academy issues. The recording is outstandingly vivid, even by Decca/Argo standards with the Academy, and for this Jubilee reissue the set has been remastered from three discs (as on the original full-priced Argo issue) to two, with matching chrome tapes.

(i) *Bassoon concertos: in A min., RV.498; in E min., RV.484; in F, RV.489; in B flat, RV.502;* (ii) *Flute concertos: Op. 10, Nos. 1 in F* (*La Tempesta di mare*)*; 2 in G min.* (*La Notte*)*; in A min., RV.108 and RV.440; in G, RV.436 and RV.438; in D, RV.427 and RV.429; in C min., RV.441;* (ii; iii) *Double flute concerto in C, RV.533;* (iv) *Oboe concertos: Op. 11, No. 6 in G min.; in C, RV.447 and RV.450/51; in A min., RV.461; in D, RV.453; in F, RV.455; in F* (*P.457*)*; in A min.* (*P.463*).
(M) *** Ph. 6768 015 (5). I Musici, with (i) Thunemann, (ii) Gazzelloni, (iii) Steinberg, (iv) Holliger.

This five-record set is a cheap way of acquiring some noteworthy Vivaldi. By far the most remarkable music here is to be found in the *Bassoon concertos*, which are as richly inventive as anything in Vivaldi's output. He wrote thirty-seven concertos for this instrument, as opposed to fifteen for flute and nineteen for the oboe. Somewhat disproportionately, the *Bassoon concertos* occupy only one record here as opposed to two each for the flute and oboe concertos. But there are good things among them, too, and some fine playing from all the soloists. Yet fine though such favourites as *La Notte* and *La Tempesta di mare* are, it is the *Bassoon concertos* recorded here that leave the strongest impression of originality and power. All in all, this is a most rewarding set and can be strongly recommended. The performances are all superbly accomplished and the recordings impeccable.

Bassoon concertos: in A min., RV.498; in B flat, RV.504; in C, RV.472; in C min., RV.480.
**(*) Chan. ABR/*ABT* 1057 [Musicmasters 20018]. Thompson, L. Moz. Players, Ledger.

Robert Thompson turns a genial eye on these four concertos and he is warmly and stylishly accompanied. He is rather forwardly balanced, which tends to detract from any subtlety of effect, but the performances are direct and agreeably fresh. The sound is natural and the cassette has only fractionally less upper range than the disc.

Cello concertos: in C, RV.398; in G, RV.413.
(M) *** DG Sig. 2543/*3343* 517 [2530/*3300* 974]. Rostropovich, Zürich Coll. Mus., Sacher – BOCCHERINI and TARTINI: *Concertos.****

Performances of great vigour and projection from Rostropovich. The playing is superbly brilliant and immensely strong in character; it may be somewhat large-scale for Vivaldi's two quite short concertos, but undoubtedly every bar of the music comes fully to life. Splendidly lively accompaniments and excellent recording, bright and clean, yet with no lack of depth. The tape transfer too is admirable.

Cello concertos: in C, RV.400; C min., RV.401; G, RV.413, A min., RV.420; B min., RV.424.
*(*) Erato STU/*MCE* 71453. Lodéon, Paillard CO, Paillard.

The five concertos recorded here are more than mere routine Vivaldi; indeed the cello seems to have inspired him to considerable heights of imagination. The performances, however, are not in the very first flight. Frédéric Lodéon is a sensitive artist who plays with refined tone and musicianship and the Paillard ensemble have the advantage of modern instruments, but the playing is lacking in polish and affection, and faster movements tend to sound a little routine. The recording is excellent.

Cello concertos: in C, RV.400; in C min., RV.401; in B min., RV.424; (i) *Double cello concerto in G min., RV.531;* (i; ii) *Triple concerto for violin and 2 cellos, RV.561* (all ed. Malipiero).
*** HMV ASD/*TC-ASD* 3914. Paul Tortelier, L. Moz. Players, Ledger, with (i) Maud Tortelier, (ii) Manzone.

The performances here are strong and alive, the slow movements expressive without being over-romanticized. Philip Ledger directs the full-bodied accompanying group and provides a continuo with some flair. The playing is undoubtedly stylish, although the overall effect is not aimed at the 'authentic' lobby, rather at those who seek primarily a warmly understanding response to the composer's inspiration and readily communicated musical enjoyment. The sound is excellent and the cassette splendidly clean in focus.

Cello concerto in C min., RV.401.
(M) **(*) DG Arc. Priv. 2547/*3347* 046. Storck, Seiler CO, Hofmann – BOCCHERINI and TARTINI: *Concertos.***

Originally part of a Vivaldi anthology, Klaus Storck's excellent performance of the *C minor Concerto* has been recoupled with other works for the same instrument. The Vivaldi is the highlight of the collection, for it is played with assurance and flair. The recording is good, if not distinguished. The treble needs smoothing on disc; the cassette is preferable, vivid yet less strident on top.

Cello concerto in C min., RV.401; Double cello concerto in G min., RV.531; Double concertos for cello and violin: in A, RV.546; in B flat, RV.547; Concertos for two cellos and two violins: in D, RV.564; in G, RV.575; Harpsichord concertos: in B min., RV.168; in C, RV.112 and RV.116; in E, RV.131/2; in F, RV.137; in G min., RV.156; Violin concertos: in E (L'Amoroso), RV.271; in F, RV.542; Double violin concertos: in A (L'Eco in lontana), RV.552; in A min., RV.523; in B flat, RV.525 and RV.527; Triple violin concerto in F, RV.551; Quadruple violin concerto in B flat, RV.553; Concertos for strings: in A, RV.158; in C, RV.114; in C min., RV.119; in D, RV.126; in D min., RV.129; in E min., RV.134; in F, RV.138 and RV.141; in G min., RV.153, RV.154 and RV.157; Sinfonia in G, RV.149;

Sonata a quattro in E flat (Al santo sepolcro), RV.130.
(M) *** Ph. 6768 014 (6). Various soloists, I Musici.

These performances presumably date from the early 1970s; only the first of the six records has appeared before in the UK, though they have surely been issued separately elsewhere. There is much distinguished playing, particularly in the *Violin concertos*; Pina Carmirelli's account of the *E major* (*L'Amoroso*) is beautifully warm and to be preferred to its predecessors on record (even Grumiaux's). There is a varied, well-planned sequence on most of these discs, except perhaps for the last but one, which offers instrumental concertos without soloists. The music is far from unrewarding but is best not heard all in one go. The last of the six records has some relatively unfamiliar and often unpredictable music, forward-looking and searching. The playing throughout is highly polished without being excessively bland, though in the couple of instances where direct comparison arises with the Academy of St Martin-in-the-Fields, the latter sounds fresher. Given the excellence of the recorded sound and the reasonableness of the outlay (the cost works out at rather less than medium price), the rewards of the set are clear.

(i) *Cello concertos: in G, RV.414; in G min., RV.417; in A min., RV.418 and RV.420.* (ii) *Orchestral concertos: in C, RV.556 and RV.558; in G min., RV.576 and RV.577.* (ii; iii) *Viola d'amore concertos: in F, RV.97; in D, RV.392; in D min., RV.393–5 and RV.540; in A, RV.396; in A min., RV.397.*
(M) *** Ph. 6768 013 (4). (i) Walevska, Neth. CO, Redel; (ii) Dresden State O, Negri; (iii) Giuranna.

These four records contain some good things: Bruno Giuranna's accounts of six concertos for the viola d'amore, joined in the case of two other concertos by *obbligato* instruments: P.266/RV.540 is with lute, and P.286/RV.97 is also for two horns, two oboes and bassoon. The third record is taken up by concertos for miscellaneous instruments and includes the fine *Concerto per la Solennità di San Lorenzo*, all of these with the Dresden orchestra; and the last, and in some ways most interesting of all, is the disc devoted to four cello concertos, superbly played by Christine Walevska with the Netherlands Chamber Orchestra. There is a lot of interesting music here, and the recordings are as excellent as the performances.

Chamber concertos: in D, RV.84; in D, RV.89; in G, RV.102; in A min., RV.108. Sonata in D min. (La Follia), RV.63.
*** DG Arc. 2533 463 [id.]. Col. Mus. Ant.

Vivaldi's *Chamber concertos* (works for more than one solo instrument and bass continuo) are far fewer than his concertos for solo instruments: Ryom lists only thirty-nine, twenty-three of which are of undisputed authenticity. Indeed, the *G major Concerto* recorded here (RV.102) is arguably not by Vivaldi himself. The best-known of the set is the *A minor Concerto*, which is given a performance of great verve and life; and much the same might be said of the remaining pieces in this anthology, three of which are not otherwise available. This is Vivaldi playing at its best with all the keenness and delight of first discovery. Excellent recording of some charming music.

6 Flute concertos, Op. 10 (complete).
*** O-L DSLO/*KDSLC* 519 [id.]. Preston, AcAM.
*** Ph. 9500/*7300* 942 [id.]. Petri, ASMF, Marriner.

Stephen Preston plays a period instrument; a Schuchart, and the Academy of Ancient Music likewise play old instruments. Their playing is eminently stylish and yet both spirited and expressive, and they are admirably recorded. The cassette has marginally less refinement in the upper range than the disc but is otherwise of good quality.

Whereas Stephen Preston uses a baroque flute and Severino Gazzelloni (see below) a modern instrument, the young Danish virtuoso Michala Petri uses a modern recorder. At least this, like Gazzelloni's set, gives us the opportunity of hearing these concertos at present-day pitch. Michala Petri plays with breathtaking virtuosity and impeccable control, and she has the advantage of superb recording. In the slow movements – and occasionally elsewhere – there is more in the music than she finds, but the sheer virtuosity of this gifted young artist is most infectious. The cassette matches the disc closely. The upper orchestral range has slightly less bite, but the solo recorder has fine naturalness and presence.

6 Flute concertos, Op. 10; Flute concertos: in A min., RV.108; in D, RV.427; in C, RV.429; in G, RV.436; in G, RV.438; in A min., RV.440; in C min., RV.441; in A min., RV.445. (i) *Double flute concerto in C, RV.533.*
(M) *** Ph. 6768 147 (3). Gazzelloni, I Musici, (i) with Steinberg.

For those who do not want the set of the Opp. 11 and 12 concertos (or who bought them separately in the mid-1970s), Philips offer Gazzelloni's 1969 recording of the Op. 10 plus a variety of other flute concertos, including a diverting *Double concerto in C.* All this is of high quality, but not for continuous listening!

(i) *6 Flute concertos, Op. 10.* (ii) *6 Violin concertos, Op. 11; 6 Violin concertos, Op. 12.*
(M) *** Ph. 6768 012 (4). I Musici, with (i) Gazzelloni, (ii) Accardo.

Severino Gazzelloni's version of the six concertos, Op. 10, has been in circulation throughout the 1970s and its merits are well established; it is probably a safer recommendation for the general collector than the authentic rivals, good though the best of these is. The Opp. 11 and 12 concertos are perhaps of uneven quality, but the best of them are very rewarding indeed, and played so superlatively by Salvatore Accardo they are likely to beguile the most unwilling listener. These were all available separately in the mid-1970s; this set is one of the most desirable of the Vivaldi Edition.

Flute concerto in C min., RV.441; Piccolo concerto in C, RV.443.
(M) *** Argo ZK 82. Bennett, ASMF, Marriner – BACH: *Flute concerto, BWV 1056; Suite No. 2, BWV 1067.****

Both these admirable performances are taken from Argo full-priced collections – see below. The sound is first-class and if the couplings are suitable this is a bargain.

Guitar concerto in C, RV.425; Double guitar concerto in G, RV.532; Concerto for 4 guitars in B min., RV.580; Concerto in A for guitar, violin, viola and cello, RV.88.
(M) **(*) Ph. Seq. 6527/*7311* 042 [Mer. 75054]. Los Romeros, San Antonio SO, Alessandro.

These are all good performances, well played and recorded. The accompaniments are alert and the balance is generally realistic. These works were all originally conceived for the mandolin, but they sound well in these formats, though not all the music is especially memorable. Vivaldi's concertos of this kind are often more effective when grouped in a miscellaneous collection with varying solo timbres. However, guitar and mandolin enthusiasts should find this satisfactory, for the recording is excellent, both on disc and on the high-level cassette.

Lute concerto in D, RV.93; Double concerto in G, RV.532.
(*) RCA RL/*RK* 11180 [ARL 1/*ARK 1* 1180]. Bream, Monteverdi O, Gardiner – HANDEL and KOHAUT: *Concertos.*(*)

The *Lute concerto* receives a first-class performance here from Julian Bream, and he is very well accompanied. The slow movement, with its delicate embroidery over a glowing texture of sustained strings, is particularly fine. In the arrangement of the *Double mandolin concerto* Bream is able by electronic means to assume both solo roles. This too is a highly effective performance, though the exaggeratedly forward recording balance makes the solo instruments sound far larger than life and negates much of the dynamic contrast with the accompanying group. Otherwise the sound is lively and full-blooded, and the high-level cassette matches the disc closely.

Oboe concertos: in C, RV.451; in D, RV.453; in F, RV.455; in A min., RV.461; in F (P.457).
*** Ph. 9500 299 [id./*7300 568*]. Holliger, I Musici.

These five concertos, all sharply contrasted with one another, show Vivaldi at his most inspired. Holliger, with lively accompaniment from I Musici, gives delectable performances, endlessly imaginative, beautifully recorded.

Orchestral concertos (con molti stromenti): in C, RV.556 and RV.558; in G min., RV.576–7.
(M) **(*) Ph. 7503/*7313* 071. Dresden State O (members), Negri.

These recordings come from Volume 7 of the Vivaldi Tercentenary Edition (6768 013 – see above). The allegros are busy and bustling. The opening *G minor Concerto* was dedicated to its Dresden performers, though not the present group! The most interesting work is the last to be played (RV.558) with its delicacy of scoring for flutes, chalumeaux, mandolins, theorbos, violins 'in tromba marina', and cello. Elsewhere the complicated orchestrations suggested by the composer are not followed to the letter, with trumpets introduced – rather effectively – into the *Concerto in C*, RV.556. The playing is alert, the sound is lively, on tape as well as disc, but overall these works are more interesting for their ingenious scoring than for the music they contain.

Piccolo concertos: in A min., RV.108 and RV.445; in C, RV.443–444.
** Cal. CAL 1630/*4630*. Beaumadier, Nat. O of France, Rampal.

The documentation for this collection leaves much to be desired as three of the four concertos are incorrectly detailed. Jean-Louis Beaumadier, however, is an accomplished soloist and the music is worth having: RV.444 and RV.108 both have striking slow movements. With the use of a piccolo rather than a recorder, the overall effect is robust (Rampal's accompaniments are alert and spirited). The playing has plenty of personality, even if ultimate points of style are neglected. The recording is vivid, the soloist well forward. The cassette is highly modulated, with hints that a slightly lower level would have brought marginally more refinement.

Viola d'amore concertos in A min., P.37; in D, P.166; in A, P.233; in D min., P.287.
** Erato STU/*MCE* 70826. Calabrese, I Sol. Ven., Scimone.

Viola d'amore concertos in F, P.286; in D min., P.288; in D min., P.289; (i) *Concerto for viola d'amore and lute in D min., P.266.*
**(*) Erato STU/*MCE* 70827. Calabrese, I Sol. Ven., Scimone, (i) with Crisoforetti.

Nane Calabrese is an excellent player, even if the viola d'amore does have its limitations, which one notices more readily when listening to a set of concertos. One of the drawbacks is the contrast with the orchestra, which, using modern instruments, makes an ample sound compared with the more meagre tone of the soloist. Not all these concertos are masterpieces, but the quality of invention is often surprisingly high and the *F major Concerto*, P.286, which uses a wind accompaniment, is outstanding. The second disc offers the more interesting collection.

MISCELLANEOUS COLLECTIONS

L'Estro armonico, Op. 3: Concertos Nos. 2 in G min.; 11 in D min. Flute concerto in G min. (La Notte), Op. 10/2; Oboe concerto in A min., RV.461; Concertos for strings: in C min., RV.120; in D min. (Madrigalesco), RV.129.
*** Chan. ABR/*ABT* 1008. Soloists, Cantilena, Shepherd.

Cantilena and Adrian Shepherd are fortunate in that television appearances have made them widely familiar in the UK. Their performances of baroque music in general and Vivaldi in particular are stylish without being self-consciously so. They use modern instruments and pitch, and are not afraid to express emotion, investing some of the slow movements with greater feeling than some collectors may like. However, this anthology of well-known Vivaldi is eminently well played (perhaps without the last ounce of finish sometimes), thoroughly musical and admirably recorded. It should give pleasure. The cassette transfer is clear and clean, the soloists well focused; but on tape the upper strings are rather lacking in body.

L'Estro armonico: Concerto No. 10 in B min. for 4 violins. The Four Seasons; Bassoon concerto in A min., RV.498; Flute concerto in C min., RV.441; Double horn concerto in F, RV.539; Double oboe concerto in D min., RV.535; Piccolo concerto in C, RV.443; Double trumpet concerto in C, RV.537; Violin concerto in B flat, Op. 4/1; (i) *Gloria in D.*
(M) *** Argo D 240 D 3/*K 240 K 33* (3). Soloists, ASMF, Marriner, (i) with Vaughan, Baker, King's College Ch., Willcocks.

Those not wanting to invest in the larger ASMF Vivaldi collection (see above) might consider this instead. Very reasonably priced, it includes *The Four Seasons*, plus an attractive array of wind and brass concertos, with the invigorating *Gloria in D* as a bonus on the last side. The recording is first-class on disc and cassette alike.

L'Estro armonico: Concerto No. 10 in B min. for 4 violins. La Stravaganza: Violin concerto in D min., Op. 4/8. La Cetra: Double violin concerto in B flat, Op. 9/9. Double trumpet concerto in C, RV.537; Cello concerto in C, RV.401.
(M) **(*) Decca Ser. SA/*KSC* 21. Soloists, ASMF, Marriner.

A more than acceptable reshuffling of performances recorded between 1965 and 1978. This means that the sound balance and quality alters between the items although it is always lively and clear. (On the cassette version the *Double trumpet concerto* is shrill.) Performances are all of good and sometimes very good quality, but the juxtaposition of works has no special felicity.

L'Estro armonico: Concerto No. 10 in B min. for 4 violins. Flute concerto in C min. (*La Notte*), *Op. 10/2; Mandolin concerto in C, RV.425; Double mandolin concerto in G, RV.532; Recorder concerto in C, RV.444; Double trumpet concerto in C, RV.537.*
(B) *** CfP CFP/*TC-CFP* 40353. Soloists, Toulouse CO, Auriacombe.

A lively clutch of very agreeable concertos (those for mandolin being piquant in timbre rather than memorable in invention), and they are vividly played and very well recorded. The balance is rather forward, but this has produced an excellent cassette transfer: the disc has only fractionally more range at the top. Several of these works are available in at least one other collection, but this anthology makes a satisfying whole, diverse in colour and substance. A bargain.

Bassoon concerto in A min. RV.498; Flute concerto in C min. RV.441; Oboe concerto in F, RV.456; Concerto for 2 oboes, bassoon, 2 horns and violin, RV.369.
*** Argo ZRG/*KZRC* 839. Gatt, Bennett, Black, Nicklin, Timothy Brown, Robin Davis, ASMF, Marriner.

This issue will give enormous pleasure. The playing is splendidly alive and characterful, with crisp, clean articulation and well-pointed phrasing, free from over-emphasis. The work for oboes and horns is agreeably robust; the *A minor Bassoon concerto* has a delightful sense of humour, while the flute and the oboe concertos, if not showing Vivaldi at his most inventive, are still very compelling and worthwhile. The recording is a model of clarity and definition and has striking richness and atmosphere too. This is one of the very finest Vivaldi collections on disc or tape.

(i; ii) *Cello concerto in E min., RV.484;* (iii) *Sopranino recorder concerto in C, RV.443;* (iv) *Concerto in D min. for viola d'amore and lute, RV.540;* (v; ii) *Double violin concerto in A* (*Echo*), *RV.552.*
(M) *** DG Priv. 2535/*3335* 200. (i) Fournier; (ii) Lucerne Fest. Strings, Baumgartner; (iii) Linde, Emil Seiler CO, Hofmann; (iv) Frasca-Columbier, Yepes (guitar), Kuentz CO, Kuentz; (v) Prystawski, Höver.

The *Cello concerto* is an arrangement by Vincent d'Indy and Paul Bazelaire of a sonata for solo cello, and a very good concerto it makes, played here by Fournier with *élan* and obvious enjoyment. The *Double concerto in D minor* also makes an alteration to Vivaldi's original, very effectively substituting a guitar for the lute. It is an excellent performance, as is that of the *Echo concerto*, which has both subtlety and delicacy of phrasing. Hans-Martin Linde is in excellent form, and his playing is perkily vivacious. With good recording throughout, this collection is very enjoyable. There is an excellent cassette transfer.

Double cello concerto in G min., RV.531; Double flute concerto in C, RV.533; Concertos for strings in D min. (Madrigalesco), RV.129; in G (Alla rustica), RV.151; Double trumpet concerto in C, RV.537; Concerto for 2 violins and 2 cellos in D, RV.564.
*** O-L DSLO/*KDSLC* 544. AcAM, Hogwood.

Not everything in this issue is of equal substance: the invention in the *Double trumpet concerto*, for example, is not particularly strong, but for the most part it is a rewarding and varied programme. It is especially appealing in that authenticity is allied to musical spontaneity. The best-known concertos are the *Madrigalesco* and the *Alla rustica*, but some of the others are just as captivating. The *Concerto for two flutes* has great charm and is dispatched with vigour and aplomb. The recording is first-class throughout, and readers with an interest in this often unexpectedly rewarding composer, whose unpredictability continues to astonish, should not hesitate. Performances and recording alike are first-rate; but on tape the sound is coarsened by too high a transfer level.

(i; ii) *Flute concerto in G min. (La Notte), RV.439;* (i; iii; iv) *Concerto in F for flute, oboe and bassoon (La Tempesta di mare), RV.570;* (vi; v) *Double horn concertos in F, RV.538 and RV.539;* (iv; vi) *Concerto in C for 2 oboes and 2 clarinets, RV.559;* (i; vii) *Sopranino recorder concerto in C, RV.443.*
(M) *** DG Arc. Priv. 2547/*3347* 060. (i) Linde; (ii) Zürich Coll. Mus., Sacher; (iii) Schmalfuss, Klepac; (iv) Munich CO, Stadlmair; (v) Neudecker, Spach; (vi) Winschermann, Schmalfuss, Michaels, Schöneberger; (vii) Emil Seiler CO, Hofman.

An attractive anthology. The combination of characterful solo playing and vividly forward recording gives the music-making an essentially robust communication. Hans-Martin Linde is memorably agile in the *Sopranino recorder concerto* (played on an authentic instrument) and the works for mixed wind are nicely balanced. Altogether an entertaining and generous concert. The high-level cassette matches the disc closely although on side two the *Double horn concerto*, RV.539, loses some of its focus because of the resonance.

(i) *Guitar concerto in D, RV.93;* (ii; iii) *Flute concerto in G min. (La Notte), RV.439;* (ii; iv) *Recorder concerto in C, RV.443;* (v) *Double trumpet concerto in C, RV.537;* (vi) *Double violin concerto in A (Echo), RV.552.*
(M) ** DG Priv. 2535/*3335* 630. (i) Behrend, I Musici; (ii) Linde; (iii) Zürich Coll. Mus., Sacher; (iv) Seiler CO, Hofman; (v) Scherbaum, Haubold, Hamburg Bar. Ens.; (vi) Soloists, Lucerne Fest. Strings, Baumgartner.

Entitled *Gala concert in Venice*, this collection gathers together five contrasted concertos from diverse sources. The *Echo concerto* is particularly well managed, and Hans-Martin Linde proves a sprightly soloist in the works for flute and recorder. The sound is variable but always good, and the tape transfer is satisfactory, although the focus slips a little in the *Concerto for two trumpets*.

Double horn concerto in F, RV.539; Double oboe concerto in D min., RV.535; Concerto in F for 2 oboes, bassoon, 2 horns and violin, RV.574; Piccolo concerto in C, RV.443.
*** Argo ZRG/*KZRC* 840. Soloists, ASMF, Marriner.

The musical substance may not be very weighty, but Vivaldi was rarely more engaging than when, as here, he was writing for wind instruments, particularly if he had more than one in his team of soloists. This delectable record makes a splendid supplement to the earlier one in the series from the Academy (ZRG/*KZRC* 839 – see above). Beautifully balanced and vivid recording, and a generally excellent equivalent cassette.

Mandolin concerto in C, RV.425; Double mandolin concerto in G, RV.532; Orchestral concerto (con molti stromenti) in C for 2 flutes, 2 salmo, 2 violins (in tromba marina), 2 mandolins, 2 theorbos, cello and strings, RV.558; Concerto in D min. for viola d'amore and lute, RV.540; Concerto for 2 violins and guitar, RV.93.

**(*) DG 2530 211/*3300 207* [id.]. Soloists, Kuentz CO, Kuentz.

An intimate programme, for late-evening listening, with a mellow recording to match. The *Mandolin concertos* are beautifully recorded, the miniature sound of the solo mandolins truthfully captured, the duet concerto having a gentle charm. RV.540 and RV.93 were intended for the lute rather than the guitar, but Yepes is persuasive here, particularly in the slow movements. The concertante work, RV.558, rounds off the programme effectively. A pleasant rather than a distinctive concert. There is a good if not outstanding tape transfer, not as fresh and open as some DG cassettes.

Double mandolin concertos: in G, RV.532; in C, RV.425; Concerto for 2 mandolins, 2 theorbos, 2 flutes, 2 salmo, 2 violins (in tromba marina), and cello, in D, RV.558; Concerto in B flat in due cori (con violino discordato).

*** Erato STU/*MCE* 70545 [id.]. Bianchi, Pitrelli, and soloists, Sol. Ven., Scimone.

Vivaldi's invention in the two *Double mandolin concertos* is fairly conventional, but the music is spirited and there is compensation in the diverse effects of timbre, so that both make agreeable listening. What gives this collection special appeal is the fine performance of the *Concerto 'con molti stromenti'*, RV.558, which offers a fascinating variety of textures including salmo (early clarinets), and using mandolins balaleika-style in the *Andante*. The recording is admirably detailed and the first movement has the vitality and colour found in Bach's *Brandenburgs*. The *Concerto in due cori* also shows Vivaldi at his most imaginative. It makes another attractive contrast and offers music of considerable character. The playing is excellent throughout and the recording besides clarifying textures also provides a suitable ambience. The high-level cassette is also lively and full.

CHAMBER MUSIC

(i) *6 Cello sonatas, Op. 14;* (ii) *Il Pastor fido (6 Sonatas for recorder, harpsichord and cello);* (iii) *6 Violin sonatas (for violin and continuo), Op. 5.*

(M) *** Ph. 6768 750 (8). (i) Gendron, Sibinga, Lang; (ii) Veilham, Verlet, Lamy; (iii) Accardo, Gazeau, Canino, Saram.

Mellifluous playing from Salvatore Accardo in the Op. 5 *Sonatas* of 1716–17, four being solo sonatas with continuo, and the remainder being trio sonatas. The music is not, however, as interesting or inventive as the *Cello sonatas*, which Maurice Gendron recorded in the late 1960s (the only recordings here that have been released before). *Il Pastor fido* is given a straightforward and intelligent reading without recourse to the variety of instruments used by Hans-Martin Linde and Eduard Melkus on Archive (now deleted). This is a useful and valuable set, well worth the modest outlay.

Concerto in C for oboe, violin and organ, RV.554; Concertos for violin and organ: in D min., RV.541; in F, RV.542; in C, RV.766; in F, RV.767.

** Erato STU/*MCE* 71060. Alain, Toso, Bonelli, Sol. Ven., Scimone.

Vivaldi was ever experimenting with textures for his concertos and the combinations here involve balance problems for the engineers which have been solved by placing all the soloists in an artificial forward balance. The *Concertos for violin and organ*, RV.541 and RV.766–7, are the most spontaneously inventive works; RV.554 is busy, with much polyphonic interweaving, but is less interesting as music. The performances are assured and lively and the recording vivid on disc and tape alike.

12 Sonatas for 2 violins and continuo, Op. 1; 12 Violin sonatas, Op. 2 (complete).
(M) *** Ph. 6768 007 (5). Accardo, Gulli, Canino, Saram.

These sonatas are not otherwise obtainable, and in any case it is unlikely that Accardo's performances, so ably supported by Bruno Canino and Rohan de Saram (and in Op. 1 by Franco Gulli), could be surpassed in terms of fluency, musicianship and sheer beauty of tone. The shadow of Corelli still hangs over the earlier set, but much of the invention is fresh, and collectors will find unexpected rewards in both sets.

Sonatas for lute and harpsichord: in C; in G min. (arr. from *Trio sonatas*).
(M) **(*) RCA Gold GL/*GK* 14139. Bream, Malcolm – BACH: Trio sonatas.**(*)

These works were originally Trio sonatas for lute, violin and continuo, but as the violin part doubles much of what the lute has to contribute it can be omitted without problems arising. The music is pleasingly lightweight and makes attractive contrasting material for the Bach works which form the coupling. The performances are fresh and imaginative and the sound equally crisp and clear on disc or cassette, although the balance is perhaps a shade too forward.

VOCAL MUSIC

Choral music: *Beatus vir* (2 settings, *RV.597–8); Credidi propter quod, RV.605; Credo* (2 settings, *RV.591–2); Dixit Dominus* (2 settings, *RV.594–5*), with *Introductions, RV.635–6; Domine ad adiuvandum me, RV.593; Gloria* (2 settings, *RV.588–9*), with *Introductions; RV.639 and 642; In exitu Israel, RV.604; Kyrie, RV.587; Laetatus sum, RV.607; Laudate Dominum, RV.606; Lauda Jerusalem, RV.609; Laudate pueri, RV.602; Magnificat* (2 settings, *RV.610–11*); *Sacrum, RV.586.*
(M) *** Ph. 6768 149 (7). Marshall, Lott, Burgess, Murray, Daniel, Collins, Finnilä, Finnie, Rolfe Johnson, Holl, Thomaschke, John Alldis Ch., ECO, Negri.

This is a splendid collection which, over a very wide range of works, presents lively, stylish performances, beautifully recorded. Any lover of Vivaldi is likely to be astonished that not only the well-known works but the total rarities show him writing with the keenest originality and intensity, for there is no question of routine inspiration as there can be in Vivaldi concertos. The seven discs are also available in three separate boxes (see below).

Beatus vir; Canta in prato (motet)*; Dixit Dominus; Domine ad adiuvandum me; Gloria in D; In furore* (motet)*; Introduction to Dixit Dominus; Juditha triumphans* (oratorio)*; Kyrie; Lauda Jerusalem; Magnificat in G min.; Nulla in mundo pax; O qui coeli* (motets)*; Salve Regina in C min.; Te Deum.*
(M) ** Ph. 6768 016 (8). Various soloists, choruses and orchestras, Negri.

This volume from the Vivaldi Edition devotes three of the eight records to the massive oratorio *Juditha triumphans*, and also Negri's earlier Berlin versions of the *D major Gloria*, the *C minor Salve Regina*, a spurious *Te Deum* and the double-choir version of the *Magnificat*, recorded with inferior sound in 1965. The rest duplicates the seven-record box of Vivaldi choral works (see above), which makes a far better investment if the oratorio is not a first essential. Negri is a stylish and sympathetic interpreter of Vivaldi (having obviously learnt from his 1965 Berlin recordings); he draws lively performances from his excellent English team.

Beatus vir, RV.598; Credo, RV.592; Dixit Dominus, RV.595, with *Introduction, RV.635; Gloria, RV.588,* with *Introduction, RV.639; Laudate pueri, RV.602; Magnificat* (2 settings, *RV.610–11*).
(M) *** Ph. 6769 046 (3) [id.]. (from 6768 149, cond. Negri).

Taken from Negri's seven-disc box of choral works (see above), this three-disc selection offers superb performances of an admirable group of rare works; mostly these are less well-known versions of texts that Vivaldi set more than once, as for example the *Dixit Dominus* and *Gloria*. In the piece described as an *Intro-*

duction to the *Gloria,* Linda Finnie sings with spectacular virtuosity; the other soloists too are splendid, and the choir captures the dark Bach-like intensity of many passages contrasted with more typical Vivaldian brilliance. First-rate recording.

Beatus vir, RV.597; Motets: *Lauda Jerusalem* (for 2 sopranos and double choir); *Nulla in mundo pax sincera* (for soprano).
**(*) Erato STU/*MCE* 71003. Smith, Stampfli, Huttenlocher, Lausanne Vocal Ens. and CO, Corbóz.

The *Beatus vir* is a stirring piece, not otherwise available except as part of Negri's Philips box, and the *Lauda Jerusalem* likewise forms part of this compilation. Only in *Nulla in mundo pax sincera* is there competition, and that from Emma Kirkby and the Academy of Ancient Music. In this performance modern instruments are used and produce a warm, well-focused sound. The acoustic is spacious but not cavernous and the performances are vital and musical. Readers would be as well off with the Negri – and, in the long term, this will doubtless prove the more satisfying investment. However, those who want to collect this repertoire separately will find these performances very acceptable even if at times they fall short of the highest distinction. The cassette is generally successful, full and quite clear.

Dixit Dominus, RV.594; Stabat Mater, RV.621.
** Erato STU/*MCE* 71018. Saque, Silva, Ihara, Serafim, Lopes, Lisbon Gulbenkian Foundation Ch. and O, Corbóz.

The *Dixit Dominus* is not otherwise available except as part of the Philips Vivaldi Edition where it is conducted by Vittorio Negri. The Lisbon performance is pleasingly old-fashioned with robust tone and modern instruments, but it is performed in a cavernous acoustic (that of Sao Vicente da Fora Church in Lisbon), and though a warmth and space are desirable, some readers may find this too much of a good thing. The *Stabat Mater*, thought to have been composed at great speed, is the more affecting piece. In spite of the woolly acoustic, the solo singers and instrumentalists are fairly well focused, though Naoko Ihara has a bigger vibrato than we like. Although the focus of the *Dixit Dominus* is not absolutely clean at the opening of the tape transfer, the sound is generally satisfactory, lively and well balanced.

Gloria in D, RV.588; Gloria in D, RV.589.
*** Argo Dig. **410 018-2**; ZRDL/*KZRDC* 1006. Russell, Kwella, Wilkens, Bowen, St John's College, Camb., Ch., Wren O, Guest.

The two settings of the *Gloria* make an apt and illuminating coupling. Both in D major, they have many points in common, presenting fascinating comparisons, when RV.588 is as inspired as its better-known companion. Guest directs strong and well-paced readings, with RV.588 the more lively. Good, warm recording to match the performances. There is a vividly detailed chrome cassette, but the upper choral focus is not quite as clean as the disc, and a treble cut is useful to smooth the sound. On compact disc the added clarity is never clinical in sharpening detail, and the overall ambient atmosphere is most appealing.

(i) *Gloria in D, RV.588;* (ii) *Nisi Dominus in G min., RV.608.*
*** Erato STU/*MCE* 71200. E. Bach Fest. Ch. and Bar. O, Corbóz, with (i) Jennifer Smith, Bernadin, Barham, (ii) Watts.

Vivaldi's less well-known version of the *Gloria* (shorn of the three-movement *Introduction* on a non-liturgical text) makes an attractive coupling for the *Nisi Dominus*, which is sung beautifully here by Helen Watts, arguably more apt for this music than a male alto. In the *Gloria* Corbóz may encourage his soloists to a little too much operatic expressiveness, but with fine recording and baroque orchestral playing on authentic instruments this can be recommended to those who fancy the coupling.

Gloria in D, RV.589.
(*) Argo ZRG/*KZRC* 505 [id.]. Vaughan, Baker, King's College Ch., ASMF, Willcocks – PERGOLESI: *Magnificat.*(*)

Gloria in D, RV.589; Kyrie, RV.587 and Credo, RV.591.
*** Erato STU/*MCE* 70910 [RCA AGL1 1340]. Jennifer Smith, Staempfli, Rossier, Schaer, Lausanne Vocal and Instrumental Ens., Corbóz.

Gloria in D, RV.589; Magnificat, RV.611.
** HMV ASD/*TC-ASD* 3418 [Ang. S 37415]. Berganza, Valentini-Terrani, New Philh. Ch. and O, Muti.

(i) *Gloria in D, RV.589;* (ii) *Nulla in mundo pax.*
*** O-L DSLO/*KDSLC* 554 [id.]. Christ Church Cath. Ch., Ac AM, Preston with (i) Nelson, Watkinson, (ii) Kirkby.

Magnificat, RV.610.
(*) Argo ZRG/*KZRC* 854 [id. LP only]. King's College Ch., ASMF, Marriner – BACH: *Magnificat.*(*)

The freshness and point of the Christ Church performance of the *Gloria* are irresistible; anyone who normally doubts the attractiveness of authentic string technique should sample this, for the absence of vibrato adds a tang exactly in keeping with the performance. The soloists too keep vibrato to the minimum, adding to the freshness, yet Carolyn Watkinson rivals even Dame Janet Baker in the dark intensity of the Bach-like central aria for contralto, *Domine Deus, Agnus Dei*. The choristers of Christ Church Cathedral excel themselves, and the recording is of demonstration quality, on cassette as on disc. The solo motet provided for fill-up has Emma Kirkby as soloist coping splendidly with the bravura writing for soprano.

Michel Corbóz, a fine choral conductor, gives a lively performance of the *Gloria*, and his version is aptly coupled with two other richly rewarding liturgical settings by Vivaldi. The *Kyrie* is magnificent, with its four soloists, double chorus and double string orchestra. This is very welcome as the first in a whole series of Vivaldi's choral music. The professional singers of the Lausanne choir are generally admirable, and the soloists are sweet-toned. Good, clear recording.

The Willcocks version uses comparatively small forces, and save for the occasional trace of preciosity it is very stylish indeed. It has an excellent team of soloists and is very well recorded. Some might feel the exaggerated consonants are tiresome, but this is unquestionably a most acceptable performance. There is a very good cassette. The slight blurring of the focus by the King's acoustic is not serious and the solo voices have a natural presence. The orchestral introduction is arresting in its vividness.

Although the HMV Muti record and the Argo King's coupling with Bach both list Vivaldi's *Magnificat*, these are two quite different versions of the same basic work. Muti offers the more expansive score, including extended solo arias. The Argo recording shares some material, such as the opening chorus, but here the music is on a much smaller scale. Ledger opts for boys' voices in the solos, such as the beautiful duet, *Esurientes*, and though the singers are taxed by ornamentation, the result has all the accustomed beauty of this choir's recordings, set warmly against the chapel's acoustic. This makes a fascinating and attractive coupling for the grander Bach setting of the *Magnificat*. The transfer to tape has been quite well managed but this is not one of Argo's finest cassette issues; the choral sounds are not always completely clear in focus.

Muti's approach, both in the *Magnificat* and in the *Gloria*, is altogether blander than the Argo performances. His expansiveness suits the larger-scaled *Magnificat* better than the *Gloria*, which here lacks the incisiveness and freshness of the Argo performance. The HMV cassette is not recommended; the sound is congested at peaks.

(i) *Nisi Dominus* (*Psalm 126*), *RV.608; Stabat Mater, RV.621; Concerto for strings in G min., RV.153.*
** O-L DSLO/*KDSLC* 506 [id.]. Ac AM, Hogwood; (i) with Bowman.

These performances are vital enough and there is no want of stylistic awareness. James Bowman is a persuasive soloist, though since Vivaldi probably wrote these for the Pietà, a Venetian orphanage for girls, readers might prefer to turn to Helen Watts in the *Nisi Dominus*. Probably the best thing about this disc is the concerto, an engaging work whose charms benefit from the authentic instruments. The recording is cut at a higher level than usual and does not always reproduce with maximum smoothness. The cassette, however, is of excellent quality, smooth, yet clear.

OPERA

Opera overtures: *Armida al campo d'Egitto; Arsilda regina di Ponto; Bajazet; Dorilla in Tempe; Farnace; Giustino; Griselda; L'Incoronazione di Dario; L'Olimpiade; Ottone in Villa; La Verita in cimento.*
*** Erato STU/*MCE* 71215 [id.]. Sol. Ven., Scimone.

Vivaldi's 'opera overtures' were conceived as mere sinfonias, scarcely related to the character of each work. These eleven make a lively and surprisingly varied collection, splendidly played and recorded. But it may be as well not to play them all in sequence.

L'Olimpiade (complete).
*(*) Hung. SLPX 110901/3. Kováts, Takács, Zempléni, Miller, Gáti, Horváth, Káplán, Budapest Madrigal Ens., Hungarian State O, Szekeres.

It is delightful to find, in the first Act of this long-neglected opera, a choral adaptation of an idea we know very well indeed from *The Four Seasons*. It is good too to find that Vivaldi, though very much bound by the conventions of his time – not least in the complications of the plot about royal love affairs in ancient Crete – had real freshness in his arias at least. The pity is that this Hungarian performance, recorded in clean-cut stereo, with sharp divisions between left and right, is rhythmically so heavy that any sprightliness of idea is undermined. The recitative – relatively little for the modern listener to swallow – is taken heavily too, with the singers adopting a nineteenth-century style. Quality of voice varies markedly, allowing only a limited recommendation.

Orlando furioso (complete).
*** Erato STU 71138 (3). Horne, Los Angeles, Valentini-Terrani, Gonzales, Kozma, Bruscantini, Zaccaria, Sol. Ven., Scimone.

Though the greater part of this opera consists of recitative – with only fifteen arias included on the three discs, plus one for Orlando borrowed from a chamber cantata – it presents a fascinating insight into this totally neglected area of Vivaldi's work. Scimone has heavily rearranged the order of items as well as cutting many but, with stylish playing and excellent recording, it is a set well worth a Vivaldi enthusiast's attention. Outstanding in a surprisingly star-studded cast is Marilyn Horne in the title role, rich and firm of tone, articulating superbly in divisions, notably in the hero's two fiery arias. In the role of Angelica, Victoria de los Angeles has many sweetly lyrical moments, and though Lucia Valentini-Terrani is less strong as Alcina, she gives an aptly clean, precise performance.

Tito Manlio (complete).
**(*) Ph. [6769 004 (5)]. Luccardi, Wagemann, Hamari, Finnilä, Marshall, Trimarchi, Lerer, Ahnsjö, Berlin R. Ch., Berlin CO, Negri.

Vivaldi claimed that he wrote this massive score in a mere five days, which sounds improbable even for him. The inspiration of the set numbers, most of them short, simple arias, is generally lively, and they are attractively spiced with obbligato solos. The very overture sets the classical scene well, with its *pomposo* trumpet-ful style, and the main snag for the modern listener is the sheer length, which achieves Wagnerian proportions. Unlike the other Vivaldi opera issued in tercentenary year, *Orlando furioso*, this one is given uncut except for some snipping of secco recitatives, which still make up a very substantial proportion of the whole. The performance is crisp and stylish, sympathetically directed by Negri and with generally excellent solo singing, though with women taking three male parts it is hard to follow the story, as the timbres are not as distinct as they might be. The recording quality has an attractive bloom on it, so that with patience the set can give pleasure. This set has been withdrawn in the UK, but it remains available in the USA.

Voříšek, Jan (1791–1825)

Symphony in D.

** Ph. Seq. 6527/*7311* 129 [id.]. ECO, Mackerras – DVOŘÁK: *Czech suite.***

Voříšek is the nearest the Czechs got to producing a Beethoven, and this remarkably powerful work has fingerprints of the great German composer everywhere, yet manages to retain its own individuality. The slow movement is especially fine, and after an attractive scherzo, the finale has something in common with that of Beethoven's *Fourth Symphony*. But the music is nothing like a carbon copy, and one feels that temperamentally Voříšek had much in common with Beethoven, to be able to write so convincingly in such a similar idiom. There used to be a splendid performance of the work on Supraphon by the Prague Chamber Orchestra, and the newer version by Mackerras is rather lightweight by comparison. It is a neat, small-scale performance, with characteristically lively tempi, and Philips provide good, clean sound. The cassette transfer is first-class; the resonance offers no problems.

Wagner, Richard (1813–83)

Faust overture.

(**) Ph. Dig. 6769/*7654* 089 [id.]. Concg. O, Dorati – LISZT: *Faust symphony**; BERLIOZ: *Damnation of Faust.*(**)

Dorati's account of Wagner's *Faust overture* is perfectly acceptable, but it is unlikely to gain wide currency as it is harnessed to an indifferent performance of Liszt's *Faust symphony*. Edo de Waart's San Francisco recording – see below – coupled with Wagner's early *Symphony* is a much more obvious recommendation.

Overtures: Die Feen; Der fliegende Holländer; Tannhäuser (with *Bacchanale*).

** Ph. Dig. **400 089-2**; 9500 746/*7300 831* [id.]. Concg. O, De Waart.

The special interest here is the rarely heard (and rarely recorded) *Die Feen overture*, written when Wagner was twenty for his first completed opera. It is agreeable music, cast in the same melodic mould as *Rienzi*, if less rumbustious in feeling. All the performances here are warmly spacious, lacking something in electricity (the *Flying Dutchman* – which uses the original ending – sounds too cultured). The digital recording faithfully reflects the acoustic of the Concertgebouw, with its richly textured strings and brass, and resonant lower range; but some listeners might feel a need for a more telling upper range.

Siegfried idyll.

*** DG 2707 102/*3370 023* (2) [id.]. Berlin PO, Karajan – BRUCKNER – *Symphony No. 7.****

(M) *** DG Sig. 2543/*3343* 510 (as above, Karajan) – SCHOENBERG: *Verklaerte Nacht.****

*** Ph. 6769 028/*7699 113* (2) [id.]. Concg. O, Haitink – BRUCKNER: *Symphony No. 7.****

*** Decca Dig. **410 111-2**; 410 111-1/*4* [id.]. ECO, Ashkenazy – SCHOENBERG: *Verklaerte Nacht.****

*** Erato STU/*MCE* 71333. Lausanne CO, Jordan – R. STRAUSS: *Metamorphosen* etc.**(*)

Karajan's account is unsurpassed and is available in two different couplings. Though many will choose Bruckner, the mid-priced Signature issue offers also a superb account of Schoenberg's *Verklaerte Nacht*. The string section of the Berlin Philharmonic produces rich and radiant tone in both works and the recording has fine body and detail on both LP and tape (in both couplings).

Haitink gives a simple, unaffected reading and draws playing of great refinement from the Concertgebouw Orchestra. There is very little to choose between his account and Karajan's with the same coupling: both have a simplicity of expression and a tenderness that will leave few listeners unmoved. The Philips cassette transfer is made at quite a high level and the quality is first-class, with clear detail and plenty of bloom on the sound.

The honeyed warmth of Wagner's domestic inspiration, its flow of melodies and textures that caress the ear, are superbly brought out by Ashkenazy. Warm, full recording to match the playing, especially on compact disc. The chrome-cassette transfer too is one of Decca's best, matching the LP closely.

Armin Jordan's version with the Lausanne Chamber Orchestra is very persuasive, opening and closing tenderly but with a passionately volatile climax. The central horn solo is rather thick in articulation, but otherwise the playing is beyond serious criticism, and the recording is rich and atmospheric. The Erato coupling is quite different and may suit some collectors better than the Bruckner or the Schoenberg. The Erato cassette is transferred at a high level and the sound is well focused and full.

Siegfried idyll; (i) *Adagio for clarinet and strings.*
(*) Argo ZRG 604 [id. PSI]. ASMF, Marriner, (i) with Brymer – R. STRAUSS: *Metamorphosen.**

A good performance of the *Siegfried idyll* in the chamber form that comes close to the one Cosima would have heard. It will not appeal to everyone, particularly in the passages for single strings. The middle section will also strike some listeners as a bit on the fast side. Of course, there are sensitive touches, and the engineers produce a good sound picture. The *Adagio for clarinet and strings* (see also below) is a useful fill-up and incidentally an excellent piece for a quiz.

Siegfried idyll; Lohengrin: Prelude to Act I; Die Meistersinger: Prelude to Act I; Tristan und Isolde: Prelude and Liebestod.
(M) *** DG Priv. 2535/*3335* 212 [id.]. Berlin PO, Kubelik.

There is some marvellous playing here from the Berlin Philharmonic, and the recording is spacious and realistically balanced. Kubelik's readings are expansive and relaxed rather than gripping, but the *Siegfried idyll*, if a little cool at the opening, is beautifully shaped and, like the *Tristan* and *Meistersinger Preludes*, is built to a satisfying climax. The cassette transfer is very successful. If the level is on the low side, a slight cutback of treble is possible to minimize the hiss.

Symphony in C.
(M) **(*) DG 2543 817 [id.]. Berlin PO, Gerdes – PFITZNER: *Symphony.***(*)

Symphony in C; Faust overture.
*** Ph. Dig. 6514/*7337* 380 [id.]. San Francisco SO, De Waart.

Wagner's *Symphony in C* was written when he was still in his teens, and though the thrust of ambition, the sense of challenge, is clear enough, there are few fingerprints that one could positively identify as Wagnerian. Nonetheless with its echoes of Weber and Mendelssohn it makes an attractive piece, well worth hearing. Gerdes' version is direct and well recorded, and interestingly coupled.

De Waart's version of Wagner's teenage symphony gives this often clumsy but always confident and memorable exercise in symphonism a spaciously paced, beautifully sprung reading with melodies presented in Schubertian glow. The *Faust overture*, equally well played, makes an apt if unoriginal coupling. Excellent recording. The chrome tape is slightly bass-orientated, but is clear as well as full-bodied.

ORCHESTRAL COLLECTIONS

Der fliegende Holländer: overture; Götterdämmerung: Siegfried's Rhine journey; Siegfried's funeral music; Lohengrin: Preludes to Acts 1 and 3; Die Meistersinger: Prelude to Act 1; Dance of the apprentices and Entry of the masters; Parsifal: Prelude to Act 1; Das Rheingold: Entry of the Gods into Valhalla; Rienzi: over-

ture; Siegfried: Forest murmurs; Tannhäuser: overture; Prelude to Act 3; Tristan: Prelude and Liebestod; Die Walküre: Ride of the Valkyries.
(M) **(*) HMV SLS 5075 (3). Philh. O, Klemperer.

In the LP age bleeding chunks of Wagner would seem less appropriate, although the already large (and growing) collection of purely orchestral excerpts suggests an equally wide public for this kind of record. Certainly Klemperer's readings, solidly concentrated, are characterful enough to stand presentation in a box like this. The six sides present a fascinating comment on the composer.

Overtures: Der fliegende Holländer; Rienzi; Tannhäuser (original version). *Lohengrin: Prelude to Act I.*
(M) **(*) HMV SXLP/*TC-SXLP* 30436 [Ang. (d) RL/*4RL* 32039]. Philh. O, Klemperer.

It is good to have Klemperer's view of Wagner. Most of the performances here and on the two companion issues have the kind of incandescent glow found only in the interpretations of really great conductors, and the Philharmonia plays immaculately. But judged by the highest standards Klemperer falls just a degree short. The recordings have been remastered and successfully freshened, but they originally date from 1960. The cassette transfer – made at a high level – is lively, but at times the ear senses a slight constriction in the bass, which is not as clean as the upper range.

Der fliegende Holländer: overture; Lohengrin: Prelude to Act III: Die Meistersinger: Prelude to Act I; Parsifal: Preludes to Acts I and III.
*** HMV ASD 3160 [Ang. S/*4XS* 37098]. Berlin PO, Karajan.

Fine performances of course, given richly ample EMI sound. There is urgency and edge in *The Flying Dutchman*, and the string-playing in the *Parsifal preludes* is nobly shaped; yet the last degree of tension is missing. *Die Meistersinger* is weighty, yet lacks the expansive glow of the very finest recorded accounts. Nevertheless a considerable achievement.

Overtures: Der fliegende Holländer; Die Meistersinger; Tannhäuser (original version). *Tristan und Isolde: Prelude and Liebestod.*
*** Decca **411 951-2**; SXL/*KSXC* 6856 [Lon. 7078/*5*-]. Chicago SO, Solti.

An attractive collection of Wagner overtures superbly played and brightly recorded. Except for the *Flying Dutchman overture*, these are newly made recordings, not taken from Solti's complete opera sets. So this is the self-contained *Tannhäuser overture* from the Dresden version, and the *Liebestod* comes in the purely orchestral version. Perhaps surprisingly, comparison between Solti in Chicago and Solti in Vienna shows him warmer in America. The compact disc has been digitally remastered.

Der fliegende Holländer: Overture; Die Meistersinger: Prelude, Act I; Tristan und Isolde: Preludes, Acts I and III; Liebestod. (i) *La descente de la Courtille* (chorus).
*** DG Dig. 2532/*3302* 086 [id.]. O de Paris, Barenboim; (i) with Ch.

Barenboim's is a warm and sympathetic collection of overtures and preludes plus the instrumental version of Isolde's *Liebestod.* The oddity – which gives the sparkle of surprise to the record – is *La descente de la Courtille*, written by Wagner in Paris for a vaudeville by a wealthy patron. The jolly processional piece, complete with chorus, sounds more like Offenbach than Wagner with dashes of Weber thrown in. Barenboim made the recording (full but not ideally spacious) soon after he had conducted the first ever recorded performance. The high-level tape transfer matches the LP closely.

Overtures: Der fliegende Holländer; Rienzi; Tannhäuser (with *Bacchanale*).
(M) (*) Decca VIV/*KVIC* 30. VPO, Solti.

The Vienna Philharmonic are driven very hard by Solti, and the result sounds unnecessarily frenetic. The sound balance does not help; it is very fierce, with fizzy strings. Indeed the climax of the *Tannhäuser overture* verges on distortion.

(i–ii) *Der fliegende Holländer: overture;* (ii–iii) *Rienzi: overture;* (iv–v) *Tannhäuser: overture and Venusberg music;* (iv; vi) *Die Walküre: Ride of the Valkyries.*

(M) *(*) Decca SPA 468. (i) New Philh. O, (ii) Paita; (iii) Neth. R. PO; (iv) LSO; (v) Leinsdorf; (vi) Stokowski.

This collection is notable for Leinsdorf's performance of the *Tannhäuser overture and Venusberg music* which is vivid enough, and Carlos Paita's excellent version of the *Rienzi overture*. The other two items are less impressive, and the recording of the *Flying Dutchman overture* has one or two rough moments.

Götterdämmerung: Dawn and Siegfried's Rhine journey; Funeral march. Lohengrin: Preludes to Acts I and III. Die Meistersinger: Overture; Dance of the apprentices. Die Walküre: Ride of the Valkyries.

(B) *** CfP Dig. CFP/*TC-CFP* 41 4412-1/*4*. LPO, Rickenbacher.

Karl Anton Rickenbacher, formerly principal conductor with the BBC Scottish Symphony Orchestra, here makes an impressive recording début. He secures first-class playing from the LPO with the strings at their peak in the radiant opening of the *Lohengrin Prelude* and the brilliantly articulated scalic passage at the opening of the *Dance of the apprentices*. This is chosen – rather ineffectively – to end the concert, but this is the only real criticism of a first-rate bargain collection. Rickenbacher's tempi are far from stoically Teutonic and he presses the music on convincingly, yet retains a sense of breadth. Some might feel his pacing of the *Die Meistersinger overture* is fractionally fast, but the lightweight impression is partly due to the digital recording balance which is wide-ranging and clear, but lacks something in opulence in the lower middle and bass. This is not untruthful. Many concertgoers will be familiar with hall acoustics that have the same effect. The cassette matches the disc very closely, losing only a little of the transient bite (noticeable on the cymbals), although the transfer level is necessarily modest.

Götterdämmerung: Siegfried's Rhine journey. Parsifal: Prelude to Act I. Das Rheingold: Entry of the gods into Valhalla. Siegfried: Forest murmurs. Tannhäuser: Prelude to Act III. Die Walküre: Ride of the Valkyries.

(M) **(*) HMV SXLP/*TC-SXLP* 30528 [Ang. (d) RL/*4RL* 32058]. Philh. O, Klemperer.

The *Tannhäuser* and *Parsifal* excerpts are outstanding – characteristically spacious and superbly played. *The Ride of the Valkyries*, without the concert coda, ends rather abruptly; and in the other items the level of tension is somewhat variable. The recording has transferred well to cassette: side two (with *Parsifal* and *Tannhäuser*) sounds exceptionally full and vivid.

Götterdämmerung: Dawn and Siegfried's Rhine journey; Siegfried's death and funeral march. Das Rheingold: Entry of the gods into Valhalla. Siegfried: Forest murmurs. Die Walküre: Ride of the Valkyries; Wotan's farewell and Magic fire music.

*** HMV Dig. **CDC 747007-2**; ASD/*TCC-ASD* 3985 [Ang. DS/*4XS* 37808]. Berlin PO, Tennstedt.

(M) **(*) Decca VIV/*KVIC* 48 [Lon. CS/*5*-6970]. Nat. SO of Washington, Dorati.

(M) *(**) Decca SPA/*KCSP* 537 [Lon. STS/*5*- 15565] (without *Wotan's farewell and Magic fire music*). LSO, Stokowski.

(M) ** CBS 60102/*40*- [MY/*MYT* 36715]. Cleveland O, Szell.

The first digital orchestral collection from *The Ring* is recorded with demonstrable brilliance. With steely metallic cymbal clashes in the *Ride of the Valkyries* and a splendid drum thwack at the opening of the *Entry of the gods into Valhalla*, the sense of spectacle is in no doubt. There is weight too: the climax of *Siegfried's funeral march* has massive penetration. There is also fine detail, especially in the atmospheric *Forest murmurs*. The playing itself is of the finest quality throughout and Tennstedt maintains a high level of tension.

But the brass recording is rather dry and at times the ear feels some lack of amplitude and resonance in the bass. However, the grip of the playing is extremely well projected, and the degree of fierceness at the top is tameable. The chrome tape lacks some of the glittering bite of the disc (the cymbal transients less telling), but the balance overall is richer without much loss of detail. Many will prefer the quality here, and certainly this is demonstration-worthy in quite a different way. The *Magic fire music* at the end of side two is especially impressive in its cassette presentation. The compact disc seems to emphasize the dryness in the bass, and while detail is clear there is a lack of richness and bloom.

Dorati's selection from *The Ring* is essentially dramatic. The *Ride of the Valkyries* comes off especially well, as do the three excerpts from *Götterdämmerung* (with a superbly played horn solo in *Siegfried's Rhine journey*). But in the final scene from *Die Walküre* the lack of richness and body of the string tone that this orchestra can produce limits the effect of Dorati's eloquence; and it is the brass and wind playing one remembers most in the *Das Rheingold* and *Siegfried* excerpts. Nevertheless, with brilliant Decca sound there is much that is exciting in this collection, and the programme is well balanced. The cassette transfer is of high quality, impressively full-bodied and brilliant.

Stokowski's record was first issued in 1966 and was not one of Decca's more successful Phase Four recordings. In *The Stereo Record Guide* we complained at the time of superficial brilliance and no real compensating weight in the bass. On this reissue the sound is slightly smoother but hardly refined, and in some ways the balance of the cassette is preferable, often richer, with more body to the strings, although there are moments of coarseness. However, the performances are what count and this is vintage Stokowski; he is at his most electrifying in *Siegfried's funeral march*. This issue is primarily for Stokowskians, and they will not be disappointed.

From Szell brilliantly played performances, and there are certainly some spectacular moments. But the recording has achieved its brilliance at the expense of weight at the bass end, which needs boosting. The music-making sounds much better on tape than on disc, for the transfer is one of CBS's best, with the upper range slightly smoothed, yet with no loss of vividness.

Götterdämmerung: Siegfried's funeral music; Final scene. Das Rheingold: Entry of the Gods into Valhalla. Siegfried: Forest murmurs. Die Walküre: Ride of the Valkyries; Wotan's farewell and Magic fire music.

* Decca Dig. **410 137-2**; SXDL/*KSXDC* 7612. VPO, Solti.

There is nothing at all distinguished about Solti's 1983 compact disc of *Ring* excerpts – issued to coincide with the opening of his *Ring* at Bayreuth. The effect is of an unmusically balanced hi-fi spectacular. Brilliance and high dynamic contrasts, with every strand made artificially clear, emphasize unattractively aggressive performances, notably the first item, the *Ride of the Valkyries*, with none of the bloom and flair which marked John Culshaw's classic *Ring* production of over twenty years earlier. The performances – with vocal parts at times transcribed for instruments – are bold and strong, but show little warmth of any kind. The chrome cassette matches the LP in its range, but the crystal-clear CD is least attractive of all in demonstrating that crude brilliance is not enough in these scores.

Die Meistersinger: overture.

(M) ** Decca VIV/*KVIC* 37 [Lon. STS/5-15589]. VPO, Mehta – LISZT: *Les Préludes; Mazeppa* **(*); TCHAIKOVSKY: *Marche slave.* **

Mehta's performance is well played and quite acceptable, but the recording lacks expansive qualities, although it is vivid enough, with disc and cassette sounding very much the same.

Götterdämmerung: Siegfried's funeral march. Siegfried: Forest murmurs. Tristan und Isolde: Prelude to Act I. Die Walküre: Ride of the Valkyries.

**(*) Sheffield Lab. LAB 7 [id.]. LAPO, Leinsdorf.

This direct-cut disc combining four

unedited performances has enjoyed a considerable vogue since it was first issued in 1977. Certainly the sound is admirably balanced and cleanly defined, yet it is without the exaggerated sharpness of outline which affects some digital issues. The performances have plenty of life and impetus (there is none of the inhibition one might have expected when there is no chance of correcting mistakes), and Leinsdorf achieves considerable passion at the climax of the *Tristan Prelude*. However, the body of tone produced by the Los Angeles strings does not match that of the Berlin Philharmonic in similar collections, and while the brass has both brilliance and sonority in *Siegfried's funeral music*, even here there are several instances where other recordings have greater weight and amplitude.

Lohengrin: Preludes to Acts I and III. Die Meistersinger: Overture. Rienzi: Overture. Tannhäuser: Overture.
*** HMV Dig. ASD/*TC-ASD* 143578-1/*4* [Ang. DS/*4XS* 37990] Berlin PO, Tennstedt.

Klaus Tennstedt here shows something of the Klemperer tradition with these essentially broad and spacious readings, yet the voltage is consistently high. The opening and closing sections of the *Tannhäuser overture* are given a restrained nobility of feeling (and there is absolutely no hint of vulgarity) without any loss of power and impact. Similarly the gorgeous string melody at the opening of *Rienzi* is elegiacally moulded, and later when the brass enter in the allegro there is no suggestion of the bandstand. In the Act I *Lohengrin Prelude*, Tennstedt lingers in the pianissimo sections, creating radiant detail, then presses on just before the climax, a quite different approach from Furtwängler's but no less telling. The Berlin Philharmonic are on top form throughout and the digital recording is both refined and brilliant, if without a glowing resonance in the middle and bass frequencies. The XDR cassette is generally faithful, though inner detail is less sharp.

Lohengrin: Prelude to Act III. Die Meistersinger: Overture; Dance of the apprentices; Entry of the masters. Tristan und Isolde: Prelude and Liebestod. Götterdämmerung: Siegfried's funeral march.
(M) **(*) HMV SXLP/*TC-SXLP* 30525 [Ang. (d) RL/*4RL* 32057]. Philh. O, Klemperer.

After a zestful account of the *Prelude to Act III* of *Lohengrin*, the rest of the programme is given characteristically measured tempi. The plodding Mastersingers seem a bit too full of German pudding, and the *Tristan Prelude and Liebestod* does not have the sense of wonder that Toscanini brought, though the feeling of ennobled passion at its climax cannot fail to communicate. Throughout there is never any doubt that one is in the presence of a great conductor. The orchestral playing too is first-class, and though the recording lacks something in sumptuousness at the climax of *Siegfried's funeral march*, this remains well worth considering at medium price. The cassette transfer is strikingly vivid and full-bodied, quite the equal of the disc.

Parsifal: Prelude and Good Friday music.
(M) **(*) DG Priv. 2726 054 (2). Bav. RSO, Jochum – BRUCKNER: *Symphony No. 7*.***

Splendid playing and first-class recording, which although it comes from the early days of stereo does not show its age. There is the most beautiful string and brass tone here. Perhaps the last degree of mystery is missing from the *Prelude*, but the *Good Friday music* has a moving serenity, especially in the closing pages. A good coupling for a highly recommendable Bruckner *Seventh*.

Das Rheingold: Entry of the gods into Valhalla; Tannhäuser: Overture and Venusberg music; Tristan und Isolde: Prelude to Act III; Die Walküre: Ride of the Valkyries.
(B) *** RCA VICS/*VK* 2015 [AGL 1 1336]. Symphony of the Air and Ch. with female soloists, Stokowski.

This record makes a fascinating bargain, a truly Stokowskian Wagner record, with the singers totally subservient to the conductor's lusciously rich orchestral conception. That is the only possible description of the string-playing both in the *Tristan Prelude* and in the *Rheingold* extract. This kind of approach – dedicated to sensuous beauty of sound alone – misses the inner quality of the music, and the closing pages of the *Venusberg music*, wonderfully rich, are dedicated to aural sentience. But with exciting performances of both the *Tannhäuser overture* (with vivid detail in the middle section) and the *Ride of the Valkyries*, this is highly recommendable, even if the recording itself is not always a model of refinement. The chrome cassette is very successful, every bit the equal of the disc.

CHAMBER MUSIC

Adagio for clarinet and strings.

(M) *** Decca Ace SDD 249 [Lon. STS 15408]. A. Boskovsky, members of V. Octet – BRAHMS: *Clarinet quintet.***(*)

(M) **(*) Argo ZK/*KZKC* 62. Brymer, Allegri Qt – BRAHMS: *Clarinet quintet.***(*)

There seems no doubt now that this piece, long thought to be by Wagner, is by Heinrich Baermann, a clarinet virtuoso of the early part of the nineteenth century. In any event it undoubtedly has charm and, as in the Boskovsky version, it serves as a useful fill-up for the Brahms. Brymer and his colleagues give an eloquent and polished account, though the Boskovsky remains the preferred version.

VOCAL MUSIC

'Wagner on record 1926–42': Wesendonk Lieder. Excerpts from *Der fliegende Holländer; Lohengrin; Die Meistersinger; Parsifal; Rienzi; The Ring; Tannhäuser; Tristan und Isolde.*

(***) HMV mono RLS 7711 (7). Melchior, Schorr, Leider, Bettendorf, Rethberg, Lehmann, Lemnitz, Ralf, Roswaenge, Janssen, Muller, Austral, Widdop, etc.

Between 1926 and 1932 with the arrival of electrical recording there was a Wagner explosion, magnificently celebrated here with fifty-six out of a total of sixty-four items. The brightness, firmness and immediacy of the singing, so vividly conveyed, will amaze the modern listener, for musical values are paramount. When today it is almost taken for granted that a Wagner baritone will growl or wobble on indeterminate notes, and Heldentenoren will strain in agony at times, the clarity of pitching, the absence of wobble or even intrusive vibrato are a joy. Lauritz Melchior is the great hero, matched by the superb bass-baritone of Friedrich Schorr, but comparable openness and sweetness of sound come from the Yorkshireman, Walter Widdop, and in the Lieder-like singing of Herbert Janssen and Gerhard Husch, both as Wolfram in *Tannhäuser*. The transfers from 78 r.p.m. are superlative.

Wesendonk Lieder.

*** HMV ASD 3260 [Ang. RL/*4RL* 32017]. Baker, LPO, Boult – BRAHMS: *Alto rhapsody****; R. STRAUSS: *Lieder.***(*)

(M) **(*) HMV SXLP/*TC-SXLP* 30556. Norman, Gage – POULENC: *Songs***(*); SCHUBERT: *Songs.****

Janet Baker gives a radiant performance of the *Wesendonk Lieder*. From the very first phrase the concentration and imagination are firmly established, and the expansive view of *Stehe still* makes that song far deeper than usual, with no hint of sentimentality. The range of tone colour is ravishing, and Sir Adrian draws comparably beautiful sounds from the LPO. Glowing recording quality.

Jessye Norman's early 1970 recording of the *Wesendonk Lieder* (with piano) may not have the depth of her later orchestral recording for Philips (see below), but there is an appealing freshness and natural intensity, matched by faithful observance of markings, as well as the natural beauty of the voice, well caught on a recording still fresh.

Wesendonk Lieder. Arias: *Der fliegende Holländer: Jo ho hoe!; Traft ihr das Schiff; Senta's ballad. Tannhäuser: Dich, teure Halle; Allmächt'ge Jungfrau. Tristan und Isolde: Mild und leise.*

** Hung. SLPX 11940 [id.]. Sass, Hungarian State Op. Ch. and O, Korodi.

Though the accompaniments are indifferently played and recorded, Sylvia Sass with her characterful singing makes ample amends, whether in the operatic excerpts – with each heroine sharply distinguished – or in the *Wesendonk Lieder*, where the foretastes of *Tristan* come out well. As ever the vocal line is disturbed by the occasional ugliness of tone, but the command of Sass as a Wagnerian is never in doubt.

(i) *Wesendonk Lieder*. (ii) *Götterdämmerung: Prologue: Zu neuen Taten; Heil! Heil!* Act III: *Starke Scheite schichtet. Die Walküre,* Act II: *Prelude; Nun zaume dein Ross; Hojotoho!*

(M) ** Ph. 6570/*7310* 931. Nilsson (i) LSO, Sir Colin Davis; (ii) with Windgassen, Adam, Greindl, Bay. Fest. O, Boehm.

The excerpts from the 1967 Bayreuth recordings of the *Ring* find Nilsson at her most commanding, superbly matched by Windgassen in the *Götterdämmerung* duet. The *Wesendonk Lieder* recording of five years later brings surprisingly flawed and unstylish singing. Fair recording, with a low-level cassette lacking upper range.

(i) *Wesendonk Lieder*. Arias: *Lohengrin: Einsam in trüben Tagen* (*Elsa's dream*). *Parsifal: Ich sah' das Kind. Die Walküre,* Act I: *Der Männer Sippe; Du bist der Lenz;* (ii) Act II: *Siegmund! Sieh auf mich!*

(M) *** Decca GRV 11. Flagstad, VPO, (i) Knappertsbusch, (ii) Solti (with Svanholm).

Kirsten Flagstad's glorious voice is perfectly suited to the rich inspiration of the *Wesendonk Lieder*. *Im Treibhaus* is particularly beautiful. Sieglinde's solo too is magnificent, but the scale of the voice makes *Elsa's dream* seem a little unwieldy; and, fine as it is vocally, Kundry's *Herzeleide* sounds rather staid for a seductress. However, to redress the balance, for this *'Grandi voci'* reissue Decca have included also Brünnhilde's aria from Solti's 1958 partial recording of Act II of *Die Walküre*, an outstanding reminder of one of the finest Brünnhildes of our time. The other items date from 1956, and the vintage Decca recording still sounds fresh.

Wesendonk Lieder. Tristan und Isolde: Prelude and Liebestod.

**(*) Ph. 9500 031 [id.]. Norman, LSO, Sir Colin Davis.

The poised phrases of the *Wesendonk Lieder* draw from Jessye Norman a glorious range of tone colour, though in detailed imagination she falls short of some of the finest rivals on record. The coupling is most apt, since two of the *Wesendonk* songs were written as studies for *Tristan*. Though the role of Isolde would no doubt strain a still-developing voice, and this is not the most searching of *Liebestods*, it is still the vocal contribution which crowns this conventional linking of first and last in the opera. Good, refined recording.

OPERA

Der fliegende Holländer (*The Flying Dutchman*).

*** Decca D 24 D 3/*K 24 K 32* (3/*2*) [Lon. OSA/*5*- 13119]. Bailey, Martin, Talvela, Kollo, Krenn, Isola Jones, Chicago SO Ch. and O, Solti.

Solti's first Wagner opera recording in Chicago marks a distinct change from the long series made in Vienna. The playing is superb, the singing cast is generally impressive and the recording is vividly immediate to the point of aggressiveness. What will disappoint some who admire Solti's earlier Wagner sets is that this most atmospheric of the Wagner operas is presented with no Culshaw-style production whatever, merely as a concert performance. Characters halloo to one another when evidently standing elbow to elbow, and even the Dutchman's ghostly chorus sounds very close and earthbound. But with Norman Bailey a deeply impressive Dutchman, Janis Martin generally a sweet-toned Senta, Martti Talvela a splendid Daland, and Kollo, for all his occasional coarseness, an illuminating Erik, it surpasses all current competition. The cassette transfer offers vibrantly vivid sound.

Götterdämmerung (complete).

❀ *** Decca **414 115-2**; 414 115-1/*4* (5/*4*). Nilsson, Windgassen, Fischer-Dieskau, Frick,

Neidlinger, Watson, Ludwig, V. State Op. Ch., VPO, Solti.

(M) *** DG 2740 148 (6) [2716 001]/*3378 048* [id.] (coupled with *'Das Rheingold'*). Dernesch, Janowitz, Brilioth, Stewart, Kelemen, Ludwig, Ridderbusch, German Op. Ch., Berlin PO, Karajan.

*** Eurodisc **610081**; 301/*501* 817 (6). Kollo, Altmeyer, Salminen, Wenkel, Nocker, Nimsgern, Sharp, Popp, Leipzig R. Ch., Berlin R. Ch., Dresden State Op. Ch., Dresden State O, Janowski.

In Decca's formidable task of recording the whole *Ring cycle* under Solti, *Götterdämmerung* provided the most daunting challenge of all; but characteristically Solti, and with him the Vienna Philharmonic and the Decca recording team under John Culshaw, were inspired to heights even beyond earlier achievements. Even the trifling objections raised on earlier issues have been eliminated here. The balance between voices and orchestra has by some magic been made perfect, with voices clear but orchestra still rich and near-sounding. Above all Solti seems to have matured into a warmer and wiser director. He drives hard still, but no longer is there any feeling of over-driving, and even the *Funeral march*, which in his early Covent Garden performances was brutal in its power, is made into a natural not a forced climax. There is not a single weak link in the cast. Nilsson surpasses herself in the magnificence of her singing: even Flagstad in her prime would not have been more masterful as Brünnhilde. As in *Siegfried*, Windgassen is in superb voice; Frick is a vivid Hagen, and Fischer-Dieskau achieves the near-impossible in making Gunther an interesting and even sympathetic character. As for the recording quality, it surpasses even Decca's earlier achievement. No more magnificent set has appeared in the whole history of the gramophone, and Decca have surpassed themselves in the excellence of the tape transfer. The recording has been digitally remastered for this reissue. The rosette marks the overall achievement of Solti's *Ring*.

Karajan's DG set of *Götterdämmerung* has been reissued at medium price (though the older listing persists in the USA, according to Schwann).

Karajan like Solti before him reserved for the concluding *Ring* opera his finest achievement. His singing cast is marginally even finer than Solti's, and his performance conveys the steady flow of recording sessions prepared in relation to live performances. But ultimately he falls short of Solti's achievement in the orgasmic quality of the music, the quality which finds an emotional culmination in such moments as the end of Brünnhilde's and Siegfried's love scene, the climax of the *Funeral march* and the culmination of the *Immolation*. At each of these points Karajan is a degree less committed, beautifully as the players respond, and warm as his overall approach is. Dernesch's Brünnhilde is warmer than Nilsson's, with a glorious range of tone. Brilioth as Siegfried is fresh and young-sounding, while the Gutrune of Gundula Janowitz is far preferable to that of Clair Watson on Decca. The matching is otherwise very even. The balance of voices in the recording may for some dictate a choice: DG brings the singers closer, gives less brilliance to the orchestral texture. On tape the Karajan *Götterdämmerung* is issued in a 'chunky' box together with *Das Rheingold* at what is virtually bargain price. The transfers are of good quality but made at a generally lower level than the Decca Solti recordings, which are fuller and more vivid in sound.

With sharply focused digital sound, Janowski's studio recording hits refreshingly hard, at least as much so as in the earlier *Ring* operas. Speeds rarely linger, but with some excellent casting – consistent with the earlier operas – the result is rarely lightweight. Jeannine Altmeyer as Brünnhilde rises to the challenges not so much in strength as in feeling and intensity, ecstatic in Act I, bitter in Act II, dedicated in the Immolation scene. Kollo is a fine heroic Siegfried, only occasionally raw-toned, and Salminen is a magnificent Hagen, with Nimsgern again an incisive Alberich on his brief appearances. Despite an indifferent Günther and Gutrune and a wobbly if characterful Waltraute, the impression is of clean vocalization matched by finely disciplined and dedicated playing, all recorded in faithful studio sound with no sonic tricks. The chrome cassettes too are very impressive, although some will count it a disadvantage that the layout follows the discs. However, the wide range of the recording and its excellent detail are admirably captured. The brightly lit sound gives a brilliant sheen to the strings and an exciting edge to the brass, and if the voices at times are slightly hard – the opening scene with the three Norns shows this – there is no lack of bloom, and with such overall clarity and presence this projects splendidly. On the five CDs the background silence adds to the dramatic presence and overall clarity.

The Twilight of the Gods (*Götterdämmerung;* complete, in English).
*** HMV SLS/*TC-SLS* 5118 (6). Hunter, Remedios, Welsby, Haugland, Hammond-Stroud, Curphey, Pring, E. Nat. Op. Ch. and O, Goodall.

Goodall's account of the culminating opera in Wagner's tetralogy may not be the most powerful ever recorded, and certainly it is not the most polished, but it is one which, paradoxically, by intensifying human as opposed to superhuman emotions heightens the epic scale. The very opening may sound a little tentative (like the rest of the Goodall English *Ring*, this was recorded live at the London Coliseum), but it takes no more than a few seconds to register the body and richness of the sound. The few slight imprecisions and the occasional rawness of wind tone actually seem to enhance the earthiness of Goodall's view, with more of the primeval saga about it than the magnificent polished studio-made *Ring* cycles. Both Rita Hunter and Alberto Remedios were more considerately recorded on the earlier Unicorn version of the final scenes, with more bloom on their voices, but their performances here are magnificent in every way. In particular the golden beauty of Remedios's tenor is consistently superb, with no Heldentenor barking at all, while Aage Haugland's Hagen is giant-sounding to focus the evil, with Gunther and Gutrune mere pawns. The voices on stage are in a different, drier acoustic from that for the orchestra, but considering the problems the sound is impressive. As for Goodall, with his consistently expansive tempi he carries total concentration – except, curiously, in the scene with the Rhinemaidens, whose music (as in Goodall's *Rhinegold* too) lumbers along heavily. The cassette transfer is generally very successful and is notable for the warmth and bloom given to voices and orchestra alike.

Götterdämmerung: scenes (sung in German): *Dawn; Brünnhilde and Siegfried's entrance; Siegfried's Rhine journey; Siegfried's funeral march; Brünnhilde's immolation.*
(B) *** CfP CFP/*TC-CFP* 4403. Hunter, Remedios, LPO, Mackerras.

This CfP disc of highlights was made in 1972, six years before the classic complete set in English by the same artists. Vocally what stands out from Hunter's performance is the pinging precision of even the most formidable exposed notes. Here she revealed herself as a natural competitor in the international league, and her simple, fresh manner in the most intense moment of the *Immolation*, the hushed farewell of *Ruhe, du Gott*, is most affectingly caught. Remedios is also in splendid form, and Mackerras draws dedicated and dramatic playing from the LPO. An outstanding bargain, with disc and tape very closely matched; the LP has marginally more transient edge.

Lohengrin (complete).
(M) *** HMV SLS/*TC-SLS* 5071 (5) [Ang. SCL 3641]. Jess Thomas, Grümmer, Fischer-Dieskau, Ludwig, Frick, V. State Op. Ch., VPO, Kempe.
**(*) HMV SLS/*TC-SLS* 5237 (5/*3*) [Ang. SELX/*4X5X* 3829]. Kollo, Tomowa-Sintow, Nimsgern, Vejzovic, Ridderbusch, German Op., Berlin, Ch., Berlin PO, Karajan.
**(*) CBS 79503 (5) [M5 38594]. Hofmann, Armstrong, Connell, Roar, Vogel, Bay. Fest. Ch. and O (1982), Nelsson.
(M) **(*) Ph. 6747 241 (4) [id.]. Jess Thomas, Silja, Vinay, Varnay, Crass, Krause, Bay. Fest. (1962) Ch. and O, Swallisch.

Kempe's is a rapt account of *Lohengrin* which has never been surpassed on record, one of his finest monuments in sound. After all Kempe looked at Wagner very much from the spiritual side, giving *Lohengrin* perspectives deeper than is common. The link with early Wagner is less obvious than usual, and instead one sees the opera as the natural pair with *Parsifal*, linked no doubt in Wagner's mind too, since in mythology Parsifal was the father of Lohengrin. The intensity of Kempe's conducting lies even in its very restraint, and throughout this glowing performance one senses a gentle but sure control, with the strings of the Vienna Philharmonic playing radiantly. The singers too seem uplifted, Jess Thomas singing more clearly and richly than usual, Elisabeth Grümmer unrivalled as Elsa in her delicacy and sweetness, Gottlob Frick gloriously resonant as the king. But it is the partnership of Christa Ludwig and Fischer-Dieskau as Ortrud and Telramund that sets the seal on this superb performance, giving the darkest intensity to their machinations in Act II, their evil heightening the beauty and serenity of so much in this opera. In this reissue the recording, though not always as cleanly focused as it might be, has come up well. The cassettes do not match the discs in refinement.

Karajan, whose DG recording of *Parsifal* was so naturally intense, failed in this earlier but related opera to capture comparable spiritual depth. So some of the big melodies sound a degree over-inflected; and the result though warm and expressive and dramatically powerful, with wide-ranging recording, misses an important dimension. Nor is much of the singing as pure-toned as it might be, with René Kollo too often straining and Tomowa-Sintow not always able to scale down in the necessary purity her big dramatic voice. Even so, with strong and beautiful playing from the Berlin Philharmonic, it remains a powerful performance, disappointing only in relation to the finest of earlier versions. The tape layout – on three chrome cassettes, with one to each Act – is ideal and the wide dynamic range of the recording is retained with impressive clarity and range.

The CBS set, like several previous versions, was recorded live at Bayreuth. The sound is warm and generally well balanced, with bloom on the voices but with the perspective slightly distanced, which takes some of the impact from Woldemar Nelsson's sensitive but slightly undercharacterized reading. The *Prelude to Act III*, for example, is made to sound refined rather than immediately exciting. The choral sound, however, is splendid and the raptness of ritual is well conveyed. Peter Hofmann in the name part suffers at times from a slow vibrato, but the timbre is pleasing and he rises well to the challenge of *In fernem Land* in the last Act. Karen Armstrong similarly suffers from a slow vibrato and the voice is strained at the top, but the sweetness of the character still comes over. Leif Roar is a reliable Telramund, but the most outstanding singing comes from Elizabeth Connell as a formidable Ortrude, sinister and tough, yet beautiful too, with a remarkable range of expression.

For those who find Kempe's view too contemplative, and Karajan's emotionally inflated, the Sawallisch version, recorded live at Bayreuth in 1962, provides a worthwhile alternative, the more vital in its propulsive thrust over Wagner's expansive paragraphs through the presence of an audience. For that dramatic tension one naturally has to pay in stage noises, occasional slips and odd balances, but the recording captures the unique flavour of the Festspielhaus splendidly. What above all will dictate a listener's response is his reaction to the voices of Anja Silja as Elsa and Astrid Varnay. Though Silja has been far less steady on record in other sets, this is often not a pretty sound, and Varnay was firmer in her earlier Bayreuth recording for Decca in mono. Jess Thomas is here not so reliable as he is on the Kempe set, but Sawallisch's direction is superb, fresh and direct, never intrusive.

Die Meistersinger von Nürnberg (complete).

*** DG 2740 149/*3378 068* (5) [2713 011/*id.*]. Fischer-Dieskau, Ligendza, Lagger, Hermann, Domingo, Laubenthal, Ludwig, Ch. and O of German Op., Berlin, Jochum.

**(*) Decca D 13 D 5/*K 13 K 54* (5/*4*) [Lon. OSA/*5*- 1512]. Bailey, Bode, Moll, Weikl, Kollo, Dallapozza, Hamari, Gumpoldskirchner Spatzen, V. State Op. Ch., VPO, Solti.

**(*) HMV SLS 957 (5) [Ang. SEL 3776]. Adam, Donath, Ridderbusch, Evans, Kelemen, Kollo, Schreier, Hesse, Leipzig R. Ch., Dresden State Op. Ch. and O, Karajan.

(M) **(*) Ph. 6747 167 (5). Ridderbusch, Bode, Sotin, Hirte, Cox, Stricker, Reynolds, Bay. Fest. (1974) Ch. and O, Varviso.

(M) (***) HMV mono RLS/*TC-RLS* 7708 (5/*4*). Edelmann, Schwarzkopf, Kunz, Unger, Dalberg, Berg, Pflanzl, Bay. Fest. (1951) Ch. and O, Karajan.

Jochum's is a performance which more than any captures the light and shade of Wagner's most warmly approachable score, its humour and tenderness as well as its strength. The recording was made at the same time as live opera-house performances in Berlin, and the sense of a comedy being enacted is irresistible. With Jochum the processions at the start of the final Festwiese have sparkling high spirits, not just German solemnity, while the poetry of the score is radiantly brought out, whether in the incandescence of the Act III prelude (positively Brucknerian in hushed concentration) or the youthful magic of the love music for Walther and Eva. Above all Jochum is unerring in building long Wagnerian climaxes and resolving them – more so than his recorded rivals. The cast is the most consistent yet assembled on record. Though Caterina Ligendza's big soprano is a little ungainly for Eva, it is an appealing performance, and the choice of Domingo for Walther is inspired. The key to the set is of course the searching and highly individual Sachs of Fischer-Dieskau, a performance long awaited. Obviously controversial (you can never imagine this sharp Sachs sucking on his boring old pipe), Fischer-Dieskau with detailed word-pointing and sharply focused tone gives new illumination in every scene. The Masters – with not one woolly-toned member – make a superb team, and Horst Laubenthal's finely tuned David matches this Sachs in applying Lieder style. The recording balance favours the voices, which is a pity, but is otherwise wide-ranging and refined. The tape transfer is made at a relatively low level and while the sound is warmly musical it does not match Solti's Decca set in immediacy and range at either end of the spectrum. But there are no real hiss problems and the balance is good. The layout follows the discs.

The great glory of Solti's long-awaited set is not the searing brilliance of the conductor but rather the mature and involving portrayal of Sachs by Norman Bailey. For his superb singing the set is well worth investigating, and there is much else to enjoy, not least the bright and detailed sound which the Decca engineers have, as so often in the past, obtained with the Vienna Philharmonic, recording Wagner in the Sofiensaal. Kurt Moll as Pogner, Bernd Weikl as Beckmesser (really singing the part) and Julia Hamari as Magdalene (refreshingly young-sounding) are all excellent, but the shortcomings are comparably serious. Both Hannelore Bode and René Kollo fall short of their far-from-perfect contributions to earlier sets, and Solti for all his energy gives a surprisingly square reading of this most appealing of Wagner scores, exaggerating the four-square rhythms with even stressing, pointing his expressive lines too heavily and failing to convey real spontaneity. It remains an impressive achievement, and those who must at all costs hear Bailey's marvellous Sachs should not be deterred. The cassette transfer produces electrically vivid sound. There are moments when the brilliance verges on fierceness, and the focus can occasionally slip, but generally the quality combines bloom with excellent detail. The layout on four cassettes is preferable to the discs.

HMV, in setting up their star-studded version, fell down badly in the choice of Sachs. Theo Adam, promising in many ways, has quite the wrong voice for the part, in one way too young-sounding, in another too grating, not focused enough. After that keen disappointment there is much to enjoy, for in a modestly reverberant acoustic (a smallish church was used) Karajan draws from the Dresden players and chorus a rich performance which retains a degree of bourgeois intimacy. Anyone wanting an expansive sound may be disappointed, but Karajan's thoughtful approach and sure command of phrasing are most enjoyable. Donath is a touching, sweet-toned Eva, Kollo here is as true and ringing a Walther as one could find today, Geraint Evans an incomparably vivid Beckmesser, and Ridderbusch a glorious-toned Pogner who really should have been singing Sachs.

Meistersinger is an opera which presents serious problems for an engineer intent on recording it in a live performance. Not only do the big crowd scenes with their plentiful movement bring obtrusive stage noises; the sheer length of the work means that by Act III even the most stalwart singer is flagging. It follows that the Bayreuth performance, recorded during the Festival of 1974, is flawed, but the Swiss conductor, Silvio Varviso, still proves the most persuasive Wagnerian, one who inspires the authentic ebb and flow of tension, who builds up Wagner's scenes concentratedly over the longest span, and who revels in the lyricism and textural beauty of the score. It is not a lightweight reading, as some may have expected from this conductor, and with one exception the singing is very enjoyable indeed, with Karl Ridderbusch a firmly resonant Sachs (rare thing on record) and the other Masters, headed by Klaus Hirte as Beckmesser and Hans Sotin as Pogner, really singing their parts. Jean Cox is a strenuous Walther, understandably falling short towards the end, but Hannelore Bode as Eva brings the one serious disappointment. Yet she is firmer here than on Solti's set, and for all its variability the atmospheric recording gives enjoyment.

Karajan's first recording of this opera, made live at Bayreuth in limited but clear and surprisingly acceptable mono sound, stands as a masterly interpretation, in many ways never surpassed. Edelmann's singing as Sachs is satisfyingly firm and finely phrased, and Unger as David and Kunz as Beckmesser are superb too. Hans Hopf never otherwise matched this performance on record, hardly at all coarse, but it is the Eva of Schwarzkopf which reigns gloriously here, never more affectingly than in her Act III address to Sachs, achingly heartfelt. Karajan appeared at Bayreuth only one more year, Schwarzkopf never again. This historic document is also a deeply moving one. The cassettes are well laid out on four tapes. The orchestral sound in the *Overture* is a bit rough (it is much better in the Act III *Prelude*) but when the voices enter the focus improves and there is good clarity, even if the acoustic effect is dry.

Parsifal (complete).

C ❀ *** DG Dig. **412 347-2**; 2741/*3382* 002 (5) [id.]. Hofmann, Vejzovic, Moll, Van Dam, Nimsgern, Von Halem, German Op. Ch., Berlin PO, Karajan.

*** Decca SET 550-4/*K 113 K 54* (5/4) [Lon. OSA/*5*- 1510]. Kollo, Ludwig, Fischer-Dieskau, Hotter, Kelemen, Frick, V. Boys' Ch., V. State Op. Ch., VPO, Solti.

(M) *** Ph. 6747 250 (5). Jess Thomas, Dallis, London, Talvela, Neidlinger, Hotter, Bay. Fest. (1963) Ch. and O, Knappertsbusch.

**(*) Erato Dig. NUM/*MCE* 750105 (5) [750105]. Goldberg, Minton, Schone, Tschammer, Lloyd, Haugland, Prague Philharmonic Ch., Monte Carlo PO, Jordan.

Communion, musical and spiritual, is what this intensely beautiful Karajan set provides, with pianissimos shaded in magical clarity, and the ritual of bells and offstage choruses heard as in ideal imagination. If, after the Solti recording for Decca, it seemed doubtful whether a studio recording could ever match earlier ones made on stage at Bayreuth in spiritual intensity, Karajan proves otherwise, his meditation the more intense because the digital sound allows total silences. The playing of the Berlin orchestra – preparing for performance at the Salzburg Easter Festival of 1980 – is consistently beautiful, but the clarity and refinement of sound prevent this from emerging as a lengthy serving of Karajan soup. He has rarely sounded so spontaneously involved in opera on record. Kurt Moll as Gurnemanz is the singer who more than any anchors the work vocally, projecting his voice with firmness and subtlety. José van Dam as Amfortas is also splendid: the *Lament* is one of the glories of the set, enormously wide in dynamic and expressive range. The Klingsor of Siegmund Nimsgern could be more sinister, but the singing is admirable. Dunja Vejzovic makes a vibrant, sensuous Kundry who rises superbly to the moment in Act II where she bemoans her laughter in the face of Christ. Only Peter Hofmann as Parsifal leaves any disappointment; at times he develops a gritty edge on the voice, but his natural tone is admirably suited to the part – no one can match him today – and he is never less than dramatically effective. He is not helped by the relative closeness of the solo voices, but otherwise the recording is near the atmospheric ideal, a superb achievement. The cassette transfer on chrome tapes is also of the very highest quality, losing little if anything in comparison with the discs. The four CDs, generously full and offering an improved layout, are among DG's finest so far, with the background silence adding enormously to the concentration of the performance.

It was natural that after Solti's other magnificent Wagner recordings for Decca he should want to go on to this last of the operas. In almost every way it is just as powerful an achievement as any of his previous Wagner recordings in Vienna, with the Decca engineers surpassing themselves in vividness of sound and the Vienna Philharmonic in radiant form. The singing cast could hardly be stronger, every one of them pointing words with fine, illuminating care for detail. The complex balances of sound, not least in the *Good Friday music*, are beautifully caught, and throughout Solti shows his sustained intensity in Wagner. There remains just one doubt, but that rather serious – the lack of the spiritual quality which makes Knappertsbusch's live version so involving. Maybe it is better after all not to record this opera in the studio. The tape transfer is basically of high quality, and the last two Acts produce most beautiful sound, spacious, clear and full. However, the opening *Prelude* suggests a fractionally too high transfer level; there is some slight lack of refinement. This returns in the choral music of Scene 2, and then disappears – the great choral climax at the end of the Act is resplendently expansive. The layout on tape is superior to the LP format in offering Act I spread over the first four sides, and Acts II and III each complete on two.

Knappertsbusch's expansive and dedicated reading is superbly caught in the Philips set, arguably the finest live recording ever made in the Festspielhaus at Bayreuth, with outstanding singing from Jess Thomas as Parsifal and Hans Hotter as Gurnemanz. Though Knappertsbusch chooses consistently slow tempi, there is no sense of excessive squareness or length, so intense is the concentration of the performance, its spiritual quality. This of all operas is one that seems to gain from being recorded live, and stage noises and coughs here are very few and far between.

Jordan's recording with Monte Carlo forces, clean and fresh but lacking in weight and spiritual depth, was used for the controversial *Parsifal* film. Its great merit is the singing of Reiner Goldberg in the name part. Though the voice is not always well-focused Robert Lloyd's Gurnemanz brings fine singing too, more youthful-sounding than usual. Aage Haugland's Klingsor has nothing sinister in it, but rather masculine nobility, and Yvonne Minton makes a fine, vehement Kundry. Recommendable – with full, natural and immediate sound – for those who liked the film.

Parsifal: scenes.
*** DG Dig. 2532/*3302* 033 [id.]. (From above set, cond. Karajan.)

A fair selection, including the *Prelude* and the *Good Friday music*, from a superlative set with Karajan at his most intense and spiritual, atmospherically recorded.

Das Rheingold (complete).
*** Decca **414 110-2**; 414 101-1/*4* (3/*2*). London, Flagstad, Svanholm, Neidlinger, VPO, Solti.
(M) *** DG 2740 145 (3) [2709 023]/*3378 048* [*id.*] (coupled with *'Götterdämmerung'*). Fischer-Dieskau, Veasey, Stolze, Kelemen, Berlin PO, Karajan.
(*) Eurodisc Dig. **610058; 301/*501* 137 (3). Adam, Nimsgern, Stryczek, Schreier, Bracht, Salminen, Vogel, Büchner, Minton, Popp, Priew, Schwarz, Dresden State O, Janowski.

The Decca set was the first recording ever issued commercially of the opening drama in the *Ring* cycle. Solti gives a magnificent reading of the score, crisp, dramatic and direct. He somehow brings a freshness to the music without ever over-driving or losing an underlying sympathy. Vocally the set is held together by the unforgettable singing of Neidlinger as Alberich. Too often the part – admittedly ungrateful on the voice – is spoken rather than sung, but Neidlinger vocalizes with wonderful precision and makes the character of the dwarf develop from the comic creature of the opening scene to the demented monster of the last. Flagstad specially learnt the part of Fricka for this recording, and her singing makes one regret that she never took the part on the stage. But regret is small when a singer of the greatness of Flagstad found the opportunity during so-called retirement to extend her reputation with performances such as this. Only the slightest trace of hardness in the upper register occasionally betrays her, and the golden power and richness of her singing are for the rest unimpaired – enhanced even, when the recorded quality is as true as this. As Wotan, George London is sometimes a little rough – a less brilliant recording might not betray him – but this is a dramatic portrayal of the young Wotan. Svanholm could be more characterful as Loge, but again it is a relief to hear the part really sung. Much has been written on the quality of the recording, and without any doubt it deserves the highest star rating. Decca went to special trouble to produce the recording as for a stage performance and to follow Wagner's intentions as closely as possible. They certainly succeeded. Even those who are sometimes troubled by the almost excessive sharpness of definition Decca provide in complex scores – the 'Festival Hall' effect – will find that here the clarity does not prevent Wagner's orchestral effects from coming over in their full bloom of richness. An outstanding achievement, and so is the cassette version. For this reissue Decca have digitally remastered the recording.

Karajan's account is more reflective than Solti's. The very measured pace of the *Prelude* indicates this at the start, and there is often an extra bloom on the Berlin Philharmonic playing. But Karajan's very reflectiveness has its less welcome side, for the tension rarely varies. One finds such incidents as Alberich's stealing of the gold or Donner's hammer-blow passing by without one's pulse quickening as it should. Unexpectedly, Karajan is not so subtle as Solti in shaping phrases and rhythms. There is also no doubt that the DG recording managers were not so painstaking as John Culshaw's Decca team, and that too makes the end-result less compellingly dramatic. But on the credit side the singing cast has hardly any flaw at all, and Fischer-Dieskau's Wotan is a brilliant, memorable creation, virile and expressive. Among the others Veasey is excellent, though obviously she cannot efface memories of Flagstad; Gerhard Stolze, with his flickering, almost *Sprechstimme* as Loge, gives an intensely vivid if, for some, controversial interpretation. The recording is excellent but does not outshine the Decca, and neither does the tape transfer, which is coupled to *Götterdämmerung*.

The Eurodisc set of *Das Rheingold*, part of a complete cycle, comes from East Germany, with Marek Janowski a direct, alert conductor of the Dresden State Orchestra. This performance is treated to a digital recording totally different from Boulez's. The studio sound has the voices close and vivid (on cassette there is an element of hardness on top until the treble is cut back a little), with the orchestra rather in the background. Some Wagnerians prefer that kind of balance, but the result here rather lacks the atmospheric qualities which make the Solti *Rheingold* still the most compelling in sound, thanks to the detailed production of the late John Culshaw. With Solti, Donner's hammer-blow is overwhelming; but the Eurodisc set comes up with only a very ordinary 'ping' on an anvil, and the grandeur of the moment is missing. Theo Adam as Wotan has his grittiness of tone exaggerated here, but otherwise it is a fine set, consistently well cast, including Peter Schreier, Matti Salminen, Yvonne Minton and Lucia Popp as well as East German singers of high calibre. The cassettes match the discs very closely, while the CDs sharpen the focus even further, with clarity rather than atmosphere the keynote.

The Rheingold (complete, in English).
**(*) HMV SLS/*TC-SLS* 5032 (4). Bailey, Hammond-Stroud, Pring, Belcourt, Attfield, Collins, McDonall, Lloyd, Grant, E. Nat. Op. O, Goodall.

It is a practical comment on Goodall's slow tempi in Wagner that unlike other versions the *Rhinegold* from the English National Opera Company's production spreads on to four records instead of three. For the first three sides the temperature is low, reflecting hardly at all the tensions of a live performance, even though this was taken from a series of Coliseum presentations. The recording too, admirably clean and refined, is less atmospheric than that of *Siegfried*, the first of the series to be recorded. Nonetheless the momentum of Wagner gradually builds up, so that by the final scenes both the overall teamwork and the individual contributions of such singers as Norman Bailey, Derek Hammond-Stroud and Clifford Grant come together impressively. Hammond-Stroud's vivid representation of Alberich culminates in a superb account of the curse. The spectacular orchestral effects are vividly caught by the engineers, even if balances (inevitably) are sometimes less than ideal. The transfer to tape is outstanding, even among the generally high standard of these EMI English *Ring* issues. The voices have a natural presence and the detail is remarkably clear; yet there is plenty of warmth and bloom on voices and orchestra alike. The big climaxes are admirably managed, except for the very closing bars, where there is a touch of congestion. The only drawback is that the tape issue follows the discs by placing the recording on eight sides; it would have fitted comfortably on four.

Der Ring der Nibelungen (*Das Rheingold; Die Walküre; Siegfried; Götterdämmerung;* complete).

*** Ph. Dig. 6769 074 (16) [id.]. From 1979/80 Bay. Fest. productions: McIntyre, Jung, Gwyneth Jones, Becht, Zednik, Salminen, Hubner, Altmeyer, Schwarz, Killibrew, Wenkel, Jerusalem, Egel, Hofmann, Mazura, Bay. Fest. Ch. and O, Boulez.

The Boulez set will attract many who saw his version on television. It proved the most successful opera telecast ever and attracted an astonishingly large audience, at least partly because the excellent sub-titles meant that every turn of the narrative could be followed with ease. One's involvement with the characters was almost greater than in the theatre, so strong was the pull of fine acting and singing. Boulez proved a grippingly passionate advocate of the music. His speeds are fast, putting the complete cycle on fewer discs than usual (sixteen instead of nineteen), with each of the last three operas better presented for having fewer side-breaks. The four separate boxes come in a lavish package which also includes a hardback book with over a hundred pictures of Patrice Chéreau's highly controversial production at Bayreuth. Gwyneth Jones, handsome as Brünnhilde on stage, lurches between thrilling, incisive accuracy and fearsome yowls. Opposite her as Siegfried, Manfred Jung is by Heldentenor standards commendably precise and clean, but at times he sounds puny, not helped by microphone balances. But none of these obvious drawbacks can hide the fact that the recording – digital in the first three operas, analogue in *Götterdämmerung* – gives a thrilling idea of what it feels like to witness *The Ring* at Bayreuth. Boulez's concentration falters hardly once. The fast speeds convey conviction, making one ever eager to hear more rather than to contemplate. The 1980 cast was better than average. Donald McIntyre as Wotan has rarely if ever sounded so well on record, while Peter Hofmann as Siegmund is more agreeable here than he has been on other Wagner records, such as the Karajan *Parsifal.*

Among rival sets, Furtwängler – what you can hear of him in two cycles recorded live in dull mono sound – finds a greater emotional range. Goodall's English *Ring* (see below) represents the opposite view to Boulez's on tempo. Karajan on DG is richer and smoother, while Solti on Decca blazes far more brilliantly and still remains a first choice, taking everything into account. Both he and Karajan are helped by being recorded in the studio, where Boulez's live performances are beset by all kinds of stage noises, and inevitably the singing is flawed.

The Ring (*The Rhinegold; The Valkyrie; Siegfried; The Twilight of the Gods;* complete, in English).

(M) *** HMV SLS/*TC-SLS* 5146 (20/*15*). Soloists, Ch. and O of E. Nat. Op., Goodall.

The recording of Goodall's *Ring* cycle during a series of live performances at the London Coliseum was an outstanding achievement. Goodall's direction, spacious yet compelling throughout, brings the music vividly to life; singing and playing maintain the highest standards; and the clarity and richness of the recording are equally remarkable, even if balances are sometimes less than ideal. This will prove a splendid investment for those who want to hear the *Ring* cycle in English. The sound on tape generally matches the discs closely.

'The "Golden" Ring': Das Rheingold: Entry of the gods into Valhalla; Die Walküre: Ride of the Valkyries; Siegfried: Forest murmurs; Götterdämmerung: Prelude; Siegfried's Rhine

journey; Rhinemaidens' song; Siegfried's funeral music. Siegfried idyll.
*** Decca SXL/*KSXC* 6421. Nilsson, Windgassen, VPO, Solti.

This collection of 'pops' from the *Ring*, plus the *Siegfried idyll* (once available on Deryck Cooke's *Ring* lecture disc, now deleted), makes a generous disc, highly recommendable to anyone just setting out on the path of Wagner-worship. Fine performances from the complete cycle, and brilliant recording, both on disc and on tape.

Der Ring: excerpts: *Das Rheingold:* Scene 4: *Zur Burg führt die Brücke; Die Walküre:* Act I: *Ein Schwert verhiess mir der Vater;* Act III: *Ride of the Valkyries; Loge, hör; Magic fire music; Siegfried:* Act I: *Nothung!; Götterdämmerung:* Act III: *Siegfried's death and funeral march.*
(M) **(*) DG Priv. 2535/*3335* 239. (from the complete sets, cond. Karajan).

The task of selecting highlights from the whole of the *Ring* cycle is an impossible one, but no one would seriously object to any of the items on this mid-priced sampler from Karajan's DG cycle, all of them among the Wagnerian peaks. Good, generally refined recording, and the tape transfer is mostly of excellent quality, clear and expansive. The excerpts are nicely tailored so that one is never left unsatisfied after a clumsy fade-out.

Der Ring: excerpts: *Das Rheingold: Prelude; Alberich's renunciation; Entry of the gods into Valhalla. Die Walküre: Wie dir die Stirn* (Love duet)*; Ride of the Valkyries. Siegfried: Smelting song; Ewig war* (Love duet). *Götterdämmerung: Siegfried's Rhine journey, death and funeral march.*
(M) ** Ph. Dig. 6527/*7311* 115 [id.]. (from above set, cond. Boulez).

To summarize a complete *Ring* cycle on a single disc and tape is an impossibility, and although these excerpts have been quite skilfully edited they are little more than snippets, with even the *Ride of the Valkyries* cut short and Siegfried's funeral sequence left incomplete, with an unsatisfying fade-out at the end. There are excellent reminders of the excellence of Hermann Becht's Alberich and the splendid love duets of Siegmunde and Sieglinde (*Die Walküre*) and Siegfried and Brünnhilde (*Siegfried*), showing the principals at their finest, but they are frustratingly short. The sound is brilliant and the cassette notably well managed.

Siegfried (complete).
*** Decca **414 110-2**; 414 110-1/*4* (4/*3*). Windgassen, Nilsson, Hotter, Stoltze, Neidlinger, Böhme, Hoffgen, Sutherland, VPO, Solti.
(*) Eurodisc Dig. **610070; 301/*501* 810 (5). Kollo, Altmeyer, Adam, Schreier, Nimsgern, Wenkel, Salminen, Sharp, Dresden State O, Janowski.
(M) ** DG 2740 147 (5) [2713 003]/*3378 049* [*id.*] (coupled with *'Die Walküre'*). Dernesch, Dominguez, Jess Thomas, Stolze, Stewart, Kelemen, Berlin PO, Karajan.

Siegfried has too long been thought of as the grimmest of the *Ring* cycle, with dark colours predominating. It is true that the predominance of male voices till the very end, and Wagner's deliberate matching of this in his orchestration, gives a special colour to the opera, but a performance as buoyant as Solti's reveals that more than in most Wagner the message is one of optimism. Each of the three Acts ends with a scene of triumphant optimism – the first Act in Siegfried's forging song, the second with him hot in pursuit of the woodbird, and the third with the most opulent of love duets. Solti's array of singers could hardly be bettered. Windgassen is at the very peak of his form, lyrical as well as heroic. Hotter has never been more impressive on records, his Wotan at last captured adequately. Stolze, Neidlinger and Böhme are all exemplary, and predictably Joan Sutherland makes the most seductive of woodbirds. Only the conducting of Solti leaves a tiny margin of doubt. In the dramatic moments he could hardly be more impressive, but that very woodbird scene shows up the shortcomings. The bird's melismatic carolling is plainly intended to have a degree of freedom, whereas Solti allows little or no lilt in the music at all. But it is a minute flaw in a supreme achievement. With singing finer than any opera house could normally provide, with masterly playing from the Vienna Philharmonic, and Decca's most opulent recording this is a set likely to stand comparison with anything the rest of the century may provide. The tape transfer is of outstanding quality. Decca have digitally remastered the recording for this reissue.

Dedication and consistency are the mark of the Eurodisc *Ring*, recorded with German thoroughness in collaboration with the East German record company, VEB. The result – with Janowski direct and straight in his approach, securing superb playing from the Dresdeners – lacks a degree of dramatic tension, but unlike the measured Goodall in the ENO *Ring* he does not always build the climaxes cumulatively, in compensation for any loss of immediate excitement. So the final scene of Act II just scurries to a close with Siegfried in pursuit of a rather shrill woodbird in Norma Sharp. The singing is generally first-rate with Kollo a fine Siegfried, less strained than he has sometimes been, and Peter Schreier a superb Mime, using Lieder-like qualities in detailed characterization. Siegmund Nimsgern is a less characterful Alberich, but the voice is excellent, and Theo Adam concludes his portrayal of Wotan/Wanderer with his finest performance of the series. The relative lightness of Jeannine Altmeyer's Brünnhilde comes out in the final love-duet more strikingly than in *Walküre*. She may be reduced from goddess to human, but the musical demands are greater. Nonetheless the tenderness and femininity are most affecting as at the entry of the idyll motif, where Janowski in his dedicated simplicity is also at his most compelling. Clear, beautifully balanced digital sound with voices and instruments firmly placed. The cassettes follow the discs in layout (which brings at least one clumsy side-break that could have been avoided). But the transfer itself is very sophisticated indeed, though not at the highest level. The sound is secure, rich, wide-ranging and clear, and the voices sound most natural. On CD the opera's dark colouring is given an even sharper focus against the totally silent background.

When Siegfried is outsung by Mime, it is time to complain, and though the DG set has many fine qualities – not least the Brünnhilde of Helga Dernesch – it hardly rivals the Solti version. Windgassen on Decca gave a classic performance, and any comparison highlights the serious shortcomings of Jess Thomas. It only makes matters worse that the DG balance favours the voices more than the Decca. Otherwise the vocal cast is strong, and Karajan provides the seamless playing which characterizes his cycle. Recommended only to those irrevocably committed to the Karajan cycle. The tapes are issued coupled to *Die Walküre* at a very reasonable price, but the transfer has not the flair and immediacy of the Decca or Eurodisc versions.

Siegfried (complete, in English).
*** HMV SLS/*TC-SLS* 875 (5/*3*). Remedios, Hunter, Bailey, Dempsey, Hammond-Stroud, Grant, Collins, Sadler's Wells O, Goodall.

Compounded from three live performances at the Coliseum, this magnificent set gives a superb sense of dramatic realism. More tellingly than in almost any other Wagner opera recording, Goodall's spacious direction here conveys the genuine dramatic crunch that gives the experience of hearing Wagner in the opera house its unique power, its overwhelming force. In the *Prelude* there are intrusive audience noises, and towards the end the Sadler's Wells violins have one or two shaky moments, but this is unmistakably a great interpretation caught on the wing. Remedios, more than any rival on record, conveys not only heroic strength but clear-ringing youthfulness, caressing the ear as well as exciting it. Norman Bailey makes a magnificently noble Wanderer, steady of tone, and Gregory Dempsey is a characterful Mime, even if his deliberate whining tone is not well caught on record. The sound is superbly realistic, even making no allowances for the conditions. Lovers of opera in English should grasp the opportunity of hearing this unique set. The tape transfer is admirably vivid and detailed, kind to the voices, with a natural presence so that the words are clear, yet there is no edge or exaggeration of consonants. The orchestral recording is drier than in the others of the series; the brass sound brassier, less rounded than in *The Twilight of the Gods*, for instance, but not less effective. The strings, however, have plenty of body and bloom. The layout is admirable, with each of the three Acts complete on one cassette.

Tannhäuser (Paris version; complete).

*** Decca SET 506-9/*K 80 K 43* [Lon. OSA/*5*- 1438]. Kollo, Dernesch, Ludwig, Sotin, Braun, Hollweg, V. State Op. Ch., VPO, Solti.

Solti provides an electrifying experience, demonstrating beyond a shadow of doubt how much more effective the Paris revision of *Tannhäuser* is compared with the usual Dresden version. The differences lie mainly – though not entirely – in Act I in the scene between Tannhäuser and Venus. Wagner rewrote most of the scene at a time when his style had developed enormously. The love music here is closer to *Walküre* and *Tristan* than to the rest of *Tannhäuser*. The hero's harp song enters each time in its straight diatonic style with a jolt, but this is only apt, and the richness of inspiration, the musical intensification – beautifully conveyed here – transform the opera. The Paris version has never been recorded before, and that alone should dictate choice. But quite apart from that Solti gives one of his very finest Wagner performances to date, helped by superb playing from the Vienna Philharmonic and an outstanding cast, superlatively recorded. Dernesch as Elisabeth and Ludwig as Venus outshine all rivalry, and Kollo, though not ideal, makes as fine a Heldentenor as we are currently likely to hear. The tape transfer is extremely brilliant, not quite so smooth and sweet on the top as in some Decca opera sets, but very vivid. The distant choral effects are gorgeously atmospheric; the moments of spectacle come off well, though there is just a hint of roughness at times (in the *Grand March* scene, for instance). But that is judging by Decca's own very high standards: this is still first-class.

Tristan und Isolde (complete).

*** Ph. Dig. **410 447-2**; 6769/*7654* 091 (*5*/*3*). [id.]. Hofmann, Behrens, Minton, Weikl, Sotin, Bav. R. Ch. and SO, Bernstein.

*** HMV SLS 963 (5) [Ang. SEL 3777]. Vickers, Dernesch, Ludwig, Berry, Ridderbusch, Berlin PO, Karajan.

*** Decca D 41 D *5*/*K 41 K 53* (*5*/*3*) [Lon. OSA/*5*- 1502]. Uhl, Nilsson, Resnik, Van Mill, Krause, VPO, Solti.

*** Decca Dig. D 250 D 5 (5)/*K 250 K 53* (*3*). Mitchinson, Gray, Joll, Howell, Folwell, Harris, Wilkens, Welsh Nat. Op. Ch. and O, Goodall.

**(*) DG Dig. 2741/*3382* 006 (5) [id.]. Kollo, M. Price, Fassbaender, Fischer-Dieskau, Moll, Dresden State O, Kleiber.

(M) **(*) DG 2740 144 [2713 001]/*3378 069* [*id.*]. From 1966 Bay. Fest. production (with rehearsal sequence): Windgassen, Nilsson, Ludwig, Talvela, Waechter, Bay. Fest. Ch. and O, Boehm.

'For the first time someone dares to perform this music as Wagner wrote it,' said Karl Boehm when he visited Bernstein during rehearsals for his *Tristan* recording, made live at three separate concert performances. The surprise is that Bernstein, over-emotional in some music, here exercises restraint to produce the most spacious reading ever put on disc, more expansive even than Furtwängler's or Goodall's. His rhythmic sharpness goes with warmly expressive but unexaggerated phrasing to give unflagging concentration and deep commitment. The love duet has rarely if ever sounded so sensuous with supremely powerful climaxes – as at the peak of *O sink' hernieder*. Nor in the *Liebestod* is there any question of Bernstein rushing ahead, for the culmination comes naturally and fully at a taxingly slow speed.

Behrens makes a fine Isolde, less purely beautiful than her finest rivals but with reserves of power giving dramatic bite. The contrast of tone with Yvonne Minton's Brangaene (good except for flatness in the warning solo) is not as great as usual, and there is likeness too between Peter Hofmann's Tristan, often baritonal, and Bernd Weikl's Kurwenal, lighter than usual. The King Mark of Hans Sotin is superb, and the recorded sound is rich, full and well-detailed, a tribute to the Bavarian engineers working in the Herkulessaal in Munich. Three cassettes make more convenient listening than five discs, though irritatingly the end of Act II is carried over to the third cassette. Yet the sound on the tapes is among the finest Philips have yet given us in this format. Even though the transfer level is not especially high, detail is refined and the quality of voices and orchestra alike is very beautiful.

Karajan's is also a sensual performance of Wagner's masterpiece, caressingly beautiful and with superbly refined playing from the Berlin Philharmonic. At the climactic points of each Act Karajan is a tantalizing deceiver, leading you to expect that the moment of resolution will not be fully achieved, but then punching home with a final crescendo of supreme force. He is helped by a recording (not ideally balanced, but warmly atmospheric) which copes with an enormous dynamic range. Dernesch as Isolde is seductively feminine, not so noble as Flagstad, not so tough and unflinching as Nilsson, but the human quality makes this account if anything more moving still, helped by glorious tone colour through every range. Jon Vickers matches her, in what is arguably his finest performance on record, allowing himself true pianissimo shading. The rest of the cast is excellent too. A radiantly compelling set.

Solti's performance is less flexible and sensuous than Karajan's, but he shows himself ready to relax in Wagner's more expansive periods. On the other hand the end of Act I and the opening of the *Love duet* have a knife-edged dramatic tension. Birgit Nilsson responds superbly to Solti's direction. There are moments when the great intensity that Flagstad brought to the part is not equalled, but more often than not Nilsson is masterly in her conviction, and – it cannot be emphasized too strongly – she never attacks below the note as Flagstad did, so that miraculously at the opening of the *Love duet* the impossibly difficult top Cs come out and hit the listener crisply and cleanly, dead on the note; and the *Liebestod* is all the more moving for having no soupy swerves at the climax. Fritz Uhl is a really musical Heldentenor. Only during one passage of the *Love duet* (*O sink' hernieder*) does he sound tired, and for the most part this is a well-focused voice. Dramatically he leaves the centre of the stage to Isolde, but his long solo passages in Act III are superb and make that sometimes tedious Act into something genuinely gripping. The Kurwenal of Tom Krause and the King Mark of Arnold van Mill are both excellent, and it is only Regina Resnik as Brangaene who gives any disappointment. The production has the usual Decca/Culshaw imaginative touch, and the recording matches brilliance and clarity with satisfying co-ordination and richness. There is a splendid tape version too, with the clear projection of the voices against an often sumptuously glowing orchestral texture matched by the sense of perspective and atmosphere. The work's climaxes (the end of Act I as well as the *Love duet* and *Liebestod*) are impressively free and spectacular. Each of the three Acts is complete on a single cassette.

Based on the much-praised production of the Welsh National Opera company, Goodall's recording of *Tristan* was made not on stage but at Brangwyn Hall, Swansea, just when the cast was steamed up for stage performances. With long takes the result is an extremely fresh-sounding performance, vivid and immediate, more intimate than rival versions yet bitingly powerful. Typically from Goodall, it is measured and steady, but the speeds are not all exceptionally slow, and with rhythms sharply defined and textures made transparent he keeps the momentum going. So with the frenzied lovers' greetings in Act II Goodall's tread is inexorable at his measured speed and the result compelling. The WNO Orchestra is not sumptuous but the playing is well-tuned and responsive. Neither Linda Esther Gray nor John Mitchinson is as sweet on the ear as the finest rivals, for in both the microphone exaggerates vibrato. But Mitchinson never barks Heldentenor-style, and Gray in her first major recording provides a formidable combination of qualities, feminine vulnerability alongside commanding power. Gwynne Howell is arguably the finest King Mark on record, making his monologue at the end of Act II, so often an anticlimax, into one of the noblest passages of all. This may not have the smoothness of the finest international sets, but with its vivid digital sound it is certainly one of the most compelling of latterday Wagner recordings. The cassette transfer is one of Decca's very finest, outstandingly rich, vivid and clear: the atmospheric horn calls in Act II, for instance, are magically caught. The layout of three tapes against five discs is more suitable, tailoring Acts to the ends of sides. The only snag is the libretto, a straightforward reduction of the LP booklet, with much smaller print.

Kleiber directs a compellingly impulsive

reading crowned by the glorious Isolde, the most purely beautiful of any complete interpretation on record, of Margaret Price. Next to more spacious readings, his at times sounds excitable, almost hysterical, with fast speeds tending to get faster, for all his hypnotic concentration. But the lyricism of Margaret Price, feminine and vulnerable, is well contrasted against the heroic Tristan of Kollo, at his finest in Act III. Kurt Moll makes a dark, leonine King Mark, but Fischer-Dieskau is at times gritty as Kurwenal – the role he first recorded for Furtwängler – and Brigitte Fassbaender is a clear but rather cold Brangaene. The recording though full in its digital brilliance brings some odd balances and discrepancies.

Boehm's set, now available at medium price in the UK (with a cassette box universally available) was taken from a live performance at Bayreuth, but apart from such passages as the *Prelude* and concluding *Liebestod*, where the experience is vivid, the performance too often acquires tensions of the wrong sort, and Boehm's speeds are surprisingly fast. Nilsson is here more expressive but less bright-toned than in her Decca set, and Windgassen – in his time an incomparable Tristan – begins to show signs of wear in the voice. The recording favours the voices, suffering inevitably from live recording conditions. The cassette transfer is undoubtedly vivid.

Tristan und Isolde: highlights.
(M) **(*) DG Priv. 2535/*3335* 243. (from above set, cond. Boehm).

Boehm's reading of *Tristan* lacks – in the love music at least – the glowing expansive warmth one ideally needs. But a one-disc selection covering the obvious high points of the opera is welcome, and though the recording – made live in the Festspielhaus – has dated a little, this can be safely recommended. There is a good cassette transfer.

Tristan und Isolde: Prelude to Act I; Isolde's narration and curse; Liebestod.
(M) **(*) Decca Jub. JB/*KJBC* 58. Nilsson, Hoffman, VPO, Knappertsbusch.

This record was made in 1960, before Nilsson recorded her first complete set under Solti, and the performance displays less overt feelings than might be expected. But the end result is in many ways made the more impressive with the emotion of the moment conveyed by reticence and controlled power. Knappertsbusch characteristically feels for the sublime lengths of Wagner rather than seeking the cutting dramatic edge of a Solti, but with spacious recording the result is persuasive. The Act I duet (with Grace Hoffman) goes from where Isolde sends Brangaene to fetch Tristan to the fateful moment where she selects the death potion. The recording sounds vivid in this reissue, and the cassette too is of excellent quality, with a strikingly crisp overall focus, the voices vibrant against a full-bodied orchestral sound.

Die Walküre (complete).
*** Decca **414 105-2**; 414 105-1/*4* (4/*3*). Nilsson, Crespin, Ludwig, King, Hotter, Frick, VPO, Solti.
*** Eurodisc **610064**; 301/*501* 143 (5). Altmeyer, Norman, Minton, Jerusalem, Adam, Moll, Dresden State O, Janowski.
(M) **(*) DG 2740 146 (5) [2713 002]/*3378 049* [*id.*] (coupled with *'Siegfried'*). Crespin, Janowitz, Veasey, Vickers, Stewart, Talvela, Berlin PO, Karajan.

Solti's conception of *Die Walküre* is more lyrical than one would have expected from his recordings of the three other *Ring* operas. He sees Act II as the kernel of the work, perhaps even of the whole cycle. Acts I and III have their supremely attractive set-pieces, which must inevitably make them more popular as entertainment, but here one appreciates that in Act II the conflict of wills between Wotan and Fricka makes for one of Wagner's most deeply searching scenes. That is the more apparent when the greatest of latterday Wotans, Hans Hotter, takes the role, and Christa Ludwig sings with searing dramatic sense as his wife. Before that, Act I seems a little underplayed, not nearly so sharp-edged as in Decca's rival version with Leinsdorf. This is partly because of Solti's deliberate lyricism – apt enough when love and spring greetings are in the air – but also (on the debit side) because James King fails to project the character of Siegmund and fails to delve into the word-meanings, as all the other members of the cast consistently do. Crespin has never sung more beautifully on record, but even that cannot cancel out the shortcoming. As for Nilsson's Brünnhilde it has grown mellower since she made the earlier Decca recording, the emotions are clearer, and under-the-note attack is almost eliminated. Some may hesitate in the face of Hotter's obvious vocal trials but the unsteadiness is if anything less marked than in his EMI recordings of items done many years ago. Superlative recording, digitally remastered for this reissue, and a first-class cassette version.

The Eurodisc *Ring* cycle is one for Wagnerians who want to concentrate on the score, undistracted by stereo staging or even by strongly characterful conducting. Janowski's direct approach matches the relative dryness of the acoustic with voices fixed well forward of the orchestra but not aggressively so. That balance allows full glory for the singing from a satisfyingly consistent cast. Jessye Norman might not seem an obvious choice for Sieglinde, but the sound is glorious, the expression intense and detailed, making her a superb match for the fine, if rather less imaginative Siegmund of Siegfried Jerusalem. The one snag with so commanding a Sieglinde is that she overtops the Brünnhilde of Jeannine Altmeyer, who, more than usual, conveys a measure of feminine vulnerability in the leading Valkyrie even in her godhead days. Miss Altmeyer, born in Los Angeles of a German father and an Italian mother, may be slightly overparted, but the beauty and often sensuousness of her singing is the more telling next to the gritty Wotan of Theo Adam. With its slow vibrato under pressure his is rarely a pleasing voice, but the clarity of the recording makes it a specific, never a woolly sound, so that the illumination of the narrative is consistent and intense. Kurt Moll is a gloriously firm Hunding, and Yvonne Minton a searingly effective Fricka. On chrome cassettes as on the discs (which are followed by the tape layout) the sound is consistently refined in detail, the voices have naturalness and presence, yet the balance is excellent. On CD the drama and urgency of the recording have even greater bite.

The great merits of Karajan's version in competition with Solti's are the refinement of the orchestral playing and the heroic strength of Jon Vickers as Siegmund. With that underlined, one cannot but note that the vocal shortcomings here are generally more marked, and the total result does not add up to quite so compelling a dramatic experience: one is less involved. Thomas Stewart may have a younger, firmer voice than Hotter, but the character of Wotan emerges only partially. It is not just that he misses some of the word-meaning, but that on occasion – as in the kissing away of Brünnhilde's godhead – he underlines too crudely. A fine performance nonetheless, and Josephine Veasey as Fricka matches her rival Ludwig in conveying the biting intensity of the part. Gundula Janowitz's Sieglinde has its beautiful moments, but the singing is ultimately a little static. Crespin's Brünnhilde is impressive, but nothing like so satisfying as her study of Sieglinde on the Decca set. The voice is at times strained into unsteadiness, which the microphone seems to exaggerate. The DG recording is good, but not quite in the same class as the Decca – though some machines may favour things the other way round. The cassette version too is less impressive than the Decca, transferred at a lower level. It is issued, competitively priced, coupled to *Siegfried.*

The Valkyrie (complete, in English).
*** HMV SLS/*TC-SLS* 5063 (5). Hunter, Remedios, Curphey, Bailey, Grant, Howard, E. Nat. Op. Ch. and O, Goodall.

Like the others in this series, *The Valkyrie* under Reginald Goodall was recorded live at the Coliseum, and with minor reservations it fills the bill splendidly for those who want to hear the *Ring* cycle in English. With the voices balanced a little closer than in *Siegfried*, the words of Andrew Porter's translation are a degree clearer, but the atmosphere is less vivid. The glory of the performance lies not just in Goodall's spacious direction but in the magnificent Wotan of Norman Bailey, noble in the broadest span but very human in his illumination of detail. Rita Hunter sings nobly too, and though she is not quite so commanding as Nilsson is in the Solti cycle, she is often more lyrically tender. Alberto Remedios as

Siegmund is more taxed than he was as Siegfried in the later opera (lower tessituras are not quite so comfortable for him), but his sweetly ringing top register is superb. If others, such as Ann Howard as Fricka, are not always kindly treated by the microphone, the total dramatic compulsion is irresistible. The tape transfer is generally vivid. The voices are forwardly projected and the words clear, although in Act II Ann Howard's voice is given a rather hard edge. Later the moments of spectacle are well handled, although in the *Ride of the Valkyries* the internal focus of detail is less than crisp. But on the whole this is exciting sound, if lacking in sumptuousness.

Die Walküre: Act I (complete).
(M) **(*) Decca GRV 26. Flagstad, Svanholm, Van Mill, VPO, Knappertsbusch.

Flagstad may not have been ideally cast as Sieglinde, but the command of her singing with its unfailing richness, even after her official retirement, crowns a strong and dramatic performance with Svanholm and Van Mill singing cleanly. The transfer of the original three sides on to two retains the excellence (for its period) of the original recording.

Der fliegende Holländer: Senta's ballad. Götterdämmerung: Brünnhilde's immolation scene. Tannhäuser: Dich teure Halle. Tristan und Isolde: Prelude and Liebestod.
*(*) CBS Dig. 37294/*40*-. Caballé, NYPO, Mehta.

There are moments of tender intensity in Caballé's recital, illuminatingly perceptive of detail, but the singing is too often flawed, when the voice is not well-suited to the heavier roles, and Caballé disguises her weakness in mannerism. Fair recording. There is an excellent chrome cassette matching the disc very closely.

Der fliegende Holländer. Act II: *Wie aus der Ferne. Die Walküre.* Act III: *War es so schmählich Deinen Leichten Sinn: Leb'wohl, du kühnes, herrliches Kind!* (*Wotan's farewell and Magic Fire music*).
*** HMV SXLP/*TC-SXLP* 30557. Nilsson, Hotter, Philh. O, Ludwig.

Both Nilsson and Hotter were at their vocal peak in 1958 when they recorded these duets. Hotter's pianissimo in the *Walküre* excerpt as he kisses his daughter's godhead away is one of his finest moments on record. Ludwig directs immaculate performances with recording that still sounds full and rounded. There is a very good cassette with plenty of body and range.

Götterdämmerung: (i) *Immolation scene. Lohengrin: Einsam in trüben Tagen. Tannhäuser: Dich teure Halle. Tristan und Isolde: Liebestod. Die Walküre: Der Manner Sippe; Du bist der Lenz;* (ii) *Nun zäume; Hojotoho!*
(M) *** Decca GRV 24. Nilsson, with (i) Frick; (ii) London; ROHCGO, Downes; VPO, Knappertsbusch or Solti; LSO, Leinsdorf.

Nilsson is celebrated in this *'Grandi Voci'* issue by a wide-ranging collection from recitals (Elsa and Sieglinde with Edward Downes conducting, Isolde's *Liebestod* gloriously done with Knappertsbusch) as well as complete opera sets. The opening of Act II of *Walküre* comes in Leinsdorf's often brilliant version, leading to the Immolation Scene with Solti conducting. A noble collection with sound still impressive.

Waldteufel, Emil (1837–1915)

Waltzes: Dolores; España; Estudiantina; Les Patineurs; Plus de diamants; Les Sirènes; Très jolie.
(*) Ph. Dig. **400 012-2; 6514/*7337* 069 [id.]. V. Volksoper O, Bauer-Theussl.

Waltzes: Dolores; España; The Grenadiers; Mon Rêve; Les Patineurs; Pomone; Toujours ou jamais.
(M) *** Decca VIV/*KVIC* 32 [Lon. STS/*5*-15572]. Nat. PO, Gamley.

Waldteufel's waltzes have a direct, breezy vivacity. They lack the underlying poetic feeling that takes the works of Johann Strauss into the concert hall, but their spontaneity and wit more than compensate for any lack of distinction in the tunes. Undoubtedly *The Skaters* is Waldteufel's masterpiece, but *Pomone*, *Mon Rêve* and the less well-known *Toujours ou jamais* all show the composer at his best. *España* is, of course, a direct crib from Chabrier, but is enjoyable enough, even if it does not match the original score in exuberance. Rhythmic zest and vitality are the keynote of Douglas Gamley's performances. He does not forget that Waldteufel was French. There is just the right degree of sophistication and affection in the phrasing, and the fine Decca recording, made in a well-chosen resonant acoustic, has both brilliance and bloom. The cassette transfer is very successful.

Franz Bauer-Theussl's performances with the excellent Vienna Volksoper Orchestra are amiable and recorded in a generously warm acoustic. The effect is pleasing, but slightly bland. Moreover the opening of *Les Patineurs* is truncated. The famous horn solo is omitted; instead there is just a snatch of the main theme on the cello. The compact disc makes admirable if rather expensive background music, but does not differ a great deal from the LP; the chrome tape is agreeable too, though it has slightly less sparkle on top. But Gamley's Decca disc costs about a third the price and has far more brio and style.

Wallace, Vincent (1812–65)

Maritana (opera): *Overture; In happy moments; Yes, let me like a soldier fall; Scenes that are brightest.*

** HMV CSD 3651. Dunne, Deane, Hinds, O, Nelson – BALFE: *Bohemian Girl*; BENEDICT: *Lily of Killarney.* **

Maritana was first produced at the Drury Lane Theatre in 1845. Rightly, even though this selection is short, the overture is included, for it is a marvellously typical piece in the melodramatic potpourri style. It is carried along splendidly by an inherently vulgar vitality and features as its centrepiece the memorable *Scenes that are brightest*, which is also sung here, a little gustily, by Veronica Dunne. But Miss Dunne has an ample voice and better this than a soubrette style. The baritone, Eric Hinds, has a warm voice and fatherly manner (he would do Germont in *Traviata* well) and he sings *In happy moments* with the proper degree of maudlin cheerfulness. This is irresistible. The tenor is less characterful in *Yes, let me like a soldier fall* – there is no rattle of drums and cannon in his delivery – but he has a pleasant voice and this is enjoyable enough. Havelock Nelson really has the feel for Wallace's scoring, and the recording balance is equally happy, so that the orchestral colour with its flavour of the bandstand comes over well. Most enjoyable.

Walton, William (1902–83)

(i) *Capriccio burlesco;* (ii) *Viola concerto;* (iii) *Violin concerto;* (iv) *Façade;* (i) *Johannesburg festival overture;* (v) *Partita for orchestra; Symphony No. 2; Variations on a theme by Hindemith;* (vi) *Belshazzar's Feast.*

(M) **(*) CBS 79411 (4). (i) O, Kostelanetz; (ii) Doktor, LPO, Downes; (iii) Francescatti, Phd. O, Ormandy; (iv) Sitwell, Horner, CO, Prausnitz; (v) Cleveland O, Szell; (vi) Cassel, Rutgers University Ch., Phd. O, Ormandy.

Most of the performances in CBS's memorial box date from the 1960s, with Szell and the Cleveland Orchestra amply confirming their boast to be the finest orchestra in the world. They give performances of three of the later works which rebut all idea that they may be contrived rather than passionate, the *Second Symphony*, the *Hindemith variations* and the *Partita*. Ormandy in *Belshazzar's Feast* is vigorous but not quite idiomatic. He is more at home in the romantic fervour of the

Violin concerto with Francescatti. This version of the *Viola concerto* with Paul Doktor is the best available, while the coupling of Kostelanetz's vigorous readings of the *Overture* and the work written for him, the *Capriccio burlesco*, makes a good supplement along with Dame Edith Sitwell's New York recording of *Façade*, rhythmically fallible but uniquely characterful in limited mono. The *Tango* is handed over to a helper and the *Tarantella* omitted entirely.

Cello concerto.

*** HMV ASD 2924. Tortelier, Bournemouth SO, Berglund – SHOSTAKOVICH: *Cello concerto.****

** Chan. Dig. ABRD/*ABTD* 1007 [id.]. Kirshbaum, SNO, Gibson – ELGAR: *Concerto.* *(*)

The *Cello concerto*, written for Piatigorsky, is a work that has often seemed rather cool in comparison with his two earlier string concertos, but here Tortelier with characteristically passionate playing shows the composer's consistency. After the haunting melancholy of the first movement, the central scherzo emerges as a far weightier piece than most such movements, while the final variations have never before on record developed with such a sense of compulsion. This performance is also available more economically paired with Walton's *Violin concerto* – see below. The recording is vintage EMI sound, warm and full.

The idea of coupling the Elgar and Walton concertos was a splendid one, but here, as in the Elgar, the reading of Kirshbaum and Gibson is disappointing, lacking the warmth, weight and expressiveness that so ripe an example of late romanticism demands. The digital recording is also disappointingly wanting in body on disc, while the cassette lacks range and sparkle at the top. First choice for this concerto rests with Tortelier.

(i) *Cello concerto;* (ii) *Violin concerto.*

(M) *** HMV Green. ESD/*TC-ESD* 107763-1/*4*. (i) Tortelier; (ii) Haendel, Bournemouth SO, Berglund.

Two ripely romantic recordings of two of Walton's most lyrical works make an outstanding coupling on the Greensleeve label, a logical and attractive pairing. Haendel, recorded rather close, gives a sunny and warm as well as a powerful reading, strongly rhythmic in the controversially slow account of the final coda. Tortelier, more openly emotional than the dedicatee and first interpreter, Piatigorsky, yet finds greater weight in the central scherzo, more than just a dazzling interlude, while the yearning intensity of his readings of the fine melodies of the outer movements relates the piece to the opera, *Troilus and Cressida*. Recordings of 1977 and 1972 well refurbished, with a fresh, clear cassette.

(i) *Viola concerto;* (ii) *Violin concerto.*

**(*) HMV ASD 2542 [Ang. S 36719]. Menuhin (i) (viola), New Philh. O; (ii) (violin), LSO, both cond. composer.

Fine performances of both works from Menuhin, who is in reasonably good form in the *Violin concerto* and makes a very good showing in the masterly *Viola concerto*. Walton himself is at the helm and secures expert playing from the New Philharmonia and the LSO. HMV provide a musically satisfying balance and excellent sound. But many Waltonians will not approve the extremely slow account of the *Viola concerto* first movement.

(i) *Viola concerto;* (ii) *Façade suite No. 1;* (iii) *Scapino overture.*

(**) CBS 71115/*40-*. (i) Primrose, RPO, Sargent; (ii) O, Kostelanetz; (iii) Chicago SO, Stock.

Only Kostelanetz's account of *Façade* is in stereo, a bright, lively reading. The *Viola concerto* comes in the first version with triple woodwind and heavy brass (used most judiciously), but minus a harp. Primrose was always a compelling interpreter, breathtaking in his bravura, but as recorded he rarely plays softly and intonation is not flawless. *Scapino* is given in its original, longer version, interpreted by the musicians for whom it was written in 1940. The performance is dazzling except that the 78 r.p.m. sound is crumbly, fading at times almost into inaudibility. In the other two works the quality is fresh and clear. There is an excellent matching cassette. An historical curiosity.

Violin concerto.
❀ *** Decca SXL/*KSXC* 6601 [Lon. CS 6819]. Kyung-Wha Chung, LSO, Previn – STRAVINSKY: *Concerto.* ***
*** HMV ASD/*TC-ASD* 3843. Haendel, Bournemouth SO, Berglund – BRITTEN: *Concerto.* ***
(M) **(*) CBS 60287/*40*- [Odys. Y/*YT* 33522]. Francescatti, Phd. O, Ormandy – SIBELIUS: *Concerto.* **(*)

The *Violin concerto*, written for Heifetz in 1939, shows Walton at his most distinctively compelling. Even he has seldom written melodies so ravishingly beautiful, so hauntedly romantic, yet his equally personal brand of spikiness has rarely if ever been presented with more power. Kyung-Wha Chung recorded this rich work immediately after playing a long sequence of live performances, and the brooding intensity of the opening presents the first melody with a depth of expressiveness, tender and hushed, that has never been matched on record, not even by Heifetz himself. With Previn as guide, and with the composer himself as a sympathetic observer at the recording sessions, Chung then builds up a performance which must remain a classic, showing the concerto as one of the greatest of the century in this genre. Outstandingly fine recording, and a first-class cassette too.

A glowing, Mediterranean-like view of the concerto from Ida Haendel, with brilliant playing from the soloist and eloquent orchestral support from the Bournemouth orchestra under Paavo Berglund. Kyung-Wha Chung's version is wirier and in some ways more in character, but many collectors will respond equally (or even more) positively to Miss Haendel's warmth. There is an unrelieved lyricism about her tone that may not be to all tastes, but given the quality of both playing and recording (as well as the interest of the equally successful Britten coupling) this is an eminently desirable issue. The cassette is rich and has good detail (although the percussion once or twice lacks the last degree of transient crispness) and overall provides a pleasingly natural balance. This can be recommended alongside Kyung-Wha Chung's Decca version with Previn but is even more attractive in its alternative, more modestly priced coupling with the *Cello concerto* – see above.

Francescatti is balanced very closely by the CBS engineers and the brightly lit recording emphasizes his somewhat wiry tone; yet his characteristic nervous intensity is not unsuited to this work and he is given eloquent and passionate support by Ormandy and the Philadelphia Orchestra. Francescatti's playing is certainly impressive and, were the recording better balanced, this would carry the fullest recommendation. The sound is much preferable in the cassette version, which smooths the treble and takes some of the edge off the solo timbre without loss of body and detail.

Crown Imperial; Orb and Sceptre (coronation marches); *Façade: suite; Henry V* (incidental music): *suite; Johannesburg Festival overture; Partita for orchestra; Portsmouth Point overture; Richard III: Prelude; Spitfire prelude and fugue; Symphony No. 1;* (i) *Belshazzar's Feast.*
(M) *** HMV mono/stereo SLS/*TC-SLS* 5246 (3/*2*). Philh. O, composer, (i) with D. Bell, Philh. Ch.

This box, issued to celebrate the composer's eightieth birthday, gathers together most of the recordings which Walton – for many years his own finest interpreter – made with the Philharmonia Orchestra. Only three of the six sides are in stereo, but some items such as the *Johannesburg Festival overture* (given a fizzing performance) come in stereo for the first time, and the whole compilation presents an excellent and generous conspectus of Walton's achievement. Such recordings as that of *Belshazzar's Feast* have understandably remained continuously in the catalogue, but it is good to have such an important recording as that of the *First Symphony* – less electrifying than Previn's reading, but sharply illuminating – resurrected after many years of unavailability. The booklet includes many delightful portraits and splendid notes by Gillian Widdicombe. The cassette layout too is wholly admirable, with the *Symphony* and *Belshazzar's Feast* back to back on the first of two tapes, so that each work can be heard without a break. The transfers are first-class in every way. A most desirable set.

Crown Imperial (concert band version).
(M) *** Mercury SRI/*MRI* 75028 [id.]. Eastman Wind Ens., Fennell – HOLST: *Hammersmith;* JACOB: *William Byrd suite.* ***

Splendidly paced, with an organ added at the end to give a touch of grandiloquence, this performance, alert and sparkling, is part of a highly recommendable collection of music for military band. The Holst coupling is distinguished and the Gordon Jacob suite of Byrd's music is a delight. Recommended both on disc and the excellent cassette.

Crown Imperial; Orb and Sceptre.
*** HMV ASD/*TC-ASD* 3388 [Ang. S/*4XS* 37436]. LPO, Boult – ELGAR: *Pomp and Circumstance marches* etc. ***

Walton's two coronation marches make the ideal coupling for Boult's collection of Elgar marches. It was Boult who first conducted them in Westminster Abbey (in 1937 and 1953 respectively) and he brings even more flamboyance to them than to the Elgar items. The recording is immensely rich and spectacular on disc, and its wide amplitude is, on the whole, satisfactorily caught in the tape transfer, although the focus in the bass is not very clean.

Façade (an entertainment with words by Edith Sitwell): complete.
(M) *** Decca Eclipse ECS 560. Sitwell, Pears, E. Op. Group, Collins.
(M) **(*) Ph. Seq. 6527/*7311* 133. Laine, Ross, Ens. dir. Dankworth.

The classic account still available on Decca Eclipse (one of the few remaining issues on this once important label) is not real stereo, but the transcription is astonishingly successful, clear and atmospheric. The performance – still the finest ever recorded of the complete entertainment – is miraculously deft.

The Cleo Laine/Johnny Dankworth version has also now achieved a certain vintage status. It is controversial with its distinctly jazz overtones, yet one cannot think that Walton himself would have resisted such a flavour. The performance is full of individuality and character, though some may find it slightly self-conscious; but it is certainly worth sampling. The recording is vivid on both disc and tape, transferred at the highest level.

Façade: Suites Nos. 1 and 2. BACH (arr. Walton): *The Wise Virgins: Ballet suite.*
**(*) HMV ASD 3317. CBSO, Frémaux.

Walton's arrangements of movements from Bach cantatas give off electric sparks (except of course in *Sheep may safely graze*), and with superb recording Frémaux's version is most welcome. In *Façade* his manner is not quite as light and sparkling as it might be, but his rhythmic control gives a fresh new look to the music.

Film scores: *The First of the Few: Spitfire prelude and fugue; Hamlet: Funeral march; Henry V: suite* (*Passacaglia – Death of Falstaff; Charge and battle; Touch her soft lips and part; Agincourt song*)*; Richard III: Prelude and Suite.*
(M) **(*) HMV SXLP 30139 [Sera. 60205]. Philh. O, composer.

It has been said of film music that it is only good film music if it is not noticed. This is, of course, only partly true, and in recent years a striking 'theme' associated with a famous movie has often had the effect of bringing audiences into the cinema to see the action associated with it. But Walton's film scores mostly date from an earlier period, when the writing followed a long-established tradition of incidental music for the theatre. The score for *Richard III* is a good example of this. The inspiration is direct, and the individual pieces are sufficiently varied in style to make up a good suite. The score for *Henry V* is rather less striking, although the music for the *Death of Falstaff* is touching. But easily the most memorable piece here is the stirring and eloquent *Prelude and fugue* Walton put together from his music for the biographical film about R. J. Mitchell, the designer of the Spitfire. The performances on this disc have atmosphere and intensity, and if the recording is not as brilliant and clearly defined as it might be, it has plenty of warmth and colour.

Symphony No. 1 in B flat min.
(M) *** RCA GL/*GK* 42707. LSO, Previn.
**(*) HMV Dig. ASD/*TCC-ASD* 4091. Philh. O, Haitink.
(M) ** ASV ACM/*ZCACM* 2006 [None. 71394]. Royal Liv. PO, Handley.
** Chan. Dig. **CHAN 8313**; ABRD/*ABTD* 1095. SNO, Gibson.

Previn gives a marvellously biting account of this magnificent symphony. His fast tempi may initially make one feel that he is pressing too hard, but his ability to screw the dramatic tension tighter and tighter until the final resolution is most assured, and certainly reflects the tense mood of the mid-1930s, as well as the youthful Walton's own dynamism. (The composer has since told us that the tensions express a very personal period of stress in his own emotional life.) '*Presto con malizia*' says the score for the scherzo, and malice is exactly what Previn conveys, with the hints of vulgarity and humour securely placed. In the slow movement Previn finds real warmth, giving some of the melodies an Elgarian richness, and the finale's electricity here helps to overcome any feeling that it is too facile, too easily happy a conclusion. The bright recording quality (late-1960s vintage) remains impressive on disc; but on tape, although the sound remains full and vivid, the dynamics are compressed.

The malevolent demon which inhabits the first two movements is somewhat tamed by Haitink, and in the opening movement some listeners will feel that the lack of the relentless forward thrust demonstrated by both the composer's own reading and Previn's RCA version underplays the music's character. However, this HMV account offers a legitimately spacious if less exciting view, and Haitink's directness leads to noble accounts of the slow movement and finale. The bright digital recording is lacking a little in bass in its disc format, but this is less striking in the chrome cassette, which is admirable in all respects.

Vernon Handley's interpretation of this work matured when he conducted a number of performances with the Liverpool orchestra during Walton's seventy-fifth birthday celebrations. It is essentially a broad view and tends to play down the work's cutting edge: there is very little suggestion of *malizia* in the scherzo. Indeed it must be said that the reading tends to undercharacterize the music. While the first-movement climax is impressively shaped to a considerable peak of excitement, it is the orchestral brass that makes the most striking effect; the string playing lacks bite and incisiveness, both there and in the finale. The recording is resonant and spacious, and the cassette transfer is first-class.

Gibson's is a convincingly idiomatic view, well paced but with ensemble not always bitingly precise enough for this darkly intense music (malice prescribed for the scherzo, melancholy for the slow movement). Recording first-rate but with less body than usual from Chandos and with timpani resonantly obtrusive. The compact disc is somewhat disappointing, bringing out the thinness on top.

Symphony No. 2; Portsmouth Point overture; Scapino overture.
*** HMV ASD 2990. LSO, Previn – LAMBERT: *The Rio Grande.* **(*)

If Walton's *Second Symphony* prompted George Szell to direct the Cleveland Orchestra in one of its most spectacular performances on record (see above), André Previn and the LSO give another brilliant performance, which in some ways gets closer to the heart of the music, with its overtones of the romantic opera *Troilus and Cressida*. Previn is less literal than Szell, more sparkling in the outer movements, more warmly romantic in the central slow movement. In the two overtures Previn, the shrewdest and most perceptive of Waltonians, finds more light and shade than usual. The recording is oustandingly fine.

Violin sonata.
(B) *(*) PRT GSGC/*ZCGC* 2050. Nemet, Wruble – BRITTEN: *Suite.* **(*)

Walton's *Violin sonata* was written soon after the war with Yehudi Menuhin's vibrant playing in mind. It has long needed a modern recording, and Mary Nemet brings to it the romantic style and warmth of phrasing which its leisurely paragraphs call for. But the tone is not always rich enough or the intonation clean enough. Of all Walton's works this is formally one of the least satisfactory, with its two longish movements neither fast nor slow, and one really needs more positive playing if its weaknesses are to be disguised. Very welcome, all the same, at bargain price with so apt a coupling. Clean, atmospheric recording and a good tape.

(i) *Belshazzar's Feast* (oratorio). *Coronation Te Deum.*
*** Decca SET/*KCET* 618 [Lon. 26525/5-]. LPO Ch., Choirs of Salisbury, Winchester and Chichester Cathedrals, LPO, Solti, (i) with Luxon.

(i) *Belshazzar's Feast. Improvisations on an impromptu of Benjamin Britten.*
*** HMV SAN/*TCC-SAN* 324 [Ang. S 36861]. LSO, Previn, (i) with Shirley-Quirk, LSO Ch.

(i) *Belshazzar's Feast. Partita for orchestra.*
(M) **(*) HMV SXLP 30236 [Ang. S 35681]. Philh. O, composer, (i) with Bell, Philh. Ch.

Previn's is the richest and most spectacular version of *Belshazzar's Feast* yet recorded. As a Waltonian he seems to have taken on the mantle of the composer himself as interpreter. This fine performance was recorded with Walton present on his seventieth birthday, and though Previn's tempi are occasionally slower than those set by Walton himself in his two recordings, the authenticity is clear, with consistently sharp attack and with dynamic markings meticulously observed down to the tiniest hairpin markings. Chorus and orchestra are challenged to their finest standards, and John Shirley-Quirk proves a searching and imaginative soloist. Fine vivid sound. The *Improvisations*, given a first recording, make a generous fill-up. There is an excellent chrome cassette.

Whether or not prompted by the composer's latterday dictum that *Belshazzar's Feast* is more a choral symphony than an oratorio, Sir Georg Solti directs a sharply incisive performance which brings out the symphonic basis rather than the atmospheric story-telling. Fresh, scintillating and spiky, it is a performance that gives off electric sparks, not always quite idiomatic but very invigorating. Solti observes Walton's syncopations very literally, with little or none of the flexibility that the jazz overtones suggest, and his slow tempo for the lovely chorus *By the waters of Babylon* remains very steady, with little of the customary rubato. But with generally excellent singing from the chorus and a sympathetic contribution from Luxon (marred only slightly by vibrato) this is a big-scale reading which overall is most convincing. Moreover, from the very opening, with its dramatic trombone solo, one is aware that this is to be one of Decca's demonstration recordings, with superbly incisive and clear choral sound, slightly sparer of texture in *Belshazzar's Feast* than in the *Te Deum* written for the Queen's Coronation in 1953, a splendid occasional piece which makes the ideal coupling. The quality is equally clear and vivid on both disc and cassette.

The composer's performance with the Philharmonia Chorus and Orchestra obviously has authenticity too, but the choral singing here, although good, is not always so incisive as with Previn, nor is the performance so spontaneous. The recording is extremely clear if a little on the dry side, but the spectacular moments are accommodated securely. Donald Bell's contribution is a good one if not so imaginative as Shirley-Quirk's. The *Partita* was commissioned by the Cleveland Orchestra and first performed in 1958. The writing is typical of Walton's earlier style, having something of the hurly-burly of *Portsmouth Point*, and the finale, *Giga burlesca*, more than once reminds the listener of *Scapino*. The central *Siciliana* is less successful here, although generally the performance is a good one.

(i; ii) *Gloria;* (ii) *Te Deum. Coronation marches: Crown imperial; Orb and sceptre.*
(M) *** HMV Green. ESD/*TC-ESD* 106371-1/*4*. (i) Robotham, Rolfe Johnson, Rayner Cook; (ii) CBSO Ch., Choristers of Worcester Cath.; CBSO, Frémaux.

'Shatteringly apt displays of pomp and circumstance' is the delightful description of Frank Howes for the three Walton works inspired by coronations, and here they are splendidly coupled with the grand setting of the *Gloria* which Walton wrote in 1961 for a double celebration at Huddersfield, the 125th anniversary of the Choral Society and the 30th anniversary of its association with Sir Malcolm Sargent. That last work, the longest of the four, has not quite the same concentration as the others, for it represents Walton tending to repeat himself in his jagged Alleluia rhythms and jazzy fugatos. Frémaux directs a highly enjoyable performance nonetheless, but it rather pales before the Coronation *Te Deum*, which may use some of the same formulas but has Walton electrically inspired. It is a grand setting which yet has a superb formal balance (almost a sonata form) while exploiting every tonal and atmospheric effect imaginable between double choirs and semi-choruses. The two splendid marches are marvellously done too. Frémaux uses the original full version of *Crown Imperial* instead of observing the cuts suggested by Walton, which reduce it by about a third, and that is the right decision. The rich, resonant recording is apt for the music, spacious with excellent perspectives, and it has transferred surprisingly well to cassette, where the choral focus is only marginally more diffuse.

The Bear (opera; complete).
**(*) Chan. ABR/*ABT* 1052 [id.]. Harris, Yurisich, Mangin, Melbourne SO, Cavdarski.

Walton's brilliant adaptation of Chekhov's one-act farce with its array of parodies makes ideal material for LP. This Australian recording lacks some of the wit of the original-cast recording (not currently available), but with first-rate sound and clean-cut, youthful-sounding singing it is well worth investigating. The tape is vivid, but there is an occasional hint of peaking.

Ward, John (1571–1638)

4 Fantasias for viols; 1st Set of English madrigals.
*** O-L D 238 D 2 (2). Cons. of Musicke, Rooley.

Ward's music speaks with a distinctive voice free from the self-conscious melancholy that afflicts some of his contemporaries. This is not to say that his output is wanting in depth of feeling or elegiac sentiment, but rather that his language is freer from artifice. He chooses poetry of high quality and his music is always finely proportioned and organic in conception. His achievement is well summed up by Richard Luckett's note about the poems: 'Together they make up an exploration of a sombre, pastoral world, a darkened Arcadia where the shepherds' eclogues are predominantly elegiac, and pain and loss in love are shaded by a sense of the pain and loss of death.' Many of the madrigals are eloquent and they are intelligently interspersed with instrumental fantasias. Anthony Rooley does not disturb the composer's own layout of the madrigals, and one can observe the growth from three-part settings which are lighter in mood to the more searching and powerful six-part madrigals. John Ward served the Honourable Henry Fanshawe as both Attorney and Musician, and his madrigals are dedicated to him. They appeared at the end of the period in which the madrigal flourished (in 1613, to be exact) but are by no means to be regarded as representing the tradition at anything less than its finest. These performances are dedicated and eminently well recorded, though the rather close balance and the vibrato-less vocal quality make it desirable not to hear too many at one sitting.

Warlock, Peter (1894–1930)

Capriol suite for strings.
**(*) Abbey ABY 810. Scottish Bar. Ens., Friedman – BRITTEN: *Simple symphony* **(*); ELGAR: *Serenade* **; WILLIAMSON: *English lyrics.* **(*)
(M) ** HMV SXLP 30126. RPO, Sargent – HOLST: *Beni Mora* etc.; ELGAR: *Serenade.* **

Capriol suite; Serenade for strings (*for the sixtieth birthday of Delius*).
*** Argo ZRG/*KZRC* 881 [id.]. ASMF, Marriner – VAUGHAN WILLIAMS: *Concertos.* ***

In an age when early and baroque music has become so popular on record, Warlock's suite based on Elizabethan dances seemed to have lost some of its popularity, but the availability of two new recordings and one reissue confirms its vitality and appeal.

On Argo the playing of the St Martin's Academy under Marriner is characteristically polished and stylish and no less readily reveals the freshness and memorability of Warlock's inspiration. This performance is well coupled with the gentle *Serenade* written for Delius and two larger Vaughan Williams works. The recording is first-rate, and the cassette approaches demonstration standard.

The Scottish Baroque Ensemble's forthright and lively style is quite well suited to Warlock's confection of dance movements and is well recorded. The couplings are unexpected but imaginative.

Sargent's tempi are broad and he brings out the richness of harmony and the music's dignified sonority rather than investing the score with any special vitality; but with such excellent string-playing and a warm recording, this is very enjoyable.

The Curlew (song cycle). Songs: *The Birds; Chopcherry; The fairest May; Mourne no more; My ghostly fader; Nursery jingles* (*How many miles to Babylon?; O, my kitten; Little Jack Jingle; Suky, you shall be my wife; Jenny Gray*)*; Sleep; The Water Lily.*
**(*) Pearl SHE 510. [id.], Griffet, Haffner Qt, Murdoch, Ryan.

Though this performance of *The Curlew* is not so beautiful or quite so imaginative as Ian Partridge's (deleted) version, it is good to have a whole record of songs by a composer with a strikingly distinctive feeling for English verse. Each one of these songs is a miniature of fine sensitivity, and James Griffett sings them with keen insight, pointing the words admirably. Good recording.

'Merry-go-down' (anthology): *Capriol; Tordion; Mattachins. Hey troly loly lo; Fill the cup; In an arbour green; Sweet content; Prosdocimus de Beldamandis Snr. Cod-pieces: Beethoven's binge; The old codger. Peter Warlock's fancy; I asked a thief to steal me a peach; Jillian of Berry; My ghostly fader; Away to Twiver; Mother's ruin; Drunken song in the Saurian mode.* E. J. Moeran and Warlock: *Maltworms.* Oinophilus: *In good company.* Aristotle: *An observation on beer-drinkers.* Nashe: *Eight kinds of drunkenness.* Whythorne: *As thy shadow itself apply'th.* Dowland: *My Lady Hunsdon's puffe; Mrs White's nothing.* Blunt: *The drunken wizard.* Beaumont and Fletcher: *The Knight of the Burning Pestle* (excerpts). Rosseter: *When Laura smiles.* Ravenscroft: *Malt's come down; The maid she went a-milking; By a bank as I lay; Jinkin the Jester; What hap had I to marry a shrew; He that will an alehouse keep.* Anon., ed. Warlock: *Have you seen but a white lily grow?; One more river; Wine v. women; The lady's birthday.* Warlock, arr. Tomlinson: *Piggesnie.*
*** Pearl SHE 525. Ian Partridge, Taylor, Jennifer Partridge, Gray (speaker), J. Partridge, Tomlinson (piano duet).

Songs, partsongs, rounds and readings from a Warlock anthology – a delightful collection, with specially fine singing from Ian Partridge. Fascinating too are the piano duets, including parodies of Beethoven and Franck. An oddity worth investigating, well recorded.

Wassenaer, Unico (1692–1766)

6 Concerti armonici.
*** Argo Dig. **410 205-2**; KZRDL/*KZRDC* 1002. ASMF, Marriner.
(M) **(*) Ph. 6768 163/*7699 146* (2) [id.]. Carmirelli, I Musici – PERGOLESI: *Concertos.* **(*)
//(*) DG Arc. 2533 456 [id./*3310 456*]. Camerata Bern, Furi.

These six concertos have been ascribed variously to Ricciotti, Birckenstock and Handel – and were originally attributed to Pergolesi. It now seems that they were the work of Count van Wassenaer and that he lent them to Ricciotti, who played the violin at their first performance. He modestly withheld them from publication, but this did not prevent Ricciotti from going ahead and engraving them, putting the name of the then popular Pergolesi on the title-page so as to facilitate their dissemination.

Neville Marriner and the Academy of St Martin-in-the-Fields are nothing if not spacious. They bring both dignity and warmth to these remarkable pieces, and they are sumptuously recorded too. They combine opulence of tone with genuine feeling and make a clear first choice in this repertoire. The compact disc is first-class too, though it is not markedly superior to the LP. The chrome cassette is very well managed, its upper focus fractionally less clean than CD and LP. But the sound still combines fullness with delicacy of detail.

The enjoyable I Musici performances match vigorous allegros with an agreeable sentient warmth in slow movements, underlining the stylistic source of the music as being associated with southern rather than northern Italy. There is plenty of sunshine here, and the nobility in the expressive writing that has kept these concertos in the repertoire is not missed. Compared with the Argo set, this set has an economic disadvantage, but the sound is rich and spacious, as well as clear, both on disc and tape, although the cassettes benefit from a reduction of bass.

The Swiss ensemble give performances of impeccable style and accuracy, though in the slow movements they miss something of the breadth and spaciousness inherent in the writing. The Camerata players are fewer in number than the Stuttgart Chamber Orchestra, who recorded these works together with a couple of flute concertos in the 1960s, on two as opposed to one record (that set is currently withdrawn). The DG Archiv recording is excellent.

Weber, Carl (1786–1826)

Clarinet concertos Nos. 1 in F min., Op. 73; 2 in E flat, Op. 74.
(B) ** RCA VICS/*VK* 2003 [AGL 1/*AGK 1* 3788]. Goodman, Chicago SO, Martinon.

Clarinet concertos Nos. 1; 2; Clarinet concertino in C min., Op. 26.
(*) Chan. **CHAN 8305; ABRD/*ABTD* 1058 [id.]. Hilton, CBSO, Järvi.
(*) HM Orfeo **CO 67831A; SO 67831A. Brunner, Bamberg SO, Caetani.

Clarinet concerto No. 1; Clarinet concertino.
*** HMV ASD 2455 [Ang. S 36589]. De Peyer, New Philh. O, Frühbeck de Burgos.

Clarinet concerto No. 2.
(M) ** O-L SOL 60035 [id.]. De Peyer, LSO, Sir Colin Davis – SPOHR: *Concerto No. 1.* **

These are charming pieces that require, and here receive, great elegance in performance. On HMV Gervase de Peyer plays the virtuoso solo parts with studied ease, and the orchestral support is as alert and lively as one could ask for. The recordings are reasonably wide in range and produce an agreeably warm sound.

Gervase de Peyer's earlier recording of No. 2 on Oiseau-Lyre is rather dry, and the clarinet suffers slightly from exaggeration of its upper partials by the close microphone. However, a treble reduction can correct this to a considerable extent, and the piece makes an excellent foil to its Spohr coupling, with de Peyer fully up to the work's bravura, especially the infectious finale, packed with fireworks.

Stylish, understanding performances of both concertos from Janet Hilton, spirited and rhythmic (particularly in No. 1), but erring just a little on the side of caution next to her finest virtuoso rivals. With full, well-balanced digital recording and nice matching between soloist and orchestra, it certainly outshines others in sound with an excellent matching cassette. This record is generous in including the engaging *Concertino* alongside the two concertos, a piece made famous in far-off 78 r.p.m. days by a Columbia record by the Garde Républicain Band of France with the solo part played with great bravura by all members of the first clarinet line in unison.

Eduard Brunner offers the same coupling as Janet Hilton. His performances are often more romantically ardent, with a firmer line. Both slow movements come off especially well with the horn chorale in the *Adagio* of the *First Concerto* producing some lovely playing from the Bamberg orchestra. However, articulation of the fast running passages is sometimes less characterful and Janet Hilton finds rather more humour in the finales, especially the *Alla Pollacca* of No. 2. Yet Brunner is at his best in the last movement of the *Concertino*, his bravura agreeably extrovert here. Where the Chandos issue scores is in the recording which, especially on the compact disc, is more open and transparent whereas on the Orfeo CD orchestral textures are thick in tuttis.

On RCA a welcome first issue in the UK of Benny Goodman's early stereo coupling of the two Weber *Clarinet concertos*. As we know from his Mozart recordings, when Goodman plays 'straight clarinet' (his term) he strictly avoids any jazz overtones, and to be honest there is an element of self-consciousness here. But there is technical wizardry too, especially in the jocular finales. The recording balance is forward, with dated orchestral sound and an edge to the clarinet timbre, but this remains a fascinating issue. There is no appreciable difference in sound between the disc and the excellent chrome cassette.

Introduction and theme and variations for clarinet and orchestra.

(M) *** Decca Ace SDD 575. Schmidl, New V. Octet – BRAHMS: *Clarinet quintet.* ***

*** DG Dig. 410 670-1/*4* [id.]. Meyer, Berlin Philh. Qt – MOZART: *Clarinet quintet.* ***

This piece attributed to Weber is now known to be the work of Joseph Küffner (1777–1856) and is listed here for convenience. It is an effective but unimportant brief display work, essentially lightweight, and Peter Schmidl's creamy tone and infectiously fluent style make the very most of it.

The recording by Sabine Meyer and the Berlin Philharmonia is first-rate, too, and very well balanced and recorded. This coupling is available in America on a Denon compact disc [**38C37 7038**].

Invitation to the dance, Op. 65 (orch. Berlioz).

(M) *** DG Sig. 2543/*3343* 534. Berlin PO, Karajan – BERLIOZ: *Symphony fantastique.* *(*)

Weber's *Invitation to the dance* is played with great elegance and panache under Karajan and well recorded too, but it is harnessed to his earlier, unsuccessful version of the *Symphonie fantastique.* There is an excellent account of the Weber piece by Boskovsky and the Vienna Symphony Orchestra in a mid-priced collection called '*Symphonic waltzes*' (HMV ESD/*TC-ESD* 173172-1/*4* – see our Concerts section below).

Konzertstück in F min., Op. 79.

*** Ph. **412 251-2**; 9500 677/*7300 772* [id.]. Brendel, LSO, Abbado – SCHUMANN: *Piano concerto.* ***

Weber's programmatic *Konzertstück* is seldom heard in the concert hall these days, and it is a rarity in the recording studio. This version is very brilliant indeed and finds the distinguished soloist in his very best form: he is wonderfully light and invariably imaginative. In every respect, including the recording quality, this is unlikely to be surpassed for a long time. The cassette has less sparkle and transparency than the disc but is well balanced.

Overtures: Der Freischütz; Oberon.
(M) *** DG Priv. *3335 393.* Bav. RSO, Kubelik – MENDELSSOHN: *Midsummer Night's Dream.* ***

Weber's two most famous overtures, excellently played by the Bavarian Radio Orchestra under Kubelik, are included as fillers on the cassette version (only) of Kubelik's admirable record of Mendelssohn's *Midsummer Night's Dream* incidental music. This gives the cassette a great advantage over the disc, for the sound is well engineered.

Overture: *Oberon.*
**(*) Decca SXL 6830 [Lon. CS 7050]. Chicago SO, Solti – BEETHOVEN; *Symphony No. 4.* **(*)

Solti's performance is brilliantly played, with a beautiful opening horn solo. The tension is extremely tightly held, and some of the music's romantic feeling is lost with such a degree of tautness. The recording is first-class.

Symphonies Nos. 1 in C; 2 in C.
*** ASV DCA/*ZCDCA* 515 [Van. 25018]. ASMF, Marriner.

Weber's two symphonies were written within a period of two months between December 1806 and the end of January 1807. Curiously both are in C major, yet each has its own individuality and neither lacks vitality of invention. Marriner has their full measure, and these performances combine vigour and high spirits with the right degree of gravitas (not too much) in the slow movements. The orchestral playing throughout is infectiously lively and catches the music's vibrant character. The recording is first-class, and the cassette transfer is admirably bright and full.

Clarinet quintet in B flat, Op. 34.
*** O-L DSLO 553. Hacker, Music Party – KROMMER: *Clarinet quartet.* ***
(M) **(*) HMV HQS/*TC-HQS* 1395. De Peyer, Melos Ens. – MOZART: *Clarinet quintet.* **(*)
(M) ** Ph. 6570/*7310* 882. Stahr, members of Berlin PO Octet – SPOHR: *Nonet.* **(*)

(i) *Clarinet quintet;* (ii) *Flute trio in G min.* (for flute, cello and piano), *Op. 63.*
*** CRD CRD 1098/*CRDC 4098* [id.]. (i) Pay, (ii) Judith Pearce; Nash Ens.

Weber's *Clarinet quintet* is very much dominated by the clarinet; on the CRD version Anthony Pay makes the very most of its bravura, catching the exuberance of the *Capriccio* third movement (as unlike a classical minuet as could possibly be managed) and the breezy gaiety of the finale. The Nash players provide an admirable partnership and then adapt themselves readily to the different mood of the Trio, another highly engaging work with a picturesque slow movement, described as a *Shepherd's lament.* The recording is first-class, vivid yet well balanced, and the cassette transfer is exceptionally lively.

If you want to hear how Weber's *Clarinet quintet* must have sounded during his lifetime, Alan Hacker and the Music Party will be your first choice. The Gerock clarinet Hacker uses is from 1804, eleven years earlier than the first complete performance of the *Quintet.* It is not of course the smooth, mellifluous instrument that Gervase de Peyer uses in his version, and the strings do not sound as blended as one would expect in a modern quartet. Alan Hacker plays with his customary artistry and sensitivity, and the recording is clear and vivid.

For its medium-priced reissue the HMV recording has been generously re-coupled with a recommendable performance of the Mozart *Clarinet quintet.* The performance of the Weber, with its extrovert dotted rhythms in the first movement and almost bucolic scherzo, is very assured, and the bravura playing in the finale is memorable. However, there is a slight lack of warmth here, caused partly by the recording acoustic, which is vivid but slightly dry. On its original issue the cassette was disfigured by harmonic distortion caused by a marginally too high transfer level. Later copies may well have been improved in this respect.

Herbert Stahr is the soloist in the Berlin Philharmonic performance and he is at his finest in the slow movement. Elsewhere the performance, though thoroughly musical, could do with more dash. The recording is very good, on tape and disc alike.

OPERA

Euryanthe (complete).
*** EMI 2C 165 02951/4 [Ang. SDL 3764]. Norman, Hunter, Gedda, Krause, Leipzig R. Ch., Dresden State O, Janowski.

Much has been written about the absurdity of the plot of *Euryanthe*, as unlikely a tale of the age of chivalry and troubadours as you will find; but, as this fine recording bears out, the opera is far more than just a historic curiosity. The juxtaposition of the two sopranos, representing good and evil, is formidably effective, particularly when as here the challenge is taken by singers of the stature of Jessye Norman and Rita Hunter. Hunter may not be the most convincing villainess, but the cutting edge of the voice is marvellous, and as for Jessye Norman, she sings radiantly, whether in her first delicate cavatina or the big aria of Act III. Tom Krause as the villain, Lysiart, has rarely sung better, and Nicolai Gedda, as ever, is the most intelligent of tenors. Good, atmospheric recording (as important in this opera as in *Freischütz*) and direction from Marek Janowski which makes light of any longueurs.

Der Freischütz (complete).
*** EMI 1C 149 30171/3. Grümmer, Otto, Schock, Prey, Frick, Ch. of Berlin Op., Berlin PO, Keilberth.
*** DG 2720 071/*3371 008* [2709046/*id.*]. Janowitz, Mathis, Schreier, Adam, Vogel, Crass, Leipzig R. Ch., Dresden State O, Carlos Kleiber.
**(*) Decca D 235 D3/*K 235 K 32* (3/*2*) [Lon. OSA/*5*- 13136]. Behrens, Donath, Meven, Kollo, Moll, Brendel, Bav. R. Ch. and SO, Kubelik.

None of the subsequent recordings of Weber's magical opera have quite caught the atmosphere of the piece as memorably as Keilberth's early stereo set from the beginning of the 1960s. This is a warm, exciting account which makes all the dated conventions of the piece seem fresh and new. In particular the Wolf's Glen Scene acquires something of the genuine terror that must have struck the earliest audiences, and which is far more impressive than any mere scene-settings with wood and cardboard in the opera house. The casting of the magic bullets with each one numbered in turn, at first in eerie quiet and then in crescendo amid the howling of demons, is superbly conveyed.

As for the cast, Elizabeth Grümmer sings wonderfully sweetly, with Agathe's prayer exquisitely done. Lisa Otto is not ideally agile vocally, but she is well in character, with genuine coquettishness. Schock is less than the perfect tenor casting for Max, but he sings ably enough, while the Kaspar of Karl Kohn is well focused and genuinely evil-sounding. The playing of the Berlin Philharmonic has admirable polish and the dialogue is excellently done, so that even if one's German is limited, the development of the story is made perfectly clear. While the newer DG set is also very fine and has the advantage of more modern recording, the EMI quality is vivid with an attractive overall bloom.

The DG set marked Carlos Kleiber's first major recording venture. The young conductor, son of a famous father, had already won himself a reputation for inspiration and unpredictability, and this fine, incisive account of Weber's atmospheric and adventurous score fulfilled all expectations. With the help of an outstanding cast, excellent work by the recording producer, and electrically clear recording, this is a most compelling version of an opera which transfers well to the gramophone. Only occasionally does Kleiber betray a fractional lack of warmth. Although this was a very early transfer, one of the first operas DG issued on tape in Dolby form, the quality is surprisingly good, with a generally clear focus and natural projection of the soloists. The opera's closing scene is notably well managed, and here the full, vivid sound approaches demonstration standard. The layout on three cassettes follows the discs.

Kubelik takes a direct view of Weber's high romanticism. The result has freshness but lacks something in dramatic bite and atmosphere. There is far less tension than in the finest earlier versions, not least in the Wolf's Glen Scene, which in spite of full-ranging, brilliant recording seems rather tame. The singing is generally good – René Kollo as Max giving one of his best performances on record – but Hildegard Behrens, superbly dramatic in later German operas, here as Agathe seems clumsy in music that often requires a pure lyrical line. The cassettes offer demonstration quality, crisp, vivid and clear, and the tape layout on four sides is preferable to that on disc. However, the DG set with Janowitz, Mathis, Schreier, Adam, Vogel and Crass is much more enjoyable; Carlos Kleiber may have his extreme tempi in places, but his is an electrifying reading of an opera that must be played and sung for all it is worth.

Oberon: complete.
(M) *** DG Priv. 2726 052 (2) [id. PSI]. Grobe, Nilsson, Domingo, Prey, Hamari, Schiml, Bav. R. Ch. and SO, Kubelik.

Rarely has operatic inspiration been squandered so cruelly on impossible material as in Weber's *Oberon.* We owe it to Covent Garden's strange ideas in the mid-1820s of what 'English opera' should be that Weber's delicately conceived score is a sequence of illogical arias, scenas and ensembles strung together by an absurd pantomime plot. Though even on record the result is slacker because of that loose construction, one can appreciate, in a performance as stylish and refined as this, the contribution of Weber. The original issue included dialogue and a narration spoken by one of Oberon's fairy characters. In the reissue this is omitted, cutting the number of discs required from three to two, yet leaving the music untouched. With Birgit Nilsson commanding in *Ocean, thou mighty monster* and excellent singing from the other principals, helped by Kubelik's ethereally light handling of the orchestra, the set can be recommended without reservation, for the recording remains of excellent quality.

Webern, Anton (1883–1945)

(i) *Concerto, Op. 24; 5 Movements for string quartet* (orchestral version), *Op. 5; Passacaglia, Op. 1; 6 Pieces for large orchestra, Op. 6; 5 pieces for orchestra, Op. 10; Symphony, Op. 21; Variations for orchestra, Op. 30;* Arrangements of: the *Fugue* from Bach's *Musical Offering* (1935); (ii) Schubert's *German dances* (for small orchestra), *Op. posth.* Chamber music: (iii) *6 Bagatelles for string quartet, Op. 9; 5 Movements for string quartet, Op. 5;* (iv; v) *4 Pieces for violin and piano, Op. 7;* (v; vi) *3 Small pieces for cello and piano, Op. 11;* (v; vii) *Quartet, Op. 22* (for piano, violin, clarinet, saxophone); (iii) *String quartet, Op. 28; String trio, Op. 20;* (v) *Variations for piano, Op. 27.* (Vocal) (viii; i) *Das Augenlicht, Op. 26;* (ix; x) *5 Canons on Latin texts, Op. 16;* (viii; ix; i) *Cantata No. 1, Op. 29;* (viii; ix; xi; i) *Cantata No. 2, Op. 31;* (viii) *Entflieht auf leichten Kähnen, Op. 2;* (ix; x) *5 Sacred songs, Op. 15;* (xii; v) *5 Songs, Op. 3; 5 Songs, Op. 4;* (xii; x) *2 Songs, Op. 8;* (xii; v) *4 Songs, Op. 12;* (xii; x) *4 Songs, Op. 13;* (xii; x) *6 Songs, Op. 14;* (ix; x; xiii) *3 Songs, Op. 18;* (viii; i) *2 Songs, Op. 19;* (xii; v) *3 Songs, Op. 23;* (ix; v) *3 Songs, Op. 25;* (ix; x) *3 Traditional rhymes.*
*** CBS 79402 (4) [Col. M4 35193]. (i) LSO (or members), Boulez; (ii) Frankfurt RO, composer (recorded Dec. 1932); (iii) Juilliard Qt (or members); (iv) Stern; (v) Rosen; (vi) Piatigorsky; (vii) Majeske, Marcellus, Weinstein; (viii) John Alldis Ch.; (ix) Lukomska; (x) with Ens., Boulez; (xi) McDaniel: (xii) Harper; (xiii) with John Williams. Overall musical direction: Boulez.

These four discs contain all of Webern's works with opus numbers, as well as the string orchestra arrangement of Op. 5 and the orchestration of the *Fugue* from Bach's *Musical Offering.* A rare recording of Webern himself conducting his arrangement of Schubert dances is also included. Though the recording quality varies – different items having been made over eleven years – the quality of performance remains very high, and, more important, almost all these performances convey the commitment without which such spare writing can sound merely chill. What Pierre Boulez above all demonstrates in the orchestral works (including those with chorus) is that, for all his seeming asceticism, Webern was working on human emotions. The spareness of the writing lets us appreciate how atonality can communicate tenderly, evocatively, movingly, not by any imitation of romantic models (as Schoenberg's and Berg's music often does) but by reducing the notes to the minimum. The Juilliard Quartet and the John Alldis Choir, too, convey comparable commitment, and though neither Heather Harper nor Halina Lukomska is ideally cast in this music, Boulez brings out the best in both of them in the works with orchestra. Rarely can a major composer's whole *œuvre* be appreciated within so compact a span. This set can be warmly recommended to anyone who wants to understand one of the key figures of the twentieth century.

5 Movements, Op. 5; Passacaglia, Op. 1; 6 Pieces for orchestra, Op. 6; Symphony, Op. 21.
*** DG 2711 014 (4) [id.]. Berlin PO, Karajan – BERG: *Lyric suite; 3 Pieces;* SCHOENBERG: *Pelleas und Melisande; Variations; Verklaerte Nacht.****

In the four-disc collection of music of the Second Viennese School, this last disc, devoted to four compact and chiselled Webern works, is in many ways the most remarkable of all. Karajan's expressive refinement reveals the emotional undertones behind this seemingly austere music, and the results are riveting – as for example in the dramatic and intense *Funeral march* of Op. 6. Op. 21 is altogether more difficult to grasp, but Karajan still conveys the intensity of argument even to the unskilled ear. Outstanding recording quality.

5 Movements, Op. 5.
*** Argo ZRG 763. ASMF, Marriner – HINDEMITH: *5 Pieces;* SCHOENBERG: *Verklaerte Nacht.****

Where with *Verklaerte Nacht* Marriner has the best of both worlds, here, with more sharply etched writing, he cannot hope to match the original string-quartet medium in clarity and bite. The music is inevitably made more romantic, but with dedicated playing the result is deeply satisfying. Excellent recording.

Passacaglia for orchestra; 5 Pieces for orchestra; 6 Pieces for orchestra; Symphony; Variations for Orchestra. Bach: *Musical Offering: Fugue* (arr. for orchestra by Webern).
*** CBS 76911/*40*-. LSO, Boulez.

This excellent disc gathers together all of Webern's purely orchestral works recorded by Boulez for the integral edition. Balances are not always ideal, but hearing the whole range of Webern's mature career, from the *Passacaglia* of 1908 – written before twelve-note serialism was fully formulated – through to the *Variations* of 1940, one can appreciate his development the more sympathetically. Boulez in this music conveys expressiveness as well as clarity. The cassette is full-bodied and has quite good detail, but lacks the upper range of the LP (noticeable when the strings are muted).

3 Pieces for orchestra; (i) *Im Sommerwind.*
(M) ** CBS 60258/*40*-. Phd. O, Ormandy, (i) with Luisa de Sett – BERG: *Lulu: suite;* SCHOENBERG: *Theme and variations.***

The *Three Pieces for Orchestra* were discarded from Op. 10 and only came to light in the mid-1960s. Ormandy and the Philadelphia Orchestra gave them their first performance in 1967 and precede them here with *Im Sommerwind*, an early work from 1904, very much in the style of Strauss and early Schoenberg. The two pieces could hardly be more strongly contrasted. The playing is rather impressive, with sumptuous string tone and fine blended wind and brass. However, the last ounce of subtlety is missing and the two-dimensional recording must be noted. All the same the disc is worth having and there are no alternative recordings outside the Boulez complete set. There is an excellent chrome tape.

6 Bagatelles for string quartet, Op. 9; 5 Movements for string quartet, Op. 5; Slow movement for string quartet (1905); String quartet (1905); String quartet, Op. 28.
(M) *** Ph. 6570/*7310* 925. Italian Qt.

Readers who quail at the name of Webern need not tremble at the prospect of hearing this record. The early music in particular is most accessible, and all of it is played with such conviction and beauty of tone that its difficulties melt away or at least become manageable. The recording is of outstanding vividness and presence, and it is difficult to imagine a more eloquent or persuasive introduction to Webern's chamber music than this. The cassette transfer is faithful and, although not at the highest level, the sound is both warm and clear.

Weelkes, Thomas (*c.* 1575–1623)

Alleluia; Give ear, O Lord; Hosanna to the son of David; I heard a voice; Nunc dimittis (in 5 parts); *When David heard; Organ voluntary.*
(B) **(*) Con. CC/*CCT* 7591. Ch. of St John's College, Camb., Guest; White (organ) – TALLIS: *Collection.***(*)

There is some beautiful music here, and the programme provides plenty of contrast. The two anthems, *Alleluia* and *Hosanna*, are forthright and full of conviction, while *Give ear, O Lord* is appropriately more withdrawn in style. The reconstructed *Nunc dimittis* and the moving lament, *When David heard*, both show the composer at his most imaginative. The singing here is more consistently satisfying then on the Tallis side of the disc, although the anthems might have sounded more joyous. The recording has plenty of atmosphere, and there is a high-level matching tape, every bit as good as the disc.

Weill, Kurt (1900–1950)

(i) *Violin concerto; Kleine Dreigroschenmusik* (Suite for wind orchestra from *The Threepenny Opera*).
(M) *** DG 2543 808 [id.]. (i) Lidell, L. Sinf., Atherton.

Weill's *Concerto* for violin and wind instruments is an early work, written not long after the *First Symphony* and after he had finished his studies with Busoni and Jarnach. It was written for Szigeti though not first performed by him, and during the 1920s was one of his most widely played pieces. It is resourceful and inventive, the product of a fine intelligence and a good craftsman. The style is somewhat angular (as was the young Hindemith) but the textures are always clear and the invention holds the listener's attention throughout. It is splendidly played by Nona Lidell and the wind of the London Sinfonietta, and well recorded too. The *Suite* from *The Threepenny Opera* occupies the first side and is given with good spirit and élan.

Symphonies Nos. 1–2.
(M) **(*) Ph. Seq. 6527/*7311* 225. Leipzig GO, De Waart.

De Waart's readings of these two fascinating works, the first amazingly assured for a 'prentice piece, the second masterly and original, lack something in the bite and intensity which Weill demands, but with fine ensemble and first-rate solo playing presented in warm sound, it is more than a stopgap. The cassette transfer is lively and matches the disc quite closely.

(i) *Der Dreigroschenoper* (*The Threepenny Opera*): complete. (ii) Songs: *Berlin Requiem: Ballade vom ertrunken Mädchen. Happy End: Bilbao song; Surabaya Johnny; Matrosen Tango. Mahagonny: Havanna Lied; Alabama song; Wie mann sich bettet. Der Silbersee; Lied der Fennimore.*
*** CBS 78279/*40*- (2) [Odys. Y2 32977]. (i) Lenya, Neuss, Trenk-Trebisch, Hesterberg, Schellow, Koczian, Grunert, Ch. and Dance O of Radio Free Berlin, Brückner-Rüggeberg; (ii) Lenya, O, Bean.

This is a vividly authentic recording of *The Threepenny Opera*, Weill's most famous score, darkly incisive and atmospheric, with Lotte Lenya giving an incomparable performance as Jenny. All the wrong associations built up round the music from indifferent performances melt away in the face of a reading as sharp and intense as this. Bright, immediate, real stereo recording. The songs make a marvellous filler on the fourth side, and although here the stereo is simulated the sound has plenty of atmosphere. The cassettes are on chrome tape and transferred at a high level, so that the sound is extremely vivid. The packaging is good and the booklet/libretto readable.

Happy End (play by Brecht with songs).
*** CBS 73463 [CSP COS 2032]. Lenya, Ch. and O, Brückner-Rüggeberg.

Happy End, intended as a successor to *The Threepenny Opera*, yet more savagely cynical, took far longer to be appreciated. Lotte Lenya, Weill's widow, has here turned the songs into a kind of cycle (following a hint by the composer and transposing where necessary), and her renderings in her individual brand of vocalizing are so compelling they make the scalp tingle. Many of these numbers are among the finest Weill ever wrote. Text and notes by David Drew, and forward, bright recording.

The Rise and fall of Mahagonny (complete).
(M) **(*) CBS 77341/*40*- (3). Lenya, Litz, Gunter, Mund, Gollnitz, Markworth, Saverbaum, Roth, Murch (speaker), NW German R. Ch. and O, Brückner-Rüggeberg.

Though Lotte Lenya, with her metallic, rasping voice, was more a characterful diseuse than a singer, and this bitterly inspired score had to be adapted to suit her limited range, it remains a most memorable performance. This began a whole series of Weill recordings, and like the later ones this lacks atmosphere, with voices (Lenya's in particular) close balanced. Even now one can understand how this cynical piece caused public outrage when it was first performed in Leipzig in 1930. The cassettes are well transferred and excellently packaged, with a first-class booklet-libretto.

Das Sieben Todsunden (*The seven deadly sins*) complete.
*** HMV ASD/*TCC-ASD* 4402. Ross, Rolfe Johnson, Caley, Rippon, Tomlinson, CBSO, Rattle.
(***) CBS mono 73657. Lenya, Male Quartets and O, Brückner-Rüggeberg.

Rattle's moving account of this Brecht–Weill collaboration gives it a tender but refreshing new look. The key point is the casting of Elise Ross as the two Annas, the one idealistic, the other practical, who in this sharply drawn sequence visit various American cities and their respective deadly sins. The final epilogue brings them back where they started, beside the Mississippi in Louisiana; and the agony of disillusion is presented with total heartache, thanks to Miss Ross's acting. Her singing is sweet and tender, far less aggressive than Lotte Lenya's, and though Rattle's direction is sharp and analytical, the spring in the rhythm and nicely judged expressiveness of phrase give a warmth which may not please all dedicated Weill enthusiasts, but brings out the work's often Mahlerian intensity. Full, warm digital recording. Our copy of the iron-oxide cassette was unsatisfactory.

Originally recorded in mono in the mid-1950s, the CBS performance with the composer's widow as the principal singer underlines the status of this distinctive mixture of ballet and song-cycle as one of Weill's most concentrated inspirations. The rhythmic verve is irresistible, and though Lenya had to have the music transposed down, her understanding of the idiom is unique. The recording is harsh by modern standards.

Weinberger, Jaromir
(1896–1967)

Svanda the Bagpiper (opera): complete.
*** CBS 79344 (3) [M3 36926]. Prey, Popp, Jerusalem, Killebrew, Malta, Nimsgern, Bav. R. Ch., Munich R. O, Wallberg.

The famous polka set the seal on the immediate international success of this colourful updating of the *Bartered Bride* formula. Weinberger wrote it when he was thirty, but never acquired anything like the same popularity again. He went to America, where in 1967 in disillusion he committed suicide. None of that sadness comes out in the frothy mixture of *Svanda*, a folk-tale involving a robber charmer who woos beautiful young Dorotka, wife of Svanda. The supernatural is lightly invoked in a trip to hell (Svanda the charmer there) with the devil introduced. Prey (as Svanda), Popp (as his wife) and Jerusalem (as Babinsky, the charmer) make a first-rate team of principals, lending musical flair as well as vocal glamour. Ensemble work is first-rate too, most important in this opera, with the polka taken rather slowly and bouncily. Good, full recording.

Wesley, Samuel (1766–1839)

Symphony in D.
(M) *** HMV Green. ESD/*TC-ESD* 106024-1/*4*. Bournemouth Sinf., Montgomery – ARNE: *Symphonies.****

As a child Samuel Wesley, one of the celebrated family of evangelists and musicians, was described as an English Mozart. That reputation still attached to him when, in 1784, at the age of eighteen he wrote this charming if unadventurous symphony. An excellent coupling to the rare and imaginative Arne symphonies on the reverse, beautifully performed and recorded. The full, resonant sound is well caught on the excellent cassette.

Whittaker, William
(1876–1944)

(i) *Among the Northumbrian Hills: free variations for piano quintet;* (ii) *Wind quintet;* (iii) *Anthem: I said in the noontide of my days.*
**(*) Viking VRSS 001. (i) L. Soloists Ens.; (ii) Amphion Wind Quintet; (iii) L. Soloists Vocal Ens.

William Gillies Whittaker, who spent his musical life in Newcastle-upon-Tyne, is best known for his arrangements of folksongs and (in his home city) as a skilled choral trainer, a champion of Bach and of contemporary English music. His own output is yet to be fully discovered. By no means a revolutionary, his voice was nevertheless an individual one, and all the music on this enterprising record yields increasing rewards on repeated hearings. The finest work is undoubtedly *Among the Northumbrian Hills* (1918), an ambitious set of eleven variations on an original theme (although a folksong is introduced into the seventh). Each of the movements has a title, and their strong individual identity brings a sense of fragmentation, for the theme itself becomes elusive until it returns elegiacally in the closing *Farewell*. It is in the evocation of the quiet sections that the writing becomes really haunting, with *Reflections* and the curiously unearthly *Midwinter* bringing an Ives-like atmospheric feeling, although Whittaker's musical language is not in any way 'difficult'. The performance is committed and responsive and certainly spontaneous, if lacking the last degree of polish. The *Wind quintet* (1931) is easy-going in its bright colours and engagingly complex yet mellifluous part-writing. It is admirably crafted, with attractive invention, and very well played.

The anthem is a setting of Isaiah concerning the penitence of King Hezekiah after he has recovered from a serious illness. From a powerfully sombre opening, the work steadily builds to a climax as the mood lightens to combine serenity and increasing jubilation. The performance has impressive colour and fervour although the brief soprano solo sounds a little unwieldy. With generally good if not outstanding recording, this is recommended to readers looking for twentieth-century music which communicates directly without needing to be self-consciously avant garde.

(i) *The Chief centurians;* (ii) *Chorus of spirits;* (i) *Memories of the northern moorlands* (song

cycle)*; O what saw you?;* (ii) *Psalm 139; Requiem aeternam; Shine! great sun!*
❀ *** Viking VPW 003. (i) Noble, Swallow; (ii) Hallé Ch., Handford.

With superlative singing from the Hallé Choir, inspired by their conductor, Maurice Handford, to performances of tingling immediacy, this record confirms the originality and individuality of Whittaker's music. The sustained ecstasy communicated in the early (1916) Whitman setting, *Shine! great sun!*, blossoms even more richly in the radiant *Requiem aeternam* (1935), while the *Chorus of spirits* (1930) – from Shelley's *Prometheus* – hardly lacks intensity, even if its mood is basically more subdued. Whittaker's masterpiece here is his inspired setting of *Psalm 139* (in the Robert Bridges version) for chorus and semi-chorus with an ad-lib organ accompaniment, balanced very discreetly. It is a work of great range and power, vividly atmospheric, yet never predictable. The climactic cries of *'Marvellous'* (*are Thy works*) have a Waltonian impact, yet Whittaker's style is in no way derived, while the closing pages bring a spiritual intensity almost to compare with *Gerontius*. Handford's performance is superbly dramatic and expressively compelling, with the spontaneous feel of a live occasion. Moreover the acoustic of the Great Hall of Manchester Town Hall, where the choral items were recorded, produces sound in the demonstration class; the choir's finely projected pianissimo singing is remarkably well defined while the climaxes have bite yet retain a full natural bloom.

The short song-cycle, *Memories of the northern moorlands*, written in 1928, offers settings of the Northumberland poet, W. W. Gibson, which uncannily anticipate Britten in their bleak atmospheric feeling. The performances by John Noble are direct rather than especially imaginative, but they capture the spare evocation well, and Keith Swallow's accompaniments are first-rate, effectively suggesting the rippling of *Tarras Water*, in the first of the four. The other songs are worth having on record too, especially *O what saw you*, also inspired by the 1914–18 War.

But it is the choral works which resonate most strongly in the memory and which led Holst to comment that Whittaker 'writes for the chorus as if he had neither heard nor seen an orchestra'.

Arrangements of folk songs: *Billy boy; Blow the wind southerly; Bobby Shaftoe; Bonny at morn; The bonny fisher lad; Ca' Hawkie; Chevy Chase; Derwentwater's farewell; Dollia; Doon the waggon way; Felton Lonnen; Gan to the kye wi' me; The Hexhamshire lass; The Keel Row; King Arthur's servants; Ma bonny lad; Madam, I will buy you; The Miller and his sons; Newburn lads; Noble squire dance; O! I hae seen the roses blaw; The shoemaker; Sir John Fenwick's the flower amang them all; The water of Tyne; The willow tree.*
** Viking VRW 002. Denis and Eleanor Weatherley; Aitchison, Senior; Butler (pipes); Sinfonia Ch., Fearon.

It is ironic that at the time when Whittaker's own music is being rediscovered, the concert arrangement of folksongs – on which his earlier reputation rested – is becoming less fashionable. Many will feel that any embellishment of *Blow the wind southerly* (which this collection chooses as its title) cannot be an improvement on a simple unaccompanied presentation, such as Kathleen Ferrier made famous. Yet here Whittaker's choral arrangement of *The water of Tyne*, with its perceptively fluent part-writing, is certainly beautiful, while *Newburn lads* is made to sound delightfully like a peal of bells. *The willow tree* and *The Hexhamshire lass* are both polyphonically rich, yet *Bobby Shaftoe* could hardly be more simple. The Sinfonia Chorus sing them eloquently, although the resonant recording takes some of the edge off the consonants. Other arrangements for solo voice and piano are given colloquial presentation by Marian Aitchison and Denis Weatherley (especially good in *King Arthur's servants*) and they join together in an engaging duet version of *Madam, I will buy you*, a variant on the more famous *Madam, will you walk and talk with me*, but with a different tune and given a virtuoso piano embroidery by Whittaker. The remainder of the programme is ably played on the Northumbrian pipes by Richard Butler.

Widor, Charles-Marie
(1844–1937)

Organ symphony No. 5 in F min., Op. 42/1.
(M) *** HMV HQS 1406 (with Grison: *Toccata in F.* Jongen: *Sonata eroica, Op. 94*). Parker-Smith (organ of Salisbury Cath.).
** None. H 71210 [id.]. Ellsasser (organ of Hammond Museum, Gloucester, Mass.).

Organ symphonies Nos. 5 (complete); *6 in G, Op. 42/2: 1st movt; 8 in B, Op 42/3: 4th movt.*
(M) *** Saga 5439. Sanger (organ of St Peter's Italian Church, Clerkenwell, London).

Organ symphonies Nos. 5; 10 (*Romane*), *Op. 73.*
*** Ph. Dig. **410 054-2**; 6769/*7654* 085 [id.]. Chorzempa (organ of St Sermin Basilica, Toulouse).

Daniel Chorzempa provides a massive demonstration of compact-disc opulence which should send the neighbours scurrying for cover if this CD is played at full volume. He chooses some agreeable registration for the amiable, earlier music of the *Fifth Symphony*, but at times one wonders if he does not overdo the dynamic range for domestic listening, for the gentle music is distanced and atmospheric to a great degree. Nonetheless he provides a highly energetic account of the famous *Toccata* which exudes a nice mixture of power and exuberance. The *Tenth Symphony* has its structure bound together by the Easter plainchant, *Haec Dies*, and after a pleasant *Cantilène* third movement the composer gathers up the threads of the music for another weighty finale; then the rhetoric suddenly evaporates and the piece ends gently. Chorzempa makes much of this effect (and the CD background silence helps) and seems entirely at home in this repertoire. The Cavaille-Coll organ is well chosen and the recording is excellent on LP as well as CD, although on the chrome tapes there are moments when the focus roughens under pressure. However, those interested mainly in the *Fifth Symphony* (and primarily its *Toccata*) may decide that to lay out the cost of two CDs is too much to pay, when other single-disc versions can also be recommended.

Jane Parker-Smith's account is every bit the equal of Chorzempa's and she too is very well recorded on disc, especially in her exhilarating *Toccata.*

Her encores are also very acceptable: Jules Grison's *Toccata* is suitably flamboyant, and the Jongen *Sonata eroica* is a well-made if not distinctive piece, also with a spectacular finale, which is played with fine flair.

David Sanger's account of the Widor symphony is first-class in every respect and recorded with fine bloom and clarity. His restraint in registering the central movements prevents Widor's cosy melodic inspiration from sounding banal, and the finale is exciting without sounding overblown. The other symphonic movements are well done, but serve to confirm the conclusion that the *Toccata* was Widor's one masterstroke.

Richard Ellsasser is an eloquent and musical advocate, but he seems reluctant to draw on his big guns even in the the *Toccata* itself, which here is comparatively restrained. The organ in use is a large-scale one (10,000 pipes, four manuals and 144 stops), built by John Hays Hammond in a stone tower of his castle home. The recording is admirable, faithful and easy to reproduce.

Organ symphony No. 5: Toccata.
C *** Argo Dig. **410 165-2**; ZRDL/*KZRDC* 1011 [id.]. Hurford (organ of Ratzeburg Cath.) – *Recital.**** C
(B) *** PRT GSGC/*ZCGC* 2014. Downes (organ of Royal Festival Hall, London) – BACH: *Recital.****

Those wanting the *Toccata* alone could not do better than choose Peter Hurford's exhilarating version, recorded with great presence and impact on a most attractive organ, and giving demonstration quality, whether compact disc, LP or chrome cassette is chosen.

Another brilliant performance, and one costing much less, comes from Ralph Downes. The recording dates from the earliest days of stereo (1958), but was in the demonstration class then and still sounds remarkably well. The stereo readily conveys the wide spatial displacement of the organ pipes in the Festival Hall. The excellent cassette matches the disc closely, and there is no crumbling.

Wieniawski, Henryk (1835–80)

Violin concertos Nos. 1 in F sharp min., Op. 14; 2 in D min., Op. 22.
*** HMV ASD 2870 [Ang. S/*4XS* 36903]. Perlman, LPO, Ozawa.

Those who have enjoyed the relatively well-known *Second Concerto* of this contemporary of Tchaikovsky should investigate this coupling of his two concertos. The *First* may not be so consistently memorable as the *Second*, but the central *Preghiera* is darkly intense, and the finale is full of the showmanship that was the mark of the composer's own virtuosity on the violin. Perlman gives scintillating performances, full of flair, and is excellently accompanied. First-rate recording.

Violin concerto No. 2 in D min., Op. 22.
*** DG Dig. **410 526-2**; 410 526-1/*4* [id.]. Perlman, O de Paris, Barenboim – SAINT-SAËNS: *Violin concerto No. 3.****

Perlman's new digital recording of the *D minor Concerto* offers playing that is effortlessly dazzling, yet he and Barenboim create an attractively songful *Andante*, so that the scintillating bravura of the *moto perpetuo* finale sounds even more dashing by contrast. Generally good recording, with a moderately forward balance for the soloist. There is an excellent chrome cassette. The compact disc offers the usual advantages but, as so often with DG, emphasizes that the balance is artificially contrived, with the soloist too close.

Wiklund, Adolf (1879–1950)

(i) *Piano concerto No. 2 in B min., Op. 17. 3 Pieces for strings and harp; Sang till varen.*
** Cap. CAP 1165. Swedish RSO, Westerberg, (i) with Erikson.

Wiklund belonged to the same generation of Swedish composers as Stenhammar, whose enthusiasm for Brahms he obviously shared. But if his music speaks with much the same accents as Alfvén and Stenhammar, it has none of the latter's nobility, and it is essentially second-rate. But there are good things in it: the *Concerto*, which dates from the war years, is effective in its way and well laid out for the piano, though it lacks any powerfully individual quality. The *Three Pieces for strings and harp* are more simple and have an unaffected post-Griegian charm.

Wikmanson, Johan (1753–1800)

String quartet in E min., Op. 1/2.
*** CRD CRD 1061/*CRDC 4061* [id.]. Chilingirian Qt – BERWALD: *Quartet.****

Wikmanson is less well-known than Berwald and never travelled outside his native Sweden. During the 1770s he studied with Johan Martin Kraus and published a Swedish translation of Tartini's *Traité des agréments de la musique*. Three of his five string quartets survive and were published in 1801, a year after his death. They bore a dedication to Haydn, whose good offices were enlisted to assist their publication, and whose influence is all-pervasive. Indeed, at first Wikmanson's quartets seem almost too heavily indebted to his idol, but as one gets to know them better, a more distinctive profile emerges and their rewards increase. The Chilingirian Quartet give a persuasive and eloquent account of this attractive score, and with the added inducement of a valuable coupling, this issue deserves the widest circulation. Excellent recording quality; the cassette too is full and clear, although very slightly overweighted at the bass end.

Wilbye, John (1574–1658)

Madrigals: First Set: excerpts: *Adieu, sweet Amarillis; Alas what a wretched life; Cruel behold my ending; Die hapless man; Lady, when I behold* (2 versions); *Lady, your words do spite me; My throat is sore; Of joys and pleasing pains; Thus saith my Cloris bright; Thou art but young; Weep O mine eyes; When shall my wretched life; Why dost thou shoot.* Second set: *Ah cannot sighs; Draw on sweet night; O wretched man; Softly O softly, drop my eyes; Stay, Corydon; Sweet honey suckling bees; Yes sweet, take heed; Ye that do live in pleasures.*
*** O-L DSLO 597. Cons. of Musicke, Rooley.

Here we have an anthology of madrigals by one of the major figures in the English music of the period; now that Peter Pears's record of twelve Wilbye madrigals is no longer in circulation, this record must be accounted the best introduction to Wilbye's art. Indeed its removal from the catalogue would seriously impair his representation on record. The most famous madrigals such as *Draw on sweet night* and *Stay, Corydon* are common to both, and those who have the earlier LP will probably not wish to make the change. In some ways the Consorte of Musicke is less persuasive than the Wilbye Consort on the earlier disc, but there is much that gives pleasure and the recording is very fine indeed.

Williams, Grace (1906–77)

(i) *Carillons for oboe and orchestra.* (ii) *Trumpet concerto. Fantasia on Welsh nursery rhymes.* (iii) *Fairest of Stars.*
*** Oriel CRM 1005. LSO, Groves, with (i) Camden, (ii) Snell, (iii) Janet Price.

It is good to find a composer who so glowingly showed that she believed in pleasing the listener's ear. The works here range attractively from the simple, well-known *Fantasia* (rather more than a colourfully orchestrated potpourri) through two crisply conceived concertante pieces to the relatively tough setting of Milton for soprano and orchestra, *Fairest of Stars*. The trumpet and oboe works – superbly played by soloists from the LSO – both show the affection and understanding of individual instrumental timbre which marked Grace Williams's work. It is a credit to the Welsh Arts Council that such a record could be produced. First-rate recording. (If difficulty is experienced in obtaining this record, it can be ordered direct from its sponsors.)

Penillon for orchestra.
*** Oriel ORM 1001. RPO, Groves – HODDINOTT: *Welsh dances*; JONES: *Country beyond the stars.* ***

'Penillon' is the Welsh word for stanza and though Grace Williams does not use any folk material she retains the idea of a central melodic line in stanza form in her set of four colourful and imaginative pieces. Excellent performances and recording.

Symphony No. 2; Ballads.
*** BBC REGL 381. BBC Welsh SO, Handley.

Grace Williams is best known for colourful atmospheric works like the *Fantasia on Welsh nursery rhymes*, and much of her early music reflects the folk-based approach instilled in her by her principal teacher, Vaughan Williams. But in this *Second Symphony*, her most ambitious orchestral work, written in 1956 when she was fifty, she aimed at greater astringency, just as Vaughan Williams himself had done in his *Fourth Symphony*. The writing is sharp and purposeful from the start, relaxing more towards lyricism in the slow movement and the finale with its darkly Mahlerian overtones. The *Ballads* of 1968, characteristically based on Welsh ballad and *penillion* forms, also reveal the darker side of Grace Williams's writing, notably in the stark contrasts of the third ballad. Expressive, convincing performances, originally recorded for radio.

Williams, John (born 1932)

Suites from: *Close Encounters of the Third Kind* (including new music for *Special Edition*); *The Empire Strikes Back; Star Wars; Superman.*

*** Ph. Dig. 9500 921/*7300 921* [id.]. Boston Pops O, composer.

Close Encounters of the Third Kind: suite; Star Wars: suite.

(M) **(*) RCA GL/*GK* 13650. Nat. PO, Gerhardt.

Suites from: *Close Encounters; E.T.; E.T. Returns; Star Wars.*

(B) ** MfP MFP/*TC-MFP 5594.* LSO, or Nat. PO, Barber.

This Philips record gathers together John Williams's four most famous film scores in an excellent digital recording under his own direction. While the music is eclectic in style and derivation, it is undoubtedly tuneful in a flamboyant way and spectacularly scored. This record tends to sweep the field in this repertoire, but the chrome tape is transferred at a low level and the quality is sumptuous and atmospheric rather than brilliant, with a lack of crispness in the transients.

Gerhardt too has the full measure of this music and the National Philharmonic plays marvellously for him: the sweeping strings have an eloquence in the best Hollywood tradition. He shows particular skill in the *Close Encounters* sequence, creating genuine tension and evocative feeling, while in *Star Wars* the theme for Princess Leia includes a horn solo which is played quite gorgeously, while the closing section has a *nobilmente* swagger. The RCA recording is bright but not so rich as the Philips. There is a good chrome cassette, with side two slightly sharper in focus than side one.

The Music for Pleasure disc is an excellent bargain compilation, even anticipating the return of *E.T.* The performances are lively and thoroughly competent, but do not display the flair of Williams or Gerhardt. The recording is vivid but slightly dry, with little difference in sound between disc and tape. Some will not like the battle effects included in *Star Wars.*

Williamson, Malcolm (born 1931)

(i) *Organ concerto;* (ii) *Piano concerto No. 3 in E flat.*

**(*) Lyr. SRCS 79. Composer (organ or piano), LPO, (i) Boult, (ii) Dommett.

There are few more immediately rewarding records of post-war concertos than this. Williamson composed them both in the early 1960s, and they represent two clearly contrasted sides of his creative character. The *Organ concerto*, written in tribute to Sir Adrian Boult, uses the conductor's initials, ACB, as a current motif, and though some of the writing – for the orchestra as well as the organ – is spectacular, it is essentially a tough and ambitious piece, with the two powerful outer movements framing a beautiful and lyrical *Largo* for strings and organ alone. The *Piano concerto No. 3* in four movements has immediate attractions in its catchy melodies and snappy rhythms, which could make it a popular success in the line of the Rachmaninov concertos. Unfortunately this performance has accompaniment that is less than punchy, and the red-bloodedness of the writing is not fully realized. The performance of the *Organ concerto* is quite different in temperature, splendid in every way. Excellent recording.

Agnus Dei; The Morning of the Day of Days; Procession of Palms; The World at the Manger.
*** Abbey LPB 805. Holt, Thompson, Keyte, Worcester Cath. Ch., Fest. Ch. Soc., Hunt; Trepte (organ).

Williamson, devout if not always orthodox in his Christian faith, has written copiously for the church. As a Roman Catholic himself his aim has been ecumenical, with immediacy of communication taking high priority. That is admirably illustrated in all the music here, including three memorable cantatas for different seasons – *Procession of Palms* for Palm Sunday, *The Morning of the Day of Days* for Easter, and *The World at the Manger* (the longest of the pieces here) for Christmas. As in its other Abbey issues, Worcester Cathedral Choir gives lively performances, helped by the rhythmic playing of Paul Trepte on the organ. Atmospheric recording.

6 English lyrics.
(*) Abbey ABY 810. Lea, Scottish Bar. Ens., Friedman – BRITTEN: *Simple symphony* **(*); ELGAR: *Serenade* **; WARLOCK: *Capriol suite.*(*)

Malcolm Williamson is president of the Scottish Baroque Ensemble, and this delightful sequence of varied settings (mostly of poems, such as *Sweet and low*, known very well in other settings) is a tribute to that. It makes an excellent foil for the three very familiar works also included on this disc. The microphone catches a disturbing vibrato in Yvonne Lea's voice, but these are warm-hearted performances, well worth investigating.

Wolf, Hugo (1860–1903)

Penthesilea (symphonic poem).
(M) **(*) DG Priv. 2726 067 (2). VSO, Gerdes – MAHLER: *Symphony No. 9.***(*)
(M) **(*) DG 2543 822 [id.]. VSO, Gerdes (with PFITZNER: *Palestrina*: *Preludes****).

Early in his career Hugo Wolf, much influenced by Liszt and Wagner, produced this ambitious symphonic poem, and today it makes an enjoyable curiosity, if hardly one of the composer's more important works.

The DG Privilege recording (coupled with Kubelik's version of Mahler's *Ninth*) is of a lively performance from a conductor who for many years was a recording producer for DG. This recording is also available coupled to excerpts from Pfitzner's opera, *Palestrina.*

Italian serenade.
*** Decca SXL 6998. Fitzwilliam Qt – BRAHMS: *Clarinet quintet.***(*)

The Fitzwilliams give a sparkling account of this charming piece which never fails to captivate. Well-defined recording – a shade too forward, perhaps, but there is undoubted presence.

Lieder

Alte Weisen (6 poems by Keller). *6 Lieder für eine Frauenstimme. Goethe Lieder: Als ich auf dem Euphrat schiffte; Anakreons Grab; Die Bekehrte; Blumengrüss; Epiphanias; Frühling übers Jahr; Ganymed; Gleich und gleich; Hochbeglückt in deiner Liebe; Kennst du das Land; Mignon Lieder Nos. I–III; Philine. Nimmer will ich dich verlieren* (from *Suleika Book*); *Der Schäfer; Die Spröde; St Nepomuks Vorabend. Byron Lieder: Sonne der Schlummerlosen.*
(M) ❀ *** HMV SLS 5197 (2). Schwarzkopf, Moore.

These two discs contain some of the very finest singing of Wolf songs ever recorded. Walter Legge, Schwarzkopf's husband, was the force behind the first major Wolf recording project on 78 in the 1930s, but in many ways the achievement of Schwarzkopf, and certainly the vocal finesse, go even further, whether in the dark intensity of the *Mignon songs* (including *Kennst du das Land*, a culmination in every way), the lyricism of *Wiegenlied im Sommer* or the sheer fun of *Mausfallen Sprüchlein.* The recordings, made between 1956 and 1962, still sound splendid, and the glorious singing is superbly matched by Gerald Moore's inspired accompaniment.

Das spanische Liederbuch (complete).
(M) *** DG 413 226-1/*4* [2726071]. Schwarzkopf, Fischer-Dieskau, Moore.

In this superb medium-price reissue, each of the four sides is devoted to one of Wolf's Spanish volumes, with the sacred songs providing a dark, intense prelude on side one. There Fischer-Dieskau is at his very finest, sustaining slow tempi impeccably. Schwarzkopf's dedication comes out in the three songs suitable for a woman's voice, but it is in the secular songs, particularly those which contain laughter in the music, where she is at her most memorable. Gerald Moore is backwardly balanced, but gives superb support. The voices are beautifully caught in the 1968 recording, making this a classic set. Although the tape transfer is made at a low level, Fischer-Dieskau's voice is given good projection (indeed a treble cut is useful to smooth the upper range). Schwarzkopf, however, has less presence and a softer-grained focus. The layout follows the discs and there is a clearly printed booklet with translations.

Wood, Hugh (born 1932)

(i) *Cello concerto, Op. 12;* (ii) *Violin concerto, Op. 17.*
*** Uni. RHS 363. Royal Liv. PO, Atherton, with (i) Parikian, (ii) Welsh.

Hugh Wood has so far been represented on record only by his chamber music. This issue brings two of his most important bigger pieces: the *Cello concerto* of 1969 and the *Violin concerto*, first heard two years later. Wood is a composer of integrity who has steeped himself in the music of Schoenberg and Webern, yet emerged richer for the experience – in contrast to many post-serial composers. His music is beautifully crafted and far from inaccessible. Here it is given the benefit of good recording, and the performances are thoroughly committed. Those who like and respond to the Bartók concertos or even to Walton should try these.

Wordsworth, William (born 1908)

String quartets Nos. 5, Op. 63; 6, Op. 75. (i) *3 Wordsworth songs, Op. 45.*
*** CRD CRD 1097/*CRDC 4097* [id.]. Alberni Qt; (i) with I. Partridge.

Wordsworth's string quartets, thoughtful and strongly argued, deserve representation on record. No. 5 (1957, but with the finale rewritten twenty years later) and No. 6 (1964) make a persuasive case for his brand of conservative but unconventional writing, with Nielsen or Janáček among possible influences. These are given splendid performances, beautifully recorded, and are perfectly coupled with Ian Partridge's tender and sensitive singing of songs setting words by the composer's poet namesake and ancestor. The chrome cassette has outstanding presence and realism. This is very much in the demonstration class.

Xenakis, Iannis (born 1922)

Antikhthon; Aroura; (i) *Synaphai* (connexities for piano and orchestra).
*** Decca HEAD 13. New Philh. O, Howarth, (i) with Madge.

Using higher mathematics as well as a computer (slide-rule and graph-paper to hand), Xenakis manages to produce works which, more than most such avant-garde offerings, actually sound like music – a tribute to obvious imagination, which defies any kind of technique. This is a valuable collection of three studies in texture. The most ambitious of the three, *Antikhthon*, taking up a whole side, is hypnotic in its range of colour, even if it fails to get you thinking of the infinite as the composer intends. Excellent performances (so far as one can tell), and brilliant recording.

Zamfir, Gheorghe
(born 1941)

Panpipes concerto No. 1 in G; Rhapsodie du printemps; Black waltz; Couleurs d'automne.
**(*) Ph. Dig. 412 221-1/*4* [id.]. Composer, Monte Carlo PO, Lawrence Foster.

Now world-famous as a charismatic exponent of the panpipes, Gheorghe Zamfir began his musical career as an accordionist, though he immediately graduated to the pipes on reaching music school. He went on to study composition (and the piano) at the Budapest Conservatory, and then found time to become a singer with the Romanian Opera Chorus. He is best known as the composer/performer of a haunting score for the Australian film, *Picnic at Hanging Rock*; but here he turns towards the concert hall with comparable flair. If the *Rhapsodie* seems rather long for its attractive, folk-derived material, part of the blame must be laid with the conductor, Lawrence Foster, who accompanies attentively but without much thrust. However, the four-movement *Concerto* is only about half as long (16′09″ against 29′49″), and makes a much more favourable impression, with the ingenious use of harpsichord, piano and then cymbalom in the slow movement. The *Couleurs d'automne* is slightly sentimental, the *Black waltz* engagingly colourful and rather catchy. The expert solo playing can be taken for granted. The sound is excellent, too, on both LP and the vivid chrome tape.

Zelenka, Jan (1679–1745)

Capriccios Nos. 1–6; Concerto in G; Hipocondrie in A; Overture in F; Sinfonia in A min.
⊛ *** DG Arc. 2710 026 [id./*3376 014*]. Camerata Bern, Van Wijnkoop.

In this superb orchestral collection, as in the earlier Archive issue of Zelenka sonatas (see below), this long-neglected composer begins to get his due some 250 years late. On this showing he stands as one of the most distinctive voices among Bach's contemporaries, and Bach himself nominated him in that role, though at the time Zelenka was serving in a relatively humble capacity. As in the sonata collection it is the artistry of Heinz Holliger that sets the seal on the performances, but the virtuosity of Barry Tuckwell on the horn is also a delight, and the music itself regularly astonishes. One of the movements in the *Capriccio No. 5* has the title *Il furibondo* (*The angry man*), and more strikingly still another piece has the significant title *Hipocondrie* and sounds amazingly like a baroque tango. Was Zelenka both a bitter man and a hypochondriac, one wonders, for in his obscurity no one even bothered to leave a portrait of him behind. What comes out from this is that in this period of high classicism, music for Zelenka was about emotion, something one recognizes clearly enough in Bach and Handel but too rarely in lesser composers. And in his bald expressiveness Zelenka comes to sound often amazingly modern, and often very beautiful, as in the slow *Aria No. 2* of the *Fourth Capriccio*. Superb recording to match Van Wijnkoop's lively and colourful performances.

Capriccio in D; Hipocondrie; Sinfonia.
*** DG Arc. 2533 464 [id.]. Holliger, Elhorst, Tuckwell, Poutch, Bern Camerata.

These superb and invigorating works come from the Archiv box which brought such revelation about a long-forgotten master. It is not just the intriguing title of *Hipocondrie* that is original. His writing has a sharp unexpectedness one rarely finds in baroque music, and these dazzling performances – with virtuoso solo work – make a most persuasive case. First-rate recording.

Sonatas, Nos 1–6.
⊛ *** DG Arc. 2708 027 (2) [id.]. Holliger, Bourgue, Gawriloff, Thunemann, Buccarella, Jaccotet.

Zelenka, a contemporary of Bach born in

Bohemia, worked for most of his life in Dresden – another dull German Kapellmeister, you might think. But thanks to the urgent advocacy of the oboist Heinz Holliger, we can now appreciate just how vital and original Zelenka's admittedly limited genius was. In these *Trio sonatas* it is almost as though Zelenka had a touch of Ives in him, so unexpected are some of the developments and turns of argument. The tone of voice is often dark and intense, directly comparable to Bach at his finest, and all through these superb performances the electricity of the original inspiration comes over with exhilarating immediacy. Fine recording. Another set to recommend urgently to any lover of baroque music.

Trio sonatas for 2 oboes and continuo: Volume 1, Nos. 4 in G min.; 5 in F.
**(*) Accent ACC 3226. Dombrecht, Ebbinge, Bond, Kohnen, Van der Meer.

These superb sonatas first came to wide attention thanks to the DG Archiv recordings with Heinz Holliger and Maurice Bourgue. Here a talented Dutch group interprets two of the set of six on original instruments, and those who like the tang of authenticity will certainly prefer them with the piping sound of baroque oboes. Excellent recording.

Zeller, Carl (1842–98)

Der Vogelhändler (operetta; complete).
*** EMI 1C 157 30194/5. Rothenberger, Holm, Litz, Dallapozza, Berry, Unger, Forster, Donch, V. Volksoper Ch., VSO, Boskovsky.

Boskovsky's vivacious and lilting performance of Zeller's delightfully tuneful operetta is in every way recommendable. The cast is strong; Anneliese Rothenberger may be below her best form as Princess Marie, but Renate Holm is a charmer as Christel, and Adolf Dallapozza sings the title role with heady virility. There are many endearing moments, and the combination here of infectious sparkle with style tempts one to re-value the score and place it alongside *The Merry Widow* and *Die Fledermaus* among the finest and most captivating of all operettas. For English-speaking listeners some of the dialogue might have been cut, but this is an international set and it is provided with an excellent libretto translation (not always the case in this kind of repertoire). Two numbers are cut from Act III to fit the work on to two discs. The recording is excellent, combining atmosphere with warmth and lively projection of the principal characters. A disc of highlights is also available (EMI 1C 061 28829).

Zemlinsky, Alexander von
(1871–1942)

Lyric symphony, Op. 18.
*** DG Dig. 2532 021 [id.]. Varady, Fischer-Dieskau, Berlin PO, Maazel.

Zemlinsky was an influential figure in Viennese musical life and numbered Schoenberg among his pupils and Berg among his admirers. He was a friend and protégé of Mahler, who appointed him conductor of the Vienna Court Opera in 1907. His *Lyric symphony* dates from 1922 and inhabits much the same world as Mahler. It is a symphony song-cycle, modelled on *Das Lied von der Erde* and based on Eastern poetry, and its lush textures and refined scoring make it immediately accessible. The idiom is that of early Schoenberg (*Verklaerte Nacht* and *Gurrelieder*), Mahler and figures such as Strauss and Franz Schreker. Yet it is not just derivative but has something quite distinctive to say. Its sound world is imaginative, the vocal writing graceful and the orchestration masterly. Both soloists and the orchestra sound thoroughly convinced and convincing, and Maazel's refined control of texture prevents the sound from cloying, as does his incisive manner. Varady and Fischer-Dieskau make an outstanding pair of soloists, keenly responsive to the words, and the engineering is first-class, the voices being well balanced against the orchestra.

String quartets Nos. 1, Op. 4; 2, Op. 15; 3, Op. 19; 4, Op. 25.
*** DG Dig. 2741 016 (3). LaSalle Qt (with APOSTEL: *String quartet No. 1, Op. 7****).

This DG box of his four string quartets provides ample evidence that Zemlinsky – a somewhat shadowy figure – is a composer of real substance. The *First Quartet* gained the imprimatur of Brahms, to whom Zemlinsky had shown some of his other early compositions, and the last, which was written at exactly the same time as Schoenberg's *Fourth*, pays the erstwhile pupil the double compliment of a dedication and an allusion to *Verklaerte Nacht*. None of the four is in the least atonal: the textures are full of contrapuntal interest and the musical argument always proceeds with lucidity. There is diversity of mood and a fastidious craftsmanship and the listener is always held. The musical language is steeped in Mahler and, to a lesser extent, Reger, but the music is undoubtedly the product of a very fine musical mind and one of considerable individuality. The *Second* of 1915 has already appeared separately and is grand and expansive in one long movement, in the manner of Wolf's *D minor Quartet*. Collectors will find this a rewarding set: the LaSalle play with polish and unanimity, and the recording is as first-class as the admirable documentation. The sixth side is taken up by a cogently argued serial piece by the Austrian composer, Hans Erich Apostel (1901–72). His *First Quartet* of 1935 features a variation movement which uses a theme from Berg's *Wozzeck*, while the scherzo makes use of a cryptogram on Apostel and Berg's initials.

String quartet No. 2, Op. 15.
*** DG 2530 982 [id. PSI]. LaSalle Qt.

Grandly rhetorical and expansive in its single movement lasting nearly forty minutes, this work gives an idea of what Schoenberg might have done had he stayed content with the idiom of *Verklaerte Nacht* and *Gurrelieder*. Zemlinsky was in fact Schoenberg's brother-in-law, but, though he remained a close friend, he refused to follow his contemporary into full atonality. This quartet written in the years leading up to the First World War represents the composer at his most dynamic, rich in texture and argument but not self-indulgently so. Much is owed to the commitment of the LaSalle Quartet, masters in this repertory, and the recording is excellent.

Collections

Concerts of Orchestral and Concertante Music

Academy of Ancient Music, Hogwood or Schröder

PACHELBEL: *Canon and gigue.* VIVALDI: *Concerto in B min. for 4 violins, Op. 3/10. Double trumpet concerto in C, RV.537.* GLUCK: *Orfeo: Dance of the Furies; Dance of the Blessed Spirits.* HANDEL: *Solomon: Arrival of the Queen of Sheba. Berenice: Overture; Minuet. Water music: Air; Hornpipe.*
(*) O-L **410 553-2; DSLO/*KDSLC* 594.

It seems a curious idea to play popular baroque repertoire with a severe manner. Pachelbel's *Canon* here sounds rather abrasive and lacking charm; and the *Arrival of the Queen of Sheba* is altogether more seductive in Beecham's or Marriner's hands. But those who combine a taste for these pieces with a desire for authenticity at all costs should be satisfied. The highlight here is the pair of Gluck dances, very strongly characterized and making a splendid foil for each other. The sound is extremely vivid, especially on compact disc. On tape there is an extra degree of spikiness on side one of the cassette.

'Christmas concertos': CORELLI: *Concerto grosso Op. 6/8.* WERNER: *Christmas pastorella.* GOSSEC: *Christmas suite* (with chorus). HANDEL: *Messiah: Pifa* (*Pastoral symphony*). VEJVANOVSKÝ: *Sonata Natalis.* BACH: *Christmas oratorio.* TORELLI: *Concerto grosso, Op. 8/6.*
(*) O-L Dig. **410 179-2; DSLO/*KDSDC* 709.

For those needing a touch of acerbity to prevent their Christmas pastorellas becoming too bland, the present collection provides the answer. The playing has a suitably light touch (the Corelli especially so) and the programme is imaginative, though the invention in some of the lesser-known pieces is somewhat ingenuous, notably the Vejvanovský (which has the compensation of trumpets to add colour), or the Gossec, which surprises with a chorus of shepherds as its finale. The sound is first-class (though the tape loses a degree of refinement with the entry of the trumpets), with the compact disc adding extra presence.

PURCELL: *Abdelazer: Rondeau. Amphitryon: Hornpipe and Scotch tune.* VIVALDI: *Concerto in G* (*Alla Rustica*), *RV.151.* HANDEL: *Water music: suite in F* (excerpts). BACH, C. P. E.: *Symphony in C, Wq.174.* MOZART: *Symphonies Nos. 32 in G, K.318; 35 in D* (*Haffner*), *K.385.*
*** O-L 410 183-1/*4*.

This is the most attractive of the Academy of Ancient Music samplers issued so far. The brisk alertness of the opening Purcell *Rondeau* (made famous by Britten's *Variations*) sets the mood. The playing sparkles with vitality throughout, and although not all will respond to the sprightly tempo chosen for the *Air* from Handel's *Water music*, the symphonies of Mozart and C. P. E. Bach, with their tingling sharpness of string focus, are exhilarating in outer movements and expressively resilient in *Andantes.* The sound is first-class, although the chrome cassette is not as clean on top as the disc.

Academy of St Martin-in-the-Fields, Marriner

ALBINONI: *Adagio in G min.* (arr. Giazotto) *for strings and organ.* MENDELSSOHN: *Octet, Op. 20: Scherzo.* HANDEL: *Berenice: Minuet. Messiah: Pastoral symphony.* MOZART:

March in D, K.335/1. German dance (Sleigh ride), K.605/3. BACH: *Christmas oratorio, BWV 248: Sinfonia. Suite No. 3 in D, BWV 1068: Air.* PACHELBEL: *Canon in D.* BEETHOVEN: *12 Contretänze.*
*** HMV ASD/*TC-ASD* 3017 [Ang. S/*4XS* 37044].

This account of Albinoni's *Adagio* must be the most refined in the catalogue, although (as also in the gravely measured performance of the Pachelbel *Canon*) the beautiful playing is matched by a strongly characterized overall conception. One special delight here is the Beethoven *Contretänze*, with their sudden reminder of the finale of the *Eroica symphony*, but the whole programme gives the fullest pleasure and is beautifully recorded. The tape transfer is very good too.

'The Academy in concert': MOZART: *Serenade No. 13 in G (Eine kleine Nachtmusik), K.525.* GLUCK: *Orfeo ed Euridice: Dance of the Blessed Spirits.* MOZART, Leopold: *Toy symphony* (attrib. Haydn). SCHUBERT: *Rosamunde, D.797: Entr'acte in B flat.* HANDEL: *Xerxes: Ombra mai fù (Largo).* BACH: *Cantata No. 147: Jesu, joy of man's desiring.*
**(*) HMV ASD/*TC-ASD* 3375 [Ang. S/*4XS* 37443].

The highlight here is an enchanting version of the *Toy symphony* with some delightfully piquant sounds. The programme is a frankly popular one; for all the delicacy of the scoring of Handel's *Largo*, one still craves the vocal line – an arrangements sits uneasily within this kind of programme. The most famous of Mozart's serenades is graciously played, if with a hint of blandness, and the flute solo in the Gluck piece is matched by the beautiful wind-playing in the *Rosamunde* melody. The sound is of EMI's best quality on LP; originally, the cassette was slightly less refined than the disc, but may well have been remastered by now.

'Digital concert': WAGNER: *Siegfried idyll.* DVOŘÁK: *Nocturne in B, Op. 40.* FAURÉ: *Pavane, Op. 50.* TCHAIKOVSKY: *String quartet No. 1 in D, Op. 11: Andante cantabile.* GRIEG: *2 Elegiac melodies, Op. 34.* BOCCHERINI: *Quintet in E, Op. 13/5: Minuet.*
❀ *** HMV Dig. ASD/*TCC-ASD* 3943 [Ang. DS/*4ZS* 37758].

This is a hi-fi demonstration record for those who have to think of their neighbours. These generally gentle pieces are given radiant performances, recorded in digital sound with ravishingly vivid results. As in his previous Argo version of the *Siegfried idyll*, Marriner uses solo strings for the gentler passages, a fuller ensemble for the climaxes, here passionately convincing. The chrome cassette also offers very high quality, although side two, transferred at a markedly higher level than side one, has strikingly more upper range, with the beautiful Tchaikovsky and Grieg items outstanding. However, the sound on the disc is quite exceptional.

HANDEL: *Solomon: Arrival of the Queen of Sheba; Berenice: Minuet. Messiah: Pastoral symphony.* BACH: *Cantatas Nos. 147: Jesu, joy of man's desiring; 208: Sheep may safely graze; Christmas oratorio: Sinfonia.* GRIEG: *Holberg suite: Prelude.* SCHUBERT: *Rosamunde: Entr'acte No. 2.* GLUCK: *Orfeo: Dance of the Blessed Spirits.* BORODIN: *Nocturne for strings* (arr. Marriner).
**(*) HMV Dig. ASD/*TC-ASD* 143642-1/*4*.

Handel's Queen of Sheba trots in very briskly indeed, but in general the rich digital recording will strike some ears as too ample in texture for this repertoire, and the two famous Bach chorales sound almost romantic. The *Pastoral symphony* is much more stylish and the noble contour of the famous *Berenice* melody is warmly phrased. But it is the Schubert *Entr'acte* and the passionately expressive Borodin *Nocturne* that resonate in the memory.

'A baroque festival' (with various soloists): VIVALDI: *L'Estro armonico: Quadruple violin concerto in B min., Op. 3/10; Double violin concerto in A min., Op. 3/8. La Stravaganza: Violin concerto in B flat, Op. 4/1. Double trumpet concerto in C, P. 75.* CORELLI: *Concerto grosso in G min. (Christmas concerto), Op. 6/8.* BACH: *Double concerto in D min. for violin and oboe (from BWV 1060). Flute con-*

certo in G min. (*from BWV 1056*). TELEMANN: *Trumpet concerto in D; Viola concerto in G.* ARNE: *Harpsichord concerto No. 5 in G min.* HANDEL: *Concerto grosso, Op. 3/1. Oboe concerto No. 3 in G min. Organ concerto No. 16 in D min., Op. 7/4.* FASCH: *Trumpet concerto in D.*
(M) *** Argo D 69 D 3/*K 69 K 33* (3).

A superb set. The music, like the performances, is of the highest quality and there is some splendid solo playing. The sound is first-class with the cassettes generally matching the discs; only in the trumpet concertos is there a hint that the upper range is not quite so open and free as elsewhere. Highly recommended in both formats.

'The French connection': RAVEL: *Le Tombeau de Couperin.* DEBUSSY: *Danses sacrée et profane* (with Ellis, harp). IBERT: *Divertissement.* FAURÉ: *Dolly suite, Op. 56.*
*** ASV Dig. DCA/*ZCDCA* 517.

An excellent collection. The spirited account of Ibert's *Divertissement* is matched by the warmth of Fauré's *Dolly suite* in the Rabaud orchestration. The remainder of the record is hardly less appealing. Ravel's *Le Tombeau de Couperin* is nicely done, though the *Forlane* is kept on too tight a rein and one feels the need for a slightly bigger body of strings. But though not a first choice, there is no denying that it is very well played indeed, as is the Debussy *Danses sacrée et profane.* One would welcome more space round the orchestra and, considering the disc was made in Studio One, Abbey Road, greater use could have been made of its ambience. However, this apart, everything is very clear, though the cassette has slightly less bite than the disc.

'The English connection': ELGAR: *Serenade for strings, Op. 20.* TIPPETT: *Fantasia concertante on a theme of Corelli.* VAUGHAN WILLIAMS: *Fantasia on a theme of Thomas Tallis; The Lark ascending* (with Iona Brown).
**(*) ASV Dig. DCA/*ZCDCA* 518.

Marriner's newer performances of the Elgar *Serenade* and the *Tallis Fantasia* are less intense (and less subtle) than his earlier Argo versions (see below), and the highlight of this concert is Iona Brown's radiant account of *The Lark ascending.* The sound is rich and very well defined, with the cassette only marginally less sharply detailed.

'Baroque concertos': AVISON: *Concerto in A, Op. 9/11.* MANFREDINI: *Concerto in G min., Op. 3/10.* ALBINONI: *Concerto a 5 in A min., Op. 5/5.* HANDEL: *Concerto grosso in G, Op. 6/1.* TELEMANN: *Tafelmusik, Set 2: Concerto in F.*
(M) *** Decca Ser. SA/*KSC* 10.

This was one of two LPs that launched the Academy of St Martin-in-the-Fields as a recording group in the early 1960s. This particular field of small chamber ensembles specializing in performances of baroque music had previously been cornered by Italian groups, like I Musici, often restricting themselves very much to the home product. From the beginning the St Martin's group showed themselves willing to offer a repertoire covering the widest possible range; furthermore the standard of playing and care for style and detail were to set and maintain a new level of excellence by any international standards. The first disc immediately showed the wide geographical range. This, the second, dating from 1963, is even more imaginative, the delightful work by Avison a most rewarding choice; and the playing is so vivacious that even the less interesting music comes fully to life.

Concert (with (i) J. Suk, violin): (i) MOZART: *Rondo for violin and orchestra in C, K.373; Adagio for violin and orchestra in E, K.261. March in D, K.335/1; German dance in C* (*Sleigh ride*), *K.605/3; Serenade No. 13* (*Eine kleine Nachtmusik*), *K.525.* (i) BEETHOVEN: *Romances for violin and orchestra Nos. 1 and 2, Opp. 40 and 50.* SCHUBERT: *Rondo for violin and orchestra in A, D.438. Rosamunde: Entr'acte No. 3, D.797.* ALBINONI: *Adagio* (arr. Giazotto). MENDELSSOHN: *Octet, Op. 20: Scherzo.* HANDEL: *Berenice: Minuet. Messiah: Pastoral symphony. Xerxes: Largo.* BACH: *Christmas oratorio: Sinfonia. Suite No. 3 in D, BWV 1068: Air. Jesu, joy of man's desiring.* PACHELBEL: *Canon.* BEETHOVEN: *12 Contradances.* GLUCK: *Orfeo ed Euridice:*

Dance of the Blessed Spirits. MOZART, L.: *Toy symphony*. WAGNER: *Siegfried idyll*. DVOŘÁK: *Nocturne, Op. 40*. FAURÉ: *Pavane, Op. 50*. TCHAIKOVSKY: *Andante cantabile*. GRIEG: *2 Elegiac melodies*. BOCCHERINI: *Minuet, Op. 13*.
(M) *** HMV SLS/*TCC-SLS* 5267 (4).

This box economically gathers together the ASMF EMI repertoire (including the digital concert). Josef Suk makes a distinguished contribution in the lighter concertante pieces of Beethoven, Mozart and Schubert; and with excellent sound throughout, on disc and tape alike, this can be cordially recommended, for the quality of the music-making is on a consistently high plane.

'The world of the Academy': HANDEL: *Solomon: Arrival of the Queen of Sheba*. TELEMANN: *Trumpet concerto in D*. MOZART: *Divertimento for strings No. 1 in D, K.136*. HAYDN: *6 Allemandes*. ROSSINI: *String sonata No. 1*. MENDELSSOHN: *Octet, Op. 20: Scherzo*. TCHAIKOVSKY: *Serenade for strings, Op. 48: Waltz*.
(M) *** Argo SPA 101.

This sampler offers a very happy collection of lollipops. It opens stylishly and infectiously with the *Arrival of the Queen of Sheba*, and among its special delights are the spirited and buoyant finale of the Mozart *Divertimento*, the genial Rossini *Sonata*, the beautifully played Mendelssohn *Scherzo* and the elegant Tchaikovsky *Waltz*. The recording is bright, rich and natural.

'Scandinavian music': GRIEG: *2 Elegiac melodies, Op. 34*. SIBELIUS: *Kuolema: Valse triste, Op. 44. Rakastava, Op. 14*. NIELSEN: *Little suite, Op. 1*. WIRÉN: *Serenade for strings, Op. 11*.
*** Argo ZRG/*KZRC* 877 [id.].

A splendid collection of appealing and attractive music from the north. It gives us the only domestically available version of Sibelius's magical *Rakastava* (there is an eloquent version by the Finnish Chamber Ensemble on BIS) as well as the perennially fresh Dag Wirén *Serenade*. These are good, vividly recorded performances. The cassette transfer too is of outstanding quality: the sound has striking presence and realism.

'Academy encores': HANDEL: *Solomon: Arrival of the Queen of Sheba. Berenice: Minuet. Water music: Air; Hornpipe*. BACH: *Suite No. 3 in D, BWV 1068: Air*. HAYDN: *Trumpet concerto in E flat* (with Stringer). MOZART: *Serenade No. 13 in G* (*Eine kleine Nachtmusik*), *K.525. Divertimento No. 17 in D, K.334: Minuet*.
**(*) Argo ZRG/*KZRC* 902 [id.].

This is much the same sort of repertoire that Decca have previously made available in a medium-priced *World of the Academy* selection (SPA 101). The present compilation is well made, and the sound is of good quality; but even though *Eine kleine Nachtmusik* is one of the finest available versions, and the Haydn *Trumpet concerto* is also offered complete, few collectors will feel that this should be offered at premium price. The cassette matches the disc closely, except in the *Nachtmusik*, where the LP offers slightly more range and freshness.

'Greensleeves' (Folksong arrangements): VAUGHAN WILLIAMS: *English folksongs suite. Fantasia on Greensleeves*. TRAD.: *Summer is icumen in; The turtle dove; John Peel* (all arr. Hazell). *The keeper; The oak and the ash; Early one morning; The jolly miller; I will give my love; British Grenadiers* (arr. Pearson).
** Argo ZRG/*KZRC* 931 [id.].

After opening with an attractively vivacious account of Vaughan Williams's *English folksongs suite* (in its orchestral transcription by Gordon Jacob), with *Greensleeves* an appropriate encore, the programme moves on to orchestrations and elaborations (mainly by Leslie Pearson, but three scored by Chris Hazell) of melodies many of which are far more effective in vocal form. The resonance of the recording creates a rather washy effect (especially on the cassette, which is less sharply focused than the disc).

'English music': ELGAR: *Serenade for strings*

in E min., Op. 20. DELIUS: *On hearing the first cuckoo in spring.* BUTTERWORTH: *The banks of green willow.* VAUGHAN WILLIAMS: *Fantasia on a theme by Thomas Tallis.* WARLOCK: *Capriol suite.*
*** Argo ZRG/*KZRC* 945.

These performances – especially the Elgar and Vaughan Williams – show Marriner and the Academy in their finest form, with much subtlety of detail as well as striking commitment and depth of feeling. The recording remains first-rate, on cassette as well as disc.

'Favourites': HANDEL: *Solomon: Arrival of the Queen of Sheba. Water music: suite in D. Berenice: overture; Minuet.* BACH: *Orchestral suite No. 3 in D, BWV 1068.* MOZART: *Serenade No. 13 (Eine kleine Nachtmusik), K.525. Divertimento No. 17, K.334: Minuet.* HAYDN: *6 Allemandes, Hob. IX/9.* ROSSINI: *String sonata No. 1.* GRIEG: *Holberg suite: Prelude.* TCHAIKOVSKY: *String serenade: Waltz.*
(M) *(*) Decca *410 296-4.*

An attractive programme (available on tape only) that makes musical sense in its layout and is afforded playing which matches warmth with polish. But it is let down by the misjudged transfer level, which is marginally too high. For most of the time this is not too noticeable on a small stereo player or in the car, but the loss of refinement at the entry of the trumpets in the *Water music* becomes more serious in the *Overture* of the Bach *Suite* (heard complete), where fortissimos are congested.

'Adagio'

Baroque music (with: (i) Richard Hickox O; (ii) Stuttgart CO, Münchinger; (iii) ASMF, Marriner; (iv) Philomusica, Dart; (v) Lucerne Fest. Strings, Baumgartner; (vi) V. Moz. Ens., Boskovsky; (vii) A. Stringer): (i) ALBINONI: *Adagio.* (ii) VIVALDI: *Four Seasons: Spring.* (v) *Concerto alla rustica for strings.* (ii) BACH: *Sheep may safely graze; Suite No. 3: Air; Jesu, joy of man's desiring.* (i) PURCELL: *Chaconne.* (iii) HANDEL: *Arrival of the Queen of Sheba;* (iv) *Water music: Suite No. 3 in D;* (ii) *Berenice overture.* (i) PACHELBEL: *Canon.* (ii) BOCCHERINI: *Quintet in E, Op. 13/5: Minuet and Trio.* HAYDN (HOFSTETTER): *Quartet No. 17 in F, Op. 3/5: Andante cantabile.* MOZART: *Divertimento No. 17, K.334: Minuet and Trio.* (vi) *German dance, K.605/3 (Sleigh ride).* (iii; vii) HAYDN: *Trumpet concerto in E flat.*
(B) ** Decca *KMC2 9005.*

A ninety-minute selection of baroquerie, mainly designed for in-car use. The artists' roster is impressive; the sound is vivid, wide-ranging and clear, but somewhat thin on top and not always completely refined (as in the Haydn *Trumpet concerto*).

Adelaide SO, Garforth

'Great Pas de deux' from: TCHAIKOVSKY: *Nutcracker, Acts I and II; Sleeping Beauty, Act III; Swan Lake, Acts II and III.* PROKOFIEV: *Romeo and Juliet, Act I.* DELIBES: *Coppélia, Act. III.*
(M) ** Chan. CRB/*CBT* 1010.

The Adelaide Symphony Orchestra produce alert, reasonably expansive playing, but as recorded here the strings lack a degree of sumptuousness of texture. The music includes some of the more famous purple patches of romantic ballet and is certainly enjoyable in its own right. The recording is bright and vivid on both disc and chrome cassette.

Adni, Daniel (piano)

'Music from the movies' (with Bournemouth SO, Alwyn): ADDINSELL: *Warsaw concerto.* WILLIAMS: *The Dream of Olwen.* ROZSA: *Spellbound concerto.* BATH: *Cornish rhapsody.* GERSHWIN: *Rhapsody in Blue.*
**(*) HMV ASD 3862.

By far the finest of these film 'concertos' is Addinsell's *Warsaw concerto*, written for *Dangerous Moonlight* after Rachmaninov had failed to respond to the original commission. It is a first-class miniature romantic pastiche with an indelible main theme. The other pieces here have less distinction but are taken seriously and presented with commitment and flair. The performance of the Gershwin *Rhapsody* (also used in a biopic of the same title) is not as distinctive as the rest of the programme. Excellent, vivid sound.

André, Maurice (trumpet)

Trumpet concertos (with ASMF, Marriner): STÖLZEL: *Concerto in D.* TELEMANN: *Concerto in C min. Concerto in D for trumpet, 2 oboes and strings* (with Nicklin and Miller). VIVALDI: *Double trumpet concerto in C, RV. 537* (with Soustrot); *Double concerto in B flat for trumpet and violin, RV.548* (with I. Brown).
*** HMV Dig. **CDC 7 47012-2**; ASD/*TCC-ASD* 143530-1/*4* [Ang. DS/*4XS* 37984].

Maurice André has recorded a number of such collections for EMI but they have all been swiftly deleted. He is peerless in this kind of repertoire and the accompaniments under Marriner are attractively alert and stylish. The Academy provides expert soloists to match André in the concertante works by Telemann (*in D*) and Vivaldi (*RV.548*) which come together on the second side and offer much the most interesting invention. The concerto by Stölzel is conventional, but has a fine slow movement. Throughout André's smooth, rich timbre and highly musical phrasing give pleasure. The recording is first-class, with the cassette very good too, and only very occasionally less clean in its focus of the solo instrument. The CD adds extra definition and presence.

Trumpet concertos (with Ens. O de Paris, Wallez): HUMMEL: *Concerto in E flat.* TELEMANN: *Concerto in D for 3 trumpets and 2 oboes* (with Touvron, Lionel André, Arrignon, Chavana). NERUDA: *Concerto in E flat.*
** Erato Dig. NUM/*MCE* 75026 [id.].

In the famous Hummel *Concerto* Wallez's direction of the first movement is rather square (it does not compare with Marriner's for John Wilbraham – see below) and though André plays with his usual elegance of style, the work loses its genial jauntiness. The other concertos also lack distinction in the orchestral support, although the Telemann concertante work has some attractive textures. The digital recording is not as bright and clear as one might expect, though fully acceptable, as is the chrome tape which catches the solo instrument without loss of focus.

Trumpet concertos (with (i) ECO, Mackerras; (ii) H. Bilgram; (iii) M. Sillem): (i) VIVALDI: *Double trumpet concerto in C, RV.537.* (ii) VIVIANI: *Sonata No. 1 in C for trumpet and organ.* (i) TORELLI: *Concerto in D.* STÖLZEL: *Concerto in D.* (i; iii) TELEMANN: *Concerto sonata in D.*
(M) *** DG Priv. 2535/*3335* 385.

There is a pleasing variety of textures here, and in the Vivaldi, by electronic means, André assumes a fruitful solo partnership with himself. The Viviani *Sonata* with organ obbligato is an effective piece, and the slow movement of the Stölzel concerto has genuine nobility of line. In the second movement of the Telemann, André makes impressive use of a long, controlled crescendo. All in all, an entertaining compendium, with crisp, stylish accompaniments and good sound.

Trumpet concertos (with Rouen CO, Beaucamp): MOZART, L.: *Concerto in D.* TELEMANN: *Concerto in F min.* ALBINONI: *Concerto in D min.* (transcription of *Church sonata for organ*). VIVALDI: *Double concerto for trumpet and violin in B flat, RV.548* (with D. Artur).
(M) **(*) Ph. Seq. 6527/*7311* 082.

The Albinoni transcription is a delightful four-movement work, and the Vivaldi is hardly less enjoyable, although the violin takes a rather less than equal partnership in the outer movements and provides only an accompanying role in the eloquent *Largo*. The genuine trumpet concerto by Leopold Mozart is more demanding technically, but more conventional as music. The recording is more reverberant here, and on cassette the focus (hitherto excellent) becomes slightly blurred. Accompaniments are attentive rather than especially sparkling, but this is worth trying for the Albinoni and Vivaldi items.

André, Maurice, and **Brass Ens., Dart**

'Royal music of King James I'.
(M) ** Decca Ser. SA/*KSC*4.

As Thurston Dart points out in his sleeve-note, James I's wind band consisted of woodwind as well as brass instruments, and it is unfortunate that it is represented here only by brass. The music, by composers such as Holborne, Farnaby and Ferrabosco II, is diverse, the playing is lively and the recording full and brilliant. But an entire record or cassette of rather similar pieces, played by a group with unvarying tone-colour, can become a little wearisome. Listened to in sections, this music is rewarding.

Ashkenazy, Vladimir (piano) (see also under Instrumental recitals)

'Favourite concertos': TCHAIKOVSKY: *Piano concerto No. 1 in B flat min., Op. 23* (with LSO, Maazel). CHOPIN: *Piano concerto No. 2 in F min., Op. 21* (with LSO, Zinman). RACHMANINOV: *Piano concerto No. 2 in C min., Op. 18* (with LSO, Previn). SCHUMANN: *Piano concerto in A min., Op. 54* (with LSO, Segal). BEETHOVEN: *Piano concerto No. 5 in E flat* (*Emperor*)*, Op. 73* (with Chicago SO, Solti).
(M) *** Decca D 271 D 3/*K 271 K 33* (3).

These performances are discussed within the composer index. All are distinguished, none will disappoint, and this box serves well to demonstrate Ashkenazy's range. He has seldom been unlucky in his choice of accompanists. The Decca sound is first-class on disc although the quality is slightly more variable on tape with some excessive bass resonance in the *Emperor*.

Ballet

'Ballet favourites' (with (i) LSO, Monteux; (ii) SRO, Ansermet; (iii) Paris Conservatoire O, Maag; (iv) ROHCGO, Lanchbery or (v) Morel; (vi) Israel PO, Solti): excerpts from: (i) TCHAIKOVSKY: *Sleeping Beauty;* (ii) *Nutcracker;* (v) *Swan Lake.* CHOPIN: (iii) *Les Sylphides.* (iv) HÉROLD: *La Fille mal gardée.* (vi) ROSSINI–RESPIGHI: *La Boutique fantasque.*
(B) ** Decca *KMC2 9004.*

This ninety-minute tape selection is well engineered although the sound is vivid and robust rather than refined. Performances are vintage ones from the early Decca stereo catalogue, and are lively and characterful, although the Monteux selection from *Sleeping Beauty* includes his curiously insensitive, swiftly paced *Panorama.* Otherwise there is little to complain of. The highlight is undoubtedly the selection from *La Fille mal gardée* where the full, sparkling sound belies the age of the recording.

'Nights at the ballet' (with (i) RPO, Weldon; (ii) Philh. O; (iii) Kurtz; (iv) Irving; (v) RPO, Fistoulari; (vi) CBSO, Frémaux; (vii) New Philh. O, Mackerras): excerpts from: (i) TCHAIKOVSKY: *Nutcracker; Swan Lake.* (ii; iii) PROKOFIEV: *Romeo and Juliet.* (ii; iv) ADAM: *Giselle.* (v) LUIGINI: *Ballet Égyptien* (suite). (vi) SATIE: *Gymnopédies Nos. 1 and 3.* (vii) DELIBES: *Coppélia.* GOUNOD: *Faust* (suite).
(B) *** EMI *TC2-MOM 111.*

Here (on tape only) is nearly an hour and a half of some of the most tuneful and colourful ballet music ever written. Kurtz's three excerpts from *Romeo and Juliet* are most distinguished, the inclusion of the Fistoulari recording of *Ballet Égyptien* (see under Luigini above) is most welcome, and Mackerras is at his sparkling best in the *Coppélia* and *Faust* selections. Weldon's Tchaikovsky performances lack the last degree of flair but they are alert and well played. The sound is admirable both for home listening and in the car.

Baroque music

'The sound of baroque' (with (i) Royal Liv. PO, Groves; (ii) Scottish CO, Tortelier; (iii) LPO, Boult; (iv) Menuhin, Ferras, Bath Fest. O; (v) Bournemouth Sinf., Montgomery; (vi) Reginald Kilbey and Strings; (vii) RPO, Weldon; (viii) ASMF, Marriner): (i) AL-

BINONI: *Adagio for strings and organ* (arr. Giazotto). (ii) BACH: *Suite No. 3 in D, BWV 1068: Air.* (iii) *Brandenburg concerto No. 3 in G, BWV 1048.* (iv) *Double violin concerto in D, BWV 1043.* (i) GLUCK: *Orfeo: Dance of the Blessed Spirits.* (v) HANDEL: *Messiah: Pastoral symphony. Berenice overture.* (v) *Solomon: Arrival of the Queen of Sheba.* (vi) *Serse: Largo.* (vii) *Water music: suite* (arr. Harty). (viii) PACHELBEL: *Canon.*
(B) *** EMI *TC2-MOM 103.*

One of the first of EMI's *Miles of music* tapes, planned for motorway listening as well as at home, and offering about eighty minutes of favourite baroquerie, this is recommendable in every way. The sound is lively, the performances are first-class, with Bach's *Double violin concerto* and *Brandenburg No. 3* (Boult) bringing substance among the lollipops.

BBC SO

'Fiftieth anniversary concert' (cond. (i) Elgar; (ii) Boult; (iii) Fritz Busch; (iv) Toscanini; (v) Bruno Walter): (i) ELGAR: *Cockaigne overture, Op. 40.* (ii) VAUGHAN WILLIAMS: *Fantasia on a theme of Thomas Tallis.* BLISS: *Music for strings.* BERLIOZ: *Overture King Lear, Op. 4.* SIBELIUS: *Night Ride and Sunrise, Op. 55.* (iii) MOZART: *Symphony No. 36 in C (Linz), K.425.* (iv) BEETHOVEN: *Symphony No. 6 in F (Pastoral).* (v) BRAHMS: *Symphony No. 4 in E min.*
(M) (***) BBC mono 4001 (4).

This was issued (alongside Rozhdestvensky's marvellous recording of Tchaikovsky's *Sleeping Beauty*) to celebrate the fiftieth anniversary of the BBC Symphony Orchestra in 1980. The recordings were chosen from the orchestra's first decade of existence, and many of them show their interpreters in their best light. Boult's performances are splendid – the Bliss *Music for strings* is especially valuable – and many will be glad to have Toscanini's famous version of the *Pastoral symphony*, recorded in the Queen's Hall in 1937. The only comparative disappointment is Bruno Walter's 1934 set of Brahms's *Fourth*, mellow to the point of lethargy in the slow movement. The transfers (apart from the Toscanini/Beethoven) are splendidly done by Keith Hardwick and Anthony Griffith; the sound is always acceptable and often surprisingly good.

BBC SO, Sir Colin Davis

'Last night of the proms' (1969): ELGAR: *Cockaigne overture, Op. 40; Pomp and Circumstance march No. 1 in D min., Op. 39.* Arr. WOOD: *Fantasia on British sea songs.* PARRY: *Jerusalem* (arr. Elgar).
(M) *** Ph. Festivo. SFM 23033/*7304 002.*

The very British occasion of the Last Night of the Proms is admirably captured here with all its unique, innocent fervour. The stereo certainly carries the thrill of being there and both *Land of hope and glory* and *Rule Britannia* make a stunning effect. The sound is essentially atmospheric rather than clear (especially on tape) but the ambience is all-embracing. Only the rather mannered performance of *Cockaigne* carries any element of disappointment; the rest is superb, if not very generous.

'The last night of the Proms (1971/2)' (with BBC Ch., Norman, Bainbridge): BERLIOZ: *Les Troyens: Hail, all hail to the queen.* WAGNER: *Wesendonk Lieder: Schmerzen; Träume.* MENDELSSOHN: *Octet, Op. 20: Scherzo.* WALTON: *A song for the Lord Mayor's table: The contrast, Rhyme.* ELGAR: *Pomp and Circumstance march No. 1 in D.* WILLIAMSON: *The stone wall.* ARNE: *Rule Britannia.* PARRY: *Jerusalem* (arr. Elgar). *God save the Queen.*
(M) *** Ph. 6588 011/*7339 083.*

Philips followed up the success of its first record of a Last Night Prom (see above) with this conflation of concerts in successive years, 1971 and 1972. The greater part – notably the *Wesendonk songs* sung by Jessye Norman and the Walton songs from Elizabeth Bainbridge, not to mention the traditional patriotic numbers – come from 1972, but wisely the record also includes the most successful of the audience participation pieces written recently for this annual jamboree, Malcolm Williamson's 'Cassation' *The stone wall.* Not great music, but great fun for an audience. Like the first disc this vividly captures the electric atmosphere of the occasion. The cassette is somewhat disappointing: the upper range lacks sharpness of focus, especially in the climaxes of *Rule Britannia* and *Land of hope and glory.*

Berlin PO, Karajan

'Operatic overtures and intermezzi': MASSENET: *Thaïs: Meditation* (with Mutter). CHERUBINI: *Anacreon: overture.* WEBER: *Der Freischütz: overture.* SCHMIDT: *Notre Dame: Intermezzo.* PUCCINI: *Suor Angelica; Manon Lescaut: Intermezzi.* MASCAGNI: *L'Amico Fritz: Intermezzo.* HUMPERDINCK: *Hänsel und Gretel: overture.*
**(*) HMV Dig. ASD/*TCC-ASD* 4072 [Ang. DS/*4XS* 37810].

A curiously planned programme, with the *Meditation* from *Thaïs* (Anne-Sophie Mutter the gentle soloist) played very romantically, immediately followed by Cherubini's *Anacreon overture.* The performances of the Weber and Humperdinck overtures are disappointing, the first lacking electricity, the second charm. Best are the intermezzi on side two, played with the utmost passion. The digital recording here is very brightly lit, and there is a fierce sheen on the violins. The chrome tape is preferable; the sound is subtly fuller and the upper range smoother, yet without loss of detail.

'Popular German overtures': MENDELSSOHN: *The Hebrides (Fingal's Cave), Op. 26.* NICOLAI: *The Merry Wives of Windsor.* WEBER: *Der Freischütz.* WAGNER: *Der fliegende Holländer. Lohengrin: Prelude to Act I.*
(M) *** EMI Em. EMX/*TC-EMX* 41 2052-1/*4.*

This collection, originally recorded for the Columbia label in the early 1960s, was later reissued by World Record Club and then on HMV Concert Classics. Now it makes a welcome reappearance on Eminence. The performances are all superbly played and strongly characterized, and the reverberant acoustic gives them a robust (almost massive) quality, although detail remains clear. *Fingal's Cave* and the *Lohengrin Prelude* are especially distinguished, and Weber's magnificent *Der Freischütz* overture (of which there are surprisingly few available versions) is every bit as effective here as in Karajan's later digital recording, above. The sound in this remastered pressing has plenty of range (the cassette is somewhat less far-reaching at the top, but has slightly more body – it is different from rather than inferior to, the disc) and this is a most rewarding collection and excellent value.

'Adagio': ALBINONI: *Adagio in G min.* (arr. Giazotto) *for strings and organ.* PACHELBEL: *Canon and Gigue in D* (arr. Seiffert). BOCCHERINI: *Quintettino (La musica notturna di Madrid).* RESPIGHI: *Ancient airs and dances: Suite No. 3.* VIVALDI: *Concerto for strings in G (Alla rustica), RV.151.*
*** DG 2530 247/*3300 317* [id.].

Karajan's earlier performance of Albinoni's famous *Adagio* must be the plushiest ever, and in its way it is irresistible, like a particularly enticing meringue. The playing is very beautiful indeed, as it is also in Pachelbel's *Canon,* where the orchestral tone is utterly sumptuous, the harpsichord emerging through the rich textures like a piquant condiment. The *Gigue* that follows, however, is too thick-textured to sound spritely, though it remains pleasingly elegant. The Boccherini *Quintettino* is unusually evocative and most engagingly presented, while the Vivaldi concerto (which is not included on the disc) and the Respighi suite have an appealing grace. The recording is first-class and the tape transfer of very high quality.

'Meditation': BACH: *Suite No. 2 in B min., BWV 1067: Rondeau. Suite No. 3 in D, BWV 1068: Air.* MOZART: *Eine kleine Nachtmusik: Romanze.* DELIBES: *Coppélia: Ballade.* MASSENET: *Thaïs: Meditation.* CHOPIN (orch. Douglas): *Les Sylphides: Prelude; Nocturne.* SIBELIUS: *Legend: The Swan of Tuonela, Op. 22/2.* DEBUSSY: *Prélude à l'après-midi d'un faune.*
(M) **(*) DG Priv. 2535/*3335* 621.

Karajan's perfumed Bach performances are best heard as a pleasing background for the late evening, when one can admire the superbly polished orchestral playing (the harpsichord tinkling just audibly in the background). The rest of the programme is first-rate in every respect, and this anthology is more successfully compiled. The recording is resonantly atmospheric in exactly the right way, particularly in the latter part of the programme, where the performances are highly distinguished. The Debussy *Prélude* sounds quite ravishingly beautiful. The cassette transfer is very successful too.

'Digital concert': GRIEG: *Holberg suite, Op. 40.* MOZART: *Serenade No. 13 in G (Eine kleine Nachtmusik), K.525.* PROKOFIEV: *Symphony No. 1 in D (Classical), Op. 25.*
*** DG Dig. **400 034-2**; 2532/*3302* 031 [id.].

Some of the rustic freshness of Grieg eludes these artists: this is not unaffected speech. But how marvellous it sounds all the same! This is a great orchestral partnership 'making something' of the *Holberg suite*, perhaps, yet the music survives any over-sophistication and has never sounded more sumptuous and luxurious. Apart from a self-conscious and somewhat ponderous minuet, *Eine kleine Nachtmusik* sounds good too; the playing is beautifully cultured, with exquisitely shaped phrasing and wonderfully sprung rhythms. Only in the Prokofiev does one feel the want of charm and sparkle, except perhaps in the slow movement, which has grace and eloquence. The digital recording is excellent, though the balance in the Prokofiev is not entirely natural. Nonetheless a most desirable issue, particularly on account of the Grieg, especially in its compact disc format.

'Karajan digital': HOLST: *The Planets: Mars.* MOZART: *Die Zauberflöte: Overture.* OFFENBACH: *Orpheus in the Underworld: Overture. Contes d'Hoffmann: Barcarolle.* STRAUSS, J. Jnr: *An der schönen blauen Donau.* PROKOFIEV: *Symphony No. 1 in D (Classical).*
(M) *** DG 2560 016/*3309 041* [id.].

Certainly this medium-priced sampler shows the Karajan charisma and the marvellous ensemble of the Berlin orchestra to excellent effect. The sound is excellent, although on tape side two (which includes the *Symphony*) is slightly brighter and cleaner than side one. Good value, but the inclusion of Mars, which surely almost every collector will have in one version or another, slightly diminishes the appeal of an otherwise attractive programme.

ALBINONI: *Adagio in G min.* (arr. Giazotto). VIVALDI: *Flute concerto in G min. (La Notte), Op. 10/3, RV.439.* BACH: *Suite No. 3 in D: Air.* PACHELBEL: *Canon and Gigue in D.* GLUCK: *Orfeo: Dance of the Blessed Spirits.* MOZART: *Serenata notturna, K.239.*
** DG Dig. **413 309-2**; 413 309-1/*4*.

Karajan's digital baroque collection is given the benefit of beautiful sound, rich and refined. His mood is solemn, both in the famous *Adagio* and in his stately, measured view of the Pachelbel *Canon*, with the *Gigue* sprightly to provide contrast. The rest of the programme is very polished, but the effect is enervating rather than spirited. Karajan's earlier compilation (see above), if more indulgent, also has greater appeal both as a programme and in the character of the music-making. The chrome cassette is sophisticated and smooth, yet clear and full. The CD is exceptionally vivid, approaching demonstration standard.

Berlin PO, Solti

'The world of Russia': MUSSORGSKY: *Night on the Bare Mountain. Khovantschina: Prelude to Act I; Persian dance.* BORODIN: *Prince Igor: Overture.* GLINKA: *Russlan and Ludmilla: Overture.*
(M) *** Decca SPA 257.

It is fascinating to compare this concert with the similar collection Solti made with the LSO (*'Romantic Russia':* see below). The great Berlin orchestra obviously had a softening effect on Solti's vibrant musical nature, and the tightly strung nervous tension characteristic of the earlier programme has mellowed slightly here. *Night on the Bare Mountain* is splendidly exciting, yet the interpretation is a spacious one and the lyrical closing section must be one of the sweetest ever recorded. A similar radiance pervades the beautifully flowing *Khovantschina Prelude*, which is very successful, and there is sensuous orchestral playing in the *Persian dance*. *Russlan and Ludmilla* has a fraction less impetus here than in the London performance, and some may enjoy it for this slightly more relaxed air (in London the dash and virtuosity of the LSO's playing were paramount). The performance of the *Prince Igor overture* is extremely romantic, with an unexpected ritenuto for the second subject. This is disconcerting on first hearing, but one soon adjusts when the playing is so warmly committed and the recording so richly projected.

Berlin Philharmonic Wind Ens., Karajan

'Radetzky march': STRAUSS, J., Snr: *Radetzky march.* BEETHOVEN: *York march.* ANON.: *Torgau.* WALCH: *Entry into Paris.* WAGNER, J.F.: *Under the Double Eagle.* FUČIK: *Florentine.* PIEFKE: *Königgraetz; Glory of Prussia.* SCHRAMMEL: *Vienna for ever.* SEIFERT: *Carinthian songs.* HENRION: *Fehrbellin.* KOMZAK: *Archduke Albrecht* (etc.).
(M) ** DG Priv. 2535/*3335* 647 [id.].

This is taken from a two-disc collection of Prussian and Austrian marches, played with a certain characterful rhythmic stiffness where appropriate. The Austrian examples are more flexible. One does not generally hear this repertoire played with such expertise and polish, and the recording on disc is full-blooded and brilliant. We have not heard the cassette.

Bern Camerata, Füri

'The early Viennese School': MONN: *Sinfonia in B; Violin concerto in G.* STARZER: *Divertimento in C.* VANHAL: *Sinfonia in G min.* DITTERSDORF: *Sinfonia in A min.; Oboe concerto in G.* ZIMMERMANN: *Sinfonia in C.* ALBRECHTSBERGER: *Fugue for Quartet in C.* SALIERI: *Triple concerto for violin, oboe and cello in D.* WAGENSEIL: *Sinfonia in D.*
*** DG Arc. Dig. 410 599-1/*4* (3).

This set charts the musical scene in Vienna at the time of Haydn and Mozart and brings into the catalogue some music of distinct worth as well as interest. The Monn pieces are among the most valuable as well as early (he died in 1750) while the *G minor Symphony* of Vanhal and the *A minor* of Dittersdorf are hardly less fine. None of this music belongs in the same company as the finest Haydn or Mozart, but it affords an admirable perspective of their time; the performances by the Bern Camerata under Thomas Füri are most expert. The cassettes are in the demonstration class and the documentation is excellent for both media. Highly recommended.

'Boléro'

Spanish music: (i) Chicago SO, Solti; (ii) LAPO; (iii) SRO; (iv) Lopez-Cobos; (v) Montreal SO, Dutoit; (i) RAVEL: *Boléro.* (ii; iv) FALLA: *Three-cornered Hat: 3 Dances.* RIMSKY-KORSAKOV: *Capriccio espagnol.* CHABRIER: *España* (rhapsody). (iii; iv) TURINA: *Danzas fantásticas: Orgia.* (v) FALLA: *El amor brujo: Ritual fire dance.*
*(*) Decca **411 928-2** [id.].

A reasonably generous CD anthology with a playing time of just under an hour. But apart from the last two items, the performances – reviewed within the composer index – are not primary recommendations, and the digital remastering produces a spectacular impact rather than refinement. Solti's *Boléro* reaches a fierce climax and the Los Angeles recordings have a somewhat thick bass response. The *Ritual fire dance* at the end, under Dutoit and with a digital master, shows up the rest of the programme.

Boston Pops O, John Williams

'Pops on the march': WAGNER, J. F.: *Under the Double Eagle.* ELGAR: *Pomp and Circumstance march No. 1.* TCHAIKOVSKY: *Coronation march.* WALTON: *Orb and Sceptre.* GERSHWIN: *Strike up the Band.* HANDY: *St Louis blues.* WILLIAMS: *Midway.* WILLSON: *Music Man: 76 Trombones.* HAGGART: *South Rampart Street parade.* NEWMAN: *Conquest.*
*** Ph. Dig. 6302/*7144* 082.

John Williams directs exuberant performances of these highly attractive marches. The opening piece by J. F. Wagner (no connection with Richard) has splendid flair, and all the American marches are sparkling. The digital recording has plenty of weight as well as brilliance. Surprisingly, the Tchaikovsky march (although it has a good trio) is the least interesting here, but the rest are very entertaining. The cassette does not match the disc's transients, but reproduces agreeably if not very excitingly.

'Pops round the world': KABALEVSKY: *Overture Colas Breugnon.* SUPPÉ: *Overture Boccaccio.* AUBER: *Overture The bronze horse.* GLINKA: *Overture Russlan and Ludmilla.* WILLIAMS: *Overture The Cowboys.* ROSSINI: *Overture L'Italiana in Algeri.* BERNSTEIN: *Overture Candide.*
(*) Ph. Dig. **400 071-2; 6514/*7337* 186 [id.].

This lively collection, played and recorded with brash brilliance, brings together a fizzing musical cocktail. There are subtler versions of most of these pieces, but Williams can in no way be faulted for lack of bounce or vigour. The bright, extrovert qualities of performance and recording come out even more vividly on compact disc. The chrome cassette is of good quality but does not match the LP, let alone the CD, in sparkle.

'Out of this world': STRAUSS, R.: *Also sprach Zarathustra: Introduction.* WILLIAMS: *E. T.: Adventures on earth. Return of the Jedi: suite.* GOLDSMITH: *Alien: Closing title. Star Trek – The Motion Picture: Main Title.* COURAGE: *Star Trek: TV theme.* PHILIPS: *Battlestar Galactica: Main title.* CONSTANT: *Twilight zone: Theme and variations.*
** Ph. Dig. **411 185-2**; 411 185-1/*4* [id.].

Music of much flamboyance, very well played and spectacularly recorded within a flattering acoustic. Apart from Alexander Courage's quite memorable TV signature theme for *Star Trek* John Williams's own contributions are clearly superior to the rest. There is a melodic sweep and a sense of purpose that – for all the eclectic derivations of style – put these scores in a class of their own. However, the suite from the *Return of the Jedi* is less memorable than the music for *E.T.* The chrome cassette could ideally have been transferred at a higher level, but still sounds well. The CD offers an agreeable bloom on the sound, which is vivid but lacking something in brilliance in the upper range. However, the ambient warmth is very agreeable.

'On stage': BERLIN: *There's no business like show business.* HAMLISCH: *A Chorus line: Overture.* MANN/WEIL: *Here you come again.* ELLINGTON: *Sophisticated lady; Mood indigo; It don't mean a thing.* STRAYHORN: *Take the 'A' train.* LLOYD WEBBER: *Cats: Memory.* BERLIN: *Top hat, white tie and tails.* YOUMANS: *The Carioca.* SCHWARZ: *Dancing in the dark.* KERN: *I won't dance.* CONRAD: *The Continental.* RODGERS: *On your toes: Slaughter on 10th Avenue* (arr. Bennett).
*** Ph. **412 132-2**; 412 132-1/*4* [id.].

John Williams is completely at home in this repertoire. He is especially good in bringing out detail in the *Overture* for *A Chorus line*, and in the ballet score, *Slaughter on 10th Avenue*, which is heard complete and contains two of the most memorable tunes the composer ever wrote – fully worthy of Gershwin. The other items are offered in groups, tailored sophisticatedly as tributes to Duke Ellington and Fred Astaire; but equally enjoyable is the highlight of Bob Fosse's *Dancin'*, the engaging *Here you come again.* Splendid orchestral playing and excellent sound (with a very good tape), although the body of strings is not made to seem sumptuous.

Boston SO

'Great orchestral showpieces' (cond. (i) Steinberg; (ii) Ozawa; (iii) Leinsdorf; (iv) Fiedler): (i) DUKAS: *L'Apprenti sorcier.* STRAUSS, R.: *Till Eulenspiegel.* SAINT-SAËNS: *Danse macabre.* (ii) STRAVINSKY: *Petrushka: Russian dance.* (iii) KODÁLY: *Háry János: Viennese musical clock; Entrance of the Emperor.* (iv) DVOŘÁK: *Carnaval overture.*
(B) **(*) RCA VICS/*VK* 2024.

This is reasonably priced and generous. The playing is brilliant with sound to match, and Steinberg's racy accounts of *The Sorcerer's apprentice* and *Till Eulenspiegel* are infectious. He is equally at home in the Saint-Saëns pictorialism which has both sparkle and warmth. The other items are colourful enough, and Fiedler's sprightly *Carnaval* makes an apt closing piece. The chrome tape emphasizes the upper range with a touch of shrillness but is not beyond control. The focus, on both disc and tape, is slightly less sharp in the Stravinsky and Kodály items. Good value.

Bournemouth Sinf., Del Mar

English music: BRIDGE: *Suite for strings; Summer; There is a willow grows aslant a brook.* BANTOCK: *The pierrot of the minuet: overture.* BUTTERWORTH: *The banks of green willow.*
(M) *** Chan. CBR/*CBT* 1018.

Norman Del Mar draws glowing performances of these Bridge pieces from the Sinfonietta. Most valuable of all is the tone poem, *Summer*, with its highly original and evocative instrumentation. Perhaps Bantock's comedy overture slightly outstays its welcome, but it remains enjoyable in such a lively performance, acting as a foil for the lovely Butterworth idyll which is presented with radiant persuasiveness. The recording – originally issued by RCA – is excellent, full and atmospheric.

Bournemouth SO

'90th Anniversary': AUBER: *Overture The bronze horse.* MEYERBEER: *Le Prophète: Coronation march* (cond. Godfrey). SCHUBERT: *Overture in the Italian style in D, D.590* (cond. Schwarz). ARNOLD: *English dances Nos. 1, 2, 5, 6, 8* (cond. Groves). DUKAS: *L'Apprenti sorcier* (cond. Silvestri). SIBELIUS: *Legends: The swan of Tuonela; Lemminkaïnen's return* (cond. Berglund). BRITTEN: *Gloriana: Courtly dances* (cond. Segal).
(M) (**) HMV Green. ESD/*TC-ESD* 107735-1/*4*.

The first recordings here, conducted by Sir Dan Godfrey, date from the 1930s with the orchestra vigorous rather than refined in Auber and Meyerbeer. The rest celebrates the work of subsequent conductors, Berglund and Silvestri more successfully than Schwarz, Groves or Segal, but always with the freshness and colour that have been a consistent trademark of this orchestra. Good transfers on both disc and tape.

Bournemouth SO, Dunn

'British concert favourites: CLARKE: *Trumpet voluntary.* PURCELL: *Dido and Aeneas: When I am laid in earth.* SULLIVAN: *The Yeomen of the Guard: Overture.* HANDEL: *Berenice: Minuet.* ELGAR: *Enigma variations: Nimrod.* BLISS: *Things to Come: March.* VAUGHAN WILLIAMS: *Fantasia on Greensleeves.* HOLST: *The Planets: Jupiter* (excerpt). QUILTER: *Rosamund: Where the rainbow ends.* WALTON: *Crown Imperial march.*
(M) ** Chan. CBR/*CBT* 1002.

An agreeable medium-priced collection of British popular repertoire, generally well recorded, though the *Trumpet voluntary* is not clearly focused. Sir Vivian Dunn – not surprisingly, as an ex-Musical Director of the Royal Marines – is at his best in the marches. Elsewhere the performances are somewhat routine. Dunn is especially affectionate in the Roger Quilter excerpt, but treats the central melody of Holst's *Jupiter* like a hymn.

Bournemouth SO, Silvestri

'Stereo showpieces': MUSSORGSKY: *Night on the Bare Mountain.* RAVEL: *Pavane pour une infante défunte.* SAINT-SAËNS: *Danse macabre, Op. 40.* SIBELIUS: *Finlandia, Op. 26.* BORODIN: *In the Steppes of Central Asia.* DUKAS: *L'Apprenti sorcier.*
(M) **(*) HMV Green. ESD 7064.

The late Constantin Silvestri is heard at his very best here, especially in the pieces which call for brilliance. Moreover the Studio Two recording although slightly dry in ambience, does not lack breadth and sparkle and is admirably clear in detail. *Night on the Bare*

Mountain opens the concert vividly, and both the *Danse macabre* and *The Sorcerer's Apprentice* are exciting and colourful. *Finlandia* too is done with plenty of gusto. The slower pieces lack the last degree of expansiveness and poetry, but within the context of the programme they are undoubtedly enjoyable when the overall projection is so vivid.

Brain, Dennis (horn)

(see also under Instrumental recitals)

'The art of Dennis Brain' (with (i) Philh. O, (ii) Sargent or Turner; (iii) Susskind; (iv) Cantelli; (v) Galliera; (vi) Sawallisch; (vii) Kletzki; (viii) Hindemith; (ix) Brain Ens.): MOZART: *Horn concertos Nos.* (i; ii) *4, K.495;* (i; iii) *2, K.417;* (i; iv) *A Musical joke, K.522;* (ix) *Divertimento No. 15 in B flat, K.270.* STRAUSS, R.: *Horn concertos Nos.* (i; v) *1 in E flat, Op. 11;* (i; vi) *2 in E flat.* BEETHOVEN: *Horn sonata in F, Op. 17* (with Matthews). WAGNER: *Siegfried's horn call.* (i; vii) MENDELSSOHN: *Midsummer night's dream: Nocturne.* BERKELEY: *Horn trio* (with Parikian, Horsley). (i; viii) HINDEMITH: *Horn concerto.* (ix) IBERT: *Trois pièces brèves.* DUKAS: *Villanelle* (with Moore). MOZART, L.: *Concerto for hose-pipe and strings* (with Morley College O, Del Mar).
(M) (***) HMV RLS/*TC-RLS* 7701 (3).

Dennis Brain was not only a uniquely fine horn player and a consummate musician, he was also a delightful person, and the disarming geniality of his personality coupled to a rare sensibility gave his music-making very special qualities. The full range of his achievement is readily demonstrated here, and even though many of the recordings are early, the magical inevitability of his phrasing and the expressive richness of his legato timbre illuminate everything he plays, while the almost schoolboyish sense of fun is always bubbling up when the music is lively and spirited. He began his career using a narrow-bore 'French' horn without the frills, or ease of execution, of the wider-bore German instrument. The former can be heard in the superbly confident and imaginative account of Beethoven's unevenly inspired *Horn sonata* which he recorded with Denis Matthews in 1944, while the soaring richness of line of the early Strauss *First Horn concerto* demonstrates how completely he adapted to the more flexible German instrument. The articulation in the finale of the *Second* Strauss *Concerto* shows the incredible technical freedom he achieved which was to have a profound influence on following generations of British horn players and establish new standards of virtuosity and security, by simply showing what was possible. The spirited freshness of his Mozart style in two concertos by this master contrasts with the effortless bravura in Hindemith, much less rewarding music, but a *tour de force* of execution. The Berkeley *Horn trio* is well worth having, with its bitter-sweet cultured elegance, as are the chamber pieces, while it was a happy idea to include the Hoffnung-inspired hosepipe concerto. Transfers are fresh and clear on disc and tape alike.

Brass of Aquitaine and London, Harvey

'Brass at La Sauve-Majeure': COPLAND: *Fanfare for the common man.* HARVEY: *La citadelle. L'homme armé.* LULLY: *Le carrousel du Roy.* ADSON: *4 Courtly masquing ayres.* GESUALDO: *Cor mio deh non piangete.* GABRIELI, G.: *Canzon septimi octavi toni a 12 No. 13.* VIADANA: *La Padovana.* PURCELL: *Funeral music for Queen Mary.*
*** ASV ALH/*ZCALH* 926.

Impressive playing and fine recording within a well-judged acoustic. The opening Copland *Fanfare* has telling percussion and the trumpet sonorities are especially full. Adson's *Masquing ayres* are unexpectedly attractive and Harvey's own variants on the familiar medieval theme, *L'homme armé*, are certainly effective. The concert closes with the greatest music, three excerpts from Purcell's *Funeral music*. The excellent cassette matches the disc closely, and offers demonstration sound in the Copland.

Cantilena, Shepherd

'Christmas concertos': CORELLI: *Concerto grosso in G min., Op. 6/8.* FARINA: *Pavana.* WIDMANN: *Canzona; Galliard; Intrada.*

FERRABOSCO II: *Pavane No. 4.* VIVALDI: *Sinfonia in G, RV.149.*
** Chan. ABR/*ABT* 1024.

An agreeable if not really distinctive programme of baroque music. The playing is alert and stylish, and the Corelli *Christmas concerto* sounds far more convincing here than in Müller-Brühl's more 'authentic' version (see below). The Farina *Pavana* is also attractive when presented with such commitment, but the dances are lightweight and make side two less substantial. The sound is excellent on disc, marginally less refined on cassette.

'Encore': HANDEL: *Solomon: Arrival of the Queen of Sheba.* PACHELBEL: *Canon.* VIVALDI: *Concerto in A, P.231.* TELEMANN: *Viola concerto in A.* PEZEL: *Suite a 5.* BACH, J. S.: *Suite No. 3, BWV 1068: Air.* MUFFAT: *Concerto grosso (Delirium amoris):* PEPUSCH: *Chamber symphony in D min.*
(*) Chan. Dig. **CHAN 8319; ABRD/-*ABTD* 1069.

The Pepusch and Muffat pieces are welcome rarities, no less charming than the other 'baroque encores' included on this disc. The performances are not immaculate but are always fresh and well sprung, with no sentimentality in slower pieces like the Bach. First-rate recording, with the chrome cassette in the demonstration class. With an attractive ambience, this is most enjoyable in an unostentatious way. The opening *Arrival of the Queen of Sheba* is especially engaging.

Capella Clementina, Müller-Brühl

'Italian Christmas concertos': CORELLI: *Concerto grosso in G min., Op. 6/8.* MANFREDINI: *Sinfonia in D, Op. 2/12.* SCHIASSI: *Sinfonia in D.* SAMMARTINI: *Concerto grosso in G min., Op. 5/6.*
(M) * Ph. 9502/*7313* 075.

All these concertos include the required *Pastorale* slow movements to achieve their Christmas association; indeed the Manfredini work is made up of three slow movements. The *Sinfonia* of Gaetano Schiassi (1698–1754) also includes an unusual *Largo spiccato* to remind the listener of Vivaldi. Performances here offer the current view of expressive baroque string style, but the rhythmic feeling is heavy and the end result is rather dull. The sound is better on disc than on cassette where the focus is often unclear.

Casals, Pablo (cello and cond.)

'Song of the birds': TRAD. (arr. Casals): *Song of the birds; St Marti del Canigo* (with Prades Fest. O). BACH: *Organ pastorale in F; Aria* (with Perpignan Fest. O). *Organ concerto No. 3* (trans. Rosanoff). HAYDN: *Piano sonata No. 9 in D: Adagio.* FALLA: *7 Spanish popular songs: Nana* (with Istomin). SCHUMANN: *5 Pieces in folk style* (with Mannes).
(M) ** CBS 61579/*40-*.

The main interest here is the title-piece, which seems to have caught the public fancy. The rest of the programme is most notable for Casals's own vocal contributions – various grunts and expressions of ardour accompanying the playing. The recording is good but a trifle dry and the tape transfer is acceptable (not wide in range but quite convincingly balanced), even if the upper focus of the cello timbre is not always quite clean.

Chacksfield, Frank, and his **O**

'The world of immortal classics': DEBUSSY: *Suite bergamasque: Clair de lune.* SAINT-SAËNS: *Carnival of the Animals: The swan.* ELGAR: *Salut d'amour.* TCHAIKOVSKY: *Nutcracker: Waltz of the flowers.* LISZT: *Liebestraum No. 3.* RUBINSTEIN: *Melody in F.* GRIEG: *Peer Gynt: Morning.* DVOŘÁK: *Humoresque.* BACH: *Suite No. 3: Air.* ALSTONE: *Valse d'été.*
(M) *** Decca SPA 176.

The title *Immortal classics* suggests that this might be a glamorous selection, and that is certainly so. Purists are urged to keep well away, but those who like to wallow in rich orchestral textures should sample this. The arrangements are unashamedly vulgar (yet in an essentially stylish way), with Saint-Saëns's *Swan* portrayed on divided strings floating serenely as on a Disneyland lake against a reflected Hollywood sunset. The sound really is luscious throughout and each piece is ripely characterized, with Alstone's charming *Valse d'été* fetchingly lightweight at the close. The sound offers wide dynamic contrasts (inherent in the playing), with splendid detail and range.

Chandos: 'The special sound of Chandos'

Digital demonstration recordings: (i) SNO, Gibson; (ii) Janis Kelly, LSO, Simon; (iii) J. Hilton, CBSO, Jarvi; (iv) Taverner Players, Parrott; (v) Ulster O, Thomson; (vi) J. Strauss O., Rothstein; (vii) Cantilena, Shepherd; (viii) ECO, Gibson; (ix) BBC SO, Schurmann: (i) HOLST: *The Planets: Jupiter.* (ii) TCHAIKOVSKY: *Hamlet: Scène d'Ophélie.* (iii) WEBER: *Clarinet concertino, Op. 73: Finale.* (iv) PURCELL: *Dido and Aeneas: Overture.* (v) HARTY: *Irish symphony: 3rd movt.* (i) ARNOLD: *Tam O'Shanter, Op. 51.* (vi) STRAUSS, J. Jnr: *Egyptian march.* (vii) HANDEL: *Solomon: Arrival of the Queen of Sheba:* (viii): STRAVINSKY: *Pulcinella: Serenata and Scherzino.* (ix) SCHURMANN: *6 Studies: No. 5.*

C *** Chan. Dig. **CHAN 8301**; CBRD/*CBTD* 1008.

It is surprising that a smaller company should make the first digital demonstration issue in compact-disc form, rather than one of the majors. The result is a spectacular success. All the recordings are impressive (though the Purcell sounds spiky, and the oboes are balanced too closely in the *Arrival of the Queen of Sheba*). On CD there is a thrilling impact and sense of orchestral presence in the pieces by Holst and Malcolm Arnold, while the delightful Tchaikovsky vocal scena (a perfect item for a musical quiz), the Harty excerpt from the *Irish symphony* (*In the Antrim Hills*) and the Johann Strauss *March* are equally impressive and enjoyable with their different kinds of evocation. The sound is demonstration-worthy on the LP and the chrome cassette too, but the CD is breathtaking in its vividness.

Chicago SO, Reiner

'Vienna': Waltzes: STRAUSS, J. Jnr: *An der schönen blauen Donau; Kaiser; Morgenblätter.* WEBER: *Invitation to the dance, Op. 65.* STRAUSS, Josef: *Dorfschwalben aus Osterreich (Village swallows), Op. 164.* STRAUSS, R.: *Der Rosenkavalier: Waltz sequence.*

(B) *** RCA VICS/*VK* 2013.

A vintage collection with Reiner creating a magical Viennese atmosphere in Chicago, able to relax in the most beguiling way and yet never lose his hold on the tension. The *Blue Danube*, *Emperor* (a gentle, affectionate reading) and especially *Village swallows* are memorable as are the solo interchanges in Weber's *Invitation to the dance*, while Reiner's special feeling for the music of Richard Strauss is readily demonstrated in the *Rosenkavalier* sequence. Here is a case where the vivid chrome tape is preferable to the disc (where the sound quality seems slightly more dated). But both are recommendable.

Chung, Kyung-Wha (violin)

'Favourite concertos': SIBELIUS: *Violin concerto in D, Op. 47.* TCHAIKOVSKY: *Violin concerto in D, Op. 35* (both with LSO, Previn). BRUCH: *Violin concerto No. 1 in G min.* (with RPO, Kempe). CHAUSSON: *Poème, Op. 25.* SAINT-SAËNS: *Introduction and Rondo capriccioso, Op. 28* (both with RPO, Dutoit). BEETHOVEN: *Violin concerto in D, Op. 61* (with VPO, Kondrashin).

(M) **(*) Decca D 266 D 3/*K 266 K 33* (3).

It was a pity that Decca chose to include the Beethoven *Concerto* in this box which otherwise contains performances which are all strongly recommendable. For some reason Chung's partnership with Kondrashin failed to work and, though there is some radiant solo playing in the slow movement, the outer movements do not catch fire. The excellence of the Decca recording is consistent throughout the set, though the level of the cassette transfers might usefully have been higher (in the Beethoven the tape balance is bass-heavy).

Clarinet

'The world of the clarinet' (with (i) Alfred Prinz, Stuttgart CO, Münchinger; (ii) Gervase de Peyer, with Cyril Preedy (piano); (iii) Alfred Boskovsky, with members of the Vienna Octet): (i) MOZART: *Clarinet concerto in A, K.622.* (ii) WEBER: *Grand duo concertante in E flat, Op. 48.* DEBUSSY: *Petite Pièce.* HOROVITZ: *2 Majorcan pieces.* (iii) WAGNER: *Adagio for clarinet and strings.* BRAHMS: *Clarinet quintet in B min., Op. 115:* 3rd movt.
(M) *** Decca SPA 395.

Such a collection must inevitably include Mozart's *Clarinet concerto*, the most beautiful lyrical concertante work written for any wind instrument; but this (in a fine performance by Alfred Prinz) tends to put the rest of the programme in the shade. Nevertheless the music on side two is imaginatively chosen, and the individual items fit together very well. In particular the Debussy *Petite Pièce* and the two Majorcan miniatures by Horovitz make a witty closing section after the classical and romantic repertoire. The recording is first-rate throughout.

'Classical favourites'

(i) ECO, Bonynge; (ii) LSO; (iii) Solti; (iv) ROHCGO, Boult; (v) SRO, Ansermet; (vi) Stuttgart CO, Münchinger; (vii) Kertesz; (viii) V. Moz. Ens., Boskovsky; (ix) VPO, Knappertsbusch: (i) HANDEL: *Solomon: Arrival of the Queen of Sheba.* (ii; iii) *Water music: Air. Xerxes: Largo.* (iv) BACH: *Cantata No. 208: Sheep may safely graze.* (v) *Suite No. 3 in D, BWV 1068: Air. Cantata No. 12: Sinfonia.* (vi) BOCCHERINI: *Quintet in E, Op. 13/5: Minuet and Trio.* HAYDN (attrib. Hofstetter): *String quartet No. 17 in F, Op. 3/5: Serenade.* (ii; vii) MOZART: *Masonic funeral music, K.477.* (viii) *German dance, K.605/3: Sleigh-ride. Divertimento No. 17 in D, K.334: Minuet and Trio.* (ix) SCHUBERT: *Marche militaire in D, D.733/1.*
(M) ** Decca SPA/*KCSP* 510.

An agreeable collection of favourites, generally stylishly performed and well recorded, making effective background listening for late evening, or – on tape – in the car, where a consistently high-level transfer projects the music well, if keeping it all on much the same dynamic plane.

(i) Cleveland Sinf.; (ii) Cleveland O; Lane

'English music': (i) VAUGHAN WILLIAMS: *The Lark Ascending* (with Druian). DELIUS: *Hassan: Serenade.* WARLOCK: *Serenade for strings.* (ii) BACH (arr. Walton): *The Wise Virgins* (suite).
(M) ** CBS 61433/*40-*.

This collection dates from the mid-1960s when Louis Lane was a colleague of George Szell at Cleveland and the orchestra at the peak of its form. Rafael Druian is the highly poetic violin soloist in *The Lark Ascending*, and the orchestral playing, besides being polished, has both character and atmosphere, here and in the pieces by Delius and Warlock. The snag is the very forward balance, which tends to rob the Vaughan Williams of some of its evocative quality (although Druian triumphs over the engineers by achieving a fairly wide dynamic range). *The Wise Virgins* – not often recorded – sounds suitably vivid. The cassette is not as refined as the disc, but is acceptable with a top cut.

Collegium Musicum

'Bohemian wind music': FIALA: *Divertimento No. 3 in D sharp.* KROMMER: *Partita in B flat.* TRIEBENSEE: *Variations on a theme from Jirovec's Der Augenarzt; Partita in E flat.*
(M) *** Sup. 1111 2973.

Beautifully played and recorded, this is a most engaging collection for a balmy summer evening. The music is often ingenuous, but always well crafted, and has an agreeable humanity and warmth of feeling. There is humour too and plenty of high spirits. Czech musicians make a programme of this kind very much their own. Recommended.

Cologne Musica Antiqua

'Conversation galante': GUILLEMAIN: *Quar-*

tet sonata in A min., Op. 17/6. FRANCOEUR: *Sonata in E, Op. 2/6.* PHILIDOR: *L'art de la modulation: Quartet (Sinfonia) No. 3 in G.* QUENTIN: *Quartet sonata in D.*
*** DG Arc. Dig. 2534 006 [id.].

The title of the record, *'Conversation galante'*, derives from an expression used by Louis-Gabriel Guillemain (1705–70) in one of his title-pages, though not of the *Sonate en quatuor* recorded here. However, elegant discourse is what this music is, and these players convey much poise and elegance in their presentation of these pieces. Those who have little sympathy with period instruments should not be put off, for this group plays with real expertise, grace and accuracy of intonation. The textures are transparent and clean and the whole effect has delicacy and charm. It is also beautifully recorded and presented. None of the music has depth or stature, but it is delightful for all that. Strongly recommended.

Baroque concert: PACHELBEL: *Canon and Gigue.* HANDEL: *Sonata for 2 violins and continuo in G, Op. 5/4.* VIVALDI: *Sonata in D min. (La Follia) for 2 violins and continuo, RV.63.* BACH: *Suite No. 2 in B min. for flute and strings, BWV 1067* (with W. Hazelzet).
*(*) DG Arc. Dig. **410 502-2** [id.].

The Pachelbel *Canon* taken fast with squeezed notes and buzzy decoration will not be everyone's idea of fun, and the closely balanced sound is scratchy. It improves in the Bach *Suite* and this is an enjoyably fresh, lightweight performance. The Vivaldi is successful too, in its way, though the timbre here is the opposite of mellow. The recording focus in fact is rather variable and this compact disc seems to have few of the obvious virtues of the new system, except background silence.

'Country gardens'

English music (various artists, including Bournemouth SO, Silvestri; Hallé O, Barbirolli; Royal Liv. PO, Groves; E. Sinfonia, Dilkes): VAUGHAN WILLIAMS: *The Wasps: Overture. Rhosymedre.* WARLOCK: *Capriol suite.* DELIUS: *Summer Night on the River. A Song before Sunset.* GRAINGER: *Country Gardens. Mock Morris; Shepherd's Hey.* BRIDGE (arr.): *Cherry Ripe.* COLERIDGE TAYLOR: *Petite suite de concert* (excerpts). GERMAN: *Nell Gwyn: 3 Dances.* COATES: *Meadow to Mayfair: In the country. Summer Days: At the dance. Wood Nymphs.* ELGAR: *Chanson de matin. Salut d'amour.*
(B) *** EMI *TC2-MOM 123.*

A highly recommendable tape-only collection, essentially lightweight but never trivial. Barbirolli's Delius, and Neville Dilkes's *Capriol suite* are among the highlights; one notices in the latter that the sound is drier and sharper in focus here than in the source-cassette (*TC-ESD 7101* – now deleted). This gives greater projection against motorway background noise, and certainly it makes a most entertaining concert for use on a long journey, with the lively Grainger, Coates and German pastoral dances providing an excellent foil for the lyrical music. On domestic equipment the quality is vivid, but may need a softening of the treble.

Dallas SO, Mata

Concert: MUSSORGSKY: *Night on the bare mountain.* DUKAS: *L'apprenti sorcier.* TCHAIKOVSKY: *Capriccio italien.* ENESCO: *Rumanian rhapsody No. 1.*
C *** RCA Dig. **RCD 14439** [id./also LP: ATC1 4205].

One of the outstanding orchestral demonstration compact discs. The acoustic of the Dallas Hall produces a thrilling resonance without too much clouding of detail. The opening of Tchaikovsky's *Capriccio italien* is stunning in its amplitude with lustrous string timbres and brass fanfares riveting in their impact. The silences when the music pauses are hardly less telling, both here and in the equally sumptuous Enesco *Rhapsody.* These are the two most effective performances; the Mussorgsky piece is rather lacking in menace when textures are so ample. *The Sorcerer's apprentice* is spirited and affectionately characterized, yet there is no sense of real calamity at the climax. But the Tchaikovsky and Enesco are richly enjoyable, even if the latter lacks the last degree of unbuttoned exuberance in its closing pages.

'Ibéria': DEBUSSY: *Images: No. 2, Ibéria.* RIMSKY-KORSAKOV: *Capriccio espagnol, Op. 34.* TURINA: *Danzas fantásticas: Orgía.*
*(*) Telarc Dig. DG 10055 [id.].

A disappointing collection. The recording is certainly vivid, but in *Ibéria* detail registers at the expense of a panoramic view, and as an extrovert performance this does not match Stokowski's sparklingly sensuous account with the French National Radio Orchestra (deleted, alas), which is equally impressive as a recording. Here Rimsky-Korsakov's *Capriccio* has neither sumptuousness nor a compensating electricity, and one wonders why room could not have been found for all three of Turina's *Danzas fantásticas.*

Dichter, Misha (piano), **Philh. O, Marriner**

Concertante works: ADDINSELL: *Warsaw concerto.* GERSHWIN: *Rhapsody in blue.* LITOLFF: *Concerto symphonique, Op. 102: Scherzo.* CHOPIN: *Fantasia on Polish airs, Op. 13.* LISZT: *Polonaise brillante* (arr. of WEBER: *Polacca brillante, Op. 72*).
C *** Ph. Dig. **411 123-2**; 411 123-1/*4* [id.].

Addinsell's indelible pastiche is here promoted up-market, away from the usual film-music anthologies into a collection of pieces written for the concert hall, and how well it holds its own. The orchestral detail has never before emerged so beguilingly on record as it does under Marriner, and he and Misha Dichter combine to give the music genuine romantic memorability, within a warmly sympathetic acoustic. Gershwin's famous *Rhapsody* is hardly less successful, the performance spirited yet glowing. To make a foil, the Litolff *Scherzo* is taken at a sparklingly brisk tempo and projected with great flair. The Chopin *Fantasia* has a lower voltage but the closing Liszt arrangement of Weber glitters admirably. The sound is first-rate (with a very good tape) and is superbly believable in its CD format.

Dresden State O, Marriner

Orchestral showpieces: CHABRIER: *España* (rhapsody). GLINKA: *Jota aragonesa.* RAVEL: *Boléro.* TCHAIKOVSKY: *Capriccio italien.*
* Ph. Dig. **410 047-2**; 6514/*7337* 235.

The Dresden orchestra produces some excellent playing, but there is a cosiness of style in Marriner's readings that ill suits music of this kind. The sound is not especially vivid either, although the compact disc sounds fresher than the LP, and *Boléro* obviously gains from the opening background silence. But there is no drama in its dynamic expansion.

Early Music Consort of London, Munrow

'Greensleeves to a ground': ANON.: *Greensleeves to a ground.* DOWLAND: *5 Dances.* WILLIAMS: *Sonata in imitation of birds.* PURCELL: *Chaconne.* PAISIBLE: *Sonata for 4 recorders.* VAUGHAN WILLIAMS: *Fantasia on Greensleeves. Suite for pipes.* WARLOCK: *Capriol suite: Bransles.* RUBBRA: *Meditazioni.* RICHARDSON: *Beachcomber.*
*** HMV CSD 3781.

There is some enchanting music here. One would expect the Elizabethan items to steal the honours, and certainly the Dowland *Dances* (and the famous title-piece) are effective, while William Williams's *Trio sonata in imitation of birds* (1703) is charming. But most memorable of all are the Warlock *Bransles* (deliciously scored), the Vaughan Williams *Suite for pipes*, and Richardson's *Beachcomber*, with its enchanting ocarina effects. The only comparatively clumsy arrangement is of Vaughan Williams's *Greensleeves fantasia*, where the piano accompaniment is no substitute for strings. The playing throughout is flawless, and the modest instrumentation beautifully recorded.

'The art of the recorder' (with Norma Burrowes, soprano; Martyn Hill, tenor; James Bowman, counter-tenor; Robert Lloyd, bass): ANON.: *English dance* (13th century); *Saltarello* (14th century). BARBIREAU: *Een Vrolic Wesen.* ATTAIGNANT (publisher): *4*

Chansons. BYRD: *The leaves be green* (Fantasy). HOLBORNE: *5 Dances*. SCHMELZER: *Sonata à 7 flauti*. PURCELL: *Fantasia: 3 Parts upon a ground*. VIVALDI: *Concerto in A min*. BASTON: *Concerto in D*. HANDEL: *Acis and Galatea: O ruddier than the cherry*. BACH: *Cantata No. 208: Sheep may safely graze. Cantata No. 106: Sonatina. Magnificat, BWV 243: Esurientes*. ARNE: *As You Like It: Under the greenwood tree*. COUPERIN: *2 Musettes*. BRITTEN: *Scherzo*. HINDEMITH: *Plöner Musiktag: Trio*. BUTTERLEY: *The white-throated warbler*. DICKINSON: *Recorder music*.
(M) *** HMV SLS 5022 (2).

This cleverly arranged anthology shows the recorder in all its roles, from the comparatively simple medieval instrumentation, through the Renaissance to the baroque and classical periods; the delightful decorative effect on vocal music is well represented, and the collection ends with some formidable modern examples. The recording is admirably clear and forward, with a fine presence.

(i) Early Music Consort; (ii) Morley Consort

'Two Renaissance dance bands' (both dir. Munrow): (i) SUSATO: *12 Dances from 'The Danserye'*. (ii) *Dances for broken consort from Thomas Morley's First Booke of Consort Lessons*.
(M) *** HMV HQS/*TC-HQS* 1249.

Tielman Susato (who lived in the first half of the sixteenth century) left no orchestration for his *Danserye*, directing that the music should be played on musical instruments of all kinds ('as is pleasing and appropriate'). The Early Music Consort take him at his word and provide a galaxy of crumhorns, cornetts, sackbuts, recorders and string instruments, with a regal thrown in for good measure. The instrumentation is nicely varied, with the full forces employed for the set-pieces like the *Pavane la bataille*. Perhaps the playing itself is more sophisticated than sixteenth-century listeners would have expected, but it is lively and direct, and the effect is to bring the music fully back to life. The dances from Morley's *First Booke* are given a softer, more delicate instrumentation, which matches well the melancholy grace of the Elizabethan court dance style. Again the playing is committed and there are some really lovely sounds here, which the atmospheric recording sets in excellent perspective. Altogether this is a valuable and enjoyable issue, as useful for schools as for the home, where it will provide some unusual and colourful incidental music. The cassette transfer level is relatively modest to accommodate the wide amplitude of the opening *Mourisque* from the Susato dances, and this means that (especially on side one) the transients are not very crisp. But the recorders make some delightful sounds and in the Morley group on side two the quality seems cleaner.

Eastman Rochester O, Fennell

American music: CARPENTER: *Adventures in a perambulator* (suite). MOORE: *Pageant of P.T. Barnum*. NELSON: *Savannah River holiday*.
(M) **(*) Mercury SRI 75095 [id.].

John Alden Carpenter's piece was a favourite of American audiences before the Second World War and is diverting and often charming. It does slightly outstay its welcome and, though some numbers are eminently attractive, others remain amiably innocuous. The music on the reverse side is equally accessible and the *Savannah River holiday* is quite fetching. The performances are bright and breezy, and totally committed.

Eastman Rochester O, Hanson

American music: GINASTERA: *Overture to the Creole Faust*. BARBER: *Capricorn concerto*. SESSIONS: *The Black Maskers* (suite).
(M) *** Mercury SRI 75049 [id.].

The Ginastera overture is a rather good piece: it is about a cowboy who has been to see Gounod's *Faust*, and the invention is distinctly appealing. The Barber *Capricorn concerto* is less characteristic Barber than, say, either of the *Essays for orchestra* or the charming *Cello concerto*. It has a neoclassical

Stravinskian bite to it, an impression that is accentuated somewhat by the dry, spiky recording. Detail is very clear, however, and the performance lively and well shaped. The Sessions is an eclectic but effective score. At its modest price this deserves a strong recommendation: the repertoire is not otherwise available and the performances are very good. Allowances should be made for the sound which is a bit thin, particularly on the top.

Eastman Symphonic Wind Ens., Fennell

'Marching along': SOUSA: *US Field Artillery. The Thunderer; Washington Post; King Cotton; El Capitan; The Stars and Stripes forever.* MEACHAM: *American patrol.* GOLDMAN: *On the Mall.* MCCOY: *Lights out.* KING: *Barnum and Bailey's favourite.* ALFORD: *Colonel Bogey.* KLOHR: *The Billboard.*
(M) *** Mercury SRI/*MRI* 75004 [id.].

An ebullient collection of American marches, played with splendid brio and crisply recorded in Mercury's best demonstration sound. The dynamic sophistication of Meacham's *American patrol* is matched by the vivid directness of the Sousa favourites – *The Stars and Stripes* superbly done.

'Screamers' (Circus marches): HEED: *In storm and sunshine.* ALLEN: *Whip and spur.* KING: *Invictus; The big cage; Robinson's grand entree; Circus days.* FILLIMORE: *Bones trombone; Circus bee; Rolling thunder.* JEWELL: *The screamer.* FUČIK: *Thunder and lightning.* FARRAR: *Bombasto.* HUFF: *The squealer.* RIBBLE: *Bennet's triumphal.* DUPLE: *Bravura.*
(M) *** Mercury SRI/*MRI* 75087 [id.].

These circus marches are exhilarating in their fast pacing and for the sheer bravura of the playing. Karl King was official bandmaster to Barnum and Bailey and two of his pieces are included, but the Fučik march which opens side two is more familiar this side of the Atlantic. First-class recording, although the cassette has not quite the presence and transient bite of the disc.

GRAINGER: *A Lincolnshire posy.* RODGERS, Bernard: *3 Japanese dances.* MILHAUD: *Suite française.* STRAUSS, R.: *Serenade in E flat, Op. 7.*
(M) **(*) Mercury SRI/*MRI* 75093 [id.].

Grainger's *Lincolnshire posy* (a grouping of six folksongs) is wittily characterized and Fennell shows a cool affinity with Milhaud's *Suite française*, a most attractive work. The *Japanese dances* of Bernard Rodgers (1893–1968) are ingenuously pentatonic, yet the scoring titillates the ear, especially when so well caught by the recording. The Strauss *Serenade*, however, is rather less successful, the blending of timbres here is less than ideally homogeneous. There is a good cassette, though side one (with the Grainger and Rodgers) has slightly more sparkle on top than side two where the level drops a little.

Eastman Symphonic Wind Ens., Hunsberger

HANSON: *Young composer's guide to the six tone scale.* SCHWANTER, Joseph: *And the mountains rising nowhere.* COPLAND: *Emblems.*
(M) **(*) Mercury SRI 75152 [id.].

The most rewarding piece here is Aaron Copland's *Emblems*, which shows greater individuality and distinction than its companions. However, these are highly agreeable and Howard Hanson's *Guide*, scored for piano and percussion as well as wind, is expertly fashioned, as one would expect, and its invention pleasing. The dramatic rhapsody by Joseph Schwanter is hardly less well wrought; although none of the pieces in this anthology can lay claim to the highest distinction they will reward the enterprising collector and they still sound amazingly vivid.

ECO, Barenboim

'Greensleeves' (with (i) Zukerman, violin): VAUGHAN WILLIAMS: *Fantasia on Greensleeves.* (i) *The Lark Ascending.* WALTON: *Henry V: Passacaglia (Death of Falstaff); Touch her soft lips and part.* DELIUS: *On Hearing the First Cuckoo in Spring. Summer*

Night on the River. Fennimore and Gerda: Intermezzo. 2 Aquarelles.
(M) *** DG Acc. 2542/*3342* 161 [2530 505/*3300 500*].

Zukerman's account of *The Lark Ascending* is ravishing, and the spacious recording suits the music perfectly. Barenboim creates richly spun orchestral textures; some might feel they are almost too luxuriant at times, but such gorgeous sounds are hard to resist when the playing is of comparably high quality. There is a vivid cassette transfer, but the high level brings slight roughening of the focus at one or two climaxes.

ECO, Britten

'Britten conducts English music': BRITTEN: *Simple symphony Op. 4.* BRIDGE: *Sir Roger de Coverley.* DELIUS: *Two aquarelles* (arr. Fenby). ELGAR: *Introduction and allegro for strings, Op. 47.* PURCELL: *Chacony in G min.* (ed. Britten).
*** Decca SXL 6405.

This rich-toned recording was one of the first made at the Maltings, where the acoustic gives the strings of the English Chamber Orchestra a far greater weight than you would expect from their numbers. Britten drew comparably red-blooded playing from his band, whether in his own vivid *Simple symphony*, the Bridge dance or the magnificent Purcell *Chacony*. It is good to find him treating his own music expressively rather than with cool exactness. In the Delius the delicacy of evocation is delightful, while the Elgar is in some ways the most interesting performance of all, with the structure of the piece brought out far more clearly than is common. The Bridge arrangement is delightful.

ECO, Leppard

ALBINONI: *Sonates a cinque: in A; in G min., Op. 2/3 and 6.* VIVALDI: *Concertos: in D, RV.121; in G min., RV.156; Sonata in E (Al Santo Sepolcro), RV.130.* CORELLI: *Concerto grosso in F, Op. 6/9.*
(B) *** CfP CFP/*TC-CFP* 40371.

This is a charming collection of baroque concertos, played with the superb poise, sense of colour and imagination that regularly characterizes the work of Leppard with this orchestra. Other scholars may complain that Leppard goes too far in trying to re-create such works, but the result for the non-specialist listener is pure delight, particularly when recorded with such warmth as here. A bargain disc that in every way matches comparable discs at full price. The cassette too is of high quality: it has slightly less upper range, but inner detail is not lost and textures are agreeably rich.

E. Sinfonia, Dilkes

English music: BUTTERWORTH: *A Shropshire Lad* (rhapsody). *The Banks of Green Willow.* HARTY: *A John Field suite.* BRIDGE: *There Is a Willow Grows Aslant a Brook.* BAX: *Dance in the Sunlight.*
(M) *** HMV Green. ESD/*TC-ESD* 7100.

This is a collection of English music of a kind which in the age of LP has tended to be unjustly neglected by recording artists and companies. Most valuable is the Bridge tone poem, which is given the subtlest performance. Coming after the richly evocative Butterworth pieces – with Dilkes pressing the music rather harder than usual – the Bridge piece's economy of utterance is the more telling. On the reverse the *John Field suite* and the Bax *Dance* are much lighter – charming music, persuasively played if with some slight lack of refinement of string tone. However, any reservations are set aside by the success of the collection as a whole, with its fine, ripe recording, equally impressive on disc and cassette.

Fantasia

(Film soundtrack recording, cond. Kostal): BACH: *Toccata and fugue in D min., BWV 565* (arr. Stokowski). DUKAS: *Sorcerer's apprentice.* TCHAIKOVSKY: *Nutcracker suite, Op. 71a.* BEETHOVEN: *Symphony No. 6 (Pastoral)* (abridged). STRAVINSKY: *Rite of spring* (abridged). PONCHIELLI: *Dance of the hours.*

MUSSORGSKY: *Night on the bare mountain.* SCHUBERT: *Ave Maria.*
WEA Vista D/*VC* 104 (2).

For several generations of music lovers (I.M. and E.G. included) Walt Disney's *Fantasia* was a formative influence. Stokowski's musical contribution to this remarkable movie was an integral part of Disney's artistic scheme; the present recording is listed to deplore the fact that the current reprocessed film uses a new carbon-copy stereo soundtrack, efficiently directed by Irwin Kostal, but in no way equalling Stokowski's unique performances, which were the first commercial recordings ever made in stereo. Whether the reason – as has been suggested – is connected with royalties incurred by the original, payable to Stokowski's estate, or is simply an ill-advised desire to up-date the sound, the result is an artistic travesty of a great and original enterprise. This is an American commercial equivalent of the new official Soviet version of Tchaikovsky's *1812 overture* which interpolates a Communist anthem in the place of the Tsarist hymn.

Fennell Symphonic Winds, Fennell

'Broadway marches': GERSHWIN: *Strike up the Band; Wintergreen for President.* BERLIN: *There's no business like showbusiness.* RODGERS: *March of the Siamese children; There is nothing like a dame.* COHAN: *Give my regards to Broadway.* WILLSON; *76 Trombones; I ain't down yet.* ROMBERG: *Stout-hearted men.* BART: *Oliver: Consider yourself.* LOEWE: *My Fair Lady: Get me to the church on time. Minstrel medley* (all arr. Krance).
(M) **(*) Mercury SRI/*MRI* 75115 [id.].

Brilliant arrangement by John Krance, witty rather than seeking spectacle (there is no attempt to portray the *76 Trombones* of that title). The recording is very bright and brash, the performances ebullient (though the opening of the *March of the Siamese children* from *The King and I* is quite gentle). Fennell directs with flair, although this repertoire does not bring out any of his special qualities. The cassette is transferred at a low level which takes off some of the transient edge, though side two is sharper in focus than side one.

Galway, James (flute)

(See also under Instrumental Recitals)

'The man with the golden flute' (with (i) Nat. PO, Gerhardt; (ii) Goldstone; (iii) Lucerne Fest. Strings, Baumgartner): (i) BACH: *Suite No. 2 in B min., BWV 1067: Minuet; Badinerie.* PAGANINI: *Moto perpetuo, Op. 11.* VIVALDI: *Flute concerto in G min.* (*La Notte*), *Op. 10/2.* GLUCK: *Orfeo ed Euridice: Dance of the Blessed Spirits.* (ii) DEBUSSY: *Suite bergamasque: Clair de lune. The Little Shepherd. Syrinx for solo flute.* BERKELEY: *Flute sonatina, Op. 13.* (iii) MOZART: *Andante for flute and orchestra in C, K.315.*
(M) *** RCA Gold GL/*GK* 25160 [LRL1/*LRK1* 5094].

James Galway's genial charisma, the beauty of his tone, and the spectacular brilliance of his technique command the widest possible audience, yet one is left in no doubt that besides his sense of fun he possesses the keenest musical sensibility. His phrasing is masterly and its inevitability contributes a good deal towards his special gift of making the listener forget that he is often listening to transcriptions of music written with a quite different tone-colour in mind. This mid-priced reissue includes several items from the finest of his four available anthologies, *Showpieces* (see below). One of these is Paganini's *Moto perpetuo*, which shows off Galway's bravura in its irrepressible stream of notes. The famous *Dance of the Blessed Spirits* draws an appealing beauty of line and phrase, while the spontaneous little Berkeley *Sonatina* is a welcome novelty. The balance here (as throughout the concert) places Galway well forward, but the pianist, Anthony Goldstone, manages to remain in the picture. The piano, however, is rather dryly recorded. Debussy's *Clair de lune* is also given a piano accompaniment and the arrangement is clumsy, beautifully as Galway plays the melodic line. The Vivaldi concerto too is hardly refined in its accompanying detail. The tape transfer is generally of good quality, the solo flute truthfully caught, while the resonant acoustic does not blur the orchestral focus.

'Showpieces' (with Nat. PO, Gerhardt):

DINICU: *Hora staccato.* DRIGO: *Les Millions d'Arlequin: Serenade.* PAGANINI: *Moto perpetuo, Op. 11.* BACH: *Suite No. 2 in B min., BWV 1067: Minuet; Badinerie.* MIYAGI: *Haru no Umi.* GODARD: *Suite of 3 pieces, Op. 116: Waltz.* RIMSKY-KORSAKOV: *Tsar Saltan: Flight of the bumble-bee.* SAINT-SAËNS: *Ascanio* (ballet): *Adagio and variation.* CHOPIN: *Waltz in D flat* (*Minute*), *Op. 64/1.* GLUCK: *Orfeo: Dance of the Blessed Spirits.* DÖPPLER: *Fantaisie pastorale hongroise, Op. 26.*
*** RCA RCALP/*RCAK* 3011.

This collection of 'lollipops' shows the flair and sparkle of James Galway's playing at its most captivating, besides demonstrating a technical command to bring wonder: Paganini himself must have astonished his listeners in this way. The bravura pieces, including the Dinicu *Hora staccato*, Rimsky-Korsakov's *Flight of the bumble-bee* and Godard's deliciously inconsequential little waltz, are nicely balanced by the expressive music, and there are several attractive novelties. Only Bach's famous *Badinerie* seems a shade too fast, and even this is infectious. Charles Gerhardt's accompaniments are characteristically adroit, and the sound is of excellent quality on both disc and cassette.

'The magic flute of James Galway' (with Nat. PO, Gerhardt): HANDEL: *Solomon: Arrival of the Queen of Sheba.* RACHMANINOV: *Vocalise, Op. 34/14.* BACH: *Sonata in C min.: Allegro.* MENDELSSOHN: *A Midsummer Night's Dream, Op. 61: Scherzo.* SCHUMANN: *Kinderscenen: Träumerei.* GOSSEC: *Tambourin.* CHOPIN: *Variations on a theme from Rossini's 'La Cenerentola'.* KREISLER: *Schön Rosmarin.* DVOŘÁK: *Humoresque in G flat, Op. 101/7.* BRISCIALDI: *Carnival of Venice.*
*** RCA RCALP/*RCAK* 3014 [LRL 1/*LRK 1* 5131].

Galway's gift for making transcriptions sound as if the music had been originally conceived for the flute almost succeeds in the *Arrival of the Queen of Sheba*, and his exuberant roulades in the Chopin *Variations* and (especially) the *Carnival of Venice* are very fetching. The *Midsummer Night's Dream Scherzo* has an iridescent sparkle, and, among the lyrical items, Schumann's *Träumerei* is beautifully phrased. The flair and sparkle of Galway's bravura never fail to astonish, though the Bach *Allegro* is outrageously fast. The recording balances the flute well forward with an unashamed spotlight. The cassette transfer has plenty of life.

'Songs of the Southern Cross' (with Sydney SO, Measham): HILL: *Waiata Poi.* ROBIN: *I started a joke.* BENJAMIN: *Jamaican rumba.* GRAINER: *Robert and Elizabeth: I know how.* TRAD.: *Waltzing Matilda.* GRAINGER: *Molly on the Shore.* SPRINGFIELD: *The Carnival Is Over.* JAMES: *The Silver Stars Are in the Sky.* LEE: *Long White Cloud.* CARMICHAEL: *Thredbo suite.* DREYFUS: *Rush theme.* PACHELBEL: *Canon.*
**(*) RCA RCALP/*RCAK* 6011 [AFL 1/*AFK 1* 4063].

The very engaging *Waiata Poi* is a highlight here, the sort of delightful morsel that James Galway can make indelibly his own. Benjamin's *Jamaican rumba* is delightful too, and it is the quick, witty pieces that come off best here; the lyrical music tends to be less substantial. Nicely turned accompaniments and good recording. In the cassette transfer the rather soupy and unstylish version of Pachelbel's *Canon*, which opens the collection, has hiccoughs in the bass which most listeners will find unacceptable. Otherwise the transfer is full and clear, if not as refined as the disc.

'Song for Annie' (with (i) Nat. PO, Gerhardt; (ii) Marisa Robles Harp Ens.; (iii) Kevin Conneff, Irish drum): (i) MARAIS: *Le Basque.* VILLA-LOBOS: *Bachianas Brasileiras No. 5: Aria.* FAURÉ: *Dolly suite: Berceuse.* MOZART: *Piano sonata No. 15 in C, K.545: Allegro.* DENVER: *Annie's song.* HASSE: *Tambourin.* DEBUSSY: *La plus que lente.* TRAD.: (ii) *Brian Boru's march.* (iii; played on a tin whistle) *Belfast hornpipe.* (i) BIZET–BORNE: *Carmen fantasy.* TRAD.: *Spanish love song.*
** RCA RL/*RK* 25163 [ARLI 3061].

This collection, dedicated to Galway's wife, includes the John Denver song which took him into the charts (quite an achievement for a modest flute!); but otherwise the one totally memorable item here is the opening *Le Basque* of Marais. Its simple *moto perpetuo* theme registers with indelible charm and remains in the memory long after the disc has finished playing. The rest of the programme is a characteristically fetching array of clever arrangements by either Galway or Gerhardt; but one would not give this collection a first place among Galway's anthologies. The recording and cassette transfer are both well managed, although there is some lack of upper range on tape. The flute is admirably caught, even though the balance is larger than life.

'Nocturne' (with Nat. PO, Measham): DEBUSSY: *Suite bergamasque: Clair de lune. Petite suite: En bateau.* CHOPIN: *Nocturne in E flat, Op. 9/2.* HALISCH: *Dreamers.* MOUQUET: *Pan and the birds.* MASSENET: *Thaïs: Meditation.* STRAVINSKY: *Firebird: Berceuse.* FAURÉ: *Dolly: Berceuse.* BOULANGER: *Nocturne.* FIELD: *Nocturne No. 5.* LISZT: *Consolation No. 3.* GRIEG: *Peer Gynt: Morning.*
** RCA RS/*RK* 9012.

With a very forward balance to make a jumbo-sized flute, dwarfing the accompaniment, the result here is lusciously soporific and items like the *Berceuse* from Stravinsky's *Firebird* and Grieg's *Morning* from *Peer Gynt* lose their freshness. The *Nocturnes* of Field and Boulanger are the most effective items. Disc and chrome tape are closely matched in quality.

Goodman, Isador (piano)

'World's best-loved music for piano and orchestra' (with Melbourne SO, Thomas): ADDINSELL: *Warsaw concerto.* GERSHWIN: *Rhapsody in Blue.* LITOLFF: *Concerto symphonique, Op. 102/4: Scherzo.* RACHMANINOV: *Rhapsody on a theme of Paganini: 18th Variation.* LISZT: *Hungarian fantasia for piano and orchestra, G.123.*
(M) ** Ph. Seq. 6527/*7311* 114.

In spite of the hyperbole of the title, this is a pleasant collection. The soloist is sympathetic and quite stylish (notably so in the Litolff), and the accompaniments are well balanced within a spacious acoustic. The account of the Liszt is rather lightweight, but fits well with the rest of the programme. Daniel Adni's HMV compilation (see above) is rather more distinguished, but that is at full price. The Philips cassette is transferred at rather a low level, with resultant loss of upper range. It will only sound really effective on a small portable player.

'Greensleeves'

English music (with (i) Sinfonia of L. or Hallé O, Barbirolli; (ii) New Philh. O, LPO or LSO, Boult; (iii) Williams, Bournemouth SO, Berglund; (iv) E. Sinfonia, Dilkes): (i) VAUGHAN WILLIAMS: *Fantasia on Greensleeves.* (ii) *The Lark Ascending* (with Hugh Bean). (iii) *Oboe concerto in A min.* (ii) *English folksongs suite.* (i) DELIUS: *A Village Romeo and Juliet: Walk to the Paradise Garden. On Hearing the First Cuckoo in Spring.* (iv) BUTTERWORTH: *The Banks of Green Willow.* (ii) ELGAR: *Serenade for strings, Op. 20.* (iii) MOERAN: *Lonely Waters.*
(B) *** EMI *TC2-MOM 104.*

Looking at the programme and artists' roster the reader will hardly need the confirmation that this is a very attractive tape anthology. Performances never disappoint, the layout is excellent, and for the car this is ideal. The sound is a little variable on domestic equipment; at times there is a degree of edge to the treble (notably in the climaxes of the Delius *Walk to the Paradise Garden*). But often the quality is both vivid and rich, as in the title-piece and the Elgar *Serenade.* Vaughan Williams's *Oboe concerto*, stylishly played by John Williams, sounds admirably fresh. With any necessary adjustments to the sound, this is excellent value.

English music (with (i) ASMF, Marriner; (ii) ECO, Britten; (iii) New SO, Collins; (iv) LSO, Bliss; (v) Boston Pops O, Fiedler; (vi) RPO, Cox; (vii) LSO, Monteux): (i) VAUGHAN WILLIAMS: *Fantasia on Greensleeves;* (v) *English folksongs suite.* (i) ELGAR: *Introduction and allegro for strings, Op. 47;*

(iv) *Pomp and Circumstance marches Nos. 1 and 4;* (vi) *Serenade for strings, Op. 20;* (vii) *Enigma variations: Nimrod.* (i) DELIUS: *On Hearing the First Cuckoo in Spring;* (ii) *2 Aquarelles.* BRIDGE: *Sir Roger de Coverley.* (i) WARLOCK: *String serenade.* (iii) BALFOUR GARDINER: *Shepherd fennel's dance.* (i) BUTTERWORTH: *The Banks of Green Willow.* (ii) BRITTEN: *Simple symphony: Playful pizzicato.*
(B) *** Decca *KMORC 9003.*

In several respects the Decca 'Greensleeves' compilation is even more attractive than the HMV one. The sound is consistently vivid and wide-ranging, yet smoother on top. The ASMF performances are outstanding as are those by the ECO under Britten, and the music is skilfully chosen to give variety and yet make a sensible programme. The Bridge and Balfour Gardiner dances are especially welcome, and Britten's *Playful pizzicato* is a delight. Highly recommended and equally successful in the car or at home.

Hallé O, Barbirolli

Overtures: BEETHOVEN: *Leonora No. 3, Op. 72a.* MOZART: *Die Zauberflöte.* WAGNER: *Tannhäuser.* WEBER: *Oberon.*
(B) ** Precision Coll. GSGC/*ZCGC* 2038.

Four strongly characterized performances from Barbirolli with positive orchestral playing, especially impressive in *Die Zauberflöte* and *Oberon* (a fine horn solo). The strings sound thin at times in *Tannhäuser* (a recording dating from the earliest days of stereo), but they produce an electrifying pianissimo at the opening of *Leonora No. 3*. Indeed every bar of the music-making here is alive and the sound is generally full and well balanced, with the cassette matching the disc fairly closely, if slightly less refined.

Hallé O, Handford

'Hallé encores': COPLAND: *Fanfare for the Common Man.* KHACHATURIAN: *Spartacus: Adagio of Spartacus and Phrygia.* GOUNOD: *Mors et Vita: Judex.* MacCUNN: *Overture: Land of the Mountain and the Flood.* SATIE: *Gymnopédies Nos. 1 and 3* (orch. Debussy). MASSENET: *Thaïs: Meditation.* TRAD.: *Suo Gan.* BARBER: *Adagio for strings.*
(B) *** CfP CFP/*TC-CFP* 40320.

Maurice Handford and the Hallé offer an exceptionally attractive collection of miscellaneous pieces beautifully recorded. Many of the items have achieved popularity almost by accident through television and the other media (how else would the MacCunn overture have come – so rightly – to notice?), but the sharpness of the contrasts adds to the charm. The Hallé violins sound a little thin in Barber's beautiful *Adagio*, but otherwise the playing is first-rate. What is particularly attractive about this concert is the way the programme is laid out so that each piece follows on naturally after its predecessor. The cassette transfer is of excellent quality, except for a tendency to shrillness in the violins when they are above the stave in fortissimo, as in the Khachaturian and Barber items.

'Hallé encores', Vol. 2 (with Hallé Ch.): ALBINONI: *Adagio for strings and organ* (arr. Giazotto). PACHELBEL: *Canon in D.* PUCCINI: *Manon Lescaut: Intermezzo.* FRANCK: *Panis angelicus* (arr. Sandré). HUMPERDINCK: *Overture: Hänsel und Gretel.* MASCAGNI: *Cavalleria Rusticana: Intermezzo.* FAURÉ: *Pavane, Op. 50.* TCHAIKOVSKY: *Nutcracker, Op. 71: Waltz of the snowflakes.*
(B) ** CfP CFP/*TC-CFP* 40367.

Maurice Handford's second volume of Hallé encores is rather less successful than his first. Opening with a warm but not over-lush account of the Albinoni/Giazotto *Adagio* he moves on to a rather unimaginative version of Pachelbel's *Canon*, without any sort of climax, either in the centre or at the end. The Puccini *Intermezzo* and the choral version of *Panis angelicus* are restrained, and the most memorable items are on side two, with the Fauré *Pavane* and Tchaikovsky *Waltz* again both featuring the Hallé Choir. The recording is excellent, full and clear, and there is no appreciable difference between disc and tape.

Hallé O, Loughran

'French music': RAVEL: *Boléro.* DUKAS: *L'Apprenti sorcier.* CHABRIER: *España. Marche joyeuse.* BERLIOZ: *La Damnation de Faust: Hungarian march; Dance of the Sylphs; Minuet of the will-o'-the-wisps.*
(B) ** CfP CFP/*TC-CFP* 40312.

Although lacking something in charisma, these pieces are well played and vividly recorded. Chabrier's *España* has plenty of life, and the pictorial effects of the Dukas symphonic poem are well brought off. Ravel's *Boléro* is built steadily to its climax, but undoubtedly the highlight of the concert is the suite from *The Damnation of Faust*, with each piece very strongly characterized. The tape transfer is generally well managed, although the wide dynamic range has meant that the quiet opening side-drum in *Boléro* is almost inaudible at normal playback level.

'Your favourite overtures': BEETHOVEN: *Creatures of Prometheus.* SCHUBERT: *Rosamunde.* STRAUSS, J. Jnr: *Die Fledermaus.* BERLIOZ: *Le carnaval romain; Le Corsaire.* SMETANA: *The Bartered Bride.* BRAHMS: *Tragic overture; Academic festival overture.* HEUBERGER: *Der Opernball.* MOZART: *Le Nozze di Figaro.* SUPPÉ: *Poet and peasant.*
(B) ** MfP MFP/*TC-MFP* 1026 (2).

Loughran is strongest in the classical repertoire. He secures alert, polished playing in *Prometheus* while *Rosamunde* is plain-spun but effective. Predictably the Brahms repertoire shows this combination at their finest, but *Le Nozze di Figaro* does not want for lightness and vivacity. The other pieces are well mannered and perhaps a little lacking in flair, though Loughran shows his affection for the waltz tune in *Der Opernball.* The sound is well balanced and there is not a great deal to choose between discs and the double-length cassette.

Harvey, Richard (recorder)

'Italian recorder concertos' (with L. Vivaldi O, Huggett): VIVALDI: *Concerto in C min., RV.441; Concerto in C, RV.444.* SAMMARTINI: *Concerto in F.* SCARLATTI, A.: *Sinfonia di concerto grosso No. 3.*
*** ASV ALH/*ZCALH* 914.

Richard Harvey plays with persuasive style and flair. Moreover the accompaniments are unusually authentic and in exactly the right scale. The Sammartini *Concerto* is a charmer and, of the two Vivaldi works, RV.444, for sopranino recorder, is especially engaging. The Scarlatti *Sinfonia* in five movements is hardly less winning. The recording has excellent presence and a good balance, with a very lively cassette (which needs a little top-cut) to match the disc in excellence. Highly recommended.

Heifetz, Jascha (violin)

'Ten great violin concertos' (with (i) New SO, Sargent; (ii) Boston SO, Munch; (iii) Chicago SO; (iv) Reiner; (v) Hendl; (vi) RCA SO): (i) BACH: *Double violin concerto in D min., BWV 1043.* MOZART: *Violin concerto No. 5 in A (Turkish), K.219* (with chamber orch.). (ii) BEETHOVEN: *Concerto in D, Op. 61.* MENDELSSOHN: *Concerto in E min., Op. 64.* (i) BRUCH: *Concerto No. 1 in G min., Op. 26.* (iii; iv) BRAHMS: *Concerto in D, Op. 77.* TCHAIKOVSKY: *Concerto in D, Op. 35.* (iii; v) SIBELIUS: *Concerto in D min., Op. 47.* (vi; v) GLAZOUNOV: *Concerto in A min., Op. 82.* (ii) PROKOFIEV: *Concerto No. 2 in G min., Op. 63.*
(M) *** RCA RL 00720 (6) [CRL 6 0720].

Here are some fabulous performances, unlikely ever to be surpassed. Heifetz was in a class of his own, and most of the performances collected in this six-record anthology show him at his best. The ten concertos were all recorded between 1955 and 1963, and were his last word on these scores. He takes a very brisk view of the Beethoven (as he had in his earlier version with Toscanini); yet it is all thoroughly convincing, and so is his warm and more spacious account of the Brahms, beautifully accompanied by Reiner and the Chicago orchestra at its prime. The Tchaikovsky has a meltingly lovely slow movement and much virtuosity elsewhere. Dazzling too is the record of the Glazounov, which will convert any doubters to this composer's cause. The Sibelius *Concerto* is if anything even finer than the version Heifetz recorded in the 1930s with Beecham (once available on World Records) and the Prokofiev *G minor*, though not superior to the pre-war version with Koussevitzky conducting, is every bit as good and has the advantage of more modern recording. Perhaps the least impressive things here are the Mozart and the Mendelssohn, which is very fast and a shade wanting in freshness. Otherwise glories abound. This is an indispensable set, excellently transferred – and very reasonably priced.

(Richard) Hickox O, Hickox

ALBINONI: *Adagio in G min.* (arr. Giazotto) *for organ and strings. Oboe concerto in D min., Op. 9/2* (with Sara Barrington, oboe). PACHELBEL: *Canon in D* (arr. Münchinger). BONONCINI: *Sinfonia da chiesa a quattro, Op. 5/1.* PURCELL: *Chacony in G min.*
*** Argo ZRG 866.

This performance of Albinoni's *Adagio* must be among the most sumptuous available – even more richly recorded than Karajan's – yet there is no lack of refinement. Similarly the climax of Pachelbel's famous *Canon* is graduated with great skill; the Purcell *Chacony* is no less effective, and the delightful Albinoni *Oboe concerto* makes a splendid bonus. The recording too is absolutely first-class.

ALBINONI: *Adagio.* PACHELBEL: *Canon* (from above collection). MOZART: *Serenade No. 13 in G* (*Eine kleine Nachtmusik*)*, K.525* (V. Moz. Ens., Boskovsky). HANDEL: *Rinaldo: Overture; March; Battle* (ECO, Bonynge). ROSSINI: *String sonata No. 2 in A* (ASMF, Marriner).
(M) *** Decca VIV/*KVIC* 38.

The luscious Hickox performances of the *Adagio* and *Canon* come from the Argo full-priced collection above and are supported by Boskovsky's outstandingly fresh version of Mozart's *Night music*, while Marriner and the ASMF combine elegance and sparkle in Rossini. The choice of the *Rinaldo* excerpts seems curious but they are well played, and the recording throughout is excellent.

Holliger, Heinz (oboe; cor anglais)

Concertos (with Concg. O, Zinman): DONIZETTI: *Cor anglais concerto in G.* HAYDN: *Oboe concerto in C.* REICHA: *Scene for cor anglais.* ROSSINI: *Variations in C* (originally for clarinet).
*** Ph. 9500 564/*7300 713* [id.].

Holliger's outstanding DG anthology of 1966 is still available (DG Priv. 2535/*3335* 417 [139152]) and is reviewed above under the composers represented, Bellini, Cimarosa, Salieri and Donizetti (the same *Cor anglais concerto*). This newer collection is given Philips' very finest recording, richer than on the earlier disc but without loss of freshness. The cassette transfer too is of demonstration quality. The performances are wholly admirable. The Haydn concerto (which has a side to itself) is played with wonderful finesse by Holliger, and the splendid orchestral contribution directed by David Zinman makes a full-bodied and stylish contrast with the soloist. In the other three works Holliger combines fabulous natural bravura with elegance. Highly recommended.

Israel PO, Mehta

ROSSINI: *William Tell: overture.* BEETHOVEN: *Overture: Leonora No. 3, Op. 72b.* TCHAIKOVSKY: *Capriccio italien, Op. 45.* RIMSKY-KORSAKOV: *Capriccio espagnol, Op. 34.*
*(*) Decca SXL/*KSXC* 6977.

The performances here, of which *William Tell* is the most enjoyable, are well enough played and have a fair measure of adrenalin. They are vividly recorded, although the acoustic of the recording is not especially attractive. There is in fact no real distinction here; overall this concert seldom rises much above routine. The cassette is acceptable but not one of Decca's best.

(Philip) Jones Brass Ens.

'Just brass': ARNOLD, M.: *Quintet*. DODGSON: *Suite for brass septet*. SALZEDO: *Divertimento*. EWALD: *Symphony for brass*.
**(*) Argo ZRG 655 [id.].

Philip Jones' Ensemble is well known from broadcasts and for contributions to records of seventeenth-century music, but this was their first 'solo' record. The Malcolm Arnold piece is predictably jolly and agreeable and the Dodgson work is both pleasing and inventive. Ewald is the least familiar name on the disc; he was a Russian nationalist who lived from 1860 to 1935, whose style does not stray beyond Borodin but who writes effectively for the medium. The Salzedo *Divertimento* is slightly jazzy and by no means unattractive. The disc is not one which would figure high on anyone's desert island but is nonetheless a useful addition to the catalogue and one worth dipping into as a change from more familiar fare. The recording is excellent.

'Classics for brass': STRAUSS, R.: *Festmusik der Stadt Wien* (fanfare). GRIEG: *Funeral march*. BOZZA: *Sonatine for 2 trumpets, horn, trombone and tuba*. DUKAS: *La Péri: Fanfare*. JOLIVET: *Narcisse: Fanfare for Racine's play, Britannicus*. POULENC: *Sonata* (Trio) *for horn, trumpet and trombone*. SCHULLER: *Symphony for brass and percussion*.
**(*) Argo ZRG 731 [id.].

Apart from the Schuller *Symphony*, which is rather heavy going and determinedly dissonant, this is a highly attractive and entertaining recital. The Grieg *Funeral march* is uncharacteristic but impressive, and the three fanfares (by R. Strauss, Jolivet and Dukas) show in quite diverse ways the splendour and variety of colour possible when first-class brass players mass together. The Poulenc *Trio*, witty and beautifully conceived for the unlikely combination of horn, trumpet and trombone, is a highlight of the recital as is the lightweight Bozza *Sonatine*, cleverly scored and melodically fresh. Outstandingly good recording throughout.

'Renaissance brass' (music of 1400–1600): FRANCHOIS: *Trumpet intrada*. PASSEREAU: *Il est bel et bon* (arr. Reeves). AGRICOLA: *Oublier veul* (arr. Howarth). LASSUS: *Madrigal dell'eterna* (arr. Jones). VECCHI: *Saltarello*. SUSATO: *Suite of 6 dances*. BYRD: *Earl of Oxford's march*. FARNABY: *Suite of 6 dances*. GIBBONS: *Royal pavane*. *In nomine*.
** Argo ZRG/*KZRC* 823 [id.].

An attractive collection, not all of which was originally intended for brass. In fact the madrigals and keyboard dances are among the more effective numbers but the comparatively limited range of colour possible with such a group tells if the music is taken in larger doses. The recording is very good indeed, and the tape transfer level high, but there is an element of harshness in the louder, fanfare-like pieces on the cassette.

'Easy winners': music by JOPLIN; MOZART; HAZELL; MONTI; DEBUSSY; PREMRU and TRAD.
** Argo ZRG 895 [id.].

The collector's item here is an arrangement of Monti's *Czardas*, offering a display of breathtaking bravura by Ivor James on the horn. The rest of the collection is pleasantly easy-going, though it is doubtful if Mozart's *Eine kleine Nachtmusik* on four tubas has more than novelty value, skilfully done as it is. This and Scott Joplin, plus a couple of rather attractive pieces by the recording's producer, Chris Hazell, are the most striking numbers. The playing is first-class, of course, and so is the sound.

'Baroque brass': BIBER: *Sonata a 7*. ANON.: *Sonate from 'Die Bankelsangerlieder'*. FRANCK, M.: *Intrata*. HASSLER: *Intrada V*. SPEER: *Sonata for trumpet and 3 trombones*. *Sonata for 3 trombones*. *Sonata for 4 trombones*. *Sonata for 2 trumpets and 3 trombones*. SCHEIDT: *Canzona a 10*. BACH: *Chorale: Nun danket alle Gott*. *Capriccio on the departure of a beloved brother, BWV 992*. (Unaccompanied) *Cello suite No. 1: Menuetto and Courante* (arr. Fletcher for solo tuba). SCARLATTI, D.: *Keyboard sonatas, Kk.380, Kk.430, Kk.443* (arr. Dodgson). BACH, C. P. E.: *March*.
*** Argo ZRG/*KZRC* 898 [id.].

An imaginative and highly rewarding programme, even more successful than this group's earlier anthologies. The music of Daniel Speer is strikingly inventive, and the Bach and Scarlatti arrangements are highly engaging – the latter with no attempt at miniaturization. The C. P. E. Bach *March* makes a superbly vigorous coda. If you like the baroque idiom and the sound of modern brass instruments this can be recommended, though not to be taken all at once. The recording is first-class and the cassette transfer well focused.

'Festive brass': UHL: *Festfanfare.* JANÁČEK: *Sinfonietta: Sokol fanfare.* FRANCK: *Pièce héroïque.* BLISS: *Fanfare for the Lord Mayor of London.* CASALS: *O vos omnes* (trans. Stokowski). TOMASI: *Fanfares liturgiques: Procession de Vendredi-Saint.* COPLAND: *Fanfare for the Common Man.* BRITTEN: *Russian funeral. Fanfare: The Eagle has Two Heads.* BOURGEOIS: *Wine rhapsody.* STRAUSS, R.: *Festmusik der Stadt Wien.*
*** Argo ZRG/*KZRC* 912.

Another fascinating compilation, showing a remarkable background of research into usable repertoire. Franck's *Pièce héroïque* transcribes surprisingly well for brass, and there are several other works of substance here. Apart from Britten's Russian threnody, Tomasi's *Procession de Vendredi-Saint* is a powerful nine-minute piece with a hauntingly sombre atmosphere. Britten's *Eagle fanfare* reminds us of the horn variation in *The Young Person's Guide to the Orchestra.* Richard Strauss's *Festmusik* is inflated but produces a considerable variety of texture and colour. Recording well up to the standard of this excellent series, with striking depth and sonority, although the cassette has slightly less range at the top than the disc.

'Romantic brass': MENDELSSOHN: *Song without Words, Op. 102: Tarantella.* DVOŘÁK: *Terzetto, Op. 74: Scherzo. Humoresque, Op. 101/7.* LEONTOVICH: *2 Ukrainian folk tunes.* GLAZOUNOV: *In modo religioso, Op. 38.* RAMSOE: *Quartet No. 5, Op. 38.* EWALD: *Quintet No. 3, Op. 7.*
*** Argo ZRG 928 [id.].

Engagingly lightweight, this is one of the most entertaining of the Philip Jones anthologies. The Mendelssohn *Song without Words* is remarkably nimble; the unforced bravura of the playing brings an agreeably relaxed atmosphere here and in the other lollipops. The Ewald *Quintet* is harmonically unadventurous but uncommonly well scored. It is obviously rewarding to play, and the performance is impeccably stylish. Excellent recording, beautifully balanced.

'La Battaglia': BYRD: *The Battell* (arr. Howarth). BANCHIERI: *Udite, ecco le trombe* (fantasia, arr. Jones). KUHNAU: *Biblical sonata No. 1* (*The battle between David and Goliath,* arr. Hazell). JENKINS: *Newark Siege* (fantasia, arr. Reeve). HANDEL: *Royal Fireworks music: La Réjouissance* (arr. Howarth).
*** Argo ZRG/*KZRC* 932 [id.].

Most of these pieces are arranged, rather improbably, from keyboard works. Purists may reject the idea, but with Jones's brilliant band relishing the vigour and bite of the writing, the result is another in this Ensemble's outstanding series: a real demonstration record with vivid sound. The cassette is unsuccessful: the resonance clouds the sound picture and brings congestion.

'Focus on PJBE': PRAETORIUS: *Terpsichoren suite for brass* (arr. Reeve). DODGSON: *Fantasia for 6 brass.* RIMSKY-KORSAKOV: *Mlada: Procession of the Nobles* (arr. Archibald). KOETSIER: *Brass symphony, Op. 80.* JOPLIN: *Gladiolus rag.* TRAD.: *Londonderry air.* GADE: *Jealousy* (all arr. Iveson). TRAD.: *The Cuckoo* (arr. Howarth).
*** Argo Dig. ZRDL/*KZRDC* 1001 [Lon. LDR/5- 71100].

For their digital début the PJBE have assembled a characteristically entertaining cocktail. There is no reason why the famous Praetorius dances should not be scored for brass alone; here piquancy is exchanged for splendour, with Stephen Dodgson's slightly sombre *Fantasia* making a good foil afterwards. The Koetsier *Symphony* with its interweaving lines in the outer movements is superbly effective played with this kind of bravura, and the lollipops are enjoyable, though the arrangement of the *Londonderry air* is a shade over-elaborate. The sound has demonstration presence and sonority on both disc and chrome cassette.

'Noel': BACH: *Christmas oratorio: Nun seid Ihr wohl gerochen; Ach, mein herzliebes Jesulein.* SCHUTZ: *Christmas oratorio: Die Weisen aus Morgenlande.* TRAD.: *Ding dong, merrily on high; Lord Jesu hath a garden; Come, all ye shepherds; Wassail song; God rest ye merry, gentlemen.* PRAETORIUS: *A great and mighty wonder.* HOPKINS: *We three kings.* GRÜBER: *Stille Nacht.* TRAD.: *Il est né; In dulci jubilo; Jingle bells; The holly and the ivy; We wish you a merry Christmas.* WADE: *Adeste fidelis.*
*** Decca Dig. SXDL/*KSXDC* 7576.

Sound and playing here are both superb. After the floridly exuberant opening piece from Bach's *Christmas oratorio* some might feel the mood is at times rather solemn, but the unconventional arrangements become increasingly attractive with familiarity, and there are plenty of favourites on side two where there is a real sense of joy and celebration. The closing *Adeste fidelis* is suitably resplendent. The chrome cassette is very much in the demonstration class.

SAINT-SAËNS: *Carnival of the animals* (trans. Reeve). DEBUSSY: *Général Lavine – eccentric; La fille aux cheveux de lin; Minstrels; Hommage à S. Pickwick Esq., P.P.M.P.C.* (all arr. Mowat). *Golliwog's cakewalk* (arr. Hazel). SATIE: *Gymnopédie No. 1* (arr. Harvey). CHABRIER: *Bourrée fantasque* (arr. Iveson).
*(*) Decca Dig. 410 125-1/*4* [id.].

This recording has a certain novelty value, but the transcription of Saint-Saëns' *Carnival of the animals* coarsens the music and, though there is much bravura, the colouring (certainly not French) is almost Mussorgskian in places. The heaviness of the overall effect means that the wit almost all evaporates and the solo horn is no substitute for the cello in the famous portrayal of *The Swan*. The other items come off with variable degrees of success. Playing and recording are both first-class, and the chrome cassette matches the LP closely.

King, Thea (clarinet)

'The clarinet in concert' (with Dobrée, basset horn, Imai, viola; LSO, Alun Francis): BRUCH: *Double concerto in E min. for clarinet and viola, Op. 88.* MENDELSSOHN: *2 Concert pieces for clarinet and basset horn: in F min., Op. 113; in D min., Op. 114.* CRUSELL: *Introduction and variations on a Swedish air, Op. 12.*
*** Hyp. A/*KA* 66022.

A thoroughly engaging programme of forgotten music (the Bruch is not even listed in the *New Grove*), all played with skill and real charm and excellently recorded. The Bruch is a delightful work, with genuinely memorable inspiration in its first two lyrical movements and a roistering finale making a fine contrast. Clarinet and viola are blended beautifully, with the more penetrating wind instrument dominating naturally and with melting phrasing from Thea King. The Mendelssohn duets for clarinet and basset horn are no less diverting, with their jocular finales, and they too are played with a nice blend of expressive spontaneity and high spirits. The Weberian Crusell *Variations* show Miss King's bravura at its most sparkling. This is far from being an empty piece; its twists and turns are consistently inventive. The cassette is first-class, matching the disc in range and presence.

Lloyd Webber, Julian (cello)

'Cello man' (with Nat. PO, Gerhardt): CANTELOUBE: *Baïléro.* FALLA: *Ritual fire dance.* SAINT-SAËNS: *Samson et Dalila: Softly awakes my heart.* BRIDGE: *Scherzetto.* FAURÉ: *Élégie.* VILLA-LOBOS: *Bachianas Brasileiras No. 5.* BACH: *Arioso.* PÖPPER: *Gavotte No. 2.* DELIUS: *Hassan: Serenade.* BRUCH: *Kol Nidrei.*
** RCA RL/*RK* 25383.

Flatteringly recorded, with the cello forward and the orchestra in a very resonant acoustic, this programme is soupily romantic and will not be to all tastes, though the playing is lushly effective. But a song like *Baïléro* loses its innocence with such treatment, and the arrangement of the *Ritual fire dance* for cello and orchestra is pointless. The Pöpper, Delius and Bruch pieces are the highlights. The chrome tape matches the disc closely.

Locke Brass Consort, Stobart

'Symphonic marches for brass': VERDI: *Aïda: Grand March.* MOZART: *Die Zauberflöte: March of the Priests.* TCHAIKOVSKY: *Symphony No. 6: 3rd movt.* PUCCINI: *Turandot: March sequence.* GRIEG: *Sigurd Jorsalfar Homage march.* STRAUSS, J. Snr: *Radetzky march.* BERLIOZ: *Symphonie fantastique: March to the scaffold.* MUSSORGSKY: *Capture of Kars.*
**(*) CRD Dig. CRD 1102/*CRDC 4102.*

As the very opening of the ceremonial march from *Aïda* shows, this is demonstration sound on both disc and chrome tape. The natural balance is very impressive, with the trumpets slightly recessed; there is body and fine definition too, plus admirable presence. The expert playing gives much pleasure and the Grieg and Mussorgsky items are especially successful, but the two symphonic marches, though exciting, suffer from the absence of the rest of the orchestra. The percussion sparkles, without overwhelming the ensemble.

London Festival Brass, Howarth and Civil

'Festive baroque brass': SCHEIDT: *Cantus XXI: Galliard battaglia a 5 voci.* PEZEL: *Sonata hora decima No. 14.* BACH: *Fugue in C sharp min.* (arr. Howarth). ZELENKA: *3 Fanfares.* BULL (arr. Howarth): *Pavan and variations; Galliard and 4 variations; King's hunting jigg.* BACH, C. P. E.: *March for 3 trumpets and timpani.* LOCKE (arr. Civil): *Music for His Majesty's Sackbutts and Cornets: Air (Maestoso); Solemn; Allemande.*
(M) ** Decca VIV/*KVIC* 47.

The memorable item here is the Scheidt *Battle galliard* which has spectacular antiphonal effects. The recording was originally made in Decca's Phase Four system, but although the balance is forward there is an effective ambience too. It is not a collection to play all at once, but the performances are spirited and polished and there is some attractive music here. The cassette is vividly transferred, but the focus is not always as clean as on the disc.

London Gabrieli Brass Ens.

'Brass music of the Baroque': PURCELL: *Trumpet tune and ayre; Music for the funeral of Queen Mary* (with chorus). LOCKE: *Music for His Majesty's Sackbutts and Cornets.* PEZEL: *Ceremonial brass music.* STANLEY: *Trumpet tune.* GABRIELI, G.: *Canzona per sonare a 4* (*La Spiritata*). SCHEIDT: *Suite.*
(M) ** ASV ACM/*ZCACM* 2034.

By far the most attractive music here is included on the second side of this collection, with Gabrieli's *Canzona* followed by the diverse and inventive Scheidt *Suite* and then a splendid account of the solemn Purcellian *Funeral music*, with an eloquent choral contribution. The sound is well judged; the brass group is comparatively small and thus detail is clear. The cassette is not quite as clean as the disc on top, but for the most part still sounds very impressive.

LPO, Handley

'Sir Thomas Beecham commemorative concert': VAUGHAN WILLIAMS: *The Wasps: overture.* MOZART: *Symphony No. 39 in E flat, K.543.* DELIUS: *Summer night on the river; On hearing the first cuckoo in spring.* RIMSKY-KORSAKOV: *Le Coq d'or: Introduction and Bridal procession.* DVOŘÁK: *Symphony No. 8 in G, Op. 88.* (Includes part of original 1936 Beecham concert and interview between Lady Beecham and John Amis.)
**(*) Chan. *DBTD 2007* (3).

In November 1936 during a tour of Germany, Beecham and the LPO gave a concert in Ludwigshaven which was experimentally recorded on magnetic tape, using an invention only finalized two years earlier. BASF still have the master tape and part of it is included in this box, sounding very primitive but remaining a fascinating historical document. To celebrate the fiftieth anniversary of tape recording, BASF re-created the original concert programme at the Barbican in London and also arranged for Vernon Handley to make a new complete recording with Beecham's own orchestra (still including one member who was present in 1936). The quality of the chrome cassettes readily demonstrates the sophistication of the current state of the art and Handley's performances happily capture the feeling of a live occasion, with the account of the Dvořák *Symphony* strikingly buoyant and spirited. His Delius, too, shows a natural sensibility for this repertoire and he secures memorably luminous playing from the LPO who are on top form throughout. The Mozart *Symphony*, though enjoyably spontaneous, is less distinctive; but overall this celebrates a notable occasion very successfully. As a bonus we are offered (to back the original Beecham fragments) reminiscences of the great conductor in a discussion between Lady Beecham and John Amis.

LPO, Herrmann

'Clair de lune': SATIE: *Gymnopédies Nos. 1 and 2.* DEBUSSY: *Suite bergamasque: Clair de lune. La plus que lente* (valse). RAVEL: *Five o'clock foxtrot.* FAURÉ: *Pavane.* HONEGGER: *Pastorale d'été.*
(M) * Decca SPA 570.

An interesting programme is here let down by indifferent performances. The Fauré *Pavane* is very sluggish indeed, and the Debussy and Satie pieces are not much better. Indeed the music only fitfully sparks into life. The recording – originally Phase Four – is close and unnatural in balance, so that the refinement of the scoring in the Ravel and Honegger works is not seen in truthful perspective. Disc and tape are similar.

LPO, Mackerras

TCHAIKOVSKY: *1812 overture, Op. 49* (with Welsh Guards Band). GLINKA: *Russlan and Ludmilla: Overture.* WAGNER: *Lohengrin: Prelude to Act III.* MUSSORGSKY: *Night on the Bare Mountain.*
(B) ** CfP CFP/*TC-CFP* 101.

Bright, alert performances, well played and recorded. *1812* appears to use mortar-fire at the end; the effect is small-scale. The sound is brightly lit throughout. This is good value, but none of the performances is memorable. The cassette matches the disc closely and has no problems with the close of *1812*.

LPO, Pritchard

BERLIOZ: *Les Troyens; Royal hunt and storm.* DEBUSSY: *Prélude à l'après-midi d'un faune.* STRAVINSKY: *The Firebird: suite* (1945 revised score).
(B) * PRT GSGC/*ZCGC* 2022.

A quite well-played collection, given good (1969) recording. The *Royal hunt and storm* is atmospheric, and the *Firebird suite* does not lack vividness, but in the last resort this is not a memorable concert, although it may suit limited budgets. The cassette matches the disc fairly closely.

LPO (various conductors)

'Favourites of the Philharmonic': GRIEG: *Peer Gynt: Morning.* CHABRIER: *España.* LITOLFF: *Concerto symphonique: Scherzo* (with Katin; all cond. Pritchard). FAURÉ: *Pavane* (cond. Handley). BERLIOZ: *Le Carnaval romain: overture.* SMETANA: *The Bartered Bride: overture* (cond. Barbier). GLINKA: *Russlan and Ludmilla: overture* (cond. Mackerras). WEBER: *Der Freischütz: overture.* NICOLAI: *The Merry Wives of Windsor: overture.* MENDELSSOHN: *A Midsummer Night's Dream: Scherzo* (cond. Lockhart). TCHAIKOVSKY: *Serenade for strings: Waltz* (cond. Del Mar). STRAUSS, J. Jnr: *Tritsch-Tratsch polka; An der schönen blauen Donau* (cond. Guschlbauer). STRAUSS, J. Snr: *Radetzky march.* VERDI: *Aïda: Triumphal march* (cond. Davison). BEETHOVEN: *Egmont: overture* (cond. Andrew Davis).
(B) ** MfP MFP/*TC-MFP* 1001 (2).

No one can argue with the title: there are many favourite classical 'pops' here, but they do not make a concert, with overtures dotted all over the place and no attempt to create a prevailing mood or set up appropriate contrasts. All the performances are good; some are excellent (Fauré's *Pavane* under Handley, and Lockhart's *Merry Wives overture*, for instance). The recording is bright and clear, and as a sampler of the Classics for Pleasure range this is more than adequate, even though at least two of the discs from which the items are taken are withdrawn from the catalogue as we go to print. It is curious that a CfP collection should be issued on the 'popular' MfP label.

'Favourites of the Philharmonic', Vol. 2: BEETHOVEN: *Fidelio overture* (cond. Andrew Davis)*; Ruins of Athens: Turkish march* (cond. Davison). MENDELSSOHN: *Overtures: A Midsummer Night's Dream; Ruy Blas* (cond. Lockhart). MUSSORGSKY: *Night on the Bare Mountain* (cond. Susskind). RIMSKY-KORSAKOV: *Le Coq d'or: March.* BERLIOZ: *Damnation de Faust: Hungarian march.* CHABRIER: *Marche joyeuse* (cond. Davison). WAGNER: *Lohengrin: Prelude to Act III* (cond. Mackerras). STRAUSS, J. Jnr: *Kaiser waltz; Perpetuum mobile; Polkas: Annen; Champagne; Unter Donner und Blitz* (cond. Guschlbauer). SAINT-SAËNS: *Danse macabre* (cond. Baudo). DEBUSSY: *Prélude à l'après-midi d'un faune* (cond. Handley).
(B) ** MfP MFP/*TC-MFP* 41 1036-3 (2).

This follows the pattern of the first issue, opening with three overtures in a row. Again performances are reliable (those directed by Mackerras and Guschlbauer are the most striking) and recording good. The double-length cassette matches the discs fairly closely although there is slightly less brilliance, except in the opening Beethoven overture where the situation is curiously reversed – the cassette is livelier.

(i) LPO; (ii) London Festival O, Black

(i) CHABRIER: *España* (rhapsody). LISZT: *Hungarian rhapsody for orchestra No. 2.* ENESCO: *Rumanian rhapsody No. 1.* (ii) RAVEL: *Boléro.*
(M) ** Decca VIV/*KVIC* 17.

Good, well-played performances, given vivid colourful sound (originally Decca Phase Four). Stanley Black's version of Ravel's *Boléro* is compulsive – more exciting than versions by some other more famous conductors – but there is less adrenalin flowing in the other items. The forward balance is not too noticeable in a programme of this nature.

LSO, Bonynge

'The art of the prima ballerina': MINKUS: *La Bayadere; Don Quixote: Pas de deux.* DRIGO: *Pas de trois.* ROSSINI: *William Tell, Act III: ballet music.* ADAM: *Giselle* excerpts: *Act I: Danse des vignerons; Giselle's solo; Peasant pas de deux; Act II: Pas de deux.* LOVENSKJOLD: *La sylphide* (excerpts). TCHAIKOVSKY: *Swan lake: Black swan pas de deux; Sleeping beauty: Blue bird pas de deux; The Nutcracker, Act II: Pas de deux.* DONIZETTI: *La Favorita:* ballet music. TRAD.: *Bolero 1830* (arr. O'Turner). PUGNI: *Pas de quatre* (arr. McDermott).
*** Decca SET 254/5.

Although not arranged in historical order this set has the effect of showing the background history against which the great nineteenth-century ballet scores were written. Accompanying the records is a lavishly illustrated booklet about the principal dancers as well as the music. Most of the pieces chosen are attractively scored and melodic in an obvious kind of way. With this kind of affectionate playing and Decca's superb recording they sound pleasingly colourful and Bonynge bends his back over the lesser pieces to make them sound their best. The *William Tell* and *Giselle* excerpts are a little below par, but perhaps this is because the conductor adopts stage tempi and we are used to concert performances. Some of the curiosities in the second part of the collection are especially gay and vivacious.

'Pas de deux': DRIGO: *Le Corsaire: Pas de deux. Esmeralda: Pas de deux. Pas de trois.*

MINKUS: *La Bayadere: Pas de deux. Paquita: Pas de deux. Don Quixote: Pas de deux.*
(M) *** Decca VIV/*KVIC* 27.

For ballet lovers not prepared to consider the comparatively expensive two-disc set above, the present disc and tape serve admirably to show what ballet music was like in the era before composers like Delibes and Tchaikovsky took over. Bonynge directs all this music with affectionate flair and the Decca recording is both sumptuous and sparkling. Side two with *Paquita* and *Don Quixote* (each producing a striking melody) is especially engaging, with Drigo's *Pas de trois* in between, which features a romantic violin solo. The cassette matches the disc closely, though just occasionally the focus is slightly less clean.

LSO, Gibson

'Music for royal occasions': MATHIAS: *Investiture Anniversary fanfare.* WALTON: *Crown Imperial; Orb and Sceptre* (marches). HANDEL: *Water music suite* (arr. Harty): *Allegro; Air; Allegro deciso.* DAVIS: *Music for a Royal Wedding.* ELGAR: *Nursery suite: Aubade; The serious doll.*
(B) *** Pick. Dig. RL/*RLT* 7555.

This was the first digital record to be issued at bargain price, and it is an uncommonly good one, with a matching cassette of demonstration quality. It was released without any commensurate publicity fanfares to celebrate the occasion of the royal wedding and almost passed unnoticed. The programme is admirably chosen; Mathias's *Investiture fanfare* (written earlier for the Prince of Wales) is superbly crafted, characteristic of this unostentatious but highly musical composer, and Carl Davis's *Suite* is no less congenial. One cannot help smiling at the inclusion of the Elgar items, in the event suitably prescient. The marches have regal splendour and the recording appropriate brilliance. A real bargain.

LSO, Previn

'André Previn Music Festival': GLINKA: *Overture Russlan and Ludmilla.* DUKAS: *L'Apprenti sorcier.* DEBUSSY: *Prélude à l'après-midi d'un faune.* BERNSTEIN: *Overture Candide.* BARBER: *Adagio for strings.* WALTON: *Coronation march: Orb and Sceptre.* VAUGHAN WILLIAMS: *Fantasia on Greensleeves.* HUMPERDINCK: *Overture Hänsel und Gretel.* ALBINONI: *Adagio in G min.* (arr. Giazotto). STRAUSS, J. Jnr: *Kaiser waltz.* DVOŘÁK: *Slavonic dance No. 9, Op. 72/1.* ENESCO: *Rumanian rhapsody No. 1.* FALLA: *Three-cornered hat: 3 dances.*
(M) *** HMV ESDW/*TC-ESDW* 720 (2).

An admirably enjoyable collection of favourites (recorded between 1972 and 1977) demonstrating Previn's charisma at the peak of his success with the LSO. The playing sparkles and the characterization is vivid. This is one of the most attractive available accounts of *L'Apprenti sorcier* while the performances of the Debussy *Prélude* (with some beautiful flute-playing by William Bennett) and the Barber *Adagio* are also especially fine. The delectable *Rumanian rhapsody* and Dvořák and Falla dances have splendid life and colour. The account of *Candide* rivals the composer's own. The leisured *Emperor waltz* will not perhaps be to all tastes, but there is no question of any lack of spontaneity, Previn clearly enjoying every bar, especially the coda with the horn and cello melody played most lovingly. The sound varies a little between items but is always vivid and often first-rate, with excellent, lively cassettes to match the discs closely.

LSO, Solti

'Romantic Russia': BORODIN: *Prince Igor: Overture; Polovtsian dances* (with LSO Chorus). GLINKA: *Russlan and Ludmilla: overture.* MUSSORGSKY: *Night on the Bare Mountain. Khovantschina: Prelude.*
*** Decca SXL 6263 [Lon. CS/5- 6785].

Superb recording from Decca, vivid and rich, with marvellous detail and heartwarming cello tone. This version of the *Polovtsian dances* is among the best in the catalogue. The chorus in the opening dances is lyrical and polished in a characteristically English way, but when the music warms up the performance is as exciting as anyone could wish. A very fast *Russlan and Ludmilla overture* (with the LSO on the tips of their toes, but never sounding out of breath) is very diverting, and *Night on the Bare Mountain*, played without eccentricity, but with a tender closing section, cannot fail with this quality of recording. The marvellously evocative *Khovantschina Prelude* is not quite as successful here as in Solti's Berlin performance (see under Berlin Philharmonic, above), but the *Prince Igor overture* has fine dash and spontaneity, yet is romanticized by the richly recorded textures.

Los Angeles CO, Schwarz

'American string music': BARBER: *Serenade, Op. 1.* CARTER: *Elegy.* DIAMOND: *Rounds.* FINE: *Serious song.*
*** None. Dig. D 79002 [id.].

The Barber *Serenade* was first recorded in the 1960s but its long absence from the catalogue is at last rectified by this excellent issue. It is a winning piece with all the freshness of youth. The *Rounds* for strings by David Diamond is another fertile and inventive piece, which has not been available since the early days of LP. Elliot Carter's *Elegy* was originally written for cello and piano, then arranged for string quartet, and dates from 1939. It is a long-breathed and noble piece, while Irving Fine, like Carter a pupil of Boulanger and Walter Piston, composed his *Serious song* in the mid-1950s. A worthwhile issue for all who have inquiring tastes, excellently played and recorded.

Lucerne Festival Strings, Baumgartner

'Adagio': ALBINONI: *Adagio for strings and organ* (arr. Giazotto). PACHELBEL: *Canon and Gigue.* RAMEAU: *Tambourin.* PURCELL: *Chaconne in G min.* BACH: *Suites Nos. 2 in B min., BWV 1067: Badinerie; 3 in D, BWV 1068: Air. Fugue in E* (arr. Mozart). *Jesu, joy of man's desiring. The Musical Offering, BWV 1079: Ricercare.*
(M) ** DG Priv. 2535/*3335* 606.

An agreeable collection of baroque 'pops', stylishly played and recorded with full, bright sound and a style that manages to be expressive without resorting to technicolor textures. *Jesu, joy of man's desiring*, however, sounds rather dull when heard on strings alone, without the usual oboe obbligato. Disc and cassette are of matching quality.

Melbourne SO Strings, Dommett

'Serenade': ELGAR: *Serenade in E min., Op. 20.* WIRÉN: *Serenade, Op. 11.* MOZART: *Serenade No. 13* (*Eine kleine Nachtmusik*), *K.525.* BARBER: *Adagio for strings, Op. 11.*
** Chan. CBR/*CBT* 1007.

The account of the Elgar is cool (the slow movement elegiac) and with an absence of ripeness this is very much a chamber performance. The Barber *Adagio*, although beautifully played, is also without the last degree of intensity at its climax, but does not lack warmth. The famous Mozartian *Night music* is rather bland, but the sprightly Dag Wirén piece is very successful. The sound is truthful and well balanced; on cassette the Mozart (on side two) has noticeably less bite but the first side matches the disc reasonably closely.

Messiter, Malcolm (oboe)

'Oboe fantasia' (with Nat. PO, Mace): PASCULLI: *Concerto on themes from Donizetti's 'La Favorita'.* DEBUSSY: *Rêverie.* SCARLATTI, D.: *Sonata in C, Kk.159.* SAINT-SAËNS: *The Swan.* MUSSORGSKY: *Ballet of the unhatched chicks.* NOVAČEK: *Perpetual motion.* DE LA RUE: *Compte à rebours: Adagio.* PUCCINI: *Gianni Schicchi: O mio babbino caro.* KREISLER: *Caprice viennois.* JOSEPHS: *Enemy at the Door: Song of freedom.* POULENC: *Mouvements perpétuels No. 1.* YOUNG: *Stella by Starlight.*
**(*) RCA RL/*RK* 25367.

With a showcase issue of this kind RCA are obviously trying to promote Malcolm Messiter as a star oboist to catch the public fancy and match the achievement of James Galway's silver flute. Certainly Messiter can charm the ear, as in Debussy's *Rêverie*; he can also produce impressive bravura, as in Pasculli's reworking of tunes from Donizetti's *La Favorita*. There is sparkle in Kreisler's *Caprice viennois*, and an eloquent operatic line in Puccini, but in the last result this playing has not the memorability nor quite the technical flair of Galway's. Messiter is at his best in the slighter material. The recording is faithful, the oboe well forward, the orchestral strings sometimes sounding thin, and this effect is exaggerated in the high-level cassette transfer.

Mexican State SO, Bátiz

'The music of Mexico': REVUELTAS: *Sensemayá; Homage to Federico Garcia Lorca.* MONCAYO: *Huapango.* CHAVEZ: *Symphony No. 2* (*Sinfonia India*).
(M) *** HMV Dig. Green. ESD/*TCC-ESD* 7146 [Var. Sar. 704220].

The music is vividly coloured, almost garish in its bright, dazzling effects. The Revueltas pieces are splendidly scored, as for that matter is the Chavez *Sinfonia India* with its exotic primitivism. The Moncayo piece is very appealing, as indeed is everything on this disc. Striking, brilliant and extrovert music without overmuch subtlety. Good performances, thoroughly in the spirit of the music as one would expect, and exemplary recording. The chrome tape is generally successful, but side two, transferred at a higher level, has more sparkle than side one, to the advantage of the *Sinfonia India* and the Revueltas *Homage*.

Music of Mexico: REVUELTAS: *Redes; Ocho por radio.* GALINDO: *Homenaje a Cervantes* (suite). HALFFTER: *Tripartita.*
(M) **(*) HMV Green. ESD/*TC-ESD* 270031-1/*4*.

An enterprising collection given spirited and sympathetic performances. *Redes* is a film score assembled by Erich Kleiber to make a kind of symphonic poem, balancing expressive evocation with vibrant Mexican dance rhythms. *Ocho por radio* in an engagingly offbeat octet for two violins, double-bass, cello, clarinet, bassoon, trumpet and Indian drum. It is short, sparkling, and scored with lightness and individuality. Galindo's suite is neoclassical, pleasing but rather anonymous, while Halffter's *Tripartita* offers an easy-going serialism, readily communicative. With such authoritative direction, good playing, plenty of conviction and vivid sound, this can hardly be faulted, even if none of its content, save the *Octet*, is really memorable.

Monteux, Claude (flute), LSO, Pierre Monteux

BACH: *Suite No. 2 in B min. for flute and strings, BWV 1067.* GLUCK: *Orfeo: Dance of the Blessed Spirits.* MOZART: *Flute concerto No. 2 in D, K.314.*
(B) *** Con. CC/*CCT* 7504 [Lon. STS 15493].

Claude Monteux is the son of Pierre Monteux, and the joy of family music-making shines through these charming performances. By chance the disc first appeared just after Pierre Monteux's death, and there could be no more fitting memorial for so vitally happy a musician, by turns serene and vigorous; the Mozart in particular is given the sunniest performance. The recording still sounds extremely well in this Contour reissue, although the bass is somewhat over-resonant and tends to make textures ample and rich, the very opposite of the sound one would expect from the 'authentic' original instrument school. On tape the quality is less well defined at both ends of the spectrum.

Moscow RSO, Fedoseyev

'Russian orchestral showpieces': GLINKA: *Overture Russlan and Ludmilla.* TCHAIKOVSKY: *Capriccio italien; Marche slave; Sleeping Beauty waltz.* RIMSKY-KORSAKOV: *Capriccio espagnol.*
* HMV Dig. ASD 4389 [Vox C9052].

The effect of this record is crude, with the digital recording emphasizing the blatancy of the brass in the Tchaikovsky *Capriccio* which is unconvincing as a performance, dull at the opening and with forced excitement at the end. *Marche slave* and the energetic *Russlan overture* are more successful, but as a whole this cannot be recommended with any enthusiasm.

I Musici

ALBINONI: *Adagio in G min.* (arr. Giazotto). BEETHOVEN: *Minuet in G, WoO.10/2.* BOCCHERINI: *Quintet in E, Op. 13/5: Minuet.* HAYDN (attrib.): *Quartet, Op. 3/5; Serenade.* MOZART: *Serenade No. 13 in G (Eine kleine Nachtmusik), K.525.* PACHELBEL: *Canon.*
C *** Ph. Dig. **410 606-2**; 6514/*7337* 370 [id.].

An exceptionally successful concert recorded with remarkable naturalness and realism. The compact disc is very believable indeed, but the LP and cassette also offer demonstration quality. The playing combines warmth and freshness and the oft-played Mozart *Night music* has no suggestion whatsoever of routine; it combines elegance, warmth and sparkle. The Boccherini *Minuet* and (especially) the Hofstetter (attrib. Haydn) *Serenade* have an engaging lightness of touch.

'Baroque festival': PACHELBEL: *Canon and Gigue.* VIVALDI: *Double mandolin concerto in G, RV.532.* ALBINONI: *Adagio for strings and organ* (arr. Giazotto). HANDEL: *Harp concerto in B flat, Op. 4/6.* BACH: *Brandenburg concerto No. 3, BWV 1048.* DURANTE: *Concerto for strings in F min.* GALUPPI: *Concerto a quattro No. 2 in G.* SCARLATTI, A.: *Concerto grosso No. 3 in F.* PERGOLESI: *Flute concerto in G.* LOCATELLI: *Concerto grosso in C min., Op. 1/11.*
(M) **(*) Ph. 6770 057/*7650 057* (2).

Opening with a rather delicate version of Pachelbel's famous *Canon* and including also a perhaps over-refined view of the Albinoni/Giazotto *Adagio*, this is an attractively played and beautifully recorded collection, suitable for late-evening listening, especially in its tape-box format which offers demonstration quality throughout. The first half of the programme (up to the Bach *Brandenburg concerto*) is also available separately on Sequenza (6527/*7311* 104), but makes a less satisfying concert than the collection as a whole.

Munrow, David

'Medieval and Renaissance sounds' (with Reid and Hogwood): *French 13th-century Danse royale; Scottish 13th-century Danse tune; Vertias arpie* (motet). GYMNEL: *Jesu Cristes milde moder. Nowell sing we. Piper's fancy.* COEUR-DE-LION Richard: *Ja nuns hons pris. Italian 14th-century Saltarello. 16th-century Postillon. 16th/17th-century Alarm.* ASKUE: *Jig.* CUTTING: *Squirrel's toy. Wat zal men op den avond doen* (16th century). CERTON: *Bicinium Je nose etre content. Wat zal men op den avond doen* (17th century). BENUSI: *Desiderata pavana.* Music at Henry VIII's court (ANON.: *Si fortune; Consort.* HENRY VIII: *Helas madame; Taunder naken; If love now reigned; En vray amoure.*) Elizabethan popular tunes (*La Volta; Kemp's jig; Tower Hill; A Bergomask; Bouffons.*) Suite of Renaissance dances (MAINERIO: *Il primo libro di balli: Ungarescha.* PRAETORIUS: *Terpsichore: La bourée; Ballets des baccanales et des feus.* SUSATO: *Dandserye: Bergeret sans roch* (basse danse); *Mon Amy* (ronde). ANON.: *La rocha el fuso* (galliard).)
(B) *** CfP CFP/*TC-CFP* 4384 [Desto 7183/*47183*].

This splendidly planned issue – partly a recital, partly a demonstration lecture – will be invaluable to schools and libraries, but it is so reasonably priced that anyone interested in the history of our musical culture will find it an excellent kingpin for a collection of medieval and Renaissance music. Side one is given over to a gentle *sotto voce* exposition of early instruments and how they were used, including woodwind, the psaltery, regal and medieval bells. The clearly projected recording is quite admirable and the sounds are both fascinating and piquant. The voice of the commentary might have been recorded a little louder, but the words are clear, even at a distance (in a classroom, say, using a small reproducer). However, the advantage of the quiet commentary is to make the disc suitable for late-evening domestic use. Side two is divided into three sections: Music at Henry VIII's court; Elizabethan popular airs; and Renaissance dances. The instrumental music provided is colourful and entertaining (notably, in section two, *Kemp's jig*, played on the sopranino recorder with great virtuosity). Throughout the fine instrumental playing, like the excellent recording, is worthy of the project, an education in miniature.

National PO, Stokowski

'Great overtures': BEETHOVEN: *Leonora No. 3.* SCHUBERT: *Rosamunde* (*Die Zauberharfe*). BERLIOZ: *Le carnaval romain.* MOZART: *Don Giovanni.* ROSSINI: *William Tell.*
**(*) Dell'Arte DA 9003.

Stokowski made this record just before his ninety-fourth birthday, yet, as with so many of the recordings made during his 'Indian summer', the electricity crackles throughout and his charisma is felt in every bar. The Beethoven is immensely dramatic while *Rosamunde* combines high romanticism with affectionate warmth. Dissatisfied with Mozart's ending to *Don Giovanni*, Stokowski extends this piece to include music from the opera's finale. The pacing in *William Tell* is fast, but here as elsewhere the players obviously relish the experience, and if ensemble slips a little, the music-making is enjoyably infectious. The sound is extremely vivid, too.

Netherlands Wind Ens.

'Little marches by great masters': BEETHOVEN: *Marches: in F* (*Yorkscher*), *G.145/1; G.145/2; in C* (*Zapfenstreich*). BACH, C. P. E.: *Marches in F, Wq.187/1; in D, Wq.185/1; in C, Wq.185/2; in G, Wq.185/4; in E flat, Wq.185/5; in D, Wq.185/6; Wq.187/2; in F, Wq.185/3.* HAYDN: *March for the Prince of Wales in E flat; March No. 2 in C for the Derbyshire Cavalry Regiment.* HAYDN, M.: *Turkish march in C.* VRANICKY: *3 Marches in the French style; 2 Hunting marches in the French style; 4 Little marches.* ROSETTI: *March Largo from Partita in D.*
❀ (M) *** Ph. Seq. 6527/*7311* 117.

This beautifully recorded collection is an unexpected treasure. Who would think that a collection of marches could be so diverse in colour, and make such a captivating entertainment? Of course much is due to the marvellously light touch of the playing and the style with which the concert is presented. The opening music is by Beethoven, sounding for all the world like Schubert. Then follows lyrical contrast with the music of C. P. E. Bach and scoring like a Mozart divertimento. After more charming textures from Carl Philip we end side one with a perky, spirited march by Haydn. Music from his brother, Michael, begins side two, its exotic character partly created by the imaginative scoring for flutes, like sunshine gleaming on armour. Antonin Vranicky's (1761–1820) contribution is delightful: nine marches in all, each short, crisp and very galant: one can imagine the smartest of regiments here. Joseph Haydn closes the concert with a little more weight in the sound, a suggestion (only a hint, really) of the modern military band. Detailing the contents cannot convey the delights of this disc or the superbly polished playing and the recording quality itself: wonderfully fresh. Very highly recommended. The cassette only loses a little of the transient edge of the disc and is attractively balanced.

Neveu, Ginette (violin)

'The early recordings': BACH (arr. Kreisler): *Air.* CHOPIN (arr. Rodionov): *Nocturne No. 20 in C sharp min., Op. posth.* GLUCK: *Orfeo: Melody.* PARADIES (arr. Dushkin): *Sicilienne* (all with Seidler-Winkler, piano). TARTINI (arr. Kreisler): *Variations on a theme of Corelli.* STRAUSS, R.: *Violin sonata in E flat, Op. 18* (both with Beck, piano). SIBELIUS: *Violin concerto in D min., Op. 47* (with Philh. O, Susskind). RAVEL: *Tzigane. Pièce en forme de habanera.* SCARLATESCU: *Bagatelle.* FALLA (arr. Kreisler): *La Vida breve: Danse espagnole.* DINICU (arr. Heifetz): *Hora staccato.* SUK: *4 Pieces, Op. 17.* DEBUSSY: *Violin sonata in G min.* (all with Jean Neveu, piano). BRAHMS: *Violin concerto in D, Op. 77.* CHAUSSON: *Poème, Op. 25* (both with Philh. O, Dobrowen).

(M) (***) HMV mono RLS 739 (4).

The brilliant career of Ginette Neveu was cut short by an air crash, in which her brother Jean also died. This compilation offers all the material that has already been issued in the UK, such as the Sibelius and Brahms concertos and the Suk *Four Pieces*, together with a number of recordings which have not. These include the Strauss *Sonata*, recorded in Berlin before the outbreak of the war. There is a vibrant intensity about Neveu's playing that is altogether remarkable; this four-record set gives the complete recorded legacy, and its quality cannot be too highly praised. The transfers are altogether excellent and have been done with great care. The *Early recordings* title applies only to the first two records.

(i) New SO (of London), Gibson; (ii) SRO, Ansermet

'Danse macabre': (i) SAINT-SAËNS: *Danse macabre.* MUSSORGSKY: *Pictures from an exhibition: Gnomus; A Night on the Bare Mountain.* ARNOLD: *Tam O'Shanter: overture, Op. 52.* HUMPERDINCK: *Hänsel und Gretel: Witch's ride.* LISZT: *Mephisto waltz.* (ii) DUKAS: *The Sorcerer's apprentice.*
*** Decca SPA 175.

This is the reissue of an early RCA collection (recorded by Decca engineers) originally known as '*Witches' brew*', together with an outstanding Ansermet performance of *The Sorcerer's apprentice.* The recording throughout is of the highest standard, and the Ansermet account of *L'Apprenti sorcier* is unsurpassed in the present catalogue. Sir Alexander Gibson comes from the land of Burns and it is not surprising that his *Tam O'Shanter* is also a star performance. This is a brilliantly evocative piece, one of Malcolm Arnold's finest works. Gibson's orchestra bubbles and effervesces brilliantly in the rest of his programme, but the conductor seems to stir the cauldron in rather a detached way. Yet the remarkably clear and vivid sound offers its own excitements and this makes an excellent concert.

NYPO, Bernstein

'Overtures': HÉROLD: *Zampa.* THOMAS: *Mignon; Raymond.* SUPPÉ: *Poet and peasant.* ROSSINI: *William Tell.*
(M) *** CBS 60133/*40*- [MY/*MYT* 37240].

Fizzing performances from Bernstein with the New York Philharmonic on peak form. The zest and sparkle of the playing make these popular warhorses sound as fresh as paint, with brightly hued colours reflected by the vivid, resonant recording with its glittering upper range. The cassette, however, is uneven: side one is muffled, while side two matches the LP quite closely.

DUKAS: *L'Apprenti sorcier.* MUSSORGSKY: *Night on the Bare Mountain.* STRAUSS, R.: *Till Eulenspiegel, Op. 28.* SAINT-SAËNS: *Danse macabre, Op. 40.*
(M) *** CBS 61976/*40*- [Col. MS 7165].

One of Bernstein's very best records made during his regular association with the New York Philharmonic. The performances are as volatile as they are brilliant: *The Sorcerer's apprentice* has splendid momentum; *Night on the Bare Mountain* emanates a pungent rhythmic force; *Till* is portrayed with a captivatingly mercurial projection of high spirits and *Danse macabre* has striking panache. The orchestra's bravura brings superb ensemble throughout, matched with lively and colourful solo contributions from all departments. The CBS recording is characteristically forward, but there is atmosphere to balance the brightness. The cassette is lively but less refined than the disc: climaxes are inclined to sound explosive.

Orchestre de Paris, Barenboim

French music: DUKAS: *L'Apprenti sorcier.* BERLIOZ: *Le Carnaval romain: overture. Béatrice et Bénédict: overture. La Damnation de Faust: Hungarian march.* SAINT-SAËNS: *Le Déluge: Prélude. Samson et Dalila: Bacchanale. Danse macabre, Op. 40.*
*(**) DG 2531/*3301* 331 [id.].

Outstanding recording here, demonstration-worthy in its sumptuousness as well as its brilliance. The finest performance is the Saint-Saëns *Bacchanale*, with a voluptuous climax of great intensity and power. *Danse macabre* comes off well too, but *The Sorcerer's Apprentice* shows Barenboim rather unsuccessfully adopting his Furtwänglerian mantle: the heavy presentation of the main theme bodes ill for a reading which produces very broad climaxes, with unconvincing use of accelerandi to reach them. The Berlioz overtures are exciting, with the orchestra on its toes, again helped by the flattering acoustic. The cassette is extremely successful, matching the disc closely.

Orchestre de Paris, Jacquillat

MESSAGER: *Les Deux Pigeons: suite; Isoline: suite*. LALO: *Scherzo for orchestra*. PIERNÉ: *Marche des petits soldats de plomb*. DE LISLE (arr. Berlioz): *La Marseillaise* (with soloists and chorus).
(M) *** HMV Green. ESD 7048.

An utterly delectable concert, splendidly played and recorded. The Messager scores are full of charm and colour; the Lalo *Scherzo* is a first-rate piece, and Pierné's *March of the little lead soldiers* is deliciously piquant. Berlioz's arrangement of *La Marseillaise* (all verses included) for soloists, choir and orchestra is irresistibly life-enhancing, and it is done with great flair and commitment here. Highly recommended.

Orchestre de Paris, Rozhdestvensky

'A Russian festival gala': BORODIN: *Prince Igor: Polovtsian dances*. RIMSKY-KORSAKOV: *Capriccio espagnol, Op. 34; Russian Easter festival overture, Op. 36*. MUSSORGSKY (orch. Rimsky-Korsakov): *Night on the Bare Mountain*.
(B) *** CfP CFP/*TC-CFP* 4397.

A first-class collection and a real bargain too. These are exciting performances, brilliantly played. The tension is kept at a high level throughout the concert, and yet the characterization of each piece is very well done. The *Russian Easter Festival overture* is among the finest available performances of this piece, and the *Capriccio espagnol* is also outstanding. The recording is of high quality, bright, full and vivid, although the cassette is a little lacking in sparkle compared with the disc on side one (the Borodin and the *Capriccio espagnol*) but, with a rise in level, side two has greater range.

Orchestra of St John's, Lubbock

'Classical collection': VAUGHAN WILLIAMS: *Fantasia on Greensleeves. Rhosymedre*. GRIEG: *Peer Gynt: Morning*. RAVEL: *Pavane*. DELIUS: *On Hearing the First Cuckoo in Spring*. FAURÉ: *Masques et bergamasques: overture. Berceuse, Op. 56*. SCHUBERT: *Rosamunde: Entr'acte No. 2; Ballet music No. 2*. MOZART: *Divertimento in D, K.136: Presto*.
**(*) ASV Dig. DCA/*ZCDCA* 503.

A pleasant collection of essentially atmospheric music for late evening. Fine playing; tempi are at times a little sleepy, notably in the Grieg, Fauré and Schubert items, but the effect is still persuasive. The digital recording is first-class, full, clear, yet not clinical in its detail. The cassette is excellent too.

Overtures

English overtures (with (i) LPO; (ii) LSO; (iii) New Philh. O; (iv) Alwyn; (v) Pritchard; (vi) Braithwaite; (vii) Handley): (i; iv) ALWYN: *Derby Day*. (i; v) CHAGRIN: *Helter Skelter*. (ii; vi) ARNOLD: *Beckus the Dandipratt*. (i; v) RAWSTHORNE: *Street Corner*. (iii; vii) BUSH: *Yorick*. (iii; vi) LEIGH: *Agincourt*.
*** Lyr. SRCS 95.

Alwyn's *Derby Day* begins an anthology of extrovert English overtures, all brightly and breezily played, and emphatically not to be heard in rapid succession! Best-known are Arnold's *Beckus the Dandipratt* and Rawsthorne's *Street Corner*, which have been on record before, and perhaps Geoffrey Bush's *Yorick*, a lively piece that is frequently broadcast. But all these pieces are vividly played and recorded, and the rarities by Francis Chagrin and Walter Leigh are well worth having.

'Famous overtures' (various orchestras, cond. (i) Agoult; (ii) Wolff; (iii) Bonynge; (iv) Boskovsky; (v) Kertesz; (vi) Ansermet): (i) NICOLAI: *Merry Wives of Windsor*. (ii) HÉROLD: *Zampa*. (iii) OFFENBACH: *La Fille du tambour-major*. (iv) STRAUSS, J. Jnr: *Die Fledermaus*. (v) DVOŘÁK: *Carnaval*. (vi) BERLIOZ: *Le carnaval romain*.
(M) ** Decca VIV/*KVIC* 7.

Highlights here are the (unexpected) Offenbach overture, stylish and sparkling under Bonynge, Kertesz's *Carnaval* and Boskovsky's VPO *Die Fledermaus*. The rest are acceptable but not outstanding, though the sound is always good, if sometimes a little dated.

'Famous overtures': SUPPÉ: *Light cavalry; Poet and Peasant* (VPO, Solti). HÉROLD: *Zampa*. BERLIOZ: *Le carnaval romain*. OFFENBACH: *Orpheus in the Underworld* (SRO, Ansermet). REZNIČEK: *Donna Diana*. NICOLAI: *Merry Wives of Windsor* (VPO, Boskovsky). ROSSINI: *La scala di seta; William Tell* (LSO, Gamba). MOZART: *Le nozze di Figaro* (VPO, Erich Kleiber). BEETHOVEN: *Leonora No. 3* (VPO, Schmidt-Isserstedt).
(B) *(*) Decca *410 294-4*.

Like others in this Decca double-length tape series, the transfers are made at a very high level, and at times the sound becomes unrefined, notably in the two Suppé overtures. Otherwise the collection is well made with all participants on good form. Boskovsky's *Donna Diana* sparkles and there is nothing to disappoint here on grounds of performance, with judicious arrangement of items to make an entertaining group on each side. On a small player or in the car the sound is acceptable.

Perlman, Itzhak (violin)

'Virtuoso violin concertos: TCHAIKOVSKY: *Violin concerto in D, Op. 35; Sérénade mélancolique, Op. 26* (with Phd. O, Ormandy). BRUCH: *Scottish fantasia, Op. 46; Violin concerto No. 2 in D min., Op. 44* (with New Philh. O, Lopez-Cobos). WIENIAWSKI: *Violin concertos Nos. 1 in F sharp min., Op. 14; 2 in D min., Op. 22* (with LPO, Ozawa).
(M) *** HMV SLS/*TC-SLS* 5280 (3).

Perlman – in many ways the supreme violin virtuoso of our time – plays this programme with characteristic technical assurance yet he is not less sensitive to the music's poetry and romantic warmth. The Bruch coupling is especially appealing, but the two Wieniawski concertos are eminently successful too. The inclusion of the Tchaikovsky seems a curious choice: it is standard repertoire and most collectors will undoubtedly already have a version, perhaps Perlman's own individual issue. The sound is vivid on disc, but much more variable on cassette, with often a poor orchestral focus in the Tchaikovsky and Bruch, although the Wieniawski is clean and clear. The cassette layout, however, splits the *First* Wieniawski *Concerto* between sides three and four (the first movement is on side three following the Bruch *Concerto*, which makes nonsense of the advantages of tape).

Petri, Michala (recorder)

Recorder concertos (with ASMF, Marriner): VIVALDI: *Sopranino recorder concerto in C, RV.443*. SAMMARTINI: *Descant recorder concerto in F*. TELEMANN: *Treble recorder concerto in C*. HANDEL: *Treble recorder concerto in F* (arr. of *Organ concerto, Op. 4/5*).
*** Ph. **400 075-2**; 9500 714/*7300 808* [id.].

Michala Petri plays her various recorders with enviable skill, and her nimble piping creates some delightful sounds in these four attractively inventive concertos. This is not a record to be played all at once, but taken in sections it has unfailing charm; the sound is of demonstration quality on disc and cassette alike. The CD retains the analogue ambient warmth, while detail seems marginally cleaner. While the upper range is not quite as open as on recordings with digital source, the quality remains very impressive.

'English concertos': BABEL: *Concerto in C for descant recorder, Op. 3/1*. HANDEL: *Concerto in B flat for treble recorder and bassoon, Op. 4/6* (with G. Sheene). BASTON: *Concerto No. 2 for descant recorder in D*. JACOB: *Suite for treble recorder and strings*.
❀ *** Ph. Dig. **411 056-2**; 6514/*7337* 310 [id.].

The *Concerto* by William Babel (*c.* 1690–1723) is a delight, with Petri's sparkling performance of the outer movements full of good humour and high spirits, matched by Marriner's alert accompaniments. The Handel is yet another arrangement of Op. 4/6, with the organ part felicitously re-scored for recorder and bassoon. The two instruments are nicely balanced and thus a familiar work is given an attractive new look. Not a great deal is known about John Baston, except that he lived in eighteenth-century London. But his *Concerto* has individuality, its *Adagio* has distinct charm and the finale is quirkily infectious. Gordon Jacob's *Suite* of seven movements balances a gentle bitter-sweet melancholy in the lyrical writing, with a rumbustious extrovert quality in the dances. Altogether a highly rewarding concert, beautifully played and recorded. The chrome tape is in the demonstration class, as of course is the compact disc. On CD the quality of the string timbre in the Gordon Jacob *Suite* is especially real and beautiful.

Philadelphia O, Ormandy

'Wedding march and other great marches': BIZET: *Carmen: March of the Toreadors.* WAGNER: *Tannhäuser: Grand march.* SCHUBERT: *Marche militaire.* IPPOLITOV-IVANOV: *Caucasian sketches: Procession of the Sardar.* MEYERBEER: *Le Prophète: Coronation march.* MENDELSSOHN: *Midsummer Night's Dream: Wedding march.* RIMSKY-KORSAKOV: *Le Coq d'or: Bridal procession.* BEETHOVEN: *Ruins of Athens: Turkish march.* VERDI: *Aïda: Grand march.* STRAUSS, J. Snr: *Radetzky march.*
(B) *** RCA VIC/*VK* 2037 [AGL1/*AGK1* 4298].

Ormandy's zest and flair are matched here by lively and sumptuous playing from the Philadelphia Orchestra: the Wagner and Meyerbeer marches are especially impressive. The sound is good too on disc, although the chrome cassette is too highly modulated and climaxes become fierce.

Philharmonia O, Karajan

'Philharmonia Promenade Concert': WALDTEUFEL: *Les Patineurs waltz.* STRAUSS, J. Jnr: *Tritsch-Tratsch polka. Unter Donner und Blitz polka.* STRAUSS, J. Snr: *Radetzky march.* CHABRIER: *España. Joyeuse marche.* SUPPÉ: *Overture: Light Cavalry.* WEINBERGER: *Schwanda the Bagpiper: Polka.* OFFENBACH: *Overture: Orpheus in the Underworld.*
(B) *** CfP CFP/*TC-CFP* 40368.

A superb reissue from the 1960s. Both Karajan and the Philharmonia Orchestra are on top form, and the whole collection has the right infectious 'fun' quality. An exhilarating experience, partly because the remarkably sumptuous recording also sparkles vividly to match the playing. Highly recommended on both disc and cassette (they sound virtually identical).

(i) Philharmonia O, Krips; (ii) Johann Strauss O of V., Boskovsky

'Viennese enchantment': (i) STRAUSS: *Die Fledermaus: overture. Unter Donner und Blitz polka. Perpetuum mobile. Quadrille on themes from Verdi's 'Un Ballo in maschera'. Tritsch-Tratsch polka. Der Zigeunerbaron: overture.* (ii) *Wein, Weib und Gesang waltz. Auf der Jagd polka.* (i) ZIEHRER: *Wiener Bürger waltz.* (i) *Die Landstreicher: overture.* (i) *Weaner Mädln waltz.* GUNGL: *Amorettentanz waltz.* LANNER: *Die Schönbrunner waltz.* LEHÁR: *Gold and silver waltz.*
(B) **(*) EMI *TC2-MOM 121.*

Henry Krips's version of the *Die Fledermaus overture* uses a degree of rubato which now seems excessive, but otherwise his performances are vivacious and the Philharmonia playing reflects the vintage period from which these recordings come. Boskovsky's contribution is also stylish. The sound, though rather reverberant, is always good and there are some attractive novelties here.

Polished Brass, Clothier

TRAD.: *Summer is a cummin in; Greensleeves; Londonderry air.* CLARKE: *Trumpet voluntary; Trumpet tune and air.* HANDEL: *Suite from Water and Fireworks music* (arr. Clothier). PREMRU: *Divertimento.* CLOTHIER: *Shakespearian suite.*
(M) *** HMV Dig. HQS/*TC-HQS* 107771-1/*4*.

Michael Clothier – sub-principal trumpet in the LPO for the past twenty years – here directs a new group of young brass players (ten in number) whose easy virtuosity is matched by a finesse in ensemble which is hardly less impressive. Clothier has made free arrangements of all these pieces and they are by no means conventional. His own *Shakespearian suite* is highly imaginative, especially the *Rumba* (*Fortinbrass*) and *Witches' dance*. Equally the suite of nine miniatures of Raymond Premru (a member of the Philip Jones Ensemble) is attractively resourceful, notably the engaging *Blues march*. In short, this is a lightweight but highly entertaining concert, played with great spirit, and digitally recorded with fine brilliance and sonority. The precision of articulation possible with a group of this size is striking, yet the body of sound often belies the comparatively small number of players. There is a first-class cassette.

'Pomp and circumstance'

(i) Royal Liv. PO, Groves; (ii) King's College Ch., Camb. University Music Soc., New Philh. O, Ledger: (i) ELGAR: *Pomp and Circumstance marches Nos. 1 and 4. Imperial march. Coronation march. Enigma variations: Nimrod.* (ii) *Land of Hope and Glory.* (i) ARNE: *Rule, Britannia* (with Anne Collins, Liv. PO Ch.). *The British Grenadiers.* WALTON: *Spitfire prelude and fugue. Orb and Sceptre. Crown Imperial.* COATES: *Dambusters march.* (ii) PARRY: *I was glad.* (i) WALFORD DAVIES: *RAF March past.*
(B) ** EMI *TC2-MOM 105*.

Such an unrelenting stream of musical patriotism is more suitable for keeping up the spirits on the motorway than for a continuous domestic concert, although Sir Charles Groves's sturdy performances never lack character. The transfer is not too well calculated and the high level brings patches of roughness, notably at the opening of the *Spitfire prelude*, and occasionally in the choral music. This is barely noticeable in the car.

(i) LSO, Bliss; (ii) Simon Preston (organ); (iii) Grenadier Guards Band, Bashford; (iv) Philip Jones Brass Ens.; (v) Chorus, LSO, Britten: (i) ELGAR: *Pomp and Circumstance marches, Op. 39/1–5.* (ii) *Imperial march, Op. 32.* (iii) COATES: *Dambusters march.* (iv) BLISS: *Antiphonal fanfare for 3 brass choirs.* (ii) WALTON: *Crown Imperial.* (iv) BAX: *Fanfare for the wedding of Princess Elizabeth* (1948). BRITTEN: *Fanfare for St Edmundsbury.* (v) arr. BRITTEN: *National anthem.*
(M) *** Decca SPA 419.

Bliss's account of the *Pomp and Circumstance marches* is extremely lively, never sentimentalizing, yet not missing the *nobilmente*. There is a slight edge in the sound of No. 1, betraying the early stereo recording. The brass fanfares by Bliss, Bax and Britten, contrasted in range and style, are very appealing when the stereo effect is so impressive. One might have preferred an orchestral version of *Crown Imperial*, but the recording here is of demonstration quality, and Simon Preston is an eloquent advocate.

Pré, Jacqueline du (cello)

'Impressions': ELGAR: *Cello concerto in E min.* HAYDN: *Cello concerto in C.* BEETHOVEN: *Cello sonata No. 3 in A; Piano trio No. 4 in D* (*Ghost*) (with various artists).
(M) *** HMV SLS/*TC-SLS* 154596-3/*5*.

These four sides of Jacqueline du Pré's recordings, reissued to coincide with a book of tributes from friends, give a fine representative view of her mastery on record. This version of the Elgar *Concerto*, recorded with Sir John Barbirolli and the LSO, has never been surpassed, and while the Haydn in principle brings overmuch romanticism, the results have such concentration as well as beauty that the result is heart-easing. The Beethoven performances both have fire as well as warmth, the *Trio* recorded in the studio, the *Sonata* at a live performance in Edinburgh, both of them bringing out her strength of imagination even next to her husband, Daniel Barenboim. The double folder has a moving and informative tribute from her recording manager, Suvi Raj Grubb. Good transfers, with tape and disc closely matched.

Rampal, Jean-Pierre (flute)

Flute concertos (with O Ant. Mus., Roussel): DEVIENNE: *Concerto No. 2 in D.* NAUDOT: *Concerto in G, Op. 17/5.* LOEILLET: *Concerto in D.*
(M) **(*) Ph. Seq. 6527/*7311* 095.

A surprisingly enjoyable collection of concertos by lesser-known composers. The most ambitious piece – with a side to itself – is that by François Devienne (1759–1803), a work of considerable charm in the galant style. The rococo roulades of the outer movements are highly engaging, and there is no lack of agreeable melody. The work by Naudot (*c.* 1690–1762) looks back to Vivaldi and has plenty of vitality, like the sprightly concerto of Loeillet, his contemporary. Excellent playing from Rampal. The orchestral sound is slightly less refined but spirited, recorded in a somewhat over-resonant acoustic, which brings some slight loss of sharpness of detail in the otherwise well-managed cassette transfer.

Rostropovich, Mstislav (cello)

Cello concertos (with (i) Zurich Coll. Mus., Sacher; (ii) Leningrad PO, Rozhdestvensky; (iii) Berlin PO, Karajan): (i) BOCCHERINI: *Concerto No. 2 in D.* VIVALDI: *Concerto in G, RV.143.* (ii) SCHUMANN: *Concerto in A min., Op. 129.* (iii) DVOŘÁK: *Concerto in B min., Op. 104.* TCHAIKOVSKY: *Variations on a rococo theme, Op. 33.*
(M) *** DG Acc. 2725/*3374* 107 (2).

Rostropovich's performance of the Schumann *Concerto* is the finest available in stereo and has hitherto only been available coupled to a less recommendable performance of the same composer's *Piano concerto* by Sviatoslav Richter. Here it reappears in a most attractive collection that also includes the somewhat larger-than-life but irresistible Boccherini and Vivaldi concertos and a superb collaboration with Karajan in the works of Dvořák and Tchaikovsky. With excellent sound – on disc and cassette alike – this makes an outstandingly desirable medium-priced anthology. (The cassettes are ingeniously packaged in the normal style of hinged plastic box, but twice as wide as usual across the spine.)

RPO, Beecham

'French lollipops' (with (i) Fr. Nat. RO): CHABRIER: *Marche joyeuse.* DEBUSSY: *L'Enfant prodigue: Cortège et Air de danse. Prélude à l'après-midi d'un faune.* SAINT-SAËNS: *Samson et Dalila: Danse; Bacchanale. Le Rouet d'Omphale, Op. 31.* GOUNOD: *Roméo et Juliette: Le sommeil.* (i) FAURÉ: *Dolly suite, Op. 56. Pavane, Op. 50.*
(M) *** HMV SXLP/*TC-SXLP* 30299.

This is an enchanting record, full of the imaginative and poetic phrasing that distinguished the best Beecham performances. The recording is always good and sometimes excellent, with an outstanding cassette to match the disc in vividness and detail.

'Beecham favourites': HANDEL: *Solomon: Arrival of the Queen of Sheba.* ROSSINI: *Overtures: La Cambiale di matrimonio; Semiramide.* SIBELIUS: *Kuolema: Valse triste, Op. 44.* GRIEG: *In Autumn: concert overture. Symphonic dance in A, Op. 64/2.* DVOŘÁK: *Legend in G min., Op. 59/3.* MENDELSSOHN: *Fair Melusina: overture, Op. 32.*
(M) *** HMV SXLP/*TC-SXLP* 30530.

Altogether delicious performances from the old magician. They come up remarkably fresh, too, after more than two decades, a tribute not only to the artistry of Beecham and the RPO but the quality of the EMI engineering. Notable are the Grieg items: the *Symphonic dance* is utterly delectable, while his little-known overture displays an unexpected degree of colour and charm. The cassette offers sound that is slightly fuller than the disc, which has more range at the top and a fresher upper string quality.

Rousseau, Eugene (saxophone)

Saxophone concertos (with Paul Kuentz CO, Kuentz): DUBOIS: *Concerto for alto saxophone and string orchestra*. VILLA-LOBOS: *Fantasia for soprano saxophone, 3 horns and string orchestra*. IBERT: *Concertino da camera for alto saxophone and 11 instruments*. GLAZOUNOV: *Alto saxophone concerto in E, Op. 109*.
(M) *** DG 2543 811 [2530 209].

An enterprising anthology. The Glazounov *Concerto* is a late work and the best known and most often recorded of the pieces here. However, both the Villa-Lobos *Fantasia* and the Ibert *Concertino da camera* are as appealing and exotic and there is much to give pleasure. The longest piece is the *Concerto* by Max-Pierre Dubois, a pupil of Milhaud and now in his fifties – fluent, well-crafted and civilized. Eugene Rousseau is an expert and persuasive soloist and the recording, which dates from the early 1970s, is first-class.

Russian orchestral music

'1812 overture and other Russian pops' (with (i) Bournemouth SO; (ii) LPO; (iii) RPO; (iv) Philh. O; (v) Silvestri; (vi) Boult; (vii) Sargent): (i; v) TCHAIKOVSKY: *Overture 1812*. *Capriccio italien*. (iii; vii) *Marche slave*. (i; v) BORODIN: *In the Steppes of Central Asia*. (ii; vi) RIMSKY-KORSAKOV: *Mlada: Procession of the nobles*. *Capriccio espagnol*. (i; v) MUSSORGSKY (arr. Rimsky-Korsakov): *Night on the Bare Mountain*. (iv; v) GLINKA: *Overture Russlan and Ludmilla*.
(B) ** EMI *TC2-MOM 107*.

Levels have been successfully manipulated here to avoid coarseness without too much loss of dynamic range, and even at the end of *1812* (with cannon) the sound does not disintegrate as it often does in cassette versions of this piece. Silvestri's performances are good but neither especially individual nor exciting. Sargent's *Marche slave* has a lively impetus, and Boult's versions of the Rimsky-Korsakov *Capriccio* and *Procession* show plenty of character, even if there is some lack of exuberance in the closing pages of the *Capriccio*. The richly resonant recording here is well contained in this transfer, and the only real slip of refinement comes in the final climax of Silvestri's account of Tchaikovsky's *Capriccio italien*, which also has a curiously clumsy quickening of tempo in the coda.

St Louis SO, Slatkin

VAUGHAN WILLIAMS: *Fantasia on a theme of Thomas Tallis*. BARBER: *Adagio for strings*. GRAINGER: *Irish tune from County Derry*. FAURÉ: *Pavane, Op. 50*. SATIE: *Gymnopédies Nos. 1 and 3*.
(*) Telarc Dig. **CD 80080; DG 10080 [id.].

This was the digital début of both Vaughan Williams's *Tallis fantasia* and the Barber *Adagio*. Both are given spacious performances and are well structured with strong central climaxes. The recording too is both rich and clear though not finer than the sound given by EMI to Barbirolli in the Vaughan Williams (HMV ASD 521 [Ang. S 36101]) or Argo to Marriner and the ASMF in the Barber (ZRG/*KZRC* 845). The rest of the programme here is beautifully played, but with Slatkin favouring slow tempi the overall effect is a little lacking in vitality; this applies especially to the *Londonderry air*. The sound, however, cannot be faulted. It is especially beautiful in its compact-disc format.

Sakonov, Josef (violin)

'Meditation' (with L. Fest. O): HUBAY: *Hejre Kati*. GODARD: *Berceuse de Jocelyn*. TCHAIKOVSKY: *Valse sentimentale*. *None but the Lonely Heart*. STERNHOLD: *Fêtes tzigane*. MASSENET: *Thaïs: Meditation*. HEUBERGER: *Opernball: Im chambre séparée*. SARASATE: *Zigeunerweisen*. PONCE: *Estrellita*. KORNGOLD: *Garden scene*. MONTI: *Czardas*.
(M) *** Decca SPA/*KCSP* 571.

This originally had the title *Great violin*

encores, more appropriate than *Meditation*, which gives a false picture of the character of the recital. Josef Sakonov is a specialist in Hungarian fireworks and Zigeuner melodies. He plays on one of a pair of Guarnerius violins dating from 1735 (Heifetz has the other) and he certainly produces a sumptuous tone from it, helped by the forward balance of the recording (originally Phase Four). Heuberger's *Im chambre séparée* is used to show off the luscious effects possible on the lower strings of this superb instrument, while there are some dazzling fireworks in the bravura items (Sternhold's *Fêtes tzigane* a real highlight). There is taste as well as flamboyance here, and the opening melody and Tchaikovsky's *Valse* are very nicely done. With vivid sound on both disc and tape (the latter benefiting from a degree of top-cut), this is most enjoyable.

'Scandinavian Pops'

Scandinavian music (with (i) Bournemouth SO, Gerlund; (ii) Copenhagen SO, Frisholm; (iii) Stockholm PO, Bjorlin; (iv) Bournemouth Sinf., Montgomery; (v) Philh. O, Weldon): (i) HALVORSEN: *Entry of the Boyars*. BULL: *Herd girls' Sunday*. ALFVÉN: *Swedish rhapsody, Op. 19*. JÄRNEFELT: *Praeludium*. (ii) LUMBYE: *Copenhagen Steam Railway galop*. (iii) LARSSON: *Pastoral suite, Op. 19*. (iv) WIRÉN: *Serenade for strings, Op. 11*. NIELSEN: *Little suite for strings, Op. 1: Intermezzo*. (v) GRIEG: *Sigurd Jorsalfar suite, Op. 56: Homage march*.
(M) *** HMV Green. ESD/*TC-ESD* 7156.

A useful and rewarding anthology of music that often recalls an earlier gramophone era. Several of these pieces, because of their brevity, fitted conveniently on to a 78 r.p.m. disc. They are tunefully memorable and nicely scored. Järnefelt's *Praeludium* and Halvorsen's *Entry of the Boyars* are engaging examples, while Alfvén's *Swedish rhapsody* which became famous for its opening melody has a less familiar but equally attractive middle section. All are played with character and are well recorded and this disc becomes more than the sum of its parts. But what makes it indispensable is the inclusion of Lumbye's *Copenhagen Steam Railway galop*, an enchanting pictorialization of a railway train, which has a Disneyesque sense of fantasy and a deliciously light touch and which overshadows the more portentous piece of Honegger and Villa-Lobos's rather similar portrait. The performance is first-rate and the effect irresistible. With good sound throughout – sometimes a little dry but not lacking sparkle – this is highly recommendable. The cassette is not quite as sharply focused as the LP, notably in the Grieg and Lumbye items.

Scottish Baroque Ens., Friedman

'At Hopetown': TRAD. (ed. Elliott): *Airs and dances of Renaissance Scotland*. MCGIBBON: *Sonata No. 5 in G*. PURCELL: *Chaconne in G*. HANDEL: *Trio sonata in C min., Op. 2/1*. HAYDN: *12 Little divertimenti*.
** CRD CRD 1028/*CRDC 4028* [id.].

This collection offers well-established masterpieces alongside little-known Scottish music. The Purcell *Chaconne* and the Handel and Haydn pieces are given with good style and musicianship. The Renaissance dances from Scotland edited by Kenneth Elliott are a useful addition to the catalogue and are quite attractive; the sonata by William McGibbon (1690–1756), avowedly written in the style of Corelli, is not without charm. The recording is somewhat over-resonant and in the cassette form the treble needs to be tamed a little.

'Scandinavian serenade': GRIEG: *Holberg suite, Op. 40*. NIELSEN: *Little suite for string orchestra, Op. 1*. SIBELIUS: *Canzonetta, Op. 62a*. WIRÉN: *Serenade for strings, Op. 11*.
** CRD CRD 1042 /*CRDC 4042* [id.].

Good accounts of all these pieces, let down by a rather forward balance which prevents the players making the most of pianissimo markings. The quality of the cassette transfer is not particularly distinguished but is perfectly acceptable. The Sibelius *Canzonetta*, which derives from the incidental music to *Kuolema*, is beguilingly played. The first movement of the Dag Wirén *Serenade* sounds a shade untidy at times and the quality above the stave is spiky.

'Music for Drumlanrig': ALBINONI: *Adagio* (arr. Giazotto). LULLY: *Le bourgeois gentilhomme: suite.* PACHELBEL: *Canon.* BYRD: *Fantasia a 6.* BARSANTI: *Overture in D, Op. 4/2.*
**(*) CRD CRD 1043/*CRDC 4043* [id.].

Opening with a fairly free and effective version of the Albinoni *Adagio* this is a lively concert, well played and recorded. The treatment of the famous Pachelbel *Canon* is not especially imaginative, but otherwise the music-making combines a nicely judged expressive feeling with vitality. The excellent chrome cassette matches the disc closely. This is the most attractive issue by this group to date.

Scottish CO, Laredo

'String masterpieces': ALBINONI: *Adagio in G min.* (arr. Giazotto). HANDEL: *Berenice: Overture. Solomon: Arrival of the Queen of Sheba.* BACH: *Suite No. 3, BWV 1068: Air. Violin concerto No. 1 in A min., BWV 1041: Finale.* PACHELBEL: *Canon.* PURCELL: *Abdelazer: Rondo. Chacony in G min.*
(B) *** Con. Dig. CC/*CCT* 7597.

An excellent record. The playing is alive, alert, stylish and committed without being overly expressive, yet the Bach *Air* has warmth and Pachelbel's *Canon* is fresh and unconventional in approach. The sound is first-class, with little to choose between disc and cassette, the former very slightly brighter, but both well detailed without any clinical feeling. The Purcell *Rondo* is the tune made familiar by Britten's orchestral guide; the *Chaconne* is played with telling simplicity.

SNO, Gibson

'Land of the mountain and the flood': MENDELSSOHN: *The Hebrides overture (Fingal's Cave), Op. 26.* BERLIOZ: *Waverley overture, Op. 2.* ARNOLD: *Tam O'Shanter overture.* VERDI: *Macbeth: Ballet music.* MACCUNN: *Overture: Land of the Mountain and the Flood.*
**(*) Chan. Dig. ABRD/*ABTD* 1032.

The MacCunn overture, made popular by a television programme (*Sutherland's Law*), here provides an attractive foil for the Scottish National Orchestra's collection of short pieces inspired by Scotland. These performances are not as refined as the best available versions – significantly, the most dashing performance is of Arnold's difficult and rumbustious overture – but with excellent sound it makes an attractive recital. The cassette transfer is of good quality, but the comparatively unadventurous level brings a less sparkling upper range than the LP.

'Serenade for strings'

Serenades (with (i) Philh. O, Colin Davis; (ii) LSO, Barbirolli; (iii) Northern Sinfonia, Tortelier; (iv) RPO, Sargent; (v) E. Sinfonia, Dilkes; (vi) Bournemouth Sinf., Montgomery; (vii) LPO, Boult): (i) MOZART: *Serenade No. 13 in G (Eine kleine Nachtmusik), K.525.* (ii) TCHAIKOVSKY: *String serenade, Op. 48: Waltz.* (iii) GRIEG: *Holberg suite, Op. 40. Elegiac melody: Heart's wounds, Op. 34/1.* (iv) DVOŘÁK: *String serenade, Op. 22:* 1st and 2nd movts. (v) WARLOCK: *Capriol suite.* (vi) WIRÉN: *String serenade, Op. 11: March.* (vii) ELGAR: *Introduction and allegro for strings, Op. 47.*
(B) **(*) EMI *TC2-MOM 108.*

This was the finest of EMI's first release of 'Miles of Music' tapes with an attractive programme, good and sometimes distinguished performances and fairly consistent sound quality, full and clear. Tortelier's Grieg and Boult's complete version of Elgar's *Introduction and allegro* are obvious highlights, and this certainly makes an attractive background for a car journey, yet can be sampled at home too.

'Showpieces for orchestra'

(i) LPO, Boult; (ii) RPO; (iii) Sargent; (iv) Colin Davis; (v) CBSO, Frémaux; (vi) Bournemouth SO; (vii) Silvestri; (viii) Berglund: (i) BRAHMS: *Academic Festival overture.* (ii; iii) SMETANA: *Má Vlast: Vltava.* MENDELSSOHN: *The Hebrides overture.* WAGNER:

Die Meistersinger overture. (ii; iv) ROSSINI: *William Tell overture.* (v) DEBUSSY: *Prélude à l'après-midi d'un faune.* CHABRIER: *España.* BERLIOZ: *Le Carnaval romain overture.* (vi; vii) SAINT-SAËNS: *Danse macabre.* (vi; viii) GRIEG: *Peer Gynt suite No. 1: Morning; In the hall of the Mountain King.*
(B) *(*) EMI *TC2-MOM 109.*

These are all acceptable performances, but the recording, though full, is somewhat lacking in sparkle on side one. Side two is brighter, but overall this seems an arbitrary collection that does not add up to a satisfying whole.

Smithers, Don (with Instrumental Ens.)

'Courtly masquing ayres': ANON.: *Este-ce Mars (Almande).* PARSONS: *Trumpets.* BASSANO: *Oy me, Oy me dolente.* FARNABY: *A maske.* VECCHI: *Saltavan ninfe.* BRADE: *Canzon.* ADSON: *Courtly masquing ayres à 6; Courtly masquing ayres à 5.*
(M) ** Decca Ser. SA/*KSC* 16.

When originally issued by Argo, this collection was entitled 'Music of the Waits'. One tends to associate the term 'Waits' with carols, but in fact the Waits were originally medieval musicians. By the sixteenth and seventeenth centuries (from which time this music dates) they came to be the equivalent of the local village or town band. They were used, much as the brass or silver band of the industrial revolution, for adding weight and colour to local ceremonies and entertainments. However, to judge by the present record (and indeed evidence as to what combination of instruments was used is not conclusive) the sounds created by the Waits were piquant rather than sonorous. The combination here favours both wind and string colourings, the former having the most striking character. Taken in small sections the effect is fresh and convincing, but the colouristic possibilities are limited and some listeners may find that a little of this music goes a long way. The playing itself avoids too many rough edges of execution and intonation and the recording is impeccable. There is a first-class cassette transfer.

Stuttgart CO, Münchinger

CORELLI: *Concerto grosso in G min. (Christmas), Op. 6/8.* GABRIELI, G.: *Canzon per sonar primi toni.* BACH, J. S.: *Christmas oratorio: Sinfonia.* PACHELBEL: *Canon in D; Gigue.* RICCIOTTI (attrib. Pergolesi): *Concertino No. 2 in G.* GLUCK: *Chaconne.*
(M) *** Decca Ser. SA/*KSC* 20 [Lon. CS/5-6206].

An enjoyable collection. Corelli's beautiful *Christmas concerto* is especially successful and the performance will suit all but those who insist on 'original' instrumentation. If occasionally here and elsewhere there is a suggestion of the stiffness of manner that has marred some recordings from this source, it detracts little from the general appeal of the music-making. The recording is excellent, brightly lit but with an attractive ambience. The sound for Münchinger's newer (full-priced) version of the Pachelbel – see below – is even more sumptuous, but the present collection is preferable in most other respects. The cassette, however, is disappointingly rough in its upper range.

'Baroque music': PACHELBEL: *Canon in D* (arr. Münchinger). *Gigue* (arr. Seiffert). ALBINONI: *Adagio in G min.* (arr. Giazotto). BACH: *Cantata No. 147: Jesu, joy of man's desiring. Cantata No. 208: Sheep may safely graze.* HANDEL: *Solomon: Arrival of the Queen of Sheba. Organ concerto No. 4 in F, Op. 4/4* (with Bremsteller). *Overture: Berenice.*
*(*) Decca SXL/*KSXC* 6862 [Lon. CS/5-7102].

Richly beautiful recorded quality distinguishes this concert: indeed the sound is gorgeously ripe and ample. The balance is close, which does not permit much dynamic contrast in the Pachelbel *Canon*, although the *Gigue* certainly sounds gracious. If the playing possessed a compensating alertness and vitality, the romantic overtones of such a sound balance would have been minimized; but as it is, the Handel pieces are lethargic (although the *Organ concerto*, with Ulrich Bremsteller, is nicely registered), and the Albinoni *Adagio* sounds unbelievably soupy.

Stern, Isaac (violin)

'Sixtieth anniversary celebration' (with Perlman, Zukerman, NYPO, Mehta): BACH: *Double violin concerto in D min., BWV 1043.* MOZART: *Sinfonia concertante in E flat, K.364.* VIVALDI: *Triple violin concerto in F, RV.551.*
(*) CBS Dig. **CD; 36692/*41*- [Col. IM 36692/*MT 37244*].

At a time when the pursuit of authenticity has accustomed us to pinched sound in Bach and Vivaldi it is good to have such rich performances as these, recorded live at Stern's sixtieth-birthday concert in the autumn of 1980. Stern nobly cedes first place to Perlman in the Bach *Double concerto*, and in the Vivaldi he plays third violin, though there he has the bonus of playing the melody in the lovely slow movement. With Zukerman on the viola this account of the *Sinfonia concertante* is strikingly more alive than the studio recording made ten years earlier by the same artists, heartfelt and beautifully sprung. The recording is a little thin, but digitally clear. Mehta and the New York orchestra are not ideal in this music, but the flavour of the live occasion is most compelling. The chrome cassette is extremely lively, matching the disc with its close balance and larger-than-life solo images, although it does not lack fullness.

Suisse Romande O, Ansermet

DUKAS: *L'Apprenti sorcier.* BIZET: *Jeux d'enfants.* CHABRIER: *Fête polonaise.* HONEGGER: *Pacific 231.* DEBUSSY: *Prélude à l'après-midi d'un faune.* RAVEL: *Rapsodie espagnole.*
(M) *** Decca VIV/*KVIC* 34.

During the mono LP and early stereo era Ansermet was one of Decca's big stars. He worked admirably in the recording studio and his care for detail never interfered with his ability to bring almost all the music he recorded fully to life; moreover his symbiosis with the Decca recording staff produced a long series of recordings of the highest technical quality where the balance and ambient bloom combined to project the music vividly with both 'wood' and 'trees' in equal perspective. The playing of the Suisse Romande Orchestra, especially in later years, lacked a good deal in glamour and polish, but Ansermet's strong personality usually gave ample compensation. The present collection is generous and typical; it shows the strengths and the weaknesses and Ansermet's sure sense of style in French music especially where the spirit of the dance is present. The sound remains equally impressive on disc and tape.

Thames CO, Dobson

'The baroque concerto in England' (with Black, Bennett): ANON. (probably HANDEL): *Concerto grosso in F.* BOYCE: *Concerti grossi: in E min. for strings; in B min. for 2 solo violins, cello and strings.* WOODCOCK: *Oboe concerto in E flat; Flute concerto in D.*
*** CRD CRD 1031/*CRDC 4031.*

A wholly desirable collection, beautifully played and recorded. Indeed the recording, on both disc and tape, has splendid life and presence and often offers demonstration quality – try the opening of the Woodcock *Flute concerto*, for instance. The music is all highly rewarding. The opening concerto was included in Walsh's first edition of Handel's Op. 3 (as No. 4) but was subsequently replaced by another work. Whether or not it is by Handel, it is an uncommonly good piece, and it is given a superbly alert and sympathetic performance here. Neil Black and William Bennett are soloists of the highest calibre, and it is sufficient to say that they are on top form throughout this most enjoyable concert.

Thompson, Robert (bassoon)

'The twentieth-century bassoon' (with ECO, Simon): DOWNEY: *The Edge of Space* (fantasy). JACOB: *Bassoon concerto.* ANDRIESSEN: *Concertino for bassoon and wind.*
*** Chan. Dig. ABRD/*ABTD* 1033.

Although these are all modern works the idiom is not in the least intimidating. John

Downey's fantasy *The Edge of Space* intends to suggest 'remote distance and otherworldliness', but although there are certainly some unusual sounds here, there is nothing especially avant-garde. Indeed, with its episodic nature it sounds rather like a film score without a film. It has imaginative moments and the invention is quite attractive. Gordon Jacob's neoclassical *Concerto* dates from 1947 and is pleasant enough; the Andriessen *Concertino* is a little more adventurous. Excellent performances and a bold, forwardly balanced digital recording, with a vivid cassette to match.

Tortelier, Paul (cello)

'The art of Paul Tortelier': ELGAR: *Cello concerto in E min., Op. 85* (with LPO, Boult). BRAHMS: *Double concerto in A min., Op. 102* (with Ferras, Philh. O, Kletzki). DVOŘÁK: *Cello concerto, Op. 104* (with LSO, Previn). TCHAIKOVSKY: *Variations on a rococo theme, Op. 33* (with Northern Sinf., Yan Pascal Tortelier). BACH: *Cello suite No. 3 in C, BWV 1009.* and music by: PAGANINI; SAINT-SAËNS; RIMSKY-KORSAKOV; FAURÉ; TORTELIER.
(M) *** HMV SLS/*TC-SLS* 270001-3/5 (3).

Admirers of the great cellist will find little to disappoint them in this admirable anthology which assembles some of his finest concertante performances. The only inclusion that might be counted at all controversial is the Brahms *Double concerto*, and that not for any limitations in Tortelier's own contribution, but because his timbre does not naturally match that of his fellow-soloist, Christian Ferras. Some of the shorter items feature Tortelier as both composer and a family man, joined by his wife and daughter, while his son directs the Tchaikovsky *Rococo variations*. Excellent recording throughout. The cassettes, however, are disappointing, with orchestral tuttis less well focused than on disc and the upper partials of the sound not always absolutely clean.

'Trumpet voluntary'

(i) Philip Jones Brass Ens.; (ii) ASMF, Marriner, etc.: (i) CLARKE: *Trumpet voluntary.* (ii) BOYCE: *Symphony No. 5 in D.* (i; ii) GABRIELI, G.: *Canzon primi toni No. 1.* (ii) HANDEL: *Water music: Prelude; Hornpipe.* (i) SCHEIDT: *Battle suite Galliard battaglia.* PURCELL: *Trumpet tune and air.* (ii) *Trumpet concerto in E flat* (with Stringer). STANLEY: *Trumpet tune in D* (with Wilbraham; Pearson, organ). (i) BACH, C. P. E.: *March.*
(M) *** Decca SPA/*KCSP* 556.

A really outstanding collection for those who enjoy occasional pieces on the trumpet. Almost every item is a winner, and Alan Stringer's complete version of the Haydn *Trumpet concerto* is excellent. The florid playing by members of the Philip Jones Brass Ensemble in the pieces by Giovanni Gabrieli and Samuel Scheidt is superb, and there is a contrasting elegance in Purcell's *Trumpet tune and air.* Excellent recording throughout and a vivid cassette to match the disc closely.

VPO, Boskovsky

'Overtures of old Vienna': STRAUSS, J. Jnr: *Die Fledermaus. Prinz Methusalem.* NICOLAI: *The Merry Wives of Windsor.* REZNIČEK: *Donna Diana.* HEUBERGER: *Der Opernball* (Opera Ball).
(M) *** Decca Jub. JB 47.

Vivid performances given a spectacular recording. The balance is sometimes a little larger than life, but in music for sheer entertainment like this the extra projection is effective enough. The authentic Viennese lilt gives special charm to the *Opera Ball overture*; and Johann Strauss's *Prinz Methusalem*, with its well-managed off-stage band effect in the middle, is a vivacious novelty. The exhilarating forward impulse of *Donna Diana* is nicely judged.

VPO, Maazel

'New Year's concert' (1980): STRAUSS, Johann, Jnr: *Die Fledermaus: overture; Czárdás. Neue Pizzicato polka. Perpetuum mobile. Wiener Blut. Banditen Galop. Rettungs-Jubel march. Fata Morgana polka. An der schönen*

blauen Donau. STRAUSS, Josef: *Eingesendet polka*. OFFENBACH: *Orpheus in the Underworld: overture*. ZIEHRER: *Loslassen*. STRAUSS, Johann, Snr: *Radetzky march*.
** DG Dig. 2532/*3302* 002 [id.].

This record of the 1980 Viennese New Year Concert is generously full, with applause faded quickly between items. The famous *Radetzky march* sets the pattern for the concert: the performance is crisply brilliant, with well-disciplined hand-claps from the audience. Maazel is at his best in the *Rettungs-Jubel march*, written for the Kaiser, which is infectiously volatile. The performance of *The Blue Danube* departs from the sharply rhythmic manner and is unashamedly indulgent. But charm is not a strong point here, and the brightly lit recording underlines the vigour of the playing. The sound has striking presence and detail, on both disc and the equivalent chrome tape.

Vienna Volksoper O, Bauer-Theussl

'Famous waltzes': WEBER: *Invitation to the dance, Op. 65* (arr. Berlioz). LANNER: *Die Schönbrunner*. IVANOVICI: *Donauwellen* (*Waves of the Danube*). KOMZAK: *Bad'ner Mad'ln*. STRAUSS, Josef: *Dynamiden*. ZIEHRER: *Herreinspaziert* (arr. Schönnherr).
**(*) Ph. Dig. 6514/*7337* 067 [id.].

The first of two collections, this record admirably gathers together some waltzes from contemporaries of the Johann Strauss family. Each has a striking main theme and the performances, if sometimes lacking the last degree of vitality, have an agreeable warmth. Franz Bauer-Theussl's rubato is not always subtle but is often effective in its way. He is good with the atmospheric openings, indeed he shapes the main theme of Ivanovici's *Donauwellen* (*Danube waves*) very persuasively. *Invitation to the dance* lacks the last degree of characterization although, like the rest of the programme, it is well played. The resonant acoustic is effective and the digital recording ensures good detail, although the chrome tape is a little lacking in sparkle.

'Famous waltzes', Vol. 2: ZIEHRER: *Faschingskinder; Wiener Burger*. LEHÁR: *Gold and silver; Ballsirenen*. ROSAS: *Uber den Wellen*. LANNER: *Hofballtänze; Die Romantiker*.
**(*) Ph. Dig. 6514/*7337* 068 [id.].

There is some worthwhile repertoire in Volume 2 and Franz Bauer-Theussl and his excellent Vienna Volksoper Orchestra are warmly sympathetic. The rhythmic emphasis is perhaps a little stylized, but there is an engaging geniality of spirit and the phrasing of the lyrical melodies (and there are some memorable ones) is both polished and nicely timed. The recording is within an attractively resonant acoustic and the excellent digital recording provides good detail. Both records should bring a ready response from listeners familiar with the music of the Strauss family wanting to do a little exploring in the Viennese hinterland. Ziehrer and Lanner were accomplished tune-masters and the Lehár waltzes are first-rate. The chrome tapes have only marginally less upper range and, like the discs, offer quality of considerable richness and lustre.

VSO, Boskovsky

'Symphonic waltzes': STRAUSS, R.: *Der Rosenkavalier: 1st and 2nd Waltz sequences*. GOUNOD: *Faust: Waltz*. WEBER (arr. Berlioz): *Invitation to the dance*. TCHAIKOVSKY: *Sleeping Beauty: Waltz; The Nutcracker: Waltz of the flowers*.
(M) **(*) HMV Dig. ESD/*TC-ESD* 143172-1/*4*.

In his famous 1960s recordings of the music of the Strauss family with the VPO for Decca, Willi Boskovsky gave the impression that he was leading the orchestra (rather like the composer, with a violin bow rather than a baton). Here his approach, though less endearing perhaps, is more positive and strong, and these are strongly contoured performances, rhythmically firm. They have plenty of personality and are very well played. The inquiry and response at the opening of the Weber is attractively galant and all the music-making is spirited. The bright digital recording suits the style of the music-making and there is a very good cassette.

'Violin favourites'

(i) Hoelscher, Mun. RO, Wallberg; (ii) Menuhin, Philh. O; (iii) Pritchard; (iv) Goossens; (v) Haendel, Parsons; (vi) Ferras, Barbizet: (i) SARASATE: *Carmen fantasy. Zigeunerweisen.* (ii; iii) BEETHOVEN: *Romances Nos. 1 and 2.* (ii; iv) SAINT-SAËNS: *Introduction and rondo capriccioso. Havanaise.* (v) MENDELSSOHN: *On Wings of Song.* SARASATE: *Habañera.* SCHUBERT: *Ave Maria.* (vi) RAVEL: *Tzigane.*
(B) **(*) EMI *TC2-MOM 118.*

A reasonably attractive collection, not as enticing as some in this 'Miles of Music' series, but well recorded throughout. The highlights are Menuhin's superb Saint-Saëns performances (described in the composer index, above) and the more lushly recorded Sarasate, played with panache by Ulf Hoelscher. Ida Haendel is in excellent form in her transcriptions, and Ferras gives an impressive account of Ravel's *Tzigane* (in the version for violin and piano).

Waltzes

'Famous Waltzes' (played by: (i) VPO, Boskovsky; (ii) Nat. PO, Bonynge; (iii) ASMF, Marriner; (iv) Nat. PO, Gamley; (v) Paris Conservatoire O, Maag; (vi) LSO, Bonynge; (vii) VPO, Maazel): (i) STRAUSS, J. Jnr: *An der schönen blauen Donau; Accelerationen; Wein, Weib und Gesang.* LEHÁR: *Gold and silver.* (ii) TCHAIKOVSKY: *Sleeping Beauty: Waltz. Nutcracker: Waltz of the flowers. Swan Lake: Waltz.* (iii) *String serenade: Waltz.* (iv) WALDTEUFEL: *The Skaters; España.* (v) CHOPIN: *Les Sylphides: Grande valse brillante.* (vi) OFFENBACH: *Le Papillon: Valse des rayons.* (vii) STRAUSS, R.: *Der Rosenkavalier: 1st Waltz sequence.*
(B) ** Decca *410 292-4.*

An attractive double-length tape compilation, with generally distinguished performances, notably those from Boskovsky (*Gold and silver* as attractive as the Johann Strauss items), Marriner and Gamley. The very high level of the transfer, however, robs the sound of complete refinement at times, with the resonance sometimes clouding the bass at fortissimo levels. However, this sounds well enough on a smaller player or in the car.

Wickens, Derek (oboe)

'The classical oboe' (with RPO, Howarth): VIVALDI: *Oboe concerto in A min., RV.461.* MARCELLO, A.: *Oboe concerto in D min.* HAYDN: *Oboe concerto in C.*
*** ASV ACA/*ZCACA* 1003.

The Haydn concerto may be spurious, but it makes an attractive item in this collection, and the Vivaldi, a lively, compact piece, and the Marcello (by Alessandro, not his more famous brother Benedetto) with its lovely slow movement make up a good mixture. During his years with the RPO, Wickens repeatedly demonstrated in yearningly beautiful solos that he was one of the most characterful of London's orchestral players. Though at times he seems to be looking for his back desk rather than his solo spot, his artistry comes out vividly on this well-recorded disc. The tape is outstandingly vivid to match the disc.

Wilbraham, John (trumpet), ASMF, Marriner

'Trumpet concertos': FASCH: *Concerto in D.* HERTEL: *Concerto a cinque.* MOZART, L.: *Concerto in D.* ALBRECHTSBERGER: *Concerto a cinque.* HUMMEL: *Concerto in E flat.*
(M) *** Decca Ser. 410 134-1/*4*.

The highlight is John Wilbraham's outstanding account of the Hummel, but there are other attractive works here too. The Hertel is in the nature of a sinfonia concertante and is scored for trumpet, two oboes and two bassoons; while in the Fasch, Wilbraham is also joined by a pair of oboes. Albrechtsberger taught Beethoven his counterpoint and his *Concerto a cinque* features a harpsichord. As might be expected, all the solo contributions are expert, and with excellent sound this is a rewarding disc, if not taken all at once. The cassette is disappointing, with the trumpet sound never completely comfortable, though the Hummel *Concerto* (on side two) sounds more open than the works on side one.

Instrumental Recitals

Adeney, Richard (flute),
Ian Brown (piano)

'Classical flute': MOZART: *Flute sonata in F, K.13.* SCHUBERT: *Introduction and variations on an original theme, Op. 160.* BEETHOVEN: *Flute sonata in B flat; National themes and variations, Op. 107, Nos. 3 and 7.*
**(*) ASV ACM/*ZCACM* 2024.

An attractive programme, immaculately played. There is undoubtedly spontaneity here, but the players do not always exploit the full possibilities of light and shade, and they are not helped by the close balance, which minimizes the dynamics as well as giving a larger-than-life effect. However, the recording quality itself is admirably truthful, and has a demonstration faithfulness of body and presence. The high-level cassette transfer is first-class in every way, with striking projection and transparency.

(i) **Adni, Daniel;** (ii) **John Ogdon** (piano)

'Piano favourites': (i) CHOPIN: *Revolutionary study in C min. Fantaisie-Impromptu.* (ii) *Waltz No. 6 in D flat (Minute). Polonaises Nos. 3 (Military); 6 (Heroic).* RACHMANINOV: *Prelude in C sharp min.* (i) GRAINGER: *Country Gardens; Handel in the Strand.* DEBUSSY: *Clair de lune.* BRAHMS: *Rhapsody in G min.* (ii) SINDING: *Rustle of Spring.* LISZT: *Liebestraum No. 3. La Campanella.* BEETHOVEN: *Für Elise.* CHAMINADE: *Autumn.* (i) MENDELSSOHN: *The Bees' Wedding.* SCHUBERT: *Impromptu in A flat. Moment musical in F min.* GRIEG: *To the Spring. Wedding Day at Troldhaugen.*
(B) *(**) EMI *TC2-MOM 101.*

In transferring this collection to tape the EMI engineers have made electronic adjustments to produce a high level, and the sound is dry and lacking warmth. The performances are often distinguished; Daniel Adni is heard at his best in the music of Grainger, Schubert and Grieg, and Ogdon is impressive in Liszt. In the car the sound projects clearly.

'More piano favourites': (ii) BACH: *Well-tempered Clavier: Prelude No. 5. Jesu, joy of man's desiring.* MOZART: *Fantasia in D min., K.397.* BEETHOVEN: *Andante favori.* CHOPIN: *Mazurka No. 17 in B flat min.* (i) *Scherzo No. 3 in C sharp min., Op. 39. Waltz No. 1 in E flat, Op. 18. Ballade No. 3 in A flat, Op. 47.* (ii) SCHUMANN: *Nachtstück in F, Op. 23/4.* (i) DEBUSSY: *L'Isle joyeuse. Reflets dans l'eau.* (ii) SCOTT: *Lotus Land.* LISZT: *Hungarian rhapsody No. 15.* GRANADOS: *Goyescas: The Maiden and the nightingale.* ALBÉNIZ: *Tango.* (i) GRIEG: *Lyric pieces: Album leaf; Butterfly; Shepherd's boy.*
(B) *** EMI *TC2-MOM 113.*

With first-class sound this is an outstanding recital, easily the finest collection from these two artists in this format, with recordings taken from the beginnings of their respective careers. Both Adni and Ogdon are heard at their best, the former especially in the music of Chopin and Debussy, the latter communicating strongly in Bach and Mozart and playing Liszt with great flair.

'Piano moods': (i) CHOPIN: *Scherzo No. 2, Op. 32. Waltzes in A flat and A min., Op. 34/1 and 2. Études: in A flat and G flat, Op. 25/1 and 9; in G flat, Op. 10/5.* (ii) *Mazurkas Nos. 5 in B flat, Op. 7/1; 23 in D, Op. 33/2.* LISZT: *Paganini study No. 2. Étude de concert No. 3. Valse oubliée No. 1. Mephisto waltz No. 1.* (i) GRIEG: *March of the Dwarfs.* SCHUMANN: *Arabesque, Op. 18.* DEBUSSY: *Poissons d'or. Arabesque No. 1.* MENDELSSOHN: *Songs without Words: Venetian gondola song, Op. 62/5; Spring song.* RAVEL: *Alborada del gracioso.*
(B) ** EMI *TC2-MOM 122.*

There is some impressive playing again here, John Ogdon on top form in Liszt, and Daniel Adni poetic and commanding in Chopin and Debussy. But the high-level recording is dry and some of the bloom of the originals is lost.

Argerich, Martha (piano)

'In concert': CHOPIN: *Polonaise-Fantaisie in A flat, Op. 61; Polonaise No. 6 in A flat, Op. 63; 3 Mazurkas, Op. 59; Barcarolle, Op. 60; Scherzo No. 3, Op. 39.* BRAHMS: *2 Rhapsodies, Op. 79.* LISZT: *Hungarian rhapsody No. 6 in D flat, G. 244.* RAVEL: *Jeux d'eau.* PROKOFIEV: *Toccata in C, Op. 11.* SCHUMANN: *Piano sonata No. 2 in G min., Op. 22.*
(M) *** DG Acc. 2725/*3374* 108 (2).

Incandescent, fiery, full of temperament and poetic feeling, these Argerich performances give a fairly comprehensive picture of this remarkable artist. At times she is impetuous, as in the Schumann *Sonata*, but there is such extraordinary variety of colour and character here: she might even be playing completely different instruments in the Ravel and the Brahms. Very good recorded sound indeed. The cassette transfer is also first-class, the sound bold and clear if sometimes slightly dry.

Arrau, Claudio (piano)

'An 80th birthday tribute' (recordings from 1929–1960): SCHUMANN: *Carnaval, Op. 9.* DEBUSSY: *Tarantelle styrienne; Estampes; Jardins sous la pluie; Préludes.* Book 2: *La puerta del vino.* GRANADOS: *Goyescas: The Maiden and the nightingale.* LISZT: *Années de pèlerinage, 3rd year: Les jeux d'eau à la Villa d'Este, G. 163.* CHOPIN: *Tarantella in A flat, Op. 43; 3 Nouvelles études; Études Op. 25/9–12.* BEETHOVEN: *Piano sonatas Nos. 24 in F sharp, Op. 78; 31 in A flat, Op. 100.* WEBER: *Konzertstuck, Op. 79* (with Philh. O, Galliera). SCHUBERT: *Moments musicaux, D.780/1–3. Impromptus Nos. 9 and 11, D.946/1 and 3.* MENDELSSOHN: *Andante and Rondo capriccioso, Op. 14.*
(M) (***) HMV RLS/*TC-RLS* 7712 (3).

Some classic Arrau performances in excellent transfers. The Op. 110 *Sonata* is particularly memorable and in many ways more poetic than his later version for Philips. In some respects the earliest recordings (Granados, Schumann, etc.) are the most interesting and show the great Chilean pianist at his most aristocratic. His phrasing and rubati became more and more idiosyncratic over the years and are not to all tastes. In any event this is an indispensable set for all admirers of this artist; mention should also be made of a CBS compilation of four records (CBS 79354) published in Holland for sale in the US which includes a 1946 *Kreisleriana* of great poise and finesse, some remarkably atmospheric and compelling Debussy (*Pour le piano* and *Estampes*) as well as a dazzling version of the Liszt *E flat Concerto* with Ormandy and the Philadelphia Orchestra dating from 1952. Needless to say the sound quality is variable but is never less than acceptable. The cassette transfers are excellent, although in *Carnaval* there were some 'holes' in the texture on our copy. The Weber *Konzertstuck* approaches demonstration standard.

Ashkenazy, Vladimir (piano)

CHOPIN: *Nocturne in B, Op. 62/1; Scherzo No. 4 in E, Op. 54.* DEBUSSY: *L'Isle joyeuse.* RAVEL: *Gaspard de la nuit* (*Ondine; Le gibet; Scarbo*).
*** Decca SXL 6215.

Ashkenazy's records are virtually self-recommending. This recital is no exception. The Chopin *Scherzo* is played with impeccable technique and taste, and the *Nocturne*, too, is given with the aristocratic distinction one associates with him. The most memorable performance, however, is of Ravel's *Gaspard de la nuit* which seems to us the finest account of the piece since Gieseking's 78s. Marvellous playing this, and the Decca engineers have risen to the occasion with a recording of wide range and truthful timbre.

Bate, Jennifer (organ)

'An English choice' (organ of St Andrew's,

Plymouth): WHITLOCK: *Plymouth suite.* VAUGHAN WILLIAMS: *Prelude No. 2 on a Welsh hymn-tune: Rhosymedre.* GRACE: *Psalm-tune Postlude No. 1: Martyrs.* WALFORD DAVIES: *Solemn melody.* ELGAR: *Imperial march, Op. 32.* HARRIS: *A Fancy; Short piece No. 2, Reverie.* COCKER: *Tuba tune.*
**(*) Hyp. Dig. A 66033.

Cocker's *Tuba tune* is one of the most brightly colourful of today's organ favourites, and it enlivens this collection of English organ music, which includes both popular items like the Walford Davies, the Vaughan Williams and the Elgar arrangement as well as undemanding rarities like the *Plymouth suite* with each movement dedicated to a local notable. The Plymouth organ as recorded lacks brightness.

'Showpieces for organ' (Royal Albert Hall organ): BACH: *Toccata and fugue in D min., BWV 565.* THALBEN-BALL: *Variations on a theme of Paganini.* MELVILLE SMITH: *Scherzo.* BATE: *Toccata on a theme of Martin Shaw.* WIDOR: *Symphony No. 5 in F min.: Toccata.* VIERNE: *Naïades.* DUCASSE: *Pastorale.* LANGLAIS: *Fête.*
*** Uni. Dig. DKP 9007.

Splendid digital sound, clear and spacious and with striking depth. If anything Jennifer Bate overdoes the contrasts of volume and perspective possible with the recessional effect of this instrument. The programme, although it includes several warhorses, is imaginative, and the French repertoire (the Widor *Toccata* sounding lighter than usual but no less telling) is surprisingly well suited to this essentially Victorian instrument. The Thalben-Ball *Paganini variations* (apart from the finale) are for pedals only, and a *tour de force* in Miss Bate's impressive account.

Bennett, Richard Rodney (piano)

'Little jazz bird': KERN: *Nobody else but me; Up with the lark; The folks who live on the hill.* GERSHWIN: *Little Jazz Bird; Bess, oh where's my Bess.* ARLEN: *A sleepin' bee; I had myself a true love.* RODGERS: *My romance; Nobody's heart; I didn't know what time it was; Wait till you see her.* PORTER: *Miss Otis regrets. What is this thing; After you.*
** EMI EMD 107701-1/*4*.

An agreeable enough collection, very well recorded (on both disc and tape). But the playing evokes the cocktail lounge. Richard Rodney Bennett is clearly in tune with this repertoire, but although his manner is sympathetic and elegant it is also rather deliberate and has no incandescent qualities to make one forget that these memorable tunes also have lyrics.

Bonell, Carlos (guitar)

'Guitar music of Spain': RODRIGO: *Pequenas Sevillanas. Ya se van los pastores. Fandango.* TÓRROBA: *Burgalesa.* SANZ: *Espanoleta. Canarios.* SOR: *Fantasiá elegiaca.* PUJOL: *Guajira (Evocación Cubana). Tango.* TARREGA: *Sueno* (mazurka). *Maria* (gavotte). *Capricho Arabe. Gran Jota.* TRAD. (arr. BONELL): *4 Spanish folksongs.*
(M) ** ASV ACM/*ZCACM* 2003 [None. 71390].

Carlos Bonell is a bold player and he characterizes this music strongly. This is emphasized by the close microphone placing, which tends to reduce the light and shade. Yet the sound is naturally balanced and much of this Spanish programme is imaginatively played. One can hear that the soloist is seeking dynamic contrast in spite of the close microphones. The effect is undoubtedly vivid, on disc and tape alike.

'Guitar showpieces': CHAPI: *Serenata Morisca.* ALBÉNIZ: *Asturias (Leyenda).* PAGANINI: *Grand sonata: Romance and variations.* VILLA-LOBOS: *Study No. 11; Preludes Nos. 1 and 2.* VALVERDE: *Clavelitos.* LLOBET: *Scherzo valse.* TARREGA: *Variations and fantasia on themes from 'La Traviata'.* CHOPIN: *Prelude, Op. 28/7.* WEISS: *Ciacona in A.*
**(*) Decca SXL/*KSXC* 6950 [Lon. CS 7178].

Carlos Bonell has made an outstanding

digital recording of Rodrigo's *Concierto de Aranjuez* for Decca. Previously he did two solo recitals for Enigma, one of which is now available on ASV. But his firm articulation and very positive style register in this Decca recital with more spontaneity and atmosphere than the earlier solo records. He is especially good in the Tarrega *Variations*, and he plays the Chopin *'Les Sylphides' Prelude* very evocatively. At times his rhythms seem too precise, but his personality is strongly projected here and his expertise is in no doubt. The recording is equally impressive on disc and tape.

Boyd, Liona (guitar)

'Portrait': TRAD.: *Spanish romance; El noy de la mare; Greensleeves; Kemp's jig.* TARREGA: *Adelita; The music box; Lagrima; Pavanna; Andante; Lento; Study in E.* CARASSI: *Andantino.* SOR: *Andante and Study No. 2.* GALILEI: *Saltarello.* LOGY, Comte de: *Little suite.* RONCALLI: *Gavotte.* MILAN: *Pavana.* VISÉE: *Prelude and Gigue.* AGUADO: *Study No. 7.*
*** CBS 73686/*40*- [M/*MT* 36675].

Liona Boyd is a guitarist with a strong personality who undoubtedly has the gift of bringing her programme alive in the recording studio. She is truthfully recorded, but balanced very forwardly in the CBS manner, and that robs her of dynamic contrast, although she achieves a fair amount of light and shade in spite of this. This essentially lightweight collection is made up in the main of miniatures which she projects with undoubted charm. The recital makes very pleasing listening for the late evening and there is no doubt about Miss Boyd's prodigious technique, although she does not wear her bravura on the sleeve.

Bradbury, Colin (clarinet), **Oliver Davies** (piano)

'The drawing room clarinettist': WEBER: *Variations, Op. 33.* PIXIS: *Variations über des beliebte Abschiedslied von Ignaz Ritter van Seyfried, Op. 19.* ROSSINI: *Fantasia.* SPOHR: *Fantasia and variations on a theme of Danzi, Op. 61.* REISSIGER: *Duo brillant, Op. 130.* DONIZETTI: *Study No. 1 for solo clarinet.*
(M) *** ASV ACM/*ZCACM* 2011.

A highly engaging collection of display pieces. All this music is slight but equally it is all genuinely inventive, even if the Pixis *Variations* are somewhat naïve. The Weber and Rossini works are well worth having and the unaccompanied Donizetti *Study* is also attractive. Colin Bradbury plays throughout with great flair and he communicates his enjoyment. The warmly resonant recording makes his tone sound positively scrumptious and the balance is very effective. The cassette too is first-class.

'The Victorian clarinettist': LAZARUS: *Fantasia on airs from Bellini's I Puritani.* STANFORD: *3 Intermezzi, Op. 13.* WATERSON: *Morceau de concert.* KALLIWODA: *Morceau de salon, Op. 229.* LOVREGLIO: *Fantasia on Verdi's La Traviata, Op. 45.* OBERTHUR: *Le désir, Op. 65.*
(M) ** ASV ACM/*ZCACM* 2040.

This repertoire is intended to titillate the ear by its ingenuous bravura, and the sets of variations have much in common with the cornet solo of the bandstand, although the level of invention is generally higher. It is all expertly played here, but the music itself will not be to all tastes, even if Colin Bradbury's advocacy is very persuasive. The recording is excellent and the cassette too is first-class. Both give plenty of bloom to the clarinet and are well balanced.

'The Italian clarinettist': CAVALLINI: *Andante and variations on a theme of Mercadante: Una lagrima sulla tomba dell'immortale Rossini; La Calma.* PANIZZA: *Ballabile con variazioni, nel ballo Ettore Fieramosca, for piccolo clarinet in E flat.* ROSSINI: *Cujus animam.* SPADINA: *Omaggio alla memoria di Giuditta Pasta: Duetto concertante sopra motivi dell' opera Norma.* PONCHIELLI: *Il Convegno: Divertimento per due clarinetti* (with Donald Watson).
** ASV ALH/*ZCALH* 942.

All this music is florid and excites great bravura (and not only from the clarinet). But much of it is exceedingly trivial, though played here with great expertise and flair. The recording is well balanced and sounds equally well on disc or tape.

Brain, Dennis (horn)

(See also under Concerts)

'His last broadcasts' (introduced by Wilfred Parry, with Roy Plomley, Norman Del Mar, Gareth Morris, Felix Aprahamian) including: MARAIS: *Le Basque*. MALIPIERO: *Dialogue No. 4*. BEETHOVEN: *Piano and wind quintet in E flat, Op. 16* (with D. Brain Wind Ens.). DUKAS: *Villanelle* (with Parry, piano).
(***) BBC mono REGL/*ZCF* 352 [Ara. 8071/*9071*].

Opening with a winning account of Marais's *Le Basque* (a piece James Galway has since taken over), this is an engaging portrait of Dennis Brain the man (his gentle, ingenuous charm coming over splendidly) as well as the musician: Boyd Neel was said to have described him as the finest Mozartian of his generation on *any* instrument. There is no Mozart here, but his famous set of the *Horn concertos* is still available (HMV ASD/*TC-ASD* 1140). The musical items here offer quite good mono sound, though the Beethoven *Piano and wind quintet* lacks something in range and detail. The playing is superb and the background narrative well put together, including the priceless anecdote of Karajan rehearsing Mozart and finding only a motoring magazine on Dennis's music-stand.

Bream, Julian (lute)

'Lute music from the royal courts of Europe': LANDGRAVE OF HESSE: *Pavane*. MOLINARO: *Saltarello. Ballo detto 'Il Conte Orlando'. Saltarello. Fantasie*. PHILIPS: *Chromatic pavan and galliard*. DOWLAND: *Fantasia* (Fancye). *Queen Elizabeth's galliard*. HOWETT: *Fantasia*. MUDARRA: *Fantasia*. DLUGORAJ: *Fantasia. Villanellas 1 and 2. Finales 1 and 2*. FERRABOSCO: *Pavan*. NEUSIDLER: *Mein Herz hat sich mit Lieb' verpflicht. Hie' folget ein welscher Tanz. Ich klag'den Tag. Der Juden Tanz*. BAKFARK: *Fantasia*. BESARD: *Air de Cour. Branle. Guillemette. Volte*.
(M) **(*) RCA Gold GL/*GK* 42952.

The lute has much in common with the guitar, but its slightly nasal tang gives its music-making a special colour. Julian Bream achieves miracles here in creating diversity of timbre and dynamic, to say nothing of rhythmic impulse. The quality of the music he plays for us is generally high, and his projection of musical personality strong. Having said this, one must again add that a whole LP of lute music has its limitations: a few songs would greatly enhance a concert of this kind. The recording is impeccable; the cassette transfer, made at a high level, has plenty of presence and realism, but may benefit from a slight treble reduction.

'Golden age of English lute music': JOHNSON, R.: *Two almaines. Carman's whistle*. JOHNSON, J.: *Fantasia*. CUTTING: *Walsingham. Almaine. Greensleeves*. DOWLAND: *Mignarda. Galliard. Batell galliard*. ROSSETER: *Galliard*. MORLEY: *Pavan*. BULMAN: *Pavan*. BATCHELOR: *Mounsiers Almaine*. HOLBORNE: *Pavan. Galliard*.
(M) **(*) RCA RL/*RK* 43514 [LSC 3196].

Bream is a marvellously sensitive artist and he conjures here a wide range of colour, matched by expressive feeling. He is naturally recorded (the excellent cassette matches the disc closely), and if this selection has slightly less electricity than its outstanding companion, *The woods so wild* (see below), its relaxed manner is still persuasive.

'The woods so wild': BYRD: *The woods so wild*. MILANO: *Fantasias Nos. 1–8*. CUTTING: *Packington's round*. DOWLAND: *Walsingham. Go from my window. Bonnie sweet Robin. Loth to depart*. HOLBORNE: *Fairy round. Heigh ho holiday. Heart's ease*. ANON.: *Greensleeves*.
(M) *** RCA RL/*RK* 43519 [LSC 3331/*RK 1309*].

This is an exceptionally vivid recital of lute

music. The title-piece, in Byrd's setting with variations, is immediately striking, and all the items have strong individuality; the Milano *Fantasias* are particularly distinctive, both in quality of invention and in the opportunity they afford for bravura. Try *La Compagna* (No. 4), which ends side one – most fetching and exciting. The mood of gentle melancholy which is a special feature of Elizabethan music makes effective contrasts to the virtuosity, and nowhere more touchingly than in the delightful closing piece, *Loth to depart*, appropriate for such a memorable concert. The recording projects the instrument with fine realism, and the sound on tape is of demonstration quality in this latest transfer.

Bream, Julian (guitar)

'Dedication': BENNETT: *5 Impromptus.* WALTON: *5 Bagatelles.* MAXWELL DAVIES: *Hill runes.* HENZE: *Royal winter music.*
*** RCA RL/*RK* 25419.

Julian Bream here records four (of many) works of which he is dedicatee. For most listeners the engaging Walton *Bagatelles* will prove the most rewarding music, although Henze's atonal suite of miniature portrayals of Shakespearian characters is texturally highly imaginative. Maxwell Davies' *Hill runes* are certainly atmospheric and the Bennett *Impromptus* ingenious in construction. The recording is excellent and the tape transfer live and clean.

'Baroque guitar': SANZ: *Pavanas. Canarios.* BACH: *Prelude in D min. Fugue in A min.* SOR: *Fantasy and Minuet.* WEISS: *Passacaille. Fantasie. Tombeau sur la mort de M. Comte De Logy.* VISÉE: *Suite in D min.*
(M) *** RCA RL/*RK* 43520 [LSC 2878].

Bream is on his finest form here. He makes a very clear distinction between the world of Bach (well detailed and slightly sober) and the other music, which depends more on colour to make its effect. The pieces by Sanz are strong in personality, and the *Suite* by Robert de Visée, a French court lutenist who lived from about 1650 until 1725, has the most attractive invention. Sylvius Weiss, who played for the Dresden court in the mid-eighteenth century, also emerges with an individual voice, and his eloquent *Tombeau*, which ends the recital, inspires playing of elegiac nobility. The sound is excellent; disc and tape are equally impressive.

'Popular classics for the Spanish guitar': VILLA-LOBOS: *Chôros No. 1. Étude in E flat. Prelude in E min.* TÓRROBA: *Madronos.* TURINA: *Homage a Tarrega: Garrotin. Soleares. Fandanguillo.* TRAD. (arr. Llobet): *El testament d'Amelia.* ALBÉNIZ: *Suite española: Granada. Leyenda.* FALLA: *Homenaje pour le tombeau de Claude Debussy.*
(M) *** RCA RL/*RK* 43521 [LSC 2606].

This outstanding early recital, dating from 1961, places the guitar slightly back within a fairly resonant acoustic, and the effect is very like listening to a live recital in a small hall. The electricity of the music-making is consistently communicated, and all Bream's resources of colour and technical bravura are brought into play. The Villa-Lobos pieces are particularly fine, as is the Turina *Fandanguillo* (which comes at the end), and the Albéniz *Leyenda* is a *tour de force*; here the reverberation clouds the detail a little but makes an excitingly orchestral effect. The cassette and disc are closely matched, although the focus is fractionally sharper on LP.

'Julian Bream and friends' (with (i) George Malcolm (harpsichord); (ii) members of the Cremona Qt; (iii) Julian Bream Consort): BOCCHERINI: (i) *Introduction and Fandango.* (ii) *Guitar quintet in E min.* (iii) BRITTEN: *Gloriana: Courtly dances.* (ii) HAYDN: *Guitar quartet in E, Op. 2/2.*
(M) **(*) RCA Gold GL/*GK* 42753.

This rearrangement of Bream repertoire makes a most agreeable medium-priced recital. The Boccherini *Quintet* is an attractive work with an appealing slow movement; the colourful *Introduction and Fandango* comes from the *Quintet*, Op. 50/2. The Haydn work is the usual arrangement from an early string quartet. What adds piquancy to the collection is the inclusion of the *Courtly dances* from

Gloriana. The recording is good, if a little dated (it has not the presence and body of a modern recording, except in the Britten). The cassette transfer is smooth and has a natural ambience.

Bream, Julian, and **John Williams** (guitars)

'Together': LAWES: *Suite for 2 guitars.* CARULLI: *Duo in G, Op. 34.* SOR: *L'Encouragement, Op. 34.* ALBÉNIZ: *Cordoba.* GRANADOS: *Goyescas: Intermezzo.* FALLA: *La vida breve: Spanish dance No. 1.* RAVEL: *Pavane pour une infante défunte.*
*** RCA RCALP/*RCAK* 3003 [LSC 3257/*RK 1230*].

'Together again': CARULLI: *Serenade, Op. 96.* GRANADOS: *Danzas españolas Nos. 6 and 11.* ALBÉNIZ: *Bajo la Palmera, Op. 232. Iberia: Evocación.* GIULIANI: *Variazioni concertanti, Op. 130.*
*** RCA RCALP/*RCAK* 3006 [ARL 1/*ARK 1* 0456].

In this case two guitars are better than one; these two fine artists clearly strike sparks off each other. In the first recital Albéniz's *Cordoba* is hauntingly memorable and the concert closes with a slow, stately version of Ravel's *Pavane* which is unforgettable. Here Bream justifies a tempo which he did not bring off so effectively in his solo version (now deleted). On the second disc it is again music of Albéniz that one remembers for the haunting atmosphere the two artists create together. The sound of these reissues (offered at slightly less than premium price) is excellent, and the tapes have good clarity and presence.

'Live': JOHNSON: *Pavane and Galliard.* TELEMANN: *Partie polonaise.* SOR: *Fantaisie, Op. 54.* BRAHMS: *Theme and variations, Op. 18* (trans. Williams). FAURÉ: *Dolly suite, Op. 56.* DEBUSSY: *Rêverie. Children's Corner: Golliwog's cakewalk. Suite bergamasque: Clair de lune.* ALBÉNIZ: *Castilla.* GRANADOS: *Spanish dance No. 2 (Oriental).*
**(*) RCA RL/*RK* 03090 (2) [ARL2/*ARK2* 3090].

This recital was recorded live in Boston and New York during a North American tour. The sound is first-class, every bit as good as anything these artists have done in the studio. The drawback is the applause, which, though shortened in the editing, is still very intrusive on repeated hearings. The playing is of the highest quality although perhaps at times slightly self-conscious (the Granados encore has an almost narcissistic tonal beauty). As a whole there is not quite the electricity of this team's other recitals. Fauré's *Dolly suite* sounds a little cosy and the transcription of the *Variations* from Brahms's *B flat major Sextet* is not entirely effective. But the *Golliwog's cakewalk* and the Albéniz *Castilla* are highly enjoyable. The cassette transfer is immaculate, offering superb quality, clear and naturally balanced, but apart from the titles it gives no information whatsoever about the music or the source of the recital.

Brüggen, Frans (recorder)

Recital on original instruments (with Bylsma, cello; Leonhardt, harpsichord): VAN EYCK: *Pavane Lachrimae figurations. Engels Nachtegaeltje. Variations on 'Doen Daphne'.* PARCHAM: *Suite in G* (with N. Harnoncourt, gamba). CARR: *Divisions upon an Italian ground.* PEPUSCH: *Sonata No. 4 in F.*
(M) **(*) Tel. AP6/*CR4* 42050.

Frans Brüggen demonstrates various period instruments here, but three of the works are unaccompanied, which perhaps restricts the interest of this recital to recorder enthusiasts, as the appeal of the music itself is relatively limited. The *Suite* by Andrew Parcham, the *Divisions* of Robert Carr and Pepusch's *Sonata* are all engaging and are played with characteristic skill and musicianship, so that only occasionally does the ear detect the limitations of the early instruments. The recording is first-class on disc, but on cassette the unaccompanied works are slightly too highly modulated, and the focus is not quite clean; otherwise the chrome tape matches the disc closely.

Bylsma, Anner (baroque cello)

BOCCHERINI: *Cello concerto in G* (with Con-

certo Amsterdam, Schröder). *Cello sonata No. 7 in B flat* (with Leonhardt, harpsichord; Woodrow, bass). SAMMARTINI: *Sonata No. 3 in A min. for 2 cellos*. GABRIELI, Domenico: *Canon for 2 celli* (both with Koster, cello). ANTONI: *Ricercata VIII for solo cello*.
(M) ** Tel. AP6/*CR4* 42653.

The main purpose of this collection is to demonstrate the sound of Anner Bylsma's baroque cello, which it does admirably, for the recording is very clear and the chrome cassette is of matching demonstration quality. The timbre is in fact rather dry and is rather more suited to the earlier music than to Boccherini's rococo elegance, where the soloist hardly seeks to charm the ear. However, the playing does not lack either musicianship or vitality, and the rest of the programme is undoubtedly stylish, if not endearing.

Byzantine, Julian (guitar)

'Masterpieces for classical guitar': ALBÉNIZ: *Torre bermeja. Rumores de la caleta. Asturias* (*Leyenda*). TÓRROBA: *Madronos*. TARREGA: *Capricho arabe. La Alborada*. LAURO: *Vals venezelano No. 3*. VILLA-LOBOS: *Chôro 1. Prelude 2. Étude 1*. RODRIGO: *En los trigales*. BORGES: *Vals venezolano*. GRANADOS: *Spanish dance No. 5*. MALATS: *Serenata española*. FALLA: *The Three-cornered Hat: Miller's dance; Corregidor's dance*.
(B) **(*) CfP CFP/*TC-CFP* 40362.

Julian Byzantine is a thoroughly musical player; his rubato and control of light and shade are convincing. The playing may lack the last degree of individuality and electricity, and sometimes the listener may feel that the flow is too controlled, not absolutely spontaneous, but this remains an impressive recital, generous and varied in content and very well recorded. There is no appreciable difference between tape and disc.

Cambridge Buskers

'A little street music'.
(M) *** DG 2535/*3335* 471.

An unexpectedly diverting collection. The Cambridge Buskers are a duo. Michael Copley (who plays the flute and various recorders with easy bravura) and Dag Ingram (the hardly less fluent accordionist) met at Cambridge, and these recordings first appeared at the end of the 1970s. They open with the *Rondo* from Mozart's *Eine kleine Nachtmusik* which immediately establishes not only the infectious spontaneity of the playing, but also an engaging sense of timing and style. The programme ranges from Praetorius and Chopin to a witty condensation of Rossini's *Gazza Ladra overture* plus the exuberant *Galop* from *William Tell*, but also includes more obvious showpieces like Dinicu's *Hora staccato*. The recording has splendid presence on disc and cassette alike. Recommended.

Cherkassky, Shura (piano)

'The virtuoso piano': SCHULZ-ELVER: *Concert arabesques on motifs by Johann Strauss* (*By the beautiful blue Danube*). LISZT: *Rigoletto paraphrase*. SAINT-SAËNS: *Carnival of the animals: The Swan* (arr. Godowsky). STRAUSS, J. Jnr: *Wine, women and song* (arr. Godowsky). LISZT: *Polonaise No. 2*. CHOPIN: *Scherzo No. 4 in E, Op. 54; Polonaise No. 6 in A flat, Op. 55*.
(B) **(*) ASV ABM/*ZCABM* 758.

Some might find Cherkassky's playing here too impulsive, but it is glitteringly good-humoured. The *Blue Danube fantasy* has plenty of sparkle and Godowsky embroiders *The Swan* quite nicely. The impetuous quality remains in the three non-arranged pieces on side two, but the playing is so alive that one cannot but respond to Cherkassky's flair. He is brightly recorded and there is an excellent tape.

'Clair de lune'

Favourite piano music (with (i) Joseph Cooper; (ii) Katchen; (iii) Gulda; (iv) Rogé; (v) Katin): (i) DEBUSSY: *Clair de lune*. (ii) BACH: *Jesu, joy of man's desiring*. MOZART: *Piano sonata No. 15 in C, K.545*: 1st movt. BEETHOVEN: *Piano sonata No. 8* (*Pathétique*): 2nd movt. (i)

Für Elise; (iii) *Piano sonata No. 14* (*Moonlight*). (ii) MENDELSSOHN: *On wings of song.* BRAHMS: *Hungarian dance No. 5; Intermezzo in E flat, Op. 117/1.* (v) *Rhapsody in G min., Op. 79/2.* (ii) CHOPIN: *Polonaise in A flat, Op. 53;* (v) *Waltzes in D flat and C sharp min., Op. 64/1 and 2;* (i) *Nocturne in E flat, Op. 9/2; Prelude, Op. 28/15* (*Raindrop*). DVOŘÁK: *Humoresque in G flat, Op. 101/7.* (iv) LISZT: *Liebestraum No. 3 in A flat;* (v) *Consolation No. 3.* SCHUMANN: *Romance, Op. 28/2.*
(B) **(*) Decca KMC2 9002.

This is generally a most attractive recital, truthfully engineered, offering distinguished playing of a wide-ranging and nicely contrasted ninety-minute programme. The only disappointment is Gulda's version of the *Moonlight sonata*, which has an excessively deliberate opening movement and rather 'plummy' recording. Otherwise the sound is bright and clear, without lacking depth and atmosphere. Some of these performances are very good indeed.

Clarino Consort

'The trumpet shall sound': ANON.: *Hejnal Krakowski.* PURCELL: *Trumpet tune, ayre and cibell.* BLOW: *Vers. Fugue in F.* MORLEY: *La caccia. La sampogna.* HANDEL: *Concerto in B flat.* STANLEY: *Trumpet voluntary in D.* FANTINI: *Sonata a due trombe detta la guicciardini.* CAMPION: *Never weatherbeaten sail.* BULL: *Variations on the Dutch chorale 'Laet ons met herten reijne'.* BIBER: *Suite for 2 clarino trumpets.* DOWLAND: *Flow my tears.* FRESCOBALDI: *Capriccio sopra un soggetto.*
(B) ** Con. CC/*CCT* 7554.

The Clarino Consort consists of Don Smithers and Michael Laird (trumpets), Janet Smithers (baroque violin) and William Neil (organ). There is fine playing here, but the programme includes a fair amount of music for trumpet and organ. The most striking works are the Fantini *Sonata for two trumpets*, with its echoing fanfares, and the Biber *Suite* for a pair of (high) clarinos. Not all the other transcriptions are wholly convincing, but there is no lack of melody. The sound is good, and tape and disc are fairly closely matched, although once or twice the refinement of the upper range slips on the cassette, more noticeably on side two.

Cleobury, Stephen (organ of Westminster Abbey)

'Wedding favourites': MENDELSSOHN: *A Midsummer Night's Dream: Wedding march.* BACH: *Chorale prelude: In Dir ist Freude. Suite No. 3 in D, BWV 1068: Air. Jesu, joy of man's desiring.* WAGNER: *Lohengrin: Bridal chorus.* HANDEL: *Xerxes: Largo. Water music: Hornpipe.* CLARKE: *Trumpet voluntary.* GUILMANT: *Grand choeur in D.* WESLEY, S.: *Air and Gavotte.* BRAHMS: *Chorale prelude: Es ist ein' Ros' entsprungen, Op. 122/8.* WIDOR: *Organ symphony No. 5 in F min., Op. 42/1: Toccata.*
(M) **(*) Decca SPA/*KCSP* 554.

A well-played and very well-recorded collection. In the quieter, more reflective music Stephen Cleobury's style is rather introvert, and the effect is to provide a pleasant background tapestry rather than project the music strongly. Nevertheless the playing is very musical, and in the *Grand choeur* of Guilmant and, especially, the famous Widor *Toccata* the playing springs vividly to life, using a wide dynamic range very effectively. The cassette and disc are closely matched, and although the tape has been transferred at only a modest level the spectacle of the climaxes comes over without a tremor of congestion.

Cohen, Robert (cello)

'Virtuoso cello music' (with Parsons): LOCATELLI: *Sonata in D.* CHOPIN: *Introduction and polonaise brillante in C, Op. 3.* DVOŘÁK: *Rondo in G min., Op. 94.* POPPER: *Hungarian rhapsody, Op. 68; Serenade, Op. 54/2; Polonaise de concert, Op. 14.*
*(*) HMV Dig. ASD/*TC-ASD* 270017-1/4.

Virtuosity there certainly is, notably in the three Popper items, sparkling if trivial. So is the Chopin which the composer himself described as 'nothing more than a brilliant drawing-room piece'. Cohen is forwardly balanced and the effect is unflattering, giving his timbre a viola-like quality (which perhaps suits the Locatelli *Sonata*, intended for the violin). Geoffrey Parsons accompanies attentively.

Cole, Maggie (harpsichord)

'Seventeenth- and eighteenth-century keyboard music': ARNE: *Sonata No. 1 in F.* BACH: *Suite in B min., BWV 814.* RAMEAU: *L'entretien des muses. Le lardon. La triomphante.* SCARLATTI, D.: *Sonatas: in G, Kk.144; in A, Kk.212.* FROBERGER: *Suite in G min.* (Adler IX).
*** Hyp. A 66020.

Maggie Cole uses five different harpsichords, each matched in character and period to the repertoire. The result is unfailingly illuminating, and few recitals using original instruments are so patently self-justifying, particularly as the recording is admirably truthful and well balanced. The music itself is all attractive, and played with such expert stylishness and communicative musicianship, it makes a most entertaining programme.

Cologne Musica Antiqua

'German chamber music before Bach': REINCKEN: *Trio sonatas: in A min.; E min.* BACH: *Sonata in A min., BWV 965.* BUXTEHUDE: *Sonatas: in G; in B flat; in C.* PACHELBEL: *Suites: in G; in E min. Aria and variations in A. Canon and gigue in D.* ROSENMÜLLER: *Sonatas: in C; in E min.; in B flat.* SCHENCK: *Suite in D.* WESTOFF: *Sonata in A* (*La Guerra*).
*** DG Arc. 2723 078 (3) [id.].

This much-praised collection deservedly won the *Gramophone* 1981 Award in the early-music category. Here is a case where an enterprising programme of music, a good deal of it by little-known composers, is brought fully to life by expert playing – authentically stylish and accurate but never pedantic – and first-class sound, lively and very well balanced. The juxtaposition of the Reincken *Trio sonata* and Bach's keyboard transcription is characteristic of the admirable planning of the programme, which offers much to attract the ordinary music-lover as well as having specialist appeal.

Cooper, Joseph (piano)

'Face the music': CHOPIN: *Étude in E, Op. 10/3.* LISZT: *Liebesträume, G.541.* GRIEG: *Lyric pieces: Nocturne in C, Op. 54/4.* BRAHMS: *Waltz in A flat, Op. 39/15.* SCARLATTI: *Sonata in C, L.104.* SCHUBERT: *Impromptu in A flat, D935.* SCHUMANN: *Kinderscenen, Op. 15: Träumerei.* COOPER: *Hidden melodies* in the styles of Bach, Liszt, Brahms, Scarlatti, Tchaikovsky, Schumann, Grieg, Mozart, Schubert and Chopin.
*** CRD CRD 1006/*CRDC 4006* [id.].

Following the huge success of Joseph Cooper's television show, it was CRD who first had the bright idea of recording a selection of his *Hidden melodies*. There are ten of them here, and the allusions to the melodic and harmonic quirks of the concealed composers are as ingenious as ever. The pieces simulating Schubert and Scarlatti are charming, and there is real wit in the version of *Jingle bells* in the manner of ...? The other discovery that CRD made was that J.C.'s friendly musical advocacy is not dampened in the recording studio. Thus the popular piano pieces which make up the rest of the recital are no less persuasively played than his own pastiches. The Grieg, Liszt and Schumann works are particularly beautiful, and are well recorded too. The cassette transfer has been remastered and is now of high quality, matching the disc in piano timbre which is slightly mellow and soft-grained.

Danby, Nicholas (organ)

St Andrew's University organ: BÖHM: *Prelude in D min.* PACHELBEL: *Ciacona in F min.* WALTHER: *Concerto of Torelli, arr. for organ.* MENDELSSOHN: *Organ sonata No. 2 in C.* HINDEMITH: *Sonata No. 1.* WEHRLE: *Fanal.*
*** Abbey LPB 806.

A well-planned and splendidly recorded recital spanning nearly three centuries of (mostly) German organ music. The fine St

Andrews University instrument is admirably suited to this repertoire; its timbres are full-bodied yet clearly detailed within a perfect acoustic. Nicolas Danby invests all his programme with vitality. He is especially good in the Mendelssohn *Sonata*, and presents the baroque pieces simply and eloquently. The first of Hindemith's three sonatas also sounds highly effective in his hands, while the brilliant *Fanal* by the Swiss composer Heinz Wehrle (born in 1921) makes a colourful end-piece.

Danby, Nicholas, and **Peter Hurford**

'The Royal Festival Hall organ': DE GRIGNY: *Veni creator: En taille à 5; Fugue à 5; Dialogue sur les grands jeux.* ALAIN: *Variations on a theme of Jannequin.* FRANCK: *Pièce héroïque.* GIGOUT: *Scherzo.* BACH: *Prelude and fugue in C, BWV 545.* PACHELBEL: *Aria Sebaldina.* KARG-ELERT: *Impression: Harmonies du soir, Op. 72/1.* LISZT: *Prelude and fugue on Bach.*
**(*) Argo Dig. ZRDL 1012.

This record celebrates the Festival Hall organ at the hands of two distinguished soloists, Danby devoting himself to the German repertory, Hurford to the French. Performances are excellent, and though the hall is not an easy place for recording, the sound is well spread with a degree of atmosphere. There is an excellent chrome tape.

Drake, Susan (harp)

'Echoes of a waterfall': HASSELMANS: *La Source, Op. 44; Prelude, Op. 52; Chanson de mai, Op. 40.* ALVARS: *Divertissement, Op. 38.* GODEFROID: *Bois solitaire; Étude de concert in E flat min., Op. 193.* GLINKA: *Variations on a theme of Mozart.* THOMAS: *Echoes of a waterfall: Watching the wheat; Megan's daughter.* SPOHR: *Variations on Je suis encore, Op. 36.*
*** Hyp. A/*KA* 66038.

The music is lightweight and sometimes facile, but the young Welsh harpist, Susan Drake, is a beguiling exponent, and her technique is as impressive as her feeling for atmosphere. Those intrigued by the title of the collection will not be disappointed by the sounds here (the recording is excellent) which balance evocation with a suitable degree of flamboyance when the music calls for it. The Thomas evocation of watery effects is certainly picturesque as is Hasselmans' charming *La Source*, and both the Spohr and (especially) the Glinka *Variations* have considerable appeal. The cassette manages the resonance well; the sound is warm and mellow, yet definition remains quite good.

Equale Brass

'Baccanales': WARLOCK: *Capriol suite* (arr. Gout). POULENC: *Suite* (arr. Jenkins): *Mouvement perpétuel No. 1; Novellette No. 1 in C; Impromptu No. 3; Suite française.* ARNOLD: *Brass quintet.* COUPERIN, F.: *Suite* (arr. Wallace). BARTÓK: *4 Hungarian pictures* (arr. Sears).
C *** Nimbus **NIM 5004.**

There is no LP equivalent for this compact disc. It offers sound of extraordinary presence and realism and the programme (56′ including the silences between items) is generous and imaginative. The arrangements are cleverly scored and produce highly diverting results. Warlock's *Capriol suite* and the music of François Couperin seem unlikely to adapt well for brass, yet they are the highlights of the programme, alongside the engaging Poulenc *Mouvement perpétuel* and the colourful Bartók *Hungarian pictures*. The Equale Brass is a quintet (two trumpets, horn, trombone and tuba), and besides immaculate ensemble their playing is infectiously spirited and readily conveys the enjoyment of the participants so that the music-making has the atmosphere of a live concert. Each of the twenty-one items is banded. A demonstration issue.

Fowke, Philip (piano)

'Virtuoso transcriptions': BACH/RACHMANINOV: *Suite from the Solo violin Partita in E min., BWV 1006.* SCHUBERT/RACHMANINOV: *Wohin.* KREISLER/RACHMANINOV: *Liebeslied; Liebesfreud.* BUSONI: *Sonatina No. 6 (Fantasy on 'Carmen').* WEBER/

TAUSIG: *Invitation to the Dance*. GLINKA/BALAKIREV: *The Lark*. STRAUSS, J. Jnr/SCHULZELVER: *Arabesque on themes from 'The Blue Danube'*.
*** CRD CRD 1096/*CRDC 4096*.

Philip Fowke plays with prodigious bravura but treats these display pieces with obvious seriousness of purpose. The presentation is perhaps a little lacking in fun, yet brings freshness to everything included here. It is amazing how pianistic Bach's violin music becomes in Rachmaninov's hands. It is a sparkling collection, bringing out of the cupboard music which still has the power to delight and amaze. The recording is excellent and there is a splendid chrome cassette, with all the brilliance and body of the disc.

Galway, James (flute)

'Serenade for flute' (with L. Virtuosi): BEETHOVEN: *Serenade in D for flute, violin and viola, Op. 25*. BACH: *Flute sonata in E* (for flute and continuo), *BWV 1035*. TELEMANN: *Trio sonata in E min. for flute, oboe and continuo*.
(B) *** CfP CFP/*TC-CFP* 40318.

Since these recordings were made for Abbey Records in 1973 James Galway has become a star, and another member of the London Virtuosi, John Georgiadis (then the leader of the LSO), has taken up a successful solo career. It was a bright idea of CfP to make a recital out of these performances. Beethoven's *Serenade* is the best-known work of the three. The light and charming combination of flute, violin and viola inspired the youthful composer to write in an unexpectedly carefree and undemanding way. The sequence of tuneful, unpretentious movements reminds one of Mozart's occasional music, and this engaging performance is well projected by a bright, clean recording. The balance is a trifle close, but the sound is otherwise excellent. The other two works are hardly less attractive, and the playing in the Telemann, slightly more expressive than the Bach, achieves a distinction of style. On tape the sound quality has marginally less life and range at the top; otherwise the cassette transfer is first-class.

Gilbert, Kenneth (harpsichord)

French harpsichord music: CLÉRAMBAULT: *Suites Nos. 1 in C; 2 in C min*. LE ROUX: *Suite No. 5 in F*. COUPERIN, Louis: *Pavane in F sharp min*. D'ANGLEBERT: *Gaillarde et Double in C*. LEBÈGUE: *Les cloches*.
*** DG Arc. Dig. 2534 009 [id.].

Kenneth Gilbert has recorded the Clérambault suites before on Argo, coupling them with a suite of Elisabeth Jacquet de la Guerre. Readers who have that issue (ZK 64 – see above) will probably rest content, but those coming to this repertoire afresh will find much to delight them in the present Archive release, not least the engaging piece by Lebègue, *Les cloches*, which is something of a find.

Gilels, Emil (piano)

'The art of Emil Gilels': RACHMANINOV: *Piano concerto No. 3 in D min*. (with Paris Conservatoire O, Cluytens). CHOPIN: *Piano sonata No. 2 in B flat min., Op. 35*. SHOSTAKOVICH: *3 Preludes and fugues*. SCHUBERT: *6 Moments musicaux, D.780*. BEETHOVEN: *Piano sonata No. 14 (Moonlight), Op. 27/2*. MEDTNER: *Sonata reminiscenza, Op. 38*. BACH–BUSONI: *Prelude and fugue in D, BWV 532*. BACH–ZILOTI: *Prelude No. 10 in E min., BWV 855*. RAVEL: *Pavane; Jeux d'eau*. CHOPIN: *Études Nos. 14 in F min., Op. 25/2; 26 in A flat*.
❀ *** HMV SLS/*TC-SLS* 290011-5/9 (3/2).

A most welcome reissue of material that has been out of circulation for a long time. The Rachmaninov concerto dates from the mid-1950s, and although the orchestral support is less than ideal and the sound lacks the range and definition of a modern recording, Gilels's contribution surpasses even the most golden memories. It has the virtuosity and brilliance of the famous old Horowitz version that preceded it on LP, tempered with a poetry and a tenderness that are altogether unique. One often catches one's breath at the way in which Gilels shapes a phrase or colours his tone, and he almost succeeds in conveying the impression that the piano has no hammers, so supple is his sense of line. The Shostakovich

Preludes and fugues are hardly less masterly and here the sound is very good for the period (1955). The set is worth having for the Medtner alone, and its wistful melancholy and aristocratic polish resonate in the mind. Gilels is an unfailingly perceptive guide in all this repertoire: his authority and wisdom in Schubert and Beethoven can be taken for granted. His Ravel is less familiar; indeed we have had very little French music from him on records and such is its quality that one longs to hear more. This, the Medtner, Beethoven and Schubert are recorded in stereo: the Chopin and Shostakovich have a mono source. But none of this collection is to be missed by anyone who cares about great piano playing. The tape transfers are of high quality and the use of only two cassettes against three records means that the Rachmaninov concerto is heard without a side-break.

Grappelli, Stéphane (violin), **Martin Taylor** (piano)

'We've got the world on a string': She's funny that way. ELLINGTON: *Don't get around much anymore. Manhattan tea party.* LENNON/MCCARTNEY: *Here, there and everywhere. I can't believe that you're in love with me.* KERN: *Ol' Man River. It had to be you. I've got the world on a string. Daphne. Manoir.* GRAPPELLI: *Je n'sais plus.*
*** EMI Dig. EMD/*TC-EMD* 5540.

Following his series of recordings with Menuhin (see below) Stéphane Grappelli here makes a successful creative partnership with Martin Taylor, and even changes roles in the middle of side two to provide a stylish performance on the piano of his own *Je n'sais plus.* His decorative solo violin skills are heard at their most memorable in an elegant embroidery of Kern's *Ol' Man River*, but throughout the playing is fresh and rhythmically spontaneous, occupying that curious area partly derived from jazz but firmly placed within an already established European tradition. The sound is first-class with little or nothing to choose between digital disc and the excellent chrome tape.

'Guitar favourites'

(i) Diaz; (ii) Parkening; (iii) Angel Romero; (iv) Costanto: (i) RODRIGO: *Concierto de Aranjuez* (with Professors of Spanish Nat. O, Frühbeck de Burgos). SOR: *Variations on a theme from 'The Magic Flute'.* (ii) BACH: *Jesu, joy of man's desiring. Sheep may safely graze. Sleepers, awake.* (iii) GRANADOS: *La maja de Goya.* RODRIGO: *Fandango.* ALBÉNIZ: *Tango.* (iv) VILLA-LOBOS: *Preludes Nos. 1–3.* TURINA: *Sevillana. Fandanguillo. Rafaga. Homenaje a Tarrega.* (i) MOMPOU: *Canción.*
(B) *** EMI *TC2-MOM 117.*

At the centre of this tape-only collection is a warmly attractive performance of Rodrigo's *Concierto de Aranjuez* from Alirio Diaz and a Spanish orchestral ensemble. Diaz is good too in the Sor and Mompou items. The contribution from Angel Romero has less electricity, but Christopher Parkening's group of Bach transcriptions is most enjoyable, especially *Sleepers, awake*, which is presented with great flair. Irma Costanto provides the most memorable playing of all, her style very free but compellingly spontaneous and full of atmosphere and colour. The sound is excellent throughout.

Hogwood, Christopher (organ, harpsichord, virginals, spinet, fortepiano, clavichord)

'Keyboard music on authentic instruments': BULL: *Fantasia.* PHILIPS: *Galiarda passamezzo.* FARNABY: *Giles Farnaby's dreame; His rest: Farnaby's conceit; His humour.* JOHNSON/BYRD: *Pavana delight; Galiarda.* GIBBONS: *Fantasia; Italian ground; Lincoln's Inn masque; The Queen's command.* BACH, C. P. E.: *Fantasy in C; Versuch über die wahre Art das Clavier zu spielen: Sonata No. 2.* ARNE: *Sonatas Nos. 3 in G; 6 in G min.*
**(*) O-L DSLO/*KDSLC* 609.

An enterprising and varied recital featuring the small organ at Knole House, Kent, several harpsichords, two virginals and so on. The music is aptly chosen, but the first half of the programme, although very well played, is rather sober in mood. The recital springs to life at the beginning of side two with the C. P. E. Bach *Fantasy*, a bravura performance on a Heilmann fortepiano, and the rest is equally enjoyable, especially the music of Arne. The recording is first-class, although on the tape the sound of the chamber organ tends to smudge a little.

Holliger, Heinz (oboe), and **Ursula Holliger** (harp)

ROSSINI: *Andante and variations in F.* RUST: *Sonata in A.* BACH, C. P. E.: *Solo in G min. for oboe and continuo, Wq. 135; Solo for harp, Wq. 139.* BOCHSA: *Nocturne in F, Op. 50/2.*
(M) *** Ph. 6570/*7310* 575.

Several of these works are arrangements (both the Rossini *Variations* and the Rust *Sonata* were written for the violin), but the *Solo*, Wq. 135, by C. P. E. Bach (the most substantial piece) was conceived with the oboe in mind. All the music here is delightful when played with such point and style. Ursula Holliger holds the stage alone very successfully in her harp *Solo*. The recording is beautifully balanced and sounds wholly natural, with the cassette offering demonstration quality to match the disc.

Holliger, Heinz (oboe and oboe d'amore)

Recital (with Jaccottet and Cervera): BACH: *Oboe sonata in G min.* (arr. of *Sonata for flute and harpsichord, BWV 1030*). COUPERIN, François: *Les Goûts réunis: Concert No. 9 in E* (*Il ritretto dell' amore*). MARAIS: *Couples on Les Folies d'Espagne.*
(M) *** Ph. 9502/*7313* 070.

Characteristically stylish and elegant playing here. The programme is most appealing, lightweight but attractively inventive throughout. The movements of the Couperin here are given names, like *Le charme*, *L'enjouement*, *Les graces* and *La noble fierté*; and Holliger characterizes them engagingly. The continuo is of high quality and the recording well balanced and natural, with a good tape to match the disc closely.

Hollywood String Qt

BRAHMS: *Piano quintet in F min., Op. 34* (with Aller). SCHUBERT: *String quintet in C, D.956.* SMETANA: *Quartet No. 1 in E min.* (*From my life*). DVOŘÁK: *Quartet No. 12 in F* (*American*), *Op. 96.*
(M) (***) HMV mono RLS 765 (2).

A marvellous compilation. The Hollywood Quartet were all principals in film studio orchestras, and Felix Slatkin, the leader, also led the 20th Century-Fox Orchestra. The Schubert *C major Quintet* was one of the outstanding records of its day and still ranks high. They have great technical finish and perfect ensemble, and penetrate further below the surface than so many groups do. The Brahms *F minor Piano quintet* is no less powerful and thoughtful, and much the same is true of the two Czech quartets. These are classic accounts, all dating from the early 1950s but sounding remarkably fresh all the same.

Horowitz, Vladimir (piano)

'At the Met.': SCARLATTI, D.: *Sonatas: in A flat, Kk.127; in F min., Kk.184 and 466; in A, Kk.101; in B min., Kk.87; in E, Kk.135.* CHOPIN: *Ballade No. 4 in F min., Op. 52; Waltz No. 9 in A flat, Op. 69/1.* LISZT: *Ballade No. 2 in B min., G.171.* RACHMANINOV: *Prelude No. 6 in G min., Op. 23/5.*
C ❀ *** RCA Dig. **RCD 14585**; RL 14260 [ATC1 4260].

The sound Horowitz makes has not previously been fully captured on record, particularly in some of his RCA mono issues of the 1940s and 1950s. The playing is in a class of its own and all one needs to know is that this recording (especially on compact disc) reproduces the highly distinctive tone-quality he commands. This recital, given at the Metropolitan Opera House and issued here at the time of his London Festival Hall appearance in 1982, comes closer to the real thing than anything else on record. The quality of the playing is quite extraordinary.

Hurford, Peter (organ)

Ratzeburg Cathedral organ: *'Romantic organ music'*: WIDOR: *Symphony No. 5, Op. 42: Toccata.* VIERNE: *Pièces en style libre: Berceuse.* ALAIN: *Litanies.* FRANCK: *Chorale No. 3.* KARG-ELERT: *Marche triomphale; Nun danket alle Gotte, Op. 65.* BRAHMS: *Chorale preludes; O wie selig, seid, ihr doch; Schmücke dich; Es ist ein' Ros' entsprungen, Op. 122.* MENDELSSOHN: *Organ sonata in A, Op. 65/3.* REGER: *Introduction and passacaglia in D min.*
C *** Argo Dig. **410 165-2**; ZRDL/*KZRDC* 1011 [id.].

There are not many records of romantic organ music to match this in colour, breadth of repertory and brilliance of performance, superbly recorded. The ever-popular Widor item leads to items just as efficient at bringing out the variety of organ sound, such as the Karg-Elert or the Alain. These are performances which defy all thought of Victorian heaviness, and the Ratzeburg organ produces piquant and beautiful sounds. The sound is first-class on disc and chrome cassette alike, with plenty of edge on climaxes. On CD the presence and range are breathtaking.

'The organ at Sydney Opera House': BACH: *Toccata and fugue in D min., BWV 565; Cantata No. 147: Jesu, joy of man's desiring.* ALBINONI: *Adagio in G min.* (arr. Giazotto). FRANCK: *Chorale No. 2 in B min.* MURRILL: *Carillon.* WALFORD DAVIES: *Solemn melody.* WIDOR: *Organ symphony No. 5: Toccata.*
**(*) Argo Dig. ZRDL/*KZRDC* 1016 [id.].

This is slightly disappointing. The organ is a fine instrument but Peter Hurford seems on less than his best form. The famous Bach *Toccata and fugue* is taken very fast and the *Chorale* which follows sounds curiously stiff. Best are the Murrill *Carillon* and the Widor *Toccata*, taken steadily but still projecting well because the sound is so clear. Both disc and chrome tape are technically impressive.

Sydney Opera House organ: *'Great organ works'*: BACH: *Toccata and fugue in D min., BWV 565; Jesu, joy of man's desiring.* ALBINONI: *Adagio* (arr. Giazotto). PURCELL: *Trumpet tune in D.* MENDELSSOHN: *A Midsummer Night's Dream: Wedding march.* FRANCK: *Chorale No. 2 in B min.* MURRILL: *Carillon.* WALFORD DAVIES: *Solemn melody.* WIDOR: *Organ symphony No. 5: Toccata.*
C **(*) Decca Dig. **411 929-2** [id.].

Superb sound here, wonderfully free and never oppressive, even in the most spectacular moments. The Widor is spiritedly genial when played within the somewhat mellower registration of the magnificent Sydney instrument (as contrasted with the Ratzeburg Cathedral organ – see above), and the pedals have great sonority and power. The Murrill *Carillon* is equally engaging alongside the Purcell *Trumpet tune*, while Mendelssohn's wedding music has never sounded more resplendent. The Bach (taken from Hurford's other recital, above) is less memorable, and the Albinoni *Adagio* without the strings is not an asset to the collection either.

Jacobs, Paul (piano)

American piano music: BOLCOM: *3 Ghost rags.* COPLAND: *4 Piano blues.* RZEWSKI: *4 North American Ballads.*
** None. Dig. D79006.

The death (in 1983) of Paul Jacobs robbed us of a versatile and enterprising artist, who has enriched the catalogue with much out-of-the-way material. The best music here is the Copland, also available in Leo Smit's two-record Copland set on CBS, and Jacobs plays them with thoroughly idiomatic style; and the most interesting is Frederick Rzewski's brilliant and effective *Ballads*. The composer, now in his forties, is new to the catalogue and is eminently worth watching. The Bolcom *Rags* are not particularly strong pieces but Jacobs makes out as persuasive a case for them as he can. Good recording.

Judd, Terence (piano)

'In Moscow': LISZT: *Piano sonata in B min. Paganini study No. 3: La Campanella.* SCRIABIN: *Étude in C sharp min., Op. 42/5.* RACHMANINOV: *Étude-Tableau in D, Op. 39/9.*

KAZHAEVA: *Prelude and Invention.* CHOPIN: *Étude in E min., Op. 25/11.* BACH: *Prelude and fugue in B min., Book 1/22.* SHOSTAKOVICH: *Prelude and fugue in D flat, Op. 87/15.*
**(*) Chan. ABR/*ABT* 1090.

These performances were recorded live during the finals of the 1978 Tchaikovsky International Piano Competition in Moscow. The performances are electrifying in their natural bravura, and though in the studio Judd would no doubt have played with keener precision, the excitement more than compensates. The shorter pieces come in more restricted sound than the Liszt *Sonata* which takes up a whole side. Audience noises are often irritating, but the issue is a splendid reminder of a fine artist who died tragically young.

Kempff, Wilhelm (piano)

'Für Elise': BEETHOVEN: *Für Elise, G.13. Rondo à capriccio in G (Rage over a lost penny), Op. 129.* MOZART: *Fantasy in D min., K.397.* SCHUBERT: *Moments musicaux, D.780, Nos. 1, 3 and 5.* BRAHMS: *3 Intermezzi, Op. 117.* SCHUMANN: *Papillons, Op. 2.*
(M) **(*) DG Priv. 2535/*3335* 608.

This is a well-planned recital, and although the piano tone is variable (the acoustic changes strikingly on side two) it does give a fair idea of Kempff's range. *Für Elise* is simple and totally unromantic, and the Brahms *Intermezzi* are most beautifully done; but the highlight of the collection is unquestionably the really wonderful performance of the Mozart *Fantasia*, played simply but with great art lying beneath the music's surface. The tape transfer is of excellent quality throughout, clean and clear.

(i) **Kempff, Wilhelm;** (ii) **Támás Vásary** (piano)

(i) BEETHOVEN: *Piano sonata No. 14 (Moonlight), Op. 27/2; Piano sonata No. 8 (Pathétique), Op. 13:* 2nd movt. *Rondo in C, Op. 51/1.* SCHUBERT: *Moment musical No. 1 in C, D.780/1.* (ii) CHOPIN: *Nocturnes Nos. 1 in B flat min., Op. 9/1; 9 in B; 10 in A flat, Op. 32/1 and 2.*
(M) **(*) DG Priv. 2535/*3335* 639.

An attractive enough collection, obviously intended for the late evening. The performances are distinguished and well recorded, although the cassette (the obvious medium for such a programme) is transferred at an unnecessarily low level). Vásary, because of his brighter recording, is given more presence than Kempff. The selection of *Nocturnes* is attractively chosen.

King, Thea (clarinet), **Clifford Benson** (piano)

STANFORD: *Clarinet sonata, Op. 129.* FERGUSON: *4 Short pieces, Op. 6.* FINZI: *5 Bagatelles, Op. 23.* HURLSTONE: *4 Characteristic pieces.*
*** Hyp. A 66014.

A first-class anthology, well balanced as repertoire, excellently played and most satisfactorily recorded. Stanford's *Clarinet sonata* is clearly influenced by Brahms, but has plenty of character of its own. The rest of the music is lighter in texture and content, all well crafted and worth hearing.

BLISS: *Pastoral.* COOKE, Arnold: *Clarinet sonata in B flat.* HOWELLS: *Clarinet sonata.* REIZENSTEIN: *Arabesques.*
*** Hyp. A 66044.

An admirable second anthology of twentieth-century British music for clarinet and piano, most eloquently played by both artists. The Howells *Sonata* is among the finest written since Brahms, a warmly lyrical piece that brings out the instrument's varied colourings. That has Bliss's early and unassuming *Pastoral* following it on side one. Arnold Cooke's *Sonata*, strong but hardly demanding, is similarly given a pendant in the Reizenstein piece. Thea King's warm, naturally expressive playing makes her the ideal advocate not only for the music but for her instrument. Smooth recording.

Klerk, Albert de (chamber organs)

Regal, table, case, positive, cabinet and secretaire organs: PALESTRINA: *Ricercare primi toni.* FRESCOBALDI: *Ave maris stella.* SANTA MARIA: *Fantasia primi toni. Fantasia terti toni. Fantasia octavi toni.* SWEELINCK: *Von der Fortuna werd' ich getrieben.* GIBBONS: *Fancy in A. The King's Juell.* ZIPOLI: *Canzona.* BUXTEHUDE: *Wie schön leuchtet der Morgenstern.* COUPERIN, L.: *Chaconne in D min.* CORRETTE: *Vous qui désirez sans fin.* CASANOVAS: *Sonata No. 5.*
(M) *** Tel. AP6/*CR4* 41036.

Albert de Klerk provides here a fascinating survey of the development of the chamber organ from about 1600 to 1790. The earliest instrument (a regal) creates the most piquant sounds in an expressive *Ricercare* of Palestrina; later in the survey de Klerk is able to show the more ambitious sounds made by cabinet organs of the last half of the eighteenth century in fine performances of Buxtehude's chorale *Wie schön leuchtet der Morgenstern*, a sombre *Chaconne* of Louis Couperin and a set of engaging variations on *Vous qui désirez sans fin* by Michel Corrette. Albert de Klerk's mastery of articulation on these primitive instruments is astonishing, and the timbres are always attractive. The recording is close enough to catch all the mechanical clicks, but it gives each instrument great presence. The high-level chrome-tape transfer is every bit the equal of the disc, offering demonstration quality throughout.

Koopman, Ton (organ)

Noëls: DANDRIEU: *Noël de Saintogne; Si c'est pour ôter la vie; O filii et filiae.* DAQUIN: *Noëls Nos. 2 (Or nous dites Marie) and 10.* LEBÈGUE: *Noël pour l'amour de Marie; Une vierge Pucelle. A la venue de Noël.*
(M) *(*) Ph. 6503/*7313* 076.

Arranging melodies associated with Christmas, from earlier times, into short organ voluntaries became very popular in France during the seventeenth and eighteenth centuries. The tune used in *Une vierge Pucelle* is more familiar as Byrd's *Queenes Alman*, but most of the material was traditional. The music is structurally simple and gives the opportunity for elaborate ornamentation. Ton Koopman uses an attractive, rather throaty-sounding organ from Houdan, Franreich, but his playing is curiously didactic and without any kind of flair. The recording is excellent, on disc and cassette alike.

Kremer, Gidon (violin), and **Elena Kremer** (piano)

RAVEL: *Violin sonata.* SATIE: *Choses vues à droit et à gauche (sans lunettes).* MILHAUD: *Le printemps.* STRAVINSKY: *Duo concertante.* PROKOFIEV: *Violin sonata in D, Op. 115.*
*** Ph. 9500/*7300* 912 [id.].

The most interesting item on this record is the youthful one-movement *Sonata* of Ravel which Gidon Kremer plays with a charm that is not always evident in his recordings. It is a pleasure to be confronted with playing of such real sensitivity. The Ravel is better recorded than the rival account from Augustin Dumay and Jean-Philippe Collard on EMI (see above) and, rather surprisingly, more atmospheric and imaginative in its subtlety of dynamic nuance and shaping of a phrase. The two French artists focus on its youthful virility while Gidon and Elena Kremer place it within the tradition of Fauré and Franck and yet succeed in making it sound original and distinctive. The Milhaud and Satie are hardly less beguiling in the Kremers' hands and the Stravinsky and Prokofiev pieces given with great panache. What gloriously natural sound the Philips engineers have captured. The cassette is very good too, although the Ravel, Satie and Milhaud works sound rather less 'live' than the Stravinsky and (especially) the Prokofiev on side two.

Labèque, Katia and **Marielle** (piano duet)

'Glad rags': GERSHWIN/DONALDSON: *Rialto ripples.* MAYERL: *Honky-tonk.* JOHNSON: *Carolina shout.* JOPLIN: *The Entertainer; Antoinette; Magnetic rag; Maple leaf rag; Elite*

syncopations; Strenuous life; Stop-time; Bethena.
*** EMI EMD/*TC-EMD* 5541 [Ang. S/*4XS 37980*].

The Labèque duo play with irresistible bravura and dash. Scott Joplin may have frowned on their tempi (he favoured slow speeds) but the playing has such wit and conveyed enjoyment that criticism is silenced. The recording has sparkle but depth too and the cassette – although not chrome – is of demonstration standard too. This is by far the most generally recommendable collection of this repertoire.

Larrocha, Alicia de (piano)

'Favourite Spanish encores': ALBÉNIZ, M.: *Sonata in D.* ALBÉNIZ, I: *Recuerdos de Viaje Nos. 5 and 6. Pavana–Capricho, Op. 12. Tango, Op. 165/2. Malagueña, Op. 165/3. Suite espagnola: No. 3, Sevillanas.* SOLER: *Sonatas in G min.; in D.* GRANADOS: *Danzas españolas Nos. 5 and 7.* TURINA: *5 Danzas gitanas, 1st series: No. 5, Sacro-monte, Op. 55. 3 Danzas Andaluzas: No. 3, Zapateado, Op. 8.*
*** Decca SXL 6734 [Lon. CS 6953].

An entirely delightful collection of lightweight Spanish keyboard music, played with such skill and simplicity that even the slightest music never becomes chocolate-boxy. The eighteenth-century classicism of the sonatas by Soler and Mateo Albéniz makes a splendid foil for the warmer romanticism of Isaac Albéniz and the vivid colours of Granados and Turina. The record offers very lifelike piano tone, warm and natural.

Ledger, Philip (organ)

'Organ voluntaries from King's': CLARK: *Prince of Denmark's march.* SWEELINCK: *Variations on Mein juges Leben.* BOYCE: *Voluntary in D.* BACH: *Chorales: Wachet auf; Wenn wir in hochsten Nothen sein; In dulci jubilo.* BRAHMS: *Schmücke dich, O liebe Seele.* KARG-ELERT: *Marche triomphale: Now thank we all our God.* WHITLOCK: *Folk tune; Paean.* STANFORD: *Postlude in G min.* ALAIN: *Litanies.* JONGEN: *Chant de May.* DUPRÉ: *Toccata: Placare Christe servulis.*
*** HMV Dig. ASD/*TCC-ASD* 4093.

A very successful recital from Ledger, splendidly recorded, with the King's acoustic offering no problems in this first-rate digital recording. The programme is highly diverting and well balanced to provide spectacle besides charming the ear. The three closing French pieces form an engaging triptych with Alain's quirky *Litanies* leading on to Jongen's *May song*, and the Dupré *Toccata* a thrilling endpiece. On side one the Bach and Brahms *Chorales* are nicely registered and the music of Karg-Elert, Stanford and Whitlock adds comparable diversity. This recital has wide general interest and is not just for organ fanciers. There is an excellent chrome tape with side two (where the transfer level rises) reaching demonstration standard.

'Liebesträume'

'Romantic piano music': (i) Bolet; (ii) Ashkenazy; (iii) De Larrocha; (iv) Lupu: (i) LISZT: *Liebestraum No. 3; Étude de concert No. 3* (*Un sospiro*). (ii) RACHMANINOV: *Prelude in C sharp min., Op. 3/2.* CHOPIN: *Nocturne in F min., Op. 55/1; Étude in E, Op. 10/3.* BEETHOVEN: *Piano sonata No. 14 in C sharp min.* (*Moonlight*). (iii) CHOPIN: *Prelude No. 15 in D flat* (*Raindrop*). SCHUBERT: *Impromptu in A flat, D.899/4.* SCHUMANN: *Romance, Op. 28/2.* (iv) BRAHMS: *Rhapsody in G min., Op. 79/2.*
*** Decca **411 934-2** [id.].

Jorge Bolet's warmly romantic account of Liszt gives this specially assembled compact disc its title and is also the only true digital recording included in the programme. But the sound is generally excellent and the digital remastering, if producing a rather forward image, offers truthful quality throughout. The performances are distinguished and there is passionate contrast in Ashkenazy's Rachmaninov. Lupu's Brahms is rather less extrovert in feeling; generally, the recital has a nicely relaxed atmosphere.

Lipatti, Dinu (piano)

Besançon Festival recital (1950): BACH: *Partita No. 1 in B flat, BWV 825.* MOZART: *Piano sonata No. 8 in A min., K.310.* SCHUBERT: *Impromptus, D.899, Nos. 2–3.* CHOPIN: *Waltzes Nos. 1–14.*
(M) (***) HMV mono RLS 761 (2).

No collector should overlook this excellent two-disc set. Most of these performances have scarcely been out of circulation since their first appearance: the haunting account of the Mozart *A minor Sonata* and the Bach *B flat Partita* have both had more than one incarnation; the collection of Chopin *Waltzes* is perhaps most famous of all, and its legendary reputation is well earned. The remastering is expertly done, and the ear notices that, among his other subtleties, Lipatti creates a different timbre for the music of each composer.

Lloyd Webber, Julian (cello)

'The romantic cello' (with Yitkin Seow, piano): POPPER: *Elfentanz, Op. 39.* SAINT-SAËNS: *Carnival of the Animals: The Swan. Allegro appassionato, Op. 43.* FAURÉ: *Après un rêve.* MENDELSSOHN: *Song without Words, Op. 109.* RACHMANINOV: *Cello sonata, Op. 19:* slow movt. DELIUS: *Romance.* CHOPIN: *Introduction and polonaise brillante, Op. 3.* ELGAR: *Salut d'amour, Op. 12.*
**(*) ASV ACM/*ZCACM* 2002.

Julian Lloyd Webber has gathered together a most attractive collection of showpieces for the cello, romantic as well as brilliant. Such dazzling pieces as the Popper – always a favourite with virtuoso cellists – is on record a welcome rarity. The recording, a little edgy, favours the cello; the cassette transfer is vivid, with good body and range.

Menuhin, Yehudi, and **Stéphane Grappelli** (violins)

'Jealousy' (Hits of the thirties): GADE: *Jealousy.* RODGERS: *Blue Room. The Lady is a Tramp.* KERN: *A Fine Romance. Pick Yourself Up.* GRAPPELLI: *Billy. Aurore. Errol. Jermyn Street.* GERSHWIN: *Love Is Here To Stay. Lady Be Good.* PORTER: *Night and Day.* MCHUGH: *I Can't Believe That You're In Love With Me.* STRACHEY: *These Foolish Things.* BERLIN: *Cheek to Cheek.*
*** EMI EMD/*TC-EMD* 5504 [Ang. S/*4XS* 36968].

The partnership of Menuhin and Grappelli started in the television studio; their brief duets (tagged on to interviews) were so successful that the idea developed of recording a whole recital. This was the first selection, and found each maestro striking sparks off the other in style but matching the other remarkably closely in matters of tone and balance. The result is delightful, particularly in numbers such as *Pick Yourself Up* where the arrangement directly tips a wink towards Bachian figuration. Excellently focused recording, while the tape transfer is nearly always crisp and clean.

'Fascinatin' Rhythm': GERSHWIN: *Soon. Summertime. Nice Work If You Can Get It. Embraceable You. Fascinatin' Rhythm. Liza. 'S Wonderful. I Got Rhythm.* KERN: *Why Do I Love You. All the Things You Are.* PORTER: *Just One of Those Things. Looking at You. I Get a Kick Out of You.* GRAPPELLI: *Johanny aime. Minuet pour Menuhin.*
*** EMI EMD/*TC-EMD* 5523 [Ang. S/*4XS* 37156].

One of the secrets of the success of this partnership lies in the choice of material. All these items started out as first-rate songs with striking melodies which live in whatever guise, and here with ingenious arrangements they spark off the individual genius of each violinist both as a challenge and towards the players' obvious enjoyment. The high spirits of the collaboration are caught beautifully, and like the other recordings in the series this can be recommended unreservedly to anyone fancying the offbeat mixture. Good vivid sound and the high-level cassette transfer has plenty of life (although the balance is very forward).

'Tea for Two': MEYER and KAHN: *Crazy Rhythm.* GERSHWIN: *The Man I Love. A Foggy Day.* YOUMANS: *Tea for Two.*

RODGERS: *My Funny Valentine. Thou Swell.* KERN: *Yesterdays.* ARLEN: *Between the Devil and the Deep Blue Sea.* BRAHAM: *Limehouse Blues.* HARRIS: *Air on a Shoe String. Viva Vivaldi.* GRAPPELLI: *Highgate village. Adelaide Eve* (played by Menuhin on violin with Grappelli on piano).
*** EMI EMD/*TC-EMD* 5530 [Ang. S/*4XS* 37533].

This third issue shows Menuhin and Grappelli even more confident in their harmoniously clashing partnership. Inevitably, with swung rhythms the essential element of the exercise, Grappelli is generally the dominant partner, but most successful of all are the items by Max Harris, *Air on a Shoe String* and *Viva Vivaldi*, which, with harpsichord (played by Laurie Holloway) an important element, pay more than lip-service to classical tradition. Vivid immediate recording and a splendidly clean tape transfer. Taking quality of sound into account as well as the vibrant playing, this is the most attractive of the Menuhin/Grappelli collections so far.

'Strictly for the birds': A Nightingale Sang in Berkeley Square. Lullaby of Birdland. When the Red, Red Robin. Skylark. Bye, bye, Blackbird. Coucou. Flamingo. Dinah. Rosetta. Sweet Sue. Once in Love with Amy. Laura. La Route du Roi. Sweet Georgia Brown.
*** EMI Dig. EMD/*TCC-EMD* 5533 [Ang. DS/*4XS* 37710].

An endearing continuation of a happy musical partnership. The high spirits of the collaboration are caught again here, not only in the lively numbers but also in the memorable lyrical tunes like the title song and *Laura*. Superbly focused recording, with disc and chrome tape almost identical.

'Top hat' (with O, Riddle): BERLIN: *Puttin' on the Ritz. Isn't This a Lovely Day. The Piccolino. Change Partners. Top Hat.* KERN: *The Way You Look Tonight.* GERSHWIN: *He Loves and She Loves. They Can't Take That Away From Me. They All Laughed. Funny Face.* GRAPPELLI: *Alison. Amanda.* CONRAD: *The Continental.* YOUMANS: *Carioca.*
*** EMI Dig. EMD/*TCC-EMD* 5539 [Ang. DS/*4XS* 37860].

For their fifth collection, Menuhin and Grappelli are joined by a small orchestral group directed by Nelson Riddle. Aficionados might fear that this will dilute the jazz element of the playing, and perhaps it does a little at times; but Riddle's arrangements are witty and understanding and some of these tunes undeniably have an orchestral feeling. The result is just as lively and entertaining as previous collections in this series. The music itself is associated with Fred Astaire, although Grappelli contributes two numbers himself, perhaps originally intended for *Strictly for the birds*. The sound is as crisp and lively as ever, both on disc and on the excellent chrome tape.

Michelangeli, Arturo Benedetti (piano)

'Recital': BEETHOVEN: *Piano sonata No. 32 in C min., Op. 111.* GALUPPI: *Piano sonata No. 5 in C.* SCARLATTI, D.: *Sonatas: in C min., Kk.11; in C, Kk.159; in A, Kk.462.*
*** Decca SXL 6181.

Every moment of this outstanding record proclaims Michelangeli as a great musician and a complete individualist. There is a rapt concentration in the Beethoven performance: the first movement is deliberate (some find it too much so) but this deliberation increases the music's power and the forward impulse remains spontaneous. Equally the opening of the slow movement has a projection rare on a gramophone record. The Galuppi *Sonata* is slight, but captivating when so beautifully played, and the three diverse Scarlatti works have superb poise; yet Michelangeli's lightness of touch (metaphorically as well as literally speaking) in no way detracts from the music's stature and inevitability. With excellent recording this is a very distinguished collection.

Milan, Susan (flute)

'The magic flute of Susan Milan' (with Benson, piano): ROUSSEL: *Joueurs de flûte.* DEBUSSY: *Syrinx.* POULENC: *Flute sonata.* IBERT: *Pièce for solo flute.* MESSIAEN: *La Merle noire.* FAURÉ: *Fantaisie.* BOZZA: *Agrestide.*
(M) *** ASV ACM/*ZCACM* 2010.

Susan Milan is an admirable soloist in this repertoire. Her timbre seems ideally suited to French music; her phrasing is sensitive, and the control of vibrato is beautifully judged. There is bravura too, but never for its own sake (unless this is the composer's intention). The programme is imaginative and well balanced: the Roussel pieces and the Poulenc *Sonata* are especially valuable. The recording is rather resonant, but this does not prevent clarity of focus either on disc or on the excellent equivalent cassette.

Milstein, Nathan (violin)

Recital (with Georges Pludermacher, piano): GEMINIANI: *Sonata in A* (arr. Milstein). SCHUBERT: *Rondo brillante, D.895.* MILSTEIN: *Paganiniana.* LISZT: *Consolation No. 3 in D flat.* STRAVINSKY: *Chanson russe.* KODÁLY: *Il pleut dans la ville, Op. 11/3.* PARADIES: *Sicilienne.* MUSSORGSKY: *Hopak* (arr. Rachmaninov).
(M) **(*) DG Sig. 410 843-1/4.

The Geminiani is not very stylish with its bold piano accompaniment, but the Schubert is lively, and both are well played technically. Milstein comes into his own in the arrangement of Paganini's most famous *Caprice* (with variations) which he presents with tremendous dash. The Liszt too is most effective when played so seductively, and the other miniatures are all winning, particularly the vivacious *Hopak* of Mussorgsky. Excellent sound, with nothing to choose between disc and chrome tape.

'Musical instruments at the Victoria and Albert Museum'

Virginals; ivory lute; baroque oboe; baroque violin; writing-case virginals; baroque guitar; baroque flute; baryton; hurdy-gurdy; Taskin harpsichord; giraffe piano; French hand-horn (played by various artists). Narration and illustrated booklet by Carole Patey (with 53 colour slides).

Available from H. M. Stationery Office.

At the centre of this presentation is an eighty-minute cassette on which each instrument is introduced by Carole Patey with interspersed anecdotes using additional voices (after the manner of a BBC radio programme) to increase the dramatic effect. The illustrated talk is in two halves; at the end of each there is a further short recital using the instruments discussed. This is the least effective part of the tape: the playing still sounds illustrative rather than creating the ambience of proper performances. However, the production generally is admirable, entertaining and informative. The cassette is of very good quality and the recording truthful. Each instrument is naturally balanced, and the narrating voice is given a friendly forward projection. The instrumental sound lacks the very fullest frequency range (the upper partials of the baroque instruments are smoothed off somewhat), but this is not a really serious criticism: the recording remains very effective for its purpose. A simple cue sheet, for amateur or professional use, is provided so that the colour slides can be fitted to the narrative. This is a first-class idea, efficiently realized.

Ogdon, John (piano)

'Popular piano favourites': BACH: *Cantata No. 147: Jesu, joy of man's desiring.* BEETHOVEN: *Für Elise.* IRELAND: *The Holy Boy. April.* POULENC: *Mouvement perpétuel No. 1.* IBERT: *Histoires: 2, Le petit âne blanc.* CHAMINADE: *Automne, Op. 35.* MOSZKOWSKI: *Valse in E, Op. 34/1.* RACHMANINOV: *Prelude in C sharp min., Op. 3/2.* GRANADOS: *Goyescas: The Maiden and the Nightingale.* ALBÉNIZ: *Tango in D, Op. 165/2.* SINDING: *Rustle of Spring, Op. 32/3.* SCOTT, Cyril: *Lotus Land, Op. 47/1. Danse nègre, Op. 58/5.* GRIEG: *Lyric pieces: Wedding Day at Troldhaugen, Op. 65/6.*
(M) ** HMV HQS 1287.

A highly musical but rather sturdy recital, somewhat lacking incandescence in the Granados but with Ogdon at his very best in the French and English music. The opening Bach chorale immediately sets the atmosphere of rather studied care in the matter of articulation and phrasing. The piano recording is excellent.

Ogdon, John and **Brenda Lucas** (pianos)

Music for 4 hands: RACHMANINOV: *Suites for 2 pianos: Nos. 1, Op. 5; 2, Op. 17; 6 Pieces for piano duet, Op. 11; Italian polka.* ARENSKY: *Suite for 2 pianos, Op. 15.* SHOSTAKOVICH: *Concertino, Op. 94.* KHACHATURIAN: *Sabre dance* (arr. Ogdon).
(B) **(*) CfP CFPD/*TC-CFPD* 41 4438-3/5 (2).

John Ogdon's and Brenda Lucas's readings of the two Rachmaninov *Suites*, not ideally imaginative but enjoyable, are aptly coupled with other duet recordings made by them, including the *Six Pieces*, Op. 11, of Rachmaninov and the delightful Arensky *Suite* which includes the famous waltz. It is good too to have the long-neglected *Concertino* of Shostakovich and the anything-but-neglected *Sabre dance*. Fine ensemble and sparkling fingerwork. Good mid-1970s recording. An excellent bargain package.

Organ music

'Great organ favourites' (with (i) Danby (organ of Blenheim Palace); (ii) Bayco (Holy Trinity, Paddington); (iii) Willcocks (King's College, Camb.); (iv) Preston (Westminster Abbey); (v) Thalben-Ball (Temple Church); (vi) Jackson (York Minster)): (i) BACH: *Toccata and fugue in D min., BWV 565.* (ii) *In dulci jubilo.* (iii) *Wachet auf.* (i) CLARKE: *Trumpet voluntary.* WIDOR: *Symphony No. 5, Op. 42/1: Toccata.* ELGAR: *Enigma variations: Nimrod.* GIGOUT: *Scherzo.* FRANCK: *Choral No. 3 in A min.* (iv) MURRILL: *Carillon.* (ii) MENDELSSOHN: *A Midsummer Night's Dream: Wedding march.* LEMARE: *Andantino.* HOLLINS: *Spring song.* WAGNER: *Lohengrin: Bridal chorus.* WOLSTENHOLME: *Allegretto.* BOËLLMANN: *Prière à Notre Dame.* HANDEL: *Water music: Air.* (v) PURCELL: *Voluntary on the Old 100th.* (vi) COCKER: *Tuba tune.*
(B) ** EMI *TC2-MOM 115.*

Obvious care has been taken with the engineering of this mixed bag of excerpts (one of the tape-only 'Miles of Music' series), but occasionally the reverberant acoustic brings moments when the focus slips a little. For the most part, however, the sound is impressive. The programme begins well with excellent versions of the Widor, Gigout, Franck's *Third Choral* and Murrill's engaging *Carillon*, but on side two Frederic Bayco, who provides the lighter fare, is sometimes unstylish: he is very mannered in the famous *Wedding march.* But how many drivers want organ music as a background for a car journey?

'The world of the organ' (with (i) Jeanne Demessieux, Liverpool Met. Cathedral; (ii) Edward Higginbottom, Corpus Christi College, Camb.; (iii) Simon Preston, Westminster Abbey; (iv) D. J. Rees, Alltwen Chapel, Pontardawe; (v) Douglas Haas, with Württemberg CO, Faerber; (vi) Karl Richter, Victoria Hall, Geneva; (vii) Jiři Ropek, St Giles, Cripplegate): (i) WIDOR: *Symphony No. 5 in F min., Op. 42/1: Toccata.* (ii) FRANCK: *Pièce héroïque.* (iii) PURCELL: *Trumpet tune.* CLARKE: *Trumpet voluntary.* (iv) WALFORD DAVIES: *Solemn melody.* (v) ALBINONI: *Adagio in G min.* (arr. Giazotto). (vi) BACH: *Toccata and fugue in D min., BWV 565.* (vii) *Chorale prelude: Wachet auf, BWV 542. Fantasia and fugue in G min., BWV 542.*
(M) **(*) Decca SPA/*KCSP* 262.

An admirably planned recital, offering (with one exception) first-rate playing throughout and a fairly wide range of organ sound within different ambiences. The recording is excellent on disc, but the tape transfer has been made at fractionally too high a level on side one; there is some roughness in the upper partials in the Widor *Toccata* and the Purcell *Trumpet tune*. The exception to the general excellence of the performances is D. J. Rees' account of the Walford Davies *Solemn melody* which – to put it kindly – is somewhat unsophisticated.

Ousset, Cécile (piano)

'French piano music': FAURÉ: *Impromptus Nos. 2 in F min., Op. 31; 3 in A flat, Op. 34.* DEBUSSY: *Estampes.* RAVEL: *Miroirs; Alborada del gracioso.* CHABRIER: *Pièces pittoresques: Nos. 6, Idyll; 10, Scherzo-valse.* SATIE: *3 Gymnopédies.* SAINT-SAËNS: *Allegro appas-*

sionato, Op. 70; Étude en forme de valse, Op. 52/6.
*** HMV Dig. ASD/*TCC-ASD* 4390 [Ang. DS/*4XS* 38104].

An admirable recital by this highly proficient and often impressive French pianist whose reputation has suddenly soared during the last two or three years. There is much to satisfy the connoisseur here, even if not all details will be to all tastes: the Saint-Saëns *Allegro appassionato* is rather shallow but she gives it with panache and style. The Satie pieces could have slightly more sense of movement, perhaps, but few will have quarrels with her Debussy or Ravel. The quality of the recording is very truthful and realistic and admirers of Miss Ousset will find this issue a rewarding introduction to her playing. The ferric tape matches the disc fairly closely, though the upper range of the piano timbre is softer in focus.

Parkin, Eric (piano)

English piano music: IRELAND: *The almond tree; Ballade of London nights; Columbine; 3 Pastels.* BLISS: *Sonata.* BRITTEN: *Holiday diary, Op. 5.* BUSH: *Esquisse le quatorze juillet, Op. 38; Sonatina No. 1.* GOOSSENS: *4 Conceits, Op. 20.* MOERAN: *3 Fancies.* RAWSTHORNE: *Bagatelles.* SCOTT: *Sonata No. 3.*
*** Chan. Dig. DBRD/*DBTD* 2006 (2) [id.].

This two-disc collection is entitled *'John Ireland, his Friends and Pupils'*, but in its variety it provides a good cross-section of the British piano repertory over the first four decades of this century. The pity is that Ireland is not more strongly represented, though his pieces are all distinctive and attractive in their poetic way. The major items are the *Sonatas* of Bliss and Scott, both strongly argued, and the sharpness of the Goossens *Conceits*, written in 1917, makes them equally characterful. Excellent, persuasive performances and first-rate recording on disc and tape alike.

Perkins, Laurence (bassoon), **Michael Hancock** (piano)

'L'après-midi d'un dinosaur': HURLSTONE: *Sonata in F.* ELGAR: *Romance, Op. 62.* JACOB: *4 Sketches.* GOUNOD (arr. Perkins): *Funeral march of a marionette.* IBERT: *Carignane.* PIERNÉ: *Solo de concert, Op. 35.* SENAILLE: *Allegro spiritoso.* SAINT-SAËNS: *Sonata in G, Op. 168.*
*** Hyp. A 66054.

An ingenious title for a highly enjoyable recital, very well recorded (although the acoustic is a trifle over-resonant) on both disc and the excellent tape. The *Sonatas* of Hurlstone and Saint-Saëns are agreeably fluent but, among the miniatures, that Hitchcock tune, Gounod's *Funeral march of a marionette*, and Senaille's *Allegro spiritoso* (made famous by the veteran bassoonist, Archie Camden, as a filler in the days of 78 r.p.m. discs for the last side of Mozart's *Bassoon concerto*) stand out. All the playing is characterful, bringing out the instrument's elegance as well as its humour. The recording balance is very well managed.

Perlman, Itzhak (violin), **Samuel Sanders** (piano)

'Kreisler transcriptions and arrangements': TARTINI: *Devil's Trill sonata.* POLDINI: *Dancing Doll.* WIENIAWSKI: *Caprice in A min.* TRAD.: *Londonderry air.* MOZART: *Serenade No. 7 (Haffner), K.250: Rondo.* CORELLI: *Sarabande and Allegretto.* ALBÉNIZ: *Malagueña, Op. 165/3.* HEUBERGER: *The Midnight Bells.* MENDELSSOHN: *Song without Words, Op. 62/1.* BRAHMS: *Hungarian dance in F min.*
*** HMV ASD 3346 [Ang. S/*4XS* 37254].

Perlman's supreme mastery has rarely been demonstrated more endearingly than in this collection of transcriptions, one of his outstanding Kreisler series, which in almost every way runs rings round any opposition today. Excellent recording.

'Spanish album': FALLA: *Suite populaire espagnole.* GRANADOS: *Spanish dance.*

HALFFTER: *Danza de la gitana*. SARASATE: *Habañera, Op. 21/2. Playera, Op. 23. Spanish dance, Op. 26/8. Malagueña, Op. 21/1. Caprice basque, Op. 24.*
*** HMV ASD 3910 [Ang. SZ/*4ZS* 37590].

Perlman is a violinist who even on record demonstrates his delight in virtuosity in every phrase he plays. There are few more joyful records of violin firework pieces (apt for encores) than this. Excellent recording.

Perlman, Itzhak, Pinchas Zukerman (violins), **Samuel Sanders** (harpsichord), **Timothy Eddy** (cello)

Trio sonatas: BACH, C. P. E.: *Sonata in G, Wq. 157*. BACH, J. C.: *Sonata in B flat*. GOLDBERG: *Sonata in C.*
**(*) HMV Dig. ASD 4172 [Ang. DS/*4XS* 47815].

It is good that this repertoire is not the exclusive preserve of the early-music specialists, for the rich, well-rounded sonority produced by Perlman and Zukerman is in itself a joy while the expressive warmth they command, though far from what the composers and their contemporaries may have encountered, is not completely alien to the sensibility of the period. Those who want a basically nineteenth-century approach to these pieces but who would shrink from an excess of 'romanticism' need not hesitate, for the recording is as clear and warm as the playing. Those conditioned to the constraints of period style should however approach with some caution.

Petri, Egon (piano)

FRANCK: *Prelude, chorale and fugue*. LISZT: *3 Petrarch sonnets, G.158*. BUSONI: *Indianisches Tagebuch*. MEDTNER: *2 Dances, Op. 20; Dansa festiva.*
**(*) Dell'Arte mono/stereo DA 9009.

Neither Busoni nor Medtner (or, come to that, Egon Petri) are so generously represented on record that one can afford to look askance at the present issue. The repertoire derives from Swiss Radio recordings made in 1957 when Petri was already in his mid-seventies, and are mono, save for the César Franck. Petri brought individual insights to Liszt, and as a Busoni pupil his account of the *Indianisches Tagebuch* provides an authoritative link with the past, particularly now that his 1937 Columbia recording (LX 617) has passed out of circulation. He also plays the Medtner pieces with tremendous panache and conviction, and though it is clear that he is not a young man, his technique is still marvellously secure. The recordings do not sound as fresh as one would like and tend to be somewhat bottom-heavy but they still give a more than adequate idea of this great pianist.

Petri, Michala (recorder)

Recorder works (with Hanne and David Petri): CORELLI: *Sonata, Op. 5/12 (La Follia)*. LORENZ: *Variations Nos. 1 and 2 in C for soprano descant recorder*. ANON.: *Greensleeves to a ground*. EYCK, Jacob Van: *Prins Robberts Masco; Philis schoon herderinne; Wat zal men op den avond doen.*
** Ph. Dig. 6514/*7337* 166 [id.].

The transcription of the Corelli *La Follia sonata* is by far the most interesting piece here and it is played most beautifully. Much of the rest of the programme, while demonstrating breathtaking bravura from the soloist, is of minor musical interest and the music for unaccompanied recorder tends to outstay its welcome. The recording is immaculate on disc and cassette alike.

'Intermezzo musicale' (with Hanne and David Petri): HANDEL: *Andante*. COUPERIN, F.: *Le rossignol vainqueur*. LECLAIR: *Tambourin*. BACH: *Siciliano*. TELEMANN: *Rondino*. EYCK, Jacob Van: *Engels Nachtegaeltje*. GOSSEC: *Tambourin*. PAGANINI: *Moto perpetuo, Op. 11*. BRÜGGEN: *2 Studies*. HENNING: *Satie auf hoher See, Op. 52*. HENRIQUES: *Dance of the midges, Op. 20/5*. SCHUBERT: *The Bee*. RIMSKY-KORSAKOV: *The flight of the bumble-bee*. HEBERLE: *Rondo presto*. MONTI: *Czardas.*
❀ *** Ph. 6514/*7337* 324 [id.].

None of Michala Petri's recordings show her remarkable talent more readily than this. The easy virtuosity is breathtaking, with Paganini's famous *Moto perpetuo*, taken at a fizzing pace, showing amazing poise and clarity of articulation. The pieces by Couperin, Henriques and Brüggen are hardly less striking. But the programme is far more than a display of bravura. It is very well planned and the lyrical music (Bach, Handel and the engaging *Satie auf hoher See* by Christiansen Henning) are beautifully played. The recording is in the demonstration class on disc and cassette alike; the whole recital is delightful, with no sense whatsoever of monotony of timbre. Indeed the ear is led on from each piece to the next.

Pinnock, Trevor (harpsichord or virginals)

'At the Victoria and Albert Museum' (Queen Elizabeth's virginals; harpsichords): ANON.: *My Lady Wynkfylds rownde.* BYRD: *The Queenes alman. The Bells.* HANDEL: *Harpsichord suite No. 5 in E.* CROFT: *Suite No. 3 in C min.* ARNE: *Sonata No. 3 in G.* BACH, J. C.: *Sonata in C min., Op. 5/6.*
**(*) CRD CRD 1007/*CRDC 4007* [id.].

Trevor Pinnock opens this recital by playing three attractive and very colourful pieces on an instrument originally belonging to Queen Elizabeth I, who was an accomplished virginal player. It is in splendid condition and has a most attractive sound. Pinnock plays it with enthusiasm, and his performance of Byrd's extraordinarily descriptive *The Bells* is a *tour de force*. For the rest of the recital he uses two different harpsichords, also part of the Victoria and Albert Museum collection. His style in the works by Handel, Croft, Arne and J. C. Bach is less flamboyant, more circumspect, but the music is strongly characterized and boldly recorded. The Handel suite is the one which has the *Harmonious Blacksmith* as its finale. Disc and cassette are closely matched.

'A choice collection of lessons and ayres': PLAYFORD: *From Musick's Handmaid: 3 Pieces.* LOCKE: *Melothesia: Suite No. 4 in D.* PURCELL: *Musick's Handmaid, Part 2: A new Irish tune; Ground. A Choice Collection of Lessons: Suite No. 2 in G min.* BLOW: *Musick's Handmaid, Part 2: Mortlack's Ground.* GREENE: *Overture in D.* ARNE: *Sonata No. 6 in G.* NARES: *Lesson No. 2 in D.* PARADIES: *Sonata No. 6 in A.*
*** CRD CRD 1047/*CRDC 4047* [id.].

An outstanding collection, splendidly played and recorded and with a very well-planned programme. Pinnock uses a modern copy (by Clayson and Garrett) of a Dülcken of 1745. It is a magnificent instrument, and the three colourful opening pieces from John Playford's *Musick's Handmaid* immediately captivate the ear: *The Grange* is followed by *Lord Monck's March*, and last comes a miniature portrait of *Gerard's Mistress*. All three last for only 2′ 48″, yet demonstrate a remarkable range of colour and feeling. The music on the first side comes from important seventeenth-century collections and it is all of high quality. For side two we move on to the eighteenth century, and the programme is hardly less rewarding. All this music is splendidly alive in Trevor Pinnock's hands, and stylistically he is impeccable. The sound balance is very realistic on disc and cassette alike; indeed the tape is of demonstration quality.

'Sixteenth-century harpsichord and virginal music': (Harpsichord) BYRD: *Watkin's ale. La Volta – Lady Morley. Lord Willoughby's welcome home. The Carmans whistle.* GIBBONS: *The Woods so wild. Mask – The Fairest Nymph. The Lord of Salisbury his Pavin and Galiardo.* BULL: *The King's hunt. My Grief; My Self.* FARNABY: *Muscadin or Kempe's Morris. Loath to depart.* TOMKINS: *Barafostus's dream.* (Virginals) ANON.: *My Lady Carey's dompe.* TALLIS: *O ye tender babes.* RANDALL: *Dowland's Lachrimae and galliard: Can she excuse.*
*** CRD CRD 1050/*CRDC 4050* [id.].

This programme is cleverly arranged so that on each side a central section for virginals is framed by major items on the harpsichord. On side one the two virginal pieces nearly steal the show, for the engaging *My Lady Carey's dompe* is beautifully set off by Tallis's expressively eloquent *O ye tender babes*. There is some superb bravura from Pinnock in the harpsichord music. *The King's hunt* is splendidly vigorous, and *Lord Salisbury's Pavin and Galiardo* have comparable poise and elegance. Indeed everything here springs vividly to life, and Pinnock's decoration is always well judged, adding piquancy and zest to the fast pieces. As on the companion recital (above) the recording is outstanding, on both disc and cassette, and the result is irresistible.

Pré, Jacqueline du (cello), **Gerald Moore** (piano) (see also under Concerts)

'Recital': PARADIES: *Sicilienne*. SCHUMANN: *Fantasiestücke. Op. 73.* MENDELSSOHN: *Song without words, Op. 109.* FAURÉ: *Élégie, Op. 24.* BACH: *Adagio, BWV 564* (with Roy Jesson). SAINT-SAËNS: *Carnival of the animals: The Swan* (with O. Ellis). FALLA: *Suite populaire espagnole; Jota* (with J. Williams). BRUCH: *Kol Nidrei, Op. 47.*
❀ (M) *** HMV HQS/*TC-HQS* 1437.

This heart-warming record collects the recordings Jacqueline du Pré made in her teens for EMI plus the beautiful performance of Fauré's *Élégie* she recorded in 1969 with Gerald Moore for his seventieth-birthday record. There have been few performances of Saint-Saëns' *The Swan* to match this in natural, unforced expressiveness (beautifully accompanied on the harp by Osian Ellis), and the other items all have one marvelling at the musical maturity of so young a virtuoso. Excellent transfers. The cassette is naturally balanced but lacks sharpness of focus in the upper range compared with the disc.

Preston, Simon (organ of Westminster Abbey)

'Crown Imperial': WALTON: *Crown Imperial march.* CLARKE: *Prince of Denmark's march.* HANDEL: *Saul: Dead march.* PURCELL: *Trumpet tune.* ELGAR: *Imperial march.* VIERNE: (Organ) *Symphony No. 1: Finale.* WAGNER: *Tannhäuser: Pilgrims' chorus.* GUILMANT: *March on a theme of Handel.* SCHUMANN: *Study No. 5.* KARG-ELERT: *Marche triomphale* (*Now thank we all our God*).
(M) *** Argo SPA/*KCSP* 507.

A spectacular issue which is in every way successful. Simon Preston uses wide dynamic contrasts to increase the impact of his programme, and Walton's *Crown Imperial* has a panoply of sound which compares very favourably with an orchestral recording. The Vierne and the Karg-Elert items both lend themselves admirably to such flamboyance and tonal opulence. The transfer to tape is of high quality, clean, and with the wide dynamic range accommodated without stress, even when the high-level transfer takes the indicator needles into the red area.

Ragossnig, Konrad, and **Walter Feybli** (guitars)

'Music for two guitars': BARRIOS: *Danza Paraguaya.* CRESPO: *Nortena.* LAURO: *Vals venezelano.* PONCE: *Valse. 3 Mexican popular songs.* VILLA-LOBOS: *Chôros No. 1. Cirandinhas Nos. 1 and 10.* TRAD.: *Boleras sevillanas. Salamanca. Villancico. De blanca tierra. Buenos reyes. Linda amiga. El puerto. El pano moruno. Cantar montanes. Tutu maramba. Cubana.*
(M) *** Saga 5412.

This attractive recital of Spanish and South American music features a guitar duo of some personality; they make a good team and bring their diverse programme fully alive. The recording is excellent. A genuine bargain.

Robles, Marisa (harp)

'The world of the harp': FALLA: *The Three-cornered Hat: Danza del Corregidor.* ALBÉNIZ: *Rumores de la caleta. La torre bermeja.* GURIDI: *Viejo Zortzico.* MOZART: *Theme, Variations and Rondo pastorale.* BEETHOVEN: *Variations on a Swiss air.* BRITTEN: *A Ceremony of Carols: Interlude.* FAURÉ: *Impromptu, Op. 86.* PIERNÉ:

Impromptu-caprice, Op. 9. SALZEDO: *Chanson de la nuit.*
(M) *** Decca SPA/*KCSP* 348.

The artistry of Marisa Robles ensures that this is an attractive anthology and the programme is as well chosen as it is beautifully played. The recording too is excellent, although the cassette is spoiled by too high a transfer level, which produces a generally uncomfortable feeling and hints of underlying harmonic distortion.

Romero, Pepe (guitar)

'Famous Spanish guitar music': ANON.: *Jeux interdits.* ALBÉNIZ: *Asturias.* MALATS: *Serenata española.* TARREGA: *Capricho Ababe.* SOR: *Introduction and variations on a theme of Mozart, Op. 9.* TARREGA: *Recuerdos de la Alhambra; Tango (Maria); Marieta; Las dos hermanitas.* TÓRROBA: *Romance de los pinos.* ROMERO, Celedonio: *Malagueña; Fantasia.*
(*) Ph. Dig. **411 033-2; 6514/*7337* 381.

A thoroughly professional and immaculately played collection of favourites. The effect is rather calculated and sometimes a little chocolate-boxy – the virtuoso showing his paces in familiar vehicles. Of course a bravura piece like Tarrega's *Recuerdos de la Alhambra* cannot fail to make a strong impression, and the Torroba *Romance* is very beguiling too. The Flamenco-based pieces by the composer's father, Celedonio, bring a sudden hint of fire, but for the most part the easy style of the playing does not generate a great deal of electricity. The recording is very natural and sounds well in all three formats, but even the compact disc gives a touch of blandness to the focus. No information is provided about the music (except titles).

Romero, Pepe, and **Celin Romero** (guitars)

'Famous Spanish dances': GRANADOS: *Danzas españoles, Op. 37, Nos. 2, 4, 5 and 10. Goyescas: Intermezzo.* ALBÉNIZ: *Suite española, Op. 47: Granada. Recuerdos de viaje, Op. 71: Rumores de la caleta. España, Op. 165: Tango; Malagueña.* FALLA: *El amor brujo: Ritual fire dance; Three-cornered Hat: Miller's dance.*
(*) Ph. Dig. **411 432-2; 6514/*7337* 182.

Here two guitars are not appreciably better than one, for these two artists blend their music-making rather cosily together, rather than striking sparks off each other, as do Julian Bream and John Williams. The music for the most part is rather gently projected (witness the opening Granados *Spanish dance*, which does not have the electrifying impact of Julian Bream's solo version) but not necessarily the worse for that, for the playing is musical and quite spontaneous. An enjoyable collection for late-evening listening, then, well recorded on CD, disc and tape alike, although the last is transferred at an astonishingly low level.

Rawsthorne, Noel (organ of Liverpool Cathedral)

'Toccata': Toccatas: BACH: *in D min., BWV 565.* REGER: *in D min., Op. 59/5.* BOËLLMANN: from *Suite Gothique, Op. 25.* GIGOUT: from *Dix Pièces.* WIDOR: from *Symphony No. 5.* WHITLOCK: from *Plymouth suite.* MATHIAS: *Toccata giocosa, Op. 36/2.* MULET: *Carillon-Sortie; Esquisses Byzantines; Tu es Petrus.* EDMUNDSON: *Prelude No. 4.*
(M) *(*) HMV Green. ESD/*TC-ESD* 7144.

Although this was originally recorded in EMI's Studio Two system which sought to make everything seem bright and clear, the effect is far from that, with the reverberant acoustic of Liverpool Cathedral letting the music spread into a sea of sound, with poor inner detail. Moreover the French music needs a sharper timbre than this. Bach's *Toccata* suffers from clouding and the decorations of the mighty Edmundson *Prelude on Vom Himmel hoch* are rather messy. Rawsthorne plays well, although the Widor *Toccata* tends to sag in the middle, lacking strong forward impulse. Like the disc, the cassette is not well focused.

Rubinstein, Artur (piano)

'L'Amour de la vie' (music from his film bio-

graphy): CHOPIN: *Polonaise in A flat, Op. 53. Nocturne in D flat, Op. 27/2.* VILLA-LOBOS: *Polichinelle.* SCHUMANN: *Fantasiestücke, Op. 12: Des Abends.* PROKOFIEV: *The Love of Three Oranges: March.* BEETHOVEN: *Sonata No. 23 in F min.* (*Appassionata*), *Op. 57:* 1st movt. LISZT: *Liebestraum No. 3, G.541.* MENDELSSOHN: *Spinning song.* FALLA: *Ritual fire dance.*
(M) *** RCA Gold GL/*GK* 42708.

The issue of a Rubinstein recital on a mid-price label was prompted by the pianist's film biography. Some of the playing is marvellous, the melting Chopin *Nocturne*, the richly romantic yet never sentimental *Liebestraum*, and the perky Prokofiev *March*; and the collection ends with Rubinstein's favourite encore, the Falla *Ritual fire dance*, sounding for all the world as if it were originally written for the piano. The tautly tuned instrument usually favoured by Rubinstein for recording produces some shallowness of tone in fortissimos, but the great pianist coaxes a warm, singing timbre from it for the lyrical music. The cassette transfer is crisply focused and has excellent range.

Segovia, Andrés (guitar)

'Reveries': GLUCK: *Orfeo ed Euridice: Dance of the Blessed Spirits.* SCHUMANN: *Album for the Young, Op. 68, Nos. 1–2, 5–6, 9–10, 16 and 26. Scenes from Childhood, Op. 15: Träumerei. Romanza.* ASENCIO: *Mystic suite.* CASTELNUOVO-TEDESCO: *Ronsard.* MORENO-TÓRROBA: *Castellana.*
*** RCA RL/*RK* 12602 [ARL1/*ARK1* 2602].

At once intimate and gently evocative, this 1977 recital was carefully programmed so as not to strain the eighty-four-year-old maestro's resources. Indeed he shows admirable technical assurance. The music is slight, but undoubtedly charming, and is presented with great affection. The playing throughout has a degree of spontaneity rare in guitar recordings, especially where the element of repose is inherent in the atmosphere. The recording is completely real and the transfer immaculate.

'The art of Segovia' (the HMV recordings 1927–39): BACH: (Unaccompanied) *Violin partita No. 3, BWV 1006: Gavotte.* (Unaccompanied) *Cello suite No. 1, BWV 1007: Prelude; Cello suite No. 3, BWV 1009: Courante. Clavierbüchlein: Prelude in C min., BWV 999. Lute suite in E min., BWV 996: Allemande. Violin sonata No. 1, BWV 1001: Fugue in G min.* PONCE/WEISS: *Suite in A.* PONCE: *Sonata No. 3:* 1st movt. *Sonata No. 2: Canción; Postlude; Mazurka; Petite valse; Folies d'Espagne.* SOR: *Thème varié, Op. 9.* VISÉE: *Sarabande. Bourrée. Menuet.* FROBERGER: *Gigue.* TÓRROBA: *Sonatina in A: Allegretto. Suite Castellana: Fandanguillo. Preludio. Nocturno.* MALATS: *Serenata.* MENDELSSOHN: *String quartet No. 1 in E flat, Op. 12: Canzonetta.* TARREGA: *Recuerdos de la Alhambra; Study in A.* CASTELNUOVO-TEDESCO: *Sonata* (*Homage to Boccherini*)*: Vivo ed energico.* ALBÉNIZ: *Suite española: Granada; Sevilla.* TURINA: *Fandanguillo.* GRANADOS: *Danzas españolas, Op. 37: Nos. 5 in E min.; 10 in G.*
(M) (***) HMV mono RLS 745 (2) [ZB/*4Z2S* 3896].

It was Segovia's pioneering recitals in the 1930s that re-established the guitar in the public mind as a serious solo instrument. This collection consists of his early recordings made over a span of twelve years. There are many transcriptions, including a good deal of Bach, where the style of the playing is romantic (though never showing lapses of taste). What is so striking throughout this collection is the way all the music, slight or serious, springs vividly to life. Segovia had the gift of natural spontaneity in all he played, and he was in his prime at this period, so that technically this is wonderfully assured. Guitar fans will find the set an essential purchase; others will be surprised to discover that no apologies are needed for the sound, which is natural in timbre and gives the instrument a ready projection.

Söllscher, Göran (guitar)

'Greensleeves': ANON./CUTTING: *Greensleeves.* ANON.: *Kemp's jig; Packington's*

round; Frog galliard. GALILEI: *Toccata corrente; Volta.* WEISS: *Fantasie; Ciacona.* BACH (trans. Segovia): *Chaconne* (from *Violin Partita No. 2*). SOR: *Variations on Marlborough s'en va-t-en guerre, Op. 28.*
** DG Dig. **413 352-2**; 2532/*3302* 054.

Söllscher is a fine player and he is beautifully recorded (with a splendid matching cassette). His playing is very positive, but not always relaxed enough to charm. He is at his finest in the famous Bach *Chaconne* where his firm control and impeccable technique serve the music well, and then he relaxes attractively for the final item – the Sor *Variations* – and closes the recital with engaging communication.

Still, Ray (oboe), **Itzhak Perlman** (violin), **Pinchas Zukerman** (viola), **Lynn Harrell** (cello)

Oboe quartets: BACH, J. C.: *Oboe quartet in B flat.* MOZART: *Oboe quartet in F, K.370.* VANHAL: *Oboe quartet, Op. 7/1.* STAMITZ: *Oboe quartet in E flat, Op. 8/4.*
*** HMV ASD 3916 [Ang. S/*4XS* 37756].

Ray Still, principal oboe of the Chicago Symphony Orchestra for a generation, is a superb artist, a splendid foil for the three stars of string playing who complete the ensemble. This is the finest performance available of the Mozart, gently pointed but not mannered, and the recording – close and domestic-sounding – is excellent. The three companion works are no more than charming – the Stamitz clearly imitating the Mozart with a minor-key slow movement – but make an excellent coupling.

Stringer, Alan (trumpet), **Noel Rawsthorne** (organ of Liverpool Cathedral)

'Trumpet and organ': CHARPENTIER, Marc-Antoine: *Te Deum: Prelude.* STANLEY: *Voluntary No. 5 in D.* PURCELL: *Sonata in C. Two Trumpet tunes and Air.* BOYCE: *Voluntary in D.* CLARKE: *Trumpet voluntary.* BALDASSARE: *Sonata No. 1 in F.* ROMAN: *Keyboard suite in D: Non troppo allegro; Presto (Gigue).* FIOCCO: *Harpsichord suite No. 1: Andante.* BACH: *Cantata No. 147: Jesu, joy of man's desiring.* attrib. GREENE: *Introduction and trumpet tune.* VIVIANI: *Sonata No. 1 in C.*
**(*) CRD CRD 1008/*CRDC 4008.*

This collection is extremely well recorded. The reverberation of Liverpool Cathedral is under full control and both trumpet and organ are cleanly focused, while the trumpet has natural timbre and bloom. Alan Stringer is at his best in the classical pieces, the *Voluntary* of Boyce, the *Trumpet tunes* and *Sonata* of Purcell and the stylishly played *Sonata* of Viviani, a most attractive little work. He also gives a suitably robust performance of the famous *Trumpet voluntary.* Elsewhere he is sometimes a little square: the Bach chorale is rather too stiff and direct. But admirers of this repertoire will find much to enjoy, and the *Andante* of Fiocco has something in common with the more famous *Adagio* attributed to Albinoni in Giazotto's famous arrangement. Cassette and disc are closely matched.

'Toccata'

Organ toccatas (with (i) Wicks; (ii) Weir; (iii) Hurford; (iv) Preston; (v) Nicholas): (i) BACH: *Toccata and fugue in D min., BWV 565.* (ii) *Toccata, adagio and fugue in C, BWV 564.* (iii) BUXTEHUDE: *Toccata and fugue in F.* (iv) WIDOR: *Symphony No. 5, Op. 42/1: Toccata.* (v) BOËLLMANN: *Suite gothique, Op. 25: Toccata.* (iv) REGER: *Toccata and fugue, Op. 59/5–6.* (ii) MULET: *Toccata: Tu es Petrus.* DUBOIS: *Toccata.*
(M) **(*) Decca SPA/*KCSP* 583.

Highlights here are Gillian Weir's impressive account of Bach's *Toccata, adagio and fugue in C,* with the fugue superbly buoyant. She ends the collection with an equally exciting performance of the Dubois *Toccata,* an essentially genial piece. The celebrated Widor finale comes off well too, but Alan Wicks's version of Bach's most famous organ work is a shade too relaxed, and even Simon Preston cannot make the Reger Op. 59 sound other than an academic exercise. Excellent recording throughout; the tape transfer offers no problems.

'Great organ works' (played by (i) Cleobury; (ii) Karl Richter; (iii) Pearson; (iv) Nicholas; (v) Preston): (i) WIDOR: *Organ symphony No. 5: Toccata.* (ii) BACH: *Chorale: Wachet auf, BWV 645;* (iii) *Toccata and fugue in D min., BWV 565;* (i) *Cantata No. 147: Jesu, joy of man's desiring.* (iv) CLARKE: *Trumpet voluntary.* HANDEL: *Water music: Air. Xerxes: Largo.* (v) KARG-ELERT: *Marche triomphale.* (ii) LISZT: *Fantasia on BACH.*
(M) **(*) Decca VIV/*KVIC* 36.

This collection successfully embraces a wide range of styles and the spectacular pieces (notably Karg-Elert and the Liszt *Fantasia*) make an impressively powerful impact. The chorales offer welcome contrast, although the inclusion of Handel's *Largo* within a compilation named '*Toccata*' seems curious. Performances are consistent (the famous Bach *D minor Fugue* is strikingly fluent) and so is the sound, both on disc and on the excellent cassette.

Tracey, Bradford (double virginal)

SWEELINCK: *Preludium toccata.* MORLEY: *Lachrymae pavane and galliard.* LASSUS: *Susanne un jour.* TISDALE: *Coranto.* BULL: *Lord Lumley's pavane and galliard. The Prince's galliard. Preludium and fantasia.* GIBBONS: *Fantasia in A min. Ground in A min.* SCHEIDT: *Bergamasque.*
(M) **(*) Tel. AP6/*CR4* 42074.

Another of Telefunken's recital series using original instruments, this collection demonstrates the potential of the double virginal, a visually fascinating two-manual instrument nicknamed 'mother and child' because the smaller keyboard sits above its parent. The instrument here is a copy of a sixteenth-century Ruckers; it has a splendid sound and is superbly recorded – the chrome cassette and disc are alike of demonstration standard. Bradford Tracey's style is essentially robust and rhythmically strong; this suits the short dances and gives them plenty of character, but it makes the longer works seem heavy going. One feels that more imaginative use could have been made of the contrasts of colour between the two keyboards. Nevertheless this is a thoroughly worthwhile issue.

Vered, Ilana (piano)

'Piano moods': LISZT: *Hungarian rhapsody No. 2 in C sharp min., G.244; Liebestraum No. 3, G.541.* SATIE: *Gymnopédie No. 1.* CHOPIN: *Étude in C min.* (*Revolutionary*), *Op. 10/12.* DEBUSSY: *Suite bergamasque: Clair de lune.* RACHMANINOV: *Prelude in C sharp min., Op. 3/2.* SCHUMANN: *Kinderscenen, Op. 15: Träumerei.* SCHUBERT: *Moment musical No. 3 in F min., D.780/3.* BACH: *Cantata No. 147: Jesu, joy of man's desiring* (arr. Hess). BEN-HAIM: *Toccata.*
(B) *** Con. CC/*CCT* 7558.

An excellent bargain-priced recital from a fine pianist who made a gramophone début on Decca's Phase Four label and perhaps suffered from not being associated with that company's normal classical catalogue. The recording here which dates from 1977, though closely balanced, sounds most realistic and the performances are strongly characterized and show a wide range of sensibility. There is no lack of bravura, as is readily demonstrated by the excitingly brilliant account of the closing *Toccata* by Paul Ben-Haim. Overall the programme is well balanced and this is a genuine bargain.

Williams, John (guitar)

Guitar recital 1: ALBÉNIZ: *Torre bermeja.* PONCE: *3 Mexican popular songs.* VILLA-LOBOS: *Étude No. 1 in E min.* CRESPO: *Nortena.* DUARTE: *Variations on a Catalan folksong, Op. 25.* SOR: *Variations on a theme of Mozart, Op. 9.* SEGOVIA: *Oración study in E. Estudio. Humorada.* TANSMAN: *Barcarolle.* GRANADOS: *La maja de Goya.* LAURO: *Valse criollo.*

Guitar recital 2: BACH: (Unaccompanied) *Cello suites Nos. 1 in G, BWV 1007; 3 in C, BWV 1009.* SCARLATTI, D.: *Sonata in E min.,*

Kk.11. SCARLATTI, A.: *Gavotte.*
(B) **(*) Decca DPA/*KDPC* 579/80. Recital 2 only: (M) SPA/*KCSP* 592.

This collection dates from 1959 and was originally issued (in disc form) on the Delysé label. When Decca took over the catalogue the material was remastered and rearranged into this double-recital format, with the classical items (Bach and Scarlatti) in one group and the other devoted to the mainly Latin material. John Williams's playing shows complete technical assurance and his keenly intelligent mind provides concentration even in the trifles (he is nowhere more beguiling than in the little Tansman *Barcarolle*). There is undoubtedly a lack of temperament in the Spanish repertoire, but the playing is never dull; the control of colour and dynamic keeps the music alive. The Bach suites, arranged by John Duarte, are transcribed into keys suitable to the guitar: No. 1 is transposed up a fifth to D and No. 3 down a third to A minor. They are played soberly and conscientiously, and some may seek more flair: yet the thoughtfulness of the music-making, with its conscious use of light and shade, is certainly impressive. The recording is of high quality; it does not sound in the least dated. Discs and cassettes are virtually identical. As can be seen above, the second recital is also available separately.

'The best of John Williams': BACH: *Lute suite No. 4: Gavotte.* GRANADOS: *Spanish dance No. 5.* FALLA: *The Three-cornered Hat: Miller's dance.* ALBÉNIZ: *Asturias.* TARREGA: *Recuerdos de la Alhambra.* VILLA-LOBOS: *Prelude No. 2.* PRAETORIUS: *La Volta.* TELEMANN: *Bourrée alla polacca* (with instrumental group). SCARLATTI, D.: *Sonata in E, Kk.380.* SAGRERAS: *El Colibri.* TRAD.: *El Testamen de Amelia.* LAURO: *Valse criollo.* PONCE: *Scherzino Mexicano.* VIVALDI: *Guitar concerto in D* (with ECO).
(M) **(*) CBS 61843/*40*- [(d) M/*MT* 31407].

The best of John Williams spans just over a decade of recording with CBS. Much of the material here has previously been available on a now deleted compilation called *Greatest hits.* The anthology is an essentially popular one and although it concentrates on Latin repertoire there is a leavening of baroque (including a short concerto by Vivaldi), and even a contribution from Praetorius. For those who are not guitar specialists it represents excellent value, although not better than the more extensive and better-balanced anthology in the Decca set above. The recording is excellent and the cassette transfer is acceptable, though not as crisp as some of John Williams's full-priced tapes; the orchestral detail in the Vivaldi is unrefined.

'Spanish music': ALBÉNIZ, I.: *Asturias; Tango; Cordoba.* SANZ: *Canarios.* RODRIGO: *Fandango.* TÓRROBA: *Nocturno.* GRANADOS: *Valses poeticos; La Maja de Goya.* ALBÉNIZ, M.: *Sonata in D.* FALLA: *Danse du Corregidor; Fisherman's song; Miller's dance.* TÓRROBA: *Madranos.* TRAD. (Catalan): *La nuit de Nadal: El noy de la mare.*
*** CBS 72860/*40*- [M/*MT* 30057].

This is easily the most electric of John Williams's solo recitals and it provides one of the most exciting records of Spanish guitar music in the catalogues. The opening of Albéniz's *Asturias* is gently atmospheric and then slowly the music is led to crescendo into a flashing climax. The same bright-eyed sparkle of conscious bravura emerges again and again throughout the disc, and the programme is cleverly planned to give contrast where needed. For instance, side two opens with a marvellous performance of the delightful *Sonata in D* by Mateo Albéniz (not the famous Isaac) of great dynamic subtlety; then follows Falla's rhythmic *Corregidor's dance* from the *Three-cornered Hat*, and with a magical mood change comes a hauntingly registered transcription of the lovely *Fisherman's song* from *El amor brujo.* It is this interplay of mood, created with the spontaneity of a live recital, that makes this vividly recorded disc so memorable. There is a good cassette.

'More Spanish music': TARREGA: *Recuerdos de la Alhambra.* GRANADOS: *Spanish dance No. 5.* TÓRROBA: *Aires de la Mancha.* VILLA-LOBOS: *Preludes Nos. 2 in E; 4 in E min.* ALBÉNIZ: *Sevilla.* SOR: *Variations on a theme by Mozart, Op. 9.* FALLA: *Homenaje.* MUDAR-

RA: *Fantasia.* TURINA: *Fandanguillo, Op. 36.*
*** CBS 72950/*40*-.

John Williams plays Spanish music not in a direct, intense manner (like Yepes, for instance) but thoughtfully and evocatively, with instinctive control of atmosphere and dynamics. His approach can be heard at its most magical in Turina's *Fandanguillo.* The sophisticated use of rubato and colour in the Granados *Spanish dance* is almost orchestral and very effective. Above all the playing sounds spontaneous, and (as the restrained virtuosity of the famous fluttering *Recuerdos de la Alhambra* readily shows) Williams's technique is phenomenal and always at the service of the music. There is some superb pianissimo evocation in the Villa-Lobos *Prelude*, while the control of rubato is at its most subtle in the middle section of the Albéniz *Sevilla*, which ends side one. The recording is clear and immediate and is admirably transferred to tape.

'Music from Japan, England and Latin America': YOCOH: *Theme and variations on 'Sakura'.* DODGSON: *Fantasy-Divisions.* PONCE: *Sonatina Meridional.* VILLA-LOBOS: *Chôros No. 1.* LAURO: *Valse criollo.* CRESPO: *Nortena.* SOJO: *5 Venezuelan pieces.* BARRIOS: *Danza Paraguaya.*
*** CBS 73205/*40*- [M/*MT* 35123].

An exotic and lively programme and not an insubstantial one. The Dodgson piece is by no means lightweight, and it makes a good foil for the Villa-Lobos *Chôros* which it follows. In his programme note John Williams draws the parallel between the guitar and the Japanese koto, and certainly the *Sakura* variations transcribe effectively to the Western instrument. The Venezuelan pieces are inventive and colourful too. Williams is a superbly assured and stylish advocate, and the recording here has fine presence, with an excellent tape transfer.

'John Williams and friends' (with Carlos Bonell, guitar; Brian Gascoign, Morris Pert, marimbas and vibraphone; Keith Marjoram, bass): VIVALDI: *Double guitar concerto in G* (originally for 2 mandolins). DAQUIN: *Le Coucou.* BACH: *Cello suite No. 3: Bourrée. Cantata No. 147: Jesu, joy of man's desiring. Trio sonata in C, BWV 1037: Gigue.* TELEMANN: *Bourrée alla polacca.* PURCELL: *Trio sonata No. 11 in F min.* MOZART: *Adagio (for glass harmonica), K.356. Piano sonata No. 11 in A, K.331: Rondo alla turca.*
* CBS 73487/*40*- [M 35108].

There is nothing inherently wrong in using an offbeat instrumental and percussive combination for a concert of mainly baroque music, so long as the chosen timbres do not rob the music of vitality. But this collection is too soft-centred by half. Bach and Vivaldi are vitiated by marimbas – at least as presented here – and only Daquin's *Le Coucou* (although it sounds chocolate-boxy) begins to justify the experiment. For the rest the flabby sounds created will appeal only to the listener more oriented to 'pop' than the concert hall. The recording is good, but the cassette transfer is not very crisp.

'The guitar is the song': TRAD.: *Wraggle-Taggle gypsies; Hajrá Kati; Ssák egy Kislany; Queen of Hearts; Petronella; St Patrick's Day; Búącállan Buidhe; Scarborough Fair; Carnaval; Seis por derecho; Over the sea to Skye; Mashilaé; Music box tune; Waly waly; Shenandoah; So we'll go no more a-roving.* CORDI: *Catari, catari.* DE CURTIS: *Tu ca'nun chigne.*
**(*) CBS 73679/*40*- [FM/*FMT* 37825].

A highly agreeable collection of folk material, essentially lightweight but undoubtedly tuneful, played with John Williams's usual flair and technical expertise. The recording is forward but very realistic in both formats.

'Recollections': ALBÉNIZ: *Sevilla. Tango.* SCARLATTI, D.: *Sonata in E, Kk.380.* RODRIGO: *Concierto de Aranjeuz: Adagio* (with ECO, Barenboim). LAURO: *Valse criollo.* BACH: *Jesu, joy of man's desiring. Lute suite No. 4, BWV 1006a: Gavotte.* BARRIOS: *Maxixa.* VILLA-LOBOS: *Prelude No. 1.* GOWERS: *Stevie.* TÓRROBA: *Madronos.* GRANADOS: *Spanish dance No. 5.* THEODORAKIS: *3 Epitafios.*
**(*) CBS 10016/*40*-.

This collection is made up from older recitals (which are currently coming under the deletions axe). The arrangement of items is not especially felicitous, and the overall effect does not achieve the evocative nostalgia suggested by the title. Indeed the Bach chorale has an unstylish accompaniment. However, much of this playing is of high quality, and it is cleanly recorded, with the disc rather more refined than the cassette.

'The John Williams collection': VILLA-LOBOS: *Prelude No. 1 in E min.* DOWLAND: *Fantasie No. 7.* BARRIOS: *Madrigal Gavota.* RODRIGO: *Concierto de Aranjuez: Adagio* (with ECO, Barenboim). BACH: *Cantata No. 147: Jesu, joy of man's desiring.* ALBÉNIZ, M.: *Sonata in D.* ALBÉNIZ, I.: *Asturias.* PAGANINI: *Caprice No. 24, Op. 1.* GRANADOS: *La maja de Goya.* MOZART: *Piano sonata No. 11 in A. K.331: Rondo alla turca.*
**(*) CBS 73784/*40*-.

This is a further shrewd compilation made from John Williams's earlier recordings and it deserves to be a best-seller. Opening atmospherically with Villa-Lobos, the programme shows this artist's wide talents at their best. Whether in the charmingly ingenuous sonata by Mateo Albéniz or the lyrical intensity of the Rodrigo *Adagio* (marvellously played) or the sheer electricity of Isaac Albéniz's *Asturias*, Williams is totally compelling. The drawback for some will be the Bach and Mozart pieces with marimbas and vibraphone ad lib., taken from *John Williams and friends* (see above). The recording has been strikingly well transferred to tape; the sound is admirably crisp and clean, and in the concerto the orchestra has good presence.

'Portrait': LAURO: *Seis por perecho; El Negrito.* CLARE: *Castilla.* TARREGA: *Recuerdos de la Alhambra.* BACH: *Cello suite No. 1 in G, BWV 1007; Prelude.* VIVALDI: *Concerto in D* (with orch.). LENNON/MCCARTNEY: *Fool on the hill.* BARRIOS: *Vals, Op. 8/4.* BROUWER: *Guajira; Danza caracteristica.* MYERS: *Cavatina.* YOCOH: *Sakura.*
**(*) CBS Dig. 37791/*40*- [id.].

John Williams's digital debut is a little disappointing. The solo items are forwardly balanced and the sound is somewhat clinical. The Vivaldi *Concerto*, recorded with a chamber orchestra, also sounds rather meagre in texture. The highlights are the famous *Recuerdos de la Alhambra*, the engaging version of *Fool on the hill* and the Myers *Cavatina*, which are given a string accompaniment and recorded more atmospherically. But most memorable of all is the delicious *Sakura*, a traditional Japanese melody with variations where, as John Williams aptly comments, the spaces between the notes are as important as the notes themselves.

Yamash'ta, Stomu (percussion)

'Recital': HENZE: *Prison song.* TAKEMITSU: *Seasons.* MAXWELL DAVIES: *Turis campanarum sonantium.*
*** O-L DSLO 1.

An exciting issue, revealing Yamash'ta as a major creative artist. Henze's remarkable *Prison song* was written especially for him. Whether or not it is a masterpiece, the performance here is totally compelling. The words of the poem (from the *Prison Diary of Ho Chi Minh*) are mixed in with a pre-recorded musique concrète tape, and to this the percussionist adds his own rhythmic commentary. Yamash'ta both recites (if that is the word – the vocal delivery is quite different from anything one might expect) and plays, and the result is an artistic *tour de force*. Toru Takemitsu's *Seasons* is strong in atmosphere, but does not quite match the imaginative quality of Peter Maxwell Davies's *Turis campanarum sonantium.* In this work (lasting a whole side) Yamash'ta creates and holds the strongest possible tension and builds a climax of tremendous power. The Decca recording is flawless – truly demonstration-worthy. This is a record not to be missed by those interested in twentieth-century avant-garde music.

Yepes, Narciso (guitar)

'The world of the Spanish guitar': VILLA-

LOBOS: *Chôros No. 1. Prelude No. 1.* TARREGA: *Recuerdos de la Alhambra. Capricho Arabe.* TURINA: *Garrotín. Soleares. Rafaga.* TÓRROBA: *Madronos.* SOR: *Variations on a theme by Mozart, Op. 9.* ALBÉNIZ: *Torre bermeja. Granada. Asturias. Rumores de la caleta.* FALLA: *The Three-cornered Hat: Miller's dance.*
(M) *** Decca SPA 179 [Lon. STS/*5*-15224].

Narciso Yepes's characteristic fluency and the natural freedom of his style are immediately noticeable in the opening Villa-Lobos pieces. This playing has striking temperament and the improvisatory flair which can give the solo guitar its special magnetism. The recording is not new and the solo image has less body than in Yepes's more modern DG recitals, but the quality is perfectly acceptable and always true in timbre and clear in focus. The items by Albéniz are particularly colourful (notably the *Asturias*), and the flexibility of Sor's *Mozart variations* is most appealing.

'Guitar music of 5 centuries': ADRIAENSEN: *Chanson anglaise.* KELLNER: *Fantasia in C; Aria; Fantasia in D.* DOWLAND: *The King of Denmark, his galliard.* STRAUBE: *Sonata in E.* ROLDAN: *Au clair de la lune.* POULENC: *Sarabande.* GOMBAU: *Trois morceaux de la belle époque.* TURINA: *Garrotin. Soleares. Rafaga.*
**(*) DG 2531/*3301* 382 [id.].

Yepes plays with his usual musicianship in the first part of this recital, but the music springs more readily to life on side two with the variations on *Au clair de la lune* by Roldan, and here the Spanish music has striking colour and spontaneity. The sound is natural, the cassette lacking the last degree of range but well balanced.

'Spanish guitar music': ALBÉNIZ: *Suite española: Asturias. Recuerdos de viaje: Rumores de la caleta. Piezas caracteristicas: Torre bermeja.* GRANADOS: *Danza española No. 4, Villanesca.* FALLA: *El amor brujo: El círculo mágico; Canción del feugo fatuo. The Three-cornered Hat: Miller's dance.* TURINA: *Sonata, Op. 61. Fandanguillo, Op. 36.*
(M) *** DG Acc. 2542/*3342* 157.

An extraordinarily successful recital, the playing full of electricity and immediately communicative. The opening *Asturias* immediately commands the listener's attention, and the atmospheric *Fandanguillo* of Turina and the Granados *Villanesca* are equally telling. The Falla ballet excerpts are uncannily orchestral in their colour. Highly recommended and very well recorded.

Zabaleta, Nicanor (harp)

'Spanish harp music of the sixteenth and seventeenth centuries': (Sixteenth century) CABEZÓN: *Pavana con su Glosa.* MUDARRA: *Tiento para harpa.* PALERO: *2 Romances.* ALBERTO: *Tres IV.* CABEZÓN: *Pavana Italiana. Diferencias sobre la gallarda Milanesa. Diferencias sobre el canto de caballero.* (Seventeenth century) ANON.: *Seguidillas.* RIBAYAS: *Bacas. Folias. Paredetas. Pabanas. Hachas.* HUETE: *Canción Italiana con diferencias. Canzión Franzesa. Monsiur de la Boleta.* RODRIGUES: *Tocata II para arpa.*
(M) *** DG Arc. Priv. 2547/*3347* 049.

Although the harp was in use in Renaissance Spain, much of this music was more likely to have been heard on the vihuela or guitar, and thus textures are simple. Zabaleta plays everything on a modern harp, yet his taste is impeccable and matched by stylistic sympathy, so that nothing sounds out of period. Of its kind this is faultless, and with immaculate recording (on both disc and cassette) it can be recommended to all but those seeking the cascading roulades of nineteenth-century harp writing.

Zaradin, John (guitar)

WEISS: *Ballette.* FRESCOBALDI: *Air and variations* (arr. SEGOVIA). LAURO: *Valse criollo.* ALBÉNIZ: *Granada* (arr. Tarrega). MALATS: *Spanish serenade.* RODRIGO: *Concierto de Aranjuez* (with L. Philomusica O, Barbier).
(B) ** CfP CFP/*TC-CFP* 40012.

Classics for Pleasure had the excellent idea of coupling their recording of the Rodrigo *Concierto de Aranjuez* (reviewed above) with a recital by the soloist. His playing has plenty of character, and there are some attractive miniatures here. The recording is good and the tape transfer well managed, faithful and with bloom as well as clarity.

Vocal Recitals and Choral Collections

Ameling, Elly (soprano)

'Grandi voci': Arias from: BACH: *St John Passion; St Matthew Passion; Easter oratorio; Christmas oratorio.* HANDEL: *Messiah.* HAYDN: *Little Organ mass; The Creation.*
(M) *** Decca 410 148.

This Ameling collection is generous and concentrates on eighteenth-century repertory recorded in the 1960s, when her voice was at its sweetest and brightest and her technique ideally fluent. Many of the items come from complete sets which still hold their place in the catalogue. Excellent recordings for their period, with the vocal timbre freshly caught.

Ameling, Elly (soprano), **Louis van Dijk** (piano)

'After hours': GREEN: *Body and soul.* GERSHWIN: *Embraceable you; The man I love; My cousin in Milwaukee; Someone to watch over me; I got rhythm.* PORTER: *In the still of the night.* KOSMA: *Les feuilles mortes.* KATSCHER: *When day is done.* RODGERS: *With a song in my heart.* BLAKE: *I'm just wild about Harry.* DUKE: *Autumn in New York.*
*** Ph. Dig. 6514/*7337* 284 [id.].

The title of Elly Ameling's collection of cabaret songs is *'After hours'*, and anyone who thinks of her as a rather demure singer, sweetly innocent in Schubert, will be surprised at the magnetism which can bring out the pure beauty of melodies by Gershwin or Cole Porter. Sentimental songs work better than brightly rhythmic ones like *My cousin from Milwaukee*, above all one of the loveliest of Gershwin's songs, *Someone to watch over me.* Van Dijk's pointed accompaniments often have a flavour of Debussy or Ravel. Excellent recording. The sound on the tape is smooth, but not so open as the LP.

Angeles, Victoria de los (soprano)

'Spanish songs' (with G. Moore or R. Tarrago): FALLA: *Seven Spanish popular songs.* VIVES: *El retrato de Isabela; El amor y los ojos.* GRANADOS: *El majo discreto; La maja dolorosa; El mirar de la maja.* FUSTÉ: *Háblame de amores.* GURIDI: *No quiero tus avellanas; Jota.* TURINA: *Farruca.* VALVERDE: *Clavelitos.* TRAD. (arr. Nin): *El vito; Paño murciano.* (arr. Tarrago): *Andregaya; Parado de Valldemosa; Campanas de Belén; Jaeneras que yo canto; Si quieres saber coplas.*
(M) *** HMV mono HLM/*TC-HLM* 143587-1/*4* [Sera. S60233].

Issued just after Victoria de los Angeles' sixtieth birthday, this splendid issue celebrates her remarkable achievement in establishing this highly rewarding folk-derived material in the international repertoire. The groundwork of Conchita Supervia is not forgotten, and by comparison with that remarkable artist Los Angeles' style may seem less than earthy. But she is superb in the Falla *Popular songs* and her lyrical singing is never too soft-centred when the vocal personality is so warmly communicative, while the livelier numbers have no lack of robust life and sparkle. She is superbly accompanied by Gerald Moore, and by Renata Tarrago where a guitar is more appropriate than a piano. No reservations need be entertained over the recording which, though mono, is splendidly balanced on both disc and tape, and casts a fine bloom on the voice.

'The art of Victoria de los Angeles': MOZART: *Le Nozze di Figaro: Porgi amor*. ROSSINI: *Il Barbiere di Siviglia: Una voce poco fa*. VERDI: *Otello: Willow song; Ave Maria. La Traviata: Teneste la promessa . . . Addio del passato.* PUCCINI: *La Bohème: Sì, mi chiamano Mimì; Donde lieta usci. Madama Butterfly: Entrance of Butterfly; Un bel dì*. WAGNER: *Tannhäuser: Dich, teure Halle. Lohengrin: Einsam in trüben Tagen*. GOUNOD: *Faust: Jewel song*. MASSENET: *Manon: Adieu notre petite table; Obéissons. Werther: Air des lettres*. BIZET: *Carmen: Habañera; Seguidilla*. GRANADOS: *Goyescas: La maja y el ruiseñor*. FALLA: *La Vida breve: Vivan los que rien! Alli está! Riyendo!* Songs: SCHUBERT: *An die Musik*. BRAHMS: *Dein blaues Auge. Vergebliches Ständchen*. FAURÉ: *Clair de lune*. HAHN: *Le Rossignol des lilas*. DUPARC: *L'Invitation au voyage*. Arr. CANTELOUBE: *Baïlèro*. CORNAGO: *Qué es mi vida, preguntais?* ANON.: *Ay luna que reluces*. GRANADOS: *Colección de tonadillos; La Maja dolorosa No. 3*. Arr. TARRAGO: *Din, dan Yolerán*. RODRIGO: *Cuatro madrigales amatorios*. CHAPI: *La Patria chica. La Chavala. Las Hijas des Zebedeo*. VALVERDE: *Clavelitos*. CALLEJA: *Adiós Granada*.
(M) (***) HMV SLS 5233 (3) [Ang. SCLX/*4X3X* 3914].

This three-disc set contains a vintage collection of Victoria de los Angeles recordings, mostly made near the beginning of her career in mono sound. It is particularly valuable for the series of operatic portraits, not just those selected from her complete recordings (*Carmen* under Beecham, Massenet's *Manon* under Monteux, a delectable *Butterfly* in the first of the two versions she made) but the radiant portrayals given in separate items such as the *Willow Song* and *Ave Maria* from Verdi's *Otello*. The songs too provide an attractive cross-section of her work, including her incomparable recording of Granados's *La maja y el ruiseñor*, originally issued on 78. The remastering is well managed and the stereo transcriptions do not rob the sound of its clarity of focus.

Angeles, Victoria de los, Elisabeth Schwarzkopf (sopranos), **Dietrich Fischer-Dieskau** (baritone), **Gerald Moore** (piano)

'An evening with': MOZART: *Più non si trovano*. SCHUBERT: *Nachtviolen; Schwanengesang; Abschied; Im Abendroth; An die Musik*. ROSSINI: *Cats' duet; Serate musicale: La Regata Veneziana; La Pesca*. BRAHMS: *Der Gang zum Liebchen; Vergebliches Ständchen*. SCHUMANN: *Tanzlied; Er un Sie*. WOLF: *Sonne der Schlummerlosen; Das verlassene Mägdlein; Der Zigeunerin*. MENDELSSOHN: *Ich wollt' meine Lieb'; Gruss; Lied aus Ruy Blas; Abendlied; Wasserfahrt*. HAYDN: *An den Vetter; Daphnens einziger Fehler*.
*** HMV ASD/*TC-ASD* 143594-1/*4*.

This masterly collection, at once superbly stylish yet sparkling and at times comic too, comes from the live concert which these artists gave at the Festival Hall on Moore's retirement. The full recital set of two discs is now deleted, but this selection has most of the finest and most delectable items with the exception of Schwarzkopf's unforgettable account of Wolf's greatest song, *Kennst du das Land*. Recording still vivid and atmospheric and the cassette too has splendid presence.

Archer, Robyn, L. Sinf. Muldowney

'Robyn Archer sings Brecht': BRECHT: *Benares song; Ballad of the pirates*. WEILL: *Alabama song; Ballad of sexual obsession; Epitaph 1919; The drowned girl; Song of Surabaya Johnny; Solomon song*. EISLER: *Song of the stimulating impact of cash; Easter Day; Ballad on approving of the world; Madam's song; On suicide; 5 Hollywood elegies; Song of a German mother; The flower garden*. DESSAU: *The song of the girl and the soldier*.
*** HMV ASD/*TC-ASD* 4166.

Achieving a balance between the cabaret and concert style is not easy, yet Robyn Archer with the help of Dominic Muldowney and his accompaniments (often edited afresh) gives a sharp, compelling focus to this attractive and characterful collection. The songs of the relatively little-known Hanns Eisler and Paul Dessau make a pointful foil for the more individual and flamboyant Weill items from very much the same Berlin background. Bright forward recording on disc and tape alike.

Bach Ch., Philip Jones Brass Ens., Willcocks

'Family carols': O come, all ye faithful. Gabriel's message. Angelus ad Virginem. Ding dong merrily on high. A virgin most pure. God rest ye, merry gentlemen. In dulci jubilo. Unto us a son is born. Once in Royal David's city. Hush, my dear, lie still and slumber. WILLCOCKS: *Fanfare.* RUTTER: *Shepherd's pipe carol. Star carol.* KIRKPATRICK: *Away in a manger.* GRUBER: *Stille Nacht.* Arr. VAUGHAN WILLIAMS: *Sussex carol.* MENDELSSOHN: *Hark, the herald angels sing.*
*** Decca Dig. SXDL/*KSXDC* 7514.

An admirably chosen and beautifully recorded collection of traditional carols. Fresh simplicity is the keynote here; the brass fanfares bring a touch of splendour but the music is not over-scored. *Silent night* has seldom sounded more serene, and Rutter's infectiously rhythmic *Shepherd's pipe carol* makes a refreshing contrast, the centrepiece of side two. The digital sound is in no way clinical; indeed the resonance is perfectly judged. The excellent cassette is only marginally less sharply focused, otherwise retaining all the qualities of the LP.

Baillie, Dame Isobel (soprano)

'Never sing louder than lovely' (Anthology 1924–75): PURCELL: *Blessed Virgin's expostulation; Stript of their green. The Fairy Queen: Hark! the echoing air.* ARNE: *Judgement of Paris: O ravishing delight. The Tempest: Where the bee sucks.* BACH: *Cantata No. 208: Shall pales . . . Flocks in pastures; Cantata No. 68: My heart ever faithful.* HANDEL: *Acis and Galatea: O did'st thou know . . . As when the dove. Messiah: Rejoice greatly; How beautiful are the feet; I know that my Redeemer liveth; If God be with us. Samson: Let the bright Seraphim. Judas Maccabeus: O let eternal honours . . . From mighty Kings. Joshua: O had I Jubal's lyre.* HAYDN: *The Creation: With verdure clad; On mighty pens.* SANDERSON: *One morning* (2nd verse). CADMAN: *At dawning.* KJERULF: *Synnove's song.* OFFENBACH: *Tales of Hoffmann: Doll song.* DELIUS: *Twilight fancies.* MENDELSSOHN: *On wings of song.* TRAD.: *O whistle an' I'll come; O can ye sew cushions; Comin' through the rye; I will walk with my love.*
(M) (***) HMV mono RLS/*TC-RLS* 7703 (2).

It must be unique for a soprano's recording career to span over half a century, yet Isobel Baillie over all that time rarely if ever let down her maxim which provided the title both of her autobiography and of this collection. The first item is a test recording made in acoustic days but never followed up for some years; the last a touching and still sweet rendering of a simple folksong. In between came some dazzling displays of agility as well as loveliness, with the bright fresh timbre uniquely hers under perfect control. First-rate transfers of sound inevitably limited.

Baker, Dame Janet (mezzo-soprano)

'Songs for Sunday' (with Philip Ledger, piano): BRAHE: *Bless this house.* PARRY: *Jerusalem.* TRAD.: *Were you there.* PLUMSTEAD: *A grateful heart. Close thine eyes.* EASTHOPE MARTIN: *The holy child.* THOMPSON: *The knights of Bethlehem.* LIDDLE: *How lovely are Thy dwellings. The Lord is my shepherd. Abide with me.* VAUGHAN WILLIAMS: *The call.* FORD: *A prayer to Our Lady.* BACH–GOUNOD: *Ave Maria.* WALFORD DAVIES: *God be in my head.*
*** HMV ASD/*TC-ASD* 3981.

Dame Janet Baker's total dedication makes this a moving experience, transforming songs that would as a rule seem merely sentimental. Sensitive accompaniment and excellent recording, which has transferred admirably to tape.

'A pageant of English song 1597–1961' (with Gerald Moore, piano; Martin Isepp, harpsichord; Robert Spencer, lute; Ambrose Gauntlett, viola da gamba): DOWLAND: *Come again.* CAMPION: *Never love unless you can;*

Oft have I sighed; If thou longst so much to learn; Fain would I wed. PURCELL: *Sleep, Adam, sleep; Lord what is man?* BOYCE: *Tell me lovely shepherd.* MONRO: *My lovely Celia.* ARNE: *Where the bee sucks.* STANFORD: *La Belle Dame sans Merci.* PARRY: *Proud Maisie; O mistress mine.* BUSCH: *Rest.* WARLOCK: *Pretty ring time.* VAUGHAN WILLIAMS: *Linden Lea.* GURNEY: *The fields are full.* BRITTEN: *Corpus Christi carol.* IRELAND: *Down by the Salley gardens.* QUILTER: *Love's philosophy.*
(M) *** HMV Green. ESD/*TC-ESD* 100642-1/*4* [Ang. S 36456].

This is a uniquely satisfying recital record, beautifully recorded. The twenty songs on this record cover the widest possible range, not just in style and period but in mood, too. With the beauty of her voice and the depth of her expression in every phrase, Janet Baker explores a field which yields great rewards. The richness of the songs by Stanford and Parry, for example, may surprise many, and besides the rarities there are such established favourites as Arne's *Where the bee sucks* and Vaughan Williams's *Linden Lea*. A beautiful record, while the cassette is outstanding, giving the voice a most realistic presence.

'Favourites' (with Gerald Moore, piano): STRAUSS, R.: *Ständchen.* MENDELSSOHN: *Auf Flügeln des Gesanges.* SCHUBERT: *Heidenroslein.* SCHUMANN: *Der Nussbaum.* GOUNOD: *Sérénade.* MASSENET: *Crépuscule.* CHABRIER: *Villanelle des petits canards.* HAHN: *L'heure exquise.* BAX: *Me suis mis en dance.* SULLIVAN: *Orpheus with his lute.* PARRY: *O Mistress mine.* QUILTER: *It was a lover and his lass.* FINZI: *It was a lover and his lass.* IRELAND: *The Salley Gardens.* HOWELLS: *Gavotte.* TRAD. (arr. Vaughan Williams): *Bushes and briars.* ANON. (arr. Anderson): *Drink to me only;* (arr. Hughes): *I know where I'm going.*
(M) *** HMV Green. ESD/*TC-ESD* 102439-1/*4*.

A wholly enchanting recital that shows the sheer diversity of Janet Baker's art with captivating charm. Gerald Moore's accompaniments are a model, participating in the mood and colour of every song. The recording is excellent and sounds equally well on LP and cassette, where a sophisticated transfer retains the full vocal bloom.

'Grandi voci': BACH: *Cantata No. 170: Vergnügte Ruh'.* PURCELL: *Dido and Aeneas: When I am laid in earth.* CAVALLI: *La Calisto: Ardo, sospiro e piango;* Duet: *Ululi, frema e strida . . . E spedito* (with Gottlieb). RAMEAU: *Hippolyte et Aricie: Quelle plainte en ces lieux m'appelle?* RAVEL: *Trois poèmes de Stéphane Mallarmé.* CHAUSSON: *Chanson perpétuelle.*
(M) *** Decca GRV/*KGRC* 5.

This was originally a sampler disc prepared as an answer to EMI, the company with which Dame Janet Baker had then signed an exclusive contract. The choice of items may not be ideal, with nothing between the eighteenth and the twentieth centuries, but every excerpt – especially Dame Janet's heartfelt first recording of *Dido's lament*, and Diana's aria from *La Calisto* – conveys the singer's unique intensity, and the recordings are first-rate. The cassette transfer too is first-class, matching the disc closely.

'The art of Dame Janet Baker' (with Spencer, Malcolm, Moore, Parsons; LSO, New Philh. O, Hallé O, Barbirolli and others): DOWLAND: *Come again.* CAMPION: *Fain would I wed.* LAWES: *Dialogue between Daphne and Strephon.* MONRO: *My lovely Celia.* STANFORD: *La Belle Dame sans Merci.* BRITTEN: *Corpus Christi carol.* QUILTER: *Love's philosophy.* ELGAR: *Sea pictures, Op. 37: Where corals lie. Dream of Gerontius: Softly and gently.* Arr. HAYDN: *O can ye sew cushions.* Arr. BEETHOVEN: *Bonnie Lassie.* BERLIOZ: *Nuits d'été: Villanelle. Damnation de Faust: L'amour, l'ardente flamme. Les Troyens: Ah! . . . Je vais mourir . . . Adieu fière cité.* DEBUSSY: *Chansons de Bilitis: La chevelure.* DUPARC: *Au pays où se fait la guerre.* FAURÉ: *Fleur jetée; Clair de lune.* RAVEL: *Schéhérazade: Asie.* MONTEVERDI: *Arianna: Lamento.* HANDEL: *Messiah: He was despised. Cantata No. 1: Per trofei di mia costanza.* BACH: *Cantata No. 82: Schlummert ein. Christmas oratorio: Bereite dich.* SCHUBERT: *Auflösung; Suleika II; Die Götter Griechenlands; Wiegenlied.* LISZT: *Es war ein König*

in Thule. STRAUSS, R.: *Heimliche Aufforderung; Morgen.* WOLF: *Spanish Liederbook: Herr, was trägt der Boden hier; Die Ihr schwebet.* MAHLER: *Blicke mir nichtin die Lieder; Ich bin der Welt.*
(M) *** HMV SLS/*TC-SLS* 5275 (3).

This generous three-disc collection of recordings by Janet Baker made between 1964 and 1979 was issued to coincide with the publication of her autobiography of a year, *Full Circle.* Superbly chosen to represent the full, magnificent span of her artistry, it brings one delight after another, with other great artists drawn on as witnesses, such as Fischer-Dieskau in a Lawes duet, Menuhin in two Beethoven folksongs. Italian and French opera has limited representation in Monteverdi and Berlioz, but otherwise the selections could hardly be more searchingly characterful, and the oratorio group rightly has Elgar as well as Bach and Handel. Finally Schubert, Strauss and Wolf songs give way to two of Mahler's *Rückert Lieder*, with Barbirolli conducting, a superb culmination – *I live alone in my heaven, in my loving, in my song.* Transfers are excellent, and the cassettes are no less successful, with a good booklet provided in the tape box too.

'The artistry of Janet Baker': GLUCK: *Alceste: Divinités du Styx. Iphigénie en Aulide: Vous essayez en vain . . . Par la crainte; Adieu, conservez dans votre âme. Iphigénie en Tauride: Non cet affreux devoir. Orfeo: Che puro ciel; Che farò senza Euridice.* MOZART: *La Clemenza di Tito: Parto! Parto; Deh, per questo istante solo.* HANDEL: *Ariodante: Dopo notte. Atalanta: Care selve. Joshua: O had I Jubal's lyre. Serse: Ombra mai fù.*
(M) *** Ph. 6570/*7310* 829.

Compiled from several sources, this collection presents some superb examples of Dame Janet's mature artistry on record. No one interprets Gluck more compellingly than she, and the Handel items inspire singing that is not just moving but technically brilliant. Fine recording. Side one of the cassette is transferred at the highest level, the voice vibrant and full, but the level drops on the second side, which is clear and slightly more refined.

'Lieder' (with Martin Isepp, piano): SCHUMANN: *Frauenliebe und Leben* (song cycle), *Op. 42.* BRAHMS: *Das Mädchen spricht; Die Mainacht; Nachtigall; Von ewiger Liebe.* SCHUBERT: *Die abgeblühte Linde; Heimliches Lieben; Minnelied; Der Musensohn.*
(M) *(**) Saga 5277.

In her inspirational early song recital for Saga Janet Baker's range of expression in the Schumann cycle runs the whole gamut from a joyful golden tone-colour in the exhilaration of *Ich kann's nicht fassen* through an ecstatic half-tone in *Süsser Freund* (the fulfilment of the line *Du geliebter Mann* wonderfully conveyed) to the dead, vibrato-less tone of agony at the bereavement in the final song. The Schubert songs are not quite on this level (*Der Musensohn* a little jerky), but the Brahms are beyond praise. This is singing of a quality that you find only once or twice in a generation, and whatever the price the record should be a collector's piece. The recording is not perfect. The balance favours the piano, and the piano and voice tend to be separated to left and right. There is some distortion on the voice at loud climaxes, but Baker's artistry quickly distracts attention from any such technical defects.

'Arie amorose' (with ASMF, Marriner): arias by GIORDANI; CACCINI; STRADELLA; SARRI; CESTI; LOTTI; ALESSANDRO SCARLATTI; CALDARA; BONONCINI; DURANTE; PERGOLESI; MARTINI; PICCINI; PAISIELLO.
*** Ph. 9500 557/*7300 691* [id.].

A delightful recital of classical arias, marred only by the absence of libretti or documentation about the music beyond the titles; the notes concentrate on Janet Baker's career. The programme is cleverly arranged to contrast expressive with sprightly music, and the wide range of tonal graduation and beautiful phrasing are matched by an artless lightness of touch in the slighter numbers. The accompaniments are intimate and tasteful: there is no more fetching example than Pergolesi's *Ogni pena più spietata*, with its deft bassoon obbligato, or the short closing song with harpsichord, Paisiello's *Nel cor più non mi sento.* The recording has a warm acoustic, and the resonance is kind to the voice without loss of orchestral detail, although the tape is less crisply focused than the disc.

Baltsa, Agnes (soprano)

'Operatic recital' (with Munich R.O, cond. Heinz Wallberg): ROSSINI: *Il Barbiere di Siviglia: Una voce poco fa. La Donna del Lago: Tanti affetti; La Cenerentola: Nacqui all'affano . . . non più mesta.* MOZART: *La Clemenza di Tito: Parto, parto.* MERCADANTE: *Il Giuramento: Ah, si, mia cara . . . Or là sull'onda.* DONIZETTI: *La Favorita: Fia dunque vero . . . O mio Fernando.* VERDI: *Macbeth: La luce langue.* MASCAGNI: *Cavalleria Rusticana: Voi lo sapete.*
**(*) HMV Dig. ASD/*TCC-ASD* 4279 [Ang. DS/*4XS* 37908].

Baltsa as a firebrand among mezzos today comes over strongly. There is much exciting singing here in a wide-ranging repertory ranging from Mozart and Rossini to one of Lady Macbeth's arias and *Voi lo sapete* from *Cavalleria Rusticana.* The flaw – which grows tiresome with so many coloratura arias included – is that in rapid divisions she allows herself whole chains of intrusive aitches with unstylish results. But for fiery characterization in such music Baltsa has few rivals. First-rate recording and a good tape.

Beňačková, Gabriela (soprano)

Operatic arias (with Czech PO, Neumann) from: SMETANA: *The bartered bride.* DVOŘÁK: *Armida; Rusalka.* JANÁČEK: *Jenufa.* TCHAIKOVSKY: *Eugene Onegin* (*Letter scene*)*; Queen of Spades.* PROKOFIEV: *War and peace.* SHOSTAKOVICH: *Katerina Ismailova.*
(M) *** Sup. 1116 2843.

This is perhaps the finest soprano recital record covering Slavonic opera. In all these varied items, whether Russian or Czech, Beňačková is at her very best, with unfamiliar items like the aria from Dvořák's *Armida* and the fine Prokofiev and Shostakovich arias as compelling as the culminating performance of *Tatiana's Letter Scene.* The voice is characterfully Slavonic (without being wobbly), radiant and full, and the recording is excellent.

Berganza, Teresa (mezzo-soprano)

'Grandi voci': GLUCK: *Orfeo ed Euridice: Che puro ciel. Alceste: Divinités du Styx.* HANDEL: *Giulio Cesare: Piangerò la sorte mia. Alcina: Vo cercando . . . Bramo di trionfar.* PERGOLESI: *La serva padrona: Stizzoso mio stizzoso.* CHERUBINI: *Medea: Medea, O Medea . . . Solo un pianto.* MOZART: *Le nozze di Figaro: Non so più. Così fan tutte: Temerari! . . . Come scoglio. La clemenza di Tito: Deh, per questo istante solo.* PAISIELLO: *Nina, o sia la pazza per amore: Il mio ben quandro verrà.* ROSSINI: *Stabat Mater: Fac ut portem. Semiramide: Bel raggio lusinghier.*
(M) *** Decca GRV/*KGRC* 25.

This wide selection from Berganza's classical repertory comes mainly from recordings of the 1960s, when the voice was at its most beautiful. The musical intensity combines formidably with an amazing technique (listen to *Bel raggio* from *Semiramide*) and only occasionally does one sense a lack of warmth. First-rate recording for its period with a vivid cassette, although on tape there are hints of peaking on some climactic high notes.

'Arias by Mozart, Gluck, Handel and Rossini': GLUCK: *Orfeo: Che farò. Paride ed Elena: O del mio dolce ardor.* MOZART: *La Clemenza di Tito: Parto, parto. Le Nozze di Figaro: Voi che sapete. Così fan tutte: Per pietà.* HANDEL: *Alcina: Sta nell'Ircana; Verdi prati.* ROSSINI: *Il Barbiere di Siviglia: Una voce poco fa. L'Italiana in Algeri: Cruda sorte! Amor tiranno! La Cenerentola: Nacqui all'affanno . . . Non più mesta.*
(M) *** Decca Jub. JB/*KJBC* 98.

This recital is drawn from a number of sources covering Teresa Berganza's Decca recording career from the *Cenerentola* aria of 1959 and the *Figaro* and *Così* items of 1963, all of which won great praise when they were first issued, to excerpts from her complete sets up to *La Clemenza di Tito* of 1968. Above all one notices the consistency, the rich voice controlled with the sort of vocal perfection one associates with her compatriot Victoria de los Angeles. A most satisfying collection, well recorded and with a vivid cassette transfer.

Bergonzi, Carlo (tenor)

Arias and excerpts from: VERDI: *Luisa Miller; Il Trovatore; La Traviata* (with Joan Sutherland); *Un ballo in maschera; La forza del destino; Don Carlo; Aïda.* GIORDANO: *Andrea Chénier.* CILEA: *Adriana Lecouvreur.* PONCHIELLI: *La Gioconda.* MEYERBEER: *L'Africaine.*
(M) *** Decca GRV/*KGRC* 21.

In the 1960s there was no more stylish recording tenor in the Italian repertory than Bergonzi; and this excellent selection of his work, concentrating mainly on Verdi, explains why he was so sought after by the companies, a tenor who was also an imaginative, often thoughtful musician. It is good to have the excerpts from Joan Sutherland's earlier recording with him of *La Traviata* and items from many other sets that might otherwise be forgotten. First-rate recording for its period, with an excellent, lively tape, though here, while the sound is wide-ranging and full-bodied, the strings are given an unnaturally bright sheen.

'Famous tenor arias' from: VERDI: *Aïda; Luisa Miller; La Forza del destino; Il Trovatore; Un Ballo in maschera; La Traviata.* PONCHIELLI: *La Gioconda.* PUCCINI: *La Bohème; Tosca; Manon Lescaut.*
(M) **(*) Decca SPA/*KCSP* 535 [Lon. STS 15511].

Mostly dating from the late 1950s, these recordings of favourite Verdi and Puccini arias (with one Ponchielli thrown in) show Bergonzi in his finest form. He does not attempt the rare pianissimo at the end of *Celeste Aïda*, but here among Italian tenors is a thinking musical artist who never resorts to vulgarity. The recording, of whatever vintage, is clear and gives the right bloom to the voice. The tape transfer is full-blooded (in the opening *Aïda* excerpt there is a hint of over-modulation in the brass) and it is otherwise reliable, though sometimes (notably in the Puccini arias) it does not produce a very convincing focus for the upper strings.

Bjoerling, Jussi (tenor)

'Grandi voci': PONCHIELLI: *La Gioconda: Cielo e mar.* PUCCINI: *La Fanciulla del West: Ch'ella mi creda. Manon Lescaut: Tra voi belle.* GIORDANO: *Fedora: Amor ti vieta.* CILEA: *L'Arlesiana: Lamento di Federico.* VERDI: *Un Ballo in maschera: Di' tu se fedele. Requiem: Ingemisco.* MASCAGNI: *Cavalleria Rusticana: Tu qui, Santuzza?* (with Tebaldi)*; Intanto, amici . . . Brindisi; Mamma, quel vino.* LEHÁR: *Das Land des Lächelns: Dein ist mein ganzes Herz.*
(M) **(*) Decca GRV/*KGRC* 4.

John Culshaw's autobiography has revealed what an unhappy man Jussi Bjoerling was at the very end of his career, when all these recordings were made by Decca engineers for RCA. You would hardly guess the problems from the flow of headily beautiful, finely focused tenor tone. These may not be the most characterful renderings of each aria, but they are all among the most compellingly musical. Fine recording for its period, and a good tape.

Bryn-Jones, Delme (baritone), **Richard Nunn** (piano)

'I'll sing thee songs of Araby': COPLAND: *Old American songs: Boatmen's dance; Simple gifts.* Arr. ROBINSON: *Water boy.* IRELAND: *Sea fever.* CLAY: *I'll sing thee songs of Araby.* Arr. KORBAY: *Mourning in the village dwells; Had a horse.* Arr. JOHNSTON: *Because I were shy.* SPEAKS: *The road to Mandalay.* MUSSORGSKY: *Song of the flea.* MENDELSSOHN: *I am a roamer.* COLERIDGE-TAYLOR: *Hiawatha's vision.* LONGSTAFFE: *When the sergeant-major's on parade.* QUILTER: *Go lovely rose; Drink to me only.* PHILIPS: *The fishermen of England.*
**(*) Hyp. A/*KA* 66029.

The stentorian tones of Delme Bryn-Jones represent a continuing recording tradition established by Peter Dawson and more recently continued by Owen Brannigan. Words are usually clear and the delivery is forthright, even vehement at times, though the forward balance and resonant acoustic minimize effects of subtlety. Yet Bryn-Jones can sing with controlled expressive feeling, as the fine performance of Ireland's *Sea fever* demonstrates. There is warmth and humour too, and the Mussorgsky is splendidly spirited. The singer is at his finest in ballads like *The road to Mandalay*, sung with an imaginatively wide dynamic range. The accompaniments are first-rate and the resonant acoustic is mostly as effectively caught on tape as it is on disc. With any reservations about the basic style, the spontaneity here is undoubtedly infectious.

Burrows, Stuart (tenor)

'Songs for you' (with (i) John Constable or Eurfryn John, piano; (ii) Ambrosian Singers, Morris; Martin Neary, organ): (i) TOSELLI: *Serenata.* GLOVER: *Rose of Tralee.* WILLIAMS: *My little Welsh home.* SANDERSON: *Until.* BROUGHTON: *The Immortal Hour: Faery song.* CLAY: *I'll sing thee songs of Araby.* JACOBS-BOND: *A perfect day.* WOODFORDE-FINDEN: *Kashmiri song.* LESLIE: *Annabelle Lee.* D'HARDELOT: *Because.* RASBACH: *Trees.* MARSHALL: *I hear you calling me.* PURCELL, E.: *Passing by.* HAYDN WOOD: *Roses of Picardy.* MURRAY: *I'll walk beside you.* BRAHE: *Bless this house.* (ii) SULLIVAN: *The lost chord.* GOUNOD: *O divine Redeemer.* PARRY: *Jesu, lover of my soul.* NEGRO SPIRITUALS: *Steal away; Jericho.* DVOŘÁK (arr. Ditson): *Goin' home.* MALOTTE: *The Lord's Prayer.* ADAMS: *The holy city.* TCHAIKOVSKY: *The crown of roses.* LIDDLE: *How lovely are Thy dwellings.* SCHUBERT: *Ave Maria.* MONK: *Abide with me.*
(B) **(*) Decca DPA/*KDPC* 607/8.

'The world of sacred songs' (as section (ii) above).
(M) *** Decca SPA/*KCSP* 219.

Stuart Burrows's fresh open manner could hardly be more apt for this collection of popular songs and ballads. His is a voice which takes naturally to being recorded, and the results can be warmly recommended to anyone tempted by the selection. Some may wish that the singing was more strongly characterized, but much of this repertoire responds to a lyrical presentation. The *Songs for you* collection consists of three recitals from different sources. The second disc, which is also available separately, concentrates on sacred music, with a backing by the Ambrosian Singers; it is very well recorded and excellently transferred to tape throughout. The two recitals on the first disc and cassette have different accompanists. The recording on side one (John Constable accompanying) comes from the Oiseau-Lyre catalogue and is beautifully recorded. Side two (with Eurfryn John), like the sacred music, originated on the Delysé label and is a stereo transcription of mono, with a degree of edginess on the voice at times.

'Operetta favourites' (with Nat. PO, Stapleton): LEHÁR: *Land of Smiles: You are my heart's delight. Frederica: O maiden, my maiden. Frasquita: Farewell, my love. Paganini: Girls were made to love and kiss. Czarevitch: Alone, always alone. Giuditta: Comrades, this is the life for me.* SIECZYŃSKY: *Vienna ... city of my dreams.* ROMBERG: *The Student Prince: Serenade.* TAUBER: *Old Chelsea: My heart and I.* STOLZ: *Don't ask me why.* NOVELLO: *Glamorous Night: Shine through my dreams.* KUNNEKE: *The Cousin from Nowhere: I'm only a strolling vagabond.*
*** O-L DSLO/*KDSLC* 16.

'The simple joys of life' (with Constable, piano): TOURS: *Mother o' mine.* RAY: *The sunshine of your smile.* FOSTER: *I dream of Jeannie.* HAYDN WOOD: *Roses of Picardy.* MARSHALL: *I hear you calling me.* BALFE: *Come into the garden, Maud.* ADAMS: *The Star of Bethlehem. Thora.* SANDERSON: *As I sit here.* BUTTERFIELD: *When you and I were young, Maggie.* DANKS: *Silver threads among the gold.* YOUNG: *I give thanks for you.* TRAD.: *Danny boy.* HANDEL: *Silent worship.*
*** O-L DSLO/*KDSLC* 42.

'To the land of dreams' (with Constable, piano): AITKEN: *Maire, my girl.* PURCELL, Edward: *Passing by.* DE KOVEN: *Oh, promise me.* GREEN: *Gortnamona.* COATES: *I heard you singing.* MALLOY: *The Kerry dance.* DEL RIEGO: *O dry those tears.* PENN: *Smilin' through.* RASBACH: *Trees.* WEATHERLY: *Parted.* LATHAM SHARP: *Dearest of all.* DESMOND: *Sitting by the window.* HARRISON: *In the gloaming.* BALL: *Mother Machree.* MURRAY: *I'll walk beside you.*
*** O-L DSLO/*KDSLC* 43.

'Life's sweet melody' (with Constable, piano): NEWTON: *Somewhere a voice is calling.* VAUGHAN WILLIAMS: *Linden Lea.* RONALD: *Down in the forest.* HUGHES: *The*

stuttering lovers. HEAD: *Little road to Bethlehem.* SOMERVELL: *The gentle maiden.* TRAD.: *The lark in the clear air.* CLUTSAM: *I know of two bright eyes.* RAY: *God keep you in my prayer.* PATERSON: *The garden where the praties grow.* ELGAR: *Pleading.* GRIEG: *I love thee.* O'CONNOR: *The old house.* BARTLETT: *A dream.* FROTERE: *For your dear sake.* WESTENDORF: *I'll take you home again, Kathleen.*
*** O-L DSLO/*KDSLC* 44.

With his headily beautiful tenor voice and simple charm, Burrows makes an excellent interpreter of popular songs like these, whether from operetta, musical comedy, the English school or the straight ballad repertory. The sound is excellent and each record is valuable for its particular repertory. Especially recommendable is the selection on DSLO 16 in tribute to Richard Tauber; and the ballads are sung with an eloquent simplicity that disguises their sentimental underlay. All four collections are available on tape. The transfer of *KDSLC 16* is disappointing, the voice clear but the orchestra less well focused. *KDSLC 42* and *43* are both well managed, with good balance and natural vocal projection, but *KDSLC 44* is transferred at a very high level, which brings a degree of edginess at peaks.

Callas, Maria (soprano)

Operatic recital: CILEA: *Adriana Lecouvreur: Ecco, respiro appena . . . Io son l'umile; Poveri fiori.* GIORDANO: *Andrea Chénier: La mamma morta.* CATALANI: *La Wally: Ebben? Ne andrò lontana.* ROSSINI: *Il Barbiere di Siviglia: Una voce poco fa.* MEYERBEER: *Dinorah: Shadow song.* DELIBES: *Lakmé: Bell song.* VERDI: *I Vespri siciliani: Bolero.*
(***) HMV mono ALP/*TC-ALP* 3824 [Ang. S 35233].

This is one of the classic Callas records, ranging extraordinarily wide in its repertory and revealing in every item the uniquely intense musical imagination that set musicians of every kind listening and learning. Coloratura flexibility here goes with dramatic weight; not all the items are equally successful (the *Shadow song* from *Dinorah*, for example, lacks charm), but these are all unforgettable performances. This mono reissue is well balanced and cleanly transferred, and the cassette transfer is excellent, clear and vivid, without hardness on top.

'The unreleased recordings': VERDI: *Il Corsaro: Egli non riede ancor . . . Non so le tetre immagini; Ne sulla terra . . . Vola talor dal carcere. Il Trovatore: Tacea la notte placida . . . Di tale amor. Un Ballo in maschera: Morrò, ma prima in grazia.* BELLINI: *La Sonnambula: Compagne, teneri amici . . . Come per me serena; Ah, se una . . . Ah, non credea mirarti.*
*** HMV ASD/*TC-ASD* 3535 [Ang. S/*4XS* 37557].

The fear was that a collection of Maria Callas's unreleased recordings would include items that never appeared because of all-too-obvious vocal shortcomings (it is common knowledge that right at the end of her career Callas made duet recordings which have never been released). In fact every one of these items is richly enjoyable. The solos from *Sonnambula* were recorded as early as 1955 with Callas in her prime, if anything more relaxed than in her performances on the complete set of 1957; but comparing this (and the *Ballo* aria) with Callas's singing in complete sets, the remarkable thing is the total consistency: most details are identical. Best of all – because most revealing – are the two arias from *Il Corsaro*, recorded as late as 1969, showing the vocal technique at its most assured (particularly in legato phrasing) and the artistry at its most commanding. The recordings vividly capture the unique voice, and the tape transfer is admirably smooth, catching the vocal timbre glowingly.

'Mad scenes' (with Philh. O, Rescigno): DONIZETTI: *Anna Bolena: Piangete voi; Al dolce guidami.* THOMAS: *Hamlet: A vos jeux; Partagez-vous mes fleurs; Et maintenant écoutez ma chanson.* BELLINI: *Il Pirata: Oh! s'io potessi . . . Col sorriso d'innocenza.*
*** HMV ASD 3801 [Ang. S 35764].

If, as ever, the rawness of exposed top notes mars the sheer beauty of Callas's singing, few recital records ever made can match, let alone outshine, this collection of mad scenes in vocal and dramatic imagination. This is Callas at her very peak; Desmond Shawe-Taylor suggested this as the record which more than any summed up the essence of Callas's genius. Twenty years after its original issue it reappeared at full price and is still worth every penny. Excellent recording for its period.

'Arias from French operas' (with French Nat. R.O, Prêtre): GLUCK: *Orfeo ed Euridice: J'ai perdu mon Eurydice. Alceste: Divinités du Styx.* BIZET: *Carmen: Habañera; Séguedilla.* SAINT-SAËNS: *Samson et Dalila: Printemps qui commence; Amour! Viens aider; Mon coeur s'ouvre à ta voix.* GOUNOD: *Roméo et Juliette: Je veux vivre.* THOMAS: *Mignon: Je suis Titania.* MASSENET: *Le Cid: Pleurez mes yeux.* CHARPENTIER: *Louise: Depuis le jour.*
*** HMV ASD/*TCC-ASD* 4306 [Ang. S 35882].

To the original recital of French arias issued in 1961 this splendidly refurbished version adds Dalila's *Mon coeur s'ouvre* from Saint-Saëns' opera, not the most beautiful singing on the disc but, like the rest, extraordinarily intense. The Mignon *Polonaise* is not ideally elegant, but it is almost irrelevant to criticize Callas on detail, when the sense of presence is so powerful. Even in her complete recording of *Carmen* she did not outshine these aria performances. Recording still fresh on disc; on tape, the orchestral detail is not always sharp because of the resonance, but the voice is naturally caught.

'La Divina' (*The art of Maria Callas*): arias from: MASCAGNI: *Cavalleria Rusticana.* CILEA: *Adriana Lecouvreur.* PUCCINI: *Manon Lescaut; La Bohème; Turandot; Madama Butterfly.* PONCHIELLI: *La Gioconda.* CHERUBINI: *Medea.* SPONTINI: *La Vestale.* MASSENET: *Le Cid; Werther.* ROSSINI: *Il Barbiere di Siviglia.* BELLINI: *La Sonnambula; I Puritani; Norma; Il Pirata.* MEYERBEER: *Dinorah.* DELIBES: *Lakmé.* THOMAS: *Hamlet.* DONIZETTI: *Lucia di Lammermoor.* VERDI: *Rigoletto; I Vespri siciliani; Ernani; Don Carlo; Nabucco; Un Ballo in maschera; Attila; Macbeth; Il Trovatore.*
(M) **(*) HMV SLS/*TC-SLS* 5057 (4).

So generous a selection from the recordings of Maria Callas must inevitably bring up much exciting material, and no admirer of the singer should be without this set; but a serious shortcoming is the absence of information on the times and places of the recordings, particularly when the dates of copyright given are downright misleading. And the order of the items is by genre, which makes it still more difficult for the non-specialist to fathom which vintage of Callas recording he is listening to. But the wonders of vocal imagination here far exceed any frustrations: each side, indeed every item, brings memorable moments totally unique to Callas. The tape transfer is well managed throughout the first two tapes, the sound clear and vivid. But on side five (the Mad Scene from *Il Pirata*) the level rises and the sound becomes fierce, with bad peaking and roughness at climaxes; and throughout the last two sides the vocal quality is shrill.

'Maria Callas album': arias from: BELLINI: *Norma; I Puritani; La Sonnambula.* ROSSINI: *Il Barbiere di Siviglia; Il Turco in Italia.* PUCCINI: *Manon Lescaut; Turandot; Gianni Schicchi; Madama Butterfly; La Bohème* (with di Stefano); *Tosca.* MASSENET: *Manon.* VERDI: *La Forza del destino; Rigoletto; Aïda; Macbeth; Il Trovatore; Un Ballo in maschera.* LEONCAVALLO: *I Pagliacci.* DONIZETTI: *Lucia di Lammermoor.* GLUCK: *Alceste.* BIZET: *Carmen.* MASCAGNI: *Cavalleria Rusticana.* SAINT-SAËNS: *Samson et Dalila.*
(***) HMV SLS/*TC-SLS* 5104 (2) [SB/*4X2X* 3841].

Most of the twenty-four items in this superb collection date from the mid-1950s, when Maria Callas was at the very peak of her formidable powers. The majority come from the complete sets she recorded with such conductors as Serafin and Karajan, in London or at La Scala, but the shrewdness of the choice is illustrated by the selection of Rosina's *Una voce poco fa* in the more sharply characterful and sparkling version from Callas's 1954 recital and not from her complete set of *Barbiere*. Dates and recording venues are meticulously given, with full texts and an essay on Callas. The stereo transcriptions (many of these recordings come from mono originals) catch the voice well and the transfers are bright and clear, but the cassette transfer (especially the second tape) brings a degree of edginess. However, the level has been well calculated to avoid blasting, with only a hint of peaking at times. Do not judge the sound by the opening *Casta diva* with its fuzzy chorus.

'Operatic recital': arias from: ROSSINI: *Il Barbiere di Siviglia.* VERDI: *Macbeth; Don Carlo.* PUCCINI: *Tosca.* GLUCK: *Alceste.* BIZET: *Carmen* (with Gedda). SAINT-SAËNS: *Samson et Dalila.* MASSENET: *Manon.*
(M) **(*) HMV SXLP/*TC-SXLP* 30166.

This medium-priced collection ranges wide over Callas's EMI recordings, from a gloriously fiery account of Rosina's aria from *Barbiere di Siviglia* (the force of her enunciation of the word *ma* ('but') has to be heard to be believed) to some of her relatively late performances of French items, with the *Carmen* excerpts taken from the complete set. All of this is vintage Callas and worth collecting at the price. The cassette transfer (an early EMI master) is not one of EMI's best. Side one lacks freshness, and includes one or two moments of peakiness; side two has rather more range at the top but remains acceptable rather than being up to EMI's best standard.

Camerata of London, Simpson; Mason

'The Queen's men' (Music associated with the Earl of Essex; HOLBORNE; Sir Walter Raleigh; Sir John Souch; Sir Thomas Monson; Sir Philip Sidney).
** CRD CRD 1055/*CRDC 4055.*

An interesting idea to make a collection centred on famous Elizabethans. One does not, for instance, think of Sir Walter Raleigh as a lyricist. In the event the programme is a little let down by the rather literal presentation. Glenda Simpson – who makes a major contribution – sings freshly and often expressively, but her manner is deadpan and Barry Mason's lute solos are also rather circumspect. There is much of interest here and the recording is excellent, with disc and cassette closely matched, but the concert has a self-conscious atmosphere that detracts from the directness of its communication.

Canterbury Cath. Ch., Wicks

BYRD: *Laudibus in sanctis.* WALFORD DAVIES: *Magdalen at Michael's Gate.* WEELKES: *Give ear, O Lord.* RIDOUT: *I turn the corner; Doxology.* GIBBONS: *Hosanna! to the Son of David.* BROWN, Christopher: *Laudate dominum.* STANFORD: *The Lord is my shepherd.* PURCELL: *Let mine eyes.* WILLIAMSON: *Wrestling Jacob.*
*** Abbey ABY 817.

The singing here is strikingly fresh and the programme ranges over a wide spectrum of English music. The singing is refined yet has plenty of expressive fervour; only the Purcell seems somewhat emotionally reticent. The Walford Davies and Stanford settings are unexpectedly imaginative and enjoyable. David Flood, the organist, accompanies admirably and is well balanced, and the recording overall is excellent.

Carols: '40 Christmas carols'

Choirs of: Canterbury, Chichester, Durham, Gloucester, Lichfield, Liverpool, Worcester Cathedrals; Leeds Parish Church; Magdalen and New Colleges, Oxford; St Mary's, Warwick (various conductors).
(B) ** Abbey LPB/*LPBC* 820 (2).

An ingeniously if not always very subtly edited (fades are included) collection which includes virtually all the most familiar English carols and many lesser-known ones. The singing is always accomplished (though sometimes treble soloists are weak) and often excellent. The selection opens with the *Once in Royal David's city* processional and closes with the Willcocks arrangement of *Puer Nobis.* The sound is good on disc, but our copy of the double-length cassette suffered from occasional pitch fluctuations, although otherwise the quality was acceptable. These faults may well have been eradicated by the time we are in print.

Carreras, José (tenor)

Zarzuela arias (with ECO, Ros-Marba): VIVES: *Dona Francisquita: Por el humo.* SOUTULLO: *El último romantico: Noche de amor.* SERRANO: *Alma de Dios: Canción hungara. La alegría del batallón: Canción guajira. Los de Aragón: Cuantas veces solo.* GUERRERO: *El huesped del sevillano: Raquel.* CHAPI: *La Bruja: Jota.* TÓRROBA: *Luisa Fernanda: De este apacible rincón de Madrid.* LUNA: *La pícara molinera: Paxarín, ru que vuelas.* GURIDI: *El Caserio: Romanza.*
*** Ph. 9500 649/*7300 751* [id.].

The *zarzuela* genre has yet to make its mark outside Spain, but a collection like this has many charms. Carreras draws out the often rather flimsy melodies most persuasively, and the recording is excellent. The cassette transfer is acceptable, but the sound lacks sparkle at the top.

Arias (with LSO, Lopez-Cobos): PUCCINI: *Manon Lescaut: Donna non vidi mai. Turandot: Nessun dorma.* LEONCAVALLO: *Zazà: O mio piccolo tavolo. I Pagliacci: Vesti la giubba. La Bohème: Testa adorata. I Zingari: Dammi un amore.* GIORDANO: *Andrea Chénier: Un dì all'azzuro spazio.* PONCHIELLI: *La Gioconda: Cielo e mar.* MASCAGNI: *L'Amico Fritz: Ed anche Beppe amò!* GOMES: *Fosca: Intenditi con Dio!* CILEA: *L'Arlesiana: E la solita storia.*
**(*) Ph. 9500 771/*7300 846* [id.].

Including some attractive rarities, this is an impressive recital. Carreras is never less than a conscientious artist, and though one or two items stretch the lovely voice to its limits, there is none of the coarseness that most tenors of the Italian school would indulge in. Excellent recording.

'Canciones románticas' (with ECO, Stapleton): PADILLA: *Valencia: Princesita.* LACALLE: *Amapola.* QUINTERO: *Morucha.* FREIRE: *Ay, Ay, Ay.* ALVAREZ: *La Partida.* SORIANO: *El Guitarrico.* GREVER: *Jurame.* PONCE: *Estrellita.* LÓPEZ: *Maitechu Mia.*
*** Ph. 9500/*7300* 894 [id.].

These songs have much in common with the popular Neapolitan repertoire, and some of them, such as *Valencia*, *Amapola* and Ponce's *Estrellita*, are as familiar as any of the Italian songs. They are vigorously and quite stylishly sung here by Carreras with an operatic manner that is robust rather than seeking any subtleties. But with good recording and sparkling accompaniments this is attractive enough. The tape transfer is well managed, lacking only the last degree of brightness in the orchestra, and kind to the voice.

Neapolitan songs (with ECO, Muller): DENZA: *Funiculi, funicula; I'te vurria vasà.* CARDILLO: *Core 'ngrato.* D'ANNIBALE: *'O paese d'o sole.* FALVO: *Dicitencello vuie.* LAMA: *Silenzio cantatore.* MARIO: *Santa Lucia luntana.* DI CURTIS: *Tu, ca nun chiagne! Torna a Surriento.* DI CAPUA: *'O sole mio.* BOVIO/TAGLIAFERRI: *Passione.* CIOFFI: *'Na sera 'e maggio.* CANNIO: *'O surdato 'nnamurato.*
(*) Ph. Dig. **400 015-2; 9500/*7300* 943 [id.].

José Carreras produces refined tone here. The performances have plenty of lyrical fervour and are entirely lacking in vulgarity. The opening *Funiculi, funicula* is attractively lilting, but elsewhere some listeners will wish for a more gutsy style. The recording is first-class, and the chrome-cassette transfer is smooth and full and kind to the voice. The compact disc, however, combines naturalness with added presence, yet the sound remains warmly atmospheric.

Operatic arias (with LPO, Lopez-Cobos): from: VERDI: *I vespri siciliani; Rigoletto; Ernani; Attila.* DONIZETTI: *L'Elisir d'amore; Roberto Devereux.* ROSSINI: *Stabat mater; Guglielmo Tell.*
**(*) Ph. 9500/*7300* 977.

Though the voice is one of the most beautiful among tenors today, and the selection of items is attractively varied, Carreras here shows the occasional sign of wear and only in *Una furtiva lagrima* from *L'Elisir d'amore* is there really hushed singing. Even so, the performances are strong and committed with *Cujus animam* from Rossini's *Stabat mater* bringing a fine top D-flat. Well-balanced and clear recording, though the cassette is rather soft-grained on top.

'Ave Maria': (with V. Boys' Ch., VSO, Harrer): HANDEL: *Messiah: Hallelujah.* FRANCK: *Panis angelicus.* STRADELLA: *Pietà, Signore.* ALVAREZ: *Pregária.* SCHUBERT: *Deutsche Messe: Heilig, heilig.* BACH–GOUNOD: *Ave Maria.* BIZET: *Agnus Dei.* VERDI: *4 Pezzi sacri: Laudi alla vergine Maria.* BACH: *Cantata No. 147: Jesu, joy of man's desiring.*
** Ph. Dig. 411 138-1/*4*.

To move directly from a fresh account of Handel's *Hallelujah* to the romantic religiosity of Franck's *Panis angelicus* may not be to everyone's taste, but the contributions of José Carreras are impeccably stylish, warmly eloquent and avoid sentimentality, while the choir is in good form. Some of the arrangements are less than ideal: *Jesu, joy of man's desiring* has the chorale reinforced with a trumpet. The atmospheric sound balance is agreeable and there is a good tape.

'Love is' (with O, Farnon): BRODSZKY: *Because you're mine.* HUPFELD: *As time goes by.* FAIN: *Love is a many-splendoured thing.* HAMLISCH: *The way we were.* BERNSTEIN: *West Side story: Tonight.* GROSS: *Tenderly.* STEINER: *My own true love.* MANDEL: *The sandpiper.* LLOYD WEBBER: *Cats: Memory.* LEGRAND: *The summer knows.* DARION: *Man of La Mancha: The impossible dream.* FRANÇOIS: *My way.*
(*) Ph. Dig. **412 270-2; 412 270-1/*4* [id.].

The potency of such a splendid tenor voice unleashed in standards like *The impossible dream* and *My way* is undeniable, yet José Carreras is most impressive of all in the ballads, bringing considerable nostalgia to *The way we were.* The very opening number is given a feeling of Hollywood kitsch by his slight accent, yet lyrics are admirably clear throughout, and *Tonight* from *West Side story* projects splendidly. Robert Farnon's accompaniments are stylishly made and the recording is first-class in both tape and disc formats.

Choral music

'Great choral classics' (sung by various artists): excerpts from: HANDEL: *Messiah.* BERLIOZ: *L'Enfance du Christ. Requiem.* BACH: *Cantata 147. St Matthew Passion.* FAURÉ, VERDI, MOZART: *Requiems.* POULENC: *Gloria.* ORFF: *Carmina Burana.* VIVALDI: *Gloria.* GOUNOD: *St Cecilia Mass.* BRAHMS: *German Requiem.* WALTON: *Belshazzar's Feast.* MENDELSSOHN: *Elijah.* BEETHOVEN: *Missa solemnis.* PURCELL: *Rejoice in the Lord.*
(B) ** EMI *TC2-MOM 116.*

A wide-ranging programme, quite imaginatively selected as entertainment for the car. The changing acoustics and degrees of reverberation bring less variation than might be expected in clarity of focus. Even the *Dies irae* from the Berlioz *Requiem* (surely ideal for playing in a traffic jam) avoids congestion. The opening excerpts from *Messiah* sound a little dry, and it is a pity that Muti's (rather than Previn's) *O fortuna* from *Carmina Burana* was chosen, as the quieter moments lack clarity in the tape version. Also the King's acoustic in *Jesu, joy of man's desiring* brings a rather mushy choral quality. Highlights include the *Sanctus* from Muti's Verdi *Requiem*, the delightful *Shepherd's chorus* from *L'Enfance du Christ* and the vivid *Praise ye the God of Gold* from Previn's *Belshazzar's Feast.* Purcell's anthem *Rejoice in the Lord* is heard complete.

Christ Church Cath. Ch., Oxford, Grier

'O, for the wings of a dove': MENDELSSOHN: *Hear my prayer.* WESLEY, S.: *In exitu Israel.* STANFORD: *For lo I raise up, Op. 145; Beati quorum via integra est, Op. 38; Evening service in A, Op. 12.* MOZART: *Ave verum corpus, K.618.* WOOD: *Hail gladdening light.* BACH: *Cantata No. 147: Jesu, joy of man's desiring.*
**(*) ASV ALH/*ZCALH* 919.

This is the first of a series of records centring on English music, but usually adding some more familiar items (here Mozart, Bach and Mendelssohn) to tempt a wider audience. The recording is distanced but effective and the singing expressively strong, notably so in the music by Stanford and Wesley.

'Faire is the heaven': HADLEY: *My beloved spake.* STANFORD: *Evening service in G: Magnificat; Nunc Dimittis.* HOWELLS: *Like as the hart; Collegium Regale: Te Deum.* FINZI: *God is gone up.* HARRIS, William: *Faire is the heaven; Strengthen ye the weak hands; Bring us, O Lord God.*
**(*) ASV ZLH/*ZCALH* 935.

The second Christ Church anthology is entirely of English provenance, concentrating on the late nineteenth and early twentieth centuries. All the music here is effective, but none of it is adventurous, although both Hadley and Finzi have their own harmonic flavour. The performances are eloquent and understanding, and well recorded too (on both disc and tape), but in the last resort the lack of a really strong individuality in any of the pieces included will be a drawback for the non-specialist collector.

'Carols from Christ Church': GARDNER: *Tomorrow shall be my dancing day.* HADLEY: *I sing of a maiden.* HOWELLS: *Sing lullaby; Here is the little door; A spotless rose.* BRITTEN: *Jesus, as Thou art our Saviour; A shepherd's carol.* BACH: *O little one sweet.* TCHAIKOVSKY: *The crown of roses.* WISHART: *Alleluya.* TRAD.: *Remember, O thou man; In dulci jubilo.*
** ASV ALH/*ZCALH* 938.

There is some radiantly expressive singing here, but the programme, although containing much that is attractive (the Hadley carol is delightful, as indeed are the Britten items), is rather lacking in variety: most of the items are slow and atmospheric.

Clare College, Camb., Ch. (with O), cond. John Rutter

'Christmas from Clare': King Jesus hath a garden; Up! good Christian folk; Gabriel's message; Wexford carol; Cradle song; Child in a manger; Ding dong merrily on high; Quelle est cette odeur agréable; I saw a maiden; In dulci jubilo; I saw three ships; The holly and the ivy. RUTTER: *Donkey carol; Mary's lullaby.* DARKE: *In the bleak mid-winter.* PRAETORIUS: *The noble stem of Jesse; Omnis mundus jocundetur.* TCHAIKOVSKY: *The crown of roses.* POSTON: *Jesus Christ the apple tree.* VAUGHAN WILLIAMS: *Wassail song.*
*** Argo ZRG/*KZRC* 914.

Although the excellent Clare College Choir is recorded within a similar ambience to the King's Christmas records, the character of the music-making is very different. The effect is warmer, presenting a more colourful and romantic image of Christmas, with orchestration rather in keeping with the Christmas tree lights. The opening arrangement of *King Jesus hath a garden*, using a traditional Dutch melody, immediately sets the mood with its pretty flute decorations. Moreover John Rutter is a first-rate composer of carols in his own right and his gently syncopated *Donkey carol* is memorable. The whole programme is delightful, not always especially ecclesiastical in feeling but permeated throughout with the spirit of Christmas joy. Some of the loveliest of seasonal melodies are included, and the lyrical feeling of the music-making is very persuasive. The Argo recording is splendid, with the cassette losing only very marginally in clarity of focus compared with the disc. There are few issues that will give more pleasure than this in the late evening over the Christmas period.

Cons. of Musicke, Rooley

'Le Chansonnier Cordiforme' (collection of 43 songs from the second half of the fourteenth century): includes songs by BARBINGANT, BEDYNGHAM, BINCHOIS, BUSNOIS, CARON, DUFAY, DUNSTABLE, FYRE, GHIZEGHEM, MORTON, OCKEGHEM, REGIS, VINCENET.
*** O-L D 186 D 4 (4).

'Cordiform' means 'in the shape of a heart', and that is literally what this superb collection of songs looked like in manuscript. Dufay, Dunstable and Binchois provide the core of the collection, here given with freshness in the manner which characterizes the work of this consort. The original compiler of the anthology knew what he was doing. This is a beautiful collection which, with fine balance of discreet instrumental accompaniment against stylish singing, is consistently refreshing. A superb achievement, beautifully recorded.

'The world of early music': OBRECHT: *Ich dragne de Mütse Clutse.* ISAAC: *La lo hö hö.* BUSNOIS: *Spinacino: Je ne fay plus.* TROMBONCINO: *Ostinato vo'sequire. Hor ch'el ciel e la terra.* DALZA: *Pavana and Piva ferrarese.* TIBURTINO: *La sol fa mi fa* (ricercare). AZZAIOLO: *Sentemi la formicula.* ANON./PACOLONI: *La bella Franceschina.* GUAMI: *La Brillantina.* RONTANI: *Nerinda bella.* COMPERE: *Virgo celesti.* ANON.: *Belle tenez moy. La triquoteé. Mignon allons. Christ der ist estanden. Elslein liebes Elslein. The shooting of the guns* (pavan). *Le rossignol.* SERMISY: *Las je my plains.* LE JEUNE: *Fière cruelle.* FORSTER: *Vitrum nostrum gloriosum.* DE LA TORRE: *La Spagna; Adoramos te, señor.* FAYRFAX: *I love, loved.* ANON./WYATT: *Blame not my lute.* ANON./EDWARDES: *Where grypinge griefs.* ALISON: *Dolorosa pavan.*
(M) *** Decca SPA/*KCSP* 547.

This is a quite outstanding medium-priced collection for those wanting a sampler of one current view of authentic performance of early music. The selection is generous and enterprising, and it offers much that is piquant and ear-catching both vocally and instrumentally. Penguin Books have published independently a splendid and beautifully illustrated paperback which acts as a companion to this issue, but of course it can be readily enjoyed with the notes provided with the record or the cassette (which is vividly transferred and quite the equal of the disc).

Corena, Fernando (bass)

'Grandi voci': CIMAROSA: *Il maestro di capella. Il matrimonio segreto: Udite, tutti udite.* MOZART: *Le nozze di Figaro: La vendetta. Don Giovanni: Madamina.* DONIZETTI: *L'elisir d'amore: Udite, udite, o rustici.* ROSSINI: *La Cenerentola: Miei rampolli femmini; Sia qualunque delle figlia. L'Italiana in Algeri: Ho un gran peso sulla testa. Il barbiere di Siviglia: A un dottor.*
(M) **(*) Decca 410 163.

Recorded in the 1950s, this selection from Corena's buffo repertory is an excellent reminder of a fine recording bass, not always perfectly steady of tone but reliably sparkling in patter songs. There have been few recorded accounts of Cimarosa's innocently jolly *Maestro di capella* scena so characterful as this. Recording fair for its period.

Crespin, Régine (soprano)

'Italian operatic arias' (with ROHCGO, Edward Downes): VERDI: *Il Trovatore: Tacea la notte. Un ballo: Morro ma prima; Otello: Willow song and prayer.* PONCHIELLI: *La Gioconda: Suicidio.* MASCAGNI: *Cavalleria Rusticana: Voi lo sapete.* PUCCINI: *Madama Butterfly: Un bel dì.* BOITO: *Mefistofele: L'altra notte.*
(M) **(*) Decca GRV 12.

Crespin's voice is well caught in this Grandi Voci reissue of a recital record, first issued in 1972. Her account of the *Suicidio* from *La Gioconda* is searingly dramatic and there is an affecting version of the heroine's prison aria in Boito's *Mefistofele.* There is darkness and weight in the excerpt from *Ballo,* while for Leonora's *Tacea la notte* in *Trovatore* she floats her voice more delicately than one would expect (though the lack of a trill in the cabaletta may be counted a disadvantage). Her Verdi style is not without its shortcomings, there is occasional sliding into notes and some intrusive aitches. But this can still be recommended to devotees of this most distinctive singer.

Dawson, Peter (baritone)

'The art of Peter Dawson': excerpts from HANDEL: *Acis and Galatea; Ezio; Samson; Messiah.* HAYDN: *The Creation.* ROSSINI: *Stabat mater.* ELGAR: *Caractacus.* MOZART: *Marriage of Figaro: Now your days of philandering are over.* ROSSINI: *Barber of Seville: Hey! for the town's factotum.* GOUNOD: *Faust: Even bravest heart. Philemon and Baucis: Vulcan's song.* BIZET: *Carmen: Toreador's song.* WAGNER: *Tannhäuser: O star of eve.* VERDI: *Il Trovatore: Il balen. Otello: Iago's*

creed. Songs: SCHUBERT: *The Erlking.* GLINKA: *The midnight review.* MUSSORGSKY: *Song of the flea.* TCHAIKOVSKY: *To the forest; Don Juan's serenade.* RACHMANINOV: *Christ is risen.* MALASHKIN: *O could I tell my sorrow.* BENEDICT: *Lily of Killarney: The moon hath raised her lamp.* COWEN: *Onaway! awake beloved.* TRAD.: *Turn to me.* VAUGHAN WILLIAMS: *The Vagabond; Bright is the ring of words; Silent noon.* IRELAND: *I have twelve oxen.* MCCALL: *The chant of Bacchus.*
(M) (***) HMV mono RLS/*TC-RLS* 107705-5/*3* (2).

This fine collection celebrates the highly distinctive work of a superb singer who both made his name through records and helped to popularize the gramophone in its early days. This selection makes clear – onwards from *O star of eve* recorded in 1906 – how wide his repertory was beyond the popular ballads for which he was best known. His forthright projection and complete vocal security go with natural, characterful warmth whether in opera (side one), oratorio (side two) or song (sides three and four), including many rarities. Peter Dawson's recordings were famous for the clarity of their diction, and in these excellent transfers every word comes over in the sharpest focus, so that a fun aria like Rossini's *Largo al factotum* sparkles with humour and Schubert's *Erlking* could hardly be more dramatic in its impact – the moment when Dawson changes the colour of his voice in the dialogue between father and son is immensely telling. The cassettes are no less vivid than the discs.

Deller, Alfred (counter-tenor)

'Recital': DOWLAND: *Fine knacks for ladies; In darkness let me dwell; Sorrow stay; Flow my tears.* CAMPION: *It fell on a summer's day.* ROSSETER: *What then is love.* PURCELL (arr. Tippett): *Sweeter than roses; Epithalamium; If music be the food of love; Hark how all things; Music for a while.* HANDEL: *Alma del gran Pompeo; Messiah: O thou that tellest; He was despised.*
(M) (**(*)) HMV mono HLM 7234.

Recorded between 1949 and 1952, these performances come from early in Deller's career when, almost single-handed, he changed attitudes to the counter-tenor voice, presented it as a beautiful, not an odd, phenomenon. The mannerism of the Deller 'hoot' may no longer seem stylish, but this is warmly characterful singing still, to delight many more than historians of interpretation. Excellent transfers.

Domingo, Placido (tenor)

'Portrait': VERDI: *Giovanna d'Arco: Sotto una quercia parvemi . . . Pondo è letal. Un Ballo in maschera: La rivedra nell'estasi; Dì tu se fedele; Forse la soglia . . . Ma se m'è forza. Don Carlo: Fontainebleau Foresta immense . . . Io la vidi. Aïda: Se quel guerrier io fossi . . . Celeste Aïda.* GOUNOD: *Faust: Quel trouble inconnu . . . Salut! demeure.* BOITO: *Mefistofele: Dai campi, dai prati.* PUCCINI: *Manon Lescaut: Tra voi belle; Donna non vidi mai; Ah, Manon, mi tradisci. Tosca: Dammi i colori . . . Recondita armonia; E lucevan le stelle.*
**(*) HMV ASD/*TC-ASD* 4031 [Ang. S/*4XS* 37835].

These thirteen arias from various EMI sources give a marvellous display of glorious heroic tenor tone with no coarseness. But the collection does bring home the closeness with which EMI engineers have tended to record Domingo's voice, and the result overall is a little heavy, even in an aria as slight as Des Grieux's *Tra voi belle*. Also some of the excerpts end a little abruptly, notably the closing *E lucevan le stelle* from *Tosca*. The cassette is just as vivid as the disc.

'Greatest hits': MASCAGNI: *Cavalleria Rusticana: Intanto, amici, qua . . . Viva il vino.* GOUNOD: *Faust: Quel trouble . . . Salut! demeure; Roméo et Juliette: L'amour! Ah! Lève-toi, soleil.* VERDI: *Rigoletto: Questa o quella. La Forza del destino: La vita è inferno; O tu che in seno agli angeli. Un Ballo in maschera: Di tu se fedele.* CILEA: *Adriana Lecouvreur: L'anima ho stanca.* PUCCINI: *Turandot: Non piangere, Liù. La Fanciulla del West: Una parola sola! Or son sei mesi. Gianni Schicchi: Avete torto!; Firenze è come un albero fiorito.*

BIZET: *Les Pêcheurs de perles: A cette voix quel trouble . . . Je crois entendre encore.*
(M) *** RCA Gold GL/*GK* 14364 [AGL1/*AGK1* 4364].

This is a straight reissue of a recital disc originally made in 1974. Domingo was in top form and his voice sounds agreeably fresh, though some might feel that the sobriquet '*Greatest hits*' is misapplied here, for the programme is enterprising, even though it contains several obvious popular favourites. Highlights include the *Gianni Schicchi* excerpts, especially the sparkling *Avete torto!*, and a memorably beautiful account of the aria from *The Pearl fishers*, but overall the programme is most satisfying, the recording vivid. The chrome cassette is smooth and natural on side one but gives more presence to the voice on the second side, when the level rises. A bargain.

'Con amore': RENIS: *Un uomo tra la folla; Il coraggio di dire ti amo.* VERDI: *Aïda: Se quel guerrier . . . Celeste Aïda. Rigoletto: La donna è mobile; Questa o quella. Il Trovatore: Di quella pira.* LEONCAVALLO: *I Pagliacci: Recitar . . . Vesti la giubba.* PUCCINI: *Tosca: E lucevan le stelle; La Bohème: Che gelida manina.* DONIZETTI: *L'Elisir d'amore: Una furtiva lagrima.* MASCAGNI: *Cavalleria Rusticana: Intanto amici . . . Viva il vino spumeggiante.* BIZET: *Carmen: Flower song.*
**(*) RCA RL/*RK* 14265 [AFL1/*AFK1* 4265].

An impressive collection of operatic arias, mostly recorded early in Domingo's career, tricked out with two popular songs by Renis, charmingly and unaffectedly done. The *Aïda*, *Pagliacci* and *Tosca* items stem from complete sets, and are excellent. At this period Domingo had a degree more lightness – as shown in the *Rigoletto* arias – but did not always sing with the easy command we now expect. The different recordings catch the voice well.

'Arias': DONIZETTI: *L'Elisir d'amore: Una furtiva lagrima; Venti scudi.* PUCCINI: *Le Villi: Roberto's aria; Madama Butterfly: Love duet* (with Renata Scotto)*; Addio fiorito asil. Il Tabarro: Folle di gelosia. Gianni Schicchi: Firenze è come.* MASSENET: *Le Cid: O Souverain.* CILEA: *Adriana Lecouvreur: La dolcissima effigia.* VERDI: *Requiem: Ingemisco.*
*** CBS 74022/*40*- [M/*MT* 37207].

Taken from a wide variety of complete CBS sets including rarities like *Le Cid*, this brings characteristically consistent singing with the warmly heroic voice used with natural, easy artistry. Domingo recorded this account of the *Ingemisco* from Verdi's *Requiem* early in his career and he responded superbly to the challenge of Leonard Bernstein's slow tempo. Generally good recording. The chrome tape is vibrant but rather fierce.

'The best of Domingo': VERDI: *Aïda: Se quel guerrier . . . Celeste Aïda. Rigoletto: La donna è mobile. Luisa Miller: Oh! fede negar . . . Quando le sere. Un Ballo in maschera: Forse la soglia . . . Ma se m'è forza perderti; Di'tu se fedele. La Traviata: Lunge da lei . . . De'miei bollenti spiriti.* BIZET: *Carmen: Flower song.* FLOTOW: *Martha: Ach so fromm.* DONIZETTI: *L'Elisir d'amore: Una furtiva lagrima.* OFFENBACH: *Contes d'Hoffmann: Legend of Kleinzach.*
*** DG 2531/*3301* 386 [id.].

A popular recital showing Domingo in consistent form, the voice and style vibrant and telling, as the opening *Celeste Aïda* readily shows, followed by an agreeably relaxed *La donna è mobile.* In the lyric arias, the *Flower song* and the excerpts from *Martha* and *L'Elisir d'amore* there is not the honeyed sweetness of a Gigli, but in the closing *Hoffmann* scena the sheer style of the singing gives special pleasure. The sound is vivid throughout, on disc and chrome tape alike.

'Gala opera concert' (with LAPO, Giulini): DONIZETTI: *L'Elisir d'amore: Una furtiva lagrima. Lucia di Lammermoor: Tomba degli avi miei . . , Fra poco.* VERDI: *Ernani: Mercè, diletti amici . . . Come rugiada; Dell'esilio nel dolore . . . O tu che l'alma adora. Il Trovatore: Ah sì, ben mio; Di quella pira. Aïda: Se quel guerrier io fossi . . . Celeste Aïda.* HALÉVY: *La Juive: Rachel, quand du Seigneur.* MEYERBEER: *L'Africaine: Pays merveilleux . . . O Paradis.* BIZET: *Les Pêcheurs de perles: Je*

crois entendre encore. Carmen: La fleur que tu m'avais jetée (with R. Wagner Chorale).
*** DG Dig. **400 030-2**; 2532/*3302* 009 [id.].

Recorded in 1980 in connection with a gala in San Francisco, this is as noble and resplendent a tenor recital as you will find. Domingo improves in detail even on the fine versions of some of these arias he had recorded earlier, and the finesse of the whole gains greatly from the sensitive direction of Giulini, though the orchestra is a little backward. Otherwise excellent recording, and the chrome transfer is first-rate too, with tingling digital brass in the *Aïda* excerpt; however, the sound has a more dramatic range on side two than side one (with a rise in level). But it is on the compact disc that the honeyed beauty of the voice is given the greatest immediacy. The orchestra too gains resonance in the bass and this added weight improves the balance.

'Be my love' (with LSO, Loges; Marcel Peters, piano): LEHÁR: *The Land of Smiles: Dein ist mein ganzes Herz.* Popular and Neapolitan songs.
** DG **413 541-2**; 2530/*3300* 700 [id.].

This collection does not show Domingo at his best. The performances are lusty and the recording is not very refined, the voice projected forward and the whole presentation without subtlety. The tape transfer is vivid but coarse.

Early Music Cons. of L., Munrow

'Music at the Court of Maximilian I': SENFL: *Mit Lust tritt ich an diesen Tanz. Ich stuend an einem Morgen. Das Gläut zu Speyer. Meniger Stellt nach Geld. Gottes Namen. Ach Elslein. Ich weiss nit. Entlaubet ist der Walde. Was wird es doch. Quis dabit oculis nostris.* ANON.: *Welsh dance.* KOTTER: *Kochesperger Spaniel.* ANON.: *Christ ist erstanden.* ISAAC: *Innsbruck, ich muss dich lassen. Helogierons ous. Maudit soyt. La Mora.* FINCK: *Sauff aus und machs nit lang.* KEUTZENHOFF: *Frisch und frölich wölln wir leben.*
(M) *** Decca Ser. SA/*KSC* 6.

Maximilian I was inordinately vain. He was also shrewd enough to realize that lavish patronage of the arts would ensure that posterity would remember him. His dedicated support meant that the decade between 1486 and 1496 became a watershed for the medieval development of the German Lied. Clearly the mid-century had been dominated by the music of Ludwig Senfl (who died about 1555) and Senfl's music is rightly given the lion's share of this excellent collection. To sample the individuality of Senfl's musical personality try band four on side one, the piquant bell ringers' trio, *Das Gläut zu Speyer.* In variety of arrangement and sophistication of presentation this record represents the zenith of the achievement of David Munrow and his Consort. It was recorded in 1973 as part of a series of records for Argo, three of which (including this one) are now available reissued at a reasonable price on Decca's Serenata label. The sound is strikingly lively and vivid, with little to choose between disc and cassette.

'Ecco la primavera' (Florentine music of the 14th century): LANDINI: *Ecco la primavera; Giunta vaga bilta; Questa fanciulla; Amor; De dimni tu; Cara mi donna; La bionda treccia; Donna 'l tuo parti mento.* ANON.: *Lamento di Tristan; Trotto; 2 Saltarelli; Quan je voy le duc; La Manfredina; Istampitta Ghaetta.* ANON.: *Biance flour.* PIERO: *Con dolce brama.* TERANO: Rosetta. LORENZO DI FIRENZE: *Da, da, da, a chi'avareggia.* GIOVANNI DI FIRENZE: *Con brachi assai.* JACOBO DA BOLOGNA: *Fenice fu'.*
(M) *** Decca Ser. SA/*KSC* 12 [Lon. STS/*5-15583*].

This collection of fourteenth-century Florentine music should have a wide general appeal. Landini has an immediate approachability and this extends to much else on this fine record. No one knows exactly how or on what instruments the accompaniment would have been performed, and the Early Music Consort solve the problem with their usual combination of scholarship and imagination. The singers include artists of the distinction of James Bowman and the players are quite first-rate. David Munrow's recorder playing is virtuosic. Attractive music, expertly transcribed and played, and well recorded. The cassette too is of excellent quality.

'The art of David Munrow': 1, *Munrow as soloist;* 2, *Film music* (inc. SUSATO, CORELLI, PRAETORIUS); 3, *The small consort* (inc. HANDEL, PURCELL, DUFAY); 4, *The large consort* (inc. PURCELL, PRAETORIUS, DUFAY); 5, *Sacred music* (inc. BACH, JOSQUIN DES PRÉS); 6, *Secular dance music* (HOLBORNE, SUSATO, PRAETORIUS).
(M) *** HMV SLS/*TC-SLS* 5136 (3).

The music chosen by EMI to represent the achievement of the late David Munrow is divided into six separate groups, each carefully balanced to make a diverse and enjoyable miniature concert in itself. In the first collection Munrow himself leads. The second group, music for films, includes his own compositions and arrangements. The programme for small consort is particularly attractive, ranging from Josquin's *El Grillo* and Solange's *Fumeux fume* ('He who fumes and lets off steam'), with its bizarre accompaniment for bass kortholt and bass rebec, to expressive and lively items by Purcell and Dufay. These composers are also memorably featured in the section for large consort (Dufay's Mass *Se la face ay pale* a highlight). The sacred music is balanced by the closing secular dances, with admirable invention from Holborne and Praetorius, always imaginatively and sometimes exotically scored. The recording is of demonstration quality on disc and tape alike.

'Music of the Gothic era': LEONIN: *Viderunt omnes.* VITRY: *Impudenter – Virtutibus laudabilis.* ANON.: *Clap clap – Sus Robin.* MACHAUT: *Christe, qui lux es – Veni, creator spiritus. Hoquetus David. Lasse! – Se j'aime mon loyal ami – Pour quoy.* ROYLLART: *Rex Karole – Leticie.*
(M) *** DG 2547/*3347* 051 [from Arc. 2710 019].

Munrow's choice here (extracted from a three-disc survey, DG Arc. 2723 045) covers a period of two centuries, from Leonin's organum to the *Rex Karole* of Philippe Royllart, dating from the second half of the fourteenth century. Munrow projects this music with expressive liveliness. Its presentation is essentially conjectural, but to bring the music back to life is the most important thing, and Munrow certainly does that. The recording is excellent, with a good equivalent cassette.

'Music from the time of the Crusades': ANON.: *La quinte estampie real; Parti de mal; Chevalier, mult estes Guariz; Danse real; Sede Syon, in pulvere; Condicio – O nacio – Mana prima; O tocius Asie; La uitime estampie real; Cum sint difficilia; Je ne puis – Amors me tienent –Veritatem; la tierche estampie real.* MARCABRU: *Pax in nomine domini.* CUIOT DE DIJON: *Chanterai por mon corage.* WALTER VON DER VOGEL-WEIDE: *Palastinalied.* LE CHATELAIN DE COUCY: *Li noviaus tens.* FAIDIT, Gaucelm: *Fortz chausa es.* CANON DE BETHUNE: *Ahi! amours.* RICHARD COEUR-DE-LION: *Ja nus hons pris.* THIBAUT DE CHAMPAGNE: *Au tens Plain de Felonnie.*
(M) *** Decca Ser. 410 135-1.

Not all the music on this disc can be associated with the Crusades themselves, but in his scholarly and informative note Ian Bent does not make particular claims that it is. David Munrow's work with the Early Music Consort is justly admired, combining as it does a thorough knowledge of early music and imaginative flair. Most of the accompaniments are purely speculative (only the melodic line survives in some cases) so that listeners should be prepared to approach these lively performances for what they are, imaginative reconstructions rather than exact reproductions of what was heard in the thirteenth century. The performances like the realizations are brilliantly effective, and the record deserves the highest praise for its blend of scholarship and imagination.

Ely Cath. Ch., Wills

'Service high and anthems clear' (with Le Prevost, organ): WESLEY, Samuel: *Exultate Deo.* WESLEY, S. S.: *Blessed be the God and Father.* STAINER: *Evening canticles in B flat.* ATTWOOD: *Come, Holy Ghost.* PARRY: *I was glad.* STANFORD: *Evening canticles in G.* WOOD, Charles: *O Thou, the central Orb.*
*** Hyp. Dig. A/*KA* 66012.

An outstanding demonstration of what

well-balanced digital recording can offer in cathedral music. While not detracting from the natural overall blend, inner detail is remarkably clear and the choral tone has a fresh incisiveness to give all this music splendid life and vigour. Parry's *I was glad* is superbly done, and the opening *Exultate Deo* makes an equally strong impression. The canticle settings of Stainer and Stanford are memorable and the concert closes with *O Thou, the central Orb*, showing Charles Wood at his most eloquently expressive. This is highly recommendable in every respect, and the cassette – transferred at an impressively high level – is excellent too, though there is a hint of pulsing on two fortissimo cadences.

Evans, Geraint (baritone)

'Operatic recital' (with SRO, Balkwill): HANDEL: *Berenice: Si, tra i ceppi. Semele: Leave me, radiant light*. MOZART: *Le Nozze di Figaro: Non più andrai. Don Giovanni: Madamina* (Catalogue aria). *Die Zauberflöte: Ein Vogelfänger. L'Oca del Cairo: Ogni momento.* BEETHOVEN: *Fidelio: Ach, welch ein Augenblick*. LEONCAVALLO: *Pagliacci: Si puo.* DONIZETTI: *Don Pasquale: Un fuoco insolito.* VERDI: *Otello: Vanne ... Credo in un Dio crudel. Falstaff: Ehi! paggio ... L'onore.* BRITTEN: *A Midsummer Night's Dream: When my cue comes* (Bottom's dream). MUSSORGSKY: *Boris Godunov: Pravoslaviye.*
(M) *** Decca Jub. JB/*KJBC* 60.

This is a marvellous display of wide-ranging virtuosity, of artistic bravura such as we know from almost any performance that this ebullient and lovable singer gives. Part of Evans's mastery lies in the way he can convey the purest comedy, even draw laughs without ever endangering the musical line through excessive buffoonery. His Mozart characters are almost unmatchable – Figaro, Leporello, Papageno – while it is good to be reminded that here is a singer who can be a formidable Iago as well as the most complete Falstaff of the day. Good accompaniment and recording, and one of Decca's highest-quality cassettes, vivid vocally and with a richly atmospheric orchestral backing. Occasionally the microphone – and this is equally noticeable on disc and tape – catches a slightly gritty quality in the tone, but this is not serious enough to withhold the strongest recommendation for this representation of one of the greatest British singers of our generation at the peak of his form.

Ferrier, Kathleen (contralto)

'Folksongs and songs by Roger Quilter': Folksongs: *Ma bonny lad. The keel row. Blow the wind southerly. I have a bonnet trimmed with blue. My boy Willie. I know where I'm going. The fidgety bairn. I will walk with my love. Ca' the yowes. O waly waly. Willow willow. Stuttering lovers. Have you seen but a whyte lillie grow? Ye banks and braes. Drink to me only. Down by the Salley Gardens. The lover's curse.* QUILTER: *Now sleeps the crimson petal; The fair house of joy; To daisies; Over the mountains.*
(M) (***) Decca mono ACL/*KACC* 309.

Kathleen Ferrier's freshness and warmth in this repertoire, which she obviously loved, make this an indispensable recital, and the transfers are of excellent quality, the voice open with a natural bloom on it. Considering the source of the originals, there is miraculously little background noise. The cassette is quite the equal of the disc.

MAHLER: *Das Lied von der Erde; 3 Rückert songs* (with Patzak, VPO, Walter). HANDEL: *Judas Maccabaeus: Father of Heaven. Messiah: He was despised; O thou that tellest. Samson: Return, O God of hosts.* BACH: *Mass in B min.: Agnus Dei; Qui sedes. St John Passion: All is fulfilled. St Matthew Passion: Grief for sin* (with LPO, Boult). SCHUMANN: *Frauenliebe und Leben, Op. 42.* SCHUBERT: *Die junge Nonne. Romance. Du liebst mich nicht. Der Tod und das Mädchen. Suleika. Du bist die Ruh'.* BRAHMS: *Immer leise. Der Tod das ist die kühle Nacht. Botschaft. Von ewiger Liebe* (with Walter, piano). GLUCK: *Orfeo: What is life.* HANDEL: *Rodelinda: Art thou troubled.* MENDELSSOHN: *Elijah: O rest in the Lord.* SCHUBERT: *Gretchen am Spinnrade. An die Musik. Der Musensohn.* WOLF: *Verborgenheit. Der Gärtner. Auf ein altes Bild. Auf einer Wanderung.* TRAD.: *The Keel Row. Ma*

bonny lad. Blow the wind southerly. Willow, willow. Ye banks and braes. Drink to me only. Lover's curse (with Spurr, piano). BRIDGE: *Go not, happy day.* Arr. BRITTEN: *Come you not from Newcastle.* Arr. HUGHES: *Kitty my love.* STANFORD: *The fairy lough.* VAUGHAN WILLIAMS: *Silent noon* (with Stone, piano). TRAD.: *Ca' the yowes* (with Newmark, piano).
(***) Decca *K 160 K 54* (4).

A Kathleen Ferrier anthology on tape is most welcome (there is an even more comprehensive album of seven discs, Decca AFK 1–7), and the selection here readily demonstrates not only the amazing range but the consistency with which her radiant vocal quality lit up almost everything she recorded. The transfers have been, for the most part, well done to minimize the inadequacies of the originals, although unfortunately Mahler's *Das Lied von der Erde* suffers from the restriction of high frequencies that marred the separate cassette issue; the voice is unimpaired but the orchestra is muffled. The *Rückert Lieder*, however, emerge unscathed and are among the finest treasures here. Some of the older recordings (especially those with Bruno Walter at the piano) are also restricted, but not unacceptably so. Yet even earlier records yield a fresher sound (a highlight is Schubert's *An die Musik*, recorded with Phillis Spurr). The Bach and Handel arias (also available separately – see the composer index above) have Boult's overlaid stereo orchestral accompaniments. But among the most refreshing items here are the folksongs, sung with a simple innocence that few other singers have approached.

'The world of Kathleen Ferrier': TRAD.: *Blow the wind southerly; The keel row; Ma bonny lad; Kitty my love.* BRIDGE: *Go not happy day.* Arr. BRITTEN: *Come you not from Newcastle.* SCHUBERT: *An die Musik; Der Musensohn.* BRAHMS: *Sapphische Ode.* JENSEN: *Altar.* MAHLER: *Rückert Lieder: Um Mitternacht.* HANDEL: *Rodelinda: Art thou troubled? Messiah: He was despised.* GLUCK: *Orfeo: Che puro ciel; Che farò.* BACH: *St Matthew Passion: Have mercy, Lord.* GRÜBER: *Silent night.*
(M) (**(*)) Decca mono PA/*KCSP* 172.

This selection admirably shows Kathleen Ferrier's range, and most of her famous recordings are here (though not, surprisingly, *O rest in the Lord*). It will be treasured especially for her spoken introduction to the Jensen song (taken from a BBC broadcast), which she then sings exquisitely. The transfers are vivid and made at a high level; they seem almost to accentuate the faults of the originals from which they are taken (mostly 78 r.p.m. discs), with clicks and background noises and occasional blasting. But some items, including the Bach, Handel and Mahler, are unblemished.

'The singer and the person' (with Pears, Britten, Moore, Walter, Winifred Ferrier) including songs by: BRAHMS, PARRY, SCHUBERT, BERKELEY; excerpts from GLUCK: *Orfeo,* BRITTEN: *The Rape of Lucretia;* and the singer's own autobiographical and musical comments.
(***) BBC mono REGL/*ZCF* 368 [Ara. 8070/*9070*].

In every way this is an effective and moving tribute, including as it does Kathleen Ferrier's own spoken comments and contributions from Bruno Walter among others. There is a good deal of music; most of the recordings are primitive (the *Four Poems of St Teresa of Avila* by Lennox Berkeley, which ends the recital, sound very scratchy), but the excerpt from *The Rape of Lucretia* is especially valuable.

Fischer-Dieskau, Dietrich (baritone)

'Grandi voci': MOZART: *Le Nozze di Figaro: Hai gia vinta . . . Vedro mentrio sospiro.* HAYDN: *Acis and Galatea: Tergi i vezzosi rai.* VERDI: *Macbeth: Perfidi! all' angelo contro me v'unite. La Traviata: Di provenza il mar. Don Carlo: O Carlo ascolta.* PUCCINI: *Tosca: Tre sbirri . . . Una carrozza.* SCHUMANN: *Scenes from Faust* (excerpt). WAGNER: *Parsifal: Ja, wehe! wehe!. Götterdämmerung: Brünhilde, Die hehrste Frau . . . Gegrusst sei teurer Held.* MAHLER: *Das Lied von der Erde: Von der Schonheit.* BRITTEN: *War Requiem: After the blast of the lightning from the East.*
(M) *** Decca GRV 7.

This generous collection provides superb

evidence of the enormous span of Fischer-Dieskau's artistry, including as it does unexpected corners of the repertory. His keenly intelligent, stylish command, whether as the Count in *Figaro*, as Macbeth, as Scarpia or in the Britten recording of Schumann's *Faust scenes*, is extraordinary. It was imaginative to include the passage from Britten's *War Requiem*. First-rate recording.

Freni, Mirella (soprano)

'Grandi voci': HANDEL: *Alcina: Chi m'insegna il caro padre; Barbara, io ben io so.* ROSSINI: *Guglielmo Tell: S'allontanano alfine . . . Selva opaca, deserta brughiera.* VERDI: *Falstaff: Sul fil d'un soffio etesio.* BELLINI: *Bianca e Fernando: Ove son; Che m'avvenne . . . Sorgi, o padre.* LEONCAVALLO: *Pagliacci: Qual fiamma avea nei guardo! . . . Stridono lassù.* PUCCINI: *La Bohème: Sì, mi chiamano Mimì; Donde lieta uscì. Tosca: Vissi d'arte. Madama Butterfly: Un bel dì; Come una masca prigioniera . . . Con onor more.*
(M) **(*) Decca GRV 15.

Since making these recordings – many of them taken from complete Decca sets – Freni has expanded to dramatic roles, but her purity, clarity and sweetness in these mainly lyric roles are a consistent delight, nicely varied. Sound still fresh.

Freni, Mirella (soprano), **Luciano Pavarotti** (tenor)

'In concert': VERDI: *La Traviata: Brindisi; Parigi o cara. I Vespri siciliani: Bolero.* PONCHIELLI: *La Gioconda: Cielo e mar.* DONIZETTI: *La Figlia del regimento: Convien partir. L'Elisir d'amore: Una parola . . . chiedi all'aura.* MEYERBEER: *L'Africana: O paradiso.* BOITO: *Mefistofele: L'altra notte.* MASCAGNI: *L'Amico Fritz: Suzel, buon dì.* MASSENET: *Werther: Pourquoi me réveiller.*
(M) **(*) Decca Ace SDD/*KSDC* 578 [Lon. JL 41009].

Both artists come from the same small town in Italy, Modena, where they were born in 1935. The happiness of their musical partnership in these concert performances, recorded live, comes out in each of the duets, to which are added some attractive solo performances. The *Werther* and *Africana* items are both new to Pavarotti's repertory; sweet singing from Freni too, though her delivery could be more characterful. The recording is robust, forward and clear – on both disc and cassette – but not especially refined. Some might find the vociferous applause irritating.

Freni, Mirella, Renata Scotto (sopranos)

'In duet' (with Nat. PO, Magiera or Ansielmi): MERCADANTE: *Le due illustri rivali: Leggo gia nel vostro cor.* BELLINI: *Bianca e Fernando: Ove son; Che m'avvenne . . . Sorgi o padre. Norma: Dormono entrambi . . . Mira, o Norma.* MOZART: *Le Nozze di Figaro: Cosa mi narri . . . Sull'aria.*
**(*) Decca SXL/*KSXC* 6970 [Lon. OSA/5-26652].

The Mozart will win no award for style, but otherwise this is a fascinating celebration of the charms and vocal beauty of two singers who might have been thought too alike to make good duettists. Scotto by her latterday standards is in excellent voice, with the top more perfectly under control if occasionally squally. This account of the big *Norma* scene (ending with *Mira, o Norma*) is more relaxed and delicate than the one to which Scotto contributed in the complete CBS set of the opera. The other Bellini item is also most welcome, with its dreamy melody in compound time, and so is the even rarer Mercadante duet, with its traditional chains of thirds. Warm and atmospheric recording, with a matching high-level tape transfer.

Gedda, Nicolai (tenor)

'The art of Nicolai Gedda': Arias and excerpts from: AUBER: *La Muette de Portici.* ADAM: *Le postillon de Longjumeau.* ROSSINI: *Guillaume Tell.* BERLIOZ: *Benvenuto Cellini.* THOMAS: *Mignon.* GOUNOD: *Mirelle.* MASSENET: *Manon; Werther.* LALO: *Le roi d'Ys.* MOZART: *Die Entführung aus dem Serail; Così fan tutte; Die Zauberflöte.* WEBER: *Oberon.*

GOLDMARK: *Die Königin von Saba*. WAGNER: *Lohengrin*. VERDI: *Un Ballo in maschera*. DONIZETTI: *L'Elisir d'amore; Don Pasquale*. PONCHIELLI: *La Gioconda*. PUCCINI: *La Bohème*. CILEA: *L'Arlesiana*. VERACINI: *Rosalinda*. STRAUSS, J. Jnr: *Der Zigeunerbaron*. LEHÁR: *Das Land des Lächelns*. GLINKA: *A life for the Tsar*. TCHAIKOVSKY: *Eugene Onegin*. RIMSKY-KORSAKOV: *May night*. Songs by VERACINI; RESPIGHI; CERNEVALI; R. STRAUSS; TCHAIKOVSKY; RACHMANINOV.
(M) **(*) HMV SLS/*TC-SLS* 5250 (3) [Ang. RLCX/*4RCX* 3204].

Gedda – every producer's ideal of a recording tenor – has encompassed an astonishingly wide range of repertory in his long recording career, and these three discs represent it splendidly. From the two sides devoted to the French repertory one especially marvels at the heady freedom on top in the Adam aria, recorded early in his career. Other recordings give hints of the strain which has latterly marred that upper register but, whether in opera of many schools, in operetta or in song, this most polyglot of tenors has a seemingly innate sense of idiomatic style. This collection covers many rarities from opera sets and recital records long deleted, all splendidly transferred. The cassettes are excellently managed too, the sound smooth yet vivid.

Gigli, Beniamino (tenor)

'The best of Gigli': BIZET: *Agnus Dei*. Arias from LEONCAVALLO: *I Pagliacci*. VERDI: *Rigoletto; Aïda*. PUCCINI: *Tosca; La Bohème*. DONIZETTI: *L'Elisir d'amore*. MASSENET: *Manon*. BIZET: *Carmen; Les Pêcheurs de perles*. HANDEL: *Xerxes*. GOUNOD: *Faust*.
(***) HMV mono ALP/*TC-ALP* 1681.

For most collectors this single disc anthology will make an ideal representation of Gigli's art. The recordings all date from the 1930s and are of excellent quality. In every item his individuality is clear, buoyant and charming, using his unique golden tone (never more telling than in the Donizetti and Puccini items) with cavalier freedom. There are stylistic points to query, but the natural magnetism is consistently compelling. The recording shows a somewhat limited top, but this affects the orchestral accompaniments rather than impairing the freshness of the vocal quality. The cassette transfers are well managed, at a generally high level: the *Aïda* aria (*Celeste Aïda*), for instance, has striking presence. There are excellent notes giving the recording dates and relating the music to Gigli's career.

'Sacred songs and favourite ballads': HANDEL: *Xerxes: Ombra mai fù* (*Largo*). *Ave Maria* settings by SCHUBERT; BACH–GOUNOD; GIBILARO. SCHUBERT: *Serenade*. BIZET: *Agnus Dei*. FRANCK: *Panis angelicus*. SULLIVAN: *The lost chord*. YRADIER: *La Paloma*. LEONCAVALLO: *Mattinata*. DENZA: *Occhi di fata*. ROSSINI: *La Danza*. MARTINI: *Plaisir d'amour*. MURRAY: *I'll walk beside you*. TOSTI: *Goodbye*.
(M) (**(*)) HMV mono HLM/*TC-HLM* 7019 [Sera. S 60036].

Good taste was never Gigli's strong suit, but his way with these trifles is nothing if not winsome, with the pouting manner outrageously but compellingly used. Even at his least defensible – and the intrusive aitches in Schubert's *Ave Maria* hardly improve the music's line – Gigli emerges as a major, totally unmistakable artist. His passionate advocacy of Bizet's *Agnus Dei* (which uses a tune from *L'Arlésienne*) completely triumphs over the rather woolly recording of the accompanying chorus, while Rossini's *La Danza* has a memorable sparkle. The two closing ballads are sung in English: *I'll walk beside you* has a gloriously honeyed closing cadence. The recordings date from the 1930s, except Schubert's *Ave Maria*, which comes from 1947. Both disc and tape have good clarity and presence and there is excellent documentation.

'The art of Gigli' (1918–1946): religious arias; songs; arias and duets from: PONCHIELLI: *La Gioconda*. GIORDANO: *Fedora*. MASCAGNI: *Cavalleria Rusticana; Lodoletta; L'Amico Fritz; Isabeau*. LEONCAVALLO: *I Pagliacci*. MASSENET: *Manon; Werther*. DONIZETTI: *L'Elisir d'amore; La Favorita*. PUCCINI: *Tosca; La Bohème; Manon Lescaut*.

BIZET: *Carmen*. VERDI: *Aïda; Il Trovatore*. MOZART: *Don Giovanni*. CILEA: *L'Arlesiana*. HALÉVY: *La Juive*. LALO: *Le Roi d'Ys*. BOITO: *Mefistofele*. GOUNOD: *Faust*.
(M) (***) HMV mono RLS 729 (3).

In the rich generation of Italian tenors following Caruso, Gigli stood out as the most honey-toned and positive of character. He was a natural star, and though his musical taste was not impeccable this wide-ranging selection from his recordings for HMV – missing out an important period in the late 1920s – consistently reveals that star quality. It is fascinating to compare early and late recordings, but the marvel is the voice's consistency. The recording is smooth, but in general these transfers have too little top, robbing the voice of some of its brightness.

'The art of Gigli', Vol. 2 (1947–55): songs; ballads; arias from operettas and from CESTI: *Orontea*. MONTEVERDI: *Arianna*. ALFANO: *Don Juan de Mantua*. MASCAGNI: *L'Amico Fritz*. HANDEL: *Atalanta*. GIORDANO: *Marcella*. DONIZETTI: *L'Elisir d'amore*. PUCCINI: *Turandot*. Duets (with Rina Gigli) from: VERDI: *Otello*. MASCAGNI: *L'Amico Fritz*. BOITO: *Mefistofele*.
(M) (**(*)) HMV mono RLS 732.

It would be only too easy to underestimate the worth of this additional box of Gigli recordings. The second and third discs contain a great deal of lightweight material – Neapolitan songs, and items like *Mother Machree* and *The Rosary* which are of very limited musical interest. But Gigli sang this material with inimitable style: his *Funiculi, funicula*, for instance, has irresistible zest, and although the voice had darkened by the mid-1950s, surprisingly often the bloom comes back to give a frisson of pleasure. The set opens with a series of operatic recordings made in 1947–9 (Gigli already in his late fifties) and the voice shows an astonishing freshness: the late account of *Nessun dorma* (1949) has undoubted interest alongside the 1951 recordings of duets with his daughter. Among the treasures here is Gigli's very last session, recorded in March 1955 at the Kingsway Hall in experimental stereo, a touching close to a great career. Perhaps this is a box more for Gigli devotees than the general collector, but lovers of Italian popular song will find much to enjoy, particularly as the sound is so consistently good, open and clear at the top, and often with convincing orchestral quality too.

'The art of Gigli', Vol. 3 (1918–43): arias from: BOITO: *Mefistofele*. MASCAGNI: *Iris; Cavalleria Rusticana*. DONIZETTI: *La Favorita; Lucia di Lammermoor*. BIZET: *Les Pêcheurs de perles*. PONCHIELLI: *La Gioconda*. PUCCINI: *Tosca; La Bohème; Madama Butterfly*. VERDI: *La Forza del destino; Rigoletto; I Lombardi; Attila; Un Ballo in maschera*. THOMAS: *Mignon*. GIORDANO: *Andrea Chénier*.
(M) (***) HMV mono RLS/*TC-RLS* 7710 (3).

Gigli's tenor was perhaps the most purely beautiful ever put on record, and this wide-ranging collection – including his very first record of Boito made in 1918 – demonstrates that consistently. There are many rarities – including a whole side of pre-electric recordings, and two sides made in the late 1920s – as well as three sides of excerpts taken from complete recordings made late in his career, including *La Bohème*, *Tosca*, *Cavalleria Rusticana*, *Andrea Chénier* and *Ballo in maschera*. Gigli often indulged in unstylish tricks, scattering intrusive aitches – as here in the *Ingemisco* from Verdi's *Requiem* – but the intensity as well as the beauty of each performance marks out a master. The transfers by Keith Hardwick are superb, and the cassettes are excellent too.

'(The) Glory of Venice'

'The Glory of Venice' (with (i) Monteverdi Ch., Philip Jones Brass Ens., Eliot Gardiner; (ii) Magdalen College, Oxford, Ch., Rose; (iii) St John's College, Camb., Ch., Guest): (i) GABRIELI, G.: *Canzona: Sol sol la sol; Écoutez ô princes; L'ange dit aux bergers; Qui vîtes-vous, bergers?; Notre Sauveur; Sonata pian' e forte; O grand mystère*. BASSANO: *Aujourd'hui le Christ est né*. MONTEVERDI: *Que les cieux exultent*. (ii) BASSANO: *Salut, Reine des cieux*.

GABRIELI, G.: *Aujourd'hui le Christ est né; Peuples battez des mains; Je suis celui qui suis; Avec un grand vertu; Que je t'aime, Seigneur; Réjouissons-nous, chacun de nous.* GABRIELI, A.: *Ricercar arioso II and IV* (for organ)*; Sainte et immaculée virginité; Louez le Seigneur; Hélas Seigneur; Salut, Reine des cieux.* (i) LUPPI: *Canzon: La Séraphine.* BANCHIERI: *Echo fantasia.* GABRIELI, A.: *Ricercar del duodecimo tuono.* MASSAINO: *Canzon for eight trombones.* GABRIELI, G.: *Canzon XIII; Canzon primi toni.* MONTEVERDI: *Chantez au Seigneur un cantique nouveau; Seigneur, ne me reprenez pas dans votre indignation; Nous t'adorons, Seigneur.* (iii) MONTEVERDI: *Mass for 4 voices; Louez le Seigneur.*
(M) *** Decca D 269 D 3/*K 269 K 33*.

A splendid collection, outstanding in its field and superbly recorded on both discs and the demonstration-worthy cassettes, which are consistently vivid and clearly focused. The first record was originally issued under the title '*Christmas in Venice*' and was rightly praised for the high quality of music and performances recorded in an ideal acoustic, with ringing, sonorous brass and choral antiphonies to delight the ear (see below). Then comes a rather more expressive group of music from Magdalen, to be followed by a further programme from the Monteverdi Choir and the Jones Brass Ensemble. The collection is rounded off on side six with sacred music by Monteverdi. This makes a first-class representation of a highly fruitful period, quite amazingly diverse in instrumental and vocal colour and expressive range.

Gobbi, Tito (baritone)

'Italian opera arias and songs': ROSSINI: *Guglielmo Tell: Resta immobile.* DONIZETTI: *L'elisir d'amore: Come paride.* VERDI: *Simon Boccanegra: Plebe! Patrizi! Falstaff: Quand'ero paggio. Otello: Vanne; la tua meta gia vedo ... Credo in un Dio crudel.* CILEA: *Adriana Lecouvreur: Ecco il monologo.* GIORDANO: *Fedora: La donna russa.* CAVALLI: *Serse: Beato chi puo.* PAISIELLO: *La Molinara: Nel cor più.* SCARLATTI, A.: *Il Pompeo: O cessate di piagarmi.* MONTEVERDI: *Orfeo: Rose del ciel.* Songs by: VIVALDI; CARISSIMI; DURANTE; GIORDANO; CIAMPI.
(M) **(*) HMV HQS/*TC-HQS* 143672-1/*4*.

Reissued in the very month of Gobbi's untimely death, this varied disc has a number of treasures, most of all on the operatic side. That side makes a superb memorial, for the range of expression based on a unique range of baritone tone-colour brings equally memorable characterizations of such diverse characters as Boccanegra, Iago and the swaggering Belcore in *L'elisir d'amore*. The arie antiche on the reverse bring some exquisite performances, but some unstylishness too. The transfers are first-rate on disc, but the XDR-tape equivalent, although kind to the voice, lacks upper range.

'The art of Tito Gobbi': including Italian songs; songs; ballads; arias from: CILEA: *L'Arlesiana.* PUCCINI: *La Fanciulla del West.* VERDI: *Don Carlos; Otello; La Forza del destino; Macbeth; Un Ballo in maschera; Nabucco.* MOZART: *Le Nozze di Figaro.* DONIZETTI: *L'Elisir d'amore.* BERLIOZ: *La Damnation de Faust.* ROSSINI: *William Tell.*
(M) (***) HMV mono RLS/*TC-RLS* 738 (3).

This magnificent collection includes Gobbi recordings from three decades – the early (1942) recordings made in Italy, English-made recordings from the late 1940s and mid-1950s, and a 1965 collection of Italian songs. All are fascinating. Jack Rance's *arioso* from *Fanciulla del West* is included both in the youthful 1942 version and in a 1955 version, never previously issued, which shows how the voice had grown darker and richer and the artistry enormously intensified. Of the early recordings the most valuable is of the Death of Rodrigo from *Don Carlos*, a performance as compelling in its way as the classic one in the later complete recording. And although there is some roughness of tone and expression in places, Gobbi consistently claims attention as the most characterful and magnetic of dramatic baritones of his period. The transcriptions from 78s are well managed; some of the earliest recordings display a degree of shallowness, and the voice is not always given the fullest bloom. The transfers to tape have plenty of life and presence.

Gomez, Jill (soprano)

'Spanish songs' (with John Constable, piano): GRANADOS: *Tonadillas al estilo antiguo, Nos. 1–6.* TURINA: *Poema en forma de canciones, Op. 19.* FALLA: *Trois mélodies; Siete cançiones populares españolas.*
(M) *** Saga 5409.

Jill Gomez's delectable recital of Spanish songs, including Falla's *Seven Spanish popular songs*, is one of the highlights of the Saga catalogue. Originally this issue was spoilt by noisy surfaces, but current copies – though costing more – are now satisfactory in that respect.

Hamburg Municipal Ch., Eppendorf School Boys' Ch., Detel

'Christmas at the time of Praetorius' (with Guillaume, Krebs, Instrumental Ens.): ECCARD: *O Freude über Freud.* CRAPPIUS: *Nun ist es Zeit.* SCHEIN: *Annunciation dialogue: Maria gegrüsset seist du.* FREUNDT: *Wie schön singt uns der Engel 2 Schar.* PRAETORIUS: *Quem pastores laudavere; Wie schön leuchtet der Morgenstern; In dulci jubilo.* SCHEIDT: *Ein Kind geborn zu Bethlehem.* VARIOUS: *Vom Himmel hoch; Gelobet seist du, Jesu Christ.*
(M) ** DG Arc. Priv. 2547/*3347* 080.

An agreeably atmospheric and certainly enterprising Christmas collection with authentic performances that are gently evocative and well turned to make a pleasant background rather than impinge strongly on the consciousness. There are some well-known chorales here but much of the music is unfamiliar, including the engaging *Annunciation dialogue* sung rather cosily by Margot Guillaume and Helmut Krebs. Settings of two of the chorales are shared by several composers. Othmayr, Jacob Praetorius and Eccard combine for *Vom Himmel hoch*; no fewer than seven different names are credited to *Gelobet seist du* (one verse each). The sound (1963 vintage) is good, the cassette not quite as sharply focused as the disc.

Hammond, Joan (soprano)

'The art of Joan Hammond': Arias from PUCCINI: *La Bohème; Tosca; Madame Butterfly; Gianni Schicchi; Manon Lescaut; Turandot.* CILEA: *Adriana Lecouvreur.* CATALANI: *La Wally.* VERDI: *Un ballo in maschera; La forza del destino; Aïda.* DVOŘÁK: *Russalka.* TCHAIKOVSKY: *Eugene Onegin.* TRAD.: *The last rose of summer.* BISHOP: *Home sweet home.* COATES: *Green hills.*
(M) (***) HMV mono RLS/*TC-RLS* 290014-3/*5* (2).

The special place which Dame Joan Hammond held throughout the Second World War in British musical life is vividly captured here in excellent transfers of almost all her wartime 78s, as a rule recorded in English. The Puccini items are the best remembered, above all *O my beloved father*, which she had to fight Walter Legge to record and which went on to win her a gold disc. Vocally even more accomplished are some of the other items, recorded – usually in the original language – in the years following. The power and individuality of her voice combined with unfailing and total commitment make this a cherishable pair of discs. The tapes are transferred at only a modest level and though the vocal timbre is truthful and caught without peaking, there is some loss of presence.

Hendricks, Barbara (soprano), **Dmitri Alexeev** (piano)

Spirituals: *Deep river; Ev'ry time I feel the spirit; Fix me, Jesus; Git on boa'd little child'n; His name is so sweet; Hold on!; Joshua fit de battle of Jericho; Nobody knows de trouble I've seen; Oh what a beautiful city!; Plenty good room; Roun'about de mountain; Sometimes I feel like a motherless child; Swing low, sweet chariot; Talk about a child that do love Jesus; Were you there?; When I lay my burden down.*
❀ *** HMV Dig. **CDC 747026-2**; ASD/*TC-ASD* 173168-1/*4*.

So often spirituals can be made to seem too ingenuous, their deep reserve of feeling degraded into sentimentality. Not so here. Barbara Hendricks' vibrant identification with the words is thrilling, the jazz inflections adding natural sophistication, yet not robbing the music of its directness of communication. Her lyrical singing is radiant, operatic in its eloquence of line, yet retaining the ecstasy of spirit, while the extrovert numbers – *Joshua fit de battle of Jericho* a superb example – are full of joy in their gutsy exuberance. Dmitri Alexeev accompanies superbly and the very well-balanced recording has remarkable presence on disc and tape alike. A rare example of a record that feels like a 'live' experience. *Roun'about de mountain* is unforgettable in its impact.

French opera arias (with Monte Carlo PO, Tate): CHARPENTIER: *Louise*: *Depuis le jour*. GOUNOD: *Roméo et Juliette: Ah! je veux vivre; Dieu, quel frisson*. BIZET: *Les pêcheurs de perles: Me voilà seule . . . Comme autrefois dans la nuit sombre*. BERLIOZ: *Benvenuto Cellini: Entre l'amour et le devoir*. MASSENET: *Manon: Adieu notre petite table; Je marche sur tous les chemins; Obéissons quand leur voix appelle. Thaïs: Dis-moi que je suis belle*. OFFENBACH: *Contes d'Hoffmann: Elle a fui, la tourterelle*.
*** Ph. Dig. 410 446-1/*4*.

Starting with an exquisitely poised yet fresh and unaffected account of *Depuis le jour*, Barbara Hendricks ranges wide in her French collection, singing with style and imagination, well at home in French. Warmly sympathetic accompaniment and sound to match, with an excellent matching cassette.

Horne, Marilyn (mezzo-soprano)

'Grandi voci': DONIZETTI: *Anna Bolena: Il segreto; Ah! pensate che rivolti. Figlia del Reggimento: Deciso . . . Le Richezze*. BELLINI: *Norma: Sgombre è la sacra selva . . . Deh! proteggimi, o dio!. I Capuleti ed i Montecchi: Se Romeo . . . La tremenda ultrice*. ROSSINI: *Tancredi: Di tanti palpiti; Il Barbiere di Siviglia: Una voce poco fa. Semiramide: In si barara sciature . . . Si, vendicato*. VERDI: *Il Trovatore: Stride la vampa . . . Condotta ell'era in cappi*.
*** Decca GRV/*KGRC* 8.

This is one of the richest and most spectacular in Decca's 'Grandi Voci' series, taken mainly from recordings made by Marilyn Horne early in her career, when the voice was not only at its firmest and richest, but had a coloratura flexibility few mezzos could equal. The selection is very imaginative, ranging from popular arias to such rarities as the aria from Rossini's *Tancredi*, one of the finest items of all. First-rate recording on disc and cassette alike; indeed the tape is one of Decca's finest with plenty of range, and a wide orchestral amplitude as a backcloth for the voice.

'Live at La Scala' (with Martin Katz): ANON.: *Cloris sighed*. HANDEL: *Semele: Awake Saturnia! . . . Iris, hence away*. ALVAREZ: *La partida*. TURINA: *Farruca*. MONTSALVATGE: *Canciónes negras No. 4: Cancion cuna para dormir a un negrito*. GRANADOS: *La maja dolorosa No. 1: Oh! muerte cruel*. OBRADORS: *El vito*. POULENC: *Le bestiare*. ROSSINI: *Semiramide: Ecco mi alfine . . . Ah, quel giorno*. COPLAND: *Simple gifts; Ching-a-ring Chaw; Long time ago; At the river*. FOSTER: *Beautiful dreamer; Jeannie with the light brown hair*.
**(*) CBS 74105/*40*- [M/*MT* 37819].

A vibrantly characterful recital which ranges magnetically over the widest range of repertory. The Handel and Rossini are obviously limited by having piano accompaniment, and the lovely Montsalvatge *Cradle song* could be smoother and gentler, but the liveness of the experience is superbly caught, not least in the American songs at the end. Try the roistering Copland setting, *Ching-a-ring Chaw*. Limited, rather dry recording which is fair to the voice, if taxing.

'Italian opera favourites'

LEONCAVALLO: *I Pagliacci: Prologue* (Gobbi); *Vesti la giubba* (Corelli). PUCCINI: *La Bohème: Sì, mi chiamano Mimì; Una terribil tosse* (Freni, Gedda). *Madama Butterfly: Love duet; Flower duet; Humming chorus* (Bjoerling, Los Angeles, Pirazzini, Rome Op. Ch., Santini). *Manon Lescaut: Donna non vidi*

mai (Fernandi)*; In quelle trine morbide* (Cavalli). *Turandot: In questa reggia* (Shuard). VERDI: *Il Trovatore: Di quella pira* (Corelli)*; Soldiers' chorus* (Rome Op. Ch., Schippers). *Aïda: Qui Radames verra! . . . O patria mia* (Cavalli)*; Ritorna vincitor* (Shuard). *Rigoletto: Questa o quella; La donna è mobile* (Fernandi)*; Caro nome* (Grist)*; Zitti zitti* (Rome Op. Ch., Molinari-Pradelli)*; Bella figlia* (Grist, Gedda, Di Stasio, MacNeil). *Otello: Ave Maria* (Gwyneth Jones). MASCAGNI: *Cavalleria Rusticana: Mamma, mamma* (Fernando). BELLINI: *I Puritani: A te, o cara* (Corelli).
(B) ** EMI *TC2-MOM 120.*

Recorded loudly and vibrantly, at times rather fiercely, for maximum impact in the car, this is a generous collection of operatic purple patches. The finest performances are from Gobbi (*Pagliacci*), Freni as Mimì, Gwyneth Jones in *Otello* and the excellent excerpts from the Los Angeles/Bjoerling set of *Madama Butterfly*. Corelli makes several appearances, and his singing is best described as lusty.

Jaye Consort

'Medieval music' (with Gerald English): *'The song of the ass': Two ductias; English dance; Rege Mentem; Saltarello; Estampies 1–3; Li Maus d'Amer; Lamento di Tristan; C'est la fin; Kalenda Maya; Novus miles sequitur; Moulin de Paris; In seculum artifex; Sol oritur; Vierhundert jar Uff diser Erde; Trotto; Worldes blis; Alta; Ja nun nons pris; Die süss Nachtigall; Pour mon coeur; Estampie royale.*
(B) *** PRT GSGC/*ZCGC* 2009.

A wholly captivating concert, intended not just for the specialist collector but for anyone whose ear responds to piquant sounds and basic melodies. Indeed quite a few of the anonymous items are tunefully memorable, and played using a wide variety of period instruments they project admirably. Any concert of this nature is essentially conjectural but here problems have been solved convincingly by Francis Baines who also participates as instrumentalist. Gerald English's vocal contributions are sensitive and highly enjoyable and throughout the performances share spontaneity with scholarship. The recording is first-class on disc; the tape has less upper range on side one but is admirable on side two.

'An Elizabethan evening' (with J. Norman, Nigel Rogers, Brunt, Dupré, Beckett, virginals and organ): Entrance of players: BYRD: *In fields abroad; Galliard.* MORLEY: *Thyrsis and Milla.* FARMER: *Sweet friend thy absence; Fair Phyllis I saw sitting.* ANON.: *Sacred ende.* BULL: *Fancy.* FARNABY: *Daphne on the rainbow; Now cast down your whips; Construe my meaning.* CAMPION: *Fair if you expect admiring.* INGLOT: *The leaves be greene.* PHILIPS: *Amarille di Julio Romano.* JOHNSON: *Defiled is my name.* ROSSETER: *When Laura smiles.* DOWLAND: *Flow not so fast.* RAVENSCROFT: *Bellman's song.*
(B) *** PRT GSGC/*ZCGC* 2012.

This enjoyable anthology matches the success of the concert of medieval music by the same group. Here they are joined by a number of soloists, including Desmond Dupré and John Beckett, whose contributions are distinguished. The programme is attractively wide in range and style, from solos to madrigals with mixed ensemble and keyboard. Several of the madrigals are presented in robust 'rustic' style; others are sung simply and lyrically, such as Farnaby's *Construe my meaning* which is touching in its simplicity. The sense of a concert is engendered by opening each side with entrance music, and all the performances have an attractive sense of occasion. The sleeve, however, omits the composers from the list of titles and provides little information about the music itself. The recording is first-rate and the tape sounds very well too, although the channels are reversed.

Kanawa, Kiri Te (soprano)

'Portrait': PUCCINI: *Tosca: Vissi d'arte. Gianni Schicchi: O mio babbino caro.* VERDI: *La Traviata: E strano . . . E fors'è lui.* HUMPERDINCK: *Hänsel und Gretel: Der kleine Sandman.* MOZART: *Don Giovanni: Ah fuggi il traditor; Mi tradi quell'alma ingrata.*

STRAUSS, R.: *Morgen; Ruhe, meine Seele.* SCHUBERT: *Gretchen am Spinnrade.* SCHUMANN: *Du bist wie eine Blume.* FAURÉ: *Après un rêve.* WALTON: *Façade: Old Sir Faulk; Daphne; Through gilded trellises.*
**(*) CBS 74116/*40-*.

Her appearance at the royal wedding put the seal on Kiri Te Kanawa as a world star. Here the rich sweetness of the voice gives consistent pleasure, particularly in the Puccini and Humperdinck excerpts. But it is her portrayal of Donna Elvira that shows her personality at its strongest, although the songs also bring detailed imaginative touches and the Walton items are treasurable. There is nothing to cause real disappointment here, though undoubtedly Dame Kiri's artistic charisma has room for further growth.

Recital (with Amner, piano): SCHUBERT: *Nacht und Träume. Gretchen am Spinnrade. Rastlose Liebe.* SCHUMANN: *Du bist wie eine Blume. Stille Tränen. Soldatenbraut.* WOLF: *Blumengrüss. Kennst du das Land.* FAURÉ: *Après un rêve. Nell.* DUPARC: *L'invitation au voyage. Le manoir. Au pays où se fait la guerre.* WALTON: *Daphne. Through gilded trellises. Old Sir Faulk.*
**(*) CBS 76868/*40-*.

A fascinating and wide-ranging recital reflecting Kiri Te Kanawa's live concerts. It is good to have the Walton songs, and the rag music of *Old Sir Faulk* is delightfully characterful. For the rest the singing is tasteful, but confronting the microphone Kiri Te Kanawa presents her performances with a degree less 'face' than we know from her in the concert hall. It is perhaps a pity that slow and gentle songs predominate, but with the beauty of the voice well caught, this is still a delightful record, and one of CBS's best cassettes, with the voice naturally transferred and the piano timbre truthful.

King's College Ch., Camb., Ledger

'Music for Holy Week' by LOTTI; HORSLEY; KING JOHN IV OF PORTUGAL; GIBBONS; WEBBE-MILLER; LEIGHTON; SHEPHERD; and traditional music. VICTORIA: *O vos omnes; Videte omnes populi.* LASSUS: *Tristis est anima mea.* TAVERNER: *Dum transisset sabbatum.*
*** HMV ASD 3450.

An admirable compilation, ranging widely from the music of Victoria, Lassus and Morley to more modern contributions. The King's acoustic is not easy to capture with the smoothness that is achieved here.

'Festival of lessons and carols' (1979).
*** HMV ASD/*TC-ASD* 3778.

This most recent version on record of the annual King's College ceremony has the benefit of modern recording, even more atmospheric than before. Under Philip Ledger the famous choir keeps its beauty of tone and incisive attack. The issue of this record and cassette celebrates a golden jubilee, for these carol services started in 1919. The opening processional, *Once in Royal David's city*, is as effective as ever, and this remains a unique blend of liturgy and music. The cassette brings the advantage of an almost silent background, but is not quite as refined in focus as the disc.

'Procession with carols on Advent Sunday'.
*** HMV Dig. ASD/*TCC-ASD* 3907.

This makes an attractive variant to the specifically Christmas-based service, though the carols themselves are not quite so memorable. Beautiful singing and richly atmospheric recording; the wide dynamic range is demonstrated equally effectively by the atmospheric opening and processional and the sumptuous closing hymn. The chrome cassette handles this almost as impressively as the digital disc.

'Carols for Christmas Eve' by WOODWARD; HOWELLS; WISHART; KIRKPATRICK; LEDGER; LEIGHTON; HADLEY; MENDELSSOHN; arrangements by VAUGHAN WILLIAMS; STAINER; PEARSALL; RUTTER;

WILLCOCKS. TRAD.: *I saw three ships; O come all ye faithful.*
*** HMV CSD/*TC-CSD* 3774.

The joyful opening of Woodward's *Up! Good Christian folk, and listen* is typical of this attractive concert, which gives a new freshness to many favourites by the refinement and expressive vigour of the singing. With seventeen items included this is excellent value, and the recording is excellent on disc. When first issued, the cassette transfer was too highly modulated, leading to intermittent coarseness, but this has probably been rectified by now.

King's College Ch., Ledger and Willcocks

'The Psalms of David': Nos. 23; 42–3; 46; 65–7; 84; 93; 115; 121; 130–1; 137; 149; 150.
(M) **(*) HMV Green. ESD 107797-1.

In pioneer days the early Christians took over the Psalter along with the Old Testament teachings from the Hebrew Temple, and the Psalms have always been an integral part of Anglican liturgy. Although they are called 'The Psalms of David' it has long been recognized that the original Hebrew collection (some 150 strong) was gathered together over a period of several hundred years, and the writings are from many different anonymous hands. The Anglican settings used on these recordings have offered their composers a fairly wide range of expressive potential, yet the music itself, perhaps because of the stylized metre and the ritual nature of its use, seldom approaches the depth and resonance which is found in the music of the great composers of the Roman Catholic faith, Palestrina, Victoria and so on. The King's College Choir, conducted by Sir David Willcocks from the organ, give an eloquent account of a cross-section of the Psalter on this disc. They are beautifully recorded. Those wanting to explore this repertoire further will find it covered in depth on three earlier issues (HMV CSD and *TC-CSD* 3656; CSD 3717 and CSD 3768), all of high quality.

'Choral favourites': HANDEL: *Messiah: Hallelujah chorus.* BACH: *Jesu, joy of man's desiring.* HAYDN: *The Creation: The heavens are telling.* PURCELL: *Rejoice in the Lord* (anthem). SCHUBERT: *Psalm 23.* FAURÉ: *Requiem: Sanctus.* ELGAR: *Coronation Ode: Land of hope and glory.* DELIUS: *To be sung of a summer night on the water.* VAUGHAN WILLIAMS: *O clap your hands* (motet). BRITTEN: *St Nicholas: Birth of Nicholas.* ANON.: *There is no rose.* HARRIS: *Faire is the heaven.* WOOD: *Hail, gladdening light.* DYKES: *Holy, holy, holy.*
(M) *** HMV SXLP/*TC-SXLP* 30308.

This collection of choral lollipops, beautifully sung and atmospherically recorded, makes a most desirable medium-price reissue. The second side is especially attractive, with the sumptuous Elgar excerpt followed by music by Delius, Vaughan Williams and Britten, each full of character and acting as a foil to what precedes it. The sound is consistently excellent on disc, more variable in focus on cassette, though always acceptable.

King's College Ch., Willcocks

'Anthems from King's': English cathedral anthems 1890–1940 (with James Lancelot, organ) by PARRY; BULLOCK; BAIRSTOW; LEY; NAYLOR; GARDINER; HARWOOD; STANFORD; BAINTON; WOOD; DARKE; HADLEY; HARRIS.
**(*) HMV CSD/*TC-CSD* 3752.

An attractive and representative collection of English cathedral music from just before the turn of the century until about halfway through our own. A good deal of the writing is not very adventurous, harmonically speaking, but it is well crafted and some of it is memorable. Highlights include Edward Bairstow's eloquent *Let all mortal flesh keep silence*, the fine Balfour Gardiner *Evening hymn* and Stanford's *Beati quorum via*. The last four items, by Charles Wood, Harold Darke, Patrick Hadley and William Harris, are here especially effective for being heard together, four diverse yet complementary settings that sum up the twentieth-century Anglican tradition rather well. Excellent recording. The tape transfer is generally made at a low level but is otherwise of pleasing quality; only in the comparatively ambitious *I was glad* by Parry do the clarity and refinement of the recording slip.

'Festival of King's': ALLEGRI: *Miserere* (with Goodman, treble). PALESTRINA: *Stabat Mater.* GIBBONS: *This is the record of John.* BYRD: *Mass in 4 parts.* CROFT: *Burial service.* TALLIS: *O nata lux. Videte miraculum.* VIVALDI: *Magnificat.* BACH: *Jesu, priceless treasure, BWV 227. St John Passion: Rest calm, O body pure and holy; Lord Jesu, thy dear angel send.* BLOW: *God spake sometime in visions.* PURCELL: *Hear my prayer, O Lord.* HANDEL: *The King shall rejoice. Chandos anthem: The Lord is my light.* VAUGHAN WILLIAMS: *Fantasia on Christmas carols* (with Hervey Alan). HOLST: *Lullay my liking.* ORDE: *Adam lay ybounden.* TRAD. (arr. Shaw): *Coventry carol.* HOWELLS: *Collegium Regale: Te Deum; Jubilate.*
(M) *** Argo D 148 D 4 (4)/*K 148 K 43*.

An admirable collection of vintage King's recordings, opening with the famous version of Allegri's *Miserere* (Roy Goodman the superb treble soloist). Other highlights include Palestrina's *Stabat Mater*, Vivaldi's *Magnificat* and Vaughan Williams's delightful *Carol fantasia.* The sound is first-class and generally the cassettes match the discs closely, although some slight rebalancing may be needed. (*This is the record of John* is very forwardly recorded, which produces some temporary loss of refinement on tape.)

'Christmas music from King's' (with Andrew Davis, organ, and D. Whittaker, flute, Van Kempen, cello): VICTORIA: *O magnum mysterium; Senex puerum portabat.* BYRD: *Senex puerum portabat; Hodie beata virgo.* GIBBONS: *Hosanna to the Son of David.* WEELKES: *Hosanna to the Son of David; Gloria in excelsis.* SWEELINCK: *Hodie Christus natus est.* WATTS: *Watts's cradle song.* Arrangements by: MACONCHY: *Nowell!;* BRITTEN: *The holly and the ivy;* HUGHES: *Angelus ad Virginum;* POSTON: *Angelus ad Virginum; My dancing day;* BERKELEY: *I sing of a maiden;* HOLST, I.: *The Lord that lay;* WARLOCK: *Where riches is everlasting.*
(M) *** HMV Green. ESD/*TC-ESD* 7050.

A happily chosen survey of music inspired by the Nativity from the fifteenth century up to the present. As might be expected, the King's Choir confidently encompasses the wide variety of styles, from the spiritual serenity of the music of Victoria to the attractive arrangements of traditional carols by modern composers, where an instrumental accompaniment is added. These items are quite delightful and they are beautifully recorded. Generally the transfer to tape offers refined sound; the focus never slips more than fractionally.

'The world of Christmas': The first nowell. While shepherds watched. I saw three ships. Ding dong merrily on high. King Jesus hath a garden. In dulci jubilo. Unto us is born a son. O come all ye faithful. Away in a manger. O little town of Bethlehem. The holly and the ivy. God rest ye merry, gentlemen. See amid the winter's snow. Past three o'clock. MENDELSSOHN: *Hark the herald angels.*
(M) *** Argo SPA/*KCSP* 104.

The items in this cheap sampler of carols are taken from some of Argo's many fine recordings of King's College Choir, made over a dozen or so years. The annual carol service has after all become such a national institution that the choir's choice of carol directly influences fashion and popularity. The mixture here naturally concentrates on established favourites, all performed with the poise, point and refinement for which King's is famous, but one or two items, like *Past three o'clock*, are designed to get the listener inquiring further. No other carol collection can match it at the price. The recording is first-rate, combining ambient atmosphere with good detail on both disc and cassette.

'The world of King's' (with soloists): VIVALDI: *Gloria:* excerpt. TALLIS: *Sancte Deus.* GIBBONS: *This is the record of John.* HANDEL: *Coronation anthem: Zadok the Priest.* BYRD: *Ave verum corpus.* SCHOLEFIELD: *The day Thou gavest.* BACH: *O Jesu so meek.* ALLEGRI: *Miserere* (*Psalm 51*).
*** Argo SPA/*KCSP* 245.

This anthology is designed as a sampler of

the King's style, but in its own right it makes an outstanding concert of Renaissance and baroque choral music. The resplendent opening of Vivaldi's *Gloria* is followed by the wonderful *Sancte Deus* of Tallis. The Gibbons verse anthem, however, is recorded with a curiously forward effect, so that the singing is too much on top of the listener. Side two opens with the familiar performance of *Zadok the Priest*; the beautiful flowing lines of Byrd's *Ave verum* make a perfectly calculated contrast, and after the short Bach part-song, the concert ends with the famous King's recording of Allegri's *Miserere*, with its soaring treble line marvellously sung by Master Roy Goodman. This superbly confident piece of singing, of almost unbelievable perfection, is alone worth the modest price of the disc. The recording is of Argo's usual high quality, though the high-level tape transfer brings a hint of strain at times.

'The world of Christmas music' (with (i) Andrew Davis or Simon Preston, organ; (ii) Hervey Alan, LSO): (i) *Once in Royal David's city*. DAVIES: *O little town of Bethlehem*. TRAD.: *Blessed be that maid Mary; Infant Holy; Gabriel's message; Sussex carol; Coventry carol; Shepherds in the field abiding*. ORDE: *Adam lay ybounden*. Arr. HOLST: *Lullay my liking*. DARKE: *In the bleak midwinter*. JOUBERT: *Torches*. (ii) VAUGHAN WILLIAMS: *Fantasia on Christmas carols*.
*** Argo SPA/*KCSP* 501.

The second Argo reissue of Christmas music from King's is generously full and includes for a highlight on side two a superbly joyful performance of Vaughan Williams's *Fantasia on Christmas carols*. The sound is fresh and full. The collection opens with the famous processional version of *Once in Royal David's city*. The choir is on top form throughout the programme. The cassette is less cleanly focused on side one than on side two.

'A festival of lessons and carols as sung on Christmas Eve, 1964' (with Andrew Davis, organ).
(M) *** Argo SPA/*KCSP* 528.

The well-tried formula never fails. This was the last of the series of carol-service recordings made with this choir by Argo, and with its mixture of the well-known and the unusual it remains perhaps the loveliest of all, with fine atmospheric recording. The name of Andrew Davis, the organ scholar of the time, has since become famous throughout the world of music, and no doubt his musicianship powerfully reinforced that of David Willcocks. As in the actual service at Christmas the opening *Once in Royal David's city* is sung as a processional, and the recording reproduces vividly the slow approach of the choir. Modern carols by Peter Wishart and Peter Racine Fricker are included among the traditional ones. Two of the loveliest are *There is no rose* and *Lullay my liking*, both of the fifteenth century, the latter in Holst's inspired arrangement. The transfer to tape is immaculate. Only very occasionally is the choral focus less well defined than on the disc, and the click-free background of the cassette is an obvious advantage during the opening processional.

'Hymns from King's' (with Preston, organ): *Hark! A thrilling voice is sounding. There is a green hill far away. According to Thy gracious word. Drop, drop, slow tears. When I survey the wondrous cross. Glory be to Jesus. Up! Awake! From highest steeple* (*Wachet auf*). *Break forth, O beauteous heavenly light. On Jordan's bank the Baptist's cry. Abide with me. Holy Father, cheer our way. Glory to Thee, my God, this night. The day Thou gavest, Lord, is ended. O come, O come, Emmanuel.*
(M) *** Argo SPA/*KCSP* 553.

The King's style in hymns is more restrained than that of some other recorded collections; it is the opposite of the 'Huddersfield Choral Society' approach. The recording is admirably faithful and atmospheric, with the tape transfer lacking just a little of the upper range of the disc.

'The World of King's', Vol. 2: Once in Royal David's city. TALLIS: *Salvator mundi*. HANDEL: *Chandos anthem: O praise the Lord. Ode for St Cecilia's Day: As from the power* (finale). BYRD: *Mass for 5 voices: Sanctus; Benedictus*. BACH: *St John Passion: Rest calm; Lord Jesu, thy dear angel send. Magnificat:*

Opening chorus. TAVERNER: *Dum transisset sabbatum.* PURCELL: *Hear my prayer, O Lord.* HAYDN: *Mass No. 9 in D min.* (*Nelson*): *Kyrie.* PALESTRINA: *Hodie Beata Virgo.*
(M) *** Argo SPA/*KCSP* 590.

An excellent follow-up to *Volume 1* (Argo SPA/*KCSP* 245), this sampler centres on an earlier musical period than the HMV SXLP compilation (see above). The range of the King's achievement is readily demonstrated by listening to both discs side by side. The highlights here include the Byrd and Taverner items, the excerpts from the Haydn *Mass* and the sparkling closing chorus from Handel's *Ode for St Cecilia's Day.* Excellent sound on disc, but the quality of the cassette is uneven, with the focus sometimes rather blurred.

'In dulci jubilo': In dulci jubilo; Rejoice and be merry; Rocking; Lute book lullaby. TERRY: *Myn lyking; Joseph was an old man.* PRAETORIUS: *A great and mighty wonder; Good King Wenceslas.* MATHIAS: *Wassail carol.* PETTMAN: *A Babe divine.* HOLST: *Personent hodie; Once in Royal David's city; The infant king.* WARLOCK: *Balulalow.* TCHAIKOVSKY: *The crown of roses; Christ was born on Christmas day.* HOWELLS: *A spotless rose.* HADLEY: *I sing of a maiden.* CORNELIUS: *The three kings.* KOCHER: *As with gladness men of old.*
*** Argo ZK/*KZKC* 100.

This most recent Argo reissue offers a generous collection of twenty carols and songs appropriate to the festive season, culled from King's recordings over a period of twenty-four years from 1959 to 1983. Yet the recording has consistent excellence with no hint that items come from different periods. The sleeve and label details are reversed: side one in fact opens with *Once in Royal David's city* and contains most of the more familiar items. But the choice is wide and imaginative.

King's Singers

'Victorian collection': BRIDGE: *The goslings.* SUTTON: *Come sweet Marguerite.* PINSUTI: *Goodnight beloved.* HOBBS: *Phyllis is my only joy.* Arr. PEARSALL: *Waters of Elle.* CLARKE: *Street music.* CALKIN: *Breathe soft ye winds.* MARTIN: *Let maids be false, so wine be true.* SULLIVAN: *The long day closes.* MACY: *Jenk's vegetable compound.* BARNBY: *Home they brought the warrior dead.* STEVENS: *All my sense thy sweetness gained.* HATTON: *The way to build a boat, or, Jack's opinion. He that hath a pleasant face. The letter.* LESLIE: *Charm me asleep.* PEARSALL: *Light of my soul.* ROGERS: *Hears not my Phyllis.*
*** HMV ASD/*TC-ASD* 3865 [MMG 1117].

The polish and stylishness of the King's Singers are admirably employed in these period-piece items, most of them hauntingly sentimental. First-rate recording. However, those wanting a single sample of this talented group would do even better with the generous *Portrait* on HMV Greensleeve (below).

'Sing we and chant it' (*English madrigals*): MORLEY: *Sing we and chant it; On a fair morning; Cruel, wilt thou persevere; I love alas, I love thee.* WILBYE: *Oft have I vowed; Lady your words do spite me.* BYRD: *Is love a boy; This sweet and merry month.* DOWLAND: *Say love, if ever thou didst find; Fine knacks for ladies; Come again, sweet love doth now invite.* WEELKES: *All at once well met; Lord! when I think; Strike it up, tabor; Tan ra ra, cries Mars.* FARNABY: *Construe my meaning.* JONES, R.: *Farewell dear love.* TOMKINS: *See, see the shepherds' queen.* PILKINGTON: *Have I found her.* MUNDY: *Were I a King.* KIRBYE: *Why should I love?*
*** HMV Dig. ASD/*TCC-ASD* 4092 [Ang. DS/*4XS* 37891].

The keen precision, characteristic of the King's Singers, brings delectable performances of madrigals, finely detailed and well-characterized, mainly of popular items but including rarities like Mundy's *Were I a King. Strike it up, tabor*, true to the title, has drum accompaniment. Good clean recording and an excellent cassette, forward and clear.

'A French collection' (with Early Music Consort, Munrow): Renaissance chansons by JANNEQUIN; JACOTIN; PASSEREAU;

WILLAERT; CERTON; MORNABLE; ARBEAU; LE JEUNE. POULENC: *Songs*.
*** HMV CSD 3740 [MMG 1104].

The *French collection* makes a successful juxtaposition of Renaissance chansons and all the male-voiced choral songs of Poulenc. The guiding hand of David Munrow ensures stylish and spirited music-making here; the recording is of high quality and the transfer fresh and immediate.

'Madrigal collection': madrigals by MORLEY; WEELKES; WILBYE; BENNETT; FARMER; FESTA; HOSTIA; DE WERT; CAIMO; DA NOLA; BANCHIERI; GASTOLDI; LASSUS.
*** HMV CSD/*TC-CSD* 3756 [MMG 1105].

This madrigal collection ranges further than the newer digital compilation above, which restricts itself to English repertoire. The singing again demonstrates the usual King's finesse of ensemble and has both charm and character: the robust quality of Banchieri's *Contrappunto bestiale* with its picaresque animal imitations is well brought out. Here the recording is very forward, but admirably clear, though the cassette transfer is smooth rather than especially wide-ranging on top.

'Concert collection': madrigals by: HENRY VIII; DAGGERE; FARMER; TOMKINS; MORLEY. Sacred music by: GIACOBBI; HANDL; VITTORIA. Chansons and songs by: RIDOUT; JOSQUIN DES PRÉS; JANNEQUIN; LEGRAND; GRIEG. Traditional pieces.
*** HMV CSD 3766 [MMG 1106].

The programme of the *Concert collection* ranges from Elizabethan music to the songs of Grieg and even includes an arrangement of *Puppet on a string*. Here the group show how well they have bridged the gap between classical and popular traditions and, if occasionally the smooth homogeneity of style is in danger of devitalizing some of their repertoire, there is such consistent imagination and life in the presentation that criticism is for the most part disarmed.

'A portrait': PASSEREAU: *Il est bel et bon.* WILLAERT: *Allons*. CERTON: *La, la la, je ne l'ose dire*. MORLEY: *Now is the month of maying*. FARMER: *Fair Phyllis I saw. A little pretty bonny lass*. WEELKES: *The nightingale*. DE WERT: *Valle, che de' lamenti*. LASSUS: *Matona, mia cara*. JANNEQUIN: *Au joly jeu*. GRIEG: *Kvaalin's Halling*. MARTIN: *Puppet on a string*. TRAD.: *The Mermaid*. BYRD: *Ave verum corpus*. PATTERSON: *Time piece*. Arr. SARGENT: *Mary had a baby*. GLASSER: *Lalela Zulu* (*Ilihubo; Uhambo ngesitimela*). HASSLER: *Tänzen und springen*. MACY: *Jenk's vegetable compound*. SULLIVAN: *The long day closes*.
(M) *** HMV Green. ESD/*TC-ESD* 7103.

A remarkably generous medium-priced sampler of the King's style in a wide variety of music, from early madrigals, sung with superb understanding and polish, to more popular repertoire including the lively *Puppet on a string* and the delightful tale of *The Mermaid*. Patterson's *Time piece* represents the avant-garde, quite imaginative and a *tour de force* as a performance. The programme ends appropriately with a balmily sweet – but not cloying – arrangement of Sullivan's *The long day closes*. The recording is excellent; the cassette loses only a little of the upper-range sharpness.

'Flanders and Swann and Noël Coward'.
*** EMI EMC/*TC-EMC* 3196 [MMG 1120].

The obvious introduction to the King's Singers is the *'Portrait'* above (unless a collector is especially addicted to madrigals). But if one had to pick a single issue showing the group at their freshest and most spontaneous it would surely be the splendid compilation of the songs of Noël Coward and Flanders and Swann. The opening *Transport of delight* lives up to its name, and *The slow train*, *The Wompon*, *Rockall* and *The sloth* are all unforgettable. *Mad dogs and Englishmen* has snippets of *Rule Britannia* spliced in, and throughout the Coward numbers there is ample wit, with *There are bad times just around the corner* a *tour de force* at the end. The recording is excellent and the cassette transfer is smooth, lacking only the last degree of life and presence.

'Tenth Anniversary Concert' (recorded live at the Royal Festival Hall) *Vol. 2:* popular music, including *Ten years on; In the mood; The mermaid; Greens; I'm a train; Ob-la-di; Rag; Widdicombe fair.*
*** EMI KS 1002 [MMG 1102].

The *Tenth Anniversary Concert* can be recommended with the greatest enthusiasm. The presence of the audience means that there are spoken introductions (generally witty) and the kind of spontaneity that can only come from a live recording. The atmosphere of the occasion is splendidly caught and the recording quality is excellent throughout. The first of the two discs has now been withdrawn in the UK (it is still available in the USA [MMG 1101] and includes music by Jannequin, Byrd, Weelkes, Farmer, Banchieri, De Wert, Poulenc and Glasser). The second is a fun collection, opening irresistibly with *Ten years on* and including, near the end, the audience's own sung birthday-tribute to the group. There are many favourites here, and two most welcome encores.

Kirkby, Emma (soprano)**, Cons. of Musicke, Rooley**

'Madrigals and wedding songs for Diana' (with David Thomas, bass): BENNET: *All creatures now are merry-minded.* CAMPION: *Now hath Flora robbed her bowers. Move now measured sound. Woo her and win her.* LUPO: *Shows and nightly revels. Time that leads the fatal round.* GILES: *Triumph now with joy and mirth.* CAVENDISH: *Come, gentle swains.* DOWLAND: *Welcome, black night . . . Cease these false sports.* WEELKES: *Hark! all ye lovely saints. As Vesta was.* WILBYE: *Lady Oriana.* EAST: *Hence stars! too dim of light. You meaner beauties.* LANIER: *Bring away this sacred tree. The Marigold. Mark how the blushful morn.* COPERARIO: *Go, happy man. While dancing rests. Come ashore, merry mates.* GIBBONS, Ellis: *Long live fair Oriana.*
*** Hyp. A 66019.

Quite the most imaginative of all the records prompted by the royal wedding, this wholly delightful anthology celebrates earlier royal occasions, aristocratic weddings, and in its choice of Elizabethan madrigals skilfully balances praise of the Virgin Queen with a less ambivalent attitude to nuptial delights. Emma Kirkby is at her freshest and most captivating, and David Thomas, if not quite her match, makes an admirable contribution. Accompaniments are stylish and well balanced, and the recording is altogether first-rate.

'Amorous dialogues' (with Hill, tenor): BARTLETT: *Whither runneth my sweetheart.* FERRABOSCO: *Fayre cruell nimph. Tell me, O love.* MORLEY: *Who is it that this dark night.* FORD: *Shut not sweet breast.* LAWES: *A dialogue on a kiss: Among thy fancies. A dialogue betwixt time and a pilgrimme: Aged man that moves these fields.* GAGLIANO: *Bel pastor.* D'INDIA: *Da l'onde del mio pianto.* FERRARI: *Dialogo a due, Fileno e Lidia: Amar io ti consiglio. Amanti io vi so.* FONTEI: *Dio ti salvi, pastor.* MONTEVERDI: *Bel pastor.*
*** O-L DSLO 587.

'Duetti da camera' (with Nelson, soprano): NOTARI: *Intenerite voi, lagrime mie.* D'INDIA: *Alla guerra d'amore. La mia filli crudel. La virtù.* VALENTINI: *Vanne, O carta amorosa.* FRESCOBALDI: *Maddalena alla Croce.* GRANDI: *Spine care e soavi.* FONTEI: *Fortunato cantore.* ROVETTA: *Chi vuol haver felice e lieto il core. Io mi sento morir.* MONTEVERDI: *O come sei gentile.* SABBATINI: *Udite, O selve. Fulmina de la bocca.*
*** O-L DSLO 588.

These two records were issued separately but make an obvious pair, both concentrating on duets popular in the seventeenth century. For today's ears the repertoire is exceedingly rare; most of it is previously unrecorded. Almost every item is rewarding, although (obviously enough) the duo of soprano and tenor offers more dramatic contrast, as well as greater variety of timbre. Indeed DSLO 587 is the record to start with; its anticipations of Italian *opera buffa* are matched by the colourful settings of Morley and Lawes. But DSLO 588 also offers much that is effective and appealing, notably the contributions from Monteverdi, Frescobaldi and Sabbatini. Both issues are characteristically well documented and the accompaniments are stylishly authentic, as one would expect with Anthony Rooley in charge.

'Portrait' (with AcAM, Hogwood): D'INDIA: *Odi quel rosignuolo.* TROMBONCINO: *Se ben hor non scopra el foco.* FERRARI: *Amanti io vi so dire.* BARTLETT: *Sweete birdes deprive us never.* WILBYE: *Draw on, sweet night.* DOWLAND: *I saw my ladye weepe.* PILKINGTON: *Rest sweet nymphs.* ANON.: *The dark is my delight.* HANDEL: *Messiah: But who may abide the day of His coming. Alceste: Gentle Morpheus.* VIVALDI: *Amor hai vinto* (*Cantata, RV. 651*): *Passo dipena in pena. Nulla in mundo* (*Motet, RV. 630*): *Nulla in mundo pax sincera.* PURCELL: *Don Quixote: From rosy bowers.*
*** O-L DSLO/*KDSLC* 607.

Emma Kirkby with her boyish treble-like tone excites strong opinions both ways, but admirers of her style in early and baroque music will delight in this well-chosen sampler of her work, one side of sixteenth-century song, the other of baroque arias. Clear, bright recording to match. The cassette is extremely vivid, with just a hint on side one that the higher vocal climaxes are not accommodated with complete ease.

Lear, Evelyn (soprano), **Martin Katz** (piano)

Recital: BERNSTEIN: *Peter Pan: Who am I?; My house. On the Town: I can cook too; Some other time; Lonely town.* SONDHEIM: *Sweeney Todd: Green finch and linnet bird. Evening primroses: I remember. Follies: Could I leave you?; Losing my mind. A Little night music: Send in the clowns.*
(M) **(*) Mercury SRI/*MRI* 75136 [id.].

Evelyn Lear recorded this recital at the end of the 1970s and (apart from the famous and memorable *Send in the clowns*) it contains much rare repertoire, while preserving a memory of Sondheim's musical version of *Sweeney Todd*, which not all comers found comfortable in the theatre with its curious mixture of gory melodrama and tragedy. The Bernstein excerpts are hardly less valuable. Miss Lear understands the theatrical feeling of this repertoire, even though she treats the numbers as art songs, and one's only reservation is that the voice itself is not always completely in control with high notes sometimes under-supported. Martin Katz arranged the accompaniments and he plays them superbly, while the recording has almost uncanny presence, though on cassette the piano is made to sound bass-heavy.

London Pro Cantione Antiqua, Turner

'The flowering of Renaissance polyphony': DUNSTABLE: *Veni sancte spiritus.* DUFAY: *Flos florum. Ave virgo quae de caelis. Alma redemptoris mater.* BINCHOIS: *Agnus Dei.* BUSNOIS: *Missa L'Homme armé.* OCKEGHEM: *Missa pro defunctis.* OBRECHT: *Salve crux.* JOSQUIN DES PRÉS: *Missa L'Homme armé super voces musicales. La Déploration sur la mort de Johan Ockeghem. Huc me sydereo.* DE LA RUE: *Laudate Dominum. Pater de coelis. Salve Regina.* ISAAC: *Quis dabit capiti meo aquam. Regina caeli laetari.* BRUMEL: *O Domine Jesu Christe. Noe noe.* MOUTON: *Quaeramus cum pastoribus.* COMPERE: *Crux triumphans.* GOMBERT: *Ave Regina. Musae Jovis.* DE MORALES: *Magnificat. Emendemus in melius. Lamentabatur Jacob.* ARCADELT: *O pulcherrima mulierum.* WILLAERT: *In convertendo.* CLEMENS NON PAPA: *Pastores loquebantur.* DE RORE: *O Altitudo divitiarum.* HANDEL: *Canite tuba in Sion.* DE MONTE: *O suavitas et dulcedo.* LASSUS: *Miserere mei, Deus.* PALESTRINA: *Oratio Jeremiae Prophetae. Sicut cervus desiderat. Super flumina Babylonis. O bone Jesu.*
*** DG Arc. 2723 070 (6) [id.].

This six-record set embraces music from Dunstable and Dufay through to the late Renaissance. All of it has been issued before, and certain items appeared between our publications, and their catalogue life was so short that we had no opportunity to commend their contents to readers interested in this repertoire. The first record is devoted to Dufay, Dunstable and Binchois; the second to Ockeghem and Obrecht; the third to Josquin including his *Missa L'Homme armé*; the fourth to Pierre de la Rue and Isaac; the fifth to an anthology including Morales and Philippe de

Monte; and the last to Lassus and Palestrina. Performances are expressive and warm, and the recordings (sometimes slightly forward in balance) are on the whole very fine.

Ludwig, Christa (mezzo-soprano)

Recital (with (i) Philh. Ch.; Philh. O, Klemperer): (i) BRAHMS: *Alto rhapsody, Op. 53.* MAHLER: *Rückert Lieder: Ich bin der Welt; Um Mitternacht; Ich atmet' einen linden Duft. Des Knaben Wunderhorn: Das irdische Leben; Wo die schönen Trompeten blasen.* WAGNER: *Wesendonk Lieder. Tristan und Isolde: Mild und Leise.*
(M) *** HMV SXLP/*TC-SXLP* 270000-1/4.

This valuable, well-planned mid-price reissue brings together a number of Christa Ludwig's most cherishable solo recordings with orchestra, in which her rich, characterful singing is well matched by the distinctive accompaniment of Klemperer. First-rate recording for its 1960s period, and a splendid cassette. An indispensable issue for admirers of this artist.

Luxon, Benjamin (baritone)

'Some enchanted evening' (with Nat. PO, Hughes): RODGERS: *South Pacific: Some enchanted evening. Oklahoma: Surrey with a fringe on top. Babes in Arms: Where or when. Carousel: Soliloquy.* LOEWE: *My Fair Lady: On the street where you live.* KERN: *Showboat: Ol' man river.* BERNSTEIN: *West Side Story: Maria.* WILLSON: *Music Man: 76 trombones.* GERSHWIN: *Porgy and Bess: I got plenty o' nuttin'.* KERN: *Very Warm for May: All the things you are.* BIZET (arr. Hammerstein): *Carmen Jones: Stan' up and fight.*
*** RCA RL/*RK* 25320.

An outstanding compilation of some of the finest songs from the American musical, unsurpassed in the current catalogue. Luxon is one of the most characterful of performers of this repertoire, equally effective in a full-bloodedly romantic song like *Maria* and in the lighter and charming *Surrey with a fringe on top.* His *Ol' man river* is lyrically resonant, and *76 trombones* admirably ebullient. He is given first-class accompaniments by Arwel Hughes, and only occasionally does one miss a chorus. The recording is forward but flattering, and the voice sounds warm and vibrant. The cassette matches the disc closely. Recommended.

'Break the news to mother' (Victorian and Edwardian ballads; with David Willison, piano): SANDERSON: *Up from Somerset.* CAREY: *Nearer my God to Thee.* MCCALL: *Boots.* HARRIS: *Break the news to mother.* HATTON: *The wreck of the Hesperus.* CAPEL: *Love, could I only tell thee.* BLANEY: *Mr Bear.* JACOBS-BOND: *Just a' wearyin' for you.* SULLIVAN: *The lost chord.* WOODFORDE-FINDEN: *Kashmiri song.* HARPER: *A bandit's life.* PENN: *Smilin' through.* PETRIE: *Asleep in the deep.*
(M) *** Argo ZK/*KZKC* 42.

Benjamin Luxon has made something of a speciality of singing Edwardian ballads, whether in company with Robert Tear or on his own. The bluff hints of characterization here never step into the area of outright send-up, which on a recording is just as well, and this warmly characterful collection is guaranteed to delight any who have enjoyed this singer's recitals on television or in the concert hall. Good atmospheric recording and a splendid tape transfer, both giving the voice fine bloom and resonance and placing the piano realistically.

McCormack, John (tenor)

Popular songs and Irish ballads: TRAD.: *The garden where the praties grow; Terence's farewell to Kathleen; Believe me if all those endearing young charms; The star of the County Down; Oft in the stilly night; The meeting of the waters; The Bard of Armagh; Down by the Salley Gardens; She moved thro' the fair; The green bushes.* BALFE: *The harp that once through Tara's halls.* ROECKEL: *The green isle of Erin.* BRAHE: *Bless this house.* SCHNEIDER: *O Mary dear.* LAMBERT: *She is far from the land.* HAYNES: *Off to Philadelphia.* MOLLOY: *The Kerry dance; Bantry Bay.* MURRAY: *I'll walk beside you.* Arr. CAL-

COTT: *Drink to me only*. CLUTSAM: *I know of two bright eyes*. FOSTER: *Jeannie with the light brown hair*. SOMERVELL: *Loveliest of trees*. VAUGHAN WILLIAMS: *Linden Lea; Silent noon*. PURCELL, E.: *Passing by*. BANTOCK: *Song to the seals*. GRÜBER: *Silent night*. CHOPIN: *So deep is the night*. MALASHKIN: *O could I but express in song*. HARLINE: *Pinocchio: When you wish upon a star; Little wooden head*. CHAMINADE: *The little silver ring*. DUNHILL: *The cloths of heaven*. O'CONNOR: *The old house*.
(M) *** HMV mono EX/*TC-EX* 290007-3/5 (2).

Reissued, like the companion set below, to celebrate the centenary of John McCormack's birth, this popular compilation will immediately recapture for older readers memories of one of the greatest tenor voices of our century, while for newer generations it re-creates a legend. McCormack's voice recorded with wonderful naturalness, partly because he mastered early the art of using the microphone. These 78 r.p.m. transfers from the 1930s and '40s sound as fresh and real as the day they were made. In Irish repertoire like *The star of the County Down* McCormack is irresistible, but in lighter concert songs he could also spin the utmost magic. *Down by the Salley Gardens* and Stephen Foster's *Jeannie with the light brown hair* are superb examples, while in a ballad like *I'll walk beside you* the golden bloom of the vocal timbre combining with an artless line brings a ravishing frisson of pleasure. At times there is sentimentality, but it is balanced with absolute sincerity; even so the two songs from Walt Disney's *Pinocchio* are repertoire to which the great singer was temperamentally less suited. Though the charm remains, there is an element of kitsch. Many of the accompaniments are by Gerald Moore who proves a splendid partner. Occasionally there is a hint of unsteadiness in the sustained piano tone, but otherwise no apology need be made for the recorded sound which is first-class, while the lack of 78 r.p.m. background noise is remarkable. The biographical sleeve-note is written by Desmond Shawe-Taylor who also provides a fascinating commentary on the performances.

'The art of John McCormack': MARTINI: *Plaisir d'amour*. CIAMPI: *Tre giorni son che Nina*. HANDEL: *Semele: Where'er you walk. Il pastor fido: Caro Amor. Atalanta: Come, my beloved*. OCHS: *Praise ye the Lord*. BACH: *Cantata No. 147: Jesu, joy of man's desiring*. MOZART: *Oh, what bitter grief, K.147; Ridente la calma, K.152. To Chloë, K.524*. SCHUBERT: *Who is Sylvia?* WAGNER: *Wesendonk Lieder: Träume*. BRAHMS: *Die Mainacht; Feldeinsamkeit*. STRAUSS, R.: *Allerseelen; Morgen; Du meines Herzens Krönelein*. WOLF: *Auch kleine Dinge; Herr, was trägt der Boden hier? Schlafendes Jesuskind; Wo find ich Trost; Anakreons Grab*. TCHAIKOVSKY: *Legend*. RACHMANINOV: *Before my window; How fair this spot; To the children*. CORNELIUS: *Ave Maria*. FRANCK: *La Procession*. FAURÉ: *L'automne*. DONAUDY: *O del mio amato ben; Luoghi sereni e cari*. ARNE: *The lass with the delicate air*. ELGAR: *Is she not passing fair?* QUILTER: *Now sleeps the crimson petal*. FOSTER: *Sweetly she sleeps, my Alice fair*.
(M) (***) HMV mono EX/*TC-EX* 290056-3/5 (2).

Even though it opens winningly with Martini's *Plaisir d'amour*, this second McCormack anthology in HMV's Treasury series centres on his classical 78 r.p.m. records. From finely spun Handelian lyricism through German Lieder and Russian art songs (with Fritz Kreisler ready at hand to provide violin obbligatos for Rachmaninov), to French Mélodie and songs of Elgar and Quilter, the collection generously demonstrates the great tenor's range. His French pronunciation was hardly colloquial nor was he ever entirely at home in German, yet his contribution to the Wolf Society recordings celebrated a unique feeling for this composer, readily mirrored here; and his lyrical gifts brought striking individuality to his singing of Brahms and Richard Strauss. The characteristic directness of communication makes Tchaikovsky's simple *Legend* (*Christ in his garden*) quite memorable. In the final group alongside a lovely account of Quilter's *Now sleeps the crimson petal*, there is an enchanting performance of Arne's *Lass with the delicate air*, which projects with such spontaneous charm that it sounds like an Irish folksong. It was recorded in 1940 when the vocal technique was less flexible than earlier, but the effect is captivating. Overall the recordings span a longer time-period than the popular collection above, and include a batch of pre-electrics from 1924. But transfers are exemplary and the sound from the later records is very fine indeed. Desmond Shawe-Taylor's biographical note from the first set is reprinted, with a discerning commentary about the performances from a critic who (alongside the late Sir Compton Mackenzie) has been a lifetime admirer of the artist.

'Legendary performer' (recordings processed by digital computer): arias from HANDEL: *Semele;* MOZART: *Don Giovanni;* BIZET: *Les Pêcheurs de perles;* DONIZETTI: *La Fille du régiment.* BIMBONI: *Sospiri miei andante.* PARKINS: *Le Portrait.* SCHUMANN: *The singer's consolation.* RACHMANINOV: *When night descends.* TOSTI: *Venetian song.* BARTLETT: *A dream.* BALFE: *Come into the garden, Maude.* LEHMANN: *Ah, moon of my delight; Bonny wee thing.* Arr. HUGHES: *The next market day; A Ballynure ballad; The bard of Armagh.*
**(*) RCA RL/*RK* 12742 [CRM1/*CRK1* 2742].

Like the Caruso collections available on the same label in the USA, these transfers have been made from 78s with the help of a digital computer to eliminate unwanted resonances. The result – if anything even more vitally than with Caruso – has a living quality which makes one relish the light, bright tones of McCormack in his prime. There is some superb singing here – this account of *Il mio tesoro* from *Don Giovanni* is a classic of vocal recording – to have one appreciating the special status of the Irish tenor in his earlier career. Recommended even to those who do not usually respond to McCormack's highly individual timbre. The tape transfer is well balanced and clean, if not quite as revealing as the disc.

Medieval Ens. of L., Peter and Timothy Davies

'Ce diabolic chant' (Ballades, rondeaux and virelais of the late 14th century): SUZOY: *Prophilias; A l'arbre sec; Pictagoras jabol.* SENLECHES: *Je me merveil; En ce gracieux temps; Fuions de ci; La harpe de melodie; En attendant esperance; Tel me voit.* GUIDO: *Dieux gart; Or voi tout.* OLIVIER: *Si con cy gist.* GALIOT: *La sault perilleux; En attendant d'avoir.* ANON.: *El albion; Se j'ay perdu.*
*** O-L Dig. DSDL 704.

'Ce diabolic chant' takes its title from the last chanson on this second side, *Se j'ay perdu toute ma parte* ('If I have lost all that which was my own/it is not because of any wrong or shortcoming on my part/but it is because of this devilish song which holds sway in this land. This song is not easily dismissed/for half is lost and yet it is potent'). This admirably sums up the quality of the complex and ornate chansons written in the late fourteenth century in the wake of Machaut. Many of the pieces are anonymous and little is known about them, with the exception of Jacob Senleches. The main subject of these chansons is courtly love; the writing is distinguished by long, finely spun lines, often of some considerable rhythmic subtlety and complexity. The performers are persuasive and accomplished, projecting the character of these pieces with enthusiasm and imagination, and the recording is outstanding in its clarity of definition.

Monteverdi Ch., Philip Jones Brass Ens., John Eliot Gardiner

'Christmas in Venice': GABRIELI, Giovanni: *Canzona: Sol sol la sol; Audite principes; Angelus ad pastores; Quem vidistis pastores; Salvator noster; Sonata pian' e forte; O magnum mysterium.* BASSANO: *Hodie Christus natus est.* MONTEVERDI: *Exultent coeli.*
(M) *** Decca Ace SDD 363.

Although one could not imagine a more delightful Christmas present, it would be a pity if this marvellous collection were relegated to a purely seasonal category, for the record is one to be enjoyed the year through. The insert-note draws a picture of Christmas being celebrated in St Mark's, Venice, at the beginning of the seventeenth century with the church ablaze with the light of more than a thousand candles plus sixty huge torches and silver lamps. The note tells us also that at this time the church was hung from floor to balcony with huge oriental tapestries which provided decorative splendour and at the same time had the highly practical effect of soaking up some of the reverberation and echo. This made it possible for the antiphonal polyphony to make a proper effect.

The acoustic chosen for this recording has been beautifully managed. The richly sonorous dignity of Gabrieli's *Sonata pian' e forte* has never sounded so resplendent on disc before, and in the choral numbers the vocal and instrumental blend is well-nigh perfect. The most impressive work is Gabrieli's glorious motet, *Quem vidistis pastores*, which is used to close side one. Monteverdi's *Exultent coeli* which closes side two is even shorter, but again one is amazed by the range of expressive contrast from the exultant opening *Let the heavens rejoice* to the magically simple setting of the phrase *O Maria*, a moment of great beauty each time it recurs. Then there is Gabrieli's fine *Salvator noster*, a motet for three five-part choirs, jubilant and richly expressive in its rejoicing at the birth of Christ. One specially attractive feature of Gabrieli's writing is his individual setting of the word *Alleluia* used to close each of his pieces: the jauntiness of the style is fresh and exhilarating. This is a record not to be missed on any account: it is in every way a top-priced issue, except that it was released in the Ace of Diamonds series.

Mormon Tabernacle Ch., Condie

'The best of the Mormon Tabernacle Choir' (with Phd. O, Ormandy): arr. WILHOUSKY: *Battle hymn of the Republic.* SIBELIUS: *Finlandia: Chorale.* BACH: *Chorales: Sleepers awake; Sheep may safely graze* (arr. Walton). MALOTTE: *Lord's prayer.* BRAHE: *Bless this house.* HANDEL: *Xerxes: Largo. Messiah: For unto us a child is born.* RIMSKY-KORSAKOV: *Glory.* DRAPER: *All creatures of our God and King.* TRAD.: *Rock of ages. Sometimes I feel like a motherless child. Guide us, O thou great Jehova. Come, come, ye saints.*
(M) **(*) CBS 61873/*40-*.

These items are taken from records made over a decade from 1959 to 1969 and show the famous choir's effective range. Their natural fervour is at its most eloquent in the hymns, but they respond with appealing freshness to *For unto us a child is born*, and they are equally at home in the negro spiritual. The recording is clear and vivid, and the cassette is acceptable, if without the range of the disc.

Norman, Jessye (soprano)

'Negro spirituals' (with Amb. S.; Baldwin, piano): *Do Lawd. Ev'ry time I feel de spirit. Give me Jesus. Gospel train. Great day. Hush! Somebody's callin' my name. I couldn't hear nobody pray. Live a humble. Mary had a baby. My Lord what a morning. Soon ah will be done. There is a balm in Gilead. There's a man. Walk together. Were you there.*
*** Ph. 9500 580/*7300 706* [id.].

There is a degree of restraint in Jessye Norman's singing of spirituals which may seem surprising, but the depth of feeling is never in doubt. What she has consciously done is to tilt the performances towards concert tradition, and with refined recording the result is both beautiful and moving. The cassette offers excellent quality with plenty of range, the solo voice clear and free.

'Sacred songs' (with Amb. S., RPO, Gibson): GOUNOD: *Messe solennelle de Sainte Cécile: Sanctus. O Divine Redeemer.* FRANCK: *Panis angelicus.* ADAMS: *The Holy City.* ANON.: *Amazing Grace. Greensleeves. Let Us Break Bread. I Wonder.* MAGGIMSEY: *Sweet little Jesus Boy.* YON: *Gesù Bambino.*
C *** Ph. Dig. **400 019-2**; 6514/*7337* 151 [id.].

Miss Norman's restraint is again telling here; she sings with great eloquence, but her simplicity and sincerity shine through repertoire that can easily sound sentimental. The Gounod *Sanctus* is especially fine, but the simpler traditional songs are also very affecting. First-class recording and an excellent tape transfer. The compact disc, however, is very much in the demonstration class, strikingly natural and giving the soloist remarkable presence, especially when she is singing unaccompanied.

Opera

'Nights at the opera': VERDI: *Aïda: Celeste Aïda* (Corelli)*; Triumphal march. Don Carlos: O don fatale* (Verrett). *Il Trovatore: Anvil chorus; Miserere* (Tucci, Corelli). *La Traviata: Brindisi; Ah, fors' è lui* (Monte, Los Angeles). *Nabucco: Chorus of Hebrew slaves.* MASCAGNI: *Cavalleria Rusticana: Easter hymn* (Tinsley). DONIZETTI: *L'Elisir d'amore: Una furtiva lagrima* (Alva). PUCCINI: *Madama Butterfly: Un bel dì* (Scotto). *La Bohème: Che gelida manina; O soave fanciulla* (Gedda, Freni)*; Musetta's waltz song* (Adani). *Turandot: Nessun dorma* (Corelli). *Gianni Schicchi: O mio babbino caro* (Los Angeles). *Tosca: Recondita armonia; E lucevan le stelle* (Bergonzi)*; Vissi d'arte* (Callas). ROSSINI: *Il Barbiere di Siviglia: Largo al factotum* (Bruscantini).
(B) ** EMI *TC2-MOM 112.*

This is generally a preferable eighty minutes to the collection of *Italian opera favourites* in the same tape series (see above). Sometimes the performances are robust rather than endearing (Corelli's *Celeste Aïda* is vibrant but clumsily phrased). But there are many good things, notably the contributions of Luigi Alva, Victoria de los Angeles and Callas's *Vissi d'arte*. Vivid sound throughout, with a high transfer level, yet little roughness. However, some of the excerpts, taken from complete sets, have to be faded out quickly at the end, which tends to unsettle one's listening in an anthology of this kind.

Opera choruses

'Great opera choruses' from: VERDI: *Nabucco; Il Trovatore; Aïda.* BELLINI: *Norma.* LEONCAVALLO: *I Pagliacci.* WAGNER: *Tannhäuser.* BEETHOVEN: *Fidelio.* GOUNOD: *Faust.* BIZET: *Carmen.* MUSSORGSKY: *Boris Godunov.*
(M) *** Decca SPA/*KCSP* 296.

This imaginatively chosen collection is excellent value and offers vivid sound and impressive performances throughout. Most of the excerpts come from distinguished complete sets, notably the *Pilgrims' chorus* scene from Solti's *Tannhäuser*, which has a memorable sense of perspective. Bonynge conducts the *War chorus* from *Norma* and the *Soldiers' chorus* from *Faust*, and Karajan directs the *Coronation scene* from *Boris Godunov*. The cassette transfers are generally good and often excellent. There is a slight lack of refinement in the spectacular march scene from *Aïda*, but the one real misjudgement is the *Prisoners' chorus* from *Fidelio*, where the level suddenly rises and the sound becomes fierce, so for this item one needs to cut back both the volume and the treble response.

Operatic duets

'Favourite operatic duets' from: ROSSINI: *Semiramide.* VERDI: *Il Trovatore; La Traviata; Don Carlos; La Forza del destino.* PUCCINI: *Tosca; Madama Butterfly; La Bohème.* BIZET: *Les Pêcheurs de perles; Carmen.* BERLIOZ: *Béatrice et Bénédict.*
(B) **(*) Decca DPA/*KDPC* 517/8.

The Sutherland/Horne Act I duet from *Semiramide* is a classic by any standards, and there are other interesting inclusions here too: the Bergonzi/Fischer-Dieskau duet from Act II of *Don Carlos* (superbly exciting) and by contrast the lovely *Nocturne* from *Béatrice et Bénédict* (April Cantelo and Helen Watts). Perhaps most interesting of all, however, is the successful transfer of an early Decca mono recording of *Au fond du temple saint* stirringly sung by Libero de Luca and Jean Borthayre. The rest of the programme includes oft-used Decca items by familiar artists such as Tebaldi and Bergonzi. The closing scene of *Carmen* (Resnik and del Monaco) is vibrant enough, although hardly subtle. The sound is generally very good, though the quality is more variable on tape.

'Favourite opera duets' (with (i) Vanzo, Sarabia; (ii) Callas, Ludwig; (iii) Bergonzi, Cappuccilli; (iv) Domingo; (v) Milnes; (vi) Freni; (vii) Pavarotti; (viii) Scotto, Allen; (ix) Caballé): (i) BIZET: *Les Pêcheurs de perles. C'était le soir ... Au fond du temple saint.* (ii) BELLINI: *Norma: Mira, o Norma.* (iii) VERDI: *La Forza del destino: Solenne in quest'ora.* (iv; v) *Don Carlos: Dio che nell'alma infondere.*

(iv; vi) GOUNOD: *Faust: Il se fait tard.* (vi; vii) MASCAGNI: *L'Amico Fritz: Suzel, buon dì.* (viii) LEONCAVALLO: *I Pagliacci: E fra quest'ansie . . . Decido il mio destin.* (iv; ix) VERDI: *Aïda: La fatal pietra . . . O terra addio.*
*** HMV ASD/*TC-ASD* 3908 [Ang. S 36935].

Taken from various EMI sources this makes an attractive and varied collection, featuring an impressive range of artists and a well-chosen programme. It is good to have, for example, the haunting *Cherry duet* from *L'Amico Fritz*. But it is a pity that the famous *Pearl Fishers* duet (which opens the recital) ends without a proper cadence, so that the following excerpt from *Norma* almost seems like a continuation. The sound is vivid on both disc and cassette.

Operetta

'The world of operetta favourites': excerpts from: STRAUSS, J. Jnr: *Die Fledermaus; Der Zigeunerbaron; Casanova.* ZELLER: *Der Obersteiger.* STRAUS: *The Chocolate Soldier.* OFFENBACH: *Orpheus in the Underworld; La Périchole.* LECOCQ: *Le Coeur et la main.* LEHÁR: *The Merry Widow; The Land of Smiles.*
(M) *** Decca SPA/*KCSP* 466.

An attractive programme with a major contribution from Hilde Gueden, in very good form indeed. Other highlights include Régine Crespin's Letter song from *La Périchole* and Joan Sutherland's *Boléro* from a little-known piece by Lecocq. The collection opens spiritedly with the ubiquitous *Die Fledermaus overture* and the other overture (*Orpheus in the Underworld*) makes a suitable curtain-raiser for side two. Sparkling sound on disc; the cassette has problems with the transfer of the second overture, but is otherwise satisfactory.

Palmer, Felicity (soprano), **John Constable** (piano)

'Home sweet home': LAMBERT: *God's garden.* GERMAN: *Daffodils a-blowing.* D'HARDELOT: *I know a lovely garden.* ADAMS: *The bells of St Mary's.* SQUIRE: *In an old-fashioned town.* KAHN: *Happy summer song.* BOND: *A perfect day.* CAPEL: *Love could I only tell thee.* BISHOP: *Home sweet home.* PHILIPS: *Sing joyous bird.* TATE: *Somewhere a voice is calling.* COLERIDGE-TAYLOR: *Big Lady Moon.* BRAHE: *Bless this house.* HARRISON: *In the gloaming.* PEEL: *The early morning.*
(M) **(*) Argo ZK 97.

Though the voice as recorded is abrasive rather than warm, Felicity Palmer makes a characterful interpreter of Edwardian drawing-room ballads to make this a nice counterpart of Benjamin Luxon's ballad records for Argo. Excellent recording.

'Panis angelicus'

Sacred music: FRANCK: *Panis angelicus* (Pavarotti). BACH–GOUNOD: *Ave Maria.* BRAHMS: *Wiegenlied.* SCHUBERT: *Mille cherubini in coro* (Tebaldi); *Ave Maria.* MALOTTE: *The Lord's prayer* (Burrows). MOZART: *Ave verum corpus, K.618.* BACH: *Cantata No. 147: Jesu, joy of man's desiring* (St John's College Ch., Guest). PEROSI: *Benedictus.* BEETHOVEN: *In questa tomba oscura* (Del Monaco). BRUCKNER: *Ave Maria.* FAURÉ: *Ave verum.* BRAHMS: *Geistliches Lied* (Christchurch Cath. Ch., Preston). BACH: *Bist du bei mir* (M. Horne). GABRIELI, A.: *Ave Maria* (Magdalen College, Oxford, Ch., Rose).
(M) *** Decca VIV/*KVIC* 45.

This collection of religious kitsch will not be to all tastes, but the sound throughout is enticingly rich and clear and the performances are nearly all of a high order. Pavarotti sings the title-piece with agreeable warmth and, of the four settings of *Ave Maria*, Stuart Burrows sings Schubert's version admirably while Tebaldi is no less at home in the Bach–Gounod arrangement. There are two fine contributions from the St John's (Oxford) Choir and Marilyn Horne's *Bist du bei mir* is another highlight. Good value of its kind.

Partridge, Ian (tenor), **Stephen Roberts** (baritone)

'Songs by Finzi and his friends' (with Benson,

piano): FINZI: *To a poet; Oh fair to see, Op. 13a–b* (song collections). GURNEY: *Sleep. Down by the Salley Gardens. Hawk and buckle.* MILFORD: *If it's ever spring again. The colour. So sweet love seemed.* GILL: *In memoriam.* FERRAR: *O mistress mine.*
**(*) Hyp. A 66015.

Finzi's sensitive response to word-meanings inspires a style of setting that is often not unlike an operatic recitative. His individuality and poetic originality are not always matched by memorability, but the songs of his contemporaries and friends – even where the names are unknown – make immediate communication even on a first hearing. An imaginative collection, well sung, worth exploring by those interested in the repertoire. The recording is fair, somewhat over-resonant.

Pavarotti, Luciano (tenor)

'Bravo Pavarotti': excerpts from: DONIZETTI: *Lucia di Lammermoor; La Fille du régiment; L'Elisir d'amore; La Favorita.* PUCCINI: *La Bohème; Turandot; Tosca.* STRAUSS, R.: *Der Rosenkavalier.* VERDI: *Un Ballo in maschera; Luisa Miller; La Traviata; Requiem; Rigoletto; Il Trovatore.* BELLINI: *I Puritani.*
*** Decca D 129 D 2/*K 129 K 22* (2) [Lon. PAV 2001/2/5-].

Of Decca's three two-disc anthologies of Pavarotti, this is the obvious first choice. It provides an impressive survey of Pavarotti's achievement in the recording studio over a period of thirteen years. When he started recording for Decca, he was already a mature artist, and Tonio's aria from *La Fille du régiment* with its fusillade of top Cs is as impressive as anything, a dazzling and infectious performance. Nowhere is there an ugly note, for as recorded Pavarotti is the modern Italian tenor with the most consistently beautiful tone, and the many duets and ensembles heighten his achievement in context with his finest colleagues. Taken as a whole it is a splendidly chosen and very entertaining selection. Each performance springs vividly to life, and there are only a few fades. The sound is consistently excellent on disc and cassette alike, and the order of items is perceptive.

'Pavarotti's greatest hits' from: PUCCINI: *Turandot; Tosca; La Bohème.* DONIZETTI: *La Fille du régiment; La Favorita; L'Elisir d'amore.* STRAUSS, R.: *Der Rosenkavalier.* BIZET: *Carmen.* BELLINI: *I Puritani.* VERDI: *Il Trovatore; Rigoletto; Requiem.* GOUNOD: *Faust.* LEONCAVALLO: *I Pagliacci.* PONCHIELLI: *La Gioconda.* Songs by LEONCAVALLO, ROSSINI, DENZA, DE CURTIS. FRANCK: *Panis angelicus.*
*** Decca D 236 D 2/*K 236 K 22* (2) [Lon. PAV 2003/4/5-].

This collection of 'greatest hits' overlaps with the other two-disc collection, *Bravo Pavarotti*, but it can be safely recommended to all who have admired the golden beauty of the voice. Including as it does a fair proportion of earlier recordings, the four sides demonstrate the splendid consistency of his singing. Songs are included as well as excerpts from opera, including *Torna a Surriento, Funiculi, funicula*, Leoncavallo's *Mattinata* and Rossini's *La Danza*. The sound is very good on disc, always vibrant but sometimes a little fierce on cassette.

'My own story': arias from: PUCCINI: *La Bohème.* DONIZETTI: *Il Duca d'Alba; La Fille du régiment; L'Elisir d'amore.* ROSSINI: *William Tell; Stabat Mater.* BOITO: *Mefistofele.* BELLINI: *La Sonnambula.* CILEA: *L'Arlesiana.* FLOTOW: *Martha.* VERDI: *Rigoletto.* Songs by TOSTI, DONIZETTI, BIZET, DI CAPUA.
**(*) Decca D 253 D 2/*K 253 K 22* (2) [Lon. PAV 2007/5-].

Yet another variant on the Pavarotti theme, this time associated with his book of the same title (published by Sidgwick and Jackson). The leaflet with the records (and tapes) relates each item to the development of the singer's career. Opening attractively with Puccini's most famous two arias from Act I of *La Bohème*, the selection also includes impressive excerpts from *William Tell* and *La Fille du régiment* and ranges into less familiar repertoire. A fair number of songs are included, which lightens the overall character of the presentation. This makes an admirable supplement to either of the first two double-albums, though it would not be a first choice among them. The recording is excellent and the cassettes are of high quality, with only a very occasional hint of peaking on one or two fortissimos.

'Digital recital' (with Nat. PO, Chailly or Fabritiis): GIORDANO: *Fedora: Amor ti vieta. Andrea Chénier: Colpito qui m'avete . . . Un dì all'azzuro spazio; Come un bel dì di maggio; Si, fui soldata.* BOITO: *Mefistofele: Dai campi, dai prati; Ogni mortal . . . Giunto sul passo estremo.* CILEA: *Adriana Lecouvreur: La dolcissima effigie; L'anima ho stanca.* MASCAGNI: *Iris: Apri la tua finestra!* MEYERBEER: *L'Africana: Mi batti il cor . . . O Paradiso.* MASSENET: *Werther: Pourquoi me réveiller.* PUCCINI: *La Fanciulla del West: Ch'ella mi creda. Manon Lescaut: Tra voi belle; Donna non vidi mai; Ah! non v'avvicinate! . . . No! No! pazzo son!* (with Howlett).
(*) Decca Dig. **400 083-2; SXDL/*KSXDC* 7504 [Lon. LDR/5- 10020).

This first digital recital record from Pavarotti has the voice more resplendent than ever. The passion with which he tackles Des Grieux's Act III plea from *Manon Lescaut* is devastating, and the big breast-beating numbers are all splendid, imaginative as well as heroic. But the slight pieces, Des Grieux's *Tra voi belle* and the Iris *Serenade*, could be lighter and more charming. The compact disc gives the voice even greater projection, with its full resonance and brilliance admirably caught, but it does also make the listener more aware of the occasional lack of subtlety of the presentation. The cassette transfer is vibrant and clear, if losing a little of the CD projection.

'Gala concert' (with RPO, Adler): PUCCINI: *Tosca: Recondita armonia; E lucevan le stelle. Turandot: Nessun dorma.* VERDI: *Macbeth: Ah, la paterna mano. Un giorno di regno: overture. I Lombardi: La mia letizia infondere. Luisa Miller: Quando le sere al placido.* DONIZETTI: *Lucia di Lammermoor: Fra poco a me ricovero.* CILEA: *L'Arlesiana: Lamento di Federico.* BERLIOZ: *Les Troyens: Royal hunt and storm.* DE CURTIS: *Torna a Surriento.*
**(*) Decca Dig. SXDL/*KSXDC* 7582 [Lon. LDR/5-71082].

This disc celebrates a much-publicized appearance by Pavarotti at the Royal Albert Hall in 1982. It would be unfair to expect much subtlety before such an eager audience, but the live recording conveys the fever well. Even simple recitatives as intimate as Macduff's in *Macbeth* are proclaimed grandly, and the bright digital recording shows up some unevenness in the voice. But no one will miss the genuine excitement, with the electricity of the occasion conveyed equally effectively on disc or chrome tape.

'The world's favourite arias' from: LEONCAVALLO: *I Pagliacci.* FLOTOW: *Martha.* BIZET: *Carmen.* PUCCINI: *La Bohème; Tosca; Turandot.* VERDI: *Rigoletto; Aïda; Il Trovatore.* GOUNOD: *Faust.*
(*) Decca **400 053-2; SXL/*KSXC* 6649 [Lon. OSA/5- 26384].

As one would expect from Pavarotti, there is much to enjoy in his ripe and resonant singing of these favourite arias, but it is noticeable that the finest performances are those which come from complete sets, conducted by Karajan (*Bohème*), Mehta (*Turandot*) and Bonynge (*Rigoletto*), where with character in mind Pavarotti's singing is the more intense and imaginative. The rest remains very impressive, though at under forty minutes the measure is short. The transfer to compact disc has involved digital remastering which has resulted in slight limitation of the upper range to take out background noise. However, the vividness of the voice is enhanced in the process. The cassette is slightly more uneven in quality than LP or CD, most noticeably in the *Turandot* excerpt where the chorus is none too clear.

'King of the high Cs': arias from: DONIZETTI: *La Fille du régiment; La Favorita.* VERDI: *Il Trovatore.* STRAUSS, R.: *Der Rosenkavalier.* ROSSINI: *Guglielmo Tell.* BELLINI: *I Puritani.* PUCCINI: *La Bohème.*
*** Decca SXL/*KSXC* 6658 [Lon. OSA/5- 26373].

The punning title may not be to everyone's taste, but in recent years there have been few finer or more attractively varied collections of tenor arias than this, a superb display of Pavarotti's vocal command as well as his projection of personality. The selections come from various sources and the recording quality is remarkably consistent, the voice stirringly vibrant and clear, on disc and tape alike. The accompanying detail and contributions of the chorus are well managed, too.

'O holy night' (with Wandsworth Boys' Ch., Nat. PO, Adler): sacred music by ADAM; STRADELLA; MERCADANTE; SCHUBERT; BIZET; BERLIOZ. FRANCK: *Panis angelicus*. BACH–GOUNOD: *Ave Maria* (2).
**(*) Decca SXL/*KSXC* 6781.

It is a long-established tradition for great Italian tenors to indulge in such songs as these, most of them overtly sugary in their expression of (no doubt) sincere religious fervour. Pavarotti is hardly a model of taste, but more than most of his rivals (even a tenor as intelligent as Placido Domingo) he avoids the worst pitfalls; and if this sort of recital is what you are looking for, then Pavarotti is a good choice, with his beautiful vocalizing helped by full, bright recording. Note too that one or two of these items are less hackneyed than the rest, for instance the title setting by Adam, Mercadante's *Parola quinta* and the *Sanctus* from Berlioz's *Requiem mass*. The cassette transfer is admirably clear and clean; the chorus too is naturally caught.

'Pavarotti in concert' (with O of Teatro Comunale, Bologna, Bonynge): BONONCINI: *Griselda: Per la gloria d'adorarvi*. HANDEL: *Atalanta: Care selve*. SCARLATTI, A.: *Già il sol dal Gange*. BELLINI: Songs: *Ma rendi pur contento; Dolente immagine di fille mia; Malinconia, ninfa gentile; Bella nice, che d'amore; Vanne, o rosa fortunata*. TOSTI: Songs: *La Serenata; Luna d'estate; Malia; Non t'amo più*. RESPIGHI: *Nevicata. Poggia. Nebbie*. ROSSINI: *La Danza*.
**(*) Decca SXL/*KSXC* 6650 [Lon. 26391].

Pavarotti is more subdued than usual in the classical items here: he finds an attractive lyrical delicacy for the opening Bononcini aria, though there is a hint of strain in Handel's *Care selve*. He is in his element in Tosti, and, with evocative accompaniments from Bonynge, he makes the three Respighi songs the highlight of a recital which is nicely rounded off with a spirited but never coarse version of Rossini's *La Danza*. The Decca sound is atmospheric throughout and has transferred well to tape.

'The art of Pavarotti': arias from: DONIZETTI: *L'Elisir d'amore; Maria Stuarda; La Fille du régiment; Lucia di Lammermoor*. VERDI: *Un Ballo in maschera; Rigoletto; Macbeth; Requiem* (*Ingemisco*). ROSSINI: *Stabat Mater* (*Cujus animam*). PUCCINI: *Turandot*.
*** Decca SXL/*KSXC* 6839.

A generous and well-varied collection of Italian arias which superbly displays Pavarotti's best qualities. It is remarkable that an Italian tenor with a voice that has specific lyrical echoes of Gigli as well as heroic echoes of the greatest of his predecessors should also be a thinking and imaginative musician. Those qualities are repeatedly demonstrated here, even if at times Pavarotti's positive character takes him near danger. There is nothing weak or undercharacterized about this singing, yet it is never vulgar, and the ease with which he sings up to his top Cs and (in *Cujus animam*) up to D flat is phenomenal. Culled from different complete sets, the recordings – all with excellent Decca characteristics – are admirably consistent. The cassette transfers too are well managed, although there is sometimes a slight lack of bloom on the choral fortissimos.

Neapolitan songs (with Ch. and O of Teatro Comunale, Bologna, Guadagno, or Nat. PO, Chiaramello): DI CAPUA: *O sole mio. Maria, Marì*. TOSTI: *A vuchella. Marechiare*. CANNIO: *O surdato 'nnamurato*. GAMBARDELLA: *O Marenariello*. ANON.: *Fenesta vascia*. DE CURTIS: *Torna a Surriento. Tu, ca nun chiagne*. PENNINO: *Pecchè* . . . D'ANNIBALE: *O paese d'o sole*. TAGLIAFERRI: *Piscatore 'e pusilleco*. DENZA: *Funiculi, funicula*.
*** Decca **410 015-2**; SXL/*KSXC* 6870 [Lon. OSA/5- 26560].

Neapolitan songs given grand treatment in passionate Italian performances, missing some of the charm but none of the red-blooded fervour. The recording is both vivid and atmospheric. The tape transfer is well managed although there is slight loss of presence in the items with chorus. This certainly does not apply to the compact disc, where the recording is most successfully digitally remastered.

'Mattinata': CALDARA: *Alma del core.* CIAMPI: *Tre giorni.* BELLINI: *Vaga luna che inargenti.* DURANTE: *Danza danza, fanciulla.* GIORDANI: *Caro mio ben.* ROSSINI: *La promessa.* GLUCK: *Orfeo: Che farò.* TOSTI: *L'alba separa; Aprile; Chanson de l'adieu; L'Ultima canzone.* DONIZETTI: *Il barcaiolo.* LEONCAVALLO: *Mattinata.* BEETHOVEN: *In questo tomba.*
**(*) Decca SXL/*KSXC* 7013.

Pavarotti is at home in the lightweight items. *Caro mio ben* is very nicely done and the romantic songs have a well-judged ardour. *Che farò* is rather less impressive. The tone is not always golden, but most of the bloom remains. The recording is vividly faithful on disc and tape alike.

'Yes Giorgio' (film soundtrack recording).
* Decca YG1/*KYGC 1.*

Pavarotti's excursion into the film world draws parallels with Mario Lanza. He is even given a soupy pop song called *If we were in love*. There are operatic excerpts by Donizetti, Verdi and Puccini. The excerpt from *Turandot* with a meagre chorus is far from memorable. There are several orchestral interludes too and this really stands up only as a film memento, for the voice does not sound at its freshest. The most memorable item is a song called *I left my heart in San Francisco.*

'Grandi voci': Arias and duets from: VERDI: *La Traviata* (with Freni)*; Macbeth; I Lombardi; Otello* (with Ricciarelli). MASSENET: *Werther.* PONCHIELLI: *La Gioconda.* DONIZETTI: *L'elisir d'amore.* MEYERBEER: *L'Africaine.* PUCCINI: *Turandot.* ROSSINI: *Petite messe solennelle.* DONIZETTI: *Requiem.*
(M) *** Decca 410 166-1/*4.*

Recorded live at various performances in Italy, this recital vividly captures the atmosphere of a golden-voiced Pavarotti recital, full of flair and showmanship, displaying less vulgarity than you might expect. In the duets his fellow-citizen of Modena, Mirella Freni, makes a most sympathetic partner, as does Katia Ricciarelli in that rarity, the love duet from *Otello*, a role which Pavarotti has yet to sing on stage. Good atmospheric recording and a well-managed, vivid cassette. In both formats this is excellent value at mid-price.

Pears, Peter (tenor)**, Julian Bream** (lute)

'Sweet, stay awhile': MORLEY: *It was a lover and his lass. Absence.* ROSSETER: *What then is love but mourning. When Laura smiles.* DOWLAND: *Dear, if you change. Weep no more. Stay time. Sweet, stay awhile. Can she excuse.* FORD: *Fair, sweet, cruel.* BRITTEN: *Folksong arrangements: Master Kilbey; The shooting of his dear; Sailor-boy; I will give my love an apple; The soldier and the sailor. Songs from the Chinese* (*The big chariot; The old lute; The autumn wind; The herd-boy; Depression; Dance song*). *Gloriana: 2nd lute song of the Earl of Essex.*
(M) *** RCA Gold GL/*GK* 42752 [LSC 3131].

Any Pears–Bream recital is likely to give pleasure, and this vintage collection, recorded when Pears was at the peak of his form, is a genuine bargain with its inclusion of the Britten folksong arrangements, the lute song from *Gloriana* and the *Songs from the Chinese* to supplement the original Elizabethan collection. Here the Dowland songs are particularly fine, sung with Pears's usual blend of intelligence and lyrical feeling. The cassette transfer is of excellent quality, matching the disc closely.

Lute songs: DOWLAND: *Fine knacks for ladies. Sorrow stay. If my complaints. What if I never speed.* ROSSETER: *Sweet come again. What is a day. Whether men do laugh or weep.* MORLEY: *Thyrsis and Milla. I saw my lady weeping. With my love my life was nestled. What if my mistress now.* PILKINGTON: *Rest, sweet nymphs.* ANON.: *Have you seen but a white lily grow? Miserere, my Maker.* CAM-

PION: *Come, let us sound with melody. Fair, if you expect admiring. Shall I come sweet?*
(M) *** Decca Ser. SA/*KSC* 7.

This delightfully spontaneous recital was recorded at the beginning of the 1960s and finds both artists on top form. Pears's very individual timbre readily identifies with the underlying melancholy which characterizes so many Elizabethan songs. The sound is first-rate and the balance is equally natural on disc and on the excellent cassette.

Philharmonic Chamber Ch., Temple

'All in the April evening': ROBERTON: *All in the April evening; Nightfall in Skye.* TRAD.: *Isle of Mull; Steal away to Jesus; Dashing white sergeant; Were you there?; Banks o'Doon; Peat fire smooring prayer; Iona boat song; King Arthur; Herdmaiden's song; Swing low, sweet chariot; Crimond; Eriskay love lilt* (all arr. Roberton). *Loch Lomond* (arr. Vaughan Williams). STANFORD: *The Bluebird.* BOUGHTON: *Immortal hour: Faery song.* IRVINE: *Crimond.*
*** Hyp. A/*KA* 66064.

This is repertoire made famous over the years by the Glasgow Orpheus Choir, and most of the arrangements are by its late conductor, Sir Hugh Roberton. The performances are first-class, offering the same combination of eloquence, expressive directness and simplicity that made the Glasgow choir world-famous. The acoustic is perfectly chosen and the recording of the highest quality, whether heard on disc or the excellent matching cassette.

Price, Leontyne (soprano)

'Grandi voci': MOZART: *Don Giovanni: In quali eccessi . . . Mi trada. Exsultate jubilate: Alleluja, K.165.* VERDI: *Aïda: Ritorna vincitor; Qui Radames verra . . . O patria mia. Requiem: Libera me.* PUCCINI: *Tosca: Vissi d'arte.* STRAUSS, R.: *Ariadne: Es gibt ein Reich.* SCHUBERT: *Ave Maria.* GERSHWIN: *Porgy and Bess; Summertime.* TRAD.: *Sweet little Jesus.*
(M) *** Decca GRV/*KGRC* 10.

Leontyne Price can be heard at her finest here: the Verdi and Puccini arias central to her repertory are superbly done. It is good, too, to have her also represented in Mozart and Strauss, recorded at the peak of her career, though style there is less positive and individual. Nevertheless this very enjoyable recital is more than the sum of its parts, for the arrangement of items is well managed and the recording is first-class both on disc and cassette, one of Decca's best even though only on iron-oxide stock. The programme ends appropriately with an affecting performance of *Summertime* from *Porgy and Bess.*

'Christmas with Leontyne Price' (with V. Singverein, VPO, Karajan): GRÜBER: *Silent night.* MENDELSSOHN: *Hark the herald angels.* HOPKINS: *We three kings.* TRAD.: *Angels we have heard on high; O Tannenbaum; God rest ye merry, gentlemen; Sweet li'l Jesus.* WILLIS: *It came upon the midnight clear.* BACH: *Vom Himmel hoch.* BACH–GOUNOD: *Ave Maria.* SCHUBERT: *Ave Maria.* ADAM: *O holy night.* MOZART: *Alleluja, K.165.*
(M) **(*) Decca Jub. JB/*KJBC* 38.

There is much beautiful singing here, but the style is essentially operatic. The rich, ample voice, when scaled down (as for instance in *We three kings*), can be very beautiful, but at full thrust it does not always catch the simplicity of melodic line which is characteristic of many of these carols. Yet the vibrant quality of the presentation is undoubtedly thrilling, and it can charm too, as in *God rest ye merry, gentlemen*, with its neat harpsichord accompaniment. The sound is admirably rich and vivid, and there is an excellent cassette.

'Noël' (with Montreal Tudor Vocal Ens. and SO, Dutoit): TRAD.: *The first nowell; O come all ye faithful; What child is this?; I wonder as I wander; Away in a manger; Go tell it to the mountain; Come, o come Emanuel; O little town of Bethlehem; Un flambeau; Le premier Noël.* HANDEL: *Messiah: How beautiful are the feet; He shall feed His flock.* FRANCK: *Panis angelicus.* GRÜBER: *Silent night.*
**(*) Decca Dig. 410 198-1/*4* [id.].

Leontyne Price's first Christmas record was

a considerable commercial success, so here is the mixture much as before, though this time the choir is in Montreal and the choral singing is not always too well co-ordinated with the solo voice. Moreover the balance is not wholly satisfactory with the solo voice forward and clear, the chorus less well focused and well back, almost like a lamination. However, the warmth of Miss Price's singing of this familiar repertoire compensates for minor technical inadequacies. She is especially good in the French carol, *Un flambeau*, as well as in the spiritual, *Go tell it to the mountain*, sung unaccompanied. Disc and chrome cassette are closely matched.

Purcell Ch. of Voices; Philip Jones Brass Ens., Leppard

'Canzon cornetto': SCHEIDT: *Canzon cornetto; Courant dolorosa; Psalm 103*. SCHÜTZ: *Psalm 24; Ich beschwöre; Freue dich*. SCHEIN: *Zion spricht*.
(M) *** Decca Ser. SA/*KSC* 15.

This is a marvellous record and an admirable introduction to the work of the three great 'S's of seventeenth-century music. The Schütz is resplendent and sumptuous, proclaiming his indebtedness to Venice, while the Schein *Zion spricht* is hardly less magnificent. It would be difficult to overpraise either the music or the performances which are so much more vivid and alive than so many of the Schütz readings to reach us from Germany. Both the Purcell Chorus and the Philip Jones Ensemble respond splendidly to Raymond Leppard's direction. The recording has spaciousness, detail is well defined, and there is an excellent matching tape, although the level drops on side two.

Ricciarelli, Katia (soprano), **José Carreras** (tenor)

'Italian love duets' (with Amb. Op. Ch., LSO, Gardelli): PUCCINI: *Madama Butterfly: Bimba, bimba, non piangere*. VERDI: *I Lombardi: Dove sola m'inoltro . . . Per dirupi e per foreste*. DONIZETTI: *Poliuto: Questo pianto favelli . . . Ah! fuggi da morte. Roberto Devereux: Tutto è silenzio*.
*** Ph. 9500 750/*7300 835* [id.].

The two Donizetti duets are among the finest he ever wrote, especially the one from *Poliuto*, in which the hero persuades his wife to join him in martyrdom. This has a depth unexpected in Donizetti. Both the Donizetti items receive beautiful performances here; the Puccini love duet is made to sound fresh and unhackneyed, and the *Lombardi* excerpt is given with equal tenderness. Stylish conducting and refined recording.

St George's Canzona, Sothcott

'To drive the cold winter away' (A fireside presentation of music for merrymaking, down the ages).
** CRD CRD 1019/*CRDC 4019*.

An essentially robust presentation by a group with a piquant blend of recorder, shawn, crumhorn, citole, rebec, vielle and so on. The programme opens with *Ding dong merrily* and is nicely laced with carols, although it is not specifically a Christmas collection. The music ranges broadly from the twelfth to the seventeenth centuries and there are some pleasingly lyrical vocal items to provide contrast with the – at times somewhat strenuously enthusiastic – instrumental items. The sound is impressive, on disc and cassette alike, and no one could say that the music-making lacks spirit.

St John's College Ch., Camb., Guest

'The world of Christmas', Vol. 2 (with B. Runnett, organ): BRITTEN: *Ceremony of Carols*. JOUBERT: *Torches; There is no rose*. WARLOCK: *Adam lay ybounden; Balulalow*. Arr. SHAW: *My dancing day; The seven joys of Mary; Cherry tree carol*. WILLIAMSON: *Ding dong merrily*. TRAD.: *Adeste fideles; Up! good Christian folk; Rocking*.
(M) *** Argo SPA/*KCSP* 164.

The outstanding performance of the *Ceremony of Carols* (discussed in the Britten section, above) would alone make this worth having, but the other carols are imaginatively chosen, beautifully sung and very well recorded. The tape is excellent too. Treble voices are not always the easiest sound to focus cleanly in a cassette transfer, but the engineers have managed exceptionally well here, and the Britten often approaches demonstration quality.

'The world of St John's': music by WEELKES; PURCELL; DAVY; WESLEY, S. S.; HOWELLS; VAUGHAN WILLIAMS; MONTEVERDI; BANCHIERI; HAYDN; MENDELSSOHN; MESSIAEN.
(M) *** Argo SPA 300.

As can be heard from these recordings, St John's College Choir, trained and directed by George Guest, have run the more celebrated King's College Choir at Cambridge very close. The style, while remaining refined, is often more robust than that at King's: no suspicion here of being over-mannered. The variety of the music represented here is encompassed with confidence. The Davy and Vaughan Williams works are settings of similar words (taken from Psalm 47) and they are sung with fine vigour (the Vaughan Williams has the advantage of a jubilant brass accompaniment). The Purcell *Jehova, quam multi sunt hostes mei* is also a splendid piece, while the collection closes with an eloquent *O for the wings of a dove* (from Master Alastair Roberts) and – following after with surprising success – Messiaen's *O sacrum convivium*. They are both beautifully recorded.

'Hear my prayer' (with Peter White, organ): GOLDSCHMIDT: *A tender shoot* (carol). MENDELSSOHN: *Hear my prayer*. BACH: *Jesu, joy of man's desiring*. MOZART: *Ave verum, K.618*. STAINER: *I saw the Lord*. BRAHMS: *German Requiem: Ye now are sorrowful*. LIDON: *Sonata de 1. tono*.
(M) **(*) Argo SPA/*KCSP* 543.

The refined style of the St John's Choir is here at its most impressive in the famous Bach chorale, the Goldschmidt carol and Mozart's *Ave verum*. In Mendelssohn's *Hear my prayer*, the treble soloist sings with striking purity if without the memorability of Master Ernest Lough's famous Temple Church version (from the early electric 78 r.p.m. era). The substitution of a treble for soprano voice in the Brahms excerpt is not wholly convincing, especially as the soloist sounds a little nervous. But the choir is on excellent form throughout, and the recording is first-class, with an outstanding cassette to match the disc. The concert ends with an attractively vigorous account of an organ sonata by the Spanish composer José Lidon, which features the *trompeta real* stop with exhilarating effect.

'Christmas at St John's': GRÜBER: *Silent night*. RUTTER: *Shepherd's pipe carol*. MENDELSSOHN: *Hark the herald angels; O little town of Bethlehem; Born on earth; The twelve days of Christmas; Up! good Christian folk; Good King Wenceslas; While shepherds watched; God rest you merry, gentlemen; The holly and the ivy; Away in a manger; The first nowell; I saw three ships; Suo Gan.*
*** Argo ZRG 782.

This is first-rate in every way, a wholly successful concert of mostly traditional carols, in sensitive arrangements without frills. The singing is straightforwardly eloquent, its fervour a little restrained in the Anglican tradition, yet with considerable underlying depth of feeling. The full character of every carol is well brought out: the expressive simplicity of *I saw three ships* and Rutter's *Shepherd's pipe carol* is most engaging. The recording is excellent.

(The Choir of) **St Peter ad Vincula, Tower of London; John Williams**

'Music at the Tower' (with J. Sentance, organ): BYRD: *Sing joyfully unto God*. DERING: *Quem vidistis pastores; Contristatus est Rex David*. EAST: *When Michael heard that Absalom was slain*. TALLIS: *In jejunio et fletu*. PHILIPS, Peter: *O beatum et sacrosanctus diem; Ecce tu pulchra es*. BRITTEN: *Festival Te Deum*. PURCELL: *Jehova, quam multi sunt hostes mei*. BLOW: *Salvatore mundi*. HOWELLS: *Jubilate Deo*. TRAD. (Italian), arr. Williams: *Once as I remember*.
*** Abbey ABY 814.

Somehow one anticipates that music from the Tower of London with its forbidding history must be sombre, but these freshly extrovert yet polished performances entirely give the lie to such a conjecture. Opening happily with one of Byrd's most popular anthems, the programme ranges through a satisfying variety of styles and moods, ending with a sparkling account of the carol, *Once as I remember*. The choir is sixteen strong and very well balanced. Whether in the expressive beauty of Tallis and Blow, in the settings of Dering or Britten's memorable *Te Deum*, the fervour of the singing gives constant pleasure, as does the well-judged recording. Readers will probably guess that the conductor is not that John Williams featured in our Instrumental Recitals section.

Salisbury Cath. Ch., Seal

'Carols from Salisbury': RUTTER: *Sans day carol; Shepherd's pipe carol*. CORNELIUS: *Three Kings*. HADLEY: *I sing of a maiden*. DARKE: *In the bleak midwinter*. VAUGHAN WILLIAMS (arr.): *O little town of Bethlehem*. TRAD.: *Gabriel's message* (Basque). SHEPHERD: *I sing of a maiden; I wonder as I wander*. Arr. WILLCOCKS: *Cherry tree carol; Sussex carol; God rest you merry, gentlemen*. BACH: *Chorale prelude: In dulci jubilo* (C. Webb, organ).
**(*) Mer. E/*KE* 77068.

An attractively diverse selection of carols, though not all will like the use of soloists from the choir in four items. However, many will be glad of this source for Rutter's much-loved *Shepherd's pipe carol*, delightfully done here, while the carols on the second side make a particularly enjoyable group ending with a famous Bach *Chorale prelude*. The sound is very good and the cassette, though not transferred at a very high level, is satisfactory.

Schwarzkopf, Elisabeth (soprano)

'The early years': DOWLAND: *Come again sweet love*. BACH: *Cantata No. 208: Schage können sicher weiden*. HANDEL: *Il Penseroso: Sweet bird*. MOZART: *Die Zauberflöte: Ach, ich fühls* (in English). SCHUBERT: *Die Vogel: Liebhaber in allen Gesalten*. BIZET: *Carmen: Je dis que rien ne m'épouvante*. PUCCINI: *La Bohème: Sì, mi chiamano Mimì*. STRAUSS, J. Jnr: *Frühlingstimmen*. Folksongs: *'S Schätzli* (Swiss)*; Die Beruhigte* (Bavarian)*; O du liebs Angeli* (Bernese)*; Maria auf dem Berge* (Silesian). GRÜBER: *Stille Nacht*.
(***) HMV mono ALP/*TC-ALP* 143550-1/4.

This single-disc collection acts as a supplement to the boxed set below, although it should not be regarded merely as a pendant: it is a thoroughly worthwhile recital in its own right. A girlish quality, combined with musicianship already mature, marks all these mono recordings made in the decade after the Second World War. Pamina's aria is here given in English, charming but not the full, individual Schwarzkopf, and the Dowland would have been done very differently, less solemnly, later; but this varied and unexpected collection gives a vivid portrait of a superb artist at a key period. Four previously unpublished recordings are included. The transfers are very well managed and the tape too is admirably clear and open on top.

'Elisabeth Schwarzkopf sings operetta' (with Philharmonia Ch. and O, Ackermann): HEUBERGER: *Der Opernball: Im chambre séparée*. ZELLER: *Der Vogelhändler: Ich bin die Christel; Schenkt man sich Rosen. Der Obersteiger: Sei nicht bös*. LEHÁR: *Der Zarewitsch: Einer wird kommen. Der Graf von Luxemburg: Hoch Evoë; Heut noch werd ich Ehefrau. Giuditta: Meine Lippen*. STRAUSS, J. Jnr: *Casanova: Nuns' chorus; Laura's song*. MILLÖCKER: *Die Dubarry: Ich schenk mein Herz; Was ich im Leben beginne*. SUPPÉ: *Boccaccio: Hab ich nur deine Liebe*. SIECZYŃSKY: *Wien, du Stadt meiner Träume* (*Vienna, city of my dreams;* song).
❀ *** HMV ASD/*TC-ASD* 2807 [Ang. S 35696].

This is one of the most delectable recordings of operetta arias ever made, and it is here presented with excellent sound. Schwarzkopf's 'whoopsing' manner (as Philip Hope-Wallace called it) is irresistible, authentically catching the Viennese style, languor and sparkle combined. Try for sample the exquisite *Im chambre séparée* or *Sei nicht bös*; but the whole programme is performed with supreme artistic command and ravishing tonal beauty. This outstanding example of the art of Elisabeth Schwarzkopf at its most enchanting is a disc which ought to be in every collection. The cassette transfer too is beautifully managed and provides presence yet retains the full vocal bloom.

'The early years' (1946–55): MOZART: operatic arias. Opera scenes with Irmgard Seefried (STRAUSS, R.: *Der Rosenkavalier;* HUMPERDINCK: *Hänsel und Gretel*). Arias by VERDI, CHARPENTIER, PUCCINI. Lieder by BACH, GLUCK, MOZART, SCHUBERT, SCHUMANN, ARNE, R. STRAUSS, WOLF and arr. BRAHMS. Operetta excerpts by LEHÁR and JOHANN STRAUSS, Jnr.
(M) *** HMV mono RLS/*TC-RLS* 763 (4) [ZDX 3915].

These mono recordings are well worth the stereophile's attention, for they contain performances that in their freshness and command clearly point forward to the supreme work of the mature Schwarzkopf. The Humperdinck excerpts here (with Seefried) are the ones originally on 78 r.p.m., not from the complete Karajan recording, and it is good to hear the young Schwarzkopf as Sophie in *Rosenkavalier*, bright-eyed and alert. Previously unpublished are a strong, incisive account of *Martern aller Arten* from *Entführung* and *Depuis le jour* from *Louise*, starting unidiomatically but developing beautifully. A whole record of Mozart, one of other opera, and a third of Lieder are rounded off with operetta favourites of Johann Strauss and Lehár. Excellent transfers on both disc and cassette. The booklet provided with the tape box is admirable in every way.

'Favourite scenes and arias': WAGNER: *Tannhäuser: Elisabeth's greeting; Elisabeth's prayer. Lohengrin: Elsa's dream; Euch Luften, die mein Klagen* (with Ludwig). WEBER: *Der Freischütz: Wie nahte . . . Leise, leise; Und ob die Wolke.* PUCCINI: *Gianni Schicchi: O mio babbino caro. La Bohème: Sì, mi chiamano Mimì.* VERDI: *Otello: Willow song; Ave Maria.* SMETANA: *The Bartered Bride: Endlich allein . . . Wie Fremd.* TCHAIKOVSKY: *Eugene Onegin: Tatiana's letter scene.*
(M) *** HMV SXDW/*TC-SXDW* 3049 (2).

This two-disc folder brings together two Schwarzkopf recital records that have tended to be overlooked. The first containing Wagner and Weber is a classic, with Agathe's two arias from *Der Freischütz* given with a purity of tone and control of line never surpassed, magic performances. So too with the Wagner heroines. The second record finds Schwarzkopf keenly imaginative in less expected repertory. This was recorded eight years after the first (in 1967), and the voice had to be controlled more carefully. But Schwarzkopf's Puccini has its own individuality and she sounds radiantly fresh in the scene from *Otello*. The *Letter scene* from *Eugene Onegin* is less convincing; here the projected vocal personality seems too mature for the young Tatiana. The recording sounds splendid and has been transferred to cassette with great success.

'To my friends' (with Parsons, piano): WOLF: *Mörike Lieder: Storchenbotschaft; Fussreise; Elfenlied; Bei einer Trauung; Jägerlied; Selbstgeständnis; Heimweh; Nixe Binsefuss; Mausfallen Sprüchlein; Nimmersatte Liebe; Lebe Wohl; Das verlassene Mägdlein; Auf ein altes Bild.* LOEWE: *Die wandelnde Glocke.* GRIEG: *Ein Schwan.* BRAHMS: *Mädchenlied; Am jüngsten Tag; Therese; Blinde Kuh.*
*** Decca SXL/*KSXC* 6943 [Lon. OSA 26592].

This glowing collection of Lieder was Schwarzkopf's last record and also the last recording supervised by her husband, Walter Legge. With excellent Decca sound, the charm and presence of Schwarzkopf, which in a recital conveyed extraordinary intensity right to the very end of her career, comes over vividly. Most cherishable of all are the lighter, quicker songs like *Mausfallen Sprüchlein* ('My St Trinians reading', as she says herself) and *Blinde Kuh* (*Blind Man's Buff*). Like the disc, the cassette is superbly balanced, bringing the artists right into one's room.

Scottish Nat. Chorus and O, Currie

Christmas carols.
** ASV ACM/*ZCACM* 2043.

On the whole this is a conventional collection although with one or two attractive novelties. John Currie's arrangements are effective, though the orchestral embroidery seldom adds an extra dimension (as it does in the Clare collection) to what are essentially simple inspirations. There is some very delicate pianissimo singing which gives genuine pleasure. The programme ranges from *O come all ye faithful* and *I saw three ships* to *Little Jesus* (from Czechoslovakia) and *Ein ist ein ros entsprungen* by Praetorius.

Scotto, Renata (soprano), Placido Domingo (tenor)

Duets: MASSENET: *Manon: Toi! Vous!* GOUNOD: *Roméo et Juliette: Va, je t'ai pardonné.* GIORDANO: *Fedora: E lùi! E lui! Andate.* MASCAGNI: *I Rantzau: Giorgio si batte.*
**(*) CBS 76732 [M/*MT* 35135].

Fine, rich, mellifluous singing from both soprano and tenor in an interesting group of duets. Mascagni's *I Rantzau* may not be a masterpiece, but in its warmly lyrical way the Act IV duet is highly effective. Scotto is at her most compelling characterizing Manon, less aptly cast as Juliette. In all four duets it is the warmth of the singing rather than dramatic pointing which stands out.

Seefried, Irmgard (soprano)

'Portrait' (1944–1965): includes songs by BARTÓK; BRAHMS; MUSSORGSKY; RESPIGHI; SCHUBERT; R. STRAUSS; MOZART; excerpts from STRAUSS: *Ariadne auf Naxos; Der Rosenkavalier.* MOZART: *Così fan tutte; Le nozze di Figaro; Don Giovanni; Il re pastore.* LORTZING: *Der Wildschütz.*
(M) (***) DG mono/stereo 410 847-1 (6) [id.].

This comprehensive tribute to a much-loved singer was prepared in France and comes with a French text only, but the transfers and documentation are excellent. The set covers an impressive cross-section of Seefried's work, starting with a live recording of her singing at the Vienna State Opera in 1944 a role that she made especially hers, the Composer in Strauss's *Ariadne auf Naxos*. Opera excerpts predominate, well chosen from both live and studio recordings, but among the most cherishable items are the Lieder recordings from Mozart to Bartók, the latter's *Village scenes* included in an enchanting series of live recordings made in 1953, ending with a rapturous account of Strauss's *Ständchen*. Mono or stereo, one hardly cares with a voice so sweet and characterful.

Shirley-Quirk, John (baritone)

'A recital of English songs' (with Tunnard, Isepp or Parkin, piano): VAUGHAN WILLIAMS: *Songs of travel. Linden Lea. Silent noon.* BUTTERWORTH: *6 Songs from 'A Shropshire Lad'.* IRELAND: *My fair. Salley Gardens. Love and friendship. I have twelve oxen. Sea fever.* STANFORD: *Drake's drum.* KEEL: *Trade winds.* WARLOCK: *Captain Stratton's fancy.*
(M) **(*) Saga 5473.

Gathered together from two earlier Saga issues, this is as attractive a record of English song as you will find. John Shirley-Quirk early in his career was at his freshest, already an intense and dedicated artist, giving magic to such a simple song as Keel's *Trade winds*. The recording is limited but acceptable.

Simionato, Giulietta (mezzo-soprano)

'Grandi voci': ROSSINI: *Il Barbiere di Siviglia: Una voce poco fa. La Cenerentola: Nacqui all'affanno ... Non più mesta.* BELLINI: *I Capuleti ed i Montecchi: Deh! tu bell'anima.* DONIZETTI: *La Favorita: Fia dunque vero ... Oh mio Fernando.* MASCAGNI: *Cavalleria Rusticana: Voi lo sapete.* VERDI: *Un Ballo in maschera: Re dell'abisso. Il Trovatore: Stride la vampa. Aïda: L'abborita rivale a me sfuggia ... Gia i sacerdoti adunansi. Don Carlos: O don fatale. La forza del destino: Rataplan.*
(M) *** Decca GRV 16.

This provides a superb sampler of a singer who bids fair to achieve legendary status, an Italian mezzo with a firm, finely projected voice who could snort fire to order. This generous selection covers most of her favourite roles. Only occasionally is there a sign that a recording was made towards the end of her career. It is specially good to have her as a formidable Amneris in the Act IV *Aïda* duet opposite Bergonzi with Karajan conducting. Good recording.

Simpson, Glenda (mezzo-soprano), **Paul Hiller** (baritone)

'English ayres and duets' (with Mason, lute; Thorndycraft, viola da gamba): Ayres: CAMPION: *If thou long'st so much to learn. Shall I come, sweet love?* DOWLAND: *Fine knacks for ladies. In darkness let me dwell. Time's eldest son. Old age. Flow my tears. Now, O now, I needs must part. Come away, sweet love.* HUME: *Tobacco.* DANYEL: *Eyes, look no more.* PILKINGTON: *My choice is made.* JONES, R.: *Now what is love?* Duets: FERRABOSCO: *Tell me, O love.* DOWLAND: *Humour, say.* Lute solos: ANON.: *Piper's galliard. The Earl of Essex's galliard.*
**(*) Hyp. A/*KA* 66003.

What makes this Elizabethan recital different from others is its use of 'authentic Elizabethan pronunciation'. The dialectal flavours seem mixed, but the words come over, especially those of Glenda Simpson, whose style is admirably fresh and whose decorative runs are as delightful as they are crisply articulated. Paul Hiller is also an accomplished singer, and his melancholy manner is certainly in accordance with many of these lyrics, although some listeners may find his expressive style rather too doleful, and he misses the intended humour of Hume's *Tobacco*. But the dialogue songs go very well, and there is a general air of spontaneity here. The mid-side lute solos are most welcome. The recording has fine realism and presence, and the cassette is of demonstration vividness in its sharpness of focus.

Sopranos

'Great sopranos of our time': (i) Scotto; (ii) Schwarzkopf; (iii) Sutherland; (iv) Nilsson; (v) Los Angeles; (vi) Freni; (vii) Callas; (viii) Cotrubas; (ix) Caballé: (i) PUCCINI: *Madama Butterfly: Un bel dì.* (vi) *La Bohème: Sì, mi chiamano Mimì.* (ii) MOZART: *Così fan tutte: Come scoglio.* (iii) *Don Giovanni: Troppo mi spiace . . . Non mi dir.* (iv) WEBER: *Oberon: Ozean du Ungeheuer.* (v) ROSSINI: *Il Barbiere di Siviglia: Una voce poco fa.* (vii) DONIZETTI: *Lucia di Lammermoor: Sparsa è di rose . . . Il dolce suono . . . Spargi d'amaro.* (viii) BIZET: *Les Pêcheurs de perles: Comme autrefois.* (ix) VERDI: *Aïda: Qui Radames . . . O patria mia.*
*** HMV ASD/*TC-ASD* 3915.

An impressive collection drawn from a wide variety of sources. It is good to have Schwarzkopf's commanding account of *Come scoglio* and Nilsson's early recording of the Weber, not to mention the formidable contributions of Callas and the early Sutherland reading of *Non mi dir*, taken from Giulini's complete set of *Giovanni*. The cassette transfers are admirably managed throughout.

Souzay, Gérard (baritone)

'Baroque opera arias' (with ECO, Leppard): HANDEL: *Rodelinda: Scacciata dal suo nido; Tolomeo: Che più . . . Stille amare; Radamistro: Perfido: di a quell'empio tiranno; Floridante: Alma mia; Berenice: Si tra i ceppi.* LULLY: *Alceste: Il faut passer tôt ou tard; Cadmus et Hermione: Belle Hermione; Persée: Je ne puis.* RAMEAU: *Hippolyte et Aricie: Ah, qu'on daigne . . . Puisque Pluton; Castor et Pollux: Nature, amour; Dardanus: Voici les tristes lieux . . . Monstre affreux.*
(M) *** Ph. 9502/*7313* 081.

This collection represents one of Gérard Souzay's very finest contributions to the gramophone and shows a wide range of stylistic sympathy and taste. Not least of the disc's attractions is that it contains so much rarely-heard music, and Souzay's advocacy is such as to command its attention to the least adventurous of listeners. The disc offers excellent recording, and the cassette too is naturally balanced, giving a lovely bloom to the solo voice and capturing the agreeably warm ambience to set the accompaniment in good perspective.

Stade, Frederica von (mezzo-soprano)

'Live': VIVALDI: *Filli gioia vuoi farmi morir.* DURANTE: *Danza, danza.* SCARLATTI, A.: *Se tu della mia morte.* MARCELLO, B.: *Il mio bel foco.* ROSSINI: *La Donna del lago: Tanti affetti.* RAVEL: *Cinq mélodies populaires grècques.* CANTELOUBE: *Songs of the Auvergne: Brezairola; L'aio de rotso.* COPLAND: *12 poems of Emily Dickinson: Why do they shut me out of heaven.* HUNDLEY: *The astronomers; Come ready to see me.* THOMSON: *A prayer to St Catherine.* TRAD. (arr. Hughes): *The Leprechaun.*
**(*) CBS Dig. 37231/*40*- [id.].

This is taken from a live recital with von Stade vivacious and characterful in generally lightweight repertory. Neither the arrangement of the programme nor the close-microphone recording help to create the atmosphere of a genuine recital, but there are many gems here, including the Canteloube and the most substantial piece, the Ravel. There is a good chrome cassette catching the voice naturally, although there is a hint of peaking on one or two climaxes on side one.

'French arias' (with LPO, Pritchard) from: MEYERBEER: *Les Huguenots.* GOUNOD: *Roméo et Juliette.* BERLIOZ: *Béatrice et Bénédict; La Damnation de Faust.* MASSENET: *Werther; Cendrillon.* OFFENBACH: *La Grande-Duchesse de Gérolstein.* THOMAS: *Mignon.*
❀ *** CBS 76522/*40*- [M/*MT* 34206].

'The problem is simply how to convey her excellence in temperate language', said one reviewer of this splendid recital of varied and attractive French arias. Von Stade's is an outstandingly rich and even mezzo-soprano, and here she uses it with a rare technical finesse, so that trills and ornaments have a clarity and precision not often encountered. The range of expression is comparably wide: she commandingly compasses formidably contrasted roles, from page in the Meyerbeer and Gounod to *grande dame* in the two delectable Offenbach arias, the comedy delectably pointed but never guyed. The recording catches the voice well and the tape transfer also is of good quality, kind to the voice and naturally balanced. Side two has a higher level than side one.

Recital (with M. Katz, piano): DOWLAND: *Come again, sweet love; Sorrow stay.* PURCELL: *The Blessed Virgin's expostulation.* LISZT: *Die drei Zigeuner; Einst; Oh! quand je dors.* DEBUSSY: *Chansons de Bilitis Nos. 1–3.* Arr. CANTELOUBE: *Auprès de ma blonde; Où irai-je me plaindre; Au pré de la Rose; D'où venez-vous fillette.* HALL: *Jenny Rebecca.*
**(*) CBS 76728/*40*- [M/*MT* 35127].

The delectable Frederica von Stade is, as always, magically compelling here, both in vocal personality and in the vocal production itself. If in some of these songs Schwarzkopf, Janet Baker and others have sometimes been more positive, this memorable recital becomes more than the sum of its parts, closing with an engagingly gentle encore piece by Carol Hall. The accompaniments by Martin Katz are poised and sensitive. Good recording. The cassette transfers are clean and faithful, although the treble is not as soft-grained as on LP and there is a touch of hardness on the upper range of the voice. Our copy had 'print-through' on both sides, so that in the silences between the songs the sound on the reverse tracks could be faintly heard.

Arias (with Nat. Arts Centre O, Bernardi): MONTEVERDI: *Il Ritorno d'Ulisse in patria: Torna, torna.* ROSSINI: *Tancredi: Di tanti palpiti. Semiramide: Bel raggio lusinghier.* PAISIELLO: *Nina: Il mio ben quando verrá.* BROSCHI: *Idaspe: Ombra fedele anch'io.* LEONCAVALLO: *La Bohème: È destin.*
*** CBS 76800/*40*- [Col. M/*MT* 35138].

The remarkable ability of Frederica von Stade to identify with each heroine in turn comes out vividly. The voice is used with endless imagination and subtlety of colour, as well as great intensity and seeming spontaneity. The only reservation is that such a programme is likely to be too wearing for the listener to take all at once. Excellent accompaniment and recording, and the cassette transfer is one of CBS's best; the voice is given presence without an artificial edge, and the orchestral backcloth is full and clear.

'Mozart and Rossini arias' (with Rotterdam PO, de Waart) from: MOZART: *Le Nozze di Figaro; La Clemenza di Tito; Don Giovanni.* ROSSINI: *Il Barbiere di Siviglia; Otello; La Cenerentola.*
*** Ph. 9500 098/*7300 511* [id.].

It was as Cherubino in *Figaro* at Glyndebourne that Frederica von Stade first made her mark in Britain, at once demonstrating electrifying qualities of projection and voice. Much of that electricity is caught here, not just in Mozart but if anything more impressively still in her finely characterized and superbly sung Rossini portraits, the minx-like Rosina, the sparkling Cinderella and the agonized Desdemona, at once poised and deeply involved. Excellent, refined recording with the voice well balanced; the cassette transfer is rather more vivid in the Rossini than in the Mozart, and at climaxes there is sometimes a feeling that the amplitude of the vocal texture does not expand quite naturally.

Opera arias: ROSSINI: *Otello: Quanto son fieri i palpiti; Che smania. Ohimè! che affano!; Assisa a piè d'un salice; Deh calma, O Ciel.* HAYDN: *La Fedeltà premiata: Per te m'accesse amore; Vanne . . . fuggi . . . traditore!; Barbaro conte . . . Dell'amor mio fedele. Il Mondo della luna: Una donna come me; Se lo commando ci venirò.* MOZART: *La Clemenza di Tito: Torna di Tito a lato; Tu tosti tradito.*
*** Ph. 9500 716/*7300 807* [id.].

This attractive and varied collection is made up of excerpts from complete opera recordings. It is some tribute to Frederica von Stade's consistency that the result hangs together so impressively, each performance keenly individual and intense. Consistently good recording too, and an excellent cassette transfer; the voice sounds wholly natural and the orchestra has only marginally less life at the top than on the disc.

Stefano, Giuseppe di (tenor)

'Grandi voci': DONIZETTI: *L'Elisir d'amore: Una furtiva lagrima.* PONCHIELLI: *La Gioconda: Cielo o mar.* VERDI: *La Forza del destino: La vita è un inferno . . . O tu che in seno agli.* GIORDANO: *Andrea Chénier: Colpito qui m'avete . . . Un dì all'azzuro spazio; Come un bel dì di maggio.* MASSENET: *Manon: Instant charmant . . . En fermant.* PUCCINI: *Tosca: Recondita armonia; E lucevan le stelle. Turandot: Non piangere, Liù; Nessun dorma.* BOITO: *Mefistofele: Dai campi, dai prati.* GOUNOD: *Faust: Quel trouble inconnu . . . Salut! demeure chaste et pure.* BIZET: *Carmen: La fleur que tu m'avais jetée.*
(M) **(*) Decca GRV/*KGRC* 14.

Flamboyance rarely goes with keen discipline. As Rudolf Bing (among others) has said, if those qualities had been matched in di Stefano, we should have had a tenor to rival Caruso. As it is, this cross-section taken from his Decca recordings gives a splendid idea not just of his beauty of voice but of his power to project character and feelings. But do not look for stylish restraint in *Una furtiva lagrima*: the tear is anything but furtive. Generally good recording, but the cassette transfer has moments of coarseness at peaks.

'The world of Neapolitan song' (with New SO, Pattacini, or O, Olivieri): songs by DE CURTIS; CESARINI; LAZZARO; BIXIO; CARDILLO; BARBERIS; TAGLIAFERRI; CALIFANO; COSTA; NICOLAVENTE; and traditional songs.
(M) *** Decca SPA 313 [Lon. OSA 25065].

Di Stefano was still in magnificent voice in the mid-1960s when he recorded these popular Neapolitan songs – including many comparative rarities as well as obvious choices like *Torna a Surriento, Catari, catari*, and *Addio, mia bella Napoli*. The selection here has been generously extended, with about half a dozen extra items added to the content of Decca's original full-priced LP recital (SXL 6176). Despite the inevitable touches of vulgarity the singing is both rich-toned and charming. The recording is admirably clear and vivid.

Streich, Rita (soprano)

'Portrait' (with Berlin RIAS Ch., Berlin RO, Gabel): STRAUSS, J. Jnr: *Frühlingsstimmen*

waltz. Die Fledermaus: Mein Herr Marquis; Spiel' ich die Unschuld. Geschichten aus dem Wiener Wald waltz. VERDI: *Lo Spazzocamino* (*The Chimney Sweep*). GODARD: *Jocelyn: Berceuse.* ARDITI: *Parla-Walzer.* SAINT-SAËNS: *Le rossignol et la rose.* SUPPÉ: *Boccaccio: Hab' ich nur deine Liebe.* DVOŘÁK: *Rusalka: Song to the moon.* MEYERBEER: *Dinorah: Shadow song.*
❀ (M) *** DG Priv. 2535/*3335* 367.

Dazzling coloratura and irresistible charm distinguish this recital of vocal lollipops recorded by Rita Streich in the earliest days of stereo, when her voice was at its freshest. In the Johann Strauss items with which she was so much identified on stage, she is quite delightful, and her sparkling account of *Tales from the Vienna Woods* is no less captivating. She makes a purse of the finest silk out of Godard's *Berceuse* and is marvellously agile in Meyerbeer's famous *Shadow song*. No less memorable is Verdi's little-known *Chimney Sweep*, but the supreme highlight is the exquisitely delicate *Le rossignol et la rose* of Saint-Saëns, which she understandably chose to accompany her to Roy Plomley's desert island. The recording does not show its age unduly, although the tape transfer has occasional hints of peaking.

Supervia, Conchita (mezzo-soprano)

'The art of Conchita Supervia': Arias and scenes from: ROSSINI: *Il Barbiere di Siviglia; La Cenerentola; L'Italiana in Algeri.* MASSENET: *Werther.* HUMPERDINCK: *Hänsel und Gretel.* STRAUSS, R.: *Der Rosenkavalier.* PUCCINI: *La Bohème.* MOZART: *Le Nozze di Figaro.* GOUNOD: *Faust.* BERLIOZ: *La Damnation de Faust.* THOMAS: *Mignon.* SAINT-SAËNS: *Samson et Dalila.*
(M) (***) HMV mono RLS/*TC-RLS* 143614-3/*5* (2).

Readers who remember 78s of Conchita Supervia in Rossini – and in particular her dark brittle mezzo with its wide vibrato ('like the rattle of shaken dice', as one critic described it) sparkling in the divisions of *Una voce poco fa* – may be astonished to discover her degree of lyrical charm in other roles. Her reputation for dazzling the ear in Rossini was surely deserved (and she helped to restore *La Cenerentola* and *L'Italiana in Algeri* to the repertoire) but, as these superb recordings show, she was also an enchanting Cherubino (her singing of Mozart remarkably stylish as well as engaging). Her excerpts from *Der Rosenkavalier* and *Hänsel und Gretel* were recorded in Italian, but this seems to increase the lyrical intensity of the one and the charm of the other. No less beguiling is her seductive account of Musetta's famous *Waltz song* from *La Bohème*. What is also striking about this set is the excellence of the recorded sound. The recordings were made between 1927 and 1931 and are dated mainly by the internal orchestral balance, well reinforced with wind and brass; but the voice is as fresh as a lark, and the presence of this great artist is very real. The cassettes are no less impressive than the discs in this respect and they share excellent documentation.

Sutherland, Joan (soprano)

'Serate musicale' (with Bonynge, piano): ROSSINI: *Serate musicale.* DALAYRAC: *Nina: Quand le bien.* Songs by LEONCAVALLO, DONIZETTI, RESPIGHI, BELLINI, ROSSINI, VERDI, CIMARA, PONCHIELLI, MASCAGNI, CAMPANA, GOUNOD, GODARD, MASSENET, LALO, THOMAS, SAINT-SAËNS, FAURÉ, BIZET, MEYERBEER, DAVID, CHAMINADE, DELIBES, HAHN, ADAM.
** Decca D 125 D 3 (3) [Lon. OS 13132].

Recorded in the drawing-room of their Swiss house, this set of trifles from Sutherland and Bonynge suffers a little from dry sound. With little or no ambience it is harder to register the charm of these generally unpretentious songs, even the delectable Rossini collection which provides the title for the whole box. In many ways the most successful are the French items on the last of the three records, and the six sides are not recommended for playing at one go. But the love for this music shared by Bonynge and Sutherland is never in doubt.

'Grandi voci': BONONCINI: *Griselda: Per la gloria.* PAISIELLO: *Nel cor più non mi sento.*

PICCINNI: *La Buona Figliuola: Furia di donna.* ARNE: *Love in a Village: The traveller benighted. Artaxerxes: The soldier tir'd.* SHIELD: *Rosina: When William at eve; Whilst with village maids; Light as thistledown* (all with Philomusica of L., Granville Jones). HANDEL: *Acis and Galatea: Ye verdant plains . . . Hush, ye pretty warbling quire; 'Tis done . . . Heart, the seat of soft delight. Alcina: Tornami a vagheggiar; Ah! Ruggiero crudel! . . . Ombre pallide* (with Philomusica, Boult or Lewis).
(M) *** Decca GRV/*KGRC* 1 [Lon. JL/5-41011].

These recordings were all made just at the time when Joan Sutherland was achieving her first international success. Though in those days the engineers found it harder to capture the full beauty of the voice, the freshness and clarity are stunning. The Handel items on side two are taken from Oiseau-Lyre recordings of that time; side one has six recordings never issued before, all most cherishable, including those like *Light as thistledown* which Sutherland went on to record again. The cassette is vivid and wide-ranging with only the occasional peak on vocal fortissimos.

'The art of Bel Canto' (with Marilyn Horne, LSO Ch., New SO (of London) or LPO, Bonynge): SHIELD: *Rosina: Light as thistledown; When William at eve.* PICCINNI: *La Buona Figliuola: Furia di donna.* HANDEL: *Samson: With plaintive note.* BONONCINI: *Griselda: Che giova fuggire; Troppo è il dolore.* GRAUN: *Montezuma: Non han calma.* MOZART: *Die Zauberflöte: O zittre nicht.* BOIELDIEU: *Angéla: Ma Fanchette est charmante.* ROSSINI: *Semiramide: Serbami ognor.* WEBER: *Der Freischütz: Und ob die Wolke.* VERDI: *Attila: Santo di patria.*
(M) *** Decca Ace SDD 317.

The original two-disc recital *The age of Bel Canto* (now deleted), from which the whole of this mid-price reissue is taken, included arias for mezzo-soprano and tenor as well as ensembles. It was understandable that Sutherland's contributions to the whole, not just solos but ensembles too, should one day be hived off like this, and a very impressive disc it makes. It is good to be reminded what a fine Mozartian Sutherland is, in the Queen of Night's *O zittre nicht*, and the delightful point of Shield's *Light as thistledown* is irresistible. As for her duet *Serbami ognor* from *Semiramide*, it brings a performance of equal mastery with that in the complete set recorded by the same artists. Added to the items from the two-disc set comes a generous addition – three charming arias from the Sutherland/Bonynge records of *Griselda* and *Montezuma*. Excellent recording.

'The world of Joan Sutherland': arias from: GOUNOD: *Faust.* DONIZETTI: *La Fille du régiment.* VERDI: *Rigoletto; La Traviata.* BELLINI: *Norma.* DELIBES: *Lakmé.* CHARPENTIER: *Louise.* HANDEL: *Messiah.* STRAUSS, J. Jnr: *Casanova* (*Nuns' chorus*). COWARD: *Conversation Piece* (*I'll follow my secret heart*). LEONCAVALLO: *La Mattinata.* TRAD. (arr. Gamley): *The twelve days of Christmas.*
(M) *** Decca SPA/*KCSP* 100.

Few if any vocal bargains match this – a full hour of Sutherland at her finest, ranging over the widest possible list of items. This is of course intended as a sampler, a bait for the collector to purchase much more, and in that it should be very successful. The only pity is that nothing is included from Sutherland's most famous role, *Lucia di Lammermoor*, but the two big solos from that are presented with unrivalled freshness in the reissue of Sutherland's first recital after her great 1959 triumph (JB/*KJBC* 97 – see within the composer index under Donizetti and Verdi). The sound on disc is excellent, but the cassette is now in need of remastering. The quality on side one is generally good, but the voice tends to peak slightly on high notes; on side two the focus of the recording is less secure.

'The art of the prima donna', Vol. 1: ARNE: *Artaxerxes: The soldier tir'd.* HANDEL: *Samson: Let the bright seraphim.* BELLINI: *Norma: Casta diva; I Puritani: Son vergin vezzosa; Qui la voce; La Sonnambula: Come per me sereno.* ROSSINI: *Semiramide: Bel raggio lusinghier.* GOUNOD: *Faust: Jewel song.*
*** Decca SXL 2256 [in Lon. OS 1254].

'The art of the prima donna', Vol. 2: GOUNOD: *Roméo et Juliette: Waltz song.* VERDI: *Otello: Willow song; Rigoletto: Caro nome; Traviata: Ah, fors è lui; Sempre libera.* MOZART: *Die Entführung aus dem Serail: Marten aller Arten.* THOMAS: *Hamlet: Mad scene.* DELIBES: *Lakmé: Bell song.* MEYERBEER: *Les Huguenots: O beau pays.*
*** Decca SXL 2257 [in Lon. OS 1254].

This ambitious early two-disc recital (from 1960) remains one of Joan Sutherland's outstanding gramophone achievements, and it is a matter of speculation whether even Melba or Tetrazzini in their heyday managed to provide sixteen consecutive recordings quite so dazzling as these performances. Indeed it is the Golden Age that one naturally turns to rather than to current singers when making any comparisons. Sutherland herself by electing to sing each one of these fabulously difficult arias in tribute to a particular soprano of the past, from Mrs Billington in the eighteenth century, through Grisi, Malibran, Pasta and Jenny Lind in the nineteenth century, to Lilli Lehmann, Melba, Tetrazzini and Galli-Curci in this, is asking to be judged on the standards of the Golden Age. On the basis of recorded reminders she comes out with flying colours, showing a greater consistency and certainly a wider range of sympathy than even the greatest Golden Agers possessed. The recording too is exceptionally good with Decca brilliance never spilling over into hardness.

'Russian rarities' (with LSO, Bonynge and (i) O. Ellis): GLIÈRE: (i) *Harp concerto, Op. 74. Concerto for coloratura soprano and orchestra, Op. 82.* STRAVINSKY: *Pastorale* (song without words). CUI: *Ici Bas.* GRECHANINOV: *Lullaby.*
**(*) Decca SXL 6406 [Lon. OSA 26110].

The chief attraction among these *Russian rarities* is the brilliant coloratura concerto, which inspires Sutherland to some dreamily beautiful singing. The first movement sounds like a Russian version of Villa-Lobos's famous *Bachianas Brasileiras No. 5*, and the second movement has echoes of Johann Strauss with a Russian accent. Dreamy beauty goes a little too far in Sutherland's account of Stravinsky's early *Pastorale* (there is far too much vocal sliding), while the Cui and Grechaninov songs are accompanied by Richard Bonynge at the piano. The Glière *Harp concerto* is as easy, unpretentious and tuneful as the vocal concerto, with Osian Ellis performing brilliantly. An unusual and attractive collection, well recorded.

'Grandi voci': HANDEL: *Samson: Let the bright Seraphim; With plaintive note.* BONONCINI: *Griselda: Che giova fuggire; Troppo è il dolore.* GRAUN: *Montezuma: Barbaro, barbaro; Non han calma.* MOZART: *Die Entführung aus dem Serail: Martern aller Arten. Don Giovanni: Allora rinforzo i stridi miei . . . Or se chi l'onore; Crudele . . . Non mi dir. Die Zauberflöte: O zittre nicht.* BISHOP: *Lo, hear the gentle lark.*
(M) *** Decca 410 147-1/*4*.

Most of these eighteenth-century items are taken from Sutherland's earlier recital records, and the voice is at its freshest, most dazzling and most agile. It makes an outstanding collection in every way, full of treasures, with the sound still excellent. One of the very finest in Decca's 'Grandi Voci' series and more representative of her repertory than the earlier Sutherland issue on that label. The chrome tape catches the voice vividly with fortissimos seldom offering problems.

Sutherland, Joan (soprano), **Marilyn Horne** (mezzo-soprano), **Luciano Pavarotti** (tenor)

'Live from the Lincoln Center' (with NY City Op. O, Bonynge): excerpts from: VERDI: *Ernani; I Lombardi; I Masnadieri; Otello; Il Trovatore.* BELLINI: *Norma; Beatrice di Tenda.* PUCCINI: *La Bohème.* PONCHIELLI: *La Gioconda.* ROSSINI: *La Donna del Lago.*
*** Decca Dig. D 255 D 2/*K 255 K 22* (2) [Lon. LDR 72009].

Not all gala concerts make good records, but this is an exception; almost every item here puts an important gloss on the achievements of the three principal stars, not least in the concerted numbers. These include an improbable account of the *Lombardi* trio in which Marilyn Horne takes the baritone part (most effectively); and it is good to have a sample not only of Sutherland's Desdemona but of Pavarotti's Otello (so far not heard on stage) in their account of the Act I duet. The final scene from *Il Trovatore* is more compelling here than in the complete set made by the same soloists five years earlier, while among the solo items the one which is most cherishable is Horne's account of the brilliant coloratura aria from Rossini's *La Donna del Lago*. The microphone catches a beat in the voices of both Sutherland and Horne, but not so obtrusively as on some studio discs. Lively accompaniment under Bonynge; bright, vivid digital recording, but over-loud applause.

Sutherland, Joan, and **Luciano Pavarotti** (tenor)

Operatic duets (with National PO, Bonynge) from: VERDI: *La Traviata; Otello; Aïda* (with chorus). BELLINI: *La Sonnambula*. DONIZETTI: *Linda di Chamounix*.
*** Decca **400 058-2**; SXL/*KSXC* 6828 [Lon. OSA/5- 26437].

This collection offers a rare sample of Sutherland as Aïda (*La fatale pietra . . . O terra, addio* from Act IV), a role she sang only once on stage, well before her international career began; and with this and her sensitive impersonations of Desdemona, Violetta and the Bellini and Donizetti heroines, Sutherland might have been expected to steal first honours here. In fact these are mainly duets to show off the tenor, and it is Pavarotti who runs away with the main glory, though both artists were plainly challenged to their finest and the result, with excellent accompaniment, is among the most attractive and characterful duet recitals. The recording is admirably clear and well focused, and the sophistication of orchestral detail is striking in the *Otello* and *Aïda* scenes which close the recital, and this is especially striking on the compact disc, which, though a remastered analogue recording, gives the artists remarkable presence. The cassette too is extremely well managed.

'Duets': DONIZETTI: *Lucia di Lammermoor: Sulla tomba . . . Verranno a te. L'Elisir d'amore: Chiedi all 'aura lusinghiera. La Fille du régiment: Oh ciel! . . . Me v'là mamselle . . . Depuis l'instant*. VERDI: *Rigoletto: È il sol dell'anima*. BELLINI: *I Puritani: Fini . . . me lassa!*
**(*) Decca SXL/*KSXC* 6991.

The duet from *La Fille du régiment*, first recorded of these items from complete Decca sets, is also the freshest, sparkling and happy. In the rest, too, Sutherland is wonderfully consistent, and it is Pavarotti who in a degree of roughness, of lack of concern for detail, prevents some of the other duets from having the polish one really requires in a recital even more than a complete operatic performance. First-rate recording. The cassette too is most vivid, just a little peaky on top.

Tallis Scholars, Peter Phillips

English madrigals: BENNET: *All creatures now*. MORLEY: *Hark! Alleluia; Phyllis, I fain would die now*. VAUTOR: *Cruel madame*. GIBBONS: *Ah dear heart; The silver swan*. WILBYE: *Draw on sweet night*. WEELKES: *Hark, all ye lovely saints*. RAMSEY: *Sleep fleshly birth*. FARNABY: *Carters now cast down*. TOMKINS: *Woe is me*. BYRD: *Though Amaryllis dance*.
(B) **(*) CfP Dig. CFP/*TC-CFP* 4391.

Here, at bargain price, are polished, committed accounts of some marvellous music from an earlier English Golden Age. The singing seeks to be almost free of vibrato, and at times one might prefer a more robust and more overtly expressive effect. In consequence some items come off better than others. Tempi are well judged though, the style is never too heavy and there is much to enjoy here. The digital recording is vivid and clear and there is an agreeable pervading freshness. The definition is slightly less sharp on the cassette, with consonants clearer on the LP.

Tauber, Richard (tenor)

'The art of Richard Tauber': Songs by

WAGNER; R. STRAUSS; SCHUMANN; SCHUBERT; BOEHM; BEINES; MOSZKOWSKI; Arias from: KIENZI: *Der Evangelimann; Der Kuhreigen.* AUBER: *Fra Diavolo.* R. STRAUSS: *Der Rosenkavalier.* MOZART: *Die Zauberflöte; Don Giovanni; Die Entführung aus dem Serail.* VERDI: *La forza del destino; La Traviata.* WAGNER: *Die Meistersinger.* WEBER: *Der Freischütz.* (Operetta): STRAUSS, Johann Jnr: *Der Zigeunerbaron; Die Fledermaus.* LEHÁR: *Paganini; Land of smiles; Merry widow; Friederike; Schön ist die Welt.* ZELLER: *Der Vogelhandler.* HEUBERGER: *Der Opernball.* STRAUS: *Ein Waltzertraum.* KÁLMÁN: *Gräfin Maritza.* KREISLER: *Sissy.* STOLZ: *Madame sucht Anschluss.* SIECZYŃSKY: *Wien, du Stadt meiner Träume.*
(M) (**) HMV mono RLS/*TC-RLS* 7700 (3).

Tauber's voice was one of the most distinctive of the century, and it was sad towards the end of his career that the light repertory of operetta so dominated in the public view of him. This wide-ranging selection of his recordings, mainly from the inter-war years, helps to put the record straight, giving fair representation to his Lieder records as well as to grand opera. His Lieder-singing is always characterful and often most imaginative, but he is at times out-of-style, with cursory consideration for words. Musical line was plainly more important for him, as one realises in such opera excerpts as the tenor's aria from *Rosenkavalier*. But the operetta excerpts – imaginatively chosen here – do explain his phenomenal popularity over so many years. Transfers are immaculately done and the tapes match the LPs closely; however, many of the recordings sound somewhat primitive and there is a lot of hiss stemming from the earliest 78s.

Temple Church Ch., Sir George Thalben-Ball (organ)

'Favourite hymns'.
(M) ** HMV Green. ESD/*TC-ESD* 7136.

Opening with an ample-toned version of *Jesu, joy of man's desiring* (in which Leon Goossens plays the oboe obbligato) this generous collection – by judicious pruning of extra verses – offers, including the Bach *Chorale*, some two dozen favourite hymns: *O come all ye faithful, O Worship the king, All hail the pow'r of Jesu's name, The Lord's my shepherd* and the *Old Hundredth*, to name just a few among many favourites. Side two opens with an organ version of Stanley's *Trumpet voluntary* (sounding somewhat rough in the cassette transfer) and Walford Davies' *Solemn melody* is used as an interlude in the middle of side one. The sound is full and resonant, the focus cleaner on disc than on the high-level tape, where it is more noticeably variable. But the warmth and obvious enjoyment of the singing communicate readily.

'The Temple tradition' (with Royal College of Music O, Willcocks): STANLEY: *Organ concertos Nos. 4 in D min.; 6 in B flat.* THALBEN-BALL: *Sursum corda. Comfort ye.* WALFORD DAVIES: *Solemn melody. Tarry no longer.* WILLIAMSON: *Kerygma.* MENDELSSOHN: *Hear my prayer.*
** Abbey HMP 2280.

With royalties going to the Temple Music Trust this record celebrates a long musical tradition at London's Temple Church; and by including a new version of *Hear my prayer* it reminds us of the choir's most famous record, made in 1927 with Master Ernest Lough as treble soloist. His successor, Michael Ginn, is capable but fails to distil comparable magic, and generally the performances here (except perhaps for Malcolm Williamson's eloquent *Kerygma*) are forthright rather than inspiring. The choral recording is full but not always ideally clear. Dr Thalben-Ball is the sturdy soloist in the Stanley *Concertos* and the Orchestra of the Royal College of Music (Junior Department) provides convincingly professional support under Sir David Willcocks.

Tenors

'Great tenors of today' (with (i) Carlo Bergonzi; (ii) Franco Corelli; (iii) Placido Domingo; (iv) Nicolai Gedda; (v) James McCracken; (vi) Luciano Pavarotti; (vii) Jon Vickers): (ii) VERDI: *Aïda: Se quel guerrier . . . Celeste*

Aïda. (v) *Otello: Niun mi tema.* (i) *La Forza del destino: O tu che in seno.* (iv) BIZET: *Les Pêcheurs de perles: Je crois entendre.* (vii) *Carmen: Flower song.* (i) PUCCINI: *Tosca: E lucevan le stelle.* (ii) *Turandot: Nessun dorma.* (iii) *Manon Lescaut: Donna non vidi mai.* (ii) GIORDANO: *Andrea Chénier: Come un bel dì.* (vi) MASCAGNI: *L'Amico Fritz: Ed anche . . . oh amore.* (iv) GOUNOD: *Faust: Salut! Demeure.* (viii) SAINT-SAËNS: *Samson et Dalila: Arrêtez, ô mes frères.*
**(*) HMV ASD/*TC-ASD* 3302 [Ang. S 36947].

HMV compiled this anthology ingeniously from many sources. For example Luciano Pavarotti, an exclusive Decca artist from early in his international career, had earlier still taken part in EMI's complete set of *L'Amico Fritz*, so providing the excerpt which completes this constellation of great tenors. Not that each is necessarily represented in the most appropriate items, and the compilation does have one wishing (for example) that Vickers rather than McCracken was singing *Otello*, though that excerpt is valuable for preserving a sample of Barbirolli's complete set of that opera, short-lived in its regular issue. And although Vickers does not make an ideal Don José, it is useful to have his *Flower song*, since the set from which it comes is one of the less recommendable versions. The transfers are good, and though the recording quality is not consistent the voices are well reproduced, with warm orchestral accompaniments. Disc and cassette sound very much the same.

'Great tenors of the world' (with (i) Enrico Caruso; (ii) Tito Schipa; (iii) Beniamino Gigli; (iv) Richard Tauber; (v) Helge Roswaenge; (vi) Marcel Wittrisch; (vii) John McCormack; (viii) Heddle Nash; (ix) Lauritz Melchior; (x) Jussi Bjoerling; (xi) Georges Thill): arias from: (i) LEONCAVALLO: *I Pagliacci.* (ii) DONIZETTI: *L'Elisir d'amore.* (iii) VERDI: *Rigoletto.* GIORDANO: *Andrea Chénier.* (iv) FLOTOW: *Martha.* (v) ADAM: *Le Postillon de Longjumeau.* MOZART: *Die Entführung aus dem Serail.* (vi) MEYERBEER: *Les Huguenots* (duets with Margarete Teschemacher). (vii) HANDEL: *Atalanta.* (viii) MASSENET: *Manon.* (ix) WAGNER: *Tannhäuser* (*Rome narration*). (x) PUCCINI: *Turandot.* MEYERBEER: *L'Africaine.* (xi) BERLIOZ: *Les Troyens.*
(M) (**(*)) HMV mono HLM/*TC-HLM* 7004.

This makes a fascinating comparison with HMV's other tenor anthology (see above). No more distinguished list of tenors of the inter-war years could be assembled than this, and the items have been skilfully chosen, some entirely predictable, like Caruso's *Vesti la giubba*, Schipa's *Una furtiva lagrima*, or Gigli's *La donna è mobile*, but including such rare treasures as Helge Roswaenge's magnificent account of the bravura aria (*Freunde, vernehmet die Geschichte*) from *Le Postillon de Longjumeau.* While in the more modern recordings (like Jussi Bjoerling's 1944 version of *Nessun dorma*) the voices are not damped down, in the transcriptions from 78 the top is generally restricted to cut back the background noise of the originals. This is immediately noticeable in Caruso's opening item, and discerning collectors may feel that at times it has been overdone. The tape transfers are full and clear.

Teyte, Maggie (soprano)

'Her life and art' (with Cortot, Moore, Bowen, Muller, Alec Robertson): includes OFFENBACH: *La Périchole: Je t'adore, brigand.* PURCELL: *Dido and Aeneas: Dido's lament.* Songs by DEBUSSY, HAHN, MESSAGER, NOVELLO, PURCELL, BRAHMS, WOLF.
(***) BBC mono REGL/*ZCF* 369 [Ara. 8069/*9069*].

A vivid projection of Maggie Teyte's very strong personality. Indeed in the interview with John Bowen, Robert Muller and the late Alec Robertson she anticipates the questions and almost answers them before they are asked. Her account of her relationship with Debussy is fascinating, and although some of the vocal items are not entirely flattering and the sound is only acceptable, this has interesting documentary value.

Treorchy Male Ch., Cynan Jones

'The sound of Treorchy': THOMAS: *Fantasias*

on Welsh airs. Hymn tunes. MATHIAS: *Y pren ar y bryn.* GOUNOD: *Faust: Soldiers' chorus.* TRAD.: *Steal away. Immortal invisible. All through the night. Drink to me only. Gute Nacht. Swansea town. Were you there.* GENEE: *Italian salad.* PARRY: *Jesu, lover of my soul. Myfanwy.* HUGHES: *Guide me, O thou great Redeemer.* PRITCHARD: *Alleluya.* JAMES: *Welsh national anthem.* SULLIVAN: *The lost chord.* DAVIES: *Nant er Myreth.* Arr. VAUGHAN WILLIAMS: *Loch Lomond.* VAUGHAN WILLIAMS: *Linden lea.* CAPEL: *Love, could I only tell thee.* BACH: *Jesu, joy of man's desiring.* LIDDLE: *Abide with me.*
(B) ** EMI *TC2-MOM 125.*

The opening of this collection is ill-planned, with a piano accompaniment clattering away in a resonantly 'empty' hall. But once the choir enters, the reverberation is put to good effect, although it does mean that the cassette sound is robbed of a sharply defined upper focus. All this is less noticeable in the car, where the sonorous fullness and the characteristic fervour of the Welsh voices make the strongest impact. It is the traditional material which comes off best, especially the hymns (which may tempt a lone driver to join in!). The second half of the programme – which overall runs for nearly an hour and a half – is the more attractive.

Trew, Graham (baritone)

'Songs from a A Shropshire Lad' (with Roger Vignoles, piano; Coull String Qt): SOMERVELL: *A Shropshire Lad* (cycle). BUTTERWORTH: *6 Songs from A Shropshire Lad.* MOERAN: *Far in a western brookland; 'Tis time, I think, by Wenlock town. Ludlow Town* (cycle). PEEL: *When the lad for longing sighs; Reveille; In summertime on Bredon.* ORR: *Along the field; The Lent Lily; Oh when I was in love with you.* GIBBS: *When I was one-and-twenty.* BAX: *Far in a western brookland.* IRELAND: *The heart's desire.* GURNEY: *The Western Playland* (cycle).
**(*) Mer. A/*KA* 77031/2.

It was a happy idea to put together a collection of Housman settings not by Vaughan Williams. The Somervell cycle makes a fascinating comparison with the better-known Butterworth settings using four of the same poems. Housman chimed perfectly with a fruitful musical vein among English composers of the time to make this collection enjoyably representative of a genre still underappreciated. Specially valuable is the Gurney cycle. Graham Trew's rather thin baritone is not well suited to recording, but he is an intelligent singer and Roger Vignoles' accompaniments are models of stylish imagination, well recorded. The double-length tape is of good quality. Though the transfer level is not very high there is no real hiss problem; however, because of the level the string quartet slightly lacks presence.

Tyler, James (lute, baroque guitar, mandora)

'Music of the Renaissance virtuosi' (with Nigel North, lute, theorbo, cittern; Douglas Wootton, lute, bandora; Jane Ryan, bass viol): ANON.: *Zouch, his march.* VALLET: *Suite.* BORRONO: *3 Pieces from the Castelione Book.* CORBETTA: *Suite.* DE RORE/TERZI: *Contrapunto sopra 'Non mi toglia il ben mio'.* ALLISON: *Sharp pavin.* BERNIA: *Toccata chromatica.* KAPSPERGER: *Toccata.* PICCININI: *Toccata.* FERRABOSCO: *Spanish pavan.* CASTELLO: *Sonata.* DOWLAND: *Fantasia.*
(M) *** Saga 5438.

A civilized and rewarding anthology, far more varied in sonority than the list of contents would lead one to expect. The playing of James Tyler is splendidly musical and effortlessly virtuosic. The mandora (or mandola) is an obsolete instrument related to the mandolin; the bandora (or pandora) is a metal-strung instrument like the cittern. There is some highly interesting repertoire here, and the performances are really distinguished. The recording reproduces these subdued instruments truthfully and with no attempt to make them larger than life. Strongly recommended.

Vienna Boys' Choir

'Serenade' (cond. Gillesberger, with Theimer, piano, and instrumentalists): SCHUBERT:

Gott meine Zuversicht. Die Nachtigall. Ständchen. La Pastorella. Widerspruch. MOZART: *Due pupille amabile, K.439. Mi lagnerò tacendo, K.437. Luci care, luci belle, K.346. Più non si trovano, K.549.* SCHUMANN: *Zigeunerleben.* BRAHMS: *Nun stehn die Rosen in Blüte. Die Berge sind spitz. Am Wildbach die Weiden. Und gehst du über den Kirchhof.* DRECHSLER: *Brüderlein fein.*
** RCA RL/*RK* 19034 [PRL 1/*PRK 1* 9034].

The appeal of this collection is limited to those who want to hear German art songs freshly and ingenuously presented by a boys' choir. The singing is pleasing, at its most effective in the very simple items. Elsewhere the lack of the subtlety of response to word-meanings one expects from a solo performer brings a degree of monotony. The recording is good, and well transferred to tape.

'Folksongs of Germany and Austria' (cond. Harrer with instrumental accompaniment).
**(*) RCA RL/*RK* 30470.

This is repertoire in which the Vienna Boys excel, and they sing with a genuine spirit of innocence that is most engaging. There is a wide variety of material here, and although the planning of the layout is poor (items do not always follow each other naturally, and key changes sometimes jar on the ear) the programme itself is well chosen and of high quality. The closing hunting song (*Auf, auf zum fröhlichen Jägen*), with an appropriate accompaniment, is only one among a number of memorably vivid miniatures. The recording is excellent and the cassette transfer lively, if less refined than the LP.

'Folksongs and songs for children' (with V. CO, Harrer; Farnberger; Miller).
*** Ph. 6514/*7337* 188 [id.].

Here are some two dozen songs, many traditional and all of great charm. They are presented artlessly, but the singing is polished too and the simply scored accompaniments are very effective. The recording is admirably natural on both LP and chrome tape (although the latter has rather a low transfer level). There is a good deal of moderately paced music here and sometimes one feels that the direction could be more spirited, yet the overall effect is undoubtedly beguiling and, not taken all at once, this recital will give much pleasure.

'Popular songs and duets by Great Masters' (with Ortner, piano); dir. Harrer.
* Ph. Dig. 6514/*7337* 263.

It seems a curious idea to programme a selection of German Lieder to be sung by young treble soloists, however appropriate the subjects of the lyrics. Of course an item like Brahms's *Lullaby* has a certain ingenuous charm presented this way, but much of the repertoire here needs more sophisticated treatment, although all the singing is professional, if not always secure. The recording is good on both disc and tape.

'Merry Christmas' (with Ch. Viennensis, V. Volksoper O, Harrer): GRÜBER: *Stille Nacht.* TRAD.: *Kling, Glöckochen; Stacherl; Er is een kindeke geboren op aard; Quando nascette Ninno; Weihnachtsfreude; 12 days of Christmas; First nowell; Stille, still; Nu syt wellecome; Les anges dans nos campagnes; Andachtsjodler; Marche des rois; Ach ich bei meinen Schafen wacht.* MENDELSSOHN: *Hark! the herald angels sing.*
*(*) Ph. Dig. 6514/*7337* 318.

This record has been produced with much care, and the German titles – which will not mean a great deal to many readers – hide some of the most delightful melodies in the Christmas repertoire. The settings and arrangements, many by the conductor, Uwe Christian Harrer, are skilful. The singing is good too and the recording first-class on disc and cassette alike. The snag is the direction which is curiously stiff. Even the opening *Silent night* is made to seem over-deliberate while *The first nowell* and *Hark! the herald angels* lack jubilant fervour. *The twelve days of Christmas* (like the two above items) is sung in excellent English, yet again the deadpan delivery is disappointingly lacking in high spirits.

Vienna State Op. Ch., VPO

'Grand opera choruses' (cond. (i) Karajan; (ii) Gardelli; (iii) Solti; (iv) Maazel): (i) MUSSORGSKY: *Boris Godunov: Vali suda!* (ii) VERDI: *Nabucco: Gli arredi festivi; Va pensiero.* (i) *Otello: Una vela!* PUCCINI: *Madama Butterfly: Humming chorus.* (iii) WAGNER: *Die Meistersinger: Sankt Krispin lobel ihn! Tannhäuser: Begluckt darf* (*Pilgrims' chorus*). *Parsifal: Nun achte wohl . . . Zum letzten Liebesmahle.* (iv) BEETHOVEN: *Fidelio: O welche Lust* (*Prisoners' chorus*).
(M) *** Decca JB/*KJBC* 142.

Taken from some of Decca's finest opera recordings, this collection is self-recommending, with the reservation that the editing is not always clean (the *Tannhäuser* excerpt has to be faded out at the end). Opening excitingly with the Act IV chorus from *Boris*, the selection goes on to include arresting scenes from three of Solti's major Wagner recordings where the fervour and beauty of the singing is matched by the spectacularly fine recorded quality. The chrome tape is only fractionally less well focused than the disc, but on our copy of the cassette there was a bad patch of textural insecurity in the *Pilgrims' chorus*.

Vishnevskaya, Galina (soprano), **Mstislav Rostropovich** (piano)

Russian songs: MUSSORGSKY: *Songs and dances of death.* PROKOFIEV: *5 Poems by Anna Akhmatova, Op. 27.* TCHAIKOVSKY: *Do not believe my friend; None but the lonely heart; Not a word, O my friend.*
(M) *** Ph. Seq. 6527/*7311* 222.

This is one of Vishnevskaya's finest song records, a most welcome reissue at mid-price, though no texts are given on the sleeve, only summaries. Vishnevskaya's mastery of vocal characterization comes out repeatedly, most strikingly in the Mussorgsky. Only occasionally under pressure does the voice grow hard, though the most famous song, Tchaikovsky's *None but the lonely heart*, has its legato line spoilt by unevenness. Rostropovich with formidable piano technique provides ever-imaginative accompaniment. Good firm recording and a naturally balanced cassette.

Walker, Sarah (soprano), **Roger Vignoles** (piano)

'Cabaret songs': GERSHWIN: *By Strauss.* COWARD: *World weary.* WRIGHT: *Diss.* DUKE: *Paris in New York.* BRITTEN: *4 Cabaret songs of W. H. Auden.* IVES: *In the alley.* MALLORY: *Indian summer; Unfortunate coincidence; Words of comfort; Resume.* IVES: *The side show; The circus band.* DANKWORTH: *Lines to Ralph Hodgson Esq.; Bread and butter; English teeth.* GERSHWIN: *Someone to watch over me; I love to rhyme; The Lorelei.* DUKE: *Ages ago.*
**(*) Mer. E 77056.

The gem of this collection is the group of Britten's early settings of Auden, sharply parodistic but more deeply pointful too like the poems. Sarah Walker's cabaret style is somewhat aggressive, and is made more so by the harshness of the live recording. But once the uncomfortable acoustic is accepted, there is much to delight here, sharp miniatures that deserve a place on record, not just the Gershwin and Coward but the others too. Outstanding accompaniment from Vignoles.

Westminster Abbey Ch., Douglas Guest

GIBBONS: *O clap your hands together.* BLOW: *My God, my God, look upon me.* PURCELL: *Remember not Lord our offences; Lord, how long wilt thou be angry; O God, thou art my God.* CROFT: *God is gone up.* STANFORD: *Coelos ascendit hodie; Beati quorum via.* ELGAR: *They are at rest.* BRITTEN: *Hymn to the Virgin.* VAUGHAN WILLIAMS: *O clap your hands all people.*
*** Abbey LPB 791.

Another splendid collection of English church music ranging over three centuries, with the music happily arranged in chronological sequence. The exhilaratingly complex Gibbons setting of *O clap your hands together* (Psalm 47:1–9) was sung at the Coronations of 1937 and 1953, while Vaughan Williams's setting of the same psalm (from the Authorized Version) closes the concert jubilantly. In between there is much to enjoy, with the Purcell and Britten especially successful, but the Stanford items, especially the lovely melisma of *Beati quorum via*, are memorable too, as is the Elgar elegy (1909), a setting of Cardinal Newman with a slight *Gerontius* flavour. The recording is in the demonstration class, clear but finely atmospheric.

White, Robert (tenor)

'When you and I were young, Maggie' (with Sanders, piano): BUTTERFIELD: *When you and I were young, Maggie.* FOSTER: *Beautiful dreamer.* FOOTE: *An Irish folksong.* TOURS: *Mother o' mine.* Arr. TAYLOR: *May day carol.* SPEAKS: *Sylvia.* NEVIN: *Little Boy Blue. The Rosary.* PENN: *Smilin' through.* ROOT: *The vacant chair.* BOND: *I love you truly.* MCGILL: *Duna.* EDWARDS: *By the bend of the river.* DANKS: *Silver threads among the gold.* WESTENDORF: *I'll take you home again, Kathleen.* BOND: *A perfect day.*
*** RCA RCALP/*RCAK* 3023 [AGL 1/*AGK 1* 4891].

Robert White is a tenor with a very individual timbre which may not appeal to every ear but certainly has a special fascination for those who – broadly generalizing – like an Irish tenor sound. White is in fact American, though clearly enough (his father was a close friend of John McCormack) he deliberately cultivates his Irish sound in such repertory as this. His manner is totally unsentimental, the style pleasingly direct and fresh, full of unforced charm. Fresh, clear recording to match, and the cassette transfer too is clean, with an excellent balance and natural piano tone.

'By the light of the silvery moon' (with O, Hyman): DONALDSON: *My blue heaven. At sundown.* HUBBELL: *Poor Butterfly.* HENDERSON: *Bye bye blackbird.* ROMBERG: *When I grow too old to dream.* BAYES: *Shine on harvest moon.* EDWARDS: *By the light of the silvery moon.* KERN: *Look for the silver lining.* RAPEE: *Charmaine.* SHAY: *Get out and get under.* BERLIN: *All alone by the telephone. Remember.* JOLSON: *Me and my shadow.* MOLLOY: *Love's old sweet song.*
*** RCA RCALP/*RCAK* 6012.

Here Robert White takes a programme of 1920s and 1930s hits and with his keen, bright artistry and headily distinctive tenor gives them the status of art songs. He is helped by the brilliant accompaniments, yearningly sympathetic in sentimental songs like *Poor Butterfly*, adding jaunty syncopation in such charmers as *Get out and get under*. First-rate if obviously channelled recording.

'I hear you calling me' (with Samuel Sanders, piano): CROUCH: *Kathleen Mavourneen.* MARTIN: *Come to the fair.* LEHMANN: *In a Persian garden; Ah moon of my delight.* Arr. HUGHES: *A Ballynure ballad.* TRAD.: *Danny boy; The last rose of summer.* ADAMS: *The bells of St Mary's.* HAYDN WOOD: *Roses of Picardy.* ALLITSEN: *The Lord is my light.* MARGETSON: *Tommy, lad!* Arr. STANFORD *Molly Brannigan.* Arr. SANDERS: *Molly Malone.* CRAXTON: *Mavis.* MARSHALL: *I hear you calling me.*
*** RCA RL/*RK* 12450 [AGL 1/*AGK 1* 4895].

After the success of Robert White's first recording of ballads, it was to be expected that RCA would offer a second instalment. The result has all the disarming qualities of the first and can be recommended with equal enthusiasm to anyone charmed by this very individual voice. The recital again evokes the spirit of John McCormack by opening with a tenderly stylish account of *Danny boy*. The transfer is rather smoother and warmer than for the first recital and is generally very good indeed.

'Danny boy' (with Nat. PO, Gerhardt): O'CONNOR: *The old house.* STANFORD: *Trottin' to the fair.* TRAD.: *The harp that once thro' Tara's halls. She moved through the fair. The bard of Armagh. Danny boy. The next market day. Believe me, if all those endearing young charms. My lagan love.* O'BRIEN: *The fairy tree.* LOUGHBOROUGH: *Ireland, Mother Ireland.*

BALFE: *Killarney*. DUFFERIN: *The Irish emigrant*. CLARIBEL: *Come back to Erin*.
*** RCA RL/*RK* 13442 [ARL 1/*ARK 1* 3442].

The John McCormack repertory has become a speciality with Robert White, and here he presents a programme with an intensity of charm that the master himself surely would have applauded. Brilliant accompaniments and first-rate recording; the cassette is vivid too, and kind to the voice, although side two seems marginally less refined than side one.

'Songs my father taught me' (with Nat. PO, Mace): LOHR: *Little grey home in the West*. HAWTHORNE: *Whispering hope*. DIX: *The Trumpeter*. RASBACH: *Trees*. CLAY: *I'll sing thee songs of Araby*. FOSTER: *I dream of Jeannie with the light brown hair*. BALFE: *Come into the garden, Maud*. JACOBS-BOND: *Just a-wearyin' for you*. WHITE: *Two blue eyes*. ADAMS: *Thora*. MARTINI: *Plaisir d'amour*. MURRAY: *I'll walk beside you*. FRASER-SIMPSON: *Christopher Robin is saying his prayers*.
*** RCA RL/*RK* 25345 [NFL1/*NFK1* 8005].

Here Robert White turns back to popular ballads and sings them with characteristic, artless charm. He can be dramatically vivid, as in Dix's *The Trumpeter*, or phrase a simple melody with ravishingly warm tone. In the duet *Whispering hope* (one of the gramophone's earliest million-sellers in its 78 r.p.m. recording by Alma Gluck and Louise Homer) he sings with himself (by electronic means), disguising the colour of the 'second' voice so that it sounds like a light baritone, yet blends marvellously with the 'tenor'. A fascinating sleeve-note tells of White's childhood when one of an 'enormous collection' of John McCormack's records would go on the phonograph every time his mother put the kettle on for tea. This recital contains many favourites (described enthusiastically by White as 'belters') and they are sung superbly. The accompaniments under Ralph Mace are stylishly sympathetic, although the orchestral group is thin in numbers, perhaps appropriately. The cassette transfer is first-class, matching the excellent disc closely.

Winchester Cath. Ch., Neary

Evensong for Ash Wednesday.
*** ASV ALH/*ZCALH* 915.

This highly atmospheric record presents a service complete with prayers and responses. The main canticles, preces and responses are by Byrd, but the most striking item of all is the anthem, *Cast me not away* by S. S. Wesley, darkly intense. Outstanding singing by the choir under Neary. The cassette reflects the disc closely.

'On Tour': STANFORD: *Coelos ascendit hodie*. MENDELSSOHN: *Hymn of praise: I waited for the Lord*. HARRIS: *Faire is the heaven*. BRITTEN: *Antiphon, Op. 56b*. DUBOIS: *Toccata*. FRANCK: *Cantabile* (both J. Lancelot). HARVEY: *I love the Lord*. WESLEY, S. S.: *The Wilderness*. BERKELEY: *The Lord is my shepherd*. HOWELLS: *Nunc dimittis* (*Collegium Regale*).
*** ASV ALH/*ZCALH* 922.

In 1982 the Winchester Cathedral Choir made a tour of Canada – the first by an English cathedral choir for fifty-five years – and on the sleeve of this record (made immediately after their return home) they are shown singing against the background of the Horseshoe Falls at Niagara. One can't help wishing that someone had tape-recorded that occasion, for the Winchester choral timbre heard against that mighty background roar must have offered a unique contrast. However, the acoustic of the cathedral provides a splendid ambience for this concert of nineteenth- and twentieth-century repertoire, much of it English. The choir is strikingly rich in treble soloists. Three are needed for Britten's *Antiphon* and they sing most beautifully, as does Barnaby Lane in Samuel S. Wesley's memorable anthem/cantata *The Wilderness*. The choir too are on top form throughout and demonstrate great fervour in Herbert Howells' most famous canticle setting, from the *Collegium Regale* service. The organist, James

Lancelot, provides two enjoyable voluntaries to offer contrast, and altogether this collection is one of the finest of its kind available. The cassette is smooth and quite clear, but ideally might have used a higher transfer level; there is noticeable background hiss in the quieter moments, when the choir sustains some superb pianissimos.

Worcester Cath. Ch., Hunt

French church music (with (i) Cath. Voluntary Ch., and King's School, Worcester; H. Bramma and P. Trepte, organs): FRANCK: *Psalm 150; O salutaris Hostia.* WIDOR: (i) *Mass for 2 choirs and 2 organs.* VILLETTE: *Hymne à la Vierge.* POULENC: *Mass in G.*
❀ *** Abbey LPB 758.

It seems extraordinary that among many splendid Abbey collections of English church music it is this record of French repertoire that stands out. Widor's *Mass for two choirs and two organs* has an unforgettable *Kyrie*, which if better-known could well rival the famous *Toccata* in popularity. The two pieces by César Franck are more conventional, but very well sung; but on side two the *Hymne à la Vierge* with its creamy chromaticism is another indelible piece, while Poulenc's masterly *Mass in G* is outstanding for its combination of intensity and purity of style, with a beautiful treble solo from John Davies. The recording is in the demonstration class, and the Widor set-up with two choirs, grand and petit organs is very well managed, within the properly resonant acoustic. Perhaps the organ timbre itself is a shade too English, but it is superbly recorded.

Worcester Cath. Ch. and Fest. Choral Society, Hunt

'Favourite hymns': GLOSS: *Praise, my soul, the King of heaven.* WESLEY, S. S.: *O Thou who camest.* PURCELL: *Blessed city.* HOWELLS: *All my hope on God is founded.* VAUGHAN WILLIAMS: *Come down, O love divine; For all the Saints.* TAYLOR: *Glorious things of Thee are spoken.* WALFORD DAVIES: *God be in my head.* DYKES: *The King of love.* IRELAND: *My song is love unknown.* SCHOLEFIELD: *The day Thou gavest.* Arr. HUNT: *Mine eyes have seen the glory.* PARRY: *Dear Lord and Father of mankind; O praise ye the Lord.* TRAD.: *He who would valiant be; Immortal, invisible; Praise to the Lord, the Almighty.*
(M) *** Abbey MVP/*MVPC* 808.

The glorious British hymnal, Anglican and Nonconformist, is admirably celebrated here, in simple yet eloquent presentation of some of the finest melodies in Christendom. There are no disappointments: the tune you expect is the tune you hear. Descants are used fairly sparingly but top the melody splendidly on all occasions. There is plenty of light and shade; the style is essentially robust, while the singing itself has a proper degree of refinement. One really wants to join in. The recording is first-class and there is little to choose between disc and tape.

FOR YOUR OWN NOTES

FOR YOUR OWN NOTES

FOR YOUR OWN NOTES

FOR YOUR OWN NOTES

FOR YOUR OWN NOTES

MORE ABOUT PENGUINS, PELICANS AND PUFFINS

For further information about books available from Penguins please write to Dept EP, Penguin Books Ltd, Harmondsworth, Middlesex UB7 0DA.

In the U.S.A.: For a complete list of books available from Penguins in the United States write to Dept DG, Penguin Books, 299 Murray Hill Parkway, East Rutherford, New Jersey 07073.

In Canada: For a complete list of books available from Penguins in Canada write to Penguin Books Canada Ltd, 2801 John Street, Markham, Ontario L3R 1B4.

In Australia: For a complete list of books available from Penguins in Australia write to the Marketing Department, Penguin Books Australia Ltd, P.O. Box 257, Ringwood, Victoria 3134.

In New Zealand: For a complete list of books available from Penguins in New Zealand write to the Marketing Department, Penguin Books (N.Z.) Ltd, Private Bag, Takapuna, Auckland 9.

In India: For a complete list of books available from Penguins in India write to Penguin Overseas Ltd, 706 Eros Apartments, 56 Nehru Place, New Delhi 110019.

PENGUIN OMNIBUSES

☐ ***The Penguin Complete Sherlock Holmes***
Sir Arthur Conan Doyle £5.50

With all fifty-six classic short stories, plus *A Study in Scarlet, The Sign of Four, The Hound of the Baskervilles* and *The Valley of Fear,* this volume contains the remarkable career of Baker Street's most famous resident.

☐ ***The Alexander Trilogy* Mary Renault** £4.95

Containing *Fire from Heaven, The Persian Boy* and *Funeral Games* – her re-creation of Ancient Greece acclaimed by Gore Vidal as 'one of this century's most unexpectedly original works of art'.

☐ ***The Penguin Complete Novels of George Orwell*** £5.50

Containing the six novels: *Animal Farm, Burmese Days, A Clergyman's Daughter, Coming Up For Air, Keep the Aspidistra Flying* and *Nineteen Eighty-Four.*

☐ ***The Penguin Essays of George Orwell*** £4.95

Famous pieces on 'The Decline of the English Murder', 'Shooting an Elephant', political issues and P. G. Wodehouse feature in this edition of forty-one essays, criticism and sketches – all classics of English prose.

☐ ***The Penguin Collected Stories of Isaac Bashevis Singer*** £4.95

Forty-seven marvellous tales of Jewish magic, faith and exile. 'Never was the Nobel Prize more deserved . . . He belongs with the giants' – *Sunday Times*

☐ ***Famous Trials* Harry Hodge and James H. Hodge** £3.50

From Madeleine Smith to Dr Crippen and Lord Haw-Haw, this volume contains the most sensational murder and treason trials, selected by John Mortimer from the classic Penguin Famous Trials series.

PENGUIN OMNIBUSES

☐ ***The Penguin Complete Novels of Jane Austen*** £5.95

Containing the seven great novels: *Sense and Sensibility, Pride and Prejudice, Mansfield Park, Emma, Northanger Abbey, Persuasion* and *Lady Susan.*

☐ ***The Penguin Kenneth Grahame*** £3.95

Containing his wonderful evocations of childhood – *The Golden Age* and *Dream Days* – plus his masterpiece, *The Wind in the Willows,* originally written for his son and since then loved by readers of all ages.

☐ ***The Titus Books*** **Mervyn Peake** £5.95

Titus Groan, Gormenghast and *Titus Alone* form this century's masterpiece of Gothic fantasy. 'It is uniquely brilliant . . . a rich wine of fancy' – Anthony Burgess

☐ ***Life at Thrush Green*** **'Miss Read'** £3.50

Full of gossip, humour and charm, these three novels – *Thrush Green, Winter in Thrush Green* and *News from Thrush Green* – make up a delightful picture of life in a country village.

☐ ***The Penguin Classic Crime Omnibus*** £3.95

Julian Symons's original anthology includes all the masters – Doyle, Poe, Highsmith, Graham Greene and P. D. James – represented by some of their less familiar but most surprising and ingenious crime stories.

☐ ***The Penguin Great Novels of D. H. Lawrence*** £4.95

Containing *Sons and Lovers, The Rainbow* and *Women in Love*: the three famous novels in which Lawrence brought his story of human nature, love and sexuality to its fullest flowering.

PENGUIN TRAVEL BOOKS

☐ ***A Time of Gifts*** **Patrick Leigh Fermor** £2.95

In 1933 the author set out to walk to Constantinople. This award-winning book carries him as far as Hungary and is, to Philip Toynbee, 'more than just a Super-travel-book' and, according to Jan Morris, 'a masterpiece'.

☐ ***A Reed Shaken by the Wind*** **Gavin Maxwell** £2.95

Staying in reed houses on tiny man-made islands, Maxwell journeyed through the strange, unexplored marshlands of Iraq. His unusual book is 'a delight' – *Observer*

☐ ***Third-Class Ticket*** **Heather Wood** £3.95

A rich landowner left enough money for forty Bengali villagers to set off, third-class, and 'see all of India'. This wonderful account is 'wholly original, fantastic, but true' – *Daily Telegraph*

☐ ***Slow Boats to China*** **Gavin Young** £3.50

On an ancient steamer, a cargo dhow, a Filipino kumpit and twenty more agreeably cranky boats, Young sailed from Piraeus to Canton in seven crowded and colourful months. 'A pleasure to read' – Paul Theroux

☐ ***Granite Island*** **Dorothy Carrington** £3.95

The award-winning portrait of Corsica that magnificently evokes the granite villages, the beautiful mountains and olive trees as well as the history, beliefs, culture and personality of its highly individualistic island people.

☐ ***Venture to the Interior*** **Laurens van der Post** £2.95

A trek on foot through the breathtaking scenery and secret places of Central Africa, described by one of the great explorers and travellers of our time.

PENGUIN TRAVEL BOOKS

☐ ***Brazilian Adventure*** **Peter Fleming** £2.95

'. . . To explore rivers Central Brazil, if possible ascertain fate Colonel Fawcett . . .' – this is the exciting account of what happened when Fleming answered this advertisement in *The Times.*

☐ ***Mani*** **Patrick Leigh Fermor** £2.95

Part travelogue, part inspired evocation of the people and culture of the Greek Peloponnese, this is 'the masterpiece of a traveller and scholar' – *Illustrated London News*

☐ ***As I Walked Out One Midsummer Morning***
Laurie Lee £1.95

How he tramped from the Cotswolds to London, and on to Spain just before the Civil War, recalled with a young man's vision and exuberance. 'A beautiful piece of writing' – *Observer*

☐ ***The Light Garden of the Angel King*** **Peter Levi** £2.95

Afghanistan has been a wild rocky highway for nomads and merchants, Alexander the Great, Buddhist monks, great Moghul conquerors and the armies of the Raj. Here, brilliantly, Levi discusses their journeys and his own.

☐ ***The Worst Journey in the World***
Apsley Cherry-Garrard £5.95

An account of Scott's last Antarctic Expedition, 1910–13. 'It is – what few travellers' tales are – absolutely and convincingly credible' – George Bernard Shaw

☐ ***The Old Patagonian Express*** **Paul Theroux** £2.50

From blizzard-stricken Boston down through South America, railroading by luxury express and squalid local trains, to Argentina – a journey of vivid contrasts described in 'one of the most entrancing travel books' – C. P. Snow

PENGUIN REFERENCE BOOKS

☐ ***Roget's Thesaurus*** £2.95

Specially adapted for Penguins, Sue Lloyd's acclaimed new version of Roget's original will help you to find the right words for your purposes. 'As normal a part of an intelligent household's library as the Bible, Shakespeare and a dictionary' – *Daily Telegraph*

☐ ***The Penguin Dictionary of Mathematics*** £3.95

From algebra to number theory, from statistics to quantum mechanics, this new dictionary takes in all branches of pure and applied mathematics up to first-year university level.

☐ ***The Penguin Dictionary of Sociology*** £3.50

For students from O-level to undergraduate level, this book contains full discussions of concepts, theories and writings, with entries ranging from critical theory and behaviourism to feminism and working-class conservatism.

☐ ***The Penguin Dictionary of Economics*** £3.50

The third edition of this dictionary contains over 1,600 entries on economic terms and theory, the history of economics and its key individuals.

☐ ***The Penguin Dictionary of Botany*** £3.95

This encyclopedic reference book includes some substantial articles on vital topics as well as shorter definitions, and ranges from physiology to cell biology, microbiology to horticulture and genetics to plant pathology.

☐ ***The New Penguin Dictionary of Music*** £4.50

The fourth edition of this comprehensive dictionary covers orchestral, solo, choral and chamber music as well as opera and ballet, and includes detailed entries on composers, instruments of all sorts, orchestras, performers and conductors.

PENGUIN REFERENCE BOOKS

☐ ***The Penguin English Dictionary*** £2.95

The third edition of this comprehensive, up-to-date and unrivalled English dictionary.

☐ ***The Penguin Dictionary of Troublesome Words*** £2.50

A witty, straightforward guide to the pitfalls and hotly disputed issues in standard written English, illustrated with examples and including a glossary of grammatical terms and an appendix on punctuation.

☐ ***The Penguin Map of the World*** £1.95

Clear, colourful, crammed with information and fully up-to-date, this is a useful map to stick up on your wall at home, at school or in the office.

☐ ***The Penguin Map of the British Isles*** £1.95

Including the Orkneys, the Shetlands, the Channel Islands and much of Normandy, this excellent map is ideal for planning routes and touring holidays, or as a study-aid.

☐ ***The Penguin Dictionary of Building*** £3.95

Bricklaying, tiling, plastering, plumbing, double-glazing, security – the whole range is covered in the third edition of this popular dictionary for professional builders and home DIY enthusiasts.

☐ ***The Penguin Dictionary of Design and Designers*** £4.95

From the Renaissance goldsmiths, painters and engravers to the Bauhaus and beyond, this book provides brief biographies of leading designers, plus entries on patrons, exhibitions, institutions, movements, styles and periodicals.